The Right **School** = The Right **Job**

- As the leading media company for career information, Vault understands that your education is an integral part of your career path.

- You go to college or graduate school because you want to reach your career goals.

- In Vault's *Buzz Books*, we bring readers detailed, exclusive information about employment prospects at top schools.

- Each profile also includes exclusive information on admissions, academics, quality of life and social life at the schools.

- All information is based on exclusive Vault surveys of students and alumni at each school.

VAULT
> the most trusted name in career information™

The College Buzz Book

DREXEL UNIVERSITY COLLEGE OF LAW

Scientia, Ars, Officium

The College of Law builds on Drexel University's great strengths in practical education and technology. The College of Law prepares students for the challenges of 21st-century practice by integrating legal knowledge, practical skills, and professionalism.

At Drexel Law, you will find:

- *Co-op opportunities providing valuable practice experience as part of the academic program*

- *Small first-year classes and accomplished teachers in all subject areas*

- *Concentrations in health care law, intellectual property, and business and entrepreneurship law*

- *A newly constructed building, including a law library effectively combining electronic resources and traditional print material*

3320 Market Street, Philadelphia, PA   215.895.1LAW   www.drexel.edu/law

The College Buzz Book

EDITED BY STEPHANIE HAUSER & CAROLYN C. WISE
AND THE STAFF AT VAULT

All information in this book is subject to change without notice. Vault makes no claims as to the accuracy and reliability of the information contained within and disclaims all warranties. No part of this book may be reproduced or transmitted in any form or by any means, electronic or mechanical, for any purpose, without the express written permission of Vault Inc.

Vault, the Vault logo, and "the most trusted name in career information™" are trademarks of Vault Inc.

For information about permission to reproduce selections from this book, contact Vault Inc.150 W. 22nd St. New York, New York 10011-1772, (212) 366-4212.

Library of Congress CIP Data is available.

ISBN 13: 978-1-58131-512-7
ISBN 10: 1-58131-512-0

Printed in the United States of America

Acknowledgments

Thanks to everyone who had a hand in making this book possible. We are also extremely grateful to Vault's entire staff for all their help in the editorial, production and marketing processes. Vault also would like to acknowledge the support of our investors, clients, employees, family and friends. Thank you!

Vault would also like to thank all of the public affairs and admissions officers at colleges and universities who worked with us to ensure that the information provided by students and alumni is as accurate and placed within as much context as possible Thanks for all of your patience and assistance with our editorial process!

Table of Contents

INTRODUCTION   1

A Guide to this Guide 2

COLLEGE AND UNIVERSITY PROGRAMS AND SERVICES DIRECTORY   5

COLLEGE AND UNIVERSITY PROFILES   9

Alabama   11
Auburn University 11
The University of Alabama 14

Alaska   17
University of Alaska Anchorage 17

Arizona   22
Arizona State University 22
Northern Arizona University 25
The University of Arizona 28

Arkansas   32
University of Arkansas at Little Rock 32

California   35
California Institute of Technology 35
Claremont McKenna College 38
Mills College 41
Occidental College 44
Pepperdine University 47
Pomona College 50
San Diego State University 53
Santa Clara University 56
Stanford University 59
Thomas Aquinas College 62
UCLA 66
University of California, Berkeley 69
University of California, Davis 72
University of California, Irvine 75
University of California, Riverside 78
University of California, San Diego 81
University of California, Santa Barbara 84
University of California, Santa Cruz 87
University of San Diego 90
University of San Francisco 94

Higher LSAT* score guaranteed or your money back†

Kaplan: The smarter way to prep for the LSAT

Practice with all real questions.

Every released
LSAT question explained

ONLY AT KAPLAN

Prep with the best teachers.

High-scoring LSAT experts
to keep you on track

Make the most of your time.

Focus on the areas
that yield the most points

Accommodate your busy schedule.

More options, more convenience

1-800-KAP-TEST | **kaptest.com/lsat**

KAPLAN
TEST PREP AND
ADMISSIONS

University of Southern California 97

Colorado   101

Colorado College 101
Colorado School of Mines 103
Colorado State University 106
United States Air Force Academy 109
University of Colorado at Boulder 112

Connecticut   116

Connecticut College 116
Trinity College 120
University of Connecticut 123
Wesleyan University 126
Yale University 130

Delaware   133

University of Delaware 133

District of Columbia   136

American University 136
The Catholic University of America 139
The George Washington University 141
Georgetown University 144
Howard University 147

Florida   150

Florida International University 150
Florida State University 153
Rollins College 156
University of Central Florida 158
University of Florida 162
University of Miami 166
University of South Florida 168

Georgia   172

Emory University 172
Georgia Institute of Technology 176
Georgia State University 179
Morehouse College 182
Spelman College 184
University of Georgia 187

Hawaii   190

Brigham Young University Hawaii 190
University of Hawaii at Manoa 192

Idaho   196

University of Idaho 196

Illinois   199

DePaul University 199

Read all of Vault's College Surveys at **www.vault.com/college**–get complete surveys on 100s of colleges and universities, get expert advice on applicaton essays and and more.

VAULT CAREER LIBRARY   xi

ManhattanGMAT
the new standard

the world's largest GMAT-exclusive test preparation provider

Our Curriculum

ManhattanGMAT's exclusive curriculum was designed in accordance with our philosophy of test preparation, which centers on a balance between two competing emphases: test-taking strategies on the one hand, with in-depth content understanding on the other. The heart of the curriculum is the acclaimed ManhattanGMAT Strategy Guide Set, eight content-based books (five math and three verbal), available at the ManhattanGMAT online store; they are also sold at Barnes & Noble and Amazon.com. The set, along with three other books, a test simulation booklet, and various online resources, is provided to all ManhattanGMAT course students.

Nine-Session Preparation Courses

Meet once per week in our popular group course, either in person or live and online from your home or office.

Guided Self-Study Prep Program

We provide you with all the tools you need to succeed on your own (books, tests, access) with a little bit of help from our experts as your guide.

Private Instruction

Work with one of our expert tutors, who will design a customized program to suit your needs.

One-Day Workshops

Supplement a complete prep program with focused work in four key areas: Foundations of Math, Advanced Data Sufficiency, Advanced Quant, and/or Sentence Correction.

Free GMAT Preview Classes

New to the GMAT? Learn test basics, principles of adaptive testing, and how to prepare at an online or in-person free GMAT workshop.

Questions?

Call Student Services at 800-576-4628 or send an email to studentservices@manhattangmat.com.

Get schedules and sign up at www.manhattangmat.com or 800-576-4628.

Boston:
140 Clarendon Street
Ground Floor
Boston, MA 02116

Chicago:
222 West Ontario Street
Fourth Floor
Chicago, IL 60610

New York:
138 West 25th Street
Ninth Floor
New York, NY 10001

Southern California:
at Pepperdine University in Encino,
Irvine, Long Bearch, Pasadena,
West LA and Westlake Village

San Francisco:
870 Market Street
Sixth Floor
San Francisco, CA 94102

Washington D.C.:
1327 14th Street, NW
Suite 350
Washington, DC 20005

Global:
Live instruction online in
our virtual classroom with
students from around the
world.

Coming Soon:
Philadelphia
Atlanta
New Orleans
Miami
Houston/Austin
London

ManhattanGMAT corporate: 138 West 25th St, 7th floor New York, NY 10001 212-721-7400

*GMAT and GMAT CAT are registered trademarks of the Graduate Management Admission Council, which neither sponsors nor endorses this test preparation service.

DeVry University 201
Illinois State University 204
Loyola University Chicago 207
Northwestern University 210
University of Chicago 212
University of Illinois at Urbana-Champaign 215

Indiana   219

Ball State University 219
DePauw University 222
Earlham College 226
Indiana State University 229
Indiana University Bloomington 231
Indiana University-Purdue University Indianapolis 234
Purdue University 236
University of Notre Dame 239
Wabash College 243

Iowa   247

Buena Vista University 247
Cornell College 248
Grinnell College 252
Iowa State University 255
University of Iowa 258

Kansas   261

Kansas State University 261
The University of Kansas 263

Kentucky   267

Centre College 267
University of Kentucky 270

Louisiana   273

Louisiana State University 273
Tulane University 275

Maine   279

Bates College 279
Bowdoin College 281
Colby College 284
University of Maine 286

Maryland   290

Johns Hopkins University 290
United States Naval Academy 293
University of Maryland 296

Massachusetts   300

Amherst College 300
Babson College 303
Boston College 306

Read all of Vault's College Surveys at **www.vault.com/college**–get complete surveys on 100s of colleges and universities, get expert advice on applicaton essays and and more.

VAULT CAREER LIBRARY   xiii

Boston University 310
Brandeis University 313
College of the Holy Cross 316
Emerson College 318
Hampshire College 321
Harvard University 324
Massachusetts Institute of Technology 327
Mount Holyoke College 330
Northeastern University 333
Olin College 336
Smith College 339
Tufts University 342
University of Massachusetts Amherst 345
Wellesley College 349
Williams College 352
Worcester Polytechnic Institute 355

Michigan   359

Central Michigan University 359
Michigan State University 363
Michigan Technological University 366
University of Michigan 369
Western Michigan University 372

Minnesota   376

Carleton College 376
College of St. Benedict/St. John's University 378
Macalester College 381
University of Minnesota 384

Mississippi   388

Mississippi State University 388
University of Mississippi 391

Missouri   394

Saint Louis University 394
Truman State University 397
University of Missouri 400
Washington University in St. Louis 403

Nebraska   407

University of Nebraska—Lincoln 407

Nevada   410

University of Nevada, Reno 410

New Hampshire   413

Dartmouth College 413
University of New Hampshire 416

New Jersey   420

Princeton University 420

Rutgers University 424

New Mexico   427

University of New Mexico 427

New York   431

Barnard College 431
Binghamton University (SUNY) 434
Colgate University 437
Columbia University 442
Cornell University 445
Eugene Lang College The New School 449
Fordham University 452
Hamilton College 455
Hofstra University 458
Hunter College (CUNY) 461
Ithaca College 464
Marist College 467
New York University 469
Pace University 472
Rensselaer Polytechnic Institute 475
Sarah Lawrence College 479
Skidmore College 482
St. John's University 484
Stony Brook University (SUNY) 488
SUNY Geneseo 491
Syracuse University 494
Union College 496
United States Military Academy at West Point 498
University at Albany (SUNY) 502
University at Buffalo (SUNY) 505
University of Rochester 508
Vassar College 511
Wagner College 513
Wells College 516

North Carolina   520

Davidson College 520
Duke University 523
East Carolina University 527
North Carolina State University 529
University of North Carolina at Chapel Hill 532
Wake Forest University 535

North Dakota   540

University of North Dakota 540

Ohio   543

Case Western Reserve University 543
Denison University 546
Kent State University 549
Kenyon College 552
Miami University 555
Oberlin College 558

Read all of Vault's College Surveys at www.vault.com/college–get complete surveys on 100s of colleges and universities, get expert advice on applicaton essays and and more.

VAULT CAREER LIBRARY   xv

Ohio State University 562
Ohio University 565
University of Cincinnati 568
University of Dayton 570

Oklahoma   574

Oklahoma State University 574
University of Oklahoma 576
University of Tulsa 579

Oregon   582

Oregon State University 582
Reed College 585
University of Oregon 589

Pennsylvania   592

Bryn Mawr College 592
Bucknell University 595
Carnegie Mellon University 599
Dickinson College 602
Drexel University 605
Duquesne University 608
Franklin & Marshall College 611
Haverford College 614
Indiana University of Pennsylvania 617
Juniata College 620
Lafayette College 623
Lehigh University 625
Muhlenberg College 628
The Pennsylvania State University 631
St. Joseph's University 634
Swarthmore College 637
Temple University 641
University of Pennsylvania 644
University of Pittsburgh 647
Villanova University 650

Rhode Island   653

Brown University 653
Providence College 655
University of Rhode Island 659

South Carolina   661

Clemson University 661
Furman University 664
University of South Carolina 667

South Dakota   670

The University of South Dakota 670

Tennessee   674

East Tennessee State University 674
Rhodes College 677

University of Tennessee 680
The University of the South (Sewanee) 683
Vanderbilt University 687

Texas   691

Baylor University 691
Rice University 694
Southern Methodist University 697
Texas A&M University 700
Texas Christian University 703
Texas Tech University 706
Trinity University 709
University of North Texas 712
University of Texas at Austin 715

Utah   719

Brigham Young University 719
The University of Utah 722
Utah State University 725

Vermont   729

Bennington College 729
Middlebury College 732
University of Vermont 734

Virginia   737

College of William & Mary 737
George Mason University 741
Hollins University 744
James Madison University 747
Radford University 750
University of Richmond 753
University of Virginia 756
Virginia Tech 759
Washington and Lee University 762

Washington   765

Gonzaga University 765
University of Washington 768
Whitman College 771

West Virgina   775

Marshall University 775
West Virginia University 777

Wisconsin   780

Beloit College 780
Marquette University 782
University of Wisconsin—Madison 785

Wyoming   788

University of Wyoming 788

Read all of Vault's College Surveys at **www.vault.com/college**–get complete surveys on 100s of colleges and universities, get expert advice on applicaton essays and and more.

VAULT CAREER LIBRARY xvii

CANADIAN COLLEGE PROFILES   793

Acadia University 795
McGill University 798
Queen's University 801
Simon Fraser University 804
University of Alberta 806
University of British Columbia 809
University of Guelph 812
University of Toronto 814
University of Waterloo 818
The University of Western Ontario 821

ABOUT THE EDITORS   824

Introduction

Welcome to the fourth edition of Vault's *College Buzz Book*. In this guide, we publish extended excerpts from surveys of students and alumni at more than 250 top colleges and universities in the United States and Canada to bring you the inside scoop on the specific programs. The survey comments cover the following areas:

- Admissions
- Academics
- Employment prospects
- Quality of life
- Social life

The guide is intended to serve as a complement to other references to colleges and universities currently available that utilize school-reported data. Unlike those guides, Vault's *Buzz Books* (which also include the *The Business School Buzz Book* and *The Law School Buzz Book*) are composed almost entirely of information provided directly to Vault from students and alumni. (We asked schools to comment on the surveys after they were collected; this process is detailed later in this introduction.)

About this Vault Buzz Book

Founded in 1997, Vault—The Most Trusted Name in Career Information®—is the leading publisher for career information. We publish more than 100 guides to careers, and annually survey 10,000s of employees to bring readers the inside scoop on specific employers and industries.

In the past three years, we've extended our surveys of employees to include students and alumni because we recognize that education is essentially a component of our readers' career paths. In considering what they'd like to do for a living, readers of our guides and visitors to our web site (www.vault.com) also consider what education programs best fit these goals.

College and careers

We're excited to bring you our award-winning "insider" survey methodology to this crucial aspect of the career path. Knowing that college students keep an eye on their post-college careers when choosing their schools, we've made a special point of surveying students about employment prospects. Their comments in this area concern their perception of the relative prestige of the school, the strength of on-campus recruiting (including what type of companies recruit at the school) and the alumni network, as well as other important considerations concerning employment prospects.

Read all of Vault's college surveys at **www.vault.com/college** – get complete surveys on 100s of colleges and universities, get expert advice on applicaton essays and and more.

VAULT CAREER LIBRARY   1

A Guide to this Guide

Vault's survey process

Vault collects all of its student and alumni surveys online through Vault's proprietary online survey form. We collect surveys from students and alumni through Vault's membership base and network of members and readers at top colleges and universities. For the past three years, we have also invited all of the colleges and universities we cover to invite their students and alumni to take our survey online.

The designations of whether a survey entry was filled out by a "current student" or "alumnus/a" indicate the survey takers' status at the time the surveys were completed (i.e., if a student completed the survey in spring 2006 and graduated in May 2006, the entry would be designated as filled out by a current student, even though the student has since graduated). To provide additional context for our readers, we have also included the dates of enrollment of the student or alumnus/a and the month that the survey was submitted. They appear in that order following the survey taker's major.

This year, we asked survey respondents to include their major. When a student or alumnus/a provided a major, it is included in the survey header after the survey taker's status. Because majors differ from school to school, we have abbreviated and/or generalized some of the major titles to make them universally applicable. For example, majors such as communications, advertising and/or journalism are listed under the umbrella term "Communications."

For the survey header, *Current student, English, 8/2004-Submit Date, October 2005*: "Current student" refers to the survey taker's status at the time the survey was submitted; "English" refers to the survey taker's major; "8/2004-Submit Date" refers to the survey taker's dates of enrollment; and "October 2005" refers to the month the survey was submitted.

Vault began collecting student and alumni surveys in September 2003.

Survey questions

The survey asked students and alumni to comment on their experience at the school in five areas: admissions, academics, employment prospects, quality of life and social life. The exact questions asked are indicated below.

Admissions: Please provide a detailed account of the admissions process, including advice on getting in, interview, essays and selectivity.

Academics: Please provide a detailed account of the academic nature of the program, including quality of classes, ease of getting popular classes, grading, professors and workload.

Employment Prospects: Please provide a detailed assessment of employment prospects for graduates of your school, including prestige with employers, types of jobs graduates obtain, helpfulness of alumni network, and on-campus recruiting and internships.

Quality of Life: Please provide a detailed account of the program with respect to quality of life issues, including housing, campus, facilities, dining, crime and safety, and neighborhood.

Social Life: Please provide a detailed account of the school's social life, including bars, restaurants, dating scene, events, clubs and Greek system. Please include specific student favorites if possible.

Editing the surveys

In producing this book, our Vault editors edited surveys to remove redundant information that appeared in multiple survey responses, to strike any overly biased comments (both negative and positive), to formalize the surveys for syntax and style, and to correct egregious grammatical errors. However, it was our intent to maintain the colloquial flavor of each student's survey comments, so we retained sentence fragments, slang and other nonstandard language elements that we felt did not distract from the narratives.

School responses

After editing the surveys, we sent the edited profiles to each school for comment. We asked the schools to do the following:

- Indicate any instances where students or alumni had provided factually incorrect information (average test scores or GPAs, for example);
- Provide any information they felt would provide necessary context to specific survey comments;
- If they wished, to provide a separate 500-word narrative to be published with the profile.

We received comments from virtually every school; comments came from either the public affairs/media relations office or the admissions office, depending on the school. We have included comments next to appropriate survey sections, offset with a different font and indented to be easily recognizable as school-provided comments. Corrections within the body of the comments are enclosed in brackets. In the cases where a school provided a separate narrative, we have included this at the end of the school's entry, under the heading "The School Says."

Also note that many colleges and universities reviewed our survey profiles and indicated that they saw no factual errors and did not have any comments to add.

Read all of Vault's college surveys at **www.vault.com/college** – get complete surveys on 100's of colleges and universities, get expert advice on applicaton essays and and more.

VAULT CAREER LIBRARY   3

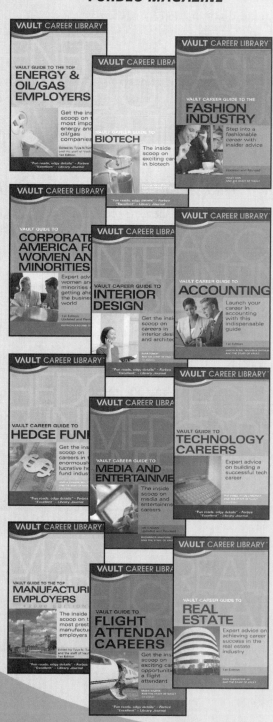

The College Programs and Services Directory

Argosy University

20 South Clark Street
Chicago, Illinois 60603
1-800-377-0617
www.argosyu.edu/buzz

Argosy University is a leading institution of higher learning founded upon the principle that relationship building is at the heart of both educational and professional success. Our academic programs focus on the interpersonal skills vital to professional achievement, while our faculty and staff nurture students' confidence - as well as competence - to thrive in their chosen fields.

Argosy University was formed in September 2001 by the merging of three separate academic institutions. The American School of Professional Psychology was founded in the early 1970s by a group of psychologists, educators, and other professionals who called for a clinical psychology degree that emphasized teaching and practical training over the research-oriented approach of the traditional PhD degree. The University of Sarasota had for more than 30 years offered degree programs in business and education to working adults through a delivery format that mixed distance learning and brief, intensive on-campus study periods. Responding to the emerging needs of the medical community, the Medical Institute of Minnesota was established in 1961 to prepare skilled allied healthcare personnel for careers in the booming medical technology fields.

Contact:
800-377-0617
auadmissions@argosy.edu

Drexel University ONLINE

One Drexel Plaza
3001 Market Street - Suite 300
Philadelphia, PA 19104
Phone: 866-440-1949
Fax: 215-895-0525
www.drexel.com/undergrad

Drexel University offers several bachelor's degrees and certificates that can be completed entirely online. It is a convenient way to earn a reputable, accredited degree, with no career interruption, commuting or fixed class hours. Bachelor's degrees are available in business, education, psychology, communications, computing technology, nursing, health services, and general studies. Undergraduate certificates include applied retail management and holistic health studies.

Drexel University is among the top 50 private, non-profit, national doctoral/research universities in the US. *U.S. News & World Report* ranked Drexel as one of America's Best Colleges for 2007. Drexel offers over 60 Bachelor's, Master's and Certificate programs in Business, Technology, Engineering, Education and more.

Contact:
Victoria Fox
Marketing Analyst
215-895-0514
info@drexel.com

Read all of Vault's college surveys at **www.vault.com/college** – get complete surveys on 100s of colleges and universities, get expert advice on applicaton essays and and more.

VAULT CAREER LIBRARY   7

College Profiles

Auburn University

Office of Undergraduate Recruiting & University
Scholarships
The Quad Center
Auburn University
Auburn, AL 36849
Admissions phone: (334) 844-4080
Admissions e-mail: admissions@auburn.edu
Admissions URL: www.auburn.edu/admissions

 ## Admissions

Current student, 8/2005-Submit Date, May 2007

Auburn University's admissions process is very easy. Auburn has a large demand, so a prospective student needs to apply at the starting application date for adequate, quick admissions. Auburn does not hold interviews, but within the application the prospective student must fill out seven short essay questions about him/herself and reasons for applying to Auburn. Before and during the application process, a prospective student and parents can visit the campus. A student recruiter walks around the campus and explains the history and purpose of the campus' buildings. After the tour, the family has the choice to meet with an academic advisor to learn more about the admissions process, the requirements for admissions, and how to improve the prospective student's chances for admission. Auburn University selects top quality prospective students by ACT/SAT scores, high school grades and GPA, and many other aspects.

Regarding selectivity, Auburn says: "All students interested in attending Auburn University are encouraged to apply. For freshmen who entered fall 2006, however, the average ACT was 24.3 and the average high school grade point average was 3.56. The acceptance criteria for students considered for admission for Summer/Fall 2008 will be based on the overall applicant pool."

Current student, 8/2004-Submit Date, May 2007

Auburn can be a selective university when it comes to out-of-state students. When I applied, the earlier you applied for admission the better off your chances were gaining acceptance. Auburn has now adopted a rolling admissions process and accepts applications year round. You should still apply early so that you can get in the pool for a coveted and hard-to-come-by academic scholarship.

Auburn mainly focuses on the applicant's GPA and ACT score and enrollment figures. Some academic areas are more selective, such as Engineering, Business, Human Sciences, majors within the College of Science and Mathematics, and Pre-Architecture and Building Sciences.

Current student, 8/2003-Submit Date, April 2006

I had a very positive admissions experience. I met with Dr. Boyd Sebra and he gave me a lot of information. He talked about the college life, as well. He told me what to expect in areas such as time management, studying and personal time. At the time, I was also interested in being a part of Auburn Athletics and he gave me the contact information when I met with him. He was very personal and made me feel like I was already a part of Auburn. Coming from Florida where the lottery makes getting into college very competitive, Auburn is everybody's safety school if they don't get in anywhere else. I picked Auburn over the University of Florida because the atmosphere at Auburn fit me better. However, I think Auburn could benefit from doing away with the rolling admissions process. They would find better applicants and raise the competitiveness. To a student from Florida, the selectivity is a joke. You can't get into a major Florida school with just a 3.0 GPA.

Current student, 8/2003-Submit Date, April 2006

Applying to Auburn was the easiest thing I have ever done. I knew that I wanted to go here the moment I set foot on campus. I was able to get automatic admission, so I was accepted within the first few weeks of my senior year. Since on-campus housing fills up so quickly, it is vital that even if you aren't sure about coming to Auburn, just sign up for housing, so in the future, you aren't stuck with having to live somewhere you don't want to. It is also important to do things as early as possible. I know that a lot of other schools are even worse about filling up too soon, but if you get it all done, it makes life a lot easier and you aren't sitting there in February wondering whether or not you got in.

The school says: "All students who have been accepted for admission must submit a $200 non-refundable tuition deposit by May 1. Students will also be required to pay a separate $60 non-refundable housing application fee. Housing and orientation is not made available to the students until the tuition deposit has been received."

Current student, 8/2003-Submit Date, April 2006

The admissions process is relatively simple compared to most schools. The application is short and concise. The school is selective, focusing on GPA and standardized test scores. The primary advice or guidelines for applicants is provided on the school's web site and in its admissions literature. The admissions recruiters who travel to college fairs and high schools are very professional and gave me a great taste of Southern hospitality. The friendly atmosphere during my campus tour was a deciding factor in my decision to attend Auburn.

Regarding admissions, the school says: "Beginning with the Summer/Fall 2008 admissions process Auburn has implemented several changes. Students still begin applying June 1; however, the first admission decisions will not be mailed until October 1. The application does require four short essay questions that may be used in the decision process. After October 1, 2007, students will receive information about their admission status four to six weeks after making application."

 ## Academics

Current student, 8/2005-Submit Date, May 2007

Auburn University has an amazing academic program. The university is composed of 12 schools and colleges and each one has its own advisors to further the student in the process of earning his/her degree. The class quality is difficult to describe. The classes are broken down into core requirements and degree requirements. The core classes tend to be difficult and the student is expected to devote quite some time to study for each class. Once the student has passed the core class, the degree class seems to be easier because the core class prepared the student for the degree classes.

The quality of the professors is up to each department. For example, the science department controls the quality of science professors. The science classes tend to be the hardest classes due to the teaching style of each professor. Some professors believe a lot of homework helps and some do not. Overall, the classroom quality is determined by the professor.

The process of registering for the classes has changed for next semester. We have a new system called Banner, which is difficult right now due to the uncertainty of the program. There are still some problems that need to be fixed in the program and the university is underway with that. Due to the newness of the program, it has been difficult to register for popular classes.

Read all of Vault's College Surveys at **www.vault.com/college**–get complete surveys on 100s of colleges and universities, expert advice on applicaton essays and more.

VAULT CAREER LIBRARY   11

Current student, 8/2004-Submit Date, May 2007

Freshman and sophomore year will mostly consist of Auburn's core curriculum. There are four semesters of English (two composition classes and two literature classes). The Mathematics courses will vary depending on the student's major. A student must complete two semesters of History (World or Technology and Civilization). Auburn's strong programs include Engineering, Architecture/Building Science, Nursing, Business and Pharmacy. I have enjoyed most of the classes I have taken at Auburn, however, the core classes seemed a bit monotonous. Freshman-level classes are very easy. However, after the first and second year, the difficulty level increases dramatically. As far as getting into these classes goes, Auburn has now instituted a new online registering system that should help with the ease of registration. I never have had problems getting into classes that I wanted. Professors at Auburn are more often than not very approachable and will help if asked. A must for incoming students is to attend class. Many times professors will give extra credit and bump you up if you are borderline on grades based on class attendance. Workload of classes: It depends on the difficulty, however, I would say no less than 15 hours per week outside of class devoted to studying; depending on test weeks, that may vary.

Current student, 8/2002-Submit Date, April 2006

The program is pretty good, in my opinion. I am in the honors college, so I have never had a problem getting the classes and/or professors I wanted—the honors college has special benefits that allow the students to register early. Depending on the college, the quality of the classes varies. I have enjoyed my upper-level classes much more than the lower-level ones because the professors usually get better with the higher-level classes.

Current student, 8/2002-Submit Date, April 2006

The classes are very large for freshmen and sophomores, in the 100s and 200s of students per class. Many of the teachers are foreign and can't speak English, making subjects like math and science VERY difficult. The classes are also very difficult to register for because they are already filled by upperclassmen. Therefore, some people mess up their four-year plan because they can't get their pre requisites done. The workload is appropriate and if you stay on track and keep up it is not too difficult. The toughest thing to learn is time management, because you have so much extra free time compared to high school. Major classes tend to be a little smaller and the teachers are more personable and easier to understand. They are also more interesting because they teach stuff you want to be learning about. The admissions department suggests that there is a 1:16 ratio of faculty to students. This is not very apparent.

Current student, 8/2003-Submit Date, April 2006

Auburn is one of those schools where getting in is easy, but staying in is hard. The classes are rigorous, but the availability of free tutoring is high. Depending on the popularity of the major, classes can be easy or hard to get into. Because I came in so many credit hours ahead, I have never had a problem getting into good classes. However, if you were registering with the rest of the students, it would be more difficult. Depending on the major, the workload can be huge or minimal. I am an engineering major and it consumes my life. I study every minute of every day and spend hours upon hours in labs. The workload is ridiculous.

Current student, 8/2004-Submit Date, April 2005

The undergraduate program at Auburn University is great. Students choose their own classes on an online system called OASIS before each semester, which enables them to get the classes and professors they want. My advice is that you run to a computer as soon as classes open up for registration because competition for the popular classes is pretty stiff. However, if you don't get the professor that you want, chances are you'll still have a good experience in another class because all of the professors here are more than capable of teaching their particular subjects. You'll find that professors grade fairly, as well, and it's very easy to keep up with your grades, thanks to another online program, WebCT. With WebCT, professors can post your grades where only you can see, as well as post messages and assignments for public viewing. Many classes require students to write several essays and other writing assignments throughout the semester, but, generally speaking, the workload is moderate.

Current student, 1/2002-Submit Date, March 2004

Auburn University provides students with a variety of 12 different schools from which to choose. Some of these are agriculture, math and science, engineering,

business, liberal arts, forestry, pharmacy, nursing and one of the Top Five veterinary programs in the United States. You have to have a pretty impressive résumé to get pharmacy, nursing or veterinary school, but all of the others are undergraduate programs, so anyone can get into those fields. Core classes can be difficult for freshmen to get, but as you move through your curriculum at Auburn, it is easier to get classes that you need.

Employment Prospects

Current student, 8/2004-Submit Date, May 2007

At Auburn, the Career Services Development Office holds job fairs, mock interviews, and helps students write their résumés. This department is able to help students with every part of a job search.

Current student, 9/2005-Submit Date, May 2007

There are lots of on-campus recruiting days for those looking for jobs and about to graduate. I would say there are at least three per semester and they seem to be very helpful. At Auburn, a lot of students are in engineering, building science, agriculture, and medicine, and all of those professions have a very high employment rate right after graduation and hold lots of prestige with employers.

Current student, 8/2004-Submit Date, May 2007

Auburn has a great networking system within the Alumni Association. It seems more and more Auburn graduates go off to Atlanta to find jobs because of the strong alumni ties there. Students with an Auburn engineering degree are almost guaranteed a job after graduation. Auburn has various internship/career fair days that are specific by college and sometimes major. Auburn's Career Development Services Center in Mary Martin Hall is a great place to go for help with résumés, interviewing and on-campus jobs. It is the student's responsibility to take advantage of these opportunities.

Current student, 8/2005-Submit Date, May 2007

Job prospects upon graduating depend a lot on what your major is. I have friends that are engineering majors and have been interning at NASA and Lockheed Martin and all have been offered jobs afterwards. I am a political science major and the department is pretty good about getting the students internships with the government in Montgomery. Business school is newer but has been receiving a ton of support from alumni, and our College of Science and Mathematics is growing exponentially.

Current student, 8/2003-Submit Date, April 2006

The career services division of the university, in conjunction with the alumni network, has established something called the Tiger Recruiting Link (TRL) for Auburn students actively seeking employment. Career services provides mock interview prep sessions and résumé help, as well as career placement testing. The university also sponsors job fairs throughout the year attended by companies such as Johnson & Johnson, Disney and Target, just to name a few. Honestly, I've found that people from Auburn end up all over from working in CNN in Atlanta to *The Today Show* in NYC. It's all totally up to the student and how far he/she is willing to go. The reputation of the alumni from the university has done wonders for the reputation of the university, itself. People expect Auburn graduates to have a good education without question. What they do with it is totally up to them, but the sky is the limit.

Current student, 8/2003-Submit Date, April 2006

Auburn has a career services center that is very beneficial for every student. If you are a freshman and don't know what you want to major in, you can go there, take a test and speak with a career counselor who will guide you in the right direction based on your interests. Also, they help juniors find that perfect summer internship by having résumé and interviewing workshops along with finding companies that may be interested in having interns. Every semester, there is a career fair where over 200 companies come in and speak with Auburn students about working for them.

Current student, 8/2003-Submit Date, April 2006

There is a lot of prestige with employers in the Southeast. Primarily Alabama, Georgia, Florida, Tennessee and Texas (the majority of students are residents of these states; therefore, alumni are also). There is a strong connection to alumni and the battle cry of War Eagle will connect anyone who belongs to the Auburn family. On-campus job fairs are visited by Fortune 500 companies for graduates and internships. The co-op program is very strong, as well. Companies recruit heavily for engineers at Auburn and recruit for many other majors, such as business.

Quality of Life

Current student, 8/2005-Submit Date, May 2007

Auburn is a very safe community and campus. We have dormitories in two locations on the campus. Around the Auburn town there are several apartments, condos and housing facilities. We also have a private dorm five minutes away from campus. Auburn has a bus system to pick up students off campus and bring them to class. Auburn has dining plans for on-campus students and the private dorm off campus also has dining plans. The dorms have resident student advisors to help with the student's life issues. We also have a student counseling service to help them transition to a college lifestyle.

Current student, 8/2004-Submit Date, May 2007

As an Auburn student, I absolutely love the campus and campus life is amazing. Auburn is a beautiful town and campus. It is called the loveliest village on the plains. The community is generally safe. Auburn currently has several new campus projects being constructed, such as a new Student Union, several dormitories, engineering buildings and research park. Recently, a state-of-the-art College of Science and Mathematics complex, and a Building Science building were completed in 2006. Housing is an issue for freshman students but the university is constructing more dorms within the next few years to combat the problem. A majority of students live off campus in apartments, condos or trailer complexes. The food on campus can be rated as fair with great need for improvement. The new student center is planned to have several new dining options.

Current student, 8/2002-Submit Date, April 2006

Life in Auburn is wonderful. It is an extremely safe town that is built entirely around the university. People are friendly, helpful and nice and housing is easy to find close to campus. There is plenty of good dining, as well, especially in the closeby town of Opelika. Campus is absolutely beautiful and green, definitely one of the best I've ever seen. I would recommend that a student interested in Auburn come and see it for him/herself to get a good idea of how great it is.is take advantage of it. But, if none of that appeals to you, Montgomery, Birmingham and Atlanta are all within driving distance.

Current student, 8/2003-Submit Date, April 2006

The quality of life is nice at Auburn. The residence hall living is comfortable. The dorms are suite style (this means no dreaded down the hall community bathrooms). It's two people to a bedroom and four to a bathroom. That is great! Freshmen are allowed to drive cars to school! Campus buildings are maintained very well with the latest upgrades of resources, facilities and technology. Auburn is a safe environment. You rarely hear of a crime on campus, or even in the town of Auburn. The campus and city police are combined to provide the highest level of security possible. They constantly patrol all areas to prevent any wrongdoings. The campus has adequate lighting and emergency call boxes, especially near the residence halls. Auburn is a major college town, though it is conservative compared to major party schools. The town practically revolves around the campus. Restaurants, shops and student apartments are in very close proximity to the campus.

Social Life

Current student, 8/2005-Submit Date, May 2007

The social life of Auburn is very diverse. We have many programs for students to attend such as concerts, movie nights and pep rallies. Off campus there are several clubs and bars to go to and several restaurants. We have a massive Greek life system for guys and girls.

Current student, 8/2004-Submit Date, May 2007

Auburn is a fun school and community with many options for entertainment. Chewalca State Park is right down the road from campus and has a waterfall. On a spring day students can be found laying out and throwing a frisbee in the quad or the large fields off Donahue Drive. Downtown offers many bars, such as Sky Bar, Bourbon St, the new Club 17-16, Bodegas, and Quixote's. There is a plethora of trendy coffee shops boutiques and restaurants within a block of campus. There is a strong Greek community at Auburn but it does not necessarily dominate campus life, but it can in certain areas such as the Student Government. The historic black Greek community is becoming more active in recent years and showing a presence on campus with activities such as an annual step show, yard shows and off-campus parties at local nightclubs.

Current student, 8/2004-Submit Date, May 2007

The main thing that drives the social scene at Auburn is FOOTBALL! During the fall, football rules every student's weekend. Auburn becomes a large city on these certain weekends. Most students are found tailgating and going to fraternity band parties on Friday and Saturday nights. The spring is definitely a more relaxed time of year, but activities can include: concerts, road trips to Atlanta, Birmingham, Nashville, Auburn baseball and basketball games as well as intramural activities.

Current student, 8/2002-Submit Date, April 2006

There is always plenty to do in Auburn, especially in the fall. Football is huge here and there is a ton of tailgating and parties during the season. There are several decent bars around Auburn, one of my favorites is the Highlands. If Auburn is not exciting enough, then Atlanta is only one and a half hours away—there are always concerts going on nearby, too. The Greek system is only as important as you want it to be; you can be completely involved in it and there are plenty of activities to consume your life; or you can forget it exists and become apart of the other 300 clubs and organizations at Auburn.

Current student, 8/2002-Submit Date, April 2006

Auburn students are very friendly and it is very easy to make friends. The Greek system is very affluent and the main social events are held by fraternities and sororities. The University Program Council (UPC) is a student-run organization that puts on many of our large events such as bringing 311 to campus and other major entertainment acts. There is still a limited number of restaurants in town, but the number has grown significantly since I arrived four years ago. There are only about four or five bars to go to but that makes it fun because you are sure to know someone no matter where you go.

Current student, 8/2002-Submit Date, April 2006

Greek life is alive around campus; however, it only includes about 25 percent of the students, thereby not making the Greek system a requirement. There is an almost equal ratio of men to women, making the dating scene thriving. Restaurants are numerous, including several that show the Auburn spirit. Some of the favorites include Cheeburger Cheeburger and Niffers.

Read all of Vault's College Surveys at **www.vault.com/college**—get complete surveys on 100s of colleges and universities, expert advice on applicaton essays and more.

VAULT CAREER LIBRARY   13

The University of Alabama

Admissions Office
Box 870132
Tuscaloosa, AL 35487-0132
Admissions phone: (205) 348-5666 or (800) 933-2262
Admissions e-mail: admissions@ua.edu
Admissions URL: admissions.ua.edu/undergraduate/

 Admissions

Current student, 8/2005-Submit Date, October 2005

Admissions wasn't that difficult. Make sure that all of your information is correct and honest. The essays aren't difficult. Make sure that your grammar is good, as well as your content. As I stated before, be honest about every answer. Make sure to include information on community service, life experiences, extracurricular activities, school clubs and plays; these topics will play a huge part in getting you acceptance into UofA or wherever you decide to attend college.

Current student, 8/2005-Submit Date, September 2005

The admissions process at the University of Alabama is done very well. Doing the application online is a much better choice than on paper. Some of the pros are that it is much easier, faster and neater. If you have horrible handwriting, the last thing you want the advisors at the university to do is try to decide what you wrote on your hand-written application.

Along with doing your application online, another great advantage is that you automatically get put into the scholarships computer. You do not have to fill out anything extra as you would if you did the paper application. Just by filling out the online application, you will automatically be signed up for every single scholarship offered by the university. Another great thing about the admissions process is the very quick response time. I believe it only took me two months to receive my acceptance letter.

Current student, 8/2003-Submit Date, April 2005

Basically, I submitted my personal information, transcripts, certificates from courses within the Marine Corps, ACT and SAT scores. Admissions is fairly straightforward, highly automated, and the admissions staff is very helpful should you run into any problems. The best advice I can give is to keep your grades up, practice and do well on the ACT and SAT. The University of Alabama currently has about 20,000 students, but plans to have about 28,000 in the next few years.

Current student, 1/2003-Submit Date, March 2005

The admissions process is pretty standard for any major public university such as the University of Alabama. The application is very simple and the only test score needed is the ACT. There are no interviews or challenging essay requirements. If you have a decent GPA and an ACT score of 18 or higher, you are in. The ACT score requirement also works on a sliding scale, so the higher your GPA, the lower your needed ACT score. I enrolled at Alabama as a transfer student and the admissions people were wonderful, helping me one-on-one and even providing me with a scholarship! Overall, the admissions process at Alabama is standard of any major institution with, perhaps, a little more personal touch and ease.

Current student, 7/2003-Submit Date, July 2004

The University of Alabama admissions is not very difficult. However, it does require a strong academic background and lots of preparation in high school. My best recommendation would be to apply early, before the admissions rush, and to attend Bama Bound in the fall or early spring to avoid long lines. There really is no interview process at Alabama. My best advice is to apply online.

> **Regarding admissions, the school says:** "At UA, we consider all applications on an individual basis. Although the average ACT

composite score for entering freshmen in 2005 was 24, we generally admit a student with a 20 ACT or 950 SAT score and a 3.0 cumulative grade point average. However, if you meet at least one of the above requirements, we encourage you to apply. For a transfer student, admission is based on the grade point average earned for your college coursework, excluding technical and remedial classes. A transfer applicant must have a grade point average of at least 2.0 on a 4.0 scale on all coursework attempted and must be eligible to return to his or her current institution. Transfer applicants who will have earned fewer than 24 semester hours (36 quarter hours) at the time they enroll at the university must also meet freshman admission standards."

 Academics

Current student, 8/2005-Submit Date, October 2005

Engineering, which is what I'm under, is really demanding. Make sure that you're getting the help you need, if you need it. There's no such thing as a popular class, all classes are challenging. You have to prepare for anything your professor assigns you. Communicating with your professors is a must. The work can be demanding at times, but if you really want something, you have to go in with a winning attitude. Taking no for an answer just will not do. You shouldn't be afraid to ask questions if you don't understand something. It's actually helpful to ask questions, it may help someone else in your class.

Current student, 8/2005-Submit Date, September 2005

This is one subject I love to talk about. The classes I have now are great. The biggest one is my economics class, which has 60 people. This let it be a personal class in which I am close with other students and my professor. It is much easier [to do much better in a smaller class.] We are able to participate on a much closer level. That way, if I ever need any help, other students are much more willing to help me because I am not just some number out of 500 students in a class, I actually have a name and they know me.

One good thing is the add/drop week. After the first couple of days of class, you are able to check online to see if there are any openings in a class you want because of kids who dropped that class. The grading so far has been good. I have had four tests so far, and I have done quite well. A couple of tests I did on a scantron, where it is multiple choice and the teacher can easily run the paper through a scanner to grade quickly. The other tests were on a computer where I was able to see my grade as soon as I finished the test. It was great!!!!

Current student, 8/2003-Submit Date, September 2005

Classes are almost always available. I've yet to have a semester when I haven't gotten the classes I want. They are highly challenging and motivating. The student-to-teacher ratio is one of the smallest in the country for a public college. Currently, we have the highest populated freshman class in the college's history. That number is expected to increase in the coming years. It should be interesting, especially since parking is currently at a premium.

Current student, 8/2003-Submit Date, April 2005

The workload is not impossible, but you will need to work hard. As far as getting into classes, I have never had a problem. It is important, however, that when it comes time to register, you do not wait until the last minute. With so many students, the most popular classes and times can fill up quickly, especially since upperclassmen get first pick. The grading system is your typical A through F system.

Current student, 1/2003-Submit Date, March 2005

The classes at Alabama are whatever you make them. There are so many majors and so many classes, a student can choose to be challenged or not. It is pretty easy for a student to get the classes he/she wants. If a student wants to take a small, discussion-oriented class or a huge lecture class, it is fairly easy to find those two opposites. Only a handful of classes are enormous and once a student gets into his/her degree program, classes get smaller and smaller.

Alumnus/a, 8/1998-5/2000, January 2005

Two of my favorite things about the program are the team projects and the accessibility of the professors. They really emphasize teamwork and, luckily, I had a great team experience. We stayed with one team our entire first year for projects in our core classes. It was great to learn each other's strengths and weaknesses. On top of that, the professors were all topnotch and were always helpful. It is great to get to know professors at that level.

Current student, 7/2003-Submit Date, July 2004

Alabama is a very large school. I would recommend registering for classes as early as possible. Know your professors, as well. Some professors and TAs are much more difficult than others, so it's important to know whose class you'll be in. Usually, your advisors can really help you know which classes to take and which to avoid. You will probably need to ask as many current students as possible about which classes to take. The Avanti members are very helpful and almost any student will be glad to give advice. Also, classes can be difficult courses but they are not impossible, just be sure to keep up. If you took honors and AP in high school, you should be more than prepared. Keep in mind that you should start out with at least 15 hours because to qualify as a sophomore your second year, you have to have 31 hours.

Employment Prospects

Current student, 8/2005-Submit Date, October 2005

Employment has a good rate. Majority of graduates of my college land jobs right after graduation. Networking is important while you're in college; that's a key into the corporate world. Internships and co-op opportunities are offered every semester. The best employment to go for is the co-op opportunities; this way, you can enjoy your job, as well as get paid. That's really helpful if you're thinking about paying your way through school or just saving money. On the other hand, internships are not bad; there's no money, but you'll get experience in different career fields with your degree options.

Current student, 8/2005-Submit Date, September 2005

This is a major subject at the University of Alabama. On the first day I entered in my classes, they said, "This is the first day of your résumé." That was very true because from there on out, I am working on that résumé to get the best job after graduation. It is amazing how many resources there are here at the university for students looking for jobs. We have what we call the Career Center here, a whole place dedicated to finding jobs. Today, I went to the career fair, which was the most amazing thing I have seen for students. There were over 300 major businesses in the room, with their employees there ready to inform me about their business and ready to take my application and get in touch with me.

Alumni are a huge contributor here at the university. There are always programs at the university where alumni come to inform us about their businesses. It is always so much easier to get a job with someone who is an alumnus from your university. They are always more willing to help you out than if you are trying to get a job with someone else. Internship programs are tremendous on campus. With the state of Alabama housing over three major car factories, interning for various positions is very easy. The university actually offers courses that you can take and get credit for where you actually intern for a semester or over the summer.

Current student, 8/2003-Submit Date, April 2005

Most graduates of the business school receive a job offer upon or even before graduation. The alumni network is out of this world and there are constant internship openings and on-campus recruiting opportunities. I have heard of very few students who have had trouble finding employment upon graduation. There are lots of job fairs and employers are constantly on campus looking for future employees.

Alumnus/a, 8/1998-5/2000, January 2005

I actually used my own resources in attaining a job after graduation. However, many of my classmates went on to very good jobs at companies like Eli Lilly,

Proctor & Gamble, Sara Lee Foods and more. They do a great job of bringing in prospective employers.

Quality of Life

Current student, 8/2005-Submit Date, October 2005

UofA has comfortable housing, on and off campus; the prices are reasonable. Adjusting to campus life is a little uneasy, but once you start meeting a few people and interacting in different student organizations, you feel welcomed. Safety is no issue at all, UAPD are on the job 24 hours a day. I feel very safe on campus. If you like keeping fit, the recreational center is an excellent place to go; it's free to students and very spacious. Intramural sports take place at the recreational center; those sports are open to anyone, no tryouts are required, all you have to do is sign up and play.

Current student, 8/2005-Submit Date, September 2005

I am actually very lucky this year. Being a freshman, I am part of the first bunch of students who are living in the new housing facility. There is a huge range [of housing,] depending on what you need. They have female only, male only, coed and there is housing for only honors students. The houses are very nice. The majority are just the one room with two beds, sink, fridge and a community bathroom.

One of my favorite facilities on campus is the Ferguson Center. This is the place where we have our cafeteria, where we pick up our mail and where we have a supply store and many other rooms. My favorite place is the cafeteria. We have what we call Fresh Foods, which is like a buffet place where there are many different types of food and it is all-you-can-eat. There are also things like Blimpie's, a Mexican place and a pizza place.

Current student, 8/2003-Submit Date, September 2005

Life is excellent; there always seems to be something to do each night of the week. I always see people whom I know on campus. On-campus housing is excellent, especially at the recently-built dorms. Parking is difficult this year, though, due to a record class of incoming freshmen.

Current student, 8/2003-Submit Date, April 2005

The quality of life at Alabama is wonderful. I can't imagine having gone anywhere else. The town is very supportive of the university and its students. Many local businesses offer student discounts for various things like dining and movies. There are always activities being offered, the campus is beautiful, crime is low, there are great facilities that are continually being improved and a lot to do out in town. Everything is conveniently located and, if for some reason something can't be found here, Birmingham is 45 minutes away.

Current student, 1/2003-Submit Date, March 2005

There is a large population of students who live off campus at Alabama. This is probably due to the sad shape of the dorms. Tutwiler dorm crams freshman girls into very tiny rooms. Paty, a large dorm for guys, is old and dirty. However, they are now addressing the problem by building three new dorms. The other buildings on campus are, for the most part, great. They are big and grand and full of Southern inspiration. The campus is beautiful, with trees and flowers growing everywhere. The giant quad in the middle of campus is great for throwing the football, running or laying out. Everyone is nice and friendly, and crime is not a big issue. There are, as with any major university, occasional cases reported around campus. But most people feel perfectly fine leaving their backpack unattended for a while.

The school says: "Enrollment at The University of Alabama is at an all-time high (23,878 students for Fall 2006). To meet this growing population, UA had six new residence halls completed by fall 2006, with two more slated for completion in 2007. Students may participate in a number of special academic programs with residential components, such as the Blount Undergraduate Initiative, a liberal arts living-learning program; Parker-Adams, which is exclusively for freshman students in the College of Arts and Sciences; and Capstone Living-Learning Community, also for freshmen in the College of Arts and Sciences. The Colleges of Engineering, Business,

Read all of Vault's College Surveys at www.vault.com/college—get complete surveys on 100s of colleges and universities, expert advice on applicaton essays and more.

VAULT CAREER LIBRARY   15

Communications and Information Sciences, Human Environmental sciences, and Nursing also have residential communities, as does the Honors College."

Social Life

Current student, 8/2005-Submit Date, September 2005

The social life at the university is a great topic to discuss. First of all, if you go to this university, there is no reason for you not to be involved with some type of activity at the university. There are over 400 types of organizations that students can join. During the second week of school, we had what we call Get On Board Day, where every single organization is out on our Quad with its tables set up, trying to get people involved. There is no maximum number of organizations that you can join.

There are so many events that go on here at The University of Alabama. Of course, as we all know, the biggest one would be our great football program, full of tradition. As a student, I had to pay $35 to get tickets for every home game. These game days are the most amazing things that I have ever seen in my life. On game day, the Quad (big grass field) is filled with people. There are vendors from local restaurants and families running around with their kids. I get goosebumps when I enter the stadium gates. It is amazing, the feeling that I can get when I am watching the event.

Current student, 8/2003-Submit Date, September 2005

The social life is incredible. The nightlife in Tuscaloosa is unique, yet familiar. There are many bars and pubs on the Strip, and almost all of them have local live music. The local music is a hodgepodge, from indie to alternative and rock. I cannot comment on all of the Greek system, but I've been to a few parties that were awesome. Dating has never been a problem either; there are tons of beautiful, single men and women all throughout the campus, from all nationalities, races and religions. The clubs almost always seem to have people dancing and enjoying the nightlife of Tuscaloosa. Student favorites include Rhythm and Brews, Jupiter Bar and Grille, The Library and many, many others on the downtown Strip. Tuscaloosa is also full of great places to eat. Depalma's, Cozy's and Cafe Venice head off the local favorites and local flavors for classier places to eat. City Cafe has some of the best country food I've ever had that wasn't my grandmother's! There's also quite a number of commercial places to eat, such as Outback and Olive Garden.

Current student, 1/2003-Submit Date, March 2005

The Greek system at Alabama dominates the social scene. While only about 10 percent of students are Greek, band parties at fraternity houses and other Greek parties are a huge part of the social scene. A student certainly doesn't have to be a member of a fraternity or sorority to have fun. Bars like 4th and 23rd bring in great bands almost every weekend—smaller bars like Innisfree and The Booth

provide a more laid-back atmosphere—and the Houndstooth was recently rated among the top sports bars in the country by *Sports Illustrated*.

Current student, 7/2003-Submit Date, July 2004

Don't come to Alabama if you don't plan to pledge. Greek life is number one at Alabama, so get your recs together and rush. Girls: get recs for EVERY sorority. You never know which house you'll end up loving. Just because a certain house has a certain reputation doesn't mean that it's true or that everyone thinks or believes it.

> **The school says:** "Campus activities include over 250 student organizations for those whose interests lie in the political, intramural and social outreach areas. The combined offerings of the UA campus, Tuscaloosa and Northport provide one of the richest cultural arts environments in the South, from the Alabama Blues Project (recognized at the White House) and blues concerts, to an outstanding celebrity music series, from the Kentuck Festival of the Arts (a nationally celebrated folk art festival) to the Bankhead Visiting Writers Series, from the Westervelt-Warner Museum of American Art to the Alabama Repertory Dance Theatre."

The School Says

UA ranks as one of the top public universities in enrollment of National Merit, National Achievement and National Hispanic Scholars. The fall 2006 freshman class accounts for 198 of these outstanding graduate students; UA ranks 13th among all public universities in enrollment of National Scholars. Six University of Alabama students have been named to the 2006 *USA Today* All-USA College Academic Team. Last year, UA had five students named to the team, and UA's combined four-year total of 20 team members leads the nation.

The University of Alabama's graduates include 15 Rhodes Scholars, 20 Goldwater Scholars, 10 Truman Scholars, eight Hollings Scholars, two Javits Fellows, one Udall Scholar and one Portz Scholar. Our student-scholars take their cues from nationally-recognized faculty who are committed to their students, and our 19:1 student-to-faculty ratio ensures that all our students have the opportunity to learn from the best. In part, this is why *Kiplinger's Personal Finance* ranked UA among its Top 100 Best Public Colleges in the nation based on quality education at an affordable cost.

University of Alaska Anchorage

Admissions Office
PO Box 141629
Anchorage AK 99514-1629
Admissions phone: (907) 786-1480
Admissions e-mail: enroll@uaa.alaska.edu
Admissions URL: www.uaa.alaska.edu/admissions/

 ## Admissions

Current student, 8/2003-Submit Date, May 2006

The admissions process at the University of Alaska Anchorage is not very inviting. It is very confusing and there isn't much help offered. There are long lines and the staff is usually less than sympathetic. If you need advice on getting in, you can see a counselor, but that may be a waste of time, too. Your best bet is to ask another student. Other than that, it is fairly easy to get into the University of Alaska Anchorage.

Getting through the admissions process is a little tricky. It is so long and the financial aid department is less than helpful. Tuition is pretty cheap, but there are a lot of very hidden fees—parking, lab, library, tutor and event fees, even if you don't participate. There is also a distance education fee if you take a class online.

Current student, 8/2005-Submit Date, September 2005

The admissions process is pretty simple if you try early. If you do not try to get in early, it gets very hard and selective. All you have to do to get in is to get your name on the list before it fills up. You do not need any essays to get in. The problem is that there are only a certain number of slots available for this program and only 12 CTI schools in the nation to train Air Traffic Controllers.

Current student, 8/2003-Submit Date, September 2004

For Alaska residents, the process of getting accepted into the university is very easy. You fill out the application and send in the fee, along with your high school transcripts and SAT and ACT scores. If you are a resident, you're given a spot, no questions asked; a lot of students travel outside the state to go to school and the state government wants to keep young people here, so offering them a spot right away is one way to do so. There are, actually, quite a few people from out-of-state, as well; the process for admissions is the same as for in-state residents.

UAA is not Princeton, so if your grades are the not the best, no worries. If you have activities that you did outside of high school—clubs, sports, community service—then that looks really good on a transcript, as well. There are no interviews needed to get into the university. It's probably good to submit an essay or two along with your application. It's good to "toot your horn," as some say. The university is not selective at all.

Alumnus/a, 8/1997-6/2003, June 2004

The admissions procedure for UAA is fairly easy. Just mail in the two-page application form with your admission fee. Essays are generic and you could copy the same one you send to other schools. If you did all right in high school, you should have no problem getting in. Actually, even if you did poorly in high school, you should get in. Good back-up school. No interview was required. The main thing about UAA is not if they like you, or even if you like them. It's if you like Alaska and the outdoor life. Not outdoorsy like Eddie Bauer, but outdoorsy like Wild America. Don't even think about going here if you don't want to be involved in things like skiing, snowboarding, mountain biking, hiking, trekking, kayaking or other outdoor activities.

Alumnus/a, 9/1992-5/1994, August 2004

It is a state school so pretty much everyone who applies is accepted. There are lots of older, returning students.

 ## Academics

Current student, 8/2003-Submit Date, May 2006

The academic nature of my program in business. The classes are OK, it really depends on which teacher you get. But I think that goes, no matter what school or class you take. If you want a popular class but did not get it, you can usually sign in at the teacher's discretion. Grading is usually up to a midterm and a final, which is really hard to work with. Workload is always heavy, it's like teachers don't understand you're taking other classes. But, believe it or not, the class with the most work is usually the one you get the best grade in.

Current student, 8/2005-Submit Date, September 2005

This program is a fast-paced, hard-study program. It is of a high quality with the utmost in technology. The classes are between 20 and 30 students. All the professors are selected based on their personal experience in the subjects being taught. There are no popular classes. When you enroll in this program, there is not a lot of picking and choosing. It is more, take this and this and at the end, you will have your degree.

Grading is mostly standardized grading. The workload is pretty difficult. This program involves learning a lot of regulations and many things that the common person has no idea about. Lots of reading and lots of understanding new concepts. One must constantly study and keep up with the work. The satisfaction makes it all worthwhile. When you look back on what you have learned, it is a lot in a short span of time and before you know it you will have a well-paid career.

Current student, 8/2003-Submit Date, September 2004

Depending on your major, your classload will vary quite a bit. For fine arts classes (theatre, dance and art) you won't worry about having to buy expensive textbooks. Art students will have to buy art supplies though. For dance and theatre classes there is some work outside of class but not much. For degrees like psychology, education and nursing (UAA's most popular degree programs), be prepared to fight the crowds on the first day that the bookstore opens. The aforementioned programs are somewhat rigorous, especially education. Be prepared to spend a lot of time out of class reading from your texts, taking notes and studying.

Grading goes by the A-F scale. Incompletes are only given in serious emergencies. (Family member in poor health, death in the family and so forth.) Most of the introduction classes are somewhat large, only because everyone has to take them for his/her degree program. As you get higher up, the classes begin to shrink in size, especially in performance classes. If you register early enough, you can get into all of the classes that you want to get into, but you may not get the perfect schedule. Often times, classes conflict with each other, so it's really good to be flexible in what you want for both classes and what time they're at. Most professors at the university are really knowledgeable and friendly. They're willing to help out students with problems that they may have with the coursework and are willing to schedule time outside their office hours to meet with students.

Alumnus/a, 8/1997-6/2003, June 2004

UAA is a small school and with a small student-to-teacher ratio. You never have a TA teaching you. It's always a professor. The attention you get from your teacher makes you think you're in a private institution. The only downside is: the classrooms aren't too hot. You have English classes next to Spanish classes. Ceramics next to Geology. Everything is very spread out.

Grading is not on a curve. If you get an F, you really earned an F. Some people have a hard time with the workload. This is because they never really ever had to study before. All classes can be as hard and as interesting as you want them to be.

Professors are very good. They are very unique, dedicated individuals who are surprisingly up-to-date on just about anything imaginable. The atmosphere is

Read all of Vault's College Surveys at **www.vault.com/college**—get complete surveys on 100s of colleges and universities, expert advice on applicaton essays and more.

VAULT CAREER LIBRARY   17

very relaxed and it's very seldom that you have a teacher who will talk down to you or treat you like an idiot. They are very respectful and very knowledgeable about their areas.

Alumnus/a, 9/1992-5/1994, August 2004

Workload was high, classes dealt mostly with psychology and anthropology, grading was not on a curve, and class quality was high. I never had a problem getting into the classes I wanted, although often I did not get the time I wanted.

> **The school says:** "UAA has just over 14,000 full- and part-time students on its Anchorage campus, with an additional 6,000 on its five community campuses located throughout Southcentral Alaska. More that 1,800 people graduated from programs at the Anchorage campus in 2005-06. The average class size in spring semester 2005 was 17.3 students with an average of 19.3 students per faculty member."

Employment Prospects

Current student, 8/2003-Submit Date, May 2006

Here in Alaska, the industries are booming, so graduates are able to go right out and get good jobs with major companies. There are a lot of career seminars and internships available, as well as many student clubs and student government. All you have to do to get a good job is say you earned a degree at the University of Alaska Anchorage.

> **The school says:** "UAA works closely with many government and industry partners to develop student internship and employment opportunities, with some programs placing 100 percent of their graduates into jobs and graduate programs each year."

Current student, 8/2005-Submit Date, September 2005

The FAA needs to higher 12,000+ Air Traffic Controllers between the years 2002 and 2012. The 12 CTI schools are only able to graduate at best 300 students a year. Do the math, they need everyone they can get. From the first month in this program, the FAA has your name and classes, and from then on, they are tracking your every academic move. So, just one month into schooling, your future employer knows who you are and what you are doing. After completing this two-year program you are then offered a job in either a center or a tower. Centers pay higher than towers and are in more need for people working in centers. Hence, most graduates are sent off to centers, but first they have to attend an eight-week course at the FAA Academy in Oklahoma. Pay differs between centers, depending on how busy they are; but the biggest pay difference is between when you are newly hired and after you are certified. This is normally a $30,000 difference, and it takes two or three years to become certified.

Current student, 8/2003-Submit Date, September 2004

Many programs have internship opportunities. Political Science has an internship in the capital for a semester working in legislative offices. Many of the popular programs at the university have excellent job offers. Nursing students could probably get a job at neighboring Providence Hospital as soon as they graduated, since the state is lacking in nurses. Education majors, after they graduate, can travel to bush villages (small towns in rural Alaska) and teach native students. Psych majors can get involved in clinical psychology after getting their master's (NOTE: UAA's Psych master's program is not accredited). Theater and Dance majors can get involved in university theatre or involved in local theater companies.

There are several resources on campus that can help students find jobs after they graduate. The most successful is the Career Services Center, which will help students decide what kind of job they want and what kind of degree they will need in order to be qualified for the job they want.

> **The school says:** "UAA's Career Services Center is a resource on campus that helps students and alumni analyze interests, aptitudes, abilities, previous work experience, personal traits, and desired lifestyle to promote awareness of the interrelationship between self-knowledge and career choice. For more infor-

mation on services offered, visit www.uaacareerservicescenter.com."

Alumnus/a, 8/1997-6/2003, June 2004

Nursing students have it made at UAA, as they are taken care of by the department. They do a lot of internships, training and job fairs. The school is right next to the largest hospital in the state and it works very well with the Nursing students. Also Psychology, Teaching and Sociology students seem to have it easy, as well. These jobs are in demand in the state.

> **UAA says:** "The fields of engineering and nursing are in especially high demand not only in Alaska, but also in other parts of the nation and the world. Graduates of these programs are likely to have many opportunities to work anywhere they desire."

Quality of Life

Current student, 8/2003-Submit Date, May 2006

Crime is pretty low, and there are campus police actually recruited from the Anchorage police department, so it is pretty safe. Good house; nice, roomy dorms with the option of a roommate. Always somewhere to eat. You can eat on campus for super, super cheap or you can go down the road to many restaurants and fast food places. Transportation is also provided for free by the University of Alaska Anchorage. Buses and shuttles will take you from place to place.

> **The school says:** "The Seawolf Shuttle services the Anchorage campus, with buses stopping every 15 minutes at each stop. UAA also partners with the Anchorage People Mover mass transit system providing city-wide free bus service to UAA students. Students can also load their bicycles onto racks on the buses. There are hundreds of miles of bike/ski trails throughout Anchorage, many in close proximity to the university allowing students to access the trail system with ease."

Current student, 8/2005-Submit Date, September 2005

The quality of life here in Alaska is perfect for this type of program. There isn't much else to do other than study, which is exactly what you need if you are to be successful in this program. There is plenty of housing. The campus and the facilities are excellent. It is in a central location of the city where you can easily shop, eat, go to movies and so on. As for crime and safety, you're in Alaska, not much bad happens here.

> **The school says:** "Anchorage is a city of nearly 300,000 featuring all the amenities one would expect in a city that size—excellent restaurants representing diverse cultures, the Anchorage Concert Association, the Anchorage Symphony Orchestra, Anchorage Opera, considerable theatre and dance performances, art galleries everywhere with city-wide monthly First Friday show openings, movie theatres, a beautiful performing arts center and an expanding museum.
>
> "Anchorage is the home of the Alaska Aces championship professional hockey team. UAA hosts the Great Alaska Shootout, one of the nation's premier pre-season college basketball tournaments. Arguably the most difficult athletic event in the world, the Iditarod Sled Dog Race kicks off in Anchorage and the city also hosts the World Championship Sprint Sled Dog Race. The Anchorage Glacier Pilots (where Nolan Ryan and Mark McGuire played summer ball while in college) and the Anchorage Bucs baseball teams are hometown favorites. Innumerable recreational sports activities are available year round—everything from softball to rock climbing to triathlons in summer and alpine and Nordic skiing, snowboarding, snowmachining and ice climbing in winter."

Current student, 8/2003-Submit Date, September 2004

Housing at UAA is nice. There are three residence halls, East, North and West, and two apartment complexes, Main Apartment Complex, known as MAC, and

Templewood. North is usually reserved for first-time freshmen. East, West and Mac are for the rest of the student body, while Templewood is for those 21 and over. There are about 900 or so students living on campus. If you live in one of the residence halls you have to enroll in a meal plan. There are three plans: five, seven and nine meals.

You can drive, walk or bike to the main campus to get to your classes. The campus is over a mile long from one end to the other. Driving can be somewhat of a hassle, especially in winter. There are usually not enough parking spaces for everyone to be happy. There are plenty of bike racks to lock your bike to if that is your preferred method of transport.

Students pay various fees when they enroll. Many of these fees pay for facilities on campus, including several computer labs, course specific labs (math lab, a reading and writing and language labs). There are several locations on campus where you can eat—the most popular being the Commons where students living on campus dine and the Lucy Cuddy Center, which has everything from Chinese to pizza to a salad and soup bar. When students sign up for a meal plan, they get "points" that work like cash. They can go to various places on campus, get food and pay for it using those dining points. It's an easy and convenient way to get something to eat when you're on the run between classes.

Alumnus/a, 8/1997-6/2003, June 2004

Student housing is very swanky. You won't ever have to share a room with anyone. You live in an apartment that is either shared with one other person or three other people. You can decorate within means, you can have a refrigerator, microwave and TV. You have ethernet in all rooms, too. Every building for housing has a computer room that is open 24-hours. Access to the dorms is secure with desk attendants in the lobby. Elevators and entry doors are card-key encoded. Visitors after 10 p.m. are supposed to be escorted by residents, but the community is so small that if you know everyone it's never a problem. Laundry is the cheapest in town.

 Social Life

Current student, 8/2003-Submit Date, May 2006

Lots of social things to do. Always parties and University of Alaska Anchorage gatherings at bars and restaurants. There are also a lot of get-togethers for shows and famous performers. My favorites are always the movie screenings of famous pictures when they put movies in the movie theatre for students to watch. There is also always some kind of group meeting where you can get free food and prizes. They also have a lot of Greek clubs and sororities. There is always something to do at the University of Alaska Anchorage.

Current student, 8/2003-Submit Date, September 2004

There are various social events that go on during the year. The biggest one is the Great Alaska Shootout, where about a dozen men and women's basketball teams compete for the top prize. This event is usually held around Thanksgiving, give or take a couple of days. Other notable events include Mainstage Theatre productions in the arts building, dance and music recitals, two art galleries, and various other sponsored events that are put on for students.

> **UAA says:** "The UAA Concert Board has also brought some very exciting entertainment to campus, including Bright Eyes and B.J. Novak from NBC's *The Office*. For more information on upcoming events happening at UAA, visit http://www.uaa.alaska.edu/campuslife/activities/."

There are six Greek organizations; three sororities and three fraternities. There is usually recruitment for these groups each semester. There are dozens of clubs to join at UAA—if there isn't a club that you think should exist, form the club yourself. A lot of the social life takes place in the dorms and off campus.

> **The school says:** "UAA currently has two sororities and one fraternity officially registered. There are also plenty of opportunities for students to get involved on campus with the more than 110 registered student clubs and organizations."

A good place to find restaurants is in downtown Anchorage, which is only about a 15-minute drive away. The city has all kinds of eating establishments, from Chinese to American to Italian, and in all price ranges. One popular place to eat is Red Robin, which has great burgers and nachos. There are also several bars around the city that cater to those 21 and over.

A non-campus event that gets plenty of attention is the Iditarod, which is held in downtown Anchorage usually in February. Dog mushers from all over the country come to the city to participate in "The Last Great Race." The race beings in Anchorage and ends in Nome, a small village on the Northwest coast of the Bering Sea. The race commemorates the journey made by mushers in the early part of the 20th Century; the town of Nome was stricken with diphtheria, and the medicine needed to save the town couldn't reach the town in time by train, so mushers gathered together and raced to Nome with the serum to save the town. (Seen *Balto*? Yup, that's Alaska!) Also popular for the outdoorsy type is the Iron Dog, which is the world's longest snow machine race, running from Anchorage to Fairbanks and back to Anchorage. So if you can't find a life on campus, you sure can find it in Anchorage!

> **The school says:** "In addition to having many things to do around Anchorage, UAA also offers many exciting entertainment opportunities, including A Cappella Festivella, Homecoming, Haunted Halloween Fun Night, No Big Heads Art Show, Campus Kick-Off, Freshmen Convocation, Martin Luther King Civil Rights Celebration and much, much more."

 The School Says

Located in the heart of Alaska's largest city is the University of Alaska Anchorage, the state's largest post-secondary institution. The campus is nestled in the middle of a greenbelt, surrounded by ponds, lakes and wildlife, and is connected to a city-wide trail system perfect for students' active lifestyles.

UAA is comprised of six teaching units at the main campus: the colleges of Education, Health and Social Welfare, Arts and Sciences, Business and Public Policy; the Community and Technical College; and the School of Engineering. There are four community campuses: Matanuska-Susitna College, Kenai Peninsula College, Kodiak College and Prince William Sound Community College.

The University is fully accredited by the Northwest Commission on Colleges and Universities. In addition, many of the colleges and academic programs are individually accredited through professional licensure organizations.

UAA offers many career pathway programs featuring associate's, baccalaureate and master's degrees, as well as vocational and professional certificates in more than 150 major study areas, including: arts, sciences, business, education, human services and health sciences. Through UAA's comprehensive curriculum, students learn practical job skills and develop a strong educational foundation that prepares them for graduate or professional schools and the workplace.

A Greek system enhances the campus environment, enriches students' lives, encourages scholastic achievement and is a positive force in the community. In addition, the University offers more than 110 clubs and organizations for students to get involved. UAA also hosts the annual Carrs/Safeway Great Alaska Shootout, featuring some of the best men's and women's basketball teams in the nation.

Workforce Development

UAA and its community partners are working together to create efficient programs to help meet the needs of high-demand career fields in Alaska. The University is focusing on workforce development and career pathway programs to help students better understand the many opportunities that are available to them at UAA and beyond.

Read all of Vault's College Surveys at www.vault.com/college–get complete surveys on 100s of colleges and universities, expert advice on applicaton essays and more.

VAULT CAREER LIBRARY   19

Collaborative Programs

UAA students enjoy an array of collaborative undergraduate and graduate programs offered between the University's campuses and other universities, including Biochemistry and Molecular Biology; Biological Sciences; WWAMI Biomedical Program (Alaska's Medical School); Clinical Community Psychology; Computer Science; Marine Biology; Engineering; and Speech and Language Pathology.

The Alaska Native Science & Engineering Program, for example, is a national model designed to effect a systematic change in the hiring patterns of Indigenous Americans in the fields of science, technology, engineering and mathematics. There are nearly 300 students studying at four participating universities in three states, along with students from two community colleges and also 40 different high schools around the Pacific Rim.

Established in 1971, the Alaska WWAMI Biomedical Program is a collaborative medical school, established through an agreement among the University of Washington and the states of Wyoming, Alaska, Montana and Idaho. Each year, 20 certified Alaskans begin their medical education in this collaborative program.

For more information about UAA visit www.uaa.alaska.edu.

Arizona State University

Undergraduate Admissions
P.O. Box 870112
Tempe, AZ 85287-0112
Admissions phone: (480) 965-7788
Admissions fax: (480) 965-3610
Admissions URL: www.asu.edu/admissions

 ## Admissions

Current student, 8/2006-Submit Date, May 2007

The admissions process is not lengthy or really scary at all compared to other colleges. You can fill out the application online in about 20 minutes and there's no essay portion, which is fantastic. Once you finish the actual application, pay the application fee depending on whether you're an in-state or out-of-state applicant, and send in your test scores and transcripts, you should get a letter letting you know if you've been admitted. They'll send you a bunch of letters in between too, letting you know what you still need to send in and what they've already received, which is nice.

Alumnus/a, Barrett Honors College, 8/2002-12/2006, May 2007

My advice would be to apply early. Get your application in by early fall of your senior year, that way you have a better chance at getting offered a scholarship. The application for admission to the Honors College included an essay and two letters of recommendation, along with test scores. The Honors College is quite selective, only taking students with high test scores and GPAs, with a focus on National Merit, National Hispanic and National Achievement Scholars.

> **The school says:** "The application process for the Barrett Honors College is a separate application process from the general university application process. Students should apply for admission to ASU first, and then apply to the Barrett Honors College. Barrett highly encourages students to submit letters of recommendation with their application for the honors college."

Alumnus/a, 8/2002-12/2005, January 2006

Their philosophy is that school should be open to everyone and if they can prove themselves freshman/sophomore year and get the grades, they can then apply to their certain programs. Just because it is easy to get in, only about half graduate. For the W.P. Carey School of Business, if your SATs and high school GPA are high enough you get a direct admit to the program, as long as your GPA stays above a 3.4. Otherwise, to get into the program, the admissions process is just like applying all over again, but a lot tougher. Reason being that the business program is trying to be recognized in the Top 10 nationally, and so far is doing an excellent job promoting themselves.

Current student, 1/2003-Submit Date, November 2005

I filled out the standard application and received an acceptance letter pretty quickly afterwards. The school in general is not extremely selective because it is so big. Everything at Arizona State University is very fast and efficient, as they need to handle so many students. I did not have to interview or write essays to get into Arizona State University in general. When I decided that I wanted to major in finance I had to apply to the W.P. Carey School of Business Finance program, which is very selective and I had to write a couple of basic essays along with my application.

Current student, 8/2002-Submit Date, December 2005

The admissions process to ASU is one of the easiest around. From what I remember I had to fill out an index card with my name, address, class rank and test scores, and from there I think I eventually submitted a transcript. I am from out of state and was also applying to schools like Stanford and California, so ASU admissions was a joke by comparison. Hardly a GPA requirement, no essays, recommendations or interview are necessary. I guess admissions is tougher if you're not in the top half of your high school class, though. On the

up side, if you are more scholastically motivated, ASU offers up tons of scholarships (which is why I'm here, it actually ended up being cheaper than an in-state school), which again require no separate application. National Hispanic and National Merit Scholars get a free ride, no questions asked. In-state students get even more scholarship opportunities.

> **ASU says:** "All students applying for admission must submit an application and the appropriate application fee. Students must also have their transcripts and test scores sent directly from the appropriate entities to the university."

 ## Academics

Alumnus/a, Barrett Honors College, 8/2002-12/2006, May 2007

The Honors College requires 36 credit hours of honors courses: 18 lower-division credits, and 18 upper-division credits. Freshmen are required to take HON 171 and HON 172 (The Human Event) their first year. The Human Event is a literature course with discussion and composition elements attached. It is taught by honors professors and class sizes are small, with a maximum of 25 students per class. Each Human Event professor has his/her own area of expertise, so read the professors bios before signing up for a class. The Human Event is challenging and eye-opening, and sets the groundwork for your future classes at ASU. This class will teach you how to read critically, and write a research or literary analysis paper. In order to fulfill the rest of the honors credits, it is necessary for students to take general courses that they would take for their major for honors credit. This is done by setting up an agreement (Footnote 18) with the professor on an extra project that will be done to earn honors credit. This allows you to create a rapport with your professor. My advice is to choose classes you are especially interested in to take for honors credit, and get them done well in advance of your senior year. Another way to earn honors credit is through the Barrett Honors College summer study abroad programs. These are Human Event-type classes held in settings like London, Paris, China, and Athens, to name a few. This is a great way to earn honors credit while seeing the world. The capstone of the honors degree is the thesis project. This can be a 50-page paper, or a research project, and so on. It all depends on which concentration you choose to research. My advice is to start early on choosing a topic and researching. Choose a thesis director who is organized and knowledgeable in your field.

Alumnus/a, 8/2002-12/2005, January 2006

Freshman year classes range in size from 25 to 500 students (yes, 500). Those classes are actually quite fun since they put a good teacher to handle it. Probably like most schools, grades are most of the time determined by the teacher. Ask around and you can get a teacher who gives nothing lower than an A, while your friend will take the same class and the class average will be a C. Once in the actual business program, quality of teaching becomes much better. However, teacher grading still varies a lot from one teacher to another teaching the exact same class. There are lots of administrators and at times it is still hard to find out who to talk to for what. Teachers' office hours are very good and sometimes it seems like they wish more students came in to talk. The workload is very reasonable for lower division classes, actually is almost too reasonable and not enough. The upper-division classes' workload is almost proportional to the grade. If you don't do the work, most likely you won't get the grade you were hoping for. There were some bad teachers, but the outstanding teachers far outshined the bad ones.

Current student, 8/2004-Submit Date, December 2005

ASU is a state school that focuses on RESEARCH, meaning it is NOT a teaching institution. However, most of the professors and instructors I have had have been excellent. They have been knowledgeable, personable, enthusiastic about the topic and available for questions during office hours or via e-mail. The grading system has recently changed to the +/- scale. This only benefits overacheivers because now if you get a B- your GPA is lower—whereas before it would have gotten the full three points of a B.

Workload for classes is such that unless you are highly organized and do not work, I do not recommend taking more than four classes at a time. Summer school and winter session are great alternatives to taking 15+ units a semester. Once you have achieved junior status, the length of time spent on assignments and extent of work expected increases. It is important to be ready for this. What you could get away with the first two years in regards to procrastination or not putting full effort in, will no longer work. Don't do what I did and learn this the hard way.

Alumnus/a, 1/2003-5/2005, September 2005

The academic program is very flexible, you can choose which area you want to concentrate on. The basic classes are a must, but even with those you get some options on what you want to take for general education classes. The professors are great, most of them with impressive credentials and still active in their field with research or publishing. It is a research facility and school so the material you learn is not just ancient history, but stuff that is being developed at this moment. The workload really depends on the professor's style and type of class. The exact sciences classes are more objective and therefore the workload is less. In those classes I usually just had to do the reading and pass the test. In the humanities field you get a lot more work because there are more papers to write and homework to turn in that affect your grade. There is usually a lot more reading with those classes.

The grading system is usually well disclosed by most professors so you know how to get the grade you want. However, I did have classes where I had no clue what my grade was until the end of the semester. The grade system used to be just ABCDF but now the teacher can use a +/- system according to his preference. Some professors let the class choose. General education classes are usually quite large and you do not get one-on-one time. You've got to take care of yourself because no one is going to come after you asking why you are doing so poorly. Once you get into the upper-level classes, they get smaller and you get more attention, but those classes fill up quickly, so you've really got to pre-register. Overall, I would say the academics are very good.

Current student, 1/2006-Submit Date, September 2005

ASU offers a wide range of majors. Many have national recognition; the Walter Cronkite School of Journalism is one of the best journalism colleges in the nation. Because it is not an overall challenging school, workload will vary drastically, depending personal choices. The minimum credit-hours required to remain a full-time student is 12 per semester. However, a more accelerated track toward your degree will require studiousness and discipline, but not at the expense of a rewarding college experience.

Current student, 1/2001-Submit Date, October 2004

Many of the academic aspects of the program depend on the college your major is in. I can speak only for the Ira A. Fulton School of Engineering and, specifically, the Computer Science and Engineering degree.

This program really gives you a bargain if you're an in-state student. Tuition is less than $3,000 a year and the program is rated in the Top 50 in *U.S. News*. Plus the department is really open and supportive, I've made good friends with professors and have benefited from small classes throughout my degree. The grading is fair. Most classes are curved but rarely to the student's disadvantage. It's competitive but not brutal and professors are willing to be flexible in emergencies, most of the time. The projects are relevant and interesting and you have the opportunity to give feedback and review your professor each semester. Workload is reasonable. If you do all the work, you get a B most of the time. If you pay attention when you do all the work, you'll get all A's.

Employment Prospects

Current student, 8/2002-Submit Date, December 2005

Job prospects for engineers are phenomenal here. One great thing about ASU is that it may not be as prestigious as schools like Berkeley or Stanford, but at the end of it all we come out with the exact same degree for way less money. With that in mind, the location of ASU provides for awesome internship or co-op opportunities right in Phoenix, with Medtronic, Honeywell, Boeing, Intel and Motorola within driving distance of the school. Utilities like APS and SRP also provide great job prospects for students.

Another plus of ASU is that what we lack in prestige we make up for in size, so tons of employers recruit at ASU looking for the top students in each class. I am a Chemical Engineering major, so many of our grads go on to work for local utilities or local companies like Intel, but others routinely accept positions at companies across the country, such as BP, P&G and Boeing, among others. Promising engineering grads are in great demand for the most part; I had a job offer on the table this past October, and I don't even graduate until May!

Internships obviously help a lot in the job hunt, and frequently people who had internships with companies end up working there after graduation. Alumni relations are much more useful if you get involved in an organization like Society of Women Engineers or IEEE, which are very strong on campus and offer great networking opportunities. Otherwise our alumni are notoriously apathetic.

On-campus recruiting can be limited for engineers (schools like Michigan and Illinois are much more popular with big-name recruiters), but events like the Career Fiesta and Super Recruiting Day are great resources; that's how I got my job offer in October. We do have internship programs and an engineering internship office, but the single best way to get a job is by being proactive and applying to lots of companies online. I worked for Boeing for three years and that's how I first got my foot in the door. Overall, it is important to start thinking about what you want your résumé to look like as early as freshman year. Leadership and work experience, especially engineering related, are invaluable when it comes time to look for a real job after graduating. A good GPA doesn't hurt either!

Current student, 8/2002-Submit Date, February 2006

ASU as a whole has a very good reputation with employers locally, with certain programs and degrees having much more widespread regional and national respect. ASU has a committed and respectable Undergraduate Career Services department that is easily accessible and very knowledgeable on any type of employment opportunities. Every fall the Career Services department hosts a week-long Career Fiesta where about 150 major employers come to recruit students graduating that December and the following May, as well as students looking for internships. There are also smaller events throughout the year with much more focused audiences for internships only for example.

I can specifically speak the most for the business programs. The W.P. Carey School of Business is the only college that puts on its own career fair event for only its students. The event is early in the spring (known as Spring to Success) generally hosts 75 to 80 employers seeking business students in particular offering full-time jobs for May graduates, as well as students seeking summer internships and co-ops.

Business school grads can find jobs ranging from general management trainee positions with run-of-the-mill companies and industries, to serious rotational programs with Fortune 100 companies, to Big Five accounting positions; and supply chain management and information systems majors are regularly placed to consultant positions with companies like IBM and Deloitte. The alumni network is not apparently active on campus, at least at the business school except for aggressive honors students who seek it out. Also, at times the very top students in each business program choose to look outside of the campus recruiting at ASU for top companies and positions. I have heard mixed reviews from these students as to whether the Business School Career Center has helped them or been useless. Many students find the best jobs through their involvement in student organizations (over 30 exist within the business school).

Quality of Life

Current student, 8/2006-Submit Date, May 2007

I lived on campus this past year and it made my freshman year and whole first experience with college so much better. Not having to commute to class makes ASU feel like so much less of a job and more of a whole experience. While the dorms are loud and cramped at times, I am so glad I made the decision to live there. Just being in Tempe is awesome—it's such a cool town that is growing

Read all of Vault's College Surveys at **www.vault.com/college**—get complete surveys on 100s of colleges and universities, expert advice on applicaton essays and more.

VAULT CAREER LIBRARY 23

tons both in size and in culture. Arizona State's Tempe campus is beautiful. Considering how many students are on this campus, it is fairly compact and always clean. The facilities are great, I love this aspect: because there are so many students, ASU has literally everything right on campus from an Olympic size pool to a travel agent to a bowling alley. Dining is decent I hear it's changing completely, but I don't think it's bad. I mean, there's a lot of variety and a Jamba Juice, which is really all I need. As for crime and safety, the biggest crime on campus is bike theft. Retrospectively, that's pretty good I think. We have a blue light system on campus, which means that there are several large poles with blue lights on them and yellow call boxes which are linked directly to the police line. So if you're ever in danger, you can run to one of these boxes (there are over 300) and press the button and speak directly into the box, which is directed to Tempe police. But honestly, this campus is very well-lit, and with this many students, there is always something going on right on campus. I've never felt unsafe on campus.

Alumnus/a, 8/2002-12/2005, January 2006

Quality of life is good overall. The main problem ASU suffers from is parking. It is almost, or it actually is, impossible to find a parking spot unless you have a decal. Even if you have a decal you still might be parking a good 20-minute walk from classes. ASU has opened up a whole new academic village for 2,000 freshmen. The later you apply for housing, the worse housing you will get. All housing on-campus is on campus and at most can be a 10-minute walk (three-minute run if you are late for class).

ASU has around 40,000 students on its main campus, the main campus is only a one mile by seven mile area. So it is a mini city in itself. With this comes the horrible lunch hour. The on-campus facilities can't handle everyone and frankly the food isn't good at all, not enough healthy options. But there are TONS of places to eat that are just a five- to 10-minute walk.

> The school says: "This fall ASU has launched several new dining options, including additional dining options across the Tempe campus. Additionally, all ASU campuses offer a variety of meal choices to meet student's personal preferences."

Current student, 8/2002-Submit Date, December 2005

Car break-ins are pretty common, but otherwise I have never felt unsafe here. Even as an engineer walking home at 4 a.m. from the computer lab, I have never felt threatened at all. For those who do want company walking out to their car though, Safety Escort Service is available to golf cart you wherever you want to go on campus until about 1 a.m. every night. Very nice when you need to get from South Campus to the North Campus frats on foot. Overall, when the awesome weather in Phoenix is factored in, ASU is a pretty nice place to be, especially in December!

> Regarding safety, the school says: "ASU offers a fully accredited police department, safety presentations and workshops and more to serve the university community. To learn more about safety at ASU, see www.asu.edu/police."

Alumnus/a, Barrett Honors College, 8/2002-12/2006, May 2007

The Honors College complex is a dorm community almost exclusively for honors students. It is a great place to meet people of the same academic caliber. The honors dorms tend to be quieter, as many people are busy studying. The courtyard area tends to be a fun place for students to congregate, with the volleyball court and Barrett Bistro nearby. The only problem is that there is no apartment style living area for upper-classmen. That will all change when Barrett moves to its new complex in fall 2009.

 **Social Life**

Alumnus/a, Barrett Honors College, 8/2002-12/2006, May 2007

Because ASU is such a large school, there really is something for everyone. There is a plethora of clubs on campus that are eager for fresh faces to join. Whether you want to do student government, community service, or music—there is a club for you. Mill Avenue, located right off-campus, is a great place to go out at night. Mill is full of great bars and restaurants, and tends to be full of students Thursday through Saturday nights. Don't miss some of the great

events at Homecoming. The parade is always fun, and the Lantern Walk is a must!

Alumnus/a, 8/2002-12/2005, January 2006

Today, January 24th, 2006, it is 75 degrees outside. ASU is a very active lifestyle setting where everyone does something outside whether that be playing ultimate frisbee or just getting a tan. ASU has its main street called Mill Ave, which is a pedestrian-friendly street with all its bars, restaurants and clothing stores. Bars are everywhere, and the good thing is that almost all of them are very good. There is a no smoking law in Tempe for restaurants and bars, which in my opinion is awesome. Students will go to Mexico, California or Vegas during any weekend of the year to get away from studies. Vegas and L.A./San Diego are hour-drives going the speed limit, and Rocky Point, Mexico (the West Coast's Cancun) is about a six-hour drive.

Current student, 8/2004-Submit Date, December 2005

Social life at ASU is great! This is why many people attend this university. The Greek culture is strong, the bars are plenty and the parties are endless. If you want to go to parties and meet a ton of people join either a sorority, fraternity or the snowdevil club. The snowdevils are a club for snowboarders, skiers and the like. They plan discounted trips throughout the year and throw big parties for every occasion imaginable. Also just a 20-minute drive away is the ever-glamorous Scottsdale nightlife scene. Take the Indian School RD exit off the 101 to Drinkwater Rd and you'll find several nightclubs with dress codes and stage dancers. Also there are several restaurants, bars and pubs along Scottsdale road in that area.

Current student, 1/2006-Submit Date, September 2005

I find ASU students to be warm and welcoming. ASU students provide a socially relaxed environment, with many interesting, easy-to-know people. While there are many opportunities for interaction, the dorms are the best place to live in a student's first year. They offer the densest population of new people, exponentially increasing one's chances of meeting someone with whom he/she has a true connection.

The ASU athletics programs are some of the best in the country. And no matter what you think of school spirit as a high school student, things are completely different in college. I never liked school events or even school spirit until going to ASU. The events are full of opportunities to spend quality time with new friends, as well as a ton of fun within their own rights.

Current student, 1/2001-Submit Date, October 2004

The men and women here are absolutely beautiful, and they dress for the sunshine. Keep in mind that we're only 10 miles from Scottsdale, AZ, rated one of the best places to live by Forbes.

 The School Says

Arizona State University is building a new model for American higher education, one that is an unprecedented combination of academic excellence and broad accessibility.

ASU serves more than 63,000 students across four unique campuses in metropolitan Phoenix. Through each campus, ASU provides a cluster of related degree programs and a distinct student experience—including a campus modeled after Oxford architecture where students study in professional and liberal arts programs; a polytechnic campus focused on experiential- and project-based learning; a city campus that marries academic study with public purpose; and one of the country's largest single campuses, where students study in research-based academic disciplines and is home to the NCAA Division I Sun Devils' athletic facilities.

ASU offers more than 250 academic programs and a learning environment where personal expression is valued as much as research and discovery. 188 freshman National Merit Scholars are members of the fall 2006 class, ranking third in the nation among public universities. ASU has a distinguished faculty, whose roster includes recipients of prestigious national and international honors, including membership in the National Academy of Sciences and National Academy of Engineering and a recipient of the 2004 Nobel Prize in economics. Barrett, the Honors College at Arizona State University, was named among "The Best in America" by *Reader's Digest*. ASU's student scholars have won Goldwater, Truman and Rhodes Scholarships and have received Fulbright Grants and Marshall Scholarships for postgraduate study.

Nationally-ranked colleges and schools, award-winning academic programs, top faculty, student resources and support services position students for success and make an ASU degree a valuable investment. Students benefit from resources including libraries with holdings that rank in the Top 20 among public institutions, studios and performing arts spaces for creative endeavors, and unsurpassed state-of-the-art scientific and technological laboratories and research facilities. Students have access to extensive career services and a network of more than 260,000 alumni who span the realm of careers and can be found at the heights of corporate life, science and public service. Resident tuition consistently ranks in the lower quartile nationally, and non-resident tuition in the lower half. Because ASU is committed to expanding access, it is continually expanding programs and providing financial aid to as many qualified students as possible through scholarship, grant, loan and Federal Work-Study programs.

For admission to ASU, freshmen must meet graduation, aptitude and competency requirements. In general, high school graduates must meet at least one of the following aptitude requirements: high school GPA 3.0 (4.0 = A), high school class rank top 25 percent of class, ACT minimum 22 Composite Score (24 for non-residents), SAT Reasoning Math and Critical Reading Score of 1040 (1110 for non-residents). ASU considers applicants who have a 2.5 to 2.99 GPA or are in the top 26 to 50 percent. Some colleges/schools at ASU have higher admission criteria. Check the Admissions web site for detailed admissions requirements on specific degree programs.

Northern Arizona University

Admissions Office
Box 4084
Flagstaff, AZ 86011-4084
Admissions phone: (888) 628-2968 or (928) 523-5511
Admissions fax: (928) 523-0226
Admissions e-mail: undergraduate.admissions@nau.edu
Admissions URL: home.nau.edu

 ## Admissions

Current student, 1/2005-Submit Date, February 2007

Admissions is very straightforward. Fill out the application, pay your money and be accepted. They are trying to boost enrollment and are not competitive. You don't have to write essays or anything like that.

Alumnus/a, 8/1998-5/2001, August 2006

I was admitted to the University as an international student. However, I did not work with the International Students Office. I worked with the Office of Undergraduate Admissions. I worked with Undergraduate Admissions office and I had a great experience. Very responsive, friendly and attentive to prospective students' needs.

Current student, 8/2002-Submit Date, June 2006

Northern Arizona University made it easy for me to be admitted. First of all, during my junior year of high school I was selected for one of the many scholarships they offer. Back in that time, I did not know much about online applications, so I filled out a paper application. It was only a few pages long. I sent it in and was mailed a response within a couple of weeks. The application itself was easy with no essay questions. Some responses were necessary for housing options. I received the admissions packet, which was informative and helpful. It was well organized and listed several ways to contact them for help. My advice for prospective students would be to fill the application out online. If you are planning to live on campus, don't forget to fill out the application for student housing. I recommend doing research prior to your senior year if possible, as showing interest often leads to early scholarships as it did in my case. Other than that, it is a breeze!

Current student, 1/2002-Submit Date, November 2004

The admissions process was probably significantly different for me than for your average student who was just graduating high school. I began school when I was 30 years old so the university considered me a "senior student" meaning that I am "nontraditional" due to my age. I had no interviews to get in and SAT and ACT scores were not considered in any way (again because of my age). I did have to supply my high school transcripts and vaccination records, although my high school transcripts were not considered for my admission either. Upon entering, I was not informed or advised about the available programs for "nontraditional" students and I was not advised there were special retention programs for first-generation college students.

The admissions process was a mess, as my last name is an odd spelling and they kept "fixing" the spelling of my name, so, when all was said and done, I had five spellings of my name and two student identification numbers. It was a complete mess as nothing matched so they said they didn't have my transcripts or my financial aid information. That took quite a while to straighten out.

Read all of Vault's College Surveys at **www.vault.com/college**—get complete surveys on 100s of colleges and universities, expert advice on applicaton essays and more.

VAULT CAREER LIBRARY   25

On top of all of this, they required me to attend orientation for new students and pay $100 for it. This orientation centered around learning how to live away from your parents. I was 30 years old, I had been away from them for quite some time. So, while being a "senior student" made my acceptance easier, it did not get me out of the annoying new-student crap. The entire process was generally a huge pain and I was not impressed with their lack of organization in the admissions offices.

One piece of advice for incoming students is to get a map of the campus and study it and carry it with you. If you need to do anything with any of the administrative offices (financial aid, admissions, registrar and bursar), they are usually not in the same building and should some odd situation arise, chances are you will be sent to another office and upon arriving there they will send you somewhere else. So know where you are going and where things are. It will save you a lot of time. If you are planning on using financial aid you must set up a bank account for disbursement. They used to mail your checks to you or you could pick them up before the semester began but now they will only do direct deposit.

> **The school says:** "Orientation is not mandatory, although students are encouraged to attend to become familiar with the university and enroll in courses. Students can pick and choose which orientation sessions are most beneficial for them. Of the offices noted in the last paragraph of this survey, the admissions office is the only one not in the same building as the others."

Current student, 8/2003-Submit Date, April 2004

It was a fairly simple process. Because of my high school grades, I was accepted in without a problem. There was really nothing to it. There was no interview, and I don't believe we had to write an essay. As long as you are within the top 10 percent of your high school class, or received good scores on either the SATs or the ACTs then you are as good as in.

The harder application process comes when you have to try and get into the desired program you want to study. Certain programs require you to audition, interview and pass tests to get into the program. For instance the nursing and education programs are very prestigious and are very hard to get into.

 **Academics**

Current student, 1/2005-Submit Date, February 2007

Lower division was very easy and straightforward. I always got the classes I wanted. In the business building, scheduling was tricky at times. Sometimes you want to take a few classes in one semester but are unable to due to scheduling conflicts. I especially had this problem in the summer session. MGT 300 and FIN 311 were two classes that many other classes required as pre-reqs. The school had the bright idea to offer both classes over the summer at the same time. There are many scenarios where you would want to get these principles classes out of the way so that you can work on a dual degree or additional certificates over the year when they offer classes that are unavailable during the summer. In the business school, all professors had real-world experience and were able to coach us on how to enter the finance field.

Alumnus/a, 8/1998-5/2001, August 2006

I loved the fact that NAU is a smaller school. The student population is about 15,000 students. Major classes in the accounting program had only 15 to 30 students. Professors provided personalized attention and care to each student. Accounting program is very strong; it would not be an exaggeration to say that it is probably the strongest in the state of Arizona. We had quite a few people who scored the highest on the CPA exams on their first sitting! All was thanks to the great professors in the School of Business. Workload was very manageable. Professors were willing to work with students around their schedules.

Current student, 8/2002-Submit Date, June 2006

Because Northern Arizona University is a smaller school, the student-to-teacher ratio is amazing. I was never in a class with more than 30 students unless it was an introductory class in which there were probably only 100 students. This also makes it easier to get into popular classes. I need the one-on-one that you get from smaller classes, so it was easy to talk to professors and to get their help. In

my freshman year, I felt that my workload was sometimes a lot due to the fact that my intro classes always had a lot of homework. I recommend rationing those classes out between the years you are there.

Current student, 1/2002-Submit Date, November 2004

The academic programs at NAU are excellent and the professors can't be beat. They know their stuff and are bound and determined to make sure you know it, too. The workload, at least to me, seems rather easy and slight. The grading is extremely fair in my experience and usually extra credit work is not given. Advising isn't always the greatest and that seems to depend on what your major is. Many times, you will hear from students whose advisors told them to take certain classes only to find out later they didn't need to take them at all. However, the biggest problem with advising is that most students haven't bothered to find out what is required or to read the catalog. As for classes, of course there are the standards that every freshman needs to take: English, Pre-calculus and others.

> **The school says:** "We also have opened the Gateway Student Success Center to provide a more consistent advising experience for new students. Not all students have to take Pre-calc, but they do have to take math."

The labs for sciences fill up very quickly so if you are planning on taking one, don't wait until the last minute and hope to get an override to get in, it's just not going to happen. Also, if you are in a lab, you need to show up the first week. If you don't show up the first week, you will be automatically dropped out of the lab to make room for those who couldn't get in. Most labs are taught by other students under the supervision of professors.

> **The school says:** "The comment regarding labs taught by students is true for science labs, less true for others. The 'students' teaching the labs are graduate students."

These TAs are a valuable source of information and are extremely good at what they do. To be quite honest, if you have difficulty in a class, see your lab TA first to clear it up before you see your professor as the TAs are students too and they seem to explain things much better and more down-to-earth. They are a wonderful resource that many students don't use. There also are two learning assistance centers that have tutors for virtually any class that you may need them for. Most of them are wonderful and extremely helpful.

The university also has a number of people and programs that you can see or go to to help you with study skills, organization skills, and test-taking skills. The professors are topnotch although extremely underpaid. A huge concern on campus among students is that our professors may leave for higher-paying jobs. We are very fond of them and would like to keep them. Many of the professors are involved in research projects in a huge variety of areas. There are opportunities for students to work on research with the professors and even freshmen have the chance of being published. All the professors I have had are extremely concerned with student progress and seem to do whatever they can to help you. Just make sure that you ask—they aren't psychic!

There are a number of classes available online or as distance programs. There are satellite campuses all over the state and I think I've heard that one quarter of Northern Arizona University's students are distance program students. They also have a number of sister schools across the world so that students have student exchange opportunities. They have a number of special programs for students with disabilities and will offer special testing areas for those with learning disabilities. You can be tested for a disability on campus with the counseling and testing center.

> **The school says:** "About one-third of the students and one-fourth of the credit hours are accounted for by distance program students."

Current student, 8/2003-Submit Date, April 2004

I enjoy the academic lifestyle here at NAU. The program that I am in is very competitive but gives undergraduates the opportunity to do more work than they would get into if there were also a graduate school. The classes are mostly small ranging from 15 to 25 students, in most cases. So the professors have more opportunities to spend with individual students.

Based on what year you are it is fairly easy to get all the classes you want. The popular classes are much simpler to get if you are an upperclassman. The grading is pretty fair. The professors are good for the most part, but many leave for better pay. The workload is fair, as well.

Employment Prospects

Alumnus/a, 8/1998-5/2001, August 2006

Many potential employers from Phoenix, Tuscan and out of state, regularly attended campus events and were heavily involved in on-campus recruiting and internships. All types of jobs and internships were available to good students: public, industry and government accounting.

Current student, 1/2002-Submit Date, November 2004

Northern Arizona is well known for its engineering program and for its Anthrax research. I am told its hotel and restaurant management program is also pretty well known, so these probably hold some prestige with employers. As for on-campus recruiting, there is quite a bit. However, it seems that all the recruiting centers around the same degrees every semester.

There seems to be only an average amount of diversity as far as recruitment available. For example, I am working on a double major of biology and criminal justice with a chemistry minor and plan to go in to forensics when I graduate. I have yet to see anyone in that field come to NAU for recruiting.

As for internships, I do know that there are a number of choices and opportunities for students as long as you are following a traditional path. With my choice of degrees, I don't have many choices. I can do a biology internship or I can do a criminal justice internship, but I cannot get a forensic internship through NAU. This is rather odd if you consider that we have a pre-forensic chemistry program and it offers forensic internships but since I'm not a chemistry major, I have been told that I will have to find internship opportunities on my own.

One good resource for students is called e-recruiting, and that's available (usually for a fee but this semester it's free) at the Gateway student center. They will help set you up with mentors and career exploration.

Current student, 10/1999-Submit Date, September 2004

Every semester, the school conducts job fairs designed to help students find jobs. There is a strong requirement for work experience in many fields. Many of the professors come from careers, not merely academic positions. Some colleges are more active in helping place graduates but most departments are willing to help if you make the effort to enquire.

Current student, 8/2003-Submit Date, April 2004

Career services is really good at getting students into internships and setting up career days for students to see the options that are out there. Whether you will get a good job or no job at all also depends on what program in which you are getting your degree. Most business and criminal justice students find many internships that will help them further their careers.

Alumnus/a, 8/1992-6/1996, June 2004

NAU's School of HRM is a favorite with recruiters, including Hilton, Hyatt, Darden Restaurants (Red Lobster, Olive Garden), Marriott, Four Seasons and Ritz-Carlton. There are more internship opportunities than students to fill them and most internships lead to job offers. Jobs have been plentiful, even during economic downturns. Students who want to travel can easily do a semester abroad with exchange partners. Many jobs are in desirable resort areas.

Quality of Life

Current student, 1/2005-Submit Date, February 2007

Life is laid-back and very slow. The town is small and the workload is easy. Jobs don't pay well, but there really isn't anything on which to spend much money. Flagstaff is a place to enjoy nature and that's free. Oh yeah, the weather is very stable. It gets kind of cold in the winter but the cold really isn't that bad considering how dry it is here. Whether you like to smoke cigars in Sedona or cruise the back roads on your motorcycle, there is plenty to do if you look.

Current student, 8/2002-Submit Date, June 2006

I will be honest here when I say that cost of living was high in Flagstaff. I actually think that living off campus was much cheaper. Housing was good though, although rent was high. The campus was clean and located in the mountains, which made for happy, mountain campus students. I often read the crime report in *The Lumberjack* newspaper and sometimes laughed because the crime they reported was actually not crime. Bike theft is big, but I think that happens everywhere. Overall, I would say that NAU is a very safe and happy place to be.

Current student, 1/2002-Submit Date, November 2004

There is a very good quality of life here in Flagstaff. It is an expensive town in which to live and the wages do not compensate well; however, the diversity in this town can't be beat. We are a mountain community with a large number of activities available for nature lovers. There are a number of cultural events on campus for students to attend, but they aren't very good about getting the word out. Many students don't find out about some events until they are over, especially those students who live off campus. There is a variety of housing available: on campus, alcohol and smoke free, coed and fraternities.

Crime on campus happens, as it does everywhere, but I think it is pretty minimal considering the number of students who live on campus. The largest number of police calls are for drunk students, very few assaults. NAU has its own police force made up of state police and it has a very good response time. There are emergency boxes all over campus and they are strategically placed so that while standing at one box you can see another one. The boxes are wired directly into 911. They also have volunteers who escort students across campus at night; you just call a number and the people come and walk with you where ever you may need to go.

> **The school says:** "The campus police aren't 'state' police, but they are trained and certified through the state law enforcement academy."

There is a gym on campus that students can use. While it's certainly not huge, it does have pretty much anything you may need. It also has a rock climbing wall, racquetball courts, volleyball courts and basketball. There is a track outside of the gym and farther down there is an obstacle course if you are into that. There is an Olympic-sized pool in the aquatic center but you have to pay extra to use that—it's not included in the tuition as the gym fees are. The aquatic center sometimes hosts movies called "movies in the pool." The first movie they showed was *Jaws* and recently showed *Pirates of the Caribbean* for students floating on tubes in the pool. NAU, due to its high elevation, hosts a number of Olympic athletes looking for high altitude training. There are also counselors on campus for virtually any issue you may have.

NAU also has its own medical center that can handle an extremely wide variety of medical issues and emergencies. You can either buy health insurance from the school at the beginning of the semester that allows you to go to any doctor or you can buy insurance at the health center for about $100 per semester. There is also a pharmacy on campus that gives great discounts on meds.

> **The school says:** "Northern Arizona University's Fronske Health Center provides students accessible, convenient, cost-effective, quality, primary health care, as well as preventive and public health services. Clinical staff consists of three board-certified family practitioners, a psychiatric nurse practitioner, two nurse practitioners and one physician assistant. Lab, x-ray and pharmacy services are available on site. Fronske Health Center offers two campus health plans that cover specific services offered by the health center. The basic plan costs $45 per semester; the extended coverage plan costs $95 per semester. Students also may purchase major medical group insurance from a private vendor."

Current student, 10/1999-Submit Date, September 2004

The facilities provided by the university are small but of good quality. There are 24-hour computer facilities and fast, simple, free Internet connections in all the residences and in some classrooms. There are also wireless capabilities in various buildings. Flagstaff is a small town and the campus is near the downtown area. I believe that it is a safe place to live, on or off campus. There are occasional problems but not beyond what would happen in any college town.

Read all of Vault's College Surveys at **www.vault.com/college**—get complete surveys on 100s of colleges and universities, expert advice on applicaton essays and more.

VAULT CAREER LIBRARY   27

Current student, 8/2003-Submit Date, April 2004

The residential life and student life offices are very interested in making the quality of life better for NAU students. They send out a quality of life survey every semester in the hopes of making NAU a better place for the students. We have our own police department on campus so the crime rates are quite low. The RAs on campus are also amazing at helping to lower the crime and enhance safety as well as helping with the quality of life. The dining services are always trying to get better but really have not made too many strides toward succeeding!

Social Life

Current student, 1/2005-Submit Date, February 2007

All the fraternities live in the same dorm and are governed by the school via RAs. The nightlife is very lame—then again, I came from a city that had more than 60,000 people, so I might be biased. There are a lot of intramurals and other activities to do on your own. For example, Mount Humphreys is the tallest place in Arizona. There are plenty of other activities like snowboarding, rafting, mountain climbing and drinking down by the creek with your friends as you slide down the rocks. The city has good proximity to Vegas, Phoenix, Santa Fe and Albuquerque.

Current student, 8/2002-Submit Date, June 2006

My social life was with my friends. We would find our own fun. My friends and I often had fun hanging out at the NAU gym playing racquetball. It was a workout but also super fun. We also liked to go jacuzzi hopping at the local hotels. While I was actually there in Flagstaff, I was not old enough to go to the bars until after hours, which most bars offer from 1 to 4 a.m.; if you are 18 or older you can attend. We did that too. There are always things to do in Flagstaff, which provides for a great social life.

Current student, 1/2002-Submit Date, November 2004

The Greek system is pretty large, and there are a number of organizations for students to join. Hazing is not tolerated in any fashion. A few fraternities have their own houses, although none of the sororities do. This is because of an old archaic law that is still on the books that states if so many women live together in a house, it's considered a brothel. It sounds stupid yes, but for some reason it doesn't bother anyone and people actually enjoy telling visitors why there are not sorority houses.

The downtown area is full of any kind of bar you could hope for, the wild, the quiet, live bands, whatever you want. Many of these are combined with restaurants. On campus, they have after hours activities, free new release movies, poker and game tournaments, movies in the pool, contests and more. I know nothing about the dating scene as I am married. I know many of the students favorite places to go are the two Irish pubs in town; they are usually standing room only on the weekends much to the chagrin of the tourists. Tequila Sunrise is also a favorite, that happens on homecoming, the day of the game. I'm not sure what time the bars open but it's extremely early and students drink tequila sunrises all day until the game, that tradition began (I think) over 50 years ago.

There are a number of social, community service based, academic and cultural groups and organizations on campus for students to choose from. Anything from Prism (a gay and lesbian advocate group) to the Young Republicans can be found on campus so virtually anyone is able to find a group to suit their tastes.

> The school says: "19 of the 22 fraternities and sororities are housed in Mountain View Hall near the center of campus. This hall serves as the campus focal point for Greek life and activities. Mountain View Hall houses students from eight sororities and 11 fraternities in suite-style rooms."

Current student, 10/1999-Submit Date, September 2004

There are many different campus groups that are active on the campus and in the community. There is a Greek system that seems well developed but not overwhelming in size or character. The social scene is that of a small town—a few bars, a lot of familiar faces and occasional frustration at lack of activities. The social scene is much more active for those over 21 as there are few facilities open that are accessible to underage student. There is a historic downtown area of several blocks that has several bars ranging from Irish pub, sport bar, lounge, hip hop dancing, pool hall, wine, two local breweries on the hippy edge and several other bars. There are plenty of places to go to and the patrons tend to visit many of the establishments in one night. I recommend Uptown Billiard, for smoke-free drinking and pool, Charly's for conversation, dancing and live bands, the Moggollon Brewery for fresh brews and random music acts, and Flag Brew for dancing and sitting on their patio.

University of Arizona

Admissions Office
PO Box 210040
Tucson AZ 85721-0040
Admissions phone: (520) 621-5078
Admissions e-mail: appinfo@arizona.edu
Admissions URL: admissions.arizona.edu

Admissions

Alumnus/a, Business, 8/1999-5/2003, June 2007

The admissions process at UofA is a rather standard undergraduate admissions process: fill out forms, take the SAT and apply for financial aid. There were no interviews and if you are an Arizona resident, you stand a very good shot of being accepted. The business school, however, has its own admissions process, which you undergo as an undergraduate sophomore. Current grades are taken

into account, and you go through a panel interview with three to five alumni and school officials.

Alumnus/a, 8/2001-5/2005, February 2007

I was an in-state student with a good GPA and good SAT scores so I didn't have to write an essay or give an interview at all. Based on GPA and scores alone I got scholarships that paid for about two-thirds of my living expenses and tuition. Three friends who chose engineering got free rides.

Alumnus/a, 8/2001-12/2005, June 2006

Admissions into the University of Arizona, when compared with most California schools, is almost laughable. However, the UofA does retain its standards. Most in-state students already know that they are guaranteed admission. So for all of the out-of-state students, there are a few things they need to know. I had a 3.4 GPA and an 1190 SAT, so when I applied to 15 schools throughout California (where I'm from) along with the University of Arizona, I felt confident that I would be accepted at least to a few California colleges. I got into the University of Arizona—one out of 15 universities in my home state. Although I was bummed, this upset would be one of the luckiest and best things to happen to me EVER.

For those with a 2.4 GPA and an SAT below 1000—hope is not lost. My younger sister who had this less than stellar record was denied admission her freshman year in 2005, but after one year at the local community college, where she only received nine total units and maintained lower than a 1.0 GPA, she applied again and was accepted for the fall of 2006. How did she do it? Persistence, for one, and requesting a "comprehensive admissions review" in which a committee of admissions counselors thoroughly review certain qualifications of candidates who might be rejected only because of poor numbers. The committee looks at the character of the individual, takes into account extracurriculars, work and volunteer experience, and other various factors. My sister was diagnosed very late in her education (during her senior year of high school) with Attention Deficit/Hyperactivity Disorder (ADHD). I believe that this circumstance, which she informed the admission committee by providing thorough documentation from her doctors, as well as effectively conveying her struggles and triumphs in some of the optional short answer questions and her personal narrative.

For those with learning disabilities, the UofA has one of the best learning disabilities resource centers/programs on any university campus in the nation—SALT (Strategic Alternative Learning Techniques). You must apply to the SALT program separately from the UofA and it does cost extra money each year, but many students with learning disabilities benefit from their note-taking, tutoring and counseling students. In order to be even considered for admittance into the SALT program, you must be diagnosed by a doctor who has reached his conclusion after you have undergone comprehensive testing for learning disabilities and you must provide thorough documentation, which the SALT center judges with strict guidelines.

Current student, 8/2001-Submit Date, September 2004

The admissions for the University of Arizona is not terribly difficult. There were no essays or interviews. The only thing that is very selective is the honors college, and even that you can petition into if you feel that you should be in it but were not automatically enrolled. The Eller College of Management is an entirely different story. There are several requirements for admission. Students generally apply for upper-division standing their fourth semester, provided they've taken the prerequisite coursework and maintain the minimum 2.75 GPA. There is a fairly gentle interview to get into the Eller College and an entrance exam, but most shouldn't have much trouble with those provided that you paid attention in accounting, business math and economics. By the way, Eller College of Management on the whole is big on ethics. If you screw up, you're out.

Alumnus/a, 8/2000-5/2004, August 2004

The admissions process at UofA is very easy. If you meet one of their four criteria you are automatically accepted. This is changing, but it is one of the easiest admissions processes in the country and no essay is required. As usual, a good SAT score and GPA can make it even easier to get in and possibly be selected for one of the several scholarships available.

Alumnus/a, 1/2001-5/2004, February 2005

I began at the University of Arizona as a non-degree student and eventually transferred in after one semester. The process was not terribly difficult. I filled out the transfer application, sent in the required documentation, and kept in contact with the admissions office. The most important aspect is to keep in contact with the admissions office. The university receives thousands of applications and they are prone to simple human error (items are lost, or misplaced). No interview or essay was required of transfer applicants at the time of my application. The university's selectivity is competitive, especially for non-Arizona residents. Given the current climate and financial difficulties the university is facing, selectivity may be at an all-time high, as far as non-resident students are concerned.

Current student, 8/2003-Submit Date, September 2004

I went through the admissions process the "easy" way by transferring from the local community college to the university. There was a class called Transfer Strategies that I took that walked me through the process. I didn't have to write any essays or go to any interviews. All I did was fill out the application and sent in my high school and college transcripts.

Current student, 8/2000-Submit Date, October 2003

The University of Arizona admissions process is a rather standard and straightforward process, it is becoming increasingly more selective over recent years and out-of-state students are put to higher level of standards than in-state students. The Eller College of Management has its own admissions process during your sophomore year, during this process you have some lengthy applications, essays and an interview process to determine your admittance into the upper division levels of the business school. This process is also becoming more and more competitive and the average admission standards are rising each semester for the last few years.

Academics

Current student, Business, 8/2004-Submit Date, November 2006

Once admitted into the Eller College, the coursework is rigorous but rewarding. The first semester in the business college (typically, first semester of junior year) you work with a team on a business plan and presentation. Some of the classes are quite difficult but the teachers are fair; if you put in the time, you will get grades that reflect it. Of the Eller professors and the classes outside of the business college that I have taken, I have been very pleased. The professors in Eller really care about their students and mean it when they tell you to come in to their office hours and get help.

Alumnus/a, Business, 8/1999-5/2003, June 2007

Classes can vary dramatically in quality, depending on the professor and the college in which it is being taught. The Eller College of Management generally has good to great quality in courses and professors. MIS and Entrepreneurship are the more coveted and prestigious majors within the business school, although recently the finance and accounting majors have gained clout, as well.

The Eller College of Management undergraduate program ranks consistently within the Top 25 undergraduate business school programs nationally; and the MIS and Entrepreneurship programs rank in the Top Five nationally.

Alumnus/a, 8/2001-12/2005, June 2006

It is the ultimate school for people whose interest in academics is neither over-obsessive nor nonexistent. This makes the UofA a truly noncompetitive atmosphere. Even though the UofA maintains this laid-back atmosphere, the academic curriculum is far from lacking. The classes are not impossible, but they are challenging, and for the most part, students receive a first-rate education. What is certain: the student only gains as much as he/she puts into his/her education.

Registration for classes is based on seniority, honors, disabilities and student ID number. I was able to take every class I wanted to take, but sometimes I was forced to take classes at hours I did not want or during later semesters. For the most part, I got the classes I wanted—but not without fighting for them. If for some reason you are not up at 7 a.m. during the five-hour window you are allotted to initially register for classes online, and you miss signing up for a popular course or gen-ed requirement—you become the crazy drop/add student. You run around from class to class begging professors to sign your drop/add form.

Lower-division courses, mainly gen-eds, are made up of 300-person lectures that break out one day a week into sections of 25 people. Coming from a senior class of 160 at a private Catholic high school, I loved these classes. Upper-division courses, mainly your major and minor courses, are much smaller and many are given in an open-discussion setting, which, by the time I figured out what my major was, I enjoyed even more. Choosing a major and receiving advice/help from the university regarding this matter, or almost any matter, is basically nonexistent. In a school of 30,0000—everything operates bureaucratically and you can and will get lost. At the UofA it is just as common to graduate in December, after four and a half years, as it is to graduate in May, after completing the standard four years. If you are undecided—find help and find help early! A lot of people say you don't have to decide until your junior year—but they are wrong. Decide early, so you don't end up with all lower-division credits that aren't worth anything to graduate.

I have had bad professors and I have had amazing professors—you'll find that anywhere. The workload is average and the library is definitely a social scene—more crazy things happen there than at any of the parties going on only a mile

Read all of Vault's College Surveys at www.vault.com/college—get complete surveys on 100s of colleges and universities, expert advice on applicaton essays and more.

VAULT CAREER LIBRARY   29

away. Grading is average—I usually got better grades than I deserved. Beware of your grades and academic probation during your freshman year because UofA does have one of the largest freshman drop-out rates. Many people have a little too much fun and forget that they are actually there to learn.

Current student, Business, 8/2001-Submit Date, September 2004

If you can, get into the Honors College and stay in it. It will allow you to register following only athletes and seniors. This especially important if you want into the best gen-eds, as they tend to fill up quickly.

The MIS program is ranked third in the nation, but don't let that scare you, the classes aren't excessively difficult. Once in the Eller College of Management, the core classes are auto-enrolled for you, so you won't have to worry about not getting into the classes in which you're interested. The professors are very nice and good at teaching. However, some courses will be taught by grad students whose abilities run the full gamut. This is a program where you can get a 4.0 if you work hard at it; however, it is not extremely common. Your first semester in the business school will be the busiest semester of your entire life, however, it too is workable and once you get done with it you'll have a very workable courseload (12 to 15 units). Electives are not terribly hard to get into and, in my opinion, are often more interesting than the core classes.

Entrepreneurship was by far my best experience at the University of Arizona, it is very hands-on and results-driven. You must have attained advanced standing in the business college to apply to add the entrepreneurship major. It is extremely competitive, but if you get into the program, you won't regret it. Don't count on getting in unless you have at least a 3.0 GPA and leadership experience. They are really looking for people who are on the right track to starting their own successful business venture. Also, going into the application process, you should already have a feasible idea for a new business because they will ask you about it. Also, plan on working with your entrepreneurship team (whom you will choose) over the summer over on the feasibility study.

The mentality of the program is that once you're admitted into the program, you start working on your business plan. Your first semester in the program will be built around creating the business plan and VC presentation. You should plan on meeting outside of class more than you meet in class. You will be very busy and at times it can be stressful; however, this will actually make you value the program even more. At the end of the first semester you will give a mock VC presentation that will be a big portion of your grade. The second semester is a lot less stressful. The focus is on starting your company, you essentially will simulate the first couple years of operations throughout the semester. You will also have the opportunity to travel and compete with your business plan. At the end of the semester you will compete with the other UofA teams marking the end of the entrepreneurship program.

Current student, 8/2003-Submit Date, September 2004

The professors whom I've had so far have all been excellent. They are very knowledgeable in their fields. Getting into classes hasn't been a problem, but some classes are only offered in one semester (either spring or fall) and that can cause problems. Grading has been fair as far as I've seen. Many professors offer extra credit papers or assignments to help cushion test grades.

Employment Prospects

Alumnus/a, Business, 8/1999-5/2003, June 2007

Upon graduation employment opportunities varied in location and opportunities. Your major, GPA and internship experiences usually drove you toward or away from certain opportunities. A majority of the positions at the career fairs are from employers who come from Arizona or Southern California. Generally speaking, going east for job opportunities can be a little difficult, unless you look to start with a national company and transfer to another location.

Both the business school and the university at large have a diverse and active campus recruiting center that has employers regularly interviewing and recruiting for both internships and positions post-graduation. Some of the more well-known employers include, Gallo Wines, IBM Global Business Services, Accenture, PricewaterhouseCoopers, KPMG, Deloitte, Microsoft, Boeing,

CEMEX, CIA, Protiviti, Intel, Honeywell, Motorola, Pulte and various other real estate (both commercial and residential) developers and investment companies.

Current student, 8/2004-Submit Date, November 2006

Each school year there are two career fairs that feature many of the Fortune 500 employers that come to UofA to recruit the top students. A large majority of them also hold information sessions on campus to tell about the jobs they are there to hire for as well as have job interviews through the campus Career Services. The campus Career Services, free to UofA students, helps students to tweak their résumés and search for jobs for which they qualify. Of the recruiters I have spoken to, most believe UofA to be a great place to recruit from and believe that good quality students come from the college.

Alumnus/a, 8/2001-12/2005, June 2006

Most recent graduates are hired through on-campus recruiting through Career Services. The range of major companies is extensive and a number of grads obtain entry-level positions with various real estate and building companies, such as Pulte, Coldwell Banker and CB Richard Ellis. Other grads rely on the extremely helpful alumni network, which is accessible also through Career Services.

Current student, 8/2001-Submit Date, September 2004

The campus and business college both do a lot to ensure that you have good opportunities for getting jobs, internships and co-ops. There are both campus-wide and business school career services departments. The two programs by the campus-wide department, Transitions and Connections, enable you to search for current job opportunities, campus recruiting schedules (both interviews and info sessions), and a whole booklet of more services. There are also résumé and cover letter checks, workshops, mock interviews and one-on-one meetings available by the campus-wide department. The business school offers many similar opportunities plus more; however, they are only available to business and pre-business students, I believe. They are also working on a library of career-related books and materials.

The University of Arizona name carries great prestige with nation-wide companies, however, we are generally not recruited at by the elite few that look only at the Top 10 business schools in the nation. A few of the companies that recruit very hard (in my opinion, I cannot speak for them) at our business school are Cintas, Gallo Vinery, Honeywell, General Mills, Philip Morris and more.

There are also several career fairs on campus both by the UofA and individual colleges and student organizations. But these are pretty typical for colleges.

Quality of Life

Current student, 8/2004-Submit Date, November 2006

When choosing between UofA and other schools, the UofA environment brought me here. It has a campus feel—students are always on campus playing football, throwing the frisbee or sitting around with their friends. Even in my third year, it still seems like I am in a movie from time to time. It is gorgeous, and a little too good to be true. I even have friends from the gorgeous state of Washington who believe the campus to be spectacular. The dorms truly have improved in the past few years; the new dorms being put in on campus are spacious and also in a perfect location. Recently, the campus put money into building the integrated learning center that is open almost 24/7 and has computers and rooms for group meetings. The UofA is very accommodating to students and it shows that they are trying to make us happy. Dining on campus is actually great, there is a large focus on health with there being multiple delis on campus and also smoothie shops. Off-campus housing is not as great, while there are nice apartments all over, they are not as safe as I would like. I have never been scared or felt unsafe, but cars are often stolen and broken into. I recommend buying a security system for your car.

Alumnus/a, 8/2001-12/2005, June 2006

The campus is beautiful and clean. The dorms are almost all brand new and have top-of-the-line facilities. The majority of freshmen live on campus in the dorms and after freshman year, most of the student body moves to off-campus living, such as fraternity/sorority houses and/or the amazing, brand-new apartment complexes with personal gyms, tanning beds, pools, coffee shops, late night dining and fashion boutiques. Along with utilities, this is all included and only total to about $350 to $400 per month. Another great thing about living in Tucson as a starving college student—life is cheap. Cost of living is unimaginably cheap, especially when compared to my friends at USC, who live in cramped two-bedroom, nasty apartments for $900 per month and go out to bars with $30 cover and $10 Jack and Cokes. My senior year, I lived in a seven-bedroom house, with my six best friends, which had two kitchens, six bathrooms, and huge living and eating area, and massive bedrooms—and closets, all for only $450 a month, after utilities. Going out to bars four nights a week would be expensive anywhere else, but Tucson. $2.00 drinks every night and two for $2.00 Tuesdays keep bar tabs below $20 almost every time.

Current student, 8/2001-Submit Date, September 2004

If you are an undergraduate student planning on living on campus, plan on getting an apartment after your sophomore year. I was a resident assistant for a year, so I've seen the ins and outs of residence life. In my experience, I've only seen one person get into a dorm after his/her sophomore year. The old dorms are typical dorms, but the new dorms, La Paz, Puente and others, are beautiful and very spacious. However, you will pay more for these newer dorms. The campus is very nice, however, there always seems to be construction of some sort somewhere—it's been this way since I've been here (three years) but hopefully they'll be done soon. We have a beautiful student union and bookstore (supposedly the biggest in the nation at one point). There are numerous on campus resources for students (Kaplan, copy center, post office and health center).

Tucson is not the best place in the world at night, and you should not plan on walking alone, even on campus. The area is well lit in the major traffic areas and the police support is sufficient, but it's just not a good idea anyway. If you're going to get an apartment off campus, try to stay north of Broadway, as south of Broadway tends to be the bad area of town. The biggest problem with the UofA is parking (by far) if you want to park in zone one (outside parking all over campus) you will probably end up on a huge waiting list. Garage permits are better, but still not great (and are four times more expensive). As for dining, don't worry about it. There are plenty of places to eat, but if you're looking for "healthy" food, your options are reduced to the Hillel Center's Oy Vay Cafe and the main student union's Cactus Grill, and expect to pay more.

Social Life

Current student, 8/2004-Submit Date, November 2006

The social life here is quite fun. I spent my entire freshman year at parties with friends. However, there are also people who do not spend every night partying. After my freshman year, I calmed down to start working more on school and I have found friends who live that lifestyle, as well. There is never a night that you cannot find a party to attend. The Greek life on campus often hosts parties and with the houses on campus, freshmen, sophomores, juniors and seniors are often there. If you are coming to the school without knowing many people, I think that it is a great idea to get into the Greek life; I am not in it, but I think that for some people it really helped them fit in. I recommend doing your research before and trying to get an idea from an upperclassman about the reputation for the sorority/fraternity since it is often hard to tell if you are just meeting them going through recruitment. There are hundreds of clubs on campus in which to get involved. There will be events held on campus just to learn about them and to see where you fit in.

Although I am not 21, the bars on University Drive are going to be a great deal of fun in a few months. There are multiple bars that after 10 p.m. Thursday through Saturday are the place to be. One of the best things about UofA is the school spirit, whether we are playing horribly in a game or fantastic the UofA fans are right behind the athletics and always ready for fun. There are many events on campus for those who don't like sports, as well. In the Union, there are improv troops that perform as well as a theatre that often has pre-screenings of movies and TV shows for $3 or less. I went to a pre-screening of the first three episodes of Season Two of *The O.C.* for free and got gifts from Victoria's Secret. I did not have to do anything other than show up early.

Alumnus/a, 8/2001-12/2005, June 2006

The University of Arizona has a reputation for having a social scene that is so fun that *Playboy* magazine refuses to rank the university in their annual list of the Top 10 party schools because they feel it is unfair "to rank professionals in a group of amateurs." I think that my beloved alma mater has this reputation because, in a town where there is not much to do, coeds become extra crafty when planning events and parties. The weekend starts on Tuesday, one of the biggest nights of the week, where the bars are crammed full of your 200 best friends. Most start out at Trident and end the night at Dirtbags. Fake IDs are common and fake ID tickets are even more common (it's a rite of passage almost—but NEVER use a fake ID at Dirtbags or Frog & Firkin). Go at least once to the Meet Rack and let the owner, "God," take you to the sex room and if he gives you a keychain, don't put it on your car keys, it's guaranteed bad luck for a DUI. Go at least once to The Buffet, but you can only make it there if you drink all night long because it doesn't open until 6 a.m., and if you do make it—be sure to order a sportsman from the old lady bartender and don't forget to take a coaster as a souvenir and proof that you made it. Dirtbags may be "a part of growing up" but they don't put enough alcohol in their drinks and the staff and bouncers there have little tolerance for fighting, stiffing your tab, or generally pissing them off and you could land yourself onto their temporary banned list or their "banned for life" list—which sucks because everyone and their mom goes there, literally, on graduation, at 6 a.m., in their caps and gowns, and UofA seniors binge with their parents at Dirtbags and stumble through the commencement processional.

Walking through the UofA campus might seem a little intimidating to those who are not used to seeing the most beautiful tanned people with great hair, Louis Vuitton bookbags and, the ultimate UofA must-have, oversized designed sunglasses. However (and this is the best part about UofA students), you come to realize that these seemingly superficial people are all some of the most open, down-to-earth, and plain chill people, who turn out to be the best friends you are guaranteed to have for life. What makes the UofA a non-stop party is the fact that in Tucson, the sun is always shining. Up until the week of Thanksgiving, pool parties are planned every weekend and bikinis and board shorts become more of a staple in one's everyday fashion than t-shirts. Oh, and the only pair of shoes you will ever need is a pair of rainbows or havaianas—wearing flip flops year-round is one of the things I'll miss the most. The Greek scene is pretty big at UofA, but not in the exclusive, hazing kind-of-way. More like narrowing down your first 55 best friends by the second day of school. As the years go by, you become friends with other the older and younger girls in your sorority, as well as girls from all of the other sororities. There isn't a major competition between the sororities or between the fraternities. Everyone just gets along and has fun with one another. I would strongly recommend going through fall recruitment, even if you think that you are "not the type," because you will make tons of friends and you'll realize that the clique-y and bitchy stereotypes that sororities and fraternities have at some other schools hold absolutely no truth in the UofA Greek system.

Read all of Vault's College Surveys at www.vault.com/college—get complete surveys on 100s of colleges and universities, expert advice on application essays and more.

VAULT CAREER LIBRARY   31

University of Arkansas at Little Rock

Office of Recruitment and Retention
2801 South University Avenue
Little Rock, AR 72204-1099
Recruitment and Retention phone: (501) 683-7302
Recruitment and Retention e-mail: recruitment@ualr.edu
Recruitment and Retention URL: www.ualr.edu/recruitment

 ## Admissions

Current student, 8/2000-Submit Date, May 2005

Admissions is quite easy. You can apply through the UALR web site. Some advice is to check and make sure all your information is in, such as different transcripts if you are transferring, immunization records, applications and other documents. UALR is not exclusive, there are no interviews or essays.

Current student, 8/2003-Submit Date, April 2005

The admissions process was a cinch! I went in to interview with an admissions officer and she handed me a blank application across the desk. I filled it out and handed it back and was offered a scholarship right there on the spot. She then called and set up appointments with the department chairs of the fields I was researching. I got a red carpet treatment and was sold on the school.

> **The school says:** "UALR no longer has paper applications. The application is online at http://boss.ualr.edu."

Current student, 8/2004-Submit Date, April 2005

The admissions process for UALR is completely open; thus, everyone who applies is accepted.

> **UALR says:** "To be admitted, you must have a 21 on the ACT and a 2.50 high school GPA."

However, for the Donaghey Scholar's Program, admissions is a bit more challenging. It is very important to be academically successful in high school if you wish to attend college for free. The Donaghey Scholar's Program at UALR is an interdisciplinary program that focuses on advanced reading and writing. When applying, you complete a brief two-page application, write two essays, attach a transcript and two teacher's recommendations. If the admissions council is pleased with your application, they will contact you for an interview with the program's director, a Scholar's Program professor, and a current Scholar. Selectivity into the program is based on overall academic success, not solely grades or test scores.

One great thing about the admissions process into the Donaghey Scholar's Program is that test scores do not play a decisive role in your acceptance. They are a factor influencing your acceptance, but again, they are not vital to getting in or not. As a first-year Scholar, I have really appreciated all of the material I have learned thus far. I am benefiting greatly from this program at UALR.

Current student, 8/2002-Submit Date, April 2005

Students are able to fill out an application online, and should request to have transcripts, all test scores and other applicable information to the school, in a timely fashion, either before or shortly after submitting the application. There are numerous scholarships from the institution, the State of Arkansas and other organizations that students need to inquire about at the time of the application. Most of these scholarships are based on academic merit, test performance and undergraduate and graduate program of choice—some are based on the above along with overall financial need.

Current student, 1/2004-Submit Date, April 2005

Admissions to the university requires a transcript and test scores. Admissions into the Donaghey Scholar's Program requires a transcript, test scores, awards and honors received, and two essays. 50 applicants are then selected for interviews with the director of the program, one faculty member and one student.

Current student, 8/2004-Submit Date, April 2005

My admissions process seemed very easy. I took a tour and talked to the tour guide extensively about attending, he was very helpful. He then helped me in giving me an application for the scholarship that I now have. The scholarship application was very simple, and I didn't expect to receive it. The tour guide kept in contact with me letting me know my status in the scholarship running, it really helped keep my stress level down. After I received the scholarship, I had to come get advised and tell my advisor what I was majoring in, and basically do the rest myself. It was very simple. I would suggest to anyone planning to attend to go on a tour or visit the web site. Get to know the scholarships that are available to you.

Current student, 8/2003-Submit Date, April 2005

The admissions process is very easy. The entire application is online and only the applicant's transcript, [shot records] and test scores are required in addition to the online application. There are no essays. There are, however, a few honors programs like the Donaghey Scholar's Program (requires two essays, separate application and interview) that have more requirements.

Current student, 8/2004-Submit Date, April 2005

The admissions process was pretty easy. I went online and filled out an application. UALR notified me by mail saying that I was accepted. My advice for trying to get into UALR is not much. The school is great. Do not wait until the last minute to apply. The earlier that you get notified about being accepted, the earlier you can register for your first-year classes. All of the staff is nice and will help you pick the best classes for your busy schedule. Because UALR is mostly a community school and everyone drives there, they offer a wide variety of classes to fit your schedule.

> **Regarding admissions, the school notes:** "The process for application is all online; there are no more paper applications."

 ## Academics

Current student, 8/2000-Submit Date, May 2005

There is a great student-to-teacher ratio. Most classes are small and the majority of the core classes are offered both day and night. Professors are easy to get a hold of and very approachable regarding help. We also have several labs that assist students in writing papers, math, research and language, either for free or at low cost. Workload is very reasonable. Most classes incorporate a balanced mix of groupwork, individual papers, tests and presentations.

Current student, 8/2003-Submit Date, April 2005

Most of the professors are easy to approach and available to the students. The program is perfect for me. I have plenty to keep me busy, but I'm not going to go crazy under stress and huge workloads. Registration is all online and quite simple once you've figured out how the system works.

Current student, 8/2002-Submit Date, April 2005

The classes are usually equal to the credit earned. In other words, the workload is not unreasonable. The workload is much heavier if you're a Donaghey Scholar, however. One of the most encouraging things about the professors at UALR is that every now and then, you will find a professor who earned his/her degree at UALR. That increases my confidence that this education will be worth something when I get out. The only problems I've run into, as far as getting into classes, is with online classes and Spanish classes. Many students want online courses, and even though UALR offers more each term, they fill up fast.

Current student, 8/2004-Submit Date, April 2005

The classes at UALR are great. The professors are really concerned with teaching students and helping them understand the material fully. Grading is different in every class, some more difficult than others, and the workload depends on the class, as well. As a prospective biology major, science classes tend to be more challenging than most other classes.

Current student, 8/2002-Submit Date, April 2005

The academic environment at UALR is extremely conducive to individual enrichment and achievement. Class sizes are relatively small, especially in the upper-level undergraduate and graduate-level classes, which allow students to freely interact with peers and professors alike. The Donaghey Scholar's Program is an intensive scholarship and honors program about which prospective students should inquire. Donaghey Scholars attend classes that are geared toward individual strengths and allow students to excel in many different disciplines. The academic faculty and staff are superior, and are extremely open to students' ideas and input while continuing to adapt to the changing needs of the university community.

Current student, 8/2004-Submit Date, April 2005

The class quality is good; there aren't many classes that won't keep you interested. It is extremely easy to get popular classes, the only thing you might have difficulty with is the time you want them. Grading is done differently in each class, but is usually pretty fair, and if you are having difficulty with a particular class you can always drop it. Each professor has a different teaching style, try to talk to someone who has already had the particular class you need to see which professor is the best. Workloads are very different in each class, depending on the difficulty of the class and how many hours you are taking.

Current student, 8/2004-Submit Date, April 2005

I love my classes. I was never lucky enough to have someone tell me which professors to take and not to take. I always had to guess and hoped for the best. The quality of the classes is incredible. The professors are extremely nice and willing to help. They all give you their office hours so that they can give you extra help if needed. Most professors grade very fairly, and the rest grade on a curve. I will not lie, most of my professors give hard tests, but if you go to class, pay attention and take notes they are no problem. Some studying is required, but that is expected. My workload is about in the middle. I take 14 hours a semester, as required by my scholarship. At 14 hours, though, my days do not begin before 10 and end by one. That is pretty easy, I would say.

Current student, 1/2004-Submit Date, April 2005

Donaghey Scholar's Program is a very selective program that accepts only 25 students per year. They must be full-time students. The workload is high in reading. Class sizes are small and are usually taught by a team of professors. Scholars also have the opportunity of preferred registration and are allowed to register for classes before other university students.

Current student, 8/2004-Submit Date, October 2004

The university is divided into colleges, such as the College of Science and Math and many others. The university has its individual requirements. Based on the student's major, he/she is placed into a college, where he/she is given other requirements. The quality of the classes is outstanding because the university is centered in a city and has one of the top leading medical schools. Since the university supports the medical school, University of Arkansas Medical Sciences, the courses are challenging and demand a high level of responsibility of the students.

Getting into classes is not very hard; however, the selection of classes undergoes a particular process. The seniors in the university get first choice of what courses they want to take. From there, the selection goes down grades. Freshmen choose their courses during the summer. However, majority of the students are able to get the classes they want at the times available. If a student wants to withdraw, add or change classes, the student does so on the university's web site and is instantly changed. Grading is based on the instructors, who are chosen based on their knowledge and their teaching skills. The workload is demanding of time and more challenging than what is commonly seen. This is due to the businesses that surround the university and the medical school.

Employment Prospects

Current student, 8/2000-Submit Date, May 2005

They have career and internships scattered throughout the year, so if you miss one there will be another one later on. Since we are located in a metropolitan area close to downtown, prospects for employment are quite high. Our career and counseling services are excellent in that they help you in terms of résumés, internships, employment, as well as different experiences such as seminars around the country. Almost each major has an individual job and internship fair that focuses on the individual major. Our school is well-connected to the non-profits and businesses in Little Rock. I personally had a chance to intern at the Clinton School of Public Service as well as Heifer Project International.

Current student, 8/2003-Submit Date, April 2005

As a speech pathology major at UALR, getting into graduate school really hasn't been an issue with most graduating seniors. Being taught by some of the grad school professors in your undergrad courses allows you a "leg up" in the process. There are people on campus whose actual job is to assist you in contacting those that can help you further. It's really up to the student to tap into those resources.

Current student, 8/2002-Submit Date, April 2005

Graduates from UALR have gone on to lead the state in public service, either through the state legislature or federal government, and continue to improve the communities in which they live. The College of Business at UALR is exceptional, and the graduate MBA, MPA, MBA-PhD programs have led many students on to careers with large companies in Arkansas such as Alltell, Acxiom, Tyson Foods and Wal-Mart. Our cyber college provides students with excellent career opportunities in computer technology and networking, while the education department has been singled out as one of the best in the nation. Many companies, both in-and out-of-state, frequent the campus in order to recruit new and upcoming graduates and the office of campus life frequently coordinates job fairs for students to attend while they are on campus. The newly-opened Clinton Presidential Library, the Heifer Project, the Arkansas Historical Society, Easter Seals, the United Way and the soon-to-be-opened Mexican consulate all provide opportunities in which students will value the education and networking contacts that they receive through the university.

Current student, 8/2004-Submit Date, April 2005

Every semester UALR puts on a job fair. Tons of employers or representatives of their businesses come on to our campus and tell anyone willing to listen about their company, job, or opportunities they provide. Many companies have internships, and they are all listed.

Current student, 8/2004-Submit Date, April 2005

Employers look forward to UALR graduates each year. The professors in certain departments set up internships for the students to attend that correspond with the class. Usually after the students have finished their schooling they are welcome to go back to the company where they had their internship for a full-time position.

Quality of Life

Current student, 8/2000-Submit Date, May 2005

Housing is easy to obtain near school as well as in the suburbs of the school. It's currently hard to get in our residence hall, but UALR is adding new halls and apartments to take care of this situation. There are several restaurants within walking distance of the campus, as well as a newly renovated cafeteria and student lounge within the school. I always feel safe walking around campus by myself, even to a night class. UALR police, as well as the student patrol, are always very visible.

Current student, 8/2004-Submit Date, April 2005

There is available housing for students. There are many available facilities for the students' enjoyment. There is a large dining facility with many options. There are security guards on staff at all times. There is also crime notices sent out through the e-mail service to warn students of dangers.

Read all of Vault's College Surveys at **www.vault.com/college**—get complete surveys on 100s of colleges and universities, expert advice on applicaton essays and more.

VAULT CAREER LIBRARY   33

Current student, 8/2002-Submit Date, April 2005

Although many university campuses within metropolitan areas have problems with crime, UALR is a remarkably safe campus with an excellent public safety department that is ready to assist students with any problem, around the clock. There are safety phones located all over the campus that directly connect to the Office of Public Safety, and students are alerted about any events that may have occurred which may put their safety in jeopardy. The facilities at UALR are updated frequently and, just last fall, the entire dining room area in the Donaghey Student Center was remodeled. The Donaghey Student Center boasts a fitness center with indoor swimming, cardio equipment and fitness machines, as well as a bookstore, dining areas and cyber cafe. At this time there is only one dormitory; however, construction has recently been started on a new housing facility. The campus also has a state-of-the-art facility for basketball, graduation ceremonies and other events.

> **The school states:** "The state-of-the-art basketball arena (the Stephens Center) opened in fall 2005."

Current student, 8/2004-Submit Date, April 2005

Quality of life is great around the campus. UALR is located in the heart of Arkansas. You can travel to at least two other main colleges in less than two hours, and other large cities such as Hot Springs are less than an hour away. UALR also has many activities on campus for their students. The Greek life is great, and there are many religious groups to join. Crime around the campus is at an all time low right now. If anything does happen, and it is reported, every student receives an e-mail on his/her school e-mail account that tells exactly what happened, where it happened, and what they are doing to prevent it from ever happening again.

> **The school states:** "UALR has opened a new residential facility on campus in addition to the already existing facility, which opened in fall of 2006."

 Social Life

Current student, 8/2003-Submit Date, April 2005

There is a Greek scene at UALR, but I am not involved. Many people at UALR are commuter students and have jobs outside of class. Little Rock is the capital of Arkansas and there is usually something interesting happening somewhere. Bars are mostly downtown and there seems to be some sort of festival every weekend. There are three or four theatres in Little Rock and the variety of shows produced would fit almost anyone's tastes.

Current student, 8/2001-Submit Date, April 2005

UALR has a very small Greek system and we have a great time. There is really not much to do on campus besides Greek life. In total, we have three sororities and three frats. We have a downtown district that has many bars. My frat goes down there often. Everyone I know I have mostly met through the Greek system.

> **The school says:** "UALR offers over 100 student organizations, including Greek life."

Current student, 8/2002-Submit Date, April 2005

There are many, many restaurants in Little Rock. There are even many restaurants on university, the street on which UALR is located. There are a good number of events including guest speakers and seminars in different areas of interest. We also have many active sororities and fraternities for a commuter school.

Current student, 8/2004-Submit Date, April 2005

Because UALR is located in a popular and common area of Little Rock, there are several restaurants and events in the area. UALR also promotes Greek life with a variety of fraternities and sororities. There is something for every student at UALR.

Current student, 8/2002-Submit Date, April 2005

The office of campus life at UALR is an excellent resource for all students' social needs. The office is managed by a former student and student government officer, and is very helpful in directing students to all of the activities that may suit a student's particular interests. There are many campus organizations ranging from academic to religious, to community service-oriented, as well as a Greek system. There are several restaurants and a mall close to the campus and Little Rock has many good places to eat, hang out, dance and socialize.

California Institute of Technology

Admissions Office
Mail Code 1-94
Pasadena, CA 91125
Admissions phone: (626) 395-6341
Admissions fax: (626) 683-3026
Admissions e-mail: ugadmissions@caltech.edu
Admissions URL: www.admissions.caltech.edu/

Note: The school has chosen not to comment on the student surveys submitted.

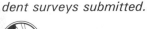 **Admissions**

Alumnus/a, 9/2002-6/2006, October 2006

Caltech is really looking for students dedicated to science. If a true love of science isn't evident through the essays, courses and extracurricular activities of the student, he/she is going to have a hard time getting in. Just having good grades in science courses won't cut it. The admissions committee wants to see that the student has a good idea that he/she really loves science. Beyond the love of science, Caltech also looks for students who will make a contribution to the Caltech community. Too many kids are brilliant in one way or another, but lock themselves in their rooms to study and play computer games 24/7. Students who have a unique talent or hobby, or who are well-rounded, in general, are considered more likely to give back to the Caltech community through participation in various campus activities. Caltech is one of the most selective schools in the country. There are only roughly 400 students admitted each year, producing an entering class of approximately 200 students.

Current student, 9/2002-Submit Date, May 2006

Caltech's application is similar to most college apps; the only thing that stands out in my mind is the final "essay" question, which is a box on an empty page that says "fill this space with something interesting." People have turned in a million different things—pictures, screenplays, cartoons, essays, musical compositions, cakes and so on.

Caltech is a very selective place, and it takes a lot to make it through here. If admissions lets you in and you're willing to put out what it takes, you can handle it. Only come here if you absolutely want to and you have a supreme desire to make it through, no matter what gets thrown at you.

That said, Caltech impresses me with its desire to take people whom one might not expect to get in: someone with a low GPA; someone with low test scores; someone without a high school diploma. Sure, they only take qualified applicants, but they're willing to look beyond numbers and pieces of paper to find people who are academically qualified and will contribute to the community in a positive manner.

There are a few current undergraduates on the admissions committee, and they try to ensure that the incoming class is both interesting and capable of getting along here.

Current student, 9/2002-Submit Date, May 2006

Admission to Caltech is highly selective. Students are evaluated on preparation, interest in math and science and initiative as demonstrated through extracurricular accomplishments. Standardized test scores are of little importance. There is no interview.

Alumnus/a, 9/2001-6/2005, May 2006

The admissions process is, well, like every other admissions process for a top-tier school. You write a couple of essays (plus an interesting "fill in the box" question that says, "Fill in the box below with something you find interesting," and gives you a box to fill in). I ended up sending in my application a week late due to my disorganization and getting waitlisted. After deluging the admissions

people with more letters of rec (including some from profs at the local state school), a pilot's license I had just gotten, and the "keep me on the waitlist" had circled about 65 times, they decided to take me.

There wasn't an interview, and Caltech takes, I think, about 13 percent of applicants. One of the cool things is that each little admissions committee is made up of a student, a prof and an admissions staff member. This means your application is read by the people who will teach you and be your peers—keep this in mind when you're applying. I was on the committee and responsible for denying a couple of people who had fine academics, but just sounded so horribly boring that I couldn't stand the thought of one of them being my neighbor.

Current student, 9/2004-Submit Date, October 2005

Caltech is usually considered to be self-selecting. That said, the admissions process is not automatic, and only about a fifth of the students who apply are admitted. The most significant component of the application is a clearly displayed passion for math and science. This passion is best displayed through the essays, clubs, recommendation letters and "the box," an empty space with vague instructions. The admissions committee contains many students and, generally, we can detect how excited the student is about math and science. Many of the students here were highly active in math/science clubs, tinkered with research at nearby universities, and took a few college classes when they had exhausted their high school's math/science curriculum. These things definitely strengthen an application. The admissions committee considers the fact that many students do not have all of these opportunities, so failure to participate due to lack of opportunity is not explicitly penalized. Failure to take hard math/science classes that were offered will be looked down upon and will likely lead to a rejection.

Caltech has no interview process, but it is highly recommended that students visit campus. The school is very self-selecting in that there are few students who have a sufficient passion for math/science to justify working as much as Caltech students do. Visiting campus will help give a better view of the workload and help students determine whether or not they really want to attend.

 **Academics**

Alumnus/a, 9/2002-6/2006, October 2006

The core requirements are unlike those at any other school. Caltech is on the quarter system, except no classes are offered during the summer quarter. Regardless of major, meaning even if a student were a History or English major (and yes, Caltech has those), he/she would still have to take five terms of math, five terms of physics, two terms of general chemistry, one term of freshman chemistry lab, one term of biology, two terms of freshman humanities (Hum courses numbered 10 or below in the course catalog), two terms of advanced humanities, two terms of intro and advanced social science, one term of freshman lab (chosen from various fields), and one term of science writing. There are additional requirements for each major beyond these core requirements. The quality of the classes depends upon the professor, but almost every class requires some help from a teaching assistant at some point during the quarter. Some profs have accents so thick it's hard to understand their English, but the departments try to have the better lecturers do the core classes. Most Caltech courses cover a semester's worth of material in a quarter, making them fast-paced and sometimes hard to follow. You have to learn to work with your fellow students early on in your school career or you will be very unhappy and probably will not do well. Caltech relies upon collaboration between students to complete coursework, a good skill to teach future scientists. It also unifies the student body since all students take the same core courses. Grading can be somewhat arbitrary depending on the professor and the class, but usually the curve is around a B or a B+. And it is a true bell-shaped curve (not just an, add ten points to each grade, curve). Most exams will have averages around 60 out of 100 points for the core classes, so students at the average normally make a B despite having failed by the numbers.

Read all of Vault's College Surveys at **www.vault.com/college**–get complete surveys on 100s of colleges and universities, expert advice on applicaton essays and more.

VAULT CAREER LIBRARY   35

Current student, 9/2002-Submit Date, May 2006

Caltech is ridiculously hard, and you have to want to be here in order to be happy. Many classes are very high quality, but a lot of the profs are here to do research rather than teach. Sadly, most classes could and should be taught better.

Since it's a small school, most classes are not offered at multiple times, so you can only take them if you can work them into your schedule. However, if you can, usually you can get in.

Professors tend to be accessible and they (or TAs) are always willing to help you learn the material better. The collaboration policy coupled with the honor code (which is actually taken very seriously here!) makes for an amazing atmosphere in which students learn from each other. Upperclassmen spend a great deal of time taking care of frosh (and s'mores and juniors, as well as each other). Homework is almost always done in groups, where people are just as concerned with learning and teaching each other how to understand things as they are with finishing the set and/or getting a few more points.

There is no grade inflation at Caltech. This creates a pretty big shock for people who were valedictorians of their high school classes and who always measured their self-worth based on the number of points over 100 they received on exams. **TECH IS REALLY HARD!** It forces people to learn to accept help, to be OK with doing their best and learning material regardless of the score they get at the end. When I was a frosh, the dean made quite a few parents angry when addressing them, saying, "I'm sorry to tell you that 50 percent of you have kids in the bottom half of the class." The point is that students at Caltech are smart already—you don't need to be the top of your class here to prove anything.

Current student, 9/2002-Submit Date, May 2006

It is extremely easy to get into just about any class, and all but a handful of classes are excellent. Grading and workload are a little stricter at Caltech than at other top schools. The average GPA is around 3.0, and students are required to take five classes a term to graduate in four years. Professors are extremely accessible outside of class, in part because Caltech has an excellent 3:1 student-to-faculty ratio. It is also far easier for undergraduates to get involved in interesting independent research projects at Caltech than it is at other schools.

Alumnus/a, 9/2001-6/2005, May 2006

Caltech is a tiny, very science-focused school. What this means is that you can basically get into any class you want. (There are perhaps three professors whose classes are even a little bit hard to get into.) It also means that you will take at least five terms of math, five terms of physics, three terms of chem (one is a lab) and a term of biology. In the interest of having slightly rounded people (well-rounded would be a lie), 12 terms of humanities/social sciences are required.

I actually really enjoyed my classes, and found the professors to be effective, but there are certainly people who would take exception to that. I think that is because they would stay up so late doing homework, they would fall asleep in class and, well, it's hard to learn when you're sleeping.

The workload is crushing. The trite expression is, "drinking water from a fire-hose"—but, while trite, it's also true. I think, however, the biggest difference between Caltech and most schools is this: at Caltech you have to work hard. It's very possible for a dedicated and hard-working person at another school (whether top-tier or a community college) to work really, really hard and learn a huge amount, and so forth. But at Caltech you don't have the option of getting your BS in drinking.

Grading is hard, too—lots of people get the first C or D of their lives. About a third of students fail a class during their stay at Tech; and these are people for whom an A- was heart-stopping in high school. That said, there are classes that have harder and easier graders—though some of the core classes have the toughest grading. The problem with the grading is that you can "fail in," or do bad enough in the core classes that you can't transfer out.

 Employment Prospects

Alumnus/a, 9/2002-6/2006, October 2006

Unfortunately, there is not much on-campus recruiting because of Caltech's small size. But occasionally companies will come to campus with the intent of hiring any Caltech grad, regardless of undergraduate major, because they know all Caltech grads have a certain skill set. Companies that often come to campus include Google, Microsoft, Northrop-Grumman and JP Morgan. The majority of Caltech grads go on to graduate school, usually to PhD programs at other prestigious colleges. My friends have gone to Stanford, Berkeley, University of Chicago, MIT, Harvard, Columbia, Yale, Princeton and Cornell, among others. Sometimes the low GPAs of Caltech undergraduates can be a hindrance to getting into graduate school or getting a job, but usually the schools and employers understand the difficulty of the school.

Alumnus/a, 9/1999-6/2003, May 2006

Caltech is designed to produce thinkers, not workers. Truthfully, Caltech does a much better job preparing students for graduate school than it does for the real world, which makes sense because more than half the graduating class will go directly to grad school. However, topnotch technology companies looking for innovative young minds recruit at Caltech every year, and you will find a large community of Caltech alumni among the aerospace companies of Southern California and the major corporations of Silicon Valley. Summer jobs at Caltech are relatively easy because every undergraduate is virtually guaranteed a research position on campus or somewhere else in Caltech's vast academic network through the Summer Undergraduate Research Program.

Alumnus/a, 9/2001-6/2005, May 2006

Caltech generates one of two responses from people: "Oh, that's the two-year trade school, right?" or "Oh My God. You went to Caltech? And you can talk?" People put folks from Caltech on a bit of a pedestal. As such, most grads don't have much trouble finding a job. I'm a bit of an oddball, starting my own business, and freelance tutoring on the side. It isn't the standard career path.

The Alumni Association is happy to help out, and they're really nice folks. Because it's a small school, there are fewer alumni, which has both upsides and downsides. The downside is that there might not be an alumnus at the company in which you're interested. The upside is that if there is, you have a pretty strong bond with him/her right away.

The other thing that should be mentioned here is that I think 50 to 60 percent of people go straight to grad school after undergrad, so for many people the employment prospects are really grad school prospects, and these are fairly good.

SURFs are also great—they're summer research fellowships, and nearly everyone does at least one, and many people do three, one for each summer.

Alumnus/a, 9/2000-6/2004, October 2004

Generally, 40 to 50 percent go to grad school and the rest find employment right away, either for permanent employment or as a break before going back to grad school. In my circle of friends, half went to grad school (MIT, Harvard, Stanford, Cal, UMich) and half got high paying jobs ($60K+). Then again, we are all engineers from Tech, so that might have tainted the results a bit. The career development center helps schedule interviews and find recruiters, has career fairs and generally helps you throughout the entire process. I suppose since Caltech is so prestigious and the academic program is so renowned, employers just come in and pluck us all.

Quality of Life

Alumnus/a, 9/2002-6/2006, October 2006

Caltech has eight undergraduate houses, which are crosses between dorms and frats. All freshmen are placed into a house through a picks process. The picks process combines a freshman's top four choices of houses with the uppclass undergradutes rankings of the freshman. In the end, each frosh is put into a house as a full member, and all freshmen live on campus in the houses their first year. Students can join other houses, but initially they are only members of the house in which they live. The houses hold social events, from ski trips to casino nights, to movie nights and parties. The house system pulls many people out of their shells by putting them with a group of people similar to themselves. Campus dining produces excellent lunches, but the dinners leave much to be desired. All students living on campus are required to be on the board plan, and many students move off campus just to avoid paying for the plan. There isn't really a student union, but most of the houses have pool tables, foosball tables, fireplaces and movie rooms available to their members. The gym is somewhat small but easy to use. The campus itself is beautiful. Southern California is always nice, and Pasadena is a relatively quiet suburb north of Los Angeles. It has the convenience of being close to the city while still having a suburban, safe feel. Crime around campus is very low, but incidents occasionally occur. Old Pasadena is one of the hotspots in Los Angeles at night, with about four blocks on Colorado Boulevard continually filled with foot traffic and some of the best restaurants in L.A.

Current student, 9/2004-Submit Date, October 2005

Opinions about Caltech's quality of life are often difficult to interpret. There is an inherent bitterness that comes with the workload and difficulty of the school. It is very common to hear people complain and joke about transferring. However, it is very much a love/hate relationship. Most of us would rather not go to any other school. There are times when we dread the workload, but we willingly bring it on ourselves and thrive on the self-imposed pressure. In the past, the administration has been very good about providing lots of goodies to offset the struggles. The undergraduate freedoms are numerous, and we are pretty much allowed to do anything on campus. There are lots of attempts to get students off campus including occasional free opera, symphony or movie tickets.

Closely linked to the quality of life is the house system. Caltech has [eight] houses, and until this year all freshmen lived in a house. In my opinion, the houses are like glorified dorms, with a little bit of a frat aspect. The first week of classes is Rotation Week, during which freshmen visit all of the houses to see which they like best. The houses each have their own traditions and culture, which basically means that each house represents a different type of nerd. Some houses are typically stereotyped as more athletic, while others are considered to be more computer-nerd oriented. Rotation Week culminates with a very complicated, secretive process by which freshmen are placed into houses. This makes Rotation Week sound almost like a rush week, but all students end up in a house and the process is designed to try to get all students in the house they would most enjoy. I find that the process works amazingly well and most people love their house. The houses are responsible for organizing weekly social events, which become very important since most people have trouble finding the time to do things outside of homework. In essence, the houses balance out the brutal coursework by providing a nice, relaxing community of nerds with whom to socialize.

Social Life

Alumnus/a, 9/2002-6/2006, October 2006

There is no Greek system at Caltech, just the house system. At Caltech, students really have to budget their time, and often that means choosing either only one night to hang out or working all weekend, depending on the time of year. I spent many Saturday nights doing math problem sets until midnight, just to watch a movie and fall asleep to cap it off. One unique aspect of undergrad life is pranking. The houses will prank each other and students even prank their friends rather often; Caltech's policy is that the prank has to be reversible, and a note has to be left so that the people pulling the prank can be contacted to reverse it.

Recently, Caltech has tried to revive the traditional rivalry with MIT. The web sites, www.caltechvsmit.com and www.mitcannon.com, detail some of the recent exploits of the two schools, assuming those web sites are still active. The dating scene is awful, as Caltech is 70 percent male and 30 percent female. But girls, don't get your hopes up: The odds are good, but the goods are odd. Couples tend to spend most of their time doing work together or wandering campus holding hands. There aren't many traditional dates around Caltech, unless one of the people really makes an effort. Delivery food is a favorite because it allows maximization of time working. Fredo's and President Thai are two favorites—Fredo's offers Italian food such as pasta and pizzas, and President Thai is arguably one of the best Thai restaurants in town—both of which deliver to the dorms. Students drink on campus, but the administration has been cracking down on underage drinking more in recent years. Still, parties often have alcohol being served by bartenders, and students can store alcohol in their rooms (assuming they are over 21).

Current student, 9/2002-Submit Date, May 2006

People at Tech are busy—it's difficult to find time for casual bar-hopping or clubbing. Still, we have to make time to hang out (on or off campus) with friends. Often this involves simple things like watching movies or playing games, but can occasionally involve beach trips, camping trips, hiking, clubbing and parties.

The house system (just like *Harry Potter*) is one of the strongest things Caltech has going for its undergrads. It is the built-in social network, the built-in safety net that is so important for the average Techer. We have family-style dinners five days a week when people can make sure they put their work away and chat about whatever they like. We pull crazy tricks to distract us from the amount of work we have to do.

Current student, 9/2004-Submit Date, October 2005

We often joke about the social life at Caltech for very legitimate reasons. The male-to-female ratio is skewed 2:1, so the dating scene is bizarre. The campus is small to begin with, so the ratio is a common complaint from both sexes. Guys complain that there aren't any girls and girls complain that there are too many nerdy guys hanging around ("the odds are good but the goods are odd"). The complaints aside, Caltech's social environment suits most of the people here. Most of us are not the types who would want to go out every night to a party. Social activities during the week include a family-style, house dinner every night followed by working on a problem set with a group of friends until the wee hours of the morning. Weekends are slightly more social since houses will often plan social activities (laser tag, bowling, picnics and movie nights). One of the highlights of the social scene is Midnight Donuts, which occurs once a term. The student body buys 800 donuts and delivers them to campus at midnight. The midnight donut crowds are some of the largest congregations of undergraduates I've ever seen here. Basically, do not come to Caltech for a social life. However, while we lack a normally defined social life, our social scene actually complements many of the students quite well.

Read all of Vault's College Surveys at **www.vault.com/college**—get complete surveys on 100s of colleges and universities, expert advice on applicaton essays and more.

VAULT CAREER LIBRARY   37

Claremont McKenna College

CMC Admission and Financial Aid
890 Columbia Avenue
Claremont, CA 91711-6425
Admissions phone: (909) 621-8088
Admissions e-mail: admission@claremontmckenna.edu
Admissions URL: www.claremontmckenna.edu/admission/

 Admissions

Current student, Political Science, 9/2003-Submit Date, May 2007

CMC is extremely selective in their admissions process. They look for excellent students. But that doesn't mean that you shouldn't apply because your GPA or test scores are below the average. CMC also tries to build a class, diverse in background, ethnicity, regional origin and interests. They want someone who will complement the other applicants they select.

Alumnus/a, 9/2001-5/2005, September 2005

The key to admission to CMC is fitting the right profile. Are you a type-A personality? Did you have a lot of leadership roles in high school? Are you interested in economics or political science? Do you dream of being a Fortune 500 CEO or senator? Then you might be the kind of student for whom CMC is looking. The school is trying to be more diverse—attract more science and humanities majors—but they will never forget the school's motto, "Leaders in the Making."

Admission to CMC is about more than just grades and test scores. This is a small school and the admissions office is being honest when they tell you that they look at every part of the application. Essays are important. Also, if you can, interview (on campus, not with an alumnus). Interviews carry serious weight, and if you're on the edge and an admissions officer likes you, they'll get you in. Some interviews are conducted by senior students at CMC. Don't be worried if you get a student instead of an admissions officer. The students' opinions matter just as much.

Current student, 8/2002-Submit Date, May 2005

I applied Early Decision because I knew that this was the only place I wanted to go. When I applied, I was in contact with some of the nicest people around in the admissions office, and had an interview with the dean of admissions, who made me feel very comfortable and not nervous at all. As I was waiting to hear on the decision regarding my admission, I got a call at work. It was Dean Vos calling me to let me know of my acceptance! He had called my house, found out that I was at work from my mom, asked for the work number and called me there. He had gone through all of that trouble to let me know personally that I got in!

As far as advice goes, I had a good GPA, and an OK SAT, but I was very involved in high school as the president of a lot of clubs. CMC likes to see leadership, and that's what you should show if you're trying to get in. Write a good essay, only interview if you know that it will help you, because it's not necessary, and if you do poorly, that could mean that you're not going to get in.

Current student, 8/2004-Submit Date, April 2005

CMC takes the Common App and a supplemental application, including a leadership essay. There is an interview process but I have heard that the interviews are informative and not evaluative. My advice for getting in is to have leadership experience in high school. CMC specializes in training young leaders, so it is important to look like CMC material. The only non-Common App essay is the leadership essay, which can be about any leader, real or fictional. Writing about a political or economic leader is always a safe bet. CMC is highly selective—I have heard that less than 20 percent were accepted this year.

Current student, 9/2003-Submit Date, April 2005

CMC is a highly selective school (20 percent) that values a well-rounded application. They look not only for good grades but to see that applicants took challenging courses, as well. Extracurriculars are necessary and hopefully you have some leadership experience. Interviews are offered, but not necessary. They usually confirm what is shown in the application.

Current student, 8/2000-Submit Date, February 2004

Interviews for prospective students are all conducted by current CMC students, which might help take the pressure off of students who are intimidated by talking to admissions officers. There is no reason to fear the CMC admissions staff; however, they are without exception overwhelmingly friendly and helpful. They really seem to enjoy their jobs, and they want to help all qualified applicants get admitted. In terms of the criteria they look for in applicants, leadership positions and a well-rounded background are high on the list. Academic achievement in high school is important, but the admissions staff takes pride in bringing students to CMC with a healthy balance of extracurricular activities, as well.

> **The school says:** "Some interviews are conducted by current CMC students, and some interviews are conducted by admissions officers."

 Academics

Current student, Political Science, 9/2003-Submit Date, May 2007

Quality professors are the hidden gem of CMC. They are anxious to advise you in your course selection, career goals and especially add to course content. They create a welcoming, engaging, learning atmosphere. Because the class sizes are small, you can interact with them on a personal level. I was late to a class recently and my professor asked me if I was OK. First, he noticed I was gone, which wouldn't happen at a bigger school. Second, he demonstrated interest in my life. I have attended dinners at professors' houses, joined them for lectures at CMC's athenaeum, and seen them attending campus concerts. The availability and orientation of CMC professors is a key element to the school's quality of academics.

Alumnus/a, 9/2001-5/2005, September 2005

Academics are tough, but if you come from a good high school, you will be prepared. There is a lot of work, and most students spend the majority of their time outside of class studying. Grade inflation is a little less at CMC than at other schools, particularly in the economics department. The government department has both easy and hard professors, but grades are generally lower here, too. It is fairly easy to get the classes you want, unless you are a transfer, and then it can be kind of tricky. The registrar's office is amazing, and they will help you in any way they can.

Alumnus/a, Economics, 8/2000-5/2004, March 2006

I think the academic experience at CMC varies greatly by department. Since the college is small, most people would believe that all students are educated similarly, but this is not necessarily the case. CMC seems to put a lot more resources into their government and economics departments than the other departments. This makes sense given that the school's reputation is built upon these areas. As such, you will find that the classes in these departments are excellent overall. The number one reason for that is the quality of the professors. CMC is consistently ranked as one of the top undergraduate economics departments in the country and it is easy to see why. The professors are not only well regarded in the economics world but are also very good in the classroom. Usually all material is explained very well in the first place, but if there are questions, the professors all have office hours and are often available even outside those set times. Importantly, most professors I had really seemed to enjoy meeting with students outside of class, and many students would routinely drop by to chat with professors about topics not necessarily related to class. The drawback to this is that since professors are available, they expect students to make an effort to seek out their help if there is a problem understanding class material. If a student does not seek help, professors will grade accordingly. This translates to grade inflation not being as common in the department as it is at other schools (and other departments within CMC). I know this sounds like I'm just attempting to justify my low grades, but trust me, it's true.

Anyways, to get through the other areas quickly: workload is reasonable, though it's definitely greater than at some other selective institutions as I found out from friends. Classes are fairly easy to get despite having a tendency to close quickly during registration. All this means is that you must see the professor and demonstrate that you really, really want to take the class, since it is ultimately the professor's decision if you get in rather than the registrar. The reason that the classes close so quickly is that classes are usually capped at 19 students, since some rankings use "number of classes under 20 students" as a criterion. This rule exists only because the administration cares about nothing other than the almighty rankings.

As for departments other than economics, some, like government, are also very well respected and have excellent professors who encourage classroom discussion and engage students (although grade inflation is rampant in that department as it is in others with the exception of econ and math). Although many classes are excellent and challenging, overall the quality of the programs is not quite as good, since not as many resources are focused in these areas.

Current student, 9/2002-Submit Date, April 2005

The school has a fine student-to-faculty ratio; I have never been in a class with more than 35 students (and that was an intro., general ed requirement class). Most of my classes have about 15 students; professors are easy to access and even take part in extracurricular activities with students (like dinners hosted at their own homes and department baseball games). The classes range from informative and dry to informative and exciting, depending on one's major. Either way, one will learn; one's mind may even be expanded.

Popular classes fill up quickly because class sizes are so small, but if you really want a class, you are bound to get it during your four years here. The workload, again, depends on the class, but I would count on a serious amount of reading and writing. You can't leave the school until you have produced a long thesis on a subject in your major. Every class will demand involvement, though that involvement will take different forms. Grading has been fair—not so inflated as at the Ivy League schools, but not unreasonable either. Econ majors will have a more difficult time getting an A than literature majors, but in both cases, the A will have been hard-earned.

Current student, 9/2000-Submit Date, February 2004

CMC can be extremely rigorous academically. The strongest departments include economics, government and history. The reading load for most classes is much larger than at other schools of its type, and the grade inflation is much lower than at other other small liberal arts schools, especially in the economics department. CMC does not have many departments that typical liberal arts colleges have, like sociology and anthropology. However, the consortium provides access to courses and majors in these areas. In fact, the consortium allows easy cross-registration, and the close physical locations and common class times allow students to utilize the opportunities available at the 5C.

Most classes are extremely interesting and well taught. Classes can be hard to get into as an underclassman, because there is a 19-person cap on many of them. However, most every class is available to everyone in their four years here. Professors are extremely available and helpful. Many students end up being research assistants for professors because we do not have a grad school. Close relationships with professors mean great recommendations, insider tips on internships and more.

Employment Prospects

Alumnus/a, 8/1999-5/2003, September 2006

Every respectable company seeks to hire Claremont students. Most if not all consulting firms, such as Deloitte, Bain, McKinsey, Mercer, E&Y, Capgemini and Accenture all come to Claremont to hire graduating seniors and hire juniors for their internship program. There is also a consulting, accounting and invest-

ment banking event that the school hosts each year where employers can set up booths and meet the students. What makes this a great event is employers and students meet before recruiting starts. This way, when an employer receives a student's résumé, he/she can put a face to the résumé. Most students graduate with outstanding job offers and nice hefty signing bonuses. Consulting and investment banking are big here, and many students work hard at securing jobs at these top firms because they know once they get those names on their résumé, they will have endless career opportunities. The school has a great Career Services Center with Career Counselors and a fully staffed office to help students find jobs, apply to graduate schools, as well as participate in community service events since some students choose to go and participate in the Peace Corps. The school helps the students a lot more than any school I have seen. The school invests and works extremely hard at marketing their graduates to companies, almost spoon feeding the students too much, but hey, that is why you pay the big bucks to go to a private college.

Alumnus/a, 9/2001-5/2005, September 2005

CMC is fairly well known on the West Coast, but if you're looking for jobs on the East Coast (not including D.C.), there will be fewer connections for you to take advantage. In general, the alumni are really helpful and supportive.

Current student, 9/2002-Submit Date, April 2005

The school has an incredible Career Services Center that strives to bring more employers (for on-campus recruiting) to campus than there are seniors in the graduating class, which means that if you want a job, set realistic expectations, and stay on top of things your junior/senior years, you will get one. Networking is huge here—we have a strong alumni network, including an Alumni Mentoring Cafe online (where we can contact alumni in our prospective fields for advice and info). Career Services keeps track of what kinds of summer internships we receive, and there are opportunities for internships in D.C. during junior year. There are a million different groups willing to fund student internships domestically and overseas, so getting a valuable internship experience while at school should not be a problem for a go-getter.

Current student, 9/2002-Submit Date, April 2005

CMC's name is known among our prospective employers, and that's what really matters. Sure, there are schools that have bigger names in mainstream society, but when it counts, CMC has a wonderful reputation. About 90 percent of pre-med students get into their first-choice school, and close to 80 percent of our alumni attend grad school within five years. We also have more CEOs, CFOs, CIOs, presidents and senior partners than I have ever heard of in our alumni base. Alumni love to recruit current students for jobs directly from their alma mater.

Current student, 9/2000-Submit Date, February 2004

CMC definitely focuses much of its Career Services on careers, as opposed to professional or graduate schools. That said, many CMCers get into top law and medical schools every year. The Career Services Center is well staffed, with many resources about internship opportunities and alumni who are willing to hear from students.

CMC may have some of the best on-campus recruiting in the country. Top accounting and consulting firms recruit here every year, including Deloitte and Touche, PwC and Standard and Poor's. Many of these companies have CMC alumni who have moved up the ranks and whose track records recommend the hiring of additional CMC graduates. I have had numerous solicitations for consulting internships, based purely on my major.

Career Services also hosts many panels and guests who talk about interning and working abroad, life after law school, and business ethics. Because of the Institute for Work, Family and Children, there are often panels about balancing careers with family life.

The school says: "In the Class of 2006, 65 percent of graduates entered the workforce, while 19 percent went directly into graduate school. However, over 70 percent of our alumni pursue a graduate degree, usually within five years of graduation. Our career services program is very strong in both recruiting and graduate school placement."

Read all of Vault's College Surveys at **www.vault.com/college**—get complete surveys on 100s of colleges and universities, expert advice on applicaton essays and more.

VAULT CAREER LIBRARY   39

Quality of Life

Alumnus/a, 9/2001-5/2005, September 2005

CMC is located in sunny California. People are always outside doing homework, hanging out and just enjoying the day. The campus is not gorgeous, but the dorms are really nice (how many other schools have maid service and give out free lawn chairs?), and the dining hall food is great (lots of vegetarian options, too). Claremont is very safe, and women can walk around campus alone at night with no problem.

Alumnus/a, 8/2000-5/2004, March 2006

Students typically live on campus all four years. The residence halls are divided into four major areas: North Quad, Mid Quad, South Quad and the apartments. The apartments are owned by the school and are open only to seniors (and juniors with multiple extra credits). They consist of a kitchen and four rooms connected to a common living area with two bathrooms. They also have air conditioning and cable TV, and are generally preferred over the dorms since you don't have to share a room.

Everything on campus is very close. The farthest I ever had to walk to class was 10 minutes, and that was the class at Pomona College. The longest possible walk within the CMC campus is probably only about five to seven minutes. CMC's compactness comes in especially handy when you have an eight o'clock class on Friday morning.

The CMC dining hall is not very good; however, things may have changed in the two years since I left. Fortunately, the school's meal plan is shared by all five colleges, so there is a lot of choice when it comes to eating. When I was there, the general consensus was that Scripps had the best food, as well as the best scenery. As an added bonus, it's closer to some CMC dorms than the CMC dining hall (Collins) is.

The safety of Claremont is not an issue. The city is very safe, in general, as long as you don't stray too far from the City of Claremont. Pomona (the city not the college) lurks nearby and is not very nice. However, like everywhere in Southern California, it's not that close and you would need a car to get there. As for Claremont, mostly old people and families live in the town itself, and boy do they love calling the police to shut down noisy parties on campus. Relations with the town are not that great, especially with the Claremont Police Department, which has a reputation for hassling students and being racist.

Besides these charming features, the town has a nice area called the Claremont Village full of overpriced shops where most college students wouldn't want to go. There are a few good restaurants though which can be good for dates. After all this, it's no surprise that social life at CMC revolves around the campus itself and that students almost never leave the five colleges.

Current student, 8/2002-Submit Date, May 2005

CMC has the best quality of life that I can say. In fact, I don't want to leave. Every Sunday, if it's warm, there are BBQs outside of the dorms, people setting up makeshift slip-n-slides down the hills, and people doing their reading on a beach mat outside. If it's raining, everyone's out on the field, splashing in puddles. Every afternoon there's a tea, with free tea and coffee, as well as pastries and chocolate-dipped strawberries. The dining hall re-opens every night at 10:30 for a study-break snack, chock full of junk food. First semester, I wanted to go see the UCLA-USC football game, and when I asked the Dean of Student Life, he told me he'd pay half the cost of my tickets. CMC will pay for everything you ask for—within reason. We have great food, maid service and a great administration; there's not much more I could ask for. The Claremont Village is a short walk away, full of great little restaurants and boutiques, but it's a bit expensive. We're about 45 minutes away from snowboarding, 45 minutes from the beach, 20 minutes from Disneyland, and depending on traffic, as little as half an hour from L.A. Kids go to Vegas and the desert all the time, too. And as far as safety is concerned, it is a very safe campus with the majority of kids leaving their doors unlocked. Sure there's the occasional incident, but it's very rare, and it usually involves a lack of common sense.

Current student, 9/2002-Submit Date, April 2005

The campus is safe; I've never felt unsafe, even walking around after dark. Housing is generally gorgeous—every dorm has its peculiar personality, but,

since I found my housing niche, I've been comfy. The campus is green and blooming year-round. (They take the grass very seriously here, and have a committed maintenance staff for the flower beds.) Southern California is really the place to be, excepting occasional mudslides and forest fires. (Our campus is completely shielded from natural disasters; it's really a haven.)

Because we are in a consortium, there are six dining halls to choose from, and plenty of local food and local color (we are near L.A.) to keep a normal student satisfied. I would not recommend having a car, especially not as a freshman or sophomore. It's just not necessary. Parties all happen on campus, but there's enough variety to keep it interesting. You will be well fed if you are at CMC. There is free food everywhere, and every day, the Athenaeum has free tea and chocolate-covered strawberries and other treats for all the students, and every weeknight there is a free midnight snack at the dining hall (attended by a lot of campus). Claremont is a bit of a sleepy town, but it's a short drive to a nightlife (should you reject the on-campus nightlife, which I haven't yet). They clean our rooms for us once a week. I'm not kidding.

Social Life

Alumnus/a, 9/2001-5/2005, September 2005

The social life is very campus based. Each dorm takes turns throwing parties (but most often the parties are in the North Quad dorms). These parties always include at least beer. There is no Greek scene. There are also bars in downtown Claremont (like the Press) for the over-21 crowd, but they're mostly filled with grad students and they're definitely not cheap. There are tons of restaurants around Claremont, and if you want something really swanky, Pasadena is only 30 minutes away.

CMC has a student center, but no one goes there because the food is bad and it badly needs to be remodeled. You're more likely to find people at the Motley (the coffee house on the Scripps campus) or the Sage Hen (the food place in Pomona's student center).

Clubs are popular, but even more popular are the Research Institutes. If you work for one of them (like the Rose or the Kravis) you will quickly become friends with the other people who do, too.

The dating scene is pretty typical. People are either in long term relationships or just hooking up. A lot of guys head to Scripps to find girls. With only 1,000 students, the school is really small, and you get to know the dating pool rather quickly (for better or worse).

Current student, 9/2002-Submit Date, April 2005

There is no Greek system here (thank goodness). Instead, social life is divided by housing into three quads (that's 12 dorms, total). North Quad residents are known for a louder, more liberal, more lax lifestyle (it's the party quad). South Quad is quiet, clean, but generally amiable. They migrate north on Friday nights but have a quiet place to retire to. Mid Quad is, believe it or not, somewhere in the middle—for people who don't mind noise but don't mind quiet either. There is not much formal dating on campus, but I really shouldn't talk about dating because I am jaded and would be unfair. There is a good guy/gal ratio, so you might just find what you are looking for.

Most people drink on campus, but the Village (downtown Claremont) has some cozy little bars and restaurants. A few standout parties every year include the Foam Party (at which a great spigot blasts mountains of foam onto the dancing crowd all night—wet and wild); Monte Carlo (our formal party, complete with a live Big Band and some fine gambling); and Long Tall Glasses (another formal 5C party, this one with champagne and roses). But generally, Thursday nightclubs and Saturday theme parties are highlights of the weekends. It might get routine, but at least the parties are outdoors and the alcohol is free.

> **Claremont McKenna says:** "The Associated Students of CMC (ASCMC, the student government) pays for alcohol."

Current student, 8/2002-Submit Date, May 2005

The social life revolves around campus. I think something around 99 percent of kids live on campus, and the school does a lot to make sure that the kids have fun. It's great seeing kids who were arguing about Aristotle's rhetoric as applied to George Bush and then playing Beirut outside of the dorms a few hours later. The school pays for great bands like Gavin DeGraw and The Roots; they pay for fun things on Thursday nights like mechanical bulls and inflatable obstacle courses, and they take us to baseball games and Knotts Berry Farm. There's a ton to do when you're not doing your homework.

The School Says

Claremont McKenna College, a member of The Claremont Colleges, is a highly selective, coeducational, residential, liberal arts college. Founded in 1946, CMC is a school with a clear-cut mission: to educate students for responsible leadership in business, government and the professions. Offering a strong grounding in the liberal arts with an emphasis on economics, government and international relations, CMC attracts students who approach education pragmatically and who intend to make a difference in the world. Richard Vos, Dean of Admission and Financial Aid, states, "CMC's curriculum is at the crease between the academic world and the real world. Additionally, through our participation in the consortium, our stu-

dents benefit by having the best of both worlds: a small, residential, liberal arts college within the larger context of The Claremont Colleges."

Research is an integral component in the CMC experience. Every CMC student is required to complete a senior thesis. And our 11 on-campus research institutes offer students the opportunity to work side-by-side with CMC faculty, studying issues including leadership, international relations, financial economics, human rights, work and family, government and public affairs, and environmental management. Students also participate in a wide range of co-curricular activities including study abroad, Washington, D.C. program, athletics, debate, performing arts, student government and community service projects.

CMC students get results, as well. One of every eight CMC graduates now holds a top management post, and more than 70 percent pursue an advanced degree in law, business, medicine and other fields within five years of graduation. Our strong recruiting and placement services help students land positions in top companies around the world.

Mills College

Office of Admission
Mills College
5000 MacArthur Blvd.
Oakland, CA 94613
Admissions phone: (800) 87-MILLS or (510)430-2135
Admissions fax: (510) 430-3298
Admissions e-mail: admission@mills.edu
Admissions URL:
www.mills.edu/admission/undergraduate/

Admissions

Current student, 9/2007-Submit Date, May 2007

I loved how I got to know my admissions officer throughout the college admissions process. During an interview, I was so surprised at how much she knew about me. They made sure that I visited the campus at least once and that I had a host. When I was accepted, I received continuous calls from Mills to answer any questions about my college decision. All these factors showed that they cared about their students and definitely made an impact on my decision.

Current student, English, 8/2005-Submit Date, May 2007

The admissions process was very simple. I was asked to fill out an online application and then send in a graded writing sample. About a week later I was accepted and eventually had an interview. The interview was very informal and we just talked about what I was looking for and what major I was thinking about doing, things of that nature.

Current student, 8/2005-Submit Date, May 2007

I applied to Mills College using the Common Application and it was the first school from which I heard back. I think Mills is looking for enthusiastic applicants; if you can make a certain part of your application shine despite not-so-perfect grades and show that you are really dedicated to Mills, your application will definitely be considered. Spend time on your essay and don't be afraid to let yourself shine through. Mills is a community of unique women, and that should show in the essay. I don't know if Mills looks very selective on paper, because it is a pretty self-selecting school. Most of the applicants know that Mills is a top choice and have worked hard during their high school career, so we have a high acceptance rate, but that isn't because it is an easy school.

Current student, 8/2004-Submit Date, May 2006

I chose Mills because if its admissions process. The school was very warm and welcoming. I felt like they really wanted me to be there. The school has a good reputation so there is some selectivity. I would suggest simply being yourself when you write your essay. The school also values students who are involved in their community, so community service is a plus.

Alumna, 8/2002-5/2006, May 2006

Mills sent me beautiful photo brochures when I was considering applying, and when I arrived for a campus tour the environment was even more beautiful than I had imagined. The admissions officers were warm and friendly and conducted a casual, laid-back interview. They are academically quite selective, but are especially drawn to unique students with unconventional approaches to learning and living. Mills values strong, radical and eccentric women.

Current student, 8/2004-Submit Date, May 2006

The best advice I can give on getting into Mills is to be you. The Mills community values the individual and the admissions staff members are most impressed by those that believe in who they are and have a clear passion in their life. Let your application reflect your passion.

They also understand that no one is perfect. If you don't have a 4.0 GPA, you aren't automatically discounted. Mills looks at every aspect of a person before making a decision.

I highly recommend an interview. The interview for me was more like a chat than an interview. In addition to increasing my chances of getting in, my interview helped me realize just how perfect a fit I was for the campus. Your essay should also be a reflection of your personality. Submit something that is attention-grabbing and a true reflection of you. Mills is selective enough to keep the student body at a high academic level.

Current student, 8/2003-Submit Date, May 2006

The admissions office was in contact with me the whole time I was applying. They were always available to answer questions and provide information. The essay is not a personal statement but a graded essay, which makes the application so much easier and less stressful. I was able to interview with an alumna in my area and it was super-easy to arrange. It felt like the admissions office really knew me as a person and not just as a number in a file.

Read all of Vault's College Surveys at www.vault.com/college—get complete surveys on 100s of colleges and universities, expert advice on applicaton essays and more.

VAULT CAREER LIBRARY   41

Current student, 8/2002-Submit Date, April 2006

The admissions process at Mills is very hands-on. While I was considering applying, I called the admissions officers a few times and they were very helpful about answering questions and putting me in touch with current students with whom I could talk. Mills has a relatively high acceptance rate, partly because it is self-selecting because it's a women's college—generally, very intelligent women with strong academic backgrounds apply to Mills!

The early admission program is not binding, which is great because you can know as soon as December if you've been admitted, but still wait to hear from other schools, if you'd like.

 # Academics

Current student, 9/2007-Submit Date, May 2007

Academics are great and by this I mean the professors are very accessible and the classes are small, so discussion is definitely encouraged. The classes are academically challenging and interesting, so I am always learning something new. The workload is somewhat heavy, but the purpose is to challenge the students, and this is what I want from a college.

Current student, Biology, 8/2006-Submit Date, May 2007

I have just loved most of my classes, and there have been enough seats for all students who wanted in, as far as I know, except for PE and art. The professors are wonderful, and very helpful and available to students. Grading is strict but fair. Workloads in the sciences, at least, are very demanding. Science labs are a particular weak point, at the general/elementary chemistry/biology level.

Current student, English, 8/2005-Submit Date, May 2007

Academic nature is hard but not overwhelming. As in most schools, some classes are better than others. But for the most part, I am very happy with my classes. Grading is appropriate.

Current student, 8/2005-Submit Date, May 2007

Mills is pretty traditional in the way that classes work, at least that is my impression as my first year ends. Professors give grades, not written reviews, but many professors prefer to be called by their first name. Despite the low average class size, there are plenty of larger (30 to 40 students) lecture classes, especially intro classes. Mills has a really weak foreign language program, which is unfortunate, but we are adding a beginner's Chinese program starting next semester. The quality of classes is good and stimulating, but it also just depends on the professor. Sometimes I feel like the workload at Mills could be a lot harder than it is. It seems like for most classes there are three big papers per semester, but besides that, there isn't a lot of work, just a lot of reading. Some people have a harder time than I do, especially if they are science majors.

Current student, 8/2004-Submit Date, May 2006

The workload at Mills is intense. They really do prepare you for graduate studies. You will find that a lot of students are tired by the end of the semester. For the most part, the professors grade fairly. I haven't had a professor who was not willing to spend extra time outside of class with his/her students if they requested it. Class discussions can be interesting.

Alumna, 8/2002-5/2006, May 2006

Though some introductory courses (e.g., Intro to Psychology, Ethnic Studies and Economics) fill up quickly, professors respond well to motivated and persistent students, and often spaces open up after the first week or so. These classes fill up quickly because they are required for higher division courses in particular fields, and also because Mills values small class sizes and the ability of students to often work one-on-one with professors.

Classes are usually discussion rather than lecture based and the average class size is around 13 or so. The largest class I have been in was around 30, while the smallest was where I was one of four in a philosophy class where the discussions and level of intellectual stimulation was amazing. Some of the best professors at Mills (and in the world) are in the Ethnic Studies and Women's Studies departments.

Current student, 8/2004-Submit Date, May 2006

The academic programs challenge both your quantitative skills and your imagination. In my experience, the practical and the theoretical blend together to present each subject in an engaging form. Every class offers something unique and valuable. The class discussions leave you thinking about them days later. It's very common to continue a class discussion two days later when you run into a fellow classmate at the Tea Shop.

While Mills keeps class sizes small, if you need to be added to a class, the professors are very lenient about adding students. Professors at Mills are unlike at anywhere else I've encountered. They are here because they love teaching and are always happy to have another person with whom to engage in their classes. The grading practices are exceedingly fair. Professors are willing to help you grasp the material in any way possible.

The workload is fairly heavy for each class but not impossible. Each class requires many hours outside of class, but the subject matters are so engaging, the time seems to fly by. The work is never busywork. It is always very relevant and stimulating.

Current student, 8/2003-Submit Date, May 2006

The classes are all pretty small, which makes for an amazingly productive learning environment. You really get to know your professors and they are always available and willing to help you. The work is difficult but there is always a TA or the professor to help you keep up, they really want you to do well. For the most part, it is pretty easy to get the classes you want; and because the professors are so accessible, it is really easy to petition to get into a closed class.

Current student, 8/2002-Submit Date, April 2006

Classes here are small, which means you get more chances to talk and interact with your professor and fellow students. Popular classes are sometimes difficult to get into because they are kept small, but once you establish a relationship with a professor, she is more likely to let you in.

Another thing to remember is that some classes are only offered every other semester or every other year, so it's important to take them when they pop up! The workload is definitely challenging, but manageable. Professors are accessible when you need help and extensions.

 # Employment Prospects

Current student, English, 8/2005-Submit Date, May 2007

It seems like Mills graduates have very important, high-up jobs. Employers are very excited to hear about prospective Mills grads.

Current student, Psychology, 8/2006-Submit Date, May 2007

As a freshman with little interest in summer jobs, I have had little personal experience with the employment prospects. However, I have heard that the alumni network is very useful, and I have seen that our career center is very active in providing job and internship opportunities.

Current student, 8/2004-Submit Date, May 2006

Mills is well known and respected, but the school itself does not have recruiting for graduates. You really have to do your own grunt work and apply yourself if you're interested in a internship. The career center could use a lot of help.

Alumna, 8/2002-5/2006, May 2006

Mills alumnae connect all over the world to help one another find personal and professional contacts. By talking to other students, professors and graduates and utilizing the free career and graduate studies counseling at Mills, students can learn about unique and enriching internships and careers. Mills graduates create a sisterhood of support and networking.

Current student, 8/2004-Submit Date, May 2006

Being an alumna of Mills College opens up doors. I recently had a conversation with a female executive who, upon discovering I was a current Mills student, said that was enough to get an interview in her company. Mills is such a prestigious place with a long, rich history and such amazing woman attendees, the reputation is unparalleled.

Mills alumnae always want to be involved, both with current campus issues and with individuals. They stay connected and are quite a force to be reckoned with. Mills also has a fantastic career center. They will answer any question, no matter how small. The departments are also a great help in placing students into internships in their fields. As an undergrad at Mills, the department will help you get as much career experience as you can, which increases your chance of employment following graduation. A Mills degree definitely prepares you for working in the real world.

Current student, 8/2003-Submit Date, May 2006

There are a multitude of job opportunities after graduation. There are opportunities to work on research projects with professors and publish your research. Professors send out information about jobs that are opening. The career center is a great way to network through alumni and learn how to write a résumé and be good in interviews.

Current student, 8/2002-Submit Date, April 2006

The career center at Mills is a great resource. They do a lot to help students get internships while at Mills, which can lead to great jobs afterwards. Many programs have internships as a requirement during senior year, which also helps students find good jobs after graduation. Employers in general like to hire women from women's colleges because they know they've had a rare chance to develop their academic and leadership skills in a supportive setting.

Quality of Life

Current student, 9/2007-Submit Date, May 2007

Life quality is very accessible for incoming students. I was shocked that Mills freshwomen got the best dorm on campus, which is divided into living-learning communities. This helped me transition into college life because immediately I formed a community bond with my classmates.

Current student, English, 8/2005-Submit Date, May 2007

Life issues are sometimes blowing out at our school. Sometimes I think women make too big of a deal about certain things. Housing is amazing. I love the fact that we get our own rooms and they are really nice. The campus is old and beautiful. I love having class in Mills Hall. The neighborhood is not that great outside campus, but we haven't had any really big problems.

Current student, 8/2005-Submit Date, May 2007

Mills can be sort of boring sometimes. The campus is small and a lot of people leave on the weekends. Any parties that happen on campus are small and have to remain quiet. However, the women that come to Mills are the most amazing women you will ever meet. They are determined, intelligent and profound. Housing is really great for the first year. Students live in beautiful dorms and have their own rooms, but sophomores get screwed and have to live in crappy dorms. The dining options are minimal, but it is such a small school. You can always get a healthy meal in our dining hall, and there are vegetarian and meat options. I never feel unsafe on campus, even in the middle of the night.

Current student, 8/2004-Submit Date, May 2006

The campus is beautiful and very relaxing. The facilities are in good condition. My main issue is a lack of parking. Parking on campus can be a real hassle. The dorms are OK, but there is room for improvement. Dining is not that great in the cafeteria, but we do have a small cafe that offers some pretty good options. The campus is safe. It is located in an urban environment and I advise all students to take the same precautions that they would with any big or mid-sized city like Oakland.

Current student, 8/2003-Submit Date, May 2006

You get a single (unless you request a double) if you live on campus, and the rooms are a pretty good size. There is also on-campus apartment and co-op living. The campus is absolutely gorgeous. The only resource it is missing is a health center on campus. The neighborhood around the campus is really fun if you know where to look. There are a lot of really cool little pockets in Oakland in which to hang out. It's a real city, so no one should walk around by them-

selves, especially at night, but there's great public transportation to help get you around.

Social Life

Current student, 9/2007-Submit Date, May 2007

For a small school there are always activities going on for different ethnic celebrations, speakers, presentations and so on. There is a plethora of clubs to join, and it is really easy to create one. The fact that there is not a Greek system on campus makes it so much easier to focus on school work.

Current student, English, 8/2005-Submit Date, May 2007

This school has an awesome location. Located close to Berkeley and the city, students are able to do pretty much anything they feel like. If you are into the party scene, you can go to Berkeley and do frat things, and if you're not into that and you like clubs, there are art galleries you can go in to the city. I love it.

Current student, Psychology, 8/2006-Submit Date, May 2007

The social lives of students from Mills College are mostly what they make of it. Mills has no Greek system, and is opposed to any sort of closed clubs or societies. However, it has many clubs, from religious (such as Workers of Faith: Christianity, and the Pagan Alliance, to ethnic (such as APISA: Pacific Islander), to interest (such as Dumbledore's Army: Harry Potter and 'Zines: book arts). Many events, primarily artistic performances, also occur. If campus life is too boring for students, there is also a shuttle that takes students to a BART station, as well as to UC Berkeley campus. Dating at Mills can be an issue for some, and not a problem for others. Some students seem to bring new people back to their dorm room every week, while others have steady partners, and still others complain that Mills is a convent. As an all-women's college at the undergraduate level, those who prefer heterosexual relationships can find dating hard, and the college does not attempt to fix this "problem." It should be noted that there is an obvious LGBTQQI presence on campus.

Alumna, 8/2002-5/2006, May 2006

Mills is an all-women's college and has no sororities or Greek system. The campus is pretty quiet, and although Mills is not at all a party school, groups of women gather together constantly in the Tea Shop, outside on the grass and in the forest areas on campus, and in the large living rooms and libraries of the residence halls.

Women at Mills are active volunteering in the community, working together in campus organizations (political, spiritual and social), and in activist work. Mills has many events and dances throughout each semester. Popular dances include the Drag Dance and the Fetish Ball. Whether at an event or enjoying the beauty of the campus at night, Mills provides a rare opportunity for women to feel safe within a community of other women.

The dating scene at Mills, though sometimes dramatic, is one of the school's best assets. Women coming to Mills can expect to find one of the most lesbian-friendly campuses in the world. Being a women's college in the San Francisco Bay Area provides students entering Mills, whether just graduating from high school or resuming their education later in life, the opportunity to befriend, date, love and possibly marry some of the finest and most extraordinarily talented, intelligent and caring women the Bay Area has to offer.

The School Says

For more than 150 years, Mills College has shaped women's lives. Offering a progressive liberal arts curriculum taught by nationally renowned faculty, Mills gives students the personal attention that leads to extraordinary learning. Through intensive, collaborative study in a community of forward-thinking individuals, students gain the ability to make their voices heard, the strength to risk bold visions, an eagerness to experiment and a desire to change the world.

Read all of Vault's College Surveys at www.vault.com/college—get complete surveys on 100s of colleges and universities, expert advice on applicaton essays and more.

VAULT CAREER LIBRARY   43

Nestled on 135 lush acres in the heart of the San Francisco Bay Area, Mills College is a hidden gem. Its idyllic setting might—at first glance—belie the pulse of activity that beats within its gates. Drawing energy from the college's location, Mills students connect with centers of learning, business and technology; pursue research and internship opportunities; and explore the Bay Area's many sources of cultural, social and recreational enrichment. On campus, students enjoy a variety of eclectic events ranging from experimental music concerts to inspiring talks by notables such as U.S. Senator Barbara Boxer, Gloria Steinem, Chilean author Isabel Allende and Sally Ride, the first American woman in space.

Ranked sixth among top colleges in the west by *U.S. News & World Report* and sixth among "Great Schools, Great Prices," Mills is an excellent academic choice for students who are intellectually curious and interested in making a difference. Renowned faculty members lead the learning process with an innovative curriculum that recognizes multicultural values and the perspectives of women. Students choose their courses of study from more than 40 majors, or may even design their own major with careful faculty guidance. With a student-to-faculty ratio of 11:1 and class sizes averaging only 15 students, students are expected to have opinions and to express them. They may also have the extraordinary opportunity to work with professors in their research, gaining hands-on experience while earning their degrees.

Mills is also recognized as one of the Best 366 Colleges by The Princeton Review and one of the "Top 50 colleges for African Americans" by *Black Enterprise* magazine. *Washington Monthly* ranked Mills 36 out of 202 institutions based on the college's community service, research spending, quality of preparation for graduate education and social mobility.

As the college motto—"one destination, many paths"—suggests, students are encouraged to follow their own course in an academic environment enriched by students of different backgrounds, ethnicities, cultures, ages and mindsets. You can be who you are, or discover who you are, in an environment that values the testing of creative and intellectual limits, where voices find confidence and purpose, and where diversity leads to knowledge. Mills women discover their best selves and emerge confident and prepared to lead in whatever field they pursue. Mills graduates are authors, composers, lawyers, professors, ambassadors, news anchors, governors, congresswomen and activists.

If you are serious about your education, curious about the world, and burning to make a difference, Mills will give you both the resources and the space you need. Find out more about Mills College today.

Occidental College

Office of Admission
1600 Campus Road
Los Angeles, CA 90041
Admissions phone: (800) 825-5262; (323) 259-2700
Admissions e-mail: admission@oxy.edu
Admissions URL: www.oxy.edu

 Admissions

Current student, 8/2004-Submit Date, November 2006

For my personal essay, I basically just wrote about how poor my family was, how bad my high school was, and how I prevailed despite all these obstacles. Oxy is known for their financial aid and the school takes in a lot of low income students. I think the school also recommends having an interview. They are not necessary, but it's a good opportunity not only to get to know some faculty members and see the campus, but also for them to get to know you.

Current student, 8/2005-Submit Date, May 2006

The admissions process was very student friendly and not overly taxing. Interviews are relaxed and informative for both parties, and my interview gave me my first feel for the communal, cooperative atmosphere that I love about Oxy. Although the interview is optional, I highly recommend it. Your application also serves as the basis for merit scholarship consideration, which is really nice because many schools require additional paperwork for such scholarships. The essay is also very straightforward; I used my personal statement from the Common App. People likely to be selected for Oxy are motivated, dynamic people with wide-ranging interests and goals. Most successful applicants have a strong academic record coupled with devotion to extracurricular activities.

Current student, 8/2003-Submit Date, May 2006

Having worked in the admissions setting, I have become familiar with the application process. For most students, applications are reviewed twice by two different admissions officers from the January deadline until early March. If a discrepancy arises between their two decisions, then the application goes to committee. This entails communal review of the application by most of the admissions officers. Since there are only eight admissions officers at a small school like Oxy, they take a very personal approach to making admissions decisions. They don't only accept students who have a perfect SAT score or have all A's. They truly consider the entire picture that the student's application paints: test scores, grades, extracurricular activities, volunteer/job experience, personal statement, an interview evaluation (if present) and other personal circumstances. As one admissions officer has said herself, Oxy looks for "well-lopsided students to make a well-rounded class" each year. The admissions staff definitely takes one's unique achievements and experiences into account.

Interviews are optional, and interview evaluations become a supplement to the application. A bad interview is not held against a student, but unless you think your interview will be stellar or that it will add another dimension to your application, you might decide to skip the interview. Since most people are nervous in interviews, it's often difficult for the admissions officers to assess the student's personality during the interview.

The school is generally need-blind, unless one is an international student.

Current student, 8/2005-Submit Date, May 2006

The admissions process is fairly easy to go through. The first step is actually filling out the application, which can be done online or by requesting a paper application from the school. Occidental is a small school with only about 1,800 students, so when it comes time to completing those college essays or blurbs, it's best to be unique enough to stand out, but also to get your main points across without going on and on. Two letters of recommendation are also required, and I suggest asking teachers who know you fairly well. An interview is recommended with the application process, and I would highly recommend it. It gives you a chance to meet some of the people in the admissions office, and these people actually look at your application. Remember, an interview can only help you and it can give you a chance to explain in more detail what is on your application. You can apply for Early Decision by December or Regular Admission, which is in January. The college will send you little reminders when they have received your application, and the rest is up to the school from there.

Current student, 8/2005-Submit Date, January 2006

I think that the essay is the most important part of the admissions process. I recommend that a junior in high school get a professional to assist them in drafting and revising their essay. The essay is what makes you stand out. Many people get good grades and play sports or an instrument, but few people can write an extremely good essay. I think the interview is not that important; all you have to do is not say or do anything outrageously stupid, just be polite and act normal and interested in the school. Have a few questions ready to ask the interviewer. I would recommend applying to as many schools as you can. That way, when May rolls around, and you have to decide where to go in the fall, you are more likely to have some choices. Applying to the most selective schools is worth a try, but make sure you have some back-ups that you wouldn't mind going to. Don't stress too much, if you worked hard and did your best, there's nothing you can do but wait. Occidental is selective, but not intimidatingly so. It has around a 45 percent acceptance rate.

Current student, 8/2000-Submit Date, February 2004

The admissions process at Occidental impressed me when I visited as a second-semester high school senior. At Oxy my interviewer talked about how applications are carefully looked at, and how character is evaluated more than simply by the numbers. I think Oxy takes the essay into greater consideration than most other schools do. This is representative of Oxy in general—it is a school that attempts to encourage and aid the individual student.

 ## Academics

Current student, 8/2004-Submit Date, November 2006

I'm doing an IPS (independent pattern of study) for Cultural Studies/Foreign Language Studies. If you have declared a major, you can easily get into any class for that major. However, if you have not declared, and a class you want to take is full, you have to show up to that class as if you are enrolled in it, and wait for someone to drop it or schmooze with the teacher enough for him or her to let you in. I would say the science classes, math, and all the other basic classes that you have to take are the ones that fill up the fastest. We also have this program called the Core Program that is designed to help the incoming freshmen learn to write at the required level of the school, but I think it is really dumb. You get to pick the topic of your core class, which is one class the first semester and then one seminar and colloquium (comprised of two classes: one lecture and another group discussion) on a different topic the next semester.

Alumnus/a, 8/2003-Submit Date, September 2006

There are some great professors and some bad ones. My classes were always writing based and I had to write a ton. Faking it isn't that easy to get away with. Discussion is also really important.

Current student, 7/2005-Submit Date, June 2006

So far, I've really enjoyed my classes. They've all been very different, as I am undecided regarding my major, so I've really tried to get a good view of what's out there by taking everything from journalism to theater, to anthropology, to English, to Spanish, to history, to education—and that's just in my first year! My professors have been really accessible and helpful, and my classes have been really small (15 to 25 kids, usually). My journalism professor was actually an editor for the *Los Angeles Times*, and he even held class at his house once, which is something college books always brag about, but I never thought actually happened. My classes have been challenging, but at a manageable level, and I've loved being able to talk over assignments with other students, whether they live in my hall or across campus.

Current student, 8/2005-Submit Date, May 2006

Reggie, the online registration program, is a very frustrating thing. It is very strict about scheduling and class availability. It makes getting into popular classes seem impossible when realistically, one only must go see the professor teaching the class. The frosh Core Program tries to emphasize dialogue in the class, but in my experience, I found that professors do not know how to lead a dialogue and prompt—so many times dialogue classes become lecture classes. My lecture classes were all very satisfactory; I always felt that the professors had the right balance between lecture and questions. The professors are also very easy to get into contact with, if not physically, through e-mail or the telephone. The workload really depends on the student and the classes he/she is taking. I found that I took very reading-intensive classes, which also meant lots of papers. Whereas, a lot of my friends were taking classes that weren't reading intensive, and thus, did not have as many papers as I did.

Current student, 7/2004-Submit Date, May 2006

Sometimes when enrolling, you can't get every class you want at the time, but every time I have e-mailed a teacher, they have let me in the class. Grading is very fair, classes are very challenging but not impossible. It's not that easy to get A's, but teachers are always available and willing to help. Most of my classes have had students who are willing to discuss topics and fully participate.

Current student, 8/2003-Submit Date, May 2006

Oxy prides itself on the small class sizes. While most classes tend to be about 20 students in size, the first-year writing seminar has 16 students maximum. Courses that are requirements for several majors usually have larger numbers of students (for example, Organic Chemistry courses can have up to 35 students). Luckily, no teacher's assistants (TAs) teach at Oxy, so all the teaching and assistance comes straight from a professor. Professors tend to be extremely generous with their time during office hours. Also, the professors know who students are, as class sizes are kept low.

Getting into these full classes is not difficult. The popular classes have size caps (at about 35 students), but that number can be exceeded. Although it may take a student his/her first year to figure this out, a quick e-mail to the professor of the class usually is the key to getting in the class.

As for the workload, it varies depending on the student's major. Science majors spend a lot of time in labs, in class, and doing research, whereas some of the social science majors (e.g., sociology) have typically had somewhat of a lighter load. Currently, faculty have been meeting to discuss equity between the majors.

Current student, 8/2005-Submit Date, May 2006

Most of the professors go out of their way to get to know the students in their classes. I have personal relationships with many of my professors, and all of those relationships are positive ones. They are eager to work with and help students understand concepts better, and their expectations are fair. The issue I have is getting into classes. Sometimes you really have to force your way into classes. I respect and appreciate the college's pledge to keep class sizes small, but it's frustrating when nothing in your major is open to you from the get-go.

 ## Employment Prospects

Alumnus/a, 8/2003-Submit Date, September 2006

If you want to get a job when you graduate, start looking early and you will. Most Oxy grads intend on going to grad school, but a lot work for a few years first. A lot of graduates don't have plans, but I'd say they end up finding something. Oxy has good connections, but you have to take the initiative.

Current student, 7/2004-Submit Date, May 2006

When looking for an internship this summer, the Career Development Center helped immensely. They read and corrected my cover letters and résumé, and helped me navigate through the alumni network. All of the alumni were very supportive.

Current student, 8/2003-Submit Date, May 2006

While 70 percent of Oxy students go on to graduate school within five years of graduating from Oxy, most find jobs in their downtime. Occidental College is definitely known in academia, and the Career Development Center on campus has made sure to market Oxy students' skills maximally. Some students opt to participate in the Peace Corps or a program like Teach for America. Some of the scientific research students decide to do a post-baccalaureate program or work

Read all of Vault's College Surveys at **www.vault.com/college**—get complete surveys on 100s of colleges and universities, expert advice on applicaton essays and more.

VAULT CAREER LIBRARY **45**

as a research assistant at places like the City of Hope. Some students go into the work force permanently. This year, one economics major has been hired by a major financial corporation to be a bond trader.

If a student wants to explore the possibilities, the internships are overflowing. Most students partake in an internship during the junior and senior years. Our majors interested in the entertainment industry often intern at one of the movie studios.

The school hosts several on-campus Career Days and has guests from the plethora of professions visiting Oxy throughout the school year.

Current student, 8/2000-Submit Date, May 2004

In my graduating class, people got excellent jobs at Goldman Sachs, Bear Stearns, Mercer, KPMG and B of A Securities. If you're coming to Oxy and wanting to do investment banking or consulting after graduation, don't expect much from the Career Development Center. However, if you're willing to go the extra mile and initiate with employers, recruiters respond very enthusiastically to Oxy students.

Oxy has a fantastic grad/professional school placement rate, and professors really go to bat for you. I have friends graduating and matriculating at schools such as Harvard Med, Stanford Law, UCLA Law, the Harvard Kennedy School and others. The list really does go on and on. Graduate and professional schools respond (surprisingly) very, very favorably to Oxy students.

Current student, 8/2000-Submit Date, February 2004

If students take advantage of the career center, it can be extremely helpful for them. I have gone to workshops and career fairs and had conferences with the advisors, and have received great advice from those who are helping me in my job search. The counselors go to great lengths to set students (who pursue it) up with alumni or internships. The Walk in My Shoes program pairs up students with a professional in the student's field of interest, for a day of shadowing. I will be doing it for the first time next month.

Quality of Life

Alumnus/a, 8/2003-Submit Date, September 2006

In my opinion, housing at Oxy is pretty bad. The dorms are old, and since the school has gotten more popular, there has been a housing shortage. Now they are building a new dorm, but when I was a freshman they crammed three kids into a room made for two. Not a good way to ease the transition into college. Perhaps the new dorm will make it better, hopefully.

The food is pretty good. However, the dining hall hours are pretty shitty. If you are a vegetarian, the staff is super accommodating.

The neighborhood is not sketchy: it has a lot of character and flavor. The only tip is that you shouldn't walk around alone at night. But Eagle Rock isn't really an exception: No matter where you are in the world, you shouldn't walk around alone at night.

Current student, 7/2005-Submit Date, June 2006

I always feel safe on Oxy's campus, and Campus Safety (Campo) is always willing to drive students from school to near-by residences off campus. I probably would not walk around Eagle Rock alone at night, but I have done it with just one other friend (again, probably not the safest idea, but it didn't seem scary at the time).

The food is great at Oxy, and our dining staff is amazing—they are all so friendly and helpful, and absolutely willing to go out of their way to make every meal the best experience possible. As a picky eater and a vegetarian, I have found plenty to eat and satisfy my appetite all year, and I look forward to returning to campus to see all my friends in the food services.

Our campus is beautiful. The buildings are always kept clean on the inside and outside, and the landscaping is lovely. I am always very proud to show visitors our campus.

Current student, 8/2005-Submit Date, May 2006

I was lucky and received good housing. There are dorms with big rooms (Erdman, Chillcott, Haines and Newcomb) and residence halls with tiny rooms (Braun). All the residence halls, though, have great housekeeping. They are very friendly. The campus has various organizations—Programming Board, Office of Student Life, Student Activities Center and Intercultural Community—that put on great events for students. Events include but are not limited to: dances, dialogues, speakers, food, competitions and *The Vagina Monologues*. The facilities are all right. The pool could definitely use an upgrading. It's a 25-yard pool with six lanes, kind of disappointing. The weight room is small and has a very limited amount of machines. The soccer field is put on the top of campus and has very bad spectator bleachers. Patterson, the football field and track, is very nice and has very impressive fan seating. The softball and baseball fields are both very nice, but the baseball field is, like the soccer field, at the far end of the campus and has very bad spectator seating. I love the food at Oxy, there is always fresh fruits and vegetables. The grill provides meats for the meat lovers, the pasta bar can make almost any type of pasta one could ask for, and the sandwich bar makes the best sandwiches I've ever eaten in my entire life. I have only heard of a few incidences of crime on campus. On campus I feel very safe and often walk alone at night.

> **The school says:** "Occidental's proposed master plan, currently pending before the City of Los Angeles, includes plans for a new Olympic-sized pool and upgrading the soccer fields with, among other things, new spectator seating. The new Field Turf surface on the football field allows use by the soccer teams, as well as lacrosse and other club sports."

Social Life

Alumnus/a, 8/2003-Submit Date, September 2006

Social life is very disappointing at Oxy. There's a little thing called the "Oxy bubble." Basically everyone forgets about the real world and only cares about the high school-like drama that happens on campus. Getting off campus is impossible if you don't have a car. And even if you do, finding people to go with you is difficult. Everyone seems to be content just having Oxy. When I started at Oxy, there was a vibrant off- and on-campus party scene. Now, there are occasional dances where everyone gets wasted.

If you are a non-drinker, the social life at Oxy must be awful. Student life is trying to work on more programming, such as open mic nights and off-campus events so that people don't have to drink. But drinking is a very popular activity.

For non-weekend activities, a ton of people volunteer to fill up extra time. Extracurricular activities are big and people at Oxy generally tend to be over-involved or not involved in anything.

Current student, 7/2004-Submit Date, May 2006

The social life is amazing. There are always off-campus parties at named houses within two blocks from school. There are also themed dances and parties on campus. These are the events where a majority of the school attends and you see everyone you know. Some favorites are Da Getaway, a casino night, the winter formal, Club Oxy, and the sororities and fraternities put on about five themed dances per year (Toga, Doctors and Nurses formals). Dorm life is also very social; there are always pre-parties in the dorms or houses very near the campus.

Current student, 8/2005-Submit Date, May 2006

The social life is not spent in bars; it actually happens best within the dorms as you form close friendships and relationships with the people you live with. There are many fantastic restaurants in both directions from the college in Pasadena and Glendale. For less expensive dining, even the surrounding Eagle Rock and Highland Park area has wonderful, moderately priced dining. A favorite for Oxy students is 21 Choices in Old Town Pasadena. The dating scene is very much on campus, with many others dating off campus. There are always events sponsored by the college or clubs like movies, picnics or even a Chocolate Seder held by the Hillel Club on campus. The Greek system usually puts on events off campus. On campus, the dances are most popular with Sex on the Beach and Splatter being some of the favorite dances of the year.

The School Says

Founded in 1887, Occidental is one of the few nationally ranked liberal arts colleges located in a major city. With 1,800 students drawn from 45 states and 26 countries, Occidental's diversity is a vital part of its academic excellence. Pell Grant recipients make up 19 percent of the student body; 17 percent are first-generation students; 37 percent are students of color; more than 70 percent receive some form of financial aid. Occidental students regularly win major national scholarships and fellowships, which, in 2005-06, included a Truman, a Marshall, four Fulbrights, two Goldwaters, and a Coro Fellowship. The College's undergraduate research program—recipient of a 1998 NSF Integration of Research and Education Award—was cited as one the country's best in a 2001 study sponsored by a consortium of private foundations. Hundreds of Occidental students collaborate on research in a wide range of fields with the College's superb faculty, who have been honored by the Dreyfus Foundation, the Mathematical Association of America, the American Chemical Society and other national groups for their teaching skills.

Occidental is at the forefront of interdiciplinary, intercultural education that takes full advantage of the resources of one of the world's great cities—Los Angeles—to enhance classroom education. Civic engagement has been woven throughout the academic program, not only in coursework, but through a long-standing commitment to identifying new opportunities for hands-on student research, internships, and volunteer projects. Students live and attend classes on a 120-acre hillside campus designed by famed architect Myron Hunt. Noted for its beauty and favored as a Hollywood location for 85 years—Occidental has been featured in dozens of movies and television shows, most recently *Monk*, *In Justice* and *The L Word*—the heart of the campus is the oak-studded Quadrangle and the College's original Beaux Arts academic buildings. A founder of intercollegiate athletic competition in Southern California in 1894, Occidental has produced conference champions too numerous to list, All-Americans numbering in the hundreds, and dozens of Olympians, world-record holders, and national champions.

Pepperdine University

Admissions Office
24255 Pacific Coast Hwy
Malibu, CA 90263
Admissions phone: (310) 506-4392
Admissions fax: (310) 506-4861
Admissions e-mail: seaver@pepperdine.edu
Admissions URL: seaver.pepperdine.edu/admission/

Admissions

Alumnus/a, Mathematics, 8/2000-5/2004, March 2007

Pepperdine wants to see that you are committed to spiritual growth, whether that is through Christian spirituality or otherwise. This commitment should be reflected in your essays.

Alumnus/a, 8/2000-5/2005, September 2005

The process is like that of any other college; however, I would highly recommend flying/driving over for an interview if you are good in person. You will meet someone face-to-face who is going to be before the board of admissions, or at least have significant input on your file when it is being reviewed. Pepperdine is becoming more desirable recently, but after five years in the place I have noticed similar types of students without fail, which is either due to a controlled admission or self-selection. I often talked with the Dean of Students, and they are looking for what almost any other school is: Students who have shown some sort of excellence in the past, something that sets them apart from the others, really anything—ping pong champ to Motocross—but something that makes them unique and indicates that they will make Pepperdine look good in the future.

I would really stress the importance of some type of achievement, academic or personal, but something very noteworthy—I had many friends waitlisted or denied even though they had very strong GPAs at great schools and good SAT scores, but they were somewhat bland on paper—Pepperdine wants something special.

All together I would say it is more selective in certain ways than UC schools but less selective on a raw numbers basis; they are looking for character, first and foremost.

Current student, 8/2005-Submit Date, September 2005

The admissions process is fairly straightforward and easy if you start planning ahead. You need a couple of references, and an interview greatly helps your chances of being accepted. Try to contact somebody at the school and get connected to them to increase your chances of being accepted. Pepperdine is fairly selective, so you need to have pretty good grades and fairly high test scores. Athletic program is good but not great, so there is potential of getting in because of sports.

Current student, 8/2004-Submit Date, March 2005

Admissions was a simple online process. There were no interviews, but there were several essays required. The fully-employed BSM program didn't seem particularly selective.

Alumnus/a, 8/2000-5/2004, October 2004

It's amazing how competitive the admissions process has become for universities, and mine was no different than most. For my school, doing an interview was optional. Unless your GPA is off the charts and you have recommendations from the likes of the Pope and the Dali Lama, I highly recommend going for an interview. Admissions counselors of course have to consider what is on paper, but they are much more likely to admit you to their university if you have a great personality and they like you. For your essays, try not to be generic. Try not to give canned answers. Remember that these people have to read thousands and thousands of essays. Do something a little different. Try your best to be unique.

Alumnus/a, 6/1996-12/1999, May 2004

The form itself is pretty basic. Fill it out and include a heart-wrenching essay. Be sure to include your picture for the school files. I don't know anyone who attended who school who did not provide a picture. Then call and set up an interview.

Read all of Vault's College Surveys at **www.vault.com/college**—get complete surveys on 100s of colleges and universities, expert advice on applicaton essays and more.

VAULT CAREER LIBRARY   47

Academics

Alumnus/a, Mathematics, 8/2000-5/2004, March 2007

It is easy to get into classes at Pepperdine because it is such a small school. It is also nice that their General Education program does not have to be taken in any particular order, so you can wait to take a boring class until you absolutely have to. Some classes/professors are better than others, but overall, I found the quality of teaching to be much better than my experience at a state school. Additionally, because the classes are so small, you really get to know your professors, which is nice when it comes time for recommendations.

Alumnus/a, 8/2000-5/2005, September 2005

The school programs are what you make of them. I was a business major and I experienced some frustration over the simple hoop-jumping type of teaching. It is not as dynamic as it could be and often resorts to more base-concept learning rather than a realistic approach to things. If one does have a passion for the study, then, yes, you will learn much, but I am trying to say you cannot expect it to cater to you, the classes aren't that involved. The quality, though, is high.

Grading is very liberal, and most professors are so nice they want to give good grades. Grading is pleasant, to say the least; I got mainly B's, a 2.98, and I never did homework ever, ever, ever. Getting popular classes is easy if you're smart, just do it the second the registration gates open! Or even better: if you're an athlete you get to start a week early!

Current student, 8/2005-Submit Date, September 2005

They have a liberal arts program that has you take a wide variety of classes. At first it seems like overkill, but it helps you figure out what you want to major in. After your GEs you can pick exactly what you want. Classes are good and there are plenty of really good teachers. Be sure to ask which teachers are the best, because there are a few bad teachers. Grading depends on the teacher; some are way easy and some are really hard. So far my workload is fairly minimal and have plenty of time to do other things.

Alumnus/a, 8/1997-4/2001, October 2005

I earned my BS in Sports Medicine from Pepperdine. The program was one of the most grueling programs I have ever encountered. The first week of class, the Sports Medicine faculty sponsored a retreat. At that retreat, we planned all four years of education (coursework, extracurricular activities). At the retreat, the faculty made it known that they would be treating us as master's students. They would be trying to weed us out by making the coursework as detailed and difficult as possible. The classes were of a high caliber. Each professor expected the most out of each of us, for every class we enrolled in. Courses must be taken in specific order, or there will be no way to graduate in four years.

The beauty of Pepperdine was that it was small in numbers, so there was a very close relationship with the faculty, and although they stated they wanted to weed us out, they also desired success. Faculty, on many occasions, invited me to their homes to aid me in grasping a certain concept, or just to get to know me. Workload was rigorous, especially when involved in sorority/fraternity life, athletics and working a job; however, it was still possible. It was made possible by the faculty who worked with us on a regular basis to make sure we were getting the most out of our education.

Current student, 8/2004-Submit Date, March 2005

The BSM program is designed for working professionals and strives to be relevant to the situations faced by students in their positions. The difficulty and quality of the classes vary from professor to professor. The workload is demanding, as all of the students in the BSM program are also working full time. Very little time is left for a social life.

Alumnus/a, 8/2000-5/2004, October 2004

For the most part, as at any top university, the hardest part is getting in. Depending upon your major of course, once you get in, you'll most likely find the courses to be acceptable in quality but not as challenging as you expected. So much of the educational experience is about the professors. If you have great teachers who are passionate about what they teach, then the quality of classes is greatly improved. However, if you have over-qualified, highly intelligent professors who have neither a passion for teaching nor for the subject being taught, you will find the quality of those classes to be very low, indeed.

Workload and grading, again, all depend on the teacher. In my opinion, a teacher should give a workload that requires consistent effort, forward planning and outside thinking. However, some teachers just give loads and loads of busywork just because they can. There are also other teachers who don't seem to know what a workload is and let their students coast by barely achieving the bare minimum.

 ## Employment Prospects

Alumnus/a, 8/2000-5/2005, September 2005

Post-graduation is not the time to look for a job. Pepperdine is prestigious enough that if you have the goods on your part (intellect, passion and drive) then it can open the doors for you.

Conversely, I would warn that the school alone is not enough for good jobs—it's amazing how many qualified go-getters there are, scrambling for jobs across the States. It's really up to you and your skills. I would say also to elaborate on my earlier principle—that the good jobs are all about getting a foot in the door, ahead of time! If you get an internship somewhere you would like to work, then show them who you are. This is the ticket for good jobs, many of my friends have gone this route and attained jobs.

Alumnus/a, 8/1997-4/2001, October 2005

One great thing about my Pepperdine degree is that it continues to increase in value. Although we were ranked 52nd in the United States when I graduated, we have since moved up to 47th and are still climbing. Pepperdine, known for its amazing campus, Church of Christ affiliation and personal attention (small classes) is growing in prestige with every passing year. When I got my present job, the fact that I was a Pepperdine alumna greatly impressed my interviewers, and was a big topic of discussion during the interview. I have maintained contacts due to my sorority affiliation, which have provided many career opportunities, as well. The alumni office is constantly in contact with me, and I receive one or two publications each month, notifying me of changes to campus, classes and faculty. The alumni office also sends out a yearly alumni update brochure. It tells of accomplishments of fellow alumni, and allows all to stay in touch with the university.

Alumnus/a, 8/2000-5/2004, October 2004

Of course, the higher ranked your university is, the better your chances for obtaining higher paying positions. The biggest factor in employment prospects is demand. It doesn't matter if you graduate at the top of your class from the number one university. If there is no demand for your skills, then there will be no work. Employment possibilities depend completely on the field you are going into. It is a good idea to get a good internship your second semester of your senior year and work as hard as you can. Hopefully, as the semester nears the end, you will be offered a job.

 ## Quality of Life

Alumnus/a, Mathematics, 8/2000-5/2004, March 2007

The campus housing and dining is, by far, the best of any college campus to which I have been. You can't beat living in a dorm surrounded by palm trees and views of the ocean. I would feel safe walking alone on Pepperdine's campus at any time of night, even as a female.

Alumnus/a, 8/2000-5/2005, September 2005

Absolutely glorious! Just do a campus tour, and I would say you will see 70 percent of the vibe—it is not hard to understand, especially with a small student body. Housing is fine and if you want to move off campus, group with friends and you can score beachfront places for not much at all. Try not to live in the Canyons; the commute is like doing some *Lord of the Rings* voyage every day, and it sucks in Calabasas and anywhere back there. Crime is nonexistent, save for burglary in Malibu. Quality of life is great! Food is OK, but the town is littered with high-priced amazing cuisine, which should be taken advantage of.

Current student, 8/2005-Submit Date, September 2005

Quality of life is very good at Pepperdine. Pretty relaxed and laid-back in a fairly peaceful campus. Housing is really good and the dorms are real nice. Plenty of room, especially if you're used to having a big family. The campus is extremely nice and well kept. Several different facilities are open to all of the students. The cafeteria always has a good selection, but is slightly pricey. The neighborhood is extremely safe, and there is no crime.

Alumnus/a, 8/1997-4/2001, October 2005

Dorm life was pretty good at Pepperdine. Every student had a meal plan for the cafeteria, which was one of the most grandiose cafeterias I've ever seen. There were two stations for each meal, where food was cooked to order right in front of you. Quality was excellent, and students were always provided a well-balanced meal. There is an on-campus coffee shop, equipped with computers hooked up to the Internet (for late-night studying and socializing). There is an on-campus hangout called the HAWC that has a big screen TV, pool tables and ping-pong tables. Each dorm is equipped with a central lobby. Each typically has a fireplace and TV. Each suite (four bedrooms, eight students, two bathrooms, one living room) is equipped with Internet access and cable. There is a public safety office that takes care of all campus safety. They make regular patrols around campus, and through the buildings. Crime rate is very low. Laptop theft would be the most common crime.

Alumnus/a, 8/2000-5/2004, October 2004

The university was amazing in terms of food. We had a gourmet cafeteria with freshly made cakes and pastries and meals like salmon, shark and pork tenderloin. The quality of housing depended on how much money you had. All of the housing was definitely sanitary and livable. But if you could afford it, really, really nice housing was also available. Most of the students agreed that after they graduated, their quality of living was going to go down.

Alumnus/a, 6/1996-12/1999, May 2004

The student housing is very nice. Nicer than the housing at any college I have visited. The neighborhood is very safe and it is very easy to become involved in the community. Malibu is a wonderful place to live. The food on campus is OK. There is no fast food on campus.

Dorms are not coed. A person of the opposite sex cannot be in your room before 10 a.m. or after 10 p.m. There are a lot of rules at Pepperdine that you will not find at your standard college. However, breaking rules creates a lot of fun and drama, which every college student needs. All my fond memories of the school involve my friends and I breaking some silly rule.

 Social Life

Alumnus/a, Mathematics, 8/2000-5/2004, March 2007

Since Pepperdine is a dry campus and many students are from the L.A. area, it can be hard to find things to do on campus. Many of the in-state students go home on the weekends, and lots of freshmen have cars, so if you don't have a car, you are literally stuck on mountain. I recommend bringing a car and/or making friends with someone who has a car. There is a beach within walking distance, but just be ready for a hike. Lots of students are involved in UM (University Ministries) and other church-related activities. Other students like to hit the Hollywood scene on the weekends.

Current student, 8/2005-Submit Date, September 2005

Social life is really good at Pepperdine if you choose to be outgoing. Several restaurants are in the surrounding area, both formal and fast-food chains. Dating scene is fairly open, all types of people from which to choose. Tons of events through the college and the school is close to all types of sporting events and concerts and stuff like that. There are several clubs and there is the Greek system, but not too many of them. Going to the beach is fairly popular with all the students or heading out to the promenade and pier in Santa Monica.

Alumnus/a, 8/1997-4/2001, October 2005

Pepperdine is a dry campus. Students are not permitted to drink on campus, or return to campus intoxicated. For each incident, a student receives a write-up. After three write-ups, the student is expelled. The most social place on campus would have to be the cafeteria and the common area outside of the cafeteria. The common area is where sorority and fraternity groups "paint the rock" (a symbol of school pride); it is a popular meeting place for students before they leave campus to go to nearby Santa Monica's Third Street promenade, the Santa Monica Pier or Hollywood for a night of dining, dancing and drinking. Local restaurants range from the karaoke bar at Thai Dishes restaurant, and local Malibu Yogurt in the heart of Malibu, to Jerry's Deli in Woodland Hills. The Greek system is more of a club system than a real Greek system. There are no sorority/fraternity houses (due to a mandate from the city of Malibu). A popular form of entertainment is the very-nearby beach. Good surf-spots, beach volleyball, sun practically year-round and midnight bonfires at Port Mugu beach.

Alumnus/a, 8/2000-5/2004, October 2004

The Greek life was very different than at most schools because there were no Greek houses. All of the sororities and fraternities were interspersed. It was a dry campus, so drinking wasn't permitted, though, of course it went on. The dating scene was pretty much nonexistent. Because there were so many more girls than boys at the school, the boys never really saw the need to settle down. That was on the one hand. On the other hand, there are a lot of couples who are engaged or married by second semester of their senior year. So basically people either weren't dating, or they were getting married. One great thing about the school was the service opportunities. There were tons of chances to volunteer for Habitat for Humanity, or spend time with kids, or do service work through the campus church. It is a relatively conservative school.

Alumnus/a 6/1996-12/1999, May 2004

No bars. No football team. The basketball team and water polo team are pretty good, but don't lead to the excitement that a football game provides. A large gay population, so not a lot of dating members of the opposite sex. Malibu Inn used to be the cool place to hang out, but it is pretty lame now. Restaurants do not last long in Malibu. A national Greek system has been on campus now for the last five years. Being a part of the Greek system is the best way to meet other people and have a social life. The school has a very active Church of Christ group.

Read all of Vault's College Surveys at **www.vault.com/college**—get complete surveys on 100s of colleges and universities, expert advice on applicaton essays and more.

VAULT CAREER LIBRARY   **49**

Pomona College

Admissions Office
Sumner Hall 333 N. College Way
Claremont, CA 91711
Admissions phone: (909) 621-8134
Admissions e-mail: admissions@pomona.edu
Admissions URL: www.pomona.edu/admissions/

 Admissions

Current student, English, 8/2004-Submit Date, May 2007

Pomona is a very selective school. Prospective students need to have stellar grades, scores, extracurriculars, essays and so on. An interview is definitely a good idea, whether on campus or with an alum in your hometown, as it can provide the admissions staff with an even better idea of who you are aside from all the numbers and essays. Pomona students are strong-willed, open-minded, curious and motivated—not necessarily exactly sure what they are going to do with it all yet, but excited to learn and find out. In the end, as it is with any of the top schools these days, getting in is a matter of hard work, persistence, dedication, charisma and good luck.

Alumnus/a, Economics, 8/2003-5/2007, May 2007

The admissions process at Pomona is quite simple if you start early and know what to do. The biggest thing at Pomona is not to try and be somebody you're not or try to fit some cookie-cutter idea of who you think has the best chance of acceptance. What you need to do is focus on something that separates you from other applicants and plays to your strengths. For example, I was probably ranked in the top 20 percent in my high school for GPA, but because I focused on how I took more AP courses than anybody else in my high school and how much I enjoy challenging myself I was accepted over kids with higher GPAs and SATs.

Alumnus/a, Philosophy, 8/2002-5/2006, May 2007

Use the Common Application along with a few optional forms. I used an athletic supplemental form to highlight my desire to play basketball in college. The college was extremely selective, but I was never discouraged by that when applying because I felt comfortable when visiting. My interview was more like a conversation than an interrogation. Received excellent advice telling me to make every word in my college essay compelling, so that's what I strived for and I think that's what made me stick out from thousands of applicants.

Current student, Biology, 8/2004-Submit Date, June 2007

The admissions process was purportedly very difficult. SAT scores were expected to be in excess of 1450 if one wanted to surpass the mere average. The most important advice I was given was that it was imperative for a California resident, or rather anyone within a reasonable traveling distance, to interview, despite the fact that the interview itself was an optional part of application procedure. The interview was conducted by one of the members of the senior class interview team, as I believe are most, if not all. Essay options were and continue to be fairly open ended. There is, however, a substantial amount of weight placed on the two personal statements, given that the school is very small and a certain politically correct and socially active student body is highly desired. Since my admission, selectivity has only increased further. This school is likely one of the most selective, if not the most selective, liberal arts school in the country. You must make the right impression with the admissions committee if you want to be admitted. Students with superior scores and admissions to Ivy League universities are often denied admission here.

Alumnus/a, 8/2001-5/2005, March 2007

When I applied, Pomona was very selective and it has become even more so since then. You need good grades in tough classes and good test scores, but admissions is not formulaic in any way. Write essays that let your personality shine through, and definitely interview, if possible. At a small school, it helps to show them what makes you unique—they are trying to build a community, not just admit the very best students.

Alumnus/a, 8/2001-5/2005, March 2006

Pomona is very selective. They look for strong grades, challenging coursework, high scores on standardized tests and unique extracurricular accomplishments. You should definitely interview. Either an alumni interview or an on-campus interview is fine. Since the school is small, they want students who will help form a vibrant, productive, and fun community, so make sure that your personality comes out in your essays.

Current student, 8/2002-Submit Date, January 2004

You really have to sell yourself. Since you may not have a chance to interview, you need to realize that everything the office is going to know about you will be from a piece of paper. Put down everything you want them to know about you.

 Academics

Current student, English, 8/2004-Submit Date, May 2007

Generally, classes are very good, but any individual student's assessment of any one class is going to depend on his/her personal interests and biases, obviously. Academics are truly difficult, but always in varying degrees. It was a shock and a challenge to jump into Pomona's rigorous academia right after the cushiness of high school, but well worth the hard work. The academics push you to work harder and perform better, and I think for the majority of students, it really pays off. Grading, again, depends on the professor, but usually I have found it to be fair and honest. Grade inflation is sometimes a problem, but it's a nation-wide one with which we are all trying our best to deal. I have received very few grades that I thought were unfair.

Professors are actively accessible and open. They always have office hours and are ready and willing to help students with anything and everything. Most have a real genuine interest in getting to know their students on a personal level, and are enthusiastic about their subject and expertise.

Getting very popular classes is hard. There are some classes (e.g., History of Jazz) that are basically offered to seniors only. But other than that handful of classes, you can almost always get into the classes you want. Even if a class is full when you register, most professors will let you in if you talk to them and show up the first day, and the second day and so on.

Alumnus/a, Philosophy, 8/2002-5/2006, May 2007

Philosophy, politics and economics—a hybrid major that has difficulty in coordinating the three departments, but luckily the small-school aspect made it work extremely well. I received a lot of one-on-one attention from professors in and out of my major, which is what allowed me to pursue topics throughout my major that were interesting to me. For example I wrote my thesis on the model of NBA ownership, blending my love of basketball, with an in-depth look at a unique ownership model through the lenses of philosophy and economics. After my first year, I never had any trouble getting into any classes. I missed one entry-level econ course second semester freshman year, because the professor I wanted was full, so I waited and took him the following semester. The only problem I had in scheduling classes was narrowing all the courses I wanted to take into four years. My workload was balanced with basketball and the great social environment of a close-knit community. Grading was always in a manner that allowed for individual growth as professors took the time to grade and even discuss papers with me at length. It is not uncommon to re-write a paper with the professor's blessing because you went in the wrong direction or simply wanted to start over.

Current student, Biology, 8/2004-Submit Date, June 2007

Specifically, the student body concentration in terms of majors of choice is divided into approximately 30 percent natural sciences, 30 percent social sciences, and a remaining large concentration of humanities majors with other scattered majors, as well. Academics are difficult but manageable. That is, if you are a humanities or social sciences major. The science program is extremely difficult. Majors may require [as many as] 15 or 16 classes.

Labs are mandatory for the majority of classes, but are not extra credits. They are simply required components of the class. Thus, it is extremely difficult to manage or rather sculpt a class schedule around the required four-hour labs that occupy many afternoons. Nonetheless, professors are topnotch. The registration process itself is a little hectic, as the school has not adopted online procedures. Instead, students crowd into a tiny room in the registrar's office as academic assistants struggle to move the line along while keying into the system the desired classes for each student. The workload is difficult but manageable. Certain semesters are more hectic than others, especially if you are a science major forced to load up on extra lab classes in a given semester.

Alumnus/a, 8/2001-5/2005, March 2007

In your first couple of years, getting the classes you want can be tough, but it is not as bad as it is at big schools; such problems don't force students to take longer to graduate. Most professors are quite good, and a decent number are downright inspirational. Overall, the school provides an intellectually invigorating and supportive atmosphere. Classes are much smaller than they are at big schools, although they aren't especially small by liberal arts college standards. Some departments, like chemistry and history, are incredibly strong, while others, like biology, physics, and economics, have disappointed many students. However, due to the liberal arts orientation of the school, students of any major can get a topnotch, well-rounded education.

Current student, 8/2004-Submit Date, February 2007

There is a range of quality and popularity of majors at Pomona. Economics is very popular and strong, so are Spanish and most of the sciences (although not biology). American history is very strong but not as popular as other majors. In general, classes are small and easy to get into, though for the lower-division classes in popular majors, it can be more difficult. Most professors will let you into a class if you show up and do the work, regardless of whether you have the prerequisites or the class is capped. Class quality is generally good. Most classes are a lot of work and pretty rewarding, though there are some duds around.

Alumnus/a, 8/2001-5/2005, March 2006

Pomona's curriculum is strictly liberal arts based. The school does not offer any business-oriented or professional training classes. Classes tend to be quite small and involve a lot of student participation. It can be difficult to get popular classes, but that varies from department to department. Grading tends to be fairly generous in humanities, arts and social sciences but tough in the sciences. Workloads are similar, though history and fine arts can be extremely time-consuming, as well. Professors vary from inspirational to horrifically incompetent; the one constant is that the vast majority are warm, helpful, friendly people. The quality of classes ranges tremendously depending upon the subject matter and the quality of the professor, but the average class at Pomona is fairly rigorous and stimulating.

Employment Prospects

Current student, English, 8/2004-Submit Date, May 2007

From what I have heard, employers generally are impressed with a degree from Pomona. Graduates get jobs all across the board after Pomona. Many go on to great grad schools, and we have an impressively high med school acceptance rate. A lot of graduates also receive fellowships, awards and grants to research, study, or travel right after graduation (Fulbrights and so on). The Career Development Office is amazingly helpful—they have an extensive alumni network that can provide summer jobs, internships, and post-graduation opportunities. They are incredibly active in bringing on-campus recruiting, hosting career fairs, and facilitating jobs/internships/anything else.

Alumnus/a, Economics, 8/2003-5/2007, May 2007

Employment prospects at Pomona are very diverse mainly because the career paths of its graduates are so diverse. While I chose to pursue a career in finance and Wall Street, I had good friends going to L.A. to start a band and others going to study at Cambridge on prestigious scholarships. You'll find out that while the average citizen has never heard of Pomona, the people who need to know will know when it comes to post-graduate employment. If they haven't heard of Pomona, it won't be a problem because a well-worded and practiced spiel on Pomona will render any employer concerns empty.

Alumnus/a, Philosophy, 8/2002-5/2006, May 2007

Pomona College, although may not have the shock value of a Stanford or Harvard, carries with it the same weight in academic and professional settings. Several of my classmates, including myself, postponed our employment by going on a fellowship—Rotary, Watson or Fulbright. Other classmates chose to take jobs where they were offered signing bonuses on Wall Street. Others chose to enter Teach for America and others went on to graduate school. I'd say of my 350-odd fellow graduates that we pretty much have the world of career choices in our pockets. I've had friends use alumni to tap into the television industry and I myself was in touch with the NBA via a Pomona alumnus.

Current student, 8/2004-Submit Date, February 2007

Most recruiting on campus is for regional companies, though not all. Larger national consulting and financial firms are very present on campus. The career development office on campus can be very helpful if you have a plan (for example, you know you want to work in a specific field, but do not know how to find internships or market yourself). People end up working all over the globe at great jobs. I know people who are banking in England, teaching in China, doing research in South America and so on.

Alumnus/a, 9/1998-5/2002, March 2004

Pomona has a good enough name that it helps with employment at big companies/law firms and for grad school graduation. Smaller places, though, are less likely to be familiar with it, even in Southern CA. All of my friends got decent jobs after graduation, though, everything from Peace Corps to investment banking in New York. I'd say the name of the school doesn't hurt, but I wouldn't count on it for getting a job. (Though Pomona alumni do love to hire other Pomona grads, it seems. Totally utilize the alumni database in the career center for contact information, everyone I talked to was really nice and really helpful.)

Quality of Life

Current student, Economics, 8/2006-Submit Date, May 2007

The quality of life is great. The sponsor group system places incoming freshmen into groups of 10 to 20 with two sophomores to watch over and guide them. The sponsor groups do activities together (like discussing a book assigned over the summer and going to see on-campus speakers) before school starts, and live next to each other for the rest of the year.

Also, Pomona has made cultural and class diversity a big priority, and not just in terms of admitting students of different backgrounds. Pomona works hard to make sure that students who are already admitted feel welcome and included. Freshmen must attend two diversity discussions a year, and activities like the Pan-African festival are widely attended by students of all races. Pomona College has an extremely politically correct climate. One complaint that I have is that the mainly liberal student body does not do enough to make conservative students feel welcome. Pomona needs more conservative speakers.

Current student, English, 8/2004-Submit Date, May 2007

The vast majority of students live on campus, with a handful living off campus in surrounding houses. On-campus housing is great: it's comfortable, clean, the housekeeping staff is friendly and wonderful, and there is generally enough space for everyone. We're going through something of a housing crunch right now, but everyone is guaranteed housing for all four years. The hardest right now is to be a rising sophomore—they get last pick of housing and are often bumped to the deferred list after room draw. Only two dorms have air conditioning, which can be uncomfortable for everyone else in August and May, but it's not terrible.

Read all of Vault's College Surveys at **www.vault.com/college**—get complete surveys on 100s of colleges and universities, expert advice on applicaton essays and more.

VAULT CAREER LIBRARY 51

Alumnus/a, Economics, 8/2003-5/2007, May 2007

The quality of life at Pomona is the best aspect of the school. As I've described it to many people, you almost have to try not to be happy at Pomona. It seriously takes effort. After visiting several similar schools, I'm positive that Pomona has the best combination of smart but normal kids who you can have great conversations with. Also, within a two-hour drive at Pomona you can do anything you want to do. For example, you can go to downtown L.A. comedy clubs, go sea kayaking, or of course visit the beach and ski slopes in the same day.

Current student, Biology, 8/2004-Submit Date, June 2007

The quality of life at Pomona is stellar. Immediately upon entering the college, students are placed in what are called, sponsor groups, consisting of approximately 12 to 16 first-year students and two sophomores. Each sponsor group lives in a hall together for their first year of college, and provides an immediate social network and base from which to expand. Students are very friendly, receptive and politically correct to everyone on campus. Housing facilities are very nice, as many students receive their own room. The school is actually in the process of building more housing options. The campus and the facilities are topnotch. The school has the biggest per-student endowment of any college in the country, and therefore, new facilities are constantly being built and older facilities are constantly being renovated. The school is directly adjacent to the Claremont Village, which provides great options for eateries, cinema and the like. The neighborhood is usually safe.

Current student, 8/2004-Submit Date, February 2007

Having visited friends and family at other colleges, the Pomona quality of life is unmatched. Dorms are large and new. They are well maintained and if something goes wrong, it gets fixed. My shower broke this semester and was fixed the next day. The housekeeping staff is so good that they even clean the private bathrooms in suites, no matter how messy. The campus is like an oasis. The groundskeepers all deserve medals. Being in Southern California, the weather is great. It is February and about 70 degrees. It hit 80 last weekend. Crime is rare and I don't know of many real problems on campus. One thing that I would say needs improvement is the town near campus. The college knows this, though, and is working with locals to improve it.

 Social Life

Current student, English, 8/2004-Submit Date, May 2007

Since Claremont is so sleepy, there really is not much of a social life off campus. Our outdoor group, On The Loose (OTL) sponsors subsidized or free trips to national parks, beaches, mountains and so on, almost every weekend. Pomona also sponsors frequent trips into L.A. to see plays, go to museums, festivals, special events, concerts and so on, as well.

On campus, there is always something going on—a concert, recital, performance, party, debate, meeting, reading, lecture—every day and every night. And if nothing much is going on at Pomona, there is always something at one of the other four colleges (Pitzer, Scripps, Claremont McKenna and Harvey Mudd) within walking distance. There are alcohol events and sub-free ones, as well. There are two frats, but they are very small and throw one small party per week—Greek life is basically nonexistent.

There are two annual school-sponsored events that everyone looks forward to, in particular. In the fall, there's Harwood Halloween, which is a big concert and an after-party. In the spring, it's Smiley 80s, a giant 80s bash with a cover band and huge dance floor. Costumes are mandatory for both events.

Alumnus/a, Economics, 8/2003-5/2007, May 2007

The school's social life is mostly campus based but there are groups of students who go off campus all the time to enjoy the wide variety of activities within reasonable range of the school. The school spends a ton of money on alcohol for large campus parties, several of which are the biggest parties of each semester. However, the most common activity is drinking in small groups in dorm rooms without going crazy. The alcohol policy enforcement is fairly lax, which is fine because the student use of alcohol is not overboard and is actually quite reserved.

Alumnus/a, Philosophy, 8/2002-5/2006, May 2007

Social life is especially campus-centric. It is great for your first couple of years, but does get repetitive by junior and senior year. Luckily you go abroad and come back more mature and looking for things different than your typical alcohol-consuming college party. However, if effort is made, there is always something to do and students do have access to the surrounding Los Angeles community, but only those with specific interests, like music or theatre, exercise that option. Restaurants and bars are upscale and not catered towards college students, although a new downtown area is opening and appears to be more attractive to budget concerned college students. For serious club goers, we simply hit up L.A. There is basically no Greek system at Pomona, the frats/sororities are essentially clubs and don't dominate life at Pomona, but do contribute by throwing regular events. School sponsored favorites include Death by Chocolate—the school spends thousands on a chocolate binge. Other notables are the alternating weekly senior-junior socials and symposium.

Current student, 8/2004-Submit Date, February 2007

The college pays for students to throw parties. If you do the paperwork and submit a proposal, student council will provide a space, beer and some snacks. It is pretty amazing. Pomona just renovated a couple of the party spots to make them nicer, so now they are pretty cool. Parties are often outside because the weather is no nice. Part of the reason for this is that there are no frat houses or bars, so there would be nowhere for students to party without it. Students also throw parties in the dorms, which are fun.

Alumnus/a, 8/1997-5/2001, April 2005

As a residential college, the social life tends to be on campus with lots of parties and socials. Student concerts are great; we have several a cappella groups that perform on a regular basis during late-night snack, which always makes for a great study break. There are frats, but they're not your typical Greek system—as there are no national fraternities on campus. It's important to have a car, though, because there is so much that you can miss out on if you never leave campus. L.A. has great clubs and it's a shame to miss out on them. Dating has its ups and downs—again, if you don't find what you're looking for, check out the other four liberal arts schools nearby. A nice gym, intramurals and impromptu ultimate frisbee help keep the student body in shape. Last but not least, there's a great Outdoor Life Club that organizes hikes and trips—a definite favorite amongst the student body.

 The School Says

Pomona College is one of the nation's premier liberal arts colleges. Located in Southern California, on a campus where ivy and palm trees coexist under sunny skies, Pomona offers an environment for intellectual development and personal growth that is second to none. Pomona College is a place for people who are venturesome by choice, people who want to make a difference and are prepared both to dream big and to work hard in order to grow.

Pomona offers its 1,500 students—evenly divided between men and women—a comprehensive curriculum in the arts, humanities, social sciences and natural sciences and when they select their majors, students distribute themselves remarkably evenly among these disciplines.

Whatever course of study they choose, students have the opportunity to work closely and collaboratively with professors who are also top scholars in their fields. Students and faculty challenge each other in laboratories, classrooms, and co-curricular activities, and everyone benefits from the energy generated by such sharp and eager minds. Friendships forged among Pomona faculty and students frequently endure far beyond the four years of college.

Few institutions can match Pomona's ability to combine such intimate qualities as an average class size of 14 with such large-scale resources as a two-million-volume library. The quality of Pomona's facilities—from art studios to physics labs—often surprises visitors who expect that, as colleges go, smaller means "less." As the founding member of The Claremont Colleges, a unique consortium of seven independent institutions on adjoining campuses, Pomona offers its students the best of both worlds—the richly personal experience of a small, academically superb liberal arts college and the breadth of resources normally associated with major universities.

As a residential college, Pomona provides a rich social environment that deepens the intellectual life of the campus. Students challenge and learn from one another not only in the classroom but in daily life. On-campus housing is guaranteed, and very few students choose to live anywhere else. The extraordinary ethnic, economic and social diversity of its student body, as well as the unusually broad range of national and international origins of the students, gives Pomona a broader mix of backgrounds than just about any comparable educational institution.

The Board of Trustees believes that the college's student body should be drawn from a pool composed of the most intellectually capable and academically committed college bound students in the nation. From that pool, the college should select students for its entering classes who represent a rich cross section of backgrounds, talents, experiences and perspectives and who offer significant prospects for achievement and leadership at the college and after their graduation. This is essential to the creation of a lively and stimulating educational environment that will prepare graduates for life in a changing world.

Pomona empowers its students both in and out of the classroom, providing the tools and support they need in order to take advantage of the wide variety of opportunities before them.

Our location—within an hour of the Pacific Ocean, the Mojave Desert, the San Gabriel Mountains and the city of Los Angeles— informs and shapes daily life at the College.

San Diego State University

San Diego State University
5500 Campanile Drive
San Diego, CA 92182
Admissions phone: (619) 594-5200
Admissions URL: www.sdsu.edu/prospective.html

 Admissions

Current student, Chemistry, 8/2004-Submit Date, July 2007

The admissions process was very simple. One must fulfill the required high school courses, take the SAT or ACT exams and then apply. The school tends to look at extracurricular activities as one of its main indicators. It is important that one have items on the application from outside of school.

Current student, 9/2003-Submit Date, March 2006

The admissions process is very basic: fill out required applications, have a fairly decent SAT score, make sure all forms are in on time and wait. No interview, no essay—selection is solely based on your high school GPA and SAT score. I've heard a lot of people say that it is becoming more and more difficult to get into SDSU because of its sought-after location and social scene—minimal 3.5 GPA and 1100 SAT score. So, keep your grades up in high school and do your best on the SATs (take them as many times as you can).

Current student, 9/2005-Submit Date, February 2006

SDSU is what I regard as a popular yet competitive school. It is way above a community college in terms of prestige. SDSU does not require a 4.0 GPA in high school; I was admitted with a 3.2. The essay I wrote was the short-and-sweet type, but packed with very specific and determined goals of what I want to do. Even if I might not have written how I really feel, it showed determination and maturity.

Current student, 8/2003-Submit Date, May 2006

I applied to San Diego State as a transfer applicant. The application process was basic and when the time came around for acceptances I found I didn't get in. The reason I was rejected was that allegedly I had not completed all the English requirements (I had). So I called the enrollment office to ask about this mix-up, to which they replied, I must have put down the incorrect course numbers on my application. I was confused as to why my math and science courses numbers had no trouble, but my English ones of the same format did. So they re-evaluated my application given my correct transcript and accepted me. The reason of rejection is important in my case, for if I hadn't called I would never have gone to SDSU. Before transferring, I visited a counselor who recommended I com-

plete all my general education requirements before transferring. By completing GE requirements you can receive a GE certificate that cannot be denied from another California State University. This eliminates most of the transfer hassles. Upon acceptance into SDSU, I found the transfer orientation programs to be redundant. I felt they were aimed to someone who had never looked through the school catalogue themselves. I found the advisor to be unhelpful, though my experience at my previous school was not much better. When it comes to transferring, I find advisors to be inadequate. I found more information by reading university-provided material and online resources than I ever found from an advisor. My advice to a transfer student: do the research yourself, ask other students and transfer students about their experiences because the schools seem to only be concerned with students who enrolled as a freshman and have stayed. This is something I also heard from other transfer students at other schools. Mainly the key for transferring is: Fulfill all requirements, make sure you won't lose credit for past classes and research the transfer process.

Alumnus/a, 9/1998-12/2002, September 2004

SDSU requires a 3.4 GPA and a good SAT to get in. For foreigners, it requires high TOEFL results and proof of some kind of graduation with honors from the country you graduated from (e.g., for French students, SDSU requires a French Baccalaureate "avec mention"). You have all four years to pass the entry-level placement tests (English and math) or you can even take classes that will waive that requirement. As for selectivity, send in your application ahead of time if you want a chance to be considered. SDSU has become very competitive!

Current student, 8/1998-Submit Date, May 2004

Because San Diego State University is a California State University, you can apply for admission to the school at the same time you apply to other California State Universities. The application is practically 10 pages long, but the personal statement part is really easy—there isn't one. There are no interviews, and there are no essays. What is important are your GPA, your SAT scores and your extracurricular commitments. Currently, at SDSU, the average GPA for an entering freshman is 3.5. If you feel confident about all those things, then the most important piece of advice I can give you regarding admissions is to send your application in as early as possible! Whether they tell you so or not, admissions is done on a rolling basis: first come, first served.

Current student, 8/2003-Submit Date, April 2004

I would first like to say I was a transfer student to San Diego State (SDSU). I transferred from Santa Barbara City College (SBCC). The admissions process was very easy for me to understand. The counselors at SBCC steered me in the right direction from the moment I set foot on the campus. I began taking classes that would transfer directly to SDSU. Their advice to me was key, and I felt that it helped me be selected for admission. In fact, two of my friends were not

Read all of Vault's College Surveys at www.vault.com/college—get complete surveys on 100s of colleges and universities, expert advice on applicaton essays and more.

VAULT CAREER LIBRARY   53

accepted. Both had higher GPAs than I did; however, I had taken more classes that would transfer to SDSU. The actual application was very easy to understand and easy to access. There was the option to complete the application on the Internet, which was a huge plus. Overall, the admissions process went very smoothly.

Academics

Current student, Chemistry, 8/2004-Submit Date, July 2007

The classes are very difficult to get into, especially for sophomores who have last pick of classes. For freshmen, seniors, and juniors, it is not as difficult because they get priority. Overall, the quality of classes is very good. Individually, it is difficult to measure quality because it is dependent on the instructor. GPA is evaluated on a curve. Grading is subject to change by the professors throughout the semester. The workload depends on how many units a course is worth. Three units of one course is moderate in difficulty. Any course worth more than three units requires a lot of time and contains a heavy workload.

Current student, 9/2003-Submit Date, March 2006

I would say that the academic nature of the program is not difficult by any means. Go to class, pay attention, do a little cramming before exams, and most can maintain a B average. I found the workload for the majority of the classes to be minimal and the grading to be fair (most professors grade on a bell curve). All programs at San Diego State University are impacted; therefore, it can be very difficult to get into classes—expect to crash at least five times within your academic career at SDSU. The business program at San Diego State University is fantastic. There are many professors who are very successful business people and have a lot of real-life information to offer students. I do enjoy going to most classes.

Current student, 9/2005-Submit Date, February 2006

A student's regular semester includes 16 credits, normally five classes. The first four semesters would normally include general education courses that are a requirement for graduation: basically mathematics, RWS (English) and history. Picking classes one wants is limited to one's ability to compile an online wish-list of classes before registration, and registering for classes within a day or two maximum of when they're able to register. Waiting a week to register for my classes left me scrambling to get into classes I didn't even want. In other words, the popular and most necessary courses fill up extremely quickly. Consider 30,000 students, one quarter freshmen (7,500 freshmen), two good RWS professors with 200 spots available. They fill up. The majority of classes are quality classes—qualified, knowledgeable professors, respectable difficulty and challenge, and required adult-level maturity in class. The grading depends on the professor, some give a letter grade up every time you hand in a revised essay, while others are stone-cold, red-pen freaks. Same goes for the workload, the professor will recommend how many hours per week of studying normally necessary for a student to pass the class. The average is at least an hour and a half per night for each course.

Current student, 8/2003-Submit Date, May 2006

In my opinion, SDSU has an excellent art program. My only problem with the program is how it's designed so you can only take a few art classes a semester (not full time), because of all the pre-reqs. As a transfer student, having completed all my GE I had to take extra filler classes to keep myself in school full time. Though I loved those classes, this delayed my impending graduation and caused me to lose some of my financial aid because I had enough credits to graduate (though my degree requirements were not met). For some classes the prerequisites are understandable, for others I think it's a way of keeping class sizes down. Workload is heavy, but it's expected. The work is challenging and quick, but it's to my benefit. The professors are informative and helpful. Some are biased, as always in art, to their personal taste rather than the quality and improvement in a student's artwork. Some of the lower-division art classes are taught by grad students. Depending on the grad student, this could be a good or a bad thing.

Alumnus/s, 9/1998-12/2002, September 2004

The undergraduate program at SDSU is put together well, although some majors have a higher ranking than others. International business, for example, is ranked seventh in the nation and is the perfect choice for students looking to expand their horizons to the international level. Thanks to a productive, efficient and friendly department, this program is certainly going to get in the Top Five within the next couple of years. Very highly recommended! Of course, the problem with that is how impacted classes get. But most of the upper-division business, regional and language classes are solid and provide great preparation for the outside world. Be prepared to study a lot, especially for your business classes and upper-division language classes (you will be required to read a book a week in the language you have studied, and you'll be tested on that). One of the key factors of this department is that you are required to do an internship abroad or study in another country for a semester. It's a great opportunity to visit and discover places you always dreamt of visiting.

Current student, 8/1998-Submit Date, May 2004

Pretty much every major at SDSU is impacted, which means that you must apply and qualify to declare it. Some of the impacted majors are extremely competitive. For example, to get into the business program, you must have a 3.5 GPA. To complete certain BS degrees, such as accounting, biology or engineering, you must immediately declare the major in your freshman year, and follow a very rigid academic course schedule in order to graduate on time. The arts programs do not offer a very large selection of classes, mostly because they are poorly funded, but some of the theatre classes provide valuable experience. The film major is difficult to get into because it is so popular, but it affords great hands-on experience and great networking opportunities. The criminal justice and public administration majors both offer a lot of great internship opportunities through the school; indeed, several of the teachers are actually working in the field now, and merely teach part time. The English and comparative literature departments offer a plethora of classes, but the MFA (master of fine arts) program is unstructured. The athletics department is well funded.

Unless you are a freshman or a graduating senior, it is hard to get popular classes. Most students have to crash at least one of their required courses. And professors accept crashers by this criteria: class standing, number of units and whether you are declared in the major. Most undergraduate classes are easy, especially the general education classes. If homework is given in these courses, it is often busywork. Once you are done with GEs and begin taking classes that are major-specific, the content is more important, and the work gets a lot harder. Unless you're in a BS-related degree, there are usually not lots of written homework assignments; rather, there are readings assigned on the honors system, and the big grade determiner is based on performance on major midterms, essays/papers and the final (and you had better keep up with the readings).

Current student, 8/2003-Submit Date, April 2004

The academic nature seems to be very similar to the other schools I have attended. In fact, this is the fourth college I have attended. I attended Pacific University in Forest Grove, Oregon, directly out of high school. I transferred after one semester back home to Green River Community College in Auburn, Washington. I went there a semester, then transferred to SBCC for two years. The quality of instruction seems very good, and the professors are more than willing to speak with students, whether that be in person or via e-mail. As far as getting classes, this seems to be a slight problem. There are many students at SDSU, and it can be difficult to get the class schedule you want. Not necessarily the classes you want, but the times you want. I haven't had a problem getting the right classes; it's just that my schedule will be all over the place with different times and days.

Employment Prospects

Current student, Chemistry, 8/2004-Submit Date, July 2007

Throughout undergraduate years, one is able to pursue many research opportunities at San Diego State University. This allows one to enhance the chances of landing the job of one's choice upon graduation. The school also provides assistance for job placement and internships. Throughout the semester, the school will have several job fairs tailored to students who are searching for internships.

Current student, 9/2003-Submit Date, March 2006

Join academic clubs (Finance and Investment Society, Criminal Justice Club and American Marketing Association). All of these clubs allow you to network with other students with similar interests, and most have weekly guest speakers from top firms in San Diego (great opportunities for obtaining an internship/job). There's also a career fair every semester with companies from all over the U.S.

Current student, 9/2005-Submit Date, February 2006

San Diego State University used to be the Number Two party school in the U.S., and employers often thought twice about hiring from San Diego State, except for business and nursing, which have always been respectable. But things have changed, and SDSU is now a well-recognized institution, with very respectable degrees. Sometimes it feels like the on-campus recruiting and internships are everywhere. They've flooded the place, and San Diego State's graduate programs are just as good as their undergrad programs.

Current student, 8/1998-Submit Date, May 2004

There is a great career services department on campus at SDSU. It offers students the chance to sign up on a school web site that sends regular career opportunity updates. It also hosts many workshops in which students can learn about graduate schools and programs, entrance exams, how to write a résumé, give a strong interview and more. There is a campus-wide career fair every semester. Many companies come to recruit on campus and give presentations and interviews in the career services building. There are many great career and internship opportunities that are available simply through the different academic departments. Most of the professors have worked in the field before teaching or currently do both, and provide valuable network resources to interested students. It is true that SDSU does not hold the same prestige as a name school as some of the universities of California or the private schools, but once you are out of college, companies are more interested in your work experience in the field and your references.

Quality of Life

Current student, Chemistry, 8/2004-Submit Date, July 2007

The quality of life at San Diego State University is very good. There is plenty of local shopping and events at school so commuting is not a problem for those living on campus. The school is also centrally located in the San Diego metropolitan area allowing for easy access to beaches and other popular areas of the city. Crime has been a problem in recent years mostly in the areas of auto theft and underage drinking. The school has developed programs that allow people to have escorts from night classes on campus. Generally, there is poor police presence in the parking structures, so this is where many of the crimes take place.

Current student, 9/2003-Submit Date, March 2006

San Diego is a great city, some say it's the best city in the U.S. The weather is great, you're always 15 minutes or less from the beach, downtown is beautiful, great shopping, too many restaurants to count, many great places to live (on and off campus). Crime is here, crime is everywhere, but I wouldn't say it's very noticeable.

Current student, 9/2005-Submit Date, February 2006

San Diego State University is an exciting environment to be in. There are lots of people who live on campus, and being in a fraternity or sorority is a must for anyone who really wants to experience college life. The campus is beautiful: Spanish architecture along with modern buildings; well vegetated with palm trees, parks, fish ponds, sun and shade any time; it is a pleasure to walk on campus. The surrounding neighborhood is teeming with college life and activities, and everything is close by: Mission Valley Mall, Mission Bay, affordable housing, two Starbucks on campus, alternate school bookstores.

Current student, 8/2003-Submit Date, May 2006

I've never stayed in campus housing, though I've stayed in apartments in the college area. The main problem is cost. San Diego is an expensive city in which to live no matter in which part you live. The first apartment I stayed in was about a five-minute drive from school. The neighborhood is not one in which you feel comfortable walking alone at night. Currently, I reside a five-minute walk from campus and the neighborhood is loud with students doing various activities. Crime at SDSU has risen and the party scene is explosive. SDSU does provide night safety for its students and there are blue lights scattered across the campus. Personally, my only problem is the cost of living, everything else is something I think would come with any university.

Current student, 8/2003-Submit Date, April 2004

The quality of life is absolutely amazing. I have friends who live in the dorms, and they are very nice, and the people who work there are very friendly. Campus facilities are also very up-to-date. The workout center (Aztec Recreation Center or ARC) is amazing with nearly brand-new equipment, nice basketball courts, a rock climbing wall, bowling, racquetball and the list goes on. The staff is also very helpful and courteous. I haven't heard of any problems concerning safety on campus or around the school. I'm sure there have been problems, but nothing major of which I am aware. The quality of life easily scores five out of five stars.

Social Life

Current student, Chemistry, 8/2004-Submit Date, July 2007

The school has activities for everyone. One of my favorite activities is going to the free movies that premier on campus. Movies are premiered before they even hit theaters, which is great. The school has one bar on campus, and there are more within five miles. It is easy to find a date at San Diego State University, but most people are not in it for the long run. They are just there to have fun and enjoy others' company.

Current student, 9/2003-Submit Date, March 2006

SDSU has been ranked within the Top 10 party schools in the U.S. for over 10 years. Clubs and bars are everywhere (even on campus, Monty's); Pacific Beach (PB) and downtown are the hotspots with bars/clubs on every corner. We find any and every excuse to party here (Mardi Gras, St. Patrick's Day, Labor Day, 4th of July and The PB Block Party are huge events in SD) and you'll find that most students try not to have classes on Fridays because our weekend starts Thursday night!!! When the weather is great you'll find minimal attendance in your classes and a lot of people at the beach.

Current student, 9/2005-Submit Date, February 2006

SDSU, although now more academically focused then in years past, still loves to party. The male-to-female ratio is a 2:3, and there are all types of people you can imagine. Strong sports teams, clubs for virtually anything, and always someone looking for a study group. SDSU offers any type of social life for which you're looking, and there's always someone who wants to meet you. Check out the adjacent restaurants and bars, like the famous Woodstock's Pizza.

Current student, 8/2003-Submit Date, May 2006

Woodstock's is a small pizza place that is packed with SDSU students; the popular night is Thursday. Thursday is the night when parties start and the weekend picks up. Effin's is also a popular Thursday night pub. There is a huge Greek system here, but of no interest to me. I find a lot of students go to house parties, which mainly involves needing to know someone or someone who knows someone who's throwing a party. Tijuana is a big hit for those under 21. There is an SDSU organization that provides safe transportation to and from the Mexican city. While it does have its risks, the bars are packed with 18- to 20-year-olds. Everyone seems to have one horrible TJ story, but if you're going to go across the border, don't forget your ID and don't go by yourself.

Read all of Vault's College Surveys at **www.vault.com/college**—get complete surveys on 100s of colleges and universities, expert advice on applicaton essays and more.

VAULT CAREER LIBRARY   55

Santa Clara University

Undergraduate Admissions
500 El Camino Real
Santa Clara, CA 95053
Admissions phone: (408) 554-4700
Admissions fax: (408) 554-5255
Admissions URL: www.scu.edu/ugrad/

 ## Admissions

Alumnus/a, Business, 1/2003-Submit Date, May 2007

Typical essay and application format. I had a personal tour of the campus by the assistant dean of the business school. SCU is not incredibly selective, but many of my friends, including myself, passed up Ivy League and Top 20 schools to take advantage of the small size and intimate nature of SCU.

Alumnus/a, 9/2000-6/2004, May 2006

The admissions process is fairly straightforward. No essays, no interviews. As long as you meet the academic requirements (found on their web site and other publications), just apply and wait to hear back. SCU is good about following up with students who are admitted.

SCU has a strong focus on diversity and giving back to the community, so if you are struggling academically, I urge you to volunteer as much as possible to pad your application.

> **The school says:** "Santa Clara University does require students to submit an essay with their application materials. The Personal Statement is looked at to determine a student's writing ability and also to help us better understand who the student is. We want to know more than just a student's grade point average or their SAT/ACT scores."

Current student, 9/2004-Submit Date, January 2006

The admissions process was detailed, but well organized. As soon as you are accepted, Santa Clara University does everything it can to make you feel right at home. That feeling really seems to stick with you, as it has for me for the last year and a half. This university seems to value either a high GPA or a high SAT score, but both aren't really required. Santa Clara has been working hard to build up their athletic image recently, so having a lot of athletic experience might also give you an edge while applying.

Alumnus/a, 9/1999-12/2002, January 2006

I was a borderline student at a Jesuit high school and I needed recommendations from some alumni and a Jesuit priest to get admitted. The best advice I can give anyone who wants to attend Santa Clara is to go visit the admissions office and the financial aid office by yourself before they decide whether or not to admit you. I visited these offices and I received a monster financial aid package from Santa Clara. This was the deciding factor in my attending the university. After I graduated I had $10K in student loans. That's it. Not many students visit financial aid, but the aid office has ties with admissions, and they want to help students who care to take the time to visit the office without their parents in tow.

Alumnus/a, 9/1998-6/2002, December 2005

The admissions process was fairly basic at SCU. They require an essay, usually of a lighter nature. They are getting tougher on admittance, but just because it is becoming more popular. The average SAT is around 1200 and the GPA around 3.6. Interviews aren't mandatory, but I would definitely recommend heading over and visiting the campus (it's gorgeous!) and meeting with admissions, as they can easier put a face to a name. I met with them the summer before senior year as I was coming off summer school to amend my D+ and pre-calc (not a SCU qualifier) and needed advice and recommendations on my application after all of that. Needless to say, showing them my concern and proving to

them I was out to correct the grade was helpful in the admissions process, and I was admitted in the first round.

Current student, 9/2003-Submit Date, April 2004

I had to write an essay on a topic, and I had about five topics from which to choose. Then I had to write out a résumé with all of my past activities and jobs. It was a very selective process because there are only about 4,000 students at this school. If I had any advice on getting in, it would be to nail your SATs and have good grades. This isn't a school that will let you in just based on athletic abilities. Also, make sure your essay is original and worth reading. Make it exciting, and follow whatever guidelines people give you regarding the proper format.

Current student, 9/2003-Submit Date, March 2004

A very vital part of the admissions process is being honest and unique. The readers do not want to hear the same comments from the prospective applicants, but instead want to know what you can contribute to the school and the community. The essay can be simple but must tell the reader who you are and what you value. Something that sparks their interest or keeps them reading is the key to a good essay.

 ## Academics

Alumnus/a, Business, 1/2003-Submit Date, May 2007

I've talked to friends at many other universities and SCU is comparable, if not more demanding, than many other schools. Enrollment is based on units, so getting classes can be tough, but most professors are willing to add students. The professors here are one of the best assets of the university. As an undergrad, I had dinner at the dean of the business school's house multiple times, and my capstone professor took every group out to dinner separately. I never had a TA and a majority of professors are always available during office hours and even give their home phone numbers.

Alumnus/a, 9/2000-6/2004, May 2006

Class sizes are small, which is nice. You will receive a lot of one-on-one attention from professors and peers. After four years, the only drawback is it starts feeling like high school again. Workload varies from class to class, but expect to be challenged. If the curriculum is interesting, then classes shouldn't be a problem. Otherwise load up on caffeine and study your butt off.

As for obtaining popular classes, if you prioritize your classes, you won't have a problem. You may not always get your class of choice, but as long as you have alternates ready, you can register for your first pick another quarter. If worse comes to worst, you can always sit in on a class for the first couple of days and hope that other registered students are no-shows.

Current student, 9/2004-Submit Date, January 2006

Santa Clara University uses the quarter system, which has some good and bad results when compared to the semester system. On the plus side, you learn a lot more because in the end you take a lot more classes. This is also a plus because as soon as a class begins to become boring and repetitive, you take your finals, get a break and then come back to a whole new set of classes. The downside of the quarter system is the time schedule when school is in session. You get an extra few weeks before classes begin in September, but they end about a month later in June. In my opinion, the quarter system really isn't that bad. I can't believe how much I have learned over the course of four quarters.

Alumnus/a, 9/1999-12/2002, January 2006

Santa Clara is extremely underrated academically. My professors were excellent and I personally had dinner with 11 of them. The class sizes are small, and although there are a few professors who are more suited for research and publications, the vast majority of professors are there to help the students, one on one, after class. Santa Clara also emphasizes excellent writing skills developed through constant essay writing. I even wrote an essay in one of my math courses.

Alumnus/a, 9/1998-6/2002, December 2005

Because the school is relatively small (about 4,000 to 5,000 undergrads), the class sizes range from 12 to 40, with the most being around 25. You get to know the professors, the graduate assistants and each other quite well, which is great because your friends will expand further than your floor mates. Santa Clara academics are pretty stringent, as it is always well ranked, and though it isn't out of reach, they do make you work in your classes. I would say 90 percent of my professors were excellent and the other 10 percent, for one reason or another, were still pretty good. Overall, I know I received a great education and was confident upon graduation that I was ready.

Current student, History, 9/2003-Submit Date, April 2004

Classes are very hard to get, which seems to be true everywhere. Whatever I end up with, I love, because the teachers are great, and the work is often interesting and challenging. My grades are A's and B's, and the teachers here are outstanding. The workload is unlike anything I have seen before. I always have hundreds of pages to read per week. That is not uncommon. All my friends who have other majors spend the same amount of time on schoolwork, whether it's a group project or papers.

Current student, 9/2003-Submit Date, March 2004

The school offers many classes in numerous areas. The school tries to accommodate everyone and make sure that the desired classes are available. Because of the small size, many people choose the same classes due to the ease of the workload, lenient teacher, or a good class time. The teachers are very helpful, and there is definitely a sense of a one-on-one relationship versus lecture-hall style.

Alumnus/a, 9/1997-6/2001, February 2004

Very strong academics in business, pre-law, and engineering. I have heard that the sciences are a little weaker. For the most part, classes are small, with few larger than 40 students. The workload is heavier than at other campuses but not overwhelmingly challenging. Professors are very approachable, and it is easy to get extra help.

Employment Prospects

Alumnus/a, Business, 1/2003-Submit Date, May 2007

Large numbers of tech companies recruit through the business school. Special programs provide guaranteed paid internship placement after junior year. A large number of business majors work in corporate finance or for a Big Four accounting firm. The retail marketing program is also very good and provides jobs in the HQs of large retail companies. There are over 50,000 alumni in the Silicon Valley/Bay Area alone. Most are very willing to help out current students and other alumni. It is a close-knit community, and many alumni stay involved with the school.

Alumnus/a, 9/2000-6/2004, May 2006

The Career Center is great. They host a semi-annual career fair with many large organizations, both local and from out of town. They also provide on-campus interviewing and other tools/resources that can help you transition from school life to work life.

Alumnus/a, 9/1999-12/2002, January 2006

Select your major wisely. Santa Clara makes it easy to transfer between majors within your school (e.g., Business, Arts and Sciences and Engineering), but be sure to meet with the appropriate academic advisors if you're thinking of changing from theater arts to finance. I have friends who graduated with English-type degrees who had some trouble finding jobs outside of the Bay Area. Santa Clara's undergrad engineering and business schools have job fairs where the majority of students receive their first job in the $50K to $60K range, depending on the type of work and your job skills. The alumni network made a big step in developing in Circle in 2005, which networked a large number of recent graduates. I have caught up with students whom I hadn't seen since graduation, and I even obtained a quality job offer through in Circle's web boards.

Alumnus/a, 9/1998-6/2002, December 2005

Santa Clara Graduates are not only all over, but they essentially run the Bay Area. The network is large and like a family. Broncos stick together and when I moved out to the East Coast, I connected with the network and found a few who were able to help me network to land a complete career change. Always willing to help out, SCU alumni are the heads of industry and want to see other grads succeed. Out of all of my friends from other schools, all are amazed at the connections I have because of my school. Senior year, the Career Center is extremely hands-on with the students regarding guidance, events and career fairs, and on-campus interviews are abundant. Career fairs are packed full of alumni and companies (especially in the San Francisco Bay Area) take them very seriously. They want SCU grads!

Current student, 9/2003-Submit Date, April 2004

The Career Center is great, as everyone is willing to work with you on your future. There are many internship possibilities through the campus web site, and you can always get a job on campus. There is often a recruiting squad on campus. They set up booths and have people from local businesses of all kinds talking to people about their futures, what they need and what kind of internships they could get. It seems that people often take advantage of these opportunities and end up getting a lot of valuable information for whatever career they want. People are often enlightened by something new and exciting they hadn't thought of, and they end up going in a completely different direction with their work.

Alumnus/a, 9/1997-6/2001, February 2004

The Career Center and other internship and job opportunities are great. Even as an alumnus I have been able to go to free workshops, and I have access to the alumni directory, which is probably the biggest help of all. Even better, most alumni feel a strong connection to the school and want to help other alumni get jobs.

Quality of Life

Current student, 9/2004-Submit Date, January 2006

Housing is great on campus at Santa Clara University. Each dorm seems to offer its own little perks, which helps to make choosing one a game, in and of itself. The big thing to remember is to get your housing information sent in as soon as possible. If you don't, you may have to spend the year surrounded by students with extremely different viewpoints than your own. Other than that, the dorms are a great place to meet people. Some of my current best friends lived on my floor last year.

Alumnus/a, 9/1998-6/2002, December 2005

SCU is gorgeous, surrounding a 150-year-old mission. The gardens are like a beach when the weather is nice (which is often in the fall and spring) and the whole campus is well kept. There are newer dorms and older dorms, (the newer go to the upperclassmen who choose to stay on campus) and the older dorms are still very comfortable. A new library is being built and the athletic facilities are less than five years old and great. The campus is always under renovation, so there is always something new and exciting coming (the alumni love to donate and give a lot of money to make sure that campus has a big wow factor). The dining hall is pretty good and there is a pretty good number of places to go for off-campus alternatives (even if you don't have a car).

The neighborhood is residential, with the direct surrounding areas inhabiting students, so it is pretty safe and comfortable. Downtown San Jose is nearby, the beach is 30 minutes away, San Francisco and Monterey are an hour a way at most (and the train to S.F. goes right by campus!).

Alumnus/a, Business, 1/2003-Submit Date, May 2007

Most freshmen and sophomores live on campus. The food is pretty good as is the variety for a smaller school. Off-campus housing is very close and easy to find but expensive. The neighborhood isn't the best, but it is largely made up of SCU students with only a few outsiders, although minor thefts can be an issue. There is currently a new library under construction and ground was just broken (May 2007) on the new business school that will be a landmark building on campus. The campus is smaller, but very scenic and well laid out. The basketball gym is new and very nice and the workout facilities are top rate.

Read all of Vault's College Surveys at **www.vault.com/college**—get complete surveys on 100s of colleges and universities, expert advice on applicaton essays and more.

VAULT CAREER LIBRARY   57

Current student, 9/2003-Submit Date, April 2004

Campus is great, surrounding housing and apartment complexes are very nice, and the area is very safe. The facilities are always kept current, and the neighborhood is great. The dorms are nice. There is no such thing as a long walk on this campus because it is so small, and the dorms circle the campus. The main center on campus with the cafeteria and bookstore is great. It is brand new and has everything you need, and people always hang out around there in between classes.

Current student, 9/2003-Submit Date, March 2004

The neighborhood is very appealing to college students. There is an abundance of off-campus housing, which is located right next to the school and the dorms. There are many neighborhood-like houses that have block parties, keep a sense of familiarity and provide safety. The dorms look like condominiums and have easy access to the gym, the pool, the dining hall, the academic buildings and all the other facilities. They are very well maintained and protected. The campus is beautiful, serviced daily and kept clean and attractive. This is pleasing to the tours that come by almost weekly.

Alumnus/a, 9/1997-6/2001, February 2004

On-campus housing is much nicer, though older, than on other campuses. Most students stay on campus for their first two years and then move off campus for their remaining years. In an effort to make housing more affordable for upperclassmen, the university has opened new housing. The food is above average and allows many options in the meal selection. By utilizing a point system, students use points like money. This is much better than other schools that make students buy complete meals. The campus is very safe. Besides the occasional bike theft, you can't find a much safer place. I would leave my laptop in the library while I went to the cafeteria for several hours to meet with my friends. It wouldn't even be touched.

 # Social Life

Current student, 9/2003-Submit Date, March 2004

The social life at the school is very simple but extremely fun and comforting. The Greek system is not affiliated with the school, but there are three fraternities and three sororities. They are very involved in the community and offer many social benefits for students. The sports at the school are not greatly followed, but the men's basketball games and soccer games are always very intense and favored. The students definitely participate and show their school spirit for these games. The big night to go out during the week is Wednesday and then the weekends. Many people go to the two bars located within walking distance. An awesome band from our school plays on certain nights, and brings a large crowd to watch.

Alumnus/a, Business, 1/2003-Submit Date, May 2007

Santa Clara is relatively quiet, but San Jose is five minutes away and S.F. is a little more than a half hour. You can always find something to do on the weekends. There are tons of events in the area as far as sports go, and SCU has a relatively big name concert come to campus every year. There are a few main bars that students frequent, and restaurants range from hole-in-the-wall Mexican food to steak and lobster within a five- to 10-minute drive.

Current student, 9/2004-Submit Date, January 2006

Santa Clara University doesn't have the best social scene around, but then again, I rarely spend my evenings bored in my room. There always seems to be something to do on or around campus. A good back-up place to hang out is a place on campus called The Bronco. It's sort of like a late-night sports bar. There are televisions everywhere, brick oven pizza and other food items are sold, and they even have pool and ping pong tables. There is even a bar for those students who are over 21 years old. Every week or so, concerts are even held in the Bronco.

Alumnus/a, 9/1999-12/2002, January 2006

You meet most of your friends during your freshman year. The dating scene is excellent; however, be careful not to date too many people at first because the school is small and everyone knows each other's business. The students at Santa Clara take care of themselves and are attractive for the most part. Students get free access to Malley gym, basketball and volleyball courts, and the pool. Intramurals at Santa Clara are great.

Alumnus/a, 9/1998-6/2002, December 2005

The Greek system was ousted a few years back, but it is still underground—though it is definitely not necessary to belong to it. Most students live right off campus, so you're friends are always nearby. There is a grocery store across the street, great pizza, fast food and Mexican food all around campus. As for parties, SCU's are great! There is a network of regular party houses with lame names like Blue House and Jail House. As a whole, the area is very college-y while still being a large metropolitan area, so there are great places to head out to dinners and many areas around town to go bar-hopping. There are, of course, some great dive bars around school and there is a beer and wine bar on campus. The Hut is notorious and alumni love it, as well as parents on student-parent weekend. The Hut hosts dads and grads every year, which is where you go drinking with your dad at 6 a.m. on graduation morning. The social scene is very fun and very dynamic and not a whole lot of dating goes on, as is the case in most colleges, but it doesn't seem to bother anyone!

Current student, 9/2003-Submit Date, April 2004

Since we are very close to downtown San Jose, there are many choices for nightlife. Bars and clubs are all over. There are many movie theatres in the area, and more than enough great restaurants. The student favorites are probably the local bars and the local movie theatres. And there are always new and interesting places to eat and visit—perfect for dates.

 # The School Says

Santa Clara University, a comprehensive Jesuit Catholic university located in California's Silicon Valley, offers its 8,047 students rigorous undergraduate curricula in arts and sciences, business, and engineering, plus master's and law degrees. Distinguished nationally by the second-highest graduation rate among all U.S. master's universities, California's oldest higher-education institution demonstrates faith-inspired values of ethics and social justice. More information is online at www.scu.edu.

Stanford University

Stanford University
Undergraduate Admission Office
Montag Hall
355 Galvex Street
Stanford, CA 94305-3020
Admissions phone: (650) 723-2091
Admissions fax: (650) 723-2846
Admissions e-mail: admission@stanford.edu
Admissions URL: www.stanford.edu/dept/uga/

 ## Admissions

Current student, 9/2002-Submit Date, December 2006

Stanford likes well-rounded candidates (exceptional academic record, active in extracurricular activities, leadership potential, and if possible, some really unique thing about your candidacy: winner of certain national/international competition, specific skills and so on). There is no interview. Recommendations should be from those who can speak very highly of you and know you well, ideally not only academically but also how you can contribute to Stanford's academic class and how you fit within the campus.

Alumnus/a, 9/2002-6/2006, November 2006

Stanford, as you know, is among the most selective institutions in the nation. Stanford does not conduct interviews; therefore, the essays have an added importance. It is really important for students applying to make sure they show a true love of learning and that they give an accurate description of themselves in each piece of the application. The admissions staff is very interested in getting to know the applicants as well as it can through the application materials. The best advice is really just to be yourself and show how you have a passion for learning and intellectual exploration.

Current student, History, 9/2003-Submit Date, May 2007

The admissions process at Stanford is changing a bit next year since it will be using the Common Application rather than its own as it has in the past. While I appreciate the effort to make the admissions process less stressful in this way, I think this is unfortunate because the Stanford application was fair and thorough.

Nonetheless, Stanford is a school that without question gets applications from the most competitive high school students. Stanford is a school made up of bright students who are motivated by more than just the desire to get good grades. They stay very active outside the classroom in both academic and non-academic ways. Your application should demonstrate passion for the things you've done in high school.

Alumnus/a, 6/2001-6/2005, September 2006

Stanford is all about the well-rounded individual. They do a really good job of weeding out most of the arrogant, snobby, close-minded people you might expect to find at an expensive private school. A 1600 SAT doesn't mean you'll get in—they want to see community service, something different. They really do a good job of creating a diverse mix of the freshman class and create a different atmosphere for incoming freshmen.

Current student, 9/2003-Submit Date, November 2006

Stanford admissions places a higher degree of importance on the essays. I know a good number of people who get into [other Top Five schools] every year but get rejected from Stanford, which has led me to conclude that there's some sort of personality trait Stanford looks for in its admissions essays. Character strengths include: being able to pick yourself up after a failure, being proactive in seeking out opportunities (as that's what most of your Stanford career will involve), passion for an extracurricular activity or cause and so on.

Alumnus/a, 9/2002-Submit Date, October 2006

Being well rounded on your résumé with committed activities is a perk. Get someone who actually knows you to write a cover letter. If you have a pre-assigned counselor, go and talk to him/her and introduce yourself. The personal essays are probably the most important since this is the only place where your voice gets heard—the struggles you've gone through, why you're unique and can contribute to the student diversity on campus, and of course it can make up for (or at least explain) any bad test scores or grades.

Alumnus/a, 9/2001-6/2005, May 2006

There is no typical Stanford student. The admissions office is not trying to match you up with an ideal student they have in mind—rather, they are really and truly interested in getting to know who you are. The admissions process realizes that every student is unique. Don't write what you think admissions officers want to hear—write, as clichéd as it sounds, sincerely and from the heart. If you're writing about your passions and interests, if you're revealing yourself in your essays, you're doing what the admissions officers want to see. There are no interviews in Stanford's admissions process. It's a very competitive school—this year, for the Class of 2010, Stanford admitted about 2,400 from about 22,000 applications, putting the admit rate at less than 11 percent. Stanford looks for intellectual vitality—the compelling applicants are those in whom the admissions officers see a love for learning and a passion for ideas.

Alumnus/a, 9/2001-6/2005, November 2005

Stanford is an extremely selective school. The admissions process involves completing an application with several short answers and an essay. An interview was not required. High school GPA, SAT scores, AP classes and extracurricular activities are taken into account in the decision process. Advice: take the hardest classes you can in high school and work hard to achieve all A's. Join a few extracurricular activities and show your dedication to them throughout high school. The application essay is extremely important and will distinguish you from all other 4.0, 1500+ SAT scores out there. Students from outside CA will have an advantage since Stanford is 40 percent from CA and the school aims to have representation from all 50 states and many countries.

 ## Academics

Current student, History, 9/2003-Submit Date, May 2007

Above all, the one thing that characterizes the undergrad experience at Stanford is balance. No matter what you want to study, Stanford boasts an outstanding department in that area. Students can take comfort in knowing that if they come in thinking chemical engineering and eventually declare in sociology, they won't be sacrificing their education as a result. There is no competition to get into any major here; students study what they want. Finally, Stanford is a very collaborative place. Students are almost universally willing to study in groups and work with their peers on assignments, something that is encouraged by professors when appropriate. The emphasis here is on learning not on breaking the curve.

Current student, 9/2004-Submit Date, February 2007

At Stanford, classes are generally topnotch. The professors are typically brilliant, but some are awful lecturers. Freshman year is somewhat pre-programmed for most students (with IHUM and PWR, as well as prerequisite math and science courses for the large number of students who are looking to pursue engineering or medical careers). Getting into classes is easy, with the exception of a few of the introductory chemistry classes and labs. My best piece of advice would be to take a freshman seminar and look to open your second year with Sophomore College. Both of these programs are great ways to get an in depth look at a subject and get to know professors with whom you may want to build research or advisor relationships.

Current student, 1/2003-Submit Date, December 2006

Class sizes are far larger than advertised on the brochure materials. As a freshman and most likely a sophomore, your average class size will be over 100. If

Read all of Vault's College Surveys at **www.vault.com/college**–get complete surveys on 100s of colleges and universities, expert advice on applicaton essays and more.

VAULT CAREER LIBRARY   59

you are an engineer, econ, human biology or hum bio major this trend will stay the same all throughout your four years, which makes the benefits of going to this private institution somewhat diminished. Professors on the whole are too busy and important to really care about undergraduates with one or two exceptions. Don't expect them to remember names or your face. Grading is the one area where Stanford stands out significantly from its top-tier peers. Stanford has very little grade inflation.

Current student, 9/2002-Submit Date, December 2006

Quality of classes and professors are superb; some of the best in the country. Grading is fairly lenient (depending on the class and the professor). Workload depends on how much you want to get out of it and your target GPA. You can still change your major until end of sophomore year: a very diverse academic curriculum.

Current student, 9/2003-Submit Date, November 2006

The academic rigor of Stanford is just as one would expect from one of the top schools in the country. Most departments at Stanford are well-connected, have great faculty and provide great opportunities for research. Grading is usually done on a curve. The workload is a bit more than you would have in a semester-system school, but the advantage of the quarter system is that you get done with horrible classes in a flash! Some departments, such as the economics department, are a bit on the impersonal side, mainly because of the size of the department and the professors' preoccupation with research, rather than mentoring future economists.

Alumnus/a, 9/2002-Submit Date, October 2006

Intro classes are large, but in general, you can get into most classes. Only small lectures have capped sizes, and you might need to write an essay to get in. The workload is pretty intense. If it's a social science class, there'll be lots of reading. If it's more technological (math and science), then expect tough problem sets. Overall, study groups help out a bunch. Grading is usually curved to a B+ average. Profs have office hours and many are really helpful, so take advantage of them (of course, be respectful and come to them with legitimate questions).

Alumnus/a, 9/2001-6/2005, May 2006

Classes are challenging and of high quality with a reasonable to high workload. Usually, students have no difficulty whatsoever (even as underclassmen) getting into classes they want. There might be a couple occasions where students are turned away in the interest of keeping the class size small and the classroom environment intimate. But these students do get priority when they are upperclassmen for the few classes that do that. Professors are wonderfully friendly and accessible. Freshmen have myriad ways in which to get to know professors through special academic programs, such as Freshman and Sophomore Seminars and Sophomore College—both programs have full-time professors who are eminent in their fields (Nobel Laureates, Pulitzer winners among others) teaching these classes. These are also small classes capped at 12 to 16 students—in fact, 75 percent of classes here are 15 students or fewer. Freshmen and sophomores can partake in these small classes through these special academic programs even before they declare their major. Student-to-faculty ratio is 7:1 but if you count the faculty of the graduate schools of education, law, business and medicine, the student-to-faculty ratio is 4:1. This latter ratio is far more accurate because undergraduates can take classes with graduate school professors and many of these freshman seminars are also taught by graduate school faculty.

Current student, 9/2003-Submit Date, October 2005

Generally, classes are fairly interesting. Class size varies greatly by discipline and class type—intro and required classes for majors can be enormous, but seminars can be tiny. Basically, you can get into any class you want, but that means good classes can be huge. Grading isn't too bad—I believe the average GPA here is a 3.4. Workload is manageable but varies according to major. I'm an American studies and biology double major and I definitely work harder for bio. I have pulled a fair number of all-nighters during finals but, generally, that's my fault.

Employment Prospects

Current student, 1/2003-Submit Date, December 2006

Basically, Stanford, like its Ivy League peers, acts as a glorified vocational school where elite firms do most of their recruiting. Job prospects, especially for those who take even just a handful of quantitative classes are extremely good. Students who neglect their grades, fail to network and take only non-technical courses still do OK.

Current student, 9/2003-Submit Date, November 2006

A lot of the top firms in every industry come to Stanford to recruit. The Career Development Center (CDC) does a stellar job with keeping students informed of work opportunities, both in the U.S. and overseas. There are career fairs every quarter, and the CDC offers résumé look-overs, practice interviews and other services to help students in their job application process. The same goes for internships. Stanford's location in Silicon Valley means that there are lots of opportunities to intern and work full time in startups, tech firms, VC firms and so on. There are also tons of fellowships in public service.

Alumnus/a, 9/2002-Submit Date, October 2006

The prestige factor of Stanford has been really helpful. The alumni network is pretty strong and can get you far since you're essentially part of the "family." Recruiting on campus is rampant in certain seasons , but the most important part about getting a job is networking: simply meet more people and let them know you're looking and what kind of job you want.

Alumnus/a, 9/2001-6/2005, May 2006

The Stanford name goes a long, long way! Students get a variety of different jobs after they graduate. Our location in the heart of Silicon Valley and our connections with many Silicon Valley companies are especially useful for students looking for jobs in technical fields. Lots of Stanford graduates work at or start these companies. For example both Google and Yahoo were founded by Stanford alumni. The alumni center maintains a database of alumni in various fields who are interested in connecting with current Stanford students interested in that field—a very useful resource. We have several job fairs every academic year with recruiters from different fields (technical, public service and liberal arts) coming in to recruit Stanford students, in particular.

Alumnus/a, 9/1997-6/2001, March 2006

Despite the numerous majors available, it seems that during autumn recruiting season during senior year, everyone not pre-med ends up going for management, consulting or investment banking jobs. Stanford is a large enough name that most of the top management consulting firms and investment banks will come on campus to recruit undergrads. I, myself, went through on-campus recruiting and received a very generous full-time offer from a major management consulting firm with a substantial signing bonus. I have heard from my co-workers that my starting pay package was higher by approximately $5K because of the Stanford name.

Even after graduation, the Stanford name carries substantial weight. When going to a new client or working with new people, there tends to be respect for your abilities just because of the fact that you went to Stanford for your undergraduate studies.

Quality of Life

Alumnus/a, 9/2002-6/2006, November 2006

Housing is guaranteed on campus for four years, which is great. You don't have to worry about finding an apartment or signing a lease or anything. Laundry and phone service are included in our student fees, so you don't have to worry about collecting quarters. All the facilities are great. They just built a new gym on campus that has a rock climbing wall. There is virtually no crime because Stanford is kind of like its own town. It has its own zip code and everything.

Alumnus/a, 9/2002-Submit Date, October 2006

There have been some housing crunch issues on campus, but I was never affected. Dorms are usually the squares, mostly doubles and triples, but dorm life is usually very happening, depending on in which one you land. Dorm food is similarly hit-or-miss with some years being better than others in different places. Row houses are more coveted and difficult to get into based on the draw number or lottery system (and only available for sophomores and up). These houses have their own personal chefs.

Alumnus/a, 9/2002-Submit Date, October 2006

Ever heard of "the bubble"? Stanford is suffering in spades. Because it's basically like a nine-month summer camp with some classes and a bit of winter rain thrown in, you lose track of reality and you get really comfy (yet also antsy) by staying on campus. But there are lots of student groups, guaranteed housing all four years, some of the best college food available in the world, low crime, great restaurants off campus. A little isolated, as it is 45 minutes from San Francisco, and because Palo Alto (the nearest "city") closes down around 8 p.m., but if you've got a car and some devotion, you can make all of California your oyster. Oh, and once you turn 21, there's obviously more stuff to do.

Alumnus/a, 9/2001-6/2005, May 2006

94 percent of undergraduates live on campus (5 percent are abroad any given year, so only 1 percent actually live off campus). The residential community on campus is very tight-knit. There are over 70 different housing options and housing styles for students—co-ops, self-ops, apartment style, suites style, four class dorms, all freshman dorms, ethnic theme houses, academic theme houses, Greek houses and so on. Freshmen are required to live on campus and are assigned to either an all-freshman dorm or a four-class dorm, depending on interest. For later years, students can decide to live with friends and enter the draw (housing lottery) together as a group. Dining options vary with the kind of housing you have. Stanford Dining provides the dorm food and is actually pretty good—they have fantastic salad bars and also make specific provisions for vegetarian, vegan, halal and kosher food. They also have a peanut-free eatery on campus for people with allergies. We have magnificent athletic facilities that are open to all students. Stanford is a fairly enclosed campus and not really integrated with Palo Alto. The campus is 8,180 acres, and so we function as a small town—we have our own zip codes (two), our own police department and our own fire department. The campus is pretty safe; there is a SURE golf cart escort service for anyone who wants to get from place to place at night. The only major problem is bike theft (there are 12,000 registered bicycles on campus).

Social Life

Current student, History, 9/2003-Submit Date, May 2007

While it would be absurd to suggest that Stanford is a party school, it's a very fun place to be. Greek life is present but not dominant. There are tons of student groups to join and nearly everyone does. Palo Alto is not a college town but there are great restaurants and a good number of cool bars. Most of all, Stanford students have fun. To put it simply, Stanford offers not only one of the best educations in the country, but also one of the most fun college experiences. I know that nearly all my friends at other schools are amazed when they find out what a social place Stanford is.

Current student, 9/2004-Submit Date, February 2007

Off-campus entertainment is a little hard to come by (even the movie theater requires a car to get to) and most of it is expensive (particularly the good dining spots). Still, you learn the good college places quickly and the area ends up being enjoyable. The best bar in the area is Blue Chalk, which offers some good pool and a full menu, as well. Many students prefer the 750, which has the benefit of being on-campus and hosting parties before and after major sporting events. There is very little Greek life on campus and those frats that do exist are looked down upon by the majority of students. Overall, you're probably best off if you stick with a close-knit group of friends for fun.

Current student, 9/2003-Submit Date, November 2006

Stanford's social life is mainly a bubble for undergraduates with tons of campus parties and on-campus entertainment events. University Avenue in Palo Alto (about five minutes from campus) is where all the restaurants are, ranging from Starbucks and cheap eateries to highly expensive, posh restaurants. Dating scene is simply so-so with most students clinging to partners for their entire four-year period at Stanford for fear that they'll never find someone better in the somewhat abysmal pool (which they usually do after graduation). We have most of the major frats and sororities represented on campus. Stanford has many quirky traditions, like Full Moon on The Quad (where all freshman line up in the main quad and get kissed by upperclassmen), Exotic Erotic and so on, which keep students occupied and well socialized throughout their entire undergraduate experience.

Current student, 9/2003-Submit Date, October 2005

Social life revolves around campus. Students don't often go to nearby bars (except for the weekly Pub Night for seniors), and the party scene is dominated by fraternities. When you read about the small percentage of students in Greek housing, be forewarned—it's kind of misleading, especially because a large portion of the social people here are Greek. There are also other fun parties held by row houses, which are frequented by older students, many of whom have sworn off frat parties.

The School Says

Founded in 1885, Stanford University is recognized as one of the world's leading research and teaching institutions. Stanford is known for its entrepreneurial character, which it draws from its Western location, proximity to Silicon Valley and from the legacy of its founders, Jane and Leland Stanford. As a result of this legacy, imagination and creativity have flourished as the university has pursued its mission of discovery.

Stanford has attracted one of the most accomplished faculties anywhere. Its current 1,770 faculty members, for instance, have won 17 Nobel Prizes, four Pulitzer Prizes and 24 MacArthur Fellowships. Because of its faculty, Stanford is uniquely positioned to pursue interdisciplinary solutions to the world's most daunting problems. Their areas of academic excellence cross disciplines and range from the humanities to social sciences to engineering and the sciences. Stanford's 14,000 students—7,500 graduate students and 6,500 undergraduate students—are drawn from the most accomplished and talented worldwide.

There are seven schools at Stanford, including the:

- Graduate School of Business
- School of Earth Sciences
- School of Education
- School of Engineering
- School of Humanities and Sciences
- Stanford Law School
- School of Medicine

There also are 13 independent laboratories, centers and institutes, including the innovative Stanford Program for Bioengineering, Biomedicine and Biosciences. Commonly known as Bio-X, it is an ambitious interdisciplinary biosciences research effort. Among the university's special research facilities is the Stanford Linear Accelerator Center, which is dedicated to research in photon science, particle physics and particle astrophysics. The Stanford Medical Center includes the Stanford School of Medicine, Stanford Hospital & Clinics and the Lucile Packard Children's Hospital.

Stanford offers an intellectually challenging environment centered in one of the most dynamic and diverse areas in the world. Stanford is located on 8,180 acres on the San Francisco Peninsula midway between San Francisco and San Jose. The university's campus overlooks San Francisco Bay and is characterized by quadrangles of California Mission-inspired buildings of local sandstone with red-tiled roofs. 94 percent of undergradu-

Read all of Vault's College Surveys at www.vault.com/college—get complete surveys on 100s of colleges and universities, expert advice on applicaton essays and more.

VAULT CAREER LIBRARY   61

ates live on campus, as do about 55 percent of graduate students and 30 percent of faculty members.

From its outset, Stanford has been nontraditional: coeducational in a time when most private universities were all male; nondenominational when most were associated with a religious organization; and avowedly practical, following the Stanfords' objective, "to qualify its students for personal success, and direct usefulness in life." With a 7:1 student-to-faculty ratio, Stanford emphasizes close interaction with faculty in its undergraduate program. Annually, 1,600 first-year students are chosen from about 22,000 applicants. Stanford looks for distinc-

tive students who exhibit energy, curiosity and a love of learning in their classes and lives. Academic excellence is the primary criterion for admission.

Stanford's 177,341 living alumni include two U.S. Supreme Court justices, as well as well-known academic leaders, astronauts, scientists and inventors, business leaders, government officials, athletes, journalists and actors. Stanford's entrepreneurial spirit has helped spawn an estimated 3,000 companies in high technology and other fields.

Thomas Aquinas College

Admissions Office
Thomas Aquinas College
10,000 North Ojai Road
Santa Paula, CA 93060
Admissions phone: (800) 634-9797
Admissions e-mail: admissions@thomasaquinas.edu
Admissions URL:
www.thomasaquinas.edu/admission/index.htm

 ## Admissions

Current student, 8/2003-Submit Date, April 2006

Thomas Aquinas College currently has a rolling admissions process, which means that there is no set deadline for applying; they take applications and have a waiting list until all of the positions for the following year are filled. All students begin as freshmen in the fall, unless they are returning to the program. The earliest students can apply is the first semester of their senior year.

When I applied, I was advised to have my application in before the end of March. Although accepted, I was eighth on the waiting list. Freshmen this year said that the waiting list began at the end of January. The school is becoming more well known and so there are an increasing number of applicants.

The application is in depth, including three essays. The college focuses on the applicant's desire for the program and his/her ability to complete the challenging curriculum. They want to know your study habits and interests, what your family thinks about your education, and that you are able to think clearly and logically.

If you really want to be at Thomas Aquinas College, tell them why!! Sometimes, students who don't meet the requirements on the first try re-apply, or they sometimes can arrange for an interview during which they can appeal and hopefully convince the admissions board.

The entire application must be submitted in full before being considered: essays, SAT scores, transcripts and letters of recommendation. The letters of recommendation are intended to demonstrate the applicant's academic strength since the program is rigorous, and a strong character is also an asset because the entire campus lives together—community life is a huge component of the four-year program.

Current student, 9/2004-Submit Date, April 2006

The admissions process consists of writing several essays covering topics, such as why you want to be admitted, what you hope to gain from the program and your experience with reading books (an important subject since the curriculum is geared around the greatest books of the western world).

SAT and high school transcripts are, of course, required, as well. Although the average SAT here is around 1310, many students here did not score that well. The admissions process here is more than just a number-crunching game. They are careful to look at every application as coming from a real person and to consider special situations. I was out of high school for almost 10 years when I completed the application processs.

> **The school says:** "In fact, the freshman average SAT score is about 1290 (combined score from the Critical Reading and Math portions of the test), while the middle 50 percent of our students scored 1190 to 1370."

My advice for someone wanting to enter this program is quite simple: ask yourself some basic questions, such as, "Am I really interested in challenging myself and doing the thinking necessary to come to an understanding of the greatest minds in history, or am I applying here because my family thinks it is a good idea?" and "Am I ready to be in a very conservative environment that values truth and order, where there are, for example, curfews and dress code requirements, or am I so given over to the lax morals of the modern age that I am unable or unwilling to abide by these relatively strict codes?" If a person answers these questions by saying that they are not ready for the challenge and that they are not willing to be in an atmosphere where social activism, moral relativism and liberalism has little or no place, then this is certainly not the school for them.

Beyond this, it should be understood that non-Catholics are welcome here. Although this college is proud of its Catholic identity, it is a place of learning that is open to all people who will form the future of this country, Catholics and non-Catholics alike.

Current student, 8/2004-Submit Date, April 2006

The admissions process was relatively simple, involving a series of essays concerning the curriculum, spiritual life, family life and literature. It being a small school, the selectivity is increasingly more difficult as more applicants are received. There was no interview, although the admissions office is very helpful in contacting you and willingly receptive of your questions and concerns.

Apply early, write honestly and take advantage of the willingness of the admissions office.

Current student, 8/2004-Submit Date, April 2006

Thomas Aquinas College uses a rolling admissions process, so that they have no due dates, but begin a waiting list once positions fill up. I wrote maybe a dozen short essays, as specified on the application, submitted standardized testing scores and provided recommendation letters, finishing sometime in February the spring before I hoped to enroll, made it on a waiting list and was offered a spot before the summer. I don't know enough about the admissions process to offer any advice or judge their selectivity.

Academics

Current student, 8/2005-Submit Date, April 2006

Everyone does the same basic program, so there is no problem getting the classes you want. There is more difficulty getting the tutor you want, since all you can do is ask. The classes are very good, though the excellence depends heavily on the tutor and section.

> **The school says:** "Students attend class in 'sections,' which are groups of no more than 20 (the average is closer to 16)."

The grading varies from tutor to tutor, on whether they think you have learned the material. The tutors with whom I have had experience are all good, but it depends on which class they teach. The older tutors are better than the newer ones. The workload is pretty heavy, since we mostly read books in their entirety, not in bits and pieces. But it can be kept under control.

> **The school says:** "At most colleges, 'tutors' are grad students who help a particular professor. At Thomas Aquinas College, however, all the members of the teaching faculty are called 'tutors' because we see them as guides who lead us through the texts of the real 'professors' (Plato, Aristotle, St. Thomas, Homer, Einstein, O'Connor)."

Current student, 8/2003-Submit Date, April 2006

Never having attended any other post-secondary institution, I cannot vouch for myself, but I am constantly reminded that TAC is one of a kind. It's very different from high school in that the classes all have purpose. The curriculum is universal: there are no electives and though students can request to have or not have certain classmates or tutors, there is no guarantee.

Class sizes range from 16 to 20. The seminar method is very good for the most part, but the one class I have with 20 students is challenging because not everyone can speak as much as they would like to. The school needs another classroom building and some additional staff, but that won't be for the next few years, as there are currently other initiatives underway (a chapel and faculty/office building).

> **The school says:** "The College had as many faculty members as were needed to teach all the students last year. Three new members of the teaching faculty were hired this year, giving us more than we need and so a few of them are teaching classes as a team.
>
> "We have just enough classroom space at the moment, with all available rooms being used virtually all of the school day (which runs from 8:30 a.m. to 3:30 p.m. with a two-hour break from 11:00 a.m. to 1:00 p.m.). We will be building another classroom building, and it will be nice to have a new building to spread out a bit, but it's not urgently needed. The College has made a point to build permanent residence halls, a library and classroom buildings (of which there are two) before beginning work on a faculty office building—the students' interests are always put first around here!"

In addition, and worthy of note, the campus has an academic atmosphere—a stifling experience for some and thrilling for others, while many have moments of both—and so your outside-class time is also intellectual. The education is the kind you have to want for its own sake, not just for a job later on. It's for you as a person. Grades cannot be the main focus, and many of the tutors are not particularly concerned with them.

> **The school says:** "While it is true that the College encourages students to focus on their studies and let the report cards take care of themselves, it should be noted that tutors work to grade students appropriately in every class they take."

Most of the learning is verbal (in-class discussions), papers are infrequent (junior year you only write two, one per semester), there are no midterms, and exams are a hell-week because you've learned so much! Still, exams are only meant to

be an opportunity to review and are more stressful for those who do not participate in class.

The tutors here are incredible. They are very intelligent and are available outside class for discussions about anything. Many of the students get to know the tutors personally, and tutors host the students they teach each semester for a dinner. Thanksgiving and Easter break are also opportunities to hang out with the tutors and their families for students who stay on campus.

Current student, 9/2004-Submit Date, April 2006

Everyone at Thomas Aquinas College takes the same classes. There are no majors or minors here since the focus of the program is on the greatest works of Western Civilization. This program gives one the tools that one needs to reason and to articulate the fruits of reason, something that is necessary to every human endeavor.

Every student has Theology (which is given pride of place as the queen of the sciences), Philosophy (focusing especially on Plato, Aristotle and Saint Thomas), Mathematics (directly from the original sources, such as Euclid and Appolonius), Laboratory (focusing on the development of scientific thought from Aristotle to the modern age), Latin (in freshman and sophomore years beginning with Wheelock's Latin Grammar and then leading, in sophomore year, to translation of the Latin of Martin of Denmark and Saint Thomas) and Seminar (an evening discussion once a week on works that don't fit otherwise into the program, such as great works of literature and history, Herodotus, Thucydides, St. Augustine's Confessions, Plato's Republic and works of poetry.

I am currently in my sophomore year and I can honestly say that the tutors (known in other schools as professors—here the philosophy is that the professors are the great authors themselves and by discussion and thought we may come to an understanding of these texts under the guidance of tutors who are themselves well experienced in these great works) are totally committed to their jobs and to helping students in every possible way to come to a fruitful understanding of the texts under consideration.

Every day, tutors join students at all three meals and discuss these texts and other matters with students. There is a real concentration here on the individual and his or her search for the truth. Tutors know your name and really watch your participation and guide your thought during and after the classes.

Current student, 8/2004-Submit Date, April 2006

The academic life here is like none other. There are classes of 17 to 19 that are constant. That is, you're assigned to be in the same class with the same people the entire year. Although, for your weekly nighttime Literature Seminar, you have a different section.

Homework involves two or three hours a night of reading original texts for discussion the next day and one or two hours a night studying mathematic propositions to be demonstrated in front of the class. Grading is based on participation in class, one paper per year and finals. However, it is a loose grading system with no definite paradigms.

> **The school says:** "Freshmen write five papers, Sophomores four, Juniors two and seniors write and defend a senior thesis. Grades are based on classroom participation, quiz grades, written work (papers) and end-of-semester finals. The grading system has been well-considered and appropriately varies by subject (e.g., in some subjects quizzes are weekly or even daily events, while in others you may not have them)."

Current student, 8/2004-Submit Date, April 2006

Thomas Aquinas College has a set program—four years without choices to make, although there are varying optional seminars offered on the side now and then, depending on interest, but nothing very substantial apart from the regular program. The regular program involves full-time classes every semester, including one two-hour evening seminar per week the first two years and two in the final two years. Seniors write a thesis and defend it before a board of three faculty members before graduating.

Classes are held in the seminar method—all students are divided into sections of 15 to 20 people who take all of their classes together, discussing material assigned for study and directed by a professor. Each class has one final exam at

Read all of Vault's College Surveys at www.vault.com/college—get complete surveys on 100s of colleges and universities, expert advice on applicaton essays and more.

VAULT CAREER LIBRARY   63

the end of the semester, and an oral evaluation is given to each student individually by all of their professors together in the middle of each semester. Writing is rather minimal, with five papers required freshman year, four sophomore year, two junior year and only the thesis senior year.

The material studied in the regular program is almost beyond improvement. We study the great books of Western Civilization, with emphasis on philosophy and theology, with special emphasis on Aristotle in view of the last two years of Theology class, which are spent studying the Summa Theologica of Thomas Aquinas in Latin. Aquinas is recognized by many popes as the Universal Doctor of the Church and recommended as the basis of Catholic education, hence the focus of Thomas Aquinas College. Language classes involve two years of beginning Latin, mostly to prepare students for Aquinas—other works are read in translation.

The program is definitely unique and not easily summarized, but the school web site offers helpful information, and the admissions counselors are quite willing and helpful. A summer program is available for discerning high school students, and visitors regularly stay for a few days to experience classes and campus life and to familiarize themselves with the program.

Employment Prospects

Current student, 9/2004-Submit Date, April 2006

Graduates from Thomas Aquinas College have the advantage of a broad liberal arts background that is suitable to just about any field a graduate would wish to enter. Many students go on to graduate work in various fields, including law, medicine and religious life. Graduates from TAC are generally well regarded at the most prestigious universities in the world, including Harvard and the Ivy League schools.

Students thinking of attending here, however, need to understand that the degree does not give them an area of specialty. Specialization (majoring in certain subjects), while having the benefit of giving a greater understanding in a particular field, has the disadvantage of not allowing the student to focus on how to think and reason, how to come to an understanding of the more important questions of life itself and one's purpose in it. Generally, however, employers seem to respect a liberal arts degree from TAC because of its challenging nature, yet this is no guarantee of immediate employment.

Since TAC does not provide specialization in particular fields, one may have to attend training or further college-level education in a certain field before being considered for employment. This is a small price to pay, however, for having a truly classical education that sets the mind free to explore the big picture.

Current student, 8/2004-Submit Date, April 2006

Most graduates are able to find a job easily, based on the quality of life that is nurtured at the campus. There is a morality and nobility to the people that attend this school that is unique in the job market today. This school teaches you to be a hard worker, obedient, competent and team-oriented. With the establishment of the new Career Placement Office, job hunting is made much less arduous and much more successful.

Current student, 8/2004-Submit Date, April 2006

I've heard that the largest groups of alumni become either lawyers or religious leaders. Several go on to graduate school, although anything besides maybe philosophy, theology and perhaps literature would require more undergraduate classes first. Other students go on to such varied things that their experience at Thomas Aquinas seems not to lead directly to them.

As this suggests, Thomas Aquinas College offers a liberal arts program in the classical sense—our studies are "artes liberales" rather than "artes serviles," which would be primarily ordered to serve some end other than themselves; professors stress that our program is just a beginning, intended to develop methods and habits of study to equip students for a life of "negotium otium," the "unleisurely leisure" that the lover of wisdom, Cicero, alludes in the beginning of the third book of his work, *On Duties* (which we read in the sophomore seminar).

Quality of Life

Current student, 8/2003-Submit Date, April 2006

The dorms are beautiful and well furnished, and the grounds are incredibly well kept. At any given time of year, there is something blooming and beautiful. Campus is probably the safest place I've ever been, with maybe the exception of watching out for mountain lions and poison oak when hiking in the hills out the back door of the dorm. But then, I can't really complain about having the Los Padres National Forest as a backyard.

Meals are served regularly in the St. Joseph Commons, and snacks like bread, cereal, fruit, coffee and drinks are available all day long (all of which is included in your room and board so unless you want a specialty drink from the coffee shop, you don't have to pay). The food, by the way, is prepared by a company called Bon Appetit. It's not like Mom's, but it's pretty darn good. My biggest complaint is the lack of a good chilling spot, but the student lounge will hopefully be refurnished in the next couple of years.

Current student, 9/2004-Submit Date, April 2006

The campus is in a rather quiet area in the mountains between two small- to medium-sized towns in California, Santa Paula and Ojai. The scenery is beautiful, with mountains and nearby streams for hiking and exploring. The campus is beautiful with old-style Spanish architecture, and work is currently underway for new buildings, including a large church.

The food here is generally very good. There are three meals a day with no selection. Given the small size of the campus, it is not practical to have a cafeteria-style meal plan, so a private company is contracted to do the cooking, which is actually better than I expected.

There aren't many places for recreation on the campus, which is a slight drawback. There are, however, a tennis court, basketball court, and an athletic field where students often play soccer and football. There is a ping-pong room and a room with a pool table (which is almost always in use). Individual dorms may have a few games or activities available, but generally this is not the focus.

The campus is fairly close to the beaches, however, and many students take advantage of this to make their own recreation! There is a full-time security guard stationed to watch the gates. Often hikers go past the campus to hike in the mountains, but this presents few problems.

Current student, 8/2005-Submit Date, April 2006

In the mountains of Southern California—it's amazing!! The dorms are beautiful and welcoming. In the winter, we sit in front of the fireplace and study together, and in the spring we sit outside on the lawn. The chapel is always open and the chaplains are easy to get hold of.

I'd say the quality of life is joyful—joyful that we are so blessed to live in such a beautiful place and to be studying the truth in such a beautiful way. The food is great and we don't need meal tickets or anything. I feel absolutely spoiled—just walk right in without having to cook for myself, eat and leave without having to clean up. I wish living at home was like that.

Because the campus is so small, it's very easy to make friends really quickly. I was a relatively shy person, but after the first week or so I already felt at home with the people around me.

Current student, 8/2004-Submit Date, April 2006

Almost all students live on our small, somewhat rural campus in the hills of Southern California, about 20 miles from the ocean. As we have less than 400 students, everyone will be at least visually familiar, and more outgoing persons will probably know very nearly everyone by name.

A cafeteria provides meals three times a day, with a coffee shop available for snacks in between. Three Roman Catholic chaplains provide mass three times a day with opportunities for confession before and after each mass.

> **The school says:** "The College recently hired a fourth full-time chaplain. All are Roman Catholic priests from these orders: Oblates of Mary Immaculate, Jesuit, Dominican and Norbertine."

Dormitories are always off limits to the opposite sex. Curfew begins at 11 p.m. on weeknights and at 1 a.m. on weekends. Dorms are comfortable and not too crowded; students are hired as maintenance personnel. Television is not allowed on campus, and movies are supervised by student prefects in each dorm. Alcohol is not allowed on campus.

The school says: "The College serves alcohol to those over 21 at formal dinners and other social occasions."

Sports are strictly intramural and student organized; our campus has a soccer field, a few volleyball courts, one tennis court and two basketball courts. Hiking trails in the Los Padres National Forest adjacent to campus provide nice recreational opportunities.

Social Life

Current student, 8/2005-Submit Date, April 2006

Most socializing goes on in the Commons and cafeteria. The only restaurant-like place on campus is The Coffee Shop, which is also a favorite haunt. The activities directors show movies most weekends, and there are five major dances a year, the Halloween Dance, Christmas Dance, Mardi Gras Dance, Spring Dance and the senior fundraiser, Chez Martin, besides other smaller dances. There is a lot of dating.

There is a very good school choir that sings for masses and graduation and does two concerts a year, sometimes including a musical. There are also other choirs on campus that have their own concerts. There are performances by individuals at Schubertiades a few times a year. There are at least two acting groups, The St. Genesius Players and The Society of the Mask, both of which put on good plays this year.

The school says: "'Schubertiades' are informal musical performances put on by terrifically talented student musicians a few times each year. They began as informal occasions in the backyard of a musically inclined member of the faculty, but their popularity quickly outgrew his backyard, and so they were moved to the campus. Any student with musical talent is welcome to perform (vocalists, pianists, violinists, cellists—even a chamber orchestra plays). Schubertiades are so named because Schubert held these kinds of informal gatherings of musicians in his home and was famous for them."

Current student, 8/2003-Submit Date, April 2006

If you want a social life other than school-related conversations with your classmates, you must find it off campus. Campus offers the occasional volleyball, basketball, soccer or softball game, but beyond that, not much more.

The school says: "While no sports teams play at off-campus venues, intramural sports are a part of daily life for those who are interested: basketball is played virtually every day of the year, soccer is probably the second-most-played sport this time of year, and ultimate frisbee, volleyball, flag football and others (including croquet) are played semi-regularly. The College employs a student athletic director, whose job it is to organize sporting events/tournaments. In addition, the College employs two other student activities directors whose job it is to organize on- and off-campus events, including dances, games, tournaments, trips to concerts, baseball games and other off campus venues. There is also a college choir, a theater group and a few informal clubs to which students belong."

Current student, 8/2003-Submit Date, April 2006

There's definitely a counter-culture here, for starters. Many freshmen go through an intense period of media withdrawal their first semester. There is one TV at the chaplain's residence where students can watch sports and a big TV in the student lounge for weekend movies.

Dancing is huge here, and there is an absurd number of talented musicians. But the quality of life is of a different sort than anywhere else I've visited or heard of: where else do you here Gregorian chant pumping out of the guys' dorm as

you head off campus on a Friday night? How many college students know how to fox trot and swing?? And the movies in the lounge have to be of a certain calibre. It's a different experience, certainly, and takes some major adjusting for some, but overall, the quality of life is high as the college strives to offer a taste of the intellectual life to its students in a Catholic environment.

The people on campus are very friendly. Given that there are between 360 and 400 students, all living in the dorms and eating, working and studying together, you can't help but know each other. If you love to sit around and talk about the big questions of life, it's an awesome place to be because you can pick up with anyone in any year and have a great discussion. If you're really into the party scene, MTV style, you might just go out of your mind. But if you're looking for a place to stretch your mind and see the best that humanity has to offer, come and visit. It's worth the trip to see for Thomas Aquinas College for yourself.

Current student, 8/2005-Submit Date, April 2006

The students, by the end of the week, are very much in need of a relaxing weekend to hang out with friends. The dating scene can be difficult sometimes just because the campus is so small. So if you try dating someone but it doesn't work out, unfortunately, you are forced to see them around campus almost every day. But it can also be just a good way to nurture friendships. They keep our events calendar pretty full with lectures, concerts, dances, sports games and plays. I'd definitely say we've got a fair balance between academics and social life.

The School Says

Thomas Aquinas College is unique among American colleges and universities. We hold with confidence that the human mind is capable of knowing the truth about reality, that living according to the truth is necessary for human happiness, and that truth is best comprehended through the harmonious work of faith and reason. We understand the intellectual virtues to be essential to the pursuit of truth and to the life of reason it presupposes, and we consider the cultivation of those virtues to be the primary work of Catholic liberal education.

The academic program designed to achieve this goal is comprehensive and unified—and it includes no textbooks or lectures. Through all four years of their studies and in every course—from philosophy, theology and math to science, language and music—students actually read the greatest written works in those disciplines, both ancient and modern: Homer, Plato, Augustine, Newton, Maxwell, Einstein, the Founding Fathers of the American republic, Shakespeare, T.S. Eliot and, in particular, Aristotle and St. Thomas Aquinas, to name a few.

Instead of attending lectures, small groups of students gather around tables for careful inquiry in tutorials, seminars and laboratories guided by members of the teaching faculty, who are called ,"tutors," because the college understands the real "professors" to be the authors of the Great Books under consideration.

The curriculum challenges students to a disciplined scholarship in the arts and sciences indispensable for critical judgment and genuine wisdom. One mark of the program's effectiveness is the success that so many of the graduates have in a wide variety of professions, careers and vocations. Nearly one-third have attended graduate and professional schools in a wide array of disciplines; among them, philosophy, theology, law and the sciences are most often chosen.

Students interested in experiencing the college's curriculum and unique learning environment are encouraged to contact the College Admission Office for information on the two-week Great Books Summer Program for High School Students held each summer. Call now at (800) 634-9797 or e-mail us: admissions@thomasaquinas.edu.

Read all of Vault's College Surveys at www.vault.com/college—get complete surveys on 100s of colleges and universities, expert advice on applicaton essays and more.

VAULT CAREER LIBRARY   65

UCLA

UCLA Undergraduate Admissions
and Relations with Schools (UARS)
1147 Murphy Hall, Box 951436
Los Angeles, CA 90095-1436
Admissions phone: (310) 825-3101
Admissions e-mail: ugadm@saonet.ucla.edu
Admissions URL: www.ucla.edu/audience/future.html

 Admissions

Current student, 9/2006-Submit Date, June 2007

UCLA focuses on GPA (usually above 4.0), extracurricular activities, and the essays. There are three essays, one of which I believe is five pages long and the other two are a little shorter. On the essays, it is best to focus on one's struggles and how one overcame those struggles.

Current student, English, 9/2005-Submit Date, June 2007

The admissions process is the same for all the UCs. I did not have an interview for this school since it is a public school. I felt the essays were pretty standard. I think that there are many well-rounded students here. It seems there is a good cross-section of students who were involved in all kinds of high school activities and have many achievements across the board. While UCLA does admit a lot of quality students, they are still very selective in their process and it was very difficult to get in. I think something like one in 10 students are admitted, so they obviously have their pick.

Current student, 9/2006-Submit Date, June 2007

I feel that UCLA looks for well-rounded people, not just book smarts and high SAT scores. Make sure to show how involved you are with leadership groups and community service, and allow your essays to stand out with your personality. Think of something genuine, but not typical, to write about.

Current student, Biology, 10/2005-Submit Date, June 2007

As of 2007, UCLA has adopted a holistic approach to screen applications. This means that the same person will look at an applicant's academic accomplishments, his/her jobs/leadership/hobbies/community service, and the personal statement. About 22 percent of applicants were admitted to UCLA for the 2007-2008 academic year. Candidates should convey their well-rounded personality in all three major parts of the application, thus proving that they can do well academically, have the potential to become good leaders and are willing to give back to the community, and show their enthusiasm and reasons for seeking higher education at UCLA. Prospective students should consider applying for the UCLA Alumni Scholarship if they meet the minimum GPA requirement.

Current student, Psychology, 9/2005-Submit Date, May 2007

The admissions process was relatively simple compared to other schools. There were no interviews and all you basically did was fill out a questionnaire with name, parental information, background, grades, and extracurricular activities. There were three essays. The most important one was about personal hardship. With UCLA's new holistic admissions process, it is important that you make it clear why you want to come to UCLA, why you would be privileged to come to UCLA, and what coming to UCLA would mean to you. I'm not saying that you should make up a hardship, but it is important to highlight any sort of struggle in your life or anything that would make attending UCLA a significant accomplishment for you. The school is very selective. More people apply to UCLA every year than to any other school. It is important to set yourself apart with your essays. Every applicant has the same basic grades and GPA, so the essays really play a large role.

Current student, 9/2003-Submit Date, May 2006

UCLA looks for students who show exceptional leadership abilities. I graduated top of my class from a public high school in Northern California. I think

UCLA stresses grades over SAT scores because grades show more of an incentive on the student's behalf. But most of all, UCLA looks at extracurricular activities. I started what is now the largest community service club my high school has ever seen. I also formed a diving team to compliment my high school's swim team. Your run-of-the-mill extracurriculars aren't necessarily enough to grant you admission to UCLA. They truly seem to look for students who go above and beyond in all aspects of their lives.

Current student, 9/2005-Submit Date, May 2006

The admissions process was fairly straightforward and definitely easier than a lot of the private universities. There were only three short essays, which was a great time saver. The only downside to such a process is that the admissions process is more impersonal. As a result, a lot of good students get rejected, while a lot of average students are accepted instead. I think that, of the essay questions, the most important is the one about personal hardship. The admissions officers seem to place a lot of importance on overcoming obstacles or, on the contrary, taking advantage of the opportunities that you do have.

> **UCLA says:** "Academic qualifications are the single most important factor. However, UCLA's holistic review process places emphasis on leadership accomplishments and individual characteristics that demonstrate special talents and qualities, including qualities related to overcoming personal obstacles, a process that helps ensure a highly-qualified and diverse student body with only one common denominator—a commitment to excellence."

 Academics

Current student, Business, 9/2006-Submit Date, June 2007

The professors here are geniuses and, for the most part, they are concerned with student learning. If they're not, their TAs are. I've learned a lot from the classes here. They're challenging, and that's what makes me a better student. Grading is usually pretty fair. Most professors curve. Workload was overwhelming at first, but you get used to it.

Current student, 9/2006-Submit Date, June 2007

The classes are large but supposedly only for the first two years. Even still, the large lecture classes are not inconvenient—there are usually smaller section classes that help a lot, and it is not hard to follow along/hear the professor even in a big class.

The workload is pretty hefty—lots of reading and out-of-class work. However, students usually do not have many hours actually in class, so doing work out of class is not very hard. It's all about time management.

Current student, English, 9/2005-Submit Date, June 2007

I think that all the classes are very high quality. Many of the professors are the tops in their fields and it's great to take classes with such amazing professors. While it is hard to get some very popular classes, or classes in high demand because of university requirements and GEs, there is always a chance to get what you need. The grading and workload really vary and depend on the class you are in and the professor you have. Overall, I would say the workload is pretty fair and you are able to keep up with it, even though it is demanding and time consuming. While grading does vary, most of the time if you put in the effort and the work, grades will reflect it.

Current student, Biology, 10/2005-Submit Date, June 2007

UCLA is a research university and that is both a positive and negative aspect. On one hand, students have numerous opportunities to explore in different research fields directly or indirectly related to their fields of study. All faculty members have proven themselves in their respective fields and usually have multiple publications. On the other hand, the classes are rather large in most cases and can range from a capacity of 20 students in seminar settings, to a capacity of 350 students in huge lecture halls. Teachers also tend to be busy because of their research and might not always be available for the students, especially in large classes. Overall, there is an infinite number of classes to satisfy the interests of all the students. The workload is generally challenging, especially for new students, because of the fast pace of the quarter system. Some classes can become impacted, especially in very popular majors such as psychology or political science. Students with priority registration will find themselves at an advantage when signing up for classes.

Current student, Communications, 9/2006-Submit Date, June 2007

For the most part, my classes are interesting and on topics that interest me. The quality is good, but it is difficult to get popular classes. Both of my majors (communications and political science) are very popular, so I have to really vie for those classes. Grading is fair and professors are accessible. The workload, so far, has been less than high school.

Current student, Political Science, 6/2006-Submit Date, June 2007

UCLA is highly challenging. At the very least, each class requires lots of memorization or very strong analysis skills. It is important to be an independent student and to be able to self-teach. It is difficult as a freshman and even as a sophomore to get into very popular classes. There is a ton of reading for almost every class. I really like the teaching structure. Large lectures are very nice for instruction, and then you have the opportunity for extra practice, individual help, or you can gain a deeper understanding of the material in your section. The TAs are highly qualified; many are even more interested and just as qualified as the professors themselves. Grading is usually very fair and professors generally look at averages of the class to determine grades. Office hours are also very helpful and every professor or TA I have encountered is excited to help me at these times.

Current student, 9/2003-Submit Date, May 2006

The general education classes aren't very insightful—while they do give you a gist of what an area of study can offer, most students are in them to get them over with. The upper-division classes, however, are great. They are very interesting and many of the professors are enthusiastic about their area of study, making for better lectures. Because of this, many professors want their students to do well and provide as much assistance as they can give. The professors also understand that grades are important, so they mostly grade on a curve. The workload depends on one's major, but it is manageable. The workload still allows for a social life and club life. Although UCLA is a large university, I've never really had issues getting into a popular class. Especially because of the quarter system, if you don't get a class one quarter you can get it another, and you eventually end up in the classes you want, despite their popularity.

> **UCLA says:** "At UCLA, you get more, and sooner—immediate, first-year access to a virtually limitless selection of studies that only a world-class university can offer. Undergraduate studies at UCLA include national award-winning programs: freshman clusters for interdisciplinary study, more than 200 specialized seminars for freshmen, opportunities for individual research that begin as early as freshman year, and a renowned Honors program that features comprehensive academic counseling to tailor your individual academic career. All of this in addition to the more than 3,500 courses available to undergraduates."

Current student, 9/2005-Submit Date, May 2006

Getting into popular classes always proves difficult. Because you are only allowed to sign up for 10 units with your initial pass, it is often hard to get the third or fourth classes that you want during your second pass. The quality of classes is high. Even though many lectures are quite large, I have found that the professors can still be engaging, concerned with student learning, and personal. It is especially helpful that most large lectures also meet in smaller discussion sections. Grading is most often fair, and I have not run into a professor or TA who grades unfairly. Though a lot of work is assigned, it is never advisable to do it all. You have to learn to pick and choose what is important. For some classes, there is no possible way that you could do all of the reading. Though it seems overwhelming at first, you will do well if you learn how to pick out the important facts and assignments.

Employment Prospects

Current student, English, 9/2005-Submit Date, June 2007

I think that there are many prospects for graduates because the school has such a great reputation. They also have many different alumni connections, workshops and networking to help students and graduates find jobs in their prospective fields. They are many different fairs that also help students with their résumés and find internships and jobs in the community and their home areas.

Current student, Political Science, 6/2006-Submit Date, June 2007

UCLA has the James West Alumni Center which has upwards of 5,000 alumni looking to give UCLA students opportunities. E-mails are constantly sent out about internships, and there are many on-campus jobs to build up a résumé for later careers. UCLA is highly prestigious and employers know that UCLA students are independent, self-motivated and bright.

Current student, 9/2003-Submit Date, November 2006

Career Center is excellent. Lots of students, so the job search is kind of competitive. There are many good career fairs, some even tailored to specific majors (e.g., accounting, engineering and so on). However, it seems that with so many people and so many companies in one place, it is mainly a way to get an idea of what is out there, and not to actually find a contact or get a job. However the career center web site is excellent in terms of job listings, résumé submission and interview scheduling.

Alumnus/a, 9/1997-9/2001, August 2006

UCLA has a lot of resources to help students find and prepare for the workplace, but like everything else at UCLA, you have to really make the effort to find and use these resources (such as the Alumni Association and the Career Center). They aren't going to come to you! In some ways, I think this is why UCLA is such great preparation for "the real world"—navigating the waters of a large, metropolitan research university can teach you how to be resourceful, to make yourself stand out and how to forge connections. The many extracurricular activities at UCLA provide excellent professional training; I was told by one potential employer (who later offered me the job) that the leadership experience I had gained through student activities at UCLA was more impressive than the kind of leadership experience a lot of people accumulated throughout their entire lives. Because UCLA is like a small city (over 50,000 students, faculty, and staff), employers are impressed with people who can stand out there.

The alumni network is most helpful for those who want to live and work in California after graduation, although there are alumni clubs of various size and activity in other cities, as well.

Current student, 9/2003-Submit Date, February 2005

A UCLA degree has always carried prestige, no doubt even more so today because the university has become even more selective in the past years. The alumni network is very strong and often hosts programs to enforce its presence in the student body, such as the Dinners for 12 Strangers Program, in which 12 people from all different backgrounds meet for dinner and are given the opportunity to network and get to know each other. Another resource that students can turn to is the career center, which is in the same building as the internship office. Here, students can seek help and internship resources, speak with career counselors about career options and even take career personality tests. Making appointments with career counselors is very easy and recommended over regular academic counselors.

Quality of Life

Current student, English, 9/2005-Submit Date, June 2007

I am only a sophomore, so I have never lived anywhere except the dorms, although I will be moving off campus next year. I have loved living in the dorms. The atmosphere and the people have been absolutely great, and I think it has been the perfect college experience. While the residential halls (the only place I have lived) are small, the community and social life make up for that. The dining halls are also wonderful. They are delicious and the all-you-can-eat makes every meal great. They have a wide selection of meals and foods that is constantly changing, but that I always love.

Read all of Vault's College Surveys at www.vault.com/college—get complete surveys on 100s of colleges and universities, expert advice on applicaton essays and more.

 VAULT CAREER LIBRARY   67

The neighborhood is great. I always feel completely safe going out and there is hardly any crime. Of course, I would never go walking anywhere at night alone, as I am a girl and that is sort of always iffy, but there are campus escorts who are available to walk you anywhere you want to go. The facilities are also really great here. Overall I think there is a really high quality of life here, and it is kept up really well.

Current student, 9/2006-Submit Date, June 2007

The housing facilities vary in their newness and location, but they are definitely clean and sanitary. The dining hall food is ranked Number Two in the nation and is very good, with lots of variety between eating in the dining halls and getting food to go at several cafes. The dorms are usually pretty quiet, as RAs roam the halls at night to prevent excessive, disruptive noise for those studying. The quality of life is great, allowing for those living on campus to be able to be very social but still productive in school.

Current student, Political Science, 6/2006-Submit Date, June 2007

There are a few different choices for housing, so you can choose one that suits you best. The food is ranked top in the nation. The campus is extremely safe, and I have never felt threatened or scared on campus even at night. Westwood is beautiful and fun. There are lots of great places to eat and shop. Santa Monica and Venice are a short bus ride away so the beach is always an option, too.

Current student, History, 9/2006-Submit Date, May 2007

Located in Westwood and neighbored by Beverly Hills and Bel Air communities, UCLA is a picturesque school. Life here is good, in part because the weather is always so nice! Housing for undergraduates is extremely nice. Many of the buildings are newly remodeled and our dining services are number two in the nation! Crime and safety is hardly a problem here, and UC campus patrol is extremely on-the-ball.

Current student, 9/2003-Submit Date, May 2006

The dorms are one of the details that sold me to UCLA. The elevators smell lemon fresh, as there's a maid service that cleans the dorms once a week. I stayed in a dorm where I had my own bathroom within the room that I shared with two roommates. Even the bathroom was cleaned once a week by the maid service, and the dorm room resembled a hotel room. The food attached to the dorms at UCLA has been compared to students' home cooking. While I didn't think it was quite up to par with my mom's cooking, it wasn't far off. The Wooden Center, our campus gym, includes personal televisions on much of the workout equipment. The campus backs into Sunset Boulevard and Bel Air. The location is amazing, and the lack of crime is incomparable to most other universities.

Social Life

Current student, Biology, 9/2006-Submit Date, June 2007

Greek system is very strong at UCLA. Big frat parties are on Thursdays because the majority of people go home on the weekend. Westwood is a 10- to 15-minute walk away with so many restaurants, movie theaters and bars. If you have a car, everything is fewer than 20 minutes away. If you don't, there is an extensive bus system that can take you all around L.A. for about 25¢ as a UCLA student.

Current student, Biology, 10/2005-Submit Date, June 2007

UCLA has the smallest UC campus and yet the most students on it. This makes UCLA a very dynamic campus with over 900 student groups and organizations on campus. Events and activities are always happening on campus, even at night. There are free sneaks for upcoming movies, all kinds of dance/martial arts/sports classes offered at the gym for a very minimal amount of money, outdoor adventure groups, many events celebrating various cultures, as well as numerous opportunities to join dance groups or musical groups. The Greek life is also very involved with the campus. Aside from partying, frats and sororities often sponsor events on campus and support others off campus. There are major events on campus that involve the entire student population, and those include Blue and Gold Week, Spring Sing, Bruin Bash, Dance Marathon and others. Westwood is a very student-friendly city with plenty of restaurants from which to choose. There are two major movie theatres and three bars where students can go. The Office of Residential Life also puts on events for students living in the dorms, and those include All-Hill Halloween, Dormal, DDR tournaments, musi-

cal performances and other activities. The diversity on the UCLA campus is also impressive. UCLA definitely has a great social life that any student can enjoy.

Current student, 9/2006-Submit Date, June 2007

I am in a Panhellenic sorority and I would really recommend it to someone who wants an easy way to meet people. There are really fun activities that spawn from it, which are not only with your own sorority, but also include lots of community service projects with all fraternities and sororities, events to meet boys and just a lot of good networking. I am not over 21, so I do not know the local club/bar scene, although I know we have two bars in Westwood, and many people go to Sunset strip for some of the Hollywood clubs where celebrities go. L.A. is the perfect place for young adults!

Current student, Political Science, 6/2006-Submit Date, June 2007

The social life at UCLA is amazing. Greek life is big, but it is definitely not necessary to join a fraternity or sorority. Most students are interested in gaining an education and making friends, going out and having fun. UCLA puts on many incredible events that are either very cheap or free for students such as the recent Jazz and Reggae festival. Bruin Walk is always teeming with people promoting events, clubs, and free movie screenings, so there's always something to do and some way to get involved. There are two major bars in Westwood, Brew Co. and Maloney's (now O'Hara's) that many students go out to on weekends. There are so many restaurants in Westwood that your options are unlimited.

Current student, 9/2004-Submit Date, May 2006

Fabulous social scene. There is just the right balance. It is not always crazy, but when you need something to do there is something not far away. Hollywood has the most happening clubs, as well as Maloney's in Westwood, and Fraternity row. The Undie Run has become a tradition on campus every quarter. At the end of the quarter, during the Wednesday of finals' week, students strip down to their underwear and run down Gayley (frat row) and Landfair.

Current student, 9/2003-Submit Date, May 2006

There are two bars in Westwood that could be better. But Westwood offers great dining! There is such a wide variety to choose from. There are always parties on Thursday night, whether in the apartments or the frat houses. The Greek system is very active in the social scene on campus. A big part of the social life at UCLA surrounds the athletic department. Football and basketball games are very popular. When it comes to the social life on campus and in Westwood, student favorites would have to be the cookies at Diddy Riese, the food at Damon and Pythias (a Greek restaurant), the burgers at Buck Fifty's, pint night at Maloney's, football games at the Rose Bowl, and the undie run during finals' week of every quarter.

The School Says

UCLA is big. That size is part of its DNA, part of its promise: 24,800 undergraduates. 3,800 faculty. 5,000 courses. 130 undergraduate majors. 109 academic departments. 800 student organizations. 11 graduate schools. More offerings in art, music, culture and sports than are available in most cities.

UCLA is a university with the size and scope to allow for unimagined diversity, unmatched breadth and depth of scholarship. Opportunity and possibility? Limitless.

UCLA attracts, challenges and empowers a performance-based elite. Students are drawn to UCLA by the opportunity for contact with a renowned faculty of teacher-scholars.

Your undergraduate experience at UCLA can begin with an innovative program that involves you in a stimulating multidisciplinary exploration of a challenging and timely topic. The UCLA Freshman Clusters engage students in year-long learning communities that introduce freshmen to distinguished UCLA faculty, and emphasize interdisciplinary teaching and learning.

The Fiat Lux freshman seminars provide you with a valuable forum for students and faculty to engage in critical thinking together. Fiat Lux offers more than 200 seminars each year that bring the talents and expertise of the faculty at a premier research university into a small classroom setting.

The opportunity to participate in research is one of the benefits of attending a research university. Each year, thousands of students participate in research at UCLA. Many of them create important publishable work in close collaboration with senior faculty—often as early as their freshman year. You can create new knowledge by working one-on-one with top faculty, or by enrolling in seminars, research tutorials, and departmental honors programs.

Interested in getting academic credit for meaningful work in the diverse communities of Los Angeles? Service-learning courses, community-based research and credit-bearing internships are cornerstones of undergraduate education at UCLA. Or, you can apply for the minor in Civic Engagement, the only one of its kind in the country.

There is no typical UCLA student or faculty member. The only common denominator is an appetite for excellence.

University of California, Berkeley

Office of Undergraduate Admissions
University of California, Berkeley
110 Sproul Hall #5800
Berkeley, CA 94720-5800
Admissions phone: (510) 642-3175
Admissions fax: (510) 642-7333
Admissions e-mail: ouars@uclink4.berkeley.edu
Admissions URL: www.berkeley.edu/applying/

 Admissions

Current student, 1/2003-Submit Date, January 2007

The admissions process is rigorous with a holistic application review. You must be a top student to be accepted. SATs and GPAs have to be at the top 5 percent of the class to have a good chance.

Current student, Economics, 8/2003-Submit Date, September 2006

According to *U.S. News & World Report*, the most recent admissions rate was 25 percent and 100 percent of those admitted graduated in the top 10 percent of their high school class. Thus, the admissions rate may seem pretty high but the pool of applicants is very high quality. You have to write an essay, provide GPA, SAT I scores, and SAT II scores (for two or three exams, I can't remember). There are no letters of recommendation or interviews.

My best advice as to how to get in is typical: get good grades, get excellent test scores, write an amazing essay, and last but of great importance, do things in high school that really set you apart from other students (president of the science club doesn't really cut it, in my opinion).

Current student, 8/2004-Submit Date, October 2006

Berkeley is looking for unique individuals who take initiative. It doesn't matter what you do, they just want to see that you follow your passions.

Current student, Social Sciences, 1/2005-Submit Date, May 2007

Great grades and test scores are really important when it comes to getting into Berkeley, but being passionate about something in high school will definitely set you apart from the thousands of other applicants. It doesn't have to be working with a congressman or being president of a huge club. Some people will write about the hardships they overcame in their personal statements, but I wrote about my love for creative writing. After showing my personal statement to one of my high school English teachers, she claimed it would be a key factor in my getting into college. Berkeley is known for its diversity, and they want to admit people who love to do a wide range of activities, apart from just studying.

Current student, 8/2003-Submit Date, November 2005

UC Berkeley uses the UC Common Application, same as the rest of the UC schools. Berkeley places more weight on the personal statement, and likes to see

some unique character traits, or something that will help the admissions officers see you as more than just a stock potential student. There is no admissions interview, except for the Regents and Chancellors Scholarship. I found that interview to be extremely relaxed, and needed no extra preparation for it. Berkeley tends to be very selective, but in a very different way than other schools. They tend to de-emphasize scores, and try to select students for a varied and unique campus atmosphere.

Current student, 8/2002-Submit Date, October 2005

The college application process is incredibly stressful. However, the University of California's process is much less stressful than the process for private liberal arts colleges. For UC students, the primary factor for admissions is GPA and SAT scores. Luckily, I went to a high school with many AP classes, which allowed me to have a GPA well over 4.0. The UC GPA calculation also uses a straight A, B, C, D scale not taking into account minus or plus grades, which also boosted my GPA. In addition to my GPA, I was in an environment where I had access to SAT preparation.

This is not to say that GPAs and SAT scores were the only important factors in my admissions. I was also incredibly active during high school, attempting to have as many extracurricular activities to put on my application, and earn as many honors and awards as possible. I feel that my essay for the UC application was well written but not something I am particularly proud of. It was good enough for UCs but not good enough to get me into any of the Ivy League schools I applied to, in spite of my high GPA and SAT scores. I think that is the main difference between UC applications and private school applications. Being a Californian, I have an edge in the UC application process, and my GPA and SAT scores were in the top percentiles of all applicants. In addition, each class at UC Berkeley has several thousand students, increasing the odds of acceptance. UC Berkeley did not conduct any interviews, which I think would be impossible considering the huge number of applications they receive every year.

Alumnus/a, 8/2001-5/2005, December 2005

UC Berkeley uses the one general application for all UCs. There is a personal statement/essay required in the application, and this is an important part of the application because it gives better insight into you as a person. There is no interview in the admissions process, so the only place you can tell the Admissions Committee who you are as a person is through the essay. UC Berkeley is highly selective. You can increase your chances of being admitted by getting good grades, high SAT scores, and being active at school or in the community. My SAT scores were average, but I got really good grades in high school, which I believe made up for the mediocre SAT scores. I was involved in some activities during high school (although, by no means I was not the team captain or the president of a club). I don't think you have to be stellar in all categories (grades, scores and activities) because I certainly wasn't. UC Berkeley considers a lot of other factors, so definitely apply if you feel that you have something to offer.

Current student, 8/2001-Submit Date, September 2004

The UC application system is very convenient; there's only one application for all campuses. I applied online to UCSD, UCSB, UCLA and UCB. The UC sys-

Read all of Vault's College Surveys at **www.vault.com/college**—get complete surveys on 100s of colleges and universities, expert advice on applicaton essays and more.

VAULT CAREER LIBRARY 69

tem does not require interviews and only requires one personal essay. The State of California has a guarantee system that the top 4 percent of a graduating class is granted admission to a UC; however, it may not be the UC of one's choice. Make sure that your personal essay tells admissions something about you that they cannot find out through your transcripts and application.

 **Academics**

Current student, Economics, 8/2003-Submit Date, September 2006

Well, I don't think it would be any surprise if I told you that academics at UC Berkeley are very tough, particularly if you take the courses in your major that are known and structured to be particularly tough.

Most of the lower-division classes have huge class sizes (200 to 400). The standard difficulty, upper-division classes in the economics major were smaller but still big (80 to 100). The graduate preparatory classes in the economics major tended to be very small to small (15 to 40). Where there is consistently high quality though is in the Graduate Student Instructors (GSI) who teach discussion sections—this is where the real learning goes on. All of my GSIs were amazingly brilliant and A-class instructors (for my professors, only the first characteristic was consistently true).

Current student, 5/2003-Submit Date, November 2006

Great professors for the most part but it matters a lot in which field you are. Science programs are topnotch.

Current student, 8/2004-Submit Date, October 2006

Overall, I think that it is a great balance. Getting good grades can be competitive, but it is not impossible. Teachers are very accessible and it isn't terribly hard to get into the classes that you would like.

Current student, 8/2000-Submit Date, October 2006

For the most part, very rigorous courseloads and requirements; grades are definitely earned. Not difficult to get desired classes if you stick it out, but definitely some work/stress involved. Very good classes, for the most part, with reliable, informed professors; I always learn a lot and get a lot out of each class I take. Grading is usually adequate; I feel each grade I receive is fair, including the B's and even the C's. Workload is heavy, for the most part; I always have work to be doing, and there are some times when I just won't get to everything that I need to get done. This gives me a feeling of always reaching, and when I succeed it's usually despite my failure to read each and every assignment.

Current student, Social Sciences, 1/2005-Submit Date, May 2007

Because of the way the process of signing up for classes works, upper-division students will get to enroll in courses before younger students. My major advisor is very sympathetic, and somehow we always end up getting into the classes we need.

Current student, Sociology, 1/2003-Submit Date, August 2006

I was a transfer student, so my first year was rough! However, the next year it got easier. Once you figure out how professors want their papers written it gets easier to format. Above all, please please please go to GSIs' and professors' office hours, not only do they help you figure out the tough essay, math, physics, and so on problems, but they see your dedication and remember you. This comes in handy when you are at a borderline grade or need a letter of recommendation.

Current student, 8/2003-Submit Date, November 2005

Berkeley has a fantastic selection of classes. While the classes for some paths (EECS, MCB) are extremely competitive, and therefore might be a little hard to get into (at least the introductory classes), the large majority gave me no trouble at all. I found myself with a lot of free time, despite the fact that I took over 20 units almost every semester. There's plenty of work, but it's manageable. As with any school, there are some sub-par professors and graduate students, but the majority of professors I had, I enjoyed. Of course, as a public school, classes are larger than might be desired, but I found this was hardly an impediment to getting to know professors. If you so desire, office hours are always provided, and can be very helpful and personal. Most professors actually ask students to come to office hours, even in the 500+ person lectures. While Berkeley boasts one of the highest number of Nobel Laureates in the country, none teach undergraduate classes.

Current student, 8/2002-Submit Date, October 2005

When I came to UC Berkeley I put myself on the pre-med track, signing up for huge calculus and chemistry lectures. My chemistry class had at least 500 students in it, making establishing a relationship with the professor nearly impossible. While we had more intimate relationships with our GSIs, it was still a very impersonal situation. I have found that many of my classes at UC Berkeley have been too large to form relationships with the instructor or professor. This is not to say that the classes were not useful. I learned a great deal from many of the larger lecture courses. My first year of classes was quite easy for me, coming from a small, private all-girls school. However, as I have moved into more specific classes in my major, the work has also gotten more specific and I have had to work harder. Luckily the classes in my major are not impacted, so it is not very difficult to get into them.

However, for some people who have to get into very popular courses, registration can be stressful. Especially for those who have yet to complete university-wide requirements—the American history classes, American cultures classes and the writing requirement courses. These classes often fill up early on in the registration process, and if you don't signup for them as soon as you can, it is likely you will not get in. Some of these courses only have 20 to 30 spots in them and when there are thousands of students who need them, it is very difficult to secure a spot. I have been lucky to find a major that is relatively small and has allowed me to forge good relationships with my professor and my advisor. Psychology majors and econ majors have one advisor for hundreds of students; my advisor, on the other hand, counsels maybe 40 other students, maximum.

Current student, 8/2001-Submit Date, September 2004

At UC Berkeley, students are allowed to take one-third of their units Pass/Not Pass, meaning not for a letter grade. Most of the lower-division classes are large (200 to 700) people. Registration for classes can be quite frustrating because it's usually difficult to get the classes you want. Many students load up on units so they can shop classes and then drop the ones they don't want. Because of course shopping, classes fill up quickly and students have to be put on the waitlist. The 8 a.m. lectures and discussions are easiest to get into, unless it is a very popular class, because no one wants to get up that early. The first few weeks of the semester are always full of scheduling chaos, but students have up until the eighth week to add or drop classes. Grading cannot always be fair because papers are not always graded by the professor. Assignments are usually graded by graduate student instructors (GSIs) who run discussion sections. Sometimes you get the easier GSIs, sometimes you don't. The workload can be tough, especially if you are involved with clubs and organizations. Depending on your major, count on a lot of reading or hours working on problem sets.

 Employment Prospects

Current student, 1/2003-Submit Date, January 2007

Maintain 3.5 GPA or over, and the doors will be wide open. The Berkeley name is prestigious and will be highly regarded in all employment situations. Recruiters, superiors and co-workers alike recognize and appreciate the Berkeley name.

Current student, Economics, 8/2003-Submit Date, September 2006

I have friends who went to work at very prestigious finance firms (e.g, Goldman Sachs), consulting firms (e.g., Deloitte), tech firms (e.g., Apple), studios (e.g., Dreamworks), and went on to do graduate work at great places like UCSF and UPenn.

Current student, 5/2003-Submit Date, November 2006

The alumni network is huge—there will be alumni at any large firm in which you are interested; however, because it is a large public school, it can be impersonal, and these connections are not always useful. For certain areas, such as science and undergraduate business, there are student groups that provide a lot of support and training for interviewing and preparing for the job market. The Career Center on campus is also useful; however, don't expect a lot of personalized attention or support.

Current student, 8/2004-Submit Date, October 2006

Berkeley is the best public school on the West Coast as far as recruiting goes. Companies recruit highly from Cal.

Current student, 8/2000-Submit Date, October 2006

I feel that a Berkeley degree will open many doors in the employment process, though these will mostly be for business, engineering and science types. These are Berkeley's strongest perceived subjects, and are accordingly respected.

Current student, Sociology, 1/2003-Submit Date, August 2006

Berkeley seems to impress everyone, but what you need is experience to finish getting your self in the door. Berkeley degrees help you get the foot in the door, but experience seals the deal. Get internships!

Alumnus/a, 1/2001-8/2003, December 2005

Overall, I think the Berkeley name carries a decent amount of weight, regardless of the major from which you come. My experience has been that graduating from Berkeley has gotten me at least a foot in the door to many interviews, but I don't think in competitive fields, that alone it provides a significant boost to one's résumé. This may vary among departments, but my general experience has been that the alumni network, while expansive, is not very tight knit and, as such, not as helpful as it could be. On-campus recruiting events occurred year-round and were plentiful while I was there. The Career Center was a very valuable resource to me; the counselors I spoke with were generally very knowledgeable and helpful.

Current student, 8/2002-Submit Date, October 2005

The Cal Career Center has a job listings web site and also hosts many fairs where recruiters for business majors and engineering majors can meet and sign up for interviews with companies. Advisors are also available to guide students to resources. The alumni network also posts fairs; however, many of these services are not advertised as well as they could be, meaning that the students must do some research to find and get access to them.

Quality of Life

Current student, 8/2000-Submit Date, October 2006

I like the dorms, though they're not as fancy and well equipped as at some schools. They are very comfortable, though. There are accessible health workers, RAs and lots of places for food, and I feel that all my possible needs are taken care of. The neighborhoods are not necessarily safe, but I've never had any problems.

Current student, Social Sciences, 1/2005-Submit Date, May 2007

The housing at Berkeley is only mediocre. They are not glamorous in the least and it is very expensive to live in Berkeley—both on campus and off campus. The food served at the dining halls is getting better and better every year, though. The buildings on campus, on the whole, are actually very aesthetically pleasing. Many of the lecture halls are very comfortable and are equipped with different technologies. Although Berkeley is not exactly the safest city, there is a lot of attention to student safety. There is a program called Bear Walk, where you can be escorted from any location on or near campus to another location. There are also emergency phones placed in many locations on and around campus.

Current student, 8/2002-Submit Date, October 2005

Going to school in Berkeley is expensive. Compared to many of the other schools, housing is much more expensive. Rent is often well over $700 per month, per person. I know some people who pay $1,200 per person, every month. On top of this, most Berkeley landlords require that students pay their utilities—water, electricity and garbage. On top of this there is the added cost of Internet access and cable television—which no college student today can live without. At least not my housemates and me. Most students live off campus, as university housing is only guaranteed for the first year of enrollment. So dorm life is not a big hit. However, even those students who live off campus utilize the universities dining facilities, which have vastly improved since my freshman year.

In the past three years Cal dining has gone from absolutely disgusting to pretty good. I know many people who opt to purchase a dining plan, even though they live off campus and have kitchens. For many, this is an economical purchase as access to groceries is difficult. The only grocery store that is close to most students is very expensive and getting to and from the store with all of the groceries is difficult via public transportation.

Campus is about a half-mile walk from my house, but then there is the added distance of getting to where you need to go on campus, I probably walk three-quarters of a mile each way to my classes. But it's good exercise. One of the pitfalls of Berkeley is the large number of homeless people. Telegraph is lined with bums and literally crazy people, making it a street many people avoid. In addition, People's Park has become a campground for many homeless people, so it is rarely used by the students. I don't feel particularly unsafe. Cal provides security monitors at the dorms and late-night walkers/drivers to take students from campus to their homes if they are by themselves and feel unsafe. There is also the blue light system that is present on many campuses that students can use to call the police from various locations.

Social Life

Current student, 1/2003-Submit Date, January 2007

With Berkeley campus' proximity to S.F., it's a good place for studying, relaxing, clubbing in S.F., or partying at the frat houses. Housing is [disappointing], although the new dorms are very, very nice. Diversity is quite amazing at Berkeley, although the Asian population is very well represented on campus, accounting for roughly 40 percent of the student population. The campus has a large number of student groups of varying interests, so whatever you do, you'll find your niche.

Current student, Economics, 8/2003-Submit Date, September 2006

You must try these places: Chez Panisse, Kiralas (Japanese), Gregoire's take out (French). For once or a few times a week: Ichiban (Japanese), the new BBQ place on Oxford/Fulton and Bancroft, Sushi House in Alameda. Good for frequent eating: Cheese Board, Dessi Dog (a hot dog stand at Telegraph and Bancroft), the taco stand at Telegraph and Bancroft, Hoa Hin (regional Vietnamese chain), Rubios (seafood Mexican chain) at Bay Street shopping center in Emeryville, Bangkok Noodle by Union Square in San Francisco. Artsy events and famous people come often to speak at Zellerbach Hall.

Current student, 8/2000-Submit Date, October 2006

There are at least three bars within a block of campus, and lots and lots of restaurants everywhere. Naan N' Curry, Thai House, Gipsy's Italian, Cafe Intermezzo, Raleigh's Pub, Beckett's bar, Kip's, Blake's on Telegraph, Cafe Strada, Cafe Milano, and many more are all within a block of campus, and Zachary's Pizza and Cheeseboard Pizza are within 10 minutes of campus. There are so many restaurants! The Greek system is fairly active, and there are parties I hear of every weekend. Campus clubs also put on a lot of events during the week, and S.F. is so close that anyone bored of the Berkeley scene only has to take a BART ride to the city. I really enjoy the social life here.

Current student, Social Sciences, 1/2005-Submit Date, May 2007

The food is cheap and plentiful in Berkeley. Some student favorites are Yogurt Park, where the yogurt flavors change every few days, Top Dog, which is open well into the night, and Blondies. The Durant food court has a variety of places to suit a whole group of friends with differing tastes. There are plenty of opportunities to attend fraternity or sorority parties, but I find that many people will just hang out with their friends at their own apartments on a Friday night. On the whole, people will be too busy studying to deal with dating. Berkeley is not exactly known for its attractive students either.

Current student, 1/2003-Submit Date, November 2005

Go Greek! The Greek life is fun when we aren't on moratorium. There are over 46 Greek houses on campus, 36 fraternities and 12 sororities. The university is invasive in Greek life though. The campus is huge and near the city of San Francisco, so frequent weekend trips to the city are not uncommon. Kips, Blake's and Bear's Lair are hip bars, but you'll find better quality farther west on Shattuck Avenue. Parties are few and far between, and the gateway to a social life is through the Greek system.

Read all of Vault's College Surveys at www.vault.com/college—get complete surveys on 100s of colleges and universities, expert advice on applicaton essays and more.

VAULT CAREER LIBRARY   71

Current student, 8/2001-Submit Date, April 2004

The school has over 300 different student groups and there are always activities in which students can participate. There is a bar on campus, the Bear's Lair, which is a popular gathering spot for students on Friday afternoons. The other bars in Berkeley are not all impressive, yet are still frequented by students, particularly on Tuesday and Thursday. Some say the dating scene is nonexistent and that people come here with "Berkeley vision," meaning that everyone here is un-datable. I do not think that is entirely true. The Greek system has its presence on campus, yet it is not domineering, as it is in some colleges. Some favorite student activities include the Bonfire Rally, the Big Game, hikes up to the Big C, noon concerts by a cappella groups, and just hanging out on memorial glade.

University of California, Davis

Undergraduate Admissions & Outreach Services
178 Mrak Hall
University of California, Davis
One Shields Avenue
Davis, CA 95616-8507
Admissions phone: (530) 752-2971
Admissions e-mail: uaos@ucdavis.edu
Admissions URL: www.ucdavis.edu/future_students/

 ## Admissions

Alumnus/a, Psychology, 9/2001-6/2005, July 2007

The admissions process was simple. As with the other UCs, you just fill out the application and submit it along with your transcript and essay, then wait for a response. No required interview. Just be sure your essay is organized, well-written, stylistically creative, and conforms to the topic well. Although this process is deceptively simple, admission into UCD has been getting tougher within the last few years. Along with a strong GPA and SAT, UCD looks for applicants who are well rounded and have shown leadership qualities. The latter two are especially important, as they can make the difference for someone who's in or out.

Alumnus/a, 9/2003-6/2006, January 2007

Because the UC application does not take letters of recommendation, I would urge applicants to spend extra time on their personal statements. It's the only soft factor at which the admissions committee can look. Put effort into making your voice come out in the statement. As an out-of-state applicant, it was a bit more difficult because of the quota system for non-residents.

Current student, 9/2005-Submit Date, January 2007

I was a transfer student and had a Transfer Admission Agreement (TAA) and had already finished my IGETC, so it was a pretty easy process for me. There were a couple of essays for the application, mostly for scholarship purposes. About half the students I meet are transfers.

Current student, 9/2004-Submit Date, December 2006

From high school, it is quite difficult. The freshmen I have met usually came out with a 3.9 GPA and an 1100 SAT score. There is no interview and, just like all UC applications, you must submit a series of essays along with your application. The transfer and freshman application essays are different as the transfer tends to target more accomplishments and freshmen are based more on academic achievement.

Current student, 10/2002-Submit Date, October 2005

The admissions process did not take a long time to complete. There is no interview for undergraduate programs. I got into Davis with a 3.7 GPA, involvement in campus clubs, sports and other activities. I advise applicants to focus on grades first, then join honor societies (National Honor Society, California Scholarship Foundation). Also, participate in community service organizations, such as Boy Scouts of America.

Current student, 9/2004-Submit Date, November 2005

The admissions process includes a basic application and personal statement. The application asks for not only your personal info and grades, but also asks about part-time jobs, community service and extracurricular activities you might have done. These last three sections are more important than you may think because the university strives to create a balanced, well-rounded student body that can contribute to the campus and community in various ways. My average high school GPA was only about 3.3, so I know that my participation in community service, part-time work and extracurricular activities gave me the boost I needed to be accepted. The personal statement is also vital in helping you stand out and relaying your personality to the admissions officers. They look for people who are honest, resilient and optimistic; so share an experience that affected your life in some way and truly helped you to develop as an individual.

Current student, 9/2004-Submit Date, April 2005

I was admitted into the University of California, Davis because my application was tagged by the water polo coach there. He saw me play in a few games and thought I was pretty good, so he tagged my application, and that is why I was accepted. I did not have very strong grades, but I excelled in athletics. I think that if it were not for my athletics, I would most likely not be at Davis.

> **The school says:** "All applicants must meet faculty-approved admissions criteria. All freshman applicants are given a comprehensive review that rates them on 15 academic and non-academic criteria. Although the academic criteria weigh most heavily, the admissions policy also acknowledges characteristics such as special talent, extraordinary achievement, leadership potential, and exceptional backgrounds."

 ## Academics

Current student, 9/2004-Submit Date, November 2006

The professors here are pretty good, but remember that they were primarily hired because of their research, not their teaching skills. If you want to do undergraduate research in any science field, this university is for you. There are plenty of opportunities for research and internships. It can be difficult to get into classes at the time you want them, but it is not difficult to get into the classes you want, in general. They have very strong biology, environmental science, nutrition, political science and agricultural science programs.

Current student, 9/2003-Submit Date, November 2006

Academic classes are relatively easy to get into if you are a declared major and they are in your major. Popular classes are a little harder to get into, but as you gain units, this gets easier and there is always the option to waitlist. Class quality is generally good. As you move from lower division to upper, the classes get smaller and the instruction gets a little more specific.

Current student, 9/2005-Submit Date, January 2007

Classes are large, but it's easy to get to know professors if you attend office hours. Most of my professors have been excellent. Workload varies, but expect between 13 and 17 units a quarter if you want to graduate on time—generally four classes not including extra stuff (PE, music performance and so on). Popular classes include Beer Brewing, Tractor Driving, and History and Folklore of Food (FST 10). Grading is generally curved, and different for every class, but for some classes you will have to work hard to earn an A.

Current student, 9/2004-Submit Date, September 2006

Davis is not an easy school. Many students who graduate in the top 5 percent of their high school class have found themselves struggling to get a 3.0 their first quarter, but it does get easier with time. Workload is decent, again depending on class and professor. There are several professors who have won honors and awards and are absolutely remarkable. Grades tend to be fair, with math and science classes having curves that help students. And as for classes: there are waiting lists for some classes, but during the four years, everyone has an opportunity to get into their dream class (Bowling PE).

Current student, 10/2002-Submit Date, October 2005

As a freshman, it is hard to get into popular classes, but as an upperclassman, it becomes easier because your registration time is earlier. The biology program is very good; the classes are put together well for the most part. There are many classes that have over 200 people, but this is made up for by the availability of professors. Most professors or lecturers have multiple office hours, respond to e-mails and are willing to make appointments with students. Most classes are curved, but the difficulty of grading depends on the lecturer. The workload expected for each class is usually proportional to the number of units a class is. However, for science labs there is much more work involved than the units received. The seven series for physics is very poor, this is the required series for non-physics and non-engineering science majors. The program is based on discussion labs; there is no textbook, and the quizzes and tests are written in a format that is not used during the lectures or labs. It is very difficult to study for the class because there is not much material to study.

Current student, 9/2004-Submit Date, November 2005

I am an undergrad in the College of Letters and Sciences and my major is American studies. Basically, you have to satisfy the overarching college requirements and those of your chosen major. The L&S requirements help you attain an excellent general education background and your major helps you focus on your interest. Quality of classes has been outstanding; the teachers are down-to-earth, reasonable, approachable and friendly people who are eager to get to know you and sincerely want you to learn. Teachers here demand an engaged style of learning in which the student is an active participant in the classroom and a critical reader of text.

My experience with workload has been reasonable in every class, and I have taken classes ranging from Film Studies to Spanish, to Nature and Culture, to Anthropology. The university seems to be aware of its most popular classes and it offers multiple sections for students. Also, with two registration appointments before each term, students are given the opportunity to get on waitlists if the classes are full. Also, if you are on a waitlist when the class begins, teachers are very willing to add you to the course if you express sincere interest.

Current student, 9/2004-Submit Date, April 2005

I never got very good grades in high school; however, now that I am at UC Davis, I have been doing very well. I got a 3.9 GPA my first semester. It is pretty easy to get into the classes I want. I can always fill up my schedule and get as many units as I need. I find most of my classes pretty challenging, but I find the professors very helpful. I really enjoy my teacher assistants. They are very helpful and always make learning the material a little bit easier than my professors do. I find the discussion sections that I have very helpful to my learning because we always discuss what we learned in class a little bit more in depth.

Current student, 9/2000-Submit Date, February 2004

Overall, the classes are decent. The grading is pretty harsh all around. Mostly you get a lot of A's and B's with a fair share of B+'s. All science majors are very good. Liberal arts is improving. I am an international relations major. Most classes are large, which makes it very hard to know your profs. I am a senior and my smallest class has 80 people. Popular classes can be hard to get, but eventually you get your classes. The best thing about Davis is we have the largest study abroad program of all the UCs, and if you plan correctly, you could spend almost two out of four years abroad in a wide variety of countries.

 # Employment Prospects

Alumnus/a, Psychology, 9/2001-6/2005, July 2007

Employment prospects are decent. Since UCD doesn't have the clout of a UCLA, sometimes the school misses out on the big companies. But UCD does have on-campus recruiting from major companies in the Sacramento area. And with the UCD Medical Center, the Capitol, and topnotch research facilities nearby, good internships aren't hard to come by. Good luck if you want to be in business or accounting though. The school does have a business major, but since it's under the guise of Managerial Economics, prestigious companies, such as PricewaterhouseCoopers, are less willing to recruit from the school since little is known about the program. In general though, job prospects and internships are good and plentiful, but you have to go the extra mile if you want them.

Current student, 9/2004-Submit Date, November 2006

UC Davis has a good reputation among employees in the area. Some of the top biotechnology companies are constantly recruiting at the school. There are lots of resources to find internships and jobs.

Alumnus/a, Sociology, 9/2004-12/2006, May 2007

Again, it really depends on your major (social science majors may tend to have a harder time getting a job after they graduate). I don't see many engineering majors not get a job in their major within six months, so that is a positive sign. UC Davis is a very well-respected school and one of the Top 50 universities in the nation. The alumni network is no more than average versus other universities. One reason is just the sheer number of alumni; there is no close-knit atmosphere that comes with being an Aggie (school mascot).

Current student, 9/2005-Submit Date, January 2007

There are lots of on- and off-campus employment while you're in school. The Internship and Career Center is amazing and holds tons of workshops on writing résumés, interviewing, finding a job and more. They bend over backwards to find students internships. If you complete 40 hours during a quarter it can also be notated on your transcript. There are career fairs every quarter with over 100 companies recruiting both undergrads and grad students.

Current student, 9/2004-Submit Date, November 2005

The campus has an Internship and Career Center with very helpful peer and adult advisors who are eager to help you fulfill your career and internship goals. I have had personal experience with this center and was very impressed with the dedication of the advisors and their efforts in helping students. The advisors are even divided up into separate career categories so that the person who helps you is somewhat specialized in your interested area. The campus has career fairs every year, and I have attended one of many seminars that are organized to help students prepare résumés, develop communication skills and prepare for a professional environment.

Alumnus/a, 3/2001-6/2003, December 2004

They have the largest career and internship center in the country, but they also have the largest student body of all the UC campuses. The Internship and Career Center is also divided by career type, which can be helpful. For example, there are different people in charge for agricultural careers, liberal arts careers and business. There are also recruiters from the Peace Corp and the foreign service that have regular office hours. There is a Washington Center where the campus will help students find internships in D.C. during the summer. In addition, since Davis is only 20 minutes away from Sacramento, the state capital, many students will do an internship at the capitol or state agency at some point during their time at Davis. 90 percent of the people I know, including myself, ended up going to grad school after they graduated.

Quality of Life

Current student, 9/2003-Submit Date, November 2006

Davis is probably one of the best towns in which to go to school. The food is amazing, and the downtown atmosphere has that perfect, small-town feel. There is plenty for students to do and Davis is a very social college town. Sacramento

Read all of Vault's College Surveys at **www.vault.com/college**—get complete surveys on 100s of colleges and universities, expert advice on applicaton essays and more.

 VAULT CAREER LIBRARY   73

is just 20 minutes away and San Francisco and Tahoe are very close, too. Housing is great and easy to find: anywhere from apartments to houses to lofts over the downtown stores. Campus is also good, with a brand-new recreation hall and several more stadiums and activity places being built right now.

Alumnus/a, Sociology, 9/2004-12/2006, May 2007

Housing is somewhat pricey as rent for a room within two or three miles of campus range from $400 to $600 a month. The dining commons was recently revamped, so it is one of nicest I have seen compared to all the other UCs I have visited. The food is also topnotch. The campus architecture is rather bland. Except for the Mondavi Center, there is no landmark building that stands out. The facilities are solid overall as there's always a place to study, go on your laptop or just take a nap, from the Silo to Memorial Union. The City of Davis is very safe.

Alumnus/a, 9/2003-6/2006, January 2007

Many people think that Davis is a boring place with nothing but cows initially. (By the way, you can't really go cow tipping. It's a myth.) However, don't under-estimate this yuppie college town. There's a lot this place offers. You really need to live here to appreciate it.

There's a great arts scene here. We have the multi-million dollar Mondavi Center, which attracts world-class artists. If you're into classical music, it's nice to know that last year Mondavi played host to stars such as Itzak Pearlman, Lang Lang, and Cleveland Orchestra. In addition, there are many great bands that play in the CoHo on Thursdays and Friday nights.

For a tiny college town, there's also quite a selection of food. There's the famous Fuji's all-you-can-eat sushi buffet for about $10 (go early, the wait is usually over an hour long), and for health foodies, there's Pluto's for salads, Delta of Venus for vegan food, and the Co-op grocery store for organic products.

Davis is also a "city on bikes." If you like biking, it's your perfect city. I biked everywhere. There are bike lanes and places to park your bike everywhere you go. You can stay fit while going to class.

Current student, 10/2002-Submit Date, October 2005

Off-campus housing can be challenging to find. There are not many apartments that allow animals, and if they do, there is a $300 to $500 deposit required. The town has a very safe environment, and it's a good place to raise children. There are many places for fine dining and cheaper dining. The campus has one restaurant on it, a gym, many fields and multiple swimming pools. The city is clean and streets are well lit. There is a green belt area with a bike and running trail. Davis is surrounded by farmland and is not a very large city.

Current student, 9/2004-Submit Date, April 2005

I really enjoy living here at UC Davis. I find the dorms very nice. They are always clean, and my dorm is perfectly placed in between the weight room and the dining commons. The campus is always clean, and there is a lot of nice landscaping around all the time. I really like the campus and how flat it is. It is nice not to have to walk up a bunch of hills just to get to class. I usually skateboard to all of my classes anyway though, it is nice being on wheels when the terrain is flat because I have to put forth very little effort to get where I am going. So that is nice. Overall, I would have to say that I really like the Davis campus and I think the school does a great job of cleaning it and keeping it clean.

Social Life

Alumnus/a, Sociology, 9/2004-12/2006, May 2007

Compared to the rest of the UCs, social life is rather below average. There is a number of good bars in very small, downtown Davis. The dating scene is good just because it is a college town. There are lots of quality clubs and the Greek life is average compared to other colleges. Picnic Day is probably the biggest event in the City of Davis and the school. It is the largest student-led event in the nation. Downtown Davis is closed for that event. But generally after 11 p.m. even during the weekends, there is very little to go except if you to Sacramento. Also, because the police are very strict here, parties can't really get too crazy or large.

Alumnus/a, 9/2003-6/2006, January 2007

UC Davis has a great social scene. People are friendly and really ready to help each other out. There's a lot to do at night and during the weekends.

There are tons of clubs and organizations to join. I recommend joining to find your niche. The school is quite big, and if you don't invest some time/ energy into meeting people, you're really losing out. If you like student government, check out the ASUCD and try joining a commission. If you're career minded, try groups, such as Pre-med AMSA, Phi Alpha Delta Pre-Law Frat, or the Pre-Pharm Club.

Once you're 21, the bar scene is great. Because everything is within walking distance of downtown, you can easily go bar hopping. There's something for every night. The drinks are also quite cheap in comparison to Sacramento or San Francisco.

Current student, 9/2005-Submit Date, January 2007

For bars, the Graduate is pretty popular. Restaurants aren't bad, and pretty cheap. Lots of Greek life, but it's not crazy like some schools, and if you're not interested, it's easy to avoid. The bowling alley on campus is popular, as is the craft center. There's also an equestrian center. There are lots of lectures, art shows, musical events at the Mondavi Center, clubs to belong to and other stuff going on to keep busy.

Current student, 9/2004-Submit Date, September 2006

For a small town, Davis has a fairly large number of bars that have themed nights and are sometimes free of cover. The university has just under 200 different student organizations and clubs, and has the largest intramural sports program in the country. Greek life is also varied. About 10 percent of students are part of Pan-Hellenic/IFC sororities and fraternities, but there are dozens of professional, cultural and community services fraternities and sororities also on campus.

The school says: "The university has over 450 student organizations and clubs."

Current student, 9/2004-Submit Date, November 2005

Davis is a small college town and it has a few restaurants and bars, most of which are not known to anyone outside of the community. There is however, one favorite bar, called The Graduate, that hosts many different themed nights/events. There is a good splash of dining options, my personal favorite is Pluto's, which has great made to order salads—it is very affordable and is designed for the health-conscious but poor student. There is also Dos Coyotes, which I have heard is a fabulous Mexican restaurant. The dating scene doesn't have a really strong presence. I work at Starbucks and I see more customers there studying than on some form of a date. There are many campus clubs available for a wide range of interests based on sports, hobbies or academia like snow-skiing, chemistry or astronomy. There is a very popular Greek system that was even featured on an MTV reality show a couple years ago.

The School Says

jobs in their chosen fields and nearly 40 percent were studying for or had completed a postgraduate degree.

Students gain invaluable leadership skills at UC Davis. They run a host of key campus services and events, including the Unitrans bus system, the campus post office, the Coffee House dining service and the annual campus open house, Picnic Day, which draws more than 50,000 alumni, parents and friends. Each year more than 1,000 students in more than 250 countries gain an international perspective through UC Davis Education Abroad Center program, while the Internship and Career Center helps more than 6,000 students obtain internships, making it one of the largest campus-wide academic internship programs in the country.

UC Davis faculty are leaders in addressing fundamental societal concerns, such as world hunger, health and the environment. The university's researchers are working to find solutions to global problems such as avian flu and West Nile virus, while others are in the national spotlight raising public awareness about the importance of strong levees, healthy food and alternative energy sources to sustain our world.

The university's commitment to providing a challenging, attentive and research-enriched education creates a dynamic learning environment for both students and faculty. Nearly every faculty member at UC Davis is engaged in original research or artistic endeavors, which results in an enriched classroom experience for its undergraduates. In fact, more than half of its students work on a research project with a faculty member in the course of their undergraduate education.

The UC Davis Health System serves 33 California counties, more than 50,000 square miles and more than 5 million residents. It includes a 576-bed teaching hospital, one of the nation's leading medical schools, a physician network and affiliated community hospitals. It operates the region's only Level I adult and pediatric trauma center, a cancer center, a children's hospital, transplant services, an Alzheimer's center, an institute for neurodevelopmental disorders and a burn center. The UC Davis Veterinary Medical Teaching Hospital cares for more than 32,000 small and large animals each year. Veterinary Faculty care for patients in surgery, oncology, nutrition, behavior, dentistry, food animal medicine and other specialized veterinary services.

University of California, Irvine

University of California, Irvine
Office of Admissions and Relations with Schools
204 Administration
Irvine, CA 92697-1075
Admissions phone: (949) 824-6703
Admissions fax: (949) 824-2711
Admissions URL: www.admissions.uci.edu

 Admissions

Current student, 9/2004-Submit Date, October 2006

I completed an online application. The day it was due, the system malfunctioned and everyone was paranoid about getting it in on time. Irvine granted us an extra day because of this. There were three essays (one long, two short). I was told to list all of my high school courses with the grade, extracurricular activities, volunteer work and work experience.

Alumnus/a, 9/2000-6/2004, May 2006

UC Irvine has gotten more selective as more people wish to attend the prestigious school. If you wish to go to UC Irvine you need the typical good grades and SAT scores, which is normal for any college institution. However, due to the increasing number of students applying to the UC System, you should participate in many extracurricular activities so you can stand out from the normal applicant pool. The typical deadline for any UC application is November 30. And a response of acceptance or rejection will be mailed out by March. After being admitted you have about a month's time to determine where you wish to attend, and if you wish to attend UC Irvine, then you will need to fill out a residency form for those who are California residents, as well as submit your Statement of Intent to Register (SIR). A student's acceptance also depends on which major he/she declares or if he/she does not declare a major. The most competitive majors are biological sciences and information and computer science. These two are the most difficult majors to be admitted in at UC Irvine. Although UC Irvine has been increasing the amount of admitted students, they continue to increase their stringent admissions standard.

Current student, 11/2004-Submit Date, November 2005

Admissions includes an application complete with entrance essays on why I thought I was a good candidate to attend University of California, Irvine. The

second essay was about an experience I had had that made me want to choose the major in which I was interested. University of California, Irvine is a fairly competitive school, so getting in is not easy. The school receives many applications and only a small percentage of students are accepted. I have found that calling the admissions and getting a responsible party on the phone helped me to obtain admission.

Current student, 9/2005-Submit Date, September 2005

When applying for admission to UCI, I filled out the online application along with three essays asking what my intended major was, any special qualities, talents, skills, or experiences I have had that I would bring to UCI, and any information I'd like to share with the university about my academic record. As a transfer student from Saddleback Community College, by maintaining a 3.0 grade point average or higher and obtaining 60 transferrable units, I was pretty much guaranteed admission to UCI. No interviews were necessary.

Current student, 9/2003-Submit Date, September 2005

I was valedictorian in high school so I got accepted into the Campuswide Honors Program and received the Regents Scholarship, which is a full ride. If you are in the top 10 of your school, you should get the Regents scholarship. As far as getting in, a 3.85 (weighted) with a 1900 SAT score should be fine.

Current student, 9/2003-Submit Date, October 2004

Standards are getting higher. You must be well rounded, including various activities outside of school, aside from clubs and organizations of affiliation. A 3.5 grade point average may not be enough for admission into the University of California, Irvine as most students received grades much higher than that. Although the ranking has changed periodically throughout the last couple of years, UCI remains in the Top 40 in the nation, among all national universities. Students who attend this school have a great sense of pride even though the school's mascot is an anteater.

Current student, 9/2003-Submit Date, May 2005

The admissions process is quite simple: you apply online. UCI is a competitive school to get into, it just depends on what major you are applying for. There are no interviews. From what I have understood about the essays, they shouldn't be a sob story about what happened to you, UCI wants to know how they can benefit from you attending their school. Their selectivity is high, it's a competitive school, as mentioned before. I would advise taking AP or honors classes before applying to any UC school, and of course having a good SAT score. But most-

Read all of Vault's College Surveys at **www.vault.com/college**—get complete surveys on 100s of colleges and universities, expert advice on applicaton essays and more.

VAULT CAREER LIBRARY   75

ly, what admissions looks for is individuals from whom they feel UCI can benefit, either in the future, or while they are students at the university.

Academics

Current student, 9/2004-Submit Date, October 2006

Workload is tough, but it's college. If you're a sociology and psychology double major (like me), there will be tons of readings. This campus is really research-based. The professors' primary concerns are their research and not necessarily the students. But they are brilliant. Lots of classes are huge (100 to 300 people). And most of those come with small discussion groups (20 to 30 people), which are completely useless and are run by the TA. If you like lectures and no special attention, it will work for you.

Alumnus/a, 9/2000-6/2004, May 2006

I went to school between 2000 and 2004 and I never had trouble getting my classes. There is a ranking system UC Irvine uses regarding class sign-ups that gives priority first to athletes, honor students, disabled students, seniors, juniors, sophomores and then freshmen. Of course, like many other colleges, the popular classes fill up fast. So, I suggest people to take many courses or summer courses to up their amount of total units so they have priority to sign up for classes over other individuals. The quality of education is topnotch. You will no doubt be educated by the best individuals in their field. All my professors had PhDs and published many of the textbooks that we were using. All the professors were great and I enjoyed all of them. All professors offer office hours and I encourage you to go and introduce yourself to your professors. This will prove useful when you need a letter of recommendation for grad school or future employment.

Grading is pretty standard for all professors. Most professors employ a curve based on the average scores of students. This can be helpful and sometimes hurtful. The workload is very doable and manageable. Many professors assign two midterms and a final and a paper somewhere in between. Also, some professors just do a midterm and a final and weight them 50/50. The competitiveness of the student body is not severe. Many students are friendly enough to discuss their paper ideas or to share class notes if you ask nicely. Most, if not all courses you take, will include a discussion course or lab course in conjunction with your lecture. Some professors make it mandatory to go to discussion and some do not, but I insist that everyone should attend. There are many distinguished faculty at UC Irvine and the biological sciences and information and computer science schools are very well known.

Current student, 11/2004-Submit Date, November 2005

Since I came in as a transfer student, getting classes was much easier than getting popular classes as a freshman. As far as I have experienced, the professors grading my work are fair and accurate. However, I would like to add that it is the teacher's assistants who do most of the grading and not the tenure professors. TAs are students themselves enrolled in their PhD programs.

Current student, 9/2002-Submit Date, October 2005

The workload is a lot harder than high school. Some of you may need to change your study habits. The more lower division the course, the more people there will be. During the first year of your major, it will be really hard because the major is trying to weed out people. It's to see how much you want to be in that major.

Current student, Biology, 9/2002-Submit Date, March 2006

I am currently an undergraduate with a goal toward a bachelor's in biology. While the breadth of courses I took throughout the first two years attending the university (humanities, psychology and math) were very small discussion groups, the biology courses were not nearly up to par. There would be a lecture of 400+ students in the lecture hall, and the lecturer would have difficulty speaking English. More importantly, they were more interested in going back to their grants and research than teaching the class, and consequently their tests were of low standards, usually having nothing to do with what they lectured about. And trying to get into the classes in the first place? That was a talent of its own accord. Almost all were waitlisted, and being a commuting student, I needed to get my classes on as few days as possible so that I could continue to work and pay the gas bills I acquired through the course of a month. That just wasn't a

possible outcome for this school, and I usually ended up going four to five days a week with perhaps only one class on two out of those four days. It's a lot of driving for just one 50-minute lecture.

Current student, 9/2003-Submit Date, October 2004

Some very good professors. Three members of the faculty have received Nobel Prizes in their respective fields. Courses are challenging and interesting. Many professors have received compliments for speaking their mind instead of simply relaying facts. Students still, however, feel the need to take easy classes to speed through the college process with a decent grade point average.

Current student, 9/2003-Submit Date, May 2005

The undergraduate program at UCI is excellent because it provides majors in all different fields for one to choose from. The academics here are awesome, excellent. We have excellent professors with great backgrounds, in all majors and fields. The popular classes can fill up quick, and they usually give priority to the seniors. The workload, just like any other college campus, is a lot. Grading for science and math classes is usually based on a curve, but for other classes it is not.

Current student, 9/2003-Submit Date, September 2004

Sometimes it's really hard to get into the classes you want. Classes at a UC are very different from classes in high school. In high school you could get by without doing any work, but in college (for most students) you can't breeze by, you have to do some kind of studying and put a lot of effort into it. Grading is usually negotiable. A lot of times your professor will base the grades on a curve, so you may think you're doing horribly, but you end up not doing so badly, after all. It's good to find out which professors are good and bad, because sometimes how well you do in a class depends heavily on your professor. Some people may think a class is a lot easier than someone else who's taken it by a different professor, only because one professor was extremely difficult and the other was easy. There is usually a lot of reading in all the classes, but some people can get by without having to do any of it. I'm not one of those people.

Employment Prospects

Alumnus/a, Pre-med, 9/2003-8/2006, December 2006

UC Irvine has a very supportive Career Center with job and internship opportunities; however, I got all of my internships from other sites, such as monstertrak.com, or other independent internship programs. If you're serious about advancing your career, you'll take advantage of all that. Career Center is really good about helping with your résumé.

Current student, 9/2004-Submit Date, October 2006

As far as getting jobs after graduation and internships, the university has a wealth of resources and people waiting to help you. But you have to be willing to help yourself and not just sit around and wait for it. There is a great alumni network also.

Alumnus/a, 9/2000-6/2004, May 2006

Employment is great, but you must have self transportation to get around. The City of Irvine is home to many high-tech companies, as well as prestigious law firms. The City of Irvine has vast lands for expanding and large amounts of rentable office space. Major law firms have at least one office in Irvine if not in the vicinity. There are bi-annual career fairs where many companies around Orange County come and set up informational booths and accept résumés from students. For engineering students they have a separate career fair, although it is open to everyone. Some notable companies at the engineer career fair include Lockheed Martin, BAE, Boeing, L3 and Northrop Grumman. The standard career fair they have for the rest of the students does not have many notable companies, yet it is still useful for any upcoming graduate to visit.

Also, the Career Center is magnificent, and many students are not aware of the value the Career Center can provide. There are very professional and informative people working in the Career Center, as well as offer a vast amount of job resources for you to review. The Career Center offers free seminars and workshops for students. These seminars and workshops include résumé help and mock interviews. There is a great alumni center, but requires payment of fees prior to graduation in order to use their services. Many students go on to prestigious positions at engineering firms and in biotech fields. Other social sciences and social ecology students work in civic positions or work for public municipalities.

Current student, 11/2004-Submit Date, November 2005

Unless students make time to address the issue of what they will be doing after college and research the question with the college Career Center, their options at the end of college are slim. College students are perpetually putting off dealing with the reality of a job search until the question literally becomes inescapable. At UCI, the alumni network is nonexistent, however there is quite a bit of on-campus recruiting for blue-collar positions. Internships are available but are fairly competitive.

Current student, 9/2002-Submit Date, March 2006

As an undergraduate, the university only points you toward their graduate schools and internships they have offered under their professors. I was never very much interested in those, as my goal is pharmacy school, and that is not currently offered at UCI.

Quality of Life

Alumnus/a, Pre-med, 9/2003-8/2006, December 2006

I love Irvine, a very safe, gorgeous city and very easy to live in! You will definitely need a car to get around though. This is not an urban environment, so if you're normally from a big city like NYC or downtown L.A. and love those areas, this may be a rough adjustment. Housing is decently priced for college apartments, and better! For the price, you get very new housing, big spaces, parking, amenities and so on. UCI has one of the highest-rated campus housing in the nation. Just go visit, and you'll see for yourself. Shopping and dining is great too, but you have to get used to the area before you know all the cool places to go. Don't forget neighboring Newport Beach, Costa Mesa, and Laguna Beach. These are all great cities by the ocean! They have a great gym, too, which I guarantee is nicer than the gym you're going to now.

Current student, 9/2004-Submit Date, October 2006

This past year the university was unable to accommodate all incoming freshman and many rooms became triples and quads. Now they are saying that they're guaranteeing housing for first- and second-years next year. This is at the expense of third- and fourth-years who they're going to kick off campus. Dining is fine. Study spaces are scarce as our student center is being rebuilt for the next year and a half. It's very safe on campus. There are police and campus security at all hours, everywhere.

Alumnus/a, 9/2000-6/2004, May 2006

Life can be boring going to college and living in a small suburban city. However, the beach is about 15 minutes away and neighboring Los Angeles is a short 45-minute drive. Also, there are many activities in cities like Huntington Beach and Newport Beach, which I feel are more college student oriented. Having a car is a must in Irvine, because the public transportation in Orange County is very limited. The campus at UC Irvine is beautiful and is in the shape of a circle, which makes it easy to cut across campus if you're running late for a class. The city of Irvine itself is very safe. Therefore, the possibility of being cited by a police officer for a small infraction, such as jaywalking, is greater.

Housing is plentiful at UC Irvine. There are two main housing units for freshmen. These include Middle Earth and Mesa Court. I lived in Middle Earth and I found the layout of the dorm to be more of a large apartment complex rather than a dorm. I suggest living in Mesa Court. It is more homey and provides a more intimate and interactive experience. After your freshman year, the chances of living in a dorm are less, but UC Irvine offers great accommodations for upperclassmen. Parking is horrible at Campus Village because the parking lot for the residents is small and the extra parking spaces are shared with student commuters and residents of Campus Village.

There are two other units of housing that are on campus but a little far from the main campus known as Vista Del Campo and Vista Del Campo del Norte. These are great places to live. It is cheap and each person has an individual lease and are only responsible for their own rooms. Rent is cheap and all utilities are included. This is your typical apartment life and even though it is sort of on cam-

pus, it feels as though it is in a world of its own. Apply early if you wish to live here because space is limited. Parking is plentiful, and they have a sand volleyball court and swimming pool within a five-minute walk of the UC Irvine gym. If you don't make it into Vista Del Campo there are many off-campus apartments within walking distance to UC Irvine, albeit very expensive. There are plenty of apartments, condos, and houses to rent out in Irvine, and the farther you go away from Irvine, such as in neighboring cities of Costa Mesa or Tustin, rent get progressively cheaper.

Current student, 9/2003-Submit Date, May 2005

Housing at UCI is great compared to other UCs. UCI has many apartments surrounding the school at walking distance. Also, we have shuttles to take you around the school and back to your apartment. Our dorms are very nice, we have two sets: Middle Earth and Mesa Court. The UCI campus is known to be beautiful, for it is built around a huge park where many students love to take naps in between classes. The facilities such as dining on campus are good, we have dining halls for the dorms, but anyone can buy a food pass for a year. Also, we have cafeterias with Carls, Jr., sushi and Subway. Also, we have an on-campus pub that is a famous gathering for UCI students. Irvine is rated one of the safest cities in the United States so, no need to worry about crime here.

Social Life

Alumnus/a, Pre-med, 9/2003-8/2006, December 2006

No football team, but people are involved in other things like clubs and the Greek system. It isn't hard to find your niche. If you're career-oriented, there are lots of business/career clubs to join. If you like partying, there are clubs that share your interest. Just put some effort into finding what you're comfortable with, and you'll be set.

Current student, 9/2004-Submit Date, October 2006

The worst thing about Irvine is the social life. We are a commuter campus and most people go home for the weekend. There is no college town or much to do in the vicinity of the campus. So the social scene can be pretty dead. But you make of it what you will. Most people still have a blast, but it's definitely something that should be improved upon. Many people are very involved on campus to make up for this, so that's pretty cool. We have lots of clubs and dedicated people.

Alumnus/a, 9/2000-6/2004, May 2006

Everyone is pretty friendly, and there are numerous clubs and social events that the school sponsors. There is a diverse range of clubs, such as ethnic clubs, religious clubs, political clubs and educational clubs. If you wish to join a club, you will find one that interests you. There are also many fraternity and sorority chapters that you may join. They vary from educational to social organizations as well as ethnic-oriented fraternities and sororities. UC Irvine also hosts many different screenings of upcoming blockbuster movies, as well as live concert events featuring popular mainstream artists. These events are open to the public, but as a UC Irvine student you have priority when purchasing tickets and receive a student discount. Many popular movies and popular musical artists have been displayed and have performed at UC Irvine.

Also, our sports teams have been doing well and should not be looked over. Any chance you may have to watch a basketball or a volleyball game, you should not hesitate to go see one. The dating scene is very good at UC Irvine, and people are always eager to find companionship or to meet new people. The best way to meet people is through your dorm experience during your first year. And after that, you can expand yourself into clubs or other school-oriented functions. The campus will open their new and improved student center in 2007 or 2008 with a variety of restaurants and a pub. The pub will offer many different kinds of draft beer, imported and domestic.

Current student, 11/2004-Submit Date, November 2005

Greek life seems to be well and alive at UCI. As far as favorite hang outs, there is a plaza across from campus that includes many cafes, a gym and other restaurants students tend to frequent. UCI students are extremely social, and classes encourage students to get into groups to study bud do homework. There are always events going on at the University. Flyers are e-mailed out and students actively participate. Marches and demonstrations against and for political events are held almost weekly. Booths supporting religious clubs sometimes hand out

Read all of Vault's College Surveys at **www.vault.com/college**—get complete surveys on 100s of colleges and universities, expert advice on applicaton essays and more.

VAULT CAREER LIBRARY   77

flyers along the cirle road. As far as the dating scene there is not much of a push and it does not seem to hinder students from finding dates. Being, like I mentioned previously, a social school, much dating goes on.

Current student, 9/2003-Submit Date, May 2005

The bars surrounding UCI are great because of our excellent location right next to Newport Beach. Also, we are close to South Coast Plaza and Fashion Island, which are excellent fashion spots for those shopaholics out there. The restaurants in Newport are really nice, as well as the ones at the shopping places. UCI holds a lot of events annually, such as an event called Waysgoose at which we have all of our clubs and organizations set up in our park and have other events for the incoming freshmen to take a tour through. We have many different clubs on campus suiting basically every single interest out there. Our Greek system is Panhellenic, so it is national. Also, our Greek system is known for throwing excellent parties, such as on boats in Newport Beach and at clubs, of course.

The School Says

Since its founding in 1965, the University of California, Irvine has combined the strengths of a major research university with the bounty of an incomparable Southern California location. In fewer than four decades, UCI has become internationally recognized for efforts that are improving lives through research and discovery, fostering excellence in scholarship and teaching, and engaging and enriching the community.

With more than 23,000 students, 1,300 faculty members and 8,100 staff, UCI is the fourth-largest campus of the University of California system. Increasingly a first-choice campus among students, UCI was fifth in undergraduate applications in a recent survey of U.S. public universities and, for fall 2003, the campus admitted the most academically competitive freshman class in its history. Orange County's third-largest employer, UCI also is an economic engine powering prosperity in the region and generating an annual economic impact on the county of $3 billion.

A top-tier research university

UCI is a center for quality education that honors classic instruction while incorporating the best new scholarship. *U.S. News & World Report* consistently ranks UCI among the nation's best public universities, and achievements in the sciences, arts, humanities, medicine and management have garnered numerous other national rankings. UCI is the first public university with faculty who received Nobel Prizes in two different fields—chemistry and physics—in the same year.

Interdisciplinary research, a UCI hallmark, is evident in the California Institute for Telecommunications and Information Technology, or Cal-(IT)2, the International Center for Writing and Translation and groundbreaking instructional programs in biomedical engineering, global cultures and other collaborations.

Committed to the community

UCI reaches beyond the classroom and laboratory to solve societal issues and support human development. In the health sciences, UCI is noted for its research into cancer, neurosciences and the genetic underpinnings of disease. UCI Medical Center is Orange County's only university hospital and Level I trauma center. A new university hospital, to be completed in 2008, will create a landmark center for medicine that integrates patient care, teaching and research with advanced specialty-care facilities.

UCI continues to build mutually beneficial partnerships with the community. With generous private support, the campus recently opened the Department of Earth System Science's new John V. Croul Hall, a center for research into global warming and other environmental issues, and is enhancing the main library, a valued community resource that was renamed the Jack Langson Library to honor its benefactor. To meet future enrollment and facility needs, some $1 billion in construction projects is underway or planned, surpassing all other growth periods in UCI's history.

With the goal of becoming a flagship UC campus and one of the nation's very best universities, UCI will continue to inspire excellence as it fulfills its research, teaching and public service missions in the decades ahead.

University of California, Riverside

Office of Undergraduate Admissions
1138 Hinderaker Hall
Riverside, CA 92521
Admissions phone: (951) 827-3411
Admissions fax: (951) 827-6344
Admissions e-mail: ugadmiss@pop.ucr.edu

Admissions

Current student, Sociology, 9/2004-Submit Date, June 2007

Most, if not all, of my admissions process was completed with the help of the counselors at my high school. Without their direction, the process would have been far more difficult. I would have run a greater risk of not presenting as strong of an application as I did had I not been aided by the counselors. The UC system was not involved in the application process, unlike private schools that actually interview their applicants rather than reviewing them on paper. My admissions essay was an essential element in the UC application.

Alumnus/a, 9/2003-9/2006, October 2006

Not as selective as UCLA. Have a solid GPA above 3.0 and an SAT score higher than 1100, and you will be fine. There is no interview. As I recall, you only need one application and essays to apply to as many of the UCs as you want. You also need to take the SAT Subject Tests. Aim for scores of 600 or higher.

Current student, 9/2003-Submit Date, March 2007

The application process was fairly simple: one application and essay. The university was not very selective, but I do know a few people who have been rejected. I submitted my application once to all UC schools and was able to streamline the application process; however, the school didn't recruit and, from what I know, it does not heavily recruit outside the Riverside area.

Current student, 8/2005-Submit Date, May 2006

The process was completed online and was easy. Advice on getting in: talk to the department in which you are interested in person. This is so that you can give a good impression, they will remember you, and they will give you advice on how best to get in. Also, this gives you an opportunity to find out if the program is right for you. Also, it is very important to talk to students in that program, as well as to get their impression of the department.

Current student, 9/2004-Submit Date, May 2006

Like the other UC schools, you fill out an application, write an essay about your personal life, give SAT scores and wait a few months before hearing back. UCR is one of the easiest UCs in which to be accepted, so it is almost guaranteed if you have fulfilled the UC requirements in high school. However, every year the school is becoming more competitive and the population is growing, so admissions may be more difficult now.

Current student, 9/2003-Submit Date, April 2006

The admissions process is fairly straightforward. The directions are easy to follow, and the best thing to do before filling it out is to read it over first to help guide you through the final process. A decent GPA of about 3.5 will pretty much guarantee entrance to a UC campus, but you cannot rely solely on academics. You must be a well-rounded student and have a good involvement in extracurriculars, such as sports, honor societies, clubs and possible job experience. Essays are a good way to convey who you are, but be sure to be concise and not to drone on or go on tangents. Stay on task and seek help from a counselor to help you write your essay to be sure that the page reflects who you are and what you have to offer the school you wish to attend. UC campuses are very competitive and the top students are pretty much what they take with occasional exception. To better your chances of getting in, apply with a less popular major or as undeclared, then change your major once you enter. This will give you a better shot of getting around the mass competition seen in fields of science and other largely popular majors.

Current student, 9/2004-Submit Date, April 2006

The UC System has a universal application for all of its 10 campuses. It consists of general application and a statement of purpose that requires a student to answer three short-answer questions. Selectivity varies with each campus but, overall, you should be in the top 4 percent of your graduating class, have good standardized test scores and have extracurricular activities under your belt. The more selective campuses will want a well-rounded person who can still get good grades while under the pressure of multiple activities.

Alumnus/a, 9/2000-8/2004, April 2005

The admissions process to the UC System was very much standard. Other than school transcripts and SAT scores, a personal statement was required to be considered for admission. Outside educational sources advised us to put a great deal of effort into writing an outstanding personal statement as this would be the last part of a prospective student's application that could possibly distinguish it from the many other students'!

Current student, 9/2003-Submit Date, November 2004

Basically, if you have over a 3.0 and you have a lot of extracurricular activities you're already in. Just make sure you have a backup in your essay because that is what makes or breaks your application. Just make sure you meet the requirements to get in. Interviews are pretty easy. Just make sure you speak clearly, as well as stand strong on whatever they ask, since it is about you, and speak the truth. Nothing is worse than telling a lie and being punished for it (being kicked out of UCR). Be prompt, on time and clean.

UC Riverside says: "No interviews are required."

Academics

Alumnus/a, Sociology, 10/2002-6/2006, June 2007

At the University of California, Riverside, the thing I enjoyed the most about the academics was that you really got to know your professors. The university really provides an intimate setting for the students and they really care about you obtaining a wonderful education.

Current student, Sociology, 9/2004-Submit Date, June 2007

After finding out about ratemyprofessor.com, it made class scheduling far more time efficient and predictable. The evaluations online have been quite accurate based on my class schedule, the workload, and my expectation of the professors. That agent alone has made class scheduling a more comfortable experience. I have no anxiety about what to expect from a class. If I have no choice but to take a difficult professor, then at least I have time to prepare and approach the course with a determined mindset. The quality of the classes themselves is quite different from department to department. In regards to the sociology department and its courses, there is a profound difference in the lecturing style of the professors.

Current student, Business, 9/2004-Submit Date, May 2007

I work very hard in all my classes. Depending on the program, students will be challenged in every class. The majority of the classes will be taught by a knowledgeable faculty. All students will be able to get into all the classes they want.

Current student, Business, 9/2004-Submit Date, May 2007

The quality of the instruction is fairly good; professors are extremely knowledgeable and have the background to back it up. As far as getting into popular classes as an undergraduate, I have gotten into predominantly all the classes I have requested. The grading is extremely fair, and the workload is manageable.

Current student, Business, 9/2003-Submit Date, June 2007

Academically, if you do not study, you will not get an A and sometimes not even a B. Sometimes, the teachers do not even care and just want you to learn on your own. With a low GPA, you will have a hard time getting into the good classes. The workload varies based on what teacher one gets and for what grade one is aiming. The upper-division classes are of higher quality. They are smaller in class size and the teachers for those classes care more about the students. Moreover, UCR has great faculty. They are really nice and answer any questions.

Alumnus/a, Business, 9/2003-9/2006, October 2006

They have a topnotch business administration program. Getting the classes you want is doable if you enroll on the day of your enrollment date. Workload is difficult but manageable. Grading is hard but professors are always available in office hours to help you along the way. You will come out of this program learning a lot of valuable things. But some professors have accents that are difficult to understand.

Current student, Women's Studies, 9/2004-Submit Date, May 2006

The majority of the classes I took were of high quality, and I was enthused to be enrolled, especially in the Women's Studies department. I think the Women's Studies program is amazing. There was only one class I wanted to take that was too full to allow anyone else in. Otherwise, getting the classes I wanted at times that worked for me was fairly simple. Creative Writing, however, proved difficult to enroll in when it came to the classes I needed and wanted. There were never enough workshop courses offered, especially in fiction. Many required classes overlapped each other so I could not take as many as I needed within one quarter. The workload and grading for both departments were usually fair along with the professors, again, especially in Women's Studies.

Current student, 9/2004-Submit Date, May 2006

The classes are fun, stimulating and interesting. They are hard and rigorous, involve a lot of studying but a lot of application and use of common sense. Rather than in high school, where you just take a test and memorize things, you may be required to think critically, write in many different formats, think and analyze your answers, learn to argue and support your views, and to become involved, hands-on, with sciences and engineering. Getting the classes you want can be difficult since popular classes fill up quickly. The professors are engaging and always willing to help you outside of class (during office hours) and are willing to involve you in research, which is a key component of UCR. The grading is fair among all the classes, some harder than others, but it just takes hard work and determination. You can't get by just by being smart.

Current student, 9/2002-Submit Date, May 2006

The UC is a quarter-based system, so classes move really fast. If you don't keep up with the reading, which is a lot for a full-time student, you will fall behind. If you want to be involved in extracurricular activities, you really have to learn how to manage your time. If you register before people in your class, then it's easy to get the popular classes. But when you are a freshman, it's very hard. The professors are good, most of them are PhDs and professionals in their fields of study. It's hard to get A's.

Read all of Vault's College Surveys at www.vault.com/college—get complete surveys on 100s of colleges and universities, expert advice on applicaton essays and more.

VAULT CAREER LIBRARY   79

Employment Prospects

Alumnus/a, Sociology, 10/2002-6/2006, June 2007

After graduating, I had no problem finding a job. Not only did I find a good job, I found one I like. The university provided me with lots of internships so that I was well qualified and prepared for the workforce.

Current student, Business, 9/2004-Submit Date, May 2007

If you are a business major, you are guaranteed to graduate with a job already waiting for you, whether in financial advising or sales.

Current student, Business, 9/2003-Submit Date, June 2007

Not much prestige will come from graduating from UCR. There are job fairs, but no one too prestigious tries to recruit us. Some are lucky, of course; it depends on how you work it. I personally got a job as a logistics assistant, but worked hard and was able to move up.

Current student, Women's Studies, 9/2004-Submit Date, May 2006

Through the Women's Studies program I was able to intern at the Riverside Area Rape Crisis Center. I completed two internships there and am currently employed by the RARCC. This opportunity was one of the most important of my life. It created numerous subsequent opportunities, not only occupationally but mentally and emotionally, as well.

Current student, 9/2004-Submit Date, April 2006

There are several job and internship fairs throughout the school year that bring in amazing companies and government institutions. The student affairs officer in your major will also send e-mails announcing job/internship opportunities that are major specific. I found out about both my research internships in mathematical physics from my student affairs officer. Your academic counselor can also offer advice on work/graduate school, depending on what field you want to go into. I also have found that some of the professors with whom I communicate regularly will keep an eye out for interesting internship/research projects that I might enjoy if they know what my tastes are. Again, through being proactive, making friends with your professors and listening to their advice, you will get even closer to success.

Quality of Life

Alumnus/a, Sociology, 10/2002-6/2006, June 2007

I always felt safe on and around campus. We have a police station on campus, an escort service for students who have late classes, as well as a well-lit campus so safety was not an issue for me. On-campus housing is actually the best out of all the campuses I visited, and the food in the residence halls is great.

Current student, Sociology, 9/2004-Submit Date, June 2007

All the construction that is currently underway at the UCR campus has hinged some of the dining services at the student common area, which impairs the food choices at a student's lunch breaks. I am expecting the new student common area to be a full service area for the students as soon as it opens.

Current student, Business, 9/2003-Submit Date, June 2007

Living in Riverside was boring. To stop the boredom, your only outlet would be the gym, but it's the best gym ever. Housing was OK and not too expensive. The dorms are new and there is plenty of housing surrounding UCR. The cost of living isn't high at all. The campus is nice and big and does not lose to any other UC. You will fall in love with it within a year. The campus isn't too big or too small.

Alumnus/a, Business, 9/2000-6/2004, June 2007

Housing for all first-year students is great. Most of the housing is new and very well organized for student life support. The construction on campus moves fast and in phases to avoid prolonged delays for on-campus pedestrians.

Alumnus/a, 9/2003-9/2006, October 2006

Clean campus and surrounding streets. I recommend living on campus or very close to campus. Very cheap housing is available. You can get your own room in a four bedroom house for less that $500. Do not live in Moreno Valley (a city next to Riverside). It is a few miles away but the commute is horrible. You will be stuck in bumper-to-bumper traffic every day.

Current student, 9/2005-Submit Date, May 2006

Dining is not bad most of the time, although I have found Lothian usually has better dinner options than A&I, and A&I triumphs over the Lothian cafeteria with numerous lunch options. Also, if a student does not like either places, they can go to the commons to eat. Depending on the meal plans everyone purchases, he/she is given amazing flexibility on where and when to eat. Students are informed by e-mail of important events, and the police force is very alert. Also, the dormitory facilities are filled with people and are very secure (forced entry from the outside is difficult). Housing is great, and Lothian, A&I, and Pentland all offer ample opportunities not just to study but also to socialize. They all need keys to get in while some of the facilities need electronic cards that are handed out to the students early on in the year.

Current student, 9/2002-Submit Date, May 2006

Freshmen are guaranteed housing in the residence halls. Living in the residence halls is a once-in-a-lifetime experience that should not be passed up! Food served in the residence halls is actually pretty good although it can become mundane. The campus has a cozy atmosphere and is very warm and welcoming. Students are extremely helpful and friendly to each other. It has the Ivy League education but the small-town feel. You're able to see friendly and familiar faces throughout the day just by walking through the campus. The facilities are great. Going to the recreation center offers ample programs and equipment for all to use. Everything is still extremely new and is constantly being upgraded. Computer labs are up-to-date and very helpful. Computers are fast and lines for the computers are not that long because there are lots of computers available. There are multiple computer labs. The libraries are excellent. Helpful resources are available and study areas are comfy. The neighborhood around the campus is extremely safe. The campus police department is within walking distance and available whenever help is needed. Campus safety escorts are available for students who want or need someone to walk with to cars, residential halls and apartments.

Social Life

Alumnus/a, Sociology, 10/2002-6/2006, June 2007

There is always some event occurring on campus, whether it is a concert or just a bunch of the student organizations hanging out. Since Riverside is centrally located, there is also a lot to do surrounding the campus. You could actually go snow boarding, surfing and hiking in the same day.

Current student, Sociology, 9/2004-Submit Date, June 2007

UCR is a dry campus in that it does not serve alcohol; hence, we do not have any bars on campus. However, I do not feel that the lack of alcohol on the campus restricts or limits the student life on campus. I enjoy my time on campus, and if at any time the campus has nothing to offer in my line of interest, then the neighboring cities are always an outlet.

Current student, Business, 9/2004-Submit Date, May 2007

I am in the Delta Gamma sorority here and I love the Greek system and all the events in which we participate. If I had to choose to join again, I would have picked to go Greek and most especially Delta Gamma, there are a couple of clubs around that make it easier for students to attend events, there are usually parties happening on Wednesdays, Thursdays and Fridays.

Current student, Business, 9/2003-Submit Date, June 2007

The social life was OK. Food and bars were pretty basic and nothing flashy. There's a gay bar. The restaurants in the area are coming up with lots of nicer places since I first arrived at UCR six years ago. The best place to eat is Los Jilbertos which is down the street on university, across from BOA. There is a Casino about 25 miles east, and on the way, there is a Big Red Barn that services the best all-American food ever. There aren't really a lot of night clubs. But they do cater to a variety of people. There is Incahoots (80s, indie) and Sevillas (Hiphop). Dating Scene is OK. I found my girlfriend at UCR.

Current student, 9/2004-Submit Date, May 2006

The Greek system is a lot of fun and a time commitment, but it is also not for everyone. You have to be motivated and committed and able to balance it with the rigors of school. Since Riverside as a city sucks, you have to go to L.A. or San Diego for the bars and clubs. Or Vegas is a few hours away. The mountains are close, as well as the beaches, so if you really want to get away, there is plenty to do. The statement is true: "In the middle of nowhere, but close to everything." Riverside is rapidly growing so it is not a deserted town. Palm Springs is close by, as well. Again, there are restaurants nearby but nothing out of the ordinary. There are lots of good taco shops near campus that students like. There are lots of clubs in which to get involved, but beware, there are a lot of things not offered; it is up to the students to make it happen. If you are an outdoor freak, Riverside is not the place to be. The dating scene doesn't seem to differ much from high school, only that people are more free and have more time to have fun.

 The School Says

Centrally located in the heart of Southern California, UC Riverside provides the resources, facilities and technology of a major university while offering the personalized attention and intimate feel of a much smaller school. A member of the prestigious UC system, UCR generally accepts students ranked in the top 12 percent of California's high school graduates and offers excellent programs in engineering, natural sciences, social sciences, humanities, arts, business and education.

UC Riverside's beautifully landscaped 1,200-acre campus features a 160-foot bell tower, 40-acre Botanic Gardens, acres of orange groves and numerous newly constructed academic, residential and administrative buildings and facilities—including the brand-new $50 million Student Commons. UC Riverside has also received authorization from the UC Regents to proceed with plans to construct a new School of Medicine. The school is expected to open in 2012.

Founded in 1954, UC Riverside offers several unique academic programs including one of the few undergraduate environmental engineering programs and the only undergraduate program in creative writing in the UC system. At the graduate level, UCR offers an M.F.A in writing for the performing arts, the nation's only doctoral program in dance history and theory, and a PhD in comparative literature with a concentration in science fiction, science and literature.

Noted for its diverse student body, UC Riverside has some of the highest minority and overall graduation rates among schools of similar size and demographics, according to the Education Trust. UCR's University Honors Program offers exceptional students extracurricular academic activities, while first-year learning programs help all freshmen make that critical transition from high school to college. Noted UCR alumni include Nobel Prize winner Richard B. Schrock, Pulitzer Prize winner Steve Breen, and Stefani Schaeffer, winner of the latest season of Donald Trump's "The Apprentice."

Every Wednesday, live bands play outdoors during lunch, and a student-programs board offers movies, concerts and fairs. Last year's concerts included Ludacris and a free concert, HEAT, that featured Lupe Fiasco. The campus runs a cultural arts program that brings professional performers such as Laurie Anderson, Margaret Cho and David Sedaris. The college boasts a lively Greek community, while nearby University Village offers a wide variety of restaurants, coffee houses, gaming rooms and a movie theatre.

UCR's athletic teams compete in Division I and, in '06-'07, the Highlanders claimed two Big West Championships in major team sports: men's baseball and women's basketball. For weekend athletes, a Student Recreation Center offers a health club atmosphere with sand volleyball, weight and athletic machines, and intramural leagues, all included in the normal student fees.

The campus home page is at www.ucr.edu. Prospective students should also check out www.My.UCR.edu.

University of California, San Diego

Admissions Office
9500 Gilman Dr., 0021
301 University Center
La Jolla, CA 92093-0021
Admissions phone: (858) 534-4831
Admissions e-mail: admissionsinfo@ucsd.edu
Admissions URL: admissions.ucsd.edu/

 Admissions

Current student, 9/2003-Submit Date, May 2007

The admissions process is pretty straightforward; you fill out a University of California (UC) application. It is one application that includes all the UC campuses and you check off the specific UC schools to which you want to apply. One essay is attached for all the UC schools. The required essay is not very long. There is no interview process. The school is selective compared to other UC campuses. It is ranked third among the UC schools, after UC Berkeley and

UCLA. The majority of freshmen have a GPA of at least 3.0, somewhat high SAT score (in the 1200 and above range), and extracurricular activities.

Current student, Biology, 9/2006-Submit Date, April 2007

The admissions process is very straightforward; it's done entirely by points. You get a certain number of points for your GPA, a certain number of points for your SAT scores. If you're worried about low grades though, a good essay is the key. It's a public school, so the nice thing is that there's only one application for all the UCs. Just remember though, UCSD has a college system, and when you apply, you pick the college to which you want to go. Ranking the colleges is important: it has to do with what General Education requirements (core classes needed to graduate) and where you'll live on campus your first two years.

Current student, Psychology, 9/2004-Submit Date, April 2007

I feel like for the admissions process, it isn't necessarily about your GPA, SAT scores, or things like that. It is more about your uniqueness, what makes you different from everyone else. I feel like the personal essays are very important and applicants should take the essays very seriously and use the opportunity to let them shine. If a person is only about logistics, then nothing sets you apart.

Read all of Vault's College Surveys at **www.vault.com/college**—get complete surveys on 100s of colleges and universities, expert advice on applicaton essays and more.

VAULT CAREER LIBRARY   81

Alumnus/a, 9/1999-6/2003, September 2006

Admissions process is straightforward like most schools. Note that you need only to complete one application for all the UC schools. You also need to rank the colleges within UCSD on the application. These colleges don't affect your major but do determine where you live and your GE requirements. SAT scores and GPA are very important! Also, some majors are impacted, meaning you can be accepted into UCSD but denied into the major. Impacted majors include computer science and bioengineering. You will need over a 4.0 and 1400 to get into these majors.

Alumnus/a, 9/2001-6/2005, January 2006

Admissions is becoming more selective as UCSD climbs the ranks to become one of the top colleges in the United States. Just make sure you do well in your classes and have a lot of extracurricular activities. The admissions process should be the same as all UCs. There is no interview to get into the school, just an application and [personal statement].

Current student, 9/2003-Submit Date, February 2005

UCSD is a top-tier school in the University of California system, so it's pretty selective. UCSD receives the second-highest number of applications, right behind UCLA (the last time I checked). The UC application process is the same for all the schools. If you aren't accepted the first time around, you can always opt to go to a community college in California and then transfer to the UC school of your choice. UC schools are very friendly to transfer applicants.

Current student, 9/2002-Submit Date, June 2004

There's an online application with general questions about GPA, plus an essay section. I was in the top 5 percent of my school, so I got in automatically. But if you haven't got a good GPA or SAT score, you can still get in if your essay is good. Several of my friends did. So they aren't just looking at grades, they do actually look at the whole person.

> **Regarding admissions, UCSD says:** "GPA requirements are based on grades in the UC's 'a-g' courses. California residents with a 3.0 or above satisfy minimum requirements if they achieve a correlating score on SAT/ACT tests in the UC Eligibility Index. Admission is very competitive and students must exceed minimum requirements. The most recent SAT averages were in the 600s for each section, the average GPA was 4.06, and the average transfer GPA was 3.42. There is no admissions interview.
>
> "Transfer students at the junior level are welcome; 95 percent of UCSD's transfer students come from a California community college. To be competitive, applicants need to present an academic profile stronger than the minimum UC admissions requirements and should complete lower-division preparation for their intended major.
>
> "UCSD's undergraduate colleges—Eleanor Roosevelt, Earl Warren, Thurgood Marshall, John Muir, Revelle, and its newest, Sixth—bring a neighborhood atmosphere to this large research university. The colleges have their own general education requirements, residence halls, educational philosophy, academic advising. Students from all colleges attend classes together throughout the campus."

 ## Academics

Current student, 9/2003-Submit Date, May 2007

A majority of the classes have large class sizes between 200 and 300 students in each class. This makes it difficult to have one-on-one interaction with the professors, but the professors have office hours you can attend if you need individual attention. Many of the engineering or science professors are here for research rather than teaching. The workload is dependent upon the class and professor, but a majority of engineering and science classes have heavier workloads than liberal arts classes. For most classes, the grading system is based on a bell curve. Popular classes are easier to get into if you have more units. The registration time for getting into classes is based on the number of units a stu-

dent has. If you are a junior or a graduating senior and the class is one of your required major classes, you are far more likely to get moved up on the waitlist and get into the class you need.

Current student, Economics, 9/2004-Submit Date, April 2007

Economics is the second-biggest major on this campus, behind biology. Economics receives large and steady funding to recruit great researchers. The downside is that some researchers are not the best at teaching even though they are very knowledgeable. The upside is that opportunities to do research, which in turn helps build excellent relationships with the faculty members, are always available. Classes are usually pretty big, so the waiting list can be long and sometimes underclassmen have a hard time getting into the class they want. Luckily, most required courses are offered at least two times a year. Also, UCSD allows students to take the equivalent classes at other UCs with transferable credits.

Current student, Engineering, 9/2004-Submit Date, April 2007

It is relatively easy to get into classes. If you are waitlisted, the professor usually allows you to add, except in lab classes. It is harder to get into really popular classes, such as Human Sexuality. You have to get an early enrollment time to get it.

Current student, Biology, 9/2006-Submit Date, April 2007

All classes are taught by professors and are fairly simple to understand. Discussions are helpful and almost all TAs come prepared and have a good understanding of the material. Popular classes may be hard to get if you are a freshman or sophomore, especially GEs, due to registration priority. The grading is always fair and directly correlated with effort, and the professors are always willing to help. The workload may be extensive sometimes, taking into consideration that you have three other classes also.

Current student, Psychology, 7/2005-Submit Date, April 2007

The quality of the classes on this campus I considered to be superior. I really do feel like I am receiving an adequate education at this university. Although the workload may be a little overwhelming at times, in the end, it is bearable and rewarding.

Current student, Biology, 9/2006-Submit Date, April 2007

The biology department is pretty great here. The classes are interesting and almost all of the professors are famous for something. It's pretty easy to get into classes, mostly because biology classes have larger numbers of students in them, simply because the biology majors are very popular here at UC San Diego. The grading is all right—if you do the work, and know the material, you should do fine. Our school has a laid-back atmosphere with a competitive undercurrent that you wouldn't necessarily pick up on unless you really cared about that sort of thing.

Current student, English, 9/2003-Submit Date, September 2005

UCSD is a challenging school, to say the least. I am currently an English major with a minor in public health, aiming to go to medical school. While it has never been a problem for me to get into my major classes or my minor classes, trying to add into some of my pre-medical classes has been a matter of luck (e.g., Organic Chemistry). The workload at this school is large but not impossible. It's very important to stay on top of your classes, especially since it is on the quarter system. I have found that while upper-division classes are harder, your chance of getting a good grade in the upper-divisions is better than in the lower-divisions. The professor lectures for the lower-divisions, but it is the TA who is grading you. Course and Professor Evaluations (CAPE) publishes a book that evaluates all the classes offered and the professors/TAs who teach them, each year. It is only $3 at the bookstore and worth every penny.

> **The school says:** "Many of UCSD's academic departments are nationally ranked, particularly in the arts, humanities, social sciences, and engineering fields. *U.S. News & World Report* ranks UCSD eighth among public universities and colleges.
>
> "The student-to-faculty ratio is 19:1. The five most popular majors are Biology, Economics, Psychology, Political Science and Bioengineering. There are extensive opportunities to study, research or volunteer abroad."

Current student, 6/2005-Submit Date, September 2005

The classes, as a whole, are pretty easy. I work a full-time job and take a full courseload. I have maintained a high enough GPA (about a 3.7). Getting the classes I need has been easy enough. The quality of professors is acceptable. In that, I mean professors of classes, such as chemistry and cell biology, are usually PhDs and have a strong grasp of their material. Other classes are often taught by grad students. In my experience, these classes are a waste of time. I usually drop the class once I realize that. Workload is typical of any college class and I have no complaints.

 Employment Prospects

Current student, 9/2003-Submit Date, May 2007

The Career Services Center offers a great access to internships, alumni and employers. There are job fairs throughout the year, where employers come and try to recruit students to fulfill part-time, full-time and internship positions.

Current student, Biology, 9/2006-Submit Date, April 2007

There are many employment prospects due to the great number of job fairs organized by the Career Services Center. Although it is true that the science and engineering majors get more prospective employers, the other humanities majors can find jobs also through our Port Triton online system and the Career Services staff. Internships are readily available due to the number of flyers posted and connections professors have with alumni. The alumni network is also of good size due to the school's location in one of California's major cities. Qualcomm is a major contributor because its founder is an alumnus of the school and is located nearby. Irwin and Joan Jacobs donated money to the school and the engineering school was named after them. The prestige is close to that of UCLA and it is a rather well-known school compared to others.

Alumnus/a, 9/1999-6/2003, September 2006

UCSD does have some name recognition but not as much as other Top 30 schools. However, with that said, UCSD graduates are regarded very highly. San Diego is fraught with start-up biotech companies. UCSD excels in that niche area. Its bioengineering program is top in the nation! This means that as a graduate of UCSD in bioengineering, you can expect to land a job paying $60K at some local biotech company. I would say this is slightly above average compared to other top schools.

Current student, 9/2003-Submit Date, January 2006

The school attracts a lot of engineering firms. If you're an engineer, you shouldn't worry about employment if you keep the grades up. If you're majoring in something else, make sure you have internship/work experience while you're in school, so you won't have trouble finding work afterwards. The school has a career web site where employers submit job listings.

Current student, Humanities, 9/2003-Submit Date, September 2005

UCSD is a science-oriented campus. I have found it hard to find internships and jobs as a humanities major, but the Career Services Center and Port Triton have been very helpful when it comes to locating internships or discussing future plans. Each quarter, there is a job fair on Library Walk where recruiters from companies, such as SAIC or Northrop Grumman, come to accept applications from hopeful students.

> **UCSD says:** "New graduates enjoy an average starting salary of $41,000. Graduate/professional school draws 40 percent of graduates—the top academic areas chosen are engineering/computer science, law, education/counseling, and medicine. The Career Services Center provides assistance: self-assessments, job fairs, career panels, interview practice."

 Quality of Life

Current student, 9/2003-Submit Date, May 2007

Housing differs for every student, depending on the college that accepts you. At this university, all the students are divided up into six colleges, making it difficult to interact with those who are not in the same college. For the most part, the housing is not overcrowded and the rooms and living areas are spacious. The campus is large and is mostly a walking campus. Some people skateboard, bike or skooter around campus. The dining halls in certain colleges are better than others. There is not much selection of food in the main part of campus. Everything around the campus is very spread out.

Current student, 9/2005-Submit Date, May 2007

The campus is excellent. The classes are too far from each other. The neighborhood is very safe. It is quiet and not too busy; it's just right for a college community.

Current student, Engineering, 9/2004-Submit Date, April 2007

There are six colleges, each with its own housing. For the first year, the dorms are set up in suites. There are singles and doubles in the dorms. The apartment dorms only have doubles on the Warren campus. You start with 1,800 meal points, which act as money for the cafeterias. There are cafeterias on each campus, each with its own little specialty. There are a couple of places that stay open until 1 a.m., which is good for the late-night studying. Off-campus housing is not that bad. There are free shuttles that go to the campus. There is a lot of housing close to campus.

Current student, Biology, 9/2006-Submit Date, April 2007

The campus is pretty much safe and crime-free. Housing is of good quality, although overcrowding is an issue for my year. The campus, facilities, dining and living areas are always sanitary and comfortable. The neighborhood that surrounds the campus is pretty laid-back and quiet, although rush hour creates traffic.

Current student, Psychology, 7/2005-Submit Date, April 2007

Although many unexpected accidents may occur, I feel extremely safe living on campus. I feel safe and glad to see and know that there is all day and night security covering many perimeters of our campus.

Alumnus/a, 9/2001-6/2005, January 2006

Chill. The weather is great and everything seems so slow-paced. It's very easy to get lazy. The beach life is amazing. Crime shouldn't be a problem since the school is located in an upper-class community. However, there are occasional car thefts. On-campus housing is nice, depending on the college (the newer, the better). The food is decent, but it's not buffet style. I guess that's a good thing since you won't become overweight. RIMAC is one hell of an athletics facility. It's like L.A. Fitness on steroids. Athletics—terrible. Results in low school spirit. The school does not offer any athletic scholarships. It would be nice if UCSD had a Division I football team or a Division I basketball team.

Current student, English, 9/2003-Submit Date, September 2005

UCSD is in La Jolla, one of the wealthiest, safest neighborhoods in San Diego. UCSD's housing is certainly the best I have seen so far, out of all the other UC campuses I have visited. Maintenance for the apartments or suites is very prompt if you are in need of anything. Dining facilities are clean and the food is pretty good. They will always offer a vegetarian dish of some sort. The campus is also within walking distance to the beach! On campus, the Price Center (which is actually in the process of re-expansion) has great eateries such as Rubio's, Subway, Panda Express, Wendy's and a Tacone Wraps. There is also a place called Shogun's where you can get sushi, and a cafe with computers and wireless.

> **UCSD says:** "Each college has residential life staff and student resident advisers to facilitate friendships and social life. There are 11 dining facilities around campus, some open late-night, offering specialty meals including kosher and vegan. The on-campus shuttle is free; so are city bus passes for students.
>
> "The famous Stuart Art Collection of outdoor sculptures gives a distinctive look to the campus in neon, bronze and stone. The landmark library, named after Theodor 'Dr. Seuss' Geisel, holds the world's largest collection of his art and books; it is one of 10 libraries on campus.
>
> "The Student Services Center building allows students to take care of all their business matters in one central location: Admissions, Registrar, Cashier, Financial Aid, Campus Tours,

Read all of Vault's College Surveys at **www.vault.com/college**—get complete surveys on 100s of colleges and universities, expert advice on applicaton essays and more.

 CAREER LIBRARY **83**

and more. Other services include: Student Health Center, Academic Support, Cross-Cultural Center, Women's Center. Expansion is underway on the Price Center and Bookstore, creating a 'heart of the campus' for relaxing, shopping and dining."

 ## Social Life

Current student, 9/2003-Submit Date, May 2007

The school greatly lacks in a social life. There is a Greek system, and a number of sororities, fraternities and clubs. Because everyone is divided up into one of the six colleges and the campus is spread out, it is difficult to interact and meet new people unless you live on campus, join clubs, sororities or fraternities. Good restaurants, bars and clubs are difficult to access without a car. There are a number of restaurants, bars and clubs around La Jolla. Pacific Beach, Mission Valley, Downtown San Diego and Mira Mesa are some of the areas close by that offer shops and restaurants. However, near the campus, there is a lack of areas where a large majority of students can gather, hang out and relax. The event most students look forward to is Sungod, which is the biggest event on this campus.

Current student, 9/2005-Submit Date, May 2007

The events on campus are good. I love the annual Sun God Festival. Also there are plenty of clubs out there for any interest.

Current student, Economics, 9/2004-Submit Date, April 2007

There are quite a few cuisines and fast food restaurants on campus. There are lots of fraternity and sorority events weekly. There are also lots of Christian fellowship meetings weekly, as well. A lot of students are involved in at least one club. Also, there is a movie theatre that puts on movies with low prices for students. The Mendeville auditorium hosts performances of UCSD students and other famous performers. The La Jolla Playhouse is located on campus and students can buy a 10-ticket pass to see various musicals and plays for a cheap price.

Current student, Psychology, 9/2004-Submit Date, April 2007

San Diego has an awesome social life all close by. The downtown, Gaslamp District, all those areas are all really hip and fun places to be at night. It is really great to join on-campus organizations. They really help network you and help you to meet a lot of people and friends. Everybody should be as involved as they can; it'll make college a lot more worth it and memorable.

Alumnus/a, 9/2001-6/2005, January 2006

Make sure you join an organization or fraternity/sorority. That's the only way to meet people. People get comfortable with their group of friends after the first year. If you're 21, you can drive to Pacific Beach or Downtown San Diego. Great places to go bar hopping or clubbing. Tons of great restaurants and local eateries in San Diego.

Alumnus/a, 9/2002-9/2005, January 2006

UC San Diego is notorious for having a terrible social life. I think it's the heavy workload combined with the competitiveness of all the students that creates this sort of atmosphere. If you really want to better your social life, I recommend joining a club or, even better, a sorority or fraternity. I knew I had to when I realized the only people I ever went out with were my roommates and their friends. I joined AKPsi—a professional coed business fraternity. I enjoyed it a lot (aside from the lack of diversity), I got to meet tons of new people and most of them within my major. The best thing about being part of an organization is that you meet people who want to extend their college life to something other than academics.

> **The school says:** "UCSD hosts quarterly celebrations, including the popular spring Sun God Festival. Frequent concerts, first-run movies, 30 fraternities and sororities, and 450 student clubs balance the academic life. In sports, NCAA teams in Division II have won 29 national championships. Tennis courts, swimming pools, and sessions in dance, yoga, wellness and a lot more highlight UCSD's recreational life—and yes, you can walk to the beach."

University of California, Santa Barbara

1210 Cheadle Hall
University of California, Santa Barbara
Santa Barbara, CA 93106-2104
Admissions phone: (805) 893-2881
Admissions fax: (805) 893-2676
Admissions URL: www.admissions.ucsb.edu/
UCSB URL: www.ucsb.edu

 ## Admissions

Current student, Computer Science, 9/2006-Submit Date, April 2007

It was pretty easy to get in. All you need is an above average GPA and an above average SAT score to do it.

Current student, Mathematics, 9/2006-Submit Date, April 2007

Admissions at UCSB are relatively selective, and there are not any interviews for the large majority of majors, so you are accepted based on your application. They really do read your essays, so it is important to spend time on the essay, making sure that admissions really gets a sense of who you are. Express your passions and the ways you have gotten involved in high school and in your community. Much of the admissions process is online, so it is important to check your e-mail and admissions status online.

Current student, Sociology, 9/2006-Submit Date, April 2007

As a transfer student I felt that the admissions process was very fair, and not overwhelming. The application is identical for all UCs, which make the process much easier when applying to more than one campus. My admissions process was somewhat unique. I initially missed the UC APP deadline, and thought that I would end up spending another year at a CC. However, UCSB offered an extended application deadline for Santa Barbara City College students (the local CC). Having this opportunity gave me a second chance, and I am truly grateful to UCSB for this. As far as advice, I would say that the most important part of the application is the essays/responses. The questions are short, simple and open to a wide variety of answers. Be honest, passionate and real. Although the prompt calls for a traditional response (e.g., discussing strengths, and overcoming weaknesses), it is important to tell a story that demonstrates who you are apart from your academic record. Although you may not have the top GPA, well thought-out, passionate essays do set a student apart from the rest.

In regards to selectivity, UCSB is becoming increasing popular, and thus more selective. In a recent statistic put out by the admissions office stated that for the 2007-2008 school year about half of 40,000 students who applied were admitted, and the mean grade point average was 3.98.

Current student, 4/2004-Submit Date, October 2005

Transferring from a community college is a breeze if you have good grades. On the other hand, I transferred with a high GPA, but a buddy of mine transferred with a 2.7 GPA at the same time. I get the feeling UCSB is in the process of diversifying its student body. If you are trying to get in from high school and get rejected, it's a great idea to attend Santa Barbara City College first. You will be in fairly close vicinity to the UCSB campus, and get an idea of what life is like for a UCSB student, while paying a significantly lower tuition and having less pressure. A high GPA is very attainable at SBCC, which ensures admission to UCSB most of the time.

Current student, 9/2003-Submit Date, September 2005

Extracurricular activities are worth a substantial amount in the admissions process, so don't worry if you have only a 3.2. Obviously it helps to do well on SATs, but if your GPA and extracurriculars are pretty good, bad SAT scores won't matter as much. Make sure the personal essay is just that; don't borrow an idea from a sibling or friend because it won't sound sincere.

Current student, 9/2004-Submit Date, March 2005

The admissions process to this university consists of an evaluation of the GPA and SAT scores, plus a written response to three essay questions. Students are asked to write about a quality or personal accomplishment they feel will be a real contribution to the university. Students must also write about how their involvement in an academic organization or extracurricular activity has helped to shape their personality. The last topic is open-ended. I suggest that students write about interesting events. Use a writing style that will reflect you as a person. Because the admissions officers do not have the opportunity to interview a student in person, make the essays memorable.

Current student, 9/2002-Submit Date, April 2005

The admissions process is much more difficult now than it was, even when I applied just three years ago. The best advise I have is to find a school guidance counselor or teacher who can walk you through the applications and writing samples. Having a well-rounded life helps an incredible amount in admissions, so get involved in something other than just your classes. Universities want to have students who will somehow enrich the campus. On the essay, make sure you play up your strengths while identifying what your weaknesses are and what you are doing to better them.

Academics

Current student, Computer Science, 9/2006-Submit Date, April 2007

You've got to sign up for the popular classes at the first chance that you get. You can get along at UCSB with a pretty easy workload, if you budget your units wisely. Some professors are great, but others are simply horrible. It is pretty easy to switch between sections and lectures, as long as they're not full.

Current student, Sociology, 9/2006-Submit Date, April 2007

The academic programs UCSB offers are just as diverse as the school's party scene. The university is home to many Nobel Laureates, as well as esteemed scholars. The quarter system is rigorous and can be overwhelming at times. Although 12 units are considered full time, most, as encouraged by the college, take 16 units or more (four courses) during the quarter. There is not much downtime, and keeping up is imperative to your success. That said, if you do put in your time and moderately attempt to remain on par with the fast pace, you will get a handle of it and be able to excel. I was overwhelmed at first, but I have been able to consistently walk away with A's.

In addition, all of the professors I have encountered have been exceedingly fair and accommodating. Again, the workloads, due to the short quarters, can be overwhelming, and vary from class to class. Luckily, most of the popular upper-division courses are large classes (over 300) and often offered during each quarter. Lower-division required courses, such as writing and so on, are more difficult and often there is difficulty getting into these courses. However, the majority of the courses are large in order to accommodate the large college population.

Current student, Mathematics, 9/2006-Submit Date, April 2007

UCSB is a research university, and much of the instruction is theoretical rather than technical. Most of the classes in which I have enrolled have challenged me to analyze critically and to think outside the box. There are many outstanding lecturers, though the TAs are sometimes under-qualified. For the most part, I have gotten all the classes I've wanted. Even on the first day of classes, I would talk to my professors or TAs and they would try to make room for me. Grading

is fair, and it is not extremely hard to get A's in classes. The workload is what you make it. Though most students average at about 16 academic units, many take only 12, which is a very light courseload.

Current student, 9/2005-Submit Date, December 2006

The workload is manageable; you just have to make sure you attend classes and get all your reading done on time. If you need extra help, seek tutoring or start a study group. I came in to an impacted major, so it was hard getting the classes I wanted at first. The professors are all good. They encourage you to think outside the box, and you learn things you have never learned before.

Alumnus/a, Biology, 9/2001-12/2005, April 2007

Almost all the professors are great. Some GE classes can be hard to get into, but most upper-division requirements are not full. There are many weed-out classes, especially in the sciences, so be sure you are going to focus in on them; otherwise, you may be booted out of your major.

Current student, 9/2003-Submit Date, September 2005

Most of the material is excellent across the board. The biggest difference is in the professor teaching the class. Some profs are really dull and just stand behind the podium lecturing from a lectern while others walk around doing demonstrations and gesticulating wildly. Popular classes (those starting at 10 and 11 a.m.) are really hard to get if you're unfortunate enough to have a late registration date. If you're in the honors program, you have an earlier registration time than the rest of the students, and upper-division students can register earlier than lower-division. Different professors have different ways of grading; some grade on the curve and others just use raw percentages.

Current student, 9/2002-Submit Date, April 2005

Students here really work together; we help each other rather than compete for better grades. However, grades in most classes are curved. Class quality depends on the professor. Most are pretty good and care about teaching. Find good ones if you have a choice—try sitting in on a class. TAs are important. If you don't have a good one, switch sections ASAP. Getting into the class I want has never been a problem, as long as I remember to sign up on time. Even if a class is full when you try to enroll, you can usually crash on the first day. Workload depends on your choices, especially major. Engineering is a lot of work: plenty of homework, although it's usually only about 20 percent of your grade, and hours and hours of labs.

Current student, 9/2004-Submit Date, March 2005

The undergraduate program at the College of Letters and Science provides students with a wide range of classes from which to choose in order to meet general education requirements. Registration into some classes is difficult because seniors get priority. However, students have the option to crash courses, i.e., arrive at the lecture hall on the first day of instruction and obtain an enrollment code. The professors are very approachable. All of them have office hours and, if there is material that is hard to understand, professors welcome and encourage students to stop by and ask questions. Because many of the undergraduate courses are large, one-on-one attention is difficult.

Employment Prospects

Current student, Mathematics, 9/2006-Submit Date, April 2007

There are many resources for internships. We also have job fairs and lectures by practicing professionals. Many alumni are eager to lend their advice, and the Career Services on campus are excellent.

Current student, Sociology, 9/2006-Submit Date, April 2007

The campus does have many alumni and graduate career resources, such as GauchoLink. Also, within the majors there are several internship opportunities.

Alumnus/a, 9/2002-6/2004, May 2005

There is some on-campus recruiting. Most of it I found through the English department's listserv, which I signed up for when I decided to major in English. You can drop in to have your résumé reviewed or to get help with your cover letter. Their web site also has a listing of job postings. I've had friends who seemed to have some luck with the Career Services.

Read all of Vault's College Surveys at **www.vault.com/college**—get complete surveys on 100s of colleges and universities, expert advice on applicaton essays and more.

VAULT CAREER LIBRARY   **85**

Current student, 9/2001-Submit Date, April 2004

There are numerous career fairs and presentations going on throughout the year, and the career center has a vast amount of information to help you out. Info sessions range in topics from résumé and cover letter help to career info sessions that feature alumni talking about their careers and answering your questions. I've never gone there without them being a big help.

Current student, Computer Science, 9/2006-Submit Date, April 2007

Being one of the second-tier UCs, graduating with a degree from UCSB comes with plenty of prestige to get your post-graduate career off and running.

Current student, 9/2001-Submit Date, February 2004

UCSB accounting has been named a target school by all of the Big Four accounting firms and is recruited by many of the midsize firms. Employers like UCSB students because of how prepared they are coming into the workforce with a good accounting background. It is also noted that UCSB accounting grads are desired because of the social skills they develop in school.

Current student, 9/2000-Submit Date, September 2003

Because Santa Barbara does not have a business school, I feel that employment with top financial employers is more difficult. The closest thing they have here is a business economics degree with an accounting emphasis. Because of this, the Big Four recruit very heavily on our campus. Due to this I have had an opportunity to intern for one of the Big Four, and next year I have an employment opportunity with the firm.

Quality of Life

Current student, Mathematics, 9/2006-Submit Date, April 2007

UCSB is located adjacent to the Pacific, and I cannot imagine a more beautiful location. Many of the campus facilities are older but well maintained. The older dorms are not so nice, but the newer Manzanita Village is beautiful and spacious. The dining commons are excellent, though it is easy to tire of them into the quarter. The small Isla Vista community is very old and lacks aesthetic appeal, but it offers a variety of interesting shops and restaurants. More appealing is the famed State Street, only a 15-minute drive away. On State Street, there are numerous movie theaters, hundreds of shops, and an innumerable number of excellent restaurants and cafes.

Current student, Sociology, 9/2006-Submit Date, April 2007

There are several housing opportunities; however, the unfortunate high cost of living in the area often poses a problem. The community, as a whole, is relatively safe and is regularly patrolled, almost to a point of overkill, by foot patrol during active week and weekend nights. The campus is large, and bikes and other wheeled transportation are a major part of the campus landscape. In addition, the campus is less than a five-minute walk to the beach, which is a major plus.

Current student, Computer Science, 9/2006-Submit Date, April 2007

The dorms are great (especially San Nicolas). And the dining is an all-you-can-eat buffet. Biking is the number one method of transportation, but with the campus being only about one square mile and the bus system being free for students, that's all you'll need to bring. The number one crime on campus is bike theft, though, so just buy a good bike lock, and you'll have no reason to worry about crime on campus.

Current student, 9/2005-Submit Date, December 2006

Housing is hard to get in the small college town, but you will have a good social life. Is an expensive town in which to live, but you can totally make it with good friends. The recreation center has awesome facilities, and you can play a sport at almost any time of the day.

Current student, 4/2004-Submit Date, October 2005

UCSB boasts a brand-new gym, and is continually adding more and more structures to the campus to expand its facilities. In particular, the new student resources building will be an invaluable resource to any new students once it is completed. The quality of life at UCSB is wonderful. The campus is set on the ocean, with parties going on every night in nearby Isla Vista. Despite all the

drinking, most people are friendly drunks. Rarely has there been a violent dispute emerging from the late-night fun.

Current student, 9/2002-Submit Date, April 2005

The on-campus dorms are absolutely amazing, as they have views of the ocean from the dorm room. The campus, itself, is pretty amazing, too. Everyone rides their beach cruisers to class, and it is a very laid-back atmosphere. We have brand-new rec center facilities that are very nice and a new dining hall that is supposed to be pretty good. Most students move off campus to neighboring Isla Vista after freshman year. IV is right next to campus, which makes it awesome because you can wake up five minutes before class, hop on your bike and make it on time. The landlords here like to rip off students and pack as many as they can into houses, so IV is pretty crowded, but it is also really fun because all of your neighbors are your age. Like any campus, there is crime, but it is mostly just bicycle theft, so lock your bike.

Social Life

Current student, Computer Science, 9/2006-Submit Date, April 2007

The social life is amazing! Getting good grades and having the best time of your life is much easier here than any at any other university in the world!

Current student, Mathematics, 9/2006-Submit Date, April 2007

It is often said that UCSB is the most well-rounded school of all the UCs, in that we are not only academically competitive but also have social skills. There aren't many 18-over bars, but Isla Vista is never short on parties. While UCSB is a party school, you will also find a large handful of people here who don't like to party. With a student body as large as ours, it is easy to find people with the same interests and preferences that you have. The Greek system is a considerable part of the UCSB community, and many people on campus are involved in some sort of club. There are many interesting events on campus, ranging from free movies at the IV Theater to concerts and food fairs.

Current student, Sociology, 9/2006-Submit Date, April 2007

The social scene is very lively and diverse, which has continued to fuel its standing as one of the top party schools in the nation. The immediate college community, Isla Vista, is compacted with several bars, restaurants and clubs that offer entertainment well into the night every day of the week. From Thursday to Sunday nights, you can find throngs of students walking the streets hopping from bars to house parties. Along with the party scene, UCSB also offers a variety of student activities, such as Friday night movies, improv comedy, lectures and clubs. In addition, a local company that offers a $6 bus ride into Santa Barbara allows the 21-and-over crowd to enjoy the downtown Santa Barbara club and bar scene. Within a few blocks, Santa Barbara's downtown area contains more than 30 that offer a mixture of live music, packed dance floors, great food and drinks.

Current student, 4/2004-Submit Date, October 2005

There are some great eats near campus, but if you really want to delight your palate, downtown Santa Barbara is the place to go. It boasts gorgeous restaurants with a classy atmosphere. The food will surely impress. Your wallet will be a little sore after one of these outings, though. Madison's is a great place to go for a drink. It's a sports bar that's always lively. Thursday is when all the student specials are going on, so make your plans for that night. There is not much of a Greek system at UCSB. I think that's good because at UCSB, we're pretty much a big group of students who accept each other.

Current student, 9/2003-Submit Date, September 2005

There are plenty of frats and clubs on campus, so finding friends/dates isn't that big of an issue. In many cases it's made easier by the alcohol that flows freely in Isla Vista, especially at parties and large club gatherings. The favorite local pizza joint is Woodstocks, although the more common midnight food is found at Freebird's, which has burritos and nachos. Isla Vista doesn't have much in the way of restaurants as it's a high-density college town (supposedly 9,000 people/square mile). For a real restaurant experience, you have to venture out into Goleta, which has establishments such as Denny's, Outback and The Elephant Bar.

The School Says

Located on 989 scenic acres overlooking the Pacific Ocean, the University of California, Santa Barbara combines breathtaking natural beauty with enormous intellectual vitality. UCSB is one of only 62 research-intensive institutions elected to membership in the Association of American Universities. The distinguished 900-member faculty includes five Nobel Prize winners and scores of elected members or fellows of prestigious national academies and associations. The campus is also home to 12 national centers and institutes, eight of them sponsored by the National Science Foundation.

UCSB enrolls some 19,600 students, about 2,600 of them at the graduate level, and offers more than 200 majors, degrees, and credentials through its five schools and graduate division. Competition for admission is at an all-time high. In recent years the campus has enrolled the most academically competitive and ethnically diverse classes in its history. More than 25 percent of all applicants had a high school grade point average of 4.0 or higher.

Applications to the university for undergraduate study are taken online at www.ucop.edu/pathways or via paper. The application includes a written personal statement.

A high school diploma is required for freshmen and the GED is accepted.

High School Subject Requirements:

- History/social science—two years
- English—four years
- Mathematics—three years required, four recommended
- Laboratory science—two years required, three recommended
- Foreign language—two years of one language other than English required, three years recommended
- Visual and performing arts—one year required
- College preparatory electives—one year required
- Entrance examinations:
- Either the SATR or the ACT test with writing and two SAT Subject Tests are required for freshman admission
- The SAT Subject Tests are sometimes used for placement and/or counseling.
- All tests must be taken by December, and the scores must be received by January.

University of California, Santa Cruz

Admissions Office
University of California, Santa Cruz
1156 High Street
Santa Cruz, CA 95064
Admissions phone: (831) 459-4008
Admissions e-mail: admissions@ucsc.edu
Admissions URL: admissions.ucsc.edu/

Admissions

Current student, 9/2005-Submit Date, May 2007

I think that the most important part of the application process is the essays. If you have a good essay and you are within all of the other requirements, then you will definitely be accepted. All UC schools are competitive and it is getting more difficult to be accepted. Make sure that you meet all of the requirements, and all extracurricular activities definitely help. Anything that makes you memorable or different from the rest of the students applying will help you gain acceptance.

The school says: "Although the personal statement is considered, the most important components of the application process are the academic factors: courses taken, GPA in UC-eligible courses, and standardized test scores."

Current student, 9/2005-Submit Date, May 2007

The admissions process for UCSC is just like any other UC with the standard UC application. I chose to do my application online, which was easier than on paper. While it was easier to apply online, the web site was still cumbersome and slow. There was no interview. The essay portion of the application is probably the most difficult. There are three: two short and one long. The shorter essays are more difficult because you have to decide what is really important and what is not.

Regarding essays, UC Santa Cruz says: "Starting with applications for fall 2008, the personal statement requires answering

two questions, not three, for a combined length of about 1,000 words."

UCSC is not that selective, but I was surprised when I found out some of my classmates were rejected. They took AP classes just like me, but didn't get into UCSC. I attribute most of my college admission success to extracurricular activities.

Regarding selectivity, the school says: "UC Santa Cruz has become steadily more selective over the years, and is expected to become even more selective. Unfortunately, we have had to turn away many fine applicants. We encourage anyone who is interested in attending UC Santa Cruz to meet and exceed the academic standards for UC eligibility. Again, although extracurricular activities are considered, the most important components of the admissions process are the academic factors."

Current student, 9/2006-Submit Date, May 2007

The admissions process for the UC system is fairly straightforward, and is done primarily online. You submit one application for the entire system, then select to which campuses you want your application sent. The application involves around three essays, each with fairly generic prompts (what you have achieved academically, what you will bring to your college and so on). My impression, however, is that it is mostly a numbers game. Do well on your SATs and SAT Subject Tests, maintain a good GPA, try to do extracurricular activities, and write decent essays. Santa Cruz is one of the less selective universities in the system, but can still offer a really good education.

Current student, 9/2005-Submit Date, May 2007

The admissions process for UCSC included a straightforward form that must be filled out. I was admitted as a junior transfer from a community college in Southern California (Ventura College). I found there was a gap in information about what classes I should take before being admitted to UCSC as a transfer. My advice to future transfers would be to contact the university directly (this applies to any university) and ask them for the information, because the community colleges are not guaranteed to have the most up-to-date information, nor are they guaranteed to care about getting you transferred to the college of your choice.

Read all of Vault's College Surveys at **www.vault.com/college**—get complete surveys on 100s of colleges and universities, expert advice on applicaton essays and more.

VAULT CAREER LIBRARY   **87**

Current student, 9/2004-Submit Date, September 2005

Getting into any of the UCs is very similar. On the UC web site there is an online application, you can apply to multiple UCs at once. To enroll, you must complete some background questions about your education, e.g., your grades, your SAT scores, any awards you have won and extracurricular activities, and write three essays. I believe the three topics are: "What is an extraordinary thing you have done in your life?" "How will you contribute to your campus life?" and "What sets you apart from other applicants?" or something of the like. Two of the essays are short, one is long. You get to choose which one is long and which ones are short. You should really get an outside reader to edit them before eventually pasting them into the text boxes provided in the form.

> The school says: "Starting with the application for fall 2008, the UC application includes two personal statement prompts. Prompt Number One: Describe the world you come from—for example, your family, community or school—and tell us how your world has shaped your dreams and aspirations. Prompt Number Two: Tell us about a personal quality, talent, accomplishment, contribution or experience that is important to you. What about this quality or accomplishment makes you proud and how does it relate to the person you are?"

Depending on what you plan to study, UCSC varies from easy-to-get-into to extremely difficult. Check the department web sites on www.ucsc.edu for specific admissions requirements for that major, and if you can't find any info, write to one of the department counselors. They're also the people to ask on what courses you can take in high school to help your major.

> The school says: "UC Santa Cruz admits students campuswide, not to specific majors. There are majors at UC Santa Cruz with selective admissions criteria, but this does not affect students' admission to the campus."

 **Academics**

Current student, 9/2005-Submit Date, May 2007

I have yet to have a problem getting into my classes, but I am also in a major that many students do not even consider. The class size is pretty large and until about the third year, you will not be in a class smaller than 50 people. It's hard to get to know your professor, but if you work at it and go to office hours, then you won't have a problem. Professors are usually pretty lenient on grading; there is often a very large curve and if you work hard, then getting an A is definitely a possibility.

Current student, 9/2006-Submit Date, May 2007

It's difficult to get into popular classes, but if you try to get in repeatedly for a few quarters, you should have no difficulties. Also, if you get in contact with the professor within the first week of the class and continuously ask him/her about open space, he/she will believe you really want to be in the class and favor you over other students who simply complain about not being able to register.

Current student, 9/2006-Submit Date, May 2007

Santa Cruz has the potential to provide an exceptional academic experience, but only if you are in the right program. My experience in the School of Engineering has been nearly all positive, but I have heard of other programs that are simply not supported. If you want a larger breadth of material to study, you are going to be better off at a larger school. Don't be fooled by the relaxed attitude of the student body: the workload can be extremely heavy at times; it really depends on which classes (and how many) you choose to take.

Current student, 9/2005-Submit Date, May 2007

The nature of my major is a combination of business analytics and computer science. The focus is equally shared between the two topics, and they are detailed enough that if I wanted to pursue a career in either field, it would be very easy to assimilate into a wide range of jobs. The lower-division classes can be tedious and to some extent boring, whereas the upper-division classes are very interesting and extremely challenging.

Current student, 9/2005-Submit Date, April 2006

Well, UCs are the top state schools, apparently accepting only the top 12 percent of high school classes. People who come to them are smart and thus, the classes here are challenging. Naturally, some are easy because they are introductory courses (lower-division), or because you might be very smart in that area, but there is always room to improve, and there are plenty of difficult courses to challenge you. Getting into classes is based on your grade level and GPA, so keeping your grades up and applying as soon as they let you is important. There is a wide range of professors, but the one thing they do have in common is that they all know what they are talking about and are skilled in their fields. Workload is manageable, and depends on what grades you want to achieve and which classes you are taking, just like anywhere else.

Current student, Psychology, 9/2004-Submit Date, September 2005

The Santa Cruz psychology BA is focused more on research than clinical work. The psychology department is very popular, and many students take psychology on as a second major or minor in addition to the number of students who opt for the intensive psychology program over the normal psych program. Students take a wide variety of courses from the cognitive, social, personality and developmental subfields. In addition, Statistics, Research Methods, and Field Research classes are required to graduate. There are also optional courses, such as the Field Study course, and the teaching aid to the Psych I course. On top of all the classes, Psi Chi is a campus group for psychology students. Psychology is very popular, it can be really hard to get into classes, especially as a freshman. You have to make sure there are no holds on your accounts and that you stay in good academic standing and keep up with your units. It's not uncommon for people to stay and extra quarter to a year to complete their degrees. The grading system is still confusing to most teachers, UCSC switched over to grades only a year or two ago. Professors are nice, however, depending on who you get, the workload can vary from light to overwhelming. Check www.ratemyprofessors.com before enrolling in a class to see what a teacher is like.

> The school says: "UC Santa Cruz began using a traditional 4.0 grade scale, in addition to giving performance evaluations, in 2001."

Current student, 9/2004-Submit Date, March 2006

The academics at UC Santa Cruz are very interesting. Most introductory classes (e.g., Intro to Sociology) are pretty basic but are interesting if you just want to learn a little about the subject. It can be very difficult as a freshman to get into popular classes, but as you move up in years, your enrollment time gets closer to the beginning and registration is easier. Grading is on an A, B, C, D scale and you can take up to one quarter of your total classes on a pass/no pass scale. Professors tend to be really interesting and committed to their work. Oftentimes, they have a strong interest in helping students understand the material and further their learning. Workload depends heavily on the course but tends to be anywhere from one half hour to one hour of reading each assignment; and usually either a few papers or a mid-term or two per class. Although finals can be scary and stressful, they are definitely designed to be doable with a full workload. Typically two or three days of studying per class gets the job done.

 Employment Prospects

Current student, 9/2006-Submit Date, May 2007

UCSC (I am told) is quickly growing in prestige. Once considered a consortium of hippies, it is quickly growing in stature and respect, especially its engineering department. There is an increasing number of companies and organizations that talk to students about internships and jobs, and the university is extremely good about providing research opportunities for undergraduates.

Current student, 9/2005-Submit Date, May 2007

Internships are something that UCSC is all about. They are also all about undergraduate research. Many majors require an internship or independent research project. This allows students to make contacts who will help them after college. I took a class with the vice-mayor of the City of Santa Cruz who offered anyone taking his course an internship. I can't think of very many places that can offer those kinds of connections.

Current student, 9/2005-Submit Date, May 2007

The information systems management major prepares me for a wide range of jobs. Any company that either makes technology or uses technology (computers, Internet and so on) to make something or provide a service, any company that meets one of those criteria would be an excellent match for me as an ISM major (e.g., Microsoft, Google, Intel, Nike, Seagate, Sun, Disney and Sony). The limit of what I can do with my degree is limited by how I think I can apply my knowledge to the job at hand.

Current student, 1/2005-Submit Date, March 2005

Many students at UCSC end up doing research and going to graduate school. The campus does, however, provide an excellent resource for job placement assistance. The school is regarded as one of the best research organizations in the country, and the Marine Life Center is perhaps the best in the country to do research. Because of the Mediterranean-type climate in the area, one will not find more unique job opportunities than in Santa Cruz. A study ranked UC Santa Cruz 11th in the nation among public campuses for the quality of its research productivity. In the study, UC Santa Cruz ranked first in the assessment of productivity in the social sciences and sixth in the arts and humanities index. In surveys by the Institute for Scientific Information measuring per-paper impact, UC Santa Cruz ranked first in the nation for its research in the field of space sciences and second in the world in the physical sciences.

Quality of Life

Current student, 9/2005-Submit Date, May 2007

I think that the housing and dining are very good. Living on campus is very fun and very much like a typical dormroom. Students get to choose where they live so, oftentimes, they are happy because they got to choose. Dining halls are very good and have a lot of options for vegans and vegetarians. We also have an all organic locally grown salad bar. We also get a lot of produce from the off-campus farm. The neighborhood is very safe and most students live off campus in apartments for their last two or three years.

Current student, 9/2006-Submit Date, May 2007

The atmosphere and the people are absolutely amazing, and I feel very safe here.

Current student, 9/2006-Submit Date, May 2007

One very important thing to consider about UCSC is that it is situated in a veritable forest. Virtually everywhere you walk, you are surrounded by trees. This can be extremely comforting after working on homework; it provides an extremely calm atmosphere. The housing is separated into 10 residential colleges, each with fairly distinct moods. Inter-college activities are fairly uncommon; you tend to stick mainly to your own college. As such, your experiences with housing and dining may vary, depending on which one you select. My impressions have been mostly positive, but it is also important to note that even though your residential college may make it feel like you are in fact at a small university, trying to change how things are run/asking for different amenities can be frustratingly difficult. Many requests are inevitably killed in the giant bureaucracy that the UC system is famous for. That being said, the campus is extremely safe, and what is provided is enough for a very comfortable experience on campus.

Current student, 9/2005-Submit Date, April 2006

I love my school! Living in dorms your first year is something I highly recommend. You meet all sorts of great friends, and it gets you used to college life. Plus, your RA is usually a great way to get to know the college and get settled in. My campus is fantastic!! It's gorgeous, and people are always astonished when they visit. Plus, it's really big, which is great. I love having a big, diverse campus, and I could rave on and on about my campus forever, because I love it. (Being a mountain biker helps, too.) Our meal plan is all-you-can-eat whenever you want to eat, which is excellent in every way except controlling your weight. We have a great gym to take care of that, though, and we have an extraordinary amount of vegan, vegetarian and organic options, and tons of healthy food to go with the hamburgers and pizza. The neighborhood is great, and Santa Cruz is a fantastically funky place to live.

Current student, 9/2004-Submit Date, March 2006

The UC Santa Cruz campus is divided up into 10 different colleges, each with a different focus of academics (e.g., environmental studies, political science). Students who attend UC Santa Cruz are required to take a one-quarter-long course about the area of focus of the college, and then do all of their affiliated paper work for their college. On-[campus] housing is amazing, there is a view of the Monterey Bay and the entire school is immersed in the Redwood trees, it's like being in the middle of Muir woods while you are studying in the library! Dorms are pretty nice, and the cafeterias serve organic lettuce!

Social Life

Current student, 9/2005-Submit Date, May 2007

We have no Greek system and our sports are very small. A lot of people date and are in long-term relationships at our university. We have one under-18 club. Parties are all around and there are bars. The restaurants are amazing and if you like to go out, then I definitely recommend checking out the restaurants in the town. My favorite restaurant is Little Tampico and my favorite bar is Rosie's.

> **The school says:** "UC Santa Cruz does sponsor fraternities and sororities as social clubs, but there is no Greek housing on campus."

Current student, 9/2006-Submit Date, May 2007

UCSC's campus is huge, so it is actually very difficult to reach downtown Santa Cruz without the aid of a motorized vehicle. The university does have a contract with the SC Metro system, and it is easy to catch a bus downtown. Once there, you can find a plethora of different restaurants (some are extremely good), shops, plus a few bars and nightclubs. Even though there are a few sororities and fraternities available to join, Greek life is so strictly controlled by the city of Santa Cruz that they are effectively nonexistent. The layout of the University keeps the residential colleges fairly separate, but once downtown it is easy to run into people you know, or to meet new ones.

Current student, 9/2005-Submit Date, May 2007

The Greek system is slowly gaining in popularity, but most people party with their friends.

Current student, 9/2005-Submit Date, April 2006

The social life is great. I have no shortage of friends here, and some of my best friends I've made have been just from leaving my door open and socializing with people on my floor. Downtown Santa Cruz is a great place that has all sorts of things to do if you get bored on campus. Either way, you'll be able to find something to do here, and if you don't, you probably aren't looking hard enough. The Greek system is present, but they don't really do much. If you want to party, join the Ski and Snowboard Club—they know how to do it right. And if you're not a partier, there's still plenty for you to do here, too.

Current student, 9/2004-Submit Date, March 2006

Social life at UC Santa Cruz has something for everyone. There is a wide range of political activities, outdoors activities and nightlife. At Santa Cruz, there are a few sororities and fraternities that throw parties, a Ski and Snowboard Club that throws parties and regular old house parties. There are also lots of bars and restaurants with nightly drink specials such as Two Dollar Tuesdays where all cocktails are $2. Many students are involved in political rallies, fundraising, lobbying and petitioning and you often see people doing political activities on campus.

The School Says

Welcome to UC Santa Cruz, where our students are empowered to make a world of difference. UC Santa Cruz combines the resources of a major research university with the academic and student life opportunities of a small college. Undergraduates have the opportunity to engage in in-depth learning while pursuing research and scholarship with leading figures in their fields. Described as one of the most beautiful campuses in the

Read all of Vault's College Surveys at **www.vault.com/college**—get complete surveys on 100s of colleges and universities, expert advice on application essays and more.

VAULT CAREER LIBRARY   89

world, UC Santa Cruz has a reputation for excellence, with rigorous, nationally ranked undergraduate and graduate programs.

Many academic programs at UC Santa Cruz, such as computer game design, are in newer fields that focus on interdisciplinary thinking. At UC Santa Cruz, undergraduates conduct and publish research, working closely with faculty on innovative projects. In addition to their academic work on campus, many students take advantage of the variety of opportunities available for fieldwork, internships, and travel abroad. UC's Education Abroad Program offers opportunities to live and study in 34 different host countries around the world.

UC Santa Cruz includes the Jack Baskin School of Engineering, a forward-thinking new professional school with strengths in biotechnology, information technology, and nanotechnology. In 2007, the Baskin School introduced a new undergraduate major in bioengineering.

All undergraduate students, whether they live on or off campus, are affiliated with one of 10 residential colleges at UC Santa Cruz. Each college provides academic support and sponsors events that enhance the intellectual and social life of the campus, in addition to housing students in small-scale residential communities. Every college community includes students with diverse backgrounds and academic goals. College affiliation is independent of choice of major and assignments are based upon space availability.

More than 100 student organizations on campus cover a wide range of interests, including ethnic student organizations and clubs based on cultural, intellectual or social interests.

In addition to 14 men's and women's NCAA intercollegiate teams, UC Santa Cruz offers a wide variety of athletic clubs and intramural leagues, plus a busy, year-round recreational program. In fact, *Outside* magazine ranked UC Santa Cruz first out of 40 colleges "that turn out smart grads with topnotch academic credentials, a healthy environmental ethos, and an A-plus sense of adventure." The campus is located on over 2,000 acres of redwood forest and open meadow overlooking the Monterey Bay, and opportunities for outdoor sports—such as mountain biking, surfing, and hiking—abound.

The intensive undergraduate experience at UC Santa Cruz prepares students well for careers or further study in graduate school, and graduates have achieved success in a variety of fields. Well-known alumni include Industrial Light & Magic cofounder Malcolm Blanchard, president of California State University, Sacramento Dr. Alexander Gonzalez, and Maya Rudolph, a *Saturday Night Live* cast member with a recent role in *Shrek the Third*.

For more information, see admissions.ucsc.edu.

University of San Diego

Admissions Office
5998 Alcalá Park
San Diego, CA 92110
Admissions phone: (619) 260-4506
Admissions e-mail: admissions@sandiego.edu
Admissions URL: www.sandiego.edu/admissions

 ## Admissions

Current student, Pre-med, 8/2006-Submit Date, February 2007

For transfer students, the admissions process is different and easy! Very few transfer students apply—fewer than 2,000 and almost half are accepted. But I was a good candidate with a 3.7 GPA and a lot of extracurricular activities. No interview, about two one-page essays about yourself and one letter of recommendation: a very short application. And if you are a minority, you're in, since there relatively few minorities.

The school says: "USD is committed to increasing its ethnic diversity through the recruitment of well-qualified students of color."

Current student, Psychology, 9/2002-Submit Date, May 2006

The USD admissions process consists of a standard application requesting information on general background information, GPA and SAT/ACT scores, as well as extracurricular activities, such as club involvement, sports and volunteer activities. There is also a personal essay that the prospective student is required to write, which can be chosen from around six or seven options. Overall, I didn't find the application process too demanding and only minimally stressful. Also, USD has become much more selective since I applied four years ago, as have most universities. When I was a prospective student, the general acceptance rate was approximately 50 percent, while this incoming freshman class has a much lower rate of around 35 percent. Obviously, the more that can be done

to boost your application, the better chance you have of staying in the running. And if all else fails and you aren't accepted, there are several students who attend a junior college to boost their grades before re-applying, and most have been very successful at being accepted.

The school says: "USD's acceptance rate is about 49 percent, making it one of the more competitive universities in the country."

Current student, 9/2003-Submit Date, February 2007

The admissions process gets more competitive every year. Seeing as how I had a very strong GPA and SAT in high school, I did not take the essay as seriously but tailored it to sound service-oriented rather than my standard essay that I had sent to public schools and non-religious private schools. The application process is not too bad when compared to some privates that had five-step applications but was a bit more difficult than the UC applications, which were standardized.

The school says: "USD offers the Common Application, an option that allows students to apply to many schools at the same time."

Current student, 1/2003-Submit Date, October 2005

Grades are important to the admissions process. I was accepted to a good university in Florida, joined the military and was not accepted when I first applied to USD as a transfer student. Once I got my GPA above 3.0, however, I was accepted. I feel it was important to get to know the admissions officers personally and have interviews with them so they could remember me. But the grades remained the key factor.

Current student, 8/2003-Submit Date, January 2005

The admissions process at the University of San Diego (USD) is very smooth. I sent in my fully completed application early with my transcripts and a couple of letters of recommendation and received a response in a prompt manner. The required essays are very simple and to-the-point, no psychological or nerve-racking questions. The admissions process does not require an interview, which is good. Selectivity of admittance is being raised every semester; it is getting harder and harder to get admitted.

Current student, 8/2003-Submit Date, June 2004

I first applied to the University of San Diego as a transfer student. Applying was easy. The application consists of general personal information along with three essays, and includes applications for school-sponsored scholarships. Minimum requirements to be accepted are a 3.0 GPA or above out of high school or college, being in the top 50 percent of class, and leadership/service/athletic participation are pluses. The essays are about a page each in length, and were not mentally taxing.

Currently, I believe USD accepts roughly 30 percent of its applicants. There is no interview in the application process. If you are applying straight from high school, expect to hear promptly and receive tons of valuable information. However, if you are a transfer student, be sure to call and get all the information you can, especially about registering for classes because you will be forgotten.

> **The school says:** "We accepted 46 percent for Class of 2010; 60 percent for class of 2009. Regarding transfer students, the minimum requirements are as follows—a 3.0 GPA and at least one year of college work. There is no requirement regarding class rank."

Academics

Current student, Economics, 9/2003-Submit Date, November 2006

Generally speaking, the academics were good. Some of my general education classes were easy while others demanded some real studying. Small class sizes especially once you get into your major. My largest class was 60 students and that was for art history. My smallest was in my major with 16 students. If you need to see a professor for help, they have office hours and are there for the students. Educating is their number one priority. I was an econ major and enjoyed my professors.

Current student, Pre-med, 8/2006-Submit Date, February 2007

The good thing about classes is that they are small, 20 to 30 students, which is good for school discussions and professor feedback. Grading depends on your professor, but most are very easy in grading, and since classses are small, they get to know you. Workload is minimal; you are able to get a good five classes and receive all A's if you study appropriately.

Current student, 9/2003-Submit Date, February 2007

The academic aspect of this institution is phenomenal. I have yet to be taught by a TA (except for a language class, which was done away with two years ago anyway) and nearly every professor knows me by name. Some of the professors are extremely accomplished. As a political science major, I have a professor who survived the Holocaust and went on to teach at Harvard, advise President Kennedy during the Cuban Missile Crisis and went before the UN to try to avoid the war in Iraq. Although this is not what the profile of every professor is, nearly all of them are PhDs from very good institutions. The workload ranges from extremely heavy for upper-divisions to fairly sparse for some of the easier GEs. Don't be scared off by the religion requirement if you are not religious because you can take cool classes like Hinduism, Buddhism, or even Cults and Fringe Religions.

Current student, Psychology, 9/2002-Submit Date, May 2006

Being a psychology major, I will admit that I have had some trouble at times with getting into classes, as psych is one of the most popular majors on campus, in addition to being one of the most impacted. Although I had trouble getting into some of the classes that I wanted, I always got into a class that was required in my major and didn't have any semester when I was falling behind because I wasn't enrolled in one psychology class or another. Although the average class size at USD is approximately 20 to 25, with 30 generally being the maximum, the psych department tends to have its average closer to 40 simply due to limited professors to teach required courses.

I found almost all of the professors whom I have had here to be wonderful. There are always exceptions to the rules, but most professors are very well-versed in the subject they are teaching, whether it is a GE or upper division, and around 98 percent of the professors here have their PhD. I have never once had a teacher aid in any of my classes, for which I am incredibly thankful. Because of the small sizes of the classes, it is very easy to get to know your professor on a more in-depth level, and most are more than willing to help during office hours. In addition to helping with undergrad work, this helps to build relationship, as well as providing you with references that actually have the ability to honestly talk about you by knowing you more personally.

Being that USD is a private university, the classes are rather rigorous, and I have found that it is essential to study fairly hard for most of my classes. It has been my experience that it is rare to be enrolled in an easy, kick-back course, although I have experienced a couple. With that, I know from both first-hand experience and talking with various professors that the hard-workers are well-noted and that effort has been known to be taken into consideration when calculating final semester grades. For example, I had one class that, regardless of my intense interest in the subject and my seemingly endless effort at doing the readings and work, I couldn't do better than a D on the tests. However, I was in the professor's office a minimum of two days a week going over things to make sure that I understood the material. Because of this effort, regardless of the actual grade that I ended up receiving on the tests, he knew first-hand how hard I had worked in the class. He allowed me to do a little extra work, and I ended up with an A in the class, a grade that must be earned in his courses. Some professors assign more work than others, but I've found, as a whole, that most are relatively fair in the workload that is laid out on the syllabus.

Current student, Business, 8/2001-Submit Date, April 2005

I am in the business school and am disappointed with how things work here. There are three basic majors: business administration, business economics and business accounting, and that's it! You cannot specialize beyond that. Freshmen entering now will be able to specialize but that is new. The only thing I like is that you receive a BBA when you graduate, which is rare. The classes you have to take as a business admin major are broad. You have to take a little bit of everything, which is good but bad because I end up having to pay for classes that I will never use again. Grading is tough and professors are hard. Workload is tolerable but heavy. Don't even think about getting a good teacher if you do not register early!

> **The school says:** "USD's undergraduate business program is currently ranked 46th on the list of the top 50 programs by *BusinessWeek* magazine. USD's is the only ranked program in San Diego County and is the 4th highest-ranked program in California. In the fall of 2007, the school introduced two new majors, marketing and finance along with eight new minors including international business, management, real estate and supply chain management."

Current student, 8/2003-Submit Date, January 2005

The 60 units of general education requirements are easy to get into, even the popular ones. The upper-division classes and business classes are taught well. Teachers pay very close attention to students and are always ready to help. Class size is usually very small, which provides for a better learning environment. The grading depends on each teacher; some are harder than others, but the popular classes and teachers are well known and their classes are not very hard to get into. Most of the business teachers are professionals who have been very successful in their careers.

Employment Prospects

Current student, Economics, 9/2003-Submit Date, November 2006

Within the San Diego region, the university has a good reputation, but certainly doesn't carry weight like larger, nationally known schools, so don't expect to get recognition based just on name. Networking is key. I was from Central California and found a job in the Bay Area at PricewaterhouseCoopers. I don't think school recognition was key. There was on-campus recruiting, but I didn't use it.

Read all of Vault's College Surveys at **www.vault.com/college**—get complete surveys on 100s of colleges and universities, expert advice on applicaton essays and more.

VAULT CAREER LIBRARY   91

Current student, Pre-med, 8/2006-Submit Date, February 2007

Maybe one or two prestigious employers show up for on-campus recruitment. Career Services does have a lot of other jobs and internships available for students.

Current student, 1/2003-Submit Date, October 2005

The career center is great, but the options for business graduates could be better. Most jobs are for accounting firms and there are only a few (literally) jobs available for non-accounting positions. Of course, there is a lot of competition for these two or three jobs because everyone wants them. The listings for jobs seem long until you weed out the abundant door-to-door cutlery salesman and Peace Corps jobs.

Current student, 8/2003-Submit Date, January 2005

In San Diego, the school is very popular and ranks very high in prestige. The school is currently working hard, raising the prestige nationally and is doing a good job at it. The internship program is one of the best; I got internships with Merrill Lynch and Smith Barney through the internship coordinator in the school. Career Services are available for free to all students, current or alumni. The newly built alumni center is also a great way to meet fellow Toreros from the working world.

Current student, 9/2003-Submit Date, July 2004

In addition to periodic career expos, the campus has an excellent Career Services department, with loads of information, contacts and even a periodically updated database. Another advantage to attending this school is the alumni interest in current students and their entry into the workforce. Personally, I was just given an internship with a local sports team by a former USD student.

Current student, 8/2003-Submit Date, June 2004

There are career prospects abound at USD, especially in the political science and history departments. The school holds functions weekly when you can mingle with people in your career choice, ask questions and get a feel of where you would like to take your degree. There is a whole office devoted to job and internship opportunities and the people there are very friendly and helpful. USD offers many internship programs to places like Washington, D.C., Sacramento, CA, and foreign countries. In addition, USD has a very prestigious reputation, especially in Southern California.

 Quality of Life

Current student, 9/2003-Submit Date, February 2007

The housing on campus is above average for your freshman dormitory and sophomore apartment. Most people move off campus to either the beach or Mission Valley their junior and senior years or live in very nice on-campus apartments. The campus is probably one of the most beautiful in the nation. The dining ranges from mediocre (the Grille) to really good (La Paloma) although the range of choices is not as great as at a huge public school. The neighborhood is not too bad, although you might avoid going too far north or east by foot if you are concerned. It is ideally located between downtown and the beach, which is a definite plus.

Current student, Economics, 9/2003-Submit Date, November 2006

San Diego has great weather, good shopping, the beach for surfing or other water sports, plenty of good bars and so on. The campus looks like a postcard—super clean, and the facilities are nice. Student housing is nice enough. Most students live on campus their first year and then move to the beach or off campus. There is a commuter element to the school. The campus has a low crime rate and great lighting. They've upgraded the facilities within the last couple of years, so there is a real gym. Dining on campus was acceptable. Housing can be expensive since it is Southern California.

Current student, Psychology, 9/2002-Submit Date, May 2006

I have lived in campus housing for four years and have been very satisfied by the experience. In fact, many of the housing areas that are provided are much larger than many other campuses, including freshman housing. All campus apartments are fully furnished and, with the exception of freshman dorms, provide a fully-equipped kitchen. Due to the high number of incoming students, new housing facilities have recently been built in order to provide more students the opportunity to live on campus. Although housing is no longer guaranteed for four years, freshmen are still required to live on campus for the first year, although they are also permitted to have cars, something that few universities grant freshmen.

The campus is very safe, almost too safe at times, with public safety on constant watch. Although it is comforting to have them in case of an emergency, generally the only emergency that occurs is underage drinking.

> **The school says:** "In an effort to maintain a safe and secure campus, USD's department of Public Safety maintains a high degree of visibility on and around campus and works closely with Residence Life personnel."

Current student, Business, 8/2001-Submit Date, April 2005

Housing is outdated and there is never enough to accommodate all students; therefore, we have apartments and dorms built for two that are housing three and four. Safety is good. The campus is beautiful—facilities are adequate the surrounding neighborhood is run-down but relatively safe.

> **The school says:** "In the fall of 2007, USD completed a new residence hall with 250 beds allowing for the reduction of the number of students in many rooms and more single-bedroom housing units for upperclassmen."

Current student, 8/2003-Submit Date, January 2005

The University of San Diego has the most beautiful campus in the world. I do not think that any other school comes close in comparison to the beauty of the campus. The buildings of the school are all built in the Baroque style and are very comfortable. Campus living is very nice, there are building in the center of the campus and buildings on the east end of the campus near the beautiful football and baseball fields. There is a state-of-the-art gym facility where most NBA stars come work out in when in town—the Lakers made our basketball court their home this summer for training. There are several restaurants and a Starbucks on campus. The school is very safe and crime is really not an issue here.

 Social Life

Current student, Economics, 9/2003-Submit Date, November 2006

Plenty of beautiful women to date but some might be a bit spoiled. The Greek system was a little weak at the time. Freshmen hit TJ and usually grow out of that phase quickly in favor of house parties or bars at Pacific Beach, depending on age. The Gaslamp district and downtown have really been developed and are a lot of fun. Old Town is just around the corner from USD for tons of Mexican food. La Jolla is uptown if you have cash to spend. School spirit is lacking when compared to a school like Santa Clara, in which students go to the basketball games and get behind the school. USD has more of a commuter school feel.

Current student, Psychology, 9/2002-Submit Date, May 2006

USD is located in one of the best areas one can ask for as far as entertainment and social life go. Although our campus is a dry campus, so there are fewer large-scale parties, people don't have a hard time finding things to do and places to do them. The campus is located 10 minutes or less from pretty much everywhere. It takes approximately five minutes to get to Sea World, 10 minutes to Mission Beach, Pacific Beach, La Jolla and downtown. San Diego has a huge number of things to do, both during the day and at night, so there's almost never a lag. A popular spot for those over 21 is a restaurant just down the hill that serves great margaritas at happy hour, along with free appetizers. It's located in Old Town, which has some of the best Mexican restaurants in San Diego. Pacific Beach also has a wide variety of clubs and bars that are packed pretty much every night of the week. Downtown there are bars, dance clubs like Cafe Sevilla which is great for salsa dancing, restaurants, and Seaport Village right along the edge on the water.

For those who aren't of age, there are still plenty of places to go. There are three large malls, all of which have movie theaters, as well as a plethora of restaurants and beach excursions to explore. There are tourist areas at almost every turn and plenty of sand to lay out on or water to surf in. When it comes to campus events,

Associated Students and other clubs and organizations put on a variety of things. There is usually a big concert on campus once a year, holding groups, such as Maroon 5, the Roots and Jack Johnson, in the past.

Greek life is not as large as other universities, and they do not have their own houses, but that doesn't mean that they are any less prominent on campus. There are five sororities and five fraternities from which to choose, and a large percentage of people participate. There are many prominent clubs on campus, and people can almost always find something that peaks their interest. There are Christian clubs, FUSO (Fillipino club), BSU (Black Student Union), United Front, which is multicultural, and Community Service Learning, which participates in several organizations and does a lot of work in the community. Overall, as long as a student wants to do something at almost any time, it usually isn't too hard to find.

The school says: "Possession and consumption of alcohol is permitted by persons 21 years of age or older in private rooms within University Residence Halls, where at least one assigned resident is at least 21-years-old."

Current student, 9/2003-Submit Date, February 2007

The social life is pretty mixed. It is largely what you make of it due to the fact that there aren't fraternity/sorority houses for huge parties, although most fraternities have houses that are just unofficial places where parties happen on a regular basis. The Greek system is pretty good for not having houses with fraternities and sororities having events on a regular basis at local clubs and venues and most fraternities doing an annual trip to Las Vegas for their formals. The bar scene in Pacific Beach and the Gaslamp District is comparable to Bourbon Street in New Orleans, but you can't really get by if you aren't 21. The three most frequented bars for juniors and seniors are in Mission Beach. These are: the Pennant, the Beachcomber and the Sand Bar. Restaurants? You name it, San Diego has it.

 ## The School Says

University of San Diego offers a values-based education rooted in Roman Catholic ethics and tradition with a solid foundation in the liberal arts. The university is committed to advancing academic excellence, expanding liberal and professional knowledge, creating a diverse and inclusive community and preparing leaders dedicated to ethical conduct and compassionate service. USD is a coed residential university serving students of diverse backgrounds from across the country and across the world.

Chartered in 1949, the University of San Diego has been dedicated to providing a superior education that recognizes men and women as creatures of God, and to continuing examination of Catholic tradition in contemporary life. USD's 180-acre campus, Alcalá Park, overlooks San Diego's Mission Bay and the spot where Father Junipero Serra celebrated the first Catholic Mass in Alta California more than 230 years ago. Like California's oldest city, the university took its name from San Diego de Alcalá, a Franciscan brother from Alcalá de Henares, a monastery near Madrid, Spain. The Spanish Renaissance architecture that characterizes Spain's five-century-old University of Alcalá serves as the inspiration for all buildings on the USD campus.

USD enrolls approximately 5,000 undergraduate; 1,400 graduate, and 1,200 law students from the United States and from more than 50 countries.

USD offers bachelor's degrees in over 35 diverse majors, as well as master's, doctorate, JD and LLM degrees. USD is also a member of Phi Beta Kappa, the oldest and most prestigious academic honor society in the United States. We are one of only 270 chapters nationwide.

Admission to USD, which consistently ranks among the top schools in the United States, is highly selective. USD received more than 10,500 applications for approximately 1,100 undergraduate openings in fall 2007.

At USD, community service-learning is an integral part of our mission to educate the whole person. The Center for Community Service-Learning enlists USD students, faculty, staff and alumni in service projects with the community. The center believes participation in these partnership projects helps create a lifelong commitment to promote social change and justice.

USD student athletes are champions, on and off the court. They compete on 16 NCAA Division I intercollegiate teams. USD is a member of the West Coast Conference for nearly all sports except for football, which participates in Division I-AA in the Pioneer Football League.

This fall, the University of San Diego inaugurated the Joan B. Kroc School of Peace Studies, the only school of peace in the nation, bringing the university's total number of schools and colleges to six. Other academic divisions include the College of Arts and Sciences and the schools of Business Administration, Education and Leadership Sciences, Law, and Nursing and Health Science.

Read all of Vault's College Surveys at **www.vault.com/college**–get complete surveys on 100s of colleges and universities, expert advice on applicaton essays and more.

VAULT CAREER LIBRARY **93**

University of San Francisco

Office of Undergraduate Admission
2130 Fulton Street
San Francisco, CA 94117-1046
Admissions phone: (415) 422-6563 or (800) CALL-USF
Admissions e-mail: admission@usfca.edu
Admissions URL: www.usfca.edu/acadserv/admission

 Admissions

Alumnus/a, Political Science, 8/2003-5/2007, May 2007

The USF admissions process is certainly difficult. Though USF lacks a formal interview process, a lot of weight is placed on recommendations, essays and community involvement.

Current student, Liberal Arts, 8/2004-Submit Date, May 2007

The admissions process at USF is a lot more interactive than lots of other schools to which I applied. When I introduced myself to the admissions director my junior year in high school, he actually remembered me when I went to visit the campus my senior year. I applied Early Action in order to get my college applications out of the way. The essay was simple, and after working for the admissions office, I realized how much the essay counts. Our admissions directors always said that they would rather have a mediocre student with character, than a straight-A student without a personality. The mission of USF is: "to educate minds and hearts to change the world," and your essay is your chance to showcase your dedication to that. USF has been my dream school since the eighth grade, so needless to say I was elated when I found out I was accepted. My advice to future applicants would be to use the essay portion as a way to let the admissions counselors know about you, that's who they care about.

Current student, Political Science, 8/2005-Submit Date, May 2007

The University of San Francisco was very open willing and more than happy to help me with any questions I had about what needed to be done to get into school. I never had to wait on the telephone more than five minutes, which immediately made me know that this was a school that was focused on the student and making their experience most memorable and easy.

Current student, Nursing, 8/2006-Submit Date, May 2007

At a college fair, I met a college counselor who was very helpful in providing me with information on how to apply and visit the school. Upon scheduling a tour, the student tour guide was very knowledgeable about the campus and school and gave very honest answers to my questions. As I applied, I constantly stayed in contact with an admission counselor who was always willing to help me. She returned my e-mails in a timely manner. The admissions staff made my application process extremely easy.

Current student, Psychology, 1/2005-Submit Date, May 2007

I believe the essay is the most important part of the application. USF has a very holistic method of looking at the applications, and they believe that a good answer to the essay question makes all the difference in the world.

Current student, 8/2002-Submit Date, January 2006

I attended a college fair in high school and signed up for various colleges for them to send me more information so my college application was sent to me by mail. I basically just needed to fill out the application and ask for recommendations from two teachers, as well as write a personal statement and an essay, for which the school provides you with a question that the applicant has to answer. Since my school is a private, Jesuit school, the essay question was based on the school's mission and what and how I would do to put forth their mission and represent the school. I don't remember if they had a length requirement for the essay (I don't think they did), but I wrote as much as I could. However, my advice for getting in is to be clear and not to be too repetitive in the essay, and also try to get everything done as early as possible. The GPA you needed to get in is 3.5 and the University of San Francisco administration, I think, selected as

many people as they could that met the requirements. However, I'm not really quite sure how they select their students.

> **The school says:** "USF's average GPA is a 3.49. In addition to high school transcripts and standardized test scores, we also consider an academic letter of recommendation, extracurricular activities and an essay."

Current student, 8/2002-Submit Date, December 2004

USF is becoming more selective every year as it is trying to improve to compete with other Jesuit schools like Georgetown and Boston College. I applied as a transfer after my freshman year at another college. There is one person who controls the transfer admits and that is Charles Skinner. Go and see him, make up an excuse to personally deliver a transcript or something because he is your ticket in. However, for those applying regularly, I would suggest making your essay focus on social justice because the Jesuits, and USF in particular, are very concerned with SJ.

> **USF says:** "In addition to our University Evaluator (Charles Skinner), there are also transfer admission counselors who can work with you one-on-one and assist you through the admissions process."

 Academics

Alumnus/a, Political Science, 8/2003-5/2007, May 2007

The classes are generally good. The professors encourage discussion, though many are particular towards one view over another. The choice of classes is great, and even as a freshman, I never had problems getting into classes. The grading can be hard, as many classes have a great deal of requirements.

Current student, Liberal Arts, 8/2004-Submit Date, May 2007

The older you get, the easier it gets to enroll in the classes you want. At USF, you can always get the classes you need, though. It's also very helpful that every semester you're required to meet with your advisor before registration. The workload is not too overwhelming; you really learn how to improve your time management skills during your freshman year. The classes are of a good quality; of my six semesters to date, I've never been upset with a class or professor. The grading is similar to high school, as well—A through F or Pass/Fail.

Current student, Nursing, 8/2006-Submit Date, May 2007

As a nursing student, I feel our curriculum is extremely challenging. I have never been taught by a professor who did not have his/her doctorate. It is fast-paced and an overwhelming amount of information; however, the faculty members make sure to leave their office doors open and are more than happy to answer questions or clarify material.

Alumnus/a, Business, 8/2002-5/2007, May 2007

I need to say that professors at the University of San Francisco are great, they care about what the student truly feels and if he/she is learning. Also they are very easy to reach either by their personal phone or office phone. They also have office hours each week to help students with any questions. Since my second year, I went to my advisor for registration and registered all my classes online with no problems at all. Very easy and quick process, and I got all the classes I needed each semester. The grading systems are different for each professor; however, every professor is very understanding and cares about the students. As long as you did your best in the class, finished all the work they assigned and showed them that you really worked hard in the class, you will get a fair grade. The workload depends on the classes you are taking, but generally, the workload is not much at all.

Alumnus/a, Environment, 8/2003-5/2007, May 2007

The classes are definitely wonderful. The professors show real enthusiasm for the material, which causes the students to give undivided attention to the class.

If you have a junior or senior standing, most popular classes are easy to get. However because the school is such a small school, it's very easy to get any class you want. Most professors show enthusiasm and really care about their students and the importance of learning. The workload gets a little tough when it comes to the science classes.

Current student, 8/2002-Submit Date, January 2006

The academics at the University of San Francisco primarily focus on the nursing program, since it is a nursing school; however, I'm not a nursing student. Our school is very good, considering it's a private school so our campus isn't as huge compared to other campuses. Therefore, the average size of a class ranges from about 10 to 40 students (unless it's a seminar class, which could hold up to 90 or so).

> **The school says:** "Please note that we have three traditional undergraduate schools/colleges, with nursing being the smallest with about 600 students—so the comment that USF primarily focuses on nursing is misleading. The other two schools/colleges are Arts and Sciences with an enrollment of about 2,900 and Business with an enrollment of about 1,200."

The grading varies with each professor. Some professors are more easily approachable than others, and I think if you really know a professor well, the class is easier. The workload varies depending on the subject. The writing classes of course will have more writing assignments. But it could also depend on the professor because they have different teaching styles. Some just like giving tests and no papers and some just like giving papers and no test, and many do both.

Employment Prospects

Alumnus/a, Political Science, 8/2003-5/2007, May 2007

During my four years at USF, the City of San Francisco provided many opportunities for both internships and employment. Once a student reaches senior status, USF provides a lot of feedback for employment and post-college options. It is a supportive environment that encourages a variety of options.

Current student, Nursing, 8/2006-Submit Date, May 2007

Finding a job after college is not a problem; the university provides so many opportunities for students to begin internships. The Career Services Center is very helpful, but it is up to the student to show interest and initiative.

Alumnus/a, Business, 8/2002-5/2007, May 2007

The Career Services Center at the University of San Francisco is very helpful; they are there to help all students with their résumés, interview practices, and every semester they host a career fair day, where almost 100 employers come to USF campus to meet all the students who need an internship or full-time job. The Career Services Center also provides mock interviews where real employers come to campus to practice interviews with students. The Career Services Center web site is also linked with MonsterTrak, which is a national career web site.

Alumnus/a, Environment, 8/2003-5/2007, May 2007

Most employers hire you when they hear that you attended USF, especially those around the city. The Career Services Center at USF is very helpful in finding internships and jobs, as well as helping create a résumé and cover letter.

Current student, Psychology, 1/2005-Submit Date, May 2007

As time goes on, USF is gaining more and more prestige. I feel like as a graduate of USF I am entering the workforce with a leg-up on most other graduates purely because of the school from which I have graduated. I am proud to have gone to USF and I know my diploma means something, and so will my employers.

Current student, 8/2002-Submit Date, January 2006

Based on what I've experienced in the Career Services Center, they have a lot of information for the different majors in our school. They have a bunch of binders, for each major, that are full with job opportunities and internships. They also have a bunch of brochures and career planning handbooks, as well as flyers and other information that are free to students. I think it's useful and helpful. I know that you can also schedule an appointment with a mentor or advisor at the Career Services Center to discuss anything you need or want to know about the career you want to get into. I believe they help guide you in the right direction, or at least give you some options to choose from.

Quality of Life

Alumnus/a, Political Science, 8/2003-5/2007, May 2007

The quality of life is great. Living in San Francisco is one of USF's great aspects. The neighborhood is great, with easy access to downtown, the park, and many neighborhood restaurants and bars. Though the neighborhood is great, the on-campus housing is small and considered over-priced by many students. Though the housing is expensive, USF works hard to promote overall happiness in the cramped spaces. The neighborhood is safe and there is little crime in the Inner Richmond district of San Francisco.

Current student, Liberal Arts, 8/2004-Submit Date, May 2007

On-campus housing is limited, but guaranteed for freshmen and sophomores. Parking is limited, so it's not recommended that students bring cars, although it is allowed. Dining is expensive, but good, and included in room and board. Safety on campus is pretty good; however, USF is located in the center of a big city. One just needs to be aware of their surroundings, and take appropriate precautions when walking at night.

Current student, Nursing, 8/2006-Submit Date, May 2007

The university is more than 150 years old, so the campus is not in the modern condition it should be; however, the library is state-of-the-art, and more and more buildings are being remodeled.

Current student, Business, 8/2006-Submit Date, May 2007

At the University of San Francisco, finding friends and housing is simple and a great experience. My freshman year was great having lived in Hayes Healy (freshman housing hall). The university pairs people by the qualities they share. Although my freshman year is over, I have several memories that I will be able to share throughout my lifetime with friends and family.

Current student, History, 8/2005-Submit Date, May 2007

Personally, living in the dorms was a great experience because it allowed me to meet a lot of people I might not have otherwise. As a freshman, I lived in Hayes-Healy, which is the best freshman dorm on campus. I met a lot of new people and learned about sharing a room with someone. Unfortunately, I had a horrible roommate with whom I did not get along, but the Office of Residence Life made it very easy for me to move to another room. Despite that situation, I became good friends with the people on my floor and even found my roommate for sophomore year across the hall!! Sophomore year I moved into Phelan, an upperclass dorm, and also had a great opportunity to move in with a lot of new, interesting people. The facilities of USF are really nice and clean and the University does a good job of maintaining them with up-to-date equipment and technology. Additionally, the campus is really safe with a great Public Safety department that is run by a former SFPD chief and a number of our officers are actually SFPD!

Current student, Psychology, 1/2005-Submit Date, May 2007

On-campus housing has been wonderful. I have had the opportunity to meet so many different people, and I have learned an incredible amount of patience and decorum that comes from living with others. I would love to live on campus all four years, so I am very upset that as a senior housing was not available to me.

Current student, 8/2002-Submit Date, January 2006

I commute to school from across the Bay, so I never really get the chance to actually experience the on-campus lifestyle; however, I've had friends who did. I've heard good and bad stories. Basically I think the majority of the students at my school feel that they don't get as much as they paid for (our tuition is very high). The food is OK; there's a lot to choose from; however, you can get easily tired of it if you've been there long enough. The good thing about going to school in the City of San Francisco is that you can find anywhere off campus to eat at because there are lots of cuisines in the city. I know that our school has its own crime and safety department called Public Safety. I think it's good because they offer assistance when needed. For example, if it's late at night and you're

Read all of Vault's College Surveys at **www.vault.com/college**—get complete surveys on 100s of colleges and universities, expert advice on applicaton essays and more.

VAULT CAREER LIBRARY   **95**

walking all the way across campus, you could call the Public Safety number to ask for someone to walk with you. I know there's also blue lights around our school with call boxes. And there's also services for off-campus students who may need a ride to the BART (metro) station, but you need to pay for tickets.

Social Life

Alumnus/a, Political Science, 8/2003-5/2007, May 2007

USF offers more to do than students could ever complete. Bars, restaurants, clubs and on-campus activities fill planners and PDAs. The dating scene at USF is interesting, as it is 65 percent female. San Francisco is an amazing city for education!

Current student, Liberal Arts, 8/2004-Submit Date, May 2007

Social life on campus is fabulous considering its location. Bars, restaurants, clubs and events off campus are amazing—it's San Francisco. Yet the dating scene on campus, as well as the availability of clubs, organizations and Greek life is wonderful. You can be involved in as many or as few organizations as you want. USF just wants you to get involved, both on campus, and off campus in the community.

Current student, Business, 8/2006-Submit Date, May 2007

San Francisco is a great location for everything and anything, especially the University of San Francisco, which is in the middle of the city. There are all types of restaurants and activities to do in the city. My favorite place is Sushi Hana on Van Ness; it's the place to eat if you're a sushi lover like myself! There is the Italian district for pasta lovers, Chinatown, Japantown for the Asian palates. You could even go to the bridge any day to enjoy the gorgeous scenery. I would have to say that picking the University of San Francisco for my four years in college is the greatest first step in my life!

Current student, History, 8/2005-Submit Date, May 2007

At USF, the City of San Francisco is at your disposal! Golden Gate Park is down the street as is the beach and a quick 10 minute ride on MUNI will land you in the middle of downtown. However, if going out to some of the state's best bars and restaurants really isn't your thing, then there is plenty you can do on campus. There are over 320 clubs and organizations on campus that focus on all kinds of different activities. And although we do not have a huge Greek system on campus, it is still very important to the students who are members. I am a member of Delta Zeta sorority and have had so many wonderful adventures over the past few years with my sisters. We have gone paintballing, go-kart racing, toured the city, held socials and done a lot of philanthropy, as well. The nice thing about USF social life is that you really can make it into whatever you want it to be. If you want to be a party animal then go ahead but if you just want to hang out with your friends in the dorm and watch movies, then that's fine too!

> The school says: "USF offers over 100 different types of clubs and organizations, including culturally-focused clubs, community service and Greek organizations, professional and honor societies, as well as intramural and club sports."

Current student, 1/2004-Submit Date, November 2005

Buses go around all San Francisco, so transportation is really easy. Lots of restaurants and bars around. Clubs are downtown, which takes 30 minutes to get to by bus, or 20 minutes by car.

Current student, 8/2002-Submit Date, January 2006

Since I live off campus across the Bay, I don't get to experience the social life around school. The school used to have its own bar open to students 21 and over, but recently they took that out. We don't have as many Greek organizations, or at least we don't have the widely-known Greek organizations. Most of the Greek organizations we do have are academic sororities/fraternities, though there are some social ones. Since we live in the diverse city, we have a lot of cultural clubs/organizations. Each semester we have club fairs and involvement fairs and each club/organization advertise and promote their events through the Department of Student Activities.

The School Says

Make your world better—start here

The mission of the University of San Francisco is to educate the minds and hearts of leaders who will change the world. Whether your goal is to be president of a country or a corporation, a lawyer, nurse, teacher, doctor, or scientist, your USF education will set you on the path to success. We are located in one of the great cities of the world, have an outstanding faculty and draw on the centuries old Jesuit tradition of rigorous education of the whole person. USF will provide the knowledge and skills to help you build the vision and character you will need to succeed.

Since our founding in 1855 as San Francisco's first University, USF has graduated men and women who have contributed to the growth and development of the City, our country and the world. We recognize the importance of educating the whole person, and understand the time you spend in the classroom needs to be balanced by social and service activities and opportunities on campus and in the community. By living and studying with students from all socioeconomic, cultural and ethnic backgrounds, and by experiencing the surrounding community, you will take what you learn in class and apply theory to practice in the real world.

USF offers both undergraduate and graduate programs through its six schools and colleges for its 8,500 students. At the core of your USF experience will be our academic programs as you join our 4,600 traditional undergraduates enrolled in one of our 68 majors and concentrations offered through the College of Arts and Sciences and the Schools of Business and Management and Nursing. USF is in the top 10 percent of national universities and 34th for the proportion of classes offered with 20 students or fewer. Our School of Business and Management is in the Top 100 Best Undergraduate Business Programs.

One of the qualities that distinguishes USF from almost all other schools is the diversity of our students. This characteristics offers a unique learning experience, both inside and outside the classroom. You will learn from, and about, other people and cultures in your residence halls, at the Crossroads Café, at the gym and of course, in the classroom. Our dedicated faculty know that the more varied the backgrounds and experiences of those with whom you interact, the richer your education will be. USF students come from all 50 states of the union and over 70 foreign countries. USF is ranked 14th among national universities for the ethnic diversity of its students and for the number of international students who enroll.

University of Southern California

USC Office of Admission
File No. 51158
Los Angeles, CA 90074-1158
Admissions phone: (213) 740-1111
Admissions fax: (213) 821-0200
Admissions e-mail: admitusc@usc.edu
Admissions URL: www.usc.edu/admission/undergraduate/

Admissions

Current student, 8/2004-Submit Date, May 2006

Getting into USC is very selective, especially based on the program to which one applies. When I applied as a freshman, I applied to the architecture school, which was very highly competitive and required a portfolio submission in addition to the application. For the main college, there was no interview, but the essay was very important to the application. To get in, the essay should be focused, both the long and short answers. Recommendation letters are also very important, but they should be from people who really know you, not just anyone. I also advise people to turn in their applications in by the scholarship deadline so they can be considered for merit-based scholarships.

Current student, Business, 8/2004-Submit Date, March 2007

I was a transfer student, and it's easier to get in that way. Either way, it's still selective: I had a 3.5 GPA (still in the lower regions of their acceptance norm from what I hear) and lots of activities on my résumé. I made a contact in the business department and went and talked to him about joining the program if I was accepted, which was the reason I applied to USC anyway. He put me into contact with an admissions director, with whom I was able to speak that day. I'm assuming that this opportunity for face time helped, as that director personally stayed in contact with me and let me know how my application was progressing. USC is all about networking: use that to your advantage.

Current student, 8/2004-Submit Date, May 2006

The best hint for getting in is diversify. Everyone who applies to USC has good grades and test scores. In fact, pretty much anyone who would consider USC or who is applying to that caliber of university has the grades and test scores to get in wherever he/she wants. The thing that it comes down to is exracurriculars and essays. The well-rounded, driven student is whom USC is looking to admit. They are ambitious and adventurous. They have their feet solidly on the ground and they know how to take the reins in their own lives. They have a wide array of interests and a passion for getting results. USC has an optional interview available in its admissions process. As it is optional, it clearly does not weigh in as heavily as the other facets of the application students submit. It's a great way for students to connect with the university and feel they had a personal experience in applying, but grades, test scores, extracurriculars and application essays are more heavily weighted. USC is among the most selective universities in the country and every year it is getting harder and harder to get in. A lot of the time, you'll hear current students or alumni say, "I wouldn't be able to get in today. These kids are all really smart. They have certainly upped the ante."

Current student, Business, 8/2004-Submit Date, December 2006

The admissions process requires a written essay, and an interview is optional. The university seems to be getting increasingly selective as it has climbed the undergraduate rankings. USC is private, so they don't discriminate against people from out of state, as do the UC schools, though it does seem that it is somewhat easier to get in if you are from in state. During the application process, you can call the school and speak to an advisor who will answer any questions you may have. Though these lines can be very busy at times, the advice is usually very helpful and prepares you well for getting in.

Current student, 8/2002-Submit Date, May 2006

Admission to USC has become increasingly selective over the past few years. Like other top schools, freshman admission is a subjective process that takes into consideration grades, test scores, essays and extracurricular involvements. Transfer admission, on the other hand, focuses solely on academics. It's important to have good letters of recommendation from teachers/counselors with substantial information in them. There is a common misconception that letters from alumni will help the process, but the admissions committee doesn't seem to care much about who signs the letter, but what it says instead. Long time commitment to a number of extracurriculars is favored as opposed to stacking your résumé with random clubs in your last year.

Current student, 8/2005-Submit Date, September 2005

I had to write approximately two essays, not including one of journalistic intent for the program to which I was applying. The admissions process is very selective, and only about [25] percent of those who apply are admitted each year. Do not be passive in your application process. If you have a gift, differentiate yourself from others. I would definitely say, be aggressive, contact the school and financial aid offices often, and learn as much about the programs offered to show interest. It also helps to mention every opportunity you had to serve your community and surroundings. I did not have to interview. However, financial aid was very difficult at the beginning. Admissions and financial aid aren't linked per se, but I would recommend settling your aid after you are admitted, as will probably occur anyway.

> **The school says:** "USC recommends applying for financial aid in parallel with the admissions process. Although our admissions process is strictly need-blind, applying for aid early makes the entire process go more smoothly.
>
> "USC administers a robust financial aid program. Undergraduate financial aid includes need-based grants, merit scholarships, low-interest loans, and work-study. USC has a long tradition of meeting 100 percent of the USC-determined financial need for those undergraduate students who satisfy all eligibility requirements and deadlines."

Academics

Current student, Business, 8/2004-Submit Date, March 2007

As with most schools, it can sometimes be a crapshoot. I've had some of the best and worst professors here, but overall I think professor quality is good. Some of the core business classes seemed lame and tedious at the time, but looking back, it is actually fairly necessary to gain knowledge of these different areas. I kept hearing that the business program was pretty easy and that no one studied, but I was definitely challenged, and I studied a lot. The workload, especially group projects with schedule coordination nightmares, can get insane.

Current student, Business, 9/2003-Submit Date, October 2006

For the most part, it was easy to get the classes that I needed before they filled up. In some cases, certain time slots would fill up if you weren't fast enough though. I was in the undergraduate business program, and many of the classes were well over 30 students per class. There are several mega-sections in which the professor gives a lecture and then the class is split up into smaller sections with teacher assistants to discuss the subject matter from the main class. Grading is based on a curve that exists throughout the Marshall School of Business.

Current student, Business, 8/2004-Submit Date, December 2006

The business program at USC is fairly rigorous and competitive. One of the complaints among the students is the curve used in all introductory business classes, which is based around a 2.85 average. While this does reduce any occurrences of grade inflation, it has many disadvantages. Students from other

Read all of Vault's College Surveys at www.vault.com/college–get complete surveys on 100s of colleges and universities, expert advice on applicaton essays and more.

VAULT CAREER LIBRARY   97

universities may find it easier to get higher grades because they don't have such a curve and when it comes time to interview for jobs, they look like they have performed better even though two universities' grading scales are hardly comparable. Because of the curve, some professors squeeze the range of grades, making sure that no one gets too poor of a grade, but at the same time, ensuring that almost no one gets an exceptional grade. The quality of classes is good, especially in the upper-division classes and across the board in the accounting program (a separate school from the business school). The accounting classes are much smaller and have a more intimate nature. After starting the accounting track, you tend to be with the same people in all of your classes, which allows people to get to know each other better. The smaller class sizes also help the relationship between student and teacher and allow for a better teaching environment. Some of the introductory business classes are 300 people in size, which can have a negative impact on the ability of the professor to provide a valuable learning experience.

Classes can be difficult to get into at times, but overall, it is not really a problem. The professors are for the most part very qualified and good at teaching, though there are always going to be exceptions. In one of my upper-level finance classes, my teacher was a former CFO of a notable, large public corporation. His real world experience was very valuable in the classroom.

Current student, 8/2002-Submit Date, May 2006

Classes at USC have become increasingly competitive. Students are guaranteed to get the classes they need to graduate in four years, though you may have to settle for an 8 a.m. class your first semester. The large majority of classes are 50 students or less, and honors programs are available if you'd like to participate in even smaller courses. Professors are required to teach undergrad courses, and most of them are into it, and can be a great resource for either career leads or grad school recommendation letters. The academic culture on campus is high and continues to rise.

> **The school says:** "Students at USC have little problem getting the courses they need, when they need them. However, we are not able to guarantee that this is always the case."

Current student, 8/2004-Submit Date, May 2006

Every class I've ever needed has been available to me. Scheduling has always gone smoothly. While I do have large lectures, there is still plenty of time to meet one-on-one with the professors as they have office hours. I've always been able to get additional help if I need it. I've never felt that I've been graded unfairly and grades usually always reflect the amount of time and effort put into the assignment. The workload is definitely enough, although sometimes general education classes are harder and more demanding than I feel they should be.

Current student, 8/2004-Submit Date, May 2006

One of the best opportunities of going to the University of Southern California is that all core undergraduate classes are taught by tenured, full-time faculty. No full-time tenured faculty is exempt from teaching undergraduates. Critics of this practice usually ask university leaders, "why would you spend the money to do this?" We in turn reply, "why not?" The cross-disciplinary approach at USC is one of its finest attributes. The university prepares you with breadth and depth and also prepares you for multiple careers, not just one. You can major and minor in whatever you'd like and can take very interesting classes in any program that is offered to all undergraduates, not just students in that program. The classes are challenging yet fun and you learn a lot from every class, which makes you a better-informed and educated citizen, ready to leave the university and give back to the world due to everything with which the university has provided you.

 Employment Prospects

Current student, Business, 8/2004-Submit Date, March 2007

USC's reputation precedes it. This is one of the best schools around for its pre- and post-graduation networking opportunities. The Trojan Network has helped me to gain job interviews, interviews for class projects, internships and business clients. On-campus recruiting is very helpful, and many top companies from all over are represented at the job fairs and through the career center job site. USC is very involved in making sure its business graduates find placement.

Current student, 9/2003-Submit Date, October 2006

There is an on-campus career center that offers advice and sponsors workshops and information sessions for students. There is also a bi-annual career fair, in which employers can come to the campus to find student job seekers and set up interviews. USC is a big name in Southern California and often holds quite a bit of weight with local employers.

Current student, Business, 8/2004-Submit Date, December 2006

I have been very impressed with the employment opportunities after attending USC. The biggest advantage for getting a job is having employers that recruit on campus. Sometimes employers only consider students from their core schools, which are the schools where they recruit. USC has seen more and more high profile, prestigious companies coming to campus to recruit. USC has seen more and more companies from some of the most popular business jobs including accounting, consulting and investment banking. All of the accounting firms heavily recruit at USC, and USC has a premier accounting program. Bain and BCG have started to consider and hire students from USC, while McKinsey does not. Other smaller consulting firms also recruit on campus. Almost every investment bank has recently recruited students from USC. All of the top-tier bulge bracket banks consistently hire students, as do middle market firms and boutiques. However, these firms primarily recruit for the west coast and usually only interns who are given full-time offers at banks and have the option to go to New York. Among the smaller firms, it is easier to get to New York.

Current student, 8/2004-Submit Date, May 2006

It's called the Trojan Family, and from what I hear, there is no other alumni network across the country that can compete with the power and influence of the one we have at USC. Even though there are only about 250,000 graduates out there, they occupy some of the most powerful and influential positions in the country. They operate in law, medicine, theater, film, music, politics, communications, journalism and sports. Being on campus for a football game is testament enough to how strong the alumni base at our school is. Thousands of people tailgate on campus on home football Saturdays and thousands more sell out the Coliseum to see our team play. Even at 80 years old, they are still making the trek down to campus to support their alma mater. With that kind of enthusiasm remaining in the hearts for their college sports team, their willingness to help and support current Trojans with any simple favor is astounding. Whether it is to open the door for an interview with a prospective employer or to hire a fellow Trojan for the summer, they are open and willing to lend a hand in any capacity that they can.

An undergraduate I know has just landed a full-time job as an account executive for KTLA. Another one of my friends, who has not graduated yet, is currently working on the set of two major network television shows as an integral part of the production process. Every week I hear about opportunities to network with major corporations and former Trojans through the Marshall School of Business career source e-mail postings. Every semester there is the Career Fair on campus where over 160 corporations come looking for employees and interns and provide an invaluable networking opportunity to students. As I tell people who ask me about the post-graduate employment opportunities, you can't walk around campus without tripping over a networking opportunity any given day on campus. USC is rife with employment opportunities and that, if there was a one, is our golden asset.

 Quality of Life

Current student, 9/2003-Submit Date, October 2006

Quality of life is very good with a variety of food options, well-run housing facilities, and the school's own police force. The neighborhood is known for being in a rougher part of the city, but the school manages to keep the area around the school very safe and comfortable for the students. Beyond the school, the City of Los Angeles has unlimited opportunities for students to branch out and explore the city and everything it has to offer. USC football is a major event, largely due to their recent success and provides a way for students to experience the spirit of the school.

Current student, Business, 8/2004-Submit Date, December 2006

The campus is beautiful and has great facilities and housing. I have nothing negative to say about the quality of life at USC except for the surrounding neighborhoods and crime. USC is located in a high-crime area, but the university has a strong Department of Public Safety and works very hard to make students safe.

Current student, 8/2004-Submit Date, May 2006

90 percent of freshmen live on campus and a large number of students live directly north of the campus in university-owned housing. The university wants students to get to know each other, and will actually have themed floors at the dorms, such as having students in the same major all living on the same floor or students from the same part of the world, all living on the same floor. Efforts will be made ensure that students are paired with roommates who have similar interests and likes, and the resident advisors are very helpful in ensuring that students are able to find their way around the university. They will even take their students out on the town and show them the many fun activities there are to participate in in the greater Los Angeles area.

> The school says: "Closer to 95 percent of freshmen live on campus."

Current student, Business, 8/2004-Submit Date, March 2007

Off-campus housing is ridiculously expensive. I pay close to $1,000 for a studio. Property management companies know they can get away with these exorbitant prices because there is a housing shortage, and students can't move that far away without problems (questionable neighborhoods on one side and expensive downtown housing on the other side). Food on campus is pretty good; they've got lots of options. Food in the surrounding area is horrible. Besides every fast food restaurant one can think of, I think the only sit-down options are a Denny's, Sizzler and a food court.

Current student, 8/2001-Submit Date, November 2003

Because USC has such a small campus (it is bounded by four major Los Angeles streets), the housing situation can be somewhat of a problem for many people. It definitely seems as though the lack of available student housing for all undergraduates significantly hinders the school's ability to offer its students a true, four-year residential college experience. However, a large number of students decide to live in off-campus housing within one or two blocks of campus. Though rent ranges, a one-bedroom apartment can run for anything from $450 per month to $1,000 per month, depending on the location and amenities. (Keep in mind that parking is a much coveted commodity in the downtown Los Angeles area, and some apartment complexes do not offer it.) USC also has a serious parking problem, but it offers multiple on campus parking structures and has off campus parking for those who live in off campus, university-owned housing. In general, parking can be very problematic, but it should never be enough of an issue to seriously dissuade you from bringing a car to campus. USC also allows freshmen to bring cars to school.

> The school says: "The vast majority of undergraduates live within walking distance of campus, in both USC-owned and privately-owned facilities. With such a high percentage of students living on campus and in the neighborhood, the college experience here can most definitely be described as residential. USC is by no means a commuter school."

 ## Social Life

Current student, 9/2003-Submit Date, October 2006

There are many social opportunities for students to engage in, including a very robust Greek system and numerous clubs and social organizations. Housing options offered by the school are often run as communities where students get to know each other and participate in group events. In the business school, many classes involve group projects in which students are able to work together and form relationships that often extend outside the classroom.

Current student, Business, 8/2004-Submit Date, December 2006

The social life at USC is very strong. The Greek system is very popular and is responsible for a lot of social events. The bar scene is mediocre at best unless you want to go downtown or to other hotspots around Los Angeles. However, I

haven't heard many USC students ever complain about the social life. If anything, students find it too easy to have a good time. And USC is in Los Angeles. If you are willing to drive, you can find any kind of social venue that you want.

Current student, 8/2004-Submit Date, May 2006

The Greek system is very strong. About 20 percent of the undergraduate student body is a member of a Greek organization. The social life is fantastic; there's always something to do. Homecoming is probably the most amazing weekend of all because there are so many things going on in addition to the big game. Football season, in general, is incredible. We're a tight community, which makes the social aspect of the university very strong.

Current student, 8/2004-Submit Date, May 2006

USC recruits students who are leaders and want to pursue leadership positions while they are at the university. There are hundreds of clubs and organizations, and the Greek system is the largest, percentage-wise, west of the Mississippi River. There is a plethora of things to do in Los Angeles, and there are always concerts, speakers, charity events, club events and sporting events right on campus. Many of the dorms are situated around the main quad of the campus, a very social area where students congregate and enjoy themselves in the Southern California sun. The beach is not far away, and downtown is only approximately 10 minutes north. The location is perfect to receive a world-class education while enjoying the college experience, one that you will always cherish and never forget.

Current student, 8/2004-Submit Date, May 2006

USC has lots of choices when it comes to a social life. There are many scenes in which a student can choose to partake during his/her time here. There is a busy and active Greek system, as well as other party circuits within different streets and student groups. This gives students many choices regarding with whom they wish to socialize, in and around campus. Additionally, all of L.A. is available for entertainment options. Theme parks, restaurants, clubs, and major events are all in driving range, including skiing and the beach. Many students will dine at restaurants and bars all around the L.A. area but will frequent Hollywood clubs the most. There is a bar on campus and a club across the street that allow for students to socialize within the area on most nights.

 ## The School Says

What does it take to be an educated person in the 21st Century? And where do you get that kind of education? An undergraduate education at USC will prepare you for what lies ahead. The 21st Century will be filled with challenges. Will you be ready?

USC is committed to excellence in undergraduate education. Top-ranked programs in virtually every field offer an experience that combines breadth with depth. In our global environment a USC education will equip you to flourish in the dynamic environment you will encounter.

Student life at USC is exciting and filled with choices. USC is a "college with a conscience" (Princeton Review, 2005). Each semester, thousands of students and hundreds of faculty volunteer and do research in our surrounding communities. There are over 600 student organizations at USC, along with Division I athletics and intramural sports. Theatre and music performances, movie screenings and speakers' series fill each semester.

USC is located in one of the world's greatest and most diverse cities. Los Angeles is a focal point for art and culture, and home to industries from entertainment to electronics, manufacturing to medicine. Los Angeles is a fascinating urban laboratory offering USC students unmatched social and cultural experiences, as well as internships and other learning experiences. Los Angeles' diversity is mirrored in our student body: USC enrolls more African American undergraduates than any other research university, public or private, in the entire western United States; USC enrolls more Latino undergraduates than all but one other

Read all of Vault's College Surveys at **www.vault.com/college**—get complete surveys on 100s of colleges and universities, expert advice on applicaton essays and more.

VAULT CAREER LIBRARY   99

private research university in the country; USC enrolls more Asian undergraduates than any private research university in the entire country; and, USC enrolls more international students than any other college or university in the United States.

The Trojan Family includes alumni, students and parents, faculty and staff. It is a community of shared values: free inquiry; initiative and experimentation; caring and respect; commitment to service; respect for diversity; ethical conduct. With alumni networks in every corner of the world the Trojan Family is truly lifelong and worldwide.

USC received approximately 34,000 freshman applications for fall 2006. 25 percent of these applicants were accepted. USC's fall 2006 incoming freshman class was comprised of 2,763 students from 45 states and 57 countries. Their average un-weighted high school GPA was 3.7 and the middle 50 percent of the class had SAT scores between 1920 and 2180. 51 percent of our freshmen came from California. 53 percent were students of color and 21 percent were students who have been historically under-represented in higher education (African American, Latino, Native American or Pacific Islander).

Colorado College

Admission Office
Cutler Hall
14 East Cache La Poudre Street
Colorado Springs, CO 80903
Admissions phone: (800) 542-7214 or (719) 389-6344
Admissions fax: (719)389-6816
Admissions e-mail: Admission@ColoradoCollege.edu
Admissions URL: www.coloradocollege.edu/admission/

Note: *The school has chosen not to comment on the student surveys submitted.*

 Admissions

Alumnus/a, 9/1999-9/2003, February 2006

Admissions is tough, but I would encourage people to apply, even if the numbers aren't too encouraging. This is especially true if you come from a good high school and have good recommendations.

Alumnus/a, 9/1997-5/2001, February 2004

The Colorado College admissions process is comprehensive. The selection process involves reviewing academic preparedness, recommendations, test scores and civic involvement outside of the classroom. Because of the unique nature of Colorado College's Block Plan, where classes are taught in blocks of three and a half weeks, admissions counselors look for students who will not only succeed academically, but contribute to the college community.

There is a strong emphasis on writing at Colorado College. I strongly encourage prospective students to take the most rigorous writing courses available before applying. The selection process is competitive.

Alumnus/a, 8/2000-5/2004, July 2005

The school is fairly selective and getting more selective as time goes on. SAT or ACT scores are required and SAT Subject Tests are really moot. I suggest only submitting your best score (either SAT or ACT) as both are not required. An interview is not required.

The two most important things on your application are your essay and your résumé. The essay and résumé need to say something about you, proving that you have some singular, amazing and special thing that separates you from the rest of the 4.0 high school geeks, while also showing that you are human. Everyone who goes to CC scores above 1200 on the SAT, was class representative and most played sports, so mention those but don't linger. If you were a debater, explain how that shaped your life. If you were an actor (which is another common denominator), explain how/what you have done has changed you in some way. People who get in—and are "shining examples of the new classes"—are people who did cell research at a cancer institute, who pioneered high school queer-straight alliances, who rescued a missing child, who campaigned for environmental reconsideration at their local landfills (which, come to think of it, is probably on a lot of résumés, too).

Basically, your essay, which ultimately is slightly more important than your résumé, needs to show that you are an individual—CC is a school of individuals.

 **Academics**

Alumnus/a, 9/1999-9/2003, February 2006

The Block Plan can be intense, but you don't have to worry about finals week like at other schools. I liked the system and had some excellent professors, as well as a few who could have been better. Overall, I give the academics good marks. Having dinner at your professor's house is not a rare experience, and a few professors can even be talked into a game of flip cup.

The advantage of taking one class at a time is that you can really focus on the material and get involved. Most non-lab classes meet from 9 a.m. to 12 p.m. with a 10-minute break in between. On occasion, classes will meet again in the afternoon, but normally this time is spent reading or enjoying the outdoors (with the reading done at night).

Some professors give challenging workloads, but I have found that those classes generally turn out to be better in the end. Normally homework ranges from two to four hours of reading/writing a night with the occasional heavier load for papers. Really, you tend to get out of it what you put into it.

Alumnus/a, 9/1997-5/2001, February 2004

Academics at Colorado College are unique, different and cutting-edge. Courses are taught for three and a half weeks; [this system is] also known as the Block Plan. There are a total of eight blocks throughout the academic year and a half-block offered during winter break. Students are provided the opportunity to study one course at a time rather than shuffling three or four courses like most traditional semester or trimester systems. The block plan allows for intensive seminar discussion, field work and traveling abroad. Students enjoy Block breaks, a five-day break at the end of each block. Colorado College offers a variety of classes taught by professors who are genuinely interested in the quality of education it delivers to their students.

Professors are supportive of student interests. Most classes are open to all students and the availability is often determined by popularity. Popular classes tend to have more students enrolled than others. Grading is based on academic performance. Professors hold a very high standard for academic success, so grading can tend to me hard but reflects the work invested in completing the task.

The workload varies from course to course. Science-based courses tend to have a significant workload due to lab requirements and field trips. Other courses, like Southwest Studies or European Literature, will have significant emphasis on reading, writing and class discussion.

Alumnus/a, 8/2000-5/2004, July 2005

The school, like any, is what you make of it. While typically, it is impossible to skate through CC without learning a good amount, it is definitely possible to feel like a bloated intellectual sponge if you apply yourself correctly. The amazing thing is that anyone can take any class that they want (as long as the pre-reqs are fulfilled), and professors readily push students to maximize their education. The hallmark of CC is the block plan—which is amazing—where students only study one class at a time for three and a half weeks. This allows students to focus on one class and one class only, and provides certain opportunities afforded no where else.

Geology students can spend a month in the Grand Canyon studying water erosion. Astronomy students can go to the Baca (the other campus in the San Luis Valley), where they can see the Milky Way with their naked eyes. Theatre students can participate in a Drama Away and spend a month in London or Greece studying/seeing professional theatre. As a Drama student myself, I completed a Production Practicum, which put me in New York working on a professional show, getting school credit and getting paid at the same time (all while living in Greenwich Village free of charge). Even some math students get to go to Chicago for a block or two. The list goes on and on.

Additionally, due to the nature of the scheduling, top research and professionals act as guest lecturers and teachers because instead of taking a whole semester of time to come to a school like at a more traditional school, they can just spend a month or so at CC. Recent favorites have been Gretchen Cryer, Toni Morrison, Correta Scott King, Eric Schlosser—this list too, goes on and on. The classes, in short, are great. And even if you hate a course, suffering through three and a half weeks is a lot easier than a whole semester.

Read all of Vault's College Surveys at **www.vault.com/college**–get complete surveys on 100s of colleges and universities, expert advice on applicaton essays and more.

VAULT CAREER LIBRARY **101**

Another unique facet comes to registration. Students are given 40 points a semester to bid on classes. That means that if in one semester, you want to take Astronomy, Calculus III, Biochemistry II and Environmental Economics, then you might bid 20 points on Astronomy (a pretty popular class with no pre-reqs), 10 points on Enviro Econ (a moderately popular class with no pre-reqs) and five on the other two (which both have a few pre-reqs and are typically geared toward people within a certain major).

Professors are great. Most are published and most are significantly recognized in their field. About a third of the professors work in a professional capacity as well (my advisor, for example, is a professional Broadway director). Workload can be intense if not at times ridiculous. My first class ever, I had to read a book each night and memorize approximately 1,000 art slides. Languages are very tough, as it is especially difficult to learn a language in one to two months—they are, however, taught usually in an immersion style. Lab classes are also difficult, as you have a three-hour lecture every morning followed by a three- to five-hour lab, topped off with massive readings in the evening.

The Environmental Sciences program is probably one of the best in the country.

Employment Prospects

Alumnus/a, 9/1999-9/2003, February 2006
CC is a strong school with good alumni contacts, but it is small. The Career Center staff there, however, is very friendly and approachable.

Alumnus/a, 9/1997-5/2001, February 2004
Colorado College alumni, in my opinion, are well rounded and extremely resourceful when it comes time for careers. The Career Center at CC offers seminars, trainings and discussions on the best approach to getting a job and provides skills on how to interview and write a résumé. The Career Center also provides updated information on internships and facilitates campus recruiting.

Alumnus/a, 8/2000-5/2004, July 2005
Again, this is what you make of it. I know plenty of people who did nothing during school to get a job and are working at low-end jobs, but an equal amount of people who took advantage of career services or job fairs have great starting jobs in everything from foundation work to consulting.

A lot of people get jobs in the political, financial or education fields. So, probably a third have low-paying jobs, a third have great entry-level positions and another third go on to graduate school (the route that I took). In the end, it is all what you do while you are at CC.

Quality of Life

Alumnus/a, 9/1999-9/2003, February 2006
CC offers both excellent housing and some rather poor housing. My first year, I lived in a freshman dorm and enjoyed it a lot, but could never live in it again. I did choose to live on campus all four years, spending two of them in on-campus apartments, which I quite liked. The campus is attractive and offers exceptional views of Pikes Peak. Garden of the Gods, a fantastic geological wonder, is also less than a five-minute drive away and Cheyane Canyon makes for a good afternoon outdoor destination.

Though CC is in Colorado Springs, technically a city, C. Springs does not resemble an East Coast city. It really feels much more like a large town that sprawls out in every direction but west, where the mountains block it. To walk from CC to downtown takes between five and 15 minutes, and I hear a new public shuttle service is starting up for those who prefer not to exert themselves. Downtown, you can find around 10 bars, some restaurants and some bookstores. Though the bars are close, most CC students tend to party on campus and only frequent them on occasion.

Alumnus/a, 9/1997-5/2001, February 2004
Colorado College is a safe place to learn. Set at the foothills of the foothills of the front range of Colorado's Rocky Mountains, CC's location is pristine. On-campus housing is available to all students. Upperclassmen are encouraged to consider on-campus housing. However, off-campus housing is also available. The college campus is beautiful with facilities for indoor and outdoor recreation activities. Dining services at CC is provided by Marriott. The food selection is better than most colleges' and caters to all types of diets.

Alumnus/a, 8/2000-5/2004, July 2005
Student housing is both a blessing and a burden at the same time. Because CC is a residential college, it requires students to live on campus for three years (with certain, case-by-case exceptions). There are some who opt to live on campus all four years. While the first two years may seem criminal—dorms are dorms, after all—the third year makes the wait worth it.

CC recently constructed amazing apartment-style dorms. While there are many variations (from solo studios, to one ridiculous hexa-plex), the typical apartment features four single rooms, a shared kitchen and bathroom and a two-story, lofted living room with fantastic views of the mountains and Washburn field (where they play soccer).

Housing, like class registration is also very democratic. People are assigned random lottery numbers, grouped according to the amount of credit/time spent in dorms that they have accrued (for example, sophomores' numbers are worse than juniors').

Dining is fair. There are many options, and I cannot stress enough that after a while, students definitely complain, but compared to most other schools, our dining options are way above normal (there are so many organic, vegan and other alternative options, for example) and the dining plans are pretty flexible.

The neighborhood is just north (within walking distance) of downtown Colorado Springs, which is small enough to feel safe, yet almost big enough to get away in. The neighborhood is very safe, and if you feel like you need it, there are many options to choose in assisting one's need for safety, from student to campus security escorts. There is also a downtown shuttle (run in cooperation between CC and the BBB) that runs from CC to the far end of downtown and back again, so people do not have to walk late at night.

Facilities are topnotch. They have just completed a new science building, renovated the major academic building that houses the social sciences and are breaking ground on a ground-breaking performing arts center.

Social Life

Alumnus/a, 9/1999-9/2003, February 2006
There are lots of great outdoor opportunities. I went backpacking on most Block breaks and some weekends. Weekend ski trips are common, but it helps to have a car. Without one, exploring CO and UT becomes much harder. C. Springs is a fun but strange and conservative city, while the college is very liberal. Drinking is a favorite pastime, but frequent lectures, intramural sports, art classes and community service activities offer a strong alternative.

Alumnus/a, 9/1997-5/2001, February 2004
The social life at Colorado College is often governed by official parties throughout the year, hosted by the three fraternities and four sororities. My favorite parties include DU Sucks and Hollywood, sponsored by the Kappa Sigma Fraternity. I also enjoy the annual Drag Ball sponsored by Empowered Queers United for Absolute Liberation. Other organizations host a number of parties, as well.

The Greek scene at CC is low-key. Although they sponsor some of the most favorite parties, it represents about 15 percent of the student population with three fraternities and four sororities. Other events include dance, theater, music concerts and lectures. In my opinion, the dating scene is low-key. Colorado College is five city blocks from downtown Colorado Springs. Bars, shops and coffee houses line Tejon Street in downtown Colorado Springs.

Alumnus/a, 8/2000-5/2004, July 2005
Warning: If you don't want a healthy social life, CC may not be the place for you. During the week, everyone devotes major time to academics, but once the weekend sets in, there is pretty much non-stop partying Friday to Sunday. Most parties are set at off-campus houses. That means (typically) seniors or frat hous-

es throw parties, which are either open or invite-only (some are invite or seniors only until midnight, like the senior parties I'll discuss in a moment). However, a decent number of people head downtown to bars (two favorites are Old Chicago and Tony's).

Once you are a senior, there is this thing called the senior calendar. First and eighth Block (the first and last month) of senior year, the seniors produce the senior calendar in which every single senior house throws a theme party on every night of the block. Themes range from the bland "Pimps and Hos" (keep in mind, there are at least 10 "Pimps and Hos" parties during the year, come on Kappa Sig, get an original idea), to the awesome "Senior Prom 1985."

Wooglins is a seasoned favorite restaurant of CC students and is located across the street from the humanities building. Division I Hockey is huge at CC, so is DI Women's Soccer. The debate team is one of the best in the country. There really isn't a dating scene. The campus is constantly sponsoring major events. The Greek system isn't huge, but is definitely felt on campus.

All in all, students at CC are the Harvard-type without the Harvard-type competitive, boring sobriety.

Colorado School of Mines

Admissions Office
1600 Maple Street
Golden, CO 80401
Admissions phone: (800) 446-9488
Admissions e-mail: admit@mines.edu
Admissions URL: www.mines.edu/admiss/ugrad/

Note: The school has chosen not to review the student surveys submitted.

 ## Admissions

Alumnus/a, 8/2000-5/2005, February 2006

Admission to Mines is a demanding endeavor. The number one criterion is your curriculum at your previous school. If you took college prep courses in high school and did very well in them, they will help you with a spot at the Colorado School of Mines. Great Standardized Test scores on the SAT or ACT will also greatly improve your chances. Less emphasis is placed on occasional interviews and essays, as well as extracurricular activities.

Current student, 8/2002-Submit Date, February 2006

CSM is a hard school to get into. If you are in the top 20 percent of your class you will have a good chance. They are more concerned with your math and science ACT scores over reading and English. You can get an application online and there are no personal interviews or essays.

Current student, 8/2003-Submit Date, January 2005

Colorado School of Mines is a very selective school, but if you do well in high school and score well on the ACT or SAT, they will seek you out and give you incentive to go to the school. For instance, they send out what's called the Golden Scholar Application, which waives the admissions fee and the need for an admissions essay to those students who would be especially valuable at their school. They will often focus the most on your math and science scores on the standardized tests, much more so than your English or reading scores and your high school GPA because it is almost strictly an engineering school, so naturally these are the fields in which they're most interested.

Alumnus/a, 8/1999-12/2003, September 2004

Admissions at the Colorado School of Mines is not the same as it used to be. I remember when people would think it was a very selective school and you were oh-so-lucky to get accepted. However, after being there for my long four and a half year tenure, I realized that things had changed. More and more people were accepted who, in my opinion, had no business being at Mines in the first place. It works out in the end, because those who aren't keen on being there will drop out within the first year, most likely. Keeping this in mind, I also want to make the point that the quality of the school has not declined one bit. Colorado School of Mines will inevitably turn you into "a helluva engineer!"

Alumnus/a, 8/1998-5/2004, August 2004

Admission is relatively stringent, based on high school GPA and SAT/ACT scores. Typical ranges are 3.5 and above for high school GPA, and ACT scores above 29, SAT above 1350. Math and science skills are definitely favored over English and humanities. One advantage noticed by a lot of potential students is the absence of an essay on the application.

Also of note is the lack of required interview; however it is generally a good idea to set up an interview and discuss any weak spots in your application with the entrance counselor so that those can be addressed. This is also a good time to take a campus tour and see what the school is really about.

Current student, 5/2003-Submit Date, July 2004

To get into this school you should do well on your math and science scores of your ACT and SAT tests. You should also have above a 3.5 GPA. Lastly, apply early into your senior year of high school. As long as you show an aptitude for math and science and apply early you are a dead lock to getting in.

 ## Academics

Current student, 8/2003-Submit Date, February 2006

The strong academics of Mines is what most attracted me about the school. Our largest lecture on campus holds only 200 students (as opposed to 500 to 600 at other institutions) and most classes have only 20 people. I have never had any trouble getting into the classes I've wanted, and usually the professors will work with you if you have any difficulty. The accessibility of professors also makes the tough curriculum at Mines much more bearable. All classes are taught by professors, and professors always hold office hours every week if you need additional help. The workload at Mines is very heavy, but you're going to college, it's not supposed to be an easy ride. The community between students, professors, and local community makes it not only bearable, but incredibly enjoyable.

Alumnus/a, 8/2000-5/2005, February 2006

As I went through the programs offered at Mines, the focus was always on academics. There were many outside opportunities to get a well-rounded college experience, but your academic work would likely suffer if you spent too much time with these. The work you do at Mines is very difficult, but it is rewarding if you complete it. Working with peers is a common and often smart choice when doing challenging homework and studying at Mines (especially for tests). The classes were all well grounded to a principle of science that helped you develop and train your thought process as an engineer. As far as getting popular classes, although Mines is a relatively small school, you must be very punctual and register early to have a definitive shot at being in some of the more sought-after courses.

Current student, 9/2004-Submit Date, February 2006

Intense engineering focused academic nature. This school will make it very easy to be a successful engineer in any field. Very efficient and successful learning

Read all of Vault's College Surveys at **www.vault.com/college**—get complete surveys on 100s of colleges and universities, expert advice on applicaton essays and more.

VAULT CAREER LIBRARY   103

methods are used. These include a question and answer-based lecture where each student has a remote assigned to them and they answer questions in class. These are not graded. So a question is presented and you are given a certain amount of time to work on it with people seated near you. Then the results from the class are projected for everyone to see. The professor then can give different explanations as to why the answer is correct and clear up any misinterpretations immediately instead of waiting to find out on a quiz or test. Popular classes seem to be somewhat easy to get into. Grading is fair and debatable. If you show that you put forth a large amount of effort professors will usually be generous in grading giving you that extra 1 or 2 percent to get a letter grade higher. +/- grading is not something you have to worry about here. So if you get all A's, it's a 4.0 no matter what. Workload is constant but definitely manageable. I play lacrosse and put about four hours a day into that and still do fine.

Current student, 8/2002-Submit Date, February 2006

This school is very strong academically. It is very challenging but very rewarding when you graduate. I am currently studying general engineering with a mechanical specialty. The engineering department is very well organized. I have always gotten into every class I wanted. One complaint is the electives per specialty, but that's due to the nature of the degree. I think for the most part the grading is fair. Sometimes the professors can be a challenge to understand because they are so smart but have little teaching skills. The workload is very heavy at this school, but it gets easier as time goes by because you learn good time management. I was also a student-athlete which made the workload even heavier, and I found it doable.

Current student, 8/2003-Submit Date, January 2005

The academic standard at Colorado School of Mines is notoriously high and challenging to even the brightest of students. All teachers are well qualified and are nearly always available for help in and out of class. The student-to-faculty ratio is relatively low (13:1) which makes it easy to gain a personal relationship with the faculty members and more easily succeed in class. The most popular classes are the freshman classes, which are required for all majors, and if you don't take them your freshman year, it can be difficult to get into them as a sophomore or later. Grading is at times overly strict, but it varies widely, depending on the professor and course. The workload is usually fairly heavy, but good habits such as note-taking and paying attention in class help greatly to cut down on extraneous study time.

Current student, 5/2003-Submit Date, July 2004

The classes at this school are very informative and interesting. It is hard to get a desired class early in your career but you will get them in your junior and senior years when it counts. The professors are fun and care about your learning. The degrees at this school are ABET accredited. If you apply yourself to the classes and follow the professors' instructions, you will do fine.

Most exams are given at night so that class time is not taken up. There is also the academic excellence workshops that meet once a week for most freshman and sophomore classes. These workshops meet at night and some upperclassmen who did well in these classes and have high GPAs will work with you on professor-selected examples. They say that people who take these workshops get a letter grade higher than students who don't. Also, there are very few English classes offered because this is a science school. However, there are a lot of lab reports, and they will critique your English and writing skills, so beware.

The class sizes are small in your upper-level classes. When you are first starting out, you will be in classes of about 150 students with a 20-person recitation period. When you get into higher-level classes, there are only 20 to 30 students. Also keep in mind that there are very few days off. We are in school on Labor Day and the Wednesday before Thanksgiving. Some professors are nice about it and will call class off and some won't. Be prepared for that.

 ## Employment Prospects

Current student, 8/2003-Submit Date, February 2006

I have not talked to anyone who has had any difficulty in finding employment. Between two huge career fairs, connections through professional organizations and an incredibly active Career Center (with great online services) Mines' students have incredible resources at their fingertips. Most students also get intern-

ships (very well paid!) over the summer. Internships not only let students get a chance to participate, hands-on, in industry, but also learn what they like and do not like for the future.

Current student, 9/2004-Submit Date, February 2006

We have a very helpful Career Center open to all students. They helped me put together a very powerful résumé. We have job fairs where hundreds of companies show up and give students large amounts of information about companies. Many of my friends have received internships from these fairs. Two of my older friends didn't even have to look for a job. They were sought after by many companies and had their pick. They got to choose where they wanted to work and how much they wanted to make. It seems getting a job is usually not a problem for anyone who attends this school.

Current student, 8/2002-Submit Date, February 2006

Mines is very prestigious in the eyes of most companies. I have personally gotten several opportunities based the education I gained from Mines. The placement rate is very high. I haven't known many students who found it difficult to find a job. The Career Center on campus does a good job helping students find jobs as well as internships. The alumni network is always helpful in industry. Most graduates from Mines can do just about anything they want because they have proven they can be taught. Most graduates go to engineering firms, but some also go on to grad school, law school or even medical school.

Current student, 8/2003-Submit Date, January 2005

Mines has an excellent reputation with employers, and consequently, has an extremely high percentage of students who have already accepted jobs before they even graduate. For instance, it is widely thought that a C- average at Mines would be considered an A- average at most other, not-as-challenging schools, and therefore employers tend to snatch up all Mines graduates, not just those at the top of their class. Also, internships are widely accessible, and employers are constantly on campus generating more interest among students for their particular company. The alumni network is definitely present at Mines, but not really involved in the job placement of graduating students. Most engineering students obtain jobs with companies such as Lockheed Martin, Boeing, Hewlett Packard, and numerous other IT and engineering companies. Starting salary usually ranges around $45,000 per year for engineering students.

Alumnus/a, 8/1999-12/2003, September 2004

A degree at the Colorado School of Mines is exceptional in several different areas. Engineering, of course, is the most popular major and the degree is highly respected. While in school, even during the drop in the economy, Mines students have better chances of getting hired than most. The salaries given are usually much higher than average also, which is good.

Every semester an event is held called career day. Many companies are taking résumés and talking with students to get an idea of who they might hire for internships, co-ops and even full-time positions. While this is mainly being done online now, career day is still held each semester so students can meet people from the companies to which they have applied.

 ## Quality of Life

Current student, 8/2003-Submit Date, February 2006

The campus is absolutely beautiful at Mines. It is small enough that you can get from one side to the other in 10 minutes, but considering the number of students, it is huge. Another great thing about the Mines campus is how close it is to everything—the mountains, downtown Denver, and Boulder are all within a 30-minute drive. As for safety, I have never felt any danger on or around the Mines campus—it is an incredibly safe community. Only freshmen live on campus (the residence halls are normal and nice—right on campus so no driving required) and upperclassmen have no problem finding reasonable housing in the surrounding neighborhoods or in the school-owned apartment complex—Mines Park. This is where I live and love it—everything is clean and always works, you can access your files on campus, and high-speed Internet and cable are included. There is also a frisbee golf course! Like the residence halls, the slate cafe (the main cafeteria) is only used by freshmen. It recently got a major facelift and looks wonderful (beautiful, if you can describe a cafeteria like that).

As for the food, I never had any trouble finding something I liked—there are always lots of options.

Current student, 9/2004-Submit Date, February 2006

Housing is adequate and plentiful. Fair prices are offered that compare well to nearby alternatives. Our campus is growing constantly with students' opinions kept in mind. We are receiving a new rec center with a climbing wall next year. There is always something good to eat, it might not be in the cafeteria, but we have two other dining areas where you can get fresh cooked meals that are included in your meal plan. As far as safety is concerned, we have a fairly small campus which is under constant protection from our school-hired police.

Current student, 8/2002-Submit Date, February 2006

The campus is a bit older in style but has very up-to-date technology. They have been improving housing the last couple of years, as well as learning and social facilities. The dining on campus has also improved a lot over the last couple of years, offering a wider variety of food. The area is very safe in Golden. The campus police do a very good job but the neighborhood make their job very easier. Golden is an older, upper-class town and there is very little crime.

Current student, 9/2001-Submit Date, February 2006

The school does an excellent job at providing housing to international students and freshmen. If you choose not to live on campus, there is always housing located around Golden. The facilities are underway to becoming somewhat competitive with other institutions. Unfortunately, I will not be around here to enjoy the new facilities being constructed. The crime and safety, as far as I've witnessed, is very safe and quiet. Parking violations are the majority of offenses about which anyone ever hears.

The school keeps its students on their toes (as far as expectations and workload) and definitely isn't meant for students wanting to skip classes and have a true college experience.

Current student, 8/2003-Submit Date, January 2005

A wide range of on-campus housing is available, including standard dormitories, six-room suites, single and family apartment-style living, Greek housing, as well as numerous houses for rent in the neighborhood. The campus itself is well laid out and beautifully landscaped, and is well maintained year-round. Most facilities are modern, though some are aging, but remodeling takes place every year, so there really aren't any old-feeling buildings. There are numerous restaurants very close to campus, as well as three different locations on campus with set meal times for residents. Crime is negligible to none, and safety is enforced by actual police officers around the clock.

Social Life

Current student, 8/2003-Submit Date, February 2006

There are always lots of activities on campus. From Friday Afternoon Club comedians every week to Engineer Days in April (the best fireworks in the world—seriously) there is always something to do if you have time to feel bored. The dating scene is unique, to say the least—it is hard to be anything else with a ratio of three girls to every 10 guys. However, with all the surrounding schools (CU, CSU, DU, Colorado Christian and Regis) the dating scene is redeemed. A lot of people are in the Greek system. There are seven fraternities and three sororities. The sororities just got new houses last year—they are more like mansions with huge kitchens and monster, flat-panel TVs. Colorado Mills Mall is within a five-minute drive and provides an array of options for movies, restau-

rants and shops. As for bars, the favorite bar has to be Coors Lab—three free beers to anyone over 21 right at the Coors Brewery.

Alumnus/a, 8/2000-5/2005, February 2006

Social life is one of the more challenged aspect of the school. As the guy-to-girl ratio is about 4:1, many guys have a difficult time finding a date (as if most engineers don't already). Local bars become regular spots for many upperclassmen, but a far better scene is about 10 miles away in the heart of Denver. Greek life is also very active on the Mines campus.

Current student, 9/2004-Submit Date, February 2006

If you know what you want, social life is great. If you can handle not being around girls all the time, which is the generally the case, then you will have a lot of fun. I think we have the second-most clubs of any college in the nation, second to Air Force Academy. If you know or find something you love, you will have no problem finding other people who love the same things. Intramural sports are probably my favorite part of this school. Even if you aren't good at sports, you could have fun playing any sport you could imagine. With light competition in soccer, frisbee, racquetball, foosball, frisbee golf, real golf, volleyball and many other sports. Club sports also offer an extremely fun alternative. I play club lacrosse, and we are involved in a very competitive league that includes teams across the nation. The school gives us a lot of funding even though we are only a club. I get to play against my good friends in Malibu and Los Angeles too! Restaurants in the immediate area are limited, but Denver (20-minute drive) has anything you could imagine. Dating scene for men is below average only because the ladies are a little underrepresented. But if you find a girl up here you know she is going to be smart, probably loves the outdoors and is down-to-earth. Also, Boulder is a short 20-minute drive to all the partying/party chicks you could want or imagine. The Greek life seems to be awesome. I have many friends who enjoy the frat Beta, including two past presidents. One of my good friends is the president of her sorority and loves it.

Current student, 8/2002-Submit Date, February 2006

I really enjoyed the social aspects of the school. Because Mines is a smaller community, you get to know people on a personal level. There are tons of clubs and intramurals on campus, and a lot of people get involved. There are tons of restaurants around Golden and you are only 20 minutes from downtown Denver with tons of great bars and dance clubs. The dating scene on campus may not be as great as bigger schools, especially for the guys. There are three guys to every girl. Which is great for the girls, and all the guys are respectable. For the guys, there are a lot of nice girls on campus, but there are a lot of other colleges around where many of my friends date girls (CU, Metro and DU). All in all, I could have never chosen a better school to offer such opportunity in all areas of life.

Current student, 8/2003-Submit Date, January 2005

The school has a much larger population of males than females (ratio 3:1), so at times the dating scene seems a little bit scarce. Despite that, there are numerous clubs on campus that organize social events every day and night of the week, so there is always something to do. Also, intramural and club sports bring students together and give them a chance to make many friends. Most classes recommend working in groups, which also boosts social activity. Events happen year-round and usually draw huge crowds consisting of most of the student body. There are many sororities and fraternities, all of which are very close knit but more than open to visitors. Students always look forward to E-days every year, a spring break celebration where there are comedians, live performers, musicians, and usually one nationally known band or musician, for little or no cost. Stress-relieving events are planned around exam times to ensure the students don't focus too much on studies and not enough on fun.

Read all of Vault's College Surveys at www.vault.com/college—get complete surveys on 100s of colleges and universities, expert advice on applicaton essays and more.

VAULT CAREER LIBRARY   105

Colorado State University

Office of Admissions
8020 Campus Delivery
Fort Collins, CO 80523-8020
Admissions phone: (970) 491-6909
Admissions URL: admissions.colostate.edu/admissions/

 Admissions

Current student, 8/2003-Submit Date, December 2005

Colorado State has a rolling admissions process, so the sooner you apply, the sooner you'll know your admission status. Applying online was very easy. My advice is to apply as early as possible; it feels a lot better to have all your applications turned in as soon as you can. You'll feel relieved that at least that part is over. In your essay, just be yourself and talk about your strengths.

Current student, 1/2002-Submit Date, December 2005

As a transfer student, I was not required to take an entrance exam or evaluation. The university looked at my credits from my transfer institution and my high school GPA along with my ACT score. I was required to go through entrance counseling, which was basically a counselor helping me pick my classes for my first semester at CSU.

Current student, 8/2002-Submit Date, November 2005

The admissions process was comprised of three parts. The first is the general application process, followed by several essays on goals and aspirations. The university also inquired about past grades and activities. Advisors at the university were very willing to assist potential students in finding the right program at the university to fit their needs.

Current student, 8/2005-Submit Date, November 2005

When I applied to CSU, I was transferring and received some helpful advice from my current professors, who were alumni of CSU. I applied online, and even though it was a long process, it's best to take your time. Especially when writing essays and applying for in school scholarships, think it out and get help from peers and teachers. Reference letters will take you a long way, so pick teachers who are fond of you.

Alumnus/a, Interior Design, 8/2001-5/2005, October 2005

The application is probably easiest done online. Depending on your high school GPA, as well as your score on the ACT (Colorado State Schools do not require you to take the SATs), you will land somewhere on a chart that will tell you if you are admittable or not. This chart is on the Colorado State University web site, www.colostate.edu. Even if it says that you do not have automatic admittance you can still attempt to get in, with letters of recommendation and essays. Any extracurricular things you can do to enhance how you look on paper will help.

You will have to fill out an application and pay a fee to admit it. This process took about six weeks for me (this was four years ago) I was admitted to a program called ACCESS, which is a probational acceptance. I had to prove that I wanted to be there my first semester, you have to do at least average to stay. There are usually around 100 people who try to get into the interior design program every year, and about 40 are accepted. The program is becoming much more popular, and there are more and more people applying.

Current student, 8/2004-Submit Date, December 2004

The admissions process at Colorado State was fairly simple. There was an application to turn in that included a list of activities and awards. The essay was optional, but I highly recommend that you take the time to write it. Having an extra edge can never hurt. The college is not very selective because it is a state school, but make sure you do a good job with the application anyway, so that if you qualify for any scholarships, you have a better chance of actually receiving them.

Current student, 8/2002-Submit Date, September 2004

Applying to CSU was a relatively easy process. I turned in letters of recommendation from my Physics and Biology teachers. I thought that these would be quite appropriate since I was applying to the College of Natural Sciences. Also, the essay is a time to prove that you are a dedicated and motivated student. They do not want to accept students who will reflect poorly on the school.

There are many colleges within the university, and it is your job to decide the college in which you are most interested. Each college has specific admissions and graduation requirements. I was an average student, with a GPA of 3.4. I had a lot of extracurriculars, as well as a strong desire to learn. I think that CSU was able to recognize this through my essay.

Overall, I wouldn't stress over grades to the point where you are limiting yourself to which colleges you apply. I would strongly recommend getting letters from the teachers who you feel know you the best and who can prove that you are a dedicated student. Getting an A in a class doesn't guarantee you the best letter, but letting the teacher know that you worked hard for the grade you earned does.

Also, make sure that your essay is strong, and that your future goals, motivations and reasons for your ambition come through nice and clear! Good luck! Most of all, don't stress!

 Academics

Current student, Business, 8/2003-Submit Date, November 2006

Once in the College of Business, it is easy to get the classes needed for graduation. However, the university core classes that you need to graduate are difficult to get during the time slots you want in freshman year. The classes in the College of Business are very small, normally about 45 students—some lectures of about 150 students. The professors are all experts in their fields with the exception of a few. Professors are really easy to talk to outside of class whenever you need extra help. The program is leaning less towards lectures and more toward case-study class, which I feel really teaches you how to apply the concepts you have learned to be successful.

Current student, Biochemistry, 8/2003-Submit Date, December 2005

I'm a junior biochemistry major (I was a chemistry major for a year) and I loved both departments. I've had some terrific professors who will answer questions you have about the class and who care about how well you're learning the material. The workload has definitely increased this year, but most of my professors are great when I have questions or concerns. The program is tough, but I've had a pretty good experience overall. Some of the popular classes fill up really fast; however, when you get up into the upper-division courses and there's only one section, it can be really stressful if it fills up. There're always overrides, though! Most professors will give you the override.

Current student, Construction, 1/2002-Submit Date, December 2005

The construction management program is the nation's largest and one of the most highly regarded of its type. It has faculty with many years of construction experience, as well as substantial academic achievement. Once a student is fully in the program as a junior, classes are typically always open, but with the growing department, it is getting more difficult to get into the classes if you do not have much seniority. The workload is fairly time-consuming. Most of our classes have labs that require equal or double the workload of the lecture.

Current student, 8/2002-Submit Date, November 2005

Academics are taken very seriously at CSU. In my opinion, class quality largely reflects the teacher's ability to engage the class. Popular classes are different for every intra-university college (e.g., Liberal Arts, Applied Human Sciences and Engineering). Several classes fill up fast, not because of the popularity but because of the core required classes the university mandates for freshmen. Many professors at CSU are nationally recognized for their research and teaching abilities. The workload for class obviously depends on the class. Foreign languages, for example, merit a large workload.

Current student, 8/2002-Submit Date, September 2004

My classes within the College of Natural Sciences are packed. CSU is known for the veterinary sciences, so classes such as Organic Chemistry and General Biology are going to have anywhere from 100 to 200 students in them! My roommate, on the other hand, is a business major, where the upper-division classes are much smaller (anywhere from 20 to 30 students).

At CSU, you will be required to take a freshman seminar class that is a fairly small class depending upon your major (mine had 20 students). Here, you will be directed in the right path to a successful academic experience at CSU. Every class is what you make of it, if you attend class and actually enjoy what you are doing (OK, maybe not the hours of studying afterwards) you will certainly benefit!

Most of my exams are multiple choice and a few are short answers. I was able to take a Gross Anatomy course at CSU, where the exams were certainly not just multiple choice. Instead, we had a minute to identify a labeled body part on a cadaver. This class has certainly been one of the highlights to my personal experience at CSU.

An advisor is assigned to each student and that advisor is there to help you through your four years at CSU. Also, most students think that they will finish their undergraduate degree and meet the requirements by the time fourth year rolls around. This is not always the case. I am not sure of the actual statistics, but a lot of students take longer to complete their degrees. This is normal, unless you decide to take summer school, but who really wants to do that?!

Current student, Busines, 8/2004-Submit Date, December 2004

I am currently a business student with a minor in economics and I enrolled in the Honors program. I have not really gotten into the business classes, but I will next semester. The Honors program provides priority registration, so it makes it much easier to get your desired classes.

The awesome thing about Honors is that it does not involve a lot of extra work, but you still get the benefits. The seminars are not extremely hard. They're typically fun and full of discussion, so you learn without having to stress over grades and assignments. In my regular classes, the professors are all very good at setting up office hours for you to come and visit if you need any help.

The grading is typically based on a curve, so I find it to be very fair. The workload in my classes outside of the Honors program tends to be heavier. These are mostly lecture classes, so there is a lot of studying involved. The grades are based solely off a few tests, so it's important to study frequently in order to get a good grade. I probably spend about four hours doing schoolwork outside of class each day. Many days I can even afford to spend less, but as tests approach, I tend to spend a little more on my academics.

Employment Prospects

Current student, Business, 8/2003-Submit Date, November 2006

The College of Business is great at this. They have different meet-the-employer sections every week of the year; where you get to listen to employers talk about their companies and collect résumés for scheduled interviews on campus. The university also has two major carrier fairs during the year, where hundreds of employers from around the U.S. show up, and the majority of them are looking for business students. The College of Business has someone on staff to assist you in finding internships, as well. We are currently ranked 83rd out of 1,300 business schools in the U.S. Therefore, the graduates are highly favored.

Current student, Biochemistry, 8/2003-Submit Date, December 2005

We have career fairs every semester and grad school fairs also. They're informative and nice to attend. We have a great biochemistry department (and the chemistry department is also wonderful). Advisors can help point you in the direction of where you may want to work when you're done with your degree. The department also sends out information on internship opportunities.

Current student, Construction, 1/2002-Submit Date, December 2005

Because our program has been around for almost 60 years, we have over 230 employers recruiting from our school annually. Our department has a 100 percent job placement for its graduates because the program's reputation is such that any student from CSU Construction Management is a good job prospect. Because we have a mandatory internship requirement to graduate, each student has the opportunity to network and start looking for a job long before their senior year.

Current student, 8/2002-Submit Date, November 2005

CSU has a strong Career Development Office that aids students in their efforts to gain a respectable job. In addition, there are many job fairs, as well as graduate school fairs during the fall and spring semester. The alumni network has been growing strong in the past few years. Many alumni are willing to assist their fellow university graduates to obtain a wonderful career. Internships are available in almost every department on campus, as well as co-op programs. I was able to intern at the State Capitol last spring through the political science department.

Current student, 8/2002-Submit Date, September 2004

CSU has a Career Development Office that offers many international and national internships. There are many resources offered at CSU; it is just a matter of using those resources! There are people all over CSU who will give you insight as to what you can do to make it into graduate school—especially medical and veterinary school. CSU also offers prep classes for major exams such as the MCAT and GRE that are hundreds of dollars cheaper than any other organization's. It is a group of dedicated professors (whom you will have likely had in the past) who help to give students a review of what they need to know for the exams.

Current student, 8/2004-Submit Date, December 2004

The types of jobs available completely depend on your major. Many graduates have gone on to be employed by prestigious employers. We have a Career Development Office on campus to help students find jobs and internships, and make connections. Utilizing this resource is a great way to ensure snagging a good job upon graduation. As far as business is concerned, CSU has one of the Top 100 business programs in the nation, so employers express an interest in our graduates.

Quality of Life

Current student, 8/2003-Submit Date, November 2006

Fort Collins was just ranked the Number One city in which to live in the U.S. by *Money* magazine. I think that tells you that the life in Fort Collins is great, with low crime and plenty of recreational facilities and schools.

Current student, 8/2002-Submit Date, November 2005

CSU has a great student community. The City of Fort Collins is built around the university, giving a lovely college-town feel to this beautiful city. There is a blend, however, of business professionals and college students in Fort Collins. Housing in Fort Collins is targeted toward students around the university, while the majority of residential families live on the outskirts of the town. The community has several picnics and other social events that bring both traditional families and students together to discuss pressing issues with regard to the community.

Current student, 8/2005-Submit Date, November 2005

Fort Collins is one of the safest, beautiful and people-friendly towns in the U.S. The campus includes of about 10 different dorms, each with certain educational aspects directed at them (which helps a lot when you need a study-buddy). A large library, great recreational center and tons of clubs to join are just some of the great aspects of CSU. Health and wellness services are available on campus, including psychiatrists to dermatologists, all willing to help out the students. CSUPD is available on campus 24/7 for our own safety; and programs like Safewalk and Ramride help out students in need when walking on campus alone at night, or to prevent drunk driving.

Read all of Vault's College Surveys at www.vault.com/college–get complete surveys on 100s of colleges and universities, expert advice on applicaton essays and more.

VAULT CAREER LIBRARY   107

Alumnus/a, 8/2001-5/2005, October 2005

If you begin at CSU as an incoming freshman under 21, you are required to live on campus for the first year. I can tell you that it is typical university living, with a little above-average food (that still gets old as it would anywhere) and the living facilities are tolerable. This is not about having a palace. It is about becoming acquainted with your new life. This is where I met the friends I had all through school and will have for the rest of my life. It's only a year, have fun with it.

Otherwise, there are plenty of living spaces near and around campus; some are good and some are bad. I have had anywhere from one to four roommates, all have their ups and downs, but whatever you are looking for, you just have to look—you'll find it.

The community is great!! Very accepting of the college culture, lots of people from 18 to 25, but there is a diversity of age. Not so much diversity. Fort Collins is unfortunately very "whitewashed." But is not unaccepting, it is in Colorado and that is what most of the state is like. The town grew from a place based on agriculture, very laid-back and fairly liberal.

All I can say is, I could not have asked for a nicer, safer place to live and receive my education.

Current student, 8/2004-Submit Date, December 2004

The quality of life at CSU is pretty good. I am currently living in the dorms, and my room is fairly nice. I do have a roommate, but we each have a large closet and a comfortable bed. There's plenty of space in our room for us to have a stereo, TV, our own computers and desks, a small refrigerator and a microwave. The dining halls are much better than I had originally expected.

Our food is ranked fourth in the nation. There's a wide variety of food served each day, and basic foods, such as cereal, bagels, grilled cheese, hot dogs and hamburgers, are always available. A meal pass gets you to eat in any of the dorms, which creates more variety. Meal plans are available for both on- and off-campus students.

The neighborhood is also a fairly safe one. There aren't many incidences of crime, and most of the safety issues arise from drunken college students. I personally have not had any safety issues. We also offer programs, such as Safewalk, so that you can have somebody walk you home at night any time you feel you might be unsafe. Campus police also help create a safe environment.

 ## Social Life

Current student, 8/2003-Submit Date, November 2006

There are probably 100 different clubs in which you can get involved on campus. Additionally, the nightlife scene is great. There are plenty of bars and clubs all within a close distance. There are cab services, and on the weekends and Thursday nights, free rides home are offered by the school program, RAM Ride. Some of the favorite bars in town are Tony's, Tail Gate Tommy's and Road 34. We are also the home of some of the most favorite brewers, such as New Belgium Brewery, Odell Brewery and Anheuser Bush. If you like drinking and enjoying brewery tours, I don't think there is a better place to be.

Current student, 8/2003-Submit Date, June 2006

I don't know much about the Greek system; it wasn't really my scene. Old Town is so great for shopping, socializing, eating, drinking and having a blast. There're so many things to do in the span of just a few blocks. The social aspect of this town is great. Bands come and play in the summer in the middle of Old Town and tons of events come to the Aggie Theater. Sullivans is a fun bar, as are Coppersmiths and Lucky Joe's. Microbrewed beer is a favorite of a lot of people, as well.

Current student, 8/2005-Submit Date, November 2005

You don't even have to go off campus for a great meal; the dorms offer varied types of cafeterias and the central student center has various chain fast-food restaurants. Meeting people wasn't a challenge for me at all, and I'm considered relatively shy. Attending parties and events around campus is great for meeting people. On-campus events, like free movies and cultural nights are always a really fun experience, too. The Greek society on campus is great; they host events and fundraisers, like spaghetti nights, which are great for volunteer work and helping out the community.

Alumnus/a, 8/2001-5/2005, October 2005

The City of Fort Collins offers quite a bit in the line of a social life. It has a lot of bars, mostly college-type bars, but they are on a wide spectrum. Some are strictly pick-up bars where many of the people involved with Greek life hang out (e.g., Washingtons, Suite 152 and Zydagoe—where you can dance on the bar) and then there are more laid-back, pub-type bars (Lucky Joe's, Trailhead and Stakeout).

This is a town that loves its beer. There are tons of microbreweries in town and a Budwieser plant 10 minutes away. Fort Collins is the home of New Belgium, O'Dells and Fort Collins Brewery, which all offer beer tours for those 21 and up.

There are quite a few art galleries in town, first Friday of every month they have hors d'oeuvres and stay open longer for a nice evening out.

Restaurants—all I can say is, you won't have to go far to find whatever you want. Tons of restaurants, many of which are locally owned. Some legends that need to be had if you go include, Pizza Cashba, Pickel Barrel and Big City Burrito. Those will become staples in your diet, I'm sure.

There is a bar on campus called the Ramskeller. It serves real beer, and they try to have events like trivia, date night, poker and things like that to keep students entertained. There is a club for pretty much anything and there are fairs to make it easy to join. If there isn't a club for something you what to be a part of you can start your own. It is really easy, and they walk you through the process.

Most people really enjoy the town, I hope you do, too

United States Air Force Academy

HQ USAFA/RRS
2304 Cadet Drive, Ste 200
USAF Academy, CO 80840
Admissions phone: (800) 443-9266
Admissions fax: (719) 333-3647
Admissions e-mail: rr_webmail@usafa.af.mil
Admissions URL: academyadmissions.com/

Note: *The school has chosen not to comment on the student surveys submitted.*

 Admissions

Alumnus/a, 6/1999-6/2003, February 2006

Very rigorous process. Competitiveness varies somewhat by state. You must have the endorsement (a nomination) of one of your senators, or your congressman. You must pass a fitness test and medical screening, and your high school record should reflect leadership, community involvement and physical fitness.

A high GPA and SAT score do not guarantee admission, but most admitted students have very good grades. If you're a standout athlete, get in touch with the coach of your sport at the school—they can help you in the admissions process.

Current student, 6/2002-Submit Date, July 2005

The United States Air Force Academy, located near Colorado Springs, Colorado, is one of the most highly selective undergraduate universities in the nation. One of five federal service academies and one of three of the nation's armed forces academies; selection is exceptionally competitive.

Out of roughly 10,000 applicants per year, only 1,500 are offered appointments, and of those, approximately 1,200 to 1,300 enter with each new class. Applicants must meet stringent academic, medical and physical criteria in order to be considered prospective candidates. A battery of Department of Defense medical and physical tests must be passed by each applicant and submitted with the application. In addition, federal service academies, such as the Air Force Academy, require a federal nominating source for each applicant. This source can be a U.S. Senator, U.S. Representative, the Vice President of the United States or the President of the United States (military dependents only).

The purpose of the Air Force Academy is to develop the officer corps—the next generation of Air Force leaders. When screening for potential candidates, the admissions office seeks individuals who have developed leadership qualities. Although academic (SAT, ACT, GPA) and physical test scores are weighted heavily, extracurricular activities are also given strong consideration. While being a part of many clubs and sports reflects versatility, the Academy would prefer leaders over joiners. Leadership positions such as class president, Eagle Scout, team captain, drum major, AFJROTC commander and Civil Air Patrol officer reflect highly on an applicant's character.

Despite the fact that a majority of candidates wish to become Air Force pilots, flight time is not necessarily a requirement, nor is it given additional weight. The Air Force will conduct its own flight training upon selection of pilot candidates during the second class (junior) year. Flying is an important part of the Academy, but it takes second place to world-class academics and military training. Having a private pilot's license, however, does open doors to such exciting programs as the Academy's Intercollegiate Flying Team.

Part of the admissions process involves working with a local Admissions Liason Officer (ALO). More often than not, these are volunteers who are retired Air Force officers and graduates of the Academy. The ALO assists with completion of necessary forms and tests, but it is up to the individual candidate to be proactive regarding his or her application. The ALO will conduct the initial interview and assist with the application process to include preparation for the congres-

sional interview. In both instances, applicants should remember to relax and appear both professional and focused. Demeanor and personal appearance (dress, hygiene) are just as important as SAT scores. Certain questions will also almost certainly arise each time, such as "Why do you want to go to the Air Force Academy?" and "What do the Air Force core values, 'Integrity First, Service Before Self and Excellence in All We Do' mean to you?" Applicants should be well-prepared and have a good idea of how they will respond in order to minimize anxiety and be as professional and confident as possible.

The Academy's admissions office requires only three essays. The responses should all be relatively short (approximately one paragraph) in order to fit in the provided space. The questions are along the same lines as the aforementioned interview questions. The purpose of each essay is to ascertain each applicant's character, desire to attend and ability for written communication. Spelling and grammar count.

If an applicant is not selected for the incoming class the year of his or her high school graduation, he or she may be selected for admission to the Air Force Academy Preparatory School—a one-year academic, athletic and military program located on the Academy's grounds—in order to increase likelihood of admission the following year. There are approximately 150 students enrolled in the Prep School each year, and virtually all who decide to re-apply for the Academy gain admission.

In addition, there are several other privately funded preparatory schools that feed into the Academy for which an applicant may receive subsidized funding. Besides the Academy, the Air Force Reserve Officer Training Corps (training programs at most major universities) and the Officer Training School (for those already holding an undergraduate degree) are alternate routes to receiving an Air Force commission. An applicant may be admitted at any time between the ages of 17 and 22 upon in-processing, so one should not give up if denied during the first year of application.

Alumnus/a, 7/1999-5/2003, June 2005

The service academies have some of the most competitive admissions processes in the country. They are looking for students who not only are academically sound, with good test scores on the ACT and SAT and graduating near the top of their class, but who are also well rounded enough to participate in other activities, such as sports. It is much better, however, to be really good at a certain activity and be in a leadership position than it is to just participate in many different activities and never be really good at any of them. Also, an applicant must be medically qualified for military service. The Academy is looking for well-rounded leaders, not just those who are book smart.

Alumnus/a, 6/2000-6/2004, March 2005

The Air Force Academy requires a Congressional nomination, Academy acceptance board, interview process, application papers with essays and the usual jazz. Must be in high academic standing and a well-rounded person to get in. Also have to pass a physical fitness test, as well as a medical review, to get in.

Quite astringent process to be accepted, then there is a six-week Basic Training at the Academy the summer before you begin.

Current student, 7/2003-Submit Date, September 2004

Getting into the USAFA is very competitive. You must be above average in all areas (GPA, sports, extracurricular activities and SAT/ACT scores).

Candidates who pass an initial application process must acquire a nomination from their state Representative or Senator. After receiving a nomination, then the candidate's whole application is reviewed by the Air Force Academy Board of admissions. One out of 10 prospectives will then be offered an appointment.

Read all of Vault's College Surveys at **www.vault.com/college**–get complete surveys on 100s of colleges and universities, expert advice on application essays and more.

VAULT CAREER LIBRARY 109

Academics

Alumnus/a, 6/1999-6/2003, February 2006

Workload is huge—you'll stay busy. Way more hours than is normal elsewhere. For the most part, classes are very good and instructors will work with you after class to help you with things you don't understand. The engineering and math departments have the highest reputations. The management, political science and behavioral science departments are very good. Just know that the school is less focused on the liberal arts overall. So even if you're an English major, you'll take lots of science, math and engineering classes as part of the core curriculum.

20 hours plus can be normal for any given semester. You can take some classes in the summer to help with the workload. Electrical engineering students may be particularly challenged to fulfill all their degree requirements.

Current student, 6/2002-Submit Date, July 2005

The United States Air Force Academy is a nationally accredited, exclusively undergraduate university. First and foremost, however, it is a military training institution that involves intense training exercises, programs and regulations. With that being said, the academic workload is also rigorous. On average, students (called cadets) are subject to a four-year program that must be completed in exactly four years, which includes between 150 to 175 credit hours, dependent upon the individual cadet's academic program.

Upon graduation, each cadet earns a Bachelor's of Science degree, regardless of in which of the 33 academic majors the cadet specialized. Academic majors range from aeronautical engineering to fine arts and humanities, but the diverse and technically intense core curriculum ensures that each graduate has received a strong background in science and technology in order to operate successfully in the Air Force.

Although classes can be demanding, class sizes are small and instructors are readily available for additional help. On average, class size is between 15 to 30 cadets. Most instructors are graduates, and an overwhelming majority are active Air Force officers who provide career advice along with instruction. By placing at a minimum of 150 credit hours into four years along with military training, workload is naturally overwhelming, even for the most disciplined of cadets. The Academy, however, is designed to offer a challenge to those who seek it.

There is not much flexibility in class selection once an academic-major track is selected, as the core curriculum takes up so much time that in order to satisfy requirements for each major, most classes are already outlined for each cadet. However, depending on the cadet's major and the number of classes that he or she validates upon entry, that cadet may have more free space for elective courses as an upperclassman.

In addition to academic courses, cadets are required to take a variety of physical education classes, as well. The fourth-class (freshman) year requires Physical Development, Boxing or Wrestling for men, and Self Defense for women; the third-class (sophomore) year requires Swimming and Water Survival; and the second-class (junior) year requires two semesters of Unarmed Combat.

Every year, including the first-class (senior) year, cadets are required to take a lifetime or a team sport as a class, unless they are intercollegiate (NCAA) competitors. In addition, intramural competition is required each semester (again, unless a cadet is an intercollegiate athlete), as well as a Physical Fitness test and Aerobic Fitness test. These requirements, however, do not award academic credit as the physical education classes do.

Alumnus/a, 7/1999-5/2003, June 2005

Most students take five or six, sometimes seven, classes a semester, with an average of 18 to 20 credit hours. Each class usually has 20 students or less, with very easy access to the instructor whenever a student needs help (no TAs here). As a result, the quality of academic instruction is very high, and I was given the opportunity to intern one summer with a technology firm where I was leaps and bounds better able to handle engineering situations than my colleagues from other schools.

So, it's a high workload, awesome professors, grading varies on the type of class, and it's no problem to get the class you want if you have the time (there are many

classes in the core curriculum and many classes associated with your major, so not much room outside of that).

Alumnus/a, 6/2000-6/2004, March 2005

Small classes, usually no more than 10 to 15 students, with many upper-level courses having only three or four per instructor. [Instructors are well qualified and varied, and many] make themselves available for extra instruction if necessary—hard academics overall, large courseload to include military classes and physical training classes, mandatory intramurals and intercollegiate opportunities.

Many different majors and minors to choose from, but a strong core class load in science, engineering and math, so everyone graduates with a Bachelor's of Science, in whatever degree you have.

Current student, 7/2003-Submit Date, September 2004

Academics at the Air Force Academy are very rigorous and broad. You will take classes in every field of study possible. Classes are relatively small, so that students can be given the attention they need to succeed. Teachers are always available for extra help when needed. Grading for various classes depends on the subject. Most classes are contract graded, while some others are graded on a curve. All classes are challenging, and students must actively study to succeed.

Employment Prospects

Alumnus/a, 6/1999-6/2003, February 2006

School is highly thought of and is supposed to rank just behind the Ivy Leagues. On-campus recruiting is not really applicable—everyone serves in the Air Force for five to 10 years after graduation, but many leave the military for other careers after their initial commitment ends.

Grads are consistently leaders in whatever field they enter—the alumni network is helpful for visibility on what everyone is doing and finding contacts within a particular industry or company.

Current student, 6/2002-Submit Date, July 2005

Upon graduation, each cadet is guaranteed a job and a second lieutenant's commission in the United States Air Force. To Air Force officers, regardless of commissioning source, the Academy is the Harvard of the Air Force. Each graduate is required to fulfill a five-year commitment (longer for pilots, navigators, air battle managers, doctors and lawyers due to additional training costs), but after the commitment is fulfilled, graduates are able to separate from the Air Force and pursue careers in the private sector.

Competitive advantage for graduates pursuing civilian positions is high due to the level of training received both at the Academy and in the Air Force on today's leading technology. Military discipline and leadership ability are also prized, thereby leading graduates to be highly sought after.

The graduate community is an extremely tight-knit one due to common experiences and the exclusivity of the institution. To date, there are approximately 46,000 graduates of the Academy since the first graduating class of 1959. The Association of Graduates (AOG) is almost identical to those of the U.S. Military Academy at West Point or the U.S. Naval Academy at Annapolis. The AOG is exceptionally helpful in connecting the graduate community and helping graduates find either careers after the Air Force or new employees for civilian corporations.

During a cadet's time at the Academy, each summer involves an internship at one of the many bases across the world from the United States to Germany to Korea to even Hawaii and Alaska. Each three-week internship introduces the cadet to day-to-day Air Force operations and life as an Air Force officer. In addition, competitive cadets may be selected for national research programs (NASA, the Pentagon and the Kennedy Library) and/or post-graduate opportunities (e.g., Rhodes Scholarship, Truman Scholarship and Olmstead Scholarship). Graduates who proceed immediately to post-graduate work will incur an additional service commitment, but they will concurrently serve their initial commitment while pursuing another degree. The same would apply if a graduate were to pursue an advanced degree some time after graduation. Either way, the Air Force will subsidize higher education expenses more often than not.

Alumnus/a, 7/1999-5/2003, July 2005

100 percent employment in the Air Force upon graduation; extremely high prestige among employers, and a great alumni community to belong to. Half of all graduates go on to fly airplanes and half of all fighter pilots have graduated from the Air Force Academy. Other popular jobs include contracting, acquisitions and managerial-type positions within the Air Force.

Alumnus/a, 6/2000-6/2004, March 2005

We get paid a salary for attending, but are not allowed outside work except in special situations. There really isn't time for an outside job though. The pay isn't much, but is adequate in relation to the amount of time you are allowed outside, which slowly increases over your four years at the Academy. There is also a great loan opportunity towards the end of your junior year, usually dubbed a "car loan," which can be used for anything at an incredibly cheap interest rate; and since there is no tuition, you wont have student loans!!!

Current student, 7/2003-Submit Date, September 2004

A degree from USAFA is highly prestigious. Every student will owe a commitment to the Air Force for a minimum of five years following graduation. This is because every student is on a full scholarship, and this is the Air Force's way of getting something for their money. Opportunities after the Air Force are endless. Registering with the Association of Graduates distributes your information to a plethora of employers who want to hire USAFA graduates.

 ## Quality of Life

Alumnus/a, 6/1999-6/2003, February 2006

Housing—everyone lives in dorm rooms on campus. Not fun. And it's the military, so he/she has to be clean all the time. Very sterile. Heating can be poor in the winter. Some of the rooms are old, and snow will blow through cracks in the window and pile up in the room.

The campus is pretty, you see the mountains every time you step out the door. Dining is at a common hall. The food is mediocre but all 4,000 students sit down and eat at the same time.

Current student, 6/2002-Submit Date, July 2005

The Academy is a military training institution located on a military base. As such, the normal college experience is largely absent. Despite the fact that there are military restrictions that leave each cadet with relatively little freedom and independence, all basic needs are met.

Housing is provided in on-campus dorms for the entirety of a cadet's time at the Air Force Academy. Uniforms are required on a daily basis, but are provided at each cadet's expense through a fund set up specifically for that purpose.

Meals, medical, dental and hygiene services (haircuts) are also at the expense of the cadet, but are unlimited after a fixed amount has been automatically deducted each month from the cadet's salary. Since a cadet is not allowed to seek additional employment, a monthly stipend is provided. The amount varies from $100 to $660 per month, depending upon the cadet's seniority.

The dorms, dining hall, gym and grounds are all topnotch, provided for and maintained at public expense. Due to the importance of the Academy to national defense, security is also at an extremely high level. Air Force Security Forces troops protect and monitor the base and campus, and all cadets are subject to security procedures (anti-terrorism) training. The crime rate is virtually zero on campus.

Alumnus/a, 7/1999-5/2003, June 2005

No crime and a very safe campus. Quality of life gets better each year (everyone has to enter as a freshman) as you progress, but that is by design. Ultimately, you're getting paid to go to college, and room and board is provided. Everyone, however, must live in dorms, usually with a roommate, the entire four years.

Alumnus/a, 6/2000-6/2004, March 2005

Well-kept dorms, military standards, no off-base housing, gated base at the heart of the Rocky Mountains in Colorado Springs. Cadet bar on campus, excellent gym and athletic fields.

There are regular uniform and room inspections, have to wear uniform every day, march to lunch and at various parades throughout the year. Dining facility is decent, and breakfast and lunch are mandatory. Dinner is optional—you can eat at the dining facility, but there are a couple other options, as well, including delivery.

There are also mandatory summer programs, each three weeks long, of which you have to have at least two every summer (broken into three blocks of three weeks), so you only get three weeks off during summer leave. You get two weeks off for Christmas, and about a week each for spring break and Thanksgiving.

Current student, 7/2003-Submit Date, September 2004

All students live in on-campus dorms. Room and board is all included under the full scholarship. Students at the USAFA are actually paid a small amount every month. During freshman year, students rarely will leave campus.

Life at USAFA keeps everyone busy enough as it is, so there is not a whole lot of reason to leave campus. Opportunities on campus provide recreation and sports activities that could keep anyone occupied.

Some students may complain about quality of life because of the fact that all students are required to wear a uniform to class. All classes require mandatory attendance to each lesson and there is no tolerance for skipping. The dining hall on campus is rated one of the best in the country, students are required to attend breakfast and lunch meals all, at the same time. This requires an enormous dining room facility where food is actually brought to your table for you.

 ## Social Life

Alumnus/a, 6/1999-6/2003, February 2006

Social life is nonexistent. No Greek system or restaurants. It's a military base. Some students date one another, but keep in mind the school is something like 85 percent male.

School keeps all students very, very busy, so the time to date and really have a healthy social life is limited for everyone. I think social development is somewhat stunted during these years, which is why the stereotype of grads who can't stop talking about "the Academy" develops. Some adopt their association with the school as the only means of defining their identity.

Current student, 6/2002-Submit Date, July 2005

A cadet's time is almost always already scheduled on a day-to-day basis, leaving little time for personal recreation or enjoyment. The time that is available, however, is spent in the company of extremely close friends that are developed through a bond of common experience. When cadets go out on the town, people take note.

There is a small food court (Arnie's Food Court) with a separate bar (Hap's Bar) for those of age in the student union building, which is also home to various shows, concerts and dances during the year. As a cadet progresses in seniority, he/she also sees an exponential increase in freedom to explore neighboring Colorado Springs and Denver. Colorado offers a wide variety of outdoor activities, such as skiing, hiking and camping. Denver and Colorado Springs are also comparable to other major metropolitan areas of their size and include a wide variety of restaurants, bars, nightclubs, theaters and social activities. Many popular concerts come through the Denver Metropolitan Area, and there are more activities than one knows what to do with. However, cadets may also take advantage of special military rates on recreational activities or concerts, or sometimes be privy to exclusive military events.

The dating scene is limited within the student population, as it consists of 80 percent males and only 20 percent females. There is also a restriction that fourth-class (freshman) cadets may only date within their class. The upper three classes, however, are free to date each other. More often than not, however, cadets will date civilians either from their hometowns or from neighboring cities in Colorado. Both Colorado Springs and the Denver area are home to many college campuses, including the University of Colorado and Colorado State University, which are very popular places to party and meet people.

Read all of Vault's College Surveys at **www.vault.com/college**–get complete surveys on 100s of colleges and universities, expert advice on applicaton essays and more.

VAULT CAREER LIBRARY   **111**

Almost every interest category, sport, or religion offers a supporting club at the Air Force Academy, and most needs can be accommodated. The Academy realizes it is important for cadets to find their niche and that diversity in interests must be cultivated to produce high-quality officers. Funding is largely provided by the Association of Graduates.

There is no Greek society at the Academy, but similar factions are drawn within each cadet squadron, a coed group of approximately 120 cadets that lives in the same geographic area of the dorms. The entire cadet population is divided into 36 squadrons, each of which contains its own specific command structure and leadership opportunities.

Alumnus/a, 7/1999-5/2003, June 2005

There is one bar on campus, reserved mostly for juniors and seniors. No Greek system. After that, it's what you can make of it in Colorado Springs. Denver is not far away, either. The hardest part the first two years is finding rides off campus, since you're not allowed to have a car until junior year. It's kind of the price you pay, but I will tell you it's all worth it after graduation.

Alumnus/a, 6/2000-6/2004, March 2005

What social life? It's a military college. Nah, Colorado Springs has quite a few bars and clubs, and Denver is only an hour away full of all the amenities of a big city. Skiing and snowboarding in the mountains is always a good time on weekends, as is camping, hiking and fly-fishing. All outdoors stuff is available including whitewater rafting, horseback riding, mountain climbing, sky diving and more. There is no Greek system, but there are numerous clubs and lots of activities on base to fit anyone's taste.

Current student, 7/2003-Submit Date, September 2004

The Air Force Academy is composed of approximately 80 percent male students. The 20 percent female population presents little opportunity to date extensively on campus as a male. However, the cities of Colorado Springs and Denver provide almost limitless opportunities for dating and other activities (clubbing, bars, theme parks, concerts and sporting events).

The various clubs offered at USAFA provide for many opportunities to go skiing and snowboarding, horseback riding, kayaking and rock climbing. There is never a shortage of social things to do. The trick is finding the time.

University of Colorado at Boulder

Office of Admissions
University of Colorado at Boulder
Regent Administrative Center 125
552 UCB
Boulder, CO 80309-0552
Admissions phone: (303) 492-6301
Admissions URL: www.colorado.edu/prospective/

 ## Admissions

Current student, Finance, 1/2003-Submit Date, October 2006

I transferred to the University of Colorado in January of 2003. The school is becoming even more selective, but if you are a minority, make sure to use that to your advantage. The school is continually looking to diversify its student body. Write yourself a solid essay because I have heard that the admissions people look long and hard at these.

> **The school says:** "We look for students from a wide range of diverse backgrounds. We seek students from a wide variety of cultural backgrounds, first-generation students, students with unique talents, those from underrepresented geographic areas, and those who will make contributions to the campus community. We feel a diverse community benefits the educational goals and well-being of all of its members."

Current student, 8/2003-Submit Date, October 2006

CU is not extremely competitive as far as admissions. A solid SAT score and a decent high school GPA should get you admitted. Selectivity is higher within the business and engineering schools but not too high, in general. CU is a quality school for good students.

Current student, 8/2005-Submit Date, May 2006

I highly recommend writing an essay. When I applied, I submitted two essays, which I believe is the reason that I got an academic scholarship. I also recommend sending in your application as early as possible.

Current student, 8/2004-Submit Date, May 2006

The admissions process for an in-state student (as I am) is not too difficult. Especially because I was guaranteed admission based on my test scores and high school GPA. The application is not too lengthy, and there is an optional recommendation and/or essay. I turned in an essay, simply because we worked on them in my senior year English class. I received my acceptance letter two weeks after submission.

Current student, 8/2005-Submit Date, May 2006

As an in-state student with a certain GPA and test scores, you are guaranteed admission to CU. However, CU is becoming increasingly selective for in-state students, and a number of my friends who did not have the GPA or test scores were waitlisted and only a few actually got accepted. For out-of-state students the requirements are more rigorous.

Current student, 8/2005-Submit Date, May 2006

The essay is not required but is definitely recommended as it provides a chance for the student to describe him/herself and set him/herself apart. The application is relatively quick and very easy to do online, and notification of acceptance is usually prompt. The housing applications are easy, as well, and are based on a first come, first serve basis. As far as selectivity, the school is not incredibly selective. However, individual colleges can be more selective, including the engineering school and the Leed's School of Business.

Current student, 8/2003-Submit Date, May 2006

As an out-of-state applicant, my admissions process to the University of Colorado-Boulder was a bit more in depth than a potential in-state student. After filling out the generic documents about my grades, accomplishments and test scores, I had to write an essay about why I wanted to attend school at CU. I had to prove not only why I deserved to go there but what I would bring to the campus. It wasn't required but it was encouraged. Always a competitor, I poured my energy into crafting an essay that would distinguish myself from others and prove to the University of Colorado that not accepting me would be a mistake.

Current student, 8/2003-Submit Date, March 2005

The admissions process is simple. Getting into the school is one thing—have good enough grades and/or high enough test scores (ACT/SAT) and you're in. What's hard is getting financial aid. Get some good letters of recommendation, participate in a lot of extracurriculars (especially things having to do with awareness and diversity). It also helps to know which particular school you want to attend or major you want to pick. Art, music, business, engineering? Then contact one of the professors and meet with him/her and discuss the school and the program, and ask him/her for advice about applying. He/she may be able to put in a good word for you. If you want to be a music major, practice, practice, practice! If you're good enough at your instrument, you can get a lot of good financial aid. Especially if your instrument is in demand.

The school says: "To receive early notification of their financial aid eligibility, students should complete the Free Application for Federal Student Aid (FAFSA) as soon as possible after January 1, whether or not they know if they've been admitted to CU-Boulder at the time. For speed and accuracy, we recommend that students complete the FAFSA online. See: www.colorado.edu/prospective/freshman/apply/finaid.html for further information on applying for financial aid and scholarships."

Current student, 8/2003-Submit Date, April 2006

In-state students should apply, as they are likely to be accepted. Out-of-state students go through a more competitive process. Entrance essays should be sincere and open—it makes a difference. The admissions process is fast if you are on top of all your required documents. First generation college students should apply for the McNair or TASC programs for scholarships. Apply for all scholarships.

Academics

Current student, 8/2003-Submit Date, January 2007

Most classes are relatively straightforward. Some of the professors have strange teaching methods, but they seem to work, for the most part. They all make themselves available for out-of-class help, and those who do go tend to do much better than those who don't. The work will creep up on you if you don't keep up with it, and there are some points where assignments or projects will be very difficult, but it's more or less manageable. Classes aren't too hard to obtain if you register when you're supposed to. The grading depends on the professor but is usually fair.

Current student, 8/2004-Submit Date, May 2006

I have thoroughly enjoyed my classes at the University of Colorado. I was hesitant to attend, as I was worried they would not be challenging enough, but I have found that not to be the truth. There is also the option of taking classes through the honors program, which offers an additional challenge if you are eligible. Scheduling can be a pain sometimes, as it is all done online based on the number of credits you have. However, waitlists move fairly quickly, and generally you can work it out to get into the class you need. Your advisor is also your best friend when it comes to scheduling. They can definitely prove to be quite helpful when it comes to being on the borderline of getting into a class. Grading varies from class to class. In my experience, the lower-level classes have larger grade adjustments than the upper-division courses; however, it depends on the professor. I have thoroughly enjoyed my professors here. They are knowledgeable, approachable, and genuinely interested in your progress and education. All in all, the academics here have exceeded my expectations.

Current student, Finance, 8/2003-Submit Date, October 2006

The academic program is solid. Lower-division classes tend to be very large but often with quality professors. Some majors are harder than others, but many courses within the business school are not extremely difficult. Getting the right classes can be a pain, but you can usually manage it.

Current student, 8/2005-Submit Date, May 2006

The academics are very good. CU is the kind of school where you can sign up for five 300-person lectures every semester and not get a great education, or you can choose to get involved. The more and more things that you do at this school, more and more doors will open for you. If you choose to get involved in anything and you choose to take smaller classes you will get so much more for your money.

The school says: "Although CU does have large lecture classes, the majority of the classes are small in size. Over two-thirds (68 percent) of regular class sections have less than 30 students in them, and 85 percent of class sections have less than 50 students per class."

Current student, 8/2005-Submit Date, May 2006

CU is a big state school with a party reputation; therefore, I went in with the idea that classes were going to be 1,000-person lectures that no one went to, and that it would be so much easier than my IB classes in high school. While there are larger (100 to 200 people) lectures that depend on your initiative to attend, the majority of classes are smaller and rigorous. College requires a complete different academic mindset, even for the most diligent and determined high school student. As a freshman, four out of my first 10 classes were large lectures, but the rest had fewer than 40 students.

Current student, 8/2003-Submit Date, May 2006

I've been very happy with the academics at CU. I've had world-class professors and decent class sizes with few exceptions. I've even had the chance to work with one of our four Nobel Laureates. Some of the intro freshman classes can be a bit tedious or large, but this can be mitigated for the most part by residential academic programs (RAPs), the honors program and careful class selection. Even in the large classes, the professors are very open to meeting with students individually and providing individual support. I really feel like I've gotten one of the best educations in the country. I am also a member of the Presidents Leadership Class (PLC), a premier leadership development program, and have learned and been challenged immensely both in and out of the classroom through PLC.

Current student, 8/2004-Submit Date, April 2005

The academics at CU are actually quite good. It still provides a superior undergraduate education. The philosophy department faculty is quite good, despite many of the better scholars having recently departed. The major requirements are difficult enough to be rigorous but not incredibly difficult. The core requirements for any BA are not that hard either, but you are required to take quite a bit of upper-division classes. All in all, you are forced to get an above-average education, and there is plenty of opportunity to get a great one. The procedure for graduation with honors, for example, requires a written thesis defended in front of a board of several faculty members from within and without your department—CU tends to expect their better undergrad's to be like grad students, and there are opportunities to take graduate classes for undergraduate credit if you seek them out.

The student-to-faculty ratio is not great. Most classes are quite large, and getting into the smaller seminars can be quite difficult. However, a great professor in a lecture hall is far better than a poor professor in a seminar. There are plenty of good profs in every department too, and I have yet to have had what I would call a bad professor. Some will be boring, of course, and very few will have the time or desire to get to know most of their students personally. Overall, though, the academics at CU are topnotch, especially if you make the effort.

The school says: "For comment on CU-Boulder's class size, see above. The average student-to-faculty ratio, based on faculty FTE to student FTE is approximately 17:1."

Employment Prospects

Current student, Finance, 8/2003-Submit Date, October 2006

Finance majors have great prospects when graduating from CU. Dedicated career counselors can help you network with the right people and get a job.

Current student, 8/2002-Submit Date, May 2006

The Career Services Center at CU is excellent. They have some of the best help on writing résumés and interviewing. The really are amazing. They have workshops, and you can make appointments for individual help, as well (like for a mock interview, they will tape you and go over it afterwards so you can see how you act).

There are career fairs happening on a regular basis and I know several of my friends have gotten jobs through that. They also have tons of internships and a web site to facilitate all of this. I know people who have gotten everything from jobs in labs to working with the state.

I also know that our school has a good reputation, and at least in my department, they are known for being a strong school. I will be getting paid to go to grad school and I know that being from here didn't hurt.

Current student, 8/2004-Submit Date, May 2006

Employers who are not from the Colorado area do not seem to understand fully that there is validity to the degree received at CU. Local employers understand

Read all of Vault's College Surveys at **www.vault.com/college**—get complete surveys on 100s of colleges and universities, expert advice on applicaton essays and more.

VAULT CAREER LIBRARY **113**

that there are very hard-working students from CU who are worthwhile employees. Also, very few companies other than purely business/managerial types interview and present on campus. Liberal arts have a hard time finding employers willing to present on campus.

> **The school says:** "We have a nice mix of companies hiring locally and nationally. In general, the focus is on industry rather than on major, and many of those industries are looking to hire CU graduates from every discipline (including Arts and Sciences). The types of companies who utilize career fairs are often ones looking for many candidates from each school. Different types of opportunities (including those that may be more interesting to Arts and Science majors) are conducted on a smaller scale through our online system. We encourage students and recent graduates to take advantage of all types of services, not just the big flashy fairs. See Career Services homepage for further information: careerservices.colorado.edu/."

Current student, 8/2003-Submit Date, May 2006

Questionable prestige given recent scandals, but if anyone bothered to look, they'd recognize the excellence of our amazing scientists and researchers; billions in grants. Also our psychology program is extremely comprehensive and many of our classes are the basis for standards used by other schools. The alumni network is huge and extremely active, especially for employment after graduation. Lots of internship possibilities, many paid.

Current student, 8/2000-Submit Date, December 2003

There is a valuable tool called Buffalo Trak that serves as an online résumé submission and job-finding service. There are two big career fairs, one in the fall and one in the spring. These are somewhat helpful, but usually don't result in serious job prospects. The accounting and finance programs are a step above the others in terms of on-campus recruiting. There are a barrage of on-campus interviews in the fall and spring for students in accounting and finance. Firms like Wachovia, Ernst and Young, PwC, Merrill Lynch and others conduct interviews.

> **The school says:** "Working career fairs is an art form. Some companies use them as screening interviews while others are more informational. We recommend students follow up with prospective employers and certainly use our online system (now called CSO—Career Services Online) in addition to the fairs, rather than relying wholeheartedly on either."

 # Quality of Life

Current student, Finance, 1/2003-Submit Date, October 2006

Campus is one of the most beautiful you will find any where in the nation. Surrounded by mountains and streams, the outdoor adventurer is never bored. The safety is unsurpassed. Women feel safe to walk home alone at night , and you can even get away with not locking your door. Wouldn't want to live anywhere else.

Current student, 8/2003-Submit Date, November 2006

The campus is one of the most beautiful in the world. Facilities are modern and accessible, though housing is often dated. Boulder is an accessible town with great dining, recreational opportunities and almost zero crime. Denver is just over 30 minutes away and easily accessible by bus.

Current student, 8/2003-Submit Date, January 2007

Freshmen almost always stay at the dorms which are all on, or very close to, campus. The campus is very nice, as well as the facilities, and the handful of cafeterias serve food that is more than palatable. The surrounding neighborhoods, are very nice. They can get a little sketchy when you get away from the town a little, but the area around the campus is very pleasant. Safety doesn't seem to be much of an issue.

Current student, 8/2005-Submit Date, May 2006

One of the perks of being a student at CU is definitely the quality of life. You couldn't ask for much more than this campus offers. The campus is beautiful. Not only is the whole campus comprised of beautiful architecture, but anywhere

you walk, you have a beautiful view of the Rocky Mountains. The weather is another advantage. Almost everyday is sunny, and the change of seasons never allows for boredom with the weather.

On-campus housing is pretty much only for freshmen. The dorms are an essential part of the college experience. You get to meet so many new people from so many different places. There really isn't one bad dorm on campus. No matter in which dorm you live, everyone seems to think that the one in which they lived was the best. The quality of food in the dining halls on campus is not the greatest, but it seems that dining services has made an effort to improve the variety of food offered. My biggest complaint is that they don't offer enough nutritious foods, such as vegetables. After freshman year almost all students move off campus, to wherever they choose. The only problem is that Boulder is an extremely expensive place to live, relative to most college towns. However, if you move out of walking distance of campus, you can find some very good deals. For the most part, Boulder is very safe. Boulder is also very environmentally friendly.

Current student, 8/2005-Submit Date, May 2006

Housing on campus is more than adequate and probably similar to many other college campuses. The food is pretty good most of the time, and there is always good food available in at least two or three of the seven dining halls on campus. The Boulder area is an amazing place with numerous activities to do. Intermediate skiing is only 45 minutes away and seven expert resorts are about and hour and 15 minutes away. In Boulder itself, people enjoy world-class rock climbing, hiking, biking, running, rafting, backpacking and snowshoeing. Boulder is a very active city, and it's definitely one of the most beautiful places to go to school in the world. The town itself is incredible, as well. Everyone is friendly, laid-back and loves Boulder—it's definitely a great place to live.

Current student, 8/2003-Submit Date, April 2006

Housing is expensive, but living in Boulder is worth every penny. The campus and city are second-to-none in beauty—particularly in the fall and spring. It just comes alive! Boulder offers tons of amazing food and nightlife. Generally, Boulder is an incredibly safe place, but as in any college town, there are still creepy people. You have to be vigilant—girls need to stick together, or walk with males after dark. Unfortunately, just like any other city, women should not be walking alone at night. For freshmen, dorm life is very enriching and a great time to meet lifelong friends. This is where you will find roommates for the following year and a social network which will likely last long after freshman year.

 # Social Life

Current student, 8/2003-Submit Date, November 2006

Bars in Boulder are increasing in size, popularity and diversity as the city vies for nightlife-goers from around the Denver-metro area with Denver itself. Bars in the city are not as dominated by students as most college towns, as Boulder hosts many young professionals. Pearl Street and The Hill are favorite hangouts, with loads of fun and funky student haunts and more trendy restaurants and lounges. The dating scene is nonexistent, and those who do date are relegated to the Greek scene. The Greek system does not dominate CU social life; there is a thriving independent house party circuit, where one can head out for an evening, heading from house to house with kegs in the bathtub and Kanye West on the stereo. On larger Fridays and Saturdays, residential streets from 11 p.m. to 3 a.m. resemble pub crawls in other cities. Thursday and Saturday nights are the biggest nights to go out, followed by a much quieter Friday. CU home football games dominate the weekend; everyone within a 30-mile radius essentially gets increasingly blitzed as the game nears, climaxing with a win or loss at Folsom Field. The city then essentially becomes an enormous hangover afterwards, with very few house parties, bar hoppers, or people on the street afterwards. A big win can rejuvenate party-goers to make it off the couch one more night, while a big loss can do exactly the opposite.

Current student, 8/2003-Submit Date, January 2007

There are many good bars and restaurants that are less than a mile from campus, as well as a few concert halls. As far as favorites, I guess it depends what you're into. For pizza, you can go to Cosmo's or Abo's Pizza and get a 28" pizza. There are many good places to get sandwiches. Some of my favorites are Half Fast Subs, The Cheba Hut, and Snarfs. If you want your food delivered to you, almost everywhere delivers until 2 a.m., but if they don't deliver, you can call a service called Restaurant Runners who, for an extra $3, will order, pick up and deliver the food to your residence. If you're into finer dining, the Boulder Chophouse always has great food. The Greek scene is big, but not huge. Guys who aren't involved with a frat can't usually go to the parties; obviously it's different for girls. The frat parties are fun, but there are a lot of restrictions that they have now.

Current student, 8/2005-Submit Date, May 2006

For those of us who are under 21, the social life mostly consists of house parties. Greek life at CU is big, but not so big that you are out of the loop if you are not involved. No matter what type of activities in which you are interested or what kind of music you like, you will have no problem finding people with the same interests as you have. For the part of the student population that is over 21, the bar scene is very big. Most students go to any number of bars on Pearl Street on the weekends. Connor O'Neil's, The Foundry and Trilogy, just to name a few, are bars frequented by CU students. The Fox, a small venue on University Hill, frequently has musical performances that are also very popular. Boulder also has tons of great restaurants. The Boulder Dushanbe Tea House is a must-see. The teahouse was a gift to Boulder from Tajikistan, and not only is it a beautiful work of art, they serve great brunch and dinner. There's a ton of great shopping and dining on Pearl Street.

Current student, 8/2005-Submit Date, May 2006

The campus is only about 12 percent Greek, so their presence is definitely there (if you seek it out) but not overbearing like at many other schools. There are over 300 clubs in which to get involved on campus, including Boulder Freeride—the ski and snowboard club and largest college club in the U.S. There are tons of great restaurants within walking distance with many foods from which to choose. There are also tons of bars and clubs within the Boulder area, and the clubs in Denver are a 30-minute bus ride/drive away. Generally, Boulder is a great town with lots of activities, and it is definitely not a college town where everyone leaves on the weekends; there is so much great stuff to do!

Current student, 8/2003-Submit Date, March 2005

There is a ton of stuff to do in Boulder. Hiking, biking, rafting, kayaking, bird watching, protesting, clubbing, bar hopping, partying, going to concerts, you name it. There are several different concert venues. You can get hooked up with a religious group or church, there are tons of them, too! Opportunities to volunteer, such as a youth hostel, nursing home, open-mic nights, poetry slams, snowboarding and skiing. There is an awesome bus system, every CU student gets a free bus pass for unlimited rides all year long. It goes all over town. There are 300 days of sunshine a year. Riding your bike and using the bus is all you need if you want to stay in Boulder. It's fun, you get in shape and it saves money!

Regarding social life, the school comments: "There is an abundance of social activities available to students at CU-Boulder that have nothing to do with bars. More than 300 student clubs are active, addressing a wide range of academic, political, social, religious, and recreation interests. Entertainment is easy to find with the Colorado Shakespeare Festival, CU Opera, the College of Music Artist Series, faculty and student concerts and lectures, the CU Art Galleries, the International Film Series, the University of Colorado Museum, the World Affairs Conference, and many multicultural opportunities. The Student Recreation Center is one of the finest facilities of its type in the country. It includes swimming pools, an indoor running track, multi-use gymnasiums, saunas, weightlifting equipment, an ice rink, aerobics studios, handball/racquetball courts, tennis courts and a climbing wall.

"CU-Boulder was one of the first universities to begin addressing alcohol abuse and underage drinking in a systematic way. One of the programs, A Matter of Degree, is outlined at www.colorado.edu/alcohol/."

Read all of Vault's College Surveys at **www.vault.com/college**—get complete surveys on 100s of colleges and universities, expert advice on applicaton essays and more.

VAULT CAREER LIBRARY 115

Connecticut College

Office of Admission
Connecticut College
270 Mohegan Avenue
New London, CT 06320-4196
Admissions phone: (860) 439-2200
Admissions e-mail: admission@conncoll.edu
Admissions URL: http://www.conncoll.edu/admission/

 Admissions

Alumnus/a, Business, 8/2002-5/2006, October 2007

I think it was very important to visit the school to see what it really had to offer. In the same way, I think that it was very beneficial to have an interview to show CC what I had to offer. I applied Early Decision because this was a school that I really loved. I know that CC is very selective, so I made sure to turn in any optional material in addition to all of the requirements.

Alumnus/a, Visual Arts, 8/2003-5/2007, October 2007

Though the college is highly selective, the admissions staff is extremely friendly, helpful and patient. I would definitely recommend an interview, as the college highly values the information gathered through that process. Students who are creative, bright, self-motivated, enthusiastic and active clearly have an edge when it comes to gaining acceptance.

Alumnus/a, Business, 8/2003-5/2007, October 2007

The admissions process entails personal essay, high school transcript, a question about "Why Connecticut College?" and optional SAT scores, SAT Subject Tests or ACT scores are required, as well as an optional interview. The essay and transcript are the most important pieces. The interview can help provide more information about a candidate as well as determine the fit with Connecticut College. The best advice is to be yourself in your application and definitely in your interview! There is a link on the web site called "Essays that Worked," which is helpful to look at if you're stuck on the personal statement. Conn is selective but it's not impossible to get in. The admissions office is looking for a well-rounded student body as a whole, but it doesn't mean each individual needs to be perfectly well-rounded. Conn wants passionate students who will become passionate leaders and will live the Conn motto "liberal arts in action." Students are very active on campus and drive change.

Current student, Political Science, 8/2004-Submit Date, October 2007

Admissions tries to be as personal as possible, but that requires action on the part of the prospective student. Open houses, tours, info sessions, interviews—it is all available, and [underrepresented students] who might not otherwise be able to afford travel expenses, there is a funded explore weekend.

When looking at applicants, the admissions committee considers high school transcript and essays first. The student's record of achievement is extremely important—if he/she cannot excel in high school, he/she is less likely to thrive in college. The essay is a piece of personal expression—you don't have to go over the top, but the more personal it is the better. Check out the school's web site "Essays that Worked" section which highlights favorite essays from past years. Supplemental information like DVDs, dance performances and art work are only important in the context of academic pursuits. If they go to the art department or dance department for evaluation it is OK, but don't send all of this to admissions initially.

> **Connecticut College says:** "Students who desire their artistic talents to be considered as part of the application process are encouraged to meet in person with departments, preferably during the fall of their senior year. Applicants may submit arts materials directly to the Office of Admission by the admission deadline only if travel to Connecticut College for an on-campus review is cost prohibitive. In such cases, arts faculty may be

asked to participate in the evaluation of submitted materials. Submission requirements are listed in the college Course Catalogue and the Supplement to the Common Application."

Conn continues to get more and more competitive. Show a true interest in the school and a specific program or opportunity there and you will be far more likely to get noticed by the admission committee. No school wants to be just another school to which the student applied.

Alumnus/a, Business, 9/1999-5/2003, October 2007

The admissions and application process was fantastic! Admissions representatives went to my high school to provide more information on the college and give out their contact information if we had any questions. The admissions office was very receptive to questions and extremely responsive. Admissions Fellows, current student leaders, interviewed prospective students and offered unabashed advice on the admissions process and what makes the college great. It was great having that personal touch.

Connecticut College is already a premiere and selective private, liberal arts school, but is constantly maintaining its charm and re-inventing itself to bolster its selectivity. Connecticut College looks for a diverse array of students centering on scholars who not only show academic prowess, but also balance their academics with leadership, performing arts, community service and citizenship in an evolving global world.

Alumnus/a, 8/2001-5/2005, October 2005

I worked as a Senior Admissions Fellow at Conn during my senior year, so I spent a lot of time interviewing applicants and selling the school to anxious parents. No surprise, the admissions process at Conn is comparable to that of most small liberal arts colleges on the East Coast. The first step is the supplement to the Common Application, which basically just starts a file for you at the admissions office. About a month or so later, you submit your actual application which includes your essay, teacher recs, transcript, [counselor recommendation] and the application itself. Fortunately, Connecticut accepts the Common App, which will save you considerable time and effort if you are applying to more than one school.

There are a couple aspects of the admissions process at Conn that often confuse potential applicants. The first is SATs. Connecticut College doesn't require that you take the SAT, and it is not held against you if you decline to submit SAT scores. The best way to approach this is simply to take the test and then see if your scores are comparable to the average score of last year's incoming class (about a [1330] or so). If you scored at or above this mark, you may as well submit them as they can only help your application. Similarly, students coming from nontraditional backgrounds (e.g., home schooled or from high schools without traditional grading) would be well-advised to submit your SAT scores even if they are a little below the class average. This will demonstrate that, although you come from a nontraditional background, you can still compete on more standardized modes of assessment. Three SAT Subject Tests are required of all applicants.

> **The school says:** "Connecticut College requires two SAT Subject Tests or the ACT. The SAT is not required but can be submitted and considered if requested by a student."

The second non-required but highly recommended aspect of the Connecticut College admissions process is the interview. An interview isn't mandatory but, unless you are extremely inarticulate or trying to hide some obvious character defect from the admissions committee, it is almost always a good idea. First, it demonstrates that you are interested enough in the school to make the extra effort to come in to interview. Most importantly, your interview (along with your personal essay) will help differentiate you from a pack of applicants who look very similar on paper. Connecticut is a selective school (34 percent acceptance rate) and a surprisingly large percentage of the applicants would do well there and are, in fact, probably qualified for admission. Many students are coming from upper-tier public high schools or private schools, and nearly all of these students have impressive academic resumes studded with the requisite extracurricular activities, community service projects and interesting summer experiences. So, while an interview won't make up for poor grades or mediocre teachers recs, it will help you stand out from a well-qualified crowd.

So how do you differentiate yourself during an interview? Trite as it sounds, be yourself. Interviewers are looking primarily for depth and passion. What do you care about? Are you interested in what you've been doing in school and can you talk about it in a way that conveys some depth and intelligence or did you just take a bunch of classes because your college counselor told you to? What have you read recently, what pisses you off about the state of the world, do you really think Quentin Tarantino is a better director than Scorsese? Basically, a good interview resembles a good conversation and a competent interviewer will not be afraid to let the conversation drift into an area in which you are interested as a way of gauging the depth of your interest and knowledge. For instance, if an applicant mentioned that he/she was interested in politics or environmentalism or literature, I might ask him/her for an opinion and then simply let the conversation take off from there.

Thus, don't say that you are interested in something that you aren't prepared to talk about. Also, don't spend too much time reciting your qualifications. The admissions committee can get that from your written application. Above all, be relaxed. Most interviewers are students and would prefer an interesting, laid-back conversation as much as you would (an awkward interview is uncomfortable as hell for everyone involved). A little humor will go a long way, as will self-confidence.

Academics

Alumnus/a, Physical Sciences, 8/2003-5/2007, October 2007
With the exception of a few 100-level classes (Bio 105, Psych 101) nearly all classes are small (fewer than 20 students). All classes are taught by professors, there are no TAs! Classes are challenging but generally not overwhelming. Teachers understand that students attend a four-year residential college as much for what they learn outside of the classroom as what they learn inside. There are numerous research opportunities and study abroad is really popular.

Almost every student develops a close friendship with at least one teacher, if not more. It is not unusual to see teachers in dining halls and even the campus bar eating and dining with students. This really leads to a community atmosphere on campus.

Alumnus/a, Business, 8/2003-5/2007, October 2007
I loved my classes and professors at Conn. Conn takes an interdisciplinary approach to academics. Therefore, it is easy to double major or combine different types of subjects that other schools would not allow you to combine easily. Conn even has majors that are interdisciplinary, such as international relations and environmental studies, which combine classes from different departments into one major. There are four interdisciplinary centers that offer a certificate upon completion. Students apply to these centers separately and complete two classes with the center in addition to an internship after junior year in that area. These centers are very popular and give students the freedom to explore their interests. The centers include: CISLA (Center for International Studies in the Liberal Arts), PICA (Public Policy), CCBES (Conservation Biology and Environmental Science), and CAT (Center for Arts and Technology). Faculty and administrators [have recently developed] a center for race and ethnicity. Classes are easy to get into. The registrar is easy to talk to; there is very little "red tape" at Conn. And if the registrar can't get you into a class, if you ask the professor and sit in on the first day, he/she will usually let you in. Professors realize that students have lives outside of class, so the workload can be pretty easily balanced with extracurriculars. However, there will always be times that are busier than others with papers and mid-terms to take. If you find you are not being challenged enough, there are always additional research and "independent study" options to pursue a subject you're passionate about. Professors are easy to talk to and have weekly office hours. Professors will often offer to talk outside of office hours, as well, whether its over a cup of coffee or at their house for dinner. [More than half of the] students study abroad and the classes are easily transferred back to earn credits at Conn.

Current student, Political Science, 8/2004-Submit Date, October 2007
Academics are fairly hard but not impossible freshman year. They get much harder as students get older. Teaching is amazing—if you are bored in class it's your own fault! There are tons of options and enough room in the schedule to take extra classes, get into a variety of classes and explore outside of the major. Grading varies widely, but on the whole a serious workload is the norm for good grades. Classes are not usually hard to get into because majors are so diverse over the school population.

Alumnus/a, Business, 9/1999-5/2003, October 2007
Connecticut College offers excellent professors who oftentimes develop an outstanding relationship with students due to the small class size. Sometimes it can be difficult getting into some of the more popular courses in economics, government and psychology, particularly with the more notable professors going on sabbatical or abroad.

Grading and grade inflation often depend on the professor, as professors with the reputation of easy graders in difficult courses often find their classes full and waitlisted. The rigors of the academics varies between course, professor, and major, but overall the quality of the academic experience is phenomenal. It is strongly complemented by lectures and common hour discussions that center on local, national and global issues.

The workload is what you make of the college experience. Many students can "get by" with mediocre effort, but miss the broad array that Connecticut College has to offer. The college offers an assortment of personal, professional and educational development both inside and outside of classes in the form of lectures, discussions, focus meetings, and numerous academic and social organizations and clubs.

Alumnus/a, 9/1999-5/2003, August 2006
My average class size at Conn was smaller than my average class size in grad school, but a lot of that depends on the courses you choose. Be selective. I often took classes I wasn't necessarily interested in beforehand because I knew they were taught by a professor I'd like. Most faculty members are very approachable and fair. However, there are a small number who will base your grade on their personal opinion of you or your beliefs. Thankfully, most of those profs don't seem to last more than a year or two.

Academics are about what you would expect—the workload is challenging, but not overwhelming, and the material itself is fairly difficult. The toughest thing was probably registering for classes, because due to the school's size some courses are not offered on a regular basis or fill up very quickly. I found that was usually not a problem in 300- or 400-level courses, though.

Alumnus/a, Sociology, 8/2001-5/2005, October 2005
Overall, I was very satisfied with the tenor and quality of the academic environment at Connecticut College. It's a selective school, and most of the students there are smart and fairly motivated. The workload varies from class to class, but most students work pretty hard. Likewise, grade inflation varies from department to department and from professor to professor. For instance, the chemistry, biology, and government departments are known to be tough while the history and sociology departments have some easy classes. (There's no shame in this, I was a sociology major. OK, some shame.)

The faculty are also excellent. While I had one or two bad profs, most of my teachers were very good and actually cared about the craft of teaching (as opposed to just their research). Perhaps most importantly, most students are actually engaged in their classes and care about what they're learning. I would like to see more students who feel this way, but many do, as evidenced by the amount of student-run extracurricular clubs, publications and so on.

Employment Prospects

Alumnus/a, Physical Sciences, 8/2003-5/2007, October 2007
The Office of Career Enhancing Life Skills (CELs) is one of the best things about Conn. They provide every student with the opportunity to get a $3,000 stipend toward an unpaid internship after his/her junior year. My internship turned into a full-time job (I was hired by my current company in January of my

Read all of Vault's College Surveys at www.vault.com/college—get complete surveys on 100s of colleges and universities, expert advice on applicaton essays and more.

VAULT CAREER LIBRARY 117

senior year). CELS also helps every student gain the skills for a successful career by insuring they know how to make a résumé, cover letter, and going over any necessary interview skills.

Alumnus/a, Business, 8/2002-5/2006, October 2007

I had three job offers before I graduated from Connecticut College. All in financial services and consulting. The school's Career Enhancing Life Skills (CELS) office works with students to polish their résumés, prepare for interviews, and make connections. I think the CELS office has done a wonderful job with both current students and those who have graduated.

Alumnus/a, Visual Arts, 8/2003-5/2007, October 2007

Conn's internship program is probably the best I've ever heard of. Each student is free to enroll in the CELS program, which not only provides mentoring and counseling services for job hunts, résumé creation and so on, but also awards each student a $3,000 tax-free stipend to spend while completing an internship in the summer between the junior and senior year. My internship was among the most educational aspects of my entire college experience, and I certainly wouldn't have been able to do it without CELS. After graduation, the alumni office is very helpful in making connections and networks, both of which are invaluable during job searches.

Alumnus/a, Business, 8/2003-5/2007, October 2007

Conn has a great career office called Career Enhancing Life Skills (CELS). Each student is assigned to a CELS counselor during his/her freshman year. Each student is given the opportunity to complete a series of workshops and get funding from the college of up to $3,000 to complete an internship after his/her junior year. The college realizes that not all students can take off a summer from paid employment and offers a stipend to compensate that. The internship allows students to apply their background in theory into something concrete. Students often do their internships abroad; I did mine in London. CELS also works with the four centers to help those students find an internship and work it into their career goals. However, CELS does not find the internship for you, which makes the job search process more doable. CELS teaches you how to find an internship or job, how to write a résumé and cover letter, and how to interview and present yourself to employers. Conn is involved in several recruiting consortiums in nearby cities. Employers also come to campus to recruit directly and present information sessions to interested students. Conn alumni will often return to speak on panels about their careers as well. Conn alumni are happy to help with the job search process and they are easily found through our online alumni directory. Many students will go straight into jobs after college, and many go to grad school. About 50 percent of students will have gone to grad school within five years of graduating from Conn. The rest of the students go into the Peace Corps, fellowship programs or other similar programs.

Alumnus/a, Business, 9/1999-5/2003, October 2007

The career counseling office offers an extensive alumni network who cross-cut many different barriers and professional paths. These alumni are very receptive and willing to help young alumni and current students find employment and an internship.

Internships are a major drawing point to Connecticut College. Few schools in the country offer such an amazing program for professional development. By fulfilling several career workshops and meeting with the Career Enhancing Life Skills(CELs) office students become eligible for a $3,000 stipend for an internship during the summer after their junior year. Many of these internships boost résumés, provide needed life experience, and job opportunities after college. Personal and alumni connections are beginning to add to alumni recruiting. Many graduates obtain solid jobs outside of college in fields ranging from community activism, government, law, economics, the arts, and sciences to name a few. Connecticut College uses the liberal arts education to fully benefit them in their new careers and often advance quickly in their respective professions.

Quality of Life

Alumnus/a, Physical Sciences, 8/2003-5/2007, October 2007

Quality of life on Conn is high. Although the buildings are old-ish, they are very homey. All dorms are freshman through senior and coed, so it is inevitable that you will be friends with people from grades other than your own. One thing that

some students should beware of: coed bathrooms. Sounds strange but is really only weird for the first two days of frosh orientation.

The campus is beautiful with an amazing view of the Long Island Sound that will stick with you long after you leave school. The arboretum is an great resource for classes, as well as a great place to take a hike or have a picnic. The dining halls are as top notch, from Harris (the main dining hall) to Freeman (the vegetarian dining hall), all the staffers are friendly and the meals are wonderful. Keep an eye out for Lobster and Steak night as it is a highlight of the fall semester.

> **The school says:** "Connecticut College exists in a singular environment known as the Connecticut College Arboretum, which offers a quality of life and conservation classroom unique among liberal arts institutions. The Arboretum's very diverse 750 acres include the landscaped grounds of the college campus, as well as the surrounding plant collections, natural areas and managed landscapes."

Alumnus/a, Business, 9/1999-5/2003, October 2007

The experience at Connecticut College certainly is what you make of it. Everyday there are opportunities to enhance both your experience academically, socially, artistically and athletically. Afternoons and evenings offer various lectures, discussions, and ways for students to impact the campus. At Connecticut College, students are empowered by one of the nation's topnotch Honor Codes, and a unique style of shared governance that grants students a major say in every aspect of student life.

New London often receives a poor reputation, but truly is a "diamond in the rough." More and more students and faculty venture into New London, which offers excellent dining opportunities, restaurants, great beaches, art galleries and festivals. It truly has something for everyone! Transportation is difficult at times, but the college offers a Camel Van shuttle system (which is sometimes unreliable). Taxis are also inexpensive and many friends are willing to drive the three minutes off campus to downtown New London.

Current student, Political Science, 8/2004-Submit Date

Most students live on campus, so there is a good sense of community. All classes are equally distributed in the dorms so there is no freshman housing. Dining hall is good and smaller dining rooms offer different food which is a nice change from the huge dining hall. President Higdon is making a huge effort to restore the dorms and facilities and there is already significant improvements to campus in the last year. Crime in minimal and for most of my time at the college I have kept my door unlocked—I've never had anything stolen.

The honor code works both socially and in academics. So no cheating or lying, and everyone in the dorms has respect for quiet hours and privacy. The student government association, student activities council and judiciary board all structure the honor code outside the dorms and the students have an amazing amount of influence in the life of the college, the administration and alumni networks.

> **Connecticut College says:** "Over the next 10 years, Connecticut College will invest $53 million in renovations and infrastructure. The college just completed $9 million in renovations to classrooms and residence halls."

Alumnus/a, Business, 8/2003-5/2007, October 2007

Conn was my home for four years; that's why I chose it! Almost all students live on campus. The dorms are mostly coed and they house all ages of students; thus, freshman live with seniors, juniors, and sophomores. I prefer this to having an all-freshman dorm. With taking introductory classes, freshmen will easily meet one another but it's more difficult to meet upperclassmen. The orientation program for freshmen before upper classmen move in is also great and enables freshmen to feel ownership of the campus. The campus is beautiful and small and tight knit. One of my fears of going to a liberal arts college was feeling claustrophobic with the same people, same buildings, etc. but I did not find that to be the case. Additionally, most students ([50 to 55] percent) go abroad, which allows them to come back excited and with a new worldly perspective. Conn is located in New London, CT, which is not a booming city. However, it improved even in the four years that I was there. New London is located two hours south of Boston, [two and a half] hours north of New York City, and 45 minutes south of Providence. Students have the opportunity to travel and visit other friends on the campus but campus does not empty out on the weekends. I always feel safe on campus, even walking back from the library at 2 a.m. when it closes.

Social Life

Alumnus/a, Physical Sciences, 8/2003-5/2007, October 2007

Social life at Conn is all about staying on campus and being with friends. There is no Greek life, so don't expect any wild frat parties. However, kegs are permitted in the dorm common rooms (with approval from the Office of Residential Life), and the parties are fun but usually under control. Campus wide parties, such as Festivas (think winter holiday party meets semi-formal) and Floralia (spring concert held the first weekend in May), are the highlights of the year. The whole campus goes out to these events and they are good old fashioned college fun.

Most weekends students can be found hanging out in their rooms drinking a few beers with friends or at the on-campus bar, which has probably 10 to 12 beers on tap. The Student Activities Council does their best to get students to come to events, and there are things to do every weekend, if you choose to. Conn is really all about making the choices that you want. If you choose to do something, the College will generally support you. Conn is a place for pro-active people who really want to lead themselves down a path of education, rather than following 40,000 other ants.

Alumnus/a, Business, 8/2002-5/2006, October 2007

Cro-bar is the only bar on campus, but alcohol was allowed in dorm rooms if the student was of age. Most of the partying occurred on campus, but if you wanted to go to the bars Mystic and New London had a few places and many people went to Mohegan Sun or Foxwoods casinos because they were so close. Mystic and Groton had a ton of great restaurants that were only five to 15 minutes away. Margaritas, Olios, Paul's Pasta and Bravo to name a few. If you want to go clubbing, plan on going to Mohegan Sun or driving to NY, Providence or Boston.

Alumnus/a, Business, 8/2003-5/2007, October 2007

The social life at Conn is mainly made up of keg parties in dorms on Thursday and Saturday nights. These parties are thrown by sports teams, clubs, or groups of friends. Everyone is invited. Friday nights are more low-key; a band comes to campus every Friday night and students often eat off-campus for Friday night dinner. There is a bar on campus in the student center called the Cro Bar. Students who are 21 will occasionally go off campus to bars in the town but it is not the norm. Not all of the social life revolves around drinking. Many speakers and performers have come to campus. Students are also very involved in clubs, sports and student governance. There is no Greek system, which is generally a good thing. The culture is very open and everyone is invited and welcome at all events. The dating scene is hard to describe; it seems like students are either hooking up or dating for the long-term. Students often date students at other colleges, as well.

Alumnus/a, Business, 9/1999-5/2003, October 2007

Cliques do exist but cross-cut many groups. Oftentimes, you will find freshmen and seniors, athletes and artists, student leaders and partiers intermingling. It is common for many of these students' interests to overlap. The community and college have many events that appeal to a large group of students—from celebrating culture, religion, diversity, scholarship, leadership or empowering students to solve local, national or global issues. There truly is something for everyone at Conn!

New London offers a wide selection of restaurants that offer delicious food at respectable prices. Many students have several favorite restaurants in New London, nearby Groton, and Mystic. Student favorites for bars and restaurants include Hot Rods, The Tavern, Hannafins, Brown Derby and many more! There are too many great restaurants to list.

Connecticut College offers a very strong, active, and empowered student government that looks to impact and improve the campus on issues ranging from small to great. The SGA has been extremely involved in the community, leading blood drives, orienting freshmen to the community in their New London 101

tour, raising money for OxFam, and working with students, faculty, staff, and administrators to formulate policy on campus.

Alumnus/a, 9/1999-5/2003, August 2006

There are a lot of great activities on campus, but they get repetitive after a while (except for Camelympics, which is a yearly competition in a variety of athletic and other endeavors that is held at night and preferably with a lot of drunk contestants). There aren't any great bars or clubs in the area and campus alcohol policies have been getting stricter. After a while you will have to make your own fun.

The School Says

Situated on the coast of southern New England, Connecticut College is one of the nation's leading private, coeducational liberal arts colleges. Our dynamic, intellectual community lives and learns on a 750-acre hilltop campus with historic granite architecture and views of Long Island Sound and the Thames River. Since its founding in 1911, this small liberal arts college has offered a challenging academic curriculum that fosters a lifetime of learning and community involvement. Our alumni have earned distinction in virtually every field. Our student body includes 1,900 men and women from 45 states, Washington, D.C., and 71 countries. 40 percent of students are men, and 20 percent are students of color (15 percent domestic).

Connecticut College is distinguished by interdisciplinary studies, international programs, funded internships and a commitment to faculty-student research usually found only at large universities. We are global in scope. 55 percent of our students participate in innovative international and national programs to study away or abroad. We give our students unparalleled access to funded internships and research opportunities in the U.S. and throughout the world. The college offers more than 50 majors and more than 1,000 courses in 27 academic departments and interdisciplinary programs. Top anticipated majors are Biology, English, Government, International Relations, and Psychology. The student-faculty ratio is 9:1. The college has 162 full-time professors; 89 percent hold a doctorate or equivalent. All classes are taught by professors.

Our 85-year-old honor code, a fundamental distinction, underpins all academic and social interactions and creates a palpable spirit of trust and cooperation between students and faculty. There is no Greek system. The college has been nationally recognized for our service-learning programs and cited as a "College with a Conscience" by the Princeton Review for fostering social responsibility and public service. We are on the Peace Corps' 2006 Top 25 list of volunteers produced among small schools. We meet the high standards of membership in Phi Beta Kappa and the Watson Foundation List. Graduates have won prestigious post-graduate honors, awards and fellowships, including Fulbright, Luce and Truman Fellowships.

Leo I. Higdon, Jr., the 10th president of Connecticut College, took office on July 1, 2006. We have a long tradition of operating the college as an environmental model by initiating and implementing innovative policies that promote environmental sustainability. We manage the entire 750-acre campus—forests, ponds, gardens and main campus—as an arboretum. Our athletes compete in the NCAA Division III New England Small Colleges Athletic Conference (NESCAC) with Amherst, Bates, Bowdoin, Colby, Hamilton, Middlebury, Trinity, Tufts, Wesleyan and Williams. Since the 1970s, our mascot has been the Camel.

Read all of Vault's College Surveys at www.vault.com/college—get complete surveys on 100s of colleges and universities, expert advice on applicaton essays and more.

VAULT CAREER LIBRARY 119

Trinity College

Admissions Office
300 Summit Street
Hartford, CT 06106
Admissions phone: 1-860-297-2180
Admissions e-mail: admissions.office@trincoll.edu
Admissions URL: www.trincoll.edu/prospectivestudent/

 ## Admissions

Current student, Cultural Studies, 9/2004-Submit Date, October 2007

The Trinity College admissions process is designed to take into account all aspects of the student. There is an optional interview that helps the admissions committee get to know the student. There is an essay and, of course, high school grades and the transcript are important, as well.

Current student, Liberal Arts, 9/2006-Submit Date, October 2007

What drew me to Trinity most in the beginning was the amount of candor with which the administration used to describe the college. As one of many institutions I visited in the Northeast within a weeks time, Trinity stood out by showing concern for helping prospects with the entire college selection process, rather than focusing on convincing seniors to choose Trinity. They presented what I needed to make an informed decision, rather than persuading me with just the positive aspects. So visiting and attending information sessions in person not only allowed me to get a feel for the school, but allowed me to assess the character and philosophy of the faculty, which isn't always evident at other places.

Having an interview definitely helped me get in at Trinity, considering I didn't have the best grades. The interviewers are not intimidating, and although it's always important to emphasize past accomplishments, I felt as if they were most concerned with who I am as a person. As a smaller college, Trinity has the advantage of being able to offer this opportunity.

Trinity's most prominent concern at this time is to enrich the student body by diversifying in every way possible. So, although academic merit is important (mostly A's and B's in high-level classes), I wouldn't automatically count out a person who doesn't have the best grades. I can't presume to know what the admissions office is thinking, but they seem to gravitate toward a well rounded class rather than seeking out the "best" individuals one by one. So, exceptional talent outside the classroom is almost equally as important. As a small college, fostering a positive community environment is as vital to an institution's success as the level of merit that exists among those who inhabit it. Trinity accepts the Common Application, which has only one essay, so they can't help but assume it's your best work. This was another aspect that helped me get in because I was able to express a creative way of thinking, to which they seemed very receptive.

Alumnus/a, 9/2000-5/2004, March 2007

Trinity allows or at least at the time allowed the use of the Common Application. I took APs and SATs and SAT Subject Tests, all of which helped. I think what they are most looking for is interest. I wanted to play on the soccer team there so I went and visited three times. I went to meet some of the professors and went to some of the classes. I think this was the largest help in the application process. More than just knowing who I was by name and that I went to high school and did well, they got to meet me and they knew exactly what I was going to do once I enrolled.

> **Regarding admissions, the school says:** "This year Trinity welcomed 576 first-year students, selected from the largest applicant pool in the college's history. Members of the first-year class come from 33 states, plus the District of Columbia and 15 foreign countries. The incoming class includes 22 percent students of color. Trinity has a strong commitment to increasing racial and cultural diversity on campus. "

 ## Academics

Current student, Economics, 9/2004-Submit Date, October 2007

It is hard to get into popular classes here, and depending on the department, it might also be hard to find a wide array of classes. Often, your lottery number will decide which classes you will be able to get into.

Current student, Cultural Studies, 9/2004-Submit Date, October 2007

Trinity College academics are highlighted by the close student/ faculty relationships. With such small class sizes, students are really able to get to know their professors and learn in a more interactive and personal way. Professors are the top in their field and opportunities to do research are endless.

Current student, Liberal Arts, 9/2006-Submit Date, October 2007

The majority of the professors at Trinity are fantastic mentors. I would feel comfortable going to speak to any of my current professors individually, both for academic concerns as well as personal advice. They may not always have the answers, but they will try to point you in the direction of someone who can help. I've always been impressed with the faculty here, and although I have heard that some have personal agendas, I have yet to encounter this phenomenon. Each of my professors has his or her doctorate or is currently working towards it. They're also aware of events around school and attend sporting events to watch their students.

The music department is small, and doesn't have a lot of course options or professors. Many students take classes from the department to satisfy distribution requirements, and therefore the more serious students don't necessarily get as much out of some courses. A consortium exists between Trinity, University of Hartford and St. Joseph's College where students can take classes and transfer the credit back to Trinity easily. This arrangement is useful to arts students because the Hartt School at University of Hartford provides many more options. The neuroscience field is fairly new, but the classes are innovative and facilitate hands-on learning opportunities. Courses, from biology and chemistry to psychology and philosophy, are incorporated into the major, ensuring a rich and self-directed educational experience. The sciences in general encourage undergraduate research; all an interested student needs to do is ask a professor, and they'll have the unique chance as an undergraduate to help in the lab and potentially be published.

The only instance in which I feel grading doesn't always reflect the amount of knowledge gained is in large lecture classes, which there are very few of. The majority of classes are seminars or lectures with only 12 to 30 people. Regardless, students never feel uncomfortable about asking questions. The workload seems slightly above average, but I never feel overwhelmed. The more motivated a student is to succeed, the heavier the workload will be because there is never a shortage of information to learn on any given subject. The professors are happy to facilitate those who want to go above and beyond. Supplemental instruction sessions are held a few times a week in the more difficult courses, and have proven to be a huge help to students.

Upperclassmen get first choice for classes, meaning the most popular classes are often difficult to get. If an underclassman wants a class desperately enough, he/she can chase down the professor and have a decent chance of getting in. Students have to be proactive about getting the courses they want because there is often only one section of a class offered only one semester during the year. Just because a course is in the catalog, doesn't mean it will be offered that year. Sometimes elective courses for major requirements aren't offered for over a year or two. Students double major in areas like engineering and math or biology and neuroscience, but it is more difficult to study across disciplines, like theatre and chemistry, because the courses are scheduled at the same time. I chose Trinity primarily for the academics, and I have yet to be disappointed. It has all the qualities for which small colleges strive

Trinity has a five area distribution requirement (humanities, social sciences, fine arts, logic and reasoning and natural sciences) which assures a sound liberal arts education. They also require a certain level of proficiency in logic and reasoning, as well as writing, which may be accomplished before arriving. This can be determined through a combination of application materials (the essay), AP/IB tests, and short tests taken prior to the start of freshmen year. Writing 101 and math 101 must be taken, usually as a freshman, to satisfy these requirements if deemed necessary by the college.

Alumnus/a, Math/Economics, 9/2000-5/2004, March 2007

I completed two majors at Trinity: Mathematics and Economics. The quality of these classes is very high. The teachers are used for more than just math majors since mathematics is required to a certain point of all students enrolled. This amounts to classes between 15 and 20 students for Calculus I and II and lower-level classes. Every higher-level class within the math major had fewer than eight students. If you want to learn math and have a full professor who can spend and entire afternoon answering your questions and working with you to get through complicated math problems this is your school. No TAs—none.

Economics is the most popular major at Trinity. For that reason, the class sizes are somewhat larger at all levels than the math classes above. Lower-level econ classes will have between 15 and 25 students depending on the teacher and the class. At the highest levels class sizes are not allowed to be above 10. They won't ever tell you that. Due to the popularity of the economics major some none core classes can be difficult to get into. Econ majors will always be able to get into any class they need for graduation.

Alumnus/a, Theater and Dance, 8/1998-5/2002, March 2004

In general, Trinity is an amazing, academic school, even down to their theater degree, which I believe is really rare in a theater program. All classes are top quality, even the fun ones like Food in Italian-American Culture and the Math of Games and Gambling. They have a very detailed process of getting into popular classes, and it's very fair. As for grading—you get what you give. If you are as good a student as you were to get into the school, you should do fine. Unless you're in a disgustingly hard major like econ or poli sci. Professors at Trinity are amazing—nothing else needs to be said. Workload is a typical college workload.

> **Regarding academics, Trinity says:** "Trinity has a strong First-Year program and each year about 500 students participate in the Community Learning Initiative (CLI), which links students with individuals and organizations in Greater Hartford. Study Away and other global study opportunities are integral parts of a Trinity education including Trinity's campus in Rome, eight Global Learning Sites, Trinity/La MaMa/NYC, and the Trinity Shanghai Semester. Trinity, a liberal arts college, has a number of special curricular opportunities and offers study in Human Rights, Engineering, Environmental Science, and Public Policy and Law."

Employment Prospects

Alumnus/a, English, 9/1995-5/1999, October 2007

Trinity's alumni network is very strong, and willing to help recent graduates whenever possible. Graduates find themselves in a competitive position for jobs. Many graduates move to Boston, New York, and the West Coast. The Career Services Office helps students with the job search process throughout the undergraduate years.

Current student, Cultural Studies, 9/2004-Submit Date, October 2007

The Trinity College Career Services Office is a great resource on campus and organizes networking receptions, résumé workshops and mock interviews. Trinity students are well prepared after their education here to enter the workforce or graduate school competitively.

Current student, Liberal Arts, 9/2006-Submit Date, October 2007

The more popular paths out of Trinity include careers in finance and graduate schools (about half). Many further their education in law and medicine, with impressive acceptance rates. The Career Services Office is constantly holding information sessions and recruiting services with employers from nearby cities like New York and Boston nearly every week. Trinity's alumni are generally very successful, so they certainly play a more prominent role in employment of new graduates than the average college or university.

Alumnus/a, Math/Economics, 9/2000-5/2004, March 2007

I graduated during a downturn in the market and hiring was scarce. However, once I got out into the world and started looking around, everyone knew Trinity and it does appear to be well-respected. I have never found finding a job difficult. Then again I was a math and economics major.

Alumnus/a, Theater and Dance, 8/1998-5/2002, March 2004

I don't think Trinity is the place to go for a career in theater unless you want an academic theater career. There are very limited job and internship opportunities for Theater majors there. There was absolutely no campus recruiting for my major. As for prestige that it has given me: as in anything, there is prestige in the fact that you get a degree from a very good college, and that you went to college at all. But for theater majors, there really isn't any career placement. As for every other major, I obviously don't know as much, but I do know that senior year the Career Services Office was always packed with my friends. The counselors are very genuine and willing to help and really easy to set up appointments with. There is very good support for job-hunting.

> **Regarding employment prospects, the school says:** "Roughly half of Trinity students participate in internships in Greater Hartford including business, nonprofits and the special Legislative Internship program, which brings students into the State Capitol. In addition, special programs for students preparing for graduate school, such as the Health Fellows program, and our Career Services office, which features alumni interaction both in person and online, provide students with opportunities for career exploration and recruitment."

Quality of Life

Current student, Liberal Arts, 9/2006-Submit Date, October 2007

The campus is easy to navigate, and one can walk from one end to the other in slightly more than 10 minutes. A few have bikes or skateboards, but most walk. Most everyone has been to the gym at one point or another, and I would guess well more than half are frequent visitors. Housing right now is a little tight with the renovations underway of the biggest dormitory on campus. The college guaranteed housing for all four years in the past, but is no longer in a position to do so. Since the college is a rather concentrated community, this makes life a little more difficult for those forced off campus. There are many apartments available surrounding the campus, but as in any city, walking alone and after dark poses some risk. The campus itself is beautiful and has plenty of green space, but right on its doorstep is the rougher side of city life.

There is a lack of indoor common space at the college. When the weather is nice, many students take advantage of the quad and athletic fields. Winter draws everyone indoors, making the lack of common space a reason for a bit of isolation during these months.

The Mather Dining hall has just been renovated and is likely one of the premier facilities in the area. It has strict hours, though, and two other more modest eating facilities are open more often. There is no 24-hour facility or form of variety store. Some snacks and bottled drinks are available in the Cave and toiletry essentials for sale in the bookstore, but most need to venture off campus for more extensive shopping (and lower prices). A movie theatre on campus is a major benefit, and members from the outside community come for showings.

Current student, Cultural Studies, 9/2004-Submit Date, October 2007

Residential life at Trinity is spectacular. I have always felt safe on campus and am very satisfied with my housing on campus.

Alumnus/a, 9/2000-5/2004, March 2007

They have several dorms, which are hotel quality in the rooms. In my opinion, freshman dorms are awful even compared to other schools in the area and the Northeast that I visited. After freshman year, the dorms improve immensely. Senior dorms and 21 plus dorms are all excellent in quality. Crime and safety can be a problem.

Read all of Vault's College Surveys at www.vault.com/college—get complete surveys on 100s of colleges and universities, expert advice on applicaton essays and more.

VAULT CAREER LIBRARY 121

Alumnus/a, Theater and Dance, 8/1998-5/2002, March 2004

Trinity's quality of life when I went there was amazing. I know it's changed a lot since then. Housing is great. The campus is beautiful. Facilities are very good. Dining is good—at least I thought it was, but I know everyone did not agree with me because everyone has different standards. Neighborhood is not so good. There is a lot of crime in Hartford and campus safety is a constant issue on campus that has been going in circles for so many years that at this point doesn't really seem to be solvable.

> **Regarding quality of life, the school says:** "Students are involved in community service, athletics, as well as in campus clubs, the student newspaper and student government. Many students volunteer at the campus Boys and Girls Club, as well as the new Koeppel Community Sports Center/Rink where community children learn to skate. In addition to internships, students are able to enjoy cultural, dining and shopping opportunities in the Greater Hartford area, as well as in New York and Boston. Our trained campus safety team oversees an emergency notification system, campus shuttle and electronic key system, as well as provides regular safety updates."

 Social Life

Alumnus/a, English, 9/1995-5/1999, October 2007

Trinity offers a wide range of social options to fit all tastes. Access to the City of Hartford expands the choices, but there is plenty to do right on campus. Greek life is present but does not dominate. Sports are big.

Current student, Economics, 9/2004-Submit Date, October 2007

There is a raging party scene here at Trinity and you can find something fun to do every night of the week. Students often go downtown to bars a few nights or to frats and off-campus parties.

Current student, Liberal Arts, 9/2006-Submit Date, October 2007

Although I have already seen a change in the student population during my stay at the college, the majority of the student population is from the Northeast and generally well off. Much of the social scene centers around Vernon Street, where most all the fraternity and sorority houses are located. This could take some getting used to for those not familiar with this lifestyle, which can be a source of turmoil freshman year.

Students at Trinity don't generally take part in long-term relationships. They prefer the no-strings attached lifestyle and there doesn't seem to be an identifiable "dating scene."

Parties of all types are the main source of entertainment on campus. Alternative events occur, especially in the arts, but are not well recognized or advertised. The Trinity Exchange is a daily e-mail that informs the student body of happenings around campus, but is often ignored. The student activities committee throws a few school sponsored parties throughout the year such as the welcome back dance with a live band, the 80s dance and spring weekend, with another more prominent guest artist. The Fred is a dormitory which fosters an alternative type of community. It is organized by students and is intended as a social contrast to that of Vernon Street. They often hold screenings of independent films with discussions afterward. Their off-beat Friday night events are what they are most known for.

Most stay on campus for entertainment because the community directly surrounding it does not provide many options. The Tap is a popular bar near the hockey rink just off the south side of campus. There is also a mall nearby and the Bushnell Theatre, which hosts many prominent plays and musical performances.

It is easy to start a club on campus and there are many to take part in, such as the skiing club, karate club, young republicans/democrats, fencing club and many more. There are several a cappella groups on campus, which play a prominent role in the extracurricular activities scene. Squash matches are the most highly attended sporting events, followed by football, then basketball and baseball.

The Quest program is an optional outdoor orientation program held prior to each school year. Incoming freshmen with upperclassmen leaders hike, canoe, camp, climb and rappel in the wilderness for a period of time in the summer. They also participate in a two day long solo experience. It serves as a fantastic transition to the college life, introducing freshmen to other new students and upperclassmen mentors, as well as allowing them to challenge themselves both physically and mentally.

Current student, Cultural Studies, 9/2004-Submit Date, October 2007

Trinity has a great campus on which to live and have fun. There are so many weekend activities and students are very involved in clubs, sports, and cultural organizations so there is always something fun to do.

Alumnus/a, 9/2000-5/2004, March 2007

Social life has two different possibilities at Trinity: in dorm and in frat. There is one bar off campus that everyone goes to every weekend. It is a dive. The frat scene is very welcoming to all students. Some freshman, as well. Don't bother eating off campus since the food on campus is wonderful. There is a restaurant called the Bistro which has surprisingly good food. It is somewhat expensive though if you are on the dining plan. You get flex dollars for the bistro but it doesn't always add up to a full meal.

Alumnus/a, Theater and Dance, 8/1998-5/2002, March 2004

The school's social life, like any college, is focused and centered upon drinking and partying. That's it. When you get to be a senior, a lot of seniors go off campus into Hartford to go to bars downtown occasionally just to get off campus and to get away from the freshmen. The restaurants in downtown Hartford are really great. As for the dating scene.... well... it's really unique at Trinity. For whatever reason, Trinity has become really only a "hook up school" and when you find couples it's really rare and really surprising. It's really easy to stay single for all four years. The school does a decent job trying to promote and provide non-drinking social events. Unfortunately, there is little interest based on the traditions of Trinity. Clubs in Hartford rock!!! The Greek life is kickin and in full. Every year there is a threat to shutting them down on campus, but the truth is that they have been such a great part of the school's history that everyone knows that without them it would lose a lot of it's alum support. Favorite frat parties include Tropical, Calypso, the Spring Weekend semi-formal, Halloween parties, Miami Vice, Get Leid, Avalanche, Los Pantalones, Pimps N Hoes, Heaven N Hell and more! When there is an excuse to have a party, the frat houses will have one. And they're usually all theme parties and/or dress up parties, and they are all annual traditions. There is huge campus upset when one gets cancelled because the house is on probation.

> **Regarding social life, Trinity says:** "Trinity is a community of learners that prides itself on welcoming people from a wide variety of social, economic, geographical, religious and family backgrounds. Trinity supports Cultural Houses, the Zachs Hillel House, the Queer Resource Center, 'The Fred'—a student-run campus living alternative—and approximately 18 percent of students participate in Greek organizations."

 The School Says

Trinity College, one of two national, residential, liberal arts college located in a capital city, offers unique opportunities for combining classroom instruction with experiential learning and student-faculty research. Whether studying engineering, human rights, neuroscience or one of the 38 majors that integrate hands-on research, students expand their education through intellectual conversations and campus activities, engage with the city through internships and community service, and explore the wider world through our eight Global Sites. The most visible and newest manifestation of Trinity's commitment to urban and global engagement is the launch of the Center for Urban and Global Studies (CUGS), the first center at a U.S. liberal arts college to have an integrated urban-global name and focus. With all of its outstanding outreach programs, Trinity College has been recognized by Campus Compact, in association with

Princeton Review, as one of the top schools in the country dedicated to civic engagement and social responsibility.

Among other programs Trinity offers first-year students the opportunity to focus on Cities, Guided Studies, Interarts, and as well as an outdoor leadership program called Quest. Students may enroll in an Interdisciplinary Science program, neuroscience, environmental science, public policy and law, human rights, or a five-year engineering and computer science program in partnership with Rensselear at Hartford.

About 40 percent of Trinity students participate in intercollegiate athletics and even more play intramural sports. Trinity athletic teams regularly achieve high levels of success. Recent standouts include the men's squash team, which has won the College Squash Association team championship nine years in a row, and the women's squash team, which won the Howe Cup in 2002 and 2003. The men's team was recently honored by Connecticut Governor M. Jodi Rell at the Capitol for its outstanding achievements during the 2006-07 season. Four-time NESCAC champions, the football team has won 38 out of 40 games over the last five seasons. In 2006-07, the men's cross country, men's basketball, baseball, women's lacrosse and women's rowing teams each earned trips to the NCAA Championships, while the men's rowers won NESCAC and New England titles. While these and other teams post solid records on the playing field, the emphasis at Trinity remains on the scholar/athlete, and members of many teams also receive recognition as outstanding students. In 2006-2007, 22 Trinity student-athletes earned All-American honors and 55 were named to NESCAC All-Academic Teams.

Approximately 38 percent of Trinity's undergraduates receive some form of aid from the College; an additional 4 percent receive further financial assistance from federal, state and private funds. For prospective students, the best way to determine if Trinity is a good fit is to visit the college. See www.trincoll.edu for more information.

University of Connecticut

Admissions Office
2131 Hillside Road, Unit 3088
Storrs, CT 06269-3088
Admissions phone: (860) 486-3137
Admissions e-mail: beahusky@uconn.edu
Admissions URL: www.admissions.uconn.edu

Admissions

Current student, Sociology, 8/2004-Submit Date, May 2007

The admissions process was fairly easy. UConn uses the Common Application, and one of the essays allows you to ask yourself a question and answer it. I found this extremely effective because it allowed me to express myself not only through the answer but the question itself. When I was applying, I also received a phone call from a current student who answered all my questions about the school, and helped ease my nerves about applying.

> The school says: "UConn does not use the Common Application; we use CT Mentor, a user-friendly online application process."

Current student, Education, 8/2003-Submit Date, May 2007

I applied to UConn through Early Action as a pre-teaching major. I had my application submitted before Thanksgiving. The application process was easy. The instructions were straightforward. I only went to my guidance counselor to send my transcripts. UConn was my first choice, so it was the first application I completed. I knew I wanted to pursue education and I spoke to several UConn students in the education program about their experiences. There was no interview for undergraduate admissions to UConn. The essay was very similar to the essays for other college applications. I only wrote one essay for all my applications and it was two pages long. To be honest, I don't remember what I wrote about. I had two English teachers read over it for me. I was notified of my acceptance in mid January, which is a benefit of Early Action (non-binding). Since it was my first choice school, I did not have to worry about the application process the rest of my senior year.

Current student, Biology, 8/2005-Submit Date, May 2007

The best advice I can give would be to start the admissions process early. Start by taking a general campus tour and information at the Lodewick Visitors Center. The student tour guides are extremely knowledgeable and helpful in presenting information about UConn. In the fall, come back for the Husky-for-a-Day Program, in which you are paired up with a current UConn student who has the same or a similar major as you do. There is a fall open house to attend, as well. Apply directly to the school/program/college in which you want to major, as it is easier to be accepted directly from high school. The two exceptions are the School of Education and the School of Pharmacy, for which you fill out an application in your sophomore year. The application is all online. Spend as much time as you can on the essay, as it is the most important part.

Current student, Business, 8/2006-Submit Date, May 2007

UConn is becoming a much more competitive school than its past reputation implies. The application was relatively simple, and the essay [required]. There was no interview process. I made it into the Honors Program, but there is no application for this; they select who they want based on admitted students.

Current student, Mathematics, 8/2004-Submit Date, May 2007

Because I knew that if I got accepted I would be going to UConn, I applied Early Action. If you are in the same situation, I encourage you to do the same. Applying early takea some of the pressure away. When I attended an open house, I made an appointment to speak with an admissions counselor. This was one of the best things that I did when I was going through the admissions process. The counselor with whom I spoke introduced me to a major I had never heard of, and I will be graduating in December with that degree.

Current student, 8/2003-Submit Date, May 2006

The admissions process included an application specific to UConn. They do not accept the Common Application; however, it doesn't matter because the essay question can easily overlap with essays written for other colleges. There is a variety of essay options, and I believe that the last one tells you to write about a question the student wishes UConn had asked. No interviews are given but we are told to really focus on making our personal essays stand out. UConn has become increasingly selective and rightfully so! I always tell my younger friends applying to focus on their grades, but to also get involved and be well-rounded. UConn seems to look for a complete-package student and doesn't just let SAT scores dictate everyone's admittance. They look for versatile people who will make an actual contribution to the campus and student body.

Current student, 9/2004-Submit Date, May 2006

$70 application fee was one of the more expensive ones when I applied. There are no interviews (because there are almost 20,000 applicants) and the essay can be on any topic. The earlier you apply, the better, since UConn has an admissions process very similar to rolling admission; that is, they do not wait until all the applications are in to accept students. They review your application when they receive it. Thus, if you apply earlier there will be more spots available.

Read all of Vault's College Surveys at **www.vault.com/college**—get complete surveys on 100s of colleges and universities, expert advice on applicaton essays and more.

VAULT CAREER LIBRARY **123**

UConn has been becoming more and more selective, especially the Storrs branch, which is pretty competitive right now. State residents are in tough competition to attend the Storrs branch, and many B to B- high school students get accepted only at a branch campus. Out-of-state applicants number about 10,000 now, and they compete for as little as 1,000 spots.

> **The school says:** "UConn receives about 11,000 applications from out-of-state students; one-third of the students enrolled in the UConn community are from out of state."

Academics

Current student, Biology, 8/2005-Submit Date, May 2007

The workload was much more difficult than I anticipated. I expected to excel with ease, as I had previously done in high school. It took some time, but I realized that if I wanted to do well, I had to work harder than ever—which I did. As I moved forward in the program, classes were easier to get into because my selection date was sooner. One thing I did have to accustom myself to was the fact that every professor is different. One must acclimate themselves to the style of the professor in order to do well. Once you've figured this out and you work hard, you can do well.

Current student, Education, 8/2003-Submit Date, May 2007

Neag School of Education is a competitive program. I applied into the School of Education the spring semester of my sophomore year. The application process included an application, essay, résumé and interview. The program is looking for students committed to education with experience working within schools. I was admitted into the program and began my education classes my junior year. I was accepted into an integrated bachelors/masters program (five-year program). I have been extremely happy with the School of Education. I never had any problems getting into classes and my class sizes varied. I had some courses with 20 students, others with 12 students, others with 50 or more students. The classes incorporated state-of-the-art technology and included guest speakers, experts in their area. It also emphasized discussion, student-centered learning, and groupwork. The professors are accessible and devoted to their profession. I have met some of my professors' families and have made strong friendships with others. Along with the classes and strong faculty, I had a clinical every semester in a variety of schools and age groups. Throughout my student teaching, I had a very supportive network of people, including an advisor and supervisor. I felt the program prepared me for student teaching and gave me the support I needed. I have just graduated with my bachelor's in education, and starting this fall, I will begin my master's degree in education.

Current student, Health, 8/2005-Submit Date, May 2007

Academics at UConn are full of opportunities. There are over 100 majors with a chance to create your own curriculum through our Individualized Major Program. For each major you have an academic advisor who may also serve as one of your professors. This gives you the chance to interact with him/her on both the personal and the academic levels. For classes there are many ways one can customize one's schedule to one's likings. There are numerous openings in classes held at various times and offered by more than one professor in many cases. The average class size is about 30 students. This number does include our large lecture halls, having up to 300 students, as well as our discussion classes. Grading is fair based on the level of the class, as well as the requirements. Professors are very open and offer various ways for students to get help. There are online discussion boards, weekend review sessions, as well as office hours. To be considered a full-time student, one needs a courseload of at least 12 credits, but the average student takes five three-credit courses per semester to end his/her four-year career with about 120 credits.

Current student, Animal Science, 8/2004-Submit Date, May 2007

Academics can be both rigorous and easy. There is an honors program for students who would like the additional challenge in coursework, which also requires a thesis. The classes are very hands-on, particularly in my major, animal science. Web-CT is used in a variety of classes, which enables students to speak with other students in the class in a closed chat room and get class handouts, syllabi and notes. Professors are available, willing to work with you, and very understanding. There is a variety of different classes and different times; so for the most part, if you don't want an 8 a.m., you can usually work around

that, or if you want all your classes in the morning, you can usually plan it that way. Classes vary from 50 minutes to three hours depending on the number of times they meet a week. The average class meets for a total of three hours a week over three separate meetings. Classes are signed up for through People Soft, an online computer system which allows you to see up-to-the-minute availability of classes, times, professors and course descriptions. Academic advisors are assigned to each student, and the advisor will help you to decide which courses you should take in order to fulfill the requirements for your degree program. Advice: Make sure you plan out your entire degree program during freshman year or before, so that you can make sure you have the pre-requisites for the courses that you will eventually need to take.

Current student, Business, 8/2006-Submit Date, May 2007

In the Honors Program, classes are relatively small (usually about 20 students), which is great at such a big school. Even non-honors classes aren't too bad, because huge lectures usually have a small discussion section once a week. It can be hard to get popular classes, but this all depends on the date you get to pick. If you make sure you pick classes as soon as you are able, your chances of getting everything you want are much better. There are so many students that it's impossible for everyone to get exactly what he/she wants. Grading is different depending on the professors. I've had some who use big curves and include participation and some who use your three exams and nothing else. I haven't had any bad experiences with professors, but obviously they are all different. The workload usually consists of a lot of reading for most classes. Obviously there are often lengthy papers in some classes. Depending on what you take, you may have to do work constantly or you may have very little.

Current student, 8/2003-Submit Date, May 2006

Students' freshman and sophomore years are spent completing general education requirements—general classes all students are required to take before getting into the classes for their major. These first two years, students will find themselves in a few lecture-style classes of about 200 to 250 students (taught by a professor). These meet twice a week and then break up once a week into a discussion section of about 25 students that is led by a teaching assistant (TA) who has graduated from UConn or another school and is pursuing a higher degree in their field (master's, PhD). These discussion courses do not teach anything new, but review what was said in lecture.

The classes are challenging, but professors and TAs are concerned about their students and will help in whatever capacity. The classes a student needs usually are not that difficult to get, but an underclassman (freshman, sophomore), may find that his/her classes are early-morning ones since the later times are scooped up by the juniors and seniors. Grading is fair. Exams may occur a few times a semester or twice (midterm, final), and papers and projects are frequent, as well. Professors and TAs are good about getting back grades and can also post them on WebCT, an online program that allows them to post notes and grades and even has a discussion/chat function that students and professors can use to talk about course material, set up study groups or prepare for exams. There is a lot of work (especially reading), but with great time-management skills it is no problem to balance school, work and relaxation. The FYE (First-Year Experience) course that many freshmen take their first or second semester at UConn reviews those types of skills, along with study skills, utilizing library resources, finding your way around campus and getting involved.

Employment Prospects

Alumnus/a, Health Professions, 8/2002-5/2006, May 2007

UConn provides students with the opportunity to sign up for E-Recruiting where students can post their résumés online for prospective employers to view. There are also job fairs on campus where students are able to meet with representatives of various companies and give their résumés to representatives of jobs in which they may be interested. Other opportunities students are eligible for include graduate assistantships with professors at UConn or applying to other graduate schools.

Current student, Political Science, 8/2004-Submit Date, May 2007

A strong percentage of our students is able to find very good jobs upon graduation. UConn is a school that's come a long way in the past 10 years, not just with basketball, but with academics and research, as well. Employers recognize this, and that goes a long way. The Alumni Association and Career Services work very well together to create opportunities for undergraduates to find good jobs upon graduation with different workshops and career fairs held each semester.

Current student, Health, 8/2005-Submit Date, May 2007

Because of great services such as Career Services, students can prepare for life after college. Career Services offers job-shadowing programs, résumé writing seminars, as well as an annual Career Fair. Students can visit the office at anytime in their academic career and even after they graduate. Through sponsors of various programs students can also get involved in internships that will most likely lead to a full-time position upon graduation. Employers such as General Electric, Pfizer, The Hartford, CVS Pharmacies, General Motors, United Technologies and so on all look to hire UConn graduates. Many of our programs have 90 percent placements rates for their graduates, with the NEAG School of Education having a 100 percent placement for all of their master's recipients. Because of great study abroad programs, students may even have the opportunity to travel and work over-seas.

Current student, Mathematics, 8/2004-Submit Date, May 2007

I am going into my senior year, and this summer I will be participating in my second internship. After my senior year, I got a paid internship (with housing included) in Boston with an international company. This summer, I will be doing the same with a different company in Hartford. I have no worries about UConn helping me find a job when I finish my undergraduate career.

Current student, 8/2003-Submit Date, May 2006

UConn programs have high graduation and placement rates. Each individual school (e.g., business, education) have counselors to help students find jobs or internships. UConn also provides many on-campus recruiting opportunities through job and activity fairs, bringing employers to campus to talk to students. Alumni also attend these to talk to current students about after-college opportunities. The school of business has many student break-out rooms that include a table, chairs, TV and video camera. These rooms are used for mock interviews where students can practice their interviewing skills with a counselor or professor and watch the video for feedback. Many employers come to campus to interview students for jobs and internships in these break-out rooms. The State of Connecticut recently granted UConn $2.3 billion ($1 billion over 1995-2005 and another $1.3 billion over 2005-2015; $2.3 billion over 20 years) to improve all UConn campuses (Waterbury, Hartford, Avery Point, Torrington, Stamford and Storrs), as well as their graduate and professional schools (law, social work, medicine and dental medicine). The improvement to on-campus academics and infrastructure has been incredible and really show employers that the education we're receiving is a fantastic one.

Current student, 8/2002-Submit Date, May 2006

I always felt that Career Services was willing to meet students half-way. They hold two Just In Time career/internship fairs, various seminars regarding résumé and cover letter writing, have an extensive web site that allows for ERecruiting, and an entire office dedicated to finding students jobs and internships. Students, in turn, need to take the initiative to attend their seminars and prepare for the career fair in order to begin their network.

Overall, I felt I had a positive experience with Career Services. They were helpful when I posed questions and extended themselves frequently beyond the call of duty. Some students felt that the companies were too business-oriented and there was not enough recruiting for other types of jobs within the medical field, for example. Most of the employers were also from the Northeast, and I had trouble making contacts with organizations who were not centrally located. There were also vast differences between the prestige of the 150+ companies that visited the campus each year. In other words, GE Capital visited, but so did a chain of grocery stores I had never heard of before. The list of companies was suddenly widdles to approximately only 10 for which I actually wish to work.

Quality of Life

Alumnus/a, Health, 8/2002-5/2006, May 2007

On-campus housing is really nice at UConn. Over 70 percent of the students at UConn live on campus. Most freshmen and sophomores live in dormitories, while upperclassmen live in recently built on-campus suites or apartments.

These new living arrangements are competitive and students must enter a lottery in order to choose housing. Most of the time, students are able to live where they choose, which is nice. Other facilities on campus include the gym which is free to all students, but is kind of small for the school population and it gets really busy before spring break in March. We also have an on-campus movie theater that plays really recent movies, Jorgenson Center for the Performing Arts where many comedians and theatrical performers visit, Gampel Pavilion where many basketball games are held, and a new student union filled with a cool cafe and several places to eat.

Current student, Liberal Arts, 8/2004-Submit Date, May 2007

Get involved in campus activities, clubs and research. There are plenty of opportunities to do these things. Campus may seem very big at first; however, once you adjust, it really is not as big as it may first seem. When planning classes make sure to take a look at the location so that you are not crossing the entire campus in a period of 10 minutes. The campus is very safe. There are emergency call buttons located in various places on campus and can be reached quickly in an emergency. All dorms are locked and can only be entered with the student ID of the student that lives in that building.

There are plenty of places to study in the library, including rooms that are open 24 hours of the day. Online databases are also available so that you never have to go to the library to do research. They are accessible anywhere in the world through the university's network address.

Make sure to get your housing deposit for enrollment in as soon as possible so that you can obtain the housing you would like. Food on campus is actually very good. There are multiple dining halls on campus and any student can eat in any dining hall they choose. There are always the basics of hamburgers, grilled cheese, deli, and salad, but in addition, hot entrees and a made-to-order station. Kosher food, hallal and vegetarian options are all available. Public transportation is free to all students, as well as the university bus line which is also free and goes around campus.

Current student, Health, 8/2005-Submit Date, May 2007

Campus is very fun-filled each and every day. Housing options of dormitories, suites, and on-campus apartments allow for friends to be around days, nights, and weekends. There are 19 different residential areas and 96 percent of them are coed by floor. There are single-sex residential halls available, as well. Typically as a freshman, you will live in a traditional dorm with one roommate. But as you progress, there are opportunities to live in a triple, single or quad. All of our facilities have been remodeled to state-of-the-art buildings through our $2.3 billion grant that helped to renew the infrastructure of all UConn facilities. Each residential area has its own dining hall. Meal plans allow for students to dine at any dining unit, as well as use the points system to take meals with them when necessary. Also, there are cultural dining units, such as the NOSH Kosher kitchen and the Muslim food station. The UConn community is very safe with our own police and fire departments. There are blue lights with call boxes all across campus in case of any kind of emergency. There are campus shuttles and escort services to provide students with transportation between 6 a.m. and 12 midnight (buses) and escort from dusk to 2 a.m. The UConn campus is like home with friends always close by. Even the students living in off-campus apartment complexes are part of campus life with their own apartment shuttle bus line. Campus life is fun and safe—providing lasting memories and lasting friendships.

Current student, 8/2002-Submit Date, May 2006

UConn 2000 and 21st Century UConn have brought great changes to the university—everyone can attest to that. New buildings are opening frequently, and the campus gives off an aura of cleanliness and friendliness. Some programs, of course, still feel that they are not being considered within the processes, but students do not understand that each building project triggers another (i.e., you cannot tear down one building until you complete another, which is to be preceded by another). In time, all departments will have been touched in some way and no one should feel they were left out of the $2.3 billion investment.

The biggest complaint that most students have is, "we only started calling it Storrs when we added the second one." There aren't many retail outlines or fine-dining facilities from which students can choose. It should be noted that we are 30 minutes from Hartford, 20 minutes from Manchester, 90 minutes from Boston and 75 minutes from Providence, and these cities provide lots for students to do

Read all of Vault's College Surveys at www.vault.com/college–get complete surveys on 100s of colleges and universities, expert advice on applicaton essays and more.

VAULT CAREER LIBRARY   125

on extended breaks and weekends. Moreover, UConn is building a downtown UConn, which students expect to bring a higher quality of life. In the mean time, we keep ourselves entertained with UConn Late Night, SUBOG events, high-class preforming artists, cheap athletic tickets, and the events sponsored by our own clubs and organizations.

 ## Social Life

Current student, Sociology, 8/2004-Submit Date, May 2007

Although Storrs truly is in the middle of nowhere, the campus is a city unto itself. There is a series of bars, restaurants and other stores all in walking distance. The new student union has a food court, a movie theater that shows two movies a weekend for only $2 each, a game room and so much more. There are also over 300 organizations that constantly plan events. I have attended everything from learning to roll your own sushi, a Matisyahu concert and Lewis Black's latest comedy show, to being auctioned off for a date at a local bar where all proceeds went to charity. While we do have a strong Greek system, they don't take up the entire social scene. They are amazing to hang out with, but for people like me who don't desire to be a part of the Greek community, you can easily not be affected by them. If students are looking for specific areas to visit, check out Tequila Cove (best margaritas ever!), the student union theater and food court (specifically the Good Earth and its Mediterranean salad), D.P. Dough, and any event at the Jorgenson theater.

Current student, Political Science, 8/2004-Submit Date, May 2007

UConn has a lot of different opportunities to meet and have fun with other people. There are over 300 different clubs and activities in which to get involved, where you could meet others. While there is a number of area bars, there are not as many sit-down restaurants. The university is aware of its rural setting, and works to offset this by providing a lot of different events and services on campus for its students, whether it be different concerts and comedy shows in Jorgenson, or athletic events like the basketball games, or even the late-night programs put on in the student union. We're about 15 percent Greek, with different social, academic and service fraternities and sororities on campus. As for the dating scene, I'm sure it's just like any other college campus.

Current student, Health, 8/2005-Submit Date, May 2007

The social scene on campus is one that is increasing each year. This year we were pleased to have our student union with our Union Street Market and Food Court. In our student union, or the "U" as it is affectionately known, all six of our cultural centers show the diversity we have across our entire student body. They provide different events, both social and academic, including Coffee Houses, book talks, holiday celebrations and dances. The student union also has a board of governors known as SUBOG, which is responsible for all the events held throughout the academic year. SUBOG sponsors concerts, lectures and the weekly event, Husky Howl. Also, athletics are a very big part of being a UConn Husky. SUBOG also sponsors the road show buses to both football and basketball events. Involvement can include on-campus employment with over 5,000 student job opportunities; to volunteering and community service, as well as intramural sports and clubs. We have over 300 clubs and organizations. We have everything from your national honor societies and Greek life with sororities and fraternities, to some peculiar groups, such as the Peanut Butter and Jelly Club and the Old Man Sports and Leisure Club. There is something for everyone: musical groups, such as The Conn Men and the Voices of Freedom Gospel Choir, dance teams and major clubs. You can even create your own! Campus night life offers bars for the 21-and-older crowd, as well as other areas for the younger crowd. There are concerts and shows held at the Jorgenson Center for the Performing Arts at reasonable prices. Classes and activities will get you involved, and you will meet great friends with whom you will build lasting friendships and relationships.

Current student, Business, 8/2006-Submit Date, May 2007

The social life is great. There are always parties, usually off campus. Many are held by fraternities. There are a few bars on campus, but those aren't as popular as the house parties. Favorite nearby restaurants include Chang's Garden and Wings Express, which delivers the best chicken wings you've ever had. There is basically a club for any interests, from skydiving to photography, and the newspaper, radio station, and TV channel are all very reputable and exciting ways to get involved. There are seven a cappella groups on campus, which are all awesome and so much fun to watch. If you sing, you should definitely try out for one. There are also a few drama clubs and dance groups. There really is something for everyone. We have many fraternities and sororities which do a lot of good philanthropic events and have a lot of fun.

Wesleyan University

Admissions Office
The Stewart M. Reid House
70 Wyllys Avenue
Middletown, CT 06459-0265
Admissions phone: (860) 685-3000
Admissions fax: (860) 685-3001
Admissions e-mail: admissions@wesleyan.edu
Admissions URL: www.wesleyan.edu/admission/

 ## Admissions

Current student, 8/2003-Submit Date, December 2006

Wesleyan is pretty selective. They accept the Common Application with no supplement, which is great. Interviews can be arranged on campus or with alumni across the country. Essays are really important, and you want to try to find something off-beat about you that sets you apart. Weird does not equal bad at Wes.

Alumnus/a, 8/2001-5/2005, October 2006

Be original. Have a strange talent (ice hockey goalie, successful online comic strip or food co-op leader). Be passionate about your hobbies and academics. Make meetings with department heads, as well as the admission interviewer. If you know someone who went there, have them put in a good word for you. Write an amazing college essay. If you are an artist, share your portfolio with the department. If a teacher or coach wants to work with you, they will be your most effective cheerleader to the admissions crew. If you don't get in your first year, go to your second-choice college and then apply to Wesleyan again. It seems much easier to transfer into the school than to get in as a freshman. Transferring is not typical, so it shows admissions how passionate you are about the school.

Alumnus/a, 9/2001-5/2005, October 2006

Admissions at Wesleyan, like at so many other small liberal arts schools, is as difficult to predict as it is to be accepted. The essays and interview should be used to show individuality, as well as drive. Wesleyan students should be adamant about being leaders and enacting social change, both on and off campus.

Alumnus/a, 8/2000-5/2004, March 2005

The admissions process was pretty straightforward. I used the Common Application and was able to use my generic essay. However, I chose to include an additional essay, which I felt gave the admissions staff better insight into my background. Wesleyan looks for a diversity of students from different backgrounds and different views. Applicants who can demonstrate something that sets them apart from the next person gives them an admissions edge. The admissions staff was very helpful in answering questions. I would highly recommend setting up an interview, whether it's on or off campus. The admissions office has many alumni across the country with whom you can meet in your hometown.

Wesleyan offers many open houses and information sessions to familiarize students and their families with the school. The school also hosts, WESFEST which is an entire weekend devoted to pre-freshmen, or as we called them, pre-frosh, in the spring. This is an excellent opportunity for prospective students to be a Wesleyan student for the weekend—stay overnight with a Wes student, attend classes, and party with students! During this weekend, parents can also attend informational sessions and seminars about financial aid, housing, and student life. Selectivity is very high and is getting more selective every year.

Alumnus/a, 9/2001-5/2005, October 2006

Wesleyan accepted the Common Application. It was easy to apply, but getting in is more difficult. I did not have an interview, but I know that many other Wesleyan admitted students had interviewers with alumni or with students at the school. The school is selective in terms of grades and test scores, but it also looks for other things—participation in student groups, creative projects and volunteer work.

Current student, 8/2000-Submit Date, March 2004

I was a Wesleyan University tour guide, so I am well aware of insider information. The acceptance rate is challenging, about 29 percent. There is a committee that reads through the applications and gives each application a rank. Diversity is a factor. We try to pull students from every part of the country, and every part of the world. Although standardized test scores are important, it is definitely the overall package that is considered. For example, if one school does not offer Advanced Placement classes while another does, we will try to figure out how outstanding a student is within the context they are given—in other words, how they used the available resources and how much they challenged themselves.

The interview is optional and is not as big a factor as is a job interview. In other words, it can help or hurt you, but if you do not interview well, it's better to stick with the written application. Essays should be creative, unique, but mature and insightful. Wesleyan is a very unique school that is looking for self-motivated students, students who are passionate about something, students who are interested in making a difference.

Academics

Current student, 8/2003-Submit Date, December 2006

There are a lot of wonderful classes and professors here. However, sometimes getting the class of your choice can be difficult, especially if you are an underclassman who has not yet declared a major. There is a significant amount of grade inflation here as anywhere, but professors can also be really tough and expect a lot from their students. For a liberal arts college, we have a fantastic science program with incredible research opportunities for undergrads. Wesleyan classes will definitely change the way you look at the world.

Alumnus/a, 9/2001-5/2005, October 2006

The workload is generally very fair. Professors are knowledgeable, enthusiastic and extremely available. Most classes are small, outside of the entry-level science and psychology classes. Students at Wesleyan tend to be interested in what they study, largely because there are very few required classes, and even those can be avoided. This leads to active discussion and a great learning experience. Getting popular classes in the government department is difficult, especially if you are not a government major. Getting other courses is not so difficult.

Alumnus/a, 9/2001-5/2005, October 2006

The academics at Wesleyan are very strong, but vary greatly depending on the department. The language departments are experiencing cutbacks currently, and thus although the courses in these departments are great, the selection is quite limited. The most popular classes are very difficult to get into, although seats are generally reserved for non-majors and non-seniors. The grading varies greatly by professor, and the workload is what you make of it. It is very easy to get by with a small workload because of the ease with which classes can be added/dropped and the straightforwardness of the professors and their syllabi.

Current student, 8/2000-Submit Date, March 2004

One of the biggest downers about this school is class registration. It is often very difficult to get into very popular classes, and there are many restrictions as to who can get into what courses. With that said, there is a drop/add process through which it is relatively easy to get most of the classes you weren't able to get through the regular online registration process. One reason the registration process is so troubling is the following: basically, you sit in front of a computer, listen to a countdown, and then the students who click the fastest and have a lot of luck get the classes they want first. This is in stark contrast to other universities, where, for example, you can bid points on classes you really want so that professors know you have genuine interest (because if you use all your points on one class, you don't have much left to bid on others).

The academic program is very self-determined. You can make it as challenging or relaxed as you want. If one semester you are bogged with extracurriculars, you can choose to take three classes instead of four, and take the fourth class during summer when you have more time. However, only up to two classes are available to be received per summer and one per winter. There are no summer or winter sessions for regular undergrads here on the campus. The classes, with the exception of big intro classes, are small. Class size ranges from two to 150, but most are on the smaller end.

Alumnus/a, 8/2001-5/2005, October 2006

You have to plan ahead to get the best classes. Talk with professors, make friends with seniors you admire—they have been through it all recently and will have the best advice on which courses to take. Figure out with whom you want to work, and then make sure they are not planning a sabbatical in the next four years. Feel free to take a year off and do a year-long internship or travel. The school is flexible about taking time off. This is sometimes a good approach to insure you take all the classes you want and get into the department you want. For example, the film department is extremely selective and you may have to be patient to get into a class or be accepted by the major.

The best learning is done out of class. Take advantage of volunteering for student films, college radio, or in the costume shop. The radio station is a great resource, as well. You can also learn a lot by starting your own magazine at school (you can receive the funding to publish it, as well) or offering to be a teacher's assistant.

Alumnus/a, 8/2000-5/2004, March 2005

Wesleyan offers a plethora of courses within the liberal arts framework with the ultimate goal that graduates will be well rounded, well grounded, and know how to think, not what to think. No matter what the major, Wesleyan encourages students to explore a wide variety of courses. The classes are very small, excluding introductory science courses. All professors are very dedicated and easily accessible and willing to meet with students during scheduled office hours. Every professor I had was willing to meet with me outside those hours if I e-mailed or called him/her a few hours in advance.

With regard to registration, it was a bit of a chore to get into the most popular classes—but if you were persistent, you could get into most. The best thing to keep in mind is that if you don't get into a course one semester, keep trying. Priority is given to upperclassmen, so you are more likely to take the popular or cool classes, such as dance, art and film classes your junior and senior years. Workload is pretty intense but not to the point of being oppressive. Most students are able to get their work done during the week and still have a social life. Grading is very straightforward—not many curves unless its a science class. The professors do not bend over backwards to give A's in any subject area, you have to work for it.

Employment Prospects

Alumnus/a, 8/2001-5/2005, October 2006

Forecast looks good as long as you network. The name of the school will go a long way. Extracurriculars are more important than grades. Students seem to either volunteer—Teach For America or Peace Corps—or move to hip cities (San Francisco, L.A., NYC, Boston, Seattle, or Portland, Oregon) after school. The more folks you know in your town after college, the better connections

Read all of Vault's College Surveys at www.vault.com/college—get complete surveys on 100s of colleges and universities, expert advice on applicaton essays and more.

VAULT CAREER LIBRARY   127

you'll have—the more eyes and ears looking out for you. Wesleyan has a great alumni career network, too.

Alumnus/a, 8/2000-5/2004, March 2005

Most Wesleyan graduates take their liberal arts education seriously and explore nonprofit, public interest, travel and fellowship opportunities after graduation. This is because most Wesleyan students are do-gooders and are not looking for immediate big bucks when they graduate. Many pursue graduate and professional degrees within three years after graduation. Wesleyan has a phenomenal economics department, and econ majors gain employment at top investment firms upon graduation.

Wesleyan also offers an extensive alumni network—binders upon binders of Wesleyan alumni willing to speak with students are in the Career Resource Center. The Career Resource Center has a lot of materials, but it is up to the student to put in the work to find a job or internships. The center offers on-campus recruiting and transportation to job fairs. But again, it is really up to the student to make note of these opportunities and pursue them. Oddly, I found that the Career Resource Center was more helpful after graduation—I get frequent e-mails with job openings, fellowship opportunities and internships.

Current student, 8/2000-Submit Date, March 2004

The school has a very prestigious name on the East Coast, especially the Northeast. However, in Los Angeles, for example, they don't know Wesleyan as one of the best liberal arts colleges in the country. That it is extremely exclusive and academically rigorous.

The CRC (Career Resource Center) is one of the best run organizations/offices on campus and it is a huge resource, both for current students and grads. You can use its resources even 10 years down the line, simply because you are an alumnus/a of the school! Most students here are known; however, for being unemployed after college for a couple of years. They are known, too, for not knowing exactly what to do when they graduate even in their last months as a senior. In other words, this college isn't as career-oriented as other universities. It doesn't have a business program like a public university would have, for example.

Alumnus/a, 8/1996-5/2000, September 2003

The Career Resource Center has improved dramatically over the years. Many companies (McKinsey, BCG, Goldman Sachs and Lehman Brothers) recruit on campus nowadays, despite Wesleyan's small size and out-of-the-way location. The alumni network is very strong—people are very willing to help current students out in seeking opportunities and mentoring. Aside from the business world, students interested in nonprofit work, teaching, politics and film have also been very successful in securing opportunities.

 Quality of Life

Current student, 8/2003-Submit Date, December 2006

Housing at Wes is awesome, with your pick getting progressively better as you go through the years. Seniors normally end up in campus-owned houses of their very own in which they live with their friends, porches and back decks included. We just got an amazing new gym, and in general, I'd say we have fantastic facilities. Like at most schools, there is some town/gown tension, but most of us believe that Middletown is generally a safe place to be.

Alumnus/a, 9/2001-5/2005, October 2006

The campus is beautiful, but not all of the housing options are so comfortable. Rooms in low-rises tend to be very tiny. The high-rise is dark and both are located next to low-income housing developments. The Butterfields are slightly removed and the room size is decent. The lounges are sparse and outdated, and occasionally the school has turned the doubles into triples. The Foss Hill dorms seem somewhat nicer. Clark Hall was recently renovated and is pretty nice, aside from the fact that most rooms are doubles. There are new dorms being built, which seem very nice. The only drawback is that in the past, seniors have had the opportunity to live in houses, but due to the cost of maintaining the houses, the school has begun to phase them out. This is still probably a change for the better as the school does not seem capable of maintaining the housing locations. Dining at Wesleyan is generally sub par. MoCon, the freshman dining

hall, is really bad, despite some recent improvements. There has been discussion of new dining facilities, which should ameliorate the situation.

Current student, 8/2000-Submit Date, March 2004

Most students are happy to be here. However, at some point a lot of us get tired of Wesleyan culture. It is highly political here, and most people would consider themselves political activists. Issues are always pressing, and political correctness is almost a prerequisite to have a conversation in public. Housing is decent. Food is not so great.

The campus is really beautiful, and there is a change of seasons (not seen for those of us from the West Coast). The surrounding town is quaint and nice in certain ways, but don't expect the amenities of a big city at all.

Alumnus/a, 8/2000-5/2004, March 2005

The Wesleyan student body is very friendly, open-minded and noncompetitive. It's a very, very diverse campus. The dorms are like small communities, and most students live in singles. However, the all-freshman dorm that was renovated two years ago has mostly doubles. Most students move into houses or town houses their junior and senior years. The campus is very small and everything is accessible.

The only negative is the small campus center, but it is going to be moved to a larger facility (the old gym) in the next few years. The athletic center was also just renovated and has indoor tennis courts, an indoor pool, basketball courts and huge fitness center, as well as squash courts, saunas and hockey arena. Campus food isn't that great, but there is a good market on the campus where you can purchase food with your points. There are also some amazing restaurants right around the campus, delis, Thai, Italian, Indian, Middle Eastern, Tibetan and Mexican. The neighborhood is fairly safe. There are very few safety incidences, most occur on the weekends at off-campus housing locations. Public safety is available and helpful and will be found parked at many corners all over the campus, 24 hours a day.

 Social Life

Current student, 8/2003-Submit Date, December 2006

Middletown has some really great restaurant choices, and some cool bars with great happy hours, if that's what you're into. People don't really date here, you're either just hooking up, or what we like to call, "Wes-Married." There is pretty much a club for anything, and it's really easy to start one if you can't find what you're looking for. The three frats are there if you want them and pretty easy to ignore if you don't.

Alumnus/a, 9/2001-5/2005, October 2006

There are restaurants nearby, but students don't go out for nice dinners too often. Wednesday night is bar night, which seems to be most popular with athletes and their friends. The dating scene is typical for a college-not much dating. There are random hookups and then practically married couples. There are always interesting events on-campus concerts, plays, club meetings, activist events, movies, parties and so on. Greek life is not big. There are only four fraternities and one sorority. The fraternities do throw parties, which seem to be more popular for freshmen and sophomores. There are also two societies—Eclectic and Alpa Delta Phi—which are coed groups with their own houses on campus. They host a number of events, and Eclectic's parties tend to be attended by the largest number of students. Upperclassmen tend to host and go to house parties, but with houses being phased out slowly, that will eventually change.

Alumnus/a, 9/2001-5/2005, October 2006

Most of the social life is on campus. There are a few bars about which little can be said, and there are wonderful restaurants that often close too early. There are no clubs, very few events worth speaking of aside from plays and on-campus bands. The Greek system is very small, but very welcoming.

Alumnus/a, 8/2000-5/2004, March 2005

Social life is mainly limited to the campus. There are a few bars on Main Street that have drink specials but they are mainly during the week. Gatekeeper has $1.50 draft nights on Wednesday. Most students choose to stay on campus because there is no transportation to these bars aside from their own cars. There are also only four fraternities on the campus, so the Greek life isn't that dominant. Those involved with the Greek scene tend to party within this scene, but they host campus parties every weekend for the entire campus. Also students attend or throw house parties or room parties. The campus also has a great performing arts center and theater, every weekend musicians, dancers, singers and bands perform. Most shows offer discounted tickets for students. There are also a lot of student-run, student-directed and student-performed shows. There are campus events for students who are not into the drinking scene. The Wesleyan Cinema offers a film series throughout the week and weekend, classic films and new films. There is something for everyone on this campus—anything goes! Seriously, go to Wesleyan and you'll know what I mean!

Current student, 8/2000-Submit Date, March 2004

There are limitless events on campus. There is always a club to join or a cause to follow, even something as insignificant as a club from being born in the Midwest to a Boogey Club, that goes around and dances in random places at random times. The students love Foss Hill, where they hang out when it's warm. Students admit that they sometimes skip class to sit and hang out with friends on the Hill, or maybe watch a baseball game on Andrus field. As far as athletics, it's not a very big school for attending games. Two-thirds of or the students are, however, some type of athlete, whether that be at the collegiate level or intramural/club level.

 The School Says

In his inaugural address in 1831, Wesleyan's first president, Willbur Fisk, stated that education serves two purposes: "the good of the individual educated and the good of the world." This enduring vision of a Wesleyan education has guided us for 175 years. At Wesleyan, we prepare our students to face a rapidly changing world with confidence and the sense of responsibility to want to make the world a better place.

Our faculty engage students by bringing their own intellectual lives into the classroom. Nationally recognized as scientists and scholars, they are teachers whose experience and high standards inspire students to achieve. Working closely with these teacher-scholars, Wesleyan students develop their critical thinking skills, their abilities to analyze scientific and social phenomena, their imaginations, and their capacities for ethical reasoning. Many Wesleyan students explore their own academic projects in partnership with members of the faculty.

Wesleyan's approach to education is at once highly individualistic and academically rigorous. Our programs are demanding, yet students accomplish them out of genuine, personal drive. We expect students to develop their own unique programs of study—programs that reflect each student's own interests and are uniquely developed with the help and encouragement of our faculty. Wesleyan offers more than 900 courses and 46 major fields of study from which to choose.

Wesleyan's positive, open and diverse environment encourages personal growth and intellectual independence. At the same time, the richness and energy of Wesleyan's campus life reflect the shared engagement of Wesleyan faculty and students with issues current in world affairs, the sciences, the social sciences, and the arts. Our students both pursue their own interests and celebrate the accomplishments of their fellow students in the lab and the studio, on the playing field, and in service to the community.

Wesleyan has many ties to its home city. Middletown, Connecticut is located along a bend in the Connecticut River about midway between New York and Boston. It mingles white- and blue-collar industries and a diverse residential mix. Main Street features restaurants, clothing stores and a new hotel. Students enjoy dining at the city's ethnic restaurants and can choose among Mexican, Japanese, Thai, Indian, Italian and even Tibetan options. Our students are active volunteers, especially in the local schools. On average, they provide over 30,000 hours of service each year. A favorite volunteer location is the new Green Street Art Center, a community facility founded by Wesleyan in the city's north end, which offers classes and workshops for children and adults in music, visual arts, dance, theater, literary and media arts.

Wesleyan's 2,700 undergraduate students come from 48 states, the District of Columbia and the Virgin Islands, as well as 46 foreign countries. They are a diverse group racially (26 percent are students of color) and economically (42 percent receive student aid); and 12 to 15 percent of students are the first generation in their family to attend college. Our ratio of students to faculty is 9:1.

Wesleyan graduates are successful in every profession imaginable, including law, science, medicine, business, politics and the creative arts. They are often leaders and innovators in their fields. Here are just a few of the university's prominent alumni: Bill Belichick '75, head coach, New England Patriots, winner of 2002, 2004 and 2005 Super Bowls; William Blakemore '65, correspondent, ABC News; Amy Bloom '75, author of *Come to Me, Love Invents Us*, and *A Blind Man Can See How Much I Love You*; Dominique Browning '77, editor-in-chief, *House & Garden Magazine*; John Hickenlooper Jr. '74, mayor, Denver, Colorado; Sebastian Junger '84, author of *The Perfect Storm* and *Fire*; Herb Kelleher '53, founder, chairman, and former president and CEO, Southwest Airlines; Theodore Shaw '76, president and director-counsel, NAACP Legal Defense and Education Fund; Beverly Daniel Tatum '75, president, Spelman College, and author of *Why Are All the Black Kids Sitting Together in the Cafeteria?*; Joss Whedon '87, creator, producer, director and writer for "Buffy the Vampire Slayer", and screenwriter for *Speed* and *Toy Story*; Dar Williams '89, folksinger.

Read all of Vault's College Surveys at **www.vault.com/college**—get complete surveys on 100s of colleges and universities, expert advice on applicaton essays and more.

VAULT CAREER LIBRARY **129**

Yale University

Office of Undergraduate Admissions
P.O. Box 208234
New Haven, CT 06520-8234
Admissions phone: (203) 432-9300
Admissions fax: (203) 432-9392
Admissions e-mail: student.questions@yale.edu
Admissions URL: www.yale.edu/admit

 Admissions

Alumnus/a, Sociology, 9/2003-5/2007, June 2007

I didn't have an interview. I wrote three essays. I found the admissions process very organized and smooth. I applied to the early admissions. I got waitlisted and then found out I got in. I think the best thing for me as a rather shy high school senior was attending the pre-frosh weekend. This allowed me to meet new people and just get comfortable with the surroundings.

Alumnus/a, 9/2002-5/2006, March 2007

Nuts and bolts: basic application, two (short) essays, alumni interview (optional but highly recommended), on-campus interview (optional), teacher recommendations, usual standardized tests. All students who apply are at the top of their class academically—it helps to have something that makes you stand out from the crowd of valedictorians and so on. For example, I am a violinist and submitted a CD of my work. Also, please note that Yale is not looking to fill a class with smart, boring people—they will definitely take a person with good (but not perfect) grades.

Alumnus/a, 8/2003-5/2005, August 2006

Yale seeks a diverse crowd of people, and standing out from the many applicants is the most important admissions criterion. Many potential applicants stress out about having perfect on-paper credentials, when in fact Yale is looking for interesting people who represent themselves as people who will contribute both intellectually and to school culture. The essays are the most important part and can make up for relative weaknesses in your application, which is very beneficial for applicants from nontraditional geographic locations and backgrounds. Interviews are pretty negligible and nothing to stress over.

Current student, 9/2002-Submit Date, October 2005

The admissions process is difficult. The most important thing is making yourself stand out by focusing on an individual activity, accomplishment or other significant characteristic about which you are proud. Although academic prowess is important, other talents are what will get you in the door. Use the essays and the interviews to showcase whatever it is that makes you unique and what you will be able to contribute to the diverse campus.

Current student, 9/2004-Submit Date, July 2006

Everyone at Yale has a "wow factor" and that's exactly what we call it. You know that if the admissions rate is under 10 percent, then the students that you are mulling around with in New Haven are not run-of-the-mill; and one day you're in the middle of good conversation and you discover that your colleague spent a year with New York City Ballet before attending or speaks nine languages, or starred in a movie opposite Meryl Streep and Angela Basset (all of these stories I have encountered) and you say, "wow." Any potential applicant should keep this mind. Every Yale person has it. So in order to be a viable candidate, you need a passion, not just an activity that would make anyone go, "wow." Making this the common thread throughout your application is more important than anything, though with such stiff competition scores, GPA and a relative diversity of interests and experiences are also important.

Current student, 9/2004-Submit Date, January 2005

Yale is an extremely selective institution. In order to get in, an applicant must have extremely strong SAT scores and grades to be considered in the first place.

However, the best way to ensure admittance is to have a "hook" that makes it impossible for Yale to pass you up. A "hook" would include anything from working in a medical research laboratory to being a national champion in some esoteric discipline. The interview is not important and mostly serves to educate the prospective student about life at the school. Essays are extremely important because they represent many applicants' sole means of demonstrating that they possess a personality. Try to write vividly in such a way that you reveal your unique personality.

Current student, 8/2001-Submit Date. April 2004

Having well-written and unique essays, as well as personalized (preferably glowing!) recommendations are what an applicant should focus on most. SATs and high GPAs are important, but Yale gets so many applications from really smart kids that you have to make yourself stand out in some other way. If you are really interested, I would recommend applying early, as the acceptance rate for Early Action applicants is significantly higher than normal admission rates. Yale uses a standardized application nowadays, but [you should] personalize yours for the school and let them know that it's your first choice. Attend any interviews that are offered to you.

> **The school says:** "Single-Choice Early Action candidates are evaluated in the same way as are those who apply Regular Decision. The admission rates are different because the applicant pools are different."

Current student, 9/2001-Submit Date, December 2004

Yale is so difficult to get into these days, with an acceptance rate hovering around 9 percent. It honestly takes a lot of luck—an outstanding GPA, a high SAT score (average is around 1490) and great extracurriculars. Remember, to get into Yale, your application must convince an admissions representative that you would flourish here. Your application must have a "story." I'm not sure how to explain this, except that your application should all fit together and have a theme. Ultimately, your application must convince an admissions rep to be your advocate in front of the rest of the admissions committee, and then this rep must be able to convince the others with your application that you are Yale material.

 **Academics**

Current student, 9/2001-Submit Date, December 2004

Academics are outstanding. Sure, I've had my gut classes/classes I wish I'd never taken, but most professors are honestly interested and engaged in teaching undergraduates. I have had countless meals with my professors, many of whom are really famous. Many classes at Yale give me the sense of "sink or swim," not in a bad way, though. The professors expose students to difficult material, and students must put the work into the classes to get A's. However, Yale students are always willing to help each other. There's a sense of healthy collaborative competition. Sometimes grading can seem very arbitrary, especially in non-science courses. Just be sure to warm up to professors/TAs.

Alumnus/a, Sociology, 9/2003-5/2007, June 2007

Grading was tough—most classes graded on a curve. Therefore, even if you got a 95 on a test or a paper, it didn't mean you got an A. I found some of the professors aloof and more involved in their own work—publishing or whatever. However, I had at least a couple of professors each year who were open, available for advice and helpful with work. I didn't have trouble getting into classes but I always registered as soon as possible. The workload was high at all times. However, being organized helped a lot. And not procrastinating on my school work left me with time to work and have fun.

I found the classes to be of high quality, but I have to say that you get out what you put in. Some people just put in enough to get a B or even enough to get an A, but they just stayed in the realm of regurgitation. Then you had other people who really dove into the classes and got everything they could out of it. Yes, it sounds insane to study even when you don't have to, but college is a once-in-a-lifetime opportunity to immerse yourself into learning and to figure yourself out!

Alumnus/a, 9/2002-5/2006, March 2007

Students do not have to choose majors until the end of sophomore year, and after that, it is fairly easy to switch. This makes it easy to explore new avenues—but be sure to get in core courses that you might need, such as calculus, basic chemistry or basic English. Class quality is good for the most part, because of the shopping period. Students can shop classes for the first two weeks of each semester without actually signing up for the class, allowing them to sample class quality. Beware though of traditionally required classes—professors are less motivated to make them good because students have no choice as to whether or not to take them (i.e., Econometrics for econ majors). Workload is what you make of it—for me, it could have been worse. Some people worked harder than I did, and others less. There are many people at Yale who are able to take really hard courses and do very little work, because they are far more brilliant than you thought humanly possible. However, no one is competitive, and competitiveness is frowned upon—one major quality that made me choose Yale over other top-tier schools.

Alumnus/a, 8/2003-5/2005, August 2006

Professors are incredibly accessible. My experience has been very good, as I've been able to work with professors outside of the classroom in research settings. Knowing your professor not only in the classroom but also in research and socially enhances the quality of Yale academia. Yale academia shapes all students as people who can think analytically and argue their positions. Discussion as well as argument is the very nature of the academics, and this teaches beyond the details of the material. Grading is fair, classes address very broad and diverse subjects, professors topnotch. Workload is primarily dependent on what you want from your education, the goals you set out for yourself and how hard you want to work. Most Yalies take their academics very seriously and enjoy added responsibilities of harder classes. Very few Yalies shy from taking hard classes, and many strive to get into and do well in advanced classes in their early years.

Current student, 9/2004-Submit Date, January 2005

It is extremely easy to find great classes taught by famous professors. All of my classes are special—the students are brilliant and the professors continually amaze me. Grading is pretty lenient because the professors figure that if you were outstanding enough to gain entrance into Yale, you deserve at least a decent grade. The workload depends largely on the courses you take. You can take the hardest courses and not have any time to sleep because you are so overloaded with papers and reading. However, many students can cater their courseload to how hard they want to work.

Current student, 8/2001-Submit Date, April 2004

The classes here are, for the most part, amazing. The professors are topnotch, if in some cases a little quirky. The workload and grading can vary quite a bit between classes, but Yale allows its students to shop classes for two weeks before deciding what they want to take, so you can get a sense of what the class will be like (in terms of lectures, grading policy and workload) before committing to it. Though some small seminars can be hard to get into, generally speaking if there's a class you want to take and you have taken the pre-reqs (providing there are any), you can take it. In the case of huge, popular lectures, Yale is very open to shuffling classrooms to make room for all interested students.

Employment Prospects

Alumnus/a, 8/1993-5/1997, January 2007

Excellent. But don't think all you have to do is graduate and then sit around and wait to be offered jobs. The race to succeed in life never ends. Yale isn't an end, but a beginning. Use summer breaks for internships to explore interests and skills. Attack on-campus recruiting opportunities with the same gusto you did the Yale admissions process or you won't get into your top-choice employer. Remember, you're not the only one graduating from Yale or an Ivy League school.

Alumnus/a, 8/2003-5/2005, August 2006

The Yale name and degree go a long way. The medical school, law school, graduate school, investment banking, and consulting routes taken by many Yale students are a testament of Yale students to take and perform well in analytical, high-caliber roles. Yale's alumni network is incredibly helpful and accessible, although Yale does a poor job letting alumni know about it.

Alumnus/a, 8/1999-8/2003, June 2006

Top graduates from Yale get employment offers from the best companies in the country. Career Services is very helpful, especially if you plan on going into the traditional Ivy League professions. I personally took a more non-traditional route and had very little interaction with Career Services. The alumni network is very supportive in just about every field; people are very proud to call themselves Yalies and will help out a fellow Yalie at the drop of a hat. The Yale Club of New York is quite an amazing resource for someone who moves to New York City after graduation; it is located right next to Grand Central.

Current student, 9/2002-Submit Date, October 2005

Employment prospects for graduates are great—many of the top companies and firms recruit heavily at Yale. There is also an extensive alumni network that encourages students to take advantage of Yale connections. The on-campus career center is helpful in finding finance-oriented jobs, but more limited in its capacity to help students looking for other, more diverse careers.

Current student, 9/2001-Submit Date, December 2004

Excellent, excellent, excellent. The only concern I have is for those interested in pursuing careers other than investment banking and consulting right out of Yale. While Undergraduate Career Services does an all around excellent job, I believe they could do a better job by offering to help for a broader range of career choices. However, the Yale network is amazing—upon coming to Yale, you instantly join a tremendous network of many powerful alumni willing to help a young Yalie.

Quality of Life

Alumnus/a, 9/2002-5/2006, March 2007

Yale's system of residential colleges (similar to Oxford and *Harry Potter*) hugely affects all aspects of school culture—quality of life, campus feel, facilities, dining and so on. All students are assigned to a four-year college upon Yale matriculation—usually, they live within that college all four years, eat in that college's dining hall and so on. Each college has about 100 people in a class, and has a master and dean. Facilities quality varies fairly widely based on what college you are in, although Yale is renovating all colleges (one per year) to bring them up to par with each other. Crime/safety: New Haven is perceived as being dangerous. For some parts of town, this is true. For the Yale campus, for the most part, this is not. All colleges and student areas are locked with key card only access, and there are buses to take students from place to place, especially at night. (Although, many students don't take advantage of them because they are not always convenient.) Keep your wits about you and you will be fine. Housing is guaranteed for all four years.

Alumnus/a, 8/2003-5/2005, August 2006

Every Yale student misses Yale terribly in the first year out. This speaks to the quality of life at Yale. The diverse crowd of people, all of whom are very capable and interesting, is the best part of Yale. The residential college system really brings people together, especially seen in hindsight. Facilities are for the most part good. Crime is a bit of an issue in New Haven. I certainly had my run-ins with crime.

Current student, 9/2004-Submit Date, January 2005

The residential college system is one of Yale's defining qualities. It makes students feel like a very integral part of Yale because they can be known within their rather small residential college. Within the ivy-covered walls of these glorified dorms are rooms pretty much like any other college. However, one extreme exception is the basement entertainment room filled with flat-screen TVs, pool tables and video games. The food is amazing and the catering service makes sure that the food does not become too repetitive. The campus is stunning—all the buildings are in the Gothic style. The city of New Haven, despite popular

Read all of Vault's College Surveys at **www.vault.com/college**—get complete surveys on 100s of colleges and universities, expert advice on application essays and more.

VAULT CAREER LIBRARY 131

belief, is actually quite nice and filled with high-end eateries and ethnic restaurants. Shops range from Banana Republic to J. Crew. However, like any city in America, New Haven does have bad areas that students are advised to avoid at night.

Alumnus/a, 9/2000-5/2004, March 2005

The residential college system is unique and one of the highlights of living at Yale. It fosters a sense of belonging and friendly rivalry without divisiveness. I enjoyed the only all-organic dining hall in the university, so the food was amazing, although at times, monotonous (which is true of any dining hall). The surrounding neighborhood is dangerous but campus is very safe.

> **The school says:** "Crime has decreased substantially in recent years in urban areas nationwide, including New Haven. Crime statistics gathered by the government are available that allow the public to compare cities and regions around the country."

Current student, 9/2001-Submit Date, December 2004

Yale dorms vary, from squalor to palatial. Wood floors and wood molding/siding are the norm, with marble bathrooms. The renovated colleges (Branford, Berkeley, Pierson and Timothy Dwight) are amazing. Each college has a dining hall, weight room, library, TV room, common room, and other amenities unique to certain residential colleges, such as Silliman's climbing wall. Dining hall food is great the first few months, and then you sort of get tired of it. I feel perfectly safe in New Haven, and I think most students do, too. New Haven is a great town and very lively even late at night during the week. This is due in large part to the university insulating itself from the rest of New Haven by purchasing land around campus and developing it. However, Yale does strive to foster good town/gown relations.

> **The school says:** "While some of Yale's highly regarded residential colleges have been renovated more recently than others, there is little difference in housing quality from college to college. All students on campus live in comfortable settings."

 ## Social Life

Alumnus/a, 9/2002-5/2006, March 2007

Not much of a Greek system because of the residential college system—I'd say only about 10 percent of the student population is Greek, and maybe 7 percent live in Greek housing. Dating scene: most people say they are too busy to have long-term relationships, although I did it myself for three years. New Haven has surprisingly good food around town—one street has four different Thai places within a block, all differentiated based on food, service and so on. My favorite is Thai Taste. Also, people rave about Naples Pizza, but I prefer Yorkside—more food variety, better pizza, and a more central location.

Alumnus/a, 8/1999-8/2003, June 2006

Social life at Yale is sprawling. A majority of the partying happens on campus or at the few fraternity houses. There are tons of events sponsored by undergraduate organizations that range from very cheap to free. The dating scene is adequate, though people tend to prefer random hookups at parties over casual relationships, but Yale definitely has its fair share of serious, going-to-get-married-within-a-year-of-graduation relationships, as well. Bars and clubs that rank among student favorites include: Toad's, Bar, Rudy's, Hot Tomato's, Richters, Anchor, Anna Liffey's and Sullivan's.

Current student, 9/2002-Submit Date, October 2005

The social life ranges from kids going out five nights a week to local bars and clubs (Bar, Toad's Place, Vivas and Hula Hanks) to students who hang out with friends in a dormroom once or twice a week. There's pretty much a scene for any personality type here. There are a lot of good restaurants around New Haven, with a wide variety of different cuisines. Unfortunately, the dating scene is not booming. The first two years of school, very few people dated. By junior and senior year, however, dating became more prevalent. The Greek system is limited. Although there are a few frats and sororities, their presence on campus is minimal. Athletic teams dominate the bar scene instead. Senior year, senior societies are also a source of social life.

Current student, 9/2004-Submit Date, July 2006

Yalies are very cultured. We like to party as much as we like to attend the theater or an a cappella concert. There is a wide range of activities in which to engage, from the quirky to the traditional. The best perks are the intimate parties in someone's suite or apartment and master teas, when distinguished guests have meet-and-greets with the students at the master's house. Yale is drenched in tradition, as well, and I love that. The architecture and amenities are breathtaking. It is truly a once-in-a-lifetime experience.

Alumnus/a, 9/2000-5/2004, March 2005

Since Yale is isolated from large cities, most of the social life is located on campus at frats, colleges and local bars/clubs. This is especially good for the first two years for the consummate "college experience." But junior and senior years can be a bit boring and redundant, especially if you don't have a car like the majority of people. New York is close enough. Favorite bars/clubs: Toad's (all roads lead to Toad's on Wednesday/Saturday nights); the aptly named Bar (great pizza and their own microbrewery), the famous Sally's and Pepe's pizzerias—there's no shortage of pizza in New Haven—Louie's Lunch (for the original hamburger—don't ask for ketchup!). There is no dating scene—mostly married or just hooking up. Fun school events like 80's Safety Dance, Casino Night, and of course, The Game (vs. Harvard), which inspires the most excess of the year. Secret societies are also a time-honored tradition for seniors.

Current student, 8/2001-Submit Date, April 2004

The Greek system is not very large, though it is present. Any student can either ignore frats or rush everything and embrace the Greek life; it's up to him/her. It's a rare weekend when there're no parties to attend, and there are often large campus-wide events such as Casino Night, Winter Ball and Spring Fling. The dating scene isn't the greatest, as casual dating doesn't seem to really exist, though there are both a large number of dedicated couples, as well as random hookups. There's a wide variety of restaurants for all budget levels, time constraints and taste buds. The Thai in New Haven is especially good, and there are two places that claim to have invented pizza and hamburgers, respectively. I don't know if they're telling the truth, but the food sure is good. Bars and clubs: there's a bit of everything, whatever atmosphere you want, you can find it.

University of Delaware

Admissions
116 Hullihen Hall
Newark, DE 19716
Admissions phone: (302) 831-8123
Admissions fax: (302) 831-6905
Admissions e-mail: admissions@udel.edu
Admissions URL:
www.udel.edu/admissions/viewbook/apply/

 ## Admissions

Current student, Visual Arts, 8/2005-Submit Date, May 2007

UD has become a very popular university, receiving about 22,000 applications this past year. They accept about 9,000 and expect between 3,000 to 4,000 students to enroll in the incoming freshmen class. Admissions looks at class choices and pays attention to the level of difficulty in a student's high school schedule. They want to see a student taking challenging classes and not slacking off his/her senior year. AP and honors classes are a plus. They also look at your extracurricular activities. They want an involved student, not somebody who just sits in his/her room and doesn't participate in anything. Admissions understands that SAT scores are not always the best representation of academic performance, so they are less important than the other factors. Interviews are optional, but they don't always help. There are essays on the application. There are also essays on the honors program application.

Current student, English, 9/2005-Submit Date, May 2007

Delaware has definitely gotten hard to get into. It's important to have good essays, recommendations and extracurricular activities. Judging from other people who have gotten in, Delaware seems to value community service highly, as well. Obviously, grades and SATs are also important.

The standards are probably a lot more rigorous. For out-of-state students, as Delaware has recently started a new program that basically guarantees any student from Delaware who meets minimum criteria, admission.

Alumnus/a, Engineering, 8/2002-12/2006, May 2007

Using the Common Application was helpful to save time and UD's supplement to the Common Application wasn't exhaustive. Arriving on campus for a tour or an open house is an incredible experience. The admissions office makes it a point to put its best foot forward with their admissions counselors and student tour guides. Overall, a very positive admissions process.

Alumnus/a, Political Science, 8/2003-5/2007, May 2007

The Delaware admissions process is rigorous. Students are required to provide high school transcripts, letters of recommendation (two, but more can be provided, after five though, admissions officers will probably stop caring to read them), an essay describing a particular challenge or an explanation of your desire to attend UofD, SAT or ACT scores, and general statements explaining activities and jobs. Interviews are only used when the admissions staff is having a difficult time making a decision and they require personal interaction to help make a decision. They will contact you; you do not contact UofD for an interview. The selection process is intense; they read over everything and take grades, SAT scores and HS activity into consideration. By no means do SAT scores determine admittance. Admissions looks at everything, if a student has stellar GPA in high school but poor SAT scores and few extracurricular activities, they probably won't accept that student. You must be wellrounded!! Also, the admissions office has a "commitment to Delawareans." Personally, I believe this program to be lenient towards Delaware residents. In an attempt to expand the number of DE residents at the university, Delawareans are probably given a break. Again, to get into UD, be active in high school: join clubs, maintain a job and work for your town. Also, keep your grades up, your SAT scores high, and give the university exactly what it asks for on the application: no more, no less.

Alumnus/a, 9/2002-5/2006, May 2007

The admissions process is not difficult. I recommend getting into the Honors Program. It is not that hard to maintain honors status and it looks great on résumés. The essays are your usual college application essays. UD is becoming more and more selective as a state college. It used to be the fallback school for anyone from Delaware, and now, even students who live in the state are not being accepted. I also recommend going into the school with a major selected. It is easier to switch majors than enter as an undecided. That is how lots of kids end up being here longer than four years.

Current student, Education, 9/2004-Submit Date, May 2007

I applied to UD when they had Early Decision. Now they don't have that, but the process is still very similar. It takes a long time to hear whether you've been accepted or not, but it's worth the wait. I feel like UD is the only school I applied that actually looked carefully at all of the admissions materials I sent. When I got to UD, I became a tour guide, and some of the admissions counselors actually recognized my name from my application. You have to appreciate a team that looks at more than just your rank and file!

Current student, Biology, 8/2004-Submit Date, May 2007

Make sure you write a good essay. That probably counts the most. Your grades and GPA are factored in, but a good essay can help people who may not have as strong of an academic record. Take AP classes; they show commitment and help you gain intro class credits. Interviews are not necessary. .

Current student, Psychology, 8/2005-Submit Date, May 2007

As a transfer student, my admissions process was a little different. I had to write about why I wanted to transfer to the University of Delaware. In the essay, I included what I did not like about my other college and how I thought the University of Delaware could improve my future. As an in-state student, I realize that I probably had an easier time getting in than other applicants. However, the university is becoming very selective as the years go on.

Current student, Physics, 8/2005-Submit Date, May 2007

There was no required interview. The Common Application was accepted. The Honors Program had a separate application that required additional essays. The school is very selective in choosing its students and screens the applicants fairly well.

 ## Academics

Current student, History, 8/2004-Submit Date, May 2007

Most of the classes here have been very good, and the professors are always helpful. While there are those classes that you should avoid, for the most part, classes are stimulating and provide a lot of information. The workload is tough, but the professors are more than willing to help if you get stuck. They are required to have office hours and many times will be available by appointment if necessary. All of my professors have been accessible and friendly. Grading is generally fair, and some professors do grade on a curve. There are some classes that are easy A's, but for the most part, professors do not pad grades, and you have to work for what you want.

Current student, Pre-med, 9/2005-Submit Date, May 2007

UD has become a lot harder to gain admittance to over the past couple of years. They really want UD to have an excellent reputation. Workload really depends on what you pick and, of course, some majors are easier than others. Getting into classes isn't too bad as long as you have an early registration appointment. It's all done over UDSIS, which has good sides and bad sides. It's good because you can get your classes right away, but it's bad because you have to be one of the first people online and sometimes the site crashes because so many people are trying to login.

Read all of Vault's College Surveys at www.vault.com/college—get complete surveys on 100s of colleges and universities, expert advice on applicaton essays and more.

VAULT CAREER LIBRARY 133

Alumnus/a, Education, 8/2003-5/2005, May 2007

Though a big university, my major still made me feel as if I were part of a small community. The department of education at Delaware is quite prestigious for the East Coast, and they are always trying experimental ways of teaching future educators. I was a member of a new cohort for learning to teach science to students in an exciting way. There was a lot of hands-on experience.

Current student, Visual Arts, 8/2003-Submit Date, May 2007

Most teachers use a standard grading system: 93 and up is an A, 90 to 92 is an A- and so on. The university, however, sometimes does require that for a class to count towards you major, you must get at least a C-. My experience with professors at this university leaves me pretty impressed, on the whole. Most of the professors are very helpful and will give you as much help as you need when asked. Many will work, one-on-one after class when they have time.

Current student, Business, 8/2003-Submit Date, May 2007

The only weak department is the math department. Most majors only require a few math classes, but they are rough because most of the math classes are taught by graduate students who do not speak English very well. There are tons of majors from which to choose with varying degrees of difficulty. The engineering department is by far the best the University has to offer. Business, political science, HRIM, and exercise science are also very good.

Alumnus/a, 9/2002-5/2006, May 2007

The Business program at UD is fantastic and the reason why I ultimately decided to attend the school. Most of the professors have had experience in the business world, run their own businesses or have held high-up positions in big companies. They know what they are talking about, and you can learn a lot from them. The business classes are mostly hands-on application. Exams usually ask for application of the class subject matter—no memorization of facts. There is also a lot of teamwork and projects. The workload is not excessive. Grading and difficulty depends on the professor, but I never had anyone who graded unfairly. Popular classes are much easier to get into when you are a junior or a senior.

Current student, Business, 8/2005-Submit Date, May 2007

The business school has some core classes that are difficult, especially math-oriented courses which you must take. Most professors I have had have been good, some not, and some excellent, but overall I am pleased and impressed. Workload depends on the course; sometimes you have a lot to do and sometimes you don't need to touch the book in order to get a B at least. Signing up for classes is based on the amount of credits you have, and you can usually get the classes you need.

Current student, Engineering 9/2003-Submit Date, February 2007

Engineering is the most difficult and well-known program here. However there are more than 200 other programs for students to choose from, including nursing, marketing, East Asian studies, mathematics and education. Good grades will not come easily from most professors, although there is that small bunch where little work is required in order to give you an A. Registration is through a live system based on seniority, so upperclassmen will have an easier time getting desired courses. Classes, for the most part, are small, as (there is a 14:1 student-to-teacher ratio). Introductory classes can hold up to as many as 200 students, while some classes can have only four to six people. Workload is manageable, depending on major, and every professor I've had has been understanding and welcoming.

 ## Employment Prospects

Alumnus/a, Education, 9/2003-5/2007, May 2007

We have many services on campus to help with employment. The Career Services offers free help sessions for résumé writing, interview skills and so on. They hold many job fairs for different majors, many times throughout the year. The alumni network is always around—one of my friends just got an interview because she was a graduate of UD, and an alumnus was looking at her résumé. Many different majors have service-learning components or internships in order to gain work experience. For example, nurses do rotations, Hotel Restaurant and

Institutional Management majors work in our on-campus restaurant and hotel. Our education majors are out in the schools.

Current student, Engineering, 8/2005-Submit Date, May 2007

Many big companies are attracted to UD, so there are immense opportunities. There are career fairs and a Career Services Center where you can learn more about your future. There is a site called e-recruiting where companies post jobs and internships. As a sophomore, I was able to get a few interviews with major companies (Exxon-Mobil and so on) and get a highly paid internship at Air Products. This is due to the status of UD, especially for their chemical engineering students. The sky is the limit, and out of the 2007 chemical engineering class, the top pay was offered by Exxon-Mobil for over $70,000.

Alumnus/a, Computer Science, 8/2002-6/2006, May 2007

There were several career fairs that I attended at the end of my senior year, and I did my fair share of networking that way. I was actually hired the April before I graduated because my employer found my résumé in the university's résumé book and gave me a call. The career center is really helpful, with tips on writing your résumé, doing interviews and making basic contacts. They are also very good at helping you choose a major, I hear.

There are lots of different internship opportunities offered through the school, as well. I had a friend who interned in Florida at Disney World for two semesters and another who was a hospitality major and interned at the school's hotel for a while. If you work hard and look carefully, there's something to benefit anyone's career at Delaware.

I graduated just about one year ago, and nearly all of my friends and roommates have some type of job related to the major of their choice. Again I would say if you try to make the most of your time at school, you'll do well when you get out.

Alumnus/a, Chemistry, 9/2002-5/2006, May 2007

Lots of employment opportunities. Scouts come often—you just need to set up your seeking-employment account. Students actually post résumés and employers call you to speak to you about the job, not the other way around!

Current student, Education, 8/2005-Submit Date, May 2007

Graduates of my school get jobs immediately, for the most part. There are stats available online, but I believe something like 80 percent were employed within six months of graduation, with the rest either to pursuing higher degrees or still looking.

Alumni of UD are constantly saying how much they love the school, and I have gotten offers from complete strangers who graduated from UD for things from jobs to discounts on cars.

Current student, History, 8/2002-Submit Date, May 2007

The University of Delaware holds numerous career fairs for students with many recruiters from all over the East Coast. The University also has a Career Center for students that offers advice, career guidance and other types of advice. A degree from the University of Delaware holds a high status amongst employers all over the United States. Academic Advisors also provide good information and insight to students about internships concerning their major. Most graduates receive entry-level jobs at large, well-respected companies with the understanding that advancement opportunities are plentiful. Students who graduate with engineering degrees are highly recruited and receive higher starting pay than most other graduates.

 ## Quality of Life

Current student, Business, 6/2003-Submit Date, June 2007

The judicial system is the only department I ever had a problem with at Delaware. The rules and regulations for drinking have become so strict that you have to be careful even if you're 21. They have a "three-strikes" policy where they usually expel you from school on the third strike. The kicker is that if you ever need an ambulance for alcohol poisoning, you get an automatic two strikes.
.

Alumnus/a, Visual Arts, 8/2004-6/2006, June 2007

The facilities and the campus are breathtakingly beautiful. The music department just completed the David and Louise Roselle Center for the Arts, a building that houses the music department and the robust theater department, providing state-of-the-art facilities for both. Practice rooms are plentiful; there is a fantastic proscenium theater for plays. At this time There is no suitable performance venue for the UD Orchestra, although two small concert halls, a recital hall and a bizarre gymnasium-style rehearsal hall/performance venue exist.

The campus is gorgeous, with a mostly uniform, red-brick that dates back to the original college, established after the Revolutionary War. (then called, Newark College). There are many historical artifacts, like Elliot Hall, Newark's oldest building and the undergraduate advising center, and Memorial Hall, where the names of all UD's war veterans are on display. UD's library is one of the largest university libraries in the country, and it has just about everything for which you could be looking, with new texts being added constantly. There is a sizeable computer center in the basement, and technology access is widespread. Wireless Internet is available, as well as tech centers in many buildings. The housing is ever improving, with new dormitories just finished on the nearby Laird campus. Dorms generally include air conditioning, and there are three, full dining halls with reasonable prices for off-campus students and a good selection at each.

There are many blue-light public safety phones throughout campus, especially in areas that may be less secure. All dorms are single-point entry with key card access, and there is a strong (one might say annoying) UD police and public safety presence on campus. As a lifelong resident of the city of Newark, I can attest to it being a fairly peaceful college town, where most people enjoy the vibrancy that the students bring to the town. There is a lot of inexpensive housing throughout the city, and the immediate area around campus is absolutely wonderful.

Current student, Visual Arts, 8/2004-Submit Date, May 2007

New residence halls have been built on campus, and existing structures have been cleaned up. The maintenance staff is exceptional. Delaware's campus is always green and well kept. It's actually so nice that students spend a lot of time out on the green (the mall on main campus). Public Safety keeps the campus very safe. There is also a system of blue lights in place. In order to gain access to the residence halls, you must have an access card. The Newark Police are also active in protecting students.

Alumnus/a, Education, 9/2003-5/2007, May 2007

I loved my time at UD. Housing is guaranteed all four years, and there is plenty of on-and-off campus housing—something for everyone. Campus is beautiful and always maintained! Maintenance is pretty good; you call them and they will come help you with whatever is wrong in your building. There are four dining halls, and you can eat at any one you want. They post the menus online so you can choose where you would like to eat. The food is good, and they have staple options at every meal.

Current student, Engineering, 8/2005-Submit Date, May 2007

Newark, DE is a college town: the majority of the people you see everyday are students. There have been a few instances of violence, but I have never felt unsafe; Everywhere on campus is well lit and they have call boxes. They have been building new dorms on the north campus, which are very nice and provide an alternative to the usual communal bathroom-type dorms. They are suites with two people to a room and two rooms connected by a bathroom. There are also the normal communal bathroom-type dorms in which many people also like to live. There are a few gyms and a bus system that runs until 3 a.m., often during class times, less often at night. The dining halls are the one thing that I don't love; many times I would find myself eating cereal because the food choices were not great. They had premium nights when they would cook really good food, but you had to pay more. The brunch was always good on weekends. When living in the Christiana Towers, the on-campus apartments, a dining plan was not necessary, but it was everywhere else. There are good alternatives to the dining hall, such as the Trabant University Center and Perkins. Trabant has different food choices, such as sushi, Quiznos, Chick-fil-A, and others. Basically the campus is great and people love being here.

 # Social Life

Alumnus/a, Visual Arts, 8/2004-6/2006, June 2007

UD is fed (literally and figuratively) by Main Street, which is basically the northern border of campus. Here, there are five bars that have some restaurant capacity, several really good restaurants, including Home Grown Cafe (also a bar), Cafe Gelato (also ice-cream), Cucina di Napoli (great Italian food), and Ali Baba's (best Middle Eastern food). There are three pizza joints, a burrito hole, a Pita Pit, a Panera Bread, a Coldstone Creamery and a really mediocre diner (Korner Diner). The Iron Hill Brewery is a microbrewery and restaurant where you can take your parents, or business colleagues who want to interview you. There is also a campus restaurant run by the Hospitality program.

There are several excellent shops on Main Street, as well, including Rainbow and Wonderland Records, Crystal Concepts (for your incense, tarot card, and magic rock needs), Days of Knights (for Magic Cards and Battlestar Galactica merchandise), and several boutiques for vintage clothes and jewelry. There is a movie theater that is very inexpensive and has some huge theaters. There are several cultural events provided by UD. The Bob Carpenter Center has hosted Ludacris, Korn, Garbage, Dane Cook and probably a bunch of others I can't think of immediately. The Trabant Center has hosted the Upright Citizens Brigade a few times in the last year, and regularly has comedians and cultural exhibitions. There is also a movie theater on campus, showing things like The *Life Aquatic*, and often anime, for a small price.

The Greek system on campus is fairly vibrant, with many major fraternities and sororities housed on and near campus. I was a member of Phi Mu Alpha Sinfonia, the national music fraternity; Sigma Alpha Iota, its sister sorority, is also active. The campus is dry, so most fraternal activities tend to be low-key or off-campus, although I noticed quite a few drunken people in my classes during Greek Week. Pi Kappa Alpha is a popular fraternity, as is Sigma Phi for girls. There are many many clubs to join on campus, and there is a large endowment to fund activities that promote drug-free activities. There are many Christian ministries on campus, as well as a Hillel Center. The greatest advantage UD has is being located halfway between Washington, D.C./Baltimore and New York/Philadelphia. Aside from the cultural offerings of Delaware and Wilmington, one can pay $5.50 to ride the train into Center City Philadelphia and enjoy the many attractions there, including the Philadelphia Orchestra, South Street, the Art Museum and Old City.

Alumnus/a, Chemistry, 9/2002-5/2006, May 2007

Homecoming is allowed to have tailgating tents again. Lots of fests throughout the year, Skidfest, Wilbur fest, Capel fest and so on. There are lots of day-drinking with friends and live music. Bars on Main Street are pretty good—lots of beer for cheap—Shaggys, Deer Park, East End, Home Grown; even Margaritas Pizza has beer on tap. Great intramural sports too. People take it very seriously and it's very fun. The gym is Greek, with an indoor rock climbing wall, volleyball, basketball courts, pool, free weights, machines, cardio and so on. There is a shirt rule: no tanks allowed at the gym. It's a great idea because you don't have to see people's bodies, and it keeps the machines cleaner! You can't beat the location, 45 minutes from D.C., 40 minutes from Philly, one and a half hours from NYC, 40 minutes from MD. Hungry for a cheesesteak, you'll be back in time for the new *Grey's Anatomy*!

Current student, Education, 8/2005-Submit Date, May 2007

House parties are the main events at UD. Any given night of the week, there are parties to attend. Often, there are bus trips to clubs in nearby Philly and Baltimore. A fair number of bars are in Newark, although the bouncers go by-the-book. Dating isn't as prevalent as hooking up, but there are plenty of eligible students on campus. Concerts come each semester, with HelloGoodbye being the most recent. Preakness is a big deal, as are tailgating for football games, Cinco de Mayo and Greek Week, for the Greeks. Greek life is not as popular at UD as it is further south, but about 15 percent of students are involved in it. There are currently eight Pan-Hellenic sororities and 14 IFC frats, along with numerous non-social, or special-interest or Greek organizations.

Read all of Vault's College Surveys at www.vault.com/college–get complete surveys on 100s of colleges and universities, expert advice on applicaton essays and more.

VAULT CAREER LIBRARY   135

American University

American University
Admissions
4400 Massachusetts Ave, Northwest
Washington, D.C. 20016-8001
Admissions phone: (202) 885-6000
Admissions fax: (202) 885-6014
Admissions e-mail: afa@american.edu

 ## Admissions

Current student, 8/2004-Submit Date, May 2006

AU's application process was similar to others. They have a great and easy online application form, and you will be required to send in an essay, usually personal in nature, with topics such as; obstacles you have overcome; and the like. AU's standards have been gradually going up in the past years, so admissions are becoming more and more selective.

AU is, no doubt, very expensive, but unless your parents are really rich, the AU Grant is your friend. However, you will still need to be prepared to take out loans, loans and more loans. When you get notification of acceptance, this will be accompanied by a financial aid, award package.

Current student, 9/2004-Submit Date, May 2006

American University accepts the Common Application, which is nice, and requires no personal interviews (though I imagine they may help in some instances). Advice on getting in? Do well in high school—get good grades and have some interesting extracurriculars. Doing well on SATs is also helpful ,though it does not seem to be the deciding factor. Also, take SAT Subject Tests—particularly math, writing. AU likes people who take them, and they can also help you skip a few classes in the university math requirements (beware, though, Statistics is hard). As far as college essays go, it seems to me that the better-written, the better. Also, creativity seems to be a plus. I know when I wrote my college application essays, I was a bit nervous because they ended up being quite political and interesting, but American University loved them! They were calling my high school advisor—before I was even formally accepted—to encourage me to attend American University.

Current student, 1/2003-Submit Date, May 2006

I would definitely recommend a campus visit and alumni interview, although they are not required. AU is becoming more selective. In fact, at a recent alumni event our former president quipped, "Most of you would not be able to get into AU if you applied today!" The campus is beautiful, and D.C. is a great place to visit with several colleges to compare and contrast.

Current student, 8/2005-Submit Date, May 2006

The essays did a good job of letting me express interest in something I was passionate about, a large plus. I live far from D.C., so I did not interview. I really liked how quickly they got back to me, and the scholarship offered through the honors program was a big perk. If you are applying for a social sciences major, having some sort of volunteer job which is socially active is really attractive to the admissions office. Almost everyone you meet here worked for an election or Darfur Awareness.

Current student, 8/2005-Submit Date, May 2006

The admissions process is simple and free if done online. No interview was required. Each year the process becomes more and more selective, and there are many upperclassmen who say that, given the standards now, they couldn't have gotten into American. AU looks for students who not only show potential in the classroom but have a strong desire to change the world and help out in their communities, and they look for this desire during the application process.

Current student, 8/2005-Submit Date, May 2006

American University wants to see activism in their incoming students. They want to see unique high school activities, leadership and community involvement, especially in politics. The essays, like all other colleges, are just to see writing skills. The content is semi-important, but the grammar and style are key. A slightly above-average GPA coupled with high school activities will secure an admission. The amount of money granted depends on higher levels of selectivity.

Current student, 8/2004-Submit Date, April 2005

The admissions staff is very helpful and always available to answer questions. Admissions offers many opportunities for students to visit campus, both before and after their application has been submitted. Extracurriculars are very important, as well as a solid GPA. Interviews are not necessary. Essays are a way for a student to stand out in a pool of qualified candidates. American University selects only the best of the best; students are all qualified and are unique additions to the campus. Admission to AU is getting harder every year.

 ## Academics

Current student, 9/2004-Submit Date, May 2006

Getting into classes can be frustrating. AU is a smaller school, and because of that, there may be only one or two sections of a particular course you're looking to take, including the popular ones. As a rising junior, I have not yet gotten into my top two choices of classes. You are required to take 10 general education courses from five curricular areas, as well as completing a math and English requirement. In my opinion the gen eds are fairly easy classes and lacking in depth and creativity. The English requirement is difficult because you are graded with very high standards. Professors are generally approachable and available, with the university requiring that they keep office hours each week. As far as the workload, it depends on the classes. I have about three hours of homework a night, while my roommate rarely does any.

Current student, 9/2004-Submit Date, May 2006

I must say that the academic programs are great. The professors—especially the full-time professors—are amazing people—UN advisors, EPA scientists and ex-ambassadors. And if you don't know it yet, the professor makes the class—any subject can be wonderful or terrible depending on who is teaching it. Grading and workload also primarily depend upon the professors. What is really great about AU, though, is that teaching evaluation surveys actually affect the status of professors' jobs! Why is this good? The truly terrible, know-nothing professors don't last! Still, American University is a serious academic school—the workload is far more severe than anything at a "party school." Really, though, it's worth it. Oh, and as far as getting into classes you want—it goes by number of credits earned so it is a bit tough in the beginning (which doesn't really matter because you are taking general education at that point) but it gets easier. For a small school, American University offers a lot of variety, which definitely decreases the number of sections for any given class, but if you are willing to take something in the meantime and wait for a class, you can always get it. People often drop a class, or even if the don't, you can petition the professor to let you in the class (which they will usually do unless it violates fire code—in which case, sometimes they will even switch to a larger room if there is enough interest).

Current student, 8/2004-Submit Date, May 2006

Overall, there are lots of great professors at AU. They are very accomplished in their fields and have the advantage of having many connections, so it is not uncommon to have ambassadors and other extremely accomplished individuals coming to the classroom. Very popular professors fill up pretty quickly, so it may be difficult to get into a popular class until your junior or senior year when you can register before freshmen and sophomores. AU's general education requirements can be frustrating sometimes as you ponder what Biology and

Physics courses have to do with your Political Science degree, but it's required, so the best thing you can do is check professor ratings online and get the best professor possible.

Grading depends largely on the professor. Some will fail you for more than three absences, although most do not adhere to this rule. Provided you show your face in class on a regular basis, do the assigned readings, and demonstrate a decent amount of understanding, your chances of getting a high grade in most classes is good. Again, workload will depend on the professor. You will find most classes require a couple of major papers and, of course, exams.

Current student, 8/2005-Submit Date, May 2006

The classes at American University offer the highest standard of academics. The professors push students to meet their full potential in a wide range of interesting courses and subjects. Sometimes, underclassmen may miss out on the most popular classes, but by their junior or senior years, they will be able to take the classes about which everyone raves. Though many classes and majors have large workloads, it is well worth it, and the professors never give work just for the sake of assigning it. The professors are excellent and very knowledgeable—many are currently involved professionally in their fields of expertise, and they pass on the most recent information to the students. The professors at American are always open to students and encourage students to talk to them. In fact, some professors will give students their cell phone numbers and home addresses. Many professors at AU are highly recognized for their work. Some examples of such amazing professors include Julian Bond, James Thurber and Akhbar Ahmed.

Current student, 8/2005-Submit Date, May 2006

The academic nature of the school is intense. The first year, advisors guide the class-selection process and general education classes are required. These low-level classes allow students to get a feel for the academic standards of college without incredible pressure. It is very difficult for an underclassman to get popular classes because registration opens earlier for those with more credits. It is practically required to sit at the computer at midnight, right when classes open, to try to get the popular classes. Grading and workload depends on the professor. Generally, there is significant reading and writing due each day of class. For every hour of class time, there is about an hour and a half of work.

Current student, 8/2004-Submit Date, April 2005

The undergraduate program is very well designed so that students take a variety of subjects during their general education classes, as well as having majors which allow students to pick and choose classes that would most interest them. Classes are all of high quality. Professors know, and most often love their subjects and can provide students with information never found in any textbook.

As experienced professionals in their fields, many have excellent connections or run internships that engage students, both inside and outside of the classroom. Popular classes are fairly easy to take. Grading is very fair, but if you receive a good grade, you know that you worked for it. Workload varies by class. Some are more demanding than others, and classes require different skills. In one class, a student may need to only read books and write papers, whereas in another, trips into the city, videos and discussion are included in the classroom. Overall, academics are rigorous, professors are excellent and grading is fair.

Current student, 9/2004-Submit Date, April 2005

The academics are the best part about American. My classes are small (anywhere from 10 to 50 students), the teachers know our names, and opinions are meant to be shared. Discussion is encouraged, and the professors are passionate and know what they're talking about. As a political science and literature double major, I have government professors like the head of the NAACP and White House aides for classes, and my literature professors are leading scholars and thinkers. They are engaging and excited about their topics. I am particularly fond of the College of Arts and Sciences here, where departments are small (most students at AU are in the schools of public affairs, international service, business or communications—not CAS) and highly personal. It really is a community of scholars.

 Employment Prospects

Alumnus/a, 9/2004-5/2006, November 2006

American University has an outstanding reputation among employers in the fields of international affairs and public policy. Many students have gone on to stellar careers with the U.S. government and nonprofit organizations in the capital and overseas. AU has very strong connections to its alumni parishioners, and many students participate in prestigious student career-experience programs.

Current student, 9/2004-Submit Date, May 2006

There is a lot of on-campus information on internships and employment. There are job and internship fairs at least twice a year and a full-time, super helpful Career Center. Graduates of AU go on to do lots of things—a good number first go into Peace Corps or the like. Many end up working for the government—especially in divisions like the CIA. Many also end up as high-ups in Multinational Corporations. Some end up as ambassadors, UN advisors or professors. American University definitely looks good on paper.

Current student, 8/2003-Submit Date, November 2005

I have not known one senior who did not have some sort of plan after graduation. By this I mean, they had a job offer, were enrolled in graduate school or decided to take time off. And the jobs they received right out of undergrad are nothing to scoff at. Several graduates end up working on the Hill for a Representative or Senator. Others end up at the top lobbying firms, accounting firms and nonprofits. I do not know anyone who has used the alumni network to receive a job, but there are definitely alumni who have great jobs and would be willing to help out.

Current student, 9/2004-Submit Date, April 2005

Grads can stay in Washington, go to amazing graduate or law schools, run for public office, go abroad (AU is one of the top Peace Corps and CIA recruiting schools in the nation), or work for the *Associated Press*, *New York Times*, or anywhere in the world. The alumni network is always running, and there are networking receptions every week, it seems.

Current student, 8/2002-Submit Date, April 2005

The Career Center is amazing! They hold a job and internship fair once a semester, which brings in over 120 employers from all over the D.C. metro area. The Career Center also has career and internship advisors specific to each of the schools within the University that guide you through the process of finding an internship or job, from editing your résumé to holding mock interviews to help you hone your interviewing skills. The center has pamphlets on everything, from how to write a résumé to networking techniques.

They hold multiple networking events each semester when current students can meet and network with alumni in the area. Many local businesses and departments of the federal government contact AU specifically for interns and recent graduates to fill their open positions because of the good experiences they've had in the past. AU grads have gone on to work for the federal government, major news corporations, and for international firms. I can't say enough good things about AU's Career Center!

 Quality of Life

Alumnus/a, 8/1998-5/2002, May 2006

AU is a safe campus generally. It is still located in an urban area, but upper NW D.C. is largely residential, well lit and quiet. There are blue lights all over the place, an optional campus safety escort program, roving Public Safety patrols, and 24-hour, secured access to all the dorms. As a former RA and dorm desk receptionist (those responsible for monitoring the 24-hour secured access to the dorm) I can tell you that security is taken very seriously. While it is not the best option to walk alone at night on campus, I did it many times over four years and never felt unsafe or threatened whatsoever.

I lived on campus for all four years—two years as a resident and two years as a Resident Assistant (RA). There are five dorms located on main campus: Letts, Anderson, Centennial (South Side) and McDowell, Hughes and Leonard (North Side). I lived for two years on the North Side (McDowell) and two years on the

Read all of Vault's College Surveys at **www.vault.com/college**–get complete surveys on 100s of colleges and universities, expert advice on applicaton essays and more.

V\ULT CAREER LIBRARY **137**

South Side (Letts). North Side tends to be a bit quieter than the South Side, and you'll find a lot of athletes, international students and honors students living in these dorms. The South Side is a bit more loud and the dorms are larger. You'll tend to see more Greek members living on the South Side—just look for their letters in the windows. It really doesn't matter which side you live on—they both have their own personalities, and there is a good chance that you'll spend a lot of time on both sides of campus.

Alumnus/a, 8/1998-6/2002, May 2006

The campus itself is quite lovely, though a trek from downtown D.C. Students are typically not allowed to have a car until they are upperclassmen and are therefore dependent on public transport, which is no big deal in D.C. once you get to it. To that end, the university operates shuttle buses that run between campus and the Metro on a regular basis, but infrequently on weekends. Otherwise, the walk takes about 20 minutes through a dark, residential neighborhood. After that Metro and buses will take you anywhere you want to go, which is what makes D.C. so livable. Don't be afraid to learn the bus system. Often, buses run directly past campus and can significantly cut down your commute.

Current student, 8/2004-Submit Date, April 2005

American University is a true college campus. Housing is very good; rooms are larger than most colleges and have built-in storage units to maximize space. Dorm bathrooms and kitchens are cleaned daily, and overall, the dorms are clean and well maintained. Campus is beautiful and revolves around a quadrangle where students congregate and where many events are held.

Academic buildings, the spiritual center, library, student union and more surround the quad so students need not go far to find what they need. Dining at AU is excellent. The food available in the dining hall is delicious and of much higher quality than most colleges'. With an emphasis on freshness, AU understands that its student body is rather diverse in what they want to put in their body and offers vegetarian, vegan and many other types of dishes. The neighborhood that surrounds AU is mostly residential and beautiful. Due to patrols by public safety and the area in which AU is located, crime normally does not occur, and almost everyone feels safe on campus.

Social Life

Alumnus/a, 9/2004-5/2006, November 2006

AU offers a quiet, pretty campus with popular student clubs like the ballroom/swing dancing club. In addition, AU students make use of all Washington has to offer: free museums, fascinating political speakers, inexpensive concerts and so on.

Alumnus/a, 8/2001-5/2005, May 2006

AU has a variety of programs in which students may get involved. To name just a few, there is the Kennedy Political Union, which hosts famous and notable speakers, fraternities, sororities, community service clubs, language clubs and sports clubs. There is definitely a good variety of student organizations in which to become involved.

There are restaurants galore because a benefit of going to school in a big city is the variety of culinary choices. There are amazing restaurants near campus and in the city, and AU students will become familiar with them very quickly.

Current student, 8/2005-Submit Date, May 2006

This might be the one area where AU is somewhat lacking. It is a dry campus, even for students over 21, and there are no bars near the university, though by using the Metro system, some are easily accessible. There are some great restaurants around the university and are easily accessible via public transportation. As the population of AU is about 60 percent female and 40 percent male, some girls find the dating scene difficult . Also, estimates of the homosexual male population hover around 20 to 25 percent. Greek life is alive and well here at AU, with over 20 percent of students involved in social Greek organizations. The campus has almost 200 recognized and official clubs in which students maybe involved.

Current student, 8/2005-Submit Date, May 2006

D.C. is filled with different social events. Adams-Morgan is a haven to tons of different restaurants. Clubs are also downtown but not as popular among D.C. college students, especially under 21. Most parties are in the dorms or frequently hosted by frats but with an open-door policy. Greeks make up about 30 percent of AU and are generally well respected and inclusive. The Kennedy Center has free performances every night and Guapo's and Neisha's restaurants in Tenleytown are popular dining places as well as party sites.

Current student, 8/2002-Submit Date, April 2005

Social life at AU revolves around the D.C. scene. Our own section of D.C., being more residential, does not offer a lot in the way of bars or clubs. About a 10-minute bus ride from campus is Dupont Circle, which has great bars (Cafe Citron) and bookstores (Kramer Books). Dupont Circle and Georgetown are where you typically find students on Friday and Saturday nights.

Georgetown's M Street has the best bar scene for students in D.C. Jazz clubs and nightclubs are all within walking distance, as well as great restaurants, such as Five Guys and Bistro Francais. AU sponsors many of events on campus from the different clubs, as well. The Kennedy Political Union brings political speakers, such as Bill Clinton, John Edwards and Mikhail Gorbachev to campus. Greek life on campus is pretty lacking. There are no houses on campus, but there are frat parties off campus, which are pretty popular. However, Greek life does not rule over students very much.

The School Says

Innovative. Rigorous. Interdisciplinary. American University (AU) invites it's more than 11,000 students (equally divided between undergrad and graduate) to engage in learning that's energetic and intellectually stimulating. AU is home to a close-knit, supportive community. We're small where we need to be. Big where it makes sense to be—Just the right environment in which bright, curious minds thrive. You'll sharpen your reason and your ability to express and defend your ideas. You'll also grapple with ideas you've never encountered before,-and form your own opinions.

Our business, international studies, law and public affairs programs are ranked highly nationwide. The Katzen Arts Center provides academic space for AU students studying the performing and fine arts, and boasts a 30,000 square-foot museum that features art and performance installations by local, national, and internationally-known artists. The Greenberg Theatre hosts quality theater, music and dance performances by the AU arts programs and professional companies for the AU and Washington, D.C. communities. Our academic programs combine theory with practice, and our faculty is comprised of noted scholars who are practicing professionals in their fields. All are teachers, and all teach undergraduates. You can choose from an interdisciplinary curriculum with over 70 programs in the arts and humanities, business, education, international studies, public affairs, sciences and social sciences.

The top 15 percent of admitted students are invited to join the university honors program. Academically outstanding students are automatically considered for merit scholarships when they are admitted. The average undergraduate class size is 23, and the student to faculty ratio is 14:1. Not just a political town, Washington, D.C. offers internship and job opportunities in nearly every field. About 80 percent of all students participate in at least one internship. AU Abroad offers more than 100 study abroad programs in 33 geographic locations around the world. Our Washington Semester Program brings students to campus from universities around the country for internship and seminar courses, ranging from American Politics to Journalism and from International Business to International Environment and Development.

AU has seven residence halls on the main campus accommodating about 3,300 students. The recently renovated Nebraska Hall will house 115 students in suite-style apartments. Each apartment will have two, three or four single bedrooms clustered around a common area containing a living room and kitchen, and each apartment will have its own bathroom shared by the residents of the apartment. Most rooms are for two students and have two complete sets of furniture, and have computer network and telephone access. Laundry and cooking facilities are available on each floor. Some residence halls have special interest floors, such as the honors floors and the community service floor. With over 160 student clubs, frequent on-campus speakers, and social events including entertainment and sports, there are many activities for you, right on campus. AU sponsors 16 intercollegiate teams to compete in the NCAA Division I as members of the Patriot League. You may also participate in intramural and club sports and work out in a first-class fitness center.

The Catholic University of America

620 Michigan Ave, Northwest
Washington, D.C. 20064
Admissions phone: (202) 319-5305 or (800) 673-2772
Admissions fax: (202) 319-6533
Admissions e-mail: cua-admissions@cua.edu

 ## Admissions

Current student, 8/2003-Submit Date, June 2004

The admissions process is not difficult. If you have average grades and some extracurricular activities, you should get in. The architectural, nursing and music programs may be more selective due to their reputation.

Current student, 8/2002-Submit Date, June 2004

I applied to Catholic online via their online application on their web site. I had to fill out information about myself, including an essay and several letters from teachers. Also, because of my major, I had to audition at the actual school. The school, itself, is highly selective. Admissions is based on GPA, SATs, essays, letters, interview and audition.

Alumnus/a, 8/1993-6/1996, March 2004

The written process, essays and interviews were fairly standard. I found it easy to apply and get in. In fact, the whole process, from the time I applied to the time I started my first class, was less than three weeks!

 ## Academics

Current student, 7/2003-Submit Date, August 2006

Very good quality faculty and facilities. International environment. Stimulating social life. Very challenging coursework.

Alumnus/a, 8/1989-6/1993, November 2005

Academic quality was very high. Generally, classes were instructed by faculty holding PhDs. Classes were engaging and of high quality.

Current student, 8/2003-Submit Date, June 2004

If you are an upperclassman, you can pretty much get into any class you want. If you aren't, good luck (although you can often weasel your way in). The grading system varies, as do the professors and workload. Architects are always at the studio. Music students are always at class. Biology students are often studying. Nursing students have long clinicals and a rigid grading system. .

Current student, 8/2002-Submit Date, June 2004

I am in a rigorous academic program at my school. I average 21 credits per semester. I personally never had a problem getting into the more "popular" classes, because registration is dealt with online. Grading is very fair and reflects the amount of work you put into the class. I have always found working and communicating with my professors easy. They are generally eager to help you in all of your work in the class. My workload is reasonably heavy because of the amount of classes I take. The nature of my program is highly competitive and selective in terms of the students who are allowed to continue in it every year.

Alumnus/a, 8/1993-6/1996, March 2004

Quality of classes was excellent, although it was widely known that some programs were rated better than other programs. I never had an issue getting into the classes I desired, other than in the School of Art, with classes such as Pottery and Painting. Due to very limited space in the studios, these classes had waiting lists each semester. A distinguishing mark that sets the Catholic University of America apart is that they require comprehensive examinations prior to graduation. Depending on your field of study, these exams require a full semester, just for preparation.

 ## Employment Prospects

Alumnus/a, 8/1989-5/1993, November 2005

Graduates are well prepared for employment prospects and take a wide variety of positions. The internship program is strong on campus, and the on-campus recruiting program is popular. Alumni network is very active.

Alumnus/a, 8/1993-6/1996, March 2004

At the time I attended the Catholic University of America, Internet usage and even simple e-mail accounts were just starting to be used. Due to this, job placement was difficult and involved a lot of running-around. I assume that this aspect of the university is different now.

Regarding employment prospects, the school says: "The Catholic University of America provides extensive online career services support for both students and alumni through our web site at: careers.cua.edu. CUA posts over 2,000 internship, work-study, part-time and full-time positions each year. Site contents also include links to popular job search engines, job fair schedules for both on- and off-campus events, resources for career exploration and graduate school searches, as well as an alumni career network. Students access the Internet via

Read all of Vault's College Surveys at **www.vault.com/college**—get complete surveys on 100s of colleges and universities, expert advice on applicaton essays and more.

VAULT CAREER LIBRARY 139

Ethernet connections, available in all residence halls and computer labs across campus. Wireless access is also available in the library, university center. In addition, career services offers more traditional support through career counseling, assessments, workshops, résumé and cover letter critiques, and interview preparation."

Current student, 8/2002-Submit Date, June 2004

This summer, I received two internship opportunities within the field of work I hope to pursue. My school is highly regarded in the career path in what I am working. The teachers in the school push us to consider all options within our field in order to maximize career prospects. It's a very goal-oriented and career-driven major.

 ## Quality of Life

Current student, 7/2003-Submit Date, August 2006

Campus life was very safe (private security). In addition good dorms, edible food, good transportation, proximity to Metro station, and its easy to find neighborhood housing.

Current student, 8/2003-Submit Date, June 2004

The quality of life at Catholic is good. Housing is a pretty bad and stressful process, and leaves some people happy and others devastated. The dining hall is OK. It offers a decent selection, and the food isn't bad. Once in a while, it gets boring, and you just have to indulge off campus.

The campus is not the safest. It is located in Brookland. It's D.C., though, so this isn't anything out of the ordinary. They have security guards and lights throughout campus to help make it safer. As long as you don't travel alone, you are usually OK.

Current student, 8/2002-Submit Date, June 2004

The school is located in a rather rough neighborhood. However, the campus and housing are fairly safe. I have never personally had any problems. Housing includes many different styles of living on campus, including traditional dorms, quads, trailers and apartments. There are new dining facilities. The facilities are rather nice, but the food, itself, leaves much to be desired.

Alumnus/a, 8/1993-6/1996, March 2004

Housing is fairly standard to slightly below standard. The university campus is set in an area of Washington, D.C. that is crime-filled. There are daily crime alerts posted around campus, and police are always in the area. After hours, there are many phones available from which you can call security to escort you around, if desired. Although you need to be aware, I never felt particularly threatened or scared.

> **Regarding quality of life, the school says:** "The Catholic University of America is located in D.C.'s historical Brookland neighborhood, which was voted one of the 'Best Places to Live' in the D.C. Metropolitan area by *Washingtonian Magazine* in April 2002. In fact, according to statistics published by the National Center for Education Statistics, The Catholic University of America ranks as the safest campus among the major private universities in Washington, D.C. (NCES, 2004)."

"The CUA campus is bustling with activity at all hours of the day and evening. In addition to the 2,650 undergraduate students, over 3,600 graduate and law students, most of whom are working professionals in D.C., keep campus vibrant and secure in the evening. Additionally, the National Shrine of the Immaculate Conception adjacent to the CUA campus welcomes over 700,000 visitors each year.

"The Brookland-CUA Mertrorail stop and CUA's parking areas offer students safe and convenient access to the university. The Department of Public Safety patrols the 194-acre residential campus 24 hours a day, seven days a week. The CUA Blue Light/Emergency Phone Systems located throughout campus enable students to immediately contact the Public Safety if needed. Residence halls are equipped with magnetic key entry accessible to CUA students only and hall monitors ensure a safe environment for students within the dormitories."

 ## Social Life

Current student, 7/2003-Submit Date, August 2006

Great bars around, lots of dating going on, good shows, good theater, lots of fraternities. Good football games, excellent library and great bookstore. The shrine is big, beautiful and stately. If you can't get a good education and have the time of your life here you are dead anyway.

Current student, 8/2003-Submit Date, June 2004

Catholic has been dubbed a "drinking school with a Catholic problem." If you are interested in a social life here, you will have no trouble finding one.

If you are interested in drinking, you will fit in great here. A good portion of the students will be out partying at local bars three nights a week. Also, some houses hold parties on the weekends.

If you are not interested in drinking, Catholic University of America is a great place. With a Metro stop on campus, you can be down in the heart of D.C. in 15 minutes. There are more monuments and free museums to see than you will ever have time to visit. For sober fun, the House holds outings on Friday nights to places such as the circus, ice skating, hockey games and more.

D.C. provides a great diversity of food from every ethnic background you can imagine. The options are endless.

Current student, 8/2002-Submit Date, June 2004

D.C. is always alive. There are always bars, restaurants, clubs and events to attend. There are no frats on campus, but other schools in the area have them. D.C. offers many different types of social setting, whether you enjoy art and museums, cultural food and restaurants, or watching sports in bars. Many favorites include restaurants in the DuPont Circle area.

Alumnus/a, 8/1993-6/1996, March 2004

The Catholic University of America was ranked by *Playboy* among the Top 10 party schools in the nation! Students, while serious about their studies, were also there to party hard. Almost everyone I knew—myself excluded—would arrange their class schedules around karaoke nights and ladies' nights at the local bars. School-sponsored events and clubs were really lacking participation.

The George Washington University

Office of Admissions
The George Washington University
2121 I Street, Northwest, Suite 201
Washington, D.C. 20052
Admissions phone: (800) 447-3765 or (202) 994-6040
Admissions fax: (202) 994-0325
Admissions e-mail: gwadm@gwu.edu
Admissions URL: www.gwu.edu/admissions.cfm

Admissions

Alumnus/a, 9/2003-5/2006, September 2006

Admissions process required one essay, one recommendation and a standard application that took me about a week to put together. An optional essay detailing your hardships in high school or anything in your file that isn't obvious to the university is read and considered. I didn't interview, but I have been hearing that more applicants are accepting the optional interview to boost their application. School is very big on rising in the *U.S. News* rankings, but the administration won't say that is the goal. Therefore, ACT/SAT score is huge, along with ranking in the top 10 percent of your class. In addition, the university tries to get as many applicants as possible to increase their selectivity. I witnessed this in high school when I received tons of materials in the mail asking me to apply, even a fee waiver. GW also recruits heavily outside of the East Coast and takes pride in fielding students from every state and dozens of countries. Therefore, in my essay and application, I played up my experience living abroad and other things that made me a unique candidate.

Current student, Political Science, 9/2005-Submit Date, April 2007

The process was less difficult then other programs'. The school is very numbers-based, so strong SAT and grades are required. Interviews are not necessary as they don't really have an effect on your admission. The essays are right from the Common Application and the supplements are relatively similar to most other programs. The selectivity has gone up every year for the past five, but if you resemble anything like a decent student, you have a pretty good shot at being selected for admission.

Alumnus/a, 8/2000-12/2003, March 2007

The admissions process was straightforward: standard application, GPA, SAT, essays, rec letters. My impression is that the school is becoming more selective, but basically they place the most weight on the SAT and GPA. I was admitted to the Honors Program, which involves meeting higher academic thresholds and probably more scrutiny. I did not interview, but borderline candidates should, to improve their chances of admission.

Current student, 8/2005-Submit Date, May 2006

They accept the Common Application form plus a supplemental essay about why you would like to attend The George Washington University. I went down to visit, which they ask on the application form. In addition, an area representative visited our school, and I made it a point to go. If they go to your school, I would absolutely recommend attending the information session. They take your name and talk to you about admissions. It lets them know you're serious about attending their college. I would say the selectivity is fairly high. It also depends on the school to which you apply. The Columbian College of Arts and Sciences is easier to get into than, say, the Elliott School of International Affairs.

Alumnus/a, 8/2001-5/2005, May 2006

The admissions process was pretty straightforward. Definitely try to apply for scholarships, you never know how it may turn out. In 2001, there was a Presidential Arts Scholarship, and they had students apply for a $15,000 per year scholarship. At the greeting for the audition, one of the professors stated that if you got this far, getting into GW was pretty likely. Second, I would suggest Early Decision. Third, be creative. If you had any type of work published, or if

you have a poem or short story from English class, definitely send that in instead of the regular essays. I feel like they look for students who have done different things, or who think differently from the rest. Finally, don't miss the deadlines, and remember the second part of the application essay.

Current student, 8/2003-Submit Date, February 2005

GW, short for The George Washington University, has become increasingly selective over the last 10 years. They consider SAT scores very important, along with overall high school GPA and extracurricular involvement. A large portion of undergraduates have invested considerable amounts of time in community service, so that is vital to getting in. Also, they're looking for students who can qualify for advanced-standing credits (AP Classes, CLEP), however that is not the be-all and end-all. There are other factors. Successful applicants generally have SAT scores well into the 1200s and 1300s, and a class rank in the top 10 percent. GW also maintains a significant number of waitlisted students, and people get admitted from there. It is also an advantage to visit the campus (Foggy Bottom or Mount Vernon).

Current student, 9/2001-Submit Date, April 2005

It has gotten considerably harder to get into GW over the past few years, not just percentage-wise but in terms of the caliber of students applying. The honors program is particularly hard to get into, with a lot of weight placed on the special essay the program requires. A lot of people in the honors program turned down higher-ranked schools (I turned down Georgetown and Johns Hopkins) to come to GW, because they just loved the feeling they got on this campus. Interviews are optional but can really help.

As a senior, I was selected to help conduct interviews for the admissions office, and so I have seen the process from the inside. There are a lot of really outstanding students who want to come to GW now; on the other hand, plenty of people get in who are basically sub par.

Academics

Alumnus/a, Political Science, 8/2002-5/2006, June 2007

In my opinion, there is no better place to study political science on the planet. GW's international affairs school is literally right across the street from the state department and two blocks from the White House. Many of my classes were taught by professors literally walking out of work from the state department and into our classroom to discuss current foreign policy issues—an experience that cannot be matched anywhere else. There are no better teachers than those who lived what they are teaching. GW has several professors who are former ambassadors teaching about the conflicts and regions of the world they served in. I have never had a problem getting the classes I needed. Others did, but that is usually a product of lazy registration. Grading is difficult—professors expect a lot from their students, workload is not overly stressful except during finals and midterms like all other colleges.

Current student, Political Science, 9/2005-Submit Date, April 2007

In my opinion, the school does not spend enough money to get the quality teaching it needs to fill its expensive buildings. The Columbian College of Arts and Sciences has a full set of general requirements that usually take up most of the first two years. There is also a mandatory writing class, required of all freshmen which was surprisingly helpful. Once you get past the 100-level courses, the classes become more interesting but still lack where other similar schools excel. The political science program is very popular and is one of the better programs in the country. Getting certain professors is really hit-or-miss as you can get lucky in the class selection process. Grading seems to be fair as most teachers tell you exactly what they require and stick to the syllabus. There are a select few teachers who deviate from the rules and create new guidelines halfway through the semester. The workload is light if you want to skate by, like many do, but to do well, you'll need to work.

Read all of Vault's College Surveys at **www.vault.com/college**—get complete surveys on 100s of colleges and universities, expert advice on applicaton essays and more.

VAULT CAREER LIBRARY   141

Alumnus/a, Economics, 8/2000-12/2003, March 2007

Students are smart on paper but lack intellectual curiosity. There are individual professors who are great, but the programs, as a whole, are average. Popular classes may be difficult to get if you are a political science major. There is grade inflation, and the workload is average.

I majored in economics and minored in mathematics. I also took several high-level science classes. The economics department has some strong professors; stick with them to get the best education and contacts for a career. The math department was weaker. Similarly, the sciences have a few good professors, but the school lacks the facilities needed for a strong program.

Alumnus/a, 8/2000-5/2004, May 2006

GW was a very academic school where your class size seemed to match the workload. Popular classes were extremely hard to get. Most of the time, the class would be full, and the only way to get in would be to attend the first class and hope the prof would let you attend. Grading was generally fair. I've never actually experienced a really horrid prof. They told you the expectations for the class in the first few sessions, and then they'd figure you knew what was expected. If not, they made clear they were always open for questions during office hours. Well, I guess that can be true for everything except the math department. The math department was never a highlight department for with whom I spoke. The professors were so hard to understand. Professor evaluations for the math department, by the time I was a senior, actually had a question devoted to the professor's ability to speak clearly enough to be understood. Workload for all my classes was quite high. It wasn't unusual to have three books to read in a period of two days. I learned how to skim and learned it fast. Coming from a slower-paced, rural public school this was extremely hard for me to do. I actually spent most of my time feeling overwhelmed.

Alumnus/a, Biology, 9/2001-5/2005, May 2006

The university's biggest school is by far the Elliot School of International Affairs. The Columbian College of Arts and Sciences, which I attended, offers a broad selection of courses with highly qualified professors in all fields.

> The school says: "The Columbian School of Arts and Sciences is the largest school at GW."

Above the introductory level courses, class size pretty much drops to a maximum of 70 students. This makes it difficult to take some of the most popular classes, but the professors are as helpful as can be about letting more people in when you solicit them on the first day of the semester. Come prepared: bring your pink add/drop form already filled in and ready for the professor to sign. The registration process is done online, with spots being held in classes so that even those with the latest registration date (entering or second-semester freshmen) still have options. The first time I registered freshman year, I got all the classes for which I asked, and I was always able to get into those I really wanted to take. Professors practice curving or not depending on their personal beliefs. Several professors whom I had over my four years announced on the first day that they would give as many A's or D's as they felt were merited. Professors are mostly helpful and accessible out of class, although there will always be the boring ones and the fascinating ones inside the classroom. As a pre-med, I expected a huge workload; however because I was never overwhelmed by work or felt I had to lock myself away in the library, I only went for a BA in biology. There was time to have a life and still get work done.

Alumnus/a, 8/2001-12/2004, April 2005

GW has some great faculty and huge opportunities within the city. In one of my classes, we had a guest lecture from the White House Chair of the Environmental Quality Council. Another professor taught essentially the same class he teaches to GW students, to new foreign service officers at the State Department. Researching in the Library of Congress is amazing. That said, it's also possible to slack off and get by at GW. Criminal Justice is by far the easiest major in the Columbian College, and undergraduate business students are well known for complaining about wimpy "group projects" when everyone else is writing massive papers or studying for finals.

When you are enrolling for popular classes, it certainly helps to be an honors student. Otherwise, being determined and having a good relationship with your academic advisor are key. The school administration is a bureaucracy, so it certainly helps to make a four-year plan during your freshman year and then keeping track of your credits as you go.

Employment Prospects

Alumnus/a, American Studies, 1/1999-5/2003, May 2007

Most people seem to get jobs straight out of internships. Everyone at GW interns at one point or another, so we graduate with job experience. In my field (museum work), there are tons of GW alumni around and the school is well-regarded. Most people I know didn't have too much trouble getting a job after graduating.

Alumnus/a, Political Science, 8/2002-5/2006, June 2007

I was recruited by a local financial consulting company and hired before graduation. I had been planning to take three to six months off to travel, but was offered compensation superior to what others around me were getting, so I couldn't turn the job down. The fact that I was recruited for a finance job with a political science degree speaks volumes for the level of respect given to a GW alumni.

Alumnus/a, Business, 1/2003-Submit Date, June 2007

GW wasn't a target school for top investment banking jobs, but it was very good for accounting and middle-office banking jobs. With the help of my professors, other business fraternities and particularly SEO, I was able to secure an internship.

Current student, Political Science, 9/2005-Submit Date, April 2007

The career office helped to put me in touch with numerous companies for an internship after my freshman year. Graduates tend to get very good jobs right out of school, and within a year, mostly everyone who was looking for a job, seemed to have one. People know GW as an up-and-coming school, and many major companies come to recruit on campus. The location of the school is excellent being near some of the most important political and financial institutions in the U.S. Political and financial jobs seem to be the favorites of most graduates. The alumni network helps as much as it can, but there doesn't seem to be much of a connection between students and alumni.

Alumnus/a, 8/1999-12/2002, May 2006

A huge benefit of GW is that the school is in the heart of D.C., and semester internships are always available. A lot of people from the International Affairs school stay in D.C. after graduation and work all over the city. Many people decide to work for think tanks or nonprofits, but plenty of people work for the government.

Alumnus/a, 8/2001-5/2005, May 2006

One of the ways GW compensates for it's less-than-mouth-watering academic program is with its second-to-none location, squeezed between the White House, the State Department (where I interned), and the K Street lobbyist corridor. When you walk into a campus party or bar, the natural question to ask is "So who do you work for?" For this reason, every single graduate I know landed a sweet gig immediately after graduation because we were all offered jobs by at least one of the companies where we interned (and many in the private sector and in other cities besides D.C.). The career center/alumni network is there, but I don't know anyone who used it. GW students, by nature, are extremely urban, networking-savvy, and self-motivated.

Quality of Life

Alumnus/a, American Studies, 1/1999-5/2003, May 2007

Housing and dining are overpriced, but the location can't be beat. You're walking-distance from most places in D.C. you'd want to visit, and it's probably the safest area of the city. Dining options seem to change every year but never really improve. Lots of rooms have kitchens, so people cook. The campus may be a city campus, but it has two great quads where everybody hangs out. People also go to the National Mall, right near by, if they need more space. The library overflows at finals and is severely lacking in humanities books, but the exchange with other university libraries works very well and quickly.

Alumnus/a, Political Science, 8/2002-5/2006, June 2007

You won't find better or more fun campus housing. At least five different police squads [are in the area] (FBI, Secret Service, MPD, UPD and State Department Police); needless to say, it's a very safe campus. Dining options change every year because they can't quite figure out what students want, but all-in-all it's usually pretty good. It is a constantly improving campus with new facilities being built all of my four years there. Not to mention constant access to all of the culture and variety that D.C. has to offer—it's in a prime location, next to Georgetown, and downtown and national mall and museums are easily accessible. Let's not forget that with its prime location, GW gets a lot of famous guest speakers on campus, so many in fact they can be hard to find.

Current student, Political Science, 9/2005-Submit Date, April 2007

The quality of life is adequate at GW. The building of the GW campus has been at the forefront of GW development plan, and the creation of new facilities is at the top of the list. The facilities are truly topnotch, including a brand-new, $52 million business school that was just made two years ago. The housing is very hit-or-miss, with newly-renovated gems and 20-year-old holes. The school is working hard, though, to create the finest dorms in the country and has a reputation—its dorms are like palaces. I've been to other schools, and the rooms here really are that much better. The dining options here are incredibly unorthodox. There is no official dining hall, but rather the school has linked up with surrounding food chains and services. You use your GWorld student ID, which acts like a credit card, and you can purchase food from over different locations. The food is on the unhealthy side, ranging from Wendy's to Quiznos. The neighborhood is really the finest in D.C. Surrounded by trees and only four blocks from the White House, the location really could not be better. Its a major draw for students who choose to come to this school.

Alumnus/a, 8/2000-5/2004, May 2006

Quality of life is excellent at GW. I don't know if you've seen the dorms, but they are the best I've ever seen by far. Luxury is not an issue for students. The campus is basically a city campus, with its own little charms. The quad and plaza provide nice park-like settings for students. So much so that on weekends, they are both filled with the little children of those who live in the Foggy Bottom neighborhood. The facilities are excellent and constantly being updated or bettered in some way. I don't think GW students lack anything. There is even adequate computer space in the many computer labs. I don't think dining will ever be an issue again for GW. The GW food plan can now be used on campus and at almost every off-campus restaurant. The neighborhood is a historical district in D.C., and though I'd love to say there is a wonderful relationship between those who live in Foggy Bottom and the school, it just isn't possible. Many who live in Foggy Bottom fear the expansion of the school and have done all in their power to prevent it. They are quite good, though, in keeping their anger for the school from the students. Most realize that expansion has nothing to do with the students and are quite pleasant when you get to know them. They also realize that it's a great place to find babysitters. I think the campus is very safe. There is the University Police Dept. which does a great job on campus. If something happens, it would not be hard to find help. GW has a great location being only [four] blocks from the White House. On campus, I've met and seen off duty Secret Service, D.C. Police, and even FBI dining at the J-Street food court.. The biggest scare the area had was probably 9/11, and though it was scary, I'd say that knowing that all of the top police forces were not far away was actually a comfort.

Current student, 1/2005-Submit Date, May 2006

The dorms at GW are incomparable. They just built a new freshman dorm, named Potomac, which is right across from the other freshman dorm, Thurston. Almost all freshman rooms have their own bathrooms. When people move off campus, they find either nice apartments or places in Georgetown. The dorms are truly amazing. Each student receives a Gworld card that is good for almost all restaurants around GW.

Alumnus/a, 9/2000-5/2003, April 2005

Let me say this (especially after having been at a few other colleges)—GW treats its students like royalty. The dorms are immaculate (for dorms), the food choices are great (which includes a gourmet market where one can use his/her meal points if he/she feels like cooking instead of eating prepared food), and the atmosphere is (once again) supportive! To name a few amenities, GW provides its students with ample living space, dishwashers, cleaning ladies, cable ready

rooms, air conditioning, just to name a few things I have come to long for at my new university.

One special event every semester is called "Midnight Breakfast;" it occurs the week of finals and professors come at night to make the students breakfast (fuel to study all night) as a midnight snack. The gym at GW is the finest athletic facility in D.C.; it has five floors which include a pool, a basketball court, an indoor track, state-of-the-art machinery, a weight room, TVs to watch at every workout station, and fitness classes. The neighborhood surrounding GW is probably the safest in D.C., but D.C. is not the safest city and any student at GW should be aware of that. There is an extensive campus security network and vans that will drive students home at night (or around campus), which helps students not to feel "locked down" after nightfall.

The campus itself is as beautiful as can be expected. The school sacrifices much in the way of a truly defined "campus" in exchange for its prime real estate (four blocks from the White House, six from the National Mall, and about a mile from the U.S. Capitol and Supreme Court). Most of the buildings are plain greyish yellow concrete, but tend to look nicer on the inside.

Social Life

Alumnus/a, 9/2003-5/2006, September 2006

Nightlife is slow in the Foggy Bottom area, but a quick cab ride puts you in the more lively places of the city. Washington offers good places to eat and socialize, but it usually requires getting off campus, which is easy to do. There is a Greek system that stays to itself, and they aren't a presence unless you seek them out. Great people who were interesting and fun. Making friends is very easy.

Current student, Political Science, 9/2005-Submit Date, April 2007

The social life is severely lacking for anyone under the age of 21. The party scene seems to be full of life when you first arrive on campus, but after three weeks it becomes the same thing over and over again. The clubs are mostly 21 and up and are very strict with IDs. The fraternity and sorority scene is relatively small, making up just 12 percent of the community. The restaurants in the neighborhood are some of the nicest in the city, and the school is within walking distance of Georgetown. The dating scene is rather difficult, as most of the students seem to keep it casual and avoid relationships. Being in D.C., there is never a lack of things to do, including the Smithsonian and monuments. There are always events going on around the city and on campus because GW attracts some of the more famous acts. The bar scene is a staple of the GW community ,and many of the upperclassmen frequent bars, such as McFadden's and 51st State.

Alumnus/a, 8/2002-5/2004, May 2006

As they say, those who work hard, play harder. With so much academic pressure, GW students really let loose. On any given night, you can find at least one good party in every dorm. There are plenty of bars within walking distance and everyone drinks, regardless of age or tolerance. There aren't many couples at GW, students just hookup.

Being in D.C. is a huge plus for GW. Georgetown shopping is a five minute walk. Restaurants of any kind you could imagine can be found within walking distance. There are plenty of dance clubs all around the city and several great concert venues. There's the Wizards, the Capitals, the Redskins, all just a Metro trip away, as well as GW sporting events. Of course, there are the monuments and museums, and you can always find interesting little hidden spots all around the city to explore. There are also all sorts of events going on year-round, festivals, farmer's markets, book fairs, Presidential Inaugurations, rallies, anything you can imagine.

Alumnus/a, 9/2001-5/2005, May 2006

The Greek system is not very developed at the school, mainly because there are many other outlets for social activity. Clubs like Platinum and Pure attract a crowd of students weekly. Georgetown is replete with bars. The Chinatown area is newly renovated, with many interesting options. Perhaps the all-time favorite is the Adams Morgan area with its many bars and restaurants that are always packed on the weekend. Make sure you stop for greasy pizza before heading off to the afterparty!

Read all of Vault's College Surveys at **www.vault.com/college**–get complete surveys on 100s of colleges and universities, expert advice on applicaton essays and more.

VAULT CAREER LIBRARY 143

Alumnus/a, 9/2000-5/2004, April 2005

The social life at GW is definitely what you make of it. As a first-year alumnus, I can say that my friends and I are constantly reminiscing about our GW experience. Since it is a big school and we live in a city for college, you have to put a lot of effort into meeting the group of friends with whom you will ultimately end up crying at graduation. I absolutely adored my friends. We had the best time, especially senior year, when we were all 21 and could hit the area bars.

For people who want the more traditional route, we have a Greek system, they live on Greek Row, so they have a visible presence on campus and offer a different social experience if you choose. Favorite local bars and restaurants are Froggy Bottom Pub, Garretts, Big Hunt, Lucky Bar, Front Page, First Edition—the list goes on! There are so many student favorites, and what you will find is that your group of friends will develop its own favorite spot in the area, where you can walk in and the bartenders know you and where you feel comfortable. That is why D.C. is so nice for college, it is small enough that you don't feel lost.

Dating scene is really dependent upon what your scene is, but like most colleges there is a lot of random hooking up and serious dating going on. Basically, my GW experience was great, and it took graduating from there to realize how lucky I was to have the best paid, four-year vacation for which I could have ever asked. I made memories and friends there who are perfect for me. On our last night at GW after graduation, all my friends got together at the Lincoln Memorial in the darkness and just sat there and looked out over the city for the last time together. Moments like that are priceless and I would tell anyone looking at GW to know that he/she would be lucky to call it his/her school!

Georgetown University

37th and O Streets, Northwest
Washington, D.C. 20057
Admissions phone: (202) 687-3600
Admissions URL:
www.georgetown.edu/undergrad/admissions/

 **Admissions**

Alumnus/a, 8/2000-5/2004, January 2007

It is highly selective. I was a transfer student from and had an interview with a Georgetown alumnus in the area. Additionally, I did not have stellar grades in high school but had a 4.0 at UMass and did extremely well on my SATs. The process was difficult, but Georgetown made it much easier by constantly keeping in contact with me and giving me access to various faculty members throughout the process to see if Georgetown was the right fit for me. I knew the major and major subfield I wanted to get into at Georgetown (within the School of Foreign Service), so I put together a convincing argument using my background to show why I wanted to enroll in that major, and I believe that was the chief reason for my admittance. Identify why you really want Georgetown above other schools, and with a little help from grades, I think that goes a very long way.

Alumnus/a, 8/2001-5/2005, September 2006

If all you aspire is to end up in a corner office on Wall Street, consider this express lane closed. Hardly anyone gets into Georgetown without demonstrating a desire or effort to improve society. Don't confuse a commitment to social justice with closed mindedness to political diversity; bi-partisanship is the unspoken fourth of Georgetown's values, after honor, duty and faith. Students do serve on admissions committees (and yes, we read everything). Admissions committees are also school-specific, so unless you're applying to the College of Arts and Sciences, you had better have a good reason why you're applying to your particular school.

Current student, 8/2003-Submit Date, October 2005

The admissions process includes a written application with a supplemental essay and a regional interview with an alum. Tours are given at the university twice a day, as well as on the weekend, but are limited during the coldest months of the year. The admissions committee likes to see an applicant's sincere interest in the university, so I encourage an applicant to do sufficient research before applying. Once accepted, new students can come to Georgetown for a weekend hosted by the Georgetown Colmission Ambassador Program. Here, they can view dorms, observe classes, and get a better understanding of the university before making final admissions decisions.

Current student, 9/2004-Submit Date, October 2005

Georgetown University is about the education of the whole person. The students who go here love philosophy, theory and international politics. So, when you are writing your essays, really get across that you have strong passions and desires that complete your non-academic side. The best way to get that point across is getting an early interview. Georgetown accepts about 20 percent of its applicants making it the 11th most difficult college to get into.

Alumnus/a, 8/2000-5/2004, September 2005

Getting into Georgetown is comparable with getting into any of your other top-tier schools: they want it all. The application asks for a résumé, SATs, SAT Subject Tests, transcript and personal essays, as you would expect. But since Georgetown is super-selective, and getting more so—more kids apply each year but the university can't really expand unless it wants to fall into the river—you really have to try to do something to make yourself stand out. It's a Jesuit school, so if you have a passion for volunteering and social justice, play that up. I also recommend having fun with the personal essay part. No one wants to hear another story about how you learned to appreciate what you have while working at a soup kitchen or how your grandma inspired you. When I applied, the application asked for a one- to two-page essay introducing yourself "creatively or narratively." I wrote a free-form poem about myself. My friends said I was crazy. I got in. I'm not saying my poem was the only factor, but considering I was mid-range in all other statistics, I figured the risk was worth it.

Georgetown is unique in that you apply to individual undergraduate schools (School of Arts and Sciences, Foreign Service, Business or Nursing). While I found it was fairly easy to switch schools once you are in the college—come on, who really knows what they want to do when they are 18—be sure to appear passionate about the school you are selecting, even if you know you could fit into three. It makes you seem focused. Also, be sure to highlight strengths necessary for that school. Your entrepreneurial nature or your being a calculus whiz should be at the top if you're going for the business school; the fact that you aced your SAT Subject Tests in Spanish and French will go over better for the School of Foreign Service.

Interviews are done by alumni, and while they are considered in the application process, they aren't too important. Mostly, just show up looking neat and excited about the school. Alumni do the interviews for free, so you are mainly dealing with gung-ho Hoyas here who love their school. Show excitement, ask questions, and all will be good. I did work in the admissions office, so I can say that admissions have some of the "good old boy" feel to them. You get extra "points" for having a legacy (daddy's name can help you) and the admissions office has "arrangements" with the big-name boarding schools (so the Phillips-Exeter or Taft name will help, too). That said, I came from a no-name Western Pennsylvania public school; my parents went to local public colleges, (my name means nothing in the grander world outside my town), but I got in. Yes, it is hard to get in, but the school does do a good job of trying to get a socioeconomically, racially and ethnically diverse class. They're not going to hold it against you that you didn't take 15 APs when you went to a public school that only offered five.

Academics

Alumnus/a, 8/2000-5/2004, January 2007

The great thing about Georgetown is availability. The relatively small class sizes and the professors are always available. It's easy to get popular classes as long as you make sure you don't wait until the last minute to register. If you don't get the class initially, make sure you are first in line to e-mail/call/see the professor and passionately state your case, why you want to get into his/her particular class. One bad thing about the business school was that different professors definitely graded on different difficulty scales.

Alumnus/a, 8/2001-5/2005, September 2006

Academics are very school-specific, which is why each committee (other than the College of Arts and Sciences) looks for a demonstrated commitment to its area. There is a common university core that most students complete by the end of their second year. Most students ultimately end up appreciating this because it forces them to take courses they would not otherwise have completed. Each school also has its own requirements. Overall, smaller schools will allow you more flexibility and facetime with administration and teachers. However, even the larger schools don't really have any large classes. Grading varies by teacher, class size and school. A good rule of thumb is that in the business school, everyone wins, Organic Chemistry students deserve their fate, and Foreign Service students like to read anyway, so the fact that they get a lot of it is fine, and Nursing students are very busy saving lives (and are guaranteed jobs anyway). Somehow we all have time to meet at the bar (The Tombs). Professors all have office hours and always are willing to set up special office hours.

Current student, Social Sciences, 8/2005-Submit Date, June 2007

The academics are tough. It might not seem that way sometimes, since a lot of the classes I take are just reading and lectures. But if you're prone to procrastination like me, when midterms and finals roll around, you realize how much work there is to be done. Course reading loads are heavy, and can go upwards of 1,000 pages a week. That being said, the professors are phenomenal. A lot of them have real world experience, which is awesome in the classroom. So far, I've taken classes with a former assistant secretary of defense and a senior fellow at the Brookings institute.

Current student, Political Science, 8/2003-Submit Date, April 2007

Georgetown recently adopted a new grading scale of A, A/B, B, B/C, D, F. It is supposed to help the A/B students who were getting B's before. While it is somewhat academically rigorous, the average school GPA is somewhere above a 3.0. I would say one to four hours of homework a night is average. There are always people to help (free tutors, the writing center, study sessions with paid student instructors). I have always gotten into every class I wanted. As a freshman, it is harder, but after that, it gets much easier.

Alumnus/a, 1/2001-5/2005, November 2006

Class quality is what you make of it. If you are willing to engage your professors and make the time to go in during office hours, the quality of the classes are superb. Professors at Georgetown are there because they want to be. In all of my four years, I was never intimidated or shy about going in to see a professor when I was having a problem. The workload is bearable. However the environment at Georgetown is competitive. Everyone with whom you're in class wants the A, so be ready to work for it.

Alumnus/a, 2/2002-5/2005, October 2005

As an undergraduate program, GU provides a great variety of courses in its requirements. It aims at truly developing a student who has a strong liberal arts background. Students are encouraged to take foreign language and culture courses (ranging from Arabic to Basque). Also, there are a number of minors

and regional studies certificates students can add to their undergraduate work. Also, the human element is emphasized by having internship and volunteer programs for students in different fields of interest, especially education and politics. While popular classes often have enrollment issues as seniors are given priority, this is balanced by GU's commitment to keeping class sizes small, anywhere from five to 20 students per class, and providing a number of interesting core requirement courses within each discipline. For instance, to fulfill a literature requirement, East Asian Literature. is an option, in addition to the usual American and British genre courses. As far as professors go, GU attracts some of the best. Most have ample office hours and encourage student participation outside of class (like honors thesis research). GU students carry a large workload, and that said, know how to enjoy D.C. to the fullest on weekends.

Current student, 8/2002-Submit Date, December 2005

The quality of the classes and professors is extraordinary. Most students will get the classes for which they sign up because most of the popular professors teach multiple sections of the course. Georgetown has tough grading expectations because the administration does not want the school to be accused of grade inflation.

Current student, 1/2003-Submit Date, July 2006

The institution is truly committed to undergraduate study—no graduate students teach courses, and professors are generally approachable and interested in teaching. The academic environment is rigorous and intellectual but not competitive or cutthroat. There is a unique combination of intellectual rigor, practical application and service/ethical influence, which makes the undergraduate experience here compelling. The school has the resources of a major university but fosters the atmosphere of a liberal arts college. The Washington, D.C. location, with its unique resources in government, policy, business, medicine, science, and technology, is integrated into the academic and social life of the undergraduate experience in ways not found at most other universities.

Employment Prospects

Current student, 8/2003-Submit Date, December 2006

We have high prestige and placement within Goldman Sachs. Other investment banks recruit heavily, as well. Georgetown is the best university in the D.C. area—local employers can find very talented people without paying much to fly graduates in for interviews and exploratory events.

Alumnus/a, 8/2001-5/2005, September 2006

The alumni network is strong and most people enjoyed their time on the Hilltop. It's D.C., and Georgetown students are Georgetown students, so opportunities abound.

Current student, Political Science, 8/2003-Submit Date, April 2007

The Center for Calling and Careers is an excellent resource available to students providing networking, résumé help, business card services, internships, and so on. They put on various seminars throughout the year and are very helpful.

Alumnus/a, 1/2001-5/2005, November 2006

On-Campus recruiting is awesome for the financial industry, consulting, healthcare, NPO and government employers. If a student is interested in another arena, the Career Center has a database of posted jobs for a wide variety of careers. However, if you're not sure about what you want to do or where you see yourself, their best advise is: figure it out.

Current student, 1/2003-Submit Date, July 2006

Students have no problem getting into top-ranked graduate programs and professional schools (the fact that all of the pre-med students get into medical school and anyone who wants to go to law school can make the atmosphere at the school unusually friendly and noncompetitive—a refreshing approach and experience to academic study). Most students will find little problem finding a job if that is their direction—the Career Center is a phenomenal resource. The alumni network is extremely helpful in providing advice, leads and jobs to the graduating senior—the Hoya network is powerful and committed.

Read all of Vault's College Surveys at **www.vault.com/college**–get complete surveys on 100s of colleges and universities, expert advice on applicaton essays and more.

VAULT CAREER LIBRARY 145

Current student, 8/2002-Submit Date, March 2005

From my own experiences and what I have heard from my peers at other schools, Georgetown has one of the best on-campus recruiting systems. The career center sends out weekly e-mails regarding upcoming speaking panels, workshops, events and deadlines, and works with alumni in setting up students with internships. In the McDonough School of Business, there is the MSB Mentor Program, in which second-, third- and fourth-year students who apply are grouped with former Georgetown graduates who work in their fields of interest. Throughout the year, these groups meet in various environments. Each mentor has a different framework they like to follow, but students often come away having had a first-hand look at a day in the life of the career they could one day have, advice on applying for jobs, interviewing skills, network-building and even internships. Many of my peers who are graduating this year have already accepted jobs with top banking firms in New York and L.A., lobbying groups, or positions in some of the best law schools.

 ## Quality of Life

Alumnus/a, 8/2001-5/2005, September 2006

Georgetown students know how to have a good time. With any luck, Hoya basketball will be even better this year, and it will be a great time. Of course, on the Hilltop, a good time often means we work hard but drink a lot. Housing is tolerable. It's either an on campus dorm or apartment, or a house in the neighborhood. Rent is expensive; however, unlike other area schools, you're getting the prettiest and safest neighborhood. It helps to have U.S. Senators and Congressmen living down the street. Dining is what you can expect from college dining halls. However, a serious nightlife has always existed on M Street (a 10-minute walk from the front gates), which is full of restaurants and bars. There are churches, temples, and prayer rooms in or by the university, as well as chaplains and imams from each of the major faiths. The field house (gym) could be better, but it serves its purpose and is pretty big. Overall, it's a relatively small campus, so you never have to walk more than 10 minutes to get to class.

Alumnus/a, 1/2001-5/2005, November 2006

Campus life is fantastic. So much fun!! Especially for first- and second-year students, dorms have been recently renovated and the communities set up there are wonderful. Dining halls at Georgetown are decent, though the surrounding area offers tons of different dining options. Campus feels very safe, though the surrounding area has had a recent problem with petty crime. Students shouldn't walk off campus alone at night; common safety measures are a must. Most of the permanent residents of Georgetown don't mind the students too much, though they would prefer less partying off campus. The gym at Georgetown leaves much to be desired; although, if you're a regular, the most it's ever used is the week after Thanksgiving and the month before spring break.

Current student, 9/2004-Submit Date, October 2005

Georgetown has one of the most beautiful campuses in the nation. It's a classically collegiate ivy-covered buildings, with picturesque groves of flower and trees, with open quadrangles and numerous fountains. The neighborhood is relatively safe. Georgetown has every ethnic type of food of which you can think and the shopping is great! Georgetown University is a Jesuit school with a Catholic background. Many of the students have a Catholic background. This makes issues like contraceptives and gay pride prevalent issues. However, the University does a good job to service many different religions.

Current student, 9/2001-Submit Date, March 2005

There are many good on-campus housing options; however, the administrative office is a mess, and students constantly complain about how disorganized and unfair the housing lottery and selection process is. Students are guaranteed two years of on-campus housing but typically get three years and sometimes four. The campus is amazing. The buildings (except the library) and grounds are gorgeous, and Georgetown has an enormous "flower endowment" that ensures beautiful flowers cover the campus. Spring at Georgetown is surreal—students all wear pastel polo shirts and sundresses while sitting on the front lawn, and flowers are everywhere.

Athletic facilities for students are adequate—Yates Fieldhouse has basketball courts, a crappy indoor track, free weights, weight machines, and a number of

treadmills and stationary bikes. It isn't the nicest place, but it has all the essentials. The two on-campus dining halls are nice—one is new and the other was just renovated, but the food is terrible. There is little variety. The Georgetown neighborhood is incredibly nice and upscale: Kerry, Edwards, and others live within blocks of campus. Downtown Georgetown, M Street, has tons of upscale retail stores, bars and restaurants. Georgetown is a great place to live, with the only drawback being the lack of public transportation near campus. I have always felt completely safe on campus, though.

 ## Social Life

Alumnus/a, 1/2001-5/2005, November 2006

Georgetown has an awesome social life. The student body at Georgetown wholeheartedly believes that if you work hard, you play hard. Hoyas play hard and love basketball. Any new student should definitely get a set of season tickets, you won't regret it. Overall, there's a bit of something for everyone. The campus is large enough that you won't know everyone. But by the time you're a junior and have chosen your major, you will know everyone in your classes. Which is wonderful, studying in groups is one of my favorite pastimes.

Alumnus/a, 8/2000-5/2004, January 2007

We have a great social life. If drinking is not your scene, you are in Washington D.C. There is a ton of stuff to do and see, like museums, history, government buildings and white water rafting in West Virginia, as well as hiking and rock climbing.

There is no real Greek system at Georgetown, although there is a quasi-Greek system for Foreign Service and Business School students.

Current student, 9/2004-Submit Date, October 2005

Georgetown has many bars and restaurant within walking distance or just a cab ride away. Some of the best clubs include Dream, Lulu's, and the 1819 Club. There are many great date ideas, such as the 9:30 Club, the Kennedy Center, and D.C. Improv. The school actually has a policy that forbids Greek societies to exist and holds strong repercussions for hazing. As far as student activities go, we have over 100 clubs and societies on campus, some of which include *The Hoya*, which is the oldest collegiate newspaper and the Philodemic Debate Society, the oldest debate society in the nation—in which Scalia took part. The largest clubs on campus are the International Relations Club, College Democrats and College Republicans. The Corp is the largest student-run organization in the country, and the Georgetown University Student Investment Fund is the largest student-run fund.

Alumnus/a, 8/2000-5/2004, September 2005

The Georgetown area gives you more of your prepster scene, while a short bus or Metro ride takes you to Dupont Circle (hipster places and a good gay scene) or Adams Morgan, where there's definitely a bar for every taste. For any Hoya, though, The Tombs is the bar. Tucked under a fancy-schmancy 1789 Restaurant, the Tombs offers pitchers and bar fare and is ruled by Hoyas (and nostalgic alumni). Wednesday night marks the start of the weekend with 80s night (beer + 80's music = bliss) but the Tombs will always be like your Cheers: by the time you're 21, you can go there and be sure to find people who know your name and are always glad you came. Restaurants around the school run from good places at which to gouge mom and dad for a pricey meal, to plenty of places for cheap sandwiches. Fall in love with Little Cafe's hummus and pita, swoon over Booeymongers subs and heavenly cinnamon coffee, and swing by Bangkok Bistro for reasonably priced, non-greasy Thai food.

One more thing: Georgetown has a reputation of being home to a bunch of rich, snotty white kids. We call them Jane and Joe Hoya. They wear pearls, polos with the collar popped up (Ralph Lauren, of course) and $200 Seven or True Religion jeans. And there are plenty of Jane and Joes. But that's not all it is. There are plenty of international and middle class kids just trying to make it through and hippies and artists and other loveable weirdos. You just have to be willing to go out there and meet them. As a less-than-rich, kinda goofy kid, I was sure I was going to leave Georgetown after a week. Then I found other goofy kids on my newspaper, and like-minded liberal nuts at my job and other Italo-philes studying abroad. Now, my college pictures show a U.N.-worthy spectrum of races and ethnicities, and dreadlocked nuts and just plain normal, fun people. Point being, Georgetown is big enough that you shouldn't assume "everyone is rich" or everyone is anything. There are kids like you there, and they're awesome, funny and smart, so have fun finding them instead of worrying.

Howard University

EM/Admission
Howard University
2400 Sixth Street, Northwest, Room 111
Washington, D.C. 20059
Admissions phone: (800) 822-6363
Admissions fax: (202) 806-2763
Admissions e-mail: admission@howard.edu
Admissions URL:
www.howard.edu/enrollmentmanagement/admission

 ## Admissions

Current student, Psychology, 8/2003-Submit Date, February 2007

Not a tough application. There's also an essay option for people who want/need a scholarship. Interview is not required. It is a very open-minded application. They look for talented, well-rounded individuals who show leadership skills. They accept a diverse student body and are willing to take people who may have bumps along the way.

Alumnus/a, 9/1999-5/2003, November 2005

Initially, the admissions process was fairly easy . I sent in my application and received an acceptance about three months before I went to school. When I got there, the validation process was crazy. They seemed very unprepared. The lines were extremely long, and after we would stand in one line for an hour, we would have to wait until we reached the front to find out we were in the wrong line.

Current student, 8/2004-Submit Date, July 2006

The admissions process is fairly easy with the application, essay, two letters of recommendation and, of course, the $45 application fee. My advice to anyone who is serious about going here is: (1) ensure that you send everything at the same time; and (2) apply for Early Action because otherwise you'll be waiting until forever for Howard to send you an acceptance letter.

Current student, 8/2003-Submit Date, June 2006

In applying to Howard University one must provide: (1) a completed application; (2) two recommendations (one from a guidance counselor and the other from a professor); (3) official transcripts; (4) ACT or SAT scores; (5) and a personal statement. The personal statement usually has a question about continuing the Howard legacy. In writing a personal statement I advise one should know some Howard history. The application process was a lot smoother than I anticipated, university officials were willing to answer any questions I had. I also recommend applying early in order to receive an Early Decision and calling to check the status of your application to avoid any issues.

Current student, 8/2000-Submit Date, May 2005

The admissions process includes completing a standard application and a personal essay. At the time I applied, I found the admission office to be extremely helpful in providing assistance. Any questions I had about applying to Howard were answered by numerous professors, alumni and administrators. Therefore, I felt welcomed throughout the entire application process. Unlike many other selective schools, Howard is known to take a chance on some students. Historically, the mission of the university has been to help those who may not have been provided with the same access to educational opportunities at prior academic levels. In turn, a student is nurtured and allowed to subsequently flourish and become a scholar. Also, for exceptional students, they are eligible to enter into one of the many honors programs offered at Howard. These programs provide additional academic rigor.

Current student, 8/2003-Submit Date, April 2005

The admissions process was an enlightening experience on its own. Howard University has been known to be a very selective school, and so I wanted to make sure that I stood out from the rest. I spent a lot of time on my application, especially my essay, making sure that it was the best that I could do. I had one of my teachers proofread it to check for any mistakes. I think that my academic achievements spoke for themselves and really aided me in getting into Howard.

Current student, 8/2003-Submit Date, January 2004

When you send in your information to Howard, make a copy of everything. My admissions process went pretty smoothly, but HU is famous for screwing up paperwork. I applied to Howard, Early Action, and I found out that I was accepted very early. I advise anyone who is serious about the Mecca to apply early and not procrastinate. Work hard on your entrance essay, and make sure that your application is very neat, orderly and up-to-date. If Howard fails to tell you about your acceptance status, do not panic. Keep calling the university until you can, and ask them about the status of your application. They will eventually tell you, even if it is two months before school starts. Just don't be discouraged by the many mishaps caused by the administration, because in the end, it will be worth it.

Alumnus/a, 8/1999-5/2003, September 2003

Being admitted to Howard University had to be one of the most trying times of my life. I had decided that it was the university I most wanted to attend, and I was not going to allow anything to get in the way. I had spoken with alumni and my counselor about best practices for admission into my first choice. I applied for early admission as I was advised, and my application was, in my opinion, flawless. I sent my application in November, and I did not receive a decision until July. There were no interviews. My essays we real. I have been told that I am an excellent writer by many of my peers, so I believe that my heart goes into an essay, and those reading it pick up on how I feel. It was a long waiting process for me, but I am glad I got in, no matter how late I received the acceptance. My SAT score was not the best upon graduation from high school, so they heavily weighed a lot of other things, and I made the cut.

Patience is a virtue in the whole admissions process, and I learned that. I believe it has made me a better person, and I did not look back. I will say that if anyone is thinking about attending the university, exposure is the key. If you take that extra step to get in (i.e., attending summer programs, speaking with current students and alumni), things will definitely be easier for you.

 ## Academics

Current student, Psychology, 8/2003-Submit Date, February 2007

Many professors are considered favorites, and it's tough getting into their classes. The grading is simply: A, B, C, D, or F, or Pass/Fail for some classes. There is no A+ or A-. The professors are generally strict, but caring, kind of like your parents. Most don't baby or coddle you, but are willing to help if you talk to them during the office hours. Many of the classes are traditional lecture style,

Read all of Vault's College Surveys at **www.vault.com/college**—get complete surveys on 100s of colleges and universities, expert advice on applicaton essays and more.

VAULT CAREER LIBRARY **147**

and others are open discussion. The students work hard, but they don't necessarily compete with each other in a way that's frustrating. The workload varies depending on your program. Some people's schedules are relatively lax, and other people's, (e.g. engineering majors), have little time for much but studying.

Current student, 8/2003-Submit Date, June 2006

The coursework at Howard is challenging, but it is not impossible to do. As one gets used to one's workload, it gets much easier. Workload is dependent on your major and your classification. In trying to get in popular classes, it is generally easier for upperclassmen to get their classes of choice. Registration at Howard is a week long process, and students register on different days based on classification. For example, honors students register on Monday, seniors on Tuesday, juniors on Wednesday, sophomores on Thursday, and freshmen on Friday. Generally, grading is standard; 100 to 90 percent is an A, 89 to 80 is a B, 79 to 70 is a C, 69 to 60 is a D and 59 and below is Failing. Professors vary from mediocre to excellent, and people are open to recommending good teachers. Howard is very fair about grading. If a professor gives an unfair grade and refuses to change it, students can file for a grievance and plead their case to the judiciary committee to get it changed.

Current student, 8/2000-Submit Date, May 2005

Academics at Howard are top priority. Classes are interesting, challenging and eventful. Howard is a blend of cultural concepts that may seem at odds—urban hip-hop and the academy. However, Howard represents the best of both. Numerous scholars and political leaders frequent the university. Through online registration, it is easy to register for classes with a preferred professor. Professors can be stringent in their expectations from students, but the grading system is fair; students receive what they earn. And for students who may struggle with classes, additional help is never hard to find. Howard's mission is to train and produce the best and brightest students.

Current student, 8/2004-Submit Date, April 2005

The academics here rival that of the Ivy League institutions. The School of Communications and the School of Business are rated among the top in their fields. However, there are some classes that are of low-quality, just like there are at any other school. The registration process is annoying, and not registering early ensures that you will probably get stuck with the worst classes at undesirable times. Most of the professors are very knowledgeable about their craft. The workload isn't too heavy, but time management is key.

Current student, 9/2001-Submit Date, April 2005

When I first arrived at Howard, it was difficult to get used to because everyone in the class was competitive. There were no people who shined more than others because everyone was operating on a elevated level. The classes are very open, and the teachers are somewhat helpful. One thing I can say is that in each and every class, you will get the African-American perspective no matter what the nationality of the professor. Howard is wonderful for teaching culturally enlightening things in classes from Calculus to Cultural Anthropology. The workload is heavy when you first get here because most students are encouraged to take 16 to 18 credits per semester. With time, the work gets easier.

Current student, 8/2003-Submit Date, January 2004

The academics at HU range from excellent to satisfactory. There are some teachers who don't want to be in class that much, and they miss almost as many days as some of the students. But most of the teachers are not like this. I am a political science major, and all of my poli sci teachers have been superb and really felt a passion for the subject. Howard also offers an education that is fit for a black student who is really trying to make it in this cruel world. They teach us about who we are and where we come from. They also try to keep the campus as politically active as possible, and we learn a lot about world affairs.

Alumnus/a, 8/1999-5/2003, January 2004

As at most schools, the business school classes ranged from absolutely fabulous to mediocre. I found many teachers to be inspiring, entertaining, excellent at explaining, and engaging. A great teacher should be able to impart knowledge, answer questions, have high expectations of students, and, at the bare minimum, keep students awake.

My workload at Howard was demanding at times, but I think it taught me how to manage my time and find balance.

Leadership opportunities were ample at HUSB. The student government, clubs, honors program, fraternities, sports, sororities and innumerable other activities provided students with the ability to step up and take on leadership roles.

Communication and teamwork are very much stressed at HUSB. Each year the freshman class is divided into several small groups. Each group is adopted by a different corporation. The groups work together throughout the year to do projects, presentations, company site visits, and so on, which are aimed at preparing students for the business world.

 Employment Prospects

Current student, Psychology, 8/2003-Submit Date, February 2007

Every summer, I do some type of research or internship, and everywhere I go, I hear about Howard University. Howard alumni are everywhere, and HBCU alumni (Historically Black Colleges and Universities) consider Howard a sister school. There are career fairs, internship opportunities, and graduate school fairs often. Howard U has a special relationship with Monster.com, and Howard students are considered the cream of the crop. Many students go on to graduate school immediately after. Students in the School of Business generally have a job waiting for them upon graduation due to their rigorous internship program requirements.

Current student, 8/2004-Submit Date, July 2006

There are several job fairs at Howard University between the School of Business and School of Communications. The School of Business was ranked Number One School for Minority Recruitment by the *Princeton Review*. Both schools have high recruiting rates for internships and jobs straight out of college.

Current student, 8/2003-Submit Date, June 2006

The opportunities for employment from Howard University are endless! Howard graduates work literally everywhere in any given field. Many top-tier companies come to Howard to find good prospects. It is important to keep your eyes open for these opportunities because so many companies come to Howard, it can be easy to become jaded and miss out when a company of your interest comes to the campus. Internships are easy to obtain because after your first year at Howard, you will be prepared. Many students maintain internships during the semester. I have friends (Howard alumni) who work on Wall Street at any given investment bank, in insurance, as buyers, at advertising agencies—you name it and a Howard student or graduate is doing it. Along with the year-long recruiting, Howard has four career fairs per year. There are also career seminars in the evenings all year long. Although Howard has very notable alumni, they are not as helpful as one would hope. The good news is that the alumni network is strengthening.

Current student, 8/2001-Submit Date, April 2005

I was tired of turning down jobs. Howard is in corporate America, the entertainment industry and any other field of interest you can imagine. Howard's presence is felt, and the alumni network is fantastic.

Alumnus/a, 8/1999-5/2003, January 2004

The opportunities at Howard University for career placement and development are limitless. Scholarships and internships from corporations abound, the most prestigious companies are there recruiting regularly, and students are taught how to dress, speak and present with confidence in any business setting. Students interact with company reps at formal dinners, presentations, information sessions and seminars. There are university-wide and school-based career development offices. Private companies, corporations, government agencies, nonprofits and professional schools attend the career and graduate school fairs in huge numbers, recruiting for new-hire positions, analyst programs and internships. Workshops and speakers' bureaus are regular at the school and give students exposure to recruiters, alumni and other company reps. There isn't enough focus on entrepreneurship, but if you are looking for a corporate job, especially in investment banking, accounting, marketing, pharmaceuticals or entertainment, Howard is absolutely the place to be.

Quality of Life

Current student, Psychology, 8/2003-Submit Date, February 2007

One of the biggest problems at Howard is the administration. The administration here is tough to navigate and bureaucratic, and in my experience, unfriendly. It is located in the middle of D.C., so as in any major city, precautions should be taken against walking alone, especially at night. There is a vibrant homeless community in the Howard University area. Housing is limited and many students live off campus. The facilities and buildings are decent, but could stand some improvement. The campus is well integrated into the D.C. area, so many dining options are available outside of cafeteria and restaurants on campus. Chic-fil-A is on campus. There are: a campus restaurant, two campus cafeterias and a convenience store.

Current student, 8/2004-Submit Date, July 2006

Housing is always a problem with Howard, mainly because of its environment and lack of space for building more dorms. There is good access to off-campus housing through the school. Soul food Thursday is always a good thing for the Cafe, and the Punchout is the home to Chick-fil-A, a pizza parlor and a burger joint. Because it is in Washington, D.C., there are several issues with crime and safety. It's definitely one of the larger problems with the university, partly because it is an open campus.

Current student, 8/2003-Submit Date, June 2006

Howard University is an old school. Thus, many of the facilities are old. Some buildings are newer than others, depending upon the individual school in which one is studying (Business, Arts and Sciences). There are about eight different dorms to choose, all with very different personalities. For example, The Bethune Annex in a very quiet all woman freshman/sophomore dormitory, while Meridian is a coed party, mainly sophomore dormitory, which is not directly on campus (the only off-campus dorm, provides a shuttle). Howard is not in the best neighborhood. It is important to be smart and aware of your surroundings.

Alumnus/a, 8/1999-5/2003, January 2004

Safety is a serious issue at Howard, which is located in the heart of urban D.C. There is a shortage of on-campus housing, but off-campus housing isn't necessarily difficult to obtain. Shuttle buses are available to transport students to and from the Metro station, dorms and various campus locations.

Alumnus/a, 8/1999-5/2003, September 2003

The campus is beautiful. It is a peaceful place, which I believe holds the most diverse group of individuals, and it shows in our successes. The school is not located in the best part of the country, but being near our national government made it a little better. The facilities could have been better, in my opinion. A lot of buildings look worn and tired inside . They could definitely use some work, but I believe that the university president is working to raise money for change even as I type.

Social Life

Current student, Psychology, 8/2003-Submit Date, February 2007

Howard University produces students who are well educated who also know how to party! Most of the partying doesn't occur on campus, however. It happens in local clubs, lounges and cafes. Popular student hangouts include Love, the Nightclub (they have a college night), H20 (21 and over), Platinum, and BusBoys and Poets, a spoken word cafe. House parties are popular. Students go to the movies in Chinatown for the most part; there are also a lot of popular restaurants for Howard students there. Many of the students hang out in the Adams Morgan area also.

Current student, 8/2004-Submit Date, July 2006

There is always something going on at Howard. Step on the Yard at noon on first Friday, it is definitely on and poppin'. The Yard is always a fashion show. The Diner is a hit in Adams Morgan, and near campus is Negril and, of course, Five Guys, where you can find the best burger anywhere! People do often date at Howard, but because we're broke college students, it's nothing extravagant. Homecoming, of course, is the biggest event of the year, and Luda said it best, "can't miss the Homecoming at Howard." Many Greek organizations were started here, so it is an active and large part of campus activities.

Current student, 8/2003-Submit Date, June 2006

Howard University is a very social school. If one decides to come here, one needs to be prepared to balance academics with social life. Because Howard is in Washington, D.C., there is always something to do. There is an abundance of clubs, restaurants, on-campus events and political debates. There is something for everyone's individual taste. Dating at Howard is hard but the opportunity is definitely here. The female-to-male ratio is 10 to one. If you know anything about Howard University, I am sure that know the magnitude of Homecoming. This is the biggest social event of the year and it is one week long. Some people think that people are excited because celebrities come to our Homecoming, but you can see a celebrity on any given day (in the Café, on the Yard, also known as the runway). The social life at Howard is great, but it is important not to lose sight of why you came to college (to get an education!). The Greek life at Howard is huge, five of the nine Black Fraternities and Sororities were founded at Howard. Howard is social, but the history at Howard is what I am most proud of.

Current student, 8/2003-Submit Date, April 2005

Howard University is an extremely active school, whether it is political or social, there is always something going on at Howard University. Being in a city like Washington, D.C., there is always something new to see and experience, so there is never a dull moment. There are many clubs, bars and restaurants that are unique, so every day is an adventure. The Greek life is very important at Howard University, and many organizations were started at this campus.

Current student, 8/2000-Submit Date, May 2005

Howard's social life is vibrant and fun. Once classes are over, students are able to have fun with friends on campus or throughout Washington, D.C. Howard is the home to five of the nine historically black, Greek fraternities and sororities; therefore, there is a large Greek presence at Howard. From throwing parties to helping out in the local community, Howard's Greeks help ensure that Howard is a home for its students and the residents of the community. Dating is never a problem at Howard. Whether through mutual friends or a chance run-in, students commonly date and enter into relationships. In fact, many people meet their future husbands or wives while attending Howard.

Alumnus/a, 8/1999-5/2003, January 2004

I found the social scene at Howard University to be absolutely amazing, energizing and fun. The parties at Howard were wild and memorable, to say the least. Every day out on The Yard was like a fashion show. And every day something is going on at Howard, from yard-fests to television shoots, preview movies, famous speakers (Colin Powell, Jesse Jackson, Al Gore, Larry Ellison and Jay-Z), fashion shows, concerts, step shows, political rallies, community service (and I mean a lot of it!), homecoming, football and basketball games. Many of the black sororities and fraternities were founded at HU. Howard is teeming with talented, articulate successful people (students and professors) from all around the country and the world. The mixture of cultures, attitudes, backgrounds, perceptions and experiences make for very interesting classes and synergies on campus. It gives the school a more international perspective.

Being in the nation's capital allows students incredible access to political figures, institutions and organizations that impact the rest of the world. D.C. also has several other schools and a great nightlife. Also, I met great friends at Howard with whom I still keep in contact today.

Read all of Vault's College Surveys at **www.vault.com/college**–get complete surveys on 100s of colleges and universities, expert advice on applicaton essays and more.

VAULT CAREER LIBRARY   149

Florida International University

Office of Admissions
P.O. Box 659003
Miami, FL 33265-9003
Admissions phone: (305) 348-2363
Admissions URL: admissions.fiu.edu

 Admissions

Current student, English, 8/2006-Submit Date, April 2007

I was a transfer student, so the admissions process seemed easier: I did not have to write an essay, and was able to apply online. I had a high GPA and a high ACT score, which got me in, but I got the sense that FIU considers other factors, as well. They are selective but not too selective. An interview, in most cases, should not be necessary.

> **Regarding admissions, the school says:** "Students compete for admissions based on the incoming academic profile of applicants. Admissions requirements vary for freshman and transfer students."

Current student, 8/2006-Submit Date, April 2007

I decided to attend on-the-spot-admissions, which, if you want a quick decision, is really good; however, gives you the, "yes," or "no," on the spot. Pretty much, you sign up on their web site: www.fiu.edu, and you go to "future" or "prospective students," and click on admissions or you send a letter or e-mail to their undergraduate admissions office. A lot of people will tell you to bring everything you own that represents you, like your social security card, a copy of your bill, your transcripts and so on. I don't recommend doing that because they are only going to look at certain documents, and the more you have, the easier it is to become disorganized. What I recommend bringing is a clean, neat copy of your transcripts, your original SAT scores, your license or ID, a copy of your immunizations record, and the completed the application forms. As long as you have this in a neat and organized manner, and you have a decent SAT score and GPA, there's no reason you would not get in.

> **FIU says:** "On-the-spot decisions are based on the academic profile of the student."

Current student, 8/2006-Submit Date, April 2007

The undergraduate program is one of the easiest to get into. Those with minimal requirements will likely get in. However, certain programs, especially the nursing program, are very competitive for entry.

Current student, Biology, 8/2006-Submit Date, April 2007

This was probably the simplest school to which I applied. I applied online and was required only to answer a few short essay questions right on the form. They asked for the usual documents, such as my high school transcript, my SAT scores, and I gave my résumé, too, but I think that was optional. They are pretty open with their selectivity as long as you show you are willing to work hard. For example, if you have relatively good grades but not so good test scores they will admit you but make you take remedial courses over the summer for the parts of the test you missed. I liked it because I got to know the campus beforehand. Also, I've heard they like out-of-state applicants.

Current student, Business, 7/2005-Submit Date, April 2007

The admissions process is not always an easy one, especially when you are so stressed out from your soon-to-come high school graduation. First, you take the SAT or ACT, then you must do well in high school classes in order to have a good GPA, which will be weighted with your exam scores to determine whether you are a good candidate for that particular university you wish to get into. Finally, try to put extracurricular activities such as sports or clubs to which you belonged. Also, write down all your achievements during your high school years, such as awards and sports. Even community service, helps when appli-

cations are reviewed. Don't stress anymore; simply let them decide, and hopefully it'll be in your favor. Good Luck!

Current student, Computer Science, 9/2006-Submit Date, April 2007

Being an international student, I depended on the Internet for admissions information. Believe me, all the information you will need with regard to admissions requirements and the process, is online, just take the time to surf through. The only grey area was information regarding the evaluation of international credentials.

> **The school says:** "International students are required to submit foreign credential evaluations, which are accepted from a NACES-approved organization."

 Academics

Current student, Political Science, 8/2006-Submit Date, April 2007

Well, the ease of classes depends on the type of class you are taking and what level of class it is. Sometimes professors can become very frustrating. Some of them are pretty straightforward and attentive to your needs while others refuse to assist you with questions you may have. The best thing to do is check ratemyprofessors.com before entering a class, and definitely trust the other students who posted bad comments about a professor. Usually, the bad comments a professor receives are true! The grading also depends on the professors you get. For example, some professors deliberately make their grading scale a little easier than usual and sometimes can curve on exams while others stick to the basic scale.

Current student, English, 8/2006-Submit Date, April 2007

The English program at FIU is outstanding. I have had professors who have graduated from Harvard and Yale, among others, and indeed, they are intelligent, often brilliantly so, encouraging and caring. Unlike other (ironically higher-ranking) universities where the professors concern themselves primarily with research, FIU's professors focus on instruction. I have never had a TA teach a class. Classes depend wholly on the professor: some are challenging, and others are not. Availability of classes seems to be good, except in the summer. The grading scale varies; FIU's grading scale considers an A to be any score between 93 to 100, but many professors still use the 90 to 100 scale. Workload depends on the nature of the class and the professor.

Current student, Physics, 1/2002-Submit Date, April 2007

Some courses were easy especially at the beginning of the program. However, as my major coursework started, the workload became great. In all, getting desired grades was something somebody definitely had to earn. Getting popular classes was sometimes difficult—if you don't sign up early, you might not find an opening in all the desired courses. Professors ranged from great to lousy, with an average of, about, good. All in all, the academic aspect was good but not great.

Current student, Nursing, 9/2006-Submit Date, April 2007

The intensity of the Anesthesia program at FIU has been frequently compared to a medical residency. Classes are well taught by clinically practicing faculty (not found in many nursing graduate programs). Once accepted to the program, classes are well mapped out, and any issues with registration are easily solved by the program coordinator. There are usually less than 40 students accepted to the program every year, so individual attention is given freely.

Current student, Engineering, 8/2006-Submit Date, April 2007

The classes you take at FIU are extremely demanding. The professors assign a great amount of work, but it is completely necessary. It is all about managing your time and planning out a schedule that is effective and healthy for you. The professors are also extremely helpful. They are always willing to meet with you, one-on-one, during their office hours, so make sure you take full advantage of that opportunity. It is also vital that you plan out your classes ahead of time so you can get into the classes you want. Becoming a part of the Honors College can also help you attain the classes you want.

Alumnus/a, Engineering, 8/2002-12/2006, April 2007

Generally the classes are large in the lower division. This is to be expected, once again, due to the University being a public institution. As you move up in your degree, the classes become smaller and smaller. At the highest levels of your degree, class size tends to be around 30 to 40 students.

Employment Prospects

Current student, English, 8/2006-Submit Date, April 2007

FIU is best known for its business program, and its graduates often have no problem getting jobs. FIU's journalism graduates have gone on to work for CBS, *The Sun-Sentinel*, among other prominent companies. The career center is available and useful for students when it comes to finding a job. There are often several job fairs on campus throughout the semester.

Current student, Nursing, 9/2006-Submit Date, April 2007

Many students have submitted applications with well-recognized anesthesia providers for educational sponsorships in exchange for a two-, three-, or four-year work commitment after school. FIU graduates are well respected as competent anesthesia providers. The FIU program, above other local programs ,requires a higher caseload of patients, so the FIU graduate is proportionally more prepared for jumping into work upon passing the state licensure exam.

Current student, Visual Arts, 6/2006-Submit Date, April 2007

On-campus recruiting and internships are amazing at FIU. Most of the people working in these offices have had hands-on experiences with the people providing internships and job opportunities. With a good attitude and proper people skills, you could definitely use these resources to your advantage. They'll cater to your every need and help you get where you want to be in the job world.

Current student, Social Sciences, 1/2005-Submit Date, April 2007

Employment prospects are promising in each and every program under the umbrella here at FIU. Job fairs are held regularly on campus are so that students can get a bird's eye view of what to expect in their careers. Most of all, through internships, the students gain plenty of experience with hands-on skills in their particular majors.

Current student, Communications, 8/2004-Submit Date, April 2007

There is a system set up so students can get credit for internships in the field, but the internship needs to be procured by the student him/herself without much help from the university. There are internship fairs, but the positions are usually for the management track of advertising, PR or journalism. There are clubs on campus that provide networking opportunities with advertising agencies off campus at student/agency mixers, but these clubs frequently have dues.

> **The school says:** "The School of Journalism and Mass Communication provides advertising and public relations students with the opportunity to earn three credit hours toward their degree by completing an internship in the field. Students locate internships in one of three ways: by obtaining internship announcements from FIU's Career Services department, by inquiring with faculty, or by approaching a company directly. Internships can be paid or unpaid; students must document a total of 300 hours of work during the semester and prepare a portfolio for review in order to receive credit. For more information, contact (305) 919-4578."

Quality of Life

Current student, English, 8/2006-Submit Date, April 2007

The food is awful, but the housing is excellent: the buildings are new, technologically-savvy and safe. Only about 8 percent of the students live on campus, so while there exists an active student life, it is not as much of a party school as

it could be. Most students go off campus to party: South Beach, Coconut Grove and so on.

Alumnus/a, Business, 1/2006-Submit Date, April 2007

I leave 20 minutes away from the campus, so it is really easy to commute to school. Florida International University offers a wide variety of facilities to students, from great dining areas to a great library where students can stay after hours to study or work on projects.

Current student, Biology, 1/2006-Submit Date, April 2007

I feel safe on campus. I take classes at night and on Saturdays because of work. There are times when I leave campus at 1 a.m. and I always see police officers patrolling the parking lots and the buildings. Both campuses are located in good neighborhoods, and there are emergency call boxes throughout campus. There are more things to do on South Campus than there are on North Campus, but there are buses from North to South and vice-versa. If you don't want to drive, the ride takes one hour each way. I live off campus but the dorms are pretty neat, the typical college housing. Both campuses have gyms and aerobic classes are offered for students only. The cafeteria on North Campus closes really early but there is a Publix, Subway, Friday's and Costco all about five minutes away. The facilities are well maintained. There are plenty of vending machines around campus if you don't have time to sit down and eat.

Current student, Business, 6/2004-Submit Date, April 2007

It depends on the campus you attend. If you want a small, quiet, calm campus, then the Biscayne Bay campus is for you. The University Park campus is very large and more of a typical, large university. The neighborhoods are safe, and crime in the area is low. Overall the FIU campuses are placed in safe environments. FIU also has their own police monitoring the school daily.

Current student, Business, 6/2005-12/2008, April 2007

I live in my own apartment. The campus is in excellent condition. I like the campus very much. It's full of modern sculptures, and it's very big. I find it relaxing for a studying environment. Facilities could be better, but even though it's an old campus, I think that it is very well-maintained. Dining services you have are the following: Subway, Einstein Bagels, pizza, sushi, Burger King, Pollo Tropical, Starbucks, Café Bustello and a big all-you-can-eat bar, which is actually very good and healthy. The neighborhood is OK; the traffic is a mess during the peak hours of the day. The biggest problems of all are the parking places. There are not enough parking spaces. I usually wait 10 minutes to find the right one.

Social Life

Current student, 6/2006-12/2006, May 2007

There is wonderful diversity here, almost 70 percent minorities, so this was a terrific experience for a boy from Nebraska. My roommates were all great guys. We mostly studied and played video games in our spare time. I was a member of Panther Rage and attended all football games. My roommates took me to lots of clubs and to South Beach.

Current student, Health, 8/2006-Submit Date, April 2007

There is always something going on, everyday so there is never a boring day at FIU. The game room is there for pool and computer games, video games, ping pong; tournaments are held there, as well. The restaurants in school provide good service and they have a variety of restaurants from which to choose. Pollo Tropical opened in 2006, and is now my favorite on-campus restaurant, other than Burger King, Gracie's Grill, or the sushi place. If you want to join any fraternity, sorority, or club, feel free to do so. I am in a club called Indian Student Association, and we welcome not only Indians but also anyone else who may want to join.

Current student, Environment, 8/2005-Submit Date, April 2007

There is a bar on campus, believe it or not. The school is located near a highway that's a direct route to all the hottest clubs in Miami. Many free concerts of very popular performers occur here. Many speeches are given by the country's hottest stars and even the most prestigious politicians.

Read all of Vault's College Surveys at **www.vault.com/college**–get complete surveys on 100s of colleges and universities, expert advice on applicaton essays and more.

VAULT CAREER LIBRARY **151**

Alumnus/a, Nutrition, 8/2004-5/2006, April 2007

Since FIU is located in Miami, FL there is a lot to do at night. There is Coconut Grove and South Beach, which tend to be the hotspots at night. There are endless activities in the city with regards to bars, clubs, and nightlife. The parties last all night and go on into the early morning. The dating scene at FIU, should be pretty easy, meaning people of both genders tend to be really outgoing and friendly. Every person I have met has been super nice. The university has an endless list of clubs and organizations that one can join. The clubs try to recruit new members annually and try to promote themselves at club fairs within the school.

Current student, 5/2005-Submit Date, April 2007

I am a member of the Golden Key International Honor Society. The school has several Greek affiliations that promote community service and brother/sisterhood. The different groups and organizations promoted many events around campus. I love their advertisement methods, with the decorations around campus and the gatherings they have. The school is always decorated because of different events, which really makes the campus fun, young and enjoyable.

 The School Says

Florida International University is Miami's first public four-year university. Our powerful record of innovation and research continues to improve the quality of life in our communities.

History and Growth:

FIU was founded in 1965 and opened for classes in 1972 with 5,667 students—the largest opening day enrollment in U.S. collegiate history. Today, it has more than 38,000 students, almost 1,000 full-time faculty and approximately 124,000 alumni. FIU is one of the 25 largest universities in the nation, based on enrollment.

Programs:

The university offers more than 200 bachelor's, master's and doctoral programs in 22 colleges and schools:

- College of Architecture and the Arts
- School of Architecture
- School of Art and Art History
- School of Theatre, Dance and Speech Communication
- School of Music
- College of Arts and Sciences
- College of Business Administration
- School of Accounting
- College of Education
- College of Engineering and Computing
- School of Computing and Information Sciences
- Honors College
- School of Journalism and Mass Communication
- College of Law
- College of Medicine (2009)
- College of Nursing and Health Sciences
- College of Social Work, Justice and Public Affairs
- School of Social Work
- School of Criminal Justice
- School of Public Administration
- School of Hospitality and Tourism Management
- Stempel School of Public Health

National Recognition:

FIU is the youngest university to have been awarded a chapter of Phi Beta Kappa, the nation's oldest and most distinguished academic honor society. FIU recently ranked among the best values in public, higher education in the country, according to *Kiplinger's Personal Finance* magazine's 2006 survey, "100 Best Values in Public Colleges." FIU ranked among the Top 50 nationally for in-state students and among the top 100 nationally for out-of-state and international students.

Faculty:

95 percent of the university's full-time, tenure and tenure-earning faculty hold doctorates or the highest degrees in their field.

Athletics:

FIU's intercollegiate athletic teams compete in the National Collegiate Athletic Association (NCAA) Division I, the nation's most competitive college sports division, the Sun Belt Conference and Conference USA. 17 sports programs are offered, including football (Division I-A), basketball, track and cross-country, soccer, volleyball, softball and baseball.

Research:

FIU emphasizes research as a major component of its mission. Sponsored research funding (grants and contracts) from external sources for 2005-2006 totaled $92 million. The University is ranked as a Research University in the High Research Activity category of the Carnegie Foundation's prestigious classification system.

Arts and Culture:

FIU has emerged as one of South Florida's major cultural assets, offering programs to both students and the local community. Several of its programs are nationally renowned for their excellence.

Campuses:

FIU has two campuses, the 344-acre University Park campus in western Miami-Dade County, and the 200-acre Biscayne Bay Campus in northeast Miami-Dade County. The University also has an academic site in Broward County, FIU Broward-Pines Center in Pembroke Pines.

A major research facility, the 40-acre Engineering Center is located near the University Park campus. The Downtown Center, located in downtown Miami, offers graduate level business courses for busy professionals.

Florida State University

Office of Admissions
A2500 University Center
Florida State University
Tallahassee, FL 32306-2400
Admissions phone: (850) 644-6200
Admissions fax: (850) 644-0197
Admissions e-mail: admissions@admin.fsu.edu
Admissions URL:
www.fsu.edu/students/prospective/undergraduate/

Note: The school has chosen not to comment on the student surveys submitted.

 ## Admissions

Current student, 8/2004-Submit Date, November 2006

The admissions process at FSU was fairly simple. One can either fill out the application on line or in paper format. I completed mine the old-fashioned way and I heard back roughly around the same time as other students who applied online. The application was run of the mill: résumé, letter of recommendation and essays. When I was accepted, I received an e-mail and a nice folder with a certificate of enrollment. I thought it was very special and a lot of my other friends who applied to different schools were shocked at how hospitable the admissions committee was. After getting in, while I was deciding between two schools, I received roughly five phone calls from current FSU students welcoming me to FSU and asking if I had any questions or concerns. I thought this was so nice and no other university did this. That friendliness and caring about me as a student are what made me decide on coming to FSU!

Alumnus/a, Music, 8/2001-5/2005, June 2007

For my major, through the School of Music, I had to go through a rigorous audition and interview process that was actually separate from the university application process.

Current student, 8/2004-Submit Date, September 2005

Admissions was typical of the major public Florida universities. I applied to FSU online via its online application. It was a relatively quick and painless process. I wrote three possible essays on subjects like a vacation that influenced my life or some aspect of my life. Another topic was about a school program in which I was involved and how it made me the person I am today. They aren't too selective. I received notification within two weeks of the application date.

Current student, 8/2002-Submit Date, October 2005

Now, more than ever, universities are looking for a well-rounded student. Not only should you have a high GPA, but you should also be involved with school sports, clubs, community service and a part-time job. There is no interview, only an online application. I recommend you apply early. Many people tell you to do Early Decision, which is different than just applying early. In Early Decision you apply and if you are accepted you attend that university. I wouldn't recommend this choice because you obviously limit your options. Also, many people say that you should apply for summer because it's easier to get into. That's not true but it is a good idea to go during summer because you meet people before you get a full classload, there are more parties, and parking on campus is easier. For your essays, be candid. Just be honest and make sure you check spelling! They love minorities, use that to your advantage—ask about scholarships. Make sure you are on time with all your paperwork, especially housing and tuition.

Current student, 8/2003-Submit Date, November 2004

The admissions process for Florida State University is straightforward. An average GPA ranging anywhere from 2.7+ and an SAT of 1000+ have a fairly good shot at getting accepted. There are no required interviews and the essays are the same as any state school. The only advantage Florida State offers is in-state stu-

dents pay much less for tuition than any out-of-state student. Florida State is a school for those who can't afford to pay out-of-state fees, so the student body is made up of a lot of in-state students looking to get a higher education at a minimal cost.

Current student, 8/2002-Submit Date, December 2004

To be admitted, a student must have a high school diploma and graduate with a 2.5 GPA or higher. You fill out a form with a $20 fee, plus provide two essays from a choice of three to five topics. Letters of recommendation are not required. FSU is required to meet a certain quota of minority students, including international students.

Current student, 8/2003-Submit Date, March 2004

It is actually very simple: just send your SAT scores, transcript and a brief essay to the school, and remember to keep abreast of what is going on. The key is to be honest and to submit your information as soon as possible, as FSU gets a lot of applications. Oh, and please get your housing done as soon as possible because they often overbook, leaving you with no place to live. When you get there, wear comfortable shoes, because there is a lot of walking.

 ## Academics

Current student, 8/2004-Submit Date, November 2006

From the beginning of my freshman year until now, the majority of my academic professors has been amazing. All of them have cared about me as a person first and then as a student. Getting into classes is difficult for students with less credit hours, e.g., freshmen and sophomores. I am in the honors program at FSU and we get priority registration, which has been a huge blessing. The grading scale is not the best here at FSU. We have the minus and plus system. The workload has been difficult but that is what college is all about. Overall, the academic community at FSU has been very nurturing.

Alumnus/a, Music, 8/2001-5/2005, June 2007

I thoroughly enjoyed my academic life at FSU. Most of my undergraduate academic classes were taught by graduate assistants, but that was not a problem. I enjoyed learning from them. Although I must admit, my favorite liberal arts academic class was Women in Literature. The only class I wish was offered as a general liberal arts class is finance.

Current student, Business, 8/2003-Submit Date, November 2005

Liberal studies classes are pretty easy. My upper-level business courses are challenging, but the teachers are happy to help during their office hours. Getting classes is no problem for me because I get priority registration for being in the Honors Program. Workload isn't too bad as long as you plan things out, some points in the semester however, leave little time for anything other than studying.

Current student, 8/2002-Submit Date, October 2005

FSU has some amazing programs! Luckily if you don't know which program to take advantage of you have two years of general AA classes to get out of the way before you must decide on your major. As for registering for classes, here are a few things I wish someone had told me before I got here. (1) The classes are numbered by level of difficulty. Classes that are in the 1000 are easiest and they continue up from there. As a freshman 1000s and maybe some 2000-level classes are acceptable but 3s and 4s are not recommended. I made the mistake of taking CCJ3001, AMH2000, and PSI3324 all my first semester! (2) Even if you think you are a morning person now, you won't be once you hit college 8 a.m. is too early! Go for classes later in the day. (3) College classes are the best! They are really interesting and therefore more fun to learn and you do better. Don't be afraid to talk to the teachers in their office hours; they love that. (4) We have a saying here "Five is Fine" you can handle five classes and not overload yourself. Of course this is different for everyone but four or five classes is the norm. (5) Registration windows open based on how many credits you

Read all of Vault's College Surveys at **www.vault.com/college**—get complete surveys on 100s of colleges and universities, expert advice on applicaton essays and more.

VAULT CAREER LIBRARY **153**

already have. So, if you know older students, their windows will open up before yours. Ask them to save popular freshman classes for you before the freshman window opens, then plan out when they will drop and you will add those classes once your window opens. This way you have a better chance at getting what you want. (6) Know your professors, not just your classes. Pickaprof.com and similar sites are very accurate places to find out about your teachers before you even step foot in the classroom.

OK, I think that's all. FSU is a blast, but you need to maintain a good work/play balance!

Current student, 8/2003-Submit Date, November 2004

Almost all upper-level classes at FSU are taught by well-trained professors who have extensive background in the subjects they teach. Many of the lower-level classes, however, are taught by grad students because of the simplicity of the class and the sheer number of classes offered by FSU. The ease of getting popular classes is difficult because of the number of students. However, thanks to drop/add week and a new mandatory first day attendance policy, it is possible to get a class even if it filled up five minutes after registration opened. Resourceful students can almost guarantee that they can have their ideal schedule perfected by the end of drop/add week.

Alumnus/a, 8/2000-4/2004, December 2004

This is another area in which FSU varies widely depending upon certain facts. As a research one institution, FSU boasts some extremely impressive professors, especially in some of the science departments. However, these professors are often engaged in research and do not teach many classes. Nevertheless, some of FSU's programs are nationally renowned. These include computer science, physics and meteorology departments, among others. Its film and theater departments are also widely regarded as some of the best in the Southeast United States, and are extremely difficult to get.

The rest of the departments, such as most of the liberal arts departments, are considered on par with most major universities. While a department may not be a national shining star, most, such as the English department, are graced with a few truly brilliant professors who aren't so busy researching that they can't teach some classes. Students will find that many of their entry-level requirement classes are pretty miserable. They are usually massive and taught by TAs. They are easy to skip if that is your ambition, but they are hard really to learn and retain something from unless you make an honest effort.

Current student, 8/2000-Submit Date, May 2004

Undergraduate students at Florida State University are required to participate in liberal arts studies. This requires students in their first two years to take classes in literature, history, multi-ethnicity and so forth. Classes in the science and math areas are very challenging, with a high failure rate for those whose academic minds are not equipped for such subjects. Popular classes fill quickly as soon as registration opens. Grading, as I have seen it over the past four years, seems to have gotten lax. Professors are more willing to give in to the high failure rate in some classes by offering ways out to improve grades without hard work. There are several extremely talented and distinguished professors at FSU. The workload is only as challenging as you make it for yourself.

 ## Employment Prospects

Current student, 8/2004-Submit Date, November 2006

I know that there is a variety of opportunities for FSU graduates. The graduate programs for some departments are among the best in the nation, so the available experiences are very large. Teach for America has a a strong presence on campus and has new members every year. There are at least half a dozen career fairs that occur throughout all times of the year that are always looking for new college graduates.

Current student, 8/2002-Submit Date, October 2005

There is a great Career Center here. I'm graduating soon and I have had them help me with résumé building, mock interviews and networking for job interviews. I don't know much on statistics, but I know that each individual school has amazing records for job placement especially our School of Hospitality.

There are always lots of job fairs and expos going on and there are a million and one internship opportunities.

Current student, 8/2002-Submit Date, December 2004

There are tons of on-campus recruiters and it is very easy to get an internship. Most FSU grads I know got jobs right out of college. A close friend, a double business major, got six job offers and took the job in Columbus, OH, at the Nationwide Insurance world headquarters. Having a degree from FSU does not get you a whole lot of prestige and most start on the low-paying aspect of work. But there are exceptions. The alumni network is helpful if you're in the right place and have the right major, and our alumni are awesome.

Alumnus/a, 8/2000-4/2004, December 2004

The bigger the university, the more the post-graduate prospects can vary; and FSU is enormous. I know that a fairly high percentage of FSU undergraduates go on to grad schools, which is a pretty good indicator of the quality of education you can get at FSU if you apply yourself. Exceptional students from FSU have gotten into the best grad schools in the nation and won the highest possible awards (Fulbright and Rhodes Scholars aplenty).

There is a very high-quality Career Center that gives you access to programs that you can use long after graduation, and a whole database of FSU alumni that are looking to hire recent FSU grads. As a whole, FSU isn't going to stack up in prestige against, say, an Ivy League school, but the advantage of a large school like this is that people who apply themselves can earn higher awards within the school itself. So if you can say you were in the top 10 percent of your class, then that is going to boost your résumé, naturally. FSU has so many departments that the types of jobs you can obtain after school are limitless. The Career Center can be really helpful here if you're not sure where to go next.

Current student, 8/2001-Submit Date, June 2004

There are employment prospects everywhere in the world. Some may fit your desires better than others. Florida State has a great gradient of local careers available to start students off in the real world with an excellent foot in the door. Internships are widely available in all fields, and students are highly regarded and invited. Recruiters are constantly on campus looking to reach those interested students. Employers have developed a superb relationship with students and honor their needs for education and training before they take on the full-time commitment. Career placement opportunities are extremely available through the career center, which provides tips and guidance for interviews, résumés, contacts or simply career ideas.

 ## Quality of Life

Current student, 8/2004-Submit Date, November 2006

FSU has some of the nicest facilities for campus recreation. They are always in the process of renovating and rebuilding to keep up with the fast growth. A freshman is not guaranteed on-campus housing, which is a little difficult; but if one applies on time, one should have a high chance of getting housing. The food on campus is improving every year. FSU has a lot of tradition and the students and surrounding areas of campus realize that and try to incorporate that to their fullest potential. I love my life here at FSU; even if parking is a pain, the atmosphere is wonderful!

Current student, 8/2003-Submit Date, November 2005

Off-campus housing can be hit or miss. Large student apartment complexes are pretty safe, but a lot of neighborhoods right next to campus are pretty rough. Everything on campus is pretty nice and safe.

Current student, 8/2002-Submit Date, October 2005

Housing can be tricky. There are lots of renovations going on. For now avoid Kellum and Smith Halls, both are old and gross. The only benefit to them is they are on the same side of campus as the gym so you're more inclined to go. LOL. The campus is extremely pedestrian friendly. You can walk anywhere but if you don't want to, the bus system is great. The Leach Center (gym) is fantastic!!! It's three stories with great equipment and classes and it's not too busy. Food on campus is good, too. There are lots of options all over campus so you don't have to worry about getting to a certain spot like a food court to eat, although we do have a food court that is centrally located. We are lucky in that FSU has a place called The Rez, which is a large area of land with a lake where you can go canoeing or play volleyball or just hang out. You can also talk to Campus Rec about trips that groups of FSU students go to that are adventurous. Every year they go skiing and white water rafting and hiking all for decent money. FSU also has some amazing tech classrooms. We also have an online classroom-type deal where you can check all your grades online, talk to teachers and e-mail other students from class. As for the neighborhood, it's lacking. Girls should never walk alone at night!!! I cannot stress this enough. I would not recommend anyone walking/jogging anywhere off campus especially!

Current student, 8/2003-Submit Date, November 2004

The quality of life is definitely an A. Almost all of the on-campus housing has been renovated, so you can enjoy a quality dormitory with clean facilities. The campus itself is very well-kept. The facilities are all cleaned daily and the computer rooms and libraries have been updated with some of the latest hardware money can buy. Crime is relatively low, given that Florida State is not only located five minutes away from the capital, but the entire City of Tallahassee has grown into a college town. A good majority of the residents who live around Tallahassee are students seeking out higher education. There are two universities and one community college located no more than 10 minutes away from one another.

Current student, 8/2000-Submit Date, May 2004

I lived in the residence halls all four years at FSU. I am very glad I made the decision to remain in the heart of the campus. I was able to have easy access to any and all campus events, without ever having to worry about added time commuting back to campus or getting ready. The student union was one of the most comfortable places to hang out, and everything was at my fingertips—places to eat, a computer lab, the post office, the bank. There is a large feeling of tolerance and liberalism on FSU's campus. Students have free speech regardless of sex, race or religion, with rarely any riots or disturbances.

 Social Life

Current student, 8/2004-Submit Date, November 2006

FSU's social life is always flourishing. There is always something going on around campus with the 400+ sum student organizations. There is never a dull moment!!! The strip is a local pastime for college students on nights and weekends. The athletics of FSU are always a big hit throughout the year, even if we are having an off season, people bleed garnet and gold!!! There are so many wonderful local scenes to check out being in the capital city. There are two other higher education institutions and that adds to the diversity of the town. Greek life at FSU is big but not the only thing with which students who are looking for a social group can get involved with. There will never be a dull social life for FSU students!

Alumnus/a, Music, 8/2001-5/2005, June 2007

I was very involved in social activities at FSU. My friends and I worked very hard in the theatre and music schools and would often go out to clubs and bars on the weekends to relax and let off steam. I personally preferred the bars and

clubs a little farther away from campus because the college crowds could get a little rowdy. But every once in a while I would go out to Tennessee Street, the premiere party spot, and visit the bars. Potbellies, a local bar, had happy hour starting as soon as classes let out on Fridays. That was always a hotspot for socializing. Tallahassee is such a wonderful town because the college life is there at hand, but there is plenty of culture as well. Kool Beanz is one of the nicest restaurants in town, and a great place to take a date. Cafe Cabernet is a great spot for a formal event involving dinner, dancing to live music, and drinks. There is definitely plenty to do in Tallahassee and at Florida State.

Alumnus/a 8/2002-12/2005, February 2006

I really enjoy the campus events, such as comedy nights and movies at the Student Life Building. There was always something to do, no matter what your preferences and the students and organizations sponsoring them did a fantastic job at advertising and publicizing.

Current student, 8/2002-Submit Date, October 2005

It is what you make it! If you love to party, there's always somewhere and someone with whom to party. If you like to stay in, there are quiet neighborhoods and dorms. I love the clubs here because the people in them are all college students, mostly from FSU. You inevitably run into a ton of people you know and it's a blast. Also, the clubs and bars know how poor college kids are and have constant specials. Greek life is pretty big, but it's not everything. Again that's a matter of to what you choose to expose yourself. Game days are huge! The whole town is in on it and the alumni are big supporters. There's nothing more fun than tailgating at Indian Village. It's a huge block party like no other school has. We pride ourselves on beating our biggest rivals UF (Gators) and UM (Canes). The town itself can be impressive if you are from somewhere really small, but I'm from Miami so it's difficult to compare. I will say that FSU has a lot of Southern culture so expect lots of sweet tea and camo. It's got great hospitality and a love for country.

Alumnus/a, 8/2000-4/2004, December 2004

Where to start?! Once again, Tally has so much to offer the college student that it's easy to forget that you moved to there to get an education. (Don't say I didn't warn you!) If you're into the Greek scene, have no fear. There are more sororities and fraternities than I could possibly count; social, academic, religious, career-oriented; you name it. The aforementioned student life building and exhaustive list of clubs and organizations is also a real asset. Tally has bars that have been listed in national magazines (some of ill repute!) as being in the Top 10 college bars in the country. Namely Bullwinkles. Vinyl Fever is a music store that is also nationally renowned (music snobs beware: you can easily devastate your life savings in this store; it really is amazingly good).

There's a surprisingly good indie and underground music scene in Tally, given that on the exterior it's such a frat-daddy-type town. Those with more transgressive tastes should check out the Beta Bar. The best coffee shops are All Saints Cafe and the Black Dog. Poor Paul's has the cheapest beer and the best specials in town. Brothers is the main gay/lesbian club (if you swing that way). The dating scene is, well, essentially a town full of post-adolescent single kids who are all looking to have as much fun as they can.

Read all of Vault's College Surveys at www.vault.com/college—get complete surveys on 100s of colleges and universities, expert advice on applicaton essays and more.

VAULT CAREER LIBRARY 155

Rollins College

Admissions Office
1000 Holt Ave.
Winter Park, FL 32789
Admissions phone: (407) 646-2000
Admissions e-mail: admission@rollins.edu
Admissions URL: www.rollins.edu/admission/

 Admissions

Current student, Economics, 8/2003-Submit Date, October 2005

When I enrolled, an interview was not necessary. I think my essay helped me a lot as it gave more depth to my application. I also feel that my SAT score helped greatly as my GPA was not very high. I applied Early Decision but did not get in until the second round of Regular Admission. The school has become increasingly most selective with each year since my enrollment, with both the required GPA and SAT scores rising.

Alumnus/a, English, 8/2001-5/2004, November 2004

I had a very easy time getting into Rollins. Actually I never applied coming out of high school because it had a reputation for being a country club that offered classes. After spending a year at a freezing cold university up north, I wanted to come home and Rollins was the only major Florida school still accepting applications. I applied, wrote the essay, and sent in recommendations. It was very easy and I received my admissions notice three weeks later. Most students have SATs in the 1050 to 1250 range and I had a 1260 with a 3.65 GPA. The statement of purpose is very straightforward, but much attention is paid to it. The admissions office is very friendly and I believe the woman working there is still Ginger. She is very helpful and will answer any and all questions during the application process.

> **The school says:** "Our combined SAT scores for the middle 50 percent range from 1090 to 1260."

Current student, 11/2002-Submit Date, May 2004

The admissions process was rather simple. It consisted of sending in one of three types of forms. Early decision (where you sign an early contract saying that you will go to that school of accepted and reject all others), Early Action (same as regular just at an earlier time) or regular entry. The essay was one that dealt with a significant event or series of event in ones life that made them the person they are and how the person they are can add to the academic and social life of the campus. I got in with a 4.0 GPA and 1210 SAT, I was not interviewed but I have spoken with the dean of admissions from time to time and was even called to be told that I was accepted into the school. My year was supposedly one of the most selective years the school ever had.

 Academics

Current student, Economics, 8/2003-Submit Date, October 2005

I am doing an economics major. There is a high level of understanding needed, but the workload is not high. Exams are hard, but due to the nature of most of the courses, there is less emphasis on essays and more on exams and class participation. Professors put emphasis on students giving their views and opinions. At Rollins all the classes are small and there are no lecture courses in large rooms. Grading can be tough, of course this depends on the course, but most students have to work very hard to get A's. The majority of the professors have doctorates and teach interesting course subjects.

Alumnus/a, English, 8/2001-5/2004, November 2004

I was an English major and film minor at Rollins and had a wonderful experience. The professors are topnotch and carry several awards in their fields. The

approach at Rollins is small classes, discussion, and a hands-on education. Professors are there whenever you need them and I actually became better friends with my professors than students. While the professors are always there to help, the workload is enormous, especially if you take a course such as American Literature. If you really can't make a deadline, show your professor the work you've done and he/she will usually extend the deadline.

The department relies heavily on essay tests and multiple choice tests are shunned. Some professors such as Henton, Boles and O'Sullivan double as film professors or speakers so if you have an interest in film and English, you've come to the right place. I've taken classes at Duke as part of the TIP program, at Davidson College, American University, Columbia University (for film) and spent a year at the University of Pittsburgh. The professors at Rollins College blow them all away because they have patience, energy, and a genuine interest in the education of their students. The library is mocked as "Club Olin" because people dress up to be seen in the computer lab. Rollins may be the only place on the planet where stilettos are considered "study tools."

Current student, 11/2002-Submit Date, May 2004

The professors are amazing. Probably the best thing about it all is that I can go into their offices any time they have office hours and sit down and have a chat. The availability of the professors in Rollins college is probably the key strength of the college. I personally have never had any trouble getting into the classes I wanted, especially when they have to deal with my major.

Grading is fair within the college but a little unique for they grade on a plus/minus system where one can receive an A- or a B+ depending on the exact percentage of one's grade. On average, this has hurt more than helped my overall GPA being that A-'s are a frequent thing on my final grades. The workload is very difficult for me. This is directly a result of my major but other majors don't always have it so easy either. Being that Rollins professors can take so much time on their students the resulting effect is that there is a lot of homework dished out.

 Employment Prospects

Current student, Economics, 8/2003-Submit Date, October 2005

There is high prestige associated with Rollins College, as it is known as being a small school with high quality programs and professors. There is great career service department, which helps set up internships and job interviews. There are a number of college fairs in the area, to which the college provides transport. Rollins College is a highly recognized college in Florida and I would assume is also known by most top corporations.

Alumnus/a, English, 8/2001-5/2004, November 2004

There are several high-powered Rollins alumni. Many students already have jobs waiting for them after college because of family connections. Jane Cordray from career services is very helpful with résumés and returning e-mails, but there just aren't that many good opportunities that come through when you compare it to other schools. I just checked Rollins' interview track schedule today for the month of November and there were only 10 opportunities. No one I've met is really impressed when you tell them you graduated from Rollins and it's a shame because some students really work hard there and the professors are doing all they can.

Current student, 11/2002-Submit Date, May 2004

Career resources is a department that I don't use as frequently as I should. But I have heard that it is an excellent source of information for applying to grad schools, workplaces and summer internships. Its database is directly connected to Monster.com where internships can be looked up online. Many of my friends have gone off to additional schooling, such as law school or med school, rather than into the work force directly. Their successes are usually attributed to the internships they got that were researched through the career resource center.

Quality of Life

Current student, Economics, 8/2003-Submit Date, October 2005

There is a host of things to do both on and off campus. The dorms are relatively big compared to those I have seen at other colleges. The bathrooms are large and are kept clean. The dining hall is excellent, as are the facilities, such as the soccer field and swimming pool. The pool is a great hang-out spot during the day in between or after classes. There is a number of clubs, organizations and sports on offer. There are eight tennis courts, the gymnasium holds two basketball courts and a full gym.

Alumnus/a, English, 8/2001-5/2004, November 2004

Housing at Rollins is tremendous. Everyone at the college complains because half of their homes are on MTV *Cribs* and moving to campus is quite a change of scenery, but when compared to other colleges, the housing is great. The cafeteria is also topnotch (for a college cafeteria of course) and has a wide variety of offerings every day. There is also Diane's, which offers salads, soups, sandwiches and other light foods. People working at Rollins are very friendly and understanding. The gym is below average, though. While the building looks great and has televisions, which most campus gyms don't have, the equipment stinks. Most gyms these days use Nautilus, Cybex, or power strength equipment and Rollins' gym uses some old stuff from the 80s that looks like they bought it at Chuck Norris's yard sale. There are only two precor running machines and there's always a wait to use them.

The neighborhood is as safe as it gets. The campus police and Winter Park police hang around waiting for things to happen, but nothing ever does. I think the biggest emergency we ever had was that a drunk kid flipped over a golf cart, which was more entertaining than threatening. The campus is beautiful and most dorms overlook the lake, so you really couldn't ask for anything more. The only reason I moved off campus was because it was cheaper to do so.

Current student, 11/2002-Submit Date, May 2004

This issue has both its yin and its yang. I ended up living off campus rather than on due to the price of living on campus. I save $2,000 a year living off campus. The food at the school gets pretty boring pretty fast and cooking at home is just so much better. If you live on campus, you eat breakfast, lunch and dinner in the cafeteria (we call it Beans) where there is a variety of food depending on the day of the week with occasional events on holidays like before Thanksgiving. Dave's Down Under is the late-night eating place that is open until 2 a.m. and consists of mostly fried foods like cheeseburgers and chicken strips. And finally there is the C-store where people can buy overpriced grocery food on their food accounts. Dorm life is fun but it is like a kennel cough, if one person gets sick the whole building can get sick and that gets annoying. The one strongly redeeming attribute to living on campus is that you are on campus. You always hear what parties are happening and have a consistently satisfied appetite for social engagement. Crime is an occasional problem, such as random vandalism or someone stealing a bike, but it is not a constant, pressing issue.

Social Life

Current student, Economics, 8/2003-Submit Date, October 2005

The area outside the campus is very nice, with lots of restaurants and shops within walking distance. Downtown Orlando is only 20 minutes away by taxi. All the college bars are walking distance from campus. Everyone knows each other. There is a number of fraternities and sororities and there is interaction between them all. Going to nightclubs is less popular than going to bars. Fiddler's Green is the local Irish-themed college bar that hosts trivia during happy hour and is always packed on nights out, which run from Wednesday through Saturday. Bars are usually a late night-scene with most people pre-gaming at house parties of students.

Alumnus/a, 8/2001-5/2004, November 2004

It's a country club and the students are proud of it. The social circles are small and everybody knows everybody, but it doesn't mean they'll talk to you. There's a lot of staring, pointing and gossiping. There is also a lack of diversity. They use statistics to show that according to percentages, Rollins is diverse, but when you consider there's 3,700 students the actual number of minority students is very small.

> **Rollins says:** "There is a total enrollment of 3,478 students, with a 25 percent minority rate."

I hated the social life at Rollins, but that's because I'm not a big fan of the Greek system, which really dominates campus life. Even though I had a few "confrontations" with certain fraternities on campus, most of my friends are in fraternities. You just can't get away from them at Rollins. I never pledged and most of my friends held out till sophomore or junior year, but in the end pledged.

The dating scene is pretty funny because there're only like four or five couples on campus, but everyone still seems to find a way to percolate from time to time. The two popular bars are Fiddler's and Bistro. Fiddler's is awesome and I still go there because they have over 20 beers on tap, live Irish bands, Curtis Earth trivia during happy hour, and great food. Wow, they should hire me to do marketing. Downtown Orlando isn't a great downtown either. The bars are sweatboxes and there aren't really any good hangouts. If you come from NY, Chicago, L.A., or any other city with some decent nightlife, you might struggle with Orlando. There are some nice places to eat on Park Avenue, which is basically on campus, and there's always the Winter Park Village five minutes away as well that has nice restaurants and a huge Regal Cinema.

I'm a big sports fan and knew coming into Rollins that there weren't any major sports teams, but I thought I'd get over it. I never did. Most students are from Massachusetts, so it's cool if you're a Red Sox fan. There is also a large NY contingent so Octobers are interesting. Many students aren't knowledgeable about sports though and life can be boring for a sports fanatic. There's always the Orlando Magic.

Bottom line, if you like Greek life and country clubs, this is the place for you. I can't say I regret going to Rollins because the professors were wonderful and the college administration is helpful and caring. Dean Nielson is tremendous. I loved the *Sandspur* (Rollins College Newspaper).

Current student, 11/2002-Submit Date, May 2004

Above all else the social life of Rollins is Greek. The Greeks throw the parties. Dating at Rollins is rather superficial and usually consists of one-night hook-ups. Much of the time large groups of people will head into downtown Orlando and party at the clubs like Antigua. One of the more popular places is Fiddler's, which is about 10 minutes walking distance from campus and is basically a restaurant and bar where people can get a beer and a meal and just hang out. The main club that organizes all of the events at Rollins is a club called ACE (all campus events) and they organize everything from campus wide BBQs to the Greek Olympics where all the Greeks compete in a series of events to win a prize. At Rollins the frats throw the parties, which are usually a lot of fun such as ATO's Swamp Party where everyone dresses up like they're in the military and starts dancing and drinking away. Or TKE's Playboy mansion party where everyone dresses up like their going to the Playboy mansion (rooms included).

Read all of Vault's College Surveys at **www.vault.com/college**–get complete surveys on 100s of colleges and universities, expert advice on applicaton essays and more.

VAULT CAREER LIBRARY **157**

University of Central Florida

University of Central Florida
4000 Central Florida Blvd.
Orlando, FL 32816
Admissions phone: (407) 823-3000
Admissions fax: (407) 823-5625
Admissions e-mail: admission@mail.ucf.edu
Admissions URL: www.admissions.ucf.edu

 Admissions

Current student, Mathematics, 8/2004-Submit Date, June 2007

As a National Merit Semifinalist, I received a letter from UCF offering a full-scholarship and automatic acceptance to the university, as well as to the Burnett Honors College and the LEAD Scholars Program. After visiting, I filled out the State University System Application, and I was accepted a few weeks later. However, don't be fooled, as UCF is increasing in selectivity, boasting an average freshman SAT score of 1201 this past year, and its Honors College has an average SAT score of 1350.

Current student, Business, 8/2004-Submit Date, June 2007

UCF gets more selective every year. The admissions process is comparable to that of other state universities, and involves a formal application and two short essays. Interviews are not required. This is a great institution for people looking for scholarships. After already being awarded the highest number of Bright Futures awards, I received an invitation to the Burnett Honors College and three scholarships, without ever applying for any of them, based only on my application information.

> **The school says:** "The submission of two short essays is highly recommended but not required."

Current student, English, 8/2003-Submit Date, June 2007

The admissions process was great for me. I didn't know that I wanted to go to UCF when I completed my application but I had heard great things. Upon writing my essays and turning in my application, I decided to check out the campus. It is unbelievably beautiful and my orientation guide is actually now a good friend of mine! The people were extremely friendly and there was a kind of optimism that everybody seemed to have for where the school was going to be in a few years. Having been here for four years, I can see why! Things have changed in remarkable ways. The campus is so much more beautiful now (even more beautiful than it already was!) and I am so glad I made the decision I made. UCF is much more selective now. When I came, it was not as hard to get into and it is now the second-hardest school in the state, with an average SAT of over 1200 and a GPA of over a 3.6. I truly believe the difficulty to get in has increased due to the demand that is growing to be a Knight. There is really no better choice for an undergraduate degree.

Alumnus/a, Political Science, 8/2003-5/2007, May 2007

The admissions process at UCF is well run from what I have seen and heard. Follow the advice online and you should be fine. Completing the online application is one of the best options. I did not need to interview; I am not sure if that will change. I doubt it, since UCF is such a huge university.

> **The school says:** "The most efficient and effective way to receive assistance regarding your application is to contact the UCF Office of Undergraduate Admissions directly."

Try to use your essays to tie your whole application together, and refer to highlights in the other materials you are submitting. Admission to the university is getting more difficult ever year. UCF should probably no longer be considered a back-up option for the average student. It certainly does not deserve the reputation of being a back-up school—it has well outgrown that. As a note, if you have the grades, apply to the Burnett Honors College. It is by far the best way to go to school at UCF. You have access to smaller classes, early registration and special attention which will help you thrive and get connected early on.

Current student, Liberal Arts, 8/2004-Submit Date, March 2007

Normal forms about GPA, SAT scores and extracurricular activities. There are a few short answer essays. No interview is required. Best advice would be to be honest during the essays. A good GPA and SAT score are the main things, but being well-rounded with extracurricular helps. Look into the Honors College if you apply and qualify! It has been a tremendous asset. Also, there are Pegasus Scholarships that are given based on GPA and SAT scores (you don't even have to apply for them!) which most Florida schools don't offer.

Current student, 8/2004-Submit Date, April 2006

As an up-and-coming and rapidly growing school, UCF is growing increasingly more selective in admissions. In general, it is comparable to other state universities in Florida, admitting 41 percent of FTIC students, and having average freshman GPA of 3.6, 1180 on the SAT, and 25 on the ACT. If a student is borderline, I would strongly recommend completing the optional essays. Sometimes, these can also lead to university scholarships. In addition, the earlier a student applies, the better off he/she will be.

Current student, 8/2004-Submit Date, September 2005

Have a high GPA, apply early and write the essays to help your chances of getting in. This college is selective and chooses only those with high grade point averages who have been active in school with such things as clubs and sports. Volunteering and community service activities are also another plus.

Current student, 8/2002-Submit Date, April 2004

Admissions used to be very easy, but with the increased popularity over the past five years (1999 to 2004), UCF is becoming more selective. Essays are optional, but you should write one, because if you are neck and neck with someone, it could determine whether you get in or not. A B average is the standard cutoff, with a few lower GPAs accepted as a result of SATs, ACTs or other factors. The top 400 or 500 students accepted into the freshman class are invited to join the Honors College, although other students can download applications for consideration.

> **The school says:** "Admission to the Burnett Honors College and LEAD Scholars Program requires applications separate from the application for undergraduate admissions. LEAD Scholars invites all first-time-in-college freshmen to apply. Admission to the program is selective and based on previous leadership experience, community service, academic performance and perceived potential, and interest in leadership and service."

 Academics

Current student, Engineering, 8/2004-Submit Date, June 2007

Now that I am a senior, I can say that the only rigorous thing about engineering is time management. I enjoyed the classes and felt the progression of learning from one class to another was good (I never felt unprepared for a new course). However, most engineering courses require you to do lots of homework problems. So if you are taking five engineering courses, think about how much homework you had in your most difficult math class in high school, and multiply it by five. Engineering homework can also be frustrating, especially when you have 20 homework problems and get stuck on problem number one.

The professors were generally good. Most were very informed about their subject matter. TAs do become your best friends though, because if you don't understand what the professor is saying in class, chances are you're not going to understand what he/she is saying in his/her office hours. I did find that many professors cared a lot more about their on-campus research than they did about their classes—but I think you will find that at any university. I never had trouble contacting a professor or getting a professor to review a test with me.

Current student, Mathematics, 8/2004-Submit Date, June 2007

Classes at UCF come in all types. I have taken one class in a large lecture hall with 170 students, and the professor managed to teach the material well, learn the names of many students, including mine, and have ample availability to help students outside of class. Some courses, especially introductory and General Education Program courses, are this large. However, most of my classes have ranged from eight or 10 to 30 or 40 students. Professors try hard to challenge students to learn as much as they can in the time allowed. An average workload is five classes, which is manageable. Classes are not that hard to get into because the registration system allots seats in classes for freshmen at each registration session. Classes within each major are usually easier to get into, especially once students near the end of their undergraduate careers. Also, students who maintain over a 3.5 GPA are eligible to register for three semesters at once, while other students must wait until the end of the fall semester to register for the spring term.

Current student, English, 8/2003-Submit Date, June 2007

The academics at UCF are challenging. From my experience, professors at UCF really care about what they do and are passionate about their research. If you are looking to do research, UCF is hands down the best place to be in Florida for undergrads. Classes are big though at first, but once you progress, they get a lot smaller. I'm an English major and although the English program here has way too many students per faculty member, I still have been able to get to know my professors really well. In fact, I had coffee with the [department chair] of the English department the other day. Professors make themselves very available and are extremely kind, which shows that they are passionate about education rather than just making money. The workload is definitely tough, but the average student should have no problem as long as he or she studies and balances out his or her social life. The grading is mostly on a +/- scale of which I am not too fond. Getting into popular classes has not been hard for me at all. I've always managed to get the classes I want, so I certainly don't think that's an issue.

Alumnus/a, Political Science, 8/2003-5/2007, May 2007

UCF is a large campus, which implies large classes for the general courses. These courses are easy to get into but fill up fast, which means you need to register as soon as possible to get the times you prefer. Your first year, try to go see the professors in your smallest classes. These professors usually like to talk with students, even though they do not have lots of time for individual attention with so many in their classes. Gen Ed courses help you learn what college is like and prepare you for your higher courses.

Grading is determined by your professors within bounds set by the university. This means you may have one professor who uses a +/- scale, one who uses a 90 to 100 is an A, and another who requires you to get a 92 or higher for an A. The lesson is: Always read the syllabus! Professors will consider rounding your grade if you have worked hard. Always ask!

Current student, Advertising, 5/2004-Submit Date, March 2007

The individual major I chose, advertising, is partnered with public relations at my school. The major is limited access, meaning you are only accepted into the major if you apply and meet the GPA requirement set each semester. The classes within my program have been very beneficial and the same can be said about my professors. Registration is one flawed part of the university, which recently decided to go with multiple-term registration, which only stresses out students more.

Current student, Engineering, 8/2005-Submit Date, March 2007

Most of the classes are very interesting. Because I am a part of the Honors College, I get to register on the first day that classes are open. I have never had a problem getting the courses I need. Also, athletes, LEAD Scholars, and several other programs students get to register early for classes. After that, the registration goes by class standing and GPA. However, most people do not have too much trouble getting the courses they need because many open up later and there are always some over-rides if a course is vital to graduation. Everyone can choose his/her workload, however, the engineering workload keeps a full load of classes every week. We do have the +/- grading here, which can hurt or help your grades. All of the professors I have met have always been very helpful and willing to meet after class for extra help.

Alumnus/a, Humanities, 8/2002-12/2004, August 2006

Since I've graduated, registering for classes has changed. Now, you must register for two semesters worth of classes, meaning you have to have your full school year planned out, which sounds horrible to me because you have to take into account possibly not doing well in a class and failing but also needing that class as a pre-req. So you can see how it might get complicated or frustrating. If large classes don't suit you, I would start at a community college and then transfer. I was a humanities major and the classes had anywhere from 12 to 35 students depending on the class. The teachers were excellent and it was pretty easy to get into those classes just because there aren't that many humanities majors. The workload was OK, you just have to enjoy reading and writing a lot.

Current student, 8/2004-Submit Date, April 2006

Students begin their program with General Education (GEP) classes from English, math, science and social studies. Students generally take two years to complete this, but if they have credit from AP, IB or dual enrollment, they may finish the requirements earlier and begin their major coursework. GEP classes are larger, taught by either professors or TAs, and generally adhere very strictly to the corresponding textbook and schedule. They are usually easier and more straightforward than upper-division classes. In contrast, upper-division classes are usually taught by tenured faculty and are more discussion-based, paper-based and relaxed in atmosphere, but they usually have more difficult exams. In most classes, students who attend class regularly, read the textbook, study the material, complete assignments and ask questions when necessary can earn high grades. Professors come from all over the world, so they may have heavy accents, but they generally are very knowledgeable about their subject and helpful to students.

Ease of getting popular classes varies throughout the school. There are usually ample sections of GEP courses, but students who register later may have difficulty getting into the time slots they want. Depending on the major and college, upper-division classes may be small and fill quickly, or they may be open only to majors and therefore easy to get. The average workload is five courses. Students in the Burnett Honors College have access to smaller, more intimate courses with higher quality faculty, and they receive the privilege of priority registration.

Current student, 8/2004-Submit Date, April 2006

As an Honors student, I would definitely recommend applying to the Burnett Honors College. I feel that my Honors classes provide much more depth, especially because of the smaller class sizes. One of the areas that needs improvement at UCF, though, is the availability of classes to students. However, when you do get into the classes you want, you can create a pretty amazing schedule for yourself. Overall, I have been very satisfied with the quality of professors at UCF. I believe that any student who is serious about his/her education can succeed at UCF. UCF has an amazing amount and variety of resources to help students succeed in their academics. UCF's tutoring programs are very efficient and plentiful.

 Employment Prospects

Current student, Mathematics, 8/2004-Submit Date, June 2007

UCF, is in Orlando near NASA, Disney, Lockheed Martin and more, and has ample internships, co-ops, research opportunities and other hands-on experience available to students. Job fairs and career fairs are held frequently and Career Services is open during normal business hours to help students gain such opportunities, prepare for interviews, tweak their résumés and so on. Alumni and university staff are extremely helpful and willing to help students pursue these opportunities.

Current student, English, 8/2003-Submit Date, June 2007

With Orlando being so close to UCF, employment is unbelievably easy. I currently work for a commercial real estate company and it is unbelievable how many UCF grads I meet working downtown. There are many alumni who love giving internships and jobs to Knights in all sorts of various fields, and the transition process from college to the workforce is very easy, since the central business district is only minutes away. I know almost all of the colleges (especially the College of Business and Engineering) help UCF students find internships

Read all of Vault's College Surveys at **www.vault.com/college**–get complete surveys on 100s of colleges and universities, expert advice on application essays and more.

VAULT CAREER LIBRARY **159**

and oftentimes provide them. I have never met anybody who has had a difficult time getting an internship. Everybody in Orlando seems to know about the prestige UCF is accumulating by the day, and the reputation of the school is topnotch in the whole Central Florida area. There are also various job fairs that the school hosts where there are various big-name employers.

Alumnus/a, Political Science, 8/2003-5/2007, May 2007

UCF has many partnerships with local businesses. The Career Services department provides significant aid to students as they prepare for the professional world. Locally, some of the best business partnerships are in the areas of simulation and technology, engineering, nursing and teaching (UCF will have a medical school opening soon).

Try to get in touch with graduates through your department. They can often put you in touch with someone doing what you want to do. Through the Honors College, I got in touch with a graduate using his political science degree at the U.S. Department of State. There are plenty of opportunities for internships through your department. There are several job fairs on campus every year, as well. The UCF alumni association also facilities career searches and helps you make contact with graduates. Become a member of the alumni association when you graduate!

Current student, 1/1999-Submit Date, April 2005

I believe that employment prospects for UCF graduates are great if you're planning on staying in the Central Florida area. The school has done great work in establishing partnerships with local industries, and this is often reflected in the number of graduates who are hired by various local companies. On the same note, however, I feel that there is a lot of work to be done to establish the school as a top recruitment source on a national level. The prestige with employers right now does not extend beyond the state level, and work needs to be done to build prestige in the eyes of large national and multinational corporations. I have had to deal with this issue personally within the last year while searching for a job outside of FL. I think that the main cause of this problem is the school's relatively young history and its small alumni network. As time goes on I have no doubt that this problem will be alleviated.

> **The school says:** "In 2005, Career Services and Experiential Learning hired five new staff members to focus on developing new employer recruiting partnerships locally and nationally. In 2007, CSEL began to focus on developing partnerships with 'Employers of Choice,' including Fortune 500 and other industry leaders. Since 2005, more than 3,000 new employers have begun recruiting at UCF, including leading national employers such as Microsoft, Georgia Pacific, Sony, GE, CIA, EPA, Bank of America, Earthlink, GlaxcoSmithKline, Hilton and Turner Broadcasting."

 ## Quality of Life

Current student, Engineering, 8/2004-Submit Date, June 2007

The facilities on campus are absolutely incredible. All of the buildings are less than 50 years old and most of them are brand new! State-of-the-art technology is employed in almost all of the buildings. Flat-panel screens are installed in hallways so students can catch up on the news as they are walking from class to class. Many on-campus labs have the newest equipment. In engineering, student organizations get their own offices in the engineering building (most other organizations are housed in the student union). The gardens and landscaping are well manicured and you always have that postcard, picture perfect view of campus.

The Marketplace (our dining hall) has the best breakfast buffet. Omelets, pancakes, waffles, fruit, cereal: it is divine for $4!!! I always loved the food I had there, no matter what the meal, but breakfast was always the best. It's a great place to meet people, too! The student union area has many fast food choices, with more to come. You can generally get what you want, but it is just as expensive as if you went to the place off campus.

Current student, Mathematics, 8/2004-Submit Date, June 2007

Housing facilities are beautiful. All residence halls and apartments are suite-style containing double and single rooms. Many facilities, such as Academic Village and the Towers, are relatively new, and living there is a pleasure. My on-campus furnished apartment has four single bedrooms, two bathrooms, a kitchen and a common room. We also have access to a state-of-the-art gym. The Marketplace is the dining hall, which provides sufficient variety for students who utilize it on a daily basis. Another one is under construction. In addition, there are three Subways, a Burger King, a Sbarro, a mini convenience store, Geoffrey's Coffee, a Natura's Table, Red Brick Pizza, Reflections and more on campus. There have been a few crimes in the past few months, but the campus police and residence hall staff do an excellent job making students feel as safe as possible.

Current student, English, 8/2003-Submit Date, June 2007

UCF on-campus housing is amazing. There is no school in the state that has on-campus housing like UCF. The dorms have maids who come once a week to vacuum and clean the bathrooms! All dorms have AC (unlike most Florida schools) and the on-campus dining hall is a hotspot for people who do and don't live on campus. The facilities are all new and UCF has done an exceptional job creating an environment that fosters community, such as the new on-campus leisure pool and retail center near the new basketball arena. To sum up the quality of life, everybody at UCF is excited about what is going to happen next year with the new on-campus stadium, basketball arena, and so many other things the university is committing, like a new medical school that is going to change the entire city of Orlando. The campus is beautiful, especially at night when it is all lit up, and the fountains and grassy fields provide the common student with so many chances to relax. I believe the quality of life at UCF is really unmatched . Another factor regarding UCF that I think all students should consider is safety. UCF is very safe, with a very enhanced security system on campus and a shuttle system that students can call to be escorted via golf cart anywhere on campus.

Alumnus/a, Biology, 8/2003-Submit Date, March 2007

All housing buildings are suite style, so there are no communal bathrooms! They are all new (or recently renovated) and very convenient for class. The new stadium looks amazing and the arena will be brand-new next fall, as well. The gym has state-of-the-art equipment, recently replaced after the 2004 hurricanes. They offer many group classes, outdoor ropes courses, a rock wall and a resort style pool!!

There are blue lights around campus for safety and it's generally well-lit. The campus police patrol the streets and have been known to give jay walking tickets on occasion. Parking has greatly improved over the years, and there are eight garages on campus!

Current student, Engineering, 8/2005-Submit Date, March 2007

I think that we have some of the best housing here at UCF because we are able to live on campus in dorms or apartments. The rooms are new, clean and good-sized. In the off-campus housing, there are some issues with crime depending on where you live; however, there have never been any problems on campus or in most of the off-campus housing. The campus also has almost every activity possible. There are clubs for juggling, chocolate, sports (noncompetitive and competitive), music and much more. These organizations offer many different opportunities to meet people and have fun outside of courses and work.

Current student, 8/2004-Submit Date, April 2006

Most students at UCF have a high quality of life. The campus is beautiful and dynamic, filled with welcoming, happy and involved students. There are clean, suite-style residence halls available to freshmen, and on-campus apartments available for upperclassmen. Since most students in residence halls share rooms, the buildings usually contain community study rooms and kitchens. Students in the apartments live in groups of two or four, get their own bedrooms, and share the bathroom with one roommate, and the kitchen and living room with all of their roommates. Maids clean the dorms and apartments weekly. Resident assistants and housing staff work hard to maintain a safe, fun, educational campus safe for students to live and study. The Marketplace, Cafeteria is located near the residence halls. It has cereal and drink dispensers, a soup and salad bar, two entree stations, omelet station, a sandwich area, and a grill in the back with pizza, burgers and other items. Students with meal plans also receive flex dollars that they can use at other venues on campus, including Chick-fil-A, Island Grill, Java City and Reflections. There is also a Subway, Einstein Bagels, Smoothie King, Sbarro, Starbucks, Baha Burrito, a hot dog place, a convenience store, and a restaurant called Wackadoos.

Social Life

Current student, Engineering, 8/2004-Submit Date, June 2007

The biggest event on campus is Homecoming. It is a week-long event that will rock your world, ending with the biggest tradition at UCF, Spirit Splash! Friday afternoon, all the students get to do the one thing they've wanted to do the entire year:—jump into the Reflecting Pond! It is a crazy party of rubber duckies and splashing! If you want to make friends at UCF, it's very easy—get involved with a student organization that participates in Homecoming. Tons of work goes into a group's success at Homecoming, but you will have lots of laughs and great memories. I just can't believe that anyone who participates in skit night wouldn't make friends with the others in the skit. There's painting, dancing, acting, speaking, service events and so on, all during the week of Homecoming, and each year it is my favorite experience. This year on comedy night Bob Saget came to entertain the crowd. He was great!!

I am proud to be a part of the Greek system at UCF. I would highly recommend that you do a year without it, though, only because there is so much more to experience at UCF outside of Greek Life. There is so much more to explore on campus. I do feel that Greek Life has contributed to my stay at UCF very positively. I have met lots of people and really feel like I have done everything there is to do here. Greeks have great parties and go out together to the local bars. The socials with other fraternities and sororities are fun, too! But like I said, I think it is best to wait a year and get a grip on things.

Current student, Business, 8/2004-Submit Date, June 2007

There are about 10 popular bars and several smaller pubs within a few miles of campus, and such. The most popular places close by are the Knight Library, Knightly Scoop, Devaney's Too and Pounders. People go out every night of the week. For looking to get more dressed up, downtown Orlando is only about a 15-minute drive away and has more high-end clubs. Anyone over 21 hangs out on Wall St., mostly at Big Belly Brewery, Chillers and Latitudes. Other clubs include Antigua, Club Paris, Dragon Room and Tabu. (These lists could go on and on.) The nightlife is great.

Our Greek system is one of the largest and best in the nation. Check out http://greeklife.sdes.ucf.edu. Socially, this is the best way to meet people and get involved at UCF. Also, Pleasure Island (at Downtown Disney) is good for the 21-and-up crowd. As a random comment, we have a huge event funded every year by SGA called Universal Knights, where tickets are handed out to get into Islands of Adventure. It's pretty amazing, and so is living close enough to go to the theme parks on a regular basis. The dating scene is the same as at any university. Lots of single people, everywhere, who aren't necessarily looking for a significant other.

Current student, English, 8/2003-Submit Date, June 2007

Being in Orlando is obviously a huge advantage. There is an entire downtown where students can go to socialize and party and do whatever it is college students love to do. Personally, I love to use the downtown area to go on dates and get to know people better. There are some amazing restaurants that are actually quite inexpensive (and lots of expensive ones too!), you just have to find them.

I joined a fraternity when I was a sophomore, I can say that the Greek system at UCF provides a tremendous amount of opportunities to socialize and enhance one's involvement in the community. There are lots of bars nearby if you are really into the typical college scene. The Knight Library, Devaney's Too, and Pounders at the three biggest bars nearby. One of my favorite places is El Cerro, where I can get excellent Mexican food, an unmatched margarita, and an awesome time with my friends.

There are two large movie theaters within 10 minutes of campus, and Orlando has big concerts every week. If you are into shopping, there are also at least five malls within a half hour, some of them being extremely high class. Whether you are into large, mainstream concerts or underground, indie music, Orlando is a hub for good music, with House of Blues and other famous venues close by. Oh, and I don't even think I need to mention Disney and all of its benefits (Downtown Disney, the Boardwalk) and Universal's Attractions, too (like Citywalk, where Jimmy Buffett's Margaritaville is located!).

The School Says

The University of Central Florida's talented and diverse student body is attracted by its beautiful campuses, extensive undergraduate research and service-learning opportunities, experienced faculty members and exciting campus life.

UCF is the sixth-largest university in the nation, with more than 47,000 students; and the academic quality of UCF's students continues to increase as the university grows in size. UCF anticipates that a record 43 National Merit Scholars will enroll in fall 2007, and the average SAT score of first-year students exceeds 1200.

UCF is an academic and research leader in modeling and simulation, optics, computer science, nanotechnology, education and many other disciplines. Students benefit from exceptional internship opportunities in fields such as business, engineering and education, and service-learning partnerships with Junior Achievement, Orlando-area schools and many nonprofit organizations.

Hospitality management majors study on a new campus located near the nation's second-largest convention center and several of the nation's best-known theme parks. Pending accreditation, a new College of Medicine will open in 2009 and will be part of a burgeoning health sciences cluster in Central Florida.

UCF supports partnerships that focus on student development and learning in a safe environment where students can lead healthy and productive lifestyles; develop leadership skills and a sense of civic responsibility; and support diversity and inclusiveness.

The UCF Knights will play their home football games on campus for the first time in fall 2007 in the new, 45,000-seat Bright House Networks Stadium, and a new 10,000-seat arena that will host basketball games and concerts is also opening this fall.

Read all of Vault's College Surveys at **www.vault.com/college**–get complete surveys on 100s of colleges and universities, expert advice on applicaton essays and more.

VAULT CAREER LIBRARY **161**

University of Florida

Office of Admissions
201 Criser Hall
P.O. Box 114000
Gainesville, FL 32611-4000
Admissions phone: (352) 392-1374
Admissions URL: www.admissions.ufl.edu/ugrad/

 Admissions

Current student, 8/2003-Submit Date, December 2006

Florida continues to strive for academic greatness and is increasingly selective when admitting prospective students. However, solid test scores on the SAT or ACT will help immensely, as will letters of recommendation from UF alumni or boosters. I'm an out-of-state student, so the criteria were even more difficult. If you have doubts about getting accepted into UF, I also recommend applying for the Summer B session. Fewer students apply for this, as most high school seniors expect to start college in the fall, so the admissions criteria are a bit more relaxed.

> **Regarding Admissions, UF says:** "Admission to the University of Florida has become more and more selective each year. Because the number of applications far exceeds the number of spaces available for any term, we must make fine distinctions between many good applicants. All applications receive a comprehensive review of academic and non-academic information, including an evaluation of the high school record, standardized test scores (SAT or ACT), essay, honors, awards and extracurricular activities. The Office of Admissions is committed to employing equitable admissions process to ensure all applicants a thorough review of selection criteria."

Alumnus/a, 8/2001-8/2006, October 2006

While UF claims that it is becoming increasingly selective, it is still easy to gain admittance. Due to the volume of individuals who wish to attend, UF considers GPA and SAT score first and then everything else. However, individuals with high levels of involvement in high school are considered even if their GPA and SAT scores are lower than average. If you are not an excellent candidate, applying for a summer semester will make the process easier. Additionally, there are special programs for various ethnic groups tied to certain majors, like engineering, that one can attend with a lower GPA and SAT score.

Alumnus/a, 8/2002-12/2005, February 2006

The admissions process was very easy. I am a resident of Florida, so I had a three-page, simple application. I filled it all out on the last day and gave it to my guidance counselor, who sent it in to the University of Florida. The whole process took roughly two hours. The school is selective but I was in the International Baccalaureate (IB) program, which the school loves. I had no problem getting in, and I think only one student in my IB class of about 50 who applied to the University of Florida was not accepted. There was no interview and the essay was short if there was one, I don't remember exactly. SATs are important, as UF is concerned with rankings, as is every school, and a large component is the SAT score.

Current student, 8/2001-Submit Date, November 2005

As a MINAMBA member, and Minority Ambassador at the University of Florida, I spend much of my time with admissions officers. The University of Florida, like many schools today, is looking to increase minority enrollment. But contrary to popular belief, UF is only looking for the best of the best, for the leaders and over-achievers. There have been many with 3.5+ GPAs who have been turned away, which is mainly due to the fact that UF is beginning to cap or decelerate undergraduate admissions and increase graduate admissions in an effort to rise even farther in the rankings. Although GPAs and test scores matter a great deal, a mediocre essay can demolish or bolster. It has often been said,

but let me reiterate:—The essay is crucial. You want to show them that you are a good writer, that you are articulate and well-rounded, and to show different sides of yourself. Your ability to do this is especially key for undergraduate admission.

Current student, 8/2004-Submit Date, October 2005

University of Florida weights students on their GPA, SAT scores and involvement in high school. Florida focuses on creating a strong well-rounded institution with students of many different backgrounds, race and educational experiences. The university looks for leaders among high school seniors who were highly involved in extracurricular activities and managed to keep their grades up in accelerated courses, such as advanced placement or IB programs.

Current student, 7/2001-Submit Date, October 2004

Getting in was no problem. I graduated high school in the Daytona Beach area with an International Baccalaureate Diploma. At the time, the University of Florida, highly regarded students graduating with this diploma. From what I can tell, the admissions board has become more selective since then. The classes are becoming harder and the incoming freshmen are smarter is what I keep hearing.

Current student, 8/2002-Submit Date, December 2004

The admissions process for in-state applicants was comparable to other in-state schools. There were two basic essays required on topics, such as "Describe a challenge you experienced and how you handled it" and "Describe a situation that changed you and why." There were no interviews. Requirements are getting more selective every year. Right now, National Merit attendance is a school priority, so those students are almost always ensured admission.

Current student, 6/2002-Submit Date, April 2005

The first step is getting your application in as soon as possible. UF is a very competitive school, so the earlier the better. Your SATs, GPA and even HS extracurricular activities will play a role. Another point of advice I can give is to make sure you contact the admissions office. Speak with an advisor there and strike up a rapport. And lastly, set yourself up for success and work hard in HS, it's only going to get harder in college.

 Academics

Current student, Engineering, 8/2003-Submit Date, December 2006

I'm a civil engineering student with an English minor. The workload for engineering consumes much of my free time, but I have found a good balance with fraternity life, campus involvement and study habits. UF has a great engineering program, which is evident in the quality teachers I have on a consistent basis. Several UF professors are nationally known and recognized in various engineering organizations. Many freshmen take a light courseload (12 credits) their first semester to acclimate to the extremely social fall at the University of Florida. Personally, I re-took Calculus I in college even though I tested out of it in high school to ensure that I could handle the work to come. Getting into large classes (Economics, Calculus, Chemistry, Physics, Elementary English,) is fairly easy, but you must ensure you don't miss your registration time, which is given to you on ISIS (Integrated Student Information System). Several freshmen get into trouble because they don't meet with their advisor prior to registering for classes, which develops a hold on their records preventing them from registering. Failing to get into a class can really hurt a student's graduation schedule at UF, so I recommend any students here stays close with his/her advisor and does not miss any registration deadlines. To put some numbers to the above information: As an engineer taking 15 credits per semester, I can expect to spend about 18 hours a week, in class, at least, (some three-credit classes meet more than three hours per week), and another five to 15 hours per week studying.

Alumnus/a, 8/2002-5/2006, September 2006

For the most part, academics were not too strenuous but definitely not for slackers. Sometimes hard to get into popular classes, especially if you haven't taken a lot of hours yet. Since the university is so large, many of the basic undergrad classes are taught by grad students; the smaller, more specialized classes are lead by professors. You do have to make an effort to get one-on-one attention by going to office hours or using the free tutoring resources that the university offers.

Alumnus/a, Pre-med, 8/2003-7/2005, March 2007

Academics are challenging. It is not too difficult in that it is not designed to make students fail, but it is designed to help challenge students to put in the extra effort if needed. Academics are very organized and structured.

Quality of classes is great. There is a number of teachers who care about a students success. They do more than just make sure the student achieves a passing grade. They want the student to learn and apply both knowledge and skills to his/her future. The larger classes are a bit more difficult. They are not personalized and the online classes makes attendance slim. The professors of the larger classes are not as involved with the students. They are more involved in their research and leave the teaching assistants to help the students out.

Alumnus/a, Marketing, 7/2001-5/2005, July 2006

I was a marketing major and felt that the business program was pretty simple. Most of the general business classes can be watched on TV or on the Internet, so there is rarely a need to go to class in person. Exams are scheduled in lecture halls throughout campus to accommodate thousands of students in a single class. Once you get into the classes specific to your major, there are much smaller class sizes of 20 to 30 people and you are able to get more interaction with the professors. The marketing program is ranked Number 12 in the country and has some really outstanding faculty.

Alumnus/a, Business, 8/2002-12/2005, February 2006

Many of the classes are taught online. You can go to the live lectures but very few people do. It all comes down to how you do on three or four tests. In many of your main classes, they have begun to add more homework/quizzes. The professors are very good, for the most part. I would definitely recommend getting to know them as early as possible. I was in the business school and never had a problem getting the classes I needed. The workload was bearable, not too hard.

Current student, 8/2004-Submit Date, October 2005

Popular classes are nearly impossible to get unless you have some kind of inside connection through a staff member. Registration priority is given first to honors students, and then to other students based upon the total number of credit hours taken and passed. As a freshman, you will be stuck taking terrible electives, so I'd recommend trying to get all the Gen Eds out of the way and registering for more popular classes later on.

Workload for courses varies by which course. Some classes are taught strictly over the Internet (Electronic Platform or EP classes) and require very little work. Some students don't watch these classes or buy the book, and instead opt to purchase Smokin'Notes which are like *Cliff Notes* for a class and will almost guarantee that you get an A.

Current student, 8/2000-Submit Date, March 2005

Since UF is such a big school, you have to learn how to take care of yourself. We have anywhere between 27,000 to 35,000 undergrads on and off campus, so professors and advisors do not have time to hold your hand and explain everything to you. If you need hand-holding, make sure you want to major in one of the smaller colleges where the advisors have time to talk to you one-on-one. That's not to say that if you want to have your hand held, you can't make it happen. Make appointments so you can get the same advisor every time, go and see your professors in their office hours. They will help you, but like I said, you have to put in the effort.

Getting into classes can be a problem as registration goes by the grade level. So freshmen coming in with no credits pretty much get to pick classes after everyone else. It's not that bad, though the administration does make an attempt to save spots in core required classes. But don't even bother trying to get into any of the easy athletic classes (Bowling, Aerobic Dance, Football, Soccer, Baseball) until you're at least a junior or an athlete. Grading depends on the professor.

Some classes, your entire grade depends on three or four tests over the whole semester; no HW, no attendance, nothing else. Others take everything into account, some don't have exams at all, just classwork and activity grades. Some teachers also grade on the bell curve, which sucks for you if you have a 94 and 20 people have higher grades because you will still get a B.

 ## Employment Prospects

Current student, 8/2003-Submit Date, December 2006

A UF degree garners great attention from employers. At the ultimate extreme, there are some building construction employers that will only hire UF graduates because of the quality of that particular program. Since UF is so large (about 50,000 students), employers are always available to give information and recruit college graduates. Our Career Resource Center is very helpful; and since UF is so big and there are so many alumni, many times graduates find that the people interviewing them are gators, as well. I receive about three e-mails per day from my advisor regarding internship or job opportunities, so there is no dearth of information about the job market at UF.

Alumnus/a, 8/2002-5/2006, September 2006

The employment prospects vary greatly depending on the individual college you are in. There are career fairs hosted every semester (although most of the fairs are for business or engineering students), and the Career Resource Center offers a lot of classes and info for all fields. The university carries a high prestige, especially within the state, but some of the prestige varies by the program in which you are enrolled. Most of the grads I know got jobs either before graduation or within two or three months of graduation.

Alumnus/a, Pre-med, 8/2003-7/2005, March 2007

The employment prospects are great at the University of Florida! UF is a well-known school and the quality of students who come out of UF is known amongst employers. Every fall and spring semester, the top employers and top companies come out to UF for the career fair and hold multiple on-campus interviews and information sessions about employment at their company.

Graduates obtain all types of jobs for all kinds of positions. UF has a very strong and well-known business school. Its accounting program is one of the top programs in the country. UF's engineering program is also one of the top programs so graduates come out with very successful careers. Graduates can take all kinds of jobs from sales positions to design, to analyst. It really depends on what a company is looking for, but usually they look for the top quality from University of Florida students.

Alumnus/a, 7/2001-5/2005, July 2006

UF provides exceptional career resources. There is a Career Resource Center on campus that offers career counseling, mock interviews and résumé guidance. There are two job fairs on campus each year that attract some fantastic companies from all over the country. Many companies do on-campus interviews throughout the year. Most students complete at least one internship before graduating, if not more.

Current student, 8/2004-Submit Date, October 2005

The University of Florida is without a doubt the most prestigious school in Florida. Regional employers recognize this and have been hiring students for years. We are starting to gain exposure from major national employers (in business: Goldman Sachs, Bain & Co.). The alumni base is extremely dedicated to hiring graduating Gators, so this is a huge driver for UF hiring. Internships result in the majority of hiring for people, so you want to land a great internship during the summer after your junior year.

The school hosts a biannual career showcase that most of the employers attend. I would also recommend making yourself known to tenured professors and getting on their good side. I have received more than 20 interviews or offers through referrals from professors in the business school.

Read all of Vault's College Surveys at www.vault.com/college–get complete surveys on 100s of colleges and universities, expert advice on applicaton essays and more.

VAULT CAREER LIBRARY **163**

 Quality of Life

Current student, 8/2003-Submit Date, December 2006

Freshman dormitories are not of high quality, although they are very social. Since UF does have so many undergraduates, living accommodations are certainly not the best in the country. Other housing, like apartments and duplexes around campus, however, can be extremely nice. Several apartments boast a main pool with balconies, courtyards and plush vegetation. UF's campus itself is very nice, as the facilities are old, traditional brick buildings that give the students a sense of belonging to something that has been around for a long time. The football stadium here is the best in the country. I've traveled to several other large colleges (Texas, LSU, Clemson, Wisconsin), and all stadiums pale in comparison to the Swamp, which is by far the nicest and loudest.

Alumnus/a, 8/2002-5/2006, September 2006

The campus has over 7,500 students living there, plus an additional 2,000 or so grad students living in special grad/family housing. The on-campus housing is well maintained and sponsors many events throughout the year. There are also plenty of apartment complexes in town. Lots of food facilities are on campus, from cafeterias serving buffet meals to fast-food places like Wendy's, to a nice, sit-down buffet restaurant in the student union. The campus has its own police department with lots of units on patrol and security devices like phone poles scattered all over campus. Off campus, security isn't quite as high, but for the most part as long as you follow common sense and avoid certain high-crime areas, crime isn't a problem.

Alumnus/a, Pre-med, 8/2003-7/2005, March 2007

Quality of life at UF is not spectacular, but it is nice. Since Gainesville is primarily a college town, many students seek housing off campus and thus live on their own outside of the university influence. The city is aimed towards students, as that is the main population, so quality of life is enjoyable at the least. Not too big or crowded, and the schedules of restaurants and many stores are nearly perfect for the student lifestyle.

Current student, Pre-med, 8/2004-Submit Date, December 2006

The biggest thing I have to say about housing is that renting an apartment at UF costs the same amount of money as a dorm room. I like the variety of dining options at UF, although a great deal of these places are more suited for younger students, as some dining places do not accept credit cards. They only accept cash and whatever the credit system is used for Gator Dining. The campus seems safe to me. I don't feel like it is unsafe to walk around campus at night because most of the campus is well lit. The campus facilities are impressive. Between the South West Recreation Center, Lake Wauberg and the sport facilities, UF's facilities are more than adequate.

Current student, 8/2002-Submit Date, May 2006

The dorms on campus are social and respectable. Students, typically freshmen and some sophomores, live in the dorms the first year or so and are exposed to dorm-wide activities that cater to students. The campus is beautiful and always clean. There are several large dining halls on campus as well as a student union that provides food from various franchises (e.g. Wendy's, Subway, an Italian eatery, a Chinese food and sushi bar, and a coffee shop). The student union is the hub of campus and is open quite late. There are at least four large libraries on campus that are open into the early morning, as well. There are emergency lights and phones on every corner of the university and almost never any crime on or around campus.

Current student, 8/2002-Submit Date, December 2004

Gainesville, Florida is a town centered around the University of Florida and its students. Housing is available on campus, but is primarily available for only first- and second-year students. However, there is a multitude of apartments within walking distance of the school and the efficient RTS bus system is utilized by the majority of off-campus students, since parking is so limited on campus. The facilities at the school include two state-of-the-art recreation facilities, two dining halls, several tennis courts and pools, six libraries and two computer labs.

The school says: "There are nine campus libraries that hold more than 4 million volumes and include the George A. Smathers Libraries, the Health Science Library and the Legal Information Center. The largest is Library West, which houses the humanities and social sciences collections, and features group study rooms, a digital media center, faculty studies, graduate studies, training rooms, public computers and a variety of study areas on six floors."

The latest closing library is only open until 1 a.m. on weekdays. There is one 24-hour computer lab, but it is difficult to find any open seats during finals weeks. The Gainesville police department and student government have been working on initiatives to make the campus safer, including increased lighting around campus and more blue light police responders. Two additional after-hours buses will pick up students and transport them anywhere on campus, and more university police department cars patrol after dark.

Social Life

Alumnus/a, Communications, 8/1998-12/2002, July 2007

University of Florida has a very diverse and active social life. There are parties almost every weekend, and the Greek scene is prevalent. Within walking distance of campus are a row of nightclubs and bars to which many can walk for a fun night out.

Gator Growl is also an enjoyable annual event for which thousands of students, faculty, alumni, family and fans gather to rally some team spirit for the Florida Gators. This event is a paid seating event and includes live entertainment, speeches, guest appearances by local celebrities and a spectacular light show. Even if you are not into the football games, you have to attend Gator Growl at least once to experience the best of student life.

Current student, 8/2003-Submit Date, December 2006

Since Gainesville is a college town, the local bars treat it as such and do not overcharge for drinks. There are drink specials every night at different places and bottles range from $1 to $2. Ladies night is every night and bars rarely even need to advertise it. We have two main areas to go out: midtown (traditional bars and heavy Greek attendance), and downtown (several more clubs, larger venues, and Gainesville residents more expensive than midtown). I am a male and the women here are some of the most beautiful and intelligent in America. Getting a significant other is no problem, especially in your sophomore year when you are more accustomed to college life and have matured some from your high school self.

I am a huge proponent of going Greek at UF. I did so my freshman year and the connections, social experiences, friendship and leadership opportunities are unparalleled. Fraternities and sororities have some kind of social event—whether amongst themselves or the community—every week. They do service and philanthropies as well, and boast higher average GPAs than the overall student body. Going Greek offers the student a more close-knit sense of community in a student body of 50,000, networking in a smaller group. Specific restaurants and bars to attend are: Bars—The Swamp Restaurant (bar by night restaurant by day, this is the signature place of UF), Sloppy Gator, Grog House, Gator City, Lillian's, Rehab, Whiskey Room, and Rue Bar; Restaurants—Liquid Ginger (delicious Thai food, best I've ever had), Ballyhoo, Bonefish, Dragonfly (sushi), Pita Pit (late night), and of course Hooters.

Alumnus/a, Pre-med, 8/2003-7/2005, March 2007

Social life is excellent at UF. Enough cannot be said about the social life at UF. Plenty of on-campus events bring many people together. The many groups and organizations bring people together with common interests and backgrounds. Making friends and having a social group is never a problem. The sports teams at UF have been doing great as of late, which also brings the entire student body together and all have a great time.

There are plenty of bars in the city—none on campus, but plenty to go around downtown and in other areas. These are all ranges of restaurants from high class to fast food, whatever a student may desire. Dating scene is also good as there are plenty of social events to meet new people. Again, enough cannot be said about UF's social life. A student can have a great time and also receive an education to help excel far in the future.

Current student, 8/2003-Submit Date, October 2005

Downtown Gainesville is full of social activities. Bars and clubs close at 2 a.m., which is usually a great bummer. There are buses that shuttle students to and from campus and other student-populated areas in Gainesville—anything to keep people from drinking and driving.

There are about 63 different Greek organizations—not including the honors and academic organizations with Greek letters. The options range from the Divine Nine (historically African-American fraternities and sororities), to Kappa Phi Lambda (the new Pan-Asian interest sorority), to Delta Delta Delta (a social sorority). There are four Greek councils—the two social councils, the National Pan-Hellenic Council, and the Multicultural Greek Council.

Student organizations are very popular here on campus. There are over 400 registered student organizations, from the Rock Paper Scissors Club to the Falling Gators (sky-diving club), to the Hispanic Student Association.

There are also two places—the Institute of Hispanic-Latino Cultures and the Institute of Black Culture—where all students can come, hang out, eat free food and learn about different cultures. These are great places for new freshmen, where they can meet future friends and have some help adjusting to college life.

Current student, 8/2002-Submit Date, December 2004

Gainesville is a town centered around its students. Restaurants, bars and clubs all cater to the student population with reasonable covers, drinking specials and late hours. The Later Gator bus route will transport students for free from campus area locations to downtown Gainesville where most of the bars and clubs are located. Additional bars and clubs are located on University Avenue., just across the street from the college stadium.

There is also a multitude of trendy restaurants serving foods ranging from sushi, to Mexican food. Student organizations are easy to join or establish. There are literally hundreds of different organizations meeting any type of interest imaginable. Because there are so many different school clubs, there are several student events every day and evening at the school. From prominent guest speakers, such as President Bill Clinton and documentarian Michael Moore, to philanthropic activities, such as Dance Marathon, there are always interesting events for students to enjoy.

There is also a massive Greek network. Sorority and fraternity members comprise the most organizationally active students on campus. They hold many events throughout the year, though they are often closed off to non-Greek students. And of course, one of the best aspects of attending the University of Florida is the football games at our Swamp stadium. The Florida Gators have just signed on a new coach, Urban Meyer, who has high hopes of leading the Florida Gators to another SEC championship. There are some more upscale clubs (guys have to wear collared shirts, dress pants and no sneakers allowed) but for the most part, just throw on some jeans, flip flops and a cute shirt, and you're good to go.

The School Says

The University of Florida ranks among the top public research universities in the United States. In 1985, Florida became a member of the Association of American Universities, the prestigious higher-education organization comprised of only 63 public and private institutions in North America.

UF's Honors Residential College at Hume Hall was the first honors residential college designed and constructed specifically for honors students in the United States. In 2006, UF's incoming class had an average 3.99 GPA and 2241 SAT score. Its freshman retention rate of 94 percent is among the highest in the U.S. UF admitted 1,049 International Baccalaureate graduates for the 2004-2005 academic year, more than any other university in the world.

The University of Florida and the City of Gainesville have much to offer the more than 50,000 students who pursue an education here. UF consistently attracts world-class symphony orchestras, Broadway plays, opera and ballet performances. Among UF's artistic venues are a permanent collection of more than 6,000 original works, the largest natural history museum in the Southeast, musical and theatrical centers, two television stations and four radio stations. The McGuire Lepidoptera Center at the Florida Museum of Natural History has a collection of 8.5 million butterflies and moths, making it the largest in the world, with about 100,000 more specimens than London's Natural History Museum.

On the athletic front, Florida is, of course, well known for its national championship basketball and football teams. However, there is much more. UF has ranked among the nation's 10 best athletic programs in each of the last 20 years. Florida couples its strong intercollegiate sports program with more than 50 intramural and club sports ranging from badminton to wrestling. More than 90 percent of students take advantage of the numerous outdoor courts and playing fields, and the various indoor facilities on campus.

The UF student body follows an honor code and is voluntarily committed to the highest standards of honesty and integrity. The learning experience at UF continues outside the classroom through a myriad of activities and services that include resources for students with disabilities, judicial affairs, Greek life and multicultural affairs. Counseling and career resources are also available.

The Reitz Student Union serves as a clearinghouse for student organizations and activities, as well as a place to meet. It houses an art gallery, movie theater, video game room, bowling alley, numerous restaurants and more. When school is in session, every Friday night is Gator night, when offerings can include free movies, bands, dances, billiards and more.

Read all of Vault's College Surveys at www.vault.com/college–get complete surveys on 100s of colleges and universities, expert advice on applicaton essays and more.

VAULT CAREER LIBRARY   165

University of Miami

Admissions Office
P.O. Box 248025
Coral Gables, FL 33124
Admissions phone: (305) 284-4323
Admissions URL: www.miami.edu

 ## Admissions

Alumnus/a, 9/1999-5/2003, November 2006

Miami is dedicated to improving its ranking to get into the Top 50. This isn't a secret, they state it openly on their web site, and I often read about it alumni e-mails. I got in with a good SAT but a weak GPA that had an upward trend.

Alumnus/a, 8/2000-5/2003, April 2006

The admissions process was nerve-wracking, because you are not sure what they want. After I was accepted, I realized that they just wanted well-balanced students, which meant knowing when to have fun and when to buckle down to get work done. The only stressful part of the admissions process was my interview for a full-time scholarship because it meant that I would be attending a prestigious, private university absolutely free!

Current student, 8/2003-Submit Date, April 2006

Admissions counselors visited my high school to present the University of Miami. I was impressed by the presentation and visited the campus before my high school junior year. I was introduced to the Summer Scholar Program by the admissions representative. During the summer, high school students can enroll in this program. Not only do the high school students earn college credits, but by living in the dorms for six weeks, they can survey the school. I was impressed; University of Miami became my first choice during the college application process. When meeting with the admissions representative, I was given guidance for my application. It helped to take my grades with me because the admissions representative was very encouraging. The application included a primary form and a secondary form. The secondary forms included four short essays. I chose the Early Decision option and had an offer on December 15, with an academic scholarship.

Current student, 8/2004-Submit Date, January 2006

The admissions process was something that I felt was very important. I took my time, especially with the University of Miami because it was my primary choice, to fill out all application and recommendation requirements with extreme detail. Since they were going to be deciding between hundreds, maybe thousands of kids with exactly the same grades, I felt I should list anything and everything that might give me an advantage over other students. Do not be afraid to submit everything, since you never know what might catch their eye. Include all sports, jobs, clubs, additional schooling or skills, or any other programs of which you might be a part. GPA and SAT scores alone are often not enough to give you the edge over other students. For the essay, pick something personal, something that will let them know your character, and stick to the length requirements. I wrote about my high school varsity ice hockey state championship and about a problem that occurred in my family and how we got through it. For the recommendations, pick someone who got to know you as more than just a student, maybe someone who was a coach. I did not have to interview; I only had to complete an application with my transcripts and SAT/ACT scores.

Current student, 8/2001-Submit Date, January 2005

It seems like the admissions process has grown increasingly competitive since I first entered the school. I arrived with eligibility to be an honors student my freshman year. However, now incoming freshmen have to achieve higher academic standing in high school in order to apply for honors admission. Also, the University of Miami has been raising its SAT and ACT standards over the past four years. I did not have to interview when I was a freshman, nor did I have a high SAT score (I had a 1020). Rather, I believe the school looks for diversity in academic and athletic areas.

UofM seeks the creative student who offers something unique to the university. For example, I was the senior editor of my yearbook in high school, captain of the varsity soccer and softball teams, and an honor roll student. I think Miami wants students who can adapt to various situations. Diversity is the key word. Finally, Miami has a lot to offer for students with disabilities. I myself was offered disability services and have been involved in this department for four years now. Students with disabilities will find their needs met at the University of Miami.

Alumnus/a, 8/1999-12/2002, December 2003

The University of Miami is great because it offers merit-based scholarships, not just scholarships based on financial need. I attended the university and got a half ride without even having a single interview, just through test scores, grades and academic performance. The essays were by no means difficult. If you do the best you can before applying, they take care of the rest for you. It's easy, painless and, ultimately, handsomely rewarding.

 ## Academics

Alumnus/a, 9/1999-5/2003, November 2006

Quality of classes is good though I have nothing to compare them to except high school. Poli sci and business school classrooms are amazing. Every student gets a leather chair! Professors are decent, some good ones, some bad. Many of them were focused on their own research and not as much on teaching. I guess that's true at most places. Getting into popular classes is not a problem, for the most part. Grading is fair. Workload is pretty light for social sciences. Lots of time to do whatever you want. Your classmates will probably be your biggest let-down if you're a brainy type. Although there are a few really smart people among them.

Current student, 8/2003-Submit Date, April 2006

As freshmen, students are required to take the English and Math core courses required for a BS. A student may declare his/her major/minor at the end of freshman year. There are some students who are enrolled into the general honors program right from the first day of school. Based on my freshman grades, I was inducted into the general honors program. Along with general honors, the university has a departmental honors program for approved programs in junior and senior years. The honors classes have small class sizes; about 10 to 15 students or fewer. The pre-med department advises students on which track they should follow if they are interested in going to medical school after graduation. I am an environmental health science major, chemistry minor and I follow one of the suggested tracks for pre-med studies. The pre-med department head also helps student with medical school applications and recommendations. Besides a pre-med advisor, each student has an advisor based on major. This system helps students graduate on time. Most professors at this university are helpful, flexible and want you to do well. The professors are graduates from the top-ranked schools in the nation and expect a high standard from their students. Grading is usually tough, with an A at 95 percent. Some professors tend to favor the bell curve, which is not popular with the student body. Workload depends on the professor and course; it varies. For BS students, the hard classes are Organic Chemistry and Physics. Both of these classes have tough professors who show no mercy. A lot of students come to hate these classes. If a professor is not up to the standard, his/her contract is not renewed. Surveys posted online for most professors, help the students pick their teachers. To get into the popular classes, a student needs to register early. Though the honors classes are small, the regular classes for the general science subjects are large. MyUM (formerly known as Easy), the student web site, is efficient enough to help the large classes run well. MyUM also keeps the students informed on their academic status, financial aid, parking, residence halls and meal plans.

Current student, 8/2004-Submit Date, January 2006

The pre-med program at the University of Miami is great. They have six- and seven-year programs that commit you to their medical school from the beginning. The six-year program is something which you come into college. If you meet the requirements, you can join the program. This is an extremely intense program and requires a lot of work and dedication. The seven-year program is based on your first-year GPA and requires an invitation from the school after your freshman year. I am taking a pre-med track with a biology major. My core classes are science, mostly large lecture hall classes. The popular classes are usually not a problem to get; however, it is often hard to get the time you desire. As you become an upperclassman, this is not a problem. I feel that the quality of classes are great; the teachers are all extremely knowledgeable and, for the most part, always willing to help. To achieve A's you have to work hard, but if you do the required reading and study a little each day, it does not get overwhelming. If you do your work, join study groups and don't leave everything to the last minute, you can achieve great grades.

> The school says: The pre-med program is currently seven or eight years as of fall 2004-05.

Current student, 8/2001-Submit Date, January 2005

I am a double major, which is required by the School of Communication. I major in both advertising and international studies. Roughly 98 percent of the professors at my school have their PhDs. Also, Miami offers an intimate class setting with a low student-to-teacher ratio. Since there are only 20 to 30 people in each classroom per teacher, this allows for a better academic environment with high interaction and participation for each student. Each student (if he/she chooses) can easily have a personal relationship with the professor which greatly increases the rate at which a student is able to learn and the ability of the teacher to reach each student individually.

> The school says: The students-to-professor ratio is 13:1.

Alumnus/a, 8/1999-12/2002, December 2003

Honors students have easy access into any classes because they get to register before the other students. That was a big plus, and a lot less of a hassle. Other students always had difficulty. English and creative writing professors are top-of-the-line published writers, easily approachable and generally kindhearted. The anthropology department is also top-of-the-line, encouraging, helpful and understanding. In general, all the professors are well studied, easy to reach and willing to help.

Alumnus/a, 8/1999-5/2003, September 2003

The University of Miami is the perfect place for learning both inside and outside of the classroom. Depending on the major there is quite a variance in terms of workload. Sociology is a common easy major, and engineers and nurses have it tough, often being required to carry an 18-credit minimum. The quality of classes varies depending on how each individual qualifies the word "quality." I prefer smaller classes, which are very common at the University of Miami. However, be careful: There are weeding-out classes in some departments that are large lecture halls of over 100 people and often involve a massive curve. To improve the quality of classes and relationships with professors, join the honors program if you have the grades as a sophomore or incoming freshman. The University of Miami is also usually great about having enough sections of popular classes to satisfy the student body. The earlier you register, the easier it is, and the registration system isn't horrible.

Employment Prospects

Alumnus/a, 8/2002-5/2006, November 2006

The Toppel Career Center is amazing. The job selection is especially good if you are a business major. I got two summer internships and my post-graduation job by attending the career fairs and using the Career Center resources.

Current student, 8/2003-Submit Date, April 2006

I am proud to be a University of Miami senior. Though I have no experience with seeking employment after graduation I do have experience interviewing with medical schools all over the country. I am sure not just my effort but the name tag, "University of Miami" had a role in me being accepted to three medical schools.

Current student, 8/2001-Submit Date, January 2005

I believe there are plenty of employment prospects at the University of Miami. Since I have been a senior, I have been inundated with e-mails offering me jobs for both of my majors. This is due to the fact that we have an online résumé that our school submits to different businesses around the world (all four years we attend). Also, we have incredible alumni and the University of Miami is considered by most employers to be a credible, highly academic university.

Alumnus/a, 8/1998-5/2002, December 2003

Career Services is there, but you must make the effort to keep up and know what services they provide and sign up before deadlines. Even alumni can benefit from The Toppel Career Center. Every service is there for the asking; just stay informed.

Alumnus/a, 8/1999-12/2002, December 2003

They are very willing to help, but unfortunately there were never any big opportunities for my major. I got a great internship through the university and learned a great deal from my boss, which I will carry with me through the rest of my corporate life. I use these skills every day. Career Center resources are endless, but you have to be willing to do it the way they want you to do it.

Quality of Life

Alumnus/a, 8/2002-5/2006, November 2006

I felt very safe on campus. It's a beautiful, cozy campus. It really feels like paradise. It is filled with endless palm trees and exotic plants. The campus has everything: a convenient store, pharmacy, health center, fitness center, post office, cafeteria, food court, Starbucks, Subway, TicketMaster, religious centers, tennis courts, swimming pools and more.

Current student, 8/2003-Submit Date, April 2006

University of Miami has good housing with numerous dorms, double and single rooms and apartments that can hold six students. All the student housing is on the campus with security guards, wall and gates. The university has open and garage parking for resident students. Non-resident students have metered parking. The bookstore and gift store are in the same space, thus making it convenient to shop. Along with the meal plans, the university has a food court and one upscale restaurant on campus. The university is located in Coral Gables, Florida and is not in a safe neighborhood, in my opinion. Most of Miami is not a safe neighborhood. The university tries to keep its campus safe with 24-hour security guards and has only one manned gate after 11 p.m. open for traffic.

> The school says: "The campus safety information is posted at miami.edu/public-safety/safety-matters-0506/safety-maters-0506.pdf"

Current student, 8/2004-Submit Date, January 2006

The housing for me has been a great experience. In my freshman year, I lived in the dorms where most freshmen live. Although these are not the nicest dorms on campus, they are the best for meeting people. Since most freshmen are in the dorms, everyone is in the same situation and looking to meet friends. Some of my best friends now are from my floor last year. You get to know everyone on your floor very well, if that is what you want. There are also on-campus apartments, that are very convenient, but I would recommend living in dorms and meeting people with whom you feel comfortable living with before getting an apartment. The cafeteria food is very good and offers a wide variety. I can always find something good in the cafeteria. There is also a Subway, Burger King, Starbucks, Sushi Tsunami, Chinese food, deli and Mexican food located around campus where you can pay with dining dollars given at the beginning of the semester based on your meal plan or with your own money. In my experience, I have always felt extremely safe. In each dorm, there is a student guard who sits at the entrance from 10 p.m. to 8 a.m. every day.

Read all of Vault's College Surveys at www.vault.com/college–get complete surveys on 100s of colleges and universities, expert advice on applicaton essays and more.

VAULT CAREER LIBRARY 167

Current student, 8/2001-Submit Date, January 2005

I lived in the dorms, my freshman year. I think they were above and beyond my standards (although I lived in the nicer ones of the bunch). Each dorm room shared a bathroom with only one other dorm room, and there are plenty of single dorm rooms offered. The living situation in the dorms is pleasant. The apartments are nice; however, most students opt to live off campus after their freshman year. The housing around the university is very nice and affordable. Parking is one of the most inconvenient aspects of the university. Many commuters and students receive parking tickets, and there are rarely enough parking spaces due to Coral Gables parking laws and permits. Students must carry quarters in their cars at all times! The campus is beautiful. I often say that our president must spend more money on landscaping than the international studies program that I attend. Either way, I have to admit we have one of the most beautiful campuses in the world, filled with palm trees and perfectly mowed lawns. Crime is somewhat of an issue outside of the radius of campus. On campus, however, there are few incidents reported and most students feel safe walking around at night. There are phones located all around campus in case of an emergency.

Alumnus/a, 8/1999-12/2002, December 2003

The campus is like a resort. It is absolutely spectacular for the art lover, the writer, the partier, the poet. Even the food in the cafeteria was good. I actually miss the stir-fry. I never felt more safe walking alone in the dark anywhere. The neighborhood is upscale and rich in terms of people, culture, opportunities and variety. There is always a place to go and something to do, day or night. It is great for the beach, the culture, the people, the weather, the architecture, everything. It's much better to go to school here than to live and work here. Four years is plenty.

Social Life

Current student, 8/2004-Submit Date, January 2006

The social life on and off campus is everything a student could want. Since it is located five minutes from Coconut Grove (location of bars, clubs and restaurants) and 20 minutes from the famous South Beach, the nightlife is always amazing. There are many people on campus that work as promoters, so you always know what is going on at clubs and bars. The football games are extremely fun and always packed with students, alumni and fans. Many bands come to play at the on-campus auditorium. This year, Green Day came and Fall Out Boy is coming soon. Greek life is also a big part of this university. The fra-

ternity/sorority housing is located close to classrooms. There are more than enough fraternities/sororities to match anyone's personality. There is a bar/restaurant on campus that does sell alcohol, it is not a dry campus. You are allowed to have alcohol in your dorm room if you are of age. There always seems to be something going on. I have had so much fun here and never once have I wished I had chosen to attend a different school.

Alumnus/a, 8/2002-5/2006, November 2006

Miami has everything. If you want to relax, you can spend your weekends lying out at the beaches yearround. The same goes for any outdoor sports (besides mountain climbing and skiing), since it's 70 to 80 degrees all the time.

If you like the club and bar scene, you can spend your nights partying until sunrise. Unlike most people, I lived on campus all four years with no car. Still, I never got bored and could always find something to do. The school provides transportation to the beaches and the local nightlife.

Current student, 8/2003-Submit Date, April 2006

The Miami beach is popular with the university students. Rathkeller on the campus is popular, along with some small restaurants just outside the campus. Because of Tri-Rail station just outside the campus gates, the students travel as far as Fort Lauderdale for good dining, shows and recreation.

Current student, 8/2001-Submit Date, January 2005

I sometimes wonder if the whole purpose students come to the University of Miami isn't of the social life. The City of Miami has everything to offer, including amazing clubs, bars, restaurants and city events, such as fairs, festivals, art clubs, dances and concerts. The Greek life at UM is also flourishing and steadily growing for such a small student population. I really don't see how any student couldn't find something to love in Miami.

Alumnus/a, 8/1999-12/2002, December 2003

Social life is out of control. Crazy frat parties, great bars, a million people to date, every niche you could imagine to find yourself in and more. The Greek system is stereotyped and intimidating, but where is it not? It's close to Coconut Grove and South Beach for clubs and bars galore, not to mention frat row. You can find whatever you want to do somewhere and close by. The Tavern, a particularly cramped, old bar in the Grove, is just that, but it's a great place to meet frat guys and sorority girls. Great 80s music, hard rock, sports on the TV. Go to Fat Tuesdays for daquiris, Hooters, the Cheesecake Factory, Moe's for beer, the beach if you want to spend more money. Thursday nights in the Grove is really where it's at.

University of South Florida

Admissions Office
4202 E. Fowler Ave., SVC1036
Tampa, FL 33620-6900
Admissions phone: (813) 974-3350
Admissions URL: www.usf.edu/admissions/

Admissions

Current student, 1/2003-Submit Date, August 2004

Admissions to USF is painless. It is a state school and really looks at grades and SAT scores and gives priority to students graduating from Florida high schools. Calling the Admissions Office can be challenging. People are not especially helpful. There are more than 30,000 registered students and there is little time for school employees to provide excellent service to students.

Financial aid works well as long as you have no problems. It is hard to receive assistance from people over the phone. The registration, admission and finan-

cial aid processes can all be accomplished online. This is relatively new to USF. It simplifies things for the students, but also contributes to the anonymous feeling that students experience.

> **The school says:** "Total enrollment is 45,056 students, 34,036 of which are undergraduates. The Tampa campus enrolls 38,521 students, 28,846 of which are undergraduates. The remaining students are enrolled at one of the university's regional campuses located in St. Petersburg, Lakeland and Sarasota."

Alumnus/a, Business, 1/2003-5/2007, June 2007

The application can be filled out online or printed out and turned in physically. The main key is to turn in your transcripts as soon as possible, whether from another college or high school. The second step would be to enroll in the campus tour visit. Even though it's an hour and 15 minutes of walking,g it is more than worth it. The following step should be to sign up for an orientation date. One thing to take into consideration is what kind of student you are. You are one of the following: a transfer with an associate's degree from community college, a transfer without an associate's degree, or a high school student, also known as first time in college. Deadlines, vary depending on the type of student you are. The selectivity varies as in: The higher the SAT, ACT, the lower your GPA can be, and vice versa. Also, if you apply before December 31, you are automatically submitted for scholarships.

Alumnus/a, 8/2001-5/2006, May 2006

The school is pretty easy to get into. Sometimes I hear it's getting harder to get in and sometimes I hear it's getting easier. All I had to do was fill out the college application. A woman at a college fair said that my SAT scores and GPA were a little above average, and that I did not need to attach an essay to the college application. So I didn't. Some people did, and some people didn't and they still made it into the school. At times, I think they accept everybody but I don't know. I don't know anyone who has applied here and been rejected.

> **The school says:** "When reviewing applications for admission, USF reviews high school curriculum, cumulative GPA, and SAT and ACT scores. For fall 2007, the middle 50 percent ranges for the freshman class were 3.44 to 4.0 on the high school GPA, 1060 to 1230 on the SAT and 23 to 27 on the ACT; 55 percent of our freshmen ranked in the top 20 percent of their high school class. Of the nearly 21,000 students who applied to USF in 2007, only 50 percent were offered admission to the freshman class."

Current student, 6/2004-Submit Date, November 2005

The University of South Florida is not a very selective school. I was a transfer student, so the admissions process was very easy for me to complete. I filled out an admissions application with a fee and also wrote a one-page essay. There is no interview required. All in all, the process was really simple and quick. There isn't a lot to do on the student's end but he/she must stay on top of the admissions department, as well as any other department helping him/her to ensure everything is entered into the system correctly. If you are transferring, make sure your transcripts are sent to the school in a timely manner and it would be good to keep an extra copy of certified transcripts just in case something were to happen during the process of admissions.

> **Regarding transfer admissions, USF says:** "USF welcomes close to 8,000 transfer students each year and has been cited by *U.S. News & World Report* as the top campus in the country for students transferring from another college."

Current student, 8/2005-Submit Date, October 2005

I first applied to the university and then waited for my acceptance. I had to mail in transcripts and all documents required. I made trips down to the university to get my name known and I met with counselors to set up financial plans and see what my options were. I selected University of South Florida as a second option to University of Florida because they have an excellent medical school. When selecting a school, you must be aware of cost of attendance, what kind of programs they offer and if you think you would do well at that university or school. Visiting the campus and doing campus tours also help you get a better perspective of the school and see if it is right for you.

Current student, 8/2004-Submit Date, February 2005

The admissions process was fairly straightforward and simple. There was the standard application, which I completed online, along with an essay. Within a few weeks, I was accepted. I applied to a few other schools, and USF is where I had the best admissions experience. They judge students fairly, based on grades, extracurricular activities, awards and honors, and college aptitude tests.

> **USF says:** "Freshman applicants should submit the following: an application for admission; a non-refundable $30 application fee; official high school transcript; official SAT or ACT scores (including SAT essay or ACT writing); and official GED or TOEFL scores, if applicable."

Alumnus/a, 1/2002-2/2004, September 2005

The admissions process to University of South Florida is not as painful [the process to] the junior college I attended. This school was helpful—as they were small enough to really care about the students. Getting in is as simple as filling out the application and dropping by the Admissions Office to drop off the application. Speaking to a counselor prior to applying helped the process.

 ## Academics

Current student, Education, 8/2005-Submit Date, June 2007

I have been extremely pleased with every single class I have taken at USF thus far. All my teachers have been passionate about their work as educators, yet see their students as equals. I have yet to come across a teacher who was not more than happy to spend some time out of class to discuss things in further detail. Because my professors are passionate about what they are teaching, I am passionate about what I am learning.

Alumnus/a, Pre-med, 8/2003-5/2006, December 2006

I was in the communication disorders department. We have some of the best faculty in the country. We are doing graduate and undergraduate research. The faculty and staff are also professional, on time and graded fairly. I also felt very comfortable with my professors in some general education classes. They were knowledgeable, easy to get along with, and if you took the time to get to know them, they would do the same for you.

Current student, 8/2002-Submit Date, October 2005

Overall, I wish the academics were a little better. As a business major, most of my basic classes are very large survey classes with over 200 students. Some of those classes have smaller labs, which really helped a lot, but in general, survey classes are very difficult environments in which to learn anything. As a member of the Honors College, I have smaller classes for some of my AA requirements, capped at 25 I think, but it may be smaller. I also get first day registration, which is really nice in a school this size. Many of my friends have difficulty getting the classes they need. Many majors don't open up enough sections or seats to accommodate demand.

Alumnus/a, 8/2000-8/2004, January 2006

Some programs have outstanding levels of teaching and teachers, and others much less so. The education, psychology and engineering programs are outstanding, ranked high on the nation's scale. The arts, however, are incredibly under-funded and the facilities are archaic. The level of teaching somehow survives in spite of this, and the students have a basic foundation readiness for the outside world. The quality of classes is good; but like 80 percent of the schools in the nation, the quality of education is directly related to level of challenge, and the level of responding to that challenge (self-motivation). Usually, by talking to professors and counselors, it is easy to find which classes are cakewalks and which are harder. Do you want your degree to be a ribbon or a reflection of attained educational enlightenment?

Current student, 6/2004-Submit Date, November 2005

Pretty easy-going classes. Getting into popular classes usually isn't a problem because there are waiting lists or you are able to go to the first meeting and request to take the place of someone who is absent. This usually requires a little legwork but will result in getting into that class. Grading is usually fair. Workload becomes increasingly more time-consuming but not very difficult. The semesters are mapped out for you beforehand but normally, students just make their own schedules according to what fits in their personal schedules.

Current student, 8/2005-Submit Date, October 2005

I am in the undergraduate program, majoring in bio-medical science. It is semi-easy to get into the classes you desire if you are quick to register when registering becomes available. My professors are very fair in their grading habits and the workload is, for the most, part manageable. I have to put in about an hour of reading for each hour I am in class to keep up with the course. There are also Internet sites that offer very helpful information with which to study and keep with school.

Alumnus/a, 8/1998-5/2004, April 2005

Academics at USF is usually ranked as an B+ in national rankings, but I would probably say that this is a bit low. I was a marketing major, and any and everything to do with the College of Business is an A+. The latest technology is present in every classroom and the professors are as good as it gets—most professors gave great office hours and many gave personal numbers to all the students to reach them at any time for emergency assistance.

The classes were always very well-organized and interesting; professors generally did a good job of making it interesting and easy to learn. In my five years

Read all of Vault's College Surveys at **www.vault.com/college**–get complete surveys on 100s of colleges and universities, expert advice on applicaton essays and more.

VAULT CAREER LIBRARY   **169**

at USF, I didn't have one class I wanted or needed that I didn't get. If the section is full, contacting the professor would allow him/her to open up a slot (this is a little-known fact), but professors enjoyed teaching even more when they were teaching people who were eager to be involved in the class.

Current student, 1/2003-Submit Date, August 2004

The women's studies program is academically challenging. The professors require excellence from students. USF is a commuter school that caters to working students. This is changing. So, many classes that used to be available to students in the evenings are now only available during the day. Classes often fill up early, so it is difficult to get the classes one needs. There seem to be fewer classes and more students. The professors are available to students, but make no special effort to provide support.

> **The school says:** "With 75 percent of USF students living within a two-mile radius of campus in a region called 'Bulls Country,' USF prefers to refer to students who do not live on campus as residents of an extended residential community."

 Employment Prospects

Alumnus/a, Business, 1/2003-5/2007, June 2007

With a degree in accounting from USF you will get a job. The Career Center offers multiple options for students. Résumé critiquing, interview building through virtual and live representatives. They also provide a system for employers to view your résumé and virtual interview online. The Career Center allows you to receive e-mails on job fairs, job placements, as well as using several different tests for those not sure on what to major. The career center also offers etiquette dinners for a minimal fee. There are many networking opportunities through Beta Alpha Psi (accounting) and Alpha Beta Psi (business). PricewaterhouseCoopers is a huge supporter of Beta Alpha Psi.

Current student, Education, 8/2004-Submit Date, May 2007

The University of South Florida is one of the most underrated universities in the Southeast, if not the country. Our graduates go on to lead extremely successful lives in all fields of the world. Some of our graduates are Major League Baseball club managers, successful politicians and former Miss Americas. USF is growing in popularity, and it is becoming known.

Current student, 6/2004-Submit Date, November 2005

All of the employers in the area usually come to the engineering building and set up a presentation table in order to attract any students searching for employment. There are internships available, which are both paid and unpaid if a student wants to go that route. Most of the employers in the area are also listed with our Career Center located on campus. We are able to join by paying $10 and uploading a current résumé to the database. This allows us to be in contact with employers in our area that are looking for part-time workers, full-time workers and interns.

> **Regarding on-campus recruiting, the school says:** "More than 800 employers visit USF each year with the intention of recruiting graduating students. Companies who routinely hire USF graduates include American Express, Bank of America, Black & Decker, Citigroup, Department of Homeland Security, GE, IBM, Microsoft, NASA, New York Yankees, Proctor and Gamble, Tampa Bay Buccaneers, Universal Studios and Walt Disney Corporation."

Alumnus/a, 1/2002-2/2004, September 2005

The school, I believe, is looked at as a great local university. I have not heard of anyone having any problems getting a job after graduation. The alumni network programs are great. They help keep their contacts available after graduation. Many internships are available in large companies throughout the Bay area, like Raymond James Financial, Franklin Templeton and Raytheon.

> **The school says:** "According to the U.S. Department of Labor, Tampa is the top city in the nation for job growth. The USF Career Center offers many services to students during their job search process, including job search coaching, advising servic-

es, online job listing service, campus recruitment fairs, networking fairs, resources for letters of recommendation, practice interviews and online job resources."

Alumnus/a, 8/1998-5/2004, April 2005

USF is very well respected in the local community, as well as the state and regional areas. The school lacks a little awareness on the national level, but this will change with increased research money and increased sports program performance (it shouldn't matter but it does, plus sports bring in a lot of money to the university to better programs and campus life). Graduates have an extensive network of on-campus recruiting and internships available to them. The organizers work very hard to get a comprehensive gathering of employers to provide excellent quality opportunities for those who are looking. There are huge on-campus recruiting events, what seems like monthly, and the big names from national firms always show up (again, excellent brand awareness and marketing by the organizers of these events). The great part about the university is it is in a major metro area and this means the alumni don't need to leave to find jobs. There is a huge alumni network present in the Tampa area and throughout the Southeast. Graduates can stay local and get about as good a job as they would find in any market across the nation.

Alumnus/a, 1/2003-12/2003, February 2005

The University of South Florida offers a Career Center. I would encourage students to register there. It enables your résumé to be on file and allows companies seeking employees to search the database to find prospects. While on file there, I received many e-mails from companies interested in interviewing me. You may also get information on internships and co-ops through the Career Center. Two times a year, USF hosts a job fair. This provides the opportunity to meet potential employers and find out information on many companies in a short amount of time. Career fairs can get very congested with students; I would recommend getting there early, dressing appropriately and having copies of your résumé available.

 Quality of Life

Alumnus/a, Pre-med, 8/2003-5/2006, December 2006

USF is an up-and-coming school. We are one of the youngest state universities and research university. The atmosphere on campus is fun and safe. The school is building lots of new housing, with more apartment and suite styles. There are always activities going on around campus and there is something for everyone in which to get involved. The Tampa campus is absolutely beautiful and is growing every day.

Current student, 8/2006-Submit Date, September 2006

Housing is nice but expensive. The campus is big but there are buses that take you almost anywhere on campus and even out to the mall on Fowler Avenue. The meal plans are OK, but you have to watch out because the food in the dining places is not too healthy. It does not seem like a dangerous place, the most common crime is the stealing of bikes, but that's it.

Current student, 8/2005-Submit Date, October 2005

Housing is excellent at USF. The dorms have to be the nicest I have seen. Apartment-style living on campus is nice, as well. They usually do a good job of matching roommates . Dining is pretty good. There is a good selection of food, ranging from Italian to subs, to smoothies. Campus is pretty safe, and there are police who monitor it 24 hours a day. I personally live off campus because it is cheaper and the places are nicer. You also are not limited to eating strictly with your meal card on campus. You can eat wherever you want.

Alumnus/a, 8/1998-5/2004, April 2005

USF is located in North Tampa, bordering New Tampa, and it is a nice area with little crime. Campus police are always present and very approachable. Campus housing has been constantly updated and renovated; in addition, there are several new dorms now open. Greek housing hit the university two years ago and the houses are topnotch. Moving to the Big East sports conference has its benefits—all upgraded facilities will be done by the end of summer. On-campus dining offers all the big national names and campus dining halls have very good food and offer a wide variety of options. Beautiful Florida doesn't hurt quality of life any either.

Current student, 8/2004-Submit Date, February 2005

The USF campus is exquisitely beautiful. The landscape is littered with palm trees and water fountains, one building on campus even doubles as a waterfall. The food at USF is better than average, not gourmet but usually fairly tasty. The dorms on campus are well maintained and clean. While they do lack a certain element of style on the inside, they are quite functional and not aesthetically demeaning. USF is located in a relatively safe area, about 10 miles from the heart of Tampa.

Current student, 1/2003-Submit Date, August 2004

Parking is always a challenge. This hurts even more because the cost of parking is more than $100 a year. Athletic facilities for students are great. There are yoga and aerobic classes free for students. The track, tennis courts, pool and weight rooms are always full. The bookstore on campus is nice. Lots of nice coffee shops and restaurants, too.

Campus is safe overall. Students have to make wise choices, though. USF is in the middle of an urban area, so it is about making sure that one is not alone at night. There is an on-campus health clinic available to all students. Student health insurance is available for about $1,000 a year. The feeling at USF is one of anonymity. The campus is huge and students are just one of 10s of 1,000s.

 ## Social Life

Current student, Business, 1/2003-Submit Date, June 2007

There are many bars around campus and there will be a Beef O'Bradys on-campus in 2008. The new Marshal Center should be finished by summer of 2008, and it is amazing. There are hundreds of organizations on campus of which I am involved in the Beef Studs, Wakeboard Club, Surf Club, Volunteer USF, and Sigma Phi Epsilon. SPE is the largest fraternity on campus with the highest GPA. We are also the intramural champions for 2006-2007. We offer a game room with seven pool tables, and a free printing service. The Greek life is becoming more and more popular on campus. There are over 44,000 students at USF, so it would be impossible to list all of the activities.

Current student, 8/2002-Submit Date, October 2005

Depending on age, there is quite a bit of nightlife in Tampa. If you are under 21, there is always Ybor City, with tons of 18-and-up clubs (and some good bars if you are 21). I think that USF still runs a bus down there at night for students. All you have to do is show a student ID. I can get really rowdy, and there are always police everywhere. Twice a year, they have huge celebrations down there with wall-to-wall people, Guavaween (around Halloween) and Gasparilla (around Mardi Gras). The day parades are fun, but the night parades are too much for me. For those 21 and up, there is Channelside, which is a complex with bars and clubs, much more upscale than Ybor. Mostly young professionals go there.

Alumnus/a, 8/2001-5/2006, May 2006

There is always something going on on campus. They have movies on the lawn every week. They show movies that either just came out on DVD or haven't quite yet. Dating is dating. You meet people all the time. Most people are nice. It's definitely not a hard place to meet someone. There are so many events, like concerts and carnivals and free food and music, all the time. The best is Patio Tuesday, which happens on Tuesday from 11 a.m. to 2 p.m., and they give away free food, prizes and other stuff like build-a-bears, airbrush pics, key chains and photos.

Alumnus/a, 8/2000-8/2004, January 2006

Social life is as crazy as you want it to be. There are many frats and sororities. There are clubs, organizations and restaurants, and the dating scene is as crazy as you want it to be. There are many events, especially on or near campus. WWE? Counting Crows? Weezer? There's good stuff. Ybor City: A million bars, a million drinks and as scandalous as you want it. It's a college student's dream world, surrounded by a lower income residential area which can create some tension on occasion. It is a crazy area, especially at Gasparilla. a huge event like Mardi Gras, but in Ybor City (20-minute drive from USF), where people show skin, drinks are aplenty and fun is all over the place.

Current student, 8/2005-Submit Date, October 2005

My roommates and I enjoy going to local bars. Two of our favorites are Diggity Dogs and the bowling alley located right next door to our apartments. Everyone from our complex usually goes and hangs out there and plays beer pong, sings karaoke and socializes. I have found everyone to be very nice and kind of family oriented. The restaurants around are great, as well. Carrabba's is a lot of people's favorite spot. They have great food and casual dining. A fun spot is always Hooters. The game is usually played there and we all go to hang out, and socialize and watch the game. It is a lot of fun. I have only lived here for two months, so I haven't been to all of the hotspots but I know Tampa is filled with them. Ybor City has a lot of good, fun places, but you have to make sure to go with a group of people to be safe down in Ybor.

Alumnus/a, 1/2002-2/2004, September 2005

The social life is great. With beautiful beaches and so many popular bars and restaurants near by, it is never boring. The Greek system has also increased so much that they are being compared to the larger universities in Florida. Some favorite places to dine and drink are Bennigan's, Ale House (ladies night free drinks Thursday nights), Channelside, Ybor City and much more.

Current student, 8/2004-Submit Date, February 2005

For those who are not so apt to stay out until three in the morning on the weekends, there are Florida's beautiful beaches. USF is located about 20 miles away from one of the most popular Gulf Coast beaches in Florida, Clearwater Beach. Speaking as a heterosexual male, I feel the need to inform other male prospective students of the vast array of beautiful females who flock to the Florida area. Not only is there a plethora of social activities outside of the school, there are many within the school. On campus, there is a concert, dance, movie or some kind of social gathering practically every night. The student government at USF is working steadily to keep the students busy when they are not studying. Greek life is also a great aspect of USF, as there are well over 40 different fraternities and sororities from which to choose.

Read all of Vault's College Surveys at **www.vault.com/college**–get complete surveys on 100s of colleges and universities, expert advice on applicaton essays and more.

VAULT CAREER LIBRARY 171

Emory University

Office of Admission
Emory University
200 Boisfeuillet Jones Center
Atlanta, GA 30322-1950
Admissions phone: (404) 727-6036 or (800) 727-6036
Admissions e-mail: admiss@learnlink.emory.edu
Admissions URL: www.admission.emory.edu

 ## Admissions

Current student, Business, 8/2005-Submit Date, June 2007

As part of my admissions process, I did many things, including visit the campus, go to information sessions, sit in on a class, and meet with an Emory rep at my high school. I've heard from many sources that coming all the way to Atlanta to visit is a big thing for Emory because they like to see interest and effort from out-of-towners (I am from MA). I did not interview but my brother also went to Emory, which helped me as a legacy.

> **The school says:** "Emory considers applications based on a combination of academics and extracurricular. In terms of activities, we look for leadership roles and dedication to a few specific activities. Emory encourages prospective students to take advantage of as many aspects of our admission program as possible. This may range from meeting with an admission officer at your high school or at an evening program, visiting the campus, viewing our video, or contacting us for information. A student who has clearly researched the university and has a strong interest is a higher priority in our review. However, visiting campus is not a pre-requisite for acceptance, it is simply one way for you to demonstrate interest, and more importantly, a great way for you to form your own perspective and opinions of the school."

Current student, Chemistry, 9/2004-Submit Date, June 2007

Emory's admissions are definitely getting harder as its popularity grows. As a rising senior, it's amazing to hear how the overall qualifications of the freshman class are so much higher than many of the students in my year. Based upon that, my advice would be to make sure you visit and make sure you seem focused. Emory works hard on keeping a socially diverse community, so bring something to the table that will contribute here. Don't just dabble in everything.

Current student, 8/2005-Submit Date, March 2007

Apply early. Emory has a program called Emory Scholars that is a need-blind scholarship program. Being a Scholar has so many benefits: you pick housing before the rest of your class, you pick classes before the rest of your class, and there are also various retreats and programs for Scholars. I applied early to Emory but did not apply to the Scholars program because I did not know all that much about it. In the 2010 class, more students decided to come to Emory than expected so the selection process for the Class of 2011 will probably be more competitive.

> **Emory says:** "Students interested in merit scholarships must be nominated by a high school official for the Emory Scholars program. Each school is permitted to nominate up to four students for the Emory Scholars program and the application deadline is November 1 of the senior year."

Current student, History, 8/2004-Submit Date, March 2007

The admissions process is fairly straightforward. Like most schools, you submit an application, transcripts, letters of recommendation, extracurricular résumés—the usual. Emory's admissions works hard to make personal contact with potential applicants, so don't be surprised to see an information session at your high school or to receive an invitation to a local presentation by an admissions coun-

selor. That said, you also have to show Emory that you're interested in being there. I'd recommend ordering the video visit, especially if you can't visit in person. That way, you show interest and get a great picture of what campus is actually like at the same time. It may not be a perfect substitute to a live visit but it's better than static pictures. There really is no big secret to getting in, you've simply got to make it clear what you will contribute to the Emory community and what sets you apart. The people reading your application are also reading thousands of others, so don't be afraid to be a little different and to stand out. Also, you could have a 2400 SAT and a 4.0 GPA and it won't make a difference if you haven't done anything other than study in high school.

Emory is incredibly selective—its ranking allows it to be—so by no means is this an easy school to get into. However, many students here say that they were surprised to get in, so I'd recommend going for Emory, even if it's your reach school. Some comment that Early Decision lowers the admissions bar, which is only half true. While the standards for admission are still the same, the pool of applicants in which you are competing is much smaller, making it a great deal easier to stand out in the crowd. I'd venture to say that a significant portion of the students at the school got in via EDI or EDII.

Current student, 8/2004-Submit Date, May 2006

One of the things that the Emory Office of Admission holds in high esteem is whether you have visited the campus. I would recommend taking a trip to Atlanta, and making sure to stop and sign in at the admissions building so that they have a record of the visit. Obviously, Emory is a very academically competitive school, and the application process gets tougher every year. Like with any university's application, I would suggest emphasizing the fact that you have committed yourself to something. Emory is not looking for the kids who spread themselves thin across 19 different sports, musical groups, and after-school activities. Emory is a very diverse campus with hundreds of student groups, and the Office of Admission is looking for people to occupy all of those different spaces.

Current student, 8/2003-Submit Date, April 2005

I like how the Office of Admission was always ready to answer questions. I was definitely one of those applicants whose mother would make him/her call to make sure he/she didn't need anything else in his/her application, and the counselors with whom I spoke were very nice and helpful. They were never annoyed that I called and would often take time to answer several questions, without giving one-word answers. The only thing I didn't like was that they don't do interviews, since that was usually my strongest area.

Being involved in the Office of Admission now, I like to see how well-rounded students are greatly favored over students who just got really high test scores but weren't really involved in anything outside of academics. Emory prides itself on having a socially active community with students who will add to the ever-changing Emory environment, so admissions counselors don't want to see people who aren't likely to be involved on campus.

 ## Academics

Current student, Political Science, 8/2005-Submit Date, June 2007

Academic programs at Emory are truly fantastic! Students and professors demonstrate enormous commitment to their studies and particular fields. Emory professors, like the students, are overwhelmingly enthusiastic about sharing knowledge of their subject with other students and colleagues. After class, I, along with so many students, walk out feeling excited and feeling as if each class is worthwhile to increasing my knowledge. I love the learning environment here more than I can express! Professors really do care about their students and show it by meeting with students after office hours and by setting up meetings to improve students' work in class. Getting into popular classes can be difficult, but most professors will overload students. Grading depends entirely upon the professor, as does the workload. However, with a class comments system, stu-

...dents have a general knowledge of the class structure, professor's demeanor, grading scale and workload. You are never blind going into an Emory class-room.

Current student, Chemistry, 9/2004-Submit Date, June 2007

Many people who have gone to Emory will talk about the General Education Requirements (GERs). Although their purpose is noble (to make students take classes in different areas), it is kind of overboard. I admit that I have had great classes that I would not have taken if not for the GERs, but there are a lot of them, and ones like PE still bother most students as a waste of time. In terms of difficulty, major can make a big difference. For example, I've heard business school classes are not difficult, but they have a curve that makes it difficult to get a great grade. My friend who is a history major says it's a piece of cake, while my fellow chem majors complain how impossible our major is. Most classes and professors have review sessions and TAs which makes it very easy to get extra help if you need it.

Current student, 8/2005-Submit Date, March 2007

Classes are picked based on a bidding system. The number of points you put on each class is compared to that of others and you get the classes. Some of the upper-level popular classes are difficult to get into simply because of supply and demand. A number of spots of the popular introductory classes are held so that freshmen may get into them. Due to the diverse majors at Emory, the workload varies. There are some classes where I have 100 pages of reading a week, and others where I have 30. Usually, one has enough time to get involved in extracurricular activities and accomplish homework with time to spare. Grading varies dramatically by professor. Some professors inflate grades, while others do not. Professors are approachable; if you go to office hours or schedule an appointment, the professors will make time for you, so that you can talk to them.

Current student, Pre-med, 8/2004-Submit Date, May 2006

I tell myself every day how lucky I am to be at Emory. Emory epitomizes a liberal arts college, but we really have the best of both worlds: a strong research environment and programs in the natural sciences, plus strong programs in the arts and humanities. The most popular classes are probably some of the GERs (General Education Requirements), the great PE classes like Backpacking, SCUBA and Stress Reduction and Meditation, and the upper-level Political Science course that former U.S. President Jimmy Carter sometimes teaches. A large percentage of classes are taught by full professors (95 percent), and 98 percent of professors hold their terminal degrees. Depending on your major, your introductory courses can be either small or large. The pre-med courses are the biggest; they are usually between 100 and 150 students. Most classes are really small once you get into your major. This is wonderful, because it means you will be able to develop a good rapport with your professors. What sets Emory apart from other schools with similar academics is the willingness of students to help each other. Rather than classes that are so competitive that no one wants to help you understand things, the emphasis is really placed on the class working together to triumph over the difficult concepts or subject matter. One of my classes freshman year even made T-shirts that said, "I Survived Freshman Organic Chemistry." You should expect to have a lot of work and reading outside of class, but it is not so overwhelming that students don't have time to do other things outside of academics. Most students participate in several of the 250+ student clubs and organizations, and many students (like me) choose to spend their free time engaged in more academic pursuits, like doing research.

> **The school says:** "90 percent of classes are taught by full professors and 99 percent of Emory professors hold the terminal degree in their field."

Current student, History, 8/2004-Submit Date, March 2007

Academics at Emory are simply topnotch. At very few other institutions can you learn from huge names like the Dalai Lama, Jimmy Carter and Salman Rushdie, as all three have had professorial appointments at Emory. While the big name teachers are great, the rest of the faculty is the heart of the academic program, and they cannot be beat. We have dozens of faculty who are the top in their fields. Yet remarkably, the vast majority of the professors at Emory are legitimately interested in their teaching, and their research comes second. This creates an undergraduate experience where you don't feel rushed through and treated like mindless drones, but rather professors take a personal interest in your success. It isn't unheard of for a professor to invite his class over to dinner at his house, or to have creative venues for classes. I've had classes held at museums, baseball games, restaurants, movies and even a trip into nature, and there are countless other places where others have learned.

Current student, 8/2004-Submit Date, May 2006

While it is competitive to get into Emory, the classroom attitude amongst students is never competitive. People are always willing to share notes, discuss topic, and form study groups. Emory is very good about creating a rigorous academic environment but also provides every student with the tools needed to succeed. Free peer tutoring and mentoring, office hours and advising programs are topnotch at Emory. I have never been taught by a TA at Emory. My professors are renowned in their fields and are not kept tucked away for the graduate students only. They are passionate, knowledgeable and very, very accessible. I spent the first three months of a seminar not knowing that my energetic and humble professor was a Pulitzer Prize winner. The professors here are not out to get you, but to make sure you walk across the stage at commencement having exerted your Emory education to its highest capacity. They also really take the time to become involved in your life outside of the classroom and get to know you as an individual.

Alumnus/a, Business, 8/2003-Submit Date, September 2006

Emory, to me, is one of the easiest "smart" schools. If I were to recommend anything, it would be to try and attend the business school. It really prepares you to enter the corporate world right out of college. Workload obviously depends on the class. Organic Chemistry is going to be a lot more work than an intro microeconomics class. But no matter what class, teachers here are fairly nice and really try and help you through your problems. Only downside is that most lower-level classes are taught by graduate students. Class selection is relatively easy at Emory. Each student is assigned bid points, freshmen with fewer points and seniors with the most. More senior students get to bid on assigned classes first. So even if you don't get a class when you are younger, chances of getting the class later in your collegiate career are very high.

 ## Employment Prospects

Current student, History, 8/2004-Submit Date, March 2007

Employment prospects from Emory, and especially the Goizueta Business school, are probably among the strongest if not the strongest in the Southeast. The finance industry recruits heavily at Emory, especially since Goldman Sachs just named the business school a recruiting target. Additionally, accounting firms are big recruiters for interns and for full-time associates.

If your classmates aren't heading to one of the big three (med, law, or public health), they probably are going to be entering the workforce. Following finance jobs (stock analysts, bankers and more), marketing and accounting, as well as lab work in the sciences, are probably the most popular. Many students return to their hometown or neighboring big city (New York, especially) after graduation, but a large portion actually choose to stay in Atlanta to work. Once outside of Emory, the alumni connections stay strong, with alumni associations in many major U.S. cities that help you continue to network and maintain job prospects.

Alumnus/a, 8/2003-Submit Date, September 2006

Emory is a Top 20 school. Obviously, this helps with post-college recruiting. Granted, Emory is no Harvard, but having a degree from here comes with some clout. Furthermore, the undergraduate business school is ranked fifth, which definitely can add weight to your résumé. This is especially true for smaller firms and firms in the Southeast (particularly Atlanta). Also, its reputation in the medical community makes it a great school for those pursuing a career in medicine. Lastly, although some people say they had a positive experience with the Career Center, mine was sub par. However, I hear the business school students get spectacular guidance and support.

> **The school says:** "In the most recent *Business Week* rankings released March 2007, Emory University's Goizueta Business School's Bachelor of Business Administration program ranked fourth in the nation."

Read all of Vault's College Surveys at **www.vault.com/college**–get complete surveys on 100s of colleges and universities, expert advice on applicaton essays and more.

VAULT CAREER LIBRARY 173

Current student, Business, 8/2004-Submit Date, April 2007

Employment depends on major. Most Emory undergraduates go on to graduate school. Business school graduates often go into investment banking, consulting or accounting. The alumni network at Emory is also helpful with navigating career opportunities, and plenty of recruiters come to campus for interviews and information sessions.

Current student, 8/2004-Submit Date, May 2006

Our undergraduate business program was just ranked fifth in the nation. There is a huge number of high-paying jobs for graduates of the program, particularly in the Southeast. Applicants who are pre-med also have a very high success rate in their application to the most prestigious medical schools. There are ways to get involved with alumni, including an alumni mentoring program and a program called Dinner with 12 Strangers, where students sign up to attend dinners hosted by former alumni living in the Atlanta area. This program is also a great way to meet your peers. An Emory degree is probably more valuable if you plan to stay in the Southeast, but that is changing.

Alumnus/a, 8/2000-5/2004, April 2006

Employment depends on how assertive you were—I was able to land an internship at a prestigious national nonprofit during my senior year in college. I now work there full-time. The requirements called for a graduate student in communications, but my résumé and the Emory name, I am sure, helped me leap that hurdle. The alumni network is not where it could be formally, but there is definitely support of alumns: informally if you look for it. This is especially true. in the Atlanta area. Emory also hosts a slew of career fairs, some better than others.

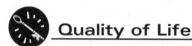 **Quality of Life**

Current student, Political Science, 8/2005-Submit Date, June 2007

Emory students enjoy a very high quality of life. Housing, while it can be frustrating finding any, is up to date. Emory requires that second-year students live on campus, and this significantly contributes to Emory's cohesiveness providing a positive beginning college experience. Facilities, whether the library, gym, dining areas or technology labs, are phenomenal! Students take every advantage of what Emory has to offer in this respect. The campus is incredibly beautiful and often, especially in the fall and spring, you see students utilizing the campus grounds to the fullest extent. People are laying out on the quad reading books, students are playing ultimate frisbee and grilling out. Emory is very safe, as well. If any crime has been committed on campus, students are notified very soon afterwards. Emory is great about maintaining the security of the campus and the Emory police department is always on hand and immediately responds to any kind of emergency.

> **Emory says:** "More than 70 percent of Emory students live on campus, and all first-year students live together in first-year residence halls. After the sophomore year, upperclass students can choose to live off of campus, but many prefer the sense of community that on-campus living provides. Every residence hall room features air-conditioning, phones with voice mail, cable hook-ups, ethernet connections, and carpeting. New residence halls are under construction, with ten freshman living complexes being built in eight years. One of the 10 new residence halls opened in fall 2007 with two to three more opening in fall 2008.
>
> "Upperclass students who remain on campus may live at Emory's newest housing complex, the Clairmont Campus. The Clairmont Campus combines private, spacious living accommodations with such amenities as a cafe, computer workstations, an outdoor Olympic-sized pool, clay tennis courts, a full gymnasium, and a workout facility."

Current student, 8/2005-Submit Date, March 2007

Emory is currently rebuilding a lot of the freshman halls. Upperclassmen live at the Clairemont Apartments, which are really nice. There is one freshman hall that is almost complete and other projects will be starting soon. The campus is beautiful and the warm weather in mid-March is fantastic. Most of Emory has just been rebuilt or refurnished or is in the process of it, so almost all of the facilities are nice and there are a lot of places in the buildings where you can go study or sit and talk in. Cox Hall has a food court that is really good. There, we have Chik-Fil-A, Pizza Hut, Burger King, a sushi stop and a sandwich place, amongst others. Dooley's Den is also a really good place to eat because they are open until 2 a.m., and great for food at all times of the night.

Current student, History, 8/2004-Submit Date, March 2007

The freshman year experience is critical to life at Emory. The dorms are relatively small by number of occupants, and the rooms tend to be very generously sized. The freshman hall usually makes up most of your friends, as well as the locus for programming about adjusting to college life. Various programs provide fun interaction with hallmates and RAs, as well as a program called the Sophomore Advisor, which includes a mentoring big brother who looks out for you and helps you with any questions you may have. These sophomores live as members of your hall community and are readily available, as are resident advisors, though RAs tend to be viewed more as hall police than advisors. As an initial acclimation program to Emory, all freshman dorms participate in Songfest where they get up with the rest of the dorm and scream and dance their heart out in hopes of winning the coveted trophy that ends up displayed proudly in the winning dorm. Many at Emory rank Songfest as one of their most vivid memories of their four years.

Campus is gorgeous, especially in the spring. There's a joke that more money is spent on flowers than anything else on campus because it seems that there is never a wilted flower and that the vegetation is always being updated. The architecture is fascinating and very nice. Unlike your typical Gothic college campus, Emory's architecture is warm and friendly, and very contemporary. Not to be missed is the view from the 10th floor of the library stacks, where you can go out on a wraparound balcony and see all of campus, as well as downtown, midtown and Buckhead.

Current student, 8/2005-Submit Date, April 2006

Emory has done an excellent job of creating a quality campus environment and is only improving by encouraging a walking environment on campus and a unified central campus grounds. Facilities are amazing, state-of-the-art and encourage academic learning. Overall, the quality of housing has been excellent. Improvements in upperclassman housing are amazing and groundwork for a unified freshman housing quad provides even better prospects for housing on campus. Overall dining choices on campus has been excellent, though limited hours are a weakness and improvements in late-night dining are needed. The main campus dining could also use improvements in the quality of food. Neighborhood crime is limited and safety precautions are of the highest degree. If crimes do occur, the school is quick to announce concerns for student and faculty safety.

 Social Life

Current student, Political Science, 8/2005-Submit Date, June 2007

Emory's social scene is improving year after year. It gets better with each semester! Atlanta provides so many great restaurants, bars, clubs, sporting events and arts events. Students really take advantage of the Atlanta scene. Emory students have their token favorite bars like Maggie's and Famous Pub. You can always expect to see other students there late at night and into the wee hours of the morning. The Greek system is huge at Emory. While only one-third of students are involved in it, members of Greek life typically become campus leaders in every other area also. Greek life is pleasantly different from most Greek life at other schools. Girls in different sororities are still friends despite their respective allegiances, as are guys in different fraternities. Emory students often go to clubs together. A former student has established a business that rents out clubs entirely for Emory students. These set club nights provide wary students with a sense of security knowing that those at the clubs are all Emory affiliated. It also allows for more community bonding! Students here study hard, but also know how to play hard. Everyone at Emory seems to have a nice balance of academics and social life.

Current student, 8/2005-Submit Date, March 2007

The freshman social life revolves around Frat Row and Emory club nights. As you get older, the social life comes to revolve around local bars and Atlanta because Atlanta does have a great nightlife. Due to the proximity of Atlanta, there are many different restaurants around. I use a Zagats to find my restaurants

...ut you can always use word of mouth and/or a *Daydreamer's Guide to Emory*. *The Daydreamer's Guide* has all of the best places to go and do things, and gives suggestions about restaurants, nightlife, shopping, day trips, and so on. Greek life is only 30 percent of students, but it can seem like more at times. It is not like typical Greek life because most people have friends both inside and outside of the system. Emory puts on events weekly. Emory clubs put on events for students all of the time. These events usually raise money for a cause. Wonderful Wednesdays is an old tradition that was brought back last year. It used to be that classes were cancelled on Wednesdays as a break in the middle of the week. Now it is just a big event where clubs promote different activities and sponsor the day with food and entertainment in the middle of campus. Dooley's Week is also a big week. Dooley is Emory's unofficial mascot. During his week, if he comes to your class you are let out for that day.

Current student, History, 8/2004-Submit Date, March 2007

One place that students go for night-time entertainment is Taverna Plaka in Buckhead and Nicola's near Emory, which turn into rollicking parties with music, dancing and lots of laughs after you finish your meal. Speaking of dancing, every Thursday night, a promotion company run by students rents out a nightclub for Emory night, and charges between $10 and $20 per person for the opportunity to cut loose in a normally 21-and-over club if you're 18 or older. Additionally, Emory itself throws two big parties, one per semester. In the fall, there is the semiformal Homecoming ball, and in the spring, Dooley's Ball. Dooley is an unofficial mascot of the university, and there is a week in his honor every spring, culminating in a Halloween in April party on McDonough Field with music, food, and many intoxicated, costumed revelers. It has become a contest for some to see who can come up with the most outrageous costume—last year someone came dressed primarily in body paint and nothing else. Definitely not a celebration for prudes, it is probably the most fun that is had on Emory's campus all year.

Second to that in fun, however, is the annual Freshman Semi-Formal, where freshmen get gussied up and (for the past three years) come to a giant ballroom in the Fabulous Fox Theatre for a night of dancing and appetizers.

Current student, 8/2003-Submit Date, December 2005

The social life at Emory starts freshman year, revolving around Fraternity Row and the frat houses that regularly hold parties. Greek life is huge at Emory, with almost more than a third of the student body involved. And within the Greek community is a strict hierarchy, with certain sororities and fraternities clearly more desirable. Next year they are building the first-ever sorority houses, which will be located across the street from all the fraternity houses on the Row. Greek life here is a strange hybrid of Southern and Northern frats/sororities, but they are definitely not your stereotypical participants. It becomes more important to be a part of the Greek community sophomore year, mostly to meet the right people and stay away from the freshmen. Junior/senior year, it's all about the Atlanta bar scene, with Maggie's Bar and the midtown area dominating social life. Students at Emory definitely do date, but, hooking up is an important part of interacting with the opposite sex.

> **Regarding social life, the school says:** "Emory students are involved in over 230 diverse clubs and organizations, including artistic, athletic, international, media, professional, religious, service and social groups. Because students live on campus for the first two years, campus involvement is enhanced by a close-knit living community and by numerous programs and events sponsored by the school during the week and on the weekend. So whether you join Outdoor Emory, Volunteer Emory, Concert Choir or Greek life, there's always plenty to do! And Atlanta is just minutes from campus, offering unlimited social, cultural and intellectual opportunities."

The School Says

Emory University is an inquiry-driven, ethically engaged and diverse community whose members work collaboratively for positive transformation in the world through courageous leadership in teaching, research, scholarship, health care, and social action. The university is recognized internationally for its out-

standing liberal arts college, superb professional schools, and one of the leading health care systems in the Southeast.

Atlanta: A Favorite College town

Emory is enriched by the legacy and energy of Atlanta, whose downtown area is just 15 minutes away. Emory's location along the Clifton Corridor, which also includes the U.S. Centers for Disease Control and Prevention and the American Cancer Society, helps to foster dynamic collaborations that establish Emory as a major public health center.

College within a University

There are 11,781 students enrolled at Emory, about half (6,587) pursuing undergraduate degrees and the rest enrolled in graduate and professional programs. A palpable sense of community and social connection exists on campus and, because of Emory's intimate size, students are nurtured in a way that is not possible at larger institutions.

Diverse Undergraduate Education

Emory expects its students to do well and also do good for the world. Undergraduate programs in humanities, sciences, business and nursing allow Emory students to explore their talents. Students choose between two campuses for freshman and sophomore years—either the main campus in Atlanta, or in Oxford, where the school was originally founded. By junior year, all students take classes on the main Atlanta campus and continue with liberal arts courses or apply to the highly regarded business or nursing schools.

Liberal Arts Learning

Emory encourages students to push intellectual curiosity. From excellent teaching in small classes to lectures from prominent scholars, to opportunities for study abroad, research and internships, Emory provides a rich setting for learning.

- The curriculum is grounded in the liberal arts, providing an education of across-the-board strength that emphasizes writing well and connecting ideas.

- Students can choose from over 75 majors, 55 minors, nine pre-professional programs, 10 four-year combined bachelor/master degrees offered in 10 disciplines, and two combined degrees in engineering.

- The honors program enables qualified seniors to conduct intensive research in the subject of their choice.

- Study abroad for a semester or summer programs that span the globe.

Expert Faculty Who Love to Teach

- Average class size: 18 students.
- Student-to-faculty ratio of 7:1.
- 88 percent of classes have fewer than 40 students.
- 98 percent of the 700 professors hold their field's terminal degree.
- Unique seminar-style classes of 15 students at the first-year level.

Discover Emory University

Emory receives more research funding than any other university in Georgia and also has a long tradition of emphasizing fine teaching. It is the most ethnically and religiously diverse university of the Top 20 national research universities and is the only one that remains religiously chartered. Emory was founded by the Methodist Church in 1836 in Oxford, Georgia, where Oxford College of Emory University continues today as a two-year liberal arts division of Emory.

Read all of Vault's College Surveys at **www.vault.com/college**–get complete surveys on 100s of colleges and universities, expert advice on applicaton essays and more.

VAULT CAREER LIBRARY   175

Georgia Institute of Technology

Georgia Institute of Technology
Office of Undergraduate Admission
Atlanta, GA 30332-0320
Admissions phone: (404) 894-4154
Admissions fax: (404) 894-9511
Admissions e-mail: admission@gatech.edu
Admissions URL: www.admission.gatech.edu

 ## Admissions

Current student, 8/2004-Submit Date, May 2006

I would absolutely recommend that all prospective Tech students visit the campus. It wasn't until I visited campus that I really got a feel for Tech's atmosphere—serious about its academics but not all nerds. Also, I believe, my informal campus interview is the reason that I was accepted to Tech. When I explained everything I had done in high school, my admissions counselor came to see me as a person rather than a set of test scores. She actually asked for my cell phone number and as I was walking back to my car, she called me and told me that I had been accepted. Admissions does place great emphasis on SAT scores, but even more important are your AP credits and grades. Most people come to Tech with at least some AP credits. If your SAT scores are not stellar, as mine weren't, use the essay to convey either your strong personality or dedication to science and technology. As far as selectivity, Tech truly is the MIT of the South—except much less expensive and with great sports teams. While it's not a household name outside of the South, Tech is rigorous and requires its students prove their intellectual stamina before admission. I definitely see Tech becoming more selective in the future.

Current student, Computer Science, 1/2003-Submit Date, June 2007

Princeton Review's web site has the detailed statistics. But you should be a top student in your high school and score high in the SAT at the minimum. I went to a community college and aced a bunch of classes before transferring to Tech. It worked out just fine for me. You need to know that engineering is what the school is all about. I was a computer science major and I feel like I chose the school because of that.

Current student, 6/2003-Submit Date, September 2006

You will need decent SAT scores (especially in math if applying to the engineering program), as well as the basic application, including an essay. No interview is required. Medium selectivity: This school is not MIT or CalTech, but it is the best engineering school in the Southeast. Tuition is not overly expensive. In fact, Georgia Tech has been ranked as a best bargain in some college guides I've seen. And if you are from Georgia, HOPE Scholarship (B average in high school) will pay for your tuition. Getting into Georgia Tech has never been the hard part. It's staying in and getting good grades that makes this school challenging.

Alumnus/a, 8/2001-12/2005, September 2006

They rely mostly on SAT and GPA scores but are starting to emphasize well-rounded students. Alumni recommendations are not technically considered, but I know it doesn't hurt and they do look at them.

Current student, Engineering, 8/2003-Submit Date, May 2007

Rolling admissions lets students know early whether they got in. Math SAT scores were very important. The essay was a tiebreaker. GT admits students based on a formula, including GPA and test scores, so any numerical aspect of your application is heavily weighted.

Current student, 8/2001-Submit Date, May 2005

I feel that Georgia Tech is very selective and its only downfall is that it is a public state university. Out-of-state students find it more challenging to get in, although the process is rather easy. The essay plays a large role in the admissions process, but the actual application is very concise. You need to highlight your most outstanding high school achievements because the efficiency of the application only allows five extracurriculars. For the overachievers at Georgia Tech, this is sometimes difficult.

 ## Academics

Current student, Computer Science, 1/2003-Submit Date, June 2007

Georgia Tech is well known as a demanding school. But you can learn a lot in the process. Those who manage to study hard all four years will graduate with honors and have the future ahead of them. It's worth the hard work. Some professors can be nit-picky, but it's such a gigantic school that you should always expect a few professors who think they are all that.

Current student, 6/2003-Submit Date, September 2006

It's a tough school with very competitive students. The students always know which are the easier classes and those fill up quickly. There is a good mix of large lecture courses (over 200 students) and smaller classes (around 20 to 30 students). There are many weed-out classes at the freshman and sophomore level; however, grading for upper-level classes is much fairer. Degree requirements are plentiful, making this a five-year school for many.

Professors often seem more concerned about their research projects than teaching. However, if you can find a great professor, latch onto him/her. You will be glad you did.

Current student, Engineering, 8/2003-Submit Date, May 2007

Classes are very difficult and scheduling can be tough. Everything is on a curve so do not get discouraged with test scores themselves. The workload is very intense and studying with friends is a must if you want to graduate. Word is a collection of old tests and quizzes, which is very helpful in passing classes. Large weed-out classes are very demanding and throw a ton of information at students very quickly to see if they can comprehend it all.

Current student, 8/2005-Submit Date, February 2007

Georgia Tech is very difficult. This is certainly one of Tech's drawbacks. Until you get into really upper-level courses, there is little to no discussion in class. Some departments are nicer than others, though. The management program is really nice, with great facilities and interesting classes. Computer science also has great facilities that were just built.

Current student, 8/2004-Submit Date, May 2006

Since the school is ranked the 37th institution in the nation and the ninth public, academics are understood to be rigorous. The classes are tough, extraordinarily but manageably so. Registration is done entirely online, and time tickets open up based on the number of hours earned. The workload is a little above average for an engineering school, but manageable once you know how to handle it. The student government association has a good course critique for checking out the GPAs of all the professors who have ever taught before on campus, and is an essential resource during registration. All professors and TAs are required to hold office hours, and are usually good about scheduling appointments or offering help to those who ask for it.

Alumnus/a, Public Policy, 7/2001-5/2005, May 2006

There is no joke about it, Tech is a difficult school. I have never worked harder than the four years I was there; but it was well worth it. I was a public policy major, so most of my classes were smaller in size. I had great relationships with the majority of my professors and I found most of them willing to answer my questions and assist me on a regular basis. I don't agree with all the core classes we are required to take and I oftentimes found it difficult to register for the required classes. The workload at Tech is steady throughout the semester with major projects, papers and tests grouped together in the weeks before break and he end of the semester. These are without a doubt the most stressful times of the semester.

Alumnus/a, 8/2000-6/2004, May 2006

I was always able to get the classes, teachers and time slots I wanted. The quality of faculty in your upper-level undergrad classes is excellent and world-class. The introductory teachers are average. The workload is tough and a student should be willing to work seven days a week to keep up.

Current student, Architecture, 8/2004-Submit Date, May 2006

I am in an architecture program. My freshman year, I got some core classes out of the way like Calculus, Computer Science (which everyone is required to take), English, History and, of course, my introductory classes into the College of Architecture. The classes are definitely challenging, but between provided tutors for students in the Freshman Experience program and really smart friends, there is plenty of help to make it through. My workload is a little different from some other majors'. I spend a whole lot of time in studio working on my architecture things and it can be difficult keeping up with studio work along with the workload for other classes. Grades are in no way inflated at Tech. An A is not a common thing. We also don't have any fluffy classes like Volleyball or Ceramics that count towards your degree. There are critiques available on a lot of classes and professors so you can see what a professor's GPA is, how many people withdraw from the class and grade distributions, which is really helpful when registering for classes. All professors and TAs are required to have office hours so they are available to students.

Employment Prospects

Current student, Computer Science, 1/2003-Submit Date, June 2007

Employment prospects are terrific. Several departments even hire top undergraduate students as teaching assistants to hold recitation lectures for the lower-level classes as they become juniors and seniors. Needless to say, it helped me a great deal when applying to graduate schools later on. I ended up receiving a doctoral fellowship offer at the Johns Hopkins University, while most either go on to other graduate programs or start a rewarding career immediately. Most of my friends and co-op buddies got multiple job offers prior to graduations. It's a wonderful school to go if you want to have a bright future, and I'm hyping it.

Current student, 6/2003-Submit Date, September 2006

As one of the top engineering schools in the country, job prospects are very good. Our career fair is one of the best college career fairs. Almost every person I have known has gone to the career fair and at least gotten interviews. Co-op program is very popular. Jobs range from private engineering companies, to government engineering, to consulting and more. We have a great alumni network with alumni clubs all over the country.

Basically, unless you have absolutely no interviewing skills and just a terrible résumé, you should be able to find a good job after graduation. Companies, especially in the South, find a Georgia Tech education very desirable.

Current student, Engineering, 8/2003-Submit Date, May 2007

A degree from GT has wowed everyone with whom I have interviewed. Since it is very difficult to graduate (only one-third of freshmen, finish), the alumni network is very tight. There is an instant bond when meeting an alumnus/a since you both went through a very tough process.

Current student, 8/2005-Submit Date, February 2007

People tend to get really great jobs after graduating from Tech. People do generally have pretty low GPAs upon graduation, and that can be a difficult obstacle when job hunting.

Current student, 8/2001-Submit Date, May 2005

The network of people I have met through Georgia Tech is outstanding. I have been involved in the most amazing co-op program, which has offered me a world of opportunities I may not have gotten otherwise. The starting salary of students from Tech tends to be higher than the expected averages for each major, and most students are offered many interviews. Tech helps with these interviews and résumé writing through the career services department. In addition, internships

and co-op companies often come to campus for interviews, which makes it easy on the students.

Quality of Life

Current student, Computer Science, 1/2003-Submit Date, June 2007

Atlanta is a decent city. It's no New York City or Chicago but you can have fun. You need a car to get around. The train/subway doesn't really get you many places. Traffic gave me a headache. For many years, I was a Yellow Jacket. The mayor has done a lot of great things for the city, and crime is no longer a big deal compared to what was going on before the Olympics. Since it's the state capitol, you can get involved in local and state politics and meet influential politicians of the state, as well. The city itself is a liberal oasis of the state, if not the South. Being a liberal intellectual, I had a great time.

Current student, 6/2003-Submit Date, September 2006

New construction has transformed this once average campus into a beautiful one, with a new management building, bookstore and health center.

Although I have never lived in the on-campus housing, I've heard that the rooms are beyond tiny. On-campus food is OK, but the Chik-Fil-A rocks!

Safety is always a concern when talking about an urban campus. For the most part, crime is low and police are plentiful, but occasional incidents occur.

Current student, Engineering, 8/2003-Submit Date, May 2007

The campus is nice and extremely safe even though some surrounding areas are not. Joining the Greek system is a must, since it practically runs the social part of the college. The quality of life is very high, besides studying a large amount of time. Most people are very easy-going and helpful. The athletics on campus are huge and in fall everything is about game day.

Current student, 8/2005-Submit Date, February 2007

On-campus housing is really tight on space. This year they started moving three freshmen into two-man dorms because they underestimated the demand they would face. This seems to be a problem every year. Living in freshman housing was fun, and we did our best to raise hell in the halls. If you have a choice, live on East Campus. East Campus is where the Greek system is and generally where all your friends will be. West Campus is the retirement home. Dining is OK, but you'll be sick of it by the end of your freshman year. There are tons of great restaurants really close by to break up dining hall blues.

Current student, 8/2004-Submit Date, May 2006

The location of the school is ideal—in the middle of the city in its own oasis. The on-campus atmosphere is very collegiate, and the school is less than a mile from many of the sights in Atlanta. Violent crime is not a problem on campus, and most students agree that they feel safe on campus, even at night. The upperclassman housing is all new, built for the athletes during the 1996 Olympics. The freshman dorms leave something to be desired, but are the same as most colleges' freshman dorms. There are many dining options available on campus, on the outskirts of campus, in Technology Square, in downtown and midtown. Several options are also open late or 24 hours.

Social Life

Current student, Computer Science, 1/2003-Submit Date, June 2007

Georgia Tech has a lot of fraternities. The co-op programs also link students together because a bunch of kids work for the same company for semesters. As far as off-campus activities go, you should not have to worry about what Atlanta has to offer. It's a city that is still booming.

Current student, 6/2003-Submit Date, September 2006

You will have a great social life if you are female. I believe the ratio is about 3:1, guys to girls. Hence, parties are often sausage fests. Greek life is very prevalent.

There are lots of great restaurants and bars nearby. Ru-San's, also known as the McDonald's of sushi, has great happy hour deals on temaki ($1 a piece).

Read all of Vault's College Surveys at www.vault.com/college–get complete surveys on 100s of colleges and universities, expert advice on applicaton essays and more.

VAULT CAREER LIBRARY   177

The on-campus student center is a great hangout for study groups and just general meeting up. Lots of students cram this place before tests and exams.

Current student, Engineering, 8/2003-Submit Date, May 2007

Dating is tough because of the male-to-female ratio, but it is getting better. Join a fraternity or sorority if you plan on being social at all during your four, five or six years in undergrad. The Greek system is extremely good; it is a large social network and runs most aspects of student government, as well.

Current student, 8/2005-Submit Date, February 2007

Go Greek. Tech is a blast if you are involved in a fraternity or sorority, but if you're independent you'll find yourself with nothing to do. Atlanta is a big city, but the nightlife isn't made for college students. There are some fun bars that people like to go to, but your best bet is to join a fraternity and raise hell with your brothers. Tech always brags about its work hard, play hard attitude, and that's right on. People put in ridiculous hours studying, but when the time comes people go nuts.

Current student, 8/2004-Submit Date, May 2006

25 percent of the campus is Greek. Many students, both Greek and non-Greek, enjoy the Greek party scene. Tech Square provides a good option for campus dining, and during the fall, the campus is lively from football game day action (Division IA ACC school). There is plenty to do on campus—the student just needs to go out and do it. Rocky Mountain Pizza (just off campus) and Peachtree Tavern in midtown Atlanta are popular student hangouts. Lots of student involvement opportunities on campus, and lots of campus events put on. Lots of concert venues in Atlanta, several in close proximity to campus.

Current student, 8/2001-Submit Date, May 2005

Fraternities and sororities are the throwers of most on-campus parties. They provide the most active social life Tech can offer. In addition, Geroga Tech offers different programs to all students many times a year, such as the Ludacris concert for Philanthropy Day last month. Local bars and clubs are very popular, although there are very few college nights because of city laws. This leaves those students under 21 on campus on the weekends instead of in the city. Over 23 percent of students here are in the Greek community, which is above the national average.

Also, Tech sponsors over 400 different organizations—everything from the sky diving club to the lasagna eating club. If you can't find your niche here, you weren't looking. Favorite student bars: Peachtree Tavern and Moondog's. Favorite student restaurants: Fellini's Pizza and Rocky Mountain. Favorite ice cream place: Jake's Ice Cream. Favorite club: Compound or Eleven 50. Favorite place to shop: Lenox Mall. Favorite sports place: Turner Field for the Braves games. Favorite theater: The Fox. Favorite Tech events: concerts, like Ludacris.

The School Says

Georgia Tech is a competitive university. The criteria used in determining an applicant's qualifications for admission includes: satisfactory evidence of scholastic promise based on the applicant's academic record; scores on selected tests of aptitude or achievement; and evaluation of the applicant's personal statement, leadership and activity record. All qualified students are equally welcome to seek admission to Georgia Tech. All applicants may apply for and accept admission confident that the policy and regular practice of the institute will not discriminate against them on the basis of race, religion, sex or national origin.

Although we like to know if an applicant has had relatives who attended Tech, it does not impact the acceptance decision.

Because the academic environment at Tech is challenging, students have a multitude of support programs that include tutorial assistance, study groups, and mentoring opportunities. The university has a 92 percent retention rate from the freshman to sophomore years, demonstrating that students who are qualified for admission will succeed at Tech.

Georgia Tech strives to recruit a diverse student body that includes in-state, out-of-state and international students. Qualified in-state students receive the HOPE Scholarship in Georgia, which pays for tuition and some fees, but it is not a full ride. Students must maintain a B average to retain the HOPE Scholarship from semester to semester.

Tech has changed from the traditional days of "an engineering school" to its current ranking as one of the nation's best public universities. Women now make up 30 percent of the student body. The institute has expanded and continues to cultivate top-ranked programs in architecture, sciences, management, computing and liberal arts, as well as maintaining its reputation as a global leader in engineering.

From its beginnings more than a century ago, Georgia Tech has established a tradition of excellence in technological research, as well as education. The institute is well known for its high academic standards and stands among the top ranks of U.S. research universities with a clear vision for leadership in providing a cutting-edge, technological education for the 21st Century.

Georgia State University

Admissions Office
Sparks Hall
P.O. Box 4009
Atlanta, GA 30302-4009
Admissions phone: (404) 651-2365
Admissions fax: (404) 651-4811
Admissions e-mail: admissions@gsu.edu
Admissions URL: www.gsu.edu/admissions

Admissions

Current student, 8/2006-Submit Date, August 2006

Sent in application and received acceptance. It was that simple. Luckily I got a scholarship, or I wouldn't have been able to attend.

Current student, 8/2003-Submit Date, May 2006

I just had to submit and pay for my application online. There was no admission essay or anything—just sent in my SAT and ACT scores separately. Once I got in, I went to the two-day orientation. It was an advertisement for the Freshmen Learning Communities.

Alumnus/a, 8/2000-5/2004, November 2005

GSU has horrible organization. I got accepted but I had to call about 10 times to find out. They forgot to send me my letter. The process was simple—no essay, just an application form. I have heard it has gotten a little harder to get in because the school's reputation is really taking off. If you apply, make sure you make copies of everything and do not be afraid to follow up with the admissions office!

> **The school says:** "Georgia State has experienced tremendous growth in the number of applicants and enrollees in the past several years. As a response to the growing interest of students, the university has streamlined the enrollment process with the One Stop Shop. This One Stop Shop allows students to get information in person at one location and via the Web through their university e-mail account for questions concerning admissions, financial aid, registration and student accounts."

Alumnus/a, 8/2000-8/2004, November 2004

My main reason for applying to Georgia State was the HOPE Scholarship here in Georgia. I really wanted to go to school out-of-state but my parents told me it was on me to come up with the money. Looking back now, I'm glad they made their stand. Back then it was relatively easy to get accepted as long as you had good grades—I had a 3.3 GPA out of high school—but now I'm sure they are much more selective, as their image further improves. I don't even recall worrying about essay questions. I'm sure those AP classes in high school helped smooth my admittance, as well.

Alumnus/a, 1/1997-6/1999, May 2005

The admissions process was thorough, but not grueling. Georgia State is designed for motivated students who have other commitments, like a job or family. They want strong academic candidates, but allow lots of leeway for focusing on other things. With that said, the school requires well-thought-out, well-written admissions essays, and interviews are preferred but not required. Most students admitted probably have a 2.5 or higher in high school and score at least 1000 on the SAT.

> **The school says:** "Georgia State University is attracting more traditional freshmen. For fall semester 2005, 8,317 first-time freshmen applied and 5,150 were accepted, and 5,127 undergraduate transfer students applied with 3,136 accepted. Enrollment for fall semester 2005 was 25,945 (19,004 under-

graduate, 6,941 graduate). The average SAT score for entering first-time freshmen was 1094."

Academics

Current student, 8/2003-Submit Date, May 2006

The classes are pretty good. There is a huge option of classes and times for flexible scheduling, for the most part. Most of the professors I have had have been great. Hard work pays off. The workload is not that bad. Especially compared to other schools in the area, such as Georgia Tech or Emory. I really enjoy the academics. They are right up my alley. The J. Mack Robinson College of Business is very popular. Some of the more upper-level classes have attendance policies, which are hard for many of the students to follow.

Alumnus/a, 8/2000-5/2004, November 2005

The program was great! They offer a lot of relevant classes, and they offer them at a lot of different times. Since Georgia State began as a predominantly commuter college and because it is in the middle of downtown Atlanta, they seem to be understanding that most students have jobs in addition to the classes they are taking. The quality is good, but you should really try to ask around about the teachers and find out what teaching method you like the best. There isn't a whole lot of consistency. Some take attendance, some don't. Some offer only multiple choice testing—some are more project based. The workload is manageable, and the best thing I experienced was the professors' willingness to work with students who went out of their way to meet with them and discuss what they wanted out of the class or what they were struggling with.

Alumnus/a, 1/1997-6/1999, May 2005

Georgia State is a fairly large school within an urban setting that attracts very high-quality professors and associate staff. The required freshman classes can be large, but not 500. Think of a large auditorium for English 101 filled with maybe 100 students. Getting morning classes and night classes can be tough because the majority of students work during the day. It is important to register very early if possible.

The grading was surprisingly tough in all of my classes, but the professors allow for remediation and offer support. TAs are also often available for tutorials insome of the tougher subjects. The workload was manageable and very practical. The professors know that most of the students work and want to provide assignments that are authentic and can translate to the real world.

> **Georgia State says:** "The university offers a pre-planned schedule of courses in various interest areas called Freshmen Learning Communities. Each FLC enrolls about 25 students and is proposed and led by staff and faculty advisors. Being a part of this community provides a forum for discussion of new ideas, makes registering and advising easier, and creates a rich freshman experience, helping students quickly get to know fellow students, faculty and upperclassmen."

Alumnus/a, 8/2000-8/2004, November 2004

Going to school in the city, I got a lot out of learning about urban politics, public administration, sociology, and policy analysis. A lot of the books could be found in the libraries of one of the nearby schools (GSU, GT, Emory) and actually proved useful for other classes if you bought them. Even though I don't consider myself the hardest worker, I did much better academically in my junior and senior years. The teachers were usually fair and open-minded.

The downside of this particular school is the lack of pre-requisites offered each semester and the timing. You could always count on having night classes once a week at least (4:30 to 7pm, 7 to 9:45pm) and you had to stay on your toes before each semester to make sure you took the stuff you needed to graduate on time. I know a lot of people who, for some reason or another, didn't do that but

Read all of Vault's College Surveys at **www.vault.com/college**—get complete surveys on 100s of colleges and universities, expert advice on applicaton essays and more.

VAULT CAREER LIBRARY 179

I managed to finish up in four years despite missing a semester. Summer school helps you keep pace, even the dreaded mini-mesters.

On the flip side, the night classes helped if you worked parttime or if you were getting back into school. A lot of times I was one of the youngest people in my classes and one of a few non-transfers. GSU has always been good for people to come to up their degree, but more and more people actually start and finish there now. Other electives you choose can be in just about anything, and I even got to cross-register at Georgia Tech to cover an elective requirement. I also took a bunch of real estate classes, which led me to pursue real estate development as a career.

Current student, 1/2002-Submit Date, July 2004

Its classes are pretty easy, depending on the professor. Generally, there is always a curve. In the business classes, the coursework becomes much tougher, with a heavy reliance upon technology and team-based projects. You have to be fast in registering for classes, and oftentimes the school does not do a good job announcing when signup begins. To get the good classes, you need to be always monitoring when registration starts and what your exact time slot is. Have your classes picked out before you are due to register, and that will ensure you get the best classes. Also, they have a program called Statware (which you can access from GSU's web site). This gives you the grade distribution of every teacher over the past 30 semesters, divided by class and section.

> Regarding academics, the school says: "When compared with the experiences of freshmen at other schools in Georgia and in the United States, results from the National Survey of Student Engagement for 2005 indicated that Georgia State freshmen had more incidents of: (1) participation in class discussions; (2) working with other students on a class project or report; (3) including diverse perspectives (different races, religions, genders, political beliefs) in class discussions or assignments; and (4) participation in a community-based project as part of a regular course."

 ## Employment Prospects

Current student, 8/2003-Submit Date, May 2006

I do not really know what others that have graduated from GSU have achieved, but I got a beneficial co-op position two terms through GSU. I think a lot of people go to GSU for their MBAs. I am sure they get rewarded in the business world for their accomplishments at Georgia State.

Alumnus/a, 8/2000-5/2004, November 2005

One of the best things about GSU is location—internship opportunities throughout the city open up and post all over the campus. I got my first three internships with major international companies all because of Georgia State. The only problem I had was that the advisors were pretty useless. You have to take the initiative yourself. Make sure to talk to professors and peers before you use the advisors.

Alumnus/a, 8/2000-8/2004, November 2004

Naturally, most of the students in my school went after public-sector jobs with the exception of those in the HR specialization. The required internship forces you to be proactive in a good way and the listings through the University Career Services were helpful. Georgia State is very popular with MBA students and its prestige seems to have grown every year. The main thing is to be proactive though job hunting because, quite frankly, if a job is advertised at school, literally 27,000 students have access to it. The University Career Services only does so much and their career fairs have always been weak compared to GT's or Emory's. Talking to professors helped establish connections to the local area and the school posted a good number of internships.

> The school says: "Georgia State University now provides services through two career centers, one for undergraduates and one for alumni. New graduates can take advantage of services from both centers. Some of the services offered to alumni include programs, workshops, networking events, access to

career fairs and an online system for résumé posting, worldwide job postings and personal career advisement."

Alumnus/a, 1/1997-6/1999, May 2005

Locally, the employment prospects are great, although Atlanta is home to several excellent top schools. Georgia Tech, Emory and Agnes Scott probably provide a challenge for Georgia State grads in many areas, but in the fields of human resources, criminology and economics, GSU ranks very high. One of the nation's top economists is on staff at Georgia State and gives that department lot of clout.

Current student, Accounting, 1/2002-Submit Date, July 2004

The accounting department recently hired a full-time person to help with hooking GSU accounting grads up with jobs. He is a former recruiter from Deloitte and his responsibility is simply to labor on behalf of GSU students to get them the best jobs possible. The accounting department does a good job preparing you for the real world. Forget about getting a job with the Big Four unless you're a part of Beta Alpha Psi. GSU just recently restarted BAP, and it has grown to over 100 members in the past two years. This has propelled GSU onto the recruiting front stage much faster than anyone expected. Most students do internships while getting their 150 hours. GSU is in the heart of Atlanta, so it is a great place to go to school and work part-time.

 ## Quality of Life

Current student, 8/2003-Submit Date, May 2006

The GSU housing is OK. It is a lot bigger than most dorms. It was the housing for the Atlanta Summer Olympics. Downtown Atlanta can be kinda scary for some; but during the day with other students there, it is fine. I hear a lot of complaints about the transportation system to and from the dorms—they are not exactly near campus. But they seem a lot better than when I went. I had to take MARTA all the time, and this required a lot of walking.

> The school says: "Georgia State University will open 2,000 new student housing units in the heart of campus for fall semester 2007. Students will be able to walk to classes, the library and all points on campus. Future plans include Greek and other student interest housing on campus and another development for 2,000 students just off of Decatur Street."

Alumnus/a, 8/2000-5/2004, November 2005

Safety is something the school needs to work on. Theft was a problem, but they have increased security since I graduated. They are also building additional housing, which should be good for future students. Dining—you are pretty much on your own. The dorms now have kitchens, which is really nice, but there is no meal plan. There is a health department and a fantastic gym. A lot of Georgia State is being built up really well.

Alumnus/a, 8/2000-8/2004, November 2004

I didn't stay on campus but I wanted to. I still visit the fairly new rec center to work out. Most of the campus housing is actually near GT, with the university lofts restricted to older, married and international students. School of Policy Studies finally got its own building after being housed in three separate buildings near the heart of downtown. It's something for alumni to be proud of as the school expands into the city like the rest of the universities. It's best to ride MARTA to school and avoid parking near Turner Field or shelling out a few bucks every day for parking. I never felt threatened on a campus, but then again I'm a guy in pretty good shape.

> Georgia State says: "Georgia State University will open a new on-campus housing complex this fall for 2,000 students. A central plaza will link four towers offering apartment-style housing with street-level retail. Plans for even more on-campus student housing are underway.
>
> "The university's police department is the largest campus police department in Georgia and was the first campus police department in the state to achieve the distinction of 'Certified Law Enforcement Agency' from the State of Georgia Law

Enforcement Certification Program. The university's proactive approach to preventing crime has succeeded in minimizing criminal activity on campus, while promoting a strong sense of awareness and safety. As a university located in the heart of downtown Atlanta, Georgia State is not alone in efforts to prevent and combat crime. The downtown area boasts several agencies assigned to provide security, and the university police have strong working partnerships with these agencies."

Current student, 1/2002-Submit Date, July 2004

Not much of a campus life because it is a commuter school. However, you can have one, you just have to pursue it. It doesn't happen naturally like at UGA. Housing on campus is actually a mile off campus (where the dorms for the athletes during the 1996 Olympics were). Those dorms are not great, with many complaints about lack of Internet access and one central unit that gives heat in winter and air conditioning in summer. Once the A/C is on, it is not going off until winter. Once the heat is on, it is not going off until summer. At the main campus, the buildings are old but continually being renovated. The neighborhood is safe, but it is downtown, and walking through campus at night should be done only with a friend.

Current student, 10/2002-Submit Date, May 2004

Downtown Atlanta is very interesting place. It is something to experience first hand. The student housing is not next to the campus but close to it. There are a lot of rumors about what activities go on in the dorms. Lots of action for those interested in things of that nature. The campus is very nice for being located downtown. There are enough police for every person on campus, so crime isn't that big of a problem.

 Social Life

Current student, 8/2006-Submit Date, August 2006

Georgia State is centered on social life. There are bars, restaurants, dance clubs and many other things that encourage students to socialize and realize the diversity of the school.

Current student, 8/2003-Submit Date, May 2006

It is kind of difficult to make good friends at GSU in my opinion. Everyone just comes and goes, almost everyone seems to commute and do his/her own thing. As for the Greek activities, there are some fraternities and sororities, but they are not very traditional. They don't even really have houses on campus, which is weird to me. I just go over to Tech, where I made friends when I studied abroad, to party and have a good time. The people there are not as dorky as you hear they are.

The school says: "There are more than 250 student organizations. Becoming actively involved with other students on campus can greatly improve the quality of your student experience. One way that Georgia State has fostered bonds among students is through the Freshmen Learning Communities. Here's what students have told us:

'I'm glad I joined the FLC. It helped me make friends that I've stayed with the whole time I've been at GSU.'

'I thought I might feel overwhelmed when I first got to GSU, but the friends I made through my FLC made it feel like a family.'

'All my friends from high school kept saying, "Why are you in an FLC? You're wasting your time." But now I've got the 3.5 GPA, and none of them are even close. They lost their HOPE Scholarships, too.'

'I'm not sure the FLC made me stay. I was already focused. But it did help me academically and made me want to stay.'

'Registering for the FLC helped my GPA. It taught me how to study, how to study in groups and work with other students on projects. It also taught me how to be more connected with my teachers. I wouldn't have a 4.0 without it.'"

Alumnus/a, 8/2000-5/2004, November 2005

As a big city school, Georgia State lacks something of a traditional campus. All the facilities, clubs and Greek life are there, but they don't really advertise and the Greek organizations don't have houses. If anything is lacking at GSU, it is a traditional college social life. That was something I missed, but the appeal of living downtown and making my own social life was a little more appealing than a chance to be in a typical sorority or fraternity. The dating scene, events and bars are great because you are right in the middle of a huge city. There are tons of concerts and tons of bars. The theater is pretty popular and in the next couple of years, GSU is going to have a football team, which should increase social life activities dramatically.

Alumnus/a, 8/2000-8/2004, November 2004

Georgia State is trying very hard to fight the commuter school image it has had since it began as a night school about 85 years ago. Being in the city is nice, except most of it shuts down after 5 p.m. The 24-hour diner at one of the new classroom buildings is a nice touch. Never got into the Greek scene or most clubs because I worked 20 to 40 hours a week while in school. The upside is you can always find something going on in Atlanta.

Current student, 1/2002-Submit Date, July 2004

Tons of small businesses have opened up restaurants in the area because we have 30,000 students at GSU. The hotspot is Sidebar, right behind the Aderhold Building, which has first-class food and Stella always on tap. After finals (or before), that is the place to go. The Greek system is small but very active. It does a lot of off-campus activities because most people live off campus.

Current student, 10/2002-Submit Date, May 2004

GSU is located in downtown Atlanta, so there is a very good chance to meet some interesting people. The campus population is around 20,000 students from very different backgrounds.

 The School Says

Comments from Georgia State University alumni and students:

From a 2004 graduate: "College is about getting to know yourself. No other place is better to do that than Georgia State. On an everyday basis, you learn to live in one of the largest cities in America and interact with thousands of people who can be very different from you. You will definitely learn the keys to success in the business world and with other cultures. You can enroll at Georgia State unsure of your future and graduate with a degree that ensures your success."

From a sophomore, enrolled 2004-Submit Date: "Georgia State is a very diverse school that provides a great environment for students. I've had the chance to meet and get to know different kinds of people from all over the world. It really opens your eyes and helps you grow as a person."

From a junior enrolled 2003-Submit Date: "Before I came to Georgia State, I thought the classes would be huge and I wouldn't get to have any one-on-one time with my professors, but I was wrong. The classes are not too big and the professors are so helpful. They want you to ask questions and participate in the class. I also like that the focus is more on academics than sports, which is what I was looking for."

From a senior, enrolled 2002-Submit Date: "Georgia State has been a great experience for me. I've made so many friends here through my classes and campus activities. It's so easy to get involved in things you're interested in. I live in the lofts on campus with most of my friends. Campus housing is like having your own downtown apartment only cheaper, plus you meet a lot of people. And the rec center is right down the street—it's really nice and it's free."

From a freshman, enrolled 2005-Submit Date: "I would advise any incoming students to attend the INCEPT orientation pro-

Read all of Vault's College Surveys at **www.vault.com/college**—get complete surveys on 100s of colleges and universities, expert advice on applicaton essays and more.

VAULT CAREER LIBRARY   181

gram. This is a huge university, and right away, I feel like I belong. I knew I wanted to major in biology, so I signed up for the Immunology Freshmen Learning Community at INCEPT. My first semester in college, and I'm already working in the lab with one of the top immunology researchers in the country."

Morehouse College

Admissions Office
830 Westview Drive
S.W. Atlanta, GA 30314
Admissions phone: (404) 681-2800
Admissions e-mail: admissions@morehouse.edu
Admissions URL: www.morehouse.edu/admissions

 ## Admissions

Current student, Business, 8/2002-Submit Date, June 2007

I wrote an essay in addition to the application process. My mother attended the sister school, Spelman, so I made sure to mention that, and I also made myself visible to the admissions office by becoming active in the alumni affairs for my local city and speaking with the dean of freshmen about the programs offered. Presently, students must submit an application and interview. My best advice for those students choose Morehouse for their undergraduate education would be to do well on your SATs, actively seek out information on pre-student programs with the college, get in touch with your local alumni chapter president, and visit the campus so that you can get a good idea feel for the institution.

Alumnus, 8/1997-5/2002, December 2004

This school is fairly selective in its admissions process. Being the only all-male school for African-Americans, there are a lot of high-caliber students who apply.

Alumnus, 8/1999-5/2003, November 2003

The admissions process was pretty straightforward. In fact, I finished the application in roughly two hours. However, the process has become much more competitive as the school is beginning to get noticed around the country. With a decent GPA (roughly 3.0) and SAT scores (1100), acceptance should not be a problem. Administratively, the school can be slow. Do not feel brash by continuing to call regarding acceptance decisions or receipt of application materials.

Current student, Business, 8/2000-Submit Date, August 2005

The admissions process for Morehouse was much more simple than I thought it would be. The most important issue was the actual application, including the essay. My high school GPA was rather high, so I focused on making my essay as truthful yet interesting as possible. Thinking about college should start freshman year of high school, as opposed to junior or even senior years. Unless there is an interview process, all that sets you apart from the rest is how you look on paper. GPA calculation starts the first day of school, and it is much easier to keep it up, than to bring it up. The essay should be very well written but (truthful). It will hurt your chances of admission if you fabricate a story or opinion. Admissions officers are trained to sense these fraudulent essays a mile away.

Current student, 8/1998-Submit Date, November 2003

The admissions process was not complicated at all. One thing about Morehouse College is that you'll be surrounded by some of the brightest African-American male minds in the country. That is hard to find elsewhere.

 ## Academics

Current student, Business, 8/2002-Submit Date, June 2007

Morehouse is a small, private and all-male college. The classes are generally smaller than those of larger universities, thus making them a lot more intimate. Students are able to engage with professors for a quality education. You feel more like a student than a number. The workload is rigorous. It is a competitive educational atmosphere. Major classes do fill up; however, there are two neighboring schools (Spelman and Clark Atlanta), where students are able to cross-register.

Current student, Business, 8/2000-Submit Date, August 2005

I am a business administration major with a concentration in finance. The first two years were mostly filled with a core curriculum, consisting of history, math and English. While some business courses were offered at the sophomore level, they were core business classes. The well-rounded curriculum of a liberal arts institution sets a good foundation, making the major concentration courses that much easier to grasp.

An emphasis has to be placed on developing good study habits, another thing that should be started early in high school. The core classes, given a good study habit, enable you to set boundaries, organize massive, oftentimes unrelated courses, and prepare you for more detailed and tedious upper-level classes.

Alumnus, 8/1997-5/2002, December 2004

The school's curriculum competes with any top program in the country. It is designed as a liberal arts college providing students the opportunity to learn various disciplines before embarking on committed educational paths.

Alumnus, Economics, 8/1999-5/2003, November 2003

Morehouse College is not a noted school for nothing. As an economics and math major, the classes were rigorous and professors were knowledgeable about their academic interests. The books used were similar to those at any Ivy League school and the technology, although below par, has been receiving much funding lately. In addition, the requirements are in line with those needed to succeed in your chosen career.

Current student, 8/1998-Submit Date, November 2003

Don't fall into the trap that Morehouse College is easy because it is a HBCU. The coursework is demanding and most majors will have you pull all-nighters. The teachers demand the best from you.

 ## Employment Prospects

Current student, Business, 8/2002-Submit Date, June 2007

There is an excellent career center offered at Morehouse, as well as in the Atlanta University Center, that Morehouse students can utilize. As a business major, my experience is that there is continuous training for interviews, résumés, and internships with some of the country's leading organizations.

Current student, 8/2000-Submit Date, August 2005

I believe this factor is the strongest and most driven by Morehouse College. The business department has many classes to prepare students for corporate America, as well as heavy ties with companies' feeder programs. Having a strong alumni base in corporate America helps tremendously with interning and gaining the inside track. Interning is definitely very important, and should be considered for sophomore and junior summers. Internships are an excellent way to apply what you've learned during the year in real-life settings. The internships will set you apart from classmates who just worked or went to summer school.

Alumnus, 8/1997-5/2002, December 2004

Whether an individual wants to enter the business community, a graduate program or a nonprofit, Morehouse bridges the educational gap between theoretical and practical perspectives. As an alumnus, I meet other alumni doing so many different things within different industries across the country.

Alumnus, 8/1999-5/2003, November 2003

Morehouse College is like a labor market. There are two tiers, primary and secondary. Getting into the primary tier is a function of both academic accomplishments and, on some level, schmoozing. The job opportunities are diverse and plentiful. I had internships on both the buy and sell sides as well as a high-level nonprofit. In addition, the top-tier graduate programs (for any field) are interested in the students. In a recent *Wall Street Journal* article, Morehouse ranked 29th in the total amount of its graduate students attending Ivy League institutions per year. In addition, companies, such as Goldman Sachs, Morgan Stanley, Merrill Lynch, Glaxo Smith Kline and McKinsey, recruit heavily and often. However, if you are in the second tier lower than 3.0 GPA, I would advice a switch to a larger state school because you will find $22,000 per year wasted.

Current student, 8/1998-Submit Date, November 2003

If you do well at Morehouse, you can have any job you want when you graduate.

Quality of Life

Current student, Business, 8/2002-Submit Date, June 2007

Morehouse has been in the process of updating its facilities, and there are now new housing developments, computer labs and a new business building. Crime is relatively low on campus. It's been my experience that the Morehouse police are always visible and the dorms are pretty secure.

Current student, 8/2000-Submit Date, August 2005

The college life is one that builds strong character, especially once the initial fright of new surroundings settles. Extra care has to be taken to ensure safety off campus. Traveling in pairs or groups is a must, as freshmen are easy prey to criminal activity.

Alumnus, 8/1997-5/2002, December 2004

The school's surroundings provide a great quality of life because it is in the heart of Atlanta and there are three or four other institutions within walking distance. Furthermore, students are able to enjoy the activities throughout the rest of Atlanta—that is if they have an automobile.

Alumnus, 8/1999-5/2003, November 2003

The quality of life at Morehouse varies. On average it is on par with any other school. The school has invested in beautiful new housing facilities and increased protection. The surrounding neighborhood is not the greatest, but the school does a good job of keeping wanderers away from students.

Current student, 8/1998-Submit Date, November 2003

Expect a lot of expansion in the near future.

Social Life

Current student, Business, 8/2002-Submit Date, June 2007

For those students who are familiar with what an HBCU is, then you know it's non-stop fun, parties, frats and several other extracurricular activities and programs.

Current student, 8/2000-Submit Date, August 2005

Restaurants are the best in Atlanta. Once public transportation is mastered or a car is assumed, many dining opportunities are afforded. Getting away from campus is essential, as sometimes you get sick of seeing the same people. It's also another character builder and a way to practice crucial social skills not learned in the classroom.

Alumnus, 8/1997-5/2002, December 2004

Social life is the best bar-none for an African-American student. There is no other city that provides the types of opportunities with so many positive people in one area.

Alumnus, 8/1999-5/2003, November 2003

The social life at Morehouse is what you make of it. The Greek organizations are back and as lively as ever. Spring (and sometimes fall) rush are exciting times. In addition, Atlanta is a great city with a vibrant nightlife. Restaurants, clubs and cultural events dot the week's calendar.

In addition, Spelman College is across the street and, trust me, there are no finer women in the world than there. Not only are these women beautiful, but they are smart and well-to-do. They more than makeup for the lack of females at Morehouse. However, if confident women with a touch of brashness do not float your boat, then Agnes Scott, Brenau, Emory and GA State are all within a 10-mile radius. The dress and attitudes at Morehouse and Spelman take some getting used to. The dress is flashy but classy, be prepared to see people wear clothes matching in every way from head to toe. Morehouse College is the school for the African-American bourgeoisie.

Current student, 8/1998-Submit Date, November 2003

It's Atlanta. Enough said.

Read all of Vault's College Surveys at **www.vault.com/college**—get complete surveys on 100s of colleges and universities, expert advice on applicaton essays and more.

VAULT CAREER LIBRARY 183

Spelman College

Admissions Office
350 Spelman Lane S.W.
Atlanta, GA 30314-4399
Admissions phone: (800) 982-2411
Admissions fax: (404) 270-5193
Admissions e-mail: admiss@spelman.edu
Admissions URL: www.spelman.edu

 Admissions

Current student, 8/2005-Submit Date, May 2007

If a student has participated in a pre-college program at Spelman, her parents have connections with administration, and/or if she is a well-rounded student, there should be no problem with admission. Interviews are optional. Someone who did not perform well in high school should schedule an interview so the college won't make a judgment based on her tarnished record. The college is selective. Taking summer classes for college credit and AP/IB classes in high school is a plus. When you get in, know that you are among the brightest women around the world. One's college essay is not required to consist of huge words and deep expression. Allow the reader to understand your story, be creative, use light humor and, in some manner, set yourself apart from others.

Current student, Psychology, 8/2006-Submit Date, May 2007

The admissions process at Spelman was a smooth one. Spelman College looks for well-rounded students who participate in community service, as well as extracurricular activities, while maintaining a presentable GPA. I did not have an interview, but I was allowed to speak with administration when I came to visit Spelman's campus the spring semester before I was accepted. Since Spelman was the only college to which I applied, I spent an ample amount of time writing my essay to ensure that I would be accepted. The essay prompt I chose was quite easy to respond to, being that it focused on my love for Spelman. I absolutely loved the very idea of Spelman and therefore I poured my heart in the essay, which I feel greatly impacted Spelman's decision to allow me the privilege of being a Spelmanite.

Current student, Economics, 8/2006-Submit Date, May 2007

Spelman is a very selective liberal arts school for women. It has three programs for admission: Early Decision, Early Action and Regular Decision. Early decision is legally binding and you must attend Spelman, while Early Action simply notifies you a bit earlier of your acceptance. Be very creative when writing your essays because the admissions committee wants to see who you are; women who apply to Spelman are at the top of their class, so you want to say something that makes you stand out.

Current student, Psychology, 8/2006-Submit Date, May 2007

Because it is a liberal arts college, it looks at more than your grades. It is good to put effort into your essay to let a bit of your personality shine. Spelman is very selective, so make sure you show something about yourself that separates you from the rest.

Current student, English, 8/2006-Submit Date, May 2007

There's a basic application and essay. They are looking for high GPAs, high test scores, college prep courses, IB, AP, the works. They want you to stand out; they are very selective. Maybe 10 percent of applicants are accepted. It will help if you have a cause that you are passionate about—Spelman wants to help you achieve your goals to make the global community better, not just be a degree on a wall.

Current student, Psychology, 8/2004-Submit Date, May 2007

Spelman is a very competitive school to get into. To apply to Spelman, I had to fill out an application and write an essay. I didn't have to do an interview. I would advise any student applying to Spelman to make sure that she not only meet the academic criteria, but that she also make herself stand out from the other candidates. The essay is an opportunity to present herself to the college. Spelman likes women who are ambitious and who will be leaders and innovators.

Current student, Psychology, 8/2004-Submit Date, April 2007

Scholarships at Spelman are limited. There are five Presidential Scholarships and about 65 Dean's Scholarships awarded each year. The best way to get one is to apply Early Action: this is a non-binding early admission option that will let you know by December 31 whether you were admitted or deferred admission to the regular pool. Early action gives you two chances to get in and also puts you in the early pool to be considered for scholarships. I would also apply for any outside scholarship for which you are eligible early in the game, as Spelman may look more favorably on you if you bring outside money.

Current student, 8/2004-Submit Date, May 2006

There are no interviews; therefore, your essay needs to be on point. Each year there are two questions and the applicant only has to answer one. When writing your essay, just make sure that you are honest and that the content and mechanics are correct. Have an English teacher or counselor review your application letter. Even better, have two or more review your letter!

The most important aspect of applying to Spelman is the scholarships. When you fill out an application, you are immediately put in the pool to receive a scholarship from the school. If you come for a tour or A Day in Your Life, an event to tell you all about Spelman, the admissions staff will tell you that scholarships are given to the person who has a decent SAT, a good GPA, involvement in school and community service. To get a scholarship at Spelman, and a good one, an applicant must have an outstanding SAT score. To receive a Presidential Scholarship, an applicant must have a 2400 out of 2600, while having a 3.5 or higher GPA. For a Dean's Scholarship, an applicant must have a 2200 out of 2600, and a 3.5 GPA or higher. Therefore, please make sure you get those SAT scores up there. Other than that, they have the Bonner Scholarship that pays everything, but you must fill that out separately and you do not get the application until you are accepted to the college.

The college accepts approximately 500 to 600 entering students each year out of about 5,000+ applicants, so acceptance is very selective for this small liberal arts college.

 Academics

Current student, Education, 8/2006-Submit Date, May 2007

It is extremely hard to get popular classes. If you want all of your classes, you should register on the first day possible. The classes are relatively small; therefore, you can get close with the students, as well as the professors. The grading system is complicated; If you are good with time management, the workload is pretty light.

Current student, Economics, 8/2006-Submit Date, May 2007

The academics here are unlike anywhere else. You are able to feel as if your professors really care about you and whether or not you are actually learning the material. Some of the more popular majors are biology and psychology because Spelman creates excellent female physicians.

Current student, Psychology, 8/2004-Submit Date, May 2007

Academically, Spelman is challenging. Of course, some classes will be harder than others, but overall, you need to work hard to get good grades. Fortunately, there are many resources on campus to help you in areas where you need it, such as the Learning Resources Center, the Writing Lab and student tutors.

Current student, Computer Science, 8/2004-Submit Date, May 2007

Academics at Spelman are ranked very highly, which was one of the reasons I chose to attend Spelman. Because of the small enrollment, one is able to receive more one-on-one attention from professors concerning all aspects of the class, as well as speak with upperclass-women about what courses to take and from whom to take them.

Current student, English, 8/2006-Submit Date, May 2007

The academic workload is rigorous. They expect you to do a lot of work outside of class (they call it the "fourth hour justification"). Expect late nights, lots of papers regardless of the major, and individual thought. You will need to analyze critically for success.

Current student, Sociology, 8/2005-Submit Date, May 2007

Understand that we are a liberal arts school, so that's the limiting factor of our programs. There are no business major programs, fashion design programs and so on, but you do have the option of creating your own major and you can enroll at any class in the Atlanta University Center. Morehouse College has a business major and Clark Atlanta University has a fashion department. Every professor I have ever had encourages all students to come to his/her office, and this is doable because of the small class size. No one will be overlooked unless she chooses to be by not attending class and even the professor will know. When choosing your schedule, choose early because we are all students who desire to get every class we want, and being a small class, some classes are only offered at two different times during the semester and may not return until the next year.

Current student, Psychology, 8/2004-Submit Date, April 2007

Academically, Spelman is wonderful. The professors have rigorous classes and yet they care about the individual progress of each student. Classes are rarely larger than 30 students, and professors typically learn the names of all their students, as well as their writing styles and particular strengths and weaknesses. There are also a lot of alumnae who teach here, and who understand the unique position of Spelman students. Nevertheless, our professors are diverse and from unique backgrounds who all bring something important to the table.

Since this is a small liberal arts college, classes are typically held between 8 a.m. and 5 p.m.. There is the occasional evening class, but that will rarely be a class needed for a major, and will most likely be an elective course or a special interest course. Therefore, attending Spelman's classes is difficult for part-time students who work full time during the normal work day.

While cross-registering at Morehouse and Clark offers classes with male students, there is something very rewarding about being in all-female classes. It is an empowering thing, especially in classes where oppression and social justice are major themes (which, given Spelman's mission, is nearly every course, even some math and science).

Current student, 8/2004-Submit Date, May 2006

Academics at Spleman College are excellent. It is hard to get into the popular classes that everyone needs because there are not that many openings. The grading is fair, depending on your major.

Employment Prospects

Current student, 8/2004-Submit Date, May 2007

Everyone receives weekly, sometimes daily, mass e-mails about internships, fellowships and information on post-grad employment. Most graduates attend graduate school, others obtain excellent careers, such as Teach for America, pharmaceutical sales rep, or pro buyers for large corporations, such as Macy's.

Current student, 8/2006-Submit Date, May 2007

I can't even begin to describe all the opportunities that are just waiting for you when you come to Spelman. In every field, recruiters from the best grad schools and the best companies come on a regular basis to recruit our students. Seniors are lining up jobs and internships with everyone from Goldman Sachs to Pfizer and everything in between. The alumnae are a huge part of the success of the current students. Quite a few comeback often to offer advice in the fields they have pursued and sometimes even offer internships to a few students. On campus there are quite a few programs specifically geared towards helping students

reach specific career goals like the Office of Science and Technical Careers (OSETC) and there is Career Planning and Development that also helps those in every major.

Current student, Psychology, 8/2005-Submit Date, May 2007

Spelman's Office of Career Planning and Development is extremely helpful in connecting current and past Spelman students with potential employers. There are job fairs every semester and employers come specifically to Spelman to recruit the best all throughout the year. Also, Career Planning helps students get summer internships. There is a staff of about five to eight people whose sole job is to get internships and jobs for Spelman students and alumnae.

Current student, English, 8/2006-Submit Date, May 2007

Spelman provides a lot of prestige if you use the opportunities they give you in undergrad to build your résumé. The name is not enough, but it will help you get an interview, especially if another Spelman sister works there. The alumnae network is very tight, internships are bountiful if you have a good GPA, and the grads get into good entry-level positions. However, these jobs will sometimes require relocation.

Current student, 8/2004-Submit Date, September 2004

Spelman has an Office of Career Planning and Development that actively works to help students get not just jobs after graduation but internships. The school year just started about six weeks ago and already we've had so many corporations and companies come to recruit on campus: Teach For America, Goldman Sachs, PricewaterhouseCoopers, the list goes on and on! Spelman is highly recognized with employers because, CPD is very committed to getting students involved with early career development (they are always inviting us out to their office and talking to us whenever they see us), and we have alumnae who are very committed to Spelman and love to hire Spelman alumnae. Our name is very prestigious and valued with companies all over the country. There is always someone from some large corporation or government sector on campus recruiting Spelman students.

Spelman is really good about getting internship opportunities for students. These students go all over the country and world; they work at NASA during the summers, research on university grants, and work for the national government in public policy. I'm constantly amazed by the places these young women go and what they have done there. Our small size makes it easier for career placement officers to develop a close relationship with students, and to meet their specific needs. There are certain internships that companies have created specifically for Spelman students, or that they consistently want to have Spelman students fill.

Quality of Life

Current student, 8/2006-Submit Date, May 2007

There are quite a few programs on campus that try to ensure the safety and well-being of the students like SHAPE, which stands for Student Health Awareness and Peer Education, and others along that line that just deal with everything from safe sex practices to positive self image and self esteem. Housing is set aside only for freshmen and for everyone else there is a lottery system that is sort of stressful but fair. The classroom facilities, as well as the rest of campus buildings, are well kept and therefore able to serve their purpose. Now the food, I am not going to lie, can be pretty bad, but you can ask almost any college students anywhere and they would say the same. We are in the process of working with the cafeteria staff to change a few things, though, so hopefully things will be looking up.

Current student, English, 8/2006-Submit Date, May 2007

Living here is not for the faint of heart. There are challenges for some of the most simple of tasks. Many of the freshman dorms don't have air conditioning, and most of them are many decades old. It adds to the traditional feel, but sleek and chic they're not. The food is edible and there are lots of choices, especially for vegetarians, those with special dietary needs or who don't eat beef/pork. The campus is located near public housing facilities, so the surrounding neighborhood is sometimes not the safest of places. Don't walk around alone if it isn't absolutely necessary.

Read all of Vault's College Surveys at **www.vault.com/college**–get complete surveys on 100s of colleges and universities, expert advice on applicaton essays and more.

VAULT CAREER LIBRARY **185**

Current student, Psychology, 8/2004-Submit Date, April 2007

Housing on Spelman's campus was a mixed experience. I lived in the residence halls for two and a half years, one and a half of those years as a resident assistant. The housing staff was friendly and helpful and the experience of meeting a cohort during my first year remains friends throughout my years at Spelman, including my roommate, was priceless. However, in my opinion, the facilities are not great. Most of the residential halls are decades old and don't even have electronic card entry—we use keys. There are no suite-style rooms, although Spelman is fixing that; most of the residence halls don't even have air conditioning, and there is a long list of appliances we're not allowed to bring (refrigerators, microwaves, hot plates, George Foreman grills, candles, incense, it goes on.)

They've been getting much better with the food, so now I actually look forward to eating rather than dreading the cafeteria and getting cereal for dinner again. The options for vegetarians and vegans are slim, and I wouldn't suggest getting a meal plan if you live off campus: I just pay the $3.75 when I want a meal (it's buffet-style). There's only one cafeteria, although with the new residence hall they're planning to build another one.

Current student, 8/2005-Submit Date, May 2006

Housing could use some improvements, such as air conditioning. The classrooms are nice and accommodating. The science center is fully equipped with all the technology a student might need.

Current student, 8/2005-Submit Date, July 2006

Campus is very beautiful and well kept, flowers year-round, constant grooming. Very safe, no need to worry about any safety issues with 24/7 public safety officers on a gated campus. Housing is average, no air conditioning in freshman dorms, no refrigerators allowed. Main cafeteria food is decent, while there is a tastier option, "the grill," with a card of up to $25 each semester. Several facilities, the science center open 24/7 with a computer lab, MIT help center, tutors in every department, no need to worry about academic help. Deans available for meetings upon request, extremely resourceful.

Social Life

Current student, 8/2004-Submit Date, May 2007

Although there is an all-male school literally across the street and a coed university on the other side, as well as a plethora of other surrounding colleges, the dating scene is still sub-par, to say the least. I believe the social student events around campus are interesting (homecoming week is the best, founder's day week-long events are good, too.) There is a coffee shop the underclassmen enjoy, as well.

Current student, Economics, 8/2004-Submit Date, May 2007

In my opinion, Atlanta is the number one college town. There is a lot to do and see all the time. Especially in the infamous Atlanta University Center. Well, let's just say, we definitely know how to party!

Current student, 8/2006-Submit Date, May 2007

Now, despite what some may think, this school is beyond social. You can walk on this campus everyday of the week and find more guys than girls, just hanging out. Not to mention there is always some group or club having its week and hosting some sort of party or social on campus, especially in the spring. In the fall the big thing is going to the clubs, which actually provide transportation to and from their facilities, which is great for freshmen since we aren't allowed to have cars the first year. Besides that, there are three or four malls within 30 to 40 minutes from the school and those are popular hangouts also, and of course the movie theater is a good place to go, too. Dating is kind of interesting. Sometimes things can get a little heated when girls find out one boy from Morehouse or Clark has been dating two girls. The college community is small here, so everyone knows each others businesses or is a part of others business and doesn't know it, but most of the time the drama is limited. Like I said, lots of groups to join: the newspaper staff, student government, we have a group that plans events for students, students who bring health awareness issues, and regional clubs based on where you are from (e.g., Texas Club, Tri-State). Basically you name it, we probably have a club for it or you can start one if

you'd like. There is not an overwhelming amount of Greek Life but at the same time it is an option for those who choose.

Current student, 8/2004-Submit Date, May 2006

There are over 300 organizations in the Atlanta University Center for a student to get involved, so there are no excuses when it comes to being involved. The clubs range from religious clubs and SGA, to clubs for majors and clubs for career interests.

There is a coffee place and mini grocery store out on Morehouse's car deck called Jazzman's and they have some food and excellent smoothies and coffee. There is the grill at Spelman and Clark Atlanta. There is also a grill type place on Morehouse's campus.

There are people in relationships and dating, but most of the dating-type activities occur off campus.

There are events like every day on either one of the three campuses. These range from spoken word performances and concerts, to seminars and parties. There is always something to do around the AUC. There are also club nights that begin on Thursday and usually end on Saturday, and charter buses come to pick students up and drop them off at the end of the night. When it comes to church on Sunday, charter buses are there on Sunday morning and many of the churches serve lunch. However, if you want to stay on campus, there is church service at each of the schools on Sunday beginning at 10 p.m.

The biggest event on any Historically Black College and University (HBCU) campus is homecoming. There are events every day of the week, including a fashion show, concert and coronation, and these all lead up to the homecoming parade and game. And even after the game, there are club events.

The Greek system is very big here in the AUC. Many people believe that they run the campuses. If you decide to do a Greek organization here at Spelman, do not expect it to be easy. There are so many females trying to get into basically two organizations, it is hard to get into any of them. Important info.: If you want to join an organization, keep your mouth closed. Do not let anybody know, especially the Greeks, that you want to join the organization. That is all I can give you on that.

The School Says

Celebrating its 126 year legacy, Spelman College is a private, independent, liberal arts, historically Black college for women. Founded in 1881, Spelman is the only historically Black college in the nation to be included on the *U.S. News & World Report's* list of Top 75 Best Liberal Arts Colleges—Undergraduate, 2007. To build on its legacy and become even more competitive, the college launched Spelman ALIVE, a five-prong initiative that promotes academic excellence, leadership development, improving our environment, visibility of our achievements and exemplary customer service.

Spelman is part of the largest consortium of historically Black institutions of higher learning in the world. Its four partner institutions include Clark Atlanta University, the Interdenominational Theological Center, Morehouse College, and Morehouse School of Medicine. Spelman shares cross-registration with its undergraduate partners. They also share the Robert W. Woodruff Library.

Five minutes west of downtown Atlanta, Spelman sits on a historic campus of 32 acres, dating back to 1883. There are 25 buildings, including Sisters Chapel, Giles Hall, Packard Hall, Rockefeller Hall and Reynolds Cottage. The Camille O. Hanks Cosby Academic Center was dedicated in 1996, and a new state-of-the-art science center houses classrooms and labs.

For 126 years, Spelman College has empowered women to use their talents fully to succeed and to better the world. The college boasts outstanding alumnae, including Children's Defense

Fund Founder Marian Wright Edelman; U.S. Foreign Service Director General Ruth Davis; authors Tina McElroy Ansa and Pearl Cleage and actress LaTanya Richardson.

With a student to faculty ratio of 12:1, more than 83 percent of the full-time faculty members have doctorates or other ter-

minal degrees. Annually, nearly one-third of Spelman students receive degrees in the sciences. The students number more than 2,186 and represent 43 states and 34 foreign countries.

University of Georgia

Admissions Office
Terrell Hall
Athens, GA 30602-1633
Admissions phone: (706) 542-8776
Admissions fax: (706) 542-1466
Admissions e-mail: undergrad@admissions.uga.edu
Admissions URL: www.admissions.uga.edu

 ## Admissions

Current student, 8/2006-Submit Date, September 2006

If at all possible, do the early admissions process. It takes fewer than 10 minutes and is well worth your time because all you have to fill in is your SAT scores and general information. I, however, missed this deadline by one day and was stuck filling out the regular decision application, which meant I found out later than the rest of my friends had to fill out the full application, which was extremely long. I had no interviews before coming or being accepted to this institution and the essays were long and difficult (at least more difficult than other universities applications). UGA is pretty selective; however, this I learned when I got here. Many in-state children of alumni did not get in this year, and if you are from in state, you are on the HOPE Scholarship. However, us out-of-stators are expected to pay the high out-of-state tuition.

Current student, History, 7/2003-Submit Date, June 2007

Getting into Georgia has become more difficult every year. The Honors Program at Georgia is probably one of the best programs of its kind in the United States. When I got in, the average SAT score was 1420. Now, I believe it's 1480. There is no interview process.

Current student, 8/2003-Submit Date, January 2007

I believe the admissions process was very easy. The school (back in 2003) had the option of completing a paper application or an online application, which was very convenient. There was no interview required as part of the admissions process, but it did require two essays. The essays were fairly easy to write and did not require any thinking outside of the box.

Alumnus/a, 8/2001-5/2006, December 2006

The admissions process is fairly simple and if you have a good SAT, and 3.5 GPA and you were in at least three or four clubs and maybe played a sport, you will get in. Also there are exceptions to the rule when it comes to the SAT score if your GPA is very high.

Current student, 5/2003-Submit Date, April 2005

The admissions process at the University of Georgia is the longest that I had to complete before coming to college. The application is very detailed and has an extensive policy. A recommendation is required from someone that you know from your school or in the community. The essays are 500 words long on topics that you may not want to write about and they seem to deal with your morals and opinions. There is no interview required. The personal information that is required is very extensive and asks everything from what you have participated in while in high school and everything that you may do while not in school. It takes about a month before the university notifies you if you are accepted.

Current student, 8/2002-Submit Date, February 2005

I applied here as a transfer student, and had a wonderful experience applying. The application was very easy to fill out, and as a transfer applicant, there were no essays to write. Everyone to whom I spoke, whether it was about classes, tuition or my application, was very friendly and willing to help me out. The best piece of advice when applying is to be organized. Be familiar with any information they may need, like your social security number, ACT scores, SAT scores, GPA and your transcripts. Also, be on time. If there is a deadline for your application, which there is, turn it in early. There were no interviews just the application.

Current student, 10/2003-Submit Date, November 2004

Don't write what you think they want to hear, write about what you want. Every year, it becomes harder and harder to get in. So, turn your application in early. Also, it is very important to keep a high GPA, around 3.75, and get a mid-high score on your SATs (around a 1240 at least). If you get in, pay to reserve your spot immediately.

Current student, 8/2003-Submit Date, June 2004

Pretty easy to get in. It is getting harder every year with more good students staying in Georgia to take advantage of the HOPE Scholarship. If you have a decent SAT and GPA, you shouldn't have a problem. I think they still look at legacy information. Apparently, the essay portion of the application is growing in importance. The university, by charter, must have 84.4 percent of its students from in-state. Out-of-state students usually have a much harder time getting in. A 1390 SAT score and 3.8 GPA got me in from out of state and I think you can get in with less.

 ## Academics

Current student, 8/2006-Submit Date, September 2006

The quality of classes that I have been able to observe so far is pretty good, but I do think that high school prepared me well for college classes and curricula. As a freshman attending the second to last orientation session, my experience with the ease of getting popular classes was that it wasn't easy at all; however, drop/add week helped a little with that problem and I was able to pick up two classes then that I hadn't been able to earlier that summer. Grading has just changed this year with a test-program of a plus/minus system. Because I am in the Honors Program, the professors are mostly the top of their respective fields, which is extremely nice to have. The workload is similar to that in high school; except, you must study in advance and read a lot!

Current student, History, 7/2003-Submit Date, June 2007

The Honors Program is incredible, and some of the regular classes can be quite challenging. That being said, Georgia can be as difficult or as easy as you choose to make it.

Current student, 8/2003-Submit Date, January 2007

The academic program can be either difficult or easy depending on your major. The journalism and business schools are very competitive. I found the quality of classes to be rather high. I have been very satisfied with many of my business courses. As far as the ease of getting popular classes, it can be difficult sometimes due to students who qualify for early registration who may sometimes prohibit older students (juniors/seniors) from getting some classes they

Read all of Vault's College Surveys at **www.vault.com/college**—get complete surveys on 100s of colleges and universities, expert advice on applicaton essays and more.

VAULT CAREER LIBRARY 187

may want. For example, I am a senior in my last semester and am just now taking an intro religion class that has a majority of freshmen.

Alumnus/a, 8/2001-5/2006, December 2006

All academic programs at UGA are becoming increasingly more difficult. The president of the university and many of the program deans are hiring better professors (from Ivy League or Top 10 schools), and the workload for most programs has increased and become more strenuous if you try to take a full load of classes. Also many of undergrad majors and graduate majors are highly respected, for example, the business school, public administration, education and few others are Top 20 or 30 programs.

Alumnus/a, 8/2001-5/2005, March 2006

If you want to study abroad, UGA has excellent programs. The Oxford program is absolutely fantastic, and inexpensive, as well. No kidding, UGA probably has the best Oxford program behind Columbia, as you can take classes at any college you want, as long as a Don there is willing to teach you. Most other programs are restricted to one college, or to a few, and are always far more expensive.

If you go to UGA and care about the quality of your education, get into the Honors Program (it is really hard to get into once you are at UGA, better to be in it from the start). The Honors Program is like a different school.

Current student, 5/2003-Submit Date, April 2005

The quality of classes depends on the professors. It is very hard to get a good class if you are not an Honors student because they get all the good teachers. The Honors students get to pick classes first because their classes are supposed to be harder. The grading is fairly reasonable because there is room for improvement in some classes. There are classes that don't give anything but one test and a final. Also, the workload depends upon the teacher because there are classes where the only thing the professor does is lecture and expects you to come to class later in the year and pass a test and eventually a final. Some professors give out homework all the time just to keep you busy and do not take it up or grade it.

Current student, 8/2002-Submit Date, February 2005

Most lower-level classes consist of 150 to 300 students. If that class size is too large for you, I would suggest applying to the Honors Program. This will give you first dibs on most courses, as well as provide you with smaller, more personal classes. There will still be some cases in which you will have to be in a large class, but overall they are not that bad. UGA has some of the best professors, all of whom are very willing to help you out in any way they can. I have had professors want to meet with each and every one of his 300 students, even if it was just for five minutes. Overall, it is not too difficult to get into popular classes. Again, if you are in Honors, it will be easier. Or, if you are an upperclassman, it will also be easy. The grading depends on the teacher, but most are very fair. They give you a syllabus labeling each and every assignment and its worth. The overall workload is not too bad, depending on your courseload. There will always be those weeks when there are a number of tests or papers due, but it has never been unbearable.

Current student, 8/2003-Submit Date, June 2004

Despite being a larger school, the University of Georgia is one of the elite public schools in the nation. This holds true for the program I am participating in right now, which is a bachelor's in political science program. Being a second-year student, it is much harder for me to get popular classes, as the university performs class registration based on credit hours. In other words, people with the most credit hours at the school get first choice of their classes.

The grading system is pretty uniform throughout the school with an A-F, A being a 4.0, B being a 3.0 and so on. The professors are nice enough, but it is harder to get to know them in very large classes, such as the classes the university provides in the first several years of a student's education. The workload is not too bad, probably not any worse than six to seven hours per week, depending on the intensity of a student's class schedule.

Employment Prospects

Current student, History, 7/2003-Submit Date, June 2007

There seems to be a real polarization: either my friends are working at Lehman Brothers and JP Morgan, or they're moving back with their parents for a few months until something comes up (which is not necessarily a bad thing; we have the rest of our lives to work).

Current student, 8/2003-Submit Date, January 2007

I believe the employment prospects are very good. Our Career Center is very helpful in providing resources for students. There are always employers interviewing on campus for graduating students, as well as for current students who are seeking internships.

Alumnus/a, 8/2001-5/2006, December 2006

Excellent employment prospects if you excel and network. The Career Center holds interviews with many of the top companies in the U.S. Last year alone, Goldman Sachs, Booz, Merril Lynch, Suntrust, Morgan Stanley and couple of other I-banks, all Big Four accounting firms and dozens of other companies interviewed at the Career Center. In addition the Career Center helps students with internships and part-time jobs. There are so many UGA grads working good jobs that a degree from UGA can get you decent interviews in the Southeast.

Alumnus/a, 8/2001-5/2005, March 2006

As with many large schools, career prospects are pretty much a result of your own work and ambition. Large career fairs are held once each semester, and some schools and major programs hold their own smaller career fairs (e.g., a Risk Management and Insurance career fair). Some programs send out résumé books to prospective employers. Very involved and well-connected students (e.g., SGA presidents) receive their own personalized career placement, but the rest of the student body has to fend for themselves.

Current student, 8/2002-Submit Date, February 2005

Every semester UGA has excellent career fairs where over 100 companies are represented. We also have a strong Career Center that helps students with their résumés, helps find internships, and also gives advice on how to act during an interview. The Career Center does whatever it can to help you find the type of job you are looking for and is very successful in doing so.

Quality of Life

Current student, 8/2006-Submit Date, September 2006

I am currently living in a high-rise dormitory, which it is not the nicest but it will do for my first year. All the facilities besides the high-rise dormitories are, however, extremely nice and if they are not new, are currently being updated. Dining is amazing in the dining halls (they are award winning and well deserving of those awards) and the availability of variety is always there and you can usually find what you are craving. The neighborhood, because of the poverty level in Athens-Clarke County, is, say, sketchy at times; however, the police are always searching to help keep the crime down and help students feel safe.

Current student, 8/2003-Submit Date, January 2007

The dining hall is one of the best dining halls in the nation. There are many options to suit anybody's tastes. We also have special dinners where we may be served lobster, steak and crab legs. The housing is also very nice on campus. Many of the dorms are centrally located on campus making it very easy to catch a bus to class if you don't feel like walking. The dorms are equipped with heat, air conditioning, cable, phone line, everything a college student could want. I have lived on campus all four years and would not change it. I find that it is a lot more convenient than an apartment because of the various student organizations in which I am involved. I also think the dorms are very safe because they are equipped with a biometric hand scanner—students must swipe their ID card, and place their hand on the scanner to be let in the building. There are also several dorms with 24-hour desk staff to watch people who enter the building.

Current student, 5/2003-Submit Date, April 2005

Housing is very good because there are new dorms that have enough room for all the students who decide to live on campus. Students are allowed to pick in which dorm they would like to stay. The safety of the student is taken care of by the university's police department and there are call boxes all around campus for easy access.

Current student, 8/2002-Submit Date, February 2005

Athens is a wonderful college town. There is plenty to do both on and off campus. Downtown Athens is literally right across the street. UGA is a very safe campus and it has officers on campus and on duty around the clock. Not only does UGA provide housing for a reasonable price, it also helps students find jobs when needed, such as being an RA or desk assistant. UGA has a wonderful, state-of-the-art exercise facility, the Ramsey Center. It has workout rooms on two floors, an indoor pool, an indoor track, basketball courts, racquetball courts and so much more. The dining halls are also very good. The meal plan is reasonably priced with unlimited service. This year, a brand-new dining hall was opened, expanding a student's choices.

 ## Social Life

Current student, 8/2006-Submit Date, September 2006

Athens does have the most bars per square foot of any city in the United States; however, the social life does not completely revolve around downtown. Most bars are now 21 and up simply to enter, so I cannot get into a lot of them. Athens does have a great music scene, and there is at least one good concert every single week, such as Pat Green, Sister Hazel, Widespread Panic, Nelo and others. The Greek system is definitely prevalent here on campus through charity work, Milledge Avenue, football game days, and intramural sports, but it makes up less than 20 percent of the student body, so it definitely doesn't rule campus life. Clubs are awesome, abundant, and it's easy to get involved. Recently UGA hosted a Student Activities Fair to allow students to explore all possibilities of every club on campus and how to get involved, overall a great idea. Restaurants downtown are delicious and reasonably priced. Late night favorites include The Grill, Pita Pit, Little Italy, and Gumby's, while normal favorites include Five Star Day Cafe, Weaver D's, Transmetropolitan, Doc Shey's, East-West Bistro, and Harry Bisset's New Orleans Cafe & Oyster Bar.

Alumnus/a, 8/2001-5/2006, December 2006

In my opinion the university is not a party school anymore, due to the school's becoming more academic. The weekend/party time at UGA prior to 2003 was Tuesday through Saturday (maybe Sunday) but now it's a Thursday to Saturday

bar scene. The downtown bars are student favorites, but if you are minority some are not that friendly. Downtown restaurants are good but parking is a nightmare sometimes. The Greek scene is huge but can be exclusive if you are not a member or know members. There are some big-name bands and has-beens that visit the campus/downtown from time to time. And there is every type of club you can think of or you can make up your own (seven people needed, I think).

Alumnus/a, 8/2001-5/2005, March 2006

I visited dozens of colleges, both during my college search and while attending UGA. Athens is the best college town in the country if you like warm weather, great live music, cheap beer and Southern girls (better than Austin, which is really the only comparable town). UGA is pretty easy in terms of academics, but you can make it challenging with high courseloads and graduate courses. Be ready for lots of frat guys in pick-up trucks and blonde sorority girls who will all be exclusively wearing date night shirts, but that isn't all of UGA. Greek life is around 20 percent, but because fewer non-Greeks go out downtown, the effective ratio is closer to 40 percent when you go out. That said, UGA is big enough that you can find whatever you are looking for, and Athens townies are quite different from your average UGA student. Game days are really fun. Even if you think you are too cool for them and you hate football, if you just get into it a little bit, it is really fun. Only drawback is having Athens inundated with away team fans. The bars rock, the live music scene can't be beat, Greek parties can be fun, and game days are the key social events.

Current student, 8/2002-Submit Date, February 2005

The Greek system is huge here. If you are at all interested in joining a fraternity or sorority, this is the place for you. Students generally come early to begin rush before classes start, but it is worth it. Downtown Athens is right across the street. There are over 60 bars, and a number of little shops and restaurants. It is the place to be Thursday through Saturday nights. For those who don't want to go downtown, the university also offers Dawgs after Dark, a program on Friday nights that allows students a place to hang out, play games and have fun—free of alcohol. There are also a number of events put on, especially during football season. There are concerts for homecoming, pep rallies, as well as other activities. The restaurants in and around Athens are wonderful. They cover just about every and any kind of food one could want. Plenty deliver, but most are just walkaways. Most students enjoy downtown. With many restaurants with free wireless connections, students will spend afternoons down there doing work. They will also spend their evenings at restaurants or checking out the bars. Again, the Greek system is also very popular with students here at UGA.

Read all of Vault's College Surveys at **www.vault.com/college**–get complete surveys on 100s of colleges and universities, expert advice on applicaton essays and more.

VAULT CAREER LIBRARY   **189**

Brigham Young University Hawaii

Admissions Office
55-220 Kulanui Street
Laie, HI 96762
Admissions phone: (808) 293-3738
Admissions e-mail: admissions@byuh.edu
Admissions URL: w3.byuh.edu/admissions

Admissions

Current student, 8/2004-Submit Date, July 2006

The admissions process is fairly easy, all you need is a good enough ACT score, a recommendation from your local ecclesiastical leader, and two short 200-word essays on general topics that are easy to discuss. The selectivity is the tough part, because it is a small school, not everyone who applies is accepted.

Alumnus/a, 12/2001-8/2004, February 2005

I went to their web site, www.byuh.edu, and started filling out the international student application form. There were about six to eight sections and some essays. The school was very specific when asking the applicants why they wanted to be admitted to BYUH. The school is owned by the Mormon Church, and so being a Mormon was a big plus, but this is not to say that other applicants of other denominations were not equally welcomed.

Alumnus/a, 1/1994-12/1996, February 2005

The admissions process was a long, difficult process but well worth it. It included countless interviews, grade reviews, scholarship opportunities and lots and lots of paperwork! Any advice on getting in would be never to give up and try your hardest every day as if it was the best thing that you had ever wanted in the world! Have a positive attitude and prepare for the interviews by doing research and questioning former college graduates. Essays should come from your heart and be the best of your capability. Write as if this is your only chance to prove yourself and accomplish your dreams.

Alumnus/a, 1/1999-1/2003, August 2004

Freshmen from mainland U.S. have a hard time getting in. It is easier for transfer students and people who have returned from LDS missions. The best tip for getting in is to convince them that you want to graduate there and won't just be there short-term. Fall semester is the hardest time to gain acceptance.

Academics

Current student, 8/2004-Submit Date, July 2006

The nature of the academics at this school is subjective because it is such diverse school. Getting popular classes is fairly easy and they have a very good Web registration program that makes it even easier. Grading is fair and easy to understand. The professors are awesome, of course you are always going to have some that just honestly suck, but for the most part, it is always interesting to hear a Christian outlook on various subjects like science and history. The workload depends on your major, I think some are lighter than others.

Current student, 1/2003-Submit Date, October 2005

The classes are really great because they were small. This allowed for one-on-one tutoring with the professors. The School of Business is the best. Marketing, finance, enterprenuership and communications are all integrated, and companies are formed, giving you the real feeling of how businesses operate in the world today.

Alumnus/a, 12/2001-8/2004, February 2005

The quality of classes was excellent because of the size of the classes. Most classes averaged around 20 students, so the quality of education is very good. The professors were very close to their students. They are very easy to approach and they help the students in whatever they can. The workload was sometimes overwhelming, most especially my English classes. But I'm grateful for it, though, because I learned a lot.

Alumnus/a, 1/1994-12/1996, February 2005

Brigham Young is known for its strong religious values and respectful reputation. The quality of the classes is phenomenal and the professors are amazing. Signing up early and focusing on the classes you need are the key. Handling your workload is all about focusing and getting your priorities straight. Homework is a must and you have to be disciplined about keeping up and staying ahead of your work. You should always shoot for the highest grade and expect the most out of yourself.

Alumnus/a, 1/1999-1/2003, August 2004

Excellent academic program, especially in science, international cultural studies, English, ESL and TSEOL. We had small classes and great professors! I was never in a class bigger than 50 students. There was an excellent honors program with great lectures, discussions and weekly activities. The business programs were good and there were lots of things going on academically besides classes. We had weekly lectures from successful business-people. Humanities focused school. Mostly very conservative professors. Lots of readings posted online. Good phys ed program.

Employment Prospects

Current student, 8/2004-Submit Date, July 2006

Graduates from our school have really good employment prospects because the school is such a diverse place—when you graduate, you can pretty much always have a contact wherever you feel like working in the world. The graduates get awesome jobs and the alumni are very helpful with this process, there are also always people coming to the campus and doing workshops or offering internships globally.

Alumnus/a, 12/2001-8/2004, February 2005

A great number of international students go back to their native countries for internships arranged by the school and their trip back and forth is sometimes also paid for by the school.

Alumnus/a, 1/1994-12/1996, February 2005

You have many opportunities to obtain internships and have access to on-campus recruiting at BYU. It is very important to get involved in all areas of your field, looking for an open door of opportunity. Graduates continue to be very successful and they improve the community with their knowledge and skills from their education at BYU.

Alumnus/a, 1/2000-5/2003, August 2004

Fairly prestigious school. 100 percent acceptance rate to dental schools. Decent campus recruiting, good career center with help finding internships. I found a paid summer journalism internship in San Francisco. Good theatre program, though not much variation in professors there. Good pre-med program. School of Business, and hospitality and tourism and teaching programs are probably the most notable. Some of my friends have landed good computer jobs from the technical programs, too.

Quality of Life

Current student, 8/2004-Submit Date, July 2006

Housing is subjective—on campus is all right, the dorms are small but it gives it a more family-like feel. The off-campus housing is all fairly close to campus and the town is small and safe so there are always people around, walking, skateboarding, biking to and from school and even until late at night. The quality of life in the little town can't be complained about, it's very country, laid-back and relaxing.

Alumnus/a, 12/2001-8/2004, February 2005

The quality of life is amazing in a sense that you are right in the heart of Hawaii. The only thing that I despised during my stay in BYUH was the quality of dining. The cafeteria lacked the skill to prepare quality and nutritious food. Facilities are quite impressive except for the biology department, which needs some upgrading. The sports facilities are very good. Crime is not as rampant as in bigger cities and colleges but burglary is an issue.

Alumnus/a, 1/1994-12/1996, February 2005

The quality of life is outstanding at BYU. They have strict values that must be observed by all students. There is a dress code, conduct and overall attitude expectancy of all students. Housing is safe, clean and very well maintained by the staff. Facilities are beautiful and always welcoming to the students and visitors.

Alumnus/a, 1/2000-5/2003, August 2004

Dorms and married student housing are decent, as is the cafeteria food. Seasider Cafe has pretty good food, too—great prices. Subway, McDonald's, Domino's, and L&L (Chinese) are the only restaurants close by. Off-campus housing isn't the best. Crime is almost nonexistent. Lots of people ride bikes, skateboards or scooters to school; you can definitely get by without a car. There are gorgeous beaches closeby. Rated Number One surfing school by *Surfer Magazine*. Beautiful campus. Nice hiking, SCUBA, snorkeling, surfing, reef fishing and mountain biking in the area.

Social Life

Current student, 8/2004-Submit Date, July 2006

It's a Mormon school, so there are no bars and not many restaurants that close to campus, as the school is set on the North Shore of Oahu out in the country, but the social life is all the better for it. The dating is more creative, as there is a lot to do with the ocean and hiking, lots of outdoorsy things to do. Some of the favorites are, of course, surfing and picnics, and skydiving is an interesting one that a group of at least 40 new students do every summer. The school events and community things are always well attended. Especially with the Polynesian Cultural Center, there are always functions going on.

Alumnus/a, 12/2001-8/2004, February 2005

School dances are held every Friday night. School activities are held on a regular basis like Food Fest, culture nights, Students with Guitars, and professional concerts. All these events are so much fun to attend. There are not too many fine restaurants and bars near the school premises because BYUH is located in the outskirts of Oahu. But students who have cars will usually go to Waikiki or Honolulu during weekends if they opt for a nightlife. It only takes about an hour to get to the city. But the good thing about BYUH is that the beaches that surround it are more than enough to enjoy a bonfire with fellow students. Since the school population during regular semesters is only 2,300, everybody seems to know everybody as the semester progresses. Because of this, everyone seems to be afraid to ask someone out. But in my case, I can't count the girls whom I've asked out on a date. And among all the girls I've asked out, there were only three who I dated for more than one week.

Alumnus/a, 1/1994-12/1996, February 2005

The social life at BYU is centered around the school's religious values. There are school dances, clubs and a lot of dating that is safe and simple. There is excellent communication between students and friendships that build into some marriages. Some student favorites are climbing the mountain to the word sign BYU, having friends over for dinner and visiting the local LDS Temples around

town. Students look out for one another and there is little crime to worry about. The dance clubs are safe and play mostly uplifting music and don't serve alcohol. The restaurants are locally owned and are mostly LDS members who treat the BYU students with respect and offer a wide variety of delicious meals. Brigham Young is a wonderful school to attend and anyone would be lucky to get the chance to go to college there.

Alumnus/a, 1/2000-5/2003, August 2004

This is a no-alcohol campus. Social life is varied and very interesting. Lots of on-campus entertainment and social life. Students go to the movies, to see plays, music and dancing. School-organized dances take place off-campus and are great dates! There are lots of clubs—mostly cultural—like the Southeastern Asian club. Food Fest is the highlight of each semester, where you can try lots of different foods from several countries for a low price, plus live entertainment. The best thing about this school is that it is about 40 percent international students—people from over 60 different countries (though largely Polynesian and Asian countries). Amazing cultural experiences await you! About two girls for every guy. Hot dating scene. No Greek system on campus. Polynesian Cultural Center nearby. Culture night and talent night are big draws. Movies are shown on campus every weekend, plus there's one small theater in town we like to call "The Big Screen TV" that only plays two movies a week. Hukilau and Waimea beaches are favorite hangouts. Plenty to do. An hour drive to Honolulu and Waikiki.

The School Says

Brigham Young University Hawaii is located in Laie, Hawaii (population 7,000) situated 35 miles north of Honolulu on the island of Oahu. The 100-acre campus is nestled between lush mountains and an ideal shoreline. The average annual temperature is 77 degrees F (25 degrees C); the average annual precipitation is 23 inches (584 mm).

This top-ranked four-year undergraduate university has an enrollment of 2,400 students who represent 70 different countries and cultures: 26 percent from Asia, 22 percent from the Pacific, 16 percent Hawaii, 32 percent U.S. mainland, and 4 percent from elsewhere. About 94 percent are members of The Church of Jesus Christ of Latter-day Saints.

The school is part of the LDS Church Educational System, which serves almost half a million people worldwide in higher education, seminaries and institutes, elementary and secondary schools, and continuing education and literacy programs. In addition to BYU-Hawaii, the system includes BYU in Provo in Utah, BYU-Idaho, LDS Business College in Salt Lake City, and elementary or secondary schools in many countries, including Mexico, Fiji, Indonesia, New Zealand, Tonga and Western Samoa.

BYU-Hawaii has consistently been ranked by *U.S. News & World Report* (fourth in 2007) in the top tier of universities in the Western United States. *Consumers Digest* magazine ranks BYU-Hawaii as best value in the U.S. Tuition/books and living expenses average $13,800 total cost per year per student. A firstrate curriculum, featuring excellent programs in business, education, computers and technology, the sciences and fine arts.

Special study options include: accelerated study, cooperative education, double major, dual enrollment of high school students, ESL, exchange student, honors, internships, liberal arts/career combination, teacher certification, Army, Air Force ROTC.

Among the support services offered are: learning disabled program, writing center, learning center, tutoring, remedial instruction, pre-admission summer program, reduced courseload and peer counseling.

Read all of Vault's College Surveys at **www.vault.com/college**–get complete surveys on 100s of colleges and universities, expert advice on applicaton essays and more.

VAULT CAREER LIBRARY **191**

95 percent of BYU-Hawaii students are on some type of financial assistance including scholarships, grants and loans. Financial aid in the form of scholarships awarded for academics, art, athletics, music/drama and other private scholarships is available.

BYU-Hawaii is closely linked with the Polynesian Cultural Center (PCC), the Number One paid tourist attraction in Hawaii. The PCC provides employment opportunities for hundreds of students who would ordinarily be unable to afford a college education. Over 30 percent of BYU-Hawaii students help pay for their educations working at the PCC in a variety of positions including: performers, guides, and food service personnel.

Approximately 90 percent of BYU-Hawaii students are employed part-time while earning their four-year degrees—either at the Polynesian Cultural Center or on the BYU-Hawaii campus. Jobs on campus include janitorial and grounds crew work, cafeteria help, technical support, lab assistants, and general office work.

BYU-Hawaii students excel in athletics competition, as well as in the classroom. In the NAIA and more recently, in NCAA Division II, our teams have compiled 19 total national titles in volleyball, tennis and rugby. 20 percent of BYU-Hawaii's 150 student athletes are international students. Intramural sports include: badminton, basketball, bowling, cross-country, football, golf, racquetball, swimming, table tennis, tennis, track and field and volleyball.

University of Hawaii at Manoa

General Office
2500 Campus Road
Hawaii Hall 202
Honolulu, HI 96822
Admissions phone: (808) 956-8111
Admissions URL: manoa.hawaii.edu/admissions/

 Admissions

Current student, Marine Biology, 8/2004-Submit Date, August 2006

It seemed to be very easy to gain acceptance. The application process was minimal and survey-like! Be careful if you are a transfer student. The University of Hawaii is known not to accept credits. Keep all of your syllabi. You will need them for the appeal process, usually you can successfully appeal transfer credits!

Current student, 8/2004-Submit Date, June 2006

As an out-of-state applicant, the criteria are straightforward (2.8 GPA and I can't remember the minimum SAT requirement). I, however, had a 2.68 GPA and consequently was initially denied admission. Like most things here at UH, though, all it takes is some perseverance to get what you want. Because most people here are so casual and laid-back, a little initiative goes a long way. For me, it took a couple of phone calls to admissions staff, and accepted I was!

Current student, 8/2004-Submit Date, September 2004

The admissions process was fairly simple. First of all, you'll have to submit your SAT scores (ACT is also an option depending on what you're comfortable taking) along with a health clearance form indicating that you have up-to-date tuberculosis and measles vaccinations. There isn't much more until you've been contacted by the school's admissions department. You will need a transcript completed through your senior year of high school or a diploma or GED evident form proving that you've gotten through high school.

There is no essay to worry about, which is definitely a plus. It's definitely a great choice if you're living in the state prior to applying because tuition is a great deal lower.

Current student, 9/2004-Submit Date, October 2005

Well, first I attended the meetings held when the representatives of UH came to talk to prospect students. When I expressed an interest in applying to UH, I went directly to my counselor to see what I need to do. First of all, I had to get my SATs done and I took it three times only reaching the required math score.

However, I was assured that I had a likely chance of being accepted even without a passing reading/writing score. Every student is required to submit a record of his/her tax return and proof of a TB test. After applying for UH and being accepted to the university, I had to take and pass a series of required placement exams in order to qualify to register for classes such as Math, Chemistry and English courses. For the English placement, students are required to write an essay on a given topic. For math, students must pass with a certain score to take a math class at UH. And so on and so forth for other required placement exams.

Current student, 8/2003-Submit Date, September 2005

From the time you take your SATs (minimum 1020 for Hawaii residents) to getting your acceptance letter, it is definitely a roller coaster ride. However, UH often waives its SAT requirements for those with athletic abilities or with higher high school GPAs. The process of getting into UH is definitely not as rigorous as those Ivy League schools, so you learn to appreciate the fast process of applying and finding out whether you got admitted or deferred.

 Academics

Current student, Marine Biology, 8/2004-Submit Date, August 2006

Word to the wise. This school used to be a mandatory five-year school and although that is not the case anymore, many of the programs have not changed to four-year programs, so it is hard to get out of here in four years! I have found that this school gives you the runaround about a lot of things, so when you talk to people try and get an absolute answer and write things down, like names and phone numbers, so that you can find that person again.

Current student, 8/2004-Submit Date, June 2006

Having never attended another university, I don't really have a frame of reference for the rigor of the academics. It's obviously not MIT here, but it's certainly not high school. You are expected to meet the basic requirements in all your classes, and for the most part, I'd say they are fairly standard college requirements. In college, you get what you're willing to put into it. If you want to invest the time here, you can find some great professors who are willing to help, and I guarantee you'll come out having maximized the experience and learned everything you could. If you just want to pass, then you can probably put in some minimal effort and do so.

I can tell you that it is not easy getting the classes that you need, let alone the ones you just want for pure interest. Classes fill up fast, and often underclassmen are left with the dregs. In addition (and I'm sure this happens at other colleges, but I had no idea when I first came here), upperclassmen will sometimes hold a seat in a class for an underclassmen, then free the seat when it is the underclassman's turn to register, or after everyone has already registered. I object to the practice, personally, but if you want specific classes, I suggest you make some friends among the seniors and the juniors. Your other option, and this is how I do it, is persistence. Generally, if you keep checking enrollment levels on a regular basis, you'll catch the seats that open up when people start dropping. And people always drop. If that doesn't work, sometimes speaking to the professor or the advisor for the specific department helps.

Grading is done fairly, for the most part, and the workload is standard. Professors/Instructors generally leave much to be desired, in my opinion, but there are a few great ones. Take the time to talk to people (hopefully, you've found your upperclassman friends by now) and find out which professors are good and which it is best to avoid. Also, utilize your good professors. When you find the good ones, there are no limits to the amount of time and effort they are willing to put in to help you out.

Current student, 8/2004-Submit Date, April 2005

The University of Hawaii has many diverse academic programs ranging from architecture and marine biology, to business and law. However, it is difficult to be enrolled in a class that you want if you do not have upperclassman standing. Most classes tend to be large (30 to 300), but you can find smaller discussion groups and labs if that suits you. Professors grade both on a curve and regularly. It is not hard to excel in your classes if you are focused and assertive in reaching your goal. The staff tends to be kind and supportive and will help you if you ask them.

Current student, 8/2004-Submit Date, September 2004

Classes vary in size, some in small classrooms and others in lecture halls where 300+ seats are occupied. Registration dates are given far in advance so that getting the classes is not hard.

Professors all run their classes differently, with grading and type and quantity of work. The teachers are, for the most part, friendly and always try their best to help their students achieve their goals.

Current student, 8/2000-Submit Date, September 2005

Popular classes like guitar and golf are impossible to get unless you are at least a junior. The university is generally understaffed and there are not enough classrooms to accommodate the increasing student population. Incoming freshmen register last and sometimes cannot get into freshman-level classes, such as English 100 and History 151.

Workload obviously varies from class to class. Professors are generally friendly. They are happy to work in Hawaii, although not necessarily for Hawaii. In the spring of 2002, the professors went on a strike for about two weeks. Talks of another strike surface from time to time. Unfortunately some of them are not native speakers of the English language and therefore hard to understand.

Current student, 9/2004-Submit Date, October 2005

The classes here are quite varied. Some of the classes I have taken have been great, with instructors who really seem interested in educating. But others, and they are in the minority I should add, have been quite tedious, with professors who really don't seem to care about education, or even the subject they teach. But on the whole, most classes and teachers here are pretty decent.

Grading is quite standard (A through F). Getting good classes can be tough at times, I know I've had a few I wasn't able to get into, but if you need to take a certain class you should be able to do it within the next two semesters. The workload is just like any other college, it seems to be normal college-level work.

Current student, 8/2003-Submit Date, September 2005

Personally I am in the ICS Program (Information Computer Science) and it is one of the more difficult majors at UH. As with all schools, there are many difficult classes and some easier "GPA booster" classes. Since enrollment is at its highest in years, the availability of classes is very limited. Upperclassmen have the ability to register for classes first, and then it progresses down to the freshmen class, which by then don't have many available popular classes. Getting classes is difficult if you are an underclassman.

The University of Hawaii just recently implemented the +/- system with the goal of having a more accurate system of grading. Professors at UH tend to be friend-

ly and very helpful, but again, as with all schools, you always have a few bad apples. The workload at UH for specialized majors probably averages to about 10 hours of studying per week on top of daily homework assignments and projects. Overall, the academics at UH is quite average compared to the rest of the nation.

 # Employment Prospects

Current student, 8/2004-Submit Date, June 2006

As an accounting major, I can only speak for the College of Business Administration and the School of Accountancy. Prospects for employment are excellent. On-campus recruitment leaves something to be desired, but what you should know in the CBA is that you have to join the clubs. I don't know how it is at other colleges, but here firms recruit heavily through the different on-campus organizations. Great clubs to join in the CBA are the honor society in your major, if there is one, or the general club for your major. It is true that this will generally lead to employment in-state, but as far as accounting goes, if you have what they want—the grades and the personality—once you get to know the recruiters (which is what being in these clubs is all about), most national firms are willing to set you up wherever you want to go so long as there is a need there. And right now, there is a pretty much a need everywhere for accountants.

Current student, 8/2004-Submit Date, April 2005

I do know for sure that Pearl Harbor is recruiting many engineers, especially electrical engineers. We also have a fantastic business and marine biology program due to the fact that we are in the middle of the Pacific and have many opportunities for business ventures and biological studies.

Current student, 8/2004-Submit Date, September 2004

There are many internship opportunities available, particular in the business and administration building. As you walk down the hallways in this area of campus, you'll see posters and flyers with varied job and internship opportunities, most of them up to date for the current year.

Current student, 8/2000-Submit Date, September 2005

The only place where graduating from UH can be an advantage is Hawaii. The locals tend to favor locals, and there is only about three degrees of separation between you and everyone else if you live in Hawaii. Many locals care more about the high school that you attended, rather than the college. On-campus recruiting and internships are mostly for local jobs.

Current student, 9/2004-Submit Date, October 2005

Graduates from UH are open to a wide range of post-college employment opportunities. Graduating from UH is, first of all, as good as having any other university-level degree, in that it shows employers you have the dedication and willingness to complete college, and therefore should make a pretty good employee. But UH is quite unique to most other American schools in that its setting, Honolulu, Hawaii, is literally a melting pot for cultures all across the Pacific and Asia. Going to UH will open your eyes to many other cultures and peoples that you would just never get to meet at most other colleges.

Current student, 8/2003-Submit Date, September 2005

Graduates from UH move on to get local jobs depending on their particular fields. ICS majors often work for small firms or start their own companies. A lot of them move away to the mainland for better opportunities working with Fortune 500 companies. Around 20 percent of the students continue on to grad school. UH's alumni network lacks a lot of funding and ability to bring in money from alumni of the school.

 # Quality of Life

Current student, 8/2004-Submit Date, June 2006

I live off campus in a house with three roommates. Housing is expensive out here, but I think it's worth it not to live in the dorms. There was a huge housing shortage the last two years, but I think enrollment has declined just slightly to where it's not that much of an issue anymore. The neighborhood is pretty safe, and there's a lot of options for off-campus housing.

Read all of Vault's College Surveys at **www.vault.com/college**–get complete surveys on 100s of colleges and universities, expert advice on applicaton essays and more.

VAULT CAREER LIBRARY 193

Eating on campus is mediocre—there's Taco Bell, Pizza Hut, Subway, Paradise Palms (which reminds me of airport cafeterias), Bale (Vietnamese sandwich shop), Yummy's (Korean barbecue), and a vegetarian place called Ono Pono. With the recent (fall 2005) addition of Govinda's (a newer, better vegetarian lunch truck), which serves you an excellent entree, salad and dessert for $4, I'm much happier now to eat on campus. It is hands down the best deal I have found for food in Hawaii. Nearby off-campus hotspots for eating include Volcano Joe's and Magoo's. It's all relative, but being from New York, eating in Hawaii, is greatly overpriced and, other than Japanese and Korean, very mediocre.

That's one other thing you should know if you're from out of state. Everything in Hawaii is much more expensive than it is stateside. Prices when you first get here will make your jaw drop. But, hey, that's the price you pay to live in paradise. And the beautiful weather and sunshine mean there's plenty to do here that doesn't cost a dime.

Current student, 8/2004-Submit Date, April 2005

Dorm life is fun and helpful in distracting you from everyday academic life. Many parties are present in the dorms helping to elevate the social mood of the dorms. I have never seen crime being committed on campus and I have been in school from 6 a.m. to 6 p.m. studying. Dining services are plentiful, offering various ethnic cuisines. The campus is aesthetically pleasing, thanks to the large number of trees and wildlife growing on campus.

Current student, 8/2004-Submit Date, September 2004

Crime is definitely one of the least worrisome problems you'll find at UHManoa. The campus is very clean, as many of the students and faculty keep it in great condition. You won't find litter on the ground anywhere.

As for housing, there was a shortage of on-campus dorms for the students with the rising numbers in enrollment. This is a problem that's in the process of being solved.

Current student, Marine Biology, 8/2004-Submit Date, August 2006

The university is old as are the dorms. The housing really isn't that expensive; however, you get what you pay for. Although it is quite a bit cheaper to live on campus and easier to get housing, the facilities leave a bit to be desired. The on-campus food is pretty good, but the cafeteria stinks. They always have the same old stuff! It all tastes the same after a while, which is no fun. I find that the fact that there is no A/C in the dormrooms frustrating. Days get really hot here and all you want is a cold place to go. However, the classrooms are air conditioned and they are cold so bring a sweatshirt to class. Make sure that you get your housing app in on time because on-campus spaces are limited and if you turned in your paper work in late, you are out of luck basically. I found that out the hard way!

Current student, 8/2000-Submit Date, September 2005

Everyone complains about the housing and the parking. The majority of students are commuters, yet there is simply not enough parking to go around. Underclassmen have no chance at getting a parking pass. Instead, some of them get to the parking structure at 6 a.m. and sleep in the car to get a spot. There is also not enough housing. Rooms and furniture are very old. They will be building new ones in 2007.

Generally, crime is very low. However, there has been a string of rape and sexual assault cases over the past year. On-campus eateries are way overpriced. Bale (Vietnamese sandwich restaurant) is in my mind, the only eatery on campus worth your money. There is one bar on campus with a decent selection of drinks. The neighborhood is not much of a college town.

Current student, 9/2004-Submit Date, October 2005

The facilities here could use some work. The campus leaves a bit to the imagination, it's nothing special I should say. The dorms are basic, some buildings are very old though some are brand new. None have air conditioning, which can be a bit cumbersome when living in Hawaii. But all in all, I like it, and all the little problems are small enough that you really shouldn't mind that much.

Current student, 8/2003-Submit Date, September 2005

Housing on campus is quite an issue at UH. With enrollment being higher than ever, dorms and housing are almost nonexistent. The number of students from out of state is on the rise, so housing for them is priority for the direction of UH.

With this type of mentality, the local students are getting the shaft and are forced to commute or live off campus for a much higher price. Safety is a big concern for the chancellor of the school and she is very proud of UH. Campus crime is very low.

Social Life

Current student, Marine Biology, 8/2004-Submit Date, August 2006

There is little to no Greek life on campus, so that means few parties. If there are parties, the RAs are all over it so it is best to go into town. Honolulu has a huge nightlife that will satisfy any need! There are tons of bars and clubs that do college nights where you don't have to pay cover if you go to school, there is also a huge program for designated drivers in the area: you get free non-alcoholic drinks! It is really hard to have a car here since parking sucks on campus. It is really hard to get a parking pass, let along find a space if you have the pass. I recommend a moped. They are quick and easy to use. They are not too expensive and are cheap to fill up with gas!

Current student, 8/2004-Submit Date, June 2006

It all depends on what you're looking for. UH Manoa is very definitely a commuter school and, as such, has little in the way of campus social life. I think there are maybe five total fraternities and sororities. I'm an uber-geek, so I prefer it that way. I didn't want a school with a large Greek system, nor did I want a huge party school. Sports are the main attraction on campus, the big ones being men's and women's volleyball and football. Tailgating is popular at the football games, and since the state doesn't have an NFL team, pretty much everyone comes out for football games.

Other than that, there are tons of trails to hike on the island, and of course endless water sports—surfing, body boarding, kayaking, paddle boarding, open water swimming, and there's a very large and active triathlete community. Again, it's kind of about what you're looking for in a school. I love how easy it is to be athletic here, and how easy it is to find a community of people with whom to do your sports.

There is one place on campus that serves alcohol, Manoa Gardens, but it is a very odd place, and I don't really know anyone who hangs out there. Down a couple of blocks from campus, there's a cluster of about four bars—Eastside Grill, Magoo's, Red Lion, and another one I can't remember. Magoo's is the most popular one among students, and it's not bad. The food's decent, the beer's cheap, and the crowd is friendly.

My personal favorite events on campus are the movies they show sometimes on Friday nights, and the arts and crafts events they hold sometimes on Fridays, as well—glass etching, glass fusion, raku firing, and make your own stuffed animal around the holidays. Like I said, I'm an uber-geek.

Current student, 8/2004-Submit Date, April 2005

We offer many extracurricular activities, such as various clubs, band, orchestra, sports, intramural sports, and martial arts. The campus center is where most people hang out and provides numerous opportunities for encounters with the opposite sex. I am personally in the band playing the saxophone. Everybody has been friendly to me and I am presented with opportunities to meet people who have helped or given advice that helped with my college life.

Current student, 8/2004-Submit Date, September 2004

There's a wide variety of students with dozens of ethnic backgrounds who attend this school. You will see just about every race represented on and around campus. There's great food provided courtesy of restaurants located around campus, including Taco Bell, Pizza Hut, Jamba Juice, a vegetarian cafe and others that many seem to enjoy. There's a gaming hall where students and friends can enjoy games of pool or different coin-operated arcade games. There's also a lounge with a big-screen TV where students can enjoy regular cable television.

Campus center is home to music played throughout the day by a local DJ.

Current student, 8/2000-Submit Date, September 2005

Greek system not very active—only one frat house, although a recently formed chapter of Kappa Sigma has been recruiting a large number (100+) of members.

About 80+ registered student clubs. The ones that are the most active are the Pre-med Association, Golden Key and most of the business clubs.

The Leisure Center is especially popular with students from out of state/country because it rents out surfboards and other beach equipment for a reasonable price. You can also sign up for surfing classes and neighboring island trips there.

Restaurant (order at the counter) across the street called Volcano Joes has some decent sandwiches, salads and pizzas—and it's BYOB. Farther down the street are popular bars Eastside Grill, Magoo's and Red Lion. Beer price and selection at Magoo's cannot be beat. Magoo's is a very popular hangout. Eastside Grill draws a loyal older crowd. DJs spin at Red Lion on weekends. In the same lot as Red Lion is an ice cream store called Bubbies. Ice cream is a little pricey, but worth the price.

No popular nightclubs in immediate area. Clubs are in the downtown area (10 minutes by car). Popular clubs: Pipeline Cafe, Venus Nightclub, Ocean Club, O-Lounge, Feng Shui.

Current student, 9/2004-Submit Date, October 2005

It's great. With all sorts of different people from all over the world in Honolulu, there are all kinds of things to do, from Waikiki to the North Shore, many of Hawaii's greatest attractions are within a 20-or-30 minute drive from campus! There is no Greek system at this school, save two frat houses, but out here no one really cares about that kind of thing anyway. It's just a different kind of school than most universities. Also, most of the people here are great, while you may hear horror stories about angry locals, the truth is that most Hawaiians are very, very warm, welcoming people who make you feel right at home no matter where you're from.

The School Says

A research university of international standing, the University of Hawai'i at Manoa is a land-grant, sea-grant and space-grant institution. Manoa creates, refines, disseminates and perpetuates human knowledge; offers a comprehensive array of undergraduate, graduate and professional degrees through the doctoral level; carries out advanced research; and extends services to the community.

Located in Manoa valley on O'ahu, our university was founded in 1907 as a land-grant college of agriculture and mechanic arts. The College of Arts and Sciences was added in 1920, and we became the University of Hawai'i at Manoa to distinguish from the other campuses in the UH System. More than 20,000 students are enrolled in campus courses and via distance delivery. Classified as a Carnegie Doctoral/Research University-Extensive institution, Manoa offers 87 bachelor's degrees, 87 master's degrees and 51 doctorates. We offer professional degrees in law, medicine and architecture. 69 percent of Manoa students are undergraduates, 57 percent are of Asian or Pacific Islander ancestry, and 56 percent are women. The campus is accredited by the Accrediting Commission for Senior Colleges and Universities of the Western Association of Schools and Colleges. 54 degree programs are also accredited by appropriate professional agencies.

Manoa's special distinction derives from its Hawaiian, Asian and Pacific orientation and unique location. These attributes foster unique opportunities for study in tropical agriculture, tropical medicine, marine sciences, astronomy, volcanology, botany, evolutionary biology, comparative philosophy, education, languages, urban planning, cultural studies in Pacific/Oceania, performing arts, second language studies, and international business. We have four faculty in the National Academy of Sciences, one member of the National Academy of Engineering. Our extramural funding places us in the Top 25 of U.S. public institutions with annual extramural funding in excess of $400 million. Nearly all of the units at Manoa have developed strengths in Hawaiian, Asian and Pacific studies, which have created an international reputation for the university. We are widely recognized as the best university in the U.S. in these areas, and we have recently been invited to become a Confucius Institute by the Chinese Ministry of Education.

Manoa also offers instruction in more Asia-Pacific languages than any other U.S. institution of higher learning. We have five Title VI Centers: a National Foreign Language Resource Center, three National Resource Centers (East Asian, Pacific Islands, Southeast Asian), and a Center for International Business Education and Research. Students are provided special opportunities for research, service learning, and co-curricular activities in Hawaiian, Asian and Pacific studies. The beauty of Manoa valley provides a backdrop for a unique and inviting campus, and Hawaiian, Asian and Pacific traditions are well represented throughout the campus. An authentic Japanese tea house and garden grace the campus, as do a replica of a Korean king's throne hall and a Hawaiian taro patch. Off-campus facilities include the Lyon Arboretum, the Waikiki Aquarium, several marine facilities, numerous agricultural research centers and cooperative extension offices, and the world-famous telescopes atop Mauna Kea and Haleakala.

Our fall 2007 classified freshman profile had a mean GPA of 3.41. We attract students from all over the world, and we are proud of the large number of students enrolled in our study abroad programs throughout Europe, the Pacific and Asia. A new dorm is being constructed on campus with 850 beds. Vast major renovations and beautification projects are planned for the near future.

Read all of Vault's College Surveys at **www.vault.com/college**–get complete surveys on 100s of colleges and universities, expert advice on applicaton essays and more.

VAULT CAREER LIBRARY **195**

University of Idaho

New Student Services
PO Box 444253
Moscow, ID 83844-4253
Admissions phone: (208) 885-6163 or (888) 8-UIDAHO
Admissions fax: (208) 885-4477
Admissions e-mail: nss@uidaho.edu
Admissions URL:
www.students.uidaho.edu/futurestudents/

 ## Admissions

Current student, 1/2004-Submit Date, January 2006

I was a transfer student. I don't really remember much of admissions, just filling out the paperwork. The hardest thing, actually, was getting my previous college to send an official transcript to UI. They charged me almost $15! I guess every college does that. They also just needed my SAT scores. It is a very easy school to get into.

Alumnus/a, 8/2002-12/2005, January 2006

Applications are available online or at state schools. Applications are easy to fill out and require SAT/ACT scores. Selectivity is not too high, considering a GPA above a 3.5 makes ACT/SAT scores irrelevant.

Current student, 8/2003-Submit Date, January 2006

I completed a detailed application with a few short-answer questions. Then I submitted standardized testing scores and concurrent enrollment transcripts, as well as an official high school transcript. All of my questions throughout the process were answered clearly by calling the school's toll-free number. It was a quick process and I received my answer very quickly (within two weeks of applying).

Current student, 8/2004-Submit Date, January 2006

Idaho has a fairly simple application process. A short essay describing extracurricular activities and clubs, along with your high school transcript and test scores are all that is necessary. I would suggest also applying to the honors program.

Current student, 8/2003-Submit Date, May 2006

Based mainly on grades and SAT scores, not too rigorous. There are no interviews or essays needed.

Current student, 8/2003-Submit Date, September 2005

The University of Idaho is a fairly easy college to get into. They are a lot more lenient towards things such as high school grades than many other universities. They also have a very up-to-date web page at www.uidaho.edu where a lot if not all of your questions about the school can be answered. There is also an online application that can be filled out under the student section.

Current student, 1/2005-Submit Date, November 2005

The admissions process was relatively smooth and fairly painless. The application to the school was shorter than many that I had previously filled out. There was only a short section for the essay part and the rest was standard. UI also has pretty easy qualifications for the WUE, which made it nice, as well. There is no interview and the chances of acceptance are fairly high. The people are very nice and cooperative, as well.

 ## Academics

Current student, Liberal Arts, 8/2006-Submit Date, July 2007

The academics are far beyond what other colleges in Idaho have (I know; I have attended three of them). The professors here want their students to do great things and are willing to lead them in the right direction. This is not a school that simply wants your tuition money to spend on random equipment for the athletic teams, but rather it is a school that wants students to graduate and be successful in the future. Plus, there are computers littered throughout campus and wireless everywhere. We may be in the middle of nowhere, but we are connected to the world.

Current student, 1/2004-Submit Date, January 2006

My program, secondary education, is complicated because you have to have a major (other than education) then take about six or seven education courses. I found the courses lacking in consistency, organization and overall completeness. The professors and instructors are just as they are at any school, some good some bad. I found that the best tended to be either very strict or very laid-back. The less good instructors tended to be undecided on how to teach effectively as well as manage the course. I don't think this particular department has its ducks in a row yet.

The grading, again, depended on the instructor. One odd element of this university is that they don't give + or - on grades. You are just given a B if you got between 80 and 89 percent. The workload depends on the professor, as well. The one professor I had who gave the largest workload happened to be an excellent professor and I learned the most in his class. Workload does not necessarily mean a good class, though.

It was pretty easy to get into the classes I wanted, though I am a history teaching major and most colleges offer a plethora of history courses. The hardest class to get into is Yoga! Since we register through seniority, seniors register first and usually take all the Yoga classes before anyone else can.

Alumnus/a, 8/2002-12/2005, January 2006

Getting in classes is competitive and most students will apply immediately when academic blocks are removed. The school excels in the areas of business, agriculture and engineering, and thus, classes in those fields are of high quality.

The workload for classes is dependent on the level of difficulty of the course and what the instructor expects. Most class workloads vary and in an average semester, a student will have a mix of classes ranging from heavy workloads to the bare minimum weekly.

Current student, 8/2003-Submit Date, January 2006

Classes can often be troublesome to get as a lower-level student, but as class status changes, the chance to register earlier is available. The professors are very helpful here at UI, if a student attends class on a regular basis, individual help is much more likely to be achieved. Professors' grading scales vary by pedagogy and the level of the class. If a student is taking a 100-level class, the difficulty level is low and the grades reflect kindly on the student.

Current student, 8/2003-Submit Date, January 2006

The 100-level classes vary from extremely large (200+) to very small (10). After meeting with an advisor, students are able to register online or if that process is challenging, their advisor can register for them during an advising session. Upper-division classes are typically smaller and range from 10 to 100 students.

Waitlists are used but usually the professor can allow more students in after the semester begins. (I have never been excluded from a desired class.) The professors are available during office hours and are always willing to make private appointments.

The information studied is current, relevant and usually interesting. In general, the courses are high quality, the workload is appropriate, the grading is reliable and the classes are worthwhile.

Current student, 8/2004-Submit Date, January 2006

Professors are very approachable and take genuine interest in students' success. Enrollment in the honors program ensures early registration privileges and almost always guarantees you'll get the classes you want. Workload and grading are typical. You get the grade you work for.

Current student, 8/2003-Submit Date, May 2006

This is a very liberal arts school. We have very good freshman classes. We are noted for our engineering, business and forestry schools. Most of the money and focus go into these programs. There are some very good professors, but they would be better if they were required to get some training on teaching before being able to teach.

Current student, 8/2003-Submit Date, September 2005

The academics at the University of Idaho are good. Many of the programs, such as engineering, are recognized among some of the best. I am currently enrolled in electrical engineering and am enjoying the teachers and way things are taught. I also have a roommate in mechanical engineering and another in civil engineering who also like their schooling here.

The classes are challenging enough to get you to where you need to be, but not too much to handle that you want to drop out. Likewise, the grading depends on how hard you work, and if the class was obviously too hard for the students, the teachers will grade the class so the students still get the grades they deserve.

Enrolling for classes is also easy since it can be done online. You may run into some problems getting into classes if you are late registering. However, the teachers are very good about getting you into the classes you need if you show up to the classes, despite not being enrolled in them, and talk to them afterwards about your situation.

Current student, 1/2005-Submit Date, November 2005

The quality of the programs is very high, although it can vary depending on the program of interest—some better than others. Whether you get into the classes you want depends fully on your grades in school and the classes in which you want to enroll. The professors aren't really easy on students, but they are there to help the students and ensure they earn their grade. Workload depends on the classes, as well.

Alumnus/a, Political Science, 8/1990-12/1994, September 2003

Well, as a political science major, I can honestly say that I truly loved my degree program. The only regret that I have is I wish I had had more of an opportunity to partake in the scholastic activities within the department of political science. Because of my commitment to my intercollegiate sport, I did not have the opportunity to bond with fellow political science students. However, the experience I did have was extremely positive.

My professors were topnotch and very approachable, which was important to me. The class availability was good, as registering for popular classes, especially with my limited schedule, was relatively easy. The workload for the higher-level courses was as expected, but not overwhelming.

Employment Prospects

Current student, 1/2004-Submit Date, January 2006

While the employment prospects for the College of Education are great, I'm not sure about others. I have yet to meet an education major who didn't find a job after his/her internship if he/she looked. Internships are also required and assigned by the College of Education., so those are pretty easy to get, as well. I've yet to see what the quality will be, but I imagine you get as much as you put in.

The Career and Professional Planning Center is really great. They help with résumés, interview workshops, internships and more. They are also incredibly friendly and helpful in getting connections.

Alumnus/a, 8/2002-12/2005, January 2006

The alumni network at UI is a strong one and alumni stay connected to the university post-graduation. The campus does a great job with joint job fairs with Washington State University. Most students are from the Northwest and do not seem to find it too difficult to obtain a job. Out of state, employers are generally interested in students from Idaho since it is not too common.

Current student, 8/2003-Submit Date, January 2006

UI is very proactive in getting employers on campus to meet with students. The prestige is, of course, not anywhere near that of a highly accredited private school, but our engineering programs are some of the best in the Northwest. We also have a very strong architecture program that is looked upon well by many future employers.

Current student, 8/2003-Submit Date, January 2006

The University of Idaho has an extremely large and very active alumni association that works very hard to maintain respect for UI graduates and helps new graduates network. The headquarters is located on campus and works with the Career and Professional Planning services to help grads.

Graduates from the University of Idaho go on to many types of professions and graduate schools here and all over the world. We have a great resource on campus, Career and Professional Planning, that aids all students in finding jobs during and after their college careers.

Current student, 8/2003-Submit Date, September 2005

There are many employment prospects in the engineering program. They require students in the program to take a class that is solely for preparing a good résumé, making you aware of job opportunities and even requires you to sign onto an Internet site where you can search for employers and internships. The university also has a staff that will help any time with any questions you might have about finding a job or getting a job.

Current student, 1/2005-Submit Date, November 2005

The University of Idaho is very on top of employment opportunities. They are frequently sending e-mails of upcoming job fairs, work study programs and a wide variety of employment opportunities. The head of the department of Biology often sends e-mails of internships and job opportunities within the program.

Quality of Life

Current student, 1/2004-Submit Date, January 2006

I live off campus, always have, so I know little about housing or dining. We do have new dorms called the Living and Learning Centers that I have heard are very nice. I have only eaten in the coffee shops and Commons, but I can honestly say the food is pathetic. The university dining situation is more set up for students living on campus who have dining cards than those off campus.

Alumnus/a, 8/2002-12/2005, January 2006

Crime on campus is very small, but it is not completely safe and the university and student life have worked to keep students safe. Greek life on campus is strong, with 13 fraternities and nine sororities. Campus residence hall life has improved with the building of new facilities.

Food courts/halls are available across campus with three coffee shops. The campus boasts a large student rec center, recently built within the last five years, with a two-level facility and rock climbing edifice.

Current student, 8/2003-Submit Date, January 2006

The Moscow area is one of the safest places I had ever been. The community is based around the university and is no larger than 25,000. People leave their doors unlocked with no worry of crime. Campus living is an excellent way to start a college experience at the University of Idaho. We have a strong Greek and residence life system, which are extremely helpful in building a strong feeling of community and an excellent method for networking.

Read all of Vault's College Surveys at www.vault.com/college–get complete surveys on 100s of colleges and universities, expert advice on applicaton essays and more.

VAULT CAREER LIBRARY 197

Current student, 8/2003-Submit Date, January 2006

The University of Idaho is the pride and joy of the local community, which is built around the college. Our campus is very safe and the local police force adequately meets all of our safety needs. The neighborhoods vary from large, new apartment complexes to old neighborhoods full of turn of the century homes and everything in between.

On-campus housing provides a wonderful setting to succeed academically and is comparably priced to the local apartments. We also have a very active Greek community that provides on-campus housing for many of our students. On-campus dining is great with hundreds of dining options and it is constantly working with students to improve. Our campus and facilities are beautiful, and vigilantly maintained. The centerpiece of our campus is the administration building with its sprawling lawn and its beautiful clock tower, but we are still growing. We recently completed the state-of-the-art Teaching and Learning Center, which provides high-tech classrooms and lecture halls for students in all majors.

Current student, 1/2005-Submit Date, November 2005

Quality of life is very high here in Moscow. The dorms are nice, they have new on-campus housing for older students and exchange students. There is also a wide range of restaurants in town from fast food to high quality. Crime is low, I don't know of any instances of when I or someone I know have been victims of crime.

Alumnus/a, 8/1990-12/1994, September 2003

The quality of life in Moscow, ID was very good. Coming from a small town in Colorado originally, moving to Moscow for four years provided a good transition to college life. The surrounding community provided an excellent backdrop. Restaurants within walking distance of the school were plentiful, the neighborhoods were friendly and inviting, and there wasn't the animosity that is sometimes present in small college towns between the students and the residents. The campus was beautiful and the facilities were solid with a new library being built during my final year. I wish I could have been there to use it.

 ## Social Life

Current student, 1/2004-Submit Date, January 2006

This is quite a party town. There are no bars on campus, but students generally have house parties on campus. The worst thing about these parties is the enormous amount of underage drinking. If you are 21, you don't want to go to these parties, especially ones that get busted.

ASUI and the student clubs always have something going on, it is best to check with them if you need something to do. We also have LCD screens all over campus displaying what events are happening. There is one club in town, The Beach, and it is 18 and over. Good for dancing and the country swing night on Thursdays are fun. It isn't that great for over-21ers. It does have an awesome Tabbycat (cross-dressing) Show.

There are four bars in town: John's Alley (very seedy), The Garden (a great place with a no smoking section), Mingles (nine pool tables!) and CJ's (a hip-hop club). I prefer The Garden because it is built in the lobby of an old hotel and always has a lot of people in it on the weekends. Another bar just outside of town, The Slurp n' Burp, is awesome for food and Monday night football. It has an older working-class crowd normally.

Current student, 8/2003-Submit Date, January 2006

To be perfectly honest, the community does not lack in the variety of things to do. There are multiple bars in the community, of all different persuasions; a number of quality restaurants in the area; and three or four movie theaters. The theater program on campus often has a play running and there are often local bands playing at the bars or parties. Washington State University is only 10 miles away and that community also offers a large number of events. Homecoming week is a big event at the University of Idaho. We have a bonfire and a small parade before the football game. In the spring there is an annual Renaissance Fair, which is a favorite of the community.

Current student, 8/2003-Submit Date, January 2006

Moscow, Idaho is a town made for college students. Dating is easy with so many options; we have ice skating, bowling, movie theaters and there's always someone new to meet. When it comes to events, there is a surprising number here. ASUI, our student government, hosts free concerts on campus like Reel Big Fish and Blues Traveler, and there're sporting events almost every single week.

The Greek system is very popular on campus and provides housing and social activities for thousands of students. On a typical weekend, you can catch a play, attend a sporting event, dance at a club, watch a movie with friends and catch a party at a Greek house.

Current student, 8/2003-Submit Date, May 2006

Considering our school is one of the Top 10 party schools, the social scene here is hoppin'. Even if you don't party, there are lots of groups to which you can belong. The coffee shops around here provide for a lot of hang-out places. I think it helps that we have another college so close to us.

Current student, 8/2003-Submit Date, September 2005

The social life at the university is pretty good. There is not much to do as far as amusement parks or big clubs to visit, but there are plenty of other things to do. We are located by many other towns where you can travel to do these things. That is also a plus at this university. We are located about 10 minutes from WSU, about an hour from Lewis and Clark, an hour from Gonzaga and about an hour from Northern Idaho. This gives students plenty of places to visit.

There is also a big Greek system at this school, which is how most of the students spend their time. Although the University of Idaho is known as a big party school, there are still plenty of activities that come through and that the university puts on that students can choose to do if they please.

DePaul University

Loop Campus (main office)
1 East Jackson Blvd., Suite 9100
Chicago, IL 60604-2287
Admissions phone: (312) 362-8300 or (800) 4DEPAUL
Admissions URL: www.depaul.edu/prospective_students/

 ## Admissions

Current student, 9/2004-Submit Date, October 2006

DePaul accepts students based on a standard application and one or two essays. The essays were pretty standard topics. DePaul, though, was not very selective. As the largest and, in my opinion, most liberal Catholic university in the country, it really lives by the core of Catholicism: "universal." It is very inclusive and was one of the trend-setting universities at the turn of the century to admit women and blacks. So although it is not exactly difficult to get in, that does not mean that they do not take many things into account. For example, DePaul officially has the most diverse student population in the country, which makes for a very exciting and cultural campus life.

There is no mandatory interview for admission. I did have an interview with a counselor the fall of my senior year to get a feel for the staff at DePaul and speak with someone internally. I thought it was really helpful, especially when returning and knowing a familiar face of an admissions counselor.

Current student, 9/2004-Submit Date, January 2006

I applied as a transfer student to DePaul, but I also applied while I was a senior in high school. Granted, I transferred to DePaul from another four-year university with a high GPA, but it appears as though they accept anyone. There are a lot of people who transfer in from community colleges after two years. Classes aren't easy so I am not sure everyone lasts while they are here, but I have never heard of anyone not being accepted.

Current student, 9/2003-Submit Date, November 2004

Getting in was not as difficult as I thought it would be. I am a re-admit student, so I'm not really sure how long the normal process takes. I understand that DePaul is quite selective for new students, and a little less selective for transfer students. I think that I wrote an essay, and that it wasn't too hard to write, but I am really not sure of what their standards are for the entrance essay. As with any school, I would say go to community college first and get good grades, and then try to get involved in lots of extracurricular and volunteer activities.

Current student, 8/2002-Submit Date, March 2004

In high school, a representative came from DePaul University and talked to anyone who was interested in applying to DePaul. From there, I was given an application, which included three essays and the typical demographic information along with letters of recommendation. The essays, as I recall, were more along the lines of why I wanted to go to DePaul and what I have been involved in. There was no interview for the application.

Current student, 4/2003-Submit Date, May 2004

The admissions process is unique among the universities and colleges I have attended or researched, in that one must qualify through study to become fully matriculated.

Current student, 1/2002-Submit Date, June 2004

DePaul is not very selective in admitting transfer students. The general requirement to get into DePaul as a transfer student is to have a GPA of at least 2.0. Once a student is admitted, he or she could have a hard time getting all the courses transferred from the previous school. This depends on the college office that the student is transferring into and the quarter that the student is transferring into. I transferred to DePaul in the winter quarter. I had to send in my transcript three times until they finally received it. Once, they even lost my transcript when I delivered it to them in person. Overall, the admissions process is very stressful.

DePaul says: "DePaul University seeks a highly motivated, academically well-prepared, and diverse student body. We value individualized attention for each and every student and guarantee that your application will be reviewed carefully by admissions representatives. DePaul's Office of Admissions reviews an array of criteria in selecting the transfer class. Foremost is the applicants' academic performance and preparation, followed by personal characteristics and experiences. Additionally, admission is dependent upon the applicant's selected major; however, all transfer students applying to DePaul for undergraduate admission are required to have a minimum cumulative grade point average of 2.0 for consideration. The necessary minimum GPA is higher for our competitive majors than noncompetitive majors, with the College of Commerce, School of Music and the Nursing completion program requiring a 2.5 GPA and the School of Education requiring a 2.75 GPA for transfer admission consideration.

"Coursework completed at a college or university that is accredited by a regional accrediting association with a C or better, that corresponds to a course in content and credit value is generally accepted for credit at DePaul University. As a general rule, major courses taken at another institution will be evaluated for applicability after a transfer student enrolls at DePaul."

 ## Academics

Current student, 10/2003-Submit Date, September 2006

The School for New Learning (SNL) is a program for adults over 24 years old. All classes are very challenging and the instructors are extremely helpful. There are lots of writing tasks and presentations to complete. However, these skills are required at all workplaces.

Current student, 9/2004-Submit Date, October 2006

As a member of the University Honors Program and Strobel Program (Honors Accounting), courses are definitely not laid-back. I always have homework in every class, whether it's reading, assignments, studying for a test, or just reviewing. Professors are hit or miss. I have had professors whom I currently worship and others, of whom I would gladly dispose. I have never had a professor grade unfairly or unjustly. Often, they adjust percentage requirements for grades, e.g., an 88 percent would be an A in a very difficult course. In the University Honors Program, courses are capped at 20 students, which is great. It allows for more interactive discussion, more teacher-student attention, and greater relationships among students. As a Strobel student, I get to register first (with the athletes), so I have never not gotten my first choice schedule. One warning: As DePaul is on the quarter system, courses seem much more overwhelming. Four (or five in my case) courses in 10 weeks is a lot. Teachers do not exactly go slowly either. I have never missed a class without giving my teachers at least one week's notice. Ditching is basically out of the question because we move so quickly. It's really important not to fall behind, because before you know it, it's midterms and then finals.

Current student, 9/2004-Submit Date, January 2006

DePaul is on the quarter system, which means you take four classes a quarter, which is 10 weeks long. There are three quarters a year and there are opportunities to take a December intercession class and there are two sessions in the summer to take classes. Classes at DePaul are small, about 30 to 40 people maximum, and from my experience in the business school, my professors are professionals who have retired or who teach as they work, which means you receive much more real-world information. The workload at DePaul is tough if you don't keep up. The quarters move really fast and if you don't stay on track, you will not do well. I really prefer the quarters at DePaul, though, as you can take more classes and figure out which subjects you really do enjoy.

Read all of Vault's College Surveys at **www.vault.com/college**—get complete surveys on 100s of colleges and universities, expert advice on applicaton essays and more.

VAULT CAREER LIBRARY   **199**

Current student, 9/2003-Submit Date, November 2004

The quality of classes is excellent overall. They are all quite challenging, and the academic tone is quite serious at DePaul, but the students definitely know how to have fun. As for as class selection, it is not very easy to enroll in popular classes, and a lot of classes are only offered once per term. Also, I don't think that DePaul offers as many choices as it should, considering that its enrollment is well over 20,000 students. They should definitely add some more classes, especially the more common ones that everyone needs to take.

Also, the transfer system is terrible. If you took a class at a prior school, chances are it won't transfer. I had to repeat the exact same class I took at another school just because they wouldn't transfer it to DePaul. They say that they are working on it, trying to improve it, but I find that hard to believe. Overall, professors are good—mostly older and tenured, I believe. Normal workload is four classes (16 credit hours). I don't think I'd recommend more than that.

Current student, 8/2002-Submit Date, March 2004

All our registering is online, which is convenient if you have access to a computer at the time that you are supposed to register. Usually if you are at the end of the registration days, you will not get the classes you want, because our class sizes here are really small. But you can always find a friend who registers earlier, so try and have him/her hold a class for you. There are also class descriptions available for all classes, but it is surprising because a lot of the time, the descriptions do not match up to what the professor teaches. As for grading, well, that most certainly varies by teacher, but every teacher always has a syllabus explaining how he/she grades and what he/she is looking for, so the grading method is never really a surprise. The workload is always tough because it is a 10-week quarter. Everything here is at a faster pace than most schools because of the quarter system. But I love having the quarter system because that way you get a taste of so many different classes. Also it is convenient in that if you do not like a particular class so much, you know that in a matter of 10 weeks it is over!

Current student, 4/2003-Submit Date, May 2004

The academics are outstanding. The coursework is rigorous, and since it is online, an added element of rigor is included. The same courses, texts, instructors, papers, assignments and other evaluation and grading methods are used at SNL as in the traditional campus. Additionally, graduation is not predicated upon units required for graduation, but rather competencies. The university has set forth a set of 50 competencies that the student must accomplish (regardless of how many college credits may be required to do it), regarding the scientific world, lifelong learning (including mathematics, writing, critical thinking, research and collaborative learning environments), a focus area (students choose an area of concentration), arts and ideas (creation, expression and interpretation of art, artwork, literature, music) and human community (dealing with social sciences). 50 competencies are required, and two competencies may be attached to most courses, if appropriate. Transfer courses gain one competency each.

This is a very unique and innovative way of looking at education, and this appeals to me, an adult learner, greatly. DePaul was the first to do this, and now several other universities are following suit. Plus the big name of DePaul is a huge advantage.

Employment Prospects

Current student, Accounting, 9/2004-Submit Date, October 2006

As a Strobel student and accounting major, employment prospects are the least of my worries. I currently have a new job with a hedge fund firm. I am in the midst of second round interviews with at least four different firms for an internship next summer. Our e-recruiting web site, networking via student clubs (like Accounting Club and Beta Alpha Psi), and faculty resources make finding a job much easier than any homework assignment. Many DePaul alumni (at least in the field of accounting) currently are CEOs, CFOs, partners of accounting firms, and many more executive-level positions. Ledger and Quill, an accounting alumni group, awarded over $200,000 in scholarships last year to students who are accounting majors. DePaul has a strong alumni-student relationship and makes sure that its products or assets—students, are well taken care of.

Current student, 9/2004-Submit Date, January 2006

I was very surprised with DePaul's Career Center. They have an ASK mento program that connects graduates and alumni with people in similar fields fo practice interviews, advice, networking or just simply mentoring. It is surprising how many alumni are willing to help and volunteer their time. On-campus recruiting is basically geared to Chicago companies, a lot of Chicago companie have DePaul alumni.

There is a lot of help in the Career Center for getting jobs and internships résumé help, and networking events, but you do have to seek it out.

Alumnus/a, 9/2003-6/2005, November 2005

After graduating from DePaul, I was literally bombarded with business intern ship proposals and job offerings. A degree received from the university is very helpful but not as much as the on-the-job, real-life experience you get while stil being in school. Alumni network and the on-campus recruiting school sector both participate quite actively in the school life. These services are often advertised and referred to in many classes, during discussions considering caree opportunities.

Current student, 8/2002-Submit Date, March 2004

Our Career Center is awesome, but only if you know how to use it. Many students here are frustrated with it because a little work needs to go into it in orde to get something out of it. The Career Center staff is great in the respect tha they are willing to sit down with you and help you build your career path and fil you with knowledge on how to look like the best candidate out on the market. personally went into the office one day, sat down and learned the entire process of how to get an internship, went home, went online and registered, and put up my revised résumé, and within three days I had two offers. They are that good I believe this is because DePaul has a well-known reputation in the community, and the businesses and organizations know that DePaul produces quality students, ones they want working for them.

Current student, 1/2002-Submit Date, June 2004

DePaul has a great Career Center, which offers a variety of events, workshops and networking opportunities. Several employers, such as Deloitte and Touche, Nation Futures Association and Morningstar, recruit students from DePaul and participate in on-campus recruiting. Additionally, it provides a database of jobs that is accessible to its students and alumni.

Quality of Life

Current student, 9/2004-Submit Date, October 2006

A few years ago, DePaul students were selected as the happiest by the (*Princeton Review*). The quality of life is pretty great. Being in the city can be overwhelming, but Lincoln Park, the location of our main campus is primarily residential and manageable. Of course things like the sound of the EL, the dirt and grime of the outdoors, and the virtually nonexistent social life for under-21-year-olds are all deterrents to us students. Despite those, though, there's so much at our fingertips by being in the city: plays, comedy clubs, concert venues, museums, the lake, shopping, businesses, the planetarium, the aquarium and so much more. I always feel safe on campus, thanks to public safety and our safety buzzers. Public Safety patrols from 6 p.m. to 6 a.m. every day throughout the entire year, responding to emergency calls and even acting as a free taxi for students. If a student is out late, studying or drinking, public safety will pick him/her up and drive him/her home (as long as it is within campus limits). Once a student steps off campus, though, especially at night and/or when alone, it does become more dangerous. However, that goes for any location: big city, suburb or small town. As long as students steer clear of the poorly lit streets while alone or not completely sober, there's not much to fear.

Current student, 9/2004-Submit Date, January 2006

The campus is beautiful. There is a campus located in the Loop and a campus located in Lincoln Park, which is a 15-minute EL ride. You receive a U-pass so all public transportation is free. Housing is expensive but very nice. It is often cheaper to live off campus but if you want to meet people, you really need to live on campus as DePaul in the Loop is a commuter school. The gym is awesome nd brand-new. The neighborhood is the trendiest in the city and a wonderful place to live.

Current student, 9/2003-Submit Date, November 2004

DePaul students are the happiest in the nation! This is because the campus is gorgeous and well taken care of, housing is luxurious, the neighborhood is beautiful, and the campus is extremely safe, considering it's in the middle of Chicago. The quality of life at DePaul is excellent.

Current student, 8/2002-Submit Date, March 2004

DePaul has a very diverse community of students, which DePaul does a great job emphasizing. Housing is lacking due to the lack of room; hence, no one is guaranteed housing, not even freshmen. The facilities here are topnotch. All the classrooms equipped with the state-of-the-art technology, which makes presentations by the students and professors a breeze. The Lincoln Park campus neighborhood is gorgeous, but is not excluded from crime. DePaul does a decent job warning new students that crime still occurs in the neighborhood and tells them how to be safe. There is public safety available for students all the time. The Loop Campus is beautiful, as well, and is in the heart of the Loop, which makes things very convenient.

Social Life

Current student, 9/2004-Submit Date, January 2006

DePaul has a social life only if you live on campus. There are sororities and lots of events that bring people together on campus—in Lincoln Park, but there are a lot of people who see themselves living in Chicago and going to school rather than living at DePaul. DePaul is definitely a bar school.

Alumnus/a, 9/2003-6/2005, November 2005

Social life at DePaul flourishes. Restaurants, bars and clubs welcome students with variety of advertising and discount packages that are widely distributed in school entertainment areas. The school newspaper *Depaulia* keeps the students up to date with all the entertainment activities that are going on in the Chicago area. There are many clubs established, which recognize students' common interests and hobbies as well as their cultural heritage.

Current student, 9/2003-Submit Date, November 2004

There is a lot to do around DePaul. I'm a commuter student, so I don't do a whole lot around campus. I remember spending some time at the Gin Mill, and going to Midnight Madness a few years ago. I'm not sure of much else. As far as I know, the social life is pretty good. There is not much of a Greek row, but there are sororities and fraternities.

Current student, 8/2002-Submit Date, March 2004

Lincoln Park is the root of where the bars are. Kelly's Pub, Irish Times and O'Malleys are the local pubs. There are exotic and new age bars around, with plenty of entertainment and low prices for the college kids. Greek life is unlike what you'd find at the big state schools, especially since there are no Greek houses. But there is still a presence of Greek life on campus.

The food around here is amazing. It's Chicago, for crying out loud. Everything you need is within walking distance. Thai, Italian, Chinese, Mexican, you name it, we've got it. Demon Dogs, Tomato Head, Llades, Potbelly's, Noodles in a Pot and Penny's are a few of the have-to-go places. But there are hundreds, so we are never in short supply of places to go. And don't worry about 24-hour joints, because Clark's is the happening college diner.

DeVry University

Admissions Office
One Tower Lane
Oakbrook Terrace, IL 60181
Admissions phone: (866) DEVRY-34 or (866) 338-7934
Admissions URL: www.devry.edu/admissions/overview.jsp

Admissions

Alumnus/a, 6/2003-6/2005, April 2006

I first heard about DeVry University when one of their representatives came to my high school. I filled out a form, expressed interest in attending the school and the representative came to visit me at my home. The application process was very easy and they did everything to make sure that I was getting all of the financial aid and scholarships for which I was eligible. After filling out some initial information, I visited the campus and took an entrance exam; the exam

took about an hour and was very comprehensive. I scored well on the exam and was accepted to the school.

Current student, 9/2004-Submit Date, November 2005

It was fairly easy to get into the university. They required transcripts, of course. I did interview with an administrator, but it was more to see if I would like the school [than for the school to see if they like me].

Current student, 1/2005-Submit Date, December 2004

The admissions process consisted of visiting the main campus in downtown Philadelphia and meeting with a DeVry university counselor. First, there was a pre-interview process that made sure that I was serious about getting involved in dedicating myself to becoming a full-time student again. Then, there were many forms to fill out, including personal information and financial information. Then I had to take an admissions test for prior skills in math, English and basic knowledge skills. Next was meeting with a financial aid counselor who directed me in making sure I could afford school and set up on financial calendar for me to make reasonable payments. That was the process for admissions.

Read all of Vault's College Surveys at **www.vault.com/college**—get complete surveys on 100s of colleges and universities, expert advice on applicaton essays and more.

VAULT CAREER LIBRARY 201

Current student, 11/2003-Submit Date, April 2004

When I went into the admissions interview, they informed me that all I needed was to score high enough on the entrance exam, which consisted of reading, arithmetic, algebra and an essay. After I scored high enough, I was admitted. The admissions process is not the most stringent in the world, but the true weeding out comes within the first two semesters. After you hit the third semester, over half of the students with whom one starts will no longer be there.

Current student, 7/2002-Submit Date, March 2004

I first heard about this school through a DeVry representative. They visit local high schools and educate students about the university. I wasn't really planning on attending this school, and I thought I would most likely end up at CSUN, but I received a call from someone in admissions and ended up having an interview with their representative for my high school.

It would take approximately three years for me to graduate instead of the normal four years, if I attended part-time every semester. He even told me that I could qualify for a scholarship because of my high SAT scores. I filled out paperwork immediately after the interview to enroll. A couple weeks after, I found out that I would receive the Dean's Scholarship, which would cover $1,000 of the tuition for each semester, and I also qualified for the Presidential Scholarship, which pays for the full tuition. I missed the deadline to submit the essay for the Presidential Scholarship because my parents were out of town, and I needed them to fill out some of the paperwork, but my representative came to my school and told me that he had spoken to the university director and that they would give me an extension if I completed the essay that day. He brought over all the paperwork, I typed up an essay and I faxed it from school.

A couple days later, I got a call while I was at work saying that I received the full scholarship. My advisor is the best. Since I got the scholarship, I didn't have to go through the tedious process of financial aid, which made the admissions process run smoothly. I now work here on campus and help students, new and continuing, with the registration process, trying to make it run as smoothly as it did when I first came to this school.

Academics

Alumnus/a, 6/2003-6/2005, April 2006

I was enrolled in the electronic engineering technology program at DeVry University. While the general education classes sometimes had 30 to 40 students in one class, the technical class sizes were relatively small. The personal attention I received from each of my professors had a major impact on my ability to grasp the information being presented quickly. All of the professors were extremely knowledgeable and went beyond teaching from a textbook by incorporating real-world experiences into the lectures. Each technical class had an accompanying lab, which proved to be an invaluable part of my education. The hands-on experience provided by each of the labs sets students from DeVry University apart from most major universities.

Current student, 9/2004-Submit Date, November 2005

The school's flexibility with classes is amazing. Not only do they have classes on weekends, but they also have evening courses, accelerated courses, online classes and hybrids (combination of any two). It is a more technical school but does offer other types of programs with a combination of technology. So far, the only classes that have really challenged me have been the math courses. Many of my credits are transferred from a community college. Thankfully, the school took many of my transferred courses.

Alumnus/a, 6/1999-7/2002, June 2004

Telecommunications management required students to take classes such as Algebra, Statistics, Financial and Managerial Accounting, Economics, Law, Career Building, Project Management and more. Most of these classes also required labs that students had to take in conjunction with the class and more often than not would be counted as a separate grade from the lecture class. Consequently, one could pass the lecture portion of the class and fail the lab or vice versa.

The pace of the classes was pretty quick and would be difficult for students who did not have any background in the field. The workload was heavy but bearable.

The best and most difficult teachers taught during the day and most of the teachers who taught at night were adjutants who were either new hires or had day jobs in the field. Getting popular classes is pretty easy if you register early, otherwise it could be difficult to get into a closed class.

Current student, 7/2002-Submit Date, March 2004

Because this campus is small with a student population of just over 1,000 students, the class sizes are not at all as large compared to the ones at the big state universities, which makes the student/teacher relationship even better. We have an academic support center with student and professor tutors to help with most majors; however, there are no tutors for accounting. Students can also make appointments with their professors or e-mail them with any questions or problems they may be having.

Alumnus/a, 7/1997-6/2000, September 2003

The academic structure at DeVry is one of the most unique I have seen. You are in a set program with set classes. There is very little flexibility. You have the choice [of going to classes] in the morning, afternoon, evenings or on weekends. You generally attend all of your classes with the same group of people. However, their hands-on approach truly does work. And 95 percent of the time your professor will be in the room to assist with any problems you may come across. In addition, they have faculty assistants who can also help.

On an extra note, most classes are team oriented. You will be placed or have to choose a small team of about five to work with on your projects for the entire semester. My advice is to choose your teammates carefully! If you are the only worker in a group of slackers, you will either have a lot of late nights playing catch up or your grades will suffer.

Alumnus/a, 6/2002-6/2003, September 2003

80 percent of my experience with the professors was excellent. I had professors who had excellent, real-life scenarios they were involved with in actual companies. Some professors over-test, with major exams every single class session. Some under-test, with just a midterm and final, for which they gave you the questions a week ahead of time.

The grading policy is up to the professors, some are harder than others, but generally the grading was pretty fair. All except the one who does not believe in A's (as he stated), so the highest achievable grade with him was a B.

The workload can be intense. The program is accelerated, so it covers the same material twice as fast. This can lead to a quick burnout if you're a slow worker and can't catch up.

Employment Prospects

Alumnus/a, 6/2003-6/2005, April 2006

Career Services at DeVry University is dedicated to helping students find a job, even long after they have graduated. Each semester, employers like Lockheed Martin and Rockwell Collins visit the campus to recruit the best and the brightest. Most of the people I know who graduated in my program acquired a job within three or four weeks of graduation. The average starting salary for people in my program was in the range of $40,000 to $55,000.

Alumnus/a, 6/1999-7/2002, June 2004

The campus always had companies that came to recruit recent graduates or students who were just about to graduate. There is Career Services that gives students access to advisors in their chosen career fields and keeps in touch with students with prospective employment via e-mail or verbal leads and posted job opportunities.

Current student, 7/2002-Submit Date, March 2004

Every term, we have part-time and career job fairs on campus, where many nearby businesses and retailers come to recruit prospective employees. We also have a Career Services center that helps students in job placement, and they also have literature on things like how to format your résumé, depending on what type of business or what major you are.

There is also a job board that has a current listing of nearby jobs, including information on the location and pay, and students can find more information about

ese jobs at Career Services. Jobs on campus are also posted on the job board
there are students looking to work on campus who are eligible for federal work
tudy. One of each major's course requirements is to take a career development
lass where you basically learn interviewing skills and how to build a career
ortfolio to take with you to job interviews.

Alumnus/a, 7/1997-6/2000, September 2003

think we all know the career prospects for the computer field these days. By
aying that, generally DeVry does do a good job of putting its students a cut
bove the rest. When attending career fairs, you are expected to wear a suit,
ring your résumé and conduct yourself as a professional. And DeVry offers an
ntire class devoted to finding a job. This includes how to dress, act, even what
o say on interviews. They offer mock interview services, as well.

ven with all these pieces, the one thing that was most helpful to all of those who
id find jobs was to volunteer for an internship. If you work in your field while
ou go to school, your chances of getting hired are much better than if you
orked at just a regular job or didn't work at all.

Regarding career opportunities, the school submits two alumni comments:

I needed some form of training and I felt DeVry was a very good place to start. If I hadn't gotten that degree, I never would have gotten the job I have now. I have nearly tripled my income since starting with the company. It's done wonders for me both financially to support my kids and as a person. I'm not just a mom, I have a career.

Sunday Aiyash, Alumna
Associate of Applied Science, Electronics and Computer Technology
1999

I absolutely would not be where I am today without DeVry— working as a nuclear engineer for a major corporation. I thought it was impossible. I certainly did not dream of where I am today. DeVry made it all happen. DeVry graduates have a skill that a lot of college graduates don't have. They possess something different. We're set apart from typical graduates.

Rodney Winterland, Alumnus
Bachelor of Science, Electronics Engineering Technology
2001

Quality of Life

Alumnus/a, 6/2003-6/2005, April 2006

Because DeVry University is a small private college, many of the problems associated with larger universities do not exist. While DeVry does not have on-cam-
us dorms, they do offer reasonably priced student housing in apartment com-
lexes very close to the school. Crime is almost nonexistent on the campus; dur-
ng the four years that I was there, I did not experience or witness any criminal
cts. The campus is very nice and all of the classrooms and labs are equipped
with state-of-the-art technology.

Current student, 9/2004-Submit Date, November 2005

The area is pretty safe. A few miles from the school itself is where things can
et a little more hectic, but so far seems like a safe town. Housing is OK, not
ypical. The school offers apartments, not dorms, in two different areas. The
housing is not just students, but actual families live in the same buildings. It is
hard to find a student in the housing areas, most commute.

Current student, 1/2005-Submit Date, December 2004

Attending school online does not exactly allow students to be directly affected
by outside distractions. Although online students are primarily working from a
personal computer in the privacy of their own homes, students sometimes have
to meet on campus for discussions and projects with teachers and other students.
I feel very safe on the campus and there is also around the clock security on the
campus for extra protection.

Current student, 7/2002-Submit Date, March 2004

There is no campus housing here, like at some of the other DeVry campuses, so
this is basically a commuter school. We are located in a fairly safe, residential
neighborhood. We do have a bulletin board in our commons with listings on
rooms, houses and apartments for rent, and we also have a listing of web sites
where students can search for places around campus. We have two malls close
by and several restaurants and shopping centers, so if students have several hours
between their classes, there is always somewhere to go.

Alumnus/a, 7/1997-6/2000, September 2003

There are a few clubs and organizations for those who are interested in similar
activities and such. But you will find that your immediate classmates will be
closest to you here. Given the fact that you spend at least four or five hours a
day (not counting group projects) with these people for three years. Facilities
are kept up to date. And they are available at most hours.

Social Life

Alumnus/a, 6/2003-6/2005, April 2006

The social atmosphere of DeVry is not as exciting as most universities'. If you
are looking for a party school, DeVry is definitely not it. There are only a few
clubs on campus, but the social atmosphere is great because the small population
makes it possible to know and associate with almost everyone at the school.

Current student, 9/2004-Submit Date, November 2005

The school does not have any school-sponsored events or social life. The city
itself has a big social life because it is surrounded by many other universities.
There is a downtown area near the city and it is where you can find the most
social life.

Alumnus/a, 6/1999-7/2002, June 2004

Unlike a traditional university, the social scene in terms of a Greek system is not
available. Students can join clubs pertaining to their fields of study and attend
meetings. Students can purchase lunch and/or breakfast from the cafeteria but
alcoholic beverages are not served.

Current student, 7/2002-Submit Date, March 2004

The key to having a great social experience here is to get involved. There are
many organizations here on campus, including an anime club, bowling club,
Christian club and we even have a fraternity and sorority, of which I am a part,
that are the first chartered Greek organizations in DeVry history.

Every second week in the beginning of each term, we hold a Welcome BBQ
where students can get free food, and this gives students a chance to see the different organizations the school has to offer. This is also a great opportunity for
the organizations to recruit new members.

We also have an tri-campus picnic coming up, which is an event for all three
Southern California DeVry campuses, and every January/February, we have a
tri-campus winter formal.

Alumnus/a, 6/2002-6/2003, September 2003

When thinking of school-sponsored social activities, keep in mind, it is a small
school, so don't expect the quantity of things you'd find a major university. The
school has approximately 20 clubs that function on campus, but that's about all
I know about it. Between the classes, exams and full-time work, I did not have
time for much else.

They do a yearly retreat, free of charge, for new (incoming) students, sponsored
by the school, at a mountain ranch above Capistrano in Orange County. The
retreat is nice, but a lot of work. I was not new to college, but quickly realized
that this retreat was designed for those who were. The three day (over a weekend) retreat, was broken into sessions and ran a strict time schedule. Sessions
included studying habits and how to be a successful student. For team building
exercises, they created six teams. Each team was responsible for cooking a meal
for the rest of the group.

Read all of Vault's College Surveys at **www.vault.com/college**—get complete surveys on 100s of colleges and universities, expert advice on applicaton essays and more.

VAULT CAREER LIBRARY 203

Illinois State University

Admissions Office
Campus Box 2200
Normal, IL 61790-2200
Admissions phone: (309) 438-2181 or (800) 366-2478
  or (309) 438-2006 (TTY)
Admissions e-mail: admissions@ilstu.edu
Admissions URL: www.admissions.ilstu.edu/

 ## Admissions

Current student, 8/2004-Submit Date, October 2006

I transferred into ISU, and I felt that the admissions process went by quickly. I didn't feel as though I waited months to find out and they even gave me an approximate date of when I would hear back. I was originally accepted as a general student and when I called to find out why, I was informed that I needed one more class that I had to take that summer. However, I would have liked the letter of acceptance to inform me of that information. As for the essays, I suggest one of two things. Either sit and write whatever comes to mind even if it has nothing to do with your topic (you can always go back and edit it later), or plan out what you are going to say. Make lists, charts or pro/con lists if that is what it takes. They look for organization and logic in your writing.

Current student, 6/2003-Submit Date, December 2005

I hear every year it's getting more difficult to get into my school; I was rejected from a few Big 10 schools and this was my safety school. That being said, I did excel in many subjects in high school with very competitive grades. My ACT score was 28. I would now be considered very average in an incoming class of freshmen. At the time I was a little above average.

Current student, 8/2004-Submit Date, September 2005

Basically, the admissions process for ISU was simple. I just had to fill out an application form, including my GPA from high school and my SAT grades.

Alumnus/a, 1/1999-1/2003, January 2005

I was given a grant and matching loan. Later, I participated in the track program and was given a scholarship. It varied from semester to semester. All participants had to have a C average and NCCA ruling to be considered.

Current student, 8/2003-Submit Date, October 2004

When I applied, it took a while to get a reply. I went to the financial aid office and applied for loans to attend the school. After I got accepted, I looked for places to live. Dorms were my primary option until I saw what Farm House Fraternity had to offer and it was much cheaper to join them, so I did.

Current student, 8/2003-Submit Date, June 2004

Application to ISU is really quite simple. It includes filling out an application and writing an essay. As long as you have good grades in school and write honestly in the essay, you have good chances of acceptance. I was accepted with a 25 on my ACT and a graduating GPA of 3.77. Most students at ISU graduated in the top 25 percent of their high school class. Things get a little more foggy when you talk about getting into your particular major. From applying to being accepted, to registering for classes, this aspect is a bit more confusing and time-consuming.

Current student, 8/2002-Submit Date, June 2004

Admissions is still fairly easy. If you want to get into the special education program, or really any other education major, it may get more strenuous.

I transferred from a community college with a 4.0 GPA into the business school, so obviously I segued quite easily. They took 69 of my 73 credit hours, and I finished my BS in 1.5 semesters. They're efficient in their transfer relationship with community colleges.

 ## Academics

Status: Current student, 8/2004-Submit Date, October 2006

The workload is a lot of reading. Make sure that you can devote one or two hours a night to reading for your classes. I only had one less-than-great experience with a professor, but I would still rate him highly. I also had phenomenal experiences with professors who have helped me during their office hours and one who made numerous appointments with me so that I could pass the class. I feel that the professors at ISU really care about what their students are doing. I frequently visit these professors just to keep them up to date on my progress. The program itself is very focused and it is nice when many of your classes touch on the same or similar subjects because you end up doing better on tests and quizzes because of repetitive information. I felt that as long as you do the work and go to class, you should have little to no difficulty getting good grades.

Current student, 6/2003-Submit Date, December 2005

It is very difficult to get into my major classes due to limited availability. I have needed overrides since my sophomore year for every major class. The quality of the math programs range from very interesting and intriguing to poorly taught and hardly planned out. I have had professors for my classes who are also my academic advisors. Classes are cancelled frequently during registration week because the professor has multiple responsibilities. There are commonly teachers who will not meet with you after class. This may be because the math department is grossly in need of new teachers and understaffed.

Current student, 8/2003-Submit Date, October 2005

ISU is an excellent school if you want to pursue a career in education. The advising is very helpful, and the workload is fairly moderate depending on which classes you take.

Current student, 8/2004-Submit Date, September 2005

The first two years everyone takes general education classes, which are required by the university. Students complain that some classes are not relevant to what they want to focus on for their future career. On the other hand, it helps those students without a major decide what interests them.

Quality of the classes is average. Some classes are small, encouraging student-teacher relationships, and others are large lecture halls. Here, quality goes down since teachers and students don't touch base individually because there are too many students. Getting popular or easy classes is difficult. Those are the classes that go the fastest. So it all depends on when your registration date is (if you have early registration, you get lucky!).

Grading is acceptable. Some classes have their own separate way of grading, which sometimes confuses the class. Professors are average. Professors are strict, others are easy. The workload is horrible! It seems I have no time for anything else. Some students say the workload is OK, but if you want to get an A in the class, studying takes up a lot more time.

Alumnus/a, 1/1999-1/2003, January 2005

Classes were about 30 people total. Attendance was 50 percent of your grade. Your grade had to be above a C in departmental majors and no more than 30 hours outside of university for a total of 127 to graduate. You needed to establish a rapport with professors. Some 400 classes, as I remember, were shared with graduates and the assignments were demanding.

Current student, 8/2003-Submit Date, October 2004

Getting into the criminal justice program is easy. The classes are somewhat easy if you are interested in criminal justice. Classes that I am interested in are Organized and White-Collar Crime, Alcohol, Drugs and Crime and Correctional Institutions. They are really easy to get into and they are fantastic classes that I highly value. I recommend these classes to anyone at ISU. Gen ed classes aren't too difficult as long as you do your work and study. I recommend any agricultural class that's in the 100s or 200s. They are fun and easy, even if you are city folk.

Current student, 8/2003-Submit Date, June 2004

Most of the GE classes I have taken have been of very good quality. The professors are all very good, especially in the music and teacher education departments. Grading has been fair, although sometimes the expected workload is unreasonable. I have found the chemistry program to be notably sub-par, but most people do not go to this school for chemistry anyway. The College of Business is very good and will certainly bloom in the years to come, as the new College of Business [building] is almost finished. Generally, grading depends on the professors, but generally I have not had any problems with the grading system being too strict or too lax.

Current student, 8/2002-Submit Date, June 2004

Few ISU graduates become research analysts, attorneys or successful entrepreneurs; most alumni work at medium-sized and large corporations. ISU skillfully teaches how to create and deliver presentations and sell your ideas, and they provide a fair amount of focus on the technical side of business.

If you're interested in sales or marketing, ISU is the place to go. It has a great reputation as a sales school, and the professors who teach the marketing and sales classes are prima in their efforts.

 ## Employment Prospects

Current student, 8/2004-Submit Date, October 2006

At ISU there is a career and internship fair every semester. Many companies show up for these fairs and there are even fairs specifically geared towards specific schools/colleges. Currently, I have not had the opportunity to participate in these activities, but I did visit one and I thought it was very helpful.

Current student, 6/2003-Submit Date, December 2005

As an education major, I hear that our employment rate is very high. I will soon learn more about this upon my graduation. Illinois State University is renowned nationally for its outstanding education program. I feel very strongly about entering the education field in the upper echelon of pay.

Current student, 8/2004-Submit Date, September 2005

I am an elementary education major. I have an advantage to future employment because ISU started out as just an education university. They are known for their education curricula. ISU also provides programs that are helpful. For example, PDS (Professional Developmental Schools) is an education program that allows students to student teach for a whole year, instead of the regular one-semester student teaching.

Current student, 8/2003-Submit Date, October 2004

I am currently looking for a position in corrections in Illinois or Colorado. There are always career days that help you decide what internship or job you would like to secure. ISU also has a great employment program that will send out your résumé to everyone.

Current student, 8/2003-Submit Date, June 2004

Internships are prominent at ISU, and many graduates are placed into well-paying jobs immediately following graduation. I have personally known people in the music business major being hired by Yamaha through internships. Internships are literally a phone call away, and most of these resources can be found on the web site, which is a very useful hub of information. Many seminars are held for each major several times during the year regarding job placement and paid work experience.

Alumnus/a, 8/1999-5/2001, September 2003

The school did hold a few career expos with multiple employers. The school also had an online job search engine where students and employers could meet and set up interviews. I did not have much luck with either. The economy was on the downturn when I graduated, so I had a hard enough time trying to find a job and I did not receive much help from ISU.

 ## Quality of Life

Current student, 8/2004-Submit Date, October 2006

As I live in the dorms, I feel that the quality of life is relatively high. The buildings are well maintained and all but East Campus are located right on campus. East Campus is about two to five minutes away. As for the dining, I feel that we have an excellent selection and quality of food. The meal plans are set up nicely and there is always the option halfway through the year to change your meal plan. At the end of the year, any money left on your meal plan will be reimbursed to you. The campus is extremely nice because 90 percent of the buildings are located in one quad. Every building is pretty much within 10 minutes of the others, on foot.

Current student, 6/2003-Submit Date, December 2005

I try not to walk alone after dark. This is not an extremely safe campus. In an attempt to make the campus safer, there are several emergency booths on campus.

> Regarding crime and safety, the school says: "A summary of every police report is made public—nothing is kept secret. ISU is known for its low crime rate."

Current student, 8/2004-Submit Date, September 2005

Housing here is average. Rooms are small (but what college dorm rooms aren't!), electric plugs work well, but the cable doesn't come in at all! The campus is beautiful—the perfect size, well-kept, trees and flowers, buildings cleaned. Dining facilities barely have a good selection of healthy foods. Mostly unnutritional foods are served (in my opinion), like Chinese, Mexican, Italian and grill. The neighborhood is small, with crime being very low. I always feel safe wherever I go.

Current student, 8/2003-Submit Date, October 2004

ISU has plenty of living opportunities. Utilities are not paid for but they are cheap. There are a lot of apartments in the area owned by the school, which are cheap and offer free utilities—definitely take advantage of that!

Current student, 8/2003-Submit Date, June 2004

The dining services at ISU are the best I have seen on any campus. I have many friends in college, and ISU surely has them all beat in dining. Dorms are dorms; nothing too great there. The campus is beautiful, and crime is generally not an issue. From Subway to Chick-fil-A, to Donzello's Pizza, to Ben and Jerry's, you can swipe your card at a variety of places, including the general cafeteria where you can munch on some very good food.

Current student, 8/2002-Submit Date, June 2004

Bloomington/Normal has about 140,000 people when you include the school's population. Normal, the northerly twin city, is a college town and super-conservative. This stems from the large number of State Farm (B/N is their international HQ) employees who live in Normal; they're constantly worried about car accidents, violence and so forth, so they control the city autocratically.

B/N has everything you need as far as restaurants, malls and recreation. Just watch out for those nasty winters.

 ## Social Life

Current student, 8/2004-Submit Date, October 2006

Bloomington-Normal has the highest growth in restaurants and bars. There is so much to do that I couldn't list it all.

Current student, 6/2003-Submit Date, December 2005

Social life is rather slow unless you are 21. There used to be many varieties of fun. The local police are notorious for breaking up any large house parties.

Current student, 8/2004-Submit Date, September 2005

There are many social groups to join, from democratic programs all the way to sororities and fraternities. There are enough bars around for entertainment and drinks (maybe too many!). It seems that's the only thing people do on week-

Read all of Vault's College Surveys at www.vault.com/college—get complete surveys on 100s of colleges and universities, expert advice on application essays and more.

VAULT CAREER LIBRARY   205

ends! Events held by the university are always fun alternatives to the bar scene. Lots of them are very interesting to our age group.

Alumnus/a, 1/1999-1/2003, January 2005

The school had a recreational facility in the student union. In the surrounding community of Normal, it was a dry county, meaning there was no liquor allowed in the community. However, just up the street in Bloomington, there were lounges, taverns and social clubs. There are plenty if fast food and dining restaurants in town. There was no fraternity life when I was there—no Greeks on campus, just interest groups, such as the Delteen's and Pacesetters. There was a curfew on campus of 1 a.m. on the weekends. I enjoyed movies, bowling and intramural programs such as track, football and swimming.

Current student, 8/2003-Submit Date, October 2004

We have a rec center that has pool and bowling. As far as bars go, there are good ones where there is a great atmosphere, such as Foul Shots, the Pub and downtown altogether. As far as Greek systems go, there is a variety of options for people to choose from, I joined a small-town fraternity called Farm House. It was the best thing I ever did. In the dorms, there are plenty of things to do, poker tournaments and parties are commonplace. If you are big into partying, there are plenty of places to hang out. If you are not big on partying there are plenty of events in the dorms to attend, which are a good time. I should also mention the athletic events at ISU. There is always a good crowd for all the events and the students in the student sections have a great time and have chances to win prizes frequently.

Current student, 8/2003-Submit Date, June 2004

I have met more people at college than I have ever met before. Dorm life is quite an experience. Restaurants include most of the typical ones: Burger King, Taco Bell and so forth. But there are also many local chains that cater to college students, offering good food at low prices. Though I am not yet 21, I hear the bar scene is a very good place to meet intelligent college people looking to secure their future and have a good time, as well.

Alumnus/a, 8/1999-5/2001, September 2003

The nightlife at ISU/Bloomington was wonderful. Before I turned 21, there were two bars close to campus that we could visit. After I turned 21, the place to go was downtown Bloomington. Some of the bars of note included Bogie's, Rhino's, Fat Jack's, Club 110, Elroy's and in downtown Normal, we used to always go to the Stadium Club. I really enjoyed the bar scene at school.

 **The School Says**

Comments from Matt Kiesewetter, current student:

"The chemistry department at Illinois State has only 135 students, most students do not attend Illinois State for the chemistry program. This mundane statistic cannot be justifiably extrapolated to conclude that our chemistry program is sub-par. My choice to attend Illinois State was made, admittedly, by happenstance. In hindsight, however, I could not have made a better choice.

"The instruction, starting from day one in the freshman lecture courses, is conducted by faculty members who are readily available to assist students personally. As a freshman I experienced a 14:1 student-to-teacher ratio, a ratio that only improved as I progressed through the program (ultimately reaching 5:1). As good as the classroom and laboratory portions of my undergraduate education are, the most alluring asset of our department is the research program.

"The PhD caliber of our program is not hindered by the fact that our department does not offer a PhD, and, in fact, the small size of our program allows undergraduates in chemistry at ISU to have excellent research opportunities. I was trained to use the most advanced analytical equipment, all available in-house, while conducting independent research at the cutting edge of chemistry. In essence, the small size and superior quality of our program allows undergraduates to receive an experience unlike that offered by other schools of our size. My proof as to the quality of our program is the fact that personal interaction with two faculty members is a routine and cherished part of my day. Such interactions, and the superior instrumental and chemical training that I have received, has resulted in the publication of my research in chemistry journals of the highest regard; one of said publications was recently honored with a selection as an Editor's Choice in *Science Magazine* (July 16, 2004 issue)."

Comments from Carl Kasten, alumnus, BA in social sciences, 1966:

"Illinois State University has more than 1,100 alumni who are attorneys. Their pre-law graduates have been accepted to more than half of the Top 25 law schools in America, with two accepted to Harvard for this fall semester. Of the two, one received a full scholarship. For the past five years, Illinois State University has had students accepted at Yale Law School. The university also numbers many alumni who have become judges. Through its Pre-Law Advisement Center, the university offers a pre-law mentoring program and advisement about law school admissions processes, LSAT preparation and financial aid. Illinois State students participate on a Mock Trial Team and have competed and won nationally. A Pre-Law Advisory Council, comprised of alumni lawyers and judges, assists the university with all aspects of pre-law education and interacts with students."

Loyola University Chicago

Admissions Office
320 N. Michigan Avenue
Chicago, IL 60611-2196
Admissions phone: (312) 915-6500 or (800) 262-2373
Admissions e-mail: admission@luc.edu

 ## Admissions

Alumnus/a, 8/2002-5/2006, February 2007

The Loyola admissions process was incredibly easy. In fact, during the year I applied, essays were not even required as part of admission. My fee was waived for applying online, and I received my admissions decision within a reasonable amount of time. Admissions and financial aid personnel were available to answer questions. I highly recommend taking the campus tour and spending some time in Chicago before making a decision to apply. Loyola's main strength is that it is a part of Chicago, and you can't know the school without knowing the city.

Current student, Biology, 8/2006-Submit Date, May 2007

Loyola has a rolling application deadline. They have no set deadline for turning in admission applications, but in order to qualify for scholarships and get into a preferred housing assignment, students would do best submitting their applications as soon as possible—preferably before March and no later than May.

Current student, 8/2002-Submit Date, February 2006

I completed the Early Action application that is due prior to the general admission application. By doing this, my application was given priority and I was notified about my acceptance before the general applicants. There was a one-page essay requirement. I believe the essay asked us to write about a unique experience (overcoming adversity, a life changing event). There was no interview, but I recommend sending a résumé-like description of what activities, club, awards and jobs you were involved in and/or received during high school.

Current student, 8/2002-Submit Date, January 2006

Easy process. Send in your application early, they respond fairly quickly. They are becoming more and more selective in order to rise within the *U.S. News* rankings. They seem to be failing because every year they have been sliding down the rankings.

> **The school says:** "*U.S. News & World Report*'s 2008 edition of *America's Best Colleges* again ranks Loyola University Chicago among the top national universities, and also names Loyola as a best value in education. Only schools ranked in or near the top half of their categories are included."

Current student, 8/2001-Submit Date, April 2005

People who are not familiar with Loyola Chicago seem to think that it is a highly selective school; however, that is not the case. Many students are accepted through a fast-track application that Loyola Chicago sends out to prospective students. This shorter application is only one page (front and back) and has an optional essay. Interviews are not a common part of the admissions process due to the lack of selectivity. Supposedly, Loyola Chicago is cutting back on freshman admission and raising its standards, but this doesn't seem to be happening very quickly. However, Loyola Chicago is very good with scholarships. Not only do many students enter with academic scholarships, but during freshman year they are also giving the opportunity to increase the number by attaining a certain GPA. This is a great way to motivate freshmen to achieve high grades their first two semesters and it is a great relief for many parents paying for their education.

Current student, 1/2002-Submit Date, November 2004

I found the admissions process to be relatively easy but not altogether problem-free. As a transfer student with a high GPA, I was approached by LUC and

offered a great scholarship. There were no complicated forms to fill out. From discussions with peers, I know that the admissions process is not as extensive as at other schools. LUC has become more selective, especially in their business school. Overall, if you have a decent GPA, you should have no problem.

Current student, 5/2004-Submit Date, April 2004

I was looking for a college with an excellent criminal justice program and was eager to leave Georgia. The admissions process was somewhat difficult. Their criminal justice program is highly selective, and I was on nerves waiting for admission. I had a 3.71 GPA but was still concerned that my extracurriculars were not up to par. I was finally admitted in January 2004 and received a $9,000 scholarship, the highest available for a transfer student. I was very proud of myself and the work I have accomplished as an undergrad.

Current student, 8/2004-Submit Date, January 2004

I applied to Loyola at the beginning of October using the fast-track application. I did not need to enclose the $25 processing fee, nor did I have to write a new essay. I filled everything out normally and sent it in. I was to receive a response before Thanksgiving, but it came the day after. I was accepted. I was a fairly good student with a 3.3 GPA and a 23 on the ACT, and was applying for a major in biology. I did not receive a scholarship, most likely because my GPA was below 3.5. My advice is to apply early, keep that GPA above a 3.5 and keep excelling in school!

 ## Academics

Alumnus/a, 8/2002-5/2006, February 2007

My professors were dedicated, knowledgeable and approachable. They embraced the opportunity to get to know their students personally and really worked hard to teach and treat everyone fairly. I started having trouble toward the end of my career at Loyola, however, as I found the class sizes, especially in the psychology department, growing to unimaginable proportions. Popular classes included students sitting on the floor. Whereas, as a freshman, I was enrolled in 101 classes with 25 people, as a junior, I took part in a 300-level course with 100 participants. Workload, on the whole, was quite manageable, and I benefited from the projects and papers I was required to write and didn't feel my work was just there for the purpose of doing something.

> **Loyola University Chicago says:** "Loyola's average class size is 29 students. The student-to-faculty ratio at Loyola is 13:1, which is far below the national average."

Current student, Biology, 8/2006-Submit Date, May 2007

At Loyola, students are required to undergo a curriculum of classes known as the core curriculum classes. A degree of enjoyment can be obtained from these classes, as they teach on a variety of subjects such as anthropology, philosophy, literature, psychology and the like. Some of these classes can count toward major credits, as well. The biology major curriculum is perhaps one of the most difficult. Not because the subject is difficult, but getting into classes poses quite a problem at times. This major requires 68 credits for completion, and due to the large number of biology majors at the school, it is difficult to get into all the required classes. Labs often fill up the fastest, and are the most difficult component as they are the practical application of scientific knowledge. The workload at Loyola depends on the major and classes the student takes. As a biology major or pre-med concentration, the student should expect a large amount of studying to be done throughout the week. Don't be discouraged by the large amount of work to be done, however. The instructors are very understanding and look forward to visits from students. E-mails are appreciated, as well, for students who don't prefer face-to-face confrontation.

Current student, 8/2001-Submit Date, February 2006

The majority of the classes I've taken while at Loyola have been great. There has been the odd exception here and there but that is to be expected. I was in the

Read all of Vault's College Surveys at **www.vault.com/college**–get complete surveys on 100s of colleges and universities, expert advice on applicaton essays and more.

VAULT CAREER LIBRARY 207

honors program throughout my undergrad years and therefore getting classes was a breeze because honors students were allowed to register first.

Current student, 8/2002-Submit Date, February 2006

It depends on which program you are looking to get into—nursing is very competitive. If you are trying to get into the nursing program, your chances of getting in are better straight out of high school than transferring in. It is basically impossible to get into the program as a transfer. Business seems to be pretty easy from what I have seen, heard and experienced. The physics program is very demanding and intense, but the professors are very helpful, patient and engaged with the students. The physics dept is great. Math is touch and go. There are some great professors. It is impossible as an underclassman to get into the popular classes unless you are in the honors program or an athlete. The fun and popular classes go to juniors and seniors. The quality of classes is hit or miss—some are great, some are horrible. Grading is subjective according to the professor, some don't care about attendance while others include attendance in your grade.

Current student, 8/2002-Submit Date, January 2006

It is easier to get classes if you're in the honors program because they get the first pick of the courses they want, so do the athletes. It's harder to get the classes you want if you're a freshman because you get to choose your courses last, unless you're in the honors program.

Current student, 8/2001-Submit Date, April 2005

The academic nature varies greatly depending on a student's major. A communications student will receive fewer challenges than a biology student. The pre-health track at Loyola Chicago is hard and intensive. The core curriculum is large but manageable. The university recently completed a core evaluation and a new core curriculum was instituted in the fall of 2004. The core gives students exposure to a variety of classes including theology, social sciences, mathematics and more. Registration becomes easier as a student earns more credits. Incoming freshmen have the hardest time getting into classes because they are the last to register. Grading seems to be quite consistent across the board, but there are always some professors with tougher grading requirements than others. Overall, the academic atmosphere seems to be much more relaxed than what one might imagine at a private university.

Current student, 1/2002-Submit Date, November 2004

At first, I found the core business program too extensive and unnecessary, but as I got deeper into the program, I realized the value of taking such classes. I was impressed by the continuous improvement of classes and offering of more cutting-edge courses. The workload is substantial but not unfair. The professors are generally wonderful, professional and helpful. The only downside is that the class timings don't always tend to work well. Also, as time has gone on, we have changed from a four day week to a five day week. It isn't too bad but it just takes some adjustment on the part of the student. I have also found that the variety of classes offered at the business school has been pretty skimpy. Very often, you will have to wait till the following semester to take a class that you need. Often this is inconvenient because you are trying to finish your core in your last semester. The classes, however, are definitely interesting since many professors bring in speakers from the outside world, which leads to recruitment, as well. (We had a senior person from Gatorade come in and talk to us.)

 Employment Prospects

Alumnus/a, 8/2002-5/2006, February 2007

Although Loyola tends to suffer from an inferiority complex, being surrounded by University of Chicago in the south and Northwestern University in the north, I have never had a problem getting a job or opportunity with my Loyola education. Alumni are eager to help and support current students, and are active in all manner of Illinois business, government and nonprofits. On a trip to Springfield, Illinois for lobby day, my classmates and I were astonished to discover that nearly 20 percent of Illinois' legislative bodies had some sort of Loyola tie. Loyola graduates are strongly committed to service and the community, and last year, Loyola had an incredibly successful class of students accepted into the Teach for America program, as well as several Fulbright Scholars.

Current student, 8/2002-Submit Date, February 2006

Our school is great at providing job fairs and opportunities for employment. Th[e] School of Education requires clinicals as does the nursing program, and these ar[e] great opportunities to get your foot in the door with a school or a hospital. Sinc[e] we have a medical school, it is to the pre-med student's advantage to apply earl[y] to Loyola's medical school. There are also career life classes offered to help stu[dents] discern what areas of study and careers would be of interest to them. Ther[e] is also a Career Development Center on campus that helps students with place[ment] into jobs and internships.

Alumnus/a, 8/1999-5/2005, November 2005

Graduating from Loyola Chicago is awesome if you're looking for a job i[n] Chicago. The alumni resources available to you are unlimited. They hold jo[b] fairs constantly and business students who graduate with fair grades have n[o] problem breaking into finance. Outside of Chicago, there is not as much recog[nition] as supposed to a Northwestern student. Internships are plentiful i[n] Chicago as long as you do your own research. Unlimited supply of opportunit[y] in this city.

Current student, 8/2001-Submit Date, April 2005

It seems that a degree from Loyola University Chicago is still considered a pres[tigious] accomplishment. However, the job market has not been great lately an[d] a degree from Loyola Chicago doesn't seem to give much of an edge. Many cur[rent] seniors are struggling to find a job. Yet, it depends upon the degree. Loyol[a] Chicago has a phenomenal nursing program. In addition, nurses are in hig[h] demand. Therefore, nursing students have little difficulty finding a job—sam[e] with elementary education majors. However, for students with an English communication or psychology degree, the job search is a much tougher process[.] The Career Development Center is helpful in terms of cover letter and résumé advice. However, the on-campus job fairs are not very good. Employers ar[e] almost all from the financial field, which leaves all non-business students out i[n] the cold. Chicago is rich with diverse business opportunities. Loyola Chicag[o] needs to tap into these resources to benefit students.

> **Regarding the Career Center, the school says:** "In addition to its Business Career Center, which provides School of Business students with career assistance, Loyola's Career Development Center works with students from all majors to help them achieve their personal and professional goals. The Career Development Center sponsors many career fairs throughout the year, attracting employers from many prestigious businesses and organizations. Also, the Career Development Center is available to students even after graduation. To learn more about the Career Development Center and employment statistics, visit: *LUC.edu/career*."

Current student, 1/2002-Submit Date, November 2004

I found that through a certain business fraternity, I was able to gain an internship with a top financial company. I was also contacted by several other people through Loyola's Career Development Center. Depending on which group you choose to become a part of, there are numerous opportunities to network. Also, LUC hosts many talks, forums and lectures that students can attend and network. I know that Ernest and Young recruited at LUC and six out of seven people were offered employment at that time.

 Quality of Life

Alumnus/a, 8/2002-5/2006, February 2007

Housing on campus is wonderful and a really great way to get to know other people. While some of the rules for students living on campus can seem a little harsh, it's understandable that Loyola's urban location necessitates a bit of extra security. That said, I don't think that the campus safety program is entirely on the ball. They're really trying, but it takes very long to attend to calls. The Rogers Park neighborhood is relatively safe; it's still not a good idea to walk home alone, especially if having been out to the bars for the night. Loyola offers a taxi service for students studying or out late at night, but it can get quite bogged down on snowy, rainy or cold days. The location by the lake is perfect, and the downtown campus is really stunning. Shuttle service connects the two campus-

...s, and public transportation is very easy to access. Really, quality of life at Loyola is great.

Current student, Biology, 8/2006-Submit Date, May 2007

Loyola has a wonderfully diverse group of students. Everyone comes from different backgrounds. The school is very accepting of all races and religions and promotes awareness of other cultures, as it is a Jesuit school. Although it is a Catholic-affiliated school, there are places of worship for Jews, Muslims and Hindus, as well. Loyola requires that freshman and sophomore students live on campus. I believe they do this to ensure that students are familiar with the campus around them and that they form a close relationship with their fellow students. However, due to the increasing number of incoming students each year, Loyola often has a problem finding housing assignments for its students. The assignments are picked through a lottery system, and students with the lowest number stand the best chances of getting into the residence halls of their choice. Freshman housing assignments are chosen at random.

> **Regarding housing options, the school says:** "Loyola recently opened two new residence halls: Regis Hall at the Lake Shore Campus on the shore of Lake Michigan, and Baumhart Hall, a 25-story high-rise at the Water Tower Campus in the heart of Chicago. More than 3,800 Loyola students reside on campus, and many upper-class students enjoy apartment living in and around the Lake Shore Campus."

Current student, 8/2001-Submit Date, February 2006

Housing—who doesn't complain about the size of on-campus housing? The dorms are of course small, and sharing a room can wear on you, especially if you don't get along with your roommate. The rules were very strict in the dorms (I felt like I was at boarding school at times) and inconsistent, at best, in the on-campus apartments. The campus is nice. Lack of anywhere for sports clubs to practice was a pain, though. It is nice having campuses that are condensed. It makes it a whole lot easier and faster to get around. Dining isn't bad. It wasn't that great to be eating in the cafeteria day in, day out, for a full year. But once I was out of the dorms and able to choose whether or not to eat in the caf it was good, albeit the complete lack of vegetarian options—even the vegetarian options were prepared on the same surfaces as meat products. The area isn't the greatest, but I love it. Crime and safety is an issue. Anyone going to school in the city just needs to be smart about how he/she travels around. Although the school does offer a campus shuttle service (8-RIDE) at night, it is entirely unreliable.

> **Loyola says:** "Like most Jesuit universities, Loyola University Chicago is located in an urban environment, giving students many opportunities to experience the benefits of living in a major American city, including learning how to interact with and serve others in different communities. Loyola offers safety orientation sessions, neighborhood tours and several other initiatives to help students learn how to be savvy and smart as they get involved in their new community. For more information, visit: LUC.edu/safety."

Current student, 8/2001-Submit Date, April 2005

Housing is constantly improving at Loyola Chicago. A new dormitory was just constructed and was ready for use in fall 2005. There are many options for students and there is housing available for upperclassmen, as well. However, most juniors and seniors choose to live off campus in the Rogers Park area. Much like housing, dining services are on the up-and-up. A new cafe-type dining area was created this spring (2005) in one of the classroom buildings. In addition, a new mini-mart store was added to one of the housing buildings. At the downtown campus, an improved dining facility was opened in the fall of 2004. In addition, plans to create housing for students at the downtown campus are in the works. The main campus (Lakeshore) is beautiful. Located right on Lake Michigan, there are beaches nearby and in the spring and summer, it is gorgeous. There are lots of trees and flowers, and Loyola Chicago does a lot to keep up with the landscaping. Unfortunately, the surrounding neighborhood (Rogers Park) is not very safe. Students should never walk alone at night without carrying pepper spray or something similar. On campus, things are extremely safe and campus security is always present. Wander a few blocks off campus and it is an entirely different story. It is an unfortunate location for such a beautiful campus.

Current student, 5/2004-Submit Date, April 2004

I moved to Chicago the first week of April. The environment is a complete 360 to what my suburban life was. The hustle and sheer awe of such a remarkable city is somewhat daunting. I have a great apartment that sits on the city overlooking the Hancock Building and with beautiful views of the lake. I feel safe; like anywhere else, there are the good parts of a neighborhood and some shady areas, but my area is clean and seems to attract desirable residents. The food also has to be commended. I have had some of the best meals here, from Sushi Samba to McCormick's and Smitts, to great deep-dish pizza.

Social Life

Alumnus/a, 8/2002-5/2006, February 2007

The bars, restaurants and clubs around Rogers Park are not worth mentioning. Hamilton's, the local bar and student favorite, is famous in the Chicago culture for being a place to pick up underage women, and Carmen's Pizzeria is less than stellar. Leona's Restaurant and Deluxe Diner are also good student hangouts, but sometimes on the pricey or hard-to-walk-to-in-the-snow side. But why stay in Rogers Park when you can hop on the EL any time of the day or night, and experience all of Chicago? Downtown is fabulous, with many jazz and blues clubs, places for dancing and great bars. The theater district is great, and every weekend there's something new playing. New students especially like the shopping on Chicago's Magnificent Mile. I love Chicago in the spring, fall and summer, when there are free music festivals and concerts, as well as fireworks every weekend during the cold winter months.

> **The school says:** "Chicago boasts thousands of dining options, and while Loyola students have access to public transportation that will take them all over the city, there are also numerous restaurants and cafes in the Rogers Park neighborhood. For a detailed listing of places to go in Rogers Park, visit: LUC.edu/communityrelations."

Current student, 8/2001-Submit Date, February 2006

Social life is good. Bars around the area are total dives but fun in their own right. Restaurants are few but it's not difficult to find more options. Dating scene is fine I guess, the male-to-female ratio is definitely in the guys' favor (for heterosexuals). The gay scene is OK. Boystown and Girlstown are just short distances away. Some events are fun, some are lame, some are borderline. There is a club for everything and if there's not you can start one. Greek system is pretty much a joke.

Current student, 8/2001-Submit Date, April 2005

Social life is not an area in which Loyola Chicago excels. The main campus, including all student housing, is located in a far north neighborhood (Rogers Park). There is not a lot to do in the area. There is one bar that all students go to, especially on Thursday nights. There are not a lot of restaurants in the area. Luckily, students receive a U-Pass that allows them unlimited rides on public transportation, so getting to fun areas of the city is not very difficult. Greek life does exist on Loyola Chicago's campus, but it is not a strong presence. There are four nationally affiliated sororities and four fraternities. It is a beneficial experience to take part in Greek life; because Greek life is not very big, these students get to know one another quite well and it provides a good social network. Club sports and intramurals are pretty popular at Loyola Chicago.

Current student, 5/2004-Submit Date, April 2004

Chicago is the social capital of the U.S. There is a rich, eclectic group of people who migrate here. Every bar and social scene is different from the last. The diversity of life is what really drew me to this place. I have found it especially easy to talk to people here. I lived in the South for the greater part of my life and found the people to be somewhat stuffy and closed-minded. The campus and its surroundings are inviting for all walks of life, and it is truly a multicultural setting.

Read all of Vault's College Surveys at **www.vault.com/college**–get complete surveys on 100s of colleges and universities, expert advice on applicaton essays and more.

VAULT CAREER LIBRARY 209

Northwestern University

Office of Undergraduate Admission
Northwestern University
P.O. Box 3060
Evanston, IL 60204-3060
Admissions phone: (847) 491-7271
Admissions e-mail: ug-admission@northwestern.edu
Admissions URL: www.northwestern.edu/admissions/

 Admissions

Current student, Pre-med, 9/2004-Submit Date, January 2007

Gaining admittance to Northwestern is as difficult as to any Top 20 college in the United States. High school students should have an excellent GPA and SAT scores ranging from the high 1300s to the low to mid-1500s. Northwestern has an application rife with essays; I knew fellow peers who quit before making any attempt of completion. However, if completed thoroughly with grammatical and logical integrity, a student would probably be placing himself or herself at an advantage.

Current student, 9/2003-Submit Date, September 2006

The application at Northwestern is notorious; do not let this discourage you from applying. It was, without question, the most painful part of my entire time there, and once you are accepted, you and your classmates will all joke about the experience. Some applicants receive interviews and others do not, but you should not worry one way or the other. Most interviews are based around location and convenience than interest in any particular student.

Current student, 9/2003-Submit Date, November 2006

I applied Early Decision. The essays are intimidating simply because of the whole college admissions process but they are good questions and not abstract or extremely difficult to answer.

Alumnus/a, 9/2002-6/2006, October 2006

The application was nothing out of the ordinary. There were some short-answers, which were fun and interesting to write.

Current student, 8/2004-Submit Date, October 2006

I found NU's process to be the least difficult compared to other universities. The process can be done online in the fall through the deadline, which I believe is early February. The short essay questions were much more interesting because students create them and they were quite diverse and interesting, unlike the other, blander essays that I had to write. They really give the applicant an opportunity to express him/herself and truly show his/her individuality. No interview necessary, so your essays and application will often be the only real peak that admissions will have into your life and your world.

Current student, 9/2005-Submit Date, October 2006

This school has the longest application of any that I completed, but it seems to really try to learn as much as possible about applicants. Apparently, it helps to take the SAT Subject Tests and do interviews.

Current student, 9/2002-Submit Date, January 2006

Northwestern is a selective institution, of course. It is important to go to NU to get a feel of it, not so much for getting into the school, but for just getting a good feel. In touring campus, the prospective student will have the opportunity to relate his or her experience into his or her essays, e.g., one of my essays talked about how my ideal college culture very much mirrored that of Northwestern's. I was able to get away with saying this because I had toured the campus and spent the night. Interacting with students is important. Another vital feature of the program is the interview process. I have heard that many prospective students do no interview—everyone should interview!! Interviewing gives applicants an opportunity to distinguish themselves and personalize their essays, in a

sense giving their applications flare. In your interview, it is essential that you relate much of what you say back to why Northwestern would be a good fit.

Current student, 9/2003-Submit Date, March 2005

The admissions were pretty standard for a Top 20 school. Enter all your SAT scores and other achievements. There were a lot of essays and they were not easy to write, but were not horrible either. I found that the questions asked were pretty entertaining to answer. There were no interviews or things like that, so it took less time. Another important thing to realize is that if you apply early to Northwestern, then you can't apply Regular Decision, as well. So if you get denied in early admission you are denied in the regular admission, too. So don't try to rush through your application just to get in it before the early admission due date.

Current student, 9/2002-Submit Date, January 2005

The best way to get into Northwestern is to show in your essays and activities that you have something at which you are great. They claim that they want their students to have passions, but truly they are trying to find the most skilled individuals capable of being true leaders as opposed to good workers. I never had to interview, I am in CAS so I don't see this as a necessity. The school seems to be selective enough—about or above 1400 SAT, and some athleticism. I have yet to meet more than a handful of people who lack some sort of athletic background. I imagine this is because Northwestern is seeking dynamic individuals and team players as opposed to bookworms (although we also have those here too). For your essays, it just matters that you write well and are creative and witty. Northwestern has the most unique application, and that is because they want students who aren't run-of-the-mill intelligent, they want the intelligent ones who are also graced with personality.

 Academics

Current student, Pre-med, 9/2004-Submit Date, January 2007

Northwestern works on a quarter system: more classes, more exams, more stress, yet more rewards. Like any college, there is a hierarchy to getting popular classes. If, for instance, you're a freshman, you will most likely not procure a spot in the professional class, Investment Banking. However, you will be able find a slot in equally good classes across a variety of majors. Professors always teach in lectures, while smaller details are sorted out by teaching assistants; however, professors are always willing to meet. Grading is mostly based on merit, as it should be. If you slack: B; if you exert some effort: B+; and if you really try, expect an A- to A. The workload will vary according to your school of choice; engineers normally have a greater workload than an English major. Choose your battles.

Current student, 9/2003-Submit Date, September 2006

The academic experience at Northwestern was wonderful! If you pick your classes well, then you will be provided the opportunity to work with some of the leading researchers in the field. The biggest mistake that students make is not engaging their professors outside of the classroom. Northwestern provides all of the resources necessary to prepare you for any field, and the breadth of classes is unparalleled.

Alumnus/a, 9/2002-6/2006, October 2006

The academics are very strong. In the quarter system you take a lot of classes, which is both good and bad. The professors are high quality to really want you to learn. There is a lot of groupwork and the environment is conducive to learning.

Current student, 8/2004-Submit Date, October 2006

NU can be tough, hands down, but in a very intellectual and beneficial way. The academic challenges here will train you to pursue whatever career you desire. The sciences are known to be trying, especially if the pre-med and engineering track are where your interests lie. As a philosophy major, I feel that we have a strong department, and I think that could be said for the majority of the departments that are lesser known than our theater, journalism and other programs. As a Lib Arts student, I've taken a number of classes outside of my discipline, one of the requirements that I love about the university. I've taken a five-person Chemistry class, as well as 100-person Sociology class, finding both types of classes to be enlightening due to the surprising availability of our professors. If you want to get into a class, you can, though maybe not your first year, as seniority rules. Workload gets tougher with seniority, as well, but setting a strong base in early years is important, especially balancing extracurricular with academic responsibilities. In general, the kids here are very active, on campus and off, so there's a plethora of opportunities that often can supplement your academic pursuits.

Current student, 9/2005-Submit Date, October 2006

The quarter system is brutal. There is a ton of work and not enough time to do it all. But, for the most part, you learn a lot. Grades are tough. Everyone here is smart, so curves don't play as big of a role as they do at other schools.

Current student, 9/2003-Submit Date, December 2005

The biggest factor with Northwestern academics is that it runs on the quarter system and so you will take three sets of classes and three sets of finals each year. This tends to make classes faster paced, but the impact of each class on your overall GPA is significantly lower than at other schools.

The average student takes four classes and workload depends very much on his/her major. Poli sci students can expect a lot of reading, which only needs to be read by finals, while math and econ students have weekly problem sets. The workload is very correlated with the majors.

Getting into classes should not be a problem. Since there are 12 required classes (distribution requirements), if you don't get into a class you want you simply fill it up with one of these (so you don't waste a class). Obviously, getting into classes of your choice gets significantly easier as you become older. Timing of registration is broken up into three slots, so each year you will have one early slot, one mid slot and one late slot. Very even registration process.

Current student, 9/2003-Submit Date, February 2004

Northwestern is a major research university, and as a consequence, some of its professors are more oriented toward research than they are toward teaching. On the whole, they're good teachers, and even when they're not, there is something to be said for studying with a preeminent researcher in a particular field. There are a handful of excellent teachers, teaching both introductory and upper-level courses.

Employment Prospects

Current student, Pre-med, 9/2004-Submit Date, January 2007

Generally, employment prospects out of Northwestern are good. The university is considered a pre-professional school and many undergraduate economics degrees are courted by local investment banks like Goldman, UBS, Lehman and Morgan Stanley. Career fairs are held most quarters and the Career Services offers help with résumés, cover letters, interviews and so on. Many undergraduate students who major in fields like history, political science and international studies will prepare themselves for law school. Here again, most of the necessary accessories to finding a job are provided by Northwestern through things like Career Cat.

Current student, 9/2003-Submit Date, September 2006

A Northwestern degree will open many doors for the hard workers who succeed in their time there. Many recruiters come through campus and the alumni network provided helps a great deal in the Midwest and across the country. Friends I know went to the best law schools, medical schools and graduate schools in the country. Others went on to work for the top firms in both private and public enterprises.

Alumnus/a, 9/2002-6/2006, November 2006

The NU degree is very good. Coming out of NU, you can go anywhere. With that said, if you want to go to Wall St., the Ivies provide a slightly better opportunity, but if you want to be in Chicago or some other area of the country that is not New York, NU provides a slightly better opportunity.

Current student, 8/2004-Submit Date, October 2006

NU carries a lot of weight, in general. I've found the alumni network here to be rather strong and the ability to contact alumni via our alumni association very easy. I've used it to meet at least two lawyers so far, and they've helped me in a number of ways (e.g., recommendations, perspective and contacts). On-campus recruiting is pretty effective, as well. We have a number of career fairs throughout the year, and there are always smaller sessions in many fields, though consulting and other economics-related fields host the bulk of these. That said, it often takes some initiative to find opportunities for internships and such to prepare for post-grad, but the resources are definitely here.

Current student, 9/2002-Submit Date, January 2006

You must take your own initiative to get jobs. Our Career Services does help, but they will not do it for you. Use alumni as networking tools and career databases to help facilitate finding a job. It is important to explore internships in fields of interests prior to graduation, which will strengthen the opportunities for securing a full-time job in your area of choice.

Current student, 9/2000-Submit Date, January 2004

The school is on the quarter system, so it is difficult to come across summer internships that align with that time schedule. However, there are cooperative programs and field studies that help the students get placed in internships and jobs. Prestige is high with employers in business and journalism fields. For engineers, the school is small, so getting your name out there is more difficult. Very prestigious for law school, med school and business school, though.

Quality of Life

Current student, Pre-med, 9/2004-Submit Date, January 2007

The quality of life at NU is good. You've got all the resources of a large city in proximity and the administration has done a sufficient job of quelling students' complaints about the student center by adding a Starbucks. Crime is relevant, but usually only to off-campus residents, which is a decision most students make for their junior and senior year. Fraternities and sororities enjoy most of the social limelight and it's easy to find a right fit due to Northwestern's policy of Winter Quarter Rush.

Current student, 9/2003-Submit Date, September 2006

It's cold, but if someone were not to pick a school based solely on weather, then they would be making one of the more foolish mistakes of their lives. The people and opportunities to which Northwestern students are exposed are fantastic and the friendships you make and the experiences you share will impact the rest of your life.

Alumnus/a, 9/2002-6/2006, November 2006

The quality of life is good. Campus housing is decent. The campus is beautiful and the fall and spring are amazing. The facilities are all pretty good and the dining halls have been improved dramatically. Evanston is a good city that has a lot in terms of restaurants and stores, and Chicago is so close by and provides so much. I always felt safe on campus but like anywhere you go, you should always use common sense and be smart.

Current student, 8/2004-Submit Date, October 2006

Housing is very diverse and fits most types of students whether they like to party or like their free time. That, however, can suck if you have friends on the other sides of campus, as sometimes you don't see people from other parts of campus that often (the only real example is between North and South). Dining can get bland after a while, but there's a downtown area right south of campus with a host of other options. Safety has been an issue as people have gotten mugged quite a bit the last few years, but this year's committee is implementing new strategies, including surveillance cameras and more staff in halls.

Read all of Vault's College Surveys at **www.vault.com/college**—get complete surveys on 100s of colleges and universities, expert advice on applicaton essays and more.

VAULT CAREER LIBRARY 211

Current student, 9/2005-Submit Date, October 2006

Housing is basic housing as far as dorms go. Residential colleges are very nice, but you pay for the luxury. Dining is good, but you do get sick of it after a year or so. Evanston is not extremely safe, but on and near campus University Police and Evanston Police keep it very safe.

Current student, 9/2002-Submit Date, January 2006

Life is what you make of it. This is to say that you may pursue your interests on this campus. There are those who love I-banking and those who like participating in student government; whatever your interest, go out and explore the offerings. There are tons of clubs! Housing is OK—if you like partying, go up north and if you are more into community atmosphere go with the res colleges. SPAC is the gym on campus and is nice—it's up north. Blookquist is the gym down south. There is some crime around NU, and it is important to walk with others at night and utilize campus safety services.

Current student, 9/2003-Submit Date, December 2005

Food is not very good. This is a problem because when it gets cold, you lose motivation to go into Evanston and eat out. Plus, food is getting ridiculously expensive and the meal plans there may be the biggest ripoff you've ever seen.

South Campus is generally for your more artsy, music, sorority girl student types, while North Campus is more your frat boy, party types. South Campus dorms are more community oriented, North Campus more party oriented.

Facilities are excellent if you ever decide to make a trek up to use them.

Social Life

Current student, 9/2003-Submit Date, September 2006

Social life at Northwestern is whatever one hopes to make it. Chicago offers all of the arts, plays, food and other amenities that any great city has to offer. Northwestern, situated just a train ride away, has a vibrant campus with the best theatre scene in the country, wonderful dance troupes and great comedy. The involvement in extracurricular activity often seems like a requirement with a vast majority of the campus being involved in multiple activities. There are Greek parties both on and off campus. A vibrant theater community is always willing to have a good time, and Evanston is host to several bars that are packed most every weekend.

Current student, Pre-med, 9/2004-Submit Date, January 2007

The social life can be a drag sometimes, but only if you really try not to have a good time. With Chicago so near to the campus, few students have an excuse to complain. There are many music venues within short EL range from campus including The Metro, The Riviera, The Aragon Ballroom, the Vic and so many more. A small investment in research will yield a great many fun opportunities. Evanston even boasts Nevin's and Bar Louie, two very suitable bars.

Current student, 8/2004-Submit Date, October 2006

Greek is big here, but as a non-Greek there's a number of other things to do that won't make being non-Greek a big issue. There are about four bars that people frequent in Evanston, and of course Chicago is just a 30-minute train ride away. The campus always has some sort of event, some academic and quite a few that are social. This sometimes keeps people on campus too much instead of checking out Chicago. As a black student, the community is vibrant and there's always something going on. Though I have strong ties to the community, it is extremely easy to branch out, and this goes for all prospective students. You can easily find a niche, but there's always something else out there to keep you intrigued and enjoying yourself.

Current student, 9/2002-Submit Date, January 2006

If you really want a good social life I'd join a frat or sorority. Other than that, the bars include the Duece every Thurs and P-Moon and Bar Louie—The ASG restaurant guide helps tons in finding restaurants to eat at—and there are plenty in Evanston! Dating is here—people always seem to complain about it, but people do date.

Current student, 9/2003-Submit Date, December 2005

The social scene leaves much to be desired. It's not a state school so you won't see a lot of raging keggers. The party scene is essentially what you make of it. Early in your NU career, you will hit up as many parties as possible and later in your NU career, you will hit up the bars.

Current student, 9/2003-Submit Date, February 2004

I'd be lying if I said there was a typical Northwestern student. In fact, because of the diversity of the academic and extracurricular programs here, there are several types of students: athletes, Greeks, theatre majors, extracurricular overachievers, future corporate titans, lawyers of America and activists. You name it, we've got it. This can result in a slight balkanization of the campus, since people tend to divide along certain lines here and like sticks with like. But the upside is that even the most unique students can find a niche and meet other students like them.

University of Chicago

University of Chicago
Office of College Admissions
Rosenwald Hall 105
1101 East 58th Street
Chicago, IL 60637
Admissions phone: (773) 702-8650
Admissions fax: (773) 702-4199

Admissions

Current student, 9/2004-Submit Date, January 2007

They use their Uncommon Application. I don't remember much anymore except for the unique and interesting essay questions. But there is always the option of handing in one of your own topic, which is what I did and I actually used my Common Application essay. I did not have an interview. Selectivity is not as high as the Ivy Leagues. Students joke that people who didn't get into Ivy Leagues come here, but then there are others for whom University of Chicago

was a first choice. Overall, I think they look for the entire picture of who you are and having some "uncommonness" in your application helps.

Current student, 9/2004-Submit Date, October 2006

While admissions procedures use the same modes of data-finding as all other colleges, the type of student likely to get attention is peculiar. The University of Chicago is a cerebral place looking for cerebral candidates; most people here are serious scholars, not future business execs in training, and usually serious scholars are accepted. Most students take up a course of study simply because they are passionately interested in it. The University of Chicago takes "the life of the mind" seriously, and successful candidates will, too.

Current student, 9/2004-Submit Date, September 2006

The UofC essay is designed to be different. Have fun with it, but don't go overboard. I have a friend who submitted a 10-page essay brimming with philosophical mumbo jumbo. He didn't get in.

I had a mediocre interview the first time and spoke with an admissions counselor about my experience when he visited my high school. He promptly scheduled me for another interview.

Current student, 9/2005-Submit Date, September 2006

The admissions process at the UofC relies heavily on the essays and the interview. The essays, which range from the wacky (the infamous "How does a giant jar of mustard inspire you?") to the deeply philosophical (ranging from a variety of social justice issues to questions based on Zen sayings), are designed to provoke a critical self inquiry. Creativity of approach, depth of meaning, and method of self criticism are inherent in the essay questions. As for the interview, admissions officers are prone to asking rather outlandish questions, like, "If you had a conjoined twin and had the option of undergoing an operation that may or may not kill your conjoined twin, who would you consult for an opinion?"

The school gives little admissions preference to athletes.

Alumnus/a, Pre-med, 9/2002-6/2006, March 2007

The admissions process at the University of Chicago was rigorous and time-consuming; however, it was interesting and fun at the same time. The essays offered an opportunity to be creative with your personal story, interests, intellect and previous education. The mailings were clever and witty, full of facts about Chicago, Hyde Park, the community and culture, and of course the eccentric student population, activities and organizations. I applied Early Action and I was deferred. I didn't give up. I contacted my regional academic adviser weekly and told him about my on-going accomplishments the spring of my senior year (Intel International Science Fair, state mock trial, science research competitions, state track and field). I didn't expect to get in because I knew how cutthroat the admissions process is, but I received my acceptance letter in May.

Current student, 9/2003-Submit Date, March 2007

They just want an interesting person with whom they can share the university. You can be a little weird, nerdy, whatever. Show that you are smart, that you have an interesting opinion on something, and that you are probably pretty fun to talk to. They want people who will reform scholarship because they see things differently.

Current student, 9/2004-Submit Date, February 2006

Be unique! The University of Chicago is a place where eccentricity is the name of the game. The Number One thing the admissions office looks for is the quality of your writing in the essays, while also checking to make sure you have the grades and test scores to back it up. A highly selective, world-class university.

Current student, 9/2003-Submit Date, May 2005

True, it's not as hard to get into UChicago than it is to the Ivies, but Chicago is very self-selective. Many students don't want what the university prides itself on: a rigorous academic experience. Visit the school and feel it out. If a tour, class visit, the architecture or chat with current students don't hook you, then UChicago is probably not the place for you. If you really want to get in, let your interviewer know exactly why or make a point of it in your essays. Set yourself apart; the admissions counselors want to enjoy the essays they read.

Current student, 12/2004-Submit Date, May 2005

I think that the most important part of the University of Chicago's admissions process is the essay. We pride ourselves on the unusual essay topics that find their way onto the application each year, and the admissions office wants to see that the applicant put time into his/her essay. Don't do what everyone else would do—be unique when answering the essays.

Test scores and GPA are also factored in, but the essay is very important. The interview is also considered carefully. The interviews are usually low-key and fun; the interviewers are, like everyone here, very smart and interesting to talk to. I think the applicant pool is very self-selecting; because of the school's reputation for difficult academics and a sluggish social scene and because the application is more difficult than other schools' only people serious about their academics even apply.

Academics

Current student, 9/2004-Submit Date, January 2007

Very, very academically intense. Workload is heavy and due to its quarter system, if you don't start right away, you will be likely to fall behind. And midterms can start in the third week of the quarter. For me, it has been pretty easy to get into popular classes by getting a pink slip signed. It might be because they are lecture classes. The more famous professors are very willing to let you in (as long as there are seats in the room, and even maybe try to get a bigger room) but it's not the same for small discussion classes. The registration system isn't that good though. Grading depends on class and professor.

The core system, although you hear some students complaining about it, is necessary for gaining a liberal arts education. Most importantly, it gives you the tools to be able to read academic literature in different fields that are not your major.

Current student, 9/2004-Submit Date, October 2006

The core curriculum includes a set of classes that all undergraduates must take. There is some free range; unlike Columbia or Princeton, all underclassmen will not take the exact same course as everyone else. Undergrads do, however, need to choose a multi-quarter sequence in the social sciences, the humanities, "civilization studies" (essentially history), the biological sciences, the physical sciences, mathematics, and fine art. Some of these requirements can be fulfilled by transfer credit, AP scores, and on-site testing, but everyone takes a Hum (pronounced "Hume;" undergrad jargon for "humanities sequence") and social science sequence.

The professors are every bit as serious as the students they teach. Most students' lives are made full enough simply from schoolwork, which includes foreign language drills, problem sets, papers and reading. Don't be scared though: If you actually belong at the UofC, you will find all of it perversely fun.

Courses are amazingly intimate in the humanities and social sciences. Science, math and econ (the exception among the social sciences) courses are usually large, lecture-style courses with very little opportunity to get to know professors. But in Hum and other soc courses, you can get to know your professors really well and even genuinely befriend them.

Current student, 9/2004-Submit Date, October 2006

Classes are generally small, barring some science lecture classes. While they are more intensive than you may find at a state school, anyone who can manage his/her time will have no problem with taking on the workload and involving him/herself in extracurricular activities. The strong point of the university is that we offer classes that range from Introduction to IR, to Conflict Theory and Aikido, so there's something for everyone.

Current student, 9/2005-Submit Date, September 2006

The quality of classes is typically excellent. Professors often take pains to accommodate student learning needs. They offer very long office hours, are easily accessible, often invite entire classes to their homes for dinner, and are open to new ideas. At the end of each course, students are asked to evaluate the professor, the teaching assistant(s), and the course curriculum. The administration reviews these evaluations and an instructor's course evaluations typically improve each year. Very few classes are taught directly by TAs, who typically lead discussion sessions and are rigorously chosen from a talented pool of graduate students. Some core classes are taught by highly qualified PhD candidate students. The largest class size does not exceed 65.

Popular classes are very difficult to enroll in because typical class sizes usually do not exceed 25.

Current student, 9/2003-Submit Date, March 2007

Greatest and best university in the world. In most departments, every single professor I've had has made and continues to make innovations in his field that change the way everyone else thinks about scholarship. This is particularly true of economics: It's the greatest department that has ever existed anywhere, ever. Anthropology classes, biology classes, history classes, math classes. Once a week for the last four years, I have experienced short moments of epiphany when I have been made to realize my professors' brilliance.

Current student, 9/2002-Submit Date, October 2005

Rigorous academics. Chicago is famous for having an extensive core. This is a set of 13 courses that every student must take and the set of classes looks a little something like: three social sciences, one or two art/music/drama classes, two or three humanities classes (depending on how many art classes you take), two or three civilization classes, one or two math classes (you will test into generally

Read all of Vault's College Surveys at www.vault.com/college–get complete surveys on 100s of colleges and universities, expert advice on application essays and more.

VAULT CAREER LIBRARY 213

one of four levels), two or three physical sciences, and finally two or three bio-logical sciences. Then you have nine to 13 courses for your major. And finally six courses open for electives (many of which can be filled with AP credits, only fours or fives though), for a minimum total of 28 courses to graduate. Classes are very small. My smallest was three people including me, and my largest was 100, but most discussion classes are no more than 20. Classes are what you make of them. They are largely discussion based and you will have to sit through a lot of pointless remarks made by that "kid" who always has to hear the sound of his own voice. But at the same time, you are sitting with peers who are extremely smart and talented, and conversation usually flows in that direction. Professors are awesome. They are always willing to help and hold extra office hours. Sometimes graduate students teach lower-level courses or weed-out classes and those will be the worst you will have to endure. I've never had a problem getting into a class, but I have seen instances when it has happened, usually due to poor planning on the student's part. Workload is heavy, but you soon realize what things you have to read/do and what things are OK if skimmed over.

Current student, 9/2003-Submit Date, May 2005

Believe them when they say that the main focus at UChicago will be your academic life—that's why you're in school. The academic environment is described as "intense" but it doesn't mean that the academics are all-consuming. One of the best things about UChicago is the quality and accessibility of the professors, the student-to-faculty ratio is 4:1.

Employment Prospects

Current student, Economics, 9/2004-Submit Date, January 2007

As an economics major, I can only speak of internships and jobs mostly in investment banking and consulting. Top firms come for on-campus recruiting. Career Advising & Planning Services, I think, does a decent job if you are proactive. They help with your résumé, cover letters, and interview skills. But you definitely have to go to them and make appointments or go for walk-ins. They are pretty available. They do have resources not only for finance but also for other industries (nonprofit, government, journalism and sciences). If you ask, they will be able to direct you to resources. Alumni network, from what I have seen, seems pretty good. And they are easy to contact and alumni are willing to help you.

Current student, 9/2004-Submit Date, October 2006

Prestige with employers: doesn't matter. The University of Chicago has always been one of the premier institutions of higher learning in the United States since its inception, and is only likely to gain more prominence among lay people since it broke the Top 10 in the *U.S. News & World Report* rankings. But, as most of us know by now, that doesn't really matter to employers, who primarily want to know how competent and experienced prospects are.

Graduates mostly stay in academia. But anyone who doesn't can securely pursue any position he/she wants, whether it's an econ major trying to land an I-banking job with Goldman Sachs or an English major who wants to work in the PR office of a nonprofit.

Current student, 9/2005-Submit Date, September 2006

The university also has a special program called the Metcalf Internships. These paid internships are specifically reserved for UofC students and are closed to all outsiders. Over 200 big-name employers (ranging from JP Morgan to Human Rights Watch) are available for these internships, which are often designed for students majoring in the respective disciplines.

Undergraduates are actively engaged by CAPS beginning with their freshman year in the college.

Alumnus/a, Pre-med, 9/2002-6/2006, March 2007

Job fairs consisted of prestigious financial and consulting companies and organizations, community advocacy/volunteer opportunity, Peace Corps, Teach for America, law firms, and governmental organizations like the FBI, CIA or Dept of State. These organizations and recruiters think very highly of UofC students, their ability to think, strategize and problem solve and work hard. Often, the main criticism is students have difficulty socializing and being interactive, but

they are still very driven and motivated. On-campus recruiting is huge for the financial sector. Most of my jock, frat guy friends are in the investment banking, hedge fund market making close to six figures by their second year in the job market. Many of my friends went straight on to law school, graduate schools and med schools, some on scholarship or research grants, others taking out another $120,000 in loans (without financial aid). However, students who really want a job out of school, no matter what their BA or BS was, can land a pretty sweet paying/ interesting job somewhere in the world. It is just difficult not to feel inferior to the world around you, by your peers and your ability to co-exist in a non-isolated non-campus environment.

Current student, 9/2004-Submit Date, February 2006

The UofC is a well-known name among employers, especially those in the City of Chicago. The Career Advising & Planning Services office has many connections with alumni to whom students have access and great summer internship opportunities for current students. On-campus recruiting happens year round, but many students choose to go to graduate school after undergrad. Since so many students at UofC are economics majors, financial services and consulting jobs are hot for the recently graduated.

Current student, 9/2001-Submit Date, May 2005

I think that employment is a big issue right now at our school. Not only are we a liberal arts college, we are THE liberal arts college, without even an engineering school. It sometimes seems like we specialize in the impractical. I'm a medieval studies and a religious studies major; I would feel un-employable were it not for my leadership skills and web design experience from my part-time job. As for those English majors who don't do any student clubs, I feel bad for them.

Quality of Life

Current student, 9/2004-Submit Date, January 2007

Housing is OK but there is a lot of variance. Some dorms are much nicer than others. It sometimes feels unfair to be paying the same amount of money for some dorms, but I guess each dorm has its own advantages. They are building a new dorm, which I think should be nice (at least clean and new). Campus is, I think, nice although not one of the most beautiful. And since it is in Chicago, it does get freezing cold and snows at odd times of the year. When weather is grey, which it often is, it gets very dreary. We have nice computing facilities on campus, not necessarily at dorms (although there is wireless), and printing is definitely not free. Dining, I would say, is average compared to other schools. I have eaten at worse dining halls in other colleges. They have different sections but within the section, there isn't much variety. It's good once in a while but if you eat it every day, you will get sick of it. But then, that is probably true with most dining halls. There are kitchens (community or otherwise) in most dorms. Chicago neighborhood won't necessarily make you feel safe but I've never really felt scared despite the crime reports. In any case, university police are all around.

Current student, 9/2005-Submit Date, September 2006

The university housing system is divided as follows: each dormitory is divided into a series of houses that consist of 30 to 80 students. Each house has its own character and personality, as does each dormitory. There is a variety of dorms on campus, ranging from neo-Gothic architecture to big-name architect designed buildings. Students are placed into houses based on a written personality form that covers all sorts of questions on personality and personal habits. Singles, doubles, triples and quadruples are all available to all years of students.

Dining hall food is generally good. The university has strived to improve dining facilities and food quality over the last decade. As the president of the food services company, Aramark, sits on the board of trustees, dining fare includes organic, vegan, vegetarian, kosher and Halal cuisines quite well.

Current student, 9/2003-Submit Date, March 2007

College is hard. I mean, you want college to be hard, right? You don't want to finish college and say, "Well, that was easy." And the neighborhood sucks, but you'll have stories about living in the ghetto. On a larger scale, the bigger neighborhood is Chicago, which is a great city. It's cold. Everyone will complain about that a lot.

Current student, 9/2002-Submit Date, October 2005

Quality of life, ah yes, we have some of the nicest dorms I've ever been in. I've been here for four years and haven't had to share a bathroom with more than three people. The dining halls are arranged by house and you typically end up eating with the same 30 or so people for most of your first year. The food at one of the dining halls has been named second best in the country. You can have anything from Indian to vegan, to a custom gourmet salad. The desserts are from the Cheesecake Factory. The campus reminds me of Hogwarts: Gothic arches, huge trees, and at least one squirrel every square foot. A new gym was opened last year and it has a beautiful Olympic-sized pool and a bunch of shiny workout equipment. There is an indoor track in another building with indoor basketball and squash courts. While on campus, you feel really safe, but once you venture three blocks or more in any direction, save for going east since you run into the lake, things start getting a little sketchy. I never walk alone at night if I'm off campus. A bike will be your best mode of transport.

Social Life

Current student, 9/2004-Submit Date, October 2006

As goes the stereotype, the social life is not what you'd find at a state school. There are weekends without parties and is a dearth of attractiveness. That being said, it's what you make of it. It's normal for people to enjoy themselves, and everyone finds a niche. While you might describe Dartmouth or Princeton as preppy, I think you'd describe UofC as hipster.

Current student, 9/2005-Submit Date, October 2006

The Regenstein Library is where students spend most of their time. If you can you had a great weekend.

Current student, 9/2005-Submit Date, September 2006

It is often heard, "fun comes to die" at the UofC. This is not the case. Although academics are very intense, students regularly take advantage of the City of Chicago's wide variety of cultural and social offerings. The university has worked with the Chicago Transportation Agency (CTA) to provide multiple bus routes to Chicago's extensive subway system and bus routes to popular neighborhood destinations throughout the city. It is sometimes difficult to break through the UofC's social wall, but the campus is never quiet, never empty, and always full of events. Though Greek life does exist, it is often muted compared to other activities on campus. Fraternities host large parties on a weekly basis. DOC Films, the student-run film group, is the nation's oldest such group and schedules a highly envied series of movies every day, often including world-premiere screenings of big name and art house movies.

Hyde Park has a large variety of restaurants and bars though a bit removed from campus. The variety of restaurants is quite wide, ranging from Thai to Middle Eastern. Favorites include the Medici (called the "Med" by most students), Cedars, and The Snail.

Alumnus/a, Biology, 9/2002-6/2006, April 2007

The social life of UofC students varies enormously from nonexistent to party-animal. I wouldn't recommend either of those extremes if you want to stay sane and stay enrolled, but there is plenty of room in the middle. There is a small Greek presence on campus if that interests you. In addition, there are numerous clubs and RSOs you can join, as well as intramural sports and musical groups. You would have to walk quite a distance to find an actual bar, but alcohol is definitely not hard to come by: My dorm had a weekly drinking night, and I have a feeling most other dorms did, too.

Current student, 9/2003-Submit Date, March 2007

Most people end up in pathologically long-term relationships eventually. I'm not sure, but I expect this characterizes most of our generation. It's the kind of place where you leave the library at 2 a.m. to go have sex with your girlfriend, and then you wake up to walk with her to the library.

Current student, 9/2002-Submit Date, October 2005

Don't know anything about the Greek system except for the fact that if you are really looking for it to be a big part of your college experience, don't come to Chicago. Less than 10 percent of the student body goes Greek, and most are looked down upon by the rest of the school. Social life, yeah, that's not so great either. We do have parties, though, usually a frat will hold one, but they charge $5, which is an outrageous fee.. The ultimate frisbee team throws some of the best parties on campus, and you can usually get in free or at a discounted rate if you come dressed in theme. They are known for random acts of nudity, but it's all in good fun. OK, so you wanna know where to get liquored up, eh? If you are under 21, get a fake so you can go to Jimmy's, the local pub where you are almost always sure to see a familiar face. The bartenders are super nice and will usually put your mixed drink in a pint glass if you tip well. A frat on campus holds Bar Night every Wednesday in the basement of their dingy house where you can get imported bottles for $2 (if they haven't raised the price). Mostly first-and-second years go to Bar Night. If you are interested in something, chances are someone else on campus is as well and you can form a club if one doesn't already exist. I almost forgot: Coffee shops are huge on campus.

University of Illinois at Urbana-Champaign

University of Illinois at Urbana-Champaign
Office of Admissions and Records
901 West Illinois Street
Urbana, IL 61801-3028
Admissions phone: (217) 333-0302
Admissions e-mail: ugradadmissions@uiuc.edu
Admissions URL: www.oar.uiuc.edu/

Admissions

Current student, 8/2003-Submit Date, April 2007

The admissions process is highly selective. The school does not feel it has to recruit actively and therefore appears snobby to interested students. Try to ignore this impression as much as possible because it really is a great school where you'll grow both in and out of the classroom tremendously. It is important to take as many AP

or honors courses as you can. They really weed people out based on GPA and ACT score, so if you can focus on working as hard as you can on those two things you are putting your energy in a good area. Also, make yourself stand out in your essay. What makes you, you, right now? Is there something you are really passionate about? It is better to focus your passions and not feel like you have to be involved in everything in high school in order to be admitted. Admissions really seems to like people who have some unique passion. They want you to bring something diverse and unique to the classroom so I think it would be a good idea to show how you want to learn from the others around you on campus and how you want to contribute to the education of your fellow students, as well.

The school says: "Our admissions counselors are happy to take phone calls and e-mails to help any prospective student through the application process. We also provide monthly online chats and a blog to connect prospective students to the Illinois community. Feel free to check our Illinois Near You link at, www.oar.uiuc.edu/future/ILnearyou/index.html, to find the Illinois representative for your area."

Read all of Vault's College Surveys at www.vault.com/college—get complete surveys on 100s of colleges and universities, expert advice on applicaton essays and more.

VAULT CAREER LIBRARY 215

Current student, Biology, 8/2004-Submit Date, April 2007

The admissions process involved writing essays along with sending standard application materials, such as a high school transcript and ACT or SAT scores. More students have ACT scores because of the high number of in-state students. Therefore, taking the ACT may allow you to be ranked against other students more accurately. The school is pretty selective for a public institution, but they take other factors into consideration so that GPA and test scores are not everything.

Current student, Engineering, 8/2004-Submit Date, April 2007

The admissions process at the University of Illinois-Champaign is rolling, which means that's it's your best bet to apply as early as possible. The UofI is a public school, so there's no interview, and it's not that selective (depending on what major you apply towards). Since there's such a wide pool of applicants, your grades and your SAT/ACT scores play a big role in differentiating you from other applicants.

> **Regarding admissions, the school says:** "Admissions is not on a rolling basis. We have two decision dates. The first decisions will be posted online at 5 p.m. CST on December 14, 2007 for Priority Applicants who have all of their materials postmarked to us between September 1 and November 10, 2007. Final decisions for applicants who apply between November 11, 2007 and January 2, 2008 will be posted online at 5 p.m. CST on February 15, 2008. Some priority applicants may be deferred and, therefore, will not hear a final decision until the February date. However, they are still making their application stronger by applying early. Select programs through the College of Fine and Applied Arts may not have decisions until March due to audition and portfolio reviews."

The UofI is by no means as competitive to get into as an Ivy League school, unless you plan on applying to the one of the selective colleges, such as the College of Engineering. Based on my personal experience, I think that if you're slightly interested in majoring in some type of engineering, and you have good test scores (about 30-to-31 ACT), but you're not definitely sure if it's for you, you should apply to a major in engineering off the bat, because it's much easier to change your major from engineering to something in the College of Liberal Arts and Sciences than the other way around.

Current student, 8/2003-Submit Date, April 2006

Pretty standard. Grades, test scores, extracurriculars, personal statement. There is a decent amount of variation in the school's selectivity because of its focus on many types of diversity. Students who can prove their worth, whether in grades or extracurricular activities, will be accepted. The Campus Honors Program has an independent admissions process, as well.

> **The University of Illinois at Urbana-Champaign says:** "The application for admission is the same application used when considering students for the Campus Honors Program and other honors programs on campus."

Current student, 8/2005-Submit Date, April 2006

I applied pretty early on. It was a little hard because I had to write two short essays for the application. I didn't get them checked out by any teachers, so I was hoping they were good enough. My sister and I sent in our applications around the same time. She found out pretty quickly that she got in, but I didn't find out until more than a month later. I was very nervous about that, but in the end I got in, so it was all right. I know that UofI is very selective. But it mainly depends on which program you want. It's a lot easier to get into UofI if you apply as an undecided major rather than try to get into the College of Business, which is very competitive. I applied as a biology major, so I didn't have any problems with that.

> **The school says:** "Last year we began only having two pre-set decision dates. If you applied by our Priority Filing Date, you can view your decision online on December 14, 2007 at 5 p.m., CST. If your application was completed after November 10, 2007 or you were deferred on December 14, then you may view your decision online on February 15, 2008 at 5 p.m., CST. The official decision will be sent through the U.S. mail."

Alumnus/a, 8/2002-5/2006, November 2006

Admissions process consistent with those of other large public schools—fairly selective with the top 10 percent of Chicago suburban students accepted. The University of Illinois accepts substantially lower ACT scores from lower performing school districts in southern Illinois and inner-city Chicago. The abilities of accepted students are generally high; because the school is large, ACT scores are weighed more heavily than at smaller, private schools where there is more time for the admissions department to read essays, and so on.

Academics

Current student, Business, 8/2004-Submit Date, April 2007

I am in the College of ACES within the UofI. My experiences with professors and classes have been nothing short of amazing. Even all the way up to the deans, they have all been supportive. I truly feel the quality of education at the UofI is one of the best in the world.

Current student, Communications, 8/2005-Submit Date, April 2007

The classes are small in my area of study, which is very nice. I am greatly prepared and feel ahead of others in similar programs outside of my college. The university does a great job diversifying classes, as well. Most classes are 20 to 25 students but some can be as large as 700. It is not always easy to get into popular classes, but with proper scheduling of one's semester plans this becomes easier. As long as students go to class and do their homework, workload is not terrible. Although you must work, the work seems valuable and worthwhile. Also, all of the instructors and professors I have had are extremely knowledgeable and willing to assist with any needs. Plus, they are very responsive to e-mail, which I consider a must!

Current student, Engineering, 8/2004-Submit Date, April 2007

The great thing about going to a big public university is the class selection. There are so many different types of classes you can take, and sometimes the best ones are the hardest ones to find. There's a wine tasting class that is really good, but of the ones I've personally taken, I recommend HORT 100, which is a horticulture class on fruits and vegetables. It's one of the most interesting classes I've taken in my undergraduate career. (Who knew that tomatoes were ruled a vegetable by the Supreme Court because they're generally eaten as part of the main meal, rather than as desert?)

For the most part, it's pretty easy to get into popular classes. Honors students get the opportunity to register before all over students, so if you had a high ACT score, look into the James Scholar Program. I've never had any major difficulty getting into classes I want, but sometimes if a class is required for all the students in a major, it may be a little tough.

Grading is usually on a curve, and generally it's not too bad. In engineering classes, the grades are very low on exams (averages are usually 50 to 60), so you get used to low grades. Most of the time, professors are reasonable when it comes to grades, although in some classes I have heard stories about professors curving down. But overall, as long as you put in some effort and turn in your homework, it's not difficult to pull off A's or B's.

Alumnus/a, Liberal Arts, 8/2002-5/2006, March 2007

It was easy to get into the classes I wanted, even those that were popular. Freshman and sophomore years had many required classes in my curriculum so taking fun classes like ice skating and photography did not fit into my schedule until junior and senior years. If there was a problem getting into a class, students could talk to professors or departments to get a spot. It is really easy to enroll through the online system and see how many spots are left in classes and what times and professors are available. Class selection is based on number of credit hours, so older students usually have a better selection. Classes were challenging, yet allowed students time for extracurricular activities. Workload depended on the class and college the class was within. Business or engineering majors had more technical work than education majors, for example.

Current student, Psychology, 8/2003-Submit Date, March 2007

The Speech Communication courses are awesome! They are smaller classes and for the most part, you are with tenured professors who actually know what they are talking about. The psychology program is awesome. We have some awesome faculty working in the department. Make sure to figure out the type of psychology you are into early so you are able to take a lot of classes in that area (e.g., biological psychology vs. industrial-organizational psychology).

Current student, Education, 8/2006-Submit Date, March 2007

Adjusting to the academic processes on campus was relatively easy. At orientation, each student works with his/her advisor to select courses and go through the course registration system. The more hours you accumulate, the easier it is to get the classes you want and need for your major. If you are able to join an honors program on campus, the early registration and honors courses are a great benefit to your academic development. Professors have been great to work with, grading has been fair, and the workload has been stressful at times, but not unmanageable. Pay close attention to your syllabi and go to class!

Current student, 8/2004-Submit Date, March 2005

At the UofI, they say that for every one hour spent in class, you are expected to do about three hours of outside work. For some classes this is accurate and others it is not. I think it is a good way to be prepared to work knowing that it will take up a lot of your time. I enjoy most of my classes but they are relatively large.

I have been here for two semesters and have taken 11 classes. My smallest was about 20 students and largest almost 700. As an undergrad this seems to be the norm. In addition, you really cannot expect to get the exact classes you want your first year. Upperclassmen have the first choice and the freshmen kind of get what is left. Yet, there are so many classes offered that this has not been a major problem. Grading, I find, is usually fair and the professors make themselves very accessible through office hours and e-mail. This is very important because the classes are rather large.

> **The school says:** "There are many classes/sections only open to freshmen, with 19 students per class."

Employment Prospects

Current student, 8/2003-Submit Date, April 2007

If you want to work in Chicago or the Midwest, Illinois is a very highly respected school and it'll get your résumé looked at longer than others. People know Illinois for engineering and business. Because of this, they know the school so people not in those programs can benefit, too. The Career Center here coupled with the world's largest alumni network allows for students to find internships and jobs that suit them if the student seeks out those resources and uses them. No one will hand anything to you, but there are things you will hear about on campus and you just need to get yourself together to go utilize those options. There is a lot of on-campus recruiting for business and engineering jobs and governmental positions, as well. There is a huge law school open house day when schools come and that is a great help, as well. For being in the middle of Illinois, one would think the school wouldn't be somewhere companies or organizations want to come but they make the trip here because of the outstanding reputation of Illinois graduates.

Alumnus/a, Mathematics, 8/2001-5/2005, April 2007

While I did have friends who were not offered employment related to their programs of study after graduation, I think that is much more a reflection of the job situations for all students than specifically UIUC students. I've heard from many people and employers that they really like UIUC graduates because not only do they have strong academic backgrounds, but they are also well-rounded individuals who are much more down to earth than their academic counterparts from other prestigious universities. Also, students at UIUC are also experienced in working with diverse people on teams, projects, organization, and so on. I definitely feel that I was set up for graduate school having graduated from UIUC.

Current student, Business, 8/2004-Submit Date, April 2007

The UofI has multiple career fairs that focus on people's interests. I have found numerous employment opportunities for me in sales, marketing, merchandising and management.

Current student, Finance, 8/2003-Submit Date, February 2007

The College of Business really helps you prepare for employment even prior to graduation. The alumni network is amazing and on-campus recruiting and internship opportunities are endless. There are tons of workshops to help students polish their résumé and fine-tune their interviewing skills. I have found them extremely useful in helping me move forward.

Quality of Life

Current student, 8/2003-Submit Date, April 2007

The towns of Champaign and Urbana are huge supporters of the university and there are tons of things you can do to learn more about the community and more students should utilize those things. Housing is packed, so get your requests in early. The housing division is strong and allows new students and transfers to make friends and get involved. Getting involved in the beginning is essential in order to feel connected on such a large campus and it is also important to make yourself well rounded and successful upon graduation. Campus buildings are a mix of old and new, but renovations are taking place. The campus is not the safest place and definitely has crime like most American cities of around 100,000 people. I wouldn't suggest anyone walk around late at night or the early morning without a partner, Safe Rides and other campus services plus tons of cabs that are very cheap are a great way to be a smart and safe citizen, like in any city. Acts of intolerance have been happening on campus as well but the student body is asking for change and lots of exciting changes are taking place, so students wanting to be a part of social change would be happy here.

Current student, Psychology, 8/2004-Submit Date, April 2007

In respect to quality of life issues, I think this university rates very highly. I live in private certified housing, so I have a different experience than most in regards to the dorm life, but overall, I hear mostly good comments about housing. The facilities are great here, ranging from an amazing center for the performing arts to organizations that host famous guest speakers.

Current student, Business, 8/2004-Submit Date, April 2007

The UofI has the largest Greek system in the world. I found my place in a house with similar interests to my own. The campus is big and beautiful, always clean. Champaign-Urbana is a smaller community; crime has not been an issue for me.

Current student, Biology, 8/2004-Submit Date, April 2007

Facilities are maintained well, and there are many projects underway. A new business building is being constructed. There is a plan to build a new, state-of-the-art dining facility for the Champaign Residence Halls within the next couple years. Eventually, all of the Champaign Residence Halls are going to be rebuilt. Also, the larger intramural building (gym) is in the middle of a large-scale renovation project. Not to mention the football stadium is being renovated.

Current student, Business, 1/2007-Submit Date, June 2007

Housing is very easy and affordable. I have been in both the dorms and apartments. The dorms are a fun environment to meet different types of people and create new relationships. They are coed and both boys and girls can enjoy the company of each other. The RAs of the building are assigned two per floor and are very helpful. I had some trouble in the beginning with my roommate and my RA gave me a lot of advice about handling all the situations and also about the options of moving dormrooms.

Current student, 8/2002-Submit Date, April 2006

I think the university housing is fairly average. It is definitely not as nice as some other schools but it was not necessarily bad either. It is simply average. There are private housing options for dormitories and those are very nice and spacious. While I was in the dormitories, I would judge the food as below average. Most students live in apartments by junior year. There are numerous apartments available in a wide range of pricing and locations. I think the cost of living in apartments is fair. In addition, I feel you can find a very nice apartment in excellent condition. Also, most apartments are furnished, which is very convenient. Although you are not in a major metropolitan area, there are still plenty of dining options. In addition, there are plenty of different stores so that you are always able to purchase what you need.

Read all of Vault's College Surveys at **www.vault.com/college**–get complete surveys on 100s of colleges and universities, expert advice on application essays and more.

VAULT CAREER LIBRARY **217**

Social Life

Alumnus/a, 8/2002-5/2006, March 2007

Social life is great at UofI; something for everyone. Students can study, attend seminars, musicals/plays/other productions at the Krannert Center for the Performing Arts, go to the Krannert Art Museum, go to dinner on Green Street or downtown Champaign or Urbana, go out to the bars, stay in on their residence hall floor to socialize with friends, go on retreats with their registered student organizations (there are over 1,000!).

There are many types of bars and students can enter at age 19. It is fun to go out with friends, and if you didn't want to drink that's OK, too. Murphy's and Legends are fun for the junior and senior students, as well as going into downtown Champaign, which has had remarkable improvements over the years.

There are lots of registered student organizations on campus, from sororities and fraternities to the Falling Illini, which is a skydiving club. There is really something for everyone, and students enjoy getting involved. There is also the Illinois Leadership Center where students can enhance their leadership abilities to improve themselves, their campus and their future. The Greek system is great. So many different chapters to get involved with, and again, something for everyone. Greeks talk to non-Greeks and don't think of themselves as supreme.

Current student, Biology, 8/2004-Submit Date, April 2007

The social life is good on campus, even if you do not belong to the Greek system. While the university has the most Greek life activity of all universities, there are many other ways to meet friends. There are nearly 1,000 registered student organizations, and there are many bars on campus. There are also many religion-based groups, with many options for Christians. At the beginning of the year, an event called Quad Day is held, and all kinds of groups look to recruit members.

Current student, Finance, 8/2003-Submit Date, February 2007

Our school has an enormous Greek system (I believe we're ranked Number Four, at least that was the record in 2004). Other than that, we have a variety of restaurants and bars on Green Street. The clubs on campus also features a younger crowd (students mostly). I would recommend going downtown (Champaign) if you are over 21 just to get a piece of mind.

Current student, 8/2004-Submit Date, March 2005

If you are smart but love to have a good time, Illinois is the place for you! There is way more to do here than people think. There are many little restaurants on campus that cater to college students. There are so many bars here it never gets old! People go out every night of the week and campus is always hopping. Not to mention you only have to be 19 to get in to the bars in Champaign!!!! KAMs is the home of the drinking Illini and is always hopping, especially when sporting events are happening.

There are always things going on besides drinking activities. There are musicals, comedy shows, fashion shows, beauty pageants, a cappella concerts, movie nights, anything you can think of has happened here—even a drag show! My favorite group to see is The X-tension Cords. They are the best a cappella group ever! Also if all else fails in your planner, we have the best basketball team in the nation and that is incentive enough to come to school here! It is mad here during basketball season. The Orange Krush is the best cheering section in the country!!!! What other cheering section raises money for charity so they can sit on the floor at basketball games?!?!?!

 The School Says

The University of Illinois at Urbana-Champaign is a place of excellence, innovation and tradition. More than 2,000 Urbana-Champaign faculty members lead 40,000 undergraduate, graduate and professional students in a process of discovery and learning in 16 colleges and schools and more than 80 research centers and labs. Faculty and students pursue projects with other top scholars from around the world and across disciplines. Campus resources include the nation's largest public university library, outstanding centers for the arts, and many world-class research facilities, including the National Center for Supercomputing Applications, Beckman Institute, Institute for Genomic Biology and Siebel Center for Computer Science.

Illinois provides a diverse learning environment: Students and faculty members from more than 120 nations, and a choice of 150 undergraduate programs of study. Students find opportunities ranging from participating in research or studying abroad, to leading one of more than 1,000 student organizations.

11 University of Illinois alumni have gone on to win Nobel Prizes. Of 12 Nobel Laureates who have served on the faculty, two were honored for work undertaken at this university. In addition, three graduates of University High School have received Nobel Prizes. Illinois faculty members have won Pulitzer Prizes, Tony Awards, and memberships in the nation's elite academies of arts and sciences. In fall 2003, Illinois became only the third American public university, and the 11th institution in the world, ever to have two Nobel Prizes (in different fields) awarded to members of its faculty in the same year. And, only months before Professor Anthony Leggett was awarded the Nobel Prize in physics and Professor Paul Lauterbur was awarded the Nobel Prize in medicine/physiology, a third faculty member, Professor Carl Woese, won the Crafoord Prize, the Nobel equivalent for biology. These are the instructors and mentors of Illinois students.

Ball State University

Office of Admissions
Lucina Hall
Muncie, IN 47306
Admissions phone: (800) 482-4BSU or (765) 285-8300
Admissions e-mail: askus@bsu.edu
Admissions URL: www.bsu.edu/admissions/

Admissions

Alumnus/a, 8/2003-5/2007, May 2007

As a high school student, I made sure that I took several AP courses and maintained high grades in those and regular classes. My grades, in addition to my SAT scores, helped me gain acceptance to Ball State and the Honors College. For my major, I needed to audition into the department of theatre and dance. Criteria and requirements for auditions were different then, but it involved performing monologues, singing selections from musical theatre songs and learning and performing a dance routine. If anyone wants be a part of the new musical theatre program at Ball State, I suggest that the quality of your grades and your performances be no less than excellent.

Alumnus/a, 8/2003-5/2007, May 2007

The admissions process was fairly simple when I applied. There was an application and request of transcripts and ACT/SAT scores. Based on my scores and transcript, I was awarded a half-tuition scholarship. I know the selectivity for admittance has increased since I enrolled.

Current student, Finance, 8/2004-Submit Date, May 2007

Not a very hard school to get into, but underrated as far as the educational experience goes. Average SAT score is right around 1050. Interviews and essays are not part of the admissions process. Basically, if you fit the minimum requirements, you will be accepted. I toured the campus on October 1, turned in my application within a week, and received my acceptance letter before Halloween. As long as you didn't slack off completely in high school and were involved in a few extracurriculars, you should get in with no problem.

> **The school says:** "The average SAT score for the 2007-08 freshman class is approximately 1560 for the SAT test with the writing section."

Current student, 8/2003-Submit Date, May 2006

I had to apply to both Ball State and the College of Architecture and Planning. Applying to Ball State was very easy and I was almost immediately accepted into the Honors College. Personally, I would accept an offer to go to the Honors College if it's extended to you because you get scheduled sooner, you have more class options, and you can avoid some of the university core classes that are not always so great. It was a little more challenging to apply to the College of Architecture and Planning, which required an essay, and a portfolio was optional. If you are interested in applying to CAP, don't do it last minute! Early applications are best!

> **Ball State says:** "Beginning with the 2008-09 freshman class, students must now complete a separate application for the Honors College."

Current student, 1/2003-Submit Date, January 2006

The admissions process was extremely easy. There are no essays required unless you want to be in the architecture program. Ball State is trying to shed its unearned image of being Indiana's third choice school, where one goes if one can't get into IU or Purdue, by becoming more selective.

Alumnus/a, 8/1999-8/2003, February 2005

Admissions process (as far as I can remember) included an essay, application and a certain score on SATs and GPA from high school. There was no interview process. You also have chance to be enrolled in the Honors College, which includes some of the best classes that I took in college.

> **The school says:** "Beginning with the 2008-09 freshman class, students must now complete a separate application for the Honors College. Students admitted to the Honors College may receive the Presidential Scholarship, which covers one-half of in-state or out-of-state tuition."

Current student, 8/2000-Submit Date, July 2004

I researched quality design schools near my hometown of Chicago. I selected Ball State and proceeded to show them my high school portfolio. Ball State is one of the Top 10 architecture schools in the country, so the process was extensive. They do a great job of selecting candidates with the most pre-requisites.

Many students don't get accepted to the first-year program that enables incoming selected students to be exposed to the design professions of urban planning, architecture and landscape architecture all in your first year. Those students must reapply until they are accepted. I was advised to give each profession a look at because professors told me many students change their minds. It was important to choose which fit my personality best.

Academics

Alumnus/a, Finance, 8/2003-5/2007, June 2007

The classes at Ball State are great. Since its focus is educating students, professors usually are there because they enjoy teaching. Many times they seem to pride themselves on knowing their students personally. I prefer small class sizes and when signing up for classes, the system tells you how many spaces total there are in the class so you are able to sign up for the smaller sections. The classes themselves are challenging and may seem a bit daunting when you first start, but if you try hard and work, you find that you can do much more than you thought. The classes I took at Ball State have directly prepared me for work in the real world. (I am in accounting and information systems.)

Current student, Communications, 8/2005-Submit Date, May 2007

Really, the telecommunications classes depend on the professors. All of the classes, in my opinion, are of high quality, but the grading and the difficulty relies totally on how the professors want to teach that class. I have had professors ease me along every step of the way, and I have had other professors who have basically just handed me a camera and said, "Go," no advice on what to do or how to do it. But in both scenarios, I have learned a tremendous amount. Sometimes the workload is overwhelming, but this is to be expected—after all, this is college. The grading is usually fair, although sometimes I have had professors with a bit of a different grading scale. Academically, I think Ball State has a wonderful program to offer.

Current student, Finance, 8/2004-Submit Date, May 2007

I have yet to have an extremely hard class through three years at BSU, but a number of courses have definitely been challenging. I have had a professor teach every course (never had a TA) which is nice, and every single one of them has been available to help me outside the classroom. I have thoroughly enjoyed the classes within the Millier College of Business that I have taken, but the Honors College courses leave a little bit to be desired. If you're an Honors student, you get priority class scheduling, which helps get into the courses that you want and need. The most people I have had in a class is about 100 in a lecture hall for one of my core classes that everyone has to take. Within my major, class size is typically around 30 to 40 people. The grading has been pretty fair all the way around; I don't think I've received a grade that I didn't deserve thus far. Your workload really depends on how involved you are outside of the classroom

Read all of Vault's College Surveys at www.vault.com/college—get complete surveys on 100s of colleges and universities, expert advice on applicaton essays and more.

VAULT CAREER LIBRARY 219

with extracurriculars. For the most part, though, anywhere between 12 to 18 hours is very manageable for students.

Alumnus/a, 8/2003-5/2006, May 2006

Getting into the more popular classes at BSU is tough. Using the electronic system makes it difficult for priority scheduling and gaining permission to classes. My major classes were very valuable, but I didn't appreciate the core classes very much—I think it would have been more valuable to allow students to select core classes that pertained to their area of study rather than from astronomy, chemistry or NREM when none of the above related to their area of study.

Alumnus/a, 8/2003-Submit Date, May 2006

There is strength in the Ball State academic programming. Once into higher levels and more depth into majors the classes are very small and provide personalized attention by the professors. The professors make classes challenging and incorporate many different styles of teaching and medium to make the material interesting. Getting into classes is not very hard at all—departments will try to help you out personally if you don't get a class you are required to take. Grading is unbiased and I feel that students are well aware of their grades. Workload varies among classes. Some core classes offer a lot, while others don't. It all depends on the professors. I know in my higher-level classes, the workload definitely increases, mostly including presentations and papers instead of standardized testing.

Current student, 8/2000-Submit Date, April 2005

The academics at Ball State are fair, but can always use improvement, especially the courses required for the core curriculum that is part of the required track of classes for every student. I think that the professors are hit or miss with regard to popularity and grading, but for the most part they are very fair and of high quality.

The class size is amazingly small compared to other universities. I have had only three or four classes that have been larger than 30 students, but most of my classes are smaller classes and spread out to fit into my schedule. The workload is average, but I think more and more, the professors are giving large projects at the end of the semester instead of small projects throughout the semester, which makes the end of the semester stressful for everyone.

Employment Prospects

Alumnus/a, Finance, 8/2003-5/2007, June 2007

The Career Center is a great resource for getting a job. It was easy to use its resources and someone was always willing to help. I got my résumé critiqued and attended many on-campus interviews with prospective employers. It was an on-campus interview that led to the job I hold now.

Alumnus/a, 8/2003-5/2007, May 2007

The connections the professors in the journalism department have are unbeatable. Often my professors would send me inquiries for job applicants that were sent just to him or her to send to appropriate students. The program's reputation is outstanding—often employers came from as far as Washington State to campus to interview. Professors took care of you. If you didn't have a job or internship by April, they took you under their wings to help you get one. You always had to do the nitty gritty and pull your weight, but they made the contacts and placed you.

Current student, 8/2002-Submit Date, May 2006

On-campus recruiting and internships are very expansive at Ball State. They are always offering a job fair and the Career Center is available and advertises well. I have not had experience with the alumni network as of yet. I know that graduating from Ball State in certain colleges is seen as higher than others (architecture, teaching, business, journalism).

Current student, History, 8/2004-Submit Date, May 2006

The Career Center is great and will edit your résumé and help you get interviews with companies. Annual job fairs are also held where you can bring your résumé. I find that my professors normally have career advice for me about after I graduate. With the history major, I do not find a lot of job connections, but the

people in the business department, architecture and communications are always networking.

Current student, 8/2002-Submit Date, October 2005

From what we are told as students by both our professors and visiting professionals in the field of architecture, finding jobs after completing the architecture program is as easy as saying, "I went to Ball State" (not literally that easy, but the point has been made). Alumni are extremely helpful, often times they visit to perform presentations, seek students interested in internships (during the career fair) and other professional gestures. During field trips to locations of splendid examples of architecture, the school usually takes the students to visit one or more offices/companies either run by alumni or where some alumni have become employed. These are extremely beneficial to students, providing excellent opportunities and making it very easy for dedicated students to grab a foothold in the professional world.

Current student, 8/2000-Submit Date, April 2005

There are several departments and majors that are very successful when graduating and finding a job—specifically, telecommunications, architecture, education, music and any business major. Most of the students graduating from these majors find jobs immediately after graduation or even before and go directly from college to their full-time position.

The alumni network is very strong and connected to the university within some departments, but there are others that have very little contact or connection with the alumni from their college.

Quality of Life

Alumnus/a, Chemistry, 8/2003-7/2006, May 2007

Housing was fantastic. I lived on campus my entire undergraduate career. Food was good, crime was minimal in the surrounding city, and access to local attractions was very easy as the city provides free public transportation to Ball State students.

Current student, Environment, 8/2004-Submit Date, May 2007

Ball State is nestled within the quiet community of Muncie, IN. Students feel right at home in the residence halls, as the university is constantly revamping the community setting within the halls. Currently there is a new residence being built and another will be built with the completion of Park Hall. We have many options within campus housing (semi-private rooms, double rooms, honors halls and campus apartment options). The living environment on campus is very nice. We have SURF halls (Students United to Remain Free from drug, tobacco and alcohol use, Green halls (environmentally friendly halls), 21-and-over halls and Wellness halls for an active lifestyle. All recreation facilities are free for student use. Ball State also has professional chefs within their dining facilities so students never go hungry with many options to choose from on campus. Campus is very safe; there are 15 emergency call boxes located around campus and a full-scale police force on campus. Any crime that is ever reported usually happens off campus.

Current student, 8/2002-Submit Date, May 2006

The university is in the nice part of town and there is almost no crime on campus and very little in Muncie as a whole. On-campus housing has a full range. BSU is really trying to get housing fixed up. The biggest problem is dorm food, which everyone complains about everywhere.

> **The school says:** "A new residence hall recently opened in fall 2007, and another new residence hall is in the initial stages of construction."

Current student, 8/2004-Submit Date, May 2006

I always feel safe on campus. I will walk alone by myself at night and I do not worry. The housing and dining facilities are very nice and are always open. I am a vegetarian and they have always been helpful, finding me the foods that work best in my diet. My freshman year I loved the residence halls because all the friends I made were my neighbors. I always love how the campus looks. Facilities does a great job at keeping up the campus.

Current student, 1/2003-Submit Date, January 2006

Ball State is the most wireless campus in the nation. They also have an over-whelmingly good residence life program, with many students staying in the dorms from the time they arrive to the time that they graduate (I'm one of them). The campus is laid out in a very linear fashion, with most all of the campus buildings on one street, making it easy to walk to class. In fact, one could make it from one end of campus to the other in about 15 minutes, not an easy task for most large public universities. Dining is wonderful. There are dining services in all residence halls but one, Beeman/Demotte. Overall, there are [12] different places to eat on campus, and all of them take dining cards as well as cash.

> **Regarding dining, the school says:** "Ball State students can eat at any of 12 dining locations on campus, including Woodworth Commons, a recently renovated dining facility offering a variety of food choices."

The vegetarian options leave a lot to be desired, but the options that you do have are much better that what one would find off campus. But don't walk around alone at night.

Current student, 8/2003-Submit Date, February 2006

I live off campus, and safety is sometimes an issue. I am close enough to campus to be considered "in campus district" so you would think that it would be somewhat safe, but there are a lot of local people wandering around at all hours of the day and night.

Social Life

Alumnus/a, Finance, 8/2003-5/2007, June 2007

Muncie may seem like a small town with not much happening, but that is wrong. I came from Chicago and was scared of being bored every weekend. However, I found that Munie is a great town with wonderful people. All freshmen should leave campus and McGalliard Roadand explore Muncie. I loved the coffee shop, The Blue Bottle, and the restaurant, The White River Landing, in downtown Muncie.

Current student, Environment, 8/2004-Submit Date, May 2007

Ball State has many activities for students to choose from. We have over 300 student organizations on campus, from Greek life to professional student organizations, to special interest groups. At Ball State we have 22 fraternities and sororities as well as 10 National Pan Hellenic Council organizations on campus. There are endless activities for students to participate.

Current student, 8/2002-Submit Date, May 2006

The university is not directly associated with the bars right off campus, The Village, but many believe since it is so close to campus that it is a part of it. The bars and other drinking scenes do provide entertainment for students all nights of the week and weekend. You must go about two to three miles to reach any good restaurants. This requires the student to have access to a vehicle. This is also the case for the movies and clubs. Ball State does over the superb Late Nite @ Ball State program, an alcohol-free party on campus on Saturday nights. It offers free food, entertainment, giveaways and so much more free to students. This is a great way for students to get out on Saturday nights and enjoy being with their friends and having fun. The Greek system has drastically gone downhill since I've been here. I started out in the Greek system and got out within one and a half years. I felt that I was pressured to take time away from my schoolwork and volunteer work to participate in things that I didn't feel were important. I see the different groups and just do not see them as solid groups that live up to their expectations with their national committees or the university.

> **The school says:** "Ball State students can ride the MITS (Muncie Indiana Transit System) bus for free with their student ID. The bus stops all over campus and will take students to the mall, movie theatres, restaurants, Wal-Mart and Target."

Current student, 8/2003-Submit Date, May 2006

I am very social at Ball State. Greek life is small, but is a lot of fun for people who are involved in it. Roughly 10 percent of the campus is Greek. Males have housing and females have suites, which are glorified living rooms. With over 80

women, our chapter, can barely fit, so we use other campus facilities. There have been a lot of restaurants slowly coming to Muncie, but they are always full. They definitely could support more. There are plenty of things to do on campus, like Late Night programs, which occur every Saturday from 9 p.m to 1 a.m. The bars are always busy and there are many off-campus parties to attend. Students enjoy getting Carter's hot dogs at 2 a.m. in the Village while hanging out with friends. Homecoming is a blast, with events like Air Jam (lip sync contest, which is sold out every year in the big auditorium), talent search, bed races, the parade and the game. Athletics are improving—students get in free to all events with an ID, so it's always got a good crowd.

It's a big school with a small state of mind. It's not too big, and it's not too small—that's how we like it.

> **Regarding diversity, Ball State says:** "Ball State was recently recognized as a university committed to diversity by Minority Access. The university earned the honor largely due to work done through the many centers and institutes established on campus and its many programs and policies that promote diversity and multicultural awareness."

The School Says

Innovation in teaching and learning is a tradition at Ball State University. This tradition brings people, ideas and extraordinary resources together to redefine academic excellence: what it is, how it is achieved, and the outcomes it produces.

At Ball State, bright, curious students excel in an intellectually energetic environment—one that challenges, yet supports. Classroom learning is crystallized and extended by relevant, intense, hands-on experiences beyond the classroom. These immersive learning experiences—found in every academic college and in special centers—are a hallmark of the Ball State experience.

In addition, Ball State is a magnet for active and respected scholars who are master teachers. Professors here take advantage of small class sizes and motivated students to foster a spirit of personal exploration and engagement. They leave doors open, give out phone numbers, answer e-mails, start blogs, keep regular office hours, and reach out to students every day.

Our faculty take creative risks—and encourage their students to do the same—while collaborating with them on meaningful projects in and out of the classroom. Ball State's leading technological resources raise the caliber and extend the reach of our students' experiences. The result: Students emerge exhilarated, self-assured, and well prepared to meet the shifting needs of a dynamic future.

In 2007, Ball State was named among the nation's "Best Value Colleges" by The Princeton Review. In addition, the university has several nationally recognized programs. For the fourth consecutive year, *U.S. News & World Report* ranked Ball State's undergraduate entrepreneurship program among the Top 10 in the nation in 2006. The landscape architecture department was ranked as the nation's seventh best undergraduate program and the Midwest's best graduate program by *Design Intelligence* in the 2007 edition of *America's Best Architecture and Design Schools*. The architecture program was ranked 13th in the nation overall and seventh for best value in architectural education by *Design Intelligence* in the 2004 edition of *America's Best Architecture and Design Schools.*

Read all of Vault's College Surveys at **www.vault.com/college**–get complete surveys on 100s of colleges and universities, expert advice on applicaton essays and more.

VAULT CAREER LIBRARY 221

DePauw University

Office of Admission
101 East Seminary Street
Greencastle, IN 46135-0037
Admissions phone: (765) 658-4006 or (800)447-2495
Admissions fax: (765) 658-4007
Admissions e-mail: admission@depauw.edu
Admissions URL: www.depauw.edu/admission/

 ## Admissions

Current student, Physics, 8/2004-Submit Date, January 2006

Some advice for getting in: Be honest about yourself and don't be afraid to show off what you did in high school. Some students shy away from telling colleges all about their accomplishments in high school, feeling that they are being too much of a braggart. Don't be afraid to toot your own horn. You have to tell them how great of a student you are and make them want you. But don't get too carried away. Be honest. Don't tell them you are a Civil War buff if you can't even remember how the Civil War started.

If the application asks you for an essay, write what you know. Don't try to impress them with big words or long sentences. They won't buy it. Don't try to make them believe you know more than you do. If they ask you what you want to do after college, don't tell them you want to be a particle physicist and then go on about how you want to revolutionize the world with particle physics when you don't even know that protons, neutrons and electrons are not the smallest particles in the world (there are even smaller particles than those, I know because I really am studying to be a particle physicist).

Also, be confident in interviews. They really just want to get to know you and see that you are the perfect student for DePauw. Honestly, interviews are actually quite fun. I enjoyed my interview for an honors program. We spent maybe 10 minutes on my application and then 50 minutes just talking. DePauw professors and administrators are not scary people. So don't be scared. Just have fun.

Current student, 8/2004-Submit Date, October 2005

DePauw is a fairly tough school to get into. It is helpful to have a high GPA and SAT scores of over 1300 [on the Critical Reading and Mathematics sections.] It is also extremely helpful to take part in many extracurriculars activities during high school. Minorities have an easier time of getting in to help diversify the school. Interviews and essays are very important also. These can make the difference of getting in or not.

Alumnus/a, Music, 8/1998-5/2002, April 2005

Contact the admissions office at DePauw and they will send you information such as admissions catalog, scholarships, financial aid, sports, clubs and academic programs. I auditioned for the School of Music. There are a number of audition weekends when many prospective students come to audition and this can be very competitive. During these weekends there are many activities that prospectives can attend such as master classes, an opera, facilities tours and sample lessons with different teachers. The practice rooms are open to use throughout the weekend.

In order to be accepted into the music school, you must first be accepted into the College of Liberal Arts. The application included a few essays that are important to give the school an idea of you beyond transcripts and GPA/test scores. DePauw has made it onto *U.S. News & World Report*'s Top 50 small liberal arts colleges and therefore is becoming increasingly selective. They seem to be looking for well-rounded students and place a high value on volunteer activities and service.

Alumnus/a, 8/2000-5/2004, December 2004

DePauw has a straightforward admissions process. They've become increasingly selective (even since I attended) due to an immense grant they received from a wealthy alumnus/a. The up-side is that they have a simple-to-use and fair scholarship matrix: Just enter your GPA and SAT and you can see what kind of academic scholarship you will receive. Most (if not all!) receive aid, so don't let the $30,000+ price tag deter you too much.

> **The school says:** "DePauw no longer uses a scholarship calculator. Our Scholarship Committee reviews all admissible candidates for merit awards. Our process is more holistic in nature and rewards students for their academic accomplishments. If a student applies online, the application fee is waived. However, there is a $40.00 fee if a Common App paper application is submitted."

DPU looks for strong essays from high school. I received my acceptance letter along with a personal note regarding the high quality of my high school essay. Choose a paper about something other than literature. Everyone writes lit. papers in high school. I took an interdisciplinary philosophy/humanities course in high school, and used an essay from it. It was unique, with college-level themes.

 ## Academics

Current student, 8/2004-Submit Date, January 2006

Academics at DePauw University are rigorous. There is no such thing as an easy class at DePauw. Every class challenges you. The classes are small (usually 20 people or so, sometimes fewer), so getting individual attention is very easy. The professors are very willing to meet with you after class to help you with anything with which you have trouble. They have a genuine desire to teach students and really want every student to get something out of class every day.

The workload can get very heavy sometimes. It all depends on the kind of classes you take. English and other humanities typically have a lot of reading, sometimes 100 pages of reading a night. Science classes have a lot of problem sets, which are packets of problems that can sometimes take several pages to answer.

Registering for classes is easy for some and difficult for others. What happens at DePauw University is that we split up the alphabet into several groups and rotate which group gets first choice of classes. This is done by the students' last names. Some semesters students get exactly what they want. Other semesters it may be hard to get the classes they want. If you can't get into a class through the registration process, you can typically go to the professor's office and ask to be added to the class roster and if the professor agrees, you are given a special code to put into the online registration form and you are added to the class even if the class is filled to capacity.

Grading differs among professors. The standard here is if you try your best and do all the homework, there is a good chance that you'll get a good grade. All the professors here are fair, and if you have a problem with your grade they are usually willing to listen to your case and maybe even compromise if they believe you have presented a good argument.

Alumnus/a, 8/1998-5/2002, April 2005

DePauw's academic program is very rigorous. Most of the class sizes are small—five to 30 students per class. There are some larger introductory classes in the sciences that can reach 50, but that is rare. There is also the option to have independent study classes at the upper levels where you work one-on-one with a professor. Classes meet for an average of four hours a week. Night classes are available.

Most students find that they are able to get into the required classes in their major with no difficulty. Classes are prioritized according to their status as an introductory or prerequisite class or upper-level section. The course catalog points out the priorities for registering for each class. There is online registration, which makes it very easy.

Grading depends on each individual professor. Most professors follow the attendance policy that only allows three unexcused absences per semester. DePauw is lucky to have many high-quality professors who are dedicated to teaching rather than research. The small class sizes are great for getting to know professors, and many professors invite students to their homes. The workload is intense, compared to larger public state schools. Some majors have heavier workloads than others, and science classes spend at least three hours per lab class in the lab.

Current student, 8/2004-Submit Date, October 2005

This is a tough school academically. The classes are very good and most of the teachers are highly knowledgeable in their departments. Strong lectures are given. The workload is pretty heavy at times. You are expected to have a full-time load, with work combined with class time. So if you have class for 15 hours a week, you should have 25 hours of homework a week.

It is tough to get the classes you need as a freshman or sophomore. Classes are fairly small and this is the reason it is tough to get classes, so the class size stays small and effective. Grading is usually fairly tough in most classes. There are professors who rarely give out A's.

> **The school says:** "The university guarantees graduation within four years of matriculation to DePauw in standard four-year degree programs. The student has primary responsibility for knowing the graduation requirements and planning adequately to meet them. Should a student follow the course of study agreed upon with his/her academic advisor and not be able to graduate within eight consecutive semesters, tuition will be waived for any subsequent coursework necessary for graduation."

Alumnus/a, 8/2000-5/2004, December 2004

The best part of DePauw is its professors. I don't know how they manage it, but the administration obtains some of the best in the country to settle in good ol' Greencastle, IN. Profs have reasonable workloads and great time-off opportunities, which puts them in great position to be enthusiastic teachers.

Also, class sizes are exceptionally small. This was great for me because I prefer discussion-based classes. However, if you don't want to speak up or you want to skip class, then forget DePauw. You'll rarely be able to slide through courses with your eyes half-open or without having done the reading. On the other hand, you will learn the material.

The largest course I took had 25 people, and it was Intro to Psychology. I had one course (Shakespeare) with only seven people! Even in the sciences, courses are small. Outside the sciences, lectures are unheard of. All courses are interactive.

The workload is what you make it. There's a saying at DePauw that you can get a C without doing much, a B by just using your head, but you have to bleed books to get a full A.

Because profs are so accessible, you'll rarely have a problem getting into a course you want. You may have to a wait a semester for a very popular course (such as Intro to Creative Writing). Speaking of creative writing, DePauw's program is second-to-none. It is possibly the best prep college for future literary artists in the country. Every year DePauw grads are accepted and attend the best MFA programs in the country with full scholarships.

DePauw's fellowship programs are also second-to-none. Media, management and science fellows have incredible opportunities to intern with giants in their fields. The Honor Scholar Program will also give anyone with grad school in mind a leg up with its intense courseload and notorious "ho-scho" thesis in the senior year.

Studying abroad is a strongly encouraged and widely available opportunity. DPU recognizes that you might want a semester out of Indiana. I spent a semester in Cork, Ireland and a summer in Florence, Italy, and my course credits transferred seamlessly with the help of DPU's International Center. The financial aspect is quite simple as well: pay DePauw tuition, DePauw pays your university. Easy as pie.

Finally, without exception, DePauw's academic program has a clear focus on composition. Every student (aside from School of Music students) will write several papers in each class. 300-level courses usually require three four- to six-page papers and one term paper. Plus or minus one short paper for 200- and 400-level courses.

Bottom line: If you want to hone your analytical and writing skills while developing a close connection with other students and faculty in the classroom, DePauw is a great choice.

 Employment Prospects

Current student, 8/2004-Submit Date, January 2006

At DePauw, we have a really strong alumni network. Alumni are typically very willing to help a graduate find a job. Alumni come to DePauw all the time (we even have an alumni house where they meet). Students can even leave their résumés at the alumni house for alumni to look at if they are looking for new employees.

Internships are also a big deal at DePauw. The university stresses internships and studying abroad. They want everyone to get the chance to try out a career before he/she leaves campus and find out that maybe he/she want to do something different. Alumni are also a big help with finding students internships. We have a Career Center as well, which is a great resource for finding internships.

The kind of jobs that graduates obtain are with some of the elite companies in the world. Some of these companies come here to find graduates. It says a lot about the school when the employers come here looking for their next executives.

Current student, 8/2004-Submit Date, October 2005

This is the biggest incentive of coming to DePauw. The school gets you well integrated with employment opportunities while in school by setting up many internships for semesters or winter terms. The alumni support is very strong and they will almost always be able to get internships set up for current students. Many DePauw alumni have very prestigious jobs, making it possible to find a good or high paying job directly out of college.

Alumnus/a, 8/1998-5/2002, April 2005

DePauw has a very extensive Career Center with databases for alumni and employers. DePauw-graduated employers are always eager to hire other DePauw alumni. Many employers come to the campus for interviews each year. DePauw is also unique in its off-campus internship and study abroad programs, which help students make connections that very often lead to employment.

Alumnus/a, 8/2000-5/2004, December 2004

The key to having a great job lined up after graduation is taking advantage of DePauw's excellent connections through internship opportunities. The Career Center is proactive about getting students involved in internships. DePauw's unique winter term (sometimes called a January term) creates great opportunities with companies without taking a lot of time or money for either the student or the company.

The various fellows have even more exceptional available internships, ranging from Eli Lilly to CNN, to MTV, DePauw students have interned with plenty of big leaguers.

While I was not in a Greek house, my understanding is that being in one also yields great connections with other Greek alumni. That's a consideration if you're die-hard about finding the best career (which I wasn't).

Read all of Vault's College Surveys at **www.vault.com/college**–get complete surveys on 100s of colleges and universities, expert advice on applicaton essays and more.

VAULT CAREER LIBRARY   223

Quality of Life

Current student, 8/2004-Submit Date, January 2006

I would say that the students here have it pretty good. For food, we have a food court in the Union Building, a cafeteria-style place in the basement of a dorm, which is all-you-can-eat for around $6, a place called The Duck that serves nicer meals (steaks and such) and has a place off to the side with a bar for those who are of age.

> **The school says:** "DePauw indeed still has the Hub, which is most popular because of its food-court style dining. After a summer of renovations, we have opened The Longden Market, a made-to-order café and convenience store where students can get hamburgers, sandwiches and entrees. Alongside the Longden Market is The Den, a new social space for students, equipped with pool tables, shuffle board tables, flat screen TV and quaint areas for relaxation. The Den also has a room designed for live acts and bands—Tracks in The Den—is its own concert series. In its very short time of existence, The Den has become a popular hangout for our students."

There are two main housing areas: South Quad and North Quad. South Quad has Hogate Hall, Humbert Hall, Bishop-Roberts Hall and Longden Hall. North Quad has Lucy Hall and Mason Hall. There are singles, doubles, triples and quads. The singles are only in one particular dorm called Hogate Hall. Hogate Hall has the suite-style setup. Each floor has eight suites. Each suite has two doubles and two singles with a common room in the middle. I lived in Hogate Hall my freshman year and I loved it. My suitemates and I are best friends now. I really liked the suite-style dorm because there was always a place to hang out together.

A lot of my other friends lived in the typical dorms where it was just a floor of doubles. They loved the setup because you could yell down the hall to a friend and see what they were up to. Everyone always had their doors open and everyone just loved to be able to call down the hall and see what other people were doing. We're a pretty safe campus so people don't feel afraid to leave their doors unlocked or even open. We keep an eye out for each other.

Speaking of crime and safety, we have a great police force. They are always willing to help us with anything we need, even if it's just to walk with us across campus at night after studying for hours in the library. They are typically really good about getting to you very quickly. This is easy because our campus is small. Also, they alert everyone to any problems on campus and publish their activity log on the DePauw web site for anyone to see.

The most common crime that occurs on campus is alcohol violations by students who are not of age. But of course, this happens on every college campus, so it's nothing new. There are people who go around to parties and try to stop the underage drinking, but they can't be everywhere at once. For those who are caught, they are taken to court (DePauw's court, we do have one, and sometimes state court).

DePauw has a plethora of services available for students who have personal issues. We have counseling services in the [Wellness Center]. The RAs are always willing to talk to students. First-year students also have mentors to whom they can always talk. This is part of the DePauw First-Year Experience. It's a mentoring program where upperclassmen are mentors to a group of students. They answer any questions about college life, where to go for the best pizza in town, and are just there to talk to if students have any problems at all.

> **DePauw says:** "DePauw has recently opened a Wellness Center that houses both health and counseling services. The center is staffed with a physician and physician's assistant and supported by four full-time nurses. In addition, four professional counselors are also on hand to meet with students about mental and emotional issues."

Professors actually know you by name and can tell someone else a little bit about you. Some of them become great friends. I've gone to a couple of my professors' houses for parties and picnics. They really are more than just teachers. They put forth the effort to get to know you as someone other than their student.

Current student, 8/2004-Submit Date, October 2005

In my opinion, housing is the worst part of the quality of life here. The campus is beautiful and clean in a nice small town. The facilities are all well above average and DePauw is known for its technological advancements compared to other schools. The dining is about what it should be for a school this small. There are a few choices of places to eat ranging from a buffet, to a commons, to a nice restaurant. Crime and safety is really not a problem on this campus and rarely worried about by students.

> **Regarding housing, the school says:** "DePauw's residence halls are all air-conditioned. Furthermore, DePauw has a variety of living units that one can choose between after the first year. Besides the traditional residence halls, one can opt to live in a Greek house, if affiliated, or university-owned apartments or houses. These living units provide a smaller atmosphere where students typically have their own room, but share common spaces with only a few other peers. DePauw is 100 percent residential, but with optimal living environments students have many options."

Alumnus/a, 8/2000-5/2004, December 2004

Greencastle is small and so is DePauw. The pros and cons of this are the same across any similar school, so I won't go into the details.

The campus is truly magnificent. It's undergone drastic construction in the last 10 years in order to become very Ivy League looking. The Greek houses are exactly what you think of when you think Greek fraternity house—old, very large, very brick and stone—and they add to the campus' traditional feel. If for no other reason than to see the campus, you should visit. Facilities are top of the line. There's Wi-Fi in every academic building and ethernet hook-ups spot every wall of every building, academic or residential.

Generally, I found it a nice, quiet place to live, work and study. However, I know a lot of people left for Indy most weekends because it was simply too dull at DePauw. Most people stay, though. We like our, as we called it, DePauw Bubble.

Bottom line: DePauw has traditional building exteriors with high-tech interiors combined with great residential buildings and decent food (not so good if you're a vegetarian).

 ## Social Life

Current student, 8/2004-Submit Date, January 2006

This campus is very, very Greek. The last I remember, the statistics said that we were 70 to 80 percent Greek. Of course, to have a social life you don't need to be Greek and those who are Greek don't look down on Independents. Independents still go to parties and hang out with Greeks. It doesn't really matter if you're Greek or not. There is no pressure to drink at all. All frats offer drinks without alcohol, so there's no reason for non-drinkers not to have fun on a Friday night after a stressful week of tests and papers. Because of the party scene here at DePauw, the dating scene is very good.

The only downside about DePauw being in a small town is the lack of good dating sites off campus. At bigger campuses that have a lot of restaurants and clubs just off campus, it is easier to get away from school and go on a date somewhere. But since we're in a small town, that's hard to do sometimes, especially if some students don't have extra cash to spend on gas to go to Indy. But because of this, students have gotten really creative. Once, a couple of my friends went on a date in the Nature Park that's on the west side of campus and had a sunset picnic and afterwards just sat and looked at the stars after the sun went down. The stars are great out here because we don't have all the city lights.

> **Regarding Greek life, DePauw says:** "Actually, 68 percent of DePauw students are affiliated with a fraternity or sorority. Our Greek system provides tremendous leadership and service opportunities for our student body and doesn't solely exist as a social option."

Current student, 8/2004-Submit Date, October 2005

This is another plus side of the campus. There aren't too many bars, but The Den is a campus-owned bar that has live music and a nice restaurant where school meal plans can be used. There aren't too many restaurants on campus but Marv's is very well known, even for those that don't go to DePauw who have visited before.

Dating isn't a big part of social life at DePauw because there aren't too many places to go out on a date. Events range from sports to bands coming to play on campus, very well-known people come to speak, including Peyton Manning, Mikhail Gorbachev, Paul Bremer and many others.

> **The school says:** "For the fall of 2007, DePauw's speaking engagements include Robert F. Kennedy, Jr., Ralph Nadar, and well-known feminist author, Bell Hooks."

There is a club for nearly every interest on campus. We have the Number One Greek campus in the nation with about [70] percent of the students being Greek affiliated. This is the dominant part of the social life on campus.

Alumnus/a, 8/2000-5/2004, December 2004

What makes DePauw's social life different from most (even small) schools is that it has one of the most pervasive Greek systems in the country. I did not join a house. This gave me a pretty immediate label of the informal but oft-used Independent. I was very, very happy not to be in a house, but I'll be the first to admit there's less to do if you're not in one. The good thing about having 85 percent of the students in a house is that the process is not nearly as vicious or selective as other schools where only the elite are in a house. Pretty much, if you want to be in a house, you can, with very rare exception.

Drinking is a big part of Greek life, but the administration has been cracking down on that, in light of recent drinking-related accidents.

People joke that nobody actually dates at DePauw. Instead, people hook up and then sort of move on. It's a small school and gossip is pervasive. I met my boyfriend at DePauw, but he graduated by the time our relationship got going, so the social scene didn't even enter into our relationship. Four years later, I'm glad I found him, but I can't think of many other prospects at DePauw.

There are plenty of clubs at DePauw. The two biggest clubs are JC (student Christian organization) and United DePauw (for gay, lesbian, bisexual students and their allies), although there are plenty of other clubs.

Bottom line: It is what you make of it. Even though I wasn't in a Greek house, I found best friends. It seemed to me everyone else did, too.

> **The school says:** "The Interfraternity Council (IFC) and Panhellic Council (Panhel) are the two largest student organizations. Furthermore, DePauw has over 100 clubs and organizations that are very diverse in nature. Some other popular student organizations include the Rock Climbing Club, College Mentors for Kids, College Republicans, College Democrats and Dance Marathon, just to name a few."

 The School Says

DePauw University, founded in 1837 by the Methodist Church, is a private, selective, coeducational, residential and undergraduate liberal arts college. It is nationally recognized for a distinctive liberal arts approach that links intellectual rigor with life's work through extensive internship opportunities and study abroad programs.

The DePauw School of Music provides an opportunity for conservatory-level training within a liberal arts and science environment—enabling students to have the best of both worlds. With 130 students majoring in music and nearly 400 College of Liberal Arts students participating in lessons, performances and ensembles, DePauw has a rich musical arts community.

The campus has 36 major buildings on 695 acres, including a 520-acre nature preserve, located 45 miles west of Indianapolis. Historic East College, built in 1877, is listed on the Register of Historic Landmarks.

DePauw functions under a 4-1-4 academic calendar, two 15-week semesters separated by a four-week winter term in the month of January. This term allows students to investigate learning in nontraditional ways. Students may choose among internships, faculty lead off-campus study projects, service projects, research, independent study, on-campus classes and projects at other universities. Winter term fosters creativity and independence by providing room for experiential learning.

There are five honors programs that offer internships, research opportunities and/or independent study for exceptional students: Honor Scholar; Information Technology Associates Program; Management Fellows; Media Fellows and Science Research Fellows.

U.S. News & World Report has ranked DePauw in the top tier of national liberal arts colleges for seven consecutive years.

DePauw ranks eighth among over 800 liberal arts colleges as the source of top business executives, according to Standard & Poor's.

DePauw ranks 16th among private liberal arts colleges as the baccalaureate source for PhD degrees in all fields, according to a 1995 survey by Franklin & Marshall College.

60 percent of DePauw students complete more than one career-related internship.

DePauw University is among the Top 10 colleges and universities in the United States for sending students to study abroad, according to Open Doors 2004, the annual report on international education published by the Institute of International Education (IIE) with funding from the State Department's Bureau of Educational and Cultural Affairs.

DePauw enjoys all the benefits of NCAA Division III athletics: a high level of participation, a focus on the student-athlete and a proud tradition. DePauw fields 11 women's and 10 men's intercollegiate athletic teams in the Southern Collegiate Athletic Conference, comprised of 12 schools in eight states. The annual football game between DePauw and Wabash College, called the Battle for the Monon Bell, has generated national TV coverage and has earned DePauw a place in the National College Football Hall of Fame. In 2007, DePauw's women's basketball team won the NCAA Division III National Championship. Also in 2007, student Liz Bondi was named the Honda Division III Collegiate Woman Athlete of the Year for her role with the women's basketball team and for capturing the NCAA Division III women's single's tennis championship title.

The 132,500 square foot indoor tennis and track facility opened in February 2001 and served as the host site for the 2003 NCAA Division III Men's and Women's Indoor Track and Field Championships. The center provides competition and practice venues for several of DePauw's athletic teams, also serving as a recreational facility for the DePauw and Greencastle communities.

Read all of Vault's College Surveys at **www.vault.com/college**–get complete surveys on 100s of colleges and universities, expert advice on applicaton essays and more.

VAULT CAREER LIBRARY   225

Earlham College

Admissions Office
Earlham College
801 National Road West
Richmond, IN 47374
Admissions phone: (800) EARLHAM (327-5426)
Admissions e-mail: admissions@earlham.edu
Admissions URL: www.earlham.edu/admissions/

 ## Admissions

Current student, Political Science, 8/2004-Submit Date, June 2007

My three years at Earlham have taught me that people are accepted and rejected for good reasons. If you're a resident of Indiana, a racial minority, a practicing Quaker or a recruited athlete, you're starting out on the right foot. But I've still seen applicants who fit into all of these groups get rejected. I fit into none of them. But I had a solid transcript that showed improvement throughout high school. I also took the SAT Subject Tests and did well on them. But as it turns out, Earlham didn't really care. Standardized tests, as a whole, aren't terribly important from my perspective. But just by looking at past and current Earlham students, I would say that a résumé with volunteer work, after-school employment or world travel would catch the eye of the admissions office. Earlham isn't looking for people who sit on their tailbones all day. If you're driven, if you've got a cause, and if you're looking to grow, then Earlham is the place for you.

Alumnus/a, 8/1999-6/2003, May 2007

I found that the most important parts of the process were the essays and interviews. GPAs vary so widely nationally, and many of my friends did poorly on the ACT. However, if you can demonstrate that you are seeking truth and are eager to learn critical skills, it will probably improve your application. Earlham is a unique place, and I always felt that we were looking for a certain student, not just the ones with high test scores but the ones who can contribute to the community. Also, when interviewing or visiting campus, be interested and show some personality. If you are interested in the school, they tend to be interested in you. I always believed that if you seem lackluster, then you won't be the dynamic student they want to admit.

Alumnus/a, Social Sciences, 8/2003-6/2007, May 2007

Having worked for admissions, I can tell you that Earlham does an excellent job of considering prospective students as human beings rather than relying on standardized test scores and grades to guide acceptance decisions.

I would say that visiting Earlham and interviewing dramatically increases your chances of acceptance; Earlham wants to admit students who will actually come.

The admissions counselors are very down-to-earth and unimposing. Interviews are more informal than at most schools (don't worry about dressing up or putting on an act: just be yourself).

Currently, over 25 percent of students are non-white or international. Earlham continues to increase the number of minority students, particularly from urban areas. This is pretty impressive for a Quaker school in the middle of Indiana.

> **The school says:** "In the fall of 2006, Earlham's enrollment included 12 percent minorities and 9 percent international students."

Current student, 8/2004-Submit Date, May 2006

I wouldn't call Earlham an incredibly selective school; the applicants tend to be pretty self-selecting. In the past, factors like personality and personal fit with the school have been just as important factors in admissions as SAT scores and class rank. However, because the number of applicants has been steadily increasing in recent years, Earlham has been faced with the choice of either becoming more selective or admitting more students than it can provide for.

Good grades are definitely key in the admissions process, but so are a lot of other things. Earlham likes people who are self-motivated, interested in finding a place in the world and enthusiastic thinkers. For essays, I would say write about something that truly reveals a piece of who you are, something that you are passionate about. Past admitted student essays have covered everything from international experiences to significant figures in your life, to being gay, to a detailed plan to change the packaging system in America so that hot dogs and buns come in equal numbers in the packages.

Interviews are pretty valuable, I think, just because they provide a chance for the college to get to know you outside of the heartfelt essay. It's not that we are looking for you to perform backflips trying to impress us—we just want to know more about you and try to gauge whether you would be a good fit for our college.

 ## Academics

Alumnus/a, 8/1999-6/2003, May 2007

With only one exception, I have never been told that I cannot take a class in the last eight academic semesters. Class size, however, is bigger than it should be—classes of 50 kids aren't rare (but they are uncommon). However, students don't want to take big classes, professors don't want to teach them and administrators don't want to offer them: They have been taking remedial steps in the past few years and the problem is getting better. I love my professors. Also, the only two professors who I genuinely thought were terrible no longer teach here. All of them want to meet with you, want to engage you in their classes and want to help you develop important skills. They read drafts of papers, have dinner with you at their houses, join card games, watch films; they really are accessible and dynamic. We are a small college, which means we can only offer so many classes. I don't think we offer too few classes, but who would ever complain about more? The workload is heavy. It really is a 40-hour-a-week job to take classes. Toward the end of the semester, it is a great deal more than that. However, I find them all rewarding and the work really does help you seek truth wherever it may be.

Current student, English, 1/2004-Submit Date, May 2007

Classes at Earlham are not easy. Professors will work with you one-on-one, but they will not allow you to slide by without studying or doing your share. Some students think because Earlham's admissions process is not all that selective, that classes are not going to be hard. This is definitely not true and students should prepare to be very challenged here.

Current student, 8/2004-Submit Date, May 2006

While Earlham may not be a name-brand university, I definitely believe that its academic programs are among the most rigorous you'll find. Earlham's approach to education is very think-outside-the-box-oriented, and I have definitely found myself learning to think in new ways over the past two years as a direct result of the critical analysis I have learned at Earlham. You learn to cover all your bases and to look at questions from different angles.

My personal favorites are the small (15 to 20 or fewer) discussion-oriented classes. Every Earlham student takes reading- and writing-intensive courses his/her first year, and I think those are very helpful in preparing students for the next three years of their liberal arts education. There are opportunities to study diverse topics, and I think the variety of courses offered is very impressive for such a small school. I loved my first-year seminar on the manifestation of different forms of love in society, and my class on the political poetry of Latin America—great stuff that I really had no idea I could study until I came to Earlham.

Like any school, some classes are better than others. For the most part, professors are great, but there are some that will get on your nerves just like at any other institution. I do think Earlham is pretty special because of the absolute enthusiasm of its professors about helping the students learn as much as possiple and pursue their interests. I was amazed by the level of support I got from various professors last semester when I told them I wanted to design my own major; they not only met with me numerous times to discuss how to best channel my interests into a coherent program, but also talked with one another in their spare time to make sure their advice was consistent. I don't think that's something you find at most schools.

Also, at the end of every semester Earlham students fill out an evaluation of each course they take and the professor who teaches it, and these evaluations are taken very seriously by the college. It's nice to feel that you can affect the way the class may be taught in the future. For most Earlham classes, there doesn't tend to be a huge problem with people not being able to get in. I'd say applied art classes like Ceramics or Weaving are the hardest—you really have to be an art major to have a good chance of getting into those. Some introductory classes get pretty big, but I never heard of anyone being flat-out turned away from a class.

Grades are grades—you get them, many people really care about them, for some they're not that important. People don't really talk about grades with each other—the focus tends to be much more on the class itself. The workload is fairly steady. Some people get away with hardly ever doing homework, while other people seem to live in the library. I think the workload is whatever you put into it, but the people who put more into it get more out of it.

Current student, 9/2002-Submit Date, April 2006

I find Earlham to be an academically rigorous institution, especially when I talk with my friends at large state schools who tell me that they only have a midterm and final exam or paper in their classes. Earlham boasts of having smaller class sizes, and we do. My smallest class consisted of four students; my largest [started with] 60 and I'm sure some students dropped it along the way. On average, I would say that my classes are between 20 and 30 students.

One of the great things about the small class sizes at Earlham is that you really get to know the faculty members who are teaching you. I think the best advice I received my first year was that you should make an effort to go see your faculty outside of class, make time to go and meet with them, regardless of how you are doing in the class. The reasoning was that it showed the faculty that you were interested and cared. I have done that each semester, and I have a great relationship with the faculty teaching my classes. Not only that, but they are much more flexible when it comes to needing an extension or asking for extra help.

> **Regarding class sizes, the school says:** "While only 6 percent of Earlham's classes have 35 or more students, the average class size is 17. Most students experience classes that are both larger and smaller than this while enrolled."

I really do love the faculty at Earlham. I have great relationships with professors whom I've never even had, but have met through friends of mine. The faculty is interested in our lives and futures. As a graduating senior, I have had so many meals and check-ins with professors who are trying to make sure that I feel confident and ready for what awaits me after Earlham and who want to let me know that they've appreciated having me here. I think that aside from having to say goodbye to my peers, the hardest part about graduation is going to be saying goodbye to my professors. One of the things that can be frustrating about small classes is that there is way more homework, projects and assignments than you would get at a larger school.

 Employment Prospects

Alumnus/a, 8/1999-6/2003, May 2007

We have a wonderful Career Development staff. They are part of a much broader phenomenon at Earlham—experiential learning. The huge percentage of students who study abroad for a semester are all required to hold internships in foreign countries. Likewise, our summer vacation is a full 15 weeks long, which, in my experience, made me more competitive for summer internships (because I had more time to offer). There is a beautiful Quaker principle that says: "Looking inward we are compelled outward." The time we spend on campus is, in some respects, a time to gather ourselves to go off campus (for semesters, summers and after graduation) to seek truth and be a lifelong learner in uncon-

ventional ways. Many of my friends are working for prestigious UN Organizations, faith-based lobby groups. But more commonly (because I am still young) most of us go off to graduate school. As an application to PhD programs (mind you, before I even had my BA) I was accepted with full funding to three schools. Many faculty at these schools commented upon the strength of our reputation, and when talking with the prospective graduate cohort, I did not feel underprepared in any way—that is very impressive given how many of that cohort had master's degrees.

Current student, 9/2002-Submit Date, April 2006

I think this is the hardest question for me to answer. I think that employment prospects for graduates of Earlham are pretty high. It is my understanding, though, that many Earlham students head on to graduate school or take a year off to go live abroad, travel or pursue some interest. In the last few years, we've had at least one graduating senior receive the prestigious Watson Fellowship, and a couple who have received Fulbright Scholarships.

> **Earlham says:** "Part of why Earlham students have had great success earning national awards is the work of the college's Graduate Fellowship Committee, which assists students in seeking grant and foundation funding for both undergraduate and graduate pursuits. The college was ranked 20th among 549 bachelor's degree-granting institutions producing Fulbright Scholars in a 2005 article in *The Chronicle of Higher Education*."

The alumni network has been very useful for me. I have many people whom I have been able to contact to talk about their job and whether I think it is an area that I would like to work in, and I have had many alumni offer to help find me a job. There is not much on-campus recruiting from what I have seen, though the CIA did come a little while back. We have a Service Learning and Career Development Center that is very helpful in terms of looking for jobs and internships and helping you prepare for interviews and with résumé writing.

I feel like Earlham is much better known and prestigious in the academic community, but that it is becoming much better known in the business world. This could also be because it seems like no matter where you go there is someone who went to Earlham or knows someone who did. In most majors at Earlham you are required to do some sort of internship, field study or volunteer experience, which allows you to create connections with a business or organization, and frequently these can help you find a job after graduating. Employers who know Earlham know that an Earlham graduate is someone who can do a task without being supervised, and without having to be given detailed instruction.

Earlham obviously feels that its graduates are well prepared for working, as it frequently hires recent graduates to work in admissions, alumni development, the president's office, as off-campus program leaders and as teaching assistants. Earlham graduates obtain a variety of different jobs. I know people who are working with environmental awareness groups, others who are working in their state representative's office and others who are doing specimen-collecting for the federal government. There are also a number of students who are teaching, whether it be with Teach for America or in private schools. Some students go on to the Peace Corps, others move home and work somewhere locally. There is a student who graduated last year who is working with the MacDonald's Corporation in Russia.

 Quality of Life

Alumnus/a, Liberal Arts, 8/2003-5/2007, June 2007

I have found that I lived a very good life at Earlham. People complain sometimes about its location in middle-of-nowhere Richmond, IN, but I beg to differ. Earlham is located in beautiful country. Cities like Indianapolis and Dayton are easily accessible. Smaller cities like Fairfield, Springfield and Oxford are within easy reach, as well. On campus, the dorms are decent and comfortable. Students are able to interact with each other. The Office of Residence Life is overworked, but they do a good job of trying to meet students' needs. There is always someone willing to help if you need a ride to the store, the doctor, or just some time away from campus. The school spends a lot of effort to ensure that speakers, musicians and other interesting acts are able to come to campus to

Read all of Vault's College Surveys at **www.vault.com/college**–get complete surveys on 100s of colleges and universities, expert advice on applicaton essays and more.

VAULT CAREER LIBRARY **227**

engage with students, and help them in their engaging with each other. From Renaissance music to top-of-the-line underground hip hop, from human rights activists, to slam poets and comedians, there is always someone interesting at or about to come to Earlham. We like to complain about the food, and it would not really be college if we did not, but really, food services is just fine. There are lots of options to choose from even for vegans and vegetarians. And if one gets tired of the meal plan, one can opt to eat at the co-op or cook for oneself!

Current student, Political Science, 8/2004-Submit Date, June 2007

Earlham's 800 acre campus is a dream. The front 200 is occupied by simple, Quaker-style buildings. The other 600 is known as the back campus. It's all undeveloped land and gets a good amount of use from students. I love to go running back there. I always find a new trail. I'm originally from Massachusetts and I'm a guy who likes four, distinct seasons. When students arrive in late August, it's still hot and muggy. Every dorm room has a box fan in the window. But January can bring a blizzard. Luckily dormitories are close to academic buildings so you never have to trudge too far. Residents of Earlham Hall are lucky: They can check their mail, play pool and dine all without stepping outdoors. But for most of the year, students want to be outdoors. Folks studying or playing a game of soccer are always using the center field, known as the Heart. Campus facilities are in good shape. Earlham has consistently been building ever since I got on campus. The Wellness Center is tops. Even the library, as dated as it is, still gets the job done. Most dorms follow a simple layout: A corridor spans the length of a building and is accompanied by a line of double-occupancy rooms. Earlham built its first suite-style dorm last year. I hate it. The old style encourages community in the dormitories. As a first year, I found it impossible not to make friends. Richmond, Indiana is your typical economically depressed Midwestern city. There's not much in town for students to do. I enjoy going to symphony performances. But there's little in the way of music or even restaurants for students to go to. World cuisine is especially absent. Richmond is home to crime and it has occasionally affected Earlham.

> **The school says:** "The City of Richmond, located along the National Road the pioneers traveled in the 1800s, has an interesting heritage related to the jazz recording industry. In the 1920s, 30s and 40s, the Gennett Record Company recorded such jazz greats as Hoagy Carmichael, Louis Armstrong and many others. The college publishes a student-edited *Earlham Guide to Richmond* that explores historical facts and describes many local gems, from museums and cultural entertainment to eateries and unique shopping options."

Current student, 8/2004-Submit Date, May 2006

I'd say Earlham has a better situation than most in terms of housing. While my friends at bigger schools have had to find apartments and commute to campus after four years, I and all other Earlham students are guaranteed housing for all four years. Most of the rooms are pretty nice, although some of the rooms in the older dorms definitely leave something to be desired. However, Earlham has been putting major effort into dorm remodeling recently, and the results are really nice.

After the first year, students can also choose to live in one of a number of themed houses (such as International house, Quaker House, Peace House, Jewish Cultural Center), language houses or friendship houses. Most of the time it's fairly easy to get a living assignment you're happy with, although housing is determined through a lottery system, so absolute satisfaction is not necessarily guaranteed.

Earlham students love to complain about the food, although I'm sure we have it better than some. While there are always vegetarian options, many people say that it's difficult to eat a balanced vegetarian diet if you're eating every meal in the dining hall. However, if you're willing to be creative, you can always find something you'll want to eat—and since we pay by the meal rather than by the item, we don't run out of points at the end of the year and have to live off ramen. Many people cook for themselves at least some of the time, especially upperclassmen. There's also an on-campus co-op with organic food and other natural products available for purchase.

Social Life

Alumnus/a, Liberal Arts, 8/2003-5/2007, June 2007

Social life: Hmm. Earlham students are adept at making their own quirky sort of fun. Examples include cookie-making scavenger hunts, impromptu library dance parties, playing random pranks in academic buildings, exploring the steam tunnels and making campus movies. Richmond, truth be told, does not have much of a nightlife. We entertain ourselves on campus pretty much. But it is indeed entertaining! The school brings in musicians and so on, so there are frequent school-sponsored concerts, and these are usually good. Student groups also perform with incredible frequency (I wonder why they don't have any homework). Weeknights are usually spent catching up on homework, depending on to whom you talk. Weekends are for playing—cheering at athletic events, watching movies, visiting a city nearby. Earlham is a dry campus, which means that alcohol is not allowed on campus. The reality is somewhat different. There are some bars that Earlham students will visit in Richmond. With regards to dating, it's a small place. That makes dating very complicated. If you do date at Earlham, you are no more than three degrees of separation from having dated every single individual who has been an Earlham student for about eight years. It's that scary. People do date, though. Scarily, many Earlham alumni end up as happily married couples. It's cute. Students are nice and friendly. There is always something to do, somewhere to go, someone to hang out with. It's definitely not like being in a big city, or any sized city, but it's not a bad experience. In fact, it's quite a charming scene.

Current student, English, 1/2004-Submit Date, May 2007

There is no Greek life at Earlham. Many students attend concerts on campus—I would say that live music is a huge part of the social life at Earlham. There are lots of student bands who play either in Runyan or in the various college houses. The bars in Richmond are OK, but really only on nights when they are populated with other Earlham students. Otherwise, many local, creepy old men tend to frequent them and it's not as much fun. The dating scene is OK, but it is a small school so obvious problems arise, such as having to run into exes, dating your friends' exes and so on.

Current student, 8/2002-Submit Date, January 2006

There aren't a lot of things to do in Richmond or on the campus but hang out with friends. This is really not a very social place because most of the time we are working—no joke. But the campus does give us a free movie night and bowling to hang out with friends and such. Very fun, though you just have to make it fun by yourself here.

> **Regarding social life, the school says:** "For those students who don't have a car and choose to stay on campus, Earlham offers an abundance of activities. Many students report finding it difficult to fit in all of the things they'd like to do. An Artist and Lecturers series brings many well-known performers and speakers to campus each year; more than 60 student-run clubs and organizations are available—many of which focus on Earlham's diverse ethnic and religious groups; 16 intercollegiate sports and several intramural sports programs involve 40 percent of students; student government, in addition to involving a wide range of students in leadership and decision-making responsibilities, sponsors several events and activities each semester; and active performing arts ensembles present a lively calendar of concerts and theatrical productions. In addition, a student-run newspaper, radio station and yearbook complete the program."

The School Says

Students of many races, religious backgrounds, economic levels and ethnic traditions join together on Earlham's Midwestern campus. The college's 1,200 students represent 47 states and 61 countries and share an experience rooted in the Quaker values of tolerance, equality, justice, respect and collaboration. Earlham has long been dedicated to advancing the causes of social justice and equality and in building the conditions for a more peaceful world.

Earlham's commitment to engaging students with a changing world is at the heart of its mission. The college was founded in 1847 by the Religious Society of Friends (Quakers) and to this day believes that a strong liberal arts education is the best intellectual preparation for life. Earlham graduates have distinguished themselves in careers in science, medicine, law, business, higher education, and social and humanitarian service.

Earlham's faculty members fully invest themselves and their talents in undergraduate teaching. They are highly accessible to their students. Many students and faculty members collaborate on scholarly projects, working together—often exchanging the roles of teacher and student—in classroom settings, the library, the laboratory and even the coffee shop. They share their scholarly work in classroom discussions, in poster sessions, at regional and national conferences and in scholarly publications.

Coursework at Earlham is demanding and rigorous. Students master challenging content and are encouraged to consider the application of skills and ideas to work, personal life and a broader society. At Earlham, learning is expected to make a difference.

Classroom learning goes hand-in-hand with experiencing the diversity of the world. More than 70 percent of Earlham students participate in exciting off-campus programs in more than 20 different countries and throughout the United States. Recently, the Association of International Educators recognized

Earlham's commitment to the importance of global thinking by naming the college a recipient of the prestigious Senator Paul Simon Award for Campus Internationalization.

Closer to home, more than 60 percent of Earlham students learn through volunteer service in the local community. Through the Service Learning Program, students annually provide more than 40,000 hours of valuable service to community agencies and individuals.

Life at Earlham is not all work, of course. Students participate in performing arts ensembles, 16 intercollegiate sports and over 60 student-run organizations. They enjoy the recreational and fitness facilities of the Athletics and Wellness Center. Earlham's Equestrian Center offers a student-operated equestrian and stables program. Students and faculty alike take full advantage of a rich offering of visiting performing artists, convocation speakers and both popular and classic films.

A belief in the essential worth of every person is reflected in the structure of campus governance and the consensus-based decision-making process. Students are members of college-wide committees and have a say in community life.

Earlham alumni are making an impact in all 50 states and in 56 countries as scientists, teachers, lawyers, ministers, executives, physicians, writers, concerned leaders, involved citizens and caring parents working for the common good.

Indiana State University

Admissions Office
Tirey Hall 134
Terre Haute, IN 47809
Admissions phone: (812) 237-2121, (800) 742-0891
Admissions fax: (812) 237-8023
Admissions e-mail: admissions@indstate.edu
Admissions URL: www.indstate.edu/join_us/

 ## Admissions

Current student, 1/2003-Submit Date, January 2006

The admissions process is fairly basic: You make an appointment with the admissions office go and fill out the necessary paperwork, you will then be contacted by your advisor for your major. You need to set up an appointment with them and they advise you as to what courses you need to take. There wasn't an interview for me. I came in as a transfer student with 96 credit hours. I had a lot of trouble with lost transcripts, not recognizing previous degrees, due to this my financial aid was significantly lower than should have been. It seemed that there are too many cooks in the kitchen. The offices do not communicate well with each other and getting to the bottom of a problem or issue is extremely difficult and time consuming. They do not respond to calls in a timely manner and every time you talk to someone you get a different response.

Alumnus/a, 1/1999-12/2003, December 2005

Indiana State had a fairly easy admissions process by phone (quick and easy). Getting in was fairly easy, as I didn't have to undergo an interview or essay to be selected.

Current student, 8/2003-Submit Date, November 2004

I entered Indiana State University as a transfer student from another local (two-year) college. Admission for me entailed providing a complete transcript and an application fee of $25.

Current student, 8/2003-Submit Date, March 2004

I started looking for schools I would like to attend my junior year of high school. I went to a college fair held at my high school and chose the colleges that interested me. I had filled out at least 10 applications and had gotten accepted to most of them. I was deciding between two colleges, Indiana State University and University of Southern Indiana. I went on tours of each and decided that I liked ISU. I was pleased with the environment it provided, how close it was to my home town and the academics. My advice on getting into college is to work hard throughout high school and fill out applications to colleges that are realistic for you.

If you are like me, already out of high school and looking into getting into college, and maybe your grades weren't too good during high school, there are many programs you can participate in to help get into college. Many colleges have programs where you attend a community college or a trade school for the first semester, and if you do well, they accept you into their college. I didn't have to go to any interviews or fill out any essays, but if you do, I would suggest you dress to impress, and get your essays proofread over and over until they are perfect. I got into college quite easily, and I wish all of you the best of luck in getting into college, as well.

Current student, 8/2003-Submit Date, September 2003

I filled out my application on the web site and waited to hear from the school. After waiting several weeks and hearing nothing, I sent an e-mail asking about the status of my application. When I heard back from them, they finally told me they were waiting on my transcripts for classes I was transferring from other schools. I followed up with my schools to make sure the transcripts were sent. After waiting another couple of weeks, I still hadn't heard anything, so I sent in another e-mail. I was then informed they had received the transcripts from one school but were still waiting for the information from the other. I again followed up with the second school and contacted ISU again the following week. That time I was told that I had been accepted. However, I was not given any information on how to get signed up for my classes, which were starting in two weeks. So I sent another e-mail and told them that I was interested in the dis-

Read all of Vault's College Surveys at **www.vault.com/college**—get complete surveys on 100s of colleges and universities, expert advice on applicaton essays and more.

VAULT CAREER LIBRARY **229**

tance education program and wanted to know how to get signed up for classes. When I heard back, I was terribly dismayed because I was told that I would need to be on campus that Friday for a seminar. I was told that I should contact the distance education department that I was interested in directly and see what could be worked out. Once I got in touch with this department, everything went as smooth as silk! I got signed up for two classes (even though it was such short notice), and things have been going great since!

 Academics

Current student, 1/2003-Submit Date, January 2006

The workload is a lot of hands-on activities. Classes that are not in the program tend to be more difficult to get into and the professors are more impersonal in class. I found that if you take time to show them that you have a genuine interest in the class and succeeding in the course, they are more than willing to give suggestions, check work before you turn it in and give extra credit. In the HRD major, you work closely with groups, peers in the class, and going out and interviewing other professionals in the field. You have to be ready to put time and effort into the course: your participation and interest plays a large part into your grades. Also, because you work closely with groups, you need to pull your weight or the whole group's grade can and will suffer.

There are lots of options for courses to make them work for your schedule. This particular major offers all of the classes on the Internet and the majority of the classes are also offered late in the afternoon or evening to help accommodate people who work during the day. Advisors work to get you the necessary courses. They are commonly out of the office or hard to get ahold of. As of spring 2006, the classes and grading seem to be reasonable.

Alumnus/a, Aviation, 1/1999-12/2003, December 2005

The aviation program is one of only three in the state. The classes are fairly easy because the instructors are former students with expertise in the field. The classes are scheduled with plenty of openings, since only a small percentage of the campus is aviation tech oriented. Professors can be fairly hard, but fair. The workload can be between one and three hours, nightly for each credit hour a student is in class.

Current student, 8/2003-Submit Date, March 2004

Indiana State University, in my opinion, has a very good academic program, mainly because of the environment it provides. Indiana State University has a student body of about 11,000 students, so it's not too big but not very small either. Many of the classes I take range from 15 to 100 students, but I have only two classes that are near 100 students. Even with large classes, I feel like I'm only in a class of 20 students. The professors do a good job of maintaining a small classroom feel by making jokes and including the class in discussions and lectures. As long as you register early, it is very easy to get into popular classes. This year I am a freshman, so I got the last pick of classes, and I even registered a week late and got into a very popular history class. This class has almost 100 students, and every seat is full. The professor also only teaches one session of this class, so as you can see, it is relatively easy to get into popular classes. Most professors, their grading and the workload will be about the same no matter where you attend college, depending on the year and severity of your classes.

Current student, 8/2003-Submit Date, September 2003

I am only beginning this program, which is a distance education program. My registration process was easy once I got in touch with the appropriate people. However, when I received the list of classes that I needed to take, it did include a note that the required PE class tends to fill up quickly for distance education. I have been finding the classes interesting and the workload to be manageable even while working full-time, commuting four hours each way on weekends, teaching pre-school classes at church on Sunday, performing a part-time job of "mystery shopping," and home-schooling my daughter. Needless to say, scheduling is an important part of my life!

  **Employment Prospects**

Alumnus/a, Aviation, 1/1999-12/2003, December 2005

The people who do graduate with a 3.0+ are almost guaranteed a job, because the commercial airline's mandatory retirement age is causing a surplus in openings. Indiana State's aviation program is also a springboard to students looking to further their aviation program at Purdue University, which is considered, by some, to be the leading aviation program in the country. The professors and the students are mainly only in one building used for the aviation tech courses, so it is easy to find your classes and professors' rooms for extra help. A lot of the aviation students will work with the certified flight instructor program and start teaching other students how to fly, and get paid while doing it.

Current student, 8/2003-Submit Date, September 2003

The program I am enrolled in is human resource development. This seems to be one of the most promising fields currently, since all businesses and government agencies will have needs for staff in this area. I believe this training, in addition to my training and experience in information technology, will help me diversify and expand my job opportunities.

Quality of Life

Current student, 1/2003-Submit Date, January 2006

The campus is safe and security is commonly seen. There is constant improvement to the campus and buildings. Housing in the junior and senior buildings is fairly nice. The underclassmen have no air or personal bathrooms. When you are in a 20-story building in July, this makes for a miserable summer.

Alumnus/a, 1/1999-12/2003, December 2005

The campus is clean, although there is little parking during the midday times; there are dorms, plenty of off-campus housing and fraternities. There is a food court with Taco Bell, Burger King, Subway and many other places to eat, including the traditional college dining halls. There are fountains, quad areas, good sports and state-of-the-art libraries. They still have a closed-in smoking room inside of the library, so students who smoke don't have to freeze when they light up in the winter.

Current student, 8/2003-Submit Date, November 2004

Indiana State University is located in Terre Haute, Indiana. There are huge limitations on shopping, entertainment and recreation. Housing is easily accessible and readily available to those with the money to rent or buy them. There are rentals very close to campus, whose landlords rent solely to students because they charge each student individual rent. The campus here is not very big and generally easy to understand. Parking is ridiculous! The dining hall leaves room to be desired, in my book. However, there are several different fast-food restaurants within the commons located right in the center of campus where you can get just about anything you might want to eat. Neighborhoods vary from high class residential subdivisions on the outermost areas of town, to the ghetto located right smack in the middle of town and subsequently a matter of a few blocks from campus. Therefore, crime and safety could be better and they could be worse.

Current student, 8/2003-Submit Date, March 2004

Indiana State University has a great quality of life. There is everything you could possibly need on campus, including 24-hour computer labs, workout facilities, dining halls, different programs and a security office including emergency posts around campus in case you need help. The neighborhood surrounding the university is pretty safe from crime and robbery. On campus it is very safe; I feel comfortable walking around at night by myself. I have never seen or heard of robbery, mugging or any other crime committed on campus so far. To increase safety, the students need keys to get onto their floor during the day and keys and a university ID to get into the buildings at night. Overall, the campus has many available facilities that the students can use at almost any time.

Current student, 8/2003-Submit Date, September 2003

My program is a distance education program, which allows me to listen to the classroom presentation and discussion on the Internet according to my schedule. This was essential due to the busy schedule my family and I lead. While the cost of the classes is a little higher than on-campus classes, the convenience makes pursuing more education possible.

Social Life

Current student, 1/2003-Submit Date, January 2006

There are several bars and restaurants in the area that the college students frequently visit. The Terminal, Simrell's and the Dog House are favorites of the students. There are many sororities and fraternities on the campus. There are many activities that you see going on just walking to and from classes—there are dramatizations, bands playing, free food, surveys to take. The commons is filled with popular fast food and the bookstore is also there in case you need to grab something for a class in a rush.

Alumnus/a, 8/1999-12/2003, December 2005

There are fitness areas, intramural sports, bars around campus, and a great Greek system. The Ballyhoo Pizza King and Simrell's are two great bars to come back to for homecoming. They have a trike race in the fall (like Indiana University's little 500), and a tandem bike race in the spring. The area also has Olympic Dream Team member Larry Bird's Boston Connection, which is a great medium priced restaurant/hotel. One of the drawbacks to the town is the fact that it can get a smell to it on some nights. I don't know what causes it but you do eventually get used to it. There are some great fishing areas within short driving distances for bass, bluegill and big catfish.

Current student, 8/2003-Submit Date, November 2004

The social life of Indiana State revolves around the sporting season at hand. There are several restaurants and bars within a two-block distance from campus. The dating scene here seems very bland. There does always seem to be an event of some kind going on. The locals make a very big deal about the events happening on campus and make it a big deal to include the campus in their own events. There are literally clubs from A to Z at ISU. You name it, you will find it active at ISU. The fraternities and sororities, of course, have their own system and a large multitude of them.

Current student, 8/2003-Submit Date, March 2004

The social life at Indiana State University is very diverse. There are different programs and meetings that you can attend for either fun or academic reasons, as well as restaurants and parties to attend if you just want to hang out with your friends. Indiana State University isn't the best campus for a social life compared to larger universities that have movie rental, bars and restaurants sprinkled throughout campus. Although we do not have those facilities, we do have a lot of fun on and off of campus.

Current student, 8/2003-Submit Date, September 2003

Because I am a distance education student, I do not access any of the school's social activities. However, I am from the city where the school is located and do know that there are numerous activities and events available for the students. The college campus is centrally located, with the downtown area within walking distance. There are several bars and restaurants convenient to the campus that are extremely popular with the students. I am not familiar with the Greek system, however.

Indiana University Bloomington

Office of Admissions
300 North Jordan Ave.
Bloomington, IN 47405-1106
Admissions phone: (812) 855-0661
Admissions fax: (812) 855-5102
Admissions e-mail: iuadmit@indiana.edu
Admissions URL: www.admit.indiana.edu

Admissions

Current student, Business, 8/2005-Submit Date, May 2007

I basically just applied like everyone else. I applied online and as early as possible. I also returned my housing application early to ensure I would receive the one I had requested. My biggest piece of advice is just to do everything early.

Current student, Business, 8/2005-Submit Date, May 2007

Not hard to get in. No essays, no interview, not selective. A decent SAT and a 3.0 GPA and you're in.

Current student, Nursing, 8/2005-Submit Date, May 2007

While sitting in on an IU admissions office information session, I knew immediately I wanted to apply to the university. Furthermore, once I toured the campus I was certain Bloomington was an amazing college town. The application took great thought but minimal time, as no recommendation letters or essays are required! IU Bloomington has rolling admissions and I received a, "YES, you're in," envelope within two weeks. Though admission to IUB is becoming more competitive by the year, I strongly encourage students with even the smallest inkling to apply.

Current student, Business, 8/2003-Submit Date, December 2006

As an international student, the admissions process at IU is fairly simple compared to other schools of this size and caliber. The online applications are simple to fill out and do not include of a personal statement or an essay. A great deal of emphasis is paid to SAT scores and high school transcripts. Many merit scholarships are given out based on those criteria, as well, similar to the one I received. IU is not a very selective school with acceptance rates around 75 percent. Certain programs at IU, however, are quite selective, such as the music and business undergraduate programs, which are both consistently ranked in the Top 10 nationally. In order to be accepted to IU, students should concentrate on grades. Extracurriculars may help compensate for below par grades but students who are around their class average in GPA terms should face no difficulty whatsoever. The standards are slated to become more selective in a few years, however.

The school says: "While most students are admitted to the university division as freshmen and then certify or apply to their school of choice later (usually at the end of the freshman year), some students are offered direct admission to their school of choice. Students who are offered direct admission are academically competitive and have a strong sense of what they want to study."

Current student, 8/2004-Submit Date, April 2005

The admissions process is a breeze; no essay is required. SAT or ACT scores should be relatively good but I wouldn't worry too much about them. They seem to look more at your actual grades. The admissions form is very simple and their response time for early admissions was OK.

The school says: "Over the past several years, admission to IU has become more selective, and SAT/ACT scores are consid-

Read all of Vault's College Surveys at **www.vault.com/college**–get complete surveys on 100s of colleges and universities, expert advice on applicaton essays and more.

VAULT CAREER LIBRARY   231

ered more in the process than in the past. In addition, IU does not have an Early Decision policy. However, we begin rolling our decisions early in September."

Academics

Current student, Biology, 8/2004-Submit Date, May 2007

IU provides quality classes with professors who are knowledgeable and well respected in their fields. The professors are very approachable and eager to help students succeed. The grading procedures vary from class to class with some classes being curved while others are not. The grading procedures I have encountered have been fair and represented what I had learned in the class. The workload tends to depend on your major and the number of classes taken. For example, as a science major, I take difficult science courses that require a good amount of studying that may not be necessary with other majors.

Current student, Business, 8/2005-Submit Date, May 2007

As you move up in how many classes you've taken, the ease with which you can get into the class you would like becomes better and better. Classes are of high quality and professors truly know what they are talking about. They care about the students and are always there to help. Classes are rigorous, but you will finish feeling a sense of accomplishment. The workload is not overwhelming, unless you choose for it to be, and you have plenty of time for other activities.

Current student, Nursing, 8/2005-Submit Date, May 2007

IU has superb academics in a broad range of subjects ranging from top-ranked business and nursing programs to the Number One music school in the nation. Classes are challenging, as they should be. With few required classes, IU is flexible. Freshmen register the summer before classes begin, but are still able to register for popular classes, as slots are reserved for the incoming students. Of the two years I've been at IU, I have been able to register for all of the classes at the top of my list.

Current student, Pre-med, 9/2003-Submit Date, February 2007

The classes are good depending on professors. Kelley has a lot of high qualification professors. However, you have to know how to choose them and study hard in order to benefit from them.

The accounting and finance classes are particularly harder than other majors. With this, IU has the pride of being one of the best placements in these two areas, especially in the Mid-West. Many don't make it through accounting and decide to change majors. However, it is easy for you to have more than one major in Kelley with the right coursework.

The grading is harsh, and full commitment is needed if you want to earn the grade you want.

Current student, Business, 8/2003-Submit Date, December 2006

Classes at IU vary in size and quality, as is the case with huge schools, such as IU. Many classes consist of a two lecture sessions with professors and one discussion section with a TA. Students can air their thoughts in these discussion sections and discuss the material they've learned in a more comfortable environment. Registering for classes is automated and done online. It is a prioritized process with seniors getting the first chance at registering for classes and then juniors, sophomores and so on. Again grading can vary with some professors not paying much emphasis on grades and allotting more A's than is normal. In the 100-and 200-level classes, close to 70 percent of students receive A's and B's, in my experience. IU has a great faculty base with experienced professors from all over the globe with varying backgrounds. This factor always enriches the in-class experience. The workload at IU varies from major to major, but in general, students follow the rule that in order to get an A, students need to spend an equal time outside of class as they do in class.

Current student, 8/2003-Submit Date, November 2005

Mixture of large lectures for my general ed requirements, and generally much smaller classes for major classes (10 to 30 in journalism school). I personally loved the mix, and the ability to choose with some classes whether to take a large lecture with a small discussion or to take a 60-person lecture with no discussion. Classes I disliked were because of content (not my area of interest, but required)

not because of professors. Also, good variety in topics courses. If you made th effort, professors were very approachable and personable. Almost all seeme very interested in teaching, especially for a research university. Registration based on hours earned, as at most public schools. I had some challenges gettin the perfect schedule at classes and times I wanted but never had problems get ting into required courses or key courses I really wanted. Participated in gra pact program (not sure if it still exists) but definitely didn't need it. Workload as much as you make it. Honors classes were challenging and gave great oppo tunities for close student-professor interaction.

Current student, Business, 8/2003-Submit Date, December 2005

The Kelley School of Business here at Indiana has been nothing short of out standing. The opportunities available rival those of Ivy League schools, at fraction of the price. The faculty realizes that we don't have the reputation t compete with schools like Harvard and Wharton, so they make up for it wit preparation.

Current student, 8/2004-Submit Date, April 2005

The program so far seems challenging but I don't feel as though I am losing m mind. Everything is done online, so getting classes and accessing information easy. Professors at the 100 level seem to be well trained and I haven't yet had professor who doesn't have some form of proficiency in teaching. Getting int classes depends on the amount of time you have spent at IU. The longer you ar here, the earlier you get to register. As a freshman, you may have difficulty th first semester getting the exact classes you want but you will be able to get you core freshman classes out of the way your first year.

Employment Prospects

Current student, Business, 8/2005-Submit Date, May 2007

Alumni help tons with jobs after school. Also, especially through the Kelle School, you take classes that teach you how to interview and recruiters come i looking for IU students. You can get interviews just by going to this schoo Graduates obtain good paying jobs with chances to move up or move on t greater things.

Current student, Nursing, 8/2005-Submit Date, May 2007

There are numerous services at IU to assist graduates in finding employment Not that they need help with an IU degree in their hand! The Caree Development Center will help students write up and edit résumés, provide jo listings and hold career fairs for a variety of professions. The Kelley School o Business is phenomenal; several corporations interview Kelley students on cam pus.

Current student, Pre-med, 9/2003-Submit Date, February 2007

Midwest is huge for IU. The placement for Fortune 500s is great in the Mid west. There are also special workshops for top elite students in accounting an investment banking if that is something one wants to pursue. Those in thes workshops are almost 100 percent guaranteed positions in consulting or invest ment banking. However, as mentioned, those who are determined and able t enter the workshop are among the top of the top students not just in Kelley bu throughout the nation. Many have competed nationally in certain cases and hav come back as top performers.

Current student, 8/2002-Submit Date, December 2004

There are so many employment opportunities that I don't know where to begin There is an office on campus that specializes in preparing students to enter th job force by helping them decide on a career area, tips on interview and résumé techniques, and many job fairs and interview and application opportunitie through the Career Development Center. In addition, all of the schools an departments have their own internship opportunities and are great resources fo researching jobs. Lastly, there are many on-campus interviews, job fairs an recruitment opportunities held at several locations, at different times during th school year. They are well-advertised, easy to find and well worth the time spen at them.

Current student, Biology, 8/2004-Submit Date, May 2007

The campus programs involved in employment for graduates are great in m experience. The Career Development Center has several different services tha

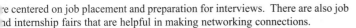

re centered on job placement and preparation for interviews. There are also job
nd internship fairs that are helpful in making networking connections.

Quality of Life

Alumnus/a, 9/2002-5/2006, February 2007

The overall town of Bloomington is amazing. There are so many places to live.
I chose to join the Greek system, but it is absolutely not a must on this campus.
There are tons of amazing rentals (homes, apartments, dorms and so on) that sur-
round the campus.

Current student, Biology 8/2004-Submit Date, May 2007

We have one of the most beautiful college campuses that I have ever seen.
Beyond academics, the campus is what made me choose IU. It is very wooded
and full of green spaces to enjoy in all seasons. There are several housing
options from dorms and apartments on campus to apartments and houses
throughout Bloomington. The dining halls offer a variety of choices and I never
have trouble finding something that I want to eat. IU offers state-of-the-art facilities including all of the latest computer and Internet technology, as well as up-
to-date research equipment in the laboratories. Bloomington is a great town to
live in—full of friendly people and environmentally friendly. It is a small setting with little trouble with crime. IU does quite a bit to ensure the safety of its
campus. It is patrolled by IUPD, Bloomington PD, and the state police. There
are also services that will give you rides to your dorm at night, which is very
helpful.

Alumnus/a, 8/1999-5/2003, November 2005

Bloomington seemed small at first, but I fell in love with it once I got off campus to explore more. The small college town charm is perfect. Good options for
ethnic food, though this is largely limited to a couple of options of each fare.
Always felt safe, don't know of anyone who didn't. Most students move off
campus after first year—some dorms were old and needed air conditioning, but
they were in the process of updating when I was there.

Current student, Business, 8/2003-Submit Date, December 2006

Bloomington is an extremely safe town. I personally have never had to experience any kind of crime aside from drunken vandalism, which may possibly occur
but is by no means widespread. Campus police are extremely efficient and very
strict. IUPD, as the police is known, are actually police officers in training and
therefore as good as the Bloomington police. Campus housing is comparable to
other regional schools. Many different halls exist and are best described as
decent. They are well maintained, however. The furniture in the dorm rooms is
adequate but again nothing more. The food served in the dining halls has been
an issue for many incoming freshmen who have to live on campus and purchase
the meal plan. Not enough variety exists on campus in food available and the
only restaurant where meal points can be redeemed is McDonalds. Athletic
facilities at IU are superb, though. Tennis courts, running tracks, soccer field and
basketball courts are spread out all over campus. Two massive sports complexes all exist where Olympic-size pools, multi-use courts and gyms are present.
Equipment can be rented for free for students. Athletics are very big at IU and
the basketball program, in particular, is the pride and joy of Indiana. The campus is beautiful and very scenic with many green open spaces.

Current student, 8/2004-Submit Date, April 2005

I recommend starting at the lowest meal plan—you can always add more if you
wish. Most people have excess meal points and have to use them on worthless
things at the end of the year. Meal points can be redeemed at the food courts in
the dorms and a variety of other places. They are not able to be used at the
library and the IMU. If you live in the Kirkwood area, housing can be more
expensive. The on-campus dining facilities offer a variety of options, including
Greek and Chinese. There are two large food courts with plenty of options.
Meal points can even be redeemed at a local McDonald's. The area is relatively safe and I know no one who has had problems. I do hear about the occasional incident in the student newspaper. Parking is available for everyone, although
as a freshman, you probably won't get parking close to the dorms. The parking
tickets are a bear, so be careful where and how you park.

Social Life

Current student, Business, 8/2005-Submit Date, May 2007

The social life is definitely a huge part of IU. It is there if you want it, but if you
lack in self control to stay in and do homework, it may be hard to get the grade
here. IU has over 500 clubs and organizations and the campus is only 20 percent Greek. This leaves a wide range of activities in which to get involved. You
can make a big school small, but you cannot make a small school bigger.

Current student, Biology, 8/2004-Submit Date, May 2007

Bloomington revolves around IU, making it a great college town. There is
always something to do on or off campus. There are lots of restaurants to choose
from, including a whole street full of ethnic restaurants. Dats is my most recent
favorite with authentic Cajun food, but if you're looking for the best pizza in
town, I would head to Mother Bear's. We have everything from academic clubs,
to service-oriented clubs, to clubs just for fun. Personally, I like the Biology
Club and the Swing Dancing Club. The dating scene is alive and well on campus. IU is a great atmosphere to meet new people. There are also several bars
for the over-21 crowd. There are places to sit and chill like Nick's and also
places to go and dance like Upstairs. There are also places that have live music.
The Bluebird and Jake's are two campus favorites.

Alumnus/a, 9/2002-5/2006, February 2007

The social life is the best you can find at any college in the country, hands down.
Bloomington is the ultimate college town with a variety of things to do any day
of the week. It not only has a great bar scene, but is also very culturally diverse.
From Kirkwood to the quarries and Lake Monroe, you will never be bored in
Bloomington. The campus is great in the fall (tailgating is always a student
favorite) and spring brings Little 500, the greatest week of college!

Current student, 8/2002-Submit Date, November 2005

Such a wonderful school and a perfect college town. Kirkwood is the downtown
area and has great restaurants and great college bars. Nick's English Hut is a
campus tradition. There are so many clubs and organizations to be a part of that
make being on this campus so much more fun. The Greek system is strong and
really has made my college experience.

Current student, 8/2004-Submit Date, April 2005

IU has a major social life. It doesn't matter what day of the week it is, there is
always a party to go to and you'll enjoy every minute of it. The union offers tons
of stuff like bowling, pool, movies and just about anything else you could possibly want.

The School Says

IU is recognized as a school that provides outstanding academics and a quintessential college experience. Indiana University
is the perfect place for students who can appreciate the fact
that there are more than 320 degree programs offered (many
ranked as the best in the nation), organizations to join (there are
more than 400 clubs and student organizations), and thousands
of cultural events. If you choose this school, you'll find all kinds
of ways to indulge your interests—even if those change several times over the course of four years.

There is an institutional philosophy to provide personal attention
to students in and out of the classroom. While professors won't
hold your hand, they are committed to teaching undergraduates
and are there if and when you need them. IU has outstanding
student support services, especially for freshmen. These
include academic support centers offering free tutoring in each
of three residential neighborhoods, one-on-one academic advising, an exploratory services office, and freshman interest groups
that connect like-minded students from the first day of the
semester.

IU students come from all 50 states and from more than 130
countries. There is diversity not only in geography, but also in

Read all of Vault's College Surveys at **www.vault.com/college**—get complete surveys on 100s of colleges and universities, expert advice on applicaton essays and more.

VAULT CAREER LIBRARY **233**

race, religion, and political persuasion. Our students are leaders and go on to do great things. 15 career services offices provide contacts for internships and jobs after graduation. Our Health Professions and Prelaw Center works with students interested in medicine, dentistry, optometry and law schools.

Located an hour south of Indianapolis, the Indiana University campus is regarded as one of the most beautiful in the nation. The Town of Bloomington is consistently named one of the top college towns in the country, as well. Students are very much a part of our vibrant, friendly community.

Some of the most notable majors at this institution are those in business, music, languages, communications, education, the social sciences, the life sciences, informatics, and the hard sciences.

Notable alumni include Jane Pauley—broadcaster, Kevin Kline—actor, Joshua Bell—violinist, Michael Uslan—executive producer, James D. Watson—Nobel Prize winner, Tavis Smiley—PBS radio talk show host, Mark Cuban—business mogel, Jim Morris—Executive Director of the United Nations World Food Program, and Will Shortz—editor of the *New York Times* crossword puzzle.

Indiana University - Purdue University Indianapolis

IUPUI
Office of Admissions / Enrollment Center
Cavanaugh Hall 129
425 University Blvd.
Indianapolis, IN 46202-5143
Admissions phone: (317) 274-4591
Admissions fax: (317) 278-1862
Admissions e-mail: apply@iupui.edu
Admissions URL: enroll.iupui.edu/ec/

 ## Admissions

Current student, 1/2003-Submit Date, April 2006

Prepare well before college. Find your direction in life during high school. Join social groups, volunteer groups and other clubs while attending high school; the more extracurricular activities you are involved in, the better. Find a mentor early in the process of developing your career. Finding someone who has already paved the avenue in a field in which you are interested could potentially save you a lot of time and money in the long run. Mentors will not only give you advice in the field you hope to join, but will also offer helpful hints and tips that will surely increase the likelihood of your future successes. If you have set your mind towards a particular field you find interesting, don't stray away from your intentions. If your mind is set, go forth in putting your best effort in your academics and your extracurricular activities. Everything you do could potentially aid in getting you into an elite collegiate establishment.

Alumnus/a, 1/2002-5/2004, May 2005

Choosing to attend IUPUI was a last-minute decision I made after attending a university away from home for one semester. My decision was based on the fact that I could attend IUPUI and live with my parents, thus cutting down on some educational costs. IUPUI was very accommodating to my situation considering I did not decide to leave my former university until December, and by the time classes started for the spring semester at IUPUI (around the first week of January), I was already accepted and enrolled in my desired classes. The application for admission is very terse, short, easy to understand and formatted to find out only the necessary information in considering your enrollment to their university. The advisors are exceedingly willing to help you out in any way necessary. The application requires a short essay (I believe it was along the lines of "Who has had the greatest influence on your life," "What will you bring to the university"), the essay and application was not nearly as complicated as 75 percent of the other college applications I had completed. After I was accepted, I was able to contact an advisor over the telephone who walked me through the admissions process and ensured that I would be ready to go to class along with the other students on the first day of classes for spring semester. This was amaz-

ing considering I had only given them about two weeks notice! I was highl impressed, I must say!

Current student, 8/2003-Submit Date, October 2004

The admissions process was pretty simple. I was a former student of anothe university. Given that, the only thing I had to do was act as a liaison betwee my previous university and IUPUI. The admissions office was very helpfu every step of the way. They gave me phone numbers to call and specific thing I should ask of my former school.

Current student, 6/2002-Submit Date, May 2004

Admissions process included an application (academic history, family informa tion, financial information). No interview was necessary, although the universi ty does make use of this tool. Essays are not necessary unless an individual i applying for the graduate programs. The university is not very selective. It is major commuter campus and has a very diverse student population.

Current student, 8/1998-Submit Date, October 2003

I submitted my application online and dropped off my application fee the nex time I was in town. At the time, they didn't accept payments online but I believ they do now.

 ## Academics

Current student, 1/2003-Submit Date, April 2006

Classes are/were designed to build one's character in the real world. Teacher would assign projects that one would see in one's working career. All classe were formatted in this regard. The projects assigned demanded long hours an rigorous attention to detail in design and practical implementation of scripting Many deadlines were impractical but were somehow met in the end.

Alumnus/a, 1/2002-5/2004, May 2005

I consider IUPUI to be a top academic institution because it combines the cur ricula of two top universities: IUPUI and Purdue University. The best part i that it is all located on one campus (you don't have to travel to Bloomington o Lafayette) and you can get the education you desire in a big city setting. I gues one downfall of this is that the campus is very popular, and therefore enrollmen is constantly high—if you don't get registered for classes early, you may not b able to get into the classes that you want most. I recommend meeting with counselor, and they are very good at doing their best to make sure you get th classes you want and need. IUPUI has adopted a pretty universal grading stan dard that applies to most of its classes. The basic 90 to 100 A, 80 to 89 B, an so on. This is a pretty good grading scale, although some professors do differ The thing that I admire most is IUPUI's professors—most all of the professor on campus have had work-related experiences in the fields they are teaching This really helps in their ability to provide you with real-world insight and the ings that a book cannot teach. Because IUPUI is almost a totally commuter campus, it does host a lot of nontraditional students. Professors are very understanding of this fact and administer a workload that is not overbearing; one that definitely provides you with a strictly need-to-know viewpoint—there is not a lot of busywork going on at this institution. However, these professors require a lot of hard work from their students (I admire this tremendously; if you get a degree at IUPUI, you have definitely earned it, it has not been handed to you).

Current student, 8/2003-Submit Date, February 2005

I believe that the quality of classes at my school is pretty decent. There are a lot of classes that are smaller-sized and have one-on-one student-teacher connection, but then there are also those that are lectures and have a lot of students with little connection between the student and teacher. I believe that when I have a smaller class size, I am able to do better in my classes. I am able to learn better when the teacher can be more focused on what we need to learn rather than just teaching the material. The grading in the big classes seems to be a little more lenient than it is in the smaller classes because they want you to be able to get out of the class and move on to the next. When you are in the smaller classes, they feel that you receive more attention so they aren't really that lenient.

Current student, 8/2003-Submit Date, October 2004

I am currently working on getting an associate's degree in interior design. The program is a great one! I can't say so much for the instructors, and frankly the students either. Since this is a secondary location, and a joint effort for Indiana University and Purdue University, I don't think there is as much time spent locating professionals to lead the classes. On many occasions, a person from that line of work was placed into a classroom. Now, I agree that information from your field of work is great, but not everyone is a teacher. This program seems to be more of a self-taught one. I will also admit that there are a select few instructors who are legitimate instructors and have a lot to offer. Unfortunately, everyone else knows who these people are, too, and it can be a mad dash to get into their classes. I know because I waitlist them if I can't get into their class. Grading can be very lax. I hate to say it, but I think because they don't have professional instructors, there is a lack of appreciation for good work. It seems that they are afraid of giving bad grades! The workload is heavy but manageable! I actually enjoyed working on the projects assigned! It can be difficult to hold a full-time job while studying this field because each project requires so much. Although it seems that you need to in order to finance the supplies required! You really need to be driven and self-motivated in this program.

Current student, 6/2002-Submit Date, May 2004

The nature of the program is very conducive for learning and utilizes a high level/quality of technological services for students. The quality of classes varies with the level of coursework one has. The lower-level (freshman) courses have more busywork than upper-level courses. However, the professors and teaching assistants are all knowledgeable in the courses they teach and make time to help students. Getting into popular classes can be difficult as a freshman because so many people try to earn their general education requirements. Sophomore year and up, everyone's popular classes are concentrated in their particular area of study and students can usually get into any class with ease. In general, the grading system is fair and clear. The grading styles vary from professor to professor, but the system is always the same four point GPA scale, letter grades/points awarded. Professors are as diverse as the students. The professors are not just at IUPUI to pursue their own agendas, most of them are really gifted at teaching. Sadly, the workload for freshmen is compiled of mostly busywork. As students move into their sophomore year and up, the workload increases significantly but the work is more interesting.

 Employment Prospects

Alumnus/a, 1/2002-5/2004, May 2005

IUPUI holds a lot of prestige with potential employers because of the university affiliation. For example, when you graduate, your degree will not read IUPUI, but it will read either Purdue University or Indiana University, depending on which school your degree is from. No matter which school your degree is from, both schools hold a lot of prestige with not only local companies like Eli Lilly, but also with nationwide companies such as NASA. The medical program at IUPUI (through Indiana University) hosts one of the nation's largest medical programs, boasting the medical complex containing Riley Hospital for Children, Wishard Hospital, and many other well-known facilities. I also know that students in this medical program get hands-on experiences at these facilities, including internships and future employment and career opportunities. IUPUI also hosts several job fairs throughout the two semesters at which students can meet with potential employers, fill out applications for employment, and gain real-world experiences all within one day of a job fair on the campus lawn.

Current student, 8/2003-Submit Date, February 2005

There are a lot of employment opportunities around Indiana. The way that you can get into these jobs is through internships and knowing people within the company. Getting anything anymore is all about who you know and the different connections that you have. Within the next year or so, I will be able to start my internship and hopefully get in with a company for which I would enjoy working and be offered a position once the internship is finished.

Current student, 6/2002-Submit Date, May 2004

Career prospects for students depend on the department they are in. Students have many resources available for career planning; however, few really take advantage of this early. The medical/science/engineering job and internship opportunities are incredible. Jobs and internships for more liberal arts-oriented students are available, as well, but must be sought out. The campus provided opportunities for students in the writing center, the speech lab, the peer advising offices of any department, teaching assistant positions and many other opportunities. The school has many nationally and internationally renowned programs (aviation, engineering, business, medical studies, journalism, music). For students interested in these areas, little needs to be done in the area of recruitment. College representatives and mail (snail mail/e-mail) are other recruitment methods used by the university. The career placement resources are impressive and fulfill a high level of benefit to the students who utilize them. There is also a wealth of graduate school information presented by the career center. Students can have walk-in or scheduled appointments but they have to make them.

 **Quality of Life**

Current student, 1/2003-Submit Date, April 2006

The academic field is not an easy one. There will be many sleepless nights. Critical deadlines are what push you to your edge in college. When attending college I was living off campus, which played to my advantage. The cost of living was much cheaper than many of the colleagues and classmates. However, I did miss out on the fraternization of the college scene.

Alumnus/a, 1/2002-5/2004, May 2005

I know that IUPUI is currently under construction and expanding its campus to include new buildings for certain schools of studies, new housing and so forth. From my standpoint, IUPUI is helpful because it does not require you to live on campus at all, not even your first year. This is really a help to students who are nontraditional, or to students who already live in the area. Since IUPUI receives funding from two major universities, it is always expanding and developing state-of-the-art facilities. Recently, IUPUI built a new building for the following schools: new media, law and Herron School of Art. IUPUI is located in the heart of downtown Indianapolis, and therefore is easily accessible through the bus system. Also, it is within walking distance of many city parks, government buildings, restaurants and museums. IUPUI prides itself on having a good security program. There are several call stations located around the campus for help, and also security officials patrolling at all hours. Being a single female, I have always felt safe on this campus.

Current student, 8/2003-Submit Date, February 2005

The quality of life is pretty good. The only bad thing is that, I have to work and go to school full time. I live in an apartment with my fiancée about 25 minutes away from school. It gets a little difficult keeping up with my schoolwork, working and taking care of my fiancée and dog.

Current student, 8/2003-Submit Date, October 2004

IUPUI has very few buildings for campus housing. They recently started construction of a new dorm building that should be open soon. It is, I guess, more of a growing community college. There are a few places surrounding the school

Read all of Vault's College Surveys at **www.vault.com/college**—get complete surveys on 100s of colleges and universities, expert advice on applicaton essays and more.

VAULT CAREER LIBRARY 235

for dining but not many. The neighborhood is great, it's quiet and seems to be pretty diverse.

Current student, 6/2002-Submit Date, May 2004

The campus is always packed but it is a commuter campus. The student life is not that impressive compared to residential campuses but the university continues to develop new opportunities for student life. The campus is located in the heart of Indianapolis, so there are always activities taking place. On campus, many clubs and organizations are available to students. Housing is still being developed. The housing that is provided is very up-to-date, as are the campus facilities. The dining areas on campus are just OK. Because the city is so close, many students buy food around town. The crime and safety of the neighborhood is surprisingly safe. There are patrol police who really keep an eye on everything and there are cameras in public areas and around buildings. As always, there are dangers anywhere, common sense goes a long way.

 Social Life

Alumnus/a, 1/2002-5/2004, May 2005

IUPUI has a unique social life because the majority of the students do not live on campus. This means that unless you live on campus, it can be difficult to get directly involved with student life and activities (even though there is a vast range of activities available). Like I stated before, IUPUI is located in the heart of downtown Indianapolis, so there is never the issue of not having anything to do. Circle Centre Mall is within walking distance (a four-story shopping center), Indiana State Museum, Eiteljorg Museum, NCAA Hall of Champions, RCA Dome (Colts), Conseco Fieldhouse (Pacers) and lots more!

Nightlife is very popular in Indianapolis, and if you frequent many bars, it is normal to run into a lot of students with whom you probably have classes at IUPUI. On Meridian Street (also within walking distance), there is a strip of bars popular to college students that many times host college nights (get in free with your college ID), including Tiki Bob's, Have a Nice Day Cafe, The Lotus, Jillian's, Howl at The Moon, Six and a local favorite called The Pub. Also a college

favorite is the Town of Broad Ripple, about a 15-to-20 minute drive, hosting [a] variety of bars and nightclubs lining one entire street of the artsy town. The mid-week favorite getaway for college students is the Vogue in Broad Ripple, whe[re] an old theater turned nightclub. On Wednesday nights it's Retro Rewind, fea[-]turing songs of the 70s and 80s, well drinks for $1.50 and Miller Lites for 75¢

Current student, 8/2003-Submit Date, February 2005

The social life is pretty nice. The campus is located downtown and that is whe[re] a lot of bars and clubs are. There are a few Greek organizations on campus. [I] enjoy going to the bars and hanging out with my friends and fiancée. It is fun [to] go and have a couple of drinks and listen to bands. There is also a little tow[n] called Broad Ripple people like to go hang out. I have never been there, b[ut] from what I've heard, it is a pretty hopping place.

Current student, 8/2003-Submit Date, October 2004

The Greek system is new and budding! Although there are few to select from[,] it's becoming more and more popular! Indianapolis has a lot to offer any co[l]lege student. There are three great and popular towns to bar hop in: downtow[n,] Broad Ripple, and Castleton, each providing its own flare of clubs, bars an[d] restaurants. There's Ugly Monkey, Lotus, Have a Nice Day Cafe, The Vogu[e,] Rock Lobster, LandSharks, Velvet Lounge, Vapor Room, and Champs, just [to] name a few! And, there's a pretty good selection of willing participants in th[e] dating scene. That's not all: there are plenty of other activities, including a[ll] sorts of festivals, philanthropy organizations, concerts and football! Go Colts[!]

Current student, 6/2002-Submit Date, May 2004

Bars and restaurants are very numerous and within walking distance of the cam[-]pus. The dating scene is very active and people seem to get connected wit[h] whomever and whatever they want. Events in the city (sports, arts, music) ar[e] always taking place but there are also many university-hosted activitie[s.] Students interested in specific areas can usually find something going on. The[re] are a lot of clubs but the activity level depends largely on what club one [is] involved in. Most, however, do make a good effort to be active. Developme[nt] of campus housing has brought Greek systems. There are several very activ[e] Greek groups on campus and more are in their first stages of development.

Purdue University

Purdue University Office of Admissions
Schleman Hall
475 Stadium Mall Drive
West Lafayette, IN 47907-2050
Admissions phone: (765) 494-1776
Admissions fax: (765) 494-0544
Admissions e-mail: admissions@purdue.edu
Admissions URL: www.purdue.edu/Purdue/admissions/

 Admissions

Current student, Engineering, 8/2004-Submit Date, June 2007

Purdue's application process was quite simple. I applied online and since they have rolling admissions, I was accepted a few weeks later. I applied early, which is why I received an answer so quickly. I met with a Purdue representative who came to my high school and asked a few questions about the university, but most of my information came from the information sent to me by the university before applying.

Current student, Engineering, 8/2006-Submit Date, June 2007

In comparison to other admissions processes, Purdue's process was very straightforward. It entailed filling out a traditional information form which included all personal information, high school information, past experience information, and completing a short essay encapsulating why the applicant is

interested in Purdue and a glimpse at what he/she expects his/her future to loo[k] like. As far as I know, Purdue is not one of the most selective schools; howev[-]er, it does value the applicant's credentials very highly. Throughout the applica[-]tion time and even after admission, Purdue was very good at contacting me, pro[-]viding all necessary information, and providing many different ways to have an[y] questions answered.

Alumnus/a, Liberal Arts, 8/2003-Submit Date, May 2007

I came to Purdue during one of the organized visits. I remember there were sev[-]eral workshops available, such as time and money management. At the end o[f] the day we had the unique opportunity to submit our admissions applications[.] An admissions advisor sat down with me right away and went over my applica[-]tion. We talked about what program I wanted to be admitted to and the status o[f] my application.

Current student, Business, 8/2004-Submit Date, May 2007

The selection process at Purdue University was actually very simple. The appli[-]cation process did not involve any essays or exams other than either the ACT o[r] SAT and in some cases they even waive the application fee. They offer rolling admissions so you find out right away if you have been accepted and they ar[e] very accommodating of their students, especially minorities like women in engi[-]neering.

Current student, Cultural Studies, 8/2004-Submit Date, May 2007

Purdue is a public land grant university, which means that the rigor of the admis[-]sions process depends on where you live. If you are from Indiana, especially th[e] West Lafayette area, and have a functional human brain, then you are more o[r] ess guaranteed entrance. The reason for this is that, as a public land grant school, Purdue is forced to accept a certain number of Indiana residents, no matter how unqualified they are. If you're from outside the state, however, Purdue can be a very difficult college to crack. Here are a few tips that can ease your trials if you are applying from out of state: Don't apply to the colleges of engineering or science right away: they are needlessly picky (instead try going through liberal arts and then transfer); talk to the admissions officers in person or on the phone as much as you can (Purdue is thoroughly wired and as such, you can be lost in the digital shuffle); and be completely honest about yourself during the process because Purdue's admissions staff possess great BS detectors.

The school says: "Academic preparedness is Purdue University's primary consideration in evaluating admission applications. Purdue does not guarantee admission to anyone, nor does the university use a different set of admission criteria or expectations for Indiana residents versus nonresidents."

Current student, Biology, 8/2003-Submit Date, April 2007

Purdue is becoming more selective due to its recent reduced enrollment and higher tuition. The application is still one of the easiest of all Big 10 universities to complete; it's a single page and there's no essay required. But don't let the easy application mislead you, Purdue is a challenging school with a competitive applicant pool and a distinguished reputation. Purdue has a number of programs for prospective students and admitted students to check out what Purdue has to offer. Purdue's for Me, Introducing Purdue, Day on Campus, and other programs offer parents and students a preview of what Purdue undergraduate life is like. Some academic schools are more challenging to get into than others, but it depends on incoming class size and the faculty/staff assigned to teach that year.

Current student, 8/2002-Submit Date, October 2005

Getting into the school was pretty easy, especially when I was an active participant at my high school. I also had a high GPA of 3.8, SATs of 1250 and I was both a basketball player and a football player. However, getting in required a lot of prep. I interviewed with my school advisor as well as talked to advisors at Purdue. From what I noticed, Purdue welcomes all students and generally accepts a high percentage of students because it feels that people can change.

Current student, 8/2003-Submit Date, December 2005

The application was very simple and easy to understand. There were no interviews or essays for the program. Krannert School of Management does not fully accept a student until he/she has completed all pre-management courses and obtained a 3.0 GPA in those courses. This is where most students fall short and choose another path of study. Once in upper-management, the professors are much more open and approachable to students.

Current student, 8/2004-Submit Date, April 2006

Admissions was not a very arduous process at Purdue. In fact, it was much the opposite. Purdue has a rolling application system, so your application gets processed as soon as you submit it. You can apply online fairly easy. Depending on which school you're applying to, you may or may not have to submit essays. Purdue offers Days on Campus for prospective students. These day trips to the campus offer a great deal of information regarding requirements for acceptance and expectations once accepted into the program.

Academics

Current student, Engineering, 8/2004-Submit Date, June 2007

There is a lot of homework in my engineering courses. I easily spend over 10 hours for a class assignment that is due at least once a week. When taking over three engineering classes, that becomes very time consuming. I never really know what my grade is because it is curved at the end of the semester. It is not uncommon to get below 50 percent on an assignment or exam and still be doing above average. In my non-engineering classes the work is not nearly time consuming or hard.

Current student, Economics, 8/2005-Submit Date, June 2007

I am an agricultural economics major, which looks at all types of economics with emphasis and examples in the agricultural industry. This helps students from rural and farming areas better understand economics and how markets work. Some classes can be dry and a little boring; however, some professors have taken the material and made it exciting and easier to relate to. When signing up for classes, make an appointment with your adviser at least a week before scheduling classes begin if not earlier. Make a mock schedule of the classes you would like to take, and then make sure that you do not have any classes that overlap, or have class conflicts. If you do, then you will have to wait until next semester, or try to take it at a different time. As soon as you show your adviser your schedule, then they can write the classes down for a scheduling run, and you are done. Schedule early, and it won't give you as many headaches. Grades could be improved because every professor has a different program he/she likes to use to keep grades, if he/she uses any program at all. Always take a class that is easy and enjoyable for you each semester. That will not only help your semester GPA, but it will also give you something to look forward to twice or three times a week. Believe it or not, if you go to class, take notes, pay attention, and study your notes/extra reading, you can get an A or B in about any class.

Alumnus/a, Pre-med, 8/2003-Submit Date, June 2007

Getting into classes is relatively easy, especially since Purdue has a program of study for each designated major and concentration. There may be waitlists for especially popular classes, such as wine tasting or bowling, but most students usually get in.

Current student, Education, 8/2003-Submit Date, May 2007

I am an English education major. The majority of my classes were through the school of liberal arts with additional education classes. The English classes and upper-specified English education classes challenged my thinking and pushed me to work diligently on projects, papers and assignments. My instructors were amazing. They were available and knowledgeable on their subject matter and educational issues. Popular classes were sometimes difficult; there is still a class I would have loved to take but could not fit into my schedule. Workload was manageable.

Current student, Business, 8/2004-Submit Date, May 2007

Although getting into Purdue was very simple and did not require much work, the school itself is a fantastic institution that is very difficult to remain enrolled in. During the first week of my engineering courses, around 60 percent of my class transferred to different majors. It is a very tough school but is highly regarded for its excellent teachers and curricula. Due to the drive of students and professors, the school has risen on all academic charts, and employers have noticed. Just beware of professors not teaching your courses—teaching assistants are very difficult to work with and not many speak English very well.

Alumnus/a, Liberal Arts, 8/2003-Submit Date, May 2007

The wonderful thing about Purdue is that throughout your study, you will always see familiar faces in the students and the faculty. However, you always have the opportunity to meet new people by taking electives to explore courses beyond your specific major. The workload is greater than that of high school, but the key is time management. A break between classes is an ideal time to work on or complete an assignment. I have found that it is so easy to get to know my professors by just stopping by for a chat or getting help with an assignment. They were always eager and willing to lend a helpful hand.

Current student, Cultural Studies, 8/2004-Submit Date, May 2007

On my first day at Purdue my academic advisor told me that, while she is there to help, I have to be the one to plan my own career. The whole school operates on this mentality. So in everything from your freshman meal plan to arguing some extra credit in a course, you will be the one doing all of the work. That level of independence is probably the most difficult thing about Purdue. After that, your stress level depends on your professors. Most of them realize that your core classes are hard enough and will take it easy on you, in particular during your first year. Each semester you'll likely find that one or two of your required courses take up the majority of your time. It's perfectly normal; just be sure to adjust your schedule accordingly and give effort where effort is due. I do think that too many courses are taught by teaching assistants who have a formidably weak grasp of the English language, and I believe this is true of all academic programs at Purdue.

Current student, 8/2004-Submit Date, May 2006

Being a double major in history and political science, I see two completely different departments. Inside the history department, the classes are usually quite

Read all of Vault's College Surveys at www.vault.com/college—get complete surveys on 100s of colleges and universities, expert advice on applicaton essays and more.

VAULT CAREER LIBRARY **237**

large. The popular classes are near impossible to get, such as History of Rock and Roll, unless you are a senior. The professors do not know you, and the classes are a blur unless you are in a 400-level or obscure class. Political science is a completely different story. Smaller classes and lots of student-professor interaction, where the odds of having the same professor twice are quite good. Certain classes are tough to get, such as the international law classes, because of the professor. Overall, the quality of classes in both departments is quite good. Most of the professors have written their own books, and as a senior I have only had one political science class taught by a teaching assistant. And he was in his 50s, and going back to school to work on his doctorate anyway. Overall, do not let the engineers tell liberal arts student that they have way more work, it's not true, liberal arts students work just as hard as anyone else.

 ## Employment Prospects

Current student, Business, 8/2005-Submit Date, June 2007

Purdue graduates are regarded highly. There are many job fairs that welcome companies from various career fields to the campus to meet the students. This is a great way for students to meet representatives from the companies and better understand what the company is all about. The companies also look for interns during college, and interview for job positions after college. The alumni network is great within the college, and many alumni give back by promoting the hiring of Purdue graduates.

Current student, Engineering, 8/2004-Submit Date, June 2007

Purdue hosts the largest student-run job fair for technical majors of any university with 300+ companies in attendance. These companies are all looking to recruit Purdue engineers, computer scientists and so on. Last I heard, the average starting salary for a chemical engineer from Purdue was about $55,000. We are strongly recruited for full-time and internship offers. A very diverse group of industries recruit on campus. Oil and gas companies and personal products and food all come to convince Purdue students to work for them. It is pretty great when seniors are getting four or five full-time job offers, and as an underclassman, I had interviews with five or six different companies for internships. If you graduate from Purdue you are set for a great start to a career.

Current student, Education, 8/2002-Submit Date, June 2007

There are many job prospects for the new graduate and the connections made while at Purdue are numerous. There is a large alumni network that will help with job connections if sought out by the new graduate. There are also many opportunities on campus, such as Teacher Recruitment Day and the Center for Career Opportunities.

Current student, Education, 8/2003-Submit Date, May 2007

Purdue is such a well-known name, people sometimes think it is Ivy League. This is a huge advantage in the work field. Purdue's education is accredited and well-respected in the field of education. The recruiting events on campus are large and helpful. The CCO (Career Counseling Office) provides numerous opportunities to get résumé assistance, set up interviews, work on co-op, and find internships.

Current student, Business, 8/2004-Submit Date, May 2007

Purdue has the best job fairs of any campus I have ever. Not only do we have the largest student-run job fair, we have at least two job fairs for every college each semester and sometimes they even overlap! I have gotten three internships from Purdue's job fairs since my freshman year and it seems that most of my peers have had the same experience.

 ## Quality of Life

Current student, Business, 8/2005-Submit Date, June 2007

I am a member of a social professional fraternity. Housing consists of two to five people per room, depending on room size and closet space. We have a library in which quiet hours are enforced 24/7. We also have a computer lab consisting of four communal computers, as well as a laser printer, fax machine, and photocopier. The facilities are kept in good order and it is one of the cleanest fraternities on campus (a student in one of my classes thought it was a sorority

because it was so nice). We have our own cook who serves lunch, snack, an dinner, Monday through Thursday. She serves only lunch on Friday, and sh always keeps lunch meat (and anything else you ask for) for the weekend Many of our members go home on the weekends to work on their farms. Th house is always locked at night, and is well looked after on the weekends. W have little crime in our part of campus.

Current student, Engineering, 8/2006-Submit Date, June 2007

Life at Purdue is nothing short of amazing. I lived in the residence halls fresh man year and am living there again this coming year. They are clean, safe an fun. Many of the residence halls have dining halls attached, which make mea times very convenient. The dining halls are clean and not over-crowded Campus is gorgeous and clean. Not to mention, I have never failed to feel safe even when walking at night. I know the procedures and phone numbers neces sary in case of an emergency on campus. When I made my college decision Purdue's campus definitely played a major part. The fact that campus is set apa from the city gives all of campus a safe and confined feeling, which is good West Lafayette is a beautiful town, despite its location in the middle of Indian farmlands.

Alumnus/a, Pre-med, 8/2003-Submit Date, June 2007

Housing is really easy to find on campus, as new residence halls and apartmen buildings are being built. Freshmen should definitely live in residence hall because it's the best way to meet people at such a big school; however, it is no required. The dining halls are awesome (especially in comparison to othe schools), and the options are great, even for vegetarians and vegans. Four bran new dining halls have been built in the last five years. Campus life is grea there's always something to do, either bowling, movies, parties, the bars, fre salsa lessons, free speeches or presentations. There's an apartment fit for ever student, some old, cheap and run-down, some brand-new, spacious and ove extravagant, with prices ranging from very cheap to very expensive.

Current student, Cultural Studies, 8/2004-Submit Date, May 200

People in West Lafayette often refer to Purdue as a "bubble." The school boast one of the safest campuses in the world despite an undergrad population of wel over 38,000. Just the same, there are the same dangers here as anywhere els and the campus community does a terrific job of watching out for one another.

Purdue's campus is beautiful in the fall, spring, and summer, but an absolute ter ror for the four months of Indiana winter. Despite snow drifts up to seven fee the school almost never declares a snow day unless the state governor forces th administration to do so. Luckily, Purdue pays for free buses that run almost al the time in loops around campus, so it's usually only an eight-minute wai between rides.

 ## Social Life

Current student, Engineering, 8/2004-Submit Date, June 2007

A third of the campus is Greek. Greek life is huge with a lot of events caterin to that crowd not to mention all the philanthropies that each house sponsors. I you decide to go Greek, your social calendar will always have something on i which is a lot of fun. If the Greek scene isn't for you, there are lots of off-cam pus housing available. Grab your best friends and move into an apartment There are a few good bars nearby with Harry's Chocolate Shop as a favorite an the Neon Cactus on Thursdays for Piano Bar night. The restaurants are varie in style from pizza joints to Indian, Mediterranean and Thai. There are a hug number of clubs at Purdue catering to everything from ski and snowboarding t sky diving, to Habitat for Humanity. The male-female split is just under 50/5 with a male dominance, but dating has never seemed to be a problem. I woul say the dating scene is healthy, very healthy.

Alumnus/a, Pre-med, 8/2003-Submit Date, June 2007

Bars are awesome, there are only cover charges at two bars; the rest have n cover and great drink specials. There's fabulous food on campus, from the quic burger and fries at McDonalds, Triple X or Pappy's, to the fabulous milkshake of Triple X and Pappy's, the delicious pizza at Jake's and Villa, and the grea sandwiches at Oasis. We have more cute little independent coffee shops than w do Starbucks, such as Village Coffee Shop, Vienna Coffee Shop and Cafe Roya who all offer free wireless Internet. With fabulous food and great drink specials ake's wins for the best bar. Harry's Chocolate Shoppe has the strongest drinks, though you pay a little more for the drinks, but it's a fabulous place to be. Breakfast club, a Purdue tradition where the bars open at 7 a.m. on home football game days, and students dress up in costumes and wait in line at 5 a.m. to get into the bars, is the best tradition ever. Fountain runs and sledding down Slayter Hill are equally as fun. The dating scene is great, as Purdue has approximately six males to every four females. Clubs are fantastic, there's always something for every student, and if there isn't something you like within the 620 student clubs, you can create your own Purdue club after getting the OK from the Student Organization Committee.

Current student, 8/2003-Submit Date, May 2006

Purdue has an active social scene. The student government and residence hall councils put on many activities during the year. I am not 21 so I can't go into specifics on the bars, but most people enjoy them. Some are known as being more social then others so you have to find which ones you like. There are many restaurants around town. Some have special things they do like Trivia Night at Buffalo Wild Wings. I have not done much dating here, I met someone early freshman year and we have dated for about a year and a half. Many of my friends are in serious relationships and one is married. So the potential is there, and I was not popular in high school by any definition. Purdue has a large Greek system if you go that route. We have about 50 fraternities and 26 sororities. They cover most majors and groups. There are some bad apples in the bunch so if you go Greek do your homework on them, and they are not all like the ones in *Animal House*.

University of Notre Dame

220 Main Building
Notre Dame, IN 46556-5602
Admissions phone: (574) 631-7505
Admissions fax: (574) 631-8865
Admissions e-mail: admission.1@nd.edu
Admissions URL: www.nd.edu/prospect/

 Admissions

Current student, Business, 8/2006-Submit Date, April 2007

The admissions process at the University of Notre Dame is similar to any other highly selective university. The quality of an application relies on SAT/ACT scores (SAT Subject Test scores are not required), high school GPA, extracurricular activities and athletics, and finally a personal statement. For my personal statement, I chose the essay prompt that allowed the applicant to choose his/her own topic. I felt that my SAT scores and GPA were strong enough that I didn't need to impress them with my personal statement, but simply not damage the quality of my application with it. I wrote an essay about the issue of ethics and its relation with cultural and religious relativism. I guess the greatest advice I can give on getting into Notre Dame is to apply Early Action. Although the office of undergraduate admissions tells its prospective students to apply early only if they are in the top 10 percent of its previous applicant pool (top 1 to 2 percent of high school class and 1500+ on SAT), one's chances of getting in are much better when applying early. To understand why this is, you have to understand that Notre Dame is only one of 10 schools in the nation that accept less than 50 percent of applicants, and of those accepted applicants, more than 50 percent enroll in the university. Most applicants are applying to Notre Dame as their first choice. Consequently, the admissions office realizes that they will fulfill their desired enrollment size without accepting a large applicant pool. Understanding this, one can see that during the regular admissions process, Notre Dame has the luxury of denying very well-qualified applicants because they know the Early Action applicants are going to enroll. So, in short, I guess the best advice I can give is apply Early Action, it is not binding and if you don't get in, you still have the regular admission to fall back on.

Alumnus/a, 8/1999-5/2003, August 2006

Admissions these days have become so tricky and hit-or-miss it is difficult to give advice other than the general, "Work hard and get good grades and test scores in high school." However, I think that with highly selective schools like Notre Dame, the essay is a key part of the admissions process. With so many candidates who are smart enough to do well at Notre Dame, the essay is the only way to make yourself really stand out. So my advice would be to take the essay very seriously, not only should it be written well, but it should provide insight into you as a person and how you are going to make a unique contribution to the ND community.

Alumnus/a, 8/2000-5/2004, August 2006

Admissions process was relatively painless, although the school does not use the Common Application. Essays are somewhat unique to the school and may have a religious spin on them. I recall a topic that included a Papal statement on mine.

Interviews are neither required nor expected. Selectivity has become continually harder over the past five years, as demonstrated by climbing GPAs and SAT scores for entering classes. Admissions seems to favor students with strong service/extracurriculars and participation in varsity athletics.

Current student, 8/2003-Submit Date, April 2006

Notre Dame certainly has its pick of the best students of the best in the country and nation. Personally, I was at the top my class academically, had great essays and letters of recommendation, and was very involved. I was waitlisted initially, but in mid-May, I was accepted. I would say that if you have challenged yourself in high school and are a well-rounded individual, at least apply to ND, even though the statistics get better (and scarier) each year. Your odds are slightly better if your parent(s) went here and even better if you are a student who can contribute to diversity at ND. The best part is that once you are admitted and come to ND, SAT scores, GPAs and all that crap doesn't matter anymore. People don't go around asking about that kind of thing, but rather accept that everyone here belongs here and has something unique to add to the Notre Dame family.

Current student, 8/2004-Submit Date, April 2006

You can apply either for early acceptance or regular admittance. You have to have a competitive GPA, and it is good if you have taken as many AP classes as you can. It is also important to have a high SAT score, and write a good essay. There is no personal interview. It is very important that you have been involved in a lot of extracurricular activities in high school.

Alumnus/a, 8/2000-5/2004, March 2005

Notre Dame's application is fairly typical for Top 20 schools. There is no interview. Notre Dame looks for well-rounded students in particular. A student interested in Notre Dame should have a high GPA (above 3.7) and SAT or ACT scores (above 1400 for SAT), and be involved in activities, clubs, sports, and/or service. The more extracurriculars you are involved in, the better. Also, good recommendations and well-written essays are key. Make sure your essays are interesting and try to point out distinguishing characteristics about yourself in them.

Current student, 8/2003-Submit Date, April 2004

My SAT was 1360 (20 points above the average for my class). That's important because my GPA was pretty low, owing to the fact that my school used a different scale. However, I found out that the reason I was accepted was my commit-

Read all of Vault's College Surveys at **www.vault.com/college**–get complete surveys on 100s of colleges and universities, expert advice on applicaton essays and more.

VAULT CAREER LIBRARY **239**

ment to community service. As a school, Notre Dame is pretty lenient. Your SAT may be below par, but if you have a good GPA and service to make up for it, then they might let you in. Of course, if you're a terrific athlete, then you'll have a much better chance of getting in if your GPA wasn't good. Interviews are not required, but the admissions officer was pleased when I asked for one anyway. So ask, even though you won't have to interview.

 ## Academics

Current student, 8/2003-Submit Date, November 2006

Overall, the academics are whatever you make them out to be. The first semester can be overwhelming for some students who are not used to getting a lot of work, but overall I felt that it was pretty manageable. After the first semester, you are free to choose whatever classes you want, though Notre Dame does have a lot of general requirements, which makes sure you have a broad array of classes. The classes vary depending on the teacher you get, but overall if you research your classes well before registering, you can find really interesting classes that challenge your mind.

Current student, 8/2003-Submit Date, April 2006

Notre Dame is a challenging school academically, but it is as challenging as you want to make it. There is quite the workload of reading and papers and pre-class preparation, but you will quickly realize how much work is necessary to get the grades you seek or will be content with. Students at ND do care a lot about their grades and GPAs, but it is refreshing to find that people are hardly selfish. For example, if you have a final exam and the professor gives you the 10 questions ahead of time, it is quite easy to find a group of your peers with whom you can split up the questions, make up a study guide, and learn and study efficiently. People want to succeed, but not at others' expense. For an arts and letters major (film, television and theatre), there are fascinating classes offered and the amount of work necessary is not too strenuous. All professors come to ND knowing that it is both a teaching and research institution, so they are very present, often giving out cell and home phone numbers or creating AIM screen names. Even the hardest classes to get into because of excellent professors are possibilities if you make a call or send an e-mail. Professors are certainly one of the unknown treasures of going to ND.

Alumnus/a, 8/2000-5/2004, August 2006

Academics are rigorous, although students are still able to enjoy themselves thoroughly. For proof of this, just go to any of the popular off-campus bars on a week night. Certainly however, some schools, such as engineering and architecture, have more strenuous workloads than others.

Teaching quality is excellent for the most part. Moreover, students have access to thorough teacher profiles on the student-run web site, ndtoday.com, which helps when selecting courses. The business school stands out for its faculty and has received many accolades for excellent instruction in various rankings.

Alumnus/a, 8/1999-5/2003, October 2005

Every student is very highly focused on academics at ND. Some of the top professors in the nation teach here, and you are sure to be in several outstanding courses each semester with professors who know what they are talking about. It is often tough to register for popular classes, especially in the business school. Workload varies by course, but expect to have an average of six to 10 hours of work each day outside of class. Grading is tough, but by no means brutal. There is not much evidence of grade inflation, like you see at other highly respected academic institutions. You definitely have to earn your A.

Current student, 8/2003-Submit Date, April 2004

Getting a good class all depends on your DART time (the time you're allowed to register for classes), which is decided by lottery. I got a really good one and had no problem getting my classes. Other students were not so lucky, and a friend was stuck with a calculus class that she wasn't required to take but was the only one left. If you do nothing but study (no extracurricular activities) the workload will be light. But almost everyone does something else, so yeah, you'll go to sleep very late, but there is no cause for all-nighters. The professors here are super-nice. They don't like to fail people and try to make lots of time for you. They're also (generally) lenient with extending deadlines. Grading is fair. Getting below a B except for in math/science is hard. However, getting an

A is pretty difficult if you don't commit yourself to perfection in everything yo do in that class. Classes are pretty interesting. I haven't had a professor wh was a complete dud. They all try to make you like it, but this might just b because I pick my professors very, very carefully, by reading the reviews offere at ndtoday.com. This is the key to having good professors.

> **The school says:** "The course registration process changed in 2005 and is no longer called DART. Under the new format, which is considerably fairer, a date and time are assigned to students, which begins the registration process. Their opportunity to register then continues 24/7 until the seventh class day. Registration times are spread over a two-day period for each undergraduate class. First day registrations, within class, rotate between even and odd student ID numbers."

Current student, 8/2001-Submit Date, September 2004

The best part about the university academic program is the first year of studie program. It really ends up being very similar to a fifth year of high school a most students take another year of classes in math (calculus), science, foreig language, and English (everybody is even required to take PE). The plus of thi program is there is plenty of time to choose one's major and there is very littl penalty for switching majors during the second year. Rigor of courses and grad ing is definitely dependent on the major one selects, but most people seem to ge along fine. Grade inflation is beginning to become a major point of contentio amongst faculty members and dean's list and graduation honors have bee tweaked to reflect an ever-climbing average GPA.

Current student, 8/2000-Submit Date, September 2003

Quality of classes depends on the teacher. As a general rule, class quality is phe nomenal—professors love what they teach, and students do participate in class

In the first year, there are a lot of core requirements (e.g., swim test, physica education for two semesters, at least two math classes, two science courses, tw writing courses). It's religiously and philosophically oriented, so you have t take two philosophy and two theology courses, which are very hard classes, b the way. Notre Dame cares about a well-rounded education, so there are require ments in virtually every department of the university—sciences, languages, soci ology, arts, you name it. Although in freshman year, kids are simply not inter ested in the classes because they are only requirements, as you move up the lad der kids get more and more into the classes.

Since most non-freshman classes are small (limited to 45 students), getting int a popular class may not be easy and depends on your seniority and luck in th class registration lottery. Registration in Notre Dame takes about three weeks— one class per week starting with seniors, then juniors and sophomores. You ar assigned a time and a day to register online through a lottery in your own class Classes fill up on a first come, first serve basis. So, if you're a to-be sophomor in a relatively small department like economics—forget about it, you'll only b able to get the classes with the non-English-speaking professors. Differen schools might also try to trample your way when you try to take a class in a dif ferent department than the one in which you're enrolled (unless, of course, yo want to take a course in the School of Arts and Letters, which is a free-for-all).

Grading is extremely fair—you get for what you deserve. If you did bad work you get a bad grade. If you worked hard, you get a good grade. Grade inflatio is very mild, but usually there is curving and opportunities for extra credit although not very much.

Workload is enormous! Teachers will gladly assign a fewer than 100 pages o reading plus homework per class, and for some majors there are papers du every couple of weeks. Teachers also check on your homework, and it's usual ly part of your grade.

 ## Employment Prospects

Alumnus/a, Business, 8/1996-5/2000, April 2007

The greatest strength of ND lies in its culture of family that pervades all areas o study and all generations of students. The alumni network is tremendous and expansive, with ND grads all over the country and across the globe in extreme-

successful positions and influential jobs. In terms of jobs grads obtain right out of school, it seems the possibilities are pretty high to get attention from tier-one financial firms, especially for jobs in Chicago.

Current student, Business, 8/2006-Submit Date, April 2007

One of the main reasons I chose Notre Dame over some other highly selective universities was the advantages that the alumni network offers after graduation. The Career Center offers two career fairs with many corporations there offering both internships and full-time employment opportunities. Beyond that is an alumni networking online database that allows students to contact alumni in a desired field or city that enables possibilities of both career advice and internship opportunities. Additionally there is an online database that informs students of all internship opportunities of on-campus recruiting businesses. The top names include Goldman Sachs, Morgan Stanley, Lehman Brothers and Citigroup.

Current student, Political Science, 1/2003-Submit Date, April 2007

First, the alumni network at ND is incredible (I've heard that it's the largest out there, but I can't say for sure). I think our career services and placement people are doing a fantastic job—they are both knowledgeable and accessible.

As far as prestige goes, Notre Dame is pretty topnotch. Just as a crude indicator of that, we usually score around Number 20 on *U.S. News & World Report*. It's definitely a school of which a recruiter has heard.

Notre Dame especially resonates with government recruiters and other employers for whom professional ethics and integrity are crucially important criteria. We occasionally hold government-specific recruiting events. Our business ethics program is first-rate. Aside from those fields, I think our graduates do particularly well in philosophy/theology and architecture.

Current student, 8/2003-Submit Date, April 2006

Notre Dame has the largest alumni organization of any American university, and this will undoubtedly help you after graduation, especially if you are a business major and/or want to stay in the Midwest. We have career fairs to which employers will come and recruit—employers that do not typically attend career fairs or recruit at campuses. The ND Career Center is very helpful, too, and there's a multitude of alumni connections you can utilize. Personally, I am a journalism minor and wanted a summer internship. So my professor, who is also news director at a local radio station, created a summer position for me and I applied for funding from the Career Center, meaning I will be paid for an internship that didn't previously exist and wouldn't have paid at all. This is the type of opportunity that exists for those who seek it out.

Alumnus/a, 8/1999-5/2003, October 2005

ND is a prime recruiting ground for some of the country's top companies including IBM, Accenture, GE, Target and Microsoft, among hundreds of others. Each semester's job fairs have nearly 100 companies and the student turnout is always large. The Career Center hosts a lot of workshops and on-campus interviews. Most of the job hunting was done on my own, though they do offer quite a few resources to help. The alumni network is one of the finest in the country. ND grads hold some of the top positions at companies all across America, so no matter where you want to end up after graduation, you will be able to find a Notre Dame grad willing to give you a shot. And of course, their loyalty to ND should give you a leg up on the competition.

Quality of Life

Alumnus/a, Business, 8/1996-5/2000, April 2007

Probably 75 to 85 percent of students live on campus their first three years and then moving off for your senior year is the thing to do; in that sense the school is kind of old fashioned. There is no Greek system and everyone strongly affiliates with the dorm where they live, which mimics the Greek system in some ways. The atmosphere on campus is serious and reverent, but still fun loving to an extent. Dining halls, relatively speaking, are great. The dorms are historic and cool with each one usually having a long and storied past/tradition, they are well taken care of and the school does everything it can to make living as comfortable as possible. On-campus crime is virtually nonexistent. I cannot imagine a safer campus, and I am sure there are statistics out there somewhere that support that claim. The university has done a tremendous amount of building in

recent years, so most of the classroom buildings are great, and even the old ones aren't bad.

Current student, Business, 8/2006-Submit Date, April 2007

The housing issue at Notre Dame is certainly unique compared to other universities. The majority of the student body lives on campus in the single-sex dorms until senior year. The campus is stone and stone-colored brick, with several beautiful open quads, which are constantly home to sports and laying out studying. In the center of campus, God Quad is filled with old trees with the golden dome and the basilica among them. Dining on campus is limited beyond the dining halls. However, with this being the case, the dining hall food is tolerable compared to home cooking, and fine dining compared to most other universities. Facilities on campus are springing up all over under the direction of recently inaugurated President John Jenkins. Among the scheduled and recent constructions are a brand-new science building, a new law school, a new Center for Social Concerns building, and a renovation of the Joyce Athletic Convocation Center (the home of the Notre Dame basketball team).

Current student, 8/2003-Submit Date, November 2006

Notre Dame's campus and dining halls are amazing. There is just something special about being on Notre Dame's campus. The residence halls are outdated, however; if you get lucky and get into one of the newer dorms it is pretty nice, but the older dorms have not been remodeled.—Some do not have air conditioning or elevators, which you can live without, but the small space just drives you crazy. Notre Dame has two gyms—one is newer and very nice, while the other one feels like being in an old high school gym. South Bend does not have a very good reputation—yes, it can be boring, but overall it's what you make of it. You can find a lot of things to do (we have one of the only Olympic white water rafting facilities) and as far as safety is concerned, no, it's not the kind of community that most kids who attend Notre Dame are used to, but it's not that unsafe—you just have to be smart about it. It's a huge learning experience to live off campus and definitely a valuable one.

Alumnus/a, 8/1999-5/2003, October 2005

On-campus life is tremendous. While there is no Greek system, the single-sex dorm environment creates very strong camaraderie, similar to frats and sororities. The dining halls have been ranked some of the top in the country, but like anything, even too much of a good thing can spoil it. The campus is one of the prettiest in the world, with religious symbolism and nature coming together to form a tranquil learning environment. ND is in somewhat of a bubble when it comes to interacting with the surrounding South Bend community, though the Center for Social Concerns does a lot to reach out to the community. Volunteerism is huge, with probably nine out of every 10 students committing time to some volunteer project.

> **The school says:** "One of the most common—and justified—complaints among Notre Dame students for decades has been the lack of a 'college district' with shops, restaurants and coffee houses next to the university. That is about to be addressed. Notre Dame is negotiating with a developer to begin construction during the 2006-07 academic year on Eddy Street Commons, a retail and residential district adjacent to the south side of the campus. The project will include about 85,000 square feet of retail and restaurant space, as well as a hotel and a variety of residential units."

Social Life

Current student, Business, 8/2006-Submit Date, April 2007

The social life at Notre Dame is centered around the unique housing arrangement. The 27, and soon to be 28, single-sex dorms where most students reside until their senior year create a fraternity environment within each dorm. The absence of actual Greek life is replaced by these dorm/fraternities. While most students party within their dorms, they eventually make it out to an off-campus house party or the bars. The student favorite bars and restaurants off campus are CJ's, Club Fever, The "Legendary" Linebacker, and Rocco's.

Read all of Vault's College Surveys at **www.vault.com/college**–get complete surveys on 100s of colleges and universities, expert advice on application essays and more.

VAULT CAREER LIBRARY 241

Current student, 8/2002-Submit Date, April 2006

Drinking is a part of Notre Dame culture—do not let people tell you differently! Lots of tradition here: *Rudy*, Rockne, The Gip, blah blah blah. Football is awesome—buy the student season tickets. OK bars. Favorite social events: SYR's (dorm dances), tailgating, kegs 'n' eggs, pigtostle, senior week, rally in the alley and more. No Greek system. Freshmen must live on campus. Many seniors, some juniors, live off campus. Closest off-campus housing is Turtle Creek (all students and the rare townie).

Current student, 8/2003-Submit Date, April 2006

We call the ND campus a bubble, since it is very disconnected from South Bend, thankfully. There are a good number of parties on campus and off if that is what you're after, but it's also very easy to find a circle of friends even if you have no interest in typical college weekend activities. Dating and gender relations are somewhat strained because of same-sex dorms. And we have rules called "parietals" that restrict late-night visitation and over-night guests of the opposite sex. Kind of annoying, but that's the biggest complaint of your average ND student. But you can move off campus for independence if you wish and those limitations are a thing of the past. Drinking at bars is a 21+ thing only, if you want to avoid the heavy hand of the South Bend excise police, a force created basically to curb underage drinking by ND students. But once you're 21 and you want to go out, there's a bar for you. Most ND students head to a specific bar on weeknights, and weekends and football weekends are a free-for-all. There is no Greek system at ND and that's a good thing, if you ask most students. The residence hall system takes the place of Greek life, so all the pride and community without hazing or forced drinking. If you don't want to drink at ND, that's totally cool, but be prepared to be confronted with it at football tailgates, in your dorm, and in everyday conversation. ND students work hard and play hard.

Current student, 8/2001-Submit Date, September 2004

Social life is an issue that has been covered in much depth in the school's editorial pages. Gender relations is a major point of dissatisfaction, as the university often treats its undergraduates as middle-schoolers when it comes to social interactions. Nevertheless, most students find a way to have fun despite the absence of on-campus bars, restaurants and clubs. Dorm life takes up most of the slack as a liberal alcohol policy allows students to throw parties in their dorm rooms.

Current student, 8/2003-Submit Date, April 2004

There is no Greek system. Lots of people drink, but mostly during the weekends, and almost no one does drugs. Dating is very Catholic with curfews that keep the opposite sex away from dorms (all are single-sex) after 12 a.m. on the weekdays and 2 a.m. on weekends. Intramural sports are very big. People work like nuts on the weekdays and wind down on Friday and Saturday night. Of course, football is big, too.

Current student, 8/2000-Submit Date, September 2003

Since South Bend is a small town, university officials know everything and control everyone in the city. If you're busted at a bar, expect to hear from the university. I live off campus, and I had a few parties broken—not by cops, but by actual university officials. For those who are 21, the situation is a little better. Some of the campus favorites are Heartland (a big dance club), the Library (jock bar), the Linebacker and Corby's, which has an older crowd (often you'll find your TAs hanging out there). The Legendary Boat Club—a classic underage bar that sold $1 pitchers of beer, played bad 80s music and still lives in the memory and hearts of all students—is no more at Notre Dame thanks to Res Life, which was able to bust the place last year. However, word is out that they will come back in a year or so.

The school says: To say that South Bend is a small town is disputable. The population for the total metro area is 268,000.

The School Says

The University of Notre Dame, founded in 1842 by a priest of the Congregation of Holy Cross, is an independent, national Catholic research university located adjacent to the city of South Bend, Indiana, and approximately 90 miles east of Chicago.

Admission to the university is highly competitive, with more than five applicants for each freshman class position. 69 percent of incoming freshmen were in the top 5 percent of their high school graduating classes.

The university's minority student population has tripled in the past 20 years (to 21 percent), and women, first admitted to undergraduate studies at Notre Dame in 1972, now account for 47 percent of undergraduate and overall enrollment.

The university is organized into four undergraduate colleges—Arts and Letters, Science, Engineering, and the Mendoza College of Business—the School of Architecture, the Law School, the Graduate School, 10 major research institutes, more than 40 centers and special programs, and the University Library system. Fall 2006 enrollment was 11,603 students overall and 8,352 undergraduates.

One indicator of the quality of Notre Dame's undergraduate programs is the success of its students in postbaccalaureate studies. The medical school acceptance rate of the university's preprofessional studies graduates is 75 percent, almost twice the national average, and Notre Dame ranks first among Catholic universities in the number of doctorates earned by its undergraduate alumni—a record compiled over some 80 years.

The Graduate School, established in 1918, encompasses 46 master's and 23 doctoral degree programs in and among 35 university departments and institutes.

The source of the university's academic strength is its faculty, which since 1988 has seen the addition of some 500 new members and the establishment of more than 200 endowed professorships. Notre Dame faculty members have won 29 fellowships from the National Endowment for the Humanities in the past eight years, more than for any other university in the nation.

At Notre Dame, education always has been linked to values, among them living in community and volunteering in community service. Residence hall life, shared by four of five undergraduates, is both the hallmark of the Notre Dame experience and the wellspring of the university's rich tradition. A younger tradition, the university's Center for Social Concerns, serves as a catalyst for student voluntarism. About 80 percent of Notre Dame students engage in some form of voluntary community service during their years at the university, and at least 10 percent devote a year or more after graduation to serving the less fortunate in the U.S. and around the world.

With 1,250 acres containing two lakes and 137 buildings with a total property replacement value of $2.2 billion, Notre Dame is well known for the quality of its physical plant and the beauty of its campus. The Basilica of the Sacred Heart, the 14-story Hesburgh Library with its 132-feet-high mural depicting Christ the Teacher, and the university's newly renovated 128-year-old Main Building with its famed Golden Dome are among the most widely known university landmarks in the world.

Wabash College

410 West Wabash Avenue
Crawfordsville, IN 47933
Admissions phone: (800) 345-5385 or (765) 361-6225
Admissions fax: (765) 361-6437
Admissions e-mail: admissions@wabash.edu
Admissions URL: www.wabash.edu/admissions/

 ## Admissions

Current student, Biology, 8/2003-Submit Date, May 2007

The admissions staff works very hard to recruit a great class each year. They give a lot of personalized attention and always make sure to seek out students across the country, from varying backgrounds. While an essay is not required, it is strongly encouraged and helps the college get a better feel for a student's abilities.

Current student, Liberal Arts, 1/2005-Submit Date, April 2007

After filling out an application, I wrote an essay on a prompt given by the college. I visited the campus several times and once was interviewed by a member of the admissions staff. As I recall I received my acceptance letter in December of my senior year of high school and enrolled that fall.

Current student, Psychology, 8/2004-Submit Date, April 2007

Our admittance selection process is rather rigorous and selective because we are a very small school. Wabash has to be selective, they will choose individuals for their accomplishments both academically and extracurricular alike. This makes it one of the best institutions in the nation. Our school will accept you for you, not for your 4.0 GPA. I was a student selected to attend Wabash College. I graduated valedictorian (as did about most of Wabash); however, I was not selected because of that, I was selected because I also had a very intense social life. You need to show someone that you are smart, not that you can regurgitate information. GPA is worthless at our school. I chose Wabash over Harvard, and I would do it again. This institution is productive and one of the most productive in the world. We do what is right.

Current student, Biology, 8/2004-Submit Date, April 2007

The admissions requirements have recently changed, moving the essay from required to optional, but everything else has essentially remained the same since I applied. The fee was waived as long as you met with an alumnus or one of the counselors and he/she signed your application. The best way to get in is to do well in high school academically, be well-rounded, and do moderately well on the SATs, basically what it takes to get into any small, private college with some selectivity. There is no interview for direct admission, but talking to counselors would be highly advantageous, and they will call you often enough to give you those opportunities. Wabash is fairly selective, but I'm not sure if there are minimum requirements for admission or denial. There are many interviews for scholarships given by the school, along with weekends of testing and interviewing to receive scholarship money.

Current student, Mathematics, 8/2003-Submit Date, April 2007

I had no problem getting accepted. The application form was easy to fill out and I sent them a sample of my writing. I applied Early Action so I got my decision back as early as February.

Current student, History, 8/2006-Submit Date, April 2007

At Wabash College, the number of applicants keeps increasing every year. Make yourself interesting on your application by being involved in school and out-of-school activities. Make sure to look into whether your school accepts AP credit or not. Wabash College does not just give you credit, they will place you into the next class higher and if you get a good grade in the higher class then you will get that credit and another credit for the class you tested out of with the AP credit.

Current student, Psychology, 8/2003-Submit Date, April 2007

The application was pretty basic, a couple of broad based essays and an online application. I remember getting lots of literature on programs and opportunities that were available to the current students, as well as lots of literature about the wonderful alumni body that Wabash College has. I also received individual letters from really successful alumni who encouraged me to contact them if I had any questions and told me a little about their experience at Wabash. I believe Wabash is fairly selective, having a little over a thousand applicants and accepting around 300 or so with a hope of filling a class of 225 or so.

> **The school says:** "Wabash received 1,450 applications, accepted about 700, and will enroll a class of approximately 250 new students each year."

Current student, 8/2004-Submit Date, November 2006

The admissions office does a bang-up job of recruiting prospects, hosting a number of Wabash visit days for recruiting and inviting everyone on campus to participate. Additionally, admissions counselors make numerous off-campus visits throughout the country in hopes of spreading the good word about Wabash. Overall, the admissions process is quite selective, but even with that, many students feel that the hard part begins once you walk on campus. The school is well endowed (ranking, on a per-student basis, among the Top 30 colleges in the nation), so merit scholarship money is readily available for anyone who qualifies. It is also a lure for students who might otherwise choose a public education were it not for the generous financial package offered for attending Wabash. Athletic coaches are particularly savvy at recruiting good athletes who are also smart, since a Division III school does not offer scholarship money specifically for athletes. At Wabash, student athletes are students first and athletes second. My experience is that admission is especially likely for an out-of-state prospect, since over half of the student body hails from Indiana. Other potential students who would improve the diversity numbers at the college might also merit additional consideration.

 ## Academics

Current student, Biology, 8/2003-Submit Date, May 2007

A great academic program with a liberal arts focus. Students are challenged in courses across the curriculum and often find areas outside of their original intended area of study for a minor.

Current student, Psychology, 8/2004-Submit Date, April 2007

If you want to take a class at Wabash you can, you will have the opportunity. Rigorous or not you will be challenged. We have one of the most balanced staff in the world. For example, there is a club on campus called the Sphinx Club, to which I belong. It selects one professor a week to be a guest speaker at our chapel on campus every Thursday. This not only strengthens the relationship, but also allows for the intellectual walls to be eliminated.

If you want to find a professor on campus, you can, and if not they have all probably given you their cell phone numbers and house phone numbers. That is why Wabash is academically rigorous—the relationships that allow challenges to be made. For example, I had a professor who knew I could write an A paper on Christianity, but he challenged me. He just addressed me and suggested, why don't you write on Hinduism or Mormonism?

Current student, Biology, 8/2004-Submit Date, April 2007

The academics at Wabash are very intensive. Even the 100-level classes will give plenty of reading and writing assignments, and with the small class sizes here, you rarely will get by without doing most of the reading. It is a liberal arts college; therefore, it is required to take classes from all divisions and most departments, giving every student a well-rounded education. The biology department is fairly highly structured, with a known sequence for the first two years and electives thereafter. Getting into classes with desired teachers is hit-

Read all of Vault's College Surveys at **www.vault.com/college**—get complete surveys on 100s of colleges and universities, expert advice on applicaton essays and more.

VAULT CAREER LIBRARY 243

or-miss, some of the classes have no cap and therefore are easy to get into; others cap classes at 10 to 15 students and are fairly competitive. There are a number of classes that contain study abroad opportunities, with classes taking trips to Prague, Rome, Germany, England and Mexico, along with other locations, both in and out of the U.S., all within the last year.

Current student, Psychology, 8/2003-Submit Date, April 2007

Classes at Wabash were always taught by the professor, there were no TAs or anything like that. The classes were small, usually no more than 20 students and in the upper-level classes there were at times six to 10 students in each class. The professors were readily available for questions and general discussion about the class, outside of class, and they often encouraged you to stop by and talk if you had any questions. The classes were a little rigorous, but it was made easier by the availability of the professors. There was an issue about getting into some of the more popular courses, since Wabash is so small, many times only one section of a particular course was offered and so that course often filled up rather quickly; however, if you absolutely had to take it you could—ask the professor if he/she could let you in and most of the time he/she would.

Current student, Mathematics, 8/2003-Submit Date, April 2007

Scheduling is very easy and there are a lot of interesting courses to choose from. The academic nature is very rigorous: expect a lot of outside work. The professors are more than willing to put the time in to help you out, though. If you show your professors that you care and are putting an appropriate amount of work into the course, you will take home a grade that you are happy with.

Current student, 8/2004-Submit Date, November 2006

Incoming students are welcomed well before arriving on campus in the fall of their freshman year. During the summer months, each one of us was given a list of freshman seminar offerings and asked to select topics in order of preference. Each seminar was limited to 12 to 15 registrants From the very beginning, Wabash is committed to helping each student become successful. Although you may plan to major in mathematics, if the seminar topic that catches your eye is about video games (yes, there was such a topic), your advisor could end up being a professor in the drama department. You don't have to stay with the same advisor for all four years, but most students find that every Wabash professors is equally familiar with the liberal arts curriculum and requirements to fulfill each major, as well as complimentary courses outside one's major to encourage a well-rounded graduate. Such depth and breadth of knowledge might not be the case for professors at a larger school; nor would the number of advisees assigned to a particular professor be as small.

Most classes are small and interactive, as professors employ the Socratic Method, meaning that they drill you on what you read the night before to make sure you understand the requirements for class preparation before continuing with the lesson of the day. Professors know each student's name by the end of the first week of classes, and most professors take the time to get to know even more about each student before the end of the semester. It is not uncommon to have faculty members routinely participating in campus clubs and sporting events alongside their students, yet students still retain a great amount of respect for their professors. Not only are all freshmen invited to meet the college president at his house soon after their arrival, students receive similar invitations to professors in their department throughout their Wabash years. These rapport-building interactions create an environment where each student, being treated like a gentleman, is expected to act like a gentleman. As a result, campus crime, insubordination and plagiarism are almost nonexistent.

At Wabash, nearly a quarter of our students participate in a study abroad program, whether it is a program directly sponsored through Wabash itself or a program offered through another U.S. school. I chose to take a summer program studying philosophy in Greece, where I was able to walk in the footsteps of Socrates, Aristotle and Plato while studying in the cradle of philosophy's birth. For those who choose to participate in a Wabash-sponsored program, whether overseas or merely at another U.S. school, a Wabash student's financial aid will be applied to the cost of his off-campus study, making the cost comparable to a semester's tuition at Wabash.

Besides the demanding curriculum, Wabash requires that each senior successfully complete oral and written comprehensive exams at the beginning of their last semester in order to graduate, something that is fairly unique in the undergraduate community. These comp exams are specifically tailored to each student

and his course of study over his years at Wabash, so a double major and/or major and minor student will have his exams specifically designed based on th courses he took. There are usually three faculty members who evaluate a student's comprehensive performance, one professor from your major department along with two other professors. Such academic preparation and affirmatio provides any potential employer with the assurance that each Wabash grad ha met a measurable standard of achievement and been certified with a seal o approval. Such means of accomplishment are well-documented in many nation al publications that consistently rank the Wabash academic experience one of th tops in the country. I couldn't have asked for a better academic environment.

Employment Prospects

Current student, Biology, 8/2003-Submit Date, May 2007

Simply one of the best alumni programs in the country. Graduates are foun everywhere and will do anything and everything to help you out. Personally, found the alumni not only helped me get started on the application process, bu also gave me guidance up until I accepted a job in the pharmaceutical sale industry: a highly competitive field into which three of this year's graduates wil be heading.

Current student, Liberal Arts, 1/2005-Submit Date, April 2007

Many graduates of Wabash have the great opportunity to work for highly presti gious companies and firms due to the colleges' intense network. It is not uncommon that our students will work for an alumnus for some time before they go t graduate school or pursue a greater position. In addition, students are able to use the resources of the Schoder Center on campus to help them with résumés, finding internships and establishing careers.

Current student, Biology, 8/2004-Submit Date, April 2007

Employment prospects are very good, with students frequently being hired by Teach for America, Eli Lilly and other big corporations, many based out o Indianapolis and Chicago. Most graduates are able to find a job of some sor directly out of college, with examples of people going directly into multiple areas. Also, placement into professional and graduate school is often very high The recent medical school placement rates have been near 90 percent for the las couple of years.

Current student, Mathematics, 8/2003-Submit Date, April 2007

There are a lot of internship opportunities with the college over the summer in the various departments and programs. Alumni contacts are very friendly and open to offering advice and/or guidance. We don't have a great deal of name recognition, so the employers and grad schools we attend are, in the majority less recognized. But people who work hard enough can easily get the big names We have very close ties with Eli Lilly and Co., which is a great place to work.

Current student, Business, 8/2005-Submit Date, April 2007

Success out of college is amazing here. You hear every year about students who were offered jobs into some of the most amazing companies around. I am an employee at our career services office and I know firsthand the helpfulness that alumni offer to students through internships, presentations, mentoring and so on. On campus we have hundreds of different events that are centered around employer recruiting and internships.

Quality of Life

Current student, Liberal Arts, 1/2005-Submit Date, April 2007

Life at Wabash is quite nice. Located in Crawfordsville, Indiana, the school has the fortune of being a member of a small community and not the hustle and bustle of the city. Students live in fraternities, dormitories and off-campus housing. Many of these residences owned by the school have been recently renovated and meet the specifications of the student in the year 2007. Some of our buildings are old; however, they have been fairly well maintained and continue to service our students' needs.

Current student, Biology, 8/2004-Submit Date, April 2007

The campus is small, and has 10 national fraternities located on it. All of the fraternities are going through renovation plans, with six of the 10 living in new or newly renovated houses and the other four in the plans for the same. All of the fraternities have their own dining rooms and hire cooks, hence the food is different depending upon the living unit. All independents eat at one dining facility, and the food is pretty good for cafeteria food. Independent living is not as new as Greek living, but every room on campus has phone, computer and cable lines for all the occupants of the rooms. Rooms are different depending upon the living unit, but most are fairly spacious.

Current student, Psychology, 8/2003-Submit Date, April 2007

The town of Crawfordsville is a Midwest industrial town, there is not a lot of crime and there is not a lot of things to do outside of campus. On campus the living situation is a little sticky right now. Our campus is 55 percent Greek life and 45 percent independent. This has changed from recent years, where the Greek life was more like 70 percent of the campus. Because of this issue, the independent living units are old and out of shape. [The school keeps] building these brand-new, magnificent fraternity houses that cost millions of dollars, while often times neglecting the outdated and over-cramped independent units. On campus, all fraternities have their own kitchen so they eat at their house. The independent students eat at the dining hall on campus, which is also outdated and cramped.

> **The school says:** "The fraternity building and renovation projects are part of a long-term, 10-year plan that started before current students arrived on campus and will continue for the next three years. Independent residence halls were renovated prior to the start of the fraternity renovation campaign, and one residence hall received a $2.4 million renovation this summer (2007) and is ready for occupancy this fall."

Current student, Rhetoric, 8/2003-Submit Date, April 2007

Wabash is extremely safe. In four years I have not heard of any type of violence on campus. Never have I been fearful of anything on campus. The small campus size makes that possible.

Current student, History, 8/2006-5/2010, April 2007

Wabash College is a school of about 870 students. Crawfordsville is a very small town of, I think, about [14,000] people, which is out in the middle of nowhere, so the town is very peaceful. The campus is only like three or four small city blocks wide. It is very small campus and it takes only five to 10 minutes to get anywhere on campus.

 ## Social Life

Current student, Biology, 8/2003-Submit Date, May 2007

The 10 national Greek fraternities provide a great deal of social life, along with the student senate-sponsored campus activities committee, which has recently hosted such acts as Lewis Black, Guster and OAR. Several local bars are within walking distance and offer drink specials to students, and for those who wish for a greater social scene, Purdue, Indiana, and the University of Indianapolis are all within an hour's drive.

Current student, Psychology, 8/2004-Submit Date, April 2007

Whenever I try to explain the social life of Wabash, I comment on three things: academics, sports and women. During the week academics and sports are all you have time for, and frankly there is not enough time. You read an average of five to eight hours a night and practice an average of two to four hours a day depending on the sport. This leaves no time for women, which is fine. We study hard and play harder! When the weekend rolls around, if you are not playing a sport then you are going to support and cheer. Then at night, the parties begin. What woman in her right mind wouldn't come to an all male school on the weekend? The odds are in her favor. The social life is amazing and the camaraderie even better. There are also weeks when we have additional parties during the weekdays, but the professors usually know that in advance and make papers due the week before. Amazing.

Current student, Visual Arts, 8/2003-5/2007, April 2007

Crawfordsville has several local bars to choose from, as well as many fast food restaurants. There are not many regular restaurants; however, local growth is promising.

Men who desire to pursue a relationship are typically able to meet women from nearby institutions. The college environment is largely conservative, but there is a small homosexual community.

The college sponsors many events, including a wide range of speakers, visiting artists, musical events, theatrical events and art displays. A large portion of the student government budget is spent on a nationally recognized musical act each semester or year.

Current student, Psychology, 8/2003-Submit Date, April 2007

Wabash is all male, so there is not a lot of dating that happens on campus. Purdue University, Butler University, DePauw University and Indiana University are all within an hour drive with some, like Purdue, being about 20 minutes away. So often many students go to another campus for at least one weekend night, usually Friday. Most students then return to campus on that Saturday and there are usually social events such as fraternity parties or national acts (usually concerts) or sporting events. There are not a lot of local bars that students go to, there are a couple local tavern-type places but mostly if a student wants to go out, he goes to another campus!

Current student, 8/2004-Submit Date, April 2006

There are numerous clubs that men can get involved in on campus. Plus, we only have one rule on campus and that is the Gentleman's Rule, no constitution or governing body or rules at all. We govern ourselves accordingly and act as gentlemen at all times on and off campus. We enforce these within ourselves and it has never been a problem since 1832.

 ## The School Says

Wabash College pursues its mission of educating men to think critically, act responsibly, lead effectively and live humanely in a residential liberal arts setting. The college of 870 students is small by choice, to better foster personal relationships between faculty and students. Alumni of Wabash are extremely loyal and involved in all areas of the college.

While Wabash's curriculum is strictly liberal arts in nature, the college offers a number of distinctive programs that allow students to augment their studies with experiential learning. Some of the programs include:

Immersion Learning Trips—Each year, over 100 Wabash men will travel around the world on Immersion Learning Trips. Tied directly to liberal arts coursework, the trips take students and professors to the source of the material being studied. Over the course of 10 days, completely immersed in the subject matter with faculty guiding every step, students emerge culturally enriched with a deeper appreciation for the subject. All expenses are paid by Wabash.

Summer Business Immersion Program—Each summer, 12 Wabash students spend eight weeks on campus learning all aspects of business, from creating a business plan to marketing and advertising products and services. Alumni and state business leaders provide instruction, while students simultaneously work on community business and marketing challenges. The capstone experience is a student's two-week experience working in a local business or industry. Students are chosen from a large applicant pool and are paid a generous stipend.

Collaborative Research—Each summer, many Wabash students remain on campus pursuing paid internships that allow them to work hand-in-hand with faculty doing cutting-edge research. Not only do students become involved in the work, but they are

Read all of Vault's College Surveys at **www.vault.com/college**—get complete surveys on 100s of colleges and universities, expert advice on applicaton essays and more.

VAULT CAREER LIBRARY   245

also partners in the research and are routinely published in national academic journals.

Lilly Endowment Indiana Internship Initiative—This year, 32 Wabash students participated in paid internships in businesses and nonprofit agencies across the State of Indiana. The eight-week program allowed students to apply the economics and liberal arts coursework in a real-world setting. Each participant received stipends ranging from $2,000 to $3,000 from Wabash.

Small Business Internships—Through the generous donation from an alumnus, Wabash students have the opportunity to work with small business owners and get paid a generous stipend for the experience. The alumnus believes concepts gathered in small business settings are applicable to business at the highest possible level.

Washington, D.C. Externship Program—Each spring, a carefully selected group of students are chosen to travel to Washington, D.C. to engage in an externship program hosted by Wabash alumni who work in business, law, politics, and public service. Students spend whole days with their alumni hosts and are often housed with the alumnus during the week-long experience.

Study Abroad—In addition to Immersion Learning Trips, each year about 25 percent of the college's junior class chooses to study abroad in traditional yearlong or semester-long programs.

Wabash men have studied in over 50 programs in 30 countries; the student's financial aid and scholarships travel with him.

Buena Vista University

Admissions Office
610 West Fourth Street
Storm Lake, IA 50588
Admissions phone: (800) 383-9600
Admissions e-mail: admissions@bvu.edu
Admissions URL: admissions.bvu.edu

Admissions

Current student, 2/2003-Submit Date, November 2004

The application required that I write an essay. A preview day was planned for me to check out the college and for them to meet me. We all stayed a night in the dorms before we even knew we were accepted. I love being here now because I have so many friends. My interview was very basic, not scary at all. The woman I chatted with made me feel like I was just chatting with my mother on the phone or something.

Alumnus/a, 9/2000-11/2002, November 2004

I had no problems getting into the school. I went to a school in the same conference for a year and all my credits transferred. It is easy as long as you keep everything organized and talk to the right people.

Alumnus/a, 9/2000-11/2002, September 2003

Admissions was easy. Getting my transcripts was a pain but I think that happens everywhere. I had pretty good grades before entering. I entered with a two-year AA degree.

Academics

Current student, 2/2003-Submit Date, November 2004

The professors are great to work with and if you don't like them there are many tutors at the college to help you out. I have been to the tutors myself and they are great. I love being here and learning as I have fun.

Alumnus/a, 9/2000-11/2002, November 2004

Classes were easy to get into. Class sizes are small so you get a lot of one-on-one attention. Grading was good—overall, I had one bad professor who liked to be a drill sergeant who gave me a B for an average of 96 percent.

Alumnus/a, 9/2000-11/2002, September 2003

I went to a center where they sent a professor each week. It was nice; the classes were very small. All of the students knew everyone's names, teachers included. Getting into classes was no problem. Grading was good; workload was fine.

Employment Prospects

Current student, 2/2003-Submit Date, November 2004

I am fitting in really well here and I think I know what I want to do when I graduate in four years because of my experience at my internship.

Alumnus/a, 9/2000-11/2002, September 2003

The college said they would help me find a job but I didn't need help, I started my own business. Internships were possible but I did not do one.

Quality of Life

Current student, 2/2003-Submit Date, November 2004

I live in a dorm on campus. It is a wonderful place but I wish the rooms were bigger. I know of some people who live off campus and they say that they wished they could live in the dorms so they wouldn't have to drive.

Alumnus/a, 9/2000-11/2002, November 2004

Everything was great. Campus felt safe. It's very beautiful with lots of labs and places to study. Dorm life was fun.

Alumnus/a, 9/2000-11/2002, September 2003

Life was good. Classes were at night so you could hold a full-time job and carry on with your normal life.

Social Life

Current student, 2/2003-Submit Date, November 2004

There is a bar in town that is called Malarkie's. It's fun but I like all the clubs and stuff on campus. There are over 1,000 clubs—maybe even more. I would like to join more of them but I just don't have the time with my studies and the clubs in which I am already involved. On the weekends they have exercise stuff to do, sports, movies, games, and even a game night when we all stay up and play board games and even Twister.

Alumnus/a, 9/2000-11/2002, November 2004

I am very sociable. I went to the bars and out to eat.

Alumnus/a, 9/2000-11/2002, September 2003

School was great. There weren't any clubs on campus. We would all meet for food after class sometimes.

The School Says

Buena Vista University offers a comprehensive educational adventure, balancing traditional liberal arts studies with innovative professional experiences. Founded in 1891 by the Presbyterian Church, U.S.A., the college has grown to an enrollment of approximately 1,300 undergraduate and graduate students on its main campus in Storm Lake, plus an additional 1,500 students at 15 branch sites throughout Iowa.

Several features set Buena Vista University apart from other colleges:

- A unique and welcoming campus in picturesque lakeside surroundings—our 60-acre campus is situated on the shores of beautiful Storm Lake, a 3,200-acre natural lake in the northwest Iowa city of Storm Lake, population 10,000. The university is dedicated to providing the best educational facilities in the region, including the $9.5 million Lamberti Recreation Center and the $26 million Estelle Siebens Science Center.

- A nationally recognized leader in innovation—in 2000, BVU became the first truly wireless community in the nation. We provide our students with their own notebook computers and wireless Internet access, allowing them to go online anytime, from anywhere on campus. This not only puts a world of information at their fingertips, but also enhances their learning opportunities both

Read all of Vault's College Surveys at www.vault.com/college—get complete surveys on 100s of colleges and universities, expert advice on applicaton essays and more.

VAULT CAREER LIBRARY 247

in and out of the classroom, giving them the skills they need to compete in today's global economy.

- A distinguished teaching faculty provides students with practical academic experiences that lead to meaningful careers and lives—with a balance between traditional liberal arts courses and innovative experiential learning opportunities that require the practical application of knowledge, the BVU curriculum prepares students for successful careers in their fields of study. Quality, personalized teaching is emphasized and recognized at BVU.

- A dedicated and caring community of learners committed to preparation for a life of service—by integrating service-learning opportunities into the academic curriculum, providing volunteer opportunities in the co-curricular program, and fostering a culture of respect, equity, fairness and collaboration, BVU honors its founding motto, "Education for Service," and prepares students for leadership and service in their communities.

- Access to high-quality educational programs for adult learners throughout Iowa and beyond—for over 30 years, the BVU Centers program has offered students of all ages the opportunity to complete their education at 15 campus sites located throughout the state. BVU's Graduate Program allows working teachers the opportunity to obtain a master's degree while balancing family life and career. BVU also offers an online bachelor's degree completion program in business administration.

- The Buena Vista University curriculum is designed to produce graduates who are prepared to live responsibly and joyfully, fulfilling their promise as individual humans as well as their obligations as citizens of a global community. Our bold vision of what an education should be is creating bright futures for BVU students.

Cornell College

Office of Admission
600 First Street SW
Mount Vernon, IA 52314-1098
Admissions phone: (800) 747-1112 or (319) 895-4477
Admissions fax: (319) 895-4451
Admissions e-mail: admission@cornellcollege.edu
Admissions URL: cornellcollege.edu/admissions/

 ## Admissions

Current student, Social Sciences, 9/2006-Submit Date, June 2007

The admissions office was the most dedicated and persistent office with which I worked. I had multiple in-depth phone conversations with my representative, which eventually persuaded me to make a trek to visit the school. Once here, I saw the dedication of the admissions office in action throughout the entire campus. The community is unique in making one comfortable while on campus as well as offering many resources to access vast amounts of information about the school.

> The school says: "The Office of Admission offers opportunities to communicate with current students, faculty and staff. Students may customize their campus visit through an individual appointment or attend a Preview Day."

Alumnus/a, Psychology, 9/2003-6/2007, June 2007

Cornell is a fairly selective school and the average ACT score is rising each year. They do not give out sports scholarships; however, almost all students who attend the school receive some sort of scholarship money either for academics or a specific discipline. One thing to note when going into an interview is to stand out from the others interviewees. Personally, when my interview was conducted, I had recently cut 17 inches off my hair, donated and dyed it and told my interviewers thus. He was so taken aback by how excited I was to have done that (in addition to good interview in general) that I won a full tuition scholarship because he remembered me and something interesting about me, as well.

> Cornell College says: "Each year, Cornell reviews approximately 3,000 applications to fill the 360-student first-year class. The middle 50 percent of ACT scores for admitted applicants is 24 to 30; 1150 to 1350 for SAT scores. Approximately one-third of admitted students are offered an academic scholarship,

which range from $10,000 to $20,000 per year. 80 percent of students are awarded need-or merit-based financial assistance.

Alumnus/a, Biology, 9/2002-12/2005, June 2007

Cornell College is a fairly selective school. I would definitely recommend interviewing with an admissions counselor even though it is optional. The essay is extremely important: Make sure it contains no errors and that you have placed a lot of thought into it before submitting the application.

> Regarding interviews, the school says: "An admissions interview is not required, although the admissions staff attempts to interview every applicant for admission. Interviews are offered on campus and off campus in more than 40 metropolitan areas each year and others are conducted by phone."

Alumnus/a, Biology, 8/1999-6/2003, June 2007

Cornell's admissions process was very easy. I applied using the Common Application, which meant I didn't have to spend extra time personalizing my application. I had to interview on campus for my full scholarship, though they no longer use the interview process to select recipients. Throughout the process the admissions office was very friendly and more than willing to provide any information I needed to help me decide whether Cornell was right for me. My graduating class included many very talented individuals, and the school is working toward becoming more selective as the number of applicants increases.

Alumnus/a, Mathematics, 8/2003-6/2007, June 2007

The admissions process is very personal, and the staff is wonderfully friendly. Many of the admissions counselors are recent alumni who can offer detailed, helpful insight into all aspects of life at Cornell. An interview is not required, but may be helpful in assessing whether the school is a good fit for the student, more like an interview conducted by the student rather than by the admissions staff, but it may soon be required as the school is becoming increasingly selective.

Advice on getting in: Demonstrate that you are a motivated student in and out of the classroom. Cornell has a strong academic program but is also a vibrant community of talented students active on campus, in the community, and across the country. Most importantly, though, be honest with yourself and with the admissions staff in your evaluation of whether you would be happy and successful at Cornell.

Alumnus/a, English, 8/2003-6/2007, June 2007

The only reason I applied to Cornell was because they waived the application fee and gave me a free T-shirt; I had all ready been accepted to my school of choice and thought a free T-shirt was pretty cool. I was extremely candid in my application, especially in the essay where I choose to respond to the question of what literary character has had the greatest impact on me (Charlie Brown!). Since I wasn't planning on going to Cornell I felt no stress about having to show what an amazing person I was. Ironically the silly essay that showed my true personality is exactly what Cornell wanted and their persistence at my attending their school convinced me to go. I realized that the school I had initially planned on going to only accepted me because I pretended to be something I wasn't; Cornell knew who I was from the very beginning and they liked it!

Alumnus/a, Physics, 8/2003-6/2007, June 2007

The admissions process when I applied was a bit unique, and if you did it by a certain date, there was no application fee. Honestly, this was one of the major draws for me, as my parents weren't willing to pay for anything at the time, and Cornell seemed like a good school. I sent in my application, and heard back within two weeks that not only had I gotten in, but also that I received a very large scholarship. I would recommend that anyone who is applying to Cornell uses the Common Application, as it makes it much easier to apply to more than one place, especially since this is becoming a much more accepted application at higher ranked schools.

Alumnus/a, Biology, 8/2003-6/2007, June 2007

Admissions made itself fairly accessible to me, including two meetings in my area with my admissions counselor. Acceptance to Cornell has never been only for the elite, and lower matriculation in recent years has allowed most students admission. But the better applicants receive large scholarships so it is definitely worthwhile to put together a good application. Generally, test scores and grades are used as guidelines in admission criteria and scholarships, but the writing samples and person-to-person discussions seemed much more of a basis for the big decisions. Admissions is well-organized, and they work hard to get the students they want.

Alumnus/a, Biology, 8/2003-6/2007, June 2007

The school does a great job of examining the person as a whole. It looks at what the student has to offer, and makes a calculated decision about the student. While standardized tests do matter, they are not the top priority. Interviews are very casual and because I know the school is still fairly selective, I feel very proud of myself for just being admitted.

 # Academics

Alumnus/a, Sociology, 9/2001-5/2005, June 2007

Cornell provides a rich academic experience. Cornell's class schedule is One-Class-At-A-Time (OCAAT). Students take one class for 18 class days, or three and a half weeks. After each class there is a four-day weekend and on the following Monday you begin a new class. I loved learning in this environment! The classes are very hands-on and no class has more than 25 students. The small class size and OCAAT provide an opportunity to really get to know your professors. Professors do an awesome job at making themselves available to students. The workload can be heavy because you are completing a semester's worth of material in 18 days, but it is also manageable.

Alumnus/a, Psychology, 9/2003-6/2007, June 2007

A few of the things that students love about Cornell are the small, intimate class sizes and the open communication with professors. Classes are capped at 25 students and none of them are taught by TAs. Most professors prefer to be called by their first names and several even give out their home phone numbers for any students who may find trouble with their work after class hours. Workload and class time often depend on the class (math, sciences, and foreign languages usually have four to five hours of class time per day while philosophy, religion and English often only have two); there is usually between one and five hours of homework a night, averaging about two to three. Sometimes highly popular classes are difficult to get, but all students have equal opportunity to attempt getting into classes, with the exception of some seniors. There is a bid system in place granting each student 90 points to distribute amongst his/her nine classes and the highest bidders of each class may enroll until it is full. This system generally works well with few exceptions and most students can finish double majors within four years.

Current student, Psychology, 8/2004-Submit Date, June 2007

The quality of each class is from good to outstanding. The classes are small and the professors not only post their office hours on the syllabus but give you their home phone number if you need something when you are working on a paper at 11 p.m. at night.

Alumnus/a, English, 8/2004-6/2007, June 2007

It's fairly difficult to compare Cornell's academics to those of any other institution. The One-Course-At-A-Time schedule allows students to be very focused on a single subject, but at the same time, find easy ways to connect the subject to related fields. I would say that Cornell's humanities classes were a heavier workload than some students might be used to only because of the condensed schedule. At the same time, I felt that this setup allowed a much more intimate connection to the work and more open atmosphere in the classroom.

Alumnus/a, Biology, 6/2001-5/2005, June 2007

I loved OCAAT. I wouldn't have done college any other way. It allowed me to travel, study and work in Bolivia, the country where my father was born and raised. Although I was a biology major, I loved the fact that I was able to take a variety of classes, like Anthropology. OCAAT isn't easy—you have to be able to stay on top of things. Grades are not just handed to you because the professors know how rigorous OCAAT is. The workload depends on the class—upper-level science classes require more time in the lab and classroom while some anthropology classes only meet in the mornings because of the amount of reading.

Alumnus/a, Cultural Studies, 9/2003-6/2007, June 2007

The BA program has several general requirements; however, they are left open for the student to decide how to fulfill these requirements. Four humanities courses, two social science courses, a writing course, two science courses, and a foreign language requirement comprise the general requirements. A Cornell student needs 32 course credits to graduate; 21 of these must be outside one specific major field, ensuring that a broad liberal arts education is achieved. The classes are of the highest quality mainly because the professors are so passionate about teaching in their fields, and teaching in a system which fosters extended discussion and critical thinking. Getting into courses is relatively easy; students are usually able to enroll in their desired courses. The professors are extremely fair yet challenging when it comes to grading and workloads. I have found that professors who assign a great amount of work usually teach you the most, and I have found that I come out of that class having gained far more knowledge than in other classes with less challenging workloads.

Alumnus/a, Biology, 8/2003-6/2007, June 2007

Cornell's academics are well suited to its student body. The brightest students can find a challenge in many courses while being a "big fish in a small pond." These students can often find work doing summer research and projects with professors. At the same time, profs are very accessible to all students who desire one-on-one attention. While professors direct their efforts in a "teach-to-the-top" fashion, students who struggle academically are able to maintain reasonable grades and derive a great deal from courses. Many courses maintain smaller sizes of 10 to 15 students, but the more popular majors consistently find courses at or over cap. The workload is generally determined by the amount of effort students wish to apply: a 4.0 requires a great deal of work, but a 3.5-3.75 can be attained with substantially less effort.

Current student, Education, 9/2004-Submit Date, April 2007

In my experience, I would say that Cornell has a wide range of classes. There are some classes that keep students working on homework, papers, projects and so on all day every day, and there are others that give students a great deal of free time. Grading is more or less even across the board; I have never been in a situation of unfair grading or had professors grade wildly different than others. It is fairly easy to get into popular classes because of our add/drop process. Also, if students want to take a class that is full, professors can sign them in.

Read all of Vault's College Surveys at **www.vault.com/college**–get complete surveys on 100s of colleges and universities, expert advice on applicaton essays and more.

VAULT CAREER LIBRARY **249**

Employment Prospects

Alumnus/a, Biology, 8/2003-Submit Date, June 2007

Cornell has a great new internship program called the Cornell Fellows Program, which provides high-level internship opportunities solely for Cornell students. Several students have been successful getting job offers from the companies where they completed their fellowships. I personally completed a fellowship at the Translational Genomics Research Institute, where the individuals with whom I worked encouraged me to come back to the company after graduation, though I turned them down to attend a doctoral program. Several of my friends have had great luck getting into medical school and other graduate programs. Other friends who are trying to find jobs seem to be having less luck and don't seem to be well-prepared to apply for jobs. If asked, professors on campus can be a great resource for connecting students to alumni and other contacts who may be able to provide job opportunities. My fiancée was able to find multiple job opportunities though a Cornell professor in his major department.

Current student, Social Sciences, 9/2006-Submit Date, June 2007

The school has developed many programs to help equip students for success after leaving campus. The alumni office works diligently with students before they even leave so that they feel a strong connection to their alma mater once they do graduate. The Cornell Young Alumni (CYA) program works with students within the first 10 years of graduation through supporting local alumni chapters and sponsoring parties for people to gather. The Engagement Program offers fellowships for students to experience a variety of fields from government to nonprofits, to marketing and many more. Career Services offers services in internships (which often count for academic credit) and externships (mini-internships over spring break).

Alumnus/a, Sociology, 9/2001-5/2005, June 2007

Cornell has a program called Cornell Fellows. Students apply to be placed with specific companies, organizations and agencies. These prestigious companies, organizations and agencies have developed a relationship with the college and the fellowships are competitive. I moved to Arizona after graduation and although most employers had not heard of Cornell College, they were impressed with my public speaking, problem solving and communication skills! I thank Cornell for giving me those skills! Many students go on from Cornell to obtain post-graduate degrees; others work in the field they studied at Cornell.

> **The school says:** "Cornell College annually awards 30 to 40 Cornell Fellowships. These are funded, high-profile internships. Any Cornell student may utilize the block plan to arrange a meaningful internship experience essentially wherever his/her interest would best be served, in a national or international location."

Alumnus/a, Psychology, 9/2003-6/2007, June 2007

Employment prospects upon graduation are generally good, depending on how much effort is put forth beforehand. There are internships and work-related programs available for credit and students sometimes obtain full-time employment with these companies after graduation. Job fairs, alumni services and networks, and career counseling are also readily available to students. Additionally, many students continue on to graduate school immediately following their undergraduate work.

> **Cornell College says:** "Approximately two-thirds of Cornell graduates complete a double major or a major and a minor. Through the college's multi-faceted undergraduate research, internship and off-campus study programs, graduates can offer substantial résumés to graduate schools and employers."

Current student, Biology, 8/2004-Submit Date, June 2007

Cornell graduates have very few problems finding employment after their years at Cornell. Our graduates are very attractive to potential employers and from what I've seen, alumni can be very helpful in this process. Internships are great on the block plan. Instead of taking time away from multiple classes, students at Cornell can devote their entire day for the whole block to working at an internship.

 ## Quality of Life

Alumnus/a, Psychology, 9/2003-6/2007, June 2007

The quality of life at Cornell is great for students who are seeking a smaller school that contains a close-knit community. Almost all students live on campus all four years of their schooling ranging from traditional college dorms to college-owned suites and apartments. Since the campus is fairly small, most students are within a 10-minute maximum walk (usually closer to two to five minutes) from each other. Although some of the facilities (including both housing and academic buildings) are historic, old, and somewhat rundown, there are others that have been built during this past year. While living together builds a close community, so does eating together. Since the class schedules are essentially the same for all students (9 to 11 a.m., 1 to 3 p.m.), the cafeteria is open for lunch for a one-and-a-half hour period during which the majority of students dine. The cafeteria has been recently renovated (and will continue receiving renovations in the near future) and has had dramatic improvements in the past three years. With such a close and trusting community, most students feel entirely safe both on campus and off. The grounds are well-lit, the dorms are locked in the evenings and campus safety employees will provide an escort to whoever calls for one.

Alumnus/a, Biology, 6/2001-5/2005, June 2007

I never felt unsafe at Cornell. I would stay up late studying and then take midnight runs through downtown without ever feeling threatened. The college is in a very nice, friendly town with people who are really interested in every Cornell student. I was involved in the Adopt a Student Program, where the local Catholic church had a Cornell student over for dinner. I ended up being the family's babysitter and still talk to them today.

Alumnus/a, Environment, 8/2002-6/2006, June 2007

The Town of Mount Vernon is relatively quiet and very safe feeling. It is a small town with a more traditional development plan. You can walk to everything you might need (groceries, pharmacy, bank, post office, doctor, dentist and so on). This is a huge plus for living in Mount Vernon. On-campus quality of life is average to above average. The housing is good, and new dorms are being opened most every year, providing students with more options. I always felt taken care of, though the food could use an upgrade.

Current student, Education, 9/2004-Submit Date, April 2007

Although our dorms are old, living in the dorms is generally a pleasant experience. There is a variety of different dorm cultures, so students are able to find the dorm that fits their interests best. Cornell seems like it does not have crime—there is of course crime on campus, but it is at a very low rate and students feel quite safe here. The dining service is the worst part about Cornell. There are few appetizing options available and there are days when students eat cereal for both meals because there is nothing else even remotely appealing. Being a vegetarian on campus is particularly challenging because the dining service does not offer a wide enough variety of protein options.

> **Regarding dining options, the school says:** "Within the past year the cafeteria, located in The Commons, has been completely renovated. In addition, dining options have been enhanced in direct response to student feedback. A vegetarian option is provided at each meal."

Current student, Social Sciences, 9/2003-Submit Date, April 2007

The campus is historic, and because it is in a small town, crime is nearly nonexistent. Housing is mostly dorm-style, though other options are growing. It is a residential campus, meaning that only a select few seniors can live off campus. Facilities are kept in good condition, and the college is constantly improving the existing facilities.

 ## Social Life

Current student, Social Sciences, 9/2006-Submit Date, June 2007

The school offers New Student Orientation as an immediate way to make friends and become familiar with other new students as well as student leaders. After this, though, if you are not one to party, it can be difficult to find quality relationships. After spending time feeling it out, though, you can find a group with which you feel close. Through all of this, it is clear that the school does have many cliques. Going to meals seems more like high school than high school itself. Dating in campus happens, but it is hard to find someone when there is such a small campus to choose from. There are many events on campus, although you need to make an effort to understand what is going on. Student senate does a great job of supporting the interests of students through funding. Greeks make up around one-third of campus and are viewed differently by everyone. There are no national affiliations for the groups, which means each group has total control. Since the school is in such a small community, there is not a lot to do. Drinking tends to be a student favorite on the weekend. There are three bars downtown but they only serve the purpose of drinking, not a place to dance or party. If you want to do something, the best option is to go to Iowa City.

Alumnus/a, Sociology, 9/2001-5/2005, June 2007

Cornell student life is very vibrant! Cornell has about 1,100 students, because of the small size, students know one another and take interest in athletics, music, theatre and student organizations programming. All concerts, athletic events, plays, art shows and other events that take place on campus are covered by tuition and students are not charged admission fees. About one-third of Cornell students participate in Greek life and Greek life is a large part of Cornell's social scene. All fraternities and sororities are local, not national. There are a few fast food restaurants and pizza places in town. There is also a fine dining restaurant in Mount Vernon called the Lincoln Cafe; it is one of the best restaurants in Eastern Iowa. There are several bars on Main Street in Mount Vernon and on the weekends the bars are full of students. Even though Mt. Vernon is very small, it has a bowling alley and movie theatre. Iowa City (home to the University of Iowa) and Cedar Rapids are both less than half an hour away from Cornell. Iowa City and Cedar Rapids have many bars, restaurants and clubs.

Alumnus/a, Psychology, 9/2003-6/2007, June 2007

There are plenty of social activities and places to go, both on and off campus at Cornell. On campus, there are several fraternities and sororities that have parties and events for both members and non-members. There are also certain organizations on campus, such as PAAC and Dark Purple, which are geared towards on-campus entertainment. PAAC (Performing Arts and Activities Council) invites speakers, artists and musicians and organizes their own events ,such as Casino Night and Bowling Night, at Cornell and in the surrounding towns. Dark Purple hosts late-night events, specifically aimed at non-drinkers, such as Night Games and late night movies. There are an additional 70+ organizations that range anywhere from lacrosse to math club and more can be created when someone's interests are not included. Although it's a small town, there is still plenty to do in Mount Vernon. Some favorite bars are Northside and Chameleon's and students can be found at either of these places any day of the week. The Lincoln Cafe is a well-known and delicious local restaurant where people can head for a nice meal before catching a family-friendly show at the Bijou theatre and heading to Fuel, the favored coffee shop. And if nothing peaks interest from these options, Cedar Rapids and Iowa City are larger college towns just 25 minutes away. Students can find just about anything they're looking for either on campus, in town or nearby.

The School Says

As a nationally acclaimed four-year, private liberal arts college, Cornell College's distinctive One-Course-At-A-Time (OCAAT) academic calendar provides extraordinary opportunities in the classroom, on campus and around the world.

Located on a wooded hilltop in Mount Vernon, Iowa, Cornell has been grounded in the liberal arts since 1853. Our academic program is built around OCAAT, also called the block plan. Instead of taking multiple courses simultaneously, students immerse themselves in one subject for three and a half weeks. In an academic year, students can take up to nine of these "blocks" on a range of subjects—essentially one course each month from September to May. Each course counts as one credit, but is the equivalent of four-credit hours at a semester-based school. It takes 32 credits, or an average of eight courses per year, to graduate in four years.

Typically, more than 95 percent of Cornell graduates complete their degree requirements in four years or less; the majority finish with a major and a minor, if not a double major. Two-thirds of Cornell graduates pursue graduate school in medicine, law, business or education. Cornell's academic rigor is further reflected in the fact that we are one of just 270 colleges with a chapter of Phi Beta Kappa, the nation's oldest scholastic honorary society.

At Cornell, classes are small—averaging 16 students—and a professor (not a graduate assistant) will help you explore a single academic subject. Faculty members only teach one course per block, so you will have their full attention. In fact, we believe the level of one-on-one interaction between our faculty and students is unparalleled among other top colleges and universities in the nation. Students choose from more than 40 majors and one-of-a-kind pre-professional programs, including Dimensions for pre-medical and health professionals; the Berry Center for Economics, Business and Public Policy studies; pre-law; and more. Or you can design your own major.

OCAAT's flexibility allows our students to engage in courses, high-profile internships, and programs that travel out of state or overseas for a week or even a month without worrying about missing other classes. Many of our students study overseas in two or three locations and still graduate in four years.

Cornell's student body of about 1,150 comes from almost all 50 states and dozens of different countries. Almost all of our students live on campus, which is listed entirely on the National Register of Historic Places. More than half of our students are involved in the performing arts, two-thirds in service projects, and about one-third in athletics. Cornell competes in 19 sports as part of the NCAA Division III, ranking among the Top 15 colleges in NCAA Postgraduate Scholars. And we have more than 125 student-run organizations and activities.

Loren Pope's "Colleges that Change Lives" and "Beyond the Ivy League" feature Cornell among the country's best colleges. And *The New York Times* named the college one of 20 "stealth powerhouses." Cornell also is annually recognized in such college guides as *Barron's*, *Insider's Guide*, and *The Princeton Review*.

Read all of Vault's College Surveys at **www.vault.com/college**–get complete surveys on 100s of colleges and universities, expert advice on applicaton essays and more.

VAULT CAREER LIBRARY **251**

Grinnell College

Office of Admission
John Chrystal Center, 2nd floor
1103 Park St.
Grinnell College
Grinnell, IA 50112
Admission phone: (800) 247-0113 or (641) 269-3600
Admission fax: (641) 269-4800
Admission e-mail: askgrin@grinnell.edu
Admission URL: www.grinnell.edu/admission/

 Admissions

Current student, 8/2003-Submit Date, May 2006

Grinnell is a highly-selective school, and since it was named the best overall college by *Newsweek* [in 2004], there are now more and more applicants every year, and the SAT/ACT scores keep rising. To get into Grinnell, high school record is a very important factor, besides standardized tests, extracurricular activities and essays. Grinnell treats all the prospective students (we give them the nickname of prospies) on an individual basis. The overnight stay program offers them the opportunity to shadow a current student, live in the student dorms, have individualized campus tours, go to classes and meet with professors and staff. Grinnell also offers interviews abroad with alumni. It's really easy to find someone to talk to when you are abroad. In recent years, Grinnell has been trying to promote more diversity by recruiting more students of color in the incoming class, and [Grinnell offers great financial assistance].

Current student, 9/2002-Submit Date, May 2006

The admissions office at Grinnell is staffed with the nicest and most helpful college employees at any institution with which I had contact during the college application process. Since I was applying from half-way across the country, it was very helpful for them to set me up with an interview with alumni with whom I could talk about Grinnell [so that I wouldn't have to come to campus.] After I was admitted, Grinnell offered wonderful accepted student weekends. They were great about transportation from the airport and setting me up with two great hosts. There were lots of informative and recreational activities on that weekend and I had a great time, which convinced me to come to Grinnell College!

Current student, 9/2004-Submit Date, April 2006

As a liberal arts school, Grinnell College views students as a whole person, and tries to select students from a variety of backgrounds. The school is very selective and Grinnell applicants are typically academically driven and have a strong high school record in addition to extracurricular interests. Grinnell accepts the Common Application and the admissions staff is very friendly and welcoming to students.

Current student, 8/2003-Submit Date, April 2006

Grinnell has very high standards for who they admit, both academically and from a social consciousness perspective. They look for students who are not exclusively bookworms but rather those who have shown commitment to community involvement—Grinnell is a residential campus and has a long history of social activism. The admissions process for me was interesting because I applied as part of the Posse Program. However, all applicants are required to write essays and send in letters of recommendations along with transcripts and such. The interview process is optional but highly encouraged.

Current student, 8/2002-Submit Date, May 2004

I applied to Grinnell using the online Common Application. This simplified the application process for me, because I was applying to a number of different schools. I visited campus twice and spoke to admissions counselors, who were a great help in establishing Grinnell as my school of choice. I recommend staying a night at the school to get a feel for the social atmosphere and the student life in general, but don't stick with your host the whole time. Go do your own thing and meet lots of people, so that you can get lots of information about the school. Grinnellians are very positive toward prospective students and are more than willing to tell you all about the school.

Current student, 8/2002-Submit Date, February 2004

Grinnell College was helpful throughout the admissions process. They were receptive to my questions and offered an admissions fee waiver. My application included slides and essays on why I was specifically interested in a liberal arts education. Grinnell is fairly selective. Academic performance in high school as well as test scores and extracurricular activities are taken into account. For students who have performed strong academically in high school, Grinnell generously offers scholarships. It is one of the few need-blind schools that offers to meet every student's [institutionally determined need] while offering merit aid.

> **The school says:** "50 percent of the admission decision is based on the quality and performance of a students high school curriculum, 25 percent of the decision is based on an ACT or new SAT and 25 percent based on co-curriculars, teacher recommendations, the essay and the interview (optional)."

 Academics

Current student, 8/2003-Submit Date, May 2006

Admittedly, Grinnell requires hard work. The workload is not all that overwhelming, but professors have very high expectations and really work hard to engage all the students. The quality of classes is amazing, and with a [1:9] faculty to student ratio students get a lot of personal attention and personal contact with the professors. Most professors make themselves really available and some would invite students to their homes for meals or an afternoon tea chat. Popular classes are not usually hard to get into, since there are many interesting classes available and students have a variety of interests. All classes are taught by professors, no TAs, and they are all engaged in both teaching and research. It is very common to do research with a professor in his/her field of expertise during the semester, and there are different independent studies or mentored project programs available during the summer, in which students get a stipend and the great experience of research. Some students will have the opportunity to be a co-author with the professor in published journals. There is a scholars convocation every Thursday morning. Also lots of programs sponsor seminars (in almost every department, including science departments that offer weekly seminars, bringing scientists engaged in cutting-edge researches to campus). With endless resources, the wonderful facilities, professors and staff and alumni, Grinnell offers the most amazing academic experience one can ever imagine. Or if you want to study abroad, Grinnell has many connections and encourages students to participate in the off-campus programs all around the world.

Current student, 8/2002-Submit Date, May 2006

I've never been shut out of a class. I've always gotten the classes I wanted, though not always the section. The classes are of superb quality. They vary from lecture-based to discussion-based although introductory courses do tend to involve more lectures. The average class size for introductory classes is 25, and for non-intro classes, the mean is 20. The largest class I ever had was an Introduction to Economics course taught by the most popular professor of economics. The class had 55 students and the professor knew everyone's name in a week or two. The smallest class I've had was a five-person chemistry class, although I also did a senior thesis where both (two) of my advisors met with me on a weekly basis; so you could say that I had a one-person class with two professors. A senior thesis or project is not required by the college, but some majors do require such a course. In fact, the college has no requirements at all (i.e., no core curriculum or distribution requirements) except that everyone has to take a [first-year] tutorial in their first semester. Over the summer, incoming first years submit their top five choices for tutorials out of roughly 30 choices. Tutorials range from the History of Baseball, to a course focusing on the works of Tom Stoppard, to a course taught by the genetics professor on the consequences of genetically modified foods. A major has to be declared by the end of one's second year, but, of course, you can always change majors. Students may study abroad junior year or first-semester senior year. Roughly 55 percent of our students study abroad at some point, and typically only for a semester.

The professors at Grinnell are wonderful. Generally, they are supportive, understanding and helpful. However, the professors tend to grade harshly. The current opinion on campus is that Grinnell has less grade inflation than many of our peer institutions. Professors do not have qualms about giving a student a C, or even failing a student, although it is hard to fail a course at Grinnell if you are trying because the professors and academic advising give students a lot of support. Additionally, while Grinnellians are competitive internally, we all strive and work very hard to do the best we possibly can academically, we are not competitive with other students. Typically, I find that I have so much to do, that I can only afford to go out one night per weekend and that I spend the other night studying simply because I'm so busy. While I think that's typical of most students, I could also cut back on activities and have more free time.

Current student, 9/2002-Submit Date, May 2006

Grinnell is an academically rigorous institution, something on which we pride ourselves. Professors expect a lot from their students, but they also provide a plethora of resources to get help. Additionally, the small class sizes allow for lots of contact with professors, which pretty much every professor I have had, loves to do. Professors are here to teach, more than to research, which is great for students. Because professors expect a lot from their students, getting A's is not always to be expected. But professors are not unreasonable, and when an A is deserved, you will get one. Another important thing about academics at Grinnell is that students love to learn. It is often hard to separate the classroom from the student. Students engage in discussion about their academics outside of the classroom and are interested in learning through lectures and other venues outside of the classroom.

Current student, 8/2004-Submit Date, May 2006

The academic program at Grinnell is extremely difficult. Professors expect a lot out of their students, and as a result students have a very large workload but also end up gaining a lot from their classes. Professors are difficult, but always helpful and happy to meet with their students. In such a small town, it is hard for the professors to go too far away, so they are almost always available to the students. As a second year, I've dined at about three professors' houses so far. Grading is very subjective, depending on the nature of the professor. I have never been denied a class that I wanted.

Current student, 8/2003-Submit Date, November 2004

Generally, grading is very hard. The workload is very intense; you are definitely here to learn something. Classes are great because they are all small, and you get lots of attention from your professors. The only drawback is that professors will know if you skip a class. It's not too hard to get into the popular classes, the only problem comes with fitting them into your schedule. So if you are planning to do a double major or with a concentration, do plan at least two years ahead, since some courses are only offered in alternate years. If you are a science student, you will be very happy here, since you will get grants and funds for projects you propose to do. You will get professor's personal attention and supervision and instruction on your projects. I think this is unique about Grinnell because the college has one of the top endowments and only focuses on undergraduate students. So as a college student, you will have the opportunity to develop some very precious research experiences.

Current student, 8/2002-Submit Date, February 2004

Academics at Grinnell are amazing. After four semesters I have yet to have a class with more than 26 students. The majority of my classes have been with 16 students or less. I've gotten to know all of my professors pretty well and have been to several of their houses.

Grinnell is a very demanding school. If you are taking a full courseload of 16 credits or more, expect to be working late into the nights. Professors, while expecting a lot, are generally very understanding. They are often willing to offer extensions, as long as they know that students are not taking advantage of their permissiveness. I've had some amazing professors. The best are more geared toward teaching than research—they are also the ones, for some odd reason, who produce the most interesting research. Certain professors have naturally gained a strong reputation and therefore have the most popular classes. One class I

took, History of U.S. Immigration, had about 50 sign up for a class whose maximum was 25. If students e-mail the professors prior to preregistration and claim true interest, the professors often let them in the class.

Grinnell offers many research opportunities for students. Students can do additional independent research related to a course they're taking (a "plus-2"), as well as independent readings, summer research, or mentor advised projects (MAPs), where they work one-on-one with a faculty advisor to create a thesis-level production. Sciences are topnotch, and the majors often brag about the facilities. Other departments are generally very strong, especially history and Russian. Grinnell recently renovated the arts building and has state-of-the-art performance facilities and a fabulous art gallery. Every two years Grinnell offers a course where students curate a professional gallery showing. We are currently working on setting up an exhibit for an entire set of Francisco Goya's Disasters of War prints. The academics were probably what most drew me to Grinnell. I feel challenged every day and at the same time feel supported by my peers and professors.

 ## Employment Prospects

Current student, 8/2003-Submit Date, May 2006

While about 30 percent of Grinnell students go straight to grad school, making Grinnell one of the biggest grad school feeders, a lot of students choose to work in many different professions. The incredible alumni network offers externships (where you shadow a successful alum for a week) starting your first year. Students can also get a $2,400 grant from Grinnell for the summer internships if the company does not pay. On-campus recruiting brings companies from New York, Chicago and many other big cities to campus every year for the seniors.

Current student, 8/2002-Submit Date, May 2006

Grinnell does a great job of helping students with their post-collegiate careers. 80 percent of Grinnellians go on to graduate school within five years. 30 percent do some type of service work. We have the highest enrollment in the Peace Corps per capita, Grinnellians do really well in Teach for America, and Grinnell even runs its own Peace Corps-esque program called Grinnell Corps. The Career Development Office also has a bunch of internships for students to do over the summer, so most Grinnellians graduate with the real work experience for which employers look. As a senior, I've found that most of my peers have gotten their top choice for whatever it is they want to do after graduation. A bunch of students are going abroad to teach English, while others are going off to law school, medical school and other things.

Alumnus/a, 8/2002-12/2005, April 2006

Grinnell is well known for its network of alumni, and it makes efforts to maintain this network. If you don't already know someone from Grinnell in a place to which you're moving, the alumni department will find someone and put you in contact with him/her to help you find a job and a place to live.

Grinnell is not as widely known as it likes to think it is, but it has a very good reputation among those people who have heard of it. It's kind of hit or miss. There is some recruiting on campus, but not a whole lot; Grinnell seems mostly geared to prepare its graduates for more academic work, rather than entering the workforce. Mock interviews and career advising are offered, but don't expect the campus to be crawling with Microsoft recruiters.

Current student, 8/2002-Submit Date, May 2004

Grinnell has many career opportunities available in the Career Development Office. This office assists with résumé writing and making connections in the field of the student's interest. Having spoken with a number of Grinnell alumni, I have found that graduates from Grinnell go on to pursue exciting and rewarding careers in a number of different areas, from documentary film making to Peace Corps to presidents of other colleges.

Current student, 8/2002-Submit Date, February 2004

About 50 percent of the student body works immediately after Grinnell. The rest either do volunteer programs, such as Peace Corps or Teach for America, or go on to graduate school. As a student, I can only speak of experience with internship opportunities. I recently sought out an internship with one of the best-known architecture and town planning firms in the nation. The firm recognized

Read all of Vault's College Surveys at www.vault.com/college–get complete surveys on 100s of colleges and universities, expert advice on applicaton essays and more.

VAULT CAREER LIBRARY 253

Grinnell and offered me an internship. Grinnell offers grant programs where students like myself can apply for grants to go along with my internship. I am currently applying for $2,400 through the college, the maximum allowed. The Career Development Office is very helpful. They list job and internship opportunities throughout the year.

Quality of Life

Current student, 8/2003-Submit Date, May 2006

The campus is an incredibly safe place, as is the town of Grinnell. Students get to pick their rooms and roommates starting the second year, and seniors have the option to live off campus. There are language houses available, hosting seven to 10 people each, where students can apply to live if they want to practice the language with native speakers, who are at Grinnell for the teaching exchange program, or with fellow students who are also interested in the language. There are also themed houses available, such as music houses and international gourmet houses. All the facilities are user-friendly and very convenient. The town relationship is great, too.

Current student, 9/2002-Submit Date, May 2006

The campus has first-class facilities in every regard and currently a great deal of expansion is occurring, which means within the next 10 years the campus will have a number of brand-new, beautiful facilities including a centralized dining hall and campus center, and an expanded science center and athletic center. As part of a small town, Grinnell is in a very safe neighborhood where it's OK to walk around by yourself. The dorms are very comfortable and of adequate space, which means that most students don't mind living on campus for the traditional three years, or even for all four years. The dining hall is also great. There are lots of vegetarian and vegan options, a permanent salad bar, cereal bar and sandwich bar. There is also a movement going on campus right now to have dining services purchase more local foods, which is an important economic, environmental and nutritional issue.

Current student, 8/2003-Submit Date April 2006

As a city kid, the size of Grinnell was a real challenge my first year because I had to adjust to living in small town Iowa. The residential life experiences makes up for it. We operate on the philosophy of self governance allowing for students to be on equal footing with the administration with regard to how we want our campus to be. Instead of residential advisors, we have student advisors. They are volunteers who live on every dorm floor and are responsible for maintaining the integrity of the communities that develop. There is a brand-new campus center due to open in the fall and we also have a new gym. The dining isn't too bad and with the opening of the new campus center, there will also be a new dining hall and supposedly more meal options. Grinnell is a safe town but the relations between students and people who live here could be strengthened. Nevertheless, it's a much safer community than where I grew up.

Current student, 8/2002-Submit Date, February 2004

The quality of life at Grinnell is very high. There is very little crime. Grinnell is a residential college, therefore most students live on campus. Freshmen live with upperclassmen, creating a learning environment where students from different backgrounds and experiences interact on a daily basis. The campus is beautiful, especially in the fall and the spring. The winters [can be brutal]; expect subzero weather [from time to time.] One of the reasons I personally chose Grinnell was the opportunity to live in middle America and experience small town life (I wanted to experience something radically different from my hometown, Miami). The college offers many volunteer opportunities to work with the town and foster a relationship with the locals.

The campus has been undergoing major construction in the last few years. By the time the majority of the construction is completed, Grinnell should have some incredible facilities, among the best in the nation. Being one of the richest liberal arts colleges, Grinnell has been able to fund these mammoth projects without the use of bonds and without raising the tuition too radically.

Social Life

Current student, 9/2002-Submit Date, May 2006

One of the great things about Grinnell is that because it is in such a small town both the college and students at the college realize that they have to create their own fun instead of being able to rely on a city for activities. The college does an excellent job of bringing in a wide range of events including plays, movies, lectures and concerts. Student organizations, with funding from the college, bring in many of the same events, as well as create their own fun through many different kinds of themed parties. There is no Greek system on campus, which means that all events are open to everyone—it's really one big family here. Also, the campus is primarily residential with only 150 students living off campus, which means that the community is very tight knit. Grinnell is a very work hard, play hard environment.

Current student, 8/2004-Submit Date, May 2006

Grinnell is unique in that we do not have Greek life on campus. We have an unwritten policy that students should not be excluded from groups. This policy even applies to our varsity sports, there are no tryouts for the teams. Grinnell is also unique in that it is literally in the middle of cornfields. Thus instead of having bars or dance clubs, we have the town pub. Surprisingly though there is always a lot to do. Our weekends are busied with shows and speakers and many themed parties. Some of our favorite annual parties include Disco, in which everyone gets decked out in disco clothes, and the guys start growing their chops months ahead of time. We also have Mary B. James, which is named after an alumna and taken literally: mary be james—it is our cross dressing party. Thus despite the odd location Grinnellians keep themselves extremely busy, and manage to have a lot of fun. There are quite a few couples on campus, but you rarely hear of people going on dates.

Current student, 8/2002-Submit Date, May 2006

The social scene at Grinnell is different than what I assume it is at other colleges. There isn't much to do in town, so the college spends a lot of money to provide programming on campus, such as bringing in bands, movies to our on-campus movie theatre, and providing non-alcoholic programming every weekend. In addition, there's usually an all-campus party once a weekend, and several theme parties (Underwear Ball, Mary B. James (cross-dressing party), and our twice a year formal, Waltz) spread throughout the year. Students over 21 frequent the pub in town, which is owned and operated by a Grinnell alum, and Wednesdays are unofficial pub nights. A lot of students assert that there isn't a dating scene, but there is, it just isn't prominent. Student groups and clubs are very active, and it is incredibly easy to start your own and get funding for it. In addition, there is not a Greek system at Grinnell. And personally, I don't think we are lacking in any way for not having one. That was one of the many reasons that Grinnell appealed to me. My favorite student group is called Alternative Break. Over each of the academic breaks, this group organizes volunteer trips all over the country. My sophomore year I participated in a Spring Alternative Break in Boston. We stayed with an alumnus and worked in soup kitchens, food banks and homeless shelters. It was an amazing opportunity and really opened my eyes to the social issues facing our country. Then this year I led a trip of my own to Omaha, where we focused on issues facing troubled youth in an urban environment. The reason I love alternative break is that it gives students a chance to actually go out and get something done in the world instead of just talking about it in the classroom.

Current student, 8/2003-Submit Date, November 2004

On-campus activities are great—crazy parties, free movies, excellent guest speakers. The town is kinda dead. Dating is awkward on campus, after all, it's a small campus. Though successful long-term relationships are not uncommon, the problem occurs when you break up with someone but have to see him all the time. Grinnell is very liberal in terms of homosexuality. Everywhere is queer friendly, and no one is ashamed of being gay.

Current student, 8/2002-Submit Date, February 2004

Grinnell offers a unique social life. Situated in the middle of Iowa, the college has to bring its own sources of entertainment. The college brings in everything from ballet to alternative rock concerts to jazz to hip hop shows. The hot spot on weekdays is the Pub, which now regularly checks students' IDs. Themed dance parties at the Harris Center are thrown almost every weekend. The most popular are Halloween, Spring and Winter Waltz, the Haines Underwear Ball, Disco and Mary B. James (the cross-dressing party). The college has no Greek life, which is better, because all students are invited to all the events. There are over 150 student groups on campus. Though we're in the middle of Iowa, students often discover that there is too much to do and not enough time.

 The School Says

Grinnell College is a place where independence of thought and social conscience are instilled. The four-year college experience is viewed as an academic journey where students are able to explore their interests and build knowledge. The strong advis-

ing system ensures that the experience is comfortable but challenging; that students are challenged academically, but supported along the way. The path to graduation from Grinnell often includes internships, off-campus study, and mentored research.

Rather than seeing Grinnell College's location in a small-town in Iowa as a detriment, the college sees this as a benefit. Students are attracted to Grinnell not because of the city nightlife, but rather because of strong academics and the close-knit community. This community is intellectually engaged and creative. Strong bonds form between faculty and students, ensuring that students do not feel lost in a crowd. Friendships and connections made at Grinnell often last a lifetime.

Iowa State University

Office of Admissions
Alumni Hall
Ames, IA 50011-2010
Admissions phone: (515) 294-5836, (800) 262-3810
Admissions fax: (515) 294-2592
Admissions e-mail: admissions@iastate.edu
Admissions URL: www.admissions.iastate.edu/

 Admissions

Alumnus/a, 8/2002-5/2006, November 2006

Admissions did not seem difficult. The minimum scores were not high, and there were no interviews or anything too painful. As long as you were a good student in high school, it shouldn't be a problem getting in. They aren't that selective.

Current student, 5/2004-Submit Date, October 2006

It's a state school, so as long as you have a GPA that's above 2.5 and an average ACT or SAT score you should be safe. There was no essay or interview for general admission, but I recommend applying for as many scholarships as you qualify for. If you can get an interview for a scholarship, you're gold.

Current student, 8/2003-Submit Date, October 2006

Getting in isn't too hard and ISU offers some great scholarships. Great engineering and design school. The business and law programs are on their way up as well.

Current student, 8/2003-Submit Date, September 2006

The admissions process was very straightforward. The online application was easy to fill out and they contacted me about admission shortly after I submitted my application. However, information for on-campus housing was not straightforward. They did not tell me until three weeks before school that I had housing on campus and where I would be living. I did not receive orientation information either.

Current student, 8/2005-Submit Date, September 2006

The admissions process was pretty painless. Colleges are doing everything online now. The Honors Program required a simple essay on three items you would take with you into space.

Current student, 8/2004-Submit Date, September 2006

The process is fairly simple. I just submitted my ACT scores to Iowa State University. They then sent me a package for admissions. You fill it out, send it in, and pay the fee. That's about all it takes. So long as you're in the top 25 percent of your class and got an 18 or higher on your ACT, you shouldn't have a problem getting in.

Current student, 8/2004-Submit Date, November 2005

The admissions process here at ISU is done completely online through a link at the school's web site. There are not any essay questions with the application, however qualified students for the freshman Honors Program are required to write an essay. Once you have applied, the freshman Honors College will notify you if you meet the necessary requirements.

Current student, 8/2005-Submit Date, November 2005

Getting into Iowa State University really wasn't that difficult in my opinion. I started out planning to come here and enter the College of Engineering, which is one of the toughest programs to get into. There were no interviews or essays I had to complete. I happened to be in the top 10 percent of my class with a GPA of 3.7 in high school. However, this is not all necessary. I believe you have to be in the top 50 percent of your graduating high school class with a GPA of 2.5 or greater. Also, I had a 26 on my ACT test. I think the minimum ACT score they look at is around 18. I filled out the application, mailed it in, and was informed that I got accepted shortly there after. I would say that the admissions process at Iowa State University is very simple and easy to understand.

Current student, 8/2003-Submit Date, April 2005

The admissions process was fairly easy. There is an orientation the summer before you enter when you tour the campus, find out where you're living, and talk to your advisor who asks you what you want to do and helps you to find the right classes. My advice on getting in is to have a decent GPA in high school and be sure to take the ACT (perhaps twice) to maximize your score. Since this is a large public school with a diverse set of colleges, as long as you're a fair student in high school, odds are pretty good that you'll get into whatever program you choose.

 Academics

Alumnus/a, 8/2002-5/2006, November 2006

There was a high stress on academics. I was in the computer engineering program, and it was a very demanding major in terms of the amount of work required. However, the quality was high, and each class offered something unique and helpful to gain a broad understanding of the field. Grading standards often depended on the professors, but most were not interested in giving out all A's and B's. They graded according to how well they thought you mastered the material they wanted you to learn. Expect to work quite hard and spend a lot of time on homework for an A. At times, with a selection of classes, the workload can be very intense in combination with other activities. It would probably be much more manageable but less interesting if there was no outside involvement.

Current student, 5/2004-Submit Date, October 2006

Intro courses are usually big lectures that are designed to weed out students who are not right for the field. These courses aren't usually very engaging. In my

Read all of Vault's College Surveys at www.vault.com/college—get complete surveys on 100s of colleges and universities, expert advice on applicaton essays and more.

VAULT CAREER LIBRARY 255

opinion, big lectures can be interactive and should be to some extent. However this system of teaching has a long tradition and will be here for some time, unfortunately.

Higher-level courses are similar to a high school class of 20 to 30-something students. Students are more comfortable asking questions in class as well as outside of class. Some instructors are very good about meeting outside of class to help students.

Workload depends on your field. As a design student, there is not a single week where you can get to bed before 3 a.m. But if you manage your studio courses and academic courses ahead of time, you'll feel much more organized and prepared.

Overall quality of classes is average. Every now and then you'll get stimulating teachers. I've had some fantastic ones in political science, sociology and psychology. But if you're unlucky, you will get teachers who are not as challenging or excited about the subject.

Current student, 8/2003-Submit Date, October 2006

Variety of professors. You have to be careful who you get but it's easy to find someone who you like and fits your style; just ask around. Classes seem to be in line with other universities and the requirements are also similar. Getting into classes is no problem if you are in the Honors Program, but for those who aren't ,make sure you develop a flexible four year plan.

Current student, 8/2002-Submit Date, September 2006

Science courses are rigorous and grading is fair. The workload is not overwhelming, but appropriate. The quality of classes has been excellent in the science fields. Getting into classes is easy with honors or other special status.

Current student, 8/2005-Submit Date, September 2006

The academic aspect is challenging, though there is always help available. Study opportunities are announced and supplemental instruction is provided. I have not had a problem getting into classes. The scheduling system allows for easy rearrangement of classes. Advisors are friendly and helpful. The workload keeps you busy, but you can easily stay on top of it if you prioritize. Most professors are very competent and helpful.

Current student, 8/2003-Submit Date, September 2006

Iowa State University is a university with high expectations. There are high expectations of students, and students equally have high expectations for staff and faculty. The class content is of high quality. Upper-level classes have smaller class sizes and the learning is more one-on-one. When registering for classes, it can be difficult to get the classes you need. Workload is progressively heavier in higher level classes and often includes group projects.

Current student, 8/2004-Submit Date, September 2006

Regarding the political science department, all texts and material are adequate. The lower-level classes are not difficult if the student studies according to professor's expectations. Most classes are easy to get into; some upper-level courses can be difficult, and in these cases, students typically must put off taking them until they're upperclassmen when they receive registration seniority. If students study as recommended, an average student should be able to attain a C or B in upper-level courses. To receive an A in these courses requires either extra study or special skills that most students do not have. Most professors are thorough and approachable, some are inspiring.

Current student, 9/2004-Submit Date, December 2005

We have some of the best teachers at ISU. The classes are the highest quality classes for my major. It is sometimes hard to get into some of the easier classes that are just electives but the university helps you get into required classes. The professors are awesome. They will help you out as much as they can throughout the class. The workload can be as demanding as you want to make it. It all depends on your classes and your major. My personal workload was extremely hard this semester because I am on an ISU team.

Current student, 8/2002-Submit Date, November 2005

I am in the biology program, which is an excellent course of study. As an underclassman, it was more difficult to get classes at the times I wanted them, but there were almost always seats open in the classes at another time. I recommend joining the learning community for your major, which will ensure that you get

into the classes you need to graduate on time. There are a few classes on campus that are notoriously difficult to get into. You will have better luck getting into these as a junior or senior. Grading differed significantly between professors, departments and the different colleges of ISU. The workload is what you make it, by choosing how much of a challenge you want to give yourself. All of my professors have been very approachable and willing to answer questions and help me out.

Current student, 8/2003-Submit Date, November 2005

The academic program is very self fulfilling. Classes are clearly in a progressional order. The quality of classes is of the highest caliber. Getting into classes is never a problem; they scale them respectively every year to accommodate the right number of students. Grading is based on the teacher. There are easy professors and hard professors, but all help you to learn the material in their own way. You get a fair amount of work, but nothing more than you should expect for college classes. They do expect you will only be doing college and do not take into account other circumstances, but when you talk to the professor then he/she is usually flexible with special cases.

 Employment Prospects

Current student, 5/2004-Submit Date, October 2006

Iowa State's engineering school appears to be relatively prestigious. So is its reputation in science. The College of Design has an average reputation although they'll try to tell you otherwise. Most designers from the college will most likely go on to work for a small firm. That's not to say there aren't great designers that come out of the college.

Current student, 8/2003-Submit Date, October 2006

Great career service programs for engineering and business. They're slacking on the LAS side; however, they offer great speakers and seminars on how to succeed in your area. Good companies come in and recruit, especially in the Des Moines Business (insurance) area along with national engineering firms. There are some great career fairs early on in the semester with a good selection of companies; you just have to be prepared and do a little homework on what you are looking for, and an internship/job opportunity is no problem. Just make sure you get involved on campus and keep a decent GPA.

Current student, 8/2004-Submit Date, September 2006

Job placement efforts are outstanding through the university. Job/internship fairs, seminars, workshops, and so on are readily available. Students who have solid GPAs and social skills have a high probability of reaching the plateau they desire. Job type and prestige depend on major, but technical students advance especially well.

Current student, 8/2003-Submit Date, September 2006

There is a career fair that allows students to meet employers and interview for jobs. There is also CMS, which is an employment network, through which jobs are posted for which students can apply. Also, individual clubs sometimes sponsor companies to meet students, and these events serve as networking.

Current student, 8/2004-Submit Date, November 2005

Each college has its own career services. The College of Engineering hosts the second largest career fair in the country in the fall and spring. Opportunities such as co-ops, internships and summer work experiences are highly encouraged by the faculty and they are very helpful. I was fortunate enough to have received a co-op position my sophomore year. Companies such as NASA, Boeing, Lockheed Martin and Hamilton Sundstrand are just a few that recruit here.

Current student, 8/2005-Submit Date, November 2005

The job outlook for students graduating from Iowa State University is great. Iowa State hosts the nation's largest indoor career fair, so there are definitely resources right at your fingertips here. Graduates of Iowa State work at companies such as General Mills, IBM, John Deere, 3M and Texas Instruments, to name a few.

Quality of Life

Alumnus/a, 8/2002-5/2006, November 2006

The campus can't be beat. It is beautiful and it is obvious that the school cares about its appearance. There are many university housing options to suit every student's desires and lifestyle. More new residence halls have been built in the last couple years, so they are always trying to appeal to the interests of students. The neighborhood is very safe and I never felt uncomfortable, even walking through campus late at night. There are always security people available and there is a number to call if you ever need it.

Current student, 8/2003-Submit Date, October 2006

Athletics are starting to improve (thanks to a great new athletic director), and we have a great president who is good at looking ahead. The campus town is the downside (not much for businesses but bars and tattoo places), but the campus itself is wonderful and beautiful. Campus housing is good and we have a great sports recreation program: one of the best in the country!

Current student, 8/2002-Submit Date, September 2006

Housing is excellent and the city provides many amenities without the hassle of a big city. Entertainment options are adequate and the city is very welcoming. Campus is beautiful and easy to navigate.

Current student, 8/2005-Submit Date, September 2006

Housing is good. The community in the residence halls is very diverse. There are several options for university housing: double dorms, singles, apartments, family apartments and so on. The food is good and fresh and there is plenty of it. The department of public safety does a good job especially with education and awareness.

Current student, 1/2001-Submit Date, November 2004

Ames is a relatively small place, with Des Moines being 40 minutes away by car, and Minneapolis three and a half hours away. There is no regular bus service between Ames and Des Moines.

Central campus is like a park, and the campus was ranked as one of the 25 most beautiful campuses in the nation. There is a man-made lake on campus with two swans kept by the university. Generally, the campus is safe and problem-free.

Wireless Internet is accessible throughout most of the campus, and dorms are all equipped with free cable TV and high-speed Internet. Rooms are small though, and dining service has came a long way. The traditional line cook concept has been abolished in the biggest dining hall, and it is like a cafe right now, with different kinds of food from which to choose. The recreational center is nice, and there are bowling lanes on campus.

Social Life

Alumnus/a, 8/2002-5/2006, November 2006

There is a strong social aspect to the college. The town is largely focused around the university, so events are readily available. Concerts and cultural events occur continuously. Also, there are hundreds of clubs and interest groups for practically everything you can think of, so there are endless ways to get involved. Welch Avenue, which is right by campus, has many bars that are popular hangouts. The Greek system is strong, so they host parties on the weekends as well. The nearby restaurants are largely catered to the fast lifestyle of college students. However, there are several nicer places nearby and more in other areas of Ames.

Current student, 8/2003-Submit Date, October 2006

We have the best Greek system ever, if you are looking for that. Bars are OK but must be 21 and up. Restaurants are improving and Des Moines isn't too far away. The school is a nice trip away from Minneapolis, Omaha, Kansas City or Chicago, so you can always take a break and head to a city if you feel like it. As far as dating goes: there are a lot more guys (60 percent) than girls on campus but it's starting to even out. Students love the intramural sports program and going to sporting events. Cyclone Alley makes ISU basketball fun and exciting, and there is a club for every type of interest.

Current student, 8/2004-Submit Date, September 2006

The school brings in many big-name speakers, comedians, and bands. The Greek system is strong and vibrant. There is a fair number of restaurants, many bars and decent number of other entertainment centers (e.g., theaters) within walking distance of campus. There are many restaurants and a suitable number of entertainment centers within the larger City of Ames.

Current student, 9/2004-Submit Date, December 2005

Ames has a great social life. There are at least 10 bars within walking distance from any part of campus. We also have great restaurants in town and surrounding areas. Whatever you feel like eating you can find it here in Ames. The dating scene is awesome. There are so many people in Ames in our age groups making it so easy to date. Also by living on campus you meet so many different people who are very datable. There are so many different events throughout the university. You can see plays, bands, movies—whatever you could ever think of, ISU will have it. We have clubs of all sorts. If you are into animals, religion, human rights, health, politics, anything. The Greek system is awesome at ISU because they are so involved with the university. They hold different events at their houses as well as parties. This is one the coolest Greek systems I have ever seen! Students love to hang out at the bars as well as just on campus. There is so much to do that you can have something new every day of the year. You can go bowling, to a movie, to eat, to drink, to study, anything at all you can do.

Current student, 8/2005-Submit Date November 2005

This university has over 25,000 students. You can meet a lot of people very easily. Most everybody here is very friendly and open to meeting new people. There are always parties going on on the weekends, and they are easy to find. There are many different fraternities and sororities you can join. They do many different interesting activities throughout the year, also. Right by the university are many bars and small restaurants. This is a very exciting town in which to live.

Read all of Vault's College Surveys at **www.vault.com/college**–get complete surveys on 100s of colleges and universities, expert advice on applicaton essays and more.

VAULT CAREER LIBRARY **257**

University of Iowa

Admissions Office
107 Calvin Hall
The University of Iowa
Iowa City, IA 52242-1396
Admissions phone: (800) 553-IOWA
Admissions URL: www.uiowa.edu/admissions/

 Admissions

Current student, Business, 9/2005-Submit Date, May 2007

The admissions process at the University of Iowa is a very simple one. Either you meet the index required for admission and are accepted, or you do not and are rejected. As I am a resident of Iowa, my index score needed to be over 95. To calculate my index you would take the percentage of the high school class I was ahead of in GPA, plus two times my ACT score. As this number was over 95, I was accepted.

Current student, Communications, 8/2004-Submit Date, May 2007

After sending in my ACT information, I requested information from the office of admissions located on campus. After hearing back from them, I completed the admission application. This can be done with the paper materials they send you, an online application, or a printed application obtained from the admissions web site. This application needed to be submitted by a certain date. Along with the application, the university needed ACT/SAT scores sent by the testing agency, high school transcripts sent by the high school, and college coursework transcripts from the college institution. Finally, I had to pay a $40 application fee. When I applied, I sent a letter of recommendation accompanying my application. After applying you will be given a Hawk ID and password to access your admissions profile where you can track your application. After submitting your application, you are automatically admitted if you meet the class rank or admissions index requirement. Iowa residents must rank in the upper 50 percent of their high school class or present an admissions index of 95 or above. Residents of other states must rank in the upper 30 percent of their high school class or present an admissions index of 100 or above.

Current student, Education, 8/2002-Submit Date, May 2007

As I recall, admissions was done on a first-come-first-served basis, so it's a good idea to get application materials in early. This also gives you time to look into scholarship opportunities that may apply. It was a while ago when I did this, but I don't remember the application being terribly hard to fill out, just a little time-consuming.

Current student, 1/2003-Submit Date, January 2006

Top 50 percent of high school graduating class and ACT scores over 18 for general university admissions. Business school admissions require an application, essay on "why you want to be in the College of Business and what your career goals are." Additionally, applicants must have a minimum 2.75 GPA, résumé and completed all core courses.

Current student, 9/2002-Submit Date, January 2006

The admissions process was very easy. All I had to do was fill out a simple one- or two-page questionnaire that included a few short essays regarding my college plans and career goals. A few months later I found out that I was accepted. Following my acceptance letter, I later received applications for housing and meal plan contracts. The admissions process never required an interview of me, and honestly I do not feel that the selection process was very selective at all. I am pretty certain that anybody with a high school GPA of 3.0 or better and a 20 or higher on the ACT would get accepted if they were an in-state student. I am not sure how difficult it is for out-of-state students to get accepted to the University of Iowa, but it will be at least somewhat harder. My advice to anyone who wishes to get into the University of Iowa: Don't be lazy and make sure that your grades in high school are decent, and do your best on the ACT. Getting in is the easy part, being successful in college is far harder.

Current student, 8/2005-Submit Date, September 2005

There was no personal interview or essay. The college is fairly open and admissions accepts all graduates from Iowa high schools. This affects the graduation rate, but is good for equal access. I did speak with admissions personnel, they gave me personal attention and helped me pick out coursework that would suit me. My high school and community college grades were a positive factor in getting admitted, and they enabled me to join the Honors Program immediately.

Current student, 9/2004-Submit Date, September 2005

The admissions process first started by completing the online admissions profile and then obtaining my high school records and having ACT test scores to be sent to the school. Most schools, including the University of Iowa, really look for solid GPA, class rank and ACT/SAT score. Having very good scores on all of these, I was very confident that I would be accepted and even did well enough to get a scholarship. I did not have to complete any essays or interviews, but did have to take a mathematics placement test.

> **The school states:** "To apply for admission as an undergraduate, students need to submit an application with the $40 application fee, a final high school transcript (freshmen submit a sixth semester transcript) and transcripts from all colleges attended. The Colleges of Business, Nursing, and Education require additional materials. No letters or essays are required for freshman admission."

 Academics

Current student, Communications, 8/2004-Submit Date, May 2007

I believe the academics at Iowa are great. There is a very wide selection of classes. The registration process is based on the number of credit hours (the way the university awards credit) a student has. Because of this, some of the major-specific courses are harder to get into for entering first-year students, yet most first year students tend to take mainly general education courses that remain open throughout registration. The professors of all classes seem very interested in teaching the material they teach making the classes very enjoyable. The university has a standard grading scale that provides an easy way to calculate your grades throughout the semester. Many professors grade on a curve though allowing for your grade to increase slightly at the end of the semester. The work load depends on the student's schedule, both semester hours taken and which classes are taken.

Current student, Business, 8/2006-Submit Date, May 2007

The workload is moderate, but heavy at times. I believe a student must put in a substantial amount of time to be successful . I am a student who has early registration, so it is easy to get the courses I want. I have not been really unhappy with a class thus far. I like most professors and attend almost every lecture. Grading is competitive. I believe, however, that if I put in enough work, I will be happy with the grade I receive, so grading is not unreasonable.

Current student, Business, 8/2005-Submit Date, May 2007

I feel that the academics are very solid at the University of Iowa. I think that many of the general education classes are not as strong as they could be, but the major coursework has been very strong. Usually, it is relatively easy to get the classes that you need and the grading in classes is very fair. I think that many professors do a great job, while others don't. Overall, my experience has been good at the University of Iowa.

Current student, Pharmacology, 8/2005-Submit Date, May 2007

There are so many academic options available at the University of Iowa. As an incoming student, I was amazed at the number of different courses on different topics I had never heard of before. I can whole-heartedly say that my electives and general education coursework were enjoyable, interesting and definitely beneficial to my degree. The classes I have taken have been of high quality, led by professors and teaching assistants who know the subject matter very well and enjoy discussing the material. Some classes may be harder to get into than others, but all the waitlists and adding class procedures are laid out well and professors are willing to try to get additional students into their classes. The workloads and grading for classes seem very fair and are very clearly stated on the very first day of class.

Current student, Engineering, 8/2006-Submit Date, May 2007

Classes are never easy, but they are not impossible. With the right frame of mind, amount of time spent on homework, and diligence to ask for help, any class is manageable. There are plenty of sections for each class, but sometimes if you register late, you might not be able to get the class you want.

Current student, Business, 8/2003-Submit Date, October 2006

As far as the business program goes, you have to work your way into the school by your junior year if you want to graduate within four years. The beginning courses are fairly large but overall, professors are more than willing to help you out individually if you approach them. It is a fairly competitive program to get the best interviews for internships and full-time jobs, but if you get involved on-campus it is very easy to succeed at Tippie. The best professors are allocated to the more important core business courses, and overall, they are excellent. You will be stuck with a TA for most of the lower-level classes and might find it hard to understand exactly everything being taught. The workload is pretty standard from what I have heard about most Big 10 schools. You will definitely have some free time and will find a lot of distractions if you do not keep yourself busy.

Current student, 9/2002-Submit Date, January 2006

The academic program is quite good. The College of Liberal Arts and Sciences is the program that most people enter into initially. This college contains the largest number of possible majors, and suits most students well. For most freshmen and a large number of sophomores, the class sizes will be large (200+ students). Don't worry, it doesn't take long to adjust. You do need to come prepared to pay attention and take notes, regardless of your classmates' habits. I feel that the grading at Iowa is relatively liberal compared to other schools. A+'s are worth 4.33, and if you are one of the students who can get those, a 4.00 GPA is by no means out of reach. Most of the professors are willing to work with you outside of class if you need help, but if you don't go to ask for help, then don't expect any. The workload totally depends upon your major, as well as how good of a student you wish to be. For those who wish to excel, then the workload will be hard no matter what the major. Seeing that people are way more laid-back and mature in college, it is generally pretty easy to fit in and find a group of friends.

> **The school says:** "80 percent of undergraduate classes have fewer than 30 students. There are some classes with lectures of 200 students or more but all lecture courses have discussion or laboratory components where students meet in much smaller groups."

Current student, 1/2002-Submit Date, October 2004

The business school is probably one of the most underrated business schools in the world. There is virtually no barrier between the MBA students and undergrads. We actually compete within student organizations. MBA-level professors teach finance courses to undergraduate students. Throughout the semester, students research selected public companies from macro to micro and compete for the opportunity to present to a board that then makes equity investments in the endowed portfolio. Essentially we perform a comp analysis, organize a pitch and deliver. Note that these courses, taught by MBA-level professors, are the same professors who teach the MBA finance students; this department is ranked seventh in the world by *The Financial Times*. Iowa business students are making a name for themselves in bulge-bracket investment banks and the Big Four accounting firms. Accounting grads have an unbelievable placement percentage. The undergraduate program's primary goal is to develop students who can speak and write professionally, analyze and research effectively, and learn more than the foundations of basic technology. The college is truly unique and professional.

Employment Prospects

Current student, Communications, 8/2004-Submit Date, May 2007

The university has just built a new building to house its very effective career center. This center does everything from helping students pick a major, to helping students obtain jobs. The university's Employment Expo allows graduates to post résumés that employers search for future employees. Many students may even apply for jobs within the university community. Not enough can be said about how helpful the University of Iowa's Career Center is, and how much they do.

Current student, Business, 8/2005-Submit Date, May 2007

Going into business, there are multiple businesses that are always on campus trying to recruit graduates for jobs, and undergrads for internships. I feel that Iowa has very close ties to the commercial world, which in turn makes it easier for a student to be ready for the business world when he/she leaves.

Current student, Business, 8/2003-Submit Date, May 2007

Graduates of the College of Business have a wide variety of employment prospects. The network of employers provided by the University of Iowa is both very large and very strong. Many employers from the State of Iowa specifically seek out University of Iowa graduates because of their superior work ethic.

The types of jobs that College of Business graduates obtain vary with the student's major. Most accounting students pursue employment with one of the Big four accounting firms, many of which are conveniently located in the Chicagoland area (only three hours from Iowa City). Most other majors will find a variety of employers that are seeking out MIS, marketing, management, and finance majors. I would venture to guess, though, that a large number of students end up around the Chicago area after graduation.

Current student, 8/2003-Submit Date, October 2006

On-campus recruiting has definitely improved with the addition of the Pomerantz Career Center. It provides an excellent resource for the employers to come in and do on-campus interviews. There are definitely opportunities to interview with very prestigious firms if you make the extra effort to distance yourself from your peers all four years of college. The alumni from Iowa are pretty loyal to the school and you will find plenty of job offers if you stand out from your peers. Also, it is essential to land a good summer internship your junior year. This will ensure that you have some good experience under your belt and you might receive an offer. It gets much more difficult to get interviews if you have not done so. Accounting is huge at Iowa and graduates get offers from the Big Four firms. If you excel in finance, you definitely have the rare opportunity to interview with some prestigious investment banks and consulting firms. The Hawkinson Institute of Business Finance is an excellent way to get access to these companies that normally do not recruit at Iowa.

Current student, Business, 1/2002-Submit Date, October 2004

As a finance major, I have every opportunity in the world. I've met with people from Credit Suisse First Boston, Houlihan Lokey Howard and Zukin, Piper Jaffray, Harris Nesbitt, Lincoln Partners, Accenture, The Gallup Organization, The Monitor Group and Hewitt Associates—and the list goes on. The alumni network? Excellent. We have a Student Alumni Board, with students who have graduated in the last four years, come and recruit us; they have all built exceptional reputations at their respective firms, which makes it easier for current students to get interviews. The Student Alumni Board represents firms such as Goldman Sachs, Credit Suisse, First Boston, Harris Nesbitt, Northern Trust, Monitor, Hewitt, Aegon, among others. Our undergrad program draws the best firms from New York City.

Quality of Life

Current student, Education, 8/2005-Submit Date, May 2007

I love Iowa City. The campus is intertwined with the community giving students more of a city feel while still having a close-knit community. The residential halls are some of the best I've seen anywhere, and the facilities around the entire campus are great!

Read all of Vault's College Surveys at **www.vault.com/college**—get complete surveys on 100s of colleges and universities, expert advice on applicaton essays and more.

VAULT CAREER LIBRARY   **259**

Current student, Business, 9/2005-Submit Date, May 2007

Quality of life in Iowa City is great. There is very diverse series of restaurants in Iowa City, offering very casual dining and also very formal dining. Crime and safety doesn't seem like a big issue, and between Iowa City Police, campus police, and recent precautions added to ensure campus safety, I am not worried about traveling around the city at night, or any other time of the day. I feel safe and comfortable anywhere in Iowa City. There are tons of places to live in Iowa City, stretching from downtown to distant places in the surrounding area, and all of them I feel are nice places to live. Facilities on campus are all of very high quality, and some are still being renovated to make even better.

Current student, Business, 8/2006-Submit Date, May 2007

I love the campus. Housing is centrally located and I only had to walk about three blocks to my farthest class when I lived in the residence halls. The downtown area and campus meet, so a car is not necessary, and everything is easily accessible. The downtown area also has great restaurants unique to the area, and excellent boutiques for shopping. The wonderful people are my favorite part of college life at Iowa. The residence hall experience was a great way to meet people.

Current student, Pharmacology, 8/2005-Submit Date, May 2007

The University of Iowa and Iowa City community is an amazing place to spend four or more years of your life. There is such a wide array of culture and activities to enjoy on every corner. University Housing offers students several buildings on campus in which to live that all have their own benefits and special qualities. Each building is staffed with extraordinary staff, from resident assistants to hall coordinators, to custodial and maintenance staff that genuinely cares about each and every resident that lives in the building. In general, campus is simply gorgeous. There is no better sight than walking to class early in the morning with the golden dome of the Old Capitol shining in the sun. Buildings are situated conveniently within each program and have all the facilities and resources necessary to hold any level of coursework. Dining is provided in several places throughout campus. Each location is convenient, cost-conscious, and offers quality food for any taste. Also, several groups and organizations are continually making an active effort to maintain safety on campus and in the Iowa City area at all times.

Current student, 8/2003-Submit Date, January 2007

The University of Iowa does a great job of balancing outstanding academics with a great social scene. The on-campus dining facilities at Hillcrest and Burge residence halls are brand new and the University just approved the construction of a $69 million state-of-the-art Recreation and Fitness Center. Downtown Iowa City has a lot of offer with shops and restaurants, and there are plenty of activities on campus, from concerts to movies playing in the student union.

Current student, 1/2003-Submit Date, January 2006

Iowa City is a great college town. The university's facilities are among the best in the country. Computers and Internet access are readily available throughout the campus, as are study areas and other student services. Over 100 student organizations are available to serve a variety of interests and offer excellent leadership opportunities. Housing on and off campus is readily available in every form, from apartments to dorms, to co-ops, all of which are reasonably priced. Apartments usually cost $250 to $500 a month depending on location and quality. Crime is nonexistent and the area is very safe. Dining ranges from fast food to bars, to fine dining. Additionally, the university operates two large cafeterias in the dorms that are open to all students and has cafes in many university buildings.

> **The school says:** "In fall 2007, there were more than 400 recognized student organizations on campus."

 ## Social Life

Current student, Pre-med, 8/2005-Submit Date, May 2007

There are over 50 bars in the downtown area that is located directly on the campus. They vary in the way that they are set up; many are dance clubs at night and eateries during the day. These are great areas for social gatherings and most of the bars are 19-and-older, which means that you can go into the establishment if your over 19 but still cannot drink unless you're 21. I do not participate in the Greek system, but have many friends involved and in most cases they enjoy it.

Current student, Business, 9/2005-Submit Date, May 2007

If desired, the bar scene in Iowa City can be a great time. As the bars only require persons to be above 18 years old, many people enjoy hanging out in the bar environment, dancing and having fun. Many restaurants downtown turn into the most popular bars at night, and on certain nights of the week, the downtown area can be very crowded. Dining, is very diverse, and provides a great selection for all types of people. Dating scene in Iowa City is great, as the bars downtown are very popular, many people can meet and mingle with tons of new people every night. Many events are available in Iowa City, and the university does a great job of providing the city with very famous types of entertainment from around the world. Greek life isn't as popular at the University of Iowa as it is elsewhere, but those involved seem genuinely to enjoy it.

Current student, Business, 8/2006-Submit Date, May 2007

The downtown is alive 24/7. The restaurants are unique to the downtown area and there are hardly any chain restaurants. The bars are a great place to gather and are very popular. On warm days, local musicians can be heard in the pedestrian mall. There are so many clubs and activities that anyone can find a niche. The Greek system is strong and contributes a lot to the university, but only 1 percent of students are involved in Greek life. This way, there are so many more things going on that are not affiliated with Greek life, and being in a chapter is not essential to having a great social life.

Current student, Communications, 8/2004-Submit Date, May 2007

With over 400 student organizations on campus, there is something for everyone. Some student organizations include the Campus Activities Board (CAB), which puts on free events such as movies and stand up comedians. One other popular student organization is SCOPE productions, which brings live music to the University of Iowa campus. SCOPE has put on big name shows such as O.A.R, Kansas, Jack Johnson and Metallica just to name a few. Another great aspect of the University of Iowa is its close proximity to downtown Iowa City. Downtown Iowa City is located directly across the street from the Pentacrest, the heart of the university. Downtown provides many dining establishments, bars, clubs, novelty shops and bookstores. Some favorite downtown establishments include the Summit, Brothers, Pancheros, Taco Bell, The Sports Column, Active Endevors, Third Base, One Eyed Jakes, Iowa Book and the Prairie Lights Book Store. Iowa also has a Greek system. While not very big, only containing about 12 percent of the student population, it is a strong social community on campus.

Current student, 8/2003-Submit Date, January 2007

Iowa tailgating is also far wilder than most of the other Big 10 schools. Hawkeye fans wake up at the crack of dawn to drink on game days and all of Iowa City turns into one big party. By just walking down the street, past parking lots and past bars, you constantly witness an almost Mardi Gras like atmosphere and it is not uncommon to witness alumni taking beer bongs and playing flip cup with students.

Current student, 1/2003-Submit Date, January 2006

Iowa City has to rank among the top college towns for social life. The downtown area has over 40 bars in a four block area that includes a pedestrian mall. As mentioned above, a variety of dining options is available to fit all tastes as is a variety of student clubs. The Greek system is strong, but not dominant. Students can enjoy a great social life without being Greek. As a school that is nearly 50/50 men to women, the dating scene is strong.

Kansas State University

Office of Admissions
Kansas State University
119 Anderson Hall
Manhattan, KS 66506-0102
Admissions phone: (800) 432-8270 or (785) 532-6250
Admissions fax: (785) 532-6393
Admissions e-mail: k-state@k-state.edu
Admissions URL: consider.k-state.edu/admissions/

 ## Admissions

Current student, Animal Science, 8/2005-Submit Date, November 2006

Kansas State University's admissions process is very simple. Fill out the admissions application, send in the application fee along with your ACT scores and any previous transcripts and that's it.

Current student, 8/2003-Submit Date, September 2006

The admissions process was a very simple process. The application included the basic information, including high school involvement and so on. There was no interview. The admissions representative that was assigned to my area (out-of-state) was amazing. She always remembered my name, major and hometown. She would send me information that she thought might be useful or interesting to me. The dean of student life was also an amazing person. He always made my family and I feel that we were of utmost importance to the university. I would get post-cards, visit invites and so on, constantly. The recruitment and admissions process at K-State was really what made me feel at home and want to be part of K-State.

Current student, 8/2005-Submit Date, February 2006

To get into this university, I had to fill out an application. A couple of weeks later I a got a letter of acceptance from them.

Current student, 8/2002-Submit Date, February 2006

Getting in is very simple. Four years ago there was an easy online application and a minimal application fee. I'm sure this has probably been updated to be even easier. You have to meet one of three requirements to be accepted, and these are: (1) score a 21 or higher on the ACT; (2) rank in the top third of your graduating class; or (3) complete the Kansas pre-college curriculum with a 2.0 GPA.

K-State accepts all students who meet these requirements; however different colleges have their own requirements. For example, the College of Education requires a minimum of a 26 on the ACT.

Current student, 6/2000-Submit Date, February 2004

I applied in 2000, the last year of guaranteed entry (i.e., any graduate from an accredited Kansas high school was guaranteed admission). Admission is now slightly more selective, but as long as you complete a rather easy set of core requirements, you're pretty much guaranteed to get in.

Alumnus/a, 8/1999-5/2003, December 2005

Plan the university visit late in the spring of your high school junior year. Send your high school transcript and a letter of introduction to the the dean of the college at which you are looking, requesting an interview and full college department tour.

Sit in at least six classes. Meet at least three other students who are currently in the major/program that you are looking into. If possible, arrange to stay over for two or three days and tag along with one of the students for a full 48 hours during your visit. This should include classes, and all social and living aspects. The key is to immerse yourself in the university, culture, classes, curriculum and social life as much as possible.

Then, revisit and do the same senior year and then make your decision. You must spend as much time immersed in as many elements of Kansas State and the appointed program that you are interested in to make the best possible decision.

 ## Academics

Alumnus/a, 8/2002-5/2006, November 2006

Classes were of high quality. I feel I learned a lot in all of the classes. Workload was medium. If you stayed on top of things, it wasn't very difficult to handle. Most of the time classes were easy to get into. I didn't have much problem because I was ahead of most people in hours, so I got to enroll earleir than most. Professors were competent and knowledgeable.

Current student, Animal Science, 8/2005-Submit Date, November 2006

The animal science program at Kansas State University is one of the very best in the nation. As expected, it is considerably more challenging than any program you will find at a junior college or smaller university. The professors are industry experts and are very successful and knowledgeable in their fields. The grading and workload are fair and the facilities are some of the best available at a land grant institution. They don't just teach you facts, they teach you how to comprehend the facts and put them together to have greater overall understanding of animal agriculture.

Current student, 8/2003-Submit Date, September 2006

The academic programs are similar to a buffet. Although it is a large university, there is so much freedom to pick and choose courses and majors/minors. As many of the classes overlap, I was able to complete three majors and two minors in just two years. There is an open option program that allows younger students to have the freedom not to be in a specific major, but still get the general requirements done in the meantime. Freshman year is really the only time that it is a little bit more difficult to get into the classes you want, but there are waiting lists. I was only waitlisted once and I ended up getting into the course. The grading is very fair; it is based on an A, B, C, D and F scale with no plus or minus. The professors really care about their students, and always have an open-door policy. The professors come from all over with amazing life experiences to share with students. The workload is what I had anticipated. You do have to focus, and there is homework and studying, but it isn't so overwhelming that it consumes every minute of every day.

Current student, Health 8/2005-Submit Date, February 2006

I am currently enrolled in Human Nutrition. I am going to use this degree as a pre-dentistry degree. It is easy to get into classes that have a popular teacher. It was difficult to find that out, though, your first semester here. I think that the classes are very high quality. Grading is very fair as most is done by TAs.

Current student, Engineering 8/2002-Submit Date, February 2006

The engineering program is not easy. It requires a strong work ethic and serious dedication. Classes in the engineering college are not difficult to get into; enrollment is based on the number of credit hours you have. Some of the pre-reqs for engineering classes fill up quickly, however there are usually several sections available and enough people will drop a class in the first week so you can usually enroll.

Some professors are very good, others could use some [guidance]. I've really enjoyed the good ones, but have been frustrated with the bad ones. The workload in engineering is a lot, yet manageable. Several of the engineering departments have their own computer labs where you can work with others in your classes, and these are open 24 hours a day.

Current student, 6/2000-Submit Date, February 2004

Easy. The quality of the professors varies by department. Political Science and English are very good. Once you get above 75 or so credit hours, you can get into pretty much anything you want, even the popular classes. Grading and

Read all of Vault's College Surveys at **www.vault.com/college**—get complete surveys on 100s of colleges and universities, expert advice on applicaton essays and more.

VAULT CAREER LIBRARY **261**

workload varies by professor, but I've had a 30-hour-per-week job throughout college, and had no problem maintaining a 3.4 GPA.

Alumnus/a, 8/1999-5/2003, December 2005

Kansas State University is a major land grant university with tremendous diversity. Everything from architecture to bakery science, to vet medicine, to business. I am originally from Massachusetts. It is a great cost option to expensive East Coast schools. You have many options to change and switch majors once you are there. The education is great.

Professors are fair but challenging academic workload. Lots of choice in classes and electives. SAT 800 or above will do well.

Employment Prospects

Alumnus/a, 8/2002-5/2006, November 2006

Job placement is very good, and a number of employers like graduates. The alumni network is good, and on-campus job fairs are very helpful. We rank high in food science placement, engineering, architecture, and others.

Current student, Animal Science, 8/2005-Submit Date, November 2006

Employers respect a Kansas State University diploma. The largest agricultural corporations in the nation routinely recruit and offer internships to Kansas State University students.

Current student, 8/2003-Submit Date, September 2006

We have something called Career and Employment Services here at K-State. It is a free service to students, and it helps with résumés, interviews and job placement. They are really helpful in getting students prepared for the real world. We also have an amazing alumni center. It is a brand-new facility that welcomes alumni with open arms. They do a great job of keeping in touch and knowing what their grads are doing. We also have an on-campus job and internship fair that helps students network with big corporations all over the nation and get interviews on the spot.

Current student, 8/2002-Submit Date, February 2006

Employment prospects for the College of Engineering are very good. We are told that K-State graduates are highly sought after, and they appear to be very esteemed at the workplaces we visit.

While the selection of companies is somewhat limited to the Midwest, more and more employers are looking at K-State for their new hires. Everyone in my class with over a 3.0 GPA had multiple job offers in the fall semester of their senior year. Our starting salaries are all above average.

The alumni network is great, they are all proud of where they came from and would like to see more K-State graduates in their workplaces. The on-campus recruiting is also very good, and has lots of employers at the career fairs. Working with the on-campus recruiting office is a very good way to gain employment at K-State. Internships can be difficult to obtain, but if one is persistent and presents themselves well opportunities are available.

Quality of Life

Current student, Animal Science, 8/2005-Submit Date, November 2006

Kansas State University is located in the "Little Apple": Manhattan, Kansas. Manhattan is a hidden jewel in the Midwest. It is nestled in the Kansas River valley at the northern end of the beautiful Flint Hills prairie region. Kansas State University is the smallest of the Big 12 schools yet the community does not lack in amenities. The crime rate is low, the sports teams are nationally recognized, apartment housing is abundant, neighborhoods are tree lined and peaceful and dining options are more than adequate.

Current student, 8/2003-Submit Date, September 2006

K-State is one of the friendliest places on earth. The Midwestern values and welcoming students and faculty are like no where else. I remember walking around on campus one of the first days of school looking like I was lost, and about five students came to see if I needed help finding where I was going. K-State has

become more than a place to go to school, it has become a community. I love walking around and seeing familiar faces and knowing that I'm important to the university. Housing is great. There is a wide variety of residence hall options as well as an outstanding Greek life and off-campus housing options. The food is great in the dining halls and the campus is very safe.

Current student, 8/2005-Submit Date, February 2006

There is an extremely low rate of crime here. I live off campus in a fraternity so I am not sure what is it like on campus, but I like the off-campus life. The housing is good, but the meals need to be improved a little bit.

Current student, 8/2002-Submit Date, February 2006

Kansas State has a fabulous environment in which to live. Older residence halls are being converted to suite styles, which is popular with today's freshmen. The campus is fairly small and can be traversed in 15 minutes in all directions. There are lots of green spaces to study on so the walk to class is pleasant. There are some new buildings on campus and some old, yet all are very functional.

The campus is very safe, even at night. Dining halls have very good meal programs, most of the food comes from K-State suppliers (for example, beef and dairy) and fresh bread comes from the baking department. The student union offers a variety of places to eat and accepts credit cards, even for small purchases, which is very convenient for today's student.

Current student, 6/2000-Submit Date, February 2004

Dorm housing is pretty typical. The campus is safe, there's very little crime. Manhattan has little violent crime also. Off-campus housing is fairly expensive for Kansas.

Social Life

Current student, Animal Science, 8/2005-Submit Date, November 2006

Kansas State University offers a large Greek system and enough clubs and events to keep busiest socialite happy. We have an active bar scene and shopping district known as Aggieville, which is full of eclectic stores, pubs and eating places including Chinese food, American food, Tex-Mex, Cajun, BBQ and three pizza joints.

Current student, 8/2003-Submit Date, September 2006

Just off campus is a place called Aggieville. It is a few blocks packed with places to eat, bars, little unique shops and more. It is the center of college life here in Manhattan. Manhattan isn't the largest place, but it definitely is a fun place to hang out. We also have a mall in town, as well as chain stores, such as Staples, Best Buy, Target and so on. The Greek system is one of the best in the nation. Just this year we added two fraternities and the sorority system is growing by the year. All the houses really work together and support each other. Some favorite places students go are Kite's Bar and Grill, Tubby's, Rusty's, So Long Saloon and O'Malleys.

Current student, 8/2005-Submit Date, February 2006

There are a lot of restaurants in Manhattan. I do not know about the bars since I am not 21. There are plenty of opportunities to party elsewhere, though. The Greek system is very strong. There are also many events that you have the opportunity to attend, as well as many clubs to join.

Current student, 8/2002-Submit Date, February 2006

The social life is fabulous, with a great bar district within walking distance of campus. Included in this bar district is Rusty's Last Chance, voted the Number 12 sports bar in America by *Sports Illustrated*.

There is also a park and rec center close to campus, and a natatorium on campus for recreation. Many students are actively involved in student organizations whether they are Greek, department/college clubs, religious organizations or things like bowling leagues. There are also tons of intramurals for students to participate in. The Greek scene is very active and Greek students hold 60 percent of the campus leadership positions.

Current student, 6/2000-Submit Date, February 2004

Aggieville has all the bars you could ever want. Many restaurants in town, too, of good quality. I particularly recommend Little Apple Brewery and Whiskey Creek.

The University of Kansas

KU Office of Admissions and Scholarships
KU Visitor Center
1502 Iowa
Lawrence, KS 66045-7576
Admissions phone: (785) 864-3911
Admissions e-mail: adm@ku.edu
Admissions URL: www.ku.edu/admissions/

Admissions

Current student, Liberal Arts, 8/2003-Submit Date, April 2007

The admissions process is detailed but not impossible. Applying for the Honors Program and for scholarships is the most time consuming part. With everything online now, it is very user–friendly. As far as interviewing and essays go, it is best to be honest. Be sure to share true but appropriate things about yourself. Come prepared! Prepare answers before you go into an interview and you feel more confident.

Current student, 8/2003-Submit Date, September 2006

Getting in was fairly easy. I applied early and was accepted by Halloween my senior year. There are no early admissions, just rolling deadlines. Apply early to get good housing options!

Current student, Sociology, 8/2006-Submit Date, April 2007

KU's admissions process is one of the most efficient that I encountered when applying for colleges. As an in-state student, it was simple to go online at www.ku.edu and follow the online tutorial for applying. As soon as an e-mail and letter were sent concerning acceptance, it was simple to continue using the web site to finish the other necessary steps.

Current student, Cultural Studies, 8/2005-Submit Date, April 2007

The admissions process at KU is relatively simple. The application is online and it's quite easy to fill out. No essays are necessary for simple admittance, but if you are interested in receiving a scholarship from the university, essays are required. There are no interviews, and generally speaking KU is not incredibly selective, as long as you attended a Kansas high school.

Current student, 8/2003-Submit Date, September 2006

The admissions process was a wonderfully guided process. There was nothing confusing or intimidating about it. I applied early in hopes for a scholarship and the questions posed were appropriately insightful. The best way to get in is to be honest and show ambition to succeed.

Current student, 8/2005-Submit Date, May 2006

Getting into The University of Kansas is not that difficult. If you meet certain pretty easy requirements (which are a result of the school being state funded), you will be admitted. There are programs at the university that are a little more difficult to be admitted to, such as the Honors Program, which requires an average (old) SAT score of 1400 and a pretty good (3.5+) high school GPA. To be admitted to the business school, students must apply after completing the pre-business requirements, which are Financial Accounting I, Managerial Accounting I, Micro and Macroeconomics, Business Statistics and Introduction to Information Systems. If a student passes all of these requirements with a 2.5 GPA, he/she will be guaranteed admission to the business school. If not, he/she must hope the rest of his/her application is competitive. The pre-business class-

es can be weed-out classes, so students should be prepared to work hard in them. Not doing homework or not studying for one test could cost admission to the B-school. And remember, just because KU is easy to get into doesn't mean it's easy to stay at.

Current student, 9/2004-Submit Date, May 2006

To get into the School of Business you have to have a 3.0, mostly in the business classes, as well as a required 60 hours. I would suggest that one take the required classes when a freshman or sophomore because you have to fulfill some required classes to get into the school. I suggest that you should take the majority of the required classes to get in before the semester that you are applying. This is to make your GPA higher. For example, if you are taking most of them the semester you apply and then only have taken one, and not done so well in that class your GPA only stands for that one class.

Current student, 8/2003-Submit Date, November 2005

There were no interviews. The application process was easy and only included essays if you were applying for scholarship. Transcripts, ACT scores and recommendations were all I needed. It is more selective for out-of-state. I think you have to probably be in the top third of your class, OR have a 22 or higher on your ACT OR have a GPA above a 3.0 to get in if you are in-state. If you are out-of-state it is a little more strict, but I have not known many people that have had problems with this usually.

Current student, 7/2002-Submit Date, January 2006

I was an in-state applicant, which means that I had to get in no matter what, based on minimum Kansas Regents requirements (I was in the top third of my high school class and I achieved a 19 or higher on the ACT). I believe the school is working on being more selective for out-of-state students in an attempt to raise our current ranking (somewhere around 36 among public colleges). There was no interview and the application only requires an essay if you are applying for scholarships.

> **Regarding admissions, the school says:** "The University of Kansas has a long and respected tradition as a top public university that demands the best of its students. Your high school academic, extracurricular and community activities are part of the information you will be asked to submit in your application, as are standardized test scores. Requirements for admission will vary depending on whether you have attended other colleges or training schools, are reapplying to the KU or are applying to certain departments or programs. There are two ways to apply: You can fill out your application online, or you can download an application from the KU web site and mail it in. New freshmen and new transfer students can apply for admission and first-year scholarships in this one application."

Academics

Current student, Communications, 8/2003-Submit Date, April 2007

Large classes are expected during the first two years as general requirements are completed. Once I got focused in my majors, journalism and political science, the classes were smaller. In the White School of Journalism and Mass Communications the classes are very personable and the faculty does wonders trying to assist students.

Read all of Vault's College Surveys at **www.vault.com/college**—get complete surveys on 100s of colleges and universities, expert advice on applicaton essays and more.

VAULT CAREER LIBRARY 263

Current student, Sociology, 8/2006-Submit Date, April 2007

Speaking with regards to liberal arts and general education requirements, my classes to this point have been the perfect balance of challenging and interesting. The great thing about our classes is that with virtually any class, the student has the choice between learning in an environment with 15 to 20 other students or 500 to 1,000 others. The professors are all great and knowledgeable in their subjects and the graduate teaching assistants work well in a more limited capacity with the undergraduate students.

Current student, 8/2003-Submit Date, September 2006

I am a political science major. KU is liberal arts oriented, so you take a lot of general education classes your first two years especially; these classes can be a pain to get into. Once you're in more of your major classes, it is easier to enroll. Professors are great and always willing to talk to you during their office hours; they are very helpful. Grading depends a lot on which professors you get or which graduate teaching assistants you get—some can be easy some can be hard. Overall workload isn't too bad; expect to do the usual two hours outside of class for every hour you spend in class, that's a pretty universal rule here.

Current student, Cultural Studies, 8/2005-Submit Date, April 2007

I have always found that KU is academically very pleasing. I love the courses and the instructors. There have been basically no classes that I haven't enjoyed. I feel that it is generally easy to get into popular classes, because the administration understands the popularity and opens a lot of sections of the courses, so more can take the course.

Current student, Engineering, 8/2004-Submit Date, April 2007

The engineering program at KU is wonderful. We have a full staff of qualified professors who care very much for the students. Research is very much encouraged and has strengthened my academic experience incredibly.

Current student, Spanish, 8/2004-Submit Date, April 2007

I have had a wide experience with classes. Several that I just took to fulfill a general education requirement actually ended up being some of the most interesting classes I have ever taken. I've also had one or two that I thought would be amazing just fall short. The workload really depends on the student and how much time he/she is willing to put in. For the most part, students who attend class regularly and complete assignments will be able to get a C or a B. Even though KU is a public school, earning an A does require quite a bit of work. My class sizes have ranged from a 1,000–student accounting lecture to a five-person seminar about national identity in Latin America. I feel like students have to seek out individual attention, but faculty and staff are more than willing to help and guide you along.

Alumnus/a, Political Science, 8/2004-12/2006, April 2007

Being a Political Science and Sociology major, most of my classes were contemporary and had some effect on current issues. Since I had already completed my general requirements, I only took upper–level classes. Most of those classes had 30 people or less. All of my professors were willing to work with me and were there if I needed help. I remember having to call some of them at home and they were always willing to give the extra help. My professors knew how to keep our attention and most of the time the workload was pretty even in every class.

Current student, 8/2003-Submit Date, September 2006

As a senior, the workload has increased with each year. It is not too intimidating as a freshman, yet it takes a lot more determination than high school. There are classes from 1,000 people to classes with 20. Since this is such a big school, you need to make your own effort in order to succeed with precision and timeliness. You are required to see advisors twice a year as an underclassman, but after that, it's all up to the individual. The professors are fantastic. I have been surrounded by many great minds. They make you think for yourself with an appropriate amount of guidance. You have to read the text and go to class to do well. A lack of effort will show on your grades because the exams cover everything. All of the individual schools are very welcoming. Some are very difficult to get into, but that is a reason they are the best in the country (pharmacy is Number Two, for example). KU makes you fully prepared for the real world and work force.

Current student, Business 8/2005-Submit Date, May 2006

For all the business classes I have taken, the quality of education has been great. As one of the top business schools in the nation, KU employs some of the best faculty members who really know what they are doing. Many employed faculty members are people who have actually worked in the field before coming to teach, which is important because it provides an insight into the real-world requirements of the job. It can be hard to get into popular classes if you are not flexible, but if you leave some wiggle room in your schedule you will be able to take all of your requirements. Students should be prepared to work outside of class for the business classes. Expect a few hours of homework each week for each class. For example, in Financial Accounting I, a student can expect close to three hours per week of homework, and that is if they are understanding the material and are able to do it with relative ease. Intro to Information Systems homework can be around the same timeframe. While this may seem like a lot of homework, it is important to note that by doing the homework, it helps better prepare the student for tests.

Current student, 9/2004-Submit Date, May 2006

Getting into a specific class at KU depends on when your enrollment date is. Based on how many hours you have, KU determines when you will enroll for the following semester. Students who have the most hours are the first to enroll and so on down the list. The grading aspect depends on the professor. Most of the classes determine your grade based on the tests and final. Most classes, including math of some sort, include homework in your grade as well. The professors are amazing and always willing to help out their students any way they can. The workload is heavy in some of the upper-level classes, but it all depends on how the student manages his/her time. If you manage time well, you will be fine.

> **Regarding academics, KU says:** "The University of Kansas offers more than 190 majors in 11 undergraduate schools. As a freshman, you can be admitted to the College of Liberal Arts and Sciences (which encompasses 53 academic departments) or the Schools of Architecture and Urban Planning; Engineering; or Fine Arts. The other schools admit upperclassmen. Historically, KU students have built an impressive record of scholastic achievement. A total of 25 KU students have won Rhodes scholarships since that award's inception. Many KU programs rank in the top 25 for public universities. KU also has one of the oldest Honors Programs in the country."

 Employment Prospects

Current student, Sociology, 8/2006-Submit Date, April 2007

The potential for finding a job after KU is extraordinary! There are various programs (such as Jayhawks on Wall Street) that group KU students with successful professionals outside of the campus and the various career programs located within the Lawrence campus. The opportunities to improve one's résumé are staggering. The Alumni Association at the University of Kansas provides an excellent opportunity for willing alumni to be involved with their Alma Mater and help current students achieve great things during and after college.

Current student, 8/2003-Submit Date, September 2006

Employment prospects are pretty good, especially if you want to stay in Kansas. If you're from out of state you will need to do a lot of networking that people who want to stay in Kansas won't have to do.

Current student, Cultural Studies, 8/2004-Submit Date, April 2007

A lot of KU graduates stay in the Midwest, but I have friends who have gone all over the world after graduation. Kansas City, Chicago, Denver and Dallas seem to be the most popular. A lot of student organizations on campus can help students find jobs after graduation by being involved during their four years at college.

Current student, 8/2003-Submit Date, September 2006

What's great about KU is the feeling of tradition and home. The alumni are always involved and continuously make opportunities for students. Several of my friends have gotten amazing internships and jobs from alumni in prominent ities like New York and L.A. In the White School of Journalism and Mass Communication, there is a great career center and I receive e-mails on a weekly basis featuring new opportunities. One thing KU particularly prides itself on is its connections on the international realm. The study abroad programs are very popular and make for great opportunities. You can make a lot of connections around the world if you want to. When seeking a job or interview, employers know the University of Kansas. It sticks out. We are the number one research university in the Midwest. We have one of the most recognizable symbols (the Jayhawk) and the statistics show how well the university is and how it is continuously improving.

Current student, 8/2001-Submit Date, March 2005

Job fairs are definitely intimidating, but it's in your best interest to come in a suit and tie, résumé in hand, and give it your best shot. The two major job fairs—one in the fall and one in the spring—are quite helpful in trying to obtain gainful employment before graduation. Although it is very competitive, even if you aren't able to receive an interview, it's a great experience overall. The on-campus recruiting and job database system that is set up online is very easy to navigate and is very helpful for students looking for a job. When it comes time for you to find a job here at KU, the simplicity network that you will be using through career services is a great tool.

As far as the prestige goes for the employers, I'd say that the majority of companies that come here is reputable. With exceptions of a few employers that recruit on campus and attend the job fair, there wouldn't be many companies that at least wouldn't consider. To the best of my knowledge, it seems as if many students end up in sales positions, internships after senior year, or were able to gain employment through the internship that they had in their previous years.

I'm still currently looking for a job, but I'm still pursuing that avenue because after investing four years of my time and energy into getting a degree, I'd like to try to end up somewhere where my skills and knowledge will be valued. Although there are a number of employment prospects on campus through the year, you have to be the final one to say what kind of job you want and how bad you want it. You can have a job, or you can work hard to obtain the career that you want and you deserve.

> **Regarding employment prospects, the University of Kansas says:** "The University Career Center does an excellent job of preparing students for the work force. The center offers workshops throughout the year on résumé writing, interviewing, and job searching. In addition, the center hosts career fairs each year with top recruiters from companies nationwide. Several schools, including journalism, business and engineering, have their own specialized career centers."

Quality of Life

Current student, Communications, 8/2003-Submit Date, April 2007

I did not know anyone when I arrived at KU and I can say that Lawrence is now my home. I rarely return back to the Washington, D.C. area where I grew up because I enjoy Lawrence so much. I lived in a fraternity for three years and now live in an off-campus apartment. The town is gorgeous and is not "stereotypical Kansas."

Current student, Sociology, 8/2006-Submit Date, April 2007

The KU and Lawrence communities are some of the easiest in which to live. There are numerous housing options (great residence halls, scholarship halls, off-campus housing and a tremendous Greek community), a newly opened student recreation center that has near-future plans to expand, great surrounding neighborhoods that provide housing for students as well as a proximity to campus, and of course all the great dining along Mass Street. Lawrence is a very open city with a highly accepting atmosphere and opportunities to get involved in a variety of community organizations.

Current student, 8/2003-Submit Date, September 2006

I definitely would recommend the dorms freshman year, you meet a lot of new people there. Go for a traditional dorm; they are a little more social than the suit dorms are. Campus is beautiful, and if you haven't visited, you should. Most of

campus has a wireless network and is technologically up to date; some buildings aren't there yet. Dining is great, after you live off campus for a year or two you will miss the dining hall. Food on campus, not in the dorms, is really good too; there is a lot of options. There is little concern with safety, especially in the dorms; when going out at night, just be smart about your decisions and you will be fine.

Current student, Biology, 8/2006-Submit Date, April 2007

I live in the all-girls' dorm, which is on the North end of campus and I have never felt unsafe walking to and from the library or the Union at night. KU has a good safety system. Campus dining: what can you really say about this? Feeding mass quantities of people, obviously the food isn't going to be amazing, but I think KU does a good job. The all-girls dorm is a little lacking, but the main dining hall for the dorms on Daisy Hill (Mrs. E's) is pretty good. Has nice selection. Campus facilities (libraries, buildings, gyms and so on) are fantastic! I love going to the library and working out at our Rec Center.

Current student, 8/2004-Submit Date, May 2006

I live in a scholarship hall, which is a fairly big part of this campus and a fantastic place to live. We have a great community. The campus is very beautiful, and the university takes pride in keeping it up and making it look nice. Hopefully, you like hills and walking up them, because a lot of that is done here. If you want great calf muscles, come to KU. We have a brand-new rec center that is beautiful and convenient. The neighborhood is that of your typical college town, but KU has taken the necessary measures to make this a safe place to live.

Current student, 9/2004-Submit Date, May 2006

KU has an amazing housing program. We currently have eight residence halls on campus and a great student-run bus system that runs throughout campus and the City of Lawrence. There are many off-campus apartment complexes that cater to KU students. Campus seems huge when you first step foot on it, but everything is compacted into one street, so you're not running all over the place attempting to get to classes on time and whatnot. As far as dining goes, there are three dining halls for all of our residence halls and multiple restaurants and fast food places strategically placed all over campus. We also have the KU Police and multiple safety options all over campus to keep students safe 24 hours of the day.

Current student, 9/2004-Submit Date, May 2006

Housing around here is fairly inexpensive, which makes it more accessible for students who cannot afford to live a high quality life. We have excellent on-campus housing with tons of options for students with different preferences. This allows for students to be happy no matter what you want. The facilities are very nice, yet some recently have needed some repair and maintenance needs to be done. Dining on campus is great. We have recently added a new on-campus food center, which includes Pizza Hut, sandwiches, salad bar and Asian food. This is in addition to our food at the Union and Burge Union, as well. The neighborhoods are fairly safe with not much crime going on.

> **Regarding quality of life, the school says:** "Getting involved at KU is practically impossible to avoid. KU's eight residence halls house 275 to 900 students, and its scholarship halls house about 50 undergraduate students each in a cooperative living arrangement. Residents share cooking, household and hall government responsibilities. Even if you live off campus, there are 500 student organizations to join, a brand-new multicultural center, study abroad opportunities, undergraduate research experiences and community service projects. You can do anything you dream at KU."

Social Life

Current student, Cultural Studies, 8/2005-Submit Date, April 2007

The social life at KU is amazing!! There are so many clubs on-campus and organizations in which students can partake. It really enhances your college experience. Most students at KU are involved in clubs or social organizations, such as Greek life, Scholarship Hall life and so on. There are a lot of amazing restaurants in Lawrence, especially in the downtown area. Speaking of down-

Read all of Vault's College Surveys at **www.vault.com/college**–get complete surveys on 100s of colleges and universities, expert advice on applicaton essays and more.

VAULT CAREER LIBRARY 265

town, we have amazing local shops, coffee shops (Lawrence has amazing coffee!), restaurants, and bars within that area. It's the best place to go to spend your afternoon/evening/weekend/whatever! You will always have fun downtown, no matter what you do and the area is gorgeous.

Current student, 8/2003-Submit Date, September 2006

The Greek system is huge here; if you think you would like it at least try it for a little while. There are plenty of other options to meet new people, get involved in a student organization; you will meet some of your best friends here. Much of KU's social scene revolves around drinking. Favorite bars include: Quinton's, The Sand Bar, The Bar and It's Brothers. A freshman favorite is Liquid, which is more of a dance club. The dating scene is pretty big, but no more so than at any other college. Mass Street is a great place to go out to the bars or grab something to eat; there are plenty of local restaurants to try and plenty more bars to find the one that you like the best.

Current student, Cultural Studies, 8/2004-Submit Date, April 2007

Lawrence has something for everyone including the frat boy, the beatnik, the intellectual, the JoCo brat, the screamers and the farmers, you name it. Downtown is vibrant and has a wide variety of local stores which is a nice contrast to the sprawl of suburbia in Kansas City. And, if you do need something from a chain store, Kansas City is only 30 minutes away and has everything you could possibly need.

Bars are awesome. Mass Street has an English Pub (The Red Lyon) with free darts and popcorn, a huge dance club (Abe and Jake's in an old factory on the river), a local brewery (FreeState, with amazing food and even better beer), and a number of laid-back sports bars. There's also the Holy Trio at 14th and Tennessee with the Bull, Hawk and Wheel, all three of which are Greek traditions and right next to campus. The Crossing is also right next to a sub shop right across the street from campus, just in case students need to start celebrating right away.

Downtown restaurants include almost any ethnic food you could possibly want: Mexican, Thai, Greek, Italian, South American, Mediterranean, and even a whole slew of good old fashioned burger and pizza joints. Musicians stop in Lawrence a lot, despite any disparaging comments made by John Mayer on national television: The Shins, Guster, the Wallflowers, Dierks Bentley, and Hanson have all stopped by in the past two years.

And last but definitely not least, we have athletics. This town breathes basketball. James Naismith was the first coach at KU. That's right, the dude who invented the game started it here and started a killer tradition that includes Wilt Chamberlain, Dean Smith, and Danny Manning. My parents both went to KU

and were so huge into basketball that I have never missed watching a KU game during the NCAA championship, even when we would spring break in Hawaii, Costa Rica, or Disneyworld. The history is cool, but watching the team now is even better. Camping out for seats in Allen Fieldhouse is something that everyone has to do, but it's also really fun to watch the game in a restaurant, bar, or house with your friends.

Current student, 8/2005-Submit Date, May 2006

Lawrence is a more or less safe town with lots of places to go out and party. If you do not like the party scene, do not attend KU. There are loads of bars and restaurants. I believe the university has something like 400 clubs and there is some kind of event either sponsored by a club or Student Union Activities every weekend. The Greek system is pretty wide spread at KU and I believe something like 25 percent of students are involved in it. Sports are also a major part of KU. Favorites include attending KU basketball games at Allen Fieldhouse (although they say student tickets are limited, I have never had a problem using my sports pass to attend a game) and football games at Memorial Stadium.

> **Regarding social life, KU says:** "Lawrence has the friendly atmosphere of a small town with the amenities of a big city. The town is known for its arts scene—there are dozens of music venues, galleries and theatres—and its shops and restaurants in the beautiful downtown area. Lawrence has public swimming pools, more than 30 parks, a library and several museums. Topeka, the state capital, is 25 miles west of Lawrence, and Kansas City is about a 40 minute drive to the east."

 ## The School Says

The University of Kansas is a major public research and teaching university. The KU campus will offer you energy and excitement throughout the year. As a part of the Jayhawk family, you will learn traditions such as the Rock Chalk Chant, Waving the Wheat and singing the Alma Mater with your fellow Jayhawk fans. KU is recognized nationally by college guide books as a "best buy" university for the high quality of its programs and faculty and its reasonable tuition rates. At KU you can find your passion—in the arts, the sciences or anything in between. More than 40 KU programs are nationally ranked, many in the Top 10. KU truly is a great place to be.

Centre College

Admission Office
Centre College
600 West Walnut Street
Danville, KY 40422
Admissions phone: (800) 423-6236 or (859) 238-5350
Admissions e-mail: admission@centre.edu
Admissions URL: www.centre.edu/web/admission/

 ## Admissions

Alumnus/a, 9/2002-5/2006, May 2006

Centre is becoming increasingly recognized nation-wide, and thus more competitive. Applicants should possess an excellent high school academic record, strong extracurricular activities and an understanding of what a liberal arts education is all about. Your personal statement is, of course, vital to the process, and an interview with an admissions counselor helps the school get to know you personally.

Current student, 1/2003-Submit Date, May 2006

The thing that initially struck me about Centre College was how inviting they were throughout the application process. Obviously, it is a very demanding academic institution with a competitive application process to match, but it seemed like they were very willing to listen to me and share what it would take for me to come to Centre.

From what I remember the actual application was very cut and dry. My best advice on filling it out would be to take your time and include everything in which you were involved, along with all your awards and achievements. For the essay, think about the fact that there will be many many applicants writing about, the same topics. Be yourself, but in doing so let your personality and interests shine through. Make your essay memorable.

Obviously, the most fun and down-to-earth part of the application was the interview. I felt very comfortable when I went in to talk to someone from Centre. It was not an interview as much as it was a conversation about who I was and where I was coming from compared to where I wanted to be. Once again, throughout all of your college application process just be yourself, and if the right fit for you happens to be Centre, I hope to see you around campus.

Current student, 9/2004-Submit Date, May 2006

I actually work in the Admissions Office, so I know somewhat how the process works from the inside. First of all, it helps to apply Early Action—this is non-binding, and you find out sooner. Why worry until mid-March when you can find out in mid-January?

Having an interview is a definite plus. If the grades or activities are on the low side and the candidate isn't good on paper, the counselor can fight for an individual during the decision process. Centre is all about personal education, even during the admissions process. Visit campus and sit in on a class. Spend the night with a current student, take a tour and have lunch with other students. Talk to people. Come with questions—intelligent questions you really want the answers to. The interview is usually painless, a time for the counselor to put a face with an application.

Have as many people read over essays as possible. Every opinion and critique counts. Do not send in essays that have not been proofread. Also, these counselors are reading hundreds of essays. Be creative. Come up with your own topic or your own twist. Make it as interesting as you are.

As far as selectivity, Centre is fairly selective. The school is looking for multidimensional people who will add to the campus. Candidates can add to the campus through a particular interest in a club or organization, their academic excellence or through their leadership.

Current student, 9/2005-Submit Date, May 2006

Centre accepts applications via paper or Internet, with the application fee waived when applying over the Internet with the standardized Common Application online. The average ACT score is around a 27 or 28, and Centre is selective about which students are admitted.

Centre College gives out loans and gives a hefty sum of financial aid each year to its students. It is optional to come interview, and the odds of receiving financial aid increase greatly if one has an interview. The staff in the admissions office is friendly and the interviewer has a one-on-one interview with the applicant that lasts about an hour. Although some people dress up for this, the interview is rather a casual conversation about life, goals, extracurricular activities and what one is looking for in a school. Usually before or after an interview there is a tour led campus by student volunteers who show potential students the entire campus while telling general history about the college and what it has to offer.

Those who send in applications earlier will receive their entrance status in January while the second set of letters informing an applicant of admission status is sent out in April. Financial aid letters are sent along with acceptance letters.

Current student, 8/2002-Submit Date, May 2006

I found out about Centre through the trumpet world—that's what I play. Vince DiMartino, the former president of the International Trumpet Guild, teaches here. I also discovered that Centre was a very high-ranked school and had the strong liberal arts background I was looking for, so I decided to visit. Once I came here, the campus and all of the amazing people I met blew me away. Although I was getting Ivy League mail from institutions, they couldn't compare to what Centre had to offer in terms of personal education and atmosphere. I did binding Early Decision and I've never doubted my decision once.

Current student, 8/2004-Submit Date, May 2006

The admissions process was very straightforward. Application was fairly general. No interview was required. Besides having the appropriate grades and test scores, I simply wrote down every single club and activity with which I was involved in high school. Centre College has the reputation of being fairly selective, so any extra activities or groups that you are involved with is going to be beneficial.

They give you quite a few options for the essay, and my advice would be to pick a topic that is unique to you. Everyone can write about how they idolize their father, but pick something off the wall that will stand out, and this will further help to distinguish yourself from others.

 ## Academics

Alumnus/a, 8/2001-5/2005, May 2006

The quality of classes at Centre never ceased to impress me. I believe I spent my first year of college wondering how they thought I was intelligent enough to be a student there because I was so impressed with my professors' wealth of knowledge and high expectations of students' contributions to class discussions and quality of analytical writing. My favorite part of classes was always the discussion that stemmed from ideas from reading rather than just discussing readings at face value—particularly in government classes where all theories could be applied to the "what if" situations of the current or future times based on past occurrences.

While getting into some of the more popular classes was sometimes not guaranteed, most of those classes are offered once every year, so you have several chances during your time on campus to try again. This was particularly true with some art classes, some practical life classes on family life, and some English or

Read all of Vault's College Surveys at **www.vault.com/college**—get complete surveys on 100s of colleges and universities, expert advice on applicaton essays and more.

VAULT CAREER LIBRARY 267

history classes with popular professors who always assigned interesting projects or took fun field trips with the class.

The workload takes some definite adjustment from high school, but you quickly learn your professors' true desires and pick up on what can be considered supplemental to the true assignment. That being said, most professors are realistic as to understanding that students are in intensive classes and extremely active on campus, for the most part, so they understand that we will take from the class what we choose.

Current student, 9/2004-Submit Date, May 2006

There are no two ways about it: Centre is a hard school. Classes are small and the professors are topnotch. Students assess their instructors at the end of each term, so if professors aren't performing well, the deans and the professors find out about it and try to improve it.

Classes, for the most part, are not lecture based. You are expected to have read material before coming to class and then to participate in discussion. We have no speech class because you are expected to have a presentation or project in every class. Professors won't let you slack off. With classes being capped at 30, they take attendance with their eyes.

Professors have been known to call students or go to their rooms to get them out of bed. They are the best part of the college. The professors strive to foster personal relationships with their students, including dinners and teas at their houses on a regular basis. Just because a professor likes a student does not guarantee that student a good grade. Grading is fair, but tough. Everyone knows the professors from whom it is almost impossible to get an A—they're usually the best and most popular.

Certain popular classes can be difficult to get into, but usually you can talk to the professor and get in or get in during another term. And you will have homework. Students read every night and work on projects and papers and math and economics problem sets. The library is a very popular place.

Current student, 8/2002-Submit Date, May 2006

Centre has no grade inflation—and this is something to be proud of. It is a tough little school, but the professors really care about you and want you to do well. The classes are great—there perhaps was only one class out of the 50 or so that I took that I did not like—and that is saying something. CentreTerm provides invaluable experiences in classes such as Basketball as Religion and abroad trips to Vietnam, Russia and Barbados among many others.

Current student, 9/2005-Submit Date, May 2006

Centre's academic program is known to be rigorous, but well worth the tuition and the amount of time spent in class/preparing for class. Each year at Freshman Orientation, incoming students meet with professors and talk about what subjects he/she likes and sets up a schedule of classes.

Later during the summer, freshmen receive notice of who their academic advisor is; this is the professor who teaches the subject the student expressed most interest in. I was interested in art, so I was paired with the art history professor. The academic advisor meets his/her group of students during the five school days that freshmen are required to be on campus before school begins. The professor takes the group to his/her house and serves dinner and talks about the summer reading that all freshmen are required to do. The academic advisor helps students get into classes and aids in the choosing of classes to complete all general requirements and a major program. Because of the academic advisors, Centre guarantees that all students will graduate within four years or the fifth year is free.

Classes are fairly easy to get into, and it is unusual for people to be pushed out of classes. We are on somewhat of a trimester schedule, with two long semesters with the fall semester lasting from September to December and the Spring Semester from February to May. The month of January is called CentreTerm, and students take only one class during this month that meets for three hours a day. The idea to to be able to dedicate all of one's time to explore in-depth one specific field.

The workload is heavy, but the professors are personable and friendly and are willing to meet and talk if there are any problems with the workload. Professors take part in the students' lives by coming to football games, art exhibits and other student-centered events, and because of this, professors are thought of more tha[n] just teachers in the classroom but also friends and mentors.

Alumnus/a, 9/2002-5/2006, May 2006

Centre provides a personal, applicable and intensive education for every studen[t]. Classes are incredibly small (mine averaged around 15) and the professors a[re] outstanding. Each one is personally invested in students' educations and always willing to work outside of class to help anyone out. Grading is difficu[lt] and the workload would be overwhelming for the average college student. A 4[.0] GPA at Centre is about a 3.5 anywhere else because standards are set so high. [It] is not unusual to actually utilize the "one hour in class equals three hours out [of] class" method of studying. We push ourselves and expect the professors to pus[h] as well.

Current student, 8/2004-Submit Date, May 2006

The workload is tough, challenging and time-consuming, but by no means is [it] impossible or overwhelming. It gets close to the line of being too much, b[ut] never crosses. Classes are great because you get so much individual attentio[n] from professors. They are so eager to work with the students. I will write the[m] an e-mail and ask them a question, and within minutes I will get a respon[se]. They know you by name and their office doors are always open.

Popular classes are not a terrible problem. Throughout your four years at Centr[e] you should be able to get into any class that you want, and if somehow you don'[t] the administration is more than willing to work with you to solve the proble[m]. Grading varies with professors just like any college or university (we do have th[e] system). You will get a well-rounded education here with the general require[-]ments. Even the classes within one particular discipline have aspects th[at] include many other disciplines. For example, in economics classes you ma[y] have a laboratory portion and have to write lab reports as if it were a chemistr[y] class.

 ## Employment Prospects

Alumnus/a, 9/2002-5/2006, May 2006

Centre is notorious for its alumni network, dubbed the Centre Mafia. There ar[e] invaluable contacts who help in securing employment; many visit campus sev[-]eral times during the year to conduct interviews and accept résumés. Moreove[r] Centre students land amazing jobs; the fact that a school of our size has histori[-]cally produced vice presidents, a Supreme Court Chief Justice, and the founde[r] of the Hard Rock Cafe, just to name a few distinctions, is revealing enoug[h]. Lastly, Centre offers a wealth of internship opportunities (each student is guar[-]anteed an internship) and provides funding to many students.

Current student, 9/2005-Submit Date, May 2006

The most impressive statistic our school boasts is the acceptance of pre-med stu[-]dents. All of the students who completed the pre-med program in the school an[d] were members of the pre-med society at our school were accepted into medica[l] school. Centre holds job expos, has a web site and sends out e-mails about sum[-]mer opportunities and post-graduation jobs.

Alumni often help out in finding jobs for graduates. Career Services on campu[s] meets with students and helps them look for jobs. Centre College offers a pro[-]gram called Centre Futures. To be a part of this program, one needs to meet wit[h] a Centre Futures advisor for about a half an hour each semester. If one is in thi[s] program (which is open to everyone), Centre guarantees one will graduate i[n] four years, study abroad and receive an internship.

Alumnus/a, 8/2002-6/2006, May 2006

The Centre Commitment provides that every student can go abroad and have a[n] internship and graduate in four years. Career Services is geared toward findin[g] internships for Centre students and helping students move on with employmen[t] after graduation. During my time at Centre I participated in three internships— one at a nonprofit in Danville, one at a nonprofit directed by a Centre graduat[e] in Nashville, Tennessee and one on Capital Hill in D.C. in my Congressman['s] office.

The alumni are extremely dedicated to Centre and will do anything to help out [a] Centre student—after all, Centre is always in the top of the percentage of alum[ni] i giving rankings. A number of students go on to graduate school at places like Harvard and Johns Hopkins Medical School, and students who take jobs end up at Toyota, among many other places. Centre students also regularly receive Fulbright Fellowships, Truman Scholarships and Rotary Ambassadorial scholarships.

Current student, 8/2002-Submit Date, May 2006

Our alumni network is amazing and even a little scary. It seems like any profession in the U.S., and even Europe and Asia, there are Centre grads who know someone to get you an in. I'm amazed at how prolific they are. Also, the Centre Promise guarantees an internship before graduation, so anyone who wants one gets one. I've actually had three.

It seems like everywhere Centre grads go, they leave such a positive response that they are eager to hire more graduates, despite coming from such a small school in Kentucky. I don't really know about recruiting since I'm going to law school (Ohio State, with a scholarship), so I didn't participate in that kind of thing.

Quality of Life

Alumnus/a, 8/2001-5/2005, May 2006

Centre is not a suitcase college. People stay on campus on the weekends, which makes living on campus very fun and important. All freshmen must live on campus and most students choose to do so all four years. Cowan (the dining hall) is as much a social scene as it is a food establishment. People go there two or three meals per day to catch up with friends, find out what is going on that weekend or cram with a group for an upcoming test.

The housing is nice and campus is kept looking spectacular year-round (sometimes it feels like they mow every day)! Danville as a town is small, but growing in its options for food and activities. It has that small, Southern town charm that is very inviting and safe. I never once felt unsafe at Centre in my four years there. Everyone knows everyone and we look out for each other. If you visit the campus and you feel like people are looking at you funny, it's simply because we all know and recognize one another so we know when someone is on campus who normally wouldn't be there. All residential buildings now must be entered by swiping your student ID so outsiders must be accompanied by a resident.

They have just remodeled the library and the athletic center so they are wonderful. Very welcoming and a comfortable environment to study and work out.

Current student, 1/2003-Submit Date, May 2006

I have felt safe from the day I first set foot on Centre's campus. The campus security is always there to help out, whether it's simply unlocking a door when you forgot your key or giving you a lift to your dorm late at night. Plus, the students tend to look out for one another. We walk with each other across campus at night and check on each other just to see how things are going. I was also surprised at how friendly and outgoing President Roush was when I first came to Centre. During Freshman Orientation, he invited all of us to his home for a cookout and greeted every last one of us personally. It's this kind of thing that sums up the quality and security of life at Centre College.

Alumnus/a, 9/2001-5/2005, May 2006

Living on campus was great! It was such a rich and diverse community, and I always felt like you were living with your best friends. I never felt unsafe on campus, except when I was with some of my friends and they wanted to do something stupid, but that was an aside.

My senior year was great because I was able to move into a large apartment that the school owned for no extra cost, it was on a beautiful street with professors as neighbors, and just across the street from campus. Dining was OK, it got rather dull after four straight years. The school is located really close to downtown Danville, so it was a pretty section of town. All in all I loved living at Centre.

Current student, 9/2005-Submit Date, May 2006

Centre College has nice residential facilities, with all freshmen living in single-sex dorms. Upperclassman students are eligible for singles, off-campus housing, apartment housing and co-ed housing. There are two main dining facilities and one coffee shop. The library and gym are both completely new and remodeled. Centre is walking distance outside of the town. Crime rates are low, and the campus has a department of safety that takes care of any crime issues on campus.

Current student, 8/2002-Submit Date, May 2006

Centre has a high quality of life. Danville is one of the 50 Best Towns to Live in in the U.S., and it is very safe, idyllic even. 98 percent of students live on campus so there is a very strong sense of community. Our new College Centre really goes far to improve this. There is one main dining hall, so students get to interact on a regular basis in a non-academic setting. Also, the professors usually live in Danville and many staff members live near campus, so they are around a lot, making Centre more than just the students, but everyone involved in the Centre experience.

Social Life

Current student, 9/2005-Submit Date, May 2006

Centre is in the middle of a dry county, but it is a damp school. There are no bars around but the county next to ours is a wet county so alcohol is available. Restaurants also serve alcohol, but there are no bars.

The Greek system is very active at our school with over [50] percent of all students Greek affiliated. Centre holds free concerts, activities and a spring carnival. Although Centre may be a small school in a small town, it keeps students busy.

Dating at Centre is hard because it is such a small school, but still possible. A little less than 20 percent of Centre students end up marrying each other. Although there are no clubs in Danville, Centre is 45 minutes away from Lexington which has clubs, bars and a shopping district. Many students go to Applebee's in town or Cheddar's in Lexington on Friday and Saturday nights. Just because the students are residing in a small town, they are by no means confined there.

> **The school says:** "A number of restaurants in Danville have bars."

Current student, 8/2002-Submit Date, May 2006

The Greek system is unlike any other. Most fraternity parties are open to the entire campus, and a good number of students attend them. Favorites include Phi Tau's Air Guitar and the SAE's Graffiti party. Close to half of the women on Centre's campus are in one of four sororities: Alpha Delta Pi, Delta Delta Delta, Kappa Alpha Theta or Kappa Kappa Gamma.

The music organization Centre Encore, and the service fraternity, Alpha Phi Omega, are also very active on Centre's campus. The Student Activities Council also puts on multiple events throughout the year, including carnival which has brought acts such as Ben Folds and Pat Green in past years. One of the most well-known activities on campus occurs during Greek Week, Spring Sing, where all of the Greek organizations perform songs for the president and other judges on the steps of Old Centre (the main administrative building and symbol of the college).

Current student, 9/2004-Submit Date, May 2006

Greek life is huge at Centre (usually about 60 percent of campus). To a certain extent, it does dominate weekend activities. The great thing for non-Greeks (like me) is that all the events are open. There is no list, and everyone is welcome. Dating and social interactions are a little bizarre at Centre, but it is a small campus where everyone knows everyone else. People will talk.

Outside of Greek life, there are more than 100 campus clubs and organizations, ranging from political interests to community service to intramural sports to mock trial. I usually have meetings three nights a week. It's hard not to be involved on campus. Danville and Boyle County are moist. All of the sur-

Read all of Vault's College Surveys at www.vault.com/college–get complete surveys on 100s of colleges and universities, expert advice on applicaton essays and more.

VAULT CAREER LIBRARY 269

rounding counties are dry or moist (dry = no alcohol at all, moist = alcohol by the drink only). The restaurants are decent, but the same selection can get old. Students' favorite events include the Welcome Back Concert, Carnival and Carnival Concert.

Current student, 8/2002-Submit Date, May 2006

The Greek system is huge at Centre, over 50 percent. It's not elite and scary like at larger schools, but is more like a group of friends who volunteer and hang out together who happen to have the same values. Centre dating is a little weird since the student body is so small, but it works since 20 percent of the student body marries another Centre grad!

There are always things going on on campus, like movies on the lawn, concerts, panel discussions, art exhibits and intramural sports. While Centre does not have a bar scene since Boyle County isn't wet, there are the Danville classic restaurants that students love. Guadalahara serves up a mean margarita and quesadilla for under $7. Applebee's and O'Charley's both serve alcohol and have the usual fare for a little more money. If all else fails, the 24-hour Wal-Mart serves as entertainment in the rare occasion that students are bored and looking for something to do.

 ## The School Says

Founded in 1819, Centre College is a *U.S. News* Top 50 national liberal arts college. Centre was recently named the Number One educational value among American colleges by *Consumers' Digest*. Centre has one of the nation's Top 10 study abroad programs and is known for having America's most loyal alumni. Over the past two decades they have given annual financial support at a rate higher than that of any other college or university.

Centre makes a promise to all its students: we will provide a challenging, personal education that will enable you to achieve extraordinary success in advanced study and your career. And

we back up our pledge of individualized, timely education with The Centre Commitment. If students meet the college's academic and social requirements, they are guaranteed an internship, study abroad and graduation in four years; otherwise, they receive up to a year of additional study tuition-free.

Centre enrolls approximately 1,175 students from throughout the U.S. and several foreign countries. The college's students are highly motivated and accomplished. They typically rank in the top quarter of their high school class, with about 60 percent in the top 10 percent of their class.

Centre offers a full range of traditional majors, and we encourage self-designed majors, so you can create a program that perfectly fits your abilities and interests. Students frequently earn two (and occasionally even three) majors during their four years at the College.

Centre faculty are dedicated teachers. They challenge and support their students in and out of the classroom. 98 percent hold their PhD or equivalent.

The average class size is 18 and virtually no classes are larger than 30.

Within 10 months of graduation, 96 percent of Centre students are employed or engaged in advanced study.

Centre has a beautiful, 150-acre campus. Buildings are predominately Greek Revival in style and 13 are included in the National Register of Historic Places.

Centre's study abroad program is ranked ninth in the nation by *U.S. News*. More than four of five of the college's students study abroad. We have campuses in England, France and Mexico, with exchange programs in Japan and Northern Ireland. Three-week study opportunities are available in virtually all parts of the world.

University of Kentucky

Admissions Office
100 W.D. Funkhouser Building
Lexington, KY 40506-0054
Admissions phone: (859) 257-2000
Admissions fax: (859) 257-3823
Admissions e-mail: admissio@uky.edu
Admissions URL: www.uky.edu/UGAdmission/prospective/student.html

Note: The school has chosen not to review the student surveys submitted.

 ## Admissions

Alumnus/a, 8/2000-5/2004, December 2005

The admissions process for the undergraduate program was simple. I completed the application packet, with required attachments, and was accepted. I also received a good deal of scholarships. Make sure you apply for scholarships. The university was not very selective when it came to admissions.

Current student, 8/2003-Submit Date, April 2005

The admissions process for physical therapy school was pretty intense. There are sections for essays, past transcripts and extracurricular activities. There i also an interview process if you get past the first step of the application process You will meet with two professors in the department and they will question yo about yourself and your goals. Don't be nervous for the interview. The professors are very laid back and appreciate it if you ask them questions. It's chees but true. Just relax and be yourself.

Current student, 8/2000-Submit Date, December 2004

Applying to the university is not nearly as time consuming compared to othe universities in the area. There is one optional segment in which a student ca submit a personal statement as to why they should be considered for acceptance No teacher recommendations are required.

Current student, 8/2003-Submit Date, August 2004

It was very easy to get into UK. I had a previous background of schooling a another college so everything transferred over very nicely. The application wa very easy to fill out, the essay question was not hard at all. Just make sure tha all the information is filled out completely and there should be no problems.

Academics

Alumnus/a, English 8/2000-5/2004, December 2005

I thoroughly enjoyed all but three courses throughout my four full-time years of study at the University of Kentucky. My teachers were phenomenal. Mandatory introduction courses, including biology and English, were surprisingly helpful and interesting. The university requires a semi-broad cross-field study at the introductory level. This can be a great opportunity. I do not recommend the College of Education—I found this program very weak. However, I had considerable contact with the English and political science programs (I majored in both) and found them to be excellent programs with helpful teachers. It was a bit difficult to register for some courses, but I was always able to get courses by the time I needed them. Grading was definitely fair. I was able to earn a 3.975 with consistent work. The workload can easily be managed, though it takes everyone some time to adjust to college academics. I was able, with difficulty, to handle seven courses in one semester. However, students should take only four classes their first semester, because it takes a while to get the flow. Many students can maintain part-time jobs with such workloads.

Current student, Physical Therapy, 8/2003-Submit Date, April 2005

The classes in the physical therapy program are all laid out for you. The classes are pretty good but the program needs organizational help. Most of the professors are great but they all have their quirks. The actual content isn't that difficult but the program is very intense. You are in class from 8 to 5 usually and that is the hardest part to get used to. And it is straight through the summers, that's a big blow. They are very tough with rules and grades.

Current student, 8/2000-Submit Date, December 2004

There is a huge number of classes available at the university. In terms of quality, it all depends on what specific section a student tries to get into. Some professors are extremely technical, while others offer a very relaxed class atmosphere. The relaxed professors' classes will usually fill up very quickly leaving few students stuck in sections that are not their top choices. Overall, if a student registers on time, he or she will be happy with the course selection available regardless of class year.

Alumnus/a, Nursing 8/1987-6/1991, November 2004

The classes at the university built on our knowledge and continued our education toward our nursing degrees. The classes were very large and impersonal, but the clinical groups were smaller and more one-on-one. Because the classes were so large, it wasn't difficult getting into the classes you needed, again the basic course work was completed at another college. Grading was fair. The system was geared toward weeding out those who could not do the work. The clinical professors were great with few exceptions but you had to know your stuff when you went to clinical—they would help but would not go lightly on those unprepared.

Current student, Animal Science, 8/2003-Submit Date, August 2004

My program (animal science) is wonderful. The teachers are so friendly and helpful. It is a very demanding program but you learn a lot. The classes are very easy to get into. There are not many people in the program at one time so the classes that you pick are usually still open so that you will be able to get in. The workload is moderate. It all depends on what schedule you make for yourself and if you plan to work at the same time while going to school.

Employment Prospects

Alumnus/a, Political Science 8/2000-5/2004, December 2005

From what I know, a degree from the University of Kentucky carries the basic prestige of graduating from college. The degree shows that you worked and achieved at the collegiate level. However, a degree from UK does not necessarily represent excellence compared to other universities. If you are living in Kentucky or don't intend to compete nationally, this degree would easily be sufficient, but if you have higher goals, this university might not be enough. With this degree, however, I was able to earn a full ride plus teaching assistantship at the University of Colorado Political Science PhD program, one of the better programs in the country. People at the University of Kentucky were generally helpful.

Alumnus/a, Education 8/1983-5/1987, September 2005

I remember UK had an excellent educational job fair the spring of my graduation. I actually got an offer out of that fair. But let's be honest. There's a teacher shortage, I hear, and a good recommendation from your supervising teacher can help as much as anything else. That being said, UK is the largest state school in Kentucky, and has a decent education program—which, as I said, I believe they've toughened. As far as actually helping me get my job, I don't believe UK itself was much help—except for the excellent job fair. On the other hand, I didn't seek much help either. I was employed full time by the following fall because there was an opening where I had completed my student teaching.

Current student, Physical Therapy, 8/2003-Submit Date, April 2005

The professors will tell you that our school is really well-known and has a good reputation but I think that's all relative. Physical therapists are in demand again so we will all probably get jobs. We have clinicals to introduce us to the working world which are very helpful. We can get jobs in either outpatient clinics, acute care hospitals or long-term care facilities.

Current student, Business, 8/2000-Submit Date, December 2004

The business fair at the school is fairly decent with a number of regional offices representing firms like Merrill Lynch, IBM and Morgan Stanley offering presentations. Overall, the recruiting process may be difficult for a student trying to work somewhere outside of Lexington. Many students end up going to graduate school, while others find regional work at prestigious locations.

Alumnus/a, Nursing 8/1987-6/1991, November 2004

The university is highly regarded in Kentucky. Although there are several other nursing universities in the area, it is not difficult to find a job. Most of the graduates are working in hospitals both locally and from their home towns after passing boards. I believe there was a 5 percent fail rate on boards the year I graduated. The campus did hold job fairs in the university hospital as well as other places. There is an alumni network that offers info on jobs and news.

Current student, Animal Science, 8/2003-Submit Date, August 2004

In my program there are always big companies coming in and recruiting people that are ready to graduate to come into their business. The internship opportunities are plentiful. If you graduate with an animal science bachelor's degree from UK you will get a job. There are no questions asked.

Quality of Life

Alumnus/a, 8/2000-5/2004, December 2005

In general, the University of Kentucky is a safe and fun place to be. Lexington is not a huge town, but there is plenty to do. I had a wonderful experience with campus housing. There is a big decision for incoming students to make when it comes to housing. South campus is party campus: this is good because there are lots of parties to attend and because south campus is also close to the library (a 20-minute walk from north campus). However, living on south campus can be difficult because it is nearly impossible to escape the parties when you want some quiet time to study or be alone. It is also easy to get in trouble on south campus. On south campus, you will probably live in one of two towers: there isn't much feeling of community there and you have fire alarms many, many times all through the night. North campus, on the other hand, is closer to a lot of classes, though not all. North campus is where most of the honors students live, although you do not have to be an honors student to live there. There is a real sense of community, you can know almost everyone in your building, and there is plenty of opportunity to hang out together off campus and get some quiet when you want to. I personally lived on north campus and loved it. I was also a resident advisor there. Remember, resident advisors are there to help you adjust to college life. Use them as resources. Security has really tightened up at the university, for good and for bad. I always felt safe, but things do happen sometimes. Dining is good, but when you eat the same things for a year, it's bound to get old. Just expect it to. South campus has slightly better food, but you don't have to live there to eat there. You have lots of opportunities living in campus housing. Get involved.

Read all of Vault's College Surveys at www.vault.com/college—get complete surveys on 100s of colleges and universities, expert advice on applicaton essays and more.

VAULT CAREER LIBRARY 271

Current student, 8/2003-Submit Date, April 2005

Housing is always a problem in undergrad, I hear. But if you are willing to walk a ways or buy an expensive parking pass, you can find really great places to live. There is a decent bit of crime on campus and in Lexington. You definitely have to be safe and cautious. The physical therapy school just got a new building and our facilities are great. Lexington has a ton of great restaurants and entertainment.

Current student, 8/2000-Submit Date, December 2004

The University of Kentucky has been named one of the friendliest campuses in America, and for good reason. The teachers are incredibly helpful and the activities offered are endless.

Alumnus/a, 8/1987-6/1991, November 2004

The school is located in downtown Lexington. The area, though not crime free, is a safe place. The housing is co-ed, but there is also a number of houses that rent specifically to students. There are many fast food restaurants around as well as casual dining places, but the campus food and cafeterias are good. The school is very large and until you get into your major there, it's hard to really meet and get to know people—you never seem to see the same people twice.

Current student, 8/2003-Submit Date, August 2004

I didn't stay on campus but there are so many dorms and sororities. If that is your cup of tea, then you will have such a great time. The facilities are great especially the library. It seems as though UK never runs out of room for anyone except at basketball games. There are many officers around campus at night to make people feel safe and it is very well lit. UK offers many extracurricular activities that don't include sports.

 ## Social Life

Alumnus/a, 8/2000-5/2004, December 2005

There are bars in Lexington and some students frequent them. I have never experienced this part of Lexington's social life, but I can tell you that you aren't going to find the kind of nightlife in Lexington that you would in larger cities. If this is important to you, go somewhere else. There are lots of fraternities and sororities on south campus you can join, and that comes with a full social life of parties. There are lots of restaurants to enjoy: mostly chains, not many grass roots kinds of places. There is an opera theatre you can enjoy and the university does a good job of providing lots of arts entertainment for very reasonable prices. There are some good light restaurants around campus like Jimmy John's (subs) and the big mall is only about 10 minutes away from campus.

Current student, 8/2003-Submit Date, April 2005

Lexington is definitely a college town and there are young people everywhere. I love McCarthy's, Fishtank, Trump's, BW3's and Cheapside's. Good places to eat are Macaroni Grill, Panera, Qdoba, Mai Tai and Pazzo's. The Greek system is huge on campus. There are tons of events that the student government puts on.

Sports at the University of Kentucky are a huge deal. Football games are a great time, especially the tailgating. The team is never that good but the games are a great time. Basketball, of course, is huge at the University of Kentucky. Our team is always really good and the games are so much fun to watch. Students can enter the lottery for student seats in the Eruption Zone for only $5 each. There is tons of school pride on campus. Everyone wears University of Kentucky apparel all the time.

Alumnus/a, 8/1987-6/1991, November 2004

There are many things to get involved with at UK. The school is located right in the heart of Lexington and it seems the town has grown up to accommodate the students. There are tons of clubs, restaurants and events occurring there all the time. UK is well known for its basketball, and during basketball season the city is full of mania. The school is big and there are lots of opportunities to meet new people, whether in groups or individually. The Greek system is there but I never participated in it.

Current student, 8/2003-Submit Date, August 2004

The bars around campus are great. They have awesome specials and each one has a different thing going on each night. Like ladies' night, karaoke night and two for two night. The events are endless and there is always something going on almost every night. The favorite things for students to do are go to the bars if you are of age but if you are not then the fraternity and sorority parties are fun also.

Louisiana State University

Office of Undergraduate Admissions
110 Thomas Boyd Hall
Louisiana State University
Baton Rouge, LA 70803
Admissions phone: (225) 578-1175
Admissions e-mail: admissions@lsu.edu
Admissions URL: www.lsu.edu/lsu4me

 ## Admissions

Current student, Psychology, 8/2004-Submit Date, April 2007

I filled out an application online. I was then informed that the university received my application and needed transcripts and such. Once I sent those in, I was informed of my acceptance based on my academic success. They base acceptance on ACT/SAT scores, GPA and extracurricular activities. I didn't have to write an essay or do an interview; however, I believe you have to do those things if you are borderline.

Current student, Business, 1/2006-Submit Date, April 2007

Simply have ACT or SAT scores sent to university along with official transcripts and fill out brief application. As long as the student meets the test score and GPA requirements, he/she is accepted.

Current student, Communications, 8/2003-Submit Date, April 2007

LSU is mostly concerned with your GPA, SAT or ACT score, and involvement. There is no interview process. A short essay was required. Advice to incoming students: study hard and get involved. Involvement looks great on any admissions form.

> **The school says:** "An essay is no longer required for university application, scholarships or honors college."

Current student, Business, 8/2004-Submit Date, July 2007

The admissions process was pretty straightforward, and the counselors were nice. If you're from Louisiana, the process is even simpler. ACT score is a big factor in determining admittance and scholarship recipients. That said, some people do get scholarships even if they don't meet the ACT requirement, so the rules are flexible if you have lots of extracurricular.

> **The school says:** "LSU's Office of Undergraduate Admissions awards scholarships based on a prospective student's GPA, ACT/SAT score and his/her extracurriculars."

Apply early and attend spring testing if you're invited! You can test out of all the low-level courses people complain about being forced to take.

Current student, 1/2003-Submit Date, March 2007

When I got into LSU, they took anyone from LA with an ACT of 21 and a high school GPA of 2.5. The standards have changed a lot. It used to be almost automatic that you would get into LSU. Now, I believe it's a little more difficult. There are no essays or interviews. It's strictly based on your HS performance and test scores. The Honors College requires an essay, but all you have to do is pull some strings and pretty much anyone can get in to the Honors College if they want to. It's not hard to get into LSU, and certainly not hard to graduate.

Current student, 8/2004-Submit Date, May 2006

I had to fill out all of the application process information as well as send them a copy of my transcript and ACT score. The requirements were a 22 or better on my ACT and a GPA of at least 3.0 in high school.

> **The school says:** "As an advisory, the fall entering class of 2006 had an average ACT of 25.1, 1183 SAT with more than 74 percent having a high school GPA of at least 3.4/4.0."

Current student, 8/2005-Submit Date, April 2006

The university provided scholarships. In order to receive one, students have to submit an SAT exam, a TOEFL exam (for international students) and write a personal essay. The selection process was rigorous and it filtered the most prospective students. The easiest way to get into any college is to perform well in your high school as that is the single most crucial deciding factor when you apply to a college. LSU is no exception in this case. Interviews also improve the chances of one getting selected in the university but with LSU, interviews are not necessary although they are recommended.

> **The school says:** "TOEFL exam scores and personal essay are required for international student scholarship applications."

Current student, 8/2005-Submit Date, October 2005

Make good grades, get good ACT scores and write a good essay. Being from LA helps. Obviously, the more involved you were in high school, the better chance you have of getting in, or getting a scholarship. Really try hard on the ACT. Take prep courses if you need to. It's important, and not hard if you put forth the effort. Basically, you make decent grades, you submit an application that reflects your hard work, you show good ACT scores (24 or above helps tremendously) and you'll have a very easy time getting in, and a decent chance of getting some sort of scholarship. Just apply yourself, and you'll get what you want.

 ## Academics

Current student, Honors College, 8/2006-Submit Date, April 2007

LSU can be the university that you want it to be. The Honors Program offers smaller classes with accelerated material for those wanting to learn as much as they can. Other classes' level of difficulty depends on the teacher. There are requirements to what a teacher has to teach and assign but it is up to them if they want to teach the bare minimum or add what they think is important. Most of the time your grades reflect the amount of work you put into a course. Also, the professors are always available to help you or answer any of your questions during their scheduled office hours. Popular classes do fill up fast, but because of the priority scheduling most seniors get the classes that they want.

Current student, Business, 8/2004-Submit Date, July 2007

You get out of LSU what you put into it. LSU's Honors College, where the class sizes are much smaller and the work much more demanding, is nothing to be scoffed at. If you can be successful in a place with 25,000+ students, you can be successful anywhere.

You can squeeze by without doing (or learning) much, or you can work hard and learn a lot. It's your choice, but the quality of the class is directly related to the work you put into it.

Honors students get to pick their classes first, which all but guarantees they'll get what they want. Then it goes by seniority, which is determined by number of hours. Take as many as you can early on so as to put yourself ahead of your peers. You will thank yourself later.

Grading is fair and not extremely challenging. Top-tier employers expect state school grads to have a 4.0 or close to it, so always work for the A's.

For the most part, professors are very nice and helpful outside of class. Just like every other school, there are a few bad apples. Avoid them by asking advice of older friends.

Current student, 1/2003-Submit Date, March 2007

Classes are very hard to schedule, especially if you're a freshman. LSU has way too many students and not enough instructors, let alone professors. Expect class sizes from 60 to 900 students in your first year. Literally, 900 students can be in a class at one time taught in a huge auditorium. Luckily, I'd finished all my basic

Read all of Vault's College Surveys at **www.vault.com/college**—get complete surveys on 100s of colleges and universities, expert advice on applicaton essays and more.

VAULT CAREER LIBRARY **273**

courses when they started that. LSU is very easy if you're a decent student. I didn't go to class for my first two years and made a 3.5 every semester. I read a lot, though. Most professors are strictly textbook, and there are many under-performing students to help you out on the curve if you study at least a little. Expect many multiple choice tests and little retained knowledge. Essay tests are apparently reserved for History, English, and WGS classes, unless you get lucky

. Current student, Engineering 8/2004-Submit Date, May 2006

LSU has some of the most challenging curriculums in the nation. Our internal auditing program is the best in the nation. Our architecture and interior design degrees are nothing to snuff at either. They are among the best in the nation. LSU also has a very strong engineering program. I know this from personal experience. It has pushed me to new levels I never thought I was capable of. LSU scheduling is all electronic, which makes scheduling faster and easier. The professors are all highly qualified individuals with multiple degrees and most have their doctorate degrees. The workload is heavy but an education of this caliber should have such a workload. LSU is also leading the nation in technology. With its flagship agenda in mind LSU will, in the next few years, be tripling their technology base in search of a better technologically academic environment for its students.

Current student, 8/2005-Submit Date, April 2006

The classes vary from as few as 20 students to as many as 100 students. However, the professors are very friendly and very helpful. The university offers a large number of choices to choose when selecting classes. The grading system is fair where by grades get curved when the whole class performs poorly (no curving down). Getting an A or a B is not very hard as long as one is willing to put in the efforts and not spend too much time partying. Generally workload is not an issue as long as one is up to date with one's work. However, if one wastes too much time on other things, then this might become an issue.

Current student, Engineering, 8/2001-Submit Date, September 2005

I'm a mechanical engineering major so our classes are rather easy to get into. We have the eighth best ME department in the country, and are one of only three in the country to require a prototype design from concept to manufacture to get a degree. If you need to get into a class that's full, just e-mail the undergraduate coordinator and he'll stick you in it. However, the ME department operates under a lockstep program, so if you have to drop certain classes, it will put you back a full year instead of a semester. But lockstep can be good because since professors only teach the required courses once a year, it frees them up to teach more electives. The computer engineering program is ranked third in the country, and the College of Engineering as a whole is pretty good.

My psychology major friends all have a very hard time getting into their classes because it's one of the most popular majors on campus and lots of non-majors take the courses as general education social science electives.

Freshman math and English courses have increased in size five-fold (from 20 students to 100). Most of the work is done by computer in those classes, and I hear it's pretty hard to get in contact with the teachers. It's part of the former Chancellor's plan to make LSU a flagship university. Most students (and teachers) think it sucks, but the powers that be have decided to stick with it.

Employment Prospects

Current student, Communications, 8/2003-Submit Date, April 2007

Everywhere you look on campus there is another flyer for some kind of internship. Counselors and professors are very helpful if you are in need of guidance post-graduation. The good thing about going to LSU is that everyone around the country knows LSU. Once you become an alumnus, your family grows to an infinite number. Mention that you are an LSU graduate around another former Tiger and there is an instant bond.

Current student, 1/2003-Submit Date, March 2007

LSU has a lot of oil companies recruiting and local businesses. There are no placement services offered, but Career Services will tell you everything you already know about a résumé and interview if you'd like.

It would be nice if they had real placement services like most other universitie do but there are just too many students.

Current student, 8/2004-Submit Date, May 2006

The LSU alumni association provides many opportunities for after college employ ment. Alumni are always looking for LSU students in their job market. Tha reminds me of that LSU is one of four schools at which the national governmen looks for D.C. employment after college. So if a job with the government is wher you see yourself, I would recommend LSU as a place to consider.

Current student, 8/2001-Submit Date, September 2005

There is a career day every semester and recruiters come to accept résumés. It' pretty much a huge job fair. Career Services on campus gives students every opportunity to get a job/co-op/internship. They come in and speak to classes conduct mock-interviews, host a job-posting web site, actively help you with job search, and much more. I honestly believe that if you leave LSU without job, it's your fault because they do everything in their power to place you some where.

Current student, 8/2002-Submit Date, February 2005

There are many opportunities for LSU students to meet with prospective employees. LSU holds several career fairs and also has a career center that wil help you with just about anything you need. Internships are stressed as very important, and the school will help you obtain the right internship for you major. The alumni of LSU are very involved, and more than willing to help students.

Quality of Life

Current student, Honors College, 8/2006-Submit Date, April 2007

The quality of life at LSU is wonderful. Most freshmen live on campus and it is quite an experience. The residential halls are not the best quality but the experiences you have in them are worth sharing a bathroom with 20 other people The rest of the students can choose to live in houses and apartments that can be found throughout the Baton Rouge area for all budgets. In addition, the bus routes that go from most apartment complexes to campus eliminate the hassle o having to drive to class. LSU's campus is stunning. Where else can you walk to class under the shade of the century old oaks and flowering trees? The buildings may not all match or be from the same era, but they are all pretty in their own way.

Current student, Business, 1/2006-Submit Date, April 2007

Many residence halls are available to students as well as upper-class luxury apartments within walking distance and/or bus ride. Fast food is available or campus, including Blimpie, Pizzahut, Chick-fil-A and so on. Other options such as Louisiana style food, are available and are buffet quality.

Current student, Communications, 8/2003-Submit Date, April 2007

Over the past couple of years Baton Rouge has been growing right before ou eyes. Apartment complexes, gyms, restaurants, you name it, and it is all being built somewhere near the edges of campus. Living in a residential hall is recommended to all freshmen. The people you meet there will become friends for life. You are close to all of you classes, you don't have to fight for a good parking spot, and dining halls are close by. In general Baton Rouge is a safe place.

Current student, 1/2003-Submit Date, March 2007

Dining at LSU is mediocre. I've seen much better at other universities, ever other state schools. Greek life is huge at LSU, so if you want to join a sorority or frat, you have lots of options.

Current student, 8/2004-Submit Date, May 2006

The campus is one of the most beautiful in the nation. You enter campus passing the LSU lakes and enter into a oak tree wonderland that is known as LSU The campus just seems to grow on you. Every day I find a new reason why I love this campus. The housing is moderate. There are plenty of dorms but I would recommend getting an apartment off campus. Campus dining is OK but the food around LSU is excellent. Cane's is by far the landmark food of the LSU campus. It is a chicken tenders place that got its start here, and if it isn't one of ne top fast food places in the nation by the time I am 30, I will probably cry. Crime is relatively nonexistent.

Social Life

Current student, Honors College, 8/2006-Submit Date, April 2007

My favorite part of the LSU social life is Saturdays on game days. It is on these days where LSU legendary tailgaters come out in masses. It is truly amazing how the campus transforms itself into the largest picnic ever. Everywhere you walk there are tents set up where people are having a good time. You could walk up to any one of these places and they would welcome you with open arms to eat as much cajun cooking as you can handle.

Current student, Psychology, 8/2004-Submit Date, April 2007

School social life is big. You meet so many people and there are all kinds of events, like free concerts, drive-in movies, pancake dinners and athletic events that are out of this world! Bars are pretty big around Baton Rouge, but I don't go out very much. It's pretty easy to meet new people in Baton Rouge. We have over 350 organizations on campus and if you can't find one for you, you can start one if you get together five people and a constitution. Most students on campus love football games, obviously! There is nothing better than Death Valley on a Saturday night in Louisiana!

Current student, Communications, 8/2003-Submit Date, April 2007

LSU offers over 300 organizations in which students can get involved on campus. The Greek system is one of the best in the country. They are very involved on campus and loyal to their brothers and sisters. LSU students can go out to a bar or club any night of the week and find a crowded bar. Drink specials, live bands, karaoke, and plenty of students looking to have a good time are what you'll find all around the city at night.

Current student, 1/2003-Submit Date, March 2007

The Greek system is overwhelming. It's impossible to miss the decked out sorority girls. Tigerland is where most freshmen go out, and the Greek crowd hangs. It's a pit of drunken masses resembling Bourbon Street at Mardi Gras.

Also, your favorite bands from the 90s will play most nights whether covered or the real thing. There are lots of restaurants in Baton Rouge, but not many late-night joints: only two or three, really, if you don't count Waffle House. People seem to be getting married all the time, so I suppose the dating scene is alive and well.

Current student, 8/2004-Submit Date, May 2006

LSU has one of the most prevalent night lives with plenty of opportunities to have a good time. The main going out sector is known as Tigerland which includes about seven bars. These are not nightclubs, but rather old-time bars with open areas for just talking, dancing and drinking. The women at LSU are some of the top in the nation as well. It is true what they say, Southern women take the cake.

Alumnus/a, 8/1999-5/2003, November 2005

The social scene at LSU can't be topped. We were in the Top Three party schools of the *Harvard Review* for three years while I attended and Number One my sophomore year. (Some things you don't forget.) Saturday nights are football games and win or lose—usually we win—it's always a party. Dating scene—I met my wife at LSU. Greek system: I wasn't involved, but several of my friends were and had a blast. Bars, Tigerland in general from Thursday to Saturday.

Current student, 8/2001-Submit Date, September 2005

Chimes is the best restaurant around campus—always good for that Cajun food. Reggie's is the best bar, but all are pretty good. There are lots of fraternities and sororities, depending on what you like; although I don't know the specifics of the Greek system because it's not really my scene.

Football rules the campus. Death Valley is the place to be on Saturday nights in the fall, but freshmen rarely ever get tickets, so I wouldn't bother trying. The ticket policy changes every year based on who's elected to student government, so freshmen (and anyone else who didn't get tickets) can buy them from another student. LSU only sells season tickets to students, so if you only want to go to a few games, buy the set and sell the rest.

GEAUX TIGERS!

Tulane University

Office of Undergraduate Admission
210 Gibson Hall
6823 St. Charles Avenue
Tulane University
New Orleans, LA 70118
Admissions phone: (800) 873-9283
Admissions fax: (504) 862-8715
Admissions e-mail: undergrad.admission@tulane.edu
Admissions URL: www2.tulane.edu/admission.cfm

Admissions

Current student, Business, 8/2003-Submit Date, May 2007

The admissions process is interesting because the admissions counselors get to know the prospective students when they come in for a visit. The admission counselors are very hands on. It is good to know that Tulane gives out more scholarships than any school I know of. I think about half of my friends are on scholarship. You fair a better chance of getting in if you come down to visit and get to know the admissions counselors on a face-to-face level.

Current student, 8/2005-Submit Date, May 2007

Tulane University is admissions process is very user friendly. The easiest way to apply is online with the Early Action option. (This is different from Early Decision; it is non-binding.) The application deadline is usually earlier for the online application, but you find out about your acceptance before most universities have even started accepting Regular Decision applications. That definitely helps take the pressure off.

> **The school says:** "We offer Early Action and Regular Decision. The Early Action application is due November 1st, and is non-binding. Regular decision applications are due by January 15th. One of the good things about Early Action is that we will give you a decision by December 15th. No matter when you apply, you have until May 1st to make a final decision."

As with most universities today, Tulane wants to see that you are well rounded and dedicated to your passions. Make that clear in your essays. This is the time to express yourself, use it to your advantage! Tulane calls its essay a "personal statement" for a reason!

According to the Princeton Review, Tulane's average GPA is a 3.45, average SAT is a 1320 and average ACT is a 30.

Read all of Vault's College Surveys at **www.vault.com/college**—get complete surveys on 100s of colleges and universities, expert advice on applicaton essays and more.

VAULT CAREER LIBRARY   275

Current student, 8/2005-Submit Date, May 2007

I found the admissions process at Tulane a lot less daunting than at many comparable schools. I don't think an essay is required unless you are applying to a special program or for a specific scholarship. Tulane is also very generous with money and tends to give accepted students very generous scholarships and financial aid. Don't be discouraged by the price—if you are competitive academically, Tulane will help make it affordable. Also, you definitely need to visit campus to appreciate Tulane.

Current student, 8/2005-Submit Date, May 2007

Tulane pays equal attention to standardized test scores, high school GPA and the essays. None of those categories stands on its own in the admissions process. Tulane students are smart, motivated people who strive to achieve greatness in and out of the classroom, as well as maintain a balance between social and academic arenas. If that's you, then you're in, provided your standardized test scores and high school GPA are stellar. However, since Katrina there are more students applying to Tulane with the false hope that we have lowered our standards to rake in more money. This is absolutely not true.

The school says: "Tulane's admit rate is roughly 40 percent."

Current student, 1/2004-Submit Date, May 2007

Tulane admissions is similar to other Top 50 schools. There are no interviews at Tulane; however, I definitely would suggest visiting the admissions office and meeting with a counselor to ask questions. I definitely recommend visiting the campus because that is the best way to see if you feel a connection with the school. The essay is pretty simple. Basically, you just have to write a maximum 500-word essay on anything. I recommend writing about something that is important to you or something that changed your life.

Current student, 1/2006-Submit Date, May 2007

The admissions process is fairly standard. Tulane makes an effort to make students feel wanted. They send certain students pre-filled out applications in August that they can send back free of charge and without an essay and hear a decision within a month. Regardless of Early Decision, Early Action or Regular Decision, all students are considered for academic merit scholarships, which Tulane is fairly generous about giving.

Current student, 8/2004-Submit Date, May 2007

I applied to Tulane Early Decision. I went to a "Tulane Day," a program they have for seniors before being accepted. They had different programs that day, including a tour, panel and lunch. After visiting the campus and the city, I knew this was the place for me. I definitely would go visit the campus if you are unsure; it really shows what the school and the city are all about. The selectivity has increased since I applied, mostly because we are much more well-known because of Hurricane Katrina. Right now, we are about back to the numbers we had for admission pre-Katrina. There are no interviews available, but you can meet with an admissions counselor, which I would highly suggest as well because they are incredibly helpful and knowledgeable about Tulane.

 **Academics**

Current student, Political Science, 8/2003-Submit Date, May 2007

Political science at Tulane is a great program. The city provides a great learning resource for students and there are tons of political science internships in and around New Orleans. The classes are really interesting and the teachers foster good discussions. The professors are probably the best part. They are always at their office hours and will meet with you at any time. They don't just sit at the front of class and lecture; they really try and engage with students. Getting into classes is never a problem, even if you can't get into the class initially, you can get on the waitlist or just ask the professor to add your name.

Current student, 8/2005-Submit Date, May 2007

One of Tulane's biggest pros is the class size. You will rarely have a class with more than 20 people; if this does happen, it is usually a 100-level science class. There is a huge variety of classes to take at Tulane, from African dance to Creole language classes, to your basic economics and calculus classes. There is no such thing as a bad class at Tulane. Yes, the class may be difficult or the professor

may grade a bit harshly, but the actual material of the class will always be informative and useful.

The school says: "Tulane's average class size is 22, and our student-to-faculty ratio is 9:1."

Registering for classes is all done online. It is very simple and problem free. You can see how many people are already signed up, which professor is teaching which class, class times and locations all on the Internet before and while you are registering. If a class you want is full, you can see the professor to ask to be allowed in. They are generally very accommodating as long as you have a legitimate reason for wanting this class. You will never be left out of a class you need. Classes like Hip Hop and Urban Culture and Guns and Gangs are very popular and therefore are difficult to get into; professors for these courses are probably less accommodating because they know you only want to take their class because it's cool.

Advisors: Tulane lacks a bit in this area but they are restructuring the advising department so it will improve. Freshman advising is better than upperclassman advising, so that's not a problem. After freshman year, it is best to head to a major advisor or even a favorite professor in your department for help.

I am on my third university (Katrina semester I went to Syracuse University and I studied abroad for a semester in Paris) and Tulane has the best and most helpful professors I have seen. They are always willing to go the extra mile for a student. For example, a professor in the French department held an extra class every week of the semester out of his own time for the students not understanding the material. Another professor of mine made a huge dinner for us over finals week to help us relax (and the home cooked meal, a rare thing in college, was a plus too).

Although Tulane may be a party school, you won't find a student here who doesn't care about his/her studies. Our motto is work hard, party hard and that is evident with the work ethic (and party ethic) of students at Tulane. Someone is always willing to help you out if you miss a class or ready to form a study group the night before the big test.

Workload really depends on your major. Most students at Tulane have two majors and almost everyone is either pre-med, pre-law or pre-something. In general, the workload is rough and the gorgeous weather and the huge parties don't help either. Honestly, if you don't have good time management skills, don't go to Tulane. If you do, then have no fear. There is always someone to study with so you won't be the only one missing the kegs and the crawfish boil at the levee.

Current student, Business 8/2005-Submit Date, May 2007

I'm in finance and have found the program to be excellent. If you are thinking about majoring in business (especially finance or accounting) make sure you check out the Burkenroad Reports at Burkenroad.org. It's a very high-profile hands-on equity research program where students provide Wall Street like coverage over small to mid-cap companies in the South that don't get a lot of Wall Street coverage. The Reports look amazing on résumés and provide a unique topic to discuss during the intense finance interviews. I don't think there is another program like this anywhere in the country.

Current student, 8/2003-Submit Date, May 2007

Most of the classes at Tulane are relatively small (around 25 to 30 students) and therefore students receive lots of individual attention. I've also taken many seminar classes, where I have had only eight students in the classroom. The quality of both the classes and the professors is unbeatable. The professors make themselves very accessible and are always willing to give you some extra help, or just talk during office hours. You can usually get the courses that you want to take, just maybe not during your first year. The workload is sometimes pretty hard, especially in the upper-level classes—the trick is to balance the workload with your crazy social life.

Current student, 8/2005-Submit Date, May 2007

My favorite aspect of the academic culture at Tulane is the easy accessibility of professors. Tulane's small-school feel, when combined with its big-school opportunities, make it the perfect atmosphere to get to know faculty mentors at the forefront of their fields. Professors are always available and eager to answer questions and help you out with whatever you need. Classes are pretty easy to get into. Some classes, mostly those like General Chemistry and Introduction to Macro and Microeconomics that come in two semesters, are only offered in the fall or spring. Grading is fair, not inflated. The workload is rigorous and great preparation for the working world.

 Employment Prospects

Current student, Political Science, 8/2003-Submit Date, May 2007

Many employers come to Tulane and recruit our students. There are two big job fairs during the year, one in the spring and one in the fall. Also, the Freeman School of Business hosts Freeman Days in Houston, New Orleans and New York City. The B-school will hold career fairs for Tulane students in these cities so that employers can see Tulane students in other cities.

Current student, Business, 8/2003-Submit Date, May 2007

I really like the fact that I have had options to work all across the country because of the strong connections the school has. Tulane alumni live everywhere and are very willing to help out undergrads. The opportunities are pretty limitless. I am going into investment banking but also have friends going into trading, financial advisory, hedge funds and consulting. Prestige with employers is strong; I interviewed for a job where I was the only non-Ivy Leaguer there other than a guy from Stanford.

Current student, Business 8/2005-Submit Date, May 2007

As a finance major looking to Wall Street, I have found a solid alumni network in New York. For a Southern school, we have an excellent finance program, which gets a lot of recruitment on campus. If you are a finance major looking to stay in the South, Tulane is definitely the place to be. Our finance majors get a leg up because of the Burkenroad Program, which brings a lot of recruiters to the campus. As a sophomore, I was proactive and attended final round interviews for internships in New York, San Francisco, Dallas, Houston and New Orleans; I received several offers. I will be taking an internship in New York doing equity research. So there are definitely good job/internship prospects coming out of Tulane, but it helps if you are proactive about it. However, there aren't always as many recruiters on campus from the North and West as some people would like.

Current student, 8/2005-Submit Date, May 2007

The career center at Tulane is amazing. As a pre-med student, I was offered the opportunity to mock interview with an administrator from the local hospital, facilitating a great career connection. You can't escape the people who work at the career center because they're always trying to get you to go to a résumé workshop or to apply to an internship you'd be great for. As a result, I acquired an internship at L'Oreal as a sophomore.

Current student, 8/2003-Submit Date, May 2007

I knew that I wanted to go to graduate school, and working on an honors thesis my senior year (individually with one of my professors) helped me to prepare for grad school and to be accepted. My professor was so helpful: editing my statement, helping me to select schools and so on. I also utilized the career center, where they updated my résumé and made it look more professional (and gave me a free T-shirt to boot). So, come next fall I'm going to be starting a PhD program in Management and Organizations. Most of my friends who have graduated have found employment that they enjoy, and a good deal of my friends this year have jobs lined up in various fields (finance, real estate, banking, art gallery work).

 Quality of Life

Current student, 8/2005-Submit Date, May 2007

Bob Dylan once perfectly described this city: "You can live in a lot of places but New Orleans is the only place that lives in you." New Orleans is one of the most interesting cities in America. It is filled with a heart and soul that rivals no other. Once you live there, you will never want to leave.

Tulane is located in the Garden District in New Orleans. The campus is across the street from Audubon Park, the largest park in New Orleans. The Garden District is the most beautiful area of the city. Tulane is on St. Charles Ave., surrounded by mansions, gorgeous green grass and flowers.

The first thing to realize about Tulane is that it is a school in a city. Fact, there is crime in cities. Tulane is no less safe than any other school with the same type of location. If you keep your eyes and ears open, you will be fine. If you are stupid and go walking through the ghetto (which is nowhere near campus by the way) at night by yourself, you will not be fine. There are campus police that patrol within a one-to two-mile radius of campus. Also, post-Katrina Tulane expanded its police force.

The campus is moderately small. The academic quad located at the front of campus is where most of the class buildings are located. This is a grassy lawn with trees and benches. In warm weather many professors hold classes outside to take advantage of the gorgeous Louisiana weather. Leaving the academic quad you pass by the new business school, a state-of-the-art building with a lot of high tech equipment. Continuing on you pass the brand-new university center that has study lounges, a food court, a bar, a spa, stores, and tables outdoors that are always crowded with students. In front of the UC is another quad where people play sports, lay out to get some sun, and do homework. Newcomb quad is next to the UC quad. Surrounding Newcomb quad are more class buildings. Language, art, dance, and theater classes as well as others are held in this area of campus. The rest of campus is the dining and housing facilities.

Tulane has recently taken many steps to improve its housing options. There are huge freshman dorms that are typical to any college campus. These dorms have been or are currently being renovated. Tulane also has an honors dorm, a wellness dorm, a girls-only dorm, and Wall Residential College. This is a unique housing opportunity modeled after the colleges at Oxford and Cambridge. Wall provides many leadership opportunities such as dorm president and community service chair. JL, the all-female dorm, is also a great option for girls. It is farther from classes but closer to the bars and parties.

Bruff dining hall is where freshmen go to eat their meals. Meal plans are required for freshmen and most upperclassmen who live on campus also enroll in some type of meal plans. Bruff has hot meals, a salad bar, a sandwich bar, a cereal bar, a fruit bar, a grill, a pizza bar and a vegan section. On Mondays for lunch there is always red beans and rice, the traditional New Orleans Monday lunch. On Fridays for lunch there is gumbo, another New Orleans favorite. Along with Bruff, the UC has a food court, Le Gourmet is a take out restaurant on campus that sells yummy wraps, quesadillas, and sandwiches, and two PJs coffee shops are located on campus.

Tulane's state-of-the-art Reily Recreation Center is perfect for anyone looking for a good workout. It has a massive weight room, an indoor track, tennis courts, racquetball courts, four gyms, an Olympic-sized pool and a social pool (you can always find students here studying and getting a tan).

Current student, 8/2002-Submit Date, March 2005

Housing is quite a bit nicer at Tulane than, say, at a state school. I always feel very safe on campus because of all the TUPD (Tulane University Police Department) officers around, making sure everyone gets home safe and sound. The surrounding neighborhoods can sometimes be troublesome areas; however, if you listen to the safety precautions offered at orientation and anything else you'll go to on campus, you'll be fine. As far as facilities, Tulane always has the latest technology and the gym is amazing. There are a number of places to eat on campus, some of which are open all night for those late-night study sessions.

 Social Life

Current student, Political Science, 8/2003-Submit Date, May 2007

New Orleans is, hands down, the best city in the world in which to go to college. There is always, always, always something to do, whether on campus or off campus. Greek life only consists of 30 percent of campus. You don't have to go Greek to have fun at Tulane, but it's there if you want it. All fraternity parties are open to all students, and the sorority scene isn't the typical Southern sorority scene. The girls aren't catty and there aren't rivalries between the houses. Plus, girls don't live in the sorority houses, which adds to the mellow quality.

Read all of Vault's College Surveys at **www.vault.com/college**–get complete surveys on 100s of colleges and universities, expert advice on applicaton essays and more.

VAULT CAREER LIBRARY **277**

Current student, Business, 8/2003-Submit Date, May 2007

The social life in New Orleans is outstanding. At Tulane we constantly say that the social life is stressful. Students can get into bars at the age of 18, and there are around 10 bars within walking distance from the freshman dorms. There are always concerts of every genre but students seem to love taking in some local jazz when possible.

Current student, 8/2005-Submit Date, May 2007

Not all of New Orleans' bars exist on Bourbon St. Around campus be sure to check out The Boot (which Tulane is known for, don't miss happy hour on Wednesdays and Fridays with three-for-one bottled beers and three-for-one cocktails—200 of your closest friends are guaranteed to be there), the Palm's for a classier evening (OK not that much classier) and the bars on Maple St. including Phillip's (Thursday night is Lady's Night), Vera Cruz for amazing margaritas and queso, and Bruno's and the new Bruno's. If you have a car, there is always Magazine St. The Bulldog has specials on pints on Wednesdays and you get to keep your glass. Balcony Bar and Le Bon Temps are also favorites. Don't miss F&Ms on Thursdays after 1 a.m; make sure to eat the cheese fries. Next door to F&Ms is Grits, a grimy but fun bar that has free hurricanes for girls on Friday nights. If you do want to check out Bourbon (and you should), don't miss Pat O'Brien's piano bar, The Cat's Meow for karaoke, and Bourbon cowboy for a mechanical bull.

Plenty of restaurants are within walking distance of campus. Try Vera Cruz for Mexican food, Fresco's for take-out, Reginelli's for pizza, and Camilla Grill for burgers and pecan pie.

Current student, 8/2005-Submit Date, May 2007

Everyone really becomes involved in the culture of New Orleans and it is really a great time to be a part of this city. Life post-Katrina has not changed much for Tulane. Tulane students spend most of their time either Uptown or downtown around the French Quarter. These are the two historic areas of the city are on high ground and were the least affected by the storm. I have never found much reason for Tulane students to venture into the badly damaged areas except to do community service. If you are interested in making an impact on your community, New Orleans is definitely the place to be. There are countless great opportunities to make a real impact and not just accumulate service hours.

Current student, 8/2002-Submit Date, March 2005

Tulane is consistently ranked as one of the Top 50 (and sometimes in the Top 10) party schools in the nation. There is always something going on during every night of the week. There are tons of bars that offer a wide variety of drink specials, and each has a different crowd that hangs out there. The most popular bars include the Boot, Quills and Friar Tuck's. These are the bars that are 18+ and all freshmen can get into. Upperclassmen have a lot more options with bars like Bruno's, Madigan's, Miss Mae's, and the Palms. The bar scene on campus is really active, and drinking at bars is almost as cheap (and sometimes better) than buying alcohol on your own. The majority of the social life isn't at the bars though.

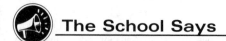 **The School Says**

Founded in 1834 and reorganized as Tulane University in 1884, Tulane is one of the most renowned comprehensive research universities in the nation.

Among national universities, Tulane is known for its emphasis on undergraduate teaching and accomplishments in research.

The same senior faculty who break new ground in research regularly teach freshmen and sophomores. With fewer than 6000 undergraduates, Tulane gives each student the personal attention and teaching excellence typically associated with much smaller colleges, while providing the state-of-the-art facilities and interdisciplinary resources usually found at much larger universities. Close student-teacher relationships pay off—graduates frequently win prestigious fellowships, and many go on to graduate or professional school in their chosen field.

Undergraduates choose from over 70 majors in the schools of architecture, business, liberal arts, public health and tropical medicine, and science and engineering. Nearly all of Tulane's faculty members have earned the highest degree in their field. Over one-third of classes include less than 10 students. Tulane is one of only a few research institutions in the country where almost all undergraduate courses are taught by full-time faculty, each of whom is highly respected in his or her field.

Tulane students come from all 50 states and many foreign countries. More than 75 percent come from over 500 miles away. On average, over 50 percent of each incoming class graduated in the top 10 percent of their high school class and present outstanding test scores. But Tulane students are much more than just quantifiable credentials. Tulane attracts students with wide-ranging academic, athletic and social interests.

More than 200 student organizations offer something for everyone. Student government, pre-professional societies, performance opportunities, student media, public service, and other organizations bring students together to meet, motivate and make a difference both on and off campus. Student groups offer numerous opportunities to gain leadership experience. On the field, students can choose from a number of intercollegiate, intramural and club sports programs. Facilities include the Reily Student Recreation Center, a $10.5 million state-of-the-art gym including an indoor track, indoor and outdoor pool and sun deck, racquetball courts, weight room, saunas and a refreshment bar.

The $40 million Lavin-Bernick Center for University Life is a brand-new addition to the campus, featuring a food court, Barnes and Noble bookstore, FedEx Kinkos and an Aveda salon.

The university is situated on 110 acres in the Uptown neighborhood of New Orleans, four miles from the city's downtown. The unique culture and history of New Orleans permeates the Tulane community with the unique music, food, art, language, and literature of the city. Following Hurricane Katrina, the university underwent a spectacular renewal: renovating facilities and restructuring academic programs. The academically-oriented public service component of the curriculum offers unprecedented opportunities for students to take their studies and research into the real world—it's learning in action. Work in health care. Teach in schools. Study the environment. Enliven the arts. Help plan a community.

More information can be found at admission.tulane.edu

Bates College

Bates College Admissions Office
23 Campus Avenue
Lewiston, ME 04240-6098
Admissions phone: (207) 786-6000
Admissions fax: (207) 786-6025
Admissions e-mail: admissions@bates.edu
Admissions URL: www.bates.edu/admissions.xml

 ## Admissions

Current student, 9/2003-Submit Date, March 2007

Bates is very selective. They pick people who have a specific passion or talent and have followed it mostly. Of course, those people also have excellent grades.

Alumnus/a, 9/2000-6/2002, April 2006

Applying to Bates was fairly straightforward. I recommend visiting the campus and scheduling an interview with a student at the admissions office. They tend to put a good word in to the admissions team if they really like a prospective student. Bates likes well-rounded kids. If you play a sport, it is highly advisable to talk to the coach—they have pull when it comes down to admissions. The essays are standard and if you put a lot of effort and enthusiasm into getting in ,the school really takes notice.

Current student, 9/2001-Submit Date, February 2004

Bates is seen as a very selective school, but I found them to be lenient. They didn't penalize me for the fact that I had received a few poor grades during high school. My interview was conducted with a current student and offered a chance for me to ask questions of the interviewer. It was very relaxed, and helped me to see why Bates was a good fit for me.

Bates doesn't [require] SAT scores. You can add them to your application if you like, but I think it shows that the institution understands that some students don't do well on standardized tests. Show that you are a well-rounded student, and tell them what you are really passionate about. A student in 30 clubs is often less interesting than a student who dedicated his or her time and energy to two or three, as this shows a real interest and commitment. I wrote the required two essays and then added a third one I had written because I felt it said a lot about me.

Current student, 1/2000-Submit Date, February 2004

Bates doesn't require standardized test scores. You are evaluated on things like GPA, class rank, recommendations and interview. Bates is looking for students who want to change things and are willing to take the initiative. Must show strong leadership skills with a humanitarian agenda.

 ## Academics

Current student, 9/2003-Submit Date, March 2007

You will almost never be deferred from a class because too many people want it. Bates is very rigorous; however, some majors are easier than others (religion, American cultural studies and so on). The sciences will work you hard but are very interesting.

Alumnus/a, 9/2000-6/2002, April 2006

Bates operates on a two semester system with a much shorter academic term in the month of May, called short term. Students typically take four classes a semester and are required to fulfill requirements in other departments outside their major in order to graduate. There is no language requirement. Seminar classes are the best ones to take—they really rock if you get the right professor. You pretty much have your pick of a class—registration is online and even if you don't get in, it is common for a professor to let you in if you show up for the first few classes. Workload is what you make of it—usually you have required reading every night and papers every two weeks—sometimes you get the readings done, sometimes not. Oh and take Intro to Astronomy—walk in the park and really funny teacher!

Current student, 9/2001-Submit Date, February 2004

Bates follows the pattern of most liberal arts colleges. [Bates requires three courses or short-term units in the sciences, including two in a department-designated set, three in the social sciences also with a set, and five in the humanities.] The school is small enough that you can establish a relationship with each of your professors, but some of the seminar classes are big enough that you can blend in if you need to. While the student-to-teacher ratio is somewhere around 10:1, most professors teach only [two or three courses per semester], so in reality [classes average 17] students. Sometimes they are smaller for more specialized courses, and sometimes much bigger for more popular ones.

It is a good idea to get your requirements done early, as the rush to get into 100-level sciences often makes them difficult to get into. I am taking the most popular course on campus right now, which has the largest allowed enrollment. There are 140 students, but we meet in small groups for discussion once a week. I don't know how he does it, but the professor knows the names of most of the students and is always available during his office hours to answer questions or to talk about the reading. Most of my professors encourage students to come in and visit during their office hours, and I have found that to be my favorite part of a small school. The downside is that because it is fairly small, your options for classes can seem limiting.

At Bates most students go abroad for at least a semester, and the school encourages students to try new programs. It is usually easy to fit a study abroad into your schedule unless you are a bio major, although my friend managed to get the bulk of his classes out of the way freshman year and went to study in China for a semester. The major requirements vary greatly between departments, and some departments are more lenient than others. I would say that most students come to Bates with an idea of what they would like to study and then change their minds when they find a great professor in another department.

The workload can be very heavy at times, but I find that grades almost always reflect the energy put into the class. Every student must complete a thesis [or comprehensive exam in his or her major] to graduate, which is difficult but often rewarding. It also gives you the chance to work one on one with a professor and often leads to great job recommendations.

Current student, 1/2000-Submit Date, February 2004

This is a very academically rigorous school. Professors look for improvement and are there to help you. You can get into almost any class you want, and should base your selection on the popularity of the professor.

 ## Employment Prospects

Current student, 9/2003-Submit Date, March 2007

Bates has an excellent OCS, however you have to take the initiative to get help. It is there if you want to use it though. The only thing it lacks is information for niche careers (e.g., pharmaceutical consulting) or specific grad programs (e.g., MS in Infectious diseases).

Alumnus/a, 9/2000-6/2002, April 2006

As far as I know, Batesies are very helpful to each other upon graduation. I have friends working for IBM, as an assistant gallerist in New York, writing for a travel magazine in Paris, and working for a health supplement company in Miami. Senior year you get a few workshops from the college on how to be recruited for employment. Also, companies visit the campus on a very regular basis.

Read all of Vault's College Surveys at www.vault.com/college—get complete surveys on 100s of colleges and universities, expert advice on applicaton essays and more.

VAULT CAREER LIBRARY 279

Current student, 9/2001-Submit Date, February 2004

The school Office of Career Services is supposed to be a great resource, but I have never been. We have recruiters once in a while. I have friends who do internships with alumni every summer, and I have been told that the school has a great reputation with employers. I spent the past summer living on campus and doing an internship with one of the offices here, which was very fun, and I learned a lot. I also was able to meet a lot of the administration here.

Current student, 1/2000-Submit Date, February 2004

There are a lot of summer internship possibilities that the Office of Career Services can help you with, along with alumni connections. Bates has a good reputation with many law and medical schools.

Quality of Life

Current student, 9/2003-Submit Date, March 2007

Housing is excellent. The only thing to watch out for is Smith (all freshman dorm) your first year. They are currently re-doing certain dorms and the dinning facilities. The food is excellent.

Alumnus/a, 9/2000-6/2002, April 2006

It is your quintessential college campus—the housing is either dorms or houses, with the option of living off campus your senior year. I recommend living in Frye Street Union—it is the nicest house on campus. The pool is beautiful, the academic buildings are stunning, the running track leaves a little to be desired though. And sometimes it is hard to get a workout in on the treadmills as there are few and always in use. The cafeteria is typical college food—off campus there are a couple of options and Portland is only 30 minutes away. Everyone eats in the dining hall, so it is a good place to see your friends and to catch up on gossip. The town is not very nice—the campus is the main economic draw but while I was there I never had a safety problem. It is not a place I would walk around at 3 a.m. alone but the few times I did so I was never bothered. Everyone on campus looks out for each other and the campus buildings are locked up at night.

Current student, 9/2001-Submit Date, February 2004

Housing can be good or bad. Some freshmen are put into quads, which can be really cramped. I managed to get a huge double. Usually they are really good about matching roommates; I only knew two people on my floor who didn't get along that well. Freshmen are put into freshman-year centers where they have a junior advisor to help them choose classes, learn things about the campus, and help settle any domestic issues that arise. After freshman year, students can pick their own roommates and enter a lottery system. Singles are a little difficult to get until junior year, and no one may live off campus until senior year. Even then, most students live within three blocks of campus. I really like that; it keeps people active and involved at all hours. There are a few major dorms, and then [several] streets of Victorian houses converted into dorms. There is also the option of a theme house, of which there are probably seven a year. All of the members of the house are involved in a common theme (or are friends of people involved in that theme). This year there is a performing arts house, a community service house, an environmental house and many others.

The dining is amazing. They do it all here at the school and take suggestions from students seriously. They buy from local farms and [also recycle food] waste [through a local] farm. Our dining [services have won recognition for environmental sustainability]. Not to mention that it is pretty good. Like anything it can get old after a while, but I've experienced dining at some of my friends' schools.

The facilities are OK. We have a few beautiful buildings and a few old ones that need a little help. There are computer labs, but while students are working on theses it is difficult to get a computer. Sometimes they hold classes in the labs. If you use a Mac, however, you will have more options than you know what to do with.

The neighborhood isn't great. The town has been in a depression and is just now beginning to recover. It is as safe as any city might be. We have a few security problems each year, sometimes fairly major, but I think that the school really works to keep things up. The town itself is a nice place to work with. I am able

to tutor Somali children after school, and I have friends that work at the elementary schools.

Current student, 1/2000-Submit Date, February 2004

It is very cold here, so be prepared! Also, most students stay on campus although there are lots of volunteer opportunities. The housing is decent, and most students stay on campus all four years.

The Bates campus is beautiful all year long, but be prepared for cold. Some students come to visit during the late spring and don't realize that it can be absolutely freezing in January.

Social Life

Current student, 9/2003-Submit Date, March 2007

Bates has a no hard alcohol policy on campus. Other than that, Bates is relatively lackadaisical when it comes to alcohol consumption within reason. Security is mostly there if there is a complaint or for student safety reasons. Since Bates is located in Lewiston (not that exciting of a town), the college is pretty good about providing activities for students.

Alumnus/a, 9/2000-6/2002, April 2006

Partying consists of drinking in dorms or drinking in bars. Pub 33 is the place to go if you are cool and want to mock the Bates experience over a Guinness and a game of pool. There are a couple of clubs downtown that are more of the dance party hook-up scene. The kids who like to drink usually throw a kegger in a house off campus and the others like to drink in groups of four or five in their rooms. Dating is really nonexistent—you are either a couple or you hook up randomly with guys on the weekends—which start Wednesday, by the way. Kids are into sports and drink like fishes on the weekend. Favorite sports are basketball and lacrosse. Newman Day is craziest school holiday—a day in January where kids try to drink 24 beers in 24 hours. Favorite drinking game is beer pong. New England preppy all the way baby or it's "I'm into Phish and wear dreads and I drive a Prius". A few eccentrics in between. It was an entertaining experience.

Current student, 9/2001-Submit Date, February 2004

The school isn't located in a very active city, so most activities remain on campus. There is no Greek system (there never was), and I find that people are generally very open to meeting others. I have never felt out of place at a party, and because the school is fairly small, it is easy to meet people and then run into them again. The dating scene is OK, although the downside to the small school is that you can't avoid anyone. There are two or three bars a few blocks from campus that most seniors go to Thursday and Friday nights if there isn't a lot going on by way of campus events (although it is rare to have a free weekend).

There are a lot of clubs, and I would advise any new student to join one or two. It is a great way to meet people. Every student is automatically a member of the Outing Club, which organizes hikes, canoe trips and other activities for anyone on campus. The sports teams are fun, and I know that people enjoy going to hockey games and sometimes the football games. I do a show at the radio station (which I love).

There are a lot of activities every weekend, as clubs sponsor dances, parties and games. This weekend alone, the radio station ran Trivia Night (an all-night trivia game that ends at 8 a.m. in the dining hall), which over 100 students were involved in. On Saturday night the community service theme house held a party with two campus bands performing, and Sunday the improv comedy group performed. There was also an ice fishing trip, a five-band punk concert, a knitting circle and more than a dozen parties. The film board also gets movies each weekend, which students can go to for $1. There are local restaurants, but students really need a car to go anywhere.

Usually you can find a friend with a car, but most people stick to campus for lack of transportation. A few times a semester one club pays for two buses to Portland so students can go to the bars there. There are also a few concerts a year on campus.

Current student, 1/2000-Submit Date, February 2004
There are no sororities or fraternities. There are campus-wide dances almost every Friday and Saturday nights and great concerts. There are a couple of popular bars nearby, and the dating scene is decent for such a small college.

Bowdoin College

Admissions Office
Burton-Little House
5000 College Station, ME 04011-8441
Admissions phone: (207) 725-3958
Admissions fax: (207) 725-3101
Admissions URL: www.bowdoin.edu/admissions/

 ## Admissions

Alumnus/a, Physical Sciences, 9/1999-5/2003, May 2007

If you have an opportunity to visit the campus, please take it! During the college admissions process, it is as equally important for you to get to know the college as it is for the college to get to know you. At Bowdoin, the people make the college, so please take a campus tour, interview, attend a class, eat in the dining hall and talk to people. The Bowdoin admissions process reflects the type of school it is—two people read your entire application (essays and grades and extracurriculars are important) and the admissions policy is need-blind.

Current student, English, 8/2006-Submit Date, May 2007

I transferred into Bowdoin College. To do this, I had to complete the Common Application as well as the Bowdoin College transfer supplementary application. This called for a total of two essays. The transfer process into a small liberal arts college is extremely selective, as such schools have very high retention rates. For admissions—particularly transfer admissions—the strongest case is made by your academic record. Demonstrated interest, a good interview, strong essays and extracurricular success are very worthwhile, but grades are the most important factor in admissions.

Current student, 9/2003-Submit Date, March 2005

Although I was a good student in high school, some of my grades, mostly those from my science and math courses, were rather low. Due to these grades, I was considered to be a bit below Bowdoin's standards. As a result of this, I was deferred from Early Decision. My interview process had gone exceedingly well, however, and I formed a bond with an admissions rep who explained to me that the college wanted to see the transcripts from my senior year in order to see if I could apply myself in the Bowdoin setting. As they needed the grades from the entire year, I also got waitlisted for Regular Decision. I did not find out that I had gotten into Bowdoin until July 2nd, weeks before I would later enter a pre-orientation trip in August.

My best advice that I can give students in high school who are applying is to be persistent. Although colleges are interested in your grades and test scores, it's "the little extra" that will move you past others. I kept a good, casual rapport with Bowdoin throughout the admissions process, continually letting them know that I was interested in their school. I worked hard my senior year, something that was particularly difficult due to the senioritis that many others were feeling. But it paid off! I will admit that the Bowdoin I applied to is less competitive than today's Bowdoin. However, I think that Bowdoin, as opposed to many other colleges, really looks at the integrity of the students it admits.

Alumnus/a, 9/1999-5/2003, December 2003

Bowdoin's admissions process is fairly standard, utilizing the Common Application and its primary essay as the basis for analysis. In addition, applicants are required to submit a supplemental essay that describes the positive impact that a secondary school teacher has had on his or her development. A strong supplemental essay will focus on an isolated example of the teacher's influence, preferably with ties to both academic and personal development. The trick is to provide an account that highlights the teacher's unique style, and the way that they personally connected with the applicant.

Interviewing is not required, but, obviously, provides the applicant with the opportunity to speak with a representative from the admissions board and to show his or her extreme desire to attend Bowdoin. Bowdoin is annually recognized as one of the nation's most selective schools, and an applicant who seriously wants to enroll there should do everything in his/her power to assure that his/her application is polished, the essays are perfect, and that his/her credentials will place him/her among the top percentage of applicants in the country.

 ## Academics

Alumnus/a, Physical Sciences, 9/1999-5/2003, May 2007

Academics are rigorous and you are expected to work hard and care about your classes; in return, your professor knows and cares about you. Classes are typically about 10 to 25 students for introductory classes and often drop to five to 10 students in upper-level classes.

Current student, English, 8/2006-Submit Date, May 2007

The word for classes at Bowdoin would be "accessible." I have not had any difficulty in getting the majority of my first choice classes, if not all of them, and this success rate only increases as you gain seniority and declare a major. Classes are small, not intimidating, and so far my experience with professors has been extremely positive. Professors are easy to get in touch with, happy to meet, and very enthusiastic about their subjects. Professors want you to do well and are more than happy to give assistance. Workload is respectably sized and undeniably rigorous, but if you manage your time well it is manageable with time left over for a social life and extracurriculars.

Alumnus/a, 9/1999-5/2003, March 2006

Academics are topnotch at Bowdoin. Students generally want to learn and develop intellectually. The professors, for the most part, are excellent. Any school will have duds who are only at an institution because they bring in huge grant money, but Bowdoin prides itself on having great professors who want to teach first and do research second. Grading at all top schools is fairly shady in my opinion. Did I find myself saying "was this really A-caliber work?" Yes, of course. But these institutions need to compete with each other by maintaining some sort of grade inflation. Everything is fair in my opinion. Workload varies with a major. I was a humanities major taking the pre-requisite pre-med classes, so my workload was intense, a combination of papers and tests. The classes are great. They have the standard variety, but also offer ones that make you think outside of the box to prepare you for work in the real world. Certain departments are stronger than others. The chemistry, government, economics, history and English departments are all nationally renowned. But the education, visual arts, music and foreign languages are all lacking.

The school says: "Bowdoin is experiencing a resurgence in the arts, propelled by new and renovated theater facilities, a 280-seat state-of-the-art recital hall and music practice space that opened in May 2007, and by a $21.8 million renovation of the Walker Art Building which houses the Bowdoin College Museum of Art (slated to open in October 2007). Bowdoin's new dean

Read all of Vault's College Surveys at www.vault.com/college—get complete surveys on 100s of colleges and universities, expert advice on applicaton essays and more.

VAULT CAREER LIBRARY 281

of academic affairs, Cristle Collins Judd, is a member of the music faculty and a renowned music theorist. In addition, the American Musicological Society has recently relocated to Bowdoin."

Alumnus/a, 9/1997-4/2001, September 2006

Topnotch education! Having attended an Ivy League school for science graduate work, I can confidently say that Bowdoin's academic experience exceeds anything found at its Ivy League peers. At Bowdoin faculty are 100 percent committed to teaching and that makes education exciting! Bowdoin is true to its liberal arts mission.

Current student, 9/2003-Submit Date, March 2005

Class setting at Bowdoin is unparalleled. In the first year at Bowdoin, each student has the option of taking a first-year seminar, a class with intensive writing and discussions, a priceless introduction to the college grading system, and writing guidelines, as well as a way to allow students to feel more comfortable in college classroom setting. In my experience I have been incredibly successful getting the classes I want at Bowdoin, . There have been times, of course, when I have not gotten into a class, but I always remained on the waitlist for that class, and the teachers usually adopt the idea that if there is space for students, then they can teach to the number of chairs in the room. I think that's a great outlook.

The teachers here are so dedicated to helping their students. Students are continually reminded of office hours, and teachers often write private notes to certain students to remind them that they are there for the student's use. The workload at Bowdoin is light enough so that one can get by by doing the minimum, but heavy enough so that it requires a lot of work to reach an A in some classes. Of course, some teachers are harder than others, but for the most part, it is not too hard to stay at a 3.0 or higher.

Alumnus/a, 9/1999-5/2003, December 2003

Bowdoin is a liberal arts college in the truest sense, and all academic disciplines have well-accomplished professors and interesting course options. The school's most popular majors are English, history, economics and biology. In order to receive the most value for the price of education, students should take classes in a variety of disciplines during their first year and really get a sense of what they find interesting.

Bowdoin benefits from very small class sizes, especially in its advanced levels. There are definitely classes offered annually that are recognized as the most popular, and that are generally quite difficult to get into as an underclassman. Many of these classes are popular because of the professor and his/her grading and teaching methods, and are often times nice compliments to the intense coursework of the higher level classes taken by upperclassmen.

Expect a hefty workload at Bowdoin, especially in disciplines such as economics, psychology, and any of the natural sciences. Grading recently changed, adding plus and minus to a formerly straight letter system. There are few pushover courses at Bowdoin, and professors are tough but fair in their grading.

 ## Employment Prospects

Alumnus/a, Physical Sciences, 9/1999-5/2003, May 2007

The Bowdoin network and reputation is strong throughout the U.S. and abroad. As a Bowdoin graduate, particularly if you have involved yourself in the campus community, you will be well prepared to take on a challenging job.

Current student, English, 8/2006-Submit Date, May 2007

The Career Planning Center has a fantastic reputation in helping graduating students find jobs and current students find internships. There is also an online database that uses a search function to help students locate internships and jobs based on interests and skill sets. The alumni network is spectacular; alumni are very involved with the school and happy to help out Bowdoin graduates.

Alumnus/a, 9/1999-5/2003, March 2006

Graduates of Bowdoin tend to have success getting jobs, particularly in New England where the Bowdoin name carries a significant amount of prestige. Bowdoin grads tend to go into a variety of industries. They range from the typical consulting and financial sectors, along with education and science to non-

profit and community service-based corporations. Bowdoin is a target school for certain companies, but due to its small size and liberal arts nature, is not a target for other companies (Goldman Sachs, McKinsey). But Bowdoin definitely has alumni representation at those types of companies. Bowdoin has tremendous success of getting its students into [high] caliber professional and graduate programs based upon its reputation. One thing I wish I knew about Bowdoin before applying Early Decision was that the Bowdoin Career Planning Center is not helpful. They give no support to alumni past one year post-graduation. And within that first year, they only give you a 15-minute phone call. I'm currently making a career change from medicine to another field and have received virtually no help from Bowdoin and have had to do it all on my own. Other liberal arts colleges of the same prestige level give support and career counseling to all of their alumni. The network of Bowdoin alumni in the Northeast is terrific. We seem to all look out for each other and help one another as best we can. But, the drawback is that the online network from the career center is awful. It is not kept up to date and makes it very difficult to contact alumni who work in areas you are interested in. I've been able to contact other Bowdoin alumni in my career search just out of personal connections.

Alumnus/a, 9/1999-5/2003, December 2003

In the Northeast, employers certainly recognize Bowdoin as one of the preeminent schools in the nation. Especially in Boston and New York City, a Bowdoin alumnus can expect to run into many more fellow alumni than they may expect from such a small school, and networking is therefore a very useful technique in these areas. Based on personal experience, Bowdoin is not very well-known outside of the Northeast, and can make the entry-level job search a bit tougher than expected.

Many big-name employers will recognize the school for its academic excellence, but the lack of an alumni base in non-Northeastern areas of the country give employers little else than name recognition as a basis for their knowledge of the typical Bowdoin graduate.

> **The school says:** "While it is true that 40 percent of Bowdoin alumni live and work in New England, that leaves a majority of alumni in other parts of the country (11 percent, for example, live in the far west). This means that the alumni network is expanding throughout the country."

The Career Planning Center does a fine job of assisting upperclassmen in their job searches by introducing them to the resources that can be used most effectively in contacting employers. A number of Portland, ME, Boston and New York employers recruit on campus, but not quite as many as one might see at a school closer to these cities. Nonetheless, because of the number of high-quality employees produced by Bowdoin, an employer will hold a degree from the school in high prestige.

 ## Quality of Life

Alumnus/a, Physical Sciences, 9/1999-5/2003, May 2007

On the edge of campus is Brunswick, a small and charming town with excellent restaurants and amenities. 30 minutes away is the unique city of Portland and just over two hours away is Boston. Five miles south of campus lies some of the most beautiful coastline in the world, ideal for kayaking, hiking and relaxing.

Most students live on campus because options abound and Bowdoin has a very personal community. Another plus is the food—ranked Number One in the country for several years in a row and with highlights such as local organic produce, lobster bakes and extensive options.

Current student, English, 8/2006-Submit Date, May 2007

The facilities on campus are very new or newly renovated. There is a lot of growth and development around campus, and facilities are all new, clean and cutting edge. Dining services have the best reputation in the nation for a reason: staff is extremely personable, food is prepared by the kitchen staff rather than purchased through a distributor, and the variety and quality is exceptional. Bowdoin has a very positive relationship with the town of Brunswick, as community members my take classes at Bowdoin, and Bowdoin has a large number of outreach and community service programs. It is a small, friendly town and both campus and the surrounding area are extremely safe.

Current student, 9/2003-Submit Date, March 2005

Bowdoin students are spoiled with housing at the minute they enter the college. The freshman bricks are spacious, well-designed and comfortable living spaces. Something like 96 percent of Bowdoin students live on campus, and this is not because of a lack of choices off campus. The college just has great choices for its students. The campus is a beautiful place in any season. The fall is gorgeous with the foliage, the winter icy and cold, but majestically alluring. And spring is spring. You just can't say anything bad about spring.

Alumnus/a, 9/1999-5/2003, December 2003

First-year students are fortunate to live right in the center of campus in very large dormrooms (all of which have been fully renovated in the last two years). It is a wonderful way to assimilate students, with close proximity to all necessary resources including the student union, workout facilities, dining halls, and most academic buildings. First-years are offered the choice of living in a substance-free dorm, as well as the option of living co-ed by floor as opposed to co-ed by room. Sophomore housing is not as nice, since the housing lottery favors upper-classmen and forces sophomores to move out of their majestic first-year rooms into smaller, but adequate, rooms. Juniors and seniors are allowed to live off campus, an option taken by many who choose to enjoy living within driving distance on Maine's gorgeous coastline. Still, the majority of upperclassmen choose to live on campus.

Bowdoin's campus is picturesque, with an expansive quad amidst a red brick enclosure of first-year dorms, academic buildings and [two] museums. The campus is situated in the center of Brunswick, and the every building is easily accessible and reachable on foot. Parking is an issue because of very limited on campus parking space which is reserved for faculty.

Recently rated as the Best College Food Program in America by Princeton Review, the Bowdoin College dining service provides students with the best quality on-campus dining imaginable. They always impress with their selection, and are sure to accommodate each dining nuance. There are two dining halls on campus, as well as Jack Magee's Grille, which is great for a late night snack or a study break. Meal plans are offered in 19, 14 or 10 per week packages.

Social Life

Alumnus/a, Physical Sciences, 9/1999-5/2003, May 2007

Friend groups at Bowdoin tend to be very diverse, mixing different academic majors, athletic teams, arts and music interests, and so on. Recognizing the engaging and unique community that the school creates, students are proud to be at Bowdoin and alumni are loyal.

Current student, English, 8/2006-Submit Date, May 2007

The school's social scene is very accepting. There is no Greek system, but the unique Social House system at Bowdoin takes the perks of a Greek system without many of the drawbacks. Social Houses are upperclassman housing—though dorms are also widely available. There are eight Social Houses, each of which is affiliated with one of the freshmen dorms. Social Houses are responsible for helping freshman get oriented at the beginning of the year, and throughout the year are required to have a certain number of events and activities, often in the form of parties. The selection for Social Houses, however, is done by Res Life, and thus not peer-driven and consequently there is no hazing or inherent cliquiness. The school makes a good effort to bring activities, speakers and performers to campus. Common Hour is a time every Friday when no classes are scheduled and the college brings a noteworthy speaker to campus—past speakers have included Robert F. Kennedy Jr. and Art Spiegelman. The party scene is very accessible—larger parties are hosted at Social Houses, but many students have their own parties in their dorms. There is a number of restaurants in Brunswick, but most of the town closes down fairly early. However, Portland is a big city that is only about half an hour away, and as many kids have cars, it is easy to get down to the city and get in a better nightlife scene.

Alumnus/a, 9/1999-5/2003, March 2006

Bowdoin students like to party. But that partying doesn't go much beyond the on-campus apartments, off-campus houses and other living situations. There is no dating, just random hook-ups. There is no Greek system, but instead a social house system that is still growing. It has been slow to take life but is a good idea in principle and will most likely become more popular as the years go by. Bowdoin-Colby hockey games a popular with students as well as the Brunswick folk. Ivies weekend is a time to booze it up as well.

Current student, 9/2003-Submit Date, March 2005

For a small town in Maine, Brunswick has a lot of choices. In terms of bars, there are three or four bars within walking distance of the college. Past the boundary of Brunswick is Portland, which is about a half hour away from the campus. The bar scene in Portland has been often regarded as one of the best for a small city in the U.S.

The Bowdoin campus is always bustling with activities. Students try hard to be involved. Much of the events, however, are centered around athletics. Bowdoin is a very active school. Games, matches and meets are well-attended, and the fan base is excited and energetic. The dating scene at Bowdoin is nearly nonexistent, however recent strides have been made in order to resurrect it. As it is a small campus, relations can often be strained due to the rapid spread of gossip. There is no Greek system at Bowdoin any longer, instead, it is replaced by what is called the social house system. Although created in order to stop the negative aspects of fraternities, the house system is only in its first few years running and has thus not done its best to retain the better aspects that the Greek life bring college living.

The School Says

Our curriculum articulates a blueprint for a liberal education designed to inspire students to become world citizens with an acute sensitivity to social differences and an understanding of the natural and artificial world.

Students are required to take courses in natural sciences, mathematics, social sciences, humanities and fine arts; however, the content of the newly required courses reflects a sharpened examination of issues vital to a liberal education in the 21st Century. The requirements are also designed to help students hone their written and analytical skills, deepen their aesthetic judgment, use varied forms of informational resources and create multifaceted solutions to complex problems.

Exploring Social Differences draws from courses spanning multiple disciplines, including sociology, history, Asian studies, environmental studies, gender and women's studies and economics. These courses are designed to help students examine characteristics of social differences, such as gender, race, class, ethnicity, sexual orientation, religion and environmental condition, and analyze how they shape societies, history and the global environment.

Mathematical, Computational or Statistical Reasoning addresses the data-driven nature of the 21st Century by requiring students in courses as wide-ranging as economics to psychology to use quantitative and symbolic methods to describe, explain and model the world around them.

The distribution requirements also include one First-Year Seminar to develop intellectual capabilities through communication; one course on Inquiry in the Natural Sciences; one course on International Perspective; and one course in the Arts.

Bowdoin offers a minor in gay and lesbian studies, and recently added interdisciplinary majors in Latin American Studies; Eurasian and East European Studies; and English and Theater. Bowdoin also added an emphasis on service learning to the curriculum in about one-third of the departments which allows stu-

Read all of Vault's College Surveys at www.vault.com/college–get complete surveys on 100s of colleges and universities, expert advice on applicaton essays and more.

VAULT CAREER LIBRARY   283

dents to apply knowledge gained in the classroom to real-world problems while helping a local community group.

All of the first-year residence halls have been renovated in the past two years, converted from two-room triples to three-room quads or two-room doubles. A fully renovated art museum, with one of the nation's oldest collegiate art collections, re-open in October 2007. A new 280-seat state-of-the-art music recital hall opened in May 2007. Plans are also underway to build a new hockey arena for 2008.

Bowdoin is also a leader among colleges and universities on issues of sustainability. In May 2007, Bowdoin signed the American College & University Presidents Climate Commitment, committed the college to reducing sharply and eventually eliminating all of its global warming emissions. In 2006, Bowdoin announced that it will purchase 100 percent of its electricity from renewable, or "green," sources. This announcement followed other steps at Bowdoin aimed at improving sustainability and promoting conservation. These include converting our boilers to burn more efficient and lower-impact fuels; significant investments in geothermal heating; student competitions to reduce energy consumption in residence halls; replacing college-owned vehicles with ones that use hybrid technology; and our own community organic garden providing food to our Number One rated food service. Bowdoin was awarded Silver Status certification under Leadership in Energy and Environmental Design standards for conservation and sustainability features in our two newest residence halls. Environmental literacy and stewardship are discussed in our classrooms and students are encouraged to explore ecological problems and solutions. All of this important work is significantly supported and influenced by our students who, after all, will inherit a planet made better by the conservation and sustainability efforts we put in place today.

Colby College

Office of Admissions and Financial Aid
4800 Mayflower Hill
Waterville, ME 04901-8848
Admissions phone: (800) 723-3032
Admissions fax: (207) 859-4828
Admissions e-mail: admissions@colby.edu
Admissions URL: www.colby.edu/admissions

 ## Admissions

Current student, 9/2005-Submit Date, December 2006

Admissions process is relatively easy and fast. When I applied in 2005, I used the Common App and a few more supplementary application forms. Colby was probably the first college acceptance notification I received and they seem to want to set a good first impression on their prospective students. The admissions process was probably one of the best and fastest of all the schools to which I applied.

Current student, 9/2002-Submit Date, November 2005

The admissions process is similar to any other college's. It's been a few years, and I know that the admissions criteria and forms have probably changed quite a bit. When I applied during the fall of 2001, I submitted a Common App and then had an interview (supposedly a big deal at small schools). The standards for admission are higher now than they were when I applied. I believe that the median SAT score is [1410]. [Though the majority of students come from public schools,] many students come from boarding/prep schools.

Alumnus/a, 9/2002-5/2006, October 2006

The admissions process is competitive, but only about half the students viewed Colby as their first choice. I knew a lot of kids who applied Early Decision, but I also knew just as many who applied to other liberal arts schools as their first choice schools.

Current student, 9/2002-Submit Date, July 2004

Fill out the admissions form completely and accurately. Add everything you can that you think will help you get in. Don't be shy; if you joined a club for a month or two, then tell them about it. Schools want to see students who are well-rounded and willing to try new things. The interview process only helped, but it is not mandatory. In order to have an interview I had to visit the school, which showed them that I had a serious interest in attending. I found the whole process to be a little tedious, but it was well worth it because I really wanted to go to Colby College. It is a highly selective school that takes everything into consideration, so it is important to write good, well proofread essays. They did not make the essays very difficult, in fact they were open-ended, meaning they wanted to read creative answers that caught their attention. They asked about important personal experiences and life choices that you have made. They wanted to get a feel for the student and see unique responses, because those are the ones they will remember.

Alumnus/a, 1/2004-5/2006, June 2006

Colby is very selective. It may be difficult to get into Colby, but the process is a breeze and the counselors are great. I think Colby, focuses on the essay and activities portion of the application the most.

 ## Academics

Current student, 9/2005-Submit Date, December 2006

A Colby education gears you for whatever future profession you would like to pursue. The professors are intelligent, caring and personable. The study abroad program, in which about 70 percent of Colby students take part, broadens your horizons. Classes are usually small in size (most are about 20 to 30 students). And there is really nothing to do but to study at Colby. So the students are actually very studious although it is hard to find competitiveness amongst students that prevails in larger top ranking schools. I've heard some Colby students say that Colby was like a smaller version of an Ivy League, but with less of a culture of competition.

Current student, 9/2002-Submit Date, November 2005

Generally classes are quite small, but I've been surprised by how difficult it has been to get into many classes. The general education requirements make academic life quite a pain, and are approached unenthusiastically by students. Some professors are wonderful, while others are just plain awful. I've been lucky enough to have engaging and great professors. There is a fair amount of work if you take your academics seriously. Most students make good use of the libraries on campus.

Alumnus/a, 9/2002-5/2006, October 2006

The academics actually did live up to the cliché of what you would imagine from a school where students brag about "babysitting for professors" and "having beers at the bar with professors." While those two things aren't exactly academic, they do indicate an environment where you have true access to professors and co-exist with faculty in a small, relatively secluded, intellectual environment—there were a lot of kids who really were passionate about the "intellectual pursuit" of the liberal arts degree.

Current student, 9/2002-Submit Date, July 2004

Colby is a difficult school to get into because it has a prestigious academic program that demands a lot out of its students. Students at Colby have to work hard to receive good grades but I have had no problem motivating myself to do well. I believe that the reason for this is because I enjoy the courses I am taking and professors always find time to meet with students. Most classes are very small, giving you a lot of personal attention. I had two classes last semester with a total of six students. Personally I enjoy the attention I get from professors. It makes me feel like they care about me and my future. Because Colby is a small school, getting into your preferred classes is very easy. I have had no problem there. Some professors grade harder than others—in certain classes—but this mainly occurs in intro classes, where professors try to weed out students who are not suitable for further study past the intro level. Every major/class is different, as far as workload. Majors in high demand tend also to produce the greatest workload. Overall, professors treat students like adults and let them decide how much effort they want to put into their class. They are fair and the workload can be a lot, but every student who puts forth the effort will get through it.

Alumnus/a, 1/2004-5/2006, June 2006

Academics are the reason for coming to Colby. Colby personifies the liberal arts experience. Professors are perfect.

Employment Prospects

Current student, 9/2005-Submit Date, December 2006

Colby is well respected throughout the New England region, especially in the Boston area. However, when you speak nationally or internationally, I would be impressed if someone recognized Colby. But it seems like Colby grads are doing well in whatever professions they are in. (And Colby students are known to go after wide variety of different things after graduation.) Colby does very well in terms of grad school placement. If you are in the top 10 percent of your Colby class, you will be very well prepared for any grad program. Colby's economics program is also topnotch, so there are many alumni who are in the finance field. The newly built Diamond Building for social science is an example—Bob Diamond is the CEO of Barcap.

Current student, 9/2002-Submit Date, November 2005

Depending on your area of study, employment prospects are either great or ridiculously awful. Econ majors have the best prospects and by far the most support, while humanities majors seem to wallow in a maze of confusion.

Alumnus/a, 9/2002-5/2006, October 2006

Recent graduates pursue a wide variety of jobs and higher degrees. Most of the jobs that the Career Services Office put their biggest effort into were financial analyst/consultant positions. SG Cowen, Barclays, IBM Consulting, and Cambridge Associates came to campus to interview, with "invites" to interview with companies that also interviewed at Bowdoin and Bates. I have six or seven close friends working at banks, such as UBS and Barclays, as well as consulting firms, such as McKinsey and Cambridge Associates. (However, note that half of those jobs were landed through family connections.)

Current student, 9/2002-Submit Date, July 2004

A bachelor's degree from Colby will help anyone find a job. Career services at Colby gives personal aid to all students to help them find jobs after they graduate. The school keeps students informed about new internship opportunities in the summer or after graduation. They provide a lot of resources for students to tap into and search for the best job or internship. A degree from Colby is something that employers consider prestigious. Colby College opens doors for its students and gives them many options for future careers. I am very happy with my school because I feel that it is helping me option a successful future.

Alumnus/a, 1/2004-5/2006, June 2006

Career services is great. They work with students and cater to individual needs. Colby's prestige is high in New England and with employers. If people have heard of it anywhere else, they are very impressed; however, because it so small, many people haven't heard of it. The best employers should know the Colby name.

Quality of Life

Current student, 9/2005-Submit Date, December 2006

The food is good, housing is good, campus is one of the prettiest. People don't really worry about being robbed or getting things stolen. People are nice. The first two months of school feel like heaven weather wise.

Waterville doesn't have the lifestyle that you would find in larger cities. It gets cold in the winter. Gym is pretty far away if you live near Foss. And very far away if you live in the Gardens, but you can take the shuttle van.

Current student, 9/2002-Submit Date, November 2005

The quality of life on campus has been steadily declining since I began school here in 2002. The campus is situated away from the town, so there is minimal crime. Housing can really be unfortunate if you're unlucky (everyone is encouraged to live on campus, and there is a lottery system to decide how rooms are allotted). Colby needs to build more dorms—they've been converting lounges into rooms for the past few years and recently had to rent a facility off campus to house 60 to 80 or so students. Food is great, but dining hours have been shortened since my first year and one dining hall has been closed on the weekends. Facilities are OK, but could use improvements. Currently, the school is undergoing a lot of construction, which is a pain for all the students who have to put up with the noise, lack of parking and rerouting while knowing that they'll never enjoy the fruits of all this labor.

Alumnus/a, 9/2002-5/2006, October 2006

Kids generally kept busy between extracurriculars, schoolwork, athletics and so on.

Current student, 9/2002-Submit Date, July 2004

The campus is beautiful and the dining halls are ranked among the best in the nation. I eat in the dining halls at least twice a day. There are three dining halls on campus, so the food does not get repetitive. The dorms are cleaned every morning, although some can get trashed on the weekends. There are dorms that are quiet and substance-free, so they always remain very clean and in excellent condition. I feel very safe on campus because it is a small campus with its own security team.

Alumnus/a, 1/2004-5/2006, June 2006

Life is good. Intellectual cultivation amongst the Maine backdrop is perfect.

Social Life

Current student, 9/2005-Submit Date, December 2006

People are very friendly. Parties start early and end fast. Colby does not have the Greek system, so usually the parties are smaller in size. Dana dorm, West quad and Frat row are usually better for parties. There are no nightclubs and people usually have dorm parties. Sometimes the student government invites popular bands or singers for concerts or has dances at the Cotter Union. Loudness weekends and a few other special days, like St. Patrick's Day, can get big and crazy.

Current student, 9/2002-Submit Date, November 2005

Social life has plummeted. The police are very stringent about shutting down off-campus parties and fining students accordingly. On-campus social events are limited and oftentimes unappealing to most students. There is a pub on campus that is popular a couple of days out of the week. There are quite a few clubs, but no Greek system. There are a couple of dives off campus that students like to frequent, no clubs to speak of, and a handful of fairly good restaurants. Generally, it's a very apathetic scene.

Alumnus/a, 9/2002-5/2006, October 2006

Social life varied probably more than anything else. It sounds a little meatheadish, but I am not sure what the kids who didn't drink alcohol did for fun. The school tried hard to manufacture fun, but (as is generally agreed upon) school sanctioned functions that liken to your 8th grade dances aren't that fun. Waterville offered a couple small bars, but typically the local bar scene did not embrace the preppy Colby kids in pink Lacoste shirts. For the most part, first-

Read all of Vault's College Surveys at www.vault.com/college–get complete surveys on 100s of colleges and universities, expert advice on applicaton essays and more.

VAULT CAREER LIBRARY 285

years (yes, it's Colby and the administration refuses to use the term "freshmen") and sophomores partied 10-at-a-time in multi-room dorm rooms, with the exception of the socially ambitious underclassman boys and cute underclassman girls who ventured to the off-campus house parties. (It sounds very frat-like, but the fact that the parties were simply "house parties" and not "frat house parties" really made for a more laidback environment.) Juniors and seniors primarily partied at these house parties at friends' places off campus, which typically were located within a five to 10 minute drive from campus.

Current student, 9/2002-Submit Date, July 2004

The social life at Colby is pretty good. It does not have an excellent bar scene and for the most part students stay on campus to have parties. The school sponsors many parties during the school year and the rules and regulations on consuming alcohol are lax. Colby has an assortment of people and the great thing about the school is that anyone who comes here can find people with the same interests. The school does a lot to try and get people to meet different kinds of people and it starts with orientation where all of the incoming students spend four days participating in an outdoor trip. This trip gives freshman students a chance to meet other first-years before they actually start classes. It eases their way into college. I had a great time on my orientation. Colby has a great deal of clubs and groups to join. No one is left out at Colby; everyone finds their own niche.

 The School Says

Colby is one of the top liberal arts colleges in the country. Established in 1813, it is also one of the oldest. In 1871, Colby became the first previously all-male college in New England to admit women. Admission today is highly selective; 63 percent of the Class of 2010 ranked in the top 10 percent in high school. 88 percent were in the top 25 percent.

Academics are the core of Colby. Achieving excellence in undergraduate liberal arts learning is Colby's central mission, and the Colby experience is, first and foremost, about the life of the mind. Colby's academic program is fueled by a dedicated and passionate faculty, first-rate facilities and amenities, and close interaction between professors and students—the faculty-to-student ratio is 1:10. The academic program, with 53 majors, 25 departments and 11 interdisciplinary programs, is

the heart of the Colby experience. There is a dedicated emphasis on progressive, innovative teaching techniques; project-based learning and research are incorporated throughout the curriculum. There are four academic divisions—the natural sciences, the social sciences, the humanities and the division of interdisciplinary studies, which encourages distinctive, innovative courses of study. Colby operates on a 4-1-4 calendar with a unique one-month January term during which students focus on a single course, independent project or internship.

Colby's 1,800 students come from virtually every state and more than 65 foreign countries. In 2005, Colby was presented the Senator Paul Simon Award for Campus Internationalization, recognizing its emphasis on study abroad programs, the international diversity of the student body and faculty, and the ways global issues permeate the curriculum. The Institute of International Education annually ranks colleges by the number of students who go abroad for international study. Each year, Colby shows up near the top of that list. At Colby, study abroad is encouraged and, for some majors, it is required. Two-thirds of Colby's students study abroad for at least one semester.

Colby also is a leader in environmental awareness and has won environmental awards for its commitment to sustainable practices on campus, including an Environmental Protection Agency (EPA) Environmental Merit Award and two Maine Governor's Awards for Environmental Excellence. All new building construction on campus is in accordance with green industry standards. These attributes befit a prestigious liberal arts college located on 714 acres in the heart of Maine, a state rich in natural resources and steeped in a tradition of respect for ecology and the environment.

Colby is known for its friendly, welcoming campus atmosphere and close-knit community. The pace of life is brisk and there is a rich roster of activities and organizations for students, including 32 varsity teams, 11 club sports, and a robust intramural sports program. Community service is an integral part of campus life, too, and the student-run Colby Volunteer Center coordinates dozens of service programs. Civic engagement and awareness are built into many parts of the academic program.

University of Maine

Office of Admission
5713 Chadbourne
Orono, ME 04469
Admissions phone: (877) 486-2364
Admissions URL: www.go.umaine.edu/

 Admissions

Current student, Legal Studies, 8/2006-Submit Date, March 2007

I was given a referral by my brother, an RA at the college, to apply to the school because he said it had good programs. From there, I went to my high school guidance counselor where he gave me the information and financial aid forms I needed, showing me the programs available at the school. I then took it upon myself to research the school by visiting the web site. I wasn't too sure about what I really wanted to do. I was interested in the law though because I had some bad experiences when I was a teen. I looked into that program; the classes were exactly what I was looking for. I liked what I saw so I applied. I had to send in an application about the reasons I wanted to attend college and this col-

lege in particular. I also had to tell them why I would be a good student attending their college and what goals I hope to achieve by graduation and after. They asked for why I specifically chose this degree to study for and I must have had good reasons because I was accepted within six to eight weeks. I began the financial aid process, followed up by a lot of paperwork and a move to the campus at the beginning of the 2006 fall semester.

Current student, 1/2003-Submit Date, July 2006

I am an international student and at first I was afraid to apply, but as soon as I contacted them, they walked me through the process. You can either apply online at the university web site or you can have an application mailed to you. The advice for international students is to have a high TOEFL score; the higher the score, the easier it would be to get accepted without an English course requirement. The minimum score is 550 on the paper-based test.

Current student, 9/2003-Submit Date, October 2005

I was a part of the Upward Bound program at the college for two years before I applied. I believe this helped greatly in my acceptance. I filled out the application, including an essay, and was accepted shortly thereafter. I did receive a lot of advice on filling out the application and essays from my counselors at Upward

Bound. For the most part, the college doesn't seem to be too hard to get into, but you do need to maintain decent grades to stay in and qualify for future programs.

Current student, 8/2001-Submit Date, May 2004

The admissions process varies widely at the University of Maine, depending on the state you are from and the degree you plan to pursue. Students from Maine will find the admission standards at the University of Maine to be quite low. An average to slightly below-average SAT score and GPA will get you in. Those from out of state will find the process more challenging, but will likely be admitted with average to above-average SAT and GPA scores. Those who intend to pursue an engineering degree will find they need high scores to attend; the University of Maine has a very popular engineering program. Most students majoring in something other than science or math, or undecideds, will find the University of Maine to be relatively easy to get into.

> **The school says:** "In fact, UMaine's SAT averages significantly exceed both national and state averages; the student's comment suggests that all UMaine students could, statistically speaking, have average or below-average SAT scores. That doesn't make sense."

There is no interview requirement at the University of Maine. An essay is required, but it can be on a topic of your choosing. The University of Maine is very fast when it comes to getting back to you on your application. It was the first school I heard back from, by well over a month. That makes it a good school to apply to, even if you don't plan to go, because it takes the pressure off to know you got in at least one school.

Current student, 8/2001-Submit Date, March 2004

A student must have good grades from high school and reasonable SAT scores to get himself or herself accepted into the University of Maine system. Each Maine school has its requirements. But you should first of all decide which of the Maine system schools you are interested in, then apply. A student should apply for scholarship. A student should also follow up with admissions by calling frequently to check his or her status.

Academics

Current student, Legal Studies, 8/2006-Submit Date, March 2007

Each class is different in its own way and I think that is why it is so easy to learn. Each teacher his/her own way of teaching, some better than others, but I learn something every day in each class, big or small. I enjoy how they don't just have teachers, but they have actual police officers, investigators and detectives as the teachers of each class. Depending on what the police official specializes in, that is what they teach. The college has a very calming setting. It is on the coast of southern Maine and you can see the ocean from almost every building. It is always good to see the ocean before you go to class at 8 a.m.. The grading is average, classes are average, and the workload is about average. The scheduling is set up very nicely though, where you can choose to take school five days a week, three days a week, two days a week or one, which makes it very easy to make a personal life.

Current student, 1/2003-Submit Date, July 2006

The academic programs are very competitive and leave little room for laziness. Most departments will have a requirement of 120 credits to be able to graduate. Most people take five years to graduate instead of four. Concerning the classes, you can either [have] lecture class or recitation, the enjoyment of either depends on the seriousness of the subject, the popularity of the subject and the professor. Seniors are the first ones to register, then juniors and so on, which makes it easier for seniors to get into the classes they want. The grading system is the letter system, but the range in which the letter [includes] is at the discretion of the teacher. The workload will mostly depend on the class level and the subject matter.

Current student, 9/2003-Submit Date, October 2005

I'm majoring in broadcast journalism, and so far the workload has been bearable. The most intensive part is going out to interview people and get stories. Generally the class quality is very good, and most professors are easy to get

along with. Grading seems fair, but that all depends on the individual professor. As far as getting popular classes, it's easier to get them each year you attend. The seniors get first pick at classes, then juniors and so on. I've not really had a hard time getting classes that I want though. Most students stay up past midnight to apply for classes on the first day application becomes available. This is to ensure that they get their first picks.

Current student, 8/2001-Submit Date, May 2004

Classes at the University of Maine are excellent. They are as in-depth and challenging as any you will find. However, keep in mind this is not a good thing for all students. Well under 50 percent of those admitted graduate in four years, and around 40 percent never graduate at all.

I have never not been able to get into a class in my three years at the University of Maine. The main problem is getting classes at the times you want, not getting in. Most popular classes offer an option to take the class online, so if you need a class, you will almost always be able to get it.

Grading works on the traditional four-point system. Typically, most grades are primarily based on test scores. As mentioned above, getting good grades at the University of Maine can be tough, but generally the grading system is very fair.

The professors at the University of Maine tend to be very good. They also usually teach classes themselves, rather than handing the duties off to a teaching assistant. They are always available to help.

Current student, 8/2001-Submit Date, March 2004

Classes are not difficult if a student pays attention. The quality of teaching and classes is very good, because the professors know students by their names. The professors let students experiment and try applied knowledge, which enhances the learning capabilities of the students. Practical work and research are carried out to promote hands-on experience and knowledge.

Current student, 9/2003-Submit Date, March 2004

Classes are readily available. Classes are small in size, and difficult but enjoyable. Two of my four classes are online. Classes are available early in the morning and are open until as late as 9 p.m. I find that a big plus. They offer free tutoring for anyone who is interested. The tutoring is available during a varied number of hours and is easy to access. I have to give a lot of credit to the English tutor who made English not quite as tedious as I thought it was.

The workload varies from class to class. My English classes give me the most work; second is psychology. The most popular teachers are the ones who are lenient about homework being in on time. Many will not accept late work. The least popular teachers have been the ones I have learned the most from. People don't like them because they are so strict, but they make sure you are doing what you are supposed to be doing. That's not true of all the teachers. Some are not that way. Many teachers figure you're an adult and you know what you are supposed to do. They don't push you to achieve. They just tell you what to do and leave it up to you. That method makes it easy for some to slack.

Employment Prospects

Current student, 1/2003-Submit Date, July 2006

The university has an excellent career center and usually students receive career opportunities according to their majors. There is also a very good web site where UMaine students can look for careers after graduation or internships for the summer. The biggest employer in Maine is the state government. If you plan to stay that will probably be your next employer, but most people leave and go settle somewhere else.

Current student, 9/2003-Submit Date, October 2005

The degree does look decent when applying for a job off campus. As far as employment opportunities for everybody, it really depends on the degree obtained, and the attributes that particular person has. Also the school offers many work study programs for students. I've worked for the same office for the three years I've been here and enjoyed it very much.

Read all of Vault's College Surveys at **www.vault.com/college**–get complete surveys on 100s of colleges and universities, expert advice on applicaton essays and more.

VAULT CAREER LIBRARY 287

Current student, 8/2001-Submit Date, May 2004

Job and internship opportunities depend completely on the major you have. Since the University of Maine is a fairly large school, each department takes care of its own students. As a general rule, most departments are very good at finding their students internships. Many majors even require an internship, which they find and set up for you. Because there is a small city nearby, and there are no other quality four-year schools in the area, it is easy for University of Maine students to find internships, because they have essentially no competition from students at other schools. This is one area where the school's isolated location actually pays off. All in all, internship opportunities at the University of Maine abound.

Campus recruiting is quite good at the University of Maine, as it is at most large schools. There are typically three to four large job fairs each year, with numerous employers from many fields of work.

The University of Maine has very high prestige among employers within the state of Maine. Out-of-state employers, however, view the University of Maine as just another state university. Basically it depends where you intend to work; if you wish to pursue a career in Maine, there are very few schools that can rival the University of Maine in prestige with employers. If you intend to work out of state, the University of Maine will likely be considered average to low-average.

The University of Maine has a large career center that provides students with any type of job resource they may need. This includes placement, information, help choosing the right career, and anything else you might think of.

Quality of Life

Current student, Legal Studies, 8/2006-Submit Date, March 2007

I stayed on the campus in a dorm for the first three months. The dorm was nice, a single room that looked at the ocean. I was surprised and I liked what I saw the day I moved in. While I lived there, it was peaceful. There weren't many problems; it almost seemed a little unreal. The housing is nice and the campus is set up nicely on the coast of southern Maine where you can see the ocean from every building. The dining services are better than I expected. They have very good food, but they could have more of a change in the food every meal. I also worked in the cafe on the campus and the campus cafeteria just up until recently. The neighborhood is in a very good part of town. It isn't known for much crime or many problems. The security is good at the school also, which is good to have in mind while attending. The school is inviting and open to all new and different people, which is why I like it.

Current student, 1/2003-Submit Date, July 2006

Life in Orono is pretty safe. Apartments are very affordable. For those who choose to live on campus, they will have meal plans that will give them access to the dining commons. There are three dining facilities and they are located near the dorms. Campus rooms are usually two bedrooms but residents also have the option to request a one bedroom by paying a little more. Dorms are not co-ed. Each floor is either all male or all female.

Current student, 9/2003-Submit Date, October 2005

I lived on campus for my freshman year only. The housing was fair, but could have been better. Many of the students in the dorm were inconsiderate of the others living there, and the dorms were often messy. The dining commons weren't bad, but they were pricey, and you weren't compensated for meals you didn't eat. Our campus police are usually quite busy, but mostly they are dealing with parties and bad drivers. I live in an apartment complex now that is right off campus. I enjoy it very much.

Current student, 8/2001-Submit Date, May 2004

The dorms at the University of Maine are quite nice. Since the town of Orono, where the University of Maine is located, is technically an island (it is surrounded by two rivers), law prohibits any building reaching over four stories in height. This keeps the size of the dorms reasonable, so you feel as though you know all those with whom you live. All dorms are co-ed, and are nice and clean. Each dorm has at least two full-time janitors assigned to it, so they tend to stay

quite clean. All dorms are within easy walking distance of dining areas and classes.

The campus is very nice. It is its own entity and is completely separate from the town it is in. This makes for a very quiet campus relative to the size of the student body. The buildings are all within walking distance, and there is a large central mall or park area. This is another advantage of the school's isolated location, the campus is well planned and provides a nice environment.

The campus has very nice facilities of all types. The class buildings are nice and fairly modern. There is a post office, bank and any other such service you can think of. The athletic facilities are good, but a little out of date. However, a new stadium and field house are currently being built, so that should be rectified soon. The field house should be done halfway through 2005, and the stadium a year or so later.

The University of Maine is a very safe campus. This is because the campus security force is comprised of actual police officers, not simply hired security. This is somewhat rare for most colleges, and makes for a safe campus. The state police barracks also happen to be located in the town, which also keeps things safe. Most will find this a good thing, but beware, if you get caught doing something wrong at the University of Maine, you get in trouble with real police, not just campus authorities, which generally means a larger fine.

Social Life

Current student, 1/2003-Submit Date, July 2006

Orono is a pretty small and sometimes things to do can be hard to find. In downtown Orono however, you find Mexican and Thai restaurants, for example, and the main town bar. On Saturday night, students who are usually under 21 go to Ushaia, which is the most popular and only nightclub. Bangor, which is about a 10-minute drive away from Orono, is a bigger city and has way [more] to offer. There are countless restaurants, a big shopping mall and many bars.

Current student, 9/2003-Submit Date, October 2005

The school offers many on-campus activities, including concerts, religious activities, movies, clubs, fraternities and sororities and so on. The local bars are very popular. As far as the dating scene, I don't get involved with many of the programs on campus. The nightlife seems to be one of the more popular things. Many of my classmates are always up late partying or socializing, and pay for it during classes the next day. Thirsty Thursdays also seem to be a popular night for students to go out and drink.

Current student, 8/2001-Submit Date, May 2004

There are numerous campus events. The most popular, by far, are the hockey games. The University of Maine has one of the nation's best hockey teams, which plays in a fairly small arena. This combination creates a rowdy atmosphere and great fun. I'm not really even a hockey fan, but I would never miss a game because it is such fun. Each spring there is also a music festival known as Bumstock. It is two-day music festival that draws surprisingly good bands. Over the years many big bands have participated, from the first big band to play, The Grateful Dead, to the most recent, Eve 6. It's also free, which is a plus. It's not every day you can be front-row for a headliner and not pay a dime. In the warmer months there are also numerous free barbeques that are well attended.

Current student, Legal Studies, 8/2006-Submit Date, March 2007

The school holds monthly dances, local get-togethers, concerts and comedy shows on the campus. There is a local bar just off the campus which most 21 and up people visit that go to the school. The restaurants are nice and unique. There are some of every kind in every part of the city and they are plenty close to the campus if you have no vehicle. The shopping centers, stores, and sales you can find are great and of course, we are located just 10 minutes from the Maine Mall, of which I take advantage! There is always something to do on those days you don't have class and places to go to study the days you do.

Every type of club you can possibly imagine exists at the University of Maine, far too many to list. One club of note is the Outing Club, which provides a free ski cabin at Sugarloaf to students.

There is an active Greek community at the University of Maine. It is moderately sized, and seems to be quite fun. It is not, however, as important to the University of Maine culture as it is at other schools. At many schools, Greek life is very large and important, but that is not so much the case at UMaine.

 The School Says

As the flagship university of the University of Maine system, UMaine offers the range of programs and services befitting a comprehensive university, including an Honors College, modern research facilities, and the state's largest library and government document repository. Maine's largest liberal arts institution is also the home of the state's only NCAA Division I athletic program. UMaine's five colleges meet the changing needs and challenges of the state, its students and practicing professionals (Business, Public Policy and Health; Education and Human Development; Engineering; Liberal Arts and Sciences; and Natural Sciences, Forestry and Agriculture).

UMaine has statewide responsibility for those educational, research and public service programs associated with its designation as the state's land-grant university and sea-grant college. In the spirit of its land-grant heritage, UMaine is committed to the creation and dissemination of knowledge to improve the lives of its students and of Maine citizens in their full intellectual, social, economic, artistic, and cultural diversity. As a sea-grant college, UMaine is dedicated to conducting research and communicating information on the wise, humane use and conservation of marine resources.

The University of Maine's 1,100-acre campus enjoys an ideal physical setting on the banks of the Stillwater River in Orono, Maine. It is 10 minutes from Bangor, Maine's third largest city. Because of its natural beauty, safety, and affordability, Bangor is consistently ranked as a highly desirable place to live. Fifteen minutes from an international airport, Orono is also adjacent to an interstate highway (I-95), only an hour from Bar Harbor and Acadia National Park, and within an easy drive of several major ski resorts. Despite these convenient travel connections, it sits at the edge of the last great expanse of undeveloped lakes, forests and streams in the Northeast. The UMaine campus serves as the cultural and performing arts center for the area, as well as the home of Division I men's and women's Black Bear athletic teams. Through Cooperative Extension and other outreach efforts, UMaine has a physical presence and employees in each of Maine's 16 counties. It also has major outreach and research centers and forest holdings statewide.

Read all of Vault's College Surveys at **www.vault.com/college**–get complete surveys on 100s of colleges and universities, expert advice on applicaton essays and more.

VAULT CAREER LIBRARY   289

Johns Hopkins University

Office of Undergraduate Admissions
Johns Hopkins University
Mason Hall
3400 North Charles Street
Baltimore, MD 21218-2683
Admissions phone: (410) 516-8171
Admissions fax: (410) 516-6025
Admissions e-mail: gotojhu@jhu.edu
Admissions URL: apply.jhu.edu/

 ## Admissions

Current student, 9/2005-Submit Date, May 2007

Hopkins admissions is extremely selective and the essay plays an important role. It is important to be creative and to think outside of the box. Hopkins seeks well-rounded and intelligent students who will benefit from the type of comprehensive education the school provides.

Current student, 9/2004-Submit Date, May 2007

I was waitlisted and then admitted to Johns Hopkins. My best advice would be to pursue actively schools you want to go to if you are put on a waiting list. Send them an updated résumé, an extra letter of recommendation, a CD of performed music, or whatever you can send them to show that you are really interested. It will pay off in the end.

Current student, Cultural Studies, 9/2006-Submit Date, May 2007

I applied using the Common Application with the Johns Hopkins supplement. Hopkins is very selective, and they look for students with a complete background and an interest in many different things. Interviews are recommended but not required, and you interview with current students. I did not interview. The most important thing to show on your application is that you are a hard worker who is interested and involved, and who can handle Hopkins and put the education and opportunities to good use.

Current student, Pre-med, 9/2006-Submit Date, May 2007

Let's face it: it's true you should earn the highest GPA and standardized test scores that you can. You have to show you can handle the academics at Hopkins. For the same reason, try to have as challenging a courseload as possible in high school. But still, you can't just study and expect to receive an admissions letter from Hopkins. While you should do well in academics, you should also prove that you're an individual. Show that there's something in addition to academics about which you're passionate. Be a person to take initiative outside the classroom and make a difference in the world!

Current student, Sociology, 9/2003-Submit Date, April 2007

The admissions process for JHU is a highly selective one. Our incoming freshman class consists of 1,200 students. A complete application includes an essay (Common Application or Hopkins Application), transcript, résumé, standardized test scores and two recommendations. Interviews are not required and are conducted on campus with a current student who is a junior or senior.

> **The school says:** One counselor recommendation and one teacher recommendation are required, as well as two essays. Alumni interviews off campus are also available.

Current student, Engineering, 9/2005-Submit Date, April 2007

Applications for admission are read based on geographic location. There is an optional interview process, but not coming for an interview will definitely not have an adverse effect on your chances of getting in. Hopkins has its famous "$10 essay" every year. Students have the option of writing the essay or sending in something they made with $10, about which I can only say don't send in something that people won't want to touch, because then you definitely won't

get in. Every year, more and more people are applying to Hopkins, which mean it gets more selective each year. Unless you're one of the 100 best lacrosse players in the nation, you're going to need a very strong résumé to get in. On a final note, going on a tour will not help you get in, so while tour guides love people who ask questions, don't think they can help you gain admittance.

> **Johns Hopkins says:** "The essay question has changed to: Communities define our lives. Those you are born into, those you make yourself, and those you fall into by accident—communities of all types influence us and help shape us. Describe a defining community in your life and what it means to you."

Current student, 9/2005-Submit Date, May 2006

I applied to JHU randomly because I live in Baltimore and thought it was wort a shot, but basically I planned on being rejected. In fact, there was no doubt i my mind I would be rejected. Now that I go to school here though I'm realizin that admissions is a holistic thing. There are students here who had OK grade in high school but excellent SAT scores and outstanding dedication to extracu ricular programs. I think the personal skills shown through the essays are also huge factor. Essays that show you are passionate about something, and are di ferent from the other essays—that is what they are looking for. They want sma kids who are interesting. They don't want a bunch of genius nerds. They turne down the valedictorian at my high school for example, but accepted me (I' barely in the top 10 percent).

Current student, 9/2005-Submit Date, May 2006

It's difficult to be admitted to the university, as it is one of the most competitiv in the nation. The place to find solace is that Hopkins has a holistic view o admissions, in that they look at everything. They may reject a 2400 [SAT] an accept an 1800. It is because they look at the whole person. I recommend look ing at the admissions web site, especially Hopkins Interactive, in order to gai an appreciation for student life and for the admissions process.

 ## Academics

Current student, 9/2005-Submit Date, May 2007

Hopkins academics are dictated by the student's major, so classes and difficult differ from student to student. Getting into popular 101 classes tends to be easy but getting into popular upper-level classes can be difficult. The classes are o the highest quality, and the professors take a serious interest in the success o their students. Grading differs from professor to professor, as does workload.

Current student, 9/2004-Submit Date, May 2007

It's very easy to get into classes because there are only [4,400] undergraduates especially compared to other schools where I've heard of people having to tak five or six years to graduate because they can't get into English 101. Also because we don't have required courses but only distribution requirements, yo can always take classes that actually interest you. You don't have to take Englis 101. You can take a creative writing class in the writing seminars department o you can take another writing intensive course on Shakespeare or British author instead. As far as workload is concerned, it really depends on the individual an the semester.

Current student, Cultural Studies, 9/2006-Submit Date, May 2007

If you have trouble getting into a class that you'd like to take, the professors ar very accommodating and willing to make space for you if you show an interes in the class and go on the first day to get their permission. Grading, again, real ly depends on the class and the professor. There are lecture classes, which mee in big lecture groups about twice a week and in a smaller section of about 20 people led by a graduate student or teaching assistants once a week, and small er classes that do not have sections.

Current student, Biology, 9/2004-Submit Date, April 2007

The classes, for the most part, are taught by true leaders in the field who are surprisingly accessible. Office hours are a great time to visit your teachers and get, essentially, personal tutoring. There is a rumor that the undergraduate population is overshadowed by the graduate population, but this is completely false. These assumptions are probably based on the famous reputation of the medical school, which is second only to Harvard. However, the medical school campus is in a completely different part of the city than the undergrad campus—there isn't any overshadowing going on. There are four undergrads for every grad student on the Homewood campus, so the grad students aren't able to overshadow. In fact, they're usually the ones teaching sections (smaller versions of the lectures) and teaching you lab techniques in whatever research job you've managed to snag.

Current student, Engineering, 9/2006-Submit Date, April 2007

The program at JHU is often rather competitive. However, if you are having issues in any class, everyone will offer you help. Professors and teaching assistants are very approachable and very flexible with when they will meet with you. Most programs have recommended schedules, so it is easy to fit everything into your semester. The classes are hard, but you learn a lot, and is easy to see how relevant this information is to your future job. Smaller classes are hard to get into early on, but if you talk to the professor, he/she will often find ways to get you in. Otherwise, it can usually be fit in later. The grading is fair, and many of the harder classes are graded on a curve. However, hard work is required to succeed at Johns Hopkins University.

Current student, 9/2005-Submit Date, May 2006

As far as the Herculean effort I was warned I would have to exert to accomplish anything, it couldn't be further from the truth. Surprisingly, I have found the classes enjoyable and above all, manageable. The professors are accessible and classes relatively easy to get into. Large lectures break down into smaller sections with TAs who are willing to help you out as much as you need them, which is comforting in the imposing atmosphere of such a notoriously cutthroat academic environment.

Current student, 10/2005-Submit Date, May 2006

Hopkins is a very challenging place, but the academic experience here is one of a kind. Majority of the classes are amazing, taught by the world's leading professionals and intellectuals. Although majority of the professors are incredible, a prospective student should speak with current students to find out which courses are most popular. In sum, even though the workload is difficult and intense, the [breadth] of information and experiences are phenomenal.

 # Employment Prospects

Current student, 9/2005-Submit Date, May 2007

Hopkins has the highest rate of grad school admissions of any school in the country. 90 percent of pre-med students are admitted to medical school, and 95 percent of pre-law students are admitted into law school.

> **The school says:** "86 percent of first-time medical school applicants from the Class of 2006 gained admittance."

Hopkins students obtain high profile jobs at large companies all over the world. In addition, Hopkins has an extensive alumni network that provides many opportunities. Also, the pre-professional advising office is quite helpful.

Current student, Biology, 9/2004-Submit Date, April 2007

In terms of employment, Johns Hopkins is quite the prestigious name to have on a résumé. There are many on-campus job fairs for juniors and seniors to get internships and jobs. The proximity to Washington, D.C. provides a range of employers, especially in fields like consulting. The employment office is great at helping to edit résumés and prepare you for interviews (They'll even stage mock ones for you!) However, it should be pointed out that Johns Hopkins has an extremely high portion of its graduates go on to graduate school—one of the highest percentages in the country. The pre-professional advising department (which deals with applications to medical school, law school, business school) is extremely good at what it does.

Current student, Pre-med, 9/2004-Submit Date, April 2007

Many of the nations top employers look at Hopkins grads as prepared above their peers to continue into the workforce. The jobs range from research to finance and the alumni I know are more than willing to lend a hand with either networking or job preparation. The on-campus events are helpful as well. The Career Center works diligently to get some of the top names in most industries to come to campus.

Current student, Social Sciences, 9/2004-Submit Date, May 2007

The best reason to attend Hopkins specifically for IR is to try to get into the five-year BA/MA SAIS program. According to recent IR publications, SAIS is the Number One school only for a terminal master's program. To get into SAIS from Hopkins, all you need is a GPA of 3.5 or above, fill out a two-page application, and get approved from the vice dean Steven David. SAIS graduates get good jobs in the government, nonprofits and so on, due to a good education with famous faculty and a vast alumni network in the D.C. area. This is probably because SAIS is located near DuPont Circle, in Washington, D.C. However, many graduates work in New York as well.

Current student, 9/2005-Submit Date, May 2006

Percentages for admissions into law and medical schools are ridiculously good for Hopkins graduates. I had to learn them for the Hopkins tour guide society and I am always so excited to share with prospective parents and students how well Hopkins grads fare post-graduation. Also, I have used the alumni network to seek out summer internships and just to talk to people who graduated from Hopkins with my major and see what they are doing with their lives now. It is an accessible and fascinating resource available to all undergrads and post-grads.

Current student, 9/2002-Submit Date, September 2005

The Career Center does a good job in assisting students with job hunting and career management. The school also offers a comprehensive networking system with alumni which provides details of their current employers and contact info.

Since our school does not have a business school, big-name business companies don't always come for on-campus recruiting. This is surely a disadvantage for students who are interested in pursuing a career in business, but I heard that the situation is significantly improving recently. For example, companies like Goldman Sachs, Lehman Brothers, Legg Mason Wood Walker and Citigroup are much more actively recruiting Hopkins students because they realize engineering students from our school can be great assets to their companies with our training in quantitative analysis.

> **The school says:** "The Johns Hopkins Carey School of Business opened its doors in January 2007. The school has plans for a five-year bachelor's/master's program."

 ## Quality of Life

Current student, 9/2005-Submit Date, May 2007

Hopkins is always improving its housing situation and should offer housing to all undergrads within the next few years. Crime and safety is another issue on which Hopkins is focused. In the past few years an extensive security system including cameras, emergency lights, and security officers has been activated. Charles Village, the area of Baltimore in which Hopkins is located, is a nice quiet area of town where there are plenty of restaurants and services within walking distance of campus.

Current student, 9/2004-Submit Date, May 2007

Housing is great and is improving every year. We have a brand-new dorm called Charles Commons that houses 600 sophomores, juniors and seniors. It's great and beautiful! It also has a dining hall, Nolan's, which is amazing! I even eat there and I'm a rising senior. The neighborhood, Charles Village, is really up-and-coming in terms of getting new restaurants and stores all the time. We have a new Starbucks, Chipotle, Cold Stone Creamery and so on. Crime is a small problem in the surrounding area but the Hopkins security guards patrol the area all around campus, so students feel really safe even late at night. I've never had a problem nor do I know anyone who has ever had a problem with security, crime or safety.

Read all of Vault's College Surveys at www.vault.com/college–get complete surveys on 100s of colleges and universities, expert advice on applicaton essays and more.

VAULT CAREER LIBRARY   291

Current student, Cultural Studies, 9/2006-Submit Date, May 2007

Housing is only guaranteed here the first two years, but the school is really making an effort to improve the housing situation. There's a good variety of places to live, and I have no complaints about any of the dorms. The campus is beautiful and a nice size, made up primarily of three quads. The neighborhood has a good number of amenities, such as markets, a bank, a dry cleaner and a movie rental, all within short walking distance of campus.

Current student, 9/2005-Submit Date, May 2006

The three-block radius around Hopkins is a generally safe community, and the Hopkins police patrol the area well. Once outside that area, you are in the heart of Baltimore, so you must be aware that it is a city. Housing around the campus is easily attainable for students and is not too expensive.

Current student, 9/2005-Submit Date, May 2006

Freshmen are all grouped together on the main campus, which is definitely conducive to a socially thriving freshman year and efforts are being made to incorporate more students in on-campus events. I have found it very possible to manage a full class schedule with sorority life, a social life and participation in various clubs on campus. The facilities are generally up to date; however, it lacks a general student center and the sense of belonging to one big university is somewhat lacking. Hopkins is located in a city, and therefore common sense and general precautions go a long way. As long as one makes prudent decisions and utilizes the free shuttles around the neighborhoods, [one will] never feel as though one's safety is seriously compromised.

Social Life

Current student, Political Science, 9/2005-Submit Date, May 2007

Social life is pretty underrated at Johns Hopkins. It's obviously much different than that which would be found at a big party school, but it's not terrible or non-existent either. Baltimore has a lot of cool bars, micro pubs, clubs and so on.

Current student, 9/2005-Submit Date, May 2007

Hopkins has a very tightly-knit Greek community with Greek organizations available to all students. Also, there are plenty of bars and restaurants in the area.

Current student, 9/2004-Submit Date, May 2007

Again, because Charles Village is really an up-and-coming area, there are new restaurants and bars in the area. There are no clubs in the area, but students often go down to the Inner Harbor, Canton, or Fells Point to go clubbing. Personally I am in a sorority and it's a lot of fun, but only about 20 percent of the student body is involved in Greek life. It is by no means the only thing to do on campus but it is a lot of fun. As for student activities, there are so many that I can't possibly name even a small portion of them but there is everything from political groups to movie groups, to theater and comedy groups, musical groups and so on: everything you can think of. Also, if you want to start a club that doesn't already exist, you always can write a proposal to start your own.

Current student, Cultural Studies, 9/2006-Submit Date, May 2007

There are a lot of things to do off campus, including a few pubs in the neighborhood (PJ's, Charles Village Pub, Rocky Run), and there are great restaurants, clubs and bars in the city. Baltimore is pretty small and getting around is very easy. Greek life is not a make-or-break-your-social-life thing here, but fraternities do host a lot of parties and events that students can attend.

Current student, 9/2004-Submit Date, May 2006

Baltimore is a bar town. Even though Hopkins has a reputation of very serious students, the athletic teams and Greek life dominate the social landscape. Although a minority of students participate in Greek life, a majority of those who go out frequently are members of fraternities or sororities. Not a lot of places to eat around campus, but there are plenty of great places downtown.

Current student, 9/2005-Submit Date, May 2006

The social life at Hopkins is what you make of it. Many upperclassmen gather at bars that are across the street from campus, making it an easy social scene. Baltimore has a great ethnic culinary scene that has been interesting to sample. Hopkins guys are, well, not the most attractive as a rule, but there are some to be found. Also, there are at least six other less nerdy colleges surrounding Hopkins with a seemingly endless supply of good looking young men. The Greek scene is not mandatory to have a social life, but it definitely helps. It narrows down the size of your class and the school into a nice group of people you can call your friends. The sorority-fraternity relationships are very close. However, it doesn't have to be the only thing going on in your social life. That is the nice thing about Hopkins; you can be affiliated with the Greek system, but it certainly doesn't define you, because everyone is involved in so many things.

The School Says

Ever since its founding in 1876, Johns Hopkins has made the undergraduate experience all about exploration. This is a place that attracts students eager to pursue new ideas, discoveries, and directions-wherever they might lead.

From Beowulf to bioengineering, archaeology to astronomy, independent learning spans every discipline. In fact, Hopkins is one of the few schools where undergraduates receive grants and awards to support their original projects. Whether you know where you're headed or want to keep your options open at first, at Johns Hopkins you'll find faculty, academic, and pre-professional advisers ready to help you find the path that's best for you. Internships, independent projects, study abroad—because Hopkins puts so much emphasis on real-world learning, you're a step ahead of your peers from other schools when it comes to that first job interview or graduate school. Chances are, you'll already have had some actual experience in your chosen field of study or profession.

Student life is centered around our 140-acre, spacious, green campus. Events pack the calendar all year long with music, theater, guest speakers, art exhibits, live comedy, film, dance, and athletic events, not to mention all the culture and entertainment you'll find throughout the city. Located in Baltimore, Maryland, Hopkins is in the heart of the busy New York-Washington, D.C., corridor, within easy reach of the most important and exciting cities on the East Coast. Baltimore itself offers all the amenities of a major urban center but retains the easy lifestyle and neighborliness of a smaller city. Nicknamed "Charm City," it has a unique flavor and a character all its own. People are friendly and take pride in their city; they also go out of their way to make everyone who comes here feel welcome.

United States Naval Academy

Admissions Office
117 Decatur Road
Annapolis, MD 21402-5018
Admissions phone: (410) 293-4361
Admissions e-mail: webmail@usna.edu
Admissions URL: www.usna.edu/Admissions/

 ## Admissions

Current student, 7/2003-Submit Date, March 2007

It was a very difficult admissions process. You have to be interviewed by a Blue and Gold officer in your hometown as well as by someone on your congressman's or senator's staff. They really focus on leadership and ethics; you must demonstrate both of those to succeed. They will ask about your desire to serve in the military as well, so be prepared for that.

Alumnus/a, 6/1997-5/2001, January 2006

The admissions process is difficult, because you have to apply through two separate sources: the school and a person who can nominate you. To be accepted into the Naval Academy, you have to be accepted by the school itself, and receive a nomination from an appropriate source. Those sources include: Vice Presidential nomination, Senate nominations and Congressional nominations. The list of potential nomination sources and the process for seeking one, are listed at the Academy Web Page, or a Blue and Gold Officer can help you find and learn about them. Of note, in some states, it's harder to receive a nomination than others. While almost all states are represented in a given USNA class, there are always a high percentage of students from MD, VA and CA. So if you're from a state like MD with a small number of potential nominations, the competition can be quite fierce.

Interviews: from my own experiences and others this process is formal, but can vary widely, especially for the nomination side of the process. You'll end up going to a congressman's or senator's office and being interviewed from someone on their staff that the duty has been assigned (can't imagine that's a great job when most probably aren't USNA alumni).

Other than that, the process is similar to the other colleges and universities with regards to essays.

Alumnus/a, 6/1999-5/2003, September 2005

Very competitive. Requires a nomination from a U.S. Congressman or Secretary of the Navy. Each candidate must write essays and qualify on a well-rounded academic and athletic achievement background. Scoring above average on the SAT is almost a requirement.

Midshipmen were admitted from every state in the nation as well as Washington, D.C., Puerto Rico and Northern Marianas. The Class of 2009 also includes 11 international students from the following countries: Guyana (two), Honduras, Ireland, Malaysia, Maldives, Mauritius, Philippines, Singapore, Taiwan and Thailand.

Student body/council/government president or vice president—9 percent. Class president or vice president—9 percent. School club president or vice president—25 percent School publication staff—24 percent. National Honor Society—59 percent. Varsity athletics—91 percent. Varsity letter winner—85 percent. Dramatics, public speaking, debating—85 percent. Leader of musical group—9 percent. Eagle Scout/Gold Award—13 percent. Boys/Girls State or Nation—14 percent. Reserve Officer Training Programs—10 percent. Sea Cadets—2 percent

Current student, 8/2003-Submit Date, April 2006

Must request application from school. It is a very tough school to get into. You have to receive a nomination from a congressman or senator. Need to have high

grades, SAT scores, active in sports and other activities, not in trouble with the law, basically all around person. Over 14,000 students apply each year, but only 1,200 are accepted. The application takes a long time to fill out due to all the different parts that are required. You also have to get a physical from a military doctor.

Current student, 7/2003-Submit Date, December 2005

The United States Naval Academy is a difficult University to get into,and includes a multi-step process, but it is not impossible. Each person who applies to the United States Naval Academy must meet four main criteria. They include: (1) a congressional nomination; (2) being medically qualified; (3) being physically qualified; and (4) being academically qualified

(1) The congressional nomination varies from each state, and even the different congressmen from each district. Some congressmen only ask that you send a letter requesting their nomination, while others send you an application to be filled out, complete with essays, letters of recommendation and an interview. The congressional nomination is a difficult step to becoming qualified to enter the Academy, however, there are ways around getting your congressman to nominate you. If for example, you are to get a Letter of Assurance (early acceptance letter), then as long as you are medically and physically qualified, the academy can find other sources to get you a nomination. Sources such as the congressman from districts in other states in which no one applied.

(2) Being medically qualified is mainly out of your hands. You get numerous physicals, and several things can disqualify you, but like I said, if something is going to inhibit your ability to be an effective leader in a high stress environment, than I am sorry, but you are out of luck. However, for those who want to press their luck, you do have the option of applying for one of the limited number of medical waivers to get in without meeting all of the medical standards.

(3) Being physically qualified is pretty obvious. There is a basic physical fitness test, including a kneeling basketball through, max pull-ups, sit-ups, pushups, a shuttle run, and a standing long jump. If you ask me, this doesn't really show your overall physical fitness level, but these are the standards that the academy has set.

(4) The most difficult part about getting in is most definitely being academically qualified. With a average SAT of about 1300, and a majority of all entering students being in the top 20 percent of their senior class, the bar is set high. However, there are, as with all universities, exceptions to the rules. There are a limited number of spots for student-athlete recruiting, as well as the admissions department's pushing for the most diverse student body possible, including students from all 50 states, and usually over 10 foreign countries. Don't let this all scare you away though, there are also numerous prep school programs set up for students who are sure they want to go to the academy, but didn't quite have the grades the first time around. The academy will even help pay for it! Did I mention that the Academy itself is free?

 ## Academics

Current student, 7/2003-Submit Date, March 2007

The academics are very tough, especially if you aren't an engineer or scientist. Most of your classes focus on either naval needs or hard sciences and engineering. It challenges you to be very intelligent on a broad variety of subjects, which is great. It is easy to get the classes you want and overall the professors are pretty good, although sometimes they can be too tough.

Alumnus/a, 6/1997-5/2001, January 2006

No matter what you major in you will graduate with a Bachelor's of Science. Many argue that everyone at USNA receives a degree in Naval Science, and the major is more like your concentration. Since you will receive a BS, be prepared to take lots of math, engineering and science regardless of your major (even the poets have to be able to do calculus). When you have an economics degree, but have taken classes in Weapons Systems Engineering, Naval Architecture,

Read all of Vault's College Surveys at www.vault.com/college—get complete surveys on 100s of colleges and universities, expert advice on applicaton essays and more.

VAULT CAREER LIBRARY 293

Electrical Engineering, three semesters of calculus and so on and so on, you can honestly say you have had a minor in math/science/engineering (at least you should be able to). Also of note, everyone has to declare a major by the end of the freshman year (can be changed, but it can be tough).

The classes most people have problems with are the hard math/sciences: freshman chemistry (highest failure rate), physics (sophomore year) and differential equations. These classes provide the most failures.

Workload: this is somewhat major dependent, although everyone is guaranteed to take 21 hours at least one semester. The engineering and science majors tend to take a lot of hours every semester, and with tons of labs it can add up quite quickly. The humanities and social science types tend to come in a little lower on average, say 17 to 18 hours a semester, and with fewer labs (leave that to the techy types).

When you add this to the leadership, ethics and other academy specific classes, you get a well balanced and unique education.

Alumnus/a, 6/1999-5/2003, September 2005

The Naval Academy's philosophy of education stresses attention to individual students by highly qualified faculty members who are strongly committed to teaching. Classes are small, with an average size of fewer than 18 students. Our 600-member faculty is an integrated group of officers and civilians in nearly equal numbers. Working together closely, these military and civilian faculty member form one of the strongest and most dedicated teaching faculties of any college or university in the United States.

Current student, 8/2003-Submit Date, April 2006

Workload is very high. All students must take at least 15 credits a semester and the required courses (even for English majors) include chemistry, calculus, physics, electrical engineering and others. Quality of classes are great, teachers very willing to meet for extra instruction. Each student has to meet with an academic advisor before registering for classes to ensure that he/she is on track and gets the classes he/she needs and wants. Requesting professors and classes is easy and you have a good chance at getting whom and what classes you want.

Current student, 7/2003-Submit Date, December 2005

The level of academics at the Academy can be paralleled with that of the Ivy Leagues. Most classes are smaller than 30 students, and all are taught by either military professors or civilian professors with Doctorates. There is no such thing as a professor's aid, and each and every teacher is available for help after classes on almost a daily basis. The workload is difficult, but there are always people available to help, and interested in helping you understand the material. There are three types of majors:

Group 1: Engineering majors. Group 2: Mathematics and Sciences majors. Group 3: Humanities majors (English, history, economics)

Alumnus/a, 6/1999-5/2003, November 2005

Very science and math oriented even though I majored in history. I took three calculus classes, one statistics, two electrical engineering, one systems engineering, two physics, two chemistry classes, navigation, professional and ethics classes pertaining to the Navy. The classes were small averaging about 24 people. Sometimes it was hard getting the teachers you wanted because of popularity of classes. The professors were always available if you needed help and looked favorably on you if you were having trouble and got help. There was a tremendous amount of work. All kinds of papers, projects, not to mention the activities that we had to participate in (e.g., training underclassmen). The summers are filled with professional programs that allow for experience in the fleet as well as opportunities to travel to many places (this is all considered part of the training/academic regimen at the Academy). I went to Japan once and Russia twice. You can do study abroad programs, fleet cruises on submarines and ships or fly, as well. Also, you can train the incoming freshmen over the summer.

Employment Prospects

Alumnus/a, 6/1997-5/2001, January 2006

Alumni network: a common saying amongst academy grads is that it can be a bad place to be, but it's a great place to be from! This is because the academy connection is one that spans worldwide and is a bond that few other schools ca match. As a military officer, soon to transition out, the alumni network h already proven its worth. If you want to work for a certain company or go to certain school, all that needs to be done is call or e-mail an alumnus/a and you' bound to get the inside scoop and a leg up in the process. If he/she can't he you, he/she knows someone who can. There are many USNA grads wi advanced degrees who go on to get great jobs with high salaries, but half tl time, it's the alumni network that landed them the position, not the advance degree they worked so hard to get. I can't say enough about the alumni! You find them in many, many fields. There's a high percentage in consulting, eng neering, IT, real estate, MBA programs, entrepreneurs, finance, HR and mai more.

Current student, 7/2003-Submit Date, December 2005

Well, this is an easy one. When you graduate the United States Naval Academ every graduate earns a Commission into the United States Navy or Marii Corps, depending on the service selection process. Every newly commissione officer is then committed to a minimum of five years of service as an officer either the Navy or Marine Corps. However, you can choose to stay in the mil tary for a career, in which case, several other opportunities arise. You will t given the opportunity to go back to school and get your master's, as well as ga great tools that can be used in your life after the military. If you decide that aft five years, you have had enough, you already have gained wonderful leadersh skills and a great education that will surely make it easy to land a good job o in the corporate world.

Alumnus/a, 6/1999-5/2003, November 2005

100 percent. Employed by the U.S. Navy or Marine Corps. With the milita you can choose to fly jets, drive submarines or ships, be a Navy Seal or expl sive ordinance disposal. The military allows to fly or go infantry. After the m itary, an Academy education looks very good on a résumé. They allow intern ships during the summer. The Navy provides help in finding jobs after retir ment. The alumni network could help but it isn't a foregone conclusion. Alum are involved in all facets of society from government to business. Regardles someone coming from the Academy will have the opportunities to do wh he/she wants.

Alumnus/a, 7/2000-5/2004, April 2005

Following graduation, every single graduate is guaranteed a job in the U.! Navy. There is a commitment of five years to be a surface warfare office marine, submarine officer or any restricted line officer. Pilots and naval fligl officers have a commitment of eight years after they get their wings, which a their qualification pin. It takes about two years to get wings. All of these jol are very prestigious in that you are serving your country. The Naval Academ is free to attend because you will repay them by your officer commitment aft graduation. Following your commitment, you can either opt to stay in the serv ice or get out. For those officers who get out, they have no trouble getting ar job of their choice, because of the leadership experience that they got while serv ing in the military. There is a network that will help officers who want to get ou of the Navy or Marine Corps to find civilian jobs that suit them in an area tha they would like to live in.

Quality of Life

Current student, 7/2003-Submit Date, March 2007

Quality of life is OK. The housing takes some time to get used to because ever midshipman lives in the same building called Bancroft Hall. They used to n have air conditioning but that has recently changed, which makes it much, mucl much better. You aren't allowed to have a television in your room, but that help you focus on academics and mingling with your classmates. Given the stri honor code guidelines and the expulsion that violators face, crime is not an issu at the academy.

Alumnus/a, 6/1999-5/2003, September 2005

It would be impossible to predict what four years at the Naval Academy wou be like for you personally, but we can describe our philosophy and the daily lif you can expect. Only when you experience the exhausting rigors of Pleb Summer, only when you face the responsibility of commanding other midshi en and only when you throw your hat into the air at graduation will you really now what the Naval Academy experience is all about. Your four years at nnapolis will be tightly structured. While there are many ways you can pursue our individual areas of interest, a four-year program is required of all midshipen.

udents from all over the world regardless of ethnicity or gender are treated qually at the Naval Academy. You will live and learn with a very diverse and lented group of people. The Naval Academy program is designed to challenge very student. Life within the Brigade of Midshipmen, or student body, will be ifferent from anything you have experienced. First, Naval and Marine Corps fficers must be persons of honor and integrity; therefore, while training to chieve your commission you must abide by the Naval Academy Honor oncept. Your regimented daily schedule will challenge you morally, mentally, nd physically. All midshipmen must participate in athletics. The Naval cademy also has many extracurricular activities that allow midshipmen to xpand their horizons outside the classroom and off the athletic field. lidshipmen are encouraged to take part in religious services should they hoose. Finally, midshipmen enjoy regular active-duty benefits and pay comensurate with their rank. All these components of Naval Academy life serve o build the whole person.

current student, 8/2003-Submit Date, April 2006

ood, lodging, initial uniforms, computer and even a stipend each month are upplied. There are many restrictions on when students are allowed to go out. hey get better as you proceed through. We all live by an honor code and that eeps crime down a ton, can leave $100 on your desk and not worried about getng it stolen. Campus is kept very clean and neat. Downtown Annapolis is rithin a two-minute walk from the entrance to campus. If you do not like havig to answer to someone (i.e., the military), then this place is not recommend-d. We live in dorms all four years of school and have to adhere to the rules set orth. We do have curfews, which can be annoying, but we get used to them.

current student, 7/2003-Submit Date, December 2005

he campus is beautiful, the facilities are wonderful, and Annapolis is a safe eighborhood and a great place to go on the weekends. But, this is a military chool. Anyone who is seriously considering this university needs to understand e commitment he/she is making. Quality of life here is what you make it, and elieve me, it is difficult to see light at the end of the tunnel when you are a eshman. But, quality of life here has a lot to do with privileges, which are ken away when you arrive as a freshman, and are slowly given back to you ver the next four years.

Alumnus/a, 6/1999-5/2003, November 2005

veryone had to live in the dorm all four years. The campus was big enough and rovided things to keep occupied. It was extremely safe. Plenty of places and iings to do for physical activity. Plenty of places to study. The life is very stricted but lessens with time. The first year the student is allowed one day out week (Saturday). The second year student gets two days as well as three weekids (leave friday, come back Sunday). Third year students get four days and x weekends. Fourth year students get every day and nine weekends per semesr. Expect to study a lot. You cannot go home every weekend.

Alumnus/a, 7/2000-5/2004, April 2005

t the Naval Academy, all expenses are paid, and you get a paycheck every onth. This makes the quality of life in your time off very good. You are never e typical broke college student. Every midshipman (student at the Naval cademy) lives in Bancroft Hall, which is a very large dorm. Each bedroom has eds, desks, closets, a shower, and a sink. There are floor toilets. The living is itegrated because all students live with their companies (organized groups of bout 120 with 30 from each class). The campus of the Naval Academy is beauful. There are beautiful buildings everywhere, as well as monuments and other istorical structures. It is so beautiful that it is included in part of the tour of hisric Annapolis, Maryland. The campus is situated right on the Severn River ear the Chesapeake Bay.

s far as physical fitness facilities are concerned, there is more than enough pace for every student to work out. There are at least four gyms with weights nd aerobic equipment. There is an indoor pool, track, plenty of turf fields for ecreation, a whole lot of grass fields for recreation, tennis courts, an indoor limbing wall and much more.

As far as dining goes, every student eats breakfast and lunch in King Hall which is inside Bancroft Hall. All 4,000 students sit down and get served at the same time. Dinner is served in King Hall buffet style, or you can eat in either of two small restaurants: Steerage, which is also in Bancroft Hall or Dahlgren, which is next door to Bancroft Hall. There is also the option to go out into downtown historic Annapolis for dinner, if you are either a junior or a senior. The party scene in Annapolis is very good. There are tons of bars and pubs to go to and the neighborhood is well kept and very safe.

 Social Life

Current student, 7/2003-Submit Date, March 2007

The dating scene sucks as women only make up 10 percent of academy. No Greek life, although football weekends get pretty fun. However, they now breath-alyze all students, even if you are not driving and if you blow higher than a .08, you face conduct action. Bars are nearby in downtown Annapolis, as well as many other colleges including Georgetown and Maryland and Towson. Plenty of ladies there to go chase after.

Current student, 8/2003-Submit Date, April 2006

Around 15 bars within a two- to 10-minute walk from school. Tons of restaurants there, as well. Close to D.C. and Baltimore with plenty of colleges to visit. We have over 30 clubs, but no Greek system. Great social life when we have the time. Girls like guys in uniforms. There are two movie theaters in town and several golf courses. If you enjoy boating, there are boating and sailing clubs you can join. Every year we have an International Ball where many single, foreign girls come here to meet and dance with the midshipmen (that's what we as students are called here).

Current student, 7/2003-Submit Date, December 2005

The social life at the United States Naval Academy consists mostly of groups, clubs, and sports teams as a freshman. It is not until you become a sophomore, junior and senior, that you begin to realize that there is a wonderful little town called Annapolis only about a five-minute walk outside of the gates of the campus. Annapolis has great nightlife, and is filled with bars and restaurants for all different tastes. It is a great place to go on a date, or just go out to celebrate a friend's 21st Birthday. As far as Greek life is concerned, it is nonexistent, with the exception of one or two academic fraternities, but can you really call those frats?

Current student, 6/2003-Submit Date, November 2005

The school is located in downtown Annapolis, Maryland just a walk away from at least 12 bars. 20 miles North is Baltimore and 25 miles west is Washington, D.C. Plenty of things to do plenty of girls to meet. No fraternities. There are 90 or so clubs, sports teams and other organizations that you are able to join. They go from chess club to varsity football. Anything you want they have and if they don't then you can start it.

Alumnus/a, 7/2000-5/2004, April 2005

There are limited social events at the Naval Academy simply because it is about 80 percent males. However, each year they bus in a few hundred foreign girls and have an International Ball. It is a very big deal. We have the normal social events like tailgaters before every football and lacrosse game. We have a Homecoming Dance and a Ring Dance, which is for the juniors who just got their class rings. The whole school is very school spirited so a lot of the social events at school are sporting events.

Outside of campus social events, downtown Annapolis has a great bar scene with about 20 bars of all sorts. There are restaurants of all price ranges and we are a 30-minute drive to the Baltimore Harbor or an hour from Washington, D.C. Most students at the Naval Academy have a boyfriend or girlfriend. About half of the students date outside of the student population while the others date within.

There is no Greek system at the Naval Academy, but we are said to be the biggest fraternity in the country. Each year there is a croquet match against St. John's College, which is also in Annapolis. All of the students tailgate and picnic on the lawn at St. John's and everyone gets dressed up. It is the highlight of a lot of the students' years. Favorite bars and restaurants for students at the Naval

Read all of Vault's College Surveys at **www.vault.com/college**–get complete surveys on 100s of colleges and universities, expert advice on applicaton essays and more.

VAULT CAREER LIBRARY 295

Academy are: Armadillo's, McGarvey's, Riordan's, Griffen's, OBrien's and Acme. There are a slew more, but those are the bars and restaurants that have the most events catered towards students.

University of Maryland

Office of Undergraduate Admissions
University of Maryland, Mitchell Building
College Park, MD 20742
Admissions phone: (301) 314-8385 or (800) 422-5867
Admissions e-mail: um-admit@deans.umd.edu
Admissions URL: www.uga.umd.edu/admissions/

 ## Admissions

Current student, 8/2002-Submit Date, November 2006

The admissions process is rather standard for this state school. Since I applied in 2002, things might have changed. From looking at my peers, it seems that Maryland residents have a very large advantage in gaining admission at the university. The school is slightly more selective in admitting out-of-state students.

Current student, 8/2003-Submit Date, February 2006

The admissions process was typical of most schools. Instead of the Common Application, Maryland has its own application process that consists of a pre-application with a few screening questions and then the second application that gets to the meat of the candidate. Essays can cross over from the Common Application but the option is also given to create your own question and answer it. SAT Subject Tests were not required. Standards for in-state students were much easier than for out-of-state students but the caliber of all here is extremely high.

Current student, 8/2004-Submit Date, September 2005

You should take a lot of honors classes in high school and AP classes, if possible. The more credits you come to school with, the easier your time will be in college. Grades and SAT scores are both important and being an athlete helps a lot too, especially if you are planning on playing at the school.

Alumnus/a, 5/2001-5/2004, September 2005

The admissions process was simple. I did not need to submit an SAT score because I transferred from another university within the Maryland system. I only needed to write an admissions essay and I received my letter of acceptance thereafter.

Current student, 9/2001-Submit Date, April 2005

A great deal of my personal time at Maryland has been spent dealing with admissions issues. As a campus tour guide, information session presenter and Visitor Center employee, I speak to prospective students and their families regularly. My advice would be to apply to Maryland before the priority deadline of December 1. This guarantees you will receive a response by mid-February; however, applying early is not binding. Maryland has a large student population and an even larger pool of prospective students. The essay is a great way to showcase your individual accomplishments and personality traits with the admissions counselors. Be as creative as possible! Maryland has become more and more selective but students who pass through the process provide the community with a committed, involved and intelligent campus.

Current student, 8/2003-Submit Date, December 2004

You can apply either online or request an application to be mailed to you. strongly recommend applying to UMD by December for the priority applicatio date, which is not binding if you're accepted. This is the best way to get int programs like Honors, Gemstone or College Park Scholars. Gemstone is th hardest, then Honors, then Scholars. UMD is getting a little more selective wit the rising popularity of basketball and football. It is a Top 50 school, and is eas ier for in-state students to get into. Interviews are not required, and essays ar optional but helpful. GPA, SAT and extracurricular activities are more impor tant, though. Make sure to take your application seriously, and double chec everything, from your information to your spelling and grammar. You ca declare a major when applying, or declare undecided, which is also known a Letters and Sciences.

Current student, 8/2001-Submit Date, October 2004

Admissions the University of Maryland, College Park have become tougher i the past decade. The school has been making efforts to increase its student base so as a consequence you can expect admissions standards to ease up a bit.

The easiest way to get in is to get your Associates Degree from a Maryland Stat Community College. If you get an Associates Degree from any Maryland Stat Community College, even with a 2.0 GPA, you are guaranteed admission.

Current student, 8/2003-Submit Date, April 2005

I came in as a transfer student and had no problems. But I have heard that it i hard to get in as an undergraduate. I would recommend having extracurricula activities to show for your high school years along with a good GPA. Las school year (2003), I think the average incoming freshman GPA was 3.87. came from an accredited journalism program so I was automatically accepte into the Maryland accredited journalism program, which was a big plus an saved me a lot of time.

 ## Academics

Current student, 8/2002-Submit Date, November 2006

I have completed programs in biology (physiology/neurobiology) and physic There is a world of difference between the two programs and this is reflecte campus-wide. Beyond obvious differences in the difficulty and complexity o the material, the physics department simply places more demands on the studen For example, physics homework sets can take 10 to 20 hours to complete Likewise, laboratory reports must be substantive and clearly written. This is i contrast to the typical biology course, which places relatively few demands o the students and the opportunity to distinguish oneself from his or her classmate comes only through examinations. The objective of the physics department is t engage the mind of the student. The biology department is largely just a pre medical preparatory program. Several biology faculty members have gone as fa as to say that the biology program is catered toward pre-med students, thus th tremendous emphasis on rote memorization.

In both departments, the grading for various courses is heavily dependent on th professors teaching them. Students who do equivalent work for different pro ssors in the same course may receive drastically different grades. Most hysics courses only have one section, one professor, per semester. This is con-asted to the typical biology classes that may have several sections and be ffered by various professors. The overabundance of students taking biology ourses means that they usually fill up rather quickly, regardless of the number f sections available.

Current student, 8/2003-Submit Date, February 2006

Vithin the business school, all of the professors are of the highest caliber. They vere previously leaders in the economy and migrated to academia. They offer ast prospectives and diverse backgrounds that allow students to get a better rasp of the material and see the real-world application rather than just the con-eptual ideas that are presented in the textbooks. All classes have required texts nd readings but going to lectures amply prepares most for the exams. The lasses you're supposed to take are easy to get into and the schedule is flexible o that morning or afternoon classes can be eliminated for employment and/or ocial obligations.

Current student, 8/2004-Submit Date, September 2005

he classes are really big, so you have to work hard to get anything out of them; o one is there forcing you to do work. All of the professors I have had have een, for the most part, at least excited, passionate teachers.

Current student, 1/2005-Submit Date, May 2005

rom my experience, most 100- and 200-level general lecture classes (psychol-gy, maths) were very big (100+ students). TAs are hit or miss whether or not ley are helpful. It is important to be able to handle your own schedule as far as tudying and assignment/test dates. Some classes inherently conflict in the cheduling (foreign language and math, for me), so be ready for that.

Current student, 8/2001-5/2005, October 2004

he academic program at the University of Maryland, College Park is above verage for a state school. Many freshman classes, specifically in engineering, hemistry, and biology are designed to weed out students.

he undergraduate business program at the R.H. Smith School of Business is asy. At the upper-levels, most professors give out only A's or B's. Also, the vorkload in the business school is significantly less than the A. James Clark chool of Engineering. Compared to the engineering school, students in the usiness school get better grades and do less work. In addition, the business chool is much less competitive and cutthroat than the engineering school.

ietting popular classes is nearly impossible until you are a senior unless you are n athlete. Students with higher credit levels get priority in picking classes. .lso, athletes get the greatest priority in picking classes. Furthermore, at orien-ation the advisors have no idea what they are talking about and will sign up stu-ents into any class that has room, be weary.

Alumnus/a, 8/2000-5/2004, May 2005

ince Maryland has a lot of students, it is almost definite that at some point dur-ig your time you will be put on a waitlist or hold file. Unless you are up to umber 15 in a small 30-person class, usually you have a good shot at getting nto the class. Many people switch their schedules or drop the class, even arough to the first few weeks of classes. Hold file is a bit different because it neans you are registering for a class that is not within your major. You will only e granted admittance once the waitlist has depleted. Since registration is deter-nined by the number of credits you have, upperclassmen register first.

Aaryland is unique in its method of grading. They use plus and minuses, but do .ot calculate it into your final GPA. Therefore a B, B- and a B+ are all a 3.0. Aany students believes this hurts them, but it actually can help. For a student ike myself, I fought hard for the A- and reaped the benefits of an A. I am not .ositive when and if they will change this policy, but I can assure you for as nany times as you get a +, you will get a -. It all works out in the end.

he school is lucky because of the close proximity to Washington, D.C. My Aacroeconomics teacher was a part of President Clinton's cabinet. All in all, I vas very fond of and impressed by my professors throughout my time at school. /ery rarely would students be taught by a teaching assistant (TA), but they were .lways on hand to help the professors. The instructors genuinely seemed to care nd were very eager to help those students who asked.

As with every school, the workload is quite different from high school. However, the only time I ever felt overwhelmed was during midterms or finals. Unfortunately, the school coordinates finals as best as they can, but many times you might have two or more finals in a given day. Policy states that if you have three in one day you may reschedule one of those finals. Also, as you get more into your major, the professors sometimes work the schedules out themselves. Throughout the rest of the semester I would say that a few hours each night was enough to cover all of my classes' workload.

Current student, 8/2003-Submit Date, April 2005

This university is demanding. I was surprised by the number of papers we were required to write. Even introductory classes have papers, which are a great learning tool and make for a better learning experience than just taking three tests. The discussions each week can get monotonous but I think you would find that anywhere. You really can get to know your TA. If not in class, there is a good chance you could run into him/her on campus. Getting classes was never a problem for me and if you do your work and try, grades aren't a problem. I recommend getting to know your instructors and let them know you are a con-scientious student. The workload is semi-heavy but you are getting a stellar edu-cation so it is worth it.

 Employment Prospects

Current student, 8/2002-Submit Date, November 2006

The school is relatively devoid of prestige with employers. Most of the more prestigious investment banking firms do not even interview with UMD students. The alumni network, though relatively unimpressive, is helpful for many. The large amount of scientific research done in the proximity of UMD make it a friendly place for students seeking science-related jobs. Most alumni find plen-tiful job opportunities, though they are relatively localized to Montgomery County and D.C.

Current student, 8/2003-Submit Date, February 2006

The employment prospects in the business school are outstanding. Top-tier firms such as PwC, Ernst & Young, UBS and UPS are on campus daily at the Employer of the Day table. The Career Center posts job and internship oppor-tunities and has a convenient web-based system to apply and drop résumés. Courses are offered to tweak résumés and prepare students for business dinners. There is even a business golf course that teaches students the fundamentals of making a deal on the links. If you do well in school and aren't an idiot the career staff will find you a job.

Alumnus/a, 5/2001-5/2004, September 2005

There is an active Career Center on campus, which, even upon graduating, con-tinues to work with you to fit you into your ideal working environment. UMaryland grads receive a wide range of opportunities and the alumni network is very vocal in terms of recruitment and retainment. Every student is encour-aged to find a meaningful internship at some point in the academic career, but at UMaryland, they actually help you to land the perfect one.

Alumnus/a, 8/2000-5/2004, May 2005

The university has a fabulous Career Center that will help all students find internships, co-ops or full-time jobs. Additionally, it has an amazing career web site where you can search and apply for positions. These positions are posted by the Career Center and many host on-campus interviews. There are larger career fairs throughout the year, but many students choose to go to their particular school's fair (e.g., business, engineering).

Personally, I took a semester off of school in order to complete a co-op for Johnson & Johnson (which I found at our career fair). A co-op is a full-time position for five to seven months in order to get better experience before exiting school. To help me graduate on time, the university offers credits to those who complete a certain amount of working hours in a semester. I was able to get six credits for that co-op.

All of my friends were able to obtain jobs straight out of college with the help of the school. The only people that were met with challenges were those indi-viduals who wanted to work out of the Maryland/D.C./Virginia area. It just takes

Read all of Vault's College Surveys at **www.vault.com/college**—get complete surveys on 100s of colleges and univer-sities, expert advice on applicaton essays and more.

VAULT CAREER LIBRARY 297

a little more effort. I got a job in New York City and am proof that it is possible.

Current student, 8/2003-Submit Date, December 2004

Recruiting at UMD is excellent especially for business, engineering and computer science majors. Large companies come to the school, but a lot of small companies come as well. Internship prospects are also great, with career counselors and advisors always available for appointments to help you. Recruiters often come to campus to do first-round interviews for both full-time and part-time jobs and internships. Often, there is a second round on campus too, or at the company site along with final rounds if needed. Internships often help you gain full-time employment there post-graduation. And if not, internships are probably the most important thing you can put on you résumé. The Career Center has a formal alumni network, so you can look up people who have careers to which you aspire. You can then use their contact information to set up an informational interview or quickly ask them a question.

Alumnus/a, 9/1999-5/2003, October 2003

Current students are lucky. Many former students, who are now in the corporate world, are sending their HR reps to the school. Some firms that recruit finance undergrads from campus for internships and full-time positions include Lehman Brothers, Legg Mason, JP Morgan, T. Rowe Price, Marriott, GE, IBM, Morgan Stanley and Freddie Mac. In addition, the office of career management is awesome; the advisors there are extremely helpful. Maryland's resources just keep getting better. Recently, the school opened up a financial markets lab. This lab is state-of-the-art and allows students to use the same real market data and software that I-bankers and traders use on Wall Street (info from Reuters and Bloomberg).

Quality of Life

Current student, 8/2002-Submit Date, November 2006

Housing is atrocious at the University of Maryland. College Park is not your archetypal college town. In fact, there is a lot of hostility toward college students by residents of the neighborhoods surrounding the campus. This hostility is probably understandable given the frequent rioting and other boisterous behaviors undertaken by UMD students on a regular basis. The campus and its facilities are lovely, and new buildings are continually being added. Crime and safety is a concern on and around campus. Fortunately, nearby towns of Hyattsville and Greenbelt allow the students to procure affordable housing and avoid some of the crime that plagues College Park. Whether this is a favorable option for many is debatable, as it has the effect of taking one out of the college scene. Maryland is definitely a campus where it pays to have a car.

Current student, 8/2003-Submit Date, February 2006

Life in College Park is good. Social opportunities are everywhere. Bar life is great and the beer is cheap. The dorms are typical college dorms but the upperclassman housing is incredible. The gym is state-of-the-art and only overcrowded during the first week of the semester when students still have ambition. The dining halls offer the best personal pan pizzas I ever had. If they delivered, I would never graduate. As with any major city, there is crime but by walking in a group you'll be OK. For three years now I haven't locked my door and nothing has come of it. College Park is a great place to be.

Current student, 8/2004-Submit Date, September 2005

On-campus housing is similar to that of any other college, small dorms with community bathrooms and lounges for freshmen and sophomores, and then small apartments or quads for upperclassmen. There are numerous off-campus places to live, such as houses and apartments. There are several on-campus dining areas, such as diners, a cafeteria-like area with fast-food restaurants, and several small cafes. The Diner on North Campus, South Campus Diner and several of the small cafes on campus accept meal points, which are included in housing fees. This makes life a lot easier since you don't have to carry cash every day to get a bite to eat. Also, there are two convenience stores on campus, which accept Terrapin Express or Terp Bucks. (Terp Bucks are included in Resident Meal plans, and Terrapin Express is like a debit card, where you can add money either online or at the Terrapin Express Office.)

The crime rate here is very high, and although campus administrators are trying to make it safer, there is no way to escape the crime in College Park. Some safety features are the blue lights that are all over campus. If you press a button on these lights, an alarm goes off and police are notified of the location. There is a UMCP police force, that patrols the campus and right around it, along with the Prince George's County Police who are always present and make life feel safer. After a certain time at night, all entrances to campus are guarded, and anyone entering must show a university ID, or else a regular ID and their license plate number, car type and name is taken. This makes it a little harder for just anyone to get on campus

Current student, 8/2003-Submit Date, April 2005

Housing is not a highlight for the University of Maryland. First of all, if you are a transfer, on-campus housing is almost nonexistent. You are the last priority and get bad placements. Dining is normal—just like any other dining. College Park has great neighborhoods but I wouldn't walk by myself at night, especially to the Metro; drive there. We have had a lot of crime on campus this semester but we are in a major metropolitan area. I feel safe walking around campus after dark, just not around the city.

The workout facilities are great! We have a huge rec center and then smaller gyms on the other side of campus that are really nice. It usually only gets busy right before spring break and the beginning of each semester. We also have an outdoor pool with sand volleyball courts where lots of people hang out. I think it holds like 400 people and sometimes there are lines to enter. That is really great. The union is great. It has a movie theater, bowling alley, arts center, food co-op with healthy options, food court and convenience store. The Jewish center is a nice option for people who need Kosher food. There are a lot of churches around campus, as well as the chapel that has weekly services.

Social Life

Current student, 8/2002-Submit Date, November 2006

Bars are limited: only two or three in town for a population of 30,000 undergrads. Restaurants are national franchises and a few unimpressive local ones. As with many Northeast schools, the dating scene consists of either inebriated hook-ups at one of the three local bars or simply meeting through mutual friends. Events on campus are usually centered on sporting activities.

Current student, 8/2004-Submit Date, September 2005

There are vast numbers of clubs and groups to join here, and Greek life is extremely prevalent. Often Greek groups are in charge of many activities that go on on and around campus. There are several bars that are popular: Cornerstone, Bentley's, Santa Fe and Lupos, which are all within the same block of each other and about three minutes from campus. There are groups for anything you can imagine: religious groups, athletic groups, recreational groups (skydiving, ski/snowboarding), and all engage in exciting activities. There are club and intramural sports teams for which anyone can sign up, and are a lot of fun. I am on a intramural soccer team, which is co-ed with a bunch of friends. We play once a week for four weeks and then a tournament starts.

Alumnus/a, 8/2000-5/2004, May 2005

D.C. is only about eight miles away, which usually takes 20 minutes by car. You may also take the Metro (campus buses take you to the station two miles away) into the heart of D.C., Reagan Airport and Arlington, VA. Many weekends we would take cabs into D.C. to go out for the night and it is important to play "let's make a deal" with the cab drivers. Usually, you can spend less than $8 a person to get into the city. Baltimore is 30 minutes away, but it is a quick and easy drive up 95. Many times throughout the year there are special events where buses are rented to bring us to Baltimore for the night. This is ideal for an individual who wants both a city life and a campus.

Please note: College Park police are very strict on the use of fake IDs. There is a more than likely chance that your ID will be taken away and you can be slapped with a $500 fine.

Greek life was my favorite part about Maryland. There are 14 sororities and numerous fraternities. We have 14 houses on Fraternity Row (three sororities and 11 frats). Fraternity Row is beyond fun, especially in the warmer weather.

t all times you are met with different sporting activities on The Row. Formal sh is in the spring, which allows you time to get to know the different chap- rs. Although this is usually a distressing time for the rushees it is quite inter- ting how people just wind up in the right chapter for them!

reek life offers the best leadership opportunities around. I was president of my rority, which was both a challenging and eye-opening experience. This better epared me for the business world. Once a semester, fraternities pair up with rorities, pick themes and we battle (Greek Week in spring and Homecoming in e fall) in various activities including sports, talent shows, relays and decora- ns. This is usually the most eventful week of the semester because of the con-

stant flow of activities and the promise to meet many new people. Greek life provides great opportunities to participate in philanthropies, alumni events, as well as parties.

I don't think I need to mention our amazing basketball team and brand-new arena to replace Cole Field House. The Comcast Stadium is two years old and topnotch. During the fall the campus is filled with tailgaters before our football games. With a new alumni center, it promises to be even larger in the upcoming years. Important note: students get free tickets to basketball and football games. More on-campus activities consist of Maryland Day, movie nights, beach vol- leyball tournaments, ice cream socials and almost anything you can think of.

Read all of Vault's College Surveys at **www.vault.com/college**–get complete surveys on 100s of colleges and univer- sities, expert advice on applicaton essays and more.

VAULT CAREER LIBRARY **299**

Amherst College

Office of Admission
Box 5000, Amherst College
Amherst, MA 01002-5000
Admissions phone: (413) 542-2328
Admissions e-mail: admission@amherst.edu
Admissions URL: www.amherst.edu/admission/

 Admissions

Current student, 9/2001-Submit Date, February 2006

Very competitive admissions, but the college actively recruits under-represented minorities and other hardship candidates. For a small college, some parts of the admissions process were none too personal, but still more human than big schools. No interviews. Essays are extremely important, and excerpts are shared with permission with the other students at freshman orientation. Very selective elite college. Try to find a "hook" to make your application stand out. This college cares deeply about every student, and this starts from the very beginning of the admissions process. Considering the overwhelming number of applications for admission, the administration functions efficiently and fairly at all times.

Current student, 9/2005-Submit Date, October 2005

The admissions process is the same as any other college. Amherst is very selective and you should have an interesting essay. My advice on getting in is to have good SAT scores and good grades in high school. Amherst doesn't give interviews, but if a member of the admissions office comes to your area, you should get in contact with him/her.

Current student, 8/2003-Submit Date, December 2004

Amherst College uses the Common Application, which is pretty easy. They also have a supplemental essay, which is creative, but not too bad. I do think they could update their admissions process a little—nothing was computerized, and there was more (physical) paperwork than other schools. Also, they were a little late in contacting me about getting in. Other than that though, it was a relatively easy, and painless process.

> The school says: "You can now apply online to Amherst."

Current student, 8/2000-Submit Date, February 2004

Amherst uses the Common Application and a supplemental essay, with about three topics from which to choose . There is no interview. Amherst is very selective. I think the current overall acceptance rate is about 16 to 17 percent. Amherst says it looks for well-rounded, intelligent people who will add to the quality of life and diversity of the campus. Honestly, recruited athletes are given preferential treatment in admissions and so are legacies and underrepresented minorities. Amherst is also really generous with financial aid.

Current student, 8/2001-Submit Date, January 2004

In terms of selectivity, Amherst is in an elite group of schools, with an admissions rate similar to the "lower Ivy" schools. SAT scores above 1400 (and often 1500), top quality high school activities, and a high class rank are the norm for applicants, and are usually a necessary but not sufficient condition for admission.

Amherst, like most top schools, accepts the Common Application. However, there is also a required supplement with an additional essay. Generally, the student is provided with three essay prompts and must choose one. Of the three, there are generally two more mundane questions about leadership or a current issue, and then a third question that is intentionally ambiguous. When I applied, I used the third question, which I believe gave me more of a chance to show some creativity. Generally Amherst sends two groups of Regular Decision acceptance letters—usually a small group of letters sent to a small fraction of the class in mid-March, and then the rest of the batch in early to mid-April.

Amherst, unlike most schools, has neither alumni interviews nor on-campu interviews.

Alumnus/a, 8/1997-5/2001, November 2003

The Amherst admissions process is a bit of a black box, like those at other higy ly selective schools (the college admits to admitting 18 percent of applicants 2003). There are certain GPA and SAT score benchmarks (86 percent of accep ed students were in the top 10 percent of their high school classes and scored average of 1422 on the SAT), but at Amherst, admissions criteria go well beyor the numbers. Amherst is a small college of 1,650 students who are in direct cor tact with their professors each day. As such, the unique aspects of each stude are prized, and Amherst takes extra care to consider extracurricular activitie interesting life experiences, well-written essays, and any other ways in whic applicants may stand apart.

Application essays tend to be more on the philosophical side (responses to qu tations from Sartre or narratives of your life philosophy), and their impact shou not be underestimated. Amherst maintains active recruiting programs for exce tional athletes, underrepresented minorities, economically disadvantaged st dents, gifted artists and children of alumni. If you fit into any of these cat gories, contact the admissions office early and it is very likely to help yo chances. Interviews are not offered, so your ability to come across as bright an interesting through your application and the materials you provide to support is key.

 Academics

Current student, 9/2001-Submit Date, February 2006

The curriculum is open, with no core curriculum. This goes with the who approach of Amherst to entrust each and every student with considerable pe sonal responsibility for themselves and others, ready or not. Maturity is incu cated, like it or not. The academics are demanding, but not unbearable. The pro fessors are almost without exception outstanding teachers. The classes are high quality, and are generally exciting (at least in part because the student act ally selected to be there during registration). Classes are very small, so there some anxiety about getting into the most popular ones with the most awe-inspi ing teachers. Yet rarely is any student actually denied admission. Grading rather tough, the workload is as demanding as would be expected at such an ed cational institution, and students are expected fully to fulfill their responsibiliti in their coursework in a timely manner. There is an honor code, which increasingly being enforced. But all-in-all, students are well-rounded, with tim and energy for extracurriculars, including sports.

Current student, 9/2005-Submit Date, October 2005

The academics are challenging, and you will be working a lot if you are admi ted. You take four classes per semester. One of my teachers admits that he on gives B's. It's pretty easy to get into the classes you want though. I would sug gest a balance of science/math courses and humanities courses. By doing thi you won't overload in reading or labs, and you will have a good balanc Amherst has a great first-year seminar program, in which all incoming freshme participate. I recommend War or Secrets and Lies. Every week, there are speak ers who come and speak about current issues, too.

Current student, 8/2003-Submit Date, December 2004

Amherst College provides an excellent academic atmosphere, with small class es, caring professors and a wonderful open curriculum (which means there ar no core requirements). Professors are generally always available and pretty eas to contact. Also there's this awesome program called TYPO—Take You Professor Out. The school pays for you and a group of friends to take one c your professors (per semester) out to dinner at a restaurant in town. It's a won derful opportunity to get to know professors on a more personal level. I'v found that the professors here genuinely want to get to know their students an care about their education.

Current student, 8/2000-Submit Date, February 2004

Amherst is widely regarded as the best liberal arts college in America, usually along with Williams and Swarthmore. The professors here are excellent, and there are no TAs or graduate students teaching. All of my professors know my first name, and it's great to be able to stop by their offices and chat. With few exceptions, professors go far out of their way to be available to students.

That said, Amherst is small—around 400 students per graduating class—and so the diversity of the curriculum is not what you'd get at a much larger institution. However, that's never really been a problem; classes are interesting, and with no distribution requirements and few prerequisites, you can find what classes interest you and take them. Major requirements are pretty lax, too: usually around eight to 10 classes required for a major.

Current student, 8/2001-Submit Date, January 2004

Amherst provides a topnotch academic experience, with departments that are first-rate. Particularly popular are the English, history, political science and economics majors, each of which boasts several excellent professors with first-class credentials.

Amherst, like most top schools, has a moderate level of grade inflation, but still provides a rigorous workload. Students are driven but not overly competitive.

Alumnus/a, 8/1997-5/2001, November 2003

Once you are at Amherst, the academic environment is surprisingly low pressure. Amherst students are not a terribly competitive lot, and the work is usually manageable enough that maintaining a decent GPA (B+) does not require holing up in the library for the entire semester.

Those who attended larger high schools, especially, will be surprised at the personal nature of the education. You will be part of a class of around 450 students, and your individual courses will rarely exceed enrollments of 20 to 30, and will often be as small as five to eight. With all but the most popular classes, you'll have no trouble getting into the sections you want. For particularly tough-to-get courses, you'd be advised to take them early; in a backwards-logic system, Amherst usually gives enrollment preference to underclassmen.

You will likely have a close relationship with your academic advisor, with whom you will meet at least twice a year to plan your courses for each semester (advisors are assigned according to the likely majors you list on your application, so you may end up with the same advisor for all four years). Outside of the formal advising system, you will find that nearly all of your professors will try to get to know you personally and will be eager to provide advice on courses, social life or anything else you wish to discuss (visits to professors offices are encouraged, and a visit to the home of a particularly engaging professor is not unusual).

No matter what major you choose, you are sure to be impressed by the quality of the teaching. Amherst enrolls only undergraduates and employs only professors, so even introductory courses are taught by full professors, not grad students or teaching assistants. Your grades are given individually, and professors are generally accommodating of reasonable requests for extensions on large assignments. The well-equipped libraries and language lab, as well as the computer center and ethernet connection in every dorm room, ensure that you will have all necessary academic resources at your disposal.

Employment Prospects

Current student, 9/2001-Submit Date, February 2006

Excellent employment and postgraduate prospects, especially on the East Coast. The West Coast still has little recognition of such a small, though outstanding, private college. But even those employers who do not immediately recognize Amherst's incredible academic reputation, upon just a little inquiry, come to realize what a valuable graduate has been produced. Amherst is very prestigious, and its reputation can be easily exploited with prospective employers and grad schools.

Current student, 9/2005-Submit Date, October 2005

Amherst has a great career center; they have weekly programs from study abroad programs to internships, to law school panels. Part of the reason I chose

Amherst is because I want to go to law school and Amherst has an excellent rate of getting their graduates into law schools. The alumni network is extensive, during the winter break, certain alumni host students in their homes and allow them to extern with them. During the school year, you can also participate in activities with the alumni, like having dinner with them or going apple picking.

Current student, 8/2000-Submit Date, February 2004

Amherst is pretty well-respected, and many top employers recruit on campus, like Bain and McKinsey in consulting, and Morgan Stanley, JP Morgan and UBS in finance/banking. The job market has slim pickings for the past couple of years with the poor economy, but things are looking up this year. I'm a senior and was hired for a management consulting position starting next year. The career center can be useful, but only if you make the effort to use it—they're not going to set you up with a job unless you make the effort.

The alumni network needs some work, but if you can get in touch with an alumnus/a, he/she will most likely go out of his/her way to help you and give you contacts. Lots of Amherst graduates go to law and medical schools each year, and are accepted at all the best graduate schools. Also there are usually a couple of Fulbright scholars, Goldwater scholars, and occasionally a Rhodes scholar. For its size, Amherst is definitely over-represented at top schools and in scholarship winners.

Current student, 8/2001-Submit Date, January 2004

In terms of employer prestige, Amherst is roughly on the same level as any Ivy. On-campus recruiting is excellent. As far as I-banks and consulting firms go, nearly every top company recruits on campus, including Bain Consulting, Goldman Sachs and JP Morgan. There are very few top firms that do not. Blackstone Group and McKinsey are two notable exceptions, but they also do not recruit at many other Ivies and top universities. The size of Amherst is a huge advantage here, as there is less competition, and alumni are far more eager to help students than those at larger schools (probably because there are many fewer people hitting them up for favors).

For professional schools, Amherst is at an excellent level. I have seen the LSDAS reports of Amherst student success in admissions to med and law school, and the results are fantastic, adjusted for Amherst's size, Amherst is better represented at the Top Six (HYSCCN) law schools than any other top university besides HYP. The last calculated average LSAT score for Amherst is a 162, which is on the same level as the Ivies besides HYP (whose averages are a point or two higher). Medical school admissions are another strength—see www.amherst.edu/~sageorge/guide1.html for more info on this.

As far as PhD programs, Amherst students also do well. As most grad students can tell you, professor recommendations are incredibly important, and Amherst's size and teaching-focused faculty makes it much easier to get to know professors. I have often found it quite surprising how eager professors here are to meet with students, and how flexible professors are regarding office hours.

Alumnus/a, 8/1997-5/2001, November 2003

In general, Amherst enjoys a great nationwide reputation, and many of the top consulting and financial firms send representatives to the campus in the fall to interview juniors and seniors for summer or full-time positions. For those not seeking a junior professional career, the career center is well staffed and you can schedule appointments to plot a strategy for finding jobs in whatever field you are interested. Outside of finance and consulting, many students regularly enter teaching, research, nonprofit and government jobs, with 80 percent of Amherst grads continuing their study in graduate or professional schools at some point in their lives.

The Amherst alumni network is strong; with a 65 percent giving rate, Amherst has the largest proportion of alumni who donate money of any school in the country. The career center maintains a database of alumni in every career field, and any who you contact will usually be happy to offer advice, and perhaps even an interview or internship.

Read all of Vault's College Surveys at **www.vault.com/college**–get complete surveys on 100s of colleges and universities, expert advice on applicaton essays and more.

VAULT CAREER LIBRARY   **301**

Quality of Life

Current student, 9/2001-Submit Date, February 2006

For a small college, there are many opportunities for living the good life. The exclusive on-campus housing is quite adequate, and is being aggressively improved. Upperclassmen enjoy frat-type, sumptuous housing, with many single rooms. For studying, the library is large and accommodating. Wireless Internet has arrived for all dorms. Campus dining is just adequate and unimaginative, even boring. For a small town, Amherst does provide adequate commercial and retail services for the average student, including diverse dining. True (violent) crime is rare, but there are the usual property offenses (vandalism and theft) for even a small, wealthy college.

Current student, 9/2005-Submit Date, October 2005

The food in the dining hall isn't that great. I eat out frequently. The campus is pretty safe. The freshman dorms are all nice except for Plaza and Waldorf, they are trailers. James and Sterns are the nicest because they were built two years ago. They are really open and have huge common areas. The library is really big and the staff is very helpful. The library has many computers available for use. It is usually open until 1 a.m.. You can check out books and movies not only from the Amherst library, but also from other nearby colleges.

Current student, 8/2003-Submit Date, December 2004

Amherst is a great, safe place with that small, New England town feel. There's plenty of nature, with a lot of breathtaking scenery, but it isn't in the middle of nowhere, since the University of Massachusetts (a huge school) is two minutes away. Besides UMass, there are three other colleges in the area. Housing is excellent—it's guaranteed for all four years, and the dorms are very nice (I know this because I've visited a lot of friends at other schools). The campus is beautiful and well-kept and the food isn't even all that bad (it could be better, but hey, it's college). The thing I like most about Amherst College, above all, is the sense of community. It's small, so you get to know and become connected to a lot of people. And most people, I've found, are really well-rounded, nice, and chill. Everyone is very self-driven, but no one is super-competitive.

Current student, 8/2000-Submit Date, February 2004

I'd say that most people at Amherst are pretty happy. The food isn't bad (people complain, but people complain wherever they go). The housing leaves a little to be desired, but the school is currently remodeling and building lots of new dorms which should be great. There are also lots of old, beautiful frat houses from the late 19th-early 20th centuries that have become student housing.

The town of Amherst is cute and quaint, but not a big city by any stretch of the imagination. UMass Amherst is right down the street, so there are tons of good restaurants around, some cute boutiques and plenty of bookshops. Also, Northampton (where Smith College is) is the next town over, and it's a great spot with better nightlife, great restaurants and good shopping. Amherst has a pretty safe campus. It's not difficult to know almost everyone on campus, which can be a positive or a negative—on the one hand, there's a distinct community atmosphere, since you live, eat, and go to class with the same group of 1,600 people, but on the flipside, there's no anonymity. Everyone knows your business.

Social Life

Current student, 9/2001-Submit Date, February 2006

The social life is not thrilling, given the relative size and isolation of the campus and community (small-town America). But there are a few other small and large colleges nearby that permit socializing opportunities. Dating is more casual than not, more hook-ups than commitments. Alcohol consumption is central to most social occasions, on and off campus, and can be characterized as rampant. The school administration permits experimentation, in concert with its commitment to encouraging the maturization process among its students, but concomitantly expects responsible behavior and will make offenders responsible for their screw-ups. Students find the social life adequate, if not equal to that of a party school.

Current student, 8/2003-Submit Date, December 2004

The social life is pretty good, there's always something to do, whether it's school-sponsored or club-sponsored event (of which there are lots) or just someone's party in a dorm. Amherst is by no means a party school, but there are some pretty good parties here. Fridays are usually pretty dead because a lot of people have sports games on Saturday mornings, so Thursday and Saturday are the big party nights. There are no frats or sororities here (besides the few off-campus underground ones). As for restaurants, everyone loves Antonio's pizza because it's fast, cheap, and delicious. There are plenty of other great restaurants here; everything from crepes to Indian to Thai, there's something for everyone in any price range.

Current student, 8/2001-Submit Date January 2004

Social life is generally centered around parties on campus. Although TAP (a weekly party sponsored by the social council) has been curtailed to the point that there is generally only a TAP party every few weeks or so, the social council sponsors a lot of events, some of which are well-attended. There is a bar scene, but most bars in town are very strict about IDs, so it is generally restricted to seniors. As part of the Five College Consortium, there is free bus service to the other four colleges (which are anywhere from five to 40 minutes away by bus). Students often go to parties at other schools, especially Smith and Mt. Holyoke. There is an underground Greek system that tends to host fairly prominent parties every month or two, but in general it has very little influence on social life. I would say no more than 4 to 5 percent of guys on campus are involved with the frats, which are officially banned by the college, by the way.

Current student, 8/2000-Submit Date, February 2004

For such a small, selective college, Amherst has a reasonable party scene. There are four underground frats (not recognized by the college) that occasionally sponsor parties. I'd say that most of the on campus party scene is organized around the sports teams. Playing a sport at Amherst is almost like being in a frat or sorority. Your social life becomes organized around the team if you play, which a lot of people do.

I'm not crazy about the bar scene in town, because they're mostly dive-ish college bars, but if that's your thing, they're there for you. The college sponsors bar nights for the senior class and underage bar nights (no alcohol) for the underclassmen. Those are usually fun, because you see lots of your class out in a non-Amherst context. I'd say the most popular bars are probably Barsie's (Barsellottis), the Monkey Bar and McMurphy's.

There isn't a lot of traditional dating at Amherst. It seems that people either are in a committed relationship or hook up on the weekends, without a lot of gray area between the two.

There are tons of active clubs and organizations on campus, and it seems like everyone is involved in at least one. They range from affinity groups to dance groups to community service to political affiliation groups to improvisation. There's definitely something for everyone.

Babson College

31 Forest Street
Babson Park, MA 02457-0310
Admissions phone: (781) 239-5522 or (800) 488-3696
Admissions fax: (781) 239-4006
Admissions URL: www.babson.edu/ug

 Admissions

Alumnus/a, Finance, 9/2003-5/2007, May 2007

The first step of the admissions process is visiting the school and learning about what it has to offer through one-on-one interviews or personal tours. I chose to do both and upon my first visit to the college, I knew that it was the right choice for me. After walking around campus and viewing the classrooms, campus centers and dorm rooms, I was brought back to the admissions office to sit down with a senior undergrad and discuss what I was looking for in a college and how Babson might be the right fit. This interview also gave the school an idea of what type of student/community member I would be.

After deciding that Babson was the school I wanted to attend, I applied Early Action and heard back in early February with an acceptance. The application was fairly basic, and asked you to write an essay as well as describe your accomplishments up to that point in your life.

Alumnus/a, Finance, 9/2003-5/2007, May 2007

Babson is becoming a very hard school in which to be accepted. With an incoming class of roughly 440 students, the admissions office is looking at each student's individual application in great detail. Most important is the high school transcript for a student. Incoming students typically are expected to take honors/AP courses. While the transcript is most important, Babson also places a strong emphasis on a student's college essay. The college essay is looked at closely by the admissions office. Write about something that nobody else will write about. Keep in mind there are over 3,500 applications each year and only 2,000 are accepted! It's very hard to get in, so you need to think about what makes you different. The admissions office is looking for students who have held leadership positions at their high schools. They can see through the students who inflate their résumés if they have no leadership positions in their organizations. Quality over quantity is key. At Babson interviews are optional for prospective students but highly recommended. They are mainly an opportunity for a prospective student to learn more about Babson from a student intern in the admissions office or an admissions counselor.

Current student, 8/2004-Submit Date, November 2005

The staff at Babson was very friendly. They not only invited us to the school but also set us up with current students to live with them for a day and even attend their classes. We were shown around campus to look at the different facilities and were brought to events where we learned about why we should apply. The essay was enjoyable to write. We were writing to our roommates if we were to be accepted to the school. Babson is pretty selective in terms of grades and student activity. They are very welcoming to international students and they promote a very competitive and diversified community.

Current student, 9/2003-Submit Date, December 2005

The admissions process is typical to most schools including the Common Application, a specific essay (choose one of two) and a supplementary essay. The specific essay was to write about a person or time in your life in which you were greatly inspired to create change and the supplemental was to write about why you wanted to attend and why you were a good candidate for Babson's undergraduate program. The essays were each around 500 words. There is an optional interview, which is highly recommended. Babson, is ranked as the Number One entrepreneurial school in the country and takes a wide array of students mostly concentrated from the Northeast and Florida. It also has a huge international presence. A lot of wealthy internationals send their children to Babson to learn how to take over the family business while others go to start

their own from solar-powered trash cans to nonprofits, to big city flower boutiques. They really want smart, savvy, clever and creative students who are going to drive change, so the interview is recommended. Typically students go to the interview and flaunt a business they started in high school: Internet start-ups, delivery services, catering companies, and even artists who started an after school kiosk to sell pottery in a mall. They also have students who are straightforward business students who want to work in the corporate world at investment banks or larger firms, like GE and Hewlett Packard. The average high school GPA is around 3.6 to 3.8 with SAT scores of 1250 and up (on the old scale). The SAT Subject Test requirements are Writing and Math but they won't help you dodge a class.

> **The school says:** "The average SAT range for admitted students this year was 1780 to 2050. We do not require SAT Subject Tests but we do recommend the Math."

AP exams are big and many students come in and waive 12 credits thanks to them, they are being seen more and more as the standard to have and a disability not to have. To receive credit a score of 5 is usually needed. APs like Calculus (AB/BC), Economics, and English look especially good as there are heavy math requirements, eight credits of English (reading writing) minimum and a breadth of economics at Babson. Most people who apply really want to go to Babson as it is a very unique program so don't be too optimistic about the waiting list. If you don't get in first round, transferring is an option after one full year at another school. In the fall around 100 apply and 40 percent get in, in the Spring about 50 apply and 20 get in. Transfer process is identical, but credits aren't easy to transfer. The school overall is around 2,000 students, around 25 percent international and they usually always get in.

> **The school says:** "Typically, the total undergraduate population at Babson is between 1,700 and 1,800 students, currently it is 1,776, and international students comprise 20 percent of the class on average."

As of now, Babson is boosting its athletic program so athletes interested in business should look here (basketball, soccer, baseball and running; no football). There is also an inner-city program to grab smart and hungry kids from inner Boston and city areas that are disenfranchised. The standard good grades and good SATs don't bode well at application, being a standout is really important.

 Academics

Alumnus/a, Finance, 8/2003-5/2007, May 2007

The first two years of the program are highly integrated, rigorous and challenging. If you aren't ready to put in time, don't bother coming here. That said, this education, like any other, yields only what you put into it. You can get away with minimal effort, but you won't excel at that level. There are plenty of chances in our small community to excel, and academics are perhaps the best chance. The varied course selection available in the last two or three years of the program allows the students to round out their competencies and pick a concentration or two. The first two years are all about knocking off core requirements, exposing you to all the aspects of business and finance, economics and management and more. The true power of our program comes in the first year program FME: Foundations of Management and Entrepreneurship, where you and 29 other classmates build a business from the ground up with a grant from the College, donate all profits to charity, and learn how to succeed—and fail—in a real business environment. The second year has two semester-long projects in teams of five or six, where three classes are intertwined, so you can see how all the parts of a business interrelate. Who cares about grading? Every Babson student. We're all hungry to succeed, and ready to either make it big on our own with a venture or get a high-paying job with a big firm right out of the gate. Everyone is concerned with his or her respective career. All Babson students complain about workload, but the truth is it isn't that different from anywhere

Read all of Vault's College Surveys at www.vault.com/college—get complete surveys on 100s of colleges and universities, expert advice on applicaton essays and more.

VAULT CAREER LIBRARY 303

else. You get out of it what you put into it. The professors are great. You won't ever find another school where you can graduate from a prestigious school while having a personal relationship with multiple professors throughout school and beyond. I have eight professors' cell phone numbers and maintain consistent contact even now. Remember: You can't skip class at Babson, because professors know everybody's name in their classes, and attendance is taken. A last note is important: Don't bother applying if you aren't ready to work with others collaboratively. If you can't respect the opinions of others and be willing to find the right answer, you won't do well here. If you're too timid to speak up with a good idea, you won't do well here. We're all about creating an open society.

Current student, 8/2004-Submit Date, November 2005

The workload is pretty intense at Babson. Starting with freshman year, we have a year-long interactive management class where we team up with 30 students and receive $3,000 to start a business. At the same time we were presenting our ideas to our peers and faculty, we were learning material in accounting, IT, management and sales. Grades are very competitive in Babson because the average GPA is a 2.7 (B-) but because of the amazing faculty and small classrooms, they provide us with a lot of help and insights to what we should be doing or where we can get additional tutoring or help. We sign up for classes online and sometimes it is difficult to get the classes that we want but, if we speak to the professors, sometimes we can still get into a class even if it is full. That is why Babson being a small college is useful.

Current student, 9/2003-Submit Date, December 2005

Classes are always under 40 but usually between 15 to 30. The rooms are elevated with cushioned chairs, new desks and high-speed Internet for your laptop (Babson gives you a new one every other year, fully hooked up). FMEs and IMEs are taught by a team of teachers that integrates assignments and projects and sometimes teaches together, which is awesome because these teachers are not academics usually. Finance teachers come from places like Fidelity and worked at investment banks. Economists worked at the IMF, World Bank or premiere financial institutions. There are no teaching assistants and no Friday classes. Work is rigorous, but not busywork. Teamwork is expected as each course has many group assignments. Example: in IME II you visit a place like Pepsico and Zildjian Cymbals and are given a plant tour and then present a project on the financial health and strategy of the company (20+ pages, 40 percent of grade). For IME III you participate in a team for a company as consultants and make a proposal and present it (Blockbuster going to Video On Demand is an examples, 30 pages, counts for each IME III class by varied weight). The teachers make the classes, though. A number of teachers are tenured so you get consistency in advanced coursework. They all want to be there and teach this innovative curriculum, so it is rare you find an unenthusiastic teacher and everyone has worked in relevant field. Another example is a services marketing prof who specializes in distressed service oriented business marketing. Entrepreneurial classes are huge. A real-time case study with a start-up is hands on, and there is an "apprentice class." There is a summer and two-week winter session with courses like Japanese Business Culture and Contract Law for the entrepreneur. Other entrepreneurial classes include, nonprofits, family business and many more. Many classes use text books that were specially written by teachers for their class only, so don't expect to see "Fundamentals of"—unless you are taking CPA track accounting course. Other classes include negotiations, which is the most popular class at Babson taught by a corporate consultant specializing in mediation. It is so popular the teacher went from one three-hour session for 30 students a week to four sections, one a day. That is commitment to teaching and she is a phenomenal teacher.

Current student, 8/2001-Submit Date, April 2005

The nature of the academic work at Babson is rigorous. Students should be prepared to do a lot of groupwork. There are relatively few easy classes at Babson and teachers hold students to extremely high standards. One can expect at least three hours of work a night and even more in freshman and sophomore years. The business curriculum and entrepreneurship classes are second to none and students will leave with a skill set that will make them successful as soon as they graduate. Also there is a number of unique opportunities for Babson students including starting your own business in a first-year program, the management field consulting experience, and the Babson college fund where students invest part of the school's endowment.

Employment Prospects

Current student, Finance, 9/2004-Submit Date, June 2007

I am sitting here writing my responses as a soon-to-be senior and I've alrea[d] had two great internships. Internships are much desired and strongly encourage[d] at Babson. My first internship was as a sophomore, and I went all the way [to] London to work for one of the Top Five global consulting firms. Babson st[u]dents are very attractive to employers. Employers know how hard we've work[ed] at school and how integrated our curriculum is. They know we understand t[he] whole business approach to a problem and that we know what the different co[n]sequences to our decisions will be for every department within the business.

I think Babson's strongest assets are the alumni. The reason Babson students g[et] fabulous jobs is because students have gone before us and done extremely we[ll] and paved a path of gold, if you will. Every year we have over 600 internshi[ps] posted through our e-recruiting system at Babson, and by the time we gradua[te] there are more jobs posted than there are graduates! To say Babson students a[re] readily employable is a no-brainer. If I think about all the friends who are work[ing] right now, they're all working at companies like Lehman Brothers, Harr[is] Williams, Deloitte, Accenture, MetLife Investments, KPMG, PWC, Proctor [&] Gamble, General Electric and so on. Babson students are ready to hit the grou[nd] running and are more than qualified to work at any world-class firm.

Alumnus/a, Finance, 9/2003-5/2007, May 2007

Babson's reputation in the business world is global. It is amazing to hear ho[w] well regarded this school is by international students who spend their four yea[rs] here. The majority of my friends went into finance or accounting and have jo[bs] with a topnotch investment banks or Big Four accounting firm. Students al[so] leave with marketing jobs at MTV or working on the entertainment marketin[g] side of the NFL. Students even decide to start their own businesses. I worke[d] with the Center of Career Development in my sophomore year. They helped m[e] with my résumé and held a mock interview with me. I interned with an accoun[t]ing firm in my junior year, then received a full-time offer before my senior yea[r.] I also worked for Babson alumni on my audit engagements, so there is stro[ng] networking for a small school.

Current student, 8/2004-Submit Date, November 2005

Most Babson alumni have great jobs coming out of college. Most alumni work wi[th] great business firms in banking, accounting, finance, marketing, management a[nd] also entrepreneurship. Babson has many great connections with big companie[s] such as PricewaterhouseCoopers, Morgan Stanley, L'Oreal, Lindt and Merr[ill] Lynch. We also have a Center for Career Development where they help us g[et] internships, teach us how to write the perfect résumé and how to network. We eve[n] have a Career Expo twice a year for big companies to come and recruit us. Babso[n] is definitely the place to be if you want to go into the business world.

Current student, 8/2001-Submit Date, April 2005

Getting a job out of Babson begins long before senior year. Depending on yo[ur] field, it is very important to find a summer internship. This is a tough situatio[n] for a number of reasons: in marketing, you'll need to take a non-paying inter[n]ship if you'd like experience at a major firm. For accounting and finance, if yo[u] don't have an internship after junior year at a major firm, chances are very sli[m] that you'll be able to find employment at one of those firms until very late in[to] your senior year. Personally, I varied my experiences between IT, marketing a[nd] entrepreneurship and was able to get a job in marketing at a major IT firm by t[he] first week in March. I believe this was made possible by the fact that I diversi[fied my résumé, but was also able to back it up in person by understanding wh[at] the employer wanted to hear. The most important thing to remember is that [if] you're smart about it, you'll get a job. The resources on campus played a mini[mal role in my job search—except that they provided the link between m[e,] employer and Babson on their e-recruiting online site.

Current student, 8/2001-Submit Date, April 2005

Recently Babson has taken a giant leap forward in terms of prestige with employ[ers. The reputation of the school is growing on Wall Street and the alumni networ[k] is becoming increasingly helpful. There is a lot of competition for investment bank[ing, consulting and marketing jobs coming out of Babson. Most students who don[t] choose these routes are trying to start their own companies. The Center for Caree[r] Development is very helpful and the number of top employers coming to campu[s] to offer jobs and internship is greater than ever before.

Quality of Life

Alumnus/a, Finance, 8/2003-5/2007, June 2007

Wellesley is a fantasy town: clean, quiet and wealthy. Little to worry about for crime. Police are over employed! I love the campus—it's beautiful. Dorms and food are solid compared to most schools. Love the proximity to Boston, even though this hurts social life a bit.

Alumnus/a, Finance, 9/2003-5/2007, May 2007

I had a great living experience all four years on campus. The facilities staff does a great job keeping the school looking great. You'll be wowed when you come to visit campus, especially in the fall, since it'll be hard for you to find a leaf that hasn't been raked. Students are placed in a freshman dorm with all freshmen, which was helpful to me since I got to meet people going through the same experience. There is also a lot of specialty housing for students. If students are interested in entrepreneurship, the outdoors, finance, culinary arts, women's leadership arts, media—there are towers for each of these interests. I'm already missing the dining hall. It's all you can eat, which is great but you'll love the stir fry bar. The Dining Hall Staff does a nice job of listening to your requests. It may be tough for vegetarians but if I know the Dean of the Undergraduate school, this won't be the case for long. There are also a few other cafes on campus that are nice. Reynolds has some American food and Padinis is mainly Italian food. Campus Public Safety may be on the strict side, but Chief Jackson is a very good man who is working to improve the relationships between the officers and students. Some of the officers are involved in organizations on campus. An officer, helps with the Babson Dance Ensemble as the advisor.

Current student, 9/2003-Submit Date, December 2005

Quality of life is very high. Babson is located right in Wellesley, a dry town, hence Babson's own zip code so they can have a pub. Wellesley is an higher-income suburb 15 minutes from Boston. There is nothing fun in town but everyone goes to Boston anyway. Babson and surrounding towns are incredibly safe and the only blip on the radar is when a student parks for more than 15 minutes in the visiting parking. The campus is beautiful and often over the top. Everything is modern and wireless Internet is everywhere. With a lot of executive programs and companies visiting, a lot of money is spent on gardens, newly paved roads, expensive lamp posts and freshly painted everything. The library has flat panel TVs with CNBC, and dual LCD display computers everywhere and separate computer labs that are 24 hours a day. There are many group meeting rooms and adequate space for a small campus. Don't look for fiction other than *Harry Potter*. As always, Sodexho handles dining. The area is huge and while the food isn't great, it is up there. There are two other food cafes and a coffee shop in the library and Reynolds, which has tables, TVs, meeting rooms and pool tables. Unfortunately, most places close at midnight, so delivery Dominos, Thai, pizza, Chinese) is clutch. Campus is immaculate and very clean, the service staff is friendly and incredibly good. The dorms are pretty nice, and there are mostly singles and doubles and specialty living. Fraternities and sororities have seven towers (15-person units) with a living room and kitchen and others can apply for specialty housing (entrepreneur tower, investment tower, women's leadership tower, and outdoors activity tower). There are suites for juniors and seniors (five people, kitchen and living room). Resident Assistants are very laid back compared to most schools and let things like alcohol go but will slam you for other questionable activities. The best perk is parking, there is enough for some students to have two cars, which a bunch do.

Social Life

Alumnus/a, Finance, 8/2003-5/2007, May 2007

Lots of restaurants everywhere in Boston makes it easy to go off campus for food. Nick's Pizza is a great take-out place. The calzones are life savers for every Babson student. Lemon Thai and Tian Fu are Thai and Chinese food that every Babson student orders from all the time. They all deliver. Wellesley has lots of sandwich shops and small restaurants. Another 20 minutes away there are hundreds of restaurants all over Boston. The campus has a pub, Roger's Pub, named after our founder, who was part of the Prohibitionist Party—can't make that up. It serves beer on tap at a relatively cheap price. The pub has a great hang-out atmosphere to watch the Red Sox play on a big screen TV or talk. It's always crowded on Thursday and Friday nights. Speaking of that, we have a three-day weekend, making it great to party on weekends, as well as go home if you feel like it.

Current student, 9/2003-Submit Date, December 2005

This is a rough patch for Babson. The school is very fragmented. Most international students live off campus and they all go to clubs like Aria and Venue on the weekends and are only seen in class. This group is discernable by cell phone chatter, cigarettes, designer clothes and sunglasses when they aren't needed. Then there are the Greeks that have been increasing in numbers. Tau Kappa Epsilon, Sigma Phi Epsilon, AEPi (Jewish fraternity) and Theta Chi have charters. They aren't really known for their parties like at most schools, with the exception for Tau Kappa Epsilon who throws the best Halloween, around the world and themed events. It is probably the only place that is always open to hanging out at 3 a.m. They are the smallest and most selective but are long rooted in campus fraternities that had their charters revoked. Sig Ep is the largest and most open. There are three sororities: Sigma Kappa, Kappa Kappa Gamma and a new one, Chi Omega. They are small and less popular than most schools. They don't have parties most likely because people wouldn't go to them. Most girls view the sororities at Babson to catty, elitist and discriminatory in terms of recruiting.

Current student, 8/2001-Submit Date, April 2005

As previously alluded to, public safety keeps a watchful eye on the party scene. They usually allow parties to go on until someone calls in a noise complaint (which happens more often than not) or it seems to be getting out of hand. Getting caught with a keg or beer ball is an easy way to get kicked off campus, especially if under-agers are clearly at the party.

The problem is that you are 15 miles Southwest of Boston without very close public transportation. There is a bus that goes in at 10 p.m. and comes out at 2 a.m., but that is only one night a week. So you've got to either constantly find a designated driver (and deal with parking in town) or party on campus. In addition, the curriculum is so intense at times, that one of the only ways to release and feel better is to drink. Not the healthiest of lifestyles.

Campus life and the campus activities board do a nice job of planning certain weekends, such as Winter Weekend or Spring Weekend. Bands come, we have events on campus, and public safety seems to get a bit more lax. OCL and CAB also try very hard to bring entertainment to campus regularly, but it gets difficult after a while to find someone who will come to a 1,700 student campus with a low budget. Pub nights are the main event of the week, where everyone goes down to the on campus pub and drinks until it closes at midnight. Nothing special.

> **Regarding social life, Babson says:** "Significant strides have been made recently in response to student life concerns similar to the above comments. In addition to more shuttle options available to popular destinations in and around Wellesley and Boston, Babson has formed a partnership with Zipcar to provide additional vehicle accessibility throughout the year. Many student common areas including dorm lounges and the Reynolds Campus Center have undergone a facelift to improve functionality and accessibility. Among the improvements include flat screen televisions, new casual furniture and additional gaming options. The Reynolds Campus Center will also be open late-night Thursday through Saturday evenings with dining options and Roger's Pub will now be open on Friday nights. Within the Webster Athletic Center, improvements have included the addition of new cardio equipment, a state-of-the-art Cardio Theater system that includes five flat-screen televisions with closed circuit sound, new ceiling fans to improve air circulation, a new lighting system, new flooring, as well as several additional weight equipment upgrades."

The School Says

Our approach to education is unique. We believe (as do our graduates and their employers) in the value of an interdisciplinary approach combined with experiential education. And because we're the most innovative, integrated, entrepreneurial business school in the world, anything is possible with a degree from Babson!

Read all of Vault's College Surveys at **www.vault.com/college**–get complete surveys on 100s of colleges and universities, expert advice on applicaton essays and more.

VAULT CAREER LIBRARY **305**

Babson is a residential college and is a 24-hours-a-day, seven days-a-week community alive with intellectual, cultural, athletic, and social activities. Approximately 83 percent of the undergraduate student body live on campus in thirteen residence halls. Housing options include coed residence halls, fraternity and sorority housing, and substance-free, multicultural, entrepreneurial, and other-themed housing.

Babson's beautiful 370-acre campus is in Wellesley, Massachusetts, 14 miles west of Boston, a city renowned for its cultural and recreational opportunities. More than 60 colleges and universities bring more than 250,000 college students to the Boston area, making it one of the world's best college towns for cultural exchange and research.

Babson College is an NCAA Division III school, and most of the College's intercollegiate teams compete in the New England Women's and Men's Athletic Conference (NEWMAC). There are 22 men's and women's varsity sports teams, with additional club and intramural sports available to all students.

The undergraduate curriculum integrates core competencies, key business disciplines, and the liberal arts into foundation, intermediate, and advanced programs. Babson's core competencies include rhetoric, quantitative analysis, entrepreneurial and creative thinking, global and multicultural perspectives, ethics and social responsibility, leadership and teamwork, and critical and integrative thinking.

Because of Babson's close-knit community, students are able to form close relationships with the faculty. Of the nearly 230 faculty members, more than 150 of them are full-time, and over 90 percent of the full-time faculty members hold a doctoral degree or its equivalent. Faculty members are accomplished entrepreneurs, executives, scholars, authors, researchers, poets, and artists, who bring an intellectual diversity that adds depth to Babson's educational programs and offers students a rich, challenging experience. Babson's student-to-faculty ratio is 14:1, with an average class size of 29. Most importantly, faculty members teach 100 percent of the courses.

Babson also offers special programs to help you take advantage of additional learning opportunities. Babson students can take a course each semester at one of the other area colleges, including Brandeis University and Wellesley College, for full academic credit. These off-campus programs offer greater access to liberal arts courses, including a wide range of foreign languages. In addition, Babson has a partnership with the Franklin W. Olin College of Engineering, an independent institution that opened in 2001 and is located adjacent to Babson. Babson and Olin are collaborating academically in order to provide extraordinary opportunities in technology-based business, including joint academic and research programming, engineering, and entrepreneurial thinking. Babson's vibrant study abroad program enables students to spend either a summer or one or both semesters of their junior year overseas at a college or university. Currently, 37 programs are offered in 20 countries, and full academic credit is given for approved management and liberal arts courses.

For more information, please visit www.babson.edu/ug

Boston College

Office of Undergraduate Admission
Devlin Hall 208
140 Commonwealth Avenue
Chestnut Hill, MA 02467-3809
Admissions phone: (617) 552-3100 or (800) 360-2522
Admissions fax: (617) 552-0798
Admissions URL: www.bc.edu/admission/undergrad/

 ## Admissions

Current student, 6/2003-Submit Date, November 2005

Looks more into overall academic achievement than single SAT score or GPA. In the essay, if you state importance of Jesuit university and emphasize how you want to incorporate spirituality into education, that's a huge bonus point. Also, if you're from a Jesuit high school, that's a plus, too.

Alumnus/a, Finance, 9/1999-5/2003, March 2007

Boston College seems to prefer students who are very active in extracurricular activities. Rumor has it that most of the companies that recruit on campus do so because they recognize that BC students are very social and could be expected to easily pass the "airplane test" (i.e., would you like to spend an eight-hour flight sitting next to this person?). For me the admissions process was as follows: contact BC to ask for an application, fill out the application, mail it in, and wait for a response. Otherwise there was nothing to it. I applied with a 3.4 GPA and a 1290 on the SATs. One of my friends for the same high school that I went to applied with the same stats but didn't get accepted. I think my essays made the difference.

The school says: "Hardly anyone applies using paper forms any more. Boston College has a fully automated online application available from its admission web site based upon the Common Application. For those who have completed the Common Application already, Boston College is a member. BC requires a supplemental application in addition to the Common Application. The Supplemental Application should be submitted first."

Current student, 9/2003-Submit Date, November 2005

Selectivity is increasing. Interviews are not required and the essay is just the Common Application essay. The application itself is not difficult. BC gives preference to those who do community service as it is a Catholic school that pushes service and global justice.

BC says: "While Boston College does give due consideration to applicants who do community service, we place primary weight on academic excellence and a demonstrated passion to make a difference in the world in any chosen endeavor."

Current student, 9/2002-Submit Date, May 2006

The admissions process was based on GPA, essay, SATs, recommendations and extracurricular activities. The most emphasis was placed on GPA and extracurriculars, including volunteering and athletics. Boston College does not offer interviews. The selection process is very difficult as they only accept roughly [7,700] students out of 26,000 applicants.

> **The school says:** "This year Boston College received nearly 29,000 applications and are Number 20 in selectivity among national universities. We do look for well-rounded students who may be future leaders in their chosen fields. Athletics is considered only among students being actively recruited by coaches."

Current student, 9/2003-Submit Date, October 2005

BC admissions is very selective, and is getting increasingly more difficult as the years go on. BC does not give personal interviews or at least BC doesn't officially give personal interviews. Rumor is if you know someone, you can get an interview. The application consists of the Common Application and a personal BC application that contains mostly demographic information. The only essay is the one required by the Common App. For the 2003 pool—the numbers for Arts and Sciences turn out like this: there were [2,200] spots for about 22,000 applicants. Another common rumor on campus is that it is much harder to get into the College of Arts and Sciences, but much harder to graduate from the Carol School of Management. Students apply to the particular college they want to go to, which include Arts and Sciences, Management, Education, and Nursing. BC has Early Action—which does not require the student to go to the school if they are accepted. It is a great way to show the university that you are interested, and even if you are deferred to Regular Admission—if you maintain a strong interest (send updated work/personal info over Christmas break) it ups a student's chances of getting in Regular Decision.

> **Regarding Early Action, BC says:** "It is a myth that students can increase their chance of admission by applying Early. We go to great lengths to make certain that students who apply during Regular Admission are not in any way disadvantaged. Students should apply Early Action if that want substantive feedback on their admissibility and to give them time make plans to apply to other institutions. Students who apply Early Action and are accepted have until May 1st to make their enrollment decision."

Current student, 9/2001-Submit Date, January 2005

The admissions process at Boston College is very selective; and often family legacy and administrative connections can be decisive in whether or not a student is accepted. Interviews are not [part of] the admissions process.

> **The school says:** "Legacies receive some preference in selection, yet candidates should not consider these connections 'decisive.' All applications are read holistically and a legacy relationship is just one factor."

The admissions counselors claim that the key to acceptance at BC is using every opportunity in high school. BC looks for excellence: graduation at the top of one's class, challenging course schedules with an abundance of AP courses as well as ample extracurricular activities. BC is a very selective school, but continued contact with your region's admission officer can better your chances of acceptance.

> **Boston College says:** "Continued contact with you admission officer will <u>not</u> increase your chances of acceptance."

Current student, 9/2000-Submit Date, April 2004

Boston College has been an up-and-coming school ever since Doug Flutie threw the winning touchdown pass against Miami. Because of this, it is harder and harder to get in every year. In order to get in it is important to be well rounded, with an emphasis on community service. Boston College is a Jesuit university, so they are looking for people that will live up to the ideals of learning and com-

passion. Community service, a good GPA and good SAT scores are a good combination to get into this school.

In terms of GPA, the student should have above a B average. Students with a higher GPA will have a better chance of getting in, even if their SAT scores are lower, because it shows that they can work hard and do well. Doing well in Advanced Placement classes is something at which BC admissions looks closely. If they see you can do well in an AP class, they will think you can do well at BC. In terms of the SATs, your score should be [over 1,350]. Many kids here have scores above 1,400, but those kids that don't have such a high score are kids that did a lot of community service, have high GPAs or are minority students.

> **The school says:** "Students should have an A- or higher average."

Being a minority student will definitely help you get into BC. There is a large majority of white Catholic students here, and admissions is looking to make the student body more diverse. If you come from a lower-income area, BC will make exceptions to its admissions criteria. For example, I know my freshman roommate was from a disadvantaged area, and he only had an 1,100 on his SATs [and yet BC met his full financial need].

> **Boston College says:** "While being a minority student may be a plus factor, candidates should keep in mind that the pool of prospective minority applicants to Boston College has expanded greatly. The latest incoming freshman class is 28 percent minority, so the above statement is out of date. We will also take into consideration economic disadvantage if candidates show that they have overcome such obstacles to excel."

 ## Academics

Current student, 9/2004-Submit Date, October 2006

Great classes, intelligent students and inspiring teachers. They're working harder to attract even better faculty. They just bought a new building on Commonwealth Avenue for faculty to live. If you're in the business school, you can expect to work hard and do a lot of team projects.

Alumnus/a, Finance, 9/1999-5/2003, March 2007

The classes were fine. I can't remember feeling overwhelmed or unsatisfied. I wouldn't say that it was challenging. As long as you do your homework, you can expect to do well in most classes. The workload is probably about the same as most universities at BC's level. You can expect to spend at least four hours per day on homework assignments. There were very few classes that I got shut out of.

Alumnus/a, 8/1999-5/2003, March 2007

In my experience, the process for getting into classes was very fair. Students are randomly assigned a time for registration, with the seniors getting the earliest times and the freshmen getting the latest. Some popular classes do fill up quickly, but spots often open up during the first week of classes ("Drop/Add Week") and, on occasion, another section of the class might be added. The quality and popularity of professors vary. BC has a web site maintained by the student government where students can read reviews of professors and post their own. I found these to be very accurate and very helpful—it is something I wish I had known about before freshman year, since I wound up taking two professors who were very poorly rated. There is a number of core requirements that all students must fulfill. Often, you can use AP credits to get out of them, but I would advise freshmen to take at least one core course in their first semester—such as writing, a language, or a survey course (Modern History would be a good choice). I made the mistake of passing out of a lot of core courses and taking on an advanced courseload my first semester. I found it more difficult to adjust and keep up with my work than my friends who were taking mostly core classes.

Current student, 9/2003-Submit Date, November 2005

The core curriculum is rigorous and entails [one] course in math, two in philosophy, two in theology, two in science, one cultural diversity, [two in] English (with one being Freshman Writing Seminar), two in social science and [one] art. The business core requires Financial Accounting, Managerial Accounting, Basic

Read all of Vault's College Surveys at **www.vault.com/college**–get complete surveys on 100s of colleges and universities, expert advice on applicaton essays and more.

VAULT CAREER LIBRARY 307

Finance, Principles of Marketing, Management and Operations, Strategy and Policy, Organizational Behavior, Statistics and Micro and Macroeconomics. Being in the undergrad business school leaves very little room for other electives because the two core curricula and major courses take the bulk of one's schedule. The finance and accounting is rigorous and the marketing and general management majors are weaker, information systems is very unpopular.

Current student, 9/2003-Submit Date, October 2005

BC is an academically challenging school, but it's worth it. The professors are great, many are participants and leaders in their fields of study. Despite hectic schedules, professors will find time to meet with you and help you—the catch is you are responsible for initiating it. There is a variety of classes. A student organization has put up a web site that allows students to grade and comment on professors, classes and workload. Before registering for a class, most students check out their alternatives. BC's drop/add period as well allows students some flexibility. Also, students can take classes in just about any school or field in which they are interested without majoring in it. For classes that fill up quickly (registering is done by class year), students are advised to see a professor and ask for an override, which are commonly granted. BC endeavors to provide a Jesuit education for all of its students. Although classes are without Catholic overtones, students easily grasp the idea that professors are aiming at the education of the whole person. Classes that encourage and require outside community service, as well as guest speakers and academic lectures all aim to invoke students with a sense of spirituality (not necessarily Christian spirituality) but a sense of living for others. Social justice and service are important for BC students both inside the classroom and out.

Current student, 9/2001-Submit Date, January 2005

The values of a Jesuit liberal arts education are strong at BC, with a heavy emphasis placed on its core curriculum. Students are required to take courses in writing, literature, philosophy, theology, math, arts, social science and foreign language unless [AP or IB qualifying scores] can be provided to excuse a student from any of these requirements. The core curriculum is an asset, not a hindrance, since it forces students to explore varying arenas so as to make a more informed decision about the correct major to pursue.

Courses are relatively small, with a lot of one-on-one interaction with professors. Courses aren't often taught by TAs, and generally only entry-level courses are held in large lecture halls. Grading is not inflated, but good grades are definitely not hard to come by if you put in the required effort. Professors are generally great and enthusiastic about their subject matters, as well as very open to students' input and needs.

 Employment Prospects

Current student, 9/2004-Submit Date, October 2006

I'm going into investment banking. I have a few offers in banking and two offers from the Big Four accounting firms but not sure where I'll end up. Companies want BC students. There are information sessions literally almost every night in September from the major financial companies trying to attract people who are committed, competent, and can still handle being around clients; and BC has that.

Alumnus/a, Finance, 9/1999-5/2003, March 2007

It depends on the year, but some of the top management consulting firms and investment banks recruit at BC. Make sure to attend recruiting events and take advantage of the Eagle Link recruiting web site. Also, even though I am an alumnus, the Career Center continues to help me with my career decisions. The alumni network is also really helpful. Most of the people whom I have contacted have been eager to offer guidance and advice.

Alumnus/a, 8/1999-5/2003, March 2007

The Career Center is helpful if you take advantage and use it right. Many students go in to have their résumés reviewed and then sit back and wait, which doesn't produce results. There is a number of available resources—résumé critiques and practice interviews being the most popular. Many major companies recruit on campus—such as the top investment banks and a number of Fortune 100s. The Career Center does make students aware of who is coming on campus, although looking back I think additional information was provided within

schools. For example, the investment banks typically come on campus to recruit in the early fall. The School of Management students were all informed and prepared, much more so than the average Arts and Sciences student. However there are lots of great companies recruiting at BC, as well as a lot of alternative options, such as Peace Corps, Jesuit Volunteer Corp and Teach for America.

Current student, 9/2003-Submit Date, November 2005

Strong finance and accounting program. Accounting majors with over a 3. GPA have a solid chance at the Big Four Accounting firms. Investment banking is growing stronger with JP Morgan, Goldman Sachs, UBS, Deutche Bank, Bank of America and Citigroup actively recruiting. Barclays, Bear Stearns and Lehman have a weaker presence but do recruit. Asset management and private banking are strong in BC. JP Morgan and Goldman Sachs recruit heavily for those fields. Buyside has less of a presence, minus Fidelity Investments, as Peter Lynch, the famed money manager was a BC alumnus and Fidelity is based in Boston. Alumni are very helpful because they want Boston College graduates to be able to compete with Ivy League students. The on-campus recruiting is convenient because Boston is a city they visit anyway. Marketing is the weakest area for employment. Many go to advertising firms, but that is about it. Very few go to corporate marketing departments. Many strong students end up going to schools with stronger MBA programs, increasing their desirability among top financial services firms.

Alumnus/a, 9/1999-5/2003, January 2005

Boston College has a great image in the business world. When you say you went to Boston College, either the employer knows someone who went there or they have had some sort of great experience with a graduate from Boston College. This directly adds to your chances of being hired at a well-known firm. The school does a great job helping you through the first steps of finding a job.

The only students who had problems had them because they didn't make an effort. Boston College has everything to offer, but you must be willing to put in your time and interests. The Career Center will not come to you, and the amazing alumni network will not check in just to make sure that you have a job. Once you make the first step, then Boston College services can do almost all the rest.

 Quality of Life

Current student, 9/2004-Submit Date, October 2006

Incredible. Everyone is fun, intelligent and well rounded, which makes living around BC a once-in-a-lifetime opportunity. They are working to make more rooms available on campus and I'd say where they really need to focus on is building better student facilities. Right now where BC is at in terms of athletics, volunteer opportunities, and its grade of students I can't think of a better place for an intelligent sociable person to be.

Alumnus/a, Finance, 9/1999-5/2003, March 2007

The campus is attractive and the accommodations are comfortable. The only complaints came from the freshmen who had to live on Newton Campus, which is located about one mile from the main campus. Others enjoyed the experience because it gave them an opportunity to bond with other freshmen. There are some particularly comfortable accommodations, but there is a lottery that decides who will get the opportunity to live in them. Most juniors live off campus, where housing is expensive, but as long as you have several roommates, it's not too bad.

Alumnus/a, 8/1999-5/2003, March 2007

BC is unique in that students are very eager to live on campus. All students are guaranteed three years of housing, with about a fourth of each class given four years housing. The vast majority live on campus freshman, sophomore and senior years. Junior year students move off campus or go abroad. BC is the only school I know of where students clamor to live on campus senior year. I can't explain why, but that is just how it is.

Current student, 9/2003-Submit Date, October 2005

BC is located within the City of Newton. Last year, Newton was voted the safest city in the country. It is a very upscale neighborhood. All students are guaranteed three years of housing, and the top percentages get four years. Students are not required to live on campus, though. Those students who live off campus or go abroad, are assisted throughout the entire process by the Office of Residential Life—Off-Campus Housing Department (which links students with realtors who are more than happy to drive students to all the best listings) and the Hovey House, which assists students with study abroad programs. BC has programs in over [171] countries. As for dining, BC has seven dining halls—which include three main dining halls, a gourmet sandwich bar and a chocolate bar—with 13 flavors of chocolate ice cream! The mean plan allots students $1,850 a semester for students to use in any of the dining halls. There are no set times for meals like at other schools. The food quality is pretty good for college food, and there is quite a bit of variety. Just stay away from that chicken in the salad bar, it tends not to taste so good, especially after sitting out for hours. As for on-campus facilities, BC has a large gym/recreational area, diving pool, regular pool, sauna, ice rink and football stadium. We also have a computer lab, free of charge for all students, and especially good if you have a lot of printing to do. There are also [seven] libraries at BC. On-campus resources include counseling, a 24-hour infirmary, academic advising and financial aid assistance. Although BC is a Catholic and fairly conservative school, they are open to view points from all sides of the political/social spectrum. BC has been trying very hard of late to increase diversity. Homosexuality and race issues have been brought to the administration by students.

Current student, 9/2003-Submit Date, May 2004

BC has excellent housing on campus. Freshman students are split between the main campus and a satellite campus about one and a half miles away with a shuttle bus service. The satellite campus has its own cafeteria and is also home to the law school. I was housed on the main campus but never heard many complaints from the Newton students. Often they developed more friends as a result of the shuttle bus ride. Most students were typically only guaranteed three years of on-campus housing. Junior-year students rent apartments in the surrounding Allston/Brighton area or go abroad. [98] percent of seniors return to campus for senior year. BC is aggressively upgrading and building more housing.

> **The school says:** 50 percent of students are guaranteed three years housing.

The food is top quality; friends from other schools were always jealous. The dining services recently won a worldwide award. Meal plans are on a dollar basis rather than a meal basis. You pay for each individual item you purchase. Many surrounding businesses now accept the dining card as a type of debit card for food, dry cleaning and so on.

Newton is one of the safest communities in the entire United States. I never felt unsafe walking around campus, even very late at night.

 Social Life

Alumnus/a, Finance, 9/1999-5/2003, March 2007

There's no Greek system, but there are plenty of parties. As a matter of fact, students from many other nearby universities can be seen at BC just about every weekend. Even people from MIT and Harvard can't stay away from BC parties. BC also has a reputation for an attractive student body. I guess that depends on what you're looking for. Mary Ann's is the hot-spot nearby. They used to have free wings and $1 drinks on Fridays in the afternoon. You can expect to wait in line for about an hour most nights if you want to show up late. Most of the parties are in the dorms or off-campus apartments.

Alumnus/a, 8/1999-5/2003, March 2007

BC is a big school, and I think as a result, most friendships are formed between dormmates in freshman year. There are a lot of clubs that students can join, which is a good way to expand one's social circle. Service is a big part of life on campus—there are lots of big volunteer groups, and a class open to sophomores called PULSE that combines theology and philosophy and requires service in the Boston area for several hours each week.

A few other things: Football is big—during home games, it seems the entire school is out tailgating or attending the game, regardless of whether or not they are fans of the sport. One thing that has changed is the tailgating policy. You used to be able to tailgate through the whole game, so many people didn't even buy tickets and just hung out outside the stadium. Now, everyone has to be

inside before the end of the first quarter and tailgating after the game is restricted. Still, I'd recommend that freshmen buy season tickets—they are very affordable and the games are attended by almost the entire student body. BC does not have a Greek system. There is no "dating scene" at BC (in the traditional sense of going out on dates with a few different people). Students are either single or in a relationship. Students tend to go straight from being friends into a full-blown relationship. There is a lot of emphasis on appearance at BC, especially for women. When I was there, there was a "BC look" that was considered the standard of attractiveness—this essentially translated to being about 5'5", 115 pounds, with blond highlights, and a wardrobe from J.Crew and Abercrombie. There are no bars on campus, although alcohol is allowed. There are all kinds of restrictions and requirements for throwing parties, which must be registered with the RA, but that doesn't stop people from partying.

Current student, 9/2002-Submit Date, May 2006

The social scene for freshmen, sophomores and juniors is mainly off-campus parties or dorm parties. The senior's social scene includes many of the local bars, including Mary Ann's, the Kells, Kinvara and An Tua Nua. Of course, we also like to go downtown to the bars in Fanueil Hall. And on campus, we party in the Mods, which are the famous senior modular homes with backyards and grills.

Current student, 9/2003-Submit Date, October 2005

While there is no Greek scene at BC, students make up for it by having parties related to certain sports groups or clubs. BC students often stereotype themselves saying, "We work hard and we party hard." Off-campus junior housing is where most freshmen and juniors go to on the weekends. Sophomores tend to hang out in their large eight-person suites, while seniors, who live in the Mods (the BC version of on campus condos), tend to have parties on their lawns. Clubbing at places like Roxy, Avalon and Axis is big, especially because the city is only a 15-minute T-ride away. But if you want to stay local, Mary Ann's is definitely the "BC bar," only about a five-minute bus ride away. Dating at BC—not so big, especially for the underclassmen. However, hooking up at parties is very big. Hooking up is random and casual at BC to the point that it is common to be woken up the next morning, hung over and searching Facebook trying to find out the full name of the person you had hooked up with the night before. A lot of college guide books describe BC as clickish and looking like "all the students just stepped out of a J.Crew Catalog." The clickish part I would have to disagree with, and if all the students appear to be wearing J.Crew it is only because J.Crew gives BC students a 10 percent discount on everything. I believe the high level of alcohol use at BC has to do with a lack of options. Although BC does have a variety of student groups (like a cappella groups and sketch comedy) that put on shows in the evening, BC is lacking the outside talent that a lot of other universities manage to pull in. It seems like other schools bring in popular musical groups or real comedians to perform—BC does this rarely. In the cold Boston winter the 15-minute walk to the T, which stops running before 1 a.m., doesn't seem worth it, especially when taking a cab is so expensive. In some ways students feel stranded on campus, without other alternatives. And alcohol, in general, makes a person feel warmer than he/she really is. It gets very, very cold here!

> **The school says:** Recent school-sponsored entertainment venues included Chris Rock, Dane Cook and Kanye West.

Current student, 9/2003-Submit Date, November 2004

There's always something good going on around campus. The Mods (modular apartments, senior housing) are the places for all the big parties. Also, most juniors live off campus, so lots of parties rage on all weekend at apartments and houses nearby without any RA interference. There are several popular bars in nearby Cleveland Circle (Mary Ann's, Roggie's, Cityside) and many many more just down Comm. Ave. on Harvard Avenue and the surrounding area (The Kell's, Kinvara).

 The School Says

Boston College ranks among the top universities in the country based upon admission selectivity. In each of the past two years, over 26,000 candidates have applied for 2,250 openings in the

Read all of Vault's College Surveys at **www.vault.com/college**–get complete surveys on 100s of colleges and universities, expert advice on applicaton essays and more.

VAULT CAREER LIBRARY   **309**

freshman class. Just under 30 percent of applicants were admitted.

Top overlap competitors for applications include Georgetown and Notre Dame, as well as Ivy League institutions. Thirteen of Boston College's Top 20 overlap application competitors are considered Top 25 institutions by *U.S. News & World Report*.

The mean SAT score for students admitted to the Boston College Class of 2009 was 1371, and the mean SAT score for enrolling students was 1322. Students who perform well in rigorous secondary school programs are most competitive for admission. The Admission Committee also values leadership, engagement with school and community activities, and evidence of intellectual vigor as expressed in teacher and guidance recommendations.

Boston College is one of 28 Jesuit institutions spanning the United States. Founded 450 years ago by Ignatius of Loyola, the Jesuits bring a distinctive character to undergraduate education. Students develop strong critical thinking and communication skills through a liberal arts core curriculum. They also encounter the problems of society through service learning opportunities, and they are encouraged to respond to these problems in meaningful ways. Graduates of Boston College should be competent professionals, as well as good citizens of the world.

As an academic institution, Boston College is best defined as a medium-sized university with 9,000 undergraduates. Students enroll in one of four undergraduate colleges: College of Arts and Sciences, Carroll School of Management, Lynch School of Education, Connell School of Nursing. The student-to-faculty ratio is 13:1 and the median class size is 23 students.

Faculty at Boston College are active scholars in their respective fields who are committed to undergraduate teaching. The departments of chemistry, physics, biology, economics, political science, English, and sociology are particularly strong. The pre-medical and pre-law advisory programs place the majority of their graduates in these professional schools.

The undergraduate population is geographically and ethnically diverse. All 50 states are represented at Boston College, as well as 60 foreign countries. Approximately 25 percent of students are from AHANA (African-American, Hispanic, Asian, Native American) backgrounds.

Finally, the socioeconomic diversity of the student body is ensured through Boston College's commitment to need-blind admission and its ability to meet the full demonstrated need of every admitted student. The university will award nearly $70 million in need-based grants to undergraduate students during the 2007-08 academic year.

Boston University

Office of Admissions
121 Bay State Road
Boston, MA 02215
Admissions phone: (617) 353-2300
Admissions fax: (617) 353-9695
Admissions e-mail: admissions@bu.edu

Note: The school has chosen not to comment on the student surveys submitted.

 Admissions

Current student, Economics, 9/2003-Submit Date, April 2007

There is a way to get a Boston University degree if you feel that you may not get into CAS or ENG or any of the other four-year colleges—try College of General Studies. It is a two-year program after which you apply to a four-year college. From the College of General Studies you can transfer into any other college with a lower GPA requirement. There is no required interview. The essay is standard. Since this is such a large school, acceptance is more numbers based.

Alumnus/a, 9/2001-5/2005, April 2006

I applied to the School of Hospitality and was accepted with ease. In fact, I applied one month after the deadline and was still admitted. However, the business school and communication school are very competitive. BU admissions rule of thumb: If you are not accepted to your desired school, you are put into General Studies, which is similar to a junior college within BU. It is a two-year program.

Current student, 8/2003-Submit Date, February 2006

Almost like a professional recruitment process. Pick out a few things that make you stand out from the rest and elaborate. I was an international student, and my experiences outside of school, like acting and community service, helped sell my application. I suggest you get some good recommendations from your teachers; I know they helped me to a great extent.

Current student, 9/2003-Submit Date, February 2006

The admissions process was standard fare for competitive institutions, accepting both the BU application and the Common Application with a supplement. The one very confusing aspect, the gravity of which was not addressed in the application, is to which school the applicant is applying. Boston University has 13 individual colleges, ranging from a College of General Studies (nicknamed "Crayons Glue and Scissors" for its initials) to a School of Management. Criteria for acceptance and level of competitiveness vary drastically for each school, so seek more information!

Alumnus/a, 9/2002-5/2003, December 2005

I was a transfer student, so I completed the online application for transfer students. I did not interview at the school, but I did have to write an essay and provide transcripts from my previous college. I have heard that the transfer selection is pretty tough, but my grades weren't so great from my previous school and I still got accepted. It is competitive but also so huge that they can accept more students than some of the smaller schools.

Current student, 9/2003-Submit Date, August 2004

The admissions process is a bit more involved than the average state college admissions program. As the school is private, they ask for more detailed information. They look at the level of writing in the essay responses, which is highly important to BU in all areas of study, as well as the creativity and believability of the responses. Of the entire admissions process, one of the most important aspects is the transcript, which details not only grades received in high school, but what type and level of courses the high school student chose to take. Advanced Placement and International Baccalaureate classes are very important as the school likes to see that the student has chosen to challenge him/herself. Also, the school likes well-rounded students who excel not only in academics but in sports and community service/extracurricular activities.

Current student, 9/2002-Submit Date, April 2004

Students do not need to interview as part of the admissions process. There are many options for completing the application. The easiest way to apply is by submitting the online application. Students can check the status of their applications online and see if they have submitted all the required forms. Remember, time is of the essence for any required documents, especially those related to financial aid.

It has become harder to get into BU, due to the increasing numbers of applicants and their qualifications. It is not necessary to have done many extracurricular activities in high school. If a student has a good academic record, he or she has a good chance of being accepted.

Academics

Alumnus/a, Economics, 9/2002-5/2006, April 2007

Probably the number one asset of the university is the sheer number of great professors. The university is somewhat under-rated by the *U.S. News* rankings because of its low alumni donation ratio and the existence of the College of General Studies. It's very easy to get a broad education at BU and the university is very flexible in terms of double majors/minors/dual-degrees and also awarding AP/IB credits. I think another great feature about the University is the strong study abroad program that is fully integrated into the curriculum of the major schools on campus.

Current student, 9/2003-Submit Date, February 2006

As a political science major, I am part of one of the more popular disciplines at the school (along with psychology and international relations), yet ease of use, as far as the department, remains admirably high. The professors are accessible and the level of instruction is noteworthy. Survey classes, as expected, are large and impersonal, but higher-level classes are more seminar-style, offering good amounts of professor-student interaction. Workload in those upper-level classes is commensurate with the specificity of the course (e.g., a class on the European Enlightenment has 2,500+ pages of reading, all of which is from 18th century texts). Class selection is made much easier because of the WebReg online registration system, which means no lines and no waiting—registration is a breeze, though in the more popular majors, many of the seminars go fast.

Alumnus/a, 9/2002-5/2003, December 2005

The liberal arts classes were excellent. A lot of great classes with great teachers and classes are generally available. The workload varies from class to class, but BU provides a great booklet of student reviews on classes, so you can determine if the class would be a fit. Classes are generally available, but be sure not to miss your sign up time and to get a signature from your counselor for all upper-level classes. Since the school is so big, there are always other classes you'll want to take if you don't get your first choice.

Current student, 9/2003-Submit Date, August 2004

Boston University is an excellent school for academia. I chose the school primarily for its courses and the excellent professors. The primary difference between the professors at BU and most other colleges is that the professors at BU have acquired many years of experience in their chosen field. One professor of journalism used to be a correspondent for the *Washington Post* and had also taught journalism courses as such prestigious schools as Harvard and Yale. The education offered at BU is unparalleled by any other school, in my belief.

Current student, 9/2001-Submit Date, July 2004

There are many schools within the university. You'll have to fill out a separate application for certain schools. There are majors for whatever your interests may be. Even if you don't know, you could enroll at any of the school's as an undecided major. The quality of classes depends on what major and school you get into. You may have large classes like 50 to 100 people or small classes like 10 to 15 people. There is limited space for classes so getting into a popular class may be hard especially if you are an underclassmen. Upperclassmen have priority.

Grading at this school is very hard. The administration watches for grade inflation. Some schools have tough workloads while others do not. It just depends on what you choose. As for professors, some are great and some are not. It's the luck of the draw.

Alumnus/a, 9/1997-12/2001, September 2003

Depending on to which school you applied your classes and experience will differ. BU is such a huge school that there is bound to be extremes. The College

of Communications emphasized lots of writing and social sciences—barely any math or science classes are required for graduation. The College of Arts and Sciences runs the gamut of courses. There are hundreds of classes to choose from and some are obviously very different from others. Classes are selected on a lottery basis. You get numbers at the end of each semester and depending on your number (and seniority with seniors getting first dibs) you can register for classes over the telephone and online.

Classes in CAS can be huge—hundreds in a class. You'll also get small classes—10 people even. It all depends on the class. If you're taking courses with a school, like the College of Engineering, then those classes will be smaller with 15 to 30 students.

Professors are approachable. Teaching assistants however, can be trickier. They are often busy themselves since they're grad students. Grades are often dependent on a handful of assignments so take it all seriously! Workload is manageable but can be a little heavy sometimes. No one ever has a lot of time on their hands. There is a student guide that is published each year—you can use that to get inside information on how most of the classes work and what the workload is like. It's called, *The Source.*

Employment Prospects

Alumnus/a, Pre-med, 9/2002-5/2006, January 2007

There are opportunities for prestigious jobs after graduation from the School of Management, but only for a handful of students who really excel academically, which is very difficult. The school claims there's no grade deflation, but after you get B after B with that ever illusive A just out of your reach, the students tend to think otherwise. Many students never even break a 3.0 GPA, so be wary of scholarships where you have to keep a 3.2 or better, few students keep them after their first semester. But there is a Career Center inside the School of Management that does a really great job at attracting top employers, especially for the accounting and finance majors. PricewaterhouseCoopers, Ernst and Young, Merrill Lynch, Accenture, Deloitte, GE Finance, Unilever, IBM Consultants, State Street, CIT, and JP Morgan are just naming a few. You won't find the Ivy-League companies like Goldman Sachs and Lehman Brothers though.

Current student, 9/2004-Submit Date, December 2006

I know that the School of Management and College of Communication offer great alumni network, conferences, and seminars. SMG helps you with your résumé and brings in people from Deloitte to do mock interviews. There have been many famous COM alumni, such as Howard Stern.

Current student, 9/2003-Submit Date, February 2006

Employment prospects from the university are good, with the sole but very real challenge that BU grads are competing with grads from other Boston-area schools, including MIT, Harvard and Tufts. BU, though, makes a point of having career fairs, though they are surprisingly poorly attended.

Current student, 9/2003-Submit Date, December 2005

Since Boston University is such a huge school, there are graduates from BU all over the country in all different industries. Boston University reads well on paper and will definitely help you find a job. The school offers good college counseling and a great alumni network.

Current student, 9/2003-Submit Date, August 2004

The school is very active in working with students toward internship possibilities and opportunities. BU acknowledges the importance of hands-on experience for any and all career types and does its best to help students acquire these positions, so that they may network and have better opportunities upon graduating from the undergrad program at the university. As for the College of Communications, and more specifically, the journalism major, BU is very unique in that it offers its undergrads the opportunity to intern one semester of their junior or senior year as a credentialed journalist in Washington, D.C. while taking classes. Their work is sent to papers around the nation and published, while the students gain invaluable insight and network with people a great deal to help set them up for job positions upon graduation of the university. This is the only program like it offered for undergrads in the nation.

Read all of Vault's College Surveys at **www.vault.com/college**–get complete surveys on 100s of colleges and universities, expert advice on applicaton essays and more.

VAULT CAREER LIBRARY 311

Quality of Life

Alumnus/a, Economics, 9/2002-5/2006, April 2007

BU is a very undergraduate student-friendly place. You get to live in the heart of the ultimate college city. All the new housing going up is great and the gym that opened up in the last year is probably the best university gym on the East Coast. They do a good job controlling crime—though the guest policy is a little restrictive. Just don't come to BU looking for the big green campus.

Current student, 9/2003-Submit Date, February 2006

Quality of life is unimpressive as a whole. The school has a commuter feel and the administration—especially the housing department—has a Gestapo mentality. Undergrads are treated as a necessary annoyance, a meal ticket of sorts for the grad kids and the research aspects of the school. Certainly do not expect to be coddled, because that's not going to happen! BU is most advisable for academically minded, independent and emotionally stable kids.

Alumnus/a, 9/2001-5/2003, December 2005

The student body is great, the teachers and academics are great, but the administration is lacking. They treat the students with disdain and mistrust and it often feels like you are in high school, not college. There is a definite disconnect between the two. A lot of the dorms are run like a prison in that you can't have visitors past certain times, you can't have overnight guests of the opposite sex and there is a lot of redtape as far as getting people in and out of the building, even BU students from other dorms! Best to get an on-campus apartment with less security than one of the main tower dorms.

The food is excellent. The cafeterias are great and the campus offers many restaurants for a great variety on the meal plan. You can get Starbucks, Jamba Juice, pizza, fruit, Ben and Jerry's, McDonald's and other fast food meals on the plan if you use the flex point option. They have a late-night grill in certain dorms, as well. The cafeteria has a huge selection of food and lots of seating.

Current student, 9/2003-Submit Date, August 2004

As BU is basically right in the City of Boston, the security on campus is very strict and actually rather effective in helping keep the students feel safe. Nearly all on-campus residences have security desks in the front of the buildings that are manned 24 hours a day. The housing facilities range from being average in quality to the high quality apartment-like housing that is available for mostly upperclassmen and perhaps a few very luck underclassmen. Dining is some of the best in the nation, from what I've heard, and they offer a great variety of food for all kinds of diets, whether vegetarian or not. Dining hours are very convenient as well.

Current student, 9/2003-Submit Date, May 2004

Housing is a great experience, especially if you're cool with your RA. West Campus is the best campus, period. It is the most sociable part of BU. I really enjoy it; it surrounds Nickerson field. The dining is great. Currently, West Campus has the newest dining hall, which is the best in the whole school. The campus itself is very city-like. Basically the school is placed vertically throughout Commonwealth Ave, and it looks nice. It seems as if Boston University is a neighborhood instead of a college.

Social Life

Alumnus/a, Pre-med, 9/2002-5/2006, January 2007

Greek life is minimal as many students choose the Boston background for their social scene. Hockey is a popular sport that gets a lot of school spirit, but don't expect the kind of face-painting fans at other Division I football schools. BU doesn't even have a football team. You will find a lot of international activities though. Most BU students are either living in another country and just came to the U.S. for BU or they were born in another country, but recently moved to the U.S. At one point I was in a team project and I was the only American on the team. One of my favorite activities was Casino Night, which is put on by the School of Management government association. BU is a very large school, but the School of Management does a really great job at creating a close-knit community within the school so you don't feel lost in the crowds.

Current student, 8/2003-Submit Date, February 2006

The Greek system is a minority, and being part of one means nothing. You can have as much fun being in a frat/sorority as you can if you abstain. There are bars/clubs of all types, from the $14 martini to the $1 beer. One thing that makes this a great city is that it has some form of entertainment for everyone. From the cinematography geek who likes obscure foreign films, to the Prada miniskirt dressed blonde, to the Greek jock who likes beers in a frat house, to any other niche in between, this city can cater. The dating scene does not get more attractive than it does in Boston. 50 universities and colleges providing half a million mostly single students between 18 and 24 years old who are dying to go out for a drink and forget about exams/papers/projects—go figure! It doesn't get any easier than this!

Current student, 9/2003-Submit Date, February 2006

The Greek system is functional, but just barely. Only about 10 percent of Terriers are involved, and all houses are (far) off campus. The administration accepts, but does not actively support, the Greek system. Social organizations are weak in general, and interaction among students is not actively fostered by the school. Unless, as a freshman, one is placed in one of the mostly-freshman dorms, he/she may go the first year not meeting more than a dozen or so people. Likewise, the New England mentality (read: icy) is quite present here, so don't expect warm smiles from strangers, or even smiles at all!

Alumnus/a, 9/2001-5/2003, December 2005

Boston is a great college city with lots of young people, bars and things to do at night. It is literally a few blocks away from Fenway and the heart of Boston. The T is easy accessible for anything you want to do. The nightclubs, where most concerts take place, are also right around the corner. The school is located on the Charles River and it is really beautiful in the spring time to see the building lit up and the rowers on the river. There is great shopping just a few T stops away and also the Boston Commons where people can hang out when it's warm. There are a lot of local CD stores and clothing stores that appeal to college kids. Boston has a lot to offer the tons of students in the area.

Current student, 9/2001-Submit Date, July 2004

The social life is great. Since there is a cluster of schools, you meet a lot of other students. Fenway Park is just around the corner. There are bars at just about every block. The school is not too far from downtown so there is a great variety of restaurants and clubs to choose from. The Greek system at BU is not too big. There is a few but it is not a big deal.

Current student, 9/2002-Submit Date, April 2004

The school is really diverse. Students come from all over the United States and many foreign countries as well, so there is plenty of opportunity to learn about different cultures. Students have numerous options for entertainment nearby. There are many clubs and bars within walking distance. Also, students can attend major events around Boston, such as the Boston Marathon. The Greek system is not that big at BU and seems less important than cultural clubs and academic organizations.

Brandeis University

Admissions Office
P.O. Box 549110
Waltham, MA 02454-9110
Admissions phone: (781) 736-3500 or (800) 622-0622
Admissions fax: (781) 736-3536
Admissions e-mail: sendinfo@brandeis.edu
Admissions URL: www.brandeis.edu/admissions/

Note: The school has chosen not to review the student surveys submitted.

Admissions

Alumnus/a, Mathematics, 8/2002-5/2006, April 2007

Every year Brandeis is becoming more and more selective. It's an excellent school, and more people are starting to realize that and apply.

About 25 percent of students are from Massachusetts, and another quarter are from New York, so your best bet is not to be from those areas. If you can't help it, you'll need an excellent transcript (including extracurriculars).

Standardized test scores are used less in admissions and more in financial aid. Simply put, if you get a 1500 or above on your SAT (old scoring, obviously), you will get offered merit-based money. It was this sort of offer that drew me to Brandeis, and I know the same is true for many of my friends and acquaintances.

Current student, 8/2005-Submit Date, December 2005

It was very important to write a good essay. I put a lot of effort in writing a coherent essay that reflects who I am and what college admissions expects from a prospective student. I felt quite confident about the interview. The interview went very well and I felt it may have made a difference in my application. I did not have much control over the rest, such as my high school grades and extracurricular activities.

Alumnus/a, Economics 8/2000-5/2004, March 2005

I am an international student, and for international students, the competition for financial aid is intense. I had significantly higher SAT scores than the school's average, and got a relatively large amount of financial aid. That said, I still feel that Brandeis is more generous with financial aid for international students than other schools that have a similar ranking. I think that SAT scores, class rank, and personality fit are the most important factors for admissions. You have to be an interesting person to get in, and I have seen candidates with better academic credentials than mine get rejected.

Alumnus/a, 8/1999-5/2003, November 2004

Brandeis gets more competitive every year. Good grades and test scores are imperative, but an interesting background is also helpful. In addition, the university is extremely committed to diversity including geographic (a large percent of students are from Massachusetts and New York, as well as New Jersey and California). The interview is a small part of the process but there are alumni all over the country who do them. However, I recommend doing it on campus if at all possible. The admissions office is extremely well-organized and staffed. They bend over backward to help and recruit. Also, Brandeis has excellent merit-and need-based aid packages.

Alumnus/a, 8/1999-5/2003, September 2004

The selection process at Brandeis has become more and more competitive. As a liberal arts school, a large amount of emphasis is placed on the essay/personal statement portion of the application. High SAT/ACT scores and a demonstrably good academic history are also important.

Alumnus/a, 8/1999-5/2003, April 2004

Brandeis is becoming more and more selective. They accept many international students, people from all 50 states, and people with something special about them. They look far beyond just grades—a difference that I think makes Brandeis really special. They want to see that you are a unique person with a history of interesting experiences, and they like leadership. Although competitive scores are important, they are not the last word. My SAT scores were low, but I had interesting and unique activities that they obviously considered highly.

Academics

Alumnus/a, Mathematics, 8/2002-5/2006, April 2007

Brandeis is an academic school—while that may sound like a redundancy, it's the truth. The focus of the school, above and beyond extracurriculars or athletics, is academics.

To that end, we have excellent faculty, tiny classes and moderate workloads. I rarely had poor classes, and when I did, it was usually because I was in one of those classes that had so many enrolled students that they'd broken it into sections for TAs to teach (which only happens with calculus and writing seminars).

Surprisingly, the hardest classes to get into are gym classes. The fun ones (Karate, Dance Dance Revolution) are tiny and go quickly. Similarly, language classes are hard to get into. But for the most part, Brandeis is small enough (3,200 undergrads) that you can nearly always get what you want.

Current student, 8/2005-Submit Date, December 2005

I am an undergraduate student. I think I want to major in politics, so I am trying to take courses in this field, but otherwise I am trying to get a wide range of courses. For instance, I am taking a course in philosophy as well as one on international relations. So far, I feel the classes are good but demand a lot of work. However, I am getting good grades. Professors at Brandeis University are very committed to their work. It was not hard to get in the classes that I wanted because there are so many from which to choose.

Alumnus/a, Economics 8/2000-5/2004, March 2005

Your academic experience depends entirely on your major. The school has a very strong pre-medical science program. However, there are almost no engineering classes, and the computer science department also has limited course offerings, and very few opportunities for research. I was an economics major, and the economics program is growing. Brandeis also has a young business school that is closely linked with the economics department, so there are opportunities to take graduate-level courses, as well as undergrad courses taught by business school professors. The economics major is also very flexible, so it is up to the student to take more rigorous or challenging courses. As for the humanities, the politics department is fairly strong. Other departments vary in their strengths.

Alumnus/a, 8/1999-5/2003, November 2004

Brandeis has relatively few required courses, but all programs are topnotch. It is a major research university with the size and feel of a small college. It is particularly strong in the sciences, both research and pre-med, and many students come here for this. However, the arts, particularly theater, are some of the best departments too. There is a strong commitment to cultural studies particularly surrounding the Middle East, partially because of the school's Jewish heritage. Most students have multiple majors and participate in interdisciplinary programs. Also, the school has some of the best graduate schools and undergrads have access to their resources. In addition to the sciences, this includes the Heller School for Social Policy and the International Business School. Class sizes are getting bigger, but there is a lot of academic flexibility.

Read all of Vault's College Surveys at **www.vault.com/college**—get complete surveys on 100s of colleges and universities, expert advice on applicaton essays and more.

VAULT CAREER LIBRARY 313

Alumnus/a, 8/1999-5/2003, September 2004

The general education requirements are few and far between. Often the most common complaint was finding a course to fulfill the "writing intensive" category. Outside of the sciences, many courses do not carry pre-requisites, and advanced classes are easy to get into. Most classes are small (six to 15 students) and are discussion based (especially in the social sciences and humanities). Many professors will expand their maximum number of students for upperclassmen. Professors are understanding but professional and foster positive relationships with their students. Workloads can be intense, but Brandeis has a (proportionately) very high percentage of double and triple (yes, triple) majors.

Current student, 1/2000-Submit Date, April 2004

Certain programs, such as biology, biochemistry and neuroscience, are very strong. Other programs, such as economics, are growing stronger, with, the addition of a business minor, and the establishment of a business school. A word of caution: Investigate the programs in which you are interested beforehand. In a small school, people who end up in weaker departments or majors are disappointed.

The professors are always accessible outside of the classroom; this is a major advantage of attending a small liberal arts school. Research opportunities are available for undergrads in both the sciences and the humanities. Another major strength that is always overlooked is the school's commitment to developing student leaders through the orientation program, and the resident advisor program.

Alumnus/a, 8/1999-5/2003, April 2004

In pretty much every department at Brandeis academics are exceptional. I studied science and psychology, and, our lab classes and others were incredibly rigorous. We have a truly distinguished and knowledgeable faculty: every class is absolutely taught by a professor with master's and PhD. Brandeis even has somewhat famous people teaching, like Stuart Altman from the Clinton Administration teaching about the American health care system in conjunction with Dr. Their, president of Partners Health care, or Robert Reich teaching Wealth and Poverty.

The teachers are completely dedicated to their students. I was impressed with their responsiveness to their students and availability, even on weekends. I have become very close with some professors through the extra time I spent working one-on-one with them outside of the classroom. I got so many recommendations for medical school that I had too many!

While I was taking classes I was cursing at the workload we were given, which does vary from class to class, honestly. But when I got through it, I was amazed at how much I had learned, especially in comparison to students at other colleges, as my friends reported. After Abnormal Psychology, I was reading case studies and diagnosing based on the DMS IV with newfound analytical skills. I designed and conducted an experiment and wrote a full APA publication-style paper with poster session, a skill that I used from that point forward in all of my writing.

 Employment Prospects

Alumnus/a, Mathematics, 8/2002-5/2006, April 2007

Brandeis pulls a lot of weight with some employers (generally those in the Northeast) and not at all with others. If I get: "Brandeis—that's in New York, right?" one more time, I may blow a gasket. We're a top tier-school, but some people outside the Boston area have never heard of us.

I'm sorry to say that the on-campus recruiting prospects are quite dim for many careers. While the career counselors are certainly very helpful people, there just are not enough career fairs or chances to meet with employers. However, if you want to go onto medical, dental or law school, Brandeis has fabulous connections with all the top schools in those areas.

Current student, 8/2005-Submit Date, December 2005

There is a Hiatt Center on campus that helps graduates to find jobs. I believe that this organization is effective and that there is also a strong alumni support. The school has a good amount of prestige around the country. Graduates obtain a wide variety of jobs, often not directly related to their majors.

Alumnus/a, 8/1999-5/2003, November 2004

The school is famous for getting a well above average number of students int professional and other graduate schools. A large number of students continue o to law and med school or get master's degrees. There are job and career fairs i Boston and New York and there are good networks within certain fields. It ca be hit or miss, but most students have great options when they graduate.

Alumnus/a, 8/1999-5/2003, September 2004

The Brandeis career center boasts an 80 percent rate of success in placing stu dents who utilize their resources. Unfortunately, their online job boards ar somewhat limited outside of financial and educational fields. Many program offer or require internships that provide valuable experience and contacts fo placement after graduation. A large percentage of Brandeis graduates go on t notable law, medical and graduate schools before looking for a job.

Current student, 1/2000-Submit Date, April 2004

The career center staff is very helpful. In a slower economy, however, fewe recruiters come to campus, so it is up to students to reach out to prospectiv employers. Being in the same location as extremely competitive schools, suc as Harvard and MIT, is also a little bit of a disadvantage when it comes to recruit ing. Additionally, a very large percentage of the student body heads to graduat school right after graduation, so students who are seeking jobs at graduatio have to be self-motivated.

Alumnus/a, 8/1999-5/2003, April 2004

Brandeis has an office for student career development. They have an extensiv web site with tips on résumé writing, interviewing and job application, with link to job search engines accessible only to Brandeis students. People from compa nies and internship programs actually recruit Brandeis students through th career center, and it seems there are job and internship fairs every week. Ther is free one-on-one career counseling available as well.

The career center was an invaluable service, and I don't know how I would hav prepared for my life after college without it. People definitely regard Brandei graduates very highly. Anyone knowledgeable about academia has heard o Brandeis and its good reputation. I even traveled to a medical school interviev in rural Missouri and was greeted with respect for Brandeis' undergraduate pro gram. I work at Brigham and Women's Hospital in Boston now, in conjunctio with Harvard Medical School—the reputation that Brandeis gives you is defi nitely a major advantage.

Quality of Life

Alumnus/a, Mathematics, 8/2002-5/2006, April 2007

Brandeis is possibly the safest place in the world. My second night as a fresh man, I walked the length of the campus at 4 a.m. and felt perfectly at home.

On-campus housing is mediocre and harder to get than it should be. They'r slowly revamping the housing—tearing down the old and putting up new—bu your best bet as an upperclassman is to live off campus. It's possible to get apart ments that are closer to campus than some of the on-campus housing, which i what I did my senior year. It was cheap and just as livable as the dorms.

The dining halls are a pleasant surprise for vegetarians/vegans. They actually provide options.

Current student, 8/2005-Submit Date, December 2005

Housing is very good and there is little crime on campus. Dining hours are no very flexible and the food is mediocre. The facilities are good, but not excep tional.

Current student, 1/2000-Submit Date, April 2004

The housing situation has improved with the opening of a new 220-bed, state of-the-art residence hall in 2003. Now, over 90 percent of students are able to obtain on-campus housing. Housing is assigned based on randomly generated lottery numbers, so the situation can get tense for people who get worse numbers and have to depend on friends to pull them into suites or doubles. I, however, have been able to obtain on-campus housing for all four years, so getting hous ing clearly isn't impossible.

Alumnus/a, 8/1999-5/2003, April 2004

Brandeis is probably the most impressive in the area of student life. Problems with meal plans, housing shortages and other policies through the four years that I attended the school were responded to by the administration with such haste that I have seen and benefited from all of the changes made during my stay at the university. I am truly amazed at how important the school thinks its students' opinions are and its responsiveness.

Dorm life is great—there are so many options for students and multiple cafeterias that accepts certain student meal points for every food need, including a kosher cafeteria, a late-night snack and pizza/sandwich store, and a coffee shop with fancy Starbucks-esque drinks and bagels. I was always very pleased. Campus safety is not even an issue! There are police on campus around the clock, and we have a student-run emergency medical corps with trained EMTs who are ready to respond to any emergency and call in paramedics or an ambulance when needed. I was part of that club, and I can tell you that our response time was pretty fast—at all hours of the night! We also have a van service that will bring you into downtown Waltham until late and pick you up.

 ## Social Life

Alumnus/a, Mathematics, 8/2002-5/2006, April 2007

There is no Greek system at Brandeis, except for the tiny percentage of people who skate around the system and have unrecognized frats. They're not the typical 'Deis students.

Waltham is renowned throughout Massachusetts for its excellent dining, and it's a well-deserved reputation. Every possible ethnicity is represented there.

Waltham is also home to a few bars, several of which are popular student hangouts, especially the Iguana Cantina: on Thursday nights, if you buy a drink, you get as many free tacos as you like.

The dating scene is interesting. Even for those non-matrimonial-minded among us, Brandeis seems to be the genesis for a lot of marriages. People tend to date one person for a long time rather than multiple people for short periods.

Current student, 8/2005-Submit Date, December 2005

The social life is a little bit lacking. The town has some good restaurants. There is a wide range of restaurants, some nice as well as some quick eats. The dating scene is not great.

There are four fraternities and two sororities. They are not recognized by the school and are somewhat of a joke. There are many diverse clubs, which suit the interests of anyone. Also, if one wants to participate in a club that does not exist one can do so by creating it. The school is very supportive toward such an ini-

tiative. I have friends who want to start a French Club and the administration has shown itself to be very supportive of the initiative.

Alumnus/a, 8/1999-5/2003, November 2004

Social life at Brandeis is good. There is a good mix of going to Boston and staying on campus for social opportunities. In addition, clubs are extremely active, but Greeks are not, so there are a lot of friendship networks that form. There are several all-school big parties each year, but mostly socializing happens on a smaller scale. The school runs free transportation to Boston and Waltham on weekends, which is great, and in addition many students have cars. But the heart of the social scene is parties on and near campus, as well as with activities and clubs.

Alumnus/a, 8/1999-5/2003, September 2004

Outside of religious functions, Brandeis seems to be lacking in social skills. The Greek life on campus is almost universally considered a total joke, and students prefer studies to parties. Deficient public transportation makes going out difficult for those students who would like to (trains only run until midnight or 1 a.m.) and cars seem to be an absolute necessity. There is, however, a large number of clubs and activities that take place on campus. For the activist group, organizations abound to nurture debate skills and campaign reform efforts.

Current student, 1/2000-Submit Date, April 2004

Greek life does exist [in some instances off campus], but fraternities and sororities are not officially recognized by the school. There is a very wide range of clubs with which you can get involved, if you are willing to make the time and effort. A lot of people complain that there isn't enough to do on campus, but I believe that that claim is not justified. In short, people who enjoy organizing club activities, or going out to a dinner and movie with friends, are much happier at Brandeis than people whose idea of fun is getting drunk three nights a week with their fraternity or sorority.

Alumnus/a, 8/1999-5/2003, April 2004

You will actually probably hear that Brandeis is filled with overly studious people who never socialize. I don't know where this stereotype came from, but that is the furthest thing from the truth! Not only are the over 200 clubs on campus with students active in arts, cultural activities, sports and other organizations, but there are many events, plays, arts and dance shows, and many dancing and clubbing events. There are $1 big-screen movies shown, as well. I had so much fun at Brandeis!

There are bars in downtown Waltham that students attend constantly, and we even have an on-campus restaurant with a bar that hosts many fun events. The international club hosts a clubbing event called Patchanga twice every semester. It is the most popular event on campus—people even come from other colleges, because it is huge. We have unique shows like the Liquid Latex Show, which I participated in two years. Students choreograph pieces and get painted in liquid latex costumes.

Read all of Vault's College Surveys at www.vault.com/college–get complete surveys on 100s of colleges and universities, expert advice on applicaton essays and more.

VAULT CAREER LIBRARY   315

College of the Holy Cross

Admissions Office
Fenwick Hall, Room 105
1 College Street
Worcester, MA 01610
Admissions phone: (800) 442-2421 or (508) 793-2443
Admissions fax: (508) 793-3888
Admissions e-mail: admissions@holycross.edu
Admissions URL: www.holycross.edu

 ## Admissions

Current student, 9/2005-Submit Date, August 2006

Admission to the college is difficult. The college particularly looks for kids who really stand out in high school. The school is begging for individuals. Find a way to stand out in high school, maintain solid grades, write an interview that will make you stand out and appear unique and have at least one solid recommendation. The school has become very selective recently, so just because it's not an Ivy League, don't expect to be accepted even if you're Ivy League material.

Alumnus/a, 8/1995-5/1999, September 2006

Holy Cross is highly selective, and becoming more so. Last year, applications jumped by 41 percent over the previous year, making the acceptance rate just 34 percent. Part of the increase in application numbers could be due to the school's decision last year to make submission of SAT and ACT scores optional. HC has always stressed performance in a challenging high school program (e.g., lots of AP and Honors courses with good grades) over standardized test scores. Nonetheless, the majority of this latest class were in the top 8 percent of their graduating classes.

Interviews are optional in the admissions process, but as one of the admissions counselors likes to say, "If you don't go for an interview, you're a moron." You should absolutely use every opportunity the college gives you to express your enthusiasm and be a face—not just a name. This summer, HC started offering optional seminars for high school students on the applications process, interview skills, and essay-writing. If you can make it, take advantage!

Early Decision is a good option if you are sure you want to go to HC. If you're waitlisted, keep in close contact with the Admissions Office. Send them new information on awards, community involvement and so on. The more you prove that you're interested, the more likely they are to admit you off the waitlist.

Current student, 8/2004-Submit Date, July 2006

The Admissions Office holds a ton of dinners and special events for prospective students. It looks really good to go to these events and stay in contact with the admissions faculty. I was a B- student with only a 1090 on my SAT and I bombed my SAT Subject Tests, but I showed that I was really dedicated to Holy Cross and that I would do all that I could to be a student there (even though I wanted to go to another school). I went to almost every prospective student event and I also scheduled overnight visits. You want to make sure they know who you are. Everyone in admissions is really, really nice and helpful and putting in the time will only serve to be beneficial—who gets anything without putting in effort?

Current student, 8/2000-Submit Date, March 2004

There is an application, which must be filled out and submitted. I applied Early Decision, which meant that if I got accepted I would be obliged to attend. They reviewed the application, which asked for such information as high school coursework, activities and recommendations from teachers. An interview was encouraged, but not necessary.

There was a choice of essay topics. The one I chose was actually rather fun; I had to write a letter to the person I was going into high school. I felt as though I could do a lot with that type of an essay. Some of the other options included who your role model was and which person you would meet, alive or dead, given the opportunity. Within two months, they sent me a letter in the mail granting me acceptance.

This school is very selective. Many students who attend here came from private Catholic high schools, and a good deal of us were in the top 10 of our class. Community service is also an aspect on which is heavily focused.

Alumnus/a, 8/1999-8/2003, May 2005

SAT of about 1200 required, as well as a good essay. I also went on an interview, which they recommend. Extracurriculars, community service, and other unique experiences are a plus. Early Decision is an available option.

> **Regarding admissions, the school says:** "Beginning with the class entering Holy Cross in the fall of 2006, the submission of standardized tests (SAT, SAT Subject Tests and ACT) is optional for admission."

 ## Academics

Current student, 9/2005-Submit Date, August 2006

A few years ago, the school was ranked as one of the Top 10 Most Overworked schools in the nation. It pays off, however. You really have to work for solid B's, and A's are not for everyone, even standout students. Academics can be described in one word: tough.

Alumnus/a, 8/1995-5/1999, September 2006

Holy Cross is an exclusively undergraduate liberal arts institution. The curriculum involves distribution requirements, not core classes. That means that you do have to take two semesters of a foreign language, two science/math courses, two English/literature, one history, one philosophy, one religion, one arts course, one cross-cultural studies course, and two social sciences. It's a Catholic school, but that does not mean that your religious studies distribution has to be in Catholicism. Courses within your major can count to complete distribution requirements. It sounds like a lot to ask, but it's really not hard to do in your four years at HC.

Students take four classes per semester. You can choose to take an additional course (for credit or as an audit) but your advisor has to approve your decision to add to your courseload.

Classes are demanding. Humanities classes require a good deal of writing and lots of reading. The science classes almost all include an additional lab during the course of the week. Teachers do not tolerate slackers, nor will your peers. That said, the competition that you'll find at Holy Cross isn't cutthroat; it's supportive. You enter into a community of learners who are genuinely excited about what they're pursuing, even if the teachers are tough graders.

HC almost guarantees that you'll get the courses you need to graduate. If you don't graduate in four years, almost 100 percent of the time, it's because you took time off or failed a class. It's not because your advisors steered you wrong or because you got closed out of a class you needed.

The student-to-teacher ratio at HC is 10:1, and the only people without terminal degrees in their fields are the foreign TAs who moderate the language speaking labs. They are enthusiastic about office hours and are known for being very accessible. Often, professors will cultivate promising students by involving them in their own research. More than 12 students each year are published along with their professors on research papers.

If HC doesn't offer the major you want, you can create your own with the help of your advisor. For example, one student created his own architecture major by combining math, fine arts, history and art history courses. He also studied abroad for a year, where he completed an independent study project on the architecture of European castles. The faculty is very supportive about initiatives like this.

Current student, 8/2004-Submit Date, July 2006

This school is really tough, especially for students coming from schools that don't adequately prepare them for college. If you want to have at least a 3.0 GPA, then you're going to have to study for at least two hours for each class. Not studying like memorizing but most classes have a lot of reading and note taking. It really depends on the professors, as well. I've had some really bad professors. Then I've had professors, who will sit down with you for as long as it takes to make sure that you can do well. Most of the professors I've met are very understanding, especially toward freshmen. They're not stupid, however, and they will be very frank and blunt with you if you start to slip up. It has been my experience that professors tend to grade tough but they're fair and they will sit down with you and help you figure out ways to improve your grades. If you put in the work they don't want to see you fail. Classes are either fun or boring, depending on your interests, and getting good classes depends on your definition of what good classes are.

Current student, 8/2000-Submit Date, March 2004

The academics at this school are very challenging. The professors assign a lot of work, and require a lot of critical thinking and reflection in the work. Among the most difficult majors are the sciences, which emphasize a discovery approach in the labs. Most of the professors are very friendly and charismatic. This being such a small school, professors know their students by name and are able genuinely to take interest in their college careers and personal lives. Classes are mostly easy to get into—preference is given to seniors first and then juniors, sophomores and freshmen. There is random selection among the classes. Grading is difficult. Generally it is pretty easy to get a B, but getting an A requires a lot of hard work and effort.

Alumnus/a, 8/1999-8/2003, May 2005

There is a heavy but manageable workload. Classes are never larger than 30 to 40, and are often smaller, so there's great attention to students from the professors. Professors encourage office visits, and really care about the students. A good variety and range of classes are offered, and it's very likely that you'll get the classes that you want. There is an option of getting signed into a class by the professor if you are unable to get in through regular registration. Classrooms are in new buildings with great features.

 Employment Prospects

Current student, 9/2005-Submit Date, August 2006

Holy Cross has some of the best career planning people in the country. HC alumni love to give HC students jobs, and HC does a great job of making sure kids find jobs that will pay good money, so in turn Holy Cross will receive money from alumni later on.

Alumnus/a, 9/1973-5/1977, February 2004

If you want to go to medical school, go here. If you want to go to law school, go here. If you want to be an accountant, go here. Holy Cross is well known as a great school in New England, NY and NJ and pretty much down through MD. They also produce excellent high school teachers and a wide variety of career options. Federal agencies love Holy Cross. 90 percent or more of graduates go on to post-graduate degrees.

Current student, 8/2000-Submit Date, March 2004

This college is very prestigious. Its pre-med program is quite well known and respected among medical, dental and veterinary schools. They frequently have internship and job opportunities. They use e-recruiting to apply to jobs through the school. They usually have employers come to campus to recruit, and they have a career counseling center to help students with their résumés, cover letters and to find jobs.

Alumnus/a, 8/1999-8/2003, May 2005

Holy Cross has one of the best alumni networks. The school is small enough to foster a great sense of community, and alumni and current students all share a sense of pride in the school, so alumni are always willing to help. Internship pro-

grams and study abroad programs are available. Many go on to graduate studies, and the rest find jobs with relative ease—anything from accounting to teaching. There are on-campus recruiting opportunities.

 **Quality of Life**

Current student, 9/2005-Submit Date, August 2006

Life is OK at Holy Cross. Worcester is kind of a run-down city. There are some great eating spots, as well as some nightlife. Bars like Irish Times and Raw-Bar are popular spots for kids. Drinking is a big deal, but as a non-drinker I can say that I have found plenty to do and plenty of accepting students at Holy Cross, even though it has a stereotype of being a conservative, uptight school. It's small, but big enough so that you don't know everyone, but you get to feel popular everywhere you go. Kids are friendly in one-on-one scenarios, but when they form in groups, sometimes people can get cliquish. The dorms are pretty solid, and the grossness of the dorm, depends on where you end up (Mulledy is awful because of freshmen; Healy is nicer). Then there are non-hill dorms, which are apartments and suites for the upperclassmen. The food is average college food, though we're about to get a Cold Stone Creamery on campus.

Current student, 8/2004-Submit Date, July 2006

Like any place, there is the good and the bad. The good is that many people here are friendly, at least the ones I know. Freshman year housing kind of stinks because they stick you with random people, but if you have roommate issues Res Life will do whatever it can to resolve them. I had a terrible roommate my freshman year, but we worked it out and she was placed in another room and my BFF moved in with me. The most crime on campus is drunken foolishness. There is simply something about alcohol that makes boys want to destroy things. Weekends can get loud and crazy and dorms are usually fined hefty fees because of property damage but other than that, living on campus is great. You get to do pretty much whatever you want and laundry is cheap.

Current student, 8/2000-Submit Date, March 2004

I think, this campus is liberal for a Catholic school and the quality of life is pretty good. A lot of the students have a lot of money and are kind of spoiled. There is a heavy drinking culture on and off campus, but there are things to do if you don't drink too. Housing on campus is guaranteed to those who want it. The rooms are much bigger than at other schools, and there is a new apartment complex for seniors. All the facilities are awesome. The dining leaves a lot to be desired, but then that's probably the case at any school. Generally the surrounding neighborhood is very safe.

Alumnus/a, 8/1999-8/2003, May 2005

There are many student organizations with which to become involved. The campus is beautiful, especially in the spring. It's a wonderful community environment. There are two main dining areas on campus, as well as a coffee shop and lobby shop. Campus safety is good, and van services are available to many places in the Worcester area. On-campus housing is available all four years. A new senior apartment building opened in fall 2003, and is a very popular choice for upperclassmen. Some students also live off campus, usually within walking distance.

The Holy Cross basketball team has done quite well in recent years, and has gone to the first round of the NCAAs in three of the past five years. They are at the top of the Patriot League. Other sports include swimming, football, lacrosse, soccer, rugby and field hockey.

 Social Life

Current student, 9/2005-Submit Date, August 2006

Social life is OK. The school does not do enough to put on events to stop kids from drinking. But, they do offer transportation to malls, Providence and Boston for weekend visits. The football team is average to bad, but the basketball teams are good. The dating scene is fairly nonexistent. You either hook up or get married. There is no Greek life. Spring weekend is usually pretty cool: carnival, big music events, combined with the fact that everyone is done with classes gives it a good feeling.

Read all of Vault's College Surveys at **www.vault.com/college**–get complete surveys on 100s of colleges and universities, expert advice on applicaton essays and more.

VAULT CAREER LIBRARY   **317**

Alumnus/a, 8/1995-5/1999, September 2006

Though the culture is dominated by students who drink (there are a lot of off-campus parties on Caro Street and the surrounding areas), there is plenty to do for students who don't. Favorite bars include The Irish Times. Worcester has a bunch of great restaurants, concentrated on Shrewsbury Street and including 111 Chop House (expensive), Cafe Dolce (delicious desserts), and Junior's Pizza. A great place to make your parents take you is The Sole Proprietor on Highland—excellent but pricey seafood. For a cheaper meal ($6 to $11), there's Mediterranean Cafe, which is behind the campus on Millbury St., a great option for a home-cooked Italian meal. If you're into music, try Ralph's Diner on Grove St.—a very funky joint with taxidermy on the walls, where gritty bands play. For bigger bands and tours, the DCU Center is right downtown.

Current student, 8/2004-Submit Date, July 2006

Some days the social scene is pretty hot, others it's not. It all depends on with whom you hang out. If you're like the rest of the campus, then you'll have a great time getting smashed every weekend and screaming and destroying property. If you were brought up with a modicum of self respect, you'll find that the invite-only parties are always hot. It's like the saying goes: "work hard, play harder." Holy Cross embodies that sentiment but I think it's great living here and the people I've met here are awesome. I wouldn't trade my experiences here for anything in the world. They could ease up on the homework though, because that puts a real damper on the social life.

Current student, 8/2000-Submit Date, March 2004

The social life is fairly active here. There are a lot of on-campus parties and also off-campus parties. Generally students pregame in their rooms on campus and then move off campus for the parties. There are lots of restaurants just a few miles from the campus. There are chain restaurants, but mostly there are a lot o privately owned restaurants, which are really tasty. I don't know much about the bars.

There are a lot clubs and organizations here. There are no Greek organizations. Specific student favorites are the SPUD program and the SGA. SPUD stands for Student Programs for Urban Development, which is a community service organization, and SGA stands for Student Government Association, which sponsors a lot of programs on campus. In addition, there are several immersion programs where students can travel to other countries or areas to help the poor. There is a good study abroad program for junior year, as well.

Alumnus/a, 8/1999-8/2003, May 2005

Very good social life, although no Greek system since it is a Jesuit school. There are many bars and restaurants a short cab ride or drive away from the school. Bars often cater to Holy Cross students by offering discounts and drink specials on certain nights of the week. Bars will often hire Holy Cross students to attract the college crowd. The Worcester Centrum hosts several concerts and other events throughout the year. Great bars include Mahoney's, Irish Times and Plantation Club; popular restaurants include Flying Rhinos, Pizzeria Delight, and Corner Grill

Emerson College

Undergraduate Admission
120 Boylston Street
Boston, MA 02116-4624
Admissions phone: (617) 824-8600
Admissions fax: (617) 824-8609
Admissions e-mail: admission@emerson.edu
Admissions URL:
admission.emerson.edu/admission/undergraduate/

 Admissions

Current student, Communications, 9/2005-Submit Date, April 2007

The admissions process at Emerson is great. The Early Action option on the application is a great way to go, with a decision being sent to you just a month after submitting your application. Overall, the application process is pretty painless. They also don't require interviews, which takes some stress off the process. The best part about the program is the campus visit/tours. The tour guides are the best I've ever encountered, extremely knowledgeable and helpful.

Alumnus/a, 9/2000-6/2004, September 2005

I applied for early admission and had an interview. This demonstrated my sincere commitment to attending Emerson. I also auditioned for the theater program. A good audition and a good interview can certainly do a lot for your chances of being accepted. The essay is standard, SAT scores count, but a good interview or transcript can makeup for bad scores. In my case, I had good SAT scores and a poor transcript, and I believe it was my audition and interview that put me over the top and got me into Emerson.

Current student, 9/2003-Submit Date, April 2005

I requested an application be sent to my house after I checked out the school's web site, as referred by a friend. It was a fairly typical college application with the exception of questions regarding which extracurricular activity meant most to me; and whom, within the media I admired and why. The essay asked about what my own personal background could bring to the Emerson community, but I think I may have submitted an essay on a different topic because I thought the

question they asked was a bit lame. I did not go on an interview because it wasn't necessary (and I never even visited the school until I eventually moved in). I don't know how different the selectivity is today compared with two years ago when I applied, but I don't know if I would be accepted if I were to apply this year with the same GPA that I acquired in high school.

Current student, 9/2003-Submit Date, April 2005

Apply early. It can be an advantage to have your application reviewed first, as many of the programs fill up quickly and scholarships will still be available. Make sure your essay is well thought out and make sure that it shows the committee that you are applying to the appropriate program. The writing programs are very competitive and require a writing sample.

> **The school states:** "Writing samples are recommended, not required."

Alumnus/a, 6/1999-12/2003, May 2004

The process was quite simple. I heard from many friends who were going to college in the Boston area that it is easier to transfer than start as a freshman. Interviews at Emerson are not required, and I never actually had to interview to get into the school. I did, however speak with many students at parties on my own and through social events that were set up through the school, which ultimately led me to transferring. I wrote the essay in one night; need I say more? I hear that it is more difficult to get into Emerson now as opposed to four years ago. I know that you need to have a good SAT score and strong grades to be selected.

Current student, 9/2002-Submit Date, April 2005

When I applied to the college, I had no idea what to expect. I thought I had a decent chance of getting in because I had a really good high school GPA. The best thing to do to get in is to have really good grades and be involved with a lot of stuff in high school. This is because, at Emerson, you will need to be involved with many extracurricular activities, so they obviously want people who are already used to that.

Make sure you write a really good essay; I edited mine nine times before I sent it in because I wanted it to be perfect. They ask a specific question for a reason because it shows them what type of person you are so answer it very truthfully nd make sure there are no mistakes in your spelling or grammar. Be creative with it.

The admission counselors are extremely helpful and if you have any questions they will definitely answer them for you. Also, students do work in the office and are trained to be extremely knowledgeable as well so pretty much any question you have will be answered if you give them a call or come in for a meeting. There aren't interviews (except for some performing arts students) but you can speak to a counselor any time to get your questions answered. The application dates are pretty strict, as well.

ust be truthful with everything and show your enthusiasm for the school and hey will love you. Test scores are somewhat important but they look at everything you send in so don't worry if you didn't do as well as you had hoped.

Academics

Alumnus/a, 9/2000-6/2004, September 2005

The staff is quality. The theater program is rightfully renown. Grading is fair and impartial. The workload is light, and classroom dynamics are good. Small class size helps nurture a good learning environment. Overall, Emerson is a place where one can drift by and get a degree without too much effort, but also a place where if you put enough into it, you can leave with an Ivy League-level education.

Alumnus/a, 9/1999-5/2003, October 2005

If you get a [550] or higher on the SAT in math, you do not need to take math at Emerson. If you complete three years of high school language, you do not need to take language. Only one science class is required and I thoroughly enjoyed mine. The classes are small, 15 to 20 students, and essay heavy. The performing arts program is topnotch and requires full commitment. There is a lot of reading and writing at this school.

Current student, 9/2003-Submit Date, April 2005

The classes are amazing, and I mean it. The largest class I've ever had was one with roughly 60 students, and that's still small compared to other schools. With the exception of maybe one or two classes within a school year, all my other classes have been 20 students or fewer. I knew my professors well, and they knew me, too. My professors made themselves available always, despite what subject they taught. They would give their phone number, e-mail address, and even their AIM screen name. All my teachers have been very knowledgeable in their field and some are working in the media business so they can tell you all about the real world. I never feel like an anonymous face in a crowd.

Grading is tough and fair. It's different at Emerson because instead of being graded on a 10-page essay, you may be graded on a five-minute short film shot with a DV camera, which takes up a comparable amount of time as writing a paper, if not more. Workload tends to increase as projects and homework assignments pile up in class, and that's not including all the extra co-curricular activities that people get involved in. Registering is pretty tough and you just have to luck out if you may want a specific class. It gets easier as you become an upperclassman, and isn't that the same case for all schools? But fear not, because students get into all of the classes they need.

Current student, 9/2002-Submit Date, April 2005

The academic program is extremely good. You have to take two writing classes your freshman year and then you need to take some philosophy classes, history classes, and other general education type of classes. The highest number of students that will be in a class is about 60. Most of your major concentration classes are about 17. This lets you get to know all your teachers extremely well.

Registration is done online, so you never have to wait in a line to sign up for classes but upperclassmen get preference on registration times. Most really popular classes are available, however sometimes photography classes are a little hard to get into. You can take classes at Mass College of Art, Berklee College of Music, the School of the Museum of Fine Arts, Boston Architectural Center, and Boston Conservatory.

Grading is different depending on which professor you have. Some teachers will have tons of work to do and some won't. The classes where you will get the most work are in your major because they are training you to get a job. They will make you work and you better be able to take criticism, because the teachers will be brutally honest with you.

Most professors will give you their home phone number or their cell phone number and will tell you to call them if you have any problems. And a lot of teachers still work in the field in which they teach. One of my journalism teachers was the assignment editor for a local news program and still taught my class twice a week and it was a great experience. Most lecture classes have a midterm and a final, but many other classes have final projects to work on. Final projects are the best thing ever because you don't have to go to class on your final day and you can do all the work on your own time instead of taking a test. And it shows how you do with what you want to be doing in the future.

No one really ever talks about their grades either so there isn't pressure from other students to get good grades, but the pressure comes from wanting your work to be as good quality as other students in your class. No one really complains about their grades all because most students realize when they are going to get a job no one is going to ask them what their GPA was in college.

Current student, Communications, 9/2005-Submit Date, April 2007

The communications program at Emerson is based very much on professionalism. All of our classes within the curriculum encourage and support real-world thinking and professors treat students as associates or equals. The workload includes lots of team projects, which again equate to real-world situations and support leadership.

Alumnus/a, 6/1999-12/2003, May 2004

Overall, I would give the program an average score. It really depended on the [faculty you had] and how much you wanted to challenge yourself. The classes were hands-on in that we were actually put in real-life situations with almost every class. I actually hold a speech degree, which focuses on advertising, marketing and public relations. We were required to take many public speaking classes, which taught us how to write speeches and create presentations in various settings. The program did a pretty good job of simulating what the real world would be like.

It wasn't that difficult to get the classes I wanted. Most of them were required, and so it mainly came down to making sure you fulfilled the core curriculum for your major. There are, however, classes outside of your major that I imagine would be a bit more difficult to get into, but I think that as long as you sign up as early as you can, you should be fine.

For the most part, I feel like the teachers graded fairly. I think it is sometimes difficult for the teacher to say which student's work is better, [for instance when a marketing grade] is based on coming up with good ad campaigns and writing press releases. It is just a matter of opinion. I understand that there are fundamental strategies, which need to be present in marketing and public relations; however, some teachers were set in their ways when it came to strategizing the best idea. I guess you would find that at any school.

Employment Prospects

Alumnus/a, 9/2000-6/2004, September 2005

If you're planning on a career in film or television, Emerson is a great place to start. Their Career Services staff is extraordinarily helpful. The theater program is widely respected, and many graduates I know have found good work in the field. I have friends who are now acting and directing professionally who graduated only two years ago. Every degree program at Emerson is geared toward real-life, career-oriented skills. Emerson grooms students for careers in their chosen fields; in that way, it is sort of a vocational liberal arts school. The film, radio and television programs are all very hands-on. A film degree from Emerson demonstrates that a student knows how films are made; how the writing process works, how funding is obtained, and how a shoot is organized. With nearly 40 percent of the student body at Emerson studying film, it is a great place to start a career in that field.

Read all of Vault's College Surveys at **www.vault.com/college**–get complete surveys on 100s of colleges and universities, expert advice on applicaton essays and more.

VAULT CAREER LIBRARY **319**

Current student, Communications, 9/2005-Submit Date, April 2007

We have very high job-placement rates at Emerson because of the professional atmosphere that is here on campus. Everyone is very career-oriented, and very focused on gaining relevant skills for the years after graduation. The Career Services offices and alumni networking opportunities are incredible.

Current student, 9/2002-Submit Date, April 2005

If you come here for one of the programs other than performing arts, I don't want to say you will be guaranteed a job, but you will be trained better than any other institution in the country for whatever field in which you want to be. Our TV majors get to solve their problems and make all their mistakes while in college instead of making them while working on a production in the real world. Students have already been through the toughest criticism they can take in class, so if a producer starts yelling, they know what to do when out in the real world. In journalism, they teach you how to look on camera, how to write and edit your news stories. And this is taught by teachers who have been working in the field for a long time.

One of my teachers actually brags that all her students get jobs because of how tough she is with them. And I don't think she is lying. Our alumni base is excellent—employers will look at what you have done because of all of the great alumni who have come out of here. Some recent graduates that I know work for an MTV show, one worked for a late-night talk show, and a few work for small TV or radio stations. I'm sure there are people who have better jobs, but I just don't know what they are. If you come here and work hard in your classes and in organizations, you will get a job. There is really not too much to worry about.

Alumnus/a, 9/1995-12/1999, May 2004

This school has amazing career prospects. That is actually one of the reasons I chose it. In every field, the school offers [a study abroad program in the Netherlands]. They also have an internship program for seniors in Los Angeles. Because so much of the school's focus is in the entertainment field (broadcasting, film, television), [you are given the opportunity to position yourself in Los Angeles with] an internship where you will earn anywhere from two to 16 credits. They have housing and available internships ready for the Los Angeles students when they come out. [Academic] classes are offered with the program as well. Many students find quick job placement after their internship is over.

Emerson College is considered one of the most wired schools in the nation. It has also been called the Ivy League school for misfits. It is most definitely well regarded by employers. Good, strong, hard workers come out of that school, and people are becoming more aware of it every day as this little campus builds popularity throughout the U.S.

Quality of Life

Current student, Communications, 9/2005-Submit Date, April 2007

We have the best of both worlds, being a small, focused school with all the benefits of being in a major city. Boston is incredible and Emerson really uses Boston as part of its campus. Classes will often go to museums or sites to do on-site projects or to learn something relevant to current events. The dorms are huge, the food is good and the neighborhood is fine. Make sure to use the buddy system at night, but that's just common sense.

Alumnus/a, 9/2000-6/2004, September 2005

Housing on campus is limited (roughly [half] of Emerson students live on campus), but the City of Boston has plenty of affordable housing. The location is safe during the day and somewhat dangerous at night. Students tend to move in groups, and there are very few incidents reported each semester. A student's safety depends mainly on his or her living situation. If you live in Dorchester, you are less safe than if you live in Back Bay, obviously. Most Emerson students tend to live in the suburbs of Allston or Brighton, which are very safe areas. Living on campus, however, is probably the safest housing for an Emerson student as the dorms are secure. Dining facilities on campus are adequate.

Current student, 9/2003-Submit Date, April 2005

Topnotch. I live in the dorms and they are always nice. Never any problems with heat, water, mice—anything. Dining hall food is fairly standard and I don't have any complaints. Other kids complain but that's just because they eat too

much and feel gross about it. After all, it's buffet style eating. We live right in downtown Boston, a block away from Chinatown, the Theater District, swank shopping areas, and just about everything. Boston is a city, so you just have to be prudent about safety. Obviously, you don't want to be out walking alone in the park at 3 a.m. If you are smart and sensible, you should never run into any problems feeling unsafe. Besides, the public safety office is located right in the lobby of the main building and they are always on call.

Current student, 9/2002-Submit Date, April 2005

Emerson is a pretty safe place. We are in the middle of a major city so sometimes there can be issues but our public safety officers do a good job of keeping us safe. There is enough housing for about half the student body but we have an off-campus service office that is second to none and has found students apartments within days. Most upperclassmen choose to live off campus, so housing is guaranteed for freshmen and most sophomores. After that, there's a lottery done by computer.

Our facilities are second to none as well—we have three beautiful theaters for performing arts majors including the Broadway-style Cutler Majestic Theater. Our TV studios are brand-new as well so you will be working with the latest technology; they are great at keeping up-to-date with what is being used in the workplace. But like everything else, you will only get out of it what you put into your work.

Social Life

Alumnus/a, 9/2000-6/2004, September 2005

Greek life is barely visible on campus. The student body is overwhelmingly liberal. Many people are politically active. Because, as Emerson puts it, "the city is your campus," the nightlife, dating, bars and restaurants of Emerson are the same as Boston's. At Emerson, Boston truly is your campus. And Boston is a relatively small city with plenty to do. Bars abound, as do music venues and clubs. Big bands regularly come through and play bigger venues like the Fleet Center or the Tweeter Center. Red Sox games are a popular pastime for college kids. Also, because the Boston area boasts more colleges and universities than almost any other place in the world, there are a ton of young people to meet and socialize with across the city.

Current student, 9/2003-Submit Date, April 2005

Boston is insane because there are always parades throughout the year for the sports teams (like the Pats and Sox), the Boston Marathon, the Boston Underground Film Festival, and tons of other events. Greek life here is pretty much a joke. Only 5 percent of our entire body is involved in them and we don't have houses for obvious reasons. Just goes to show that if you come to Emerson, you don't have to join a frat or sorority to have a social life. My personal Emerson favorites are the comedy troupe performances, walking around the Boston Common and Public Garden, the North End (the Italian area), being able to escape to the other Boston colleges within 20 minutes on the subway, and going to the stores that offer amazing student discounts.

Alumnus/a, 6/1999-12/2003, May 2004

There were many places students went to on the weekends. A lot of students would go to the Middle East Club to see live shows or TT The Bears in Cambridge. I think many students socialized with other kids from different universities as well. I had a lot of friends that went to Boston University. Boston was a great city in which to go to school, because there are so many people there doing the same thing as you, and it is a great place to meet people.

Current student, Communications, 9/2005-Submit Date, April 2007

There is a lot going on all the time, both on campus and in the city. There are several local venues where you can find lots of Emerson students hanging out, and if you're tired of the same old bar, there are so many more to check out. Again, all the benefits of a small school combined with the major city's activities makes for a perfect balance.

The School Says

Since its beginning in 1880, Emerson College has been a place for those unique students for whom thought and experience overlap: thinking is linked to doing. At Emerson, students discover their perspectives and put them to use. A rich liberal arts curriculum is paired with concentrated studies in all areas of communication sciences and arts, giving students here the perfect balance of knowledge and know-how.

Emerson in Boston

With dozens of institutions of higher education, Boston is arguably one of the country's best known college towns and the city contains a wealth of diversions ranging from scenic harbor cruises, Boston Pops concerts, and neighborhood festivals to baseball's Fenway Park, book and music stores, and the legendary Boston Marathon. An international center for technology, finance and medicine, Boston is a world-class city. Yet, with a population of around 600,000, it is manageable and easily navigated on foot.

Emerson's campus is located on Boston Common in the heart of the city's Theatre District—within sight of the Massachusetts State House and walking distance from the historic Freedom Trail, Boston Public Garden, Quincy Market, Chinatown and numerous restaurants and museums.

There are more than 60 student organizations and performance groups, 13 NCAA teams, student publications, and honor societies at Emerson. Hundreds of academic internships exist throughout Boston and in major cities across the United States, including exclusive placements through the College's Los Angeles Center. The College also sponsors study abroad programs in The Netherlands, Czech Republic, and Taiwan, as well as and course cross-registration with the six-member Boston ProArts Consortium.

Facilities

Emerson is home to WERS-FM, Boston's oldest noncommercial radio station; the historic 1,200-seat Cutler Majestic Theatre; and Ploughshares, the award-winning literary journal for new writing. More than 1,300 students are housed on campus, some in special living/learning communities such as the Writers' Block and Digital Culture Floor. There is also a fitness center, athletic field and new gymnasium. Our 14-story Piano Row College Center and Residence Hall just opened to rave reviews and current construction projects include extensive renovations to the historic Paramount Theater complex (to be completed in 2009).

We also possess the highest quality visual and media arts equipment, including sound-treated television studios, digital editing labs, audio post-production suites with analog and digital peripherals, industry-standard software, and a professional marketing suite/focus group room. There are two radio stations, seven on-campus facilities and programs to observe speech and hearing therapy, and an integrated digital newsroom for aspiring journalists. Our Tufte Performance and Production Center houses performance and rehearsal space, a theatre design/technology center, makeup lab, costume shop and television studios.

Hampshire College

Admissions Office
Hampshire College
893 West Street
Amherst, MA 01002
Admission phone: (413) 559-5471
Admission fax: (413) 559-5631
Admission e-mail: admissions@hampshire.edu
Admissions URL: www.hampshire.edu

Admissions

Current student, 9/2005-Submit Date, June 2007

The admissions process at Hampshire was different from that of the other schools to which I applied. On most applications my primary concern was how my GPA and SAT scores would measure up to the other thousands of applicants, I knew that Hampshire focused less on the numbers and more on who I was at the core. Because of this, I invested a great deal of time and energy into the creative aspects of my application. I made a point of writing a strong essay specifically catered to my Hampshire application, seeking out a college interview, and touring the school multiple times to ensure that it was the right fit for me.

Current student, Education, 7/2006-Submit Date, May 2007

Hampshire admissions is about showing your individuality and ability to take the initiative. The application is a combination of the Common Application with a few essay supplements. The essay questions are unique, so no copying and pasting other application essays! Having an interview is highly recommended but not mandatory. Hampshire is becoming more selective as more people begin to apply, but as long as you can argue for yourself you shouldn't worry.

Current student, Education, 9/2003-Submit Date, May 2007

I found the admissions process to be really helpful—from the people I spoke with in the office to the publications I received in the mail—I really felt like the admissions office cared about its prospective students.

I think that something I worked really hard on as I applied was to ensure that I set myself apart from the other applicants. I made sure that my writing samples were strong and I also had an interview. Having an interview was really helpful because it was also a time for me to learn more about Hampshire.

Current student, 9/2005-Submit Date, May 2007

Interview! This was certainly the most important part of the admissions process for me. The interviews are a great way to show that you are a good fit for the school, but also for you to ask any questions you might have in a one-on-one situation. The interviews run like conversations: they are comfortable and really allow you to show why it is you should be at Hampshire. Additionally, the student interns in the office are great: they actually answer your questions truthfully.

Current student, 9/2004-Submit Date, May 2007

I felt that Hampshire was pretty much self-selecting. Beyond that, I think they were really just looking for those who would be most successful at the school. So, the interview was really important. Even though they were important to my mom, standardized tests were pretty much irrelevant to the Hampshire admissions process. Basically, put your best foot forward, be passionate about things, let it show and, if you can, have an interview. If you can't make it to the school, there are probably alumni interviewers in your area, or admissions counselors who travel to your region. I found the admissions staff extremely helpful, don't hesitate to give them a call if you have any questions!

Read all of Vault's College Surveys at **www.vault.com/college**—get complete surveys on 100s of colleges and universities, expert advice on applicaton essays and more.

VAULT CAREER LIBRARY   321

Current student, 9/2004-Submit Date, May 2007

I applied Early Action and visited the school after I had submitted my application. When I visited, I toured the campus and interviewed with one of the admissions counselors. The tour I had was decent, but nothing extraordinary. My interview was actually really great, I appreciated the questions that my interviewer asked and I felt at the end that she really listened.

Alumnus/a, Chemistry, 1/2003-4/2007, June 2007

It's easy. I would suggest writing about weird or alternative topics and including radical thinking, staying with social change or revolution or issues dealing with humanity and so on. The most important part of your application is the writing. Write it well and revise, revise, revise.

Academics

Current student, 9/2005-Submit Date, June 2007

The Hampshire education is different. With no tests, no grades, and entirely self-designed majors, the academic focus no longer becomes a number game for students. Students complete each course with a final semester evaluation. This is a narrative evaluation from the professor evaluating the student's progress in the course. With an evaluation, there is no cap on excellence. Whereas an A is the highest of honors at most schools, an evaluation always leaves room for growth.

The no-test-no-grade system also means that classes are small, and professors must pay particularly close attention to all students. At Hampshire, student-professor relationships are built on trust and ongoing communication. This is key to the success of such an independent academic program.

Current student, Education, 7/2006-Submit Date, May 2007

We have no grades and no majors. Students receive narrative evaluations at the end of each semester from their professors. The academic structure is divided into three Divisions. Division I is the first year. This is time to try out different classes and professors and to explore your interests. Division II is called the concentration and lasts two years. It is a combination of eight classes, internships and study abroad opportunities. This is when you should begin to narrow down your interests into one area. Division III is your fourth year. You have to write almost a whole graduate school thesis in one year. The topics are quite varied from inventing a snowboard for paralyzed people to ethnography of a South African apartheid primary school. To make sure that no student gets lost with all the academic freedom, each student has two advisors. These advisors are professors from Hampshire or the other four colleges in the five college consortium (Hampshire, Amherst, Smith, Mount Holyoke and UMass Amherst).

Current student, Education, 9/2003-Submit Date, May 2007

The academic program is very self-directed, which is something that works for some people, but does not work for others. We create our own academic programs here so it demands that students are motivated and passionate about learning.

The classes are usually pretty specific and very interesting and they are primarily all small and lecture based. The workload is definitely heavy, but not unmanageable.

The professors are incredibly invested in each student and they are just as excited to learn from us as we are from them. I never thought that I would've had such close and comfortable relationships with my professors.

At Hampshire, we also do not have letter grades. Instead we get narrative evaluations from our professors who describe in detail our performance in the class and the individual pieces of work that we completed. These are much more specific and helpful than getting generic letter grades.

Alumnus/a, Chemistry, 1/2003-4/2007, June 2007

If you plan to major in art or writing, you will have a very difficult time getting into classes you want. Writing concentrators only get to take one writing class a semester, and oftentimes these classes are only offered once. However, any other school is a safe bet, and certain professors you will find are qualified and ready to help.

Current student, 1/2005-Submit Date, September 2005

The classes and professors are excellent although they may seem obscure. It more "get what you give" than other schools because you do not receive grade You are required to do a lot of homework. Students are often found at 9 a.m. their way to class bleary eyed and proclaiming "I was just up all night preparing for this class!" or "I just finished my 10-page paper on the Effect of Colonialis on Latinos in the United States now."

Alumnus/a, 9/1999-9/2003, January 2005

It is a very unique college academically. Classes are very discussion-based. We don't have GPA systems. Professors are very approachable. We don't use tex books but original texts. Interdisciplinary activities are very strong Hampshire. There is a program called CBD, Culture, Brain and Developmen They very generously sponsor students who are interested in combining cogni tive science with cultural studies (or any humanities). The school is very arti tically oriented, and also politically. There are a lot of activists on campus. B recently, the school seems to put forth efforts in developing the science depar ment.

> **The school says:** "The sciences are also very strong and encour-age student-designed research and activism."

Employment Prospects

Current student, Education, 7/2006-Submit Date, May 2007

We have CORC, or Career Options Resource Center. It is an amazing resourc that connects students with all internships and graduate schools. We have rough ly 8,000 alumni and most of them are really willing to work with current stu dents.

Current student, Education, 9/2003-Submit Date, May 2007

The on-campus resources for job opportunities, internships and graduate school are incredible and I have utilized them quite a bit. My impression is that man graduates use their Hampshire education to start their own businesses, wor within the arts or teach. I feel as if Hampshire is great preparation for the re world, and I feel ready to go out and put my degree and knowledge to good us

Current student, 9/2004-Submit Date, May 2007

Hampshire has an excellent Career Options Resource Center and I am on i database to receive lists of internships, graduate programs and employmen opportunities via e-mail. Every single day I get this list of 10 to 20 job oppo tunities that all sound great. They also include opportunities with alumni in th film, theater, art and music industries. They also offer a limited number of sum mer internship grants, which I was lucky enough to receive this year to do a internship in my area of study that I wouldn't have been able to do otherwise because it is unpaid.

Current student, 9/2004-Submit Date, May 2007

We have a Career Options Resource Center on campus to assist students in find ing internships and employment while students and after graduation. This offic coordinates with alumni in this process as well. Generally, I believe that stu dents have access to the jobs that they desire and have help in getting them.

Quality of Life

Current student, Education, 7/2006-Submit Date, May 2007

Most students joke that we all go to: "Camp Hamp." The school is surrounde by 800 acres of beautiful forest behind us as well as a running farm (with lla mas). But it is never isolated because a five-minute bus ride away is UMass an Amherst with thousands of other college students. Typically students a Hampshire are classified as extremely liberal, but of course there are hundred of different facets of liberal. By no means do we all think alike. Hampshire i also an extremely safe campus. There is very little crime that happens, beside the occasional bicycle theft.

Current student, Education, 9/2003-Submit Date, May 2007

At Hampshire we have dormitories, which are the best way to meet people the first year, and then most upperclassmen move into the on-campus apartments. Both of these are great options and allow for people to live with people with whom they are close.

This is a pretty safe campus, and there are lots of people who are here for our safety when and if we need it.

Current student, 9/2005-Submit Date, May 2007

The campus facilities are often no-frills, but that is not to say they don't provide: Hampshire students have access to everything they need. They are also welcome to use many of the resources (libraries!) at the other four schools in the consortium. The housing situation is excellent; even during times of housing crunches, Hampshire students have more space than they would at almost any other academic institution. The dining commons are, well, institutional. They are not spectacular, but there are enough options and ways to customize your food that you can make things work (plus, you usually only have to deal with them for a year, then you live in on-campus apartments where you can cook whatever you want). As a female student, I have never felt unsafe at Hampshire. While it is, of course, important to exercise common sense (i.e., don't walk around in the woods alone at 3 a.m.), Hampshire's campus is very safe and has little crime.

Current student, 9/2004-Submit Date, May 2007

This part of the U.S., the pioneer valley of western Massachusetts, is a wonderful area full of art and cultural activities in addition to many outdoor recreational opportunities. The campus is not gorgeous, but it is well used and loved by students. Housing consists of two dormitory buildings and three neighborhoods of on-campus apartments. These allow for the most rewarding social activities in which a group of people negotiates how to share space (and maybe food and so on). The campus facilities that exist are sufficient for student life, but the students and the administration both acknowledge that the student body would like to have more space and more flexible spaces for gathering, meeting, performing and so on.

Current student, 1/2005-Submit Date, September 2005

Housing is awesome because once you get out of the dorms (usually after a year), you can live with people you like in an on-campus apartment in one of the three little villages. Most of the population lives in these. They have bathrooms and kitchens and living rooms. Sometimes people let the apartments get a little disgusting, but come on, what else is new? Some apartments are theme based; for example, there is a greenhouse mod, a kosher mod, a women of color mod, a vegan mod and so on.

Social Life

Current student, Education, 7/2006-Submit Date, May 2007

There is no Greek life at Hampshire. Hampshire is a very mellow school that enjoys outdoor adventures and listening to music. There is a bar in town but it is frequented mostly by UMass and Amherst students. The dating scene depends on your particular sexual orientation. We have a wide variety of students here and most seem to find someone.

Current student, Education, 9/2003-Submit Date, May 2007

We have a ton of student groups on campus, ranging from more academically geared groups to others that are just for fun. Additionally, since we are located in the Five-College Consortium, we are able to utilize the activities, classes, libraries and various other resources at those other schools.

We do have parties, but they are not the central form of social life here. There are also tons of restaurants and bars within 10 minutes of our campus, and we have a free bus system that links Hampshire with the other schools in the area as well as with the nearby towns.

Current student, 9/2005-Submit Date, May 2007

There are dozens of amazing restaurants from which to choose in Amherst and Northampton featuring just about every kind of cuisine you can imagine. The social situation at Hampshire is amazing—students can sit down for lunch with a total stranger like it's no big deal. Most everyone is friendly and everyone is funky in one way or another. The student population is also very active: People genuinely care about what is going on in their community.

Current student, 9/2004-Submit Date, May 2007

The local towns have a lot to offer in terms of dining, museums, bars and so on. There are four other college campuses in the immediate vicinity making for a robust student oriented economy. Between these campuses there are always lectures, performances, movies and concerts happening. On campus, students put on shows or bring in acts regularly throughout the year (both live, and exhibited work). Students on campus organize groups around a variety of issues from Local Food to Circus performance. These clubs are a vital part of campus life. There is no Greek system on campus, but individual halls or houses host parties throughout the year.

Alumnus/a, Chemistry, 1/2003-4/2007, June 2007

Social life really is a caring, awesome experience and you meet interesting people and have a lot of fun. Nothing really happens outside of the "Hampshire Bubble," and leaving the campus is more of a quest for most students.

Current student, 1/2005-Submit Date, September 2005

Other college kids come here to party. It's where people are happy, always wanting to dance and the campus public safety stays out of the way unless they are needed. In order to have a gathering of over 25 people you must technically register your party otherwise it can get shut down, but this rarely happens. If you have two 21-year-olds you can register it as a party where alcohol will be served. Rowdy drinking/dance parties are sometimes held in strange locations such as the cultural center or even the dining hall.

The School Says

At Hampshire we are proud to be a leader in innovative education. A few radical, yet simple ideas lie at the heart of a Hampshire education:

- The best education grows out of a student's own interests.
- Pre-set majors and academic departments restrict student and faculty inquiry—the most fertile and interesting ground often touches on many disciplines.
- Grades limit students' imagination and development—students learn more from individual narrative evaluations of their work.
- Students who take responsibility for their learning will learn more.
- Students should use their education toward the greater good. Hampshire's motto is Non Satis Scire. (To Know is Not Enough.)

Students progress through Hampshire in three stages, or Divisions. In the first year (Division I) students explore their interests by taking courses of their choice, including at least one in each of Hampshire's five interdisciplinary Schools of Thought. In Division II, the second and third years, they complete an individual concentration of study, in close consultation with a Committee of at least two Hampshire professors. In the fourth year (Division III) each student completes an original project, again, working closely with two faculty members. Students submit a portfolio of their work and retrospective at the end of each Division. Faculty members provide narrative evaluations at the end of each course and a comprehensive evaluation at the end of the concentration and the final project. About a quarter of Hampshire students incorporate off-campus study into their work, and most complete one or more internships and/or independent study. With the approval of their committee, students can spend a semester or more engaged entirely in independent study anywhere in the world. Past projects

Read all of Vault's College Surveys at **www.vault.com/college**–get complete surveys on 100s of colleges and universities, expert advice on applicaton essays and more.

VAULT CAREER LIBRARY 323

have taken students to Kazakhstan, Turkey, China and Cuba, among many other countries.

Hampshire students make extensive use of the courses, libraries and cultural activities at Amherst, Mount Holyoke, Smith and the University of Massachusetts. The Five College Consortium offers free bus service to the five campuses and easy open-stack access to a combined 9 million library volumes.

Several interdisciplinary programs support student and faculty interest and research. The Culture, Brain and Development Program cre-

ates new courses and supports student and faculty work at the intersections of neuroscience, anthropology and psychology. The Global Migrations Program looks at many different aspects of today's unprecedented movement of people across national and cultural borders. Others include Critical Studies of Childhood and Learning and the Civil Liberties and Public Policy Program.

Hampshire graduates work in a large variety of fields, including health care, education, communications and the arts. They are disproportionately successful in two particular areas: earning PhDs and founding their own businesses.

Harvard University

Office of Admissions and Financial Aid
8 Garden Street, Byerly Hall
Cambridge, MA 02138
Admissions phone: (617) 495-1551
Admissions fax: (617) 495-8821
Admissions URL: www.admissions.college.harvard.edu/

Note: *The school has chosen not to comment on the student surveys submitted.*

 Admissions

Current student, 9/2004-Submit Date, January 2007

In general, I am just going to reiterate that the Harvard admissions process is clouded in mystery. Although a clear pattern of good grades and good activities (and yes, for some, good lineage) can be seen from my group of friends, I believe that Harvard bases its admissions process largely on the potential it sees in its candidates. I don't believe that interviews count for a lot in the admissions process (I think this is just Harvard's way of filtering through the people who might have obvious behavioral or attitude problems). As for essays, I believe that is the component that makes or breaks the admissions process (at least for me specifically). I've encountered many kids in high school who boast a similar résumé to me (in terms of grades, class standing and activities), but I believe writing a personal essay gave me the oomph to stand out. I am going to be absolutely honest and say that I am a typical run-of-the-mill Harvard student (as in I have all my bases covered in terms of grades and activities, nothing exceptional or spectacular, I've done "enough" for grades, standardized testing, and activities that each of these factors will not damage me in the application process). But in order to take that extra step across the gap between the accepted and the waitlisted, I think students should put in extra effort into their essays and try to be themselves. Talk about what specifically interests them. Anecdotes are helpful, especially personal stories about failure and then growth in character. There is definitely a gamut of topics that can be explored: ethnicity, favorite childhood cartoons, weight loss and so on. I think the key point is not necessarily to go out of your way to impress the admissions officers by listing all your accomplishments (he/she is very aware of that already because he/she has seen the rest of your application), but the goal of the essay is for him/her to get to know you better.

Current student, 9/2003-Submit Date, October 2006

The admissions process involved filling out a Common Application along with a Harvard supplement; then there was a local interview, one-on-one with an alumnus for about 45 minutes. Obviously the process is selective, and I'm not sure how much advice there is to give on getting in—there is no formula. Some kids are well-rounded, others are very talented in one area. Important things to note, among many others, in the application are both how the school can help the applicant develop and how the student can contribute to campus.

Alumnus/a, 9/2002-6/2006, September 2006

The admissions process is standard. It consists of a regular application (recommendation letters, transcript, brief résumé, essays), and also includes an interview. While I cannot claim any great insight into the admissions process, it certainly did seem from the makeup of the class that there are "types" of students the college is looking. Almost everyone is very, very smart, but there are few which many who may have helped themselves because they did something distinctive in high school, or could paint themselves as a type—social, interested medicine, interested in politics, first-generation American and so on.

Alumnus/a, 9/2000-5/2004, August 2006

The admissions process is pretty standard at Harvard. Students fill out Common Application form and send it to the admissions office along with recommendations and a personal essay.

Harvard is, without question, extremely selective; when I applied for admission for the fall of 2,000, the applicant pool numbered roughly 19,000, with only 2,000 students gaining admission. Of the applicants, roughly 85 percent were academically qualified and over 2,000 were the valedictorians of their high school classes—all in all, some pretty stiff competition. Apparently, the number of applicants is steadily rising while the number admitted remains constant which means that the process is getting even more difficult. For this reason, is important to make yourself stand out to the admissions committee. Make sure that your recommendations are thorough and glowing, and that your essay says something interesting about you; mine was about growing up in the restaurant industry and although I had all the credentials to get in (valedictorian, editor of the school paper, president of numerous organizations and varsity basketball player), I truly believe that my essay was what set me apart from all of the other qualified applicants. At the end of the day, you want the admissions committee to remember you out of the myriad candidates with straight A's and 1500s SAT scores.

Alumnus/a, 9/2001-6/2005, April 2006

The admissions process includes the Common Application, a supplemental application and an interview process; the interview is not optional. The application also includes essays. My recommendation is that students should always add supplemental materials—clippings of high school newspaper articles they've written, local articles in which they may have been featured, projects they have produced—to the application. Harvard's interview is notoriously tough—perhaps because it's mandatory—and my advice on this is to try and schedule it after interviews with other schools so as to feel more comfortable with being interviewed.

Current student, 9/2003-Submit Date, April 2005

The things for which they look are: good grades, commitment to a few extracurriculars, something unique about you and the potential to succeed later on. Interviews are more to gauge how the candidate will get along with others and how well he/she will be able to thrive in a college environment. As for essays it's best to be original and write about something interesting in your life. Harvard is very selective and will probably jump on any little error to eliminate candidates. They look for people who have done extraordinary things or for people who are very well-rounded.

Academics

Employment Prospects

Alumnus/a, Economics, 9/2002-6/2006, June 2007

The classes are pretty standard and the faculty is largely very good, but the true power of a place like Harvard is the learning opportunity that exists around you each day in the form of the other students. Every undergraduate at Harvard has done many things and done well at many things, and the students represent a unique opportunity to learn a great deal about everything from their experiences to the way they study, to the way they attack certain situations. The power of Harvard lies in its spectacular student base, not in its ivy-clad walls.

Current student, 9/2003-Submit Date, November 2006

Harvard is a lot of work. Generally most classes are pretty intense. As a freshman or sophomore, the chances of not getting into a popular class are high. However, shopping period (before actual classes begin) will allow you to preview your classes and change them if you don't like them. This means that most people are satisfied with the classes that they do end up selecting. Grading is not standard at all. Some classes are graded very lightly and others aren't.

Alumnus/a, 9/2002-6/2006, September 2006

While the academic quality of all of the classes is very high, there are always the more and less rigorous courses within a field of study. One of the consequences of this is that grade management becomes a relatively simple proposition—one simply picks the courses that are clearly within one's range. However, most students choose to challenge themselves, and there are always classes that promise to do so—if not in the undergraduate curriculum, then in the graduate classes, which are generally open to qualified undergraduates.

The high quality of the classes, thankfully, is in no way limited or slanted toward one field or area of study. There are excellent courses in science, math, physics, writing and philosophy. The ambitious student will find it worthwhile to seek out excellent courses in other disciplines. For example, physics and math concentrators often dip into the advanced microeconomics course, which is, unsurprisingly, primarily an applied math class. Similarly, economics, philosophy and history concentrators often switch to social studies for their sophomore year to take the superb sophomore tutorial, and then switch out afterwards. Also, students from all disciplines, but the humanities and social sciences in particular, often take tutorials (small, specialized courses taught in seminar style) from other concentrations when space in them is available (it often is).

Current student, 9/2002-Submit Date, September 2005

Some of the best professors around—when it comes to publishing academic papers. Not necessarily the best teachers, although there are many very good ones to be found. Getting into the classes you want is rarely a problem. Harvard students tend to flock to easy, low-reading, somewhat interesting classes, so the better a class looks on paper, the less attention you'll be getting in the course. When it comes to workload—well, this is Harvard. Everyone knows that everyone else is doing their papers the night before they're due, and that they'll turn out to be very good. If you want to stand out you'll have to be either brilliant, or do a little more than the minimum you did in high school.

Alumnus/a, 9/2000-6/2004, October 2004

Being at Harvard is really, really humbling. I arrived having attended a very small public school, thinking I was of extraordinary intelligence. Then I met the professors. They are absolutely the most intelligent people I have ever met in my life. A lot of people talk about what it takes to be a Harvard student. You should instead be talking about what it takes to be a Harvard professor. But the main part of being a Harvard professor is research. This is a research institution. Graduate students outnumber undergrads two to one. There is a ton of pressure on the professors to publish.

Contrary to popular belief, almost everyone I've met is more than happy to help you out with homework or tutor you voluntarily or give you the answers straight out. Though the classes are curved, I didn't really get a sense of cutthroat competition. There are a few students like that, but they're quickly ostracized. Most students are really helpful.

Alumnus/a, Economics, 9/2002-6/2006, June 2007

Coming out of Harvard, you are presented with virtually limitless opportunities which begin with but certainly do not end with the school's Office of Career Services. On-campus recruiting for investment banking and consulting jobs is overwhelming—there is virtually no limit to the access you can get to these jobs. However, if you are interested in other things such as film, entertainment and so on, you are going to have to look a lot harder and receive less help than on the finance/consulting end of the spectrum.

Current student, 9/2004-Submit Date, January 2007

Employment is one thing that Harvard can definitely boast about. It opens the door to many job opportunities. The employers are extremely prestigious (some of them recruit exclusively at top Ivy League schools) and there's very few companies that will say "no" outright to a Harvard student seeking an internship or a job (unless of course, they're looking for employees with more experience or graduate students). The only possible nick in the Harvard plate is that it is liberal arts school, so certain programs that seek students from specific trades might be turned off by Harvard's general curriculum. But most of the time the prestige is able to supplant these requirements. Harvard has a nice Career Services office and there's also many other ways to pursue internships. For example, the IOP (Institute of Politics) helps place students in government/policy related internships each year, as does specific regional-focused centers such as the Rockefeller Center (for Latin-America). For science students, many students op to stay on campus during the summer and work with professors (for some fellowships, housing and stipend is provided). Harvard also offers a vast number of fellowships for students interested in exploring different subjects or students who are interested in working in nonprofits. Most of the seniors with whom I have interacted chose the route of either: pre-professional/graduate school, Teach for America then law school, or I-banking/consulting. Of course, there are always exceptions to this rule, but I feel that the vast majority of Harvard students are interested in these pursuits. On-campus recruiting definitely does ease (or maybe stress) undergraduate life. During junior spring and senior fall, students have the opportunity to apply to a vast number of internships online. Many students use this system to obtain prestigious summer internships or after-graduation employment. Most of this online recruiting system focuses on the profession of consulting and I-banking.

Current student, 9/2003-Submit Date, December 2006

Only the top companies recruit at Harvard, and the employment prospects are unbelievable. With that being said, it sometimes seems like everybody's either entering investment banking or consulting, which can be bad for people who have more diverse interests that are less centered on making so much money.

Alumnus/a, 9/2002-6/2006, September 2006

In general, employment prospects are very good. While I do not know the exact numbers, a large portion of the graduating class that is looking for employment (a large number are interested in graduate studies or fellowships of some sort) find it through on-campus recruiting. The process is primarily focused on those who want to get jobs in finance or management consulting, but there are a lot of firms from other fields that recruit as well, including advertising, computing, economic consulting and retail management.

Alumnus/a, 9/1998-6/2002, November 2005

The pedigree from a top Ivy League school is unmatched as far as getting you in the door for most employers. However, that's where it ends. Once you're there, it's up to you and your skills to land the job and be successful. On-campus recruiting consists mainly of finance, investment banks and consulting firms. Many other recruiters are few and far between on campus. For those opportunities you need to do your own networking and self-promotion.

Alumni networks are very helpful. I have lived in three cities since graduation and the first thing I do is find the local alumni chapter and get involved. They are generally quite helpful and eager to help you succeed. I have found that generally for business networking, the Harvard Business School alumni are more helpful. For personal and intellectual networking and assistance, the undergrad alumni chapters are great.

Read all of Vault's College Surveys at **www.vault.com/college**–get complete surveys on 100s of colleges and universities, expert advice on applicaton essays and more.

VAULT CAREER LIBRARY **325**

Quality of Life

Alumnus/a, Economics, 9/2002-6/2006, June 2007

Harvard is lucky to be located in one of the best college cities imaginable. Cambridge is loaded with shops, stores, restaurants and bars of all flavors, while also being a very short ride (15 to 20 minutes) from all that Boston has to offer, as well. My on-campus housing was spectacular and that will only improve in the years to come with the planned expansion into Allston and the new undergrad dorms that go with it.

Current student, 9/2003-Submit Date, October 2006

You live in a freshman hall in Harvard Yard your freshman year with all of the other freshmen in the Yard. After that, you block with up to eight others and are assigned an upperclassman house, where you live for the next three years. Although living on campus is only mandatory the freshman year, only a small minority (maybe 5 percent) choose to move off-campus. This means that house communities are strong and that there is a lot of activity going on around campus all the time. Campus is around Cambridge, near Boston.

Alumnus/a, 9/2002-6/2006, September 2006

In general, housing is excellent, especially in comparison with other schools (at least in my experience). It may not be as luxurious as small liberal arts colleges, but it is generally quite sufficient. That said, there are some issues. First, luck of the draw plays a major role in determining housing quality, as the buildings on campus (due to their age) are not uniform at all. Excellent housing, for example, can be found in the three Quadrangle Houses, as well as Leverett, Quincy and Mather. Unsurprisingly, those are the newer houses, and are lacking a bit in "Harvard spirit," at least as far as their architecture is concerned. However, the housing quality more than makes up the balance.

Alumnus/a, 9/2000-5/2004, August 2006

In general housing is very good and about 97 percent of students live on campus throughout their four years of college because besides the rooms and suites being generally attractive and spacious, it is simply more convenient and cheaper to live on campus than to rent an apartment in notoriously expensive Cambridge. All first-years live in Harvard Yard and are assigned to an upper-class house before sophomore year rolls around. Students spend the rest of their time at Harvard at their house (a system based on the Oxford/Cambridge model of colleges). Choosing a rooming group at the end of freshman year can be traumatic and people conduct all kinds of strange rituals to get into the house of their choice (for example, many want to end up near the Charles River as opposed to one of the houses on the Radcliff Quadrangle), but once the dust settles and people move into their houses, they are usually happy with the way things turn out and with their house community, in general. Each house has its own dining hall (where the food is generally above-par), its own gym and several common spaces. Some houses have added amenities like dance studios, theater stages and photography studios.

Alumnus/a, 9/2001-6/2005, April 2006

Once you find your community quality of life at Harvard is great. Freshman year can be isolating, but after that most people find their way. Housing is guaranteed for four years, and it is generally very good. There are, from time to time, reports of assaults in Cambridge of Harvard students, though overall this doesn't have a great impact on the quality of life.

Harvard also recently updated the gyms in each of the residential houses and doubled the equipment in the Malkin Athletic Center, which has been a boon for campus life. Lastly, the dorm food is generally good, though one naturally grows tired after four years of the same cycle of food. Kosher dining is available every evening at Hillel.

Social Life

Current student, 9/2004-Submit Date, January 2007

Restaurant choice is limited to Indian, Greek, Thai, Chinese, Mexican (if we call Felipe's Mexican) and American food. Dating scene is rather lousy; most people who are dating usually start dating by freshman year and continue on for the rest of college. The rest of the people grow desperate, hook up and stay single. Events wise, Harvard does not host that many events. Clubs are a huge deal at

Harvard (how else will its students beef up their résumés?) and a significa[nt] amount of time is usually dedicated to them. The major clubs on campus a[re] probably the *Crimson* (student newspaper) and IRC (international relatio[ns] group broken up into different Model UNs, and the *Harvard Internation[al] Review*—student publication). Of course other clubs exist, and students partic[i]pate in them with varying degrees of intensity. As for the Greek system, it's n[ot] a huge deal at Harvard for guys (guys rely on a Final Club system, which is sim[i]lar to a fraternity), but for girls it may be helpful to join a sorority and ma[ke] some connections.

Current student, 9/2003-Submit Date, October 2006

Harvard Square is dominated by Harvard students, so there are lots of near[by] bars (walking distance) and restaurants. The dating scene can be whatever o[ne] makes it—there are plenty of serious couples and there are plenty of very cas[u]al relationships. The Greek system is peripheral to the Final Club system, a pr[i]vatized version of fraternities. Clubs (dancing, not final) can be found in Bosto[n.] Student favorites are local bars and final clubs.

Alumnus/a, 9/2002-6/2006, September 2006

Social life at Harvard depends a lot on your particular circle of friends an[d] acquaintances. In general, social life on campus is dominated either by even[ts] thrown (either formally or informally) by members of particular student organi[i]zations, by campus-wide events thrown by the student government, or by the fr[a]ternities, sororities and finals clubs on campus. As few fraternities and soror[i]ties have their own space, the latter scene is mainly dominated by the old-mone[y] all-male finals clubs.

In general, however, most people find the social scene to be very good, if occa[a]sionally a bit repetitive because Cambridge is not quite a city. However, wi[th] Boston a T ride away, there is always a remedy to that repetitiveness.

Alumnus/a, 9/2000-5/2004, August 2006

Social life is what you make of it at Harvard. Some students took full advantag[e] of all of the opportunities for fun offered to them. I also knew students wh[o] barely ever went out, which is a shame because for those who like an urban env[i]ronment, Harvard's location is really fantastic. Cambridge is a fun city and very manageable, and Beantown is right across the Charles River (a 10-minu[te] T ride away from Harvard Square). There are all manner of bars and restauran[ts] in Harvard Square, and more adventurous souls can wander to Inman Squar[e] (lots of ethnic restaurants), Central Square and Davis Square (quirky, indepen[d]ent bars and shops). Harvard Square also has plenty of restaurants and bars, b[ut] because it is so famous and the rents are so high, it is teeming with tourists an[d] tends to be much more commercialized. Some of the students' favori[te] Cambridge hangouts include Red Line bar, L.A. Burdick's cafe (for awesom[e] hot chocolate and coffee), Dali (amazing Spanish tapas), and Pinocchio's (f[or] good take-out pizza and subs). Those who easily get tired of the Cambridg[e] scene can find any number of things to do in Boston, from the swank nightclu[b] scene on Boylston Street, to the raucous college bar scene on Lansdowne Stree[t] to the romantic restaurants of the North End (Boston's Little Italy), to the var[i]ous Irish pubs that dot the city, and the list goes on and on. Sports enthusias[ts] can take in baseball games at Fenway and watch the Celtics and the Bruins, a[s] well as the annual Beanpot college hockey tournament, and those looking for [a] little getaway can hit the Berkshire hills to the west, Martha's Vineyard and Cap[e] Cod on the shore, Vermont and New Hampshire for skiing, Maine, Canada an[d] so on. There is no shortage of things to do, and Boston is the ultimate colleg[e] town. As for the social scene, students tend to work hard during the week an[d] party hard on the weekend, and the only true Greek scene exists with the fina[l] clubs and the few fraternities and sororities on campus. In the end, though, the[re] is something for everybody.

Alumnus/a, 9/2000-6/2004, April 2005

There are plays, performances and events hosted by student groups every week[end]. In fact, there are so many of these that clubs often have to book venues a[s] far as one or two semesters in advance. Most of these events are of high quali[i]ty and attended by both students and residents of Cambridge. Admission gene[r]ally doesn't exceed $12 for students.

Favorite events among students include the spring formals, Cultural Rhythms ([a] day of cultural celebration with cultural performances, ethnic food booths and [a] celebrity host or hostess) and Arts First (a campus-wide celebration of the art[s] with student bands, performances, students' art displays and workshops).

Massachusetts Institute of Technology

Office of Admissions
Massachusetts Institute of Technology
77 Massachusetts Avenue, Room 3-108
Cambridge, MA 02139-4307
Admissions phone: (617) 253-4791
Admissions e-mail: admissions@mit.edu
Admissions URL: web.mit.edu/admissions/

 ## Admissions

Current student, 8/2003-Submit Date, November 2006

When I got in, the admit rate was 18 percent. The class of 2010's admit rate was 13 percent. MIT has gotten to be extremely selective in the four years I've been here. They are looking for maybe 10 percent of those "pure geniuses" who win the International Math/Physics/Chemistry Olympiads, but otherwise, they want well-rounded students who are passionate about math and science. For example, my admissions essays were pretty nerdy—I calculated the amount of rice I ate over my childhood and linked that to how I was brainwashed to a math/science degree.

Students submit a few short essays (150 words of less) and then a long essay. This year's topic was "Speak about something you do just for the fun of it." The Institute focuses on students who aren't study machines, but who work very hard at whatever they're passionate about. There is also an interview with an educational counselor. Usually these interviews are pretty informal, and the school uses them to gain insight into your personality. They want to see that you can express your ideas and work on a team, since a lot of engineerin is team-focused. The admissions team keeps an honest blog about the process. It's good to read through it.

Current student, 9/2004-Submit Date, January 2007

The admissions process is fairly straightforward. While traditionally they have emphasized the SAT math section and SAT subject test scores in science and math, the committee has become much more focused on looking for well-rounded individuals with an exceptional capacity to manage time efficiently. They seek go-getters beaming with intellectual curiosity and extremely sharp analytical skills. Many first-year students bring with them meaningful high school work experience or independent research experience that reflects their commitment to math, science or engineering. Mechanics of the essay certainly come ancillary to the voice of the student. MIT students have character, enthusiasm, energy and are usually willing to try anything out of curiosity. The committee also seeks demonstrated maturity, as they know the first year is a lot to handle and adjust to: an experience that can hardly be prepared for.

Current student, 9/2005-Submit Date, August 2006

Admissions process MIT offers an Early Action as well as a Regular Decision program. Applying Early Action is non-binding. The deadline is earlier, but you are also notified early (around mid-December). You are free to apply to other Early Action programs that are not binding or Early Decision (for instance, you can choose to apply EA for MIT as well as Caltech, but not MIT and Harvard).

Most students are chosen from the Regular Decision pool. The admissions rate for the class of 2009 was around 13 percent, which represents a 3 percent decline over the past five years. The admissions process includes your application (general info, test scores, recommendations, mid-year report, grades, essay) as well as an optional interview, either on-campus or with alumni in the area. You are notified of your acceptance in late March.

Throughout the process, MIT has many resources for you to use—the my MIT portal is one, through which applicants apply online, network with fellow students after they are accepted or check their application status. MIT also tries very hard to make the admissions process less stressful by making it a very human process. Admissions counselors and several undergraduate students use blogs at www.mitblogs.com to speak about their experiences, themselves and MIT.

Current student, 9/2002-Submit Date, September 2005

The admissions process is pretty standard, just like any other top-level school. Clearly top scores and grades are important. For the areas in which you can set yourself apart (e.g., the interview and essays), be aware that MIT is focusing more and more on well-rounded people. Remember that you must be strong in technical and science areas—be sure to bring that out in whatever you are writing or with whomever you are interviewing. However, the image of the MIT nerd, while still applicable, is becoming less so. More people are into sports, into music and into community service, and this trend is intentional. Make yourself out to be well-rounded, but with a strong enjoyment of science, and you will improve your chances. Also, high-schoolers may have heard that more schools are keeping track of contact attempts such as e-mails and phone calls to admissions officials. MIT is one of those schools.

Current student, 8/2002-Submit Date, April 2005

In order to be admitted to MIT, you must have both good test scores, and have done something interesting. According to *U.S. News & World Report*, MIT is the most selective undergraduate university in the nation. With around a 16 percent admissions rate, everyone is smart, and many smart people aren't admitted. The key to getting in is having a hook, such as having participated in the research science institute (RSI) summer program at MIT, having placed in the Siemens Westinghouse competition, or having done something else notable in your free time. As I had done none of the above, I spent a summer in high school working at MIT as an intern (called an undergraduate research opportunities program researcher). I was able to use a recommendation from that summer to assist in my admission.

 ## Academics

Current student, 8/2003-Submit Date, November 2006

Students' experiences vary based on their major. Freshman year is a very humbling experience. Half the semester is pass/no record, which gives students a chance to adjust to being in college. Talk advantage of pass/no record to explore Boston and make friends! Coming off pass/no record is difficult—don't overload on classes because you still don't know how to study for MIT tests.

There are three majors that are well-respected on campus due to the pace and intense workload. These are Aerospace Engineering, Electrical Engineering and Computer Science, and Physics. Still, about 30 percent of students in each year are enrolled in these majors. Although difficult, EECS is the most organized, well-run and best-taught major, in my opinion. We have an amazing repertoire of professors—Oppenheim (the god of digital signal processing), Abelson and Sussman (founders of Scheme and revolutionized the way CS is taught), and more. There is probably a 1:1 ratio of faculty-to-students. The professors love interacting with students, but they can be hard to approach. You will often work directly with professors on research and they really do take you under their wing.

I was scared of the bell-curve grading when I came here, but it has become my best friend. Most engineering classes are B-centered. You get a B if you get the average, plus or minus the standard deviation. There are tons of resources to help you do well. The Institute is committed to helping students graduate, and it shows.

Alumnus/a, 9/1999-5/2003, October 2006

I think MIT students are very fortunate in being able to take the classes they want, both in terms of having a substantial amount of freedom within each major to choose classes of interest, and being able to get into the classes they choose. The workload is not too bad. Professors are consistently brilliant and prominent in their fields, but do vary in their ability to teach classes and accessibility. Grading may seem harsh to those who are used to getting straight A's.

Read all of Vault's College Surveys at **www.vault.com/college**—get complete surveys on 100s of colleges and universities, expert advice on applicaton essays and more.

VAULT CAREER LIBRARY 327

Alumnus/a, 8/2002-6/2006, March 2007

Double majored in Chemistry and Biology. Luckily they overlapped a lot so I didn't have to take too many extra classes. Grading is relatively easy. Most people get B's with average effort. Popular classes are lotteried and most classes are very well taught and it's usually easy to see professors during office hours if you really want.

Current student, 9/2004-Submit Date, January 2007

Academics are tough, grades are competitive, particularly in pre-med fields, and the workload is frequently overbearing. However, collaboration is encouraged and academically necessary for survival for most students. Professors are typically hit or miss; some are great, others are terrible, few are mediocre. Classes with ineffective professors are scarcely attended, and students usually find other ways to learn the material through recitations, study sessions or tutoring. Academic support for any class is pervasive, though it may not be directly from the professor. The onus is usually on the student to find whatever help he/she needs. Responsibility and dedication to coursework will almost always be rewarded with favorable grades. The class registration and enrollment system is slick; the school only very rarely restrict students from taking certain classes.

Current student, 9/2005-Submit Date, August 2006

People are extremely collaborative at MIT. There is practically no competition among students, and it is very easy to find someone to help you with an impossible problem set at 4 a.m. Everyone goes through it together, and upperclassmen are amazing. All dorms have freshmen through seniors, so it's very easy to get academic and career advice from down the hall.

Current student, 9/2002-Submit Date, September 2005

The academics are topnotch and difficult at MIT. All the stories of students staying up night after night doing work are true. The philosophy of MIT is that other schools teach you 100 things and expect you to remember 80 percent, while MIT teaches you 1,000 things and expects you to remember 20 percent. If the previous statement didn't make sense to you, MIT is not the place for you. Classes tend to give lots of work, and grade inflation is not prevalent. The business school tends to give more A's, on average, than the science and engineering schools, and you'll probably see more C's and D's than at any other top-tier school. Despite the stressful academic environment though, students always feel like they genuinely learned and nearly always feel a solid sense of accomplishment after a solid all-nighter. Popular classes are generally easy to get into. I've never heard of anyone wanting to take a class that they could not take. Professors are known for being especially accessible, even the well-known ones. While inevitably, there are a few professors more interested in furthering their own research than in teaching undergraduates, the majority are eager teachers of the next generation.

Current student, 8/2003-Submit Date, November 2004

Excellent programs. Sloan School of Management's undergrad business program is a hidden gem—you get to interact with Sloan School MBA students, unlike other top business schools that are quite segregated from undergrad. The essence of MIT is our appetite for problems—especially those big, intractable, complicated problems whose solutions make a permanent difference. As an undergraduate, you will spend a lot of time preparing yourself to face the challenges of the world through your course work. From the core subjects of your first year, to the intense focus of your major, to the fresh breeze of IAP and any electives you explore, MIT offers lots of new ways to use your mental tool kit and keep the edges sharp.

MIT also believes passionately in connecting young people with the fresh ideas and practical experiences of leading-edge research—which is the driving idea behind a wildly popular MIT institution known as the Undergraduate Research Opportunities Program (nicknamed UROP, pronounced "YUR-op"). By the time they graduate, close to 80 percent of MIT undergraduates participate in frontline research, side by side with senior faculty and graduate students.

 Employment Prospects

Current student, 8/2003-Submit Date, November 2006

MIT is extremely well regarded by employers. Alumni are always willing help students find a job at their company because they know you've prov yourself at MIT and will be successful in anything in the future.

Last year, 33 percent of students went into finance or consulting. This h become a new trend. Many engineering majors will go into finance or consu ing because the engineering gives them the quantitative/analytical skill set blaze the crowd. The top consulting/finance/engineering company heav recruit at MIT. Our career fair boasted 300+ companies in attendanc McKinsey has consistently employed more MIT students each year than a other company. Many EECS students go to Google, Microsoft and Oracle. A major banks recruit at MIT: JP Morgan, Goldman Sachs, UBS, Morgan Stanl and Lehman. MIT students are top picks on Wall Street, but only if you ca prove through the interviews that you're not socially awkward.

Current student, 9/2004-Submit Date, January 2007

Hundreds of companies recruit on campus during fall and spring. Internships a plentiful, even for sophomores. The availability of research positions on can pus helps many students start building their résumés from the day they arrive c campus. In short, getting a job was a piece of cake. From Wall Street banks hedge funds, to consulting firms, to leading engineering firms and startup employers yearn for the technical skills MIT students possess, particularly tho majoring in computer science and engineering. Finance and consulting repr sent the most popular industry destinations of graduates, but many also go in engineering positions in industries such as software, biotech and industrial ma ufacturing. The alumni network is extremely strong, with a terrific searchab database. Alumni are eager to help current students by answering questions c connecting them to jobs.

Current student, 9/2005-Submit Date, August 2006

The top employers of MIT graduates include Google and Goldman Sach Whether you are interested in computer science/electrical engineering or financ or consulting, MIT is a great institution to attend. It is a brand name amon schools, but that's not all. As someone once said, coming from MIT, peop assume you are intelligent. However, they also assume you are a geek with r social skills. Now, we know that is untrue. It is much easier to convince som one that you are not a nerd than it is to convince them that you are intelligent.

The MIT ICAN web site links up alumni who are willing to be contacted by st dents for any sort of advice or help. The externship program sets up studen with corporate internships over the Independent Activities Period (four weeks i January where you can decide to relax and go home, take a class on campus, d seminars, or work). About half of MIT graduates go on to professional or gra uate school, and the other half enter industry. Of those, the major industries a engineering and finance/consulting.

Current student, 9/2000-Submit Date, October 2005

Employment prospects out of MIT are excellent. MIT has a lot of prestige, an people will respect your analytical skills, your work ethic, and ability to take c many things at once. People get jobs in anything they want, as long as they s out and look for opportunities. On-campus recruiting is very, very extensive— we have been getting five to 10 companies daily that come on campus for firs round interviews. Frankly, you will not have exposure to so many recruiter elsewhere. The same goes for internships, where many companies will come MIT looking to hire full time by first giving them an internship. Admittedly, is a lot more competitive to get an internship.

Current student, 8/2002-Submit Date April 2005

Very good. Over 80 percent of students will eventually go to graduate schoo The average undergrad makes $50+K instantly upon graduation. Very prest gious employers, such as Microsoft, Google, Apple, Goldman Sachs, UBS, Fore Citadel and Bain make a large effort to recruit at MIT. There is a large and help ful alumni network with an online directory for easy access. On-campus recrui ing is plentiful.

Quality of Life

Social Life

Current student, 8/2003-Submit Date, November 2006

MIT doesn't have a mandatory dining plan. The dorms with cafeterias have a preferred dining plan. You pay $300 a term and get half price on all the food. The food is pretty healthy with lots of variety day-to-day. Some dorms have kitchens, and most students cook their own food. You can choose your dorm, so [p]ick that reflect your desire for cooking.

[T]he neighborhood is safe, but if you wander a few streets over, you'll hit the bad [ar]eas of Cambridge. Campus police are always available if you have an emer[g]ency or just need a ride home at night.

[A]lumnus/a, 9/1999-5/2003, October 2006

[Q]uality of life is pretty great. The dorms all have their own personality so you [c]an choose which one fits best. The campus does not have a classic university [fe]el, but it's highly indicative of the quirky nature of MIT. I've never had prob[le]ms with crime and safety, even in Random Hall, which is a little bit north of [ca]mpus in Cambridge.

[C]urrent student, 9/2004-Submit Date, January 2007

[O]verall students usually enjoy their lives at MIT, but mid-semester exam week [an]d the last two weeks of the semester are certainly exceptions. Students are fre[q]uently stressed out, but often the types of students who attend live off of this [k]ind of pressure.

[T]he campus is quite isolated from the rest of the Cambridge community, which [im]proves safety and policing. Housing is very much reflective of the social and [a]cademic needs of students, offering a whole spectrum of living arrangements [an]d social environments. Dorms are almost entirely along one street, which [m]akes them very safe. Dining is á la carte, which promotes healthy eating, but [is] not great socially.

[C]urrent student, 9/2005-Submit Date, August 2006

[Y]ou get to choose which dorm you want. Each dorm has a different culture, and [M]IT gives you information about that before you enter the lottery. If you do not [li]ke your dorm or roommate, you can choose to change. It is not assigned—MIT [h]as a special residence exploration period after orientation, before classes start, [to] show you your options and so you can change. Some dorms are suite-style, [o]thers are all singles. Some have kitchens on every floor, others with commu[n]al kitchens for everyone. Some have in-house dining halls. Those that don't [te]nd to have more kitchens.

[S]ome people don't like the campus architecture, but no one can say it's not [u]nique. It has one of the best sculpture collections in the country. The grounds [a]re extremely well-kept, and shoveled during the winter. We have multiple [li]braries, including a music library with comfortable chairs and headsets to lis[te]n to relaxing music. Bose was founded by MIT people, so it donates speakers [f]or all the school's sound systems.

[W]e have no required meal plans, but if you live in a dorm with a dining hall, you [a]re required to enroll in Preferred Dining, where you spend $250 each semester [t]o get 50 percent off all campus dining halls. Otherwise, there are restaurants in [t]he student center, food trucks, campusfood.com, and lots of great restaurants [w]ithin walking distance in both Cambridge and Boston.

[C]urrent student, 9/2000-12/2005, October 2005

[I] can't say much about the housing, as I lived in a fraternity right off the bat when [I] came to MIT. Freshmen are no longer allowed to live off campus their first year, [b]ut many of the dorms have some very cool people. Dorms have a lot of parties, [an]d pretty good ones for that matter. The facilities are just great. The sports com[p]lex could not be any bigger. Whatever activity you are interested in, you will find [a]t MIT. Anna's Taqueria opened up in the student center recently, and that's just [s]ome great, cheap, college food. There is no crime around MIT, and for the most [p]art you are safe, not much happens as far as dangerous activities.

Current student, 8/2003-Submit Date, November 2006

MIT is heavy on the Greek system. 50 percent of boys and 25 percent of girls are affiliated. They usually aren't your normal frats and sororities. Most of the normal students go Greek, so it's not the crazy lifestyle as in other colleges. Frats hold many parties on the weekends, and while not super big, they are well-run, with lots of alcohol, and pretty fun. Students from other colleges even come here to party.

My favorite restaurants around the area are: Thailand Cafe (small cheap Thai place about five minutes from MIT), India Quality (best Indian in Boston), Pour House (near the Pru.: half price burgers on Saturday nights), Bertuccis (near campus), Borders (two subway stops away in Harvard Square: best frozen margaritas).

Alumnus/a, 9/1999-5/2003, October 2006

There is an incredible range of people yet there are enough groups out there, whether it's Greek, dormitory or clubs, that it's easy to find other people with whom you can really be (become?) yourself during your time there. On-campus dining is not bad. There are cafeterias in a bunch of locations as well as La Verde's Market, plus a couple of options in the student center, and lunch trucks. Off campus, there's a whole range of places to get good food in the Cambridge and Boston area. For ice cream, there are JP Licks, Emack and Bolio's, Toscanini and Christina's. There are also nice restaurants close to campus in Cambridge, such as Cuchi Cuchi and Salts.

Current student, 9/2004-Submit Date, January 2007

Greek life is quite strong; many students live in off-campus fraternities, sororities and independent living groups. The administration and MIT Police are supportive of safe parties and not likely to break up a party as long as it appears under control. Students have easy access to the bars, clubs and restaurants of downtown Boston and the Fenway neighborhoods, which are popular among students. Student groups frequently organize harbor cruise trips, formals and ski trips. There are several campus pubs frequented mostly by graduate students. Fraternity parties are generally very inclusive of anyone who wants to come. Several dorms are known for partying, others not so much.

Current student, 9/2005-Submit Date, August 2006

Over half of all MIT males join a fraternity, and one-fourth of MIT females join a sorority. We also have independent living groups and co-ed fraternities as well. The party scene is amazing. Every Thursday to Saturday, you can find parties. However, if that's not your scene, what makes MIT great is that you can find people who will go barhopping with you, but you can also find people who will stay in and watch a movie or even build a catapult with you.

Dating at MIT has been very fun (at least for me). It's very easy to get to know someone through school, but it's also great to meet people at parties. Because MIT fraternities throw the best parties in Boston (if you don't believe me, ask anyone at Harvard, Boston University, Wellesley, Boston College, Tufts or Northeastern), it is also very easy to meet someone outside your academic sphere and strike up a conversation with them.

Current student, 9/2000-Submit Date, October 2005

You will be surprised when you come here and see all the different types of people who are here. While half the students are the stereotypical dorks you would imagine when you hear the name MIT, the other half are just regular, down-to-earth folks who just happen to be smart. It is in the Boston area, so you have all the nightlife of Boston. Parties happen all the time, and there are so many restaurants around. There are around 30 frats at MIT, so if you are looking at joining the Greek system there is bound to be a house in which you fit. Also, you can find clubs/teams/organizations in which to do any activity you might be interested in. I've seen people who put on full set of armor (metal and everything) and hitting themselves with swords every once in a while. I've seen martial arts practicing in the fields. There's a ton of varsity sports here, and also a myriad of club sports. You can play intramural sports, as well. Also, there is an incredible number of academic societies and groups.

Read all of Vault's College Surveys at www.vault.com/college–get complete surveys on 100s of colleges and universities, expert advice on applicaton essays and more.

VAULT CAREER LIBRARY 329

Mount Holyoke College

Admissions Office
50 College Street
South Hadley, MA 01075-1488
Admissions phone: (413) 538-2023
Admissions fax: (413) 538-2409
Admissions e-mail: admission@mtholyoke.edu
Admissions URL: www.mtholyoke.edu/adm/

Note: The school has chosen not to review the student surveys submitted.

 ## Admissions

Alumna, 9/2002-5/2006, October 2006

Pretty painless. MHC is looking for well-rounded students. They no longer require the SAT, but if your scores are good, it doesn't hurt to report them (although I doubt they consider the scores much). Essays should be well planned and well written. Avoid first person essays if possible. Instead, be creative and discuss an idea, a movement and so on. The admissions are "more selective" but not "most selective." For instance, MHC admissions are on par with the other Seven Sisters (maybe not quite as selective as Wellesley), and on par with other co-ed liberal arts colleges but not as tough as the Ivies or the top liberal arts schools (e.g., Williams, Amherst, Middlebury, Bowdoin).

Current student, 9/2004-Submit Date, January 2007

Mount Holyoke is a fairly selective college, but what they look for the most is whether you are a good match. The admissions process is all about getting to know you—SAT scores are optional, so it's more about your essays, recommendations and about what you are passionate. They are looking for women who are driven to make a positive change in the world.

Current student, 9/2005-Submit Date, February 2006

The essay questions were different from most college applications. With other college essays, it was easier to come up the corny and fake answer that one feels will appeal to the admission officers. These questions forced you to be real, and creative. I liked that. I think I was rewarded for presenting the real me. MHC looks for students who are diverse; they pride themselves in their so-called diverse student population.

Current student, 9/2005-Submit Date, October 2005

This school is considered to be highly selective. The fall of my senior year I had an interview on campus with a student, and met with the representative when she came to my high school. My essays dealt with responsibility and caring for the community in which I live. I applied regular admissions, and was informed of my acceptance in early April.

Alumna, 9/1999-12/2002, March 2005

Mount Holyoke has a unique admissions process. The essays are different from those of other universities. Hence, it is not possible to use the Common Application. It was fairly selective when I applied. However, in recent times, I believe acceptance rates may have gone up. The college has stopped requiring submission of SAT scores and that has negatively affected the college's ranking, though I am unsure whether it has affected the quality of the student body. Students applying should try to get in touch with current students at the college. I knew it was a right fit for me because I felt a connection with the students with whom I got in touch. Everybody was very helpful and nice and that was a reassuring feeling.

Current student, 8/2004-Submit Date, August 2004

Everyone in the admissions office was really friendly. The dean of admissions even wrote personal handwritten notes throughout the year. There was also the added bonus that if you applied online, there was no application fee. The process ran quite smoothly. Being an all women's college, they are looking for women who will take advantage of all they have to offer. The college is very selective which means they accept only about 40 percent of their applications. If you want to get in, you should have pretty much A's in high school, but that isn't absolutely necessary. Test scores are not that important. Personal interviews, essays and the application are all very important. The most important thing is to just be yourself. They are looking for interested, engaged and motivated young women.

 ## Academics

Current student, 1/2003-Submit Date, December 2006

Academics at Mount Holyoke are rigorous. Classes are quality if students put in the effort to attend class (class participation and attendance is key to success), do the readings, and seek guidance from professors or the Speaking, Arguing and Writing Program, also known as SAW, which assists students with writing and public speaking. The faculty and visiting faculty are superb and Mount Holyoke students also have the opportunity to take classes in the Five College Consortium that includes topnotch schools such as Smith College, Amherst College, Hampshire College and the University of Massachusetts Amherst. Average student-to-faculty ratio at Mount Holyoke is about 10:1. With that ratio, faculty can easily assess students interests and needs and are highly accessible if the student engages in discussion and asks for help when needed. Grading is fair and an A grade does not come with mediocre effort by any means!

Alumna, 9/2002-5/2006, October 2006

Professors are very interested and involved with their students. They are accessible and ready to help you out. The classes are, for the most part, interesting and engaging and it's not difficult to take the classes you want to take, even as a first year. The workload varies from department to department and course to course, but on the whole MHC is rumored to have one of the heftiest workloads around. Whether that's true or the students just do everything that is assigned (a rarity at many colleges, I think), I'm not sure. Regardless, I find the workload challenging but doable.

Current student, 9/2004-Submit Date, January 2007

I've never not been able to take a class I wanted to take. Classes vary in quality and difficulty from professor to professor and subject matter. The workload is strenuous and demands a lot of writing outside of lecture. Grading is generally fair, reflecting how much work and effort you put into the class.

Current student, 9/2005-Submit Date, February 2006

The academic program is very strenuous. If you are a dork, or enjoy doing lots of work then MHC is for you. People take classes very seriously and the workload is sometimes overbearing. If you took AP or IB courses, then you are used to this type of workload, but if not, be prepared. The professors are nice. This a science school, and the science program will either make you or break you. The classes are small and intimate.

Alumna, 8/1999-12/2002, March 2006

I found the workload challenging, but I was also on an accelerated program there. Professors and the community at large is very nice, welcoming, helpful. Easy access to professors. It was more or less easy to get into the classes that you wanted.

Current student, 9/2005-Submit Date, October 2005

The offered classes cover a range of topics. Also, if Mount Holyoke does not have a course that a student wants to take, it is very easy to register and take a class at UMass, Amherst, Hampshire and Smith. The classes are of very high quality, with a system that is designed only to keep excellent professors. At the end of each semester, students fill out anonymous evaluations of the professors which are read by the dean and the professor a few weeks after the course is finished. These evaluations are kept until the professor comes up for tenure, and are looked over at that time as part of the way to decide if the professor deserves

ure or not. While some classes are capped at 16 or 18, this benefits the stu-
nts so that class sizes are kept down to reasonable sizes. Many courses are
ered in both fall and spring semesters, and from one year to the next. The
orkload depends on which classes one takes. Generally, though, with good
ne management, it can be done. It does take up large amounts of time.

Current student, 1/2001-Submit Date, February 2004

is school offers challenging academics and wonderful, caring professors.
ere are 47 departmental and interdisciplinary majors, including an option to
sign one's own major. Majors of current students are: 32 percent humanities,
percent social sciences, 26 percent natural and applied sciences.

Alumna, 9/1999-12/2002, March 2005

ound it pretty easy to get into all the classes that I wanted to take during my
ne there. Popular classes (intro-level classes) can end up becoming quite
rge—I took a couple of intro-level classes that approached 100 students. I took
rd courseloads during my time there; I was trying to graduate early with a dou-
e major, so I found the workload challenging. However, people manage to bal-
ce workload with extracurriculars and a social life. I preferred the depart-
ents of one of my majors over the other. In general, there are a couple of
partments that are good. Biology is one of them; economics is another; dance
another. The professors, for the most part, are very approachable and con-
nial. They always have office hours and are willing to make time for the stu-
nts.

Current student, 8/2004-Submit Date, August 2004

ost of the professors are excellent, and dedicated to teaching (there are a few
d apples, but every college has those). The workload is very challenging. Be
epared to do a lot of reading and writing. Professors expect a lot of their stu-
nts, but the rigor is actually one of the most popular things about MHC. The
ofessors are all available and eager to help out. There are also lots of extra-
ademic programs (such as the SAW Center for speaking, arguing and writing
at helps students write papers and formulate arguments, and the Center for
areer Development that aids students in finding jobs and internships). Mount
olyoke is also a member of the Five College Consortium, so that if a student
ants to take classes that Holyoke doesn't offer, she can go to any of the other
ur colleges in the immediate area—UMass Amherst, Hampshire, Smith or
mherst.

 Employment Prospects

Current student, 1/2003-Submit Date, December 2006

ount Holyoke is Number One for graduating women with the highest number
PhDs held in the sciences and social sciences. Mount Holyoke graduates go
to pursue graduate study at top-tier law, graduate, business and medical
hools. Directly after graduation, alumnae often go into investing banking,
aching, public service careers, research assistantships and government posi-
ons. Students from Mount Holyoke also are involved with international oppor-
nities such as the Fulbright (15 students in 2006 were considered Fulbright
holars), Freeman-Asia, Peace Corps, Aerators and Teach for America. The
umnae from Mount Holyoke are easy to find with the new online system called
FENET provided by the Alumnae Association of Mount Holyoke to track
umnae offering internships, jobs and housing for students and fellow alumnae.

Alumna, 9/2002-5/2006, October 2006

epending on for which sort of employment you're looking, the Career
evelopment Center can be your best friend. If you're looking for something in
e business world (like investment banking or consulting or something), then
HC can offer plenty of contacts with companies like Goldman Sachs or
avigant. MHC also has a strong program in the natural and physical sciences,
if you're looking for prospects in the biotech industry, or wanting to work in
chem lab, they can probably hook you up. It seems that most students go to
raduate school (if not right away, within two to five years) and generally the
DC and professors are pretty helpful with getting into med school, law school
the graduate program of your choice. There are also plenty of opportunities
help you study for your GMATs, CATs, LSATs and GREs. The alumnae net-
ork is very strong—something most people don't realize or take advantage of
ntil they're walking in the Laurel Parade the day before graduation. The CDC

has a number of resources for helping you find an internship, but again, it
depends on for what you're looking. If you're looking for an environmental
studies or geology internship or job, you're better off accessing your professors
for those disciplines.

Current student, 9/2004-Submit Date, January 2007

Everyone from top investments banks, such as JP Morgan and Goldman Sachs,
to government agencies, such as the CIA, recruit on campus. Mount Holyoke
grads have their pick of the top firms. The alumnae network is very strong, with
alumnae willing to go out of their way to help you out. With a liberal arts degree,
you really can get a job in any field.

Current student, 9/2005-Submit Date, October 2005

There is a center on campus that helps facilitate interactions between students
and future employers, so that students can get either internships or jobs right
after graduation. Internships during the summer and during January-term are
very popular, and many jobs stem from those internships. The alumnae are very
involved in the school, and are willing to help out any woman from here.

Alumna, 9/1999-12/2002, March 2005

The common complaint of a lot of graduating seniors was that a lot of the
recruiters that came to our campus consisted of financial institutions and investment bank organizations, and so on, which left a lot of the majors in the sciences
and arts with less choices. Although the Mount Holyoke connection (the alumnae network) is strong, it was always a scramble for the international students to
obtain internships and full-time jobs because a lot of employers during my time
did not want to deal with the issues of sponsorship of visa and hence, preferred
to hire American citizens. Mount Holyoke produces a lot of bright and talented
students. I know a lot of people who went onto prestigious organizations,
though: Goldman Sachs, Fidelity, Microsoft, Merrill Lynch, JP Morgan,
Barclay's, Morgan Stanley, NERA and so on. I also know people who went on
to work for Teach for America, the Peace Corps and others.

Current student, 8/2004-Submit Date, August 2004

Many graduate schools and companies actively recruit Mount Holyoke graduates. They are known as hard-working, dedicated, motivated and intelligent. I
would say that going to a women's college is a really wonderful idea. In a co-
ed setting, males often end up dominating in classes. Women here have really
amazing self-confidence and gain so much from their friends.

 Quality of Life

Current student, 1/2003-Submit Date, December 2006

Mount Holyoke is located in South Hadley, Massachusetts, a suburban-rural
town where crime is low and safety is absurdly high. Mount Holyoke is in the
process of building a new dorm that will continue to be like other dorms but will
be larger and will include suites and wireless Internet. For a small, liberal arts
college campus, facilities are superb for there consists of a Dance and Sports
complex with a great number of tennis courts, weight-training machines, treadmills, an Olympic size pool and equestrian center. It is home to one of the oldest and fastest growing libraries in the nation. Dining varies for the menus hardly change but almost every dorm specializes in breakfast brunch; for example,
dorms offer crepes, home made waffles, and smoothies. Every month there is a
sushi special in the campus center and one thing Mt. Holyoke prides itself for is
the Kosher/Halal dining center open to all. Vegan and vegetarian food is easily
obtainable and delicious. Every special occasion and holiday is celebrated with
a "gracious" dinner, which include a restaurant-like menu and silverware in
every dining hall.

Alumna, 9/2002-5/2006, October 2006

The dorms are great. For the most part, they have spacious rooms and they are
in the process of constructing a new dorm that should open for the '08-'09 or the
'09-'10 school year, if things go according to schedule. The older dorms have a
lot of character. The community isn't as centered around in which house you
live (though it was that way at one point) the way it seems to be at Smith or the
way it is at Harvard. But the campus center offers a pretty central location for
people to get together to build community. There are also heaps of traditions
ranging from milk and cookies to founders day, to Laurel Parade, to mountain
day, to May Day celebrations and many more. The traditions are a point of

Read all of Vault's College Surveys at www.vault.com/college—get complete surveys on 100s of colleges and universities, expert advice on applicaton essays and more.

VAULT CAREER LIBRARY 331

bonding for the student body. There's not much to do in South Hadley itself (a little movie theater and take-out Chinese). But the Five College Consortium offers a lot in the way of classes to take as well as social connections—there's a free bus that runs between the colleges, so it's pretty easy to get to Amherst for shopping and men and restaurants and bars, as well as a normal size movie theater. It's not necessary to have a car, but having one definitely improves the quality of life (especially social life) as you're no longer restricted to the bus schedule to get to Amherst, NYC (about three hours) or Boston (about an hour and a half). Also, with the Consortium, there are plenty of extracurriculars and clubs with which to get involved.

Current student, 9/2004-Submit Date, January 2007

Housing is great, with beautiful dorms and relatively good food. The campus is consistently ranked one of the most beautiful in the U.S. by the Princeton Review. The facilities are truly state-of-the-art, with the exception of the gym. South Hadley is a quiet town, so safety is not really a concern.

Current student, 9/2005-Submit Date, October 2005

The housing options are varied, from singles to quads, very old buildings to modern buildings. The sizes of the rooms vary as well. Freshmen are in either doubles, triples or quads. The room sizes are livable, but not always comfortable. All dorms have a living room on the first floor. In the living rooms, there is a piano, and many couches on which students study. Also, they may request to hold private parties of 50 or less people. Some clubs meet in the living rooms of the dorm. All of the dorms offer continental breakfast Monday through Friday. Only three dorms offer all three meals, seven days a week. Other dorms offer a variety of services, many with dinner Sunday through Thursday, and lunch Monday through Friday. All of the dorms offer what is known as M&Cs or milk and cookies, Sunday through Thursday, from around 9/9:30-10/10:30 p.m. While it may sometimes only be celery sticks and graham crackers, it offers a study break. There is always milk and tea available. The neighborhood is very safe, as is the campus. Campus Safety patrols all of the campus all hours of the day, driving around in their Suburban.

Current student, 8/2004-Submit Date, August 2004

At MHC the dorms are beautifully maintained, spacious and well laid out. I have no reason to complain. Some of the rooms don't have such good lighting, but that is a small issue. The food is quite decent, and they offer kosher and halal dining. The campus is easily maneuverable (in other words not too big) and also well-groomed and pretty. Facilities are amazing, especially the brand-new science facilities. The area (South Hadley) is unexciting, but North Hampton and Amherst are 20 minutes away, so you if you're looking for a downtown, you can drive or take the free intercampus buses over there. The campus is incredibly safe. There are very few problems with dorms and quality of life issues.

Social Life

Current student, 1/2003-Submit Date, December 2006

Mount Holyoke has over 150 student organizations, academic clubs and honor societies, arts organizations, club sports, community service, dance, entertainment, peer education, political and activist organizations, and publications. All are student led and run! There are cultural centers on campus open to all students. Our cultural centers offer students a place for learning and supportive community. The centers are open to all members of the Mount Holyoke community, and most have space that can be reserved for special events. These include Asian Center for Empowerment, Betty Shabazz Cultural Center, Eliana Ortega Cultural Center, Zowie Banteah Cultural Center, and the Jeannette Marks House.

Alumna, 9/2002-5/2006, October 2006

Men can be found in Amherst at Hampshire College, Amherst College and UMass. Also, girls date men from other regional colleges like Dartmouth, Middlebury, Yale, Harvard, Tufts, and the other Boston-area schools. Not much

for bars or restaurants in South Hadley, but Amherst and Northampton both ha plenty and are only a 20-minute bus ride away. The campus is fairly quiet most weekends. A few years ago there were two big parties, one in the fall a one in the spring. In the fall there was Las Vegas night, and in the spring a "tra eling" party called Three P's where you traveled amongst the houses who names began with P. I don't think Three P's still happens (at least it didn't l year), but Vegas night is not to be missed. There are also plenty of parties at cultural houses (Betty Shabazz is the cultural house for black students and Ortega House is for Latina students and the ACE house is for Asian students, name a few). There is no Greek life. The rugby team throws good parti There's also the "network," which is the social organization on campus. Th put together "Thursday night edge" with local bands performing at the camp center and "something every Friday" where something happens every Friday the campus center. Additionally, the college offers a free concert in the spri (with people like Eve, Kanye West and The Bravery). Also, off-campus parti at the other colleges are popular—like Amherst's Luau at the beginning of school year and Hampshire Halloween and Smith's Debauchery party (usua in the spring, I think).

Current student, 9/2005-Submit Date, February 2006

People are too serious about work, and sacrifice social life for work. If you wa a social life, then you must be a slacker. The dorms are quiet on weeken There is zero to do in South Hadley, but we are a bus ride away from UMass a Amherst. However, still it's not the most happening place, but it can help. you want a taste of a city, Springfield is the place to go; however, it's hard to g there if you don't have a car.

Current student, 9/2005-Submit Date, October 2005

There is no Greek system on campus. The adjacent small shopping complex small, but has a few expensive restaurants. There is also a movie theater, wi usually three or four movies showing. There is one shop that has less expensi items, and caters toward the college. It is even possible to use the College O card, or the debit card, there to make purchases. For the weekends, many st dents choose to leave campus and visit the other four colleges in the area. The is a bus system that leaves every 40 minutes that drives to all five colleges, a runs to about 2 a.m. Thursday, Friday and Saturday. This takes students in Amherst town, where there are a few bars and restaurants and shops. Conce come through the Five-College area frequently, and students can find out abo events through a web site.

Current student, 8/2004-Submit Date, August 2004

The towns of North Hampton and Amherst have better bars and restaurants a are thus suited to a social scene. Mount Holyoke, though, is pretty self-sustai ing. Students hang out in the dorms, in the campus center and so on. As women's school, the dating scene is pretty small, although the lesbian scene larger than at most co-ed colleges. There are no sororities. There are enoug clubs, events, musical and theater productions to last a lifetime. The only pro lem is deciding which one to go to on any given night. There were a good 10 11 clubs that I would have loved to join, but I had to limit myself to three.

Mount Holyoke has a fabulous sports program (Division III). One of the best all the women's colleges in the country. MHC also has the largest percentage international students of all liberal arts colleges in the country. Religious life fairly pronounced, but there is no single religion that dominates. MHC has re gious services for almost every religion, including the major branches Christianity, Judaism, Islam, Buddhism, Hinduism, Baha'i, Wiccan, among ot ers. There are many campus traditions that make life for new students fun, f example, "elfing." Each freshman is assigned a sophomore "elf" who leav random notes and small gifts for her frosh throughout the first semester. Eac student also receives a plant when she arrives on campus, and is supposed to tak care of the plant, and it comes to symbolize her growth on campus. Milk an cookies is teatime at three o'clock every afternoon, which gives students a brea from their studies and the opportunity to socialize a bit. Mount Holyoke is rea ly incredibly welcoming and has a warm and intellectual community.

Northeastern University

Office of Undergraduate Admissions
Northeastern University
150 Richards Hall
360 Huntington Avenue
Boston, MA 02115
Admissions phone: (617) 373-2200
Admissions e-mail: admissions@neu.edu
Admissions URL: www.northeastern.edu/admissions

 Admissions

Current student, 9/2004-Submit Date, April 2006

I'm in the College of Engineering (COE), which is the most selective college (in terms of SAT and high school GPA) at Northeastern University. The process is fairly simple and uses a general college application. I had to answer one essay question that was "describe my greatest moment," or something along those lines.

No interview required for undergrad programs. In the past few years this school has gotten a lot more difficult . SAT scores in engineering went from a 1250 average in 2004 to a 1310 in 2006.

> **The school says:** "SAT scores for incoming freshmen in the College of Engineering for Fall 2004 and 2006 were 1269 and 1273."

I would recommend applying Early Action if you really want to get into NEU. If you get accepted, you're not obligated to attend the university, like Early Decision.

Current student, 1/2004-Submit Date, March 2006

The admissions process for Northeastern University was basically the same as all of the other four-year private universities/colleges to which I applied except for a few things. The advice I have to offer regarding getting accepted includes: Maintain grades in the B+ to A range in high school; and if transferring from another college or university, make sure to get quality recommendation letters from teachers/professors or even current/former employers. Be involved in as many extracurricular activities as possible during high school or college; if transferring, especially try to be involved in an activity/club/student organization in which you can take on a leadership role. Prepare for the SATs by attending preparatory courses and take the SAT as many times as possible to acquire a decent score (1200 and above is probably acceptable for this school). If you are applying to a very specialized or specific program like mine (speech language pathology and audiology), it is very helpful to have some type of experience with the field (e.g., something involving working with children with special needs). Always try to include information about yourself that would make you stand apart from other applicants. I had to write one long essay and a few shorter essays as part of my application and my advice is to be honest and really try and pull from your experiences and give the admissions committee some insight into who you are. The selectivity of this school increases every year as more and more people are applying. I think that coming to the school and being interviewed can also be very helpful in getting accepted. It shows that you are truly interested in the university.

Alumnus/a, 9/1999-5/2003, September 2005

The admissions process is similar to any other college or university. Northeastern offers a wonderful Alternative Freshman Year option, where if your SATs and/or high school GPA weren't great, you might still be admitted based upon the school believing you have potential to succeed at this school. They have a normal fee for the application process, just like most schools.

Current student, 9/2003-Submit Date, March 2005

At Northeastern admissions is rolling, so I was accepted into the university one month after I applied. I never did an interview with anyone and my essay was the same one I used for all colleges to which I applied. I was ranked 26th in my high school class and got 1260 on my SATs.

> **The school says:** "We no longer have rolling admissions (for a few years). Our deadline is January 15th, and students receive a response starting March 15th. Early Action deadline is November 15th."

I got accepted into the college of my choice as well. If you do not get into your major but get accepted into general studies, you should enroll. This way you can do an internal transfer. This program is very strong and you might need more time to get adjusted to the college life anyway. I wouldn't be worried about the five-year verses four-year issue because believe me, you are going to want longer than four years and your friends at college will all be doing the same thing.

Current student, 9/2003-Submit Date, September 2004

Northeastern has become much more selective these past couple of years, and the competition for admission is getting harder. Definitely maintain a lot of diversity within the activities and clubs in which you participate, and work hard to get a good SAT score. If in your essay you try hard to appear like a diverse student who can bring a lot of different things to the university, it will help your chances.

Current student, 9/2003-Submit Date, September 2004

The admissions office was very helpful. They sent many brochures to help lead us step by step through the process. There was very little confusion and the help lines were great. They answered all my questions quickly and efficiently. A lot of scholarships are also available and the process doesn't require any extra paperwork, which is great for those busy seniors.

 Academics

Alumnus/a, 9/1999-5/2004, March 2007

In general, the quality of classes at Northeastern is great. The professors are extremely intelligent and educated in their subject matter. For the most part, the class sizes are generally around 30 people, therefore making it somewhat easy to develop a relationship with other students, as well as the professors.

Signing up for classes at Northeastern is fairly easy. There is a set date for each student to sign up and as long as you have the classes you'd like picked out and sign up on that day, most of the time you will receive the classes you wanted.

The majority of the professors grade fairly, but there are of course a few on each end who are either much easier, or harder than most. The workload is fair and can be heavy at times, but generally nothing that isn't manageable.

Current student, Engineering, 9/2004-Submit Date, April 2006

I am finishing my sophomore year this week, and the program has been great. Freshman year, you take more standard classes, then sophomore year, take classes in your concentration. For example, as a mechanical engineering student, I have started to take classes that directly relate to ME.

Most classes are great. Some are boring, but most get the point across in clear fashion, which many engineering programs have a difficult time doing.

Engineering classes are not popular to students outside of engineering, therefore, it's easy to take the courses you need to take, at a time that fits your schedule.

Read all of Vault's College Surveys at **www.vault.com/college**—get complete surveys on 100s of colleges and universities, expert advice on applicaton essays and more.

VAULT CAREER LIBRARY **333**

Workload is heavier in engineering than other colleges, excluding pre-med and sciences. However, I try to get my work done during the week so I can enjoy my weekend.

Current student, 9/2005-Submit Date, January 2006

The rigor of the courses really depend on which courses you take. So far, I have been taking mainly science courses, such as chemistry and biology. These courses require you to take supplementary lab courses. The science curriculum is fairly rigorous, and the professors are great. They are always available to you. Grading here is similar to most other universities with a 4.0 equating to an A, a 3.0 to a B and so on. Registration can be all done online, which is just wonderful! Classes can fill up quickly though.

Alumnus/a, 9/1999-5/2003, September 2005

Northeastern offers great class sizes. The professors are great, highly knowledgeable and fun to listen to and learn from. The classes are of high quality. Many of my professors have written their own book on the topics of the class. I had a lot of respect for my professors, and always felt they respected me. They had good office hours and were available when I needed them. I never had a problem getting classes I needed when I needed them. The advisors are very helpful with keeping you on track. The class sizes for courses in my major were on average 20 students. Classes that everyone needed, like Psychology, were more like 100 students, but that was very rare. In the summer, if you choose to go to school, you can choose to go only three days a week, allowing you to enjoy still the summer weather. The library is relatively new at Northeastern. It also has a system where you can request books from many other libraries in the area, like Boston University or Boston College. There are many computers in the library.

Current student, 9/2003-Submit Date, March 2005

Although Northeastern is a university, I feel a close connection with my fellow classmates because in the College of Communications, there are about 100 students in my year. We are all very close, and the classes are small and interactive.

The professors are very accessible and the workload is challenging but reasonable. Getting into the popular classes is difficult, but if you keep in close contact with your academic advisors, you will increase your chances. It is very important to keep a good handle on your time-management skills because there is so much offered at Northeastern.

Current student, 9/2003-Submit Date, September 2004

So far I have been impressed with the academics at Northeastern. In the business school, of which I am a part, the program starts off with an excellent introduction to business course that shows you all aspects of business and helps you become more acquainted with which route you might want to take.

Classes are in nice, comfortable settings, and encourage participation and group projects rather than just lectures and tests. I haven't had trouble getting into the classes I need, and it hasn't been confusing figuring out which ones I do need. Overall, it is a pretty strong, structured program.

Current student, 9/2003-Submit Date, September 2004

Very well organized schedules, not too fully loaded on any day more than another, great enthusiastic professors who enriched the classes. A great system to get everyone a well-rounded education with certain required classes in each field of study, no matter your major or minor. The grading systems differ between each professor but for the most part they seem equal and fair with the exception of some math classes for which the final is a largely significant part of the final grade.

 # Employment Prospects

Alumnus/a, 9/1999-5/2004, March 2007

At Northeastern the employment prospects are great. I received a job offer from one of my former co-op employers before I began my senior year, and started upon graduation. Northeastern has numerous contacts at different employers, especially in the Boston area. Northeastern offers co-op opportunities that are great opportunities not only to build your résumé, but also to start a career.

Current student, 9/2004-Submit Date, April 2006

Because of the co-op program, Northeastern has many connections. GE, J&[Boston Scientific, Gillete, just to name a few companies. Then tons of sma[labs/design firms. Plus, the jobs are not just in Boston. They exist all across th country, even across the Pond. The co-op/internship program is the best in th U.S.

Current student, 9/2005-Submit Date, January 2006

The co-op program at Northeastern is the best in the country, according to U.[News & World Report. If you opt to do the co-op program, you will typical[graduate in five years with some great work experience already under your be[This looks great on a résumé and for applying to graduate school/me[school/law school. You go on co-op for six months at a time, starting in yo[sophomore year.

Alumnus/a, 9/1999-5/2003, September 2005

Northeastern offers co-op opportunities were you go to school for six months [year (sophomore to senior years, and you go to school for a total of five year[and work six months a year at jobs that are in your career field. Your advise[offers many jobs from which to choose and you are then required to set up inte[views with the companies you find interesting. After the interview process [complete, you choose the job that you want and begin working within week[The student has the option of working consecutively for three or six month[The co-op programs offers experience in interviewing, and is a great opportun[ty to make good money and get great experience working in your field [study—something that most college graduates lack. It also allows you to stay [school yearround instead of having to return home to your parents.

> **The school says:** "We no longer offer three month co-ops. The standard is six months."

Current student, 9/2003-Submit Date, September 2004

Northeastern has an excellent co-op program. After the fall semester of you[sophomore year, you alternate six months on a co-op job and six months in clas[This way you are getting multiple opportunities to experience real, well-pa[jobs before you graduate and while you are still in the learning process. So [you realize that you really don't like doing something, you can switch soone[rather than later, instead of after you have already graduated. Also, you usual[get to have three different co-op jobs before graduation. Because [Northeastern's vast connections, opportunities for these jobs can be almost any[where around the world.

Current student, 9/2003-Submit Date, March 2005

Northeastern is a cooperative learning environment and most students work f[the two recommended years over the course of their five-year program. It give[us quite the edge against other universities that don't offer this. A lot of peop[continue working at the co-op where they worked during college. You will b[working real jobs in real professional work environments. If you are career-ce[tered and work-oriented this is the school for you.

If the thought of taking four more years of general classes sounds dreadful [you, don't go to a liberal arts college, come to Northeastern where you lear[practical skills for a practical life.

Current student, 9/2000-Submit Date, January 2004

Northeastern is a great way to start off your career, thanks to the well-establishe[co-op program. Even during tough economic times, it does well placing kid[with some good companies. We have internships with top firms, such as Bosto[Consulting and GE, and we have small internships where you can get a sma[company feel. The employees come back for NU kids every semester, whic[says a lot. The co-op program can make you cry from frustration and happines[when you get that six-month internship paying $18 an hour and a full week [paid vacation. After college, many kids go back to the companies with whic[they co-oped. I am graduating this year, and the career services is trying its be[to network for postgrad jobs. I am quite impressed. The resources are here [you are willing to use them. We do have many career fairs for almost all of ou[majors throughout the semesters. Many kids get their jobs here or at least ne[work.

Quality of Life

Current student, 9/2005-Submit Date, January 2006

The freshman dorms are nothing special. Most rooms are about 8x12 feet and are shared with a roommate or two. It's best if you get along with your roommate because if you don't, the chances of you getting moved to another dorm are slim. When you come to orientation, you'll learn a lot about how to stay safe in this part of Boston, as Northeastern is next to Roxbury. It is not particularly safe to walk around alone at night as there are a few muggings. The dining halls are nice, but the food does not change and you basically get the same thing everyday except during parents' weekend. And the food isn't exactly the healthiest either, but the Marino Center is one of the best gyms I've ever seen and you can burn off all the calories you consumed from the dining hall food. Everything is within walking distance: the Pru and Newbury Street are about a 10-to-15 minute walk. If you can't walk, the T is right on campus on the Green line. You can literally go anywhere around here. There are a lot of restaurants and shops to keep you entertained. There isn't much of a nightlife around here, but Boston is still a great city.

Alumnus/a, 9/1999-5/2003, September 2005

Boston is a great city with little crime. I always felt very safe there. There are many things to do and see in and around the city. There is a great history and diverse culture here. You don't need a car due to the great transit system. You can even use the commuter rail to get to other areas of Massachusetts. The school offers cafes and other spots to get food and drinks throughout the week. The cafeteria program works well for freshmen who still live in the dorms. I lived off campus for my last three years of schooling and used the train to get to campus. It was cheaper and more private than living in the dorms. NU does have a new 14-floor dorm with great views of the city.

Current student, 9/2003-Submit Date, March 2005

At Northeastern the housing is among the highest rated. After freshman year, all housing is apartment style. The food is fantastic and available until late hours. There is so much to do in and around campus because it's in Boston and we have our own safety force and crime is closely monitored.

I currently live in a single apartment in an apartment-style residence hall and I have my own kitchen, a huge living room with two couches, a bedroom with two beds, my own bathroom so I don't have to share with 60 other people. I am living better than I did before college and the only way to afford living in this highly expensive city is by being a student or being rich. So take advantage of being a student and get yourself to Boston!

Current student, 9/2000-Submit Date, January 2004

The on-campus housing is improving. In my four years here, I have seen five new housing buildings go up. Very impressive, since NU is right in Back Bay, and property is not cheap. Many kids live off campus after their freshman year to save money. I would say the average rent off campus is around $750 a month. Some pay less and the kids who are wealthy pay much more. The gym is state-of-the-art. It is safe at Northeastern. If you live behind the university, it is a little more unsafe, as well as if you live near Fenway Park. You have to keep in mind that it is Boston. With any major city comes risk, but if you are aware of your surroundings and do not walk alone at 4 a.m., you will be fine. The university also offers campus police who will actually come pick you up if you need them too, free of charge.

Overall the classrooms are good. Some buildings are nicer than others, but how nice does a place where you sit down and take notes have to be? The freshman dining hall is good. It has two different cafeterias, with options like stir fry, pizza and the usual cafeteria food. In addition, there are lots of reasonably priced pizza and pasta restaurants for when you get tired of the cafe. If you have money to dine out, Boston offers a great selection of food and many varieties. Overall, I have been happy.

Social Life

Current student, 1/2004-Submit Date, March 2006

Northeastern is in the center of Boston, one of the biggest college cities in the country. There is always something to do here. There are tons of bars and restaurants all around; one of my favorites is right on campus (Connors) and is always fun to go to. The dating scene is great because there are tons of students from other colleges all over. There are also tons of clubs that are fun to attend and there are always campus-sponsored events. There are sororities and fraternities but I am not involved with them really. There is so much other stuff to do.

Current student, 9/2003-Submit Date, March 2005

This is the place to be for socializing. There are hundreds of restaurants within reach, nightclubs within walking distance, upscale places and romantic pathways along the Charles River for dates, pizza joints open late and a lot of bars and coffee shops with live entertainment. I cannot imagine being bored in this city. I would go crazy at a small suburban campus because there's nothing to do there. But in Boston, you have everything at your fingertips.

There are at least five transit systems that run directly through our campus. We have access to the Green and Orange Line of the MBTA, the commuter rail that runs out to the suburbs, the buses go into and away from the city, and if none of those work for you taxi services frequently go through campus.

Current student, 9/2003-Submit Date, September 2004

Being in the middle of Boston, there is a lot of social life here. There are tons of clubs, bars, restaurants and shopping areas all over the place in pretty much any form that you would want. Being in Boston, you're also in the middle of pretty much the biggest college city in the nation, so there are tons of people your age.

The Greek system is not huge at Northeastern, but it does exist. Usually those parties happen at various apartments since there isn't really room for any fraternity or sorority houses. Some favorite student spots are Fenway, where the Red Sox play, Landsdowne Street, which has multiple clubs, The Roxy, and shopping places, like the Prudential and Copley, Newbury Street, Downtown Crossings and Faneuil Hall.

Current student, 9/2000-Submit Date, January 2004

The social life is Boston. Almost no frats or sororities, but there are a few. The nightlife is a lot of fun; whether you just want a college bar, trendy club, Latin bar or hole in the wall, you can find it. There are a few Northeastern bars, such as Our House East and Connor Larkins, where you run into the same people almost every weekend. If you come to Northeastern, you will most likely live here in the summer after your freshman year. It is really great in the summer. Classes are laid back, and you can travel with friends up to Maine or down to the Cape in no time.

Northeastern can be overwhelming at the beginning. There is such a mixture of cultures and students, it might seem hard to fit in at first. But once you do, you will be glad you stayed with all the opportunities Northeastern offers.

The School Says

Founded in 1898, Northeastern University is a private research university located in the heart of Boston. Northeastern is a leader in interdisciplinary research, urban engagement, and the integration of classroom learning with real-world experience. The university's distinctive cooperative education program, where students alternate semesters of full-time study with semesters of paid work in fields relevant to their professional interests and major, is one of the largest and most innovative in the world. The University offers a comprehensive range of undergraduate and graduate programs leading to degrees through the doctorate in six undergraduate colleges, eight graduate schools, and two part-time divisions. For more information, please visit www.northeastern.edu.

Read all of Vault's College Surveys at **www.vault.com/college**–get complete surveys on 100s of colleges and universities, expert advice on applicaton essays and more.

VAULT CAREER LIBRARY   335

Olin College

Franklin W. Olin College of Engineering
Office of Admission
Olin Way
Needham, MA 02492-1200
Admissions phone: (781) 292-2222
Admissions fax: (781) 292-2210
Admissions e-mail: apply@olin.edu
Admissions URL: www.olin.edu/admission

 ## Admissions

Current student, Engineering, 9/2006-Submit Date, October 2007

The admission process at Olin is intense to say the least. There are definitely high admissions standards. The essays are some of the most challenging—and that is only to get to Candidates' Weekend! Olin looks for passionate, interesting people. The essays are an excellent chance to display that passion are as important as extracurricular activities. The first cut is to a group of about 150 students. Olin then pays for you to fly up and spend two days interviewing and learning about the school. At Candidates' Weekend, you will participate in a design challenge, as well as individual and group interviews. The key to doing well at Candidates' Weekend is to be yourself. Ditch the parents and chat with all the current students. Believe it or not, every student can submit positive or negative comments on every candidate. That is certainly a little intimidating but it is also really cool. It gives you a chance to see if you will genuinely fit into the community here. I guess the big keyword is passion. If you exhibit passion in your extracurriculars, essays and interviews, you will do just fine.

Current student, Engineering, 9/2006-Submit Date, October 2007

The admissions process has two parts. Like any undergraduate college, you first apply by submitting your high school transcript, teacher recommendations, test scores and essays. The admissions team looks at all of these things and, as I understand it, selects students whom they think have achieved some level of academic success and have shown an interest in non-scholastic activities—in other words, a pretty typical college admissions process. They select about 180 students to come to Olin for Candidates' Weekend, a weekend of interviews, team building activities, information sessions, and some other random things. This second round of the process looks at your personality, and how you would fit at Olin College. From the candidates chosen, some number are admitted (based on the expected acceptance rate, which I don't know), so that the next class is made up of approximately [70] students. Olin focuses on having passions outside of school, which could be a sport, music, fixing up junk cars, or pretty much anything. There is also a fairly significant focus on community service. Overall, they look for students who would not make narrow-minded engineers, but who have a good sense of a bigger picture, students who don't just build something, but think about its impact on the world, how to market it, and how to make sure it is really something that will help the user.

Alumnus/a, Engineering, 8/2001-5/2006, October 2007

Olin is definitely a highly selective school. This year alone, there were over 1,000 applications for the 75 or so spots in the freshman class. The admission process is split into two phases. The first phase is fairly traditional: students submit test scores (SAT or ACT plus two SAT Subject Tests—either Math I or Math II and a science subject of the student's choice), get teacher recommendations (two are required and a third optional), write essays (there are two essays, one of which is aimed at finding out the applicant's passion—it better not be doing homework!), and submit a high school transcript.

As far as advice on getting in, I can only say be honest. Grades and test scores are important, but they are not everything. Olin looks for unique and well-rounded people to create the "Renaissance" engineer.

Current student, Engineering, 8/2006-Submit Date, October 200

Olin has a two-tiered admissions process. First, like any other college, we tak applications that involve essay questions and the like. Then things get different Of the applicants, approximately [180] are invited to visit the campus for one of two Candidates' Weekends. CW serves both to let the applicant get to know the school, and for the school to get to know the applicant. There are team projec and presentations about the school. This is similar to some schools' admitte students' weekends, save that there are two interviews, one individual and on group, that ensure that the applicant really fits Olin.

Alumnus/a, Engineering, 8/2002-5/2006, October 2007

Olin's admission process is selective, but designed to make sure that Olin is good fit for the student as much as that the student is a good fit for Olin. Goo scores, and involvement in a variety of activities during high school, will hel you, but not seal the deal. Olin looks for individuals with passion—prospectiv students who have shown a desire to learn and an ability to get excited abou their interests. It's also important that students are sure they want to study eng neering; Olin has excellent opportunities for cross-registration with other inst tutions (Wellesley, Babson, Brandeis), and offers a wide variety of classes, bu the focus of the institution is on engineering.

Alumnus/a, Engineering, 8/2003-5/2007, October 2007

The admissions process at Olin was created to ensure that Olin would admit no only the best, brightest and most talented students, but also those who are th best fit for the school. Like any other college or university, Olin's applicatio consists of a generic form (name, hometown, grades, standardized test scores volunteer/extracurricular activities and so on), two essays, and letters of recom mendation. The essays really provide a chance for the student to shine through These applications are sifted through in great detail before being narrowed dow to approximately [180] students. Each of these students is flown to Olin ove two weekends to meet the Olin community, be interviewed (individually and i groups), and get a feel for how they would fit in at Olin. At this time, the aca demic excellence of the students don't matter; all that matters is whether the stu dents demonstrate the characteristics that truly make Olin students great: ded cation, passion for Olin and a love of learning.

 ## Academics

Alumnus/a, Engineering, 8/2001-5/2006, October 2007

Olin was created to revolutionize engineering education and it's doing just tha Students not only take the standard engineering math and science classes, bu they also apply that knowledge to hands-on projects starting in their first semes ter at Olin. Not only is this a fun way to learn, but it also makes the materia more meaningful and easier to absorb. Olin also places a big emphasis on desig and entrepreneurship, which are two areas about which the industry loves engi neers to know.

The classes are pretty intense—make no mistake, you will work at Olin—an you end up learning a lot. Part of it has to do with the fact that the professor teaching at Olin are incredibly focused on the students. They are there to teac and because Olin is so small, students receive a lot of individual attention from professors (most of whom like to be called by their first name). In addition, ther are no graduate students, which means all the research is done by undergrads.

The grading depends on the professor and the class. The math and science class es tend to be tougher than the humanities classes. You have to work for an A but it's pretty hard to get anything lower than a C.

I should also mention that Olin has cross-registration agreements with Babso College, Wellesley College and Brandeis University, which means that Olin stu dents can take any class at those institutions. Talk about options! There's eve a shuttle that goes between Wellesley and Olin.

Alumnus/a, Engineering, 8/2003-5/2007, October 2007

Olin is hard and demanding but other students and professors provide a lot of support to students. One of the most unique and distinguishing features is our curriculum. We teach engineering in a totally novel way—focusing on team-based projects, interdisciplinary learning, and a do-learn mentality. Because of the small nature of the school, getting classes is never a problem because you will always have a chance next year. Our professors are some of the most dynamic and interesting people I have ever met—incredibly accomplished, but human to us. We call most of them by their first names and develop very close relationships because of the small size of the school.

Current student, Engineering, 8/2007-Submit Date, October 2007

The education at Olin is an intensive immersion in the skills an engineer now needs. In addition, Olin is dedicated to producing a "new type of engineer," one who is not limited to in-depth knowledge about physics, math and so on, but who can effectively communicate ideas, organize design projects and otherwise apply his/her brilliance in the real world. Freshman year's curriculum includes a Design Nature class, in which students design and build a bio-inspired hopper, using Solidworks software and machine shop tools along the way. In addition, the Integrated Course Block (ICB) consists of physics, calculus/math, engineering of compartment/distributed systems, and an introduction to programming component. The goal of this is to teach the various components in an integrated fashion so that students may understand where the mathematical concepts they learn apply in physics, how to model these behaviors in programming (MAT-LAB), and how to apply general concepts of systems to specific physical problems. Finally, there is an arts, humanities, and social sciences foundation, which in the past has included digital photograph, health and the urban environment, Islam and the West, creative writing, fundamentals of anthropology and much more. The rest of the Olin education is dependent on the particular student. Olin is particularly strong in mechanical, electrical, and systems engineering, though bioengineering and materials sciences are well-represented among the faculty and course offerings.

In general, classes are project-based, following the belief that to truly understand concepts, students must use them and accomplish given tasks with them. Classes are taught by professors with impressive academic backgrounds, many hailing from MIT, Harvard or similarly high-caliber schools. All of them are extremely capable, not only in their own fields, but interdisciplinary. As a small school, with total enrollment at around 300, entrance into your desired classes is almost guaranteed. Class sizes max out at around 25 and are on average lower as they become more specialized. As such, there is much one-on-one attention from professors. They also make themselves very available, and often request feedback from students about how the course is going. The Olin workload is considerable, though almost all students still find plenty of time to participate in extracurriculars and enjoy college life.

Alumnus/a, Engineering, 8/2002-5/2006, October 2007

Classes are hard, and students work hard to succeed. That said, there is a focus on teamwork and collaboration, and professors encourage students to get help and not just struggle in solitude. This leads to a friendly and supportive environment amongst students, and makes the workload bearable. Popular classes are not usually too hard to get; when there's a lot of competition, professors will sometimes be flexible and allow extra students to take classes. The professors are excellent teachers who chose Olin because they wanted to teach undergraduate students. They make themselves very available, get to know their students, and go above and beyond to help their students succeed.

Current student, Engineering, 9/2006-Submit Date, October 2007

Olin is a small college, with a limited number of professors. This can make getting some classes difficult in a given semester. However, my experience has been that if you don't get a class the semester you want it, you can almost always get it the next semester. Courses that are prerequisites for things are pretty easy to get. The wonderful thing about Olin is the professors. The professors are all extremely accessible—they make themselves easy to contact, have office hours and tend to know their students.

Classes aren't tiny, as many classes that might have 12 students some places have maybe 20 or 25 here, but there are no classes with more then 30 students, there are no giant 101 classes in which you never even meet the professor, and even in large classes, the professors make an effort to really be accessible. Professors

often join student tables in the dining hall at lunch, and several professors even live on campus and host events for the student body.

The workload is pretty intense, but it is an engineering school, so it's about what you'd expect. A lot of the work, particularly in the first two years, is project based, as opposed to problem set based. Classes vary in intensity and quality, but in general they are all fairly difficult and informative.

 # Employment Prospects

Alumnus/a, Engineering, 8/2001-5/2006, October 2007

Current alumni work at Google, ESI, Yahoo!, Raytheon, DEKA, IBM, iRobot, BostonScientific, HP, J&J, Texas Instrument and many other prestigious companies, and the opportunities are getting better every year, due to the expanding alumni network. Since Olin is tiny, students tend to form close relationships with their classmates. This means that alumni are really motivated to help seniors find jobs.

Olin has the Office of Post Graduate Planning to help students find jobs after graduation and internships during the summer (a lot of Olin students do internships during the summer). There is also a push for on-campus recruiting (there is a career fair every year), and industry officials often attend Olin's Expo (a day at the end of each semester when students show off their projects). Expo is a great opportunity to get a job or an internship.

I also want to emphasize that not all graduates go into industry. About a third of the first graduating class went on to grad school, be it in engineering, science, law, medicine or business. Olin students also receive prestigious fellowships, such as Fulbrights, IGERTs and NSF GRFs.

Alumnus/a, Engineering, 8/2003-5/2007, October 2007

Some high-profile employers can't get enough Olin employees. Many technical companies (HP, IBM, Mathworks, Sylvania, Google) recruit on campus, even though there are only 75 graduates per year. Many students choose to go top research graduate schools (Stanford, MIT and Harvard Business School get the most). There is little to no alumni network to date, though that will change! Because the school has little reputation, employment tends to be at a personal level. Many students choose to work with small companies, however, as the culture may be a better match. Every year, some go to law school or medical school. As a whole, Olin graduates go do a huge variety of things.

Alumnus/a, Engineering, 8/2003-5/2007, October 2007

We've only graduated two classes, but we've had alumni go on to work for well-known companies, such as Google, GE, Raytheon, Northrup Grumman and smaller smart-ups. We have alumni pursuing Fulbrights and receiving scholarships to attend some of the most prestigious educational programs in the country in engineering, education, medicine and law.

Alumnus/a, Engineering, 8/2001-5/2006, October 2007

Since Olin only graduated its first class in 2006 students have to work hard to make sure employers understand Olin. The number of interested employers keeps increasing and this year's career initiatives day had more recruiters than ever before. Prestige is increasing especially at companies where Olin students have started working. Olin students are developing a reputation for being able to work without much supervision on things they have never done before.

Alumnus/a, Engineering, 8/2002-5/2006, October 2007

I'm now in a competitive graduate program at MIT, and had several competing opportunities when I graduated. On-campus recruiting options abound, as Olin focuses on project-based and team-based activities that provide numerous opportunities for industry guests to connect with students.

As one of the first alumni (Olin has only existed a few years; I was in the first graduating class!), the alumni network is still being built. That said, we're eager to help each other, and very supportive of both alumni and students. I know that several current students and alumni have already found jobs and internships through alumni networking. Graduates have gone into competitive graduate programs at Oxford, Stanford, MIT and other excellent schools, along with obtaining a number of excellent job offers and positions from Google, IBM, the Woods Hole Oceanographic

Read all of Vault's College Surveys at **www.vault.com/college**-get complete surveys on 100s of colleges and universities, expert advice on applicaton essays and more.

VAULT CAREER LIBRARY 337

Institution, iRobot, Boeing and numerous other industry leaders. I would rank employment prospects as excellent and improving.

Quality of Life

Alumnus/a, Engineering, 8/2003-5/2007, October 2007

Olin treats its students extremely well. There are beautiful and modern facilities that are brand-new. The dining hall is superb compared to other colleges because of the small student body size, but it is still college food. The dorms are fully wired and are either doubles with private bathrooms or suites (six singles) with a common living room and two private bathrooms. Both come with refrigerators and microwaves, and all the necessary furniture. The campus is small (only five buildings), so getting around takes almost no time, which is great when you wake up late for class or it's snowing/raining. The neighborhood, Needham, is incredibly safe because it is a small suburban town.

Alumnus/a, Engineering, 8/2003-5/2007, October 2007

Olin's dorms were compared to palaces by the Princeton Review, which I believe gives a good description of how wonderful the living spaces can be. Olin is located in Needham, probably one of the safest places in the universe, and besides that, everyone at the school abides by the Honor Code. My favorite story to tell about the Honor Code is that once, a student tried to test it by leaving a $20 bill on a table in one of the dorm lounges. A few weeks later, the money was still there because of the respect Olin students show for other's property. Although Olin is in no way perfect, I do not know of any other place where I could leave my laptop sitting in the library while I went to the cafeteria for lunch.

Current student, Engineering, 8/2007-Submit Date, October 2007

Housing consists of doubles or suites with private bathrooms and plenty of space. None of the dorms are more than six years old and all facilities have the latest technology and safety equipment. The entire campus has wireless Internet. The dining hall is a buffet with gourmet quality food. Crime is essentially zero, because the Honor Code is in effect, and it is common practice to leave belongings in public space, because there is no chance that it will get stolen or misplaced. Needham is a small suburb, and next door Wellesley is equally safe.

Alumnus/a, Engineering, 8/2001-5/2006, October 2007

Everything at Olin is really new, and the dorms can't be beat. Most freshmen and sophomores share a large room with a bathroom. Juniors and seniors can live in suites—six single rooms with a common lounge area and two bathrooms. The dining hall has great food, but it's the only option to eat on campus and it can get old.

The small size of the school is both a blessing and a curse. On the one hand, going to Olin can sometimes feel like being in a bubble and you'll probably be able to recognize a classmate from 200 yards just by the way they walk. On the other hand, you'll forge incredibly close friendships with your fellow classmates, faculty and even staff. Students who struggle with the small size of the school (as I did) can go to neighboring Babson College (a five-minute walk) to make new social connections or just to grab some different food. Babson also has great workout and art facilities.

Alumnus/a, Engineering, 8/2002-5/2006, October 2007

The on-campus dormitories are very nice, especially the six-person suites. The dormitories are only a few years old, and have been well taken care of to date. The facilities are topnotch, including a scanning electron microscope, advanced machine shop, fully outfitted materials science lab, and required laptops for every student.

Alumnus/a, Engineering, 8/2003-5/2007, October 2007

The facilities are excellent, and very well cared for. The community is clean and respectful of the campus because it is so small and intimate, and there is a feeling of ownership. Dorm rooms are comfortable and every room has its own bathroom (suites have two). Most importantly, the food is fantastic! The dining hall staff listens to student suggestions and has a great relationship with the student body.

Social Life

Alumnus/a, Engineering, 8/2002-5/2006, October 2007

Olin's social life is vibrant, with a diverse and supportive student culture. That said, it is a very small school, and prospective students should be aware that with only 300 fellow students, you will know each of them. This means that the school is very tight-knit and supportive, but it can be claustrophobic for some. There are some nice restaurants nearby in Needham and Wellesley, and a number of events both on-campus and at neighboring colleges Wellesley and Babson.

Current student, Engineering, 8/2007-Submit Date, October 2007

With Boston within a T-ride and neighboring college campuses of Wellesley and Babson, there is as much of a social life as one could desire at Olin. There are no fraternities or sororities, but Man Hall is a fine substitute if you want parties and general entertainment. Everyone knows each other on this small campus, so there is a real feel of community. Everyone looks out for one another, and you only need to ask for rides to get help.

Alumnus/a, Engineering, 8/2003-5/2007, October 2007

There are always events happening on campus and these are well attended by the student body. We often talk about the "Olin bubble" because it is so easy to get caught up in everything to do at Olin. There are tons of clubs for the number of students (about a club per six students) and all it takes is four people to start a new club and obtain funding. We are close to Wellesley and Babson and are invited to most of their events, too.

Alumnus/a, Engineering, 8/2001-5/2006, October 2007

Dating is tricky. The school is really small so there's no escaping your ex. There is little casual dating, so people either have flings or really committed relationship. With that said, about a a third of the student body has an on-campus relationship, another third has a significant other off campus and the rest are not involved.

There are many clubs at Olin and the Student Activities Committee throws some fun events on campus: dances, music events and outdoor movies.

Alumnus/a, Engineering, 8/2001-5/2006, October 2007

There aren't any bars or restaurants on campus aside from the dining hall, which is generally quite good. With such a small campus, some of us say Olin is like one big frat/sorority. In the first year with only 75 students there were 36 clubs formed, so a lot of students are involved in a lot of groups and organizations. The most popular are the community service organization, SERV, and the drama organization known as the Franklin W. Olin Players or FWOP. Olin students attend many of the events on campus and usually also attend many events/performances Olin students are a part of either on Babson's campus or around the Boston area.

Alumnus/a, Engineering, 9/2003-5/2007, October 2007

Students work hard, but also have fun. You can find people who share your interests, but you also are able to learn and try many new activities through your friends. The community of people at Olin, including the students, faculty, staff and administration, are what make Olin really stand out to me.

Smith College

Northampton, MA 01063
Admissions phone: (413) 585-2500 or (800) 383-3232
Admissions e-mail: admission@smith.edu
Admissions URL: www.smith.edu/admission/

Admissions

Current student, 9/2004-Submit Date, January 2007

Recently Smith has begun to accept only the Common application with supplements, such as guidance counselor's recommendation, SAT or ACT scores, two teachers' evaluation, mid-year report and high school transcript. Interviews are not required but I would recommend one because a good interview increases your chances of getting in. Most interviews can be set up with a local alumna in your area or on campus, if you prefer. Because Smith is a liberal arts women's institution, the admission is very selective. Applicants should show a desire to succeed and a willingness to grow. Applicants should show what they will contribute to the Smith community as a whole and why they choose Smith of all colleges.

Alumna, 8/1996-12/1999, March 2006

I applied as a transfer student. Approximately 75 seats are held each year for incoming transfers. The application process proved straightforward and the admissions office was exceptionally helpful. As an alumna, I am working now with the local chapter of my alumnae association to recruit young women interested in Smith. We provide opportunities for students to meet with alumnae and learn more about Smith from our best resources—our alumnae. Smith is highly selective, but prides itself on looking at the whole student and not just the numbers posted on the student's application. As such, the admissions committee seeks well-rounded individuals who demonstrate spark—that is, women who stand out because of a passionate interest in learning and other aspects of their lives. I highly recommend that applicants interview both at the school and with an alumna. In terms of essays, Smith demands considerable writing skills from its students, so I advise applicants to make certain that their application essay is strong and reveals—through showing, not telling—something interesting about themselves.

Alumna, 9/1995-6/1999, March 2005

Smith has a fantastic network of alumnae who assist with screening students. Typically you will have an interview with a local aluma but a campus interview is also preferred. While the average SAT scores at Smith are high, Smith tends to be more flexible than many schools—if a student has demonstrated academic excellence and/or other talents, Smith seems to hold that above test scores (in many cases).

Alumna, 9/1993-1/1997, January 2005

Focus on what is unique about Smith for you; in which programs, resources and events will you be involved—why do you want to go Smith over another college? Why are you the right person for Smith? What makes you stand out over everyone else? For the essay, choose something that is unique to you. I had taken a year off. I focused on how that year had helped me grow and become more focused on my education.

Alumna, 9/1999-9/2003, November 2004

Admissions was fairly competitive, as is normal for colleges of this caliber. I submitted SAT scores of 1400 and SAT Subject Test scores of similar levels for three areas—math, English and Spanish. I applied in time for early admission and wrote only one essay and had four teacher recommendations (although I think only two or three were required).

Alumna, 9/1994-5/1997, October 2003

I applied to transfer to Smith. I have been told that transferring to top schools is easier than trying to get in from high school. I think this could be a myth as far as Smith goes, however. I have known multiple, highly qualified people who did

not get in as transfer students. Anyway, I interviewed with a school-appointed admissions counselor and met with students. The interview was a little stressful because they really want to know why I wanted a women's college and why Smith specifically.

Alumna, 9/1999-12/2002, October 2003

I applied Early Decision. It was fairly straightforward: application, essay (I believe I got to choose a topic), interview with an admissions person and an optional campus tour. I interviewed on campus.

Alumna, 9/1991-6/1995, September 2003

Smith is a very selective school, but as a women's college, statistically it admits a much larger percent of its applicants than similar co-ed schools. A full application, essays and interviews are required. Regional alumnae interviews are helpful, both with informing the applicant in the decision-making process and boosting chances of admission. I strongly recommend a campus visit, as the property (a national arboretum) is beautiful and the atmosphere compelling. A visit sealed the deal for me.

Academics

Alumna, 8/1991-5/1995, November 2006

The classes are challenging, there is no other way to put it. I attended a rigorous high school, and Smith classes were the next logical step in the progression. I mention this because my friends who attended nearby universities, such as Ivy League, found the classes easier than at my high school—they were partying on weekends and I was in the library. However, once I got used to the fact that I would need to continue to forge ahead I loved it—the classes are small, the faculty truly cares about each student's education, and I figured out how to balance everything without too much trouble.

Alumna, Psychology, 9/1999-5/2003, June 2007

Very high academics, though not as competitive as larger institutions. Very unique group of classmates who are more interested in the ideas being discussed than in one-upping each other. Classes are taught by the professors, not grad students, which is a huge plus. Also professors treat students as future colleagues, and are mainly very approachable, and invested in a student's education.

Current student, 9/2004-Submit Date, January 2007

Smith is very different in its approach to academics in that there is an open curriculum. The only requirements outside of your major are a writing intensive course to be taken your first year and half of your credits must be outside of your major. You will create your own curriculum with the help of a faculty advisor. Classes are easy to get into. In most cases, you will get into the classes you choose, but priority is given to upperclasswomen and majors, in the rare cases that the class is full. Most professors will try and make a way for you to take their class if you really want to get into it. Professors are very helpful and you never will be taught by a TA. Professors make an extra effort to get to know all of their students. Classes are relatively small, the largest class numbers in a popular major introductory class may have about 100 people, but not often. One growing popular major is Engineering Science, which focuses on the fundamentals of all engineering, while still gaining liberal arts studies. It is the first all-women program of its type. The workload is what you make it. It can be a very demanding workload but Smith offers all the resources, tutoring and writing help needed to succeed in your class studies.

Alumna, 8/1996-12/1999, March 2006

Smith provides a demanding liberal arts education. There is a tremendous variety and diversity of classes from which to choose—I never experienced difficulty getting into a course. For admittance to some senior seminars, however, I did have to complete an application process. In my entire time at Smith, I never came across an incompetent professor (I mention this because I've attended many schools since Smith and I've never encountered the same caliber of teach-

Read all of Vault's College Surveys at www.vault.com/college–get complete surveys on 100s of colleges and universities, expert advice on applicaton essays and more.

VAULT CAREER LIBRARY 339

ing that I experienced at Smith) or a professor who didn't believe that a student could succeed. Almost all of the classes are small; my largest class was comprised of 65 students, but most held approximately 12. Grading at Smith is difficult—A's are reserved for students who produce publishable quality material in a class (or at least, this was the case in the English classes). Perhaps the best way to put it is that you do have to go above and beyond the workload on the syllabus to earn the top grades. However, faculty members are so accessible and the camaraderie among students is so strong that it is not difficult to find people to study with or get help from. Education is always about what you make of it, but Smith provides more resources (truly accessible ones) than any of the other institutions I've attended. In addition, Smith participates in the Five-College program, so students can take classes at UMass Amherst, Amherst, Hampshire and Mount Holyoke. It isn't always easy to arrange an exchange class (simply because of class schedules), but many people take advantage of this. Essentially, you get access to classes at five schools for the price of one.

Alumna, 9/1995-6/1999, March 2005

As a college prep school graduate, I felt much more prepared for the rigorous academics at Smith than many of my public school counterparts, but the academic workload was still completely overwhelming in my first year. Academic advisors are professors and often give in to what you want to do, as opposed to advising you that, for example, four survey courses can be completely overwhelming to a first-year student. There were rumors floating around that the workload at Smith was second only to MIT. It sure felt like it, but was well worth it in the end.

Alumna, 9/1993-1/1997, January 2005

Very competitive. Most classes are small, anywhere from eight to 20 students. There are some lectures that are larger. High quality classes and professors. Many professors are doing research work in addition to teaching. Many professors provide outside hours and the larger lectures often have smaller group times with an assigned professor. High workload with challenging classroom environment and instructors. Ease of getting into popular classes is determined by your major and year. For example, if you want to take an art class but you are not an art major, you will be chosen after all the students in the major get the class. However, if you register early enough, you still have a good chance. Smith is part of the Five College Consortium, which adds to its diversity and choices. You can take classes at any of the other five schools in the area. This includes Mt. Holyoke, UMass, Amherst College and Hampshire.

Alumna, 9/1994-5/1997, October 2003

The workload was enormous compared to the school from where I transferred—a large, well-respected university. The classes range in difficulty, but every professor asks students to think outside the box. Because the students are so aware and politically charged, class discussions can get really heated. I looked at this as a plus. I learned a lot from my peers. It can be hard to get into really popular classes, but professors have the right to let a student in. So, if one has a compelling reason for taking a class, one will likely get in. The professors are also very available to students. There is a neat program where professors come to dinner at houses. There isn't this great juvenilization of students going on. Professors at Smith are incredible because they (generally) don't see their job as just teaching; they are there to guide young women into mature adults who are also armed with a fantastic education. There is a huge push for sciences at Smith that continues today. The school really prides itself on debunking myths that females aren't proficient in math and science. There are also no distribution requirements unless one is trying for Latin honors. So, the academic program is quite flexible.

Alumna, 9/1999-12/2002, October 2003

Most classes have no space limits, so it is generally pretty easy to get the classes you want, assuming they fit into your schedule. Some courses have annoying prerequisites, especially in the economics department, where you have to take about four classes before you can do virtually anything else in the department. I had a couple of very small classes (fewer than 10 people), but popular classes can be over 50 people, which makes discussions difficult. Cross-registering among the five colleges is not as easy as they make it sound, but lots of people do it. Just be prepared for a lot of red tape with the five-college system. Smith, in general, became much more electronic in recent years, and a lot of things can be done online, such as registration and housing lottery. The classes are all taught by professors—TAs help only with extra help sessions. I never once

encountered a TA during my time at Smith. Professors vary in quality but are fairly accessible. Smith does not consider vocational courses to be worthy of degree and will not give credit for business, journalism or other profession-specific courses (except education).

Employment Prospects

Alumna, 8/1991-5/1995, November 2006

I earned a BA in Comparative Literature, and was a solid student with a 3.6 GPA. When I graduated, I had acceptance into a Top 10 master's program in English Literature at a major university; an au pair position in Milan, Italy; and a job offer for an entry-level editorship at Random House. I ended up choosing grad school, but any of those paths would have been valuable and interesting, I believe. The Career Development Office at Smith is absolutely amazing. I have continued to turn to them for assistance at various forks in the road in my career and they have always provided exactly what I needed to get to the next level.

Current student, 9/2004-Submit Date, January 2007

A Smith degree is something of which to be proud. Many employers think highly of Smith College. Because of the liberal arts curriculum, Smith grads go into an array of fields. Smith has an amazing alumnae network. Alumnae are very active in the Smith community and are always willing to help a Smith student find internships, jobs and just about anything. Many of the grants Smith awards for financial aid come from alumnae donations. The Career Development Office also works directly with alumnae to post job opening and provide mentors. Smith is dedicated to seeing all grads and undergraduates succeed. All students get a $2000 stipend to use to work at any unpaid internship they would like. This is given to ensure that students are able to access funding for summer internships to foster their career exploration. One of the reasons I chose to attend Smith was because of the amazing resources and opportunities for employment after graduation.

Alumna, 8/1996-12/1999, March 2006

Since the Class of 2000, every student at Smith receives a paid internship as part of her tenure at the school. Additionally, the Career Development Office (CDO) assists both students and alumnae with career development at all stages. The alumnae network is incredibly strong (with graduates like Betty Friedan and Gloria Steinem, how could it not be?) and it is easy to make connections with other alumnae. I think the school's reputation speaks for itself—all the best companies actively recruit students.

Alumna, 9/1995-6/1999, March 2005

Smith graduates are held in the highest regard. If a woman is willing to devote four years of her life to her schooling in an all-women's academic environment, she undoubtedly is devoted to an exceptional education and a secure future via her career. Smithies are pursued for a wide variety of positions after graduation, including career spots in finance, teaching, nonprofit, sales and marketing. Smith's CDO (career development office) helps with every aspect of the job hunting process, and the network of Smith alumnae is also a very strong force in hiring and advising Smith graduates.

Alumna, 9/1993-1/1997, January 2005

There is an intensive recruitment period on campus including some Fortune 500 companies. It can be more difficult if you are interested in more nontraditional or nonprofit careers. Smith prides itself on its alumnae network and its Career Development Office, touting that they are always a resource for alumnae regardless of where they are in their lives. Smith has started some superb programs over the past few years to assist in internships. The Praxis program has made internship funding more accessible and the possibility of internships more available. In addition, the CDO provides suites for interviews, if needed.

Alumna, 9/1999-5/2003, November 2004

The alumnae network at Smith is amazing. It offers high prestige with employers—graduates get wonderful jobs—my best friend got her statistical demographics job through an alumnae connection (not a friend before the network). The Career Development Office helps you get good internships, too.

Alumna, 9/1994-5/1997, October 2003

The Career Development Office is a wonderful resource for students and alumnae. The active alumnae networks are also a huge help. The school does a great job bringing in recruiters during the senior year. Students also have access to any recruiters that go to Amherst, UMass, Hampshire and Mt. Holyoke. This means students have access to a large array of employers and graduate admissions officers. Also, Smith has a Praxis program, which allows students to do an internship paid by the school over one summer. This is a huge advantage for graduates, because it allows students to take unpaid internships that they might not otherwise get to take. As we all know, these internships can turn into future jobs.

One very great advancement that has occurred since I graduated is the new Women and Financial Independence program offered to students and alumnae. When I left Smith, I had no clue how finances really worked. I think a lot of women leave college not knowing this stuff because of some of the old-school mentality that women don't need to know how to finance things, what a 401k plan is and how to pick a good one. The school has made great strides to arm women with this information regardless of one's major. These are the commitments that make Smith a very unique and wonderful place for women.

Quality of Life

Current student, 9/2004-Submit Date, January 2007

Smith has a beautiful campus. There are many new buildings mixed with the old campus feeling. A new state-of-the-art sports facility was built with TVs at every machine, full pool, indoor track and many more facilities to meet your every athletic need. The campus is very welcoming; it is very much looked at as a home, not a campus. Students live in houses that have anywhere from 43 to 70 students. All dining is in house and prepared by house cooks. 15 houses have dining but if you are not in a house with dining, you are most likely right next to a house that does. It is a loved tradition that every house has tea in the house living room once a week. There are many other traditions within houses but each is unique and traditions vary from medieval dinners to house apple picking trips. It is a very open, yet safe campus.

Alumna, 8/1996-12/1999, March 2006

Smith has a unique campus system. Instead of traditional dorms, students live in houses. These houses become invaluable communities—students feel like they truly have a home versus a dorm. Candlelight dinner is held every Thursday night and tea is served every Friday afternoon. There is a wide variety of houses from which to choose, ranging in size from seven people to 70. The best part about Smith is that it has a large number of single rooms available; after first year, you're pretty much guaranteed a single if you want one. The campus is beautiful, designed by Fredrick Law Olmstead, the same person who designed Central Park. The City of Northampton, of which Smith is a part, is a thriving New England town. Although it is small, it has a variety of restaurants, shops and entertainment. For a great history and description of the town, read Tracy Kidder's *Hometown*, a non-fiction book about Northampton. For those who prefer large cities, Northampton is approximately two hours hours from both Boston and New York and one hour from Hartford. There are no crime issues of which I'm aware—as a student there, I rarely locked my door and I never felt unsafe either on campus or in town.

Alumna, 9/1999-9/2003, November 2004

The housing is pretty good and most of the social life is in the houses, so choose wisely. I had a great house, Chapin House, which had 70 women. The houses are in different parts of campus and have very different feels. So for example if you live in the main quad (like Wilder or Gardner, where maybe 50 percent of the housing is), it feels pretty preppy, but if you live on the main campus, like Chapin House or Haven-Wesley House, the feel is much more liberal and open-minded and engaged. The campus is beautiful and has very little crime. The dining options are somewhat limited, although if you go downtown, there are a lot of places to eat, including several wonderful Italian restaurants and three Thai places (the one on Pleasant Street is much better than the one on the Main Street).

Alumna, 9/1999-12/2002, October 2003

The dorms are great. I had a big single all four years. Food is also excellent. Hardly anyone lives off campus, both because the dorms are awesome and because you have to give a good reason why you need to live off campus in order to get permission (such as being married, having children or living with your parents). They make a big deal out of safety, but it is not a dangerous area, and while I was there, I never heard of any crimes other than graffiti. Sometimes there is racial tension. I have not seen the new campus center, but it is supposed to be beautiful, and I'm sure it has really enhanced life on campus. It is hard to have a car at Smith, because there is virtually nowhere to park it.

Social Life

Alumna, 8/1991-5/1995, November 2006

You need to be prepared for the fact that Smith is a women's college. I came from a large, public, co-ed high school—so this was quite different. I took classes at Amherst College for three of my four years, and in that way had regular interaction with guys during my college years. However, I didn't date regularly, which was partly because I was so busy with classes and my other activities (including my wonderful friends at Smith), and partly because I didn't meet a lot of them and didn't arrive at Smith with a boyfriend already. For me, this turned out not to be a big deal at all. I ended up meeting my husband after grad school, and actually, in retrospect, I'm glad I had the time in my life that I did not to worry about my dating life so much and explore the rest of life. At Smith, I would go out with my friends every Thursday and Friday nights to one of the local bars or to a movie. Favorite ice cream place: Herrell's (amazing!); Favorite bar: Packard's; Favorite restaurant: Circa. Enjoy!

Alumna, Psychology, 9/1999-5/2003, June 2007

Wonderful town. Plenty of guys from the surrounding colleges, or up visiting from Yale or Harvard. Having them around on weekends is a treat, not having them around during the week means you can be serious about your studies.

Current student, 9/2004-Submit Date, January 2007

Located in the City of Northampton, MA, there are many great restaurants, movies theaters, art museums, bars and shopping in the area. The only downfall is if you are from a big city, Northampton does not seem like a city. I am used to the Philadelphia nightlife so I had a hard time adjusting to small city life where everything closes early, but it grows on you. There is no Greek system on campus but you are able to pledge at UMass Amherst, which is only 20 minutes away by bus, which we are able to ride for free. There five-college area will be of advantage if you want an active social and/or dating life. The surrounding colleges consist of Hampshire, Mt. Holyoke, Amherst and UMass Amherst. Smith students are able to take classes, join groups and use any facilities at the surrounding colleges. In all, Smith does have parties and boys do come, but the social life surely suffers due to the academic workload and the all-women setting.

Alumna, 8/1996-12/1999, March 2006

This list could be endless. The newly built student center is a great place to start. Then there are bars, diners (Whateley's is not to be missed!), restaurants, including: Bella's vegetarian, Fresh Pasta Co., Teapot (Japanese), Thai and Amanouz (Middle Eastern). Breakfast favorites like Sylvester's (Northampton's tribute to Sylvester Graham, inventor of the Graham cracker!), ice cream at Herrel's (homemade!), coffee houses like the Haymarket or the ubiquitous Starbucks, Thorne's marketplace. Two independent movie theaters including the Academy of Music (one of the oldest theaters in the U.S.), and that's just in Northampton! Within a 10-mile radius, you have the towns of Hadley and Amherst and West Springfield—all of which have their own wonderful restaurants, bars and shops. And lest a student be concerned about the fact that Smith is a women's college, fret not! As a Smithie, you get the best of both worlds—you can go to class in your PJ's and then go to Amherst to see the boys at night. There is no lack of opportunity for dating, whether you're straight, gay, bi, whatever. Anything goes.

Alumna, 9/1995-6/1999, March 2005

Smith is part of a Five College Consortium in Western Massachusetts. The other four colleges are Amherst, Mt. Holyoke, Hampshire College and the University

Read all of Vault's College Surveys at **www.vault.com/college**—get complete surveys on 100s of colleges and universities, expert advice on applicaton essays and more.

VAULT CAREER LIBRARY **341**

of Massachusetts Amherst. This facilitates many opportunities for socialization. Harvard, Dartmouth and Bowdoin are all within reasonable distances from Smith, so many students will travel between schools on the weekends. Smith students host parties in their houses on the weekends, and many fraternities will attend or send their pledges. Smith is located in Northampton, which has a very unique population and town setting. The dining options are exceptional and the town is as quaint as it is radical.

Alumna, 9/1999-5/2003, November 2004

The social life is mostly based in the houses, but also includes a cappella jams, plays, soccer or tennis matches, and other fun things. A cappella jams are very popular with the students. There are four main a cappella groups: The Notables, The Smithereens, The Smithenpoofs and The Vibes. There is also a comedy/dance group called Crapapella that is really funny (although a few people find them annoying). Sports are fun but not huge, and there's no football team. No frats or sororities are fine because of the great in-house bonding.

The School Says

Smith College's New England campus is located on 147 acres of tree-lined paths and streets. Larger than most liberal arts colleges in the United States, Smith provides unique resources and outstanding facilities including: the Smith College Museum of Art, widely acknowledge as one of the most important art collections at an American college; a new campus center; the largest undergraduate library system of any liberal arts college in the country; a state-of-the-art fitness center; extensive performance facilities; and a multi-building science complex of teaching and research laboratories and classrooms. Smith also has begun construction of Ford Hall, a science and engineering facility that will be a hallmark of Smith's leadership in science education for women.

Tufts University

Bendetson Hall
Medford, MA 02155
Admissions phone: (617) 627-3170
Admissions fax: (617) 627-3860
Admissions e-mail: admissions.inquiry@ase.tufts.edu
Admissions URL: www.tufts.edu/home/admissions/

 ## Admissions

Current student, 8/2005-Submit Date, May 2007

Many of the students are extremely intelligent but extremely normal at the same time. I think Tufts looks for students who look like they could be CEOs or be the next Isaac Newton on paper, but who sound like "real people" in their admissions essays. I have also noticed that many kids didn't have exceptionally high GPAs in high school, but did have high SATs. We are always looking to increase our diversity, so if you can bring a different race, culture or something else to campus, that could be a plus.

Current student, Engineering, 9/2005-Submit Date, May 2007

Like most selective schools, Tufts requires a strong high school career and good scores. On the other hand, Tufts also seems to have a little more respect for unusual applications or students. The essay is definitely an important aspect of the application, and making it unique is important. I know one admissions officer who keeps a folder of his favorite essays. He also jokes that he reads so many essays about service trips to central America that he feels like everyone just got on a plane together. Additionally, since Tufts is trying to change the admissions process with a new application, they want more creativity and personality to come through the application.

Current student, Psychology, 9/2005-Submit Date, May 2007

Tufts is very selective. There has been a big surge in the number of applicants (I believe about 80 percent increase in last 10 years), and as the quality of applicants applying to the school gets better and better, it's increasingly becoming hard to get into Tufts.

The school puts strong emphasis on internationalism and active citizenship, so I think the admission officers like it a lot when they see an applicant's commitment to community service, activism, and involvement in various extracurricular activities. Tufts really encourages its current students to become active citizens, and I myself was this type of high school student when I applied to Tufts—not an all-A student, but very much involved in community service and extracurricular activities.

Current student, 9/2006-Submit Date, May 2007

Tufts was a moderate reach school on my list of possible schools. A little less difficult to get into than an Ivy, Tufts seems to have a certain set of criteria to get in. They love to emphasize globalism, public service and innovative ways of thinking. If you feel as though you have something to say and you have the time, definitely do the supplemental essays. Tufts looks favorably on creative and interesting responses and if you've done something cool, talk about it. I did an interview with an alumnus and almost immediately he told me that the interview doesn't count for much. I found it more informational rather than helpful for getting in.

Current student, 9/2005-Submit Date, May 2006

Tufts is one of the most selective universities in the States. Solid academic records and SAT scores are obviously very important, but I feel like Tufts admission officers put a lot of importance on factors other than the academics. Essays and extracurricular activities that you have done in your high school are highly regarded, as it is in these aspects that the officers are able to know what the prospective student is really made out of. I especially feel this way because my friend who had better grades than me in high school got rejected while I was admitted.

Also, the university put a great emphasis on philanthropy and active citizenship, so perhaps the officers will like people who have shown commitment to various service activities. Also it should be mentioned that renowned psychologist Robert Sternberg became the dean of arts and sciences at the university, and there have been talks about a change in the application. It has been mentioned that Tufts plans to withdraw itself from the Common Application and implement its own distinct application that will be based on Sternberg's triarchic theory of intelligence (the theory states that human intelligence is divided into three sectors: analytical, creative and contextual). Therefore, the new application will continue to put emphasis on the strict grades and scores of an applicant (analytical intelligence), but it will also consider applicant's creativity and adaptive skills.

> **The school says:** "While we continue to explore the ways that Sternberg's theories of human intelligence can be incorporated in our admissions evaluation, there is no plan to withdraw from the Common Application at this time."

Current student, 9/2005-Submit Date, May 2007

Getting into Tufts is not easy—it is a steep admissions process. The most important aspects are definitely originality, creativity, unconventional intellect and your extracurricular activities. Tufts isn't looking for just book-smart kids, but individuals who truly have something to bring to the university. Tufts prides self on being a service school with a global conscious and it seems literally very student is trying to save the world in some way. In my opinion the essays re the most important part and can really make or break you. It is important to e yourself in them and not drown your answers in pretension. I suggest trying to get to know your admissions officer and really doing your research on the chool before applying.

Academics

Current student, 9/2006-Submit Date, May 2007

ypically classes are small and intimate, which is really nice. Something to keep n mind is the extensive six-semester foreign language requirement and the ight-course distribution requirements to graduate. AP or IB credits are essenial if you don't want to spend your four years focusing on graduation requirehents. Besides that, I absolutely love the professors here. There's a lot of readg, but typically not a lot of work to hand in if you're into social sciences or humanities. As a freshman, it's hard to get popular classes, so really focus on equirements, which will free you up to take popular classes later on. Lastly, here's the Experimental College, which offers some of the most fascinating lasses on campus, such as History of Rock and Roll.

Current student, 9/2005-Submit Date, May 2007

very single professor I have had is amazing. Most classes are small intimate ettings with eight to 12 students. But even in the big intro classes with over 100 tudents, professors are always accessible and caring. I've had many professors eek me out if I do poorly on a test or paper to check up on my well-being. I've ad dinner at many professors' houses along with my classmates, and grabbing coffee or sharing a cigarette with a professor is not an unusual thing. rofessors at Tufts are genuine in their concern for the students and for the dvancement of the university. Tufts professors are all accomplished and really vork toward creating global citizens.

Current student, 8/2005-Submit Date, May 2007

ufts is rigorous and rewarding. Tufts has the opportunity of an enormous esearch university with the community of a small liberal arts college. The vorkload is tough. The professors are unbelievably talented and approachable. he coffee houses (Brown & Brew, The Tower) are free if you go with a profesor. One complaint that you will always hear is that Tufts grades too hard. This s probably true, but it depends on the class. There are academic events going n nearly every day at Tufts. Check out the Fares Lecture Series and the Institute or Global Leadership.

Current student, 8/2003-Submit Date, May 2007

ufts is academically rigorous. There is a substantial number of general requirenents, falling into foundation and distribution requirement categories. Certain lepartments are more challenging than others, but all professors are well qualiied and expect a lot from their students. I definitely have felt that the quality of ourses here is above average, and while grading may be difficult in some courss, the amount of knowledge and understanding that I have taken away from lasses has far exceeded any concern over grades.

Alumnus/a, 8/2003-5/2006, August 2006

By and large, Tufts does not have grade inflation. This infuriates some of the nany hard-working students, who feel like their superior work is only granted a neek A- or B+ on their transcript, while some students down the road might ave it a little easier. The truth? Yeah, other schools may inflate grades more han Tufts, but A's are easily attainable if the student works hard.

Professors are extremely accessible, I've had multiple dinners and extra meetngs with professors in any subject, from econ to Chinese. Classes are smaller han big schools, and language classes are capped at 17 students, with many of he upper-level language classes having enrollments of 10.

Current student, 9/2005-Submit Date, May 2006

Tufts' academics are first class. For the first time, I have actually wanted to go o class because I enjoy learning about the subject material and because my professors are so energetic, engaged and concerned with students' progress. Professors do all that they can to help students succeed. I have had professors who gave me their home phone numbers and encouraged calls at any hour of the

day or night. Other professors have scheduled review sessions during their weekends and will stay at the review until every single question is answered, regardless of how long it takes. Larger classes (mostly introductory classes) break down into recitations (discussion groups) or lab groups weekly, which allow students to discuss material in much smaller groups and not rely on lecture as their only way to learn. One of my largest classes, biology, was videotaped daily so that students could go to the library and re-watch lecture to clarify confusing concepts. I really feel like the professors go out of their way to give students all the resources they need to succeed.

The workload was intense. Time spent studying per night varied, but on average was probably between two and a half and four hours. On Sundays, the campus is pretty dead because most students are studying. Getting into classes has been challenging at times. However, when shut out of a class, many professors will let any student who demonstrates interest or who shows up the first day into their class. Although getting shut out of a small class as an underclassmen can be frustrating, upperclassman usually don't face this problem. There is very little cutthroat competition between students. Most students are willing to help others, form study groups, share notes and work together. Professors encourage student collaboration.

Current student, 9/2003-Submit Date, May 2006

The classes range from 10 students to 100 students per class. The professors are hand selected and are some of the most motivating people you will ever meet. The beautiful aspect of Tufts University is that unlike major research schools or large state schools, it is focused entirely on the student. There are several resources for getting extra help, including resident tutors, academic resource center, free weekly tutoring, extended TA office hours, recitations, professor's office hours, writing workshops, campus-wide review sessions, online library of old exams, and group discussions. Even more focused on the students, the university creates a second class or moves it to a larger room or offers the same class at a different time when a class becomes too popular. Usually, the older you are, seniors vs. freshmen, the earlier you get to register for classes. If you were accepted to Tufts, then you should have no problem with most of the classes except for the more difficult IR and science classes that require almost three hours per day of studying per difficult class. Total workload, given you've had a chat with your different faculty and student advisors, will probably be one very difficult class, one difficult class, and two to three easy classes, which would give you about five to eight hours (depending if you paid attention in class) of homework per day. Keep in mind, this is an estimate of the numbers of hours you need to get at least an A- in the class.

Employment Prospects

Current student, Independent, 9/2004-Submit Date, May 2007

There are such great academic resources on this campus. I think one reason students might not get jobs or internships is because they don't take advantage of all that Tufts offers. I have an internship funded by a Tufts Career Services grant for $3,500 this summer (sweet!), plus Tufts seems to always be offering jobs, especially for the summer. I've already made so many connections through Tufts and the Urban and Environmental Policy and Planning (UEP) grad school that I have no fear of not being able to a job I want after graduation!

Current student, 8/2003-Submit Date, May 2007

I definitely think that Tufts has a good name among prospective employers. People in the Boston area, especially, recognize Tufts as an outstanding academic institution and have generally been impressed with Tufts students. The job search, however, really depends on what the student puts into it. Career Services has helped to bring many employers to campus for interviews and through Recruiting. This has been helpful, although in my own experience, it appears though students who have participated in internships in the past and have networked were at a distinct advantage over other students just entering the job search without previous work experience or professional connections.

Alumnus/a, 8/2003-5/2006, August 2006

There are great employment prospects for graduates of the engineering school. Career fairs are abundant and reputable engineering employers, including name-brands like Intel, AMD, Apple and so on, actively recruit at Tufts. For those who aren't engineers, you will not find major investment banks or consulting firms at

Read all of Vault's College Surveys at **www.vault.com/college**–get complete surveys on 100s of colleges and universities, expert advice on applicaton essays and more.

VAULT CAREER LIBRARY **343**

Tufts recruiting. This is, in my opinion, the greatest weakness—Tufts is currently rapidly expanding its career resources department. If you want a top-tier job, you aggressively will have to pursue employers such as Goldman or McKinsey your sophomore or junior year and hope to land an internship to get on track with them. Don't plan on seeing those recruiters at Tufts.

Current student, 9/2004-Submit Date, April 2005

No doubt about it, as it experiences its modern-day renaissance, Tufts is a hot school. A degree from this institution is prestigious, but I truly believe that even in another five or 10 years, it will become that much more impressive. Most graduates apply to graduate school; we have acceptance and matriculation rates that are significantly higher than the national average (for example, 83 percent of Tufts students who apply to law schools are accepted).

The alumni network is particularly helpful; any day of the week, students can log on to a web site full of hundreds of alumni contact names. Almost every day, prominent graduates return to Tufts and hold forums and seminars. With its proximity to Boston, Tufts offers amazing internship opportunities that can be fulfilled for credit or experience.

While there isn't that much on-campus recruiting, Tufts is regularly invited along with a handful of other elite institutions to career consortiums in New York and D.C. Finally, if you come to Tufts, you'll acquire more than a degree, you'll have four years of transformative education that prepares you for our ever-expanding global society.

Quality of Life

Current student, Engineering, 9/2005-Submit Date, May 2007

I think the Tufts campus is nice but a tad segmented. There are two or three different "feelings" on campus that all depend where you are. Uphill is a more traditional liberal arts feel, while downhill is a tad more contemporary and free form. This is also where all of the newest buildings are, which kind of adds a new place on campus. Even though there is a somewhat physical divide between Uphill and Downhill, it's not an actual separation in the students or campus life. Housing is guaranteed and required for freshmen and sophomores and then most students choose to move off campus and or go abroad for a semester or year. There is a new push to encourage more seniors to move back on campus by adding a new building and converting an old building to all singles for seniors.

Current student, Independent, 8/2006-Submit Date, May 2007

Tufts really makes an effort to take care of its students, and it shows in the quality of life. Housing isn't provided all four years, which is a complaint, but the residential life office makes it easy to find off-campus living, and the dorms that are available are really nice compared to most other schools. Many dorms have big rooms, private bathrooms, and there are apartments and suites. The location couldn't be better. Davis Square in Somerville and Boston Ave. in Medford are great places to grab dinner, run errands, or see a movie, and the T is a 10-minute walk from campus or a five-minute ride on the shuttle. Right on the Red Line, the Davis Square stop is 10 minutes from Harvard and 30 from downtown. Food at Tufts is really good and there are tons of options, you can even order take-out or delivery from local restaurants on the meal plan. The gym could be bigger, but it's open to all students, which is nice. Overall, quality of life at Tufts is excellent.

Current student, Independent, 9/2004-Submit Date, May 2007

Quality of life is good, but not stellar. Housing can be stressful, and the dorms are pretty basic. There's an Uphill-Downhill feud (I used to be pro-Uphill until I moved Downhill.) and a variety of living spaces—apartments, dorms, all-female floors and houses, specialty housing, student organization housing and so on. Though the trees are planted in straight lines, in spring and fall campus is heavenly. Everyone's out on the lawn playing frisbee or having picnics, and the library roof provides a great place to hang out and check out the Boston skyline. The food is really good compared to other campuses; it took me three years to get sick of it! It sounds negative, but really that's a pretty long time. There are two dining halls, a campus center with two places to get food, and a funky Oxfam Cafe Uphill. The downside is that Hotung Cage in the campus center is expensive, but points aren't really money anyway, right? I've always felt very safe on campus.

Current student, 9/2003-Submit Date, May 2006

The location of Tufts is great—we have our own campus, yet have the entire Ci of Boston right at our fingertips. As you get older, you start to explore mo areas, but there is definitely enough to do on campus. The housing lottery wa a pain for the year I had to deal with it, but they changed it for the better su posedly, which will be good. A lot of housing options provide variety for ever one. Compared to some schools I have visited, Tufts has great food. But eatir it for every meal is quite repetitive. Luckily, we have alternative food options the dining halls and a wonderful points system to balance everything.

Current student, 9/2005-Submit Date, May 2006

Tufts' dining hall is known to be one of the best. There are themed nights, lik African Night or Indian Night, but often the food in the main dining halls ge repetitive. Not to worry though, because Davis Square (10 minutes away b walk), Porter Square (one T stop away), and Harvard Square (two T stops awa; provide a wide range of cuisines. Dorms are all pretty nice and spaciou although some (e.g., Wren, Haskell halls) can be a bit disappointing. New gy equipment and computers have been upgraded, and campus-wide wireless co nectivity is underway. Tufts University Police Department has won camp safety awards, provides Safety Escort service any time of the day, and whe called for an emergency, they are very prompt and helpful. Medford is a nic quiet and safe suburb anyway, but the reliable TUPD adds further feeling of saf ty for the student body.

Social Life

Current student, Independent, 8/2006-Submit Date, May 2007

At Tufts social life is really what you make of it. Some students complain, bt it's a lot more than what I expected from a selective, small, liberal arts schoo Greek life plays a big role in the social lives of freshmen because it's an eas way to meet people and their parties are always open to the whole student bod; Lots of students attend the parties but very few are actually members of Gree organizations. Favorite restaurants include Anna's, Redbones and J.P. Lick's f dessert. Good date places are Dom's in Little Italy and Antonia's in Davis. Tuf is categorized as a "hook-up school" because lots of students are too busy to b interested in real relationships. While lots of students tend just to-hook up o the weekends, there are plenty of students who are dating or in relationships, a well. Tufts also sponsors great social activities that are actually really popula and well-attended. Fall Ball and Winter Bash are two school-wide dances hel in the gym (think high school homecoming, but without dates). The school als sponsors two concerts and then Spring Fling, which is a full day concert ever on the President's Lawn. The concert board manages to get really good per formers, too. Also, Tufts is famous for the yearly NQR on the last night of fa semester. Social life is really what you make of it at Tufts, but there is some thing to make anyone happy.

Current student, 8/2005-Submit Date, May 2007

Davis Square is a hidden gem with dozens of restaurants and even some bou tiques. It's an incredible place to hang out on a nice day. And you can hop o the T at Davis and be downtown in 15 minutes. It really is perfect. Social lif on campus is very diverse. There are students who hang out playing boar games with their friends, students who go to acoustic guitar shows at the coffe shop, and students who go to bars and party at the frats. No matter what make you happy, there will be something going on to entertain you.

Current student, 9/2005-Submit Date, May 2007

Tufts is known for not having the greatest social life or the most attractive peo ple. The dating scene is practically nonexistent. We have a few bars nearby, bu most people who are of legal age go into Boston for nightlife. Even Boston i not that great for a college town; clubs are very strict, and everything close down by 2 a.m., which Boston is currently trying to change to 1 a.m. Howeve Boston and surrounding areas have very good food, shopping, theatre, art and s on. Also, Tufts provides tons of activities and other events. We have man; famous speakers, from Madeleine Albright to alumnus Peter Gallagher. Tuft students tend to be ridiculous overachievers who fill their free time with ever; club in sight. There are so many interesting student organizations that it's har not to fill up your time with club activities. The Leonard Carmichael Society which houses dozens of community service clubs, is the largest student organi

ation on campus. Tufts Dance Collective is the most popular dance group, with
ver 300 members. A cappella is also very big here. I think maybe 14 percent
f students are involved in the Greek system. There's no pressure to join, but
veryone knows people in fraternities and sororities. Frat parties are a large part
f the weekend social scene.

Current student, 9/2005-Submit Date, May 2006

have so much fun at Tufts during both the week and weekends. Almost all stu-
lents stay on campus during the weekends because there is so much going on.
Boston offers amazing social opportunities—restaurants of every cuisine and
price range, shopping, educational activities (Tufts students receive free admis-
ion to the Museum of Fine Arts), clubs and sporting events. I think students use
he city more than they initially plan to because there is always more to explore
nd because there are so many college students in the city. Davis Square (where
tudents access the T), Teele Square and Powderhouse are all within walking dis-
ance from campus and all have fun, inexpensive bars and restaurants. Personal
avorites include El Guapo, a bar that attracts a young crowd, and Tip Top Thai,
 delicious and inexpensive Thai restaurant. J.P. Licks is a delicious ice cream
hop in Davis Square. Tufts has several fun coffee shops on campus where stu-
lent bands play. Every year we bring in famous speakers and well-known
ands. This year, for Spring Fling, Guster came to play. The Greek system at
Tufts is present, but does not dominate the social life and only a minority of stu-
lents are Greek. Greek parties are open to everyone and there is no tension or
listinction between Greek and non-Greek students. My favorite activities on
ampus were Tufts traditions that brought the whole campus together—the
Naked Quad Run, the Tufts-tonia Carnival and Spring Fling.

 ## The School Says

Tufts University's focus on innovation and progressive thinking took root at its founding as a liberal arts college in 1852. Today, Tufts is recognized as a premier university dedicated to educating new leaders for our changing world. Superb teaching and world-class research equip graduates to address multi-faceted challenges around the globe. Creative cross-school collaborations and multidisciplinary centers engage students in seeking solutions to complex economic, health, political and environmental issues even before they graduate.

Each year, Tufts enrolls 8,500 students from across the U.S. and more than 100 countries who attend classes on the university's three campuses in Massachusetts (Boston, Medford/Somerville and Grafton) and in Talloires, France.

Tufts' highly regarded undergraduate, graduate and professional programs are offered at the School of Arts and Sciences, Graduate School of Arts and Sciences, School of Engineering, the Fletcher School of Law and Diplomacy, School of Dental Medicine, School of Medicine, Sackler School of Graduate Biomedical Sciences, Friedman School of Nutrition Science and Policy, and Cummings School of Veterinary Medicine. Tufts' unique Tisch College of Citizenship and Public Service is an innovative educational model that works across all schools and disciplines to energize the theory and practice of active citizenship.

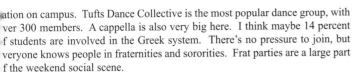

University of Massachusetts Amherst

Admissions Office
37 Mather Drive
University of Massachusetts
Amherst, MA 01003
Admissions phone: (413) 545-0222
Admissions e-mail: mail@admissions.umass.edu
Admissions URL: www.umass.edu/admissions/

 ## Admissions

Current student, Business, 9/2006-Submit Date, April 2007

The admissions process is simple, fill out the appropriate application, which is available online or by request. I was applying for the Isenberg School of Management, which is highly competitive and I transferred from a community college that provided a business compact program with UMass so that the transfer and acceptance into the school was fairly easy. Make sure to fulfill your requirements beforehand. When writing the essay, creativity is key; try to stick out in the minds of the readers. UMass has become increasingly more competitive and the selection process is getting more and more difficult. Do not hold back, let them know who you are, and include all your strong qualities!

Current student, Biology, 8/2004-Submit Date, April 2007

The admissions process for UMass is similar to most large, public universities. There is a UMass-specific application that can be found online and the school also accepts the Common App. Since application numbers are so large for each entering class, there are no formal, evaluative interviews required for admittance. The components that make an applicant most desirable for admittance are solid SAT/ACT scores, solid high school grade point average, and a well-written personal essay. The strongest essays will address growth as a learner or plans for the future—admissions readers have read countless stories about applicants' deceased grandmothers and state-championship sports teams. An essay that is

unique and honest is best, since this is a replacement for the formal interview and a way for UMass to get to know the applicant. Also important for boosting an applicant's prospects are extracurricular activities such as work, volunteering, clubs, sports, and music. The school's selectivity increases each year, as can be seen by the annually increasing average SAT/ACT scores and GPA of the first-year class.

Current student, Pre-med, 8/2004-Submit Date, April 2007

UMass is no longer the safety school that it is often thought to be; admissions is not "highly selective" but more and more students are being declined as it searches for a higher caliber of student. The process is very easy and painless, especially now that UMass is accepting the Common App. Online updates keep you informed as to the progress of your application. Some majors are harder to gain acceptance to than others (e.g., School of Management, Sport Management, Nursing, Engineering and Computer Science).

Current student, Communications, 1/2003-Submit Date, April 2007

The admissions process for UMass Amherst is pretty standard. I heard that the school is becoming more competitive with the admissions process and it is a lot harder to get accepted now. The essay was a standard essay and not very stressful. I believe it had to do with a personal experience. Most of the students here have received average and above grades and have been involved in extracurricular activities throughout high school. My best advice would be to get involved in something. Maybe a charity, sports, or even start a group or club if there is nothing available to you. Make sure you have someone proofread your essays and application. It is best to proofread it, let it sit for a day, then go back to it later because you will notice your mistakes more. Also, read your essays out loud, oftentimes if you trip up on your words, the sentence may not make sense. I would say that the selectivity at UMass would be a challenge for students who did not perform well in high school. They are open minded with SAT scores, so I wouldn't worry about them. Overall, it was pretty easy.

Read all of Vault's College Surveys at www.vault.com/college–get complete surveys on 100s of colleges and universities, expert advice on applicaton essays and more.

VAULT CAREER LIBRARY 345

Current student, 9/2003-Submit Date, October 2005

I believe that the admissions process depends more on personality than straight technical indicators such as GPA or SATs. Although the latter are both important and should always be taken seriously, conveying your personality, goals and outlook on life in college admissions interviews and essays are a significant deciding factor in your ultimate acceptance.

In the essays and interviews, one should be sure to include details about sports, clubs and other leadership roles with which one was involved during high school. Like a job interview, the admission interviewer doesn't want to just talk about grades, but rather, knowledge taken away from the class. How is your outlook on life? Are you a positive person that can face adversity in your years at college. (Hint: you almost undoubtedly will face some during your first semester after talking with many friends.)

Current student, 11/2002-Submit Date, January 2006

The admissions process was very straightforward. There are many students to show you around campus and to speak to you about the opportunities in a university so large. There was not much advice given on how to get in because the admissions employees are so busy with the thousands of applications arriving at site. This essay was the most practical of all the essays I had to write to get into school. "Why do you think UMass would be a good school for you?" was basically what it asked. Just yesterday I also applied for the master's program here at UMass in Molecular and Cellular Biology, they wanted to know how the university and myself would benefit from the research that I will conduct. It was difficult to narrow it down to the specifics, but as I get to know the faculty here, they become more personal and have helped me along the way.

Academics

Alumnus/a, Business, 9/2003-5/2007, June 2007

The Isenberg School provides a selective business program with outstanding resources and opportunities. I did not have much trouble getting into popular classes within my school; and if I did, I found it easy to get permission from instructors and administration. However in comparison to many of the other classes I took outside the Isenberg School, I found that there was a lack of resources that could enrich the academic experience further. Nevertheless every class I took at UMass was a quality; I felt confident with the material and information provided. Generally the faculty members were committed to the students and overall I would say my experience was a positive one.

Current student, Business, 9/2006-Submit Date, April 2007

Due to the fact that UMass Amherst is so large, the availability of classes can be difficult and frustrating. It is extremely beneficial to look and prepare a list of the classes you are hoping to get into and register immediately once your appointment time has come. I have found that I enjoy all of my professors, and have learned so much in all of my classes. Grading has always been fair, and professors are always available when you need extra help. The workload can vary, there are some classes where the workload can be difficult and some where the workload is fair. Nothing you can't handle though.

Current student, Biology, 8/2004-Submit Date, April 2007

The undergraduate program at UMass is most benefited by its size. With 88 majors from which to choose, including the bachelor's degree with Individual Concentration ("Build Your Own Major"), it is nearly impossible to find a course of study not suited to one's interests. UMass offers nearly 3,000 courses every semester. This tremendous offering is further supplemented by an additional 2,000 courses that are available through the Five College Consortium. The Five College Consortium is available to all UMass students after the first semester and includes prestigious colleges such as Amherst, Hampshire, Smith and Mt. Holyoke.

The quality of classes can vary depending on a student's learning style. Introductory-level and general-education lectures can run as large as 450 student. Generally these classes are subsidized by a weekly discussion section of no more than 30 students as well as available office hours for one-on-one interaction with professors or teacher's assistants. Many professors and TAs hold review sessions before exams and are willing to give feedback on grading. The

opportunity to get into smaller classes increases greatly in upperclassmen year or before, depending on the department of study.

In larger lectures professors have many different styles. Expect that most lectures in intro courses will be done in PowerPoint format or by hand-written overhead projector. Most times lecture notes are posted online, but this is at the professor's discretion, and is typically not an adequate substitution for missing class. Attendance for some lectures is tracked by Personal Response clickers, or remotes used to answer multiple choice questions that are administered randomly during classes.

Current student, Pre-med, 8/2004-Submit Date, April 2007

I have never had any issue getting into the classes that I want. Classes are usually on the smaller side (30 to 40) students and only a few intro classes are large (200 to 300). All profs. have office hours and teaching assistants will hold review/discussion sections once a week for small groups of students, not the entire large class. Also, we use the Personal Response System (PRS). It is like polling the audience in "Who Wants to Be a Millionaire" and the prof can see how well the class understands the material, some will also use this to take attendance, so it helps with getting you motivated to go to class.

Current student, Communications, 1/2003-Submit Date, April 2007

I became a communications major the end of my sophomore year. You have to take two core classes before getting accepted. They are the basics Interpersonal Communication and Introduction to the Media. At first, the program starts off a little boring but then as you delve into the information and diversity of the courses it becomes very eye-opening. I am happy with the classes I took at UMass. They ranged from Advertising, Public Relations, Health Communication, Religion and Popular Culture, Children, Teens and Media, Media Audiences, Argumentation and Debate. The classes were very interesting and I really believe I got a well-rounded education.

The only way to get into popular classes at UMass is if you research what courses you want to take before your enrollment appointment. Also, there is a pecking order at UMass. Seniors enroll before juniors, juniors before sophomores and so on, so course choices can be limited. If you go to the class on its start date, you can usually sign up for a waitlist. I recommend taking as many small classes as you can. All of the larger classes have standardize testing, multiple choice that is. You get a lot more out of smaller classes and better grades. Workload is too easy for freshman and sophomore year. Once junior year comes, it is like a slap in the face.

Employment Prospects

Alumnus/a, Business, 9/2003-5/2007, June 2007

Within the Isenberg School it is rare to find a senior who doesn't have at least one or two prospective employment opportunities after school. There is a tremendous amount of support and networking available to the students from alumni, internships and partnered companies. However, I have found that students outside Isenberg also have had many opportunities for employment due to campus resources, such as career fairs, career services and e-recruiting.

Current student, Biology, 8/2004-Submit Date, April 2007

Employment prospects for UMass graduates are vast. The Career Services Department is available to prepare students for these opportunities and does so by hosting résumé-writing workshops, career fairs and grad school fairs. They also provide connections for participating in internship and co-op programs.

With total enrollment of nearly 25,000, UMass has a strong alumni network. By mandate, 70 percent of students must come from Massachusetts, which means that the New England area has an especially high concentration of UMass grads. Departments regularly contact undergraduates with opportunities for research or internship opportunities.

Current student, Business, 9/2004-Submit Date, April 2007

The UMass Amherst Hospitality Department is very well-known by many companies in the industry. They have people from the Disney College Program come to have people work for them and to recruit. They also have companies such as Starwood, Omni and Marriot doing on-campus interviews and informa-on sessions. There is a campus-wide career fair as well as an HTM career fair that this year almost 100 companies attended.

Current student, 11/2002-Submit Date, January 2006

There are great opportunities for students who graduate from UMass Amherst. This university has an excellent school of business, and excellent programs in the sciences and engineering. We also have a pre-school that is open for our students to complete education degrees here and also for students who want to pursue a career in hotel management, for we have a hotel in the center of our campus where these students are able to receive hands-on experience. As for my major, we have an overwhelming number of labs where we gain our experience. From this I was able to secure an internship position at Wyeth, one of the largest pharmaceutical companies in the world. There is also a huge fair where all the companies that want interns arrive and set up a table for us.

Quality of Life

Current student, Biology, 8/2004-Submit Date, April 2007

For traditional, non-commuting students, living in the residence halls is mandatory for the first and second years. The housing options are many and play to diverse personalities and lifestyles. The largest residence area, Southwest, houses half the on-campus population. Southwest is reminiscent of city-style living and includes five high-rise towers. Smaller areas, such as Orchard Hill and Northeast, are intended to be more academically focused and quieter. North, a residence area for upperclassmen, was recently completed. This area features four-person suites with two bathrooms, a kitchen and a living space, as well as less direct university supervision.

The campus is best described as a walking campus. It is fully accessible, with areas and buildings with the most traffic (including the Student Union, library and Campus Pond) located in the center of campus around this central ring. The six residence areas and the five dining commons are located. On the outermost perimeter of campus are located athletic fields, parking lots and connections to the surrounding area.

The neighboring community is exceptional. Downtown Amherst is a short walk or bus ride away. The strip includes many colorful hometown bookstores, boutiques, restaurants and bars and a minimum of corporate storefronts. The large campus is nestled in the middle of Western Massachusetts farm country, so Amherst is the epitome of a college town. Nearly all those living in the town when school is in session are in some way related to UMass or one of the nearby schools. Crime and safety have become a concern since UMass was ranked one of the most violent campuses in the nation, but this is a vastly overstated claim. There have been isolated incidents in the past, but no more than one would expect from a large university. Crime statistics are inflated since all crime is reported directly to the university police and is not shouldered by local police as would occur in a city setting. I have never felt more unsafe walking the streets of UMass than I have walking the streets in my suburban hometown.

Current student, Pre-med, 8/2004-Submit Date, April 2007

The dorms are not amazing, but they are a dorm similar to any university. Campus is a great place to be with tons of stuff to do—music, concerts, theater, sports. Events are really cheap (only $5 to $15) and sporting events are free for students. Basketball, football, ice hockey and lacrosse are popular. Food is good always a lot of options and that way it never gets boring, which is important. Crime does of course happen (we have 24,000 students) but no more than you would expect. Mostly just petty theft but I have never felt unsafe on campus. Our cops are real cops—not rent-a-cops—so people do not mess with them and because of that, campus is safe.

Current student, Business, 9/2004-Submit Date, April 2007

On-campus housing isn't the best. I was friendly with each of my roommates freshman and sophomore year, however I was not placed with someone in my year. Freshman year I lived with a junior art major and sophomore year I lived with the junior nursing major. The rooms are decent sized, however the number of things you can do with your furniture is limited. (I was forced to keep my dresser in my closet.) The new on-campus apartments are nice because they have privacy; however, they are still working out all the kinks in the system (the central air and heating still aren't responding to the thermostats in the apart-

ments). They are also extremely expensive for the area for the amount of space you get. UMass has award-winning dining commons, and the majority of the time the food served is good. However, I got tired of the repetition and if you didn't like one or two of the options or were trying to eat healthier (such as low carbs), it would be hard to do. There are little nutrition cards by most of the food items but no one bothers to fill them out, so you get the name of the food and not much else. Housing in the Amherst area is extremely affordable. I am renting an apartment in a house next year with three other people for $435/each, plus utilities. The town of Amherst is also very nice. The downtown is awesome for walking through and there is almost no tension between the Amherst locals and the college students. For anything you can't find in downtown, the Route 9 Strip has all the big chain stores, so you are sure to find it there. I feel very safe at UMass. I had no problems walking across campus at night and do so often for color guard practices.

Current student, Communications, 1/2003-Submit Date, April 2007

The people in town are really nice and helpful, they tend to look out for the college kids. On-campus housing is forced for two years and then you are pushed to move off campus. There are downsides and positives to both. On campus is really fun, and you stay involved with friends and university events. It really is a party school! There were parties of 5,000 people plus on farms, and an insane amount of drinking. If you are uncomfortable with this I wouldn't attend this school. Off campus is a time where everyone starts to grow up a little and focus more on school; however, there are still parties, lots of them. Many also head to the bars off campus. It is hard to get work done in the dorms so the library is recommended. Overall, it is positive.

Social Life

Current student, Business, 9/2006-Submit Date, April 2007

Social life is great in Amherst. Northampton and Amherst are known for great restaurants and bars. Judies, Pasta e Basta, and Bueno y Sano are all great restaurants in Amherst. There are always parties being held around campus. Events are held constantly especially in the spring when the weather begins to get nice again. The Greek system is huge on our campus, they are extremely active in and around the community.

Current student, Biology, 8/2004-Submit Date, April 2007

The social life at UMass is vibrant. Though the administration deplores the pseudonym "Zoo Mass," many students are more than dedicated to keeping that nickname accurate. UMass is the third largest residence campus in the country, not including the thousands of students who live in nearby apartments and houses. Downtown Amherst has a great nightlife, though some may feel stifled by the 1 a.m. last call. The popular Amherst bars are Delano's, McMurphy's, ABC, and The Spoke. When the crowds let out at 1, the party generally takes a break to grab a slice at the renowned Antonio's pizza, right on the downtown strip. For under-agers, partying requires more discretion. The university is strict in its enforcement of drinking policy. Public drinking is not tolerated and enforced, but certain areas, such as Southwest, tend to be known for partying. Off-campus parties are frequent. Apartment complexes like Puffton, the Townhouses, and others along with student-rented homes and fraternity houses occasionally provide grounds for massive, Hollywoodesque (sometimes exceeding 2,000 people) parties.

Events are never in short supply, as UMass is home to roughly 250 registered clubs. These clubs include social, academic, religious, cultural, sporting, and political organizations. Advertisements are easily found on the school web site, on the dining commons tables and in *The Daily Collegian*, the UMass newspaper. Also included in the registered clubs are all Greek life organizations. Currently, Greek life at UMass has a sub-par reputation, with only 3 percent of the student body participating in fraternities or sororities, but the administration is interested in positively increasing its presence on campus.

Current student, Pre-med, 8/2004-Submit Date, April 2007

There are a few party scenes at UMass. The dorm parties, which happen a lot, house parties, bars and no parties. The great thing about UMass is our size—we have something for everyone. If partying is not your thing then you don't have to. We have so much more to do than party (movies, concerts, sports,

Read all of Vault's College Surveys at **www.vault.com/college**–get complete surveys on 100s of colleges and universities, expert advice on applicaton essays and more.

VAULT CAREER LIBRARY **347**

dances/social, off-campus trips, great food, hiking biking and skiing). But if you want to party (in a dorm, at a house, or in a bar), you can do that, too.

Current student, Business, 9/2004-Submit Date, April 2007

There are a lot of parties in the area. There are four other colleges close by, not to mention the fact that UMass has about 20,000 undergrads so the parties are pretty inevitable. There are lots of bars in downtown Amherst. There are some that are pretty nice (ABC Upstairs) and some that are a little dirtier. There is also a pool hall about a five-minute drive from the center of town that is generally fun to go to and play pool; however, in order to walk through the door in all of these places, you have to be 21or older. There are lots of nice restaurants in Amherst center. Lots of small local ones, then if you are looking for a familiar name you can go out to the Route 9 Strip. They have Applebee's, Chili's and Panera Bread out there. The Greek system isn't that big at UMass. This past year the campus bought the land that three or four frats were located on and bulldozed their houses. Now the frats are more scattered than they were. The fraternities and sororities will do events every so often, but most of the time they are just attended by other Greeks. There is always something going on campus. My favorite is the "Something Every Friday" program. Movies that have just recently left theaters but have come out on DVD yet Mass will screen on Friday and Sunday nights. The showings are free to everyone and there is free popcorn and soda as well. There are clubs for pretty much whatever you are interested in. I went to a couple of dance classes with the Ballroom Dance Club. I am also a member of the Science Fiction Society and borrow books from its library. I was a member of the UMass Minuteman Marching Band in the color guard but now I just participate in the winter color guard program called Color in the Cage. The program got the name because the show we put on at the end of the year happens in the Curry Hicks Cage, one of the gymnasiums on campus.

 The School Says

A nationally-ranked research university, the University of Massachusetts Amherst has experienced a steady rise in undergraduate applications over the past three years. The academic profile and diversity of the entering class has also increased, with some students admitted directly into Commonwealth College, the university honors college.

Beginning fall 2005, UMass Amherst began an Early Action admissions program, with applications due November 1 and students receiving a response by December 1. A new waitlist program also accommodates the increased applications. Concurrent with the growth in applications, the campus is currently undergoing $650 million in campus construction, and is in the process of hiring 250 new faculty.

Offering over 85 undergraduate majors, UMass Amherst complements classroom academics with unlimited opportunities for career development through internships, practicums, field or co-op experience and clinical assignments. A recent survey of graduating seniors indicates that almost 60 percent of undergraduates participated in one of these co-curricular opportunities. UMass Amherst students also enroll—at no extra charge—in courses at nearby Amherst, Hampshire, Mount Holyoke and Smith Colleges. These five colleges participate in open library borrowing, a meal exchange and a free bus system connecting all campuses.

UMass Amherst provides pre-medical advisers for all students interested in medicine, dentistry, veterinary medicine, chiropractic and other allied health fields. Other notable undergraduate programs include Chemical Engineering, Computer Science, Electrical and Computer Engineering, Finance and Operations Management, Linguistics and Psychology. Chemical Engineering is ranked fifth in U.S. in 2003 by the Institute for Scientific Information and 22nd by the National Research Council. The College of Engineering hosts the Chemical Engineering and Electrical and Computer Engineering majors. Undergraduate offerings were ranked 51st among Best Engineering Programs Where the Highest Degree is a Doctorate in 2004 by *U.S. News & World Report* in the National Universities-Doctoral category.

Computer Science ranked ninth in the U.S. in 2003 by *Science Watch* magazine and 18th nationally by the National Research Council. Electrical and Computer Engineering ranked 29th by the National Research Council. The Isenberg School of Management hosts the Finance and Operations Management major. Isenberg's undergraduate offerings were ranked 75th among Best Business Programs and Departments in 2004 by *U.S. News & World Report* in the National Universities-Doctoral category. Linguistics ranked Number Four in quality of faculty and Number One in quality of education (presumably PhD) by the National Research Council. The department has been consistently ranked among the Top Four in the country. Psychology: Ranked Number 27 by the National Research Council. Across all areas of academic study, a recent survey of graduating seniors indicated that more than 25 percent had secured a job related to their major. Almost 20 percent of graduating seniors were planning on attending graduate school immediately after graduation, while more than 36 percent would attend within two years.

Wellesley College

106 Central Street
Wellesley, MA 02481
Admissions phone: (781) 283-2270
Admissions fax: (781) 283-3678
Admissions e-mail: admission@wellesley.edu
Admissions URL: www.wellesley.edu/Admission/

 Admissions

Current student, Economics, 9/2003-Submit Date, May 2007

Admissions was very organized. There were a few essays. Wellesley is not too selective; it's more like candidates are self-selective. I think 40 percent was admitted out of the total pool, but then there are very few applicants who are truly average. Most are pretty smart, and many are kids/relatives of alumnae.

Current student, Int'l Relations, 9/2003-Submit Date, December 2006

The admissions process is very competitive. However, it is very important that you schedule an appointment with one of the admissions personnel, because it will help a lot. Wellesley is a very small school, and if you do well on your interview, it will boost your application quality a lot. Be sure to show lots of enthusiasm about Wellesley and try to bring as much extracurricular activity experience as possible. Essays are one of the important aspects for Wellesley. To do well on the liberal art college, writing ability is crucial, and you will be writing a lot of essays in Wellesley. So be sure to put lots of effort in writing essay, and Wellesley likes the theme of "diversity." If you can show something about diversity and your academic excellence, it will help a lot.

Alumna, 9/2000-6/2004, February 2006

I almost didn't apply to Wellesley, and I would have missed the best four years of my life. I knew it was a great school, but I was not interested in a women's college experience. My mother insisted that I apply, so I filled out the Common App and scheduled an interview. Since I didn't want to go there, I was very relaxed and confident during the interview—I considered it a practice. I think that really helped me, because confidence is something that is highly valued within the Wellesley community. When visiting the campus, I was struck by how helpful everyone was. A student did not just point us to a place we could buy food, she walked us over and recommended a dish. Students waved at our tour guide. This experience was no fluke, I would later discover—Wellesley is a happy, friendly place. It's also very selective, and admission is only getting tougher. You need good grades and good SATs, but the most important thing, I think, is that you demonstrate that you are a woman who can communicate and who possesses the charisma to lead others in the future. Good luck!

Alumna, 9/2000-5/2004, November 2004

I took advantage of Wellesley's unique Early Evaluation option. The process is non-binding, yet you're given early notification of chances for admission (likely admit, reject or waitlist). Interview: I didn't have one, but had many classmates who did. Personal essay is extermely important. Don't ruin your chances by neglecting to proofread! Selectivity: so-so. If you have mediocre SAT scores, but have a knock-out essay, there's a good chance that you'll get accepted. I cannot emphasize this enough: spend time perfecting your personal statement!

> **The school says:** "Wellesley considers a student's personal essay, secondary school record, recommendations and standardized test scores to be very important factors in its admission decision."

Alumna, 8/2002-6/2006, November 2006

The admissions process was not bad at all. I didn't do the optional interview and the application was just the Common Application with some supplemental forms. I believe the main thing they look for is leadership skills. They want to see through your essay and extracurriculars that you want to make a difference

in the world and would be a good leader. They are not as selective as the Ivies, but still very selective. They want to see leadership qualities basically. They want to see somebody who is driven and knows what she wants.

Current student, 8/2002-Submit Date, September 2004

I found Wellesley's application to be very simple, especially for a school of this caliber. The packet arrived with everything I needed to apply for admittance and for financial aid. They were firm on the dates, but understanding about mail problems. I visited Wellesley before I decided to attend, and everything was well-run—from the tours to the information session, to the interview. The admissions office gave the distinct impression that my visit and my application were important to them, which I didn't always get from other schools. I knew my admissions counselor by name and received letters from current students once I had been admitted. Wellesley also has an interesting program called Early Evaluation, which told me I would "likely" be accepted. It was lovely to find this out in early March rather than in mid-April.

Alumna, 9/2001-5/2004, September 2004

When I was applying to schools, I believe that I naively believed in my invincibility. I applied to mostly Ivies, a state school and Wellesley. Most of my friends who ended up at Wellesley, and myself included, had intended upon going somewhere else and were left with Wellesley as the only available option. This is not to say that there were not the few students at Wellesley who had intended upon going to Wellesley ever since they were born and absolutely loved the idea of an all-women's college nestled in a back-country, suburban utopia complete with lake and hills. At that time, Wellesley used the Common Application, which was very simple to fill out if you had applied to Harvard (which I didn't). Luckily, the essay question was very similar to most other essay questions.

 Academics

Current student, Int'l Relations, 9/2003-Submit Date, December 2006

If you planned to have a good, relaxing college life, then Wellesley isn't the right place. About the academic program, Wellesley has good and challenging liberal art courses. Art history, political science, economics, psychology are the popular ones. The MIT cross-registration program allows students to take courses at MIT. Wellesley students can take all the MIT classes they want, and you can pursue a degree from MIT as well. The professors are extremely dedicated, and they push students to go beyond their abilities. Workload is a lot. You will be required to study everyday, and some weekends as well. However, you will really learn a lot from Wellesley.

Alumna, 8/2002-6/2006, November 2006

The academic environment was what I enjoyed most at Wellesley. The teachers are wonderful and they are always willing to help students. The classes are pretty small so it's very easy to get one-on-one attention. The workload is fair and grading is competitive but still pretty fair. I have never had a problem in terms of getting classes I've wanted, so I think Wellesley does a really good job in meeting the demand of students.

Alumna, 9/2000-6/2004, February 2006

Classes at Wellesley are usually small, except for some introductory-level science or art history courses, and even those usually break into smaller groups or labs for discussion purposes. Students do the reading and come to class prepared to discuss it in detail. Sometimes the workload can be very heavy—I am someone who had a lot of trouble writing papers in advance, and often found myself spending the night in the library to get things done. Friends with better time management skills had an easier time, but midterms and finals are a busy time of year for everyone. It can be hard to get into the most popular classes, but if you can demonstrate to the professor of a full class that you really want or need it, he or she will usually work something out. The professor are excellent: they are a brilliant group of people, and they still inspire me with their knowledge and most especially their continuing curiosity. Some of my friends formed close

Read all of Vault's College Surveys at www.vault.com/college–get complete surveys on 100s of colleges and universities, expert advice on applicaton essays and more.

VAULT CAREER LIBRARY 349

relationships with certain professors, but while I found them to be very helpful about answering e-mailed questions, I didn't develop a friendship with any of them.

Alumna, 9/2000-5/2004, November 2004

Quality of education is topnotch. Professors are very approachable and willing to help. Office hours are a great thing; learn to take advantage of them early on. I never had any problems getting the classes that I wanted due to over-capacity issues; if anything, time conflicts screwed me over. Workload: Regardless of what you decide to major in, you're not going to earn a Wellesley degree without buckling down and doing some serious work. Wellesley is definitely not a place for slackers.

Current student, 8/2002-Submit Date, September 2004

Most of Wellesley's classes are difficult. There are no easy classes. Even classes designed to fulfill distribution requirements (which we have in spades—distribution requirements, that is), like biology for non-majors; these aren't coasting classes. The professors expect a lot from Wellesley women. Grades are important to the students here, and we work hard for our grades, but the administration is making an effort to curtail grade inflation, so there is a fear of falling grades. Depending on your major and the level of classes you take, classes meet twice a week for 70 minutes and usually there is a significant amount of homework each class—p-sets, reading, lab reports. It is difficult to get into some of the more popular classes that have caps at 20 or 25 (Wellesley's effort to keep small classes abundant), but most classes are offered at least twice in any given four year period, so students can usually get into these in-demand classes in their junior or senior year.

Alumna, 9/2001-5/2004, September 2004

The academic program is of course what Wellesley is known for. Because it is a smaller school, the classes are smaller than most large universities throughout all levels. Wellesley begins with 30 to 40 at 100 level (beginning) courses to six to 12 people at seminar (advanced) levels. The largest gripe I had about the Wellesley academic program stems from exactly why the school is so small—a smaller college means fewer professors and a smaller breadth (and depth) of study. As a result, independent study is very popular at Wellesley, but depends entirely on your personality and your professor.

> **Wellesley says:** "More than 85 percent of classes, including many introductory-level courses have fewer than 30 students."

I labeled my program as accelerated because I finished college in three years. I had two A.P. credits and received two credits for spending a summer abroad in China after my first year. As you can imagine, a good number of ambitious young women at Wellesley accelerate by a half year or year—definitely more so than at other schools. It saves money and time, but if you have any reservations about leaving early, it's not the right thing for you. This decision should also depend on how much you would like to get involved in the college community and if you want to begin a career where a junior year summer internship is essential.

 ## Employment Prospects

Current student, Economics, 9/2003-Submit Date, May 2007

Wellesley grads are well regarded in investment banking. We have alumnae (or more like teams of alumnae) from most large investment banks to do recruiting here. Many alumnae join Wall Street bulge brackets upon graduation (I won't be surprised if it's about 20 percent of the economics majors—we are target school for many BBs). Slightly less recognized in consulting, but still a number of alumnae work in top firms like McKinsey and BCG. Others go into places like the Fed.

Current student, Int'l Relations, 9/2003-Submit Date, December 2006

Wellesley students go into variety of places. Grad school—most pursue law school, med school, and grad school in public policy or poli sci. Wellesley has a very good reputation of sending people to the top grad schools.

Jobs—investment banking and consulting firms are two major ones. Many to IBs and Consulting firms come to Wellesley for recruiting. Other popular jo sector is public sector. A lot of poli sci major tend to lean toward NGOs.

Alumna, 9/1988-5/1992, March 2005

Because Wellesley is a liberal arts college, alumnae go in many different directions after graduation. It is a prestigious alma mater, and the "Old Girl" network is very strong—a friend and classmate of mine looks to Wellesley first when selecting summer interns. There is an expectation that alumnae will become leaders in whatever career they pursue. Many alumnae obtain post-graduate degrees, MBAs and JDs are popular.

Current student, 8/2002-Submit Date, September 2004

Wellesley sends so many people into the world of business and finance (about an eighth of any given graduating class is composed of economics majors,) a significant number in policy, law, and government (another eighth are political science majors), and quite a few into the medical field (about a tenth are psychology majors, and a fifth major in some scientific field). The Center for Work and Service is very helpful in getting internship (there are several sponsored by the CWS and open only to Wellesley students) and stipends are provided to many students who otherwise couldn't afford to participate in non-paid internship programs. There doesn't seem to be much of a problem for Wellesley graduates to get jobs after graduation and many go to graduate school of some sort.

> **The school says:** "Wellesley offers dozens of internships programs and hundreds of connections to individual internship opportunities. The college provides stipends, most of which are $3,000, to more than 300 students each year to enable them to pursue these experiential learning opportunities."

Alumna, 9/2001-5/2004, September 2004

Speaking as a graduate entering the finance profession, it is essential that if you know it is what you want, you prepare yourself in the best way possible. While everyone will tell you that you can get into anything with any major, you should take into consideration that it will be easier to get past a résumé screening if you have a major that has to do with your future industry. At Wellesley, you can do a double major, so some women do both a fun and functional major. Keep in mind, however, that since Wellesley's focus is more in a scholarly/academic sense than a professional sense; your economics major is not as appealing as a finance or business major from another school.

These are majors that Wellesley does not offer becasue academic training is very different from how Wellesley teaches. Wellesley has a stellar reputation among companies and individuals who have heard of the school, so the good thing is that many recruiters come to Wellesley. While it is many, it is not the same number as recruiters that may go to Harvard or MIT. To get better exposure if you are planning on going into finance or business, take a course at MIT Sloan School of Management and sign up for their recruiting announcements as well.

The most important thing is to work closely with the people in Wellesley's career office (the Center for Work and Service or CWS). Their advice is invaluable. Also, especially if you are preparing for a career in finance, begin going there early in your time at Wellesley (before junior year). This is doubly important if you are accelerated. I missed the boat by a year by not realizing that companies do junior year recruiting at Wellesley for jobs in banks. Thus, I missed the opportunity to interview for a memorable internship on my résumé. Try to make things easier for yourself in the future by putting a little effort in now.

> **Wellesley says:** "Wellesley has a very strong on-campus recruiting program. More than 100 companies interview on campus for full-time employment opportunities. The Center for Work and Service hosts a Nonprofit Career Fair and a Wellesley Women in Science Fair, both of which are attended by dozens of organizations and companies."

Quality of Life

Current student, Economics, 9/2003-Submit Date, May 2007

...ould really use some more partying. Housing is guaranteed—hence a non-...sue and our campus is beautiful. Facilities used in academic activities are gen-...ally good though we don't have a decent number of exercise machines. ...eighborhood doesn't have a college town feel: inexpensive, white, not too fun ...ut then very safe. Many find employment off-campus in town (good thing ...bout expensive town is you have expensive boutiques that need help).

Alumna, 9/2000-6/2004, February 2006

...Wellesley has an amazingly high quality of life, if you are a good fit for the ...chool. It is not a party school. Students do their homework, watch movies, go ...r walks, and they mostly leave campus to do their partying, though if you look ...ard enough you can usually find something going on. There a lot of hanging ...ut with your friends and dormmates, but if you want to meet boys you do have ...o make an effort. This is a factor you should seriously consider before making ...e choice to attend school here. You can have as much of a social life as you ...ant, but if you know you won't be happy hanging with the girls and commut-...g to the guys, if you've pictured college life as one big party with noise all the ...me and crazy antics? Wellesley is not the place for you. The town is a small ...nd pricy suburb, which limits shopping options, but there is a regular and cheap ...us to Boston (it takes about 40 minutes) and a mall only 10 minutes away by ...ar. There are grocery stores you can walk to, but the dining hall food is sur-...risingly good, with lots of healthy or vegetarian options. The academic facili-...es are incredible—new technology is everywhere and they make good use of ... On the other hand, when I was there the sports equipment was a big let-down. ...hey may have bought new machines since, but they were very limited at the ...me and there was often a wait, which I found disappointing.

Current student, Int'l Relations, 9/2003-Submit Date, December 2006

...ousing is 100 percent guaranteed, and dorm's dining hall food is OK. You can ...urvive with it. There are five dining halls, and each has its own theme, and ...ere is a vegetarian dining hall as well. The student center was newly built ...bout two years ago, and it has very good food, including fresh sandwiches, ...ushi, burgers and sauté section. Wellesley has a beautiful campus, and nice peo-...le. Very nice environment. Campus police has an escorting service at night, ...rom school buildings to your dorm.

Alumna, 9/2000-5/2004, November 2004

...Comfortable dorms, good food (especially at special college events). You'll def-...nitely walk away from Wellesley knowing what good food is! The campus is ...eautiful and serene. Dining halls are open from approx 7:15 a.m. to 6:45 p.m. ...here is a fast-food type of establishment open until 10:30/11p.m. for your late-...ight needs. However, with the development of the brand-new campus center ...which is funded by an alumna donation of $25 million, I'm sure more options ...ill become available. Just another note about the campus center: The plans ...ook absolutely gorgeous and I'm so jealous of the incoming students who will ...enefit from this much-needed structure!

...he campus itself is absolutely beautiful. Don't believe me? Rent *Mona Lisa* ...*mile*, lots of the film took place on location. As for campus safety, no worries. ...Campus police does a great job of keeping the grounds safe. You'll get the occa-...ional car full of teenage boys/frat boys that drives through the campus hooting, ...ut other than that, I never felt scared walking around late at night.

Alumna, 9/2001-5/2004, September 2004

...Wellesley is always improving its dorms and the campus. Right now, a new ...ampus center is being built. Over the summer, the last dorm that I stayed in was ...enovated. While Wellesley food is usually appreciated, I decided that I would ...ather cook for myself, so my last year, I stayed in a dorm where I could get off ...f the meal plan and cook for myself. This option was accessible because of my ...ccessibility to getting off campus. There are three options: (1) into the town of ...Wellesley; (2) into Boston; and (3) elsewhere accessible by car.

...he town of Wellesley is a five to 12-minute walk from campus, depending on ...where you start. Some people think that it is the cutest town, because it has a ...Main Street and a certain attitude of its own. Wellesley town is a predominant-...y white, upper-middle class, young family town. Those from town are either ...ery welcoming of Wellesley students, or not very friendly with anyone. Boston

is a 25 minute drive away. However, if you do not have a car, you will have to take the bus from Wellesley. During the weekdays, this is the bus that students going to class at MIT use, so it is free. On the weekends, however, the bus is $1.75 each way and often overcrowded. It's an experience riding the bus, espe-cially on a Friday night at 9:20 when everyone is dressed to go out. If you like to party, however, there is no way to get around it. The bus has its advantage in that you won't have to drive and can drink, but the bus also takes about an hour in good traffic to get to Boston.

The areas surrounding Wellesley are more suburbs, although less wealthy. The most notable is Natick, where the Super Stop n' Shop is located (24 hour grocery store), Sam's Club, Wal-Mart and a large, pleasant mall. On Saturdays, there is a shuttle that goes to the stores at Natick, $1.75 round trip. The less traveled sub-urb is Framingham, which is houses more working class families and minorities. As a result, Framingham is known as being more sketchy and most of their liquor stores are frequented as being less stringent with checking IDs (you are usually required to show a federally issued photo ID if you have an out-of-state license).

The school says: "The Lulu Chow Wang Campus, affectionate-ly known as 'The Lulu,' is a hub of activity throughout the day and into the night.

"The building houses a large dining area, cafe, bookstore, Cafe Hoop (a student-run coffee house), Punch's Alley (a student-run pub), space for student organizations to meet, large and small gathering and meeting spaces."

Social Life

Current student, Economics, 9/2003-Submit Date, May 2007

Basically most students go into Boston/Cambridge for bars, dating, partying and clubbing. Not much to do on campus. Official stance is no sororities but we do have societies here that are effectively sororities that don't live together and party a lot less than average sororities.

Current student, Int'l Relations, 9/2003-Submit Date, December 2006

Wellesley has some fun parties, however students tend to go out to Boston for more fun. Wellesley has a shuttle bus from campus to Harvard, MIT and down-town Boston on weekends. During the weekdays, Wellesley-MIT shuttle runs every hour from 7 a.m. 'til 12 a.m. for people taking MIT classes for free. On the weekends, students pay $2 for shuttle and on Saturday it runs every 40 min-utes. It is extremely convenient shuttle. Wellesley town also has a commuter rail. It is about a five to 10 minute walk from the campus depending on where you live, and about $4 for one way. It goes to Back Bay station and South Station.

Alumna, 9/2000-6/2004, February 2006

If you want to date a male, you will need to in put some effort. You need to get out to parties at MIT or Harvard, or join a club that interacts with them. There are often a few guys in classes from MIT or Babson, but they are few and the student body of Wellesley is many. You can meet people and have successful relationships at this school, but be prepared to make an effort. Wellesley is in a dry town, but there is one small bar on campus that serves only beer. There is some drinking in the dorms, but really it is not a party school and most people go into Boston really to go all out. There are more clubs than I would ever have believed, and students are encouraged to start new ones as needed. There is no Greek system at Wellesley, but there are four societies, three of which are simi-lar to sororities, and one of which is dedicated to the love of Shakespeare. It's cooler than it sounds. There is an active gay scene on campus, and it is a safe place to experiment if you are so inclined. Major events are Tower Court (a beginning of the year dance—you are supposed to meet your husband there, but I didn't), Dyke Ball (everyone goes, of all sexualities, and there is usually a line around the block of people trying to bring in their dates. One guest per student. This is kind of a costume party.), Marathon Monday (the scream tunnel!) and Spring Fling, when they usually have at least one major band come in, although the band choice usually tends to be a compromise to the lowest common denom-inator. There are other concerts and events through the year, of course.

Read all of Vault's College Surveys at **www.vault.com/college**—get complete surveys on 100s of colleges and univer-sities, expert advice on applicaton essays and more.

VAULT CAREER LIBRARY **351**

Alumna, 9/2001-5/2004, September 2004

Wellesley has no Greek system, and while there is on average one party on campus per weekend (sponsored by a student organization) it is best to go off campus if you want to party. Boston has a host of dance clubs, bars and frats, and most definitely a lively population of students from other colleges. Boston shuts down at 2 a.m.. If you are not into parties, that is the advantage of going to Wellesley. The option is very readily there to go to a movie theater in Boston or Natick, stay in and watch a movie, or go to dinner off campus. As far as large events (like concerts) go, there are not as many because Wellesley is a small school and less attractive to housing large concerts. If you enjoy folk musicians or punk bands, they are accessible in Punch's Alley, the only place liquor is served on campus. On that note, the town of Wellesley is a dry town, meaning that there are no liquor stores.

As far as dating goes, if you like women there is no better place to be; if you like men, then you must go off campus. The options are vast in that you do not need to go to a frat party to meet guys, but they are really so limited in that you must have friends of friends in a Boston-area college, or get involved in a Boston area organization or take a class.

The biggest advantage to social life at Wellesley is that Boston is nearby. Without this option, it would be very difficult to stay on campus and maintain sanity. So, while the bus is not the most comfortable place to sit on for an hour one-way, you will develop a love-hate relationship with it, speaking as one who used to ride the bus three times a weekend to get off of campus. Going to an all women's college in the middle of a wealthy, white suburb has its limitations, but it all depends on how determined you are to maintain sanity and make the best of it.

Williams College

Admissions Office
33 Stetson Court
Williamstown, MA 01267
Admissions phone: (413) 597-2211
Admissions e-mail: admission@williams.edu
Admissions URL: www.williams.edu/admission/

 ## Admissions

Alumnus/a, Foreign Language, 9/2002-6/2006, October 2007

Admission is highly selective. The student body is made up of people who not only have excellent high school grades and test scores, but can also contribute something extra to the campus community. The school is very interested in creating a diverse and involved student body, so showing excitement for participation in that community is probably important. While interviews are given, they say they're purely informational; meaning it's a chance for you to learn more about Williams, not for them to learn about you.

Alumnus/a, Economics, 9/2002-6/2006, October 2007

No interview. Common Application. Campus visit (before applying) recommended. Best to write an essay that caters to the profile of the school (it values itself as an active, if isolated, community). Best to be an active high schooler (literally, active, it is said that Williams likes athletes).

Alumnus/a, 9/1996-5/2000, September 2004

The school required a basic essay that was comparable to other essays such as "describe a significant experience or person." This is a very hard school to get into. It's right up there with Harvard. The interview was not required—very weird. This is unusual for such high tier schools. I did not interview (fortunately, I got in), but I would strongly recommend interviewing if you are on the border for getting in.

> The school says: "Interviews, as we say everywhere in our literature, play absolutely no role in admissions decisions."

Alumnus/a, 9/1993-6/1997, August 2006

The Williams admissions process has become ultra competitive in recent years. If you are not a true academic superstar (near-perfect grades and SATs and state-level awards), a recruited athlete, an underrepresented minority, a first generation college student, or a star in the arts (theater and studio art, in particular), you really need to make yourself stand out. Williams wants folks who are well-rounded and will contribute to campus in a variety of ways—admissions loves the jock/scholar/artist combo, for example. At the same time, don't spread yourself so thin that you don't exhibit real dedication to at least one area of life, whether that be science research, being a community service leader, star of all the school plays and so on. In other words, unless you have legit hook, you face steep odds. Try to make your personality come alive in your essays and peer rec-

ommendation—I know my peer recommendation really helped me out, so choose your friends wisely!

Current student, 9/2001-Submit Date, November 2004

Very difficult to get in, but manageable. Interest in the school counts for something, as does athletic and musical ability, and affirmative action (African Americans and Hispanics). Looking for interesting people in general, so send some supplementary information that lets them know more about you, a page from a sports or music program, for example, is cool. All of this is for you to get around the numbers. The safest way to get in is to be in the top 10 percent of your class and have a 1500+ SAT. Stress your passions, present yourself honestly in your essay, and do try to impress them.

Alumnus/a, 9/1997-6/2001, January 2004

The admissions office was very helpful in answering questions and connecting me with current students for real perspectives on Williams. Many students are admitted Early Decision, and you should know that it is quite competitive. You will be held over for consideration with the regular pool if you don't get in Early Decision, however.

I applied Regular Decision, primarily because of financial aid concerns—I wanted to see my full picture before accepting anywhere. The financial aid office did everything they could to help me attend Williams. They had a strong influence on my decision, because they were willing to meet the packages of other schools that had accepted me.

The admissions office always includes a few recent graduates, generally with great mix of backgrounds, so you can get a pretty good sense of different experiences at the school.

 ## Academics

Alumnus/a, Foreign Language, 9/2002-6/2006, October 2007

The quality of instruction is excellent. Professors are interesting and involved and work there because they love to teach. There are certainly times when people don't get all of their first-choice classes, but the majority of the time it's not a problem, and if it's a class you really need for your major or really want to take, you can usually talk to the professor and get accepted. Grading varies depending on department and professor, but it's much harder to get in than it is to get good grades once you're there. There's definitely a lot of work. Unlike many places, the majority of the student body spends a lot of time in the library.

Alumnus/a, Economics, 9/2002-6/2006, October 2007

Extremely rigorous. Tons of writing and problem sets. Courses were small, and accountability was high. Popular courses: math, art history, biology. Student profiles: a nice mix of pre-professionals (doctors, lawyers, bankers) and intellectuals.

Alumnus/a, 9/1993-6/1997, August 2006

In recent years Williams hired many new faculty members, lowering the student-to-faculty ratio from 9:1 to 7:1. As a result, it is very easy to get into most any class (except for a few very rare exceptions). Professors pride themselves on their accessibility, and the college funds student-professor interaction, such as dinners out, in an effort to encourage collaboration. Williams' most unique asset is its tutorial program, in which pairs of students meet with a professor for intensive, weekly sessions. Nor for the faint of heart, but if you attend Williams without taking at least one tutorial, you are really missing out on perhaps the best academic experience in the country.

Williams is strong across the board, but its strongest departments are art history, math, physics, chemistry, geology, English, econ/political economy, biology, psychology and political science. While many of these departments are prominent at other top liberal arts colleges as well, Williams' art history, math and physics departments really stand out. Asian languages are solid, while romance languages could be improved.

Alumnus/a, 9/1996-5/2000, September 2004

The academics are extremely strong and this school is recognized nationally as being the top liberal arts school in the country. For the most part quality of classes is very high—professors mostly are excellent. Some-intro level classes are fairly large however. It is pretty easy to get into almost any class you want, particularly if you speak to the professor beforehand.

I would say grading is difficult but, if you turn in a paper, you won't get anything lower than a C. But it's incredibly hard to get an A. Workload is enormous if you are going for a high GPA. Again, if you want A's, expect to push yourself nearly every weekend. If you're happy with B's or B-'s, it's not that hard to get them.

Current student, 9/2001-Submit Date, November 2004

The academics are topnotch. The liberal arts curriculum is strong across the board, especially in the maths and sciences. Certainly the best amongst liberal arts colleges. The interaction with professors is special, as well. They are always available and treat you as a colleague—a great place to develop intellectually. The French department is the only weak link in the curriculum, perhaps the best school in the country for everything else. Very open curriculum, allowing plenty of opportunities to take not too hard classes in subjects in which one only has an interest. Winter study program fits with this—a one month, pass/fail term in January where one can develop that artistic or philosophy bug one has always wanted to scratch, or go overseas to school sponsored programs in Guatemala, Morocco or Russia. Overall, an incredible place academically.

Alumnus/a, 9/1993-6/1997, June 2004

The highlight of the academic experience at Williams is access to professors, to which the school is amazingly committed. Williams recently expanded the size of the faculty to allow for more time for student-faculty interaction outside the traditional classroom confines, and the student-to-faculty ratio is now 8:1. Williams sets aside a lot of money each year to fund creative student-faculty social interaction, such as wine and cheese tastings.

> **The school says:** "Student to faculty ratio is now 7:1."

One amazing opportunity unique to Williams is the tutorial program, in which pairs of students meet weekly with a professor for intense analysis and critique of each other's independent work products. The school has vastly expanded the tutorial program in recent years.

The winter study program also distinguishes Williams from its peers, providing a chance for experimental learning without the pressure of grades during the month of January, when many other schools are closed for an extended vacation.

Alumnus/a, 9/1995-6/1999, January 2004

The classes were phenomenal. Lectures were terrific and well prepared, class size was small, workload was heavy but manageable, and there was not an issue with getting into popular classes. With no graduate students (so no teaching assistants), professors focused heavily on teaching. Since Williams, I've attended many classes in graduate school at UC Santa Barbara, MIT and Harvard, and the average quality of the classes has been significantly lower than those at Williams.

Alumnus/a, 9/1997-6/2001, January 2004

Williams is an extremely demanding academic environment. There are gut classes here and there, but in general the professors are demanding, the coursework is challenging and the workload is intense. Don't let this scare you off, though, because the professors are also extremely approachable and helpful.

For math and science classes, there is a resource center staffed by fellow students Sunday through Thursday that provides drop-in help in a very low-key, supportive environment. Most departments will match you up with some kind of tutor or discussion partner to help you out, also.

On average class size is pretty small, especially in upper-level courses. There are some larger lecture courses in psychology, econ, and the hard sciences at the intro levels. It is pretty easy to get the classes you want. Enrollment is done online, and spaces also open up after the first few days of most classes.

Not much grade inflation that I noticed. It doesn't seem too hard to get a B- or a B, but to move beyond that, you have to work. There has been some criticism that grades are too high in the math and science classes, but that tends to be the nature of any subject that has definite correct answers.

The art history department is one of the finest in the country, math profs are constantly winning teaching awards, for a small college our science grants are phenomenal, and the English, philosophy, history and political science professors are constantly referenced as experts in their fields. There is a reason Williams remains in the top three of liberal arts colleges every year.

Employment Prospects

Alumnus/a, Foreign Language, 9/2002-6/2006, October 2007

Employment prospects are very good. While the liberal arts degree doesn't prepare you to do anything specific, graduates end up in great jobs in many different fields. The alumni network is incredibly strong. There is a long list of alumni "mentors," and alumni usually go out of their way to help fellow Ephs, including giving them preference in the hiring process.

Alumnus/a, Economics, 9/2002-6/2006, October 2007

Williams has strong roots in the arts institutions, and my classmates had no trouble finding positions in banks and consulting firms. Many people paralegal. Many teach, many travel. Williams alumni are famously willing to help.

Alumnus/a, 9/1993-6/1997, August 2006

As for grad schools, Williams places as well as any school in the country. You can pretty much write your ticket to top law, medical, MBA or PhD programs with over a 3.7 at Williams, and over a 3.4 puts you solidly in the ballpark at many highly ranked programs. Williams grads also do better in obtaining fellowships than any other liberal arts school.

As for jobs, Williams places really well in certain fields, namely the art world, consulting, investment banking, and prep school teaching/coaching. Wall street recruiters love Williams grads because of their work hard/play hard mentality. On the other hand, many (generally less prestigious) employers will have never heard of Williams, much like they have never heard of other small liberal arts schools. Since most Ephs want to go to grad school or the above-mentioned areas, not a big problem, but if you have very off-the-beaten path interested, you will have to work a little harder to market yourself than you would with a comparable (but more widely recognized) Ivy degree.

Alumnus/a, 9/1996-5/2000, September 2004

Campus recruiting for jobs after graduation is very strong; again, it is recognized at a top school up there with Harvard. The career counseling center is very effective and has a great alumni network. There aren't any job or internship opportunities during the academic year available, except in the winter study period, one month in January where you can do such things, plus the summer.

Current student, 9/2001-Submit Date, November 2004

Outstanding. A core school for all of the top investment banks. Not just for econ majors, but that obviously helps with the interviews. Core school for most of the major consulting firms as well, Bain and Monitor especially, and you certainly start with your foot in the door at McKinsey, as well. The banks all recruit here

Read all of Vault's College Surveys at **www.vault.com/college**–get complete surveys on 100s of colleges and universities, expert advice on applicaton essays and more.

VAULT CAREER LIBRARY 353

heavily, so if you are interested in JP Morgan, Morgan Stanley and Goldman, this is a safe place. This is all even more true for law schools. The curriculum here prepares you perfectly for the LSAT, and most students score 170 and higher. Last year, out of the 180 person class at Yale, by far the most selective school in the country, Williams had nine students. It is a beautiful place for a future lawyer to begin his or her career. For all else, liberal arts sells. Marketing, advertising, you name it—you can get a job in it when you leave. The only program it lacks is engineering. There is a combined program with several engineering schools, and one can always pick up the math in undergraduate and then go to grad school, but if you know you want to do engineering now, go elsewhere.

Alumnus/a, 9/1993-6/1997, June 2004

Williams students and alumni are highly sought after by employers in the most prestigious fields, in particular law, consulting, medicine, academia, scientific research, investment banking and the arts. The Williams name is not as well-known as it should be outside of the traditional prestige fields like law, medicine and business, but most students have no trouble finding work or gaining acceptance to elite graduate schools. The Williams alumni network is fiercely loyal, and I was amazed at how helpful and accessible even very prominent alumni were when contacted for career advice.

Alumnus/a, 9/1973-6/1977, September 2003

The office of career counseling provides outstanding support to students as well as alumni seeking job placement and career coaching. The college has few peers in its prestige among employers and graduate schools. Therefore, many top firms tend to recruit at the campus. In addition, there is a large, well-organized and highly active group of alumni that have agreed to be helpful and involved in career placement. Many internships and summer jobs come from this source.

 ## Quality of Life

Alumnus/a, Foreign Language, 9/2002-6/2006, October 2007

Most of the facilities are top-of-the-line, and the ones that aren't are in the process of being rebuilt. There is a lot of different dining and living options, and a surprising number of freshmen (and almost all upperclassmen) live in singles. Williams is located in a very small town. It's naturally beautiful and extremely safe. The campus sort of encompasses the downtown, making it easy to walk to restaurants, coffee shops and stores.

Alumnus/a, Economics, 9/2002-6/2006, October 2007

The town is small and isolated. Most people don't bring cars, but without one, it's just you and the students. People are nice, and the administration keeps the campus going with speakers, parties and other entertainment. Skiing is nearby (there's a shuttle), which is also a nice (and close) getaway.

Alumnus/a, 9/1993-6/1997, August 2006

Wonderful quality of life, but you have to understand that this is a rural town without tons of bars, restaurants or nightlife of that ilk. Within those constraints, however, Williams offers wonderful options: many incredible hiking trails, skiing, a PGA-caliber golf course on campus, three amazing art museums within 10 minutes of campus, including Mass Moca, which hosts all sorts of great events, and the most prominent summer theater festival in the country. The Berkshires is not known as America's Cultural Resort by accident. Students also benefit from the unusual concentration of good restaurants and bars for a small town. But, again, it is a rural atmosphere and you'd better prefer views of mountains to views of skyscrapers if you choose Williams.

Alumnus/a, 9/1996-5/2000, September 2004

Crime is almost nonexistent—particularly since it is a college campus. I thought the dining was excellent, actually and I hear it's even better now. Housing is pretty cool although you must stay on campus for the first three years and only some small percentage of seniors are actually allowed to live off campus (lottery system). The campus also has great gyms and pools.

Alumnus/a, 9/1993-6/1997, June 2004

Safety is not an issue, as there is essentially no violent crime in Williamstown. Housing, facilities and dining options are all topnotch already, and the school is currently building a [$36] million state-of-the-art student center to complement

another student center completed only five years ago. Pretty much all of the facilities at Williams, including housing, have been newly built or renovated in the last 15 years, or are scheduled for renovation in the next five years. The administration is very responsive to student requests, and takes the opinions of the student body seriously.

Alumnus/a, 9/1997-6/2001, January 2004

Williamstown is the idyllic little New England village. It is a "one-stoplight town" despite what the brochures may show. You can get most necessities on Spring Street—drug store, coffee shop and barber shop. Groceries are a bit of a trek, but there is a college van service and lots of willing friends with cars.

Housing is pretty nice—mix of singles and doubles as frosh, with a guarantee of a single if you want it by senior year. You must live on campus until you're a senior, then you can apply to live in off campus apartments or in co-ops (basically school-owned houses and apartments that still provide toilet paper and basic custodial services). First-years live in entries, which are groupings of 15 to 25 students living with two junior advisors who help guide the way through the transition to college. They are not college employees, so no worries about them tattling. It's a very unique and remarkable program.

Facilities are constantly improving—they are finishing a student center for 2005 as well as a new theatre and dance complex, and the Unified Science Center was done in 2000. I believe plans are being drawn up for a renovation of the main library. There is a multicultural center, center for environmental studies, space for religious groups, and a variety of spots to hang out. One of the best things is an all-night computer lab for those last-minute papers.

There are occasional thefts but, in general, it's a safe campus and town. Safewalks are available late at night if you're nervous, and blue emergency phones can be seen anywhere on campus. Security is mostly friendly, and will often give you a warning first.

The social scene can be a bit lacking, but there are always lectures, speeches, debates, performances and more to keep you occupied. There is a cute small movie theater on the town's main street, and a few bars that cater to both locals and students. Remember, this is a small town!

 ## Social Life

Alumnus/a, Foreign Language, 9/2002-6/2006, October 2007

Because there isn't a lot of social options off campus, the students and college both make a pretty big effort to make sure there are things going on. There is one bar that a lot of upperclassmen go to, a number of restaurants (at least for the town's size), and a small independent movie theater that shows some good stuff. A lot of social life revolves around campus parties of various sizes, though there are also lots of other activities that people take advantage of to varying degrees.

Alumnus/a, Economics, 9/2002-6/2006, October 2007

A couple of bars, lots of campus-sponsored parties, and lots of close network spending time in nice public spaces in college dormitories. No Greek life, but sports teams filled that niche instead.

Alumnus/a, 9/1993-6/1997, August 2006

Bars: two on campus—the new pub opening in January '07 in the amazing new student center and the Log, which is awesome and hosts lots of fun events. Three others in town: the student favorite pub, the Red Herring, and when you want to class it up, the bar at Mezze (best restaurant in town by far). Most social life takes place at student parties and student dorms—can feel like an insular bubble, but the bonding is intense with life-long repercussions as a result. Most Ephs I know, their best friends are former Ephs as well, and whenever I'm spotted with a Williams t-shirt on the street, I inevitably have a random Williams alumni come up and introduce themselves. It's that sort of an intense place, not for everyone but those who love it (which is 90 percent of students) love it passionately.

There is no Greek system and given how small the student body is, there is simply no need for one. The school, as of 2006-07, will be divided into four "houses" á la *Harry Potter*. The verdict is still out on how that will affect social life

vorite student eaterie: Pappa Charlie's, Helen's Place, Thai Garden, Hot mato's Pizza. Hangouts: Goodrich (the smaller of the two student centers), e Log, The Snack Bar, Tunnel City Coffee (great new coffee place in town). ctivities: going to Williams/Amherst sporting events (basketball and football; particular), attending concerts and movies sponsored by all campus entertain-ent, attending student theater events or a cappella concerts (which always pack e house), going to "row house" parties on weekends, hiking/running in good eather, playing frisbee/soccer/basketball/broomball, hanging out at coffee use/snack bar. But just talking with groups of friends into the wee hours in rm common rooms is probably where students spend the plurality of their ne.

asically, Williams students, despite the relative isolation of the school, are ver lacking for things to do—the students are amazingly proactive in creating eir own fun, which more than makes up for any lack of urban nightlife to be und in the area.

lumnus/a, 9/1996-5/2000, September 2004

did very little in terms of social life because I wanted to graduate summa, but ere is a lot to do considering that there is nothing around Williamstown. There e no fraternities or sororities allowed, but all parties are open to everyone, hich is the best part so no one feels left out or less than because they are not in frat. There aren't any clubs in town, but there are some 20 minutes away and ere are plenty of restaurants, although most are pretty pricey.

Current student, 9/2001-Submit Date, November 2004

Social life is good. Not in a major city, so either outdoors stuff during the day and/or hard drinking or socializing at night. Lacks a cool bar scene, which is a shame. Dating scene: there is a surprisingly high marriage rate of Williams stu-dents. The classes are small, 500 people per a year, so people know one anoth-er. Some sleeping around, but reputations get around, and if you have a girl-friend freshman or sophomore year, it could be permanent. For guys, your prospects improve as you age, for girls, your high point is your first year, so enjoy it. There are no frats, and the school has not entirely adjusted to that fact. New York is only a few hours away, and a weekend trip there is helpful in the winter. Great winter sports scene with skiing and snowboarding, college subsi-dized and taught. Whatever you ask for, you get. If you want to have a party, the college pays for it.

Alumnus/a, 9/1997-6/2001, January 2004

You are with some amazing fellow students who find a variety of ways to enter-tain themselves. The intellectual discourse and activities outside the classroom are great.

Every student organization under the sun is at Williams—except the Greek sys-tem. And if a group you like is not here, you're encouraged to start it. Students run the campus after 4 p.m. You can definitely hone your event-planning and organizational skills at Williams. Improv comedy groups, student theater groups, a cappella groups, student symphonies and jazz ensembles provide entertainment, and usually for $1 to $5 per ticket!

Worcester Polytechnic Institute

Admissions Office
00 Institute Road
Worcester, MA 01609-2280
Admissions phone: (508) 831-5286
Admissions fax: (508) 831-5875
Admissions e-mail: admissions@wpi.edu
Admissions URL: www.wpi.edu/admissions.html

 Admissions

Current student, Engineering, 8/2003-Submit Date, October 2006

he admissions process is quite simple; the interview isn't all that important and electivity isn't extreme. The only reason, however, that selectivity isn't so high because there is a relatively low rate of applicants. Make sure the essays are nique and stand out from the crowd. Using the Common Application is the best pproach.

lumnus/a, 8/1999-5/2003, January 2007

pply online to the school and you won't have to pay the application fee of $50 hen I applied). The applications submitted online are treated the same as reg-lar applications, so don't be scared that it will be ignored or lost in the system. ther then that, the application process isn't any different from any other school, you have decent grades in high school and a decent SAT score, you should be olden.

Current student, 8/2005-Submit Date, October 2005

he admissions process was not too bad for this college. Athletics are a huge elper at this school, and can help students to get in over the extremely intelli-ent students. As long as you show interest in the school by visiting, touring and eeing various programs and possibly an overnight, you should be set. All this next to your grades, of course. A 3.0 average with extracurriculars can get you .

The essay should not be cheesy and should actually mean something to you. Write what comes from the heart but do not stray from your topic. Use it to prove a point about what changed your life or how you see this problem or mir-acle in the world today. There are many possibilities.

Current student, 8/2004-Submit Date, November 2004

I used the Common Application that I used to apply to several other schools. If I remember correctly, there were a few other supplementary questions, but noth-ing too difficult. From what I've heard, interviews aren't that important at WPI. It's a really selective school, and there's lots of competition to get in, so you need to have good grades, transcripts and references from teachers.

> **The school says:** "We do not have a supplement or any supple-mental questions to the Common Application."

Alumnus/a, 8/2000-5/2004, October 2005

Worcester Polytechnic Institute (WPI) has a very streamlined admissions process. I applied through the Early Decision program in the fall and received a decision in mid-December (the best Christmas present). (Full disclosure, I worked as a tour guide and intern in the office during my time at WPI.) Over the past few years, WPI rolled out two rounds of Early Action (non-binding) admission. Students admitted under these programs are not bound to attend WPI, they just find out whether they've been accepted earlier.

The admissions office couldn't have been more helpful. E-mails were promptly answered (keep the e-mails professional as they are included in your application file). The web site and the office are loaded with information on every aspect of the university. As an added bonus at tours and open houses, students can usual-ly try out a Segway HT (Dean Kamen attended WPI).

When I applied WPI's essay was pretty open-ended and I believe it still is. This is very nice when every other school has a unique prompt. Interviews are optional and only a small percentage of applicants request one. The staff views them as informational, but will take notes and add them to the applicant's file.

As far as selectivity, grades are the most important factor, with an emphasis on honors and AP courses. The staff takes a balanced view of grades (so that C- in

Read all of Vault's College Surveys at **www.vault.com/college**—get complete surveys on 100s of colleges and univer-sities, expert advice on applicaton essays and more.

VAULT CAREER LIBRARY 355

Spanish shouldn't torpedo your application if everything else is in order). The other four factors are test scores (old SAT inter-quartile range 1170 to 1380), recommendations, extracurriculars and personal statement.

Academics

Current student, Engineering, 8/2003-Submit Date, October 2006

Getting into classes is a piece of cake if you register early, and there is a lot of flexibility from professors to let students be admitted to classes even if they are full. The workload is pretty extreme and strenuous and most of the professors are incredibly intelligent. The labs are up to date and the TAs are usually very helpful. Once again, the workload is real intense, and difficult.

Alumnus/a, 8/1999-5/2003, January 2007

At this school academics are topnotch. The workload is horrendous, the academic program really is a lot of hard work and you will have many sleepless nights, but in the end, you really will have learned a lot of things that are necessary in the workforce. Employers know this and so does everyone else who knows anything about WPI. People will be impressed that you go there.

Alumnus/a, 6/1998-6/2002, September 2006

Generally the quality of the courses and professors is high. The project-based curriculum is integrated into most classes, and really brings real-world scenarios into the classroom. Generally, the workload is reasonable, but it's not the place to skip classes or assignments. The short terms mean that if you don't stay on top of things, you will fall behind. The good news is, even if a class is hard, it's over in seven weeks.

Current student, 8/2005-Submit Date, October 2005

The quality of the classes are exceptional. There are hardly any large classes and when there are, quite a few of the faculty members are there to assist you whenever you have a problem. The workload isn't too bad and the academics you learn in the classes are entertaining. Getting into classes, even the popular ones, should not pose a problem. The grading ranges from an A, B, C and NR. An NR means no record and the course won't show on your transcript because you did not get at least a C. The professors are nice and are always willing to help.

Alumnus/a, 8/2000-5/2004, October 2005

The academic program at WPI is intense but very user-friendly. WPI is unique from other colleges and universities in several ways. First, all undergraduates must complete three projects before graduation. Second, WPI operates on a quarter system in which students generally take three classes at a time. Third, academic advising is taken very seriously at WPI. Finally, WPI employs a non-punitive grading system that encourages students to explore courses outside of their known strengths.

The project program is what truly sets WPI apart. As mentioned above, students are required to complete three projects. The first is a project in the humanities. Students complete a sequence of five related courses on a topic, such as music, art, English and history, and then complete a capstone project worth one course. The second is the Interactive Project (IQP in WPI lingo). This project (worth three courses) examines how society and technology interact. It is also the project that most students travel off campus to complete (more on this later). The third project is the Major Project (a.k.a., MQP), which is similar to a senior thesis. This is also worth three courses. The latter two projects are generally completed in groups of two to four students and are often sponsored by businesses or nonprofits.

WPI sends a high percentage of its students abroad at some point during their undergraduate career (when I was there, I believe we had the second highest percentage in the U.S.). The quarter system dovetails with the project program to make this possible. While students have the opportunity to travel abroad for the humanities project and the MQP, most students travel abroad for the IQP (as this alumnus did).

The quarter system truly makes the project system work, as it allow students to focus their energies on the project during one term. I also enjoyed the term system because it allowed me to focus on three classes for seven weeks at a time

instead of trying to remember material from September for five finals December.

Academic advising is taken very seriously at WPI. Freshmen are assigned team of advisors (faculty advisor, peer advisor and resident advisor) at orientation that works with their residence hall floor throughout the year to make su each student adjusts well to WPI's unique program. This is especially importa because seven-week terms do not allow much time to recover for an undisc plined student. Finally, the WPI grading system consists of four grades: A, B, and NR (not recorded). NR is not really a grade because it does not show up the student's transcript. This takes some pressure off of the student if they get over their head with a course, and the curriculum allows for up to three NRs d ing the course of study. I never had to take advantage of this fact, although I w a bit nervous once or twice.

Current student, 8/2004-Submit Date, November 2004

The classes are really difficult, and the workload is even worse. But it's wo it, since WPI prides itself on its academics. We have excellent laboratories a facilities, there's even a nuclear reactor here!

> **The school says:** "The nuclear reactor on campus is very low power—it only generates enough power to run a toaster!"

When you walk through campus, you can see lots of students working on t various projects they are required to do to complete their degree. Some pa projects are actually part of the physical campus, like the water fountain in o of the main plazas. The professors are helpful and the classes are sma Worcester Polytech uses the term system, two terms per semester and each ter is seven weeks long. Watch out—these terms go by incredibly fast. A typic courseload during a term consists of three classes. This doesn't seem like a lo but you're really taking six classes per semester, which is more than the typic college student. Also, be prepared to have lots of homework and do lots studying.

Employment Prospects

Alumnus/a, 8/1999-5/2003, January 2007

Employment prospects are excellent. A lot of prestigious employers visit t campus and conduct on-campus interviews and the WPI Career Services offi web site has a lot of jobs on it. There is no doubt that if you graduate from th school you will get a good job, and get paid very well.

Alumnus/a, 6/1998-6/2002, September 2006

The project-based curriculum lends itself well to a college student's résum especially if he/she takes advantage of the opportunity to do a project abroad ar work with a major company (e.g., GE) for his/her MQP (capstone) project. I ha around six interviews the fall of my senior year with well-known companies, a ultimately had an offer in the spring.

Current student, Engineering, 8/2003-Submit Date, October 200

On-campus recruiting and internships are huge at WPI, and (particularly loca employers hold the school in a very high regard, perhaps second in the sta behind only MIT and certainly in the Top 10 in the Northeast. Students comir out of WPI generally make at least $50,000 to start and some coming out, eve with bachelor's degrees, are making in excess of $75,000 per year.

Current student, 8/2004-Submit Date, November 2004

WPI has one of the highest rates of employment after graduation in the countr I know that many graduates get hired as soon as they graduate, sometim before. There are a lot of internship opportunities, so many people have a opportunity to move up in the company before they even graduate. There's career development center on campus that is extremely helpful at finding the types of internships and job opportunities.

> **The school says:** "WPI is a nationally-ranked and known university, ranked Number 63 among the top-tier doctoral institutions in *U.S. News & World Report*. WPI students are recruited annually on campus by national organizations, such as General Electric, Pfizer, IBM, Accenture, Raytheon and more. Many students get experience at prestigious national and international

organizations through the project program. Students have the opportunity to go to one of more than 20 project centers in the U.S. and around the world. Recent project sponsors have included: NASA, Johnson & Johnson, Gillette, UNESCO and Deutsche Bank."

Current student, 8/2005-Submit Date, October 2005

This college excels in that department. 95 percent of the students who graduate from WPI get a good job immediately proceeding their academic career. The jobs usually consist of engineering, computer scientists, and others that use science/math fields.

Quality of Life

Alumnus/a, 8/1999-5/2003, January 2007

The food company, Chartwells, has its act together and the food is pretty good. The dorms are a good place to live (although somewhat expensive). Most people move into apartments after their first year simply because of the cost; it's much cheaper to live in an apartment. Like many colleges that are in a city, the WPI campus area is good, the areas around the WPI campus area are not so good, but I have never had a problem with crime and have never felt scared to go anywhere. WPI also offers a free taxi service at night; you can call them wherever you are and they'll pick you up and take you wherever you want within a one-mile radius.

Current student, 8/2005-Submit Date, October 2005

The housing is wonderful. The rooms are spacious compared to other universities and easy to move about. The halls are wide and allow plenty of students to move to and fro. The campus is small but homily and very accessible. Students may dine at various locations on and off campus. The food can get repetitive at the cafeterias, but there is a number of places you can visit to widen your range of food. Worcester is an inner-city but the campus police are everywhere at all times within a couple minutes. They are very reliable and will basically do anything a student requests if asked ranging from opening a dorm room to transporting a student to a building. There have been a few occasions when the police had to step in, but that is a rarity at WPI.

Current student, Engineering, 8/2003-Submit Date, October 2006

The campus is tiny, and the Quad is nonexistent now that a new admissions building was built. Currently, the athletic facilities are sub-par but there are plans to completely revamp that athletic system, including new field-turf fields, practice fields, a new field house and a completely renovated gym that will be completed in four stages over the next 10 years. Some parts of the surrounding neighborhood are incredibly affluent and wealthy, while the other side of campus boasts a troubled area. Generally, students are safe, but walking with a friend or two is definitely advised. The building facilities are in pretty good condition overall and the dining isn't bad. If you do dine on campus, the VIP meal plan is by far the best and even though it's the most expensive, it is fully worth its value.

Alumnus/a, 8/2000-5/2004, October 2005

The WPI campus is beautiful and well maintained. Unfortunately, the rest of Worcester is not as pristine. WPI continues to make major investments in additions and upkeep of the campus. The campus center opened in 2001 and is a hub of student activity. The residence halls are some of the best maintained that I have seen. Most of the campus is Wi-Fi enabled and the network is extremely fast. Classrooms are very up to date, and almost all have A\V presentation equipment included.

WPI's dining halls are the best that I've seen. While the food isn't home cooking, it far exceeds college food. Beyond that, the variety available ensures that there is always something good to eat even if you don't care for the main course.

WPI is surrounded by residential areas, largely populated by students, faculty and staff. Many cheap apartments are located close to campus, providing a nice option after the first year. The school also has several apartment and suite style options. While WPI is in an urban area, I always felt comfortable around campus.

Current student, 8/2004-Submit Date, November 2004

The dorms are really nice, and the people and RAs are nice, as well. The facilities are amazing. The campus center is an awesome place to hang out. There are lots of organizations to help you deal with the difficult coursework, too. There isn't an incredible amount of diversity on campus, which is to be expected at any technical school. As far as safety goes, Worcester itself isn't a very safe city. However, the WPI campus has relatively few incidents and campus crime rarely happens. There are lots of campus cops around.

Social Life

Current student, Engineering, 8/2003-Submit Date, October 2006

The City of Worcester is not great, but Boston and Providence are each only about 40 minutes away. The bar scene in Worcester isn't bad and there are some places with really cheap pitchers of Bud Light or inexpensive draft beers. A local favorite for all colleges is Leitrums, and the opening of McFadden's will most likely prove to take over as a superior place. Irish Times is also enjoyable with its bar on the first floor and dance club on the second. There are some good restaurants in the area including The Boynton, The 111 Chophouse and the Sole Proprietor. Most students who enjoy themselves on campus are either involved in athletics, Greek life or a combination of both. There is very little school spirit for athletics, which is depressing, and the poor ratio (3:1 males-to-females) certainly doesn't help. If you're a male and don't join a fraternity or belong to an athletic organization, you're more than likely either going to hate the school or love the fact that there are swordfights on the quad (seriously). Females have the ultimate deal: getting free drinks everywhere they go and being welcomed with open arms to almost every fraternity in the area.

Current student, 8/2004-Submit Date, November 2004

There's lots to do in Worcester, since there are about 150,000 college students here, and the social committee plans fun events like concerts and movies for the weekends. The students are really fun to hang out with. The campus body can be split into two categories: those students who never leave their room and play computer and video games all day, and those students who are involved in lots of campus organizations and are very social. There's an equal number of people from these two groups, so you're bound to find a clique with which you'll fit in. Everyone is very nice—I haven't really met that many snobby people here. One thing that you'll hear about a lot is the ratio: three guys to every girl. This is fine if you're a girl, but it's not a favorite topic for most of the guys. Still, with many colleges in Worcester, meeting new people isn't a problem.

> The school says: "There are 30,000 students at 10 area colleges."

Current student, 8/2005-Submit Date, October 2005

The social life is a bit different here. There are the few who lock themselves up in their dorm rooms and never come out because they are in front of their computer all day. There are also the regular kids who hang out and have a blast with their friends. There are plenty of bars and restaurants less than a 20-minute walk away from campus. Those bars and restaurants are where the dating scene usually occurs but there are plenty of parties on campus where that can occur as well.

Clubs and the Greek organization are big here as well. Almost every student is in a club or Greek organization. They meet and do what they enjoy or simply have parties. It's up to the students to do what they want.

Alumnus/a, 8/2000-5/2004, October 2005

To say the least WPI's social life is varied and unique. Students form groups around every conceivable interest from medieval combat to intramural sports, to fraternities and sororities. Greek life is a palpable presence on the campus with about half the students affiliated. Other major clubs include SocCom (the Social Committee), which sponsors a variety of events from Sunday Night Films to major concerts).

WPI's approximately 75 percent male ratio creates for an interesting dating scene. However, this is mitigated by the fact that several colleges in Worcester have ratios that are almost inverse. The most popular bar is The Boynton, named

Read all of Vault's College Surveys at **www.vault.com/college**—get complete surveys on 100s of colleges and universities, expert advice on applicaton essays and more.

VAULT CAREER LIBRARY **357**

after WPI's founder. The B, as it is called, just underwent a major renovation in 2004 that was well received.

Alumnus/a, 8/1988-5/1994, July 2004

Most college students went for pizza like Domino's and Boyton Pizza. You had to walk a distance to visit bars. Getting drunk on campus turned out to be quite easy if you had friends at the fraternities. Most activities revolved around the fraternity parties and sporting events. At these events you could mix with others. Outside sports, the campus had little to offer for clubs.

> **The school says:** "There are nearly 200 student clubs and activities, including music, theater, cultural, Greek organizations, professional societies and more. Students can always form a new club if they want to."

 # The School Says

Small classes, a flexible curriculum, hands-on project experience and one-on-one interaction with professors make learning at WPI an experience unlike any other. Students work closely together in classes and on projects, building valuable collaborative skills.

Founded in 1865 as one of the nation's first technological universities, WPI has been widely recognized for its quality undergraduate education. WPI is consistently ranked among the best national research universities in *U.S. News & World Report* and the *Princeton Review*. For the past three years, WPI has been named among the top 50 universities for best values in *U.S. News & World Report*. It was the only technological university among the 16 Leadership Institutions selected by the Association of American Colleges and Universities to serve as models for excellent practices in liberal education.

WPI offers over 35 areas of study in engineering, science, management, social science and the liberal arts leading to the BA or BS degree. New interdisciplinary programs are driven by real-world demand, like interactive media and game development and environmental engineering.

At WPI, students work on projects on campus and around the globe where classroom learning is applied to pressing real-life challenges. All students complete three projects: one in the humanities, one in their major and one working with a team to solve a problem at the intersection of society and technology—helping to bring electricity to remote villages in Thailand, or studying the bioethics of cloning, for example. Recent project sponsors include NASA, Johnson & Johnson, Morgan Stanley, the Environmental Protection Agency and UNESCO.

Besides being passionate about teaching, WPI professors are committed researchers and scholars. Eleven members of the current faculty are Fulbright Scholars. More than 40 are fellows of top national and international societies. Since 1994, 17 WPI professors have won the National Science Foundations CAREER Award, its most prestigious award for young faculty members.

With its beautiful architecture, grassy quad and ivy-covered walls, our traditional New England campus is the kind of place where students can't help feeling inspired. There are more than 200 student clubs and activities, including 11 fraternities and three sororities, and a full roster of varsity, club and intramural athletics.

Home to 12 other colleges and universities and over 30,000 college students, Worcester is a great college town. Boston is less than an hour away by commuter rail. Worcester is centrally located with easy access to Providence, New York City, the White Mountains and Cape Cod.

With a placement rate of over 90 percent, students are recruited by leading organizations such as Pfizer, General Electric, Fidelity Investments and IBM. WPI graduates' starting salaries are higher than those of many other college graduates, according to the National Association of Colleges and Employers. WPI graduates are accepted at prestigious graduate schools, including MIT, Yale University and Tufts University Medical School.

Every aspect of the WPI education is designed to help students see and solve problems in fresh, creative ways. Our mission for the past 140 years, simply put, is to give students the education they need to achieve things that really matter—in the workplace and in the world.

Central Michigan University

Admissions Office
Warriner Hall 102
Mount Pleasant, MI 48859
Admissions phone: (989) 774-3076 or (888) 292-5366
Admissions e-mail: cmuadmit@cmich.edu
Admissions URL: www.cmich.edu/Admissions

Admissions

Current student, Music, 8/2003-Submit Date, October 2006

To apply for admission at Central Michigan University, I just had to send in an application. There were no essays or interviews. However, I had to audition to get into the music program. The audition consisted of music theory, aural skills, and a playing audition on my major instrument. The playing audition not only tested my abilities on my instrument, but was also a test on how fast I learn things, how I take instructions, and how my personality would fit in with the others in the studio.

Current student, 9/2005-Submit Date, November 2006

From what I know, Central is not that selective; most people can get in with whatever their numbers are.

> **The school says:** "We carefully review each student's application. The following factors are taken into account: overall grade point average, ACT test score, rigor of high school courses, extracurricular and leadership activities, work experience, and volunteer activities."

Current student 8/2003-Submit Date, October 2005

For undergraduates the process is pretty simple. You can write special essays to try to qualify for scholarships, which is a one-day thing on campus. Otherwise, it is a basic application.

Current student, 8/2005-Submit Date, December 2005

It is pretty easy to get into the school as long as you have a 2.5 or above GPA. All I did was fill out the application given and I got a letter telling me I was in.

Current student, 9/2005-Submit Date, October 2005

I was attending a community college for my first year in college, just to get a feel for the college life. The way I got into Central was I asked my counselor at the community college about Central and two other schools. She told me to go on the CMU web site and look up anything I needed to learn, including classes, teachers and living. I decided a little later that CMU was the place for me and I filled out an application. For Central there were no interviews or essays to be written. I got a letter back in two or three weeks that told me I was accepted into CMU.

Current student, 8/2003-Submit Date, September 2005

No essay is required with an application. There is a fee of $50. The average GPA accepted is 2.5, the average ACT score is 22.

> **Central Michigan says:** "The undergraduate application fee is $35. The average accepted GPA is 3.3; the average ACT score is 23."

Current student, 8/2000-Submit Date, January 2004

A recruiter came to my high school, talked about Central Michigan University and handed out brochures of programs that they offered and other information about Central. There was just an application that applicants had to fill out. There were no essays. In 2000, I think most of the people who applied were being let in. They would not take you if your GPA was 2.5 or lower and you had a below-average ACT score. Now, I think Central is being more selective because the campus is expanding rapidly.

Alumnus/a, 8/1998-12/2002, March 2004

I started the admissions process to prospective colleges in my junior year of high school. I visited four campuses in Michigan altogether. I took a campus tour of Central and loved it! The small atmosphere was great, everything from housing (on and off campus) to bookstores, coffeehouses and academic buildings was within short walking distance. I attended a campus tour and question session, which later in my college career I gave to other prospective students. I had one application to fill out, in which my high school counselor had to write a paragraph on how he thought Central would be a match for me. I applied early, with a 3.2 GPA, and was accepted in four days. Central Michigan admissions called me at home to congratulate me on my admission.

Academics

Current student, 9/2005-Submit Date, November 2006

As an honors student, I get priority registration, which is amazing. Workload is a lot harder than high school; it's hard to stay focused.

Current student, Music, 8/2003-Submit Date, October 2006

There are lots of music classes. There are a number of one-credit classes that music majors have to take. It can be very busy and overwhelming to students. It is a large workload. I usually take between seven and nine classes each semester. The classes are all important to music majors. As a music major, the students take classes for their major in their first semester of classes, which fills up most of a schedule. This makes it difficult to take university program (general education) courses. Most of the professors in the music program are good, but there are one or two who are not good at teaching. It is easy to get into music classes, but be prepared to take early morning classes, especially in the first two years. Grading is pretty straightforward. In labs, such as piano, the professors understand a variety of skill and tend to grade on improvement.

Alumnus/a, 8/1999-12/2003, October 2005

CMU's PT program is topnotch, it is recognized nationally. It is a great program. The faculty is wonderful and very well known in the profession. The classes are tough, but you learn so much information. You always automatically get into the classes because there are only so many people in your class, so you all take the same classes together. The workload is intense, but it is a doctorate of PT program now, so it should be! During your last academic semester you have the opportunity to do a research project, which is a lot of work, but such a great experience. The grading is tough, just like the classes, but they map it out for you right from the beginning. The professors like to have fun, but only after they push you really hard in the classroom!

Current student, 8/2005-Submit Date, December 2005

My program's courses are very fun, but also very hard. The professors are very good but some just don't know how to explain the material well. It is very hard to get into the courses because they fill up fast. They are very popular! The workload can stress you out because the health courses expect a lot from you.

Current student, 8/2004-Submit Date, October 2005

Average workload is 15 credits per semester. On average professors are good. Check ratemyprofessor.com to find a good one for each course number. Classes usually aren't too big unless it is a lecture hall class. Generally getting the classes and times you want is not a problem unless you register late.

Current student, 7/2003-Submit Date, March 2004

Well, overall, I like the professors at CMU, and the classes are pretty nice. I have no complaints about the school as a whole; it's a pretty good education. The workload is not too overbearing, but you will need to do your fair share of work just like any other college. Most professors are nice and considerate. They have a great academic program here, and the core classes are laid out pretty nicely. You know from the beginning what you need to do in order to graduate, and it's very simple to plan out your schedule according to the guidelines.

Read all of Vault's College Surveys at **www.vault.com/college**–get complete surveys on 100s of colleges and universities, expert advice on applicaton essays and more.

VAULT CAREER LIBRARY 359

Current student, 8/2000-Submit Date, January 2004

The academic program is challenging. Of course, this depends on the class and professor. I think most classes appropriately challenge the students. The quality of classes is good, and so is the quality of the professors. There is a broad range of general classes to take and also many in the majors that are offered. The ease of getting popular classes depends on what level you are at and if the university will "bump" the person in. Every person's situation is different and requires different measures.

Grading is mostly fair. Some professors are easier than others, of course. The professors in my major all have PhDs and know what they are talking about. They respect students and are very willing to help a student outside of class. The workload, of course, varies from class to class, but it is mostly reasonable. Some professors expect way too much of their students, but if students devote their time, it will be worth their while, mostly.

 # Employment Prospects

Current student, 8/2003-Submit Date, September 2005

Most graduates are hired within six months of graduation. There are tons of internships available, too.

Current student, Music, 8/2003-Submit Date, October 2006

Graduates from CMU's Music Education program have a good reputation. Many graduates get jobs in the state, while some choose to go out of the state. The music degree certifies a person to be able to teach K-12 general, vocal, and instrumental music.

> **The school says:** "CMU's music education graduates have 100 percent job placement immediately after graduation."

Alumnus/a, 8/1999-12/2003, October 2005

Employment rate for PTs is very high. When I went to school, it was 100 percent. CMU PT grads are a great position for employment because of the prestige of the program. The program gets your internships for you, so that is a great bonus, as well. I belong to the alumni network and that has been great. My husband and I moved to AZ and we have met with the alumni group down here a few times.

> **Central Michigan says:** "CMU's physical therapy doctoral students have 100 percent job placement immediately after graduation."

Current student, 8/2004-Submit Date, October 2005

We have on-campus recruiting almost monthly as well as career fairs to give information on with which companies you may want to be involved. 85 percent of graduates graduate with a job in mind already.

Alumnus/a, 8/1998-12/2002, March 2004

CMU had what is referred to as Career Services, located at the heart of campus. There you can sign up for interviews for internships and careers online or by stopping in and registering. All interviews were conducted at their facility; they had six interview rooms that the employers could use at their discretion. Career Services also had a mock interview, where students could be videotaped being asked interview questions and later get critiqued on their responses. CMU held two career fairs a year for the business program; I am not sure about the others that came to campus. CMU brought top employers for students to interview with, including Coca-Cola, Pepsi, Stryker Medical, Johnson Controls, Deloitte & Touche, Marshal Fields and Target Corporation. I got my first job from an on-campus interview I received from the career fair.

 # Quality of Life

Current student, Music, 8/2003-Submit Date, October 2006

The music program is a community within the university. Most music studer live with other music students. In fact, many of the freshmen and sophomo live on the residential college floor. That is a good place to live because there a lot of support and help from people who are going through the same thir Being a music major does take a lot of time.

In regards to the university in general, CMU is a nice place. The dorms are sor of the nicest dorms in which I have ever been. The ones that I stayed in had tv bedrooms, a study, and a bathroom for four people. Off of campus there is a l of housing options. There is a lot of apartment complexes that have competiti rates. There is also a number of houses for rent. Campus is a nice place. It compact, taking between 10 and 15 minutes to walk from one side of campus the other. It also looks friendly. There is a number of facilities on camp including a new, nice library, Student Activity Center (with a gym, two pools, weight room, wallyball courts, basketball courts, and many other things), a ro wall, an art gallery, a museum, and many others. Dining on campus is eas There are residential restaurants attached to almost every dorm. There are al coffee shops, a food court and convenience stores. The neighborhood is pret safe. There are accounts of crime, but if you play it smart, you'll be fine. The are always police around in Mt. Pleasant. The CMU police also offer free rid on campus to students after dark.

Current student, 9/2005-Submit Date, November 2006

Housing and campus are great! Facilities are very well taken care of. I love N Pleasant! Crimes seem to happen off campus more than on. I feel extreme safe here.

Alumnus/a, 8/1999-4/2003, June 2006

The first year you are placed in a dormroom, normally four unknown people in a dorm that is not much bigger than a 20 square-foot room. Off-campus hou ing is nice, depending on where you stay. All apartments/housing are very clo to campus. Distance is probably less than five minutes from apartment to clas room. Campus is very beautiful and not very big. Though it is separated k grass and nice artwork. It is constructed so that most business classes are loca ed in Grawn building; rather than all over. The school dining could use mo work, but then again, when cooking for over 3,000 students; you can't expect th food to be awesome. The hours of the hall were excellent and they always ha fresh cold cuts with all the fixings. I have never, never experienced any prol lems with crime and I was always out and about doing things.

Current student, 8/2004-Submit Date, October 2005

Housing in dorms is comfortable because dorms are big and have private bat! rooms. Apartments are very inviting and open to sophomores or higher. Mar choices. Facilities are clean and accessible. I feel very safe with five differe law enforcements in the city.

Current student, 8/2003-Submit Date, September 2005

Housing is awesome, there are a lot of new dorms and apartments to live in. TI campus food is good, and there is a generally positive attitude. Not too muc crime.

Current student, 8/2000-Submit Date, January 2004

There is a broad range of housing up at Central. Of course, the conditic depends on the owner and age of the home. Most homes are in pretty good cor dition, and so are the apartments. Both are plentiful. The campus conditions ai good. They could work on the snow issue a little harder. Facilities are in goc condition. Dining depends on which dorm a person is in. In the freshma dorms, the food isn't so great. As a person gets into older dorms, the food ge better. I believe Central has a good grasp on its crime and safety. Not mar issues come up on campus. Of course, there are a few, but they are few and fi in between.

Social Life

urrent student, Music, 8/2003-Submit Date, October 2006

he school has a lot of available student organization. There are lots of Greek ganizations. There are also lots of bars and restaurants. La Señorita has daily ecials ($2.50 nacho Tuesday) and is just off campus. Most chain restaurants e in Mt. Pleasant, but there isn't a White Castle or a Panera. There are coffee ops: Kyia and U-Cup.

lumnus/a, 8/1999-4/2003, June 2006

rst, I was in the Greek system and it was a great experience in my life. It pro-ded me with a network of friends and lots of different things to do. The bars e all great because they are all within walking distance and have different emes daily. Such as, every Tuesday, everyone would go to the BlackStone for pitchers, Wednesday was Wayside, Thursday was the Bird for 90¢ shot and p, Friday's were house parties, Saturday was a mix of recovering and starting o early watching college football at O'Kelly's. As for the restaurants, the best Embers; if you take a date there, she will be impressed. The dating scene is ry easy, the ratio I think is seven girls to one guy; which means we take our ck. All the people that attend CMU are very friendly and come from a diverse ckground, which makes it cool!!

lumnus/a, 8/1999-12/2003, October 2005

he bars at CMU are fun: a lot of sports bars and a few pubs. The dating scene great for both guys and girls. The Greek system is strong on campus with lots do in that respect. Dining is good, but it is a small town.

urrent student, 8/2005-Submit Date, December 2005

here are many places to go out here. Many students hit the clubs; mostly a ace called Wayside either to have a beer or to just dance. It is very fun and you e never bored at CMU.

urrent student, 9/2005-Submit Date, October 2005

 far the social life has been very good. I have not yet joined any kind of clubs school. I have my close friends so far, and we are all getting a flag football am together, and we play poker twice a week to relieve pressure of school. ars are not an option because I'm still under 21, but we find other parties that e hop around to, to have fun on a Thursday/Friday/Saturday night.

urrent student, 8/2003-Submit Date, September 2005

here are great parties and several great bars with specials every night of the eek. There are around 20 to 30 fraternities and sororities to join. There are so clubs for just about every interest.

urrent student, 7/2003-Submit Date, March 2004

he social life is pretty good, but it's not the biggest of towns, and if you want e downtown scene and the nightlife, this isn't the place for you! There are lots restaurants, and there's a nice strip of businesses in Mt. Pleasant, but it isn't actly huge. There are a few popular bars here, but the nightlife isn't all that eat. If you have a nice group of friends to hang out with, which I do, it isn't that bad. But put it this way, when it's zero degrees outside and 10 inches of snow, do you wanna go outside and walk to a party? I don't think so. There are quite a few fraternities and sororities available here, and if you're interested you'll have no problem getting to know them.

The school says: "CMU's social scene is acclaimed mainly today for its friendliness and supportive atmosphere, which is repre-sented formally in a 'We Care' campaign initiated by students and in the work of more than 4,000 students who annually vol-unteer their time to constructively help others."

The School Says

Founded in 1892, CMU today is a multifaceted university that is shaping Michigan's future and preparing its residents for careers in a global economy.

CMU is distinguished for its supportive learning environment. The university encourages student engagement and focuses on the success of every student, ranking in the top 17 percent nationwide for graduate rate performance. 80 percent of CMU's graduates enter directly into Michigan careers.

As one of Michigan's top-choice universities—and fourth largest with 27,452 students—CMU maintains its engaging small-col-lege learning environment with distinguished professors who share a strong commitment to undergraduate teaching, research and discovery. The main campus in Mount Pleasant is home to nearly 20,000 students, including a record 2006 freshman class of approximately 3,700 and a steadily improving cumulative grade point average of 3.31. Applications for the 2006-2007 freshman class numbered a record 16,500, a 7 percent increase from 2005-2006.

CMU offers one of the best educational values in Michigan. The CMU Promise tuition program guarantees students that their tuition will not increase for up to five years—from their date of first enrollment until their expected graduation. The CMU Promise helps students and families better plan financially and enables CMU to maintain the quality and integrity of its aca-demic programs.

As a doctoral research institution, CMU offers more than 200 programs at all levels—bachelor's, master's, specialist's and doctoral. CMU's faculty members are widely acclaimed for their applied research, scholarship and creative activity. The univer-sity encourages groundbreaking new research in its 350-acre Center for Applied Research and Technology, where leading sci-entists, faculty and students conduct biotechnology research of importance to national security and American health care.

Read all of Vault's College Surveys at **www.vault.com/college**–get complete surveys on 100s of colleges and univer-sities, expert advice on applicaton essays and more.

VAULT CAREER LIBRARY 361

Michigan State University

Office of Admissions
Michigan State University
50 Administration Building
East Lansing, MI 48824-0590
Admissions phone: (517) 355-8332
Admissions URL: www.beaspartan.com

 Admissions

Current student, Psychology, 8/2004-Submit Date, June 2007

The admissions process is different for everyone! I'm working for the admissions office now, and there are definitely some things I would have done differently when I was applying. When you are applying, make sure the application is accurate from your birthday, to your name, to your social security number. Small things like this can make the process a little slower. When sending your transcripts, make sure it is an original copy, don't fax it. When sending in the application, send all your transcripts, both high school and college if you are transferring. Send in a personal statement that accurately describes you and the things you are doing in your life. When students apply here they think it's a simple process; it's not. There are many factors that need to be considered. If you have a great GPA and great test scores, you're pretty much golden. That doesn't guarantee your admittance, but they are key factors!

Current student, 8/2003-Submit Date, October 2006

The admissions process was similar to that of all the other schools to which I applied. However, because MSU is such a big school, they had options for everyone, so if you didn't take the ACT, but instead took the SAT or another standardized test, you were able to submit the information. MSU required one or two essays, an official transcript, letters of recommendation and an application.

Once admitted, I was notified very quickly. Also I did not have to submit any additional paperwork for scholarships or admission into the Honors College. As an applicant I was immediately considered for scholarships and admission to the Honors College. I received lots of information about the different programs and even in March of my senior year in high school I received a letter congratulating me for being selected as a recipient of a full-tuition (out-of-state) scholarship recipient. I felt as though MSU really wanted me to attend the university, rather than feeling like if I was begging to attend.

Current student, 8/2004-Submit Date, September 2006

MSU is becoming more difficult to be accepted into as the years go by. Our student body is becoming more and more competitive. In order to apply to MSU, it is easiest to fill out an online application. This application is very easy and straightforward, except that you do have to write an essay. Normally there are five topics from which you can choose, all of which are very basic and to which anyone can usually relate. If you are a high school senior looking to apply to Michigan State University, I would highly advise you to apply early. We are on rolling admissions, so this is key. The application is usually online early August.

> **Regarding the application essay, the school says:** "The application for admission to Michigan State University now requires students to select from the provided topics when completing the personal statement."

Current student, 8/2005-Submit Date, April 2006

The general admissions is moderately selective. While MSU has a rolling admissions process, you ought to apply by November in order to be considered for more scholarships and for membership in the Honors College. Similarly, you should apply earlier if you want to get into certain specialized colleges, like James Madison, which admit on a first-come basis. MSU does not require an interview. Only one personal statement is required.

Current student, 8/2003-Submit Date, October 2005

It is very easy to get accepted in terms of having descent grades and average test scores. I got in with 3.69 GPA and 27 ACT/1240 SAT scores. I believe that it is getting more competitive to get in though. It took me only two weeks to get an answer from State. I believe that they require essays as part of their admissions process. Get into their Honors College Program is very tough. However, they do give out a lot of scholarships if you are in the of top 2 percent of students.

Current student, 9/2005-Submit Date, January 2006

The admissions process is fairly simple. There was an online application, which took approximately half an hour to complete and had one short essay. When I applied, the essay was simple: why would you make a good Spartan? "This application is the only one you fill out for scholarships and Honors College consideration. It seems that MSU uses class rank more than ACT/SAT scores. MSU is becoming much more selective in its admissions process. At first I was not admitted to the Honors College with an ACT score in the 30s and a high school GPA over a 4.0. I have heard of people being deferred this year with an ACT score of 28 and a high school GPA around 3.2.

> **Michigan State University says:** "Michigan State University offers rolling admissions; there is no set deadline for submitting your application. Students are strongly encouraged to apply early during their senior year of high school. Applications for admission are accepted on the Web and on paper. For faster processing, apply on the Web. Freshman admission is based on academic performance in high school, the strength and quality of high school curriculum, recent trends in academic performance, class rank, ACT or SAT test results, a required personal statement (also used for scholarship consideration), leadership, talents and diversity of experience.
>
> "For admitted freshmen fall 2006, the middle 50 percent ranges are:
>
> High school GPA: 3.4 to 3.8
> ACT: 22 to 27
> SAT: 1040 to 1270
>
> "These ranges are not minimum requirements; however, they do represent the level of competitive academic achievement among MSU applicants."

 Academics

Current student, 8/2003-Submit Date, November 2006

Academics at MSU can be very intense. You really need to know how to prioritize. You also have to be willing to get help whenever you need it. The resources to do well in a class are in front of you; you just have to make an effort to grab a hold of them. Also, when it comes to choosing courses, go talk to an advisor. They will help you in any way possible.

Current student, Psychology, 8/2004-Submit Date, June 2007

When you first start classes, you aren't going to get the best times or even the best day. You settle for what there is. As your years progress, it gets way better! Each class is different. Some professors are very easy: they give you everything you need to know and that's what the class is based on. Other professors give you so much information and then the rest you have to find on your own. The workload is more than that of high school. Some classes have papers due every other day. For others, there is no homework. That all depends on the professor! Same with grading. No one grades the same—some curve some don't. There is no real trick to academics. If you want to check out a class or a professor, just log onto AllMSU.com and it's all there. Professor and class ratings!

Read all of Vault's College Surveys at **www.vault.com/college**—get complete surveys on 100s of colleges and universities, expert advice on applicaton essays and more.

VAULT CAREER LIBRARY 363

Alumnus/a, 8/2001-8/2006, October 2006

Expect to be challenged everyday. It is a lot harder than high school, but not impossible to get through. You have to know why you are at MSU, and hopefully it's more than the football season.

Current student, 8/2004-Submit Date, September 2006

MSU is a competitive school with many difficult classes. You are required to take certain integrative studies, and these can range from quite easy to crazy hard. Most classes offer a free help room in which teaching assistants go around answering students' questions. I would say that sophomore year is the most difficult academically. Workload really depends on the prof. You can check out professor ratings and comments at allmsu.com. I like the grading system at State, as it is different from most other schools. We go by grade point for every course. So, if you receive between a 90 and 100, you usually (depending on the class) get a 4.0 in that class. Doesn't matter if you get a 91 or 99. This can seem annoying when you do very well, but I think it ends up helping you more than hurting you over the years. I have learned a great deal while here, and think you can really get as much out of it as you put in. We may be a huge school, but teachers are willing to get to know you if you want them to. You can choose to be a number, or you can introduce yourself and form a relationship with your teachers. It all depends on what you want. My biggest advice would be don't buy the book unless you know you need it. You often never have to read, and books cost lots of money!

Current student, 8/2003-Submit Date, April 2006

I am in both the MSU Honors College and what is called a Living Learning program. The Living Learning option provides students with the opportunity to live with other students who are in the same major. This greatly increases students' understanding of the material, collaboration, productive studying opportunities and provides a great social circle. Although not all majors have such a program, MSU is expanding its Living Learning programs. The specific one I am in is the James Madison College, which focuses on international relations, foreign policy, social issues, human rights and political theory. All of the first-year students live in the same dorm that also houses all the James Madison classrooms and professors' offices. After freshman year, students have the option of moving out of the dorm, but many remain as I have done. Through this program I have gained some of the most important educational experiences of my life both from my incredible professors and my fellow student who have become close friends. The Honors College has also presented me with unequal opportunities to heighten the intellectual level of many of my courses, as well as skip many of the introductory courses, required for all students, and replace them with higher-level courses. I have developed close relationships with many professors because of these opportunities that will undoubtedly aid me in the future. Although the Honors College is by invitation only, it is just one example of the great programs MSU offers. MSU is an institution that is genuinely concerned about its student population. The majority of the professors I have had have been great teachers as well as people and have been fair in grading. Although there are obviously exceptions to this, I honestly cannot complain about the level of instruction I have received at MSU. At MSU, a student truly has the opportunity to make college a personal experience that fits his/her needs and sets him/her on a successful track.

 Employment Prospects

Current student, 8/2003-Submit Date, October 2006

We have a large center in the basement of our business college complex just for outside companies to recruit our students. It seems that almost ever senior has a job before second semester of his/her senior year if he/she puts in the energy to interview and research the companies. Recruiting occurs all year round, and there are tons of resources to help with the interviewing process, including mock interviews, résumé critiques and business etiquette sessions. I started off my senior year with a full-time job lined up for after I graduate. I was able to obtain this because I interned with GE over the summer and they decided to offer me a full-time position. This is just one of the benefits of being from a well-known, highly respected business college that has a reputation of producing hard-working, bright and innovative professionals.

Current student, 8/2003-Submit Date, April 2006

The alumni network and employment prospects from James Madison are wonderful. Though the majority of graduates from James Madison go directly on law school or some sort of liberal arts graduate program, there is no shortage employment prospects if that is what a graduate would like to do. James Madison has graduates in almost every professional sector, with the exception of medical or some science fields. From social researchers and NGO employee to lawyers and politicians, James Madison has a broad alumni base. Plus, James Madison has alumni career fairs that allow us to interact directly with Madison alumni and often results in job offers. I feel very optimistic about my ability begin an enjoyable and fulfilling career after I leave MSU.

Current student, 8/2002-Submit Date, April 2006

I did the grad school (medicine, in my case) thing. All of my pre-med friend got into good programs, the sciences seem especially strong at putting PhD a MD students out. Good advisors for those interested in more schooling.

Current student, 8/2002-Submit Date, April 2006

MSU has a great employment record. As an English major, I'm not exactly marketable as an accounting student. But the alumni network is extreme strong, and people you become close to (for me, the administrators of the Hono College) never lose interest in helping you find success. There are always campus fairs and events, usually divided by college (College of Business, Ar and Letters), and in the English department alone, there are smaller worksho on writing cover letters, arranging CVs and other important aspects of movi from the academic to professional world.

Alumnus/a, 9/2000-5/2004, March 2005

Michigan State has an internship center on campus that I attended and a ton job fairs every year. It amazes me that anyone could graduate from there wit out having a job before commencement. Michigan State is mostly known for undergraduate business and communication programs. Typically, students w come from these programs have no problems finding jobs, nor do those who a pursuing careers in teaching and of course agriculture and veterinary medicin The opportunity to attend graduate school for anyone in the sciences or soci sciences is good, too. Michigan State has been praised on several occasions f its superior science programs.

 **Quality of Life**

Current student, Psychology, 8/2004-Submit Date, June 2007

MSU is a great campus. The scenery is beautiful. Minus the construction, it's great place to take a walk by the river and look at the old buildings and garden The housing and dining are great. After living in the dorms for two years, y kind of miss it once you leave. The food is right there in the hall. It's so co venient and the food isn't bad at all! It's great living so close to class and oth students because there is always help! The neighborhood is great too. Everyo seems to be quite friendly and helpful! There isn't much crime. The camp seems to be quite safe.

Current student, 8/2003-Submit Date, November 2006

MSU is known for its large campus, but you can make it feel smaller by getti involved in student organizations. There are buses that run on and off camp all night and all week to help students get to their destinations. Dorms and caf terias are located in five prime locations, so it is easy to grab lunch no matt where you are.

Alumnus/a, 8/2001-8/2006, October 2006

Neighborhoods close to campus are your best living situations. The campus a neighborhoods are very friendly and welcoming. The best place to live if y are looking to make life-long friendships are the dormitories. The cafeterias a excellent, but you won't appreciate them until you move off campus.

Alumnus/a, 8/2002-5/2006, September 2006

Definitely get the dorm experience at least for one year. There is nothing e like it. With that said, there is a variety of housing options off-campus (and the is a housing fair to help you decide). The diversity of restaurants is amazi (bars too)!! Safety is always an issue with that many people, but if you are awa of your surroundings and are smart, you should be fine.

urrent student, 8/2003-Submit Date, April 2006

he housing at MSU is pretty good. I have lived in the dorms for three years
d will return next year. The accommodations are extremely livable and there
a great variety of dorms on campus. MSU has about 17 different dorm build-
gs and an extensive food service. There are cafeterias everywhere on campus
d the honestly food is not too bad . It isn't spectacular, but there are many
tions. The campus is absolutely beautiful and has sidewalks everywhere. It
an incredibly large campus, so the winter can be tiresome since the campus is
vered in snow and very cold. However, it is all worth it when the campus is
full bloom and the weather is warm. The campus and the surrounding cities
e really safe and the crime rate is very low. MSU has its own police force, so
blic safety is of the highest importance.

Social Life

urrent student, Psychology, 8/2004-Submit Date, June 2007

cial life at MSU is an understatement! There are plenty of places to go each
ght of the week! The bars and restaurants are fantastic. Right across the street
m campus, there are many places to sit down, enjoy a meal, and have a few
inks. There are plenty from which to choose. Greek life is cool too, because
at's the place to be! You get the opportunity to meet a bunch of new people in
e house and also the people that come into the house. It's great for making new
ends, or even meeting that special someone for whom you may be looking!
vents for Greek life and other MSU scenes are displayed all over campus.
here are plenty of posters and signs across campus letting you know what's
ing on in each group! My favorite part of the whole social scene is the Greek
e. Although I am not a part of a sorority/fraternity, they are great places to
eet new people! I have met a few great friends in them and it was always a
od experience!

urrent student, 8/2003-Submit Date, October 2006

he options for socializing are endless! There is a huge party scene here—the
rs are always packed and a ton of fun. There are about 10 located within three
ocks of each other, so it's a nice area to hang out. The main avenue is filled
ith shops and restaurants, all of which are great. If you're not one to party,
ere are tons of other options, as well. We have free movie screenings every
eekend in one of our large lecture halls and there are always free events going
on campus. We have tons of concerts and shows. School spirit is huge, too,
we usually have lots of events centered around sporting events (including
me awesome tailgating).

urrent student, 8/2004-Submit Date, September 2006

he social life here is great. There is always something to do, especially in the
l. We also have a good football team, so everyone tailgates and gets really
to it. Most people tailgate at the tennis courts, but be careful if you are under-
e. We have a bunch of really popular bars, including The Riv (which has
rgerama on Thursdays), Ricks, P.T. O'Malleys and Harpers. We have really
od restaurants, too. If you come here, Mennas and Flats are a must! There
e always tons of events, from free concerts to movies in Wells Hall every
eekend to random performances like Second City. There is a club for pretty
uch every interest, and if there isn't, you can start one. The clubs are a really
od way to meet people. The Greek system is really big, and most people who
in it really love it. Greek houses are spread out all over campus, and some are
cer than others. Beta is really popular for their parties, as well as Lambda Chi
d "the Taco Bell frat." State dies down a little in the winter since everything
so far away and it gets pretty cold. But, if you have a group of friends to hang
t with there is still always something to do.

urrent student, 8/2003-Submit Date, April 2006

cial life at MSU is basically what you make of it. MSU has a club for almost
y interest, an extensive intramural sports system, a large Greek community,
d a great community atmosphere. However, the student population is
solutely gigantic, so it can be easy to get lost in the crowd if you don't take
e initiative to meet new people. I have never found it difficult to meet people
re because everyone is so friendly, reflecting the Midwestern friendliness and
spitality. Also, MSU has Big 10 sports and there is nothing more exciting.

The School Says

Founded in 1855, Michigan State University has been advancing knowledge and transforming lives for more than 150 years.

Michigan State has more than 35,000 undergraduate students,
including students from every state in the nation and from more
than 125 countries. MSU was named a Top 100 Global
University by *Newsweek* magazine, furthering its reputation
worldwide as a top-ranked university with global impact.

Michigan State University has a comprehensive system of merit
scholarships, including the Alumni Distinguished Scholarship,
Distinguished Freshman Scholarship and the University Scholars
Award.

Michigan State is famously known for its lush, park-like, 5,200-
acre campus. Students enjoy the scenery throughout the year,
with both traditional and modern architecture interspersed with
the beauty of natural surroundings.

MSU features the largest on-campus residence hall system of
any single campus in the nation, providing students with a variety of living options and dining choices.

10 distinct living-learning communities exist on campus, providing students with the opportunity to live and study with students of similar interests. The newest living learning community, scheduled to debut in fall 2007, the Residential College in
the Arts and Humanities, is a program that will include literature, history, the visual and performing arts, and the study of
languages and cultures.

MSU's Honors College is one of the oldest and most distinctive
in the nation. Open by invitation only, Honors College students
are given unparalleled freedom and flexibility to explore academic opportunities and research.

Michigan State University's 200 undergraduate programs feature many nationally-ranked disciplines, including Engineering,
Business, Education, Nursing and Hospitality Business, among
others. Popular undergraduate majors include Business,
Communication, Education, Engineering and Advertising.

The Undergraduate Research and Creative Activities program
enables students to participate in original investigation, experimentation, and creative activity and presentation. Freshmen
can work independently with a faculty mentor or in faculty-led
teams across many fields of study.

25 NCAA intercollegiate athletic teams represent the Spartans,
providing both athletes and fans with exciting action throughout
the year. Teams compete in the Big 10 Conference. MSU also
features one of the largest intramural sports programs in the
country.

With 550 student organizations and 54 Greek-letter organizations, students at MSU are quickly able to find activities of interest and people to connect with.

MSU's study abroad program is one of the largest in the nation,
with opportunities to study in more than 60 countries and on all
seven continents, including Antarctica!

More than 461,000 living alumni help MSU earn its reputation
as having excellent career services and job placement programs.
More than 600 high-level organizations conducted more than
18,000 on-campus interviews in 2004. Recent campus interviewers have included Boeing, General Electric, General Motors,
IBM, Morgan Stanley, PepsiCo, Pfizer and the U.S.
Environmental Protection Agency.

Read all of Vault's College Surveys at **www.vault.com/college**–get complete surveys on 100s of colleges and universities, expert advice on applicaton essays and more.

VAULT CAREER LIBRARY **365**

Complementing campus life is the adjacent city of East Lansing where shops, eateries, and houses of worship offer Michigan State students an enthusiastic welcome. Just down the road is Lansing—Michigan's capital city, offering students a wealth of shopping, dining and entertainment activities.

Michigan Technological University

Admissions Office
1400 Townsend Drive
Houghton, MI 49931-1295
Admissions phone: (888) MTU-1885 or (906) 487-1885
Admissions e-mail: mtu4u@mtu.edu
Admissions URL: www.admissions.mtu.edu/

 ## Admissions

Current student, Engineering, 8/2000-Submit Date, April 2007

Admission to Michigan Tech is not difficult. It is beneficial to take the ACT because you can get scholarships from it but there are no complicated essays or interviews. The application process is simple and straight forward.

Current student, Environment, 8/2005-Submit Date, April 2007

Michigan Tech heavily weights the applicant's GPA from high school. They have a rolling admissions process, so applications are taken at any time. I heard back from Michigan Tech during the summer before my senior year, which was very beneficial. There are no interviews or lengthy essays, but they do have high standards for out-of-state applicants. They respect those who take tougher courses in high school, and do weigh those above easier courses that provide an easy A.

Current student, Pre-med, 8/2003-Submit Date, April 2007

Michigan Tech has a simple admissions process consisting of a free online application with a short essay section. The most important part of considering Michigan Tech as a university is to visit the campus. I was not completely set on being far from home and away from my friends, but as soon as I visited the campus I felt at home. The selectivity of Michigan Tech is very low. I believe something like 98 percent of applicants are admitted, but the courses are incredibly hard and unless a student is a hard worker, he/she will not be able to keep up with his/her courseload.

Current student, Business, 9/2005-Submit Date, April 2007

The admissions process is very straightforward. There is not a burden of paperwork to fill out. The campus tours are great, the students who show you around campus are friendly and you even receive a friendly thank you card for coming. The process of getting in is not too difficult.

Current student, Social Sciences, 8/2003-Submit Date, April 2007

Quick and painless. When I applied as an undergrad, everything was paper, but I just applied to grad school here and they have everything online now: very easy to use. You also find out if you're accepted quickly—for my undergrad application, I knew I was accepted in about a month.

Current student, 9/2005-Submit Date, May 2006

The admissions process is relatively simple. It requires an application all of the basics: name and other personal information, prospective major, extracurricular activities, high school transcript, and SAT or ACT scores. Our acceptance rate is fairly high as well, but that is only the start; you must maintain good standing once here, and that can be difficult.

When considering the ACT and SAT, overall scores are important but math a science are the main focus, seeing that we are a predominantly engineering a technology school.

Current student, 8/2005-Submit Date, May 2006

The admissions process at MTU is online and easy to complete. There were essays and the only portion that cannot be completed online is mailing your tra script. The deadline is rolling, which is convenient, but apply early for the be chance. Admission is fairly open and the university is willing to let you in ev if you are lacking in some areas. Do not be fooled, though, MTU has a rigoro curriculum and I've heard that nearly 20 percent of freshmen are forced to wit draw after the first two terms. The real test is while you're here, not while y are in high school.

Alumnus/a, 6/2000-5/2003, April 2006

At one point, I had heard that MTU accepted between 80 and 90 percent of tho who applied to the university. As long as your GPA is fair, and you did OK the SATs, you should have no problem getting into the university. Staying MTU is a completely different story. The classes are very rigorous, and ma students leave after the first year, either because they couldn't handle the clas es or they were asked to leave due to their grades.

 ## Academics

Current student, Engineering, 8/2003-Submit Date, April 2007

Classes are good and very hands on, which is why I chose this scho Scheduling is very easy for my major as our department is small enough so the is very little competition for seats in preferred classes. Mechanical Enginee had a very difficult time and often only could get in classes they wanted if th cheated the system somehow. It would be nice if more sections were availab in required courses and if priority was reconfigured. Grading is usually pret clear and fair; the instructors explain what is expected at the beginning of t semester and that is what is followed through.

Current student, Engineering, 8/2000-Submit Date, April 2007

The engineering curriculum, depending on the discipline, is largely set. There little room for choosing courses until the upper-level courses when you c choose in what you would like to specialize. In environmental engineering, t class size begins large for the basic courses but quickly become a small, co group with which you will share courses your entire time at Michigan Tec I rarely remember much trouble getting into specific courses as long as I h enough credits and exceptions can be made. The grading is tough but fair an never took a typical freshman "weeder" course that you hear about at other ur versities. Courses were difficult but not graded on curves so that everyone h an opportunity to pass. In my department the professors were personable a welcoming and we developed strong relationships during my time at schoo Schedules can be rearranged if the typical workload is too much, but most st dents can manage the amount of work required. Students are held to a high sta dard as Michigan Tech prides itself on its engineering program and the enginee it sends out into the world.

Current student, Engineering, 8/2002-Submit Date, April 2007

For the most part classes are challenging. Depending on your major, it can difficult to get into classes you need. As a mechanical engineering student.

ometimes had to rework my schedule because classes I was supposed to take according to my flow chart were already full when it was my turn to register. rading for classes really depends on your professor. Classes like perspectives d world cultures are really luck of the draw. But even classes in my major, ke Product Development, were very dependent on the professor who taught em (not just grading, but also the information that was taught).

urrent student, Business, 9/2005-Submit Date, April 2007

he academic nature is great. The classes are challenging and fair. No student ould expect to waltz in and do well. The work is necessary and the rewards e great. The ability to get the desired classes is nice also because the classes low for easy entry into them, and if you are unable to get into a class, the advi- rs and faculty do a good job of admitting you if necessary. The grading and rofessors, like the classes, are fair. The teachers impress me with their back- round and what they have accomplished and I feel honored to be learning from em. The grading is what you would expect in a college atmosphere; if you do e work that you should there will be a reward in terms of grades. The work- ad is not too bad, I have a 3.81 GPA and I study usually or work on each class n average of three to four hours each week and maybe a little more if there are xams coming up.

urrent student, Social Sciences, 8/2003-Submit Date, April 2007

or the most part, the quality of the classes is really good, I feel that almost all f the professors are willing to work with you if you have a problem. Seniors et to register first, so this year it was really easy to get into the classes I need- d/wanted to take, but it's harder as a freshman because you get whatever is left ver since you register last. However, if there is a class you need and you can't et in because it's full, you can usually talk to the professor or your academic dviser and get a waiver to be in the class, or the academic adviser may suggest n alternative class that would fulfill the requirements. The workload can get a ttle heavy sometimes, but if you learn how to schedule your time properly, you an handle it. It's a lot of hard work, but college isn't supposed to be easy, and feel like I've gained so much from attending college here.

urrent student, Engineering, 8/2004-Submit Date, April 2007

n my six semesters here, I've had a wide range of registration difficulty level, lass and professor quality, and workload. Most of the courses here are techni- al and because of that require a bit of energy and focus. Classes can be pretty ifficult. The larger general classes, such as physics and chemistry, are pretty oor quality as there are over 300 students in a classroom. But once you get past ose, the classes become more intimate and valuable. Most classes aren't hard get into. Sometimes, for the freshman English course called Perspectives, you ust have to accept whatever you can get into, but for most others, the advisers nd professors are very helpful at getting you into a class.

urrent student, Environment, 8/2005-Submit Date, April 2007

bout 80 percent of the time, undergraduate students are able to get their pre- erred class and time slot. I have never had an issue with getting any of my lasses. The professors are very down to earth people who can relate to your sit- ation. Most have doctorates, but they do not wave them above the students' eads. 95 percent of those who graduate are offered a job or continue schooling irectly out of college, thus the classes are of high quality. Each professor has is/her own grading policy, and the exams are tailored to that policy. Therefore, class with a seven-point scale will not have tougher exams than the class with 10-point scale.

lumnus/a, 8/2000-5/2004, May 2006

was in the Scientific and Technical Communication Program, which is report- d to be the best of its kind in the United States. The academics were challeng- g, but not overbearing or overburdening. There is a real emphasis on real- orld learning at Michigan Tech, which is supplemented by book learning. A reat combination of the two, with dedicated faculty, make academics at MTU uly outstanding.

Employment Prospects

urrent student, Social Sciences, 8/2003-Submit Date, April 2007

f you're an engineer, you'll have no problem finding a job or a co-op. Tech's areer center has a huge job fair twice a year, and at the last one there were over

400 employers looking for Tech students. But, if you're not an engineer, you're going to have a really hard time finding a job and you'll have to do all the leg work yourself. I've applied to positions and the recruiters are always surprised that Tech even has people in my major (social science)—they haven't even heard of us!

Current student, Engineering, 8/2002-Submit Date, April 2007

As long as you work hard while in school and make the most of your time here, there is no problem getting a job after graduation. People I know who have decent GPAs and who are involved on campus have at least two or three offers from very good employers. Alumni networks are very helpful. I have used them to pursue different employment opportunities. Our on-campus career center is amazing. Both job fairs put on are very well-organized and bring a lot of good employers to campus. They also do a lot of work to help students find co-ops and internships, as well as help them prepare to interview.

Current student, Engineering, 8/2004-Submit Date, April 2007

Employment after Tech seems like it is pretty easy. All of the students I know who are graduating have full-time jobs lined up. Most engineering students here at Tech either get internships or go on co-op while they are here so that definitely helps with job placement. We have an awesome career fair every fall when tons of companies (200 to 300) come here looking for new Tech students to hire. We also have a career fair in the spring that is a little smaller than the fall but still exceptional.

Current student, Environment, 8/2005-Submit Date, April 2007

There have been many instances where employers will take Michigan Tech grad- uates over any other institution. We have two large career fairs (over 200 employers) where the employers actively seek Michigan Tech students for careers and internships. Many internships lead to full-time positions with the company. Engineers at our school start out with jobs that can pay over $60,000 the first year. Employers of alumni from our school include IBM, John Deere, Weyerhauser, Kimberly Clark, US Fish and Wildlife Service, CCX, and many more.

Quality of Life

Current student, Social Sciences, 8/2003-Submit Date, April 2007

Tech just renovated Wadsworth Hall, the biggest dorm on campus, and it seems to be OK. I lived there before the renovation and it was awful. The food was all right, though. Campus is beautiful, especially in the summer. Most people live off campus and find housing really close. They just walk or bike to school. Houghton is a very safe town, and it's cute. If you don't like the great outdoors I wouldn't recommend coming to Tech because the majority of activities avail- able to do are outdoors. Tech has great mountain biking, snowshoeing, and cross country ski trails as well as its own downhill ski hill. Campus is also situated on the Portage Lake, and Lake Superior is only about 20 minutes away. Camping, hiking, stargazing, cliff jumping (jumping from designated areas near Canyon Falls into the river just past the waterfall, about 45 feet from where you jump to where you hit the water) are the main activities in the summer. The winter is a bit longer than in a lot of places and we get about 180 inches of snow every year on average, but it makes for great skiing, snowshoeing, snowmobiling and sled- ding. There is also a lot of wildlife—deer, bears and so on.

Current student, Business, 9/2005-Submit Date, April 2007

The quality of life depends upon where you are from and to what you are accus- tomed. I am from a larger city and am accustomed to a mall, a professional sports team and restaurants at every corner. It's not too difficult to get comfort- able with the atmosphere here, but it does take some adjustment and considera- tion of the circumstances. The facilities on campus are very good, clean and so on. The dining was good; there are multiple choices every day depending on what you want to eat. I have never had any difficulties with crime and safety and can only say that they do a good job controlling that here.

Current student, Pre-med, 8/2003-Submit Date, April 2007

I love the community of Houghton, Michigan because of the beautiful outdoors. I am surrounded by lakes, mountains, snow and trails. I thoroughly enjoy snow- shoeing, skiing, snowboarding and running. Laying by the beach is a perfect way to spend the summer here as well. I love the old homes, and affordable

Read all of Vault's College Surveys at **www.vault.com/college**–get complete surveys on 100s of colleges and univer- sities, expert advice on applicaton essays and more.

VAULT CAREER LIBRARY **367**

housing. Also, the Keweenaw Peninsula is full of history. The Quincy mines, museums, and old ice arenas add a lot of character to the city. Crime is very low, and I always feel safe in the city of Houghton.

Current student, 8/2005-Submit Date, November 2006

Houghton is one of the safest places to live. Campus feels safe even in the middle of the night. On-campus housing does not provide much personal space but it provides a great sense of community. Campus dining, unfortunately, leaves something to be desired. After a semester of dorm food, a person generally craves better nutrition.

Alumnus/a, 8/2001-12/2005, May 2006

If you're going to live off campus, most places are comparable to a shack. The cost of living is low up there (sometimes you can get an apartment for $250 a month with electricity/water/heat included) but eventually you're going to get what you pay for. The house we got had drywall cracking in the walls where there was drywall. Most houses you're going to find up there are going to have carpet much older than you, and probably older than your parents. That being said, the campus is fairly nice. You can walk from one side of the campus to the other in 20 minutes. Most of the buildings are in fairly good shape (except Fisher Hall, which really needs to be bulldozed over). The computer labs in most of the buildings are pretty nice, and several students never had to buy a computer at school. The crime rate at Michigan Tech is very low.

> The school says: "Fisher Hall has recently undergone a multi-million dollar renovation and now features wired classrooms and state-of-the-art lecture halls. A wide variety of housing is available locally at reasonable cost. Michigan Tech enjoys a low crime rate and is safe in other respects as well.

 Social Life

Current student, Pre-med, 8/2003-Submit Date, April 2007

There are several small bars and restaurants that have a lot of personality and great specials. Everyone seems to go to the same places for particular specials every day of the week. There are two terrific award-winning breweries, authentic Finnish restaurants, and several seasonal restaurants that serve fish caught in nearby Lake Superior. Students love all the bars, but especially "quarter beers" at the Uphill 41 on Thursday nights, "double bubble" at the DT on Friday at happy hour, and the Dog House, and KBC anytime before or after.

Current student, Engineering, 8/2004-Submit Date, April 2007

In some respects Tech is at a disadvantage because the technical nature of the university leads to a lack of women. For this reason the dating scene can be in shambles for the guys (although it's pretty good for the girls). Still, Tech does a good job of bringing in social events and lecturers at the Rozsa and hosting fun activities during Women's Week, Pride Week, and the International Night to really focus on minorities on campus. There are quite a few bars in the downtown area and in addition to being a fun place to hang out, they have a great history which can be seen in the woodwork and murals on the walls and ceilings. There are many extracurricular activities and clubs on campus ranging from WMTU radio to the pistol club, the four-wheelers club, and even Keweenaw Symphony Orchestra. If you are interested in something, there's probably a group for it.

Current student, Engineering, 8/2004-Submit Date, April 2007

The social life is OK. We do have our fair share of bars. Some of the local favorites are: The Downtowner (DT), The Ambassodor (Ambo), The Douglas Houghton House (The Dog), the Kewennaw Brewing Company (KBC), and the Library pub. The Ambo and the Library also have great food. We have four subways for some reason, which is cool. Jim's Foodmart is the hot spot to buy kegs for parties almost everyone goes there for their barrels. The Greek community is really cool; most of the houses have an open door and are willing to let almost anyone in. The only problem with going to a technological school is you do get a lot of people who are more introverted and like to stay in at night. But if you are a social butterfly, there is still plenty of opportunity to be social. There is also a lot of great campus events. We have a great intramural sport program. We also do this thing every year called Winter Carnival that is just a huge event with snow statues, live music and lots of other events. Plus, the residence hall councils put on a lot of events along with all of the other student organizations.

Alumnus/a, 8/2000-5/2004, May 2006

The Greek system at MTU is strong but not exclusive. An open system that very supportive of the university and vice-versa. Because of the unique env ronment in Houghton, MI, it often gets the reputation of being empty, with not ing to do. Quite the opposite is true. You can find a lot going on, if you just loo for it. Clubs, per se, do not exist, but there are a number of bars all with gre atmospheres. The area has grown in the past few years, and there is a numbe of new, familiar, chain restaurants as well as all the local favorites. T Ambassador, The Library, The Dog House and The Downtowner are a few stu dent favorites.

 The School Says

Michigan Tech students create the future in engineering, the sciences, forest resources, computing, arts and human sciences, technology and business. Approximately 6,500 students from throughout the United States and 90 nations enjoy beautiful Upper Michigan while pursuing associate, bachelor's, master's and PhD degrees. Michigan Tech is rated among the nation's best universities and as a "tech powerhouse" by the Princeton Review.

Michigan Tech has one of the nation's best forest research programs, the largest program in scientific and technical communication, and Top 10 programs in environmental, mechanical and geological engineering enrollment. The average composite ACT score for incoming first-year students is approximately 25, compared to the national average of 21.

The university provides students a number of opportunities to enhance their college experience. In the Enterprise Program, students from many majors work together on real-world industry projects ranging from video games to homeland security to hybrid SUVs. The Michigan Tech Honors Institute offers exceptional students a chance to enrich themselves through self-directed study. The Pavlis Institute for Global Technological Leadership provides training in the tools of leadership to select students in all majors.

The university is committed to student success. While the Michigan Tech curriculum is challenging, learning centers and coaches are available to augment the classroom experience.

Michigan Tech students are in high demand among employers, averaging six job interviews before they graduate. In addition to working with the Career Center to hone their job-seeking skills, they are encouraged to obtain internships and co-op jobs to gain workplace experience before they graduate. Students can also choose from dozens of international educational programs, expanding their language and cultural skills before they enter the global marketplace.

Michigan Tech's graduate programs continue to grow in stature. Enrollment is increasing, and students collaborate with faculty who are leaders in their fields. The university offers Master's International Peace Corps programs in engineering and forestry that prepare graduate students to make a huge difference in communities around the world.

Traditions include K-Day on the shores of Lake Superior, the world's largest freshwater lake. The Parade of Nations is a celebration (including food) of the 90 nations that have students and faculty at Michigan Tech. Homecoming has a hobo theme, and students dress in their worst attire and parade through campus in autos that barely run. Our biggest event is Winter Carnival, when massive snow statues emerge on campus and in the towns.

In athletics, Michigan Tech competes in the WCHA, which has produced the last five NCAA Division I National Champions.

Football, men's and women's basketball, tennis, cross-country, track, and women's volleyball teams compete in NCAA Division II.

Michigan Tech is surrounded by an outdoor recreation paradise. Students enjoy snowboarding, snowmobiling, fishing, hunting, hiking, skiing, biking and water sports in some of America's most beautiful forests, lakes and rivers. Intramural sports include everything from ultimate frisbee to water polo, and club sports range from women's hockey to paintball.

Overall, it's a great combination: an excellent education in a beautiful, safe location.

University of Michigan

Office of Undergraduate Admissions
University of Michigan
220 Student Activities Building
15 East Jefferson St.
Ann Arbor, MI 48109-1316
Admissions phone: (734) 764-7433
Admissions URL: www.umich.edu/prospective.php

 ## Admissions

Regarding admissions, the University of Michigan notes: "As of January 10, 2007, in accordance with an amendment to the constitution of the State of Michigan, the University of Michigan will not discriminate, nor grant preferential treatment to, any individual on the basis of race, sex, color, ethnicity or national origin in its admissions and financial aid processes. There are some exceptions provided in the amendment the university will recognize, including one for programs that receive federal funds."

Current student, BBA, 9/2003-Submit Date, October 2006

The admissions to the Ross School of Business as an undergraduate is quite rigorous. After completing two years of required classes, students apply to the BBA program with the grades from those classes. The application consists of a resumé, three essay questions and basic personal information. The three essays are usually similar in content each year. They are: "Why the BBA program?" "What team oriented experience do you have?" and "What kind of extracurricular activities do you participate in?" Each year there is only an acceptance rate of 30 percent; therefore, it is quite competitive to get in.

Alumnus/a, Engineering, 8/2003-5/2007, May 2007

Admissions is getting more subjective than when I was applying. You generally need a 1250 and 3.5 at the very minimum for the cutoff, unless you are a recruited athlete. Most important thing is the GPA, as UMich doesn't give a lot of weight to the SAT, like many public universities.

Current student, 9/2003-Submit Date, August 2006

The admissions process at Michigan has definitely changed since I was accepted. When I applied, it was a very simple application (just filling in vital stats about yourself) and a personal statement. I used the same one that I used for other schools. It is rolling admissions, so send yours in as soon as you can. Getting accepted earlier will also give you a leg up on housing. In the recent years, however, Michigan has upped its admissions requirements and I believe there are more writing samples.

Current student, 9/2003-Submit Date, March 2006

Michigan prides itself on admitting a talented and diverse class. In addition to a strong academic record, demonstrating leadership skills and a commitment to service activities, especially through the essays, is beneficial in the admissions process. These essays are also the chance to highlight your personal experiences and perspectives on diversity. Since Michigan does not interview its undergraduates, these essays (recently expanded to a requirement of three essays) are critical in the admissions process.

Alumnus/a, 6/2001-4/2005, June 2006

The best advice on getting accepted to Michigan is to be very, very well-rounded. Good grades or SAT scores are not the only criteria at which they look. Alternatively, if your grades are not as great as you would like them to be, don't necessarily count yourself out from getting into this school. The best advice is to be involved in plenty of activities in high school—such as volunteer work and sports But be prepared—if your grades are not that great, make sure to make up for it on your standardized tests and activities outside of school. Also note that if your grades/standardized test are not the best, you may be let in, but on the condition that you come to Michigan the summer before to take non-credit courses in order to prepare for the fall. In your essays, make sure to relate everything to personal experiences and how they will relate to your time at Michigan. Again, this is where your activities outside of school will aid you. Also, a little research about the university will show your interest in the university and help your app stand out in the crowd. Michigan is a very selective school, but as long as you are well-rounded and able to articulate this in your essays, you will have a great chance of getting accepted.

Current student, Engineering, 8/2001-Submit Date, September 2004

The admissions process to the College of Engineering is quite rigorous. It includes competitive SAT scores and essays, along with a high GPA. Since it is a public school, it is a little easier for Michigan students, but foreign and out-of-state students face private school standards. The median GPA from high school for a student attending the College of Engineering is a 3.9. The best advice that can be given for getting admission is to ensure that many AP classes are taken during one's high school career. Mainly these should include math and science classes, but computer science will also help quite a bit.

 ## Academics

Current student, BBA, 1/2007-Submit Date, June 2007

There is a "Ross curve," which varies by the type of course you are taking. Also, your GPA starts over once you are admitted to Ross. I believe the average GPA is around 3.5. This doesn't sound too harsh, but the competition is high. The strength of the student body has increased over the last couple of years and probably will continue to increase as the pre-admit program expands and the new facilities are completed. The professors have been great and I can't imagine a better advising program. The workload is fairly heavy.

Alumnus/a, Engineering, 8/2003-5/2007, May 2007

Engineering was very rigorous, I struggled the first two years, but made the dean's list in the last two years and came out with a very respectable GPA. You won't have a lot of fun in the engineering school if you want to sit back and relax all the time; however if you are serious about your career and knowledge, you will learn all you want. Most professors are very caring, despite what you might expect from a large school. They always have office hours. The key to success here is perseverance and very organized studying habits.

Alumnus/a, Engineering, 9/2002-4/2006, September 2006

The school is very used to large numbers of students wanting to get into popular classes. Psychology is the most common major of an undergraduate Literature Science and the Arts (LS&A) student, and there are many, many sections every semester for thousands of students to enroll into in the Psychology department.

Read all of Vault's College Surveys at www.vault.com/college—get complete surveys on 100s of colleges and universities, expert advice on applicaton essays and more.

VAULT CAREER LIBRARY 369

There is a wide array of opportunities to research within the university as well. The Undergraduate Research Opportunities Program (UROP) is a very valuable program for students interested in research. It helps students to get into the door and work on research projects. These projects can (and have personally) helped students get job opportunities and recognition within their department as an excellent student.

Current student, 9/2003-Submit Date, January 2007

Academics at Michigan are excellent across the board. That's what separates Michigan from the rest of the pack. Nearly every single academic program is ranked in the Top 10, and there is an abundance of departments to choose. With no general weaknesses in any area, you are assured to receive a great education no matter which field you enter, an advantage I think because most students do not know what to major in upon arriving on campus. The biggest drawback is the size of classes in your first two years. While programs are generally strong, you probably won't be able to enroll in small classes taught by the best professors until your junior year. Before that, you are indeed going to have to deal with big lecture halls and inaccessible professors. After your junior year, however, the class selection improves dramatically and the level of instruction improves markedly.

Current student, Psychology, 9/2003-Submit Date, March 2007

As a psychology major, I have mostly stayed far away from science classes, taking most of my courseload in the humanities and social science areas. Class selection for incoming freshmen is done at orientation, so get into an early session. Once on campus, class selection is roughly ordered by credits—the more you have, the earlier you get to register. Popular classes fill early and can be difficult to get into; lots of people show up on the first day of class hoping to get in and only some are successful. Michigan has distribution requirements that require at least two classes in science, humanities and social sciences, but it is easy to find classes within these general categories that will work even if you are not very interested in the category; for example, I took a Biology and Human Affairs course that counted toward natural science credit and played to my interests in social sciences. Science grading (I hear) tends to be on a curve, while my social science and humanities classes were all graded on a standard scale (94 to 100 = A, 90 to 93 = A- and so on). Professors hold regular office hours, and while some are more or less accessible than others, I was always able to connect with professors when I needed them.

Current student, 9/2003-Submit Date, March 2006

Undergraduate classes range from very demanding and rigorous to laidback and "fluffy," depending on the department, and sometimes even within departments. Popular classes are sometimes difficult to get into, especially for first-year students, as Michigan is a very large university. Be persistent. Contact the professor and explain your interest, show up on the first day and continue to show up and speak with the professor. More often than not, especially for large lecture courses, determined and interested students will be able to get into these classes. Workload and professors vary widely. Michigan's student government (MSA) runs a web site where past students rate individual professors and classes on issues ranging from workload to grading, to class discussion. This web site is accessible through Michigan's homepage and is a great resource in considering classes, as are upperclassmen in your department of study.

Current student, 9/2003-Submit Date, February 2006

There are some pretty broad graduation requirements. These include humanities, social science, natural science, quantitative reasoning, race and diversity, and upper-level writing requirements. The specifics depend upon which degree you are trying for: BS, BA or Bachelor of General Studies. But they are pretty easy to meet within four years. Quality of classes and professors varies a lot at Michigan, especially in LSA. Sometimes you'll get amazing professors, sometimes they can barely speak English. You just have to ask around to find out which classes and professor are good. There is also a survey of professors that MSA releases. If you take a pre-med, BBA, engineering or economics route, the courses are generally pretty challenging and competitive. Course registration is based upon classification. So seniors get priority. As a freshman, you may have problems registering for popular pre-requisite courses. But if you really want the course, you can often get an override. If not, you can get in eventually. Persistence helps a lot. There wasn't a course that I really wanted that I wasn't able to take while I was there. Workload depends upon you. At Michigan you can make college as hard or as easy as you like. There is also a foreign language

requirement of four semesters fluency in the language of your choice. You c also test out of some classes and use AP or IB credit from high school to exem yourself from some lower-level courses.

Employment Prospects

Alumnus/a, Engineering, 8/2003-5/2007, May 2007

I've had about 10 interviews my senior year for full-time employment. Althou the final job offer that I had picked was not through the engineering career offic I think they do a pretty good job. All sorts of companies come to recruit—t major financial, management consulting, defense, auto companies all recr heavily here. Take a look at the engineering Career Resource Center's report employers of Michigan engineering graduates and you'll see that employme prospects are wonderful. Some of the top hiring companies are Accenture, UB Boeing, Lockheed Martin, Citigroup, Toyota, Ford and GE. If you are looki for the well-rounded education for engineering or financial/consulting type jobs, this is the school for you.

Alumnus/a, Engineering, 9/2002-4/2006, September 2006

Employment prospects are pretty good coming out of the university. T University of Michigan alumni base is very large, and new alumni are given free year of membership in the alumni association and invited to events a encouraged to meet other alumni. The university has a job search site for all st dents (LS&A and engineering) and also one just for engineering graduates. T school's career center facilities are very helpful in the job search process.

Current student, 9/2003-Submit Date, March 2006

Michigan's alumni network is one of its best assets. With being such a large ur versity comes the simple fact that there is a lot of Michigan alumni scatter across the country, many in the position to be making hiring decisions. T strong school pride and sense of community that Michigan bestows upon its st dents practically ensures that Michigan alumni will be inclined to (sometim even thrilled to) mentor, assist, guide and even employ Michigan studen Additionally, Michigan is nationally recognized as one of the top public schoo in the country, and the associated prestige of such rankings and perceptions is great benefit for students competing for highly desired jobs and internships.

Current student, 8/2003-Submit Date, July 2006

The Office of Career Development is amazing. People use it daily. They pr pare us, help us look over résumés, conduct mock interviews, have appointme sign-up online, and have corporate presentations prepared for us. I can't ev explain in words how much they help us. It is truly wonderful. They make li really easy for us. You really have no excuse not to get a job after all t resources they provide.

Companies that recruit at Ross are very prestigious firms. Many investme banking firms recruit here. Michigan seems to produce a lot of investme bankers. The alumni network is great. There is an online directory where yc can search for anyone. The alumni usually have executive level positions at ve well-known companies. They're always willing to help out a fellow Wolverin

Quality of Life

Alumnus/a, History, 9/2003-4/2007, June 2007

First of all, Ann Arbor is very safe. Personally, I know I can walk alone at mi night and there won't be problems. Housing is a little tricky, since Ann Arb real estate is quite pricey if you want to live alone (oftentimes so you can study Dorms are lacking with small living spaces. I also did not like the foo Facilities are nice. There are nice lecture rooms and classrooms. There are a l of wireless spots and the technology is up-to-date.

Alumnus/a, 8/2003-8/2005, January 2007

Housing was fantastic, albeit a little pricey. Ann Arbor can cost quite a bit, b there are also areas that are a bit cheaper if you do a little hunting. All of th campus resources are wonderful, and there is a low level of crime around can pus—nothing to worry about.

Alumnus/a, Engineering, 9/2002-4/2006, September 2006

The living conditions at the university are good, but housing and crime issues are a growing concern for the area. The housing rates for the University of Michigan are ridiculous. The price for a year of room and board in the dorms was around $8,000 four years ago, and I am sure that it has gone up since. The monthly rate for the house that I lived in for three years was $3,350/month and the house cozily held eight or nine of us in it. This rent for the house was considered cheap among many of my friends.

Current student, 9/2003-Submit Date, October 2006

Dorms on campus are average. Dorm food is terrible. However, off-campus housing is relatively decent. Although rent on campus will be inflated, it is still better than living in the dorms. Crime and safety is kept to a minimum as we have three different types of police on campus. In Ann Arbor, you will be able to find any type of food you want.

Current student, 9/2003-Submit Date, March 2007

Ann Arbor is a great college town. Crime rates are low, and mostly relate to theft from unlocked doors (and of unlocked bikes). On-campus housing is centrally located (unless one ends up on North Campus, but there is regular busing down to Central). Food in the residence halls is pretty bad, but I always found something to eat. Campus itself is pretty (some buildings more than others), with lots of trees and a large central open area in the Diag where students hang out on the warm days of fall and spring. Off-campus housing is plentiful, but expensive. There are workout facilities on the south and north side of Central Campus, and North Campus has a gym as well. I am very happy with the campus atmosphere at the University of Michigan.

Alumnus/a, 8/2001-4/2005, September 2005

Many students choose to attend UMich for the sole fact that it is in Ann Arbor. And it's a damn good reason! AA has a low crime rate (though don't be surprised if things get stolen if you don't lock your doors), housing is all right on campus so students can actually walk to classes. Additionally, bike racks abound. Main buildings are close together (forming a square called the Diag), and walking to class is never a drag, but actually a very pleasant experience where you're bound to run into a friend, admire the trees, watch students toss frisbees or listen to the lovely sound of the harmonica man.

On the downside, parking is very tight in AA and housing is extremely expensive. If you want to lower your housing costs you can choose to live in a student co-op, though be forwarded many of them are wretched [dives.] As for dining, there are plenty of restaurants (both expensive and cheap) all within walking distance to campus/housing. Additionally, there is a great diversity of food (Mediterranean, Mexican) sure to please any student hoping to grab some grub between classes.

Social Life

Alumnus/a, Engineering, 8/2003-5/2007, May 2007

Sports add a lot to the social life, but I got pretty tired of it after a while. There is a lot of school pride. Saturday at the Big House is something you'll get used to doing a lot. There are museums, small shops, restaurant of every flavor, of course there are always parties on weekends if you are into that, but this is by no means a party school.

Current student, 9/2003-Submit Date, January 2007

I wouldn't recommend Michigan if you're shy and reserved. You have to find friends here, and most people do it through extracurriculars or the Greek system. If you're not outgoing, it is possible for you to get lost in the shuffle. On the other hand, Michigan is great for very outgoing people. There are endless things to do. Ann Arbor is really catered to students with nice bars, restaurants and clubs with various angles. There is a perfect fit for anyone. Obviously, the sports scene is big here, as well.

Alumnus/a, 9/1998-4/2002, September 2006

There is a club for every activity you can think of. There is a big festival at the beginning of every year where all the clubs set up table in the middle of campus and students can walk through and sign up for them. Intramural sports are also huge on campus. There are probably five different sports going at a time for all different levels of competitiveness. I was not involved in the Greek system, so I don't know much about it other than it is huge. There is a traditional Greek system and a black Greek system. The biggest events at UMich are sporting events. Campus pretty much shuts down on Saturdays during football season because everyone goes to the games. Every night of the week a different bar is where everyone goes because of the specials. Mitch's, Scorekeepers, the Nectarine, and the Blind Pig are all popular hangouts. Good Charlie's is the place to be after a football game or to celebrate your 21st birthday, and Dominick's is an open-air bar that is only open in the spring. It is where everyone goes to skip classes in March.

Current student, 9/2003-Submit Date, March 2006

In the fall, Ann Arbor, boasting the largest college football stadium in the nation, revolves around football; and attending Saturday football games is a great Michigan tradition. The downtown Main Street area offers a wide array of restaurants, from ethnic to upscale, catering to diverse tastes. In addition, the campus area has many Michigan favorites, such as the Brown Jug, Good Time Charleys, and Ashley's for pub food and drinks; Rendezvous, Oasis, and Kebob Palace for Middle Eastern food; China Gate and Sushi.com for Asian and sushi; and Pizza House for day and late-night food. The bar scene for undergrads centers on Rick's, Scorekeepers and Touchdown's for dancing; and the Brown Jug, Good Time Charleys and Ashleys for a more low-key setting.

Alumnus/a, 8/2001-4/2005, September 2005

Aside from premiere academics, UMich boasts a campus so busy with activity it would be nearly impossible not to have a social life. There are numerous clubs (outdoor clubs, engineering clubs, anti-sweatshop clubs) and even a huge festival in September to help students get acquainted with the various clubs. Additionally, some of the dorms offer special freshman programs, which can be helpful in meeting new people. There's plenty of great bars and tons of frat parties (if you're interested in that type of thing!).

Best of all though, UMich has so many events that you're never bored at night. Heck, most of the time you wonder why your academic commitments must interfere with having fun. There are tons of cultural events (super-cool if you want to take advantage of attending a university with a high diversity of students), numerous musical events (a cappella, symphony and also regular concert halls). UMich also has a great natural science museum and is conveniently located near multiple ice cream shops and comedy places. Also, plenty of really famous people come and speak at UMich and it is awesome to go hear them. Best of all, each one of these opportunities is in walking distance. Additionally, there're plenty of religious organizations (if you're into that) and numerous volunteer opportunities. You'll have so much fun at UM you'll wonder why you ever graduated (then you'll remember the tuition price and know why).

Read all of Vault's College Surveys at **www.vault.com/college**–get complete surveys on 100s of colleges and universities, expert advice on applicaton essays and more.

VAULT CAREER LIBRARY   **371**

Western Michigan University

Office of Admissions
1903 West Michigan Avenue
Western Michigan University
Kalamazoo, MI 49008
Admissions phone: (269) 387-2000
Admissions e-mail: ask-wmu@wmich.edu
Admissions URL:
www.wmich.edu/admissions/undergraduate/

 ## Admissions

Current student, Business, 1/2003-Submit Date, May 2007

Admissions requirements were as follows: above a 3.0 GPA and 19 ACT (admitted); above a 3.0 GPA and below a 19 ACT (admitted on probation); below a 3.9 GPA and above a 21 ACT (admitted on probation).

> **The school says:** "The average WMU freshman has a 3.3 high school grade point average and a 22 ACT score, but you should not view these numbers as minimum or cutoff points. WMU reviews applications based on your high school GPA, ACT or SAT scores, number and types of academic courses, trend of high school grades and other factors. Other factors include an essay or letters of recommendation, if these materials are included with your application."

Current student, Education, 7/2003-Submit Date, November 2006

I found the admissions process easy, but initially the university lost some of my transcripts and I had to call them to find out my status. I was denied because of the transcripts they lost (later found because someone misplaced them) and later admitted when the mistake was cleared up. They do have a tour but I didn't find a lot of help in the area of getting settled as a student. It was pretty much wander around and hope you find where you're going. Occasionally you'd see people passing out maps.

Current student, 8/2003-Submit Date, January 2006

The pressure of getting into college really stressed me out and worried me, so I chose to take the extra time and do on-site admissions. You bring your transcript, your application fee, test scores and your application, and then they either admit you or deny you. Of course, it wasn't official until you got the mailed letter. The admissions area is packed with nervous students, but it was definitely worth it.

Current student, 8/2004-Submit Date, October 2005

Obviously the best possible way to get admitted into WMU is to do well in high school and accumulate a good GPA. Also, the campus wants to know that itsstudents are anxious to attend the programs. If one goes to the on-campus admission, takes the tour and writes an essay on why one should be admitted, the one-on-one interview will be a breeze.

Current student, 9/2003-Submit Date, April 2005

The admissions process was smooth, and I did not feel it was overly selective. There were no essays or interviews for admission, but there were some for scholarships. The process involved simply filling out the application and sending it in on time. This enabled me to qualify for some scholarships, which was great. WMU offers excellent high-level merit scholarships, and includes an on-campus scholarship competition. This competition involved interviews and essay writing, but if you remain calm and answer truthfully, it's not too bad.

Current student, 8/2002-Submit Date, May 2004

The admissions process can be quite strenuous on a high school student. Usually in essays you want to be very opinionated. Giving your voice on the subject at hand and expressing your thoughts on paper is something that looks great to a college. For interviews, dress casually and don't overdo your own style, or it

will show on your face. Best bet is to be yourself; it can never go wrong. I'm firm believer in a firm handshake; remember to do just that. And before yc think about getting in, make sure your foundation of education is well place Take the SATs and ACTs a few times, it couldn't hurt. Make sure you know wh lies ahead in the profession you choose.

Alumnus/a, 9/1998-4/2002, April 2004

Admissions was pretty easy. I did not go to the university the year following m high school graduation because I lived in Argentina for a year. When I returne I got re-accepted right away. I do not remember writing any essays or havin any interviews.

Alumnus/a, 9/1989-12/1993, September 2003

The admissions process for WMU was very simple. I submitted an applicatio through my high school, which included a copy of my GPA and appropriate te scores, and paid the application fees. I only applied to four colleges, since the all had application fees. The process was very simple and straightforward.

Alumnus/a, 9/1997-5/2002, September 2003

Western Michigan University has undergone some major admissions change since I applied there. I think the standards have increased. But when I applie I was considered based on my whole person: leadership, sports, academics an service activities. The advice I would give is to include everything about your self in your application. This is not a school that is only interested in your log ical thinking brain.

 ## Academics

Current student, Business, 1/2003-Submit Date, May 2007

Both small and large classes. Great business school, with a brand-new buildin and solid profs. Small focused classes, which are good preparation for corporat life. Scheduling classes fills up quickly; must plan ahead and get schedule in o time, as seniority gets priority in classes. Workload is not terribly difficu (depending on which degree you are pursuing). There are lots of great profes sors.

Current student, Education, 7/2003-Submit Date, November 200

Overall, I think the program achieves its goal, but I think the process should b evaluated. A number of universities have a full-year internship and this univer sity just has a semester. A number of pre-intern assignments are done for class es, which adds to time spent in the classroom but there is a lack of teaching. believe it would be more beneficial if at the start of this program a student ha to spend some real time in the classroom to know if this was the degree they rea ly wished to follow. The grading process is decided by the department.

Current student, Engineering, 9/2004-Submit Date, April 2007

Engineering program at any university is pretty tough. Professors try to choos same textbooks used at UMich. Most of the engineering program at WMU i accredited by ABET. Chemical engineering class sizes are fairly small.

Current student, 8/2003-Submit Date, January 2006

I'm getting my degree in psychology. The emphasis at Western is primaril Behavior Analysis. I'm in my last semester of the program and I still don't know if I like it or not! Either way I have learned lots. It is very hard to get into pop ular classes, even if you talk to the professors. The grading is infuriating a Western! It goes like this: A, BA, B, CB, C, DC, D, F, so a B- is really a CB which makes it seem much worse than it is. Nobody else grades like this—Jus Western.

Current student, 8/2004-Submit Date, October 2005

WMU is basically a college full of business students. The Haworth College o Business, located on campus, is an excellent way to learn about business and th professors are amazing. WMU also has excellent teaching and art programs rading and workload can sometimes be a little stressful, but in the end it all ays off.

Current student, 9/2003-Submit Date, April 2005

very much enjoyed the industrial engineering program at WMU. The classes nd profs are topnotch, and the grading is fair. The workload varied according course and prof, but I think it is what should be expected for an engineering egree. It's not too hard to get popular classes since class sizes are set to a small ze and offered often. As a freshman, it's a little tricky, but if you are in athlet- s or the Honors College, you get priority registration, so it's worth it to apply the Honors College. The engineering program is pretty intense; I'm not sure bout other programs.

Current student, 9/2000-Submit Date, May 2004

am a finance major with accounting and econ minors, and they are good pro- rams. The business school is solid; you can learn a lot if you really work. The lasses are good, and there are a lot from which to choose. Western has a pio- eering financial planning major, so a lot of the curriculum is going toward that. can be tough to get popular classes because it is such a big school. The grad- g is easy, too easy: 92 is an A, but most classes are curved, and the professors en't very good until you get to the upper-level classes. Once you get to the ore advanced classes, they are all very experienced and leaders in their fields. he workload is nothing. If you want to go full time and graduate early from a lid school, this is the one.

Current student, 8/2002-Submit Date, May 2004

When choosing academic classes, consult the many web sites available where rofessors are graded by previous students. I would say that after you pick your asses, talk to others and make friends, ask them about other classes you may ave to take. The grading is usually fair with colleges; just as long as you go to ass and do the work you'll be fine. The workload is more than in high school, ut remember, this is your life, no more time to do easy street. Work hard now, lax later.

Alumnus/a, 9/1998-4/2002, April 2004

s a freshman at Western Michigan University, I studied abroad in Costa Rica. decided to major in Spanish and Latin American studies. The foreign language epartment was very good, and I had several outstanding professors. I also took variety of classes for my Latin American studies major, which included histo- , geography, anthropology and political science. I had a geography teacher ho was very good, and I ended up going with him and a group of students from ichigan State University to Merida, Mexico, for a study-abroad trip to study conomics and the Mayan culture. Workload at Western Michigan University aried depending on the teacher. I had some teachers who required a lot of read- g, and others who required class participation.

Alumnus/a, 9/1997-5/2002, September 2003

started out in the music theory program and changed over to English and com- unications. Both of these programs are very competitive. The professors are asy to talk to, but my advice is to research them carefully. There are some bad nes, especially in the English department. The size of classes is great. Once ou get into the upper-level classes, there are no more than 20 students in each ass, and the professors go the extra mile to make sure they are available for ou. As for getting into the classes you want, I would suggest that you always ave many back-up plans, and remember you have a lot of electives to take. rading and workloads are generally fair. Don't be afraid to use as many out- de resources as you can to help you. Western is great for providing flexible toring in a wide variety of subjects.

 Employment Prospects

Current student, Business, 1/2003-Submit Date, May 2007

ot a strong alumni network—an underrated degree. It's an accredited univer- ty and a fun place to get your degree. The business school is good, but isn't et recognized as being as good as it is by employers. The school is run fairly ell and a lot of donating alumni help to improve the facilities (brand-new engi- eering and business research facilities). Also, Kalamazoo is home to Pfizer, Merck and Stryker, so if you are looking to get into pharmaceutical and medical elds, you will have an advantage here.

Current student, Education, 7/2003-Submit Date, November 2006

The job market is not good for teachers in the area. The university does have a very nice job fair for students. Interested employers come from all over the country and are available at one location for students to turn in résumés and interview. The career office at the college will help with résumés. There is a focus panel for prospective teachers to ask questions about interviews and what they need to know.

Current student, Engineering, 9/2004-Submit Date, April 2007

Engineering major is tough to finish, but once you do, you'll make good money. Currently, 100 percent of the chemical engineering grads from WMU found jobs within a couple of months of graduation with a salary of $55,000.

Current student, 8/2004-Submit Date, October 2005

Every year, Western holds Career Day. Basically companies, such as Pepsi and Kellogg, come to the campus and hold interviews. Some people find their careers at Career Day.

Current student, 9/2003-Submit Date, April 2005

Most students are employed in the area or in the Detroit area. Some students go out of state, but not usually. Finding a job from WMU is not too difficult because we have excellent career fairs and intern recruiting programs. There are two or three career fairs per year, sponsored by different student organizations. Over 100 employers attend in a wide variety of fields. When it comes to engi- neering, most of the jobs are in automotive or supply chain fields, such as man- ufacturing, food supply or appliance networks. Popular companies include Whirlpool, Kellogg, Dana, American Axle, Delphi, Ford, Denso, Stryker and General Motors.

Current student, 8/2002-Submit Date, May 2004

Careers are easier to come by when one is at college. Job internships are usual- ly obtained with a great deal of support from the university. Not only that, but there are also job fairs on campus that recruit students on an annual basis. And if one does well with internships, it looks great on one's résumé. Jobs like to hire from within the company, and if you start out as a intern, most likely they would love to have you aboard full time. There are also online and physical bulletin boards that list job opportunities.

 Quality of Life

Current student, Business, 1/2003-Submit Date, May 2007

Good campus, laid-back/party type people. Semi-liberal. Weak fraternity sys- tem. Great and inexpensive housing and apartments. Lots of corporate-type apartments have sprung up in the past 10 years with gyms, pools, lobbies, bas- ketball courts, free Ethernet and so on. Also, on-campus housing is a lot of fun, but it seems that most students prefer apartments. The campus is pretty decent, but there could be more events and such. Great Rec Center, state-of-the-art facil- ities with pools, a climbing wall, basketball, tennis, racquetball, tracks, fitness and weights. Solid intramural sports teams that are well run and competitive. Parts of the City of Kalamazoo are dangerous, but generally campus is safe. Dorms are much better than most universities I have seen.

Current student, Education, 7/2003-Submit Date, November 2006

I'm a single mother of two and lived in campus housing. The apartments were very small. It's hard to fit two children and an adult in them. The cost was not competitive. I paid a little less than $600 a month, although all my bills were included. The best part of living on-campus was the access to campus and the bus line. I will say that little crime happened in the on-campus apartments.

Current student, Engineering, 9/2004-Submit Date, April 2007

I lived in a student apartment. Pretty cheap and utilities are included. There are also many apartments and house rentals around the campus.

Current student, 8/2003-Submit Date, January 2006

Housing is easy to find and very reasonable. You can find really nice or really not nice. There aren't enough good restaurants. Some of the neighborhoods are nice and some are not nice. There is crime like there is everywhere.

Read all of Vault's College Surveys at **www.vault.com/college**–get complete surveys on 100s of colleges and univer- sities, expert advice on applicaton essays and more.

VAULT CAREER LIBRARY 373

Current student, 8/2004-Submit Date, October 2005

The housing on campus is great. It is a very beautiful and friendly environment. Western has one of the lowest crime rates in Michigan. Although I would not recommend walking alone at night, it's just as safe as walking during the day. Words just cannot describe the campus, it is absolutely amazing.

Current student, 9/2003-Submit Date, April 2005

The quality of life is great in Kalamazoo. I feel very safe here, and housing is quite affordable. There's not much to do at clubs if you are under 21, but there are always tons of on-campus activities. The best on-campus activities include an active intramural program, student plays and art shows, active international student programs, and many different social societies. The engineering campus is brand new, and has state-of-the art facilities, such as computer labs, testing labs, automotive labs, and advanced electrical, mechanical and industrial engineering labs. The other campuses are doing extensive remodeling, such as health and human services and main campus. Most students live near campus, which is advisable since parking is expensive on campus. Off-campus housing is very diverse, and includes new apartments and historic homes with rooms for rent.

Current student, 9/2000-Submit Date, May 2004

Housing is no problem in this area. You can find decent rent at nice places within two to five minutes from campus. The facilities are nice: the business school building is less than [15] years old, and the recreation center is one of the best I've ever seen. There is plenty of campus dining and other stuff to do on campus.

Current student, 8/2002-Submit Date, May 2004

Quality of life is a thing students fear before going to college. But, most likely, one will be staying on campus in dorms one's first year. Not to worry, dorms aren't that bad—I had some of my most cherished memories in the dorms. This is where you meet so many new people and the living is quite fair. The food isn't bad, and it's always served when you're hungry. As for crime, once you know everyone on the floor with you, it's like one big family. Everyone watches out for one another, and crime is not a big issue. Same applies for safety, there's always safety in numbers.

Alumnus/a, 9/1998-4/2002, April 2004

Kalamazoo, Michigan is definitely a college town. There is much to do throughout the community, but often students do not take advantage of the unique downtown atmosphere. There are coffee shops, museums, parks and trails; however, students at WMU tend to stick pretty close to campus. There are a number of dormitories on campus, where I lived for one year. After the first two years, students usually find an apartment near campus. The facilities are good for the most part. A few buildings could use some remodeling. Parking on campus is not very convenient and costs a fortune. Crime on and near campus is pretty controlled.

 Social Life

Current student, Business, 1/2003-Submit Date, May 2007

Tons of bars (something for everyone), posh clubs, pubs, cheap eats places, fraternity/sorority hangouts and so on. Not a ton of great restaurants, but much better than a lot of campuses that I have been to. More women than men (when I attended). Fun nightlife though. Transportation can be difficult; a car is probably necessary post-freshman year. The Student Ghetto is a lot of fun. It is a huge neighborhood of students living in old homes from the 50's and 60's. Cold winters (bring your hat). Also, Chicago is only two hours away, which makes for good weekend or even weeknight trips to the Windy City.

Current student, Education, 7/2003-Submit Date, November 2006

I'm a single mother there are a number of activities for children. The Kalamazoo Institute of Art has an interactive room for kids. The Kalamazoo Valley Museum is free and has wonderful hands-on materials and exhibits for children. Parades are big around here with lots to do in downtown. A zoo is only 20 minutes away where you can actually feed a giraffe and feel its long, slimy tongue. Overall, I like this area very much. The Kalamazoo Promise also offers college help for students graduating from a Kalamazoo Public School.

Current student, 8/2004-Submit Date, October 2005

Around the campus there are endless supplies of bars, restaurants and club Everything is very youth-oriented and it is mostly students ranging from 18 24 at those scenes. We have a large variety of Greek clubs. It is just a very f place to be. No matter where one is, what one is doing, one will always have great time. It is very difficult to be bored.

Current student, 9/2003-Submit Date, April 2005

The most popular 21+ social spots include Wayside West and Firehouse. Th Greek scene is pretty popular, but by no means dominant. There are lots of cu tural activities such as museums, poetry readings and music spots. Bel Brewery, which makes well-known beer across the state, often has great mus from local and out-of-state bands. Also, Miller Auditorium at WMU offers ha discounts to Broadway shows for WMU students. The City of Kalamazoo offe lots of events during the summer and fall such as Irish Festival, Island Days ar Taste of Kalamazoo.

Current student, 9/2000-Submit Date, May 2004

Social life is awesome at Western, there are a lot of bars within five minute Downtown Kalamazoo has a lot to offer, including excellent microbrews. In th summer there are cool events downtown, like Blues Fest, Rib Fest and Regg Fest. The Greek system is big because the school has 30,000 students, but would say proportionally it's not as big as many other schools of the same siz Wayside West is the bar of choice. It's 21-and-over, but it's huge, with sever bars inside and many different dance floors and pool tables. There is a housir district that is big and has all the big house parties where you can meet a ton people. There are two main off-campus areas, one on each side of campus, ar between them you can walk to anything, including campus, good food ar nightlife.

Current student, 8/2002-Submit Date, May 2004

The social life is the best part of college by far. You will spend the best times your life going to social gatherings. If one is interested in the Greek system, the more is offered to students to do as well. The dating scene is great, there ar more people on a college campus than in high school, leaving more opportuni to meet that special someone. There are also events on campus that one coul go to and participate in all the time. Anything from kite flying to paintball, it endless fun. After you turn 21, the bars and social scene become more flavorfl and you meet other friends that always lighten the mood.

 The School Says

Students who choose Western Michigan University get an edge in work and life by taking full advantage of a school that combines the resources of a national research university with the personal attention and atmosphere often found at a smaller institution. WMU focuses on providing the tools students need to become successful alumni.

The University's topnotch academic programs, faculty and facilities attract national and international attention, as well as 25,000 students from across the country and 80 other nations. Its 237 academic programs are designed so graduates can immediately add value to their work places or enter graduate school.

At WMU, students also have countless opportunities to obtain internships, conduct research and study abroad. The educational environment is further bolstered by programs such as University Curriculum, which helps undecided students select a major; the Lee Honors College, which is one of the oldest honors programs in the nation and offers the intimacy of a small college with the resources of a major university; and BroncoJobs Plus, which puts career-development and job-search services and information at students' fingertips.

Faculty members are well-established in their fields and bring a global perspective to the classroom through their broad range of activities. They have a passion for teaching and regularly collaborate on real projects in the real world. Many conduct research and welcome both undergraduate and graduate students into their research labs or creative studios.

WMU's campus features some of the best facilities in the Midwest. Among them are a state-of-the-art science pavilion; a world-class aviation campus; specialized buildings for the health and human services college and its public-service clinics; a cutting-edge engineering campus next to WMU's Business Technology and Research Park; acclaimed fine arts venues; and a well-equipped student recreation center.

The University Libraries and University Computing Center provide campuswide access to worldwide information resources. Numerous computer labs are available, many in residence halls, and wireless computing is the norm. In fact, Intel ranks WMU second on its list of America's 100 "Most Unwired College Campuses."

There are nearly 300 student organizations to choose from, including a wide range of academic, professional, Greek and special-interest groups. The University also has nationally recognized arts programs, a lively cultural calendar, dozens of intramural and club sports, and 16 NCAA Division I-A teams.

WMU is one of the most affordable schools in Michigan. In 2007-08, tuition and fees for full-time freshmen and sophomores cost $7,260, while room and board cost $7,042. The Western Edge student/University compact makes WMU even more affordable by helping students find the right career path and earn their degrees quickly. Less time in school automatically saves money and allows students to head for graduate school or enter the job market sooner.

Some 20,000 students receive financial assistance totaling nearly $211 million. Merit-based programs include the Medallion Scholarships, which are valued at $40,000 over four years. Need-based loans, grants, college work-study and other aid options are provided for students who demonstrate financial need.

Read all of Vault's College Surveys at **www.vault.com/college**–get complete surveys on 100s of colleges and universities, expert advice on applicaton essays and more.

VAULT CAREER LIBRARY 375

Carleton College

Office of Admissions
100 North College Street
Northfield, MN 55057
Admissions phone: (800) 995-2275
Admissions e-mail: admissions@carleton.edu
Admissions URL: apps.carleton.edu/admissions/

 Admissions

Alumnus/a, 9/2000-9/2004, September 2006

Carleton is very concerned about having a diverse student body. Not only does the school want diversity in race or ethnicity, but it also wants students who are diverse in their experiences and beliefs. A few other traits the college seems to value are intellectual curiosity, creativity, uniqueness, independence, motivation, leadership, passion about just about anything legal, and people who are willing to step out of their comfort zones in pursuit of a goal or valuable experience. By carefully examining how the college markets itself and talking to current or former students, you can probably figure out many of the types of diversity and other traits for which admissions looks. For example, you can see a lot on the web site about the college's geographic diversity, both within the U.S. and abroad. Consequently, when you're thinking about what to write in your essays and what to emphasize on your application, you should spend some time identifying how your strongest characteristics match traits the college values and carefully work that information into your essay. Obviously you want to be at least somewhat subtle, and I imagine that a well-written, creative essay will make a good impression.

Current student, 9/2003-Submit Date, April 2004

I applied for Early Decision. This is a great option because it really shows your interest in the college, the admissions officers aren't jaded yet, and you're competing in a smaller pool. Plus, you find out in December. Show your originality and intelligence in your application, essay and interview. Carleton is extremely selective, and it is looking for original students who can handle the work. If you're still in high school for a while, make sure you're taking advantage of the opportunity to take advanced work. Try to take the hardest courses for which you're qualified in every subject. Most students starting at Carleton have already had some calculus, but it isn't required. In fact, some students get in with only one or two years of high school math, as long as they've made up for that deficit in other subjects.

Carleton isn't looking for well-rounded students—it's looking for students who challenge themselves, but can identify areas in which they want to succeed. The same goes for activities: don't try to participate in every high school activity. Choose a few of them, and make your time count. Become an officer or plan a significant service project. Carleton is impressed by results. Then you have to sell yourself on the application—don't try to sound either too humble or too cocky. But make the admissions officers aware that you're proud of your accomplishments.

Current student, 9/2003-Submit Date, June 2004

It is a selective school, but an interview helps a lot. Also, mention the random things you have done—we always joke that each year is more impressive and one day someone will be an underwater basket-weaver who cured cancer while biking across Africa. So be yourself, but definitely play up the individual things you've done. Volunteer work helps a lot. And if you're from a less represented state, it's an advantage.

Current student, 9/2003-Submit Date, April 2004

Carleton is a highly selective liberal arts college, with an acceptance rate of around 30 percent. I applied online in 2000, and was accepted almost immediately. Interviewing is optional, but I went ahead and talked to the director of admissions when I drove up for a visit, and eventually decided that I would accept the college's offer. The actual application is fairly typical, with a few per-

sonal essays and two or three required recommendations from employers and teachers. Carleton accepts either the SATs or the ACT exam, or both if you want to send them.

Current student, 9/2000-Submit Date, February 2004

Selectivity is very high, usually in the Top Five in national liberal arts rankings. The admissions process is rather streamlined—apply online, then interview. Obviously, a well-written essay is required. Generally, the school is known for giving breaks to independent or maverick types. They will also overlook bad grades if you are from a desired area or have high board scores.

 **Academics**

Alumnus/a, 9/2000-9/2004, September 2006

One thing about academics at Carleton that I don't think can be emphasized enough is the importance of the small class sizes. (I only had two classes that had more than 30 students and I had at least three classes that had less than 10 students.) There are two basic reasons why I think the small class sizes are important.

First, small classes allow professors to assign more challenging assignments and give more challenging exams than they otherwise would. Outside of introductory language classes, there are no busywork assignments and no multiple choice tests. It's all papers that require in-depth analysis, challenging problem sets and lab assignments, and essay/problem oriented tests where you're given a list of questions and a blue book or two.

The second important result of small cases is that it is very easy to get to know your professors. By and large they're great people who can give you advice about college, write excellent letters of recommendation, help you find good internships or jobs that fit your interests, help you to figure out what your interests are, and give you an opportunity to do research with them (which is extremely valuable if you want to go to grad school or get a job in certain industries).

Current student, 9/2003-Submit Date, April 2004

Carleton's academics are nothing if not rigorous. In keeping with the community atmosphere of the college, most classes are fairly small (usually fewer than 25 students), and 300-level seminars are particularly intense. Personally, I don't think I disliked more than a couple of professors; the quality of the faculty is outstanding. Furthermore, professors are focused much more on teaching than on outside academic work, which is an added benefit for students.

Most popular classes are waitlisted, but professors often accept the waitlisted students, depending on the number of seats available in the classroom. Grading is all over the place: some profs are easy, others are not. The workload is tough, especially for third- and fourth-year students. Seniors are required to complete a comprehensive exercise, which can be a 30-page paper, a test or lab work. Exceptional comps work is rewarded with distinction in the major.

Current student, 9/2003-Submit Date, April 2004

Carleton provides a quality education—the professors are the most dedicated and caring in the country. Also, the campus is becoming more and more diverse politically, so it is not a solely liberal campus anymore. There are no easy classes, but the more popular ones are even attainable to freshmen, because the profs are very helpful and usually let you in even if you're waitlisted. It takes a lot of work to get an A; B's are very normal. Some profs rarely give A's, so a B is about the best you'll get. The workload is difficult, but you can work around it. Of course, if you "work around it" your grade will reflect that—there's no way around that.

Current student, 9/2003-Submit Date, June 2004

The classes are terrific, and the professors are wonderful. Every professor takes personal interest in the students. Classes are never larger than 75 students (and even that is rare). You can get into most popular classes if you talk to the professor ahead of time. The workload is heavy, especially with regard to reading. Professors want you to succeed and will meet with, you if your grade isn't what you want.

Current student, 9/2000-Submit Date, February 2004

The school is highly regarded because of its profs. They are teachers first and foremost and usually very good. The grading is strict, and the workload is generally heavy, although if one wants to take history or econ classes, the workload is often less. Very few classes fill up, so getting a popular class is not hard.

Employment Prospects

Alumnus/a, 9/2000-9/2004, September 2006

If you want to go to grad school, your prospects are very good. Carleton sends many people to grad school in the natural/physical sciences, social sciences, and humanities, as well as to law school and medical school. However, if you're looking for full-time employment after you graduate, Carleton's small size and its geographic location won't help your prospects. Even within Minnesota, a surprising number of employers either haven't heard of Carleton or don't know that it's a very good school. However, most employers I know have heard of Carleton and have a very positive impression of it. Another issue is we only get a small number of employers who come to recruit on campus compared to larger campuses and campuses that are located in cities. Larger elite schools that are located in cities manage to attract many more employers to their campuses to do interviews.

I was an economics major and most of my fellow econ majors and I found very good jobs. We just had to work harder than people at certain other schools and make make use of all the resources available to us. For instance, Carleton has a great alumni network (which is basically how I found my job). Carleton students get invited to SLAC job fairs and other job fairs around the country (which is how many people I know found good jobs). Professors also have useful contacts and will help you take the time to build a good rapport with them if you do reasonably well in their classes. Carleton students can use private Internet databases to which Carleton subscribes in order to find jobs, and of course some firms do conduct on-campus interviews and I know of at least a few people who got good jobs from those interviews.

Current student, 9/2003-Submit Date, April 2004

Carleton's career center is well staffed and open for students to come in and talk to career counselors. Internships are plentiful in the Twin Cities, and companies periodically recruit right on campus. As far as prestige value goes, Carleton is ranked fourth among liberal arts colleges in the *U.S. News & World Report* survey, so that goes a long way.

Current student, 9/2003-Submit Date, April 2004

Carleton is not well known outside of the higher education world, but you can flash its Top 10 *U.S. News & World Report* rating if you like. We have a high number of students going into the Peace Corps, and the medical school acceptance statistics are excellent.

Current student, 9/2000-Submit Date, February 2004

If you are pursuing a career in finance, you are on your own. If you are looking to go on to graduate school, Carleton prepares you very well, especially in the sciences. There are alumni in very good positions who are more than willing to help.

Quality of Life

Alumnus/a, 9/2000-9/2004, September 2006

The campus and neighborhood are very safe and beautiful. The housing is of variable quality (varies from moderately nice to very nice, although unless you get lucky, you won't end up with the very nice housing until you're a junior or

senior), and the various facilities are of good quality. I think the complaints about the dining halls are somewhat overstated unless you are a vegan (I know some people who were vegans and they got by, but they certainly didn't get much variety). The main problem with the dining halls is that after a few months of eating there, the food starts to get boring. However, having cooked for myself for a couple years now, I've learned to appreciate the dining hall. Unless you want to spend a lot of time planning your meals, shopping for food and cooking your food, you're going to be hard-pressed to eat better than you will in the dining hall. I've talked to a few other recent Carleton grads who share my feelings about the dining hall.

Current student, 9/2003-Submit Date, June 2004

The dorms are great—even the least favorite one is still great. The food is notoriously bad, but the staff workers are great. It is in a small farm town, so parties happen often. Drinking is a normal thing, but the non-drinking outlets are becoming more and more prominent. There is practically no crime. The rec center is new and great. It has a climbing wall and indoor track. The aerobics room is great and has many machines. There are also many phys ed classes available. The rec center also offers classes. I took a Saturday morning yoga class. There is also a hip-hop class taught by students. The interest houses are also diverse. This year, there was a yoga house. There is a culinary house, Q and A house, Fish house (Christian), art house and more. I loved my time there.

Current student, 9/2003-Submit Date, April 2004

The one problem with a small liberal arts college in a small town is that there are very few opportunities to actually live off campus. In fact, residential life discourages it in keeping with its desire for a community atmosphere. The quality of the dorms, where most people spend their first couple of years, ranges from excellent to mediocre. Obviously, the more seniority (or friends with seniority) one has, the easier it is to get better housing. There are also numerous campus interest houses for the myriad of interest groups on campus.

Carleton's facilities are generally first-rate, especially the new recreation center's fitness equipment. There are two gyms, rec rooms in all the dorms, a campus pub, a concert hall and a roundhouse-style theater. The two dining halls and snack bar leave something to be desired, however.

Northfield, itself, is a typical Midwestern college town, although it is actually home to two colleges (the other being St. Olaf). If you need groceries, toiletries or anything else for that matter, it's necessary to drive a few miles to the local Target, as there are few options in town. Crime is not a problem at all, and the neighborhood around the college is beautiful.

Current student, 9/2003-Submit Date, April 2004

Everyone is guaranteed campus housing if they want it, and most people do—about 90 percent live in some form of college-owned housing, whether that's a dorm or a shared house. The food is better than average, there's very little crime and there are tons of activities. The area is absolutely beautiful, especially if you like hiking and/or cross-country skiing.

Current student, 9/2000-Submit Date, February 2004

The campus is in rural Minnesota, but not far from the Twin Cities. The campus is well laid-out and very pretty. The housing is above average. The new townhouses go first and are all taken by seniors. The town has numerous housing options that students can take advantage of after their second year. Safety is not an issue.

Social Life

Alumnus/a, 9/2000-9/2004, September 2006

The social scene is decent. There is no Greek system. It's usually easy to find parties on the weekend. Most of them are just normal house parties, but some are unusually fun or creative. The college also sponsors a lot of other activities. There are lots of intramural sports in which a large percentage of the college participates in. The most popular are ultimate frisbee in the fall and spring and broomball (which is amazingly fun) in the winter. There are also a lot of different clubs. If you check out the college's web site, you can get a pretty good sense of what is available. I think one of the best things about social life at the college is that you're constantly surrounded by fun and interesting people with whom you can often find

Read all of Vault's College Surveys at www.vault.com/college–get complete surveys on 100s of colleges and universities, expert advice on applicaton essays and more.

VAULT CAREER LIBRARY 377

fun and interesting things to do, even if it is just hanging out in a dorm room and talking. Most dorms and houses, especially ones where there is a large population of first- and second-year students, have a great sense of community.

A lot of people complain about the dating scene, probably because it is a little odd. There is very little traditional dating, i.e., asking acquaintances out on dates. People either seem to be involved in long relationships, which are often built from close friendships, or very short relationships (i.e., hooking up with someone at a party).

Current student, 9/2003-Submit Date, April 2004

Both drinkers and non-drinkers have active social lives at Carleton. Most social events are private parties, as there are only about two bars in town. Carleton has

no Greek system, and the students are very accepting of all types of peopl Usually the "thing to do" is take in one of the free movies, go to a student dan performance or attend an a cappella music festival. We've got clubs for ju about everything you can think of, and new ones are always sprouting u Though Northfield is a small town, arts-wise we get performers coming in all t time, either to the Cave, our small club-like venue that sells beer, or to one of t larger auditoriums. Second-run and old-school movies are shown for free eve weekend, sometimes with an audience of 10, sometimes with a wild and cra audience of hundreds. It's easier to find friends than dates, but plenty of datir goes on—a lot of Carls end up marrying other Carls.

College of Saint Benedict/Saint John's University

Office of Admission
College of Saint Benedict
Saint John's University
P.O. Box 7155
Collegeville, MN 56321
Admissions phone: (800) 544-1489
Admissions fax: (320) 363-2750
Admissions e-mail admissions@csbsju.edu
Admissions URL: www.csbsju.edu/admission/

 Admissions

Alumnus/a, Economics, 9/2000-5/2004, April 2007

They look for well-rounded candidates. It's not enough to have a great GPA any longer, but rather make sure you are involved in extracurriculars or working in addition to going to school. It shows you can manage your time and it gives you more "depth" as a candidate.

Alumnus/a, Liberal Arts, 8/2002-5/2006, April 2007

The admissions process was helpful. The college sent me information on visit days and about how to contact people with questions. I had to write one personal statement essay and provide a detailed application. I was not interviewed except for scholarships. The college was fairly selective in its acceptance because I was a valedictorian in high school but was not eligible for the highest scholarship because of my ACT score.

Current student, Communications, 8/2003-Submit Date, April 2007

CSB has a joint education process with Saint John's University in Collegeville, MN and they are known as CSB/SJU. The admissions office is joint. I remember it being one of my best admissions processes as far as visiting the campuses. Everyone was super friendly and helpful. I had a private tour of CSB, met with an admissions representative who went over the curriculum and answered all sorts of questions. After lunch with a student, we went over to SJU and had another private tour of Saint John's. After the tour, I attended a class and then met with a professor in the communications department. It was all very influential. The application process was equivalent to other schools', including personal essay and letters of recommendation.

Alumnus/a, History, 8/2001-6/2005, April 2007

The admissions process was much more selective than I had thought. The institution is often a familial one, but my family ties didn't help me as much as I would have thought. I had a 26 on my ACT and a 3.2 GPA when I had applied. The ACT score was above average for what I had read on the school and the GPA was a bit low. They kept track of my grades for the entire senior year, and I wasn't admitted until June after graduation.

Throughout this process they were very clear about what their thinking proces was and what I had to do to gain admission. In sum, getting admitted in Jur wasn't fun, but the admissions office eased the pain by being helpful and trans parent.

Alumnus/a, Communications, 8/2000-5/2004, April 2007

Admissions is fairly standard. I chose to do my application online to avoid th applicaiton fee. I was from a lower socioeconomic level, so this was a very pos itive thing. Within the application process I was pointed toward FAFSA. Whil I was awaiting acceptance I was able to complete my FAFSA application. I wa accepted to SJU, and then automatically sent scholarship information. I ende up getting a Dean's Scholarship ($5,000/year, renewable), music ($500/yea renewable), and some other grants and need-based financial aid.

> **The school says:** We do not require an application fee for any method of application.

Current student, 8/2003-Submit Date, May 2006

The school continues to become more selective every year. The admission office prefers a GPA of around 3.0 or higher and above average test scores. It also helps to have good letters of recommendation, involvement in the community and a high-quality personal statement. There are a few options for essay topics, but it is also a possibility to submit your own idea.

I participated in the program designed for out-of-state students to visit th school. The school pays for half of each student's plane ticket, and provide food and transportation to and from the airport for the weekend. Current stu dents volunteer to host prospective students and the student is able to observe class, receive tours, meet other accepted students and visit with professors and coaches in the area of interest. It was really helpful to get a taste of campus life for making my decision.

Current student, 8/2004-Submit Date, May 2006

I suggest applying early, however, it doesn't hurt you if you apply after the early application deadline. The application consists of your contact information and little bit about yourself. There is a one-page essay question that [you] will write as well as letter of recommendation from teachers, coaches or people you work with. There is a specific GPA and ACT/SAT score (but I can't remember exactly what it is) that you will need to be accepted into CSB/SJU. You do not have to take both the ACT and the SAT. Most people just take the ACT. If you qualify for specific scholarships, you would then come to campus to interview for it otherwise there is not an interview process to be accepted.

> **The school says:** "There are no specific GPA or test score requirements for admission."

Academics

Alumnus/a, Biology, 1/2000-12/2003, April 2007

Highly competitive! Professors demand that students take their education into their own hands. Professors are more than willing to help, mentor, guide and give you the tools to succeed. A lot of reading is assigned per class, and books are expensive.

Alumnus/a, Economics, 9/2000-5/2004, April 2007

The school is best known for its nursing program, but there is very knowledgeable staff in all academic areas. Students are given preference to sign up for classes based on academic standing, i.e., how many credits you have at the time (so if you take a larger load your first semester or if you have AP credits, you will have a higher standing than most others in your class). Some classes are only offered every other semester, so it is important to keep that in mind when signing up. Also, if you are traveling abroad (which is something CSB/SJU is very involved with) keep in mind which classes you will need to take so you ensure you are able to get everything done. Workload is fine—it really depends on your courseload but people always find a way to manage. Most professors are very involved, so you have access to their home phone numbers and such in case you have a question in the evening.

Alumnus/a, Physics, 8/2001-5/2005, April 2007

Each class throughout my undergraduate experience had less than 30 people. As I got further within my degree, the class size decreased where I was able to attain one-on-one teaching from the professor as needed. The faculty was quite conversational in and outside of the classroom, which made it easier to comprehend how life in a particular major would be like. The expectations of professors were high and they taught the material at optimum level. Even though my major was in the sciences, CSB/SJU made it possible for me to explore other areas and made me well-rounded through the emphasis of a Bachelor of Arts degree. A benefit to a smaller university is the capability of taking any course without difficulty. The professors were fair in their grading and were more than helpful during a time of crisis.

Alumnus/a, Biology, 8/2000-5/2004, April 2007

I loved all my classes and felt that the professors were wonderful. I participated in the Honors Program, and I was always very satisfied with those classes. The discussion in the classes was always interesting and pushed me intellectually, both inside and outside of class. For the most part, I was always able to get the classes I wanted, but some of the more popular classes are difficult to get into as a freshman or sophomore. I e-mailed the professors of some of those classes and both times they were able to add me to the class. The professors are always willing to meet with students and seem to go out of their way to help students with class and grad school/scholarships/employment concerns. The workload varies by major: I was a Nutrition Science major and spent a lot of time in labs and doing lab work, but it was almost always manageable. Grading also seemed to depend on the department. CSB/SJU also has a great study abroad program.

Alumnus/a, Communications, 8/2000-5/2004, April 2007

My class sizes ranged from eight to about 25. I don't recall having a class larger than that. The classrooms are small, cozy and inviting. A perfect atmosphere.

Standard courseload is four classes per semester (16 credit hours), with 12 considered full time and 20 being the maximum without paying a small fee. Each class is 70 minutes on a rotating six-day schedule. Week One has classes A and B on Monday-Wed-Friday, and Classes C and D on Tues-Thurs. Week Two has classes A and B on Tue-Thurs, and classes C and D on Mon-Wed-Friday. It's very simple and allows students flexibility perhaps not afforded with a five-day schedule. Many classes have labs at least once a week, ranging from one to two hours.

Current student, English, 8/2003-Submit Date, April 2007

The academic program is a fairly rigorous program although getting a B average is obtainable for most students. In order to get an A, it takes a little bit more work and dedication to the class. Getting into classes has never been a problem and even if you can't get into a class first year, you will be able to get into it if it is needed for graduation. The registrar is very flexible in helping students get into classes that are in a series and needed to move on in the following semester. The professors are extremely helpful and always willing to go the extra mile

with students, and while most assign a lot of work, they are understanding that students are in a variety of classes and at times need a break in order to continue functioning. In some of the lower-division classes, getting an A is fairly easy and it isn't until getting into upper-division classes that grading becomes more difficult.

Alumnus/a, 8/2001-5/2005, May 2006

CSB, a college for women, shares professors and classrooms with SJU, a college for men. All courses are co-educational. Class sizes are small (around 20) and the professors are wonderful. They really care about the success of each student. It is generally easy to get into the classes you need and the overwhelming majority of students graduate in four years.

Employment Prospects

Alumnus/a, Economics, 8/1999-5/2003, April 2007

St. John's/St. Ben's has a very good reputation in accounting. The Big Four accounting firms all interviewed on campus, along with several major corporations (Cargill, 3M and Honeywell). The process was quite simple.

Alumnus/a, Psychology, 8/2002-6/2006, April 2007

I applied for two jobs and received both offers. They were very good offers and CSB/SJU has a good reputation with many businesses. Companies are very happy to have students from our school working for them. The alumni network at CSB/SJU is very strong and helpful within the job search process. Many internships and on-campus recruiting events are offered. Many first-round interviews and even second-round interviews are held on the campus.

Alumnus/a, History, 8/2001-6/2005, April 2007

CSB/SJU grads have an abundance of employment opportunities. The alumni network is extremely tight in the upper Midwest and is expanding to become an exceptional national network.

All major accounting firms regularly recruit on campus, as well as Target, a Minneapolis-based company. These companies can be seen on campus often, while other Minneapolis-based companies also have good presence on campus, too.

Many grads volunteer or serve after graduation, often through Catholic organizations. There is definitely a culture of service at the school. As a result, the school is becoming a favorite with larger national and international service organizations like Teach for America, Peace Corps and JET. Fulbright scholars are also a norm for grads.

Career Services is exceptional, but under-utilized. Visit early and often and you can do anything.

Alumnus/a, History, 8/2001-5/2005, April 2007

Our alumni network is awesome! The career center is not very good unless you are a business major of some sort. Most graduates end up in finance, business analysis, or other horrible office jobs. If you are a humanities or social science major, it is much more difficult.

Current student, English, 8/2003-Submit Date, April 2007

Getting a job after graduation is fairly easy in the business-related careers If students stay within Minnesota, we have a very helpful alumni network. Our on-campus career resources are very helpful in terms of creating résumés, networking, advice on interviewing and the like. CSB/SJU is known within Minnesota as a good school from which to hire and volunteer programs throughout the whole nation also see CSB/SJU as a good school from which to draw. Graduates obtain jobs from all areas, including business, marketing, financial, volunteer positions, teaching and nursing A lot of students pursue post-graduate education.

Quality of Life

Alumnus/a, Liberal Arts, 8/2002-5/2006, April 2007

Campus life was awesome! A great sense of community was formed and there was a constant goal to strive to create true communities with diverse members

Read all of Vault's College Surveys at **www.vault.com/college**–get complete surveys on 100s of colleges and universities, expert advice on applicaton essays and more.

VAULT CAREER LIBRARY **379**

and great connections between people. Residence halls built a great base for that community and the requirement to live in them for the first two years helped build such a community.

Alumnus/a, Physics, 8/2001-5/2005, April 2007

I always looked forward to eating in the cafeteria because the baked goods were all made fresh! The best is the Bennie and Johnnie bread, everyone lives for this stuff and it is freshly baked! The options were numerous and you never got tired of it. The quality of flavor is great. Living conditions were great from freshman year. The new apartments are even better! Every year of living on campus, you are guaranteed a sink in your room. This was quite beneficial when getting ready in the morning. The location is in a minimal crime area, and you always feel safe walking at night anywhere on campus. The work-out area was a great place to enjoy others' company.

Alumnus/a, History, 8/2001-6/2005, April 2007

Facilities are exceptional and more importantly accessible to students. The campus is one of the largest in the country and is a playground for environmental scientists: an up-and-coming program at the school. The on-campus housing is great and the campus is gorgeous anytime of year. The food is good and the facilities of St. John's extend to the St. Benedict's campus, which has newer science facilities for chem and bio.

At times life can get a bit lame in Central MN, but the cities are less than an hour away, and campus brings on a good variety of speakers and traveling festivals.

Current student, Communications, 8/2003-Submit Date, April 2007

Upperclasswomen have their own bedrooms with washer and dryers in the apartment, two women per bathroom. They're gorgeous and new! We have access to two of everything—for a school of our size you can't beat it. Food is fabulous. We're in a very safe area where walking alone in the dark, although not encouraged, is still safe.

Current student, English, 8/2003-Submit Date, April 2007

CSB/SJU excels in these areas. Our on-campus housing options are great and many students choose to live on campus for all four years, especially since our upperclassman apartments are nicer than most one can get in town. Our dining facility is being replaced with the new one opening next fall and this will be extremely nice. Our campus is safe and our security department is very customer friendly and willing to help in any situation, as well as provides escorts from any spot on campus.

Social Life

Alumnus/a, Physics, 8/2001-5/2005, April 2007

There really isn't a typical Greek system. The Greek system of CSB consists of only one, called AKS Service Sorority. Their goal within the community was to provide service to the student body, the surrounding community and help out whenever possible. It was a great way to meet fellow women who wanted to make a change within the world for a better purpose. There are numerous clubs from which to participate that are quite visible on campus! Many events per weekend to choose, a specialty was always the Chapel Walk (a nature walk in the woods to a empty chapel), happy hour for those 21 and up, and of course various cultural events, such as dancing, festivals and food celebrations. As for the dating scene, there is a joint all male university, Saint John's University, which you share classes with on both campuses.

Every freshman is required to take a symposium for a full year. This is the only class where the same students remain with the same professor for the whole year. This provided great opportunities to create close friendships along with meeting people not within your selected major.

There are many mom and pop type places close to CSB/SJU, with which made life feel more like at home and many students enjoyed the delicious food. You can always have Gary's or Papa-G's pizza, and any student would just devour this in seconds! It definitely beat the typical chain pizza places by far.

Current student, Communications, 8/2003-Submit Date, April 200[?]

There are tons of events going on every weekend: dances, concerts, gam[e] shows, comedians, hypnotists and so on. The bars are a blast; it's extremely di[f]ficult for minors to get in. There are some small fun restaurants aroun[d]. However, we are 10 minutes from St. Cloud, which gives you a huge assortmen[t] of restaurants ranging from McDonald's, Applebee's, Olive Garden, Outbac[k] and so on.

Alumnus/a, Psychology, 8/2002-6/2006, April 2007

There are different activities for every person. There are two bars in town a[t] which you will often find college students. There are also a few coffee house[s] and restaurants. The college hosts many events during the week and on week[-] ends. A favorite of the students is Pinestock, which is held in the late spring. [A] band performs out on Watab Island and it is an all day event. Very fun! Th[e] football games at Saint John's are also a very big event in the fall.

Alumnus/a, History, 8/2001-5/2005, April 2007

I think it's really good for a small school. There is only one sorority and one fra[t] but they are awesome and not your typical Greeks. The bars are typical bars an[d] really fun. The dating scene is interesting because as a freshman you hook-u[p] but by senior year you're either still with that person from freshman year or sin[-]gle. By senior year, everyone knows everyone else by no more than two degree[s] of separation, so no one is new or fresh.

Current student, English, 8/2003-Submit Date, April 2007

St. Joseph has all of the bars that students attend and are all very popular. Ther[e] are four bars in town all within walking distance and they are busy on mos[t] nights of the week, particularly Friday and Saturday. There are also pizza place[s] in town that are frequented both in person and through delivery. These pizz[a] places are particularly busy after the bars close on Friday and Saturdays and sta[y] open fairly late on those evenings. Another favorite spot for students is Brothe[r] Willie's Pub, which is on our brother school's, St. John's, campus and has happ[y] hour every Friday from 4 to 8 p.m. Lots of students attend this and there is ofte[n] live music playing on these evenings. We have a lot of on-campus activitie[s] going on Friday and Saturday nights. We have no Greek life on campus. I[n] terms of other off-campus activities, we can go into St. Cloud, the nearest semi[-]large towns, where we can see movies, eat, shop and so on. Another popula[r] activity to do, strangely enough, is bingo on Wednesday nights at O'Connells[,] which is our on-campus coffee shop/evening restaurant and bar.

The School Says

The College of Saint Benedict (CSB) and Saint John's University (SJU) are nationally-leading liberal arts colleges whose unique partnership offers students the educational choices of a large university and the individual attention of a premier small college. Together, CSB/SJU provide students access to the resources of two colleges through a common undergraduate curriculum, identical degree requirements, and a single academic calendar. The colleges' 3,900 students attend all classes and activities together on two campuses.

CSB/SJU are located in a remarkable setting of 3,200 acres of woods, lakes and prairie—providing students with unique opportunities for education, recreation and reflection. Nearly all students live on campus or in the immediate campus neighborhood, providing them with opportunities for a highly engaged learning experience. A compelling sense of place and community shapes the undergraduate experience and creates a lifelong network of alumni/ae connection.

Students seek and discover an engaging and integrated learning experience. Nearly all of them complete an internship, participate in undergraduate student research, study abroad, participate in community service or participate regularly in student government, student clubs, campus publications or other student organizations.

The colleges prepare students for leadership and service in a global society. CSB/SJU provide international study programs on six continents and are ranked third among baccalaureate colleges nationally in the number of students who study abroad. More than 200 academic courses have an international component or global emphasis, and one-third of CSB/SJU faculty has led a study abroad program. The colleges enroll nearly 150 students from more than 30 countries, creating an enriching and culturally diverse global experience on campus.

The learning experience is enlivened by Catholic and Benedictine traditions of hospitality, stewardship, service and the lively engagement of faith and reason. A historic commitment to arts and culture creates a vibrant environment for creativity and community.

Macalester College

Admissions Office
1600 Grand Avenue
Saint Paul, MN 55105-1899
Admissions phone: (800) 231-7974
Admissions fax: (651) 696-6724
Admissions e-mail: admissions@macalester.edu
Admissions URL: www.macalester.edu/admissions/

 ## Admissions

Current student, 9/2003-Submit Date, May 2006

As a highly-selective liberal arts college, Macalester draws students from around the country and the world. This not only makes for a diverse environment on campus and in classes, but for an interesting admissions process. While a PF (prospective first-year) at Mac during my senior year, I met people from all over the country who were also interested in moving to Minnesota for their college years. It made moving from New York easier for me because I knew that there would be people from all over. Macalester places high emphasis on the campus visit and all the various activities contained therein. I think it is a key part of the admissions process—and when you visit, you should not only have an interview and take a tour, but also take time to meet students and sit in on a class.

Current student, 9/2003-Submit Date, May 2006

The admissions process was very simple and straightforward. Macalester College uses the Common Application with a short supplement for both incoming first-year and transfer students. The application process is explained on the web site (www.macalester.edu/admissions/applying/) and it can be submitted electronically or by snail mail. Macalester is a very competitive school and the essay is a very important part of the application. They are looking for students who have a strong interest in service, diversity, internationalism and academic excellence. An applicant should have a high GPA and good test scores as well as an interest in the school's mission: "Macalester is committed to being a preeminent liberal arts college with an educational program known for its high standards for scholarship and its special emphasis on internationalism, multiculturalism, and service to society." Early Decision applications are due in mid-November and regular applications are due in mid-January.

The school says: Students may also submit the Macalester Application online or by mail.

Current student, 9/2005-Submit Date, May 2006

Macalester, as it becomes more and more well known, is becoming much more selective. The admissions process at Macalester was no more harsh than at any other school to which I applied, and they always seemed much more friendly in my dealings with them. After I got in, they had students call my house to see if I had any questions they could answer. In terms of advice for getting in, show how much you really want to come here. Take the chance in your "Why Macalester" essay to demonstrate how much you want to come.

Current student, 9/2003-Submit Date, February 2006

The admissions process is fairly typical for a selective liberal arts school. Several essays are required; including one on why you would like to attend Macalester. Originality and the quality of an applicant's prose are important factors, as writing is a crucial part of the academic nature of Macalester College. Macalester also seeks students who believe in or share some of the values that Macalester, itself, espouses. Showing the admissions staff that your passions are consistent with the core values of the college is important, as the school seeks out students who will support and become part of the colleges mission of internationalism, multiculturalism, civic engagement and academic excellence.

Current student, 9/2005-Submit Date, July 2006

Macalester looks for smart students, but grades alone will not necessarily get you in. The focus is on diversity of experience, so if you studied abroad in high school or travelled out of the country, that's a strong selling point. Macalester is also very committed to egalitarianism and environmental awareness, so expressing interest in these topics during the interview process will earn extra points in admissions. Being broad-minded can be more important than your GPA. Early Decision strengthens the chance of admission; the college has a greater incentive to accept students during the first round because it improves the yield. This is a greater concern for colleges looking to gain recognition than those that already have a reputation for selectivity. As with any school, enthusiasm and optimism are strong selling points for students.

 ## Academics

Current student, 9/2003-Submit Date, May 2006

I love the academic life at Mac. Professors respect students and their opinions. Generally classes are small and discussion-oriented, but vary depending on the subject and course level. Ultimately, I have found all of my professors and classes to be engaging and challenging without being cutthroat. At Macalester, I have learned valuable skills that allow me to read and write critically and I know these skills will allow me to succeed in any field I choose. Getting into classes is also very simple. Registration is done online and by seniority, but almost all professors have an informal waitlist system if a class fills before you can register for it. The workload at Mac is substantial, but it's college, so it is supposed to be.

Current student, 9/2003-Submit Date, May 2006

I transferred to Macalester College my sophomore year. I was thoroughly impressed by the facilities and small class sizes. Professors did not have office hours because they were always available. Every department had a weekly department social get-together, usually tea and snacks, to encourage dialogue outside of class. Professors were focused on the students and not on their research; however, they encouraged students to participate in research during lab, January term and summer research programs. The classes were very challenging and required a lot of studying. Despite the heavy workload, I still had time to be very involved in athletics, student newspaper, and complete an internship. I completed my cousework in three and a half years because I was able to take all the classes I needed when I wanted to take them. Some professors were more popular and I had to beg to get in, but they gladly opened up spots, espe-

Read all of Vault's College Surveys at **www.vault.com/college**—get complete surveys on 100s of colleges and universities, expert advice on applicaton essays and more.

VAULT CAREER LIBRARY 381

cially to seniors. Many upper-level classes had less than 10 students and the professors were tough graders but rewarded students for their hard work. It was difficult to skip class when there were only six people in the class, but no one wanted to skip because the classes were very interesting and stimulating. Overall, I enjoyed the challenging workload but I had to work to get A's.

Current student, 9/2005-Submit Date, May 2006

Every class I've taken at Macalester has been amazing. I'm only a first-year and I've been able to get into some very exclusive classes. During registration, you might not be able to get in, but if you pester the teacher and get on the waiting list early you can usually get in to the class. Some professors grade harder than others. The economics department is notorious for being particularly harsh graders.

Current student, 9/2002-Submit Date, May 2006

The classes I've taken at Macalester have generally been exactly what I was looking for. Most of them are a great mix of interesting texts, engaging professors and lively class discussions.

As you'll find at any school, there is certainly a mixed bag of professors and classes—in terms of quality, ease and energy. I have one professor who is literally able to bring tears to students' eyes when he tells stories and displays his passion for what and who he studies. And I've had professors who bore a class to tears. Thankfully though, I've found that most of the professors I don't enjoy much have either just been visiting faculty, or have since moved on from the college. The tenured and tenure-track faculty have been great in their insights and ability to teach, which makes me think Macalester must be doing something right.

As far as grading and ease go, I've never been one to concern myself with it so much, and I think most Mac students are the same way. You'll have some professors who demand a lot, and have others who are more lax. This is simply how colleges operate. Workload has been more consistent, but still varies a lot—as it should. The great thing about a small school like Macalester is that you're almost assured of knowing someone who has had a certain class or professor before, so you can easily get specific advice and tips when it comes to register.

Current student, 9/2005-Submit Date, July 2006

Macalester is a small liberal arts college, so with the exception of one class (Drugs and Society), there are no more than 40 students in a classroom. However, you will only find 40 students in popular intro. classes, such as Psychology 101; the typical class size is between 15 and 20 students. The small size of the classes is not an indicator of difficulty for getting into them; professors are usually more than willing to let in whoever wants to join a class. Language classes are capped at 20 students, and they all include language labs with a native speaker that are capped at 10 students. The classes are challenging with a manageable workload, with the exception of some of the upper-division economics courses and Organic Chemistry, which can be described as stressful at the very least. Generally professors make an effort to keep their classes engaging, and are very accessible by e-mail and office hours. Grading varies from teacher to teacher, but in general any hard worker can manage a 3.0. While some students will toil away for eight hours a night in the library, most Mac students will do fine with an average of three or four hours of work a day. The downside of being a very liberal college is that many of the history and literature classes deal with unheard perspectives and voices, which at a small college doesn't leave much room for the classics such as intro-level American history. Another negative aspect is that there are a lot of visiting professors, making it difficult to form strong and lasting relationships with professors. However, there is a lot of choice as to which classes a student can take, so the educational experience can be almost entirely decided by the individual.

 Employment Prospects

Current student, 9/2003-Submit Date, May 2006

Macalester graduates are extremely prepared for graduate schools and have the reputation to compete with and excel over students from other universities. While at Macalester, many students participate in internships and research, which are set up through the internship office, the department or alumni con-

nections. Macalester students have a great reputation for being hard-working and motivated and are well respected. Internships and research allow students to build up their résumés and get great letters of recommendation. Students go to top graduate programs in their respected fields, such as academia, medicine, law and business at schools like Harvard, Yale, UC-Berkeley, and Mayo Medical School. Macalester ranks high for schools whose students participate in service programs, such as Teach for America, AmeriCorps and Peace Corps, due to Macalester's multicultural, international and service-oriented mission.

Current student, 9/2005-Submit Date, July 2006

When I decided to go to Macalester, my mom joked that it was a one-way ticket to grad school, because no one wants to hire a college grad from a liberal arts college. At Macalester, that just isn't the case. The most sought-after graduates are the economics majors who are often hired for investment banking starting at $120K a year. Politically minded students usually have no trouble making connections that come in handy after graduation; over half of the interns at the Minnesota capital are Mac students. Despite its size, Macalester has a big internship and career office. The internship office has connections all over the state, and doing for-credit work for a company or non-governmental organization often leads to a job offer. The career office keeps interested students up to date on job news, and helps to write and build résumés. Macalester students are known for strong principles, which make the graduates more marketable to nonprofits. The downside of Macalester is that the name is not as recognizable in places outside the Midwest. This is changing quickly, being twice named the hottest liberal arts college and twice ranking in the Top 25 liberal arts colleges in the country shows that Macalester is increasing in prestige. The degree is becoming more recognizable nationwide, and even globally thanks in no small part to Kofi Annan of the UN, our most famous alumnus.

> **The school says:** "Macalester has been ranked in the Top 25 for a decade."

Current student, 9/2004-Submit Date, May 2006

Mac is not very popular among high-end corporations and companies, but it is quite famous among nonprofits, politicians on the local level, and employers in the Twin Cities area. It is a challenge to secure a high-paying job outside the Twin Cities right after graduation; Mac students go into a variety of fields, including nonprofit work, investment banking, consulting, teaching, political campaigning and journalism. It all depends on one's major and interests.

Alumnus/a, 9/1999-5/2003, January 2004

This is a good school for advanced studies, like PhDs and JDs. In my opinion, the career department is not so great. Very few companies recruit and for business in those companies you have to have a phenomenal GPA in economics and at least a minor in math. Of course, those companies are really prestigious. However, most of the students are on their own.

 Quality of Life

Current student, 9/2003-Submit Date, May 2006

Macalester guarantees housing for students for the first two years and also requires that they live on campus. The college also provides some upperclassman housing, but cannot house all upperclassmen. Many choose to live off campus in nearby housing units with friends. The campus is relatively tiny, tucked into a pretty residential neighborhood, with Grand Avenue bisecting campus (Grand is lined with shops and cafes). Historic Summit Avenue forms the northern border of campus. Summit, is home to the governor's mansion, Garrison Keilor's home, F. Scott Fitzgerald's house, Mac's president's house, some beautiful bike and roller-blading trails, and the longest stretch of preserved Victorian houses in the country. Summit stretches all the way from the Mississippi River to downtown Saint Paul. Macalester has one dining hall in our five-year-old campus center. All students who live on campus eat in this cafeteria, known as Café Mac. The food is very good and varied, as it comes from all over the world.

Current student, 9/2003-Submit Date, May 2006

First- and second-year students must live on campus in rather large dorm rooms. There is a campus center with the only cafeteria and grill. Surprisingly the food is good and incorporates dishes from every continent. Students complain that the food gets old by the end of sophomore year, but that is to be expected at any school. The campus center and Bateman Plaza are centrally located and help create a community where students always come to eat together and hang out, rain or shine. The campus is in an urban area, so safety is always an issue but I always felt safe walking around campus. There is a Safe Walk service where escorts will take you to and from anywhere within a one-mile radius of campus, 24/7. The science facilities are generally nice and the campus is totally wireless. The science building is high-tech and nice with spacious labs, for example there are individual chemistry hoods for each student. The athletic building is very old but a new building will be completed by 2008. The art and humanities building is also older and will be renovated after the athletic building is completed. The library is a great place to hang out and study. The staff is very helpful and knowledgeable and if the library does not have a book or journal, the University of Minnesota or consortium of MN liberal arts schools has it and can lend it to Macalester through interlibrary loan for free.

Current student, 9/2003-Submit Date, February 2006

The college is a small, inclusive, almost familial community within the greater Twin Cities area. Thus you have the benefits of a small school without feeling completely isolated from the outside world. The Twin Cities are easy to get around using either car or public transportation and there is a bustling metropolis to be discovered. The cafeteria food is pretty good and the campus is beautiful both when it's warm and in bloom or when it's covered in snow.

Current student, 9/2005-Submit Date, July 2006

The housing isn't bad for dormrooms, students are required to live on campus for two years and most stay for the whole four. Two of the three freshman dorms have an exercise room equipped with cable TVs, and all of the dorms have a kitchen and lounge on every floor. First-year students are housed with members of their first-year course, special seminars only open to freshmen. This creates a feeling of unity on each floor; because each floor usually houses two first-year courses, it's very easy to get to know everyone. The beds are lofted over the desks in the freshman dorms, which creates more floor space. Students are given the choice of getting a single, which looks like a closet but offers the advantage of privacy. The upperclassman dorms are much like the freshman dorms, but quieter and more attractive. The campus is very small, from the farthest dorm to the farthest classroom is less than half a mile. Some of the buildings are connected by skyways, which becomes important when the Minnesota winter kicks in. While there have been a few muggings off campus near a sketchy liquor store, the campus, itself, is very secure and the surrounding neighborhood is quite safe. The fine arts are a little lacking, there's only one dance studio and one rehearsal hall. With the exception of the drama department, performances are generally not well-attended. The gym is like a maze, but it's being renovated. The food at Cafe Mac is pretty good for cafeteria food, Indian and Mexican food are staples. When eating at the cafeteria gets boring, there's a great Thai restaurant right next to campus, and for less money there's a Domino's and Subway down the street. The neighborhood is ritzy, so things tend to be a little overpriced in the area.

 Social Life

Current student, 9/2003-Submit Date, May 2006

Macalester has no Greek system. Our social scene is hard to describe because, ultimately, every student who comes to Macalester needs to carve out the social scene that will make him or her most happy. As on most college campuses, there is partying, but if that is not your scene, there is no pressure to do anything you don't want to do. Similarly, if you want to have a million friends or just a few, that is cool, too. Macalester has over 90 clubs—something for everyone. There are always lectures, concerts, dances and other events happening on campus. Because we have access to not one but two great cities, there are tons of concerts, restaurants, shops and clubs that students can and do utilize off campus.

Current student, 9/2003-Submit Date, May 2006

Most students enjoy their social lives at Macalester. The school has a lot of liberal students; however, there is a club called College Republicans (total members: three). The social scene is largely on campus or in nearby off-campus houses. Many students drink but not heavily; a recent health services poll showed that most students have fewer than three drinks when they do drink. Bars are within walking distance (O'Garas, the Tap and Plums) yet seniors enjoy going to downtown Minneapolis or Uptown on the weekends. However, going off campus is expensive, so most students prefer the on-campus parties. There is a variety of restaurants (Thai, Tibetan, Mexican, Turkish) on Grand Ave. near the campus and even better options accessible by bike and bus. Most students eat all their meals at the cafeteria because they are on the meal plan. The dating scene is interesting. As is common at most schools, there are many different kinds of relationships among students: girls dating girls, girls dating guys and guys dating guys. Athletes tend to date other athletes, not because they are groupies but because they are around each other so much. There is no Greek life but there are language houses and a veggie co-op that students in which can live. Sports teams function similar to Greek life; they tend to live together off campus and host themed parties and progressives. Student clubs host dances on the weekends and hundreds of students attend soccer games in the fall. Overall, Macalester is a great place to be for four years! I loved it!

Current student, 9/2003-Submit Date, February 2006

There are numerous bars in both Saint Paul and Minneapolis. Several are within walking distance of Macalester. Some favorites are the Groveland Tap, O'Gara's, Plums and the Turf Club. There is a historic theater a couple blocks from campus that shows great films. In the absence of any fraternities or sororities the on-campus social scene can be tame. Many upperclassmen and women live off campus, so there are off-campus house parties every weekend.

During the week, the Coffee News Cafe is a very popular destination for food, beer or coffee. It's got a great atmosphere, an uber-chic staff and is always packed with Macalester students. In general, Macalester's location is ideal for its proximity to almost everything a student could need or want.

 The School Says

Macalester has the world covered. Students comes from all 50 states and 90 countries to share in an experience defined by rigorous scholarship, global perspective and purposful attention to teaching. They share a sense of passion and enthusiasm about what they're learning. Math teams frequently qualify for the International Collegiate Programming Contest. The debate program has been nationally ranked among the Top 10 for decades. The labs are alive with student research aimed to address real issues ranging from medical treatment to solar cells.

The academic experience is distinctly international and intentionally local. Students benefit from living and learning in a community of bright students from all over the U.S. and around the world. Macalester cultivates the ability to succeed in a work environment defined by new challenges and change. Graduates enter the workforce with real experience in a global community, prepared to succeed in their chosen fields.

Read all of Vault's College Surveys at www.vault.com/college—get complete surveys on 100s of colleges and universities, expert advice on applicaton essays and more.

VAULT CAREER LIBRARY   383

University of Minnesota

Admissions Office
240 Williamson Hall
231 Pillsbury Drive S.E.
Minneapolis, MN 55455-0213
Admissions phone: (612) 625-2008 or (800) 752-1000
Admissions fax: (612) 626-1693
Admissions e-mail: admissions@tc.umn.edu
Admissions URL: admissions.tc.umn.edu/

Note: *The school has chosen not to review the student surveys submitted.*

 ## Admissions

Alumnus/a, Graphic Design, 8/2005-1/2006, October 2006

The admissions process began by applying online to a particular program. Once you fill out all the paperwork and send in all transcripts from your high school, you wait for an answer back, which for me took about four months. I then had to apply to my major. So I went to get advice from the guidance counselor in my college of the UofM. She helped me narrow down my major and gave me everything I needed to help me apply for my major. After the meeting, I applied online to get into graphic design. During the meeting I found out that only 100 students made it in and they only accept in the fall, I also learned it was only a four-year program, so if I had taken all my generals first then it did not matter, I still had to be there for four years. After completing my major application I had to write an essay on what I thought graphic design was, what I wanted out of this program and school, and where I wanted to be when I was done. After that I waited another two months to find out I got in. I then had to attend an orientation and then that was it. They were very helpful.

Alumnus/a, Business, 9/2002-5/2006, September 2006

The admissions process for the business school was the most competitive of all the schools on campus. Our class was about 400 students out of several thousand applicants. The program and school are expanding in the next few years to accommodate the growing demand to attend the Carlson School, but will still be competitive with admissions.

The admissions process was the UofM application, and just indicating that the Carlson School was the first choice.

They like to admit well-rounded students. Having a 4.0 GPA is not enough. You need to be involved in school or the community, have good test scores, and have a high GPA (they have turned down valedictorians because they weren't involved enough.)

Current student, Communications, 9/2003-Submit Date, April 2006

There were no essays to get into this school. Now it is a lot more difficult to get into the U. Recently, I heard that to get accepted into the College of Liberal Arts, the average GPA was 3.7 and ACT average was 26. It was no where near that when I applied and was accepted, and that was only three years ago. However, do not be turned away by that because if you have a strong record of extracurricular activities as well as a solid course schedule (i.e., Calculus over no math, just more difficult than super easy), you will be good to go. Apply early, as it will be more beneficial for you will find out earlier. Admissions is not a difficult process, unlike other schools. Simply fill out the application and you are done. It is easier now as well, since a great deal of stuff is online, so it isn't as hectic as it was years ago.

Current student, 9/2004-Submit Date, September 2005

Applying to the UofM was a fairly simple process as only forms need to be filled out. No essays or teacher referrals were necessary. While the university becoming more and more selective, an average student can be accepted based extracurriculars and choice of college (e.g., General College).

Current student, 8/2004-Submit Date, April 2005

The process for admission to the U was fairly straightforward. The process included the standard application. There was no essay portion to the application Even with average grades and being a transfer student, acceptance was not a issue. However, as a transfer student, I have had some difficulty making m transfer credits apply within the structure that the university has set up.

Current student, 9/2004-Submit Date, March 2005

The admissions process is tough here at the U. The best advice is to get a head start—apply in January or sooner. The admissions questionnaire is long, but yc should take great concern in answering the essay portion to the best of your abity. As with many other schools, the university admissions board greatly value involved students (community and school). Volunteer participation is also see as a large plus. The essays are very broad questions, yet they expect a thorough answer. There are no interviews in the admissions process here at the U. Th selectivity is very tight, but less strict in the beginning of the selection process

Current student, 1/2001-Submit Date, October 2004

The admissions process was easy, but required a lot of running around. I applie to the university and was accepted, then had to apply to the program I wanted attend, which required an entirely different application process. The proces isn't bad as long as you read the documentation—everything you need to do explained somewhere. The college staff isn't always helpful, though, becaus they don't always know what else needs to be done. If you are going to appl be sure to check and double-check with different people to make sure you hav everything done that you need to do, then read every piece of paper they giv you to make sure no one forgot to mention something.

Current student, 9/2003-Submit Date, March 2004

I participated in on-the-spot admission. This option was only extended to stu dents who participated in the post-secondary education option, which allow high school students to take courses at a university. It required an applicatio and short interest essay with activity résumé. Other information they considere was an AAR or SAR score, which was a combination of your ACT or SAT scor and your class rank in high school. Minimum requirements for these scores a set by each individual college with the university. I was admitted on the spo whereas most students go through the typical application process and wait unt spring to find out.

 ## Academics

Current student, 9/2004-Submit Date, September 2005

Academic quality is the top priority at the UofM. While popular classes do fi quickly and end up, as enormous lecture crowds, the discussion sections ar small and make a student's questions easy to answer. I've yet to have a profes sor I didn't like as an instructor. They were all extremely knowledgeable an eager to teach their subjects and help out their students. They are easy to kee in touch with through e-mail, phone or office walk-ins. Workloads vary fror class to class, though it is always made clear within the first week how muc work is expected of a student. Grades are typically curved, usually to the bene fit of all.

Current student, 8/2004-Submit Date, April 2005

There is a wide variety of courses that can be taken as the university is so large However, with the large campus size there is also difficulty in getting qualit instructors in some of the general courses. Many of the professors don't hav the greatest English speaking abilities. This can make it difficult to get question nswered in an efficient manner. Another disadvantage of the large university mosphere is that the class sizes, especially in the general education courses, eflect the overall size of the university. It is not unusual to attend courses that e well above 100 students per classroom.

lumnus/a, Graphic Design, 8/2005-1/2006, October 2006

he Graphic Design Program had very small class sizes, which was helpful in earning. The quality of the classes was not that impressive. We did not learn at much or as much as I thought we should have. It was hard to get into class-s since they were limited in how many students could get into them. The grad-g was very standard. In graphic design, they look more at quality of work ather than completion. The workload was huge. I would be up until 3 or 4 in e morning doing projects. I guess workload depends on how many classes you ke and what kind of classes. You don't want to have more than three DHA ourses, which are the design courses.

lumnus/a, Business, 9/2002-5/2006, September 2006

he program provides a broad liberal arts background the first one or two years, nd then gives a broad overview of the different functional business areas rough a set of core classes (Financial Acct., Managerial Acct., Finance, 1arketing, HR, Operations/Supply Chain, Management, Communications, and 1IS), and then allows you to focus more on your major.

enerally class quality is quite high. Professors are former/current business eaders, mostly from the Twin Cities area. They are passionate about the sub-cts they teach and are very knowledgeable. There tends to be a bit of grade aflation overall, but the students are all high-caliber and work very hard, so in art, deserve the high grades they get.

Workload depends on the class. Almost every class has at least one group proj-ct of some sort. Most classes have a project or large paper to do, and some have veekly/bi-weekly assignments.

Current student, Communications, 9/2003-Submit Date, April 2006

am majoring in public relations. However, I began my studies in the College f Agricultural, Food and Environmental Sciences (COAFES). This was con-enient as I earned quite a bit of money in scholarships. I soon transferred to 'LA, into the School of Journalism, and entered into the program (only 25 per-ent of people who apply are admitted). The classes were good, of course there vere a few that I could do without but that happens with everything. Grading vas fair—most professors will grade on a curve or help you out with extra cred-. However, if you attend class on a regular basis that is not needed.

Current student, 9/2004-Submit Date, March 2005

As for any student in college, you can pretty much determine your own work-oad. You are able to sign up for whatever classes you please, but that is the hard art here. There are so many it may become overwhelming. The academic pro-ram here is great. All the teachers are well educated and provide very intensive lasses. When signing up for classes, they go by alphabetical order and grade. 'ou don't really have a choice to register early if you are not in the designated irst spot. Register as quickly as possible in your category to ensure your best hance at getting the classes you want. You can choose A through F or pass/fail. 'ou are only allowed a certain number of pass/fail classes in your college career, o choose them wisely.

Current student, 1/2001-Submit Date, October 2004

he classes vary from huge lecture-hall classes (for required and popular class-s), to tiny classes with eight students and a teacher. Overall, I've been very avorably impressed with the quality of the teachers at the University of Minnesota. Even in the large classes, they are usually excellent at making the ubject interesting and offering their students personal attention. I've had sev-ral teachers in classes with over 60 students who not only memorized every stu-lent's name, but still remember us when we run into them on campus, two years fter we had their classes. The academic expectations are standard: some class-s are tougher than others, there's really no coasting, though, in any class. You re expected to work hard for your grades, and they seem to be increasingly strict bout giving out A's. I get the impression that the teachers were lectured recent-y about grade inflation and have decided to remedy the situation by making it ougher to get those A's.

It can be difficult to get in to popular classes in any program, and timely regis-tration and advanced class standing help a lot. I've heard some students com-plain because they were unable to get a class that they needed to fulfill a pre-requisite, which resulted in their program taking longer than it otherwise would have. I haven't had too many problems with this, although it has come up. Generally, if you show up on the first day of class, professors will let you in if there is any way they can do so. The workload is heavy, but I think it depends on what sort of grades you want. I've noticed that a lot of students find plenty of time to play.

 Employment Prospects

Alumnus/a, Graphic Design, 8/2005-1/2006, October 2006

During orientation they showed three-inch binders of many employers that they work with to help you find jobs. They have one lady in particular who helps you find jobs after college or even internships. They were helpful during orientation, so it seems like they would be there if you need anything.

Alumnus/a, Business, 9/2002-5/2006, September 2006

Undergraduate Business Career Center does a fabulous job at helping students find employment after graduation. The Minneapolis area has a large number of corporate headquarters and businesses that interview on campus, and they are focusing on bringing in more out-of-town companies as well. Most employers in the area know the Carlson School and openly admit that the students they get from there are among the best they recruit.

Current student, 9/2004-Submit Date, March 2005

There are many different schools within this university. Depending on what you're interested in determines in which school you will enroll. Carlson School of Business is here and is one of the best business schools in the nation. Graduates from this school have been shown to make six-figure incomes their first year after graduation. There are internships and recruiting all over the cam-pus, not to mention countless career shadow opportunities and workshops. The alumni network is always available to speak to with any questions a student may have.

Current student, 1/2001-Submit Date, October 2004

The University of Minnesota has a good reputation with employers, especially in journalism, health sciences, business management and political science. It is one of the Big 10 schools, and has the second-largest student body in the coun-try. The quality of the education here is widely respected, and the alumni are unusually active on behalf of the school. Every program seems to have a lot of community ties, and your teachers are often people with real-world experience and industry ties, who will tell you about jobs as they come up, and get you in touch with prospective employers in industries you are interested in working for. The university actively encourages students to pursue study abroad and intern-ships, and has a huge network of resources available for students who want to do so. The Twin Cities also have a thriving business community and one of the best economies in the country, so jobs here are (relatively) plentiful.

Alumnus/a, 9/1996-5/2000, April 2004

Excellent career services center. The Twin Cities metro area has so many large employers headquartered there, such as 3M, General Mills, Northwest Airlines, U.S. Bank, Medtronic and Target Corporation. In addition, there are two large regional investment banks based in Minneapolis, and there is a decent consult-ing presence in Minneapolis with McKinsey & Co. and Deloitte Consulting. I had three internships in college and found each of them through the career serv-ices center. There are many interviews on campus, and the selection process is automated over the Internet. Since the University of Minnesota is in Minneapolis, the ties to the business community are very tight. The ability to go to New York and do investment banking is improving as more and more students find ways to work out there. The alumni base is very loyal, and it's just a mat-ter of time before more investment banks recruit on campus. In school, I received calls from Lehman Brothers and Goldman Sachs to interview without even expressing interest in either bank.

Read all of Vault's College Surveys at **www.vault.com/college**–get complete surveys on 100s of colleges and univer-sities, expert advice on applicaton essays and more.

VAULT CAREER LIBRARY **385**

Quality of Life

Alumnus/a, Graphic Design, 8/2005-1/2006, October 2006

The quality of life around the University of Minnesota was great. There was a very diverse group, which was wonderful to be around to learn about other cultures. They treat every type of life issue, they had church, sports, academic clubs, counselors, other guidance, family problems, rape clinics, abuse clinics and homes. They had everything possible that you could think of. I stayed in a co-op (not dorms), but I visited the dorms and they were pretty average. They were small, clean, and did not allow any alcoholic beverages in the dorm, which was good. The campus was just beautiful all year round even in the winter. The buildings are old fashioned and yet there are some modern ones. There is a lot of history behind this college. The crime was low, but when anything did happen everyone was notified that same day through e-mail, just to keep us aware so we could watch out for anything suspicious. All in all, it was a great school.

Alumnus/a, Business, 9/2002-5/2006, September 2006

The business school currently resides in one building, but they are building a second to accommodate the growing program. Overall, UofM campus is large, spread over the Mississippi, but is very beautiful. Most on-campus housing is nice, mostly for freshmen, and almost all residence halls are on the other side of the river from Carlson.

Current student, Communications, 9/2003-Submit Date, April 2006

It's a good campus, nice and spread out with tons of people so you can always make new friends if you would like. There are a lot of great college-atmosphere restaurants on campus, as well as some fast-food restaurants (Chipotle!) and there are a few bars that college kids hang out. They just redesigned The Library (a bar) so that is once again a popular hang-out spot whatever night of the week. They also have a lot of really great drink specials, so you can't resist.

Current student, 9/2004-Submit Date, September 2005

Housing is terrific at the university. Dorms are convenient with there own cafeterias and laundry rooms, an excellent option for students. There are many apartment complexes and houses available for rent as well being either on campus or just off it. All are near either the metro transit bus line or the university bus line (which is free!). The UMPD are everywhere, as well as blue panic buttons, should one need it. There is also an escort service that runs 24/7 should a student wish someone to accompany him/her to and from classes. These are especially useful for night classes.

Current student, 9/2004-Submit Date, March 2005

The housing for students at the university is awesome. All of the on-campus housing is located in what we call the "super block." It is in the direct center of the campus so the freshmen and other kids on campus do not have to worry about the overwhelmingly large campus. Housing costs are very reasonable. When you live on campus (for most all of the locations) you must include a meal plan with your costs. The meals here are great; don't worry about old cafeteria food, this is much better! The crime prevention is amazing. There has not been a day where I have seen less than five cops patrolling. If there is a crime that occurs, the prevention squad sends e-mails to all students to notify them and provide them with a safe feeling of assurance. All of the facilities are well-kept and this is an absolutely beautiful campus.

Social Life

Alumnus/a, Business, 9/2002-5/2006, September 2006

Very healthy social scene. Many events on campus if you don't like going out, such as late-nights at Coffman Union. The three main areas to go out are Stadium Village (by the Superblock dorms) with Sally's and Stub and Herbs,

Dinkytown with the Library, Burrito Loco, and Blarney (this area is busiest on Thursday nights, and on hockey/basketball nights) and West Bank/Seven Corners, with Sgt. Preston's, Corner Bar, Bullwinkles, Grandmas, and Town Hall (another popular Thursday night area). Campus is also close to downtown with many other going out options.

Current student, Communications, 9/2003-Submit Date, April 2006

Campus bars are fun, downtown bars are hard to get into because they have strict dress code. There is a great deal of events happening on campus and throughout the city. Restaurants are mediocre; there are basically a bunch of chain (Chili's, Applebees), but not too many individually owned.

Current student, 9/2004-Submit Date, September 2005

The restaurants, bars and clubs abound, not only on campus, but also in downtown Minneapolis, which is only a few minutes away. Everyone loves Annie's Parlor in Dinkytown close to the McDonald's that stays open into the wee hours of the morning should anyone be hungry at those hours. The authentic Hong Kong Noodle is the most popular Asian food restaurant on campus. Both Spin and Escape, two nightclubs, are 18+ on Thursdays and are a short bus ride away. There are hundreds of clubs to join directly on campus from the Equestrian Club to Ballroom Dance Club, to Shotokan Karate. Immediately, at the beginning of the year, the Greek system asks for new pledges for their sororities and fraternities, making it very easy to join.

Current student, 8/2004-Submit Date, April 2005

The great part about being in Minneapolis and Saint Paul is that there is never shortage of activities. There are great places for nightlife, lots of people to meet, cultural events, sporting events and even lots of free or inexpensive things to do. I am not very familiar with the Greek system on campus (I'm not a member), but I know that their housing takes up about two city blocks.

Current student, 9/2004-Submit Date, March 2005

The school is located right near downtown Minneapolis where there are endless opportunities for different nightlife, whether you attend sporting events or music events at the Target Center or the Metrodome, or you hit up one of the hundreds of bars there. We are also close to many malls including the great Mall of America. There are also many bars and clubs within walking distance such as the Steak Knife or Blarney's. The Greek system here is quite large and is always recruiting new members. If there is an event at the U, you will know about it either from the graffiti chalk all over the sidewalks on campus or one of the thousands of flyers. The school spirit here is absolutely amazing, so get ready to be full of maroon and gold if you attend this school!

Current student, 8/2003-Submit Date, March 2004

Social life is great around here. There are new restaurants all the time, and there are many cafes and more. There are bars and other meetings places; they are generally placed on the outskirts of the university, but that is fine. The Greek system is pretty bad around here, as you can generally only get into the parties if you are on a list. One can always find a party on the northern side of campus and the university sponsors many events aimed at helping you find yourself at the university and develop new friendships and relationships with other people. The university has other leadership programs you could get into to plan these events as well.

Current student, 9/2003-Submit Date, March 2004

The Greek system at Minnesota is more of an addition to the social scene than a requirement. There are many bars and restaurants on campus, as well as in the downtown area only a few blocks from campus. Carlson offers clubs and organizations for every interest. We also have two business fraternities, in addition to 22 social fraternities and 13 social sororities.

Mississippi State University

The Office of Admissions & Scholarships
P.O. Box 6334
Mississippi State, MS 39762-6334
Admissions phone: (662) 325-2224
Admissions fax: (662) 325-1MSU
Admissions e-mail: admit@msstate.edu
Admissions URL: admissions.msstate.edu

 ## Admissions

Current student, Health, 8/2004-Submit Date, April 2007

Mississippi State has a wonderful admissions process! Their enrollment counselors and Roadrunner (student recruiters) make coming to a big college an easy adjustment. They were friendly and extremely helpful. When I came for my senior campus tour and college visit the admissions staff made my trip a wonderful experience.

Current student, Business, 8/2003-Submit Date, April 2007

The admissions process is pretty awesome. They have made it even better since I applied by making everything online. They also require you to do some scholarship stuff even to apply, so that really helps out up front to go ahead and already start looking at what scholarships you can get by attending.

> **The school says:** "If you wish to apply for scholarships, an online résumé is required along with admission to the university. While the scholarship résumé can be completed as part of the application process, the résumé is not required for admission to the university; only for scholarship consideration."

Not to mention, this also makes it easier for whenever you come down for a visit. You don't have to go over and talk to all these different people about trying to get scholarship money, because it has already been taken care of when you completed the online scholarship stuff. Probably the best part of the admissions process though is when you come down for your visit. Everyone is very personable. You aren't put in a big group with all these people. You meet with an admissions counselor one-on-one so you can really be more specific with your needs or wants. Another great part is getting a tour of campus. One of the Roadrunners, or student recruiters, will give you a tour of campus. They can be as detailed as you'd like, or if you just want to talk to them more about what the university is like it is a great opportunity for that.

Current student, Chemistry, 8/2006-Submit Date, April 2007

New dorms have been built on campus, called Northeast Village, and have been a huge pull for incoming students. Because of their high demand, it is very important to submit the housing application early. There are no interviews or essay requirements in the admissions process. Another important piece of advice is to keep up with all deadlines. The final application in the process is a scholarship application; after it is submitted, the Office of Admissions Scholarships at MSU grants scholarship money. However, if the scholarship application is not submitted by the deadline, scholarship money cannot be given. MSU has an Honors Program that accepts students based on ACT score and GPA. If accepted, these students are required to take at least one honors class per year.

> **Regarding scholarship application deadlines, the school says:** "Scholarship priority dates are as follows:
>
> "Freshman: Distinguished Scholarships—December 1, 2006
> General Academic Scholarships—February 1, 2007
> Transfers: May 1, 2007"

Current student, Business, 8/2006-Submit Date, April 2007

First, you fill out the college application. Depending upon your grades, you ca automatically get scholarships. There is also a scholarship application you ca fill out based on your activities. There was no essay. This was the best colle application I had to fill out when applying to college.

> **Mississippi State says:** "Scholarship awards are based on review of academic credentials such as high school grades, ACT/SAT scores and/or college credit depending on the level of education completed, as well as honors and achievements submitted on the scholarship résumé."

Current student, Biology, 8/2003-Submit Date, April 2007

The admissions process is very easy. You go online to get the application a fill it out. If you want to receive a scholarship, you fill out the online schola ship résumé before the February deadline and you will be considered for a possible scholarship that you might be eligible for. The entire process is rel tively easy and is not too time consuming.

> **The school says:** "For scholarship consideration, admission to the university and receipt of a scholarship résumé is required prior to the appropriate priority date. Scholarship priority dates are: December 1, 2006 for freshman Distinguished Scholarships, February 1, 2007 for freshman General Academic Scholarships, and May 1, 2007 for transfers."

Current student, Communications, 8/2005-Submit Date, May 2006

The admissions process is very easy. You can apply online or call and they ca send an application. Just fill out the application and send in your high scho transcripts along with your medical records. It is a rolling admissions proce and you have until August 1 to apply.

> **MSU says:** "While there is no application deadline for admission, students are encouraged to apply no later than two weeks prior to the start of a semester."

Within two to four [weeks] you will find out about your acceptance. There is essay for the application, which makes it very simple. ACT or SAT scor required. Both your grades and standardized test scores are considered, if y did well in your academics, but not so well in the tests, you can still be admitte and vice versa. For more questions, you can check o www.admissions.msstate.edu

Current student, 8/2005-Submit Date, May 2006

The admissions process was quite simple. An admissions counselor came to m high school and explained the process to our senior class. She told us abo applying as soon as possible to be considered for scholarships and such and s also gave us advice on applying for housing in order to get into the dorm of o choice. The application was quite simple. There was nothing too intimidatin no essays, only questions about GPAs, parents' info, personal info and so o Selectivity is liberal. Admissions is quite simple.

 ## Academics

Current student, Business, 8/2003-Submit Date, April 2007

As for as the College of Business and Industry goes, it is really great. There a large number of students with business majors, and a large number who tak some business classes are engineering students. Classes are good with a num ber of different professors teaching classes, especially in your lower-level class es. Once you get further along, options for different professors decrease, but th is normally good because you will have a professor who has been teaching th class for several years, so he/she really knows what he/she is doing and you lear a lot. Grading always depends on the professor, as well as the subject matter. might be easy in one class, but really hard in another. Teachers are normall

...ally good about helping you if you need it. They all have office hours when ...ou can go by and meet with them, or will set up a time to meet with you if that ...n't possible. I have been very pleased with the program.

...urrent student, Chemistry, 8/2006-Submit Date, April 2007

...is very important to me to sign up for good teachers. I like to ask older stu-...nts who have taken the classes I need who the good teachers are. It is not hard ... find out who these teachers are and sign up for them. I have been pleased with ...e professors I have had my first year of college. They are very nice and very ...illing to meet outside of class to answer any questions. Some of my classes ...ave been very large (100 to 300 people), but that has not been a problem for ...e, and it wasn't hard to adjust.

> **Regarding class sizes, the school says:** "The average class size at State is 30 to 39 students. Approximately 3 percent of the classes at MSU have 100 plus students while 13 percent of the classes have less than 10 students enrolled. The 15:1 student-to-faculty ratio facilitates the working relationship necessary for students to succeed."

...ach student takes the number of hours that works best for him/her. Because I ...m a science major, I have to take many classes that require labs. Thus, I take ...wer classes because the labs usually require a lot of work and only give one ...redit hour. It is important to figure out how you will work the hardest and best ...nd to determine for yourself how heavy your workload needs to be. A student's ...eshman year is a good time to determine that.

...urrent student, Business, 8/2005-Submit Date, April 2007

...cademics are the most important thing to take into consideration when apply-...g for college. The point of going to college is to receive a quality education. ...he Business program at Mississippi State challenges students to think outside ...f the box and ask questions. Professors, administrators and peers encourage ...ach other to excel in everything. Mississippi State is a learning environment in ...hich leaders are produced through teamwork and effective life skills as well ...nowledge through the classroom. Finding the classes that you need to gradu-...te is not a difficult task; there are enough seats to accommodate each student.

...urrent student, Biology, 8/2003-Submit Date, April 2007

...he program is a quality program. There are very qualified professors who wish ... help each and every student. Except for the rare professor, each one is will-...g to take time to help the student learn. The material is hard, but the profes-...ors grade in a reasonable manner and the tests reflect what is taught in the class. ...here is more work in some classes than others, but there are some classes that ... have a considerable workload, which should be expected in a science based ...ajor. As far as the ease of getting popular classes, it's relatively easy with only ... small number of classes being unavailable. And even then, sometimes they can ...rce you into a class if it is absolutely necessary.

...urrent student, Communications, 8/2005-Submit Date, May 2006

...he communication department at Mississippi State has five emphases: broad-...asting, journalism, theater, communication studies and public relations. Those ...rograms offer excellent opportunities. Many of the public relation students ...ssist with on-campus activities, the journalism students write for the student ...aper and the broadcasting students participate in the student-run news program. ...he teachers and professors are eager to help the students and are highly quali-...ed. In the communication major, you find professors who have worked in the-...ter, written for papers or were news reporters and know what it takes to obtain ...ose jobs.

...ISU offers a variety of majors. The engineering department is one of the best ... Mississippi. We also offer professional golf management and meteorology ...mong other typical majors.

...urrent student, Business, 8/2003-Submit Date, May 2006

...he College of Business and Industry is a great school. We have wonderful ...eachers who are extremely helpful, both in class and out. Most classes are rel-...ively small allowing you to get to know your professor and classmates really ...ell. We also have a lot of teamwork that goes on in class. Lots of teachers like ... do group projects which help prepare you for corporate America.

Employment Prospects

Current student, Business, 8/2003-Submit Date, April 2007

Getting a job when you graduate is definitely one of the most important things about college. We really have it made, because of the Career Center on campus. They hold Career Day in both the spring and fall semesters. This is where they have anywhere from 100 to 150 different employers come from all over to recruit students. They may be looking for internships, part-time, co-op or full-time employment. This is a great way to go ahead and get some experience before you ever even graduate. This sets you up for a job when you do gradu-ate. There is also a high number of employers that contact the department heads of the different areas of study looking for graduating seniors. They typically have a good relationship with the university and have been pleased with MSU graduates who have worked for them already. Also talking with previous grad-uates in your area of study can help you find a job. They might even let you know that the company they are working for has a job opening, and could even help you get that job. The people here are just so helpful and will go out of their way to help you in any way that they can.

Current student, Biology, 8/2003-Submit Date, April 2007

Graduates of my school have pretty good prospects for getting hired. The chances are higher with engineering degrees, because our school is recognized for having a very good engineering program. We have a co-op program that is open to anyone and if you use it, it drastically improves your chances of getting hired by that company. There are several on-campus recruiting events for employers, so there are a lot of chances to find a job. Because of the atmosphere at Mississippi State, the alumni form a tight-knit group that most of the time will go out of its way to help a MSU graduate looking for a job.

Current student, Business, 8/2005-Submit Date, April 2007

The international business program is well-connected with several Fortune 500 companies, including the two main employers for our internships: FedEx and Citigroup. The alumni of the program are most helpful in placing new graduates and they have shown much success in the jobs they pursued after graduating from MSU.

Current student, 8/2005-Submit Date, April 2006

There are several opportunities available for internships and part-time jobs on campus. The recruiting department is wonderful and also offers opportunities and connections after graduating. We have great alumni who make networking and connections possible. Also I like how each department e-mails interview-ing opportunities of all kinds to every student in that major.

Current student, 8/2003-Submit Date, April 2006

My advisor is always e-mailing me with opportunities for on-campus employ-ment as well as with information about internships and available local work rel-evant to my major. The job fairs hosted here attract a large number of employ-ers and many majors have separate job fairs exclusively designed for their par-ticular field. The MSU alumni are always ready to help, whether it be donating scholarship money or giving graduates quality jobs.

Quality of Life

Current student, Chemistry, 8/2006-Submit Date, April 2007

Mississippi State life is known for its rather laid-back atmosphere and campus life. Freshmen are required to live on campus, but it is honestly unlike many other colleges in the country: new dorms are still being built in the Northeast Village. These dorms have their own bathrooms and carpet floors; they are in high demand for incoming students! There are many on-campus apartment com-plexes for older students, as well. I am unfamiliar with the dining services at MSU; I do know that there are meal plans available that accommodate many of MSU's students. Perry Cafeteria is an excellent facility, offering a huge variety of food for breakfast, lunch and dinner. There is a shuttle system on campus that is very helpful for transporting students to class or anywhere else they need to go on campus. There are about four different routes; these shuttles run all day Monday through Friday, and there is also a night route, which increases safety. I feel very safe here at MSU. Police are always on campus and willing to assist

Read all of Vault's College Surveys at **www.vault.com/college**–get complete surveys on 100s of colleges and univer-sities, expert advice on applicaton essays and more.

VAULT CAREER LIBRARY 389

students all the time. Students are given the on-campus police phone number for emergencies or any situations.

Current student, Business, 8/2005-Submit Date, April 2007

Starkville is a small town, but it offers a variety of housing options, both on and off campus. There are recently constructed residence halls that are a top-of-the-line option, and there are many apartment complexes nearby. Dining on campus is really good, actually. The cafeteria has diverse offerings and doesn't taste like traditional cafeteria food that most people avoid. There are also many venues in the Union for a quick lunch. The campus seems really safe—there's a police station near the center of campus, and I feel safe running alone even at night.

Current student, Communications, 8/2005-Submit Date, May 2006

Mississippi State has brand-new housing facilities. Ruby Hall just opened August of 2005 and three more will be completed within the next year. Each room has a private bathroom and shower and is very spacious. The new halls have a coffee shop, courtyard and trash shoot. The Honors facilities will also include classrooms for the students. The older housing is very clean, but offers communal showers over private accommodations. Cleaning staff is there daily to maintain the cleanliness. Washers and dryers are available for 75¢ to wash and 50¢ to dry.

Current student, 8/2004-Submit Date, May 2006

Housing on campus is awesome; we just built one of the nicest dorms in the SEC and in the process of building three more. We have lots of living space on our campus and lots of apartments are within walking distance. The campus is incredibly friendly and safe; I have no qualms about staying late on campus and walking back to where I live. There are lots of fun dining places around and Stromboli's has some of the best pizza in America. Starkville is a college town and you can feel it as soon as you pull in from Highway 12. The locals love us and I love living here.

Current student, 8/2003-Submit Date, April 2006

The on-campus housing at MSU is wonderfully accommodating, with sink areas, microwaves and large refrigerators in the rooms; newer residence halls are hotel-like with private rooms, private baths and wireless Internet access. The cafeteria features Southern "home-cooked" food options as well as a grill that caters to students' requests for omelets, quesadillas and the like. Crime is not a very big issue at all; I always feel safe walking to and from the library at night. Campus police patrol on bicycles and are located in the middle of campus.

> The school says: "In fall 2005, Ruby Hall, a new residence hall offering private baths, was opened. In fall 2006, S. Bryce Griffis Hall, an Honors residence hall, and Hurst Hall were opened and in spring 2007 an additional new residence hall will open, completing the new Northeast Village. To supplement the construction of new facilities, Mississippi State has renovated a number of current residence halls in the pursuit to provide exceptional options for all on-campus housing."

 # Social Life

Current student, Communications, 8/2003-Submit Date, April 2007

Social life is average. Compared to the small towns where most students come from, it's pretty good. There are about six or seven bars to visit. My favorites are Mugshots, Bin 612, and Old Venice. Lots of sandwich restaurants but not too many white tablecloth places to eat. Lenny's Sub Shop is the best place to eat, in my opinion. Greek system seems to still be doing well although it's obvious our new president hates Greeks and is making it harder for us to do any activities the way we used to, e.g., Bid Day and weekend parties for Homecoming and Super Bulldog Weekend.

Current student, Chemistry, 8/2006-Submit Date, April 2007

Greek life at Mississippi State is only about 20 percent. For those who do decide to participate in Greek life, it is positive experience. There are fraternity and sorority houses on campus where students eat, have chapter meetings and live. Together they participate in philanthropic events, as well as social events. There are also many clubs and honor societies available on campus, which encourage students to get involved in activities that promote their interests. There are also

fun restaurants and bars that are typical of most college towns. Athletic even[ ] are very popular on campus, always making all students, faculty, staff, alum[ ] and families excited on game days. The Junction is a grassy area in front [ ] Davis-Wade football stadium that was opened just last year, where families ar[ ] students can tailgate and celebrate at football games. Left-field lounge is situat[ ] ed in left field of the baseball stadium where different fraternities, alumni, [ ] other organizations have set up unique trailers to enjoy the baseball games. Th[ ] Hump is the basketball stadium where MSU basketball is played and is als[ ] where concerts or any major speakers or events are held.

Current student, Business, 8/2005-Submit Date, April 2007

Starkville, where Mississippi State is located, is a nice, quaint town nestled in t[ ] heart of Mississippi. On campus, we have over 300 student organization[ ] including academic, professional, international, Greek, honorary, fine and pe[ ] forming arts, political, recreational, religious, residence life and servic[ ] Throughout the year we have many different concerts. This year we have hos[ ] ed The Fray, The Blues Travelers and Ingram Hill, just to name a few. There a[ ] so many ways to become involved on campus and in the community that yo[ ] will always have something to look forward to!

Current student, 8/2005-Submit Date, May 2006

There are over 300 campus organizations at MSU. The Greek population is [ ] percent and all are welcomed, Greek or non-Greek. Athletics at MSU are a l[ ] of fun. We are Division One in all collegiate sports. The Sanderson Center [ ] our recreational center which offers and indoor gym, Olympic-size swimmi[ ] pool and rock climbing wall among others. On campus you can fish [ ] Chadwick Lake as long as you have your license. Popular organizations are th[ ] Student Association and Campus Activities Board, which bring concerts dow[ ] town in the Cotton District. The Bulldog Deli, Bin 612, Ole Venis and the Boar[ ] Head are popular hangouts for students.

Current student, 8/2005-Submit Date, May 2006

MSU social life is the perfect size. Our bars, which are located in downtow[ ] Starkville, are lots of fun. I know almost everyone in them when I go. Som[ ] local favorites are Rick's, Mug Shots and the Boar's Head. Starkille has som[ ] of the best "mom and pop" restaurants in Mississippi. The dating scene seen[ ] to be pretty good because most of the guys here are true Southern gentlemen! [ ] am a Zeta Tau Alpha. I love MSU's Greek system. All of the sororities and fra[ ] ternities get along with one another. We are not always in competition with on[ ] another.

 # The School Says

Established in 1878, Mississippi State University offers a diverse learning atmosphere that nurtures the dreams and goals of our students. From the classroom to our residence halls, MSU supports the overall development of students by supplying them with the advantages they need to lead successful lives.

State of Mind

Serving over 16,000 students, MSU awards baccalaureate, master's, specialist's, and doctoral degrees. We have approximately 80 majors through our eight colleges and nearly 85 percent of our faculty hold terminal degrees. Our 15-to-1 student-to-faculty ratio facilitates the working relationship necessary for students to succeed.

Our enrollment represents all 82 Mississippi counties, 50 states and nearly 75 foreign countries. With over 300 student organizations, MSU offers students a variety of opportunities, both inside and outside the classroom.

The Judy and Bobby Shackouls Honors College includes over 1,000 students. Honors classes typically number no more than 20 students and are taught by some of the university's top professors.

Focusing on a global education, MSU has a variety of study abroad programs and exchanges. During these programs, students may study architecture, studio art, international business, engineering, geosciences, a foreign language or other options.

MSU has a commitment to preparing students for their futures. Along with academic advising and classroom participation, the Career Center can help students choose the right study path. It also houses the Cooperative Education Program that lets students alternate a semester of school with a semester of work.

State Your Home

Mississippi State's residence halls are not only close to classrooms, they are conveniently located near the heart of campus, enabling students to be surrounded by a multitude of activities and opportunities.

MSU is a part of the friendly community of Starkville which is home to a multi-screen cinema with stadium seating, a variety of restaurants, live music, performances, and annual festivals. And, downtown Starkville and its shops, restaurants and coffeehouses are within walking distance of campus.

State Your Spirit

The Bulldog spirit is a huge part of the experience at Mississippi State. We offer a large variety of Southeastern Conference sports. For women, we provide eight varsity sports, including basketball, cross country, golf, soccer, softball, tennis, track and field, and volleyball. Our seven men's sports are baseball, basketball, cross country, golf, tennis, track and field, and football.

For students who would rather experience that thrill of victory for themselves, the Department of Recreational Sports offers club sports and intramurals, such as flag football, basketball and softball; Rugby; cricket; soccer; lacrosse; paintball; rock climbing; fencing; martial arts; scuba diving; cycling; and hiking.

Giving students the chance to experience Greek life, Mississippi State has 17 social fraternities and 11 social sororities. Six of our sororities have campus houses, as do 13 of the fraternities, and they all participate in philanthropy and expand the college experience.

State Your Opportunities

MSU also offers a variety of academic scholarships and non-resident scholarships for qualified students. For more information, please visit admissions.msstate.edu.

University of Mississippi

Office of Admissions
145 Martindale
The University of Mississippi
University, MS 38677
Admissions phone: (662) 915-7226 or
(800) OLE-MISS (in Mississippi only)
Admissions e-mail: admissions@olemiss.edu
Admissions URL: www.olemiss.edu/admissions/

Note: The school has chosen not to comment on the student surveys submitted.

 ## Admissions

Current student, 8/2004-Submit Date, December 2006

First: submit your application with two essays and three recommendation letters. Second, submit your transcript from high school and SAT scores.

Alumnus/a, 8/2002-5/2006, October 2006

The admissions process includes filling out an application, being accepted by the university with the discretion of your final transcript, and financial aid counseling. The selectivity of the university is very high. They are looking for bright students with the potential to do great things who will be an asset to the university.

Current student, 8/2001-Submit Date, September 2005

The first time I applied for admission to the university, it was not such a bad experience. They had simple paper forms, as well as online forms that I could print out at home and mail in. I met with entrance counselors and financial aid officers before actually having been accepted to the university. The advisors gave me pointers on what kind of program I would need to look into, what school I would need to be in for my chosen major and so on.

The admissions process here was fairly smooth. I withdrew for a few semesters, and when I came back and had to apply for re-admission. It was quick and painless.

Current student, 8/2005-Submit Date, August 2005

Admissions process is easy. Fill out the application, which mostly includes your name and address and some other basics. They do ask for ACT and SAT scores. There is no interview that you have to attend to be accepted. It is a good idea, though, once you have applied and are accepted to take a tour of the school to make sure this is the place you want to be.

The only essay I had to write was for scholarships. It's a fast and easy application that mostly asks you about yourself and your high school academic history.

Current student, 8/2004-Submit Date, December 2004

Applying for college was not hard; it just took some time and effort, and was a bit of a headache. I had to go to my counselor at my high school and get all my transcripts of my SAT, ACT and grades. I had to consider what colleges I wanted to send my transcripts to that would benefit me and my degree the most. I looked up what each college had to offer and their requirements. I went around to my teachers and other influential leaders in my life that I thought would give me the best recommendations for each school.

I also wrote an essay, even if it was not required—it never hurts to go an extra mile, especially when it is for something as big as college. Then my parents and I got together, addressed my envelopes and sent all my information off to each school. We did this as early as possible because it increases your chances of acceptance.

I also had to write a résumé, which was one of the things that I felt was most important. When writing a résumé, you need to include everything about you, even if you feel it's not important, a college may see it differently. Also, the SAT or ACT scores are important when applying for college; you want to get on these beginning your junior year because if you do poorly, you can always retake them and this is a large cut-off for many colleges.

Right away I started getting acceptance letters back. Luckily, I was excepted to every school to which I applied, which was a relief, but then I had to make a

Read all of Vault's College Surveys at **www.vault.com/college**—get complete surveys on 100s of colleges and universities, expert advice on applicaton essays and more.

VAULT CAREER LIBRARY   **391**

decision on which one to choose. This ended up being the hardest thing from applying. I visited every college, met professors, other faculty and talked aside to alumni. This helped to sway my decisions. Most importantly, I looked at my career and what I felt would help me out most in the long run. I looked at the statistics of each school and did plenty of research.

Alumnus/a, 8/1998-6/2002, September 2004

The university's admissions process was one of the easiest I endured. It was primarily filling out a simple application and sending in a small fee. I did not have any recommendation letters, essays or interviews. The requirements for the University of Mississippi have increased in the past several years; however, when I went through admissions, it was fairly easy to get.

 ## Academics

Current student, 8/2004-Submit Date, December 2006

Slow paced academic program in most cases. Mostly easy classes, with few exceptional hard honors courses. Light workload. Six courses per semester is easily manageable. Very nice and patient professors. Easy class registration process with priority registrations.

Alumnus/a, 8/2002-5/2006, October 2006

The biological sciences program is intense. The quality of the classes is great. However, there are not as many classes offered as I feel should be. The earlier you register for your classes, the better the chance you have to get into the classes you want. The grading scale seems fair to me. The professors are willing to help anyone who is willing to ask for help.

Current student, 8/2001-Submit Date, September 2005

My freshman year was busy, but not really difficult. I averaged about 15 credits a semester for the first two years. I took as many core curriculum classes as possible to get them out of the way so I could start taking classes that would be required for my particular major. I met with my advisor, we looked at the course catalogue together. I decided which classes I would take, and my advisor told me the best course of action from there.

My first two years were carefully scheduled so that I could get a good jump on things. My advisor was readily available for meetings, e-mails and phone calls. She also directed me to other majors in my field. Later on, I changed my minor to a major and added another major. This was not quite as bad as it would seem. I would register for the classes that would cross-list with other required classes. I had a few problems registering for the classes my second time around, because I was coming in in the middle of the school year (all spots had been filled). That was difficult, but it worked out that I ended up with unexpected courses that served as entertainment and electives.

Current student, 8/2005-Submit Date, August 2005

If a major has been decided, then the dean of that school recommends classes that you should take. It is an easy process of getting into classes. The best way to excel in class is to attend and take notes. If the student does not understand a lecture, homework or such, the teacher has office hours of which students can take advantage. The teachers are very willing to help the students succeed and also understand what they are really learning.

Current student, 8/2004-Submit Date, December 2004

College classes are not always as hard as people make them out to be. You do have to study a lot more that you did in high school, but you also have a lot more free time to do it. In high school those wasted hours of doing nothing in school; you do not have them in college. Every minute you spend in class, you are doing something. You go to class three hours a day but every minute is full of learning. The studying is up to you. You do not want to overwhelm yourself with classes though. 15 to 17 hours is plenty. That gives you free time to go out with friends, and plenty of time to spend studying.

Certain professors are always better than others; you always want to ask around about the best professors. Grading is different, too. You usually have a couple papers that together will affect your grade, but you only have a few tests and if you do poorly on one, then you can do poorly in the class just because of that one test. Professors tend to be more forgiving than they get credit for. If they

see you put forth an effort and try, they will give you the benefit of the doubt. you are doing poorly, you can always take time and talk to the professors a they will most likely help you out.

Depending on the class is the workload; there is always going to be a certa amount of time you have to study. To get into good classes you have to regis early, though. The good classes always fill up quickly.

Alumnus/a, 8/1998-6/2002, September 2004

The academics surprised me. The classes had a very small student-to-profess ratio and even my largest lecture classes did not exceed 150 students. I major in marketing and business and the curriculum was difficult at times. I feel li I did get a quality education in the business school.

Professors were fair and knowledgeable, and the workload was sometimes ove whelming. I particularly enjoyed every business class having a PowerPoi presentation. Almost every class was a presentation class.

 ## Employment Prospects

Alumnus/a, 8/2002-5/2006, October 2006

There are prestigious firms that come to the university's college fair. Tl recruiting on campus is excellent (the best in the SEC). I recently joined tl alumni network, but have not had the opportunity to utilize it.

Current student, 8/2001-Submit Date, September 2005

There are quite a few employment opportunities and internships available, b my major is not as widespread or common as others. There is a small numb of majors on campus. I know that summer internships and university positio are available. The career center on campus has books of different job opport nities divided up by location, interest and major/field of study.

Current student, 8/2005-Submit Date, August 2005

The School of Engineering has a high employment rate. The school gets diffe ent businesses to visit, and students have the opportunity to apply to their jo or at least talk to the different representatives to get their name out there. Tl different employers definitely recommend this because once you have finishe with your degree you can have a job already lined up for you.

Current student, 8/2004-Submit Date, December 2004

I have not graduated yet, but we have a very good pharmacy school and la school. They are very old and have a lot of recognition in the South. The aren't very many job opportunities out the state but a lot of the on-campi recruitment comes from the surrounding states.

Alumnus/a, 8/1998-6/2002, September 2004

The business program required a résumé class to gain experience and to wri exceptional résumés. Many people went through the growing career center. Tl main companies that came to visit and interview from in the South.

I, on the other hand, did not go directly through the career center. My job sear began when I moved to my current place of residence. The campus did off some study abroad and internship experiences of which I did not take advantag of.

 ## Quality of Life

Current student, 8/2004-Submit Date, December 2006

Nice housing and campus environment, many parties, few crimes, easy an leisure lifestyle, low pressure.

Alumnus/a, 8/2002-5/2006, October 2006

The quality of life is great. The campus is safe and the facilities are great. think there should be a greater selection of dining on campus. Oxford is a gre community.

Current student, 8/2001-Submit Date, September 2005

The freshmen are required to stay in the dorms for their first year, unless they are local students with a local address. Therefore there are a lot of students, especially freshmen, in the dorms. The housing office administered questionaires during the summer preceding the academic year that asked basic questions such as whether or not you smoke and whether you are a morning person. They try to match you with someone similar.

My roommate was great. We had a lot of respect for each other, and that is the key to living with someone you do not really know. Of course, we became friends, but we never expected to become best friends. That is one mistake most people make that causes conflict. Do not expect your roomie to be your bosom buddy, because you each have your own lives. If it happens that you are compatible enough, a true friendship may emerge. They had room swaps available for the first few weeks of school, where you could simply write in your switch on a board in the lobby.

The dorm I stayed in was small but busy. Everyone got to know everyone else on their floor, except my roommate and me. We kept very much to ourselves, and now I wish I had been a bit more outgoing. It would have made things simpler.

However, the condition of the dorm was fair, and maintenance was timely. The dorms were secured and required a magnetic key card (your student ID) to enter. All guests had to check in and out, leaving some form of identification at the front desk. Also, there were designated visiting hours and quiet hours. They served the needs of the residents well.

Current student, 8/2005-Submit Date, August 2005

Ole Miss has a wonderful safety rate. It is very rare for there to be crimes in Oxford. There are multiple emergency pull stands where if you come across trouble, you go to one of these stands and push a button and it immediately alerts the police. The police will arrive within a minute and help you.

Housing is also very nice. The rooms are a decent size and there are multiple ways to create more room for yourself and your roommate. There are rooms available that are individual rooms, rooms with one roommate and suite rooms.

The food is also excellent. You don't have to miss out on the home-cooked meals. There are multiple types of [meal plans] you can buy. One may be five meals a week, [another, unlimited food plan so you can go and get food whenever you want].

Current student, 8/2004-Submit Date, December 2004

The dorms suck, but they are fun at the same time. You meat tons of new people. They are dirty though and are all community bath. [All-girl dorms] have visitation hours for boys, which sometimes stinks, but you also have the security of never have to worry about a boy being were he should not.

There is not really any crime, sometimes some petty theft. The town is small and is a college town. It is beautiful, though, with a old little square full of little restaurants and over-priced boutiques. The campus is beautiful and very well kept.

Alumnus/a, 8/1998-6/2002, September 2004

The campus' beauty is breathtaking and cannot be described in words. The dorms were older and needed work when I was living on campus but I believe they have come up with a new project and started renovating the dorms on campus. Oxford is a very safe community and I always felt very safe in the City of Oxford.

Social Life

Current student, 8/2005-Submit Date, August 2005

Ole Miss has a very large Greek system that I have heard to be nice, but there are lots of other things to do without being Greek. There are tons of organizations and groups you can join. There are also intramural sports to get involved in. If you like ping pong and there isn't already an intramural sport of it, you can create it yourself, it's that easy. There are tons of restaurants in Oxford and many things to do. There is a movie theater, bowling alley, shopping, billiards and so on.

Current student, 8/2004-Submit Date, December 2006

Plenty of bars and restaurants for students, many events and clubs.

Alumnus/a, 8/2002-5/2006, October 2006

If you are open to diversity, you will have a great time with anyone you meet at any place. Greek life is difficult, but extremely fun. The best clubs to go to are NightTown Billiards, anywhere on the Square and Applebee's. I preferred going to Memphis to socialize with my fiancé's family and to go to Beale Street.

Current student, 8/2001-Submit Date, September 2005

This university is one of the top party schools in the country. We have an entire subculture of partiers here. The downtown area serves as the party district. Nestled around the courthouse are bars upon bars upon clubs. In between are upscale restaurants, from black tie to Sunday ware to t-shirt and jeans.

The town is considered a mini arts mecca of the region. Famous people lived and worked/work here, adding to the mix. The campus frequently hosts concerts, outdoor events and fairs of all sorts. No matter what your ethnicity, race, sexual orientation, leisure preference, there is something for everyone. Many organizations register with the university and have posts all over the town. You can volunteer, study and party here.

Our Greek system is one of the most respected and involved systems. It is such serious business that U-Hauls can be seen on campus after rush. Local merchants cater to the Greeks by offering private showrooms for their merchandise and gatherings. Just like football, the Greek system is a way of life.

Tailgating is also one of the staples of the university. People eat, sleep and breath football (and drink beer in little discreet containers). Everybody goes to the parties and tailgating festivities.

A huge performing arts center was newly built, and hosts concerts, film festivals and major theater productions. If you'd rather see a play than watch someone play, this is the place for you. Or, if you are into the film scene, a new eight-screen theater will be gracing our town in a matter of months; the ole cinema will be used for foreign films and independents. Writers and musicians swarm here for the culture.

Current student, 8/2004-Submit Date, December 2004

During the week there are always date parties and fraternity/sorority swaps, which are always a blast. The Greek life is very large at Ole Miss. During the spring because we don't have football games, we celebrate for baseball and basketball. We also have weekend events like Derby Day that are like small little carnivals that the fraternities and sororities throw.

Alumnus/a, 8/1998-6/2002, September 2004

The restaurants are amazing, the food is the Southern style that does not go out of style! There are many bars to choose from as well, maybe too many. The Burgundy Room, City Grocery, The Library, Pearl Street, Downtown Grille, Proud Larry's, Murphy's, Sneaky Tiki and Long Shots are just a few.

The Greek system consumes about 40 percent of the campus. It is not as popular but I am positive that each and every year more girls and guys go through Greek recruitment. The student enrollment is rising every year and with the popularity of Greek institutions going away, some are opting not to go through—especially at a school where legacies count. It is a very difficult rush to go through, especially if you do not know anyone.

Read all of Vault's College Surveys at **www.vault.com/college**–get complete surveys on 100s of colleges and universities, expert advice on applicaton essays and more.

VAULT CAREER LIBRARY   393

Saint Louis University

Admissions Office
DuBourg Hall, Room 119
221 N. Grand Blvd.
St. Louis, MO 63103
Admissions phone: (314) 977-2500 or (800) SLU-FOR-U
Admissions fax: (314) 977-7136
Admissions e-mail: admitme@slu.edu
Admissions URL: www.slu.edu/admissions

 ## Admissions

Current student, 8/2004-Submit Date, September 2006

You can either send in a hard copy of the application or turn one in electronically. I believe that it was free to send one in online, but there was a charge to mail it in. The application required an essay. I wrote about what I planned to do with my life and the steps in my life that I had taken to bring me to this decision. SLU is considered a selective school, but a decent GPA (above 3.0) and ACT scores will most likely get you accepted. It's not nearly as selective as some places. To get accepted to the school there is not a required interview; however, the admissions application is also the financial aid application and there are interviews for some scholarships. I believe that the only SLU scholarship (just general: not department specific) that required an interview was the President's scholarship, which provides free tuition for four years.

Current student, 8/2002-Submit Date, October 2005

All applications were handled online through the school's web site. To submit an application, one has to submit three essays of varying degrees and topics as well as fill out a rather generic application. After your application is submitted, you are contacted and the school requests grades and transcripts from your high school. The application process is rather simple and the school provides ample financial aid.

> **With regards to their application, the school says:** "Students may apply either online or via paper applications. Saint Louis University requires only one application essay."

Current student, 8/2003-Submit Date, January 2006

The admissions process was pretty easy. I did it all online. It was quick and I could track the progress of my application on the school's web site.

Current student, 8/2001-Submit Date, March 2005

The application process wasn't any different than at other schools. You fill out the application asking general questions and you write an essay pertaining to the major you are going to study and a person who impacted your life. I suggest writing a good, emotional essay for both. Create sympathy and show passion and dedication. They are pretty selective but there is also a summer program that people can take if they are a little lower than what they would usually accept and can still be admitted into the school after completion of the classes.

> **The school says:** "Saint Louis University only requires one application essay. Though the admissions office suggests many topics, applicants may choose their own topic."

Current student, 8/2003-Submit Date, November 2004

I did not have to have an interview. I was provided with an admissions advisor who helped tell me what paperwork I needed and helped direct me toward financial aid. I received a letter of acceptance within two weeks.

Current student, 8/2003-Submit Date, August 2004

SLU has a very organized and competent admissions staff. Questions answered immediately and thoroughly. The application process is challeng enough that it weeds out students who would be a poor fit for the school. On other hand, it is not so grueling that it discourages good students from applyi Students are not put through interviews unless they are eligible for large sch arships, but interviews are available upon request to gain information about school. I would recommend applying to this school, even if you don't think y have a shot of getting into it. They accept a diverse range of students and S is not as selective as some students may think.

 ## Academics

Current student, 8/2003-Submit Date, August 2004

Classes at SLU are very well taught. Generally I have found it pretty easy to the classes I want. They offer a wide variety of classes, and programs for t matter. The classes are challenging, but still allow students to have a life outs of school. Grading seems to be very fair, and I have almost always been able achieve success in my classes at SLU. Professors are always very qualified a knowledgeable about their areas of expertise, and their workload is usually ve understandable and valuable to learning the topic.

Current student, 8/2002-Submit Date, October 2005

For the most part, the quality of the classes is very good. There are basic, gen ic classes that everyone must take, which do not add much value, but SLU ai toward building a complete person and not just a professional. When it con time to register, you better be first in line because most popular classes fill very quickly, but the school will work with you to try and get into closed cla es. The online registration for classes is not very reliable so many go to the r istration office to register for classes. The campus has switched its online reg tration program and has yet to be fully tested.

> **The school says:** "Saint Louis University encourages students to register online. However, students may also register with their academic advisors and at the registrar's office."

Grading has also just switched to curb grade inflation. The grades are now A-, B+, B, B- and so on. (Before it was straight A, B, C, D.) Now if one w to get between 92 to 90 it is considered an A- and a 3.7 on the GPA rather th an A and a 4.0.

> **The school says:** "SLU uses a four-point grading scale (A = 4) with +/- distinctions. Each professor determines his or her grading scale within department and university standards."

Professors in the higher-level courses are excellent and very well versed. For most part they care very much for the students. In the lower-level classes taug by graduate students, it is what one would expect, lack luster.

> **The school says:** "Only 11 percent of freshman classes are taught by graduate students."

Workload is medium. Some classes, mostly upper-level, require a great deal time but it is not unbearable unless one takes many difficult classes at one tir

Current student, 8/2004-Submit Date, September 2006

You will learn a lot in all of your classes because SLU has many excellent qu ity professors. It's not too difficult to get into the classes that you want if y register for them right away. The registration and classes schedules are onli through Banner. It will tell you how many slots there are available in that cla how many have been filled, and how many are left. If there was a class that y absolutely wanted to get in to, but couldn't, then you can talk to the teacher that class or the department head, as well as your advisor and sometimes get waived so that you get to take it. The professors are pretty tough but will ma re that you learned the material. That's very general, but usually before regis-ring for classes, students talk to people who are familiar with the teacher or go rateyourprofessor.com. Most of the teachers are on there if you search for ur school and you can find feedback and see how tough of graders they are d so on. The workload can get pretty tough if you load up on classes. A egree from SLU looks pretty good because everyone knows that it's a selective rivate school. Last year SLU just implemented a new grading scale so that inuses are included, so we have A, A-, B+, B, B- and so on, rather than just hole letter grades. This makes the GPA a little bit more specific from one per-n to another so that a high B (almost A) doesn't look the same as a low B lmost C). Since Saint Louis University is a Jesuit school, at least one theolo-y class is required depending on which college you attend.

urrent student, 8/2003-Submit Date, November 2004

he program involves taking two history, one fine arts, one math, three foreign nguage, two science, one cultural diversity, three theology, three philosophy d three English classes in addition to your major classes. A student must also ld a second major, a minor, a certificate program or elective classes to complete e 120 hours needed for graduation. The quality of classes varies but the upper-vel courses are always well-taught. I have two majors; one is with a large epartment and one is with a small department. Both departments are helpful ith academic advising. The amount of reading varies but was very heavy in the story and theology classes I have taken. Professors are usually approachable d willing to help if a student has a problem. Popular classes are almost impos-ble to get as an underclassman. Grading varies slightly from class to class but is roughly on the standard numeric grading scale.

The school says: "Each of SLU's schools has a different set of required core classes. None of the schools require students to have more than one major, nor are students required to complete a minor."

Employment Prospects

urrent student, 8/2004-Submit Date, September 2006

areer Services can be pretty helpful if you go to them and ask the right ques-ons. They hold mock interview days to help prepare you for real ones. They t us connected to do co-ops, internships, and get jobs both part time during hool and full time afterwards. Many times there are career fairs in which dif-rent companies will send a representative to the campus and you can interview ere or just find more information if you are looking for the future in general.

urrent student, 8/2002-Submit Date, October 2005

LU has an incredible network to find jobs. Their career center is fabulous and ill help you find an internship and job if necessary. The SLU prestige tends to e concentrated in St. Louis, not many people know of SLU outside of St. Louis, ut in St. Louis it is very well known. Employers seem to like SLU grads than ny other graduate in the St. Louis area because of the presence, alumni and net-ork it has established in the area. Jobs graduates gain span the spectrum of the b market. Most of them begin making considerable amounts of money but not x figures. The alumni network is very useful in that usually alumni like to help aduates and students out. The school puts on many programs throughout the ar, as well as has a club that incorporates alumni in many different forms. On-mpus recruiting is good and becoming great. Internships are one of the best rts of the campus, they have an innumerable number for the taking.

urrent student, 8/2003-Submit Date, August 2004

he career section of SLU is probably the most impressive. The counseling epartment is very active, and provides the students with tons of opportunities. eing in a large city, SLU has the opportunity to connect students with many big mpanies in town. Many companies are also lured to campus to hold meetings d fairs in the new student center. SLU provides students with a degree that lds a lot of weight when entering the working world, in town and out of state. st going to school here connects you with many students who will be success-l in the future.

Quality of Life

Current student, 8/2004-Submit Date, September 2006

Saint Louis University is unique because it's in an urban environment, yet the majority of the streets that previously ran through campus are now strictly pedes-trian traffic. There are lots of trees, flowers and other plants, that give it a feel of not being in the heart of the city. The plus is that there is public transporta-tion nearby, both metrobus and metrolink. Honestly, the air is not as clean as it could be because we're in the middle of a city. On-campus housing is rather pricey. Many people have found that living off campus is cheaper, but it depends on the living situation. We have five major dorms and three apartment com-plexes. The security for these is very good because you are required to have an SLU student ID to get into any of them. If you are not an SLU student, then you must be escorted by a SLU student and you have to check in. The meal plans are not very good and everyone is required to buy one. The prices are far too expensive for what we get. The cheapest meal plan per meal is about $7 per meal, whereas if you were a visitor just buying a meal from the cafeteria, you would have to pay $6. We have two major cafeterias and many other random places to eat on campus including a food court, student center, coffee shop and so on. SLU's campus is actually very safe. We have DPS officers constantly patrolling. They send us e-mails of any incidents that occur and none have actu-ally happened on campus since I have been a student here. Several have hap-pened off campus, but evidence has shown that about half of these incidents were due to the victim's intoxication. It is also safer to keep your car on cam-pus in a garage or lot than leave it at an off-campus parking meter. The parking is expensive and there is no place for visitors to park for free, but it's worth it when you know that your car won't be broken into or stolen. There are cameras at all of the lots and parking garages, with attendants at all of the garages.

Current student, 8/2002-Submit Date, October 2005

Quality of life is wonderful. The campus is downtown next to the arts district. The campus is very safe thanks to the second largest force of security officers on a campus in this nation.

The school says: "Saint Louis University's department of public safety is the third largest police force in the state of Missouri."

At times housing is difficult because of the concentration of people in a small space, but for the most part, housing is very nice, especially when compared to those of many state schools. The campus is one of the most beautiful urban if not any campus in the nation. The school obviously takes pride in its appearance and spends lots, maybe too much money on landscaping, lights, statues and fountains. Dining is campus dining, adequate but nothing like a home-cooked meal. There are plenty of options that are name-brand restaurants on campus. Crime can be a problem, but only if you wander off campus. On campus it is very safe thanks to the security force aforementioned.

Current student, 8/2001-Submit Date, March 2005

I feel extremely safe at this campus. There are more campus safety officers than city police officers and you see them everywhere. They will escort you or drive you places if you need them to. The surrounding neighborhood is a little sketchy but it is getting a lot better. Housing had some issues when I lived on campus with messing up who goes where and I think it is the biggest complaint of most students. I don't know how they work housing now, though. Before they would do it by year and GPA.

The campus is relatively small but beautiful, there are fountains and flowers everywhere. The amount of places to eat on campus could be a lot better. There are two cafeterias that serve the same food, two food courts and one restaurant. One of the food courts closes early on the weekends and the other isn't open at all and on weekdays closes at 5 p.m.

Saint Louis University says: "Although the Saint Louis University's public safety department is not larger than the city's, there are nearly 100 university public safety officers ded-icated to creating a campus environment that is safe and secure.

"Upperclassman housing assignments are determined by a number of factors, including how many semesters the student

Read all of Vault's College Surveys at **www.vault.com/college**—get complete surveys on 100s of colleges and univer-sities, expert advice on applicaton essays and more.

VAULT CAREER LIBRARY   395

has lived on campus, the number of completed credit hours and GPA.

"In addition to two cafeterias, there are three coffeehouses, two food courts, a Mexican restaurant and national chain restaurants such as Au Bon Pain and Subway."

 Social Life

Current student, 8/2004-Submit Date, September 2006

Many people belong to fraternities or sororities. There are two bars right next to campus: Humphrey's and Laclede's. They are literally right across the street and many students hang out there. Humphrey's has Penny Pitchers night on Wednesday nights, so many of the 21 and up crowd hang out there. Since we're in the middle of the city, there are many different restaurants that aren't really very far away. The places closest to us are Vito's pizza, which is a classy pizza restaurant and bar, Joe Boccardi's and Nadoz. There's also a Jimmy John's and DelTaco. SLU is about 60 percent girls, so it's great for you if you are a guy. The Fabulous Fox theatre is literally two blocks away up Grand Ave. Students are constantly getting fliers for clubs and local bands and so on, so there is always something to do.

Current student, 8/2002-Submit Date, October 2005

Social life is adequate if you get out of your room. There are two Italian restaurants, three fast food restaurants, and three bars pretty much on campus. The campus is a wet campus, meaning drinking is allowed in venues as long as it is legal.

> The school says: "Students are only permitted to consume alcohol on campus when they are 21 or over and in the presence of other students of age."

There is a very prominent Greek life because the campus is concentrated. There is a large number of fraternities and five major sororities and each one holds different, large events every semester.

> The school says: "Saint Louis University has 11 fraternities and five sororities. Greek life applies to approximately 20 percent of SLU students."

The campus brings in world-famous speakers, popular music artists for private concerts each semester and there is a golf cart homecoming parade because of the abundance of golf carts on campus. There is an innumerable number of clubs and excellent nightlife in the city that you can get to if you can find a ride off campus. The SAB (student activities board) is the most funded organization on campus and puts on events all the time for students, including comedians, festivals, carnivals and events. You can be very involved if you want to be. Its one of the most perfect sizes imaginable.

Current student, 8/2001-Submit Date, March 2005

There are only three bars [near] campus, but it is a city, so there are many more places to go. There are parties around campus but nothing really huge. The majority of guys are in a frat and about 50 percent of the girls. They don't rule the school but they can help you to get to know more people. The dating scene is pretty decent, now that we are seniors, a lot of people are dating and no longer looking. The best Wednesday (Penny Pitchers) nights are at Humphrey's and if you love dancing Laclede's is open until 3 a.m.

> The school says: "Approximately 20 percent of Saint Louis University students are involved in fraternities and sororities."

Current student, 8/2003-Submit Date, November 2004

The main bar to go to is Humphrey's, but in addition to that there is a flourishing Greek life on campus, which provides much of the students with parties to go to. The campus is located about three minutes from the St. Louis theatre district with ballets, musicals, symphonies, plays and concerts going on throughout the school year. A lot of students like to join the wide variety of clubs ranging from political to cultural. There is a good neighborhood for dating called the Central West End, which is about a five- to 10-minute drive from campus. It has a nice theater and intimate restaurants.

 The School Says

Admissions

Saint Louis University is a Jesuit, Catholic university ranked among the top research institutions in the nation and as one of the nation's best educational values for the ninth consecutive time by *U.S. News & World Report*.

Nearly 15,000 students apply for approximately 1,600 places in the freshman class each year. The average admitted student has an ACT score of 26.4 and a 3.69 GPA.

Academics

SLU offers more than 85 undergraduate majors and more than 40 graduate and professional programs including the nationally-ranked allied health, business and engineering programs.

The average class size at Saint Louis University is 25, and the student-to-faculty ration is 12 to one. In addition, the SLU Inquiry program provides another intimate class environment in which classes are limited to 13 first-year students and six returning students.

Employment prospects

More than 90 percent of recent Saint Louis University graduates report that they found employment in their chosen fields or are attending graduate school. SLU graduates can be found working at many prestigious corporations and organizations, including AG Edwards and Sons Inc., Anheuser-Busch Cos., Bank of America, Boeing, Catholic Charities, Ernst & Young and SBC Communications Inc.

Through its web database, the career department posts extensive internship opportunities and job openings. Counselors advise students on major and career selection, résumé building, and job placement.

Several of the local Fortune 500 companies, as well as top employers from across the country come to SLU every year to conduct on-campus interviews and recruit students.

Quality of Life

Saint Louis University is located in Midtown St. Louis. SLU's campus is adjacent to St. Louis' arts and theatre district and about three miles west of the St. Louis arch and riverfront. Even though SLU is in the middle of a bustling city, the campus is green and welcoming as it stretches across nearly 250 acres of flowers, fountains and lush greenery. SLU's urban campus has undergone more than $500 million in construction, renovations and beatification since 1987.

SLU has made community safety a major priority. The campus is well-lit and patrolled 24 hours a day, seven days a week, by foot, bicycle and car by its outstanding and well-staffed security department. SLU offers a shuttle and escort service to take students from one corner of campus to the other.

Social Life

Saint Louis University students are academic, social and committed to outreach. More than 100 student organizations, including fraternities and sororities, provide opportunities for everyone to get involved. The Student Activities Board brings all sorts of entertainment to SLU including recent musical acts such as Yellowcard, Jason Mraz, and O.A.R., and comedians like *Saturday Night Live*'s Seth Meyers.

Finally, Saint Louis University offers students something rare in higher education: the opportunity to study at a place where academic achievement and the advancement of knowledge unite with community commitment and Jesuit values. At Saint Louis University, students collaborate with premier scholars and

researchers, and create knowledge that will change the face of their disciplines and the lives of others.

Truman State University

Admissions Office
McClain Hall 205
100 East Normal
Kirksville, MO 63501-4221
Admissions phone: (800) 892-7792 or (660) 785-4114
Admissions e-mail: admissions@truman.edu
Admissions URL: admissions.truman.edu/

 ## Admissions

Current student, 8/2004-Submit Date, May 2007

Test scores and grades are very important. Truman is a state school, but is selective in its admissions process. Test scores are also important to the process of awarding scholarships. All students are eligible for automatic scholarships and there are a few special interest/competitive awards as well. No interview is necessary, and the admissions process is friendly and helpful, as well as low stress, which is good! Overall, the admissions process is easy compared to other schools of this caliber.

> **The school says:** "Qualifying freshmen are eligible for an automatic combined ability scholarship based on their high school rank percent or GPA percent (whichever is higher) and their national percentile of the ACT or SAT. Many competitive scholarships are available as well."

Current student, 8/2004-Submit Date, May 2007

I found the admissions office very helpful. I was pretty sure that I wanted to attend Truman, but I wasn't sure how to go about getting scholarships and completing everything that I needed. They called me several times with follow-ups and sent out several mailings to make sure I had everything I needed. They were also more than willing to answer any and all questions that I had. I had to fill out the online application, complete the placement exams for my foreign language, and submit an essay in order to qualify for admission here.

> **Truman State says:** "To apply for admission first-year students must submit an application, an essay, high school transcript, and ACT/SAT test score. Placement exams are completed as part of the registration process."

Current student, 1/2005-Submit Date, May 2007

The admissions process is quite simple. I filled out one application online and submitted my résumé, transcript and letters of recommendation. There were no secondary applications or additional forms that I had to fill out, even for scholarships. This relieved the stress of the admissions process. I found out a few weeks later that I had been admitted into Truman and that I qualified for some scholarships. I interviewed for the Pershing Scholarship, and the interview was very relaxed: they just wanted to learn more about me.

> **Truman State says:** "Letters of recommendation are not required as part of the application process."

Current student, 8/2003-Submit Date, May 2007

I recommend going for early admission, as you have the best chance of getting one of the bigger, more competitive scholarships. Truman is highly selective but has a free application, which is really nice. It has been a number of years, but I remember having to submit an essay sample of my writing and taking math and foreign language placement tests before I could enroll in courses. They were really great about notifying me of my early acceptance and when I came up for a campus tour, it was fabulous. I also had the chance to compete for a piano performance scholarship, which was a really great opportunity.

> **The school says:** "Truman has a priority deadline of December 15. Students wishing to be considered for all scholarships and financial aid programs are strongly encouraged to apply by this date."

Current student, 8/2006-Submit Date, May 2007

Truman is more selective than most other state schools. You do need a fairly high GPA and ACT score. However, they do take into account the activities in which you participated during high school.

The admissions process was very easy. You can do your whole application online, making it all very smooth. I do not remember if essays were included in the admissions process. I know I did not have to do an interview to get admitted. However, I think that interviews are required for certain scholarships.

> **Truman State says:** "Students are required to submit an essay with their application. Students selected as finalists for the Pershing Scholarship are invited to campus for an interview."

Current student, 8/2004-Submit Date, May 2007

Application was really basic and easy to fill out, no application fee. I sent in an essay from another application and mostly just had to transfer the standard application information from my applications to other schools. I don't think an interview is required; I was interviewed after I was accepted. I had a good GPA and very high test scores, which I think are the most important qualifications, but I also had lots of extracurricular involvement and job experience. Truman accepts about 75 percent of all applicants, but the applicants are self-selective because the majority of applicants are well-qualified and have higher GPAs, test scores, and involvement. I received my acceptance a week after sending my application.

> **Regarding selectivity, the school says:** "The acceptance rate for first-year students in 2006 was 81 percent."

Current student, 8/2004-Submit Date, May 2007

One of the appealing parts of Truman's admissions process is that there is no application fee! Heavy emphasis is put on GPA and ACT scores but an impressive personal statement and résumé can help get additional scholarships. Visiting campus is a wonderful way to learn about all aspects of the campus. In addition to meeting with an admissions counselor, students can go on a campus tour, sit in on a class, talk with faculty members, and stay overnight in the residence halls with a current student.

Current student, 8/2003-Submit Date, November 2006

Truman is moderately selective for a state school. It is not difficult to get in if you have been involved in high school, have above a 3.0 GPA and over a 23 or

Read all of Vault's College Surveys at **www.vault.com/college**—get complete surveys on 100s of colleges and universities, expert advice on applicaton essays and more.

VAULT CAREER LIBRARY **397**

so on the ACT. If you have overachieved in any three of those areas, they might cut you a little slack if another area isn't as good. No interview is needed, but you do have to write essays. My advice is to stick to what you know, write about a learning experience in high school, or something that is most important to you. The best part about the application process is that it's free! So you can't justify not applying.

Regarding admissions, Truman State says: "Admission to Truman is based upon high school curriculum; high school grade point average and rank; standardized test scores (ACT or SAT); special abilities, talents, or achievements; cocurricular involvement; and an essay."

Academics

Current student, 8/2004-Submit Date, May 2007

Almost all classes are challenging. There are very few blow-off classes. There are a lot of very good professors in each division, and students in particular divisions usually have their favorites. Depending on the chosen major, classes can be difficult to get into during freshman and sophomore years. Workload is generally higher than at other schools, but students are typically very high achievers. At Truman it is OK to be smart and hardworking, and while partying exists, most students see school as their first priority and are very successful. The academic community in some majors becomes relatively tight, and students and professors become more of colleagues and friends. Professors are generally very down to earth and friendly and not at all intimidating. Most encourage getting to know them personally, which is a great thing because the academics are so challenging. Knowing your professors personally does make it more comfortable in this challenging situation. This relationship is encouraged by the faculty themselves and the academic advising system in the upper classes because students work directly with faculty for their advising needs.

Current student, 8/2005-Submit Date, May 2007

This school is rock solid academically. The classes are very challenging and that's what I love about it. It is very competitive. It's nice having small classrooms because you get more one-on-one time with professors. For the most part, professors are a big help when you go to see them in their offices.

Current student, 8/2004-Submit Date, May 2007

The classes at Truman are small (around [23] students) and the professors expect a lot from the students. The average workload per week is about 15 hours outside of class. The professors are always available to assist students outside of the classroom as well. Truman is a research savvy campus and many students participate in research during their undergraduate.

Current student, 9/2004-Submit Date, May 2007

Truman is considered a liberal arts college. What this means is that students are required to take classes from a variety of subject areas, not just within your major. Students must fulfill seven out of eight Modes of Inquiry, which cover the basic subject areas: English, history, fine arts, mathematics, science and so on. Students are allowed to drop one area (hence seven of eight). So, if you are like me and hate mathematics, the opportunity is there for you to drop the Calculus Mode of Inquiry. The great thing about Truman classes and professors is that teachers really make the effort to get to know you. You won't find yourself in a lot of large, lecture-style classes taught by a TA. Because Truman is a smaller school, class sizes don't get too large and professors have more of a chance to get to know you. The class choice process is determined by the number of hours a student has. So, seniors get priority on making their schedules. This doesn't mean that freshmen are stuck with horrible classes, only that they will have a hard time getting into an upper 400-level class in their first semester. Grading at Truman depends upon the professor. Just like many academic environments, professors can choose how to evaluate their students' performance. Some teachers are harder graders than others, but some are much more lenient. Usually, the professors are incredibly understanding, and will take the time to work with you if you have a conflict, such as illness or a death in the family. When entering Truman, students should not expect to be able to party 24/7 and still maintain a 4.0. Classes at Truman are challenging compared to most universities' standards, and the university works diligently to maintain the level of excellence that is expected of its students. If you are the type of person who

wants to blow off class every day, then Truman simply isn't the place for y We take our academic standards seriously.

Current student, 8/2004-Submit Date, May 2007

Professors at Truman really do love to teach, that is why they are at Trum rather than at some larger university where their main focus would be research. The liberal arts program at Truman offers a lot of flexibility, especi ly for students who do not have a major in mind as freshmen. It can be frustr ing trying to get into upper-level major classes as a freshman or sophomore, professors generally will grant over rides and let you in if you personally them. Generally class sizes are small. Larger general biology classes can enr nearly 100 students, but break into smaller groups once a week for the lab p tion of the class.

Current student, 8/2003-Submit Date, November 2006

Truman is a school that truly gets more difficult as you progress. There is a eral arts program that requires you take different classes in many disciplin Most of these classes are harder than they should be. It seems that the prof sors are out to prove that these classes are not blow offs, and thus, getting an is like getting a brick of gold. It's not easy to do. The quality of classes is go class size is small, which keeps everyone engaged. Skipping class will severe hurt your grade in the long run. Classes get more difficult as the years pass. am currently in one class right now that requires about four or five hours group work per each class period, and half of the class failed the first exam. T is somewhat typical in the harder majors (finance, or any life science). If y want the easy way out, I recommend Communications or Health/Exerc Science. Their classes seem interesting, and the difficulty is low compared others. Art/music/visual communications are ridiculously hard, as is finance/accounting program, and biology/chemistry/and so on. Be ready work!

The school says: "Truman enrolls academically talented students and provides them with a quality education. While Truman is academically challenging, the university enjoys the highest graduation rate among Missouri public colleges and universities as reported by the Coordinating Board for Higher Education."

Current student, 8/2002-Submit Date, December 2005

For most incoming students Truman is a difficult university . Most students w come to Truman breezed through high school and have little or no study ski Study skills are a must! Classes at Truman are very well rounded, but being liberal arts school, students can get frustrated with classes outside of their maj Classes in math, science, literature, physical well-being, history and art/mu are required to graduate. Professors at Truman are well-qualified. I'd say percent have received their PhD and/or have worked within the field they teaching. Registering for classes can be frustrating because it goes by how ma hours you have accumulated. Those with the least number of hours register la It would be helpful to come to Truman having already taken classes for colle credit. Popular classes are hard to get into. The workload at Truman can overwhelming at first, but once you get the hang of it, you will feel as if you c accomplish anything.

Truman State says: "85 percent of full-time faculty have PhDs or the terminal degree in their field."

Employment Prospects

Current student, 8/2004-Submit Date, May 2007

Truman's Career Center is very helpful if students take advantage of it as resource. It plans the Career Expo every year that brings employers to us. M career choice is not helped very much by this event, but I know it is especia useful to people in business and IT career paths. The Career Center also he with internships and jobs, but a lot of internship support comes directly from students' departments and the professors whom they know best. Career cou seling is also available from the career center and the professors whom the s dents use as advisors.

Current student, 8/2004-Submit Date, May 2007

I was able to receive two internships, one for last summer and one for this summer, thanks to Career Expos put on at Truman. Despite being in the middle of nowhere, Truman does a good job of bringing employers to campus. Because of Truman's reputation and many companies' success with Truman grads, they are typically very interested in Truman students. The Career Center on campus is a fantastic resource for the job, internship or grad school search. The staff there is incredibly helpful when preparing for interviews or writing résumés and cover letters. From what I have heard, most Truman grads do not have much of a problem finding a job post-graduation.

Current student, 8/2003-Submit Date, May 2007

As a highly-selective university, Truman's name is becoming more and more well known and respected. There is a high acceptance rate for professional schools (many medical, law and dental students come out of Truman) and with Truman's internship program, it's not too difficult to be able to network with the business world for future career opportunities. There is always a Career Expo and Graduate School Fair put on by our Career Center (a wonderful resource), and they will also take the time to look over résumés, personal statements and bring in well-known writers and experts to speak to students about getting that desired job or placement. Also, Truman is working extensively at improving its alumni program.

Current student, 8/2005-Submit Date, May 2007

Our graduates have a very high employment placement after graduation. I know a lot of students participate in internships over the summers. The placement in those internships is also very high. It is fairly easy to find an internship if the student lives in or is willing to travel to a major city. Our professors will help a student find a place to intern that is good for them.

Current student, 1/2005-Submit Date, May 2007

Truman State University is a relatively new name (Northeast Missouri State University became Truman State University on June 15, 1995), so Truman may not be widely known outside of the Midwest.

> **Regarding the university name, the school says:** "Legislation went into effect on July 1, 1996 that changed the university's name to Truman State University."

Current student, 8/2004-Submit Date, May 2007

Many graduates either go on to graduate school, become teachers, or are employed by government agencies (such as the Department of the Treasury) and private corporations (such as Boeing, a large employer of Truman graduates).

Current student, 8/2002-Submit Date, December 2005

Employers in Missouri love to hire Truman students. Truman students are involved, very intelligent and well rounded. Employment prospects can be very good, depending on your major. Over 100 companies attend the Truman career fair every fall and spring to look for potential hires. Internships are required for certain majors, but anyone can look into an internship anywhere in the country. From personal experience, the two internships I have been involved with will certainly help me when interviewing for a job and when I actually get a job. Further learning outside of the classroom is highly encouraged at Truman.

Quality of Life

Current student, 8/2004-Submit Date, May 2007

Generally students at Truman are happy and live comfortably. Most of the dorms are old, but there is an extended renovation program in progress. One dorm is brand new, and beginning in fall 2007 a freshly renovated dorm will open for residents. Although buildings are old, they aren't too bad. Food is not fantastic, but it will get you by. Kirksville is a pleasant place to live and plenty entertaining if you get to know the town. It definitely has the small town feel and is generally safe. Off-campus housing still leaves a lot to be desired, but a large amount of new housing is being built. Overall, off-campus housing is affordable and easy to come by within walking distance to school.

Truman's Student Activities Board and other student organizations provide wonderful (and free!) entertainment opportunities. Because of its location in northeast Missouri, Truman students are encouraged to interact with their fellow students on a daily basis. This interaction builds a strong sense of community.

Current student, 8/2004-Submit Date, May 2007

Quality of life at Truman is nothing to complain about. The residence halls are all in decent shape, especially compared to many that I've seen at other schools! Furthermore, Truman is doing a lot of remodeling, which is only improving the campus. In general the campus is very beautiful and it is not uncommon to see students filling the quad and other outdoor areas on a nice day. Dining at Truman is typical college food, but as a non-picky eater who does not have a knack for cooking, I think it is just fine. There are several options both on and off campus for students who don't necessarily like the dining hall. The area around Truman is interesting. Truman is, in my opinion, the best thing about Kirksville. While it's a quaint town, there really isn't much there. Thankfully, Truman always has so much going on around campus that the lack of a mall, museums and so on, isn't terrible. Truman does a good job of bringing in comedians and hosting concerts so you can always find something to do! There are a few really good restaurants in Kirksville, as well as other small town features that you can't find in your typical suburban town. In my years at Truman, I've learned to appreciate Kirksville for what it is. I'm always excited to go home, but being in Kirksville is a nice change of pace. (You don't have to worry about going broke!) In terms of safety, you hear reports of theft and so on, from time to time but I have never felt unsafe in Kirksville or at Truman. DPS (Department of Public Safety) is well-known on campus and students can always contact them.

Current student, 8/2003-Submit Date, May 2007

Kirksville was probably the worst part about going to Truman. But, I did enjoy living in a small town because of the friendliness of the people in town. Also, it was cheap as dirt to move off campus into a house or apartment. Although the Truman students get sick of the cafeterias, they were great and always had something for everybody.

Current student, 8/2002-Submit Date, December 2005

Truman is located in a town of approximately 18,000 people. It is a small town. There is no mall and most people shop at Wal-Mart. Because the town is so small and does not offer much to do, getting involved with student organizations is important. Crime is very low and the residential housing is very satisfactory. It is easy to make friends in the dorms. The food is not the best, but the overall experience of living in the dorms is a necessary life experience. The campus is small and it takes little time to get from place to place. In the spring and summer, the Truman campus is very lush and green.

> **The school says:** "Kirksville has a population of about 17,000."

 # Social Life

Current student, 8/2004-Submit Date, May 2007

There are several fun bars in town (21 and up only) and restaurants all over the place. The Greek system is fabulous here, unique from other schools. There are so many strong leaders within the Greek system here; it is not at all the stereotypical system that you often see at other big state schools. Dating is never a problem because of the restaurants, movie theatre, and campus events that are held weekly by the Student Activities Board, among other student organizations.

Current student, 8/2004-Submit Date, May 2007

I don't participate in Greek life, but I know many who do. For the most part, people are pleased with their decision. It definitely helps the socially inclined who are always looking for a party and people to go with. A few favorite restaurants include Il Spazio (probably the best) and the Mexican restaurants (La Pachanga and El Vaquero). Ruby Tuesday's is also great. Many people love going to Thousand Hills State Park when it's nice out. I've camped there, hiked, swam, had picnics, studied and water-skied (you can rent boats or make friends with people who have boats!). There are so many clubs and organizations with which to become involved on campus. As freshmen, it makes sense to take your

Read all of Vault's College Surveys at **www.vault.com/college**–get complete surveys on 100s of colleges and universities, expert advice on applicaton essays and more.

VAULT CAREER LIBRARY **399**

first semester to try them all out and decide what you like. Then, in your second semester, you can become more involved with those you really like. It's possible to be a part of many. There are tons of leadership opportunities within these groups and it's great to take advantage of them: a great résumé builder! Truman's SAB (Student Activities Board) does a great job of providing events for the students. From concerts to Bingo nights to outdoor movies in Red Barn Park, they keep students busy! I'm not yet 21 so I haven't been able to frequent the bar scene, but I know it is definitely happening in Kirksville! Students love Trivia night on Tuesdays and $5 all you can drink on Thursdays at Two-Talls. Other favorites include the Dukum where there are typically concerts on the weekends (and those under 21 are allowed to these!!) and TeePee's.

Current student, 8/2003-Submit Date, May 2007

Kirksville itself is your average small town surrounded by farmland here and there, but it has the most beautiful state park (1000 Hills) and lake! It's their best kept secret: perfect for late-night stargazing, hiking on trails, canoeing on the lake, camping and more! There are also walking trails by the K-12 schools and bike routes around town. Kirksville also has quite the rustic town square, with great college bars, a coffee shop for Saturday studying, flower stores, a Hallmark, a Christian bookstore, antiques, movie theater, and more. On the main thoroughfare, there's a Wal-mart, Walgreens, Ruby Tuesdays, Taco Bell, McDonald's, Sonic, Wendy's, Burger King, a few great Chinese Buffets and Mexican restaurants. Kirksville recently passed a no-smoking ordinance to go in effect this summer, which will make the bar experience a lot more enjoyable all around, in my opinion.

As far as dating scene goes: if you're a male, you're in luck. There are a lot of ladies at Truman. It may be a bit harder for the girls to snag that special someone, but there are a lot of nice guys at Truman, so either way, you can make a lot of wonderful friends at Truman.

 The School Says

Truman has forged a national reputation for offering an exceptionally high-quality undergraduate education at a competitive price. For the 11th consecutive year, *U.S. News & World Report* has ranked Truman as the Number One master's-level public institution in the Midwest offering bachelor's and master's degrees. In addition, Truman is ranked as the second best public college value in the nation by Princeton Review's 2008 edition of *America's Best Value Colleges*.

A commitment to student achievement and learning is at the core of everything Truman does. This commitment is evidenced by faculty and staff members who recognize the importance of providing students with the opportunity to interact with their professors both in and out of the classroom. With class sizes averaging only 23 students and 93 percent of freshman-level academic courses being taught by professors, students find ample opportunity to ask questions of professors as well as interact with their multitalented peers.

Truman's academic environment is enhanced by a student body that achieves at remarkable levels. The 2006 freshman class had an ACT midrange of 25 to 30 and an average GPA of 3.78 on a 4.00 scale. In addition, numerous opportunities exist for students to engage in undergraduate research. Each year, approximately 1,200 students work side by side with professors on University research projects, gaining greater confidence, knowledge, and skill in their chosen disciplines.

With more than 230 University organizations available to students, encompassing service, Greek, honorary, professional, religious, social, political, and recreational influences, Truman students have tremendous opportunities to become involved while enrolled at the University. Truman's Student Activities Board provides popular culture entertainment such as special events like *Mythbusters: Adam and Jamie*, comic acts such as Lewis Black and the Laughing Irish Comedy Tour, and musical artists like Cake, Yellowcard, and MXPX. In addition, admission to all varsity athletic events, Truman theater productions, and Lyceum Series events is free to Truman students.

Truman is Missouri's premier liberal arts and sciences university and the only highly selective public institution in the state. The Liberal Studies Program is the heart of Truman's curriculum and is intended to serve as a foundation for all major programs of study offered by the University. Truman's mission is to "offer an exemplary undergraduate education, grounded in the liberal arts and sciences, in the context of a public institution of higher learning." The philosophy behind the Liberal Studies Program is based upon a commitment that Truman has made to provide students with essential skills needed for lifelong learning, breadth across the traditional liberal arts and sciences through exposure to various discipline-based modes of inquiry, and interconnecting perspectives that stress interdisciplinary thinking and integration as well as linkage to other cultures and experiences.

University of Missouri

Admissions Office
230 Jesse Hall
Columbia, MO 65211
Admissions phone: (573) 882-7786
Admissions e-mail: mu4u@missouri.edu
Admissions URL: admissions.missouri.edu/

 Admissions

Current student, 8/2002-Submit Date, January 2006

As a minority student, I applied, interviewed for, and accepted the George C. Brooks Scholarship, which paid the university's huge out-of-state tuition, plus $7,500 a year for four years. Selectivity is not high, though I consider this school high quality. Recently, there's been a controversy over whether the uni-

versity is admitting too many students with the aim to get their tuition mone especially given state funding cutbacks.

Current student, 8/2004-Submit Date, September 2005

Admissions was very easy. I had a 2.9 GPA from my community college. I on had to fill out an application online. There was a short essay, but no interview or anything. I did fill out a more extensive application for scholarships, but didn't get any. I did receive a grant because I was from out of state. Out-of-stat tuition is a lot, usually about $8,000 to $9,000 more than in-state tuition Establishing residency in Missouri is kind of a pain, but worth it. You have t live here for a year and work and register to vote, and they establish you as a res ident so you don't have to pay out-of-state fees.

Alumnus/a, 1/2001-5/2004, April 2005

The admissions process for UMC was a fairly painless process. A simple appl cation filed along with an essay question was all that was needed. The accep ance program is fairly straightforward. Residents of the state of Missouri ar tomatically accepted provided they meet the basic requirement of a high hool degree. For added insurance on getting in, it is a good idea to call the reg- rar's office regularly to check on your application status. This is a huge bonus your favor.

lumnus/a, 8/1999-8/2003, March 2005

is very easy if you are a Missouri resident with good grades. If you are from t of state and want to get into the journalism school, the process will involve od grades and a lot of motivation.

urrent student, 8/2000-Submit Date, April 2004

he undergraduate admissions process at Mizzou is extremely accessible and rsonal. I mailed in my application and application fee and was notified a few ort weeks later that I had been accepted. The application process is fairly sim- e. Mizzou has an automatic admissions policy for all students with a 24 or ove on their ACT. The paper application is one page, and then there is an say to write for scholarship consideration. The essay is about 250 words, and at portion is not due until December.

called the admissions office to schedule a campus visit, and the admissions aff did an excellent job of catering a visit for me. I took a detailed campus tour ith a knowledgeable current student, ate lunch with a student interested in my eld, took a tour of the journalism school, and sat through a 5 p.m. newscast at e journalism school's NBC-affiliate TV station, KOMU. Since I was interest- in broadcast journalism at the time, this was the perfect visit for me, and I ew when I left that I definitely wanted to attend Mizzou. After that, I was sent stcards and called by Mizzou students, to see if I had any questions. This ade me feel very comfortable about going to Mizzou.

uring the summer, I attended a summer orientation program, which was excel- nt. I registered for classes at that time, met fellow incoming students, spoke ith current students, and learned a great deal about the traditions, history and mpus life at Mizzou. After leaving summer orientation, I was very excited out going to Mizzou in the fall!

 Academics

urrent student, 8/2002-Submit Date, January 2006

m in the communication department, which I love. The atmosphere of the partment is wonderful, with professors who actually care about you. Most ve great availability and understanding. The classes are of good quality, but u only get out of it what you put into it. You can get out of a class with a B d not learn very much, thanks to the unchallenging standardized testing. Some asses are more challenging than others (e.g., essay exams instead of multiple oice). The workload isn't too overwhelming. There are daily reading assign- ents, but unless the class has daily or pop quizzes, students typically don't read erything until it's time to cram for exams. My biggest issue with the depart- ent is the inability to get all of the classes that I want. Since the department is t huge, class choices and times are limited.

urrent student, 8/2003-Submit Date, January 2006

here are some weak classes, and it's best to find a professor you like and take s/her classes. All the courses with labs are great—there is a lot of opportuni- to have one-on-one help. I have never had a problem getting the courses I eded or wanted. My favorites have been Strat Writing I and Design and isuals and Interactive Advertising. News and magazine students must work at local daily paper that's run by students. It is extremely stressful, but for those ho are interested in reporting, it's a great experience.

urrent student, 8/2004-Submit Date, September 2005

am an English major and I find the quality of the classes dubious. Most of the asses are no where near my expectations. Some English classes don't even quire papers. It is also difficult to get into popular classes, and in one class, I d to drop it because I would have had to sit on the floor. The classrooms are ry overcrowded and it is difficult to find help on campus.

lumnus/a, 1/2001-5/2004, April 2005

lass sizes are often decided after enrollment, this allows for an ease of getting to the classes needed or wanted. If the class size is pre-determined and is full

when you decide to register, it is fairly easy to find another section for the same lecture. In some cases, it's even possible to arrange for a new section to be given specifically to accommodate any students who may have been denied access due to class size being full.

As far as teachers go, Mizzou has some of the best in the world. It's outstand- ing in the fields of journalism and others are known worldwide. Several tenured professors are known as being in the top 10 percent of the researchers in their fields. Grading is always fair and the professors are always willing to go over the policy with you as well as answer any questions you may have about grades received.

Alumnus/a, 8/1999-8/2003, March 2005

Academically, when you are a freshman and sophomore, it is very important to get into the Honors College in order to take advantage of the best classes that Mizzou has to offer. The classes are smaller, the professors very involved, and they will challenge you and really give you a good education while you are also taking all the required general education courses, which are big lectures and not in a field that necessarily interests you. As a junior and senior, the classes will by nature be smaller, harder and more specific to your interest, and I believe that the professors are very qualified, dedicated and open to individual interaction with students. They love it when you visit their office with questions or a dis- cussion; and you receive an excellent education.

Alumnus/a, 8/1999-12/2003, April 2004

I did not enjoy the general education classes at all. The smaller ones were OK, but I did not do well in the big lecture classes at all. The classes in my depart- ment of interior design were all wonderful.

Current student, 8/2000-Submit Date, April 2004

I am a senior in the advertising sequence of the Missouri School of Journalism. Mizzou is well known for being a world leader in journalism, with many oppor- tunities that are not available for journalism students at other universities. We have an NBC-affiliate TV station, KOMU, where juniors and seniors report and anchor, just like they would after college. This gives them great experience and a step up on the competition. Our news editorial students report and edit for the *Columbia Missourian*, a newspaper that serves the community. Our magazine students write and design for *VOX Magazine*, and our photojournalism students take pictures for these publications. Students in the advertising sequence are given actual clients for whom they must create and implement a comprehensive marketing/advertising plan.

Our journalism students and graduates are some of the best in the field. Just last week, senior Mike Hall was chosen as the winner of ESPN's Dream Job, and he will work for ESPN SportsCenter already next year. Other alumni include Jim Lehrer (Lehrer NewsHour), Lisa Myers (NBC Chief Congressional Correspondent), Elizabeth Vargas (ABC), Jann Carl (*Entertainment Tonight*), and John Anderson (*ESPN SportsCenter*).

Our classes are interesting and diverse. Professors have typically worked in their respective fields before going into teaching, so they bring real-world knowledge to their students. They are extremely passionate about their fields, and pass that on to students. Since we have so many outstanding alumni in journalism, they bring in about three to six alumni guest speakers each semester to give students advice and help them make connections.

 Employment Prospects

Current student, 8/2002-Submit Date, January 2006

The university is famous for its journalism school. Employment prospects as a journalism major are great. The J-school actually has a black book of alumni to whom you have access. I have used this black book. It's invaluable. The busi- ness school also does a good job of bringing recruiters on campus. Public sec- tor jobs like Teach For America and Peace Corps have a strong presence on cam- pus.

Current student, 8/2004-Submit Date, September 2005

There are lots of internships available. However, it just depends on who you know. A lot of fraternities have good networks with which to work. The school

Read all of Vault's College Surveys at **www.vault.com/college**–get complete surveys on 100s of colleges and univer- sities, expert advice on applicaton essays and more.

VAULT CAREER LIBRARY **401**

has a good reputation. It has the Number One journalism school in the country and the Number Two residency program in the country, or something like that. It carries a lot of weight. Also, since the university is affiliated with University Hospital, you can find a job while going to school, which is nice.

Alumnus/a, 1/2001-5/2004, April 2005

The alumni network and student centers on campus are always willing to assist both alumni and current students with finding employment. The international prestige of the University of Missouri Columbia makes it easy to find employers. Graduates of the university have filled many positions from world renowned journalists to celebrities in movies and music. Brad Pitt and Sheryl Crow are both alumni of Mizzou.

Alumnus/a, 8/1995-5/2000, February 2005

The J-school is the only one to offer a BJ, other communications and journalism programs offer a BA or BS. The history and strong alumni network at Missouri is amazing. There are Mizzou alumni in probably every communications or journalism-related field and those connections are how you get in the door and ahead of the pack. J-school alumni are extremely proud and take care of their own. It's aptly dubbed the Mizzou Mafia. As a broadcast journalist out of Missouri, you can quickly get a job in the 60s to 80s ranked market (DMA) and then how quickly you move up in market size depends on your work and time there. But everybody that I know who wants to continue as a TV reporter has no problem getting a job. For broadcast, there's no recruiting. News directors don't have the time nor the money to do typical recruiting because they are usually bombarded with résumé tapes if/when they're not hiring, so having that Mizzou connection really helps catapult your work.

Current student, 8/2000-Submit Date, April 2004

The journalism school does a great job of making students aware of job and internship opportunities. They strongly suggest that students have internships the summer between their junior and senior years. Every spring, the school hosts a job/internship fair, where recruiters from Kansas City and St. Louis come to meet with students. The staff in the school send out weekly messages with job/internship postings, deadlines and scholarship information. They are always willing to meet with students to discuss job placement, and offer names of alumni who could help particular students. The Missouri School of Journalism carries a great deal of prestige and employers look for Mizzou graduates.

Quality of Life

Current student, 8/2002-Submit Date, January 2006

Quality of life is good in Columbia. Apartment housing is readily available, and neighborhoods throughout the city are relatively safe. Campus housing has been increasing over the past couple of years, with several nice new dorms being built. Campus dining offers variety, though it's expensive, and I haven't eaten at a cafeteria since freshman year, when it was required for me to live in a dorm. The newly renovated recreation center facility is incredibly beautiful. If you like working out, this university has a lot to offer. The campus is well maintained, and certain department buildings (e.g., business school) are beautiful, high-tech facilities. Wireless web is accessible all over campus. Public transportation is pretty terrible around Columbia.

Current student, 8/2003-Submit Date, January 2006

There is much construction going on throughout campus, which means big improvements and great new dorms! The new rec complex is amazing! Voted Number One for rec complexes in all of America by *Sports Illustrated*. (I work there.) Anyway, if I would had seen the rec center when I took a campus tour, I would be sold automatically. Dorm food is good, also.

Current student, 8/2004-Submit Date, September 2005

I live off campus but still near it and I have issues with the fraternities. My apartment window was broken because they were hitting golf balls randomly as a prank. Other than that, it is safe. There's no real crime. And Columbia is a nice city. It's not too crowded. A couple of new dorms were also built and they are pretty nice. The few blocks right by campus are fairly inexpensive apartment buildings, which is nice because parking is very expensive and very exclusive.

Alumnus/a, 1/2001-5/2004, April 2005

Dorms are well lit, comfortable and nearby to most class buildings. The university has its own police for along with security personnel for special events, a night patrols. Security is even put in place for school holidays when most of t students have left the campus. Campus, itself, is a beautiful garden spot w plenty of shade, trees, artwork, even its own museums. Crime is relatively lo people are friendly, and even the campus police are willing to walk you back your dorm if you feel the need.

Current student, 8/2000-Submit Date, April 2004

All freshmen are required to live on campus in the residence halls. There are residence halls, 13 of them are co-ed, four are all female and two are all ma Mizzou has a thriving living and learning community atmosphere in the re dence halls, and many of the halls and floors are dedicated to speci majors/interests. Some of these include: The World of Busine Journalism/Mass Communications, the Honors Learning Community, t Leadership Residential College and the Wakonse Service Community.

Students can also be part of smaller freshman interest groups (FIGs), where th live with students in their major, take three classes together, and take a one-ho proseminar course on college transitions and life skills. This greatly improv the academics and quality of life for freshmen.

The dining halls are very good for cafeteria food. There is a wide selection many of the dining halls have fresh salad, fruits, grilled items, pizza, deli, h entrees and desserts every day. Some are arranged in all you can eat fashion and others are on a carry out, point system base. Students can choose from me plans of seven, 10, 14, 17 or 21 meals per week. There are other eating optio on campus, such as Pizza Hut, McDonald's, Burger King, Chick-fil-A, Subwa and Italian and homestyle cafes.

Many sophomores, juniors and seniors live off campus in apartments, duplex and houses near to campus. They then get parking on campus and commu back and forth.

Mizzou is a very safe community. In fact, it is the safest campus in the Big 1 Campus is well-lit at night, and residence halls lock at 11 p.m. Students ca access their residence halls after that time by swiping their ID cards at the fro doors.

Social Life

Current student, 8/2002-Submit Date, January 2006

Columbia is a small, but eclectic city. If you're coming from a big city, y might get a little bored here. However, there's a nice mix of bars, restauran clubs and coffee shops in the downtown area, which looks like an old scho walking/shopping district. Certain places have become absolute must-sees, su as Shakespeare's Pizza and Cherrt St. Artisan (coffee shop).

Current student, 8/2003-Submit Date, January 2006

Great college town. There are many fun clubs and bars. The Greek system huge here at Mizzou and I encourage everyone to get involved with that. I w involved with Alpha Delta Pi and at first it made the huge school seem small and gave me an opportunity to meet people I wouldn't otherwise meet and atte fun parties. It also encouraged me to keep my grades up. Hapro's is the pop lar hang out on Thursdays. Friday is a great day to go to the Penguin (piano ba ladies get in free, and Saturday $2 at Campus!

Current student, 8/2004-Submit Date, September 2005

There are lots of bars and clubs. Shakespeare's is the preferred pizza place. A of downtown has really cool vintage stores and bars and restaurants within couple of blocks. Greek life is huge on this campus. There is Greek row, whi is a couple of blocks of Greek houses. Bid Day is a big deal here. A large po tion of the campus is in a sorority or fraternity. The restaurants downtown a really good as well. They are right off campus so a lot of students walk there f lunch and dinner. Many people stay right in the area, although the mall and stu is across town. The dating scene is pretty nonexistent. Most people don't ha relationships. They might date casually, but that's it.

lumnus/a, 1/2001-5/2004, April 2005

he town of Columbia, MO is full of nightlife of any and all varieties. Music, ovies, parks, festivals, coffee houses and shops all cater to the student body of izzou. On campus, the special events can be found almost every night of the eek. Clubs are easy to find and join. People are easy-going and always open fun. It really is a great school and city.

urrent student, 8/2000-Submit Date, April 2004

izzou has a strong social atmosphere. 25 percent of the student population is rt of the Greek system, and our Greek community is located in a central area campus. This strengthens the community and allows for greater accessibility om chapter to chapter. Greek students have chapter meetings every Monday ght, participate in various philanthropies, academic and athletic competitions d host many social events. Members are also extremely involved in campus tivities outside of their chapters.

ur non-Greek students are also very involved in student activities. We have the rgest student-run homecoming celebration in the nation that takes place in ctober. Our Homecoming Steering Committee plans service activities, campus ecorations, barbecues, the parade, a blood drive and much more for students, milies and alumni.

e have over 400 student organizations in which students can par take. Some the most popular organizations and committees include Homecoming, the lumni Association Student Board, Greek Week Steering Committee, Summer elcome Orientation Leaders, Outreach and Tour Team.

olumbia's downtown area (called the District) is well known for its cultural climate d great dining. Three of students' favorite restaurants include: Shakespeare's Pizza, ddison's American Grill and Flatbranch Brewery. There is also a number of bars d clubs downtown, including Deja Vu Comedy Club, Tonic, Shattered, Quinton's, ieldhouse and of course, Mizzou's famous bar, Harpo's. In Columbia, the weekend arts on Thursday, with quarter draws at Harpo's. Dancing is popular on Thursdays d Fridays, and many students go to parties on Saturdays. Mizzou is a dry campus, all events with alcohol take place off campus.

The School Says

MU teaches the people who solve problems and change the world.

The University of Missouri-Columbia was founded in 1839 as the first public university west of the Mississippi River and the first state university in Thomas Jefferson's Louisiana Purchase territory. Today with more than 28,000 students, 12,000 faculty and staff members and 240,000 alumni worldwide, Missouri's flagship university offers 265 degrees programs through 20 colleges and schools.

MU provides all the benefits of two universities in one—it's a major land-grant institution and Missouri's largest public research university. Considered one of the nation's top-tier institutions, Mizzou is one of only 34 public universities to be selected for membership in the Association of American Universities. The Carnegie Foundation for the Advancement of Teaching classifies MU among American universities that offer the most educational opportunities and the highest level of instruction.

Mizzou is the favorite classroom for the best and brightest, attracting more valedictorians, Curators Scholars and twice as many of the state's Bright Flight Scholars than any other college or university in Missouri. It also is one of only six public universities in the country with medicine, veterinary medicine and law all on one campus.

Designated as a botanic garden, MU's 1,358-acre main campus features more than 5,400 trees and 650 varieties of plants. A number of University buildings also are listed on the National Register of Historic Places.

Citizens across the state connect with Mizzou by participating in Extension programs in every county, visiting MU Health Care specialists, competing in state competitions in MU facilities and by cheering on the Missouri Tigers at athletic events. A member of the Big 12 Conference, Mizzou features the state's only division I-A athletic program, where student-athletes in 20 sports compete at the highest level nationally.

Washington University in St. Louis

ndergraduate Admissions
Vashington University in St. Louis
Campus Box 1089
ne Brookings Drive
t. Louis, MO 63130
dmissions phone: (314) 935-6000 or (800) 638-0700
dmissions e-mail: admissions@wustl.edu
dmissions URL: admissions.wustl.edu

Admissions

urrent student, 8/2005-Submit Date, October 2006

tandard admissions process—using the Common App is nice. Applying Early ecision gives you a boost. Visiting campus is a must, as WashU really likes to ccept students who have already shown interest in their campus. Very selective chool.

Current student, 8/2005-Submit Date, October 2006

I applied Early Decision and everything went very smoothly. The application was concise and simple and I really enjoyed that I got to pick my essay topic. I did not participate in an interview though the school does hold interviews for some students. It is a highly selective school.

> **The school says:** "Interviews are optional at Washington University. But we encourage students to interview and will hold one for any student who requests it."

Current student, 9/2004-Submit Date, October 2006

Admissions process was very easy. I was in constant contact with the representative for my region. I just filled out the Common Application, so the essays were easy. There was no interview process and the selectivity was high.

Current student, 8/2004-Submit Date, October 2005

The number of applicants to Washington University has increased greatly over the last decade, The application, itself, is not difficult (WashU [accepts either the Common Application or the Universal College Application]), and interviews are granted (though most of them are conducted by junior and senior undergraduates). WashU (as students call it) is notorious for waitlisting qualified applicants,

Read all of Vault's College Surveys at **www.vault.com/college**—get complete surveys on 100s of colleges and universities, expert advice on applicaton essays and more.

VAULT CAREER LIBRARY **403**

probably with motivation of wanting to increase their enrollment rates. While WashU has risen in ranking toward the more famous Top 10 universities, it still loses students to the Ivy League. Therefore, interest goes a long way with securing an acceptance.

> **WashU says:** "Interviews are conducted by undergraduate students, faculty, and staff members from across the university."

If you are a competitive applicant, it is important to demonstrate to the admissions office that you are strongly considering Washington University or that it is your top choice school. Many students are also accepted Early Decision. There are two options: fall Early Decision and January Early Decision (II), but both are binding. There are also many scholarship opportunities, some of which require special applications. While there are many students who receive need-based aid or scholarships, there are a surprising number of students who received merit scholarships (from $2,500 to full tuition). There are scholarships for many different types of people, and they are granted on grounds such as test scores/grades, overcoming hardships, excellent writing, technical or musical skill, and many more. As a Division III school, WashU does not grant athletic scholarships. There is also a program called University Scholars that will grant certain extremely qualified prospective students a guaranteed admission to one of the graduate programs upon graduation from WashU contingent on a certain undergraduate GPA and graduate entrance score. These students are released from the burden of applying to law schools, grad schools or med schools, but they are also not bound to attend WashU if they decide they want to change their minds. The Medical University Scholars program is especially competitive, as WashU's medical school is consistently ranked in the Top Three (with Harvard and Johns Hopkins).

> **The school says:** "The January Early Decision (II) is no longer an option."

Current student, 7/2003-Submit Date, January 2005

I had to fill out an application that asked a number of questions about my background and my motivation for wanting to enroll in the school. My grades and SAT scores were reviewed, and I got two recommendation letters from two different previous teachers. On top of this I was asked to write a number of essays, including what my greatest difficulties and accomplishments were. I included a personal statement about my current family situation at the time. I had an informal interview with an alumni and made sure to visit the school. Washington University is very selective and is currently ranked as the 11th best university in the country by *U.S. News & World Report*.

> **Washington University says:** "None of our applications ask for the student's motivation for wanting to enroll at the university."

 **Academics**

Current student, 8/2004-Submit Date, December 2006

I have really enjoyed almost all of my classes at WashU. The classes are hard and cover very advanced subject matter, but are very interesting and teach you a lot. I have almost always been able to get into all the classes I wanted to take, especially as an upperclassman. Even if you cannot get into a class in a certain semester, you will probably be able to take it later when you have higher priority in registering. I am in the English program, and while I have to work very hard to write all my papers, professors grade pretty easily. I have found grading to be very fair at WashU. The standards are rigorous, but if you do the work assigned and keep up with the reading, you can do very well. Professors here are wonderful and generally highly concerned for students' success. They are always willing to meet with you to try and help you with assignments and are generally very understanding about what students are going through in trying to keep up with their work. The workload is very hard. It is very stressful to keep up with sometimes, but it's very rewarding.

Current student, 8/2005-Submit Date, October 2006

The classes are the highest quality. I rarely felt challenged, in hih school and at Washington University not only do I feel challenged, but I feel like I'm provided with resources to meet those challenges. There are tons of tutoring programs and through the engineering school I even receive free tutoring hours. All of my

professors hold weekly help sessions and make themselves very available t questions. The professors are hit and miss. This semester I switched sessions a particular class because one teacher was so much easier to follow than t other. The workload is heavy but manageable if students use their time wise

Current student, 8/2005-Submit Date, October 2006

As a Biomedical Engineering student, I am very pleased with the academic c riculum. It's very challenging but fun. Classes are not hard to get into. Expe a heavy workload if you do engineering. Professors are very accessible on t whole and usually grading is fair.

Current student, 8/2004-Submit Date, October 2005

Washington University consists of five undergraduate colleges: Arts & Science Engineering, Business, Art, and Architecture. While students apply to a parti ular school, they can take classes in any of the five colleges. This highligh WashU's flexible curriculum, which allows students to double or trip major/minor or dual degree (for example, a Business degree and an Art degr or an Arts and Sciences degree and an Engineering degree). There is only o required course, which is a basic Freshman Writing and Argumentation class cu minating in a research paper. The only other requirements in Arts and Scienc are the completion of a major and the fulfillment of clusters (three classes ea in natural science, textual and historical studies, language and the arts, and soc science). These clusters are incredibly flexible, however, as students can fulf the natural science with pre-medical classes such as Organic Chemistry, anthr pology classes, math classes, or environmental science courses or language a the arts with English, foreign language, linguistic, drama or music classes.

Current student, 7/2003-Submit Date, January 2005

The classes at Washington University are very valuable but tend to grow tedio from time to time. Students will often find themselves doing work that w assigned to keep the students busy and not actually to add to coursework at han I took a lab for my Calculus II class last semester and almost nothing we did the lab actually related to the materials being covered in class. The quality, how ever, is very high and I do find myself learning a great deal. I do not think the has been a single semester where I have gotten into every class that I wanted, b one can usually get into most of the classes one desires. The grading is fair tough although the professors are fair and generally do explain what they a looking for at the beginning of each semester. The workload at Washingto University is very high and should not be taken lightly.

Current student, 8/1999-Submit Date, May 2004

The academics of the school are pretty laid-back. If you want to work real hard, there are a lot of things to learn and a lot of people with whom to stud The classes are varied. In the arts and sciences school, the quality of teaching somewhat better than the engineering school. In the engineering school, the pr fessors are there to do research, and some don't care much about the teachin aspect of being a university professor.

The sizes of the classes are varied, too. First-year classes tend to be large, b when you get into 300- and 400-level classes, usually you're in a class of aroun 20 people. It's also pretty easy to get into popular classes, as long as you're a upperclassman. With grading, again, it totally depends on the professor an class. The workload can be tremendously varied. You can get by on a day worth of work a week. But if you really want to learn a lot, you can find all sor of research opportunities, and the professors are generally helpful if you hav questions. Also, there is no boundary between different schools in the universi ty. Business school students can take engineering classes, and arts and science students can take architecture classes if they want. So the opportunity is ther for a well-rounded education.

 Employment Prospects

Current student, 8/2004-Submit Date, December 2006

Graduates of WashU go on to do almost every job possible. Our career center very helpful in finding positions and opportunities for students. They help stu dents through every step of the job finding process, from deciding what you wa to do, to formulating a résumé, to finding a specific organization. WashU is very well-known and prestigious school. Students are very high achieving an employers know this. Alumni get wonderful jobs all over the country, and man

rms come to campus to recruit people. There are constantly meeting sessions
r students to meet representatives from different employers and to network.
he career center also arranges several parties every year for current students to
eet with alumni who are located all over the country now. There are many
line resources from the career center to help students find jobs. There are
ousands of internship opportunities listed on the database.

urrent student, 8/2004-Submit Date, October 2005

ashU's name is gaining notoriety, but there are some problems with name
cognition outside of the Midwest. That said, graduates of WashU go on to
eat graduate schools and jobs in a variety of fields. The career center has made
commitment to ensure that each senior is secure in a job, graduate program, or
nsitional program (such as Peace Corps or Teach for America) by graduation,
d they have succeeded every year. As the WashU curriculum is diverse, so are
students so they go on to be leaders in a variety of fields in science, technol-
y, law, humanities, business, music, art and architecture. Companies are con-
ntly recruiting at WashU, and there is an online and paper-based database of
umni connections, jobs, and internships. It is easy to secure an internship due
the incredible listings provided by the career center, and most students will
ve completed at least one before graduation.

urrent student, 7/2003-Submit Date, January 2005

ashington University is typically viewed as a very prestigious school by
ployers and I have not had trouble finding an internship or summer job yet.
ur graduates tend to obtain jobs that they are very pleased with. One of my fra-
rnity brothers just received a job in consulting with a starting salary of $72,000
r his first year out of school. The career center is always looking for some way
another to get involved in the students' lives and have always been helpful. I
ve yet to contact any alumni for help, but I have been told that they are eager-
willing to help.

lumnus/a, 8/1999-5/2003, September 2004

ternships are easy to find if you ask professors and advisors for help. Within
ch department there are often faculty who know about internships and even
ll-time opportunities. Of course, if you are looking for a job outside the
idwest you may be looking for a while—and be prepared to nod and smile
hen your interviewers say what a nice city Seattle must be to go to school in.

lumnus/a, 8/2003-6/2002, September 2003

areer prospects are much better if you stay in the Midwest (I don't think that
e East Coast has caught on to WashU just yet). However, WashU is well
garded by graduate schools, so that might be a good way to go.

Quality of Life

urrent student, 8/2004-Submit Date, December 2006

ashU provides a great environment for students. There is an unbelievable
mount of activity on campus everyday. Physical and mental health care facili-
es are easily available. Housing is very nice. There are many different options,
d each one facilitates socialization for a student with others in their grade
vel. Also, there are certain interest related housing options, where you can live
ith people who share your interests and engage in programs with them. RAs
e very nice and helpful in letting students get adjusted to college life and show-
g them fun things to do in St. Louis. Also, we have peer advisors to recom-
end classes and professors. They have a budget for the year and take out their
visees for casual dinners and other things.

he campus is beautiful and pretty small, so getting around is really easy. The
brary is comfortable and popular with everyone, but it closes rather early some-
mes. We do not have wireless everywhere on campus, though, which can be
ally irritating when you need to use the Internet. Gym facilities are a little
cking. There are two gyms on campus and you have to pay extra to belong to
em. One is very small but nice. The other is better equipped but a little dingy
d dark because it is underground. Classrooms are very well equipped with
mputers and projectors in every one. Some have electrically controlled
ades, which is really neat. The food here is very good. There are a lot of
tions and many places to grab food around campus. There is a general buffet
ar all the freshman dorms and more specialized options elsewhere on campus.
e have Starbucks and Kaldis coffee, and really great prepared salads. There

are kosher options, too. WashU itself is very safe, and I've never felt in danger
on campus. Some of the areas around the school are a little more dangerous
though, but there are always security officers patrolling.

> **The school says:** "The library is open late almost every night of
> the week. Sunday through Thursday, it is open until 2 a.m. It's
> open on Friday until 8 p.m. and 10 p.m. on Saturday. Whispers
> Café, located at the entrance of Olin Library, is open 24 hours
> a day during the academic year.
>
> There is one athletic complex on campus, and there is no mem-
> bership fee for full-time students. There are two fitness centers
> on campus, one is within the athletic complex and the other is
> located on the South 40. There is a small fee for the use of
> these fitness centers."

Current student, 8/2005-Submit Date, October 2006

I feel very safe and comfortable at Washington University. That's not to mention that it's gorgeously maintained. Everything is always clean (even the
dorms). A wide range of food, diner hours, and locations is provided, making
meals nothing to worry about.

Current student, 8/2005-Submit Date, October 2006

Housing is absolutely phenomenal—WashU has much better dorms on average
than other places. Campus is small, but has a "homey" feel. I love it! Very safe
campus. Food is absolutely excellent compared with other universities (when I
visited a friend, I had a problem stomaching the food there). Very nice, affluent
neighborhoods surrounding most of university. Also, there is a lot of college
housing around campus.

Alumnus/a, 8/2000-5/2004, January 2006

Housing process is well organized and a large majority of the houses are less
than 10 years old and are very spacious. Residential Advisors are chosen carefully (a very prestigious honor to be selected) and the food is restaurant quality
(not kidding!). Surrounding neighborhoods are reasonably safe and full of
restaurants, bars, movie theatres, concert rooms and bowling allies. Free shuttle
transports students to grocery stores and one of the largest malls in the area.

> **WashU says:** "All full-time students now receive a U-Pass,
> which provides access to all Metro buses and the MetroLink
> light-rail system."

Current student, 8/2004-Submit Date, October 2005

All freshmen at WashU who do not live within 25 miles of campus live in the
South 40 residential area. Housing is guaranteed all four years, and 96 percent
of sophomores stay on campus. There are also university apartments and affordable off-campus housing options. Both the residential and academic areas are
well-maintained, clean, beautiful and safe. There are more computers than there
are students to use them, food is incredible, and there are amazing resources both
by the residential areas and main campus including many libraries, help desks,
and hangouts. There are over 20 places to eat on campus that are all accessible
via the meal card. There is even a hang out called Ursa's Cafe that provides free
coffee and live entertainment every Friday, has handmade ice cream, smoothies,
and crepes, and game boards with rentable pieces in the tables. Students, however, are required to purchase a meal plan and the food provided by Bon Appetit
(the campus dining services company) is often considered delicious but incredibly overpriced. Campus is very much based around the students and campus
officials are constantly innovating to create new and exciting areas. The library
was also recently revamped to include beautiful new study areas, comfy chairs,
and a 24-hour cyber cafe called Whispers. There are some dangerous areas in
St. Louis, but the WashU campus is surrounded by safe, suburban areas.
Campus security is great and includes Washington University Police Department
(Missouri police officers that only patrol WashU's campus). There are blue light
phones and students can call to have a van pick them up if they feel unsafe
(which they rarely do) walking back to their dorm or car at night.

Read all of Vault's College Surveys at **www.vault.com/college**–get complete surveys on 100s of colleges and universities, expert advice on applicaton essays and more.

VAULT CAREER LIBRARY **405**

Social Life

Current student, 8/2004-Submit Date, December 2006

I am not in the Greek system, but it is very popular here. Lots of people are involved, but it is certainly not necessary to be. It does not dominate social life in any way. There are a lot of bars around St. Louis, but you have to be 21 to get into them. Most underage students have fake IDs though.

Blueberry Hill is a bar and restaurant really close to school that is very popular with seniors. There are a lot of bars on Laclede's Landing downtown, and students go there usually on Thursday nights. A lot of people of groups rent out bars often and have exclusive parties for WashU students. Bars close either at 1 or at 3 a.m., which is really lame.

WashU is in a great area for restaurants. Students eat out usually about once a week or more. Il Vicino is a very popular Italian restaurant that is pretty cheap. Olympia is a Greek restaurant nearby that has the best gyros in St. Louis. The Loop, where Blueberry Hill is, is about five minutes from campus and there are a ton of restaurants there including: Thai, Japanese, Italian and American. There is also the Melting Pot, which is a nicer fondue restaurant that's good for dates. Modai on the Loop is a Japanese restaurant where students like to go sake bombing for people's birthdays.

There are lots of events going on campus all of the time. The most exciting two are WILD in the spring and in the fall. They are huge campus concerts that everyone goes to after partying all day. Team 31, who puts the concert on, gets pretty big names to come. We have had Ben Folds, Ozomatli, Guster and Robert Randolf. These are the most fun days all year. There is also Dance Marathon, which is a charity event in which students dance for 12 hours straight to raise money for the Children's Miracle Network. It is a really popular event. Another campus highlight is Thurteen carnival, which is the largest college carnival in the U.S. All fraternities and sororities build big structures and put on plays in them. This is a huge competition for the Greek system and a lot of fun. The proceeds from the carnival go to charity and it is a very fun week on campus.

Current student, 8/2005-Submit Date, October 2006

There's something for everyone! With sub-free dorms if students like, and a very diverse student body, no matter what you're doing you are sure to find a group of people who will do it with you. The Greek system is there if you want it but doesn't dominate the social scene. There is no pressure to join a Greek club if you don't want to.

Current student, 8/2005-Submit Date, October 2006

The Loop is right by campus and contains many different restaurants and bars. Blueberry Hill is the place of Chuck Berry—he performs there at least once a year. There are events happening all the time and the business school sponsors clubs on Thursday nights. Some students do Greek life, but it isn't over dominating on campus.

Alumnus/a, 8/2000-5/2004, January 2006

Work hard. Play hard. Weekends are booming with the noise of parties all over campus. Although Greek life before was an accessory to the social scene, the growth of the Greek system of late has started to create a clear (so sad!) division. No matter who you hang with, you go to Blueberry Hill as soon as you turn 21 because you will always find at least one good friend—that's where everyone is. Dating comes and goes depending on what year you are, often times relationships fall apart because everyone is just so busy with other aspects of college life.

Current student, 8/2004-Submit Date, October 2005

Freshmen are not allowed to have cars (and parking is often horrific), but the are four free shuttle lines to take students to nearby grocery stores, clubs, restarants, shops and cafes. Many places in St. Louis require students to be 21 older to enter, so there is a lot of under-aged drinking on campus. However, i student chooses not to drink, there are many other social outlets both on and c campus. WashU is located in Forest Park in St. Louis, which is ranked Numb Two in the nation for free cultural activities, which include a free zoo, art mus um, history museum and outdoor theatre. Forest Park, itself, is 500 acres larg than Central Park and is a common place for students to relax, run, bike, rollerblade. Students will frequently go to the Loop, which is a series of restarants, bars and shops located within walking distance of campus (about a 1 minute walk). There is also a concert venue in the Loop called the Pageant (p marily for rock), and there are many opportunities to hear a variety of mus types at nearby venues, including the Fox Theatre, which has Broadway show

 The School Says

Washington University students learn in a flexible, challenging academic atmosphere that encourages them to cross disciplines, taking courses in any of our five undergraduate divisions: arts & sciences, architecture, art, business and engineering. We also offer graduate programs in these divisions as well as law; medicine, including occupational therapy and physical therapy; and social work. This interdisciplinary environment allows students to study alongside other academically talented students from across the country and around the world in any subject that interests them. Through research projects that start as early as the freshman year, students can participate with our world-class faculty in the creation of knowledge. This academic exploration takes place in a supportive, friendly community that provides the resources to ensure success. Outside the classroom, students participate in nearly 200 activities, including community service and multicultural groups; musical, dance and theater groups, fraternities and sororities; intramural, club and varsity sports; student government; and literary groups.

We invite you to visit Washington University any time to experience these outstanding opportunities firsthand. When you visit, you may attend an admissions information session, take a student-led campus tour, have an optional on-campus interview and attend classes, sporting events, or meetings of student groups.

Applicants for fall 2008 are required to submit scores from either the SAT or ACT test. Applicants who submit scores from the ACT test may submit with or without the Writing component. We encourage all students to apply for our Academic Scholarships and for financial assistance based on family financial circumstances. This year our undergraduates are receiving nearly $60 million in university scholarships and grants.

University of Nebraska—Lincoln

Admissions Office
13 N 13th St
P.O. Box 880256
Lincoln, NE 68588-0256
Admissions phone: (402) 472-2023 or (800) 742-8800
Admissions e-mail: admissions@unl.edu
Admissions URL: admissions.unl.edu/

Admissions

Alumnus/a, Business, 8/2002-5/2006, April 2007

Admissions requirements are similar to most large, state universities. Either top 10 percent of high school graduating class, 21 or higher on ACT and you're in. Essays and résumés are required in order to be considered for all university merit and need-based scholarships. At this time one may also apply for the university's Honors Program. The Honors Program allows you to take smaller classes with the top professors. It also requires a senior thesis.

Current student, 8/2004-Submit Date, September 2006

The application process was very indicative of the competitiveness of this school. It was easy to fill out and easy to submit. When I wanted to visit the school, they were waiting for me with a free t-shirt, a sign of welcome and interviews with any administrators or students with whom I wished to talk. This was the friendliest university I dealt with and as a current student, I can attest to the effort they make to take care of their own. However, the level of competition was slightly disappointing, but it's a state school.

Alumnus/a, 8/1999-5/2003, July 2005

The admissions process is not as rigorous as other schools (mostly private ones) to which I applied. I did not apply to any other state schools, so I am not able to compare the process to that of other schools. The University of Nebraska—Lincoln is not very selective, as it is a state school. If you have the required ACT and GPA, you will have no problem getting in. The essays are still important, however, as the school offers a great deal of scholarship money. The essays were pretty typical of application essays. I'm not certain how much weight is placed on them. As far as I know, there is no required interview. The school offers a lot of opportunities for high school students to visit and see if the school is for them. A word of advice for Nebraska state residents: the State of Nebraska offers a lot of scholarship money to students willing to stay in state for college. Take advantage of this!

Alumnus/a, 8/1999-8/2003, March 2005

I applied to UNL on a whim really. I went there because I received a full-tuition scholarship. Everything about getting into UNL was so easy for me. I had great grades, great ACT scores, and I don't recall having to do any interviews. I wrote my essay and my guidance counselor pretty much did the rest. I went down to admissions office, signed up for my classes and was ready to go. I recommend signing up a lot earlier in the summer than I did. I had a 7:30 a.m. Calculus class.

Current student, 8/2003-Submit Date, March 2005

I just sent in an application and they sent back an acceptance letter. No essays. You can even apply online. The new student orientation makes getting started here easy and fun. You can meet a lot of people during orientation while getting to see the campus and signing up for classes. This is also a good time to look for where your classes are located so you don't get lost on your first day of school.

Current student, 8/2001-Submit Date, October 2004

The admissions process at the University of Nebraska—Lincoln consists of a several page application that includes questions about your personality and questions about where you plan to take your education, what you would like to get out of college, and what field you are interested in and why.

Current student, 8/2001-Submit Date, February 2004

I am a transfer student from Malaysia. I was studying in a college in Malaysia, filled out an application for the university and then I was admitted. In order to qualify for the International Student Scholarship, besides a GPA of 3.0 or above, I needed to have three recommendation letters.

Alumnus/a, 8/1998-5/2002, September 2003

Moderately selective: must have at least a 20 on the ACT or be in the top half of your class. Not sure about the GPA requirement. To apply, fill out the application, send official transcripts, official ACT/SAT test scores and the application fee. I do not believe that there is an essay requirement.

The application deadline is early summer, but the scholarship deadline is March 1. You must have already been accepted to receive scholarships or financial aid. Make sure you fill out the scholarship form, as well.

The admissions office can answer any questions or give you other information. I recommend going to a Red Letter Day on campus (a visit day), it is very helpful to see the campus and get the feel of the university. Good luck!

Academics

Current student, Pre-Vet, 8/2004-Submit Date, September 2006

I am majoring in Veterinary and Biomedical Sciences and I believe I am getting one of the best Pre-Vet educations in the Midwest, if not the country. My advisors are veterinarians, as are many of my upper-level professors. Some of the lower-level classes are large lectures where it is harder to get to know your professors, but through recitations and study instructional sections, the university manages to break it down so you're not just one in a crowd and you have the personal help you need to succeed. Grading is fair and grade inflation is not much of an issue. If you have concerns, there are advisors and department heads who will talk to you. Workload has steadily increased and every year I can't imagine being busier. This Pre-Vet program is preparing me for the best schools in the country, and it is demanding a lot of me. I wanted a competitive school and though I wasn't sure a state school could provide that, individual programs raise the bar for participating students making it more of a small college atmosphere where you really get to know the other students in your major with whom you can study and work.

Alumnus/a, 8/1999-5/2003, July 2005

The academic program was great. It was a great value for the tuition. My teachers were all great. Most of the professors I had held PhDs in their fields. Many of the professors have open-door policies, and if you need help they will do what they can to help you. Most of my professors insisted that you stop by and see them outside of class. The only bad part of the academic atmosphere is the fact that a lot of students are there to slack off and get by with C's. That is frustrating for students who actually want to learn. I think you don't get that as much in private schools, where many students are aware of the money they (or their parents) are spending to have them there. There are some classes that are pointless, but I think you get that at any school you go to. The other thing to be aware of is the fact that a lot of emphasis is placed on athletics and the athletes. I think that many of the great academic programs, such as the engineering program, get overlooked because of this. The workload was not too overwhelming, but it depends on your program. You will want to register for classes early, as they fill up quickly.

Alumnus/a, Business, 8/2002-5/2006, April 2007

Specific to finance classes, the classes were small and easy to get into the most popular classes. The workload is medium but the quality of the professors and the classes is high. Now working in investment banking, the corporate finance classes did a good job in preparing me with the analytical skills I need. Additionally, the MBA program and accounting program are ranked highly.

Read all of Vault's College Surveys at **www.vault.com/college**—get complete surveys on 100s of colleges and universities, expert advice on applicaton essays and more.

VAULT CAREER LIBRARY **407**

Current student, 8/2003-Submit Date, March 2005

Each class is different. Some are easy, some are hard, some have no work, and some are very time consuming. It mainly depends on your major. Obviously a chemical engineering degree will be more difficult than family and consumer sciences degree, for example.

Current student, Engineering, 8/2001-Submit Date, October 2004

The engineering program is very high-quality. Both the university and the department are totally committed to providing a topnotch program for students. The grading at UNL is based on a +/- system, which raises the bar in difficulty. Getting into the most popular classes hasn't been a problem for me so far; they are really good about providing enough seats for everyone that wants to take the class. They are also very good about working with students who really need to take the class, and students who don't really need to take it. At UNL, the engineering department is one of the most difficult programs of which to be a part. The workload is heavy and stringent. This is balanced out with elective classes that are designed to be somewhat less difficult. A good balance of engineering classes and electives each semester is the key to success.

Current student, Business, 8/2002-Submit Date, January 2005

I like to say that academics at UNL are really similar to other undergraduate programs. Students at private colleges in Nebraska try to say that UNL is easy, but it's not true. Students at UNL do the same work as students at the private schools. I am a student in the business college and it can be really hard to get into the classes you need. As a freshman or sophomore, classes are large and offered a lot. As a junior or senior, classes are more specialized and can be hard to get in. Also, the advising in the business college is not very good. The academic advisors are students and they know as much about the requirements as I do. Each student is issued a faculty advisor, but when I tried to contact mine, it was impossible. UNL also requires students to take lots of general classes from each area. It can get really confusing because one class will count for one area for one college, but not for another. If a student transfers from one major to another they can be set back a semester or more. Each class grades differently. It all depends on the professor you get. You can fail one class and re-take it with a different professor, do the same quality of work and get an A.

Current student, 8/2001-Submit Date, February 2004

For the actuarial science courses, there is only one section for each course and all these courses are offered once a year, plus the courses are sequential prerequisites of each other. There is no problem in getting into a class, but one needs to plan accordingly in order to graduate in four years. Students need to have discipline to do well in class, since there is absolutely no homework assignment or whatsoever, except for the three or four exams.

Employment Prospects

Alumnus/a, Business, 8/2002-5/2006, April 2007

The staff and resources of the Careers Services office are very helpful in obtaining internships and full-time employment. "Husker Hire Link" is a job board for students and alumni. However, if one is looking to work in a larger city or on the East or West Coasts, that individual must take his/her own initiative to find jobs outside the region. If your industry is not well represented in the Midwest (such as computer technology, investment banking and so on), you may have difficulties finding employers that recruit on campus.

Alumnus/a, 8/1999-5/2003, July 2005

The career center was very helpful. Internships and jobs are posted everywhere, and the career center web site is easy to use. There are always lots of employers doing on-campus interviews, and the center is good about helping you with your résumé and giving you practice on interviews. The help is there if you seek it out. I personally left the college with a good number of job offers. As for prestige, if you are staying in the Midwest, it is fine. I'm not sure what the value of your degree is if you move elsewhere.

Current student, 8/2003-Submit Date, March 2005

There are Career Services available for graduating students. Advisors are very helpful in getting you ready for what you need to do when you graduate. There are also career fairs held throughout the year, which are a great way to network

with potential employers. Thousands of part-time jobs and internships are ava able on or within walking distance of campus. Plus, Nebraska has the m national companies recruiting on campus of any school in the state.

Current student, 8/2001-Submit Date, October 2004

The employment prospects are very high for students who have graduated fr UNL. The demand for employees with the quality of personality that com from going to school in the Midwest is invaluable to many organizations. Ea year, hundreds of organizations flock to UNL to recruit students to join th companies. There are many on-campus opportunities to attend career fairs, vie job listings, as well as post your résumé on an online job search site sponsor by the university. Graduates from UNL attain high-paying and high-quality jo from employers that know what kind of work ethic is instilled in a student fr UNL. This wonderful work ethic is the key to so many students success af graduation.

Current student, 8/2002-Submit Date, January 2005

The career center on campus is great with helping students find jobs. There a two large career fairs each year. The career center also sets up on-campus inte views for different employers. The students must take the initiative, but on you talk to someone, the opportunities are endless. The school also offers a ser ice called Husker Hire Link through which students and employers can sha info online.

Quality of Life

Current student, 8/2004-Submit Date, September 2006

I've lived on campus every year and loved it. There is a lot of housing for unde graduates with good food in the dining halls and a good process of matching roommates. My freshman roommate is now my best friend. The residence ha are also located on campus, which is very convenient if you don't have a car. I've felt very safe on campus. I am never worried about walking alone at nig Lincoln provides many activities a larger city would, with the small town hosp tality and atmosphere. We have a recreation center that is a wonderful place work out, with a pool, a great equipment room and a large selection of class you can take for a student rate. The only problem is that living on campus is ki of expensive. I am now living in my sorority house on campus and it is muc cheaper. There is a large Greek life at this school and it is very easy to live the houses if you participate. If you want to live off campus, there is a ton housing all around both campuses and a busing system (for which you get a fr pass that can help with transportation. Parking is reasonable, dirt cheap com pared to East Coast schools and always within a decent walking distance where you live. There are garages if you want to avoid Nebraska winters, b it's all first come-first serve.

Alumnus/a, 8/1999-5/2003, July 2005

The University of Nebraska—Lincoln is a typical, large state school. The can pus is very pretty. If you are not from the area, be prepared for snow! Th school has built a lot of new housing units recently, so suite-style rooms a available. Dining services is nothing special; it's typical college food. The tow of Lincoln is very nice, although the area right around the campus is getting ki of run-down because it mostly consists of rental units with college kid Lincoln, although it is not that small, has a small-town atmosphere. Crime is nc that bad because of this. Lincoln is a good blend of town—it is mostly a colleg town, but it is also big enough that there is a lot to do. For those who want live off campus, housing and related costs are very affordable.

Current student, 8/2003-Submit Date, March 2005

Lincoln (population 230,000) was named the best U.S. city by a SUNY stud Lincoln has all the offerings of a large city with a small town atmosphere an there is not very much crime. I feel safe in Lincoln. Lots of housing on and o campus. The University of Nebraska—Lincoln is a true residential campus, wit 14 residence halls located on city and east campuses. All residence halls featu award-winning dining services, T3 Internet connection in every room, 24-hou computer labs, free phone with voicemail, free cable TV service, coordinate activities and events, and on-site laundry facilities. Campus is located in dow town Lincoln. There are many restaurants and fun things to do. UNL is a bi nough school to give the feeling of autonomy yet small enough to make you feel safe.

Alumnus/a, Business, 8/2002-5/2006, April 2007

Lincoln is a very safe city with friendly residents. Housing options, on and off campus, are abundant. The facilities are topnotch, including the Campus Recreation facilities. Dining is not as good as larger cities, but suffices. The city has every entertainment option you would need, including highly ranked collegiate sports and a great theater on campus. The campus also has a highly ranked American contemporary art museum.

Current student, 8/2002-Submit Date, January 2005

The campus is safe and in a great location. It's very close to a vibrant downtown with many bars, restaurants, movie theaters and other activities. Housing on campus is improving. The university offers traditional dorms and now also apartment-style housing. The meal plans are kind of limited and students don't get much choice. Parking on campus is an issue. Passes are very expensive and do not guarantee you a spot. Most students end up walking several blocks or miles from parking to class. Also, students usually rack up plenty of parking tickets while on campus.

Social Life

Alumnus/a, Business, 8/2002-5/2006, April 2007

The university has a very strong undergraduate Greek System with over 20 sororities and fraternities. These Greek houses arrange many social and philanthropic activities during the school year. Additionally, the University Program Council arranges for entertainment options throughout the school year. The school also has a great bar scene: O Street, where the majority of the bars in town are located, is only two blocks from campus. The Bar, Woodys, Iguanas and Main Street are the most popular undergraduate hang outs on the weekend. The town gathers on campus to tailgate at the bars and in parking lots for Husker football games on Saturdays. On a more academically related note, the university has over 300 recognized student organizations, including hobbies/special interest to academic honoraries.

Current student, 8/2004-Submit Date, September 2006

There is a ton of bars within walking distance of campus and I cannot explain to you how wonderful that is. It's a dry campus, which is actually really nice if you're living on campus. Parties are held off campus, and there is a cab service for students to avoid drunk driving. The Greek system has its pluses and minuses. Almost everyone can get in a house if they're interested, but at least being in a sorority can be expensive and time consuming. However, if you want the hookup for parties, go Greek. There are frat parties probably four nights a week and it will give you an excuse to wear your old prom dresses.

UNL has amazing events throughout the year, especially at the beginning. They'll have concerts in front of the Union and in August, they have Big Red Welcome where all the clubs set up booths and many organizations come to get their name out and there is a ton of free stuff, from food to t-shirts, to candy and prizes. It's really fun. There is always stuff going on at the Union for cultural events, fundraisers, philanthropies and so on. This is where it really pays off to be at a big university. There's every club you can think of and there are so many things you can do. You really have no excuse to be bored. And the football games are the most amazing things in the world. Really. The sea of red is intense and the energy alone is something no one should miss. It's fairly easy to get tickets at the student rate. Also, we have the best girls' volleyball team in the country. Basically, sports rock here and you have to go to the events. However, with my workload this year (I'm a junior), my social life is suffering. UNL makes it so you can have a balance. But as anywhere, it's all about your priorities.

Current student, 8/2001-Submit Date, October 2004

The social aspects at the university are wonderful. The university has a wonderful Greek system with over 50 percent of students involved in a Greek organization. Downtown Lincoln provides students with a bar scene unlike any other. The university offers many events throughout the year for students including free concerts, movies and dances. They are committed to providing good clean fun for students, as well as quality intramural sports for athletic students. There

are over 300 clubs and organizations available for students to join at the university ranging from the Movie Club to the Yo-Yo Club to the Institute of Industrial Engineers Club. Most students are involved in several clubs, organizations, Greek organizations, as well as a participate in intramural sports.

The School Says

10 Great Reasons to Become a Husker

1. More access to world-class opportunities.

As a major research university, Nebraska offers topnotch teaching, resources and facilities. With an undergraduate student population of just 18,000, we are smaller—and more accessible—than other top national universities.

2. Learning from professors who write the textbooks.

Nebraska faculty bring the results of their cutting-edge research to the classroom. Many are recognized leaders in their field and teach from textbooks they've written themselves.

3. One-of-a-kind Husker experience.

School spirit is contagious at Nebraska, and Big Red football is only the beginning. We're a tight-knit, residential campus with more than 400 student organizations, including 150 intramural programs and more than 20 sport clubs.

4. Exceptional guidance in selecting your major.

Nebraska offers the ideal experience for students who begin with an undeclared major—our general studies advisers have won national awards for helping students pursue their interests. We offer nearly 150 majors, with specialized programs of study to match any interest area.

5. Community of scholars.

At Nebraska, you learn from the best and with the best. Based on average test scores and high school class ranks, the past five freshman classes have been the most talented in the 137-year history of the university.

6. Enrichment through diversity.

UNL is one of just a few national universities in the Midwest and has been rated by Kaplan as a school that supports diversity. At Nebraska, our cosmopolitan campus enriches your education.

7. Lincoln—Number One U.S. City (2004 SUNY study).

Lincoln (pop. 235,000) is the second largest city in the Big 12, and art, music, theatre, state government and downtown businesses are all within walking distance of campus. Plus, Nebraska has the most national companies recruiting on campus of any school in the state.

8. Unmatched opportunities to learn by doing.

You can get true hands-on experience through our nationally acclaimed undergraduate research program. Nebraska is a leading research institution, and the only Big 12 school recognized by the Association of American Colleges and Universities for providing innovative undergraduate teaching.

9. More for your tuition dollar.

Kiplinger.com has rated Nebraska as a "Best Value in Public Colleges" for our academic excellence at a low cost.

10. Preparation for success.

97 percent of employed graduates said they were happy with the job they secured with their Nebraska degree (2005 annual graduate survey).

Read all of Vault's College Surveys at **www.vault.com/college**—get complete surveys on 100s of colleges and universities, expert advice on applicaton essays and more.

VAULT CAREER LIBRARY **409**

University of Nevada, Reno

Admissions & Records
Mail Stop 120
University of Nevada, Reno
Reno, NV 89557
Admissions phone: (775) 784-4700
Admissions URL: www.ss.unr.edu/admissions

 Admissions

Alumnus/a, Biology, 8/2002-5/2006, May 2007

The admissions process was very easy for me personally. I didn't have to write an essay or interview. As a resident of Nevada, I only had to fill out some relatively simple applications and take the SAT and ACT. I had good grades in high school and my test scores were decent. It is important, however, to pay attention to the deadlines set forth by the school.

Alumnus/a, Communications, 8/2001-5/2005, May 2007

Initially I applied and was accepted to two private schools in Southern California. However, I was not offered enough financial aid and ended up calling the UNR admissions office in Las Vegas. They were very excited to have me apply and I was accepted almost immediately.

Alumnus/a, Legal Studies, 8/2002-12/2006, May 2007

It was very easy to get in back in 2002, I'm not sure how the process is done nowadays. All I had to do was fill out an application, but there were no essays or interviews. The application was short, a page or so, and only asked general information.

Current student, 8/2004-Submit Date, November 2005

I was admitted as a transfer student from a local community college, so, for me, the process was very easy. As a transfer student, I applied online and sent my transcript to admissions. The process was fairly quick (perhaps a month) and my credits were transferred without having to haggle with anyone (although I have heard other students say that they have not had the same luck with transfer credits as I had). For students who are aiming for the College of Business, make sure to schedule early to get an advisor because they are always booked for weeks in advance.

Current student, 8/2004-Submit Date, February 2006

Admissions to the university is not tough but there are a few important things to remember. First, the required GPA for admission only takes into account your core academic classes (English, math, social science and science). Classes like [art] and home economics do not count into your final GPA. Second, make sure you apply and have all of your information turned in by the February 1 deadline. If everything is turned in by then, you will be guaranteed a specific amount of money, determined by your overall GPA and SAT or ACT scores.

> **Regarding scholarships, the school says:** "Scholarships are automatically awarded to new freshmen admitted to the university by February 1 of the year preceding their fall enrollment and who have an 'academic index' qualifying them for a scholarship. The 'academic index' is calculated using the unweighted high school GPA and the college entrance test score (ACT or SAT I)."

Finally, if you plan on living in the residence halls, you should apply and place a deposit no later than December of your senior year of high school.

> **The school says:** Students are encouraged to apply and place a housing deposit as soon as possible.

Current student, 1/2003-Submit Date, April 2006

I enrolled via the Internet and university web site. I was required to attend the new student orientation and campus tour before being admitted, but was accepted based on my GPA and SAT scores. I was notified via mail that I had bee accepted to the school. It was a pretty easy process.

Current student, 9/2001-Submit Date, April 2005

UNR is not a hard university to get into. Get the admissions form, which believe doubles as a scholarship application form, in person at the student serv ices building or online at www.unr.edu. There are no interviews or essays, as recall. Selectivity is easy—basically they take anyone who applies and ha around a 2.0 GPA. If you want something of a challenge, apply to the honor program, which mandates something like a 3.5 each semester and has some di ferent classes.

> **Regarding selectivity, UNR says:** "For admission to the university, the minimum GPA in core academic high school courses is 2.75. Starting in Fall 2008, the Nevada System of Higher Education requires a minimum 3.0 (weighted/unweighted) GPA in the high school academic core (English, math, social science and natural science).
>
> "Successful applicants to the Honors Program generally have unweighted GPAs of at least 3.65."

Current student, 1/2004-Submit Date, April 2005

I transferred from SF State. I was given great advice, from the transferrin process to advisement. The crew at UNR really helped me decide what I woul major in and the direction that I would take. They helped me to focus on wha I was good at, enjoyed doing, and apply that to a career goal.

Current student, 7/2000-Submit Date, November 2004

To be admitted to an undergraduate degree program as a regular student, yo must be a graduate of an approved or accredited high school and satisfy thes four requirements. Specific high school courses (13 units) to include English four units (with an emphasis on composition, rhetoric and American, Englis and world literature). An ACT English score of at least 20 (or SAT English scor of at least 500) also satisfies this requirement. Mathematics: three unit (includes algebra, geometry, trigonometry or other advanced math). An AC math score of at least 21 (or SAT math score of at least 500) also satisfies thi requirement. Social studies: three units (includes world history and geography U.S. history, economics, government and law). Natural science: three unit (preferably biology, chemistry and physics, with at least two in a laboratory sci ence). High school GPA: you must have an overall GPA of at least 2.5 upo graduation. You must submit ACT or SAT test scores to support your applica tion for admission.

> **The school says:** "High school GPA: you must have an overall GPA of at least 2.75 in core academic high school courses upon graduation. Starting in Fall 2008, the Nevada System of Higher Education requires a minimum 3.0 (weighted/unweighted) GPA in the high school academic core (English, math, social science and natural science)."

 **Academics**

Current student, Engineering, 9/2003-Submit Date, June 2007

I am a chemical engineering major. Chemical engineering classes are very challenging, and weed out students who are not willing to do the work. Teachers are available for help.

Alumnus/a, Education, 8/2003-5/2006, June 2007

I had no trouble getting into the classes that I wanted to take, but I also had quite a few required classes for my major (some of which were only offered one semester out of a year). Personally I found my workload to be fairly moderate and I had some professors whom I really liked and learned a lot from and others

ho were not as inspiring or informative. I would think this to be fairly typical
any program.

lumnus/a, Biology, 8/2002-5/2006, May 2007

elt that the quality of the classes was great. I often had trouble getting the spe-
fic classes that I wanted, or they were only offered at times that made it diffi-
lt to make a schedule that was conducive to working and taking other classes.
rading always seemed to be fair, and for the vast majority of the time, profes-
rs were very respectful, congenial and willing to help. There was a fair
mount of work in most classes as well as others that consisted of a very large
d small workload, respectively. All classes were very informative, and I feel
at they prepared me well for future endeavors.

lumnus/a, Communications, 8/2001-5/2005, May 2007

he undergraduate program in journalism is a great all-around learning experi-
ce. The lower-level classes, especially the writing classes, are very challeng-
g. Moreover, as the professors and instructors recognize talent, they provide
ore encouragement and coaching to prepare those students for the work they
ould like to do.

lumnus/a, Legal Studies, 8/2002-12/2006, May 2007

wasn't that easy getting into certain Criminal Justice classes since they would
nly admit a certain number of people every semester. The quality of some
asses was poor, but then there were classes that were superb.

urrent student, Business, 8/2004-Submit Date, November 2005

am a student in the College of Business Administration (COBA). The courses
ave been generally good. The professors often have better credentials then one
ight expect at a public university: the first three professors from which I took
urses at the school had earned their PhDs from Stanford, Harvard and UC
erkley. Not all professors are like that though, as with anything the best advice
to find a professor who you respect and ask him/her to help guide you. If you
hoose the right professors, you can have a very rigorous and educational expe-
ence; other students are able to find the easy teachers if they try. The workload
not bad—I work full time and take 15 credits and have been able to maintain
good GPA.

urrent student, Political Science, 1/2003-Submit Date, January 2006

have an economics minor and the professors, overall, are very qualified and
nowledgeable. In general, they are easy for me to access. You have a lot of
ading in any department you choose. For my major in political science it is
ery interesting. The sad part is that we are losing a lot of great professors due
retirement. But there some who are OK. There really are some great profes-
ors in political science.

> **The school says:** "Two new political science professors have
> been hired since 2006 and another faculty member is expected
> to join the department for Fall 2008."

urrent student, 8/2003-Submit Date, April 2006

verall, a great school. 99 percent of instructors are helpful and properly edu-
ated. There is a variety of programs from which to choose, and an array of
lasses, which are surprisingly easy to get. The workload is fairly light, depend-
ng on the course. Classes are very interesting and fun with great instructors
nost of the time. Besides that, academics are good at UNR!

urrent student, 8/2004-Submit Date, February 2006

JNR has many respected academic programs. Our journalism school is one of
he top in the nation and our mining engineering and seismology labs are some
f the top in the West Coast.

> **UNR says:** "The Reynolds School of Journalism has produced
> six Pulitzer Prize winners."

ll class registration is online. If you want to be guaranteed the professors and
lasses you want, you should try to get into the Honors Program. Those stu-
ents, as well as athletes, are allowed to register before everyone else. For
veryone else, registration is staggered by class (seniors, juniors and so on)
Grading varies from professor to professor. Typically, they grade on a +/- scale.
Jnlike high school, an A- is not worth the same weight on your GPA as an A.
ikewise, a B+ will boost your GPA higher than a B will. Check with each
espective professor and refer to the syllabus for the class. Workload tends to be

high, especially in the upper-division classes, but professors are very accessible
for help. They often give out cell phone, e-mail, home phone and other contact
information, as well as set up office hours and study times for students.

Current student, Communications, 9/2005-Submit Date, November 2005

I am in the journalism college, with an advertising concentration. I also have a
minor in the college of fine arts with a photography concentration. As far as getting into the photography classes, they are very small and very few are offered.

> **The school says:** "The Department of Art offers 10 photography
> classes."

This year, I have been very impressed with the quality of all the classes, as I have
been challenged to do my best in all of them. Grading seems fair and reasonable
thus far, and it's obviously harder than high school. The workload is a little overwhelming, because with work, school, homework, labs and extracurriculars, it's
definitely difficult to balance everything; but you do eventually learn how to
handle it all!

 # Employment Prospects

Current student, Communications, 8/2004-Submit Date, June 2007

It is easy to get a job after graduating from this school, but like any other school,
you have to have a good résumé. I am a journalism major and our J-school is
prestigious. We have a great faculty and they know a lot of higher-up's in our
profession. There is not that much on-campus recruiting from employers.

Alumnus/a, Education, 8/2003-5/2006, June 2007

The employment prospects and opportunities available for graduates are tied to
your major. I know for my major of education with a focus in history or social
studies, your employment opportunities are few.

Alumnus/a, Biology, 8/2002-5/2006, May 2007

I can only speak on personal experience, but I felt that the university was very
helpful in allowing me apply to and get accepted into dental school. There are
several organizations on campus that helped me in every aspect from obtaining
letters of recommendation to actually submitting an application. There were
numerous job and career fairs as well as workshops on numerous subjects,
including the interview process.

Alumnus/a, Communications, 8/2001-5/2005, May 2007

During the last two years of my academic program, I was queried several times
about where I was planning to work after graduation. Because the journalism
school has close contact with its alumni and donors, I was able to meet and
socialize with media executives and reporters. Through those contacts I was
offered recommendations to work abroad with the *International Herald Tribune*
or Sunbelt Communications.

Current student, 8/2004-Submit Date, November 2005

Students from the College of Business are often recruited by Fortune 500 companies, especially distribution centers because the Reno/Sparks area is a big hub
for that type of commerce. Toyota and Chrysler have also recruited from our
program recently. The alumni association is in the process of a developing new
programs to increase its utility, so it is difficult to evaluate what the alumni experience will be for future students, but it appears promising.

 # Quality of Life

Current student, 8/2004-Submit Date, November 2005

Quality of life at UNR is one of the high points. The campus is beautiful, yet
you are walking distance from downtown. Beyond that, if you have a car, Tahoe
and Truckee are less than one hour away for your skiing, outdoors or beach loving leisure. The university just finished building a new residence hall (Argenta
hall) and has expanded the dining facilities on campus substantially.

Current student, Engineering, 9/2003-Submit Date, June 2007

Local neighborhoods are fairly safe and clean. Proximity to downtown attracts
some homeless people into the area. Campus is safe. Not too many dining

Read all of Vault's College Surveys at www.vault.com/college—get complete surveys on 100s of colleges and universities, expert advice on applicaton essays and more.

VAULT CAREER LIBRARY **411**

options near campus, but there are a few good ones. Campus is very nice, especially near the Quad.

Current student, Communications, 8/2004-Submit Date, June 2007

Great quality of life all over. Our campus is beautiful, safe and is going under construction right now to make it even better. Housing is topnotch. The dining commons get old but that is to be expected from eating there everyday. Everything else is great.

> **The school says:** "The university opened the new Joe Crowley Student Union in November 2007 and the Mathewson-IGT Knowledge Center, one of the most technologically advanced libraries in the country, is slated to open in Fall 2008."

Alumnus/a, Education, 8/2003-5/2006, June 2007

I cannot speak for campus housing. I lived off campus all three years. The neighborhood isn't the best neighborhood in town, but it's far from being the worst neighborhood and they are constantly working to improve the community. I have found that the campus police are excellent at responding to problems and the campus facilities are wonderful. The campus is beautiful.

Alumnus/a, Biology, 8/2002-5/2006, May 2007

I felt that the quality of life was outstanding. I was fortunate enough to be able to live at home throughout college, but I knew many people who lived on campus or nearby. Crime never seemed to be an issue and the cost of living was very reasonable. The campus itself is currently undergoing renovation with a new library and student services building currently under construction. The facilities are more than adequate, and the university provides help for students in nearly every aspect including financial assistance and health related issues.

Alumnus/a, Communications, 8/2001-5/2005, May 2007

Reno seems to be an aspiring college town, though it is still a way off. The climate and region are very comfortable. Housing is widely available around campus. However, there is not much retail or dining available within walking distance of the university. Recreation opportunities and facilities abound.

Current student, , 8/2005-Submit Date, September 2006

Housing is way too expensive for what they give you. The campus is extremely beautiful, especially the landscape and rose gardens. Safety isn't really a concern. I walk around campus at night and I never had a problem. Everyone feels a strong sense of safety and unity.

Current student, 1/2003-Submit Date, January 2006

For college students this is a 24-hour town where coffee shops are open and restaurants as well. You have skiing and Tahoe and golf courses nearby. If you want to head to CA for a day, it is not far away.

 ## Social Life

Current student, Engineering, 9/2003-Submit Date, June 2007

Social life is fairly weak compared to other campuses. Hangouts include a few college bars (Little Waldorf, Breakaway) and downtown bars and clubs (210 North, Rumbullions, Imperial).

Alumnus/a, Education, 8/2003-5/2006, June 2007

I have found that there are many opportunities to socialize on campus. We have movie nights once a week where a new release movie is shown on campus. It is free and offers popcorn and sodas. More and more restaurants are popping up

in the area and with a new student union coming into play even more options f food will be available. Sporting events also provide a wonderful opportunity get out and socialize. We have a wonderful basketball team which the stude body is very proud of and students attend games for free. There is no lack social opportunities on campus.

Alumnus/a, Communications, 8/2001-5/2005, May 2007

As a member of a fraternity, I was well connected on campus. However, t Greek system still needs a lot of growth for it to reach its full potentia Downtown Reno offers a decent number of clubs and bars, if you're into that.

Current student, 8/2004-Submit Date, November 2005

The social atmosphere at UNR is one of the school's weak points. The camp is largely a commuter campus with little school involvement. I highly recom mend that students become involved in the Greek system as it is a closely kr group (15,000 students at UNR). The university's event center/basketball aren (Lawlor Events center) is one of the premiere venues in the city, so it is very eas for on-campus students to see great events (from Sarah McLachlan to Micha Moore and WWE recently). There are several local bars near campus but th most popular are probably The Breakaway and Pub n' Sub; and most students g clubbing, or start at least, at Brew Brother's in the Silver Legacy casino.

Current student, 8/2004-Submit Date, February 2006

For dining out, there are several student favorites. Jimmy Johns is popular wi residents because they deliver to the dorms. Also popular is Jim Boys, a gre Mexican restaurant down the street. There is plenty to do around town like jaz clubs, comedy clubs, arcades and golf. Also, Lake Tahoe is just an hour driv away and there are several ski resorts that offer discounted day passes to stu dents. UNR has over 150 clubs on campus so there is bound to be something t join. If not, the student government makes it very easy to start a club. Get 1 members, a faculty advisor and write a constitution. The ASUN will approve th club then give you a $50 start up check to help with recruitment. Overall Ren and the university is a great place to attend school. You get the opportunitie such as funding and special programs that larger schools get, yet it still keeps th small campus feel to it.

 ## The School Says

Founded in 1874, the University of Nevada, Reno has nearly 17,000 students and is one of the country's top 150 research universities listed by the Carnegie Foundation. It is Nevada's historic land-grant university, with four campuses and employees in every county in the state. The university is home to America's sixth-largest study abroad program. Created 25 years ago, the University Studies Abroad Consortium enrolls thousands of students every year from dozens of universities. The university is also home to the state's oldest and largest medical school, which extends health education throughout rural Nevada communities. While providing the classic undergraduate liberal arts education at a fraction of the price of similar prestigious private programs, the university also has nationally recognized programs in environmental literature and sciences, biotechnology, hydrology and earthquake engineering.

Dartmouth College

Office of Undergraduate Admissions
6016 McNutt Hall
Hanover, NH 03755
Admissions phone: (603) 646-2875
Admissions fax: (603) 646-1216
Admissions e-mail: admissions.office@dartmouth.edu
Admissions URL: www.dartmouth.edu/apply/

 Admissions

Current student, Social Sciences, 1/2003-Submit Date, June 2007

Dartmouth is an extremely selective institution, on par with the other Ivies and first-tier schools in admissions rates. That said, the Dartmouth admissions process is much more thoughtful than that of many other schools, it seems. Dartmouth strives to create the class as a whole and the admissions process is much less strictly numbers-based like many other schools.

My number one piece of advice is: be yourself. Just tell Dartmouth who you are, through your essays and your interview, and throughout the application process. Dartmouth students are fabulous, amazing, driven, talented, outgoing and accomplished but fabulously down-to-earth, and I think that this is determined as much by admissions as by the overall atmosphere here. Same goes for essays—be yourself. Don't try to be something you're not, don't put on airs, or be afraid to show Dartmouth who you are. Your essay doesn't have to say everything about you, but it does have to say something about you, something distinct, unique, interesting-something about your passions, about who you are.

Dartmouth has made a major change to its interview process this year. Admissions is no longer offering on-campus interviews as part of the process, but now has small group student forums, where students sit down with a current student, without parents present, and get to chat about Dartmouth honestly, openly and candidly. This change is in keeping with Dartmouth's overall attitude toward admissions: openness and transparency. Dartmouth is as interested in making sure that it's the right school for you as you are in making sure it's right for you.

Current student, 9/2006-Submit Date, May 2007

The admissions process is quite similar to other schools that follow the Common Application. Dartmouth does have a supplement, and I believe this is one of the things that makes Dartmouth stand out as a university. In the supplement, the applicant needs a peer evaluation and the applicant is allowed to write in five words what best describes him or her. I believe this represents that Dartmouth's aim is looking at the whole student, and not just the academics. We want to see what your personality is like and how your peers view you because Dartmouth College and campus is quite a community. Because of this, just getting good grades in high school and acing the SAT/ACTs does not mean you'll get in. Dartmouth is very, very selective. Dartmouth is looking for a well-rounded, ambitious applicant to add to its current student population. It's truly about character.

Current student, Social Sciences, 9/2006-Submit Date, May 2007

The admissions process at Dartmouth was straightforward. Given that they take the Common Application, it made applying easy, and furthermore, the only supplement that they required was a peer recommendation—I thought that it was a particularly unique aspect of the application process that represented Dartmouth's efforts to obtain a truly holistic view of the applicants.

When I applied, they offered both on-campus interviews as well as alumni interviews; however, for the upcoming admissions round, Dartmouth is only going to be conducting alumni interviews. Both the on-campus and alumni interviews were very straightforward, and I might even say, enjoyable. The senior and alumnus with whom I spoke were extremely friendly, welcoming, and in no way intimidating—I truly got the impression that they wanted to know more about me as a person rather than try to "scare" me as part of the admissions process.

Not surprisingly, Dartmouth is one of the most selective institutions in the nation, so they're basically looking for the "best of the best," so to speak—with a 15 percent acceptance rate, they can surely afford to do so, so do whatever it takes in order to make yourself standout. Why are you unique? What demonstrates that you've made the best out of whatever you've been given? These are all particularly significant factors to keep in mind while completing your application.

Current student, 9/2005-Submit Date, May 2007

The best thing about the Dartmouth application is the peer review component. It gives Dartmouth the opportunity to learn about you from the eyes of a friend, not just a teacher or mentor. It's important to choose an articulate friend who can accurately describe your personality and why you would be an asset to Dartmouth. Also, I loved my interview with a Dartmouth alumnus from my area. We spoke for more than an hour and the stories he shared with me about his time at Dartmouth helped move Dartmouth high up on my college list. Another nice feature of the Dartmouth admissions process is the likely letter that offers a "hint" to students who will be offered admission before the admissions letters are actually mailed. This letter can help relieve the stress and worrying involved in waiting for admissions responses. Dartmouth is one of the best colleges in the country and is accordingly very selective and becoming more so with each passing year.

 **Academics**

Current student, 9/2003-Submit Date, September 2006

Dartmouth runs on a quarter system with fall, winter, spring and summer terms. Students can pick and choose the terms that they would like to be on campus. But it is a requirement for all students (excluding international students) to be enrolled in the summer term for their sophomore year. It is dubbed, "Sophomore Summer," and although it may sound unpleasant to be spending a summer in school, it is arguably the most favorite term of Dartmouth students. Students can enjoy many outdoor activities, such as swimming in the lake (a five-minute walk), canoeing, kayaking, hiking and organic farming (all these activities are only minutes away). For those students who aren't very sporty, they can still enjoy studying or tanning on the green, constant BBQs, and the fast lines in dining halls.

Current student, Social Sciences, 1/2003-Submit Date, June 2007

The best way for me to sum up Dartmouth academics is personal attention, intense, exciting discussions, engaging professors, engaged students, and an overall sense of learning, discovery and interest not found at other schools. Dartmouth classes are small, really small, and professors are almost always interesting, passionate, exciting people who are happy to hold far more office hours than required, have students into their offices at all hours of the day to accommodate them, have BBQs at their homes after the term ends. They really take time and interest in getting to know students well and in advising students in academic capacities and more.

Dartmouth functions on the quarter system, so we have four 10-week terms, which includes a full summer term that all sophomores attend and love. It's so great to be in Hanover for the amazing weather, beautiful mountains and rivers for hiking and jumping into, and the green, littered with students reading and playing ultimate frisbee. The D-Plan, the name of Dartmouth's unique term schedule, allows students the flexibility to decide how they want to spend their time on and off campus throughout their four years here, and because all sophomores attend the summer term, they are able to replace it with a fall, winter or spring, sophomore or junior year, which they spend traveling, working abroad and getting awesome internships! Students really love the flexibility that the D-Plan allows. It also makes study abroad programs, of which Dartmouth has over

Read all of Vault's College Surveys at **www.vault.com/college**–get complete surveys on 100s of colleges and universities, expert advice on applicaton essays and more.

VAULT CAREER LIBRARY   **413**

40, and in which over 60 percent of the students participate, very easy to fit into your schedule and popular because they are 10 weeks long, just like a normal term.

Current student, 9/2006-Submit Date, May 2007

Dartmouth is not easy. The workload here is quite rigorous, depending on the types of classes you take. More often than not, however, the workload will be worth it because the quality of the class you are taking is amazing. The professors here are always available and love it when students come in during office hours. You don't even need to come in and talk about grades—you could just come in and chat with them. Sometimes, you may study really hard and the results may not be what you expected. But the professors truly take into account effort when they are grading. In the beginning, you will be focused on getting the good grades and getting straight A's. But what I have found more often than not, is that students begin thinking about learning in general with less emphasis and focus on the grade. That's why Dartmouth is not an academically competitive or cutthroat institution. The students take their academics seriously but they will not be afraid to help others in need in their classes or other classes. The class sizes are small (on average 22 students), which is great because you get a lot of individual attention if you want it. Besides introductory classes, which contain approximately 100 or so students, the professors really try to learn everyone's name in the class. No TAs teach classes here at Dartmouth. Professors teach 100 percent of the academic classes, because Dartmouth is really undergraduate focused. Even though professors do research, their main focus is on the undergraduates. You really feel like you are walking away with important information. Obviously, some classes will be duds, however on a whole, the classes are amazing with a bunch of enthusiastic professors.

Current student, Social Sciences, 9/2006-Submit Date, May 2007

Even though we only take three classes per term because we're on the trimester system, the workload is intense. Everyone works hard all the time; I can't imagine ever taking more than three classes at once because we always have so much reading and writing to do. That said, professors are incredibly friendly and caring—they're almost always willing to go out of their way to help you out whenever you need it, and it's really fantastic. A rather significant component of the tenure review process at Dartmouth is the quality of teaching as it has been ranked by the students, and it really shows (for the most part, at least).

On the whole, I would say that there isn't a real significant amount of grade inflation. While sure, there are some classes where the median grade is an A or an A-, the large majority have a median of a B or a B+. And it's not to say that you can get these grades without trying; most people have the work ethic to do what's necessary in order to achieve at least the median—you normally need to go way above and beyond to excel really.

Classes vary rather significantly in size—there are definitely a few large, lecture classes with 100+ students, but there are also a lot of classes that have less than 30 people. One thing that is particularly frustrating is that there are a few departments, such as Economics and government, that are chronically oversubscribed, so getting into the core classes in these departments can be quite difficult, and the administration hasn't done a whole lot to add additional sections. But on the whole, not getting into classes is pretty rare.

Current student, 9/2003-Submit Date, May 2006

I feel like I am receiving an excellent education at Dartmouth. I can honestly say that I attend one of the best, if not the best, college in the country. Part of what makes the academics so great is that 100 percent of our classes are taught by professors who are experts in their fields. TAs do not teach our courses, instead they occasionally lead lab sections or discussion groups in larger courses. At Dartmouth the average class size is about 25 people and it's not unusual to have classes smaller than this. The smaller class size enables students to participate in class and to receive more individual attention than if we had mainly large lecture classes. Only about 2 percent of classes have over 100 students and those are generally introductory courses like Economics 1 or Psych 1. And as I said before, these classes tend to break down into discussion sections. I think that professors' accessibilities also makes the education at Dartmouth so great and professors genuinely want to speak with their students. All professors are required to hold office hours at least once a week and many hold them two or even three times a week. In terms of registering for classes, that's very easy

because we sign up for all of our classes online. I've never not been able to get into a class that I wanted to take and if a class is full, it will probably be offered again during your four years at the college so you'll have another opportunity to take it. Grading at Dartmouth varies from professor to professor and department to department. Overall, I think that the grading is fair and objective. The work load varies as well, but although we have a lot of work outside of class, it's not overwhelming.

Employment Prospects

Current student, Social Sciences, 9/2006-Submit Date, May 2007

Employment prospects at Dartmouth, in general, could not be better. It doesn't matter in what you major or minor; employers see that you attend Dartmouth and are immediately interested in considering you as a potential job candidate. Dartmouth seems to have a particular trend with sending students into the corporate world—our number one recruiter annually is Goldman Sachs (but then interestingly enough, the number two recruiter is Teach for America). The Dartmouth name, while it might not be overly recognized by the average person on the street, definitely raises the eyebrows of those "in the know," and that's where it really counts. If you've got the Dartmouth name on your diploma, you're set for life.

Furthermore, one thing that really helps is that Dartmouth has an incredibly strong alumni network, and both Career Services and the Alumni Relations office have all of these programs to help students connect with alumni to find internships, jobs, and even just general advice about living in a new area from where a student might have grown up. They do an amazing job, and Dartmouth alumni in general are crazy about Dartmouth, and they love to take care of current students. It's pretty fantastic.

Current student, 9/2005-Submit Date, May 2007

As a sophomore, I haven't yet gone through the full recruiting process. Still, the connections with friends that I've made helped me obtain a great internship for the spring. The Dartmouth name definitely carries prestige with employers and opens doors. Career services has some great resources but sometimes the breadth of what they offer can be overwhelming. In addition, since the school is not as pre-professional as some other schools, students sometimes need to take a lot of initiative to receive the full benefits that Career Services can provide. The D-Plan—Dartmouth's unique four 10-week quarter scheduling system—can be either a blessing or a curse for getting an internship. On the one hand, being off during a certain term, say the winter, can lead to decreased competition with students from other schools in terms of finding good internships. On the other hand, companies may not have internship programs that run on schedule with Dartmouth's terms. Still, I know that the connections I make here will help me after graduation and the Dartmouth name carries a lot of weight.

Current student, 9/2002-Submit Date, May 2006

Dartmouth has one of the strongest alumni networks of any institution. One of the most popular phrases heard in describing Dartmouth alumni is that they "bleed green" (green is Dartmouth's color—the school is referred to as "The Big Green"), and this is not an exaggeration in the slightest bit. Dartmouth alumni are extremely connected to the college and they are known to go completely out of their ways for undergraduates. This puts students at a huge advantage because a significant number find internships and post-grad jobs through alumni, many of whom will only offer these positions to Dartmouth students. Not only that, but Dartmouth has extensive faculty advising, minority advising, and peer advising programs, so students are able to get the assistance they need. Every student has multiple resources at his/her fingertips, but freshmen are especially put at ease because upperclassmen are very helpful and accommodating and genuinely care about the well-being of underclassmen. Many graduates obtain a number of prestigious jobs at companies, including Goldman Sachs, Morgan Stanley, McKinsey and Bain, they attend top-ranked medical, law, business and engineering schools, they participate in Teach for American or the Peace Corps, and they are essentially competitive in all endeavors.

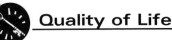

Quality of Life

Social Life

Current student, Social Sciences, 1/2003-Submit Date, June 2007

The campus is beautiful—in the middle of the White and Green Mountains of NH and VT respectively, Dartmouth itself is centered around "the green"—the big grassy town green around which are the library, administrative and academic building, and the Collis student center and Hopkins Center for the Arts. On sunny days, you'll see hundreds of kids, laying out, reading or playing ultimate frisbee on the green. The best sign of spring there is! The Dartmouth Outing Club makes getting outdoors and enjoying the area easy, with trips led every week and a number of cabins that students can rent for almost nothing! Dartmouth also has its own Skiway just 20 minutes away!

Dartmouth food is good. Consistently rated among the top dining services in the country, Dartmouth has 10 different dining halls/cafes and tons of options. From made-to-order pasta and stir fry in Collis, to a grill line, panini bar, and vegetarian options daily in Homeplate, to Kosher, Halal and Sakahara meals at the Pavilion, to typical cafeteria food (but better!) at Food Court; you'll never be hungry at Dartmouth. We've also got a convenience store where you can use your meal plan to pay for things.

Current student, Social Sciences, 9/2006-Submit Date, May 2007

Quality of life at Dartmouth is simply amazing, to say the least. People are often initially scared by the seemingly "rural" location, out in the "middle of nowhere," but to be entirely honest, it simply isn't true. For starters, Dartmouth is located in an area on the border of Vermont and New Hampshire known as the Upper Valley. About 10 minutes away from campus, in the town of West Lebanon where there's a shopping strip with a large number of chain stores—Wal-Mart, K-Mart, Best Buy, TJ Maxx, Home Depot, BJ's Wholesale Club, Panera, Friendly's, Chili's, Applebee's, Kohl's, JCPenney's and so on. So basically if you need anything, you can get it in West Leb, as we refer to it, and there's a free bus service called Advance Transit that goes right from campus to West Leb. So that's really convenient, and Hanover isn't nearly as isolated as people make it out to be. Also, we have the Dartmouth Coach, a private bus service that goes directly from campus to Boston South Station and Logan Airport five times a day, seven days a week—so it's really easy to spend a weekend in Boston if that's what you want to do.

Current student, 9/2006-Submit Date, May 2007

The quality of life here is amazing. The town is very supportive of Dartmouth College, and the town is extremely safe. I feel completely comfortable walking across campus at 3 a.m. in the morning. There are blue lights all around campus, and safety and security are always driving around, riding their bicycles or walking around to ensure safety. I love residential life and our Undergraduate Advisors. Our UGAs, similar to RAs in other schools, help us transition into college life and are always there for you if you need them. All-freshman housing is definitely the way to go. You get to know a lot of the freshmen sooner than you would expect outside of just class. The campus is just gorgeous. I just love walking around campus and recognizing that this is my campus. The resources here are fantastic—beyond words essentially.

Current student, 9/2005-Submit Date, May 2007

Dartmouth is an amazing place to be. Hanover is beautiful, even during the winter. Some students bemoan the cold and snowy New England weather in January and February, but I personally love it. It makes the campus feel more cozy and brings people together in their need to survive the occasionally frigid temperatures. Plus, it's a treat being able to take the 15 minute trip to Dartmouth's skiway after classes or on weekends. In the spring and fall, the temperatures are nice and the summers are beautiful. Campus housing is great and getting better thanks to the completion of new dorm clusters that are used primarily for freshman housing. Still, the older dorms are great and full of character—this year my dorm had a fireplace, though sadly the Office of Residential Life forbids us from using it. Most students live on campus, which keeps students close both physically and spiritually. This is an intimate campus and since there aren't many places to go in rural New Hampshire, students spend time on campus building lifelong friendships. It's great being able to walk around and see tons of people I know. Yet the student body is also big enough for me constantly to meet new people each term. My group of friends and acquaintances always seems to be growing.

Current student, Social Sciences, 1/2003-Submit Date, June 2007

Greek life is popular, and one of the major social options on campus, but is by no means the only option. Fraternities have dance parties, often fun themed parties that are attended by tons of students, not just Greeks. Also, most houses are open to anyone who wants to hang out or play pong, so the Greek scene is pretty open to anyone.

Students also spend weeknights and weekends at the Hop for their movie series ($12 pass for 20 movies!), Up ALL Night activities in Collis, Lone Pine Tavern (a cool place in the basement of Collis for food, drinks, milkshakes and studentsperformers on a regular basis), discount tickets to the Nugget, the real theater in town, hanging out in dorms, and more.

Current student, Cultural Studies, 9/2006-6/2010, May 2007

The Greek system largely dominates the social scene here. I have now learned, however, that that is not something to be intimidated or scared by. Relatively few members live in the houses, and no house has its own chef, so fraternity and sorority members eat and live with the rest of campus. This lack of exclusivity extends to the party scene, as well; it is a rule of the College that every party and event must be open to all of campus, so no one is ever turned away. Greek houses are also largely involved with community service and philanthropy and are responsible for a lot of the social programming on campus. They host dance groups, Dartmouth a cappella groups (insanely popular with students here), and visiting speakers, among many other things. *Animal House* may have been based on life at Dartmouth, but the Greek system offers so much more than the average person might think. Aside from some great restaurants and a movie theater in town, Hanover does not have much to offer socially. However, the Hopkins Center for Performing Arts brings incredible performances and some great films to Hanover multiple times a week, from Dave Chappell and Meryl Streep to Yo-Yo-Ma and Sonny Rollins. Regardless of the price for the public, all events and performances at the Hop at just $5 or less for Dartmouth students. Collis, our student center, hosts Thursday Night Salsa and Friday Night Rock, the latter being a group that brings indie bands from New York and all over the U.S. for free concerts almost every week. Despite being up in rural New Hampshire, there is never a night where there is nothing going on. I would venture to say that almost 100 percent of students stay on campus on the weekend, and with good reason.

Current student, 9/2005-Submit Date, May 2007

Frat Row is the hub of the Dartmouth social scene. As a freshman, I sometimes wished that the fraternities were not such an integral part of the school but now, as a sophomore and a member of the Greek system, my views have changed dramatically. Having no bars or clubs around means that students only interact with each other, which creates a very tight-knit community around campus. The fraternities are great places to foster friendships and despite the *Animal House* reputation that Dartmouth has, they are not the raunchy centers of hedonism that many expect (well, at least most aren't). Instead, they help build friendships and provide many community service opportunities for their members. Students are not allowed to rush until sophomore year, which enables freshmen to take their first year to decide if they want to join a house and, if so, which one. There is a house for nearly every type of person and joining a house does not mean that you only socialize with your frat brothers/sorority sisters. Members of the Greek system maintain strong bonds with friends in other houses and students who are unaffiliated. Drinking is a big part of the social scene but there isn't much pressure to drink and there are tons of people who avoid drinking all together. A cappella groups, improv troupes, movies and clubs all provide alternatives to Frat Row. The biggest on-campus organization, the Dartmouth Outing Club, provides a great way to take advantage of the stunning New Hampshire wilderness. The club also organizes DOC First Year trips for incoming freshmen, which provide the perfect introduction to Dartmouth's craziness. The trips are a five-day journey into the wilderness filled with non-stop fun and enjoyment. They are a great way to meet the people with whom you will spend the best four years of your life.

Read all of Vault's College Surveys at www.vault.com/college–get complete surveys on 100s of colleges and universities, expert advice on applicaton essays and more.

VAULT CAREER LIBRARY   415

The School Says

Founded in 1769, Dartmouth College has a rich tradition of supporting intellectual endeavors and the education of truly global citizens. As a member of the Ivy League, Dartmouth combines the best features of an undergraduate liberal arts college with the intellectual vitality of a research university. Dartmouth offers excellent graduate programs within the Arts and Sciences and in business, engineering and medicine. The professional schools, among the first established in their respective fields, have had a historic role in defining the school's intellectual values. Dartmouth encourages a love of learning and discovery in every member of our community. We celebrate the diversity of that community, which includes men and women from many different backgrounds and with a range of experiences and values.

Dartmouth has a special character and is committed to fostering the unique bonds that exist between the institution and those you learn, teach and work here. This character is rooted in the following essential elements:

- A devotion to a vital learning environment that relies on a faculty dedicated to outstanding teaching and scholarship; a talented and intellectually curious student body; a staff committed to the institution and its purposes, and alumni supportive of the pursuit of the highest ideals of teaching and learning.

- A conviction that one of Dartmouth's strengths is providing undergraduate students with close contact with faculty, small classes, and opportunities for independent study and research. Dartmouth should be a place that challenges students but also supports them in their endeavors.

- A resolve to enrich the learning experience at Dartmouth by encouraging regular interaction among members of a diverse community. A Dartmouth education should prepare students for life in a complex world, one in which the ability to understand and appreciate the differences and similarities among all people and societies is essential.

- A commitment to sustain an academic residential community that cultivates and nurtures the social, emotional, moral and physical wellbeing of its members. Dartmouth encourages intellectual endeavors, artistic expression, community service, athletics and outdoor activities, religious life, and political and social activism.

- A recognition that our setting and location in northern New England offer Dartmouth unique advantages, special traditions, and ongoing obligations related to understanding our relationships to our community and our environment.

University of New Hampshire

Admissions Office
4 Garrison Ave.
Durham, NH 03824
Admissions phone: (603) 862-1360
Admissions fax: (603) 862-0077
Admissions URL: www.unh.edu/admissions/

Note: *The school has chosen not to review the student surveys submitted.*

Admissions

Current student, 8/2004-Submit Date, September 2006

The University of New Hampshire offers the convenient Common Application form for admissions. This form is easy to fill out and takes fairly little time. Getting recommendations and a good essay are also key to getting into the university. An interview is not necessary. The university is getting more selective over the years and I recommend applying Early Action so that the admissions staff will recognize your initiative to wanting to gain admission to the university.

Current student, 8/2004-Submit Date, October 2005

The admissions process at UNH was very simple. Although the business school is a competitive program, it is very helpful with the process. No interview was necessary for me. I would suggest to any high school student applying to UNH to be honest about yourself but don't be afraid to brag about your achievements. Be as detailed as possible when writing about your accomplishments. Your essay should tell a story, but be sure to follow any guidelines given and make sure to double check for spelling mistakes. Although the school is selective, it is looking for students who are willing to work hard rather than students who are naturally smart who do not like to challenge themselves.

Alumnus/a, 9/2000-5/2003, September 2005

The application process was very [typical]. I completed a four-page applicatic that asked very general questions about my experience as a high school studen I was also required to submit three letters of recommendation, SAT scores and copy of my high school transcripts. If you are an in-state student applying UNH, you are eligible for half price tuition if you get good SAT scores (I believ it was 1300 and higher), so it is worth it to take the SATs more than once an have your highest score submitted. There was no interview requirement. On essay had to be submitted and there was a choice of three fairly generic topic I believe the essay I wrote was about my most embarrassing moment. Gener admission to UNH requires a C average GPA and strong recommendation letter Some of the departments, such as the English department or the science depar ments, require additional writing samples or letters. You may also need to tak a few classes and pass with a 3.0 or higher to be allowed to declare a major.

Current student, 8/2005-Submit Date, February 2006

I got A's and B's all four years of high school. My essay was about my experi ence racing dirt bikes and the fitness it requires. My letter of recommendatio was written by my favorite teacher.

Current student, 8/2005-Submit Date, October 2005

I was able to use the Common Application to get into UNH. I did not go to an inte view. UNH's selectivity is average—not too difficult but not easy either. I had t write a 500-word essay to include with my application. There were five differer topics from which to choose or you could choose your own. I chose my own.

Current student, 8/2003-Submit Date, March 2005

Admissions involved several different small essays. The best thing to writ about in these essays is personal experiences. One question I remember wa writing about a hero. A friend of mine who was accepted wrote about Rocky a fictional hero who meant so much more. They like to see people using thei imaginations and not just a common every day hero. I didn't have the best hig hool GPA or the best SAT scores, but I feel that I made them know what it was ke to be me.

here were no particular interviews except the interviews with your academic dvisors. Even if you don't know what major you're thinking of doing, UNH as courses designed to help show students the expectations of each major as ell as what can be expected in life after graduation, such as salary and employ-ent options. If you are thinking of a career in the engineering sciences (this cludes CS), then I suggest focusing heavily on your math skills before coming UNH. A mathematical placement test is used to determine where students are aced in the mathematical ladder (so to speak). Basic calculus knowledge fore coming to UNH is highly recommended.

lumnus/a, 9/2000-5/2004, January 2005

he admissions process, as I remember it, was fairly simple. There was a written pplication and an essay. I do not believe that they asked for written recommenda-ons. Most students are in-state students from New Hampshire with a C or better verage in high school. I don't think the university is very selective. I can only peak as an in-state student myself but UNH was a safety school for me. I never uestioned whether or not I would get in. However, it is more selective than the her NH state colleges and universities (excluding Dartmouth, of course). The stu-nt body is not very diverse so minorities and out-of-staters might have an easier ne getting in than your average middle-class white NH boy.

Academics

urrent student, 8/2004-Submit Date, September 2006

he University of New Hampshire offers over 100 majors in a variety of areas cluding business, life sciences, liberal arts, and health and human services. The asses usually begin with large lecture courses with little intimacy with the profes-r. This is typical of a medium-large university, but it doesn't really affect me. You et a certain number (called your "RAC number") from your advisor toward the end f the semester to sign up for classes for the next semester. People usually get most f the classes they want. There will always be those popular classes, for which you ill either have to be lucky and sign up early to get, or take later in your years when ou get more priority. The priority is seniors first, then down to freshmen last. The rading depends on the classes. For the large lecture courses, it is letter grading usu-ly determined by only a couple of tests. This is the same pretty much anywhere. the smaller-sized, higher -level courses, there are usually specific outlines of the rading that depend on more papers and projects and participation than the larger asses. The professors are nice and easily approachable and they all have office ours to go see them. Almost all of the professors with whom I have had to meet ave been more than happy to meet with me. The workload isn't too bad. People sually get through just fine.

urrent student, 8/2004-Submit Date, October 2005

he business school at UNH is the hardest college in the university. However, ere are a lot of options, such as tutors and TAs, available to assist you. The rofessors are great for the most part and very helpful and understanding of xtenuating circumstances. Classes are large freshman year (up to 300 students) owever class sizes get smaller. I am an athlete at UNH and we get first pick of lasses, so it's easy for me to get into what I want, but I believe most students on't have problems. Grading is on a 4.0 scale and in the business school you an't get below a C or you will have to retake the class. Workload is reasonable nd there are many classes from which to choose.

lumnus/a, 9/2000-5/2003, September 2005

majored in general psychology. The classes are taught by both graduate students nd professors. I found when registering for classes it was better to select a course here a professor was listed rather than TBA (to be announced) as these were ourses the grad students taught. The psychology program requires core classes, hich are typically 50+ students, that are offered in several different sessions every emester. Registration is determined by the number of credits you have earned so nat upperclassmen register first and then underclassmen. There is also a large vari-ty of courses in specific tracks depending on what your interest is. Course descrip-ons were very accurate in describing what the course would cover. Psychology tudents should expect to spend two or three hours per week per class writing papers

and anywhere from two to six hours per week per class doing research. Professors handed out syllabi at the beginning of each semester and then stuck closely to those outlines. Reading assignments complemented lectures and in class discussions but were not just a repeat of what the professor already talked about. Assignments were relevant to the information that was being studied and we were generally given at least one week to complete all assignments.

The professors were all very approachable both in class and around campus and also took the time to learn all of our names in the first couple weeks of class. All the professors have a requirement to continue conducting research and writing papers. They are very knowledgeable and respected in their fields. My child development professor was called to testify at court hearings as an expert and my personality professor developed a test of emotional intelligence that had him going to periodic conferences in Australia. Professors are willing to work with students to complete assignments and further topic understanding. Grading in psychology is heavily reliant on writing skills but professors often give several suggestions on how to improve your writing style and emphasize your voice. Grammar and APA style account for a good portion of your grade. Tests often consisted of both multiple choice questions and essays. Participation in class and attendance raises your average, and there was never one item, such as a test or paper, that accounted for more than 30 percent of your grade.

Current student, 8/2005-Submit Date, October 2005

I am an English/journalism major, and I am in my first semester of freshman year. So far the workload has not been bad at all; it has been very manageable. I am a varsity athlete for UNH, and it is still not too difficult to handle classes and athlet-ics at the same time. The class sizes vary a lot. However I am taking several intro-ductory level classes, which are much larger than the more specific, major-based classes. Three out of the four teachers I have this semester are excellent. I also have a tutor, which I have for free through the athletic department, and there are TA ses-sions for one of my classes with groups of five to 10 students together.

Current student, 8/2005-Submit Date, October 2005

I have found that the workload in classes is much more than high school. It's all about time management. You need to manage your time so you can get your study-ing and homework completed. The biggest piece of advice I can give is go see your professors. I made a point to go see all my professors and all of them have said that seeing them was definitely a good idea because they know who I am now.

Current student, 8/2003-Submit Date, March 2005

The computer science program is quite difficult. You will find the extent of what is learned is not offered in many other schools. I still keep in touch with friends from high school who are in different colleges, and they all tell me that UNH offers far better programs targeted toward engineering and the sciences. UNH is targeted toward giving students the very basic, low-level programming skills they will need to be able to further their development in computer science skills.

Alumnus/a, 9/2000-5/2004, January 2005

The school requires eight or so general education classes along with your major coursework. While these can be useful, especially in helping you decide a major, some people who had a specific career path in mind from day one found them to be annoying. The university is broken down into several colleges. I went to the Whittemore School of Business and Economics, so I can only speak for my expe-rience there. Popular classes were not too hard to get into because places were saved for people if they were requirements. The quality of classes varied, but over-all I was not too happy with them. WSBE lacked hands-on and real-world experi-ence. If I were to do it all over again, I probably would have chosen a different, smaller major. I have heard that most small majors require internships and actual-ly teach you hands-on skills. In the business school, you learn a lot of theory.

Employment Prospects

Current student, 8/2004-Submit Date, September 2006

Employment prospects are usually very good if you use the Career and Academic Resources in the Hood House on campus. They are very helpful there with booklets and pamphlets about part-time, full-time and summer jobs and internships as well as providing one-on-one time to review résumés, practice for

Read all of Vault's College Surveys at **www.vault.com/college**—get complete surveys on 100s of colleges and univer-sities, expert advice on applicaton essays and more.

VAULT CAREER LIBRARY **417**

interviews and so on. Career fairs and study abroad fairs are also held at least twice each semester, some according to the specific college to which you belong (e.g., College of Liberal Arts will have a specific career fair). Graduates obtain all sorts of jobs and go all over the globe. On-campus recruiting is good and plentiful as well and the internships are always available.

Current student, 8/2004-Submit Date, October 2005

Employment prospects are very good for a graduate of the UNH business school. One of my classes included an in-depth look at partner companies mostly of graduates of the UNH business school that had succeeded in the world of business. Alumni of the school talked of how prepared they felt they were for a career in the field of business and some earned jobs right out of college from organizations such as the Boston Red Sox and USA Hockey. Alumni of UNH seem very eager to help the future alumni. There are also web sites given by professors of New Hampshire business that are looking to employ graduating seniors. Internships are also available and helpful to students looking to get started in the business world.

Alumnus/a, 9/2000-5/2003, September 2005

Several people who obtained an undergraduate degree went on to graduate study programs. People who graduated in my class went on to Ivy League schools in the U.S. and abroad. An undergraduate degree in psychology can get you jobs in human resources, day care, sales and customer service or social service. After completing my degree I took the summer to evaluate prospective employers and then submitted my résumé to three social service companies. I got hired to my first-choice position with my top-choice company.

Current student, 8/2005-Submit Date, February 2006

I think UNH has a 98 percent success rate for a job when graduating. They provide excellent on-campus recruiting and internships.

Current student, 8/2005-Submit Date, October 2005

There are many internship opportunities for undergraduates, as well as exchange programs, which all provide for an impressive portfolio and résumé by the time they have graduated.

Current student, 8/2003-Submit Date, March 2005

UNH is the only school to the have the Interoperability Laboratory, which is nationally renowned for testing of cutting-edge technologies. Job placement upon graduation is near 100 percent, as Governor Benson stated his last visit to the lab. Additionally, UNH has lots of different places where one can intern. Every department on the campus has a set of mailboxes for students in that particular major. These mailboxes are used for upcoming job fairs, job events and other job opportunities as well as other interesting information. Just the other day, I was putting flyers for IOL opportunities in computer science mailboxes.

Alumnus/a, 9/2000-5/2004, January 2005

The WSBE advisors were impersonal because they had so many students. Therefore, I did not get much help with anything like discussing post-grad options. I job-searched for over six months before finding a mediocre entry-level job. I think WSBE's prestige has varied over the years. Another program is doing much better—Health and Human Services' Recreation Management and Policy recently got re-accredited and is very highly-regarded by employers. I highly recommend this major. It offers tons of hands-on experience, so you can really decide if it is something you want to do as a career. It is kind of like a business degree with a recreational focus. It is one of the best programs of its kind in the country.

As for the types of jobs people obtain, it is so varied because of the size of the school. You could graduate from UNH and get any sort of job you want, as long as you studied down that path in school. Overall, I believe UNH graduates are desirable to employers.

Quality of Life

Current student, 8/2004-Submit Date, September 2006

Housing is guaranteed as long as you don't disobey the laws or have multiple violations. Housing options are plentiful and some dorms even have themed housing options. The on-campus apartments are really nice, too. There were recently two more Gables apartment complexes built, which are very comfortable. Campus is big but not too big. Facilities are being reworked as well as some renovations are being done. Overall, the facilities are maintained pretty well. The dining options here are very good! I enjoy being delighted by the numerous and plentiful options there are. The neighborhood is nice and quiet surrounding the Durham campus, although you can tell it's a college town. Crime isn't bad at all here. I feel very safe on campus.

Current student, 8/2004-Submit Date, October 2005

Quality of life is very high at UNH. Although it is not located in a city, everything a student needs is located on or around campus. A car isn't necessary and at times challenging because parking is so bad, however on-and-off campus transportation is free for students and very good. Students often get jobs miles from campus and don't have to waste money on gas if they utilize the campus transportation system. Housing is good; construction on new dorms is underway. The food is the best part of UNH. There are two dining halls on campus and they offer a wide variety of choices, including pizza, stir fry, omelets, grill and salad. There is a wide selection and vegetarian options are good as well. Students can pick a meal plan that includes unlimited meals plus dining dollars which are good at all food locations on campus. Great for late-night study sessions. UNH is a very safe campus and the police are abundant.

Current student, 8/2005-Submit Date, October 2005

The dorms at UNH are pretty big; there is a lot of room for both roommates. However this year's freshman class is the biggest ever, and they had to make built-up triples for about 60 percent of this year's freshman student body. People are very respective of the campus and its facilities. The campus is beautiful, with lots of grassy areas where students play frisbee or wiffle ball on a regular basis. It is a very safe and relaxing environment. UNH dining is very good compared to other schools' food. There is a wide variety that changes every day.

Current student, 8/2003-Submit Date, March 2005

The campus is beautiful, the staff is always willing to help, housing is plentiful (slightly expensive) and parking is a nightmare unless you are at least a sophomore! The campus is fairly large, with academic buildings available all around campus. There's also plenty of computer clusters and online information available for whatever your needs are. You can walk into a computer cluster in the middle of the night because UNH keeps the academic buildings open all the time.

Social Life

Current student, 8/2004-Submit Date, September 2006

The school provides so many options for getting involved! The University of New Hampshire is Division I (except Division I-AA for football), so it is highly competitive. There are so many clubs and groups that range from the College Democrats to the Knitting Club. There is also a prevalence of Greek life here as well. Parties are usually good but frat parties are hard to get into unless you are female or are a member. The restaurants are all very good wherever you go. The dating scene is OK. It's hard to meet people one-on-one without partying or being a member of a sport team or club. The Whittemore Center Arena offers lots of music and comedic events come to campus. The Theatre and Dance department also offers many dance, theatre and other creative collaborations and performances throughout the year.

Current student, 8/2004-Submit Date, October 2005

Social life is pretty good for a campus of 12,000. Although the bar scene is small, there is a wide variety of places to go. Libbies Bar on Main St. is the most popular. There are few restaurants, however, Durham House of Pizza is very popular for students when late-night slices are only $1. There are a lot of events on campus. Popular attractions include $2-movie night, theater sports (improv group) free of charge, and bands or comedians that are brought in and charge between $3 and $10. The Greek system has been on the decline, however, there are about 10 frats and sororities. Theda is the most popular frat located next to Stoke (the largest dorm on campus). Parties do get broken up often.

Alumnus/a, 9/2000-5/2003, September 2005

A couple good restaurants in Durham are the Tin Palace for lunch and dinner and Young's for breakfast. The have an amazing ice cream place called the Licker

ore. There are several bars in downtown Durham that are heavily patrolled by
olice. Portsmouth is only 15 minutes away and offers good bars, like Coat of
rms and the Muddy River Smoke House. There were often several events a
eek at the Whittimore Center including sports, concerts, guest speakers and ral-
es. The Greek system has their own street where most of the houses are. They
e known for being loud, rowdy and drunk on most warm weekend nights.

urrent student, 8/2005-Submit Date, October 2005

here is a lot to do at the University of New Hampshire since it is a big research
iversity. I am involved in the Greek system and have found that it is a good
ay to get involved and meet people. There are many options for restaurants
d bars around here because there are many towns surrounding the university
d Boston is only an hour away.

Current student, 8/2003-Submit Date, March 2005

One of the best things about UNH is the diverse population of students. My
freshman year, I lived in a dorm with at least 1,000 other students and it was
excellent. I met more people my freshman year than I did my entire years in
high school! On top of that, there are plenty of frats, pubs and restaurants in the
area. Also, UNH gets lots of medium-sized venues for performing artists such
as Maroon 5, Guster and many others. Never a dull moment at UNH. If you're
into fitness, then UNH is perhaps the best place to look. Government funded,
UNH has the best gym in the area with five or six basketball courts, as well as
saunas and racquetball courts. There is also an indoor swimming pool located
across from the gym area. On top of this, there are so many intramural sports
that I can't even count, ranging from ultimate frisbee to softball.

Read all of Vault's College Surveys at www.vault.com/college–get complete surveys on 100s of colleges and universities, expert advice on applicaton essays and more.

VAULT CAREER LIBRARY 419

Princeton University

Undergraduate Admission Office
Princeton University
P.O. Box 430
Princeton, NJ 08544-0430
Admissions phone: (609) 258-3060
Admissions fax: (609) 258-6743
Admissions e-mail: uaoffice@princeton.edu
Admissions URL: www.princeton.edu/admission

Admissions

Alumnus/a, Politics, 9/2002-5/2006, March 2007

I found Princeton's application process very unique and rewarding. Thought the essays were more unusual—they asked pertinent questions that provided the applicant a sense of the school itself. In one such essay, the prospective student is asked to describe him/herself as others would potentially describe him/herself. The application did take a significant amount of time to complete, so I would suggest working early and spacing out the time dedicated to completing the application. It ensures that you notice even the smaller mistakes that can differentiate your application from a higher quality one.

Alumnus/a, Engineering, 9/2001-6/2005, April 2007

The Princeton application was fun! It included a couple of interesting short-answer questions, one longer essay, and a hodgepodge section of single or few-word answers to help the admissions office get to know you as an individual (favorite book and things like that). There are no on-campus interviews, just the possibility of a small group session with an admissions counselor. The very active Alumni Council tries to conduct alumni interviews for all applicants, and as a current interviewer (and young alum), the best thing you can do is be enthusiastic about Princeton, your interests, and why you think it'd be a great place to spend four years.

Alumnus/a, Politics, 9/2000-6/2004, March 2007

The admissions process included an application (not the Common Application at the time) and an alumni interview. Princeton is an extremely selective school, and so many applicants have extraordinary items on their applications. The key is exceptional balance in addition to an outstanding item (literally an academic or extracurricular item that makes you stand out). To get in, you pretty much need an admissions officer to say, "wow!"

Alumnus/a, Social Sciences, 9/2002-6/2006, April 2007

I applied Early Decision to Princeton, got in, and the rest is history. The difficult part of the Princeton application (they did not accept the Common Application in my day) was filling out the essays creatively and succinctly enough to stay under the word count. I would still advise people to use the Princeton Application (instead of the Common Application), especially with the demise of Princeton's Early Decision program in 2008, as a way of signaling to the admissions committee that they are serious about attending Princeton and not just filling out one more of their 20 or so applications. It is important to get across your unique personality and passion in pursuing both scholastic and extracurricular interests in your essay. You have to get across a picture of you as a desirable person to have walking around outside of West College, not as merely a strong test-taker with high grades. Remember that the admissions committee routinely rejects valedictorians and kids with perfect SATs, so make sure your application and essays stand out from the pack. Also, you must interview with an alum as part of your application—don't let the word, optional, fool you. My alumni interviewer actually called me to congratulate me on getting admitted before I had received my acceptance letter in the mail, so they are extremely involved in the process.

> Regarding interviews, the school says: "An interview is not required for admission to Princeton and applicants will not be at

a disadvantage if they happen to live in an area where our volunteers are not available."

Alumnus/a, 8/2001-6/2005, August 2006

Princeton's application is different in that there are four main essays to write a a "hodge podge" section that asks for the applicant's favorite food, scari dream and so on. For engineers, there are three additional essays to write th are more specific to science/technology. The essays are specific in their top but probing at the same time. It is very unlikely that you will be able to recy another school's essay for your Princeton application. The admissions proce is extremely selective— the normal admissions rate is approximately 10 to percent each year.

Interviews are not a mandatory requirement, and I personally was never offer a chance to interview. The opportunity will usually arise if you are located in area close to an alumnus/alumna who has offered to give an interview on beh of the school. Interview topics can range from current events to sports to ac demics. Interviewers are not given a list of questions from which to choose in fact, much information about their interviewees. This past year, as an alu na, I interviewed several students—after the interview, the interviewer is ask to complete a short form with rankings on topics such as "intellectual curiosit and "appreciation of other cultures."

Current student, Engineering, 9/2003-Submit Date, June 2005

The admissions process that I went through was not exactly easy, but not incre ibly difficult. My main advice on the application would be to start early. The are several detailed essays to complete that require a decent amount of thoug so it is not something to save until the last minute. Try to be creative, but yourself. The admissions officers are not necessarily looking for geniuses, b people who they think will positively contribute to the university communi Write about a special or unique skill you have, or something that is a passion which you have contributed a lot of time.

For the interview, I again suggest that you be yourself. My interview was rea ly casual; usually the alumni who give the interviews just want to get to kno the applicants and they won't drill you about school history. However, it woul n't hurt to have some questions lined up. This school is one of the most sele tive in the country with only a 13 percent admission rate, so your academ record and SAT scores will have to be pretty decent. However, don't be di couraged if you didn't get a perfect score or take 10 AP classes or have a 4 GPA. I didn't and I got in.

> Princeton University states: "The 2004-05 admission rate was about 10 percent."

Academics

Alumnus/a, Engineering, 9/2001-6/2005, April 2007

As an engineer, I had a large number of required courses (my freshman year wa predominantly general chemistry, biology, physics, math, and I also had to tak a writing seminar), but they were all useful and prepared me well for my uppe level environmental/civil engineering courses. All the other "fun" classes I too (history, religion, public policy, languages, music) complemented my technic focus. Professors and grad student TAs are approachable. The very popul classes nearly always have large enough caps that everyone who wants to ca enroll. A few by-application-only seminars (12 to 15 students) are competitiv but you can usually find plenty that suit your interests and fit requirements.

Alumnus/a, Politics, 9/2002-5/2006, March 2007

Academically, Princeton soared in comparison both to my expectations and experiences of my friends at other schools. Even as a freshman, I was able get into upper-level classes when I had the interest and background that enable my entry there. I found the seminars at Princeton particularly engaging, as th reading was more difficult and compelling, and the other students in the class were ready and willing to speak about these materials.

Additionally, professors were always available to answer questions about their classes and about other topics in their fields. I developed very close relationships with at least four professors, all of whom helped me with my independent work and with my application process for graduate school.

Alumnus/a, Politics, 9/2000-6/2004, March 2007

Overall, I would say it is hard to fail a class; the corollary is that it is hard to get an A. Thus, you can get by with skipping class, skimming the readings, and not applying yourself to graded work. However, you need to spend a lot of time to do well in most classes.

The most popular classes are difficult to get for freshmen and sophomores. For upperclassmen, particularly when it is your major, it is not that difficult. If you really want to get into a class, talking to the professor will get you in. An exception to this is seminars, which can be difficult to gain admission.

Alumnus/a, Social Sciences, 9/2002-6/2006, April 2007

The quality of classes is second to none. I took undergraduate courses with a Nobel Prize winning biologist (Eric Wieschaus) and economist (Daniel Kahneman), a Pulitzer Prize winning Civil War historian (James McPherson), and countless other brilliant professors who were equally deserving of such recognition. It is worth noting that there are some easy classes to fulfill every major academic requirement. If you—for example, are an English major—need your quantitative requirement completed, you don't need to sign up for calculus to do it. There are much easier ways to get the credit. Princeton is as difficult and challenging as you want to make it. There is no such thing as an easy A. The curve—which mandates that all academic departments stay at or below 35 percent A's is extremely strict in comparison to Harvard's grading patterns (51 percent A's) or Yale's (47 percent A's). The difficult curve though does not tend to lead to a cutthroat academic environment, because of the clubby social scene. Princeton students tend to help each other study, if only to improve their bicker chances at their favorite eating club.

Alumnus/a, 8/2001-6/2005, August 2006

Professors are generally approachable—most large classes have smaller "precepts" in which students are divided up into groups of nine or 10 and meet once a week (separate from lectures) to ask questions and have more interaction with professor/teaching assistant. The precepts are often where the true lessons take place—where students are free to ask questions and enter into debates/discussions, as opposed to listening to a lecturer for an hour.

The workload is difficult and heavy at times, but professors are understanding and will often grant extensions if a student has a reason for delaying a due date/exam. Most classes have little homework and are more focused on projects and exams—particularly higher-level courses, which may use only one examination to determine a student's entire semester grade.

While popular classes will fill up quickly, professors usually keep a waiting list or will expand the limit if many students are unable to enroll. All enrollment is done online, and upperclassmen have priority in signing up for classes.

Current student, Engineering, 9/2003-Submit Date, June 2005

Princeton is one of the best universities in the country for a reason; it's not easy. While it's not likely that you'll get straight A's unless you lock yourself in the library when you're not in class (and who wants to do that?), there are always people around to help. I am in the Engineering program, so my classes require quite a heavy workload of reading and problem sets. We usually do them in groups, and professors and teaching assistants hold regular office hours to help if you're having trouble.

Most classes have decent lectures, so you'll actually want to go to class. As far as getting into classes, it is not difficult to get into the required classes for your major. However, the popular classes, like Intro to Psychology and Anthropology, do fill up; freshmen rarely get into them since they are the last people to register for classes. If you really want to get into a class and it's full, simply e-mail the professor ASAP and you'll either get into the class or be one of the first people on the waiting list and you'll probably get it.

Finally, the grading system has just recently changed; now each department is required to only give a certain percentage of A's. This makes it a bit difficult if you've really worked your butt off and deserve an A by the numbers but don't get it because of the cut-off, but I've found that generally professors are pretty fair about it.

 # Employment Prospects

Current student, Economics, 9/2004-Submit Date, March 2007

If I had to use one word, it would be: amazing. For starters, the alumni network is incredibly strong and you'll always find alumni who are eager to help with anything, whether it be advice or assistance with a job search. On-campus recruiting is quite strong, especially for finance. Every prestigious company, from Goldman to McKinsey to Morgan Stanley, actively recruits on campus and takes a good number of students into its internship/full-time programs. Opportunities in the sciences and community service are also particularly strong. Upon graduation, a huge percentage of students go into finance though there are fairly strong contingents going into research and programs like Teach for America.

Alumnus/a, Social Sciences, 9/2002-6/2006, April 2007

Every top firm in NYC recruits at Princeton. The school is roughly an hour away, and the train drops you off directly onto campus. It's too convenient not to. The typical Princeton grad entering the labor force works either at a consulting firm or an investment bank. I recall seeing a statistic that 40 percent of undergraduates employed at graduation had chosen a career in finance. Other, more altruistic types will work for the State Department or Teach for America (founded by a Princeton grad, and a major recruiting success on campus). Let's just say that if you cannot find a job with a Princeton degree, you're probably not trying very hard.

Alumnus/a, 9/2000-6/2004, April 2006

If you want a job from any of the top investment banking or consulting firms, send a résumé and interviews will land in your lap. If you want a job with a government agency or a nonprofit organization, there are wonderful programs such as Princeton Project 55 and an amazing alumni network, but you will not get much support from Career Services.

> **The school says:** "Princeton's informal motto is 'In the nation's service and in the service of all nations.' Our unparalleled, no-loan policy that allows students to graduate debt free also enables students to choose careers in nonprofits. Career Services organizes job fairs throughout the year and hosts an alumni database, called TigerTracks, which connects students to career prospects through alumni."

Alumnus/a, 8/2001-6/2005, August 2006

Following Princeton, undergraduates typically have no problem finding a job. The most popular jobs recently have been investment banking, consulting and private equity—of which there is no lack of supply. Given that Princeton is very close to New York City, interviews are usually conducted first on campus and then on site. All the top banks recruit heavily from Princeton. There is also the chance to enter public service careers from Princeton—the school encourages students to enter into nonprofit jobs by sponsoring career fairs and jobs particularly geared toward those interested in nonprofit.

The alumni network is also very helpful. Many of my peers received job offers/internships through alumni. Princeton's Career Services organizes alumni in a database called TigerTracks that boasts over 100,000 alumni who are willing to talk to Princeton students about career choices and their particular jobs/companies.

Alumnus/a, 1/1998-5/2002, July 2005

The Princeton network has helped me land every job I have held. I have actually never been in a formal interview setting because the network is so strong and Princeton grads are generally very open-minded about discussing topics with you and deciding your fitness for a job, rather than subjecting you to a formal interview process.

Read all of Vault's College Surveys at **www.vault.com/college**—get complete surveys on 100s of colleges and universities, expert advice on applicaton essays and more.

VAULT CAREER LIBRARY 421

Quality of Life

Alumnus/a, 9/2000-Submit Date, April 2006

Housing at Princeton is not the highest quality of housing I've seen, in comparison to other Ivy League schools, but housing is 100 percent guaranteed. If you're looking to live in an apartment and cook your own meals in a kitchen, this is not the college for you. But since the structure of the housing system requires students to live on campus (vs. apartments off campus), it's really easy to meet new people and make great friends. It's one of the best parts of Princeton, that you will always bump into roommates, classmates, teammates and friends walking to class, hanging out in the common room and eating in the dining hall.

> **The school says:** "With the opening of Whitman College in 2007, Princeton launches a new four-year residential college system, which provides enhanced and expanded residential options for all students, including juniors and seniors."

The Princeton campus is absolutely beautiful. The Gothic buildings, the Princeton Gardens and the Chapel are among the finest I've seen on a college campus. Princeton feels completely safe from midnight to 10 a.m. I've never felt worried about my safety, whether I'm coming home from the library or from one of the eating clubs on a Saturday night.

Alumnus/a, Politics, 9/2002-5/2006, March 2007

One of the most unique aspects of Princeton is the fact that nearly everyone lives on campus. Despite being all dorm housing, the living accommodations are comfortable, and everyone is guaranteed housing. The campus offers a number of amazing facilities. The campus center is open for very extensive hours, especially during exams, and offers floors of rooms for study and hanging out. They have computer clusters all over campus that provide free computers and printing. They have free laundry services throughout campus.

Because everyone lives together, the campus is very close. People attend each other's sporting events, a cappella group arch sings, and other similar events. There is very little crime, and the campus feels generally safe. When issues come up with theft, the university is quick to investigate.

Current student, Economics, 9/2004-Submit Date, March 2007

With regards to crime, Princeton really has none. The town is quite upscale and the Campus Crime Alerts are never much more than a stolen bicycle. However, being in an upscale town has its downsides as the surrounding shops and restaurants are all fairly pricey. However, there is a shopping mall nearby (but you'll need to take the bus or drive there). Housing is guaranteed for all four years and fairly good. Many of the older dorms are being renovated while the brand-new (and amazing) Whitman College opens in fall 2007. With the infamous Butler College being razed, the housing situation is quickly improving and it was pretty good to begin with. The campus is fairly large but easily walkable and while a bike is helpful, it is by no means necessary. The campus itself is gorgeous and while the landscaping down campus often leaves much to be desired, it is usually impeccable up campus. The buildings themselves are beautiful and there really isn't much to complain about (aside from Wilson and the aforementioned Butler Colleges). The only possible negative is the construction on campus. There are several large projects occurring on campus right now, including building the Gehry-designed Lewis Science Library and rebuilding Butler College. There isn't much noise but construction equipment tends to hurt the aesthetics of the campus. The dining halls are decent but vegetarian options, while always present, often leave much to be desired. However, the eating clubs (an option only for upperclassmen) almost always have great food. Nevertheless, the dining halls are quickly improving and all of them are scheduled for renovation in the next two or three years.

Current student, Engineering, 9/2003-Submit Date, June 2005

I can't think of a place I would rather be. The environment is incredible—campus is pretty isolated, meaning that it is not spread out around a city. The campus kind of functions like a bubble; you don't really have to leave if you don't want to. However, it isn't in the middle of nowhere. There is a train station right on campus that can get you anywhere from New York City to Philadelphia, including Newark Liberty International Airport. Also, campus isn't far from major shopping centers; and again public transportation is available.

Princeton is a beautiful town, with lots of trees, squirrels, birds, running trai and what-not. Overall, it is extremely comforting and safe with a very low crin rate and emergency blue light phones all around campus, just in case. The Publ Safety Officers are very helpful—once they picked my friend and I up from t train station when we misread the schedule and missed the last train shuttle bac to campus.

Then there is the incredible Frist Campus Center, the center of life on camp (clearly). It has an eating area with everything from pizza to home-cooked foo multipurpose rooms, a convenience store, a cafe, a healthy eating lab, big-scre television, pool tables, a theater for movies and performances, classrooms, ma services and of course lots of places to study. Many, many, many hours are spe there.

Finally, dining is an interesting subject. Freshmen are randomly assigned to o of [six] residential colleges, where they live during the first two years Princeton[, with options to continue living in the residential colleges as uppe classmen.] Each college has its own dining hall, administrative staff (dea director of studies), dorm buildings and facilities. Underclassmen can eat at a of the dining halls, however. For the second two years, students have vario options: [residential colleges,] independent (provide your own food), co-o (group of people cooking for each other) or an eating club. The different optio vary in cost and convenience.

Social Life

Alumnus/a, Politics, 9/2002-5/2006, March 2007

Princeton technically outlawed Greek life, though some fraternities and soror ties still exist. They provide a nice outlet for freshmen who want to make frien with upperclassmen and get more information about the school in general.

Additionally, the bars in the Princeton area are scarce, and the restaurants a generally pricey (though fairly good). This is because social life at Princeton focused on eating clubs (unique to Princeton) and university-sponsored event The eating clubs are social and dining clubs for upperclassmen. They bring DJs, bands, karaoke and other entertainment, as well as provided alcohol [f students over 21] through the club itself. Some parties are exclusive to clu members, while many are not. These clubs allow you to make a small, clo group of friends with whom you eat and hang out on a consistent basis. You ca occasionally bring guests or swap meals with other clubs to hang out with di ferent groups of friends outside your eating club. Some students chose not join a club but still have access through friends.

Additionally, Princeton itself provides many social options. The universi sponsors concerts (of all kinds—from Third Eye Blind to pianists from aroun the world), plays (both put on by students and outside groups), dance perform ances, and other outside eating events. There are other campus wide sportin events that feature competitions between clubs and underclassmen residenti colleges. The workload is generally such that a student can attend all of thes events and still complete work if he/she wanted.

Current student, Economics, 9/2004-Submit Date, March 2007

New York and Philly are a short train ride away and one can find most anythin they want there. However, on-campus social life is dominated by the eatin clubs on "The Street" (Prospect Avenue). It goes without saying that membe of a club are always allowed into parties their club has. Parties at several of th clubs, including Charter, Colonial, Quadrangle and Terrace are always open t any student while those at Ivy, Tiger Inn, Cottage, Cap and Gown and Tow usually need passes. These are just cards that members get and can give to the non-member friends that allow them to get in. However, it really isn't all th hard to get into any party that you want. The eating clubs sometimes have a fai ly bad reputation outside of campus but most every student loves them. The definitely provide one of the safest environments for college parties and are fa from elitist or exclusive. Most every student joins a club and I do believe th most every student loves them.

Alumnus/a, Social Sciences, 9/2002-6/2006, April 2007

Princeton students like to have fun, drink and party. The stereotypical Princeton student gets blitzed Thursday and Saturday nights at "The Street"—Prospect Avenue's student-run eating clubs. He or she wears Lacoste or Ralph Lauren polo gear almost at all times. The eating clubs dominate the social scene. Their parties are by far the most popular—held at [10] mansions lining the same street—and technically off campus (though across the street from it), so the university has to take a relatively hands-off approach in regulating them. The eating clubs are student run with student officers and members. The bicker clubs often require a pass to get in, and the sign-in clubs just require that one show a student ID in order to party there on Thursdays and Saturdays.

Alumnus/a, 9/2000-9/2004, April 2006

Residential colleges offer a variety of social activities of which the weekly study breaks and trips to New York (ranging from Broadway Shows to the Philharmonic) are constant favorites. In addition, student groups fill the calendar with plays, movie nights, dance shows and concerts. For students without a car (you will be in the majority), there is a two-screen movie theater located across the street from Firestone Library that is a popular weekend destination for students.

For the final two years, approximately 80 percent of the students choose to join one of the eating clubs. They provide social activities during the weekend and three meals every day. The clubs line both sides of one street (Prospect Avenue), which allows for interaction between the clubs and keeps students from feeling isolated in the setting of their particular club.

Princeton's undergraduate clubs offer another incredible opportunity to socialize. Princetonians tend to find that their closest friends emerge from amongst the students with whom they helped put out the newspaper, led campus tours or sang underneath the arches. In addition to their stated purposes, the clubs host annual dinners, brunches, outings and, the Princeton favorite, study breaks.

The School Says

Princeton simultaneously strives to be one of the leading research universities and the most outstanding undergraduate college in the world. As a research university, it seeks to achieve the highest levels of distinction in the discovery and transmission of knowledge and understanding, and in the education of graduate students. At the same time, Princeton is distinctive among research universities in its commitment to undergraduate teaching. As freshmen, students can engage in intimate discussions with Nobel laureates and other faculty leaders of their fields.

Princeton is a leader in higher education, adopting groundbreaking policies such as a generous financial aid program that offers aid to every admitted student based on financial need. More than 55 percent of Princeton students receive financial aid and the unique no-loan policy gives students the opportunity to graduate debt free.

The university provides its students with academic, extracurricular and other resources—in a residential community committed to diversity in its student body, faculty and staff—that help them achieve at the highest scholarly levels and prepare them for positions of leadership and lives of service in many fields of human endeavor. Each incoming freshman class helps shape Princeton in new ways. Students make significant commitments of their own time, energy, and resources, and in return Princeton provides them with extraordinary opportunities to grow and learn, both in and outside of the classroom.

Princeton students often find themselves learning just as much from their peers as they do in the classroom. Informal opportunities to interact with professors, graduate students, and administrators also abound. Life as a Princeton student includes generous amounts of time for social interaction, extracurricular activities, and even for quiet introspection—perhaps on a bench in one of the many places of natural beauty on campus. Princeton is a dynamic community filled with wonders waiting to be discovered.

Through the scholarship and teaching of its faculty, and the many contributions to society of its alumni, Princeton seeks to fulfill its informal motto: "Princeton in the Nation's Service and in the Service of All Nations."

Recognized globally for academic excellence, Princeton today is a vibrant community of scholarship and learning. Recently, Princeton announced new initiatives in African-American Studies, the Creative and Performing Arts, Engineering and Neuroscience. As President Shirley M. Tilghman noted in a recent Commencement address:

"The specific components of a Princeton education have evolved over time, but our central aim has remained the same: to instill in each graduate those qualities of mind and character necessary for good citizenship and wise leadership. They include a broad intellectual curiosity that embraces open-mindedness coupled with critical thinking; respect for our moral and cultural inheritance coupled with a capacity for innovation and change; an appreciation of the shared destiny and common humanity of all peoples; and core principles of responsibility, integrity and courage."

Read all of Vault's College Surveys at **www.vault.com/college**–get complete surveys on 100s of colleges and universities, expert advice on applicaton essays and more.

VAULT CAREER LIBRARY **423**

Rutgers University

Admissions Office
Room 202
65 Davidson Road
Piscataway, NJ 08854-8097
Admissions phone: (732) 932-INFO (4630)
Admissions e-mail: admissions@ugadm.rutgers.edu
Admissions URL: admissions.rutgers.edu/

Admissions

Alumnus/a, 9/1999-5/2003, September 2006

The admissions process was rather simple. I did not have an interview and from what I recall, an essay was not necessary. As an in-state undergrad, I believe it was easier to get in. I'd say that generally if you fall into the middle of your class, you should be able to get accepted.

Alumnus/a, 9/2002-5/2005, February 2007

Rutgers University's admissions process was fairly easy. The application is very straightforward without the necessity to write an essay, which was optional. Interview was also not part of the admissions process unless requested by the prospective student.

Current student, 1/2003-Submit Date, August 2006

It is not hard to get admitted to Rutgers University. The university is big, though, and this means that it is important for prospective students to keep on top of the admissions process. A few weeks after sending in my application, I found out that Rutgers had not connected my SAT scores to my application. If I had not harangued the admissions office and found this out, I would have assumed that my grades were not good enough to gain admission and applied elsewhere.

Alumnus/a, Pre-med, 9/2001-12/2005, February 2007

Rutgers was not really hard to get into, especially as a high school senior, I had a very low SAT score, and a very high GPA, so it varies. Now it's a bit more challenging as the school is highly recognized for its football team (finally), and their rigorous and highly recognized engineering program.

Current student, 9/2002-Submit Date, November 2005

I graduated seventh in my class from high school and had a 1170 on my SAT. I kind of also applied sort of late, like two weeks before deadlines for fall 2002 admission. It was a relatively easy process. I filled out the application online and within two weeks got a notice of acceptance.

Current student, 9/2003-Submit Date, September 2005

From the day that I applied to the day that I found out I got in, I still received mailings from Rutgers, which I thought was very nice. Rutgers does make an effort to develop a relationship with those whom it recruits. My advice on how to get in—basically you need to look good on paper. You should have a good GPA and SAT scores. Furthermore, you should have a well-rounded background of clubs and activities.

Current student, 9/2003-Submit Date, March 2004

Registration is a breeze. You register online; the web site keeps you informed when your transcripts and SAT scores arrive, so you are fully informed throughout the application process. They do not have Early Decision, but have [rolling admissions], informing you [as early as the fall] if you have been accepted.

> Regarding Admissions Rutgers says: "Big changes are happening on the New Brunswick/Piscataway campus of Rutgers, The State University of New Jersey. Students arriving in the fall of 2007 will find a new system of undergraduate education on the New Brunswick campus.

"In one of the most significant changes in its 240-year history, the university has reorganized academics on its main campus, so that all new students in the liberal arts and sciences will be enrolled in a single Rutgers School of Arts and Sciences, rather than four different colleges as in the past. That means one faculty, one student body, one core curriculum and one set of admissions and graduation requirements for all students. The structure will be streamlined, but the variety expanded with 70-plus majors in the humanities, social sciences and biological and physical sciences; a choice of five distinct residential campuses, and better opportunities to customize individual educational programs through first-year seminars, a campus-wide honors program and joint-degree programs.

"The new core curriculum will encourage students to develop a broad base of skills and knowledge in writing, quantitative reasoning, natural and social sciences, humanities, interdisciplinary studies, diversity and global awareness.

"Rutgers' highly regarded professional schools will remain. One of them, Cook College is now the School of Environmental and Biological Sciences—different name, same mission. Students with a clear sense of career direction, as well as the technical, quantitative or artistic competence to excel in their fields, may also choose to apply to the Mason Gross School of the Arts, Ernest Mario School of Pharmacy, the Rutgers Business School, the School of Engineering or the College of Nursing.

"Essays are now strongly recommended for all applicants and required for those applying for scholarships or honors programs.

"For more information, visit the Undergraduate Admissions web site at admissions.rutgers.edu/"

Academics

Alumnus/a, 9/1999-5/2003, September 2006

What I enjoyed most about Rutgers' classes would have to be the wide variety of subjects that can be taken. Every class that I had was exciting and the teachers were very interested in the material. The grading was fair as I never was upset with any grades that I received and the workload was manageable even with an 18-credit semester. Scheduling the classes you wanted became easier as the years went on and sometimes it required some patience and speaking with professors to allow you into the class. Each semester I was very satisfied with my schedule and this helped me perform better academically.

Alumnus/a, 9/2002-5/2005, February 2007

Depending on the major and subject, the classes varied in size. One of the key advantages of Rutgers University was its size. As a university that included five different campuses across New Brunswick/Piscataway, the class/subject selections were unparalleled. Getting popular classes were easier for the upper-classmen as they had first choice to pick out their classes. Overall, the academics at Rutgers University were quite pleasing.

Current student, 1/2003-Submit Date, August 2006

Because the New Brunswick campus contains four geographically separate areas, getting the classes you want to fit into your schedule is very difficult. It is hard to get into some popular classes even if you're willing to build your whole schedule around them. Happily, though, I ended up in some interesting classes I would not otherwise have taken. I must say that I found the instructors at Rutgers to be excellent overall. I can think of a handful of teachers who were either mildly incompetent or seemingly uninterested in helping their students. Mostly, I had very engaging and interesting professors who genuinely desired to p their students. I found the workload to be tremendously light, and grading s fair in most of my classes.

umnus/a, Pre-med, 9/2001-12/2005, February 2007

eshman year is a breeze, but can be a bit overwhelming. You get the last pick classes, but once you get into your major, classes are easier to obtain. They ve an abundance of tutoring for large courses, especially science and math, d tons of review sessions for exams.

urrent student, 9/2002-Submit Date, March 2006

e classes I took are great but it really depends on the department. My only mplaint is that because it is a huge university, the lecture halls are huge and to me people are too impersonal.

ke the classes, the professors I've had are pretty good, some better than oth- s. Some professors can be very boring, but most of the time it is not their fault t the subject they teach. If you already have a distaste for the class or subject, u will probably not like the professor. I did however come across four pro- ssors who were absolutely phenomenal! After I had them I recommended m to all my friends. They were all from different departments: chemistry, ysics, Portuguese and Spanish. These professors love the subjects they teach d really care about their students.

is not easy getting into the popular classes if you are a freshman because reg- ration dates are different depending on the number of credits you have. sically, those with more credits get to register first and therefore have priori- In a way this is fair because many upperclassmen have to take specific class- before they can graduate or declare a major. New students have four years to to register for the class in which they are interested. The good thing about e registration process is that you can do it over the phone, in person or online. is flexibility is great if you have a rigid schedule.

urrent student, 9/2003-Submit Date, September 2005

asses are fair and kind of easy. I have learned a good deal in all of my class- As far as grading, the only thing that really upsets me is classes where the ade is on a curve comparing you to the rest of the class. Other than that, the ademics are good. Getting into and registering for classes can be a bit of a has- though. The good ole' RU screw can get to you. To register you have wake at 6:30 in the morning at the same time as thousands of other kids and get to the computer. What makes the problem worse is the lack of classes avail- le which means that when you can't get on in the morning, your classes fill up d your whole college plan gets reworked.

umnus/a, 9/2001-5/2005, October 2005

tgers is such a large and comprehensive school in many facets, and its aca- mics are no different. Class sizes range from large lectures (typically intro- ctory or pre-requisite courses) to small and intimate discussions. The faculty very diverse in the origins of their studies as well as specializations. It is often fficult to get popular classes and even the necessary pre-requisites to a given ajor. That can prove most cumbersome if a student is trying to complete cer- n studies in a given amount of time. The grading is standard and includes plus ades, but no minuses. A full courseload is considered [12 credits] per semes- r, so the workload can tend to be weighty as classes are not necessarily easy.

urrent student, 9/2004-Submit Date, April 2005

ass quality is great, especially for honors students like me. The school takes re of me and gives me special classes. I also passed out of most of my fresh- an courses, so course selection and getting classes was very easy for me. This hool is ideal for my political ambitions because it has a joint-degree program r history and political science. The professors here wrote the books, literally, education in their topics. There are a lot of TAs, but they are very knowl- geable and accessible. TAs may not speak perfect English, especially in more chnical math and science courses.

Employment Prospects

Alumnus/a, 9/1999-5/2003, September 2006

There were plenty of job fairs and the alumni network was helpful and extensive. The internship process was difficult for me. Many of the fairs had internship positions over the summer.

Alumnus/a, 9/2002-5/2005, February 2007

Rutgers University Career Service office was dedicated to serving not only just the Rutgers students, but alumni who had already graduated. The school also offered several career fairs each semester that were helpful for all students. Assistance with internships was A+ as each department of the specified major was able to help the individual student. After graduating, the support did not stop there as Rutgers University continued supporting their alumni with career services as well as alumni networks.

Current student, 1/2003-Submit Date, August 2006

I don't think employers are falling over themselves to employ Rutgers grads. The career center's seminars are helpful; it is easy to get appointments with counselors who will critique your résumé or give you interviewing help. I have not used the alumni network. Students should be sure to register with the career center so they have access to job and internship postings, as well as interviews.

Alumnus/a, Pre-med, 9/2001-12/2005, February 2007

Rutgers grads are most likely able to get great jobs, depending upon in which field you are, how you market yourself, internships, networking and so on. Johnson & Johnson is a huge fan of Rutgers grads, whatever your major. The MD/D.C./VA area favors Rutgers grads, as well. As for the farther southern states, I wouldn't recommend that move for an entry-level grad.

Current student, 9/2002-Submit Date, November 2005

The employment prospects here are pretty good. There are many career fairs or internship fairs and such where many employers of all different prestige come and participate in such as Johnson & Johnson, Procter & Gamble, Morgan Stanley and Citigroup that take in a fairly good number of graduates from Rutgers University. There are even groups, organizations and associations that you can join in your specific major/minor to help you network with possible employers by their alumni network. There are also online sites with listings of internships and jobs that help students find what they want to do. Career serv- ices office helps students with résumés, interview strategies, internship findings and the such that allow students to accustom themselves to the workforce envi- ronment before getting out there.

Current student, 9/2003-Submit Date, March 2004

Rutgers has a program for freshmen for one credit called FIG, Focus Interest Group. This allows you to meet professionals in the career area you want to explore such as communications. The class size is held down to about 20. The contacts you make through this class provide freshmen with unheard of opportunities for intern- ships. If you want to try a career, this is a stepping stone worth taking.

Quality of Life

Alumnus/a, 9/1999-5/2003, September 2006

I was satisfied with the quality of life. A car is key because usually classes are scheduled on different campuses, which requires either a car or campus bus. Plus, with New York City only 45 minutes away, there are endless possibilities for things to do. Housing is fairly expensive due to supply and demand. It's not a problem getting a place to live but the landlords are able to charge pretty hefty rents because of the number of people competing for a place to live. Crime is an issue from time to time only with those who live in New Brunswick on the out- skirts of campus. The main campus itself never has any problems. There are always plenty of Rutgers Security officers to make one feel safe. Overall, I was very happy with the quality of life on campus.

Read all of Vault's College Surveys at **www.vault.com/college**—get complete surveys on 100s of colleges and univer- sities, expert advice on applicaton essays and more.

VAULT CAREER LIBRARY **425**

Alumnus/a, 9/2002-5/2005, February 2007

The quality of life wasn't one of the highlights at Rutgers University. Dorms varied with quality as some dorms were air conditioned and some were not. Some dormrooms were three-student occupancy while other dormrooms of similar size were two-student occupancy, which didn't make sense. Rooms were quite bare. The washer and dryer for laundry for my personal dorm was down in the basement, which we called the dungeon due to its dark and gloomy appearance. The dining hall food was hard to eat sometimes due to the lack of variety. Breakfast was always eggs, toast, French toast and cereal. Dining hall quality differed from campus to campus as the campus more populated had better quality and selection of food. One thing that made quality of life easier was the bus system. Even though at night times you would have to wait 10 to 15 minutes, even 20 minutes or more, for the bus to arrive, it would be worth the trip as the campuses were separated and far away from each other. Livingston tended to have a more diverse community and transfer students, while Busch Campus had a high number of science and engineering majors.

Current student, 1/2003-Submit Date, August 2006

I have not lived on campus so I cannot address campus life issues. I feel totally safe on any campus during the day. At night I give plenty of thought to where I'll park because I worry about my safety. Rutgers is working hard to help improve downtown New Brunswick, and there definitely have been improvements since I started there. Overall I find the campus buildings and classrooms to be well kept, and I enjoy strolling through the campuses. Many of the old buildings are charming and very pleasant.

Alumnus/a, 9/2001-5/2005, October 2005

As Rutgers-New Brunswick comprises four or five separate campuses, the quality of life differs greatly between each. There are a great many different environments available to the prospective student. Certain campuses have an urban feel while others are more rural or environmentally-focused. Dining, housing and facilities are standard, with slight variations depending upon one's precise location of residence. Neighborhood crime can be problematic in areas where off-campus housing is prevalent, and often in the late evenings in very remote parking lots at the corners of campuses. Rutgers has responded in large ways to crime issues by increasing enforcement and strategizing the placement of enforcement. RU Police has also created a program for students interested in crime and security professions to train as community service officers who parole campus in pairs.

 ## Social Life

Alumnus/a, 9/1999-5/2003, September 2006

As a very large university, Rutgers has no problems when it comes to a social scene. There are plenty of on-campus bars and restaurants that allow students to let loose on the weekends. The Greek system is big but not a dominant aspect of the social scene. Another great part of Rutgers social life would have to be the events. Every year, Rutgers has a campus wide event dubbed Rutgersfest which is an outdoor free concert that includes a big-name headliner. Rutgers also has a comedy show each year that features a well-known comedian.

Alumnus/a, 9/2002-5/2005, February 2007

Social life ranked very well at Rutgers University as there were so many students at Rutgers. With a diverse crowd on campus, it was easy to find something to do without being bored. If I had to complain about social life at Rutgers, it would be not having enough time to explore all the social opportunities the school offered. Sports events were free for all Rutgers students, which was a fantastic way to have fun without spending a dime. Dating scene was definitely a perk at our school as the population combined exceeded 50,000 students and young professionals around Rutgers U area. There were clubs for almost anything, everything and anyone. If there wasn't, it didn't take much to start your own club of interest. There were events, such as new student orientation, to get students new to the school involved and aware of such orgs around the school. Greek organizations were around campus providing social events such as parties or fundraisers that welcomed most students. Grease trucks were a favorite after a hard night of partying as it provided exactly that, greasy sandwiches that quenched anyone's hunger for delicious comfort food late at night. If you wanted a night of bar-hopping, you could stay around Easton Ave. and go from bar to bar. Nightclub was a favorite for your everyday student, while Scarlet Pub was a favorite amongst your normal frat boy or sorority girl. If you wanted some fine dining or an expensive night out on town, you could go to downtown New Brunswick. Downtown provided high-end restaurants and lounges such as Frog and the Peach, Glo, Sapporo and Platinum. It was great to take a date out on, to go out with friends to celebrate a birthday with some expensive drinks and even more expensive menu of dining.

Alumnus/a, Pre-med, 9/2001-12/2005, February 2007

Great! I have met some of my lifetime friends at Rutgers. An abundance of clubs, Greek life, events, dating, religious clubs/organizations and so on. They have Rutgersfest every year—a free concert to celebrate the end of the year and unwind. Past acts have included Ludacris, Nas and Kanye West. Comedy shows sponsored by the Black Student Union are great as well—Mike Epps has been there and a few other prominent black comedians. Overall, a great social life.

Current student, 9/2002-Submit Date, March 2006

New Brunswick has restaurants, comedy clubs, theaters, live music events and many other attractions for the young crowd that walking distance from school bus stops. If you have a car, you have endless entertainment options. A great thing about Rutgers is that NYC is less than an hour by train. Thursday night is the official party night and the different sororities and fraternities always have those. Every semester the Greeks recruit new members and there is a different one for every taste and interest.

University of New Mexico

Office of Admissions
MSC06 3720
University of New Mexico
Albuquerque, NM 87131-0001
Admissions phone: (505) 277-2446
Admissions fax: (505) 277-6686
Admissions e-mail: apply@unm.edu
Admissions URL: www.unm.edu/futurestudents.html

 ## Admissions

Current student, Political Science, 7/2006-Submit Date, May 2007

The interview process wasn't a stressful experience at all. It was great because being from New Mexico I was able to apply for the Bridge to Success Scholarship, then later for the New Mexico Lottery Scholarship that pays for my full-time tuition and fees.

Current student, English, 8/2004-Submit Date, April 2007

UNM is not hard to get into. The SAT/ACT entry requirements aren't high, so students who didn't take high school as seriously as they might have can get a chance to start again. I don't know anyone whose application to UNM was refused. If you graduated from a New Mexico high school, you are eligible for some lovely scholarships, including the Lottery Scholarship (automatic if you have the GPA for it) and the Presidential and Regents scholarships (application required). As with any scholarship application, community service, leadership skills, and extracurricular activities look very good.

Current student, Business, 9/2005-Submit Date, April 2007

Admissions for in-state students is really simple. Everything is made available online, which makes the application process easier than ever. It isn't a very selective school, but essays should still be thoughtful and original. To get accepted to the university isn't that big of a challenge, but the scholarships are a bit hard to attain. It's a good thing there are so many offered!

Current student, Cultural Studies, 1/2004-Submit Date, April 2007

I applied for admission in the spring as I graduated early from high school. The application was manageable and concise. The actual process of registering for classes was a little more difficult, especially with the masses of incoming freshmen all competing for the various departments' attention.

The university is not super selective. There is a joke that you just need a pulse to get into UNM. However, I have been pleasantly surprised with the level of instruction, coursework and so on at UNM. It is no Harvard, but you definitely get your money's worth.

Current student, English, 8/2001-Submit Date, April 2007

The process was fairly simple and I applied just before the June deadline for the semester beginning in August. A standard fill-in-the-blanks application and a copy of my high school transcript were the requirements; a personal essay was optional. As I was a slightly-above average student applying to an in-state university, I wasn't concerned with selectivity; I assume most solid students would have no difficulty being accepted.

Current student, Engineering, 8/2005-Submit Date, April 2007

The admissions process was very straightforward. Since I went to high school in Albuquerque, we had several admissions counselors visit to help with applications, answer questions and promote scholarships. Admissions were simple and I was accepted, along with most of the other students from my private high school. The scholarship applications were the most difficult part because there are so many scholarships open to New Mexico students, which is a very good thing. Few people take the time to find out about them and apply for these scholarships, so if you take your time and apply to everything for which you are eligible, you are sure to be rewarded.

Current student, 8/2005-Submit Date, April 2006

As a resident of New Mexico, the admissions process was rather straightforward. My high school sent over my SAT scores and I filled out an online application. A representative from UNM eventually came to my high school and discussed more details, such as LOB Orientation and scholarships. The process was relatively painless. The scholarship process, I felt, was political. I personally know a student who was given the Presidential Scholarship solely on his résumé. He didn't have the GPA or the ACT scores to get the scholarship. Further, I personally know students with Hispanic/Native American descent who had similar GPAs and SAT scores who were awarded scholarships, and I wasn't.

Current student, 8/2002-Submit Date, April 2006

UNM's admissions process was thorough, yet very easy to do. Being a resident of New Mexico, I was given many opportunities by choosing to attend UNM. I was able to obtain the Lottery Scholarship to pay for my tuition, as well as many other in-state scholarships. I did not know how popular UNM was until I decided to apply. Many out-of-state students are competing competitively to attend. A well-written essay that includes reasons for choosing UNM over other universities and also gives a description of you as a goal-oriented student, should be included when applying. Focus on showing your individuality and how you will be able to positively influence UNM. Upon being accepted, I was able to stay at UNM for a few days in the summer to participate in orientation. I was able to take a guided tour on campus as well as learn about all of the organizations and activities that UNM offers.

Current student, 8/2003-Submit Date, April 2006

The admissions process is similar to most other colleges. No letters of recommendation are necessary. A student will be accepted with relatively low high school GPAs and ACT/SAT scores as a result of the local population being accepted to the school. Most of the NM locals have lower-than-average grades and are accepted by UNM anyway as an incentive to get a college education. So, no essays or letters required. Just apply and you'll get in.

 ## Academics

Current student, History, 8/2003-Submit Date, May 2007

The academics at the University of New Mexico differ for every department. Some are more dedicated than others and those that use a large number of graduate teachers are harder to deal with. But the grading system is fair and balanced. There are many choices for study and within each department there is a wide range of classes and activities. I think this makes the university superior because there is something for every interest and something for those who are just curious.

Current student, English, 8/2004-Submit Date, April 2007

Academics can be excellent at UNM. Many classes vary in their workload depending on which professor you get, so it's a good idea to talk to students who have taken classes recently about which section to sign up for. Many of the professors are wonderful. General freshman classes, such as Psychology 105, Astronomy 101 and lower-level science classes, often use online quizzes to help you prepare for tests. Grading depends largely on the professor: some will curve and some won't. A couple of instructors believe that a C should be the average grade and will give an A to only one or two students, but this is not the norm. Getting into popular classes, including fine arts classes and lower-level science labs, is difficult for freshmen because they must wait to register until all the upperclassmen have already chosen their classes. For some classes, especially core requirements in the sciences, extra students can get into the class by asking the instructor for special permission. As you accumulate credit hours, you get to register earlier and it becomes easier to get the classes you need or want. I recommend applying to the Honors Program at UNM. Unlike honors in high school or at many other universities, our program does not offer accelerated versions of other classes (Honors physics and so on). Instead, we have an Honors faculty

Read all of Vault's College Surveys at **www.vault.com/college**—get complete surveys on 100s of colleges and universities, expert advice on applicaton essays and more.

VAULT CAREER LIBRARY   **427**

that teaches interdisciplinary seminar classes. The Honors Program is not extra hard: most Honors classes I've taken required fewer papers than my English classes. It's a great opportunity to explore new areas and meet fun people in small classes (usually fewer than 16 students) that fit your interests. UNM's Honors Program is one of the oldest and most respected in the nation.

Current student, Business, 9/2005-Submit Date, April 2007

Academically, the business school is fairly challenging, but the professors are great (at least most of them). There is always the option of yellow carding into any classes that aren't available at the time you are signing up. Workload can be what you want it to be. Many people choose to disperse their harder classes so semesters remain manageable. Grading varies among profs.

Current student, Cultural Studies, 1/2004-Submit Date, April 2007

You get out of UNM what you put into it. I have yet to take a class that has an extremely overwhelming workload. I have been able to work between 30 to 35 hours a week, take 18 hours and be president of a club successfully at UNM. Workloads are tailored to allow students time to work, study and so on at the same time. Night classes are tailored for nontraditional students with families and full-time work schedules. UNM does a superb job of accommodating all types of students.

Current student, Biology, 8/2005-Submit Date, April 2007

UNM's classes are usually easy. Many teachers give "practice tests" that have all of the information necessary for the real test, and many times, the actual questions on the test. Popular teachers' classes fill up very quickly, but many of these teachers are glad to fill out override cards so that extra students can take their class.

Current student, English, 8/2001-Submit Date, April 2007

A plus to the English program is you pick a concentration among Liberal Arts, Creative Writing, Pre-Law, English-Philosophy, Literature and so on, so you're able to tailor (to a limited degree anyway) your major to your interests. However, there is no selectivity to the programs. The psychology department is far better organized but is too popular for its resources. The classes are large and it's difficult to find openings when it's time to register, but the special topics courses, Abnormal, Human Sexuality, Personality, Alcoholism, are much more rewarding than the freshman-level courses.

Current student, Engineering, 8/2005-Submit Date, April 2007

Like any other college, UNM is as hard as you want it to be. I am an engineering student with a concentration in Mechanical Engineering. This program and all other engineering fields are selective and very challenging. UNM is a research institution and it shines brightly because of it. I thoroughly enjoy all of my classes, my labs, my advisors and everything related to the school of engineering. It is a relatively small department, so all the ME students are treated like family. I learn a lot and I know my hard work now will be rewarded in the future. I am also involved in the FSAE Racecar Program. UNM ranks very highly in this competition and it is yet another example of how UNM can be a very rewarding and life changing experience.

Current student, 8/2005-Submit Date, April 2006

I am still completing the core classwork. I expected (as was reported to me by other college students) core classwork to be just a repeat of high school. However, I learned more in my first semester English 101 class than I had learned all together in high school. I feel that the coursework is challenging and I am introduced to new material daily. I don't know if this speaks well of UNM, or just ill of my high school but regardless, I feel the coursework at UNM is challenging. The most frustrating aspect of UNM was the transition from small high school classes to large college classes. I went from 30 year trained teachers, to having TAs in a class full of 70. The class sizes actually work to my benefit. I enjoy being anonymous. If you ever do need one-on-one help, all of the professors have always been more than willing to meet outside of class. My only complaint could be having TAs teach is troubling because they don't have any experience. Both the students and the teacher are testing the waters. For a student who wants to go to class, get the work done, and be done with it, having a TA always trying to figure it out for him/herself, is frustrating to say the least. But there is no college that won't have TAs; it's just part of the college experience. Despite my complaints about the TA system, they have all graded equally as fair as my full professors. I have been pleasantly surprised at the classes and class operations at UNM.

Current student, 8/2005-Submit Date, April 2006

UNM is not for everyone. It is a very large school and most of the classes taken by freshmen are huge—400 or 500 or more people. However, one of the benefits of a large university is that there are many high quality professors. The workload depends on how many classes you take and their subjects. I have found that the workload is quite similar to high school. In fact, my second semester was easier!

 # Employment Prospects

Current student, English, 8/2004-Submit Date, April 2007

A degree from UNM looks better than most New Mexico residents realize. People who go to high school here think of UNM as a fall-back college, but it's a distinguished institution in its own right. Several of our programs are nationally recognized, including anthropology, flamenco, the Honors Program and the school of medicine. Career Services hosts frequent events to help students find employment, including career fairs, résumé workshops and seminars on how to give a good job interview. Several departments at UNM help students find internships, and some programs, including Professional Writing, require students to hold an internship before graduation. Many of the companies that take interns from UNM tend to hire students after graduation.

Current student, History, 8/2003-Submit Date, May 2007

Many UNM graduates go on to be hired by the state's largest employers, such as Sandia Labs, Los Alamos National Labs and Albuquerque Public Schools. I have personally known many students to go to work for large companies, such as IBM, Boeing and Lockheed Martin. Many graduates go on to obtain jobs within the community of Albuquerque, jobs that they were able to attain because of internships or experiences they had while at the university.

Current student, Engineering, 8/2005-Submit Date, April 2007

UNM has a very good career placement program for all fields. Education can easily get you a job as a teacher. There are several hospitals in New Mexico that offer positions to students to gain experience, Engineering is in close contact with Sandia National Labs and other engineering firms to get you work in your field of interest. I am also a member of Phi Delta Theta Fraternity and that has helped tremendously with contacts and getting jobs as well.

Current student, English, 8/2001-Submit Date, April 2007

I will say the university seems to care about finding jobs for us once we graduate. There are numerous job fairs each year and a Career Services Center on campus that appears to be helpful. UNM is a fairly typical, large, state school, better than some, not as good as others. It's by far the best school in New Mexico at any rate.

Current student, 8/2004-Submit Date, April 2006

I am aware that the Career Services Center on campus is very thorough in holding seminars that help with career oriented questions. I recently attended a seminar on business etiquette that explained how to act when at a business party or dinner. They also hold workshops on how to write résumés and receive scholarships. It seems like they have a well-organized program to help alumni and graduates find jobs on and off campus as well as out of the state.

Current student, 8/2002-Submit Date, March 2005

I have heard from recent graduates that because of Anderson School, they received a very good job with starting salaries of $40K and up. Anderson often has recruits come in from prestigious companies such as Ford, Goldman Sachs and KPMG. There is a wide variety of recruiting and Anderson always makes it very easy to learn about the best ways to interview and what you should do in the process. In addition, I have heard from professors that companies are always looking at Anderson for students after they graduate as well as for internships. Because of Anderson I have always felt that I will be set for a job as soon as I graduate.

Quality of Life

Current student, Cultural Studies, 1/2004-Submit Date, April 2007

UNM provides tons of facilities to students including a gym, pool, recreational area and so on. The facilities are nice and modern. There is Wi-Fi around the entire campus and one can even sit at the duck pond on a nice day and work on homework.

Current student, English, 8/2004-Submit Date, April 2007

The cafeteria food is actually quite good. Very picky eaters may have trouble, but the cafeteria always has a variety of choices, including pizza, hamburgers/grill, vegetarian, Mexican, pasta, a salad bar, desserts, sandwiches, and a changing home style option that ranges from fried chicken to pot roast. You can also eat at one of the other food locations on campus, which include Chick-fil-A, a smoothie shop, Sonic, a sandwich/salad/soup shop, a coffee shop with fresh pastries, a couple of Mexican options, and a place with hot wings. The campus also has two convenience stores where you can buy snacks, prepared food and limited groceries. The apartment-style dorms have kitchens, and most people who live there cook a lot of their own food.

I have lived in the dorms on campus for three years, and they are fantastic. The older dorms (Hokona, Coronado, Santa Ana, Santa Clara) have plenty of storage space and solid construction. The newer, apartment-style dorms (Redondo Village and the Student Residence Center) have several single rooms that share a kitchen, bathroom and living area. These have thinner walls and occasional of problems, but they are also fairly nice. Even in the dorms with shared bathrooms for the whole floor, the excellent cleaning and maintenance crews do a good job of keeping the environment nice for students. The Residence Hall Association hosts plenty of activities, including free movies, inter-hall sports competitions, and reduced-price events like rock climbing and ice skating. Individual dorms may have even more activities, and you can get involved in your dorm to help plan events. Campus is well-lit in most areas, so it is reasonably safe at night. Albuquerque is small as cities go, but the campus is right on Central, so I would recommend taking someone with you to walk around at night if you are small and female like me. Cars are safe in most lots, but bicycles get stolen or vandalized occasionally; several people I know keep their bikes in their dormrooms at night.

Current student, Engineering, 8/2005-Submit Date, April 2007

UNM offers adequate housing and student facilities. Our Student Union Building is new and is top-tier from what I have seen. I live in a fraternity on the Greek part of campus. My house is very inexpensive, clean and stimulates me to get involved on campus and get good grades. With the best grades of any organization on campus and with over 2,000 hours of community service, Phi Delta Theta has really pushed me to get involved and attain a higher quality of life.

Social Life

Current student, Political Science, 7/2006-Submit Date, May 2007

As a member of the Greek system, it provided me with numerous opportunities for social events and study groups. The university is located almost directly off of Route 66, providing us with countless restaurants, bars, and so many other things.

Current student, Cultural Studies, 1/2004-Submit Date, April 2007

I believe that UNM has a good social life. There isn't a whole lot to do in the city, so parties and get-togethers are commonplace. There are tons of hip restaurants within walking distance in the posh Nob Hill and downtown is just down the road.

The Greek life at UNM is strong. There are tons of options for frats and sororities that most students will find one that fits them well.

There are tons of great organizations available on campus. I am the president of the university's Model UN Club and we travel every spring to an international conference to participate in Model UN. Students bare no cost and the entire trip is funded. There are clubs for everything: pre-med students, Turkish students,

political clubs and so on. Most students will also find a user-friendly student government with elections every semester. Campus social life is very good!

Current student, English, 8/2001-Submit Date, April 2007

The Frontier restaurant just off campus is always a favorite, as are the usual coffee shops and pizza parlors, one of which, the Brickyard, is a convenient place to drink because of its proximity to campus. There's a movie theater in the Student Union Building and the individual departments always have events happening, though they're typically ignored by the campus at large. Frequenting the bars downtown a couple of miles away is always something to do, though it gets repetitive fast. There are tons of clubs if that's your thing and most seem welcoming and happy to have new members. The Greek system isn't as big a deal as it is on some campuses; if you're not in a frat or sorority nobody cares, and if anything people tend to be wary of you if you are a member. Popejoy Hall is a great resource if you're into the arts. There's always a play to see or concert to hear. In the fall, Albuquerque has two really cool events: The State Fair (which is exactly what you'd expect: rides, corn dogs, turkey legs, farm animals) and The Balloon Fiesta, which is the largest balloon rally in the world. It's really pretty, with all those balloons in the air.

Current student, 8/2002-Submit Date, April 2006

Going to UNM is a blast because of the laid-back culture of New Mexico. Students are more likely to hang out with their friends outside than go to class, especially when the weather is good, which is 85 percent of the time. People are very friendly. There is always a lot going on at campus. Tons of parties, hanging out and eating! Many parties can be reached on foot from campus. There is not a lot to do in Albuquerque besides party, so the scene is pretty big. Music is huge in Albuquerque and so there are always a lot of concerts in town.

Current student, 8/2003-Submit Date, April 2006

Albuquerque has a decent nightlife. Many bands come here to play. I saw Three Doors Down for only $15. I have also seen Dave Matthews (twice), 10 years, Rammstein, Chevelle and Ozzy Ozbourne. Shows are always priced very well. Because of the extent of alcohol use in Albuquerque, the city shuts down the downtown area to vehicles on Friday nights. This way, people can go bar hopping in the downtown area and stumble around in the streets without fear of being run over. Making the downtown area walking only is a neat idea. Central Ave. is an interesting display. Albuquerque seems to have something for everyone. On the other hand, I don't suggest driving on Friday nights as playing Russian Roulette is sometimes safer.

The School Says

The University of New Mexico resides in the heart of Albuquerque, a city of more than 700,000 people. From the magnificent mesas to the west, past the banks of the historic Rio Grande to the Sandia Mountains to the east, Albuquerque is a blend of culture and cuisine, styles and stories, people, pursuits and panoramas. We are minutes from downhill skiing, hiking, biking, river rafting and over 300 days of sunshine provide ample opportunity for endless outdoor adventure.

UNM offers a unique campus environment with a Pueblo Revival architectural theme that echoes the buildings of the nearby Pueblo Indian villages. Albuquerque is home to the International Balloon Fiesta featuring world-renowned balloonist events and mass ascensions of up to 1,000 hot air balloons.

UNM, a Hispanic-Serving Institution, represents a wide cross-section of cultures and backgrounds. We are by far the most diverse university at the highest level of the Carnegie Classification System. UNM boasts outstanding faculty members and include a Nobel Laureate, two MacArthur Fellows and several members of the national academies. UNM faculty have been published in many professional journals including *Scientific American*, *New England Journal of Medicine*, *Nature* and many others. UNM professors have been quoted in many national publications and shared their expertise on CNN, *Today Show*, *Good Morning America*, *Nova* and other news shows.

Read all of Vault's College Surveys at **www.vault.com/college**–get complete surveys on 100s of colleges and universities, expert advice on applicaton essays and more.

VAULT CAREER LIBRARY 429

UNM's main and branch campuses offer 93 different bachelor's degrees, 68 master's degrees and 37 doctoral programs. Additionally, there are three first-professional programs—in law, medicine and pharmacy. Several UNM programs consistently rank among the best nationwide. For the 12th consecutive year, *U.S. News & World Report* graduate school rankings place two UNM School of Medicine programs in the Top 10—rural medicine and family medicine. Pharmacy and occupational therapy also made the rankings, while clinical law was ranked eighth nationally. Engineering and mechanical engineering also made the list.

UNM is consistently ranked among the Top 25 colleges and universities for Latinos by *Hispanic Magazine*. So noted because UNM is "strong in Latin American affairs and Southwest Hispanic studies. Nearly half of the undergraduate students are minorities and the law school is the most racially diverse in the nation." In addition, Hispanic Outlook in Higher Education ranks our music and dance programs among the top 25 for Hispanics.

The Health Sciences Center is the state's largest integrated health care treatment, research and education organization. Among the university's outstanding research units are the High Performance Computing Center, Cancer Center, New Mexico Engineering Research Institute, Center for High Technology Materials, Design Planning Assistance Center, Environmental Law and Policy and the Center for Non-Invasive Diagnosis.

UNM is home to the NCAA Division I-A Lobos and is part of the Mountain West conference. Lobo athletics draw fans from all-over, and the University Arena or The Pit was ranked 13th by *Sports Illustrated* as one of the Top 20 sports venues of the century. Students maximize their campus life experience by participating in over 400 clubs and organizations. And, it's a bargain! UNM has been listed among America's Best College Buys for 10 consecutive years.

Barnard College

Office of Admissions
3009 Broadway
New York, NY 10027
Admissions phone: (212) 854-2014
Admissions fax: (212) 854-6220
Admissions e-mail: admissions@barnard.edu
Admissions URL: www.barnard.edu

 ## Admissions

Alumna, 9/2002-5/2005, May 2007

From the interview to the paperwork, the admissions process was very holistic. Their supplement to the Common Application had a variety of suggested essay topics that let me both show my writing skills and give them a little bit of insight into who I am. I know they read them, since at orientation I met someone from admissions who commented on one of my application essays! The interview isn't required, but I think it gave me a chance to demonstrate the sincerity of my interest in the things I discussed on my application. In fact, it didn't really feel like an interview—more like a conversation. I think every little bit helps when applying to a college as selective as Barnard. So many people have great grades, recommendations and test scores that it's important to highlight what makes you unique and interesting above and beyond what looks good on paper. Above all, be sincere in your application. Let them know why you think Barnard is the right school for you, and hopefully you'll convince them!

Current student, History, 9/2004-Submit Date, March 2007

Barnard admissions focuses on the student as a whole, and the counselors really try to get to know the students as much as possible. This means that they look at more than just SAT scores and GPAs, but really want to know the activities the prospective student is involved in, for example. Barnard uses the Common Application but has its own supplement as well, and the counselors put a lot of emphasis on the personal statement and the short-answer questions. Interviews are not required but highly recommended, as they can help counselors learn more about the applicant and get to know her on a more personal level. What's unique about a Barnard woman is that every Barnard woman is unique, and the counselors try to select applicants who illustrate this in their applications in order to continue having committed students with diverse interests to offer each other once they arrive on campus.

Current student, Psychology, 9/2005-Submit Date, March 2007

While Barnard is the most selective women's college in the country, the Office of Admissions has never let it get to their heads. The admissions counselors devote so much time and energy towards each applicant and make it clear to each applicant that their decision will be made by the full application, not just GPAs and SAT scores. Interviews are not required and are with senior interviewers, not admissions counselors. The only advice I can give about getting in is that the applicant needs to try as hard as possible in the essay and short answers to truly reflect who she are and her individuality.

> **Regarding interviews, the school says:** "Admissions officers and alumnae interviewers also conduct interviews on and off campus."

Current student, Pre-med, 9/2003-Submit Date, March 2007

The admissions process at Barnard College offers prospective students an opportunity to get to know the campus and community. Interviews are conducted on campus in the fall as a means to supplement one's application, as well as ask questions about admissions and college life. Interviews are also available throughout the country to inquire about the school. The Barnard College application is unique because it asks diverse and personal questions in the supplemental application, allowing students to give the admissions committee a more complete picture of themselves. As a liberal arts college, diversity is essential, and therefore it is important to show one's unique qualities in the application.

Alumna, 8/1997-5/2000, March 2006

Despite its affiliation with Columbia, Barnard maintains its own financial aid, and is a lot more generous in terms of grants, by reputation and in my experience. This was a major factor in my decision to apply to Barnard College versus Columbia University—I wanted to get as much grant aid as possible, rather than being forced to take on huge student loans, while getting essentially the same degree

> **The school says:** "Barnard is a partner of Columbia University while maintaining separate admissions and financial aid offices, endowments and trustees. All financial aid awards are need-based; there are no merit-based scholarships. Demonstrated financial need is met 100 percent for four years."

 ## Academics

Alumna, 9/2002-5/2005, May 2007

I really liked The Nine Ways of Knowing, the general education requirement system. It encourages you to explore other academic areas (e.g. history, laboratory science, literature) without forcing you to take some cookie-cutter survey course. The classes were uniformly excellent. I was thrilled to find so many professors who not only taught well, but also took an interest in the intellectual development of their students outside of class. The workload can be pretty heavy, especially if you take on a lot and challenge yourself, but the professors are accessible and the other students are more cooperative than competitive, so it's manageable and definitely worth the effort. Course sizes are kept small, and some are capped and have to be signed up for in advance, but despite that I almost always got into the classes I wanted the first time around, and always got into classes I needed.

Current student, History, 9/2004-Submit Date, March 2007

Barnard is an academically rigorous environment; however, most students enjoy the challenge because Barnard students tend to be motivated women who enjoy questioning and digging deeper. The classes are very intellectually stimulating and are usually offered at a variety of times so that even popular classes aren't unavailable to students. Approximately 80 percent of Barnard classes have 20 students or fewer and TAs never teach classes. Professors hold office hours every week and are highly available and accessible to answer questions or willingly address concerns that students may have. The workload can be hefty, but students usually enjoy the fulfillment of completing it all and learning more about topics in which they are truly interested.

Current student, Pre-med, 9/2003-Submit Date, March 2007

Barnard College provides students with an academically rigorous program. The Nine Ways of Knowing are required categories that students must fulfill; however, there are hundreds of classes that can be chosen for these requirements. This allows students to personalize their coursework. Additionally, classes tend to be small and personal attention is guaranteed in class and during office hours. Professors are very clear about expectations at the beginning of each semester, making grading fair. Though the workload can be challenging, the support system among students, professors and advisors makes it more than manageable.

Current student, Psychology, 9/2005-Submit Date, March 2007

Since Barnard has access to all of the classes at Columbia University, students have way more classes to choose from each semester than other small, liberal arts colleges. Barnard classes tend to be much smaller than classes at Columbia, and professors tend to be more involved with and connected to their students as a result. Since so many classes are offered, it is not difficult to get into the classes you want to take. New York City and Columbia University draw excellent professors who are often world-renowned experts in their field.

Read all of Vault's College Surveys at **www.vault.com/college**—get complete surveys on 100s of colleges and universities, expert advice on applicaton essays and more.

VAULT CAREER LIBRARY 431

Alumna, 9/1999-9/2003, September 2003

Since it is part of Columbia University, you have access to all classes of the university. Ivy League caliber. There are waiting lists for the most popular classes, be sure to talk to the professor and sign up early. Some unique courses, including Reacting to the Past.

Employment Prospects

Current student, History, 9/2004-Submit Date, March 2007

Barnard College at Columbia University is a great place to come from when it comes to applying for jobs following graduation. Graduates go on to complete higher degrees or go straight into the workforce. The alumnae network at Barnard is very popular and graduates often offer current students and graduates opportunities because they enjoy having Barnard women working with them. The Senior Experience Conference at Barnard helps students search for jobs and expose themselves to employers during their last year at Barnard. The BC Office of Career Development also has countless resources available for students researching job opportunities and offers a lot of grants and funding for students who are still trying to figure out what they want to do in the future.

Current student, Psychology, 9/2005-Submit Date, March 2007

The Office of Career Development at Barnard is very active with currently enrolled students. They have services, such as résumé, cover letter and interview workshops, and have a database of available internships for students.

Alumna, 8/1997-5/2000, March 2006

The New York City location and reputation of the school make it easy to secure networking, internship and job opportunities in virtually every industry. I obtained a financial analyst job at my top choice firm, a bulge-bracket investment bank, during the first semester of my senior year. The Barnard and Columbia offices of career development are separate for purposes of job recruiting, so I would recommend networking and staying on top of employer information sessions and other events publicized by both OCDs.

Alumna, 9/1996-5/2001, April 2004

Career prospects are very good. There is a great Office of Career Development (in which I worked as an undergrad!); they have a good web site with lots of information and job-seeking tools. They have a recruitment program with many Fortune 500 companies, most of them in NYC. Barnard has an impeccable reputation with employers, and let's hope (for my sake!) that it stays that way.

Career services as an alumna are not as great as they were when I was there as an undergrad. Be prepared, once you graduate, to have to pay for everything, from a database search for alumnae in your field to a subscription to a Barnard-only jobs database. I wish they were a little more generous towards alumnae in terms of their services, but to their credit, they do (with the Office of Alumnae Affairs) hold many networking and informational events for young alumnae and for alumnae who are switching careers. Those events are usually free, but they're always on the NYC campus, too, so if you live somewhere else, your best bet is to contact your local chapter of the Barnard alumnae network. Both career development and alumnae affairs can help you find those people.

> **The school says:** "Barnard's Office of Career Development offers alumnae free career counseling in person, by phone or through e-mail contact to discuss career transitions, job search questions or general career planning. Counselors will also arrange for alumnae to take a career assessment exam for a modest fee and in conjunction with a counseling appointment. Résumés can be reviewed during the office's daily drop-in hours or through e-mail. Access to the alumna database is free to all Barnard graduates."

Quality of Life

Alumna, 9/2002-5/2005, May 2007

Housing is not the high point of life at Barnard. Though there are lots of nice suites, some with great views of campus and the city, and the older rooms on the quad are classically lovely, "cozy" is the most gracious way of describing t[ ] space. Some of the smaller rooms are only around 100 square feet. On the p[ ] side, Residential Life was always really responsive to problems, and, if y[ ] stayed on campus, willing to coordinate summer housing to reduce the numb[ ] of times you had to move. Additionally, they just opened up a new more lux[ ] rious dorm, so that will be a nice option for seniors. The dining hall is O[ ] though most people prefer to drop the very expensive meal plan as soon as po[ ] sible and stick to using the meal points system to buy food at other campus caf[ ] Campus is gorgeous and always well-manicured, and the neighborhood is a ve[ ] nice upper-middle class area, one of the safest precincts in New York (itself[ ] very safe, large city), full of restaurants and little shops. After leaving the neig[ ] borhood via the subway stop at the corner of campus, the entirety of New Yo[ ] City is at hand. What more could anyone ask for? Barnard has a beautiful gat[ ] campus in a friendly, family neighborhood, with one of the greatest cities in t[ ] world available 24/7 for the cost of a subway ride.

Alumna, Cultural Studies, 9/1995-5/2002, March 2007

New York City is an incredible place to live, study and play. Dorms are gre[ ] (especially by NYC standards). Barnard/Columbia is situated on the edge of le[ ] savory areas but it's very well-insulated and you never feel unsafe even late[ ] night. Barnard is all-women but you have the city around you and Columb[ ] across the street. You can even live in co-ed dorms after your first year. Dinin[ ] services are good and there are many choices for dining in the neighborho[ ] from every ethnic background.

> **Barnard says:** "Co-ed housing is possible, but in very limited numbers and is not guaranteed."

Alumna, 9/1996-5/2001, April 2004

Be prepared to live in pre-war buildings with crappy heat, rodents and no a[ ] conditioning.

> **The school says:** "There have been many upgrades and renovations done since 2007and these pre-war buildings are clean and spacious and some even offer views of the Hudson River."

Columbia and Barnard have weird, tricky rules about living in each other[ ] dorms, too. But everyone needs to live on campus, because it's just too expe[ ] sive to have your own apartment in the city.

> **Barnard says:** "While all first-year students are required to live in Barnard's Quad, approximately 90 percent of all students choose to remain in college housing. First-years live on single-sex halls, mostly in traditional double rooms. Though all first-years must participate in the meal plan, the residence halls are equipped with kitchenettes. Residence halls also have lounges (some with pianos or exercise equipment) for study and play."

The facilities are OK. There is one gym that's actually decent, Dodge Fitne[ ] Center, but that's on the Columbia campus, so I don't think Barnard can tak[ ] credit for it. People don't come to Barnard to work out.

> **Regarding fitness facilities, the school says:** "Barnard's fitness facilities include a swimming pool, weight room, track and open gymnasium for large sporting events. The weight room is equipped with variable resistance machines, free weights, upright and recumbent stationary bicycles, stairmasters and a treadmill. All students, faculty and staff are encouraged to use the facilities. In addition, the physical education department sponsors special recreational activities, such as fun runs and sports tournaments, throughout the semester. All students also have open access to state-of-the-art fitness facilities at Columbia."

The dining prospects in NYC are phenomenal, even if Morningside Heights[ ] rather hit or miss. Just go down to the East Village or the Lower East Side an[ ] you'll find wonderful, cheap dives.

Actually, the crime rate isn't that bad. Most of the people who get mugged a[ ] male college students anyway, so potential Barnard students shouldn't fe[ ] scared. Don't go walking in Riverside Park late at night, but don't be total[ ] paranoid either. Campus is usually pretty alive late into the night, every nigh[ ]

you can easily walk around and feel safe. If you don't, security has an escort service that will walk you where you need to go.

> The school says: "According to the New York Police Department, Morningside Heights is one of the safest precincts in Manhattan. Security guards patrol residence halls 24 hours a day to ensure students' safety. An escort service is also available every night from 11 p.m. to 3 a.m. to walk students to and from the libraries, residence halls, and campus gatherings."

Social Life

Current student, History, 9/2004-Submit Date, March 2007

We are located in New York City, therefore socializing is really not very difficult! Once students arrive on campus, the New Student Orientation Program (NSOP) helps them become acquainted with each other, the campuses, and the city. We have a lot of popular local restaurants and bars in our neighborhood, that are a short subway ride from various other NYC neighborhoods. The Greek system is strong but smaller than at other larger schools. We have various traditions, including Midnight Breakfast, where faculty and staff (including professors and deans!) serve us breakfast at midnight on the night before the first day of finals. Or we have Big Sub: a sub sandwich that runs across our entire campus. We have a great social community that makes being away from home a much happier situation!

Current student, Psychology, 9/2005-Submit Date, March 2007

Most of Barnard social life involves its relationship with Columbia University. Most social life is in bars around Morningside Heights, but other students choose the very small Greek scene or nightlife in New York City. The dating scene can be difficult at Barnard since it is a women's college; however, Barnard students often date Columbia students.

> The school says: "There is a plethora of performing arts, music, dance and theater clubs on campus both for students to participate in and to attend performances of."

Alumna, Psychology, 9/2000-5/2004, March 2007

Barnard was a really fun school to go to—I made many friends and participated in many activities. Because Barnard is so diverse and because of its stellar location in New York City, no matter what your interests are, you can find your niche here. There are constantly events going on on campus—spanning from social to recreational, to educational, to community-oriented. In addition, the social life expands well into the city. There are countless bars, clubs, concerts and so on to go to. And if that isn't your thing, there are always more low-key activities, such as film screenings, museums and other events. The Greek system is really not big at all on campus, and why should it be? With the benefits of living in New York City, there is no need to turn to the Greek system for campus social life. I actually found that quite refreshing, because you can honestly do your own thing at Barnard, whether that means going to a book reading with a good friend, or going out with a bunch of friends to a hot nightclub. It's all there, and you can pick what you'd like to do.

Local bar favorites within walking distance include: The Heights, West End, Nacho Mama's, and 1020. Local restaurant favorites within walking distance include: Ollie's (Chinese restaurant specializing in noodles), Nacho Mama's (excellent Mexican food), The Mill (Korean), Kitchenette (excellent breakfast, brunch and lunch), and Pertutti's (Italian). Favorite clubs/lounges of mine include: Avalon, Webster Hall (hey, five floors of music is never bad), the Copacabana, Trust and People.

Alumna, 8/1997-5/2000, March 2006

Varsity athletes at Barnard compete at the NCAA Division I level within the Ivy League, as part of the Barnard/Columbia Athletic Consortium.

Alumna, 9/1999-9/2003, September 2003

New York City—need I say anything more?

The School Says

Four characteristics distinguish Barnard College: It is a liberal arts college with a long tradition of excellence; it is partnered with a great research university; it is located in New York City, and it is a college for women. Each aspect of the college offers students unique distinctive learning opportunities. The effect is transformative.

A Liberal Arts College

Barnard's intellectual tradition has evolved over more than a century. Founded in 1889 as the only college in New York City where women could have the same rigorous education as men, Barnard has become known for its distinctive academic culture. At once challenging and nurturing, Barnard enables students to find new ways to think about themselves, their world and their roles in changing it.

Through Barnard's general education program, each student receives an education of both depth and breadth, that builds skills of analysis, independent thought and self-expression. Students take first-year seminar, first-year English, and courses fulfilling The Nine Ways of Knowing: Reason and Value, Social Analysis, Cultures in Comparison, Language, Laboratory Science, Quantitative and Deductive Reasoning, Historical Studies, Literature, and Visual and Performing Arts.

The Columbia Connection

Barnard occupies a unique niche in American higher education. Added to its status as a highly selective liberal arts college for women, it is partnered with Columbia, an Ivy League university located directly across the street from Barnard's campus. Cross-registration flows in both directions, allowing Barnard and Columbia students to take classes on either campus. Highly motivated Barnard students may take graduate-level courses at Columbia in such areas as international affairs, business, law, and arts and sciences. In the sports arena, Barnard varsity athletes compete in intercollegiate athletics through the Columbia University/Barnard College Athletic Consortium at the NCAA Division I.

Life in New York City

The Barnard experience is inseparable from the New York City experience. Morningside Heights, home to Barnard and Columbia University, is known as the Academic Acropolis and as one of the city's most diverse neighborhoods. Historic Harlem—rich in African-American history and tradition—Spanish Harlem, and the Upper West Side are short distances from campus. And the 116th Street subway stop near campus means that Chinatown, the East Village or Lincoln Center are accessible to students in minutes. Add more than 2,500 internship possibilities, and the result is a matchless college-city synergy.

A College for Women

Barnard is unequivocally dedicated to the success of women. That's immediately obvious in the way issues are considered in almost every field of inquiry, from classical studies to the history of science, or in the prominence of the nationally acclaimed Barnard Center for Research on Women.

Barnard students soon discover that their classmates are among the principal resources of their undergraduate years. Cosmopolitan in nature, the student population includes residents of nearly every state and some 40 foreign countries. One of the few generalizations that can safely be made about Barnard students is that they are diverse; a mingling of economic, regional, ethnic and cultural groups is evident in campus life.

Read all of Vault's College Surveys at **www.vault.com/college**—get complete surveys on 100s of colleges and universities, expert advice on applicaton essays and more.

VAULT CAREER LIBRARY 433

Binghamton University

State University of New York
Admissions Office
PO Box 6000
Binghamton, NY 13902
Admissions phone: (607) 777-2000
Admissions e-mail: admit@binghamton.edu
Admissions URL: www.binghamton.edu/home/admissions/

 Admissions

Current student, Social Sciences, 8/2004-Submit Date, June 2007

BU is a very selective school and it is getting more selective every year. You should definitely visit the campus, go on a tour and speak with an admissions counselor before applying. This will give you a good idea of what they are looking for. As well take advantage on the non-binding Early Action option so that you can get your decision sooner.

Current student, Biology, 8/2005-Submit Date, June 2007

Binghamton looks for very well-rounded, intelligent students who want to receive a great education. The criteria for getting accepted is increasing yearly, raising the standard of our students. While SAT scores are important, Binghamton also looks at the high school average, what courses the prospective student took throughout high school, the college essay, and extracurricular activities. The process is very fair.

Current student, 8/2005-Submit Date, May 2006

In general, the people who apply to Binghamton use it as a safety or match school (I only know one person who only applied to Binghamton). Mostly everyone who attends Binghamton does so because he/she was either rejected from his/her real first choice or realized that paying more for his/her education was unnecessary. To get in, I would recommend solid SAT scores and a good high school GPA because admissions is generally driven by numbers. Good ECs (extracurriculars) and essay wouldn't hurt though! Binghamton has become more selective in recent years, as the university has gained more clout nationally and admissions are typically becoming more difficult everywhere.

Current student, 9/2004-Submit Date, April 2006

Like any school these days, getting into Binghamton is not an easy task. Each year getting into Binghamton gets harder and harder, but don't shy away from applying. If you think you are a viable candidate, you most likely are. One piece of advice: If you are a strong student academically, it would make sense to apply to the non-binding Early Action program. Also, remember to submit the optional essay. Don't slack off. In my eyes, by not submitting the optional essay, all you are doing is showing the admissions officers that you really don't care all that much about getting into Binghamton.

Current student, 9/2003-Submit Date, April 2006

Binghamton is the top SUNY school, and as such is a little tougher to get into than other SUNY schools. But definitely easier than the prestigious private universities. The application and the essay are pretty standard, and as far as I know there are no interviews. I had a million questions when I was applying and called the admissions office—they were really helpful.

Current student, 8/2004-Submit Date, April 2006

Admission to Binghamton is very difficult, as we are the seventh most selective public school. One thing that is very important to the admissions office is the curriculum a student chose in high school. They like to see students who challenge themselves and take as many college level courses as possible. Then of course, you have to have good grades and SAT scores, but don't overlook the extracurriculars. A student with a 4.0 and 1600 on his/her SATs means nothing when he/she doesn't take any advanced courses and doesn't participate in anything outside of school.

Current student, 8/2002-Submit Date, March 2005

The process of applying to Binghamton University is fairly simple. A gene[ral] state application is filled out and sent to the SUNY (State University of N[ew] York) schools of choice. A short essay is required and visits are recommende[d] however, little else is needed. A typical applicant has a high school GPA in t[he] low-mid 90s with an SAT score between 1200 and 1300. Applicants can app[ly] directly to Harpur College (liberal arts), the School of Management, Deck[er] School of Nursing, the Watson School (engineering), or Human Developme[nt]. The engineering and business schools tend to have more competitive stude[nts] with higher GPAs and SAT scores. Binghamton University is considered the [best] of the SUNYs. SUNY, however, has a negative stigma to it, which is why [the] school is moving towards the title of Binghamton University as opposed [to] SUNY Binghamton as it had been in the past. Binghamton is an up-and-com[ing] and although it has primarily a regional reputation, the school is looking [to] obtain national prowess.

 **Academics**

Alumnus/a, Health, 8/2001-5/2005, June 2007

The classes are normally good sizes. The introduction classes, though, can [be] held in large lecture halls with over 300 students. There are a great number [of] general education classes that are mandatory in the various schools. The pr[o]fessors are generally caring and are willing to have extra office hours if neede[d]. The workload is manageable if you make sure not to fall behind, it can be mo[re] difficult for engineering and business majors. The School of Education a[nd] Human Development, which is now called the School of Public Policy, is kno[wn] to be an "easier" major with less work, more papers and fewer tests. It is ve[ry] hard to get popular classes an an underclassman because upperclassmen get fi[rst] choice, it all depends on how many credits you have.

Current student, Biology, 8/2005-Submit Date, June 2007

Binghamton offers an amazing education for a great price. The workload [is] tough, and students must keep up on their reading to do well on pop quizzes a[nd] tests. The professors are usually readily available for one-on-one time with t[he] students during office hours, and the undergraduate and graduate TAs will nev[er] introduce new material, just reinforce what was taught by the professors. As [a] freshman, it is much more difficult to get into some of the smaller, more pop[u]lar classes, and also hard to get some of the times you would prefer.

Current student, 8/2003-Submit Date, August 2006

The academic quality is excellent. Since it is a public university, there are mo[re] down-to-earth students than at a typical private university. I say this from exp[e]rience having studied for a semester at a private institution. Just like every oth[er] school, students want to put in minimal work and receive A's, which is a ve[ry] difficult practice to execute at Binghamton University. Popular classes ca[n] prove to be difficult to get into early in your academic career, but as you ga[in] seniority you have every opportunity to take any class that you want. The wor[k]load is not too difficult as long as you pace yourself and manage your ti[me] accordingly.

Current student, 8/2005-Submit Date, May 2006

I was pleasantly surprised with the quality of classes at Binghamton. Even as [a] freshman, I was in classes with only 20 students and it was very easy to get in[to] the classes I wanted. In general, the course material is interesting, and all of [my] professors thus far have been very helpful and approachable.

Current student, 8/2004-Submit Date, April 2006

The academics are very strong at Binghamton, with many programs ranked t[op] in the country. One unique difference at Binghamton University, however, [is] that there is a very cooperative environment, where students challenge and he[lp] one another and professors work closely with students, eliminating the cutthro[at] competition that breaks other schools apart. Another great aspect of academi[cs] at the university is the high caliber of faculty. It is not uncommon to be readi[ng] out research conducted by your own professor in a book that is being used across the country. Even with their commitment to research, they are very committed to the classroom. As far as getting the popular classes, it usually is not a problem, but you do have to be strategic at times. Nevertheless, the school guarantees you can get any class you need to graduate or for your major.

Current student, 9/2001-Submit Date, March 2005

The academics here at Binghamton are amazing. The professors are dynamic and engaging and are very well versed in what they teach. Many of our professors are published and 93 percent of our professors hold the highest degree in their field (PhDs). We also have adjunct professors who are people who actually work in the field and may come in and lecture about that area. An example would be a lawyer coming in and teaching a law class. Many undergraduates have the opportunity to work in research labs and get to experience hands-on many of the things that are taught right in the classrooms. Depending on the different majors, the workloads vary but Binghamton students know how to balance work and having fun. Professors are fair with grading, although each professor uses his/her own style and method of running his/her class.

Choosing classes is also very convenient and nice because students can access their DARS report online, which tells them exactly what they need to graduate, how many credits they have, and many other important facts they need to know in order to pick and choose which classes they need to fulfill all their requirements. If you ever need help with advising, there are also many different outlets: There is general advising, there is the advising from the major you declare (if you declare), there is the Career Development Center, which can help you decide what area you would like to focus your studies on and can help you get internships and job opportunities in that area. There are also DAs, or discovery assistants, who are upper-level students who are trained and there to set up tutoring hours, help you with picking classes, understanding requirements you will need and setting up programs within your dorm building to help you register.

Current student, 8/2002-Submit Date, March 2005

To be honest, getting into classes as an incoming freshman is not easy. At orientation you are among hundreds of other freshmen trying to get into the same basic classes, so spots fill up quickly and you have to be quick on the keyboard. Once you get more credits, however, registration is a breeze. Orientation was the only time I've ever been blocked from a class I wanted. Even if you're blocked out of a class because it's filled, keep trying because someone is bound to drop it the first day, so keep checking the enrollment.

The great thing about Binghamton is the general education requirements. Though they can sometimes be a drag, in the long run they are totally worth it because they give students a background in all areas, not just their major. Also, a lot of classes are not restricted to majors, so a business student can take a ton of art classes, for example. It's a great thing to get a taste of different areas of study.

I've never had a professor I did not like. Some professors are harder than others, but they are all great in their own ways.

In terms of workload, it's college, so you are bound to get a lot of work. If you don't have a lot of work, you are doing something wrong with your college experience.

Employment Prospects

Current student, Social Sciences, 8/2004-Submit Date, June 2007

Our school continuously sends graduates into some of the best jobs and graduate programs after graduation. We are competitive with Ivy League schools and some of the top business schools in the country. Our Career Development Center (CDC) is immensely helpful in getting the undergraduates ready for job interviews, internships and employment. I got my summer internship with their help.

Alumnus/a, 9/2003-Submit Date, February 2007

This school is widely regarded as an excellent school. However, it is regarded in that way especially in the State of New York, where employers are more familiar with the SUNY system.

Current student, 8/2003-Submit Date, August 2006

There is a great Career Development Center for all students, and job/internship fairs occur every semester to give students every opportunity possible to leave gainfully employed. Departments encourage internships and many give credits for programs during the fall and spring semesters that count towards your major. Some departments even require internships in order to complete the major. Many employers seem to look forward to Binghamton students since it has the conceited coin-phrase of "Ivy of the SUNYs." But, if it helps you get a job, run with it.

Current student, 9/2003-Submit Date, November 2005

As it stands, the School of Management is the third largest supplier to the Big Four accounting firms. This accolade reflects the rest of our placement, as well. I know of many employers who will only hire a Binghamton student, and others who would pick a BU student over an Ivy League graduate. I received my first job offer during the summer of my sophomore year.

Current student, 8/2003-Submit Date, November 2005

Big Four companies recruit but will only look for School of Management students. Alumni network not very helpful. On-campus recruiting caters primarily to School of Management students, which is horrible since there is only a fraction of those in the School of Management. The school should bring in more recruiters for the majority of other students from other subject areas. That is my biggest gripe about the school.

Current student, 8/2001-Submit Date, March 2005

I have a job waiting for me on Wall Street. This school caters very much to accounting majors. They have business etiquette dinners to show you which forks to use and how to taste wine. Employer fairs two or three times a semester attract the best employers, like Goldman Sachs, JP Morgan Lockheed Martin and NASA. All of them help students find jobs. Mock interviews help you formally interview, as well. Alumni are always eager to help, as well.

Quality of Life

Alumnus/a, 9/2003-Submit Date, February 2007

The weather is cold. However, otherwise it is a fine quality of life. There is a bright and active student body. The student body is involved in current political and social issues. There is a large student union to socialize and there are communities in the surrounding areas that are both urban and suburban. In addition, it's not far from Syracuse and Ithaca. Also, NYC is not so far away that you can't go for a weekend from time to time.

Current student, 8/2005-Submit Date, May 2006

Binghamton is, simply put, great for the money. As a result, lots of the students who go here are actually very smart and simply didn't want to pay $40,000+ for a year of education. Everybody at Binghamton accepts that they are here and tries to make the best of the experience. The housing is more than you would expect for what you pay: The rooms are actually fairly large, and all of the dorms are very social. The campus would benefit greatly from some gardeners and new buildings, but a large part of the unattractiveness of the campus stems from the weather in Upstate NY (it's generally cold and cloudy anywhere up north). There are lots of dining options, including Chinese, Taco Bell and a smoothie place. The campus and surrounding neighborhood are generally safe.

Current student, 9/2004-Submit Date, April 2006

Honestly, I feel very safe on the Binghamton campus. This is my second year living on campus and I have always felt safe when walking to or from other friends' dorms late at night. In terms of the quality of the housing, it really depends on where you live on campus. However, generally speaking, I would say that the quality of life in the Binghamton University residence halls is much greater than that of other schools I have visited. As a suggestion to incoming freshmen, I would get your housing preference form filled out right when you decide that you are going to attend, so that you have the best shot at getting your

Read all of Vault's College Surveys at **www.vault.com/college**—get complete surveys on 100s of colleges and universities, expert advice on applicaton essays and more.

VAULT CAREER LIBRARY   **435**

first choice residence community. I know of some people who sent their forms in late, and ended up living in a residence hall where they were not really happy, simply because it wasn't their first choice.

As a whole, the facilities at Binghamton are much better than I ever expected. I came here thinking that I really wouldn't like it because it was a state university and I didn't think that the facilities would be really nice. It turns out that I was 100 percent wrong. It is clear that Binghamton is constantly looking to the future and this shows in the fact that Binghamton is always re-modeling its facilities. For example, our newly built Information Commons, which is a computer center/reference library, is amazing. Not only is it a new, clean place for us to work, but it also provides a great resource when we have to type a research paper and need assistance from the reference librarians. Two years ago, before I started Binghamton, I never would have thought I would be saying this, but the quality of life at Binghamton is amazing. It is above and beyond, what I ever expected.

Current student, 9/2003-Submit Date, March 2005

There are new dorms that opened this year and last year. They are very nice and comfortable. Many people on campus live in suites. There are five different housing communities, each with its own identity. The housing is nice; however, signing up for housing for the following year can be a very stressful time for many students. The dining hall food is nothing special. It's an acquired taste that most get used to very quickly. Others have a hard time finding things to eat. There are many services available to students to entertain them; however, it is up to the student to find out where and what they might be. Binghamton is very safe. We have blue lights around campus with phones that go directly to the police, but I've never heard of anyone needing to use them. There are often many people out and about at all hours and for the most part it is well lit.

Social Life

Current student, 8/2005-Submit Date, May 2006

The social scene at Binghamton is shockingly diverse, considering the school is surrounded by farmland. There is a ton of popular restaurants nearby (Applebees, Outback, Friendly's), as well as some cute cafes like the Lost Dog. Despite fears of Wal-Mart being "the" place to go on the weekends, there are lots of bars or clubs to go to. The university also does a really good job at offering weekend movie specials or planning activities for those not interested in going to parties. The prominence of the Greek system depends entirely on where you live on campus (Newing has all the Greeks and they're almost unheard of in the other dorms).

Current student, Social Sciences, 8/2004-Submit Date, June 2007

There are over 200 clubs and organizations, club and intramural sports, and numerous other ways to get involved. There is a downtown club and bar scene and an on-campus event called Late-Nite Binghamton, which has free food, bowling, billiards, movies, music, and other weekly events. It happens every Thursday, Friday, and Saturday night. The Vestal Parkway, which is the road that runs by campus, has all sorts of shops, restaurants, and all sorts of other things catered to students.

Current student, 8/2003-Submit Date, August 2006

The social life is vast. From bars to frat houses, everyone is satisfied. Even if you do not enjoy that type of partying, Binghamton has a nationally recognized Late-Night program with activities ranging from movies to contests and dances. Nothing ever gets dull and people wish that the semester could last longer. The Greek system is prominently displayed but there is no pressure to take part in its activities. Clubs are rampant, one for any desire, ranging from academic clubs to cooking and game clubs. There is a niche for everyone to explore.

Current student, 9/2004-Submit Date, April 2006

What's great about the social life at Binghamton is the fact that there are no fraternity/sorority houses on campus. This makes it very easy for someone to choose whether he/she wants to get involved with Greek life or the social/party scene as a whole. Most of the social/party life goes on in what is called downtown Binghamton, which is not within walking distance from campus at all, but it is a very short drive. For party people, the campus favorites are The Rathskeller Sports Bar, and Boca Joe's/Flashbacks. On the other hand, Binghamton has a great program known as Late-Night Binghamton, where students who choose not to partake in the party scene can come and go bowling, play pool and watch new movies every week. Binghamton really has something for everyone. One of the major events at Binghamton is known as Spring Fling, which is amazing. There are so many students who come out and participate, and one can really get to see the true spirit of Binghamton. Also, Binghamton has many special events throughout the semester. For example, big-name bands, such as Green Day and Incubus, have come to campus to perform concerts in the newly built Events Center. Overall, a student at Binghamton can be as social has he/she wants to be. There are many, many opportunities for students such as myself—we just need to get up and take advantage of them!!

Current student, 9/2004-Submit Date, March 2005

The Greek system is popular but not overwhelming at Binghamton. It's easy to get involved with it or easy to ignore it. There are several places downtown to suit the interests of all students, including bars, restaurants and clubs. Some are 21 only, some are 18 to party and 21 to drink, so underage students won't feel left out or feel the need to get a fake ID. For students who choose to stay on campus, there is always something going on. A concert hosted by the Student Association or fine arts, sporting events (games are very popular and a lot of fun to go to), events hosted by the cultural/religious/political/social/academic organizations on campus, Late-Nite Binghamton—there's no such thing as "I'm bored" at Bing.

The School Says

Binghamton University is one of the four university centers of the State University of New York. Known for the excellence of its students, faculty, staff and programs, Binghamton is one of the area's largest employers and enrolls over 14,500 students in programs leading to bachelor's, master's and doctoral degrees. Its curriculum, founded in the liberal arts, has expanded to include selected professional and graduate programs.

Binghamton offers over 100 programs across its six academic divisions and is recognized as the most selective and prestigious university in the State University of New York system.

A wide range of opportunities await prospective students, including internships, study abroad, participation in any of more than 200 student organizations, honors programs, Division I athletics and attractive and comfortable housing in a safe environment.

Binghamton's faculty and students come from approximately 90 countries and 45 states, bringing with them many different cultures and backgrounds and representing a wealth of ideas to explore and enjoy. We have an excellent research library, outstanding computer facilities, a superb performing arts center, a teaching greenhouse, a wide assortment of course offerings and an Events Center. Binghamton is a highly regarded research university, yet as comfortable as a smaller school.

Colgate University

ffice of Admission

3 Oak Drive

amilton, NY 13346

dmissions phone: (315) 228-7401

dmissions fax: (315) 228-7544

dmissions e-mail: admission@mail.colgate.edu

dmissions URL: www.colgate.edu

 Admissions

lumnus/a, Biology, 7/2003-5/2007, June 2007

our high school academic transcript is the most important piece in Colgate's
dmissions process—they make that very clear. It's important to do well aca-
emically, but also it's important to show leadership and commitment to activi-
es and passions outside the classroom. Interviews are informational only and
ery application is read twice, so it's not just about your numbers. In the last
ur years, Colgate has sky-rocketed in terms of their selectivity, and in my opin-
n as an '07 Colgate alumnus, is an incredible school, so it deserves to be selec-
ve!!

urrent student, English, 8/2005-Submit Date, June 2007

olgate uses the Common Application, and has a supplemental essay. As far as
can tell, Colgate likes students with spark and personality that are apparent in
e application. Interviews don't matter in the admissions process, but Colgate
es keep track of all communication a prospective student has with the admis-
ons office. Colgate is highly selective.

lumnus/a, Liberal Arts, 8/2003-5/2007, May 2007

he admissions process is extremely personalized, and the office makes prospec-
ve students feel very important. The admissions officers really take the time to
t to know the students, so be sure to spend some time and effort on the appli-
tion. Colgate is becoming more and more difficult to get into, but they look
r well-rounded students who have something special to offer. The essays are
fantastic way to showcase personality and why you are unique.

urrent student, Cultural Studies, 8/2005-Submit Date, May 2007

olgate's application process is very straightforward—they accept the Common
pplication, with a required Colgate supplement that includes one additional
say of 250 words (a specific, creative question that changes every year—my
ar the question was "What one thing would you bring with you to Colgate if
u could only bring one thing?"). Interviews are not required and are non-eval-
tive (so don't bother). It's a very selective school. I had a 3.9 GPA, 1470
ATs, was salutatorian of my high school class, Student Council president, cap-
in of the Speech and Debate Team, officer on the Key Club Board, and volun-
ered with Habitat for Humanity, just to give you an idea. My advice: be cre-
ive! In your essay, you really need to make yourself stand out. Colgate is real-
in need of diversity, so they're looking for students who are different. If you
ay the accordion in a polka band, send them a tape. If you have blue hair, tell
em. If you spend all your free time weaving baskets, write about it. Just make
re you get across to them why you're special and unique.

urrent student, Physics, 8/2006-Submit Date, May 2007

he admissions process was interesting for Colgate University. First thing it was
ee, because I did my application online. Second thing was the question they
ked me, which was "what would you bring to Colgate?" It seemed corny at
e time but I liked the question in the end because it helped me understand
yself more. Also the campus was amazing! I don't think I have seen any other
mpuses like Colgate's, but that's not why I attended. I decided to attend
olgate because of the Colgate Connection they advertise and I have seen it
ork already because some of my friends already have internships right out of
eir first year. I also liked the fact that I could be a part of my professor's
esearch team.

Current student, 8/2003-Submit Date, June 2006

From the beginning of the admissions process, Colgate does a great job connecting with all applicants. The entire office is very accessible, and the enthusiasm of students and admissions officers really stood out to me when I was applying. Colgate uses the Common Application, but has a 250-word supplement.
Interviews are not required (or evaluative). Colgate had its largest applicant pool
ever in 2005 (8,008 applications) and its second-largest pool in 2006. Colgate
continues to attract involved, well-rounded, academically strong students, which
makes for a great campus environment. April Visit Days are held for admitted
students, and are a great opportunity to meet current students, attend classes and
get a feel for a typical day at Colgate. Overnight stays with current students can
be arranged through the admission office throughout the course of the school
year.

Current student, 8/2005-Submit Date, June 2006

From what I gathered throughout the process, and something that was reinforced
when I was offered admission, was the fact that Colgate really looks for a well-
rounded student. Of course test scores and GPA are important, but the essays are
really a chance for you to talk to the admissions staff about things you feel are
unique about you that you want to emphasize more than just your résumé.
Developing a good relationship with your dean of admissions is also a good way
to get a feel for what Colgate looks for and is all about. I felt that the admissions
process couldn't have gone smoother and the dean of admissions is absolutely
amazing. I have heard countless people tell me that he and his personal attention to every single application are the reasons that they came to Colgate. You
really feel wanted when you apply to Colgate, not like you are trying to break in,
as some other schools tend to feel.

 Academics

Current student, Cultural Studies, 8/2005-Submit Date, May 2007

This is not an easy school. The difference between us and Harvard is that we
don't have grade inflation. You have to work your butt off here. Classes are
intense and the workload can be daunting, but the professors are amazing and
class is never boring. Not one of my courses has been less than excellent.
Classes are very small (10:1 student-to-faculty ratio) and tend to be heavily discussion-based. There are no huge lecture halls, and you can't just sit in the back
and fall asleep. Your professor knows who you are. This can be good and bad.
Professors are very accessible. Office hours are regular, and it's really common
for a student to just drop in, sit down and chat with a prof, not even necessarily
about class. My calc professor happened to be really interested in theatre, and
I'm an actress, so we would often chat about plays we'd seen or read recently.
It's also common for profs to invite students over to their house for dinner. I've
had four profs do this so far. There's a really close faculty/student relationship.
Grading varies among profs, but in general it's hard to get that A. It's definitely do-able, but you really have to work. On an average day, I might do seven
hours of homework or reading outside of class time, and I have a 3.6 GPA
(roughly A-). Class registration is quite stressful, to be honest, because it's tough
to get all the classes you want. Seniors get first pick, then juniors, then sophomores, and freshmen last. Some departments are more competitive than others,
and popular classes fill up fast. However, since students and profs are so close,
it's pretty easy to go talk to a prof and get your name on the waitlist. If you're
persistent and really demonstrate to the prof that you're interested, you'll most
likely get into the class. So it all works out in the end.

Alumnus/a, Biology, 7/2003-5/2007, June 2007

The academic program is rigorous, and the faculty topnotch, although very, very
accessible and willing to help. Classes are small, so your profs know you and if
you make any effort to reach out, you will have their full attention and focus. I
consider several of my professors good friends of mine and have traveled abroad
with two of them—one in a group and one one-on-one. You can pretty much get

Read all of Vault's College Surveys at **www.vault.com/college**—get complete surveys on 100s of colleges and universities, expert advice on applicaton essays and more.

VAULT CAREER LIBRARY **437**

into any class, even if it's closed, by talking to a professor and expressing your interest in the course. In four years, I've never been locked out of a class.

Current student, English, 8/2005-Submit Date, June 2007

I find academics at Colgate to be very fulfilling. There are four core classes to fulfill—Western Traditions, The Challenge of Modernity, a scientific perspectives course, and a course on a non-Western culture. Then there are distribution requirements—two courses in humanities, natural sciences, and social sciences. These are pretty easy to fill. The core classes are a solid basis for a classic education. Workload definitely varies from course to course. Some classes you have to do barely anything for and some take up more time than your other three classes combined. Most classes I've taken have been great, taught by professors who really seem to want to be teaching. I have never had a lot of trouble getting into a class I particularly wanted to take. Grading is by no means easy, but almost always seems fair.

Alumnus/a, Sociology, 8/2003-5/2007, May 2007

The most distinctive things that I noticed about the classes is that regardless of the level, professors' expectations remained relatively high. The classes were mostly engaging, with of course a few exceptions. Popular classes are hard to get into, but professors are pretty flexible in terms of allowing students into their classes. The workload is manageable but students always have room to pursue their specific interests outside of class with the help from their professors. The grading is pretty standard; by nature certain fields allow for more subjective grading, but overall it is fair and most professors are relatively reasonable.

Alumnus/a, Liberal Arts, 8/2003-5/2007, May 2007

The liberal arts program at Colgate is what makes it a great place for undergraduates. The quality of classes is extremely high, and there is usually a really good variety of courses to choose from. There can be some difficulty getting into certain classes, but that is usually limited to specific departments that are more popular. Professors are challenging, but they are amazing. They are brilliant, supportive, interesting, accessible and fun. The workload can be tough, but Colgate students are motivated to study hard and get it all done.

Alumnus/a, 8/2001-5/2005, March 2006

Colgate offers all of its courses with a professor or visiting professor. There are no TAs and in four years I never met with one. Professors are approachable and classes are small. This is the school to go to if you want to be able to walk into a professor's office or call him/her on the phone at home if you have a research question. They pride themselves in approachability and the students take advantage of it. Course selection varies. Popular classes are tough because of class size limits and Core curriculum, but as you go along you find your niche and are able to get what want need. Above all, professors are understanding. Colgate kids work hard and play hard. It is a fun school and it is a hard school. You will have to work and you will have to write, there is no way around it, but would you want any different? There is no grade inflation and that applies across the board. It is not like some of the Ivy League where it is impossible to get a C unless you try. You will get what you deserve at Colgate and that is what my friends noticed from day one.

Current student, 8/2003-Submit Date, June 2006

The academics are excellent at Colgate. The students are very intelligent and well spoken and professors highly encourage group conversations for the most part. Professors are very dedicated to their own research, but typically make time for their students. I have had many professors go above and beyond in order to help me succeed. While ease of grading and workload totally depend on the professor, typically it is not too difficult to get a B, but one has to work hard to get an A. Most classes I feel have been beneficial to my education; however, there are a handful of weaker professors who seem to have no idea what they are doing. These professors seem to be rather few and far between, though. The really good professors' classes tend to fill up rather quickly, but if one is persistent, getting into classes never seems to be too much of a challenge.

 Employment Prospects

Alumnus/a, English, 9/2003-6/2007, July 2007

Very prestigious, many of the top firms brought alumni to interview at th school, and I got hired during my senior year during one of the alumni networ ing events.

Alumnus/a, Biology, 7/2003-5/2007, June 2007

With the depth and breadth of the Colgate alumni body—and their steadfast lo for Colgate and all things Colgate (including students!!) —finding a job is n problem. This is especially true if you are someone who likes to meet peop make connections and network. Colgate has a Center for Career Services and my opinion, its strengths really lie in helping you prepare for an interview, dec pher the details of a job offer, and negotiate your offer. You do have to be ve proactive, though, in actually finding a company you like, and getting yourse an interview.

Alumnus/a, Sociology, 8/2003-5/2007, May 2007

For the most part, the employment prospect for graduates are great. There however a noticeable emphasis on finance and investment banking—the con panies are more prestigious, the alumni are more helpful, Career Services more helpful. I'm afraid that professors are not as helpful in terms of conne tions, and the on-campus recruiting program is not as helpful as one would wi for, but overall the alumni connections that students are able to make ha proven to be very helpful.

Current student, Cultural Studies, 8/2005-Submit Date, May 200

Since I'm only a junior, I'm not too knowledgeable about this, but I can say f sure that the Center for Career Services is really great. They are really helpf with putting together résumés and cover letters, as well as finding jobs ar internships. I know a lot of people who have fantastic, paid NYC internships the business sector this summer, which they got through the alumni networ There is extensive on-campus recruiting, mostly in the economics/political sc ence side of things. Alumni are extremely useful for finding employmer Colgate grads tend to be highly successful, and highly devoted to Colgate, they are eager to help out fellow Colgaters. To give an idea of what some of m friends are doing: a French and economics major who graduated last year is no in France teaching English; my friend who just graduated with a degree in geo raphy landed an internship at National Geographic; an art history/pre-vet ne graduate is interning at the local animal hospital working with large farm an mals; I know a ton of people who have jobs in marketing. There's no shorta of help for finding employment post-Colgate. And employers definitely se Colgate on the résumé and say, "Wow."

Current student, 8/2003-Submit Date, June 2006

Employment prospects at Colgate are very high, and a big reason for this is th strong alumni network. Colgate alumni are at the top of their fields, and are ve interested and enthusiastic about helping current students. By visiting Care Services (over half of the first-year class visited last year), students can get touch with alumni worldwide. Alumni come back to campus to talk about exp riences in law, medicine, education, finance and nonprofits. Students have th opportunity to attend networking receptions with alumni as early as freshma year; my favorite such reception took place at the first Women's Summit he last fall. Dozens of alumnae returned to campus where they spoke on panels ar got to share experiences they'd had at and away from Colgate. A program calle Real World is held every January, immediately prior to the start of the sprir semester. At this program, seniors are able to meet with alumni from many di ferent fields and receive real-life advice as they prepare to graduate and enter th job market. Top job destinations for Colgate grads are business and educatio Career Services coordinates many recruiting sessions for juniors and senior and uses a weekly e-mail to familiarize students with available internships th are offered just about everywhere. 96 percent of graduates have a job, are pa ticipating in a fellowship or are enrolled in grad school one year after gradu tion. A Colgate degree holds prestige because the liberal arts education provid students with the tools to succeed in the job market—namely interperson skills, problem solving skills and the ability to communicate on paper and in pe son.

Current student, 8/2005-Submit Date, June 2006

The Center of Career Services office at Colgate is second to none. The counselors and student staff members who work there are friendly and helpful, and the alumni connection may be one of Colgate's biggest strengths. As Colgate has less living alumni than many schools have enrolled in a given year, the sense of community is much greater than at a bigger school and alumni love to come back and help; whether this is through granting an informational interview, an internship or even a job; the Colgate Connection is hugely beneficial. During the year, top-name companies and firms are constantly coming to campus to give information sessions and to recruit. Such firms as Goldman-Sachs, Merill Lynch and Morgan Stanley make a point to come, usually sending alumni to conduct the sessions and help the seniors through the process.

Quality of Life

Alumnus/a, Biology, 7/2003-5/2007, June 2007

Colgate is one of the most beautiful, well-kept, safe campuses in the country. My friends visit time and again and are always surprised by what a gorgeous campus Colgate has. The worst crime you hear of is fire alarms being pulled in dorms or the open container law being broken. The Town of Hamilton and Colgate itself have a palpable sense of community and a good relationship with one another. Colgate students are well taken care of, to say the least. Our dorms are either old with character or brand-new with all the cleanliness that comes with new buildings and our academic buildings are stunning and state-of-the-art. In the last two years, a brand-new library and brand-new interdisciplinary science building have been built.

Alumnus/a, Liberal Arts, 8/2003-5/2007, May 2007

The Colgate campus is located in a small college town, which makes a great living environment and a safe neighborhood and campus. Housing offers a variety of options, but it can be difficult to get the type that you want. The lottery system that is used is helpful in making the process fair. The dining halls are a lot of fun, and have good food. They also make an effort to offer different themed nights or healthy options for students. Athletic facilities are great, and most students on campus are involved in athletics at some level. The downtown of Hamilton also provides a great place to spend time with friends and professors, at the coffee house or one of the restaurants. Also, Colgate's newly renovated library is beautiful and high-tech, and a new science center is opening soon that will be state-of-the-art.

Current student, Cultural Studies, 8/2005-Submit Date, May 2007

The campus is gorgeous. It is on a giant hill, so there's a lot of walking and climbing involved. The facilities are great—brand-new $53 million library, a huge and impressive (and expensive) new state-of-the-art science center in construction currently, great labs, fantastic sports facilities, pleasant classrooms. This is a school with money—they've got the resources to keep a cushy campus. Landscaping and looks are important. There are three dining halls, and they're all pretty darn good. You'll be sad to leave them behind when you're a senior in an apartment with a kitchen. Housing is well kept, attractive and comfortable. Freshman dorms are the most conveniently located. Upperclassmen live in townhouses, apartments or themed houses on Broad Street (the main drag in Hamilton), all very nice, though it's a longer trek up to the academic quad on the top of the hill. There's a distinct separation between "up the hill" and "down the hill"—freshmen and schoolwork are up the hill; upperclassmen and parties are down the hill. The Cruiser is a bus that runs all over campus pretty much 24/7 to get you wherever you need to go, arriving at every stop twice an hour, which is very convenient. Although you barely need it because the campus, not to mention the whole town, is so small. Hamilton is a tiny little town, like if you were driving through you'd miss it if you blinked. Which makes it really safe. There are blue-light safety/emergency phones everywhere, and campus police are never more than five minutes away, but none of that matters anyway because there's absolutely nothing to worry about. I'm a girl and I'm perfectly comfortable walking around by myself at night in the dark. It's really safe.

Current student, 8/2003-Submit Date, June 2006

The average Colgate student is very happy, despite the long winter and daily trek up the hill. The campus is absolutely beautiful, and the strong connections between students, faculty, staff and Hamilton residents make for a tight-knit community (one of Colgate's greatest strengths). The campus is overwhelmingly safe; I can walk back from the library safely at 2 a.m. or later, and the campus safety blotter is filled with mostly trivial mishaps. Housing is guaranteed on campus for all four years. First-year housing is in six different dorms, all located up the hill, close to the student center, academic buildings and the dining hall. There are also themed housing options for first-years, which include LOFT (Leadership Options for Tomorrow), Can-Doo (a community service program), Outdoor Connections (an outdoor education program), as well as a Healthy Living (substance-free) option. The dining halls, of course, are not the same as a home-cooked meal, but have a lot of variety. Frank (the largest dining hall) holds special events like a Middle Eastern foods night and a Halloween dinner. If you have food allergies, the dining hall staff will go above and beyond to make meals for you. Students stay active through athletics (about 80 percent of students are involved), which include intramurals, club and varsity, and a great outdoor education program that runs a pre-orientation program called Wilderness Adventure, as well as gym classes, and one-day backyard adventures like a sunrise canoe or telemark skiing. The campus is currently under construction, but a beautiful library is due to be completed by the end of this year, and a new science center by summer 2007. Colgate's student body is becoming increasingly diverse in the past few years; right now, 20 percent of students come from a multicultural background. I am really pleased with the growth of cultural groups on campus just within the last few years. Dialogue circles, caucus groups, a great program called Skin Deep, a new diversity council and the first Big Gay Weekend have gone a long way to making Colgate even more welcoming and open for all students.

Social Life

Alumnus/a, Biology, 7/2003-5/2007, June 2007

The social life definitely revolves around the campus and the small town of Hamilton, which consists of four bars. The Jug is the classic late-night bar. Students never leave campus on the weekends and feel like they're missing out when they do. In four years, I have missed probably four weekends at Colgate—they're so much fun! There is definitely a Greek presence on campus—40 percent of eligible students are Greek, but the Greek system offers a very much "be as involved as you want to be" feeling. Colgate students are not a big dating group—more hook ups. There are tons of clubs and events every weeknight and weekend—honestly more than you could ever attend. Sundays are quiet and the library fills up. Colgate is truly a work hard, play hard sort of place. It sounds trite, but, coming firsthand from someone who's been there, it's true! Colgate kids are fun and smart and like being both.

Alumnus/a, Sociology, 8/2003-5/2007, May 2007

In comparison to larger schools, or colleges that are near or in larger cities, Colgate and Hamilton do not provide a huge array of choices in terms of nightlife, bars or restaurants. However, the students—though they may not admit it—take on a certain pride and ownership to their small-town bars, so much so that students become close friends with the owners and bouncers. While most students will claim that Colgate is not a dating school. I would wager that a comparable number of students do in fact date. The Greek system is visible at Colgate but is definitely not overbearing. Most students who are involved with the Greek system have many friends and acquaintances outside their particular affiliations as well as outside the system.

Current student, Cultural Studies, 8/2005-Submit Date, May 2007

We work hard, but we party hard too. Partying is a huge part of life. You won't be at Colgate a week before you find out about the Jug. The Old Stone Jug, fondly referred to as "The Jug" is the center of the freshman social scene. It's a bar, but it is open to the underage crowd as a dance club. It will be the site of many a drunken night and the beginning of countless hookups—good trashy fun. Slices, a pizza place with the most delicious pizza ever is also a very popular hangout spot. At midnight it is packed. The Hour Glass is the most popular bar, although Nichols & Beal is well-loved for its Karaoke Thursdays. The frats provide the majority of the entertainment, with parties and bands every weekend. There are, I think, seven frats and four sororities. A ton of students are involved in Greek life, but it doesn't make a huge difference if you're not. I'm not in a sorority, and I still have tons of friends and plenty to do, and a lot of my friends are in frats and sororities. There's never a shortage of stuff to do—films, lec-

Read all of Vault's College Surveys at **www.vault.com/college**—get complete surveys on 100s of colleges and universities, expert advice on applicaton essays and more.

VAULT CAREER LIBRARY **439**

tures, concerts, theatre or dance performances, workshops, art exhibits and so on. You'll never be bored. There's a club for whatever you feel like doing. There are academic clubs, tons of opportunities for volunteering, political clubs, environmental/social concerns clubs, music groups, theatre groups, and more sports than you could ever want. The dating scene is not really a dating scene, it's more of a hook-up scene. It seems like everyone is somehow connected to everyone else through a web of hookups. I know a few couples who have been in relationships for a fairly long time now, but dating is much less common.

Current student, 8/2005-Submit Date, June 2006

Being out in the middle of nowhere may seem daunting to some people, me included at first; however, it offers so many opportunities that people wouldn't have had in a suburban or urban school. Greek life is a big part of Colgate but it is in no way overpowering. Many people choose not to participate but still go to Greek parties if they want. Slices is the usual weekend hotspot—a pizza place that everyone seems to congregate to around 2 or 3 a.m. The Jug is a club/bar that is also the place to be on the weekend. Colgate's dating scenes isn't that big, it is more of a hook-up school but that's not to say people don't date. Colgate knows that it is in the middle of nowhere and does a great job of bringing things to campus. Speakers and music groups are frequently available on the weekends, often hosted by student groups on campus. Clubs are also a big part of the extremely active student body, as there are over 100 student-run clubs on campus and anyone with a creative idea and a little student support can start his/her own club.

Current student, 8/2005-Submit Date, June 2006

The social life at Colgate varies. Yes, the Greek system does have a big influence, but it doesn't have to be everything. Freshmen and sophomores enjoy The Jug, the local 19+ bar downtown that is a dancing place. For older students, Nichols & Beal is the best bet. Hookups are the most common thing on campus, but a good number of people take the step to commit to a relationship. It is rumored that many people will find their future husband or wife on campus! You rush fall of your sophomore year, so you have a whole year to make friends, find your niche, and decide whether or not you want to go Greek, which is really nice.

 The School Says

Colgate University offers the broad resources associated with a top-rated university, as well as the traditions, values and engagement of a vibrant liberal arts community. The 550-acre campus is widely regarded as one of the most beautiful in the country, with historic stone buildings sharing the striking central New York landscape with contemporary facilities. In 2007, two new $50 million interdisciplinary buildings came on line, positioning Colgate well for the future. The Case Library and Geyer Center for Information Technology reopened after a dramatic rebuilding, and The Robert H. N. Ho Science Center is sure to attract top science students. The buildings' revolutionary design has intermingled offices, study lounges, classroom spaces, and laboratories for research in biology, geography, geology, environmental studies, and physics and astronomy.

With 2,800 residential undergraduates (from 47 states and 39 countries), more than 50 academic majors, 25 extracurricular clubs and activities, an innovative program of residential education, and competitive Division I athletics, Colgate assures students a wide array of academic and social options. Colgate's interdisciplinary liberal arts curriculum features a rigorous sequence of four core courses that create a common and lasting conversation among professors and students. All courses are taught by faculty members, and the 10:1 student-to-faculty ratio encourages close collaboration on creative projects in the arts and sciences, co-authored research papers for refereed journals, field work that translates in-class learning into practice, and faculty-led off-campus study programs. More than two thirds of students study off campus, and the Institute of International Education ranks Colgate Number Three among baccalaureate institutions for the number of students who study abroad.

Colgate is a national model for supporting its community. Through the COVE (the Center for Outreach, Volunteerism, and Education), students take on complex and long-term service projects benefiting the village and Town of Hamilton and beyond. The university's Center for Ethics and World Societies engages students in discussions of urgent issues facing the international community, and strengthens the connection between Colgate and the world its students will inhabit. 20 academic courses have a service learning component.

Colgate fields 25 Division I varsity teams, and membership in the Patriot League assures fierce competition. 80 percent of students participate in varsity, intramural or club sports. State-of-the-art athletic facilities include the 10,000-seat Andy Kerr Football Stadium, the Grace Lineberry Natatorium with both Olympic and 25-meter pools, the Sanford Field House with indoor track and tennis, and the new Glendening Boathouse on Lake Moriane. A fully outfitted Base Camp on campus is headquarters for Colgate's outdoor education program, with maps and videos, as well as an equipment rental center with gear for camping, backpacking, skiing and show shoeing.

One true measure of Colgate's success is the legendary connection that students, faculty and alumni feel, not only to their classmates and college friends, but to the nearly 28,000 Colgate faithful they may meet anywhere in the world. The Center for Career Services works with alumni on programs such as Career Development for the New Economy, a nine-week course developed by a Colgate alumnus that is intended to help students determine their interests and skills, teach them how to evaluate and research career options, and show them how to present themselves effectively.

Non-evaluative, informational interviews are available for those candidates who wish to learn more about Colgate and its admissions process in a one-on-one setting. These interviews give students a chance to "interview" Colgate and to see how their interests and goals might match with a Colgate education.

Use the Internet's
MOST TARGETED
job search tools.

Vault Job Board

Target your search by industry, function, and experience level, and find the job openings that you want.

VaultMatch Resume Database

Vault takes match-making to the next level: post your résumé and customize your search by industry, function, experience and more. We'll match job listings with your interests and criteria and e-mail them directly to your in-box.

VAULT

> the most trusted name in career information™

Columbia University

Office of Undergraduate Admissions
Columbia University
212 Hamilton Hall, MC 2807
1130 Amsterdam Avenue
New York, NY 10027
Admissions phone: (212) 854-2522
Admissions fax: (212) 854-1209
Admissions URL:
www.studentaffairs.columbia.edu/admissions/

 ## Admissions

Current student, 8/2003-Submit Date, December 2006

Columbia is an Ivy League school, and as such, is pretty difficult to get into. Overall, the process was easy: all of the application was online. I lived in New York State, so I had an interview with an alumnus in my hometown. Overall, the process was pretty easy, with an application less painful than some, more painful than others.

Current student, 9/2003-Submit Date, November 2006

Columbia is an Ivy League school, and like most topnotch competitive universities, that means they are obviously expecting to see numbers. However, Columbia has been notorious for its off-beat student population, and the school does exhibit an incredible array of charismatic, passionate and extremely diverse people in all areas of life, from nationality to hobbies, to political affiliation, to academic accomplishment. Don't think that you can send in an application with all the correct numbers (i.e., perfect SATs, all AP classes, 4.0 GPA) and a middle-of-the-road, play-it-safe essay with some generic "I traveled to Latin America and saw poor people and boy, it opened my eyes to world inequality" because those admission officers have heard it a thousand times before, and have seen thousands of 4.0 GPAs. You application should take risks. You shouldn't be afraid to write an essay on something random and funny and ridiculous, if that's who you are.

Current student, 9/2002-Submit Date, March 2006

Admissions process is fairly standard. There is an option for Early Decision, which allows you to apply early and get a decision early (around mid-December). The only catch is if accepted, you must go there. I don't know what the consequences are, but I found that it's best not to test the system. It is generally considered easier to get in if you apply early (a much larger percentage of early applicants is accepted versus percentage of regular applicants). Columbia generally takes 10 to 15 percent of applicants each year, but this of course depends on the total number of applicants, which is constantly increasing.

> **The school says:** "Our acceptance rate this year was 10.6 percent and we have been below 15 percent for the last few years."

They tend to look for well-rounded individuals, as their education is based on a core curriculum that spans all subjects (literature, philosophy, music, art, history and science). Extracurriculars are important, as are grades and test scores. When I applied, essays were open-ended with no set topics. Interviews were also not required, though it appeared that borderline applicants were often asked to come in. Columbia very much adheres to Affirmative Action rules and stresses diversity. If you stress your diverse background (this can apply to anything, not just nationality or ethnic background), the ad-coms will note it.

> **Regarding interviews, Columbia says:** "We offer interviews through our Alumni Representative Committee, and they are not required. We do not ask borderline candidates to come for an on-campus interview."

Current student, 7/2003-Submit Date, October 2004

The essay is really standard. Question basics—nothing too hard. Just do n write, "I want to come to Columbia because it is NYC." Admissions office hate that. Be creative, they definitely like that. Include a picture in your appl cation, and make it a good one so they remember you (sounds strange but I kno it can help). If possible, get to know admissions officers, and applying earl helps as well.

 ## Academics

Current student, Mathematics, 9/2005-Submit Date, April 2007

The Core classes are standard, but a ton of reading. I usually get about 100 t 150 pages per week for each humanities class. Some professors are good, som are amazing, and some are terrible; make sure you go to http://www.culpa.inf before registration, since you can find all views there. Columbia has some mor ster scales, and it's not difficult to get at least an A- in all your classes. It's ver hard to do poorly, and very easy to do well. The workload is fairly light, espe cially since some of the Core classes, such as music and art, are not rigorous However, double majoring is extremely difficult with the Core, and you'll hav to plan your schedule well.

Current student, Engineering, 8/2003-Submit Date, December 200

The engineering program here is good, but be forewarned: the school is rela tively small. The curriculum is excellent, with a large portion of time devote to the famous Columbia Core.

> **The school says:** "About one fourth of courses taken by Engineering students (and one third for College students) are Core Curriculum classes."

This is a humanities program that occupies half of the first two years, the othe half taken up by basic science courses. The engineering program is also excel lent, though pretty standard. Working during engineering internships, I foun that I was on par with students from other school in terms of my technical knowl edge and prowess. The main problem with the school is that it is not well know as an engineering school. While the academics are topnotch, many companie do not immediately think of Columbia as a technical powerhouse. As a chemi cal engineering student, the curriculum was standard. I felt well-prepared t enter the workplace.

Current student, 9/2003-Submit Date, November 2006

Academically, Columbia is absolutely spectacular. I cannot tell you how man times I've signed up for a class because it looked cool and interesting and late found out that I was working one-on-one with a Pulitzer Prize winning poet. Th professors are famous, they're brilliant, and you will leave your classes dumb founded and reeling. But, on that note, Columbia is all about "academia for th sake of academia," so if you have any hope of taking courses geared at pre-pro fessionalism (like business communications, journalism, finance, accounting) you better look elsewhere because none of those are offered in the undergradu ate program of study. You will walk out of Columbia has a history, physics English, math major, as those are some of more popular ones at the school. Th first two years of study at Columbia will be filled with required Core Curriculum classes. Columbia has one of the most intense set of general requirements including things like two PE classes, so don't expect to be taking many electiv early on. On that note, it is easy to get into the classes you want as an upper classman, and because of that Core Curriculum, that will be the only time wher you can really take them. I've never had difficulties getting into a class I want ed. The humanities courses are pretty small, lectures that range from 50 to 20 people, and discussion-based "seminars" with 20 or fewer people in them Seminars are as easy to get into as lectures, so you really can pick if you wan to have a more intimate academic experience or a larger, anonymous one. Th sciences are a different story. They are usually a lot bigger, with smaller dis cussion sections and lab times that meet separate from the lecture. These require incredible workload, many of my science/pre-med/engineer friends are always stressing about the sheer volume of work they must accomplish. Grading, I find, is not that hard. To get a B+/A-, you can put in the basic amount of work. However, to get a solid A, is a different story. That is difficult.

Current student, 9/2002-Submit Date, March 2006

The first two years are focused primarily on requirements: Core Curriculum and major. It makes it difficult to experiment with electives, but you get a lot of exposure to different fields through the Core. Most Core classes are taught by TAs, and naturally some are better than others.

> **The school says:** "One third of Core classes are taught by PhD students who have completed their coursework and are writing their dissertations."

is difficult to get into popular Core sections, so if you get a bad instructor, chances are you'll just have to tough it out. Quality of classes and professors, along with grading, varies greatly from department to department. Science and engineering courses tend to have less comprehensible professors, but similarly easier grading curves. Humanities classes have high concentrations of A grades. I've had amazing classes in several departments, as well as horrible nightmare classes in those same departments, so it really is the luck of the draw. Just read the description of the course and check out the professor's reviews (there's a nifty site called CULPA—Columbia University Listing of Professor Ability). There is also a one-week shopping period in the beginning of the semester, so the best plan is to register for a bunch of classes you think you might want to take, attend all of them and then drop the worst ones.

Current student, 9/2003-Submit Date, January 2006

There are always difficult and easy majors from which you can choose. One can be a complete slacker and ace an American studies major or one can really challenge oneself and work tirelessly for a biomedical engineering degree. Overall, the engineering school is much more difficult than Columbia College (Barnard and General Studies are much easier.) Both SEAS and CC can demand much from you. As a humanities major you will read 200 pages a week per class (around four) along with a series of 10-page papers and exams for each class. CC students usually write a 40-page thesis paper senior year. Engineering is much more difficult and you usually take five or six classes a term. Upperclassman engineers take mostly grad classes with graduate students and are graded on the same curve.

Current student, 9/2001-Submit Date, May 2004

Columbia isn't an easy school. The Core comprises well over 50 credits and you can expect to spend most of the first two years fulfilling requirements. They also don't cut any slack. My reward for a 5 on the AP Calculus exam was the honors section of Calculus II at Columbia. If you don't take the next section, there is no AP credit. By contrast, that score would have earned me eight credits at another school. I must say that, in three years, I've had only one course taught by a TA. That said, in economics the TAs do all the grading, much to my dismay. I found there to be a huge disconnect between the profs' expectations and those of the TAs, which is not communicated.

Current student, 8/2002-Submit Date, February 2004

The program is obviously competitive. No matter what major you choose, if you are applying to Columbia College you will be taking the Core Curriculum. This is the distinguishing characteristic that sets Columbia apart from the rest. The Core Curriculum encompasses a solid humanities curriculum with requirements in math and science this prohibits a math major from not writing a research paper and an English major from not understanding some fundamentals of math and science.

Quality of classes within each individual department varies (I am a double major in economics and political science) and I find it extremely necessary to develop a rapport with your departmental advisor and fellow upperclassmen within your major. The quality of classes has more to do with who is teaching and less to do with the actual subject matter. Hence, if you find a good professor in your department, take every class he/she offers that falls within your degree requirements. Overall the quality of classes and the range of selection are very wide.

Employment Prospects

Current student, Mathematics, 9/2005-Submit Date, April 2007

Recruiting here is amazing, especially for investment banking/finance. All the top firms, including Blackstone and GS, are listed on our career services site for résumé drops. In addition, there are plenty of smaller funds near NYC that love Columbia, are too lazy to go to other Ivies, and choose to recruit here exclusively. The only problem about employment is that it seems as though all Columbia students want to go into finance, so sometimes the competition is quite fierce. Getting an internship, however, is not difficult at all, since it's in New York.

Current student, 9/2003-Submit Date, November 2006

Columbia is not a pre-professional school. It is, however, an extremely good school, and employers know that and don't necessarily care if you're walking out with a degree in philosophy. At the end of your senior year of undergraduate study, various employers will come to Columbia to recruit you. Columbia is notorious for feeding its graduates into Wall Street investment banks, so if you're looking to go on that track, Columbia is perfect. Also, because of Columbia's location in New York City, there are thousands of internships available for students throughout the year, and many of these can lead directly into jobs during the summer or after graduating. Because of this, alumni are very helpful—most of them have stuck around the city and post job openings for Columbia graduates only on Columbia's career services web site.

Current student, 9/2003-Submit Date, January 2006

Employment is incredibly good just because Columbia is in New York. Columbia probably has the best campus recruitment for finance internships/jobs. Columbia's employment prospects are managed by Columbia's Center for Career Education, which does an excellent job connecting students with all types of industries. CCE is really professional and helpful. They are there for the sheer purpose of holding your hand through everything.

Current student, 8/2000-Submit Date, June 2004

Going to Columbia put me in a unique position—a great one—because it's in NYC, the capital of the business world (and other worlds, too!). And since I was interested in business/finance, I was able to take advantage of the internships available at large firms. Again, like the academics, getting ahead in the realm of careers is only for independent self-starters: You have to know what you want, find out how to get it and go get it.

I found myself an internship at Salomon Smith Barney during freshman year, then at Merrill Lynch the following year and then spent over a year writing feature stories for a hedge fund journal. In January of my senior year I landed a part-time job at an asset management recruiting firm, and they asked me to stay full-time after graduation—so here I am. I got all of these jobs via the Monstertrak web site at Columbia's career services web page. The career resources at Columbia are amazing, and the school holds incredible prestige with employers. Campus recruiting is an everyday event, and Columbia students get hired—bottom line. If you don't know what you want to do, Columbia will help you there, too. Career counselors, alumni and students are available and willing to meet with you all the time. The opportunities are endless.

Quality of Life

Current student, Engineering, 8/2003-Submit Date, December 2006

The campus is fabulous, with historic and beautiful surroundings. There is always good food in the neighborhood, and downtown is a $2 subway ride away. The housing is nothing to write home about, but is generally a bargain compared to regular New York housing costs. Safety and crime are really nothing to worry about. Finally, it seems that your tuition dollars actually do buy things, as the facilities are great.

Current student, 9/2003-Submit Date, November 2006

The housing on Columbia's campus is spectacular. Living in New York City off Columbia's campus is do-able, but you wouldn't want to—for what you pay, the student housing on campus is the best accommodation you may ever have in New York City in your life—boasting things like tri-level apartments with

Read all of Vault's College Surveys at **www.vault.com/college**—get complete surveys on 100s of colleges and universities, expert advice on applicaton essays and more.

VAULT CAREER LIBRARY   **443**

sweeping views of Central Park and the Empire State Building, and studio apartments overlooking Riverside Park. Not to mention that Columbia's location on the Upper West Side of New York is extremely safe, and 24 hour security patrols the neighborhood. Your freshman year you are required to be on a meal plan, which is a good option seeing how most freshman dorms don't have full-fledged kitchens, but after that, most housing has full kitchens, so most students stay off the meal plans and opt to cook for themselves, or grab meals from the various cafes and diners lining the surrounding neighborhood. Columbia has a gated campus, full of green lawns where you can relax and throw frisbees around, so when you're living on campus, you feel like you are actually on a college campus, an extremely nice break from the over-crowded bustling city that you encounter stepping outside the gates.

Current student, 9/2002-Submit Date, March 2006

The vast majority of students (something like 99 percent) live on campus, so there is a huge social scene right here. The campus itself is small, but very academic-looking. It reminds people of old European institutions: very symmetrical architecture, large libraries with columns, imposing buildings and statues of famous thinkers (including "the thinker" by the philosophy building). The neighborhood is the Upper West Side. Many of the professors and graduate students, along with almost all of the undergrads, live within a 10-minute walk of campus. The area is filled with little restaurants and cafes, shops, bars, jazz clubs and the like. There is definitely plenty to do here on the weekends, and the subway right by campus connects you quickly to the rest of Manhattan and NYC.

Current student, 8/2003-Submit Date, December 2005

Freshmen and seniors get the best housing, sophomores the worst. I know more than a few juniors who live in walk-through doubles this year (because of an unusually large senior class). The housing itself is definitely a disappointment (compared to other universities), but as they say, it's location, location, location, and you're in the best city in the world. I feel safe walking on campus, even late at night.

Alumnus/a, 9/1999-9/2003, September 2004

Housing works on a lottery system, so if you get a good number you'll get good housing. Upperclassmen get priority, so there's hope for them even if they come up short in the lottery. Sophomores have the hardest time in my opinion, and can get stuck with a crammed single or double with one bathroom for the entire floor. I lived in East Campus, which has five- or six-person, two-floor suites, as well as doubles. I loved it there since I had a single and a kitchen and living room to share with only four other people. The dorm is located at 70 Morningside Drive; easternmost side of campus overlooking Morningside Park; within campus gates accessible by foot bridge over Amsterdam Ave. Everyone lives there—seniors, juniors, sophomores, Barnard, frats, sororities, special interest houses, even faculty members!

 Social Life

Current student, Mathematics, 9/2005-Submit Date, April 2007

Most people go bar-hopping on weekends, and there are usually frat parties on Friday/Saturday nights, as well. A lot of the fun takes place off campus but close to it, since we definitely have plenty of bars around.

Current student, 9/2003-Submit Date, November 2006

You want it, Columbia and New York has it. If you want a "college" experien complete with frat parties, Columbia has an on-campus party and social sce with a whole row of sorority and fraternity houses across the street from ca pus, occupying some of the most spacious and beautiful brownstone houses the neighborhood. Not your scene? Fine. You can always find something to off campus, from clubbing to back-alley jazz clubs, and because of Columbi connection with the city and your position as student, expect to get discounts of things like Broadway shows, and free entry into almost every single museu in New York City, as well as free tickets to concerts if you DJ at Columbia's ve own radio station, WKCR, which boasts a broadcast range of over 9 million pe ple in New York and the Tri-State Area. Are you more into the outdoo Columbia has a surf club, where you can haul your surfboard onto the subw and appear at a perfect surf beach an hour later, a hiking club that has week day trips and overnights to mountain ranges in Upstate New York, a sailing cl that practices three times a week in their very own boats on the Hudson River rock-climbing club that goes bouldering in Central Park, just to name a few.

Current student, 9/2002-Submit Date, March 2006

The Greek system, unlike at other schools, is relatively quiet here. We do ha a "frat row" on 114th Street, but only about 10 to 15 percent of students belo to fraternities or sororities. Since everyone lives near each other anyway, the seems to be little need to join a group of this kind. There are tons of stude activities and groups on campus, catering to just about every interest you c think of from political groups like the Socialists, Democrats and Republicans, cultural groups (Russian and Chinese), to activities (step team, ballroom); y name it we got it. There is a relatively new student center right on campus wi a large auditorium and cinema where the film society shows discounted film every Thursday. The bars on Broadway and Amsterdam are always crowde particularly with freshmen and sophomores. Once people get sick of that scen they start checking out the rest of what NYC has to offer.

Current student, 8/2000-Submit Date, June 2004

Social life is also a mixed bag. There are events on campus every single nig sponsored by interest groups and clubs. Dances and alcohol-based parties a also sponsored by the university on campus. However, on Wednesday night th fun begins at the West End for cheap beer and karaoke. Thursday night every one does the circuit of local bars: The West End, The Heights (for $3 margar tas), Nacho's Kitchen, Cannons (late-night 2 to 5 a.m.: mostly jocks ar groupies!); and then there's the circuit on Amsterdam Ave: 1020 (laid-bac mostly grad students and film students), SoHa (where all the freshman gir dance on the bars!), and a few others. Friday nights are kind of quiet—hom work night maybe? Saturday night it's back to the circuits.

Cornell University

Undergraduate Admissions Office
Cornell University
410 Thurston Avenue
Ithaca, NY 14850-2488
Admissions phone: (607) 255-5241
Admissions fax: (607) 254-5175
Admissions URL: www.admissions.cornell.edu

 Admissions

Alumnus/a, 8/2001-5/2005, December 2006

The admissions process is pretty standard for an Ivy League university. To get in, you just need an outstanding academic record, a focus on what you might want to major in, experience demonstrating that interest, a variety of extracurricular activities and achievements under your belt, and a fairly well-written set of essays. There isn't a mandatory interview, but it's definitely informative for a prospective student. The selectivity is high, as to be expected, but maybe not as high as some of the other Ivy schools because Cornell is so large in size.

> **Regarding interviews, the school says:** "Admissions interviews are required for students applying to the School of Hotel Administration or Architecture in the College of Architecture, Art, and Planning. Admissions interviews are recommended for applicants to Fine Arts in the College of Architecture, Art, and Planning. The college should be contacted directly to arrange the admissions interview. Interviews for all other programs are not required, nor offered."

Current student, 8/2004-Submit Date, October 2006

The essays that I had to write for Cornell were the most intensive part of the process. I think this is something Cornell really values. If you can write well, you can present yourself well in ways other than test scores and transcripts. This is also especially useful when your standardized tests are below average for admission. My SAT scores were at the very bottom of Cornell's cut-off, but I think the reason they didn't reject me was because they saw academic and leadership potential in all other areas of my application. Don't think that Cornell is cut and dry when it comes to admissions. They want to see maturity and sense of self in all areas and, of course, academic promise.

> **The school says:** "Cornell does not have a cut-off for SAT scores."

Current student, 9/2003-Submit Date, October 2006

Advice to athletes: Make an effort to find the e-mail address and contact the coach of your prospective coach. Coaches can be rather busy and there are many athletes out there, so even though you may be talented they may not have noticed you, don't take that as a sign—take action and initiate the contact via e-mail (as early as fall of your junior year). Be as specific as possible in your essays and do some background reading if possible. For example, one of the essays in my year was something similar to: "Why do you want to attend Cornell?" or "Why do you want to attend Cornell given your major?" I navigated through Cornell's site to find information about the research projects that some professors were working on, then in my essay I discussed in which labs I would like to work (contingent on my admission). Doing this shows that you are motivated, knowledgeable in the field, and most importantly, highlights the specific reasons Cornell would be the ideal school for you.

> **The school says:** "Information about Cornell athletics can be found at www.cornellbigred.com."

Current student, 8/2003-Submit Date, October 2006

Cornell University is highly selective, although selectivity does vary according to which college or program you apply, where you come from, and certain personal characteristics. I got into the College of Arts and Sciences class of 2007 with a 3.79 high school GPA and a 1520 SAT. I also had outstanding essays. I believe that choosing Cornell as my Early Decision school, and then also visiting the university, definitely improved my chances: It showed the admissions people that I was serious about Cornell.

Admissions to some of Cornell's other Colleges can be a bit easier or different. The engineering college cares far more about math than about Verbal abilities. And the State Schools: ILR, Human Ecology, Agriculture and Life Sciences, are across the board easier to get into. This is especially true for New York State residents. I would suggest, if you think that your application to the arts college may be borderline for admission, that you consider applying for a state school. The state schools teach a wide variety of things, many of which have very similar or related majors in the arts college. Internal transfer between colleges is also fairly easy, so long as you can keep your grades up in the first one or two semesters.

> **Cornell says:** "Transferring between colleges is a possibility, but not guaranteed."

Current student, 1/2006-Submit Date, September 2006

Cornell is regarded is one of the most selective schools in the country. Along with its Ivy League status, it is believed to be one of the best schools for undergraduate research. Regular decision is set for an application post-marked for January 1.

> **The school says:** "Cornell offers two admissions options: Early Decision, with an application deadline of November 1, and Regular Decision, with an application deadline of January 1.

Cornell uses the Common Application along with its own application booklet that consists of three supplementary essays in addition to the essay found in Common Application. Depending on the school to which you apply, an interview will be given. In the past, students have discovered that the school most likely to give interviews is the School of Hotel Administration, due to its infamous reputation in being a people-oriented/business institution.

SAT scores generally range from 1300 to 1590 and over 85 percent of incoming freshmen are the top 10 percent in their high school graduating class. Cornell generally admits between 22 percent and 25 percent of its applicants, with different acceptance ranges depending on the school that one applies to. The engineering school, for example, has a higher acceptance rate than the College of Arts and Sciences. Advice: Take AP or IB courses at school if at all possible. Cornell likes students who challenge themselves. Try to set yourself apart in your essay. Be detailed and descriptive on who you are and what makes you different. Get good teacher recommendations! You will find out that those are extremely important.

Current student, 8/2006-Submit Date, January 2007

One of the best things about Cornell is that they actually do look beyond SAT scores and perfect grades. Don't get me wrong, the school is extremely selective and it certainly doesn't hurt to have a 4.5 GPA and 2380 on the SAT but luckily for the rest of us, Cornell places a great deal of emphasis on personal goals and potential. I would suggest paying particular attention to the essay and short answer questions. I was never interviewed and my scores weren't the most impressive but I did pour my heart into my essay and I think that paid off. In conclusion, Cornell has been known to accept students whom other much less prestigious institutions did not admit (students like me). It never hurts to try.

Alumnus/a, 8/2002-12/2005, March 2006

I was waitlisted at Cornell after going through the regular admissions process. I think my application was very typical. I had good grades (3.9 unweighted as an IB diploma candidate), fair SAT score for Cornell (1360 in the old scoring system), and an average applicant's extracurriculars (tennis team player/asst. manager, NHS officer). I got in off of the waitlist because I was extremely persistent. I poured my heart out in a letter to the dean of admissions, had my high school counselor send a strong recommendation letter, and sent two extra teach-

Read all of Vault's College Surveys at **www.vault.com/college**—get complete surveys on 100s of colleges and universities, expert advice on application essays and more.

VAULT CAREER LIBRARY **445**

ers send recommendation letters in addition to the ones required in the application process. I then sent them another letter after graduation letting them know of all of the awards I got, how my GPA was during my last semester, and what I was up to with regards to summer and senior year activities.

 **Academics**

Alumnus/a, 8/2002-5/2006, January 2007

There is so much variation among the different colleges within Cornell (some people study painting, others study hotel management, agriculture or physics) that there's no simple answer to sum up the academic experience. As a student in the College of Arts and Sciences, I found the quality of my classes to be excellent, the faculty topnotch, and the amount of freedom and flexibility pretty great. That having been said, at any university I think that to some extent what you get out of the experience depends what you put in; although the advising system provides plenty of support and advocacy, no one is going to hold your hand or tell you exactly what to do there (and the sheer breadth of opportunity can be a little dizzying—check out the course listings online to get any idea of the possibilities for study). Looking back on my four years, I think I learned a whole lot and worked very hard to do it, but still managed to have a lot of fun. Faculty are leaders or rising stars, which is especially great for students interested in pursuing graduate study—since it's a major research university, they are hired not just to teach (and they do, for the most part, teach very well), but to be on the cutting edge of their fields, and it shows.

Alumnus/a, 8/2001-5/2005, December 2006

Cornell is tough. Although it might be the easiest Ivy to be admitted to, it might also be the hardest to survive, and get out of. The academic programs available are nearly limitless in number. Any major you can think of exists. And if it doesn't, it's in the process of being launched. The courses are incredible and the professors are brilliant. At the introductory level, you will have several large lectures, but as you climb the ladder, the classes become smaller, more focused, and more interactive. Pre-enrollment for courses can be difficult, but as you gain seniority, you have more leverage in getting whatever classes you would like. You will be sure to have a chance at every class that stirs your interest before graduating. However, a bad mix of courses can lead to an almost unbearable workload!

Alumnus/a, 8/2002-5/2006, November 2006

The academic program in arts and sciences is rigorous. They say that Cornell may be the easiest Ivy to get into but it is the hardest to get out of. They mean it. I never worked as hard as I did my freshman year, but I also really learned how to respect my independence and use my intellect in the process. It never gets easier, per say, but you learn how to deal with it. Every one of my classes was stimulating and challenging, including the ones where I wasn't that interested in the material to begin with. It's fairly easy to get into popular classes, I never had a problem. At least in the social sciences, it's fairy easy to get a B. One needs to work a lot harder for the B+ and A-, and an A is a very rare occurrence. Professors are accessible but sometimes a little pompous and into their own work. As such they are often out of touch with what a student can handle, and the workload and requirements can be rigorous. It is true that every professor thinks his or her class is the most important. On the upside, there were always a bunch of tutors and help available to students in need. I used the editing service several times and it was a great tool to fine-tune my work.

Current student, 8/2005-Submit Date, October 2006

The quality of the classes is world renowned. There are many qualified and caring professors. Being a research institution, there are also professors who only care about their own research and getting published. Students know to stay away from these professors unless the course is required. Grading is fair but competitive. If the median grade is a B in a class of 501, that means 250 students get less than a B. The quality of students at Cornell make grading competitive. Fortunately the telephone book-size course catalog is a place where students can find virtually unlimited courses in specialized areas where the class size is typically around 25 to 50 students. Plan on spending at least two or three hours per class hour outside of the classroom on homework, studying and projects.

Cornell says: "60 percent of the classes offered at Cornell have 19 or fewer students."

Current student, 8/2003-Submit Date, October 2006

Class sizes here can get very big, especially in introductory courses. Psych 10 for instance, has about 1,400 students who all meet at one time in a humongous auditorium. It is more like theatre than class! Courses here are very difficult— no matter how smart you are, there is always someone smarter! The curves are what kill you in science classes, especially introductory ones—but humanities courses are much easier. For instance, I am an English major and a pre-med, and there is about a 0.7 discrepancy between my science GPA and my major GPA. Workload is also a killer—you learn to cherish you weekends, which also leads to some pretty hard partying for a lot of students here.

Current student, 9/2003-Submit Date, October 2006

My major is biology—this major puts you into a large and extremely competitive group at Cornell mainly composed of "vicious pre-meds." Most classes are graded on a curve and I actually have a friend who won't study with other people and will never lend anyone her notes because "every person's grade effects the curve." Most people aren't that extreme but her sentiment is definitely felt throughout the major, especially in the more introductory classes freshman and sophomore year. It can be frustrating at times but often it is more of a driving force, you make friends with your peers, then compete on all your exams. In my opinion you could take a rigorous courseload at any university but what sets Cornell apart is that you are surrounded by other extremely bright and talented students, thus it is easier to spend Thursday nights studying because everyone else you know is also studying. In short, being surrounded by higher expectations and standards helps me expect more of myself, which in turn helps me achieve more.

Current student, 8-2003-Submit Date, September 2006

Although it is the easiest Ivy to get into, it definitely is the hardest to graduate from. There is no problem with grade inflation like at some other Ivies. Many intro classes are big (about 300) but professors take the time and effort to get to know students. Considering the size of some of the intro classes, they become especially competitive—be prepared to work hard your freshman year for that A. Classes are opened to seniors then juniors and downwards. It shouldn't be a problem getting into most classes, as there is a huge selection to choose from. Workload is intense, especially for those who get involved with extracurriculars as well. Most people get used to it though. Libraries are especially crowded with students studying—which is impressive considering there are [20] libraries here.

Current student, 8/2002-Submit Date, November 2005

Cornell will, without a doubt, challenge you and push you to your limits. Within the first semester, you will see how much your study habits have changed to fit a new, college environment. That's not to say that the work here is impossible. Everything is manageable, and time management is something that everyone learns. Academic programs usually progress from 300-person lecture introductory courses to smaller, more intimate, 25+ person, upper-level courses. Professors and teaching assistants will always offer office hours for help outside of class. Many even volunteer their home numbers in case you need them. Whether students choose to take advantage of these opportunities is another story. Although the large lectures may seem impersonal, these introductory courses offer valuable information for your future studies. There is, however, an answer to these large lectures—which are sections. Sections are subsets of large lectures (of about 20 students) that meet outside of normal lecture time. They put you in a more intimate environment with either the professor or teaching assistant to review the material from class or apply what you've learned. There are many classes that have great reputations on campus that many people try to get but are unsuccessful. Psych 101, Greek Mythology, and Introduction to Wines, are just a few. Some are more difficult to get than others, but as you move up in enrollment priority (by class rank—freshman, sophomore, junior, senior), they become easier to get.

 Employment Prospects

Alumnus/a, 8/2001-5/2005, October 2006

Many employers interviewed students on campus, and offered information sessions for prospective candidates. I personally attended several of these sessions, which offered me a chance to network with potential employers and figure out

The College Buzz Book • 2008 Edition

New York: Cornell University

hich fields were for me. I ended up accepting an offer from a consulting firm cause I realized that consulting is the perfect job for someone who is unsure where he/she is headed but would like to gain a breadth of knowledge. urthermore, consulting offers recently graduated students an opportunity to vel and see new places, as well as make many connections along the way, both th clients and changing teams of colleagues. Cornell engineering also has a brant alumni network, and students were encouraged to reach out to alumni for nployment opportunities.

lumnus/a, 8/2002-5/2006, November 2006

ach college has its own on-campus recruiting events and network, including a ntral Career Services office. I never felt overwhelmed because there really as such good guidance. Cornell alumni are all over the place and they are ways willing to get in touch and help one another out because of the common perience. Having a degree from an Ivy League university also never hurts. It ally gives you the competitive edge against other recent grads on the job mar- t—however, it's not everything. Employers also look at how good your grades ere, as well as your level of involvement in campus activities (Cornell offers a t of these).

lumnus/a, 8/2002-5/2006, September 2006

nbelievable on-campus recruiting and Career Services offerings—alumni net- ork was also extremely helpful. Many students go on to top firms, including vestment banks like Lehman Brothers and Goldman Sachs, as well as consult- g firms, such as Bain and McKinsey. Hotel school is world renown with a very volved alumni base and connections for graduates. The co-op opportunities in e engineering school help most undergrads find a great post-graduation place- ent and prepare them with true hands-on experience.

urrent student, 8/2002-Submit Date, October 2005

ne of my greatest joys concerning Cornell is the amazing alumni networks stablished all across the world. As a pre-law student I have used this as a foot the door for nonprofits, government offices and law firms. Cornellians are ways willing to help a fellow Cornellian. Employment prospects depend large- on your course of study. However, top recruiters hire from Cornell, so the verage pay and scope of jobs available to graduates is generally greater than at available to graduates from other universities. The Cornell name carries gnificant weight, especially in certain political realms and overseas. It always mazes me how many people know of Cornell who have never heard of rinceton or Stanford. This speaks to Cornell's international reach. We have atellites in Puerto Rico, a school in Qatar and a palace in Rome (where you can ve and study abroad). There is a wealth of information available to students oncerning job prospects and internships. Cornell sponsors a freshman extern- hip program, internship programs for all years, has small campuses in NYC and .C. (where you can go to intern while taking a few classes or doing research), nd provides an entire building to Career Services.

lumnus/a, 8/2003-12/2003, September 2004

ornell University is proud to have alumni in nearly every career field. ornellians, both past and present, can be found in various arenas, including ational government (Janet Reno, Ruth Bader Ginsberg), entrepreneurial affairs Adolph Coors), entertainment (Bill Maher, Christopher Reeve, Bill Nye), liter- ture (E.B. White, Toni Morrison), and athletics (Ken Dryden, Ed Marinaro). ornell Career Services, a free, year-round service, does a commendable job of roviding career advice and job/internship placement throughout the United tates: alumni networks, Cornell Clubs located in metropolitan areas in the U.S., nd planned meetings also provide ample opportunity to receive career advice nd meet fellow Cornellians.

Quality of Life

lumnus/a, 8/2002-5/2006, January 2007

reshmen live in dorms on North Campus, but also have an option of requesting pots in "program houses," which group together students with specific interests music, Native American culture, visual and performing arts, and so on) I lived the visual and performing arts program house and had a great time there. The ining halls are considered to be some of the very best in the nation, and the ones n North Campus are newest and nicest. The gyms are well-kept and the fit-

ness/wellness program is awesome. Although you have to pay something like $50 a semester, the fee is well worth it; yoga and Pilates courses are especially recommended.

Alumnus/a, 8/2001-5/2005, December 2006

The campus is hands-down unbeatable. The campus is so well-endowed and is tremendously vast. You'll find it hard to navigate at first, but it soon becomes your Neverland away from home. The view is breathtaking. The cold can be a bit harsh at times, but it helps in keeping you focused on your studies. The din- ing halls are the second best in the nation and crime is little to none. Dorming is a lot of fun, although many people move off campus to Collegetown during their final years at Cornell.

Current student, 8/2003-Submit Date, October 2006

Most on-campus housing is great. There has been a lot of new construction for both freshman and upperclassman housing. The dining facilities are among the best in the nation. They offer food from all over the globe to accommodate dif- ferent cultures and ethnicities. The campus is beautiful! Ithaca is one of the most scenic places I've ever been in my lifetime. This alone is one reason to come to Cornell. The neighborhood is relatively safe. We have the same aver- age crime rate as anywhere else. I feel safe walking through campus late at night. The security services offered are topnotch. If at any time you feel unsafe, there is a service to help you feel more comfortable. For example, Cornell has blue light services for students uncomfortable walking home at late hours of the night.

Current student, 8/2003-Submit Date, October 2006

All freshmen live in dorms on North Campus, which are assigned to you. You can request a single or a double, and girls can request to live in the all-girls dorm. After freshman year, people do one of three things. Many students join frater- nities and sororities, and live in their houses. Others move to apartments, usu- ally in Collegetown. Some continue to live in the dorms on West Campus or Collegetown. It isn't difficult to continue living in dorms if you want, and while the search for an apartment takes some time, most people seem to find one that they're happy with. The dorms themselves are kept in fairly good condition, and everybody seemed to be happy enough with them.

The campus is generally beautiful, especially when it's green and sunny out. Most of the buildings are old stone Ivy League types, although many of the newer buildings are ugly. Cornell has a large campus, so whatever you're look- ing for, we probably have it, from squash courts to a golf course, to gardens, to high-tech supercomputing labs.

Current student, 1/2006-Submit Date, September 2006

The housing is topnotch. Cornell is currently renovating most of West Campus and offers a myriad of contemporary facilities. Living conditions are excellent. The Residential College Initiative program at Cornell sees to it that students can live in an engaging community with professors and friends. The neighborhood of Ithaca is friendly and offers many cultural/dining options. Ithaca has been voted as one of the most "enlightened" cities in the United States, due to its housing of two main universities: Cornell and Ithaca College.

Current student, 8/2002-Submit Date, October 2005

Cornell is like a city in itself. It reaches for miles and miles across, though class- es, dorms and entertainment are centrally located, and has a bunch of things to do if you know where to find them. Collegetown has a few clubs, but is good mostly for some stores, many bars and restaurants (especially Collegetown Bagels—CTB). Housing is available on campus and off campus, each dorm about the same distance from central campus, and generally safe. There are sev- eral dining facilities, both in residential and class areas. There are 20-some libraries and five gyms (with indoor swimming pools, tennis/basketball/bad- minton/track courts). Ithaca itself has a nice downtown area with many shops, restaurants, theatres, bars and clubs called the Commons. Down Rt. 13 are com- mon stores (Barnes and Noble, Wal-Mart, Kmart, supermarkets and fast food) and there are a few shopping centers and one mall. The mall includes a Target, Old Navy, Sears, A&F, American Eagle, Payless, NY and Company, Limited, Victoria Secret, Spencers, Borders, Best Buy and other stores. The area is rela- tively safe, though people should always take care and protect themselves.

Read all of Vault's College Surveys at www.vault.com/college—get complete surveys on 100s of colleges and univer- sities, expert advice on applicaton essays and more.

VAULT CAREER LIBRARY 447

Social Life

Alumnus/a, 8/2002-5/2006, January 2007

Students joke about Ithaca being "centrally isolated," but it's not so awful to be a four-hour bus ride away from Manhattan when Cornell itself is so large and diverse. It's true that Ithaca is in the middle of nowhere, but Cornell is so huge and attracts so many interesting people interested in various interesting things that it is definitely not a humdrum place to live for four years. The fact that the university includes Colleges of Arts and Sciences, Engineering, Human Ecology, Business, Law, Art, Architecture, Hotel Administration, Agriculture, and Industrial and Labor Relations gives the student body a tremendous amount of diversity. The Greek scene on campus is big, so big in fact that there seems to be more variation among fraternities and sororities than there would be at a place where there weren't so many (i.e., they don't all fit the typical *Animal House* stereotypes). On the other hand, it's also totally possible to go there and have an active social life without being involved in that scene, attend lots of non-Greek parties and make lots of friends outside of the Greek system (I checked out frat parties maybe twice the whole time I was there, and none of my close friends belonged to such groups). If you're in the area be sure to check out The Chapter House bar on Stewart Ave. (a real classic) and The ABC Cafe next door, a great little cafe and restaurant that specializes in vegetarian, locally-sourced food. On the weekend, don't miss the Ithaca Farmer's Market down by the lake.

Current student, 8/2004-Submit Date, December 2006

There is a strip of bars to which everyone goes in an area just off campus called Collegetown, which are for the most part pretty fun. Fraternity and sorority life are big at Cornell—I didn't want to join a frat at first but ended up trying it out and loving it. There are so many houses on campus that it is really easy to find one you fit into. I would highly recommend joining a fraternity or sorority if you come to Cornell—it makes social life a lot easier and a lot more fun.

Alumnus/a, 8/2001-5/2005, December 2006

The student body is amazing. I will never have another opportunity in my life to meet so many awe-inspiring people. My classmates, teammates and so on were so diverse in experience and background. The bars and food are fantastic. Girls are surprisingly approachable considering how snobby they can appear to be on the surface. Events are non-stop and we've even had performing acts, including Snoop Dogg, The Game, Kanye West, Ben Folds Five, No Doubt, Jon Stewart, and many more performed on campus while I was in attendance. Greek life is fairly prevalent, but not forceful in any way. I personally am proud to ha been the head of Cornell's breakdancing crew, which happens to be the best c lege crew in the Northeast. Realistically, you can find a team for any inter you can possibly have.

Alumnus/a, 8/2002-5/2006, November 2006

Students at Cornell study hard and party equally hard. Until you're legal, Greek system is mostly the scene. There's a lot of drinking to be done freshm and sophomore year and generally a great social life even if you're not involv in the Greek system. I once heard that Ithaca has the largest number of resta rants per capita the United States. We were always very into trying new cuisi in town. There were a bunch of fabulous restaurants, expensive and cheap, a one can find literally anything from Kosher to Indian food in Collegetown a on campus. The bar scene is big for seniors, but I always found it a little ov rated. It gets claustrophobic because there are about five bars in college tov This means you can go out and see everybody you know in one night but it c also make for some awkward moments if you're looking for downtime.

The City of Ithaca, despite winter weather, is a great place to live in gener There's a farmer's market, several commercial and independent theatres a cafes all over the place. The gorges and plantations on campus make wonder meeting spots in the warmer months and students frequently take a book o radio and towels out to relax. Cornellians are lucky to share the solidarity both a challenging academic experience, as well as an equally exciting ge graphical context for social interaction.

Current student, 8/2003-Submit Date, October 2006

Collegetown is the spot for bars and clubs. Downtown Ithaca has more resta rants than most urban areas. There is so much diversity in the nightlife, there no reason you can't find something to do on the weekends. The Greek syste is big on our campus. It's a great way to make friends and get involved wi Cornell. There are hundreds of clubs and traditions offered to Cornell studen There are many events offered throughout the academic year. For exampl there are numerous speakers, dance and a cappella group shows, and conce from the top bands. (Snoop Dogg, Kanye West, OAR, Motion City Soundtra and many others have performed for us here at Cornell.) We have everythi from Circle K to Dance Dance Revolution clubs. Some of are traditions inclu Dragon Day, Cornell Hockey, and most importantly, Slope Day!

Eugene Lang College
The New School for Liberal Arts

Office of Admission
Eugene Lang College The New School for Liberal Arts
65 West 11th Street
New York, NY 10011
Admissions phone: (212) 229-5665
Admissions fax: (212) 299-5355
Admissions e-mail: lang@newschool.edu
Admissions URL: www.lang.newschool.edu

 ## Admissions

Alumnus/a, 9/2002-1/2005, March 2005

Lang is a particular division of the New School. All of the colleges within the university have different criteria for acceptance. I found it easy to be accepted. I came in with a 3.9 from my community college. The interview and the essay are, by far, the most important parts of the application process. Lang will take a chance on a poor student, as long as you prove you are ready to mature and that you are smart. Most Lang students are smart underachievers who think outside the box.

> **The school says:** "Admission to Eugene Lang College has become more competitive given the rise in applications over the last five years. Students who demonstrate a strong academic background, solid writing skills and a creative approach to the application process will do well in our evaluation."

Alumnus/a, 9/2000-5/2005, February 2006

The admissions process was difficult, and it was exacerbated by the fact that I was an international student. The application forms and essays were fine, but notification that I had gotten in was very delayed, and I had to call them to find out. There was also confusion about to which program I had been accepted, which was not cleared up until I arrived at school for my first semester. I applied for one program but was accepted into another and did not realize this until school began. Although in retrospect, I am glad I was in my program, I may have initially chosen a different school if I had realized I was accepted into a different program.

> **The school says:** "The admissions office has improved the application process through a new online system. International students are notified electronically of their admissions decision (in addition to an official mailing) to ensure timely receipt of information. Many forms and fact sheets can also be found on a link designed exclusively for newly accepted students."

Alumnus/a, 9/2002-5/2005, May 2005

I was in the [BAFA] Jazz and Contemporary Music program, so the admissions for that is a bit different. They require an audition, and that can be done live or, as in my case, on tape or CD. We had to choose three selections: a ballad, an up tempo and a blues song. There was an essay requirement, but it was mostly describing our history playing/writing music.

I think that at that time, they were not as selective as they are now. When I applied, there were not that many vocalists, but the three years since I have been here, the vocal program has grown quite a bit. The only advice I have for getting in is learn your songs well, learn to improvise creatively and don't try to imitate anyone. Be yourself.

Alumnus/a, 9/2002-5/2004, May 2006

I was a transfer student applicant. When I was first looking at colleges at 18, I was told to stay away from Lang because it was an adult school. This is not true

at all, Lang is undergrad with tons of kids straight from high school. When I applied, the school was flexible with the type of recommendations I used, and they looked for character. If you're a person who is more fascinating the more one gets to know you, this school wants you to show it. They value interviews, as well.

> **The school says:** "We should clarify that the New School has an adult degree program in liberal arts offered through the continuing education division, New School for General Studies."

The essays also give room for you to expand yourself on paper. A lot of people will be turned off by the idea of submitting a portfolio, but really, it's an opportunity to show how creative you can be or the type of thinker you are. This is great for anyone. Lang chooses an interesting variety of students.

Alumnus/a, 9/2002-6/2004, May 2006

I transferred from another, similar college. I applied as a transfer student and visited New York during my spring break to meet with an admissions officer for an interview. The interview was short and low-key. I was a bit nervous but it was more casual than I expected. I chatted with the student working at the desk in the admissions office and later became friends with her after I transferred when we shared a few classes.

I wrote my essay on the feminist activism I'd done at my first college, the one I was leaving. I was worried about it being slightly too angry or negative, but I also could tell that the admissions department wanted to hear that type of thing. I did well in all of my classes at the first school, so that wasn't a problem. I had the impression that it was easy to get into Lang; my main concern was whether there would be enough spaces open in the junior class for the number of transfer students, me included.

Alumnus/a, 9/2002-12/2004, May 2006

I went a bit outside the bounds with my answer to the essay question about how I learned. I didn't limit my learning experience to the classroom. I also went on an interview, which made me feel better about my prospects of acceptance. I transferred to Lang from a community college and it was the only school I applied to, so I can't really compare the admissions process to others. My acceptance letter was very late though.

 ## Academics

Alumnus/a, 9/2002-1/2005, March 2005

People go to Lang for the classes, not the socialization. It is very expensive, but you see immediately where your money goes. Classes are very small (18 student cap on most classes, 15 for writing and art classes). You develop close relationships with your teachers, which is great. However, there is a lot of face time; you cannot sit in the back of the class unnoticed. Class participation is paramount. The classes are seminar in style, not lecture. The teacher sits in a circle with the students, and does not lecture. You learn from your classmates as much as from your teachers. The students at Lang are smart, opinionated, political and different.

Testing is almost exclusively papers. In my three years at Lang, I've had three tests and countless papers. In order to graduate from Lang you must do a huge senior work, usually a very large paper. My paper was 76 pages, an average length. Be prepared, it is a lot of work.

> **The school says:** "Not every student is required to complete an individual senior work project; some academic programs now offer the option of a collaborative senior project and/or an advanced senior seminar."

Read all of Vault's College Surveys at **www.vault.com/college**—get complete surveys on 100s of colleges and universities, expert advice on applicaton essays and more.

VAULT CAREER LIBRARY **449**

The professors are wonderful, intelligent and open. It is easy to talk with your teachers and develop close relationships. The teachers decide on the subject of a class, and it can be unusually specific. You may end up studying a specific subject more closely than you care to.

The bureaucracy at Lang is terrible. It can be hard to get anything done, and your advisors are no help. Be prepared to handle your own educational track, but know that they will make you meet graduation requirements, regardless of poor guidance.

> The school says: "Lang College has created more support services for students. The professional academic advising staff at Lang College has more than doubled since this student graduated in 2005. We have also increased the percentage of full-time faculty advisors."

Internships are enormously important. The internship office is great, and most students get prime sites. Be aware that Lang is unusually political and extraordinarily liberal. While all ideas are respected, a right-wing conservative would find it hard to find a like-minded thinker amongst the students or faculty.

> The school says: "We welcome people who have different points of view to keep seminar discussions lively and to allow broad perspectives to be explored. It's not good or educationally beneficial to hear only from people who agree with you."

Alumnus/a, 9/2000-5/2005, February 2006

Academics were the best part of going to the New School. I loved the program I was in. The classes were, for the most part, of high quality, very challenging and small seminars. It was not difficult to get into popular classes but sometimes those classes would be such large seminars that the experience was not as good as it could have been.

Grading was always fairly clear. The workload is very high, with much reading, writing and other work related to the class expected each week. And because of the seminar style, if the work is not done or you do not attend class, you will fail.

Current student, 9/2003-Submit Date, April 2004

The academic program is extremely varied; the way the school is structured makes it possible to take many electives as well as core concentration courses without feeling overloaded. Likewise the quality of the courses varies greatly. It is not difficult to get into the courses that you want to be in; however, it is not uncommon that the professor will completely ignore the class description and change the syllabus midway through the semester, which can be either a good thing or a bad thing.

> The school says: "If a course description has been altered because a new instructor was hired to teach the course, this may occur at the beginning of the semester. While there may be modifications based on the pacing of the class time, it is highly unusual for an instructor to disregard the syllabus once a semester has begun."

The grading is pretty straightforward, though it is sometimes difficult to understand why a certain paper will get a better or worse grade. The workload is manageable, mostly reading and writing.

Alumnus/a, 9/2002-12/2004, May 2006

Due to the discussion-based classes and emphasis on essay writing, I feel Lang is a more rigorous school and it's a positive environment for learning. On the other side, there is a lot of intellectual snobbery and name-dropping. It's quite a relaxed environment, but you are expected to be serious about your work.

Alumnus/a, 1/2002-5/2005, May 2006

Generally, classes have a cap of 18 or 21 students (but no minimum), which is really nice. They are usually conducted as a seminar, where a professor leads the discussion but after preparing for class by doing reading assignments, students are expected to make intelligent, informed contributions to the dialogue. In some classes, class participation is a significant percentage of students' final grades. However, a lot of things vary by department and individual professor.

Some professors will really make you work for your four credits and your ʌ while some just want to see that a student did his/her work, has absorbed som thing, and became educated on the topic. But, I can honestly say that I did n have even one professor at Lang who I would say was horrible. They were a good in their own ways.

There are hardly any tests at Lang. 99 percent of the time, grades are based papers and projects, which is good and bad. For the most part, Lang really wan you to learn how to write really well, and most Lang professors will critiqu papers for writing style as well as content, no matter what the class. It can tough to get into popular classes, but it's not impossible, especially as yo become an upperclassman and get to register earlier.

Alumnus/a, 9/2002-6/2004, May 2006

I was only at Lang for my junior and senior years. It was easy for me to get tl classes I wanted, including classes at the New School for Social Research ar the New School for General Studies. I was surprised to find a smaller workloa than I'd had at my first school, but I realized—and still fully believe this—th we were assigned less (meaning less to read, shorter essays, fewer exams) in pa because the professors understood what to expect of us, as full-time students li ing in New York City. Any student in NYC, especially one who has to wor quite a bit outside of school, simply has less time to do schoolwork.

Overall, I found the academics to be less challenging than I would have like My classes really differed in terms of student participation and the quality of tl discussions—some classes were stellar, but most were disappointing in thos areas. Most of the professors, however, were just great, as educators, as thinke and as individuals.

Alumnus/a, 9/1999-5/2003, May 2006

The courses were varied and interesting. However, the way in which classe were chosen at first was stressful (the lottery process). There was an ease of ov tally or adding/dropping a class. Professors were understanding about person situations that may interfere with school production and were willing to giv alternative methods of grading and evaluating work. The workload varied fro class to class but overall there was a massive amount of reading and paperwo to be done. I did not take any formal tests during my years at Lang.

> The school says: "We no longer have a lottery process for registration. Students register online for each semester using a student information system called ALVIN."

 ## Employment Prospects

Alumnus/a, 9/2000-5/2005, February 2006

I think prestige varies, depending on the type of program you're in and the typ of job you're applying to. I have not been too impressed with the types of job my fellow students have obtained. It's a difficult market right now. The alun ni network is there, but difficult to access.

On-campus recruiting and internships are also there and I know people who wer able to take advantage of them, but they were never what I wanted. However, got good internships by finding them on my own. Now, however, I am unem ployed and looking for work.

> The school says: "Internships are available for any student with 30 credits completed, which represents sophomore standing. Internships are offered sooner than junior year."

Current student, 9/2003-Submit Date, April 2004

I found no help with finding employment through the school. Eugene Lang unlike other New School divisions, is not a very popular or well-known schoo so it holds no prestige. There are internships offered to students but they do no start until junior year. Even students in the work-study program complained o not finding campus work easily. On the upside, New York City offers countle opportunities for employment; just don't expect the school to be of any help.

Alumnus/a, 1/2002-5/2005, May 2006

The school has a really excellent internship program. I did it for three or fou semesters, and I got a lot out of it. They really work with you on an individua sis to allow you to do what you want, and get credit for it. It also has a great ffice of Career Development, with really great people, very helpful. They help th job search strategies, as well as try to hook you up with job placements. I ways thought that those were the best kept secrets at Lang—very under-appre- ated and under-valued by students.

e employers who recognize the value of Lang or the New School are limited a very specific community of people in NYC and nationwide. However, its putation is growing. But, honestly, I do not think it really matters that much. ost employers just want to see that you have a degree, and do not necessarily re where you got it.

e types of jobs people get after graduation really, really vary depending on the rson and his/her concentration. However, I should say that this is not neces- rily the school for you if you want to be a doctor, unless you are willing to sup- ement Lang classes with summer classes (for which you will get credit), or st-bacc classes.

lumnus/a, 9/1999-5/2001, May 2006

veryone I know has jobs. They are working as writers, photographers, artists, arketers, advertisers, fund-raisers and lawyers. They are all well regarded as dependent, imaginative and excellent at what they do. The secret to the alum- network is the small size of the school and the dependence of the alumni on e creative industry (arts, media and education). As a result, if you go to an ening of young artists in SoHo, you will find Lang alumni involved. And they are a certain view of the world that makes them approachable to other alum-

urrent student, 1/2002-Submit Date, April 2006

friend of mine currently works for the UN and plans on working there after aduation. Another friend who just graduated works for a nonprofit that helps meless people find resources. Another friend works at a comic book shop. y advice here is to determine if you want to go to college to get a job or to arn, or to do both.

would say that the helpfulness of the alumni network is a one on a scale from e to 10. This isn't because Lang alumni aren't nice people but because the hool has only recently begun keeping track of alumni for the purpose of net- orking. Eugene Lang College, remember, is only a few decades old. I've had o great internships that I got through Lang's internship office.

> **With regards to employment prospects, the New School says:** "Lang hired a new director of career services, who will provide much needed support to students who are exploring their pro- fessional options. In addition, the Lang Internship Program has staff designated to support students who are building their experiences through work at local community organizations, major media corporations and hundreds of other sites in NYC. The New School also provides regular workshops and career networking events to foster professional development."

Quality of Life

lumnus/a, 9/2002-1/2005, March 2005

ang is located in the best area of New York City. The Meatpacking District is e coolest place in the whole city. Amazing shopping, great restaurants, gal- ries, it is all right outside the classroom door.

While at Lang, I never lived on campus (like many of my fellow students, I had y own apartment). The dorms I have been to at Lang belonged to my friends. hey seemed nice. They had a suite: two girls to a room (two rooms) with a ared kitchen (with full-size stove and refrigerator) and bath.

here is no gym. There is a nice sized library. Very advanced computer center, most always open, with both Macs and PCs, advanced printers and flat-bed anners. Crime within the school has never been an issue, and the area is on the fer side for New York.

Alumnus/a, 9/2000-5/2005, February 2006

It was great being in Manhattan but there were also drawbacks. Housing was limited and the process for getting it was not straightforward. There were often mix-ups about where students were supposed to be. There wasn't much of a campus or dining halls, which is to be expected in Manhattan. The facilities were acceptable but not terrific. There were decent computer facilities, but not too much else to speak of. The neighborhood is very safe and easy to navigate.

Current student, 9/2003-Submit Date, April 2004

The housing is, as expected, very cramped. The dorms are set up apartment- style and are in a great location, however there are the typical New York con- cerns of mice, pollution and cramped living areas. The campus, like the dorms, is located in buildings scattered throughout Manhattan, which I like but others find it takes away the sense of community in the school. The neighborhood is extremely safe and very lively, with numerous cafes, bookstores, music stores and parks as well as two of the larger subway stops in New York, which makes it possible to go anywhere at any time.

Alumnus/a, 9/2002-6/2004, May 2006

I never lived in a Lang dorm, so I can't reflect on that. As for the facilities, I found them adequate. I love the New School's old classrooms and chairs and atmosphere. The computer labs were certainly adequate, even around finals. I love the way the buildings are spread out, and I think the shared facilities with NYU are essential. Bobst Library, specifically, was totally essential to me. The neighborhood is one of the best in the city.

Current student, 1/2005-Submit Date, April 2006

I lived in university housing during my first semester at Lang. I moved mid-term from one dorm to another. The first building I lived in was just gorgeous. However, it was in Manhattan's Financial District. After six o'clock, everything closed down. I moved to a building right off of Union Square where the rooms weren't as nice, but the location made it a fair trade-off.

We have no campus, per se. On nice days, everyone hangs out in the courtyard between classes. That's pretty much as campus-y as we get. The dining halls are next to useless. The hours suck and the food, while tasty enough, is expen- sive. I now live in my own apartment. Most kids don't remain in housing longer than a semester.

> **With regards to quality of life, the New School says:** "Eugene Lang College has an urban campus. The main academic build- ings on campus are clustered along the spine of Fifth Avenue. Classrooms, computer labs, student organization meeting areas and lecture halls are available within a 10 block radius. As the university grows, campus housing options have increased although currently only 30 percent of students live in student dorms. Student housing can be located as close as one block from classes and as far away as Brooklyn."

Social Life

Alumnus/a, 9/2002-1/2005, March 2005

Lang is not known for its social scene. There is no Greek life, and anyone who tried to start it would be laughed at. There are a few random school clubs, most- ly left-wing political groups. There is good dating scene. There is an equal mix of gay and straight, guys and girls. The gay scene is very active. The clubs and bars are great, as varied as the city.

Living in NY makes everything accessible. Take a subway to anywhere. Most people at Lang make their own social circle. People don't go to Lang looking for friends, they go to learn. The area the school is in—right near the best shop- ping and clubs, near New York University and Cardozo School of Law, not far from Hunter and Pace—means that you shouldn't have trouble meeting friends, even if they aren't from Lang. Lots of punks, party kids, alternative, freaks, gay, straight, fat, thin, rich, poor, almost any group except religious or right-wing types. Again, I cannot stress this enough: [If you are a conservative] while you will be welcome, you will not be happy. The classes, students, professors, administrators, are all very progressive. Protests are common. So are parties.

Read all of Vault's College Surveys at **www.vault.com/college**—get complete surveys on 100s of colleges and univer- sities, expert advice on applicaton essays and more.

VAULT CAREER LIBRARY   **451**

Alumnus/a, 9/2002-5/2005, May 2005

There is no Greek system, no sports teams besides intramurals, but the school is located in Greenwich Village in Manhattan. There is all kinds of nightlife within a few blocks, and much more reachable by subway. Students often throw parties at their homes, with bands and music. It is a very social scene.

Current student, 9/2003-Submit Date, April 2004

Since the school is in New York City, it is almost impossible to name every place that students find to hang out; student haunts range from anywhere between the school's cafeteria to a random bar across the river in Brooklyn! I know for cheap diner food, students will go to Joe's Diner (6th and 12th) or Veg City Diner (6th and 14th), and Park Slope or Williamsburg are two neighborhoods in Brooklyn where older students enjoy night bar life. Many students find people to date outside of the school community, although the school has a thriving gay community, so others find the school to almost be a dating service in and of itself. There are frequent parties in the dorms, especially in the Union Square building.

Alumnus/a, 8/2000-5/2004, May 2006

I made several good friends, but the school is notorious for its lack of community and no sports teams, which was fine with me. Very active political scene.

Alumnus/a, 9/1996-6/2000, May 2006

This is NY (not intended to sound NY-centric or stuck up), so there are plenty bars, restaurants and clubs everywhere you go around Manhattan and the out boroughs. There is no Greek system at Lang (thank goodness), and in terms other clubs, there weren't really any during my years there.

> **With regards to social life, The New School says:** "Student life at Lang College is unconventional. We have no athletic teams, fraternities, sororities, or marching bands. But there is an active student government, a campus newspaper and countless open mics, staged readings, student-run socials, and cultural events on campus and around New York City. The university also has a student development office that provides regular programming including boat cruises around Manhattan, an annual battle of the bands event and discount tickets to Broadway shows."

Fordham University

Admissions Office
Thebaud Hall
441 East Fordham Road
Bronx, NY 10458-5191
Admissions phone: (800) FORDHAM or (718) 817-4000
  or (212) 636-6710
Admissions fax: (718) 367-9404 (Rose Hill)
  or (212) 636-7002 (Lincoln Center)
Admissions e-mail: enroll@fordham.edu
Admissions URL: www.fordham.edu/Admissions/

 ## Admissions

Alumnus/a, 9/2002-5/2006, November 2006

Fordham is in the process of becoming more selective with each passing year, mostly due to the new president and his quest for distinction. It includes the standard college application, SATs and so on, and also takes into account extracurricular activities. Fordham's financial aid is mostly on a merit basis—ergo, those with better than average stats (and who demonstrate some need) will probably receive grants.

Current student, 8/2003-Submit Date, December 2005

Fordham University is quite close to be considered an Ivy League school. It is highly selective and was a reach on my particular list of schools. They pay close attention to grade point averages, extracurricular activities and ability to excel in their institution. The essay submitted was a general one about growth through volunteer experience. Having a broad range of interests and talents greatly helps the process.

Current student, 8/2002-Submit Date, October 2005

Work like hell in high school, take AP classes, get at least a 1350 on your SAT (old scoring style), take some SAT Subject Tests if you can. Attending a Catholic or Jesuit high school really, really helps, as Fordham is a hardcore Jesuit institution and it prides itself on it. Also, community service helps. My campus, the college at Lincoln Center, is much more selective than the other campus (Rose Hill) up in the Bronx.

Alumnus/a, 8/2000-5/2004, September 2005

The admissions process at Fordham is probably tougher than that of nearby public schools and less prestigious private schools.

Fordham sent me a fast-track application that was no more than a few pages basic questions. It guaranteed an admissions decision within 10 days, or a si ilarly small window of time, and waived the interview process.

If you are applying to Fordham, bear in mind that the school prides itself on commitment to educating the whole person. Academics are important, a frankly they're great at Fordham, but the school is concerned with each studen personal development, as well. Commitment to the service of others and to t community is also very key. Prove yourself to be not only a great student, bu well-rounded individual who is dedicated to service and is involved in his/h community.

Current student, 9/2003-Submit Date, June 2004

I wrote an essay for the admissions process. I also simply filled out the app cation and let my high school's guidance department handle it. The admissio office was quite helpful in identifying my financial situation and adjusted r financial aid to fit my current situation. Good advice would be to take AP cre its because they help you get more popular classes and they help get the housi you want. Also, you may want to try and aim for an SAT score of 1200 or mo

Alumnus/a, 6/1996-5/2000, September 2003

The admissions process was very simple and involved submitting an applicati and writing an essay about my school accomplishments, community service a why I wanted to attend Fordham University. I applied to the HEOP program a was admitted in April with a full financial aid package.

 ## Academics

Current student, 8/2003-Submit Date, December 2005

The classes at Fordham, even the preliminary core classes, are challengin They inspire the student to work harder and become open to new possibiliti and ways of doing things. The classes are excellent with well-studied profe sors, mostly PhD holders, teaching each class. Each class is kept as small as pc sible. The average class grade is based on a midterm, small assignments, eight- to 15-page term paper, class participation/attendance and a final exam.

Alumnus/a, 9/2002-5/2006, November 2006

There is an extensive core taking up the first two years. Although it can be fru trating taking all these other courses, for the most part it is appreciated by t majority. And like most other colleges, there are better programs than othe with theology, philosophy and English as the stars. The professors are know dgeable and helpful for the self-starters out there and the workload varies per major.

Current student, 8/2002-Submit Date, October 2005

The professors are a mix: Some require obscene amounts of reading and really challenge you, while others are mediocre. The most popular majors are communications, media studies, English and political science. Fordham has a core curriculum. The core takes up two years and requires you to take everything from math, to two social sciences classes, two sciences, two philosophies, two theologies, one art course, three English courses and more.

Alumnus/a, 8/2000-5/2004, September 2005

Fordham is very strong academically, requiring all students to enroll in a core curriculum of classes regardless of his/her course of study. The first two years of study at Fordham are spent fulfilling the core requirements. The last two years are spent mostly within the student's major, though there are still some cores to be completed. These core requirement classes are wonderful—be glad that you've got to take them; they will open your mind in ways you cannot yet imagine, and cultivate you as a person. Here, even an engineering student has taken French and music history, and a performing arts major has taken calculus and physics. It's a good thing. Don't start tearing up the application now—you to have your choice of classes within the core, and it is relatively easy to get your first picks here. The Rose Hill campus is great for studies in business, communications and the humanities. The Lincoln Center campus is tops for the more creative/fine arts disciplines. The professors at Fordham are passionate about what they instruct and are accessible outside of the classroom. They are also flexible and human—just reach out. While I was at Fordham, many of my professors also instructed at NYU and/or Columbia. It's topnotch.

Alumnus/a, 8/1996-5/2000, November 2004

Professors love to push students to test their limits. Do expect to be challenged and fully rewarded with a thorough liberal arts education. Fordham is a paper school. You'll come out a great writer and communicator. Grading is fair, professors are humane, and so is the workload. Classes offered are quite interesting. Professors usually know students on a first-name basis. Don't expect to be a wallflower in class. Active discussion is encouraged.

Current student, 9/2003-Submit Date, June 2004

The classes are small and grading is fair. I have never been completely unhappy with any of the classes that I got. I even registered for classes one week into school, and I was able to get classes that some people said were hard to get into. It is easy to have a one-on-one conversation with a teacher. Getting classes at first is a little hard, but it is first come, first serve. The professors are mostly amicable, and the workload is fair.

Alumnus/a, 9/1997-5/2001, March 2004

With the core curriculum, my workload was very light, and the difficulty was very minor. I had no problems getting into the classes I wanted, as FCLC is very small and provides multiple time slots for popular or core classes. Grading was typical of any college using a 4.0 system, and most classes consisted of a few assignments punctuated with a midterm and final. Professors varied greatly.

Alumnus/a, 6/1996-5/2000, September 2003

It is very rigorous freshman year, as you spend the fall semester either doing too much reading and researching, or too much writing. The spring semester, you do the the opposite. It's a very challenging atmosphere, and you have to manage your time wisely so that you don't fall behind in your classes.

Employment Prospects

Current student, 8/2003-Submit Date, December 2005

With Fordham University listed on a résumé, it is quite easy to get a job. Even when applying for part-time positions while still studying, prospective employers are quite pleased and impressed. There are numerous job fairs with special attention placed on diversity positions. Bi-weekly/weekly e-mails provide students and alumni with recent listings of all new jobs that have been posted. Additional positions are also easily accessed on monstertrak.com. The Office of Career Services is always open and provides highly organized binders with faxed job listings by category and type of position/industry.

Current student, 8/2002-Submit Date, October 2005

The business college up at Rose Hill is the only college that gets recruiting, albeit from boring accounting/finance firms like KPMG and Morgan Stanley. The alumni database isn't available online but is in a book in the library.

> **The school says:** "All of our colleges 'get recruiting' through our Office of Career Services, which arranges multiple career fairs and other networking and recruiting events on campus each year."

Alumnus/a, 8/2000-5/2004, September 2005

Fordham is a great place to be if you are looking to be recruited. It's a great school in the capital of most every business, so employers line up. If you're looking to get into a big-name company, particularly in finance, banking or communications/media, Fordham is the right place to do it. Internships are key once you graduate, and they are highly emphasized and encouraged at Fordham, where students typically begin interning for credit during their junior year. The career office at Fordham is very accessible, and holds a host of programs throughout the year, and even for alumni after graduation. Bottom line: You can get into any top company from Fordham. Many of them recruit and interview directly on campus. This is particularly true of finance/banking/accounting firms.

Alumnus/a, 8/1996-5/2000, November 2004

Fordham, being in the heart of New York City, gives students full access to top jobs and internships in the vicinity. Employers are known to say that they love Fordham students because of the broad liberal arts education obtained from their renowned core curriculum. I know students who have interned at *CosmoGirl*, Nickelodeon, K-Rock and the Chris Rock Show.

Current student, 9/2003-Submit Date, June 2004

There aren't many opportunities before your junior year of college for internships and career planning, but it is very well respected by employers. Our College of Business Administration is rated as one of the most respected business colleges in the nation. The school, itself, has a lot of prestige on a résumé and offers rather promising career prospects. If you would like, there are some programs for those who are not yet in their third year of college.

Quality of Life

Alumnus/a, 9/2002-5/2006, November 2006

Housing is fantastic, and the Rose Hill campus is beautiful. Although it is in the south Bronx, Fordham safeguards its students pretty well. The buddy system is important to use when off campus. There is very little crime on the campus itself.

Eddies (the lawn) is amazing in the spring, as most students read/eat/hang out there. The library is fantastic as well, and should be put to more use.

Current student, 8/2003-Submit Date, December 2005

Fordham University is considered a dry campus. Security is very high and in my four years here, I have yet to hear about an incident on campus. Dorms have a sign-in/sign-out policy where guests (no more than two or three per person) must be signed in between the hours of 5 p.m. and 3:30 a.m. Detailed information about each guest is gathered and all guests must be signed out by 3:30 a.m. The health office is very clean and has great hours. EMS services are readily available and housing is pretty good. The biggest complaint that students have about the school is regarding the cafeteria. It was recently renovated but the food isn't up there on the list. The salads are always fresh and pizzas are always hot out of the oven but the selection leaves something to be desired.

Current student, 8/2002-Submit Date, October 2005

No one of the same sex can sleep in your apartment/dorm, but you can have someone of the same sex over for up to three nights (this works for gay couples really well, of which there are many at Fordham). No candles either. The apartments themselves are gorgeous, but institutional looking so bring extra lamps. They're also expensive, at around $10,000 for a double bedroom for 10 months. I moved off campus because it's cheaper. The food is terrible. Don't rely on the

Read all of Vault's College Surveys at **www.vault.com/college**—get complete surveys on 100s of colleges and universities, expert advice on applicaton essays and more.

VAULT CAREER LIBRARY   453

cafe (yes, there is only one place to eat at FCLC)—go to Whole Foods and grab something. As for safety, the Upper West Side is gorgeous, rich and very safe.

> The school says: "Our Lincoln Center campus provides amazing views of NYC from dormrooms in the 20-story McMahon Hall right in midtown Manhattan. The dorms include free laundry and larger apartments than most comparably priced and located apartments in NYC."

Alumnus/a, 8/2000-5/2004, September 2005

I lived on campus and in university-owned housing off campus in the Bronx. The Bronx, as you must be aware, has a tough reputation. It is a tough place. The university itself is picturesque—really, really beautiful; people fall in love with it—but once you pass through the gates, you leave that gilded world for a very rough and dirty one. The Bronx is the Bronx, and if you are coming from suburbia you may experience some culture shock. With all that said, I, as an attractive young woman, had no problems at all living there. The school is aware of its surroundings, as well, and is extra vigilant to compensate. The school is pretty well contained within itself, so no worries. You'll get the real college experience/community, and still be a few stops from Manhattan.

Current student, 9/2003-Submit Date, June 2004

Fordham has a relatively small campus and many resources. Anything that you really need, you can get from somewhere on campus. There are six places on campus where you can get different foods. We have the Walsh Library, and it has been rated as the third-best library in the country. The residence halls are usually very likable, and upperclassmen can get off-campus housing or apartments on campus. Many of the dorms have showers and bathrooms in the rooms. Some of the freshman dorms have community bathrooms. The campus, itself, has little to no crime, yet in the surrounding area the students should use a moderate amount of caution. A little bit of advice would be that you should definitely get a meal plan that offers the most flex dollars, which is money on your school ID that gets you food at the Student Deli, The Ramskellar (Sbarro and coffee shop), Dagger John's (an on-campus restaurant) and Millennium Grille.

Alumnus/a, 9/1997-5/2001, March 2004

The on-campus housing at FCLC is gorgeous. This may have changed, but FCLC had very strict rules: no overnight visitors of the opposite gender (gay students are at an obvious advantage!) and visitors (even Fordham students) had to get a temporary pass. This caused a great distance between commuters and residents.

The FCLC campus has some beautiful, if small, grounds, considering that it's in the middle of NYC. The food is pay-per-piece and mostly healthy, so there aren't indulgent buffet-style greasy foods found in most colleges. The neighborhood is high-end residential, and although there is some crime, it is safer than most parts of NYC.

 ## Social Life

Current student, 8/2003-Submit Date, December 2005

Local bars are OK and definite hang-out spots for the younger students. There is no Greek life but there is an enormous number of clubs and organizations that appeal all political, religious and sexual views and social interests. The newspaper is fabulous and widely read by students, professors and alumni alike.

Alumnus/a, 9/2002-5/2006, November 2006

The religious life via Praise and Worship, mass, retreats and so on, is there, and quite inspiring for those looking for it.

Current student, 8/2002-Submit Date, October 2005

There are no dorm parties. Everyone goes out into the city to its numerous bars and clubs. Many people have their little social circles, usually those with whom you live, and go out with them. There is also no Greek system, but there is no

need when you have outstanding places to go (Underbar, Whiskey Park, Lott Marquee, Hudson Bar are good places). There is also a scuzzy bar nearby call Lincoln Park where law students tend to hang out. They have cheap beer.

Alumnus/a, 8/2000-5/2004, September 2005

At Rose Hill, the social life is full—and I hope you like beer! If you like drink, you'll love the life at Fordham. It's centered around parties in dorms, o campus apts, and drinks at local college bars. Occasionally you and your floc mates will pile into a Ram-Van shuttle to NYC and hit the clubs there, too, b for the most part you'll be pre-gaming with friends in the dorms, hitting an a party or two, then stumbling to local college dives. As for restaurants, you' got the city so close, and the real Little Italy just around the corner. Try son Caribbean and Latin food while you're here, too. The dating scene is not unli that of other schools. You'll probably not date locals, so it's pretty well co tained within Fordham. It's small enough that there's no room to play games push your reputation. Whatever you do will most definitely circulate. Peop who don't really know you will see you walking past and know at least a fe things about you. Note: no frats here.

> Regarding social life, the school says: "Social life at Fordham is not just centered on parties, but other activities from service to Fordham's Jesuit approach to educating the whole person, in and out of the classroom like our new Integrated Learning Communities."

Current student, 9/2003-Submit Date, June 2004

There are many restaurants on Arthur Avenue, which is quite famous for its fo and culture. There are about eight bars within walking distance of the camp gates. Dating revolves mostly around the bar scene. Many people come to co lege with significant others, but they usually don't last more than a few month although there are some exceptions. There are some cultural parades in the su rounding area. Manhattan is a subway ride away. There are clubs for anythi that you could want to participate in. I, myself, am a part of Fordham EMS a find it quite rewarding. There are also many student publications such as _T Ram_, _The Paper_ and _The Ampersand_.

Alumnus/a, 9/1997-5/2001, March 2004

There is no Greek system in Fordham, and because of this and the ridiculous v itor rules, there is almost no party atmosphere. Since the school is located NYC and a block from a major subway station, most students' social lives a outside of campus. Not too many bars or restaurants in the immediate area (ve residential), but a few blocks north there are many, and of course, the subw will take you anywhere else.

Big disappointment, as I was a part of many clubs in high school, includi debate and math. Most clubs in FCLC are based on ethnicity or sexuality. S unless you're Asian, Hispanic, black or gay, there are very few other clubs to jo (the Art Club and Business Club are the only two I can think of). My social li in FCLC was nonexistent.

> The school says: "Clubs at FCLC are widely diverse, not simply based on ethnicity/sexuality. Clubs range from the Baseball Club and Economics Society to the Pre-Law Society and the Rainbow Alliance. In addition, there are student publications and student government areas for involvement. Fordham has more than 135 clubs and organizations for students to partici- pate in."

Hamilton College

amilton College
98 College Hill Road
linton, NY 13323
dmissions phone: (800) 843-2655
dmissions fax: (315) 859-4457
dmissions e-mail: admission@hamilton.edu
dmissions URL: www.hamilton.edu/admission/

 Admissions

urrent student, Politics, 8/2004-Submit Date, February 2007

ighly selective. Best to be in top 15 to 20 percent with SAT score and top 10 rcent in graduating high school class. Huge weight paid to writing sample, as is is a college whose mission is to maximize writing skills of its graduates. As typical, better chance given to those who apply Early Decision. Though an -campus interview is not required it definitely does help your chances. This a D-III school where typical sports are not king. However, if you have some owess in athletics, make sure the coach of that sports knows you are applying.

> **The school says:** "Hamilton is SAT optional, but not test option-al. (See our web site for details.) For the 60 percent of the first-year students who recently chose the SAT to fulfill our testing requirement, the middle 50 percent range of scores are as follows: Verbal 640 to 740, Math 640 to 710, Writing 630 to 720."

lumnus/a, Pre-med/English, 9/1999-5/2003, March 2007

amilton is tough to get into. Very good grades, good scores and an interview e all necessary. Play a sport and you're in very good shape. They have elim-ated merit scholarships and have made it clear that they want to attract more ople outside their usual feeder zone—Connecticut and Massachusetts prep hools. Hamilton's admission staff wants to see more people with Hamilton as eir first choice.

urrent student, 8/2004-Submit Date, May 2006

hen I first arrived at Hamilton, I knew it felt like home. I visited the summer fore my senior year and interviewed while I was there. The interview was a mi-stressful one for me because I really cared about the outcome. We dis-ssed my extracurricular activities and summer reading books (she had read me of them). The best advice I can give about an interview is to be yourself d talk a lot—the point of the interview is for the school to learn about you, so ll yourself!

completed the Common Application and then the standard "Why do you want attend Hamilton?" question, which was extremely easy for me because I knew amilton was where I wanted to go. After reviewing all the schools I visited and oking at the selectivity of Hamilton, I decided to go Early Decision, which was ne of the best decisions of my life. It made the second half of my senior year ress-free knowing I was going to my first choice school.

> **The school says:** "As a college that stresses writing and prom-ises to improve students' proficiency in that area, the essay is an important part of the application process. Applicants are given a choice of topics for their original essay and are required to submit a graded writing sample completed for a high school course. Remember, the application essay is your chance to have a voice at the table with the admissions committee."

urrent student, 8/2005-Submit Date, May 2006

amilton College is highly selective (only about 34 percent of applicants are ccepted), so standing out in the applicant pool is essential. Interviewing with

the college is very important. At a small school like Hamilton, the college wants to have a feel for the personality of its applicants.

> **The school says:** "Hamilton's acceptance rate in 2007 was 28 percent."

Hamilton places a strong academic emphasis on writing. Accordingly, one's essays are very important. Proper grammar and punctuation is an absolute must, of course. Smooth flow and a solid writing style are very important.

Every year, a fair portion of the incoming class is chosen through Early Decision. If you're serious about Hamilton, let them know—apply ED!

Current student, 8/2004-Submit Date, May 2006

Hamilton accepts the Common Application, which involves both short-answer and essay questions. I believe Hamilton still requires a supplement, which involves some additional written responses. You will need to provide teacher recommendations, and a sample of graded written work. One of the nice things about the Hamilton app is that you don't have to submit SAT scores if you don't want to, instead you can submit the ACT and/or SAT Subject Tests.

Grades are of upmost importance, and it is essential that you are taking a demanding courseload. They do take into account the level of and commitment to various extracurricular activities. If you are interested in varsity athletics, you must contact the coach and provide all the pertinent information (stats, position); if you are interested in music, you are able to submit a tape of your performanc-es.

Interviews are optional but highly recommended, as they give the admissions office an opportunity to work with a real person rather than paperwork. Just because they are optional, don't take them lightly—come prepared. Never write about things that are obvious from the fast facts file at Hamilton. Don't say you want to go to a small school with a 14:1 student-to-faculty ratio, that doesn't show you care. Talk about things unique to Hamilton, how you can take advan-tage of them, and why you would benefit in the long-term. Remember, the admissions office is looking to create a dynamic, well-rounded class of the high-est caliber possible, show them how you fit into that.

> **The school says:** "The student-to-faculty ratio at Hamilton is 9.7:1 and for those completing the Common Application, a one-page supplement is required."

Current student, 8/2005-Submit Date, May 2006

I knew applying to Hamilton was going to be a challenge. I visited the college several times both before applying, after applying and after being accepted. One visit included an interview with a senior intern. She asked lots of questions about my academics and extracurriculars but also gave me the opportunity to ask her questions about the school.

I took both the SAT and the SAT Subject Tests, but at that point (they may have changed it some by now), Hamilton looked at the scores that reflected me the best, the SATs. I made sure to write an essay that would stand out and showed off both my personality and my writing abilities—I also took it to my parents and teachers at school to be edited. All the work paid off, I got accepted without being waitlisted. Hamilton was the best school I got into.

> **The school says:** "Students choose which standardized tests they submit to Hamilton and those options are outlined on the college's web site. If students send more than what is required, the admission committee will consider only the test scores that are most favorable to the applicant."

Current student, 8/2003-Submit Date, May 2006

Hamilton is a pretty selective school. One great thing, though, is that SATs are not required for application. You can choose to use your ACT, SAT Subject Tests, IB or AP scores instead. Hamilton encourages interviews and conducts

Read all of Vault's College Surveys at **www.vault.com/college**—get complete surveys on 100s of colleges and univer-sities, expert advice on applicaton essays and more.

VAULT CAREER LIBRARY **455**

them on campus, but can set up an interview with an alumnus/a if it is not possible for you to make it to campus.

Hamilton uses the Common Application, which makes the process a little easier. You also have the Hamilton supplement to fill out, and you have to send in a paper written in high school. If you're an athlete, artist or performer of some kind, you can send a video or some of your artistic work to admissions, as well. If you think you would really love it at Hamilton, I suggest applying Early Decision because you will have a better shot at getting in. Hamilton is very proud of the great financial aid it offers to their students.

 ## Academics

Current student, Politics, 8/2004-Submit Date, February 2007

If you dislike writing and proactive research, Hamilton will not be easy for you. Few classes have over 20 students, so the attention from professors could not be better. Professors are always accessible and eager to assist. Recently added a state-of-the-art science facility, which has quickly attracted many science majors. Hamilton has always been known for its government and economics departments. As a world politics major, I can't think of a better choice for those who seek small classes, very involved faculty and a group of students who relish learning

Current student, 8/2005-Submit Date, May 2006

The amount of variety of Hamilton's classes is extremely high. I found that compared to my competitive high school, the courses were still very demanding and challenging. The responsibility of learning the work is placed completely on the student at Hamilton. The teachers are more than extremely open to helping the students in any way they can. The writing center and the Quantitative Literacy Center are also very convenient in helping with work.

Classes at Hamilton are pretty small. However, several intro-level courses were bigger than I expected. For example, my Intro to Bio course contained about 70 students. Also, my Intro to Anthropology course had 40 kids. However, the professors still learned everyone's name and personal attention was available if I sought it. While some popular classes, such as Into to Photo, seem like they are impossible to get into as a freshman, it gets easier as you get older.

> **The school says:** "The average class size at Hamilton is 16."

Grading varies from class to class. In all the classes I have taken, the grading showed me that Hamilton's professors have high standards. In some classes, there will be several small assignments a week, while others only give you a grade for a midterm and final, or two or three major papers. I found this to be very different from high school, where I had many chances to bring up a grade. The workload at Hamilton is pretty high, depending on the classes you take. Most courses usually include a lot of reading, it is your choice to complete it but I found that failure to do the reading was detrimental to grades.

The best part about classes at Hamilton, I found, was the professors. They are passionate, friendly, very well qualified and really want their students to excel. I found that lectures many times revolved around what the students were especially interested in.

Current student, 8/2004-Submit Date, May 2006

One of my favorite things about Hamilton is the lack of core requirements. Many of my friends at other institutions spent the bulk of their freshman year taking classes they weren't really interested in. I was able to take classes that interested me immediately; this motivated me to work harder in them because I had picked them out.

Students work closely with their advisor to develop a curriculum that best fits their needs. It really made me feel like I had control over my education. Of course, there are popular classes at every school that do fill up, but professors are generally willing to cater to the needs of students and open another section if needed. If a popular class is one that you need for your concentration, professors will sign you in before registration. In general, I have found that professors make themselves extremely accessible to students. All professors hold open office hours during the week, which is a time when students can ask questions, clarify lectures or get help on assignments.

Current student, 8/2005-Submit Date, May 2006

Classes at Hamilton are both fun and challenging. Professors really take the tim to get to know each student and tailor their program to them. For example, fo my Rhetorical Act class my professor had us complete a survey one day abou what we thought our biggest weaknesses in public speaking were. At the nex class we walked in to receive a slip with a personalized assignment meant to ta get our weaknesses and improve them—the class was great and I got a lot bet ter.

Hamilton students must be prepared to work. For this last finals period, as freshman, I turned in over 45 pages of writing for three different classes (non of which was a writing intensive class—one was Linear Algebra). Although th work is difficult and requires students to stay on top of it, professors are alway there to help during class, after class, at office hours or over a cup of coffee Cafe Opus; they make it worth the effort because they help you and you reall come to respect and like them.

> **The school says:** "Hamilton students are required to complete three writing intensive courses, which are limited-enrollment courses focused on writing. Courses are offered throughout the curriculum by all departments, including those in the sciences."

Current student, 8/2005-Submit Date, May 2006

Hamilton students carry a very demanding courseload, yet in a nurturing env ronment. The professors are, by far, one of the best aspects of Hamilton's aca demics. They really extend themselves to students by making themselves read ily available through office hours and even by opening their homes up to stu dents. It is not uncommon for professors to invite a class over for dinner or movie. Class attendance is crucial, as most classes are discussion based an most professors take attendance regularly. It's hard to get an A at Hamilton. It not uncommon for students who earned A's in high school to get B's at Hamilton

Current student, 8/2003-Submit Date, January 2006

There is also an emphasis on oral communication. Although many studen dread going through it, they always love and appreciate the fact that they had do it. Many classes involve presentations and students develop public speakin skills. Such skills prove invaluable in the workforce and help you to hit hom runs on interviews. Professors are all very highly qualified and love getting know you. They have in-depth knowledge of their subjects and can answer an question or will find out the answer by the next class. They send you article about subjects you might be interested in, they are constantly publishing ne books and articles, and they travel to other schools to visit. Professors here lov eating lunch with students and it is common to see a few in the dining halls every meal. They frequently have students over their houses for dinner an come to sports and campus-wide events.

Most classes here are very difficult and challenging, but very regarding. As junior and senior, you will have no problems getting into the classes you wan As a sophomore, you can usually get three out of the four classes you want an most of the time you can get signed into the fourth. The workload is rigorou and time consuming but well worth it. Everything you read comes up in clas and all your assignments have a purpose—nothing is wasted time. Also, the are no core requirements at Hamilton, so students can take or not take whateve classes they want. Students love this aspect and you will find yourself takin courses you never thought you would, courses like Encryption, Astronomy Opera.

 ## Employment Prospects

Current student, Politics, 8/2004-Submit Date, February 2007

No matter what your field, if you have a B average or better upon graduating recruiters will flock to you. In the past, Wall Street firms, international consul ing firms and the government have recruited heavily here. More recently, muc attention has been given to grads from top technology and science employer After all, both Bristol and Myers (Bristol-Myers) are Hamilton grads, as long list of ambassadors, governors and senators. Grads who seek positions publishing and the arts are not overlooked either. Face it, Hamilton is one of th top liberal arts schools. Those recruiters who make it a point to know, know They recruit from Hamilton for a reason.

Alumnus/a, Pre-med/English, 9/1999-5/2003, March 2007

...you want to be an investment banker, this is the right school for you. Hamilton ...s a very good rep in the finance world. It has a good rep in many other fields ...t finance seems to be the source of the most successful alumni. Most alumni ...now are able to get into the grad school or field of their choice after Hamilton. ...now successful lawyers, actors, writers, media people and of course I-bankers ...m my class.

...rrent student, 8/2004-Submit Date, May 2006

...hile I was looking at schools, one thing I did not know to look for was a great ...reer Center. Looking back, it makes sense now because after spending four ...ars working hard at Hamilton, what do I want to do with my life? I got real-... lucky that Hamilton has a great Career Center. There are many counselors, ...ch with a specialization that can help students find the correct job/intern-...p/research opportunity or grad school.

... addition, there are many peer counselors who teach students how to write ...ver letters and résumés, and give interviewing advice. The Career Center web ... also offers lots of information on how to network and databases filled with ...portunities for students. I attended the Cover Letter and Résumé Workshop ... freshman year to learn how to write them (I had never seen one before) and ...ve been working with one of our counselors to gain career-related experience. ...ter my freshman year, I submitted my résumé to WCBS-TV in New York City ...d had an incredible summer working there. This summer I will be working ...th a marketing and advertising company close to my house. The opportuni-...s for students are endless.

...umnus/a, 8/1997-5/2001, November 2004

... you are familiar with Wall Street then you are familiar with the Hamilton ...afia. They own the block! Law school and an MBA programs are the most ...ughtafter graduate schools and finance seems to be the trendy after college job. ...e Career Center is wonderful and very helpful providing numerous job fairs ...d on-campus recruiting visits.

Quality of Life

...rrent student, Politics, 8/2004-Submit Date, February 2007

...all college, somewhat isolated. Dorms and facilities are all first-rate, as are ... dining halls. Lots going on socially, though, the college makes certain that ...ekends are loaded with activities. Absolutely gorgeous campus, very old ...nool with lots of stone buildings and ivy. It's been said that there is more ivy ...re than at the Ivies. Most importantly, it's a friendly school. Tough academ-... but everyone seems very happy to be here.

...rrent student, 8/2004-Submit Date, May 2006

...e quality of life at Hamilton has been great. It is a very small campus (about ...300 students), which could be seen as Hamilton's biggest weakness and great-... strength. Many people believe that seeing the same people day after day gets ...petitive but I enjoy walking across the quad and knowing three out of four of ... people I pass. The sense of community that is created is absolutely amazing. ...ving in Upstate NY without a city nearby means that everyone stays on cam-...s—Hamilton is not a suitcase school. In addition, the small class sizes are ...mething that you can only get at a small school.

...e dining at Hamilton is great—we have two main dining halls, Commons and ...cEwen. All freshmen and sophomores are required to be on the unlimited ...eal plan, which means that students can go into those dining halls as many ...nes per day as they would like (this does not help the Freshman 15 very much). ... addition, we have the diner, which offers anything a student could possible ...nt fried, and The Little Pub, which is a smaller, more intimate dining option ...r Monday through Friday lunches.

...rrent student, 8/2005-Submit Date, May 2006

...ousing on campus is pretty good. As a junior or senior it's amazing, and fresh-...an year it's not bad either. As a freshman I lived in a split double—two sin-...es with an a joining door— which was really nice. Sophomore year is the only ...ar when housing has the ability to be less than ideal—many sophomores end

up in Bundy, a building towards the bottom of the hill, most of the rooms there are singles that people can pull together so as to live next to their friends. It's just a long hike up to the rest of the campus where the dining halls, classes and other dorms are.

All campus facilities are incredibly nice, particularly the science center, which is brand-new. The food is better than at most colleges and includes a wide range of things from pizza and pasta to sushi. Still, it feels a little repetitive, and while it is never bad, it does get boring. Campus is incredibly safe, not necessarily because the campus police are really strict but more because people at Hamilton tend to be nice, good people who don't harass each other. I've walked back from a friend's room by myself at 2 a.m. on a Saturday night and never felt the least bit scared or unsafe. As a tour guide, I know that the blue light system on campus has only been used once and that was for a bee sting.

Social Life

Current student, Politics, 8/2004-Submit Date, February 2007

Active Greek system, lots of clubs, intramural sports. Varsity sports have huge fan followings. This is small-town, rural life, so movie theaters and restaurants are pretty much outside the tiny town of Clinton, but Hamilton provides jitney service to popular locales free of charge. There is so much to do on campus on weekends that few bother to venture out farther than 10 miles from campus.

Alumnus/a, Pre-med/English, 9/1999-5/2003, March 2007

People are good looking and smart but there aren't many big parties on campus anymore. It's more about smaller parties the first couple years and then about the Pub and downtown the last two years. Sports games are fun even though the teams usually lose. CAB does a good job getting good events on campus. Overall good but it is what you make of it, really.

> **The school says:** "CAB is the acronym for Campus Activities Board, which is the student-run organization that has a $200,000 annual budget to plan social and entertainment activities."

Current student, 8/2005-Submit Date, May 2006

I found this year that there is always something going on at Hamilton every day of the week. This ranges from performances to speakers, to parties. There are a few bars downtown, which the older students will go to a lot. As for restaurants, most people choose to eat on campus; however, trips to a few cheap places, such as Tex Mex or Piggy Pats, are always fun. Many times people will wind up eating at the diner, which is right in the middle of campus and open very late.

At Hamilton dating can be classified in two ways: either you are in a serious relationship, or you have an ambiguous relationship with the person with whom you are hooking up. The latter is most common, especially with the popularity of drinking and the constant opportunity to go out. There are usually always one or two Greek parties every weekend, which are open to the whole campus. These range from being regular dance parties to theme parties, to formals. There are also usually comedians, musicians or student performances going on.

Other than Greek parties, other organizations throw fun parties in the four social spaces available on campus, such as the rugby team and the Emerson Literary Society. There are also smaller parties thrown in the dorms, especially in the dark side suites and in the G Road apartments. These parties are usually themed and are really fun.

During the week, clubs are always putting on events. There are a cappella concerts frequently, which many people attend. Also, there are dance performances, student comedy troupes and student bands. Zeaskees is really popular and will often perform in the Pub on campus. The Pub is really fun, usually filled with mostly upperclassmen but everyone can go in. Other clubs range from the Hamilton Outing Club, which hosts trips and rents equipment for great outdoor fun, to clubs like yoga and knitting.

Read all of Vault's College Surveys at **www.vault.com/college**—get complete surveys on 100s of colleges and universities, expert advice on applicaton essays and more.

VAULT CAREER LIBRARY **457**

The School Says

- Students come to Hamilton to their voice. As a national leader for teaching students to write effectively, learn from each other and think for themselves, Hamilton produces graduates who have the knowledge, skills and confidence to make their own voices heard on issues of importance to them and their communities.

- A key component of the Hamilton experience is the college's open, yet rigorous liberal arts curriculum. In place of distribution requirements that are common at most colleges, Hamilton gives its students the freedom to choose the courses that reflect their unique interests and plans. Faculty advisors assist students in planning a coherent and highly individualized academic program—in fact, close student-faculty relationships at Hamilton are a distinguishing characteristic of the college—but ultimately, students at Hamilton take responsibility for their own future.

- Part of that future includes a lifelong relationship with the college. Hamilton alumni are exceptionally loyal and passionate supporters of their alma mater and the students and faculty who currently live and work on College Hill. That support manifests itself through internships, speaking engagements, job-shadowing opportunities and financial donations.

Hofstra University

Office of Admission
Hofstra University
100 Hofstra University
Hempstead, NY 11549-1000
Admission phone: (516) 463-6700 or (800) 463-7872
Admission fax: (516) 463-5100
Admission e-mail: admitme@hofstra.edu
Admission URL: hofstra.edu/Admission/

Admissions

Current student, Communications, 9/2004-Submit Date, June 2007

The admissions process was smooth and flawless. I was able to talk with counselors and deans even before I heard back about acceptance. They answered all my questions and helped solve problems with funding college. I was notified of my acceptance really early on, much earlier than most schools do today so it gave me time to make up my mind.

Current student, Political Science, 9/2005-Submit Date, May 2007

The admissions office at Hofstra is really helpful. It's a great resource during and after the process. They're always willing to re-consider scholarship decisions, not to mention are more than available for interviews and questions. They also have a great program called, Hofstra Up Close. Prospective students spend a day with a student in their major area. It's a great way for high school students to get a feel for the campus and classes. I would tell everyone to do an Up Close!

Current student, Communications, 8/2006-Submit Date, May 2007

The admissions process can be quite tedious, frustrating and long, but with the great resources provided to you and by organizing your interests and goals, the admissions process can be quick and simply. My advice when applying to Hofstra University is really to be you. During the interview process, be open, tell them something that makes you stand out from others and just be completely yourself (they love that!). During the selection process, Hofstra just doesn't base the selection on academics alone but takes other factors into consideration, such as extracurricular activities, honors, awards, essays and interviews. I just want to wrap up by saying that during the admissions process, ask tons of questions! College is going to be a place where you'll be spending the next four or even more years of your life! Take the opportunity to look into the school and, most importantly, ask questions! Even the littlest of questions can make a huge difference!

Current student, Communications, 9/2004-Submit Date, May 2007

With the admissions process, one can send in an application including one's SAT scores, as well as an essay on a topic of one's choice. Then depending on what major the student is interested in, the student can set up an interview in that specific department to learn more about what it has to offer, as well as auditions or tests the student may have to take in order to get into the program. As far selectivity, Hofstra selects about 1,300 students per year. A bit of advice ab getting into Hofstra University is to make the essay creative, and when the int view arises, be enthused and confident.

The school says: "For the 2007-2008 academic year, Hofstra received approximately 18,500 applications and accepted 55 percent of its applicants."

Current student, Education, 9/2005-Submit Date, May 2007

Definitely set up an appointment to meet with an admissions counselor! N only are they very helpful in answering questions, but they may even be able get you a few extra scholarship dollars. Take time writing your essay! Try a be abstract. Admissions counselors are always looking for things that stand o Set yourself apart from the other lousy applicants and get yourself noticed!

Current student, History, 9/2004-Submit Date, May 2007

The admissions process is competitive. The school requires a transcript, ess and SAT scores. The average SAT score has increased 100 points in the last f years, which has subsequently made the admissions process more competiti Interviews are optional, but can help a student who isn't sure if he/she would li to come to the school and are a great way for the school to get to know the app cant and the applicant to see the school.

Current student, 9/2004-Submit Date, May 2006

Hofstra University has two options: Early Action and Regular Decision. Ea Action is non-binding and the deadline is generally in mid-November. EA ap cants will receive a decision by the middle of December. It is nice to have option of Early Action because, for me, Hofstra was my first choice and kno ing which school I was attending before the holidays was great. Regu Decision is our rolling admissions process. Hofstra will take applications a accept people on a rolling basis; however, deposits and decisions are due by M 1. Hofstra really likes to look at the essay. It used to be optional and reco mended, but now it is required. This is a great opportunity to see how the app cant writes.

Current student, 9/2004-Submit Date, April 2005

Write a good essay. They don't focus as much on SAT scores as they do on yo ability to write well. List everything that you do for extracurriculars, it ca hurt. They are generous with scholarships and if you have a decent GPA, y will probably get some money. It isn't extremely difficult to get in if you'r good all-around student. I think they need to make the Honors College mo available to other students and should give them more money.

Regarding admissions, Hofstra says: "Hofstra University enrolls approximately 1,740 students each year. Students entering in the fall of 2007 had an average SAT score of 1179 and an average high school GPA of 3.37, with 74 percent earning a GPA of 3.0 or higher. Our student body is geographically, ethnically and culturally diverse, with more than 50 percent of students coming from outside New York State."

Academics

Current student, Liberal Arts, 8/2006-Submit Date, June 2007

Hofstra University provides a solid education in which any type of student can succeed. I personally am very motivated, and I am in the Honors College. The professors are always willing to work with the students to ensure their academic success, and I have always learned something valuable in all of my classes. I always know what my grades will be before I receive them because their grading policies are spelled out from the start. The workload is not too heavy; last semester I had three jobs, was in five different clubs, started a club, and still had time to go out and have fun!

Current student, Communications, 9/2004-Submit Date, June 2007

Not only my program, but all programs are extremely focused and detail oriented. The student-to-professor ratio is about 13:1 and the average class size is 23 students, enabling me to gain a lot of personal attention and make my academics reach their highest degree.

> **Hofstra says:** "The student-to-faculty ratio at Hofstra is 14:1."

Classes get easier to get in as the semesters go by, but even as a freshman I got a lot of the classes I wanted to take. There are several of the same classes offered at the same time, so more people have the opportunity to take part in them.

Current student, Communications, 9/2004-Submit Date, May 2007

The academic nature in the School of Communication is very highly rated because of exposure that a student can get as he/she goes through the program. Most of the communications classes are very hands-on and production heavy. The classes teach a communications major a lot about the media industry, and the equipment used is kept up to date with industry standards. Many of the classes are small, consisting of 15 to 25 students, so there are many times when a student may have to get signed into a particular class. Grades are based more heavily on projects and most of the learning experience comes more from the projects than the finals on hard copy. The professors are very knowledgeable and prestigious in the field, and many of them currently work or have worked in the media industry, throughout all areas of the media spectrum. The workload for a lot of the production-based and journalism classes can sometimes be a lot, but it is very beneficial for someone who wants a career upon graduating from the School of Communication.

Current student, Education, 9/2005-Submit Date, May 2007

The academic nature of most programs at Hofstra is straightforward. I have just finished my second complete year and the quality of the classes I have taken thus far has been outstanding. I truly have learned a great deal from each and every course. The professors at this university really care about their students! It's not extremely difficult to get an A, so long as you actually do the work and put aside a few extra hours to study. The workload is greater than what high school students are used to, but you need to remember this is college, and you have a lot more free time to get it all done!

Current student, History, 9/2004-Submit Date, May 2007

The history department at Hofstra is a hidden treasure for historians. While the department is small, all of the faculty have PhDs in their specific subject area. There are a number of general and specific courses available and it is not difficult to get a spot in most of them. The professors really care about the student body. All of the professors give their e-mails out to students for extra help or any questions, they all have open door hours during the week, and many will even come in on their days off for students who need help. They are also interested in students getting involved in others ways on campus. As president of the history club on campus, I have gotten a great deal of help from professors for going on trips and getting special lectures. Hofstra also has a chapter of the national history honors Phi Alpha Theta

Current student, Biology, 9/2005-Submit Date, May 2007

I am an undergraduate student in the biology program at Hofstra. My classes have been very interesting so far, and I have not struggled to get the class or the

professor I wanted. The classes here are very small, capped around 35 students. We have no massive lecture classes in any department on campus. Hofstra is a liberal arts and sciences school, so there are general education requirements, or distribution requirements, for every student. This has actually been beneficial because it has allowed me to take classes of interest out of my field of study, providing me with a well-rounded college education. I have found classes to be challenging for the most part, but definitely not impossible. The classes focus on hands-on activity and experience.

Current student, 9/2004-Submit Date, May 2006

The broadcast journalism program is extremely worthwhile, all the hard work that you put into it, you receive back. Class structure is very lax, you can choose to take core classes as a freshman or a senior, just keep in line with your requirements so you graduate on time. It is a pretty funny process, and the computers can crash on registration midnights but, honestly, if you can't normally register for a class, most professors will just let you sign in. Workload, isn't bad if you keep proper time management. Everything is very subjective—work hard, participate, and it will pay off.

Current student, 9/2003-Submit Date, May 2006

Hofstra has [21] accreditations, which means these programs are learning the same material as Ivy League students. Each student will have three to five hours of work a night depending on how much they prioritize. Students are always able to meet with professors during office hours. Upperclassmen have an earlier pick of classes for registration than underclassmen.

> **Regarding academics, Hofstra says:** "Hofstra University is a dynamic private institution where students find themselves and discover their futures in more than 140 undergraduate and 155 graduate programs in liberal arts and sciences, business, communication, education and allied human services, and honors studies, as well as law. With a student-to-faculty ratio of 14:1 and an average undergraduate class size of just 23, Hofstra offers students the individual attention they need."

Employment Prospects

Current student, Communications, 9/2004-Submit Date, June 2007

Hofstra has one of the best recruiting programs I have ever seen within a university. Our alumni are so extremely involved with our students and our services, providing easy opportunities for amazing positions for graduates of the university. We have a Career Center on campus where students have the wonderful opportunity to work with counselors who will help them build a great résumé and send it out to various employers in the students area of interest. We are located 25 miles from New York City and we are known for our wonderful schools, including business, communication, performing arts and engineering.

Current student, Communications, 9/2005-Submit Date, May 2007

Hofstra is really great with internships and finding work once you graduate. We have this thing called Pride Recruiting where businesses and interviewers tour the school and speak with interested students. We also have the Career Center on campus and over 100,000 active alumni within Hofstra.

> **The school says:** "There are 109,000 alumni at Hofstra."

The Career Center is available for help with résumés, interviewing skills, what to wear on an interview and so on. All of the advisors in every department are really looking forward to helping their kids get internships for credit while they are still on campus, as well. They will work with you in order to make sure that you finish the internship and have a positive experience.

Current student, Communications, 9/2004-Submit Date, May 2007

Employment prospects for graduates of Hofstra University are immense and many graduates are able to find jobs after graduation if they are hard-working and determined. The Career Center here at Hofstra University is a great resource because there are several job listings for every sector of communications. There have been countless Hofstra alumni members who have gone on to work at WABC AM, 1010WINS, ESPN, Sirius Satellite Radio and many more. Alumni who work at these prestigious companies come to speak to current communica-

Read all of Vault's College Surveys at **www.vault.com/college**—get complete surveys on 100s of colleges and universities, expert advice on applicaton essays and more.

VAULT CAREER LIBRARY   **459**

tions students, as well as speak with them individually, to network and make connections for internships and future jobs. There is a lot of on-campus recruiting through job fairs presented by the Career Center, as well as small programs set up by the School of Communication. Countless internships may also be set up by connections through Hofstra University professors and the Career Center. There are countless opportunities and resources available for someone who wants a career in the communications field, and all a student has to do is have ambition and goals.

Alumnus/a, 9/2003-Submit Date, April 2006

The university's Career Center sponsors career days bi-semesterly. They are beneficial to most business majors but have little to no importance to IT professionals. There is a plethora of student jobs available and with this opportunity comes the availability to network with people within your future profession. I am a prime example of this, as I got a full-time job through my networking experience within my student aide position. The university has been decreasing its turnover rate from student to full-time professional unfortunately. This has frustrated many deserving student employees. However, if you receive a full-time position, Hofstra offers to pay for college credits, which is essential for any students looking to get a free master's program.

> **Regarding employment prospects, Hofstra says:** "Hofstra offers numerous career-enhancing, life-shaping experiences. More than 400 employers from Long Island and nearby New York City visit campus each year. Students and alumni have the many resources of Hofstra's Career Center to help them realize their aspirations. More than 90 percent of the Class of 2006 was employed or went on to graduate school within a year of graduation."

 ## Quality of Life

Current student, Communications, 9/2004-Submit Date, June 2007

We are an absolutely beautiful campus, completely closed off from the neighboring town. We are a national arboretum filled with beautiful greenery and sculptures of art all over the grounds. We house over 5,000 students and we are currently in the middle of building another dormitory. We provide all different types of living: singles, doubles, triples, quads, suites and apartment styles. Housing is pretty much guaranteed so long as you deposit by the deadline. I love the dorms—they are big, they're clean, they're spacious, and you have so many opportunities to meet so many people. Laundry, common rooms and kitchens are located in all dorm houses and towers for the students to use all the time. There are about 16 dining halls on campus, all different types and you can never get bored of the food, there is so much variety. Crime and safety has never been an issue because we are gated off from the outside and we have a wonderful 24/7 security team who handles anything if something goes wrong.

Current student, Political Science, 9/2005-Submit Date, May 2007

Everything is always clean (the bathrooms get cleaned twice a day if you live in the high-rises, but if you live in a suite, you have to clean your own bathroom), and there is a safety booth staffed 24/7 and a card swipe at the entrance of every building. There's a bunch of places to eat on campus including a deli, restaurant, convenience store (open 24 hours) that has a deli counter, the student center, a bistro like restaurant, even a Sbarros. There's everything from sushi, Chinese and Mexican, to vegan and kosher options. Not to mention all the places on campus to get a cup of really great coffee!

> **Hofstra says:** "Sbarros is being replaced by Pizza Express."

Current student, Visual Arts, 8/2004-Submit Date, May 2007

The campus is gorgeous, especially in the spring. The campus has a rich Dutch tradition and in the spring there are over 100,000 tulips blooming on campus. The campus is a registered arboretum with hundreds of varieties of trees on campus. We are also the largest outdoor sculpture on Long Island.

The neighborhood is fine. It is by no means an upper-class neighborhood, but is not the ghetto. Public safety does a good job of keeping campus safe. Th are very visible on campus in their tan sheriff uniforms and hats.

> **Regarding quality of life, Hofstra says:** "Hofstra's distinctive suburban campus has 37 residence halls, which house approximately 4,200 students. Students choose from a variety of accommodations, including single rooms, doubles, triples and suites. Students can live at Hofstra year-round and will find the campus is its own community, with 17 dining facilities, a hair and nail salon, post office and full-service bank branch. To ensure the safety of students and guests, Hofstra recently installed a five-part campus-wide emergency alert system."

 ## Social Life

Current student, Communications, 9/2004-Submit Date, June 200

We are definitely a very social school, participating in a lot of Greek activiti tons of student activity events, concerts, trips to games and Broadway shows a athletics and intramural sports. The area surrounding Hofstra is great—we a right next to Garden City and East Meadow, NY, with lots of restaurants and t largest malls in America. There are lots of fun hang-out spots around this p of Long Island, but we are only a 40-minute train ride from Manhattan, so st dents seem to travel out there a lot on certain nights. Our students seem ve active in all aspects of school, especially the kids who got really involved wh they stepped in as a first-year student. There are so many different people he so there are many opportunities to meet people of all ages and races. Everyo here finds a niche.

Current student, Political Science, 9/2005-Submit Date, May 200

The social life at Hofstra is more than I ever thought it would be. There are ov 140 active clubs on campus and a Greek community that makes up about 10 p cent of our population. You don't have to be involved in Greek life to have social life, by any means. There's always something to do, and you'll go in the city constantly. They always offer discounted tickets to Broadway shov tips to museums and to Jones Beach! There are a few bars in the area, but if i not your scene, you'll still have tons to do!

> **The school says:** "There are 150 clubs and organizations."

Current student, 9/2005-Submit Date, May 2007

Hofstra's location makes it great for many different options for social even NYC is 40 minutes away by train, opening up an entire city of shows, even dance clubs, comedy clubs, athletic events and much more. Long Island itse offers the beach, several malls, numerous restaurants, bowling alleys and mov theaters. When hoping to venture off campus, there is plenty to do. Greek li at Hofstra is present but not invasive. It is available and very active for studer who choose to participate, but does not become a major factor for those wl don't.

> **Regarding Social Life, Hofstra says:** "Hofstra has a vibrant campus life, with more than 150 student clubs and organizations, including about 30 fraternities and sororities; 18 varsity sports; and more than 500 cultural events each year. Students can choose from organizations as diverse as French Club, Danceworks, and the National Broadcasting Society. Events include the popular Homecoming Weekend, festivals, readings, lectures, and a well-respected series of presidential conferences."

 ## The School Says

Whatever the dream, Hofstra University can help you get there. Hofstra is a dynamic private institution where students find themselves and discover their future in 140 undergraduate and 155 graduate programs in liberal arts and sciences, business, communication, education and allied human services, honors studies and law. Hofstra is a university large enough to have extensive academic resources yet small enough to give students individual attention. With an outstanding faculty, advanced technological resources, and state-of-the-art facilities, Hofstra has a growing national reputation. Yet our average class size is just 23, and our student-to-faculty ratio is 14:1.

Hofstra offers an exciting campus life on a 240-acre campus that is a registered national arboretum. A suburban university located 25 miles from New York City, it also offers a world of cultural and internship opportunities. Find yourself and discover your future at Hofstra University.

Hunter College

The City University of New York
95 Park Avenue
Room 100 Hunter North Building
New York, NY 10065
Admissions phone: (212) 772-4490
Admissions fax: (212) 650-3336
Admissions e-mail: admissions@hunter.cuny.edu
Admissions URL:
www.hunter.cuny.edu/prospectivestudents/

Admissions

Current student, Visual Arts, 1/2003-Submit Date, June 2007

Is very easy to get into. Simply fill out a CUNY application. This enables the prospective student to choose from other CUNY schools as backups. When I applied there was a $50 application fee. No essays or interviews were necessary.

Current student, Political Science, 9/2004-Submit Date, June 2007

The college has, in my opinion, too easy an application process. To apply, one only needs the standard CUNY application, where the prospective student checks the box next to whatever school he/she would like to attend.

Current student, Social Work, 7/2005-Submit Date, April 2007

Admission to any CUNY (City University of New York) college is really simple. There is not even an essay, which makes the school seem cheap. The Macaulay Honors College is the only college that requires an essay. All CUNY colleges require an SAT score, although the average for the regular CUNY schools is not too high. Any decent student should be able to get in. If not, transfer in (the transfer GPA has to be at least a 2.3).

Current student, Political Science, 8/2004-Submit Date, June 2007

Send in a CUNY application for general admissions to the CUNY schools or you can apply for the Hunter Honors College directly if you were an exceptional student in high school. Hunter has become more selective since I applied in 2004. The Hunter Honors College is very selective.

Current student, Political Science, 9/2003-Submit Date, June 2007

From what I remember, an application is all that is needed, SAT scores and if you have ACT scores that should be submitted, as well. Hunter pre-approves certain students and then one has to take a placement math and English test, depending on the score. The prospective student might have to take remedial classes before he/she can enter Hunter.

> **The school says:** "Hunter conditionally admits some students who then have to prove proficiency by taking a test in math and/or English."

Current student, 9/2003-Submit Date, May 2005

Generally easy to get into, but certain majors are very hard to get into, like dance and nursing. There isn't any trouble getting into Hunter, except if you're planning to enroll in the Hunter Honors College.

Current student, 8/2003-Submit Date, May 2005

When I first applied to Hunter, I did not get accepted. What I did was I went for appeals and I had to write an essay and supplied my Regents and transcript grades and then they gave me the OK!

Current student, 9/2001-Submit Date, May 2005

The admissions process was quite simple, if I remember correctly. I remember having to take a Hunter entrance exam to see at what level of math and reading I was, so that they knew what classes I needed. Choosing the classes was the confusing part, but the block program was a good start for all incoming freshmen. Although I'd say Hunter is not a hard school to get into, you do need an overall average of 85 and a SAT score of at least 1000.

> **The school says:** "On average, admitted students have an overall average of 85 and an average SAT score of 1090."

Current student, 9/2003-Submit Date, April 2005

My advice for anyone applying to the Macaulay Honors College or to Hunter College is to sell him/herself in your application. Do not be too modest about anything. You want the person to say when he/she looks at your application, "Wow, this person will be a great asset to our school."

Academics

Alumnus/a, Political Science, 1/2004-6/2006, June 2007

I came to Hunter from a more prestigious and higher ranked university, but I honestly felt that the quality of my professors was just as good, if not better at Hunter than at my previous university. It's not always easy to get into classes with the most popular professors, but if you go talk to most of them and express your interest in their class, they will usually make exceptions. The workload and grading is not easy, but definitely manageable. A lot of Hunter students work full-time while going to school full-time.

Current student, Social Work, 7/2005-Submit Date, April 2007

The professors at Hunter vary widely. Most of the full-time professors are pretty amazing. There are a few adjuncts whose classes will waste your time. This is also true with a few professors who have been in their respective departments since the 60s and 70s. Generally, though, professors are pretty good and grading is pretty fair.

Current student, Political Science, 9/2003-Submit Date, June 2007

Every class is different. The beginner's classes (intros or core requirement) will sometimes be conducted in huge lecture halls that have up to 300 students. Once the students are taking specialized classes, like Immigration, the size will hover around 25 students. There are also seminar classes at Hunter that usually have about 15 students. The workload varies from class to class. Generally speaking, there are a lot of reading and writing classes that one must fulfill before graduating. In political science we have distinguished professors who are renowned in their field of studies. All professors have office hours, when a student can stop by with questions regarding the course.

> **The school says:** "The average class size at Hunter is between 25 and 40 students."

Read all of Vault's College Surveys at **www.vault.com/college**—get complete surveys on 100s of colleges and universities, expert advice on applicaton essays and more.

VAULT CAREER LIBRARY **461**

Current student, Political Science, 8/2006-Submit Date, April 2007

I am in the Honors College and get priority for registration, so getting the classes I want has never been a problem. There are a lot of required classes to take, but most are classes I would be interested in taking anyway. For the popular classes, there are a lot of different sections, so most people don't have a problem. Professors have all been good so far, many have a lot of credentials from other schools and have written their own books and articles. Grading varies by the teacher, as does the workload, but there is definitely a lot of reading.

Current student, 9/2002-Submit Date, May 2006

The workload is sizeable depending on what courseload and field one is in. Popular classes close out quickly but it's been better the last couple of years. You get lucky if the professor curves grades. Writing classes may be intensive. Don't try taking more than one in a semester. Many classes are interesting, it really all depends on the professor and student's interests.

Current student, 8/2003-Submit Date, May 2005

Sometimes, depending on when your registration date was, things could get quite hectic. The professors are very nice and very helpful. They would spend extra time with a student if he/she requested it and they try their best to provide their aids to the student. If you take four classes per semester, the workload is not too bad. I know people who take five or six classes and still have time to sit for a cup of coffee! But like every other school, any program that you choose will be, and should be, challenging. I have been to other colleges to visit and I would have to say that the people at Hunter really, really try to see that every student succeeds.

Current student, 8/2003-Submit Date, May 2005

The first semester as a Hunter College student, you are advised to take a block program, which is a set of classes with a set theme and you stay with other students in the same block. In this way, students are able to have classes that are easy to register for and that are taken with other students. So it is easier to acclimate oneself to the college regiment and social life. Now, I have found that as time goes on the curriculum gets easier to work with and it takes time management and self discipline. Hunter College has many helpful resource centers, but everything is dependent upon the students doing something for themselves. The academic nature of Hunter College is designed to open up the mind of the student and enrich the learning process.

Current student, 9/2001-Submit Date, May 2005

Since Hunter College is one of the most diverse schools in the U.S., Hunter requires students to take several classes in the pluralism and diversity program. It's a chance for students to be more aware of their surroundings. I would say that full-time professors and associate professors are better than the adjunct professors because they provide more time and attention to the needs of the students. The workloads are not overwhelming, but enough to keep you busy. You really have to work for your grades.

> The school says: "Students are required to take 12 credits in designated courses that address issues of pluralism and diversity."

 ## Employment Prospects

Current student, Psychology, 9/2003-Submit Date, June 2007

Career Development Services is amazing. I got one of my first jobs through them and everyone is very friendly and helpful. Hunter is very well connected in the city, and provides its undergrads with various research and internship opportunities in various companies, such as ABC, Coach, Estée Lauder, just to name a few. Estée Lauder takes one Hunter students for its internship program each year and Coach interviews from two to four. The administration is very dedicated. If you get to know them and they like how you work, they will make sure you get the best internships and have a job upon graduation. Hunter is also very good at sending out an e-mail every week with different jobs, internships and scholarships available to Hunter students. Different departments have their own e-mail lists, for which students may sign up. Departments usually e-mail job opportunities out through these lists.

Current student, Political Science, 9/2003-Submit Date, June 20

Students must be proactive when looking for internships and employment. T means that the student should speak to professors, the alumni office and Car Development Services and make it clear that he/she is interested in internsh or working in his/her field of interest. If this is done at Hunter, many doors w open. Hunter loves and helps students who show initiative and ambition. T Prestigious internships will be very important when applying to prestigious fir or companies. Hunter Alumni work in a series of high-profile firms and cor rations but again, only the best and ambitious will know about the opportun of employment with these companies. Some of these companies include Coa Estée Lauder, Goldman Sachs, and I currently work (while finishing my l three classes) in the executive Office of the Secretary of State.

Current student, Social Work, 7/2005-Submit Date, April 2007

You really need to work while in college. Network with professors, get go grades, and have several internships because Hunter's reputation is not exac the best with employers.

Current student, 9/2002-Submit Date, May 2006

There have been lots of success stories for CUNY graduates. A lot of Hun alumni go on to med schools because Hunter has a very strong pre-med progra They also recently launched a course study for pre-law students, advising, me toring and events. Hunter is very close with its alumni and as part of their o reach, it tries to connect alumni mentors in certain fields with students majori in them, which has been amazing. There are lots of career fairs throughout t year, including one big one at the Jacob Javits Center for all CUNY. Car Development Services is always trying to help people with jobs, internships a inquiries into where a degree can get them. They send out e-mails and conta you to inquire about your experience at the job they helped you with.

 ## Quality of Life

Current student, Pre-med, 9/2004-Submit Date, January 2007

The college is very safe; facilities are not great but OK. Housing isn't bad eith The neighborhood is pretty busy all the time; people are all around and you c find food all around.

Current student, Political Science, 8/2006-Submit Date, April 200

I am in the dorm at Hunter College. It is a subway ride away from where cla es are held. There are lounges and kitchens on every floor, along with a ga room with printers, pool, computers, TV, ping pong and more. There is a gy swimming pool, study areas and large areas where events are held. Brookd Council organizes events like free skiing and trips to Six Flags for students. T neighborhood feels very safe but there are security guards all over and they a very tight with security as far as signing people in.

Current student, Political Science, 9/2003-Submit Date, June 200

Hunter is a commuter school. We do have dorms, but only Hunter Honor s dents and students from other states are eligible for the dorms. However, Hun is in the midst of one of Manhattan's wealthiest neighborhoods. We ha Bloomingdale's and Central Park in walking distance. It is a beautiful area w restaurants, shopping, clubs and lounges near by.

> The school says: "All full-time Hunter College students are eligible for student housing. Interested students must fill out the housing application online."

Current student, Psychology, 9/2003-Submit Date, June 2007

The neighborhood is very safe—it's the Upper East Side. I have never encou tered a problem nor has anyone I know closely. The dorm seems pretty cle and peaceful, at least at the times I've visited. Someone who lives there wou better be able to comment on it. The buildings are well-maintained and easy get around. Quality of life is good: There seems to be a good balance betwe work and play in the overall vibe of the campus. There's a lot of student life a people have the option of doing the usual commuter thing and leaving right aft class, or staying and getting involved in campus activities.

Current student, 9/2003-Submit Date, April 2005

[th]ere is one dorm for Hunter College students. There are only single rooms and, [sin]ce the the dorm is shared with graduate and nursing students; the application [pr]ocess is highly selective. Finding elsewhere in the city is difficult. Campus is [ni]ce and everything is conveniently located around the school. We have an ath[let]ic facility, cafeterias, club rooms, student lounges, and Central Park is about [fou]r blocks away. Dining in the city is great. There is a variety of places to eat [an]d you can always find something that fits your mood and budget. I will not [sa]y that the neighborhood is completely without crime, it's New York City. If [yo]u are smart, however, and travel in groups, you will be fine at night. During [th]e day, it's pretty much safe. My advice to you is to get as much as you can out [of] the city. New York City is bursting with opportunities and excitement—all [yo]u have to do is find it.

Social Life

[A]lumnus/a, Political Science, 1/2004-6/2006, June 2007

[It']s not your typical college setting in that most students commute, but everyone [ca]n find people with whom they have things in common.

[C]urrent student, Psychology, 9/2003-Submit Date, June 2007

[Hu]nter has over 100 student clubs and organizations, which as far as I know is [mo]re than any other CUNY school. Clubs are very active on campus and they [ha]ve their offices in one building. If you join a club, making friends becomes [ea]sier. Many clubs will have overlapping members and you get to know inter[est]ing people. There are a few clubs that will offer dance and martial art class[es] for free, which is a big plus. The salsa/mambo club offers free salsa classes, [the]re's a belly dance club for belly dance, an African dance club, a capoeira club, [an]d many, many more.

[As] far as dating, Hunter is 70 percent women, so it's great for those who like [w]omen but not for everyone else. Parties are not the best. They tend to be small [an]d you usually enjoy yourself more if you're part of the clubs that threw them. [U]ndergraduate student government usually throws the best parties in different [cl]ubs off campus. The good thing is it's New York City, so you can always find [a] good party off campus and don't have to depend on Hunter for fun.

[C]urrent student, 9/2002-Submit Date, May 2006

[O]ohh. The social life at Hunter is booming. Firstly, the campus is so diverse, [so] many different languages are heard in the hallways. The location of the [sc]hool is amazing—Upper East Side in Manhattan. Most everyone commutes. [Th]e location is great for going out both where the school is and even better [w]here the dorm is. The dorm life is so interconnected, everyone knows each [ot]her. Everyone in the dorm is active in school activities, clubs and student gov[er]nment, as well as working in Hunter offices. There are many social events [go]ing on at Hunter, so there is always something to do on campus. Food is [al]ways available at some event. Not much of a Greek system, but there are a [co]uple of Greek societies, huge Hillel Club, Muslim Student Association and [Hi]ndu/Indian Club. 70 percent of the students are girls. In fact, Hunter used to [be] a free, all-women's school some 60 years ago, specializing in teaching. So, [th]ere is possibility for dating but the chances are slim.

Current student, 9/2003-Submit Date, May 2005

The Thomas Hunter Building was a high school back in the day and now consists of mainly college clubs. There are also fraternities like Alpha Phi Omega, and sororities like Gamma Ce. One of the most racially diverse clubs at Hunter is the Asia Club, where students come together to share their interests or to come learn about Asian culture. Hunter Club sponsors parties at clubs or even here at Hunter almost every week. And since it is NYC, there isn't any problem finding bars or restaurants to go to.

Current student, 8/2003-Submit Date, May 2005

Hunter College is in the middle of the city and it's surrounded by museums, clothing stores, restaurants and Central Park is only two avenues away! It's Manhattan, so no matter where you are, there are always bars. A couple of blocks down is Bloomingdale's, Gap, Banana Republic, Levi's, Victoria's Secret, Sephora and much, much more. There is a variety of restaurants, including Greek, Chinese, Japanese and tons of fast food!

Current student, 8/2000-Submit Date, November 2004

There are bars in the area, but not extremely close to the school's vicinity. If they are, they are too expensive anyway. There is a wide array of restaurants all over the city. You can retrieve any type of food from Indian to Mexican, to soul food all over the city. Prices usually range from expensive to very expensive. If you are looking for fast food, there are pizzerias and delis everywhere that have sandwiches from about $5 to infinity. If you want a very good sandwich for cheap, you can go to Subway or Blimpie's or a surrounding deli in the outside boroughs and get a hero or roll for about $3. There are many clubs that students can find to relate, ranging from the gay club to the African Students Union, to academic clubs in different disciplines. The Greek sororities and fraternities exist; however, they are not as prevalent in CUNY schools as they are at other schools.

The School Says

Located in the heart of Manhattan, Hunter offers students the stimulating learning environment and career-building opportunities you might expect from a college that's been a part of the world's most exciting city since 1870. The largest college in the City University of New York, Hunter pulses with energy. Hunter's vitality stems from a large, highly diverse faculty and student body. Its schools—Arts and Sciences, Education, the Health Professions and Social Work—provide an affordable first-rate education. Undergraduates have extraordinary opportunities to conduct high-level research under renowned faculty, and many opt for credit-bearing internships in such exciting fields as media, the arts and government. The college's high standards and special programs ensure a challenging education. The block program for first-year students keeps classmates together as they pursue courses in the liberal arts, pre-health science, pre-nursing, pre-med or honors. A range of honors programs is available for students with strong academic records, including the highly competitive tuition-free Macaulay Honors College at Hutner College for entering freshmen and the Thomas Hunter Honors Program, which emphasizes small classes with personalized mentoring by outstanding faculty. Qualified students also benefit from Hunter's participation in minority science research and training programs, the prestigious Andrew W. Mellon Minority Undergraduate Program, and many other passports to professional success.

Read all of Vault's College Surveys at **www.vault.com/college**—get complete surveys on 100s of colleges and universities, expert advice on applicaton essays and more.

VAULT CAREER LIBRARY **463**

Ithaca College

Office of Admissions
Ithaca College
Job Hall, Room 100
953 Danby Road
Ithaca, NY 14850-7020
Admissions phone: (800) 429-4274 or (607) 274-3124
Admissions fax: (607) 274-1900
Admissions e-mail: admission@ithaca.edu
Admissions URL: www.ithaca.edu/admission/

 ## Admissions

Current student, 8/2004-Submit Date, March 2007

The admissions process is pretty straightforward. You apply to the general college and then are admitted into various schools within the college. Physical therapy and communications are the most reputable and also the hardest to which to be admitted. However, even if your grades or scores are low, don't worry, your best bet is to apply as an exploratory major and after a semester, apply to one of the schools once you've shown your grades at college are much better. Selectivity is somewhere around the middle; as long as you keep decent grades and stay involved, you should have no problem getting accepted.

> **The school says:** Ithaca College also has nationally renowned programs in music and theater.

Current student, 8/2004-Submit Date, November 2006

I had applied in the spring. I didn't feel overwhelmed by the process. The advice I would give any incoming student who doesn't have good SAT scores but a good GPA would be to set up an interview because even though IC looks for the all-around student, it gives admissions a face to the name.

Current student, 8/2003-Submit Date, October 2006

They take the Common Application, so it's pretty simple. I originally auditioned for musical theater, which is extremely competitive. The people are comforting and nice but the odds of getting into the theater program are like eight out of 1,000. Eventually I just applied for the Park School of Communications and wrote an essay. I showed I was very involved in the subject outside of class and had an interest in it especially for my future and was accepted. I think as long as you show you are dedicated to what you want to study and are hard-working, they will see it and it shines through for sure.

Current student, 9/2003-Submit Date, September 2006

The admissions process was pretty standard as a music student. You had to have a letter of recommendation or two and pass an audition with your application. As a recording major, I also had to have separate recommendations to get into the program, and do an interview with the professors. This was pretty standard at all the schools to which I applied.

> **The school says:** "Students applying to music, theater and some other programs must schedule an audition or interview."

Current student, 8/2002-Submit Date, January 2006

Very basic, as with other schools. I applied early admission, very prompt response. Write meaningful essays, they can tell when someone is just writing to meet their expectations. Make sure you visit the school. For some, Ithaca just isn't for them, and for others Ithaca fits perfectly. They are selective about whom they accept, make sure your SAT scores are above average, and get involved with various community/school activities. Those give admissions reasons to accept you.

> **The school says:** "Ithaca College no longer offers Early Action or Early Decision."

Current student, 8/2002-Submit Date, January 2006

From my experience, Ithaca's admissions process was moderately selective. liked that the school didn't solely rely on SAT scores. I felt that my high scho grade point average, extracurricular activities and community involvement h a substantial impact on my admittance.

Also, the essay section provided me with the opportunity to differentiate mys and I believe it was looked at closely. Interviews are not necessary but can he your chances. One thing that stood out in my mind was the speed with whi Ithaca communicated with me regarding admission and any questions I had.

Current student, 8/2001-Submit Date, July 2004

Ithaca College receives applications from around the world. Typically, son 11,300 men and women apply for 1,550 places in the freshman class. Admissi is selective, competitive and based on high school record, personal recomme dations, SAT or ACT scores, audition or portfolio for some programs. Althou neither is required for admission, Ithaca strongly recommends a campus vi and interview.

> **The school says:** Most recently, some 13,100 men and women applied for 1,630 places.

Alumnus/a, 9/1999-5/2003, March 2004

I applied to the theatre department. After attending a private boarding school CT and having a SAT score of 1370, it was no problem to get into the scho itself. Getting into the theatre department, however, was a whole other story.

I interviewed with the director of the department and with a faculty member. brought in a portfolio showing pictures of the productions I had worked on high school and a résumé. Luckily, both were extensive, and I had receiv advice on how to lay out both of them. I found the interview to be easy becau I approached it honestly, and quite laid-back. This helped to show a confiden in my work, and in myself, that the department was looking for in potential st dents.

After talking with the faculty and people who were students at the time, I rea ized that it was the place for me to attend. I was accepted into every school which I applied, and the decision was easy for me. Ithaca College was the be possible program for me to attend.

 ## Academics

Current student, 8/2004-Submit Date, March 2007

What your major is will define how much you get out of the program. Physic therapy and communications students have very hands-on programs getting work with patients or equipment as soon as admitted. The business school very tough, but highly useful for any field to at least take a few classes. T other majors are a bit easier, though students have gone on successfully to me ical school and graduate programs. The workload is truly what you make of if you try to do every reading, you will likely be overwhelmed, but the soc scene thrives here. Classes are hardest to come by in the communicatio school, but the staff is generally understanding and makes sure every class completed in time for graduation.

Current student, 8/2004-Submit Date, November 2006

The workload is not overwhelming, but for the first semester, freshman yea was very overwhelmed by everything including registering for the spring seme ter because over the summer entering into your freshman year they do it for yo But then, you have to make the transition to doing it yourself. The professors find, are helpful. The classes are small enough that the teacher can learn yo name quickly. As a freshman and sophomore, it is hard getting into the class you want, so you mainly fill in all the classes you need and then as a junior, y get to select the majority of the classes you wish to take.

Current student, 8/2003-Submit Date, October 2006

...you put in some effort, you will pass. You don't have to be a genius to pass classes. Quality of classes is usually very good in terms of professor-student ...ationship, classes no larger than 25, on average. Popular classes are hard to ...as a freshman, but if you keep trying you will get it in due time. Professor ...ality varies; most seem like newcomers to teaching at this point. A lot have ...erience in their field, but are unsure how to apply it to the classroom.

The school says: "Average class size is 15 students. Over 90 percent of faculty have a doctorate or the highest degree in their field."

Current student, 9/2003-Submit Date, September 2006

...ter transferring from recording to music education, the program became much ...re intense. I would say that between practicing and homework, I was spend-...about five hours of work outside of class any given weekday, plus we were ...class longer and had lots of time in ensembles. Throughout my time here at ...aca, I've spent an average of nine hours a week in ensemble rehearsals, so it ...lly eats up a lot of time.

...e professors, for the most part, seemed to be very fair graders. I found that ...history courses were the most difficult because they were more like standard ...demic classes with only three exams and a paper for the entire semester. This ...ant that each of these examinations had a ton of material and if you screwed ...once, it was difficult to pull yourself out of a hole.

...ink in general, the heavy workload is one of the things I like about the pro-...m because I've become much better at managing my time, and after a few ...eks, you don't really notice how intense everything is. Second semester of ...junior year was by far the busiest year of my entire life between playing a ...o recital, student teaching and proficiencies, but it was also my most aca-...mically successful term.

Current student, 9/2004-Submit Date, January 2006

...e classes at IC are great. Size is almost always small, and professors really ...ow their students. The workload is not too large but certain majors can have ...ot of work. Getting classes is not so easy but you always have a full schedule ...the end of the first week of the semester. The classes are great and every ...jor gives you a wide variety of classes in all the different schools on campus.

Current student, Art History, 8/2003-Submit Date, January 2006

...ofessors here are generally very knowledgeable and extremely friendly. In my ...jor (art history), class sizes are small and professors are always available for ...concerns or questions students have. The workload is difficult but manage-...e.

Current student, 8/2001-Submit Date, July 2004

...e psychology department offers you two different ways to approach the field. ...our BA program, you'll enrich your coursework by participating in an inten-...e, three-semester team research project. Guided by faculty members, our ...ms have studied neural activity, humor, infant perception and the effects of ...evision. Some BA students go on to medical school or graduate schools such ...Columbia, Yale and Harvard; others take jobs with human service agencies.

...u may decide to choose our BS degree in applied psychology, an interdisci-...nary blend of psychology, economics, business and communication courses. ...e BS prepares you for careers in law and organizational psychology, as well ...other fields.

...nors in neuroscience and psychology are also available. All classes take place ...our modern facility, which houses several laboratories and offers the newest ...mputers, as well as more specialized equipment.

Employment Prospects

Current student, 8/2004-Submit Date, March 2007

...aca may be a small school, but it certainly has successful graduates in every ...ld you can imagine. The Office of Career Services offers access to an entire ...abase of past graduates and their current jobs and there are always college ...rs and alumni speakers. We even have the current CEO of Disney as an alum-

...nus! Internships are a bit harder to come by, but if you meet the right people at alumni events and aren't afraid to introduce yourself to everyone, you're likely to stumble upon people willing to help you out.

The school says: "The Office of Career Services hosts career and internship fairs, and has a number of internship resources available."

Current student, 9/2003-Submit Date, September 2006

Every report I've had says that as soon as a music education major mentions Ithaca College, they move to the top of the hiring list, specifically because we are the most prepared and ready to be teachers right out of college. The hiring rate for students who look for teaching jobs is somewhere in the 99 percent range, over the past five years. The jobs that I hear about are mostly middle of the road, standard jobs in typical schools. Every once in a while, a graduate will land a job at a school for the performing arts or a school with an insane budget for their program, but mostly it's your standard suburban schools.

Current student, 8/2002-Submit Date, January 2006

Graduates obtain great jobs after graduating from Ithaca. There are, however, not a ton of great businesses that come to recruit from Ithaca. It depends more on what the student does to market him/herself, making that the most determin-ing factor in whether or not he/she gets a satisfactory job.

The school says: "Over 1,100 businesses and organizations offered more than 3,000 job and internship opportunities to Ithaca students and alumni during the 2006-07 academic year. Students and alumni also have access to thousands of job and internship opportunities nationwide through our eRecruiting sys-tem."

Ithaca has a great reputation, though, and it is looked upon as highly selective. These characteristics provide a great background for any student who graduates from the institution.

Current student, 8/2002-Submit Date, January 2006

The employment prospects coming out of Ithaca College are strong. However, don't expect great recruiting because none of the top financial institutions recruit at IC. Three of the Big Four accounting firms recruit at Ithaca, though, which is a great starting opportunity.

The best way to get a job out of Ithaca is to network with alumni. It helped me to get my first internship at Merrill Lynch, which eventually landed me a job at an investment banking analyst group among mostly Ivy League students. I'm not saying anyone can graduate from IC and get that job, but the education and career prospects are what you make of them. To give you an idea, I can name a number of institutions where recent graduates work: Goldman Sachs, Merrill Lynch, Bank of America, Morgan Stanley, Ernst & Young, KPMG, PwC, Standard & Poor's, Disney and ESPN.

The business school has a full-time internship coordinator and very helpful Office of Career Services. As a whole, Ithaca does very well in placing students in adequate jobs upon graduation regardless of major.

Current student, 8/2002-Submit Date, January 2006

Recruiting certainly lacks on the campus; however, the alumni network is absolutely outstanding and can get you into any company you want, provided you have the credentials.

Quality of Life

Current student, 8/2004-Submit Date, March 2007

There is almost no crime on campus. Housing gets better as you move up in years, as upperclassmen get access to great on-campus apartments. But even one dorm, Emerson, has a shower in every room. Dining services is convenient, though it's almost better not to have a meal plan and enjoy the variety of offer-ings available in the pub. The neighborhood is nice, just be aware that Ithaca College is on a giant hill so you will have to do some climbing to get around.

Read all of Vault's College Surveys at www.vault.com/college—get complete surveys on 100s of colleges and univer-sities, expert advice on applicaton essays and more.

VAULT CAREER LIBRARY 465

Current student, 8/2004-Submit Date, November 2006

Ithaca College is known as one of the safest college campuses. We have our own police force for the school. The first two years, students are required to live on campus. The dining halls are decent. But if I had to choose I always loved going to the terrace dining hall for Italian food or great deserts. The towers dining hall has late night foods. So you can eat as much as you want untill 12 a.m.

> **The school says:** "Students are required to live on campus for their freshman, sophomore and junior years, unless they apply for and receive off-campus approval from the Office of Residential Life."

Current student, 9/2003-Submit Date, September 2006

The dining halls are all pretty excellent here with at least one meal that you can always eat and relatively enjoy. I think the Office of Residential Life is the worst part of Ithaca College. There never seems to be enough housing for the incoming freshmen, who end up being set up in lounges, and the dorms are pretty small. The apartments offered to upperclassmen are pretty excellent, though very expensive. I currently live off campus in a house that's very close, and though it's small and mildly ugly, it's certainly comfortable, convenient and cheap. My suggestion is to move off campus.

Current student, 9/2004-Submit Date, January 2006

The housing at Ithaca is pretty nice. We have a three-year housing requirement on campus, so there are lots of options. The furthest residence hall is a 12-minute walk from center campus. We have housing ranging from singles to six-person apartments that are all well taken care of.

The dining at IC is also varied for the small campus we have. There are three dining halls on campus that provide a multitude of different foods for everyone. This is a huge vegetarian section and also a kosher kitchen. Lastly, our fitness facility is one of the most popular places on campus.

Current student, 8/2002-Submit Date, January 2006

The fall and late spring are the best times of the year. The winter is harsh, but if you enjoy winter sports (and snow in general) Ithaca will fulfill your needs. Housing can be a pain, so expect to live on campus for two years. Great apartments on campus for upperclassmen. Three large dining halls, each has its own reputation. The City of Ithaca is the best part, many festivals and art shows make Ithaca a culturally diverse place to be.

 ## Social Life

Current student, 8/2004-Submit Date, March 2007

The bar scene is nice but you won't get anywhere if you're under 21. The local clubs tend to hold holiday events and there is no Greek scene; however, Cornell is right next door and the frats are aplenty. Dating is difficult, but on-campus parties are always happening and they are a great way to meet people.

Current student, 8/2004-Submit Date, November 2006

The bars are strict downtown so you have to be 21 to get in. Usually, students start from one bar and then bar hop all night. The bars here close at 1:30 a.m. Downtown is very close to students who live off campus. There are only academic fraternities because there is no interest in Greek life at Ithaca. The party life is a mix of open house parties on and off campus.

Current student, 9/2003-Submit Date, September 2006

There are tons of bars in the area and a lot of unique and one-of-a-kind restaurants. I think I would kill myself if I didn't have a car, and my freshman year when I didn't, I felt incredibly isolated.

> **The school says:** "Tompkins County Area Transit buses serve the Ithaca College campus daily, and most routes to downtown Ithaca and elsewhere run every half hour."

Current student, 8/2003-Submit Date, October 2006

Restaurants are great. The dating scene is lacking, as are as events. Clubs are OK; there are only two and both tend to attract old townies, which can get weird

but fun with a bunch of friends. There is underground Greek system of t sororities and one fraternity but many don't know they exist.

Current student, 9/2004-Submit Date, January 2006

Ithaca as a town in a very unique environment. By going into the commons student can experience five different cultures in one night. The restaurants exotic but inexpensive and plentiful. The bars are really popular for juniors a seniors and are busy almost every night of the week. Every student has his/l favorite.

There is also a lot of live music and comedy downtown and it is mostly free. have an indie movie theater, three normal theaters and a ton of small caf There are also a few clubs around town that have theme parties and live bar that students 18 and older can attend.

At IC we do not have Greek life. Only professional societies. The Pyran Mall, which will accomplish your basic shopping needs and Syracuse is clos also closeby, for anything else.

Current student, 8/2001-Submit Date, July 2004

Ithaca is a hub of activity, and you can choose to participate in any of over I student organizations. It has options for interests in German language, comm nity service, computing, culture and a wide variety of others. Or get invol with groups like the Diversity Awareness Committee, the Bias-Related Incide Committee or student government.

> **The school says:** There are 150 student clubs and organizations on campus.

You may conduct research on campus, pairing up with a professor or other s dents to present your results. You can also get involved in the greater comn nity by working as a volunteer or intern or performing at venues like the Han, or [Kitchen] Theatres or Ithaca Opera. And if that's not enough, explore Finger Lakes region: Ithaca is on the south end of Cayuga Lake, and the gorg waterfalls and pristine vistas are inviting to trail trekkers and day hikers alik

 ## The School Says

> Located in a small, cosmopolitan city in the Finger Lakes region of New York State, Ithaca College combines the individual attention of a small, private college with the world-class facilities of a large university. The student body includes 6,250 undergraduates and 400 graduate students.
>
> Ithaca was founded in 1892 as a music conservatory and today continues that commitment to performance and excellence. Its modern, residential, 750-acre campus, equipped with state-of-the-art facilities is home to the Schools of Communications, Health Sciences and Human Performance, Humanities and Sciences, and Music, an AACSB-accredited School of Business, the Division of Interdisciplinary and International Studies, and the Division of Graduate Studies.
>
> The college offers over 100 undergraduate degree programs with teacher certification in 15 fields and a growing selection of graduate options, including doctor of physical therapy and master of arts in teaching degrees. A student-to-teacher ratio of 11:1 ensures plenty of personal attention from the award-winning faculty. Satellite campuses in Washington, D.C., Los Angeles and London, and affiliated study abroad programs in some 50 countries provide more educational and professional opportunities.
>
> An Ithaca education emphasizes active learning in the classroom and beyond. Students gain hands-on experience in the on-campus health and wellness clinics, as well as through a nationwide internship network that accommodates students of all majors. Students may also participate in dozens of co-curricular and extracurricular activities—the college has 25 highly competitive varsity teams, more than 150 campus clubs, and it holds hun-

dreds of concerts, recitals and theater performances annually. Students manage the college's television station, two radio stations, two campus magazines and a weekly newspaper—all of which consistently receive top awards from regional and national professional organizations.

Ithaca's vibrant campus is located in one of the nation's top college towns, which is enriched by neighboring Cornell University and an international population from over 80 countries. This diversity is reflected in the local cable channel's international programming, and the in places of worship, grocery stores and ethnic restaurants throughout the Ithaca area.

U.S. News & World Report has ranked Ithaca College in its Top 10 best master's universities in the north for 11 years in a row; the college ranks in the Top 10 great schools at great prices in the same category. Ithaca was also named one of the Top 100 best campuses for LGBT students by the *Advocate* College Guide for LGBT Students. 97 percent of Ithaca College graduates are employed or attending graduate school within a year of graduation.

Marist College

Marist College
399 North Road
oughkeepsie, NY 12601
dmissions phone: (845) 575-3226
dmissions e-mail: Admissions@Marist.edu
dmissions URL: www.marist.edu/admissions/undergrad/

Admissions

urrent student, 10/2004-Submit Date, December 2005

ctually, my admissions process was very easy. I transferred from Manhattan ollege in Riverdale, NY because I had a baby. All I had to do was tell Marist out my situation, they looked at my grades and courses, and accepted me on e spot.

urrent student, 8/2000-Submit Date, September 2003

he admissions process basically comes down to first selecting to which schools u would like to apply, then tailoring each application to each specific school. epending on the school, you may not have an interview. I had a short inter- ew in which I told of my excitement about attending and how beautiful I ought the surroundings were. In the essay, I talked about my family and some- ing that changed my life, something negative that I worked into empowerment my life, namely my father passing away when I was 11. Anyway, to get back track, simply write a well-thought-out essay on whatever the topic is, and n't try too hard—just be yourself. It is you they should pick, right?

urrent student, 9/2000-Submit Date, June 2004

he admissions process is on par with most other institutions of its kind. You ill have to contact the school's admissions office to receive an application. As emory serves me, there is a $25 fee.

ou will send in all your papers and write an essay describing why you want to tend. Be creative and speak frankly, but don't sound too silly. They appreci- e honesty.

ou will get an interview if they consider you, so take this opportunity to go see e school, and if you know anyone who goes there, spend a night at the school. hat way you will know what a night there is like and if it's for you. You should ve gone to see the school already and been on one of its tours, but they don't ll you everything in those tours, so ask students what they think.

emember that a college is a business, and they simply are looking for their best stomers, so figuring out what the school looks for in its applicants is your best t!

lumnus/a, 9/1995-5/1999, June 2004

was accepted as an early acceptance, which meant I was notified of acceptance December or January. As I recall, I had very good grades going in (was

ranked 12th in my high school class), but my SAT scores weren't too good (under 1000). I've heard now that they are placing a much greater emphasis on the SAT because they are getting so many more applications. So it's becoming much harder to get in.

My essay for the application was the standard "What event in your life had the most impact on you?" For this, I really just wrote from the heart (a piece on the death of a parent). It was pretty candid about my memories and how I felt at the time.

Academics

Current student, 10/2004-Submit Date, December 2005

The workload at Marist is moderate to difficult. It is college and it is what you expect of it, but since we have so much time to complete all of our assignments, it makes it easier. The classes are very educational and provide you with the knowledge you need to make it in the real world. To get the classes and professors you want, the process is very simple. Seniors get the first choice and then it goes to juniors and so on. There a multiple classes offered every semester, and I am currently a senior and have had no trouble trying to get into my classes.

Current student, Communications, 8/2000-Submit Date, Sept 2003

I am currently studying communications, which I enjoy quite a lot. I also decided to minor in psychology. The academics here are exactly what you put into them. Some classes are harder than others, and you'll know which they are. But I suggest you take the harder classes, because you will get more out of them. Classes are very well structured here, with small class sizes and very intimate class settings. I know all of my teachers, and those relationships will benefit me greatly, not only here on campus but also in real life, as many teachers have been in the industry I am attempting to break into, or know people who are.

As far as actually getting into those classes, it can be a bit competitive, but I always get the classes I want and I think most people do, too. And again, work- load ranges from light to heavy, depending on the teacher, but it is typically moderate, and you will get what you put in to it. If you don't do homework or don't care, then you'll get a poor grade, and you won't learn anything. If you do a lot of work and listen intently and ask questions, you will walk away having gotten your money's worth for your class.

Current student, Communications, 9/2000-Submit Date, June 2004

I took the communications program at Marist, and really made it more than it was. Let me explain. We had a not very functional Television Club and a pal- try program, but with increased interest and input from my class and others, we have added a lot of new classes to improve the learning experience. By far, my favorite class was Electronic Movie-Making.

The best part of the classes is the staff (I love most of them!) and the size of the class. That is the real issue I considered when picking schools. Our average

Read all of Vault's College Surveys at **www.vault.com/college**—get complete surveys on 100s of colleges and univer- sities, expert advice on applicaton essays and more.

VAULT CAREER LIBRARY **467**

class size is around 15 to 20; I could not handle a huge class of 200. Some can, but I can't learn that way.

Popular classes are given to those who need them the most, but I never had any problems getting the classes I wanted. You can get an override, which allows you to be an extra person in a full class of 15 or 20.

Grading depends on the professors. Some are tough, and others are not. Speak to your fellow students or check out the ratemyprofessor web site to get the info on those professors.

Workload is fair, but again all of these things depend on your major and classes. If you're a science major, English major or math/IT major, your workload is high. Communications, criminal justice and psych have average workloads. We don't have low workloads. But you're paying for a higher education, so why do you want to have no work?

I have a number of professors from whom I really learned a lot, not only class-work but also life lessons.

Alumnus/a, Communications, 9/1995-5/1999, June 2004

The difficulty of the curriculum varied greatly depending on your major. As a communications major (with an emphasis on TV production) I had a fairly easy time. I didn't struggle much to maintain a 3.2 GPA. On the other end of the spectrum, I knew many computer science majors who were struggling to do the same as I was. And I have to say, these were extremely smart people. It's just that they had to take four calculus classes, I think.

Alumnus/a, 9/1996-5/2000, September 2003

I was a business and marketing major. The curriculum was challenging, but the professors were fair and always available for the most part. Most classes relied on tests, which I felt was a bit contrived, especially for a business school. After all, how many times are you graded on test material once you are in the real world? I found that I achieved the most success in classes that relied upon case studies and research. Workload varied by professor, and obviously the professors who were traditionally known for their light workload had their classes fill pretty quickly come registration.

Employment Prospects

Current student, 10/2004-Submit Date, December 2005

I have to say that the alumni of Marist seem to be very successful. We are able to work one-on-one with graduates of the college who have jobs all over the world and in many different fields. Many graduates have made it very big for themselves and work in well-known fields.

Current student, 9/2000-Submit Date, June 2004

The school is intensely committed to finding you a job. I found my job through my college's career network. They still to this day send me constant e-mails about job openings related to my major.

You sign up with their service, and they post your résumé online with monster-trak. But if you don't have a résumé, don't worry, you will; they will work with you to write one.

The most important thing I did to improve my career starting ability was to intern. I had four internships. One with News 12 New Jersey, one with a local production company, one with RNN-TV in Kingston and one with CBS in New York City. It was with those internships that my employers thought I was more marketable, and I am! That's experience!

The school has a huge listing of internships, and they will help you get anything you want. They have a web site listing all the internships by geographical location.

The school is committed to finding graduates jobs, more so than most of my friends have experienced with their schools.

Current student, 8/2000-Submit Date, September 2003

We have a lot of employers wandering around our campus, usually during the job fairs. First, you should decide what you want to do, and then try and get an internship in that field. I've done two already, and hope to get a third ne; semester. They are great fun for someone like me who loves television, and th school helps you out tremendously. Marist has a lot of alumni ranking high i their respective fields, so it helps to know that, as well.

Alumnus/a, 9/1995-5/1999, June 2004

The internship program has fantastic contacts. They can help place people pre ty much anywhere they want to go. I knew a few people who were commutin to Manhattan for full-time internships at major companies (like MTV and th Radio and Television Museum). I, personally, didn't want to travel that far, so opted for an internship at a television production company in Poughkeepsie. was a great learning experience. I learned that TV production was not what wanted to do.

As far as Career Services goes, they helped me with my résumé, but I wish I ha taken greater advantage of their services. I was under the impression I could d it on my own. As I look back at it now, this was not a good idea. My advic Get to know the Career Services staff very well. They have great contacts an will do as much as they can to help you.

Alumnus/a, 9/1996-5/2000, September 2003

I didn't feel as though Marist did enough to help its students in finding pos graduate work and underclassman internships. The department often seeme disorganized. The school had an annual job fair, but the companies almo entirely represented the Hudson Valley. For a school so close to New York Cit I found this to be very frustrating. However, Marist's reputation preceded it i almost every interview I had upon graduation.

Quality of Life

Current student, 10/2004-Submit Date, December 2005

Overall, the college seems to be safe. There is not a lot of crime or issues o campus that the students are afraid of. The housing is extremely nice and received on a point basis. The better grades you receive and the more clubs yo are in, the better chance you have of getting the housing you want. The food cafeteria food and is only as good as you can imagine cafeteria food to be, b there are many cafes located around campus and they have much better quali food. Our gyms and computer labs are excellent.

Current student, 8/2000-Submit Date, September 2003

Poughkeepsie isn't the greatest town in America, but it used to be. We are ne tled in the town of Poughkeepsie, but we border the City of Poughkeepsie on o left. The city is mainly a judicial sector, with very low-income housing. Whi it does have its share of crime and poverty, I can't say that it is a problem. W very rarely socialize with them, even when we go into the city (where all the ba and clubs are). College kids dominate the area, as there are three colleges in th same town (Marist, Vassar and Dutchess CC). Housing on campus is great, ar a priority point system assures that if you are active with campus activities, g decent grades and don't destroy your current living quarters, you will get nic housing the next year. Currently, I live in Lower West Cedar, which are six-eight-person townhouses with double bedrooms. Plenty of showers, four sinl and comfortable beds make the townhouses the first choice for me. The campu is beautiful, lots of green and right on the Hudson River. I know I made the rig choice for surroundings.

Alumnus/a, 9/1995-5/1999, June 2004

Marist has a very good housing policy. It's based on what they call priori points. You get points for your grades, how many activities you participate and more. People with more points get first choice of housing. I always had very good point average, so I got to live anywhere I chose. Freshman year, lived in a typical dorm situation (Marian Hall). Sophomore year, I lived in suite with six girls (two in a room) in the Midrise Hall. There was a good siz common area and bathroom. Junior and senior years were in the Ne Townhouses; to be specific, townhouse number M2. There were four room with two people each. It was a good living situation for a college student. The was a full kitchen, which meant no more cafeteria eating (if one didn't want eat there). It had two full bathrooms, and the bedrooms were pretty big.

arist has a gorgeous campus! When I first started, though, the Rotunda had
st been completed, and for my graduation the new library was still under con-
uction and bright yellow. It has always been very beautiful. On those warm
rly spring days, you can't find a spot on the lawn that doesn't have students
ting outside studying or playing games. And in the winter we've all tried sled-
ng down the hill on cafeteria trays.

Social Life

urrent student, 10/2004-Submit Date, December 2005

e have every restaurant and store that you can think of that is in our surround-
g area on campus. On campus we also have clubs and organizations in every-
ing. The biggest organization on campus is Campus Ministry and volunteer-
g.

Alumnus/a, 9/2000-5/2004, June 2004

Ah, the social life. I made a lot of friends at Marist, and the ironic thing is, it
was a great place to be even if you don't like to go out. Obviously, people like
to go out to have a good time at bars and parties. There is plenty of that with six
bars within walking distance or $2 cab rides if that is your idea of a good idea,
but the school does so much with clubs and planned comedians (we have had
Carrot Top and Steven Lynch come to Marist in the same year) that you could
always have something to do.

And speaking of clubs, I was involved in five over the course of the year.
Serious club sports like frisbee and hockey, intramurals like volleyball, and clubs
for every major. I can't even list them all, but it's in the hundreds. My favorite
club was Marist College Television, of which I was president. That's the way to
go! And the more you do, the better it looks on your résumé.

New York University

ffice of Undergraduate Admissions
2 Washington Square North
ew York, NY 10011
dmissions phone: (212) 998-4500
dmissions URL: admissions.nyu.edu

Admissions

urrent student, Film, 8/2006-Submit Date, October 2006

n in the film program, so I had to get good verbal SAT scores and then submit
ortfolio of creative works. If they like your portfolio, they're usually willing
overlook less than desirable grades in high school. NYU is extremely selec-
e. Because of the large volume of people who apply to the university, they
n't normally conduct interviews, unless of course your intended major is a
rforming art and you have to audition. I can only speak from my own experi-
ce and say that if you're interested in the arts in general, NYU's Tisch School
r the Arts is a dream come true. You walk through the halls and hear people
nging in unison, testing lighting equipment, painting new age art and all kinds
other things. It really is a haven for people who are willing to dedicate their
es to their chosen art.

urrent student, Business, 1/2004-Submit Date, April 2007

ern is very selective, and it bases a lot of its admissions on numerical scores
ATs, GPA and so on). Your essays and recommendations can help, but if your
AT or GPA isn't high enough, they probably aren't even going to bother read-
g your essay or recommendation. You can enter Stern as an undecided major,
d I recommend that you do that, because most people end up changing the
ajor they come in with anyway.

urrent student, 9/2002-Submit Date, April 2005

YU is getting more and more selective each year. There was no interview for
mission, though. A high GPA and good SAT score will help you a lot, as will
ming from a well-reputed or feeder school. I feel like NYU really likes to
mit international students, students of international origin or students interest-
in study abroad. They are constantly boasting about how NYU sends the
st students to study abroad and how they have the most international students.

urrent student, 9/2001-Submit Date, January 2005

e admissions process is pretty straightforward. You must fill out an applica-
n (which is not very long), get three letters of recommendation, and write an
say on one of the topics provided. I don't believe that they grant interviews.
YU, although not an Ivy League school, is a top-tier school, and over the past
v years, has become extremely selective. Every year, the number of appli-

cants increases substantially. I have even heard that it is the Number One undergraduate school in the country as far as popularity; however, it is probably also
the most expensive (tuition and room and board are now about $46,000). To get
in, I suggest that you be a very well-rounded student. NYU is all about diversity, so getting all A's and scoring a 1500 on the SATs but not doing any extracurricular activities won't cut it.

Current student, 9/2002-Submit Date, May 2004

I applied to NYU through the regular admissions process. I included an essay
that I had also submitted to a number of other schools, and I got in. It was very
simple. However, this was three years ago and the school has gotten incredibly
selective since then. I doubt I would get in again if I were to apply today with
my 1360 SAT score. My sister was recently accepted just as I was, but with a
1520. The standard has gotten higher.

I think that if you can arrange for an interview, that would be the best way to go.
The NYU admissions people with whom I dealt, and most NYU people in general, are very outgoing and easy to talk to, so I would just recommend that in
general.

Current student, 9/2000-Submit Date, February 2004

The admissions process to NYU is highly selective. The average SAT score is
1350, and the average GPA is 3.7. The application is lengthy, as are most college applications. For admittance into the Tisch School of the Arts program, for
example, a portfolio is required. Admission into the Stern School of Business is
highly competitive, and the finance program is one of the best in the nation. One
of the main things NYU looks for in a prospective student is community involvement—they want to see how the student will flourish in an exciting environment
such as New York City.

Academics

Alumnus/a, Political Science, 9/2001-6/2005, April 2007

Most classes are very large and most professors are extremely knowledgeable.
You really have to make an effort to make yourself known by the professors,
since most of the discussion elements of the education take place in recitations
with teaching assistants. Many classes use the resources of the city to enhance
your experience (e.g., fine arts classes have a wealth of outside opportunities and
city planning classes encourage sitting in on a planning board meetings and touring parts of the city). Grading seems fair but you never know if it is a professor
or a lowly TA contributing to your GPA for better or for worse. Beware of the
required writing classes. As someone who got a 5 on my AP English exam and
a 720 on my SAT verbal section, I didn't really expect this class to mess up my
GPA like it did. It was the lowest grade I got during my time at NYU and it is

Read all of Vault's College Surveys at **www.vault.com/college**—get complete surveys on 100s of colleges and universities, expert advice on applicaton essays and more.

VAULT CAREER LIBRARY **469**

not from lack of trying, just poor grading and poor explanations of expectations. This may sound like it is becoming a rant but rest assured, the positive aspects of the NYU education for outweigh the negatives and some of the professors really are very caring and interesting.

Alumnus/a, 9/1999-5/2003, September 2006

The NYU College of Arts and Sciences classes are interesting, and the professors teach the classes, not teaching assistants. You are assigned a lottery number to sign up for classes, so your chance of getting the most popular ones is random. The quality of most classes is excellent, and there are so many choices that if you get a bad one, you can always drop it and go to another class. The workload is pretty average, I think. In the Stern undergraduate classes, the workload is much higher, and the students are much more competitive. One reason is that the classes are graded on a curve. The professors are generally quite good, and are often the same ones who teach in the MBA program.

Current student, Film, 8/2006-Submit Date, October 2006

The ratio of the classes is ideal, and while the material is tough, the quality of the teachers is the best in the world. If you want an education in film, come here; there's no place else you can get this kind of education. Classes are tough and this university should only be taken into consideration if you're willing to work hard. Even students who breezed by easily in high school struggle here sometimes, but it's worth the work because the quality of education that you obtain is unparalleled.

Current student, Business, 1/2004-Submit Date, April 2007

The workload is heavy. Sternies are always working in the labs, doing team projects, getting problem sets. The quality of the classes is great, though. Stern prides itself on having really good professors, and they all really try to get to know your name and help you in any way possible. The Stern curve definitely exists, though, so getting an A can be difficult in a really competitive class.

Alumnus/a, 9/2002-5/2005, March 2006

Most of the Stern classes are based on teamwork, so projects and group presentations are a must. Some of the professors are amazing, and you will hear about them when you get here. The best way to know which classes to take and not to take is through word-of-mouth. Ask your seniors and fellow classmates and you will know what is best for you.

Current student, 9/2002-Submit Date, April 2005

I am in the College of Arts and Sciences. I chose a difficult major, economic theory. The most important thing for that is to have a really strong math background and you should be good at theoretical and practical math. The classes in my major are relatively small and there is no problem getting into them, but they generally offer each elective only once every two years, so you have to plan ahead.

The professors are world-class researchers, they are just incredible and are usually well known in the field of economics. Usually, the harder the class, the bigger the curve because they don't like to punish you for taking challenging classes. The workload is really high compared to a lot of other classes, so you have to be motivated. Get to know the professors because they can help you out so much with everything from the class to your career decisions and grad school.

Current student, English, 8/2003-Submit Date, September 2004

Workload is intense as an English major. Obviously, lots of writing and reading. Very competitive due to the variety of students who attend the university. The atmosphere of the school, overall, is very directional and cutthroat. The school is very good with class scheduling and availability. Very fair in the sense that they really try to accommodate as many students as possible and will form a new course if the number of students exceeds capacity by a lot. Professors' grading is like any other professors'—some are very fair while some are extremely harsh and not understandable. Overall, professors let you know that they are there to educate and not judge.

Current student, 9/2000-Submit Date, February 2004

The academic classes are amazing. I have taken over 35 courses at NYU, and only three of them were a disappointment to me. The professors are phenomenal. They are all experts in their fields, and they know each of the student's

names. The workload is always heavy in almost any class that you enro[ll] Grading is fair. There are many popular classes; however, since the classroo[m] sizes are small, students must register as early as their registration date allow[s] There are too many great courses to miss out on—take advantage of them yo[ur] senior year.

Employment Prospects

Alumnus/a, 9/1997-5/2001, October 2006

Wasserman Center for Career Development generally takes care of everythin[g] A student in good standing with a semi-relevant junior year internship is fai[rly] assured of landing a decent job. Although true high brow, blue blood investme[nt] banks do not recruit here for the most prestigious jobs, it is not out of the que[s]tion landing a banking offer with an excellent bulge bracket bank. Also, o[ne] thing that is very helpful and something that almost everyone must do is findi[ng] an unpaid internship with major bank during the school year. One thing remember is that employers coming to NYU Stern will expect potential job ca[n]didates to have some work experience relevant to the finance industry, and th[is] is where the unpaid internship is a great help. Depending on the department, o[ne] may even receive school credit for this.

Alumnus/a, 9/1999-5/2003, September 2006

Coming out of the Stern undergraduate program, there is a great deal of on-ca[m]pus recruiting, and you have a very good chance of getting a position in a co[n]sulting or finance company. If you are going into a more nontraditional fie[ld] such as I did (international development), you're pretty much on your ow[n] However, NYU has a great reputation, and it served me well in my job searc[h] NYU also has a good Wasserman Center for Career Development, which w[ill] point you in the right direction for most career paths—mine was just a partic[u]larly narrow field.

Current student, Film, 8/2006-Submit Date, October 2006

The work placement program here is legendary. All the senior film stude[nts] already have jobs lined up for the minute they graduate. Internships are plen[ti]ful, and can often be obtained within the first semester of your freshman year you're ambitious enough.

Current student, Business, 1/2004-Submit Date, April 2007

Great. Stern has almost a 98 percent placement rate, which means that alm[ost] everyone is getting a job. All the big firms come to recruit at Stern, although i[t's] much harder to get marketing or consulting jobs, as a lot fewer firms come recruit for those positions.

Alumnus/a, 9/2002-5/2005, March 2006

If you want to work in the business world, especially in finance, no other scho[ol] can put you in a better position than Stern. Being in the heart of downto[wn] Manhattan is the single greatest home court advantage for this industry today's world, so you will benefit from the exposure just by being here. T[he] alumni are great, and the school has some pride in its business program. And t[he] on-campus recruiting is by far the best I have seen or heard of from all of m[y] friends and peers.

Current student, 9/2001-Submit Date, January 2005

Being a top-tier university in New York City puts NYU students at a great adva[n]tage as far as employment opportunities, especially within the financial servic[e] industry. All of the top firms recruit heavily from this school. At the beginni[ng] of each semester, they hold information sessions and conduct on-campus inte[r]views throughout the semester. Students can search for jobs, whether it be campus work-study, internships or full-time opportunities, through NY[U] CareerNet online. The Wasserman Center for Career Development is a gr[eat] resource and provides and abundance of information, including employer co[n]tacts, career-building workshops and career counseling. If a student is dilig[ent] enough and willing to tap into all these resources, he/she will most likely fin[d a] position.

Quality of Life

Alumnus/a, Political Science, 9/2001-6/2005, April 2007

I have always said that dorm life at NYU is based on a series of trade-offs. The farther you get from the Washington Square campus, the nicer the dorms. For example, some dorms close to campus have terrible rooms and no A/C but you can roll out of bed into class, while dorms downtown near Water Street have beautiful apartments overlooking the Brooklyn Bridge but the area dies around 6 p.m. and you have to rely on a packed, 15-minute bus ride to get to class. You are living in New York, so the average trip to the food store will cost you $50 for a few staples. But, again, you are in New York. It is the greatest city on Earth and there is never a lack of things to experience, from Yankees games, to plays and operas, to concerts, to random movie shoots on the street and great shopping. You will find yourself missing the city after you graduate even though it is a pain in the wallet.

Alumnus/a, 9/1997-5/2001, October 2006

NYU owns most of the surrounding real estate and finding housing, either university-sponsored or private, will not be a problem. Try to avoid Weinstein, as it is by far the worst of all dorms, with tiny, dusty doubles facing the asphalt-paved inner courtyard. Alumni is the best (and most expensive) dorm that is located nearby. I highly recommend the Water Street residences: Although located around Wall Street and a bit removed from classes, the living standards are unsurpassed. The rooms have floor to ceiling windows with views of the harbor, the building is relatively new, and rooms are much more spacious than anywhere else. There is a free trolley that will take one to NYU and back.

Current student, 8/2006-Submit Date, October 2006

Housing's great, and the dining halls are decent, but I'm guessing that all college food is sub-par. That's OK, though, because there are tons of great restaurants around in the neighborhood that are really cheap. Plus, your meal plan includes something called campus cash that can be used at most of the local restaurants. The neighborhood is probably the best and safest in New York. You have to walk at least 10 blocks before you wind up in a remotely sketchy neighborhood. The campus security and police patrols near Washington Square Park make you feel very safe at all times.

Alumnus/a, 9/2002-5/2005, March 2006

If you are looking for a campus atmosphere, this is not the school for you. It is basically a bunch of buildings in the middle of a city, and the entire Village is your campus. Some of the housing is good, but you have to spend a few years through the housing system to get to the good dorms by your junior or senior year. The neighborhood is safe, though, and there is plenty of activity around at all times, with plenty of eating options throughout the downtown area (the campus dining food is not too great, so I wouldn't suggest it).

Current student, 9/2001-Submit Date, January 2005

NYU doesn't have a typical campus. Most of the classroom and office buildings are situated around Washington Square Park in Greenwich Village. The dorms closer to Washington Square are freshman-only and are traditional-style with dining halls in all but one of them. The next closest dorms are in the Union Square area and are comprised mostly of freshmen also. Most of the upperclassmen live farther away in dorms in areas like the Financial District and Chinatown. Each dorm varies in its set-up, with single rooms, multi-person suites and studio apartments. A great thing about NYU dorms is that there are no communal bathrooms: Each room or suite has its own bathroom(s).

> **The school says:** "In spring of 2006, the housing lottery system was changed to give sophomore students first choice of housing among returning students, followed by seniors, then juniors. Most sophomores opt to live in the Union Square area halls. Washington Square area halls continue to be designated for freshmen."

Current student, 8/2003-Submit Date, March 2004

The quality of life is amazing for one reason: the Village. The downtown Manhattan location is vibrant, young and absolutely perfect for the energetic, cosmopolitan students. NYU students are pampered in terms of housing (you never have to experience communal bathrooms!) but the trade-off to the Manhattan address is a hefty housing bill. If you're looking for grassy knolls and classical-looking buildings, don't come to NYU. New York City is your campus. You live more like a New Yorker and less like a college student. This lifestyle is unlike any other college student's.

Social Life

Alumnus/a, Political Science, 9/2001-6/2005, April 2007

Freshman dorms are where it starts. Like many places, most people leave their doors open and wander in and out and there are tons of floor activities to get everyone acquainted with each other and with the area. Many friends are made this way and many new hangouts are discovered. Moving out to the upperclassman dorms, as one inevitably has to do, results in a far more quiet and far less social atmosphere. There are tons of cool bars and restaurants in the Village and in the city as a whole. There are tons of places to share an amazing pizza with some friends and it seems like there is always something going on to do. Greek life is restricted to a few floors of a few buildings, and sprawling frat parties that exist at some schools are not possible here. Also, the lack of a real campus and any D-I sports teams really takes away from some of the community atmosphere for which other colleges are known. It is more like living in the city but going to school rather than simply going away to college, if that makes any sense.

Alumnus/a, 9/1999-5/2003, September 2006

The social life at NYU does not revolve around the school—it revolves around the city. The Greek scene is almost nonexistent, and most freshmen will spend their time at a bar on Bleeker with a fake ID. The dating scene among students exists, but since there is so much time spent off campus, many students date non-NYU students. To be fair, the university spends a lot of time and money organizing school events. However, most students come, pick up the free stuff being offered and leave.

Current student, 8/2006-Submit Date, October 2006

There are bars, clubs, restaurants, concerts, theatres, movie houses, fraternities, and an endless supply of entertainment and interesting people right at your doorstep. You're in the middle of it all here. The fraternities are spread out all over the city and are a close-knit community. As far as dating goes, there are over 40,000 students at this university and whether you like it or not, you'll meet a whole lot of them. It's easy to meet new people and network.

Current student, Business, 1/2004-Submit Date, April 2007

The city is your campus—it's that simple. I think at Stern there is more of a community and campus building, so it's easier to make friends. But on the whole, NYU has something and someone for everyone. The Union Square area has some great bars and restaurants. I especially recommend The Union Square Cafe, although it can be pricey.

Current student, 9/2002-Submit Date, September 2005

Social life = NYC. I'm sure you've heard that a million times, but it's so true. Forget Greek life. I mean, it exists, but it's not a thing at all. I don't know anyone in a sorority or fraternity, and it's definitely not a "cool" thing at NYU. What everyone does here is New York—bars, clubs, hanging out at people's apartments. Weekends are from Wednesday or Thursday untill Saturday, and the coolest places to go are in the East Village and the Lower East Side. Ludlow Street and Orchard Street on the Lower East Side have tons of great bars, and everywhere in the East Village from 2nd Ave. east to Ave. B also has good bars and clubs. Or sometimes, when you're in the mood to get really dressed up and spend a lot of money, Chelsea is good for the clubs that you read about in celebrity magazines. I have to say, though, that as a transfer student, it's really hard to make friends. I'm lucky that I knew people in the city anyway because NYU is really not a friendly school. People just don't talk between classes. And besides the freshman dorms, the dorms aren't social either. People have their friends, but they aren't really enthusiastic about making new ones.

Read all of Vault's College Surveys at **www.vault.com/college**—get complete surveys on 100s of colleges and universities, expert advice on applicaton essays and more.

VAULT CAREER LIBRARY 471

Pace University

Pace University
Application Processing Center
861 Bedford Road
Pleasantville, NY 10570-2799
Admissions phone (Pleasantville campus): (914)773-3746
Admissions phone (New York campus): (212) 346-1323
Admissions fax: (914) 773-3851
Admissions URL: www.pace.edu/

 ## Admissions

Alumnus/a, 9/1999-5/2003, March 2006

Very easy—decent SATs and high school grades will get you in no problem, and probably with a scholarship. If you live over 30 miles from Pace, they usually give you a resident scholarship to help you pay the insane dorm fees.

Alumnus/a, 9/2001-5/2005, February 2006

Admission is relatively standard and simple. SAT scores are required. An essay is optional, and interviews are unheard of. They are not terribly selective; however, excellent SAT scores and/or grades quickly add up to many perks such as great scholarships and the ability to participate in the honors program.

Current student, 9/2003-Submit Date, April 2005

The admissions process is really quite easy. You don't even have to write an essay if you don't want to. Interviews aren't required. Admissions are on a rolling basis, so you can apply whenever you want and can expect an answer from them within a couple of months.

Current student, 9/2002-Submit Date, April 2005

Admissions at Pace University is pretty simple. They require the SATs and a good high school GPA. We have a honors program and a CAP program for those students who are exceptional and those who need help, respectively. An essay is not required but encouraged. Best advice is to get your application in before or during the fall of your senior year. An interview is not part of the application process, but you are welcome to visit or speak with an admissions representative if you have questions. You can apply for Early Decision, or just do regular admissions.

Current student, 9/2003-Submit Date, April 2005

Aside from the general application, there was an essay/personal statement that you could write. Also, a list of clubs/activities/honors was required. No interview was needed but one was recommended. I was told to do everything possible, mandatory as well as optional, and go on a tour of the campus and meet with financial aid officers. The school is somewhat selective, as they want to have quality students attending.

Current student, 9/2004-Submit Date, April 2005

The recommended date to have your application in is March 1. 73 percent of applicants are accepted into Pace. An interview is not required but is recommended if you feel you would like to speak your mind. A personal essay is required with your application. Several topics are listed or you can choose to write an essay based on any subject.

Current student, 8/2002-Submit Date, April 2005

When applying, make sure that everything is organized and go for an interview. The essay can say a lot about the student, in general—be sure to do the topic that is mandatory and then, in addition, submit an essay that tells about yourself and how you are a well-rounded student. Submitting a résumé is another good way to let admissions know what you are capable of and what your past experiences have been.

Current student, 1/2005-Submit Date, April 2005

You start off with your application. That's easy, and every school you apply has one. There is no interview to get into this school, so you need to write essay. Whether it's one that you made on your own topic or one provided you. You're also going to need recommendations. Then to make your appliction stand out from the rest, include a résumé.

 ## Academics

Alumnus/a, 9/1999-5/2003, March 2006

The computer science department was pretty good, they were just redoing t program [when I was there,] so they have made some changes for the better. T math department is really small, so students get a lot of one-on-one time wi professors. As a freshman and sophomore, it is a little difficult to get into t really good classes. Pace lets you register based on the number of credits y have, so you can take popular classes as an upperclassman. Grading is rea easy—the class curve is in all Pace classes. So if the class is really hard a everyone is failing you will probably get an A-. Not a drastic change in wor load from high school, but students need better time management.

Alumnus/a, 9/2001-5/2005, February 2006

Most classes are small and there are some excellent professors teaching. T English department, for example, pretty much has an all-star faculty whom o could expect to find only at a top school. There are sometimes lines of 200 pe ple trying to sign up for popular professors and classes. This is where the ho ors program comes into play, as honors students get first dibs on registration.

Current student, 9/2003-Submit Date, April 2005

The classes are amazing. This is mainly because they're small classes. Avera class size is 28 students and in many cases, there are two professors teaching t class. There are no TAs, which is wonderful. Every time you go to class, y can expect your professor to be there and to learn from a person who's very w educated. Most professors are experts in their fields and have experience wor ing in the subjects that they teach. You really have the opportunity to get know your professors. Classes are very relaxed and are rarely in lecture for but are mostly in the form of discussions.

Current student, 9/2002-Submit Date, April 2005

Pace has more than 100 majors to choose from. If you are not sure about wh you want to major in, we have an undecided program in our six different schoo that covers all areas and subjects, and ranges from business to computer scienc All classes at Pace have more than one section, so you can choose different tim for the same course every semester. If a class is popular and all the sections a full, the university guarantees that another section will be open, especially make sure you graduate on time. The class size at Pace is usually about 20 to students and student-to-professor ratio of 17:1. Therefore, the small class si provides a very interactive learning environment. Grading varies from profe sor to professor and usually involves a midterm and final, papers, quizzes an depending on the class, a special report or project. Attendance and class parti ipation also play a part in grading. All classes are taught by a professor at Pa and not teacher assistants. All professors are highly qualified and prominent their fields. The workload is a lot like that of any other college, but if you ma age your time wisely and set your priorities right, it is not beyond you.

Current student, 9/2003-Submit Date, April 2005

I feel that the classes here are of high quality. The professors are excellent. Th put effort into getting to know each student, and they truly want each of them succeed. They are always available for help. Many of them encourage class di cussions and groupwork in order to keep the classes fresh and exciting. Getti popular classes and/or professors is sometimes harder than any regular class. have never run into that personally because I have priority for schedulin because I am in the honors program. Grading and workload really depends the professor. Some focus more on reading, others on writing. Some choo ests over papers and projects. It varies from class to class. The work is never too overbearing as long as you do your share; however, it remains challenging for the most part.

Current student, 9/2004-Submit Date, April 2005

The classes at Pace University are very personal. The teacher-to-student ratio is 1:15, with an average class size of 25 students. Pace prides itself on having small classroom sizes so that the professors and students get to know each other. Every student has to take core classes, which can have up to 40 students. However, once students get into classes specific to their major, they can have a class of only 10 students. Professors are very personable. Many will give you their personal e-mail addresses and their cell phone numbers.

Current student, 8/2002-Submit Date, April 2005

Classes are offered in a wide variety at the 100, 200 and 300 levels for the undergraduates. The main core consist of 60 credits. As at any university, there are courses that are more popular than others, as well as professors who are preferred over others. It's easy to find the class you want, but you register for classes by seniority and if you're an athlete. You might be left redrafting your schedule, so don't be dead set on one plan. Make at least a Plan B for yourself.

Alumnus/a, Psychology, 9/2000-9/2003, October 2003

Classes were pretty small, which I wanted. They ranged from 12 to 40 students. Because I was in the honors program, I never had any problems getting the classes I needed—I always registered first. The professors were phenomenal; they were always available and eager to help. Workload was sufficient to be challenging but never unrealistic. I was a psychology major, and I feel that the program prepared me incredibly well for graduate school, which I am attending now. I learned a lot of valuable skills and got to network early on. The professors were very knowledgeable and eager to share and stimulate the class.

Employment Prospects

Alumnus/a, 9/1999-5/2003, March 2006

Pace is located in Westchester near Pepsi, IBM and several other large companies. If you are a business graduate, you will have some really good prospects. As a math/computer science major, I didn't find that Pace offered a lot of choices. I took a job at a hedge fund after graduation.

Alumnus/a, 9/2001-5/2005, February 2006

Being a business-focused school, any business-related major will feel like a kid in a candy store at the annual job fair. Other majors may have their work cut out for them, but most students are able to find good jobs after college, as well as tons of internship and part-time opportunities while they are still enrolled through the co-op program.

Current student, 9/2003-Submit Date, April 2005

The school has a good connection with its alumni, probably because Pace is located in Manhattan. Most alumni obtain jobs in the city and therefore, it is easy for them to stay in contact with current students. The Co-op and Career Services program is stellar. There are many opportunities as far as paid and unpaid internships are concerned and all students are encouraged to register with the program in order to take full advantage of these opportunities. There are plenty of job fairs, career fairs, on-campus interviews and workshops for résumé preparation and interviewing skills.

Current student, 9/2002-Submit Date, April 2005

The Co-op & Career Services Department is there to help those students find a suitable job after they graduate at any time (even if the student graduated 10 years ago). Pace has alumni in most of the top companies in the world. Every semester, we have hundreds of companies come to campus to do recruiting, workshops, presentations and so on. Pace has career fairs and seminars held by various companies such IBM, Ernst and Young and others.

Current student, 9/2003-Submit Date, April 2005

We have one of the largest co-op programs in the state and it's a great way to get started in any career. Pace really helps everyone get a foot in the door. Every year, we have at least one job fair that brings numerous businesses here, allowing you to meet with people and drop off résumés. There are countless intern-

ships, with jobs available in any major. All students are strongly encouraged and advised to go to Co-op & Career Services and make a résumé sophomore year, and start interviewing for internships junior year. The average salary for our interns is around $13 per hour. A number of students receive jobs right after graduation from either internships, student teaching or other undergrad ventures.

Alumnus/a, 9/1997-6/2001, March 2004

Pace University offers a solid education in business, which can be an advantage when you are moving forward with a career in finance. Accounting majors tend to land great jobs, as the reputation is highly recognized. The Co-op & Career Services Departments does a fairly good job of securing internships and full-time jobs for students and recent college graduates. Like most universities in NYC, Pace has legitimate connections at many big-name companies.

Alumnus/a, 2/2001-7/2003, January 2004

Pace University has a very good career program. During your senior year, you will be enrolled in the Co-op & Career Services Department, which has many tools to help you find the right job after graduation. You are able to log into the Pace Network and apply for jobs and research companies you may be interested in. Twice a year, Pace University has a career fair: one for graduating seniors and one for alumni. Each career fair includes Fortune 500 companies such as Smith Barney, Citigroup, PricewaterhouseCoopers and others. Each career fair includes about 100 employers, sometimes more. There is a high employment rate for graduates from Pace. More than half of the student population graduates with jobs, and about a quarter goes forward to graduate school.

Quality of Life

Alumnus/a, 9/2001-5/2005, February 2006

The NYC campus is composed primarily of commuters. There are many different options including trains, buses, ferries and, for the brave, even driving. NYC students can take classes at the Pleasantville campus if they wish, which offers a completely different experience from the city (including a farm, of all things).

Current student, 9/2003-Submit Date, April 2005

Housing isn't guaranteed for all four years; however, most students are commuters from the area. The dorms are very nice, but every year they get more and more expensive. It's very expensive to live in New York City on the whole, so going to Pace, while relatively cheaper than other schools in the area, is still pretty costly. The area is probably the safest in New York City. The financial district is very quiet, especially after about 5 p.m. It's not dangerous to walk around by yourself, even at night and the area is filled with plenty of places to get what you need—24-hour grocery stores, restaurants, drug stores and shopping are all located within a block or two of the school.

Current student, 9/2002-Submit Date, April 2005

Pace University Manhattan's campus is very active and has excellent facilities and resources available for its students and residents. Pace has an on-campus library with an extensive catalog of books and other multimedia. The library has a periodicals section and personal and group study rooms. Pace offers free tutoring and a writing center that helps with papers.

The campus has a gym, student lounge with 24-hour study room with Internet access, game room, movie room and dance room. The campus is wireless and has a computer resource center with computers available around the clock for students. We have different rooms to hold events and lecture halls. We have a robotics laboratory and most of our classrooms are state-of-the-art with computers and projectors that most professors use.

We have two theatres, the Schimmel Theatre run by the National Actors Theatre and the Schaeberle Studio Theater where student plays and shows are held, as well as conferences, concerts such as the Tribecca Theater and Film Festivals and various NY political sessions in which students can actively participate. We have a on-campus book store run by Barnes and Noble. We have a counselling center that offers free counselling to students by professionals. The neighborhood is very safe, as Pace is located in the Financial District of NY. The campus is secure and has security present at all entrances. You must display your ID to get onto campus and have it on display at all times while on campus. The

Read all of Vault's College Surveys at **www.vault.com/college**—get complete surveys on 100s of colleges and universities, expert advice on applicaton essays and more.

VAULT CAREER LIBRARY   **473**

main halls are monitored by cameras and the same rules apply for our housing facilities.

Current student, 9/2003-Submit Date, April 2005

There are many housing options. You can live on the Briarcliff or Pleasantville campuses. There are all freshman dorms, upperclassman dorms, honors and athlete housing. You are able to choose in which dorm you would like to live and they are all quality facilities. Each has at least one full kitchen, one laundry room, a common area and a game room. The RAs are friendly and trustworthy. The campus is scenic and calm. It's never hectic but there is always something to do. It's very picturesque, especially in the fall.

There are two dining facilities, one on each campus. They are both set up well with lots of choices in food. The cafe hours could be a bit longer; they are actually trying to set up a deli/store to be open when the cafe is not. The neighborhood is a small town, with everything you would need (groceries, 7-11, gas, bank, post office, pizza, Chinese). Overall, the area is very safe. Between security on campus and police in town, I have never felt unsafe, even at night. Security here is 24/7 and is seen all the time. We have the blue light system; security will take you anywhere you want to go if you feel unsafe, and you are only allowed access to your specific dorm, so security here is very good.

Alumnus/a, 9/1997-6/2001, March 2004

Pace offers amazing housing accommodations in luxury high-rise buildings all over the city. I understand that freshmen must spend their first year in the infamous Maria's Towers. The campus is centered in the financial district, across from City Hall. However, you might find yourself in other buildings, where Pace also holds classes and seminars. The facilities are constantly improving, but don't expect to be swimming laps in an Olympic-size pool or using any high-tech gizmos at Pace. Dining is standard, with shades of improvement as of late. Due to the many landmarks surrounding Pace, like City Hall, NYSE, Ground Zero and the Federal Reserve, expect 24-hour security on every street corner.

> **The school says:** "Maria's Tower is the freshman residence hall on the New York campus only, but the Pleasantville campus has several other freshman residence halls. The new fitness center in Pleasantville has an Olympic-size pool available to all Pace students."

 ## Social Life

Alumnus/a, 9/1999-5/2003, March 2006

Nonexistent on campus. Need to go off campus to find anything to do. Very few clubs but a large Greek population. Most of the frats/sororities live in the townhouses, making it impossible for anyone not part of the Greek system to live up there. They are very nice—room for eight people with a kitchen and laundry, so they are in high demand.

There are very few school-sponsored parties to meet people. Most of the time, people meet through friends.

Alumnus/a, 9/2001-5/2005, February 2006

Pace is located in NYC within walking distance of some of the hottest clubs, bars and restaurants in Tribeca, SoHo and the Village. Forget the keg party, we're talking sushi and $20 cocktails. The possibilities for dates are endless. For students on a budget, there are plenty of local spots like Backyard Chicken, and the venerable South Street Seaport to go to eat and hang out.

Current student, 9/2002-Submit Date, April 2005

Pace is located in downtown NYC and you are no more than 30 minutes (maximum) away from the wonderful and endless resources of the city and the world. The university has over 100 clubs and organizations, including Greek organizations, a radio station (www.wpub.org) and the school paper

(www.pacepress.org). Besides this, there is something for every desire, fro[m] academic clubs to social organizations, cultural and religious societies. Th[e] campus is very active and there are at least two events going on every day fro[m] poetry slams to comedy nights, concerts, company presentations, talent show[s,] sport tournaments, special screenings and so on. We have concerts every yea[r.] This year we had Talib Kweli and Keisha Cole. Last year, we had Kanye We[st] and the Black Eyed Peas. We also have a reggae concert featuring different re[g]gae artists. We have special shows and parties on campus almost every seme[s]ter with special hosts. The campus is always buzzing with some activity.

Current student, 8/2002-Submit Date, April 2005

We are considered to be in the suburbs of Westchester County—our Briarcli[ff] dorm sits on the edge of the Trump golf course, so you can see where expens[es] might add up. Being located 20 minutes from the central city of White Plain[s] and 40 minutes from NYC is a great benefit. There's plenty to do: movies, bow[l]ing, batting cages, nightclubs, pool halls, malls, shopping centers, day spas—n[o] matter what you're into, you'll be able to find it. The local scene in town is als[o] on the rise—the local bar and grill are the hotspots on Thursday nights, eith[er] Michael's or Paulie's. By the end of the night you will have probably made yo[ur] way to both.

Current student, 1/2005-Submit Date, April 2005

If you live on campus, you'll have more of a social life than if you don't live o[n] campus. But there are over 100 clubs, six sororities and seven fraternities. W[e] even have a commuter lounge, with TV, pool and foozball tables. We also hav[e] common hour, which is a time when no one has class. During that time, club[s] and organizations have events such as a Build-a-Bear Workshop (where the[y] gave us a bear, we stuffed it, and they gave us a Pace shirt to put on it), Dog Tag[s] (where you could write anything on the dog tag you wanted), Go Fishing for a[n] Aquarium (where you picked out an aquarium, a fish, gravel and they gave yo[u] a little packet of food), and other events that are free to students.

 ## The School Says

Pace University offers a comprehensive education combining exceptional academics, professional experience and the New York "edge."

Diverse students take advantage of Pace's college and schools in the liberal arts and sciences, business, law, nursing, education and computing. Located in Manhattan and Westchester County near world-class centers of finance, accounting, media, health care, performing arts and technology, Pace enhances the student experience with the metropolitan area's largest undergraduate cooperative education and internship program.

Rensselaer Polytechnic Institute

Rensselaer Admissions
Rensselaer Polytechnic Institute
110 8th Street
Troy, NY 12180-3590
Admissions phone: (518) 276-6216
Admissions fax: (518) 276-4072
Admissions e-mail: admissions@rpi.edu
Admissions URL: www.rpi.edu/admission/

 ## Admissions

Current student, Engineering, 8/2004-Submit Date, May 2007

I recommend that you begin the admissions process in your junior year with a campus visit and interview if possible. In the summer, attend visiting days and go to as many information sessions as possible. Write your essay on something you care about. The most important thing about your essay is that it gives a detailed picture of who you are. Going to college is about finding the best fit where you can get a great education. Rensselaer is pretty selective, but as long as you represent yourself well and express who you are, you have a pretty good chance of being accepted.

Current student, Engineering, 8/2006-Submit Date, May 2007

The admissions process is fairly straightforward at RPI. You will have to complete the Common Application, as well as a supplement. You will be given some topics for an essay, but you may also choose your own topic. In my case, I wrote sort of autobiography. Interviews are not required, but may be scheduled if you choose so. RPI is a reasonably selective school. I believe this year has about a 0 percent admissions rate. If you are applying to the architecture program or the electronic arts program, you will also be required to submit a portfolio. I would highly recommend coming to visit at least once. We also offer overnight programs for accepted students, lunch with a current student, or spending the day going to some classes/labs) with a student. It'll help give the applicant some idea of what to expect if he/she comes here.

As far as advice to get in goes, I would recommend a strong background in math and sciences. If possible, some AP or IB level courses. We take almost any AP in which you have a 4 or 5. Registration for classes is also based on how many credits you have, so if you bring in AP credits you will get to register before most of the freshman class (and thus get the classes you want at the time you want).

Extracurricular activities are also taken into consideration. Being part of a club or two, perhaps having done some community service, or even participating in athletic teams will all count towards your advantage. Big advice for any university is to start the process early. It takes longer than it seems to fill out all the paperwork. Also, turn the paperwork in as soon as you have completed it. Certain things (such as housing) will be assigned on first come, first serve basis. If you pay close attention to the stuff sent to you and follow the directions, there's no way to go wrong. Also, if you have any questions during the process, it is probably best to call our admission office (rather than e-mail) simply because that way you can obtain an immediate response.

Current student, Engineering, 8/2003-Submit Date, May 2007

I visited four different schools, RPI was the smallest of the four. I felt like I wouldn't get lost in the crowd and I could really contribute to the school. When I came for a visit with my father, a person from admissions sat down with us and let me ask any questions I still had and let me explain my thoughts on fields of study and so on. When it came down to what school to choose, it was easy to choose RPI because of the financial aid package they offered and the way I was treated on my visit.

Current student, Chemistry, 8/2005-Submit Date, May 2007

The admissions process was really quite simple. I was able to fill out the Common Application online, and send in all my high school paperwork through my counselor. My interview at RPI was with an admissions counselor, and it was quick and painless. They asked about my extracurricular activates, how I did in high school and what plans I had for my future. They also asked why I thought RPI was the place for me, and I simply said that it had many great opportunities, both academic and social, in which I wanted to engage. The process was not stressful at all, and I received my acceptance soon after.

Current student, 8/2002-Submit Date, October 2005

In order to get into RPI, you have to be pretty smart and outgoing. About [65] percent of us are in the top 10 percent of our high school classes. When applying, you must have taken math all the way up to precalculus or calculus (depending on what your high school offers). An interview is not required but I would recommend visiting the school and speaking with any of the admissions counselors while you are deciding which school to attend. An essay is required and there is usually a choice between two key topics. Admission to RPI is pretty selective because you are going up against a great pool of students. Our average SAT is 1340 at the moment, and most of us had a decent load of extracurriculars because they like to see that you can manage great grades and an extracurricular life, as well.

 ## Academics

Current student, Engineering, 8/2004-Submit Date, May 2007

I have been pleasantly surprised by my academic experience here at RPI. Before attending, I already knew RPI's reputation as a top-tier technical university, so naturally I expected the classes to be extremely confusing and the professors to be eccentric at best. What I found at RPI was a school with classes taught in a manner completely conducive to my learning style and professors who were brilliant yet dedicated to teaching. Most classes at RPI, with the exception of a few freshman year core courses, are taught in a studio setting. Studio classes are no bigger than 50 students and most often have fewer than 30. A studio class consists of about 45 minutes of lecture and instruction time and another 45 to 60 minutes of additional time to work on a current project or solve homework problems as a group. This studio setting allowed me the opportunity to practice and master the material that had just been taught. I have found that I am able to retain more information more quickly in this setting. Also, the work time in the studio has allowed me find out which subjects are difficult for me so that I can get extra help immediately.

I have yet to be locked out of a class I wanted to take at RPI. As a freshman and sophomore, in many cases I was forced to take some of the more popular classes at odd times. As a student at RPI, if you have a strong desire to take a course, the professors will make accommodations. Most classes at RPI are graded on a standard bell curve or better. This system prevents students from having a cutthroat attitude when it comes to class projects and assignments. Instead, most students at RPI are extremely cooperative with other students in their classes. The best way to succeed at RPI is to work with other students and this is encouraged. Many projects are team based and all students at RPI are required to take either leadership or professional development classes. The workload varies significantly depending on major and individual class in each major. I have found my workload to be fair and sometimes even strenuous, but I have still been able to find time to play a varsity sport and spend time with my friends. Though the work may take a while to complete, the assignments have been worthwhile and rewarding.

Current student, Engineering, 8/2004-Submit Date, May 2007

RPI is very intense when it comes to coursework. Every student on campus would probably agree that spending a couple weekends a semester studying is not uncommon. As a biomedical engineering student, I spend a lot of time taking general engineering courses, such as Strengths of Materials and Thermals

Read all of Vault's College Surveys at **www.vault.com/college**—get complete surveys on 100s of colleges and universities, expert advice on applicaton essays and more.

VAULT CAREER LIBRARY   **475**

and Fluids Engineering, as well as advanced biomedical courses such as Tissue Bio-material Interactions and Advanced Human Physiology. The classes are excellent, my professors really seem to care about the students and are always available for office hours or extra help. The professors also grade pretty fairly, if you work hard and really show that you care about the subject, you will probably do pretty well in the class. Most of my professors tell us we must work hard to fail, it is a decision you make by not participating in the learning process. When trying to make your schedule, it can be difficult to get into the exact section you want for a course, but generally if you contact the professor you can usually get in (at least that has been my experience).

Current student, Liberal Arts, 8/2005-Submit Date, May 2007

RPI is very technocentric—it should be as one of the best engineering schools in the nation. The three largest schools at RPI are the Schools of Engineering, Science, and the Lally School of Management. There are also the Schools of Architecture (which is highly respected in the field) and the School of Humanities and Social Sciences, home of the rising electronic arts major. It is usually very easy to get into the classes you want or need—if you're having difficulties, just go talk to the registrar's office and they'll help you set things in order. Grading will consist entirely of modifiers (A-, C+ and so on) by the end of next year. About 95 percent of the professors on campus have their PhD, so you'll be learning from the best minds in the nation. The work is tough and very demanding, but it is survivable; when you do survive it, you can handle anything your career will throw at you later on.

Current student, Engineering, 8/2003-Submit Date, May 2007

Every class is taught by a professor and classes are never too big. The grading system is very fair and many of the difficult courses are heavily curved. Some professors may be hard to understand or seem not as caring about the students' education. On the other hand, there are many professors who really do care about your education and you can get to know them on a very personal level, something that is almost impossible at a larger school.

Current student, Chemistry, 8/2005-Submit Date, May 2007

Being a chemistry major here at RPI has great advantages. Because the science departments are not as large as the engineering departments, the students and faculty are very close-knit. All the professors know the students by name, they give out their cell phone numbers to students in case they have questions and so on. Not only are professors required to have office hours, but RPI encourages the open-door policy (if a professor is in his/her office, he/she should leave the door open so a student may stop by), which everyone takes advantage of. I have never had any problems getting into my desired classes. Often times, classes do cap at a specific number of students, but it is always possible to go to the professor and get signed into that class. I have done this on multiple occasions, and I have never been turned away. Grading at RPI is quite fair. During the semester, professors will give you grade estimates for your exam scores and homework. If you are not satisfied with your own work, you can go to a professor and discuss your difficulties with him/her. The professors are always willing to help an interested student. As for the workload at RPI, yes, there is a lot of work. However, that's not to say it isn't feasible. As long as you don't procrastinate too long and work efficiently, there is no problem. I have never pulled an all-nighter (and I am now a senior), and I certainly plan to keep it that way. Time management is the key to success.

Current student, Pre-med, 8/2004-Submit Date, April 2007

The academics here are challenging but not impossible. While my science courseload was very much prescribed for me, I had a lot of elective space and chose to use it getting a dual major in psychology. Being in the accelerated medical program, I always got to register on the first day of registration, a huge fringe benefit. I've really enjoyed my professors. My speech communication class, perhaps the academic endeavor that was the most tangential to my courseload, had the best professor and class design I've ever had. I work hard but I play hard, too. Students design a work plan that works for them. For me, I start doing work first thing in the morning and do work throughout the day between classes. When evening comes, I relax with friends or play intramural sports.

Current student, 8/2002-Submit Date, April 2005

I'm studying within one of our unique interdisciplinary dual major programs called product design and innovation. In the program, I'm pursuing a BS in Mechanical Engineering, and a BS in Science and Technology Studies (STS) in

the School of Humanities and Social Science. In my STS classes, we look how technology affects society and vice versa. These classes are normal around 15 students, and the professors are awesome and interesting. We ha readings for each class and when we get to class, we arrange our desks in a ci cle and discuss the reading, often getting way off topic, but that's fine.

Mechanical engineering at RPI is also awesome. We have very few lectu classes—almost everything is done studio style. The way studio classes work that they are two-hour classes that meet twice a week and have between 30 a 60 students in them, your professor, and two to six teaching assistants. You w already be sitting around lab equipment (there are different classrooms and la for each class depending on what equipment is needed), and the professor w introduce new material the first hour; then the second hour, you and a partner a group will do something hands-on to apply what you just learned. This wa if you don't understand or it's not working, you raise your hand and a TA or yo prof is there within five minutes and they don't leave your side until you've fi ured it out. You leave class every day really understanding the material.

 Employment Prospects

Current student, Engineering, 8/2004-Submit Date, May 2007

RPI's job placement rate in the last decade has been outstanding. Almost all st dents who have graduated recently have been able to secure a job or been accep ed to a graduate school immediately. RPI's Career Development Center hol two career fairs annually. At these career fairs are many Fortune 500 companie as well as smaller firms (over 200 in all). These companies realize the value an RPI degree and wish to hire students before they hit the actual job mark Boeing, Bank of America and GE are RPI's three biggest employers. The enti on-campus recruiting and internship placement process is taken care of by th Career Development Center. This is an on-campus office whose only goal is jo and internship placement. Besides career fairs, the CDC holds private résum building sessions, interview practice and has an online job and résumé databas

Current student, Engineering, 8/2004-Submit Date, May 2007

A lot of graduates go right on to industry. My friends who graduated this ye went on to work for Abbott, GE, Praxair, Kimberly Clark, Exxon, Stryker, ar Boeing. There are plenty of other companies hiring RPI students. They a highly valued for their experience and performance ability thanks to our hand on learning experiences at RPI. Using the CDC is probably the best way to g a job—attend as many networking events as possible, those are always helpfu The best connection you can make for networking are your friends at RPI. Whe they go on to industry, they provide great contacts.

Current student, Engineering, 1/2007-Submit Date, May 2007

The availability of information on internships and co-op opportunities is ve high. There are job fairs and meetings especially made for students searchir for a job, whether it is permanent or just for the summer. Most students can fir internships in an area of their choice, thanks to the career fairs and the web si Red Hawk Job Link, in which all students can sign up to be listed. This web si includes a large list of employers and allows students to submit their résumés fo the employers to look at. It also allows the students to research employers befor they arrive on campus for interviews and fairs. Most RPI graduates find a jo easily before they graduate. Some students go back to the place they complete their internship, while others seek out new places and higher challenges as gra uates. Most students leaving the engineering program obtain jobs with majo companies such as Exxon-Mobil, General Electric, Westinghouse Nuclear ar so on.

Current student, Chemistry, 8/2005-Submit Date, May 2007

The Career Development Center is the place where students go to get help wit résumé building (organization, important information); etiquette training (for restaurant interview, what to order and how to eat it); and interviewing skills (th CDC will sit you down and ask you questions, all the while videotaping you, s that when complete, you can better your problem areas). The CDC also runs tw student-run career fairs, which we had over 160 different companies attend th past spring. Also available is the Red Hawk Job Link, which is like a min Monster.com. Students post their résumés on this web site so that companies ca check for qualified students. Also, what is extremely unique about the CDC i

...nat RPI alumni (10 years back or 40 years back) can always ask for help from ...hem.

Current student, 8/2002-Submit Date, October 2005

First, we have a very thorough Career Development Center (CDC) that provides many services to our students. From mock interviews to etiquette banquets, to learning how to market yourself to top employers represents just a few of the great things they offer. It helps that RPI has a pretty decent reputation with employers from IBM to GE. We are also proud to boast that we host one of the largest student-run career fairs in the nation. With over [150] companies at our most recent career fair looking to hire for co-op positions, full-time positions and internships, the students here are able to meet and network with some of the nation's top recruiters.

Quality of Life

Current student, Engineering, 8/2004-Submit Date, May 2007

The on-campus housing at RPI is nice, but in most cases not spectacular. Barton Dormitory, the newest dorm on campus is immaculate. If you apply Early Decision and have an opportunity to secure a spot in that dorm, do not hesitate. Otherwise the dormitories are fairly standard and comparable to dorms at other universities I have visited. As an upperclassman, I chose to move to an off-campus apartment. There are tons of nice apartments within a five- to 10-minute walk of campus. Since rent in the City of Troy is fairly inexpensive, if you have a group of friends who wish to live together, I would definitely suggest moving to an apartment. The on-campus dining facilities vary in quality throughout campus. The larger dining halls on campus have a great variety of different food options, including vegetarian, vegan and kosher entrees, yet the food quality is only average. The student union has awesome lunch selections, I eat there almost every day. Maxxi's deli in the union is terrific and the quesadillas at the union grill are also very popular. Campus safety is almost a non-issue at RPI. The RPI campus is isolated from the outside community by a buffer zone of off-campus apartments and family housing. While on campus the only people you will see are students, faculty, teachers, alumni and the occasional visiting family or group of high school students.

Current student, Liberal Arts, 8/2005-Submit Date, May 2007

RPI's campus is on the small side, where you're never more than a 15-minute walk or two degrees of separation away from anywhere or anyone. Housing is required of all first-year students, and there are six freshman-only dorms, as well as spots in two mixed-class dorms to choose from. The recently built Barton Hall is a favorite amongst freshmen due to its large rooms, central air, and sense of community created within each wing. Housing is guaranteed but not required of upperclassmen, and about half of them choose to live on campus instead of the myriad apartments available off campus. There are three dining halls and eight campus eateries including two large ones in the student union and six cafes spread out in the academic buildings. Most people believe that Troy, NY, where the main campus is based, is sketchy and unsafe, but that is just not accurate. Troy is full of amazing sights, eateries, mom-and-pop shops, and plenty of things to do. I have never felt unsafe walking down the hill to Troy and back, even at night.

Current student, Engineering, 8/2006-Submit Date, May 2007

Housing is somewhat above average. Most of the dorms are in very good shape, and have a maintenance crew come by regularly to check for problems and keep it in good shape. The academics facilities, such as classrooms and labs, are absolutely great. Many of them have state-of-the-art technology. We get to experiment with some pretty cool devices. On campus we have three main dining halls. With any meal plan you get, you can access all three. There is a lot of variety, and the dining halls are typically open all day (from 7 a.m. to 7:30 p.m.). Again, it is recommended that you visit campus, so as to get some idea of the environment you will be in. We have a very well-kept campus with many open grass areas, trees and plants of different kinds. It is a pleasant campus to go outside and throw a frisbee around. Being located in Troy, NY, we are also only about 10 minutes away from Albany. I think it is a nice balance between a too metropolitan area and a "middle of nowhere" area. As far as crime and safety goes, we have the public safety department, which is available 24/7, every day of the year. We also have a system of emergency boxes located around campus,

which offer direct contact with public safety. I personally have never heard of anyone who's had to use one. Public safety also offers a free escort service to students around campus or within five minutes of campus.

Current student, Engineering, 1/2007-Submit Date, May 2007

There are a decent number of places available for dining throughout the day. There is a student union center in which there is a convenience store open until midnight on a regular basis, three cafeterias for students with dining plans, one of which has late-night dining. There are many options for a student to get food, regardless of the time of day. This comes in use because students are often up very late preparing presentations or projects. The campus is small to medium in size. Most of the academic buildings can be walked to in less than 10 minutes. There are a few different section of housing, but nothing is too far. If students choose not to walk, there is a shuttle that runs continuously until 11 p.m., connecting people from parts off of campus near athletic facilities to the main campus containing classrooms and other student housing. Students can also take the city bus for free with a student ID. This brings people all around the city, allowing students to run errands off campus without needing a vehicle. The residence halls are reasonably sized, providing students with a comfortable living experience. Most people live in doubles or triples, while some upperclassmen live in suites. Some residence halls are older and have been refurbished to meet new safety codes and student needs, while others are newer and larger, some resembling small hotels. The quality of life on campus tends to be quite good. Students rarely have trouble getting a hold of things they need or doing things they want to.

Current student, 8/2002-Submit Date, October 2005

Quality of life has drastically improved since I was a freshman. With all of our new initiatives like the First-Year Experience office (FYE), our Go Be Red campaign and a highly supportive administration, it is becoming acceptable to like being here. As with any other top engineering school, the workload gets tough and it seems that there's no time to do anything else, but we are ranked Number [Two] for Most to Do on a College Campus for a reason. There are over 160 clubs funded by our union, over [35] fraternities and sororities, and countless opportunities to just link up with some great people. Residence life here has made an obvious attempt to improve the quality of living in residence halls these past few years, as well. Freshman Hill received a much needed transformation two summers ago, we have better walkways, a renovated dining hall (food provided by Sodexho), renovations to upperclassman halls and talks about adding a new residence hall or two. With the effort that the institution is giving to improving quality of life, it is easy to say that it will only get better.

Social Life

Current student, Engineering, 8/2004-Submit Date, May 2007

I love the social life here at RPI. There are plenty of things to do both on and off campus. I generally don't leave campus very often on the weekends because I have club activities, hang out with my friends, and generally always have something to do on campus. One of the nice things about Troy is the long list of restaurants you can find locally. There are tons of places you can eat, and so many different types of food you can enjoy. Most of them offer RPI students a discount, making it even easier to enjoy all that Troy has to offer. The Troy savings Bank Musical Hall also has concerts that are nice to attend, not to mention Northern Lights, Saratoga Winners, the Times Union Arena and The Egg as other venues for music and entertainment in the area. As a member of the Greek system, I really enjoy what that has to offer me socially and professionally. It is a great way to network, providing connections to numerous alumni who have contacts at at least one company.

Current student, Engineering, 8/2006-Submit Date, May 2007

RPI is known for the number of extracurricular activities on campus. Our student union (completely student run) sponsors over 160 clubs, that range from dance clubs to martial art clubs, to professional organizations, to anything you can imagine. Troy offers several coffee shops and restaurants that are often frequented by our students. Russell Sage College (an all-women university) is also very close to RPI, and there will often be interactions between both schools. This is specially good since RPI's ratio is about three guys to every girl. We also have about 32 fraternities, as well as five sororities, that often sponsor all sorts

Read all of Vault's College Surveys at **www.vault.com/college**—get complete surveys on 100s of colleges and universities, expert advice on applicaton essays and more.

VAULT CAREER LIBRARY **477**

of events. Lastly, one of my favorite things is the intramural sports program, which includes between 20 and 30 different sports. It is very easy for students to join a team or start one with their friends. We also offer five different leagues, so there is something for every skill level. The program is very popular, and it is a great way to meet new people, make friends and just take a break from studying.

Current student, Engineering, 1/2007-Submit Date, May 2007

A lot of students date, whether with people from other schools or other RPI students. It is easy to find someone with similar interests because there are over [160] clubs and organizations on campus for just about anything people are interested in. If there is not a club for something you like, the school is very understanding and allows new clubs to be formed easily. The Greek system is very popular on campus. There are different fraternities made for special interests such as a service fraternity. Some fraternities and sororities draw together African-American, Latino and Asian students, appealing to students of these backgrounds. Others are simply open to students who want to get to know more people on campus and take part in Greek events and philanthropy opportunities. About 30 percent of campus participates in fraternities.

Current student, Pre-med, 8/2004-Submit Date, April 2007

I've found every social experience I wanted here. I've gone to crazy parties and decided I don't like crazy parties. I've gone to free operas and concerts with tickets given out at school. Gone out to eat in downtown restaurants with friends. Just chilled and discussed the most random things with hallmates and friends. I've played volleyball in 24-hour tournaments, ridden horses all day in intercollegiate competitions, and am planning on walking all night for Relay for Life. I've put on dresses for military galas and fraternity formals and put on shorts and sneaker for random football or frisbee games. I've very much enjoyed my time here at Rensselaer.

Current student, 8/2002-Submit Date, October 2005

There is a plethora of opportunities to join a club at our school, and with over an $8.5 million budget, if you don't see a club of which you would like to be apart of, the union encourages you to create one. There are more than 30 fraternities and sororities on campus, and with new ones being recognized every year, this number is sure to go up. It's a middle sized campus of about 5,000 undergrad, and 2,000 grad. It's big enough so that you don't have to see the same people every day but if you wanted to, you could. There are also countless malls and so many other things to do in the Capital Region. If you don't have a car, you can just hop on the bus for free with your college ID permits.

 ## The School Says

The oldest degree-granting technological research university in the English-speaking world, Rensselaer Polytechnic Institute was founded in 1824 to instruct students "in the application of science to the common purposes of life." Rensselaer offers more than 100 programs and 1,000 courses leading to bachelor's, master's and doctoral degrees. Undergraduates pursue studies in Architecture, Engineering, Humanities and Social Sciences, Management and Technology, Science, and Information Technology (IT). A pioneer in interactive learning, Rensselaer provides real-world, hands-on educational opportunities that cut across the academic disciplines. Students have ready access to laboratories and attend classes involving lively discussion and faculty mentoring.

Rensselaer's campus, overlooking the historic and picturesque Hudson Valley, offers facilities that encourage students to become active participants in research, discovery, and the creative process. The university is home to more than 30 research centers, including one of six original National Science Foundation nanotechnology centers in the country. Rensselaer, IBM and New York State have joined in a $100 million partnership to create the world's most powerful university-based computing center, the Computational Center for Nanotechnology Innovations (CCNI), to advance the science of nanotechnology. The new $80 million Center for Biotechnology and Interdisciplinary Studies offers ample space for scientific research and discovery, while Rensselaer's newly renovated residence halls, wireless computing network and studio classrooms create a fertile environment for study and learning. The Experimental Media and Performing Arts Center (EMPAC), opening in 2008, will encourage students to explore and create at the intersection of technology and the arts.

Rensselaer infuses its curriculum with an entrepreneurial spirit that has encouraged many students to develop new products and services and start their own businesses. Several students have operated their businesses in the Rensselaer incubator, which is the first business incubator in the United States wholly sponsored and operated by a university, and later have moved them to the nearby Rensselaer Technology Park.

The student experience is enriched at Rensselaer through a wide variety of programs and services. The nationally award-winning Office of First-Year Experience introduces students and their primary support persons to Rensselaer with experiential programs even before classes begin each fall. Other Rensselaer offices offer a host of services to students, including career development and placement, cooperative education and internships, health and wellness programs, counseling, academic advising and learning assistance, writing support, and assistance for minority, international and disabled students.

Rensselaer offers excellent recreational and fitness facilities plus numerous student-run organizations and activities, including fraternities and sororities, a newspaper, a radio station, drama and musical groups, and more than 160 clubs. In addition to intramural sports, Rensselaer's NCAA varsity sports include a Division I men's ice hockey team and 21 Division III men's and women's teams in 13 sports. Women's ice hockey has been elevated to Division I. To better meet the needs of scholar-athletes, a new East Campus Athletic Village is being planned to include a new football field with seating for 7,500, a gym, a new 50-meter pool, an indoor track and field area, indoor tennis and four outdoor tennis courts.

More information about Rensselaer and its admissions requirements can be found at www.rpi.edu.

Sarah Lawrence College

Admissions office:
Sarah Lawrence College
1 Mead Way
Bronxville, NY 10708-5999
Admissions phone: (914) 395-2510
Admissions e-mail: slcadmit@mail.slc.edu

Admissions

Alumnus/a, 9/2001-5/2005, October 2006

It used to be only the Common Application as well as a required essay of your choice, plus several short answers. Interviews aren't required but recommended. They pride themselves on diversity. I feel like it is more selective than it used to be. Not as hard as Ivy League, but not easy, either.

> **The school says:** "We have never used just the Common Application. We have always had a Sarah Lawrence College application supplement that requires applicants to submit significant extra essays."

Alumnus/a, 9/2001-5/2005, June 2006

"Passion" and "Glue" are the two buzz words in admissions. The college looks for students who are passionate about their work and who will provide glue, get involved and share their energy and enthusiasm with the campus community. Writing is also a big part of the application. I've heard it said that you can write your way into the college. Sounds easy, eh? Think again. You'll also write your way out of the college, as the curriculum and progressive philosophy demands a lot of research and writing. After four solid years on campus, not only did I fall in love with the written word, but I also became completely dependent on it as a means of expression.

Alumnus/a, 9/2001-5/2005, June 2006

The Sarah Lawrence admissions process is indicative of the type of education that the college provides: It is heavily writing based.

Current student, 9/2005-Submit Date, June 2006

Sarah Lawrence is not for everyone, so you should definitely review all the information about the college and understand what type of school it really is. I did not interview or visit before I applied, but as soon as I went to see the college on admitted students day, I immediately knew it was for me. The essays for admission should be written with care but candidly, and if you are a smart individual with a drive to undertake a unique course of study, you have a very good chance of being accepted.

Current student, 8/2004-Submit Date, June 2006

Sarah Lawrence had a challenging application for me because of the numerous essays they requested you submit. Along with the Common Application essays there were two other essays, one from a previous class with teacher commentary attached, as well as an essay answering one of four questions the college asked. Also, the college recommended applicants participate in an interview at the college, with a representative of the college or with an alumnus/a. The length and detail of the application was challenging, but it was one of the most enjoyable applications I filled out because it required a certain amount of creativity and personal reflection. Retrospectively all the essays I submitted and questions I answered during the interviews seemed to help the administration find the right place for me at Sarah Lawrence once I had been accepted. It seemed that the admissions process was a way of introducing myself to Sarah Lawrence.

Alumnus/a, 9/1997-4/2001, April 2004

The admissions process is intense, with a large emphasis on well-developed writing skills. If you prefer a straightforward traditional education (i.e., the multiple-choice world), then deeply consider if you would want to apply here. The admissions board seems to like applicants who display creativity in their aca-

demic and personal lives. Write about that random experience you had when you were working as a gas station attendant. More than anything, be original. Be yourself. Sarah Lawrence College looks for well-rounded, brilliant students who want an unconventional education. You have the power to choose your path.

Alumnus/a, 8/1999-5/2003, April 2004

The admissions process was pleasant and consisted of writing a few interesting and thought-provoking essays on current and personal topics. They had a fun open house type of procedure. I remember staying with some older students who later became good friends. This was very exciting for a high school senior. Everyone was so friendly. I loved this school.

Academics

Alumnus/a, 9/2001-5/2005, October 2006

Classes don't follow the usual numbering system. You take three classes per semester (up to four if you audit), but really, each class is like taking two classes because you have to do the regular schoolwork, as well as your conference work, which is like an independent research project for each professor. It's pretty rigorous. You get very good at writing papers. It's not easy to get popular classes. You have to interview with the professors before selecting classes, which is unusual, but really helps in terms of making sure you click. Classes don't receive letter grades, instead we get page-long evaluations each semester.

> **Regarding grades, the school says:** "Sarah Lawrence students do get grades, but mainly for the registrar's record and for use by those applying to grad school."

Current student, 9/2005-Submit Date, June 2006

The college presents itself as a rigorous academic program, and I feel it holds to this. The classes are challenging, the projects are student driven and it is imperative that you pace yourself or the work is not going to get done. The classes are good, they could be better, but I took classes with new teachers who were not used to the program. It can be very difficult to get into popular classes, as they are small and assigned randomly on the computer. Some teachers provide lists of students they want in classes, but it is still possible to get "bumped" as they say. However, some teachers are willing to take on auditors without a problem. Grades do not exist, except in the registrar's office, so they are not a focus. Teachers are good at providing written and verbal feedback to make up for this. The professors are generally nice, although I did not like all my teachers or all my classes. The workload is heavy, but manageable.

Alumnus/a, 9/2001-5/2005, June 2006

Students get to know their professors very, very well at Sarah Lawrence because of the size of the student body and the conference work system. Every other week, you sit down with each of your professors for a half an hour and work toward developing a research project. I ended up becoming very close with almost all of my professors and even a handful of professors with whom I never studied. Unusual though it may be, two of them helped me get up on my feet when I was homeless after graduation.

Alumnus/a, 9/2001-5/2005, June 2006

Although it can sometimes be difficult to get into the classes you want—as class sizes are extremely small (no more than 15 students)—the challenge is worth it. The classes are the main draw of SLC, featuring small size, one-on-one interaction with your professor, heavy workload, and lots of opportunity for personal and academic growth.

Current student, 9/2005-Submit Date, June 2006

The general structure of SLC is amazing and, in my opinion, the best I've ever heard of. Each student interviews for three classes per semester, which allows he or she to meet the teacher and understand the coursework that is planned;

Read all of Vault's College Surveys at **www.vault.com/college**—get complete surveys on 100s of colleges and universities, expert advice on applicaton essays and more.

VAULT CAREER LIBRARY 479

within each class, the student then does an independent project (called a conference project) that involves research and further study coupled with one-on-one meetings with the professor every one or two weeks. The quality of education depends on what you put into it—seriously and completely. Getting into popular classes can sometimes be hard, but there are many classes to choose from, and teachers often teach similar classes, so the opportunity is not necessarily gone forever if you don't get in the first time. If you want it bad enough and love it, you will get it. Work hard, and the reward is immense.

Current student, 9/2005-Submit Date, June 2006

If you enjoy reading, writing and discussing, than this is the place for you. If you do not enjoy these things you may want to look elsewhere or learn to adapt quickly. For your workload, expect two to three hours of reading per night per class, a couple papers due per week (both long and short), and you must be prepared to lead discussions on class reading about every two or three weeks.

Sarah Lawrence focuses very much on individuality and you will be able to pick on what you do your conference work.

It sounds like too much but it is doable, trust me. Plus side to our academics: no tests or grades. You will become an excellent writer from the millions of papers you will have to write.

> The school says: "At SLC, there are occasional tests/quizzes in some classes."

The professors at Sarah Lawrence are some of the most intelligent, artistic, kind and passionate people I have ever met. Ask your teachers about their lives and you will be completely amazed. They are all truly incredible people.

Alumnus/a, 9/1997-4/2001, April 2004

As a student, you will have a huge array of interesting courses from which to choose. There is no major system because SLC wants students to have the flexibility to explore where their interests take them. As an undergraduate, you will find yourself growing immensely. SLC's academic program is built to embrace your growth. Don't be afraid to take that environmental anthropology course because you think that you need to focus solely on fiction writing. Your conference work might involve writing innovative environmental fiction.

The classes are amazing. The class size caps at 15, and as you take more advanced courses, you can find yourself with a professor in classes as small as three or four students. Before each semester begins, students arrange to interview professors who teach courses in which they have an interest. This is essential because you will be working one-on-one with professors on conference projects. Through interviewing, you can determine if you will be able to work well together and if the course is what you want. Some art courses are very popular, so be prepared to express why the class is so important to your academic and creative interests and what your very unique self will add to the class dynamic.

Alumnus/a, 8/1999-5/2003, April 2004

Academics weren't as much of a priority as self-expression. This could be a positive or a negative. I do feel it is important for a student to have discipline in a free environment such as this. It's easy to lose touch with reality and with academic goals. Sarah Lawrence is a good school for any study in the arts and provides a moderate academic balance for you if you're interested in the arts. Many of the classes lean towards liberal views focusing on the liberation of women and minorities. There is a lot of study of new and radical voices in literature, performing arts and so forth. There's not much of a science or business program.

> Sarah Lawrence says: "We have no business classes at all, but we have a strong and growing science program."

There are good language programs. Sarah Lawrence is a wonderful school if you want to write professionally. They also have a good dance program and many opportunities to perform for other students.

Employment Prospects

Alumnus/a, 9/2001-5/2005, October 2006

There is an Office of Career Counseling, as well as tons of internship opportunities in nearby NYC.

Alumnus/a, 9/2001-5/2005, June 2006

Well, I would have to say that students who graduate from SLC are very prepared to work in whatever field they wish. Many of my friends went on to graduate programs at Ivy universities; others pursued their passions by accepting jobs that came about through internships or connections. If you're proactive about your search, you'll find many, many doors are wide open. I've had great success in the employment world since graduating with a bachelor's in liberal arts from SLC. I first worked at a boarding school in New England and now teach 10th and 11th graders at an independent school in Brooklyn. Anything is possible.

Current student, 8/2004-Submit Date, June 2006

The Office of Career Counseling provides students with resources to find internships and has people who can speak with students about job opportunities, scholarships and fellowships. Also, professors often provide connections to programs and events that relate to students' areas of interest. Finding a job after graduating is intimidating, but it seems that Sarah Lawrence prepares students for choosing and applying for graduate school.

Alumnus/a, 9/1997-4/2001, April 2004

I think that if you remain in New York or in the Northeast after graduation, then many employers will be familiar with your Sarah Lawrence education. While in school, try to take advantage of as many internships and volunteer opportunities as possible. This will give you the practical life and work skills that will be marketable after graduation. Since the school is located so close to New York City, if you have an interest, then you will probably be able to find a way to explore it. SLC is popular with nonprofits, as well as publishers and writing agencies. The Office of Career Counseling is friendly, but don't wait until a week before graduation to utilize their resources. Plan a bit. Some of my friends who graduated with me are working in art, music and writing industries. Others are working in politics, education and social services. Some are living on organic farms. A few are starting their own schools and nonprofits. Some are wandering abroad.

Alumnus/a, 9/1991-5/1995, April 2004

Sarah Lawrence College has extraordinary alumni, including Barbara Walters [Alice Walker] and Carly Simon. Sarah Lawrence alumni are especially active in the film and publishing industries. The alumni association is incredibly supportive. The alumni office is often willing to put soon-to-be graduates and young alumni together with those more established in their fields. It also has an Office of Career Counseling, which provides a great deal of personal attention. There are also opportunities for community involvement.

Quality of Life

Alumnus/a, 9/2001-5/2005, October 2006

Relatively safe neighborhood with security on campus and around it. Housing was great. Facilities include a sports center, three dining areas, a new visual arts building and a science building.

Current student, 9/2005-Submit Date, June 2006

I lived in a triple in the basement of a building. At first, I was not thrilled about living with two other people in a room that was only meant for two, but I came to like it once I was able to create my own space. I'm living in the same type of building, but I have my own room, so I have to see if it makes a difference. My main qualm about housing is that it is done at random and that everybody pays the same amount of money regardless of where they live and how many roommates they have. The campus provides a lot of opportunities for students to hang out and I feel that it is a pretty safe campus. The food isn't as bad as some people will say. Sarah Lawrence is a pretty self-contained place, as there isn't much to do in the town, but there is always the city. Crime isn't really that apparent on campus, although people do report that they have had stuff stolen from them.

owever, most of the crime updates we get from the campus are incidents happening on Kimball Ave.

Current student, 9/2005-Submit Date, June 2006

ousing is good, guaranteed and safe; the RAs are mostly very kind and can listen to any questions and help mediate if necessary. The facilities are also good but this is not a place for those in pursuit of an athletic career. The food is OK, ot great, but the main dining area has a lot of character; the health food bar, on e other hand, is very good, and a better choice. There can be crime because of ur proximity to Yonkers, and sometimes there are some anti-homosexual incidents, but I have always been safe, and security generally feels present and with reach should help be necessary.

Current student, 8/2004-Submit Date, June 2006

he administration is very accessible at Sarah Lawrence so, generally, if you ave a problem, you can find the person or persons with whom you need to peak to start solving your problem. Also, the student senate is a huge organiation with many committees that students can join in order to find ways of hanging or improving the campus. Finding the right people to speak with can e tricky, but there are tons of opportunities to meet people who can direct you wards the right office, club, teacher or administrator.

While Sarah Lawrence may not have the best relationship with Bronxville or onkers, there have been many changes in the way the college reaches out to the igh schools and other colleges in the area, and since I've been at Sarah awrence, I think there have been positive changes. Bronxville is a small and ealthy community, while Yonkers is a large city, so there is a juxtaposition etween the two closest areas to Sarah Lawrence. Also, New York City is only 10-to 15-minute train ride from the college, so there are plenty of opportunies to get off campus.

would have to say that Sarah Lawrence's health services is not what it could e. While the staff works very hard, they are not very good at providing medcal attention that is effective or cost effective. While the counseling services are mazing, the nurses don't seem to have enough resources to help students with ealth problems.

Social Life

Alumnus/a, 9/2001-5/2005, October 2006

reat social life. Tons of clubs, events and parties. Bars off campus (Malt ouse, Spinning Wheel) and in nearby NYC. No Greek life, but I say all the better for it.

Alumnus/a, 9/2001-5/2005, June 2006

here is a lot of opportunity for student involvement in a whole variety of clubs, tudent organizations, public service groups and athletic teams. Plus, New York ity offers endless opportunities for students to enjoy their free time.

Current student, 9/2005-Submit Date, June 2006

he social life at SLC is a strange beast, but a lovely one. There are not many oys if you are a straight girl, but this seems to be—though often complained bout—not such a bad thing after a while. Most people go to NYC a lot—for movies, art scene and bars—and there is also a ton of campus activities and, of ourse, parties. Everyone seems to be generally respectful of each other, for the most part, and there is not a huge social pressure to drink/do drugs, though that s certainly prevalent. There is a ton of awesome clubs, and the school can be upportive of new groups holding events and bringing excellent people to camus.

Current student, 9/2005-Submit Date, June 2006

arah Lawrence has so many clubs, ranging from people who like to eat meat to mnesty International, join one!

There is no dating scene here—really just don't date within the school it is too mall. But you can always find a honey in the city.

Current student, 8/2004-Submit Date, June 2006

There are more than enough clubs at Sarah Lawrence, which in many ways makes up for the lack of sororities and fraternities on campus. There is almost

always a school- or club-sponsored event occurring, so there are endless opportunities to meet people at parties or educational events. I would have to say that my favorite club is PETA (People Eating Tasty Animals), a club that sponsors BBQs once a month in the fall and spring.

Alumnus/a, 9/1997-4/2001, April 2004

Sarah Lawrence College tends to attract students who are highly intelligent and creative but focused on individual projects. They may work like fiends on conference projects and not spend time with friends until they are finished. However, you can always be the impetus for change. Start that community garden. Organize a campus-wide play day. Man the A/V room and watch absurd films with friends. At Sarah Lawrence, all you need is a little creativity. The school will support what you want to do. There are ample bars and restaurants in Bronxville Village as well as in Yonkers. Just remember, all you have to do is take the train south for 30 minutes, and you are in the midst of Manhattan. There is no Greek system (thank goodness). There are many clubs and organizations. I was a member of the community partnerships organization, and we were involved in a lot of community projects on campus and beyond the school. With the 75 to 25 percent female-to-male ratio, dating is easiest and most diverse for lesbians, bisexuals and transgenders. As a straight, white gal, the pickings were slim. But seriously, who has time to date when you have so much writing, reading and art to make?

The School Says

Sarah Lawrence College is a model for individualized education among liberal arts colleges offering a rigorous, innovative program of study that encourages students to take intellectual risks and explore highly challenging topics as they take an active role in the planning and pursuit of their education.

Each student works with a faculty adviser, called a don, in the Oxford and Cambridge tradition, to plan a course of study and to discuss the student's progress throughout the four years. Most courses consist of two parts: the seminar, limited to 15 students, and the conference, a private, biweekly meeting with the seminar professor. In conference, students create individual projects that extend the material assigned in the seminar and connect it to their academic and career goals. In the performing arts—dance, music and theater—students' work comprises several components that together constitute a full course.

There are no majors or required courses and the college grants the Bachelor of Arts in Liberal Arts degree to all undergraduate students. Students are expected to work in at least three of the four divisions: history and the social sciences; humanities; natural sciences and mathematics; and creative and performing arts.

While transcripts of official grades are available for graduate school, written evaluations that more clearly define strengths, weaknesses and progress are provided to each student.

Sarah Lawrence has an active study abroad program and nearly half of all juniors participate. The college sponsors academic programs in Florence and Catania (Sicily) in Italy, Havana, Cuba, Paris and Oxford, as well as a program in cooperation with the British American Drama Academy in London. Students may also study in other countries around the world. Within the U.S., Sarah Lawrence College has established exchange programs with Reed College in Portland, Oregon, and Eugene Lang College, the undergraduate division of New School University, in New York City's historic Greenwich Village. Students may also combine on-campus study with off-campus fieldwork and internships at a variety of places, including art museums, theaters and hospitals and with orchestras, dance companies, publications, social action programs, government agencies and businesses.

Read all of Vault's College Surveys at **www.vault.com/college**—get complete surveys on 100s of colleges and universities, expert advice on applicaton essays and more.

VAULT CAREER LIBRARY **481**

Sarah Lawrence's student-to-faculty ratio is 6:1, one of the lowest in the country. Students work closely with an exceptional faculty of respected scholars, writers, artists, scientists, historians and social scientists. Each faculty member is a committed teacher who attaches great importance to individual work with students. 90 percent of Sarah Lawrence's faculty members in the sciences, social sciences and the humanities hold a PhD or terminal degree. Faculty members in the arts have achieved demonstrable excellence in the fields of music, dance, theater, the visual arts and writing.

Skidmore College

Admissions Office
815 North Broadway
Saratoga Springs, NY 12866
Admissions phone: (518) 580-5570 or (800) 867-6007
Admissions e-mail: admissions@skidmore.edu
Admissions URL: www.skidmore.edu/admissions/

 ## Admissions

Current student, 9/2001-Submit Date, June 2005

Unfortunately, my admissions process was not very extensive. I applied, was accepted, visited the campus and enrolled for the fall. They offered weekend visits and overnights, and when I attended it was during their Spring Fling weekend, so a lot was going on on the campus.

Alumnus/a, 9/1997-5/2001, March 2005

I applied for Early Decision, which I highly recommend because if you really want to go to Skidmore, you can apply early and find out whether you are accepted earlier than the regular applicants. To be considered for admission, you need to fill out the application, making sure to play up your hobbies and activities. Admissions counselors are always impressed by interesting students who have participated in a variety of activities.

Your essay is also very important—take enough time to think about what you want to write and organize your thoughts clearly. You also will need three recommendations, preferably from teachers or other people who know you well. Make sure to give the people you want to write your recommendations enough time to formulate their responses and mail off the letters. Also, you will need to interview with an admissions counselor at Skidmore. Skidmore is a selective college—it's obviously not at the caliber of Ivy League schools, but it is a very good school and can be selective.

Alumnus/a, 9/1998-5/2002, February 2004

One of the conveniences of applying to Skidmore is that it uses the Common Application. But that does not make it a "common" school. Even if you are using the Common App, I would suggest paying a great deal of attention to your essay. Skidmore is a very liberal institution. They value forward and creative thought and the essay should show that you would fit into this type of environment. That does not mean that if you are more conservative you should not look at Skidmore, just that perhaps it is not your ideal institution.

In addition to the essay, I suggest going to Skidmore for an interview and campus tour, and if you can manage the time, an overnight stay. From the moment I walked onto the campus, I was hooked. I knew I had to go there. The campus is beautiful and inviting, and the people are friendly and different. The interview is a great way to learn more about how you would fit in at Skidmore.

While Skidmore is not ranked as high as other similar schools academically, it becomes harder and harder to get in each year, as the students accepted raise the bar for the next class. Above all, do not apply to Skidmore as a safety school because it is not as easy to get into as it seems, and the school deserves more than that.

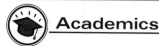 ## Academics

Current student, 9/2001-Submit Date, June 2005

At Skidmore I found the classes to be interesting and very well taught (although very liberal in nature), and I enjoyed attending them. The professors were definitely Skidmore's strong point. They were all incredibly helpful, seemed to actually care about each student's performance and I was going through a rough point in my life during these years and more than one professor took the time to talk to me and offer advice. The workloads were engaging but not overwhelming. There was always time to relax and hang out with friends.

I would say that the grading was rather generous—if you showed up and attempted to do the work, there was no way you would get lower than a C. Since Skidmore is a rather small school the good/popular classes were usually taken up if you were an underclassman student. The business program I entered was very interesting, especially their mandatory beginning class, BU 107. In it we had to research a company thoroughly, come up with a business plan that we were to follow over the next couple of years, and show how this was all to be done. Then we met with business executives, who also knew of the company and had to give a presentation. This involved using PowerPoint, other visuals and many graphs and charts. It was a great entrance into the business program for me, and really gave me a taste of what was to come.

Alumnus/a, 9/1997-5/2001, March 2005

Skidmore is a great school that offers a wide range of cool courses and majors. It offers a wonderful liberal arts education. Another neat thing about Skidmore is that is a very good school to choose if you want to study art. I minored in art and there were so many courses I could take that were taught by excellent and talented professors. Most students typically take five courses per term—the workload can be challenging but professors are, for the most part, very supportive and inspire you to do your best.

Alumnus/a, 9/1998-5/2002, February 2004

For such a small school, Skidmore has a lot to offer its students. We are one of the only small liberal arts schools in the country with a business degree (most only have economics) and a neuropsychology degree. And yet, we have an incredibly strong arts aspect to our school, including studio art, art history (featuring the new nationally renowned Tang Museum), dance, theater and music. While getting into classes is not always easy, it is something we must learn to live with if we want to keep the student-to-teacher ratio as low as it is. There are favorite teachers and classes, just as there are at every school, and eventually you will get into them if you want it badly enough.

 ## Employment Prospects

Alumnus/a, 9/1997-5/2001, March 2005

Skidmore Career Services helped me so much during my last years of college. I met with career counselors whenever I needed, and they offered insightful advice about proper résumé writing, job searching and successfully making the transition from college to the real world. Since graduating, whenever I tell prospective employers that I went to Skidmore, they are always impressed. That's a very good thing!

Alumnus/a, 9/1998-5/2002, February 2004

Career Services at Skidmore is one of the strongest I've seen. They are so help-ful in every way, from résumés to job searching. I don't know what I would have done without them!

Alumnus/a, 9/1975-5/1979, September 2003

Career Services resources were and continue to be excellent. I've had presidents and CEOs at past jobs actually shake my hand when they learned where I went to college.

Quality of Life

Current student, 9/2001-Submit Date, June 2005

Skidmore has a much better dining hall than most campuses I have visited. Student housing was also some of the best. The dormrooms were all enormous compared to other campuses', but unlike other schools, they offered nothing like pool tables or ping pong tables in the dorms.

The apartment village was also a nice touch, offering porches, grilling areas, some yard room and a nice roomy place to live. It is, however, only offered to upperclassmen, so you either had to make some older friends or wait your two years. The facilities were all topnotch. The athletic center had a nice weight room that had up-to-date equipment and new cardio machines. They have plenty of basketball courts, inside and out, a swimming pool and outdoor volleyball courts.

There is a very impressive art museum, the Tang, and the library was very nice, as well. Beautiful designs with both, and I especially appreciated the library being open very late every night.

Alumnus/a, 9/1997-5/2001, March 2005

Luckily for Skidmore students, the school is located in one of the best college towns in the country, Saratoga Springs. Saratoga has both shopping malls and cute little boutique stores lining trendy side streets. There are also bars galore and plenty of great restaurants for students on a budget. If you are from a city, you might find that the town is a little too small for your taste, but honestly it's such a pretty town and there are enough happening cafes and shops to keep most students happy and provide a welcome study break during crunch time!

Most students live on campus, either in regular dormitory-style rooms or suites. Upperclassmen can also choose to live in senior apartments with a few of their friends. Another great perk is that students—even freshmen—can keep their cars on campus. Saratoga is a very safe town—I never knew anyone at school who had a problem with safety. Campus security also does a great job.

Alumnus/a, 9/1998-5/2002, February 2004

Housing at Skidmore is above average. The rooms are large and each setup is different and interesting. Five or six people often share a bathroom, shower and two sinks, which is better than most colleges I've heard of.

The campus is constantly changing, which means technological advancements are always being made, but it manages not to disturb the beautiful surroundings. It's a perfect oasis as far as college campuses are concerned. The food at Skidmore isn't stellar, but there are always amazing options from the "make your own" section, such as omelettes, pizza, salad, waffles and ice cream sundaes. Then you have Saratoga Springs. The best college town ever. Plenty of nightlife for the party animal and culture for the studious. It is also only a few hours driv-ing from NYC, Boston and Montreal if you do get stir crazy. And Saratoga is a very safe place, which means Skidmore rarely has problems with crime.

Social Life

Current student, 9/2001-Submit Date, June 2005

Since there is no Greek system, sports teams have taken over its role at Skidmore. There is also a heavy, heavy hippie culture at Skidmore due to its lib-eral atmosphere. Drinking [can be a large] part of many of the students' lives, and the weekends can be quite fun. The bar scene is also very popular among

the party crowd, and with Saratoga's very nice downtown scene, it can be a nice weekend spot to hang out with friends. Saratoga is a beautiful area and hiking, biking and many other outdoor activities are available to whoever wants to take advantage of them. Many larger cities are nearby and weekend trips are fre-quent.

Alumnus/a, 9/1997-5/2001, March 2005

Skidmore has an awesome social scene, although if you are into the Greek scene, you may be disappointed because the school has no fraternities or sororities. I, for one, am relieved that there isn't a Greek scene because it's not something in which I'm interested. But there are events going on all week and every week-end on campus, including free movie nights, concerts, plays, lectures, exhibits and student clubs. Some of the most popular social events are the a cappella singing groups—The Bandersnatchers, The Dynamics and The Sonnateers. Their concerts were always packed. Also, we had a lot of fun events throughout the year, including Casino Night, where they set up a mock casino in the dining halls so that it looked like Vegas. Sounds cheesy but it's great fun! Also, we had a formal dance each spring, called Junior Ring, held at a swanky convention cen-ter, and a really fun Halloween party, called Moorebid (held at the Moore Hall dorm).

Alumnus/a, 9/1998-5/2002, February 2004

Saratoga is riddled with bars and places to eat. I believe it has the most bars per capita out of any college town in the U.S. But with no Greek system or major sports teams at Skidmore (two things that keep Skidmore the cozy college cam-pus that it is) sometimes the bars are needed. Desperate Annies (DA's) is a favorite among the college crowd because it is known for being the hardest bar to get into underage. This makes it the place to go once you are actually 21. Skidmore also has a ton (over 100, I believe) of clubs and organizations. Some of the favorites are the stellar a cappella groups, dance troupes and theater groups.

The School Says

We value faculty-student interactions—and they permeate every Skidmore major and program.

Great teachers but great scholars and researchers, too.

Choose from over 60 majors and minors—plus, there is unusu-al flexibility for students to self-design a major or minor.

Among the best college dorms in America and great food, too: That's what the college guide books say, and both present stu-dents and alumni tend to agree. New student apartments and newly refurbished dining halls are a campus highlight.

An extraordinary college town: Saratoga Springs isn't just horse racing and mineral springs. The range of great restaurants, bars, nightlife, shops, recreation, culture and the arts is nothing short of amazing. Plus, we're three hours from NYC, Boston and Montreal.

Beautiful and safe: Skidmore's campus isn't just beautiful but exceptionally safe and secure.

Engaged, involved students: Skidmore students perform, exhib-it, volunteer, steward the environment, travel and attend some 3,000 campus events per year—from lectures and rock con-certs to fashion shows and discussions of religion.

Read all of Vault's College Surveys at www.vault.com/college—get complete surveys on 100s of colleges and univer-sities, expert advice on applicaton essays and more.

VAULT CAREER LIBRARY   483

St. John's University

Admissions Office
St. Vincent Hall
8000 Utopia Parkway
Queens, NY 11439
Admissions phone: (718) 990-2000 (locally)
    or (888) 9STJOHNS (select option 2)
Admissions e-mail: admhelp@stjohns.edu
Admissions URL: www.stjohns.edu/admission

 ## Admissions

Current student, 9/2004-Submit Date, June 2007

I was first drawn to St. John's by all of the marketing material that I received through the mail. After I was accepted, I came on a campus tour and fell in love with the university. The admissions counselors and the student tour guides where very helpful in answering all of the questions I had. They were very knowledgeable on the history of the university, academics, financial aid, athletics, residing on campus and social life. The application process did have an optional essay that I decided to submit. The university has grown increasingly selective and is attracting more and more academically strong students. Applying here, I also knew there were plenty of scholarship opportunities that would be available to me.

Current student, 8/2006-Submit Date, June 2007

St. John's is not a particularly selective school from my experience. I was sent a special application that required no essays or recommendations. I was never interviewed, but for those more serious about admission, I would recommend it. If you really want to get into St. John's, I wouldn't recommend anything extra. Talk with an admissions counselor, tour the campus, shadow students and so on.

Current student, 8/2005-Submit Date, June 2007

I wasn't originally planning on applying to St. John's, but they bombarded me with direct mail and I eventually acquiesced. The decision to apply was the best decision I have ever made. Coming from out of state (Maryland), they made it easy for me to find out information so that I could make the right choice. I also received a very generous scholarship, which was a huge factor. My visit to the campus sealed the deal!

Current student, English, 9/2004-Submit Date, June 2007

Be yourself. Don't lie on your application. It's important to have clubs and activities to show involvement, but if you don't have an explanation why. Maybe you had a job or had to help with raising your family. And if you weren't involved in high school but want to get involved in college then say it. Do your homework about the school. Look to see the club and activities offered and talk about things that interest you. You want to tell the school how you can help it become a better and greater community.

Current student, 8/2005-Submit Date, June 2007

The application is easy, especially if it's done online. There's no interview and the essays are optional, but its best if you do them anyway. They love to give out scholarships.

Current student, 8/2003-Submit Date, March 2007

The admissions process is relatively easy. When I applied I did it through their web site and they automatically waived the application fee. I sent them a standard personal statement (that I sent to every other school). Then I was accepted. St. John's follows the Vincentian mission, a mission based on helping the economically disadvantaged, and this plays a major factor in admissions at St. John's.

Alumnus/a, 1/2003-8/2005, January 2007

Depending on the program to which you're applying, the process can vary from relatively easy to nail-biting tough. The pharmacy program has gone from being

not selective at all to incredibly selective. The Tobin College of Business admissions process has also gotten tougher over the years. Overall, admissions is too hard if you have decent grades in high school. If you have stellar grad expect either to get into the Honors Program (with nearly a full scholarship a board) or nearly a full scholarship to attend school here. The financial aid incredibly generous to those who score well and maintain high GPAs duri their years.

Current student, 1/2003-Submit Date, March 2007

Luckily, SJU has a wide range of resources and can accommodate a range of p grams not offered by other second- and third-tier schools. If a student sco below 1000 on the SAT and has below a B average, the student is not accep into a four-year degree program. Some, if they have the average, are offere spot in the St. John's two-year degree program, which is excellent and a gr bridge for smart but often immature, underachieving students. But it still mea you were not accepted.

Current student, 8/2005-Submit Date, January 2006

The admissions process was rather simple. I requested an application from school and they sent one in the mail. I had to write an essay about myself, goals, my grades and SATs had to be good. I had many teacher recommen tions, which also helped with the process. The school soon sent me an acce ance letter. Once I got into the school the freshman center was very helpful telling me what kind of grades I would need to maintain in order to be a stud at St. John's.

Current student, 1/2006-Submit Date, March 2006

Being a transfer, adult international student, I was requested to submit offic transcripts from my former college, an official TOEFL (English test) score, r high school transcript and a résumé to provide activity information after grad ation from my former college. After they reviewed my documents, they shar some questions regarding my application by e-mail and followed up by lett This was very nice since I lived outside of the country and I couldn't wait da for the letter to arrive. Once I communicated with the school's internatior admissions by e-mail and phone, everything went very smoothly and fast. A the questions were answered immediately by e-mail even after I was accepted asked my questions regarding the dormroom selections and medical insuran policy after I was accepted and admission office always replied to me with t contact information to ask those questions. I could finish everything on tir before I left country. The school admissions provided me with prompt repli with care and consideration.

 ## Academics

Current student, Marketing, 9/2004-Submit Date, June 2007

At St. John's there is a university core curriculum heavily focused on the liber arts: philosophy, theology, English, language, arts and science. There is also core within the business school. As a marketing major, I must take courses finance, management, economics and statistics, among others. Many of the pr fessors are very accomplished in their field. They do research and are regular published in newspaper articles. Also, many of these professors have worked their field before teaching at SJU. This allows these professors to relate real-world exper ence to students in the classroom.

Current student, 8/2005-Submit Date, June 2007

There is an array of majors and minors available at St. John's. There are fi colleges located within the university. The class quality is decent; it real depends on the professor who teaches the course. St. John's does have a lot adjunct professors, which is both good and bad. They are good connections your field because they may be able to help you with finding an internship. C the flip side, because they are adjuncts, it may be hard to find them on campu But e-mail is a good way of communicating with professors.

Current student, 8/2005-Submit Date, June 2007

My freshman level courses weren't too difficult, which gave me the opportunity to adjust to college coming from out of state. I learned so much in my Discover New York course, which was a huge benefit of attending St. John's. I also made connections with certain professors that continue to this day. I dreaded my first geology class, but after getting to know the professor well, I decided to minor in the subject. It caused me to think greatly about a part of my life I had previously taken for granted. Sophomore year, my business classes were much more difficult. I have been able to keep up my grades and get very involved, which has been great.

Current student, 8/2005-Submit Date, June 2007

Most of the professors are great. The classes are relatively small, so the professors usually make an effort to know your name. There is grade inflation, but where isn't there grade inflation?

Alumnus/a, 1/2003-8/2005, January 2007

The biggest asset to St. John's is its faculty of professors. Contrary to popular opinion, professors at St. John's are actually quite talented and well-versed in their respective subjects. Many, if not most, of the professors I've encountered are more about their students learning the material instead of the usual: "Take the exam; here's your grade" routine at most other research universities. Most of the professors pay careful attention to their students, and the class sizes are quite small depending on the major. The pharmacy program at St. Johns is top-notch and ranked very high.

Current student, 1/2003-Submit Date, March 2007

SJU was an awesome experience. It reportedly has gotten even better. The professors were challenging, engaging and very available. As a history and English major, I went on to take courses at NYU and degrees from Columbia and Fordham, and was more than well-prepared. Professors at those schools often inquired where I did my undergrad. I was at the top of my class at both institutions where I completed advance degrees and found SJU even more challenging than Fordham or NYU. I found my classmates at SJU intellectually equal to my colleagues at the other schools but in many ways more genuine and humble.

Current student, 8/2005-Submit Date, January 2006

I would say the quality of the classes is OK. My English professor was a very hard grader in a subject in which I think it is better to be a bit more lenient. It was not easy to get A's. Most of my professors were very helpful and I learned a lot from them. The workload for each class was moderate. My marketing professor was not very helpful, I was disappointed with his class. I basically taught myself everything in that class.

Current student, Legal Studies, 1/2006-Submit Date, March 2006

I am majoring in the legal study program at St. John's University. This program is approved by ABA and this was one of the reasons I chose this school. Class size was modest, from 20 to 30 maximum students. Every class has a computer system, which professors use for their lectures. Campus set up the wireless system and every student receives a laptop computer upon enrollment, so as students wish, they bring their own PCs to take notes and research on the Internet anywhere on the campus. There is a variety of classes and you can choose night, weekend and online classes to balance out your schedule. Professors do not give students bad grades or fail them to embarrass students, but to teach them to learn from the mistakes and overcome unexpected situations in the future. They all encourage us, suggest we grow our knowledge and skills while we are still in the school so that we are fully prepared before our graduation. Looks like only few people who wish to be paralegals major this program and the majority of students who major in legal study are planning to attend a law school upon graduation. Since we take a series of law courses, I'm sure we will be prepared to enter law school.

Current student, 1/2004-Submit Date, April 2005

Quality of professors and workload varies greatly by class. Far too often, grading is lenient, and many students get good grades who do not participate.

Regarding academics, the school says: "Students at St. John's can choose among more than 100 academic programs. Every new student receives an IBM laptop computer with full access to the university's wireless network. St. John's is the only New York-area university honored with inclusion in Intel's Top 10

Most Unwired Colleges, and our academic resources reflect this.

"Along with our varied majors, students at St. John's enjoy many unique academic opportunities. For example, all first-year students take Discover New York, a distinctive core curriculum class that uses our city as a living textbook, with students touring interesting neighborhoods, visiting museums and seeing plays. Students gain valuable real-world experience through Academic Service-Learning, course-related opportunities to volunteer locally.

"To strengthen our traditionally strong science programs, St. John's has launched a $20 million upgrade of our computer and research labs along with other science facilities. In addition, to build strong writing skills across all majors, St. John's gives students one-on-one writing assistance through our new Institute for Writing Studies.

"Personal attention in the classroom is a hallmark of the St. John's experience. With our low 18:1 student-to-faculty ratio, our internationally-known professors get to know all their students by name."

 Employment Prospects

Current student, 9/2004-Submit Date, June 2007

A St. John's degree will provide me with a wide range of employment possibilities. In the New York area, a St. John's degree is very prestigious because there are many accomplished alumni who have made a very big impact on a variety of fields. Also, the university's Career Center is very helpful with internships and employment.

Current student, 8/2005-Submit Date, June 2007

There are plenty of on-campus jobs available, but it's wise to look into them as soon as the semester begins because they fill up very fast. St. John's has a Career Center located on campus and it's resourceful to students, often holding career fairs, job seminars and so on. They help with résumé writings and even conduct mock interviews.

Current student, 8/2005-Submit Date, June 2007

Through attending alumni events through St. John's, I am amazed by the talent that has graduated from the university. I also befriended many upperclassmen and graduate students who have landed great jobs in huge companies such as Nike, Black Rock Financial, and more. I also got internship offers from great employers my freshman year, which was way beyond my expectations. Employers know that St. John's students work hard to get where they are, and have cultivated the skills to be successful anywhere.

Current student, 8/2003-Submit Date, March 2007

The average starting salary coming out of St. John's undergrad is $35K annually. They set you up with the Career Center in your senior year and there are plenty of employers who conduct on-site interviews. Among the employers who visit campus, there is Goldman Sachs (but it's for an internship), JP Morgan, law firms, banks and so on. I checked out the details on many of these employment postings and they're entry-level jobs for $30K to $35K. Additionally, there are about 20 to 30 total jobs offered through MonsterTrak job fairs in your senior year at St. John's.

Alumnus/a, 1/2003-8/2005, January 2007

On-campus job fairs usually tend to bring in local employers. However, many of my friends work for Top 25 banking companies such as Citigroup, Deutsche Bank, Goldman Sachs, JP Morgan and so on. The general student body is composed of people who are pharmacy majors, pre-med, business/finance, computer science and everyone else. Graduates from the pharmacy program are in high demand and are usually picked up by large companies such as Merck, Eckerd, Walgreen's, CVS, Pfizer and so on. Most pre-med students go on directly to medical school, or stick around and do research for a year before applying.

Read all of Vault's College Surveys at www.vault.com/college—get complete surveys on 100s of colleges and universities, expert advice on applicaton essays and more.

VAULT CAREER LIBRARY 485

Quality of Life

Current student, 9/2004-Submit Date, June 2007

St. John's is constantly looking at the most effective way to address student concerns and issues. Each year there are more and more students who want to live on campus but space is limited. To help alleviate the situation, the university has purchased of campus property for students to live. The university has undertaken many construction and master space plan improvements to provide us with a better learning environment. All of our residence halls are less than nine years old, and they are building a new student center and academic building on campus, among others. The neighborhood around the university has been attracting more and more shops that cater to the college crowd. This has provided us with an array of options of things to do off campus.

Current student, 8/2006-Submit Date, June 2007

Housing is quite nice, with some of the newest residence facilities in the country. The rooms are rather cramped at times, however, especially in Donovan Hall. It's actually nice, as I lived in Donovan my freshman year and enjoyed it, not thinking I would. Dining is sub-par but bearable, a lot of people order out with some regularity. The one dining hall is often complained of, and at times for good reason. St. John's hangs its hat on safety, especially in the residence village. The entire campus is monitored 24/7 by camera and public safety officers on patrol. Whenever you're on campus or very close-by, you should feel more than safe.

Current student, 8/2005-Submit Date, June 2007

There are always programs on campus, as long as you find them and choose to get involved in them, so you won't be bored. The area around campus is relatively safe, and is slowly becoming the college town that it has the potential to be. Lots of people hang out at the Dunkin' Donuts, which is open 24 hours, but most people head off to Manhattan for a good time. Being only a short subway ride away from the city is the best part of coming to STJ. The university provides free shuttles and all kinds of events in the city so that we all take advantage of it. And our basketball home court is Madison Square Garden! A huge emphasis is being placed on new facilities, and new buildings practically open up every year. New student townhouses, a five-story student center, and a new on-campus arena are all in the works.

Current student, English, 9/2004-Submit Date, June 2007

SJU is diverse and prides itself on its multicultural stance. I went all over the world without stepping foot off campus. I spent my summer learning the culture of people from Bulgaria and Trinidad. I was able to talk about my culture and experiences. We found common ground and we discussed issues that were larger than ourselves. We connected through family histories and love of education. And it was always safe. Public safety was around 24 hours on bike, car and foot. If I ever needed anything, they would help me. They were friendly and always said hello. The SJU staff was great and they always had kind words.

Current student, 8/2003-Submit Date, March 2007

Half the school is commuter-based. I was a commuter student, and college life basically meant what you made out of it. There were plenty of scheduled events, though—so you could definitely make a nice college life out of what's offered. The scheduled events included concerts and speakers. Nicholas Kristof of the *NY Times* was here last semester. Moreover, the student services center offered cheap $12 tickets to watch Knicks games, and affordable Broadway tickets.

Current student, 8/2005-Submit Date, January 2006

I like living on campus, although I do think security could be tighter around campus. I believe that the visitation policy is a bit too strict for people our age. My dining experience is always pleasurable. The dorms are spacious and comfortable. The quiet hours are rarely enforced, which upsets me because I take quiet hours very seriously. The RAs and RDs are very helpful and courteous, they are always around when I need help. The residence halls are always kept clean and every floor has a student lounge. The best part is there are no floor bathrooms. There is one bathroom for every five to six people, which is much better than one bath area for 30 people!

> **Regarding quality of life, St. John's says:** "St. John's 105-acre Queens, NY, campus is in a safe, stately residential community within minutes of exciting Manhattan. The 17-acre Staten

Island campus is on a wooded bluff overlooking New York harbor. St. John's ultramodern residence halls are designed with students' comfort in mind. There are ample lounges, study rooms, wireless Internet access, a Cyberlounge just for resident students and 24-hour security. Students often gather on the university's vast Great Lawn, where they chat, toss frisbees, play catch or simply study. Students enjoy a wide range of recreational facilities, including a state-of-the-art fitness center with free weights, machines, treadmills, stationary bicycles and an indoor climbing wall. With more than 180 student clubs and organizations—and our BIG EAST, Division I teams—there is always something to do on campus."

Social Life

Current student, 8/2005-Submit Date, June 2007

Social life is what you make it at St. John's. I think that the same is true at a college or university, though. St. John's has over 100 clubs and organizatio available for students to join. There is something for everyone and if there isn then you can start an organization. Student Programming Board, Stude Government, Haraya and VITAL are popular organizations/clubs on campu The university also has Greek life available. Around campus there are a numb of restaurants, take-out joints, Barnes and Noble and Cold Stone. A Manhattan is very close and easily accessible by public transportation and the S John's shuttle. There's plenty to do and get involved.

Current student, 8/2005-Submit Date, June 2007

There is always stuff going on, on campus and off, in the city! Lots of resta rants in the area have student discounts on certain nights, and the local food pretty good. My best memories have been at the Red Storm Athletic events, a I have seen some huge wins!!! Student Government's Redzone Student Sectio sponsors student events before and during all of our 17 Division I sports, wi giveaways at all the games, and sponsors away trips throughout the country f students to go and support the teams! My most memorable trips were wh men's soccer came up from behind and scored an overtime goal to win the 200 BIG EAST Tournament, or when four busloads of students went to the first tw rounds of the Women's Basketball NCAA Tournament.

I also got to see nine free Broadway shows in my first semester thanks to t Discover New York program. I have met my best friends on campus, and v always have a blast together. Our concerts have also been a blast, and the be part is that students can help plan them and work behind the scenes! Because St. John's I have met and worked with The All-American Rejects, Cia Hellogoodbye, Ne-Yo, ESPN's Howie Schwab, *ABC News*' Geor Stephanopoulos, The Yankees' Roger Clemens, and many others. I am not rea ly a partier, and the breadth of opportunities available to me makes it so I dor have to drink every night just to have fun! This is New York City!

Current student, 8/2005-Submit Date, June 2007

Well it's a dry campus, so no sex, drugs or alcohol or you're gonna get in loa of trouble, but there's always so much more to do. The sporting events on can pus are awesome, as we play some of the best college teams in the countr Student life is always giving away tickets to a Broadway show or profession sports game, not to mention giving away $5 movie tickets.

Alumnus/a, 1/2003-8/2005, January 2007

The Greek system has gained a lot of momentum over the years, and mo Greeks on campus have respectable reputations. The Greek Council mandat each organization to be proactive on campus, as well as ensures that membe maintain good academics. Most Greeks voluntarily take part in many of the o campus activities, and those who choose to go Greek usually end up getting t best overall collegiate experience.

Current student, 1/2003-Submit Date, March 2007

St. John's has a real community vibe. There is a lot of tradition at St. John's an the student body definitely connects to it. There are good bars right around can pus and lots of on-campus activities. Then, there is always NYC and our clos ness to 20 other colleges.

Current student, 8/2005-Submit Date, January 2006

The school is located in Queens, which is a [residential] area. There are many things to do off campus, including shopping, clubbing and dining. The school is also located near many subways leading to NYC, which is very convenient for someone like me who loves the city. There are also many clubs and sororities on campus. I am currently involved in the student programming board, in which we organize activities for the student body. I was also involved with OLAS and the Hispanic Cultural Society. The school has many different weekly events, such as trips to see Broadway plays, museums, shopping malls and homecomings. There is always something to do on campus whether it be plays, movies, discussions and parties.

 The School Says

If you're ready for a college that gives students a real edge for success in the global marketplace, take a good look at St. John's University.

A leading Catholic university in dynamic New York City, St. John's has everything you expect of a world-class college experience—and more. St. John's combines cutting-edge academics, a friendly campus community and outstanding high-tech resources with the most amazing study abroad options you'll find anywhere.

Choose our 105-acre flagship campus in Queens, NY, or our compact Staten Island, NY campus. By bus, subway or ferry, both residential campuses offer quick access to all the excitement of nearby Manhattan. St. John's also has a 10-story campus in Manhattan's financial district.

Founded by the Vincentian Fathers in 1870, St. John's offers more than 100 academic programs in the arts, sciences, business, education, pharmacy and allied health. Our professors are world-renowned scholars, and with our low 18:1 student-to-faculty ratio, they'll give you the personal attention you deserve.

All new students receive their own laptop computer with access to St. John's award-winning wireless network. In fact, St. John's is the only New York-area university to make Intel's Top 10 Most Unwired Colleges. St. John's further enhanced its strong science programs with a $20 million upgrade in research labs, multimedia lecture halls and other science facilities.

Our dazzling global studies options will make the world your classroom. During the semester, winter intersession or summer break, you can earn up to six credits living and learning in Argentina, Australia, Bulgaria, Brazil, China, England, France, the Galapagos Islands, Hungary, India, Ireland, Italy or Japan.

Or experience Discover the World, our amazing new global studies offering. In a single semester, you'll earn 15 credits in up to three cities for a total immersion in other languages and cultures. All global studies programs at St. John's feature specially tailored service activities that give you extra confidence while helping others.

Making our world a better place is a big part of the St. John's experience. Through Academic Service-Learning, you'll take part in course-related services activities throughout the New York area. Our active Campus Ministry also offers fulfilling service opportunities, like volunteering at local soup kitchens and helping to feed the homeless through "midnight runs."

These unique paths to your intellectual and personal growth will give you a head start in any career you choose. You'll find extra assistance at St. John's award-winning Career Center—ranked among the Top 25 college career centers by the 2006 *Kaplan Guide*.

Beyond academics, you'll enjoy all the advantages of St. John's 24/7 campus community. There are 180 student clubs, organizations, fraternities, sororities, Student Government and an active Campus Ministry that allows students to make service a part of their college experience. Of course, you'll also enjoy Red Storm Fever—the thrill of cheering for our BIG EAST, Division I athletics teams.

We invite you to St. John's in action. To schedule a visit, contact our Office of Undergraduate Admission: (888) 9STJOHNS, e-mail admissions@stjohns.edu (Queens campus); or (718) 390-4500, e-mail siadmhelp@stjohns.edu (Staten Island campus).

Read all of Vault's College Surveys at **www.vault.com/college**—get complete surveys on 100s of colleges and universities, expert advice on application essays and more.

VAULT CAREER LIBRARY **487**

Stony Brook University

State University of New York
Admissions Office
118 Administration Building
Stony Brook, NY 11794-1901
Admissions phone: (631) 632-6868
Admissions e-mail: enroll@stonybrook.edu
Admissions URL: www.stonybrook.edu/ugadmissions/

 ## Admissions

Current student, Biology, 9/2004-Submit Date, May 2007

The selection process was standard and the essay only asked for a personal statement. I also applied to the Honors College, which required a separate essay in which they asked about my most intellectual experience. The Honors College is relatively selective, but this shouldn't scare you from applying. If you think you're a good candidate, go for it. There's no interview and the scholarships that you receive are rather generous, so definitely try!

Current student, Visual Arts, 8/2005-Submit Date, April 2007

The application to Stony Brook was effortless. I applied online through the SUNY web site and filled out an application in a matter of minutes. The questions they asked consisted of a lot of personal information (e.g., support services I would like, or family information, like who went to college). The university can be pretty selective, I had a really good GPA in high school; however, my SAT scores were average, so they do not put too much emphasis on the tests. When I was accepted they sent me a very detailed brochure and admissions packet detailing all of what the freshman experience was, which was really helpful in my decision of which college.

Alumnus/a, Philosophy, 9/1995-5/2000, April 2007

The admissions process is fairly straightforward, similar to other colleges. The school is increasingly selective, and it awarded me some scholarship money. I was sold on the environment, as the campus is quite large and green (lots of tree cover). It is also easily accessible to New York City by the Long Island Railroad, which stops right on the campus.

Current student, 8/2005-Submit Date, August 2006

Stony Brook was my back-up school. I expected that I would get in, so I applied to it last. I obtained the application online, and filled it out. I was surprised that there was no essay to write and the low application fee, nor was there any interview. My guidance counselor sent all my applications with letters of recommendation, activity sheet and so on. My acceptance letter came rather quickly and was the only one I received. I cannot comment on Stony Brook's selectivity, although I will say that all the other schools that rejected me were Ivy League.

Alumnus/a, 9/2000-12/2004, December 2006

As a student of a NY school, I was recruited by Stony Brook on site at my school. There was no need for an essay. It was an on-site interview wherein you provided a copy of your SAT results along with your transcript with all your regents exam grades, as well as your GPA. It was decided right on the spot whether you are allowed in or not. I would not say that the process was intensely rigorous. It was a bit difficult to get into the computer science major. This was probably one of the most selective majors of the school. If you didn't come in with great grades, you could apply while in the school, and you must have a B+ average on two intro CS courses and one or two math courses.

Current student, Mathematics, 1/2006-Submit Date, June 2007

It is a state university, so just make sure your grades are good. It is more selective than most other SUNYs but can't compare to the prestigious private ones. No interviews required when I got in. As far as I know, extra activities and essays, besides grades, count a lot if you want to get into the honor programs or want to get scholarships. There is not so much pain in the whole process.

The international student population is huge at Stony Brook. I came here as an international student and the admissions process is a little bit different than the normal ones. Most students need TOEFL, a high school transcript, recommendation letters from teachers and a personal statement. SATs are a plus for international students but most of my friends didn't bother to take them, considering the verbal part is such a pain. As long as you have good TOEFL and high school GPA, gaining admission is not a problem at all.

Current student, 8/2005-Submit Date, May 2006

I was accepted into the Honors College at SUNY Stony Brook, which required above a [1300] on the [critical reading and math portions] of the SAT. There no interview required, but it is helpful if you would like to get a feel of the school. The essays are simple to write. In order to get into the Honors College you have to fill out a [supplemental] application and an essay. 60 students are accepted each year, so that program itself is pretty selective.

Current student, 8/2005-Submit Date, May 2006

It's basically the same as any state school. You fill out the main SUNY application and then you have the option of filling out the [supplemental] Stony Brook application, which includes an essay. For those of you who are applying to Stony Brook as your safety school and your top choices are major private schools or Ivy Leagues, think about applying for the Honors College or Women in Science and Engineering (WISE) programs. That way if you end up coming here, you'll be with kids who are at the same intellectual level as you and you'll have an automatic community going into freshman year. It's not that much more work, just an essay that's probably the same as every other one you've written and checking a box at the end of the application.

Current student, 8/2005-Submit Date, May 2006

I found that the essay has a lot to do with the admissions process. I got a lot of advice about writing an exciting essay because it would supposedly make all the difference. Later, when I got to college, admissions people told me the same thing. Transcript grades are only numbers in the end, as well as your rank and APs. The essay should be what illuminates your whole application; it should provide an account of a non-academic part of your life.

 ## Academics

Current student, 1/2005-Submit Date, May 2007

Classes can be tough, but bearing down and studying when the time calls for gives you no reason to do bad in a class. Popular classes are always tough to get into, but schedules are sometimes so flexible that if you can't get in a class one semester, you can almost all the time find a different class to take, and take the ones you missed another time. Fall and spring semesters aren't the only time take classes. Winter and summer sessions always are available.

Current student, Biology, 9/2004-Submit Date, May 2007

Stony Brook provides a relatively well-rounded curriculum, but most people know the school for its sciences. As a biology major, I have enjoyed most of courses and the workload or grading differs between classes. The introductory courses weren't very difficult, but the upper-division courses were a much greater challenge. The most difficult courses that I took were Mammalian Physiology and Animal Physiology labs, both of which I loved but had to work the hardest that I've ever worked. The professors are nice and helpful but you have to make sure that you use their office hours. As for grading, it may vary between classes, but the larger lectures are generally on a curve.

Current student, Theatre, 8/2005-Submit Date, April 2007

As a theatre arts major I am definitely a minority on campus. The theatre classes are average, about 15 to 20 people per class. The facilities are always in use which is nice and the opportunity to get your hands dirty is abundant, which is great. I had no problem getting to know the theatre department professors very well by the second semester of freshman year. Unfortunately, many of the theatre

e classes are in high demand because they also correspond to other fields of
dy, so getting into some classes is very hard. The grading system at Stony
ook is varied. As a theatre student I am not tested with paper, but with mem-
zation. I am also an Asian and Asian-American studies minor, which was a
oice I made after taking a wonderful survey of Indian dance class. I do get
says and tests in those classes, but they are not extremely hard and I do well
them. Workload, in general, varies considerably depending on which major
u are, as well as what type of person you are. Sometimes it is very easy to not
anything and just show up for tests. Other times, it is imperative that you do
that is asked of you in order to get an A. The professors I have had so far
ve all be extremely personable. All the professors in my theatre classes know
name and I call them all by their first names, the atmosphere is very relaxed.

rrent student, Biology, 8/2005-Submit Date, August 2006

y program is very intense. I intend to pursue a biology major. The workload
mmense with much reading, studying and overall preparation before and after
ch class. Nevertheless, the material learned in each class is worth all the time,
ort and sacrifice in the long run. The professors are very kind and eager to
lp. Depending on the class, there may be a long waitlist and you may find
urself sacrificing a fun but less important class for a more important one. This
ostly happens for science courses like biology, probably due to Stony Brook's
ture as a university of sciences.

rrent student, 8/2004-Submit Date, August 2006

r science classes are especially tough, Organic Chemistry in particular. We
o have to fulfill a group of DECs, as we call them, which are liberal arts cours-
    I have had wonderful professors; however, I have also had terrible ones.
ading is often fair but there are some courses that I and many others felt were
ded unfairly.

umnus/a, 9/2000-12/2004, December 2006

ofessors really depend on your major. A lot of the departments at Stony Brook
e diminished in terms of instructor talent. For example, the mathematics
partment often had graduate TAs teaching math courses due to the lack of
structors. The computer science program, however, is very good. They have
cently made the switch to start teaching in Java for most of the required cours-
and it has paid off for me thus far. It is very tough. If you can make it in, it
difficult to stay in. Most people end up downgrading to information systems,
ich is a mix of CS and business. This is a good major for those who want to
derstand business and have the IT background: ideal for those who want to
come business analysts for large banks and companies. The IS major is still a
tougher because you are still required to take some of the harder intro cours-
in the CS major. So even with that major, a lot of people end up falling down
the business major, which is far from competitive. Although they have made
ides to make it into a legitimate program, the courses are very easy and the
ndards are quite low. I have taken some courses and was surprised by how
le I learned and how easy it was. The pre-med program is also quite good.
eir affiliation with the university hospital is a definite plus since a sizable por-
n of their incoming med students are Stony Brook undergrads.

rrent student, Mathematics, 1/2006-Submit Date, June 2007

e quality of classes really differ, depending on your majors and classes you
e taking. Science, such as chemistry, biology and mathematics are killers, to
ost kids considering the big pre-med population here. The liberty art programs
e easy. It is a pain to get into some science classes, although they are 400-stu-
nt classes. Some classes are full even before my registering dates. The grades
r science classes are hard, since the smartest kids are there. The workload is
t easy. Professors are not approachable in big classes but there are always tons
TAs who are much more patient.

rrent student, Engineering, 8/2003-Submit Date, June 2006

rrently, I am in the mechanical engineering program. If you are in the pro-
am, they do not block you out of any classes because everyone is on the same
hedule. It is a little difficult, however, to get popular classes outside the major
you do not have priority registration. That comes with age or a specialized
ogram. The grading is hard for the first two years because they are using that
a weed-out technique. If you fail the class, you can't move on, so people drop
e major. The workload is extensive and monotonous for engineering until you
ach your senior year, when you do a senior design, which puts everything
u've learned to use.

Employment Prospects

Current student, Mathematics, 1/2006-Submit Date, June 2007

The employment for IT and engineering students are pretty good. It is a big science and engineering school.

Current student, Visual Arts, 8/2005-Submit Date, April 2007

Although I have not graduated yet, I do know of many people who have walked
right into jobs the moment they left campus. I have a friend who was offered a job
in his senior year as a teaching assistant to help pay for his master's in teaching.

Stony Brook is also very well-known for its biology/chemistry programs and the
medical school is in high demand. Graduating with a Stony Brook degree is very
helpful when trying to get into graduate schools. I have another friend who was
just accepted to Teacher's College in NYC to train as a biology teacher.

Current student, 8/2003-Submit Date, June 2006

It is practically impossible to obtain an internship if you live more than 15 miles
from the university because the engineering dept's connections do not reach
beyond that. Employment prospects are awesome for graduating seniors and a
large number of them decide to pursue master's degrees. These days it's easier
to look online for a job than to attend the career fairs.

Current student, 8/2005-Submit Date, May 2006

There is a Career Center on campus that offers weekly workshops on improving
interview skills, résumés and networking, and on getting internship and job
opportunities. There are several career fairs on campus, and many Long Island
companies attend.

Current student, 9/2003-Submit Date, May 2006

The university's Career Center is pretty good. There is always someone there to
help you with whatever you need. There are more business, health science and
computer science related job postings available than anything else but if you go
directly to your major department, they have major specific postings also. I get
periodic e-mails about upcoming job fairs and employers on campus, so I feel
that there are a lot of opportunities on campus if you take the time to take advantage of them. I have access to an alumni network outside of the school through
my sorority so I don't have much knowledge of the alumni network on campus.

Current student, 8/2002-Submit Date, October 2004

Graduates have a high chance of getting a job in the market because we are located so close to New York City. Most of the students of Stony Brook reside in the
metro area of NY, so it's helpful to them. There are on-campus recruiting fairs
every semester, and every week there are one or two companies that come and
try to recruit for internships and jobs. The Career Center is very helpful and they
prepare you as much as they can to allow the student to be ready for the working world. The alumni try to use their networking connections to open opportunities to their students also. They try to help out by looking for jobs and
announcing them to the students so they can look into positions if needed.
Graduates get jobs in major firms, like American Express and Computer
Associates. Medical students work at the nearby hospital, Stony Brook
University Hospital. Computer Associates has a huge bond with Stony Brook
because their CEO Charles Wang is an alumnus. He feels indebted to the school
and has given the program of computer science its prestige.

Quality of Life

Current student, Biology, 9/2004-Submit Date, May 2007

Stony Brook campus is relatively safe, but there are some areas that need better
lighting. As a female I feel relatively safe, and I have even walked back to my
dorm at midnight without any fear.

Current student, Visual Arts, 8/2005-Submit Date, April 2007

The housing on campus now is overcrowded. The residence halls are currently
at 108 percent capacity with more freshmen expected to enroll next year. The
university is trying to compensate by building another residence hall building in
the west apartments and adding more rooms to the Roosevelt Quad. What is
really cool is that upperclassmen with a GPA over 3.0 can live in the West

Read all of Vault's College Surveys at **www.vault.com/college**—get complete surveys on 100s of colleges and universities, expert advice on applicaton essays and more.

VAULT CAREER LIBRARY   **489**

Apartments, which is a brand-new set of buildings that are bigger than the normal dormrooms on the rest of campus. The upperclassmen can then choose to live in a single room (in which I will be living next semester). The rooms are clean with adjustable A/C and heat. There are several different types of dorm life. The suites are three rooms each, with two or three roommates in each; these rooms all share a bathroom and a common room. There are the corridor style residence halls, which have two roommates per room and there is a common bathroom and shower that the whole floor shares. The halls are co-ed, but the bathrooms are gender specific. The West Apartments are suites, as well, except that the suite has a fully furnished living room, two bathrooms and a kitchen.

The campus is huge. It takes me 20 minutes to get to main campus. There are buses that loop around campus going in different directions, but most of the time it is faster to walk. The facilities vary. Many of the buildings are old, but there are some that are brand-new. The humanities building is two years old and has several really nice computer labs and brand-new classrooms. Dining facilities are changing rapidly. Next year they are closing down Roth food court to renovate it completely . They recently upgraded the Tabler Arts Center cafe by adding a Dunkin Donuts. The union is getting a face-lift, too. The university is getting a new contract with a new food provider, so hopefully the cost of food will go down slightly. The food itself is a little on the fatty side. There is a lot of pizza, pasta and grilled cheese served and not enough variation in salads, but hopefully with the renovations that will not be the case anymore. Because the campus is so large, the quads have developed into their own neighborhoods. Each quad has its own event or place they can be proud of, for example, Roth has a "Roth Pond Regatta" every spring where every club races a boat made of cardboard and duct-tape across the pond. Tabler has the Tabler Arts Center, which has its own black box theatre. Each quad is huge, though. Unfortunately the campus community as a whole is pretty nonexistent. SBU pride is low despite much effort to make that not so. However, there are many events that bring the whole campus together, like the Roth Pond Regatta or Strawberry Fest, which is held every spring. Safety is an issue on every campus. Stony Brook is very well-lit at night and there are students who are hired specifically to walk people back to their dorms if they do not feel safe walking alone.

Current student, 8/2004-Submit Date, August 2006

There are plenty of activities and clubs available on campus. There is even this time period in which there are, for the most part, no classes, called Campus Lifetime, in which they run many activities.

 ## Social Life

Current student, Biology, 9/2004-Submit Date, May 2007

The best place to go near campus is Port Jefferson because it's a small town by the water and there are lots of cute little shops and restaurants to go to. As for clubbing and bars, the closest place to go is Smithtown Main Street and students can get there by train. Speaking of the train, the LIRR stops right on campus and thus it's easy to get home or travel into the city. There are some places that are within walking distance, such as Cosmos (Greek and pizza), Strawberry Fields and much more. Stony Brook doesn't have much of a Greek life, but there are frats and sororities. I personally prefer to take part in other extracurriculars, such as the Ambulance Corps and community service organizations. There is so much to do here, you just have to go out and find it.

Current student, Visual Arts, 8/2005-Submit Date, April 2007

Thursday night is a party night. There are many hotspots that people like to go to. The clubs: Myst, VIP, Bamboo Bernies and Intrigue are big. People who don't go clubbing often go to dorm parties on campus. There are different designated spots on campus that allow noise at night and those are generally the places for small parties. The clubs on campus are abundant. There are clubs and organizations for everything!! I am involved in Pocket Theatre, and undergraduate-run theatre company that puts on four to five plays a semester. I am also a member of my building's government. There are clubs for anime and Asian studies, for student activities and sports, the list goes on. There are hundreds.

Current student, 8/2004-Submit Date, August 2006

On campus they have a number of school club-sponsored dances. Off campus, I wouldn't really say it's a college town or anything, but there are a number of clubs in the area—Intrigue is a popular one. The school is not too far from the

Smithhaven Mall other shopping complexes, where there is a movie theater, well as many eateries (Friday's, Red Lobster, Friendly's and others that d[...] come to mind right now). There are also plenty of sororities and fraternit[...] some with cultural ties, others independent of an area of interest.

Current student, Mathematics, 1/2006-Submit Date, June 200[...]

The Greek system here is OK. If you are into them you will definitely find y[...] part, but if you are not, you won't be forced to get into them either. The in[...] racial dating scene here is big considering the diversity at Stony Brook. Th[...] are some good Asian restaurants around but you definitely need a car.

Current student, 8/2003-Submit Date, June 2006

The social life at Stony Brook is horrible. Everyone goes home on the weeke[...] because they all live in New York City. The closest bar to campus just clo[...] down, but everyone still goes out on Thursday nights in Port Jefferson, whic[...] like 10 minutes away. It is a small village on the water, with a ton of bars. T[...] Greek system is pretty active on campus. Everyone knows at least someone[...] a fraternity or sorority. Their parties aren't bad either, but most of the time t[...] party within the Greek system. Everyone I know gets Domino's and Chin[...] food delivered all the time.

 ## The School Says

50 years young, Stony Brook University is celebrating its evolution from a small teacher preparation college into an internationally recognized research institution. With more than 100 innovative programs for undergraduates, Long Island's only academic medical center, a satellite in Manhattan, a new college in Southampton and a thriving research/business environment, the university has come very far since its inception.

For the second year in a row, Stony Brook has been named again among the Top 100 best universities by *U.S. News & World Report*. Stony Brook is a member of the prestigious Association of American Universities, an invitation-only organization of the 62 top research universities in the nation. In addition to rising SAT scores that are at the top of SUNY institutions, the university has world-renowned faculty and researchers. In 2003, the Nobel Prize for Medicine was awarded for research conducted by Dr. Paul C. Lauterbur at Stony Brook, which led to the development of the MRI. *Kiplinger's Personal Finance* ranks Stony Brook as one of "The 100 Best Values in Higher Education" among public universities.

Stony Brook freshmen belong to one of six themed Undergraduate Colleges that offer small-group seminars and a wealth of social and academic activities that involve students in university life and ensure a successful first year. Recent additions to the undergraduate degree offerings are majors in Marine Science and Marine Vertebrate Biology, and a variety of combined bachelor/master degree programs—including an MBA program—that allow students to use graduate credits toward their undergraduate degree and complete both degrees in a five-year period.

Stony Brook's new undergraduate School of Journalism offers a major in journalism and one of the nation's first courses in news literacy, designed to help students use critical thinking to judge the credibility of the news they read and hear. Courses in print, broadcast and online journalism prepare students for an evolving multimedia future.

In the university's award-winning Undergraduate Research and Creative Activity (URECA) Program, students from every discipline are encouraged to follow their curiosity by connecting with faculty researchers and developing their own research projects, where they work side by side with graduate students, post docs and faculty. Undergraduate researchers have been the recipients of prestigious awards such as the Goldwater, Beckman and Marshall Scholarships.

Other programs of note include the Honors College, which offers high-achieving students innovative seminars, small classes and leadership opportunities. Women talented in math, science and engineering learn and work with a community of scholars in our Women in Science and Engineering (WISE) program. Scholars for Medicine, an eight-year combined undergraduate and medical degree track within the Honors College and WISE, guarantees entrance into the School of Medicine.

On Long Island's East End, Stony Brook Southampton is devoted to environmental sustainability, offering a broad spectrum of courses that include environmental studies, economics, ecology, marine science, the humanities, and many other areas. The college also offers an MFA program and is the home of the famed Southampton Writers' Conference. In New York City, Stony Brook Manhattan brings some of Stony Brook's programs to a wider audience.

The academic, cultural and research facilities at Stony Brook University provide an ideal environment for growth and the opportunity to advance knowledge that changes the world.

SUNY Geneseo

Admissions Office

College Circle

Geneseo, NY 14454

Admissions phone:(866) 245-5211(toll free)
    or (585) 245-5571

Admissions fax: (585) 245-5550

Admissions e-mail: admissions@geneseo.edu

Admissions URL: admissions.geneseo.edu/

Note: The school has chosen not to review the student surveys submitted.

 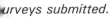

Admissions

Alumnus/a, Education, 8/2000-12/2002, May 2007

I entered Geneseo as a transfer. The process was straightforward: application, interview and letter (yea or neigh). I had to send transcripts and the usual, and was extremely happy when I found out that I had been accepted by the best, arguably, of the SUNY schools!

Alumnus/a, 8/1996-5/2000, April 2006

Geneseo is now officially recognized as the most selective of the SUNY (State University of New York) campuses. The application process consists of the standard SUNY application and Geneseo's optional supplemental application: a personal essay, letters of recommendation, an extracurricular résumé and the unique, optional parent essay. Yes, your mom, dad or legal guardian has the rare opportunity to dote on your wonderful qualities and vie for your acceptance. I think it is safe to say that with the increased competition for admission, your chances for acceptance without submitting this supplemental application are slim to none. I don't know of any fellow alumni who gained admission without submitting this and the school's selectivity has only increased since my attendance (1996 to 2000). In addition, I know several people who completed the supplemental application with the exception of the parental essay and did not gain acceptance. I can't say this is a direct correlation, but you really want to provide the admissions committee with every possible piece of information that could help.

I think that the personal and parent essays are really chances to separate yourself from the pack. If you are an honors student who is involved in several clubs and think that this guarantees admission, think again. I do not mean to sound discouraging, but everyone on that campus was an honors student and served on numerous teams and clubs. You want to put a face to your application and demonstrate your personality and what makes you unique.

Current student, 1/2003-Submit Date, February 2006

I completed the application. No essays. Current GPA required. 3.6 from transferring school. 3.0 can get you in for transfers. Will need higher if coming directly from high school. SAT over 1000 for transfers. Again, higher for high school students.

Alumnus/a, 9/1997-12/2001, October 2004

Filling out applications to any college isn't fun! Geneseo's admissions process is similar to all other NY state colleges. The one thing that makes getting into Geneseo a bit easier is there are no interviews. Geneseo is also very helpful when filling out all of the other documents once you are chosen to attend (all the financial aid documents). They actually sit down with you and fill it out, this way you know it is being done correctly.

Current student, 8/2003-Submit Date, May 2004

The first step in applying to Geneseo is to complete the general SUNY application. You can apply to up to [six] SUNYs on this form, and it is sent to a general address, and the applications are passed [distributed from there to all campus choices]. Once Geneseo receives your application, you will [be sent] a supplementary application, which is used exclusively by Geneseo. It will require that you write an admissions essay. Typically, there are three or four choices, one of which is an essay of your choice. If you are applying to many schools, it may be wise for you to choose this option because it may save you time and allow you to re-use an essay written for another school. You are given two weeks to complete and mail this supplementary application. If you apply for Early Decision, you will be notified [of the decision on December 15]. If you are [not admitted through Early Decision], your application [will] be deferred and considered for admission under the general admissions. Notification of acceptance is made in early March. If you choose to [enroll at Geneseo], you must notify the school and mail a deposit by May 1.

There is no interview required. Selectivity increases every year, and it is becoming increasingly difficult and competitive to be accepted. An average of [90 to 95 percent] and an SAT score of [1200 to 1340] are [preferred ranges for admission]. Geneseo also offers a special talent program for student athletes, [artists and musicians] who do not meet grade requirements, but [will make a significant contribution to the campus]. [Students admitted through this program are required to attend 10 hours of study hall per week.]

Current student, 8/2003-Submit Date, June 2004

Highly selective school. SUNY application followed by a second application that has an essay. Recommendations and excellent high school grades are a must.

Read all of Vault's College Surveys at **www.vault.com/college**—get complete surveys on 100s of colleges and universities, expert advice on applicaton essays and more.

VAULT CAREER LIBRARY **491**

Academics

Alumnus/a, Education, 8/2000-12/2002, May 2007

I was an elementary and special education major in the Ella Kline Shear School of Education. The faculty and support staff were highly qualified for their positions, and showed how much they cared about the proper training of the students, making themselves as available to the students as humanly possible.

Alumnus/a, 8/1996-5/2000, April 2006

Academics at Geneseo are rigorous, but if you gain admission you are most likely capable of handling the intensity. A recommendation is always to read what is required and you are less likely to fall behind in class discussion. Academics are challenging across the board, regardless of department. There is a rumor that the freshman level biology classes are made exceptionally hard to weed out students because of the high number of entering biology majors.

Classes at Geneseo are small. The largest, 100-level lecture classes hold only about 75 to 100 students and are never taught by TAs. In fact, Geneseo prohibits TAs from teaching any classes except for instructing (always supervised) at lab sessions. Once you are in upper-level classes within your major, it is rare to have a class with more than 30 people. I do believe I have truly benefited from the relationships forged with professors and students due to these small class sizes. In addition, I believe that intellectual stimulation and diving deep into subject matter is more possible in a small class environment.

Alumnus/a, 8/1994-5/1998, September 2005

The academic quality of the college is challenging. I majored in psychology and secondary education, and I had to make sure to attend all classes, complete all assignments, and participate in study groups to succeed. Most of the professors are good. I really enjoyed the classes I took during my junior and senior years, as the classes were much smaller (20 to 30 students) and it was apparent that the professors enjoyed teaching more advanced material. It was not very difficult to get the desired classes during your sophomore, junior and senior years. Freshman year was more challenging, as most students were interested in completing their core classes.

Alumnus/a, 9/1997-12/2001, October 2004

Geneseo is mainly known for its educational program (both elementary and secondary). The core classes that are required, which are required by almost all colleges, vary at Geneseo. They give you the option to choose from many different classes that will satisfy the core requirements you must have in order to graduate. This was very nice!

Current student, 8/2003-Submit Date, May 2004

Geneseo strives to offer a comprehensive liberal arts background for its students. There is a core curriculum, which each student is required to complete for graduation. The classes at Geneseo range in size from lectures with about 150 students to small, intimate classes of about 30 students. The classes are both challenging and intellectually stimulating. Professors are generally accessible and easy to communicate with. Most are very willing to work with you to accommodate any needs or concerns you may have. The registration process is done entirely online. Students receive a registration date and time. During this time students can log onto the school database and register for the desired classes. Registration time is determined by the number of credit hours a student has completed.

Current student, 8/2003-Submit Date, June 2004

Professors are very accessible and very accommodating. They are usually very helpful in getting you into a class if you don't get it during the regular registration period. Most courses have a significant workload that often requires attendance of some out-of-class meetings or events.

Employment Prospects

Alumnus/a, Education, 8/2000-12/2002, May 2007

When school districts see Geneseo on my résumé, they know that they are getting a well-trained, knowledgeable teacher with real teaching experience, as result of the practical experience that students undertake in their programs. This is not just in New York: I have even heard this in Massachusetts, where I currently reside.

Alumnus/a, 8/1996-5/2000, April 2006

Geneseo is well known for its outstanding teaching program and if you want become a teacher, schools from across the state are well aware of the stellar reputation of Geneseo's education majors. I also know someone who works in personnel capacity of a large school district who told me that applicants w graduated from Geneseo are placed "at the top of the pile." I also know that gr schools look highly upon Geneseo graduates. I have friends who went on to me school and other graduate programs at Ivy League colleges after getting the undergraduate education from Geneseo.

I am from Long Island originally. I had several internships during college, all the Rochester area. When someone from New York State heard you went Geneseo, you were treated as if you said you went to Harvard. This was the typ of reaction in the greater Rochester area. However, upon graduation, when began to look for employment in New York City, I soon found out that man employers didn't know Geneseo from Oneonta or Oswego, and that wa extremely disappointing and discouraging to me, as there is a tremendous di ference in academic excellence between these colleges. It seems that more pe ple have heard of Binghamton, I imagine, because more students from the dow state New York area attend due to its proximity. My recommendation for st dents hailing from the downstate area is instead of completing internshi upstate, trying to secure internships in New York City during the summer order to network and make the necessary connections to find employment up graduation. Unfortunately, Geneseo is lacking in its PR and marketing effort As the college continues to gain more national attention in the rankings, this w improve, but it is a regional college and if your plan is to work outside of the N area, I strongly urge you to apply to a different college closer to where you pla to live.

Current student, 1/2003-Submit Date, February 2006

Average business graduates earn $36,000. On-campus recruiting is limited b Career Services is very helpful. Interview prep is given in class and throug GOLD classes. Geneseo will prepare students for employment in various field The business program offers many opportunities for personal growth and deve opment. Examples include: business plan competitions, professional group such as an Accounting Society, Marketing Society and APICS Society. Teache are very qualified and normally have backgrounds in the field and research.

Alumnus/a, 8/1994-5/1998, September 2005

SUNY Geneseo is a well thought of school in NY State. It is one of the be ranked state schools. The education department is particularly prestigious. Mo students who complete their degrees in education can get a job, although th teaching market in the area is somewhat saturated. The school does a great jo helping students obtain internships/student teaching assignments. I rarely hea from the alumni network.

Alumnus/a, 9/1997-12/2001, October 2004

Geneseo has a great program set up for its alumni. They actually make a place ment folder while you are attending Geneseo and then when you are about graduate, you go through it and decide what you would like to keep in the fold er for potential employers to see and what you would like to remove. Genese also works with you on filling out résumés and cover letters. You then conta Geneseo and they will send it to any employer you would like for you.

Quality of Life

Social Life

umnus/a, Education, 8/2000-12/2002, May 2007

neseo, being in a rural community approximately 30 miles south of Rochester, a safe community that is still readily accessible to city life. The sense of community at Geneseo is strong: everyone will fit in.

umnus/a, 8/1996-5/2000, April 2006

ere are more stores and restaurants, which is great. Geneseo is a rural town th a resident population of 5,000. When in session, the school roughly dou-s the population of the town. Geneseo is designated a historic village and is te beautiful and charming. The campus is picturesque, with ivy-covered ldings, rolling hills and amazing sunsets over the valley. Letchworth State rk is only several miles down the road and is a great destination on weekends. wever, the rural location may seem stifling to some and a car is definitely rec-mended if possible. The nearest mall is about 45 miles away, in a suburb of City of Rochester. Rochester provides many alternatives to campus activi-s but there is limited campus bus service. Geneseo's relative isolation from pulated areas has caused some students to nickname it "the Bubble."

rrent student, 8/2003-Submit Date, May 2004

e quality of life at Geneseo is high. Facilities are well maintained and up to te. Student housing is available, and the dorms are well maintained. If stu-nts have any problems in their individual rooms or halls, residence directors, ident assistants and residence life can be contacted and notified of any prob-ns. Once a complaint is submitted, a response is generally received within 24 urs. Also, between the hours of 8 p.m. and 8 a.m., only residents of that par-ular hall are admitted. Any guests must be personally brought in. All dorms ve a swipe card system, where a student swipes his or her student ID to enter. ter 8 p.m., a social security number must be entered.

ross campus there are are blue light phones. These phones can be used to call d notify university police in the event of an emergency. University police are ick to respond to any calls. Crime in Geneseo is very low.

ere are three main dining halls: two on North Campus and one on South mpus. They offer a variety of food for students. The newest dining hall, Mary nison, is open from 8 a.m. to 5 p.m. and offers the best selection and quality food. There is also a coffee shop where students can purchase food and bev-ge in the student union and also in the library.

umnus/a, 8/2000-5/2003, October 2003

e town is small. There's Main Street, which has about three bars, three pizza ces, three sandwich places, three places to get tattoos and three tanning ces. (Yes, that's very close to an exact count.) The whole time I was there I mplained about the food (on-campus food is absolutely horrendous, and off mpus is not so good), but then again, I am from downstate New York, so I'm cky. Drive about a mile (if you pay $90 a semester to park a car on campus) d you'll come to all the requisite fast-food places, a Wegman's supermarket d a Wal-Mart. And that's about it.

lways felt safe there; there isn't much crime. Rochester is about 40 minutes rth. You can get to Buffalo in a little over an hour. Off-campus housing aver-es around the same cost as on campus, $1,500 a semester. Many juniors and niors move off campus.

gets pretty cold, well, freezing in my opinion. Not all that much snow, but eneseo is right on the top of a hill and is very windy. When I went home for ristmas break, the 32 degrees and no wind almost made me want to take off y coat.

Alumnus/a, Education, 8/2000-12/2002, May 2007

College is what you make of it. It can be a party experience, a serious academic experience, or ideally a balance of both. I feel that Geneseo provides a great opportunity for this, as I had a great time with my friends when I did not have to study.

Alumnus/a, 8/1996-5/2000, April 2006

While Geneseo is a relatively isolated campus, there are many opportunities for an active social life. There are so many clubs and activities that almost anyone can find something that is of interest.

There are many different scenes, from Greek to hippie, to sports, and most of them involve drinking heavily. Most of the open parties, however, are thrown by the Greek organizations, so it may appear that being Greek is the only way to have a good time. Greeks are very visible, and therefore, I was swayed by this during my freshman year and wound up pledging a sorority. While I don't regret my decision overall, it was mostly based on my impression that the only way to have a social life at Geneseo was to be a Greek, which is not true.

There are no on-campus facilities where students can drink, so people head to the local bars. The bar scene is rather small due to the size of the town, only five in total, and all of the bars are within walking distance of each other. There is almost no such thing as a drinking and driving problem on this campus because of the close proximity of all the establishments. There are certain bars that are notoriously easy for underage drinkers to get into and others where it's harder to get in and the population is mostly juniors and seniors. Overall, the bar scene is very casual—there are no actual clubs in Geneseo. Although students do their fair share of partying at Geneseo, this is not considered a party campus and students are very responsible for the most part and take their studies seriously. In addition, for as many students who do party on weekends, there are just as many who do not. Common nicknames for the campus were "Geek-eseo" and "Gene-zero," a reference to the extremely studious nature of the students.

Current student, 8/2003-Submit Date, May 2004

Students are able to find something to do at Geneseo. Whether it is an on-campus, school-sponsored event or a fraternity party, there is something for everyone. On Friday and Saturday nights, the school offers a program called Late Knight in the student union as an alternative for students who don't want to go to frat or sports parties. They also just opened a dance club called the Knight-Spot as another nonalcoholic alternative for students. In the town there are seven bars. Two of the bars require that you be 19 to enter and 21 to drink. The rest all require a minimum age of 21. The school has 10 sororities, eight recognized fraternities and three unrecognized fraternities. Every weekend these different organizations have different open parties where anyone can attend. Some of the more popular fraternities include Delta Kappa Tau (DKT), Sigma Tau Psi (Sig. Tau) and Phi Sigma Xi (Phigs). In town, there is a local movie theater, which offers a student discount and a bowling alley. There are three pizzerias on Main Street, Mama Mia's being the most popular. It is open until 3 a.m. and will deliver right to your dorm. Other restaurants include Geneseo Family Restaurant and the Big Tree Inn, where students can use their meal plans on Tuesdays, Wednesdays and Thursdays.

Alumnus/a, 8/2000-5/2003, October 2003

There are about 5,500 students, and about 1,000 of them go out on a regular basis. There are 10 small sororities and about the same number of frats. I pledged simply because there wasn't much else to do. The other 4,000 do seem to get somewhat involved in school clubs, but the overall stereotype of them is that it's weird to be involved. I was able to take advantage of some great leadership opportunities because there wasn't much competition.

Read all of Vault's College Surveys at www.vault.com/college—get complete surveys on 100s of colleges and universities, expert advice on applicaton essays and more.

VAULT CAREER LIBRARY   493

Syracuse University

Admissions Office
100 Crouse-Hinds Hall
900 South Crouse Avenue
Syracuse, NY 13244-2130
Admissions phone: (315) 443-3611
Admissions fax: (315) 443-4226
Admissions e-mail: orange@syr.edu
Admissions URL: admissions.syr.edu

 Admissions

Alumnus/a, 9/2002-5/2006, August 2006

I went to a BFA program for acting, which was extremely competitive and rigorous. Essentially I had to get into school twice. I had to be accepted by the university, which required high SAT scores, high grades on high school transcripts, as well as a very long application process from the university itself. I filled out over four different essays specific to Syracuse University, as well as writing my own personal two-page college entry essay that I used to apply to more than one school. Additionally, I had to be accepted to the drama department separately from the university. This process was very intense, requiring an audition of two different monologues. I competed with about 800 applicants to the department and they only accepted approximately 60 students. On the larger university scale, I was competing with literally tens of thousands of people, as the university population lingers somewhere around 15,000 people. My advice on getting into these kinds of conservatory programs within larger universities is to prepare. It's essential to feel confident about what you are doing, whether it's an audition, a portfolio or an interview with a specific department head. Breath, relax and be yourself. Let them see who you really are, don't try to pretend that you are their perfect applicant. Be proud of the work you have done and express yourself candidly, respectfully and truly. Know a little bit about the university and ask questions! You are paying them money, and although it seems like they have the power, you do! You can ask for more financial aid if you have to, or ask why they don't have certain space you think they ought to. If you are really interested in the university, make them work for you, and more often than not, they are happy to do so.

Current student, Business, 8/2005-Submit Date, July 2007

In the search for the perfect college I knew one thing was certain, I was unsure of what path of education I would study. Because of that factor I wanted to attend a large institution with numerous schools with high quality reputations. I had always heard wonderful things about Syracuse University, so it was my top choice. In order to maximize my chances with regards to admissions, I also applied to be on the track team. My essay was deeply personal and touched upon the struggles and triumphs I had faced in my life.

Alumnus/a, 8/2001-5/2005, September 2005

Well, I didn't interview and I got in fine (1250 on SATs). I forget what I got on my ACT, but I applied to 11 schools and got into 10 of them. Make sure you write essays about how you are different than other people, and the different experiences that you have encountered thus far in your life. I think this goes for many schools, but especially the larger ones like Cuse.

Current student, 8/2004-Submit Date, October 2005

I had to write an essay about part of my life that was important to me. I chose to write about my hometown and how living in a small town turned me into a person with strong morals and an appetite for education. I also had to write a 250-word essay about how I would incorporate SU's four key values into my time here. It was pretty selective, especially for Newhouse. Interviews aren't mandatory. I didn't even have one. However, I would suggest visiting for a Fall Friday. They're a lot of fun and you really learn a lot! Some advice on getting in would be to be yourself in the essay. Don't write what you think they want to hear. Everyone else is writing that.

Alumnus/a, 8/1999-5/2003, October 2005

GPA, SAT, extracurriculars, recommendations and, everyone's favorite, the personal essay. I did not interview. It is probably easier to apply to the College Arts and Sciences rather than a specialized school (School of Engineering) then transfer in if your credentials are not that great.

Current student, 8/2004-Submit Date, April 2005

I really did not consider Syracuse University as one of my top choices during college application process. I remember writing two essays and maybe a cou of short answer questions. It was a really busy time and I had my heart set other schools for which I had to spend more time working on the application remember everyone told me to keep my essays short and sweet, they should exceed a page or two. I did not have an interview for any school. A part of wished I had studied more in high school but now I'm in an excellent school a am transferring into Newhouse, which is a school here at Syracuse Univers labeled as the Number One communications school in the country.

Current student, 9/2001-Submit Date, June 2004

Syracuse is in no way a simple school to get into. It has the leading program the country for communications and has very competitive and well-rounded p grams in the fields of management, political science, IT and VPA. The m important part about applying for this school is knowing what you would like study. Many students apply for the Newhouse School of Pub Communications but are accepted to another school. However, you can alwa transfer between schools depending on your GPA and extracurriculars.

SATs are important. Essays should reflect your life, your interests and your c tribution to your community. Make sure you give them a good feeling of w you are, what you want to get out of college, and why Syracuse is a good fit you.

If you interview, remember to be yourself. Selectivity can be tough, but if y show that you are academically and culturally sound, it goes a long way.

 Academics

Alumnus/a, 9/2002-5/2006, August 2006

Being in a BFA theatre department is literally a seven days a week job. At minimum, you will be in class from about nine to five each day, with often as tle as 10 minutes between classes.

I had mostly smaller classes because I tended to stay mostly in English, mu and drama classes, all of which have smaller departments. Consequently, it w very difficult on some occasions to get into the classes I wanted, and registrati time was a nightmare. It was very competitive, and I often had to wait a year take a class I wanted. Some students were shut out of classes so consistently t they feared not graduating on time! Although I didn't have that particular exp rience, I know that it was very stressful. These were coveted places to be.

Current student, Business, 8/2005-Submit Date, July 2007

Syracuse is a school with a reputation for high quality academics. One has ability to engage oneself with as much or as little schoolwork as one wan One is rewarded for accomplishments in the classroom not only by being nam to the Dean's List and so on, but also by the ability to join the honor society one's specific major. The classes I've enrolled in have mostly had the most hi quality staff; however, a few were taught by teachers who clearly wanted to elsewhere. Professors have always been readily available, which is a factor o may not expect with classes as large as 100 or more.

Alumnus/a, 8/2001-5/2005, September 2005

The workload is a joke, don't be scared. Everyone on the whole campus pre much takes Fridays off and it's really not a big deal, professors do it too som times. The new online registration (myslice) for classes is different than the c stem and takes some getting used to but it is much better. The part about yracuse University that I loved is the whole education that it gave you. I came om a small town and this place was a huge eye-opener. It teaches you so much out people, time management, and the world and does so in a fashion that real- makes the four years fly by.

urrent student, 8/2004-Submit Date, October 2005

lasses in Newhouse are very good. Some classes in arts and sciences are over- owded, especially biology, astronomy, other sciences and math. Popular class- are sometimes hard to get, but if there is a lot of demand they sometimes form new section. Grading varies from college to college. Professors are usually derstanding and are always very qualified. Teaching assistants rarely, if ever, ach classes. The workload varies depending on the major

lumnus/a, 8/1999-5/2003, October 2005

he quality of classes depends on the academic program. The university is sep- ated into schools—School of Management, Education and so on. Popular asses can be hard to get—it gets easier as you progress. The workload is not o bad. Grading is pretty fair, and most professors are very understanding, lpful and approachable.

urrent student, 8/2003-Submit Date, April 2004

am currently an economics major on track for a BS. The quality of classes nges, but I find most of the upper-division classes have high academic quality. me classes have a relatively light workload, but most of my classes have pret- intense workloads. Most of it's pretty interesting, though. Getting into pop- ar classes can be difficult. Even as a junior economics major, I had to person- ly fight to get into each of my two economics courses this semester. I have had uble getting into, or still haven't gotten into many other popular classes, even me in the freshman division. I've been trying to get into many of these class- for over a year.

urrent student, 9/2001-Submit Date, June 2004

he best thing about the school is there are many choices—EEE (one of the best the country), finance, accounting, supply chain (not offered in many schools) d marketing. Another great thing is that you can have a double major or a dual ajor. A double major is two majors within SOM. It requires taking extra class- , typically around four or five. Having credits coming in or taking summer asses can make this possible. A dual major is a major in SOM and within other school.

nior and senior years will mostly be classes in your major. They are more in- pth and work-specific. The professors within the program can be very help- l. They are all typically approachable and require office hours. Most of the ne they have a lot of real-life experience in the field and can be the best source for careers or internships. Grading depends on the professor, but if you t the time into studying, your grade will reflect your work. Grading would in way be characterized as easy.

Employment Prospects

lumnus/a, 9/2002-5/2006, August 2006

bs in the arts are hard to come by, no matter how prestigious the university you end. Syracuse provides a showcase for selected actors and musical theatre dents that is put on for producers, agents and casting directors in New York ty. This is very helpful to bridge the gap between college and professional life, pefully setting up students with agents in order to successfully market them- lves and effectively (and hopefully consistently!) get work. For the universi- there are employment services for each academic department, all across cam- s. Syracuse University students graduate to become anything they want, nkers, lawyers, journalists, TV personalities, actors, technicians, anything they nt. We have one of the highest ranked journalism and broadcasting schools the country, Newhouse, as well as the Number One public affairs school, axwell. Our alumni network is huge and I have found enormous support since oved to New York City after graduation to pursue my acting career. I have en supported, advised and nurtured by the alumni living and working here.

Current student, Business, 8/2005-Submit Date, July 2007

Syracuse maintains an extensive career network and allows students to apply and be recruited for opportunities in externships, internships, part- and full-time employment.

Current student, 8/2004-Submit Date, October 2005

Newhouse has one of the highest employment rates in the country. They work hard with an alumni base to help graduates get jobs. Internships are a dime a dozen and there are lots of career fairs throughout the year.

Current student, 8/2003-Submit Date, April 2004

Syracuse seems to have prestige with employers. I am still a student, so I am not the best judge of this yet, but I know many people who have graduated here and have gotten good jobs right out of college. The internship program has been very useful. They have helped me find and apply for summer internships and have a very effective web site to look up internships using a variety of criteria. I have not yet begun dealing with the Center for Career Services and have no knowledge of campus recruiting yet, since I am not yet a senior.

Current student, 9/2001-Submit Date, June 2004

Careers and internships can be acquired easily, as long as you make yourself aware of the opportunities surrounding you. Job fairs are frequent throughout the year. Many top companies including GE and PricewaterhouseCoopers come and hire many students.

A career center is located in the student center, but there is also a career center specifically for management students. Classes will help you create a résumé and cover letter and prepare for interviews.

A great resource of jobs is through networking through professors. They have worked in different locations and have a good idea of where to apply. Students can find jobs in Syracuse, but many also find careers in Chicago, New York and Boston.

Quality of Life

Alumnus/a, 9/2002-5/2006, August 2006

Housing is offered in several ways at Syracuse, dorms, fraternity and sorority housing, as well as transitional housing like living at the Alibrandi Catholic Center. Also, off-campus housing is very accessible and departments find their niche of the city and all their students tend to move to that area. Syracuse isn't a very safe city, but within the campus walls, students are watched out for and taken care of. We had the blue light security system, with police officers patrolling more often than not. However, life in Syracuse itself was very tricky, and I often didn't go out because of the safety issues. It's not the most fun city, nor the most active or exciting to live in for a young person. But, there are enough things to do; there is a huge mall with everything you could want, and lots of little shops and restaurants on the campus itself.

Current student, Business, 8/2005-Submit Date, July 2007

Quality of life is highly enjoyable at Syracuse. Housing is decent, what one would expect from a college campus. The outskirts of campus are not highly aesthetic, but that is expected going to a school located in one of the most impov- erished areas of New York State. Crime and safety have had me worried at times but the school does the best it can to keep such factors in order.

Current student, 8/2004-Submit Date, April 2005

Most of my friends and I live on the Mount, which is 128 steps up from main campus. It was at first such a drag to walk up those steps a couple of times per day but we eventually got used to it. Syracuse is definitely not a safe school. Southside Syracuse, a horrible sector of the city and also known as the poorest city per capita in the country is just next door from our school. There are always fights and robberies. Housing is great, dorms are average and the RAs here are trained very well. Bathrooms in some places can afford to be renovated, but I'm not complaining.

Read all of Vault's College Surveys at **www.vault.com/college**—get complete surveys on 100s of colleges and univer- sities, expert advice on applicaton essays and more.

VAULT CAREER LIBRARY   **495**

Alumnus/a, 8/1996-5/2000, September 2003

Campus is beautiful and close to restaurants, bars and shopping. Everything is within walking distance (a car is optional, though it will be very expensive to park if you do get one). Some have complained of the campus's proximity to public subsidized housing, but there isn't much interaction between the two. There was quite a bit of panhandling on Marshall Street (near the campus), which was more annoying than dangerous. My main complaint about campus life was the noise—blasting music in dorms and from frat houses really got on my nerves. Overall, a very busy and lively campus.

Also, it gets very cold and snowy in the winter. The winters are hard-core in Syracuse. Be sure to bring good, warm boots and a coat that is wind-resistant (the wind is fierce up there). Because of its proximity to Lake Ontario, they get a lot of lake effect snow, in addition to snow from regular storm systems. If you like snow, it will be a winter paradise for you. If not, I suggest probably going somewhere else.

 Social Life

Alumnus/a, 9/2002-5/2006, August 2006

We had a local bar, Phoebe's, that we went to every Friday, were we would get together and unwind. It was a perfect place to relax, drink and eat after shows, before shows, with our families and friends. There were two other areas of the city that were fun to party in, one was Armory Square, in the heart of the city, were there were lots of restaurants, shopping and classy coffee shops to go to. It was a bit more upscale. There were nightclubs and great martini bars. Also, there were college campus bars, which boasted great deals like flip cup at Fageans, where you would flip a coin and if you got it right you got a free drink.

Classic college entertainment! It was great fun though and I had a wonderf time hanging out on campus. We also threw our own parties in the drama depar ment, which were the height of entertainment. They were always themed ar always the most fun. Favorite spots include: Sasha's (hair salon), Ambros (dinner, martinis and a great nightclub), Dinosaur BBQ, The Carousel Ma Aladdin's, and Off the Beaten Path.

Current student, Business, 8/2005-Submit Date, July 2007

Social life at Syracuse is highly entertaining. There are a range of activities engage in and nightlife is booming. There are sorority and fraternities to jo which enable students to extend their social network. Also, the area does hav downtown with suitable restaurants for even the most expensive palate.

Current student, 8/2004-Submit Date, October 2005

There are over a thousand clubs at Syracuse University, including a club f every niche. About 20 percent of students are active in Greek life. There are lo of club sports and the varsity sports compete with other Division I schools in t Big East conference. There is a multitude of bars on Marshall Street, as well other restaurants. The local transportation system, Centro, provides $1 trips the mall on weekends, where there are lots of other restaurants. Marshall Stre has good food, like the Pita Pit, and there are lots of places that deliver food un about 3 a.m. every day. Dating is easy since there are about 11,000 peop enrolled as undergrads. There are lots of events on campus. There are comed ans all the time, and academic programs. There are also movie screenings ar lots of plays and operas on campus and at Syracuse Stage, which is less than mile away. Club Tundra isn't far away and it has a lot of good punk bands con through. It's about a $10 cab ride away.

Union College

Office of Admissions
Grant Hall
Union College
Schenectady, NY 12308
Admissions phone: (888) 843-6688
Admissions e-mail: admissions@union.edu
Admissions URL: www.union.edu/Admissions/

 Admissions

Current student, 9/2002-Submit Date, June 2004

The admissions process at Union College is an important step for the prospective student in determining whether or not this college is a good fit for him/her, while at the same time helping the admissions team admit only the most qualified candidates. All applicants are required to submit a comprehensive application that includes a school report section used by numerous colleges, as well as a personal statement in which the admissions team can get to better know the applicant as a person. For instance, I wrote an essay of approximately 500 words about a person who has significantly influenced on my life. Other alternative topics include a discussion of an issue that is of importance to you or describing an experience or achievement that has had an impact on you.

The most important step in this process is the interview, which in my case took place on campus with a graduating senior from the college. This interview helped me gain insight and perspective on Union College from a student who has been there for four years while at the same time I was able to express my own reasons for wanting to attend. It was a very rewarding experience for me and helped reaffirm my interest in this college. Alternatives for students living far away and unable to attend on-campus interviews include interviews with alumni who volunteer their time because of their pride in the college and strong inter-

est in helping in whatever way they can. There is an impressive network alumni throughout the U.S. and the world who assist in this process, and aga the interview is probably as important if not more so than the actual paper appl cation.

If you are in the top percentile of your class and have worked extra hard by ta ing AP courses or other equivalent college-level courses, then you will hav made it past the first phase of the admissions process. Equally important to the is how involved you have been at your school and in the community. Due to t fact that we are a relatively small school of approximately 2,000 undergraduate it is something like a family here and everyone is encouraged to contribute much outside of the classroom as inside. Therefore, do not be shy about hig lighting your extracurricular, personal and volunteer activities throughout hi school. Work experience is also a plus because it shows maturity and internshi are often pursued by students here. However, it is of less importance than t other aspects previously mentioned. Applicants can apply as a regular freshma Early Decision or for special programs, including an eight-year leadership medicine program, six-year law and public policy program or a five-year MB program.

Alumnus/a, 9/1994-5/1998, September 2003

At the time, SAT scores were not required. The interview was highly recom mended. An overnight campus visit and an interview are the best ways for yc and the admissions office to really get to know you better—certainly better tha just test scores.

 **Academics**

Current student, 9/2002-Submit Date, June 2004

One of the unique attributes of this college is the interaction between faculty ar students. All professors are required to teach undergraduate courses and the no TAs. I have been at the college for two years now and have yet to have a professor who has not opened his/her doors to me during office hours and even his/her own time. Sometimes you will see faculty members at the campus center when you are grabbing lunch, and it is not unusual for them to invite you join them and talk. All of my professors have really taken an interest in my academic performance in their class, as well as a general interest in my career als.

ion College first opened its doors in 1795 and has a very rich history. It is the st liberal arts college in the nation to offer an engineering program. There are different majors or disciplines that a student can choose from and a wealth of er 1,000 courses. The terms run on a trimester system, in which a normal urseload consists of three courses taken in a 10-week period. Basically, this eans that there is no room to slack off because students who do will quickly l behind. Study groups are also encouraged and most are established at the tiative of the students. The motto, which has worked for years at Union llege, is "work hard and play harder." While the incoming freshmen may find a little difficult to adjust initially because of the demands and expectations aced on them, it is not beyond anyone who comes here. Tutors are often avail- le for many classes and there are language centers, as well as writing centers help students.

ter leaving here in four years, students will have completed a breadth of cours- both within their majors and far removed from their majors through the gen- l education curriculum. Each student will have taken one or more courses in e sciences, social sciences, mathematics, English and foreign language or cul- e, as well as numerous writing-based courses. This ensures a well-rounded ucation and a broad knowledge of many things.

umnus/a, 9/1999-9/2003, February 2004

e chemistry program was very good, with excellent teaching. However, it suf- red from the lack of an associated graduate school. Because of this, there were wer opportunities to take advanced chemistry courses that universities would ve offered their undergraduates.

umnus/a, 9/1994-5/1998, September 2003

ad an unusual major, interdisciplinary studies. It was a combination of eco- mics and German. The German classes were very small, sometimes only four dents, so I really had to be prepared for class. (No sliding down low in the air, everyone had to participate!) Economics is a very popular major at Union t I never had a problem getting into classes. I never had a bad teacher at nion. I had one class with about 120 students in it—it was a mandatory Intro Biology class. Even so, my professors still seemed to know who I was and en I missed class. My educational experience was one in which I always felt allenged but I never felt overwhelmed or in over my head.

 # Employment Prospects

urrent student, 9/2002-Submit Date, June 2004

ere is a career center on campus dedicated to helping students find jobs and ernships, improve their résumés, and learn of different fields and industries. so, faculty stay in touch with many graduates and are willing to help those o seek their assistance by putting them in touch with these alumni and poten- l employers. As mentioned before, there is a strong network of alumni at nion College. The college is working hard to build its name and graduates usu- y do not have a hard time finding a job. It is often said, what you get back m the college is whatever you put in and those who make the most of their perience are often rewarded with lucrative job offers or the opportunity to pur- e a postgraduate degree at some of the best universities in the world.

lumnus/a, 9/1994-5/1998, September 2003

didn't have a great experience with the recruiters, but that may be due to my ajor. The science and engineering students seemed to fare the best—lots of armaceutical companies recruit them. Anderson used to come to campus and was considered the hot recruiter. Personally, I was not impressed; I think the nderson recruiters were a joke. I had two years of work experience in banking t was not seen as a good enough candidate.

 ## Quality of Life

Current student, 9/2002-Submit Date, June 2004

Union College has extended its reach by purchasing a hotel just off campus with the goal of providing a range of housing options for students. There are also theme houses where, for instance, students are introduced to a different language or culture. Each faculty is assigned to a house and there are events throughout each term at each of these including parties and other social gatherings.

For the techies out there, there are wireless Internet capabilities at each of the dorms and there are many public computers available at the library and elsewhere for those who do not have a laptop. Students can request single dorms, doubles or suites for three or four students. It is a truly beautiful campus with great food and a comfort- able living environment. Upperclassman RAs are also assigned to each of the hous- es and assist with day-to-day matters for students, as well.

Alumnus/a, 9/1972-6/1976, February 2004

Schenectady is a wasteland, so don't expect much from the city. Most of the col- lege life centers around the frats and sororities. There is a strong feeling of us versus them between the students and the administration. Relations with stu- dents and alumni will improve greatly soon. Campus housing is not great. Off campus is inexpensive and safe.

Alumnus/a, 9/1994-5/1998, September 2003

Housing is decent, lots of opportunities to move off campus. The library is amazing, the science buildings are great. It's a beautiful campus stuck in an ugly town. Crime is minimal, although my car was vandalized once. I don't know if rapes or assaults happen; I didn't hear much about it.

 ## Social Life

Current student, 9/2002-Submit Date, June 2004

It would be an overstatement to say that Schenectady is the greatest place in the world to be. However, there are many opportunities through Union College for those who seek them. For instance, I had the opportunity of joining Big Brothers Big Sisters, and as a Big was able to go on different adventures with my Little and others in the organization such as a bus trip to a Six Flags one hour away. Also, as a member of the Economics Club, I visited New York City on two dif- ferent occasions. Finally, in the fall I will be studying in London as part of a study abroad experience.

Locally, students with transportation find more in Albany than here in Schenectady, including shopping centers, restaurants and bowling alleys. Some of that is here, as well. There is a trolley that takes students to different places and has a set schedule each week. Freshmen are not allowed to have cars and find this to be a good way to get around. Those who have been here for some time (myself included) find that overall, the social life is good because it is a closely knit community of exception- al students from around the world and together we can find lots of things to do together for fun both on and off campus.

Alumnus/a, 9/1994-5/1998, September 2003

It used to be a lot more fun when the fraternities had more free reign. If I were a parent, I'd probably feel safe sending my kids to Union. However, given the alternatives, Union is not the fun school it used to be.

Read all of Vault's College Surveys at **www.vault.com/college**—get complete surveys on 100s of colleges and univer- sities, expert advice on applicaton essays and more.

VAULT CAREER LIBRARY **497**

United States Military Academy at West Point

Admissions Office
Building 606
West Point, NY 10996
Admissions phone: (845) 938-4041
Admissions e-mail: admissions@usma.edu
Admissions URL: admissions.usma.edu

 Admissions

Alumnus/a, 6/1999-6/2003, May 2005

Although high SAT scores and high GPAs are important, demonstrated leadership potential is essential. Being a high school sports team captain or club president is a must. Expect to interview for your local political nomination (yes, you need a Congressional nomination). Expect the standard essays and recommendations. Princeton Review voted us the hardest school to get into last year.

Alumnus/a, 7/1996-5/2000, April 2005

West Point selects approximately 1,200 of over 10,000 applications. The process is rigorous in many areas, but there is no interview. The application includes a full medical exam that has many discriminators (e.g. asthma, color-blindness). Applicants also must be single, with no children and under 23 years old upon entrance. There is a physical test that includes several events measuring total body fitness. Without going into full details, just get the events and practice. Training to increase fitness is crucial, but even for those in outstanding physical shape, it is important to spend time practicing the actual events. Although not a requirement for entrance, it is advisable to be able to run two miles under 15 minutes. Otherwise, you will be miserable from fatigue and lose a lot of respect among peers.

The application is long and includes a portion for several recommendations. Most importantly, applicants must have a nomination from a Congressional representative. Securing this nomination can be difficult and it is best to work closely with the representative's office for success. West Point is primarily interested in leadership potential and math competency. It is a globally recognized institution of leadership and a top engineering school. Collect positions of leadership (varsity team captain, especially) to catch the eye of the admissions committee. Calculus and a high college entrance exam score (90+ percent) are also major advantages.

> **Regarding admissions, the school says:** "The mission of the United States Military Academy is 'To educate, train and inspire the Corps of Cadets so that each graduate is a commissioned leader of character committed to the values of duty, honor, country and prepared for a career of professional excellence and service to the Nation as an officer in the United States Army.' Approximately 10,000 applicants apply to West Point each year. Of those 10,000 applicants approximately 4,000 receive nominations. Of those 4,000 applicants approximately 2,500 are qualified medically, academically and physically. However, the average class size is 1,200. Because we have a rolling admissions process, the sooner you complete your application, the better your chance of competing for admission. Our rule of thumb for evaluating a candidate is 60 percent academic ability, 30 percent leadership ability, 10 percent physical fitness.
>
> "Although medical evaluation standards differ among the various commissioning programs of the Armed Services, only one medical examination is needed to meet the application requirements of all service academies and the four-year ROTC scholarship programs. If you are a competitive candidate, you will receive instructions for taking the qualifying medical examina-

tion directly from the Department of Defense Medical Examination Review Board at the appropriate time. You may be scheduled at an Army, Air Force, Naval or civilian facility near your home. The medical qualification is between the candidate and DODMERB, but the U.S. Military Academy admissions department can request waivers for strong candidates who become medically disqualified.

"The criteria established for candidates is set by law, Title X, U.S. Code. Each candidate must:

- Be 17 but not yet 23 years of age by July 1 of year admitted.
- Be a U.S. citizen at time of enrollment (exception: foreign students nominated by agreement between U.S. and another country).
- Be unmarried.
- Not be pregnant or have a legal obligation to support a child or children.

"Satisfactory completion of the Candidate Fitness Assessment (CFA) is one of the requirements for admission to the United States Military Academy. The Candidate Fitness Assessment consists of six physical and motor fitness events designed to measure muscular strength and endurance, cardio-respiratory endurance, power, balance and agility. It is used to determine if a candidate possesses the stamina and movement skills required to successfully complete the physical program at the Academy and perform the duties required of commissioned officers in the uniformed services. If a candidate has taken and passed the CFA for one of the other service academies, he or she can submit that CFA score with his or her West Point application. West Point will provide him with the instructions on how to prepare and how to take the test. West Point will also provide instructions for the CFA Administrator (a coach, ROTC instructor or Field Force member) on how to administer the test.

"Cadets have approximately two hours scheduled for afternoon athletics. All cadets are expected to be athletes and must participate in individual or team sports of their choice at the intramural, club or Corps Squad (Division I) Level. In addition, cadets take a semi-annual Army Physical Fitness Tests in preparation for their Army physical fitness requirements. Athletics build cohesion, confidence and foster a team spirit among cadets. This is an essential element in their leader development.

"The Candidate Questionnaire, which is a two-page document and opens a candidate's file, may be filled out online at the admissions web site. After opening a file, candidates receive the application forms. The forms that a candidate completes consist of three or four short essays, a personal data record, and an activities record, which are minimal. The other forms included with the application are to be completed by other individuals, such as a guidance counselor, three teachers (English, math and a lab science), and the candidate fitness assessment administrator (JROTC/ROTC Instructor, coach, or USMA Field Force Representative). Candidates receive a form to obtain a police record check. Sample letters are provided and available on the USMA admissions web site to use for request for nominations. West Point provides all candidates with business reply envelopes (pre-paid postage) for all the forms that candidates receive. Our entire admissions process is FREE of charge.

"Candidates should apply for a nomination from one or more of the listed sources during the spring of your junior year. You must obtain a nomination in order to compete for admission to the Military Academy. Cadetships are allocated by law to the Vice President; members of Congress; congressional delegates from Washington, D.C., the Virgin Islands and Guam; Governors of Puerto Rico and American Samoa; and the Department of the Army (service-connected nomination). Nominating officials may select up to 10 young people to compete for each cadetship vacancy they may have. At a minimum, most candidates are eligible for a Congressional nomination from their local Congressional Representative, two United States Senators and the Vice President of the United States. Candidates should apply for a nomination from each source for which he is eligible. A sample nomination request letter is provided for candidates' convenience both on our web pages and in the application instructions that are mailed to candidates. Additionally, the admissions office and/or a Military Academy Field Force representative in the candidate's area will be more than willing to answer any questions he may have.

"The United States Military Academy is a Tier I institution for higher learning, ranking with Yale, Harvard, Princeton, MIT and Stanford universities. The Military Academy was originally established in March 16, 1802 as an engineering and artillery school, making it the first engineering school in the country. Additionally, West Point is considered the premier institution for leader development. Our graduates routinely win Rhodes, Marshall and Hertz scholarships, among others, and are strong forces in the military and in civilian life."

 Academics

lumnus/a, 6/1999-6/2003, May 2005

5 percent of classes are core classes. Up until recently, cadets had to choose a ve-course engineering track (systems engineering being the most popular). lass sizes never exceed 20 cadets and average 12. Professors always have time work with cadets. The only way to fail is through lack of motivation. 75 per- nt of professors are military officers with master's degrees and the rest are vilians with PhDs. Instructors expect you to do homework before class and gularly quiz you on the reading assignments. 25 percent of most course grades e instructor points that evaluate preparation only. Just getting A's on tests esn't guarantee a 4.0.

The school says: "West Point advocates developing the whole person by providing a dynamic and integrated curriculum that balances the physical sciences and engineering with the humanities and social sciences. Graduates should be able to respond effectively to a changing technological, social, political and economic world. The Academy instills in cadets creativity, moral awareness, and a commitment to progressive and continuing educational growth. Currently 44 majors are offered to cadets so they can pursue an academic major in a discipline of their choice. The two components of the academic program are a broad, general core program that is prescribed and an elective program that is individually selected. The West Point curriculum is accredited by The Commission on Higher Education of the Middle States Association of Colleges and Schools. Six engineering programs—civil engineering, electrical engineering, mechanical engineering, systems engineering, environmental engineering and engineering management—are accredited by the Engineering Accreditation Commission of the Accreditation Board for Engineering and Technology (ABET). Additionally the Computer Science Accreditation Commission (CSAC) of the Computer Sciences Accreditation Board accredits the computer science major.

"The core curriculum is the foundation of the academic program and provides a foundation in mathematics, basic sciences, engi-

neering sciences, information technology, humanities, behavioral sciences and social sciences. This core curriculum, ranging in size from 26 to 30 courses depending on the major, represents the essential broad base of knowledge necessary for success as a commissioned officer, while also supporting each cadet's choice of academic specialization. It is, in effect, the 'professional major' for every cadet since it prepares each graduate for a career as a commissioned officer in the Army.

"The student-to-faculty ratio at West Point is approximately 8:1. A cadet not only knows his professor or instructor, but he also has the opportunity to request additional instruction when needed. Classes are small, typically numbering 12 to 18 cadets. West Point's long tradition of daily discussion and frequent grading remain unchanged. Army officers and civilian professors enhance a cadet's understanding of an academic concentration. The predominantly military faculty also helps in his professional military development.

"80 percent of professors are military officers, all with masters degrees and many with PhDs. The remaining 20 percent are civilian professors with PhDs."

Alumnus/a, 7/1996-5/2000, April 2005

The West Point program first and foremost is one of military and physical requirements as well as academic requirements. Every cadet holds a position in the cadet hierarchy and participates in a summer program involving military training (summers prior to and following freshman year). Cadets are also graded on these positions and training events. Every cadet also does sports. These include academic fitness classes, intramural or intercollegiate sports, and physical fitness tests.

West Point is an engineering school and every cadet graduates with a BS. A cadet can major in philosophy, psychology or civil engineering, but every cadet graduates with a BS. This is possible because of a required engineering core curriculum.

The core can be of several engineering disciplines (mechanical, systems), but it is nonetheless required. All cadets also take math classes including through second-year calculus. It is not difficult to get the major and classes one desires, but there is a strong mandatory workload. Nearly all of the first two years are set in stone, and the engineering core plus required classes for one's major fill almost all of the remaining two years. While it is possible to major as one chooses, it is uncommon for cadets to add to an already strong workload (16+ credit hours per semester plus military requirements, plus sports) with additional electives. Special qualities of the program include a significant amount of team projects.

Many of the freshman and sophomore, and almost all of the junior and senior, level courses are performed in teams. Professors are very involved in student conduct because they are military officers and interested in academic and professional development. Attendance to class and performing assignments are enforced by academy officials (if you miss a paper, you fail and have some type of punishment). The honor code is part of everything. While the system and the cadets are far from perfect, the honor code is very real and enforced.

The school says: "Cadets learn about and prepare for the ethical demands of officership by living under the dictates of an Honor Code. The code states: 'A cadet will not lie, cheat, steal or tolerate those who do.' Its purpose is to foster a commitment to moral-ethical excellence and an insight into the more comprehensive military professional ethic. The exact origin of the Honor Code is unclear, but it may have evolved from the code of chivalry embraced by the Officer Corps when the Military Academy was established. Colonel Sylvanus Thayer, the Father of the Military Academy, and General Douglas MacArthur helped make the code an essential vehicle for the development of character. The Honor Code demands and expects all members of the Corps of Cadets to conduct themselves with absolute integrity, both in word and deed. Cadets accept this obligation freely and with great pride."

Read all of Vault's College Surveys at **www.vault.com/college**—get complete surveys on 100s of colleges and universities, expert advice on applicaton essays and more.

VAULT CAREER LIBRARY 499

Alumnus/a, 6/1993-5/1997, September 2003

The Academy lifestyle is unique and challenging. The workload is comprised of an all-encompassing educational experience, not just hitting the books. The Academy focuses on three main aspects of development: leadership, academics, and physical development. The first two years are primarily a set curriculum of hard sciences, math and humanity classes to establish a basework from which you can seque into your major field of study. The majority choose engineering as majors, and all must at least choose an engineering track, synonymous with a minor. I chose environmental engineering due to its applicability and demand in the real world. Classes are structured with the cadets in mind and provide as much individual attention and development as possible, sometimes to the chagrin of the unprepared student. Nearly every day, cadets are asked to go to the boards that surround the classroom to work through problems and then randomly selected to explain the solutions. Needless to say, the importance of coming to class prepared is an understatement.

The professors are, from my experience, about 50 percent military officers and 50 percent civilian professors, a good mix of two disparate backgrounds and experiences that only add to the overall development. Grading is fair but tough, and competitiveness really isn't as apparent as one might think. The concept of working as a team player is thoroughly enforced and practiced, which mitigates the development of the cutthroat competitiveness present in other universities. The workload is extremely heavy, often taking a full day's worth of classes every single day of the week, followed by mandatory intramural sports and study time that culminates with lights out at midnight, with adverse action if caught studying past "lights out."

 Employment Prospects

Alumnus/a, 7/1996-5/2000, April 2005

All cadets are required to serve five years of active duty upon graduation. There are very limited programs for service in other branches of the military, and for follow up professional programs including law and medical school. The West Point Association of Graduates is ever-present and alumni are very involved in helping each other. Graduates meet annually around the world each spring to celebrate the founding of West Point. There are also parades each year at the Academy for graduation anniversaries. In addition to the alumni network, many private companies specialize in placing Academy graduates because of their marketability.

> **The school says:** "Upon graduating, a cadet will be commissioned a second lieutenant in the U.S. Army and will serve for at least five years of active duty as an Army officer and three years in a Reserve Component, a total of eight years, after graduation. The active duty obligation is the nation's return on a West Point graduate's fully-funded education. The Army has a wide variety of specialized fields called branches. Each branch has its own brand of technical and tactical expertise. Depending on the needs of the Army, and cadets' personal desires, they will pick from several branch choices that are available, including Infantry, Field Artillery, Armor, Aviation, Engineer, Signal, Air Defense Artillery, Chemical, Military Intelligence, Ordnance, Military Police, Quartermaster, Transportation, Medical Service, Finance and Adjutant General. There are specialties within several of these fields that may also be chosen. Whatever branch selected, a cadet will be responsible for the training, health, welfare, safety and morale of soldiers and for the maintenance and use of equipment. The assignments around the world will test a West Pointer's leadership and managerial skills acquired at the military academy. At the end of the military commitment, officers can choose to leave the Army to serve the nation in different capacities. These graduates soon learn that the West Point Association of Graduates is a strong family."

Alumnus/a, 6/1999-6/2003, May 2005

You owe the Army five years, period. Expect to spend at least one year in Iraq. Salary is about half as much as the degree is worth ($45K first year for 2LT), but

expect excellent job opportunities if you get out (easy to get into the top MB programs). All Army bases are in remote areas, so don't expect much of a soci or dating life while you serve. Highly rewarding if you want to lead soldiers a want to serve your country. Most of your officer peers are from lesser know schools, which can be seen as a positive or negative.

> **The school says:** "Army posts are located in both rural and urban areas across the United States and in many locations overseas, providing soldiers and families a wealth of opportunities to experience a variety of unique local cultures.
>
> "The U.S. government provides 100 percent tuition, room and board for cadet attendance at West Point. Upon graduation, cadets are commissioned as a second lieutenants in the U.S. Army, and they must serve at least five years of active duty and three years in a Reserve Component, a total of eight years, after graduation. The majority of cadets who go on to serve beyond their five year commitment, will have the opportunity to obtain a graduate degree at an institution of their choice, which is paid for by the U.S. government. Some cadets may also have the opportunity to return to West Point as part of the staff and faculty. Many cadets who receive their commission are branched in combat arms and bring their experiences, some from combat, with them back to West Point to impart to future cadets for leadership development."

Alumnus/a, 6/1993-5/1997, September 2003

The bottom line reality of those entering and graduation from West Point is minimum five-year service obligation into the armed services, with the va majority serving in the United States Army. A handful of cadets choose to ser in the other services, e.g., Navy, Marines and Air Force.

As far as internship opportunities, the experience that most correlates to a internship is what is called CTLT (Cadet Troop Leader Training) where cade in the summer preceding their senior year at the academy are able to shadow ar often act as a real second lieutenant in a regular Army unit for approximately 3 days, the position they will graduate into a year later. This is by far the mo rewarding, realistic experience in gauging what the real Army is going to be lik There are cadets that enter the Academy with prior Army or other armed force service experience while others enter just out of high school as I did. Th "internship" is valuable as it gives all cadets the unique opportunity to exper ence the real Army for a short period of time from the perspective of the junie officer, what all cadets are striving to become.

 Quality of Life

Alumnus/a, 6/1999-6/2003, May 2005

Cadets get a small salary and have no tuition costs. Food is decent, healthy a free. All cadets have one roommate in the barracks and rooms are generally lar er than most other campuses I've visited. No air conditioning in summer. Spor and academic facilities are state-of-the-art and well funded. West Point is deve oping a wireless LAN in all classrooms, and laptops will become a mandato class tool.

> **The school says:** "Cadets and faculty at West Point enjoy the benefits of a first-class wireless information technology environment. With a personal computer at every desk, and everyone connected both to a large array of powerful academic computing services and with unlimited access to the Internet, West Point has an electronic environment in which every course offered has integrated computer use. This 'computer thread' allows a cadet to make full use of his personal computer in the place where learning occurs, the barracks."

Alumnus/a, 7/1996-5/2000, April 2005

West Point is a military academy with everything one might expect. All cade live in dorms, are limited in their furniture and possessions, endure freque inspections, and live under a curfew. These restrictions lessen as cadets becon

...re senior, but are still far more restrictive than a normal college, as one might ...pect.

The school says: "There are plenty of opportunities for cadet social involvement through cadet clubs and organizations (too many to name) that meet and compete internally and with other colleges and universities. Cadet privileges for social interaction and individual time increase as cadets gain more seniority. Juniors and seniors have the most privileges, having acquired the right to wear civilian clothes when not on duty, leave post when not on duty, and bring their privately owned vehicles to West Point."

...umnus/a, 6/1993-5/1997, September 2003

...e differences between the Academy experience and a regular university expe-...nce are probably the most profound in the arena of quality of life. From the ...st day of the Basic Training BEAST summer until that graduation day four ...ars later, you live and breathe the Academy lifestyle, there is no alternative. ...e first day of BEAST summer, you gather various uniform and Army pieces ...at all piece together into an overall uniform and army field gear, which will ...come part of your life from that day forward. You will wear a uniform 99.9 ...rcent of your time at the Academy, going to class, working out, playing sports, ...dying, even sleeping. Only the upperclassmen are authorized to wear civilian ...othes on a very limited basis, basically when they are going home on leave for ...lidays or going on a weekend pass.

...e housing is one choice and one choice only: the barracks. These are actual-...quite roomy in space, with normally at least one roommate, depending on in ...ich portion of the barracks you live. They are clean thanks to the freshman ...eaning sessions and daily room inspections. The facilities are topnotch, some-...es a little over Gothic in appearance, especially during those four wonderful ...ay months of a New York winter! Spring is a very welcomed reality as green ...ppears.

...e dining hall is like no other in the world, all 4,000 cadets are fed at the same ...ne in minimal time. Each table is comprised of 10 cadets, a collection of all ...ur classes, with the two or three plebes (freshmen) acting as the "cold bever-...e corporal," or "gunner." These cadets are forced to announce to the table all ...e difference dishes for that particular meal, cut the desert (invariably a pie of ...ke is served that requires cutting into equal pieces), and serving drinks to the ...perclassmen's liking. Often the plebes rarely get to eat much of the meal, and ...they do it is after the upperclassmen are long gone. Each successive class gets ...leave the table at a different time, seniors first, juniors second and so on. The ...ebes are left to wait out the whole meal, scrounging at the last few minutes ...fore the bell sounds to exit the mess hall. The dining experience begins as a ...zy, stressful annoyance and ends as a good social gathering to hang out with ...ur friends. Once again, the dining experience at a service academy is like no ...er university in the world.

 Social Life

...umnus/a, 6/1999-6/2003, May 2005

...u will be hazed for your first year. You won't be able to leave campus regu-...ly until your third year. No party scene at all at school. Your only chances to ...eet girls are at friends' colleges if you are able to get out. Alcohol is forbidden ...barracks and to any underclassman. No sex allowed in barracks. Expect to ...end many, many Friday and Saturday nights watching DVDs with friends. If ...u realize you like to party and have fun now, don't apply.

The school says: "Hazing is not authorized at West Point. Hazing does not foster an adequate leader development environment, and it is never tolerated. Underclassmen are quizzed on 'Cadet Knowledge' that they must know. Memorizing is a useful tool that is required of Army officers and is instilled in cadets during their first year at West Point as part of leader development. All cadets may leave post during the spring, summer, Labor Day, Thanksgiving and Christmas breaks. Family members can visit cadets on designated weekends. One weekend is dedicated solely to freshmen and upperclassmen are required to leave post during this period. First class cadets (seniors) have a club for their sole use on West Point.

"The mission of West Point is to inspire and build leaders of character prepared for service as an Army officer. Cadets are expected to behave ethically and honorably and to respect themselves and others. Rules and regulations are emplaced to enforce the conduct becoming of an officer and to minimize distracters during Cadet Leadership Development. However, cadets have many clubs, organizations and facilities available to them, to include sporting events, their own ski slopes, a theater and much, much more!"

Alumnus/a, 7/1996-5/2000, April 2005

Cadets have a curfew and there is no nightlife nearby. New York City is accessible by a 45-minute train ride when cadets receive a limited pass. Clubs are prevalent, especially sports clubs. The Academy has a strong alumni network and government funding to support any club activity a student could think up.

The school says: "The Cadet Leader Development System is a demanding but professional four-year program to develop leaders of character. Life at the United States Military Academy is BUSY! Many say cadets are the busiest college students in the country. Classes, study, physical education, athletics, military duties and recreation fill many hours of the day."

Alumnus/a, 6/1993-5/1997, September 2003

The most lacking aspect of a cadet's development while at the Academy is in the social arena. Several factors play into this conclusion, the main ones being the lifestyle and workload. The regimented lifestyle requires such focus and dedication that little time remains for social activities, especially as an underclassman. The only real social activities as freshmen include going to church where cookies, punch and other snacks are served, going to sponsors' homes on post on weekends where they gorge you with food, and infrequent holidays for the opportunity to travel home (Thanksgiving and Christmas).

As far as alcohol and the assumed college party scene, it is as about as nonexistent at West Point as can be. There is one bar on post (campus) and it is called the Firstie Club (Firsties are the seniors, so-called because they are in their first class year), which is only open to seniors and only from Thurs. to Sat. No other cadets are allowed to drink on post, period, no exceptions. If one is caught drinking or possessing alcohol on post or in the barracks, serious repercussions will undoubtedly ensue. Due to its close proximity to New York City, that is probably the most common weekend retreat for cadets, although the cost of the city begins to drain the meager cadet bank accounts pretty quickly.

The final two years are the years of freedom (relative, of course) when cadets are allowed to have cars and progressively allowed more and more weekends and off-post privileges. Seniors are even allowed to leave post on what is called OPPs (Off Post Privileges) during the week, but of course must be back by lights-out at midnight, no exceptions.

Read all of Vault's College Surveys at **www.vault.com/college**—get complete surveys on 100s of colleges and universities, expert advice on applicaton essays and more.

VAULT CAREER LIBRARY **501**

University at Albany, SUNY

Office of Undergraduate Admissions
University Administration Building 101
1400 Washington Avenue
Albany, NY 12222
Admissions phone: (518) 442-5435
Admissions fax: (518) 442-5383
Admissions e-mail: ugadmissions@albany.edu
Admissions URL:
www.albany.edu/main/index_admissions.html

 ## Admissions

Alumnus/a, 8/2003-5/2006, October 2006

Admissions process was easy enough. I was told by my college counselor that I would have little chance of getting in, but I got into all four [SUNY schools], as well as a Top 40 private school; a moral in not to always listen to high school college counselors. My application essay was free-topic, so I used the one I wrote for other schools. SUNY Albany doesn't offer as much money as some other SUNY schools do though, you should keep that in mind. Selectivity is not a factor for students in the top 15 percent of their class or with an SAT score of 1280+; however, apply early. As we all know, it's never a sure bet. If you're in the mid-range, you still have a good shot of getting in, as UA has a rather nefarious reputation (recently) of admitting students over their housing limit. Keep that in mind for the time you apply, as you may be stuck in a makeshift dorm in a lounge if you apply for housing too late. SUNY Albany is a state school, as well, so there is a chance they give preference to NY residents. Also, it's really not worth it to apply from out of state, as the tuition becomes ridiculously overpriced. Best bet is to apply early, have a strong, personal essay, and don't stumble in high school, even as a senior.

Alumnus/a, 8/2001-5/2005, February 2006

This school mainly relies on you doing well in high school. They take a look at your SAT scores but they are not primarily focused on them. They do require an essay but that seemed to be just a slight deciding factor. I found this school easy to get into as it was a SUNY school and not a private school.

Current student, 8/2003-Submit Date, October 2005

The admissions process is run by the SUNY system, you use one application for all the SUNY schools. Lately, this school has toughened up its admission policies. 91 average and 1100 SAT scores minimum. There is an essay but it is optional. It has gotten more selective in the last years. The business school requires a 3.0 and you have to apply when you enter as a freshman. It is tough if you wait to apply to get into the B-school.

Current student, 9/2003-Submit Date, January 2006

The best advice I can give to getting into a college you want is to be organized throughout the admissions process. You should know all applicable deadlines and be aware of what programs and financial aid are available at each institution. I did not complete any college interviews, but at any interview, being yourself is most important. The essay you submit should be a reflection of the applicant. I would say to keep it personal and don't try too hard to impress someone in admissions with an essay that lacks character because you're trying to prove yourself the wrong way.

Current student, 9/2005-Submit Date, October 2005

Applied through the SUNY program, submitted form and was accepted because of my grades and athletics. It's a Division I school, so there are high standards here.

Current student, 9/2003-Submit Date, November 2004

Filled out the usual form (your information like name, address, phone numbe age, social security number, income information for you and your parents, yo activities in high school, why you want to go to this school) and you had to ha a transcript from high school (sealed in an envelope with the school stamp on i didn't have to have any references but you could put some in and you didn't ha to write an essay if you didn't want to but it always helps if you show the ext effort, also there was no interview unless you wanted one. This school seems be the harder SUNY school to get into but by looking at the people who go the they must not be too selective—I see a lot of people who don't really care abc college and who don't go to classes and waste away any hope for a good futu by drinking and not studying and smoking until they can't tell what's going in their lives anymore—don't do that. College is one of the best opportuniti in the world and it's not free—it's a pretty expensive trip, if I say so myself.

 ## Academics

Alumnus/a, Political Science, 8/2003-5/2006, October 2006

SUNY Albany has a surprising array of quality areas of education. I graduat with a BA in Political Science, which was my only major all through school, a my minor was in journalism. Both programs are very strong. The political s ence department has a bunch of very strong professors who all know their stu TAs are also very knowledgeable and helpful. Also, with so many other poli sc students around, you'll never have a tough time finding others to study with get advice from. The Rockefeller Institute of Public Policy encompasses t political science, public administration and criminology departments, and is very respected institution.

I am not sure about UA's science programs, as I've only taken a few, but th seem interesting enough. From my perspective, UA can provide a very stro liberal arts education if you're looking to get into government or public servi

Alumnus/a, Business, 8/2001-5/2005, February 2006

The classes are generally huge for the general education courses. It can be cha lenging to get into courses for subjects like psychology. Most professors gra on a curve, especially in the large lecture classes. The workload tends to heavier when you get into the smaller classes (a popular major at SUNY). T large lecture classes tended to be more impersonal and I enjoyed the small classes much more.

Current student, 8/2003-Submit Date, October 2005

There is a good business school, criminal justice, public policy, nanoscience a Africana depts. The workload is decent. Some classes are great, while othe are awful. Grading is on par with other universities. There are large lecture ce ters, so most popular classes are held in them. Some hold 500+ students. Ma of the 100-level classes are taught by adjuncts or TAs. Especially the ma department.

Alumnus/a, 8/1999-8/2003, May 2006

The quality of classes was very good. There was a lot of variety and options. general, the professors were very good and had office hours in which they we willing to help you improve to the degree you wanted to improve. It was ha getting into popular or lower-level classes and the system was hard. You we assigned a certain time at which you could register and this time depended up your year in school and last name. A lot of the time, the classes with the go times were full if you didn't get in there and register right away. I don't kno how else they would do this though as it's a fairly big school. The grading w pretty standard with a number of professors grading on a curve. The cur depended on how everyone else in the class was doing. If one person was doi really well and the rest were not, the student doing well would pull the curve and lower everyone's grade.

Current student, 9/2003-Submit Date, November 2004

The program has many classes to pick from. They offer languages like Russian, Spanish, Japanese, Korean, Chinese, Yiddish and Arabic. If people speak it, you can learn it here. Also, all of the required courses are hard to get into, since there are 10,000 other students who need to take all of these requirements, too. Although getting popular classes is extremely hard until you are higher in the class ranking. Everyone is trying to finish their general education credits so they can graduate on time.

Alumnus/a, 1/1998-8/2001, April 2005

SUNY Albany offers an excellent honors program in English to the top eight to 12 English majors who apply during their sophomore year. Once admitted, students enjoy the opportunity to pick any English courses (no formal requirements) from amongst their required number of credits, other than an honors seminar each junior semester and a 60 page or so senior thesis. When I was there, we were taught by one of the university's most exciting professors. If you are concerned about being challenged intellectually at Albany, see if they offer an honors program in your course of study. If they do, you will probably enjoy it. That being said, there are a lot of sharp students at SUNY Albany, but relatively few are really into their studies.

Current student, 8/2001-Submit Date, March 2004

I've noticed in my three years that the professors have progressively wanted more. And it is not just that I am in harder classes; they expect more out of us, which is good. Workload definitely increases, and getting into the classes you want is hard. However, if you're able to join an honors program, it's easy because you are automatically allowed into any class in your major. The quality of classes is good; however, I wish there were more professors teaching.

Alumnus/a, 9/2000-8/2003, January 2004

Academic programs are nationally renowned for their excellence in teaching. The following programs are exceptional: physics, sociology, business, psychology, public administration and criminal justice. The other programs range from being admirable to competent, depending on the criteria for which the comparisons are made. In the aforementioned programs, students may find class sizes ranging from 20 students to 400 students. Early and creative scheduling may allow for the escape of extremely large class sizes, but they are generally inescapable in the 101 courses, which are usually held in lecture centers, or LCs.

The course offerings are very good. It is not on par with what you will find at other top schools, but students can find intriguing course offerings taught by top faculty holding terminal degrees from the Ivy League. Getting popular classes is somewhat bureaucratic. Seniors are allowed to register first to allow for entrance into the most popular offerings. The magic of "sneaking in" is done during the infamous add/drop session, allowing the motivated underclassmen to register for the offerings that are normally full. The university does provide a large number of spaces for each level of undergraduate study, allowing students in different years to register without delay, if they plan correctly.

Employment Prospects

Alumnus/a, 8/2003-5/2006, October 2006

SUNY Albany is still a relatively unknown school at the national level, so you should always keep that in mind. However, NY State provides many opportunities and as long as you stay local you have a good chance of finding a job right out of college. Recruiters are on campus throughout the year at career fairs, as well as at the Career Development Center. Internships abound in the State Senate and State Assembly, as well as other government agencies, which all are based in Albany, the capital of New York.

Alumnus/a, 8/2001-5/2005, February 2006

Most of the employers that come to SUNY Albany are not the top companies you would expect (at least in the finance field). You will find accounting companies like Ernst and Young and tech companies like Deloitte at the career fairs that are held in the fall and spring. Other than that, most companies focusing on sales are found at these career fairs. I never did find an internship while in college. Most graduates I know had ease in finding jobs in accounting and MSI (management systems information). Jobs for majors like finance/marketing and psy-

chology were much harder to find. Many people went on to graduate school instead.

Current student, 8/2003-Submit Date, October 2005

The Career Development Center is very helpful and organized. They have a number of workshops and critique services. They hold two career fairs on campus each year. One for full-time jobs and one for internships. The CDC uses Monstertrak.com and on-campus recruiting. Even though we are a state school, some prestigious firms come, including the Big Four accounting firms, Morgan Stanley and JP Morgan. Most jobs available through the school are in NYC. If you are not a business major or related major, the school doesn't help you out with jobs, really. The CDC is very business oriented, especially accounting.

Current student, 9/2003-Submit Date, January 2006

Within my business school, there are a few professional fraternities that promise to help with networking and interviewing skills. I have not looked into these opportunities but I'm sure they're helpful when it comes to graduation. I believe we have a pretty good job placement percentage, with a few career fairs and workshops each year.

Alumnus/a, 1/1998-8/2001, April 2005

If you are interested in business, technology or accounting and do well academically, you will be OK. If you are planning to go on to a graduate or professional school and do well academically, you will be OK. If you're not quite sure what you want to do, regardless of how well you do, you're going to be in a tougher spot. Your best bet is to find the place you want to work, do an internship there during the summer of your junior year, and stick with them for your first job after graduation.

According to the experiences of myself and my friends, Albany's reputation with most people, including employers, is as a party school. But that does not mean you won't do well professionally, you just may have to work harder to get your foot in the door than grads of more reputable schools.

Alumnus/a, 9/2000-8/2003, January 2004

Many students go on to pursue graduate studies at the world's top universities. An exceptional student may be pursued by four companies after undergrad, but may decide to attend B-school. Internship opportunities abound in almost all of the major programs at the university. The Career Development Center and the respective departments have binders filled with opportunities for students who are looking for internships. A GPA of 2.5 or higher allows for students to take an internship course and work for a company through the school for a semester, which may lead to employment after graduating.

Quality of Life

Alumnus/a, 8/2003-5/2006, October 2006

The housing situation on the campus itself (not the apartments) is rather awful, as overcrowding and small rooms can make your first two years uncomfortable. It is, however, what you make of it; as long as you keep your environs clean and neat and manage to luck out with a good roommate, you can be quite happy. The Tower dorms are a bit bigger and may be preferable to the squalid low-rise dorms.

The apartment housing on Empire Commons and Freedom Quad, though, are a different story. They both offer great apartments with laundry machines and larger rooms, if you can afford them and are lucky enough to get a good lottery number. The lottery system is one of the most reviled systems on campus; your future housing is essentially the luck of the draw, unless you're chummy with an upperclassman. The Center Quads are a bit detached from the center of campus and involve a short walk. In the long run, however, it's well worth it.

Alumnus/a, 8/2001-5/2005, February 2006

The campus, itself, needs a lot of improvement when it comes to looking livelier. The age of the concrete used to make the buildings is evident, and the style they use reminds you of a desert scene. Overall, housing is best on Empire Commons (the university's apartment complex). It was first opened in the fall of 2002 and is quickly rented out every year (based on a lottery number system). These apartments can be pricey, so you might want to consider living downtown

Read all of Vault's College Surveys at www.vault.com/college—get complete surveys on 100s of colleges and universities, expert advice on applicaton essays and more.

VAULT CAREER LIBRARY   503

if you're not up for the $7,000 a year price. They are, however, a vast improvement over the traditional dorms that are small, old, and very hot (or cold) depending on the time of the year.

Current student, 9/2005-Submit Date, October 2005

They work hard to keep up the quality of the campus and it shows. Fairly large campus that has excellent athletic facilities despite not having a football stadium, but one is projected to be built by 2009. The University at Albany Department of Athletics and Recreation will provide a NCAA Division I intercollegiate athletics program for men and women committed to support the educational mission of the university. The department will strive to achieve excellence within intercollegiate competition at the highest level with deference to a continued commitment to fairness and integrity.

Current student, 9/2003-Submit Date, November 2004

The food is all right, it is catered by a company named Chartwell's and they have a campus center full of food options from Burger King, Sbarro, Au Bon Pain, Zepp's and a cafe where they have tons of live performances like unplugged and poetry readings. The campus is very safe with emergency phones spread throughout and partroling university police at night and on the weekends. During the winter months, they have everything shoveled for you so you don't have to trudge through the snow, and they have tunnels that run under the entire school so you don't have to walk outside in the snow.

Current student, 8/2001-Submit Date, March 2004

In the spring and summer, we have a beautiful campus. The winter months tend to prevail in Albany, though, so we see a lot of gray. There is not much school spirit, and it is definitely a college city. On the weekends you will see the whole school downtown. The uptown campus is in its own neighborhood, and the downtown campus is located in a fairly OK area, but I wouldn't walk by myself too often there. Crime is fairly low on the uptown campus, I think.

> Regarding quality of life, UAlbany says: "UAlbany's vibrant campus community engages students in more than 150 clubs, honor societies, a student pep band and Spirit Brigade that supports 19 Division I varsity teams and intramural sports programs."

Social Life

Alumnus/a, 8/2003-5/2006, October 2006

Most people are welcoming and friendly, not a whole lot of snobs. Albany is really not a great city for people who aren't into partying. You could literally wind up the only student in your dorms on a Saturday night if you decide to stay in, as the campus empties out to go downtown to drink and fraternize. Partying is the life of the social life at UA, and not being part of the party scene is an invitation to social awkwardness. The reputation the school has developed as one of the top party schools in the country is not unfounded.

Those who truly can't stand the party scene are not at a loss, however. There are several outlets on weekends for those enjoy the arts or just a good dinner. The Spectrum on Delaware Avenue (which is a short bus ride away from campus) is a small indie theater that provides both major first-run movies as well as less well-known and high quality movies in an atmosphere that's as homely and comforting as your own home. There are also numerous areas for weekend trips, such as Lake George and the Adirondacks for camping, Boston and New York City are both only about two or three hours away, and Montreal is about four hours away.

Current student, 8/2003-Submit Date, October 2005

The school is known as a party school, but it is not as bad as people say it is. There are a lot of bars downtown, the nicer ones are all the way downtown near the Hudson River. There is a Greek system, but it doesn't overpower the school. Under 5 percent of students are in it. There are lots of non-alcoholic activities for kids who don't drink. There are over 200 clubs and it is easy to make your own if none interest you.

Current student, 9/2003-Submit Date, January 2006

Every group of college-age people likes to have a good time, and there is decent nightlife in Albany. There are a couple of freshman bars and then the are upperclassman bars and clubs. Greek life is prevalent but I think that the b scene is more popular here. On campus, the most popular social scene would the fashion shows that are performed a couple times a year with after-parti downtown.

Current student, 9/2003-Submit Date, November 2004

There are tons of clubs to join and if they don't have one you like, you can ma your own by having 10 people sign a petition. There's a great nightlife dow town with bars and clubs. There are tons of concerts at places like the Pep Arena, Valentines and Northern Lights.

The School Says

The University at Albany is a highly selective, nationally recognized institution that offers students a deep and broad curriculum for a customized program of study. Students can choose from 54 majors in the arts and sciences, business and accounting, public policy, criminal justice, information science, pre-law and pre-health. Honors scholarships, programs and courses in many fields attract high achieving students, many of whom elect accelerated tracks for a combined bachelor/master degree. Two-thirds of graduates go on for advanced degrees and acceptance to top law and medical schools.

The university's outstanding, highly accessible faculty and award-winning advisement services give students a personalized education. The faculty offer many opportunities for research and mentoring in a richly diverse academic environment. Students can further enrich their education with the more than 300 study abroad programs available.

UAlbany's School of Business provides a solid learning foundation for highly motivated, qualified, intellectual individuals who have a strong desire to succeed. A quality, supportive faculty, challenging curriculum, and small, interactive classes (approximately 30 to 50 students once in major) fosters the growth and development of each student. Business students are highly recruited by prestigious firms and Fortune 500 companies who regard these skills as crucial to survival in the business world.

Because of its location in New York State's capital, the university also offers a multitude of exceptional internships in government, education, the arts and many other professional fields.

UAlbany students enjoy a vibrant campus life with an abundance of activities, student clubs, honor societies, cultural events, Division I varsity teams, intramural sports and resident life programs. With a 160-year history, traditions and spirit are valued components of university life.

The university provides students cutting-edge facilities that support every facet of their education, from smart classrooms, high-tech laboratories and modern art studios, to on-campus apartment-style housing. Albany is a great college city; with thousands of students from 13 nearby colleges, access to a wide range of quality cultural events, top name entertainment— and all this only a short drive to the spectacular natural and recreation centers in New York, Massachusetts and Vermont.

University at Buffalo, SUNY

Admissions Office
5 Capen Hall
University at Buffalo
Buffalo, NY 14260-1660
Admissions phone: (888) UB-ADMIT or (716) 645-6900
Admissions e-mail: ub-admissions@buffalo.edu
Admissions URL: admissions.buffalo.edu/

Note: The school has chosen not to comment on the student surveys submitted.

Admissions

Current student, 9/2003-Submit Date, May 2006

Getting in wasn't as hard as I had thought. In high school my grades weren't the greatest and my SATs were nothing special. When writing an essay for a school, whether it be to get in or for a grade, have as many people as possible read over the essay. You get better feedback that way and can fix things before submitting the essay. English teachers are the best at this.

Current student, 11/2004-Submit Date, November 2005

The application process is fairly simple for New York State residents, as it is part of the SUNY application. The extended application includes various standard questions and a number of optional essays. Completing the essays will get your application looked at above other students. Interviews are used for students who are waitlisted. With good grades and SAT scores, I would not consider UB to be terribly difficult to get into, but more so than some SUNY schools. I was accepted to the honors program at UB, which requires at 93 GPA in high school and a score of at least 1300 on the SATs. UB also offers a scholars program with slightly lower qualifications, which still has scholarships included.

Current student, 9/2004-Submit Date, September 2005

The admissions process getting into the university, itself, was not all that difficult. The essay portion was not very long and the rest of the application was pretty standard. However, the pharmacy program, for which I am applying next fall semester, is quite difficult. Only 117 students make it into the program and there is an extensive application to be accepted into the program. The essay portion is also very highly regarded when accepted into the program. All in all, the pharmacy program is a very difficult program to get into.

Alumnus/a, 8/2003-5/2006, May 2006

I entered the University at Buffalo (UB) as a third-year transfer student. I originally came from a small private school in North Carolina but decided to attend UB for its size, tuition and social life. The counselors made the transition easy and I was accepted the first time I applied. I did not lose any credits but I had to repeat some courses that UB did not believe to be set at a high enough standard. I started to look at UB in fall 2002 and applied in the spring for the following fall 2003. As a transfer student, all I needed to give was a copy of my transcript. I did not need my SAT scores because I was transferring with enough credits already.

Current student, 8/2004-Submit Date, December 2005

About 56 percent of those who apply are admitted. Admission is mainly based on your high school GPA and ACT/SAT scores. They allow you to send a secondary application after completing your general SUNY application, which takes into account previous job and volunteer experience and an essay. You are admitted directly into the Jacob's School of Management as a freshman if you indicated business administration or accounting as your declared major. In order to continue on to take upper-level business courses, you must complete seven fundamental business courses (Calculus, Macroeconomics, Microeconomics, Psychology, Accounting I and II, and Statistics) with at least a 2.5 GPA. If you

take a tour of the school, which I highly recommend, they record your visit and it does help in the admissions process.

Current student, 8/2003-Submit Date, October 2004

There is an application one must fill out in order to apply to this university. You must make sure you take the SATs (a certain score is needed for acceptance), higher level requirements, and extra activities are a plus. Also, you will end up doing an essay that is approximately two to three pages. The topic changes each year. So the admissions process is separated into two parts: application and your essay and other criteria, this is how they eliminate people.

Academics

Current student, 9/2003-Submit Date, May 2006

When it comes to classes at this school, many are fairly large lecture halls; however, most of these classes have smaller review sessions at another time during the week. The professors are flexible and willing to work with the students, most have open office hours several times a week. The workload is not too bad, but doing work every day other than homework is imperative.

Current student, 11/2004-Submit Date, November 2005

The higher-level undergrad courses have excellent professors, but many lower-level classes are taught by graduate students. There are many advisors available to help students find the right classes for their major. Students in the honors program and athletes register first for their classes, but most undergraduate students have difficulty getting into lower-level classes. Most freshmen will have large lectures for many of their intro classes besides writing. Many of the professors for higher-level classes are excellent teachers, as well as very advanced in their fields. Most professors are very willing to work with students individually. Being a large school, new students should always try to introduce themselves to professors directly and visit them during office hours.

Current student, 9/2004-Submit Date, September 2005

The academics in this [pre-pharmacy] program are quite difficult when compared to something like a business program or something of that nature. As is expected, it is mostly all science and I have had to take organic and general chemistry along with some biology classes, physics and calculus. The classes seem quite hard here. The atmosphere is quite overwhelming when you get here. Sometimes it seems like you're just a number, which is one thing I wish I could change about the school.

Current student, 8/2002-Submit Date, March 2006

Registration windows are opened in order of credits completed, i.e., students with 90+ credits completed register first, 75+ second and so on. So of course, if you're a second semester freshman or first semester sophomore, you're probably going to be shut out. Word to the wise: Online registration opens at 8 a.m., but be sure to wake up early and be in front of your computer at 7:50 a.m. and start logging in then, there must be a glitch or something because it always opens a few minutes early. Even if you don't get a class you want, if you constantly check on the status of the class, you'll probably be able to grab a seat because students drop and add all the time. Quality of classes/workload/grading varies depending on the professor. The Student Association takes surveys at the end of every semester from every student in every class and posts the results so you can have a feel for who to take and who to avoid. UB is great because it has just about every major under the sun and it's also a great research university. A lot of people come here undecided or deciding between a few majors and love it because they get to experience them and each choose, or just do several.

Current student, 8/2004-Submit Date, December 2005

UB's undergraduate business program includes a registered accounting tract and a business administration tract. Under accounting are a registered accounting and internal audit concentrations. Under business administration, there are the following concentrations: financial analysis, human resource management,

Read all of Vault's College Surveys at **www.vault.com/college**—get complete surveys on 100s of colleges and universities, expert advice on applicaton essays and more.

VAULT CAREER LIBRARY 505

international business, marketing and management information systems. The quality of the professors within the School of Management is excellent. Professors hold PhDs and MBAs from top universities and have real-world work experience with the Big Four accounting firms and some of the top financial services/I-banking firms in the world. Outside of the School of Management, professor quality can waver a bit; however, the diversity of course offerings and the fact that many professors teach the same course allows students—those who choose to put in the effort—to pick and choose among award-winning professors. The classes offered by the School of Management are enlightening and the lessons learned can easily translate into real-world work situations. As you head into your junior year you will find that many professors place students into cohort groups in order to complete assignments as a team, much as they would be asked to do in the business world. The workload is manageable. Putting in a moderate amount of work will yield a C or a low B. Only the most outstanding students who have gone above and beyond will be lucky enough to earn an A.

Current student, 8/2003-Submit Date, October 2004

The workload at UB is dependent on your major. Science and engineering majors tend to have a larger workload. The classes range from five to 350 people. Many of the science courses are in huge lecture halls of a large amount of students. Your arts (English, drama) and languages (French, Italian, Greek) tend to be in small classrooms with much fewer students. Smaller classrooms are useful for more contact with the professor, whereas larger lecture halls are good because attendance isn't required and the lectures are usually recorded online. The juniors and seniors have an easier time of registering for classes online or by phone. But, freshmen have an orientation period and course where they can comfortably adjust to new settings. The grading is from A to F and it can be changed into a numeric system. Although the campus is huge and easy to get lost in, there are maps throughout the school. The programs at UB are excellent. The teachers are helpful and the social aspect is booming, too.

Current student, 1/2001-Submit Date, April 2004

I was in the philosophy program. The material in upper-level classes is challenging. Common workload for a philosophy class, nightly reading assignments, midterm and a final, along with two five- to 10-page papers. Teachers are very intelligent. I've had teachers from Yale, Brown and Harvard. One teacher was awarded $2 million for his research. I have never had a teacher who curved. Attendance is typically optional. Class sizes tend to be around 30 to 40 students. Popular classes are easily gotten by asking the professor personally.

 Employment Prospects

Alumnus/a, 8/2003-5/2006, May 2006

UB has an Office of Career Services that offers résumé help and storage for teacher recommendations. This is the place many students look when leaving UB for help finding a job or just improving their own personal stock in the job market. There are two main job fairs each year that the college offers. These are great places to go even before your last year in school to start getting connections and learning what you will need to do in order to get the job you want. As a recent graduate I received many letters from the Alumni Association. There is a membership fee that I will be paying so I will stay in contact with UB.

Current student, 8/2004-Submit Date, December 2005

The School of Management's Career Resource Center is excellent. Each year the School of Management holds an event called Network New York for students and alumni. This year it was held at PwC's headquarters in Manhattan. Alumni from companies attend such as Goldman Sachs, JPMorgan Chase, Kraft Foods, Accenture and AIG. The Big Four accounting firms actively recruit on campus. PwC holds their annual Xact competition on campus. Other notable companies who recruit UB students include Pepsico, IBM and Lockheed Martin.

Alumnus/a, 9/1998-5/2004, November 2004

The campus Career Services is helpful to the extent that they can give direction to what companies may be hiring. They do offer quite an number of internships where you can then prove yourself to the employer to give you a full-time job after graduation. SUNY Buffalo offers a variety of majors that can lead to any perspective job offering a company may have. Seeing that SUNY Buffalo is

such a large school, usually the top tier is looked at for jobs or those who have some sort of outside connections. As for alumni, I have not felt their presence for networking at all.

Alumnus/a, 9/2001-5/2003, June 2004

When you do find Career Services, they are useful, providing mentoring, private UB job searches and personality tests. Make the staff make a connection with you. Go to every relevant Career Services event, and stop in the office regularly.

Alumnus/a, 9/2001-5/2003, September 2003

Finding an internship was difficult. The first two years, the school offers very little help, other than posting flyers of job fairs. The job fairs never pull in big name companies outside of the region. Other than companies from New York City and western New York, few big-name companies recruited from the school. The school never really offers help until the junior and senior years of college. Even then, you have to do the majority of searching and getting yourself out there. Though the Career Resource Center offers excellent help, they are unable to help you land a job outside the New York region. The prestige with employers in the western New York is excellent, but outside it is not.

 **Quality of Life**

Current student, 9/2003-Submit Date, May 2006

The North Campus, where most classes are, is in Amherst, NY, which is a very nice area, safe and quiet. This campus is the larger of the two campuses and holds the academic spine, two dormitory complexes and all of the on-campus apartments. On South Campus, you will find a few dorms, many freshmen end up living on South—it's a fun time. There are a few academic buildings on South, mostly for medical and architecture. The areas surrounding is in the process of being rebuilt, so we'll soon see how it comes out.

Current student, 11/2004-Submit Date, November 2005

UB works to provide a good environment for students on campus. The Ellicott housing complex on campus is fairly new and has great facilities for students. There are many work-out facilities on campus that are free to all undergraduate students. There are many places to eat on campus sponsored by campus dining and private venders. The school offers free counseling services to all students. There are hundreds of clubs for students that focus on sports, ethnic groups, dance, social activism and many other things. The Amherst campus is extremely safe and both campuses are constantly monitored by the university police force. As student group also offers a SafeWalk home from the library at night.

Current student, 9/2004-Submit Date, September 2005

The housing at the university is quite good. Freshmen and upperclassmen have absolutely no problem finding a place to live on campus, as there is a lot of student housing. Also, there are many programs throughout the campus just about every day to get students involved in the university. The crime is impressively low. The dining is very convenient. The facilities are also very well kept. The only complaint I have ever really had about the facilities is that the bathroom use down the hall from me has a shower that is broken and it hasn't been fixed in a few weeks, but the maintenance crew is very busy right now.

Current student, 8/2002-Submit Date, March 2006

Housing is good, I've lived in both campuses, although only in the dorms. I loved both campuses. Being from NYC, the urbaneness of South Campus made me feel right at home, and when I moved to the more suburban North Campus (Ellicott), the proximity to classes made it just as good. All the dorms are pretty good, although Governors is usually avoided, (it's kind of awkwardly located on campus), and most students live in the Ellicott Complex. Laundry, basic cable and Internet are free everywhere on campus; I've heard it's not that way everywhere. The apartments are great—they're roomy and come with every amenity you could reasonably want. I think the rates are pretty competitive with similar off-campus apartments but if you are paying more than you would elsewhere it's probably worth it because it is so convenient. Inter- and intracampus buses make getting around campus easy but be sure to check out the bus schedule especially at off-peak times.

Current student, 8/2003-Submit Date, October 2004

At UB, there are many dorms. The school is separated into North Campus, Ellicott Complex and South Campus. There is also housing on North Campus and apartments near North/South Campus for students to rent. The dining halls are very nice, very clean and large. There are also many restaurants and food places (BK, Subway, pizza places, Asian restaurants and other options). If one is bored, they may go to the commuter lounge to relax, sleep and watch TV. Or one can go to the ping pong room, arcade room, work out, play sports, go by the pond, attend sporting events and other events (numerous events occur each day). UB is very safe because we have a police station on every campus and we even have an anti-rape task force for young people in need of assistance walking to their cars at night.

Current student, 1/2001-Submit Date, April 2004

UB is located in Amherst, which has one of the lowest crime rates in New York state. UB security guards are actually police officers, so they don't mess around. The campus is huge, yet it is somewhat overcrowded. UB has a Burger King, a pizza shop, two Chinese places, a sub shop, a sandwich shop, Starbucks, CVS, a hair salon, a jewelry store, a computer store and more, all on campus. Inside the student union, there are also places to dine. UB also has both dorms and apartments only a minute off campus.

 # Social Life

Current student, 9/2003-Submit Date, May 2006

Basically, whereever you live on campus, you will be able to find a party. Word of advice, spend any time you can during the day in the library because the weekends tend to get crazy. A popular hangout for many students during the week is the student union—all the Greeks are there on a regular basis, plus there are plenty of place to eat within a five-minute walk. The Steer is a popular place for many students at the school—on Thursday nights, it's packed. If you want to do something different you could take the train downtown to Chippewa and there are crowds of people on Friday and Saturday nights. There are enough clubs and bars down there that you do not have to go to the same one twice in one month. It's nice because you can also find the right environment that you and your friends enjoy the most. Buffalo Sabre's hockey is huge up here many people go to places like Buffalo Wild Wings to watch the game.

Current student, 11/2004-Submit Date, November 2005

Students at UB are happier with the social life than any of my friends at other schools. There are many restaurants just off campus, as well as an ice skating rink, many clubs, bars and parks. There is a bus system that runs to the Main St. campus that many students use to go to the bars on Main St. Students are often found at the bars: Molly's, the Steer, or PJ Bottoms on Main St. Many students also make the short drive downtown for concerts, sporting events or clubs.

Alumnus/a, 8/2003-5/2006, May 2006

The social life of UB is one of its highlights, I believe. Whether it's a frat, sorority, club, or a Division I athletic team you wish to join, there is much offered to the students. But the nightlife in Buffalo just makes the whole college experience even better. Bars and nightclubs don't close until 4 a.m. A huge plus if you like pre-gaming at a friend's place. But the nightlife is very repetitive and gets boring after a while. One of the hotspots is Chippewa St. downtown. This is a street that is basically a strip of bars and nightclubs. Another is Main Street, which offers more bars for those students living on South Campus.

The only drawback to UB or Buffalo is the long and harsh winters. But if you can get through that, then UB is the perfect fit for you.

Current student, 8/2002-Submit Date, March 2006

UB loves to party. There are bars and clubs for everyone—really, everyone. There was a bar across the street from South Campus known as PJ Bottoms where every freshman would practically be guaranteed entry and as many cheap beers/drinks as they could handle if they just chalked their NY State IDs, but just this year it was shut down. I honestly don't know what the freshmen do now, but I'm sure they're not going thirsty. Upperclassmen, or anyone interested in anything beyond drinking warm kegs of beer, can hop on Buffalo's sad excuse for a subway that leads right from South Campus to the downtown area. Chippewa Street has tons of bars and clubs for everyone. The Greeks hold tons of house parties in University Heights (across the street from South Campus) especially in the first few weeks of the school year. The Greek system is prominent. Student clubs are huge at UB, over 100 student organizations ranging from academic clubs to anime, to people of color and international organizations. There are tons of students at UB and they're very diverse, we have sheltered kids from tiny towns, a huge NYC population, international students—every student fits in here.

Alumnus/a, 9/1998-5/2004, November 2004

SUNY Buffalo has a lot of students, which, in turn, brings a variety of activities in which you can participate. I, for one, was in a fraternity on campus, which provided me with many different party scenes, from bars to halls, to receptions. Social life is like the quality of life: it is what you make of it. There are many places to go to meet people, it's just a matter of if you are willing to put forth the effort. It will not just fall in your lap. There are plenty of opportunities, great places to eat depending on what kind of food you enjoy, sports bars and lounges. There's a place to go every night if your body can handle it.

Current student, 8/2003-Submit Date, October 2004

The Greek system is very popular at UB. It offers many social events, community service and recognition. The social life is booming at UB. There are new social events each day, such as contests, karaoke, games, movies and concerts. There are also many bars near South Campus and clubs 15 minutes away. The dating scene is booming due to the large social scene. Students enjoy the bars and the Greek system parties because of the large parties and cheap drinks. The restaurants nearby range from poor to good. Some places are small diners and pizza joints and fast food. But there is some fine dining, as well.

Read all of Vault's College Surveys at www.vault.com/college—get complete surveys on 100s of colleges and universities, expert advice on applicaton essays and more.

VAULT CAREER LIBRARY 507

University of Rochester

Admissions Office
P.O. Box 270251
Rochester, NY 14627-0251
Admissions phone: (585) 275-3221 or (888) 822-2256
Admissions fax: (585) 461-4595
Admissions e-mail: admit@admissions.rochester.edu
Admissions URL: www.rochester.edu/admissions/

Admissions

Current student, 8/2003-Submit Date, September 2006

The admissions process was relatively stress-free, at least from a paperwork level. All of the materials, along with guidelines and assistance for filling it out, available online, as well as hard paper copies. UR admissions has one of the widest ranges of SAT scores considered, to encourage students to show their individuality that cannot be seen through a test score. It is, however, difficult to get in and selectivity is growing stronger, so it is necessary for prospective student to take time and serious effort in preparing their application.

Alumnus/a, English, 9/2003-5/2007, May 2007

The admissions process was friendly. The admissions office really made it a point to get to know me as a person, not just an application. It was nice to know that all of my successes and future ambitions were being considered—not just a test score.

Current student, 9/2002-Submit Date, September 2005

Rochester was not my Number One choice, so I only applied after receiving the Bausch and Lomb Math and Science Award in high school. Despite the school's very good program, it isn't well known outside the greater Upstate New York area (in my opinion). The application accepted at the time was the Common Application, making the admissions process easy. I think the school does like looking for people who score very well on the SATs despite not having the best overall GPAs. There also is a push to limit the class size and increase diversity across campus, making the selectivity much higher each year.

Alumnus/a, 7/2001-5/2004, December 2005

The admissions process was straightforward: get the application, fill it out, write the essays and send it back with the application fee. I did not have an interview, although I hear they are now required.

> **Regarding interviews, UR says:** "Interviews are not required but are highly recommended. If a student is not able to come to campus for an interview, alternative arrangements can be made."

To get in, you should be an outstanding academic performer and have taken as many AP classes as you can handle and get high grades in them. The next most important piece of the application was the SAT score, which should at least match the average of the school. The essays were pretty standard, and if you can tweak ones you've already written to make them seem personalized for this school, they should carry you through. As you can tell, this school is pretty selective, but not as selective as the Ivy League.

> **The school says:** "We also value unquantifiable strengths, such as initiative, creativity, enthusiasm and leadership. Students can submit scores from either the SAT or ACT."

Current student, 8/2004-Submit Date, September 2005

I found the admissions process very inviting. The university holds several events called Open Campus, as well as open houses both in the spring and fall in order, to give students the opportunity to visit the campus. The tours were informative and realistic, not projecting an unrealistic view of the school. The

application process was standard but the admissions office seemed very on t of things.

Current student, 9/2005-Submit Date, November 2005

For those applying now, I believe attending classes and living in the dormitori are the most important things to do when searching and applying for colleges. is not important to look only at the name of the school because, though son schools may be Ivy League, they may not be suited for you as the academic pre sures may be suicidally high. It is important to experience it yourself for a whi before making decisions about it by attending a single class or something

Current student, 8/2003-Submit Date, May 2005

As a music major, the in-person audition with an applied faculty memb accounted for about 90 percent of the admissions process. Practicing regular was a plus. It was also necessary to enter the audition with a positive, relaxe frame of mind. Academics, although important, were not paramount in th admissions process. This only factored in if there was a close call between tw auditioning students.

> **The University of Rochester says:** "The in-house audition plays a significant part in the admissions process; however, the decision to admit, waitlist or reject is based on the entire admissions file, including the academic record."

Academics

Current student, 9/2002-Submit Date, September 2005

Heavy workload, no question. As an athlete, you really have to be balanced this school. Most programs are very well known, and if not, are certainly on th rise. Some classes are better than the others, but it mostly depends on the pro fessor. Most professors are committed to undergrads, and you can tel However, end up in a class with a professor who would rather promote his ow interest (or his grad students) and the class can be living hell. Classes fill u quickly (particularly required classes with limits), so sign up for classes ASAI

Current student, 8/2004-Submit Date, September 2005

A big emphasis is placed on the curriculum, which allows you to choose wha you want to study. Classes, aside from some introductory courses, are prett small. Even large classes meet in small groups outside of the large lecture s that the students have the opportunity to interact in a smaller environmen Professors are excited and knowledgeable about what they are teaching, man having won awards in their respective fields for excellence.

Alumnus/a, English, 9/2003-5/2007, May 2007

The Rochester Curriculum was the reason I decided to enroll. I had to comple a major and two "clusters" of related courses in the two branches outside of m major, among the humanities, social sciences and natural sciences. The progra provided freedom, but also a sensible structure that made me feel as though I' received a thorough education. I was only unable to get into one class in fou years, but after speaking with the professor of the class, was allowed in. Classe rarely fill up and exceptions are almost always made. The workload varied fror semester to semester, depending on what types of classes I took: lecture, lab c discussion. My toughest semester included a lecture/lab, a thesis, and tw intense discussion courses with heavy reading. I lived in the library that semes ter, but still had time to pursue extracurricular activities.

Alumnus/a, Engineering, 7/2001-5/2004, December 2005

As an electrical engineering major, the quality of classes was pretty good, wit lots of homework assigned and emphasis on midterms and finals. Theory an thinking were favored over rote practice, even though labs were also a part of th grade. Popular classes were not a problem to get into, as the registrar did decent job putting those classes in larger rooms. Grading was usually fair, an appealing to the professor or TA was always possible and could work in you avor. While the primary focus of professors was researching and not teaching, most had PhDs and had taught long enough to refine their material. Avoid new professors or those without tenure, as they're busy with research and have little time to develop coursework. The workload depends on your major, and in electrical engineering, it is tough but worth it.

Current student, 8/2003-Submit Date, September 2006

Academics are taken extremely seriously by everyone at UR, from coaches to deans, to students. Students have the unique opportunity to decide and develop their own curricula based upon their personal interests and desires. It is extremely rare to find any two students who have taken the exact same coursework in their four years at the college. UR also boasts one of the best teaching staffs in the country.

Professors are not pushed to publish rapidly in order to substantiate their positions at the college, so they have a greater concentration on their students and are intent on making certain they impact every student in their courses. Most students have personal relationships with their professors and, because of this, are encouraged to fulfill their potentials in their coursework not only for the grades (which are difficult but justly received), but also for complete understanding of the subject. Most students take a 16-credit courseload consisting of four classes but there are overachievers who take more than that. There is a lot of work that needs to be done for each class, but the majority of students graduate with much more than just a major from UR. Many students also take advantage of the large study abroad program. Most of my friends and I took our entire junior year abroad studying in two different places, and there have been no problems in transferring credits so we can graduate on time. Study abroad diversifies education in unimaginable ways and is an essential part of undergraduate education, which UR understands completely.

Employment Prospects

Alumnus/a, English, 9/2003-5/2007, May 2007

Many of my peers work in New York City, Boston, Washington or other large cities after graduation. Most are in jobs they enjoy. I also know several alumni at top institutions or stationed around the world thanks to fellowships and volunteer opportunities. The Career Center is a great resource: helpful and knowledgeable.

Current student, 8/2003-Submit Date, September 2006

The alumni network is pretty outstanding at UR. The Career Center is also very active. For students desiring employment within the local area, there are hundreds if not thousands of opportunities the Career Center opens up for you. Most opportunities are in economic, financial, medical or law fields. The employment prospects and internships available through on-campus sources are everything that a student makes them.

Current student, 9/2002-Submit Date, September 2005

On-campus recruiting for jobs is minimal for anyone looking to work outside Rochester, NY. The Career Center can be helpful, but you have to have the right person helping you. Once I started working with one, I was introduced to a whole new aspect of looking for a job, and she was very helpful. There are some very helpful alumni out there, but you need to push the issue with the Career Center to determine who they are. Ask around with whom it's best to work, people on campus know.

Current student, 8/2004-Submit Date, September 2005

The wide variety of jobs and forms of employment that students get after graduation demonstrate the diverse nature of the majors and interests represented on campus. Graduates receive jobs with major corporations and nonprofit organizations, as well as many things in between in fields from film to English, to engineering. Some students also pursue professional school or research upon graduation. Companies graduates find employment with include Xerox, Teach for America and Bausch and Lomb.

Alumnus/a, 9/1997-9/2001, May 2005

Science graduates can usually find jobs right away in Rochester. I've seen many of my graduating friends find jobs quickly in metro areas like D.C., Boston and NYC. Getting into grad school from Rochester is really easy, the school helps

streamline the process with a full-service career center. The alumni and senior network is really helpful, and the Career Center holds career fairs and recruitment events quite often.

Quality of Life

Current student, 9/2002-Submit Date, September 2005

Campus life is what you make of it. The dorms aren't the most glamorous, but you can still always have a good time. Once the weather gets bad, fewer people go out, but the school and Student Association work hard to run programs for students. The campus is very beautiful (with the exception of Wilson Commons) and facilities are very accessible. The dining is campus dining, probably not as bad as we make it out to be, but it's not that great.

Alumnus/a, 7/2001-5/2004, December 2005

Dining is provided by Aramark and, with a monopoly and captive audience, is overpriced and of poor quality. It's essentially like eating out for every meal at bad restaurants. The best food is served when prospective students and parents come to campus. Housing is not as bad, although there isn't always enough for students, resulting in three people sharing a room meant for two at times. A variety of housing is available, however, from traditional dorms to Greek houses, to off-campus apartments. The sports facilities are diverse and numerous, including a pool, indoor and outdoor tennis courts, a football field, a track field, indoor basketball courts, racquetball and squash courts, and an oddly square and too small soccer and floor hockey indoor court. Living off campus is cheaper, not due to housing but due to board, with grocery chains accessible by car or campus bus. Parking is notoriously bad and expensive, costing around $300 per school year to park closer to campus based on seniority, with sophomores parking more than a mile away from the campus itself. Freshmen are technically not allowed to park on campus. Free parking across the river or park is available but is a 10-minute walk to the edge of campus.

> **The school says:** "Freshmen living on campus are not eligible for a parking permit, but free buses, shuttles and Zip cars are available."

Current student, 8/2003-Submit Date, May 2005

The neighborhood in downtown Rochester is not conducive to college students; crime does happen. The dining center is run by Aramark, so it pretty much goes without saying that the food is sub-par and over-priced. In general, if you are looking for a typical college atmosphere, Eastman is not the place. Many times it feels more like a high school boarding school than a college campus, especially since the dormitory consists of one building. With that being said, however, the small community is very supportive and friendly. In short, everyone watches out for each other.

Current student, 8/2003-Submit Date, September 2006

Dining services are like all others: expensive, relatively bad for you, but with a bit of variety and vegetarian, vegan and organic options. Dorms are beautiful on the main quad but upperclassman housing leaves a bit to be desired. Rarely do students live off campus, especially students heavily involved in campus activities like sports teams, because the campus is not located in a city living-type area. The athletic facilities are great and centrally located. The campus itself is safe, patrolled by both campus security and Rochester City Police. Above all, I have yet to find a college campus more beautiful than this one.

Social Life

Current student, 9/2002-Submit Date, September 2005

On campus, students frequent the fraternity quad on weekend nights. It's great when the weather is warm, people hang around outside all night and it's great. When the snow rolls in, though, a lot fewer people enjoy making the hike there. There are usually pretty good parties in upperclassman housing and always a few off-campus house parties that are close. The bar scene is good, but not real close to campus. It is definitely a car/cab ride away, but there are quality bars on Monroe, East and Park Aves. Often on Thursdays, the Senior Class Council will

Read all of Vault's College Surveys at www.vault.com/college—get complete surveys on 100s of colleges and universities, expert advice on applicaton essays and more.

VAULT CAREER LIBRARY 509

run a bus from campus to a local bar with drink specials for the night. This is usually 21+, though. Plenty of good restaurants in the city.

Alumnus/a, English, 9/2003-5/2007, May 2007

Although the campus is somewhat isolated from the City of Rochester, bars, restaurants and shopping, the campus and student life offices do their best to compensate. It is possible to attend UR for four years without leaving campus, but then one would miss out on all Rochester has to offer. The city boasts professional sports teams, eclectic shopping and fantastic restaurants. The bus system has improved greatly and there are several opportunities to get off campus each week.

Current student, 8/2004-Submit Date, September 2005

There is a Greek life on campus, but it is by no means the end of the social scene. The many clubs on campus provide a wide variety of events throughout the year. Many events have a cultural favor that illustrates the many cultures represented on campus. There are several good restaurants in the area of varying ethnicities from Indian to Chinese, to standard American fare. Genesee Valley Park is a short walk from campus and provides students with an opportunity for outdoor activities such as canoeing and ice skating.

Current student, 9/2005-Submit Date, November 2005

Every weekend there is also something entertaining for the students to do. There are usually bands playing. Also, many discounted tickets to other concert locations, including Blue Cross Arena (major touring performances) and Eastman Theatre (classical), are available. There are also two major play companies in Rochester that are very interesting. On campus, there are two comedy troupes, a juggling troupe, five or six a cappella groups (a few nationally recognized), and various student government or organizations of entertainment. There are also several martial arts groups and various club sports ranging from table tennis to fencing.

> **The school says:** "Close to 75 percent of the undergraduate body participates in some form of organized athletic program, including varsity, club and intramural sports."

Current student, 8/2003-Submit Date, September 2006

The Greek system is very strong for guys. The main place on campus to party is the fraternity quad, which has actually existed for longer than the college. The quad is lined by six enormous fraternity houses where kids can always go for free beer and parties. The class councils and sororities often rent out bars in the city's downtown to have parties and have buses running all night long to and from the bars to transport attendees. The bars downtown are plentiful and lots of fun. Also, dining in Rochester offers delights for every taste bud. Many different Mexican, Thai, Chinese, Lebanese, Indian, Italian, Spanish and fusion restaurants are found in the city. There are numerous ones who deliver right to campus, as well. Plus, it's a lot cheaper to eat off campus in Rochester compared to in a large city like New York. There is an incredible number of on-campus groups that work to promote and instigate the development of different interests at UR. Whether you want Outdoor Adventure, Young Republicans or Polish Heritage, you can find it on campus. Sports are also very prevalent and an important part of life at UR.

> **UR says:** "The Fraternity Quad is comprised of nine houses and is a historical residential neighborhood. The initial buildings were constructed in 1930, while the newest addition was built in 1975. Once exclusively reserved for fraternities, the buildings today house a mix of fraternities and other organized special-interest living groups.
>
> "University of Rochester conduct policies and regulations, along with New York State laws, guide the event registration and management procedures of all fraternity and sorority social events on and off campus."

The School Says

Founded in 1850, Rochester is one of the leading private universities in the country, one of 62 members of the prestigious Association of American Universities, and one of eight national private research institutions in the premier University Athletic Association. Including the Eastman School of Music, the university has a full-time enrollment of about 4,500 undergraduates. Rochester's personal scale and the breadth of its research and academic programs permit both attention to the individual and unusual flexibility in planning undergraduate studies.

Along with the distinctive Rochester Curriculum to help make the most of the undergraduate years, students in the College of Arts, Sciences, and Engineering (the College) also have access to resources at the Eastman School of Music, the William E. Simon Graduate School of Business Administration, the Margaret Warner Graduate School of Education and Human Development, the School of Medicine and Dentistry, and the School of Nursing. Special opportunities include the Take Five program, which allows selected undergraduates a tuition-free fifth year or semester of academic study; Rochester Early Medical Scholars (REMS), an eight-year combined BA or BS/MD program; Rochester Early Business Scholars (REBS), a six-year combined BA or BS/MBA program; Guaranteed Rochester Accelerated Degree in Education (GRADE), a five-year combined BA or BS/MS program; study abroad; Quest courses-first-year classes designed to allow collaborative research between faculty and students; seven certificate programs; Senior Scholars Program; and employment opportunities that include a national summer jobs program and paid internship experiences.

Located on a bend in the Genesee River, the River Campus is home to almost all undergraduates who live in a variety of residence halls, fraternity houses and special-interest housing. Most of the campus is built in a consistent neoclassical architecture, yet all academic buildings are wireless, and all residence halls are wired for the Internet and cable television. Among the facilities are Wilson Commons, the student union; the multipurpose Athletic Center; and a brand-new research facility, the Goergen Biomedical Engineering/Optics building.

Rochester students participate in more than 220 student organizations, including 22 varsity teams, 36 intramural and club sports, 18 fraternities and 13 sororities, performing arts groups, musical ensembles, WRUR radio, URTV, and campus publications.

The University of Rochester seeks to admit students who will take advantage of its resources, be strongly motivated to do their best, and contribute to the life of the university community. An applicant's character, extracurricular activities, job experience, academic accomplishments and career goals are considered.

The recommended application filing date for freshman applicants is January 1 for fall admission. An Early Decision plan is available. Transfer students are welcome for entrance in the fall and spring semesters. The university accepts the Common Application. An electronic online application is available from the university's web site. Applicants for freshman admission are required to submit scores from either the SAT or the ACT. SAT Subject Test results are reviewed, but not required.

Vassar College

Office of Admission
Box 10, 124 Raymond Avenue
Poughkeepsie, NY 12604-0010
Admissions phone: (845) 437-7300 or (800) 827-7270
Admissions fax: (845) 437-7063
Admissions e-mail: admissions@vassar.edu
Admissions URL: admissions.vassar.edu

 Admissions

Current student, 9/2003-Submit Date, September 2006

Vassar is a highly selective school that relies on both hard data (test scores, grades and class rank) and personal qualities, such as special talents, accomplishments, and one's level of originality, to determine acceptance. Interviews don't count for much and are conducted off campus with volunteer alumni. The school has become both increasingly popular and selective in the past 10 years, with about a 28 percent admission rate. Early decision admissions rates are higher, though the school claims that this is because of a more qualified applicant pool. Over 6,000 students apply for freshman admission each year. Transfer admission is considerably more difficult, and only a handful of transfer applicants enroll each semester.

Current student, 8/2003-Submit Date, March 2006

The admissions process is getting even more selective. The college is actively trying to correct the 60 percent female and 40 percent male imbalance, so boys (especially if they're not from the East Coast) stand a better chance. I, personally, did not interview, but it can really help. Students who are enthusiastic about Vassar as their first choice would benefit from an interview. As far as essays go, try to demonstrate that you can think critically and creatively.

Current student, 9/2003-Submit Date, June 2005

The college is highly selective and I had an interview and visited the college far in advance of my application. I wrote an essay for the application and also included a proposal for a high school senior project in the "my space" place. I wrote at least six drafts of my essay and worked on it over the course of many months. I applied for regular admission. I believe the acceptance rate the past few years has been in the upper 20 percent range or lower 30 percent range. My SAT scores were very high, but I do not believe that this was the reason for my acceptance. Vassar seeks students who are unique and who have accomplished interesting activities or have unusual interests. My freshman year there was a world-famous magician on my hall who was traveling to St. Petersberg to participate in a show for royalty.

Alumnus/a, 9/1999-5/2003, December 2004

The admissions process was fairly straightforward, and I was able to use the Common Application to apply. I interviewed with an alumnus off campus, and the interview focused not only on my academic achievements, but also on my interests and expectations. It is very important to come across as both intelligent and dynamic in the interview, and it will certainly help to make it clear to your interviewer that you think outside the box, since Vassar is a pretty alternative school. This same rule can be applied to the application, itself. Be creative, and make it clear that you intend to make an impact at Vassar. The school has become more selective since I was chosen (though the year I applied was one of the tougher years in the past 10), though it still does not come close to the selectivity of some of the truly elite liberal arts colleges.

Current student, 9/2003-Submit Date, January 2004

The Vassar admissions process seems to become more selective every year. The Class of 2007 had a 29 percent admit rate, whereas several years before the admit rate hovered around 40 percent. Vassar seems to regard transcript, standardized test (SAT, ACT, SAT Subject Test) scores and class rank heavily; essays and recommendations are also very important. There is one long essay question;

in addition, there are a few short-answer questions. My advice is to answer each question as thoughtfully and carefully as possible. The college asks about each applicant's most meaningful extracurricular activity and his or her reasons for going to Vassar.

The interview is entirely optional, and the majority of interviews are conducted off campus—alumni contact applicants who request an interview. On-campus interviews are only granted to children of alumni.

> **Vassar comments:** "The 29 percent admit rate for the Class of 2007 was the most selective admit rate in the college's history, and the rate dropped below 29 percent for the Class of 2008."

Current student, 9/2003-Submit Date, June 2004

I found the admissions process at Vassar to be very informative and organized. Although I was unable to have an alumni interview before my acceptance, I received detailed pamphlets and letters about student organizations and academic programs almost daily. Vassar is a highly selective school and places strong emphasis on high school GPA, as well as standardized test scores. However, I found that the admissions process also focuses greatly on the opinion sections of the application. In addition to the essay, Vassar provides a "my space" section, which consists of a blank sheet of paper for the applicants to express themselves creatively outside of the standard application format. I was fortunate enough to have my "my space" section chosen to be one of the two samples presented for information sessions the year I matriculated. I am very confident that my "my space" piece strongly contributed to my acceptance. I strongly encourage all applicants to spend extra time writing a unique essay and producing a creative "my space" section. If applying, be sure to focus on individuality, originality and future aspirations. Most importantly, never think that an issue is too controversial to present. Vassar loves intelligent, opinionated and ambitious students.

 Academics

Current student, 9/2003-Submit Date, September 2006

Academic freedom is remarkable at Vassar, which requires only one quantitative course (which can be filled in psychology, economics, math or the sciences are waived with AP scores), a freshman writing-intensive course, and a language requirement (one year of a foreign language at the introductory level or one semester at intermediate, or SAT scores/AP scores). There is no core curriculum, though half of one's classes must be outside of one's major field and a quarter must be outside of the major division. If closed out of a class, it is usually pretty easy to get the instructor's permission to enroll. I have only been closed out of one class in my entire time at Vassar (I am a current senior).

Professors are uniformly fantastic, though some are easier graders than others. Our strongest departments include the art history, English, drama and film, philosophy, and history programs. Sciences are popular, as well. The college offers a number of interdisciplinary and multidisciplinary majors, such as environmental studies, geography-anthropology, women's studies, and science technology and society. Classes are tiny, with the exception of larger lecture classes such as Introduction to Art History and the English department's 200-level survey course. Most classes are discussion-based, and discussion is apt to be lively.

Current student, 8/2003-Submit Date, March 2006

Vassar classes are, for the most part, small, intimate and insightful. They do demand work, but above a certain level you are almost guaranteed a B or higher. Science classes are the exception. While I have only heard good things about the science (chemistry, physics, biology) experience, these courses are much more rigorous, with long labs and heavier workloads than social science and art classes.

Class draw is always a stressful time, but I have never been totally shut out of a class I really wanted to take. Your draw numbers are averaged over your four

Read all of Vault's College Surveys at **www.vault.com/college**—get complete surveys on 100s of colleges and universities, expert advice on application essays and more.

VAULT CAREER LIBRARY **511**

years, so it's impossible to have a terrible number every single year. I have found that it is best to choose elective classes based on the professor rather than the subject. All the Vassar professors I have experienced have been good, but some have been amazing. You'll know who they are when you get on campus, and it's definitely worth it to take a class you wouldn't ordinarily take (say, in the Russian Studies department) to experience some of Vassar's best professors.

Current student, 9/2003-Submit Date, June 2005

The academic nature is intense but relaxed. Students challenge themselves, not each other and it is all about how much you want to get out of it. The professors are amazing and always willing to take the extra step to help you in whatever way they can. All the classes are relatively small, even the intro level ones. If you want to get into a class that is full, you just have to show up and eventually they will let you in. I have never had a problem getting into a class. I am a film and sociology major and I highly recommend both departments. The film department was just enhanced by the addition of the new Center for Drama and Film, which includes beautiful facilities for both drama and film classes. Film production does not begin until junior year, but this is a wise choice on the part of the college. Making a film is extremely time-consuming and it is important to get a full academic program during the first two years of college.

The best classes I have taken at Vassar have been in the sociology department. I consider some of my classes to have been not only enriching academic experiences, but also life-changing events that have transformed my perception of the world. Students are very close with their professors and often spend time at their houses and develop meaningful friendships with them. Students are treated on an individual level and there is no chance of someone getting lost in the shuffle.

> **The school says:** "The new 200,000+ square-foot Center for Drama and Film opened in fall 2003 with professional-grade proscenium and screening theaters, state-of-the-art production facilities and greatly expanded teaching space."

Current student, 9/2003-Submit Date, June 2004

The academic program at Vassar is very liberal and provides a great deal of freedom for students to choose their academic paths. There is no core curriculum, and the only requirement for all students is a freshman course offered by multiple departments in addition to meeting one language and one quantitative requirement. Classes at Vassar tend to be discussion-oriented and fairly small. The intimate setting of these courses allows students to interact frequently with professors, which oftentimes develops into very helpful student/professor relationships that last for the duration of the four years.

Current student, 9/2003-Submit Date, January 2004

The Vassar curriculum is extremely flexible, with no core of required classes. There are only a few single-course requirements (a freshman writing-intensive course, a quantitative course and foreign language proficiency). Students can choose from a wide variety of majors, including many interdisciplinary and multidisciplinary programs, such as women's studies, environmental studies, American culture and international studies. Students have the opportunity to design their own majors, as well. The classes are all of a liberal arts nature—there are no pre-professional classes, such as marketing. Popular majors include English, biology, economics, psychology and history.

Each student, unlike those at larger universities, starts freshman year with a premajor advisor who guides him/her through course selection and academic issues throughout the year. After a student declares a major, he or she chooses a major advisor.

Students have many opportunities to go abroad or study at other schools in the U.S. About 30 percent of the junior class goes abroad each year. Vassar is a member of the 12 College Exchange Program, which allows students to spend a year or semester at Amherst, Bates, Bowdoin, Colby, Connecticut, Dartmouth, Mount Holyoke, Smith, Trinity, Wellesley, Wesleyan or Williams. Students take their financial aid with them wherever they [study off campus].

> **The school says:** "More than 30 percent of the average junior class studies abroad, and 35 percent of the most recent class."

Employment Prospects

Current student, 9/2003-Submit Date, September 2006

Vassar offers a number of career development and networking events. There an alumni networking database that students can access in order to contact alumni who have expressed interest in mentoring students and/or helping them secure internships and employment. The Field Work program allows students pursue internships for credit, and the office will place students in an organization of their choice. Most graduates (over 80 percent) pursue graduate study with five years of graduation, and 20 percent do so within one year. We have abo a 75 percent acceptance rate into medical schools and a 90 percent law sch placement rate.

Current student, 8/2003-Submit Date, March 2006

There's a popular myth that Vassar's plague of squirrels are the souls of all unemployed English majors returned to the scene of their last worldly succe The school is proud to qualify as liberal arts and condemns those departmen (film, computer science) that lean towards the pre-professional. At the sai time, the Vassar name does mean something, especially in New York publishi circles. The alumni network is also very strong, and we have ins at cool plac like Pixar.

I've found exciting internships every summer, and I think Vassar's reputation quality had a lot to do with this success. It seems like everybody who graduat ends up somewhere, if not rich and successful, then quirky and exciting. I a definitely grateful for my Vassar contacts.

Current student, 9/2003-Submit Date, June 2004

Vassar has a very helpful Office of Career Development (CDO) that is easy access by all students. Students are regularly informed of programs and ever held by the CDO through e-mail. The network of Vassar alumni also provid a great resource for career and internship opportunities (especially in New Yo City). The Field Work office allows students to acquire course credits for inter ships taken during the academic year and provides students with a multitude fieldwork opportunities.

> **Vassar says:** "The CDO's searchable database provides background and contact information for nearly 8,000 alumni who volunteer to provide career advice.
>
> "With placements ranging from Poughkeepsie to New York City, an average of 500 students each academic year participate in a field work internship for credit, and another 100+ earn credit in summer internships. In addition, the summer Community Fellows program provides a full-time stipend for 20 students to work for local nonprofits, human service organizations and municipal offices."

Current student, 9/2003-Submit Date, January 2004

Vassar sponsors a program called Field Work, in which students receive ac demic credit for completing internships and work related to their major field study. It is helpful for gaining real-world experience in students' fields choice. Law schools come to the college in the fall to recruit and speak with st dents; many companies come to campus to recruit in the spring.

Vassar seems to be highly regarded on the national scale; as one of the origin Seven Sisters schools, it was originally intended to be the equivalent of an I League school for women. After it went co-ed in 1969 (a result of declinir Yale's offer to merge), it retained its reputation as an excellent college.

Quality of Life

Current student, 9/2003-Submit Date, September 2006

Most of the dorms are outdated and in need of renovation, which the school pursuing. Campus is beautiful, park-like (an official arboretum), and easi walkable. Campus food is adequate and supplied by Aramark.

Current student, 8/2003-Submit Date, March 2006

The campus is beautiful. There is a wall around it, and I don't think anybody leaves. They're not kidding when they say 97 percent of students live on campus. Poughkeepsie isn't the nicest place but it's getting better, and I'm looking forward to a time when the school and the city are better integrated. The dining is good for the first few weeks, but it gets monotonous. There's an elected group of students that advises dining services, and every year it improves. My favorite additions are the vegan and pasta stations. They're basically a bunch of hot plates and pans where we can stir-fry.

Current student, 9/2003-Submit Date, June 2005

Housing is not luxurious but definitely adequate. The college puts a lot of care into pairing up freshman roommates and most roommates I know went on to be very close friends. Students almost always live on campus all for years and in the dorms during the first three years. Dorms become fairly tight-knit communities and each dorm is known for its specific character. ResLife is pretty accommodating when it comes to switching dorms or roommate problems. But most people stay in their original dorms because there is a certain amount of dorm pride. The campus is very safe and there are some quality restaurants within walking distance. The City of Poughkeepsie itself is not wonderful, but it has everything that a college student would need. The surrounding towns are lovely and students often take trips to restaurants in New Paltz and other towns.

Current student, 9/2003-Submit Date, June 2004

Vassar is a relatively small school (2,500 students) set in a traditional campus environment. The campus is an arboretum, as well as an academic environment. Each building carries a history that is often accompanied by a unique anecdote. However, the location of the school (Poughkeepsie) does not provide an abundance of off-campus activities. Consequently, the campus can get fairly claustrophobic. The school is sensitive to students' needs and offers various counseling facilities and support groups. Housing could use some improvement, though the accommodations are definitely livable and currently undergoing renovation.

The school comments: "The Jewett House residence hall (capacity 200) re-opened in fall 2003 after a total renovation, with similar improvements upcoming for Vassar's other historic residence halls. Upperclassmen can also now choose apartment-style living in the Terrace Apartments, Townhouses and South Commons."

 ## Social Life

Current student, 9/2003-Submit Date, September 2006

There are no fraternities or sororities at Vassar, so there are many all-campus parties sponsored by various dorms and student organizations. Clubs are active and range from a cappella groups to political organizations, publications and club sports teams. About 50 percent of the student body is involved with sports on some level, be it on the intramural, club or varsity level.

Current student, 8/2003-Submit Date, March 2006

The Mug is a popular place for students to go on campus to dance and drink. The Pub is another option, a bar in the Alumni House that features live music on Thursdays. There are a few off-campus options, but like most other Poughkeepsie offerings, these are not taken advantage of.

Current student, 9/2003-Submit Date, June 2005

The social life is very egalitarian—there is no Greek life and no exclusive social activities. The college throws the big parties of the year, which include the biggest event of the year, Halloween. There are several off-campus bars that people frequent and some very good restaurants. People with cars can explore the greater area, but a car is definitely not a major part of social life. There is not a big dating scene, people tend to hang out in small groups together. The student body of Vassar is known to be very happy and has been rated the happiest campus in the U.S. in previous years. I believe this is because college is what you make of it and Vassar allows each student to shape his/her own experience, while providing support and guidance for each decision.

Current student, 9/2003-Submit Date, June 2004

The social life primarily resides on campus. Numerous student organizations throw events every weekend including all-campus events, concerts, performances and film screenings. This year, I served on the executive board of the entertainment committee (ViCE), and we presented various musical and comedy events, such as Sleater Kinney, RJD2, The Roots and Louis Black, to name a few. Also, Vassar has an on-campus club and bar open to all students with different theme nights every night of the week except for Sundays.

Current student, 9/2003-Submit Date, January 2004

There is no Greek system at Vassar; parties are held in upperclassman housing, and each dorm sponsors an all-campus party each year (Harvest Ball, Bi-Dormal Formal and Cowboys and Catholic Schoolgirls are all names of dances ranging from the traditional to the bizarre). Prominent speakers often visit the campus; in the fall of 2003, Tom Hanks lectured, photographer Emmet Gowin gave a talk and novelist Russell Banks read from his upcoming novel.

Wagner College

Admissions Office
Wagner College
One Campus Road
Staten Island, NY 10301
Admissions phone: (718) 390-3411 or (800) 221-1010
Admissions e-mail: admissions@wagner.edu
Admissions URL: www.wagner.edu/admissions/

 ## Admissions

Current student, 8/2005-Submit Date, March 2007

When applying to Wagner College, it is vital to be a well-rounded individual. SAT scores are important, but what is more critical is your overall academic record, your assistance in your high school in clubs and activities, and your work in the community. Wagner provides its own application or prospective students can fill out the Common Application. The Common Application is extremely convenient because it can be used at multiple institutions. If you are consider-

ing Wagner College, I would highly recommend visiting the campus and taking a tour with the admissions department. It is important to find a school that is not just a good school in general but a good school for you. After the tour, prospective students should also have an interview with one of the admissions representatives because then they can put a face to the application. It also expresses your interest and allows you to ask detailed questions about the school. As far as acceptance goes, it is important to have an excellent application, and this includes the essay. Try to stay away from trite essays that only cover superficial events in your life. Really focus on an event or person that is important to you, not one you think someone else wants you to say.

Current student, 8/2004-Submit Date, March 2007

When I was first interested, I was amazed by the quality of the admissions process. Everything was done in a timely and warming matter. My counselor answered all my questions and helped me complete my application efficiently. She also directed me to all the right people for my questions concerning my possible major.

Read all of Vault's College Surveys at www.vault.com/college—get complete surveys on 100s of colleges and universities, expert advice on applicaton essays and more.

VAULT CAREER LIBRARY 513

Current student, Pre-med, 9/2004-Submit Date, March 2007

The admissions process was very unique. I had looked at four other colleges and no school was as welcoming in terms of staff as Wagner College. As soon as I showed interest in the college my senior year, my admissions counselor from Wagner met with me and began to show me everything the school had to offer. She invited me to open houses and even got me connected with the theatre department, for which I was applying. She made sure that I met the person in charge. Then after this, as the applications were being processed and reviewed, she kept me updated and advised me as my search began. As soon as I was accepted and decided to attend, she guided me through to financial aid and offered advice about residence life, campus life, and student activities. As for the actual application, it was very clear in what it asked for. I found that staying on top of what was required by calling my counselor at Wagner eased the process tremendously. Overall, I rate the admissions process at Wagner College well above usual excellence. It was the ease of the process and the warmth of the staff and student ambassadors that made my choice to attend such an easy one.

Current student, 8/2005-Submit Date, March 2007

If Wagner is one of your top choices, it would be good to get in contact with your counselor. If they know you are very interested in the college, you can come visit the school. There are many opportunities with campus-visit days and daily tours. You can even set up interviews with your counselor to ask specific questions or just so they get to know you.

Alumnus/a, 8/2001-5/2005, March 2007

Visit, visit, visit! While visiting Wagner, you will get a chance to see many of the buildings, but more importantly, you will very likely have the chance to speak one-on-one with your admissions counselor. Prepare questions. Also, take the time to ask your tour guide why he/she chose where he/she is and how his/her experiences have been so far. I think Wagner College really stands out after visiting. The campus is beautiful and the scenes of New York Harbor, Manhattan and the Atlantic Ocean are amazing! It's nice because Wagner's a small campus in a very big city.

Current student, 8/2003-Submit Date, June 2005

Visit the school as many times as possible; they have many incoming student days and events. They allow prospective students to sleep over and attend classes. The more you are involved in your school and community, the higher your scholarship will be. Nearly everyone gets an academic or athletic scholarship.

Alumnus/a, Business, 8/1999-12/2001, December 2003

Essays are not mentioned as part of the Wagner College undergraduate student selection process but I had to write an essay prior to my acceptance into Wagner College. The essay discussed topics like "Why did I want to come to Wagner College," and "Which program was I interested in enrolling and why." The only other form that Wagner requires prospective students to fill out aside from the Common Application form is the Common Application supplement. The supplement specifically asks the student "what their significant reasons are for interest in Wagner College. This is the only thing that comes near to an essay.

 **Academics**

Current student, 8/2005-Submit Date, March 2007

Wagner College stresses learning by doing and requires volunteer work in the community as well as writing intensive courses that combine ideals for different subject areas. This creates a civically engaged individual who is involved in more than just an academic experience. One thing that I can never criticize is the patience and helpfulness of the professors I have had. As a biology major, my professors are both prepared and incredibly willing to spend time with students outside of the classroom. This fact is one of the most important advantages of a small school like Wagner. Personal relationships with your professors lead to connections in the real world, internship possibilities and future career options. This has been invaluable in my academic development, and I am thankful for the kindness and caring nature of my professors.

Regarding classes, I have the most experience with the science classes. They are challenging but manageable with diligence and time management. The professors do not try to trick you on exams or have the mean average as a D. They cre-

ate straightforward and fair exams that require knowledge. Another advanta of Wagner College is how flexible the professors are and how they will help y get the classes you need. This semester, I had to take two classes that overlapp slightly, and I negotiated a very effective compromise with my professors. Th were understanding and helpful the entire time. Each major has a differe workload. In biology, there is an extensive amount of laboratory work, as w as research projects. Each major has its own facets that take intelligence a discipline.

Current student, 8/2004-Submit Date, March 2007

I love Wagner's academics. The professors are your mentors and are there help in every situation. They help with all your class needs, but also help w possible careers and internship opportunities. My professors in theatre and ed cation have been very helpful throughout my three years here and I know th will play a key element in my future career goals.

Current student, Pre-med, 9/2004-Submit Date, March 2007

Academics at Wagner are a mix of challenging and exciting that produce a gr overall product. The school is setup with several departments. It's required declare your major by your sophomore year. You take general education clas es and major classes as soon as you enter the college. It adds for an exciti workload. If you have extra space, you can take electives. Wagner is on the u system. This means that each class is worth one unit. You are required to ta nine units an academic year (over the two semesters). This results in the 36 un needed to graduate. There are several amazing and unique programs. We a one of only a handful of schools that offer Arts Administration at the undergra uate level. Our programs perform well above par and create an exciting env ronment. Classes are of good quality. They have small class sizes (fewer th 30 students), have great teacher-student interaction overall and create an enga ing environment. As for classes, it's like any other college. The seniors get fi pick, the juniors second, the sophomores third, and the freshman four However, if you get closed out of a class, you can try to ask a professor to si you in. If he/she can't, you will at some point in your years at Wagner have chance to take it. Grading is fair. Simply put, you get what you earn. Teache recognize hard work and your grades reflect that. The workload varies amo class. This creates a difference in type, amount and level. The most notable a unique idea of Wagner is the Wagner Plan, which involves a freshman learni community comprised of three classes (one in one subject, another subject clas and a writing class that combines those two), an intermediate learning comm nity that usually combines two classes, and your senior learning communit which is either fieldwork, a thesis, or both in your major.

Current student, 8/2005-Submit Date, March 2007

I love every one of the professors I've had. They are so accessible giving us c phone numbers and having reviews at whatever time of day would be best f us. They go out of their way to make sure every student gets the help he/s needs. I haven't encountered any problems getting the classes of my choice. am a sophomore and one class I wanted to take was full. I spoke to the profe sor and I was able to be signed in. The workload fluctuates from class to cla but I do not feel it's anything unreasonable. The professors I've had are all ve fair graders and I know that I deserved every grade I've received.

Alumnus/a, 8/2001-5/2005, March 2007

The professors are great. They really want to get to know you and many of the will take you out for a class conversation over dinner and drinks. I found tha learned so much more from having conversations with my professors outside class; take advantage of their office hours. The classes are small and you hav to be prepared in many of them. A few times, I was in a class with only 10 st dents. Even my larger classes only had about 25 to 30 students. The grading somewhat easy, but there is a very good group of professors who are harder ar expect more out of you. They're much better than the easy-A professors. found myself really pushing to get their approval and learning much more in tl end. The academic program is definitely unique. Right away, you're in lear ing communities, which are clusters of classes that you take with the same st dents. It's a great transition into college because you get to know the same st dents pretty quickly. Some of those students in my first semester classes becan my friends for all four years and beyond. Internships are great if you're a bus ness or arts administration major, but they need to do more if your major something else, like English or history.

Current student, 8/2003-Submit Date, June 2005

Wagner offers a different learning program, which is called The Wagner Plan. This program requires all freshmen to take a three-part class. This tailored learning experience has two different classes linked together though another class, which is writing intensive. These three classes also require volunteer or work experience out of the classroom. Then either sophomore or junior year, they take two different classes that are linked once again though a common theme. Then during senior year, they take the three linked classes again but through their major; this provides them with a hands-on internship directly dealing with their major. This is a wonderful chance and opportunity to learn in and out of the classroom.

Employment Prospects

Current student, Chemistry, 8/2005-Submit Date, March 2007

On campus there is a Center of Career Development dedicated to helping students find internships while in school and jobs after graduation. They host career fairs at least twice a semester where different employers are asked to come and speak and meet the students of Wagner College. This center will also help when writing your résumé and doing mock interviews as preparation. The experiential learning component also helps with job placement after graduation because the internship in which you will be participating during your senior year will often ask you to stay employed with them after graduation. As I am still an undergraduate, I am not sure of every opportunity offered to graduates, but in my experience so far the college has helped its students in every way possible.

Current student, 8/2005-Submit Date, March 2007

Wagner College requires an internship and/or research experience to graduate. This is one of the most important aspects of the Wagner Plan. This fact is one of the main reasons that Wagner students enjoy extensive networking options and job opportunities in prestigious companies in the Manhattan area. Business connections in politics, science, music, nursing and many more areas are excellent and alumni assist in internship acquisition. The Center for Career Development is also solely involved in connecting students to job opportunities and equipping them with résumé knowledge and interview skills.

Current student, 8/2004-Submit Date, March 2007

Undergraduates are set up with amazing internship opportunities. The Arts Administration majors are set up with full-time internships, as are the business majors. The education majors are set up with student teaching opportunities. Wagner has a large network of employers in the area and within Manhattan. They work hard to set us up with internships with these companies and many of the internships lead to possible job placements post graduation.

Current student, Pre-med, 9/2004-Submit Date, March 2007

Wagner is located in New York City. Therefore, employment prospects are endless. A lot of internships end in full-time employment. Even just the access to this large city allows for students to apply for so many jobs. With the help of Career Development and alumni, there are many opportunities. There is on-campus recruiting, as well as campus wide e-mails. They create a strong lead to future employment in your dream careers.

Current student, 8/2005-Submit Date, March 2007

There is a Center for Career Development at Wagner College. It helps students with anything from writing a résumé to mock interviews. They have even had the Crew come in to let students know about appropriate attire for interviews. Every student throughout college is involved with experiential learning tied in with the learning communities. In the senior year learning community, there is an internship for every student. Even before senior year, students can take a credit from their major and have an internship. Wagner is truly great in that it makes sure that each student is prepared for the world after college. Internships include working at MTV and NBC. A Spanish major friend of mine had an internship at Sesame Street and he also studied abroad in Spain.

Quality of Life

Current student, Chemistry, 8/2005-Submit Date, March 2007

The residence halls on campus are comfortable and larger than many colleges I visited while searching for schools. All freshmen live in the same building, which helps students make friends easier and be involved. As you become an upperclassman starting sophomore year, you have more freedom to choose which of the three residence halls you would like to live. You can pick from regular double rooms, to having a suite style where two doubles are connected by a bathroom, or another suite style where there is a very large common room connected to two double rooms. You can also request a single room for an additional price. The dining options on campus are good, offering the main dining hall with many different options: the Hawk's Nest, which is like a grill/cafe environment, and also the Wag, which is a cereal and yogurt bar. The company that is in charge of all the dining services constantly collaborates with the Student Government Association to do surveys and always changes the food options depending on student likes and dislikes. The school is placed in a very good community and security is never an issue. We do have on-campus security for added safety where you can always call for a shuttle if you do not feel safe. Other facilities, such as the gym, pool, dance studios and so on, are always kept in excellent condition and are free for student use.

Current student, 8/2005-Submit Date, March 2007

Wagner College is situated on Staten Island, a 30-minute ferry ride from Manhattan. This location makes Wagner ideal for students who desire a city experience, as well as a more residential environment. Wagner sits atop Grymes Hill and overlooks the Manhattan skyline from its residence halls. The campus is absolutely breathtaking with antique brick buildings, stately trees and an atmosphere of comfort. Wagner has three residence halls, a union with dining hall and bookstore, a library, newly designed sports center, and over a dozen other administration and academic buildings on campus. It houses a planetarium, green house, a scanning electron microscope and a transmission electron microscope. The college is surrounding by the mansions on Howard Avenue in a safe neighborhood, and is close to the beautiful Silverlake Park.

Current student, 8/2004-Submit Date, March 2007

We are a very safe school in a very safe neighborhood. The security guards are personal with the students and always aware of any conspicuous behavior. Residence Life works hard to place all the students in the best possible placements with compatible roommates.

Current student, Pre-med, 9/2004-Submit Date, March 2007

Living on campus is great! This is the type of campus where you always feel safe. We are located on our own private property but in a sense were not a "closed" campus. We do not have large fences surrounding the whole campus because we don't need them. We are located in Grymes Hill, a neighborhood not only for its spectacular views of Manhattan, Brooklyn and the Verrazano Bridge but also for its safety. The community interacts well with Wagner students and staff. We have three different dorm buildings and off-campus apartments.

Alumnus/a, 8/2001-5/2005, March 2007

The campus is beautiful! I really loved the fact that I felt at home but still a free 30-minute ferry ride away from Manhattan. My friends and I would go into Manhattan a lot to see shows, eat out, or just spend a nice spring day in Central Park. It was always nice, though, to come back to a quieter tree-lined campus. There's a good number of activities on campus, too. Division I sports, a lot of clubs, a coffeehouse where they book comedians and musicians. The food is pretty good, but it can get repetitive. Still, compared to the food I tried at a lot of my friends' colleges, it's very good. My friends from other schools always liked visiting me and eating in the dining hall. The res halls are old. The bathrooms are disgusting in the all-freshman dorm. The upperclassman hall had new bathrooms installed when I was there and they are much nicer. The rooms, though, are pretty good sizes. At first they seem very small, but you get used to them.

Current student, 8/2003-Submit Date, June 2005

The campus is small with only 96 acres but very pretty with breathtaking views. The campus is considered a closed campus, so outside crime is extremely rare. The freshman dorm building is the tallest building on Staten Island and provides

Read all of Vault's College Surveys at **www.vault.com/college**—get complete surveys on 100s of colleges and universities, expert advice on applicaton essays and more.

VAULT CAREER LIBRARY 515

wonderful views of New York City. The honors dorm has hardwood floored rooms and Jack and Jill sharing bathrooms with 24-hour quiet hours mandatory.

Social Life

Current student, 8/2005-Submit Date, March 2007

For the social butterfly, there are several bars on Staten Island that are close to the college, including Ruddy and Dean's and Bottomly's. Also, students can go to bars and clubs in Manhattan any night because the ferry runs 24 hours a day and is free to the public. The same goes for restaurants, and many students go into Manhattan to dine because of the ease of public transportation. Wagner College has over 30 organizations spanning a myriad of causes including Habitat for Humanity, Amnesty International, UNICEF and many more. Greek life is fairly popular, but there is no pressure to join a social fraternity or sorority if a prospective student does not wish to. There are seven different Greek chapters represented at Wagner College and each has its own national philanthropy that it supports.

Current student, Pre-med, 9/2004-Submit Date, March 2007

As for social life there is so much to do. Being that we are in New York City, we have access to entertainment and exciting activities all over. The school sponsors activities but there are plenty more that students do on their own. You can go to museums, see theatre (at discounted student prices), attend art shows, eat a variety of cuisines, go dancing, go to a bar, walk the streets of a new neighborhood, see the latest movies, go to huge concerts, go shopping at the mall and take walks in the park all within only a few miles of this school. There is an abundance of things and for a lot of them, you don't need a car (even though every student, including freshmen, can have one on campus). Greek life is just one part of so many choices. Each frat and sorority has its own floors with lounges in towers. There are many clubs, awesome student events and the access to so much more!

Current student, 8/2005-Submit Date, March 2007

About 15 percent of the campus is involved in the Greek life. Each frat/sorority has its own floor in one of the dorms. There are many great restaurants nearby and many that deliver to campus with a discount. There is also a Co-Curricular Center that plans activities for almost every day of the year with fun activities for everyone. They get student discounted tickets to all the latest Broadway shows for about $20. They take us skating in Central Park, museums in the city and also have movie nights right on campus.

Alumnus/a, 8/2001-5/2005, March 2007

There's not a whole lot to do on Staten Island. But, not everyone at Wagner from Staten Island. There are bars and clubs on Staten Island, but why go them when you have the whole city? There's a lot of Wagner bars in the Villa Down the Hatch, Off the Wagon and so on. If you do stay on Staten Island, the are a number of good Wagner hangouts on nearby Forest Avenue like Black D and Joedy's. There are a lot of student groups at "The Wag." Greek life is the but it's not a big deal. Theatre's pretty popular, to the point that is seems l everyone is into theatre. As far as restaurants, going to Goodfellas for pizza i must. Try the pizza a la vodka: it's won national awards!

Current student, 8/2003-Submit Date, June 2005

Most Wagner students go to the local Staten Island bars every Wednesd Thursday and Friday. Many students either stay on campus or go into the c Saturday night. Many people go home on the weekends but all the athletes always at school. The Greek system is small but involved within the scho With New York City just a ferry ride away, the possibilities are endless.

The School Says

Wagner College has received national acclaim from organizations like *Time* magazine, the American Association of Colleges and Universities, and was presented with the prestigious Hesburgh Award for faculty development. Our goal is to attract and develop active learners and future leaders.

Capitalizing on a unique geography, Wagner is a traditional, scenic, residential campus that sits atop a hill on an island overlooking Manhattan. Wagner's location allows us to offer a program that combines required off-campus experiences (experiential learning), with "learning community" clusters of courses. This program begins in the first semester and continues through the senior capstone experience in the major. Fieldwork and internships, writing-intensive reflective tutorials, connected learning, "reading, writing and doing." At Wagner College our students truly discover "the practical liberal arts in New York City."

Applicants for fall 2008 are required to take the current version of the SAT, or the ACT with the Writing section.

Wells College

Admissions Office
Macmillan Hall
Aurora, NY 13026
Admissions phone: (800) 952-9355
Admissions fax: (315) 364-3227
Admissions e-mail: admissions@wells.edu
Admissions URL: www.wells.edu/admiss/ad1.htm

Admissions

Current student, 8/2004-Submit Date, July 2006

I actually work in the admissions department as my work study job. The most important piece of advice I can give is to visit the campus. Wells has a beautiful campus and it's very easy to schedule a tour and an interview with an admissions counselor. Wells recently went coed (from female only) and is slowly growing the male population, which will be roughly 13 percent for the 2006-07 academic year.

Current student, 1/2003-Submit Date, July 2006

My admission into Wells College was not typical in comparison with most oth students. I took classes at Wells throughout my senior year in high school. F me, it was very helpful that I did well in every course I took here, and develop strong connections with my professors.

I ended up taking advantage of Wells' strong study abroad options the year af I graduated from high school; it was my art professor at Wells who wrote n recommendation into the program. After my year abroad, I decided to come Wells full time and finish my degree here, simply because I feel the educati here is unparalleled by any other institution.

Although my acceptance experience is very different from most, my advice prospective students is to pick an institution where they can see themselv thriving. If you become passionate about a school, your admissions intervie and essays will come naturally because it is not a plea to get in, rather a stat ment of why the college would be lucky to have you, and you would be equa lucky to benefit from their programs.

Current student, 8/2003-Submit Date, July 2006

When I applied, I came to a few open houses and had an interview and all that jazz. I went to a program the admissions department has in December that's kind of an open house and application day all in one. I found out that day that I had been accepted.

Current student, 8/2005-Submit Date, July 2006

If you want to get in, all you need to do is show potential. Wells is small enough that they can review each student individually and make notes about them. The selectivity isn't based upon just good grades, good SAT scores or a good essay. It's about showing that you're focused, at least that's how I got in.

Current student, 8/2004-Submit Date, July 2006

Wells isn't particularly selective if you're a good fit for the school. SATs and GPs, none of it is as important as the whole package that you present. Because of this, the interview is key. If it doesn't go well, then the admissions staff is going to make a note of your incompatibility. Show some interest, take the time to visit and interview and you stand a good chance of getting in.

Current student, 8/2005-Submit Date, March 2006

The admissions process was very simple. You needed to submit essays and go through an interview. Wells does like high SAT scores of course, but they do not put a huge amount of emphasis on them. I personally have a lower than the average SAT score, but I am pretty well-rounded and participated in various organizations and clubs in high school. Being a well-rounded student is really well looked up upon in college admissions.

 Academics

Current student, 8/2005-Submit Date, July 2006

Real average class size, seven people. Very one-on-one, you get a lot out of it. Very personal, not for the kid who likes to sit in the back row and not be noticed. You don't get left behind in the crowd. Professors are all amazing and extremely interested not only in their field but also how you as a student and person are growing.

Current student, 8/2008-Submit Date, July 2006

Across the board, my academic experience at Wells has been amazing. The average class size is 12 students, with very few classes being any larger than 20.

Most professors live in town or the surrounding area and are quite accessible, giving out their home and cell numbers along with their e-mail addresses. Wells is so small, with 450 students, that there really is no place to hide in the classroom if one hasn't done one's homework. The professors care if students have completed homework assignments, not for the homework's sake, but for the students'.

Alumnus/a, 8/2002-5/2006, July 2006

One of the greatest benefits of attending a small college environment such as Wells College is the class size. On average, our class size is 12 students. That number may increase if a student takes a beginning 101-level class; however, I have never had a class with more than 20 students. In fact, one of my senior seminar classes only had two other students in it!

All of the classes are taught by professors, not TAs. The student/faculty relationship at Wells is incredible. The professors genuinely care about their students and they want them to succeed. I remember the first day of classes my freshman year when my professors handed out the syllabi and on it were their home and cell phone numbers. My professors encouraged us to contact them if we ever had problems; either personally or academically. Truly amazing!

Current student, 1/2003-Submit Date, July 2006

The quality of education at Wells was my deciding factor in enrolling. The classes are intense and small. It is absolutely impossible to become lost in the crowd here. Every class is meaningful and passionate, you really learn more each day here and leave each class more satisfied than when you entered. The professors not only strive to know you academically, but also take interest in you personally.

Since Wells is so small, it is fairly easy to enroll in any class you want or need, although every semester or so there are those rare popular special topic classes that fill up the fastest with juniors and seniors. There is a significant workload at Wells, but it is possible. You always have access to your professor or TA, and other classmates are always willing to help you study or explain anything. It is important to know yourself and your study habits, so you can easily schedule in time to work and time to enjoy college.

The most important factor of the Wells College learning experience is the small class sizes. It is very common to have under 10 people in each class. This allows for more student to professor contact and individualized attention, as well as class discussions.

Current student, 8/2004-Submit Date, July 2006

The number of classes offered per semester can be problematic, just because the student population is so small. What this means, however, is that classes are small. You may not get into really popular classes your freshman year but you stand a good chance your sophomore year. The classes are discussion based—you can't hide in a class at Wells.

You'll also spend a lot of time reading and writing papers. If you fall behind you'll be in a world of trouble. Professors pay attention to students and many grade with this in mind. If you work really hard in a class and come up short of the next letter grade, there's a good chance that you'll get bumped up.

Current student, 8/2005-Submit Date, March 2006

Wells academics are various things. I'm not going to lie, they are hard. Yet at the same time, Wells provides every student with what he/she needs. We have math clinics and writing clinics to go to if we need help. Also, faculty here is amazing and their doors are literally always open to students. There is always a way to get in touch with your professor, like e-mail, and most professors even give students their home numbers, which is really great.

As a freshman, I can honestly say that I got into every class that I wanted. Wells is really amazing about giving you a wide variety of necessary and interesting classes. As for the workload, I do find it to be on the heavier side. Even though students do have a heavy workload, we have a lot of free time with classes. I, personally, am done at 11:30 every day and I have the rest of the day to work on my homework.

Current student, 8/2002-Submit Date, March 2006

The education that I have received from Wells is the best! The classes are small so that makes for more chances of getting your voice heard. Also, because of the class size, the professors really get to know you—you're not just a number; you're a person.

On the first day of classes when my professors handed out the syllabi, their home phone number and sometimes even cell numbers were on there! The faculty at Wells is so wonderful and always willing to help if you have a question, or even if you need to talk.

 Employment Prospects

Alumnus/a, Education, 8/2002-5/2006, July 2006

As a recent graduate of Wells College, I am finding myself searching for post-college employment. However, that search has been made easier because of the contacts and relationships I've made with people, teachers and schools through my internships. At Wells, all students are given the entire month of January off to complete an internship. Some students choose to fulfill this requirement close to home, while others take advantage of our alumni-networking across the country.

As a student in the teacher certification program, many of my internships were education centered. I was grateful of the number of Wells alumni throughout the country who were willing to provide housing for me when I was searching for internships.

Read all of Vault's College Surveys at **www.vault.com/college**—get complete surveys on 100s of colleges and universities, expert advice on application essays and more.

VAULT CAREER LIBRARY **517**

Current student, 1/2003-Submit Date, July 2006

Throughout the four years spent at Wells College, students are expected to complete a series of internships. In turn, students are allotted an extraordinarily long holiday break. Throughout the four Januarys I spent in college, three of them were spent at internships. As a result, we have a Career Development and Services Office that aids students in finding these internships.

The alumni are extremely supportive of current students and often house them during their internships in major cities, and also help them find many of their jobs after graduation. The student/alumni relationship is one of the most unique aspects of a Wells College education. Alumni are truly interested and invested in the current student body, and will go to long lengths to help them succeed.

Alumnus/a, 8/1999-5/2001, July 2006

The internship program at Wells provides students the opportunity to assess if a certain job/career is right for them. Students can do internships as early as their first year and often these internships lead toward summer employment and careers following graduation.

Current student, 8/2004-Submit Date, July 2006

Wells offers a great internship program, but the people who run it aren't as helpful as they advertise. Many students find internships through their own connections and pure luck. The internships I've done while I've been at Wells have been some of the most valuable parts of my college education.

The alumni network and its assistance with both internships and job placement post-graduation are a great asset. They're really willing to help you out, take you under their wing and give you a push in the right direction.

Current student, 9/2005-Submit Date, March 2006

One the strengths of this school is the alumni network. They are located all over the country, and are all very supportive of current students, all the way to the point of allowing them to stay in their homes while travelling.

Current student, Education, 8/2002-Submit Date, March 2006

I am a member of the elementary education program here at Wells, so when I graduate in May of 2006 I will be certified to teach, which is great! A lot of my other education major friends at other schools are going to graduate, but not be certified. Since Wells offers teacher certification, a lot of students are hired immediately after graduation.

Quality of Life

Current student, 1/2003-Submit Date, July 2006

Wells is situated in Aurora, NY, which is a very small town with virtually no crime. Hence the fact that Wells is a very safe school. We do have campus security, which does help enforce safety; they patrol campus and escort students home from academic buildings back to their dorms if they have been studying late at night and feel uncomfortable walking alone.

All but one dorm has been completely refurnished with high-quality luxury furniture and decorated by a generous alumni donation a few years ago, so they are literally nicer than living at home for some. The rooms are very big in comparison to other colleges, and is it much easier to get a single after your freshman year at Wells than at other colleges.

The campus is small, so it is not a hassle to walk from one end to the other, although it is very beautiful with a constant view of the lake. The dining on campus is all right. There are always several options of things to eat, and they provide food like salad bars, soup and sandwich bars, cereal, bagels and ice cream, so if you do not like what is being served for dinner; you have constant stand-bys to fall back on. The food quality is OK, I do think it could be greatly improved. I wish there were a lower fat content in the food; although they do always offer vegetables, sometimes I feel like there is too much fried food or food with too much grease. The quality of living at wells is extremely high, it is like a retreat because you are surrounded with so much beauty.

Current student, 8/2004-Submit Date, July 2006

Quality of life at Wells is a mixed bag. The dining hall is pitiful, and the administration shows no interest in improving its offerings. Be careful of gaining freshman 15. The dining hall is not very vegan friendly.

Housing is wonderful. The dorms at Wells are some of the nicest I've ever se and you'll definitely be comfortable in your room. They recently built a n athletic facility that is amazing, and a new science building is under constr tion. However, there are other buildings on campus that are in need of repai

The area is incredibly safe, and the neighborhood is small. There is a deli, a m ket, a library and a small downtown area. About 10 minutes down the road i larger town with a gas station and the local elementary and junior high scho Locals are friendly to students. Campus involvement needs to do a better job catering to student interests, but offerings have improved recently. Wells s dents are really good at making their own fun and coming up with creative act ities.

Current student, 8/2005-Submit Date, March 2006

I really love Wells' campus. I think it is by far one of the safest places ever never feel nervous to leave my dorm at midnight and walk to a friends on other side of campus. And if by any chance a student doesn't feel comforta with walking alone at night, security is really good at escorting students.

When it comes to dorming and such, I was extremely lucky. My roommate a I were matched perfectly and we get along really great. Wells' housing co mittee does a great job matching people up by their profiles. There aren't many problems and if there are, they are fixed easily.

Current student, 8/2002-Submit Date, March 2006

The dorms are incredible! They are like mansions—and I'm not joking! Aur is a small town, so there are not many off-campus housing options. But w would you want to live off campus when you can live in dorms like these?!?

Since we are a small campus, everyone knows each other, so it's a very sa atmosphere. Campus safety does a great job patrolling 24/7, and we do hav blue light system.

Alumnus/a, 8/2001-1/2003, June 2004

The dorms are beautiful and the views from dormroom windows are beautif However, there is no air conditioning, the heating is inconsistent, no cable in rooms (you have to sign up to watch something in the main living room), and t bathrooms are generally pretty dirty all the time. The dining hall food is bet than most.

Social Life

Current student, 8/2005-Submit Date, July 2006

Social life revolves around the Wells traditions. Not a party school, but lots drinking and smoking of pot. Dating scene is amazing if you're either male a gay female. Very open about sexuality on campus and extremely accepting gays, like a safe haven.

Current student, 8/2008-Submit Date, July 2006

Wells is half an hour from Cornell University and Ithaca College, so there's end to partying if that's the goal. However, many students stay on the We campus for the activities we bring in. Visiting poets, comedians, local ban theme dances, movie showings and a mountain of traditions are just a few exa ples of what goes on at Wells College.

Current student, 1/2003-Submit Date, July 2006

The social life at Wells is a very unique aspect of the community. It is situat in a very small town, with only one bar and a handful of restaurants. The bar naturally the favorite hangout for some students and many locals, it is called t Fargo. The Fargo also serves bar food, but at a little higher quality than wh some are used to. They served chicken wings, chili and hot dogs, just to nar a few. The special feature nights, like Fish Fry Friday, are the more popul nights.

urora also has The Aurora Inn, which is a very high scale restaurant with excel-
nt food, which is great for when parents come to visit, as it is usually too
pensive for most students to eat there frequently. Also, there is a small cafe,
orie's, which serves specialty coffees and teas in addition to sandwiches,
ups, baked goods and ice cream, since it was historically an old ice cream par-
r. It is decorated in a very cute retro style with lots of floral motifs, yet still
eping true to the ice cream parlor theme.

ll of these places are within walking distance from the college. Just outside of
e village about half mile there is an amazing restaurant, Pumpkin Hill, that is
equented by many students. The atmosphere is almost as amazing as the food,
it is situated in an old farm house, with a country French feel. The food is
licious, and affordable to students, it is a great get away.

here is no Greek life on campus, most students go to Cornell University on the
eekends to partake in frat parties if that is what they are looking for. Although
lot of students do stay on campus on the weekends to just relax with friends
ter a stressful week of work. There is an extensive number of clubs to join at
ells. The clubs are responsible for a significant number of the events planned
 campus. There is always something going on at Wells, but some students take
e weekend to go to Ithaca, and spend time in a more urban environment.

urrent student, 8/2004-Submit Date, July 2006

ells doesn't offer a lot of social activities that students are particularly inter-
ted in. Once every couple of weeks they bring in a comedian or musician, but
ese events aren't always well attended. Movies are frequently brought to camus and specific clubs host dances and events throughout the year.

raditions like Even/Odd Line (a big basketball game) and Spring Weekend are
lot of fun and bring the whole community together. Mainly 80s is a big dance
at takes place in the spring, while Disco Dodge is the biggest dance of the fall.
ost students attend these events with some amount of alcohol in their system.
ach year the school hosts a foam dance that attracts a large number of students.

haca is nearby, and students head there for big frat parties, unique restaurants
d malls and movie theatres. The nearby Super Wal-Mart is the best place for
ocery shopping, and is right near a bunch of fast food restaurants. The
riangle Diner, famous for its pancakes and omelettes, is popular with students
r breakfast. The Fargo, within walking distance of Wells, serves up cheap
er, games of pool and typical bar food. Dorie's, the local deli, offers yummy
ndwiches and wireless Internet access.

urrent student, 8/2005-Submit Date, March 2006

he social life around Wells is not that large. At first I was a little skeptical about
hether I could handle such little entertainment around us. Then I realized that
actually liked the fact that there was nothing to distract me so I could get good
ades. Also, when I do want to go out to a party place like Cornell, it's great
d only 20 minutes away. I find myself leaving campus once a week whether
 shop or eat in Auburn or Ithaca. It works out nicely, plus Wells is really good
out planning campus activities for its students.

The School Says

- Wells College is a coeducational, private, liberal arts college
  located on a beautiful 365-acre lakeside campus situated in
  the heart of the Finger Lakes Region of New York State in the

historical village of Aurora. True to its heritage, Wells maintains a national reputation for academic excellence. The college prides itself on offering one of the most collaborative
learning environments in higher education today.

- This is not your ordinary education. The Wells experience is
  deeply personal and intensely focused on superior academic
  achievement. Wells offers 16 majors and over 35 minors.
  With one professor for every eight students, professors really
  get to know everyone. The average class size has 12 students and is taught seminar-style, with discussions taking
  precedence over lectures.

- Since 1868 we've been encouraging our students to step outside the classroom. Why? Because the best education combines traditional studies with real-world experiences. Last
  year, the Wells Office of Career Services coordinated internships in 20 states, the District of Columbia, France and
  Senegal. By graduation, 97 percent of seniors had completed
  at least one internship. Your education won't stop at the edge
  of campus. Recent internships include: The White House,
  ABC Television, Aquarium of the Pacific, Rock and Roll Hall of
  Fame and Museum, Smithsonian Institution, and many more.

- Wells offers an extensive study abroad program with affiliated programs in 20 different countries. Our staff will help you
  pursue your academic interests wherever they lead you. You
  might study ecosystems in Australia's Outback or work in
  labs, film studios or research hospitals anywhere in the world.
  Although the three most popular programs are in Florence,
  Paris and Sevilla, you could study almost anywhere. We also
  work with affiliated institutions to make sure your learning
  opportunities are as rich and varied as possible. For example,
  if you find the perfect course at Cornell University or the
  London School of Economics, we'll do our best to get you
  there.

- There are also many opportunities for you to develop your
  leadership skills through over 40 different organizations
  including a literary magazine and newspaper, music and drama
  groups, and political organizations. Wells is a Division III
  member of the NCAA with intercollegiate women's teams in
  field hockey, lacrosse, soccer, softball, swimming, and tennis
  and intercollegiate men's teams in soccer, swimming and
  lacrosse. We also have an intercollegiate co-ed cross country
  team and a men's intercollegiate basketball team will be added
  during the 2008-09 academic year.

- Wells students are intellectually curious, open-minded and creative. They are comfortable expressing themselves, listening
  to others and sharing ideas. They are caring citizens of the
  world, eager to travel beyond the campus and outside their
  comfort zones. Wells students love to learn. If you love learning, you'll love the Wells experience.

Read all of Vault's College Surveys at www.vault.com/college—get complete surveys on 100s of colleges and universities, expert advice on applicaton essays and more.

VAULT CAREER LIBRARY 519

Davidson College

Admissions Office
Box 7156
Davidson, NC 28035-7156
Admissions phone: (800) 768-0380
Admissions e-mail: admission@davidson.edu
Admissions URL: www2.davidson.edu/admission/

 Admissions

Alumnus/a, Biology, 8/2003-5/2007, June 2007

Davidson has online and paper options to fill out—either the Davidson application or the Common Application (plus supplement). In terms of the written application, it is important to be yourself in the essays. Try not to make them forced or too creative. Davidson does not include interviews as part of general admissions, so the essays in your application may be the only way the school can learn about you. Writing ability is important, but it's also important to let your personality shine through. Other than the essays, Davidson puts a strong importance on the difficulty of your high school schedule. There is no single number of "required" AP or IB courses, but you should want to challenge yourself in the areas in which you are most interested. Then of course Davidson looks at your extracurricular activities. This doesn't mean that you need to join every club your area has to offer, but it does mean that you should find some passions and carry through with those. The individuals who read applications can tell if someone is simply boosting his/her résumé, so make sure the extracurricular section really reflects your interests. The last thing Davidson looks at is standardized test scores. Davidson accepts both the ACT and the new SAT, and it is strongly encouraged (but not required) that you take at least two SAT Subject Tests—math and something else.

Current student, Theology, 8/2004-Submit Date, June 2007

Davidson's admissions process is like no other in the country. Rather than weeding out applicants with standardized test scores and class rank, Davidson takes into account the whole person when considering a student for admission: one's extracurricular activities, range of interests, passion for learning and, most importantly, one's character. Essays are particularly important in the selection process, so really think about what you're writing and how it comes across.

Current student, Biology, 8/2004-Submit Date, May 2007

Davidson College accepts the Common Application, which is helpful during the application process. However, Davidson does require supplementary material, including a short essay on the value of the Honor Code and a personal recommendation from a peer of the applicant. Davidson is very selective, and the number of applicants has been steadily increasing over the years.

Current student, Social Sciences, 8/2004-Submit Date, May 2007

I first visited Davidson as a sophomore, and then again as a senior. As I drove up to campus my senior year, I looked to my mom and said, "I feel like I'm coming home." Getting into Davidson is tough, and it's getting more difficult every year. My advice would be to be yourself—the admission counselors are pretty good at seeing through over-inflated descriptions or false activities lists. If you get a chance, come visit overnight—but realize that there are lots of different student experiences at Davidson. If you don't like your host, or your host is into something you're not, ask if they know someone who may have more similar interests to you. Just because the person you stay with is super liberal or super conservative doesn't mean that the other 1,699 people are, too—there's a surprising degree of variety among student interests.

Current student, Economics, 8/2005-Submit Date, May 2007

Our typical visit program entails taking a tour, followed by an individual or group information session by one of our counselors. Overnight stays and classroom visits are encouraged. The admissions process itself is highly selective and is split into two parts. The first deals with basic student information, while the

second requires a few free responses and an essay among other things. It [is] important that a student take a rigorous high school schedule and perform we[ll] in those courses. This is a much more important indicator of how a student w[ill] perform at the college level than standardized test scores. Additionally, it [is] important that the student displays an array of interests and talents both ac[a]demically and extracurricular.

Current student, 8/2002-Submit Date, May 2006

Interviews are not required for admissions. The school is getting more and mo[re] selective. When reviewing applications the admissions officers value commun[i]ty service and involvement in activities outside of school very highly. GPA an[d] strength of schedule are also highly valued, and more so than SAT/ACT score[s].

Current student, 8/2004-Submit Date, March 2006

Davidson is really selective. When I read the prospectus, I really didn't think m[y] chances were all that great of getting in. The application has lots of writi[ng] involved. The Honor Code is a super big deal at Davidson, so there is an essa[y] that all prospective students have to write where they talk about the Honor Co[de] and how they would uphold the values of the Honor Code once accepte[d]. Davidson is also really big on service, so admissions counselors look for lots [of] service involvement from applicants. They also look for leadership and not ne[c]essarily that you were in six different organizations, but that you were in orga[n]izations that you were really passionate about and spent your time leading effo[rts] that meant something to you.

 **Academics**

Current student, Theology, 8/2004-Submit Date, June 2007

Our academics definitely challenge students, which is reflected in the sparsene[ss] of A's given out by professors. Although students often complain about grad[e] deflation, professors are generally fair graders and try to bring out the best i[n] their students. This is definitely a teaching-oriented school, and the administr[a]tion seeks professors who love interacting with students. Classes are very sma[ll] so don't come here if you don't want to go to class or participate actively [in] class. Although classes stay small (usually less than 30), if you really want [to] get into a class, most professors will try to get you into it if it's humanly poss[i]ble.

Current student, Social Sciences, 8/2004-Submit Date, May 200[7]

Davidson is tough but totally doable. Apparently, there's a rumor going aroun[d] that we work all the time and don't have any fun, which is not true. At the sam[e] time, Davidson isn't the school for you if you're looking for a school whe[re] classes are optional—the academic experience is one of the most defining par[t] of Davidson. You work hard, and you earn your degree. Professors are he[re] because they want to work with undergraduates, and they do. Nearly every on[e] of my friends has done research for a professor, in a wide variety of depar[t]ments—neuroscience, English, political science, math, history—the opportun[i]ties run the gamut. I've never had a problem getting into the classes I want. Th[e] classes at Davidson are superb, and likewise, you've earned a good grad[e]. You've got to work for an A. One thing that I think is really cool is every ye[ar] at graduation, when the honors graduates are announced, we're surprised to s[ee] funny, cool, interesting people among the top listed—the kids at the top of ever[y] class also have active social lives.

Current student, Economics, 8/2005-Submit Date, May 2007

The classes at Davidson are phenomenal. The professors are very engaging an[d] definitely "know their stuff." The average class size is [15] and we cap our clas[s] size at 32. Small class sizes allow for intimate relationships between studen[ts] and professors, and also allow for some great discussions. There are no gradu[]ate students, so all of our research is done by undergrad students. As for clas[s] registration, we have a system called "web tree" (various schematic diagram[s] one fills out with course preferences) that almost always guarantees a student[']s ideal schedule. I have never heard of anyone who didn't get the schedule he/sh[e]

nted. If a class is capped at 15, professors will allow exceptions. Grading is
ways fair, but we do not have grade inflation—getting an A requires students
go well above and beyond a professor's expectations.

rrent student, Biology, 8/2005-Submit Date, May 2007

sses are great. I say that with the knowledge that my GPA is not great but I
l like I'm getting a great education. Davidson does not just teach facts, it
ches its students how to think and work through problems. There is signifi-
nt grade deflation—I do not joke. An A is a particularly difficult thing to
hieve and as such, there were no Summa Cum Laude (4.0 GPA) graduates this
ar and only one last year.

e ease of getting classes you want is all about the numbers, since Davidson
ploys a tree-based system of choosing classes. For example, you pick class
and if you get class A then you also want class B, but if class B is unavailable
n you'll take class C; however, if class B was available then you want to take
and so on. It's a pain, but it's effective.

ere workload is excessive, each class has a general belief that you are taking
ingle course—that one. I work at least 30 hours a week on general home-
rk/studying. One thing to watch out for is that most classes move faster than
u can take notes. Just be prepared for a mental workout.

rrent student, 8/2004-Submit Date, March 2006

the most recent rankings of *U.S. News & World Report*, Davidson was ranked
mber One in workload for liberal arts colleges. Davidson is extremely
tremely challenging. Students are constantly complaining about how hard the
rk is and sheer amount of work that is assigned. I've had classes where I go
class on Tuesday and the professor assigns over 300 pages of reading and truly
pects us to have it completed for class on Thursday. Because Davidson is so
all, students are often in classes with only a dozen other students or even
ver students than that. At Davidson, there's really no way to hide from pro-
ssors. They know if you haven't done the reading. Davidson professors
pect each student to participate in each class. This is truly beneficial because
forces students to stay engaged and truly challenge themselves. The majority
classes take participation into account as far as grading. I've had classes
ere participation counted as much as 25 percent. In other classes, participa-
n has only counted for 10 or 15 percent. Professors also take attendance and
nerally have pretty strict attendance policies, so those unexcused absences
unt negatively towards your final grade. I had one class where each unex-
sed absence counted one third of a letter grade off of your final grade.
vidson is also infamous for grade deflation, meaning professors are very, very
ective about giving out A's. In most classes, I'd say a professor only gives out
e or two, but no more than three A's. Sometimes no students get an A. What
ove about Davidson classes is how truly interesting they are. We have amaz-
g professors who truly care about the students and are willing to talk to stu-
nts not only about the course, but also about life, in general. I've had several
ofessors invite me and other students over for dinner.

 Employment Prospects

lumnus/a, Biology, 8/2003-5/2007, June 2007

hatever you are interested in doing, you will find people at Davidson who are
ing to prestigious jobs or graduate schools in that area. I have friends who
ve gotten great jobs at the corporate level all over the country. I also know
ople who interviewed for medical schools like Harvard and Stanford.
rsonally, I got my dream job by networking with Davidson alumni. Others
lize our Office of Career Services, which has daily events to help edit
sumés, work on networking, look at cover letters and so on. Most important-
Career Services really wants to see you succeed and get the job you want.

urrent student, Biology, 8/2004-Submit Date, May 2007

ost Davidson grads do not have trouble getting a job after college. Most
ployers and graduate schools know how rigorous Davidson is. Most pre-med
dents get into the medical schools of their choice after Davidson. Some of the
ost recent Davidson graduates' plans include graduate school in physics, work-
g for Google, researching at the National Institutes of Health for two years
fore going to medical school, and working for Bank of America and
achovia. Also, two members of that class received Watson Fellowships,

enabling them to travel all around the world to study a topic of their choice. For
example, one will be studying how race is perceived in different cultures, particularly focusing on individuals of mixed race.

Current student, Social Sciences, 8/2004-Submit Date, May 2007

The Office of Career Services will really help you find internships, hosting
résumé workshops, mock interviews and so on. Many students use the Office of
Career Services, but they also tap into the Davidson alumni network. I'm on a
lot of national e-mail lists, and every time I find a Davidson alumnus/a he/she
always says for me to let him/her know if I'm ever in the area and he/she can
help introduce me to people. Graduates do a wide variety of things—investment
banking, medical school, Aerators, Teach for America, graduate school—so
there's not a defined formula for where you're find graduates.

Current student, Economics, 8/2005-Submit Date, May 2007

On average 60 percent of students go straight into the workforce after graduation, while about 25 percent go to graduate school or some other form of further
education. We have a very helpful Office of Career Services that aids in connecting students with internships and employers. 100 percent of our chemistry
majors have gone to the graduate school of their choice, fully funded in the last
15 years. Medical school acceptance rates hover between 95 and 100 percent. I
have seen many of my friends who majored in economics take on prestigious
investment banking jobs a few miles away in Charlotte (second largest financial
district in the nation) right after graduation.

Current student, 8/2000-Submit Date, April 2004

While most Davidson students manage to find great jobs after college, don't
expect special treatment from employers on account of Davidson's name. The
school has not yet established the connections with major employers to get on-
campus interviews or to help Davidson students' résumés find their way to the
top of the pile. With Southeastern employers, Davidson does extremely well, but
the rest of the country has not yet discovered the talent pool that Davidson provides.

Graduate school prospects are more promising, however. One law school admissions counselor to whom I talked (not knowing that I went to Davidson) commented that, "Davidson is one of my favorite schools to recruit students from,
since they better prepare their students for graduate schools than almost any
other college, including Ivy League schools." Almost every student I know who
applied to graduate school got into one of his or her top choice schools.

 Quality of Life

Alumnus/a, Visual and Performing Arts, 8/2002-5/2006, June 2007

There are lots of trees and grassy areas on campus that make it very pretty. All
the buildings are brick and there are brick paths leading everywhere. The school
also owns some property on the lake (about three or four miles away) where students can go swim, lay out on the sand/grass, play volleyball, cook out, or go
boating (the school has boats that students may rent). The campus generally
feels very safe. Everyone on campus is allowed to have a car, which is really
convenient. Parking passes are only $40 for the year and you never have to park
more than a five-minute walk from your dorm/class.

The facilities on campus are almost all new or newly renovated. The school is
constantly renovating buildings (generally over the summer so it doesn't disrupt
the students) so that none of the buildings are in poor shape. Summer of '05 they
built a new weight room and renovated the dorms at the sophomore apartments.
There are work-out facilities, computer labs and study areas open to students 24
hours a day.

Current student, Social Sciences, 8/2004-Submit Date, May 2007

I can't imagine a better place for the transition from high school to real life. At
Davidson, you don't just learn how to take classes, you learn how to be a whole
person, which I think is more important. Nearly everyone lives on campus, and
if you don't live on campus, you live just across the street, which helps create a
strong sense of community. Many professors live near to campus, as well, so
you see them walking around with their families or at the grocery store. The
campus is gorgeous and has lots of old trees and open green space. Within a 10-
mile radius of campus, you can find anything you need—Best Buy, Super Target,

Read all of Vault's College Surveys at **www.vault.com/college**—get complete surveys on 100s of colleges and universities, expert advice on applicaton essays and more.

VAULT CAREER LIBRARY 521

Panera, movie theaters—and there's a mall a little bit farther down the highway. In town, there are a couple of good restaurants (sushi, burgers and fries, pizza, Italian) and a CVS, and the perennial favorite off-campus study place—Summit Coffee, complete with a student discount. While there are a lot of off-campus options, I really like the food on campus, and the staff of Vail Commons (the dining hall) is really responsive to student requests.

Current student, Biology, 8/2004-Submit Date, May 2007

Davidson is a quiet little town and is very safe. The campus itself is also safe, not only because of the surrounding town, but because of the Honor Code. The college prides itself on its Honor Code, which is closely followed by students. The Code allows for take-home tests, which many professors use, and self-scheduled exams. In this system, students may enter Chambers, the main academic building, during either the morning or evening exam period, pick up an envelope containing the test, and then go to any classroom in the building and take the exam. Most professors use this system, except for classes where the exams are scheduled out of necessity, such as an art history class that has slide identifications as part of the exam or a music class that has a listening portion.

The food on campus has definitely improved over the past two years. Commons, the cafeteria, was renovated last summer. Also, the Union Cafe is open for all meals, and students can use their meal plan at the café for dinner. The Wildcat Den is a little sandwich place where students can use their meal plan for lunch. Last year The Outpost was reopened. This is a late-night dining facility found in the middle of Patterson Court, which is the area of campus that contains all the frats and eating houses.

Current student, Economics, 8/2005-Submit Date, May 2007

Quality of life is superb! I feel that this is largely due to the Honor Code we have on campus that states that students will not lie, cheat or steal. Benefits from this include self-scheduled, unproctored final exams among many other things. Housing is great. I imagine the average dorm size here is larger than most. Almost every student lives on campus because there is so much going on here. Also, the school does your laundry for you. We have a great union board program that is always putting on fun activities. We have no recorded violent crimes on campus. Dining is varied and really quite good. Facilities are always being updated. We have state-of-the-art research equipment.

Social Life

Alumnus/a, Biology, 8/2003-5/2007, June 2007

During the weekend, most people tend to stay on campus, with a minority of the student body heading to bars or events in Charlotte. We do have a Greek system of fraternities for the men, and non-Greek eating houses for the women. The frats and eating houses hold parties every weekend, to which all Davidson students are invited. Many of those are themed parties, some popular themes being Madonnarama, Black Light Beach Party, Superheroes Party, Glam Rock and many more. For students who do not feel like heading to these parties, there are usually other events on campus, as well. The Union hosts weekly events that include break-dance competitions, four-square tournaments, battle of the bands events, bringing in guests like hypnotists and so on. There are also movies playing on a big screen, more academically oriented speaker and events, and free food and music in other areas. The only bar in Davidson is called the Brick House. It is about two blocks from campus, and Thursday is the big night for Davidson students. Most 21-year-olds go to the Brickhouse on Thursdays, which is a nice time to see people and relax. Some people also go to bars down in Charlotte with alumni they know in the area. I never got a chance to do everything I wanted at Davidson, and I loved the fact that there were so many options.

Current student, Biology, 8/2004-Submit Date, May 2007

Davidson has an unusual policy regarding Greek life in that we currently have fraternities on campus, though no sororities. Instead of sororities, we have eating houses, which function similar to sororities. However, new members choose the house they want to join, unlike sororities that ultimately decide their membership. We currently have seven fraternities, including a Historically Black fraternity, and all but one of the fraternities have houses on campus, although no members actually live in the houses. Rather, they are used for meals, meetings, and parties. There is at least one party every weekend on the court, and there are always parties on the weekend in the senior apartments on campus. Davidson

does not have a dry campus, and the college alcohol and drug policy clos[ely] match the North Carolina laws. The Brickhouse is the local bar that is most f[re]quented by students, though there are other clubs and bars nearby that stude[nts] also go to. Some students also travel to downtown Charlotte, since it is only h[alf] an hour away.

There are many clubs at Davidson. We have different club and intramural spo[rts] such as lacrosse, soccer, basketball and ultimate frisbee. There are also ma[ny] different religious and cultural organizations, including Catholic, Methodist a[nd] Presbyterian ministries, the Black Student Coalition, and the Curry Club, [an] organization the centers on Middle Eastern cultures. There are also many se[rv]ice organizations, including the Timmy Foundation, Habitat for Humanity a[nd] the Red Cross Club. The largest student organization is Dance Ensemble. T[his] is a completely student-run organization that puts on one large dance show ev[ery] semester. Any student can participate, and the dances in the show range fr[om] hip-hop to ballet, to ballroom, to cultural dances (the most recent performan[ce] included a Bulgarian and Japanese dances).

Current student, Liberal Arts, 8/2004-Submit Date, May 2007

The social life at Davidson is limited because of its size. There are nationa[lly] recognized fraternities but no sororities. However, for the girls there are esta[b]lishments called eating houses, which are societies that one can join one's fre[sh]man year. These not only provide a meal option but also throw parties, h[old] events and do community service. A nice element to social life at Davidson [is] the fact that the parties are open to all members of campus not just Gree[k]. There is an extreme lack of bars and restaurants in the town of Davidson its[elf], but the close location of Charlotte and its surrounding areas is always a draw[ing] point. Hotspots on campus include the Union where a student organization ho[lds] events throughout the weekend, the Outpost a late-night food option a[nd] Patterson Court where the parties take place.

Current student, 8/2002-Submit Date, May 2006

There are a few bars close to campus, but only one is really frequented by st[u]dents (the Brickhouse). Most of the larger parties on campus are held by eati[ng] houses and fraternities, although there are many smaller ones in the senior apa[rt]ments. Most parties are open to all students, meaning you don't have to be a p[art] of the eating house or fraternity to come join in on the fun. There is also som[e]thing going on in the union every weekend as an alternative to the party sce[ne]. They put on fun things like midnight movies, after midnights (which is wh[en] they just give away free food accompanied by some form of other entertai[n]ment), paint your own pottery and open mic nights. Really fun.

The School Says

Davidson students pursue their studies with the college's hallmark academic vigor, while leading well-balanced extracurricular lives reflected in more than 100 student organizations, a lively social scene and a strong college union. A gender-balanced student body administers the school's revered Honor Code. An increasing population of minority ethnicity and international origin approaches 20 percent. Davidson's need-blind admissions policy currently translates to about 33 percent of Davidson students who receive need-based financial aid, with 19 receiving merit aid and 10 percent athletic scholarships. Beginning in 2007, Davidson includes no loans in its financial aid packages.

Located in a classic college town near Charlotte, NC, Davidson offers both small-town safety and city sophistication. Carolina beaches and mountains are within a few hours' drive of Davidson.

The success of Davidson's recently concluded, $250 million capital campaign is particularly evident in architectural additions and upgrades: Knobloch Campus Center includes Alvarez College Union with café and grill, convenience store, bookstore, full-service U.S. Post Office and Smith 900 Room, a venue for concerts, lectures and socials. Alvarez is also home to student government offices, student newspaper and other publications, career services and Davidson Outdoors, which sponsors excursions throughout the year to sites like the Florida Everglades and the Rio Grande. Knobloch also houses the critically acclaimed, Duke Family Performance Hall, home to the Royal Shakespeare Company's ongoing Davidson Residency, as well as other nationally renowned shows, speakers and music concerts. Sloan Music Center offers professional rehearsal and concert presentation space, and a full-service music library. Chambers Building, Davidson's main academic hall, has just been completely renovated and upgraded.

On Patterson Court, six national fraternities, three women's eating houses, a co-ed eating house, and the Black Student Coalition have dining and social facilities. In addition to sponsoring parties open to the entire campus community, members of each house are actively involved in a variety of community service projects. More than 800 students each year get involved in community outreach.

Davidson offers full athletic programming for serious athletes or just for fun. Approximately 85 percent of students participate in intramural or club sports, and about 25 percent play on a varsity team. One of the smallest colleges competing in the

Division I of the NCAA, Davidson enrolls true scholar-athletes to play 11 different varsity sports for men and 10 for women.

Davidson's core liberal arts curriculum requires courses across all disciplines—humanities, social sciences, fine arts, science and mathematics. Students choose from among 20 majors, 13 minors and 11 concentrations. Students can also design their own majors through the Center for Interdisciplinary Studies. Pre-professional programs include medicine, dentistry, law, medical humanities, neuroscience, education and engineering. Davidson incorporates a level of collaborative research that is remarkable at a four-year, undergraduate college, with students presenting papers at national professional conferences. Nearly 70 percent of Davidson students study abroad for credit during their college career.

With a student-to-faculty ratio of 10:1, the capstone of the Davidson academic experience is close relationships with professors. All classes are taught by full professors, 100 percent of whom hold terminal degrees in their fields. Average class size is no more than 20 students.

Duke University

Office of Undergraduate Admissions
138 Campus Drive
Box 90586
Durham, NC 27708-0586
Admissions phone: (919) 684-3214
Admissions fax: (919) 681-8941
Admissions e-mail: undergrad-admissions@duke.edu

 Admissions

Current student, 8/2003-Submit Date, October 2006

Applied Early Decision. I attended a public high school in the South that was not very competitive, and I think my standardized scores were kind of low. However, I believe that my essays and my recommendations were what made me stand out. I did not do an interview, only the standard application (paperwork, transcript, essays, standardized exams and so on). One of the aspects that impresses me the most about the admissions process is that it seems that the admissions team really goes over everything thoroughly. I remember when I came to Duke my freshman year, the administration held a function where new students could meet faculty and staff—including people from admissions. These admissions counselors knew us by name and could remember our applications, without having known our face. This showed me that they really got to know us through the entire application, beyond GPA and SAT scores.

Current student, 8/2002-Submit Date, May 2006

The past few years have witnessed a sharp increase in Duke's admissions selectivity. Duke, like its similarly ranked counterparts, appears to take everything into consideration. While high SAT scores and class rank are a definite plus, they no longer equate to automatic acceptance. Tailor your essay to the prompt, show passion for Duke, exhibit excellence and leadership in multiple activities, and make sure the teachers who write your recommendations actually like you and can speak well on your behalf. This advice is redundant but important.

Current student, 8/2003-Submit Date, March 2006

I was accepted before my senior year of high school began because I am an athlete. I knew that the admissions process was very difficult for the regular students, and that each year it has become more selective. The campus, reputation, social scene and weather all make Duke a top choice for students across the

country. I have noticed that many of my friends are from the Tri-Sate Area, the D.C. metro area, Texas or California. Most students are involved in extracurricular activities such as student government or community service. To simply be smart is not enough to get into this school. There are siblings and relatives everywhere, so stretch your family tree until it breaks looking for a family member or friend who attended and donates money.

Current student, 8/2004-Submit Date, December 2005

The admissions process was very rigorous. Duke is an incredibly selective school, and the application is like a long novel. A good essay is crucial to Duke admission. Duke is looking for creative essays, not an average student affirmation of themselves. Students come up with creative and controversial topics, and usually those are the ones that get admission. Interviewing, while not necessary, I would highly recommend. It not only lets the university know that you are very interested, it gives you a chance to get a feel for the school through its alumni. That being said, getting into Duke requires creativity and achievement. If you can stress both in your essay and interview, you're a leg up on the competition.

Current student, 8/2003-Submit Date, April 2005

The Common Application and the Duke supplement weren't difficult or long. Though the school is considered selective, they provide many scholarships, academic recruitment programs, and on-campus visit weekends to help you decide whether Duke is the best fit for you. Duke is about fun, passion and ambition. Anyone can fit in and admission isn't based solely on test scores, but more on the admissions committee's perception of personality and interests. Duke seeks students who are not afraid to take risks academically, as well as socially, who love to be challenged intellectually, and who are willing to learn not for the grades but for the knowledge. Don't be afraid to show Duke who you are in your application. Don't be afraid to send in slides if you are a talented artist or tapes if you are a talented musician.

Current student, 9/2001-Submit Date, January 2005

The admissions process has become much more difficult in the last three years. When I applied I only had a mid-range SAT score (high 1300s)—I do not know if this would still get me in today. Most of my friends had higher scores and almost all freshmen I talk to are above this range. I do think that my extensive experience outside of the classroom and my excellent high school education at a top-tier boarding school greatly enhanced my application. Advisor and professor recommendations are generally better from boarding schools because we have much more contact with them compared to your average applicant from a day school.

Read all of Vault's College Surveys at **www.vault.com/college**—get complete surveys on 100s of colleges and universities, expert advice on application essays and more.

VAULT CAREER LIBRARY **523**

I do think my interview at school and at Duke helped my admissions chances—I interview well and this could only add to my overall value. I would advise applicants to prepare well for these meetings. Essays highlighted my exposure to many different programs outside of school and in other countries. My GPA was relatively low (3.2). Maturity, desire to learn and a wide variety of experiences pushed me into the acceptance pool—I excelled only in languages and writing. Plus, apply early!!! I cannot stress this enough. I think Duke accepts almost a third of the class early. I applied early and I do not know if I would have gotten in during the regular admissions process. Not to mention, it was a huge relief to know where I was going in December. I spent the rest of senior year stress-free.

Academics

Current student, 8/2003-Submit Date, February 2007

Academics at Duke are generally superb given that you are attending one of the top schools in the nation. All of the professors are very accomplished—though this does not necessarily translate into being a great teacher! It may just be my own unique experience, but some of the best professors I have had at Duke are actually visiting professors (they bring in some very amazing people!)

There is no set curriculum at Duke, rather, all students follow what is called Curriculum 2000, which requires students to fulfill requirements in certain areas; however, there is a lot of variety in courses. The only requirements at Duke are Writing 20 for all first-year students and if you are in Trinity School of Arts and Sciences, you are also required to take a seminar your first year (there is one offered by every department). Fulfilling your curriculum matrix is not hard to do, as I ended up completing almost all my requirements in the first two years just by trying out a variety of courses.

You do not have to declare your major until your second semester sophomore year, which gives you a lot of time to try out different subject areas. It seems like every student has a double major, or a major and two minors, or a major and certificate and a minor and so on. The requirements for the majors vary considerably.

The workload at Duke varies at lot depending on what courses you are taking, and I definitely recommend asking around before signing up for a class. In almost all cases, it is really the professor that matters, and I always use sites like ratemyprofessor.com when choosing courses.

Current student, 8/2002-Submit Date, May 2006

Some professors at Duke are among the best instructors I've ever had. They are experts in their fields. Despite their research involvement and acuity, they take the time to answer your questions and help you understand any confusing topics.

There are also the professors who are well-respected (or even well-known) in their fields, but cannot teach very well. Needless to say, asking students who have previously taken their courses should help you when you decide which classes to take.

Current student, 8/2003-Submit Date, March 2006

Classes are small and can be easily managed with a healthy social life. Almost half of the undergrad students in the arts and science program are economics majors, and Wall Street is filled with Dukies.

> **The school says:** "Around 6 percent of Duke seniors (Class of 2007) are majoring in economics, including those who have declared economics as a second major."

The online system for signing up for classes is easy and switching in and out of classes is easy. Grading depends on the teachers, not the material. I have taken several interesting or easy classes that were recommended by friends, only to find the professors changed and so did the adjectives used to describe the class. In order to graduate from A&S, you have to complete the "matrix" composed of several types of classes you have to take. While it is a little annoying to try to complete this with your major, it is relatively easy.

Alumnus/a, 8/2000-5/2004, April 2006

The benefit of attending a school like Duke is the opportunity to study in diff ent fields and know that you will benefit from being taught by top academics each respective study. Professors can be very helpful and it is important to ta advantage of the small-sized courses to get to know them personally. Gett into popular classes can be difficult, but it is rare that you will not be able to into a schedule that you enjoy and/or get into the popular class in a later sem ter.

Current student, 8/2002-Submit Date, March 2005

Duke is pretty amazing academically. The only classes that are really big (30 ish) are intro classes in subjects like chemistry or economics, otherwise biggest classes are around 90 and those tend to also be intro classes or really po ular classes. The professors seem to be very capable of handling the bigg classes, and the quality rarely seems to suffer due to size. Some of the m charismatic professors I've had have been in classes around 70 students, a they've worked the size to the advantage of the students.

Most classes, particularly as you get higher in a subject, are much smaller a in fact, all language classes are capped around 12. Regardless of class size, professors are all happy to work with students individually, and love to get know the students in their classes. I have never experienced any professors w seemed distant from their students, or who were more focused on their ov work. The only grad students I've ever experienced have been TAs who led d cussion sections; professors have always led lectures and all other classes.

It can be difficult to get popular classes as a freshman or even as a sophomo but as you rise in seniority you should be able to get any class. It also helps be on the waitlist and talk to the professor; lots of professors will let you in a f class if you wait it out and express interest.

Duke students tend to work very hard in that they tend to double major, ta extra classes and be involved in tons of extracurriculars. The workload tends be intense, but only because the students seem to prefer it that way. You can ea ily create your own schedule that is less intense if you want to.

Current student, 8/2004-Submit Date, March 2005

The academic program is rigorous; it definitely surprised me when I arrive However, there are plenty of untapped resources to help you improve yo grades. There is the wonderful writing studio for paper help and free tuto (highly recommended). I was in the Humanitarian Challenges at Home a Abroad FOCUS program, which is an amazing way to get involved in scho Through that program, I was able to join great community volunteer activiti and had a solid application for the Baldwin Scholars program. The Baldw Scholars program has already given me an internship for my entire colle career!

> **Duke University says:** "Created in January 2005, the Baldwin Scholars program is a four-year program aimed at empowering women to change campus culture and the world beyond. Baldwin Scholars, who are chosen competitively, have the opportunity to live together, network with distinguished faculty, connect with female students, intern with Duke alumni, volunteer in the community and study in intimate seminars."

Employment Prospects

Current student, 8/2003-Submit Date, September 2006

The very best firms (e.g., BCG, McKinsey and Goldman Sachs) recruit at Duk Students with good academic track records can get highly coveted positions such firms.

Current student, 8/2003-Submit Date, February 2007

Basically, coming out of arts and sciences, if you want support, your options a investment banking, consulting, pre-law or pre-med, maybe some other gra programs, possibly working on the Hill and if all else fails, Teach for Americ Saying this, if you are interested in consulting or investment banking, the best the best do come to recruit at Duke (as for grad programs, I am sure having t Duke name helps). One cool program in the public policy department is th

ors are required to do a summer internship, and the coordinator is a wonder-
knowledgeable woman who will help place you in the best internship for
.

rrent student, 8/2002-Submit Date, May 2006

ke is one of the best undergraduate institutions for preparing you for a job in
unce or consulting, even though there is no pre-business or business major.
ke has a strong alumni network in the top investment banks and consulting
ns, and these alumni make an extra effort to hire Duke students during recruit-
season.

e school sponsors many networking sessions and dinners that you should
nd to form valuable connections.

e Career Center is excellent, as it contains a database of Duke alumni, their
upation, employer and contact information. There is also an internship data-
e and free mock interviews and information sessions to help you prepare for
uiting season.

rrent student, 8/2001-Submit Date, January 2004

e Duke Career Center is great. They make an effort to get you involved as a
t-year so that you can start making connections and networking right away.
ey have a great résumé/cover letter support staff who critiques your résumé
days a week, as well as staff who works with mock interviews. I have been
erally impressed by the employers that come to campus and, in fact, sur-
sed by the number who do. The internship opportunities seem endless, at
st in the finance fields, and I get the impression that employers do value Duke
dents for their intellect and positive attitude.

rrent student, 8/2003-Submit Date, March 2004

e Career Center is great. It is somewhat of an untapped resource. The major-
of employers that come to Duke are in finance or engineering, but the Career
nter can help you find opportunities in any industry. A lot of prestigious
ancial institutions recruit at Duke that don't recruit at other universities. Since
ke has such a large medical center, there are lots of opportunities for pre-med-
l students. Students have many opportunities for getting involved in research
.

 ## Quality of Life

rrent student, 8/2002-Submit Date, May 2006

n a tour guide at Duke, and I can say that on every single tour that I've given,
ple have commented on the beauty of this campus. Breathtaking is the only
rd to describe the inside and outside of Duke's campus. Dorms and facilities
, in general, very new and well-kept, and older facilities are constantly being
ovated or rebuilt. There are many dining options on campus and two full-
vice gyms that are included in the cost of attending Duke.

ke-Durham relations aren't the best, to say the least. However, President
odhead and the school have made efforts to reach out to the community and
ablish forums where students and Durham residents can discuss relevant
ues concerning town-gown relations. Also, a majority of students volunteer
the Durham area, but community relations can definitely be improved.

> **The school says:** "Durham is one of only a small number of U.S.
> cities with a historically strong black middle and professional
> class. The city has very close to a 50/50 proportion of Black
> and White residents, with a history of interaction among people
> of varying backgrounds and races. Race relations are arguably
> better than at most cities in the North. We readily acknowledge
> that there's still work to be done. But the truth is that Duke and
> Durham are both wonderfully diverse, and they benefit from
> being tied inextricably to one another. Opinion research carried
> out by Duke confirms that, if anything, the lacrosse incident has
> only served to strengthen the ties between the university and
> the community."

Current student, 8/2004-Submit Date, December 2005

The overall quality of life is great at Duke. The students are brilliant, yet filled
with school spirit (especially for basketball). It is a stimulating atmosphere that
fosters some competition, but unlike at many other top-tier schools, Dukies work
together and help each other. Housing situations are great. All freshmen live on
their own campus and get the chance to bond as a class before moving from East
Campus to West as sophomores. Dining is purely points based, with many different restaurants on and off campus accepting the dining plan. If you're bored
with the food that you can get on your dining plan, you're doing something
wrong. The only drawback to Duke is the neighborhood. Durham has many
good qualities, but a lot of them are overshadowed by the high crime rate.
Though Duke is an insulated bubble, Durham does not like Duke students, therefore students rarely venture off campus. Duke provides an immense amount of
security and police on campus, though. Since I've been here, there have been
absolutely no outside criminal acts committed against Duke students on campus.

> **The school says:** "Durham was named among the Top 100
> places to live in the U.S. by *Money* magazine, based on factors
> including education, housing, safety, and quality of life."

Current student, 8/2003-Submit Date, April 2005

The quality of life at Duke is unsurpassable. Just come to campus one day, see
the magnolia trees growing, the fresh grass around the chapel, the cherry blos-
som trees around Science Drive, the flower arrangements near the engineering
labs, and you will realize that Duke caters to its students more than any other.
Even Sarah Duke Gardens or the Washington Duke Golf Trail are often available
to students for exercise or for doing homework.

The athletic facilities are beyond compare. Wilson gym has three basketball
courts, ellipticals, treadmills, large screen TVs, a delicious fresh fruit/protein
shake bar and more. Housing is nice—double rooms are typically over 170
square feet large (this year mine is 226) and triples can be over 360 square feet.
Freshman year, you are housed on East Campus with a sprawling quad and
house-like residence halls. The years after, you will probably live on West
Campus in the famed Gothic architecture residence halls with friendly gargoyles,
archways, Duke stone and geometrically designed windows.

Each student must have a card to swipe into their residence hall so the dormitories are very safe. Housekeepers clean the bathrooms, hallways and trash rooms
daily. There are more dining options at Duke than at any other college. In addition to on-campus dining options (a variety of fast food, homemade and cafeteria places), your food points can go towards off-campus restaurants (some quite
classy, we order calamari all the time) that will deliver the food to your dorm. In
addition, there's a variety of international restaurants around Durham, close to
Duke, where many people can go if they have free time.

 ## Social Life

Current student, 8/2003-Submit Date, February 2007

Greek life is very big at Duke, but I think it would be a stretch to say that it dominates the social scene. Only 23 percent of men are in fraternities, and 40 percent of women are in sororities, which means most people are not Greek! There
are also selective living groups on main West that are usually themed, and in
addition to the Greek groups, they often throw parties on the weekends. Most of
the social life is centered around alcohol consumption, and binge drinking is a
large problem here as it is at many universities. Luckily, it gets a little better by
the time you are a senior. There are bars and clubs very close to Duke, but if you
are from any sort of major city you are in for a big surprise. However, they are
fine for college students and serve their purpose.

Alumnus/a, 8/2001-5/2005, May 2006

Social life at Duke is centered mainly on and immediately off campus, including
9th Street, Durham Downtown and residential neighborhoods surrounding campus. Bars and restaurants are plentiful, spanning the spectrum of price and
atmosphere. Duke is home to hundreds of gatherings, musical and dramatic productions, and academic presentations. Duke students currently administer and
run over 350 on-campus clubs. Greek life is popular, drawing almost 30 percent
of male students and 40 percent of female students. Venues popular with Duke

Read all of Vault's College Surveys at **www.vault.com/college**—get complete surveys on 100s of colleges and universities, expert advice on applicaton essays and more.

VAULT CAREER LIBRARY **525**

students include: Charlie's Grill, George's Garage, Verde, Satisfaction, James Joyce and the Federal Bar and Grill.

Current student, 8/2002-Submit Date, May 2006

Social life at Duke is a combination of that characteristic of Northern and Southern private schools. Like Southern schools, it is dominated by Greek life. Over 40 percent of women at Duke and 30 percent of men are affiliated with some Greek organization. Like the elite Northern schools, Duke's social atmosphere is very WASPy, despite its high percentage of minority students. This may be due to the school's Southern setting and atmosphere coupled with the high tuition. The social scene revolves around parties held by sororities and fraternities and football tailgates in the fall. Needless to say, if you are looking for a cosmopolitan experience, don't come here. Duke's social atmosphere breeds conformity and is not extremely welcoming for nonconformists.

> **The school says:** "About 36 percent of undergraduates participate in fraternities or sororities. Greek life is one of many extracurricular options at Duke. There are well over 300 student clubs and organizations focusing on everything from cultural, political and religious interests to intramural sports and specific hobbies."

Current student, 8/2003-Submit Date, March 2006

No Top 10 school provides the social life that Duke has. Its proximity to so many other schools allows for students to escape its small school feel, but at the same time enjoy North Carolina and the athletics that Duke is known for. Bars and restaurants are fantastic and are everywhere. Fraternities and sororities are a key to the social life, but do not dominate the scene. They usually join up to throw parties and allow members to associate with other groups.

Current student, 8/2000-Submit Date, April 2005

Social life on campus is largely dead and this is universally known on campus. It used to revolve around on-campus fraternities, but most of them have off-campus houses and throw huge parties there. Much of the campus social life used to involve alcohol, but the school has enacted policies to curb underage drinking and most people will drink behind closed doors as a pre-party and go off campus to either a fraternity party, or usually to a restaurant that is rented out by a group and converted into a nightclub. Popular night-spots include George's Garage and Shooters. Parizade's used to be another, but they recently decided not to do night-time events.

> **The school says:** "Fraternities have housing on West Campus, and about 23 percent of undergraduate men participate in fraternities. Sororities are non-residential, and about 40 percent of undergraduate women participate in sororities. East Campus, where all first-year students live, is completely dry."

Current student, 8/2003-Submit Date, May 2004

There are a handful of bars that students go to, most are restaurants by day. They are nice, well-kept and fun. There are a lot of nice, little restaurants in the area with good food and atmosphere. Not many students date, more one-night stands,

but those who do take it seriously. School sponsors some events (athlet Basketball games are really fun, but most parties are held by small groups frats. An average night at Duke ends up at a bar after pre-gaming in dorms w friends.

 ## The School Says

Duke University seeks to nurture a learning community that encourages students to question their own assumptions and engage in challenging scholarship. Undergraduates can choose courses in nearly 100 different programs, from the humanities and social sciences to mathematics, engineering nand natural sciences. Or, arts and sciences students may design their own major with help from a faculty advisor. Duke's exceptional academic opportunities, paired with a youthful sense of flexibility and a vibrant school spirit, make it unique among premier institutions.

For the most part, Duke's campus is as safe as its Gothic and Georgian architecture, colorful gardens and sprawling forest suggest. But Duke, located in an urban environment, is like most college campuses: it is not immune from crime. The university has taken numerous steps to promote safety and offers many crime prevention programs. The vast majority of crimes on campus are minor and nonviolent and can be prevented with students' help.

While Duke students are intently focused on their scholarship, they also take a serious interest in their community and the wider world. Duke students contribute more than 100,000 hours annually to community service; nearly half of Duke undergraduates study abroad before graduating, taking advantage of programs that extend from Bolivia to Beijing. The university has also committed $10 million to the Duke-Durham Neighborhood Partnership, a program that brings together students, employees, and faculty to work with nearby neighborhoods and schools.

The university provides many resources to help undergraduates succeed in the classroom and beyond graduation. The Duke University Career Center presents students and alumni with opportunities to develop skills and networks to assist them throughout their lifetime. The sense of community found among students continues for an extraordinarily large number of alumni at Duke. This sense of community contributes greatly to the ability of the center to foster career- and self-exploration, experiential education through internships and learning by networking.

East Carolina University

Admissions Office

Greenville, NC 27858-4353

Admissions phone: (252) 328-6640

Admissions e-mail: admis@mail.ecu.edu

Admissions URL: www.ecu.edu/admissions/

Admissions

Current student, 9/2003-Submit Date, November 2005

To be admitted into ECU, you must fill out an application along with mailing your transcript from former schools you've attended. No essays or interviews are necessary.

Alumnus/a, 9/1990-5/1995, April 2005

Prospective students must have about 1000 on their SATs and good grades with a lot of extracurricular activities. A short essay is required in your submission form.

Alumnus/a, 8/1992-8/1999, July 2004

ECU is a large, public university. No essays are required.

Through the years, the admissions department has become much more selective with their incoming students, especially those from out of state. My advice would be if you barely make the grade average or the SAT, make sure one of those compliments the other and that you have taken at least one to two years of a foreign language and participated in extracurricular activities (sports, other electives (e.g., music, arts, theatre) and volunteering. East Carolina University, as a whole, is a very outgoing group of people. If you are set on going to ECU and think there's a chance you may not get in, I highly suggest a trip to campus. Although it is a large student body, try to get a meeting with the assistant dean of admissions or one of the admissions counselors. They are very helpful, sweet people (and personality can go a long way sometimes). If they can't help you, they will either point you to someone who can or offer tips on how to work on your application, bringing up your GPA or SATs.

Current student, 9/2000-Submit Date, April 2004

The admissions process has changed somewhat, but when I applied I simply filled out an application that was around one page in length. The questions were basic, nothing too complicated. Shortly thereafter, I was sent a letter saying that because my mother was an alumna, I stood a good chance of getting in, which was followed by another letter, my letter of acceptance.

Academics

Current student, 9/2003-Submit Date, November 2005

Classes at ECU are moderately hard but not extreme. The quality of classes in my major is very high (recreation therapy). Getting popular classes is not hard as long as you register on time. Grading is on a 10-point scale unless you're in nursing school. Most professors are fair and will make time to sit and talk with you outside of class. The workload can seem a bit much at times, but overall it's not that hard.

Alumnus/a, 9/1990-5/1995, April 2005

Good size classes for a university; the instructors are personal and willing to help you. Waiting in lines is the most problematic part of being at such a large school. Sometimes it's hard to get the classes you want.

Alumnus/a, 8/1992-8/1999, July 2004

There are quite a few advanced departments at ECU. Consistently ECU is rated among the Top Five schools in the state in the schools/departments of business, music, art, medicine, nursing, allied health and education (ECU produces more teachers than any other college or university in the state). So if you're not sure what to major in just yet, that's OK because they have plenty of quality options to choose from. The great thing about the classes here is that they are relatively small for such a large population of students. My largest class was my freshman biology class of about 80 students, but with each semester your classes get smaller (having in part to do with choosing a major and having a more concentrated class schedule). My senior year, I don't believe I had a class larger than 35. The grading I found to be pretty fair, on a whole. If you want the more popular classes, be prepared either to stand in line at the crack-of-dawn the first day of registration or go to your advisor, explain why you "must" have this course and sometimes he/she can sign a form for you to get priority placement in a class or take you directly to someone who can go ahead and sign you up (again, a sweet disposition and a good personality can go a long way). I found the workload to be pretty fair. Of course, it will be relative to your department/major—just listen to students who have been before you (upperclassmen), they know the teachers and classes to steer clear of and the ones that are challenging, in a good way.

Current student, 9/2000-Submit Date, April 2004

My major is athletic training, which is one of the best majors here at East Carolina University. The general classes that everyone has to take are generally not too hard, and the professors range from TAs to PhDs. If you are an honor student or athlete, you stand a very good chance of getting into classes, but if you are a general student, it may be difficult to get into some of the more popular classes—those that every needs to take to graduate or those deemed as easy. Grading is on the A, B, C, D, F scale (0.0 to 4.0). Each teacher may have a different grading criteria, or may curve differently, if at all. Workload also varies by teacher and class. Once you get into your major, it's a whole new ball game: coursework tends to increase dramatically.

Employment Prospects

Current student, 9/2003-Submit Date, November 2005

The Career Center helps keep you up to date with jobs that are open in your field both full time and part time, as well as internships. Graduates obtain a range of different jobs. Advisors are the primary source for hooking you up with internships.

Alumnus/a, 8/1992-8/1999, July 2004

ECU definitely offered me every opportunity to prepare for the real world after college!! There are many different departments/offices that will assist you in this process, if you are willing to spend a little time looking at all the options. Most of this information is posted in the campus newspaper. It ranges from co-ops to job interview prep classes, to what company will be recruiting on campus that week. As far as internships go, it's usually in your best interest to check with your advisor in your department. If he/she can't help you or doesn't have the information you're looking for, try to check with the dean of your department and let him/her know you're very serious and dedicated and he/she will usually do whatever he/she can to assist you with some information at least. Personally, I was selected to co-op at Disney World (MGM Studios) my sophomore year and then had a local hands-on internship through my department (communications and broadcasting) my senior year. In the meantime I took advantage of part-time jobs offered on campus, as well as off, that were made available through our financial aid office. I also took career placement tests, job interview workshops and interviewed with different recruiters that came to campus. All of these facets helped prepare me in ways I could have never imagined without them!! Please take advantage of at least some of the services the university offers!!

Current student, 9/2000-Submit Date, April 2004

With my degree in athletic training, I can obviously pursue a career in athletic training. Internships can rage from the Wide World of Sports in Disney to NFL training camps. Career prospects are generally good, although it is recommended, as with any field in today's society, to pursue a master's before entering the

Read all of Vault's College Surveys at **www.vault.com/college**—get complete surveys on 100s of colleges and universities, expert advice on applicaton essays and more.

VAULT CAREER LIBRARY 527

job market to make yourself more marketable. Here at East Carolina, there are graduate fairs and a Career Center, but those within the athletic training program will definitely be of the most help in placing with either a graduate assistantship at another university, or an employment opportunity elsewhere (as can the National Athletic Trainers' Association web page).

Quality of Life

Current student, 9/2003-Submit Date, November 2005

Quality of life is fair. There are crime issues every so often. There are plenty of housing opportunities off campus, on campus is not so great. The gymnasium is state-of-the-art, so are the dining halls.

Alumnus/a, 9/1990-5/1995, April 2005

The cost isn't bad compared to other universities in the state. It's fairly easy to find affordable housing. The crime rate is normal compared to other large cities in NC.

Alumnus/a, 8/1992-8/1999, July 2004

My life on campus and off was quite enjoyable, for the most part. The only real issues you might encounter have to do with the weather. It's quite humid from May to October/November, so if you're not staying in a residence hall (dorm) with air conditioning, it's gonna be pretty hot. Make sure to have at least two fans in your room if you don't have A/C. On-campus housing is located in three different areas: on the hill (only resident halls and dining halls, it's close to the stadium), on the west side of campus (close to downtown, halls and the rec. center) and central campus. I lived on central campus my first two years (with A/C, thank goodness!!). Actually only by the grace of my older brother who knew someone in the housing office—most freshman don't get A/C—I'm just gonna be honest. Most of the housing has been renovated, so that's nice. I highly recommend living on campus for at least one year, it's very convenient for classes, meetings and dining, and you meet a lot of people. Finding a place off campus, once you're ready, is pretty easy. The university offers literature on this, as well as advertisements in the campus paper and on the radio. The campus itself is pretty small for such a large number of students. It's pretty flat, so no worries about hiking up a hill to get to class. It's full of trees, green grass (they're trying to make it a no-car campus, so be prepared to buy a parking sticker for off campus), squirrels, fountains, tall post-clocks, a state-of-the-art library and fitness center (with a climbing wall). There's a lot of history at our university and I think they are still trying to preserve a bit of that, which is nice.

Current student, 9/2000-Submit Date, April 2004

Housing is readily available, either on campus or off, if you act in a timely manner. While on-campus living provides quick and easy access to classes and on-campus events, off-campus living can be more enjoyable. Greenville has many restaurants to choose from, from a local flavor atmosphere like Cubbies' to chains like Outback and Red Lobster. Facilities tend to be good. The recreation center is free to all students and outstanding, and a new dining hall is currently being built on west campus. Crime is generally not an issue in areas where most students live, although that question is best answered by going to the Greenville Police Department and asking where high areas of crime are before deciding on where to live.

Social Life

Current student, 9/2003-Submit Date, November 2005

There is a lot of nightlife downtown but it can be crummy at times. Sororities and fraternities are very big here. There are lots of choices as far as restaurants, they are growing a lot. Some favorites are Chico's, Hams and Buffalo Wild Wings.

Alumnus/a, 9/1990-5/1995, April 2005

There is a big party scene in Greenville. There are a lot of great restaurants and bars and Greek houses. Greenville used to be the biggest party school in the U.S.

Alumnus/a, 8/1992-8/1999, July 2004

It's really a large university with a small college feel. Again, I'm gonna have mention personality here. ECU is home to pretty social students. While mc students are here to concentrate on studies, they're also here to become we rounded: to be social, to get involved, period. Whether it's joining one of t hundreds of clubs/groups, tailgating before a football game (by the way, footb is huge at this university, a large portion of the city is at our stadium on hor game days), applying for a job at our radio station, working at the rec. cente going to a party on Friday night or rushing a sorority or fraternity. It's a soci bunch of people, for the most part.

The school really does offer a lot: intramural sports, academic clubs, soci clubs, collegiate sports, councils, on-campus jobs, game nights, concer movies, theatre and trips. I think some of my favorite social campus memori would have to be going on a snow-skiing trip (offered by rec. services) going a movie on campus once a week, seeing Chris Rock perform, tailgating befo football games, cheering on friends in intramural sports (rugby), going to bas ball and basketball games, going to the Christmas concerts (cheesy, I know being vice president of my residence hall, going to the national conference f residence hall reps, and definitely going to Barefoot on the Mall each April (t last week before finals, they have this all-day event on this large grassy ar called "the mall" and they have food, games and events, and four to five diffe ent bands, the final band is usually pretty well known).

As far as nightlife goes, it's not bad. (Remember this is not a metropolitan city it's about 60,000 people, 20,000 or so are students.) Most students go dow town, which is within walking distance of campus. It's mainly comprised clubs, bars, restaurants and a few specialty stores. There are a handful of oth places to go in Greenville, as far as dance clubs/bars go and there are plenty other restaurants. The dating scene is really what you make it. The more y get involved, the more people you'll meet, the better your odds. I do have admit, for some reason, we seem to have a consistently good looking stude body. I'm serious. Also, if you're a male, you're in luck, the campus is ma up of 60 percent women. I have to say, if you're coming just to party or just f academics, this may not be the school for you. If you're coming for a full, we balanced experience, then this is definitely the place. I wouldn't trade a minu at ECU! (OK, maybe my cramming before finals, but that's it.) Good luck!

Current student, 9/2000-Submit Date, April 2004

You do not have to be a Greek to have an active social life, but it helps. The be fraternities are Pi Kappa Alpha and Sigma Alpha Epsilon, PiKA being t biggest on campus. The best sororities include Alpha Delta Pi and Chi Omeg There are a lot of parties at different people's houses, and the clubs are great f going out. Downtown, the Cavern is great for the under-21 crowd, while 519 more known for its 21-and-over patronage.

The School Says

personal approach to student development. It is an approach that emphasizes useful experiences that will prepare a student for the challenges of life. Learning does not end in the classroom; research is not confined to the lab. The acquisition of knowledge is not enough; it must be applied.

East Carolina recognizes that the overwhelming reason students attend college is to prepare for a career. We embrace this real world responsibility and seek to prepare our students to realize their dreams and aspirations through academic and student life programs.

Today, East Carolina is a constituent institution of the University of North Carolina and offers 106 bachelor's degree programs, 71 master's degree programs, four specialist degree programs,

one first-professional MD program, and 16 doctoral programs in our professional colleges and schools, the Thomas Harriot College of Arts and Sciences, and the Brody School of Medicine.

With a mission of teaching, research and service, East Carolina University is a dynamic institution connecting people and ideas, finding solutions to problems, and seeking the challenges of the future.

East Carolina University. Tomorrow starts here.

North Carolina State University

Office of Undergraduate Admissions
North Carolina State University
112 Peele Hall, Campus Box 7103
Raleigh, NC 27695-7103
Admissions phone: (919) 515-2434
Admissions fax: (919) 515-5039
Admissions e-mail: undergrad_admissions@ncsu.edu
Admissions URL: www.ncsu.edu/future.html

Admissions

Current student, 8/2006-Submit Date, October 2006

I applied early during my senior year of high school. I found NCSU from princetonreview.com under the counselor-o-matic web page. I was looking at schools in the NC region and I found NCSU because it was ranked highly in many opinion polls regarding many aspects of the college. The SAT average score is not difficult to achieve, but NCSU primarily bases the admissions process on the GPA. The average GPA when I applied was over a 4.0. The application was not the general application, it was their application. It was easy to fill out and the entire web site was easy to follow and it was easy to look at dates about your admissions. When I got accepted, they e-mailed me and sent me a letter through snail-mail and also updated it on the personal web site they gave me. The biggest advice I can give anyone is to focus on your GPA more than your SAT score because the admissions committee focuses on your classes and grades more than the standardized scores. I did not take an interview and I submitted a personal essay that was not required. I also submitted recommendations.

Current student, 8/2002-Submit Date, June 2006

The process was very simple when I applied. You simply filled out the request-information on their web site and submitted it. There was no required essay, though if you wanted to be considered for the honors programs you had to write a couple. I heard back from the school in mid-November. The biggest drawback to the process is that you had to pick a school to apply for. As I didn't really know what I wanted to do when I applied for school, it was very random for me.

They do have a First-Year College program, but it has a very poor reputation among the people I know who have been in it. So if you are applying, I would definitely pick a school to apply for. It allows you to live almost anywhere on campus and take whatever classes you want. Whereas the First-Year College program is very regimented and has pre-assigned housing. The school is not incredibly selective, though the average GPA was right around 4.0 when I came in. It does depend on which department/major for which you are applying; engineering is much more difficult, whereas a social science is much easier.

Current student, 9/2002-Submit Date, June 2006

NC State University recognizes that Raleigh is one of the fastest growing cities in the U.S. and welcome applicants from all over and has a huge intake every year. Good grades, a record of good behavior, a wide variety of interests, demonstrable commitment to extracurricular activities and an excellent standard of written and spoken English obviously help the application process. But if you're from NC, it is highly likely you will be accepted anyway. At the interview, apart from a confident and personable manner, well-articulated and enthusiastic answers, it is advisable to sell your interest in NC as an area to live and study, so elaborate on being the outdoors type.

NCS has one of the finest veterinary schools in the U.S., so if you are planning on studying a subject such as biology or animal sociology, it would be worth throwing in at the interview your desire to enhance and further your studies through contact with this institute.

Current student, 8/2005-Submit Date, October 2005

NC State tries to ensure that students know what they want to do before they come here. There's the option of the First-Year College (FYC) that tries to help freshmen pick a major within one year of study. A lot of freshmen feel it's a waste of time but hey, there's at least 500 kids enrolled in that program, so it must be of some value. Popular majors are extremely competitive, but you can always apply for something not so common and keep your grades up and transfer colleges within the college. Each individual college has different requirements to meet when it comes to admission.

Alumnus/a, 8/1997-5/2002, November 2004

Overall, the admissions process is very straightforward at NCSU. It consists of a basic application form asking for details of your high school performance, extracurricular activities and a short essay (500 words). At the time of my application, NCSU wasn't extremely selective, especially in comparison to neighboring schools. However, the quality of high school students has been rising significantly with the average incoming freshmen often having a SAT score of 1250 to 1300 and a GPA close to 4.0.

Alumnus/a, 9/1999-9/2003, April 2005

I took the option of early enrollment. I had a very strong academic record coming out of high school, having taken several Advanced Placement courses. Also, my extracurriculars, such as club officer and team captain, helped in my being accepted to this particular institution. This included filling out an application, then mailing the application along with the application fee to the school. I waited approximately two months for a response. At the time, no essays were necessary; however, now an essay is part of the application process. To gain admittance to particular programs and colleges, an interview may be required. Students selected to attend this university tend to have solid SAT and GPA scores coming out of high school.

Read all of Vault's College Surveys at **www.vault.com/college**—get complete surveys on 100s of colleges and universities, expert advice on applicaton essays and more.

VAULT CAREER LIBRARY 529

Academics

Current student, 8/2006-Submit Date, October 2006

The classes at NCSU vary depending on your major. As a student of the College of College of Agriculture and Life Sciences , my classes are more rigorous and time demanding than the College of Management or Textiles. The classes fill up very quickly if you are trying to register for a PE class, which is mandatory for CALS and the College of Engineering, or any popular elective such as Psychology. It is crazy trying to register for classes during orientation because so many new students are all trying to get into the same classes. You could see a class you want to add and three seconds later the class will be full and you cannot add it. Throughout the school year, it gets easier to add classes after the first week of classes have started because people drop out or switch classes. The professors I have had so far are all very fair but they are not afraid to give you bad grades. The workload is determined by how many hours you have. Many students take an average of about 15 to 16 credits, and the work can pile up very quickly. As a freshman I was surprised by the difficulty of my first biology exam because there was an enormous amount of information to memorize for just one exam.

Current student, 8/2002-Submit Date, June 2006

The academics are very good at NC State, especially considering the relatively low tuition. Most of our professors do teach at the more well-known schools close to us, Duke and UNC-Chapel Hill, showing that they are well respected in their fields. Class sizes are often fewer than 25 on the social science end of the school, except for the very beginning introduction courses, but I've heard that isn't uncommon throughout NC State programs.

Grading and workload vary a lot depending on the class you are taking, but grade distributions are made available for all courses with greater than 20 students in them at the end of the semester. This makes it much easier to pick the sections of a class where the professor may grade a little easier. However, for every major there will always be a couple of courses that everyone struggles in and the grades reflect this. The workload isn't too bad for most classes, though it will keep you busy. I have taken five or more classes every semester and done very well, though many people look at me funny when I say that around campus.

Getting into popular classes is sometimes difficult, but you can usually push your way into them by keeping up to date with the online registration system. A lot of people drop and add throughout the breaks between semesters and you can usually get in before the semester starts. Also, most teachers are willing to let you sit in on their first couple of classes and then find a spot for you as the semester goes on, even if you aren't able to officially add until later in the semester.

Current student, 9/2002-Submit Date, June 2006

As part of a degree in English, you can choose to study a wide variety of other subjects for credit to get a really balanced and broad education. You can sign up for classes as late as the start date if there are still places left. You can take classes that are entirely web based and thus allow you to organize your time much more efficiently if, for instance, you are also trying to hold down a job, look after a family or travel during your degree study. The quality of classes varies and any class that advertises itself as using the Web to post assignments or discussions is worth checking out online in advance so you can get a flavor of it. Depending on what sort of study and assessment suits you, you can tailor your choices to maximize your chances of good grades; there is a wealth of classes that primarily assess you by attendance and participation, others prefer regular quizzes and short web-forum discussions and others still depend upon coursework essays or exams.

Current student, 8/2005-Submit Date, October 2005

A lot of classes focus on engineering, but recently the university has opened up to more ideas. Common freshman classes (e.g., Biology, English) are hard to get into due to the large incoming freshman class. Some small classes are only offered during the fall semester, which makes semester planning critical. Freshman common classes are usually packed and extremely easy; however, as far as classes go they usually get smaller the more defined they get to your major. Keep in mind popular majors have fewer class openings.

Alumnus/a, 8/1997-5/2002, November 2004

The quality of academics definitely varies depending on your major. NCSU best known for its engineering, science and agricultural programs. From my personal experience as a student in the chemical engineering department, the quality of the classes is excellent. At the time I attended, the department was one Top 10 undergrad programs in the country. The curriculum is definitely a hard slog, but the education you leave with pays a lot of dividends in future career choices. The non-technical departments at NCSU are also very good, but suffer some in reputation from their more prestigious neighbors. I'd especially recommend the economics and political science departments for their quality teaching. NCSU, like most universities in the U.S., has been subject to grade inflation over the years. One of the most useful tools for the undergrads is the semester grade statistics offered on the university's web site. Before signing for classes students can check out the historical grade distribution for any class and professor, and make choices based on who's the cream puff. This is especially useful for the freshman-level classes in calculus and physics.

Current student, 8/2002-Submit Date, October 2004

The nature of the English program at NC State is very current and there are high expectations. Professors are also very personal, which makes me want to well in the class to look good to them, not just for numeric value on my GPA. Popular classes can be difficult to get, so I've heard, but I have been fortunate enough not to have that problem.

Alumnus/a, 8/2001-5/2003, June 2004

Freshmen, registering last, may have some difficulties getting into the popular classes, but as a freshman, there is a vast array of classes a student can choose from to fulfill the requirements. There are multiple classes that sound just interesting, so it should really be no difficulty.

Employment Prospects

Current student, 8/2006-Submit Date, October 2006

NCSU is known for a very high percentage of students being employed right out of college. If you are in a rigorous college such as CALS (College of Agriculture and Life Sciences) or Engineering, a student right out of college can make $80,000 a year starting out in the first year of employment. There is a club campus specifically for the alumni that can provide you with connections when you graduate. There is also an enormous amount of extracurricular clubs and programs that can provide a students with connections and internships when they leave college. CALS requires each student to participate in at least internship, community service program and makes each student create a résumé.

Current student, 8/2002-Submit Date, June 2006

I am just starting to enter the job market, but I have had two internships at relatively good institutions. My first was with the U.S. Department of State, which is a very competitive position in the summer, where my second was with Wachovia. The largest drawback is that you do have to do a lot of work on your own. No one at State is very eager to help you with your career search, so you must do it yourself. Once you do start talking to companies, though, they are often more than willing to sit down and talk to you.

Not many businesses outside of IT and engineering recruit at NC State, but will look at it if you seek them out. However, if you are interested in technology, any kind of engineering, NC State is a very strong and competitive school attend. All top-tier companies in these sectors come here to find new graduates so you can't go wrong. One of my good friends was just recruited by Microsoft as a software engineering for around $75K a year.

Alumnus/a, 8/1997-5/2002, November 2004

NCSU has an excellent reputation in the state. The Career Center on campus a real asset for the student with a large company database, regularly scheduled company recruiting visits, and widely advertised career fairs. Fellow graduates from my class have had mixed success in the marketplace, but this is more due to the poor job market at graduation. Still, most ended up in Fortune 500 companies in diverse fields like biotechnology, pharmaceuticals, industrial chemicals, petroleum, consumer goods and consulting. Although I didn't do this myself, I would highly recommend the co-op program for students interested ajoring in engineering. Co-ops offer three semesters worth of industry experience with the same company and often a job offer at graduation.

urrent student, 8/2002-Submit Date, October 2004

eing NC State on a résumé looks good to anyone as far as I know. It is not Ivy ague but it is well-respected and acknowledged. There are also plenty of umni willing to help with questions and advice as well as setting up interviews. e job fairs and career services programs at State are also well run and very lpful.

Quality of Life

urrent student, 8/2006-Submit Date, October 2006

e housing varies dramatically depending on where you are living. There are ny dorms spread all throughout the campus, and the best ones to get into are obably the central campus ones. The dorms are smaller, but there are more ople there and you can make friends easier than if you were situated in north west campus, where there aren't that many people. The campus is beautiful; ery building is made of brick. An alumnus from NCSU owns a business that akes bricks and he gives the college a ton of bricks for free as long as the cam-s can use them, so there is always something being built made out of brick hether it is a new walkway or another building. All of the dorms were reno-ted this year, so that they all have air conditioning. You can get wireless ternet in every dorm or you can connect to the campus network with an ether-t cable. You can also buy cable TV for a small price every semester. There e emergency lights in every dark part of campus, and if you call someone from ese posts, you can get an escort to take you back to where you need to go. The cort and the emergency lights make you feel more comfortable when you are alking home late at night.

urrent student, 8/2002-Submit Date, June 2006

uality of life is good off campus. I know most of our housing on campus is ry old. Many of the dorms are also being renovated with some of the new ucation bond money from the state. Dining, however, is very good. It may t be the best in the world, but it is definitely worth the price you are paying for Two large cafeterias, along with a large numbers of fast food chains, are on mpus or just a short walk away. Hillsborough Street, which runs right along e north part of campus, isn't quite what it used to be, but is still a life line for C State students looking for things to do at night with bars, some clubs and a n of places to eat. Outside of housing and dining, the campus is very nice. ost of the buildings are old, but most of them have new interiors. The school so just opened up Centennial Campus, which is an amazing new campus for gineering, computer science and textiles that is any techie's dream. I think at the biggest plus to the campus, though, is that it is amazingly safe. There e very few robberies on campus, if any, and I have never walked from a night ass to my car (about a 20-minute walk off campus) and been worried about my fety.

urrent student, 9/2002-Submit Date, June 2006

outhern hospitality is rife here, the campus is encircled by much parkland and sidential areas; it is very safe, well laid out, easy to negotiate and welcoming. me of the most beautiful residential streets are largely occupied by students d a stone's throw in any direction takes you to a fine eatery of any genre or ece of countryside. Raleigh is a growing city in the U.S. and already caters to very taste, desire and budget. You can live cheaply, safely and well here. There more than enough going on to make you have to reign in your social life for udy yet it is easy to find a peaceful spot. The mountains and the beach are ually close.

urrent student, 9/2005-Submit Date, October 2005

he housing is excellent; they are extremely helpful and the RAs are awesome. he facilities here are top of the line with the addition of the new Centennial ampus for the engineering department.

lumnus/a, 8/2002-5/2004, February 2005

aleigh is a small town and housing is not a problem. Students usually live in partments. Rent varies from $400 to $700 based on where you want to live. niversity is based on a large campus and I think facilities are really good. It

has a gym that offers many recreation areas. University dining was not really to my taste. Campus is pretty safe but there are a few incidents every year.

Social Life

Current student, 8/2006-Submit Date, October 2006

There is a huge social life at NCSU. There are a few bars right on the top of campus on Hillsborough Street that have discounts on Thursday nights, which is a big night to go out on campus. The football games are huge because we have great fans that love to support every NCSU team. There are too many restaurants to name and many of them are within walking distance on Hillsborough Street or on the other major streets surrounding campus. You can get almost any kind of food within a five-mile radius of campus and there is transportation to any restaurant or bar you need to get to. Because the school is so huge, there are constantly events going on every single night, whether it's just a group of people watching a favorite TV show or a beer pong tournament at a local bar, or a formal dance. Greek life is a big part of NCSU. Greek parties are the best places to be on Friday nights. As a Greek life sorority member, my social schedule is always full and it never gets boring!

Current student, 8/2002-Submit Date, June 2006

Hillsborough isn't quite what it used to be due to zoning laws by the city, but there is significant club life in the downtown area. While this is a long walk away, you can also find groups of students heading down there with cars. One of the biggest perks about State is that it has accepted an atmosphere of Southern hospitality among the students. You can always find someone to hang out with, or help you out with a quick errand if you need it. The school also has a huge number of extracurricular activities available. The most popular are going to basketball or football games, though there are also non-varsity sports you can get involved with if you are more hands-on like me. I play in the very nice racquetball courts very often, and have done some ballroom dancing, which was a fun experiment. Beyond this, I've also gotten the chance to go to basketball games as well as hockey games in the same arena where the Carolina Hurricanes are close to winning the Stanley Cup. There is something to do for everyone.

Current student, 9/2002-Submit Date, June 2006

There are plenty of exclusive fraternities to join, whatever club you want to be part of and whichever types of people you want to shun, you can find the clique for you, or you can join none and still be with an in-crowd. Whether you prefer dollar-sushi, Bojangles fried chicken, Alfredo's Italian, Mexican, Chinese, grills, pizza, bagels, every variety of coffee at Cup of Joes, High Street shops or community resource centers, it's all here. The Pour House in Raleigh always has good live music but it's only a drop in the ocean.

Current student, 8/2005-Submit Date, October 2005

There are plenty opportunities on campus for social events, especially in the Greek life and in the bar scene. There are plenty of bars in Raleigh. Social life is common at parties and at University Towers, a private complex that houses the rich freshmen. Just don't get caught drinking underage like my roommate and you'll be fine.

Alumnus/a, 9/2003-Submit Date, April 2005

The social scene in Raleigh is improving, with several fine establishments opening up recently in the Glenwood area of Raleigh. This part of town is about five-minute cab ride from campus. East Village is still the only good bar within walking distance of campus, but campus night buses do make stops near several other good places. The dating scene is as good as any, with several colleges concentrated in the small Triangle area. The Greek system is well established, however, not as popular here as it is other places. Most partying done by the under-21 crowd is contained to off-campus apartments. The majority of these parties go off without a hitch, but the Raleigh Police Department under the auspices of the nuisance party ordinance are quite effective at breaking up even the smallest shindigs. Most of the big events alumni of decades past remember have gone by the wayside in order to stem underage drinking and public intoxication.

Read all of Vault's College Surveys at www.vault.com/college—get complete surveys on 100s of colleges and universities, expert advice on applicaton essays and more.

VAULT CAREER LIBRARY 531

The School Says

North Carolina State University is a campus of achievers. As a progressive, research-extensive land-grant institution, NC State educates students for the 21st Century and inspires future leaders. NC State offers thousands of courses and 90 bachelor's degree programs, as well as dual-degree programs that allow students to combine varied academic interests and increase career opportunities.

We are a nationally recognized leader in science and technology with historic strengths in engineering and agriculture. But we also offer the most comprehensive design program in the Southeast, outstanding programs in the humanities and social sciences, education, management natural resources, physical and mathematical sciences, textiles and veterinary medicine. We are dedicated to providing a personalized learning environment. Our student-to-faculty ratio is 14:1, while the average class size is 35.

NC State is located near downtown Raleigh, the state capital, in the heart of the area known as the Research Triangle. This burgeoning high-tech region offers extraordinary opportunities to NC State students, and adds to the vibrancy of the campus by providing an extended learning lab right at our doorstep.

Campus life is full of possibilities. Students can choose to become involved with theatre, music, arts organizations, competitive or recreational sports, and more than 300 other campus clubs and organizations ranging from dance to equestrian skills. Sororities and fraternities create the unity and fun of Greek life, and student government provides a chance to hone leadership and political skills. Two student centers on campus offer food, lectures, cultural programs, art galleries and theater productions, as well as offices for the student-run newspapers, the FM radio station, the literary magazine, a cinema featuring first-run films and the African-American Cultural Center. Our volunteer services office can assist students in finding service opportunities both on and off campus, including international spring break service projects.

Our web site, www.ncsu.edu, provides an excellent introduction to NC State including descriptions of all our academic programs. An annual fall open house is held each year, and more personalized views of daily campus life can be arranged through Spend a Day at State programs scheduled through individual colleges. Contact the dean's office of the college you'd like to visit. Also, undergraduate admissions offers informal freshman information sessions every weekday, including walking tours, weather permitting.

For more information, go to www.admissions.ncsu.edu

University of North Carolina at Chapel Hill

Office of Undergraduate Admissions
University of North Carolina at Chapel Hill
CB #2200, Jackson Hall
Chapel Hill, NC 27599-2200
Admissions phone: (919) 966-3621
Admissions fax: (919) 962-3045
Admissions e-mail: unchelp@email.unc.edu
Admissions URL: www.admissions.unc.edu

Admissions

Current student, Business, 8/2005-Submit Date, June 2007

Essays were typical. Know why you want to be at UNC, how it can help you and how you can contribute to the school environment. They eat up diversity related stuff.

Chapel Hill is not as difficult to get into as people often make it sound. Coming from out of state, you will be facing an uphill battle: think Ivy League acceptance rates. However, the caliber of student applying to UNC is generally lower than an Ivy, so don't be too discouraged by the acceptance rates.

In-state acceptance is not bad at all. Keep a 3.5+ GPA, a well-rounded résumé/high school experience, participate in and commit to an activity for three or four years during high school and score a 1300+ on the SAT (Math + Verbal, plan on 650+ on Writing, as well).

Current student, 8/2004-Submit Date, September 2006

The admissions process is tough, especially for out-of-state students like myself. Apply early for consideration for merit scholarships, and expect multiple interviews if selected as a candidate for such scholarships. Alumni contacts are a great boost for getting in, as the school greatly values multiple generations of the same family attending Carolina. Essays were easy, one long and one short, and took no more than an hour. I had high SATs (high 1400s) and was Number Two in a class of 400 at one of the top public schools for my state. Others from my

school were waitlisted with considerably high SATs (High 1300s, low 1400 and stellar GPAs. With less than 20 percent of UNC students from out of stat this process is by far more difficult that gaining admission in-state.

Current student, 8/2004-Submit Date, April 2006

Do not be humble on your application, but be honest. Your application is rea by people who read thousands, so they can tell the fake from the real. The be thing you can do in high school is take advantage of all of your opportunitie There is no magical grade, class or activity you can have that will get you in, a they really do look at each applicant individually. A student who takes two A classes at a school that only offers three will look a lot better than a student wh took four when he attended a school that offered 12 AP classes. Be involved the school and community; take advantage of what is around you. No interview The essays are the best way they get to know you, so write your personalit Again, do not write what you think they want to hear, as they can tell the diffe ence. The school is highly selective, so be honest but write it all down.

Alumnus/a, 8/2001-12/2005, February 2006

The admissions process at the University of North Carolina does not include a interview; however, what one includes in his or her application is quite impo tant. One's extracurricular activities are weighed just as heavily as one's GP and standardized test scores. In fact, as a student, it was quite obvious that mo of my fellow classmates were former service club presidents, homecomin queens/kings, and members of the National Honors Society. Therefore, it is ve important to be as well rounded as possible. Volunteer, participate in servic organizations and show leadership. The university is a very liberal environmer in which the faculty and staff encourage their students to make differences in th world. Therefore, it is very important to show that you are capable of handlin multiple roles simultaneously. Advanced courses, such as AP, IB or fast forwar are also important. However, one should not stress him or herself with overdo ing are. At least three of these should be sufficient. Four years of a foreign la guage are also very important and will be beneficial if enrolled because one given a foreign language exam and is compelled to complete the language to certain level. Recommendations are very important and should be written b professors who can really speak favorably about one's grades, work ethic an character.

urrent student, 8/2005-Submit Date, April 2006

pplied Early Action in November of my senior year. In December, I got a
one call from the dean of undergraduate admissions telling me how much he
ed my essays and inviting me to come visit. The admissions office was so
ndly and down to earth whenever I called, e-mailed or visited. They helped
ordinate my visits so I had a student with whom to spend the night and some
sses to sit in on that were in my field of interest. I got accepted and was invit-
into the honors program, which provides additional seminar classes, special
vising, and other great opportunities to 200 freshmen each year. It's consid-
bly harder to get into UNC from out of state, but it is possible—I went to a
rmal public school in Virginia and four people in my graduating class, includ-
myself, got in. All of us enrolled.

Academics

urrent student, Business, 8/2004-Submit Date, September 2006

a business administration major, I had to reapply to my program in my soph-
ore year for admittance in the fall of junior year. The program is strenuous,
each class is considered the equivalent to an honors program. If pursuing a
BA like me, I recommend having a strong focus on academics from the begin-
ng, as well as joining several organizations early in order to attain leadership
les. Grading is right around the B range, but A's are harder to come by than
ticipated. Getting into the most popular classes is difficult, with seniors often
ing most spots as registration goes by year, not hours.

urrent student, 5/2003-Submit Date, November 2006

ademics are no breeze at this institution. Although it does vary by class, pret-
much every class I have taken at UNC has pushed my limits and taught me
nsiderable amounts. With any effort, it is easy to get into every class. I
rned early on that professors can get you into their classes if they want to and
it is the way to go. Grading varies considerably by major, so business and
rd science majors beware. UNC is making attempts to right this, but it is still
work in progress.

urrent student, 8/2003-Submit Date, April 2006

gistration for classes is all done online. That means that there are about 3,600
her students signing onto the same web site at the same time as you. I'm not
ing to try and sugar-coat it—it can be frustrating. You just have to keep on
ing to sign in, eventually you do. While that seems scary, I have almost
ways gotten the classes I wanted/needed. It's still a good idea to have a few
ck-up classes, just in case. Never try to register without a back-up class. Also,
you can't get into a class you really want to take or need to take, talk to the
ofessor. Go on the first day and sit in. Make an effort and you'll more than
ely get into the class.

e classes here are awesome. We have some of the top professors and most
ll-respected professors in the country. That's why we're one of the top uni-
rsities in the nation! No professor here wants you to fail—in fact, they all
nt you to succeed and do well both in their class and in life! (I know, that
unds cheesey, but it's true.) Professors are always willing to talk to students,
swer questions, help students out—go talk to them! They'd love to hear from
u.

urrent student, 8/2005-Submit Date, February 2006

his school is a great place for an undergraduate education. Don't be fooled by
e rumors that UNC is only for liberal arts majors. The math and science pro-
am here is very highly rated, and I have gone to sit in on similar classes at
arby universities focusing on engineering and practical sciences, only to dis-
ver that the quality of the classes at UNC is much higher. Professors here have
ch genuine interest in the subjects that they teach, so students are all the more
iven to learn and to try new subjects. Be warned, the popular classes here are
etty difficult to get. First-year students should be especially prepared to settle
r their second, third or fourth choices when it comes to registration. After the
st semester, accessing the registration system can be a hassle because it cur-
ntly opens up to all students in a particular class level at the same time, which
eans the Internet server can be jammed before you get a chance to search for
ur classes. But with a never-ending supply of interesting things to take, it's
t such a bad thing to end up in a class for which you never thought you'd reg-

ister. Some professors give frequent grade curves, others are incredibly strict. It
all depends on the professor, not necessarily on the subject. But across the
board, grading is fair in that you will get out of it what you put in. Be prepared
to have course grades based solely on the results of two midterms and a final.
Sometimes the weight rests heavily on a few grades, so it is important to keep
up with your work.

Current student, 8/2005-Submit Date, April 2006

There are general college requirements that every student must meet—two science classes, calculus, introductory English, social sciences and four semesters
of language (which a lot of people place out of based on their AP or IB scores).
Just because UNC is a large school doesn't mean you'll have large classes. We
have a lot of students, but we've also got a lot of professors. Online registration
can get frustrating, but there's plenty of time to change your schedule before the
next semester starts. If you can't get into a class, you should still go to the first
day—most professors will register students who have made the effort to come to
class instead of sending an e-mail begging to get in. In terms of workload,
there's a lot of reading but, fortunately, no busywork. Grades in most classes are
based on a midterm, out-of-class paper (usually about 10 pages), and a final
exam. Smaller classes have attendance requirements. UNC takes great pride in
its extracurricular opportunities, and the professors understand that you have
other classes and non-academic responsibilities

Employment Prospects

Current student, Business, 8/2005-Submit Date, June 2007

Alumni network at UNC is great in NC, strong in the Southeast, weak in the
West, and moderately strong in the Northeast and NYC. UNC is on the border
of schools that get strong recruitment from NYC. Nevertheless, you can make
it almost anywhere from UNC if you want it badly enough.

Current student, 8/2004-Submit Date, September 2006

Employment prospects are numerous, with a variety of on-campus recruiting
events. Both internship and career fairs are present, with specialty fairs dealing
with diversity, consulting and banking fields. Information sessions are rampant
in the fall, often with 10 to 15 per week for various positions. I would suggest
talking to professors before wasting time in the career office.

Current student, 5/2003-Submit Date, November 2006

The network at UNC is extremely strong. I just got an offer with McKinsey,
arguably the most selective employer out there, and it was through the strong
UNC contacts and the great services of UCS that I got it. UNC and its students
are being increasingly recognized by employers as having what it takes to perform at a high level in any type of work environment and thus more and more
companies and organizations are coming to UNC to get grads for their offices.

Current student, 8/2005-Submit Date, February 2006

A UNC graduate can easily compete in the job market with graduates of Ivy
League schools. The education you receive here is incredibly valuable. In addition, there are numerous opportunities throughout the year to apply for jobs,
internships, work-study programs, and other arrangements to further your competitiveness in the market. Companies frequently come to give free workshops
on applying for jobs in their field and building a résumé, and on-campus recruiting is a common occurrence. Advertisements for employers seeking UNC students or graduates frequent the local newspapers. The alumni network is also
very useful. I recommend all students join the general alumni association (the
largest student association on campus). You can join it as soon as you are a student, and the group provides support for academics, social activities, job hunting, you name it. By being a member of the alumni association, you also have
a lifelong connection to the network of UNC alumni who seek graduates to
employ. Summer internships and study abroad programs are also available and
emphasized, and several scholarship groups at UNC offer funding for unpaid
internships so that students can gain experience without the expense.

Current student, 8/2001-Submit Date, April 2004

The career center is excellent on campus, with the employers coming to you.
Interview rooms are provided, and you can sign up online. Also, there are many
online databases you can use to find jobs after graduation or for a summer
internship. The prestige factor is pretty big with employers. Usually the only

Read all of Vault's College Surveys at www.vault.com/college—get complete surveys on 100s of colleges and universities, expert advice on applicaton essays and more.

VULT CAREER
LIBRARY   533

schools that win out more on that end are the Ivies. The career center also provides students with the ability to use their resources after graduation.

Quality of Life

Current student, 5/2003-Submit Date, November 2006

The best part of the Carolina experience is the great overall quality of life. From a great college town to the restaurant scene, to the dining halls, to the athletic facilities, to housing, everything at UNC has been made with the best interests of students in mind. Anything that is not towards the top of its peer institutions, UNC is currently in the process of improving, so that it will be the best at every part of the college experience.

Current student, 8/2003-Submit Date, April 2006

UNC is a very comfortable school. The campus is beautiful (the most beautiful in the nation, according to various magazines) and Chapel Hill has been ranked America's Best College Town for many years in a row. It's simply a great place full of great people. Living on campus is also wonderful. The dorm provides you with a solid community, hall and/or suite to go back to every day. You also have an RA (resident advisor) who is there to help you, counsel you or just talk if you want. Facilities management for the campus is also great—they do their job very well, keeping the campus clean and beautiful. Also, dining halls are very social places. It's great to have a meal plan (though not required)—the food is pretty good for college food! And it's a great place to just hang out with your friends. UNC's campus is safe. UNC was actually the first university in North Carolina to have its own fully accredited police force. Naturally, you should take care of yourself—don't walk home alone at night. Instead take the Point-to-Point bus that goes all over campus. Don't leave your room unlocked—you wouldn't leave the front door of your house unlocked all day, would you? Take basic precautions and you'll stay safe.

Current student, 8/2005-Submit Date, February 2006

In general, UNC has a very high quality of life. The dormitories, for the most part, are reasonably sized and accommodating, but if you end up in a dorm on South Campus that doesn't have air conditioning (and there are plenty of those), portable fans are an absolute necessity. The campus itself is gorgeous, with all of the old buildings, architecture and landscaping that comes with being the oldest public university in the nation. Construction on various parts of campus seems to be perpetual, so you'll have to get used to taking detours as buildings are remodeled and improved. The dining facilities are some of the highest rated among public universities, and with the completion of the enormous Ram's Head complex complete with a second dining hall and a full grocery store, there is no shortage of healthy, affordable meals. Meal plans are available, though students who opt not to get meal plans can still eat in the dining halls for a flat rate and, near the end of the semester, can often get free meals as other students try to use up their remaining meal allotments. Free food is always a good thing for the perpetually broke college student, and particularly near the beginning of each semester, clubs and organizations offer so many events with free meals and information that it's easy to save money and make new friends at the same time.

Current student, 8/2005-Submit Date, April 2006

There are a lot of housing options. In addition to dorms, the Rams Village apartment complex opens in fall 2006 on South Campus. Granville Towers is near frat court and attracts the Greek crowd. There's also plenty of off-campus housing—a lot of people either rent a house with friends or live in an apartment or townhouse complex along one of our many free bus routes. Athletics are a big part of social life. We've got Division I sports, as well as club and intramural sports. Rams Head gym just opened up and it's got a climbing wall, basketball courts, a dance studio, weights and machines, and indoor track. It's a good alternative to the busier and more centrally located SRC (Student Rec Center), which has weights and machines, dance studios, an indoor pool, and squash and basketball courts. There's also a wide array of dining options. The dining halls are decent, but I love Alpine Bagel, an on-campus restaurant that serves soups, salads and bagel sandwiches and stays open until 1 a.m. except on Fridays and Saturdays, so it's a great place to grab a late-night study snack. The northern boundary of the campus, Franklin Street, offers dozens of restaurants that are priced for student budgets. A lot of these restaurants are open until 3 a.m. on the weekends. Another major bonus of going to UNC is the late-night transporta-

tion. The Point-to-Point (P2P) shuttle runs from 7 p.m. to 3 a.m. every night an established route that has stops all over campus and on Franklin Street a frat court. If you're off the route or if it's after 3 a.m., you can call a P2P van pick you up at no cost.

> **The school comments:** "Carolina has several dining facilities on campus. Franklin Street, the center of the town of Chapel Hill, has numerous restaurants and fast-food dining options."

Social Life

Current student, 8/2004-Submit Date, September 2006

Constant social scene available for any interested, especially Greek li Restaurant variety is decent, with many boutique restaurants on Franklin Str available to students, as well as several chains (Coldstone, Subway and so o There are multiple bars, but drinks are more expensive than a typical colle town.

Current student, 5/2003-Submit Date, November 2006

UNC really has a great social network. From great bars on Franklin Street, su as Lucy's and Top of the Hill, to clubs like Players and great music scenes at t Library and Cat's Cradle, UNC has something for everyone. With the openi of Memorial Hall on campus last year, there is always some great worl renowned artist coming to UNC to perform for almost nothing for studen Dating is an interesting phenomenon at UNC. It was hard for me to find som one, but I think I might be alone. A lot of people find their soulmates here.

Current student, 8/2005-Submit Date, February 2006

Franklin Street is the place to be. It stretches along the north side of campus a offers something for everyone. There are plenty of bars to be found, includi the student favorite The Deep End, with 25¢ drafts, and the Players Clu Student organizations frequently host mixers and charity events at bars and clu on Franklin Street. There are also plenty of good places to eat, ranging fro inexpensive deli food and Mexican to high-end restaurants, such as Four Elev West and the ever-popular Top of the Hill. Friday and Saturday nights are t most crowded, but any night of the week you can find Franklin Street full of pe ple. It is also the site of the annual Franklin Street Halloween party, the bigge Halloween celebration I've ever seen. Thursday nights are the standard fr party nights, and while most frat parties consist of cheap beer and girls get free, you can often find really good cover bands or student music groups pla ing in fraternity basements for free. Sororities aren't as popular, though the c ed honor fraternity is an excellent choice for people who want to get involv and meet others but aren't too eager about the stereotypical party scene th encompasses most of the other fraternities.

Current student, 8/2005-Submit Date, April 2006

With over 500 student organizations, there are always meetings and events to to during the week. A lot of our service and Greek organizations organize cha ity concerts and performances that are really great. Our performing arts theate Memorial Hall, just reopened after being renovated, and the university h brought in a lot of great acts (Wilco, Common, Lewis Black, Bill Nye t Science Guy) to encourage students to take advantage of the new venue. Near Franklin Street has a lot of restaurants (Aladdin's, Yeats, Carolina Coffee Sho Top of the Hill) that convert into bars and nightclubs in the evening. Clubs a also popular, especially Players, but also Avalon and the Saffron Loung There's also a vibrant music scene—multiple live bands perform Thursda through Sunday at The Cave, Yeats, He's Not Here, Cat's Cradle and the Librar Greek life is a part of social life, but not a big part. Only about 17 percent of t campus is Greek. Frat court is next to campus, and there are usually a few pa ties to go to every Thursday, Friday and Saturday night. Off-campus parties apartments and houses are also really popular.

The School Says

The University of North Carolina at Chapel Hill was the nation's first state university to open its doors and the only public university to award degrees in the 18th Century.

Through its teaching, research and public service, the university is an educational and economic beacon for the people of North Carolina and beyond. Our students—among the brightest in the nation—enjoy an exceptional balance of academics and camaraderie.

Carolina continues to be ranked among the top universities in the nation. Highlights from 2006-2007 rankings include:

- Fifth best public university in *U.S. News & World Report*'s annual Best Colleges guidebook. Kenan-Flagler Business School: fifth among undergraduate programs.

- First among the 100 best public colleges combining great academics and affordable tuitions as ranked by *Kiplinger's Personal Finance*. Carolina has been first six consecutive times.

- Number One "best value" among 77 schools chosen by The Princeton Review for outstanding academics, low-to-moderate tuition and fees, and generous financial aid packages.

Carolina offers bachelor's, master's, doctoral and professional degrees in academic areas critical to North Carolina's future: business, dentistry, education, law, medicine, nursing, public health and social work, among others. The health sciences are well integrated with the liberal arts, basic sciences and high-tech programs. Patient outreach programs affiliated with Carolina and the UNC Health Care System serve citizens in all 100 North Carolina counties.

In fall 2007, Carolina enrolled more than 27,000 students from all 100 North Carolina counties, the other 49 states and more than 100 other countries.

Those students learn from a 3,000-member faculty. Many of those faculty members hold or have held major posts in virtually every national scholarly or professional organization and have earned election to the most prestigious academic groups.

The Carolina academic community benefits from a library with more than 5.5 million volumes and perennially ranks among the best research libraries in North America as judged by the Association of Research Libraries. The most recent association listings place Carolina 15th among 113 research libraries in North America.

Carolina's 253,000 alumni live in all 50 states and in 133 countries. Notable alumni include writers Thomas Wolfe, Shelby Foote and Jill McCorkle; U.S. Senator John Edwards; athletes Michael Jordan, Vince Carter, Mia Hamm and Marion Jones; and journalists Roger Mudd, Charles Kuralt, Stuart Scott and Tom Wicker.

The Carolina Covenant

Since 2004, the Carolina Covenant has enabled low-income students to graduate debt-free through federal work-study and a combination of public and private grants and scholarships. For all other admitted students with a demonstrated need, Carolina guarantees to meet 100 percent of financial need through public and private scholarships, grants and loans.

This is the first program of its kind at a U.S. public university; several major public and private campuses—including Harvard and the Universities of Virginia and Maryland—have since followed Carolina's lead to offer their own programs. The Covenant underscores UNC's ongoing commitment to access and excellence.

Wake Forest University

Admissions Office
P.O. Box 7305 Reynolda Station
Winston-Salem, NC 27109-7305
Admissions phone: (336) 758-5201
Admissions e-mail: admissions@wfu.edu
Admissions URL: www.wfu.edu/admissions/

Admissions

Alumnus/a, 8/2002-5/2006, October 2006

The Wake admissions process is pretty on par with other universities of the same standing. Both SATs and GPA are weighted pretty heavily, but I have heard that the two essays are what land the many qualified applicants into yes or no piles. Wake also offers an early only choice admission, where students who have finished their junior year of high school may apply over the summer as long as it is the only place they apply. You will hear back within six weeks, at which point you are accepted or released from the agreement. Some say that candidates on the edge may have an advantage if they apply this way because admission will know that Wake is their first choice school.

Wake Forest says: "Wake Forest has combined the Single-Choice and First-Choice Early Decision plans into one comprehensive binding plan. We encourage students who have decided conclusively that Wake Forest is their first college choice to apply Early Decision; these students are given some preference in the admissions process. About 10 percent of applicants apply Early Decision each year; those students make up about 30 percent of each incoming class."

Current student, 10/2002-Submit Date, October 2005

When I applied to Wake, you had three choices: Early Admission, Early Action and Regular Admission. I actually applied for Regular Admission. I know that Wake Forest looks for service-related activities in high school, a good GPA and strong achievement in one particular area. The essays were all based on your views of liberal arts and service for the community. The top rankings say that Wake Forest has a 40 percent acceptance rate, but this is slightly misleading. I think the true rate would probably be around 30 or 35 percent. Most people who apply for Wake are self-selecting—that is, they are qualified for acceptance on average. There is a fair contingent of students who apply to Wake as a safety school in case they don't get into the Ivies.

Regarding selectivity, the school says: "Wake Forest's most recent acceptance rate is 38 percent."

Current student, 8/2001-Submit Date, September 2004

I think it is pretty much your basic admissions process. SAT scores, GPA, high school transcripts and a list of extracurriculars. It's been a while, but I think there were two rather generic essays. Interviews are not done. Wake is fairly selective. I had 1290 SAT and a 3.6 high school GPA.

Read all of Vault's College Surveys at **www.vault.com/college**—get complete surveys on 100s of colleges and universities, expert advice on applicaton essays and more.

VAULT CAREER LIBRARY 535

Current student, Cultural Studies, 7/2003-Submit Date, March 2007

I toured the campus after becoming interested. This school is very selective and has about twice as many female applicants as male. I mentioned this occurrence to the rep who came to my high school and she made sure to write my name down. Write a creative essay, mine was in the form of two short stories and narratives.

> **The school says:** "Slightly more than half of Wake Forest applicants are women."

Alumnus/a, 9/2000-5/2004, September 2004

A reputable high school in a state with low student representation is an underrated plus. Either a high GPA at public school or high SAT and ACT at a private school will suffice—Wake loves private schools unless you're in the top 25 at your public school. I don't really think the essays are that important; re-reading mine really makes me want to cringe and I think academic achievements were given more weight.

> **Wake Forest says:** "There is no preference for private schools. The majority of Wake Forest undergraduates attended public schools."

Current student, 8/2003-Submit Date, February 2004

The admissions staff couldn't be more helpful, it pays to talk to them and tell them why you are seriously interested in getting in. Go and visit the school, take a tour and fill out the card; they look to see if you showed interest. Wake is very selective, but apply early, very early, to get the best chances!

The essay is highly regarded as being important, so spend a lot of time on that one. They do also look at SAT scores and don't be surprised if you think you have a high score and don't get in, it is highly competitive. I cannot tell you how many people I met when I got here who were valedictorians of their high school graduating class!

> **Regarding admissions, the school says:** "Admission as a first-year student at Wake Forest normally requires graduation from an accredited secondary school with a minimum of 16 units of high school credit. These should include at least four units in English, three in mathematics, two in history and social studies, two in a single foreign language, and one in the natural sciences. Most admitted students will have pursued a challenging curriculum of honors and Advanced Placement courses. A limited number of applicants may be admitted without the high school diploma, with particular attention given to ability, maturity and motivation.
>
> "The admission application requires records and recommendations directly from secondary school officials. It also requires test scores, preferably from the senior year, on the SAT and/or the ACT plus writing. SAT Subject Tests are optional. Test scores must be submitted directly from the testing center. Interviews are not required but may be scheduled with an admissions officer upon request of the applicant. The admissions application deadline for fall enrollment is January 15. Applicants for first-year admission for the fall semester are notified on or about April 1. Transfer applicants are notified in late April and May."

 Academics

Current student, Cultural Studies, 7/2003-Submit Date, March 2007

Classes are hard and time consuming, but teachers are usually lenient about due dates. Just be honest and say you haven't had enough time instead of saying your aunt died. They know the difference. Classes are small, but popular classes are difficult to get into until third year. Workload is hard but manageable. Again, if you have two projects or tests going on at the same time, you will usually be able to get one professor to give you an extension. Some professors expect in you to be in class 80 percent or more of the time, so don't think you can just read the book in your dormroom and pass the final.

Alumnus/a, 8/2002-5/2006, October 2006

Students often refer to Wake Forest as Work Forest, and for good reaso Academics at Wake are difficult and require time and effort. Because clas range from 10 to 30 people, professors are usually very engaged in their clas and hold students accountable. Fortunately, this small class environment a means that professors are usually very engaged in their classes and provide h when asked. Almost every class is taught by professors, with labs being led graduate teaching assistants. Most professors choose Wake because they actu ly want to teach students, rather than do research at a larger institution, which reflected in their teaching style and availability.

> **Wake Forest says:** "Wake Forest faculty are dedicated teacher-scholars and excel in both teaching and scholarship."

Freshmen may find it difficult to register for popular classes depending on th randomly assigned registration time, but there are always plenty of alternativ Since there are so many general requirements to be completed, a freshman ca really go wrong anyway. Students don't declare a major under the seco semester of their sophomore year, so the majority of freshman and sophomo years is consumed by these general requirements.

Current student, 10/2002-Submit Date, October 2005

Wake Forest has a two-year, liberal arts requirement whereby all students m pick from divisional courses. The divisions can all be found on the Wake For web site, but in general, I would recommend coming into Wake with some A credits. It may be difficult to complete all of the divisional requirements a graduate on time.

> **The school says:** "Nearly 80 percent of Wake Forest students earn an undergraduate degree within four years."

95 percent of the professors here are topnotch. They all have PhDs and there a no TAs. Most of them are also extremely approachable, enjoy teaching, and a there for you outside of the classroom. That said, no class is easy, and y should expect to be worked extremely hard depending on the rigor of your maj Expect to go to the library every night. You stand out like a sore thumb if y don't have your work done because class sizes are so small. Grading is al slightly deflated. There are very very few A's, but a good proportion of B's. N many people fail or even receive C's. So, the grading is tightly focused arou the B range. It is difficult to get into the best classes as a freshman or soph more, but by junior and senior years it is pretty easy to get into any class y want.

> **The school says:** "There is no evidence for grade deflation."

Current student, 8/2005-Submit Date, October 2005

I have found that so far classes are not too different than high school. The ma difference is that you are required to learn much of the information by yourse By this I mean that much of what classes is lectures and note taking, and y are responsible for basically learning or memorizing the notes you have take and regurgitating them on exams. Rarely will you come across a professor w doesn't care about his or her students doing well and he/she will almost alwa make time for extra help. All the professors at Wake know their stuff and a very knowledgeable in their subjects. As far as getting classes, it depends wh year you are; it is common for upperclassmen to get most of the classes the want at the times they want. The process is done online, basically you are giv a time that you can schedule classes, seniors get priority, juniors next and so and you sit at your computer looking to see what classes are available, then whe your time comes you are allowed to schedule two classes available. The rest your classes are scheduled the next day, so as to split up different times for di ferent students; so a student who gets a late time the first day will get an earli time the next day. For freshmen and even sophomores, it can be quite hard get the classes they want, usually out of five classes they want to take they w get two of them at desired times, the rest they just have to see what is open. T grades at Wake Forest are not inflated so you do have to work for grades, th usually means studying a couple days before exams, but if you do this B's a A's are certainly attainable. In my opinion, anyone who is smart enough to g into a school like Wake Forest can definitely manage C's or better without muc effort. The workload can be overwhelming at times, homework and studyir can reach five or more hours in one day, however; I have found that a lot of t work is just reading over lectures or book passages and is not hard or time co

...ming at all. I have found myself with a fair amount of free time. Overall, the ...ogram is run pretty smoothly and the academics seem to be quite good.

...rrent student, 8/2002-Submit Date, September 2005

...ake Forest isn't nicknamed "Work Forest" for nothing. In fact, some of my ...iends have shirts that say "Work Forest, where your best hasn't been good ...ough since 1834." It's true, though, I have had classes where not one student ...as gotten an A. Wake Forest likes to deflate grades instead of inflate them. The ...rofessors are decent. Some are excellent, some aren't so good. I have learned ...ore from the good professors I have had and I overlook the bad ones. Like any ...ther school, the older you get, the more likely you will be to get good classes. ...nd beware of Calloway, the undergraduate business school, it will eat your ...ul!

Wake Forest says: "If you enroll at Wake Forest, you can expect to be challenged by a rigorous academic environment. Your professors will be dedicated to their subject matter and to stimulating discussion in class. You will be encouraged to think critically, form opinions and articulate them.

"A student-to-faculty ratio of 10:1 allows students to get to know their professors. Most classes have fewer than 25 students, and freshmen have at least two seminar classes with fewer than 16 students. With the exception of health classes and some laboratories, all classes are taught by faculty members, not graduate students."

Employment Prospects

...lumnus/a, 8/2002-5/2006, October 2006

...ake participates in a lot of on-campus recruiting, especially for financial jobs. ...any students searching for financial jobs are employed before graduation, ...any even during the fall semester of their senior year through on-campus ...ecruiting programs. Students with creative backgrounds may have more difficulty and few on-campus recruitment opportunities. Career Services is very ...elpful if you seek out their help. They also have an alumni networking system ...or students to contact alumni in their city and industry of choice. My personal ...xperience with this service was great and I was able to contact several alumni ...ho were willing to chat/offer advice about their industries.

...urrent student, 10/2002-Submit Date, October 2005

...raduates at Wake do fairly well. Many students enter investment banking or ...onsulting because the majority of companies that come to campus are from ...hose industries.

The school says: "Investment banking and consulting represent a small percentage of overall on-campus recruitment, which ranges from financial services to nonprofits."

...hat said, there are other opportunities, and Career Services is quite helpful and ...ants you to be employed. There is also a very strong alumni network, and if ...ou know what company you want to work for, there is most likely a Wake alum...us/a at the company willing and eager to speak to you about his/her job. ...mployers, once they get a few Wake students, are very confident in the univer...ity. I have heard many times that once an employer comes to campus, they ...eturn. Internships are basically up to the student and there is little assistance ...however, this is changing).

Regarding internships, the school says: "The Office of Career Services provides advice and information to Wake forest students seeking internships. Individual career counseling sessions, interest assessments and mock interviews are available by appointment. Numerous programs featuring industry representatives are held each year to introduce students to internships in a variety of career fields.

"Internship opportunities are posted through the Career Services online computerized system ECHO (Explore Career Happenings Online). Along with a national database of employer contacts, many of which host on-campus information sessions and inter-

views, students are also able to access the internship exchange, a shared database of internships from members of the University Career Action Network (UCAN), a consortium of 18 comparable universities.

"Additionally, two career fairs, one in the fall and one in the spring, bring to campus employers who seek Wake Forest students for their internships positions. These events are open to all undergraduate students.

"In the spring of 2007, the university began a program for students to intern and study in Washington, D.C. In addition, several academic departments offer students the ability to earn academic credit through internships. Networking opportunities are presented through a wide range of alumni contacts. The Alumni Career Assistance Program (ACAP), a database of nearly 2,000 alumni, and networking forums, held both on and off campus, are just two of several options for students to speak to alumni about internships."

Current student, 8/2003-Submit Date, October 2004

It seems that Wake wants all people to have jobs when graduating; however, it is only for those who want to stay in the area. Outside Wake does not get a lot of recognition because of a lot of low GPAs. They bring in a lot of recruiters; however, if you are in the accounting program, you have a guaranteed job. Alumni seem quite helpful. Graduates don't always get their preferred job. If you do not have a good GPA, good luck finding a job, your best bet is to go off to graduate school and try again; no one wants the low GPA people.

Wake Forest says: "Over a 10-year period, on average upon graduation, 31 percent of Wake Forest students go immediately to graduate or professional schools, while 60 percent go into the workplace.

"Over a five-year period, approximately 33 percent of each graduating class has historically been employed within North Carolina upon graduation. The remainder have found employment throughout the United States with 6.2 percent finding employment overseas."

Quality of Life

Current student, Cultural Studies, 7/2003-Submit Date, March 2007

Rooms are small, food plans are not good—they lack healthy options and the daily soup options always include chili. Make sure when you fill out your survey to get paired with a roommate that you think about what you will be doing as a college student and not what your sleep habits were when in high school. The campus is beautiful, safety is all right, the neighborhood could be better. Just don't go walking around alone at night. There is not nearly enough parking on campus; you will want to move off by your third year like I did. Freshmen have no need for cars, so don't bring them and take up more spaces!

Alumnus/a, 8/2002-5/2006, October 2006

Call me partial, but Wake's campus is just about one of the most beautiful places on earth to spend four years. The campus is always beautifully maintained and keeping it that way is a priority.

The dorms are also well-maintained, if not a little old. Freshmen are required to live on campus and their dorms are mostly hall style, separated male and female by hall. Sophomores are also required to live on campus, and most live in the dorms surrounding the quad, which are open courtyard style suites of six or eight. Dorms are clean (as far a dorms go) but a little on the small side. Many upperclassmen live off campus in nearby apartments or houses. Those who do live on campus either live in Greek housing or are lucky enough to live in on-campus apartments, which are new and include sitting rooms and kitchens, and often more than one bathroom.

The campus is pretty well-lit and feels safe both during the day and at night, but like all campuses has its occasional crime. The neighborhoods surrounding campus are residential and also very safe.

Read all of Vault's College Surveys at www.vault.com/college—get complete surveys on 100s of colleges and universities, expert advice on applicaton essays and more.

VAULT CAREER LIBRARY   537

Food is good, although those dependent on a meal plan may crave more variety. Winston offers pretty much everything you can think up all within a 20-minute radius.

Current student, 10/2002-Submit Date, October 2005

Housing is provided all four years and decent, although a bit moldy at times. You get HBO. The campus is beautiful and you will quickly miss the running trails when you go home for breaks. The same can be said for the facilities. One of the best attractions on campus is the unique library with its windowed rotunda. On one side of Wake Forest is a lower income neighborhood, while on the other lies upper middle-class families. Crime is usually not an issue. All entrances are guarded.

> Regarding housing, the school says: "Wake Forest University prides itself on many things, including its ability to offer exemplary housing accommodations to undergraduate students for all four years of their academic career. The Office of Residence Life and Housing, in conjunction with other campus departments, works diligently to ensure that a safe, welcoming and healthy on-campus experience is available to every member of the undergraduate community."

Social Life

Current student, Cultural Studies, 7/2003-Submit Date, March 2007

Always something to do either in Greek life (which is big) or through student union or other programs. Not many bars, but the ones we have are good. The school also sponsors events like dances and parties, which actually are very good: one is next Thursday and I'm excited for it. Most of the on- and off-campus parties are hosted by the 13 fraternities, but don't worry boys and girls, you don't have to be Greek to attend. And all drinks are always covered by the hosting frat.

Alumnus/a, 8/2002-5/2006, October 2006

Greek scene is very popular on campus and comprises most of the student body with the exception of athletes and smattering of proud independents. Social scene revolves around parties thrown on and (mostly) off campus. Most fraternities have unofficial houses nearby that can be counted on for something to do on Friday and Saturday nights. Sororities also have date functions such as formals and mixers. Intramurals are very popular and dominated by Greek teams.

Fraternities often host parties at nearby bars like Freddie B's and Ziggy's. Ziggy's also hosts small concerts and is popular with bands looking for smaller audiences to break up the series of stadium concerts and lesser known bands with large cult followings (think Dave Matthews circa 1995).

Bars rise and fall in popularity every year as does "the new Friday." But Thursdays and the following bars can usually be counted on as a general rule: Freddie B's, Ziggy's, Burke Street, Black Bear, Foothills Brewing Company, Frankie Rowland's (seniors only, on Tuesdays; Tuesdays there are martini specials and a jazz band).

No real dating scene, although plenty of couples who hook up, attend a few functions together and decide to make it official.

Current student, 10/2002-Submit Date, October 2005

Wake is a Southern school. People have an image of Wake as a preppy Southern school even though a large proportion of the students are from the North. I would recommend joining a frat as there is very little social life outside of those organizations. Exceptions being if you are into frisbee or lacrosse. All in all, you will have a good time at Wake if you are in a fraternity or find close friends with whom you spend a lot of time. The few bars are downtown near 4th Street (foothills) or on Burch Street. There are various restaurants around campus and most focus on Mexican food. La Caretta's is a favorite among students. Jimmy The Greek offers late-night fare on Friday and Saturday. Dating is not heavily present at Wake although it does occur sometimes. The main events at Wake are fraternity or sorority based, although there is a move towards school-wide events like Shag on the Mag. Like I said earlier, it is a good idea to join a Greek organization because it will provide a means to meet a good portion of the wake

population. There are no clubs in Winston-Salem, but a 30-minute drive Greensboro will provide them if you are looking for that scene.

Current student, 8/2001-Submit Date, September 2004

There aren't a lot of nightclubs and bars in Winston-Salem. The mountains close. Winston has great restaurants and they are making improvements dow town, though it's not quite there yet. Wake Forest students don't date a There are a lot of parties; on-campus parties still dominate. There is a lar Greek faction, though it's a small school so everyone knows everyone, wh has its good and bad points. It can be easy to gain a reputation and hard to lo Wake Forest students are very image conscious, so there is always someone r ning around campus or working out in the Miller Center. Also, there is a hea involvement in intramural sports.

The School Says

Consistently ranked among the nation's top universities and regarded as one of the "best values" in higher education, Wake Forest University is a private, coeducational institution dedicated to excellence in the liberal arts, graduate and professional education.

Combining the personalized attention of a small liberal arts college with the resources, technology and co-curricular opportunities of a larger university, Wake Forest is distinguished by small classes, dedicated teachers, high academic standards, a need-blind admissions policy and a tradition of service to others embodied in its motto, *Pro Humanitate* (for humanity).

With a total undergraduate enrollment of 4,255, Wake Forest has a student-to-faculty ratio of 10:1. Combined with 2,461 graduate and professional school students, the university's total enrollment comes to 6,716.

Academic resources, including libraries and information technology, are literally at the student's fingertips in Wake Forest's wireless computing environment. Libraries offer more than 1 million volumes, periodicals and microfiche, as well as advanced technology. The online catalog can be accessed from all campus buildings via the campus network or from anywhere via the Web.

A comprehensive technology plan provides students with powerful hardware and software. Upon enrollment, students receive ThinkPad computers and color printers. Computers and printers are upgraded after two years and become the student's property upon graduation. An award-winning wired and wireless campus network supports innovative online services, and provides opportunities to participate in exciting technology pilot programs.

Wake Forest ranked 30th among 248 national universities in the 2007 edition of *U.S. News & World Report's* guide, *America's Best Colleges*. In addition, the university's Wayne Calloway School of Business and Accountancy ranked 24th out of 50 undergraduate business programs in the nation. Accounting graduates rank first in the nation for their performance on the 2004 Certified Public Accountant (CPA) exam, the most recent scores available from the National Association of State Boards of Accountancy (NASBA).

Wake Forest's eight varsity men's teams and eight varsity women's teams compete in the Atlantic Coast Conference. Men's sports include baseball, basketball, cross country, football, golf, soccer, tennis and track-and-field. Women's sports include basketball, cross country, field hockey, golf, soccer, tennis, track-and-field and volleyball.

Half of all undergraduates study abroad before they graduate, either at university-owned residential study centers in London,

Venice and Vienna, or through other programs in Africa, Asia, Europe and South America.

Wake Forest gained international attention in 1988 and again in 2000 by hosting presidential debates in Wait Chapel. The university frequently features prominent speakers and concerts by nationally known artists. During recent academic years, the university community enjoyed talks from such luminaries as award-winning playwright Tony Kushner; former U.S. Rep. and vice chair of the Sept. 11 commission Lee Hamilton; award-winning poet Nikki Giovanni; Democratic strategist, author and co-host of CNN's *Crossfire* James Carville; former governor of Virginia Mark Warner; nationally syndicated columnist Leonard Pitts Jr.; and golf legend and Wake Forest alumnus Arnold Palmer. The university also hosted performances by the band O.A.R., musician Ben Folds, violinist Joshua Bell and comedian Lewis Black.

Read all of Vault's College Surveys at **www.vault.com/college**—get complete surveys on 100s of colleges and universities, expert advice on applicaton essays and more.

VAULT CAREER LIBRARY **539**

University of North Dakota

Enrollment Services
100 Carnegie Hall
250 Centennial Sr., Stop 8135
Grand Forks, ND 58202
Admissions phone: (701) 777.4463 or (800) CALL-UND
Admissions e-mail: enrollment_services@mail.und.edu
Admissions URL: www.go.und.edu

 ## Admissions

Current student, Engineering, 8/2005-Submit Date, March 2007

The admissions process is fairly easy. You go online to www.und.edu and click on admissions. The school is easy to get into, as all you need is a 2.5 and a 21 on the ACT. Then it is automatic admission. As far as costs, you're looking at about $12K a year. which isn't bad for a school with this many programs. About the same price as a community college in small Grand Rapids.

Current student, Health, 8/2005-Submit Date, March 2007

The admissions process here is relatively simple. First you must complete your ACT exam to get the score with which you are happy. You then need to get an application at a local high school or online and fill out all needed information. There is an area on the last page to write about yourself and why you want to go to school here. I recommend everyone fill this out because that will make your application unique among thousands of others' applications. You then have to have your high school transcripts sent. From this point, you wait for a letter to come in the mail. I also recommend visiting the campus before you apply because it will validate the fact that this is the right choice for you.

Current student, Engineering, 8/2004-Submit Date, March 2007

I applied and met all of the automatic admission criteria. I also attended a session in the summer preceding my freshman year called Summer Getting Started. This was a program designed for orientation and registration purposes.

Current student, Criminal Justice, 8/2004-Submit Date, March 2007

The admissions process was not very difficult. There was no essay or interview process for which I had to prepare or prepare. I was impressed by how fast I got results back from the university, notifying me of my acceptance. The process was speedy and straightforward.

Current student, Business, 8/2003-Submit Date, March 2007

UND is quite easy to get into. It is my understanding that you need a 20 or above on your ACT. You must apply and make a small payment. They have a history of taking most students who are from North Dakota.

Current student, Health, 8/2005-Submit Date, March 2007

The admissions process is simple at UND. If you have the minimum required ACT score of a 21, you should have no doubt that you will be admitted. There is no interview or recommendations needed; there is only a paper application that must be submitted with the required transcripts. An official ACT score sticker must be present on your high school transcript. If you do not have a high enough ACT score, you may still be admitted on a conditional basis. If this happens, you must maintain a decent GPA your first semester to stay in school at UND.

Current student, Education, 8/2004-Submit Date, March 2007

The application is fairly simple and straightforward. When a school visit is scheduled, prospective students get a chance to meet with a UND representative and talk about their goals and potential experience at UND. There are no essays and no major interviews in the admissions process. Only an ACT score is required, not an SAT score.

Current student, Engineering, 8/2002-Submit Date, December 200

Getting into UND requires a simple application process. Getting into the en neering school required an application, and fulfillment of certain prerequisite

Current student, 8/2000-Submit Date, December 2005

UND likes everyone who wants to go to school to get in. I had an ACT score 26 and GPA of 3.8, but I know of many people who didn't have very go scores. The application was very short, one page? There was no interview couple very short essays. Financial aid was horrible, and still is a very horrib experience for many students, just make sure everything is in order a few mont before disbursement, and don't be alarmed when you stand in the financial a line for a couple hours before the start of school. But the overall admissic process was fairly easy, they have people to help register, and like I said, th reject very few people. But you do have to live in North Dakota, and it gets ve cold in the winter.

Current student, 8/2002-Submit Date, November 2005

An application had to be mailed in along with a transcript and ACT scores. F the nursing program over 500 applicants are received each semester. An ess on a provided topic and an application form must be turned in and are review anonymously by the faculty. Approximately 50 students are selected for the pr gram each semester.

Regarding admission, the University of North Dakota has the following admissions standards:

Automatic Admission

Automatic Admission will be granted to high school graduates entering as freshmen (and transfer students with less than 24 semester hours of transferable credit) who have an ACT and GPA that correspond with the admission chart below. In addition, students must fully meet the high school core requirements—English (four units), math (three units of Algebra I or above), lab science (three units), social studies (three units).

ADMISSION CHART

H.S. GPA Range 3.50 to 4.00; 18 to 36 ACT / 870 to 1600 SAT
H.S. GPA Range 3.00 to 4.00; 19 to 36 ACT / 910 to 1600 SAT
H.S. GPA Range 2.75 to 4.00; 20 to 36 ACT / 950 to 1600 SAT
H.S. GPA Range 2.50 to 4.00; 21 to 36 ACT / 990 to 1600 SAT
H.S. GPA Range 2.25 to 4.00; 22 to 36 ACT / 1030 to 1600 SAT

Note: SAT scores considered for UND admission will consist only of the math and verbal sections. The writing section will not be measured.

 ## Academics

Current student, Communications, 8/2004-Submit Date, April 200

Once I got into my program classes, the sizes were much smaller and more per sonal. I am now able to get a better student-teacher relationship and get hel when needed. With the generals, a lot of the classes are up to about 300 in th class and it is harder to meet with the teachers. So far I haven't had problem getting the grades I want; it is a matter of how hard I study and how much tim I'm putting into it. I like to have professors who I know have good reps wit students and try to take classes from them. The workload is fair in my classes This is college—it's not supposed to be easy.

Current student, Health, 8/2003-Submit Date, April 2007

The workload has increased a lot from my earlier years, but it has gotten mor major specific and interesting. The classes are fun and interesting, some ar harder to get because some are only offered in the fall or spring. That makes tricky.

Current student, Criminal Justice, 8/2004-Submit Date, March 2007

Many general education requirements are pick-and-choose and sometimes just luck on getting a good professor who wants to truly help you succeed. Most of those classes are lecture classes and most teachers use PowerPoint. As a freshman, you get last right to classes, so you'll have to get used to doing an override of hoping the class is still open. The classes for a criminal justice major are very interesting. Only two teachers of the lot have been bad. They really help you understand all aspects of the criminal justice program. The workload is very easy. There is not much busywork and if there is, it's very easy. There are not many papers either, and most teachers just offer tests as your grade.

Current student, Education, 1/2003-Submit Date, March 2007

I believe the quality of classes is very important. The professors are willing to take the time to work with the students in a group study or one-on-one level to address any concerns. It's a good idea to be aware of the more popular classes, so you are allowing yourself equal opportunity to get in. I also feel that the workload is as manageable as you make it, using good judgment in time management and priority.

Current student, Communications, 9/2003-Submit Date, March 2007

The program is set up well, allowing students to tailor their own program to their specific needs and making it extremely easy to pick up a minor in another field of interest. Class size can make it difficult to get into the more popular lab classes, but professors are typically extremely easy to work with on this issue. Grading can be subjective at times, as many of the classes are based on writing. Overall, the program is struggling. Advisors are not typically concerned with fitting the program to the student, and professors are not as organized, disciplined or technologically knowledgeable as they should be for a program of this nature. The strongest area of emphasis is in the public relations area, and most of what I have learned has come through those specific professors. Ironically, the communication program has an extremely weak communication process with its students. E-mails are sent out late with regard to notification of upcoming events, availability of scholarships and so on, and the student council is inactive.

Current student, Business, 9/2006-Submit Date, March 2007

The classes at UND are awesome. They are generally not too big except for some lectures. Most of my classes consist of fewer than 25 students. Getting popular classes is not difficult for upperclassmen because they have first dibs. It gets increasingly harder to get the classes the younger you are. The grading system is fair. 90 to 100 is an A, 80 to 89 is a B, and so on. The professors are very intelligent. They usually have a very strong grasp on the material and present it well. The workload can be strenuous at times but this is the same at every college so I really have no complaints about the workload.

Current student, Health, 8/2005-Submit Date, March 2007

The academic nature of UND is excellent. Most professors show their passion through their methods and help you any time you ask them. It is easy to get popular classes as long as you register on time, of which your counselor will inform you. If you are a pre-med or nursing student, you should expect a larger workload because it is a hard profession and along with that comes a huge amount of knowledge to store away. Most other general education requirement classes are relatively easy as long as you keep up with your work and attend class. The grading in most classes is really fair. Most professors grade on a curved scale so if the whole class averaged a C they might curve it so most people move up to a B. They reward the people who put time into studying and show it on the tests.

Current student, 8/2002-Submit Date, March 2007

The commercial aviation program is excellent. With a few exceptions, the professors are topnotch, and all seem to have experience in the aviation industry. The grading scale is difficult (92+ is an A and in flight courses specifically, below 76 percent is failure), but because the classes are interesting, success is fairly easy to achieve.

Current student, Business, 8/2003-Submit Date, March 2007

North Dakota is known for its entrepreneurship program. It is ranked in the Top 10 nationally. The prerequisites are very easy to fulfill. The 100-level classes are quite large. They range from 50 to 200 students in some classes. As you get farther into the business program, classes shrink to under 20 students per class. The classes themselves are somewhat challenging, but when you figure out how to prepare for them, they become easier. UND is also known for its difficulty

getting a hold of its professors. However, the business department is very effective at providing students with access to teachers outside of the classroom.

Employment Prospects

Current student, Communications, 8/2004-Submit Date, April 2007

We have two career days at our school during the year when many businesses come and give out information to students looking for internships and jobs. Some students get hired on the spot; others are just looking for what options are out there. Career Services is very helpful and willing to work with all students. Internships are posted online in many of the buildings on campus, as well as job openings.

Current student, Criminal Justice, 8/2004-Submit Date, March 2007

Every semester there is a job fair where many businesses come looking for new people to work for them. Students normally dress professionally and have many copies of their résumés ready to give to hopeful employers. There is also a program on campus that helps seniors find jobs through the alumni program.

Current student, Health, 8/2005-Submit Date, March 2007

There are many opportunities for graduated students here at UND. This university has very well-respected alumni that are scattered all over the U.S. These alumni repeatedly come to UND to recruit graduating students right away. One good example is the nursing school. Our nursing school is ranked 11th in the nation, so when you graduate and are looking for a nursing job, you can pretty much pick where you want to go because there are so many calls coming in for you.

Current student, Business, 9/2006-Submit Date, March 2007

UND graduates are heavily recruited by local and national employers. The strongest degrees are accounting, aviation and entrepreneurship. Generally, with these degrees getting a job is not very hard. There are also many internship opportunities, especially in accounting and aviation.

Current student, Communications, 9/2003-Submit Date, March 2007

Internships are required for graduation from the program, and are extremely helpful in getting experience for job placement after graduation. There is an abundance of local internships available and the award-winning Studio-One news show is closely tied to the school of communication. The alumni network at UND is extremely strong and has an active student group with options to connect with alumni before graduation. The school of communication and UND have many prestigious graduates who are more than willing to hire new UND graduates. Graduates of the school typically find quality jobs before or immediately after graduation, due to their extensive internship experiences, which are conveniently built into the program.

Quality of Life

Current student, Communications, 8/2004-Submit Date, April 2007

Housing and dining on campus when I was a freshman were good. I enjoyed the dorms and they were safe to live in. The campus has a lot of safety features with the emergency phones, and lights are always on. The Greek community and some und officials take a "safety walk" throughout the campus to find areas where students may want more lights, or would feel safer walking at night if there were fewer trees in the area. Campus police also constantly patrol the streets, so it is a safe campus in general.

Current student, Criminal Justice, 8/2004-Submit Date, March 2007

The dorms are always nice and a great way to start your college experience. They are well-kept and style varies throughout the different dorm buildings. The campus is made out of mainly brick buildings and is centrally located on University Avenue. There aren't any places for class where you would have to drive to another part of campus. The dining facilities are by a meal plan system. You can purchase a 10, 14, or 18 meals a week plan. Once you use a meal, you can eat as much as you want when you go through the dining center. The City of Grand Forks is basically a college town and the neighborhoods surrounding

Read all of Vault's College Surveys at **www.vault.com/college**—get complete surveys on 100s of colleges and universities, expert advice on applicaton essays and more.

VAULT CAREER LIBRARY **541**

the university are filled with college students living just a little ways off of campus.

Current student, Communications, 9/2003-Submit Date, March 2007

UND is located in a classic college town, where life revolves around the school. The community is fairly close-knit and is supportive of the programs and students. It is a low-crime area where I have never felt unsafe. The campus is very spread out, which can be challenging in the cold winters. An efficient shuttle bus system helps deal with the problem, and even runs by some off-campus apartments and picks students up free. The facilities here are second to none, with athletic venues entirely new since 2001, and a $20 million student funded and run wellness center available to all students. The housing on campus varies widely, from dorms to apartments, and is generally inexpensive. Dining centers are a hub of residence life and are open during convenient hours. Most buildings on campus are open late, allowing students to access them whenever they need.

Current student, Business, 9/2006-Submit Date, March 2007

The housing at UND is very laid-back and social. I have had many events in my dorm that were sponsored by our resident assistant. The campus is not too large and not too small either. The only thing that is less than desirable is the weather. In the winter it gets as cold as negative 30 degrees. It is very windy and is often way too cold to go outside. Also, driving conditions, the wind and ice everywhere seem to have little affect on those in charge. Classes are almost never cancelled and I am not alone when I say that it is dangerous to be outside.

Current student, Business, 8/2003-Submit Date, March 2007

Grand Forks, although kind of boring, provides an excellent college experience. The campus is beautiful and shows you all four seasons. It can be bitterly cold in the winter; however, that cold only lasts about one or two months. The summer is very warm and dry. You can get a very nice three-bedroom apartment for under $1,000 per month.

 Social Life

Current student, Communications, 8/2004-Submit Date, April 2007

The social life is big on campus. There are a few bars not too far from campus and a majority of campus apartments. There aren't a lot of things to do in Grand Forks and that is why the bar scene is so popular for students. Just recently, we put in place what is called nightlife at UND, which are non-alcoholic events on Friday and Saturday nights available on campus. The first weekend was a huge success. Greek life is popular, as well, and it is a great way to meet people. We also have many student organizations and areas for students to get together and hang out and meet others like the student union.

Current student, Health, 8/2003-Submit Date, April 2007

I like the downtown area; there are a lot of fun places to go: Gilly's, Joe Black and Bonzers. There are a lot of restaurants as well; Green Mill, Ground Roun Applebee's, Buffalo Wild Wings, and Boston's. I am in the Greek system a we always have events going on. There is something to do every weekend a on the weekdays. The hockey team is very big here, as well, and during hock season, the games are very fun to go to.

Current student, Criminal Justice, 8/2004-Submit Date, March 200

There are plenty of bars and restaurants in this town of 50,000 people. Concer are always being put on either in Grand Forks or an hour south of here in Farg The Greek system is a strong one with 20 different sororities and fraternitie The majority of the frats and the sororities are located on University Avenue, b then there are some tucked just a little bit off of University Avenue and offer great location to the rest of campus. The overall student population's favori thing to do is drink: going out to the bars or to a fraternity or simply drinking home.

Current student, Education, 1/2003-Submit Date, March 2007

As a part of the Greek system, I have thoroughly enjoyed my social life. The are a number of events put on that get people involved and make a difference our community. The Memorial Union is a great place for social life, as well the Wellness Center and Tabula. Also, there are a number of clubs and even that include diversity and allow something for all interests.

Current student, Communications, 9/2003-Submit Date, March 200

The atmosphere at UND is centered around athletics rather than the arts. D men's hockey is the biggest draw, and season tickets are available to student Football is a fun weekly event in the fall. There are many clubs and organiza tions to get involved in at UND, and I highly recommend doing so in order t feel really connected to the campus. Involvement at any level is helpful durin the winter months when it seems the campus goes to sleep because of the col The Greek system is extremely active at UND and recruiting takes place onc each semester. Downtown Grand Forks has quickly become a favorite bar scene with several popular bars located within only a few blocks. Many UND student live in the affordable housing located above the bars in this area. Also dowr town are many smaller, eclectic restaurants and coffee houses for studying Entertainment in Grand Forks is as you make it. Occasionally larger concert make their way to the Alerus Center, but they are typically few and far betweer UND sponsors many smaller up-and-coming acts throughout the year, culmina ing in big-name musicians or comedians at the spring concert. Also a storie tradition at UND is Springfest, held annually the weekend before finals. It is gathering of all students at University Park, and has become the biggest party o the year.

Case Western Reserve University

dmissions Office
0900 Euclid Avenue
03 Tomlinson Hall
leveland, OH 44106-7055
dmissions phone: (216) 368-4450
dmissions e-mail: admission@case.edu
dmissions URL: admission.case.edu/admissions/

 ## Admissions

lumnus/a, 9/2002-5/2006, November 2006

he admissions process was very easy, which was what attracted me to the hool. At the time I applied, there was no application fee, which was a huge onus.

> **The school says:** "Case uses the Common Application. There is no application fee for students who apply online; students who apply with the paper Common Application pay a $35 application fee."

ase has been growing steadily more selective each year, but it is not nearly as lective as most schools of its caliber. I think students tend to self-select; cause of its rigorous academic reputation, the majority of students who decide enroll after being accepted are those who were also accepted into more selec- e schools. At the time I enrolled, it was a running joke among undergraduates at everyone had been accepted to an Ivy League school, but had decided to go Case because they offered excellent scholarships.

urrent student, Biology, 8/2003-Submit Date, October 2006

he admissions process was just like any other—get in scores, essays, applica- ons, all with standard prompts. I was invited to a prospective student interview, hich was enjoyable. As for advice on getting in, Case is not particularly selec- ve—decent SAT/ACT scores and grades in high school will get you in. I high- recommend taking interviews, too.

urrent student, 9/1999-Submit Date, February 2005

he admissions process is pretty straightforward. I applied online and I never d an interview. For Case, expect to get a letter of acceptance if you have an AT score of above 1200.

> **The school says:** "For Fall 2007 the middle 50 percent of admit- ted students scored between 600 and 700 on the SAT Critical Reading and Writing, and 650 and 750 on the SAT Math."

lso, if accepted, expect to get a lot of financial aid and opportunities for schol- ships as well. I didn't have an interview there, however, if your SAT score is little deficient, it might do some good to go and visit there and try to schedule interview with the dean of admissions.

> **The school says:** "Prospective students can interview with admission counselors or alumni representatives off campus."

lumnus/a, 1/2000-1/2004, November 2004

ly view on the process of entering Case Western is that it was not too difficult t not quite easy. My advice to others trying to get into Case Western is that ey should relax during the [SAT and ACT] testing, relax during the interview, d relax while they are waiting. There is nothing that compounds a problem ore than a tense attitude. The interview was also conducted in a very good for- at, and the interviewer was nice, interesting and reliable. I feel that the way in hich the interview was conducted was a profitable time for both me and for the terviewer.

Current student, 8/2002-Submit Date, November 2005

The general undergraduate admission for in-state applicants seems to be pretty laid-back and an interview was not necessary when I applied. It seems as though if you are in the top 20 percent of your high school class, you are guaranteed admittance. They really look at your SAT scores, which should range a little lower than Ivy League schools but above state school averages. The essays are pretty much open-ended personal statements and it seemed like more of a Common Application essay.

> **The school says:** "As at most private schools, in-state and out- of-state applicants are evaluated at Case Western Reserve University by the same academic standards."

 ## Academics

Alumnus/a, 9/2002-5/2006, November 2006

The typical Case student is always overloaded. Classes are rigorous. Few stu- dents receive D's or F's, but by the same token, few students receive A's. Professors expect a lot from students, and the classroom experience is entirely dependent on which professor is teaching. Some professors take their jobs as educators very seriously, and those courses are stimulating and valuable experi- ences. Others (primarily in the higher math and science courses) see teaching as an interruption to their valuable research time. While it is clear that these pro- fessors are extremely knowledgeable, it definitely can be entirely dependent on the student to teach themselves the course content: the professors are not inter- ested in babying you. Beware of team-taught courses; this usually means that you will have to learn four different teaching styles and take four entirely dif- ferent exams through the length of the course. The most valuable tool at the hands of students is the course evaluations that are included with the online scheduling option. Students should always use these evaluations to know what they are getting into with any given professor.

Current student, Biology, 8/2003-Submit Date, October 2006

The Biology program starts off as a weed-out system for the pre-meds of the pro- gram. As such, the first three core classes required by both BA and BS programs are abysmal in terms of quality, reasonability and amicability on part of the pro- fessors teaching a mish-mash of molecular, population and systems biology. In addition, there are a few courses required in the core that have limited, dubious practicality to a biologist of any field that you must suffer through, such as a semester of C++/Java Computer Programming and Thermodynamics.

After that, there is a wide array of courses available to any student primarily focused in the molecular end of biology. There are a few ecology/animal behav- ior classes, but they are not particularly advertised on campus.

Case also has the uncanny ability to schedule all the interesting classes for the Biology major at the same time, so every semester I can either take everything I'm interested in and have 11 credit hours due to scheduling conflicts, or pick up other classes I don't care about and have 19 because of how the classes fall.

The workload of any given class is reasonable, predominantly oriented around papers, presentations and exams. However, the grading of said assignments is up to the discretion of the professors, several of whom are notorious for their inconsistencies and unreasonable policies.

Should you make it past all that and manage to pick a specialization (if you intend to go to grad school, I can't speak for pre-meds) it becomes an excellent experience so long as you're not afraid to take the initiative to meet professors and get a research project going. There are some upper-level biology professors who are very reasonable and want nothing more than to support students' interests in the biolog- ical sciences. I have a professor who basically mentored me through my entire jun- ior and senior years and helped me solidify my plans for the future. It's a shame I didn't meet her sooner, because very few others seem to care.

Read all of Vault's College Surveys at **www.vault.com/college**—get complete surveys on 100s of colleges and univer- sities, expert advice on applicaton essays and more.

VAULT CAREER LIBRARY **543**

Current student, 8/2003-Submit Date, September 2006

The classes are bigger than I expected but the professors really care. The workload is crazy heavy and the grading is pretty hard. It is easier to get the classes you want as you get older.

Current student, 8/2002-Submit Date, November 2005

The workload is just as heavy as the courseloads at top-tier universities in the country. Compared to other schools, the science curriculum is heavy and difficult. Professors are not too accessible because they are often too busy with their own research (Case is a research-based institution providing tenure tracks only to professors who do research—not necessarily the best professors). Popular classes are easy to get into and grading is highly individual to the professor.

> **Based on their annual senior survey, the school says:** "94 percent of 2006 seniors said they were satisfied with the out-of-class availability of faculty. Results were similar for seniors graduating in 2003, 2004 and 2005. Nearly 90 percent of 2006 seniors said they were satisfied with student interaction with faculty and with the attitude of faculty toward students."

Alumnus/a, 1/2000-1/2004, November 2004

The academic process was one that reminded me of a school that was interested in your improvement, and also a school that wanted you to get involved with the class. The program in which I was involved was a very well-run and well-organized program. It was of such a nature that the student felt as if they were in a program that was being run by people who knew a great deal about what they were doing and what they were talking about. The professors were nice in some instances, and not so nice in other instances. That is to be expected of college professors, though. The workload was not too bad considering that this is a college course and that it is a tougher college course at that. Some nights I felt overwhelmed by the amount of homework, but I just tried to focus on the future and not dwell too much on the present.

Employment Prospects

Alumnus/a, 9/2002-5/2006, November 2006

Case definitely carries prestige in Cleveland and regionally. Although the alumni networks have appeared shaky lately due to internal politics, they are always an available resource for current and former students. The career fair is usually useless for anyone other than engineers or business majors, but career prospects are pretty good for any major, you just have to do the work of finding a job yourself. There are several excellent internship programs available of which students should take advantage, and any undergraduate who has the chance to work with a professor on research should do so. Generally professors are open to working with students, and anyone who is determined to gain hands-on experience should not have a problem doing so.

Current student, Biology, 8/2003-Submit Date, October 2006

During undergrad, jobs are abundant so long as you're willing to find them yourself. Case administration will do nothing to help you with that though they swear up and down they will. As for prestige, it depends on whom you know and what kind of work you do.

Alumnus/a. 8/2002-5/2006, September 2006

I graduated with a business degree and had six job offers from New York to San Francisco.

Current student, 8/2002-Submit Date, November 2005

Most graduates apply to medical school or engineering master's programs. I'm not too sure about the recruiting and internships available because I never took part in them. The prestige is in the local businesses/companies represented at various recruiting events.

Alumnus/a, 1/2000-1/2004, November 2004

The alumni of this university were somewhat helpful in getting me a job. The campus was equipped with a good number of recruiting and internship options, but I did not feel the need to get involved in any of those. The types of jobs that were an option after completion of the courses varied. I did feel as if I had been trained well and that I was ready to good out into the workforce.

Quality of Life

Alumnus/a, 9/2002-5/2006, November 2006

Housing has drastically improved with the addition of the North Resident Village. These dorms are more condo-like than dorm-like, and the proximity the new football field is a vast improvement. Dining is slightly better than is typically expected from college facilities, and improves every year. The great concern among students is usually crime and safety due to the close proxim to East Cleveland, which is not the best neighborhood. Overall, Case Secur does an excellent job of patrolling the area, and an isolated burglary is usua the worst of the crime on campus. Students should always be alert when trav ing at night, even in groups of two or three.

Current student, 8/2003-Submit Date, September 2006

Housing stinks the first two years and then is amazing the second two. The campus is in a bad part of town but there is a lot of campus security police and cameras to try to protect us. The dining options are OK but very overpriced.

Current student, 8/2002-Submit Date, November 2005

It isn't a very fun campus but the administration is working hard with the student body to help out with bringing the university to downtown events. Housi is great for upperclassmen—for freshmen, there are very old dorms but i almost what is expected. The food has been a problem here historically an was never happy with the vegetarian selection. There isn't an overwhelmi amount of crime—generally using common sense of caution at night is enou to stay safe. It is easy to feel like the minority at this school as a liberal a major—so be wary of that.

Current student, 9/1999-Submit Date, February 2005

Case is centered in East Cleveland, which isn't the safest place for students walk alone at night.

> **The school says:** "Case is located in Cleveland, on the east side of the city. Centered in University Circle, Case students have the opportunity to experience and enjoy numerous museums, parks, theaters, galleries and restaurants, all within walking distance."

In terms of housing, Case is currently building and expanding the housing there will be better quality of dorm rooms and a variety from which to choos They are also preparing to move the entire campus to the Northside, so wh choosing housing, it is best to choose somewhere on the Northside of camp rather than the South.

> **The school says:** "Case has changed its plans to move all students to residence halls on the Northside. New state-of-the-art residence halls on the north side are complete. But undergraduate enrollment has grown significantly in the last two years, and the number of students electing to live on campus (80 percent of all undergraduates live on campus) has also increased. Some Southside residence halls were completely renovated in summer 2006 to accommodate the increased number of students living on campus; students continue to live in north side and south side residence halls."

The quality of food is poor, though it is probably like that at any dining hall you eat their often enough. Also you don't really have accessibility to any gr cery stores or convenience stores. So if you wanted to buy your on food, a c would really be necessary to have.

Alumnus/a, 1/2000-1/2004, November 2004

The housing on this campus was of a good quality, although compared to oth colleges, it was on the lower end of the scale. My actual dormitory was a nic size, but I did not care for the bathroom facilities. I would have liked to hav had my own bathroom, so that I did not have to deal with waiting for others finish showering or using the restroom in order for me to be able to use the The dining was of sufficient quality. The food tasted good but there could hav been more choices.

Social Life

Alumnus/a, 9/2002-5/2006, November 2006

Social life consists primarily of drinking and off-campus parties. The Greek system is a network of people who enjoy structured activities and social groups, but there is no overall conflict between Greeks and non-Greeks. There is usually a different hang out bar every year. Dating can become incestuous, where one person will date several people in a given group or fraternity/sorority, simply because it can be difficult to meet people outside of a typical circle. It is more that it becomes habit to hang out with certain people than a clique problem. Typically, students form a certain social circle during freshman year and circulate within that circle through the remainder of their college career. UPB, the student programming board, always has a few great activities planned for each semester, and is definitely a resource that students should keep up on so as not to miss any great events.

Current student, Biology, 8/2003-Submit Date, October 2006

Social life is nonexistent for those on campus who don't know how to seek it out and make it happen. While there is a reasonable number of clubs and athletic groups, there are no particularly social scenes like bars or restaurants that are conveniently located within walking distance of the residential areas. The Greek system, while still the greatest outlet for social interaction, is constantly under heavy assault from the university-imposed Greek Life Committee that must approve of everything before it's allowed to happen on campus. If they don't like your fraternity, you're not doing anything for a long time.

Current student, 8/2003-Submit Date, September 2006

Greek life is pretty big. There are several bars on campus and a nice selection of restaurants near by. The dating scene is not so great with most of the prospects already taken.

> The school says: "25 percent of students belong to fraternities or sororities."

Current student, 8/2002-Submit Date, November 2005

McNulty's is a favorite bar of local students. Coventry is a really nice laid-back artsy area with a nice concert venue for fans of indie rock. Mi Pueblo is a frequented bar almost attached to the north campus dorms—very popular in the winter months when going out is not an option (not so great weather). Downtown West 6th, Warehouse District is a great place for the 21+ crowd on the weekends and the 18+ crowd on Thursday nights. West 25th houses Kanaman—a local hookah bar with special Friday nights. The Powerhouse District in the west bank of the Flats is also a nice area for parties.

Alumnus/a, 1/2000-1/2004, November 2004

I did like the social aspect of this university. The events and the scenery were a bonus addition to my experience there. I enjoyed the different restaurants around the area, and I really liked the clubs that were incorporated into the school atmosphere.

The School Says

Case Western Reserve University is recognized nationally and internationally for excellence in research, rigorous academics, and hands-on experiential learning opportunities. A private university in an urban setting, we offer more than 60 majors across the fields of arts and sciences, engineering, management and nursing. Intellectually diverse and academically flexible, our single-door admission policy means that once you're admitted to Case, you can major in any of our programs, or double and even triple major in several of them.

Experiential Learning

At Case, we believe that learning is best accomplished through hands-on experience. Internships, work placements and research projects are not just electives—they're part of a curriculum that engages students with faculty and the community. Here are some of the experiences Case offers:

- Cooperative education and internships, in which you gain full- or part-time work experience related to your major;

- Extensive undergraduate academic research opportunities, either on campus or off, at world-renowned institutions such as the Cleveland Clinic and University Hospitals;

- Study abroad programs to dozens of countries;

- Joint degree programs with the Cleveland Museum of Art, Cleveland Institute of Music, and Cleveland Institute of Art;

- Active student-faculty interaction, with 72 percent of our classes enrolling fewer than 30 students each;

- A student-to-faculty ratio of 8:1;

- SAGES, the Seminar Approach to General Education and Scholarship, a core curriculum that connects you to distinguished faculty and world-class cultural intuitions through small, interdisciplinary, discussion-based seminars.

Student Life

Located on a park-like campus in the heart of Cleveland's University Circle, Case is within walking distance of numerous museums, parks, theaters, galleries and restaurants. A few minutes on the Rapid train and you're in the heart of the Cleveland, home of Playhouse Square, the Great Lakes Science Center, the Rock and Roll Hall of Fame and Museum, the historic West Side Market area and Jacobs Field.

Our selection of student organizations is as varied as our educational programs; and while academics take priority over athletics, Case offers competitive sports in the NCAA's Division III as well as a robust intramural sports program. Our students get involved-in the arts, student government, community service, and even in shaping the future of the university.

As you might expect of a leading research university, Case offers serious technology—from our top-ranked, switched gig-to-desktop network with ubiquitous Wi-Fi to our brand-new, environmentally friendly residence halls that surround an athletic field with state-of-the-art turf.

Scholarship and Financial Aid Programs

Case is committed to making the university's high-quality education affordable through generous scholarship and need-based financial aid programs. Each year, Case awards hundreds of full- and partial-tuition scholarships and 93 percent of the entering class receives financial assistance. In most cases, scholarships are renewable for each of the four undergraduate years if high academic performance is maintained.

Read all of Vault's College Surveys at www.vault.com/college—get complete surveys on 100s of colleges and universities, expert advice on applicaton essays and more.

VAULT CAREER LIBRARY   545

Denison University

Admissions Office
100 South Road
Granville, OH 43023
Admissions phone: (740) 587-6276
Admissions e-mail: admissions@denison.edu
Admissions URL: www.denison.edu/admissions/

Note: *The school has chosen not to comment on the student surveys submitted.*

 ## Admissions

Current student, 9/2005-Submit Date, December 2006

Application was normal. I interviewed with admissions person in my hometown. He was great and wrote me several notes afterwards. This personal touch is reflective of the day-to-day reality of Denison. Denison is getting harder to get into. They still give out very good merit scholarships, although it seems fewer than they used to. I am in the Honors College, and that has been great.

Alumnus/a, 9/1990-5/1999, April 2005

The application consisted of a five-page question and answer form. Half were short answer and half were essays. Questions ranged from why you are considering Denison, what are your extracurricular activities, what awards you have received to a one-page essay describing someone whom you think is great. Three recommendations from high school teachers were required. At the time, a GPA of 3.0+ and an SAT score of 1000+ were required. I know the standards are higher now. [In 2007, the average SAT score was 1262 and the acceptance rate was 39 percent.] I was accepted based upon merit, although an interview was highly recommended.

Alumnus/a, 10/1992-5/1996, February 2005

I visited Denison in the fall of 1991. I had a scheduled tour and a scheduled interview. The school was very intimate and friendly. Our tour guide was very informed and encouraged all types of questions. My interview, I remember, went very well. I believe the reason for this was that I came to the interview with many questions that I had about this particular school. This impressed the interviewer that I took the time to research the university's policies and educational programs. I submitted an essay that I had written during junior year in English class. This was a good idea because I had my English teacher help me revise it so that it was ready for submission for college. This university, along with a few others, were so impressed with this essay that they actually included hand-written responses on my acceptance letters.

Alumnus/a, 8/1997-5/2001, October 2003

Denison is attempting to raise the caliber of the students it admits. When I applied, I had an admissions interview, an essay, SAT/ACT scores sent, Jan 15 deadline, March (maybe) acceptance, pretty traditional stuff. As it is a small school, they look for people who stand out via extracurricular activities, strong academic motives and personality. And, of course, they look for people who will bring those things to Denison, and be active on campus and in the community, and of course bring publicity to the school via their academic and social service/sports accomplishments. The best part of admissions is the huge amount of financial aid Denison gives to students. Most students can get generous need-based and merit-based financial aid.

Academics

Current student, 9/2005-Submit Date, December 2006

I am a double major: economics and environmental studies, with a minor in music. All three departments are great. The only department I've been less-than

thrilled with has been math. There is a lot of work here, and some kids underestimate that, goof off, and then flunk out. I am occasionally shut out of classes, but so far I've gotten into them the next semester.

Alumnus/a, 9/1990-5/1999, April 2005

This is a very academic school, much more so now than when I attended. I was able to experience Denison over a course of nine years, having taken a few years off between my junior and senior years. Classes were always high quality and usually small. Anywhere from four to 12 students. Admissions became much more selective after 1996 and the quality of student skyrocketed. They seemed to target more local academic talent (Ohio residents) than in the early 1990. Required classes were usually made available, but sometimes you could not get in. Grading was usually tough. Professors wanted the students to work hard and were always helpful if you showed effort. Workload was heavy: for every credit hour, there were at least three or four hours of work.

Alumnus/a, 8/1997-5/2001, October 2003

Since it is a private college, no TAs teach courses, which is a plus. Professors generally have strong academic backgrounds, and are active publishing, writing articles, participating in conferences or whatever their fields demand. The academic nature of each major varies. Everyone knew, for example, that economics and communications and sports management were the easiest majors. Not to say those departments don't have good faculty. The science programs and English department are the strongest areas, with excellent professors and many accolades. Some departments in the humanities have great academics, but no great professors. Many times the level of coursework was geared towards the middle-range student, not the high end. I had very few classes where I felt there wasn't time wasted on students who weren't prepared or really weren't with the program, those classes were fabulous, but the rest, not really. Sometimes it was shocking for example, that some foreign language majors couldn't speak the language, or political science majors didn't keep up with current events.

Some professors do show favoritism with grading. However, you will never win arguing your grade, as many students have tried, against a tenured professor their department will always stand by them. Many classes have participation grades, which are stupid. Someone can come to class, and say two basic obvious things and he/she is "participating." Attendance policies are strict, although they should be looser because it is tiring to sit with people who just regurgitate what the professor says and can't think for themselves or pay attention. Many tenured professors take advantage of their positions, and do whatever they feel like, not changing syllabus in 10 years, not teaching to the class, not devoting time to their advisees, not giving lots of time to grading, or the reading of senior research projects. Since it is a small school, you have a good chance of being able to take all the classes you want over a four-year period. To get into some full classes, I went to talk to a professor or had the registrar help me into a class. Sometimes, I had to try two or three times to get a popular gen ed requirement, like painting. Some professors are great. The great ones make it worthwhile. I knew many students, like myself, who took classes outside of their majors with great professors, and thought, why don't I change majors, because this department is much stronger than mine. Close relations can be formed with professors because of small classes, you might have a coffee or lunch with them. I still stay in touch with some professors.

Alumnus/a, 10/1992-5/1996, February 2005

Being that Denison is a college of 2,000 students, I always found it easy to get the proper attention needed. If you are searching for a more one-on-one experience with professors, then a smaller college is right for you. Each year, we were assigned to an academic counselor that met with us to ensure that you were in the proper classes and on the right path to graduation. These counselors also provided services for students who were struggling with certain classes. They also provided advice on how to get into the classes that you needed, like to start attending the class and let the professor know that you are hoping someone will drop the course so you can be added.

Employment Prospects

 # Quality of Life

Current student, 9/2005-Submit Date, December 2006

ave been invited to do a research internship this summer at Denison. I'm pret-
happy about that. I will be going to graduate school, as I think most gradu-
s from liberal arts colleges do.

Alumnus/a, 9/1990-5/1999, April 2005

aving moved to Chicago after graduation and having lived here since, I have
en contacted by more recent graduates asking about the job scene. Based on
at I have heard of their experiences, it seems Denison students are very wel-
me in Chicago in jobs ranging from banking to IT to marketing. There is a
od alumni network here, and Chicago is a great city to live in after college!

Alumnus/a, 10/1992-5/1996, February 2005

very spring, Denison held recruiting days where many companies would set up
oths at the school in hopes of talking to students and set up interviews for
ose ready to enter the working world. In preparation for these events, profes-
rs would have open office hours where you could bring your résumé for
vice. They also provided an opportunity to have mock interviews so you were
epared for the actual interview.

Alumnus/a, 8/1997-5/2001, October 2003

he career department is not a lot of help. Most of the people I graduated with
who graduated before or after me, had to do all their legwork themselves, and
ceived little or no help from career resources. They have cheesy fake inter-
ews, which don't teach you anything, and workshops that aren't helpful either.
or example, I went to them for lots of résumé help. Later I e-mailed my résumé
family members in the business world, and they told me it needed major
anges. There are a lot of successful alumni, however you'll have to contact
em yourself to make a connection. The office doesn't provide lots of helpful
ts—many lists are too general—and many people work in a field that wasn't
eir major. The campus interviews were a joke as well. I didn't go to school
r four years to interview as a department store clerk or a bank teller at a cam-
s interview. The interviews and general alumni networking are only for
vestment banking, finance and for several consulting firms.

heir are internship opportunities available to students for one to three months
ery summer. However, again, they are in limited fields, mostly unpaid and
ith some housing costs, too, which are expensive in big cities, and involve a lot
xeroxing, typing and coffee making. Real job experience? Not really. And
d a lot of people get good job offers from them? Not really. So for a lot of
ople it was giving up your summer for zero dollars and zero experience. A
w people did make connections. A few people eliminated jobs. The intern-
ips, like the alumni contacts, are limited in the fields they cover. Many poten-
l job fields don't have internships through the school, and the school is
helpful with finding internships via other sources for students.

om what I've found, most alumni with successful jobs, either are self-made—
thanks to their alma mater, have parents or family who gave them a success-
l in-track—75 percent of Denison alumni—or contacted alumni themselves
d got a connection. The biggest career encouraged is probably graduate or law
hool because they don't know what to do with all these liberal arts candidates.
e lack of a business undergraduate major, education certificate and engineer-
g major are problems for some students. That and the liberal arts degree can
ther harm you or help you by making you more diverse. However, with
day's field most people need a more specific master's degree anyway, and
me of the above students except those wanting to teach, who by state law for
blic school need a certificate, can get into great graduate programs or find
od jobs without the traditional major or curriculum. Some students find their
tracurricular involvement and close relations with professors help them into
od graduate schools. Some students also get Fulbright Scholarships, or other
vards or national honors as a result of working closely with professors.

Current student, 9/2005-Submit Date, December 2006

Denison is a great school. The kids are friendly, the profs know your name, my
biggest class has been 18 kids, the administration is no trouble at all. Housing
is on campus all four years, and you need to know that going in. There are great
apartments for seniors. All other dorms are ho-hum, but fine. Food is bad.
Because everyone is on campus, it's a tight community. Diversity could be better, but it's no worse than any other private college. I actually have friends from
about eight states and four foreign countries. The campus is beautiful and maintained perfectly. The town we're in (Granville) is not really a college town (not
a lot of bars); it's a postcard town. But it has enough to eat, and everything is
within walking distance, so we're happy. There is a big city (Columbus) close
by. It's good to have a car, but you don't have to have one.

Alumnus/a, 9/1990-5/1999, April 2005

Housing was tight. "Get thee to a broom closet in Crawford Hall," was not
uncommonly written on the housing lottery sign-up. Not the best facilities for
dormitories. But where are they ever ideal? Also, I don't think they allow off-
campus housing anymore, so that's a drag. There was one very cool alternative:
The Homestead. Check it out, it's too cool and not to be missed. Also, the dining facilities were not the best, but I hear they have improved. Many new facilities have been built in the last 10 years, like the new science and athletic centers. It has always been a safe campus, being small and well-lit with an emergency phone every couple of hundred feet.

Alumnus/a, 10/1992-5/1996, February 2005

The neighborhood surrounding the university was very safe. Set in an old suburb of Columbus, the town had one or two street lights with very old buildings.
Students either lived in dorms or in the fraternity houses. Women were not
allowed to live in their sororities as this was based on an old Ohio law that considered this to be a brothel. Every freshman was guaranteed a room and dorm
RAs were there to help incoming freshmen move in and get acclimated.

Alumnus/a, 8/1997-5/2001, October 2003

The surrounding town is a suburb, an hour from Columbus, the closest major
city. The suburb is very white (the only diverse community members are professors!), and very safe. The campus is beautiful, but has many dark corners, and
not well-lit areas. Combine the isolated areas with a dark night and drunk students, and you have a problem. There are safe-walk officers, and campus patrol,
the campus patrol. Female, minority and gay students need more education at
first-year orientation about staying safe, walking in groups and not alone, and
safe drinking practices. There is a large gay and minority and international student population for a school its size. There are a lot of other accepting faculty
and administrators and alumni and students.

Housing facilities and academic buildings are undergoing a lot of renovations,
which should make the campus first rate. The dorms were typical dorms, gross,
with old furniture and carpets, and gross bathrooms. Some older buildings probably have mold problems underneath carpets and walls. If the residential life
staff don't plan well, then the first-year class is scrunched in horrible small
rooms, two in a single, three in a small double. Residential life doesn't do tons
for the students. There are substance free and smoke free dorms available, and
one female-only dorm, although one woman said, girls' boyfriends stayed over
a lot there. Other dorms are co-ed, with same-sex roommates, and same-sex
bathrooms and floors or wings. Dorms had key card systems. You couldn't get
in without them, and after 12 p.m., if you didn't live in a dorm, your key card
wouldn't let you in that specific one. However, you can always get someone to
hold a door for you, so that's not really a good safety measure. Patrolling within dorms is minimal, unfortunately. The dining halls are constantly improving,
trying to incorporate more student favorites. It could be worse, it could be a lot
better, it could be $8.50 per meal you spent somewhere else, like a nice restau-
rant. Students have to live on campus, and most eat in the dining halls unless
they have a kitchen. This is annoying that seniors have to live on campus,
always a contention point.

Read all of Vault's College Surveys at **www.vault.com/college**—get complete surveys on 100s of colleges and universities, expert advice on applicaton essays and more.

VAULT CAREER LIBRARY **547**

Parking on campus is greatly improved with new parking deck. Townies and Granville police and students don't get along too well. Granville police are always trolling for students, following them through town on Saturday nights, bothering people, busting up parties after townies call them. Granville is dry, I think, and also has a strict no open container policy.

 ## Social Life

Current student, 9/2005-Submit Date, December 2006

Lots of on-campus activities like comedians, movies, lectures and concerts. We hang out in each other's rooms a fair amount. I play two club sports so I'm busy with that. Plus I play in two musical ensembles. Greek life is pretty much dead. No frat or sorority houses anymore—they took them away and turned them into regular dorms.

Alumnus/a, 8/1997-5/2001, October 2003

With just over 2,000 students, if you make an effort, you can meet a lot of people and see them all the time. This is good, as far as never eating lunch alone, and always seeing a familiar face. It's bad, as in people gossip a lot and spread rumors constantly and are kind of high school clique-ish. I had friends in many groups, but this is rare. Usually people stay in their groups they form freshman year, and they don't change.

Greek life traditionally has been huge on campus, because there is not much to do in Granville. Fraternities lost their right to live in their houses in the early 90s. Sororities never could because of an old law still on the books about more than three women living in a house together, gotta love Midwest conservatism. Fraternities and sororities have been under increasing pressure to cut down on hazing, illegal drug activities and bad behavior, to the point that there have been many on probation, kicked off temporarily or permanently. However, because many trustees and big donor alumni were Greek, they will never disappear. There are generally five fraternities and five or six sororities. They are all terribly stereotyped. About half of women, 60 percent are Greek, and I think one-third of men are Greek. Some Greeks are great and it can be a great social support system. However, it's also a members only club, and Greek people don't date non-Greek people, and many don't maintain tons of non-Greek friends. Many aren't even friends with people outside their own fraternity or sorority. The best parties on campus are usually Greek. Some are good students and involved on campus. Some do great community service. There are fun events like powder puff football, Greek week with games and competitions, and formals and theme parties.

There are also black sororities and fraternities, who always have great reputations but their academic standards and community service standards are so high that many students don't join. They have some small events, too. Some students of color or international students or other minorities join fraternities and sororities.

Dating at all on campus is strange. Most students have either been dating since forever, or just randomly hook up with people on weekends. The problem with Greek life is mostly labeling and bad behavior. If you choose not to be Greek, social options are limited. However, people find their own groups, e.g., the theater group, the Christian group and the swim team. Some sports are big on campus, like swimming, lacrosse, squash and club hockey. There are 200+ student organizations to choose from, everything from student government to tons of volunteer organizations, to club sports like ultimate frisbee, religious groups and honoraries. which are really great. There is a lot of drinking on campus, alcohol-free events are difficult to find. All-campus events include homecoming, parents' weekend, two drag shows, international fair, international fashion show, Gay Pride week, Greek Week, one major music concert and various other bands and groups all year round, outside campus picnics, various charity and volunteer events, various awareness events, such as free AIDS testing, fundraisers, charities, exam week midnight breakfasts, various comedians, poetry readings, karaoke and speakers on campus all the time, dance department recitals, campus film festival and campus theater. There is a campus bar and coffee house. Brand new student union with great stuff, and fast food and snacks. Gym with club sports.

The town has two bars, Brews and the Villa. No underage drinking but favs 21 and up. Local grub can be found at both bars, Elm's Pizza, Subway, Aladdin, Breakfast Eatery, a coffee shop, Blackstone's deli, the Granville or Buxton Inn for upscale food, and Victoria's Ice Cream Parlor. There are other fast food and small places between Granville and Columbus or Granville and Heath, a bigger town. There are no movie theaters nearby. The student union shows movies now and then. Students with wheels head to Heath for the nearest bad mall and dining. They go to Easton for upscale shopping, movies or eating. Few students venture to Columbus a lot, even though it is an hour, electing to stay on campus and do the same thing every weekend. Students who like dancing at clubs, go downtown to Columbus. Students who like concerts go to Polaris, or the arena downtown. Professional Hockey is downtown. Some students tailgate at OSU games with high school friends. About 45 percent of students are from Ohio. Some of them go home on weekends frequently or once in a while.

Kent State University

Admissions Office
Kent State University
P.O. Box 5190
Kent, OH 44242-0001
Admissions phone: (330) 672-2444 or (800) 988-KENT
Admissions fax: (330) 672-2499
Admissions contact URL:
www.admissions.kent.edu/contactUs.asp
Admissions URL: www.admissions.kent.edu/

Admissions

Current student, 8/2005-Submit Date, August 2006

I made the decision to attend Kent State (for the fall semester) in early August after leaving a job I had at the time. The process was very quick relative to other schools with which I'm familiar. Within three weeks, I was registered, scheduled for classes and set up with a financial aid package. Of course, the downside to this fact is the (correct) impression that admissions standards at the school are not competitive. Aside from that, the process was smooth, and many functions were completed conveniently online.

Alumnus/a, Exercise Science, 10/2003-5/2006, January 2007

Admission into Kent State was fairly easy, partly due to the fact that they tend to cater to transfer students, which I was at the time. Transfer students start with a clean slate regardless of past academic history once they are admitted. It does not matter if you had a 1.5 or 3.8 GPA at a previous institution. When you start your first semester at KSU, you begin with a 0.0 GPA. It is good and bad for me. It really depends on how you view it.

Current student, Fashion, 8/2004-Submit Date, December 2006

Overall I found that the admissions process was pretty easy. To ensure you get accepted I recommend having at least a 3.0 GPA and some sort of community service or volunteer work. Also, I recommend you work for some type of retail store and have your store manager write one of your letters of recommendation. It looks very impressive to have someone who is already fairly established in the industry recommending you to this prestigious program. (The fashion school ranks in the Top 10 fashion schools in the United States.) If you are applying to be a design major, it is crucial to send in a portfolio containing your top sketches. I definitely believe by doing so you put yourself above many others.

Alumnus/a, 1/1999-1/2003, December 2005

Study for SAT and ACT, and take them multiple times. Have as many people as possible read your essays, and try not to be too dramatic or sentimental. In an interview, be yourself and never lie. Be aware that more people are applying than can be accepted, so apply to several schools. Apply to a few out of reach schools that have program in which you are interested, then a few schools that are in your ball park and you have a 50/50 chance of getting in, and lastly a few sure thing schools. Then wait to hear from all schools before deciding, and always return info saying if you have or have not chosen that school.

Current student, 8/2005-Submit Date, October 2005

My advice would be to start early. Find out if the colleges you are applying to require essays. If they do, start them early, and get them revised by several English teachers and your guidance counselor. Take the SATs more than once, and start studying for them in the summer before your junior year of high school. For the interview, make sure you have business attire to wear, and have a teacher or parent help you prepare with practice interview questions.

Alumnus/a, 8/1998-5/2004, February 2005

KSU does not interview applicants for admission and no essays are required for the application. It is not a very selective school. If you did decently well in high school (like a 2.5 GPA or better), you'll get in. If you're accepted, you have to

schedule a PASS day, which is when you go to the school to learn more about the school and curriculum. This is when you take your placement tests to see which math and English courses you will place into. After taking the tests, you meet with an advisor and plan your schedule for your first semester's classes.

Alumnus/a, 6/1994-10/1999, June 2004

The best advice I can give on selection is to try and talk to the students who are in the field you want to study so you can get a feel for the workload and professors' expectations. Don't go away to school in Hawaii, for instance, just because you like the beach. I found the most important part of my application (other than ACT scores of course) was my involvement in local community activities. I did local theater and volunteered at the city hospital in the children's ward, and that seemed to really influence my admission. As far as the interview goes, I have to admit it has been a while, but take my advice and be yourself. Plus, after declaring your major, if you want to change it, don't do it right away. In my opinion, your first choice is usually your best one.

Current student, 7/2000-Submit Date, May 2005

Kent State was not very difficult to get into when I applied four years ago, yet it is getting much more competitive and expensive as are most schools in Ohio. I just had to fill out a short application and send it in along with my transfer from community college. If you live in OH and attend community college for a few years (even just part time) it makes it much easier to get into Kent because Ohio colleges are required to accept a certain percentage to community college transfer students each semester.

Academics

Current student, 8/2005-Submit Date, August 2006

I found many of the required courses to be blasé and pointless. I also found this to be the case at another state school I attended, however. I've never had trouble doing well in school, but the rigor at Kent is notably low by comparison. I would also note that only four of the university's programs (journalism, fashion design, aeronautics and liquid crystals) have any level of national prestige.

Alumnus/a, Exercise Science, 10/2003-5/2006, January 2007

Classes are hit or miss for the most part, which I believe is prevalent at most any school one attends. Some teachers seem to care while others seem too careless whether or not they teach you or have an impact on your life. The chemistry department is very strong at KSU, but their curriculum and tests are tough as well. They do a good job of weeding out people and for the most part do not play favorites. The psychology department is exceptional as well as the mathematics department. Their exercise science department is a bit undermanned so it is tough to get the one-on-one experience that most students pay for.

Current student, Fashion, 8/2004-Submit Date, December 2006

The quality of classes is phenomenal. They are absolutely not a piece of cake (as some would like to think). I believe they challenge you both intellectually and creatively to bring out your most excellent work. As far as getting into the best professors classes, it is not all that easy but once you become a junior and senior it will get somewhat easier for you. You also may get to know your professors on a closer level and that occasionally helps in getting into the classes you want. If you do not have any friends in this major to warn you of who to take and who not to take, I highly recommend pickaprof.com. I've used it many times and it is definitely the best thing when deciding which professor to take when you have no friends to ask. The workload of this program is not overly intensive, but it is demanding. Some classes require you to do a great deal of work, such as Visuals, Presentations, Drawing, and Product Development. Classes such as Retailing, Fashion Fundamentals, and Fashion Forecasting are pretty light on the workload. I feel it also helps to take the classes with the least number of students in them. You tend to get better grades in these classes, make more fashion friends (which comes in handy when you need to do group projects), and become friends with your professors. Unfortunately the grading scale

Read all of Vault's College Surveys at **www.vault.com/college**—get complete surveys on 100s of colleges and universities, expert advice on applicaton essays and more.

VAULT CAREER LIBRARY   **549**

is a bit tough, 93 to 100 for an A. Unlike others that merely require 90 to 100. For the most part, professors are very nice and easy to talk with. If you have any questions, don't hesitate whatsoever to ask them. They are always extremely helpful.

Alumnus/a, 1/1999-1/2003, December 2005

Until you are at junior status don't expect to get into the good or popular classes. Always take 15 hours, or it will take longer than four years to graduate and you can take up to 18 hours without having to pay extra. Always keep your options open. If another program's classes seem interesting, then take it as an elective course. Your happiness is more important than what other people think you should be doing. And lastly and most importantly do not rely solely on the work of your guidance counselor, they too make mistakes; take an active role in your education.

Current student, 1/2002-Submit Date, October 2005

In the general classes the professors were very willing to help us out if we needed extra help. Science classes were hard to get into because of limited class size. In nursing classes, the professors could seem unapproachable for extra help.

Alumnus/a, 8/1998-5/2004, February 2005

Most courses are lecture based, and many classrooms are auditoriums with large numbers of students in the class. It is not hard to get into a particular class you want, especially if you plan for it and schedule early. Most professors grade on a curve, and many offer extra credit opportunities. The workload is manageable, as long as you don't put things off until the last minute.

Current student, 7/2000-Submit Date, May 2005

The fine arts program is a bit formal and outdated in that much of the faculty is close to retirement right now. Yet, this is all about to change. They are searching for new faculty right now and want a younger staff that will have a more contemporary body of work. The classes in the first two years will be mixed with art education majors and after that you will get more personal attention from your professors because you are in smaller classes that will only include fine art majors. Basically, the first two years you are in the class with adjunct faculty and not full-time instructors. The faculty often seems overworked and angry. Yet, Kent is also very cheap compared with other liberal arts schools in the area; it is the best deal if you don't have lots of money.

Alumnus/a, 6/1994-10/1999, June 2004

Well, as you can imagine, any type of engineering is going to be math-heavy, so you have to be prepared for some serious studying. I advise taking construction management as a minor, because that's how I lived and paid for school while I was there. Of course, the bigger the city, the more chance of landing a job like that during school. In my case it involved some traveling, but the professors understood, and I took some coursework on the road. Study, study, study. That in itself will make all your classes easier.

Employment Prospects

Current student, 8/2005-Submit Date, August 2006

Again, the employment prospects are about average for a large state school, meaning mediocre to lukewarm. Some of the top graduates in accounting are snapped up for competitive program. For those in journalism, fashion design and so on, the prospects are much better. The school is very hands-on in those fields, and employers seem to recognize that. Unfortunately, the KSU study areas with the best employment prospects are also the ones with some of the lowest starting salary potential.

Alumnus/a, Exercise Science, 10/2003-5/2006, January 2007

Employment prospecting is fair at KSU. It is what you make of it since it truly depends on the person. If a student at KSU takes advantage of internships provided, then opportunities will be there. As for alumni networking, it appears nonexistent.

Current student, Fashion, 8/2004-Submit Date, December 200

The employment prospects are not the best. We do not have as many on-ca pus recruiting programs as I feel we should. In addition, the alumni network of zero help. It is required for you to complete an internship to graduate a your best bet is to intern at a company where you would want to work after gra uation. Many students get great job offers at the end of their internships or wh they apply to the same company for which they interned. The fashion sch looks very impressive to employers. They know that Kent State students ha gained incredibly extensive knowledge of the industry. They also know that students have completed many liberal education requirements and are therefo extremely well rounded.

Alumnus/a, 8/1999-8/2003, June 2006

Attend as many job fairs as you can. Practice your interview skills. Take adva tage of any co-op jobs if possible. Join a professional club related to your fie It will help you in your future job search. Also, network with as many people you field. Create a résumé. Résumés should not be longer than one page. T to work in lower-level jobs associated to your field. Although you are in scho many employers will like to see some experience. This will make you a bet job candidate.

Alumnus/a, 1/1999-1/2003, December 2005

The alumni network was not very effective for me because I moved out of sta Ask professors and other students about internships or work opportuniti Experience is the best road to receiving job offers. Begin preparation for gr school during early junior year and start research opportunities.

Alumnus/a, 8/1998-5/2004, February 2005

The ease of getting a job in your preferred field depends on your major. KSU known and well respected in certain areas, such as education, fashion design a journalism, to name a few. If you major in any of these, you will not have tro ble getting a job. Career services is somewhat helpful in job seeking. I fou advisors to be helpful in finding internship opportunities

> **The school says:** "The staff at the career services center is ready to help students plan for their future in a variety of ways. From researching careers and selecting a major, to understanding the importance of internships, preparing for graduate school and previewing available jobs, students will find friendly counselors who can help them make their long-term goals a reality. Additionally, the career services center posts on- and off campus part-time jobs and assists students in understanding how to market their experience to future employers. Kent State's career services center has been nationally recognized for recent technological innovations and for exceptional student service. Contact the career services center at (330) 672-2360 or visit www.kent.edu/career to learn more about the many services available."

Quality of Life

Current student, 8/2005-Submit Date, August 2006

I worked full time and lived off campus, so my campus experience was self-li ited. It did appear that most students living near or on campus had a lot of oppo tunities for social life. Kent is the all-American college town, with lots of ba discount stores and fast-food joints. One big selling point for the campus, a one of my favorite things about attending Kent, is the newly constructed thre story fitness center. It has an amazing range of Cybex machines, an indoor tra an Olympic pool and too much else. I've also noticed that the town and camp seem very safe.

Alumnus/a, Exercise Science, 10/2003-5/2006, January 2007

Quality of life is just about as good as it gets. Housing is clean as well as t campus facilities. Crime rate is low. Students feel safe any time of day or nig walking around the campus. It's almost too safe actually. It is a close-knit ty of community at KSU. The students are well represented by faculty and stude senate members. The voices of the KSU student are heard by all and addresse It is a clean, safe and respectful institution.

urrent student, 8/2004-Submit Date, December 2006

e quality of life at Kent State is pretty nice. The dorms are acceptable and you
 only required to live in them for two years (unlike the four that other schools
y require). None of the dorms are disgusting and I can say I wouldn't mind
ing in any one of them. I recommend Tri-Towers though because everyone I
ow who has stayed there has completely loved it and made plenty of friends
ing there. Kent is particularly liberal and does not pass judgment on people
o may be gay or bisexual. For the most part everyone gets along quite well.
e crime rate is notably very low and I feel 100 percent safe in this communi-
and am never afraid to go anywhere by myself.

e dining in the cafeteria is excellent. You have countless options of places to
or types of cuisine to eat. I gained 20 pounds my freshman year and attrib-
it all to the 24-hour diner on campus. Overall, the food is great and I sug-
st unquestionably getting a generous food plan. The campus is gorgeous in the
ing and I really like its spaciousness. All the buildings are incredibly spread
t, which can be either a good or bad thing. Not to worry though because you
 make it across campus within 15 minutes. If you choose not to walk, you
 ride the campus bus (often called the campus loop) for free to anywhere you
nt to go on campus.

urrent student, 8/2005-Submit Date, October 2005

r housing is wonderful and we are having a new dorm building built right
w. We have many programs to help new students become adjusted to living
campus. Our crime rate is extremely low. We have security on campus 24
urs a day. The dining is wonderful. We have a variety of restaurants on cam-
s and off. A lot of off-campus restaurants will take our school's flash cash.

urrent student, 1/2002-Submit Date, October 2005

r neighborhood is crime-free. Our dining is very small and limited at this
int. We have a bookstore on campus that carries everything we need at outra-
us prices.

urrent student, 8/2000-Submit Date, April 2005

e campus is nice. I like the size and the landscaping. Housing options are
o abundant. Campus is close to everything Kent has to offer. The are a lot of
od options including cafeteria foods to fast foods. They also provide legal
rvices for free to students.

 ## Social Life

urrent student, 8/2005-Submit Date, August 2006

ere are lots of opportunities to socialize. The college is constantly sponsoring
me large event in the student center or the outdoor plaza (with lots of free give-
vays, bands and so on). The town has bars, a movie theater and most of the
res and restaurants you would expect to find in a middle-class, middle-sized
wn. For bigger venues, Akron is less than 20 minutes away and Cleveland is
out 45 minutes to the north. There's also pretty easy access to Pittsburgh
bout and hour-and-a-half), and all of the cities are connected 100 percent by
ghway with no need for back road follies.

Alumnus/a, Exercise Science, 10/2003-5/2006, January 2007

The social life at Kent is great. People are really separated by "six degrees" here.
Campus life is comfortable and welcoming to all ethnicities and socialites alike.
Restaurants are located within and around surrounding areas of the Kent area.
Bars are not in short supply either. For those looking to journey out on
Thursdays they will have numerous bars to choose from. Not to mention that
Akron is just a short drive away (12 minutes). The dating scene is phenomenal.
There seem to be more girls than guys at KSU.

Current student, Fashion, 8/2004-Submit Date, December 2006

On a scale of 1 to 10, the social life is a 6.5. There are many parties, especially
fraternity parties. These can be a lot of fun but they do get old by the end of your
sophomore year. If you are interested in Greek life, the most popular sororities
are Alpha Phi and Delta Gamma. The most popular fraternities are Sigma Phi
Epsilon, Sigma Chi, and Delta Upsilon. By popular I mean the best parties and
usually the best looking. The bars are pretty entertaining and each one is seemingly different from the other. The favorites seem to be Ray's (for the after-hours
crowd), The Loft, Glory Days, The Brewhouse (Thursday nights for the under
21 crowd), and BW3's a lot of people in the Greek system hang out here). The
dating scene is pretty typical of most colleges: everyone is single. Last but not
least, Cleveland is only 45 minutes away and there are concerts and a vast number of places to eat if you wish for a small break from Kent.

Current student, 8/2005-Submit Date, October 2005

We have over 100 clubs on campus. One for every type of student. From politics to ice carving. We have several events every month. All restaurants love
students to come in, and the local bars do too. The Greek system is also great.

Alumnus/a, 8/1998-5/2004, February 2005

There are many social activities. KSU has a brand-new and very large recreation
center, with numerous basketball, indoor soccer and racquetball courts. It also
has two pools and a whirlpool. Kent's basketball teams have been very successful in recent years, making the basketball season an especially fun time of
the year. There are many bars in downtown Kent, and many people also travel
to Akron and Cleveland for the nightlife scene. There are a few restaurants near
campus, although not many. For most you'd need to drive to neighboring towns.
There are plenty of fast food establishments in and around campus, though.

Current student, 8/2000-Submit Date, April 2005

Downtown Kent is everyone's favorite. All of the bars are within walking distance of each other. People like to bar hop and party all night long. One of the
bars (Glory Days) is an all-time favorite and they provide free limo rides to the
bar. The variety of restaurants are slim. There's only a few to choose from.
Rocknes and Damon's are the best. However if you want pizza there are a ton
of options for that. Most college students are broke so they don't date much.
The dating scene is going to the bar or dinner on campus. However, you may
get lucky and get taken to dinner and a movie.

Read all of Vault's College Surveys at **www.vault.com/college**—get complete surveys on 100s of colleges and universities, expert advice on applicaton essays and more.

VAULT CAREER LIBRARY **551**

Kenyon College

Admissions Office
Ransom Hall
Gambier, OH 43022-9623
Admissions phone: (800) 848-2468
Admissions fax: (740) 427-5770
Admissions e-mail: admissions@kenyon.edu
Admissions URL: www.kenyon.edu/admissions.xml

 Admissions

Alumnus/a, English, 9/2002-6/2006, September 2007

Intensive—I was placed on a waitlist, and flew to Ohio to interview with the Dean of Admissions. We talked about Ayn Rand and Karl Marx. Then I sent in extra essays, and short fiction I had written in order to further persuade them.

Alumnus/a, History, 8/2001-5/2005, September 2007

I applied to Kenyon as a safety cool. At the time, it was pretty unknown and coming from New York City, hardly anyone had heard of it. I was the only student from my small private school to ever apply and as far as I know, no one has applied since. I attended a recruitment open house at the apartment of a current student and was in awe of the chemistry that students and parents had with one another. It seemed like everyone knew each other and was genuinely happy to be in each other's company. I left with the impression that this was not just a school but a tight-knit community. It wasn't some huge state school where you were just a number. Kenyon is not the place you want to go to if your goal is to stay anonymous. After the open house, I decided to apply. I was also applying to over 10 other schools but something about Kenyon intrigued me.

I went out to visit in March 2003 and stayed with a student I met at the open house. As soon as I came onto campus, I knew this was where I wanted to spend the next four years (arguably the four most important years of your life). It's the quintessential college campus; it exudes intelligence but not in the "we're too smart for you" kind of way. I had an in-person interview (which the college recommends, and after working as an admissions interviewer my senior year, I also recommend) with a very friendly student who seemed genuinely interested in getting to know me. After staying for almost three days (I didn't even want to leave) I knew that if I was accepted, I would make this small little rural town my home for the next four years. When I got my acceptance letter, I was shocked for two reasons: 1) They e-mailed me early because, they said, they know how anxious that time of the year can be, and 2) the letter was personally written. It wasn't a generic "congratulations" e-mail. Someone took the time out to say why they thought I would enjoy the school, what the similarities were between the college and my high school. They even referenced my application essay.

Alumnus/a, Psychology, 8/2002-5/2006, September 2007

Kenyon has one of the most detailed admissions processes. There is a multitude of well-thought-out essay and a bunch of smaller, short-answer questions. In terms of selectivity, the admissions board at Kenyon has its pick of the cream of the crop, so it only takes the top students and is looking to become exponentially harder to get into. I know that the acceptance rate over the last five years has dropped by about 40 percent. In terms of advice, I would say to interview on campus because it is recommended and Kenyon is a place you have to see to understand. Score well, work hard, and be interesting in your interview and you have a great chance of getting in.

Alumnus/a, Liberal Arts, 9/2001-5/2005, September 2007

The admissions process has definitely changed as well as become more competitive since when I applied. Kenyon looks for smart people who are also well rounded and can contribute to the campus life as well as to the academic classes.

Current student, 8/2001-Submit Date, March 2005

I sent in an application, which included my SAT, SAT Subject Tests and AC scores, my résumé, essays, recommendations and transcripts. I was asked to to Ohio for a scholarship weekend where I was competing with other stude for a scholarship. During that time, I had two interviews—one group and o private. You can interview before then, but I did not live in the state at the tim

 **Academics**

Alumnus/a, English, 9/2002-6/2006, September 2007

Utopian—everyone is passionate about what they are learning, and most classes are implicitly interdisciplinary. One semester I was taking Existentialis (philosophy), Meanings of Death (religion), Ethics and Social Justice (sociol gy), and Jazz Age literature—all of which were dealing with Nietzsche, T. Eliot, Camus, Engels, Marx, and general themes of alienation in a capitalis society. I mean, ideally, this is what a liberal arts education is all about. Certa teachers are living legends on the campus, and classes are not difficult to get in (given the small nature of the school)—except, of course, the creative writi classes for which you must submit a sample and be chosen. Worth it because t program is so well-regarded.

Alumnus/a, History, 8/2001-5/2005, September 2007

Kenyon is a great liberal arts school. It is the only place I know where teache don't really believe that you should graduate knowing what you want to do wi the rest of your life. Instead, they want you to focus on what your academic pa sions are and leave the rest until you walk out with your diploma. Most of t classes are on the small side (10 to 20 students) and the teacher knows who y are and knows your work habits. The classes are engaging, even with the mo mundane of subjects. Evening seminars, which go from 7 to 10 p.m., are usua ly 10 students maximum and they're very discussion based. There are alwa popular classes and with seniors getting to pick first, they can often fill up quic ly. Many professors, however, are more than willing to let underclassmen i even if students have to sit on the floor or on a radiator. The workload is wh you make of it. You can blow off the reading but then it shows when you ha nothing to say during your next class when everyone else is in the midst of intense and enlightening topic of conversation. Professors often have terri reading lists too, so it's not like the material is so dense that it becomes unbea able. Kenyon students thrive on being overloaded with work and it also boos camaraderie. One of my favorite memories is during exam time all your frien are sitting in the library studying and the 1:45 a.m. "nerd bell" goes off remin ing everyone that the library is closing soon and, more importantly, it's time go home and get some rest.

Alumnus/a, Psychology, 8/2002-5/2006, September 2007

Academics at Kenyon are what you make them. You are provided with some the best professors in the nation. If you are interested in political science th there is no better professor than Fred Bauman. If you are interested in Engli the you have to check out Kluge's creative writing class (one of the mo demanding classes at Kenyon). Like any school, some classes are harder tha others but you will find that every class is taught by world class professor Psychology majors should take every opportunity to take a class with Profess Levine who is a leader in his field and one of the more interesting people on th campus. The workload is immense and you will find yourself writing back-t back 25-page papers but the educational reward far surpasses any amount work. In terms of getting into classes, it can be easy or really hard. If you are an English major, you have almost no chance of getting into an upper-level clas For every other major, if you show up and talk to the professors they are pret lenient about letting extra kids into the class if they have a really strong intere Kenyon is about the education, not about capping classes.

Alumnus/a, Liberal Arts, 9/2001-5/2005, September 2007

pending on classes, workload can be easy to hard, however, in my experience
ver unmanageable. It is college, so for most things you cannot wait until the
ht before a paper or a test, so preparation is a must. Teachers at Kenyon real-
love teaching and being there. They have come to a place in the "middle of
where," which shows their dedication to the students and their studies.
asses are small and great for growth. It is not difficult to get the classes that
u want, but plan in advance! I also found that professors were rather fair in
ding and if a student showed effort before a test and essay, teachers always
k that into account.

Alumnus/a, Psychology, 8/2001-5/2005, September 2007

y academic experience at Kenyon was excellent. Professors were so accom-
dating, and were always available to meet outside of class. Additionally, the
er students were very smart, and this enhanced my academic experience. It
s rigorous, yet very manageable, and there were people to help along the way,
luding professors and classmates.

rrent student, 8/2001-Submit Date, March 2005

ofessors are very willing to help students in general and the workload is as
enuous as the program in which the student chooses to engage him or herself.
ading is fair, but if there are questions, the students are encouraged to speak
th professors, heads of departments and deans. Getting into popular classes
n be difficult, but is not impossible. In general, seniors are given priority for
rtain classes, but some great classes will only allow underclassmen to partake.
ry, very few classes allow for more than 18 students. Language classes are
en full and their maximum is 24 students, but most classes max out at 18.
me advanced classes only sit 12.

 Employment Prospects

Alumnus/a, History, 8/2001-5/2005, September 2007

nyon's alumni network runs deep. One thing that is terrific about the school
that Kenyon students love to help other Kenyon students. Even if you are
ars apart from the person you're contacting, you will never find someone who
unwilling to speak with you. Kenyon also has something called an externship,
ich pairs current students up with alumni who are in a particular field. They
t the opportunity to go work with the alums company during their spring
eak. I don't know if it's something that is widely popular, but I do know that
s there to be taken advantage of.

Alumnus/a, Psychology, 8/2002-5/2006, September 2007

I had started earlier, it might have been different, but I really think you have
be very proactive. Kenyon is a very small school, which means less alumni
n big universities. On the flip-side, every alumnus/a is willing to talk to you
d give you advice about getting a job and you enter into an alumni network
t consists of the best, the brightest and the nicest people you will ever meet.

Alumnus/a, Psychology, 8/2001-5/2005, September 2007

e people who know Kenyon, know it as a very good school that produces very
pable, intelligent and responsible graduates. Everyone I know who graduated
th me got excellent jobs, and for myself, when people see "Kenyon" on my
sumé, they are impressed.

Alumnus/a, Liberal Arts, 9/2001-5/2005, September 2007

hen I was there I did not find that the Career Development Center was very
volved. However, in my experience Kenyon alumni are so proud of their alma
ater that once you are able to contact someone in your field of interest, he/she
always willing to reach out and help. It is always important for the student to
active in working with teachers and the Career Development Center in con-
cting people in the field in which he/she wants to be a part. Graduates range
every type of job and are very successful.

Alumnus/a, 9/1989-5/1993, February 2004

nyon will teach you how to write, whether you study math or chemistry,
thropology or English. It is one of the most useful skills in the marketplace,
d one of the most rare these days. The college provides a large number of
aduates in businesses of various sorts who are willing to have an intern, and
nyon graduates seem to do just about everything from editing newspapers to

becoming pastry chefs, so this is a valuable resource and should be utilized. The
college will prepare you for anything, including law or medical school, PhD
work in various fields, business, teaching, photography, you name it, there are
people doing it. A certain amount of campus recruiting takes place, but most job
hunting is done through the careers service. Kenyon networking is excellent,
and you might find yourself invited to stay with Kenyon alumni all over the
world, if you run into them in faraway places.

Alumnus/a, 8/1992-5/1996, February 2004

The basis of training that I received at Kenyon prepared me very well for my
future career. The Career Development Center continues to be active helping
students gain exposure to the work within their chosen discipline, including participating in summer externships with professionals in their fields. The campus
life also supports a variety of different groups, clubs, and programs designed to
foster both professional identity and help students get to where they want to go.

 Quality of Life

Alumnus/a, English, 9/2002-6/2006, September 2007

The quality of life is wonderful—that said, it is also a very specific quality of
life. It's the most sincere and fulfilling environment I can think of to spend four
years. It is small, privileged and rather idealistic, but it gives back so much
experience. You have to love to learn, because that is the basis for your life here,
and then you will love the people and living within a square mile of all your best
friends. And going to the one bar on campus—I still think its the best bar I've
ever been to—it's a total dive and you can smoke inside, but isn't it the people
and conversation that make up your social life? Housing is not super, but it's all
on campus and it's all close—there really isn't a bad place to live, and once
again, it's beyond safe. You can get everything here—art, live music, theater,
sports—but you have to be looking for something a little less mainstream and be
truly adventurous. You give up a lot of traditional facets of college life, but what
you get back is hugely rewarding—and you are living in (truly) one of the most
beautiful places I have ever seen. Sunset in Ohio takes your breath away.

Alumnus/a, History, 8/2001-5/2005, September 2007

Quality of life at Kenyon is all about Gambier. The location of the college is
such that you are on a huge hill in the middle of Ohio, surrounded by corn fields
and Amish farms. The closest city is Columbus, which is about an hour, and
nearby Easton has some amazing shopping and eateries. Aside from that, there
isn't too much to do in the immediate surrounding areas. This is often the one
major bone of contention for most current students and often leads to some
heavy on-campus drinking during the winter time. Because you're in a small
town in the middle of nowhere, crime and safety is really a non-issue. Doors to
the dormitories are left unlocked and most students leave their dorms and apartments unlocked too. It's one of those community/trust things that makes
Kenyon such a great place.

Housing is getting better. Freshmen are all housed together in the freshman
quad, which is a great way to get to know your fellow classmates early on. As
you move your way up, better housing is available. Fraternities do get a bit of
an edge in that they are guaranteed housing in the older, gothic dorms on the
south end of campus (sort of the epicenter of the college). The school discourages off-campus housing, but those options are pretty sparse and undesirable
anyway. The upperclassmen apartments are spacious and accommodate anywhere from three to six students. The housing lottery occurs at the end of each
year and can get pretty dramatic so make sure you go into it with your battle
army (unless you're in a fraternity, in which it's fun to go just to watch). The
facilities at Kenyon are improving with the College's slowwwwly increasing
endowment. The new athletic center, which was opened just in the last few
years, is unreal, filled with state-of-the-art gym equipment, swimming pools,
basketball courts, squash courts, tennis courts, tracks, seminar rooms, eateries
and so on. The other facilities significantly older, but they add to the school's
charm. Several classrooms have stained glass windows dating back to the early
years of the college.

Alumnus/a, Psychology, 8/2002-5/2006, September 2007

The athletic facility at Kenyon is one of the nicest in the whole country. As a
varsity athlete and even for non-athletes, this place was truly a dream come true
(and I only had it for a semester). The area is extremely safe. I never felt

Read all of Vault's College Surveys at www.vault.com/college—get complete surveys on 100s of colleges and universities, expert advice on applicaton essays and more.

VAULT CAREER LIBRARY   553

uncomfortable walking around at 5 a.m. by myself. Housing isn't the most luxurious but it is relatively cheap and close to everywhere you need to go. The dining hall is beautiful, which makes up for the fact that the food isn't great. With that in mind, I never had trouble finding food everyday and with the dining hall always open you can eat all day long. There are also no locks or passes to go places at Kenyon (except the athletic facility), which is really cool because it shows how safe and how trusting everyone is.

Alumnus/a, Liberal Arts, 9/2001-5/2005, September 2007

Kenyon is so safe that students do not lock their bedroom doors. Anyone can get into a dorm or apartment complex. While we are always encouraged to lock our housing facilities, there is such a sense of safety, people really don't have to. Outside of the tranquil campus you can reach a more urban feeling in Mount Vernon and the trip to Columbus is only an hour away, where one of the most amazing mall centers, Easton, exists. With the new Kenyon Athletic Center as well as the main dining hall having been restructured, the quality of life on campus has drastically increased from the time that I was there. However, the special nature of Kenyon, leaves students feeling that they are a part of something that cannot be found anywhere else and that a "Kenyon bubble" really exists.

Current student, 8/2001-Submit Date, March 2005

This is a very neighborly community. A vast majority of the students do not feel the need to lock their doors at night or when they leave for the day. While there is some theft of the occasional bike, that usually is a result of a student in a drunken stupor trying to get home quickly. The campus is very safe, and campus security offers its services round the clock—offering rides or company for people walking anywhere on campus late at night. Sometimes the food is great, other times mundane, and still others unappealing. The science and math buildings are new and the equipment is pristine and regularly maintained, as is the English, drama and music departments' equipment. While the philosophy, anthropology, economics, political science and language departments do not have as much new equipment, they do have continuous access to all necessary technology and supplies. The language departments and intro. classes all demand computer access and have mandatory computer lab activity.

 ## Social Life

Alumnus/a, English, 9/2002-6/2006, September 2007

So yes, there is one bar—the Gambier Grill—and when you finally turn 21 and are allowed in, it's like Cheers, only drunker and better. The food in Ohio is not spectacular. Luckily there are a few new places on campus. I worked for three years at Middle Ground Cafe and it was my savior. Joel and Margaret (who opened the Cafe and redid the Village Inn just recently) have given so much to the village—a real coffee shop environment where kids would spend all day sitting on the couches, or all night studying at tables. The food is excellent, most of it organic and locally grown. We love them and everything they do.

Let's see, the dating scene when I was there was dominated by being "Kenyon married," which was a group that began dating the first few months freshman year and were still together upon graduation. That's the way it is at Kenyon—you develop such intimate bonds that it often feels like being married. I've heard that a ridiculous number of Kenyon couple often end up getting married and I don't doubt it. On the other hand, there is a singles' scene, but by the time you are a senior, most of the eligible students are more like your brother or cousin—that's why it's so exciting when the freshmen come. I will also say that, for the middle of Ohio, there are so many attractive and wealthy people from the East and West Coasts. I know, it's gross.

I doubt my life will ever attain the perfection that it did at Kenyon. It's like being in a dream. That said, having been in the "real world" for over a year, it is actually a dream. It is a bubble (the Kenyon bubble), a beautiful bubble, but nonetheless pretend. Full of kids from the East Coast, but its core remains a little rebellious, adventurous and pure. It is for people truly interested in a classic liberal arts education—scholars, writers, poets, and people drawn to the intensity and passion of the place.

Alumnus/a, History, 8/2001-5/2005, September 2007

With Kenyon being a school with about 1,500 students, it's very easy to make friends. Everyone knows you whether you like it or not. As a result, everyone

seems to know about everyone else's social life. With the advent of Facebook no action goes unnoticed. Because of the small feel to the school, some people would say cliques form very easily, which is true. However, the cliques int mingle freely and amicably with each other. Rivalries form but they are oft all in good fun. There are two or three bars on campus that can fill up very easily on a weekend night and provide for a great time (especially when you're paying $2.00 for a cocktail). The college is also very mindful of providing non-alcohol related events to students who choose to have a more relaxing evening lifestyle.

Restaurants are sparse, but the nearby town of Mount Vernon provides every food imaginable as well as an array of delivery options. Dating is a touchy issue at Kenyon. Hook-ups are frequent and unremorseful. Relationships are common and a source of sanity. It's pretty common knowledge that Kenyon is one of those college's where 99.999 percent of its alumni marry other Kenyon alumni. Greek life is an option for both men and women and about 30 percent of students belong to Greek organizations. Parties are inclusive, so anyone (Greek non-Greek) can attend. Some students disdain Greek life but it actually provide the backbone for much of the school's social life. Fraternity men range in personality from John Belushi in *Animal House* to *Revenge of the Nerds*. What nice about Greek life at Kenyon is that it's there if you want it, and if you dor it's easy to turn it off and pretend it doesn't exist.

Alumnus/a, Psychology, 8/2002-5/2006, September 2007

When I was there there was only one bar on campus and it was amazing. No there are two but you can't beat the prices and the drinks at the Cove (I think new name is the Gambier Grill but for those of us there before it will always the Cove). The bar has great bar food too and the service is Kenyon students a some locals who are really great people. The Kenyon Inn is the nice place to on campus but now that the Village Inn and Middle Ground are there, you ha some options.

The Greek system is huge for guys and a joke for women, but definitely r something you have to join to have fun. The independents and frat guys all par together with no divide between them. The parties are open to everyone and t scene is classic, perfect college. Dating doesn't really happen in terms of as ing someone random out for dinner. Generally people meet at parties and th continue that trend until they decide they are dating. Wednesday is the big par night at Kenyon, along with Friday and Saturday, so don't take an early class Thursdays ever. There really is no better place to go to school and I keep goi back to visit because it never changes. I would rank Kenyon as the greatest pla on earth and couldn't have asked for a better college experience.

Alumnus/a, Liberal Arts, 9/2001-5/2005, September 2007

There are two bars on campus, one is called the Cove and the other is the Villa Inn. Only 21 year-olds and over can go. Options other than the dining h include a market (groceries and small snacks), gourmet deli (sandwiches, sala breakfast), the Kenyon Inn restaurant, the Village Inn (bar-type food) and Mid Ground (health conscious food). While people do date at Kenyon, most peop meet out at parties.

Greek life—there is a variety of fraternities and a few sororities. Most sororit are not joined by the females on the campus and the sororities are not a sour of nightlife. Fraternities, on the other hand, are a huge source of the nightli Members of fraternities do not live in their fraternity houses but instead can c to live in sections of dorms that are designated to each fraternity. While ma males on campus do join fraternities, many remain independents and have sa that they do not feel like they were deprived of a social life having not joined

 ## The School Says

You can't describe a feast with a mere list of ingredients, but it's worth noting a few of Kenyon's distinctive features. Kenyon's faculty consists of superb professors, virtually all of whom hold the PhD or other terminal degree in their field. Smart and creative students with an astonishing range of interests find themselves at home here. The college boasts what we think of as a perfect smallness: Kenyon's 1,600 students thrive in small classes, have fun creating a close-knit community, and get to know their professors as teachers, mentors and friends. Professors and advisors are remarkably accessible. The average class size is 14. The student-to-faculty ratio is 9:1.

Academic life is characterized by a spirit of collaboration with other students and with professors. Kenyon offers you a thorough grounding in the traditional liberal arts and sciences, with an emphasis on critical thinking and strong writing. The flexible curriculum gives students the opportunity to go deep, through majors, individual research and group projects, and also the opportunity to go wide, through interdisciplinary programs and perspectives. Whatever their major, all seniors consolidate their learning in a capstone experience known as the senior exercise. About 40 percent of students study off campus in one of 170 approved programs in more than 70 countries. Kenyon sponsors three off-campus study programs of its own in England, Honduras and Italy.

Kenyon's stone halls and comfortable cottages occupy 1,000 acres of hilltop and shaded lawn in central Ohio, forming one of the most beautiful campuses anywhere. Founded in 1824,

Kenyon cherishes its history as the oldest private institution of higher education in Ohio. The campus is on the National Register of Historic Places. 21st Century facilities for science and music grace the campus, and a spectacular $60 million center for fitness, recreation and athletics opens in the winter of 2005.

Students lead and participate in more than 100 existing clubs and organizations, and forming new clubs is easy to do. The campus life hums at a lively pace, with a full roster of dramatic productions, film screenings, musical performances and art exhibitions. About 30 percent of students compete on varsity sports teams (11 women's, 11 men's, in Division III), and many more play club and intramural sports. More Kenyon scholar-athletes have gone on to win NCAA Postgraduate Fellowships than alumni of any other Division III school.

The Office of Admissions strongly urges interested students to visit campus and, if at all possible, seniors should interview.

Miami University

iami University
ffice of Admission
)1 S. Campus Avenue
xford, OH 45056-3434
dmissions phone: (513) 529-2531
dmissions questions: www.muohio.edu/askacounselor

 Admissions

urrent student, English, 8/2002-Submit Date, November 2006

irst heard about Miami through a mailer that I received during my junior year high school. The campus looked like a beautiful campus and the classes emed to be what I wanted. I applied in the fall of my senior year. Many of the dents here have similar GPAs averaging about 3.5 on a 4.0 scale. SAT scores d ACT scores are also above average. Most students were very involved in any activities in high school, including community service, sports, decorating mmittees, student council and many other various organizations. No inter-w was necessary for my entry because I was not expecting any scholarships special placement while attending. The essay was pretty basic. A willingness become involved in one or more aspects of the university was held in high gard. Being a minority could help greatly because Miami is not known for its versity.

umnus/a, 8/2000-5/2004, October 2006

e easiest way to get into Miami is to apply for admission into one of their anch campuses in Middletown Ohio or Hamilton Ohio. Both of these cam-ses have open enrollment, and after you complete several semesters at one of e branch campuses you can go to the Oxford Campus no questions asked. A t of the professors teach the same courses on all three campuses. Tuition on e branch campuses is approximately half of that at Oxford and all the credits nsfer with no fuss. Many students take classes at more than one campus at a me.

urrent student, 1/2002-Submit Date, May 2006

iami considers every aspect of a student when it reviews applications. While AT/ACT scores are important, it is important that a student is well rounded, ique, and has something to offer to the student body. It is wise for students ho are sure they want to attend Miami to apply Early Decision because over lf of the incoming class is accepted Early Decision during the admissions ocess.

Current student, 8/2004-Submit Date, May 2006

The admissions process at Miami is excellent. The requirements were clear cut, easy to understand, and not too time-consuming. I did not interview. I did priority notification, which was not binding, but informed me of my acceptance in much sooner than had I done Regular Decision. I really like how Miami does that.

Current student, 8/2003-Submit Date, January 2006

It is a typical admissions process. You fill out a paper application, send a high school transcript, and write an essay. You may submit an additional essay to apply for the Honors Program. Your regular application also puts you in the running for the Oxford Scholar program that offers a scholarship of $1,000/year renewable for four years. The typical ACT score is about 27. It is a school of mostly Ohio residents, but is not very selective if you have good grades and the average test scores.

Current student, 8/2005-Submit Date, May 2006

Miami University is commonly referred to as the Harvard of the Midwest. Not only is it considered one of the most beautiful campuses in the nation, but its academics rival that of the top public schools. Because of this, Miami University is known to be a highly selective university when it comes to getting in. The school isn't just looking for high GPA; it is involvement in various sports, clubs and extracurricular activities throughout high school. The more involved you are, the better your chances are of being accepted. The application can be found easily on the Miami University web site, but be prepared. The essays are definitely going to require much thought and consideration, but they aren't impossible. Just make sure everything on the application is correct and the essays are creative, thorough and revised before turning them in. Once you've shown them what a bright, well-rounded student you are, all you need to do is wait until the day when they welcome you into the Miami family!

Current student, 8/2003-Submit Date, April 2006

The admissions process was relatively easy. Just one simple essay, ACT scores and high school transcripts were all that was necessary. I didn't conduct an interview and to be honest, I'm not that sure that interviews are all that common. Typically, you can come to a campus visit but there is no formal interview process, at least not one that I am aware of. Miami overall isn't the most selective university. Someone with a 3.5 GPA in high school and an ACT between 26 to 29 should be fine.

Read all of Vault's College Surveys at www.vault.com/college—get complete surveys on 100s of colleges and univer-sities, expert advice on applicaton essays and more.

VAULT CAREER LIBRARY   555

Alumnus/a, 8/2000-5/2004, March 2005

The admissions process at Miami has been evolving over the past several years as they have been toying with tuition numbers. In doing so, they have really tried to improve financial aid and scholarship offers, which were abysmal five years ago, but now actually can make a difference. My most valuable advice here would be to keep them updated through second semester of your senior year. I was unhappy with my scholarship amount and sent them an update letter of things I had done since applying, and also pleading my case a bit. To my amazement, they made my scholarship renewable for all four years, which is what allowed me to attend.

Current student, 8/2003-Submit Date, May 2004

My main advice on getting into Miami is to start early. Go and visit the college, and you will fall in love with its campus. The campus is just one of the many things to fall in love with about this school. The admissions process was not a very difficult one. I recommend trying to set up an interview or a meeting with someone in the field into which you are looking. I think that this could alleviate some of the fears that you might have about choosing a career or a path to start down. I had a difficult time finding the right path for me, and the people were always there to help, I just had to make sure I could find them and went out of my way to make sure they knew me. The essay was not very difficult for me. I simply wrote what was in my heart and told them a story of what I thought was why I wanted to go to school there. Just tell them what you really think. If you are honest, it will show, and I think that that will really help your chances. Make sure to bring up all your good qualities. If you are a little weak in one area, that will not keep you out, because you can tell them all the other reasons that they would love to have you.

Academics

Alumnus/a, 8/2000-5/2004, October 2006

The undergraduate program at Miami is hard. Expect to study about one hour outside of class for every hour spent in class at first and then about two to three hours outside class for every hour in class for some of the upper-level courses. Some degree programs are considered much easier than others at Miami. Business, Psychology and Geography are all considered very easy to get through. Most other programs are very difficult, rigorous and thorough. The 100-level classes are generally taught in large auditoriums, with the exception of English courses. Every course after the 100 level is taught in regular classrooms with an average of 15 to 20 students per class. Most of the professors and staff are great. I rarely had a prof who didn't want to help me out with assignments. They really care.

Current student, English, 8/2002-Submit Date, November 2006

The quality of classes here is outstanding. The professors make classes both interesting and entertaining. There are always exceptions to this rule, but that is to be expected at any institution. There are a wide variety of classes available to students and many majors offered. Students at Miami are required to fulfill the Miami Plan which consists of about 32 credit hours in all disciplines. Required classes within the plan range from arts to history, to science and English. There are some classes that fit into both the Miami Plan and departmental major requirements. Classes are chosen by students via online registration. Certain classes, especially upper-level courses, have pre-requisites or hold seats for upperclassmen. The order in which students get to choose classes is based entirely on credit hours. Meaning that it is harder for a freshman to get every class he/she wants at the times he/she wants, whereas a junior or senior can more easily choose a schedule that is perfect for him/her. When I was a freshman, making a decent class schedule was stressful. Now that I am a senior, it is the easiest part of my education. Classes here have been getting more difficult over the past couple of years and the university has been cutting out some of the classes that are deemed unnecessary to higher education.

The grading at Miami is pretty fair. Large lecture classes oftentimes have departmental exams to ensure fairness for all taking the class regardless of the professor. Smaller classes can cause a few more problems when it comes to fairness. Two professors teaching the same class may require very different things from their students, which causes a gap between the two classes overall GPAs. Professors at Miami are very approachable and most are very willing to help stu-

dents with whatever is troubling them. It is not uncommon for a student to [have] lunch with a professor and aside from large lecture classes, most professors a[nd] students can exchange friendly greetings on the street because many professor[s] know their students by face and name.

The workload varies greatly depending on the student's major. Some major[s] may require a greater number of papers and have few exams, which allows [a] student more freedom in choosing how to budget his/her time. Other major[s] may require many homework assignments, reading assignments and exam[s]. This isn't really a problem.

Current student, 1/2002-Submit Date, May 2006

Miami's classes are challenging, but interesting. Professors teach the class[es] rather than graduate assistants, with the exception of lab sciences. Professo[rs] truly make an effort to meet and get to know their students. Grading is str[ict] depending on the major. A's are not handed out. The workload is pretty inten[se] for some classes, but that also depends on one's major. Scheduling is a pain, b[ut] it is usually very easy to force/add into classes.

Current student, 8/2002-Submit Date, May 2006

Miami's academic reputation continues to get better every year and most recen[t]ly the Richard T. Farmer School of Business, of which I am a part, was rank[ed] as the Number 17 undergraduate business school in the country [by] *BusinessWeek*. The professors here often have practical, real-world experien[ce] in the subjects they are teaching, so it is engaging to hear their stories and pe[r]sonal examples. Grading is challenging but fair. There has been a big push [by] administration to crack down on grade inflation and professors encourage a l[ot] of class participation to improve final grades. The thing I love most abo[ut] Miami is that a cutthroat mentality does not exist here with regards to academ[]ics. Everyone wants to do well, but not at the expense of another student. Stud[y] groups and team projects are very common and there is always someone you c[an] get notes from if you miss class.

Current student, 8/2005-Submit Date, May 2006

Professors range at Miami. They will either be forgetful and boring or the mo[st] interesting, engaging person ever. I have had some amazing professors wh[o] answer e-mails all day and night and really are interested in you as a person, n[ot] just as a kid in their class. The Western College Program is the real gem with[in] the university. It is the small East Coast liberal arts school you wish you cou[ld] have gone to, but couldn't afford. In a sea of conformity at Miami, it stands o[ut.] You learn real world, very interdisciplinary skills that otherwise would be ove[r]looked. This program makes the things you learn applicable and relevant to yo[ur] everyday life.

Employment Prospects

Current student, 1/2002-Submit Date, May 2006

Recruiters ranked Miami third in the nation for how much they like Miami grad[s.] Recruiters come to campus for two major career fairs and interview students [on] campus at the career center. The alumni network is a major support for curre[nt] students for scholarships, busing to the airport, and connections to new cities [and] jobs. In the business school, it is very popular to get an internship. Many stu[]dents have internships in order to secure a job after graduation. Students a[re] generally successful in landing jobs with companies such as Big Four account[]ing firms, Target, Proctor & Gamble, Cintas, ESPN, and many other companie[s.]

Current student, English, 8/2002-Submit Date, November 2006

Depending on the major, employment opportunities vary greatly. Business stu[]dents can easily find employment at large companies and Procter & Gambl[e] hires a lot of Miami grads due to its close proximity to the university and th[e] quality of Miami's graduates. Other majors can easily find jobs, although the[y] may not be as prestigious. Writing majors, like me, can get internships wi[th] magazines and literary publishers that can easily develop into a care[er.] Education and communication majors can easily find work in their respecti[ve] fields. Many communication majors choose to work in a political office of som[e] sort. Most jobs obtained regardless of major are entry-level. Alumni have [a] strong connection to Miami due in part to the feeling of community that Miam[i] provides.

ere are many different alumni groups and networks that help with placing
duates. Career fairs and workshops seem to be held weekly where hundreds
potential employers come to recruit for internships and permanent positions.
ese events are open to all students regardless of major or year.

umnus/a, 8/2000-5/2004, October 2006

ami is well-respected regionally. The on-campus recruiting and career serv-
s department is very good. Business degrees are very well-received with
ional employers.

rrent student, 8/2003-Submit Date, April 2006

throughout orientation, I was told how Miami is one of the original public
es. However, I am currently a junior who is looking for an internship in
estment banking and I beginning to realize that I don't have the same oppor-
ities as my counterparts at the Ivy League. Another problem Miami has is
t it has very low minority enrollment. This has major implications on the job
look since many employers who have U.S. Government contracts must have
affirmative action plan where they target institutions that have high enroll-
nts of minorities; since Miami's minority population is among the lowest in
country, it is very unattractive place to recruit.

Quality of Life

rrent student, English, 8/2002-Submit Date, November 2006

freshmen entering the university are required to live in on-campus residence
ls. Many of the residence halls are themed living communities that encour-
 students to become involved with their residence halls and the university.
sidence halls are well maintained and there are many dining locations that are
of great quality. Such great quality in fact, that students who live off-campus
ularly eat on campus because it is equally as good as a restaurant. Many stu-
nts choose to live on campus their sophomore year although they are not
uired. By the third year, most students have moved off campus into houses
 apartments. Off-campus housing is a very big business around Miami and
dents oftentimes have to bid on the house that they want. Students who live
houses name their house and place signs on the houses displaying their cre-
ve names. Some of my favorites are a green house with ivy growing on the
e that is named, The Ivy League, and a house right across the street from cam-
s that is named, Hooterville.

e facilities on campus are great. The main library is very modern and is cur-
tly adding a Starbucks in the basement. The other libraries are also very mod-
. The recreational center is a staple of many students' daily lives. It contains
Olympic-sized swimming pool, a dive tank, a large hot tub, lazy river, indoor
ck, many basketball and racquetball courts, a climbing wall, plenty of weight
chines and up-to-date exercise equipment. There are about 15 to 20 fitness
sses offered daily that range from yoga to ultimate kickboxing and dance.
ese classes cost extra, but a pass can be purchased for a fair price. The num-
 one complaint about the recreational center is that students must sign up for
5-minute time slot to use the exercise equipment due to an excessive number
users.

ami just built a brand-new ice arena with a larger hockey arena and two sep-
te broomball rinks for intramural sports. Next to the new ice arena is the uni-
rsity's first parking garage. Students are not allowed to park their cars on cam-
s (with the exception of two large parking lots on the edges of campus) until
y are a junior living on campus. Freshmen are not permitted to bring their
s on campus without special consent. This is to relieve traffic congestion and
ke the atmosphere of campus more pleasing. Handicap students and faculty
 access all buildings, but it takes some effort. Students at Miami feel safe
h on campus and uptown where the bars and restaurants are. All students are
tified of crimes that take place on and off campus through an e-mail sent out
soon as possible with suspect information and a description of the crime.

umnus/a, 8/2000-5/2004, October 2006

e dorms are pretty standard. There is plenty of off-campus housing available
 the town of Oxford. The campus is gorgeous. It looks like the typical Ivy
ague college that you see in movies and on T.V. The rec center is topnotch.

Oxford is a great little college town. Crime is relatively rare. The food is very
good. There are many choices in the dining halls. Vegetarian and vegen diets
are easily accommodated.

Social Life

Alumnus/a, 8/2000-5/2004, October 2006

The bars in uptown Oxford are typical college atmosphere places. Steinkeller's
is a great German themed bar with excellent beer. Brick Street is the place to go
if you like the club scene. Mac and Joe's is a good all-around place to get a beer.
There are good restaurants all over Oxford and in the neighboring towns.
Cincinnati is only 40 miles away.

Current student, English, 8/2002-Submit Date, November 2006

Students at Miami work very hard and party harder. There are over 20 bars and
dance clubs available to students within walking distance. The area to which
students flock for happy hour, nightlife and to enjoy a meal with friends is called
uptown. Of the 20+ bars, I would consider six of them to be dance clubs as well.
The bars are always crowded with students regardless of the night. The dating
scene seems to be lacking and most students aim instead for one-night stands
while at the clubs and bars. Most students meet dates and develop lasting relationships through classes, organizations and smaller house parties. Miami is trying very hard to deter students from drinking and have had a Friday night event
called, After Dark, for years. After Dark provides alternative fun to drinking
through game nights, casino nights, free food and a twice-nightly movie. The
ice arena offers midnight skating many Fridays and there are many cultural
events going on throughout campus. Many of the cultural events are well-
attended, but rarely sold out. Theatre department plays and large concerts are
best-attended.

Miami has a very large Greek system. There are over 50 social fraternity and
sorority organizations at Miami. Five of which got their start here. First-year
students are required to wait until their second semester to rush. Miami does this
so that students have the opportunity to adjust to college life before joining the
Greek life. I am grateful for this. Had rush happened in the fall, I may have
joined a sorority and then I my life would have been completely different. My
college experience has been everything I expected it to be and had I joined a
sorority early on, I may have never joined a club sport and then may have never
traveled as much and been able to meet as many interesting people from other
schools.

Current student, 1/2002-Submit Date, May 2006

Miami of Ohio is located in the quintessential college town with plenty to do. In
a small town, students make their own fun. There are about 18 bars that range
from sit down to club style with dancing. Each one has its own personality.
There are lots of mom-and-pop restaurants that complement the traditional fast
food favorites of college students. The Greek system is not huge, but it has a
presence. 30 to 33 percent of the students are Greek, but since the students rush
second semester, there is no segregation between Greeks and independents.
Dating is also popular on campus. Miami has an incredibly high rate of students
who get married to each other that hovers around 16 percent. Students like to go
to restaurants, such as Bagel and Deli, Pita Pit, and Brunos for a late-night slice
of pizza. Popular bars are Brick Street, 45 East, Skippers, Steinkellers and
Stadium. Brickstreet and 45 East have themed nights every night of the week,
such as Country Night, 80's Night and Ladies' Night.

Current student, 8/2003-Submit Date, April 2006

Since Miami is in the middle of a corn field, expect to do a lot of drinking in your
spare time. The Greek life here runs supreme even though they only make up
about 30 percent of the student population. Clubs are very prevalent. I competed on the forensic team (speech team), which is considered to be one of the best
in the county. If you are a guy, you will be very interested in knowing that
Miami University was ranked in the Top Five by *Playboy* for having the most
attractive female student population, so if you do go here try to date as much as
possible.

Read all of Vault's College Surveys at **www.vault.com/college**—get complete surveys on 100s of colleges and universities, expert advice on applicaton essays and more.

VAULT CAREER LIBRARY **557**

Oberlin College

Admissions Office
Carnegie Building
101 N. Professor Street
Oberlin, OH 44074-1075
Admissions phone: (800) 622-6243
Admissions fax: (440) 775-6905
Admissions e-mail: college.admissions@oberlin.edu
Admissions URL: www.oberlin.edu/coladm/

 Admissions

Current student, 9/2004-Submit Date, May 2007

Oberlin students have a unique enthusiasm, an intellectual/worldly curiosity and diverse interests. Admissions evaluates how a person would fit into the "bubble," and most students have high to very high SAT scores, over 3.5 GPAs, and try to express why they are already "Obie" in their essays. It is one of the best liberal arts colleges, and it is very selective. Many people try to visit and do interviews, and I think this helps the student more than it aids the school. Students can tell if they feel comfortable and excited here.

Current student, 9/2003-Submit Date, May 2007

The applicant pool is the "most selective" in the country. Each student applying to Oberlin is also applying to Brown, Harvard, Swarthmore, Wesleyan, and Yale. In addition, the heavy influence of international students from China, India, Eastern Europe and Africa increase the selectivity to oxygen-deprecating heights. The process includes multiple essays, test scores, interviews and serious recommendations. The holistic process aims to make sure each incoming "Obie" is prepared to think critically, study hard, engage with the world, and simultaneously be involved with music, the arts, and student activism both locally and globally. The process is Darwinian: only the strongest survive!

Alumnus, 9/1989-6/1993, January 2006

The admissions process is rather rigorous. They take the essays and the interview slightly more seriously than some places and place a strong emphasis on excellent writing skills and a social conscience. Oberlin has a proud tradition of being a socially political school and they very much welcome people who are invested in the world around them. Oberlin is definitely not for everyone—while it is a bucolic campus in northern Ohio, it is a very intense place. People study four hours a day at the minimum but socialize just as much. Make sure you visit to make certain Oberlin is right for you. They are fairly selective but a more modest SAT score (combined 1250 or less) shouldn't prohibit you from applying if you believe it's the right match. A recommendation from an alum goes a long way as well. They have slightly less endowment than some schools in terms of financial aid but will do their best to meet your needs—it can be a struggle however. It's run by a wonderfully approachable president now who is strong administrator with a scholarly background. And she cares deeply about the school.

Alumnus/a, 8/1998-5/2002, October 2004

The admissions process at Oberlin is very typical of any small liberal arts college—however, several factors are taken into account that are usually overlooked by a number of higher education institutions. Oberlin isn't a school that just talks about diversity, it is an institution that is truly committed to diversity. This could explain why many publications often name it among the most desirable colleges for African-American students. Oberlin strives to recruit well-rounded students as opposed to focusing on GPA or standardized test scores, and this shows across the student body. The thing that could help a potential student get into Oberlin the most would be complete and total honesty. The admissions staff greatly values this in students and those who are the most honest are often the ones who are accepted.

Alumnus/a, 9/1996-5/2001, August 2004

I was really impressed with one aspect of Oberlin's admissions process: an es we had to write describing why we decided to apply to the college and what academic and personal goals would be while there. I believe that was one of nicest moments of my college application process, because I had the opportu ty to reveal aspects of my self that I was too intimidated to reveal in the ap cation essays.

Alumnus/a, 8/1997-5/2002, July 2004

The admissions process was similar to most other liberal arts schools. You to fill out an application, turn in standardized test results and write an essay. interview was probably one of the most important aspects. The school is lo ing for creative thinkers who enjoy challenging traditional thought process. selectivity definitely depends on the year. It is a fairly selective school, but e if your academics are so-so you still have a good chance of getting Interesting and varied extracurricular activities are big for this admissions offi

 Academics

Current student, 9/2004-Submit Date, May 2007

Oberlin has incredible professors. They are interested in their students and p sionate about their fields of study. It takes a lot for a distinguished academic choose to be in northern Ohio, and I think this bonds students and professors a way, because there's something that draws us and keeps us here. The prof sors make themselves available and teach very good courses. Most classes very small. They can range from three students to 100. But most are betwe 10 and 22. Persistence will get you into almost any class, but there is not a co petitive environment. The workload is significant, and academic interests beyond the classroom and are extremely prevalent in the social scene. It is r orous and rewarding.

Current student, 9/2003-Submit Date, May 2007

The word on the street indicates that graduate school is a joke compared Oberlin classes. Classes at Oberlin are not merely lectures but intellectual w fare. If you want to argue the injustice of Rousseau's social contract, how ge der is a social construct, or the advantages of the free market economy, th bring your books because students and faculty are both open-minded and w ing to vocally support their arguments without hesitation. The classes are ir mate and it is not uncommon for students to grab lunch or a beer with a prof sor after class. There is a cooperative nature where students and faculty wc together to promote academic growth and development. Zero grade inflati Everyone goes to top graduate programs and those programs know abc Oberlin's zero grade inflation policy.

Alumnus/a, 9/2003-12/2006, May 2007

A teacher's enthusiasm for the material sinks right into you in the small class With plans to go to medical school and 75 percent of a Biology major compl as a sophomore, I took a class on the history and structure of the English la guage. We covered linguistics, history, and learned Old and Middle English foreign languages. Every day, the professor approached the class with a bubb mood that made the material intriguing and endlessly fascinating. Thanks to t class, I'm now an English major, though with many near switches thanks to bic ogy, classics, politics, and economics teachers who all threw themselves into classes. The classes were uniformly intense and challenging.

The registration system was at first frustrating, because it sometimes necessit ed getting approval for the class and actually talking to a professor beforehar This contributed to the notion that professors are actually people, which d turbed me as a first year. The registration system itself was a terrific learni tool. Sometimes what it took to get into that film seminar or the exclusi Middle East history class was dropping by the professor's office hours enou times the semester before along with frequent and sincere e-mailing: skills t are helpful now that I'm looking for jobs.

Alumnus/a, 9/1989-6/1993, January 2006

...e academics are very strong in this school, particularly in music (they boast a ...nowned music conservatory). The classes tend to stay on the small size and ...professors take their students seriously and make themselves readily available ...tside of class. The popular classes are popular, meaning they can take some ...aneuvering to get into. The grading is rather intense, an average student will ...t a C for doing average work—there are no courtesy B's. The workload can ...formidable so this school is not appropriate for someone who wants to get by ...ing the minimum because it will become too easy to fall behind. Half the stu...nts there arrived from the world's most prestigious private schools and they ...e ready to work.

Alumnus/a, 8/1998-5/2002, October 2004

...e workload at Oberlin depends a great deal on your major. Certain programs, ...ch as psychology are very difficult whereas the sociology program is usually ...ought of as being very easy. The quality of classes is exceptional and you can ...ways depend on your professor being available outside of regular classroom ...urs—many professors even make their home phone numbers public so that ...dents may reach them at any time and for academic emergencies. It is quite ...sy to get into the classes that you desire and the grading is quite rigid but fair.

Alumnus/a, 9/1996-5/2001, August 2004

...was a studio art major. The classes were pretty great, but then again, I studied ...der specific professors whom I knew were great people. The main complaint ...ave toward the curriculum (and it's one that even the professors share) is that ...re isn't enough technique in the instruction. Since Oberlin's a liberal arts col...ge (vs. an art school), there was an imbalance in the focus of the instruction. ...was directed toward the ephemeral, the feelings, the intention of the artist, and ...the actual craft of bookmaking, woodworking or painting was put by the way-...de.

...was really difficult to get into the popular classes. The school, at the time, did-...t have enough studio space to accommodate all the students, so unless you ...re an art major, you had to be content with being on the waiting list.

...ading was difficult, but fair. A C at Oberlin was a B anywhere else. It was ...re to have an easy teacher, and none that I knew of had that reputation; it was ...fficult to get an A, but therefore much more rewarding if/when I received a B+ ...A-.

Alumnus/a, 8/1997-5/2002, July 2004

...berlin has some very good departments and some not so good departments. ...e East Asian Studies department is a fairly strong one. It has professors who ...e really passionate about teaching. I also heard very good things about biolo-..., creative writing and religion. Oberlin is best known for its conservatory and ...environmental studies department. From what I could see, the conservatory ...excellent. The jazz department is getting better. People have mixed feelings ...out the environmental studies department. The classes are impossible to get ...o unless you are a major, and even then it can be difficult. Getting into class-...can be a challenge if they are popular. Persistence almost always gets you ...re, but it's always up to the professor. I knew seniors who couldn't get into ...sses they needed to graduate. Grading is fair and on the easy end, as well as ...orkload. But like anything, this depends on the class and the department. Over ...y four years, I took some absolutely spectacular classes and some absolutely ...rrible classes. The best approach to taking classes at Oberlin is to pick them ...sed on the professor, rather than the subject.

 Employment Prospects

...urrent student, 9/2004-Submit Date, May 2007

...berlin produces more graduate students than any other undergraduate institu-...n. Many graduates are interested in obtaining their master's or doctorate. The ...bs graduates obtain after college are just as diverse as the students themselves. ...y friends who have graduated are research scientists, sports analysts, medical ...hool students, graduate students and journalists. The students who graduate ...th honors tend to have jobs lined up before graduation, but they usually have ...veloped a specific focus. Alumni are very connected with the school and ...reer services help greatly with students and alumni networking.

Current student, 9/2003-Submit Date, May 2007

The Oberlin family is well-connected. Where a maroon and yellow Oberlin t-shirt in Central Park, out to eat in San Fran, or at ball game at Fenway, and you will find more Obies than you know what to do with. Oberlin alumni take care of the students and hook them up with internships and jobs. Moreover, the Oberlin degree guarantees you placement into a top graduate program and near-ly a handful of job offers in government, education, and social activism when your time is up. On-campus recruiting is impressive with major firms flocking to the mid-west to interview students and get their hands on potential future employees.

Alumnus/a, 9/1989-6/1993, January 2006

The alumni network is loose but the friends and colleagues I currently have are largely from Oberlin. Almost everyone I know went on to graduate school (in fact over 93 percent of Oberlin graduates do get in to grad schools of their choice). It seems to put a smile on the faces of employers, which can help open doors. On-campus recruiting is a bit weak. Most go on to graduate school and then get work.

Alumnus/a, 9/1996-5/2001, August 2004

Oberlin College itself had a wealth of employment and internship resources. They participate in the GLCA NY Arts Program (GLCA = Great Lakes Colleges Association, I think), which is how I fell into my internships.

If I meet someone "important" who knows of Oberlin, it's great. However, many people haven't heard of this place. Many employers that I have met know only of the Ivies or the local colleges.

Alumnus/a, 8/1997-5/2002, July 2004

Oberlin has enough prestige to get you almost any sort of job if you have the ambition. The only difficult thing about going to a liberal arts school is that it does not necessarily provide you with the tools for the workforce. The educa-tion provides an incredible basis for having a full and healthy life, but those first couple years out of school can be difficult in terms of finding good, challenging work.

 Quality of Life

Current student, 9/2004-Submit Date, May 2007

Oberlin is a "bubble." We are in a small town and love the school because of the people who come from vastly different regions, states, countries, backgrounds, interests and ideas. The campus is beautiful and there are lakes, an arboretum, fields and farms. The dorms and cooperatives and village housing provide a range of options for students looking for specific communities: small or large, intimate or independent, quiet or fun. I feel very safe, the campus is well-lit and there are emergency phones everywhere and we personally know the security officers. The architecture varies greatly, and although the gym is dated there is an incredible science center, environmental science center, and beautiful per-formance halls that are old and modern.

Current student, 9/2003-Submit Date, May 2007

Granted, Oberlin is not in New York City or on Wilshire Blvd. But, the subur-ban nature of Oberlin shines with students and faculty from all over the world. Not for a minute will you realize you are in the Midwest. Why? Because your so deep in work, going to your friend's recital, tutoring in the public schools, and lining up your summer internship in New York or London. During election sea-sons, the weekends are spent traveling to help with campaigns, attending rallies in D.C., or quick trips to Cleveland for concert or a ball game.

Alumnus/a, 9/2003-12/2006, May 2007

The housing at Oberlin has been nice. It wasn't beautiful, but it was entirely ade-quate, and I spent very little time in my room anyhow. It was easy to get involved in the administration, and I didn't have much of a challenge getting jobs in the ResLife office and as an RA, so I feel like I got to contribute and improve the dorms. The food on campus is terrific, and I appreciate it so much more now that I'm cooking for myself. I really miss the local, organic produce and the terrific dining hall salad bar that gets re-stocked every few minutes. The large co-op system in Oberlin also made for fun variety. I never had the patience to join a co-op full time, but I loved the chances to drop in and eat with my girl-

Read all of Vault's College Surveys at www.vault.com/college—get complete surveys on 100s of colleges and univer-sities, expert advice on applicaton essays and more.

VAULT CAREER LIBRARY 559

friend who worked in the Asia House co-op. The Asia House co-op has less variety and less time to eat than in a dining hall, but the food is fresher and more eclectic. Though I never officially joined, they're very informal and I could make up for eating there a few times a week by rolling pie crusts with a crew on Saturday nights. It was a blast. Also, the Amish people who drive their buggy from door-to-door selling fresh pies for $5 are almost entirely responsible for one of the best Friday nights I've ever had.

 ## Social Life

Current student, 9/2004-Submit Date, May 2007

Oberlin is a unique place filled with interesting, curious and engaging individuals, and that is what keeps everyone going through the winters and helps others find places that fit them better. There is a lot of creativity: music and art. It's a small campus, there is a bar downtown and a bar open late nights during the week in the student union. These are fun and lively settings, but you see all of your friends and many people you know. People like to dance and the best parties are at houses with a bumpin' dance floor and conversations in the corners, halls and outside. There is no Greek life at all, so everything is inclusive and there are six restaurants so you'll have your favorites and the staff will know them. There are always activities, lectures, film screenings, shows, concerts and performances. Because Oberlin students are very involved and have varying interests, I find myself eating at a co-op for a meal my friend planned and cooked, going to my roommate's field hockey game, my best friend's a cappella show, my co-worker's art show, a senior's fiction reading, the championship intramural softball game, and then to the town bar where I know two out of three people. This does mean that going on a date is like walking down the red carpet, but it provides a type of intimacy and community that can really make four college years meaningful and personal.

Current student, 9/2003-Submit Date, May 2007

The standard applies with house parties; however, the difference is that world class conservatory students bring the musical funk and jazz with their camp bands to entertain at the parties. Perhaps the largest resemblance to the Gre system is the co-op students, the ultimate frisbee team, and the OC Dems! Sor former high school prom kings, Oberlin just put you in the back of the line f the world-class jazz drummer and the girl who got teased for organizing com munity service events in high school!

Alumnus/a, 9/2003-12/2006, May 2007

The social life here is terrific, to the point that it makes you consider the arb trary nature of friendship. I still spend most of my time with my freshman ye roommates and the people who lived down the hall. Sometimes I feel like the people could have been exchanged with almost anybody else I've met on cam pus, and we'd be similarly close. I would have been comfortable living a hanging out in most of the dorms on campus, and the more I think about it, t more it makes me wish I had more time to spend here. Meeting girls is ea though it seems much easier when you're already dating somebody. I've had t best luck meeting girls when I'm not expecting it. Though I'd always try when I'd see a band at a house party on a weekend or at the semester camp dance parties at the college dance club, it's easier when you're working wi somebody at the college bowling lanes, or if you sit near a girl in the libra look up her address on facebook.com, and have a silent conversation insta message-ing from your laptops. But that could happen anywhere, I suppose. an arts and sciences student, one of the resources I take for granted most is t Conservatory. I tend to come across the same few dozen people in my week routine, and it's easy to forget that the Conservatory is even there. When thin feel stale, it can be nice to drop in on one of the thrice daily recitals, getting soda from the machine deep in the hallways of practice rooms, listening to v tuoso Connies (conservatory students) goofing off and playing with gara bands at parties, making them laughably talent-lopsided, or even study in t conservatory library. Forays into the conservatory can make Oberlin seem li a completely new place.

Ohio State University

Admissions Office
Enarson Hall
154 West 12th Avenue
Columbus, OH 43210
Admissions phone: (614) 292-3980
Admissions e-mail: askabuckeye@osu.edu
Admissions URL: undergrad.osu.edu/admissions/

 Admissions

Alumnus/a, Business, 9/2002-6/2006, April 2007

The interview process at OSU is pretty straightforward; the application consists of a form application (including GPA, SAT and so on) and an optional essay section.

> **Regarding essays, the school says:** "Essays are required of all applicants."

The best advice I can offer for getting in is to concentrate on your test scores, GPA, and ensure that you have participated in extracurricular activities. Ohio State is looking for well-rounded students who have not only academic potential but also leadership potential.

Current student, Business, 9/2004-Submit Date, April 2007

The admissions process was extremely easy despite the lack of an online system. With the online system available to students now, it is still user-friendly and efficient. As per getting into Ohio State, there is no interview; however, that means that you are judged by your application and that is your one chance. You are judged on your entire application, no one part is worth more than another, so be sure to highlight all of your activities, leadership, diversity (not just ethnic, but also choice of involvement, classes taken, sports, music, art, community service) and academics. If you are not strong in one area, be sure to place emphasis on another area that will balance out your weaknesses. Schools are looking for students who are well-rounded and who have more than just textbook knowledge to offer to the other students on campus.

Current student, Nursing, 9/2003-Submit Date, April 2007

I had a positive experience with the admissions process. I thought that the application was not too challenging, and knowing that they take a holistic view of your application, not just test scores and class rank, made it easier. The essays were fairly easy, and had no problem getting my application in by the early deadline.

Alumnus/a, Business, 3/2004-12/2006, April 2007

I transferred into OSU. The transfer process was very easy as long as you pay attention to the deadlines for submitting an application. It is very important to pay attention to criteria, the college requires. If you are well above those criteria, an essay really isn't worth your time. However, if you are on the border of the criteria an essay will help distinguish you from another candidate of similar measure. It will give you the chance to show what you've done outside of school and other things that may not be reflected in your application or on your transcript. OSU was known as the fall-back university when I was applying to college because "everyone" could get in. The university has become much more selective in its admissions process and if you really do what the experience of being a Buckeye it is important that you pay attention to increasing admissions requirements and do what you can to surpass those.

Alumnus/a, 9/2002-12/2006, December 2006

The admissions process seems fairly simple and Ohio State employs many strategies to recruit the best students. When I was recruited, and still today, the university uses "tele-counselors," regular students who are employed to contact recruits, answer questions and help determine their interests and impressions of the university.

The university continues to recruit better and better students, something like 11th consecutive best class of freshmen over the past 11 years. Test scores student abilities have also increased. This has thus increased selectivity Ohio State is fast losing its stereotype: "let everyone in," and is certainly becoming harder and harder to get into.

To provide access to all students, the university has employed a plan to all under-prepared students to enter a regional campus, build skills and perform ance, where they can then apply to transfer to the main campus in Columb This strategy seemed to be successful during my time at the school.

Current student, 9/2003-Submit Date, September 2006

Ohio State's application has become significantly more rigorous over the p few years. When I applied, there was an optional essay but now I believe the one or two required essays. I would certainly encourage those who are eligi to opt for the Honors or Scholars Program. The nice thing is that OSU rolling admissions so you don't have to wait until April to see if you've b accepted.

Alumnus/a, Engineering, 9/2000-6/2005, December 2006

I got in to OSU very easily, but I know now it is harder to get in. I just filled an application, sent it in and was accepted. I tried to get into the Honors Progr and was denied, even though I graduated high school with a 4.1 GPA.

 **Academics**

Alumnus/a, Business, 9/2002-6/2006, April 2007

I was impressed with the quality of the academic programs at OSU, especia given the size of the university. While some of my GEC (General Educat Courses) were in large lecture halls, my major courses were all in comforta classrooms. While at OSU I participated in the Honors Accounting Progra which pushed me to the limits of my academic potential. The skills I learned Honors Accounting, particularly related to problem solving, serve me well too in my current job.

Current student, Business, 9/2004-Submit Date, April 2007

The academics at Ohio State are absolutely amazing. It is not just a footb school. We have an undergraduate research office to provide students with re life material to supplement their textbooks; this occurs within your first year. provide students with hands-on work in their major so that they can make best decision about their major and career early on. If you do decide to chan your major, there are 170 other majors from which to choose on this camp alone (you can also create your own major). Early on, some of the more po lar classes will have waitlists, but each class you take fulfills a category: un that category, there are at least 30 other classes you can take, so view the wa list as an opportunity to branch out from what is popular and make your o path. The professors are amazing and internationally renowned—their inter tional experiences and research brings reality, culture and new experiences to classroom. The most important question is generally the size—yes, we have lectures, but they are always broken down into smaller sections of 20 student make a recitation at least one day a week so that students are not scared aw from asking questions or seeking help. College is supposed to be a challeng

Current student, Biology, 9/2004-Submit Date, April 2007

I am in an Honors Program working toward a BS in Biology. The Hon Program provides excellent professors, priority scheduling and its own advise which makes it very easy to get into popular classes. The workload is heavy classes in the major as well as general ed classes, but not overwhelming. M professors I have encountered have been ready and eager to teach and help s dents.

urrent student, Nursing, 9/2003-Submit Date, April 2007

heduling for classes is quite easy. The majority of classes that I have taken re have been great. I have had caring and passionate professors who are ways willing to meet with students and answer questions. It can be harder for unger students to get into popular classes, as our scheduling system is based a college rank. Students typically take three or four classes per quarter, which not too bad for time management.

urrent student, Political Science, 9/2005-Submit Date, April 2007

ith such a big university, there are going to be some large classes. The mis- nception is that this means you can't get help. There are also always lots of A and lots of tutor options. We get some of the greatest professors in the tion—most of them wrote the books they are teaching. It's awesome! The st part is the quarter system. You can take anything and get through it in 10 eeks. It means you get to take a lot of classes which is a great way to really ke some unusual things. I am in horseback riding right now and I love it!

lumnus/a, Business, 3/2004-12/2006, April 2007

SU is a research institute and it is important for students and applicants to real- e that. Because it is a research university many of the professors are very well ucated in their fields—they just can't communicate it to students in class. This n be very frustrating and for me, led to nights teaching myself many topics om textbooks. However, those same professors are usually excellent at swering individual questions during office hours and it is important you take vantage of those opportunities. It is difficult to get into extremely popular asses because class enrollment is based on your rank. However, the college of siness does a great job of helping get you into the classes you need during a rticular quarter in order to ensure you can keep in schedule.

nother comment I have about OSU is its size. Many people (parents especial-) are concerned about the availability of OSU professors and staff because of e size of classes. I can tell you that every professor is required to have office urs and I cannot count the number of professors who have handed out home one numbers and cell phone numbers for question purposes.

ne workload is what you make it to be. I took 21 to 23 credit hours every quar- r and graduated early. I also work 10 to 15 hours a week. This helped me to anage my time. I spent most weeknights doing homework, but was never vake past 1 a.m. (unless I wanted to be), and had my weekends to do things I anted to do. I think the workload becomes easier to manage the more you have do because you focus on getting things done when you know you are very asy. Another positive thing about OSU is the schedule of classes. Because the iversity is so big it tries to offer multiple sessions of most classes. So, if you y attention and schedule the right classes at the right times you can end up with Tuesday/Thursday schedule and have only two days of class. Or you can hedule yourself to have three day weekends every week and only have class onday through Thursday.

urrent student, 9/2004-Submit Date, December 2006

ne quality of classes at the Fisher College of Business is very good. It is more fficult to get into popular classes in the first two years but gets easier as you in ranking. Grading depends on the professor you have; and I think the GEC quirements are too extensive but you have lots of options as to which courses u would like to take to fulfill these requirements.

lumnus/a, 1/2000-6/2003, January 2007

lass quality varied from very strong to very poor. The professors who were est known and most respected often turned out to be the worst educators. Many ofessors are hired by the university due to their research abilities and are lack- g of any teaching skills. Classes became easier to get into as your class level .nior, senior and so on) increased. Being in the honors program also ensured at you were more likely to get into popular classes. Grading was generally .rly easy and professors were often willing to work with you if you needed ditional help if you showed initiative.

 Employment Prospects

Alumnus/a, Business, 9/2002-6/2006, April 2007

Employment prospects are very good coming from Ohio State. My particular experience was with the Fisher School of Business Career Services, which does an excellent job of bringing employers to campus to interview. I interviewed on campus with at least 15 companies, from various industries and was offered six job opportunities out of school. The offers my friend and I received were all very competitive offers.

Current student, Business, 9/2004-Submit Date, April 2007

Employment does not occur solely for graduates here at Ohio State. Every stu- dent who wants a job can usually find a job right here on this campus. If you want an internship or co-op experience, every major has its own office for preparing, recruiting, training and placing students into work experience. The alumni network spans the entire world producing a myriad of opportunities for students to take advantage of with ease. Most graduates can obtain a job imme- diately after graduating with the help of both of the resources mentioned above and most earn more money than those coming from other schools. I was hired as a freshman above eight professionals (all around 30 years of age) because my employer knew the caliber of the students at Ohio State.

Current student, Political Science, 9/2005-Submit Date, April 2007

Ohio State has the largest enrollment in the nation. This means a ton of compa- nies come here to look for future employees. There is also a huge alumni net- work for this reason, which OSU works really hard to keep updated to allow stu- dents to get in touch with people who may be helpful to them.

Current student, Biology, 9/2004-Submit Date, April 2007

The alumni network of Ohio State is unrivaled. The education you receive and the connections you make at this university prepare you for success immediate- ly, whether it be in continuing your education or finding employment. The Career Services Office here is also very helpful in connecting you with employ- ers and preparing for interviews.

Current student, 9/2002-Submit Date, December 2006

I've just started my job search, and there are many great employment prospects for engineers at Ohio State. The department has a great online system for sub- mitting your résumé to employers who are conducting on-campus interviews. Respected companies like P&G, GE, Microsoft and many others are always hir- ing OSU engineering students.

Current student, 9/2003-Submit Date, September 2006

Luckily OSU has a pretty extensive alumni network due to the vast number of students it graduates each year. For students in smaller departments, especially business and engineering, there are great opportunities to co-op and get intern- ship experiences and eventual job offers. For more general fields, like the humanities or social sciences, there are Career Services to assist you with résumé writing and looking for jobs, but again you must seek these services out; I have met students getting ready to graduate not really knowing how to write a résumé, so you must keep your eyes opens for these opportunities.

 Quality of Life

Current student, Political Science, 9/2005-Submit Date, April 2007

This campus is very open-minded and diverse. You can find people from all walks of life here. The housing is diverse and you can live in new dorms, old dorms and apartment-style housing—there is just about everything. The campus facilities are great. The university is always working to build the newest and best of everything. There is crime, but we live in a big city, people just have to learn to always be aware of their surroundings. Campus itself is safe and the university has a lot of ways, including free safe-rides, if you need a ride and are walking alone at night.

Read all of Vault's College Surveys at **www.vault.com/college**—get complete surveys on 100s of colleges and univer- sities, expert advice on applicaton essays and more.

VAULT CAREER LIBRARY **563**

Current student, Nursing, 9/2003-Submit Date, April 2007

Campus housing is fairly typical for college, and offers three different types of housing, specific to different areas of campus. Dining is excellent, with over 20 facilities to choose from, with great hours. University housing has programs year round to engage the students in the residence halls. There are many safety programs in place at Ohio State. We have safety poles that students can contact campus police on, as well as a student escort service that can give students rides home from campus areas at night.

Current student, Biology, 9/2004-Submit Date, April 2007

Being in a large city, some level of crime is expected and present. However, the perks of Columbus outweigh the downfalls. A large city provides access to stellar internships as well as opportunities to see shows, performances and demonstrations of diversity and culture on a daily basis. There is plenty of housing and more dining opportunities than almost any other campus in the country. We are also home to the largest recreation center on a college campus, so that you can burn off the calories from all the good food.

Alumnus/a, 9/2002-12/2006, December 2006

Ohio State continues to grow and transform its campus. Construction becomes a facet of a student's life during school because new buildings are always underway. The university has a new state-of-the-art physical education center (RPAC) and many other new science facilities. The business school is relatively new and its classrooms and amenities are often coveted by students with other majors. In addition, the university unveiled the "Gateway": a new mixed-use area including bars, the university bookstore, a movie theater, and restaurants. This area has grown quickly due to its appeal to students and is a lively area any day of the week.

Current student, 9/2003-Submit Date, September 2006

Ohio State is located in city environment and there are definitely the safety issues associated with a big city environment. I would not recommend walking home alone when it is dark. There is a campus escort service, but it takes a while to pick students up. Housing is cheaper off campus, which is a plus, but it can be loud and dirty. Dining has improved vastly since in my four years but I dropped my meal plan after my freshman year. Campus housing is hit or miss; there are many different living arrangements (suite, four-person with bathroom, two-person with community bathroom). Most of the south campus dorms have no air conditioning, which is not pleasant the last weeks of spring quarter. Upperclassman housing is better.

 ## Social Life

Alumnus/a, Business, 9/2002-6/2006, April 2007

The social life in Columbus is great because it is one of the bigger cities in Ohio. There are numerous bars, both 18 and 21 and up, and there are also great parties and tons of fun things to do. In addition, the campus provides bus service to local areas of town so you can go shopping, to the theater, to movies, and many restaurants. My favorite bar is the Ugly Tuna located in the South Campus Gateway Center and my favorite restaurant is Martinis located in downtown Columbus.

Current student, Business, 9/2004-Submit Date, April 2007

There is so much to do on this campus and in Columbus—it is unbelievable. There are bars, restaurants, retail stores and boutiques lining High Street in both directions. Greek life is around 10 percent here at Ohio State with a house for

every personality. We have our programming board, OUAB—recently voted best collegiate programming board in the nation. We have Explore Columb which brings tickets at a 50 percent discount or higher to students to enjoy acti ities around the Columbus area. You can take social dance classes, go on wee end rock climbing trips, find non-alcohol related programming, get financ help, and meet the President of Iceland all in one week here at Ohio State.

Current student, Political Science, 9/2005-Submit Date, April 200

The social scene here is amazing. There is anything you could wa Restaurants are everywhere including several Cameron Mitchell places and y can find some cool local places. There are a bunch of bars right on High Stre including Four Kegs, Panini's, Toos, Ledos, McFaddens, Ugly Tuna and S Bar. There is also a shuttle to downtown to all the bars there. The best part that we are right in a city, so you can do the campus scene or go downtown a go to places like Lodge Bar or Sugar. The Greek system is more laid-back th a lot of places, but it is growing and is a great way to meet people.

Alumnus/a, 9/2002-12/2006, December 2006

Ohio State's diversity lends itself to a diverse array of social scenes and venu for its students. The new University Gateway offers both upscale and low-ma tenance opportunities for entertainment and eating. The Ugly Tuna Saloon a Mad Mex are two favorites in this area. North of the Gateway on 15th Aven exists Greek housing where many of the university's Greek chapters live. Gre life is relatively small (6 percent) at the school, but the students have large rol in the university, such as leadership in the student government, communi involvement and so on.

Other favorites include intramural sports, which is very well-organized at t school, as well as sports. The university, Columbus, and seemingly the enti state revolve around Ohio State football. Student camaraderie during fall qua ter is incomparable and really makes the university feel connected.

Alumnus/a, 1/2000-6/2003, January 2007

Social life on campus is fantastic. There are numerous events, both related OSU and the community. Greek life is not as popular as at other schools, b there is a Greek scene. While bar life has been on the decline recently, the con pletion of the South Campus Gateway and the revitalization of the city, south campus has greatly increased the social scene. The athletic scene is one of t best in the nation. Buckeye football and Buckeye basketball are two of t strongest programs in the nation and attract a tremendous following. Go Buck

Ohio University

Ohio University
Undergraduate Admissions
20 Chubb Hall
Athens, OH 45701-2979
Admissions phone: (740) 593-4100
Admissions fax: (740) 593-0560
Admissions e-mail: admissions@ohio.edu
Admissions URL: www.ohio.edu/admissions/

 ## Admissions

Alumnus/a, Creative Writing, 9/2002-6/2006, October 2006

Admissions for OU are pretty typical: application, test scores, essay. I actually started out in the Honors Tutorial College English program, so my application process was different from the average student's. I had an interview with the head of the HTC English department where I was asked questions, such as what was the piece of writing of which I was most proud, why I wanted to be in the program and so on. HTC admissions is very selective. Overall, OU's is not. It's a big state school. It's not that hard to get in. But if you have good grades and test scores, you can generally get a scholarship.

Current student, 9/2004-Submit Date, October 2006

The admissions process for Ohio University was relatively easy compared to several other schools I applied to. There was no essay or letters of recommendation required; it was simple, hassle-free and done completely online. Selection is based primarily on test scores (ACT/SAT) and high school GPA/class rank.

Current student, Business, 9/2003-Submit Date, September 2006

I applied online for OU. There was an optional essay to write, which I did not complete. I had to mail my high school transcript and senior year grades. I had very good high school GPA and decent SAT and ACT scores, so I was not worried about getting in or being accepted.

Current student, 9/2002-Submit Date, December 2005

Getting in at Ohio University isn't too difficult. As long as you have a minimum ACT or SAT score and graduated in the top 50 percent of your high school class, you're pretty much guaranteed admission. However, the more selective programs, such as journalism, business, engineering and the Honors Tutorial College, have stricter guidelines. I'm a journalism major and to be admitted as an incoming freshman you need a higher ACT/SAT score and much higher class rank. The application advises writing an essay if you think you might be on the border of getting into a selective program, but I didn't write one as I was highly qualified, and I got in anyway. For the Honors Tutorial College, I think you have to write an essay as well as go through an interview.

Alumnus/a, Dance, 9/2001-6/2005, November 2005

Admissions to the dance department at Ohio University is like any other fine arts programs, consisting of an audition including the areas of ballet, modern, short semi-structured choreographic improvisation and jazz. The panel consists of dance professors and current students from grade levels sophomore to senior. I was fortunate enough to be on the Audition/Scholarship Panel so I was able to learn the inside scoop on what gets you in. I stress the importance of grades. Even though talent plays a major factor in your admission, it is also helpful to have decent grades. They want an artist who can function intellectually in the program, as well as physically and artistically.

Alumnus/a, 9/2001-9/2003, March 2005

The admissions process included visiting the campus after sending in an application. The visit was meant to allow me to see the campus and have an interview with a representative. The application consisted of personal information and an essay as to why I wanted to attend Ohio University. I was a transfer stu-

dent, therefore the selectivity was based on my college GPA. I started at Ohio University after two years at a community college.

Current student, 10/2000-Submit Date, May 2004

Ohio University is the union of several individual colleges that have their own individual admissions requirements. The Scripps School of Journalism is highly selective, from what I have been told. I applied to the College of Arts and Sciences (A&S) and the Honors Tutorial College (HTC). The application is straightforward, asking for ACT or SAT scores and basic academic information. Writing an essay was optional for A&S, but required for Honors Tutorial. I had high grades, so I can't say how selective A&S was. However, I have not met anybody who was rejected.

The HTC is a different animal. There is a separate application requirement, which includes the essay and academic recommendations. If you are selected for an interview, the [college] contacts you by the date they state through a letter. I was asked to come to the campus for the interview, where I was given a tour by an HTC student. The interview was conducted by the head of the major I was applying to and lasted approximately two hours. It was a pleasant experience, if a little nerve-wracking. I received a letter about two weeks later informing me that I was admitted.

> **Ohio University states:** "Arts and Sciences majors must meet the university guidelines of top 30 percent rank with 21 ACT or top 50 percent rank with an ACT of 23. There is no separate application for the Honors Tutorial College, but an essay is required."

Current student, 9/2002-Submit Date, May 2006

The admissions process at Ohio University is very simple. The application can be filled out online or on paper. There is one essay required but it is very simple. The question I was asked was, "How can education help me to accomplish my future goals?" The exams that OU requires are either the ACT or SAT. Be sure to submit your best score. I applied in September and I received my acceptance letter in October, which was a good aid in my college decision. The admissions process is more selective now, so make sure that your test scores and high school grades are good.

 ## Academics

Current student, 9/2004-Submit Date, October 2006

I feel as though this institution was and continues to be very easy for me academically. Coming from an excellent school district, I was definitely over-prepared. The quality of my classes now is definitely better than my first year, probably because they are higher-level classes and include more challenge.

Alumnus/a, Creative Writing, 9/2002-6/2006, October 2006

The requirements are set up so that you have some choice of what to take (e.g., choose one of three Shakespeare courses; choose two of three early American literature courses). Due to scheduling order (those students with the most hours schedule first, so underclassmen go last), I was actually closed out of taking any English courses one quarter. It almost happened again another quarter, but I met with my advisor and contacted some professors and got a pink slip (special permission) for a class. In general, the courses aren't overly difficult. The reading load is typically manageable. The professors are pretty knowledgeable in their areas, and I never had a real problem with anyone's grading.

Current student, Business, 9/2003-Submit Date, September 2006

The academic programs at OU are definitely intense. There are mandatory class times and about twice as much time is spent out of class on homework assignments and studying topics covered in class. The quality of each class is determined primarily on the quality of the professor. As you progress through school, it becomes easier to get into popular classes because you have seniority for

Read all of Vault's College Surveys at **www.vault.com/college**—get complete surveys on 100s of colleges and universities, expert advice on applicaton essays and more.

VAULT CAREER LIBRARY 565

choosing classes based on credit hours. Lastly, the grading scale is based on a 4.0. Again, the ease and difficulty of grading are determined by the professor, but I have never taken an easy class in college. They have all been challenging.

Current student, 9/2002-Submit Date, December 2005

Ohio University's journalism program is one of the best in the country, and definitely the premier choice for journalism education in Ohio and some of the surrounding states/areas, including West Virginia, Kentucky and parts of Michigan and western Pennsylvania. However, I found that quite a lot of professors in journalism were simply overrated. There are a few who are quite good at what they do and are also effective teachers. The rest are either professionals who are very knowledgeable about the business but aren't good at communicating that knowledge to students, or the academic types who are effective teachers but don't seem to have a lot of relevant practical knowledge of journalism as a career.

Current student, 6/2005-Submit Date, September 2005

Chemistry, sociology and psychology are all very personal classes. You can ask questions and have one-on-one time with instructors. Popular classes have online registration that's first come, first serve. Professors are great—they try and break things down to where you can understand the materials. Math 102 has a chapter and worksheets every other day so the workload is kind of rough in that class. Chemistry is a little complicated; the lab class is four hours long and some of the projects are hard to understand. We do have a class aid, who is wonderful. If you mess up, he will come and help you find where you went wrong and explain how you went wrong and how to fix it. The Sign Language class is fast paced and quite simple if you really want to learn. The professor goes over everything about 20 times in a class period, which is really good because it gets drilled into your brain and makes you understand what you are signing and reading.

Current student, 9/2002-Submit Date, May 2006

The academics at Ohio University are rigorous, but the programs offered will fit just about any interest. I am a history major and a political science minor and I have found the College of Arts and Sciences to be a wonderful college. The classes campus-wide are very well taught, and the professors are always accommodating and wonderful to speak with. Popular classes are usually easy to get into, but register for classes early in order to ensure a spot. Most professors will let you pink-slip into a class if it is full. The workload requires a lot of reading, so be prepared. It is this way with just about every class. Most professors follow a standard grading scale, with 59 and below being an F and 93.1 and above being an A. A lot of professors will take off points for skipping class, so make sure you have good attendance. Good attendance is also key to getting a good grade in a class, especially if you do not have the book for the class.

Alumnus/a, 9/2001-6/2003, December 2004

I loved my classes so much that the whole experience did not really feel like school. The classes were wonderful, as is the equipment. You heard students sometimes complain about the equipment, but I would challenge them to find better someplace else. I often had to work with worse my first year in the field as a reporter. There are six core classes every student must complete in the J-school, along with classes specific to their sequence (public relations, advertising, print, magazine, broadcast and Internet). Of the core six, I remember Language Precision being the most difficult for students, mostly because they had been ill-prepared in high school. I had an excellent high school English program and had no such problems.

 ## Employment Prospects

Alumnus/a, 9/2001-6/2005, November 2005

As for the alumni network I was amazed at how helpful everyone has been. When I first moved to NY, an alumna I had never met allowed me to sublease her apartment while she was on tour. We met, had coffee and she provided me with the best information and advice about living a dancer's life in NY. She even hooked me up with a place to get certified in pilates and called to check up on me from time to time to make sure my adjustment to NY has been smooth. I think that is how everyone is who graduates from Ohio University. Everyone is

so friendly there and that never changes once you leave. There is an unspok[en] bond between Bobcats!

Alumnus/a, Creative Writing, 9/2002-6/2006, October 2006

I graduated in June and am still searching for a job in publishing in October. [I] am unaware of any alumni network, and having a degree from OU offers lit[tle] prestige, as it is a large state school. There are occasional career fairs that co[me] to campus, but none that I knew of were geared toward my interests. As [an] English major, you can go a lot of different directions with your degree, and I [am] sure it's easier to get a job if you're looking for something less specific or co[m]petitive. Still, you're pretty much on your own.

> The school says: "In addition to career fairs on campus attend-
> ed by a variety of employers, the University's Office of Career
> Services, located on campus in the Baker University Center,
> includes major and career advising, job search assistance,
> career guides, job listings, college and graduate school informa-
> tion, and much more. For information on available services,
> visit the web site at http://www.ohio.edu/careers/students/.
> Both students and alumni can register for the Bobcat Online Job
> Search Program."

Current student, 9/2004-Submit Date, October 2006

We have regular career fairs and education fairs (the latter being for emplo[y]ment, the second for graduate school opportunities) to help students with th[eir] options.

Current student, Business, 9/2003-Submit Date, September 200[6]

Employment prospects are very positive for students graduating from [the] College of Business. I cannot speak for any other programs. The COB wor[ks] very hard to set up networking events and bring employer representatives to ta[lk] with students in different organizations and groups. I have never utilized [the] alumni network or the on-campus recruiting, but they are definitely availa[ble] and easy to access.

Current student, 9/2002-Submit Date, May 2006

OU grads generally get good jobs. Many employers interview on campus, a[nd] there are career fairs held in the fall and winter. A lot of business majors g[et] hired at these fairs, but anyone is welcome to attend. The Office of Care[er] Services is a wonderful asset to the campus. By registering with the office, o[ne] is able to access the vast alumni database and hook up with mentors; alumni [in] a particular career field who have offered to help students get started with th[eir] desired careers. Career Services will also help sharpen your résumé, send it o[ut] to prospective employers, and prep you for job interviews. It is essential [to] access the services offered through the Office of Career Services. The library [and] Career Services will also help you research jobs and find relevant internships [for] you.

Alumnus/a, 9/2001-9/2003, March 2005

Ohio University has a program developed to helped graduates get jobs in the[ir] fields. Every year they hold a college day when prospective employers come [to] campus and interview individuals in each field. In addition, OU has a high j[ob] placement percentage. The alumni are helpful in seeking out others who atten[d]-ed OU. Internships were valuable tools especially in the teaching field.

 ## Quality of Life

Alumnus/a, Creative Writing, 9/2002-6/2006, October 2006

OU has lots of dorms, which are all of pretty good quality. English majors w[ill] most likely want to live on East Green, as it's near the English building. Bry[an] Hall, a quiet dorm for upperclassmen with a certain GPA level, is right across [the] street from the English building. In my experience, the Resident Assistants a[nd] maintenance staff are very friendly and helpful. Campus is very pretty and inv[it]-ing, with red brick walkways and lots of trees. There is a large central green [on] which there are always students sitting and studying or eating lunch. The dini[ng] halls are of pretty good quality and have a variety of options. They always ha[ve] two main courses, various side dishes, a salad bar, a fast food area for things li[ke] hamburgers or chicken nuggets, and a deli area with lunchmeats. There is al[so] generally a range of desserts, fruit and cereal available.

e athletic facility (Ping Center) is great. All students have free access with eir IDs. There is a large room with machines like Stairmasters and bikes, as ell as weight machines. There are basketball and racquetball courts, a free-ights room, outdoor tennis courts, a rock climbing wall, and an indoor track. ere are lots of lockers to store personal items. For a fee you can meet with a iner or nutritionist, or take one of the many classes offered (yoga, pilates, ength training, karate and so on). There are also intramural leagues for soft-ll, soccer, ping pong and floor hockey, among others. The campus is relative-safe. The dorms lock their front doors at night. There are call boxes scattered ound should you need assistance. However, the campus could be better lit in any areas. There are your bar fights and general disturbances, but for the most rt it is a very safe campus and you won't find trouble unless you're looking r it. There were very few times in my undergrad experience that I felt unsafe.

Regarding safety, Ohio University says: "The Ohio University Police Department (OUPD) is a full-service professional law enforcement agency, with uniformed police officers patrolling throughout the campus community 24-hours a day, 365 days a year. Ohio University Police Officers patrol on foot, in marked cruisers, and on bicycle. Having a full-time law enforcement agency operating on campus allows uninterrupted safety and security, continuous customer service, and immediate response to emergency situations.

"The SAFE-T (Safe Arrival For Everyone-Tonight) Patrol Division provides a free walking escort to all students, staff, faculty, and visitors at Ohio University. The service is available every night of the week during the academic quarters. SAFE-T Patrol's mission and focus is to provide Safe Arrival For Everyone concerned about their safety on campus."

urrent student, 9/2004-Submit Date, October 2006

s an RA on campus for two years, I have had first-hand experience in dealing ith housing, the dorms and so on. There are a few dorms that have recently en renovated and have very nice living conditions. Unfortunately, there are so several halls in disrepair.

The school says: "Alvin C. Adams Hall, the new residence hall, opened on campus in fall of 2007. Renovations to existing residence halls are underway."

urrent student, Business, 9/2003-Submit Date, September 2006

the dorms your first two years on campus, you meet a ton of new people, espe-ally your freshman year. I live with my hallmates from freshman year and I ow that is the case for most students. The campus is absolutely gorgeous and e facilities are state-of-the-art and available for all students to utilize. The din-g is acceptable and even excellent some nights and there are ample additional od options uptown and around campus. Lastly, the area directly surrounding mpus is all students, so you meet and spend time with most of your neighbors well.

urrent student, 9/2002-Submit Date, May 2006

ampus life at OU is very active. There is always something to do. The dor-itories are secure and safe, and OU Police Department and Security Aides are ways patrolling 24 hours a day, but especially at night. If you are walking back om the Aquatic Center after dark, or anywhere else on campus, and you want companion for the walk to feel safer, the SAFE-T Patrol will meet you and cort you back to your residence hall. The OU library is open 24 hours a day, ve days a week. The second floor of the library is the Learning Commons, mplete with many computers and a coffeehouse.

The school says: "The university's Alden Library maintains a web site at http://www.library.ohiou.edu/find/ that allows users to search its collections, as well as view its hours of operation and other key information."

Social Life

At this time, OU is the Number Two party school in the country according to the Princeton Review. We take a lot of pride in our ranking and the parties happen often. Most students do stay on campus over the weekends in order to party—not a lot of kids go home, except for on the occasional three-day weekend.

The school says: "There has traditionally been some element of hyperbole associated with Ohio University's debatable label as a 'party school.' The university is no longer ranked among Princeton Review's Top Five party schools. In addition, a more significant measure by which to evaluate the institution may be the actual academic accomplishments and professional suc-cesses of the university's students, faculty and alumni-who have collectively won 23 Pulitzer Prizes in the past 21 years. Another indicator of academic achievement is the 45 nationally competitive awards won by Ohio University students in 2005-06, including Fulbright, Mitchell, Eisenhower and Udall awards.

"*Washington Monthly* has ranked Ohio University in the top 17 percent of public and private schools for academics/social mobility. In addition, *U.S. News & World Report* has ranked Ohio University's graduation rate performance fourth out of 257 national universities. This is the third consecutive year the uni-versity has made this category's Top 10."

Court Street and the other areas uptown are home to about 20 bars, some of which are also restaurants, so there are a variety of activities for those who are 21. For people who aren't 21, some bars will let them in with an extra cover, especially if a band is playing. Other than that, there are always tons of parties to go to, which are cheaper than bars anyway. Each bar has its own personality and type of people it attracts.

Alumnus/a, Creative Writing, 9/2002-6/2006, October 2006

There are hundreds of clubs students can join. Each fall there is a student organ-ization fair where you'll find everything from political groups, volunteer groups, sports clubs, religious groups, the arts (including modeling, swing dance, theater, comedy, choirs and orchestra), Greek chapters, foreign language clubs, the liter-ary magazine, the local radio station, student government, and many more. New groups are always being started. And yes, OU is known for its party scene. There are many bars on Court Street, and no lack of house parties. We are also home of the (in)famous Halloween block party, when Court Street is blocked off and packed with students in costume. But don't worry if you're not a drinker. I'm not, and I still found plenty to do. There are always bands playing some-where, DJs at the Union or Casa, and entertainment in the coffeehouse in the stu-dent center. In addition to being lined with bars, Court Street has many restau-rants. There are fast food, delis, bagel shops, and coffee houses. There are also nicer places nearby. Out on State St. (you'll have to drive) there are many more restaurants, as well as Kroger and Wal-Mart, and a large new movie theater. (There is a smaller one on Court that shows mainly art films.) OU has many dif-ferent Greek houses, but the campus is not dominated by them. No matter what your type, you're sure to find somewhere you fit in.

OU says: "The annual Halloween party takes place in the city of Athens, not on campus. It is not an Ohio University event."

Current student, 9/2004-Submit Date, October 2006

I'll be honest: social life here revolves around alcohol. Besides that there are a lot of great social opportunities to take advantage of. There are several great lit-tle coffeehouses (one favorite is the Donkey) that have open-mic and band nights. There's also a wide array of concerts and shows (ranging from theater to comedy to dance) to go to every week.

The school says: "The university has implemented several strategies to augment student safety and reduce high-risk drink-ing. The number of Judiciaries cases involving student alcohol violations dropped more than 32 percent in 2006-07."

Read all of Vault's College Surveys at **www.vault.com/college**—get complete surveys on 100s of colleges and univer-sities, expert advice on applicaton essays and more.

VAULT CAREER LIBRARY 567

The School Says

Ohio University—the state's first university—was founded as a place of opportunity in 1804. For the past two centuries, it has been a center for scholarship, research and creative activity. The main campus population of more than 20,000 includes students from nearly every state and about 100 nations. The university currently has more than 157,000 alumni around the world. Five regional campuses further extend university access. Ohio University offers more than 250 areas of undergraduate study. On the graduate level, the university grants master's degrees in nearly all of its major academic divisions and doctoral degrees in selected departments.

Ohio University is fully accredited by the North Central Association of Colleges and Schools and has been designated as a high activity research university by the Carnegie Foundation for the Advancement of Teaching. The university also has been cited for academic quality by such publications as *U.S. News & World Report* and *Washington Monthly*. The John Templeton Foundation has recognized Ohio University as one of the country's top character-building institutions.

Since its founding, the university has played a pioneering role in embracing the ethnic and national diversity of its students, faculty, alumni and friends from around the globe. Building upon this commitment is the Urban Scholars Program, a need-based scholarship initiative to bring talented high school students from urban school districts to Ohio University.

Our historic and charming Athens campus, part of a safe and friendly community, is a benefit and an attraction to prospective students. The importance of a residential campus goes beyond learning that takes place in classrooms and laboratories. Through participation in athletics and the arts, social activities, student organizations and community service, our students learn what it means to be involved and responsible citizens who are sensitive to global issues. Additionally, Ohio University's inclusive residential learning communities embrace cultural differences and create an environment where students of diverse backgrounds can study, live, learn and socialize together.

An Ohio University education engages students, helping them to think critically, to take a position and defend it and to translate classroom learning into hands-on education. Nowhere are these characteristics more evident than in the university's Honors Tutorial College. Founded 34 years ago, it draws upon the rich educational traditions of British universities such as Cambridge and Oxford, offering high-ability students distinctive, tutorial-based learning opportunities.

In the past 21 years, Ohio University students, faculty and alumni have claimed 23 Pulitzer Prizes. In 2005-06, Ohio University students received 45 nationally competitive awards. These honors included prestigious Mitchell, Fulbright, Eisenhower and Udall awards. Our students use these awards to travel and study in locations across the globe-from Europe and the Middle East to Africa and Latin America.

For all of the university's diverse achievements, our purpose remains straightforward: to provide a learning-centered community that broadens and deepens our students' intellectual abilities; to value excellence in both teaching and research as integral to this learning process; and to connect learning to the world around us.

University of Cincinnati

Admissions Office
340 University Pavilion, PO Box 210091
Cincinnati, OH 45221-0091
Admissions phone: (513) 556-1100
Admissions fax: (513) 556-1105
Admissions e-mail: admissions@uc.edu
Admissions URL: www.admissions.uc.edu/

Note: The school has chosen not to review the student surveys submitted.

Admissions

Alumnus/a, 9/1995-6/2000, September 2005

The admissions process was fairly simple compared to some of the other schools for which I had filled out applications. The University of Cincinnati had an SAT requirement and took into account secondary education grade point average.

Alumnus/a, 9/1999-9/2003, January 2005

The admissions process was fairly easy. I had a 3.6 GPA, and only had one interview. I also had a friend who didn't apply in time for fall classes, so he went into the continuing education program, and transferred very easily into a degree program, keeping all of his credits. The thing about McMicken (College of Arts and Sciences) at UC, is that deadlines are very early in comparison to other schools, so you have to have everything finished and ready to submit in a timely manner the winter before you plan to attend.

Current student, 9/2003-Submit Date, April 2004

It is fairly easy to apply here. You can go to apply.uc.edu/undergra DisplayAppMenu in order to apply online, which I recommend. There is a no refundable $35 application fee that you must pay by credit card or debit card you apply online. For admission, there is no essay that is required. (Howev if you are applying to CCM, you have to fill out an additional application an am not sure what is included in that.) Though particular colleges at the univ sity are highly selective some are only moderately selective. The university a whole has an open admission policy, so you can be admitted to the univers without being admitted into the college with your major. They usually let y know whether or not you were admitted within three or four weeks.

As far as placement tests go, UC prefers the ACT but accepts the SAT also. Als if you have taken any AP tests, you want to be sure to send those to UC. Speci colleges might only give you elective credit for some of the tests. (For instan engineers will get elective credit for their AP Calc test, but will still have to ta Calculus at UC.) You generally get at least some credit for any score three above.

Interviews and essays are usually required if you want to get into a speci scholarship program. For instance, the Carl H. Lindner Honors PLUS progra is a scholarship program for business students. Admission into this requires additional application (usually due in late December), multiple essays and interview.

Academics

Alumnus/a, 9/1995-6/2000, September 2005

I first started at the University of Cincinnati interested in social work, so I worked for two years to earn general and sociology-specific courses to become part of the College of Social Work. I then changed my major to a health care related field, the field of dietetics and nutrition. This encompassed science-based classes such as biochemistry and microbiology as well as anatomy and physiology. The workload was grueling at times with all of the science requirements as well as the advanced nutrition courses. At this time, I was approved for the College of Allied Health Sciences, which was located at a different location than the main campus. A more stringent grading scale accompanied the last year or so of my classes. My professors were extremely helpful and all of them made an effort to make themselves available outside of regular class hours. The head of the nutrition and dietetics department, also a beloved teacher of nutrition courses, seemed to act as an inspiration to many.

Alumnus/a, 9/1999-9/2003, January 2005

Quality of classes was pretty standard. Getting the classes you want at a reasonable time was another story. I was very happy with most all of my professors, as far as accessibility. The only real issue I had the entire time was that the choices for anthropology professors were difficult to understand due to language barriers. Grading was largely on a curve, which is a problem for some people! The size of the campus sometimes made it difficult to get from class to class in a timely manner.

Current student, 9/2003-Submit Date, April 2004

You can get the kind of classes you are looking for at UC, whether it is huge easy classes with one exam and that's the only work for the quarter or if it's a small, personalized class with lots of interaction with the professor. Though introduction classes are often large, there are many ways to receive more personal attention. If you apply for and are accepted into the Honors Program, you have the opportunity to take honors courses. These courses are much smaller, more personalized, almost always taught by a professor and not a grad student, and while being more work, it is an opportunity to get a much more positive experience. In addition, through honors you can go to seminars and lunches where professors talk with just a few students about various topics of interest (a recent one looked at life in the 1960s).

Alumnus/a, 9/1990-9/1994, September 2003

The absolutely best thing is that the co-operative education program is mandatory for all undergrad engineering programs, and the curriculum is built around it. There's never a question of missing an important class while co-oping and having to delay graduation because the class is only offered once a year! The co-op program (and some light campus employment) provided me enough money to be financially independent as a sophomore and debt-free when I graduated!

Employment Prospects

Alumnus/a, 9/1995-6/2000, September 2005

I believe that employment prospects for graduates of the University of Cincinnati were fairly good, especially if you were a part of the engineering program. The college had a very resourceful Career Development Center located on the main campus and Web accessibility that required student ID to access. The percentages of graduates achieving a position within their respective field was quite remarkable as I recall. I personally acquired an internship to achieve the advanced training and education that I needed to become a licensed and registered dietitian. The College of Allied Health Sciences Dietetics program aided the nutrition and dietetic students with their internship applications, as UC, itself, did not offer an internship through the school directly. There were also opportunities to attend presentations directed by former alumni that had secured an internship and spoke about the application process to the internship experience.

Alumnus/a, 9/1999-9/2003, January 2005

There was virtually no recruiting on campus—somewhat surprising for the size of the school. The engineering college was actually more years in length than

some other colleges offer, but the level of education was much more advanced, and so it was somewhat competitive to get into. Types of jobs were fairly run of the mill for people with whom I stayed in contact.

Current student, 9/2003-Submit Date, April 2004

UC pioneered co-ops. This allows you to alternate an academic quarter with a quarter of work. The university helps you find co-op positions (which are paid) and often these positions lead to full-time job offers upon graduation. Prestige with employers depends on the particular college, but is generally high, and very high in some areas (such as CCM and DAAP).

Alumnus/a, 9/1990-9/1994, September 2003

Again, the absolute best thing is that the co-operative education program is mandatory for all undergrad engineering programs, so: (1) the placement staff stays in year-round contact with employers; (2) your co-op placements give you experience, that is the inside track with one or more employer; and (3) you figure out fast if you really are cut out for engineering as a profession. I was well-positioned for a job after graduation!

Quality of Life

Current student, 1/2003-Submit Date, September 2005

The quality is good. The houses are nice and close to the campus. The facilities are new. There are many places to eat in the Cincinnati area, however, you have to eat by about 11 p.m. because everything closes at that time.

Alumnus/a, 9/1995-6/2000, September 2005

Housing on the campus of the University of Cincinnati was fairly standard to housing facilities that I have experienced at other universities. I personally was housed in a same-sex dorm, which was very secure and required identification of visitors and dwellers at check-in. Crime rates in the downtown Cincinnati area, although high, were never really an issue for me. There always seemed to be people roaming the campus and surrounding streets in the evening hours, and campus police and emergency services were always a call away. The dining services were typical and the food was mediocre in the cafeteria, however, with a flexible meal plan, you could dine at other facilities around the campus that were separate entities from the cafeterias. I moved out of the dorms at the end of my first year and into an apartment off campus with a roommate.

Alumnus/a, 9/1999-9/2003, January 2005

The school is largely a commuter college, so housing was odd—most of the people in the dorms were foreign students and post graduates. The neighborhood isn't the best, and it's getting worse all the time, but the campus police were visible and reliable. For the size of the school, I believe the crime rate was fairly low.

Current student, 9/2003-Submit Date, April 2004

The university is constantly building better housing. The new buildings now have suite-styled rooms that offer more privacy. However, students living in the older dorms love them too. The older, more traditional dorms have a more social atmosphere.

There are many options for food on campus. The dining halls at which students can use their meal plans actually have decent food (though I will suggest going to Siddal over Sander). Additionally, there are many restaurants both on campus and very close off campus where students may eat, too. The new student center has a Starbucks. Generally, students do not have to worry about their safety on campus. The campus is well lit and help phones are all over the place. The neighborhood off campus is a little less safe and it is wise to travel in groups after dusk. However, the campus provides a chaperone service up to three blocks off campus, so it is never necessary to walk alone. Personally, I have never felt unsafe alone or in a group at anytime, however, it is wise to take some precautions.

Alumnus/a, 9/1990-9/1994, September 2003

UC is near the crest of a bluff overlooking the Ohio River Valley and downtown Cincinnati. From the crest, there's a great view of holiday fireworks along the river. Campus has a large park nearby, and student ghetto and eating establish-

Read all of Vault's College Surveys at **www.vault.com/college**—get complete surveys on 100s of colleges and universities, expert advice on applicaton essays and more.

 VAULT CAREER LIBRARY 569

ments. Nobody can beat Cincinnati-style chili, and most of those establishments are open 24 hours a day!

Social Life

Alumnus/a, 9/1995-6/2000, September 2005

I was able to meet people quite rapidly my first year, and I think living in the dorms gave me a prime opportunity to bond with other first-year students. I rushed for a sorority at the end of my first year and shortly found myself being thrown into philanthropy events, campus gatherings and parties with other sororities and fraternities. The bar and restaurant scene surrounding the main campus was something to be desired, but downtown Cincinnati offered a variety of choices for both cuisine and social scene. My college years were some of the best years of my life that included some amazing learning and social opportunities that I will cherish always.

Alumnus/a, 9/1999-9/2003, January 2005

Social life was great. Many local businesses right off campus cater to students. Events were well-organized, and the Greek system was strong. There was always something posted at the bookstore; events were well advertised and well attended. Bars and restaurants nearby were affordable and eclectic. Very inte esting area. I didn't join any clubs, but there were many to choose from. A: said, it's a commuter college, so the clubs reflect that. When I was a freshma the Greek system was big on little sister programs for the fraternities. This w a great way to get a taste of the Greek life without having to join a sorority fraternity.

Current student, 9/2003-Submit Date, April 2004

There are over 250 student groups that you can be a part of on campus. In ad tion, if there is a group you want to start, it is relatively easy to start a group a get funding from the university. There are 32 fraternities and sororities that y can join. Going Greek is a great way to get to know many people. The Ma Street Project that is currently being completed aims to offer even more on-car pus events and put a movie theater on campus. The surrounding area has ma bars and restaurants that are usually full of UC students. Additionally, all spo ing events on campus are free with a UC ID, so many students go to these. T rec center offers fitness programs every day of the week and so it is easy to fi one to fit your schedule.

Alumnus/a, 9/1990-9/1994, September 2003

With over 30,000 students, you'd have to work hard at not having a social life UC! Even I could do it, and I was a shy dweeb!

University of Dayton

Office of Admission
University of Dayton
300 College Park
Dayton, OH 45469-1300
Admissions phone: (800) 837-7433 or (937) 229-4411
Admissions URL: www.udayton.edu/Admission/

Admissions

Current student, 8/2004-Submit Date, October 2006

The university had a rolling admissions policy. I had to submit an extensive writing sample and a letter of recommendation from a teacher. The process was somewhat selective, though not too much.

Alumnus/a, 8/2000-5/2004, April 2006

Applications for admission are reviewed for specific academic majors or, when applicable, for undeclared status in an academic division. The quality of your academic record is shown by your grade record and pattern throughout high school, your selection of courses in preparation for college, your class standing or ranking, and results of either the SAT Reasoning Test or ACT. Balanced consideration is given to all aspects of your college preparation. While no minimum grade point average, class rank or standardized test score is specified, these measures must provide evidence of your readiness for college studies in your chosen academic program. The average first-year student who is accepted to UD has a 3.4 GPA. The middle 50th percentile of our incoming first-year students receive between a 23 and a 28 on the ACT, and between a 1060 and a 1270 on the SAT without the writing component. Admission is entirely rolling, with a priority deadline date each year of January 1. Apply in September or October for best consideration. UD does not offer interviews, but it is an excellent idea to visit campus and meet with an admission counselor. This person can answer all of your questions about the university and help you determine if the school is a great fit for you.

Current student, 8/2004-Submit Date, April 2006

The admissions process was fairly easy. The application is completed online and without a fee. I personally did not have an interview or meet with a counselor, but I suggest if you are borderline on grades, you meet with one to explain your situation. I chose an open topic for the essay, but I say choose which ever you

feel most confident. Being involved in high school helped me acquire goo scholarships and I think gave me a one-up on my fellow students. Dayton h: been receiving a record number of applicants the past few years, so I sugge applying as early as possible so you can secure your spot if you are set on UI I was very happy with the admissions process and it was probably my favori out of the five schools I applied to due to the availability of staff willing to hel and ease of the process.

Current student, 8/2004-Submit Date, April 2005

The University of Dayton's application was the easiest one I filled out. It too about 10 minutes since I had already written a college essay for my high schoo senior English class. UD also responded really quickly since it has rollin admissions—it took about two weeks to get back to me. By September of n senior year, I had already been accepted to UD.

Alumnus/a, 8/2000-5/2004, April 2005

UD is a moderately-selective private Catholic university. The admission appl cation can only be done online, and there is no application fee. Students a asked to write a personal statement and to submit test scores, letters of recon mendation and an official transcript. The deadline to apply is January 1, an admissions is rolling. Students are automatically considered for academic scho arships based on the information provided in the application. An interview is n required, but a visit to campus, including a meeting with an admissions coui selor is encouraged, so that the students can get a feel for what it's like to be UD student.

Alumnus/a, 8/1998-5/2002, April 2005

The admissions process is getting more selective each year. Although an inte view was not mandatory, it was recommended. Before going for an on-site visi applicants should apply online at admission.udayton.edu and then wait for a acceptance or denial within two or three weeks. I was accepted prior to my cam pus visit, so the bulk of my visit involved speaking with financial aid reps an residence hall reps. Advice to get in: UD is a Catholic university, so commun ty service and leadership weigh heavily toward an applicant's overall accep ance. The interview should be clear and concise and normally only takes 3 minutes.

> **The school says:** "It is not necessary to apply or have an admission decision prior to visiting campus. Visits to campus are

encouraged at any point during the admissions process, even as early as the junior year of high school."

Current student, 8/2001-Submit Date, April 2005

The University of Dayton has a competitive admissions process and operates on a rolling admissions policy. UD looks at a variety of factors, including which classes you took in high school, your GPA, your class standing, your SAT/ACT scores and your involvement in school and in the community. The only way to apply to UD is online. It's easy to use and access, and the best part is that it's free! The application can be accessed at admission.udayton.edu/apply/. UD doesn't use a specific prompt for an essay; the application just asks for a personal statement. This is a great way to show off who you are and what makes you different from all the other applicants. An admissions interview isn't required, but I highly recommend scheduling a campus visit. You can tour campus, meet with admissions and financial aid counselors, shadow a current student, sit in on a class and much more. I fell in love with UD when I came to visit. The tour guide was knowledgeable and friendly, and the campus is absolutely gorgeous. You can't visit UD and decide not to come here!

Current student, 8/2003-Submit Date, May 2004

The University of Dayton is a private university. You first had to apply online, and then, if accepted, you had to go to an admissions interview. You have to take either the ACT or SAT and get reasonable scores. I had an 18, and I had to agree to tutoring in specific classes to be accepted.

> **University of Dayton states:** "Interviews are recommended but not required. In lieu of an essay on the application, UD requires a personal statement 'describing a significant achievement, experience or risk and its impact on you.'"

 ## Academics

Current student, 8/2004-Submit Date, October 2006

The curriculum is definitely a strenuous one, but can be managed effectively as long as one's time is allocated wisely. Getting the most popular classes is not always easy; seniority helps in this case. Grading depends on professors—some are easier, some are more difficult. The workload can be overwhelming at times, but again, can be managed.

Alumnus/a, 8/2000-5/2004, April 2006

Typical classes have between 15 and 40 students. It's very rare to have a class taught in a lecture hall or by a graduate teaching assistant. Faculty members typically know students' names. The UD faculty has a culture of mentoring students and creating unique opportunities. Workload varies from major to major. It's rare to be closed out of classes. The quality of teaching varies, but in the aggregate, I would describe it as above average. Grade inflation doesn't seem to be problem. UD encourages striking a balance between academic and community life—the workload is demanding, but gives you enough time to have some fun, too.

Alumnus/a, 8/2000-5/2004, April 2006

There are 70 academic majors available at the undergraduate level at UD. These 70 majors are found within four academic schools: Arts and Sciences, Business Administration, Education and Allied Professions, and Engineering. Classes are small; average size is about 27 students. Student-to-teacher ratio is 14:1. UD's professors specialize in personal attention. Grading is fair, but the curriculum is challenging and exciting. Students rarely have issue with being closed out of courses as UD is a medium-sized school.

> **The school says:** "As of August 2006, the student to faculty ratio is actually 13:1."

Current student, 8/2002-Submit Date, April 2006

I would have to say that we have some of the best and most caring professors at the school. They actually want to make sure that you are understanding the material and learning throughout the course. So if you need extra help, then it is readily available. With the average class size being 27, you have nice intimate environments. The classes that I have participated in have all been quality classes with quality professors. I have never once left out of a class feeling that I couldn't take something new from the class. Because the class sizes aren't too large, it is easy to get into the popular classes as you move along in your career at the school.

Current student, 8/2004-Submit Date, April 2006

Academics is based on each specific professor. I have been happy with all my professors thus far. My general courses seemed a bit easier. But, as I have begun to take courses for my major, I meet with professors at the top of their fields with plenty of real world experience. I like that aspect because they can offer advice for outside the classroom learning too. It is difficult to get into certain classes, so I just create backups just in case I do not get the time/professor I would like. But, I only have run into that problem once or twice. The workload depends on your courses. Sometimes, my work is done only in class, but other courses require a lot of reading and application. Grading is a university set scale, but most professors will curve the grades at the end.

Current student, 8/2004-Submit Date, April 2005

As a first-year student trying to schedule for your sophomore year, it can be a little difficult to get the classes you like because scheduling is done by credit hours. Professors are very approachable, keep regular office hours and are very interested in how their students are doing. In my intro. classes (the ones required of all students for graduation), there were never more than 40 people, and even that was considered pretty large. Most of my classes were about 20 to 30 (and the higher the level, the fewer people there are), and all my professors knew my name.

Alumnus/a, 8/2000-5/2004, April 2005

There are 70 undergraduate programs offered at the University of Dayton, along with a number of graduate programs. The most popular majors are within the College of Arts and Sciences. The School of Engineering, the School of Business Administration, and the School of Education and Allied Professions also have many popular majors. Classes are small, there are about 30 students per class, and it is rare that you would find a teaching assistant instructing the class. Class registration is an online process, but it is quite easy to get written into a class that appears to be full. In my opinion, professors grade fairly, and classes are interesting, for the most part. Workload is moderately heavy, and as with any college curriculum, it is necessary to learn how to manage your time wisely.

Current student, 8/2001-Submit Date, April 2005

Without a doubt, UD makes sure students are well prepared for life after college. All students, regardless of major, take a series of humanities-based courses, including English, history, religion and philosophy. These courses act as a foundation and help prepare students for the rest of their academic career. UD is also great in ensuring first-year students have a successful first year at college. All first-year students enroll in a one-semester seminar class, the first-year experience, which students are introduced to the university, learn about their major, receive academic and career counseling, discover clubs and organizations, and much more!

UD's academic program is well balanced. It's not so difficult or demanding that you devote your entire life to studying, but it isn't so easy that it's a joke. I have had nothing but positive experiences with my courses and professors. While I've certainly had classes that I've liked less than others, overall it has been great! The professors are available to help you after class or during their office hours, and genuinely care about you. Classes at UD are small enough (around 25 to 30 people) that you get to know your peers as well as your professor, which greatly enhances the learning experience. It also allows for discussion and group activities, which I think are much more beneficial than impersonal lectures in huge lecture halls. Grading is also very fair. Unlike some schools that grade on a curve and only allow a certain number of students to receive each grade, at UD you receive the grade you earn.

 ## Employment Prospects

Current student, 8/2004-Submit Date, October 2006

There are great prospects in terms of jobs for graduating seniors. Specifically, an organization called the Davis Center for Portfolio Management, a student-run investment center on campus, has forged relationships with firms like Merrill

Read all of Vault's College Surveys at www.vault.com/college—get complete surveys on 100s of colleges and universities, expert advice on applicaton essays and more.

VAULT CAREER LIBRARY   571

Lynch, Ernst & Young, AXA Financial, and Fifth-Third Bank. The Davis Center has dozens of alumni working at these companies who are always willing to consider students working in the Davis Center for employment after graduation. On-campus recruiting also takes place during two different career fairs held on campus during the school year. Even more so, Career Services facilitates the process by helping students find companies who may be hiring.

Current student, 8/2002-Submit Date, April 2006

One of the best programs at the school would be our Career Services Center, which focuses on helping students learn proper résumé building, interviewing skills, as well as general networking. The program also works with a long list of employers to help graduating students as well as alumni receive jobs upon graduation. Every year, our graduating students are competing for top well-known jobs because of past reputation and the quality of the graduates.

Alumnus/a, 8/2000-5/2004, April 2005

The University of Dayton is a well-known name, both for internship opportunities and post-graduate full-time employment. Graduates obtain all types of jobs, depending on their skills and ability to interview well. On campus, there is a Career Services Center, a bi-weekly intern shout-out e-mail, a career counseling center, two career fairs, and an excellent alumni network that students can use to help secure employment. The alumni network is the most helpful tool out of all of these options. Students also should expect to put a lot of independent work, research, and time into making contacts and submitting résumés—the Career Services Center can only do so much for you!

Current student, 8/2001-Submit Date, April 2005

Starting the first day on campus, students may take advantage of the Career Services Center. Career Services offers a number of services, including résumé critiques and mock interviews. Programs like Hire a Flyer and IPS Jobs connect students to employers who are offering part-time and full-time work. The alumni career network puts students in touch with over 3,000 UD alumni. The alumni in this network are more than happy to talk with students about what they did after college, their current jobs and offer tips. A large number of students participate in internships or the co-operative education program. Both programs offer students a great way to obtain hands-on experience in their fields of interest while still in college. I have continued my paid internship for the past three years and absolutely love it. I have learned so many things and gained valuable on-the-job experience.

Participating in a program like this is invaluable! Internships, which may be paid or unpaid, are available to students of any major, and some majors even offer academic credit for them. In the co-operative education programs, students alternate a semester of school with full-time work, and can earn up to enough money to pay for a semester of college! Each semester, there is a career fair, wherein about 70 companies come to campus and talk to students. Many of my friends have obtained internships, co-ops and post-graduate work through networking at the career fair. UD maintains a wonderful relationship with the community, so employers are impressed with and knowledgeable about UD graduates. In fact, over 75 percent of UD graduates are employed within three months of graduation.

Quality of Life

Current student, 8/2004-Submit Date, October 2006

The quality of life on campus is second-to-none. Students repeatedly point out how strong the sense of community is at the University of Dayton. Although the housing process can be somewhat of a pain, simply because it's a lottery system and students don't have a lot of choices when selecting their housing for the upcoming year. The campus is in a relatively safe location, and isn't too large. Overall, the facilities are well kept and up-to-date, especially with the recent addition of the $25 million fitness and recreation complex, which has been very popular among students. Dining services are pretty good (basic campus fare). Some new options have opened up, including the Emporium and Art Street Cafe, which have proven themselves popular and quite successful. Crime in the area is not too high, although venturing out into some of the neighborhoods around campus is somewhat risky, especially after dark. Public Safety (the campus police department) tends to do a good job at maintaining order and safety on campus.

Alumnus/a, 8/2000-5/2004, April 2006

Completely residential campus. Students live in UD housing all four years. N a suitcase campus whatsoever. Housing is phenomenal. UD owns over 400 si gle family homes in three neighborhoods. Some are early 1900s era homes, ne ones are added every summer. Creates a unique social environment, fosteri student interaction and involvement (porch culture). Facilities are kept up-t date. New labs, residence hall renovations, landscaping—the list goes o Strong food. Very uncommon to have violet crime on or around campus.

Current student, 8/2004-Submit Date, April 2006

UD's housing has its pros and cons. There is a new first-year dorm and plans renovate the others. But, two of the three older dorms are your stereotypical co lege, bite-size dorms. I was pleased with my room space and quality. I do su gest going random, it just makes it more fun. 95 percent of our students are re idents here, so that shows people want to stay on campus. Our upperclassm housing surrounds the campus into two neighborhoods. 95 percent of tho houses are university owned, making it easier for students to study abroad ar not have to deal with landlord issues. The food is very good here, and I am very picky eater. They cater to both greasy food lovers and health-junkies. Ea dining hall has a different menu for every meal; you can pick and choose whe you want to eat as you go. I have never felt unsafe on UD's campus. Pub safety not only includes UD Campus Police, but also the City of Dayton and t City of Oakwood (a neighboring suburb) always patrolling the campu Knowing we have many emergency blue-lights on campus makes me feel ease, as well. Public safety makes sure it is there for the students and comes duty within a minute of a call.

Current student, 8/2001-Submit Date, April 2005

The University of Dayton has one of the most unique living environments I ha ever experienced. It's wonderful! UD is a highly residential campus! Unli many other colleges, it is not a suitcase school. Most all students stay on ca pus during the weekends, which makes it a great place to socialize and meet ne friends! During their first year, students live in one of four first-year residen halls. In the second year, students may opt to live a four-person suite or a si person apartment. In the junior and senior years, students may live in an apar ment, or in one of the many houses that UD has purchased from the surroundi area. UD actually owns 85 percent of the houses that surround campus, ar there's no experience quite like living with your closest friends in a neighbo hood with your peers! As a Marianist school, UD stresses the concept of con munity. This is exemplified in the student neighborhood. On any given da you'll see students sitting out on their porch, throwing a football in the yar tossing a frisbee or playing cornhole on the sidewalk. Friendliness is the fir word that comes to mind when I think about UD. Whether you're in the stude union, on your way to class or walking home, people smile and wave at you— even if they don't know you. At UD, you really feel like you're part of som thing. It's hard to feel lost or unnoticed when everyone goes out of their way welcome you!

Social Life

Current student, 8/2004-Submit Date, October 2006

Overall, the school has a great social life, with plenty to do on weekend Several bars can be found right off campus, and the Pub in the student unic opens its doors at 4 p.m. on Fridays to serve eager students. Another popular b is Tim's, which allows 18 and up on Thursday nights—a great way to lead in the weekend. There is a sizeable strip of recently-opened restaurants withi walking distance of campus, offering a variety of dining options. There are ple ty of events taking place on campus as well, most of which are sponsored by th Campus Activities Board. Greek life is plentiful on campus, with dozens c sororities and fraternities available for students.

Alumnus/a, 8/2000-5/2004, April 2006

About 20 percent of campus is involved in Greek life, and nearly all students ar involved in service activities. Most social life happens right on campus in th student neighborhood, though there are a number of bars located on the mai street just within walking distance of campus. Student favorites include Tim' and the Fieldhouse.

Current student, 8/2004-Submit Date, April 2006

The social life at the University of Dayton is never ending. Students find a perfect way to balance school with extracurriculars and hanging out with friends. It not a big bar campus, but there are at least five from which to choose. Since most upperclassmen live in the student neighborhoods, parties tend to be open for everyone at their homes, creating an even strong bond between all class levels. With over 100 clubs and organizations, there is something for everyone. 18 percent of the students are involved in the social Greek system. So it is not a very Greek-dominated campus. Also, students do get involved in the professional fraternities pertaining to their majors. A favorite club of UD students is the Irish Club. Even if you are not Irish, you still join it. They have socials year-round and include a majority of the campus. Christmas on Campus is also a major event during the school year. Only a handful of students do not get involved with this event. UD will bus in about 1,400 kindergarten through second grade underprivledged students and make their Christmas. You can adopt a child or help with your club's booth. Either way, people don't miss out.

> The school says: "Upon arrival at the University of Dayton, students experience a strong commitment to growth as an individual and as a student. Interests, talents and needs are unique; therefore, more than 180 clubs and organizations (academic, athletic, cultural, service and social) exist on campus. Such diversity allows for achieving personal goals, establishing long-lasting friendships and enhancing individual development as a complete, well-rounded professional."

Current student, 8/2004-Submit Date, April 2005

There are a number of popular bars very close to campus, as well as the Oregon District within a few miles. Favorites include Timothy's (18 and up night on Thursdays is popular with those under 21), the Fieldhouse and Flannigan's. There's a pretty prominent Greek system, but you don't have to be involved in to make friends. Most of my friends are not in a fraternity or sorority. The Rubicon Park District is a string of restaurants and shops on Brown St. that are very popular with students, including Starbucks, Chipotle, Nothing but Noodles, and Second Time Around (a place to buy second hand DVDs, CDs, and posters really cheap). If partying out in the Ghetto (or student neighborhood) isn't your thing, there are campus activities going on most Friday and Saturday nights.

 ## The School Says

Established in 1850 by the Marianists, the University of Dayton (UD) is among the nation's leading Catholic universities, committed to educating students as value-centered leaders in their chosen professions and in society. More than 10,000 students attend UD, including 6,500 full-time undergraduate students. The student-to-faculty ratio is 13:1.

The technology-enhanced learning and student computer initiative provides every student living in a UD residence with high-speed data access to learning resources and collaboration tools. More than 70 undergraduate and 60 graduate programs of study are offered in the College of Arts and Sciences and in the Schools of Business Administration, Education and Allied Professions, Engineering, and Law.

More than 95 percent of full-time undergraduates live on campus, and the residential nature of the campus encourages active extracurricular involvement. More than 180 clubs and organizations exist on campus, including service organizations, professional clubs, honor societies, recreation/sports clubs, theatrical and musical performance groups, and fraternities and sororities. NCAA Division I intercollegiate athletics and intramural sports.

Read all of Vault's College Surveys at www.vault.com/college—get complete surveys on 100s of colleges and universities, expert advice on applicaton essays and more.

VAULT CAREER LIBRARY 573

Oklahoma State University

Admissions Office
219 Student Union
Stillwater, OK 74078-7042
Admissions phone: (800) 233-5019, (800) 852-1255
Admissions fax: (405) 744-5285
Admissions e-mail: admissions@okstate.edu
Admissions URL: admissions.okstate.edu/

 Admissions

Alumnus/a, 8/1999-5/2003, October 2005

The admissions process was fairly straightforward. I was an engineering major. I recommend applying early with the highest ACT or SAT score possible. Then you should ask the recruitment office if there are any departmental scholarships you might be able to apply for. For the most part, if you meet the minimum criteria, you will be admitted. This can be both good and bad. If you are a top student, it may mean you will be taking classes with students far from you caliber.

> The school says: "Students can apply as soon as they have completed the ACT or SAT. If the student chooses to retake either test, the highest score will be applied to their scholarship application. They will receive notification if they qualify for a greater amount of scholarship money."

Current student, 8/2005-Submit Date, October 2005

Make sure to list all extracurricular and community service activities from high school, because it looks really good, and make sure to list offices held, because it shows leadership.

Alumnus/a, 8/1992-5/1996, February 2005

Admissions procedures at Oklahoma State are very easy and even fun. They have numerous scholarship opportunities readily available to prospective students. The admissions staff is very accessible and knowledgeable about all options to help with paying for college.

There are a few opportunities for students to visit the campus and meet with advisors to help with the admissions process. The interview itself is very thorough. The student must complete several essays pertaining to academics, extracurricular activities, future dreams and general personal feelings.

> Oklahoma State says: "Students and their families can visit the our campus Monday through Friday at 10 a.m. and 1 p.m. and Saturday at 10 a.m. Students can register for tours on our web site. There are also counselors available in the Admissions Office from 8 a.m. to 5 p.m. Tours are also available on football game days. There is not an interview included in the admissions process."

Current student, 8/2002-Submit Date, January 2005

In the admissions process, you must fill out an application and inside that application there are three essays you must write. There is a panel who reviews the applications and the school is somewhat selective as to whom they let in. The essays are not that hard to write if you read the questions and just answer them truthfully.

Current student, 1/2002-Submit Date, April 2004

OSU advertises itself as a rather competitive university. However, I had no trouble at all. The admissions office staff is friendly and usually tries to work with you. I transferred and they gave me a tuition waiver to pay for my out-of-state tuition because I had over a 2.5.

 Academics

Alumnus/a, 8/1999-5/2003, October 2005

The program was very rigorous. Occasionally you would get stuck with a b professor who could make your life miserable. I recommend asking upper-le students to help plan out your class schedule and which professors to take. So of the best classes are actually taught by graduate students. Sometimes t workload can be overwhelming. There are times when multiple tests are given on the same day.

Current student, 8/2005-Submit Date, October 2005

The classes are challenging, and they move very quickly, so you have to stay top of things, and do your homework.

Current student, 8/2001-Submit Date, May 2004

I never had any problems scheduling myself for any of my classes. They we hard. I sometimes felt that I did not know what was going on, but by final exa time I was amazed at what I had learned.

Current student, 1/2002-Submit Date, April 2004

Getting into classes can sometimes be a pain. They tend to offer required clas es at conflicting times, so you have to plan out your schedule pretty well.

Professors vary widely. Some professors are great, you learn a ton in their clas es, and they're flexible on certain things. However, you also get a few profe sors who simply shouldn't be teaching because they either waste a lot of tim reading from the book, or simply don't seem to enjoy teaching and therefo don't help you even when you ask questions. Grading and workload vary fro professor to professor, but I've never had a problem with either.

Alumnus/a, 8/1992-5/1996, February 2005

Oklahoma State provides its students with a very high quality of academic Professors are very knowledgeable about their subjects and always willing help students with problems. Classes fill up quickly; however, most professo are willing to accept additional students if asked. Workloads vary depending o the professor. Generally, written papers are required in almost every field.

Current student, 8/2002-Submit Date, January 2005

In my area of mathematics, the workload can sometimes seem very hard but th quality of professors and classes makes up for the hard workload. The mo popular or common a class, the more sections or seating made available for th students. The grading in most of the classes is fair and balanced. Most of th professors can be very personable, although there are the few professors who ca be pains in the butt.

Alumnus/a, 8/1999-5/2004, September 2004

The electrical engineering program is pretty good. You learn about a lot of pro grams and processes that you will use later on in the real world. There are som professors to watch out for though, as they can be overly tough.

 Employment Prospects

Alumnus/a, 8/1999-5/2003, October 2005

Over the years I think the Career Service Office has been doing a better job wit bringing in top quality employers. I think that within engineering, the majorit of employers who come to campus are from nearby states and concentrated i the oil/gas industry as well as aerospace industry.

Current student, 8/2005-Submit Date, October 2005

Employers look very highly on students who graduate from OSU.

...umnus/a, 8/1992-5/1996, February 2005

...e job fairs for business and engineering are very good. However, because the ...ool is located in a small town, I feel it hurts the opportunities for internships.

...rrent student, 8/2002-Submit Date, January 2005

...e alumni association and on-campus job counselors can be very helpful. The ...ployers with whom I have spoken enjoy employing OSU alumni. As far as ...ernships go, I have many friends who have had some very lucrative intern-...ips with the Dell, Xerox, NSA and Intel.

...umnus/a, 8/1999-5/2004, September 2004

...e program does a pretty good job of placing students and really provides good ...portunities for the students to meet with prospective employers.

...rrent student, 1/2002-Submit Date, April 2004

...mpus has a big career services department. From what I understand, they're ...lly useful, but I haven't used them for anything yet. There are career fairs all ...e time though and they have workshops on résumé preparation and interview ...ategies.

Quality of Life

...umnus/a, 8/1999-5/2003, October 2005

...illwater is a great town with relatively low crime rates. On-campus housing ...s gotten progressively more expensive over the years. However, for non-...eshmen there are many housing options in varying price ranges. Life can be a ...tle slow in Stillwater. However, Stillwater is only about one hour from Tulsa ...d Oklahoma City. There are many dining options on campus as well as a wide ...riety of restaurants within the town. However, on-campus meal plans are over ...iced. A student will pay over $7.00 per meal on most plans.

...rrent student, 8/2005-Submit Date, October 2005

...ousing is very adequate, and the facilities are nice. There are lots of campus ...ganizations in which to get involved, and the food is really good. There is also ...large variety of on-campus restaurants. It is extremely safe, but the only prob-...m is the parking—it is very limited.

...umnus/a, 8/1992-5/1996, February 2005

...have no complaints at all in this department. The campus is very safe. As a ...oman, I never felt afraid to walk on campus at night. The campus police are ...ry visible and do an excellent job of keeping crime very low. Perhaps crime ...low because OSU does really feel like a family environment. While it is a big ...hool, everyone takes an interest in each other.

...rrent student, 8/2002-Submit Date, January 2005

...uality of life in Stillwater is great. Stillwater is centered around the campus— ...is a true college town. Campus is very clean and housing is fairly easy to come ...y. Crime is very low. Stillwater has many parks, two of which have golf cours-...s. There are four golf courses in town; one nine-hole course, two public cours-...s, and one professional level private course.

...umnus/a, 8/1999-5/2004, September 2004

...he life there is great, almost no crime. Stillwater is a small town with a lot of ...e perks of a larger city. The one thing that is rough is the cracking down on ...udent parties.

...rrent student, 1/2002-Submit Date, April 2004

...ousing standards have gone way up. Campus practically looks like an apart-...ent complex because they built a bunch of apartment style private accommo-...ations. I don't think they even offer traditional dorms anymore. Dining options ...e great. There are 11 restaurants on campus ranging from delis to bakeries, to ...ex-Mex, to pizza, to sit down restaurants, to cafeteria type things. We also have ...small store that sells grocery items for which you can use your meal swipes.

...lso, throughout town there are various restaurants at which you can use your ...eal swipes too, such as Subway and Mazzio's Pizza. The crime rate on cam-...us is higher than in the surrounding city, but that's not saying much.

Social Life

Alumnus/a, 8/1999-5/2003, October 2005

Social life is what you make of it. The Greek system is very active and does a great job of arranging co-ed events. There are many different bars and a couple of dance clubs. I think having a little more variety would be nice. My favorite restaurant in town is The Crepe Myrtle on the Strip. The girls are beautiful. Almost any major except engineering will provide you with great opportunities for dating. There is a bowling alley, a movie theater, an arboretum, many inter-national dances, and concerts nearly once a month given my the music depart-ment. There is also a great Latin dance club that has free lessons every Saturday.

Current student, 8/2005-Submit Date, October 2005

Social life is great! There is never a dull moment, and no matter what it is that you enjoy, you will be able to find an activity, or organization that is suitable for you. I enjoy the African-American Student Association.

Alumnus/a, 8/1992-5/1996, February 2005

I am member of a sorority. Greek life at OSU is fun and very beneficial for the students. It provides support on campus and off, even through alumni there are potential job opportunities. However, unlike many college campuses, you do not have to be Greek to have a social life. There are many wonderful restaurants and bars including world famous Eskimo Joe's. Tumbleweeds is a popular bar and dance hall near campus.

On Thursday nights you can barely walk through the large club. The Orange Peel is a new campus tradition bringing big talent to OSU to kick off the school year. OSU's homecoming is the biggest in the NCAA. All organizations com-pete with floats and Greeks have huge house decks.

Current student, 8/2001-Submit Date, May 2004

I was an electrical engineering major, so my social life was limited. There is a strip of bars where everyone goes. Also, the off-campus student housing is well known and everyone knows where all the parties are at all the time. Only prob-lem is that the police used to break up parties. They are expedient.

The Strip (a street with a bunch of bars on it) is across from campus. There are seven to 15 bars in the Stillwater area, but I don't drink so I can't say for sure how many. Apparently it's cool to go down there, almost everyone goes every week. There is one club called Tumbleweeds (the Weed) that plays country but also has a wing devoted to hip-hop, but that's it on dance clubs. The Greek sys-tem is huge here. Something like 40 percent of students, which is crazy consid-ering most campuses have about 11 percent Greek involvement.

Current student, 8/2002-Submit Date, January 2005

There are many bars in town and many with drink specials most nights. The Greek system is alive and well in Stillwater. There are many restaurants in town like Chile's, McAlister's, Panera Bread and the like. The town also bolsters many parks in town that are great for romantic walks to take a date on.

Read all of Vault's College Surveys at www.vault.com/college—get complete surveys on 100s of colleges and univer-sities, expert advice on applicaton essays and more.

VAULT CAREER LIBRARY 575

University of Oklahoma

Recruitment Services
550 Parrington Oval, L-1
Norman, OK 73019-3032
Admissions phone: (405) 325-2151, (800) 234-6868
Admissions e-mail: ou-pss@ou.edu
Admissions URL: go2.ou.edu

 Admissions

Current student, Business, 8/2004-Submit Date, April 2007

It is becoming increasingly difficult for students to be accepted into the University of Oklahoma. Admissions standards are being raised every few years as our president tries to bring the school into the academic elite. The application is fairly standard and students can expect to be admitted if they have the appropriate scores.

Current student, Politics, 8/2002-Submit Date, March 2007

As an Oklahoma resident, the admissions requirements were fairly straightforward. I had a 1200 on the SAT and that met one of the qualifications for admission. I applied to the university and to the Honors College simultaneously, with the Honors application requiring an essay.

Current student, Pre-med, 8/2004-Submit Date, March 2007

To apply to the university, all you must do is complete a simple application that does not include an essay. A supplement is included with the application, which includes an essay portion, but this is only used to determine scholarships. I highly suggest filling out the scholarship application as it opens many doors to the prospective student.

Current student, Liberal Arts, 8/2005-Submit Date, March 2007

The requirements to attend OU have increased over the years, however if you meet all the minimums you will have no problem gaining access. I advise any student leaders to pay extra attention to the general scholarship application. This application is comprised of three essays as well as a brief résumé of your high school accomplishments. Every year around 100 students are selected out of the more than 5,000 applications to be members of the President's Leadership Class. The organization is the best place to be for a student who desires to became a success on campus. Other opportunities are also available from this application, so take your time and make it good!

Alumnus/a, 8/1999-5/2003, November 2006

I was a transfer student from Oklahoma State University, where I had already completed two years. When coming into OU, I was told that most of my credits would transfer, but I would still need to repeat one year. This was fine with me: OU had a much more comprehensive program and I wanted to get everything they were offering. My grades weren't the best, and I was told that I would be coming in on academic probation. However, they told me what they expected of me and if I was able to bring up my grades, they would allow me to stay in the program. I did, and the program was excellent. The instructors were very attentive to each student, and if there was a student who wanted to succeed, they were given every chance.

Alumnus/a, Business, 8/2003-5/2004, July 2007

The admissions process is pretty simple. You fill out the basic high school information and write a few short essays. They are really looking for high school GPA and SAT/ACT test scores. The University of Oklahoma prides itself in having the most National Merit Scholars, so if you are one those, you will pretty much have a free ride.

Current student, 8/2005-Submit Date May 2006

The admissions process is fairly easy. The two-page admissions application is very straightforward. Also, the scholarship packet is located right behind the admissions application, so you don't forget to fill it out as well. If you prefer to work online, there is also an application available there. Either way, it's as e as any other application I've ever filled out.

> **The school says:** "We encourage all applicants to apply for admission and scholarships online. The scholarship application can be completed at the same time you complete the application for admission, or separately at a later time. We encourage students to apply early—at least by the scholarship deadline of February 1 for freshman applicants, and March 1 for transfer applicants. You can access the application for admission and the scholarship application online at www.go2.ou.edu/ and click on Admissions Information."

Alumnus/a, 8/2002-5/2006, May 2006

There is an automatic admissions process for those students who meet cert requirements. All students must meet standard high school prerequisites o lined in the application packet and online. For residents, if you have a h school GPA of at least 3.0 and you are in the top 25 percent of your class, y are automatically admitted. If you meet either of these criteria and have an A of 24 (SAT 1090) or above, you may also be admitted automatically. For n residents, the requirements are generally the same except your ACT/SAT m be a little higher (26/1170). Those students who are not automatically admit will be put on a waitlist and will be admitted based on their academic qualifi tions if there is space in the entering class. I know many classmates who ha been admitted this way and there is absolutely no stigma associated with bei admitted alternatively. Applying is fairly standard and can be completed onli Apply early as many scholarships are granted based on the admissions applic tion. Also, if you are taking both the SAT and the ACT, send both of your sco to OU as they will look at your highest score for admissions and scholarships have found that OU is fairly generous with its scholarship awards considering is an educational value already. For National Merit Scholars and students w score a 30 or above on their ACT, a University of Oklahoma education may financed completely through scholarships. Additionally, for students who well their freshman year, OU offers numerous retention scholarships (schola ships granted on a yearly basis to sophomores and above). You just have to diligent enough to look for them and apply for scholarships everywhere through Student Life, your fraternity/sorority and your major.

> **The school says:** "Admission requirements for undergraduate students may change on an annual basis. For the most current admission requirements for freshman and transfer applicants, go to www.go2.ou.edu/ and click on Admission Information. Waitlisted students (freshmen only) must meet certain performance and curricular criteria that are outlined at admissions.ou.edu/freshadm.html. Admission from the waitlist is on a space available basis with preference going to the most academically qualified applicants in the pool. For the most current information on National Merit Scholars, please reference go2.ou.edu/national_scholars/index.html."

Current student, 1/2003-Submit Date, January 2006

It is relatively easy to get into OU. If one has a high enough SAT or ACT sco one will be well taken care of by the university. I was a transfer student, and actually dealt with a lot of ill-informed and rather cold people who were n entirely helpful. Scholarships are also not easy to come by as a transfer stude Also, a statement of purpose must be included if one wants to become part of t Honors College—a minimum ACT score is required as well.

> **The school says:** "OU welcomes transfer students from other institutions. For the most current information on admission requirements for transfer students, go to admissions.ou.edu/ transadm.html. Transfer scholarship information is available at https://admrecapps2.ou.edu/apply/transferscholarship.cfm. Campus tours can be scheduled through the Office of

Prospective Student Services, (405) 325-2151 or 1-800-234-6868, or on-line at go2.ou.edu.

"Transfer course equivalency information for Oklahoma colleges and universities and some out-of-state institutions is available at www.ou.edu/admrec/tetables.htm, or by contacting the Office of Admissions at (405) 325-2252. Transfer students are encouraged to apply early in order to maximize opportunities for scholarships, financial aid and university housing. Freshmen entering the University of Oklahoma are eligible to apply to the Honors Curriculum if a) they have a Composite ACT of 29 or higher or they have a SAT Total of 1280 or higher and b) they rank among the top 10 percent of graduates in their high school class or have a high school grade point average of 3.75. Transfer students who enroll at the University of Oklahoma with 15 or more college credit hours with a cumulative grade point average of 3.40 or higher are eligible to apply.

"Additionally, all OU students who have earned 15 or more hours of OU credit hours with a grade point average of 3.40 or higher are eligible to apply to the OU Honors Curriculum. Final admission into the Honors Curriculum is determined by evaluation of this application which includes a written essay of 400 to 500 words."

Academics

Current student, Politics, 8/2002-Submit Date, March 2007

I've found that the education here at OU is what you make it. It is possible to get a better education here than at an Ivy League, but one must be an active participant in one's education. By talking to older students, one can find the best classes to take and usually there is little difficulty getting in. Professors at OU are generally very enthusiastic about engaging students. This is the greatest selling point of the university, I believe. Over the course of my time here, I have developed close relationships with over a dozen faculty members. Workload varies depending on courses, some courses are extremely demanding, others less so. I imagine this is the case at any university.

Current student, Liberal Arts, 8/2005-Submit Date, March 2007

Like any university, classes at OU are varied. There are a vast variety of programs for any student to study. Typically classes are small, but the variety of popular classes provides the opportunity for you to get into whatever class you desire. Professors are approachable and often give out home addresses and phone numbers for you to contact them when needed.

Current student, Pre-med, 8/2004-Submit Date, March 2007

Overall, the academic environment at OU is very accommodating. There are always classes available although at times it is more difficult for the underclassmen to get the classes they want because they fill up quickly. The professors are usually accommodating about opening up more seats if a course is full and there is a great demand. I also think that the professors are warm and welcoming. They provide a healthy academic community that allows students to thrive.

Alumnus/a, 8/1999-5/2003, November 2006

I was in the theatre program, and it was quite easy to take the classes I needed when I needed to take them. The professors were topnotch, very knowledgeable about the subjects they were teaching and eager to see each individual student succeed. The class sizes were small enough to allow for individual attention from the instructor, but large enough to learn from other students process of trial and error. Most of my professors were actually working in theatre during the summer. One was even working off-Broadway in New York, and would come back to Oklahoma during the school year. The teachers knew what they were teaching and knew how to dispense their knowledge to the student body.

Alumnus/a, Liberal Arts, 8/2001-5/2006, July 2007

When you take lower-division courses, the class sizes are pretty big. Once you actually get into the program, the class sizes were smaller. My smallest class had seven students and my largest had close to 250. Popular gen-ed type classes can be difficult to get into but the upper-division courses that were needed specifically for my major were not difficult. As for the professors, many did not have a big interest in their student's lives but I was satisfied with their teaching ability. The worst courses were the lower-division gen-ed requirements. The professors weren't really there to teach and the class size was too large to really get to know the professor. The grading was standard for all my classes (90-100=A and so on). I felt the workload was not very difficult. There is no "dead week," so finals were always a stressful time but other than that it usually went that you had two tests and one large paper. None of my tests were cumulative.

Current student, 8/2005-Submit Date, May 2006

Quality of classes is high at OU, especially if you are involved in the Honors College. These classes are small, generally around 15 people, so you get one-on-one time with your professor. The only problem is that unless you have early enrollment through National Merit or another program, it is a little bit difficult to get the exact schedule you want because classes fill up. However, if you check with the professors, they may be able to enroll you in their classes when another student drops out. Also, the teachers are fair in their grading and are willing to work with students whenever they need help.

> **The school says:** "OU's Honors College is one of the largest honors programs among public universities in the United States. 1,400 students participate in small classes of 19 or less. OU is one of the few public universities in the nation to cap the class size of first-year English composition courses at no more than 19 students."

Current student, 8/2004-Submit Date, May 2006

When I entered college I was really worried about what the academics would be like and how I would do, but since my first semester I have been nothing but impressed by the caliber of professors, classes and curriculum offered at this university. My classes have challenged me and really helped my writing skills, and every professor I have had has been available to help and really wants to see their students succeed. There are a wide variety of classes offered and, although workload varies from class to class, the work is very doable. There is a writing center in the library and endless resources to aid students. OU places academics first on its list, and I have been so impressed by the caliber expected of professors and students.

> **The school says:** "OU has implemented a new Freshman Writing Program that is an intensive writing and editing program for new freshmen based on the Harvard Expository Writing Program. There are now six full-time professors in the program offering 12 sections each semester. The University of Oklahoma Libraries ranks in the Top Two in the Big 12 in the number of volumes held, according to The Chronicle of Higher Education. The University of Oklahoma Library is the largest in the state with approximately 4.7 million volumes. The Lissa and Cy Wagner Student Academic Services Center will open in 2008 to bring together under one roof the main academic services available to students, including University College's Advising and Enrollment, Assessment and Learning, Freshman Programs, and the Center for Student Advancement offices as well as OU's Graduation Office and Writing Center."

Employment Prospects

Current student, Business, 8/2003-Submit Date, March 2007

Our Career Services department is exceptional. It connects you with alumni and holds on-campus recruiting out of its office. It also does résumé critiques and mock interviews.

Current student, Politics, 8/2002-Submit Date, March 2007

The University of Oklahoma is without question the premier institution in the state. Employers, particularly around Oklahoma and in the Dallas area appear to have great respect for OU graduates.

One asset of the university is a tremendous Career Services department. Students who are interested have numerous chances to interview with top com-

Read all of Vault's College Surveys at **www.vault.com/college**—get complete surveys on 100s of colleges and universities, expert advice on applicaton essays and more.

VAULT CAREER LIBRARY 577

panies on campus. Internship opportunities are also abundant through Career Services.

OU alumni are extremely eager to help undergraduates. Part of being a state university is that many people take great pride in helping students from their home state. I have found the generosity, both in time and resources, of OU alumni to be amazing.

Current student, Pre-med, 8/2004-Submit Date, March 2007

I think that one of the best parts of the university is the opportunities provided post graduation. The university has a Career Services Office, which provides résumé building, interviewing techniques and even helps to find jobs and internships. The individual colleges also help with placement of internships and post graduate careers.

Alumnus/a, Liberal Arts, 8/2001-5/2006, July 2007

If you are a business student, it is a lot easier to find a job and you get a lot more help from the school. I have a degree in International Studies and it was not easy to find a job.

Alumnus/a, Business, 8/2003-5/2004, July 2007

I landed a job with Ernst & Young and had several other prospects such as UBS, Liberty Mutual Ins Group, Halliburton and Chesapeake. The topnotch energy companies like to recruit from OU. The Big Four accounting firms that recruit from OU are KPMG, Ernst & Young and Deloitte & Touche. Numerous other firms in the Fortune 500 recruit during career fairs, which happen two or three times a semester. Internships are pretty common and most of my friends were able to get them rather easily.

 ## Quality of Life

Current student, Politics, 8/2002-Submit Date, March 2007

All freshmen live on campus in three major dormitories. This provides a unique first-year experience that I think everyone values, at least in retrospect. Affordable housing is readily available all around Norman, and safety is generally a non-issue. Students can choose from university housing, rental homes and apartments.

Current student, Pre-med, 8/2004-Submit Date, March 2007

I have not lived in campus housing since my freshman year but there have been recent updates to the facilities. The new dormrooms are completely renovated and provide a more flexible furniture arrangement. The safety of the campus is taken very seriously and especially with new blue emergency lights being placed more frequently around campus.

Current student, 8/2004-Submit Date, May 2006

So far my experience at the University of Oklahoma has been indescribable. I have met so many people from different backgrounds, have gotten involved in numerous campus activities, and made friends whom I know I will carry with me through life. Housing is required for all freshmen, and I must say that there is nothing like that first-year experience. Living in the dorms was fun and keeps students so connected because it is right there. Walking down campus at any time of the day it is obvious how much time and care is put into maintaining a rich environment to learn and to experience college. The campus is beautiful, and the student body is truly a big community.

> **The school says:** "All single freshman students under 20 years of age must live in a university residence hall for the academic year except for those who have earned 24 or more hours of college credit in residence at OU or have already lived in university residence halls for two semesters. The university does, however, grant exemptions for health and financial reasons as well as for those freshmen who choose to live at home with parents who live within nearby commuting distance."

Alumnus/a, Liberal Arts, 8/2001-5/2006, July 2007

Dorms are not very clean but you have to live in them for one year. Overall, I met a lot of friends and the food wasn't bad, so it was a pretty good experience. They also provide access to student housing in apartments throughout campus.

The housing is kind of far away and I preferred to live in a house so that I cou walk to campus. As for safety, besides petty crime, Norman is pretty safe. I ha never felt uncomfortable walking on campus late at night. The neighborho around campus is great. It is full of great old houses and lots of trees. Avera rent is $350 per person for a house. There are a lot of local restaurants and al chain restaurants by the highway in Norman.

Current student, 1/2003-Submit Date, January 2006

There is a community of dormitories quite close to campus for the freshmen, a a bus system that runs by all the university's apartments that can take students school. Parking is not advisable, as it is expensive and very competitive. T campus is lovely, and has many patrons who are constantly supporting ne buildings. It is a pleasant campus with many computer labs and wireless area too. The student union food choices are not to my liking, simply because I ha fast food. There are emergency centers on campus where one can seek help fro the OU police, but I do not know how fast response time is.

> **The school says:** "The University of Oklahoma Police Department offers 24-hour foot, bicycle and vehicle patrol, a modified 911 system, and over 150 blue light emergency phones located across campus. OU also offers self-defense education classes, free SAFEwalk and SAFEride escort services, lighted sidewalks and pathways, formal and informal safety presentations and discussions, and a variety of safety education pamphlets, posters and films."

 ## Social Life

Current student, Business, 8/2004-Submit Date, April 2007

The Greek system overshadows all other groups on campus. Nearly 30 perce of OU's students are in some type of Greek organization. This number has va ied recently due to the university's recent adoption of a no-alcohol policy for tl Greek houses wishing to be a part of the Intrafraternity council. But Greeks ar non-Greeks mix fairly well. The dating scene is very active because of the mar Greek functions and the historical Campus Corner, which is comprised of mar restaurants, bars and live music venues.

> **The school says:** "Fraternities draw 16 percent of the male student body and 25 percent of the female students are members of sororities. In January 2005, the OU Board of Regents adopted a comprehensive alcohol policy which made all residence halls and fraternity and sorority alcohol-free as well as established an extensive alcohol education program for students."

Current student, Politics, 8/2002-Submit Date, March 2007

The town of Norman is just the right size. Small enough to where the college a dominant force in the town, but big enough to where there are things like sho ping malls and movie theaters. Plus, Oklahoma City is only a 30-minute dri away; however, few students find themselves going there because there's plen happening in Norman. Campus Corner, an area where bars and restaurants ar designed for students, has been totally revitalized in the past five years. Th nightlife is great. Some favorite places are Pepe Delgado's, Louie's, 74 Victoria's, and Logan's.

Current student, Liberal Arts, 8/2005-Submit Date, March 2007

The best place to go for a wonderful social atmosphere is Campus Corne Located right across the street from campus, this four-block conglomeration c hip, trendy bars to Harold's clothing stores is the perfect place to spend a gam day afternoon or a Thursday evening out. The Greek system at OU is ver prominent. There are 11 sororities in our Pan-Hellenic system, all of which ar wonderful. I believe there are 14 different fraternities as well as multi-cultura Greek houses. The whole Greek system is respected and is a huge part of ever campus organization. However, if Greek isn't your thing, then you will hav plenty of company because 60 percent of the students at OU are not affiliate with a Greek organizations.

umnus/a, Business, 8/2003-5/2004, July 2007

>ve OU's social life. The school is not too big and not too small. OU has a
; Greek system. There is always something going on during the semester and
; a fun way to make friends if you come to OU not knowing anyone. There is
e club that is always packed with tons of people and that is Kongo's. Most of
· bar scene is located on Campus Corner, where you are guaranteed to see
neone you know. Some favorite bars: Seven47, Logan's, Louie's. As far as
ting goes, there are tons of gorgeous women around. There are too many clubs
name. I advise joining one or two. Norman has some of the best ethnic food
und. Pad Thai is the best Thai food I have ever had. Sake is a good
shi/hibachi restaurant. Pizza Shuttle is delicious and is always open late and
livers. Raising Cane's is a great fried chicken place. A great German restau-
it located 10 minutes north of campus is Royal Bavaria. They have great
rman beer made right there and the food is excellent as well. There is a lot
re good stuff to eat; these are just a few of my favorites.

The School Says

Created by the Oklahoma Territorial Legislature in 1890, the
University of Oklahoma is a doctoral degree-granting research
university serving the educational, cultural, economic and health
care needs of the state, region and nation. The Norman campus serves as home to all of the university's academic programs
except health-related fields. Both the Norman and Health
Sciences Center colleges offer programs at the Schusterman
Center, the site of OU-Tulsa. The OU Health Sciences Center,
which is located in Oklahoma City, is one of only four comprehensive academic health centers in the nation with seven professional colleges. OU enrolls more than 30,000 students, has
more than 2,000 full-time faculty members, and has 20 colleges
offering 152 majors at the baccalaureate level, 160 majors at
the master's level, 80 majors at the doctoral level, 38 majors at
the first professional level, and 18 graduate certificates.

OU offers a comprehensive educational experience to students
both inside and outside the traditional classroom setting. OU's

Honors College is one of the largest honors programs among
public universities in the United States and offers specialized
curriculum. OU is one of the few public universities in the
nation to cap the class size of first-year English composition
courses at no more than 19 students. Freshman students have
the option of taking the Gateway to Learning course, which provides a survey of the university's academic opportunities, services, and resources. The president of OU even teaches an introductory political science course each semester, which illustrates
how approachable and supportive the faculty and administration
are on campus. Students who wish to study abroad would be
interested to know that OU ranks first in the Big 12 and at the
top in the nation in international exchange agreements with
countries around the world, with 171 student exchange agreements at universities in 60 countries. OU ranks Number One in
the nation among public universities in National Merit Scholars
enrolled per capita.

In addition to academic experiences, a sense of community and
family is important at OU. This sense is broadened through programs such as the Faculty-In-Residence, where faculty members live in the residence halls among students, and OU
Cousins, which matches U.S. and international students to
share informal and social experiences. Due in part to these programs and many others, OU has won awards for new initiatives
to create a sense of family and community on campus. OU is
one of the very few public universities to twice receive the
Templeton Foundation Award as a "Character Building College"
for stressing the value of community. OU also ranks in the Top
10 in the United States in the Freshman Year Experience,
according to a national study by the Policy Center on the First
Year of College, recognizing OU's initiatives for first-year students and its commitment to put students first.

The University of Oklahoma also has a reasonable price tag,
being ranked by The Princeton Review among the Top 10 public universities in the nation in terms of academic excellence and
cost for students.

University of Tulsa

dmissions Office
00 South College
ulsa, OK 74104
dmissions phone: (918) 631-2307 or (800) 331-3050
dmissions fax: (918) 631-5003
dmissions e-mail: admission@utulsa.edu
dmissions URL: www.utulsa.edu/admission/

*ote: The school has chosen not to review the student
urveys submitted.*

Admissions

umnus/a, 1/2000-1/2004, April 2005

he University of Tulsa required a full-length application process, including fill-
g out a form for basic information, composing a lengthy essay, obtaining sev-
al references and participating in an one-on-one interview with a school
cruitment representative. TU is very selective, requiring above-average ACT
d SAT scores, and looks for other vital qualities in their students, including
adership abilities and involvement in extracurricular activities.

Alumnus/a, 8/2000-5/2004, October 2005

Pretty standard. You have to submit all the usual documents and have an interview. I really hit it off with my admissions counselor. She was great and seemed
very interested in attracting high-quality students to attend TU. It was semi-
selective but certainly not impossible.

Alumnus/a, 8/1993-5/2000, June 2004

I filled out a form with my vitals and had to send a copy of my ACT scores as
well as a copy of my high school transcript. There was also an essay I had to
write about why I wanted to be student at the University of Tulsa. I also had to
complete an audition on my major instrument in front of the music faculty. This
audition was what they used to determine the amount of scholarship, if any, I
received.

Alumnus/a, 9/1987-5/1991, September 2003

This was a very smooth process with direct interaction with the then Dean of the
College of Arts and Sciences. My on-campus tour was efficiently pulled togeth-
er, especially given that I requested the tour during the school's spring break.
The process was not cumbersome or laborious, but it was thorough.

Read all of Vault's College Surveys at www.vault.com/college—get complete surveys on 100s of colleges and universities, expert advice on applicaton essays and more.

VAULT CAREER LIBRARY 579

Academics

Alumnus/a, 8/2000-5/2004, October 2005

I studied international business and Russian. Business college was good, but not outstanding. Not extremely demanding coursework from most professors. The best thing about the school for independent-minded people, is the individual support they can obtain from professors. With the small classes, by the end of the course you have built a good, solid relationship with the professor, can ask for individual help in the classroom, or ask for support with extracurricular activities. Russian language department was small (one professor). In retrospect, a program with more depth would have been more beneficial. For a business student, I think the workload was normal. Classes increased the difficulty level substantially in the higher course levels.

Alumnus/a, 1/2000-1/2004, April 2005

The University of Tulsa required an extensive liberal arts foundation, with more intensive work in the major study area as the degree progressed. I had to take 12 hours in the major area, including several different more specified courses. It was not difficult to get good grades at TU, and I made straight A's on a number of occasions. This did not mean that the grading was easy, only that a reasonable degree of effort was required. The professors were tough and exacting, but always appreciative and respectful of student efforts.

Alumnus/a, 8/1993-5/2000, June 2004

The degree plan I was on was really a music major with an education minor, but just called one degree. There were blocks that were required by every student, but there were many classes in each block from which to choose. Getting into any class I ever wanted to was never a problem. If it was full all I had to do was get the permission of the professor teaching the class and I got in. The class size is determined by the size of the room, and there was almost always more room than the limit that was set for the class. Also, they took into account that not everyone enrolled in those classes would stay in—some would drop. The block classes were really the only classes I ever had trouble getting into.

The professors were very approachable, even as distinguished as some of them were. The class sizes were small enough that they would address me by my name, and all of the professors in my major area of study remember me, even four years later.

Grading was never something that was mystical at TU, because professors provided their grading policies at the beginning of each semester for each class. Not every class taught by the same professor has the same grading policies. If they fudged at all on the policies, it was usually to benefit the students. I always got the feeling that they would not let you fail.

Alumnus/a, 9/1987-5/1991, September 2003

Getting into classes was hardly ever a problem for me. I pretty much always got the classes I wanted, the professors I wanted, and the course schedule I wanted. Excellent, excellent curriculum—core and degree focused. My degree was a liberal arts one focused on Communications (broadcast emphasis). Finest quality of professors, in my opinion, in the land. I am still today friends with the former dean and two professors in College of Arts and Sciences.

Employment Prospects

Alumnus/a, 8/2000-5/2004, October 2005

Trying to start an alumni network for internationally interested people. Nothing currently in place other than typical alumni association. A couple of good internships out there, but Tulsa is really being hurt by companies moving to Houston (read: oil companies). Well-respected and an exceptional reputation in the region, but go outside of that area and you will have a bit more of a struggle explaining things. Career Services is not the most helpful, especially when it comes to finding something overseas. Then again, I don't know how much they have to work with in the way of companies. Overall, staying in the area is your best bet for getting respect because you went to TU, unless you study petroleum engineering. That program is internationally known and brings in a lot of foreign students.

Alumnus/a, 1/2000-1/2004, April 2005

TU is a very prominent school in Oklahoma, and graduates can anticipate mu success in terms of finding employment, as employers understand the high qu ity of the school's graduates. The sky is the limit in terms of what types of j graduates can obtain, and simply depends on the degree with which one gra ates. Students can major in anything from English to petroleum engineeri from art to mathematics, from computer science to nursing, and hundreds of o ers. The alumni relations department is invariably helpful in assisting gradua to find work.

Alumnus/a, 8/1993-5/2000, June 2004

The most help I got in finding a job came from the professor who supervised intern-teaching assignment, not the career placement center on campus. In fa they were quite ignorant about jobs in my field, saying "Have you looked in paper?" If you were in business, engineering or nursing you could find a j anywhere, but that's not the case in music education.

Alumnus/a, 9/1987-5/1991, September 2003

The university prides itself—and it should—on its career assistance programs current (and former) students. The university assisted me with my for-colle credit internship and was instrumental in the four job offers I received befc graduating the university.

Quality of Life

Alumnus/a, 8/2000-5/2004, October 2005

I think the quality of life at TU is superb. The city is big enough to have son thing going on most of the time (although it's certainly no Las Vegas). The ca pus is absolutely gorgeous and a pleasant atmosphere abounds. Housing is C in the dorms and good in the apartments. The new sports facilities are fantast As for the neighborhood, it is in an OK part of town. It could be better bui could be worse. TU really brightens up the area, that's for sure.

Alumnus/a, 1/2000-1/2004, April 2005

The housing at TU was exceptional, and they were actually building new apa ments as I was finishing my degree. The dormitories are well-maintained a easy to get into. The campus, though somewhat broad and drawn out, is alwa well-manicured and in exceptional condition. The facilities are wonderful, food is delicious, and crime is very rare. All told, the University of Tulsa i superior school with facilities and a quality of life that are second-to-none.

Alumnus/a, 8/1993-5/2000, June 2004

I never lived on campus, but the facilities were more than adequate to suit r needs as a commuting student. I was always comfortable, and there were ple ty of places on campus to study and eat, or just hang out.

Alumnus/a, 9/1987-5/1991, September 2003

Absolutely fantastic—and even more so today with all the new amenities a facilities available to current students. Great campus events, Greek society a athletics.

Social Life

Alumnus/a, 8/2000-5/2004, October 2005

There are about a zillion student-run organizations for every interest you c think of. And if there isn't one, you are bound to be able to start something. T campus definitely lacks a central meeting place. The Hut in ACAC really doe n't cut it as far as a great hang-out place is concerned. I think someone's wor ing on that, though. The students are really empowered. Very active Greek sy tem dominates activities. Still possible to have a social life without it, thougl

As far as the nightlife in the town, downtown isn't too far away from campu and that's where most of the clubs are. There are some decent bars and son karaoke places. Lots of great restaurants, though. Really like the Brookside a Utica Square areas.

...uff not to miss in the city: big Oktoberfest on the river, Christmas lights at the ...ble college, giant hands at Oral Roberts University (and other crazy architec-...re), Philbrook Museum (their Sunday brunch is an experience), Gilcrease ...useum (absolutely amazing collecton of American West paintings!), The ...rple Glaze on Brookside, wandering around Utica Square in the evening ...specially around Christmas time), going to the old-fashioned 50s-styled dollar ...ovie theater, eating at the Metro and Wendy's (both right next to campus), ...ednesdays at the Buccaneer Bar.

...lumnus/a, 1/2000-1/2004, April 2005

...e school is heavily Greek-related, with fraternities and sororities playing a ...tal role in the life of the university, and well over 60 percent of the students ...ining—Kappa Alpha Theta, Sigma Nu and Sigma Chi are the most prominent.

The campus is located in a residential neighborhood, but well within range of numerous bars, restaurants, nightclubs and other entertainment venues, like the Woodland Hills Mall, the Cherry Street Brewery and Utica Square.

Alumnus/a, 8/1993-5/2000, June 2004

Less than five minutes from campus is a district that has live music, dancing and cultural events. A place where singles know they can go to see or be seen. There are the classier places like the Bowery or Kilkinney's Irish pub, and jeans and tennies places like Full Moon Cafe. All have live music or events and the food is good.

Read all of Vault's College Surveys at www.vault.com/college—get complete surveys on 100s of colleges and univer-sities, expert advice on applicaton essays and more.

VAULT CAREER LIBRARY   581

Oregon State University

Admissions Office
104 Kerr Administration Building
Corvallis, OR 97331-2106
Admissions phone: (541) 737-4411 or (800) 291-4192
Admissions e-mail: osuadmit@orst.edu
Admissions URL: oregonstate.edu/admissions/

 ## Admissions

Current student, 9/2002-Submit Date, April 2006

The admissions process was very easy. There were no long essays to write or lengthy interviews, only an application form. They didn't even look at my SAT scores because my high school GPA was over a 3.2. All you have to do is have decent grades in high school or good SAT scores, fill out an application, and wait for your acceptance packet. I'm not from Oregon and they seem to like accepting out-of-state students, so it wasn't difficult at all.

Alumnus/a, 9/2003-6/2005, March 2006

I had completed three years at Central Oregon Community College, during which time I took all the prerequisites to transfer to Oregon State University (OSU), majoring in nutrition and food management with a dietetics option. I completed the entrance application to OSU and the summer before my transfer there, I scheduled an interview and met with the director of the Nutrition program at OSU to make sure I was on track with the courses I was planning to take my last year before transferring to OSU. I did not have to write an essay to accompany my application for admission to OSU. I had to submit a request for transcripts to all my former colleges which I attended to be sent to OSU.

Current student, 9/2002-Submit Date, August 2004

The admissions process can be done easily online. The best thing to do is to keep track of all your extracurricular activities throughout high school (and before) so you can list them all in the application. There was no interview and the essay was only for scholarship application. Students are rarely rejected if GPA is high enough (above 3.0).

Alumnus/a, 9/1996-6/2001, January 2005

This university is a public school; as long as you meet the minimum qualifications (GPA, high school, GED) then you are in. However, if you were like me and needed help financially and strived for a challenging career, there were many scholarships that the university and government financial aid offered. In my experience, I worked extremely hard in high school and took the SAT several times to do well enough for scholarships to pay for my tuition.

I was aiming for the Presidential and Laurel Scholarships offered through the university. I also was hoping to qualify for grants that are basically free money from the federal government to students who qualify. However, to be a strong candidate for either of these types of scholarships, a student's number one priority is to turn in the federal financial aid form early, which was called the FAFSA. Federal financial aid is based on a first come, first serve basis. Just as important is turning in your application of admission to the university by the deadline. Another imperative aspect for significant financial aid is to expand and develop your personal experiences.

Almost all of the scholarships I applied for wanted a candidate with a diverse background of experiences in sports, volunteer work, other extracurricular activities and a variety of work-for-pay experiences. This shows that you are ready for the college experience at OSU, serious about planning for your future and will stay in college to become a strong, contributing member of society. With that being said, you will also want to stand-out to those analyzing your application for scholarship. Focus on your strong skills, personality traits and other aspects of your person, so that OSU will be enticing you with financial aid!

 ## Academics

Current student, 9/2002-Submit Date, April 2006

OSU has some great classes as well as some fantastic teachers. When you're freshman, it is a little more difficult to get into some of the more popular classes, like Human Sexuality. If you're one of the lucky ones to be the first to register in your grade, then you have a pretty good shot at getting the classes you want. Available classes also depend on your major. The College of Business has a lot of enrolled students so some classes are hard to get into but the advisors can usually get you an override if there's a class you need to take. The workload of classes really varies by professor. I know that they try and have the same requirements for all sections of a class, but everyone knows who the easy professors are. All you have to do is ask a student who already took that class and they'll tell you from which teacher to take it. After four years in the College of Business, I really haven't had to write many papers but there are a lot of projects. Most of the professors are lenient on attendance but they stress participation, which go hand in hand. One negative about registering for classes is that it's randomly alphabetized by last name but the order never seems to change. A lot of times it doesn't seem like there is any logic to registering. You just have to cross your fingers and hope your name is first.

Alumnus/a, 9/2003-6/2005, March 2006

The academic nature of the program that I completed was very high. The quality of the classes was, for the most part, very high. I did not have any difficulty getting into my desired courses. Of course, I had registration advantage, being a junior and senior while attending OSU. Additionally, I had completed a great many courses of general nature at Central Oregon Community College, which transferred over to OSU. Grading at OSU was pretty standard (90+ = A; 80+ = B; 70+ = C; 60+ = D; Below 60 = F). I felt the professors were busy at OSU although some tried to accommodate you. The tutor help at OSU amounted to scheduling a 30-minute session with a tutor. I thought it was a very inadequate system. I found that by keeping my courseload to 12 credits each term, I could manage the study and homework needed for each course.

Alumnus/a, 9/1996-6/2001, January 2005

I was in a full-time undergraduate program. Each major, regardless of what it has basic, core classes that are required by OSU to graduate with a bachelor degree. These are mathematics, physical sciences, social sciences, health and human performance, diversity development and others. These have a tendency to have very large attendance and take place in an auditorium. Unfortunately, with this size of a class, the likelihood of getting individual attention from the professor is lowered. To accommodate this need, the professors will usually hire graduate teaching assistants (GTAs) to answer questions from the undergraduates. While the GTAs can relate to the undergraduates on a personal level—they are both students—they still don't have the same knowledge of the subject matter as the professor. Some believe that this lowers the level of education offered; others believe this is a highly convenient way of accommodating a high demand for the university.

Registering for undergraduate classes is based on an alphabetical basis. For example, for fall term, those with the last name of A through E will register on Monday, T through Z on Tuesday, and so forth. Then the rotation changes the next term. Usually the graduate students and undergraduate seniors will get first pick of any classes because many are finishing up their degree work. Of course, highly popular classes will fill up fast. Depending on the class, a student can usually override the registration system by getting a permission form signed by the professor to enter a full class. This procedure is subjective to the preference of the professor and availability of seats.

Most of the undergraduate coursework have the A through F grading system. All of your classes specifically geared toward your major has to be graded in that fashion. The basic, core university classes that all students have to take have the option on be graded on a satisfactory or unsatisfactory basis. Although, it

wned upon to have too many S/Us, I found it helpful if my courseload was
heavy.

is brings me to what establishes a full-time undergraduate student. You must
registered for 12 credit hours of classes to be considered full time. Most
ancial aid opportunities require you to be full time. It is recommended that
u average about 15 credit hours a term for you to graduate within four years,
this is what you want to do. This, of course, means that you will have some
avy terms and some light terms. Most majors have a set curriculum that dic-
e what and when you take them, so you'll have to be vigilant in following your
gram.

rrent student, 9/2002-Submit Date, August 2004

ost core classes are fairly large but when you get into specific classes (about
cond year) classes slim down in size and there is a more teacher-student rela-
nship. Some classes require recitation, which is a lab-like class where extra
mework is done in class and is monitored by a teaching assistant (TA).
metimes (more often then not) they are foreign and sometimes it is hard to
derstand their English. Grading is done on a four-point scale (A=4, B=3 and
on) and can be opted for a Pass/No-Pass (S/U) with no point value for your
edits. As long as you study for the classes you take (going to class, reading the
xt) you should pass with at least a B. Classes are registered online on prede-
rmined dates (priority is usually senior, graduate, junior, sophomore, fresh-
en). Most classes are fairly easy to get into but may require department
proval (if classes are full).

Employment Prospects

urrent student, 9/2002-Submit Date, April 2006

ch term there is a career fair where various companies come and you can turn
a résumé or just talk to them to get a feel for what the working world is all
out. Career Services is really good about being available to students and you
n sign up for mock interviews where they ask you some questions you may
me in contact with. You can also go in and have them help you with your
sumé. Sometimes companies will come to campus to do recruiting and you
n sign up through the Career Services if you want to meet with them. If you
ke initiative, there are tons of opportunities to find a job through campus. The
achers are usually really eager to help in any way possible. Internships are lit-
 more hard to come by but some companies do some recruiting for them. Your
st bet would be to see someone in Career Services because it usually has a list-
g for internships, as well as jobs. The College of Business sends out e-mails
ery month with new job listings, which is helpful. I don't have any experience
ith the alumni network but I've heard that if you have connection through an
umnus/a, you are pretty much guaranteed a job; especially if you're in a soror-
.

lumnus/a, 9/2003-6/2005, March 2006

net with an employment counselor when I neared graduation. She showed me
me sites on the computer that I could access for job searches. There were on-
mpus recruiters, but I did not hear of any in the field in which I was studying.
ne of my instructors shared with the class a couple job requests that came to
r. I did follow-up on one and went on an interview.

lumnus/a, 9/1996-6/2001, January 2005

SU has strong Career Services for students, alumni and employers to access at
ny time. The center can help you in every step in planning for your future.
here are skill testing surveys, classes on how to do a résumé, mock interviews,
dless files on internships (paid and unpaid) and an up-to-date database of job
pportunities for the motivated student.

mployers from all over enlist these opportunities for OSU students because of
e level of education a student receives there. For instance, OSU is renowned
r the quality of education within public health, agricultural sciences, oceanic
d atmospheric sciences, food sciences, accounting and others. Another exam-
e is that OSU is particularly well-known for its strong engineering programs,
hich incorporates an internship and work experience program often leading to
st-graduate careers.

Current student, 9/2002-Submit Date, August 2004

For engineering, there is a program called MECOP or CECOP, which is a
Mechanical Engineering or Civil Engineering Internship program. This requires
time during school spent working for a firm and a government agency. Some
colleges, like Geology, also offer internship opportunities where credits are
earned in exchange for work.

Quality of Life

Current student, 9/2002-Submit Date, April 2006

The OSU campus is absolutely beautiful and that was one of the reasons I decided to attend. There are tons of flowers that bloom in the spring and the campus
is small enough to walk around, but big enough that you don't feel cramped. It's
a relatively flat campus, which is nice for people who ride their bikes or skateboard. Each on-campus housing group has its own dining hall, which was nice
as a freshman because all I had to do was walk downstairs and dinner was ready.
Some of the dorms are nicer than others but they're working on updating them
all. A lot of the buildings on our campus are very old and that is apparent by the
classrooms but the College of Business building has been re-vamped a little.
Our recreation center just had a complete renovation and now it is state-of-the-
art. We have a huge weight room, two cardio rooms, three classrooms, a pool,
and many other various features. Pretty much any time of day it is full of people and it's a great place to be. It has a great atmosphere and the staff is very
knowledgeable and helpful. Our campus, in general, is very safe because we
have these blue panic buttons spread around campus that when you push one, it
immediately alerts campus security. There is a Safe Ride program that will pick
you up and take you to certain locations if you feel unsafe. I have never felt
scared on campus because it is well lit and there are usually people in or around
the buildings late into the night.

Alumnus/a, 9/2003-6/2005, March 2006

I did not live on campus, or even in the same city as OSU. I lived in a neighboring city. There were good dining facilities on campus—good choices of cuisine.

Alumnus/a, 9/1996-6/2001, January 2005

The OSU college experience can be wrapped up in one sentence: you get what
you put into it. If you are willing to pay attention to all the resources available,
all your needs will be met. There is an on-site student health center, which deals
with all health and wellness matters, ranging from flu and allergy clinics, to mental health counselors and sexual health nurses. There is ever vigilant campus
security; they have installed several emergency phones to aid those in need, cut
back overgrown shrubbery and have constant patrol watches. Corvallis is considered to be one of the nation's most bike-friendly cities. Unfortunately, OSU's
becomes target to many bike thefts, making this the highest form of crime on
campus.

What first drew me to OSU was the atmosphere and landscaping around the
campus. It was so unlike other state universities in that it had the classic feel of
a traditional college campus. In this aspect, the word traditional means decades,
sometimes century old buildings, trees and artwork, the sound of a bell tone indicating the top of every hour and large park-like areas to relax or study. One of
the coolest buildings at OSU, in my opinion, is the Memorial Union. It is the
central hub of OSU, containing student government, restaurants, a bookstore, a
ballroom, study areas and flags from all over the world. Relics from OSU's past
are illustrated in various forms of artwork on every floor of the Memorial Union,
combining OSU's rich past with today's modern world.

There are several dorms and lodges located on and around campus, each with
their own mission and philosophy. Conveniently located around the housing
complexes are several dining halls and on campus restaurants. There is also a
state-of-the-art work-out facility, Dixon Center, conveniently open during all
hours to accommodate the life a student. And of course, who can ignore the top-
of-the-line Reeser Stadium, the playing field of the OSU Beavers! I would say
that a student wanting to come to OSU must be willing to handle all types of
weather. Corvallis receives large amounts of rain every year. There are some
who can't handle many rain soaked, cloudy days. I, on the other hand, loved it!
There was also the benefit of amazing spring time blossoms around campus!

Read all of Vault's College Surveys at **www.vault.com/college**—get complete surveys on 100s of colleges and universities, expert advice on applicaton essays and more.

VAULT CAREER LIBRARY **583**

Current student, 9/2002-Submit Date, August 2004

There is some fairly affordable, quite, and nice off campus housing near OSU. I would not recommend living on campus if you are on a tight budget. You can meet people throughout the classes you take. Recently, there have been state budget cuts and an estimated cost of attendance (COA) for a resident engineering student living off campus is over $23,000. The COA includes tuition, fees, room and board, personal expenses and books. If your family income is low, then fill out a FAFSA as early as possible. You may be eligible for grants like the SEOG or Pell grant.

> The school says: "OSU residence halls and cooperative houses (co-ops) provide convenience as well as many opportunities for making connections with the university that are especially important during the first year transition to college. Research at the national and OSU studies have shown that on campus first year students have higher GPAs and are more likely to return from their first year to their second year than those who live off campus."

 ## Social Life

Current student, 9/2002-Submit Date, April 2006

Corvallis has a very active social life. There are six main bars that people go to and you can always figure out where to go depending on which night it is. Each place has a different vibe, so it all depends on what you are looking to do. Platinum is a great club to go and dance at Thursday nights, Clods is a great place to just kick back with your friends anytime, Tailgaters is where everyone goes on Tuesday for $1 beer night, and Cantina is where it's at Saturday nights for some 80s music and two-for-one drinks for the ladies. The dining options get a little old after four years because there aren't many main restaurants. There are a lot of little local places which have some great food, like Nearly Normals, but Ruby Tuesday's is really the only sit-down burger joint. There are a lot of Thai food restaurants as well as pizza joints. The campus tries to put on a lot of events, but I'm not sure how successful those are. One thing that people look forward to spring term is Battle of the Bands. There are two stages set-up in the quad with a beer garden and random food stands. It's a lot of fun and it usually has a huge turnout. I'm not in the Greek system but I know people who are and let's just say it is very active. They are always doing some event, whether it be a fun run to raise money or one of their dances. It's a great thing to join if you want constant companionship and something to identify with. They are a very strong group of people.

Alumnus/a, 9/1996-6/2001, January 2005

Fortunately, I was able to experience many of the social activities surrounding OSU's campus. Before I was 21, I was part of the Greek system. I joined my freshman year to meet new people and expand my social life. The Greek system is as diverse as the majors offered at OSU. There are some sororities and fraternities that are chartered in a house where members live. Others do not have

a house, but meet frequently at common campus areas. My advice to tho wanting to explore the Greek system, is to choose your Greek affiliation ca fully. Do not be swayed or lured into a life that you may not be comfortal with. I won't lie to you; many of the house's on Greek Row, 25th and 26 streets, near campus, are big into "functions." "Functions" usually take place a fraternity house and involve alcohol. I can't stress enough on the need to u extreme caution in this type of social situation. Always use a buddy system.

Once you are 21 and are legal to drink, there are plenty of bars in Corvallis t accommodate OSU students. There is Clodfelters, which is a popular sports b right on Monroe Street, across campus and is the place to be on Wednesd nights. If you're in the mood for some serious dancing and music, the Peacoc in downtown Corvallis, is the way to go. A popular place for those who a adventurous with beer, is the downtown bar AJ's (formerly Kell's). If you' into doing laundry at the same time as having a cold beer, Suds and Suds, King's Blvd is for you. If your looking for a unique bar with an earthy fe check out Squirrel's, in downtown Corvallis. An extra bonus to all bar patro there is a city ordinance ban on smoking in any of the bars!

For those of us who prefer an alcohol-free environment, there is always som thing happening in the campus Memorial Union Ballroom. If it's not a clu sponsored dance, there are fashion shows and flea markets. There is a univer ty theater that is consistently running plays. A big event in Corvallis is the Vinci Days, celebrating all types of art and, of course, there is always some s of sporting event happening on campus, depending on the season.

A popular pizza joint is American Dream pizza. I personally love this place! I artsy and fun and is right across the street from campus on Monroe Stre Another popular restaurant on Monroe street is Local Boyz, a Hawaiian fo place; I highly recommend food choice 14a! Just a block away from campus Nearly Normal's, a great place for organic and vegetarian cuisine. Downtov Corvallis is also home to an awesome burrito place, Senor Sam's.

Current student, 9/2002-Submit Date, August 2004

Restaurants on campus include Burger King, Woodstock's Pizza (very goc pizza made fresh), Blimpie's, Panda Express, three coffee shops and a cafeteri There are tons of small shops, restaurants and bars right next to campus (thr more coffee shops, a bar, some restaurants) and a lot more restaurants and cc fee shops around town. Learn to like coffee, it will be your best friend whe studying—hence, all the coffee shops. Nightlife is fairly dull though and seems that the Interzone cafe and the local bar is the only thing that is open town. For better nightlife it is probably better to drive to Eugene (about on hour drive) or Portland.

Reed College

ed College Admission Office
?03 SE Woodstock Boulevard
rtland, OR 97202
dmissions phone: (503) 777-7511 or (800) 547-4750
dmissions fax: (503) 777-7553
dmissions e-mail: admission@reed.edu
dmissions URL: www.reed.edu/apply/

Admissions

umnus/a, 9/2001-5/2005, May 2005

ed uses the Common Application and asks students to also provide a "Why ed?" essay to show themselves as a good match for the college. Reed does participate in the *U.S. News & World Report* rankings because of widespread satisfaction with their methods. To learn about Reed, I found Loren Pope's *lleges that Change Lives* book very helpful.

irrent student, 8/2002-Submit Date, May 2005

e application materials are just the Common Application and essay portion. e "Why Reed?" essay and the graded writing sample are the two most impor- t parts of the application.

ey're looking for originality when it comes to the "Why Reed?" essay. A nd of mine wrote about his love for giraffes and how Reed would be the place him to meet someone else with the same passion. I like to think that the missions office has a pretty good sense of humor at Reed.

ed is getting to be pretty selective in terms of admission. I guess it's selective a different way; it takes the right person to belong at Reed. If the admissions ice thinks you don't belong, maybe you really don't. I've seen many prospec- e students who would leave in a heartbeat when they find out how much a ed education really entails.

> **The school says:** "Reed College requires the Common Application, the Reed application supplement (including the 'Why Reed?' essay and graded writing sample), a school report, transcript, and teacher evaluations, and SAT or ACT scores; the Admissions office uses a holistic approach to evaluating appli- cations, taking all of these pieces into account before making a decision."

irrent student, 9/2004-Submit Date, May 2005

my opinion, it seems kind of random. They try to get a feel for your person- ty. From the people who have been accepted, they look for bright, [inde- ndent-minded] and interesting folks.

umnus/a, 8/1996-5/2000, April 2005

dmission to Reed is not just about having the numbers. Reed is looking for tellectuals who enjoy the learning process and who are passionate about being an intensely academic and uniquely creative environment. The best way to engthen your application is to take challenging courses in high school and to well in those courses. Reed also looks at essays, recommendations, extracur- ular activities and interviews. Around 45 percent of all applicants (ED and gular combined) are admitted.

> **The school says:** "The most recent acceptance rate (Class of 2011) was 34 percent."

umnus/a, 9/2001-5/2005, August 2005

nsidering its academic intensity, the quality of teaching, and average GPA and AT scores of its students, Reed College used to be a relatively easy college to t into. When I first applied in 2000, the admissions office accepted roughly percent of its applicants; by now, that number has dropped to around 30 per-

cent. Its popularity is steadily increasing and as a result, it has become a much more selective school. Like anywhere else, it helps to have good grades and standardized test scores, but Reed is unique in that the admissions office is exceptionally good at recognizing intellectual potential by looking beyond grades and scores. The famous "Why Reed" essay is very important. Interviews are helpful, but not essential. The most important part of applying to Reed is showing them how much you want to attend. If possible, elect the Early Decision option.

> **The school says:** "Reed offers two Early Decision options: ED I, due November 15, and ED II due January 2; the deadline for Regular Decision is January 15 and for transfers is March 1."

Academics

Alumnus/a, 9/2001-5/2005, May 2005

Every Reed student takes a Humanities 110 course, first semester on Ancient Greece, second semester on Ancient Rome. Reedies take a junior qualifying exam in their major as a diagnostic tool and to prepare them for their senior the- sis. Every senior does original research and writes a thesis that is bound and cat- aloged in the library.

> **The school says:** "In addition to these requirements, all students must fulfill a distribution requirement, taking a year of course- work in each of the following four groups: Literature, Philosophy, Religion and the Arts; History, Social Sciences and Psychology; the Natural Sciences; and Mathematics, Logic, Foreign Language or Linguistics."

Current student, 8/2002-Submit Date, May 2005

The classes here are the best around in all aspects one can imagine: academical- ly challenging, mentally stimulating, small and intimate, and all-around enjoy- able.

Students get to know their professors very well. Most professors leave their doors open and welcome students to enter at any time to ask questions. My math professor even taught me how to juggle clubs.

There is a lot of reading and a lot of problem solving. In my experience, one works every weeknight and most of the weekend. Rarely do we watch movies and television, and some of us only get off campus a couple of times a month.

Grades are hidden in a vault somewhere in Eliot Hall. We get grades, but they aren't published anywhere. Well, one can see his/her grades by asking his/her academic advisor. Grades are not inflated by any means. A B really is above average at Reed.

Usually, there is no difficulty in getting into any class one wishes to take. In order to sign up for Creative Writing, one must submit a writing sample to the instructor.

Here is the difference between a Reedie and another college student: a Reedie wants to take the elective courses, whereas other college students sometimes think of those classes as "a waste." One student from another college com- mented to me, "Why take the elective courses when I can take classes from another major and double major?" Why? Because we wish to be well-rounded individuals. As a physics major, I delighted in the opportunity to take linguis- tics, something I was always interested in but never got the chance to try. I still take biology classes for fun, and I plan on taking more biology and painting in the coming year.

Reedies study for the sake of learning. I have also encountered students from other schools who remarked that, "one should not attend any more classes if he/she can pass without attending the final." If your goal is to pass your classes

Read all of Vault's College Surveys at **www.vault.com/college**—get complete surveys on 100s of colleges and univer- sities, expert advice on applicaton essays and more.

VAULT CAREER LIBRARY   585

and graduate, then Reed is not for you. Reedies are genuinely interested in learning. Well, learning and debating about it later.

Alumnus/a, 8/1994-2000, April 2005

Reed academics are at the top of the top. Classes are small (average is [15] students) and are discussion based. Reed academics are traditional. Every student takes a freshman course (Humanities 110) where students study Ancient Greece and Rome (think Plato, Aristotle, Virgil). Every student writes a thesis.

Reed is very much a graduate school prep program—Reed rates third in the percentage of its graduates continuing to earn PhDs of any college or university in the U.S. (and first in biology). Reed is as strong in the sciences as the non-sciences. Reed has the only undergraduate-run experimental nuclear reactor in the country. The only classes that are tough to get into are creative writing classes. Reed professors are incredible! They treat students as junior colleagues. You will go to your professors' homes for dinner, babysit their kids, go bowling with them, as well as philosophize about classwork, life and hobbies. Reed de-emphasizes grades—there is basically no competition between students. There is great academic support (e.g., help centers, free tutoring) that does not have the negative stigma associated with it like at many other places.

Current student, 9/2001-Submit Date, November 2005

Having friends at all types of universities (from states schools to Ivy Leagues), I can say with confidence that Reed has one of the best liberal arts and science programs in the U.S. There are no classes taught by TAs and most classes are relatively small and conference based. There are a few exceptions to this: The Intro Humanities class has a lecture component with all of the freshman class and intro science classes also have large lectures but small conference and lab classes based on those lectures. I'm even taking a class right now with just the teacher and one other student and it's the best experience I've had as an undergraduate.

Classes are academically intense with lots of reading and you are expected to participate in an intelligent discussion with 12 other people on that reading for every class (but you love that stuff, that's why you came here). Though there is the occasional boring prof, by and large, they're great and the school makes sure that while there, they are just devoted to teaching (they have leaves of absence to pursue their own work). So Reed has professors who really want to teach. I've never not gotten into a class; if one is really popular they will usually add another section rather than drop students.

Grades at Reed are an interesting problem (situation?)—there is no grade inflation, the average GPA of graduates is 3.0 (and only 68 percent of the entering class graduates in six years). Grades are also not easy to see, you get a notice in your mailbox at the end of each semester that says satisfactory or unsatisfactory for each class (meaning above or below a C-) but the school make it difficult (but possible) to see your actual GPA. This is great in that the focus becomes learning rather than grades and it encourages people to be more academically daring (try different types of classes) than they would be if they were focused on GPA. However, as I'm learning now we still do have GPAs and employers care about them and may not understand that a 3.0 translates to a 3.9 or higher for these same students had they gone to a state school. Reed has a great reputation with grad schools, though, so no matter what you're GPA merely getting through Reed makes it easy to get into a great grad school. Also remember, this is a small liberal arts school so there are no practical majors (like business or accounting) and we love Ivory Tower.

> **The school says:** "The most recent graduation rate is 75 percent (six-year). Also, grades are not as difficult to see as this student suggests: you may consult with your academic advisor or request a transcript from the registrar's office, although many students choose to not ever see their grades."

Alumnus/a, 9/2001-5/2005, August 2005

As non-conformist as Reedies are, the academic program is highly traditional. All first-year students are required to take Humanities 110, a year-long survey of ancient Greece and Rome. Students must fulfill a hefty list of departmental, divisional and group requirements in order to graduate. Students come prepared to every class. The quality of the teaching is first-rate (understandable, since professors love to teach motivated, prepared and intellectually curious kids).

Students study all the time—it is a way of life at Reed. Popular classes fill quickly and preference is given to upperclassmen. Class size is rarely larger th 20, and most are conference-style. Juniors must pass a rigorous and extens qualifying examination in their major in order to begin their senior year. Seni must write a Bachelor's thesis in order to graduate, and spend all year doing All theses are bound and kept in the library. Reed employs the standard grad scale, though they are not shown to the student unless asked for. In sum, R prepares the student for graduate school.

Employment Prospects

Alumnus/a, 9/2001-5/2005, May 2005

Reedies go to Reed in order to learn to think, not as a pre-professional oppo nity. That said, a great number of Reedies continue on to graduate school, es cially PhD programs and become professors at great schools. Many Reed gr go into fields related to education and the nonprofit world.

> **The school says:** "About 70 percent of Reed graduates go on to earn a higher degree (PhD, JD, MD, or MA/MFA/MS). Reed is third highest in the nation in the production of future PhDs, and first for the biological sciences."

Current student, 8/2002-Submit Date, May 2005

A large percentage of alumni go on to graduate school and eventually earn th PhDs. The alumni network is small but mighty. There exist only about 15,0 Reedies out in the world, but the ties are strong because of the exclusivity "Reediness." If you're planning on going into academia, Reed is definitely place to be for an undergraduate education.

Alumnus/a, 8/1996-5/2000, April 2005

The highest percentage of Reed alumni are in teaching-related fields followed business (ironic as Reed has neither an education or business major). Re teaches students how to think critically, to engage in material and to have co dence in their ability to think and ask the hardest of questions. This, in my mi prepares one for employment in the greatest way possible. Versatility! On technical side, yes we have a career center and career fairs, students get inte ships all the time and our alumni network is great.

Current student, 9/2001-Submit Date, November 2005

Reed is wonderful if you want to go to grad school (med and law school incl ed), the Peace Corp or if you want to work for a nonprofit, but otherwise not good. Eventually Reed students get great jobs they love but right out of sch they tend to work at Trader Joe's for a year. The problem is we are such a sm school (and so many students do want to take a year off or pursue nontraditic al careers) that no normal companies come and recruit here. Also, one of graduation requirements is a senior thesis, which leaves almost no time for jc hunting your senior year.

Most employers haven't heard of Reed (that may change now that we've be ranked highly by [the 2006 Princeton Review] in several categories includi Number One in overall undergraduate experience), which presents proble compounded with the fact that our GPAs don't translate to traditional GPAs. T good news is that employers who have hired Reedies in the past know that are a very bright and undervalued bunch so the alumni network is very help in this regard. I found that most Reedies gravitate to socially conscious or ac demic jobs (even our lawyers tend to be in the ACLU vein) but this means th they also tend to like themselves and their jobs better than most (even if th make less money). Our graduates may not rule the business world but they d lot to make the world a better place.

Alumnus/a, 9/2001-5/2005, August, 2005

Reed is by far most useful for getting into graduate school, which is the mc popular post-graduate option within two or three years. Many students conti ue on in academia, becoming professors themselves. The range of careers a jobs Reedies explore is just as diverse as Reedies themselves. Among the mc popular are careers in government and policy-making, medicine, law, educati and medical research. The alumni network, while relatively small, is very hel ful. Alumni chapters exist in most major U.S. cities; the biggest are in L./

w York, Portland, Boston and San Francisco. On-campus recruiting and
ernship opportunities happen all the time, and are open to all classes.

Quality of Life

lumnus/a, 9/2001-5/2005, May 2005

ed's campus is beautiful and in a quiet residential section of the Portland
etro area. Dorms for first-year students are structured as divided doubles—
o rooms, one of which has access to the hall to be divided between two room-
ites ideally providing both privacy and community.

urrent student, 8/2002-Submit Date, May 2005

ousing at Reed is absolutely wonderful. Freshmen live in divided doubles and
perclassmen live in singles. Most dorms have kitchens, some dorms have fire-
ces and pianos, and all dorms have social rooms. Space in the rooms is plen-
ul—sometimes to the detriment of the student when it comes to packing it all
for the summer.

e campus is beautiful. Reed is split in half by the Reed Canyon, a body of
ater that connects water from Mt. Hood to the Willamette River. The campus
green year round, and the spring invites colorful flowers all over campus. The
ounds crew always leaves daffodil or tulip bulbs in our mailboxes in the win-
time to plant anywhere we desire on campus.

mpus dining is some of the best college food around. There's always soup,
lad and grill. At lunch and dinner times, Commons serves specialties that are
oked to order. Thursday is hot turkey sandwich day—always a favorite.

ed is generally a pretty safe place. We are run by the Honor Principle, an
[written] code of ethics kept alive through discussion. Tests usually can be
ken outside the classroom without proctors because of the Honor Principle.

lumnus/a, 8/1996-5/2000, April 2005

ousing space is generous. Most every freshman is in a divided double set-up.
pperclassmen get singles. 65 percent of Reed students live on campus. My
eshman dorm room even had a functional fireplace (note: there are not many
these). The campus is beautiful, complete with brick Gothic architecture and
24-acre nature preserve. The neighborhood in which Reed resides is upscale
d safe. The type of crime that happens on campus is usually bike and com-
ter theft—though graffitiers from off campus have been a recent issue.
afeteria food is great (in the realm of cafeteria food). Portland is an amazing
ty that has a myriad of scrumptious restaurants.

urrent student, 9/2001-Submit Date, November 2005

uality of life tends to be pretty high at Reed, the campus is beautiful (you will
ve to get used to the rain—it is Portland after all). There is very little crime
campus except for the occasional bike being stolen or car being broken into
the parking lot. Community Safety is wonderful and really there to help the
udent: they'll walk you to your dorm late at night, let you in when you forget
ur key or just chat with you when you look down. This is more important than
u might think as I've been at other campuses where students were hesitant to
ll security because they were worried they would get in trouble (for instance
an underage student drank too much or had used another substance). They are
ally there for our interests and to help us be safe and not to police us.

ining at Reed is pretty much like any other school; the food is pretty good but
ter the first six months it gets a little monotonous. A fair portion of upper-
assman students who live on campus live in school apartments where they
ve their own kitchens and the option of not having to be on a meal plan.
ousing goes from great to depressing depending on where you end up—anoth-
reason to visit the campus is the school's very accommodating system of put-
ng freshmen in the dorms they request. If you can't come to campus just make
re to request ODB, Bragdon or Anna Mann.

he surrounding neighborhood is residential and very upscale with nice parks
arby and a grocery store within waking distance (all the dorms have refriger-
ors and stoves on each floor). Portland has one of the the best public transit
stems in America, so it's easy and pretty cheap to get around town. This is a
llege with a vibrant if sometimes unusual campus life (Fetish Ball and Renn
ayre, oh yeah) so there really isn't much need to leave campus. Also, you will

be required to take six quarters of PE—a hardship for most Reedies—but the
classes are loads of fun. Who knew juggling, meditation and scuba diving certification could all be called PE?

Alumnus/a, 9/2001-5/2005, August 2005

All first-year students live in on-campus dormitories, which range in size and
quality. Some buildings are 80 years old and feature spacious rooms, beautiful
views and fireplaces, while others are rather small. No matter in which dorm
you live, you're guaranteed to develop strong bonds with your dormmates.
Reedies usually remain very close friends with their first-year dormmates. All
bathrooms are co-ed. All dorms are within a five-minute walk from the dining
area.

> **The school says:** "Although most first-year students live on
> campus, this is not a required. In addition to regular dorms, a
> number of floors each year are designated as theme dorms—
> ranging from women's only to the Outhouse (an outdoors
> themed dorm), from substance-free to the Mad Science dorm.
> Five new dormitories will open in fall 2008, allowing Reed to
> provide 75 percent of our students with on-campus housing."

Crime in southeast Portland exists but is low to moderate. There are hardly ever
violent crimes; most are thefts. Campus safety is excellent.

Social Life

Alumnus/a, 9/2001-5/2005, May 2005

All Reed student groups are ultimately funded and governed by the student body.
They are egalitarian and open to everybody. Reedies tend to be creative, bright
and a bit quirky, and student groups reflect these trends.

> **The school says:** "Each semester, students vote in a campus-
> wide Funding Poll. The 40 most popular clubs receive priority
> in funding."

Current student, 8/2002-Submit Date, May 2005

No Greek system. No football team. A cheerleading squad to mock all other
cheerleading squads. Dating scene is minimal. We're too busy studying anyway. Restaurants in Portland are excellent. Some favorites include: The Bistro
Montage (Cajun), India Oven, Papa Haydn, The Pied Cow, The Delta, Nicholas,
Otto's and Tom Yum. I personally like going to the Symphony on the student
price ($5).

> **The school says:** "Since its founding Reed College has been
> committed to non-exclusivity in student organizations. As part
> of this, we have no fraternities or sororities and no varsity
> sports teams."

Current student, 8/2004-Submit Date, May 2005

There are parties every weekend and a good number of bars around, if you don't
mind constantly bumping into other Reedies. But we have a great time when we
have the time to fit it in. Otherwise, the library is rockin'.

Alumnus/a, 8/1996-5/2000, April 2005

No Greek system! No varsity sports! We do have intramural sports (rugby, ultimate frisbee, soccer). Clubs and activities are all proposed, voted on and funded by students. There are campus clubs like on any other campus (debate,
Amnesty International, newspaper) but also Reed-specific clubs (Defenders of
the Universe, Motorized Couch Kollectiv (sic), Texas Student Union).

The intellectual nature of the academics carries over to the social—it is not
uncommon to see students in the library on Friday—it is not uncommon to see
structures like couch swings being constructed in the student quad at 3:00 a.m.
Reed is an incredibly open and sharing community. There is hardly any peer
pressure so whether you choose to go to the concert happening in the student
union or play chess in your dorm room, it is all good.

Current student, 9/2001-Submit Date, November 2005

Hmmmmm, social life. Most of social life at Reed happens in or around the
library. You will be studying most of time, most of the rest of your time will be

Read all of Vault's College Surveys at **www.vault.com/college**—get complete surveys on 100s of colleges and universities, expert advice on applicaton essays and more.

VAULT CAREER LIBRARY   **587**

spent discussing how much work you have and how much time you spend studying. You will secretly love both.

Reed does have some great social events though. There are movie nights (with a big projection screen), a pool hall on campus open till 2 a.m. every night, various balls with great music and interesting costumes and the unforgettable (unless you have "too much fun") Renn Fayre. Renn Fayre is a party at the end of the school year that starts with thesis parade, when seniors march to the registrar's office to turn in their theses, and ends three days later. During this time there is too much going on to describe here but you may be chased by naked people painted blue who are trying to hug you one morning and you will certainly see the fireworks and glow opera (a play in pitch darkness where all the actors are covered in glow sticks—much cooler than it sounds).

At most big events, including Renn Fayre, there is also the beer garden in which for a small entrance fee students over 21 can get all the free micro-brew they want. The other big event of the year is Paideia, which is the week before classes start spring semester when Reedies teach each other a variety of things in their own classes.

Social and political action clubs are also huge at Reed (e.g., Amnesty and Planned Parenthood on campus), as are weird fun clubs. There isn't much of a traditional dating scene at Reed people just tend to hook up at parties and stay together or not (wait, is that traditional now?). Little tip: avoid dormcest, dating a fellow dormie only ends in trouble even if it is really convenient.

There are no frats or sororities at Reed. If you are the type of person who thinks they might like to be in a frat don't apply to Reed—you will hate it! There are a few good bars within walking distance that Reedies do like but still most socializing occurs on campus. The bars (as almost all bars in Portland) are near impossible to get into if you are underage. Sorry, but might as well leave your fake ID at home. There is no shortage of upperclassmen who will buy liquor at the store you, though. In general I find there is less drinking at Reed than at other colleges. Reedies still drink but you just can't make it at this school if you get drunk three nights a week. Again if you are a person going to school to party think state school, not Reed.

> **Regarding Reed's Drug and Alcohol Policy, the school says:** "Reed does have a Drug and Alcohol Policy that respects state and federal laws and campus safety officers do enforce this policy. Reed's treatment of violations, however, is much more therapeutic in nature, rather than punitive."

The School Says

Since its founding in 1911, Reed College in Portland, Oregon has been an independent co-educational and nonsectarian liberal arts college that has welcomed students of any race, ethnicity, gender, class or religion. Now approaching its centennial, Reed's 1,492 students remain committed to freedom of inquiry, the pursuit of knowledge and a love of learning for its own sake.

Academics at Reed are framed by Humanities 110—a year-long study of Ancient Greek and Roman civilization, required for all first-year students—and by the senior thesis—a substantial research paper of personal interest, supervised by a faculty advisor. Between their first year and their last, students at Reed pursue a broad, liberal arts curriculum that encourages exploring connections between disciplines, rather than seeking early specialization; all students must complete coursework across a range of disciplines, although they ultimately will select a major (the five most popular are English, biology, psychology, anthropology and history). The majority of Reed courses are conducted as small conferences (with an average size of 15 students), where the emphasis is placed on active discussion rather than the passive absorption of information.

While the academic structure of Reed is, in many ways, very traditional, the college also blends this with a progressive—at times iconoclastic—side. Grades at Reed are deemphasized, and a student could graduate never knowing his or her GPA; for over 10 years, Reed has refused to participate in the *U.S. News & World Report* annual ranking of colleges, believing that such rankings are based on a mistaken "one-size-fits-all" mentality; there are no exclusive student organizations, including no fraternities, sororities or NCAA-ranked sports teams; life on campus is governed by an Honor Principle, rather than by an exhaustive set of rules and policies.

In addition to being serious and scholarly, Reedies are also quirky and creative. On Nitrogen Day students celebrate one of the universe's most abundant, and yet underappreciated, elements by reading haiku at an open mike. During Paideia (Greek for "education") students teach classes on topics of personal interest—from Underwater Basketweaving to Sock Monkey Theory. And then there is Renn Fayre, which marks the end of the academic year and is held to celebrate the completion of seniors' theses. Renn Fayre begins with a parade that runs through the library, up to the President's office, and beyond and includes events such as music performances, an interdepartmental softball tournament, fireworks and a glow opera.

Reed students come from many different backgrounds. Four-fifths hail from outside of the Pacific Northwest, including students from over 30 countries. One quarter of Reed's students are self-identified students of color and 11 percent are first-generation college attendees. Financial aid at Reed is need-based; about half of the Reed student body received aid and Reed meets 100 percent of the demonstrated need of students who are admitted to the college.

Although Reed is not for everyone, those attracted to its unique quirk, independent spirit and insatiable intellectualism might discover that it is a perfect fit for them.

University of Oregon

fice of Admissions
'17 University of Oregon
gene, OR 97403-1217
Imissions phone: (541) 346-3201 or (800) BE-A-DUCK
Imissions fax: (541) 346-5815
Imissions URL: www.uoregon.edu/prospective.shtml

te: The school has chosen not to comment on the stu-
nt surveys submitted.

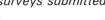

Admissions

mnus/a, 9/1999-6/2003, January 2007

e admissions process for UO was very easy and clearly detailed on the web
(uoregon.edu). The application process for UO is very similar to any other
e school. There isn't an interview process, simply the application process.
e biggest piece of advice I would offer, is to start the application process early
that you don't become overwhelmed. In all of the essays and questions just
honest, and everything will be fine.

rrent student, 9/2001-Submit Date, February 2006

pplied and was accepted. There were no essays because I had a very high
A and a very high SAT score.

rrent student, 10/2004-Submit Date, December 2005

ou have the guaranteed grade point average it is fairly easy to get in—you get
automatic spot. If you don't have that grade point average, you are going to
e to write an essay about how you will move mountains.

mnus/a, 9/1985-6/1990, October 2005

plication process made just by contacting them and filling out the form.
bmitted full packet including letters of recommendation, scholarships,
racurricular activities and SAT scores. Received admission with honors and
itation to the Honors College.

rrent student, 9/2004-Submit Date, April 2005

en applying I was trying to get into the Architecture program at the
iversity of Oregon (a Top 10 program at the time). They required an exten-
e portfolio showing skill in the field, but most of all creativity. I had no prior
hitecture experience and I feel that the creativity piece played the biggest part
my making it into the architecture program. Within my portfolio I included
ltiple pieces of art that I had completed in art classes and sketches from free
e.

mnus/a, 9/1997-6/2001, June 2004

an in-state student, the application process was very straightforward. Some
grams at UO do require essays and a more thorough application processes.
had great orientation programs for incoming freshmen, including a preview
y in the February prior to fall term, and orientation weekend where incoming
dents visit the campus for a weekend with parents and have the opportunity
stay in a dorm, take tours of campus, learn about extracurricular activities and
et older students as mentors.

rongly recommend taking part in all available activities and programs for new
dents. One program that I would strongly recommend and that helped me
come more familiar with the school and college life, was the Freshman
erest Groups (also called a FIG). This program was for the first term of
ool and prior to classes starting. You choose a group based on a subject of
erest (psychology, journalism, sociology or business). Depending on the
up you choose, you are placed with other students with the same interests and
oughout the term you have the same courses with them and meet once a week
talk about different issues and classes. There are two seniors as group lead-
who organize the meetings and prepare activities. You also have the chance

to meet with your professors once a week. This is a great way to meet people
and become more comfortable with your new surroundings.

Another aspect of college life that I would highly recommend is living in the
dorms your first year at school. This is a great experience that allows you to
meet people from all over the country and world. The people in your dorm
become your close friends and help with adjusting to this new atmosphere. If
you live off campus, it's hard to create the same network of friends that you keep
in touch with throughout your college career and beyond.

Academics

Alumnus/a, 9/1999-6/2003, January 2007

Each major has different classes and different requirements. As you progress
through school getting into classes become easier. Every professor is different
and the workload of each class is different. However, you can go online and get
a review of each professor and each class. I highly recommend checking out this
link!

Current student, 9/2001-Submit Date, February 2006

I have studied both international studies and Scandinavian studies. I spent a year
studying abroad in Norway and classes there were more difficult than they were
here on campus. As I have progressed here at the UO, it has been easier to get
into the classes I want because I register before most students. Many of my
classes are challenging and require critical analysis of traditional ways of thinking.

Current student, 10/2004-Submit Date, December 2005

The classes are a good size with a broad range of population for the various
course material. If you are a younger student you will not be able to register for
classes unless you are in the Honors College. Do not fret, as long as you speak
with the professor on the first day of class you can get in, no hassle.

Workload varies by major/professor, but expect to do as much as you like and
still get by. Professors vary in quality, half and half with lesser to good professors. If they started to pay the professors a whole lot more, I think quality professors would stream in from across the country because it is a great place to
work and study. Grading is pretty simple; most classes are straightforward about
it and you can keep tabs on it through one of several online systems and tracking devices the school employs.

Alumnus/a, 9/1985-6/1990, October 2005

Registration process has changed significantly since my time there; we used to
have to register in person for classes in a convoluted circus atmosphere, and now
you can register online.

I found the classes that met general requirements to be on the simplistic side.
Generally there were several of the same basic course offered to accommodate
different schedules; but I was able to pick up my syllabus on the first day of each
of those classes, and then only showed up for exams, while still maintaining high
grades.

The more specialized courses with a smaller student to teacher ratio generally
encouraged more participation and offered a better chance for something more
than rote learning.

My grades were high, but I question a system that would allow me to graduate
with honors while maintaining minimal participation in the process (though this
was not from choice, as I had two jobs in addition to my courseload).

Some professors were very skilled and I did learn from those, and even made a
few friends among them. Others definitely used their professorships as a platform for their own agenda—sometimes to the detriment of learning the material. Writing for other publications may generate prestige for the university, [but

Read all of Vault's College Surveys at **www.vault.com/college**—get complete surveys on 100s of colleges and universities, expert advice on applicaton essays and more.

VAULT CAREER LIBRARY **589**

perhaps there should be more restrictions on content.] Workload was on the light side.

Current student, 9/2004-Submit Date, April 2005

This particular program is what I consider a weed-out program. The professors for the first two years are trying to get rid of students who are only semi-interested or unsure if this program is right for them. I went through multiple weeks with little to no sleep in order to finish projects and meet deadlines. This was commonplace for all students in the first two years of studios, but exhausting nonetheless. Anyone who is concerned with having some semblance of a normal life while in school should think long and hard ahead of time.

Alumnus/a, 9/1997-6/2001, June 2004

My degree was through UO's School of Journalism and Communication. The first two years in the program are spent taking general courses that pre-qualify you for a specialized program. The specialized programs include advertising, public relations, newspaper, magazine, broadcasting and video production. I focused on advertising and had a great experience. All instructors and professors in the J-School have years of real-world work experience and can bring those experiences to class and apply them to what they teach.

All instructors and professors have office hours, which are open to students in their classes and allows them time to visit with their teachers, discuss exams, papers and grading. Taking advantage of these office hours is key to having a successful college career. You learn how each teacher grades (and they all have different scales) and what they expect from their students. Professors want students to be successful in their classes and in college as a whole.

Another thing that is key to having a successful college career is learning who your academic advisor is and taking advantage of his/her services and expertise. These counselors are available to help you plan out your class schedule and help to ensure you are on the right track to filling all school requirements and graduating on time.

I have friends who went through the business, sociology, psychology and education programs and all had positive experiences. Several continued their education at UO by attending the graduate programs in education and law. I am thinking about continuing my education by obtaining my MBA and would love to do this program at the University of Oregon.

 ## Employment Prospects

Alumnus/a, 9/1999-6/2003, January 2007

UO has two big job fairs each year. Many local and even out-of-state recruiters come to campus. This is a great place to hand out your résumé and make connections. There is also a Career Center. This center offers a one-credit class that teaches you how to build a résumé and cover letter. The class also teaches you how to interview. I highly recommend this class. Also, generally every major has a career fair in the spring. These career fairs are helpful because there are job opportunities in the career in which you are trying to enter. Another great resource is your professors. They are always eager to offer any advice to their students about career choices.

Current student, 9/2001-Submit Date, February 2006

I would like to teach English in a foreign country once I graduate, and then I would like to go to grad school somewhere. The Career Center at the UO is a wonderful resource. They have job postings, as well as a number of guides on how to apply for jobs, create a good résumé, and how to find what job best fits you. It is free to all students up to six months after they graduate. They also help with getting into and finding an appropriate grad school.

Alumnus/a, 9/1997-6/2001, June 2004

The UO has a campus Career Center available to all students and alumni with resources on jobs in various industries. The School of Journalism and Communication also has a resource center for careers and an internships. There are intenship coordinators at the J-School and they post and circulate all opportunities.

In the J-School and other programs, the instructors are also good resources for jobs and internships. They have work experience in their subject and often have many contacts within those fields that they share with students as network opportunities. Networking is a great way to find a job in your field. It's a about who you know!

The UO Career Center offers a Mentor Program to all junior and senior stude. This is a one-credit class that is available just about every term and is focused a subject taught at the school. You meet once a month with a leader from center and learn about writing résumés, cover letters, the interview process a networking. You work with peers to go over these things and learn tips a strategies to having a successful job search.

Another benefit of this program is the chance to meet two professionals in field(s) of your choice and conduct an informational interview with them. is a great chance to start your network and begin learning about the field y want to work in out of school or in the future. It's a great opportunity and I s keep in contact with most of my mentors.

This program is also available to alumni of UO for a small fee, but it's defini ly worth it if you are having a difficult time finding a job in your field. With economy being the way it is, it may be beneficial to network with people y know and build more relationships.

 ## Quality of Life

Alumnus/a, 9/1999-6/2003, January 2007

New dorms have just been built, and they are very nice. The dorms are loca near many of the main buildings on campus. Dorm life is safe and fun! Th are many events going on throughout the year. I highly recommend living in dorms for at least one year. A lot of social connections are made in the dorm

The dining on campus is adequate. They have many choices besides just standard cafeteria food. The food is all on a point-based system. You do need to have cash to purchase food. You simply use your student ID card as y source of money. There are plenty of food options in the dining facilities tak into consideration dietary preferences for vegetarians and vegans.

The campus is very clean and very beautiful. The surrounding neighborhoo very college like, but it is heavily patrolled by police so it is very safe as wel

Current student, 9/2001-Submit Date, February 2006

I have never lived on campus, but the facilities that I use are excellent. We ha multiple state-of-the-art computer labs, an assault prevention shuttle that v give any student a ride at any time of day, academic learning services and Braddock Tutoring Center in the business school are wonderful resources students who need help.

The rec center is a great facility with a new weight room, indoor running tra aerobics machines, multiple courts for basketball, tennis, racquetball, volleyba badminton and others. Our study abroad office has more than 100 differe study or internship abroad opportunities. We have no less than four libraries a an interlibrary loan system. We have the Yamada Language Center that he students study languages that aren't offered regularly, of which we will have next year.

Current student, 10/2004-Submit Date, December 2005

Dorms suck, super small and cramped with communal baths and showers. Fo is great. Only bikes get stolen. Good cheap food around campus, houses campus are where people live after freshman year. All the facilities, besides dorms, are beautiful and nice, conducive to learning in a high-tech environme with a feel of Oregon—frisbee players playing in a wireless network.

Current student, 9/2004-Submit Date, April 2005

At the time, housing in the dorms was sub-par. Most people's first year inclu the dorm life and then they move into a rented house for the next three-pl years. Housing off campus is extremely affordable once you have worked yo way through the sometimes difficult web of rental companies that exist Eugene.

The campus itself is beautiful throughout the year as UO and UC Santa Cruz two of the only arboretum schools on the West Coast. A heads-up for those u that are wary of rain: it rains a heap load. This does contribute to the beau- of the campus and why the countryside is so often green.

s for crime and safety, I see UO as a typical campus with its typical problems. s with most schools, most people had their bike stolen if left for too many days. elt as if the Eugene area was safer than a big city but edgier than a suburban y. Lots of students did not own cars as the campus is bike/rollerblade/skate- ard friendly. Mostly flat with some low hills, easy access to all areas whether alking or riding.

 ## Social Life

lumnus/a, 9/1999-6/2003, January 2007

here are two campus bars that are always very busy during the week and week- ds and are student favorites. The Greek system is very active and has recruit- ent opportunities throughout the year. There are many unique restaurants as ell as many chain restaurants in the surrounding areas. For all students, but pecially freshmen and new students, there are always things occurring on mpus. They have a week of welcome where there are nightly activities for all dents.

urrent student, 9/2001-Submit Date, February 2006

here are two campus bars, Rennie's and Taylor's, that a lot of students frequent. nnie's is a bit more laid back and Taylor's can get a little crazier on select ghts. There is dining all over campus.

e Erb Memorial Union (EMU), located in the heart of campus, has several od vendors including Subway, Panda Express, the Holy Cow, and several stu- nt-run stores and coffee shops. The Buzz, downstairs in the EMU, is a popu- r meeting place for various groups or any number of students. Dancing, andinavian groups, multicultural clubs and even Bible study groups meet in e Buzz. I work across the hall at the Union Market, a convenience store on mpus. Many of the student groups are housed in the EMU, such as the ssociated Students of the University of Oregon (ASUO), UO's student gov- nment; the Black Student Union; the LGBTQA, a sexual advocacy group for ; the multicultural student union and more. There is a ticket office in the EMU at has very long lines during most of the ticket releasing dates for big sporting ents, such as football, basketball and softball. There is a great club sports fice for students who want to get involved with sports but do not want to (or nnot) compete at the Division I level.

e EMU will house dances and other social events. Also, downstairs is The eak, which has pool tables, ping pong tables, a large-screen TV, a video arcade

and offers services such as locker check-out and lost and found. They have con- certs and card games and other tournaments during the week as well.

There are any number of clubs or organizations you can get involved with if you choose to do so. Lots of fun. Lots of options. I am also in a student improv troupe at the UO called Absolute Improv. We perform on campus as well as off, and we do both short form comedy (like that you would see on *Whose Line is it Anyway?*) and a long form of improv where we make an hour-long play out of only a title. The theatre department offers multiple student productions, one play on the main stage and one on the smaller stage each term. Competition for roles is fierce and it is difficult to obtain a spot in the Robinson Theatre. Many musi- cal performances are also held in the Music School's Bealle Hall (pronounced "bell"), one of the country's finest chamber music halls.

Current student, 10/2004-Submit Date, December 2005

Happening bar system close to campus, lots of nice restaurants, tons of ladies to date or to just have a good time with, good events put on by the campus groups and the ASUO, small Greek system with some cool people in it. People go to frat parties early in their college careers and tend to stick to house parties once they get off campus, however if you know people in the Greek system they will invite you to the parties they throw and that their friends throw. Weed is just everywhere, eight out of 10 parties has it there and available for those who want it.

Current student, 9/2004-Submit Date, April 2005

One side of the campus near 13th Street was where nearly all students went to hang out or eat. Max's Bar, Rennie's and Taylor's all packed in the people. Max's tended to be more of the normal college student hang out. Both Rennie's and Taylor's had the fraternity/sorority spin on them. The Greek system is rather large at the UO and has many options for students looking for a house to join. Most are conveniently located right by the 13th Street side of campus where nearly all of the businesses are located.

Maple Garden Restaurant was a fantastic family-run place that had the father doing the cooking at break-neck speed every minute of the day. Food was deli- cious and prices were very affordable. Maple Garden was the hole-in-the-wall eatery that we loved to go to whenever possible. Track Town Pizza and Pegasus Pizza were two of the best pizza eats in the entire city and deservingly so. BBQ chicken pizza was done to perfection at both locations and Pegasus has a great beer selection on tap. The Glenwood was a local house turned into a restaurant. Breakfasts here are the best. Hearty, wholesome, and reasonably priced, this was the place to take visitors from out of town when they wanted a real breakfast. Multiple organic and vegetarian options, as well.

Read all of Vault's College Surveys at **www.vault.com/college**—get complete surveys on 100s of colleges and univer- sities, expert advice on applicaton essays and more.

VAULT CAREER LIBRARY **591**

Bryn Mawr College

Office of Admissions
101 North Merion Avenue
Bryn Mawr, PA 19010
Admissions phone: (610) 526-5152
Admissions fax: (610) 526-7471
Admissions e-mail: admissions@brynmawr.edu
Admissions URL: www.brynmawr.edu/admissions/

 ## Admissions

Current student, 9/2002-Submit Date, May 2005

The admissions office at Bryn Mawr is wonderful. I dare you to try to find a college that has nicer, friendlier and more helpful people. They make an extra effort to work with applicants and answer all of their questions, no problem or concern is viewed as too silly.

After completing the essay questions and filling out the application forms, you have the opportunity to set up an interview with a college alumna. The interview can range from 20 minutes to an hour.

At first I was petrified, I wasn't sure if I could talk for an hour. The first five minutes were tough because I was so nervous, but afterwards it went great. My interviewer was friendly so I was instantly put at ease. I talked with my interviewer for about an hour—some of it we spent discussing my high school experience, as well as my hopes and expectations for college, but she also took the time to answer my questions and concerns.

When the admissions office decides to admit a student, it sends a letter and also calls. It's a wonderful idea because it makes the student feel as if she is really being welcomed into the college. You know you will be going to a school that cares about you.

Current student, 9/2003-Submit Date, May 2005

I feel that Bryn Mawr is a pretty self-selecting school—it's not somewhere you would apply to unless you were a serious student who valued academics and was looking for a strong sense of community in an atmosphere of all women. While Bryn Mawr does look for a strong academic record, I think the school also looks to select individuals who are passionate, well-spoken and diverse.

Current student, 8/2004-Submit Date, May 2005

In my case, I transferred here. I had to fill out the Common Application as well as a supplement for transfers. Be prepared to write a lot of essays if you plan to transfer here! This is a tough place to get in, but that doesn't mean you shouldn't try. They're looking for a certain type of young woman: someone articulate, determined, passionate, well-rounded, and someone who wants to better society—even while in school here. The interview was comfortable and warm. They just want to know who you are, what moves you. If this is where you want to be, be explicit. They might ask you (as they did me) why you would not prefer Vassar or Smith or Wellesley. In that case, look the interviewer in the eye: "I want to be at Bryn Mawr," and explain why.

Current student, 8/2003-Submit Date, May 2005

Bryn Mawr accepts the Common Application with a Bryn Mawr supplement. In addition, an interview is recommended. Bryn Mawr's acceptance rate is something close to 50 percent, but admissions claims that the reason the acceptance rate is so high is that Bryn Mawr applicants are a self-selecting pool. My interview was not very in-depth. It was like most of the interviews I took during my college search.

The school says: "Bryn Mawr's acceptance rate for the Class of 2011 was 45 percent."

Current student, 9/2002-Submit Date, May 2005

Being part of the Common Application, applying to Bryn Mawr was easy. addition to the Common App., I remember submitting a graded piece of writi (I submitted a fictional piece from an English class) along with my applicati essays. I remember my interviewer was really cool, had just graduated and w working in the admissions office until she found a real job. I thought my int view went poorly, just because I hadn't been very social or friendly, but app ently I was wrong. So bottom line, don't sweat the interview. Just talk ab how much you love being an independent woman and what you've done thus to prove that.

Regarding the application, Bryn Mawr says: "Bryn Mawr requires the Common Application, the Bryn Mawr Supplement, including a *Why Bryn Mawr?* essay, a school report, transcript, and teacher evaluations, the SAT and two SAT subject tests or ACT test scores. Bryn Mawr no longer requires a graded writing sample."

Current student, 8/2004-Submit Date, May 2005

I looked at over 30 colleges located throughout the East Coast. However, Br Mawr was the only school I wanted to attend. The first time I arrived on ca pus, I knew Bryn Mawr was for me. The wonderful students I met on my str throughout the campus provided me with a feeling of belonging and warm Bryn Mawr College was the last college I looked at before starting the writ application process.

Current student, 8/2002-Submit Date, May 2005

I was worried about getting into Bryn Mawr. I don't come from one of the o blue-blood families. But I worked hard in high school and it paid off. Nobo here cares that I'm from the middle of nowhere and that I don't share a nai with a senator. The only name that's important here is Bryn Mawr.

Academics

Current student, 8/2004-Submit Date, May 2005

There is only one word for the classes at Bryn Mawr: intense. The professe are amazing and really care about their students. Grades are not the purpo here, learning is. No one discusses grades, and that is nice, but everyone st wants that 4.0 because everyone here is an overachiever. The workload can tough, but in a good way. I have heard alumnae say, "Once you get past Br Mawr, everything else is cake." Popular classes can be difficult to get into a freshman, but after that you are fine, especially if you are majoring in the su ject.

Current student, 8/2002-Submit Date, May 2005

If you go to Bryn Mawr, academics will be your life—but you will love Classes are small and, after your freshman year, not too difficult to get into. T professors are extremely brilliant and well respected but always have time to s you, whether it's just to get advice or to talk about a paper. That said, the wo load is tremendous. I easily work five times harder than my friends at other c leges, but we have no grade inflation so you'd never know it. Our honor co prevents us from talking about grades, though, so they aren't the focus of m people's worries. We're so engaged in what we're studying that learni becomes primary and grading secondary. There are ample opportunities to wo with professors on research or other outside projects and Bryn Mawr will anything to help you do what interests you. The senior thesis is another opp tunity to pursue your own interests.

rrent student, 8/2004-Submit Date, May 2005

ce we're part of a few key consortiums, you can take classes at Haverford, varthmore and UPenn very easily. Between all the schools available to you, u can basically take any class.

> **The school says:** "Bryn Mawr is a five-minute shuttle ride from Haverford's campus; Swarthmore is a 20-minute shuttle ride; The University of Pennsylvania is a 20-minute ride by commuter train. The relationship Bryn Mawr has with Haverford, Swarthmore and The University of Pennsylvania gives students access to more than 5,000 course options."

re at Bryn Mawr, the classes are great. Professors are here because they are ssionate about challenging, teaching and encouraging you. They are not here st to write books (though some of them do that, of course!). The classes are all, intimate and exciting. If you don't get into a class the first time, you'll most definitely get in the second. I've never had to try twice for a class, but I ow it happens.

ading is fair—you earn what you do. Because of our honor code, nobody ks about grades here. There's no competition, except against yourself. And workload? Just right. You will work just about every day here, and you will ite papers, read and research. But, you know what? You'll will enjoy at least percent of what you do because these professors don't waste your time. You work that will help you grow and become the woman you want to be— ether in science, math, language, poli sci—whatever you love. It's a lot of rk, but it's not too overwhelming.

rrent student, 8/2004-Submit Date, May 2005

yn Mawr is notorious for the amount of work its students can accomplish, but t doesn't mean we do it without complaints. It's not uncommon to hear a shwoman discussing plans for her senior thesis, or to have a five-page paper e at the end of every week. Luckily, the professors are all incredibly proachable, and office hours are a godsend. Classes are tiny here, and chances the prof will know your name. Don't be surprised if after missing a class, u get an e-mail from your instructor asking what happened to you (particular- in upper-level courses).

rrent student, 9/2001-Submit Date, May 2005

ork here is hard, but the social zeitgeist of stress is worse. Profs expect a lot m you and won't take any crap. You end up working as hard as you can for urself, though, which makes it more stressful and more fulfilling. This is not chool for slackers.

rrent student, 9/2003-Submit Date, May 2005

asses are small and intense, and most professors are both friendly and chal- ging (the few crazies just make it interesting). Most people complain about ir workload, but they love it. Like any college, like in life, you can of course by doing the minimal requirement, or just faking through. The thing about yn Mawr women is that very few people want to or actually do that. Most ople like doing their work. Sometimes it's creepy, most of the time it's inspir- .

rrent student, 8/2003-Submit Date, May 2005

ademics at Bryn Mawr are a challenge. Each student takes approximately ur classes. This is less than most colleges because professors at Bryn Mawr d to go into greater depth. No class is ever taught by a TA. The professors e required to maintain open office hours so they can be reached by the stu- nts, and often try to entice students to attend with cookies and other goodies. ten, home phone numbers are distributed on the syllabus, and even one of my chers has invited me to dinner (twice). All classes are capped, so a popular ass is usually lotteried, first by majors, and then by class. Bryn Mawr is known r frowning upon grade inflation, and often accused of grade deflation. wever, most graduate schools recognize this, and it contributes to the power the Bryn Mawr name. The workload is immense, but Bryn Mawr teaches you w to manage it. In addition, professors are understanding, and as long as you n't abuse it, may even offer you an extension.

Alumna, 8/1998-5/2002, June 2004

The classes were truly topnotch. Popular classes are not easy to get into if they're small, like most classes there. The grading is hard. There's no such thing as a class where everyone gets an A. There was no such thing as an easy class either. Believe me, I tried very hard to locate it, and the closest thing I found was at UPenn and Haverford. The workload was intense. There's not much to do in the area, so people are very dedicated.

Alumna, 9/1995-5/1999, March 2004

The quality of the classes is high. The small classes and close attention by the professors are great. They really add a lot to the learning process. You can take courses at Haverford and Swarthmore, as well as at the University of Pennsylvania. That adds so much variety and options to those who also want to benefit from the small liberal arts college. The workload tends to be heavy. Some people say that the top graduate schools are very easy compared to Bryn Mawr. They also have frequent guest professors, which is a nice refresher to your major studies.

 Employment Prospects

Current student, 8/2003-Submit Date, May 2005

Most people in high school had never heard of Bryn Mawr, but when I told adults where I went to school, they gave me an expression of awe and respect. You will get a job after Bryn Mawr because it's that good, and I hear the alumnae network is very strong. The CDO does a good job telling seniors about job fairs, and under-classwomen about internship opportunities. We also have externships where you shadow an alumna over winter or spring break for a few days.

Current student, 9/2004-Submit Date, May 2005

Bryn Mawr is a Seven Sister School, and that carries a lot of cachet out in the world. The combined alumnae network of Haverford/Bryn Mawr is extremely powerful; the combined CDO of both schools can set you up with an amazing array of internships and an enormous network of alumnae. Because of the small size, the experience alumnae have here is often very personal and intimate, and therefore they are very willing to help the next generation of students get started out in the world. The number of firms and programs that solicit is great, and the graduate schools students go on to attend are some of the best in the world. Bryn Mawr sends more women to do PhDs than anywhere else in America.

> **The school says:** "Bryn Mawr, by percentage, is among the Top 10 colleges in the nation in the production of future PhDs, and first in foreign languages and anthropology. Bryn Mawr ranks in the Top Five of colleges that send women into PhD programs, Number One in anthropology, foreign languages and the social sciences."

Alumna, 8/1999-5/2003, September 2004

Career guidance—you have to pursue it individually. The resources are there, you just have to use them. The people at career development are nice and willing to help and make themselves very available. There are programs in place to encour-age career exploration. The externship program offers a chance to shadow alum-nae over spring and fall breaks for a week so you can learn about the careers you are possibly interested in trying out after graduation.

Alumna, 9/2000-5/2003, March 2004

I went straight to graduate school, and Bryn Mawr helped me through the entire process. However, I know that there are plenty of opportunities to shadow alum-nae, get amazing internships and summer jobs, and interview on campus with major companies. The Career Development Office does an amazing job, helping you perfect your résumé, get through that interview and pick the right job.

Alumna, 9/1995-5/1999, March 2004

Most students who graduate from Bryn Mawr go into either academia or nonprof-it work. Some also get into the profit world and have tremendous success because of the liberal arts background. We also have a network of alumnae who provide opportunities for externships in the wintertime and springtime. Bryn Mawr may not be as well known in some areas of the country, but it holds par with Ivy League institutions. There is plenty of campus recruiting, as well.

Read all of Vault's College Surveys at **www.vault.com/college**—get complete surveys on 100s of colleges and univer-sities, expert advice on applicaton essays and more.

VAULT CAREER LIBRARY **593**

Quality of Life

Current student, 9/2002-Submit Date, May 2005

The quality of life is pretty much better than you will find anywhere else. The dorms on campus are referred to as "princess dorms." For the most part the rooms are large and not overcrowded. Residential Life does not try to fit four people in a room that can only hold two. The college employs housekeepers and they do a fantastic job keeping the dorms clean. They are very friendly and it is not long before students are on a first-name basis with them.

There is very little crime on campus. We are a very close-knit community. The school has an honor code that is actually followed. The most common crime is theft. Every semester at least one student will have her wallet stolen. Most of the crimes are committed by people who do not attend the college.

Bryn Mawr has three small dining halls. You might wonder why such a small school needs three dining halls. Well, the reason is fairly simple. Having three smaller dining halls means we don't have to mass produce the food, which means the quality is 50 times better than you'd get anywhere else. Our dining halls are often receiving awards for the quality of food served.

Current student, 9/2004-Submit Date, May 2005

Bryn Mawr is renowned for its beautiful campus. It truly feels like going to school in a castle, complete with turrets, flags and stained glass—very British. The landscaping is beautiful, with sculptures, lawns, sunken gardens and more cherry blossoms than D.C. People make full use of outside space. The rooms are some of the best in any American college I have ever seen—singles are practically guaranteed as an upperclassman, and most rooms have antique details like fireplaces and window seats. You can even live in a tower! Dorms have gorgeous sitting rooms with TVs and couches, and some even have grand pianos and wonderful antiques.

The gym is not brand-new, but it is perfectly adequate for a D-III school full of active athletes. The food is also some of the best collegiate nourishment around. Haverford students regularly come to eat at Bryn Mawr's three dining halls, cafe and coffee shop. The special themed banquets are amazing, and every possible craving you could have can be satisfied. The town of Bryn Mawr is lovely; it takes less than five minutes to walk to the train station, from where other towns and Philly are just a short ride away. Bryn Mawr has everything—restaurants (both nice ones and cheap ones), bookstores, snack shops, video rentals, supermarkets, office supply stores, clothing boutiques—you name it, they have it. King of Prussia mall is only a 15-minute drive away, and the college often has shuttles.

Current student, 8/2003-Submit Date, May 2005

Bryn Mawr's housing system guarantees housing for all four years. All dorms house students of all four classes. When you enter as a freshwoman, you participate in Customs Week, a form of orientation that helps you to meet your classmates and particularly, your hallmates. Campus is quite small, and everything is within walking distance. Everyone who lives on campus is required to use the meal plan, but the food is wonderful. Our dining services are always in the running for best in the country. In addition, it is in-house and provides many on-campus jobs, including all freshwoman campus jobs. Bryn Mawr is a small town, and thus, does not suffer from a lot of crime.

Current student, 8/2004-Submit Date, May 2005

Hello singles! 70 percent of the rooms here on campus are singles, meaning that even freshwomen can have their own rooms, provided they apply to the right dorm. I live in Haffner, and love it so much I'm coming back next year as a Customswoman (someone who helps the freshwomen orient themselves during their first year on campus). Many of our dorms have wood paneling, hardwood floors, and castle-like facades that make one feel like a princess.

> **Bryn Mawr says:** "In fact, 75 percent of rooms on the Bryn Mawr campus are singles. Housing is guaranteed. However, first year students are not guaranteed single rooms and in most cases will have to share."

As far as food goes, we just won an award for our Moulin Rouge holiday dinner. We had steak. It was amazing. The school is also making an effort to cater to alternate eating styles. We always have vegan and vegetarian items in the

Haffner Dining Hall, but that is not to say those options are always appeal[ing]. Crime has not been an issue for me, at least. The honor code here makes me [feel] safe enough to leave my door unlocked most of the time. We respect each ot[her] here, for the most part, and that respect transfers to our personal belongings [as] well.

Social Life

Current student, 8/2004-Submit Date, May 2005

Social life is what you make it here. We have tons of clubs, theatre and mu[sic] groups. A lot of the socialization happens on campus in those groups. There [are] parties at Swat and Haverford fairly often that people go to. In town there's [the] Grog, Erin's Pub and Cosi. And, of course, there's Philly a short train ride aw[ay]. We don't have Greek life, but we're like one big sorority. And we have aweso[me] traditions and wonderful secrets—you have to come to know. It's a great pla[ce].

Current student, 8/2001-Submit Date, May 2005

Bryn Mawr is one big sorority. This campus has no sororities; although if tha[t's] something you really need, I hear there is some arrangement with a sorority fr[om] Villanova. There are tons of restaurants nearby and a couple of bars, bu[t if] you're a serious student, you won't be inside either of them much, as you'll [be] busy with work. That doesn't mean you won't have any social life; rather, soc[ial] life is constrained to things like mealtimes in the dining halls and the occasion[n]al weekend in which you have managed to have little work. There are so ma[ny] clubs at Bryn Mawr that I cannot list them all. You will find someone who [has] something in common with you.

Current student, 8/2004-Submit Date, May 2005

Bryn Mawr's Greek life is confined to the Classics department, and I highly r[ec]ommend taking a class or two in that field. Bryn Mawr is not a party scho[ol]; there are no daily keggers, the empty beer bottle population during the week [is] surprisingly low, and most of the aspirin consumed to treat headaches have [an] academic as opposed to alcoholic origin. That's not to say, you party anim[al] you, that if you feel the need to participate in some underaged drinking, y[ou] won't be able to find it. Haverford and Villanova are two co-ed schools in [the] vicinity where most Mawrtyrs go to party. There are occasionally dorm part[ies] but Bryn Mawr's big hoorahs are confined to two events: Halloween and M[ay] Day. I feel Halloween is relatively self-explanatory, but May Day probably is[n't] as common a holiday. The first Sunday after classes have ended, Bryn Ma[wr] women don white, participate in some medieval festivities and the proceed to [get] plowed beyond all reckoning. Even if you don't wish to consume, there [is] plenty of other fun things to do during these big holidays.

Current student, 9/2002-Submit Date, May 2005

Social life is what you make of it. Campus parties are practically nonexiste[nt] except for two huge parties that are worth attending: the Halloween party in [the] fall, where Bryn Mawr gets its reputation amongst the community as being f[ull] of crazy sexually liberated girls who will do anything. There's also May Day [in] the spring, which always has beautiful weather and everyone parties outside [all] day. There are a bunch of local bars that people go to on the weekend, like [the] Grog, Brownies, Kelly's or the Onion. Girls also go to Villanova or Haverfo[rd] parties on the weekends. Clubs are not a big deal, unless you're one of 300 gi[rls] who actually participates in campus activities.

Current student, 9/2001-Submit Date, May 2005

In terms of bars, the Grog is my personal favorite—it's within walking distan[ce], fills up fast and the pub food is great for a meal. Restaurant wise I love Lour[des] (Greek) for when my parents are in town or I want to treat myself. Otherwise [I] like Silk Cuisine (reasonably priced Thai food) and Fellini's in Haverford. T[he] dating scene is what you make of it. There are a lot of women who date ea[ch] other. Other schools are nearby, and I think it depends on your level of intere[st]. We do not have a Greek system. May Day (in early May) is a day without wo[rk]; we have several concerts and a fancy dinner on the green. We have speakers a[nd] smaller concerts throughout the year—as a small school near a city, we do[n't] usually get the big names that other schools do but your social life is only lim[it]ed by your imagination.

umna, 9/2000-5/2003, March 2004

aditions play a major part of the school's social life. There are not that many ge parties, but they do crop up occasionally. Rhoad's Halloween party (and adnor as well) are two musts while you attend Bryn Mawr. You are located on e Main Line, so there are plenty of eating and drinking locations. Make sure u hit up Peace-of-Pizza and Hope's Cookies at least once! There is no Greek stem—just you and the rest of your fellow classmates. It is single sex, but averford is just a bus ride away, and Philadelphia is just a train ride away. This cludes easy access to all of Philadelphia's clubs, bars and restaurants.

The School Says

Bryn Mawr College is a highly selective liberal-arts college in suburban Philadelphia for students who share an intense intellectual commitment, a self-directed and purposeful vision of their lives, and a desire to make meaningful contributions to the world. Bryn Mawr comprises an undergraduate college of over 1,200 women, two coeducational graduate schools and a coeducational postbaccalaureate pre-medical program.

Bucknell University

dmissions Office
ucknell University
ewisburg, PA 17837
dmissions phone: (570) 577-1101
dmissions fax: (570) 577-3538
dmissions e-mail: admissions@bucknell.edu

Admissions

urrent student, Visual Arts, 8/2005-Submit Date, May 2007

pplying to Bucknell is relatively easy. The school takes the Common pplication. As a student who was looking at other small liberal arts schools at also took the Common Application, this was perfect. I only had to fill out e Common Application and I was basically set as far as my college admissions ocess went. I think the supplemental application to Bucknell leads more stu- nts to apply as there are no extra essays required. It is basically just a check f sheet with more information such as religious preference. As far as the lmissions process goes, I know the staff is trying to make the school more lective and competitive and is accepting fewer students with each passing year. ne school is currently looking to diversify its student population, so if you me from a unique multicultural or religious background, it certainly can help ur case. An interview is not required by the school for application, however you are on campus and have an extra half hour, one certainly does not hurt. ne school likes to see that you are putting forth the extra effort to attend its formational events and to check out the campus. Anything you can do to make a extra connection is helpful.

> **Regarding interviews, the school says:** "Prospective Student Interviews are no longer part of the admissions process at Bucknell University."

ne thing that is important to the application process is your expected major. or instance, the College of Engineering is much more competitive than the ollege of Arts and Science and requires higher SAT scores and GPAs. Also, the anagement major is extremely popular, even though you are not declaring yet, ople who put down that major need to be more competitive than the regular pplicant pool. My best advice is not to declare a major on your application nless you are applying to engineering—it's tough to transfer into the school ace on campus).

hey can tell when a student is not being him/herself in his essay. My best vice is just to be yourself and recognize your flaws in your essay. The staff ants to see that you are human and that you know how to make mistakes. A nse of humor is a must. In my essay I actually admitted that there was noth- g special about me, and that is what I am looking to find out in college. I think at actually made me stand out among the crowd.

urrent student, Psychology, 9/2006-Submit Date, May 2007

looked at the school, took a tour, came back a second time to interview and me back during Bucknell's open house when I was deciding between a couple f schools. The tour guide happened also to be my interviewer as he was a sen-

ior, and the fact that we had similar interests made the interview go very smooth- ly. I really felt comfortable from the first time I stepped on campus, and the interview and tour only added to my liking of the school. The essays were not too tough, as I could use a Common App. essay for most of them, but I found the questions that were asked on the Bucknell extended part of the app. really allowed me to let my personality shine through, which made the application more enjoyable to fill out. Bucknell is pretty selective, so I was very excited when I got in.

> **Regarding admissions essays, the school says:** "Bucknell's sup- plemental application includes one required essay and one optional essay, the answers to both of which factor heavily in the application review process."

Current student, 8/2005-Submit Date, May 2007

Bucknell University has become an increasingly selective school, so getting in is no easy task. They use the Common Application and little additions to it. I had to write one long essay and complete the two prompts on the Common Application. The essay prompt from Bucknell left much room for originality and expansion, so it was not a difficult essay, which left time for perfection of the essay. I applied Early Decision, which did not require more than the regular application. Students have a better chance of getting in Early Decision than Regular Decision, but Early Decision is binding, so if you are accepted you must attend. Scholarships are offered for activities such as theatre and dance in addi- tion to sports, so extra activities in addition to great grades will help you in being accepted.

Current student, Business, 8/2004-Submit Date, May 2007

The admissions process is fairly straightforward at Bucknell. They take the Common Application with a supplemental essay. I decided to do the optional alumni interview as I figured it couldn't hurt my chances. I've heard that Bucknell likes not just smart but well-rounded students as well. I think that Bucknell has gotten much more selective during the past few years and many people ask me if I go to an Ivy. In fact, it's not but hopefully this stereotype will help me get jobs in the future.

Current student, Engineering, 8/2006-Submit Date, May 2007

Bucknell accepts the Common Application and only requires a very short sup- plement. When I went to visit campus, they kept saying there was little to no academic aid available. This made me basically rule out the school completely. When my financial aid package came, I received two merit-based scholarships. I almost did not apply and it would have been a huge mistake. Do not let them discourage you from applying if you are worried about merit aid. They do give scholarships and every year they give more and more.

> **The school says:** "Bucknell awards only a very limited number of merit scholarships; most of the $34 million in financial aid awarded to students in 2007-08 was based on demonstrated financial need."

Current student, 9/2000-Submit Date, March 2004

It's your typical four-year college admissions process. There's the application, SAT tests, transcript and essays. I'm not sure of the exact number of essays, but

Read all of Vault's College Surveys at **www.vault.com/college**—get complete surveys on 100s of colleges and univer- sities, expert advice on applicaton essays and more.

VAULT CAREER LIBRARY 595

it's either one or two. Now they have a teacher [recommendation] (something that I didn't have when I applied for 2000). It is a highly selective school. For the Class of 2007, only 38 percent were accepted.

> **Regarding selectivity, the school says:** "For the Class of 2011, the acceptance rate was 30 percent."

As for advice, I'm not sure what to say. They really do strive for diversity. If you live outside of the Pennsylvania area (and in the hot recruiting spots like Colorado, Connecticut and California), you have a better chance of getting in. My SATs and GPAs were about average, but my participation in extracurriculars and taking upper-level/AP courses were (I think) the reasons I got in.

> **Bucknell says:** "The admissions decision-making process involves many variables and, as a result, geographic distribution of admitted students varies year to year."

 # Academics

Current student, Visual Arts, 8/2005-Submit Date, May 2007

One of the reasons I chose Bucknell was for the small, individualized classes. During the first semester, each student is required to take a foundation seminar, a small class of maybe 10 students or so. The purpose of the seminars is to try to teach students how to write on a college level and teach you about plagiarizing and how properly to cite information. The introductory classes at the school are fairly large, maybe 35 to 50 students, but by no means what you would find at a large state university. As you get to the higher levels, however, class sizes dwindle down. I have classes that are only six students. Though many of the intro. classes are just lectures, as you get into the higher-level classes, professors do their best to stimulate class discussion and projects. There are still those professors, however, who refuse to stray from the PowerPoint presentation method.

> **The school says:** "Foundation Seminars are small classes that introduce all first-year students in the College of Arts and Sciences to the academic life of the university by stressing critical thinking, writing, independent learning, collaboration, and other skills central to the liberal arts."

Most of the academics at Bucknell are challenging, and the one thing that I learned is that at Bucknell, you have to learn to be an advocate for yourself. No one is going to hold your hand through a test or ask you if you need help if you are struggling. Bucknell has the resources to ensure that you can do well, such as the writing center or TA hours, but it is up to the student to seek them out and recognize that he/she needs assistance. As a freshman, it is not too difficult to get into the classes you want. Because most freshmen take intro. classes, there is not much competition with upperclassmen for such spots. However, the intro. classes, once freshman enrollment begins, do fill quickly. Do not be afraid to e-mail the professor if you have a strong interest in taking a specific class or talk with your adviser about the classes you are looking to take. They are often very good about making sure you get into the right courses for your chosen path of study. Grading at Bucknell is relatively easy. I haven't had a professor yet who grades off of a curve. I find professors at Bucknell give you the grade you deserve. If you do A-quality work, they have no problem giving you an A for the course. The workload at Bucknell is difficult but manageable. If you keep up with the class, the workload is relatively consistent throughout the semester. Students work hard, but they also make sure that there is time to relax.

Current student, Psychology, 9/2006-Submit Date, May 2007

The academics at Bucknell definitely push you intellectually, but with the foundation seminars the school does a really good job of preparing you for the work ahead. The teachers really try to help out the students as much as possible (are always there to help out through office hours, e-mail and phone), however it is up to the students to talk to the teachers if they are struggling as it is college. Getting into some of the popular classes as a freshman is not always that easy (honestly declaring your major before you come in or at least telling them a major in which you are interested is really helpful), as classes like general psychology, some biology and other popular courses fill up fast, but Bucknell tries to accommodate its students and if you talk to your adviser, he/she tries to help you out in getting the classes you want/need. Grading is very fair all around and

if you manage your time well, your workload should not be too bad. The workload is definitely different for an English major vs. an engineer, but if you can balance your time well, you can still be involved with extracurriculars and have a good social life.

Current student, 8/2005-Submit Date, May 2007

All classes I have been in (or heard about) have been appropriate, interesting and enjoyable. Classes are generally the appropriate size; for example my Organic Chemistry lecture was about 50 people, but my Japanese language class had six people. Getting popular classes can be difficult for freshmen or sophomores, but if you pursue the professor and have reason for taking the class, he/she will be happy to allow you into the class. Grading is usually spelled out in the syllabus of each course, and professors are allowed to use whatever grading scale they please (for example, a failing grade could start at 60 percent or 69 percent depending on professor). However, professors are more than willing to help you succeed in your classes and do whatever it takes to get a good grade. Student tutors are also available for every subject. From what I have seen, workload varies widely by major. Science majors and engineers have a much heavier workload than English or Humanities majors.

> **Bucknell says:** "Bucknell's academic programs are rigorous across the disciplines; students in every major must learn to balance workloads that vary from class to class and from semester to semester."

Current student, Business, 8/2004-Submit Date, May 2007

I have thoroughly enjoyed most of my classes at Bucknell. I have to say that my most rewarding classes were within the business program (my major). Students are required to take classes in a variety of different areas of business as Bucknell offers only two broad business majors (management and accounting). While I was initially disappointed at the lack of variety within majors, I believe that this has helped me in the long run because it has allowed me to become exposed to a diversity of areas of business. This has enabled me to consider aspects of business that I never would have otherwise.

In general, if you work hard within the business department you will do well. However, if you slack off, I think that it definitely shows. This is not a department where you can miss class constantly without it affecting your grades. The professors care about their students and make sure that they stay on top of their work. Grading is also generally fair and I do not think that professors play favorites. Workload is also generally fair too. You have to stay on top of your work though or you will fall behind and it is hard to recover.

Current student, Engineering, 8/2006-Submit Date, May 2007

Classes are great. The largest class I was ever in was about 130 people and that was Exploring Engineering, which every first year engineer must take. The smallest class was my English 101 class, which was only eight students. It was great and made for lots of discussion. I have never had a problem getting into classes. You may not get the time you want, but you will almost always be able to take the classes you want.

> **The school says:** "Exploring Engineering (Engineering 101), a common course for all first-year engineering students, covers basic engineering practices across the disciplines through hands-on projects and teamwork."

Grading is pretty straightforward and not overly tough but certainly not easy either. My professors have been great so far. The small classes and relatively small nature of the campus allow professors to learn their students' names and you can have a personal relationship and really get to know any professor you choose as long as you make the effort to do so. I have never had a professor who didn't know every student's name after the first couple of weeks and all professors try to get to know a little about all of his or her students. I also find that there is a good ratio of male to female professors, even in the engineering department, which at most schools is dominated by males. The workload is doable but hard. Every student has to study hard to get good grades and there is always some assignment that needs to get done, but it is not impossible and there is still definitely room for a social life.

Employment Prospects

Current student, Engineering, 8/2006-Submit Date, May 2007

There are tons of ways in which Bucknell tries to help undergraduates obtain jobs with prestigious employers. There are numerous networking events all over campus with alumni and friends of the university. There are even opportunities for freshmen to begin networking—this is an opportunity that is very valuable and not available at most schools. There are also tons and tons of internships and externships available. If a student expresses interest in one of these opportunities, the Career and Development Center (CDC) will do everything in its power to help that student. I expressed interest in the externship program that is available to all sophomores but there was not a program in my major where I live. I e-mailed the CDC and was asked to e-mail them a list of possible employers in which I was interested and they would contact those employers this summer to try and find me a place to do my externship. They are so helpful and willing to do just about anything to help Bucknellians of past and present secure employment in their field.

Alumnus/a, 8/1996-5/2000, October 2006

I can't say enough about Bucknell's networking. While a student at Bucknell, I attended the Bucknell Washington, D.C. job fair and landed a summer internship with the federal government. After graduating, I had no problem getting a job with the federal government. Many of my classmates landed jobs with Deloitte, KPMG, Accenture, and Pricewaterhouse. After working for two years, I returned to graduate school at highly selective institutions. I received full assistantships and a fellowship. I contacted three professors from Bucknell to write me letters of recommendation. All three professors agreed and wrote me excellent recommendations.

Current student, 8/2004-Submit Date, January 2006

Every person I know who graduated from Bucknell ended up with acceptance to a prestigious graduate school or became employed by a very well-paying, respected company or employer. Graduates typically find jobs in whatever field they concentrated on at Bucknell, and receive a lot of help from the Career Development Center (CDC) in doing so. The CDC also works hard to ensure that students will find valuable internship experiences if they wish to do so. The CDC is not only a service for Bucknell students, but also for alumni for the remainder of their lives.

Current student, 9/2003-Submit Date, October 2005

The Career Development Center was very helpful, and many companies came to the school to recruit. After applying to jobs through the campus web site, the majority of companies would come to the campus to conduct interviews. This was a very convenient and helpful thing when job hunting. Senior year, it is tough to get away from campus for a few days to travel for interviews. I personally also attended a few job fairs around the East Coast, which were set up by alumni and the career center. Some of them were very general job fairs, and others focused on specific areas, such as finance, teaching or science.

Alumnus/a, 8/1998-5/2002, September 2003

The Career Development Center at Bucknell prides itself on the high placement rates of recent graduates. Many companies recruit heavily out of Bucknell, including Johnson & Johnson, Ernst & Young, Deloitte and Touche, Bear Stearns, AmeriCorps, JPMorgan Chase, GE and Citibank. J&J has financially supported the business program and hosts a business case competition each year, from which it regularly recruits. Bucknell has prestigious name recognition with employers, especially on the East Coast, as well as a very loyal alumni network.

With Regards to Employment Prospects, Bucknell says: The Career Development Center regularly works with alumni to develop networking systems for current students and fellow alumni; we have a full-time person devoted to Alumni Career Services. Off-campus job fairs are held in major cities on the East Coast for the similar purposes. A new externship program allows sophomores to job-shadow and connect with alumni.

 # Quality of Life

Current student, 8/2005-Submit Date, May 2007

Campus is beautiful and the perfect size; walking from end to end takes about 20 minutes. There are about 900 students per class, and dorms are spread all over campus. There are many housing options, including singles, doubles and apartment-style living. There are fraternity houses and one sorority dorm building. Dining is very good; there are three options for dining and they all have a good variety and choices for vegetarian, vegan and fat-free options as well. Most academic buildings remain open (along with the library) for study spaces for students. The neighborhood is very small but welcoming to students. Shopping is not limited and within walking distance. Lewisburg is a very safe city, as it is in rural Pennsylvania. Local law enforcement, as well as Lewisbug police, can be seen on campus and are there to help students 24/7.

Current student, Business, 8/2004-Submit Date, May 2007

Housing at Bucknell has been great. I joined a Residential College my freshman year. My junior year I lived on my sorority hall and next year am living off-campus. Two dorms (Swartz and Vedder) are not ideal places to live but most others are very nice. Dorms are generally clean and well-kept as well.

> **The school says:** "First-year students can choose to enroll in one of six Residential Colleges, which are theme-based housing options with an academic focus on the arts, the environment, global studies, the humanities, social justice, and society and technology."

The campus and facilities are beautiful too and the most beautiful college campus I've ever seen. Dining is pretty good also. We have two options for food on campus—the Bison (a takeout place) and the cafeteria. The campus is also very safe. We have blue lights all over campus but the area in general is not dangerous. There are some safety issues every once in a while but not often as Lewisburg is a small town.

Current student, Engineering, 8/2006-Submit Date, May 2007

Housing is great. There are singles, doubles, triples and quadruples all available for freshman housing. They try as best they can to match you with a compatible roommate but it doesn't always work. My roommate and I did not get along at all and the Office of Housing and Residential Life allowed me to switch rooms with another girl on my hall who got along with my roommate. This made my year much more enjoyable and I have many friends at other universities who were stuck with incompatible roommates for an entire year and they were miserable. The campus is absolutely gorgeous. I love walking around. All of the buildings are so old and well kept. Walking around the campus I feel like a part of history. The facilities are on the edge of technology. Everything is up to date and extremely well kept. The food is good and there is a large selection. You get bored of it after eating it for nine months of the year but that's going to happen anywhere. I have never felt unsafe walking around campus. At night, in the early morning, in the middle of the afternoon, there are always people around and I always feel safe.

Current student, 9/2003-Submit Date, October 2005

Bucknell is a great place to live. All of the dorms are all relatively new, or being renovated. I lived in campus housing for three years before I moved off campus to a downtown home. The downtown area is beautiful, and the campus is one of the nicest in the country. There is a new sports facility that is probably, by far, the best in the country for a school our size. Construction continues every year to better the look and functionality of the campus.

Current student, 9/2000-5/2004, March 2004

Since it's located in a small town (and three hours from any major cities), it's very secluded. Most people either live on campus or rent houses near campus. It's a beautiful campus (Lewisburg has often been named one of the Top 100 [small] towns or something like that).

Due to the small number of students and location, all the academic buildings are within walking distance. I feel generally safe most of the time. I'm not afraid to walk around campus alone at night. The facilities are clean and pretty modern. Every classroom usually has a computer and projection capabilities. There are many computer labs. Dining is similar to most colleges. If you live on campus, you're required to have a meal plan.

Read all of Vault's College Surveys at **www.vault.com/college**—get complete surveys on 100s of colleges and universities, expert advice on applicaton essays and more.

VAULT CAREER LIBRARY   597

Social Life

Current student, Visual Arts, 8/2005-Submit Date, May 2007

People often hear that Bucknell social life is dominated by Greek life. While the majority of the students do go Greek, I think the deferred rush system ensures that Greek life is not the only thing in which students are involved. While I am Greek, I am also involved in a wide range of other activities. My sorority is used as a social outlet and a place to make new friends, but it is not the only thing I do on campus. Bucknell knows that is in a small town so the school plans as many activities as possible for students on the weekends. On any given Saturday, there are at least five things for students to do ranging from concerts to movies, to pool tournaments. This past year we had Kanye West and the Goo Goo Dolls come in for concerts. If you are an incoming freshman, be sure to do a residential college as it gives the students on the hall something to bond over other than alcohol. Lewisburg is a great college town and offers great things for students. Some popular things to do in Lewisburg include eating at the Bull Run, seeing a movie at the Campus Theater, or eating ice cream at the Freez. Fraternity and sports parties often dominate the nightlife and many upperclassmen choose to go to the bar. The school also has an on-campus nightclub that has hosted people ranging from Fall Out Boy to the Plain White Ts. Bingo and craft nights are also very popular. Students also love to rally around anything dealing with basketball, and intramural sports are also very popular.

Current student, Psychology, 9/2006-Submit Date, May 2007

The Greek system is very popular at Bucknell, and holds many gatherings that involve Greek and non-Greek members. Going to them is a great way to meet new people and being part of the Greek system from what I heard really gives you a sense of family at the school. ACE provides many events every weekend from shuttles to movies and honestly it's hard to be bored at Bucknell because even though we are a small school, there is so much going on. There are over 150 clubs from academic ones to sports that hold gatherings and keep Bucknellians lives very busy. The town is small, but there are some very cute shops and great restaurants, like the Bull Run Inn and Myas, and we have a very cute old time movie theater that plays the latest movies and has comfy couches. I am involved in rugby on campus, the neuroscience club, the outing club, environmental residential college, and Bof (Building on Foundations).

Current student, 8/2005-Submit Date, May 2007

Bars and restaurants are plentiful and some are within walking distance. They are affordable and some give discounts to students. Several delivery food services, including pizza and Chinese food, will deliver to campus. Since campus is small, everyone knows everyone else, so if you are big on the dating scene, things can get sticky sometimes. Some students date different people frequently. However, it is more than possible to avoid these situations. There is a variety of events on campus regularly, including concerts (we have had Kanye West, the Goo Goo Dolls and Jack's Mannequin this past year), intramural sports, pool tournaments, bingo, crafting, comedians and more. There is a nightclub on campus that holds a variety of events on a weekend-by-weekend basis. Greek life is prominent but can be avoided if desired. Rush and pledging does not begin until sophomore year for all students. Without the freshman class included, a huge 50 percent of the school is Greek. However, no rivalries exist between any of the fraternities or sororities, and they do not discriminate against non-Greek students. Student favorites include bingo nights, concerts, BU After Dark, and House Party Weekend.

Current student, Engineering, 8/2006-Submit Date, May 2007

There are always things going on. Every week, *The Weekender* is published and put in every student's mailbox. It details all of the events going on around campus for the upcoming weekend. Downtown Lewisburg is not exactly a booming metropolis but the people are friendly and Market Street is very cute and good for an afternoon of shopping. Greek life indefinitely a presence on campus but not being Greek does not discount you from Greek activities. House Party Weekend is great and fun and unlike anything at any other university. You just have to attend it to believe it.

 ## The School Says

- *Academic breadth and depth.* Bucknell offers more than 50 majors and 60 minors in disciplines ranging from the arts, humanities, and social sciences to the natural sciences, physical sciences, engineering, management and music.

- *Close faculty-student interaction.* Classes are small, with an average student-to-faculty ratio of 11:1.

- *Undergraduate research.* Opportunities to conduct hands-on, independent research with a faculty mentor are widely available.

- *A focus on leadership and service.* Students are encouraged to lead groups on campus and to volunteer in the local community, across the U.S., and abroad.

- *Opportunities for global understanding.* Bucknell regularly hosts visiting speakers and scholars from around the world. About 42 percent of Bucknell's students study abroad for a summer, semester, or year in order to gain a new perspective on the world.

- *Integrated living and learning opportunities.* First-year students may choose to live in one of the Residential Colleges, six theme-based housing options with an academic focus. Students live together, take a class together, and participate in out-of-class activities.

- *Quality of life.* Bucknell's beautiful and historic campus lies on the outskirts of Lewisburg, Pa., a town included in "The 100 Best Small Towns in America." The campus is safe. Public safety officers patrol campus and a comprehensive emergency preparedness plan is in place. Academic facilities are modern, with multimedia classrooms, state-of-the-art instrumentation, and campus-wide Internet access.

- *Social life.* Students attend movies or concerts, participate in poetry slams, play ultimate frisbee, or hang out with friends. Greek life is popular, with approximately 50 percent of sophomores, juniors, and seniors joining 19 fraternities and sororities. Off campus, Lewisburg presents great opportunities for shopping and dining, and the University offers periodic bus trips to New York City.

- *Great employment prospects.* 96 percent of Bucknell's graduates are employed or in graduate school within six months of graduation. The Career Development Center hosts on- and off-campus job fairs, provides interviewing and résumé support, helps students find internships and externships, and connects students to a vast alumni network.

Financial Aid Bucknell provides need-based financial aid to all qualified students whenever possible. About 65 percent of students receive some from of aid, including need-based scholarships, government grants and loans.

Admissions—www.bucknell.edu/admissions Bucknell is looking for students who are academically engaged and intellectually curious. Admission to the University is highly selective. Grades and test scores do matter, but what matters even more is a passion for learning and for life. Diversity in all of its forms is also extremely important.

Prospective students may apply using the Common Application (www.commonapp.org). Bucknell's required supplemental application includes two essay questions, the answers to both of which are essential to the admissions decision-making process. Students interested in management, economics, or engineering are encouraged to apply to that major because admission to these programs can not be guaranteed at a later time. Interviews are not offered, but campus visits are strongly encouraged.

Carnegie Mellon University

Carnegie Mellon Office of Admission
5000 Forbes Ave.
Pittsburgh, PA 15213-3890
Admissions phone: (412) 268-2082
Admissions fax: (412) 268-7838
Admissions e-mail: undergraduate-admissions@andrew.cmu.edu
Admissions URL: www.cmu.edu/admission

 Admissions

Current student, Business, 8/2005-Submit Date, May 2007

Admissions process to me was quite easy; I used the Common App and everything went through fine and fast. Since it has one of the best undergraduate business schools in the nation, I felt that the selectivity is high. Interview is not required for the application, however, I believe it is actually very helpful.

Alumnus/a, Computer Science, 8/2003-5/2007, May 2007

They mostly look for excellent math and computation skills and leadership experience. If you're smart and a leader that means that you won't be afraid to get the help you need when you're struggling, which means you're more likely to succeed. When you do succeed, you're more likely to be in a leadership position at your company, which makes Carnegie Mellon look good. Admissions looks very heavily at potential, so even if you don't have experience in the area you want to study, if you show strong potential, that's usually good enough. Definitely get an interview.

Current student, Fine Arts, 9/2005-Submit Date, May 2007

Honestly, I was more attracted to the design program than the college as a whole, and in some ways this is still true. The thing I really like about Carnegie Mellon's admissions process is that they have a program-specific tours and/or interviews for most of the departments, so it gave me a chance to get to know professors and current students in my major.

Most students applying to Carnegie Mellon have a good idea of what they want to major in (or at least think they do), so your department has some say over whether or not you get in. Many of the schools within the College of Fine Arts, for example, have portfolios or auditions and these can be a real determining factor. The thing to remember about any of the steps—essays, interviews, portfolios, or whatever else you submit—is that no one looking over your material has a specific set of qualities that they're looking for. The important thing is to just be honest about who you are and what you want do with your life.

> **The school says:** "With the exception of the College of Fine Arts, which does consider portfolio reviews or auditions as part of the audition process, applications for admission are only reviewed by the Office of Admission."

Current student, Mathematics, 8/2005-Submit Date, May 2007

My interview was very helpful because the admissions counselor with whom I interviewed gave me a lot of information about the school and answered any questions that I had. She also gave me advice about combining my interests by applying to joint programs, like the BSA (Bachelor of Science and Art) program here.

Current student, Music, 8/2006-Submit Date, May 2007

The admissions process at Carnegie Mellon is rigorous, and for good reason. The quality of the education at Carnegie Mellon is well worth the difficult application and admissions process. As a music student, the conditions of my admission depended on both academics and a portfolio of my compositions (accompanied by an interview with two members of the composition faculty). The admissions office is very willing to help students as far as answering questions, assisting with financial aid, and giving advice on the entire admissions process. I started working for admissions as a campus job, and learned some information that students applying to the university might like to know. The type of student who excels at Carnegie Mellon is well-rounded, enjoys being intellectually stimulated, and has personality enough to thrive socially. According to the admissions counselors, the essay is a very important aspect of the application. Essays should show to the admissions counselors aspects of the personalities and lives of the student applying that cannot be seen from any other portion of the application. The school is selective, so be prepared.

Current student, Chemistry, 8/2004-Submit Date, May 2007

I remember the process being pretty easy and straightforward. I had an interview with an alumnus, whose feedback was added to my file, and it went really well. I think it's good that they have alumni interview students, because I feel like after going to Carnegie Mellon, you can recognize a future Carnegie Mellon student when you meet them. I wrote my essays on pretty generic things, looking back now, and I wish I'd been more creative so that my application would have stood out more. I knew that the school was difficult to get into, and I was honestly surprised when I got in, especially after being rejected from some other comparable schools. I visited Carnegie Mellon's campus twice before making my decision, and it was raining both times but I still ended up there! The tour guides the first time I visited will always stick in my mind because they were two seemingly "typical" sorority girls who sounded somewhat ditsy, but whose majors were very impressive (I think one was a double major in computer science and physics or something).

Current student, 10/2003-Submit Date, September 2004

Predominantly academically focused, with a strong emphasis on a well-rounded individual coming into focus now. Only very strongly academically motivated students should apply, because the program is very rigorous and can leave students out of breath. Interviews really do not occur that much, while essays are very important. Selectivity is very high, with only a small proportion of students applying and even fewer getting in. Most students here were top of their class, and then they got here and got a rude shock. If you have good scores, recs and essays, you have a good shot at getting in. It helps to have good extracurriculars on the side

> **Carnegie Mellon says:** "Interviews, which are optional but recommended, are offered throughout the summer and into the fall. Carnegie Mellon receives over 20,000 applications to the university and the overall acceptance rate is 28 percent, however, selectivity among the various colleges does vary."

 Academics

Alumnus/a, Computer Science, 8/2003-5/2007, May 2007

Workload is tough, but there's a lot of help. TAs make themselves available when you need them if you can't make their set office hours, as do teachers.

Read all of Vault's College Surveys at www.vault.com/college—get complete surveys on 100s of colleges and universities, expert advice on applicaton essays and more.

VAULT CAREER LIBRARY 599

There's free group tutoring available every week for many intro and intermediate classes, and you can always ask your advisor or academic department for a private tutor, which is also a free service. Teachers make it hard and expect you to learn a lot of material very thoroughly, but the school also makes it easy to find help if you put in the effort. No one is really trying to make you fail, and that goes for your classmates, as well—they're also willing to help. After freshman year, word of mouth spreads around which teachers to avoid, so you learn the ropes as you go and whom to take/not to take.

Current student, Business, 8/2005-Submit Date, May 2007

Prestigious academic programs; high quality in every single area. About enrollment process, Carnegie Mellon uses a lottery system, so the chance of getting popular classes just depends on your luck. For grading and workload, Carnegie Mellon is quite intense. Lots of work, group projects and tests, and trust me, there is no grade inflation here. Professors are usually friendly and accessible; quality of teaching may have some differences between different professors or departments, but overall academic programs are very strong.

Current student, Mathematics, 8/2005-Submit Date, May 2007

Professors are incredibly friendly and helpful. They encourage students to come to office hours, to e-mail to get in touch, and to participate in class. I've known professors to give their cell phone numbers to students and to offer to take small groups out to coffee to get to know students outside of the classroom setting. Classes are never too big. If there is a large lecture, students have recitation on the off days, where they can relearn difficult concepts, ask questions and get extra help. I have never had trouble getting into classes, even if there is a waitlist. Usually, speaking to the department head or professor will go a long way when it comes to getting off of a waitlist, even for classes that I'm just taking as fun electives.

Current student, Music, 8/2006-Submit Date, May 2007

In the music school, which is a conservatory-style program, most of your courses in the beginning years are planned out for you. These courses fulfill basic requirements for music majors, but that doesn't mean they are boring by any means. The core music curriculum is designed to train students to be better all-around musicians, and it succeeds in doing so. As far as the general courses are concerned, the professors are very highly qualified in their fields and pay special attention to undergraduate education, which is rare for college professors. They do their own research, but their passion lies in education. The workload at the school can become intense at times, but as long as students practice time management skills, it's not too bad. It is possible for students to be very challenged academically yet still have an active social lives.

Current student, Engineering, 8/2003-Submit Date, May 2007

The mechanical engineering program (as well as most of the other programs here) is extremely intensive and challenging. It is not uncommon for those used to receiving straight A's to start getting B's and C's. Grading as a whole is not curved, and professors are more than happy to give out C's and D's. On the other hand, most professors recognize an unfairly difficult exam, and will curve grades in specific cases. The classes in general are very high quality, and the professors are great. One of the best things about Carnegie Mellon is the interest that the professors take in the success of their undergraduate students. They take more than the required time out of their day to help students do well in their courses. Also, TAs do not teach classes. They simply help professors and give the students more resources. The workload is of course heavy, but manageable. Finally, most people are able to get into classes that they want to get into, even the popular ones. Overall, the program is great, mostly as a result of the fact that the professors care so much.

Current student, Chemistry, 8/2004-Submit Date, May 2007

Most classes I've taken have been pretty quality classes, especially the math courses and the humanities courses. It has been pretty easy for me to get the classes I've wanted every semester, although I do know people in certain majors (e.g., English) who have had a lot of trouble with online class registration. The professors are very accessible, with regular office hours every week, and will almost always respond to an e-mail within an hour or so. I think the teaching at Carnegie Mellon, however, particularly in the sciences, is not put first and foremost. Some of the professors in the Mellon College of Science do great research, bring in a lot of grants, and are brilliant scientists, but are not good teachers and are kept on the teaching faculty because of the other good things

about them. The workload is immense, as rumor certainly has it, and I thi Carnegie Mellon students are some of the hardest working students in the co try. But there is still time to be a "college student" and have fun if you can ma age your time well, and are willing to get some B's here and there. The gradi I've found, is generally easier than I expected and continue to expect. Ev when I feel like I'm doing horribly in a class, I've never had less than a B si I started three years ago. And I came to the school scared that I would be behi most of the time.

Current student, Business, 8/2005-Submit Date, May 2007

The workload can be overburdening sometimes. It mostly depends on yc major. If you are a computer science major or architecture major, it is comm for you to expect to pull an all-nighter here and there. There has also been joke of "H and less Stress" in the humanities program. Most programs here a demanding, and getting at least one C by the time you graduate is comm However, with all this being said, graduating from Carnegie Mellon is favor highly in the eyes of top employers. All of the hard work pays off as many a employed by the top computer science firms, the top investment banks, a whatever company you would want to work for.

Employment Prospects

Current student, Engineering, 8/2003-Submit Date, May 2007

After an incredibly challenging academic program, the employment process one of the easiest to accomplish. Companies want us; they recruit us. We si ply put our résumés out there, and they are trying to get us for interviews a offers. Furthermore, we have some very prestigious companies that recruit fro our school, including (but certainly not limited to) Microsoft, Google, Boeir Caterpillar and Lockheed Martin. There are many job fairs on campus, biggest of which attracts around 150 companies. On-campus interviews a information sessions by companies are held throughout the year. The career ce ter at Carnegie Mellon is incredible, and provides many opportunities, signi cant assistance, advice, and also instructional sessions to aid in the process (fro résumé writing to interviews, to accepting/declining offers). Finally, alum tend to be the most active recruiters from their respective companies, and a extremely helpful throughout the process. Some alumni will send e-mails wh a position opens up at a company so that Carnegie Mellon students can get a fi bid at the position. If there is one thing Carnegie Mellon students do not ne to worry about, it is getting a job.

Current student, Chemistry, 8/2004-Submit Date, May 2007

From the stats I've heard, about 95 percent of Carnegie Mellon students have job within six months of graduation if not going to grad school, and I believe I think employers look extremely highly upon Carnegie Mellon students, ar there are tons of companies that come to recruit students for both summer inter ships and full-time jobs at our three major job fairs each year (Busine Opportunities Conference, Employment Opportunities Conference, ar Technical Opportunities Conference). Although I've never personally used tl career center, I know a lot of students who have found it very helpful. They mock interviews, are a good resource for information, and usually hold ov 10,000 first-round interviews in their offices every year.

Current student, Business, 8/2005-Submit Date, May 2007

The biggest perk to coming out of Carnegie Mellon is the career opportuniti you have during your summers here and after graduation. Employers know v work hard, and therefore they want to hire us. It is not uncommon for a busine major to be working for one of the top investment banks in New York, or con puter science major working for Google (I know an example of both). The sta ing salary is much higher than most other schools and most people have don have a problem getting internships. As a finance major, I had a good internsh after my freshman year and a better one after my sophomore year.

Alumnus/a, 1/2002-5/2006, September 2006

Carnegie Mellon students get jobs because they have a good education. But, if it was not for the amazing number of employers who come to campus, we would have to work as hard to get jobs as we had to work to get our degrees! A lot of students like to credit themselves for finding their own jobs. That's no surprise given the over blown egos of many students! But, when I look back, I realize that the professional staff members of the Career Center are the ones whom we can all credit with bringing those opportunities to us! They work hard to bring in the companies to look at the smart, talented, enterprising and bright students. Let's face it, even after that year's crop of students leave, the companies come back! Thanks to the wonderful group of women who work in the back, my interviews happened! Don't miss a stop at the Career Center!

Quality of Life

Current student, Mathematics, 8/2005-Submit Date, May 2007

The campus is in a great location. It is grassy and large, unlike many urban campuses, but it is right in the midst of Pittsburgh. There are several surrounding neighborhoods that are very easy to get to, with restaurants, shopping, museums, theaters. I like the housing system a lot. There are many options: three styles of dorms, Greek houses, and apartments both on and off campus. There are also lots of houses and apartments off campus but very close by.

Current student, 8/2006-Submit Date, May 2007

The dormitories are kept very clean, some bathrooms being cleaned every day by housing maintenance (depending on the dorm). The food on campus is pretty good for a college, and is getting better every year according to upperclassmen. What keeps the food tasting good is the variety on campus, food being sold by separate private vendors rather than a large dining hall. The food service is set up more like a mall food court than a traditional college eating facility. Pittsburgh is a very safe city, and the campus is a very safe place to be. Isolated incidents do occur, but as long as one uses common sense nothing bad should happen.

Current student, Engineering, 8/2003-Submit Date, May 2007

The quality of life on campus is fairly good. Housing is decent and there is a wide variety of options from which to choose. The campus facilities are especially good, with numerous (quality) computer clusters, many work-out facilities, and other recreational facilities. The surrounding neighborhoods are great and very conveniently located providing a lot to do for students. Finally, the campus is extremely safe, as is the immediate surrounding area. Even Pittsburgh as a whole is extremely safe as far as cities go. The dining on campus is not great, though in the past four years it has improved dramatically. Overall, the quality of life is pretty good.

Current student, Chemistry, 8/2004-Submit Date, May 2007

I think our housing is great, with lots of options including on- and off-campus apartments. Housing is guaranteed all four years if you stay within the housing system, and most students live in campus housing their entire time at Carnegie Mellon. Our campus is small, and has the feel of a close-knit community within the City of Pittsburgh. The neighborhoods surrounding our campus (Oakland, Squirrel Hill and Shadyside) are all very safe and have lots of things to do for college students (e.g., half-price food after 11 p.m. at six or seven different places in Oakland every night of the week). Dining is something that I think students unrightfully complain about. There are so many options, with over 20 different places to eat on campus, that you will find something you like. I do wish sometimes that there were more healthy options for campus dining, but overall I think the food is good and I even stayed on the meal plan my sophomore year because I liked it so much. Our police force is huge for how small our campus is, and when anything does happen, either on or off campus, the students are notified immediately via e-mail and posters around campus by the police chief (I even know his name—Chief Doyle). Also, we have a shuttle service and a program called, Safe Walk (one male and one female student will walk you where you need to go on campus 10 p.m. to 2 a.m. every day). They are decent programs, but I think the shuttle service only runs until 1 a.m., so if you live off campus, you either walk or take the city bus, which does not always have the safest stop locations. The gym facilities could use expansion or just renovation, but the facilities for group exercise classes are great. The library is good with

areas separated for group, partner and silent study, but could use more outlets, and a better wireless signal on the first floor for such a high-tech school!

Alumnus/a, 8/2000-6/2004, September 2004

Housing is limited. It is guaranteed for freshmen, but then most people move off of campus, which is cheaper and more fun! I moved off campus after my freshman year. Carnegie Mellon is at the center of several neighborhoods, each diverse and affordable. That is the great thing about Pittsburgh—living in Shadyside (a half mile from campus) is one of the nicest areas and it is very affordable in comparison to most cities in the country.

> **The school says:** "Housing is guaranteed for all four years (so long as students don't move off campus and then wish to re-enter campus housing). There are numerous options for students, such as singles, doubles, triples, quads, on campus apartments, suite-style rooms and special interest housing (though freshman typically are placed in doubles)."

The city has an extensive bus system and along with your registration fees you get a bus pass each semester that enables you to take the buses everywhere for free—even to the airport! A car is nice, but by no means necessary because the buses take you everywhere. Carnegie Mellon, itself, is very safe. Schenley Park is behind it and Oakland (Univ. of Pittsburgh) to one side, both can be dangerous at night, but use caution and don't walk alone and you're fine. Carnegie Mellon has an escort shuttle service that will bring you from campus to your front door between 10:30 p.m. and 6 a.m., and if you feel threatened, campus police will escort you any where.

Social Life

Alumnus/a, Computer Science, 8/2003-5/2007, May 2007

Close to many bars and restaurants, and down the road from the University of Pitt, so you meet many of their students when you're out because they go to the same bars. Friday night is dollar drinks at Phi Bar, which is two blocks away from campus, and Thursday nights is 50¢ drinks at Matrix, which is a club at station square that features 80s music, hip hop and techno in different rooms. There are lots of good restaurants, and great margaritas at Mad Mex, which has specials from 4:30 to 6:30 and 9 to 11 p.m. every night

Current student, Mathematics, 8/2005-Submit Date, May 2007

The social life here has a bad reputation, but it is really unfounded. About 18 percent of students are Greek, which is a good number—it's easy to not pledge, but those who want to get involved can. There are open parties here nearly every weekend, and those who want to can also go to one of the nearby universities to find a party. The university center has free, student-run events every weekend, and there are $1 movies put on five nights a week. Most students are also involved in several organizations, so that keeps them busy, as well. Some students do spend all of their time alone studying, but that is not a requirement here—it is a choice, and those who want to have a social life most definitely can.

Current student, Business, 8/2005-Submit Date, May 2007

Pittsburgh is quite a college town with many other colleges in the area. Some complain about the social life here, saying that Carnegie Mellon is made up of computer nerds who do not leave their dorms on the weekend. While there are those students here, there is plenty to do, if you want to. There are many neighborhoods in the Pittsburgh area that provide little shops and restaurants. If you are a sports fan, downtown is a bus ride away and you can catch a Pirates game at PNC Park, a Penguins game at Mellon arena, or if you're lucky enough, a Steelers game at Heinz Field. If you are into the arts, there are many places to check out in the Pittsburgh area, including many on-campus art shows. The most social students on campus often look to Greek life, which includes around 15 to 20 percent of our campus. It is there if you want it, however there are many clubs that are available to keep you busy if you do not want to participate. The most social time of the year is during our Spring Carnival. During Carnival the school is shut down for two days (runs Thursday to Sunday) and children's rides are put in the parking lot. For college students, booths (that represent the carnival theme) are created by many of the organizations on campus and also put in the Moorewood parking lot. We also have our annual buggy race, which is when a girl under five foot is put in a torpedo shaped buggy and rolled around a hill in

Read all of Vault's College Surveys at www.vault.com/college—get complete surveys on 100s of colleges and universities, expert advice on applicaton essays and more.

VAULT CAREER LIBRARY 601

Schenely Park (this is one of the most competitive events at our school!). In addition to these two events, a national comedian and national band also come in during these four days. For those, who want to go to the parties, during carnival there is a club event sponsored almost every night during carnival. These club events can be quite fun and are also thrown throughout the year. Bottom line is Pittsburgh is a great place to be. There is enough to do on Carnegie Mellon's campus alone. However, if you are not satisfied, you can go downtown and find something else!

Current student, Chemistry, 8/2004-Submit Date, May 2007

Carnegie Mellon is certainly not known to be a party school, but the social scene is what you make of it. There are things going on the Greek quad almost every weekend, and Beeler Street is a popular off-campus location for house parties. Shadyside and Oakland have some popular bars, especially Shady Grove, Hemingway's, PHI Bar, and also Fanatics in Squirrel Hill. There are always events on campus as well on weekends through a program called, Late-Night. Also, there are dollar movies on campus every Thursday through Sunday shown usually at three different times a night. The dating scene is all right, but it usually ends up that the same maybe 200 people are always out and you see them every weekend, so it becomes somewhat limited. It's nice being a girl though, because if you're decently attractive, there are basically infinite guys from which

to choose (3:2, guy-to-girl ratio: "The odds are good, but the goods are odd" There are also a lot of student organizations and clubs (over 200) and they w often have social events on the weekends (organizations have a lot of off-car pus parties at clubs in Strip District and downtown). And not to forget, t favorite after-party spot is Village Pizza in Shadyside, which has delicious b the-slice pizza for cheap prices, and is always packed with Carnegie Mellon st dents after the bars close at 2 a.m.

Current student, Engineering, 8/2003-Submit Date, September 200

Everyone is over involved, often depriving themselves of time to sleep or homework. Lots of students take on responsibilities in clubs. The dating sce is difficult because school takes up a large portion of your time. There are a fe bars nearby, but most are frequented by grad students. A lot of people g involved in the Greek system second or third year.

Alumnus/a, 1/2002-5/2006, September 2006

Join a fraternity or sorority if you want a guaranteed social life. With all t work that's piled up on you, if you don't have a reason that forces you to hav fun and let loose a bit, you won't do it. Carnival is absolutely the best time the year. So, if you make it to April, then you get to enjoy it!

Dickinson College

Admissions Office
Post Office Box 1773
Carlisle, PA 17013
Admissions phone: (800) 644-1773 or (717) 245-1231
Admissions e-mail: admit@dickinson.edu
Admissions URL: www.dickinson.edu/admissions/

 ## Admissions

Current student, 9/2004-Submit Date, December 2006

Dickinson is becoming more selective about letting students in, but they are making classes bigger and bigger. My freshman class was the largest in Dickinson history, and it has increased in size each following year.

Grades are important, as are SAT scores, but in my opinion, your essays are really what make or break you. Be personable, be witty and show enthusiasm for "engaging the world."

Also, if Dickinson is your top choice, I highly recommend doing Early Decision. You are more likely to be accepted and receive more financial aid.

Current student, 8/2005-Submit Date, April 2006

I went through admissions kind of unusually. I submitted my application before I visited or interviewed. But, I would highly encourage interviewing, not only did it reflect upon me positively, but it also made me more enthusiastic about the school. I am not really sure what to say about selectivity; I hear that Dickinson is very selective, but I was mostly worried about getting a scholarship. I wrote my essay about something that I worked very hard for in high school, and I think that the in-depth personal experience really helped me.

Current student, 8/2004-Submit Date, April 2006

As for advice for getting in, don't be one of the crowd. Get excellent grades and take tough classes, but think outside of the box when writing essays and answering interview questions. Don't think that admissions officers want to hear certain answers; they want to hear something individual and intelligent, and something that will illustrate you as being a great fit at Dickinson. Show them that you have a plan and how much you can give to the college community, not what you can gain from it.

Current student, 8/2002-Submit Date, April 2006

When I applied to Dickinson, I found their admissions program delightful. Th office works very smoothly—interviews are available with alumni and on cam pus. I remember being able to get an overnight on short notice, which was grea and convenient. As far as advice on getting in: Dickinson is a college that sui those who want to be involved and "engaged"—do your best to find out why yo want to go to Dickinson and stay away from the classic "I want to go to a libe al arts school" because it shows that you don't know the campus.

Current student, 8/2005-Submit Date, April 2006

I felt that the admissions officers were superb. They were incredibly friendl and personal. The great feeling I got from the admissions staff was actually on my deciding points for coming to Dickinson. I figured that if they love wha they do so much, then the professors and the rest of the faculty and staff mu also love it. I also felt that the students and the rest of the college communi must be as genial as the admissions staff. I believe that my feeling turned out be true.

Current student, 8/2004-Submit Date, February 2005

The admissions process was fairly simple—all I did was fill out the applicatio and complete the essay. The college required a Common Application essay an one of its own. They asked how a global education would help you grow as a individual. An interview wasn't required so I didn't have one. I don't think th college is as selective as they boast. If you attended a public inner-city schoo or if you're a minority, you should have no problem being accepted, no matte what your credentials are.

> **The school says:** "Dickinson continues to strengthen its reputa-tion as a selective liberal arts institution while increasing the overall diversity of the student body. Applications have increased by more than 1000 over the past five years to 5298 in fall 2006 while the average SAT has risen more than 50 points. The acceptance rate for fall, 2006 was 43 percent. Additionally, minority and international students now make up nearly a fifth of the student population."

Alumnus/a, 8/2000-5/2004, April 2006

I applied through the guaranteed grant process. Basically it meant that an financial aid I was awarded at the time of admission was guaranteed to me fo my full four years. I filled out a Common Application along with the supple mental application.

ighly recommend visiting the campus and getting an interview. I visited the
mpus four times and did a campus tour, formal admissions interview and an
ernight stay with a current student. I think it was a great way to get a feel for
e campus and the admissions officers to get to know you besides what they see
paper.

unique thing about my application process was that I did submit my SAT
ores to Dickinson. They don't require them for admission. However, merit-
sed scholarships are awarded for high SAT scores.

Academics

urrent student, 9/2004-Submit Date, December 2006

s with many colleges, you get what you put into your education. Most class
zes are small, and attendance is often taken. Participation is usually part of
ur grade. Depending on your major, you will have a lot of reading, papers and
me exams. In my personal experience as a Spanish and Anthropology major,
ave not been seriously overwhelmed, though things do get busy.

can be frustrating when trying to schedule classes because they want to keep
e class sizes small, but they keep admitting more and more students. The new
anner system is annoying, but that could be because it is new, and doesn't allow
u to be on a waitlist for classes.

my experience, the professors have been intelligent, engaging and caring,
ten being less harsh or strict than I would have expected from college.

urrent student, 8/2005-Submit Date, April 2006

think the classes are difficult but manageable—the first-year seminar really
ses you in. I am especially impressed with the quality of the Italian program—
have learned so much in two semesters and am now an Italian Studies double
ajor, which I would have never even considered before coming to college. I
ally love the accessibility of my professors, especially my Italian professor, by
mail or in his office, he is always there and very helpful. The workload is
eady; during midterms it can be pretty overwhelming, but there is a break fol-
wing both midterms to ease the pressure a little bit.

urrent student, 8/2004-Submit Date, April 2006

s a tough workload but manageable. It teaches you how to manage your time
etween friends, grades and extra stuff that makes life interesting. The liberal
ts program is excellent in itself; it forces students to take classes that they may
ot have taken otherwise. For example, I was "forced" to take a Medical
ociology class in order to fulfill one of the division requirements, and it was
ne of the most influential classes I have taken while at college. As a biology
ajor, I probably would not have taken a sociology class if I had not gone to a
ace like Dickinson that gets kids out of their proverbial "boxes."

urrent student, 8/2002-Submit Date, April 2006

he accessibility of courses at Dickinson has been wonderful for me. The beau-
of the liberal arts education is that it enables students to explore various cours-
s in different disciplines. I came to Dickinson with the intent to study biology
nly. I have in the last four years, however, studied both anthropology and biol-
gy and have really enjoyed both majors. Thus, the combination of my majors
as given me a broad range of insight into many academic focuses. I have never
ruggled getting into classes, even popular classes. Professors generally have
een exceptional, though I have had a few negative experiences with overly
pinionated social science professors. Grading is very fair and well outlined at
e start of the semester. The workload at Dickinson is very consistent and very
hallenging. The workload for the sciences is significantly more than that of the
umanities. In general, the workload is manageable and challenging.

urrent student, 8/2003-Submit Date, April 2006

ickinson's classes are the perfect mix of a challenging and relaxing atmos-
here. Professors are extremely accessible and personable and I believe give out
air grades on a consistent basis. If a student feels his/her grade is unfair, pro-
essors are always willing to discuss it with him/her.

Current student, 8/2005-Submit Date, April 2006

I believe that the classes are amazing, literally. I just want to take so many of
them, and it's disappointing that I can't because I can only focus on a few subjects. I enjoy many different subjects. I really feel the professors love what they
do and they are extremely accessible. If I ever have a problem with a paper or
my classes, I know that I can e-mail my professor and he/she will help me out.
They all hold office hours, but if I have class during their office hours, they will
schedule a time so that I can meet with them. The grading system is different
from high school, and I had to get used to that, but I actually like it better because
I'm not doing a lot of easy homework. The few grades I get count, and while
professors vary in grading, and some students do not like this type of grading, I
do. I know that what I am required to read or the papers I am required to write
are meaningful to both the integrity of the course and my grade. I find the workload to be very manageable. I am different from the majority of college students,
however, because I have good time-management skills that I learned in high
school while doing the International Baccalaureate diploma program. But I feel
that if you're using your time wisely, there's still plenty of free time.

Alumnus/a, 8/2000-5/2004, April 2005

The classes are fantastic. Most majors have very diverse class options.
Professors are very willing to work with students in order to tailor classes (in my
experience). Also, the majority of classes have no more than 15 students per
professor, which encourages more learning and discussion as well as increases
professor-student relationship. Freshmen, unfortunately, get first pick for classes, but good relationships with professors will allow you access to booked classes. The workload is intense, but there are only four classes per semester.
Students must take at least three classes in order to be on full-time status, but in
order to take five classes, one must appeal to the dean for permission (in which
case your academic performance will be put under the microscope). Also, there
are no credits as in other colleges. Most classes are one credit where a lot of gym
classes are a half-credit and are only half a semester.

Employment Prospects

Current student, 9/2004-Submit Date, December 2006

One thing about Dickinson is that the alumni network is really interested in helping graduates and other alumni succeed. The on-campus Career Center creates
a lot of opportunities for students to make contact with potential employers, help
to write résumés, find possible jobs and apply to them, all sorts of services.

There are e-mails sent out quite often with lists of internships and employment
opportunities. It's really up to you to utilize these resources.

Alumnus/a, 9/1999-6/2003, May 2006

This is an area that Dickinson has been working to improve. Name recognition
is considerably stronger on the East Coast than in other areas of the country,
which we are trying to improve through alumni clubs and other avenues. In general, my experience was that the majority of potential employers have respect for
a liberal arts education, study abroad, and other activities for which Dickinson is
known. But there were some instances in which employers were seeking someone with more expertise in one particular area.

Current student, 8/2004-Submit Date, April 2006

The career center at Dickinson is a great asset to the school. Even during the
first year you are here, they tell you that one day you will have to leave, and
that's where they come in. They publish a weekly newsletter called the *Toilet
Paper* that is distributed in bathrooms all over campus. The publication gives all
kinds of details about networking programs, internship opportunities, practice
interview sessions and résumé writing workshops.

Current student, 8/2002-Submit Date, April 2006

Dickinson keeps you up to date on all that is available to you. As soon as you
are a sophomore you receive weekly career updates, tutorials on how to utilize
the Dickinson alumni network and the Career Center.

Current student, 8/2002-Submit Date, April 2006

I currently work in the Internship Office as well as the Career Center and I have
found that Dickinson students are receiving a variety of opportunities, both job
and internship related. A mix of graduate programs, job opportunities and gap-

Read all of Vault's College Surveys at **www.vault.com/college**—get complete surveys on 100s of colleges and universities, expert advice on applicaton essays and more.

V\ULT CAREER LIBRARY **603**

year options describe our graduating class. The Career Center is very accessible for aiding students in exploring different fields and hosts a variety of events to promote opportunities for Dickinson graduates. Students generally receive strong jobs with a large amount of room for growth. The alumni network is fantastic, and the Career Center does a fantastic job of keeping the students in touch with the alumni network. The database that promotes jobs and internships for Dickinson is well updated and very easy to navigate.

Alumnus/a, 8/2000-5/2004, April 2005

The Career Center on campus has greatly improved since my arrival. Dickinson certainly has a great alumni relationship and the alumni networking is a great way to go in order to pursue career advice or even leads. Graduates of Dickinson are all over the world in all sorts of jobs. On-campus recruiting is very handy and there is a web site devoted to getting jobs for graduates.

Quality of Life

Current student, 9/2004-Submit Date, December 2006

Carlisle is a nice little town, and Dickinson's campus adds to the quaintness and the sense of history you have while walking around. If you're from a big city and you're used to constant entertainment, be warned. Sometimes things to get a little dull around here. The college does bring in a lot of speakers, shows movies and tries to keep things interesting.

Some dorms aren't very new, but they have been in the process of renovating, and the past couple of years have been the first for everyone to have air-conditioning! The gym is great, with aerobics, weights, racquetball courts and a pool. The cafeteria food is good with lots of vegan and vegetarian options, but after three years, it is beginning to seem repetitive.

There are definitely instances of crime, cases of assault, and drug use, of course, but generally things are safe. Public Safety is always driving around to keep an eye on things.

Current student, 8/2004-Submit Date, April 2006

The housing on campus is pretty good, but some dorms are kind of old and run down. Most kids choose to live on campus though a small percent of the senior class is allowed to live off campus. The campus, itself, is beautiful all year, and the classroom facilities are very nice. We have one major dining hall that has good food, but we still are not able to use our meal plans off campus at local restaurants. Safety has never been an issue, but there are still blue lights all over campus for security.

Current student, 8/2002-Submit Date, April 2006

Housing, facilities, dining and safety are all very positive aspects of Dickinson. Students commonly partake in elaborate conversations regarding life issues and Dickinson, as a whole, is becoming more and more diverse ethnically, religiously and racially. Students, as a whole, welcome this increase in diversity. The campus is beautiful and well maintained. Facilities, particularly library and athletic resources, are very helpful. The Carlisle community is constantly changing and in my four years at Dickinson I have seen drastic changes in the relationships between students and residents of Carlisle. Students and student groups are extremely involved with the community with regards to philanthropic service, social activities and educational resources. The quality of life at Dickinson is great; particularly within the limestone walls.

Alumnus/a, 8/2000-5/2004, April 2005

Housing is guaranteed for all four years of your college life, but many upperclassmen choose to live off campus. There are certainly many apartment complexes available. Also, creating relationships with professors will help you here, too. If you make friends with a professor who goes on sabbatical while you're a student, you may be asked to house-sit for a school year. Many of my friends were able to do this. The facilities are fantastic and state-of-the-art. The gym was just revamped about three years ago with brand-new nautilus equipment. The HUB has just finished being re-done this year—the building includes the dining hall (rated 10th in the nation the last I checked—the food is great most of the time, everyone has their off days), the school restaurant (the SNAR), the book store, the mail center, a coffee shop, the Devil's Den (mini-mart), the theater, the computer lab, the radio station and more. Crime is very low in Carlisle

and on campus. You can walk into any building on campus and put a person object down and either it will be right where you left it when you come back, someone will have put it in the building's main office. I heard of no thefts wh I was a student.

Social Life

Current student, 9/2004-Submit Date, December 2006

The school social life is largely fueled by Greek life and drinking (Delta N Kappa Kappa Gamma, Sigma Chi and so on). There are several bars, Fa Eddie's, The Gingerbread Man, The Red Devil and Alibi's (a new smoke-fr environment). These are good for hanging out, dancing, playing pool and so o There are tons of little cafes and coffee shops, as well as two movie theaters.

There are religious clubs, club sports, student government, clubs of similar inte est, like hiking, or Habitat for Humanity, a cappella groups. There are so mar things to do; you'll have to just pick a few.

Current student, 8/2002-Submit Date, April 2006

As a Greek woman, I find the Greek system to be unbelievably frustrating Dickinson. We do not receive much support on campus, though we hold ver prestigious positions nationally with our affiliated organizations. A great deal the social scene for me is involved with my sorority, however there are tons things to do both on and off campus. The restaurants are legendary, particula ly those with local character. The bars are few and far between but are regula ly packed with Dickinson students as well as Penn State's Dickinson School Law students. The dating scene seems pretty typical, though I am no expert this department. The social life is great here, though the Department of Publ Safety is a bit strict. Students here have a great time!

Current student, 8/2003-Submit Date, April 2006

There are over 150 clubs at Dickinson. Whatever people are interested in, ther is something for them. The Greek system is the perfect size because there is a option to participate in it, however it does not dominate the campus. I find the to be something to do every weekend and Carlisle is a great college town wit its bars and restaurants.

Current student, 8/2005-Submit Date, April 2006

Social life is pretty full on campus. Organizations sponsor events every week end: plays, talent shows, dances, dinners and movies. There seems to be s much on campus that I can never do everything. Greek life is not very big c campus, as only about 20 percent of students are involved, but if you're inte ested in that, of course it's easy to get involved. New movies are shown for $ every few weekends. The movies they show are ones that are just about to com out on DVD. Also, there are midnight movies, which include other option Dance parties are common in the Depot, and events are often held in the bas ment of the Quarry, which is a smaller venue than the Depot. There are som really good restaurants in town, especially Amy's Thai, which my friends and love.

Current student, 8/2004-Submit Date, February 2005

The college has so many clubs and sports (over 150) and if you can't find on that you like, you can start your own. The college brings in great bands like O Go, Ben Folds and many others. There are great comedians who come an Michael Moore was scheduled to have a discussion here but ended up cancelling The college also shows new movies for a dollar. In general, there are lots of fre or affordable activities. Greek life is huge. The college's pamphlets say that th Greek life isn't really noticeable, but it is. The fraternities have the best partie Boys are allowed to rush in the spring of their freshman year. However, girl must wait until the fall of their sophomore year to rush sororities. There are few bars in Carlisle, however there are only about three that students regularl go to. The school is a party school, which I wasn't aware of until I arrived here It has got a work hard, play hard feel to it.

> **The school says:** "Dickinson College students come from a wide variety of backgrounds. With more than three quarters of students coming from outside of Pennsylvania, including from 22 different countries, Dickinson students bring with them an assortment of individual styles, cultures, experiences and inter-

ests. This is represented by the more than 150 student organizations on campus ranging from College Republicans and Democrats, to Model UN, to African-American Society to Greek organizations. Additionally, nearly 50 percent of all students receive need based aid, with average grants of $17,711."

The School Says

As the first college charted in the newly recognized United States, Dickinson College is steeped in history and revolution. As such, Dickinson asks its students to constantly challenge what is safe and comfortable, to meet the future with a voice that reflects America and to engage the world. Dickinson is a national liberal-arts college that is enterprising in its approach to contemporary challenges and useful in its educational programs. The college requires students to cross the traditional borders of academic discipline, to witness the interrelated nature of knowledge, and to extend their studies off campus through study abroad, internships, field studies and service to community.

A Dickinson education prepares bright, aspiring young people to commit to lives of substantive contribution in fields of endeavor that are necessary to advance a globally engaged democracy, including the law, medicine and health services, scientific research, the arts, business and finance, public service, education, community service, the military and religion. It does so by weaving into the curriculum and co-curricular activities five dispositions, or habits of mind, that are the foundation of a Dickinson education: developing a global sensibility; seeking connections among people, ideas and disciplines; engaging the world, far and near; respecting civility in discourse and action; and striving for accountability and sustainability.

Dickinson teaches 13 languages and offers interdisciplinary majors in East Asian, Italian, Latin American (certificate) and Russian area studies, environmental studies, international studies, and international business and management. To facilitate its global engagement, Dickinson sponsors 40 study-abroad programs in 24 countries on six continents, and is recognized as a leading institution for international study by organizations such as the Institute for International Education. Options include academic-year programs, semester programs, summer programs and specialized programs. Dickinson is also the only undergraduate liberal-arts college in the world that conducts archaeological research and excavation at the legendary Bronze Age citadel at Mycenae, Greece.

Dickinson is also known for its hands-on approach to science education, with more than half of the college's science majors studying abroad-whereas the national average is only 13 percent.

Dickinson's 2,300 students come from virtually every state in the United States and from many foreign countries. Our students are active in more than 150 clubs and organizations on campus, including the college radio station and newspaper, performing arts, multicultural and language clubs, student government, intercollegiate athletics, religious organizations and Greek life. Nobel Laureates, Pulitzer, Tony and Oscar recipients, as well as popular musical acts and comedians, provide students with access to thought-provoking and entertaining programming through lectures, performances and interactive opportunities.

For outdoor enthusiasts, Dickinson is located near the Appalachian Trail and other areas for hiking, biking and skiing, and the college has a well-equipped fitness center with a climbing wall. If you are looking for additional world-class activities, Washington, D.C., Baltimore and Philadelphia are all within a two-hour drive, and New York City is just three hours away.

Dickinson is ever mindful of its revolutionary roots and remains committed to delivering its own brand of the liberal-arts education-academically rigorous, useful and unapologetically engaged with the world.

Drexel University

Admissions Office
3141 Chestnut Street
Philadelphia, PA 19104
Admissions phone: (800) 2-DREXEL
Admissions e-mail: enroll@drexel.edu
Admissions URL: www.drexel.edu/em/undergrad/

Note: The school has chosen not to review the student surveys submitted.

Admissions

Current student, 9/2005-Submit Date, December 2006

The application for Drexel is about seven or eight pages long with different sections for the major program types. When I first looked at the application I was confused because the co-op program was not explained. I signed up for it anyway because I knew I had the option to change my program if I wanted to. The application was relatively simple, but Drexel does not use the Common Application, so I had to fill out the same information over again. (The $50 application fee is waived if students submit their application online, so I definitely recommend saving that money—college kids need it in college.) The essays

were ones that my private high school had prepared me for. I knew my strengths and weaknesses, I had role-models, and I knew my goals in life. I also applied into the Honors College around the time of the deadline, so I feared that I might not get in, so that was probably the most surprising acceptance letter I have received. I wrote an essay in one sitting about my favorite movie and how it affected me. Once I sent my application in, I received my acceptance letter and package not long after. Joining the Honors College is one of the best decisions I have made at Drexel because as a member, I feel like I have been a step ahead of my classmates. Drexel was one of the first campuses to go wireless and they have many of their resources online. Taking advantage of that, I think, helped me receive my acceptance notification sooner. Since I did not apply into a competitive program and simply the College of Business, I did not have to interview. I have heard, from my peers in these programs, that the interview process is not difficult. The interview seemed more like a conversation, which takes a lot of pressure off the interviewee (who is probably a high school senior still trying to understand the college selection process).

Alumnus/a, 9/2000-12/2003, October 2005

The admissions process was fairly simple. You just had to fill out an application and there were some short essay questions regarding your interests and goals in life. At the time, Drexel U was admitting a wide range of students to fill its quota. Even so, they only admitted students who had above a certain GPA or

Read all of Vault's College Surveys at **www.vault.com/college**—get complete surveys on 100s of colleges and universities, expert advice on applicaton essays and more.

VAULT CAREER LIBRARY 605

who showed good potential in sports. Nowadays the selection is more stringent regarding GPA.

Alumnus/a, 9/1999-9/2003, November 2004

The admissions process at Drexel was the quickest of any school to which I applied. Perhaps two weeks after completing my application, I had an acceptance. Drexel is a large school, so the application form was rather standard and no interview was required. I can't say you need much advice to get in—as long as you did OK on the SATs (I mean maybe in the 1000s range) plus a decent essay. I'm not sure how critical Drexel's review process really is based on how quickly I was accepted. The main thing to keep in mind is that Drexel is a big school and it's easy to get lost in the crowd unless you work toward being noticed by your professors and the administration.

Alumnus/a, 1/1998-12/2001, October 2003

The on-campus interview is optional, but you should definitely do it, especially if your high school GPA or SAT scores aren't as high as what they are looking for. When I went, they wanted 1,030 or better for SAT scores. Now I hear they are looking for over 1,100. Apply on campus when you have the interview or when you're there for a tour; they waive the application fee if you do. The application was very easy, and I don't recall writing an essay for them.

Academics

Current student, 9/2005-Submit Date, December 2006

Being an Honors student, it is very easy to get into most classes because after seniors and athletes, Honors students get to register for classes. Drexel does all its class registration online, which is convenient for the students and advisors. Initially, though, it is quite a task trying to figure out how to register. Taking advantage of what the advisors can do for the students is such a benefit. They can override any issues and give the students all the information they need about their course path. Drexel prides itself on its co-op program, which allows students to intern for six months in their continuing education. Although this is a good program, students are not prepared to begin their jobs. There is a Co-op 101 class that is supposed to guide a student through the process of creating a résumé, signing up for jobs and the interview process. The class is helpful in getting the job, but it teaches the students nothing about filling out tax forms or how to interact with the executive members of a company.

On to other topics, grading totally depends on the professor, but starting this academic year (September, 2006) Drexel enforced the plus/minus system to eliminate accusations of inflated grades. Many students who got a low 90 as a class grade were against it, because that would not qualify as an A, but rather an A-. An A- is not a 4.0 GPA. Those students made a lot of noise, but their argument did not hold against the president and the academic council members. Now that the system is implemented, students have to work harder, but professors still can create their own grading system for their classes. The workload is challenging depending on the class. Personally speaking, I found the lower-level classes more demanding because there were many small assignments. The higher-levels classes required a research-intensive term paper, which was an assignment I enjoyed doing rather than several small papers.

Alumnus/a, 9/2000-12/2003, October 2005

Getting the classes you want in your program can be difficult if you're not studying business, computer programming, IT or engineering. In general, registering for classes is first come, first serve with priority given to seniors, then juniors and so on. You have to be at a computer right when registration opens, usually around 8 a.m., to make sure you can get the classes you want. And sometimes even then you can't get in because all the upperclassmen might have gotten to them already. Grading varies from professor to professor, as does the workload.

Alumnus/a, 9/1999-9/2003, November 2004

I found it easy to get the classes I wanted and to do well in them. Most of the professors are great and the accelerated pace of the quarters will make you work hard. There were a few occasional bad apples in the bunch, but that's to be expected just about anywhere. I found the range of available classes to be quite good and most of my courses were challenging without being too hard. I never felt the workload was too much, although it was definitely very challenging at times. It also depends on which program you are in. I was a business major,

which seemed much easier than being, say, an engineering major or some oth technical field. I did find it was hard to get a hold of most professors outside class time and no one ever seemed to know where the professors' offices we or when their office hours were supposed to be.

Alumnus/a, 1/1998-12/2001, October 2003

I was in both business and international area studies. The courses were cha lenging. The language classes were taught by native speakers. There were man foreign professors for other classes, though, and some were very difficult t understand. Therefore, a lot of students did not do as well as they should hav This is especially true for certain engineering classes and for Statistics.

Employment Prospects

Current student, 9/2005-Submit Date, December 2006

Although Drexel is known as an engineering school, the business students hav a lot of opportunity for employment. Being in the city, where many small an large businesses are located, helps students find jobs easily. Since Drexel ha this co-op program, they have a large database of jobs and internships availabl for all students.

Alumnus/a, 8/1996-4/2001, September 2006

Drexel is well-known in the region, and graduates usually have been on three co ops of six months each, often at three different companies. Drexel is known fo having rigorous engineering and computer programs (and increasingly, bus ness). Graduates of Drexel already have practical experience, and have littl trouble getting a decent job. Drexel took over a medical school a few years back and seems to do OK with that.

Alumnus/a, 9/2000-12/2003, October 2005

If you enroll in the co-op program at Drexel, it is a good opportunity to get expe rience in the real world. You can work for six months in your field of study an then take six months of classes. It's also a good opportunity to make som money while you are a student. If you really enjoy your job and excel at i employers will often hire their co-op employees after they graduate full time.

Alumnus/a, 9/1999-9/2003, November 2004

The co-op program is one of the biggest draws for Drexel. I had one awful co op and two great ones that really prepared me for the working world. Getting job after graduation was incredibly easy! I found most employers wer impressed with the co-op program much more so than an unpaid, part-tim internship. They were happy to find a recent college grad who already had year and a half of full-time work experience. The co-op program is well wortl it! I don't know much about the alumni network because I have never needed t use it and don't attend any alumni events. From the number of mailings an invitations I get from Drexel, though, there seems to be a pretty active alumn population, particularly in the Philadelphia area.

Alumnus/a, 1/1998-12/2001, October 2003

Drexel has a great co-op program. You can take a five-year study and have thre six-month co-op experiences. You will be working as a regular full-tim employee in your field. However, they cancelled the class they used to have t prepare students for the interview process and etiquette. Now it is up to the stu dents to seek the Career Development Center out for themselves and ask fo advice or help.

Alumnus/a, 8/1990-5/1995, September 2003

The school has a great co-op program and an excellent career placement office The school is very well respected for its engineering and science students. The major employers in the Pennsylvania tri-state area recruit from the school. There are also many corporations from all over the U.S. Many of the alumni are also working for different branches of the U.S. government.

Quality of Life

Current student, 9/2005-Submit Date, December 2006

Drexel is a city campus. Although it was rated the most unsightly campus by the Princeton Review, it isn't so bad. Drexel is going through a large renovation project to make the campus more pleasant. Students don't get the closed campus feel. Again being an Honors student made a difference in my on-campus residential experience. I lived in a suite-style dorm with kitchenettes and bathrooms in the room. I enjoyed my dorm experience because of the actual building and also because of my friendly floormates. The building also had a several events throughout the term to encourage interaction between the floors. Access to the facilities on campus is limited to students by major. For example, engineering students have 24-hour access to their labs and lounges. I am not happy with the dining facilities at all. There is a variety of food every day, but the quality and taste are not acceptable at all. As a freshman, having an unlimited plan is good for socializing, but after that cooking my own food is so much healthier. Like I mentioned before, Drexel is in the city, so students just need to be aware. Drexel provides security for anyone who wants it and there are call boxes across campus in case of an emergency.

Alumnus/a, 9/2000-12/2003, October 2005

Housing is comparable to other universities. Freshman dorms are small, though there are some suites available that are nicer. Seniors get better housing facilities, although many students prefer to move into an apartment in the area after their first year. Apartment rentals are usually affordable in the neighborhood. The campus isn't the most aesthetically pleasing, or the best planned, but it's not the worst. The campus and neighborhood are usually safe, with campus police patrolling the areas at all hours and escorts available for late nights.

Alumnus/a, 9/1999-9/2003, November 2004

Some of the on-campus facilities were lacking a bit, but Drexel is in the heart of Philadelphia! Any cuisine you could want is easily found and there is so much to do. Philadelphia has a wealth of cultural activities, museums, concerts and tons of shopping. There are also tons of options for living off campus without feeling too far apart from the campus. There is so much rental property in the area that I had an apartment every year but freshman year.

Alumnus/a, 1/1998-12/2001, October 2003

The crime rate is not too bad, but it is in Philadelphia. The campus actually starts out a block away from 30th Street Station. Housing is very hard to get after your freshman year. Also, you move often if you stay in the dorms or apartments they offer. They have built new buildings that have technologically advanced classrooms—very nice and useful. Most students say they do not like Drexel, because you always get shafted in some respect while you're putting your time in there.

Alumnus/a, 8/1990-5/1995, September 2003

Welcome to the city! You get all the great things a major city has to offer, and you do not have to worry about housing because the school takes care of that. On the other hand, you do not want to walk around flashing your wallet. You need a little common sense, otherwise you will learn that city life is tough.

Social Life

Current student, 9/2005-Submit Date, December 2006

The social life at Drexel is very active. The school does not have a football team, so our school spirit is directed to other teams, like the basketball and soccer teams. The Campus Activities Board organizes campus-wide events like ice-skating or movies for students to attend on campus. There are student organizations for every activity and if there isn't, the process to create one is quite simple. City life gives students many options for the students to enjoy themselves. Also, the art museum is a short walk away, so students can always take a walk there. Greek life is active and united on campus because there are shows and events that they are organizing throughout the year. Overall, the campus isn't huge, so lounges in various buildings become great places to socialize on campus.

Alumnus/a, 8/1996-4/2001, September 2006

Many of the establishments in the university area are less than first class, but there is an abundance of frat houses and the like. For students looking for nicer restaurants, they can wander down to the UPenn area a few blocks away. Drexel, being in the city, has the advantage that it is only a subway ride away from bar areas like old city and so on.

Alumnus/a, 9/2000-12/2003, October 2005

The Greek system is lively. There are many bars and restaurants in the area to hang out with friends. Many clubs are available for extracurricular activities. The Campus Activities Board tries to hold several different events during the year like concerts, comedians, plays, job fairs and socials. The dating scene just depends on your personal preference. There are parties going on every week on or around campus, so there's always an opportunity to get to know someone.

Alumnus/a, 9/1999-9/2003, November 2004

I was not incredibly involved in Drexel's social scene. There are no bars on campus, but plenty of pizza joints and other take-out places. The university does have plenty of fraternities and sororities, as well as a healthy athletics program and plenty of organizations. With so many other colleges in the area—and, in general, so many young people in Philadelphia—I found meeting people was really easy. The university does have a lot of events, from musical performances to movie nights.

Alumnus/a, 1/1998-12/2001, October 2003

They do have a Greek system. There are bars and clubs all over Philadelphia. Top Dog is a local favorite, located between Drexel and UPenn's campus. There are many restaurants and events both in the city and on campus. However, Drexel doesn't have many social events that have a high level of participation. I don't know about the dating scene, since I've been with my boyfriend most of my college experience, but there are many places in Philadelphia to meet people! Philly is very diverse, and so are the students at Drexel. If you do not get along with all ethnic backgrounds, you may have a rough time at Drexel, since it really is a mixture of people.

Read all of Vault's College Surveys at **www.vault.com/college**—get complete surveys on 100s of colleges and universities, expert advice on applicaton essays and more.

VAULT CAREER LIBRARY   607

Duquesne University

Admissions Office
Administration Building
600 Forbes Avenue
Pittsburgh, PA 15282
Admissions phone: (412) 396-6222 or (800) 456-0590
Admissions fax: (412) 396-5644
Admissions e-mail: admissions@duq.edu
Admissions URL: www.admissions.duq.edu/

 ## Admissions

Current student, Business, 8/2003-Submit Date, April 2007

I did not think that Duquesne was that selective of a school. Having a connection in Pittsburgh could help, but overall, it was not selective very much when I applied; however, they are starting to get more rigorous with it.

Visit the campus, even if you're from Pittsburgh and talk to students and professors, especially in the school that you actually are thinking about going into, don't just talk to people you know who go to Duquesne. It helps to have that other opinion. I never went on an interview when I came to Duquesne, but I did visit the campus twice, and I think it really helps.

Alumnus/a, 9/2002-5/2006, September 2006

Duquesne has a pretty standard admissions process. They believe in the caliber of the student both through academics and extracurricular activities. By no means am I suggesting that if you don't have the high school grades you can get in with your 100 hours of other activities. Duquesne looks for a balance, a well rounded individual, someone who can juggle schoolwork with other activities.

The best thing to do if your grades are a little low is tell them—interviews are key. For those of you who had a rough time in high school count on being able to say why (e.g., I did not do well in math because I'm an associative thinker).

Duquesne is becoming more and more selective. Be sure to study hard for the SATs to get your application noticed. With college admissions there is no such thing as overkill; if you have good grades don't think you don't need the SAT. No matter what any admissions specialist tells you, SATs do matter—it's a way of equaling the playing field. So pay attention and take a class if you have too, but take SATs very seriously. Oh yeah, never take the test cold turkey (without studying or reviewing) because every school starts to push you in the denied pile with the more tests you take, even Duquesne.

Current student, 1/2004-Submit Date, March 2006

The admissions process is what you expect from a private university with a good reputation. Good grades and scores on standardized tests are a must for successful admissions. The one thing that Duquesne does take into consideration is volunteer and religious extracurricular activities.

Current student, 9/2003-Submit Date, March 2004

I completed the standard university admissions paperwork, and interviewed with the department chair about my personal qualifications and plans for the future. Admission requirements included a number of prerequisite courses that I had to complete at a local community college prior to admission. I was also required to complete 120 volunteer hours before my application would be considered.

Current student, 9/2004-Submit Date, March 2005

For Duquesne's pharmacy program, they look for a minimum of 1200 on the SATs (I guess the "old version" now), a 3.6 GPA or above, and you must be in the top 20 percent of your graduating class. There was no interview, and a one-page essay was required. I believe there were close to 600 applicants for my pharmacy class and about 180 were selected. The program is very difficult to get into and even harder to stay in. I would not suggest this course of study to anyone who will not be 100 percent committed to it. It is a lot of work and sacrifices must be made on a regular basis such as giving up time to study for frequent exams.

> **The school says:** "The minimum SAT score for admission into the pharmacy program is 1200, a GPA of 3.5 or above, and they no longer take into consideration a student's class rank."

 ## Academics

Current student, Business, 8/2003-Submit Date, April 2007

I've never had difficulties in being admitted to a class. Professors are easy approachable, and I recommend forming relationships with them and getting know them on a first-name basis, from the very beginning of freshman year because they will help you especially when you are looking for a job.

Classes are good. I recommend at least a double major (if you are going in business), maybe even a dual major with the liberal arts school. I also total recommend studying abroad. I studied in Sydney, Australia for six months sophomore year and it was the best decision I made!

The workload is what you make of it. There were a couple of semesters whe I did 18 credits, and I still went out on the weekends; it's doable for sure. I wish though, for my GPA's sake, that I would have cared and tried harder my freshman year because it would really be nice to have that a bit higher now that I' graduating!

Alumnus/a, 9/2002-5/2006, September 2006

OK, before you read anymore of this review, understand that high school is over and you are in a different environment. Your grades, classes and professors are all different. If you did well in high school, there is no indication that you will do well at Duquesne. Also if you weren't the brightest bulb in bunch in high school, you may pull straight A's at Duquesne. A great deal depends on your motivation and also your course of study.

Alumnus/a, 9/2000-5/2004, November 2005

Duquesne has great professors, hands down. The programs that are offered are great, but I wish there were better electives. It is pretty easy to get popular professors, as long as you make your appointment early, of which is up to you take control. Grading is much easier than I thought, too. The workload intense, but you will get the grade you deserve. Workload wasn't too bad in the business school, but was killer in the sciences.

Current student, 8/2005-Submit Date, October 2005

Workload is harder than high school, but manageable. As long as you schedule things, and study and prepare for tests far in advance, you should get the grad you want. Classes are very challenging, but with hard work, the education you will receive from them will be worthwhile.

Current student, 9/2004-Submit Date, March 2005

Classes are very hard to get into because they are not yet pharmacy-specific and they require a massive workload. Most professors are nice and understanding Duquesne makes it an objective to make its students want to drop out of pharmacy because they typically like to award degrees to only about 100 pharmacy students a year.

Current student, 8/2003-Submit Date, September 2004

The academics at Duquesne are difficult. I am in the business program and the advisors make sure each student has at least 15 credits a semester to ensure his/her graduation date in four years. The classes are great, and the professors are always helpful. There are many options for class times and class days, and grading is based on the percent scale.

Alumnus/a, 8/1999-8/2003, May 2004

...e classes were great. I was in the business school. The professors knew their ...ff and had practical experience in the workplace. I could get all the classes I ...nted and the grading was fair. I learned a lot and often we studied in groups. ...was a fantastic experience. I even learned a lot in my elective courses. The ...ntent was fun and interesting. I loved the school.

...e classrooms were large enough and the media was good. The assignments ...re fair. All of my professors were very approachable for help. It was a great ...mosphere. There was a lot of groupwork. This helped us really to get to know ...r classmates. The sense of community is great. Finance was a lot of work. I ...died a lot every day but did very well. It was challenging but fun. All the ...sources are there to do well. There is tutoring available. If you use the ...sources, you can't help but succeed.

 ## Employment Prospects

...rrent student, Business, 8/2003-Submit Date, April 2007

...you want to stay in Pittsburgh, you're golden! There are so many Duquesne ...umni in the Pittsburgh area, but they are working on bringing a lot of people ...om outside the Pittsburgh area so that should help a lot. Definitely do an ...ternship if you can, and you should be able to; there's really no reason why you ...uldn't. Not only does it set your résumé apart from others, but they could end ...hiring you upon graduation!

...ofessors can totally help you score internships, too. So, if you've built that ...lationship with them, some of them will seek you out to tell you about an ...ternship they heard about. They'll be glad to help you!

...umnus/a, 9/2002-5/2006, September 2006

...ell, here lies the rub with Duquesne—it is located in Pittsburgh, PA, where ...thing happens. If you are motivated to leave the Pittsburgh area you can find ...solid starting job in a variety of places.

...n the other hand, if you can finish the pharmacy program and don't mind being ...ipped off to Arizona or New Mexico, there will be a six-figure salary with a ...xus in the driveway of your really nice house that your new employer (usual-...CVS or Walgreens or some pharmacy) has helped you find. This is were the ...oney lies, but you have to pass.

...rrent student, 1/2004-Submit Date, March 2006

...nce Duquesne is in downtown Pittsburgh and Harrisburg, many companies and ...rporations come to campus on a regular basis to interview and hire students. ...e have a huge alumni network that spans the globe in just about every country ...the world. I know the career center runs at least three career fairs with a num-...r of employers and graduate schools that participate. Not only that but ...quesne has an entire department (the Career Center in Rockwell hall) that's ...le purpose is help you find work, internships, and what not, but that is never a ...oblem since the majority of Duquesne alumni are very successful and because ...that employers are begging to hire us!

...rrent student, 8/2005-Submit Date, October 2005

...here are many opportunities for students here to get internships with important ...mpanies around the City of Pittsburgh. The school individually helps each ...udent receive the job opportunities that he/she needs.

...rrent student, 9/2004-Submit Date, March 2005

...b placement is 100 percent. If you are incapable of passing the national phar-...acy exam, Duquesne will provide to you, at no extra cost, a class that will pre-...re you to re-take the exam so that they can say have a 100 percent job place-...ent. Duquesne is well known for its pharmacy program and employers seek ...t the name when hiring.

...rrent student, 8/2003-Submit Date, September 2004

...here is a career service center that is willing to review résumés and help in any ...her way they can with internships and job placement. Throughout the year, ...ere are multiple chances to visit campus recruiters.

 ## Quality of Life

Current student, Business, 8/2003-Submit Date, April 2007

Campus is totally safe. The dorms aren't the best, but you'll make great friends there and meet everyone. Definitely live on campus—best decision. The food isn't the best, but it's edible. I don't live on campus now and I still eat on campus because it's so easy and right there.

Alumnus/a, 9/2002-5/2006, September 2006

Duquesne students like to refer to the campus police department as the Duquesne army, because there are literally 40 or more officers to patrol a campus the size of four city blocks. Just a note it is only as safe as you make it—if you do stupid things you run the risk of getting hurt, just like any city university.

Be advised that there are many sign-in policies in existence. Keep your student ID with you because that is your lifeline to get food and get back to your dorm.

The food is generally OK as university dining is concern. Be advised that the best place to go will wipe out your FLEX (extra cash that is not included in your meal plan) money, but that is normal.

The other issue is the gym, which was overrun because athletes and non-athletes had to share one area. But in 2007-2008, the non-athletes will have access to a brand-new facility that will have two indoor basketball courts and a slue of other facilities.

Current student, 1/2004-Submit Date, March 2006

Duquesne has all the benefits of a small enclosed private campus with all the features of big city. Other universities are not far away and the Strip district, South Side, and other areas of Pittsburgh are nearby. Residence life is better than most universities, campus facilities are very nice, clean and well kept, our campus is very safe and much like a small town high school (with regard to gossip!).

Alumnus/a, 9/2000-5/2004, November 2005

Housing at Duquesne is not great and expensive. You get the smallest room in really tall buildings and you can't control the air so it is always too hot or too cold, which I think is a huge annoyance. Food is decent, campus is extremely safe, facilities are nice but the gym is terrible. There really isn't any crime at Duquesne, not even really theft or anything.

Current student, 8/2005-Submit Date, October 2005

Housing is very nice here. The buildings are clean, safe and spacious. The facilities are up-to-date, and technologically advanced. The campus is very safe, even though it is in the middle of a city.

Current student, 8/2003-Submit Date, September 2004

Duquesne is in a great location—on top of a hill overlooking the entire city. I don't live there because of the cost. However, the rest of the campus, including buildings and dining services, is great. There is always campus security around whenever you need them, and the school provides an excellent counseling center, free of charge, for any student who is having psychological problems, or just difficulty adapting to college life.

 ## Social Life

Alumnus/a, 9/2002-5/2006, September 2006

About four years ago there was a bunch of bars just off of campus that would have large swarms of Duquesne students. However with a crack down by both the PA Liquor Control and the university, this doesn't happen too often. The university has made it a priority to cut down on underage drinking.

Now if you are of age, then you have a large selection of bars from which to choose around the city. As Pittsburgh boomed as a blue collar steel city there are more bars in Pittsburgh than churches in Rome. So enjoy your senior year, all the more reason to study hard in the beginning and breeze through the last few months of college in style.

The dating scene is different, as it is a Catholic school. With about 65 percent female, chances are you will find a mate if you are gentlemen. However most

Read all of Vault's College Surveys at **www.vault.com/college**—get complete surveys on 100s of colleges and universities, expert advice on applicaton essays and more.

VAULT CAREER LIBRARY **609**

of the females, although very beautiful, are already taken. But don't worry because the University of Pittsburgh is about a stone's throw away. As for the girls, don't worry: you still have plenty of guys from which to choose and the ball is still in your court.

Dances and other activities and clubs at Duquesne are pretty mediocre at best, so be warned. The best thing at the university is the freshman orientation. If you want more info call up the student director or visit their web site they are there all year round.

Also the Greek system is a fair size, not too big and not too small. It is a lot of fun if you are involved, especially if you are from outside the Pittsburgh area. But if you are not Greek, you can have a lot of fun also. The Greek system does not have fraternity or sorority houses, but they do have living quarters in the dorm building. Most of the fraternity parties are off campus at houses that are rented or owned by some of the older brothers. Housing in Pittsburgh is cheap, so it is very common to move in with a bunch of friends, Greek and non-Greek, after your sophomore year.

Most upperclassmen, about 75 percent, live on the South Side. It's usually very noisy and fun if you don't mind drinking every night. The rest of them live on Mount Washington, which is slightly more expensive, quiet and hard to get home in the icy Pittsburgh winters. However, Mount Washington has the best views of the city at night and the best seat for Steelers and Pirates fireworks displays.

Current student, 1/2004-Submit Date, March 2006

Greek life is very good at Duquesne, as I am a fellow Greek. The only drawback here is we don't have fraternity houses, but there are sections of the Towers reserved for fraternities and sororities.

Alumnus/a, 9/2000-5/2004, November 2005

The social life here is the worst. It is overrun by frats and sororities, and there is nothing to do within walking distance really since downtown is always closed. South Side, Shadyside or Oakland is where most folks spend their time for all bars, dates and restaurants.

Current student, 8/2005-Submit Date, October 2005

There is a large Greek population on campus here. There are also many restaurants and social gatherings, movies and the NightSpot.

Current student, 9/2004-Submit Date, March 2005

There really aren't any restaurants close by other than McDonald's, and bars keep getting fined for serving minors. There are about a million frats and sororities for whatever you feel like belonging to whether it be social or professional.

Current student, 8/2003-Submit Date, September 2004

It's 10 minutes from the South Side, which is known for its restaurants and bars. There are always events going on, even for commuters. And the list of Greeks is phenomenal.

The School Says

For 129 years, Duquesne University has offered highly individualized learning that enriches the heart, mind and spirit. Through 10 academic and professional schools, you can find your passion here, explore your interests, or choose a new direction.

Our more than 90 undergraduate majors and degree programs include a strong liberal arts program; we prepare students for

dynamic careers in a wife variety of fields, including business, education, forensic science, health management, music, nursing, pharmacy, science and pre-law.

With over 10,000 students and a 15:1 student-to-faculty ratio, Duquesne is the right size for students who want to work closely with their professors. Because classes are small, you will also be able to access the most modern technology in classrooms, scientific laboratories, and other living-learning environments.

Our "right-size" school allows the faculty and staff to get to know their students, but it is our caring spirit that keeps our young people safe, happy and academically productive. This family atmosphere helps students feel secure in a new environment, and inspires them to get involved in campus life.

We are also a community of volunteers, taking this spirit of caring to charitable fundraisers, service projects and neighborhood improvement works. Last year 7,602 students, faculty and staff gave over 190,000 hours to volunteer programs.

The diverse group of students who come to Duquesne gives our quiet tree-filled campus a lively vitality. Here, you will live in modern, air-conditioned residence halls with television, free laundry, Internet access and 24-hour security.

You will enjoy more than 140 campus activities, as well as fraternities and sororities, clubs, arts and entertainment-and meet your friends at our on campus Starbucks. We offer inter-collegiate basketball, football, and baseball as well as a wide array of men's and women's intramural sports. A multipurpose recreation center is under construction.

Though the campus has a small-town feel, the excitement of Pittsburgh is located just down the hill. In the city's many neighborhoods, you can experience music, art, professional sports, nightlife and shopping. Recreational opportunities for biking, backpacking, skiing or even white-water rafting are nearby.

At Duquesne, students get practical real-world experiences through fieldwork, research projects and internships at major corporations and health care systems. Many go on to one of our more than 130 graduate programs. They find that a Duquesne degree carries a reputation of scholarship and high moral standing and connects our graduates to career opportunities through an active alumni network.

Students also study abroad at our campus in Rome, Italy, or through programs in many other countries, including Australia, Ghana, England, Spain, China and Costa Rica.

It all adds up to the kind of college experience where students return to complete their degrees. About 90 percent of freshmen return for their sophomore year, well above the average retention rate. You can also discover the Duquesne college experience: where young people are transformed by a different point of view—and learn to grow.

Franklin & Marshall College

Office of Admission
Franklin & Marshall College
637 College Ave.
Lancaster, PA 17603
Admissions phone: (717) 291-3951 or (877) 678-9111
Admissions fax: (717) 291-4389
Admissions e-mail: admission@fandm.edu

Admissions

Current student, 8/2004-Submit Date, February 2006

The admissions process at Franklin & Marshall isn't much different than other comparable schools. One difference with F&M is that if you do not make an attempt to visit the college, you are seriously disadvantaged in the process and practically not considered (with the exception, of course, being if you live a plane-ride away).

Heavy preference is given to those who apply Early Decision and most scholarships the school offers are delegated at that time.

> **The school says:** "While Franklin & Marshall does have a higher acceptance rate for Early Decision, most scholarships are not given out during Early Decision. Regular Decision students have the same chance of getting a merit scholarship as Early Decision."

The option of opting out of your SAT scores if you are in the top 10th percentile of your class is tricky. The option should only be considered if your scores are well below the colleges average, otherwise it just takes away from the competitive edge of your application.

> **Regarding optional standardized tests, the school says:** "Students utilizing the Standardized Test Option can submit two graded writing samples from their junior or senior year in lieu of SAT or ACT scores. There is no minimum GPA or class rank to use the Standardized Test Option and students who use it are not disadvantaged if their other credentials are competitive for admission."

I recommend coming to the interview prepared. The interviewer likes to see that you have been seriously considering the school and already have some basic knowledge about the programs on the campus.

Current student, 8/2004-Submit Date, January 2006

The college has two Early Decision deadlines, which are convenient if it is your second choice and you apply early elsewhere. An interview is recommended, but unnecessary. My interview was painless. I liked all of the F&M admissions officers I have met. I know several people who did not have interviews and got accepted, but they lived far away (plane-ride necessary, or two days driving time).

> **Regarding interviews, F&M says:** "Interviews are highly recommended for Regular Decision and required for Early Decision (if you are within half a day drive of F&M). For those students who cannot make it to campus, the Admission Office offers regional interviews during the fall."

Showing interest in the school, including going to programs like open houses, is highly recommended. As far as essays go, I have heard of people doing creative things like writing a poem. The school does not seem to be so selective, but fairly selective—you should have good grades and good SAT scores.

> **Regarding selectivity, F&M says:** "The admissions process at F&M has become increasingly selective in the past years. The

acceptance rate this past year was 37 percent. Good grades are important, but the strength of the student's high school curriculum is equally important. The Office of Admission looks for advanced coursework (AP, IB, Honors) and increasingly difficulty of courses as an indicator that students will be academically successful."

Current student, 8/2005-Submit Date, October 2005

My father first suggested that I apply to Franklin & Marshall College. After researching the institution and finding it of high academic quality, I e-mailed the admissions office for more information. Within a day, an admissions officer had e-mailed me back with information about the college: academic programs, information on student life and so on.

I browsed the college web site and decided I wanted to visit. I again e-mailed the admissions officer and set up a tour date as well as a personal interview with her. The tour went very well as did the interview. It was laid-back and the admissions officer seemed very interested in determining if F&M was the right school for me. At the end of the interview she encouraged me to apply and even told me of some scholarship opportunities I'd be eligible for if I applied. I decided that I liked the campus and opportunities well enough to apply.

I filled out the Common Application and completed the one essay supplement required by Franklin & Marshall. Although the college is ranked as "More Selective," they accepted me!

Alumnus/a, 8/1992-5/1996, August 2005

F&M has a great program where you can apply without submitting standardized test scores (SATs) if you are in a certain percentile of your graduating class. This was perfect for me because while I am very bright and had a high GPA, my test scores weren't reflective of my potential. This is what first attracted me to F&M and I fell in love with the school at my interview.

> **The school says:** "The Standardized Test Option is available to all students, regardless of GPA or class rank."

The admissions counselor was very attentive and I enjoyed her approach of talking about current hot topic issues. Spend extra time on your essay—she had it in hand for my interview and it can get you in the "has potential" pile.

Current student, 9/2004-Submit Date, January 2005

I spent a large amount of time on my application, paying close attention to the essays. Franklin & Marshall College is a very difficult school to get into, and I am sure that my essays were the reason I was admitted. Also, my standardized testing scores were very high, which greatly increased my chances of being admitted. Also, athletics play an important role if you are a candidate for collegiate athletics.

If you want to get into college, I suggest getting the best grades you can and become involved in as many groups and activities as possible at your high school. This is extremely important as most schools are looking for people with a strong desire to contribute in a positive manner to the overall life of the college.

Alumnus/a, 7/1997-6/2001, August 2004

Franklin & Marshall has a user-friendly admissions process with an exceptional staff. Due to traffic on the NJ turnpike, I missed the tour during my first visit to F&M. The admissions office was very helpful and quickly arranged a private tour for my dad and me. F&M admissions also arranged for me to meet with the swim coach and spend a weekend on campus with current students.

My fondest memory of the admissions process was the close and supportive relationship I established with my interviewer. She contacted me later that year informing me she would be visiting my high school and would enjoy catching up with me. She also gave me her contact information, so I could call her if I had any questions, concerns, or just wanted to talk about admissions or choos-

Read all of Vault's College Surveys at **www.vault.com/college**—get complete surveys on 100s of colleges and universities, expert advice on applicaton essays and more.

VAULT CAREER LIBRARY 611

ing a college. I visited over 20 other colleges, large and small, and no other college gave me such first-class attention and service. Attending F&M was one of the best decisions I have made.

Academics

Current student, 8/2004-Submit Date, February 2006

Workload at F&M is unreal compared to other colleges. Be prepared to spend most of your weekend with reading and papers.

> **F&M says:** "F&M students do have a challenging workload. However, as long as time is managed effectively students do not spend all weekend reading and writing papers."

Pure lectures are a rare find at F&M and most professors prefer more interactive discussion-based classes. Attending class without something intelligent to add to the conversation or without doing the reading is generally frowned upon and reflected in your overall grade. This is not one of those schools where you can hope to get away with skipping class. Most professors have strict attendance policies due to the participatory nature of their classes.

Tests and quizzes are often based on class discussion and lecture as well. Although professors are challenging, they are not unreasonable. Average work gets the average grade (C's), but B's and even A's are not impossible to obtain here. All professors keep office hours and are very easily accessed on campus. It is in every student's benefit to take advantage of this as professors look upon it very favorably. Getting into some courses through the class selection can be a bit difficult, but professors are very flexible. Usually a professor will overload a class if a student speaks to him/her personally and expresses a serious interest in the class.

Current student, 8/2004-Submit Date, January 2006

Professors are very accessible. As far as grades and workload go, I think it depends on which professor you get. I recommend viewing ratemyprofessor.com before choosing classes for your schedule. Life as a science major will be harder than life as a psychology major. The difficulty of your courseload depends on the courses you take.

I have not found it hard to get into popular classes because there are often several sections available. Teaching assistants do not grade papers, which I find to be more reassuring. Classes are small and every student is highly encouraged to participate.

Current student, 8/2005-Submit Date, October 2005

As a first-year here at F&M, the academics are a sharp contrast from the easy-going living situation of the dorms and on-campus activities. The academic nature of this school is very serious and the classes are difficult. So far, my impression of the professors is that they are very well qualified and knowledgeable.

Classes are small, my largest general education class has no more than 22 students enrolled in it. Grading is extremely tough, the professors show no mercy! The workload is extensive, but you really get out of it what you put into it.

Current student, 9/2004-Submit Date, January 2005

I am currently a liberal arts student, with concentrations in English and philosophy. The classes are very small, which is a good thing and the grading is very difficult. With small classes and dedicated professors, the workload is very intense. Homework ranges from four to five hours a night.

> **The school says:** "All students are required to obtain a liberal arts background through the core curriculum. At the end of their sophomore year, students are required to declare a major."

It is relatively easy to get a popular class on your schedule and I have found that the scheduling is very easy in general. The registrar's office is very helpful in dropping and adding classes as well, and you can take up to four classes but as few as three and still maintain full-time student status. I am currently taking three classes so as to achieve the highest grades possible.

Alumnus/a, 8/1992-5/1996, August 2005

The workload at F&M is a bit out of control. Students work extremely hard pretty much around the clock. The quality of classes and professors are t[op] notch, but expect to work for every grade you receive. I never had any proble[m] getting into the classes I wanted, and even if a class was full, you can go [talk] with the professor one-on-one and he or she will most likely sign you into [the] class.

A 4.0 is unheard of. Professors are very accessible and will go above and bey[ond] to help you succeed. Most people say that F&M wants to be Ivy League a[nd] makes the academics so rigorous that only the best can make it.

Employment Prospects

Current student, 8/2004-Submit Date, January 2006

More information about internships, employment opportunities and the alum[ni] network could definitely be provided to the student body. There is minimal co[m]munication on these subjects, especially if you are not in a well-defined tar[get] group like pre-med. The school has a respectable name and reputation, so fi[nd]ing a job after graduation or getting into graduate school should not be diffic[ult].

Current student, 8/2005-Submit Date, October 2005

A degree from Franklin & Marshall College carries with it a certain prestige a[nd] level of respect from employers. As a pre-med student, I am well aware of a[nd] take comfort in Franklin & Marshall's exceptional reputation with medi[cal] schools across the United States.

Although many graduates go on to professional or graduate school upon co[m]pletion of a degree from Franklin & Marshall, those who move straight into [the] workforce seem to have no trouble landing well-paying and satisfying caree[rs.] The alumni are involved in many projects with the school, both on campus a[nd] off.

Alumnus/a, 8/1992-5/1996, August 2005

There was very little on-campus recruiting when I was a student. Most stude[nts] go on to further schooling before entering the workforce. I went directly into [the] workforce to earn money for further schooling, and found few employers w[ho] had ever heard of F&M. However, the two who had were incredibly impress[ed.] One happened to be an alumna and offered me the job before my interview sa[y]ing she knew that if I could make it at F&M, I was more than qualified and s[he] had no doubt I would be a great addition to the company. Therefore, I can tr[uly] say the alumni network is very supportive! Graduate schools think very hig[hly] of F&M alumni as they are usually aware of the academic rigors of F&M.

> **The school says:** "One-third of F&M grads go directly to grad school after F&M. Two-thirds of F&M alumni have an advanced degree within 10 years of graduating."

Current student, 9/2004-Submit Date, January 2005

Many graduates go on to graduate school, largely in the medical field. There [are] also many students who go on to engineering school as well as law school.

There is a large number of internships advertised by the school around camp[us.] In general, it seems that this school is a great place to earn an undergradu[ate] degree with the plan to enroll in graduate school.

Quality of Life

Current student, 8/2004-Submit Date, January 2006

The campus is relatively safe, though it is on the outskirts of the City [of] Lancaster (the school is not plopped down in the middle of a corn field[).] Reports of stolen property are fairly common, but this can be prevented by loc[k]ing your door. Violent crimes are not common. Safety officers are constan[tly] patrolling the campus and they are all very nice and friendly.

Housing is adequate—you can't expect much in the way of luxury from a [a] dorm room, really. There is a good gym available to all students. In my op[in]ion, dining services leaves something to be desired, but some people like [it]

od. The food is probably the same on most campuses. There are few healthy
tions, but this does not mean F&M has fewer healthy options than most other
hools.

Current student, 8/2005-Submit Date, October 2005

anklin & Marshall College is situated in a perfect location for college life.
inutes away from the small but busy downtown section of Lancaster, it is close
ough to reap the benefits associated with city life, but far enough removed for
ose same city life aspects to be a distraction. The dorms are pretty typical—
e floors are co-ed, which adds an interesting and fun aspect to the home-life
uation. The campus is very small and compact, but also very busy, with lots
do and many events, no matter what your interests. The college buildings are
autiful and with new building projects on the horizon, they're only getting bet-
.

e dining situation is also commendable. The Marketplace is the dining hall
d has a good reputation for edible food. Also there is a Quizno's, an Italian
staurant (Pandini's), a coffee shop (Jazzman's), a Mexican restaurant (Salsa
co's) and an American grill (The Sky Ranch Grill) to satisfy any and all crav-
gs while using your pre-purchased on-campus meal plan.

> **Regarding dining options, the school says:** "As of September
> 2007 there will be a KIVO (Kosher, International, Vegetarian,
> and Organic) dining option in place of Salsa Rico's and Sky
> Ranch Grill."

e campus is also minutes away from many other small, locally well-known
teries. The neighborhood surrounding the campus is very safe and communal,
e Lancaster City Police are always just moments away from any disturbance,
hough they are few and far between on this small, safe, community campus.

lumnus/a, 8/1992-5/1996, August 2005

ancaster, PA is a relatively safe city. Very few students venture too far off cam-
s, as there is little need to do so. The Park City Mall is a little over a mile
vay and any and all shopping/eating out can be done there. Campus food was
tually very good, lots of options!

orm rooms are nice, plenty of room and up-to-date. The whole campus is kept
ean, as the school is very pricey and students and parents alike wouldn't accept
ything less.

urrent student, 9/2004-Submit Date, January 2005

he quality of life at Franklin & Marshall is very good. The dorms are all very
ce to live in, and the campus is exceptionally beautiful. The facilities are all
-to-date and very pleasant to be in.

he food service isn't that bad, though it could always improve. The neighbor-
ood isn't the safest, and there are some incidents involving students being
bbed on a weekly basis. Unfortunately, this is one disadvantage to being
cated in a low-income area, but if one travels only a few miles outside of the
ancaster City area, one would find expansive farmland, which is very beautiful
d can be interesting to explore.

> **Regarding safety, F&M says:** "While crime is present on every
> college campus, F&M is very safe. During the last full year of
> statistics there was only one recorded robbery on campus."

 Social Life

urrent student, 8/2004-Submit Date, January 2006

ining clubs is a good way to meet people who have similar interests. If you
nd you'd like a club to exist that doesn't already, you can create one. There is
ot much to do besides go to parties and hang out with friends in the dorms.
ocial activities provided by the school are usually poorly attended. My favorite
chool social activity is outdoor movies, which are free.

> **The school says:** "Every weekend the school sponsors many
> activities (including movies, comedians, sporting events and
> concerts). Additionally, Lancaster City offers a wide variety of
> entertainment options within walking distance from campus."

There is a club a few miles from the school that has live music and dancing.
There are a few bars around as well. Lancaster has some cute artsy shops and
an opera house at which students can sometimes get discount tickets to see plays
and musicals. The area is also popular for outlet shopping. There is a mall about
one mile from campus. Students can take the bus downtown or to the mall, and
sometimes trips to the outlets and a bigger mall are run by the school.

The Greeks were recently re-recognized by the school, so students can expect to
be bombarded with invitations to frat parties. There is no admission price for
parties or charge for drinks. There are many restaurant options if one ventures
off campus, from Mexican to Japanese to Thai, but some of these may require a
car.

Current student, 8/2005-Submit Date, October 2005

As F&M has very recently re-recognized the campus Greek system, the fraternities are busily re-asserting themselves as a presence on campus. They host
parties throughout the week, which are very fun. The on-campus frat, Chi Phi,
has a good reputation as a dependable party place. There are bars within walking distance from campus, and many upperclassmen frequent Hildy's, specifically.

There is a wide selection of restaurants a few minutes walk from campus. Lily
on James is a good place for a casual meal or dessert, Isaac's is also a great place
for lunch. The dating scene is, as always, what you make it! Franklin &
Marshall hosts many events through the College Entertainment Committee,
including game show nights, viewings of popular movies on the weekends and
many other events throughout the week.

There are many opportunities to get involved on campus through clubs as well,
if you want to enhance your social life further. Many participate in such volunteer clubs as Habitat for Humanity, F&M CARES and Vox. There are political
clubs: College Dems, College Republicans and ALLIES, as well as academically-oriented clubs, such as Biology Club, Anthropology Club and many, many
others. As always, sports play a large role in the social life on campus as well.

Current student, 9/2004-Submit Date, January 2005

The social life revolves around the fraternities mainly, though many upperclassmen go to bars on a weekly basis. The frats are generally selective, and rather
pretentious, though they can be fun if they are holding open parties. Students
seem to be so stressed out from working that they usually want to unwind, in
other words, get heavily intoxicated on the weekends. The dating scene is weak,
and the clubs are minimal in the area, though many students drive to
Philadelphia on the weekends to seek a better social scene.

> **F&M says:** "Although Philadelphia is a short train or car ride
> away from F&M, very few students (if any) actually travel to
> Philadelphia seeking a better social scene. Quoting one student
> in response to reading this: 'I don't know of one person that has
> traveled to Philadelphia on the weekends seeking a better social
> scene.'"

 The School Says

At Franklin & Marshall College, students construct their own
education by selecting courses in each of the following areas:
Foundations; Writing-Intensive Courses; the Major (the School
offers 48, or students can create their own); Distribution;
Electives; and an Optional minor (the School offers 40). F&M
provides a graduate-type education in an undergraduate setting,
including the opportunity to conduct research. Student
research at Franklin & Marshall isn't limited to the top few or to
only scientific fields, instead over two-thirds of students do
original research before they graduate in all of the fields the college has to offer. This can lead to co-authoring articles for publication in esteemed journals and presenting your findings at
regional and national conferences.

At F&M, the professors are invested in the lives and successes
of their students. F&M professors inspire, challenge, and
engage. Whether it is facilitating an undergraduate research

Read all of Vault's College Surveys at **www.vault.com/college**—get complete surveys on 100s of colleges and universities, expert advice on applicaton essays and more.

VAULT CAREER LIBRARY **613**

project, mediating a controversial issue in class, supervising a field experience, or winding down after an exam over coffee, the faculty are dedicated to the students.

While firmly rooted in its 220 year history, Franklin & Marshall is also a college in motion, continually evolving to meet the increasingly complex changes in our world. An example of this is the brand new Life Sciences & Philosophy Building that brings together three distinctive departments—Biology, Psychology, and Philosophy—reinforcing an established environment of interdisciplinary collaboration that mirrors the finest practices in scientific inquiry today.

Outside of the classroom F&M has over 100 student clubs and organizations that range in interest from Women in Neuroscience, to Hip Hop Review, to Christians in Action, to Rude Mechanicals. Additionally, F&M is home to 27 NCAA athletics, all of which are Division III (except wrestling which is Division I and Squash, which is nondivisional).

Franklin & Marshall's residential life operates under a unique College House System. Each House contributes to the community by coordinating events every semester. From bagel breakfasts and house dinners to all-campus formals and juried photography exhibits, the College Houses have created numerous new college traditions through these many events. The College Houses have also helped to bring student and faculty interactions into the residential halls, a place where learning usually stops at the door.

Franklin & Marshall is situated on the outskirts of the City of Lancaster. In Downtown Lancaster (a 15-minute walk from campus) one can discover anything from the Country's oldest continuously run farmers market , to the Fulton Opera House, or a minor league baseball team. With a population of 56,000 and a surrounding metropolitan area of 470,000, Lancaster is an ideal college town-big enough to have a little bit of everything, and small enough so that you don't have to wait too long for it.

Haverford College

Office of Admission
Haverford College
370 Lancaster Ave.
Haverford, PA   19041-1392
Admissions phone: (610) 896-1350
Admissions fax: (610) 896-1338
Admissions e-mail: admission@haverford.edu
Admissions URL:
www.haverford.edu/admissions/home.html

 ## Admissions

Alumnus/a, 8/2002-5/2006, September 2006

Haverford accepts the Common Application, which is definitely convenient. They do require a supplemental Honor Code essay, which is pretty important given the role of the honor code in the community. Interviews are not necessary, but if you attended a prospective student weekend (as opposed to an admitted students event), it is important to keep in mind that you are still being evaluated and it is important to make a good impression. Grades and scores, are important but a good essay is always the most important thing.

Current student, 8/2004-Submit Date, May 2005

Haverford uses the Common App, but requires an additional essay on Haverford's Honor Code. Understanding the Quaker values (trust, concern, respect) on which the school is founded is key to understanding the school, and the demonstration of this understanding plays a very important role in admission. Haverford is an intellectual community with a social conscience, and integrity is valued just as much as intelligence.

Current student, 9/2001-Submit Date, May 2005

Haverford places a strong value on both academics and extracurriculars. As a very selective school, the admissions office is looking for students who are taking the strongest possible courseload and succeeding. However, they equally value the person behind the grade. Haverford is looking to develop a community with strong diversity of views and interests, but they are also looking for people who will thrive under the Honor Code and will make a valuable contribution. As a result, teacher recommendations are weighed very strongly. In addition, an interview on campus is highly recommended. If you have a perfect SAT score

and are valedictorian of your class, you may get into any school you want. B if you don't have any noticeable interests or passions outside of the classroo you will have a hard time getting into Haverford.

Current student, 9/2003-Submit Date, May 2005

It's pretty fair. They look at students as people and not as numbers only. Th are really looking for well-rounded students who can contribute to the Haverfo community once here. They are pretty selective but I think the Honor Co mandatory supplemental essay deters a lot of people who don't really "g Haverford. If you have problems answering the Honor Code essay, Haverfo may not be the best place for you.

Current student, 8/2001-Submit Date, April 2005

Haverford seeks individuality from its applicants. In addition to very stro academics, a student's personal voice is crucial to the process.

Current student, 8/2003-Submit Date, April 2005

The admissions at Haverford is pretty selective (less than 30 percent). They re ly are looking for well-rounded kids who can offer something to the school a aren't just academic. There is a supplemental essay about the Honor Code th is really important. If you can't answer the essay or don't quite know what make of it, Haverford isn't the place for you.

Alumnus/a, 9/1999-5/2003, August 2005

Haverford is a Quaker school, and hence has an all-powerful Honor Code. N only do you have to sign the Code to get in, one of your essays has to be abo your relationship with the Code. Take it seriously. A good essay can get you i

Otherwise, the school is fairly liberal and earthy, and fitting this mold in an int view (required if you live within 200 miles) helps. One part of Quaker belie holds that a group making decisions has to all be in agreement, and thus th entire admissions board has to be in consensus that you are worthy for admi sion. It's a pretty good feeling.

Academics

Alumnus/a, 8/2002-5/2006, September 2006

Classes are very rigorous; there is always work you can be doing. There a broad distributional requirements: you need to have a specific number of natu sciences, social sciences, humanities, and a social justice. These are not difficu

fulfill and can easily fall within your interests. The idea is to ensure a broad
[gen]eral education, even though you still have a specific major. Luckily, the
[co]urse offering are extensive, especially if you take into account the cross-reg-
[ist]ration options with Bryn Mawr, Swarthmore and Penn.

[It i]s important that you find out which classes are reading or writing intensive.
[Ov]erall there is usually a lot of reading. My friends in the sciences spent a lot
[of] time in labs. Essentially you are either writing papers or preparing lab reports.
[Of] course people can get away with not doing all of the assigned reading, but it
[is] very difficult to do well on an assignment that requires careful analysis of a
[par]ticular text. Finals exams are self-scheduled, which is very convenient, and
[a p]rimary part of the honor code. During finals week, there are three times each
[da]y you can take exams, and you choose. It allows you flexibility in how you
[str]ucture your finals week. Professors really get to know their students and it's
[a g]ood idea to drop by office hours. Often if you take the time to go over an
[ass]ignment, a professor will steer you in the right direction. Not to mention that
[it i]s the only way they can get to know you beyond the classroom.

[Gr]ades are not discussed, although that is slowly changing. I didn't know any
[of] my roommates' GPAs. That being said, its hard to get an A. Of course some
[pro]fessors are easier graders than others but it's often the case that a professor is
[loo]king at your individual effort and progress. It is relatively easy to get into any
[cla]ss you want. There is a lottery system, but in four years, I was never turned
[aw]ay from a class, even ones I was lotteried out of.

[Cu]rrent student, 9/2003-Submit Date, May 2005

[W]e do work hard here at Haverford, but it is in a very noncompetitive manner
[an]d because we enjoy learning, not because we want a certain GPA. Students
[he]re really focus on group and collaborative learning, with most classes being
[ve]ry intimate and actually discussing the material with profs as opposed to being
[lec]tured at. I often find myself in classes with a small round table with eight or
[so] of us at it, with the prof sitting to my right as an equal who is interested in
[he]aring what I have to say as well as what he/she wants to help us learn.

[Pr]ofs are really accessible (if you can't reach them on the phone, through e-mail
[or] office hours, you can walk over to their houses and knock on their front
[do]ors!) and teach all classes—we don't have TAs who teach class. Instead, they
[ru]n independent, completely voluntary discussion sessions where you can rehash
[the] material you learned that week or ask questions. They are usually well
[att]ended and I've learned a lot from them, as well as in class.

[Cu]rrent student, 9/2001-Submit Date, May 2005

[Ha]verford has very strong academics. Whether in the humanities, social sci-
[en]ces or natural sciences, all departments here have the same high standards. A
[str]ong emphasis is placed on discussion, which means that the classes are kept
[sm]all throughout your four years. You will get to know your professors person-
[all]y, and they will undoubtedly use this closeness to challenge you. However,
[the]y will also provide wonderful support and their accessibility makes this chal-
[len]ge very manageable.

[Ha]verford has distribution requirements rather than a core curriculum. The main
[re]quirement is to take three courses each in the humanities, social sciences and
[na]tural sciences. There is also a year-long language requirement and a freshman
[wr]iting seminar. Finally, all students must take a Social Justice class. Every
[se]mester, a certain number of classes are designated Social Justice, which means
[th]at they deal with traditionally marginalized cultures, issues of diversity and
[in]equality in the world. This academic requirement has its roots in our Quaker
[he]ritage.

[Cu]rrent student, 8/2003-Submit Date, April 2005

[Ac]ademics are awesome. We work very hard but it's not stressful due to the
[no]ncompetitive nature of the student body (due to the Honor Code), group learn-
[in]g and discussion-based classes. Most classes are small (average size is 18) and
[th]e profs are really interested in what you have to say as opposed to lecturing at
[yo]u. You end up in discussions where you are contributing as much to the dis-
[cu]ssion as your profs are. The profs are also great because they love the under-
[gr]aduate only program here at Haverford. They are interested in what you have
[to] say and want you to get to learn as much as you can in your four years here,
[wh]ether that is through hands on projects, research during the summer with them
[in] labs or praxis where you actually get to go out and do what you've been learn-
[in]g about.

Current student, 8/2001-Submit Date, April 2005

Academics at Haverford are the heart of the school. Here you can find your
niche, whether it is five other student who love the French Revolution or a prof
who spends extra time discussing a formula after class. I found my own kind,
so to speak, here at Haverford. Also, because we do not discuss grades as a general rule, there is little to no competition. It makes for a wonderfully stress-free,
healthy environment to explore academia.

Employment Prospects

Alumnus/a, 8/2002-5/2006, September 2006

The alumni office is amazing, especially considering the small alumni body.
There are networks throughout the country in major cities, offering networking
events as well as social ones. Annually, alumni distinguished in their professions
will offer externships for the small breaks (fall break, winter break, Christmas
break). For students not graduating, there is a multitude of fellowships that will
fund student projects, which in turn are very helpful for obtaining future employment.

Current student, 8/2004-Submit Date, May 2005

The alumni network is incredibly helpful—many Haverford alumni go on to
very high-up places, and the Career Development Office keeps a database of all
Bi-Co (Haverford and Bryn Mawr) graduates across the country willing to be
contacted for help getting internships and jobs. Haverford has one of the highest grad school acceptance rates in the country, and the caliber of a Haverford
education is well understood in the academic community.

Med school acceptance is usually between 98 and 100 percent, depending on the
year, with 90 percent of graduates gaining admission to their top choice med program. Law school is similarly successful, between 97 and 99 percent.

Current student, 9/2003-Submit Date, May 2005

Older graduates from Haverford are mostly male at this point (Haverford went
co-ed in 1980) and have a lot of nonprofit jobs or other types of professions that
may not necessarily have a lot of name recognition. However, they all love what
they do and are passionate about it, especially about helping out alumni if they
can. One can do internships with many of their organizations and even externships over the breaks shadowing the alumni for a few days to get a feel for what
they do.

Current student, 8/2003-Submit Date, April 2005

Because Haverford is fairly small, our alumni network isn't huge. However, the
Career Development Office is awesome at getting internship opportunities for
students, externships during the breaks with current alumni and general job
workshops ranging from résumé building to practice interviews.

Quality of Life

Current student, 8/2004-Submit Date, May 2005

Housing at Haverford is wonderful. The rooms are huge, and even freshmen
have the option of living in an apartment at the edge of campus with a private
kitchen, bathroom and living room shared only with two other suitemates. The
campus was designed by the noted Olmsted Brothers landscape architects, and
includes an arboretum complete with a beautiful nature trail, a duck pond, historic trees of diverse species, sculpture and a zen garden. It is incomparably
beautiful, with elegant gray stone buildings and long stretches of meadow and
woods on all sides.

Alumnus/a, 8/2002-5/2006, September 2006

The quality of life at Haverford is beautiful and peaceful. The housing is really
amazing. The campus is beautiful—it's an arboretum, which just means that
there are tons of trees of all kinds and there is a nice nature trail, through which
you will find people running year-round. A lot of the facilities are relatively new,
the best being the DOUG or the new athletic facility (which is amazing). There
is a great gym, a multipurpose room, squash courts, basketball courts, locker
rooms, fencing room, everything you could think of. I know the Coop (a café)
was just renovated, which is a welcome escape where you can get foods other

Read all of Vault's College Surveys at **www.vault.com/college**—get complete surveys on 100s of colleges and universities, expert advice on applicaton essays and more.

VAULT CAREER LIBRARY   **615**

than in the official dining center. They also have specialty bar, which people really do look forward to. The director the of the dining center is great. He is always open to suggestions and will incorporate recipes, ingredients and snacks that you suggest. The neighborhood is a typical suburb, very safe, clean, and nice. There are lots of things within walking distance, including a grocery store, restaurants and shops.

Current student, 9/2003-Submit Date, May 2005

Haverford has great housing guaranteed all four years. You can have a single from freshman year through senior year. The campus is beautiful, with a duck pond and nature trail (besides the fact the whole campus is an arboretum!). It's great to watch the seasons change here. We are close to anything you could need on the Main Line and 20 minutes from Philadelphia, so if you need the city experience for a day you can get it.

Current student, 9/2001-Submit Date, May 2005

Overall, Haverford's campus is gorgeous. Our campus is actually a naturally recognized arboretum that has its own separate endowment. The result is beautiful landscaping and numerous trees. The hues of autumn and the flowers of spring will take your breath away. In addition to our trees, our buildings all have a unified style that makes the campus more attractive. Rather than having different materials from different eras, all new buildings at Haverford are made with the same materials. The unity of the architecture makes this even more attractive.

Current student, 8/2001-Submit Date, April 2005

The quality of life here is superb. The dormitories are roomy and all singles are in suites so though I have my own space, I'm living with six of my best friends. The dining center is a huge social hub, as is the library and there are great student spaces on campus, including a student-run cafe. The safety on campus is wonderful—I haven't locked my door in four years and backpacks are strewn around campus constantly.

 # Social Life

Alumnus/a, 8/2002-5/2006, September 2006

The social life is really lacking at Haverford, which may or may not be a direct effect of the size of the student body (1,100, when I was there, although there is discussion of expansion). There are no sororities or fraternities on campus but the student organizations play a major role in bringing speakers, comedians, hosting parties, and livening up the social scene.

There is a sincere effort to make things fun for students but after a while you realize you know everyone and that can get a bit boring. Fortunately there are a few great resources around. First is the Tri-Co (Tri-College System—Bryn Mawr, Haverford, Swarthmore), which means that you can take classes, eat and party at any of the three campuses. There are a few local bars within walking distance. Philly is another distraction. The city has a lot to offer and is very easily accessible by train. The trains stop running at midnight however, so unless

you are willing to spilt the $25 cab fair or have friends with cars, be mindful when you will get back. There are lots of clubs, restaurants and the famo South Street. Cheese steaks are a must and Pats and Geno's are open 24 ho (great for late-night runs during finals insanity). Your social life is what y make it. There are definitely some on-campus events that everyone looks f ward to (DRAG Ball—dress in drag; Snowball—semi formal; LaFiesta—La dance with live band; and others).

Current student, 8/2004-Submit Date, May 2005

There is no Greek system at Haverford. There are a few bars nearby, althou the extreme accessibility of alcohol on campus makes off-campus drinki entirely unnecessary and usually more trouble than it's worth. Although stude won't admit it, the dating scene is actually very intense and fluid, in some wa helped and in other ways hindered by the college's small size.

Free music events are often presented in the basement of Lunt (a student dorn adjacent to the always-popular Lunt Cafe (where students go to study or c over nachos, bagels, coffee or milkshakes). Professional funk, rock, blues a jazz bands are brought in by the Federation of United Concert Series, a stude organization. Student musicians have created a vibrant musical community campus, forming (in 2005) at least 10 bands whose styles include jam rock, ha core punk, folk and jazz.

Current student, 9/2001-Submit Date, May 2005

Social life at Haverford is pretty low-key. There is not much in the way of cra parties since we do not have any fraternities or sororities. Much of the social l on campus centers around groups of friends hanging out. One popular activi is going to Lunt Cafe, a student-run cafe in the basement of the dorm, Lunt p vides a nice atmosphere for relaxing with friends and playing games. On wee ends, many bands play in the adjoining concert area. There is a range of stude bands that are mostly blues and indie rock.

In terms of off-campus activities, the most popular on the Main Line include ba and restaurants. The closest bar to one end of campus is Roache and O'Brien which students lovingly call Roaches. It's a dive all the way, which means che beer and smoky atmosphere. This used to be packed on the weekends, but rece raids by the police have driven away the underage patronage. Other popular ba include Brownies, Kelly's and The Grog, which can only be reached with a c

Current student, 9/2003-Submit Date, May 2005

Social life here is very unique. There is no Greek life, so people can attend a event they would like. Often on Saturday nights I'll end up going to three or fo separate events because students tend to support each other here, whether i going to my friend's a cappella concert or the bluegrass band my friend broug to Lunt Cafe. Lunt has concerts most weekend nights, but also has great san wiches, shakes, smoothies and treats every night of the week.

Dances are really big here—we love to get down and get really into the them whether it's Drag Ball, Screw Your Roommate or Middle School Formal. V have a lot of fun here, but it's not necessarily the traditional college scene w lots of frat parties and bar life. We have a good time with each other in a mu more laid-back party atmosphere.

Indiana University of Pennsylvania

Admissions Office
011 South Drive
diana, PA 15705
dmissions phone: (800) 442-6830 or (724) 357-223
dmissions e-mail: admissions-inquiry@iup.edu
dmissions URL:
ww.iup.edu/admissions_and_aid/admissions_and_aid.htm

Admissions

rrent student, 8/2001-Submit Date, October 2006

 be admitted to IUP, one needs to complete an application. There is no inter-
w to get into this school. Having a well-rounded background (i.e., good
des, good SAT scores and involvement in social activities in high school) will
 you at a better advantage for getting admitted.

rrent student, 9/2002-Submit Date, February 2006

e application is very self-explanatory and is also available online. The essay
 recommendations are optional. My high school guidance counselor already
 applications for IUP. I also received a wealth of information through the
il that contributed to the overall awareness of applying to the university. After
necessary paperwork is submitted, it only takes the admissions office about a
ek to make a decision and get that out in the mail. It is extremely helpful to
ow that each application for admission is reviewed on an individual basis by
ommittee. There are no magic cut-off numbers and SATs are not the only
ng being acknowledged.

rrent student, 8/2005-Submit Date, October 2005

e admissions process is not very selective. If you are a good student, espe-
lly a minority, the school will want you. Almost all students get accepted
re. If you have very low grades or SAT scores, you could still get accepted,
wever you will have to attend a smaller campus for your first year to get you
ed to college life. Then you will transfer to the main campus. An interview is
 required and an essay is optional. However, it all depends on the school you
 trying to get into. Having good grades and SAT scores are key because they
ve you more flexibility. If you don't have good scores, you may have to set-
 for a school that you may not particularly want to attend.

rrent student, 8/2005-Submit Date, September 2005

pplied for the Honors College at IUP. I had to get three teacher recommen-
tions, write three creative essays from unusual prompts, and attend an infor-
l interview. The Honors College only accepts 100 or fewer students per year,
 only 20 of them may be from out of state now (new Pennsylvania policy—
e HC isn't too happy about it since it misses out on a lot of talented people). I
s one of the lucky ones. If you live in Pennsylvania, it's obviously a lot
aper. As far as the regular IUP goes, there's a saying among some students
t if you can write your name, you're in.

The school says: "The Honors College at IUP enrolls 100 students per year. Generally 25 to 35 percent of the students are
from states other than Pennsylvania. Out-of-state, first-year
and transfer students who have at least a 3.0 or higher grade
average qualify for a substantial discount on out-of-state tuition,
equivalent to 150 percent of in-state tuition for both the Honors
College and for general IUP admission. Five states already have
a reduced tuition differential: Indiana, Michigan, Ohio, Virginia
and West Virginia. Additionally, most students enrolled receive
a scholarship and financial aid is readily available."

umnus/a, 8/2000-5/2004, April 2005

illed out an application. Writing the essay was optional and I did not write
e. There really was not much to the admissions process of this school. It was
latively easy to get in.

Alumnus/a, 5/1999-5/2004, September 2004

The admissions process entailed a submission of application, placement testing,
which assessed English and math skills, and an orientation session.

Academics

Current student, 8/2001-Submit Date, October 2006

Everything is different for each department at IUP. My department, for example, is the French and German department, which is very small (comprised of
around six professors). The quality of French classes depends on the professor,
but is usually pretty good. The German classes are impossible to take because
they're never offered, yet they still offer German as a major.

> **IUP says:** "German remains one of the options our students may
> (and do) use to complete their foreign-language requirement.
> Typically, this involves the completion of the intermediate-level
> German course. Because of declining enrollment in the German
> major in the past few years, IUP found it increasingly difficult to
> provide a sufficient number of courses that a German major
> would need to complete the program in a timely fashion. When
> these courses were offered, enrollments turned out to be very
> low. In the end, IUP decided to discontinue the admission of
> majors in German. Students who were already enrolled in the
> program at that time received the college's support to complete
> their requirements, and have since graduated. We still have a
> healthy interest among our students in German as a foreign-lan-
> guage option, but we no longer have majors in German."

Getting classes is hard in general. Many times, a major's classes are offered during other majors' classes, therefore making it harder for, say, a nursing major to
take history classes, for example. Popular classes are usually not easy to get,
because there are not enough sections open for our 14,000 students. With senior synthesis courses, it can be hard to find something that interests our college
seniors, because there are courses more in demand than others.

Workload varies. Most of the time it is reasonable, except with mass lecture
courses, like biology, where for most people, understanding the huge amount of
new material can take a much longer time. Some courses go all semester without any homework, except maybe critical thinking on the student's part.

Current student, 9/2002-Submit Date, February 2006

During my IUP career, I have never had a problem getting into a class. Our class
size average is 25 to 35 students. Registration for classes is all online and simple. If for some reason a class was full, I was always able to talk directly with
the department offering the course and it provided me with an override. As for
the professors, they are great! The university requires all professors to maintain
weekly office hours. During these hours, I never need to make an appointment
to see a professor. They are always very willing to sit and listen and help. Most
of my professors are leaders in their fields and offer assistance when needed. I
have never had a professor not know my name and I have never ran into any conflict! Some classes require more work than others. I can definitely say, there are
no easy classes!

Current student, 8/2005-Submit Date, October 2005

In college you really have to study. Most of the grades in the classes come from
exam scores. Making sure you do well on tests is the key to passing classes. If
you don't understand specific concepts in class, you should make use of tutoring
or supplemental instruction programs provided for the class. It is also a good
idea to visit your professor in his/her office. This helps them to learn your name
and also to get your questions answered. It helps to get the professor who is right
for you. Many students visit a web site www.ratemyprofessor.com to see what
others students who have already taken a certain class say about the professor
whom they had. The work is not hard, there is just a lot of material covered at

Read all of Vault's College Surveys at **www.vault.com/college**—get complete surveys on 100s of colleges and universities, expert advice on applicaton essays and more.

V∕ULT CAREER LIBRARY **617**

a fast pace. If you can manage your time effectively, then you won't have a problem.

Current student, 8/2005-Submit Date, September 2005

The Honors classes involve a lot of writing, but most of the professors are very friendly and the discussions (not lectures—it's nice like that) are informative and enjoyable. Some of the regular classes are the typical lecture type, but even in those, the class sizes are generally small. For the required courses, there are of plenty sections to pick from, so none get too crowded. Each professor's grading policy varies. Check www.ratemyprofessors.com beforehand and talk to former students in order to get their opinions.

Alumnus/a, 8/2000-5/2004, April 2005

For the most part, it was easy to schedule classes, although I had a tough time with a few of the ones needed for my degree. I had to be put on a waiting list for three of my major classes. The quality of my classes, for the most part, was high. Grading was done fairly and the workload was neither too high nor too low.

> **The school says:** "Some courses do have a waiting list. In some cases, these waiting lists are used to open another section of the course to accommodate student needs. Additional course sections are opened on a department by department basis. Overall, the University does all that it can to accommodate student academic needs to the fullest extent possible."

Alumnus/a, 9/1999-9/2003, March 2005

The quality of the education was above average. Class sizes in the lower-level classes were large enough to meet many new students, but not too large so a professor would not be able to help you. The upper-level classes were smaller in size to get more personal attention. The professors in my departments were all very professional. The professors in the biology department were all doctors. I never had one teacher's assistant teach a class, but some were often there to support the professor. The criminology department had more professors who were going for their doctorate degree. The grading was always fair and the workload was average for a college student.

I was a collegiate athlete, so I had no difficulties getting any of the classes that I needed for the semester. However, I know many friends who did have complications getting classes because they were not in sports. The system is this: the first students who get to register are nursing majors (because they have clinicals to schedule around), then athletes, then seniors, juniors, freshmen and sophomores. It is the most difficult to schedule classes that are mid-level because they are smaller in size than all entry-level classes but not a lot of people need the upper-level specialized classes. What I recommend is to make several different combinations of possible schedules so you are prepared for changing your schedule when registering. At the same time though, professors always leave seats open in classes for emergencies. Be prepared to go to a professor to get into a class you want.

Employment Prospects

Current student, 8/2001-Submit Date, October 2006

Graduates of fashion merchandising, theater and mathematics, for example, tend to have a hard time finding jobs. Graduates can usually find temporary bill-paying jobs after IUP though, such as something in sales. Other majors, such as foreign languages, education (teaching), and restaurant/hospitality management have a relatively successful rate and easy time finding a job. There are opportunities for on-campus recruiting at least twice a semester, and internships can be obtained if you know where to look and who to talk to in your department.

Current student, 9/2002-Submit Date, February 2006

Many employers in my field actually call the head of the department that I major in to see if any new prospects are graduating. IUP has a prestigious rapport with education. As a future teacher, my degree at IUP will satisfy future employers and initiate further development. As an IUP graduate, I will be able to come back at any time and take advantage of the professional development program. I will always have assistance with furthering my education, finding employment, and a general area of support to help with job transition.

Current student, 8/2005-Submit Date, October 2005

There are many internship programs that can be found on campus. Many of students who graduate have jobs waiting for them. Most of these jobs co from the internships in which the students participated. This is the reason internships are important and very highly recommended although they are required. Some majors may require internships, however the majority of th do not.

Current student, 8/2005-Submit Date, September 2005

At least in my major, communications media, Internship and Career Planning class) is a requirement, and I understand (and hope) that the professors w very hard at placing you in a suitable internship or job if you work hard enou

Alumnus/a, 5/1999-5/2004, September 2004

The program I was involved in was sociology with a focus in applied resear The career prospects for this program were high. I received a great deal of dir tion from the program faculty as to where I should pursue both an internship a a proper work environment.

Alumnus/a, 8/1999-12/2003, April 2004

IUP has a good reputation as a teacher college, but despite that, it is difficul get jobs in PA. Outside of PA, though, many states are looking for teachers. T college does offer some opportunities for finding jobs, though. There is a car center where you can search for job postings on a database, and they also of mock interviews in which they videotape the student taking an interview a give him tips to improve.

> **The school says:** "The University's Career Development Center works with students from their first year on campus with finding student employment, volunteer opportunities, and other options for gaining the skills, experiences and resources to obtain employment or admission to graduate school after graduation. Internship and job fairs are available on campus and in the region, as well as online resources to assist students in obtaining their career goals. As with anything else in life, the more effort applied, the more likely the success."

Quality of Life

Current student, 8/2001-Submit Date, October 2006

Housing is overpriced in this area. Dorms are usually more costly than living campus due to the fact that those in the dorms are required to buy a campus m plan. Meal plans are more expensive than buying your own groceries and goi out to restaurants to eat. The campus itself is its own community within Indiana community. It's very diverse and has endless opportunities, includi clubs, organizations, activities, volunteer opportunities and so on. Some faci ties are better than others, such as the newer buildings and classrooms. So buildings have no control over air circulation, which usually means air con tioning all year, even in the winter. Dining in Indiana is very good; there are l of options in such a small town. On-campus dining provides three choices locations, with a lot of small companies with their own stores, such as Quizn Starbucks, Bagel Works and so on. The neighborhood is very safe, and camp is generally a very, very safe place. Serious crimes do happen, but it only occ around once a year or so. Petty crimes, such as theft, occur more often.

Current student, 9/2002-Submit Date, February 2006

I can walk around campus, anywhere, any time of day and never feel threatene We have a blue-light security system, a strong police force and a 24-hour esc policy. The small-town atmosphere transcends on to campus providing a sa and friendly environment. Housing is currently taking a new step in satisfyi students. The university is constructing brand-new housing facilities based surveys given to current students. Campus is gorgeous! You can walk on t grass, enjoy the squirrels or forget your boots during snow season, because t maintenance staff does a wonderful job all year around! Facilities are numero regardless of what resources you need. Almost every building has an up-to-da computer lab. Our computers are equipped with all of the current programs need and very high speed. Most of campus has wireless Internet access and fr cable in the residence halls. We have three exercise facilities with brand-ne

uipment and two indoor swimming pools. Our campus provides me with a
ise of security and tight community!

umnus/a, 9/1999-5/2003, February 2006

lways lived off campus in a very nice apartment. The food on campus was
ways delicious. When visiting dorms, I really didn't like them because they
:re small and reminded me of cinder block jail cells. I was lucky enough to
d three other roommates who had the same off-campus living desires that I
l. I believe that IUP had control over crime and safety. Mostly, public drunk-
:ss or brawling in a bar got headlines. The campus was easy to get around if
u owned a mountain bike as the campus sits in between many large hills.
ving a car isn't the best idea because there is no where on or off campus to
rk it. I had over $1,000 in parking tickets during my four-year stay.

> **The school says:** "Like most colleges and universities, parking is
> tight on campus. However, the university completed in 2001 a
> four-tier parking garage that has helped to ease congestion.
> Parking on campus is free after 5 p.m. and free during semes-
> ter breaks; we continue to work to offer as much student park-
> ing as possible."

urrent student, 8/2005-Submit Date, September 2005

me dorms are nicer than others, and a few of the buildings (over 100 years
l) are badly in need of restoration. Still, the new buildings, as well as the
stored old ones, are pleasant, functional and pretty. There are three main on-
mpus dining halls to pick from: Foster, the main dining hall and buffet/cafete-
: style; Folger, a food court; and the HUB Rock II, which serves mainly fast
od, sandwiches and the like. The Pechan Health Center is out of the way and
lds odd hours, which isn't too helpful for a student with the flu. But if there
: any real emergencies, the Indiana Hospital is nearby. Crime rates are very
v, with the majority of offenses being alcohol-related. Blue emergency lights
: placed around the campus for victimized people to contact the University
lice immediately.

> **The school says:** "IUP's original building, Sutton Hall (which is
> an administrative building), is from 1875, but it was restored in
> the late 1990s. The oldest of the residence halls is 52 years
> old, and all of the residence halls on campus will be replaced or
> renovated with buildings with suite-style living and campus
> amenities on the ground floor with a 'living-learning' philosophy,
> green spaces around the buildings; all will be no more than four
> stories in height. Two new buildings will be open for students
> in Fall, 2007; by 2010, all buildings will be replaced with new
> facilities or renovated in the suite-style living format. The new
> buildings to be open in Fall, 2008 will include a comprehensive
> Wellness Center as part of the amenities space."

urrent student, 8/2005-Submit Date, October 2005

le campus is generally very safe. There is a police station located on campus
d the crime rate is very low. The rooms are very clean as well as the bath-
oms, which are cleaned every day. The buildings are very well-kept and fur-
ture is replaced when required. The town around the school is very small. The
mpus is the largest area in the town. The food on campus is not bad; there is
large selection each day, but that same selection is present every day. There is
t much variety and you will very quickly find yourself wishing for a home-
oked meal.

> **The school says:** "The university offers an amazing variety of
> food choices: several food stations are 'cook to order' in which
> you order your choice of item and see it cooked right before
> you. A typical day has individual menus in each of nine dining
> facilities/snack bars and coffee bars on campus (including a
> food court with name brand food items like Starbucks, Quiznos,
> Jump Asian Cuisine, Chick-fil-A and Zoca fresh Mex and home
> cooked meals). Several of the facilities have special events on
> a consistent basis—for example Foster Hall (the traditional din-
> ing facility) has 'spirit lifters' with special fun food items for stu-
> dents—fried veggies, milkshakes, decorate a cookie, banana
> splits, make your own waffle, a different feature Monday thru
> Thursday of every week."

A philosophy of the food service program on campus is the "Real Food On
Campus" program. It is designed to couple great food with a great atmosphere
and offers students everything from a fresh panini, a made-to-order omelet, or a
veggie sauté. Watch as your made-to-order meal is prepared fresh and right
before your eyes. Venture to one of our international or home-style stations.
Choose one of your favorites from the grill, deli or salad bar, and follow your
nose to warm chocolate chip cookies, double fudge frosted brownies and more
mouth-watering desserts.

Alumnus/a, 8/2000-5/2004, April 2005

I only lived in campus housing for two years. I really did not enjoy the dorm
room facilities. I did feel safe there, however. The campus dining was good.
There were three different dining halls. Two of them had to-go type food,
including a Burger King and a Chick-fil-A. The other was a sit-down cafeteria
style. They also had little coffee stands in the library, bookstore and other locations around campus. The bookstore was helpful for getting all the books that I
needed for class, and they also had a nice selection of items needed for dorm
rooms, gifts, and general books to read for leisure. My school also built a really nice workout gym during the second year I attended.

 ## Social Life

Current student, 8/2001-Submit Date, October 2006

Social life is probably one of the main factors that so many people like coming
to IUP. There is a good handful of bars and restaurants, though not so diverse in
the bar area. The night scene is usually only bars with dancing to one type of
music. The small number of "cultural" or "international" dining/outings are
worth checking out though. Dating opportunities are in abundance, as well as
clubs and Greek organizations. Some favorites are the Fashion Association, the
International Business Association, F.L.U.S.H. (an improv theater group), Circle
K, the Nursing Association, political groups, the Latin American Student
Organization, and many, many Greek organizations. There are so many of those
that it really is hard to keep track of the most popular ones. A favorite bar is The
Coney (also a restaurant), which has an Irish theme, where students can dance,
sit at three bars counters, play pool and other games, and sit in booths.

Current student, 8/2003-Submit Date, March 2006

There are many activities to join on campus, a lot of social life, bars, restaurant
choices, non-alcoholic events offered by many organizations. It's a good time
no matter where you go.

Current student, 9/2002-Submit Date, February 2006

Only 13 percent of our student body belongs to the Greek system. This means,
if you are into it, you can be, if not, no problem. We have a very diverse campus with over 200 clubs and organizations with which to be involved. These
range from groups that go on trips to museums, a paintball club, arts, entertainment, academics, professional, Greek and skateboarding. At IUP, there is something for everyone. With over 14,000 students, if someone is bored, it's his/her
fault. IUP's entertainment network is always providing us with current performances by modern music entertainers, comedians, movies, artists and musicals. If you are over 21, uptown Indiana has about six bars to choose from. Each
has a different atmosphere to please everyone.

Alumnus/a, 9/1999-5/2003, February 2006

The social life was phenomenal. I can't say enough about the best time of my
life! I worked at a college bar where I was always right in the middle of all the
action. The dating scene was always good for me. I really didn't like the Greek
life after turning 21 because the frats were always disgusting and the sisters were
just plain rude. I had two other major relationships in college and quite a few
flings. Partying was the only thing to do there and I did it well. The bars were
small, but they were fun. Right off campus, the best deli exists. It is called the
9th Street Deli located on 9th and Philadelphia. They have the best chicken
salad. Whenever I visit, I always get five pounds of it to take back to Philly with
me.

Alumnus/a, 8/2000-5/2004, April 2005

The bars most people attended in Indiana were located on Philly Street or Main
Street. There really weren't many bars, but the ones most visited were Coney
Island, Wolfendale's, Boomerang's and Culpepper's. With the exception of

Read all of Vault's College Surveys at **www.vault.com/college**—get complete surveys on 100s of colleges and universities, expert advice on applicaton essays and more.

VAULT CAREER LIBRARY **619**

Wolfendale's, those were also good places to eat. (Wolfendale's has no food.) There was also an Eat n' Park, Ponderosa and a Ruby Tuesday's. I would have to say the dating scene was pretty good, especially since I met my future husband there! The events were also good. They had bands like Sugar Ray, and other famous people. They also had plays and musicals, and other fun things to do. They have a lot of clubs and organizations to join. I myself, joined a community service organization that we called Delta Tau Sigma. We were not part of the Greek system, but used the Greek letters. Although my organization was not part of the Greek system, I do know a little bit about it because my boyfriend was a part of a fraternity called Phi Mu Delta. Greek life, or any organization for that matter, was a good way of getting involved with the community in Indiana.

Alumnus/a, 9/1999-9/2003, March 2005

The town of Indiana outside the university is fairly small, but the university r the town. There are about six popular bars that the students go to with a vari of places to go—ranging from dance clubs to billiards to bands. The restaur industry was expanding when I was leaving. At the time I left, the major rest rants in town included: Ruby Tuesday's, Perkins, Eat-n-Park and an O Garden was being built. Hopefully, they will continue to expand that indus but, like I said, the university is really what dominates the town and every knows that students are broke!

Juniata College

Admissions Office
1700 Moore Street
Huntingdon, PA 16652
Admissions phone: (877) 586-4282 or (814) 641-3420
Admissions fax: (814) 641-3100
Admissions e-mail: admissions@juniata.edu
Admissions URL: www.juniata.edu/admissions/

 Admissions

Current student, Social Sciences, 9/2004-Submit Date, June 2007

Juniata looks for the well-rounded student more than any other institution about which I have heard. Although standardized test scores are looked at and all of your other academic achievements are looked into those are, by far, not the most important things Juniata considers. Be involved in all different kinds of clubs and activities and tell Juniata about them all when asked. Also include any volunteer work because most students at Juniata do some form of volunteer work either before college or once they get there. In the interview the most important thing is to be yourself, because the admissions advisors know the school extremely well and also know the people who go there well. Be creative with your essay, have it stand out but still be a well-written essay. Take a chance with your writing and be imaginative. Juniata is a pretty selective school and they look for thinking that is outside the box. The interview and the essay are your only real opportunities to show who you are and that you deserve and want to be at the school, so don't hold back.

Current student, Biology, 8/2006-Submit Date, June 2007

Interviews are more casual than I had experienced at other schools similar to Juniata. The admissions counselors seemed to be genuinely interested in my academics, extracurricular activities and jobs. They also asked about my family and career goals. I would advise prospective students to participate in an internship or do community service activities while in high school. These types of activities set the prospective student apart from the pool of applicants.

Alumnus/a, Psychology, 8/2001-5/2005, June 2007

Juniata staff is extremely enthusiastic about the school, and it takes much pride in the school's increasing success. Juniata's enrollment requirements have become much higher since I applied; however, they take into account the whole person, not just an SAT score. Juniata also puts a lot of effort into financial aid, so that potential students who may not be able to afford such a great education are allowed that opportunity. To conclude, Juniata continues to put emphasis on the importance of diversity, which begins in the enrollment department.

Alumnus/a, Education, 8/2000-5/2004, May 2007

Juniata has a great staff to help with the admissions process. I highly suggest contacting an admissions counselor who will help aid in the application process. Juniata does like to interview prospective students and encourages students to

visit the campus. They like to see seniors in high school taking a full coursel including AP and Honors courses. They are not really impressed with seni who load up with study halls. They also want to see well-rounded students v are great in academics and in clubs and activities.

Current student, Communications, 8/2006-Submit Date, May 20

The enrollment staff at Juniata College is truly one of a kind. This is the o institution during my college search process that had me from: "Hello." admissions process at Juniata is very simple and the enrollment counselors above and beyond their call of duty to make a personal connection with eve prospective student. Juniata admissions takes an abundant amount of pride the institution and strongly believes that Juniata is one of the finest, private, fo year liberal arts schools in the world.

Current student, 8/2004-Submit Date, May 2006

I learned about Juniata College fairly late in the game, by virtue of a recruitm call from a coach. I visited the school as an afterthought, but was immediat hooked upon arrival at the campus. The most distinctive trait for me on that f visit was the sense of community at Juniata. I spent an overnight (which I hi ly recommend) with another student and was very impressed with how easil was able to communicate with virtually anyone on campus, including the pre dent, whom I met on that first visit.

Enrollment was very easy to work with, and the enrollment counselor w whom I interviewed is a key contact and friend of mine with whom I have c tinued to stay in touch. The competitive scholarships the school offers, as w as the merit scholarships, are both attractive features that weighed heavily on decision to attend Juniata.

 Academics

Current student, Health, 8/2004-Submit Date, June 2007

Getting into popular classes depends upon seniority and major. Priority goes those who need the class to graduate. Grading is fair here and the professe always let you know where you stand. If you need help, they get it for you. you can do better, they let you know. The professors are great too because th have an opportunity actually to get to know you and understand where you coming from, how you learn, and what your goals are outside of college. T is a huge advantage that only small liberal arts colleges can offer. The worklo for Juniata classes is fair, but may seem like a lot coming out of high school. Y do a lot of work. My rule of thumb is one hour of studying/work for every he of lecture.

Current student, Social Sciences, 9/2004-Submit Date, June 20

Every class I have taken at Juniata that is in my Program of Emphasis (POE) I been an amazing experience. My class sizes are all between 11 and 15 peo and are usually more like a discussion than a lecture. The professors in my P know what they are talking about and teach in a very hands-on way to ensure dents are learning and are able to apply the information they are learning. ...ting into popular classes is not very difficult if it doesn't matter what year ... take the class you want. Most classes are not a problem to get into any year ... there are a few that you may have to wait a year to take because they are full ...r first or second year, but you will get into the class. I have never been turned ...y from a class two semesters in a row and I do not know anyone who has. ... grading is hard but fair. Classes at Juniata are a lot of work, all classes have ...uire a lot of reading, which was the hardest thing to get used to. As long as ... space it out and keep on top of it, it is not hard to keep up. Be prepared not ...essarily for a lot of work always but always to work hard.

...rrent student, Political Science, 8/2004-Submit Date, May 2007

...iata's academic programs are very challenging; more challenging than ...iata's modest reputation would otherwise indicated. The workload is heavy ... demanding and affects all students equally. PhD professors are ubiquitous ... push students harder than most have ever been pushed. The natural sciences ...riculum, in particular, is especially challenging, with difficult core classes ...en in the first semester. While Juniata is nationally recognized for excellence ...he sciences, non-science programs have also garnered national recognition as ...ate, with students earning Fulbright, Goldwater and Rhodes Scholarships in ...ent years. As it is a small institution, there is a limit to the number of class-...hat are offered, and as a result, some programs can lake breadth. In contrast ...vever, there are special topic classes provided every year in every discipline ... offer in-depth study of a particular topic.

...rrent student, Cultural Studies, 8/2005-Submit Date, May 2007

...iata courses are usually difficult because professors are preparing you for the ... world. With that said, there are many resources available to offset this dif-...lty, including free tutoring services and professors' office hours. Professors ... always available and willing to give extra help. I have not had a class that I ...nd too overwhelming or from which I didn't learn something valuable. Since ... school is small, some classes are difficult to get in to as underclassmen, but ...ou wait until junior or senior year there are usually no problems. The work-...d is intense, but it is never too much to handle if you stay on top of it.

...rrent student, Business, 8/2005-Submit Date, May 2007

...iata is certainly an academically challenging school. All programs of study ...uniata have extremely good reputations, but we are especially known for our ...ence programs. Instead of having majors at Juniata, we have what we call the ...gram of Emphasis (POE) system. The POE allows students to have more ...xibility in what they study and students can even design their own POE. For ...mple, a student can have a POE that is Math and Performing Arts, which are ... things that you would not normally expect to study together, but the POE ...tem makes it work. Students designing their own programs work closely with ...advisor to make sure they meet all of the graduation requirements, plus their ...gram requirements.

...rrent student, 8/2004-Submit Date, May 2006

...iata works to create an interactive experience among the students and pro-...sors that differs from most colleges and the lecture style. In my accounting ...ss we worked on assignments that involved real-life situations of a company, ...ating a real-life feel for creating financial statements for a business. I have ...nd nearly every class at Juniata to be very educational and well worth it.

...e professors at Juniata truly love their jobs and it shows. Last semester, every ...fessor I had asked to be called by his/her first name. While all professors ...ve office hours, most include their home phone numbers on the syllabi and ... really can stop in at any time. The grading is laid out in great detail on the ...labus and you are often able to have a very good idea of what your grade will ...before it's posted.

...for the workload, Juniata expects a lot. From when I've talked to my friends ...other schools, Juniata assigns a lot more homework. Although they assign a ..., the culture of the people at Juniata is motivated students who might become ...essed with the workload, but have a drive and a competitive side to complete ... tasks.

Employment Prospects

Current student, Health, 8/2004-Submit Date, June 2007

I have created an immense network of possible employers from my internships and work with alumni. I will graduate with four internships, credit and non-credit, that have provided me with a broad knowledge of different occupations and fields. My friends who have graduated have been able to find jobs with the Juniata network within six months of graduation. The alumni network is great. Grads are usually really good at coming back and helping students, whether it is job shadowing, mentoring, e-mailing back and forth, or walking a résumé to a person's desk at their company. Juniata hosts a job fair every year where people find jobs and internships. Personally I have found two of my internships through this medium. Juniata's Career Services offers an excellent resource for getting a job or internships as well.

> **The school notes:** "Juniata has an extensive alumni network in place with the Juniata Career Team (JCT). This initiative, co-sponsored by the Career Services Office and the Alumni Office, has a database of more than 600 alumni volunteers willing to assist with job preparation and job search. The Alumni Office also supports regional job shadowing events where Juniata students spend a day with an alumnus at his place of employment."

Current student, Social Sciences, 9/2004-Submit Date, June 2007

Juniata has a great name with employers. Many seniors have jobs lined up months before they are ready to graduate because employers are always excited to hire someone with a degree from Juniata. Graduates also seem to start out with better paying jobs and higher status in their jobs sooner than many of the other colleges in our area. The alumni are always willing to help out graduates and provide great networking opportunities for students to reach out and meet prospective employers. They also can serve as great references for graduates whom they knew while at Juniata. Professors also create a great networking opportunity for graduates because many of the professors at Juniata are at the top of their fields and well known all over the country and many are well known in other countries. Having a good relationship with a professor is a great way to get one hand up on looking for jobs for after graduation. Juniata offers a number of great internships on the campus and many students get into internships off campus, either in town or in one of the neighboring towns.

Current student, Biology, 8/2006-Submit Date, June 2007

Graduates from Juniata obtain many prestigious jobs or go on to competitive graduate schools. It is not uncommon for a Juniata alum to be hired above other applicants simply because of Juniata's known rigorous academic program. Juniata has had a consistent acceptance rate into medical schools of at or around 100 percent.

Current student, Business, 8/2005-Submit Date, May 2007

95 percent of our students upon graduation have already accepted a job offer or are enrolled in post-graduate school. Juniata graduates obtain a wide variety of jobs including teaching jobs, the FBI, police stations, NBC and accounting firms, but there are certainly many more.

Current student, 8/2004-Submit Date, May 2006

Being located in Central PA, it's hard to bring large companies to on-campus events. With that being said, alumni have very strong ties to Juniata and keep in contact with professors about job opportunities. Juniata has an online directory of voluntary alumni who post their contact information for current students to contact for information. These alumni are separated by the field of work they are in, so students can contact people with their information they feel is valuable.

Quality of Life

Current student, Health, 8/2004-Submit Date, June 2007

The quality of life at Juniata is great. It is a small, rural community settled in the mountains of Central Pennsylvania. It is a great learning atmosphere as well as a great place to meet people and create lifelong friendships. The dorms are larg-er than most of the other schools at which I looked and they are conveniently

Read all of Vault's College Surveys at **www.vault.com/college**—get complete surveys on 100s of colleges and univer-sities, expert advice on applicaton essays and more.

V∧ULT CAREER LIBRARY   **621**

within a two-minute walk to the academic quad. The academic buildings are all within the same block. Every building is wireless and the technology grows every year. Our biology and chemistry building is second-to-none for a small school. The food is good for a cafeteria. I mean, cafeteria food is not going to be as good as mom's cooking so you can't think of it as being like that. The neighborhood is basically on Juniata's campus. It goes from town to college within a block. Juniata's safe atmosphere was actually one of the main reasons I decided to go here. No one gets harassed and campus security is excellent. There are four blue emergency light phones that go directly to security that line the school.

Current student, Social Sciences, 9/2004-Submit Date, June 2007

All students enrolled at Juniata are guaranteed housing for their time at Juniata. Campus housing, including dorms and houses, are in great condition and are constantly being renovated. All rooms on campus are fairly large compared to other college dorms and there is a good number of places from which to choose for students to live. Seniors are permitted to rent houses off campus. The campus itself is small enough so that you can get from one side of campus to the other side in about 10 minutes, but big enough so that you can find a quiet place to sit and relax if you want some alone time. There are lots of big lawns to spread out on and a lot of different facilities for whatever you are looking to do. Campus includes two sets of tennis courts and basketball courts outside, as well as a recreation center with a pool and racquetball courts for all students to use. There are two cafeterias for students and both are open seven days a week, not to mention the number of smaller cafes around campus for students to grab a bite to eat or a cup of coffee. The campus is extremely safe. Most of the buildings lock at night and campus police patrol the grounds 24 hours a day.

Current student, Political Science, 8/2006-Submit Date, June 2007

I have no complaints about the quality of life at Juniata. I don't even mind the food, seriously. We have a lot of variety and the quality is honestly decent. As far as housing, there is wireless Internet, a kitchen and washers and dryers in every dorm. The dorms are safe and the campus is safe. Everyone who visits remarks on the amazing quality of trust the campus has. In addition, the campus always looks great.

Current student, Political Science, 8/2004-Submit Date, May 2007

Juniata has always provided an excellent quality of life for its students. The campus is especially safe, with virtually no crime. The college is residential, and on-campus living for the first three years is expected (and in my opinion, preferred) with an option for living off campus granted only to seniors. The dorms are comfortable and roomy, but are older and do lack some of the modern design elements that some newer dorms at other schools may offer. The campus itself is gorgeous and well kept, with mountains surrounding the school on all four sides. The town of Huntingdon is not anything special, but does offer several good pizza places, bars and other eateries in addition to a Wal-Mart. Campus is located in the north end of town, which is primarily upper-class residential. The local community is very supportive of the school, with high local attendance for sporting events and other on-campus cultural activities.

Current student, 8/2004-Submit Date, May 2006

Students enjoy a very high quality of life at Juniata, at which crime is obsolete and housing is guaranteed. Dorms are not locked at night, creating a more comfortable and trustworthy atmosphere among students. Freshman dorm housing is very similar to other institutions', but there are a variety of options once you become upperclassmen, such as eight-person apartments, themed eight-person houses and larger dorm-style suites. 90 percent of students live on campus, and an overwhelming majority of those students stay on campus for the weekends.

> **Regarding housing, the school says:** "85 percent of students live on campus in 17 residence halls, ranging from traditional dormitories to apartments to individual homes, with co-ed, single-gender (female) and other special-interest living options."

The food is good, the best of the any school I visited, although many of my peers complain about the food frequently. I'm sure this happens at every other school though. On most nights there is enough variety to please everyone.

Social Life

Current student, Health, 8/2004-Submit Date, June 2007

The social life is what you make of it. The Juniata Activities Board bring bands, comedians, hypnotists, magicians, poets and guest lecturers. If you ca find something to do on this campus, then you are not paying attention to y surroundings. We have student-run clubs for a lot of different activities. In f it only takes three people to create a club. We don't have a Greek system, athletic teams kind of have their own scene. There are two student favorites bars that are within four blocks of the school. There are great restaurants in to too, from the laid-back imported beer hangout with Boxer's, to the more cla martini bar/restaurant with Mimi's, to All-American Pizza, Original Ital Pizza, and Dominoes all within walking distance of the school. The dating sc works out well. There's always a party on the weekend, if you're into it, there are always athletic events to attend. Students are big fans of Memories Johnny's bars, partying at the East Dormitories, any athletic event, Springf Mountain Day, Pig Roast, Storming of the Arch, the list goes on.

Current student, Social Sciences, 9/2004-Submit Date, June 20

There are also great restaurants within 30- to 40-minute drives where students frequently on weekends. State College is only a 35-minute drive from Juni and trips are made weekly for students to go dancing or out to dinner.

Current student, Political Science, 8/2006-Submit Date, June 20

The social life at Juniata has its ups and downs. The school provides a lot activities on the weekends but some are a little cheesy. The sporting events be a lot of fun though. Juniata is in a pretty small town, so there isn't much do but there are a few bars if you're over 21. However, State College and P State are only 30 minutes away, which is great. In fact, I love that I have option of a city-like atmosphere but can get away from it. We don't have Greek life, so all parties generally include anyone who wants to go. It can g little old since it tends to be the same places and people but at the same time nice that everyone takes care of each other.

Current student, 8/2003-Submit Date, May 2006

There are really two main bars that the college kids attend. One is ca Johnny's, which is more of the towny bar and then the college bar, Memor right across the street from Johnny's. The restaurants are few, but a lot of p ple will go to State College or Altoona if they want to eat a fancy meal of so sort.

> **The school says:** "On select weekends, a van service is provided through our Office of Student Activities for a minimal fee for students who are interested in traveling to State College."

Of course, dating takes place because it's a college. We have what's known JAB (Juniata Activities Board) and they have weekends when they'll sh movies, they bring bands, comedians and all of that to our campus on the we end. We have a ton of athletic clubs and academic clubs. We do not have f ternities or sororities on our campus. Everyone at our school is fun-loving a great to be around, so it's a great atmosphere.

The School Says

As competition heats up in a world economy, lasting careers will require individuals who are highly educated, globally aware, entrepreneurial and adaptable to a changing marketplace—in short, the student who graduates every year from Juniata.

Juniata is dedicated to being a student-centered college, and our 1,400 students are fully invested in cooperation and collaboration with all members of the community. For more than 35 years, with the help of two academic advisors, Juniata's unique and flexible Program of Emphasis educational plan puts the student in control, allowing them to customize their own academic program to cover wide-ranging interests or personal goals. This academic creativity enables our students to regularly win prestigious scholarships such as Fulbright, Goldwater, Davies-

Jackson, Pickering Fellows and the NCAA Postgraduate scholarship.

Juniata's engaged and accessible faculty are dedicated to teaching. In addition, they oversee extensive research programs and more than two dozen students every year present their work at the National Conference on Undergraduate Research. A hallmark of a Juniata education is hands-on learning. Young scientists learn using equipment and instruments that at other colleges often are available only to graduate students. Additionally, more than 80 percent of our students participate in at least one internship or student teaching before graduating and 40 percent study abroad.

The college's dedication to each student means Juniata excels at providing the tools to complete an undergraduate education in four years or less. Indeed, 78 percent of students entering Juniata graduate from the college and a stunning 95 percent of those who graduated in the Class of 2006 graduated in four years or less. Immediately after college, 95 percent of our graduates are employed, attending graduate school or pursuing other postgraduate activities. The Teagle Foundation has labeled Juniata an "Over Achieving College" in recognizing our exceptional postgraduate achievements and student graduation rate.

Juniata's social structure is designed to be inclusive and long-lasting. We do not have fraternities or sororities; our rich traditions are meant to celebrate our family atmosphere. Juniata students are socially aware, and they actively work to better the Juniata and local communities. Our students are busy with more than 100 clubs on campus advised by faculty and administrators. If you can't find a club addressing your specific interest, start one yourself on any topic.

Juniata has long traditions in football, basketball and baseball. We have won national championships in women's and men's volleyball. However, coursework and tests come first with our players and, more importantly, with our coaches.

Juniata students and alumni are successful. The college is one of the most oft-mentioned institutions in college guides and we are in the top tier of the *U.S. News & World Report* rankings. Just a few of our living alumni include the 1997 Nobel Prize laureate in Physics, one of the winningest coaches in National Football League history, the developer of the Chrysler Hemi engine, and six Fellows in the National Academy of Sciences.

Lafayette College

Admissions Office
18 Markle Hall
Easton, PA 18042
Admissions phone: (610) 330-5100
Admissions fax: (610) 330-5355
Admissions e-mail: admissions@lafayette.edu
Admissions URL: www.lafayette.edu/admissions/

Note: The school has chosen not to review the student surveys submitted

 ## Admissions

Alumnus/a, 8/2000-5/2004, October 2004
All the basics are required, and the Common Application is accepted, which makes things a bit easier. I was told during my sophomore year by a professor who recognized my name that he remembered my essay specifically, which leads me to believe that a strong essay can go a long way. An interview was not required, but Lafayette becomes more selective every year. High school GPA makes a big difference, as do strong SAT and ACT scores, although my SAT score was only 1290. Not bad, but not exceptional.

Current student, 8/2003-Submit Date, May 2004
Lafayette is getting more and more selective every year. The interview process is on campus and in a casual atmosphere. About three essays were necessary. Show a breadth of activities throughout high school and do something to make yourself stand out, because many of the applicants look similar on paper. Everyone who looks at Lafayette looks at some Ivy Leagues too, most are from the Northeast, and from some private school. Have something interesting to bring to the table.

Alumnus/a, 9/1984-5/1987, October 2003
Admission is pretty straightforward and comparable to any private liberal arts college. What stands out about the admissions process is that the school looks for students with social skills in addition to academic and athletic acumen, and

doesn't just pay lip service to the notion of being well-rounded. Also, since the school has been shedding the stigma of being an engineering school for decades, a strong verbal SAT score adds a bit of luster to an application. Finally, be aware that alumni are very influential in the admissions process, so an interview with an alumnus/a in addition to the admissions office can help, if the alumnus/a is close to the Board of Trustees (or preferably, on it).

 ## Academics

Current student, Pre-med, 8/2005-Submit Date, December 2006
Classes are challenging but doable if you can find the balance between work and play. The classes are small and you get to know the professors well, which is really nice and helpful.

Alumnus/a, 8/2000-5/2004, October 2004
In terms of quality of the classes, Lafayette's are certainly topnotch for a liberal arts program. Very qualified professors. Small classes. Strong emphasis on teamwork and class discussion. Classwork and homework are each challenging and must be completed in order to do well on exams. It seems overwhelming at times, but it's manageable. Getting the classes you need can be another story. There's strong competition for popular classes, and preference is often given along the lines of majors or seniority. If you stay on the professors' cases, you can usually get into what you need, though.

Current student, 8/2003-Submit Date, May 2004
The class quality is great because of the small class size, but there are not many sections for classes other than intro classes—so getting into some popular classes is difficult. The curriculum is broad-based, but there could be more majors. It seems like there are so many kids taking completely different classes who are in the same major, and who will receive the same degree. I also think that the pre-med program should be a major, like at other schools. I took more classes for pre-med than for my major. They were substantially more difficult, too. But come graduation time, nobody will know that because my diploma will only say economics and business. The workload really depends on your major. The engineers and science kids have it really tough.

Read all of Vault's College Surveys at **www.vault.com/college**—get complete surveys on 100s of colleges and universities, expert advice on applicaton essays and more.

VAULT CAREER LIBRARY 623

Alumnus/a, 9/1984-5/1987, October 2003

As with any highly competitive, small, private college, the size, quality and ease of access to classes is not an issue. The most important thing to realize about Lafayette is that it is not an easy school. Because of its high number of engineering majors, or perhaps because of its relative obscurity, the school seems to encourage its staff to operate their classes at a relatively rigorous level. I believe I can make this observation based on my experiences as a visiting undergraduate at Oxford, and based on undergraduate coursework taken at Columbia. Students are somewhat competitive with each other, but by no means obnoxious. I have also witnessed that in recent years the college embraced more than the pre-professional student, and can now make the claim to being an inviting place for those more intellectually focused. Fine arts has been making great strides in this regard. But for the pre-professionals, this is a great place to gear up for a career.

Employment Prospects

Current student, Pre-med, 8/2005-Submit Date, December 2006

Careers services are really helpful to get you into internships as well as externships during our January intersession.

Alumnus/a, 8/2000-5/2004, October 2004

Lafayette's engineering program clearly dominates in terms of recruiters' perceptions of the school. However, the school is very prestigious in the eyes of employers looking for econ majors, as well as all of the life science graduates. I wouldn't say the career counselors are the most helpful, but they do provide you with adequate avenues to contact alumni and non-alumni recruiters.

Current student, 8/2003-Submit Date, May 2004

Extensive internship/externship programs are available, networking is easy and efficient through the career services. It is really easy to get in touch with someone in the field of your choice, through professors or the career services program.

Alumnus/a, 9/1984-5/1987, October 2003

I really don't know much about these areas. I suspect that the school has come a long way since I graduated. I can say I regularly receive solicitation from the career planning office to sponsor interns. I also know that the alumni network on Wall Street is excellent and has been for a very long time.

Quality of Life

Current student, Pre-med, 8/2005-Submit Date, December 2006

It's a nice life on the hill. Most of the housing is not bad and there are even some new suites that are awesome. The gym is upscale and everyone is nice.

Alumnus/a, 8/2000-5/2004, October 2004

Campus is absolutely first-rate. Lafayette has one of the most attractive campuses I've ever seen. Visit on a nice day, and you'll be hooked—I was. All facilities are at your fingertips considering the fairly small size of the campus. Although everything is within short walking distance, it doesn't feel cramped in any way. Crime is minimal, as to be expected anywhere.

Current student, 8/2003-Submit Date, May 2004

The school is building a huge dorm next year, because it is its goal to get everybody back on campus. Usually, a lot of juniors and seniors live off campus and for whatever reason the school doesn't like this. As a freshman, you pretty much

get your choice of where you want to live, so ask around on a tour and get a f[eel] for where you want to live, because the different dorms have different cultu[re] and crowds, and in many ways form a core basis for friendships throughout [the] four years. The food in the dining halls is what you would expect for cafete[ria] food; there are a bunch of good eateries off campus though.

Alumnus/a, 9/1984-5/1987, October 2003

Housing is first class with many first-class dormitories and a number of new buildings and a great student center. I went to a particularly fine new Engla[nd] boarding school, and was shocked when I reached Lafayette and found treme[n]dous athletic, social and living facilities on such a small campus. Many of [the] frats are run-down, but I guess that applies to most schools.

Social Life

Current student, Pre-med, 8/2005-Submit Date, December 200[6]

The weekend runs Wednesday night to Saturday night. People go to frat parti[es,] sports parties, hang out with their friends, or go downtown to bars. For tho[se] who don't drink, the school has comedians, musical groups, and a lot of oth[er] activities. Everyone is involved in at least one club or sport or something.

Alumnus/a, 8/2000-5/2004, October 2004

Social life is very focused around Greek life. Personally, I felt that this add[ed] tremendously to the atmosphere around campus. Making friends is very easy [in] this sense, as parties occur pretty much every day. Smaller, off-campus parti[es] take place on the weekends in student-rented apartments. Bars are a very b[ig] part of social life as well, with three good dives on the hill, and five or so do[wn] the hill. Mother's, The Circle, Porter's and Witch Brew are all good, with [an] emphasis on Porter's and Witch Brew if you like good beer. Real great plac[es.] Small, personal, lots of fun. A lot of people at Lafayette date, but few rema[in] too serious. Random hook-ups are very common and generally are no big de[al.] Overall, Lafayette is a lot of fun. Not to mention you'll know pretty much ever[y]one on campus, which I enjoyed.

Current student, 8/2003-Submit Date, May 2004

Fraternities dominate, but the school has been cracking down hard every year. [It] won't admit it, but the school is clearly anti-Greek. Bars are so-so up the hill [a] couple pizza places serve beer at night. Most people just meet up there af[ter] going to the real bars down the hill. People are fun, but you see the same fac[es] every night.

Dating can be tough because of the small size of the school—it's pretty tough [to] avoid someone or not to see him/her if you really don't want to. The school re[al]ly lacks diversity, not to say if it's good or bad, but it's obvious.

I think that the college needs to relax with the Greek system. They have a tou[gh] alcohol patrol on weekends that they think will stop partying. Who are they ki[d]ding? Kids will find a way to party, and now on campus that's during the wee[k.] The biggest party days of the week are Tuesday, Wednesday and Thursday. O[n] the weekends people party, but it's more just hanging out at bars.

Alumnus/a, 9/1984-5/1987, October 2003

Frats used to rule the day. While still true, it is less so. If you're a guy, there a[re] too few women. If you're a woman, you may have to do too much work to ha[ve] an inordinate amount of fun. If you want a great education surrounded by se[ri]ous but gregarious peers who may even turn into great professional associat[es] some day, then Lafayette is for you.

Lehigh University

Admissions Office
' Memorial Drive West
:thlehem, PA 18015-3094
dmissions phone: (610) 758-3100
dmissions fax: (610) 758-4361
dmissions e-mail: admissions@lehigh.edu
dmissions URL: www.lehigh.edu/admissions/

 ## Admissions

umnus/a, Business, 8/1999-6/2003, May 2007

e admissions process was very typical of others I had gone through during
h school. There were open houses and meetings with admissions staff that
u were invited to attend during the entire process. You could also request an
-campus interview if you desired one. An essay was required with a choice of
ee or four different questions. I received my letter of acceptance in the same
:kage as my financial aid award.

umnus/a, Theater, 8/2002-6/2006, October 2006

ry easy. The school came to my high school and did a presentation. While
presenter was there, we scheduled an interview on campus and a tour. The
r guide was great and I applied early. Everyone was very helpful and
remely honest about all information. I knew where I was going before
ristmas.

umnus/a, 8/1999-6/2003, July 2006

ted by the *U.S. News & World Report* as a "most selective" school and ranked
st of the Top National Universities. Good essays and high SAT scores a must.
od to be in top 20 percent of graduating high school class. High school
racurriculars are a plus. AP credit a plus. Try and get a direct interview.
arity work is a major plus.

rrent student, 9/2001-Submit Date, September 2005

high has three undergraduate schools (engineering, business, arts and sci-
:es). I am earning degrees in both the engineering and business schools due
my participation in the Integrated Business and Engineering Honors Program.
r admission into the program, the key components were good SAT scores,
'A and class rank, but most of the focus was on leadership qualities, high
th/science scores, difficulty of coursework in high school (APs, honors) and
olvement. I never interviewed at Lehigh, but I know it does help because cur-
t students do the interviewing and will put in the good word for students
om they interview who are qualified to attend Lehigh. The engineering pro-
m at Lehigh is very difficult, and I venture to say that the *U.S. News & World
port* rankings do not do justice to the engineering (I was electrical engineer-
;) here at Lehigh. It is not made for the weak, and you will fail if you do not
e a full effort. Selectivity is becoming more of an issue each year due to the
her quality of candidates in the candidate pool, but I think what will make one
nd out in the application process is success in something to complement aca-
nic achievements (e.g., athletics, music, leadership activities)—basically any-
ng to show that one was involved in more than books in high school.

rrent student, 8/2003-Submit Date, October 2004

high is a place that encourages leadership among its students, so emphasis on
dership experience as a prospective student is beneficial. I recommend (as
th any university) to interview on campus in order to get a sense of the cam-
s. Lehigh has become more selective over the years, but still emphasizes a
ll-rounded individual. The ability to succeed academically and socially is
portant to Lehigh.

rrent student, 8/2000-Submit Date, July 2004

tually it was one of my safety schools so I did not bother interviewing or vis-
ng the campus. I used the standard application and did the standard essays.

My grades were probably about the B range in the advance honors courses in
high school. I took two AP courses my senior year.

Current student, 8/2001-Submit Date, February 2004

Making yourself and your résumé look good is what they look at. Try and distinguish yourself from others. This is a highly selective school, but just be yourself in the interviews.

> **Regarding admissions, the school says:** "Admission to Lehigh
> continues to be extremely competitive, offering admissions to
> approximately 32 percent of its applicants. The average SAT
> score for the Class of 2011 was 1308, and nearly 22 percent
> of incoming students are from traditionally under-represented
> backgrounds. There are more students than ever from the West
> and Southeast, and a greater percentage who have been edu-
> cated outside the United States. For admissions information:
> www.lehigh.edu/admissions."

 ## Academics

Alumnus/a, Business, 8/1999-6/2003, May 2007

The business school required you to take Introduction to Business in the first
semester of freshman year in order to become exposed to all of the various disciplines offered. Most students declare a major by the end of their sophomore
year or during the first semester of their junior year. By this time most students
have taken a class in finance, economics, statistics, accounting and management.
This makes the decision process much more rewarding.

Current student, Business, 1/2003-Submit Date, July 2006

Finance degree. Professors were decent, some were spectacular, some were sub
par. Small school so good student-to-prof. ratio. Prof always available.
Workload in business school can be rough but nowhere as tough as the engineering school. Grading is fair. Classes can be good since there are usually no
more than 30 students per class. Never had any real problems getting the classes I wanted, even the popular ones.

Current student, 9/2001-Submit Date, September 2005

As mentioned before, the engineering program is very challenging, failing courses is a definite possibility if one takes a class for granted. One of my professors
put it nicely as he said "we want you (students) to graduate and be extremely
successful and uphold the reputation of Lehigh University Engineering—so we
will not pass you unless you earn it." You can always get into a class, no matter
what people tell you, all you have to do is talk with the professor after your preliminary schedule has been made. This is sometimes overlooked as students
give up if they don't get into their preferred section/class when they first sign up
for classes each semester. It took me a semester or two to realize it, but you can
definitely get into any class/teacher/section you desire. Grading is usually pretty fair, but as far as engineering is concerned, sometimes you can give 100 percent and still not get a great grade. You're competing with other extremely intelligent individuals, and you are not just rewarded for putting in the time.
Engineering workload is a good amount, budgeting time is required, but I have
been a varsity athlete for the past four years, and have been involved in the music
program at Lehigh and have done quite fine despite time conflicts.

Current student, Business, 8/2002-Submit Date, July 2006

Academics can be very challenging at Lehigh. I am a double major in accounting and finance, which has required me to take some very challenging courses.
The school really lives up to its work hard, play hard mentality. Many students
find it easy to achieve B's, but A's are near to impossible. The top programs in
the business college are accounting, followed by finance. The most difficult
class in the accounting program is the Cost Accounting class, which is considered the weeder program. If you can't pass that class, you can't become an
accounting major. The easiest major in the business college is marketing. As a

Read all of Vault's College Surveys at **www.vault.com/college**—get complete surveys on 100s of colleges and universities, expert advice on applicaton essays and more.

VAULT CAREER LIBRARY 625

freshman and sophomore, classes tend to be large lectures with about 100 to 150 students. However, during the course of a student's junior and senior years, he or she will have classes ranging from 10 to 30 students. In classes like this, only about 10 percent of the students receive an A. Which means if you have 30 kids, only three receive an A. I found that my general classes my freshman and sophomore years were not nearly as interesting as my junior and senior year classes. I fell in love with my finance classes my senior year and really enjoyed school. The quality of classes and professors is much better at that level; however, the workload increases during the latter years. In addition, the popular classes are easier to come by as a junior and senior. I found that as a student athlete, I could register for the popular classes as a freshman, but that is not the norm. Lastly, Lehigh's business college really made a huge addition two years ago when they added a financial services laboratory. Donated by Wall Street and investment banking guru Joseph Perella, the financial services laboratory gives students the opportunity to have real-time quotes of stocks, bonds and derivatives. The lab also has the capabilities to run Thomson One and Bloomberg.

Alumnus/a, 8/2002-5/2006, May 2006

A's are possible, but they're not handed out. Professors curve around a C, and modest efforts will usually land students in that range. This is especially true for engineering students—[30] percent of the student body and one of Lehigh's strongest programs. Although the workload is intense in any discipline, professors are amazingly accessible and fair. Classes are also small, barring lectures, and I've always been able to take popular classes, whether directly or e-mailing profs to get in through a waiting list.

Current student, Business, 8/2003-Submit Date, October 2004

The workload surely challenges the student, but the material and its delivery prepare the students for applicable real-world challenges. Being a business major, I have found that the courses within my major are clear, in depth and interesting. Grading is fair, and professors offer sufficient office hours outside of class for students. The major programs within the business college are expanding, in hopes of offering students more flexibility with course choice and broadened knowledge of the chosen field and business in general.

> **Regarding academics, the school says:** "As one of the most selective universities in the country, we often attract students with an array of educational options before them. We are frequently asked, 'Why Lehigh?' We often cite an unusually diverse array of academic options (particularly for a small research university), as well as a host of other benefits; extraordinarily accomplished and committed faculty, outstanding flexibility for students to switch between Lehigh's colleges, the opportunity for undergraduates to work alongside world-class researchers, as well as the ability to avail themselves of the deeper creative, cultural and educational opportunities we offer, no matter what their major. For detailed academic information by college: www.lehigh.edu/academics."

 Employment Prospects

Alumnus/a, Business, 8/1999-6/2003, May 2007

In every employment interview the Lehigh name was looked upon positively. All of the Big Four accounting firms recruit and interview on campus and many students are given offers well before graduation. I interviewed for accounting positions after graduation and received offers in all three of my interviews. I attribute a large degree of that to the prestige of a Lehigh education.

Current student, 1/2003-Submit Date, July 2006

Topnotch school and tier-one investment banks recruit from this school, but you need to at least have a 3.5 GPA to be considered since competition from Ivy League is intense. Great job networks and alumni have proven to be very successful. If you get in with the alumni, job prospects are excellent. Recruiters come directly to the school looking to hire students. Good programs to prepare for interviews and résumés.

Current student, 8/2002-Submit Date, July 2006

Because the accounting program is so advanced at Lehigh, the Big Four recruits heavily. I found this a turn off. I prefer to be recruited by financial services.

Lehigh students will have no problem finding a job at any of the Big Four or financial services firms in controlling and operations. Unfortunately, it is v difficult to obtain a front office job in sales and trading or investment banki The best way for students to work their way into one of these careers is thro networking, which students have the opportunity to do at Lehigh. Numer trips to Wall Street are offered through classes, which gives the students opportunity to check out the firms and speak with alumni. By doing this, s dents can network and hopefully use a new relationship to open doors for inv ment banking or sales and trading. Most students seek internships during summer going into their senior year, which many times result in students hav a job come senior year. However, the downfall is many of these internships in the Big Four, not financial services.

Alumnus/a, 8/2002-5/2006, May 2006

Goldman Sachs, Bear Sterns, PwC, Ernst & Young, Deloitte—these were typical answers given by students in my senior management class when a p fessor asked what their future jobs were. This is typical of most business s dents. Engineering students can expect similar prestige in employers, altho arts and science students may have to work harder to get noticed by cho employers. On-campus recruiting typically caters directly to business and er neering, although a huge alumni network is available and eager to help in ma fields. I've contacted many by e-mail just for advice and have made some la ing contacts.

Current student, 8/2000-Submit Date, July 2004

Plenty of job opportunities. The career placement office is very good, stude just need to be proactive and take advantage of it. The career counselors will hesitate to put you in contact with high powered alumni in all sorts of differe industries. Alumni tend to be very helpful in advising and helping get inte views. I couldn't be happier with the job they did.

> **Regarding employment prospects, the school says:** "Recently published statistics by Lehigh's Office of Career Services cited the following:
>
> • 99 percent of graduates were employed, in graduate school, in the military, traveling or settled into other career-related opportunities within six months of graduation
>
> • 68 percent of graduates employed by over 260 firms, including Fortune 500, mid-size and small employers (starting salaries comparable to or greater than national averages)
>
> • 26 percent of graduates enrolled in over 70 highly competitive graduate or professional schools
>
> • 90 percent acceptance rate for allopathic (MD) medicine and 88 percent acceptance rate for law school."

 Quality of Life

Alumnus/a, Business, 8/1999-6/2003, May 2007

Freshmen and sophomores are required to live on campus, either in the Gre system or in the freshman dorms/upper-class housing. Sophomore housing determined by a lottery system with a diverse set of options from which choose. You could chose to live in a more dorm-like environment as a sop more or you can choose one of the housing options that is more similar to apartment. Many of the upper-class housing options consist of suites t include four bedrooms, a common living room/kitchen and a common bathro Most juniors and seniors who are not in the Greek system tend to live off-ca pus. It is less expensive than campus living and provides more freedo Although the Lehigh campus is extremely safe, the area around the campus experienced petty crime.

Alumnus/a, 8/1999-6/2003, October 2006

Off-campus housing is very cheap. Rent usually ranges about $250/pp to $4 (one bedroom). It gets little rough if you live too far off campus. Living sta dard is very low. Campus square is the most recently built dorm and the nic M&M is the all-freshman dorm. Most dorms are located on the hill and cla rooms are on the ground—freshmen should expect a ton of walking. I know

of universities have 24-hour cafeterias; not at Lehigh. Past 10 p.m., all on-
mpus restaurants close. Linderman is an old-style library—it's a great place
study.

urrent student, 1/2003-Submit Date, July 2006

mpus is beautiful and situated on a mountain. Housing, dining, sports facili-
s are great and the campus is self-sustaining. Town relations strained howev-
Southside Bethlehem is somewhat impoverished and at times. Good loca-
n from Philadelphia (50 minutes north) and one hour 15 minutes west of
YC. Walking around campus is tough since it is situated on a mountain.
rking is horrendous, although owning a car is advisable. Local parking
thority is a continuous nuisance. Easy to rack up parking fines if you are not
reful. School is always investing in new facilities.

> **The school says:** "Improvements to our campus included the
> addition of a pedestrian walkway, construction of a new arrival
> court and 315-space parking garage outside the Alumni
> Memorial Building, the renovation of Lamberton Hall (including
> the addition of a late-night diner and activities lounge), and the
> ongoing restoration of Linderman Library as a state-of-the-art
> home for the humanities."

urrent student, 9/2001-Submit Date, September 2005

uth Bethlehem is by no means the nicest place to live, but it is not a place
here you are scared to walk around at night. Lots of students live off campus.
e housing is cheap, plentiful, and the houses themselves are usually very spa-
us. In addition, all off-campus houses are within walking distance of the uni-
rsity. On-campus housing is phenomenal, even freshman dorms are great.
ning is pretty good on campus, but even more so off campus. Almost all the
cal restaurants and delis accept Lehigh University GoldPLUS, which is
high's student debit account that is accessed by the student ID card—extreme-
convenient and avoids having to carry cash around.

urrent student, 8/2002-Submit Date, July 2006

high sits on a gorgeous hill in South Bethlehem. If you like walking, Lehigh
for you. Don't drive because parking tickets are $35 a pop, and they nab
eryone. The architecture is really unique, and resembles an Ivy League
hool. The dorms are the usual college dorms and close to dining halls. The
wnfall is the local population. If you walk off campus, it can become a little
ngerous at night. Bethlehem is beginning to turn around. Many shops and
staurants are starting up in the southside, but the neighborhoods can be some-
hat unfriendly sometimes.

> **Regarding quality of life, the school says:** "Lehigh's Office of
> First-year Experience makes adapting to college life a breeze. A
> variety of special first-year programs, activities and exciting
> events makes it easy to make friends and adjust to the life on
> campus. The first-year program is designed to engage you
> while providing the necessary support and resources to be suc-
> cessful at Lehigh. You'll have the opportunity to participate in
> activities, attend guest speaker events and immerse yourself in
> the Summer Reading Program before you arrive on campus—all
> designed to help you develop lifelong friendships during your
> stay. To learn more about the first-year experience at Lehigh:
> www.lehigh.edu/first-year."

 Social Life

lumnus/a, Business, 8/1999-6/2003, May 2007

ny kind of extracurricular activity you would want to participate in at Lehigh
available, and if it's not, you can start it up yourself. The school is very gen-
ous about giving funding for new clubs and organizations. Students study hard
ring the semester but you will always be able to find a party at one of the frat
uses on Thursday through Sunday nights. The Greek system has a strong
esence on campus, but if you are not a fraternity member (I wasn't) the frat
uses, for the most part, are very welcoming. Not much in the way of bars in
e area, that probably has to do with the existence of over 20 fraternities on
mpus. Most students do not see the need to go barhopping.

Alumnus/a, 8/1999-6/2003, October 2006

Well known for its fraternity parties up the hill. People work hard and party
hard. McGrady's and Tally Ho are the popular bars that everyone goes to. If you
go to McGrady's, you have to try their buffalo wings; they have more than 10
favors. Check out their special, $1 drafts and $1.99 wings. Where else can you
get that? Leon's is not bad too if you like dancing. However all bars close at 2
a.m. Don't miss the deli at Goosey Gander. If you like to ski, Blue Mountain
and the Poconos are an hour away.

Current student, 1/2003-Submit Date, July 2006

Social life is good, but somewhat of a pretentious elitist group. Many students
are rich and snobby and minorities are only a small percentage of a predominately caucasian student population. Lehigh is known for fraternity/sorority life
although there is a large non-Greek population. There is more to a social life
than just drinking and partying. Dating scene is easy if you are Greek, otherwise
it can be tough at times. There are few decent bars in the town, notably the Tally
Ho and Brew Works. Many clubs to join. My favorite was crew and the radio
station. You are a god if you play football or wrestling as Lehigh is continual
first place in the Patriot League for football and ranked in the Top 10 nationally
for wrestling.

Current student, 9/2001-Submit Date, September 2005

Greek system is pretty big at Lehigh, but is being slightly phased out. The great
part of Lehigh is that people will have parties/get-togethers, and no one has to
pay. The host of the party will fund drinks, and no one is asked to pay a cent if
they attend. Frats are usually pretty welcoming, off-campus houses are very
welcoming, and people are more than willing to have a good time on the weekends. There are three or four bars right in South Bethlehem that students can
walk to (which is great when the bar closes, avoiding drinking/driving).
McGrady's pub is a new bar that opened with specials almost every night, and is
expanding its bar to the next door lot as well this year. There are tons of clubs
and organizations to get involved in, and varsity sports always welcome walk-
ons to try out. Dating scene is what you make of it, there are movie theatres
within a five- to 10-minute drive, tons of restaurants within a 10-minute drive,
and within walking distance.

Current student, 8/2002-Submit Date, July 2006

The social life at Lehigh is driven by its Greek Life. The students live up to the
work hard, play hard mentality. Joining fraternities and sororities is common
among students, especially since students are required to live on campus their
freshman and sophomore years. There really are only three bars at Lehigh,
which can become boring. The Lehigh Valley has many restaurants, some
require a car to drive to[, but many are within walking distance.] Sports are
important at Lehigh, but are mainly driven by its football and wrestling teams.
Overall, Lehigh has a solid social life, but could use a few more bars.

Alumnus/a, 8/2002-5/2006, May 2006

The Greek system is huge, but off-campus parties—especially among sports
teams—are popular as well. The party-hard mentality is taken as seriously as
studying. The week of the Lehigh-Lafayette football game and Greek Week are
especially big for drinking and festivities, but that usually just means we add the
rest of the week to the usual Wednesday through Saturday party nights.

> **Regarding social life, Lehigh says:** "95 percent of students stay
> on campus on the weekends. Whether it's sports, the arts, a
> special club or community service, we offer an assortment of
> student activities that add significantly to your experience at
> Lehigh. Even as a first-year student, you can participate in ath-
> letic competitions, land the lead in a theatre production, perform
> a solo in the wind ensemble, hold a leadership position in stu-
> dent government or join a Greek organization! Choose from
> over 150 clubs and organization, 25 NCAA Division I sports, 40
> club and intramural sports or, if you don't find your favorite
> activity, just gather a few friends with similar interests and cre-
> ate one. The Departments of Music and Theatre also offer an
> array of choral and instrumental ensembles and vibrant theatre
> production programs. For more information visit the following:
> www.lehigh.edu/activities,   www.lehigh.edu/arts,
> www.lehigh.edu/sports, www.lehigh.edu/campuslife."

Read all of Vault's College Surveys at **www.vault.com/college**—get complete surveys on 100s of colleges and universities, expert advice on applicaton essays and more.

V/\ULT CAREER LIBRARY 627

The School Says

Lehigh's distinctive 1,600-acre campus is nestled in a park-like setting where sloping wooded hills meet busy city streets. The campus lies in the pristine Lehigh Valley in Bethlehem, Pennsylvania (50 miles north of Philadelphia and 75 miles south-west of New York City). Lehigh is easy to travel to, since the campus is located near several major highways and the Lehigh Valley International Airport.

Founded in 1865 by Asa Packer as a non-denominational private university, Lehigh has expanded and grown into a nationally recognized research university offering the following degrees: Bachelor of Arts and Bachelor of Science. Advanced degrees include Master of Arts, Master of Business Administration, Master of Education, Master of Engineering, Master of Science, Educational Specialist, Doctor of Education, Doctor of Philosophy and Doctor of Arts.

Our academic programs attract the best students from around the world. As one of the most competitive universities in the U.S., Lehigh ranks in the top tier among national universities according to the *U.S. News & World Report*'s, 2007 America's Best Colleges.

At Lehigh you are offered a variety of courses to satisfy your intellectual desires, no matter how diverse. You're even encouraged to customize your course selections. Choose from over 2,000 courses offered by Lehigh's four colleges: the College of Arts and Sciences, the College of Business and Economics, the P.C. Rossin College of Engineering and Applied Science and the College of Education.

Our approach to learning is interdisciplinary in nature. We want you to build skills in your area of expertise and have the opportunity to work with others outside of your field-just like in the real world. Lehigh faculty are committed to finding interesting ways for you to interact and collaborate on projects with students outside of your major, your department, and even your college. Interdisciplinary programs at Lehigh include Integrated Business and Engineering, Integrated Degree in Engineering, Arts & Sciences, Computer Science & Business, Global Citizenship program, South Mountain College, and much more!

When you're not in class, the Lehigh campus is a hub of social activity. Like sports? The arts? Want to join a special club? Start a new student organization? No matter what your interests are, Lehigh offers an assortment of unique activities that add significantly to your college experience. You'll find more than 150 student clubs and organizations, 30 nationally recognized fraternities and sororities, 25 intercollegiate sports (Division I and Division I-AA for football), 40-plus intramural and club sports, performing arts, and a variety of faith and cultural organizations. Close ties to the Bethlehem community offer you the chance to take part in rewarding volunteer opportunities, such as tutoring local school children or helping in fundraising programs.

The intellectual diversity of our students is a key ingredient for achieving a diverse community on our campus. Academic excellence requires a learning community in which people of different backgrounds and perspectives join in the pursuit of knowledge and truth. Lehigh University is determined to prepare students to succeed in the world, and in a nation, where multiple viewpoints offer challenges and enrich our lives.

To plan a visit to Lehigh: www.lehigh.edu/visitinglehigh

Muhlenberg College

Admissions Office
2400 Chew Street
Allentown, PA 18104-5586
Admissions phone: (484) 664-3200
Admissions e-mail: admission@muhlenberg.edu
Admissions URL: www.muhlenberg.edu/admissions

Admissions

Alumnus/a, 8/2000-6/2004, April 2005

I did not have an interview at Muhlenberg. I signed up for their early admissions program and was admitted with no problem! The essay was a simple personal essay that seemed to be pretty generic. Muhlenberg is becoming more and more selective with their admissions process. My advice on getting in is to apply early, do well on your SATs and write an amazing essay. The focus at this school is on writing skills.

Alumnus/a, 1/2000-5/2004, November 2004

I visited the college about three times. I had an interview and two tours where I could ask for advice on getting in. I also spoke with my guidance counselor. At my school, they cared about how many times a student visited, whether or not they did the overnight, stuff like that because they cared about how much the student actually wanted to go to the school. You would go for an interview, send in an application and then wait to hear. The interview at Muhlenberg is optional

but if you don't want to hand in your SAT scores, which you don't have to the[n] then you have to have an interview. The essays were about moments in your li[fe] At least that is what I wrote about. Muhlenberg is listed as highly selective a[nd] most of the people in it were in the top of their classes.

Alumnus/a, 9/1976-5/1980, February 2004

Admission is highly selective. They have an innovative SAT optional policy f[or] those who have a strong academic record but who might not take standardiz[ed] tests well. The school likes to admit well-rounded individuals who have a va[ri]ety of interests (e.g., the student-performer, the student-athlete). You can ma[ke] up for some weakness in your academic record by demonstrating involvement [in] a number of different activities. I believe the campus visit and admissions inte[r]view are very important. The school is very accommodating in making the[se] arrangements. A very friendly admissions staff—they want to attract topnotc[h] students.

Current student, 8/2001-Submit Date, August 2004

Students interested in Muhlenberg should definitely go for an interview. Th[e] admissions office regards students who interview more highly than others. The[y] think it shows that the student is interested and takes the time to pursue the insti[i]tution. It is a very selective school so if you know you want to attend, definit[e]ly apply Early Decision. It is much easier to get in through Early Decision th[an] Regular Decision. As a tour guide, I have been involved in the admissio[ns] process every year since I applied.

Academics

umnus/a, 8/2000-6/2004, April 2005

ademics at Muhlenberg are wonderful. It is fairly simple to get whatever
ss you want since there are not many students to compete with! Each profes-
is different but you will learn who is difficult and who is easy. The one thing
t is constant is that you will learn an awful lot in any class you take. The
us is on writing, so you will be required to take a number of writing intensive
rses to graduate. The quality of the classes is great though! For the most
t, you will enjoy diverse methods of teaching. Each class has its own pace
d workload. You have the choice to make your weekly workload very high or
nparatively low.

umnus/a, 1/2000-5/2004, November 2004

as a self-designed major. My major was literary and visual arts; theatre and
evision. There was no writing part of their theatre program so I combined
mmunications, English writing classes, art and theatre classes. It took a long
e and I had to structure the whole thing myself with help from the guidance
nselor but it passed. Because it is a small school, it can be hard to get the
sses you want. There are no really big classes. There is only one real lecture
l. Grading is tough. It does depend on the professor. The professors at
hlenberg really take the time to get to know the students. Well, at least my
ones did. Since the class sizes are so small, I was often invited to meals with
m, or even to their homes for dinner. They also had time to meet for extra
p. The quality of classes also depended on what it was. They were very much
cussion based. The workload also varied.

rrent student, 8/2001-Submit Date, August 2004

e classes are very small at Muhlenberg. This sounds great and many times it
but the problem is that the classes tend to fill up quickly, especially the most
ular ones. I am going to be a senior and have never gotten all of my first-
ice classes. You can get signed into classes you absolutely need, but if it's
t a class you want to take, it can be difficult unless you have a good relation-
p with the professor teaching the class. The workload depends on your major.
a communication and Spanish major, I don't find the workload to be bad at
  Those in the pre-med program have a much harder workload. Professor
lity is pretty good, although you will find professors who are as very good.
ding depends on professors as well, though I have found that the grading is
.

umnus/a, 9/1976-5/1980, February 2004

ademics are challenging. Professors are high-quality. Tough workload.
ss sizes are small. Your teachers will know who you are. You have to work
 your grades. The library is excellent. Excellent lab facilities. Some nice
dern classrooms in the newer buildings with multi-media capabilities. Great
forming arts facilities. There are some more popular classes that you might
e to wait until junior or senior year to get into because of registration. Core
sses are always available. There is a strong emphasis on ethics and service as
ues. There is a good variety of interesting choices. Graduation requirements
 that each student must take at least two classes from each academic disci-
ne in addition to the major course of study. There is good support if you find
rself having academic troubles.

Employment Prospects

umnus/a, 8/1974-5/1978, October 2006

e Career Center and personnel at the college were extremely helpful in my
ployment quest. I learned how to prepare résumés, set up job interviews, and
y also provided me with several assessment tests to help me determine in
ch types of work I might be most happy and successful. I had multiple job
ers from various companies and agencies.

umnus/a, 8/2000-6/2004, April 2005

hlenberg's reputation is getting better and better each year. With a degree
m Muhlenberg, many job opportunities are waiting for you. There are many
dents who go on to grad school because they received a degree from The
rg. I believe that admissions for med school was 99 percent at one point!

Alumnus/a, 1/2000-5/2004, November 2004

In terms of future employment, they do have a Career Cneter. The connections
the school has are pretty much the same, so I had to get some connections
through talking to individual teachers, such as the head of the Theatre department, who could only give me the name of someone to talk to. Muhlenberg is
noted high in prestige with employers if they have heard of it. It is a small liberal arts school so people from far away sometimes don't know what it is. I think
100 percent of the students who graduate from the pre-med program get into
grad school. It is an incredibly hard program that really weeds through everyone who is not amazing at science. This is how it should be. In terms of on campus recruiting, it's really not great unless you want to get into the business world.
The same with internships.

> **The school states:** "The percentage of students accepted into
> medical school is overstated slightly in the comments above.
> We are consistently over 90 percent for sure, but these quotes
> are not quite accurate."

Current student, 8/2001-Submit Date, August 2004

Muhlenberg has the Career Center, which is supposed to help students find a job
or grad school after graduation. If you make an appointment and meet with a
counselor, they are helpful. The web site, however, is useless as far as I'm concerned. I wanted to participate in an internship either over the summer or during the fall semester. I found one for the fall that is in Allentown (where
Muhlenberg is). But I found it on my own because it wasn't listed on the Career
Center web site. Also, I think it's unfair that Muhlenberg makes you pay for college credit internships. It costs about $1,200 to participate in an unpaid summer
internship in order to receive college credit. In addition, many internship programs require college credit from participants. For this reason, I did not do a
summer internship.

Alumnus/a, 9/1976-5/1980, February 2004

Science/biology program is recognized as one of the best in the country. The
school has an excellent reputation with graduate schools, especially medical and
law schools with a good track record of acceptances. The teaching program also
has an excellent reputation. Internships are available with local corporations
such as Air Products and IBM. There are a number of opportunities for field
study and research for science majors. Career placement services have
improved in the last few years.

Quality of Life

Alumnus/a, 8/2000-6/2004, April 2005

Muhlenberg has two dining facilities that are kept clean and beautiful. The campus is gorgeous although small. Facilities on campus seem to be brand new
because of the upkeep. There is a new gym that was completed last year.
Housing is abundant at Muhlenberg since they just built new dorms on campus.
The surrounding area also has many opportunities to live off campus. The area
is beautiful, but since it is in the city, it is not for everyone. That being said, you
will feel completely safe in Allentown. The police and campus safety do a wonderful job keeping everyone safe.

> **The school says:** "We are in a residential neighborhood on the
> outskirts of a city."

Alumnus/a, 1/2000-5/2004, November 2004

Housing at Muhlenberg is actually really good. There is choice of all-female
housing, coed housing and coed by room, hall, side of hall or floor. Everything
really. Freshmen have this choice. A few of the dorms are falling apart because
they were supposed to be temporary, but actually those dorms go quickly in the
lottery because they are separated from campus and so it seems the students can
get away with more there.

> **Muhlenberg says:** "We are replacing the temporary dorm."

The other campus facilities are great. The gym and workout areas are amazing
now that they have a newly built center. The food is also really great. Good
variety. There are only two choices of places to eat. One is cafeteria-style and
one sort of fast food. They serve basically the same things. The rest of the facil-

Read all of Vault's College Surveys at **www.vault.com/college**—get complete surveys on 100s of colleges and universities, expert advice on applicaton essays and more.

VAULT CAREER LIBRARY **629**

ities are clean and well-kept. The neighborhood is safe if you don't go into Allentown. In the actual city part, it is in fact, not safe at all, but the actual neighborhood where Muhlenberg is is beautiful and the community actually takes part in a few projects with the school.

Current student, 8/2001-Submit Date, August 2004

Muhlenberg's campus is very pretty and housing is decent. Many of the dorms are very nice and much bigger than other schools'. The dining halls are pretty good though they do tend to lack variety. Crime isn't that big a deal on campus. As a girl, I feel safe walking around alone at night.

Alumnus/a, 9/1976-5/1980, February 2004

If you visit the school, you are going to like it. The campus is located in the quiet residential West End section of Allentown. It is a picturesque, relatively small, self-contained campus with a mix of modern and traditional architecture. Safety on campus is not an issue. Academic facilities are excellent. On-campus housing is available for all full-time students and runs the gamut from traditional dorm rooms, to shared suites to common interest housing.

The school offers a comprehensive and highly competitive program of NCAA Division III intercollegiate sports for men and women. The facilities for sports are also excellent and most are available for recreational use by students as well. There is a myriad of opportunities for extracurricular activities covering most interests. Performing arts facilities are first class. There are many interesting programs offered during each year. Parking is available for upperclassmen only. The Student Union offers decent food with a wide variety of selections.

 ## Social Life

Alumnus/a, 8/2000-6/2004, April 2005

There are many bars and restaurants in the immediate area. Dorney Park is right down the street! Muhlenberg has a good selection of fraternities and sororities on campus. I met my fiance there! We were both involved in Greek life and loved every minute of it. If you aren't interested in the Greek life, there is still plenty to do on campus and with several other colleges and universities in the immediate area, it is easy to make great friends. There are plenty of clubs to join at Muhlenberg and even if there isn't something existing that you would love to see, it is quite easy to start one up! In my four years there, I had seen many new clubs form—College Democrats, Rugby and others.

Alumnus/a, 1/2000-5/2004, November 2004

In terms of social life there is a wide variety of clubs and organizations. Stude do take part in them. Actually, Hillel (center for Jewish life) is supposedly most active and largest student organization on campus. Everyone goes to social scene there because of how fun it is and, of course, for the free food.

There really are not many choices of restaurants, bars, clubs and stuff like t because we are in a suburban area and so there really is no college town, wh really bothered me. Mostly students may go into Philly and NYC for stuff l that. Though Greek life is big on campus, not everyone has to participate. I o went to one Greek event the whole time I was there. The theater department, instance, is not heavily involved in Greek life, if at all, because we simply ha no time with performing and rehearsing. The theater department actually p vides most of the entertainment in terms of arts entertainment for the colle But we do a really good job and a wide variety of people attend.

Alumnus/a, 9/1976-5/1980, February 2004

If you are looking for excitement or a big college atmosphere, this is not yr school. This is a small college with an enrollment of just under 2,000 studer Allentown is not exactly a cosmopolitan center, but the Lehigh Valley area is bad. You are about two hours west of New York City and one hour north Philadelphia. Campus life is very quiet around midterms and during the fir exam period.

There is a system of fraternities and sororities. They have evolved over ti from the center of party life to service organizations. There are clubs coveri almost every interest group you can think of. The student body is probably as diverse as it should be but it is not completely homogeneous either. There a number of decent restaurants within a short drive from campus. It is a ve nice place to go to school, you can enjoy yourself to a certain extent, but this not a party school by any stretch of the imagination. There is a very friend welcoming atmosphere on campus. Attending Muhlenberg is a very rewardi experience.

Current student, 8/2001-Submit Date, August 2004

Greek life isn't huge at Muhlenberg. About 33 percent of students are involv in Greek life. Two frats have been kicked off campus for different reaso though I think one is being reinstated this year. For fun, students often drink their rooms or go to frat parties. After turning 21, there are more apartment a suite parties and some still go to frat parties. There are a couple bars for le students to go to. Overall, the social life isn't terrific but there's fun to be hac you know where to look.

The Pennsylvania State University

Admissions Office
01 Shields Building
x 3000
niversity Park, PA 16804-3000
dmissions phone: (814) 865-5471
dmissions Fax: (814) 863-7590
dmissions URL: www.psu.edu/dept/admissions/

Admissions

rrent student, 8/2006-Submit Date, May 2007

e admissions process for entering the university was just and fair. It was not hard as people think it is. I had no interview; in fact, all I did was complete application and submit an essay.

rrent student, 1/2003-Submit Date, March 2007

ith over [48,000] applications (the most in the country) for admission to the l, 2007 class, State College, PA became the most popular destination in the untry. Grades are weighted most heavily in the admissions process followed standardized test scores. The mean SAT for admission was around 1220. est advice is to study up and earn high marks; this university receives too many alified applicants to wade through them any other way besides the examina- n of raw data.

umnus/a, 8/1998-12/2002, September 2006

e admissions application contains no essay, which is nice. Apply early and if u have a decent SAT score, well-rounded activities, and a good GPA in high hool, you have a decent shot. Penn State enrolls about [16,000] every year, but re are so many that apply who it can be a selective process. There was no erview for undergrad.

urrent student, 8/2002-Submit Date, May 2006

ur admissions process was simple and to the point. There weren't many missions essays and they only required a few letters of reference. However, I ve found that most people with similar academic and extracurriculars with my ades and similar SAT scores who didn't do early acceptance were denied. I ink with how competitive Penn State (main campus) is, early acceptance is the st bet for incoming students.

urrent student, 6/2003-Submit Date, May 2006

e admissions process was very easy and I did it online. I know a lot of peo- e who had high GPAs from high school and high SAT scores and didn't get in d were referred to a branch campus. Penn State is pretty selective.

urrent student, 8/2003-Submit Date, May 2006

e admissions process was simple to complete, but selection of students is mplex. My year was the hardest year to get into Penn State. My advice would to try and be yourself and be completely honest. Also, try to show some inter- ed sides of yourself and show that you are personable.

lumnus/a, 8/2000-12/2004, August 2006

e admissions office at Penn State was quite determined to get me enrolled to e university. There was a slight hesitation with my parents not wanting me to that far away, but a representative from my state actually gave me a call to lk to my parents on what a great opportunity was ahead of me. So after they nsidered, there is an application fee required, which I paid. It's difficult to get to the main campus, because a lot of students from their second year on to urth or fifth year are enrolled there. So their freshman class is limited. Good PA is always a plus, especially if you have relatives, brothers, sisters or parents ho are alumni.

Penn State is a diverse university that wants students from all over the world and U.S. That's probably why they selected me from my region because they had very few students from Hawaii.

Current student, 6/2004-Submit Date, July 2006

Admissions was convenient because you apply online and you also can apply through the mail. If you have a high GPA in high school and decent SAT scores you will most likely have a good chance of getting accepted. The application doesn't have a mandatory essay, but I would recommend that you write one.

Current student, 8/2003-Submit Date, December 2004

The application was very straightforward and simple. It contained basic infor- mation that took about a half hour to fill out and review. There is no essay, although if you want to apply for the Schreyer's Honors College, they do send you a separate application after you submit the first one. Just make sure you have at least a 1100 on your SATs or something close. If you have towards the low end, make sure you apply early since it is rolling recruitment. Make sure you opt to take summer courses as a condition of your acceptance if need be.

Current student, 8/2001-Submit Date, June 2004

Personally, my admissions process consisted of only an application and short essay. I had no problem getting in as a freshman, though a few of my friends are on [conditional] admission, which means they have to attend classes in the sum- mer prior to freshman year or be waitlisted. Looking back, the transition was difficult and I would recommend taking classes in the summer to acclimate your- self to college life.

I have heard that Penn State is accepting fewer freshmen due to the lack to hous- ing and extreme growth that encourages students to enroll in one of the multiple extension campuses throughout the state. Advice on getting into Penn State: take a SAT prep course ensuring the receipt of an acceptable score and remain focused on your grades senior year of high school.

Academics

Current student, 8/2006-Submit Date, May 2007

Penn State provides a quality education with both easy and difficult classes. The workload depends upon the specific class and is necessary to succeed in the class. Most of the professors are fair and exhibit good teaching skills.

Current student, 1/2003-Submit Date, March 2007

The workload is not tremendously overbearing and the classes are usually well instructed. Some introductory-level classes are difficult because the instructors cannot possibly know who you are and that makes grading impersonal and con- fusing. The Schreyer Honors College, available to roughly 300 incoming fresh- men and additional students through the "Junior Gate Process," is one of the top in the country. It provides a small-school environment in an institution with over 44,000 students. You have the ability to schedule classes before grad students even, and you have the option to turn any course that you take into an honors course. The access to professors, smaller classes, and better job placement are all perks. Definitely worth turning down an Ivy to come here, and you get paid to boot.

Current student, Biology, 8/2005-Submit Date, May 2007

In the biology program you have to have a 2.0 to enter the major. I believe it's one of the hardest majors in the university, especially if you are trying to make it to medical school. The classes are interesting, and the professors are helpful and know what they are talking about. Grading is really up to the professor; biology classes are the normal grading range: i.e., A= 90 or better, however in the chemistry department it is different especially for one of the hardest classes I believe out there, Organic Chemistry. The workload is like any other class, there is a lot of it, and of course it is because it's college, it's your future, you need to challenge yourself to get wherever you want to be. Getting into the

Read all of Vault's College Surveys at **www.vault.com/college**—get complete surveys on 100s of colleges and univer- sities, expert advice on applicaton essays and more.

VAULT CAREER LIBRARY **631**

"popular classes" is very easy I suppose, the scheduling depends on how many credits you have. The seniors get the first pick on classes, because they are ready to graduate, then juniors, then sophomores, and then freshmen.

Current student, Communications, 8/2002-Submit Date, May 2006

I have found that Penn State's academics are topnotch (especially the College of Communications and sociology department). My advisor always went out of his way to get me into classes I needed for graduation and made sure I got the best/most popular classes. I was exposed to many activities within and around campus for a majority of my classes and we were always informed by our profs of diversity and events happening at PSU. Workload, for the most part, was reasonable. If for some reason there was too much work at one particular time, extensions were allowed on a personal basis. I utilized office hours all the time and found that profs and instructors worked with me to make sure I understood the concepts and themes.

Current student, 8/2003-Submit Date, May 2006

Penn State has an Ivy League level of education at a state college price. The academic programs are very vigorous and prepare students well for the next level in life. The workload is not easy, but doable. Popular classes can be difficult to get in but you most definitely will have a chance to take every class you want by the time you are a senior. Professors are very personable and can make a student feel like they are in a class of 20 instead of 400.

Current student, Communications, 8/2002-Submit Date, May 2006

I was a communications major and the College of Communications at University Park is absolutely outstanding. They offer so many extra lectures and panel discussions with guest speakers and the classes really do prepare you for the workforce. I was also a member of the Center for Sports Journalism, a newly developed program at Penn State, which allowed me the opportunity to meet renowned professionals and build a networking base for future jobs and internships.

Current student, 9/2002-Submit Date, Agriculture, May 2006

The classes in my major (agriculture) are typically small. Classes such as biology, chemistry and physics are usually large. The introductory biology class (BIO 110) is the largest class with 1,100 students enrolled, and only two sections. The auditorium sits up to 1,000 students at once! Most professors are personable, but some could not care less. I've only had one experience in which an instructor (a graduate student) wasn't very helpful or positive.

Current student, Engineering, 8/2001-Submit Date, November 2005

I am a chemical engineering major and I felt the courses that I needed to graduate were well laid out for me upon acceptance into the program. They had detailed plans to follow to ensure I had scheduled the right classes. All the course registration is done online and it is an easy-to-use process. I feel the courses I have taken have gotten progressively better as my academic career has progressed. As a freshman and sophomore, most of the courses are large lecture (approx 100 to 300 students) and these are a lot more impersonal and there is not the one-on-one professor interaction that some of the major courses offer. All of my professors hold weekly office hours, so the opportunity to get one-on-one help is there if you take advantage of it. The workload is high compared to other majors but I expected a high workload coming in. It is manageable as I have been able to stay actively involved in student organizations and add a minor on top of it.

 ## Employment Prospects

Current student, 8/2006-Submit Date, May 2007

Penn State students rank in the top percent of college students around the country that lands jobs following the commencement ceremonies. PSU has the largest alumni connection than other university. Having a PSU degree basically sets you up for success.

Current student, 1/2003-Submit Date, March 2007

With the largest alumni network in the world, somewhere around one in nine families has a Penn State alum in it. This is critical because they more than likely loved their time here and are always willing to lend a helping hand. Career fairs can be large and impersonal: attend smaller corporate events instead.

Definitely meet as many people as possible here, especially professors, beca they have a large list of contacts and many came from professional indus before teaching. The Smeal College offers the best placement opportunities a even has the likes of Merrill Lynch, Morgan Stanley, UBS and Goldman Sa come to actively recruits tudents.

Current student, 8/2005-Submit Date, May 2007

Penn State University is an internationally well-known, reputable, accredi university for more than a hundred years. Many graduates do find jobs quick There are many job opportunities that the campus offers to work in labs or work for professors. Internships are posted up on the web site. There are a fairs.

Alumnus/a, 1/2003-5/2006, May 2006

When interviewing, the Penn State brand was respected and well known. I h numerous job offers all across the United States. I found my employers anxic to work with Penn State and my fellow Penn State alumni willing to work w me as a future Penn State alumnus.

Current student, 8/2002-Submit Date, May 2006

I found that the web sites and recruiting I most utilized and that were most he ful toward my major (PR) were within the College of Communications. The c campus recruiting information provided online was also helpful (e.g., résur and cover-letter samples). If I was too busy to go down to the career cente could just log onto its web site and get the information I needed.

Current student, 9/2002-Submit Date, May 2006

Although I'm only 22 years old, I've already traveled to 43 states—all in o year! I have yet to visit a state or location in which nobody knows about Pe State. Penn State has the largest alumni association of any higher educati institution in the U.S. No matter where you go, you are very likely to find Pe State alumni working in some capacity. I've had internship offers with four d ferent companies. All these companies came to PSU to recruit.

 ## Quality of Life

Current student, 8/2006-Submit Date, May 2007

As a freshman, I lived in East, which contains the smallest dorm rooms on ca pus. However, the quality of the rooms is more important than the size. W that being said, the housing services catered to my every need, but one thing t I would like to see is air conditioning in the rooms if possible.

Current student, 1/2003-Submit Date, March 2007

On-campus housing can sometimes leave something to be desired. Housing freshmen is at a premium as the class sizes reach nearer to 9,000 with ea incoming class. Housing in downtown State College can be expensive compa atively, but for the most part it is reasonable (i.e., not NYC). The public tra portation ranges from free on campus to around $2 round-trip to go to the lo Wal-Mart. Most off-campus apartment complexes have their own busing or th compensate you for a public transportation pass. These residences have cheapest monthly rates and some of the nicest facilities—worth looking into, t you miss out on some of the atmosphere when you are off-campus. Also, FBI rated State College as one of the safest mid-sized cities in the world: crim other than underage citations for alcohol abuse, are few and far between "Happy Valley."

Current student, 8/2005-Submit Date, May 2007

The dining facilities are great. There are enough places from which to choo that you will not get tired of the food. The neighborhood campus environme is a great one. I have felt so safe walking around campus, and to reassure safety there are always campus police roaming the streets of the campus.

Current student, 8/2002-Submit Date, May 2006

Penn State tried its best to account for all diets within its dining facilities. I w a vegetarian my first year at PSU and I found that choices for me were wonde ful. Housing staff was always helpful, polite and smiling if we ever had que tions or issues in our dorms (e.g., broken light bulb). One reason I chose PS was based on its appearance. The maintenance of buildings and lawn care we exquisite and over four years that didn't change. Police on and off campus ma emselves available and did seminars early on in our college career to present the safety available to students. Call-safe boxes on campus every 100 feet made me feel safe and comfortable even though I was away from home (especially as a female).

Current student, 9/2002-Submit Date, May 2006

It's hard to get parking at Penn State—but not housing. Since every first-year student has to live on campus, a lot of Penn Staters stay on campus, even after they have completed their first year. It's not hard to find an apartment and roommate off campus, though. Crime and safety is probably similar to any other large campus. Over the past several years, the administration has installed a lot of lighting on campus and in the area. We also have an escort service, so if you don't want to walk back to your place alone at 3 a.m., you can always call the university police, and they'll walk you home. There are many options to live on campus—anything from suites to single rooms.

Social Life

Current student, 8/2006-Submit Date, May 2007

Penn State University Park is its own city. Everything you can possibly think of is available in State College. Popular stores and restaurants are present in the city. I love to shop on College Ave. and eat at Friday's and Red Lobster's.

Current student, 1/2003-Submit Date, March 2007

Two words: Football season. With almost 110,000 screaming fans packed into Beaver Stadium, the atmosphere is life-changing for some. On game-day weekends, State College, PA becomes one of the largest cities in Pennsylvania. Also, the bar scene is superb for the young, socially active crowd on a budget. There are few places in the United States where drinks and food can be had so readily and so inexpensively. The fine dining options are there as well with restaurants like Zola's New World Bistro (excellent, contemporary menu) or Penn State's own Nittany Lion Inn which boasts delicious entrees and topnotch chocolate desserts.

Current student, 8/2005-Submit Date, May 2007

The social life at Penn State University is the best. Even though it's not a good accomplishment for the university, but it was voted the Number Two party school in the country for 2006. There are many bars downtown where many students can go to. However, even if you are 21, it is very hard to get in. Sometimes you might have to supply two forms of ID. They are very serious about no one getting in if they are underage. There are many campus events—this campus is huge, and there is something always going on. Especially during football season, where there is always a celebration. There are many fraternities and sororities of which students can be a part. There are frat houses, mostly on Garner St., which is usually called frat row. They have the parties going on during weekends. It is hard to get if you are a guy however, unless you know a brother. There are no sorority houses; however, sorority girls live on a floor in selected dorm rooms. The dating scene is like any other, there are many many students with whom you're bound to go out on a date. There are many restaurants and shops downtown from a family-owned business, to a well-known business like Coldstone or McDonald's.

Current student, 8/2002-Submit Date, May 2006

Being Greek I was exposed early on to PSU's social scene. I found that the bars (for the most part) were kept clean and provided a great atmosphere for dating and meeting new people. G-man Tuesdays were a favorite for Greeks and specials every night at bars were catered to student budgets. The restaurants downtown had great variety concerning food and pricing. However, the shops (clothes, jewelry) located downtown were very overpriced although they were of great quality. Waffle Shop is always a weekend favorite for us (all students) especially on weekends because they are open very early (3 or 4 a.m. 'til 2 p.m.) and the food is cheap and delicious. "Freshmen think it lasts forever, seniors know it's over in an instant."

Current student, 8/2002-Submit Date, May 2006

The social life at Penn State is unbelievable. Honestly, the best time I've ever had in my life. Even as an underage student not being able to attend the bars, there are so many social events, parties and places to go on and off campus. There are tons of excellent restaurants to eat at downtown and the bars are

ridiculous. We have so much fun going out every weekend and even during the week. That's what I like about Penn State—there's always someone ready and willing to go out and have fun at any time of the day or night because everyone has such different schedules. There is something to do for everyone, whether it be sporting events, such as our amazing football games, or concerts at the BJC, or the Movin' On concert on the HUB lawn, or the nationally renown THON dance marathon. Penn State is the best place to have a collegiate career, hands down!

The School Says

The Pennsylvania State University is one of the nation's premiere public research universities. Penn State and its individual academic programs are highly ranked by such widely read publications as *U.S. News & World Report* and by numerous professional journals and peer reviews.

Penn State has 24 campuses statewide: 21 offering undergraduate education, plus the College of Medicine at Penn State Milton S. Hershey Medical Center, the Penn State Dickinson School of Law with locations at Carlisle and University Park, and the Penn State Great Valley School of Graduate Professional Studies. In addition, the World Campus offers "anywhere, anytime" learning in several undergraduate and professional master's degree programs.

Located in State College, in central Pennsylvania, the University Park campus—Penn State's administrative and research hub—is within a three-hour drive of Pittsburgh and Philadelphia, and within five hours of New York City. The University Park Airport is served by four major airlines.

Total enrollment for all Penn State campuses is approximately 84,000 students, including 42,000 at University Park. More than 600 student clubs and organizations help to personalize the campus and make it easy to make friends and connections. Big 10 athletics, intramural and club sports, and an outstanding schedule of performing arts events in music, theatre, and dance also add a valuable dimension to students' educational experience.

Penn State offers more than 160 majors within eleven academic units. Undergraduates in all fields have an unusually high number of opportunities to work with faculty in conducting hands-on research. Students can also apply to the Schreyer Honors College, which provides a comprehensive honors education unique in the United States.

The Penn State Alumni Association is the largest dues-paying organization of its kind in the country, with more than 159,000 members. With 130 chapters nationwide, the association makes it easy for alumni to stay in touch with the university and with each other. Penn State is a national leader in the number of alumni who contribute financially to their university, a clear indication of alumni regard for the education they received.

For more information on undergraduate admissions, go to: www.psu.edu/dept/admissions/

To view videos about Penn State life, go to: goahead.psu.edu

To learn more About Penn State, go to: www.psu.edu/ur/about.html

Read all of Vault's College Surveys at **www.vault.com/college**—get complete surveys on 100s of colleges and universities, expert advice on applicaton essays and more.

VAULT CAREER LIBRARY **633**

St. Joseph's University

Admissions Office
Bronstein Hall 5600 City Avenue
Philadelphia, PA 19131-1395
Admissions phone: (888) BE-A-HAWK or (610) 660-1300
Admissions fax: (610) 660-1314
Admissions e-mail: admit@sju.edu
Admissions URL: www.sju.edu/admissions/

 ## Admissions

Current student, 8/2002-Submit Date, October 2006

When I applied to the undergraduate program, the university still worked on the rolling admissions schedule. I knew I wanted to attend SJU, so I got all of my essays and recommendations done and mailed in my application in September. I knew I was accepted to SJU before Thanksgiving of my senior year. However, now they do not have rolling admissions—so the process is similar to other universities with deadlines, Early Decision, Early Action and so on.

Current student, 9/2004-Submit Date, September 2006

I applied the year SJU went undefeated, but had applied before basketball season started so I was accepted even before all the attention. This being said, I believe the process is hard in a sense. I know our SAT scores have gone up a lot since the year before me but my best advice is to attend the open-house and bring the application with you. I was accepted before Thanksgiving and had my scholarship before Christmas. I don't think we do interviews but I'm not sure and also, if you are applying to certain schools SJU uses the Common Application that will save you from writing a million essays! I did that so I was able to apply to two schools in one shot!

Current student, 1/2003-Submit Date, December 2004

SJU accepts the Common Application. I went to a strong private high school, but only had mediocre grades. I still got a scholarship because of my SAT score of 1310, and I only pay for half my college education now. If you get a 1400 or higher on your SAT, I think you pretty much get to come here for free.

Current student, 8/2003-Submit Date, May 2004

Admissions is very simple. Interviews are not that important and most schools don't require them. If you think an interview would help you out (if you are witty and good at answering questions) then go for it. It may sway the person's decision to accept you.

Alumnus/a, 8/2000-5/2004, August 2004

Saint Joseph's admissions process has become easier over the past couple of years. In order to get into Saint Joe's, you should maintain at least a 3.0 GPA in high school (although this is not a must have, for there are other qualifications that will get you in as well). For instance, if you are very good at sports, but not very academic, Saint Joe's will accept you for your athleticism. Or, if you have a low GPA, but high SAT scores, you can be accepted as well. Saint Joe's is accepting more and more students every year.

The interview process, although nerve wracking, is relatively painless. The staff is very friendly and very open to whatever you have to offer. Essays do not seem to hold too much of an impact, the most important thing is to be honest when writing them.

I think people are mainly selected on how well they seem to fit the mold of a Saint Joe's student, meaning how well will they fit in here?? Saint Joe's likes students who are really involved in high school, because they think they will be involved in Saint Joe's activities, e.g., athletics and the school paper. This also helps them determine how well you will fit in here. Most students at Saint Joe's are involved in something—it is a very sports enthusiastic school. I myself ran

cross-country and track for them (that's what helped me get into the school- almost full scholarship).

It also helps if you have relatives who attended the school, they like to acce people within the same family (and they give you a break on tuition!!).

So, basically, if you are an involved, semi-smart but look like you try hard hig school student and apply early, chances are you will be accepted into St. Joseph University.

 ## Academics

Current student, 8/2002-Submit Date, October 2006

SJU offers a great education. Because of the general education requirement students are required to take a wide range of courses. I do not know if I wou have taken a philosophy course if three were not required, and they really help me to become a well-rounded individual. Registration can be stressful, but I fe that I always had enough time in my four years to take courses I wanted to tak Some classes are harder to get into than others, but that simply means that if yc cannot get into it as a sophomore, you can probably get into it as a senic Courses are hard; there are not really any classes you can breeze through, bu professors are fair and very open to meeting with students.

Current student, 9/2004-Submit Date, September 2006

Well, I am an elementary education major and the program is amazing. We sta going into classrooms with our first education class. I think the quality of clas es is great. They offer a lot of majors and most let you have a lot of electives i let you take whatever you want. Business is the most popular major here; w have a great business school (almost all of my friends are business majors) bi you don't have to come for business. We also have great chem/bio majors ar psychology, sociology, English—the list goes on and on! Getting the "bes (a.k.a., highest rated on www.ratemyprofessor.com) teachers can be difficult a a freshman. I was lucky enough to have sophomore standing so I got the clas es I wanted most of the time. I can't think of many bad teachers and I've bee here for five semesters now. I love almost all of my teachers and I know the actually care about my education! The workload depends on your major, but fc the required classes (such as philosophy, theology, western civilization), it isn too overbearing!

Alumnus/a, 8/2000-5/2004, March 2006

Accounting faculty and curriculum are outstanding. Technology is a large focu but they also teach the fundamentals with technology so the students get a understanding of how it is done out in the workplace. In the Jesuit tradition, SJ also requires certain arts and science classes including theology, philosophy an sciences. This is a great idea because it makes the student more knowledgeab about the world and not just his/her major. Class sizes are small, which is grea for learning but difficult to get into. As an athlete, I had priority registration s I never had a problem, but I knew of others who did. Grading—not difficult, found my teachers gave little surprises. Workload—I felt it was easy, I didn't gc straight A's but did not study much to keep above a 3.5. I think my high schoc prepared me well.

Current student, 1/2003-Submit Date, December 2004

I am a business major, and the business programs are strong. Most, if not all o the teachers have a PhD and real work experience. There are few adjunct which is nice because you can get help whenever you need it. The 101 classe are fairly simple. If you're getting C's in 101, you're partying too much Getting classes is not hard. If you're a freshman, you get the bottom of the bar rel. Usually, you're not going to get into the easy electives and GEDs over 10 if you're a freshman or sophomore. My best advice is, take early classes, no on ever wants them and the teachers are in better moods. Another plus about SJI is that they have a co-op in the business school. I am in the co-op program, an I love it. Even though you have to go to school during the summer, since yot ork full-time at a company, it is well worth it. It is a paid internship. Most kids [...] between $14 and $17 an hour, and as long as you do well, you usually have [...]ew job offers after graduating. If you're a business major, do the co-op.

urrent student, 8/2003-Submit Date, May 2004

[...] St. Joe's we have good core courses. They form you into a well-balanced and [...]art man or woman. Workload is not as much as most students (in business) [...]d grading is fair. You just have to do well on the tests. Popular classes are [...]d to get into if you are a freshman, but easier as you get into a higher class. [...]ke most schools, some professors are great and some suck.

lumnus/a, 8/2000-5/2004, August 2004

[...]int Joe's has an excellent academic reputation. I myself have become quite a [...]ell-rounded person from attending this school. Saint Joe's is a Jesuit liberal [...]s university. They make you take certain classes, including philosophy, for[...]gn language, religion and sociology, plus a bundle of electives. These classes, [...]pending on your interest in the subjects, may be boring or not boring (it also [...] depends on your teacher).

[...]ofessors all have individual reputations here, like which are hard, which are [...]sy, which are more fun. It depends on how lucky you are getting the class. [...]ass sign-ups are done this way: athletic seniors first, then non-athletic seniors, [...]letic juniors, then non-athletic juniors and so on. So, freshmen who are not [...]letes will have the hardest time getting the classes they want, but as they [...]ogress, it becomes much easier. You have pretty much a 100 percent chance [...] getting the classes you want once you are a senior.

[...]asses are very good here. They teach you a lot and get you involved. Be pre[...]red for a lot of oral presentations!! Saint Joe's prides itself on its ability to [...]ve great orators. There is a capstone class for all senior business majors; most [...]ople start dreading it their freshman year because it is the most dreaded class [...] all. It is called Business Policy and it requires you to analyze a company all [...]mester and then report on it for 20 minutes!!! It takes a lot of work, but real[...] helps to prepare you for the real world.

[...]ost teachers grade using a scale on which a 90 to 100 is an A and so on down [...]e line. Hardly anyone fails out if they care, because most professors are avail[...]le almost 24/7 if you need them. The ratio of students to professors is very [...]od and there is a great chance for one-on-one teaching if you need it. [...]orkload is a lot, actually. You get usually two or three hours of work from each [...]ass, it is up to you how you handle it. Either do it right away or scramble at [...]e last minute.

[...]ottom line: if you want a good, well-rounded education, Saint Joe's is the place. [...]ou must be willing to handle a lot of work, especially if you are an athlete.

Employment Prospects

urrent student, 8/2002-Submit Date, October 2006

[...]he campus has a great Career Development Center, which is great for net[...]orking with area businesses, especially alumni, for both internships and jobs. [...]he Career Development Center hosts two extremely comprehensive Career [...]airs (one each semester), in addition to other resources, such as a Nonprofit [...]areer Fair and information on graduate schools or doing a year of service. [...]hey also host many networking nights and on-campus recruiting for various [...]ompanies. As far as internships, they publish an internship manual that outlines [...]ow to go about getting an internship as well as if your specific department [...]ffers course credit for having an internship.

urrent student, 9/2004-Submit Date, September 2006

[...] you are a business major you will have no problem finding a job. My friend [...]ot an internship with PricewaterhouseCooper as a sophomore and has been [...]sked back for next summer. Math majors are known to get jobs with Lockheed [...]artin and the like, and teachers are almost always given a position the year [...]fter they graduate. There are two career fairs each year and we get hundreds of [...]mployer search time from all around the U.S. and even the world. You do not [...]eed to stay local to get a job! Our Career Development Center also is a great [...]source for internships, co-ops and just general employment.

Alumnus/a, 8/2000-5/2004, March 2006

If you have above a 3.0, the accounting department runs an internship program in the spring semester of your junior year. All the big firms are involved and some others, as well. You are almost guaranteed an internship if you apply for the program and once the internship is completed most receive job offers, so that you have a job before you even start your senior year.

Current student, 1/2003-Submit Date, December 2004

The alumni at SJU are eager to help you. My last two internships have been with alumni. This is great because at graduation, you will probably have a few jobs lined up. There is a job fair, too. A lot of businesses from the Philadelphia area come to SJU, so there are many opportunities. The co-op office is also very diligent getting the students interviews and jobs. All my friends in the co-op program have paid jobs.

Alumnus/a, 8/2000-5/2004, August 2004

Fortunately, Saint Joe's has a good reputation for having great students. Employers usually look to our school to hire within the Philadelphia, New York and Washington, D.C. areas.

Saint Joe's has a career office but it stinks. They are always there to help guide you and help with your résumé, but they really are not good at finding students jobs. It is really up to the students' ambitions in finding a job. We do have job fairs, on-campus interviews, mock interviews and résumé workshops, but it is still very difficult. The marketing majors seem to have it made. Because our marketing department is so prestigious, students who have food marketing or pharmaceutical marketing degrees tend to get spoon-fed their jobs.

Others have quite a hard time. The percentage used to be 91 percent for students graduating to find a job, that percentage probably dropped to about 70 to 80 percent for students now. The factors that will determine job outlook are the particular student's ambition and the job market.

Quality of Life

Current student, 8/2002-Submit Date, October 2006

The quality of life at SJU is great. You have all of the convenience of living in a big city, yet there is definitely still that feeling that it is a smaller school with a distinct campus. While you have to be aware that you are living in Philadelphia, the public safety office in addition to City Ave. bike patrol and Philadelphia police work to keep the campus safe. There is a wide range of housing options including townhouses and apartment style living for upperclassmen, all of which are convenient and close to campus. The newly renovated dining hall has some great new options for students.

Current student, 9/2004-Submit Date, September 2006

Although the school is located in Philadelphia, we have a small-town atmosphere. I never felt unsafe around campus and even when walking around off-campus. Freshmen and sophomores are guaranteed housing and must live at SJU but then it is a lottery for upperclassmen. I was able to get housing this year as a junior. Also, the housing options are vast and none are slums! We are located on a major road with many restaurants and we are currently building two to be put on campus. There is so much to do by campus but you are also just a train ride away from downtown Philadelphia.

Alumnus/a, 8/2000-5/2004, March 2006

Great campus life. The key is to get involved and the university has great events that make it easy to meet people and improve the lives of others in the spirit of Jesuit education. Not what I would call a party school, but we still had some fun. Great location because you're close enough to the city without being in the middle of it. Housing is rough at times but there is plenty of off-campus opportunities. All facilities are top, they are expanding currently to take care of any housing problems. There are bad neighborhoods in close proximity but there is no reason to go there anyway. I never heard of anything happening on campus. Need more parking desperately.

Current student, 8/2003-Submit Date, May 2004

Housing is cramped. They accept a lot of students and freshman classes get bigger and bigger. My freshman year, I shared a room that with six people that was

Read all of Vault's College Surveys at **www.vault.com/college**—get complete surveys on 100s of colleges and universities, expert advice on applicaton essays and more.

VAULT CAREER LIBRARY **635**

maybe 30x15. The freshman dorms are split. There are three. McShain is the nicest one, followed by LaFarge and Sourin. LaFarge and Sourin have no air conditioning, so it is rough for the first three or four weeks of school. They just built a huge dorm, so everything should be OK next year. There is a lot of off-campus housing, which is a lot cheaper. The food is horrendous. Order food off campus often. St. Joe's just rented an apartment building about a mile away for sophomores and up to help them out with the rough living conditions.

Alumnus/a, 8/2000-5/2004, August 2004

Only good things can be said about the quality of life at St. Joe's. We have a beautiful campus, it's small, but the stone buildings and cobblestone sidewalks are gorgeous.

Dining is getting better, we offer the usuals: Pizza Hut, pasta, sandwiches, salads, baked potatoes, basically anything you want. There is an on-campus store that looks exactly like Wawa and you can get anything you want from there off your dining card. The meal plan is not cheap, however.

All our classrooms are technologically advanced, so students can plug into the Internet at every desk, and teachers can post PowerPoints up on the screen for students to take notes. We also have a computer lab for students without computers, and for those having computer problems. They are fixed right there at the front desk.

The neighborhood is dangerous, you don't go walking out alone at night. St. Joe's borders a bad area of Philadelphia. Kids have been mugged before. Now we have street cars patrolling the areas at all times. An escort will walk you to your car or take you home. They are very big on safety at St. Joe's. They have 24-hour patrol and emergency help buttons all over campus.

Parking is a bit of an ordeal at St. Joe's. They built a new parking garage to help appease some of the complaints, but sometimes if you have a car, you have to park almost 15 minutes away from campus. Some don't like to leave their cars parked in bad areas for that long. They are trying to work on that issue, but I won't lie, parking is a major major hassle.

 ## Social Life

Current student, 8/2002-Submit Date, October 2006

I was a member of Greek life on the SJU campus, and from that I was really able to be involved in a lot of different things. There is a very vibrant campus community with almost anything that you would want to be involved in available to students with the possibility of starting an organization if your interests are not met. However, Greek life is not overpowering at SJU; in fact, it only makes up about 16 percent of the student body. Students are also very involved in annual events, such as Up 'Til Dawn, benefiting St. Jude Children's Research Hospital, Hand-in-Hand, a carnival for developmentally disabled individuals, and the Thanksgiving Dinner Dance, which brings in people from nursing homes for a night of dinner and dancing. If you are 21, Old City is just a train ride away as well as Lancaster Ave. and Narberth have a lot of bars that have great specials for college students.

Current student, 9/2004-Submit Date, September 2006

We have no bars on campus, and two restaurants will be open next year. T Greek system is very small so it is not like you have to be in a frat/sorority to out/have fun. Parties occur every weekend at various apartments/houses. The are no clubs/bars nearby, but Manayunk, a hip neighborhood, is only a $20 c ride and downtown is only a train ride away. SJU sponsors non-alcoholic wee ly events called SJU Til Two and also the Student Union Board has vario events throughout the year including Tuesday night movies.

Alumnus/a, 8/2000-5/2004, March 2006

Manayunk is pretty much the campus for seniors that offers a great young po ulation with plenty of bars. Greek system is not very good, no houses a allowed on campus. There were two good frats that participated in the comm nity and university and another two that were more like *Animal House* (you f ure out by your senior year who is graduating and has jobs). The sororities a much more involved and give back to others. As an athlete I stayed out of t frats. Being close to the city, there are plenty of bars, restaurants and clubs. T only issue was where to get the money to go.

Current student, 8/2003-Submit Date, May 2004

There are a lot of bars nearby and many restaurants in downtown Phil Everyone drinks, even the service kids. There are events called SJU Til Two Friday and Saturdays, which no one goes to. There are a lot of clubs in Phil Greeks have parties all the time at off-campus houses. They are a lot of fu There are a million different clubs and activities on campus and there is de nitely one for everybody. The school has a great spirit and its basketball tea and its fans are second to none. I currently am a member of a Greek organiza tion on campus. We are unlike most other fraternities at major colleges. We a an organization that volunteers and helps out at many school events and rate the Top 10 in the country in raising money for our philanthropy. We do not ha on-campus housing for Greek organizations due to the university's ruling.

Swarthmore College

Admissions Office

00 College Avenue

Swarthmore, PA 19081

Admissions phone: (610) 328-8300

Admissions fax: (610) 328-8580

Admissions e-mail: admissions@swarthmore.edu

Admissions URL: www.swarthmore.edu/admissions/

 ## Admissions

Current student, English, 8/2006-Submit Date, June 2007

If you really love Swarthmore and know that it's the perfect school for you, then I would strongly encourage you to apply Early Decision. Swarthmore has two rounds of Early Decision admissions, with round two applications due on the same day as the Regular Decision applications. This allows students to have more time to decide if Swarthmore is truly the place they want to go.

Admissions at Swarthmore is more holistic than at other schools, where the emphasis is placed on GPA and test scores. While test scores and grades are important in the folder-reading process, what really get you in is going to be your personality, which the admissions counselors get a sense of through your extracurriculars, recommendations and personal statements (essays). What Swarthmore really looks for is intellectual curiosity—this isn't to say that they're looking for bookworms who never leave the library. Instead, they look for students whose intellectual curiosity is piqued in and out of the classroom. Swarthmore also looks for students who care about the world in which they live in, to fit with the school's teaching of "ethical intelligence." The admissions counselors are not just looking for smart kids, but they're looking for students who will use their intelligence for the betterment of their community.

Current student, English, 8/2005-Submit Date, May 2007

The admissions process for Swarthmore is pretty standard for a selective liberal arts school. The key difference is the "Why Swarthmore" essay. This part of the Swarthmore supplement to the Common App is essentially there to gauge applicants' desire to come to Swarthmore as well as their writing skills. My best advice is to be honest, and people who have a hard time finding a topic should really reassess whether they really want to come to Swarthmore.

Swarthmore College is a very selective institution, having only about 1,500 students. It is also a very unique environment of quirky, passionate intellectuals. Swarthmore is hard to get into, but if you sincerely feel like you're a good fit and would be happy at Swarthmore (with a good grades and service record), then you probably have a pretty good chance of getting in.

Social activism is also a strong part of the Swarthmore Quaker heritage. Swarthmore looks for people who are engaged and active in implementing programs of volunteerism and social change because the college has resources to nurture and develop those desire further. If you are interested in changing the world (literally) and Swarthmore is the place for you and the place to help you do it.

Current student, 8/2006-Submit Date, May 2007

Swarthmore students (Swatties) tend to be a weird bunch—in the best possible way. Everyone has some weird passion that they devote a lot of their time to. These passions may or may not be visible in the Swattie's everyday dress. It sometimes seems as though everyone plays or has played a musical instrument, speaks or has spoken a foreign language, and lives or has lived abroad. The school attracts these people like moths to a flame.

But never fear if you're normal—the school doesn't discriminate. The admissions process is proudly need blind—thank goodness, or I probably wouldn't be here—and they take the essay very seriously. Swarthmore likes to hear about "the whole person"—not just an agglomeration of statistics and extracurriculars.

Interviews are not mandatory, but recommended, and the school has alumni interviewers who can interview students who live far away.

Current student, 9/2004-Submit Date, May 2007

If at all possible, visit the school. If not, call admissions to find out how to get in contact with current students. Because it's so competitive to get into Swarthmore, the most important thing is figuring out if you're the right "fit"—which of course is an incredibly complicated thing that can't really be defined. The best way to get an understanding is definitely to talk to people already at Swat. You don't have to have straight A's or perfect test scores, but you do have to demonstrate that you're incredibly passionate about whatever it is you're interested in (or multiple things you're interested in), and that you would truly thrive in an environment like Swarthmore, where we strive to be diverse, cultivate a critical consciousness, and are collaborative in our learning processes.

Current student, 8/2002-Submit Date, October 2003

What Swarthmore looks for in an applicant is very specific: a well-rounded genius. To be honest, there's one thing common to all Swatties, they're smart as hell.

Unlike Swarthmore's peers, such as Amherst or Harvard, the admissions board at Swarthmore is not looking for a killer athlete who is only mundane when it comes to academics. It's not looking for a famous actress to boost the school's national popularity. In fact, Swarthmore is not even looking for an abnormally gifted computer geek who doesn't like smelling the roses on a sunny day. Swarthmore looks for the applicant who isn't just a state-champion athlete, but is also a genius computer programmer, an eloquent political debater, and a precocious musician all in the same body and mind.

When I first came to Swarthmore and began talking to people, I learned that one dynamic thing Swatties have in common is that they are diverse in their intellectual endeavors. Only at Swat do you have engineering/art history or physics/philosophy double majors. Even as a sophomore, I am still up in the air as to major in math, economics, English or philosophy.

 ## Academics

Current student, 9/2003-Submit Date, May 2007

Academics are important at Swarthmore and the professors do expect a lot from the students. However, there is also a lot of support available to ease students through their four years. First, and probably the most important, is that the first semester of a student's freshman year is entirely credit/no credit—this means that the focus is away from the grades and centered on, "how to do Swat." This semester was really helpful because high school can be very grade/number focused, and since Swarthmore doesn't calculate a GPA or rank students, the numbers are not important. It is more important that students know what writing a college paper is like, what professors are looking for in terms of participation and how to balance academics with sports, clubs and life in general. Time management and balance are crucial aspects of success in college, no matter where you go.

What is great about Swarthmore's courses, though, is that they are all amazing. There is no weak department, registration is based on a fair lottery and not first come first serve, and classes are not canceled due to under-enrollment. It is quite normal to have class with three people, or even to create a course that is just you and the professor. During my time here Arabic was offered as a not-for-credit class; it [is now a part of the continuing program in the department of modern languages.] It is amazing to think that this happened because a group of students was interested in learning a topic and made sure it became a reality.

When talking about academics it is also important to mention that we are in a consortium with Bryn Mawr and Haverford Colleges, so we can take any course at those schools for free and they can take classes at Swarthmore. This is great because it opens up the possibility of finding a never-ending supply of fun and

Read all of Vault's College Surveys at **www.vault.com/college**—get complete surveys on 100s of colleges and universities, expert advice on applicaton essays and more.

VAULT CAREER LIBRARY 637

interesting classes. If you do attend a course there we have a shuttle that loops between the three schools all daylong, and it's free to ride on. We also have an academic agreement with the University of Pennsylvania, and since we have a train on our campus that goes directly to their campus in less than 25 minutes, it is easy to get there (and Swarthmore foots the transportation bill and will reimburse you). I like to call it the four-for-one deal—four schools for the price of one.

Current student, 9/2004-Submit Date, May 2007

The academics are rigorous, but incredibly engaging. It's a liberal arts school, and while we don't have a core curriculum, we do have some very general distribution requirements. Grades and test scores are definitely not emphasized here—it's more about what you want to get out of your classes. The professors are all amazing and brilliant—and most of them are incredibly approachable as well. I've developed several very close relationships with my professors (as well as some of the deans). It's not very hard to get research opportunities with your professors—usually, you can get grant money for it as well. Swarthmore strives to maintain a small academic environment, so although there are a few extremely popular classes that you might get lotteried out of one semester, when that does happen, you're usually on the top of the priority list for the next time the course is offered. But, in general, getting the classes you want isn't an issue at all. There's a lot of reading, but you learn how to read the important parts—professors are also very helpful in providing reading strategies, because they admit that they don't expect you to read everything that they've assigned! What it comes down to is how much you want to engage with the material and with the other students and professor—and typically, if you're at Swarthmore, you really do care about those things.

Current student, English, 8/2005-Submit Date, May 2007

The wonderful thing about a small school is the intimate relationships you develop with professors. Swarthmore's classes are very academically rigorous, but they are also filled with facets of help and advice for when you need it. Professors have weekly office hours that they invite students to attend. I go as much to talk about my course work as about my life in general.

Classes are rigorous because of the people in them. Class discussions generate almost from nothing and can last way past the class time. Classes are also pretty easy to get into. Although popular courses are lotteried, professors are lenient and will let you into courses (over limit) if you show in the dedication and interest to really get something from the class.

Grading is serious. There really is no grade inflation at Swarthmore. The T-shirts that say: "Anywhere else it would be an A" are only half-joking. At first, it can be quite a shock for some people, especially overachievers that are used to getting straight A's in high school. The adjustment is pretty quick. You learn the ways to deal with lots of work and again, professors and fellow students are always around to help.

Current student, 9/2006-Submit Date, May 2007

Academics at Swarthmore are intense, but not impossible—not by any stretch of the imagination. Workload always depends on the class, but I rarely feel as if I have too much. Besides, ideally you are taking classes because they interest you ad that does so much for making the work go by quickly. There is an honors program at Swarthmore styled after the Oxford tutorial system, which substitutes double credit seminars for some regular courses. You can be an Honors major, minor or both. However, all students are encouraged to take seminar-style classes, even if they aren't in the Honors Program, and there are freshman year seminars so incoming students can have the experience. I highly recommend Freshman Year Seminars, I took two, and since they were capped at either 10 or 12 students (as all seminars are), I felt really involved in the class and got to know my teachers very well. Class sizes are usually pretty small; last semester I didn't have any class with more than 12 people in it, which I felt was an experience very unique to Swarthmore. Grading depends a lot on the teacher and the first semester freshman year is credit/no credit, meaning although your work is graded, no final grades show up on your transcript and they do not affect your GPA. Pretty much all Swatties think first semester rocks. There are a number of amazing professors at Swat.

 ## Employment Prospects

Current student, English, 8/2006-Submit Date, June 2007

Swarthmore graduates often head to some of the nation's top graduate schools obtain their degrees. Swarthmore is known by the top graduate schools and th top employers as being one of the best undergraduate academic environments the country. They know that the rigorous academic program will have prepare Swat grads. For example, of some of the former seniors that lived on my ha this year, one of is going to Georgetown Law, another to Cornell Law, another going to Columbia, and another is going to start work with a business firm London. Although the number of Swarthmore alumni is smaller than oth schools, the alumni network is very strong and I've known several people wh have found work through alumni. Swarthmore's Career Services Department very helpful and successful in finding employment and internship opportuniti for students and there is a Pre-law/Pre-med office that helps students in apply ing to these schools

Current student, 9/2006-Submit Date, May 2007

There is an extensive alumni network surrounding Swarthmore and a number alumni open their homes to students over the summer or offer internships an externships. Career services sends out mailings to students often and some st dents begin visiting them before senior year. They are great at helping studen find jobs, summer work, internships and so on. They also hold workshops an networking dinners and lend out quality suits for interviews. Many Swat st dents go to graduate school, and over half go within five years of leaving Swa Many students also go to medical school and our acceptance rates for medica school are around 80 percent (about twice the national average). Although no everyone has heard of Swarthmore, it has been getting more press in the last cou ple of years and I'm not worried about being able to find a job when I graduat

Current student, 9/2004-Submit Date, May 2007

There are always e-mails and reminders about alumni networking opportuniti as well as job recruiting on campus. We have a Career Services Center that' incredibly helpful—with everything from researching internships, practicing fo interviews, to getting assistance with your résumé. Swarthmore students hav incredibly high success rates at getting into graduate school programs, as well a both law schools and medical schools. If you graduate from Swarthmore, you'r prepared to do pretty much whatever you want, and there's a ton of support fo you from the institution itself.

Current student, 8/2002-Submit Date, October 2003

The majority of Swatties isn't interested in scoring big on Wall Street. Th majority is interested in helping humanity, volunteering to fight global AIDS, o fighting against the unjust actions of society, government and big corporations Not surprisingly, many Swatties become lawyers (they are often accepted to th best law schools in the country) or professors (Swarthmore ranks fourth in raw number of students who go on to obtain PhDs). Note: Swarthmore is tiny, an ranks first when you consider percentage of students who end up with PhDs.

> **The school states:** "Swarthmore is third among colleges and universities in the percentage of students earning PhDs, not first as the passage indicates."

Career placement greatly depends on the state of the economy, but I can say tha many big-name companies come to Swarthmore to recruit. Yet you mus remember what Swatties ultimately seek: greater wisdom and an end to worl suffering (I am not kidding at all!). Grad school and Peace Corps are the popu lar choices by far when it comes to post-grad decision making.

Prestige? Ask anyone who has ever heard of Swarthmore and he/she will be impressed by the name. However, people don't come to Swarthmore for its world reputation (even though my class consists of students from more than 30 countries and all 50 states). They come to Swarthmore because they know it is a utopia for gifted and passionate thinkers.

Quality of Life

Current student, Sociology, 9/2004-Submit Date, May 2007

Sharples is the only dining hall on campus, which is great. There's no confusion about where to eat or meet up with friends for meals. The only downside is finding seating for enough of your friends at peak mealtimes, like 6 p.m. Generally, though, it's not a problem, and it's great to be able to turn meals into social hours and visit with all of your friends in the dining hall. The quality of food is pretty good. It's certainly not home-cooking, but I don't think any college food is ever comparable to mom's. Sharples does do its best to buy organic fruits and veggies, cook in oil with no trans-fat, and ask for student input on food with something called The Napkin Board. Students can tack up suggestions on types of food, quality of meals, or even new recipes you'd like to see. The dining hall looks at all suggestions and works with students, which is great.

The neighborhood of Swarthmore has little to offer Swarthmore College students. With the exception of the pizza joint and the recent addition of a Dunkin' Donuts, the borough of Swarthmore only has a few stores that are of little interest to college students. The relationship between Swatties and the borough, therefore, is not strained but simply lacks any substantial connection because of the lack of interaction. The one advantage of living in a boring, upper-class, suburban neighborhood is knowing that the neighborhood is safe. As an extension, the campus itself is very safe. Of course there are still Public Safety officers who patrol campus and make sure students are safe, but the general atmosphere on campus is laid back with most students not thinking about crime at all.

Current student, English,, 8/2006-Submit Date, June 2007

Housing at Swarthmore is much better than at other colleges. I've visited friends at a variety of colleges (big state school, small liberal arts school, urban Ivy League) and their dorms could not compare to Swarthmore's dorms in terms of cleanliness, room size and appearance. The school really takes pride in placing roommates together who they know will get along—with a roommate questionnaire (sent at the beginning of June to admitted students) that lists questions beyond the standard ones and seek to understand your personality. There is a Resident Assistant on each hall and each dorm will have SAMs (Student Academic Mentors) and ITS (Information and Technology Services) to also serve as resources.

The campus is located in the nationally-recognized Scott Arboretum and the grounds are filled with beautiful flowers and trees and are well-maintained. The academic buildings are located separately from the residential buildings, which is nice because it makes it feel as if the academics aren't too connected to your life. The buildings at Swarthmore are very beautiful, each with their own distinct style, though all of them fit fantastically together.

Current student, 9/2006-Submit Date, May 2007

Housing at Swarthmore really tipped the scales for me when I visited. So many schools had dorms that were dark and festering and gloomy, while even the less desirable dorms at Swat have decent sized rooms, decent hall life and kitchens. I've single-sex housing by choice, but it really is some of the nicest housing on campus with huge rooms, and plenty of coed mingling (half of my best friends are guys).

There is no freshman housing and freshmen are put in pretty much all of the dorms with a mix of sophomores and upperclassmen who are very eager to socialize. There is only one dining hall and although the food isn't as good as some, there are plenty of options and other cafes and coffee bars to get food from on campus (and there is an ice cream endowment which means ice cream at both lunch and dinner every day!). There are also woks and frying pans in the dining hall if you feel like whipping something up using ingredients at the salad bar.

The campus itself is beautiful and intertwined with an arboretum. It is a beautiful place to walk around and I often find myself spending more time outside than in. I have always felt extremely safe at Swat and it takes me a little while to know that to say when people ask me about it because I just don't think about it that much. The town of Swarthmore is small and also very safe. The school has a health center open 24/7 which is free for all students and they also offer free, confidential psychological services to anyone who wants them. There are so many clubs and organizations here I can't begin to list them, but we pretty much have everything and they are all student run, so if anyone wants to start a club he/she can, and getting funding is very easy.

Current student, 9/2004-Submit Date, May 2007

Housing isn't anything special, but it's decent to good. The college is situated in a very small suburb with a low crime rate—the few incidents that do happen are reported, and the college is usually pretty good about getting the word out and investigating. The food is fine—some days are better than others, but there's always several different kinds of cereal, a huge salad bar, a waffle maker, an omelet maker, a wok, sandwich materials, pita and hummus and ice cream. There's a ton of different facilities as far as athletics go, and there's all sorts of campus spaces for other things, like art, music, meeting spaces, theater and dance. We have several big-screen T.V.s spread throughout campus, and all the dorms have lounges for study breaks and other events. The campus is also incredibly beautiful (being situated on an arboretum), and the Crum woods are great to walk through to clear your mind (or hold a bonfire).

Social Life

Current student, 9/2003-Submit Date, May 2007

To explain all of the social life possibilities on campus would take forever. What is important to know is that the majority of these events are funded by the college but conceived of and run by the students. This means that any club, organization, or even just a single person can create an event, apply for funding and host it on campus. It is even possible to throw a birthday party for your friend, roommate or even yourself and to get college funding as long as it is open to the entire campus. Our Quaker roots also make "equal access" really important, so everything on campus is free once you arrive. You don't pay for movies, shuttles to Philadelphia, sporting events, the gym, concerts, plays and so on: all free! Not to mention that our consortium with Bryn Mawr and Haverford Colleges is also a social agreement, so you can hop on the free shuttle to those schools and attend any of their events for free as well. There is never a lack of something to do.

The Dean's Office is also really great and they pay for a ton of great events. For example, every winter they pay for any student to go to the Penn's Landing River Rink to ice skate (this includes transportation, entrance and skate rental). They also had a trip to see the King Tut exhibit at the Franklin Institute and a tour of Chinatown (all free!). It's really nice going to a school where the administration thinks about students and actually uses the school's money to make life fun.

During the year there are also tons of traditions such as the Screw Your Roommate Dance, where you set your roommate up on a blind date and they have to dress up in costume to find their date in the dining hall. The Crum Regatta is when students make "boats" and try to see who can make it to the finish line while sailing down Crum Creek. At the end of the year we also have spring fling which includes lots of BBQs, a carnival, a music festival and other fun treats like water ice, ice cream, sushi and so on. We also have movie nights on our large lawn that are hosted by Student Council.

I can't forget the fact that we have a train station on our campus and it takes only 20 minutes to get into Philadelphia, which is filled with things for students to do. There are discounts through Campus Philly, free admission to the museums on the first Friday of the month, lots of bars, clubs, and other events going on. It's also nice to walk around on sunny days or go shopping at the various stores. Let's also not forget the sports events like the Eagles, Flyers or Sixers games. Philly is definitely a sports lover's dream city.

Current student, English, 8/2005-Submit Date, May 2007

There are always things to do on campus. Weekends have many dances and student group activities. We have three student groups: Student Budget Committee, Large-Scale Events Committee, and Student Activities Committee that are dedicated to creating fun opportunities on campus. Students are also eligible for funds to make their own activities, examples including fondue parties, Polaroid snapshots of campus sites and so on, so long as they invite everyone on campus.

Read all of Vault's College Surveys at **www.vault.com/college**—get complete surveys on 100s of colleges and universities, expert advice on application essays and more.

VAULT CAREER LIBRARY   639

Nothing that receives committee funds is exclusive. Most of the time, students just chill out on Parrish Beach (the lawn of the school) and play frisbee, bocce, and smoke hookah. The atmosphere is pretty relaxed and there is never a pressure to party and drink if you're not the type.

Current student, 9/2004-Submit Date, May 2007

The social life is pretty diverse here. There are two fraternities, and while they certainly contribute to the party scene, they in no way dominate it. There's a really cool concert space for indie bands and artists (for example, we've had Clap Your Hands Say Yeah come, as well as Mr. Lif, the Hold Steady, and more). As far as cultural and support groups go, we have the Intercultural Center, which sponsors [numerous] groups related to identity (for example, Enlace is for Latino/a students, Swarthmore Queer Union is for queer and questioning students and Deshi is a group about South Asian culture). The Black Cultural Center is a great house that serves to support black students on campus. Similarly, we have a Women's Resource Center that hosts discussion groups, has a bunch of reading material, and does other support and outreach efforts. Paces is a space that serves as a late-night, student-run cafe Sun. through Wed., on Thursday plays host to "Pub Nite" (which is a senior class fundraiser), and on Fridays and Saturdays holds parties. There are also movie showings happening all the time, ranging from independent films to just released mainstream movies. There are constantly different performing arts events happening, as well as visual arts gallery openings and concert recitals. Basically, on any given day there are about 10 different things that you could do, all of them equally exciting. As far as the dating scene goes—it's a small school. But there's always nearby Bryn Mawr and Haverford, as well as Philadelphia.

The School Says

Swarthmore has long been known as an academic powerhouse, distinguished by its deliberately small size, unique honors program, and idyllic campus. What might surprise are the breadth of the curriculum (the school offers some 600 courses a year, on par with much larger colleges) and a campus culture that eases the pressure by emphasizing collaboration over competition. On top of that, Swarthmore offers an engineering program, something of a rarity among liberal arts colleges.

There are few places with classes smaller than at Swarthmore, where the student-faculty ratio is eight to one. Three-quarters of Swarthmore classes have fewer than 20 students, and more than 90 percent have fewer than 30. Professors are deeply committed to their students, keeping their offices and sometimes even their homes open to the students.

But many Swatties will tell you that their fellow students are some of their best teachers. Everyday conversation in dorm rooms and over meals in the dining hall are as likely to center on Dostoyevsky or Middle East politics as last night's party. Students set up informal study groups and departments offer weekly clinics where students can drop in to get and give help on the week's work. The first semester of the freshman year is pass/fail, which helps ease the transition to college life.

Academic seriousness has long been a Swarthmore forte, and it remains true today as evidenced by the large number of students who win prestigious fellowships. Swarthmore students have received 138 Fulbrights, 17 Goldwater Scholarships, eight Marshalls, 78 Mellon Mays Fellowships, 13 National Endowment for the Humanities Grants for Younger Scholars, 231 National Science Foundation Graduate Fellowships, 26 Rhodes Scholarships, 21 Truman Fellowships, 66 Watson Fellowships, and 35 Woodrow Wilson Fellowships.

While this Philadelphia-area school serves as a solid stepping stone to graduate school and academic careers, increasingly, Swatties are also applying their rigorous academic training to the business world, the professions, and other careers. Among the ranks of Swarthmore alumni are Jonathan Franzen, author of the prize-winning novel *The Corrections*; Robert Zoellick, President of The World Bank; Anne Schuchat, a top scientist at the Centers for Disease Control; Justin Hall, widely recognized as the Web's first blogger; Nancy Grace Roman, mother of the Hubble space telescope, and Patrick Awuah, a former Microsoft manager who has returned to Ghana to found that country's first liberal arts college. Among Swarthmore alumni, there are five Nobel Laureates, 16 Macarthur "Genius" Fellows, and numerous Pulitzer Prize and Academy Award winners.

At Swarthmore, a commitment to academic excellence is matched by a desire to put intellectual and analytical skills towards creating a more peaceful and just world. For example, students recently have prodded corporate America to extend employee anti-discrimination policies to sexual orientation; taken on e-voting giant Diebold and won over the right to publish company memos on the Internet; begun War News Radio, a sophisticated Internet-based radio program on the war in Iraq, and launched the U.N.-recognized Genocide Intervention Network, which is in the forefront of the fight to bring to an end the humanitarian disaster in the Darfur region of Sudan.

Temple University

Office of Undergraduate Admissions
Broad Street and Montgomery Avenue
041-09
Philadelphia, PA 19122-6096
Admissions phone: (215) 204-7200 or (888) 340-2222
Admissions URL: www.temple.edu/undergrad

Admissions

Current student, 9/2002-Submit Date, April 2006

Temple's admissions process was one of the simplest I encountered when applying to colleges. Everything is clearly outlined in the application. The essay was refreshing. While it's not a terribly specific topic ("Please tell us about something that has contributed to your academic success"), it forced me to really narrow down what my academic strengths were, and how they were shaped and maintained. You'll need a strong GPA and SAT—I had a 3.19 and a 1170 back in 2002. Today, I would fall at the lower end of the range for the GPA, and at the higher end of the average SAT. I wasn't nervous about whether or not I'd be admitted. Temple did not have an interview available for prospective students when I applied.

Current student, 8/2004-Submit Date, April 2006

After receiving tons of mailings, I sifted through and started reading about the communications and theater programs at some of the more well-known schools. Temple University was my last choice prior to visiting because of the biases I attached to the institution. I thought it was too run-down and would not sound prestigious coming out of my mouth when designating my school of choice. I spoke to my guidance counselor at least once a week, being completely overzealous in perfecting my essay, recommendations and applications to all the institutions I had chosen. I picked some well-known names, but in the end realized I was being foolish. While some schools' names might sound pretty, they did not offer me the closely linked experience of both communications and theater. Temple University's state-of-the-art school for both of these was my best option. So I started reorganizing my thoughts, and started factoring in price, housing, and likelihood of great internships and opportunities. In the end, while the admissions process was lengthy, stressful and often times tedious, I found out where my priorities were (and should be) through the steps I took to complete my applications and pick my school! I couldn't be happier!

Current student, 1/2005-Submit Date, March 2006

On my visit I stayed in a dorm. Of course, I checked out the theatre department. I looked around at the facilities, talked with a professor and sat in on a class. The class was a nice size—only 12 students.

Visiting Temple totally confirmed my decision to go there. I just liked everything about it. And I felt like this was where I wanted to go.

I moved to Philadelphia and wanted to go back to school for my BA. I visited the campus and met with an academic counselor, when he told me that I would be a great candidate for admissions. I asked about price and he told me about some financial aid, which I signed up for. My interview consisted of a look back on my other schools I attended and my GPA, and of course, why I left school before graduating. I told them of a death in my family and they understood. My grades were good. My references also came through very promising. I was worried they would pass me over maybe because of my age or because I'd have to work full time while going back to school. I was accepted and here I am!

Current student, 9/2002-Submit Date, May 2004

The admissions process consists only of filling out an application. Temple waives application fees for select students. A prospective merely waits to see if he or she got in. They encourage all prospectives to visit the campus and talk with current students and teachers. There was no interview and only a couple short-answer essays. Temple is a public school, so selectivity is not as high as at some private schools. However, there is a huge influx of applicants, so the standards are being raised annually. Only a select few of those accepted then get selected for the honors program. The hardest school to get into, though, especially honors, is the business school. They have been putting a lot of time and effort in trying to make Temple Business as good of a name as UPenn Wharton Business. The rest of the schools, such as the liberal arts and education schools, are relatively easy to enter.

On a similar note, it is extremely easy to transfer from school to school. The only exception is the business school, where you need a certain GPA to get in. Plus, because the business program is so comprehensive, it is unlikely that any student would want to transfer after freshman year.

Academics

Current student, 9/2002-Submit Date, April 2006

As a communications and political science major, I find myself in two very popular programs on campus. My experience with professors has been more than positive. Many of my professors are adjuncts, which allows for so much up-to-the-minute and insider information on just how the communications and journalism world functions. I feel—and I tell my family and friends this all the time—like I am truly a more informed and more intelligent person than when I entered the university. I have been challenged both academically and personally to create work that is original in thought and style. As I'm studying two very popular curricula, so I've taken some of the most popular classes on campus. My experience with classes that and I've needed to take, and may have already been full when it came time for me to register has been generally positive. Most of the time, if you need to take a course, and it is full, simply contacting the professor scheduled to teach that course in the next semester, and gaining his/her permission to take on another student is all I've had to do to register for a popular course. Grading is fair. I've had teachers who will give just about anyone an A, and teachers who think that a grade of a C is perfectly acceptable as a "great grade." As I said before, I've had the privilege of working with many people who are currently teaching, and conducting research, or working as an anchor or as a reporter, as well. As is common, there has been the occasional professor who is very traditional, has been at Temple for a long time, and has little interest in flexibility. My workload has been heavy. I've had maybe two semesters that were not overwhelming in terms of the sheer amount of work to complete. There's a lot of reading at Temple—it's a research university, so your professors are constantly coming into new and relevant information that they find will enhance the class.

Current student, 8/2004-Submit Date, April 2006

The academics at Temple, especially in my field of communications and theater, are superb. There is no better place to study the media than with professors who either just came from management positions in the field, or are even teaching part-time and actually simultaneously working in a TV studio or radio station. The classes that I've taken and my professors have been very helpful in guiding me toward my future goals. While I had to be proactive, my teachers were very accessible and helpful—my one media management professors helped me with my internship and actually knew the head honchos at the TV studio I was writing to, and went on to write them e-mails. The grading is definitely fair for the work each student puts in. While the workload for basic classes is not too intense, if a student's attendance slacks, he/she will feel the effects. Not to mention, the selection and availability is great, and getting better. While I had a problem getting into one of the classes I had to take, I spoke to the teacher and ended up being written in as an additional student. Basically, the institution did everything it could (and more specifically my professor did her best to accommodate me).

Current student, 9/2002-Submit Date, May 2004

The general program at Temple has a lot of classes with 40 or more students, and lecture halls with 100 or more students. These classes, although a little cramped,

Read all of Vault's College Surveys at www.vault.com/college—get complete surveys on 100s of colleges and universities, expert advice on applicaton essays and more.

VAULT CAREER LIBRARY 641

are still of good quality. Temple has a requirement that all teachers have at least a master's degree in order to teach. This makes students feel more confident about their learning. TAs are used only for grading papers and focus groups for lecture halls. Popular classes are very hard to get as a freshman or sophomore, but easier the higher up you get. The workload for the general program is split 50-50. Half are really easy and actually make you feel bored and angry that you wasted your money. The other half give you so much work that your other classes might suffer. The only way to find any teacher in the middle is to ask a lot of students.

The Honors Program is more personal. There's a max of 25 students allowed per class, and all the teachers are extremely qualified. They promote a relaxed environment to ask questions (which helps a lot), and they really care about your education and helping you with any problems in or out of the class. The classes are very good, and you learn a lot if you put the time into it. Popular honors classes are relatively easy to get, since only honors students can get them. Even if one were full, though, if you show a big interest in the class, it is pretty easy to convince the teacher to squeeze you in. Grading for honors students is a little tougher, because teachers expect more. However, this gets balanced by the slightly easier workload. Teachers expect us to know (or quickly pick up) the basics of subjects, so they move on to harder, more in-depth work. This keeps pushing honors students to do better.

Alumnus/a, 9/1996-5/2000, April 2004

Temple's academic nature can be broken into two parts: the university core curriculum and your major curriculum. The university's core is a number of classes ranging from math and science to English and art history. During the initial freshman placement tests, you have the opportunity to "place out" of some of these core classes. The list of university core was a little more than half of the total credits needed to graduate. In 1996, I needed 122 credits to graduate. 64 of them were university core. Some people may see taking this many credits outside of their major to be tiresome. But I feel that is the perk of attending a liberal arts university. You do get a little bit of everything and become a well-rounded student.

I never had any trouble getting popular classes. I always registered right away, so there was never any trouble. Most basic core classes can be big. I'd guess tops 150 students. But, once you advance in your studies, classes become smaller and smaller. Grading was based on the system set up by each professor. University passing was C-. If you did not pass a class, you had to repeat the course for the grade to change on your record. I felt the workload was always manageable. I'm convinced that college studies are not difficult, only the time management of getting it all done well is hard. I had wonderful professors in both my core and major studies. They all made themselves available to me. I never had a problem or a professor whom I didn't like. I was able to graduate in four years (eight semesters). I took an average of 14 to 18 credits per semester with one big haul of 21 credits my final semester. I worked throughout college at part-/full-time jobs. I graduated with honors and a 3.5 GPA.

 ## Employment Prospects

Current student, 9/2002-Submit Date, April 2006

Philadelphia is the sixth largest city in the country, and so if a student has an interest in staying in the greater Philadelphia area, there will be little to no problem finding a place to work. Temple's name is known for several of our majors here: communications/journalism, business, anything with medicine, law, architecture and art. There are plenty of opportunities for internships, Temple even has a career office where you can go to gain information about internships in Philadelphia.

Current student, 8/2004-Submit Date, April 2006

From the day I stepped foot on Temple University's campus, I was bombarded with opportunities. From jobs to internships, to paige positions to seminars and helpful events, I never felt as though I wasn't in the know. Not to mention, we have great resources on campus to aid students in seeking jobs and preparing for interviews. We have a service that will help you prepare for an interview by taping you and allowing you to critique your performance. But aside from the services provided by the institution, I've found my teachers to be my greatest mentors—providing me with amazing advice!

Current student, 9/2002-Submit Date, May 2004

The business school seems to isolate itself from the rest of the university. Th put a lot of emphasis on getting their students to enter the professional worl They have their own career counselors who hold regular workshops and even that help business students find good internships and build strong résumés to g a solid job after graduation. In the past few years, Temple business has gott better name recognition, so more top businesses are recruiting from Templ Because of the higher standards and placing students in fields they want to ent the business school is making a good track record with employers over the qu ity of their students.

The rest of the university also has career counselors and events that help studer find jobs. These services are broader than the business school because of all t schools here, so the quality of the program would seem to suffer. Temple tri its best, though, to get its services out to the students. Some schools require st dents to do activities with career services to further push students. There a numerous internship opportunities offered to the non-business students as wel

Alumnus/a, 9/1996-5/2000, April 2004

I studied theatre and dance. Both programs focus constantly on the professio al world and encourage students to audition outside of the university. All of n professors were working professionals in the outside art world. They wou often offer positions for jobs and internships to current or newly graduated st dents. Both departments always had information in their offices for internshi and castings. Name professionals would come to speak to our department eve Friday afternoon. These speakers were always prestigious professionals, sor of them alumni. I have been out of Temple for four years now, and I am st aware of the careers of some of my fellow students and former professors. receive invites and e-mails and tips all the time. Even after four years, they a looking out for me. And now, I'm one of those working professionals! La year, I was hired by the university to teach a seminar.

 ## Quality of Life

Current student, 9/2002-Submit Date, April 2006

I have never felt unsafe here at Temple. I'm from a very small town in sou central PA, where the worst thing that could happen to you is a cow wanderi into your backyard and eating your entire garden. While I knew that I needed have a different attitude when living in a city, I never felt like I had to wor about my safety—not one single time.

Current student, 8/2004-Submit Date, April 2006

While North Philadelphia is not the safest of all neighborhoods, I feel safe ar comfortable on campus. Our professional police force is always visible, and t campus is very lit up so I don't have to worry about any dark spots where mig feel unsafe. Not to mention, there is always something going on, and someboc walking down the street, so I am never alone. I also love my apartment, as it a block off campus, and very secure. I accessed this apartment through Templ too.

Current student, 9/2002-Submit Date, May 2004

The campus is pretty nice. It is located in North Philadelphia, which is not in t best neighborhood. The city is downtown. Knowing you are on campus make it easier to meet other students and enjoy student life. There are plenty of faci ities open to students, although they are limited on the weekends. The librar and computer labs were the latest places to extend to the weekends and off later hours.

Dining at Temple will get you a mixed reaction. There are two main places eat, located at opposite ends of the campus. This is a little inconvenient, b would be even more so had they not opened little food awnings in between Plus, there are a lot of food trucks parked in the streets. The food, itself is goo at the main cafeteria. Lots of choices, good taste. The other eatery, thoug offers mostly unhealthy food that you tire of quickly.

Although the surroundings are not top quality and there are a lot of homeles people, the police do a lot to make the environment a better place. The polic always patrol the campus. They can be reached practically immediately if nee

There are blue beacons located throughout campus that have buttons that, en pressed, tell police where to go to help immediately.

mnus/a, 9/1996-5/2000, April 2004

nple University lies in North Philly. The campus grows every year. On my visit, I was blown away by all the developments. The housing is beautiful. ey have an array of options. Since Temple is in an urban setting, the majori- f students commute to campus. However, if you choose to live on campus, can choose from the freshman dorms (two per room), the residence halls ur per suite, two per room), the apartments (five per flat) and the graduate sing. All of these are newly renovated. Temple is also home to The Apollo. s is the sports arena that houses the fabulous Temple Owls.

hough Temple is in an urban neighborhood, the crime is relatively low. There o need to wander off campus. The campus is safe, so students are encour- d to stay there. I remember being told that the security on Temple's campus s the "fifth largest police precinct in Pennsylvania." Real cops keep the cam- very safe. I never had any problems. But, just so no one is worried, you are uired to take a safety seminar as part of freshman orientation.

 Social Life

rrent student, 9/2002-Submit Date, April 2006

nple's social life has improved since I was a freshman. There was nothing to on campus. We'd head down to Center City almost every weekend, or just g out in different people's rooms. Now, there's a nightclub, movie theatre, bars/restaurants and tons of events that go on Monday through Friday. wever, since I've lived in Center City Philadelphia (off campus) for two rs, I really am only on campus when I have class or have to work. Other than , my social time is spent in different parts of the city. The dating scene is rse. I never dated anyone from Temple until this year, and I'm a senior!

rrent student, 8/2004-Submit Date, April 2006

ere is so much to do both on campus and off campus in the city. On campus have a ton of restaurants and bars—including the Draught Horse (which has drafts on Wednesdays) and Maxis, with its amazing pizza and convenient ation on our main strip called Liacouras Walk. Also, many people have spa- us apartments and houses around campus, so there are always social gather- s with people you meet in classes or in organizations. The Greek system is o alive, but not the only option. While the fraternities and sororities throw ties and have socials, this is only part of the variety of activities. We have e Food and Fun Fridays at our main student center, as well as a movie theater campus and a nightclub that puts on an event each Saturday night showcas-

ing local talent, music and more. Then, of course, there's the City of Philadelphia—from South Street to Old City, to Center City, there is tons of food and fun!

Current student, 1/2005-Submit Date, March 2006

The social life is great. I didn't think I would be involved in the campus scene that much, but I find myself there a lot. I'm there for clubs and some music events. The dating scene—well, I am dating someone I met on campus after being there two months, so it must be pretty good!

Current student, 9/2002-Submit Date, May 2004

The social life at Temple can be somewhat limited. Not including downtown, where the bars and restaurants are located, Greek life and parties dominate cam- pus social life. Every Thursday and Saturday, Greek organizations (there are 10 social Greek organizations) hold parties that many students go to. Recently, one restaurant opened on campus. Temple does hold a lot of events around campus for students to go to. They range from Indian dances and music bands to poet- ry night and academic lectures. There are dozens and dozens of clubs offered, and if there isn't one that a student likes, he or she can just start up his or her own. Fraternity parties are also extremely popular.

Alumnus/a, 9/1996-5/2000, April 2004

Temple does have a Greek system that appeared to be very popular. The frater- nities had houses right on campus. I never participated in the Greek system, so I don't know much about it. However, I did go to a few of their parties. Lots of fun. The restaurants on campus were always fun to go to when there was a big break in the day. There was always plenty of variety of food choices to meet your cravings. When I was there, there was only one bar on campus. Now, I think, there are two or three.

I didn't drink much on campus, but the bars always had promotions and fun things happening. The Spring Fling was a campus favorite. All the clubs would have fund-raising stands selling food or games. There would be bands, and con- tests and fun everywhere. Very hard to go to class that day. Sporting events were always advertised. The basketball games were always popular. The music, dance and theatre schools had performances a number of times a year that were always fun. As far as Temple's clubs, there are almost too many to list. You name it, they've got it. And if they don't, they encourage you to start your own.

I don't know what to say about the dating scene. I did quite a bit of dating while I was in college, but I don't know if that's because of the university. But, sure, there were plenty of opportunities to make new friends. There was also a movie night every week that was popular. I'm sure I'm forgetting some things, but hey, that how much fun I was having that I don't remember it all four years later.

Read all of Vault's College Surveys at **www.vault.com/college**—get complete surveys on 100s of colleges and univer- sities, expert advice on applicaton essays and more.

VAULT CAREER LIBRARY **643**

University of Pennsylvania

The Office of Undergraduate Admissions
University of Pennsylvania
1 College Hall
Philadelphia, PA 19104-6376
Admissions phone: (215) 898-7507
Admissions URL: www.upenn.edu/admissions/

Note: The school has chosen not to review the student surveys submitted.

 ## Admissions

Alumnus/a, Engineering, 8/2002-5/2006, June 2007

Admissions process is very selective. They ensure that all admitted students are fully qualified in terms on intelligence and character. Furthermore, the students admitted to this Ivy League school are social, creative, and much less nerdy. They look at all SAT scores, interview some students (by alumni in your location), and look at your character in the essay. Personally, I think they take essays and scores to be the top factors. I trust the selectivity process, and the people I have met at the university are absolutely high class citizens. All of my friends SATs ranged from 1450 to 1600. I have not heard of any less. About two-thirds were valedictorians of their high school—however that does not guarantee admission and does not seem to equate to success in the school.

Current student, Social Sciences, 9/2005-Submit Date, June 2007

I applied ED so the process was fairly simple for me. You should have top grades, test scores, extracurricular activities and recommendations. I think going to a top prep school helps you at Penn too maybe more than other schools.

In terms of advice on getting in, if you have your heart set on Penn, apply ED. It will increase your chances significantly (especially if you are a legacy). I didn't interview (it is not really necessary, but I think they offer the option). I did, however, meet with the regional director of admissions when she came to my high school campus to talk with students about Penn. She was very nice and informative about the school and I think I made a good impression. I don't think it made much of a difference though in my chances.

My general essay (a page of my autobiography) was very creative, so I think you can take chances with your essay and not be afraid of ruining your chances. My "Why Penn?" essay was very specific. I talked about professors I wanted to study with and about my campus visit. Penn really wants to know that it is just not another one of your applications and that you could really see yourself being a student there.

Current student, Business, 9/2005-Submit Date, October 2006

The admissions process is extremely competitive and very selective. Most people who apply have also applied to other Ivies as well as schools like Duke, Georgetown, Stanford and so on. Most people who get in to UPenn apply Early Decision. Basically, everyone at the school wanted to be at the school. It was almost everyone's first choice, and for a good reason. I'd suggest applying early for those who know its where they want to be. On-campus interviews are only granted to legacies but off-campus interviews are available with local alumni. There are a lot of legacies at UPenn, either siblings or parents went, but not all.

Current student, 9/2002-Submit Date, September 2005

I would say that Penn has a very selective admissions process. The most important part of any admissions application is the academic transcript. One should note that the transcript is evaluated in terms of what your school offers; so if your school offers AP classes, and you don't take them, it looks bad. The next aspect the admissions officers look at is "who you are"—your extracurriculars personal statement and awards/honors. After that comes your standardized test scores. And finally come your letters of recommendation, supplementary materials (e.g., if you send in a portfolio) and the like.

Current student, 9/2003-Submit Date, November 2004

Admission into Penn is very competitive, but not solely based on numbers. notice from their brochures and letters that they value diversity and activi (they spit out numbers about the incoming freshman class like 80 student b presidents, 300 captains of sports teams and one winner of the Miss Texas be ty pageant).

My program, Management and Technology, which is a dual Wharton and en neering degree program, seems to be much more competitive in terms of nu bers. The average SAT score creeps past the 1500 mark (higher than MIT ev and most students have a load of 5s on their APs, as well as top SAT Subject 1 scores.

I never did an interview, so I don't think they're that important. Essays important. Penn wants to know why you want to go to Penn and not the ot Ivies. Best advice for getting in? Apply Early Decision. About 50 percen each incoming class is accepted early.

Current student, 9/2003-Submit Date, March 2005

The admissions process is extremely competitive, and includes two long essa multiple short answer questions and an alumni interview if available in y area; all with an only 20 percent chance of acceptance. The acceptance rate the Early Decision round is twice that of the Regular Decision round. Penn d not currently accept the Common Application. The joint-degree progra (Huntsman and M&T) are extremely competitive and include additional ess and requirements (such as an interview in your target foreign language Huntsman).

 ## Academics

Alumnus/a, 9/2002-5/2006, September 2006

Academics vary widely by program. In the most popular majors (e.g., Polit Science and Economics), first- and second-year students will inevitably end sitting through enormous lectures and sections taught by TAs (who, thou almost universally skilled and enthusiastic, are sometimes less than fluent English). In any case, every student in every school, division or department the opportunity to take advantage of the university's interdisciplinary foc Since this is one of Penn's major selling/differentiation-from-peers points, p grams for undergraduate research, advanced study in one of the gradu schools, and grant application support abound. Pre-med (or pre-vet/pre-den students can also take advantage of a fairly large pool of research assistant/ tech openings at the medical, vet and dental schools.

Alumnus/a, Engineering, 8/2002-5/2006, June 2007

I studied in the engineering program. The classes are very challenging and engineering students have the reputation of self-segregation. Grading is v harsh, however the professors are outstanding in their knowledge and fair in th judgment. The workload is high, however all students tend to find the time be social and spend time on extracurricular activities. Professors are very acc sible.

Current student, Business, 9/2005-Submit Date, October 200

I'm in Wharton, the business school which is much more competitive than college. The classes are curved which basically means that 20 percent of s dents get A's, 40 percent B's and the rest, C's and D's. For most kids, it is a c ficult transition from straight A's in high school to such a competitive atm phere. Most of the intro classes are quite large but they are all taught by prof sors, many of whom wrote the text books from which we are learning. It is pr ty easy to get into classes since it's such a large school. I've yet to have a pr lem. Basically what it comes down to is there is a lot of work and the gradi is tough but this school is not all about academics. People like having fun know that learning is a top priority.

lumnus/a, 9/2000-5/2004, March 2006

was in the College of Arts and Sciences. The school is so big that much of the ademic experience is what you make of it. Applying for classes online makes e process pretty painless. There is a course guide online that rates courses— ey are student ratings and they are usually accurate, so listen to them. The quirements of the program are flexible enough to let you study what interests u but to also taste different disciplines. The distribution requirements include o history courses, two literature/art courses, two social science courses, one ysical science, one life science, one math course and one elective course. ere is also a quantitative requirement, a language requirement and a writing urse requirement. The choices in each category are wide enough to find some- ing that interests everyone. Each major has its own additional requirements of to 16 courses. All told you need to take 32 to 36 courses, depending on your ajor. A word to the wise: try to get your required courses completed early on, they don't haunt you when you are a senior and trying to graduate!

urrent student, 9/2002-Submit Date, September 2005

e quality of the classes has been topnotch. I am often in classes with under students, and have even had multiple classes of just five students and a pro- ssor. The professors are very well-informed and are often at or near the top of eir fields. Also, most students are able to get the classes they want—the reg- ration process works quite well, and professors can let in extra students if they ant. I would say that as to the difficulty of the classes that there doesn't appear be any grade inflation, and I have often had to write 15- to 20-page research pers. Professors are willing to work with you, for the most part, if you fall ill need an extension and most Penn students will dedicate a large portion of their ne to work.

urrent student, 9/2003-Submit Date, March 2005

any freshmen and sophomores are enrolled in large lectures with 100 to 400 dents in the math, econ, psych, sociology, history and poli sci departments, d in many Wharton introductory courses. All these courses usually break up to smaller recitations (20 or fewer) taught by graduate students to go over oblems and discuss course content in more depth. Lectures are always taught full professors. As a freshman though, you will also be guaranteed to have asses with 16 or fewer students (writing courses, freshman seminars and for- gn language courses), and most upper-level classes have fewer than 20 stu- nts. Large lecture courses and Wharton courses are usually graded on a ale/curve, which may help or hurt your grade depending upon the distribution sually 65 to 70 percent A and B). This is done of course to prevent grade infla- n. The registration system for classes is extremely fair with all students reg- tration considered after a common deadline (no rolling registration). The pro- ssors are extremely knowledgeable, teach well, are accessible, and are often e best in their field. Problems often arise from graduate students in recitations ho are not always well-trained in teaching and do not speak English well.

Employment Prospects

urrent student, Social Sciences, 9/2005-Submit Date, June 2007

think everyone assumes that it is so easy coming from Penn to get jobs at top vestment banking and management consulting firms, but the OCR program is ally tough, especially for those not in Wharton. They want to see top grades e., 3.5+), previous internships, leadership positions and great interviewing ills. I think I was naive enough in high school to think that an undergraduate gree from an Ivy League school meant that finding a great job would be a ven, but I was in for a rude awakening once I got here. I think Penn has a good lationship with big-name employers in the industries popular with graduates of y League and other top colleges, but they hire relatively few Penn students out- de of Wharton. For pre-health students the appointment sometimes needs to be heduled way in advance. The job search is a tough, time-consuming process d there is no hand holding.

lumnus/a, Engineering, 8/2002-5/2006, June 2007

believe about 90 percent of the students find work before second semester of nior year begins, although among my friend all of them receive their first job fer by August of the previous year. The all employers are very prestigious due the intelligence of its students. The companies include, Morgan Stanley, oldman Sachs, IBM, Citigroup, L'Oreal, Johnson & Johnson, Sony, the CIA,

the FBI, Lockheed Martin, Boeing, MIT Lincoln Laboratory, Lehman Brothers, Boston Consulting Group and McKinsey. There are career fairs multiples times a semester in which over 200 companies come to recruit. Most students receive two to 10 offers, and have a starting pay of $50,000 plus. Most jobs are actual career paths. The alumni network is very helpful since they come to recruit on campus as a member of the hiring company. Most students, though, do spend their entire summer from freshman year to junior year doing internships of var- ious kinds.

Alumnus/a, 9/2002-5/2006, September 2006

There's also a big-fish-in-a-pretty-big-pond advantage to being at Penn if stu- dents are willing to consider staying in Philadelphia. Major newspapers, net- works, publishing houses and think-tanks are all out there for those who are less business-oriented. This isn't to say that Penn students can't or don't get the same sorts of jobs in New York or L.A. (they do), but interviewing with Philadelphia employers as a Penn student definitely gives you an extra edge. This is also use- ful when it comes to getting summer jobs/internships.

Current student, Business, 9/2005-Submit Date, October 2006

The people who graduate from Wharton do not have trouble finding jobs. Many people get prestigious jobs at Lehman Brothers or Goldman Sachs. Most peo- ple go into finance although marketing is a popular concentration as well. On- campus recruitment is legendary here at Penn. It's an extremely time consum- ing and competitive process here and most seniors are in the process if they haven't found jobs already. Internships can also be found through university services although I haven't used it.

Current student, 1/2003-Submit Date, March 2004

The Career Services Department is very strong at Penn, but make no mistake: it is oriented toward Wharton students. If you aren't seeking careers in general financial services, corporate management, consulting or investment banking, you'll probably have to do a bit more legwork. The most prestigious of firms in almost every industry recruit at Penn, and often the financial firms welcome applicants from the college and engineering as a change of pace. I don't know a single Wharton student with above a 2.9 who didn't get at least 10 first-round interviews. Most seemed to report 15 to 20. Academic route students have a number of options as well. Penn has recently been expanding and pushing its Center for Undergraduate Research and Fellowships and has brought out more fellowships and scholarships (Rhodes and Fulbright) in the last five years or so than in several decades. The university seems to have high placement rates in graduate programs, and from anecdotal experience, it's not just for the higher performing students. Many friends will be attending graduate programs at, for example, Chicago, Stanford, Harvard and sub-matriculating to Penn with mod- erate grade point averages and undergraduate résumés—Penn certainly has a strong reputation.

Quality of Life

Alumnus/a, 9/2002-5/2006, September 2006

My quality of life at Penn was excellent. Having grown up in a large city, I had the advantage of not being intimidated by Philadelphia or the rumors that tend to circulate about how unsafe it is.

The fact is, in four years of living in West Philadelphia, running all over town and walking back from center city after last call (which happens to be at an annoyingly early 2 a.m. in Philly), I never once felt threatened or unsafe. While I wouldn't recommend walking around North Philly in a Penn sweatshirt late at night, I would be confident walking about more or less 24 hours a day between 50th Street or so to the west, the Delaware River to the east, City Hall/JFK Boulevard to the north and South Street to the south. It's hard to imagine what business a Penn student would have outside of this rectangle to begin with.

Alumnus/a, Engineering, 8/2002-5/2006, June 2007

The quality of life compared to other Ivy Leagues is simply outstanding. The students are not only smart but very social. There multiple parties almost every- day. The crime rate is high, however students become used to it their first year. Campus security is also high. The housing/dining is good/fair, nothing to com- plain about. The best part about life at UPenn is its surrounding Philadelphia— brilliant history, cute great restaurants and bars (BYOBs). The student groups

Read all of Vault's College Surveys at **www.vault.com/college**—get complete surveys on 100s of colleges and univer- sities, expert advice on applicaton essays and more.

VAULT CAREER LIBRARY **645**

simply love the culture and sophistication. There is also old city (historic neighborhood), the Liberty Bell, Chinatown, and a thousand different types of shops and cafes that you will simply never get bored of the city. The city by itself is so highly recommended that you might as well go to the school.

Alumnus/a, Computer Science, 9/2001-5/2005, March 2007

Philly is a great city to live in for four years. The campus is beautiful, despite being on the cusp of the true downtown and its high-rises. By sealing off Locust Walk from cars, a true campus feeling is created. The Quad (housing mainly for freshmen) creates the perfect atmosphere for getting to know other students and relax without feeling like you have to hang out in the middle of the streets or in a club (ala New York). Dining leaves something to be desired, though they are always improving. I would recommend non-campus dining as there are plenty of food trucks and other vendors in the area—if only Penn would allow us to use our dining dollars for this food! The neighborhood is the start of West Philly, so naturally there is more crime than a rural town. I felt safe during my time there, though, because of plenty of lighting, police and campus security presence all over (and beyond) campus borders, security phones always within sight, and Penn Card only access to almost all buildings and all dorms.

Alumnus/a, 8/2002-5/2006, May 2006

Quality of life is fairly good, though work is needed on generating more campus community. Housing is awesome if you're in the Quad and great in Hill, though terrible if you're one of the unlucky few who get scattered around campus and placed in predominantly upperclassman housing during your first year. The campus is beautiful and Locust Walk, which runs right through the middle, is the center of campus life—much more so than Houston Hall, which many students don't even realize is the student center. Facilities are good, and if you're pursuing a business major, Huntsman Hall may be the best facility on any campus anywhere. While many people may have heard stories of Penn's location in a "dangerous neighborhood," it's really not that bad. Penn does have the largest police force of any school in the country and the third largest in the state of Pennsylvania. Moreover, cameras and blue-light emergency phones are present at every intersection. Safety is really not an issue, and Penn even provides a late-night "walk" service whereby security officers can accompany you if you desire.

Current student, 9/2003-Submit Date, March 2005

Big Greek scene; a real sense of a campus atmosphere within the city. Football and basketball games are well-attended. The campus is open, but there is an enclosed pedestrian pathway (Locust Walk) that gives Penn a more coherent sense of campus life. Dorms vary from 19th Century to 1970s high-rise buildings, and about half of upperclassmen live on campus. Off-campus housing is immediately adjacent to the school border and many people live in frat/sorority houses. Facilities have been well maintained, augmented and added over the last five years to reinvigorate Penn's campus and reputation. Huntsman Hall (the new Wharton building), the bookstore, Pottruck Gym, and renovations to the College Houses and Bennett Hall are testaments to this.

 # Social Life

Current student, 9/2003-Submit Date, September 2006

For the first two years, social life revolves a lot around fraterniti Upperclassmen, however, and more likely to go to bars and restaurants dov town. Plenty of great places to eat in Center City Philly, which is a five-min cab ride away. Popular bars on campus include Smoke's and Mad 4 Mex seniors, and MarBar for everyone else. Downtown there are plenty of gc restaurants and BYOBs.

Alumnus/a, Computer Science, 9/2001-5/2005, March 2007

Greek life makes up about 30 percent of students on campus, and while it i major part of life for those students, it isn't as large as at state schools. Stude in frats/sororities are often involved in many other activities, clubs and events well. There are great restaurants around campus (New Deck, Smokes, Gre Lady, Marbar, Penne to name a few) and you have the whole of Philadelp within walking/short cabbing distance. There are great bars right near camp as well (too many to list), and plenty of awesome bars/nightclubs downtown

Current student, Business, 9/2005-Submit Date, October 200(

Since the school is in a city, there are many options for the social scene. (campus, the Greek system is quite large with about one-third of stude involved. Downtown Philadelphia also has some of the most wonderful, wo renowned restaurants (including many by Steven Starr). There are plenty clubs downtown (18 to enter, 21 to drink). The dating scene at Penn is exist but most people are single and enjoying it. There are also a range of clubs fr a cappella groups to philanthropic organizations to sports clubs. There is a c for everyone however not necessary for everyone. There's plenty of stuff to at Penn besides joining clubs. A person never gets bored!

Alumnus/a, 8/2002-5/2006, May 2006

The school is notorious for its social life, especially among Ivy League schoo and it may be Penn's greatest extracurricular asset. University police rarely c students for alcohol, which is practically a campus institution at the many f ternity and house parties on weekends. There are also several bars on camp and many restaurants. Highlights include Chinese, Greek, Indian, Irish, piz Thai and more. In addition, Penn's urban location in Philadelphia often ler itself to many downtown events at several of Philadelphia's nightspots, as w as access to some of the very best and most diverse restaurants in the coun The dating scene is in full force and there are many student clubs.

Current student, 9/2004-Submit Date, April 2005

The social life here is known as among the best in the Ivy League and stude here are proud of that. We all work hard but many of us party pretty hard, well. There are, of course, all the typical groups you'd expect on a campus t cover the whole range of possibilities. Many of the people who came here loc ing to party have joined frats or sororities, but the ones that have not are at disadvantage; most parties, if not all of them, are open to everybody. There pretty stringent rules for on-campus parties that guide these frats, but luck most of them have off-campus houses that are exempt from the rules. Also, th are plenty of parties at clubs downtown, so you never really forget that you in a city.

University of Pittsburgh

dmissions Office
227 Fifth Avenue, Alumni Hall
ttsburgh, PA 15260
dmissions phone: (412) 624-PITT (or (412) 624-7488)
dmissions e-mail: oafa@pitt.edu
dmissions URL: www.pitt.edu/~oafa

The school says: "The University of Pittsburgh has chosen not to comment on the student surveys submitted. For information about current admission guidelines and profiles, visit the Office of Admissions and Financial Aid web site at www.pitt.edu/~oafa, or arrange for a campus visit by calling the Undergraduate Visit Center at (412) 624-7717 or e-mailing viscntr@oafa.pitt.edu."

 ## Admissions

urrent student, Health, 8/2004-Submit Date, June 2007

e admissions process is very simple. It's a short one-page application and en supplemental information like essays and recommendation can be added to ut are not mandatory. Anyone interested in scholarships is encouraged to sub- t supplementary documents.

urrent student, Political Science, 8/2005-Submit Date, May 2007

would describe the admissions process at the University of Pittsburgh to be one great clarity and fairness, yet still competitive. When I applied to the univer- y, I felt well-informed about the status of my application and what I needed to mplete for it, including essays, recommendations and high school transcripts. e admissions counselors were very helpful with explaining the whole admis- ns process during my campus visit to Pitt. Pitt has a rolling admissions ocess, and I heard back in about two weeks that I had been accepted. After coming a student here, I became a Pitt Pathfinder. This means that I work for e Office of Admissions and Financial Aid as a student representative and tour ide. This job is great because I have had the opportunity to observe this missions process firsthand. I can attest that the admissions and recruitment ocess at Pitt is one of professionalism, a great positive aspect of our campus, d full of Pitt pride.

urrent student, Business, 9/2004-Submit Date, May 2007

r all the schools to which I applied, I was able to do it for free. When visiting hools, most would have the option of turning in a free application on that day. applied early, and this helped me get into Pitt because we are on a rolling mission. I always suggest to prospective students to write an essay and let the mission council know that you are special, more than just a number. Everyone plying to a school like Pitt are good students, top of their class, honors stu- nts, but if you have something that makes you stand out (volunteer work, lead- ship experience) that can definitely improve your chances. I know that I was t the best student from my high school, but I got accepted to Pitt whereas oth- s more highly ranked were denied.

urrent student, Engineering, 8/2005-Submit Date, May 2007

pplying can all be done online using the university's online application. wever, a paper application can be used if preferred. A personal essay and let- rs of recommendation are not required, although they are recommended. SAT, CT and high school transcripts must be sent to the university. The application e is $45. Since the admissions process is rolling admissions, the earlier you ply, the better chances you have of getting in. So if you feel like your test ores or grades are not what you would like them to be, apply early! The uni- ersity looks for individuals who have a broad spectrum of interests. Therefore, en though you may not be the 1600 SAT, 4.0 GPA, and valedictorian, as long your application shows that you have participated in various extracurricular tivities and held leadership positions, you should have no problem getting in.

Current student, Political Science, 8/2004-Submit Date, May 2007

Pitt operates on a rolling admissions system. You can apply any time, but obvi- ously earlier applications have a better chance of being accepted for the right semester. The university had gotten increasingly selective over the past couple of years, as we are receiving more applications and more accepted students are enrolling. When I got in about half of the people who applied got accepted, now it is more like 40 percent. If you want to make sure you get in, fill out all of the essay questions and do any of the optional stuff on the application, because they really do look at it.

Current student, Health, 8/2005-Submit Date, May 2007

I used the online application, which made my process very simple. I learned of my acceptance, and then attended a fall getting ready program. It was hosted by the Pitt Pathfinders, the student tour guides. I then filled out all financial aid forms, the FAFSA and housing. Make your essay unique. My mom always told me to write it from the heart, because that's what admissions staff members real- ly want to read. They want to read essays that include real life events, and things that are important to you as the student. Not what you think they want to here. Pitt accepts about 50 percent of the students who apply, so standing out is key, especially if you want scholarship application. The best advice I can give is probably to apply early. Get it out of the way, so you can enjoy your senior year of high school without worrying about admissions. Another piece of advice is to visit schools. You really want to know the campus is like. Get a feel for the campus and its students.

Current student, 5/2005-Submit Date, September 2006

Getting admitted was done primarily online. They made it easy and you can call if you have any questions. A good reference is to call 412-624-FACT with any questions. The whole process did not take that long. To increase your chances of getting in, I would focus on your essays. These are often the distinguishing factor between hundreds of students with near-perfect grades.

Current student, 9/2003-Submit Date, September 2006

There is an online application, which is the easiest course of action, but the best advice is to apply using the old-fashioned way. This way you can include an essay, which can, if you are on the cusp, help to get you in the door. The best idea is to get the application in as soon as possible. Pitt has rolling admissions, and a limited amount of spaces, and lots of applicants. The earlier you can get the application in, the better. It's a pretty easy application, asking for a couple of letters of recommendation and an essay. The essay is key. Wax nostalgic on how you've always wanted to go to Pitt, and how it's in your blood, and you're golden. Also, avoid the application cost by touring the school. Pitt will waive the fee if you come see the campus. The tour is given by students who know what they're doing, plus they walk backwards, which is an added bonus. Apply to all the branch campuses as well, they're all nice and you can easily transfer onto Pitt's main campus. In the past years, Pitt has gotten more selective on their incoming freshman class. So if you are only accepted to a branch campus, don't take it too harshly. The average Pitt freshman now was in their top 10 percent of their graduating class, with fairly high SAT's. Compare it to getting accept- ed at Penn State main campus. Not impossible, but getting harder.

 ## Academics

Current student, Psychology, 8/2004-Submit Date, May 2007

The University of Pittsburgh offers a wide variety of classes that appeal to stu- dents of numerous diverse academic backgrounds. My psychology program consists of a group of core classes (Intro to Psych, Developmental Psych, Research Methods and so on), numerous general education requirements, a math requirement, and many upper-level psychology courses. Psychology classes are normally larger in size, but this is not a disadvantage to the student by any means. The professors are very accessible through office hours and appoint- ments, and pass out a syllabus at the beginning of the semester so you know

Read all of Vault's College Surveys at **www.vault.com/college**—get complete surveys on 100s of colleges and univer- sities, expert advice on applicaton essays and more.

VAULT CAREER LIBRARY 647

exactly what to expect throughout the term. The workload is moderate, nothing too strenuous, but challenging.

Current student, Engineering, 8/2006-Submit Date, May 2007

The academic nature of engineering at Pitt is one where during certain periods, a great deal of work is placed on your shoulders, and at other times, there is no work to do. The program is meant to simulate the working world after college. At one point, you'll be doing nothing, and before you know it, you're assigned the biggest project in your life due the next day. To prepare for this, you'll be taking rigorous classes the first year of college. The process is to push every student to the limit. Some students drop out of engineering because it is very challenging. The rewards however, in my opinion, outweigh the cost it takes to get there. All my professors loved their topics and they were very animated about the subjects. There is a handful of popular classes that you'll find in college. If you cannot get into them the first time, remember that you're in college for four years. If you really want to get into a class, from my experience, if you talk to the professor, they can usually override the system and let you in. This also works if you want a class with a certain professor and it is full. The workload as I said before is fairly intense for freshman engineers. Your grade may bounce back and forth. My advice is to get to know the professors who teach the class.

Current student, Health, 8/2005-Submit Date, May 2007

I really think Pitt does a great job with scheduling classes. We are not online with registration yet, so even though it may be a pain for advisors, the one on one time that a student experiences is tremendous. Getting popular classes is pretty easy, because they are usually large. You can usually get into a closed class if you just ask the professor, they are nice. I promise. They love seeing students really interested in their subjects. The workload from high school to college was a huge difference for me. I find it extremely hard to be self-motivated, but also find it rewarding when I do well. Grading is tough in college, but if you really want to do well in a class, help is always out there.

Current student, Business, 9/2004-Submit Date, May 2007

I am double majoring in communication and business. I like to do this because I get a good balance of math related courses and language related courses. For the most part, I feel that I have had the opportunity to learn from an experienced and passionate expert in that particular field. It is great having a teacher that is referenced time and time again within your text book and through individual research. However, I have had professors who seem to be more interested in their personal lives than in teaching, which is very disappointing. Most of these professors are extremely easy and so some students may take them for that reason. I feel like I have been graded relatively fairly throughout my college career. Most teachers allow you to set up conferences to talk about your grades and how you can improve upon them. Some professors again seem not to care. I had one professor who never e-mailed me back after I contacted him about my final grade.

Current student, 5/2005-Submit Date, September 2006

Like most large universities, you get what you make of it. There are relatively bright professors in each department. The onus is on the student to seek those out and develop a relationship with them. If you are not in the business school, it's hard to get into business classes at times but if you are persistent you will not have any problems. The workload was moderate, nothing insane.

Some classes in certain majors, e.g., neuropsychiatry and education, are notorious for getting into. Pitt still mandates visiting an advisor to register for classes so it's hard to get into some classes unless you schedule your appt very early in the class selection process. Pitt is working on improving the online course information for students via a recently installed Peoplesoft system. They expect this program to continue to increase responsibilities.

Current student, 8/2003-Submit Date, October 2006

The number one reason I came to Pitt was the strong academics offered here, and I have definitely found just that. I knew I wanted to major in science and hopefully go on to medical school, and I just could not pass up the opportunity of having a great medical system like University of Pittsburgh Medical Center literally on campus. I have been given every opportunity for research and volunteer experience, as well as clinical experience by taking certain classes at Pitt to qualify me for a paid position at a UPMC hospital. Classes in my major, which is neuroscience, are taught by the leading researchers in the field. My professors are the people who actually helped to found the science of neuroscience. Classes

are intense, especially being pre-med, but I think it is possible to do well academically and still have a life outside of the classroom, though it may not be exciting as a social life as you thought you'd have in college. Professors always willing to listen to you or answer questions, and I can't say I've really ever had a truly bad professor. Scheduling is tough as a freshman and sophomore, but as you move on into your major it gets a lot better.

 # Employment Prospects

Current student, Engineering, 8/2006-Submit Date, May 2007

Employment prospects for graduates at our school are pretty high. Most engineers partake in a program known as co-op. It is a three-semester program where a student will actually work with a company of his/her choice. Most employers hire those students who worked for them after they graduate. I also know that some employers only hire students who have co-oped in their firm. Our campus also has a job fair every year where students can set up interviews with companies. The engineering department has a very strong internship office. Some examples of places graduates work would be like Westinghouse, GM, Ford and Microsoft. I also heard that alumni are great sources for getting an "in" at a company. Alumni can put in a good word for you at various companies and I recommend getting to know a few in your field of interest.

Current student, Political Science, 8/2004-Submit Date, May 2007

There are always tons of on-campus job fairs that allow you to have valuable networking time, as well as our Alumni Association that has events throughout the year. Pitt has incredible connections to a lot of the major employers in the area, so if you are looking for internships the whole city of Pittsburgh is at your disposal, which then allows for great connections to employment later down the line.

Current student, 5/2005-Submit Date, September 2006

The career center is quite knowledgeable and readily available. Sometimes the web site is confusing because they have a ton of information readily available. Meet with a career counselor to have them break it all down. You can also take advantage of the frequent seminars the center offers. There is an average number of career fairs but the companies seem geared toward the least desirable jobs.

The alumni network is growing and they have recently enabled the online search through their database for alumni in certain industries or companies.

Current student, 9/2003-Submit Date, September 2006

The business school and the med programs are both extremely prestigious. Graduates generally do very well professionally. There is a career service at Pitt where you can post your résumé where prospective employers can look at. This applies to graduates as well as undergrads. There is a job fair every fall and spring, and internship fairs. I myself had an internship through Pitt working for the Labor Party in London. They are well-connected and can arrange amazing internship opportunities.

Current student, 8/2003-Submit Date, February 2006

It's fairly easy to get a job through the business school. Ford is a huge recruiter in finance and accounting. The Big Four (especially PwC) accounting firms stalk most of the accounting majors from sophomore year on with SOX in effect. Marketing is a little more challenging (easier to get internships, strangely). Ryan Homes, Geico, National City, Dicks Sporting Goods, Citizens Bank, PNC, U.S. Steel Pittsburgh Pirates/Steelers/Penguins all hire out of our school. On-campus job fairs are usually pretty successful.

Current student, 8/2003-Submit Date, February 2006

What you do with your time at Pitt can really determine where you will end up career-wise. I know a few people who had interviews to become Marshall Scholars, who have gained admission to some of the most prestigious graduate schools because they did more than excel academically. These people were presidents of organizations, very visible on campus and conducted independent research. Among employers, Pitt is seen as a good school. Employers know that you have had to work hard if you graduated from Pitt. I know many graduates who actually end up working for the university right out of school and I know other who have gone on to work at very high-up companies like IBM, Deloitte and Tousch, Hilton, Ford and Ketchum. Alumni are always willing to help when

y can. The university is currently working on a network to better connect stu-
...ts to their alumni. Lastly, there are internship fairs, job fairs and recruiters
...campus at least once a week.

Quality of Life

...rrent student, Health, 8/2004-Submit Date, June 2007

...r facilities are constantly being renovated and upgraded so the quality of life
...ery high. We have some of the nicest residence halls that I've seen at any
...npus. There are great dining choices on campus and a ton of other options
...hin walking distance from campus. Our campus is very safe. We have our
...n police force that is the second largest in the county. We are also patrolled
...two other police forces. All of our residence halls have 24-hour security
...rds. The university has done a lot to make sure that the campus is very safe
...l secure.

...rrent student, Psychology, 8/2004-Submit Date, May 2007

...ing a Resident Assistant throughout my college career has given me a keen
...ect on this topic. As an RA, it is my responsibility to be a resource for stu-
...ts in the residence halls. I am there to help build and promote community by
...nning programs and also enforce the policy of the residence halls (no drink-
..., smoking and so on). The University of Pittsburgh is also an extremely
...erse campus as well, so promoting diversity awareness is always a very
...portant part of my job as well. It's hard to comment on the dining facilities
...ause our entire main dining facility is being renovated for next year, but I
...ve heard very good things about it! And I couldn't ask more for campus safe-
... Being on an urban campus, it is important to use common sense, but some-
...es accidents do happen, and I feel very confident with our campus police and
...urity.

...rrent student, Engineering, 8/2006-Submit Date, May 2007

...using on campus is your regular on campus housing. As a freshman, you'll
...living in the smallest room on campus most of the time. The rooms at Pitt are
...: as small as some other places, yet they may not be as big as some other
...ces as well. The good news is that they are air conditioned. The Pitt campus
...onsidered to be a city campus but I do not classify it as a city. When I think
...city, I think of places like New York City where people are everywhere and if
...u're sitting on a park bench, they will ignore you as they walk by. Pitt is also
...t a rural campus—you will see a lot of people everyday. Pitt is a medium
...ween the two, if you were sitting on a park bench, people would walk by and
...nowledge your existence. This also adds to an air of friendliness as you get
...know the locals around Pitt. On-campus dining is not too bad as long as you
...ate a variety. If you eat at the same place everyday, I guarantee that it will
...te bad by the end of the school year. You can also eat off campus, which isn't
... bad. Around campus we have restaurants that go half-off after 11 p.m. Don't
... worried about walking around at midnight. There are usually people out and
...ut. Pitt is pretty safe in my opinion, but I still caution people to practice com-
...n sense.

...rrent student, Political Science, 8/2005-Submit Date, May 2007

...the beginning of my sophomore year, I had the opportunity to live in a brand-
...w residence hall at Pitt: Panther Hall. It proved to be a beautiful facility and
...s a nice place to stay. Our student recreation center and basketball court are
...used inside of the Petersen Events Centre. It is a state-of-the art facility, and
...a great place to watch the games and go to work out. There is a food court in
...re that also has amazing food. Our dining at Pitt is not so bad, as long as you
...n't eat at the same place all of the time. As far as crime and safety are con-
...ned, even though we live on an urban campus, I feel that we are relatively safe
...re. I do believe that you do have to use common sense: stay in groups, don't
...lk alone at night, take the university shuttles and so on.

Social Life

Current student, Health, 8/2004-Submit Date, June 2007

The great thing about the social life here is that there is something to do for
everyone. The Greek community is very active on campus but only makes up 9
percent of the total student body, so if that's not what your interested in you're
not alone. A lot of the social scene involves cheering on the Panthers at different sporting events especially football and basketball. There are also lots of
things to do off campus. Our student IDs grant us free admission to many of the
museums in the area as well as give us free transportation on the city bus system. The buses can get you anywhere in the city. There is every type of restaurant within the surrounding areas of campus so it makes it easy to try new things
or stick with old favorites.

Current student, Psychology, 8/2004-Submit Date, May 2007

Pitt's social scene is very active all the time! We live next to downtown
Pittsburgh, so we are opened up to everything that the city has to offer. Not to
mention, our own campus is like a little city in itself with endless stores, restaurants, bars, and other facilities. We also are close to Schenley Park, which is the
fourth largest in-city state park on the East Coast, which has something exciting
going on no matter what season it is. And being a Pitt student, also gives us
many opportunities for free social events around the city! There are endless
things to do here and endless people to meet!

Current student, Engineering, 8/2005-Submit Date, May 2007

Being such an urban campus greatly adds to social life during the college experience at Pitt. There are many great restaurants located right on or within walking distance of campus. Many restaurants on campus offer half-price discount
menus for late night dining (typical meal time for college students).
Hemmingway's Cafe and Fuel & Fuddle are just two of these restaurants but are
arguably the most popular hangouts for college students with The Original
Hotdog Shop (The O), Permanties, and Five Guys Burgers and Fries coming
close behind. Ginza's is a popular dance club for those underage college students on the weekends. For those of age, many bars and dance clubs are located on campus and also in larger quantities in Shadyside, Southside, Station
Square, and at the Strip. The university has a biannual carnival event where they
shut down Bigelow Boulevard and set up many carnival attractions such as
blow-up trampolines and obstacle courses for students to have fun. To cap off
the evening, they have a free concert where they bring in a big-name performer
to put on a show (recent performers being Ben Folds, Hawthorne Heights, Live
and Lifehouse). Other concerts around campus have included Dave Matthews
Band, OAR, NAS, Keith Urban, Kenny Chesney, Kanye West, just to name a
few. As for sports, Pitt football and basketball games are very popular among
students. Any students can get football tickets and it is very popular to tailgate
before games. Basketball tickets are tougher to come by, but it is possible for
any student to get a ticket to any game and attend the Oakland Zoo (our basketball student cheering section, which sits courtside for all games). Greek organizations are active on campus with roughly 12 percent of all students participating. Judging from that number, Greek life is there for those who seek to participate in it but it does not, by all means, run the social scene on campus. Give it
a shot if you are interested because you can always check out rush and decide if
it's for you or not.

The School Says

The University of Pittsburgh, established in 1787, is located on
132 acres of green lawns and hills intermingled with bustling
city streets in Pittsburgh, Pennsylvania. At its center is the
Cathedral of Learning, a 42-story Gothic skyscraper and the
tallest academic building in the Western Hemisphere.

The University of Pittsburgh is one of only 62 research institutions that are members of the prestigious Association of
American Universities (AAU). It is also home to an internationally renowned medical center, the University of Pittsburgh
Medical Center. Full-time undergraduate enrollment is 15,422;
the total Pittsburgh campus enrollment, including graduate and
professional school students is 26,860. Four regional campus-

Read all of Vault's College Surveys at **www.vault.com/college**—get complete surveys on 100s of colleges and universities, expert advice on applicaton essays and more.

VAULT CAREER LIBRARY **649**

es, located in Bradford, Greensburg, Johnstown and Titusville, share major resources with the Pittsburgh campus and offer alternative choices of campus size.

The University of Pittsburgh offers an outstanding array of academic options in its nine undergraduate schools and colleges and future opportunities for graduate and professional studies in 14 graduate/professional schools. Some other benefits for prospective undergraduates include:

- Guaranteed graduate/professional school admission to outstanding freshmen in communication science (speech disorders and pathology), dental medicine, dietetics, engineering, law, medicine, occupational therapy, physical therapy, public health, public and international affairs, social work, education and nursing.

- Hundreds of freshman academic scholarships are available to eligible students who apply for admission by January 15 of their senior year in high school. All are renewable for up to four years provided the recipient maintains full-time status and a 3.0 grade point average.

- Eligibility for participation in the University Honors College (UHC) for students in the top 5 percent of their class with 1400 or higher SAT results. (Note: UHC has an outstanding

record of graduates winning prestigious international scholarships, like Rhodes and Marshall Scholarships.)

- Extensive opportunities for learning outside the classroom through undergraduate research, internships, and volunteer work experiences.

- Engineering Co-op Program.

- PITT ARTS: university-sponsored outings linking students with museums and cultural events in the city.

- Free transportation on the Port Authority Transit bus system (including the Airport Flyer) for Pitt students with valid student IDs.

- University Center for International Studies certificate programs.

- Study abroad opportunities in more than 350 locations.

- A campus location in the very livable city of Pittsburgh, allowing easy access to experiential learning opportunities, culture, professional sports, and entertainment.

We invite you to call or e-mail the Undergraduate Visit Center at (412) 624-7717 or viscntr@oafa.pitt.edu to arrange a campus visit, or schedule online at www.pitt.edu/~oafa. For further information, contact the Office of Admissions and Financial Aid.

Villanova University

Admissions Office
800 Lancaster Avenue
Villanova, PA 19085-1672
Admissions phone: (610) 519-4000
Admissions fax: (610) 519-6450
Admissions e-mail: gotovu@villanova.edu
Admissions URL: www.villanova.edu/enroll/admission/

 Admissions

Current student, 9/2003-Submit Date, December 2006

Very difficult admissions process. Need high SATs, high school GPA, extracurricular activities. These are important because the school emphasizes community service. No interviews are held. This school was my first chose so I applied Early Action and was deferred, then I was waitlisted, then I was accepted late May. This school is very big on alumni contacts, so it is a plus if a parent, sibling, or relative attended the school prior.

Alumnus/a, 8/2002-5/2006, September 2006

Villanova doesn't really do interviews unless there are special circumstances (i.e., you're an athlete, you're super smart and might be eligible for a full scholarship, you have other special needs, special reasons). Otherwise Villanova is pretty straightforward in the admissions process: you fill out the Common Application (which they just started accepting last year) as well as a supplementary Villanova application (which means a second essay and a little more detail on your life).

Villanova has gotten progressively harder to get into. Last year I think the acceptance rate was ridiculously low. In fact, I think about 13,000 people applied for only 1,500 spots. Make sure you do well on the essay and really try to stand out. Also, make sure you've got the grades. Do not depend on legacy (i.e., your parents, siblings and so on, having gone there).

Current student, 8/2005-Submit Date, April 2006

The admissions process was rather simple—filling out the required forms writing an essay. The essay should be as honest as possible. As for the w before the admissions process, that was more difficult. It required a strong a demic background and good SAT scores. Achieving this required a lot of wo But as for the actual admissions process; just filling out the forms and awai a response.

Current student, 8/2003-Submit Date, May 2006

You have to submit an essay Villanova asks for, not a general one. Even if y don't have an excellent SAT score, make sure you have a good GPA and go extracurricular activities. I did not have an interview.

Alumnus/a, 8/1999-8/2003, January 2005

My admissions process was wonderful. I had a personal interview, which v very helpful. I remember the admissions person was impressed with my es question answers. The guided tour showed the campus but it did not reveal a thing about real campus life. My grades were borderline to get in and I think interview helped push me over the top. I was very involved in many activiti and mission work and I think that helped too.

Alumnus/a, 8/1998-6/2002, February 2004

Selectivity is very high. The admissions process has become considerably m competitive since I applied. Villanova is trying to establish itself as the pre inent Catholic university in the Northeast, and to this end its standards ha increased dramatically. The number of applicants has increased as well, so your application in on time and as early as you can.

When I applied, the essay question had to do with what you would tell y classmates at a 10-year reunion. I found this to be a breath of fresh air opposed to the traditional personal statement theme. Tips on how to get in: e excellent grades, get a great SAT score, and be very well-rounded in co-curri lar activities, especially with regard to philanthropic involvements. Good l and Go Wildcats!!

lumnus/a, 8/1995-5/1999, January 2004

dmission to Villanova has become increasingly more selective over the years,
d as a result the admissions process, especially the essay portion of the appli-
ion, has become more difficult. Gone are the days of the "where do you see
urself in three, five, 10 years?" This year's essay revolved around the
gustinian theory of "Concordia" and how the "oneness of heart" is essential
all levels of human society and all levels of relationships. The questions were
gue and obtuse and really left the applicant scratching his/her head, wonder-
g "What do they want from me?" Obviously this essay has not been popular
ong the new class of applicants, and they have let the Villanova administra-
n know it (maybe this will cause them to change their ways for next year).
egardless, this overall switch in essay tactics is a prime example that Villanova
clearly trying to raise the academic bar of who it accepts.

ere are certain core values that Villanova University desires its student to
ive for. First, the school prides itself on its distinguished pedigree as a
atholic institution and seeks for its students to demonstrate a commitment to
blic service. I cannot stress this enough, as much of the school's extracurric-
ar activities (including the Greek system) have foundations in service to oth-
s. I would suggest to any applicant that highlighting past community service,
well as community service that you plan on doing in the future, is an excel-
at idea. Second of all, Villanova holds itself out not just as a school, but rather
community within itself, and loves when they have enthusiastic students who
ll be involved in the Villanova Community.

Academics

urrent student, 9/2003-Submit Date, December 2006

ry difficult academically. Strong business school: ranked Number 19 in
usinessWeek this year. Random selectivity (somewhat based on number of
edits) for picking classes. The business school focuses on completing core
urses in the beginning of one's college education and then toward the end,
ajor related courses are emphasized. Professors are usually available outside
the classrooms, especially if you make an appointment with them. Group
lated coursework is emphasized in the business school because of the increas-
g rate of groupwork in the workforce. There is usually a lot of reading
volved in each of the classes and it is important to keep up on all the related
aterials because one can easily get behind.

lumnus/a, 8/2002-5/2006, September 2006

was in the College of Commerce and Finance (recently renamed the VSB:
llanova School of Business). There are a lot of group projects! Be prepared.
ese group projects are usually pretty interesting and often apply to real life sit-
tions (e.g., you have to invent and bring to market a new product or establish
e foundation of a business of your choice and so on); however they do require
rd work and a lot of teamwork.

asses are pretty challenging if you want to do well. That being said, I know
ople who didn't try at all and managed to pass, so it really depends on whether
u want to do well or just enjoy the experience.

urrent student, 8/2005-Submit Date, April 2006

he engineering program is a very academically intense program. The classes
quire a lot of work but are very valuable. An online teacher evaluation web
te allows for easy determination of popular professors. However, all of the
ofessors whom I have encountered so far have been ones whom I like. Getting
to popular classes is a bit difficult because there are so many different starting
mes for registration. Consequentially, if you are assigned a later time, it is a bit
rder to get into the more popular classes.

urrent student, 8/2003-Submit Date, May 2006

he class sizes are fairly small. Even lectures are small—about 50 to 100 stu-
ents. The workload can be demanding and it is not that difficult to get into pop-
ar classes. Grading is somewhat fair and the professors are OK. Some are
viously better than others.

lumnus/a, 8/1999-8/2003, January 2005

he professors were OK. They taught the subjects well, but were way behind in
chnology and did not really know what was happening in the CS real world.

The program was still very new and growing. The classes could have been better. They were too focused on programming instead of the other CS areas.

My brother was there for engineering in the 90s. He thought the engineering
department was fantastic. He learned a lot that was useful for his everyday life.
He went ROTC and has a great career in the Navy.

Alumnus/a, 8/1995-5/1999, January 2004

I was in the Honors Program as a liberal arts major. I highly recommend this
program. All classes were small (maximum 15 students, when I was there) with
excellent professors. The honors classes are more writing and reading intensive
but totally worth it, because they are not lectures but interactive seminars. As far
as ease of grades, Villanova does not have grade inflation. For example, a student who graduated with a 3.43 GPA was in the top 25 percent of her class. That
means 75 percent of students had a GPA of less than 3.43, which means students
generally got B+ or lower, not easy A's.

Alumnus/a, 8/1995-5/1999, January 2004

Depending on which college within the university you attend, the workload,
classes and professors vary greatly. Being a communications major and in the
school of liberal arts and sciences, I can tell you first-hand that in that school the
academic experience you will receive is amazing. The liberal arts school is dedicated to being exactly that—it offers a well-rounded program giving students
the opportunity to take a myriad of classes, by wonderful professors. I can honestly say that, more often than not, the teachers I had were exceptional (one even
sat with me until 4 a.m. helping me finish a project that was not even for her
class!).

I never had a problem getting to take any of the classes that I wanted. If anything, I might not have been able to take a particular class in one semester, but I
always managed to get in the next semester. Furthermore, except for very few
classes, Villanova offers a small school classroom experience on a big school
campus. I never had a class in a lecture hall with 500 students. The biggest class
I had was about 75 people, and that was only one class. Most of my classes were
20 to 30 people (or sometimes smaller). This allowed the students to have a lot
of access to professors, and allowed for a nice student-teacher relationship to
develop.

The grading and workload are pretty comparable to any other academically
respected university. You will not be able to coast through class without doing
any work, but you will be able to get your work done in time for you to enjoy
the social part of college. Like everywhere, there will be periods of projects and
finals—but they never really interfered with my good time, and I am sure that
you will manage just the same.

Employment Prospects

Current student, 9/2003-Submit Date, December 2006

Strong business contacts. Big investment banking and accounting companies
come to recruit at Villanova. The school has a database called Career Services
where one can upload one's résumé and then send them out to employee
prospects. The database shows all the available jobs related to every major, the
deadlines for each application, and the interview schedule. It also shows when
employers are coming to the school to do on-campus recruiting. The school is
big on alumni, so when searching for future employers Villanova holds a strong
bond between alumni. For example, a group of Villanova alumni started the
Morgan Stanley Investment Club.

Alumnus/a, 8/2002-5/2006, September 2006

Villanova has an awesome career center: take advantage of it! They do mock
interviews, résumé writing seminars, and a number of other career-building seminars and aids.

Villanova also has a number of on-campus interviews, career expos and so on.
We also have partnerships with several big-name businesses (J&J, Ernst &
Young and so on) unfortunately, unless you are planning on staying in the tri-
state area, it's pretty hard to find a job elsewhere. Luckily they really teach you
how to network and that's half the battle. That's how I got my job!

Read all of Vault's College Surveys at **www.vault.com/college**—get complete surveys on 100s of colleges and universities, expert advice on applicaton essays and more.

VAULT CAREER LIBRARY **651**

Current student, 8/2005-Submit Date, April 2006

Villanova has a very good post-graduate employment rate and is on good terms with many local branches of national companies. Many big-name companies, such as Lockheed Martin and other such engineering firms, have excellent relations with Villanova University. Internships are available as well.

Alumnus/a, 8/1999-8/2003, January 2005

Internships were a big deal and companies were well-represented. You could find almost anything you wanted. I had an internship lined up at my father's place of business but the recruiting office helped me get credit for it and showed me ways to make the summer internship more productive. I decided to head out on my own to California and arrived in L.A. In L.A., no one had ever heard of Villanova unless he/she were a basketball fan. It took me a long time to find a job and I had to settle for lower pay and work my way up.

Alumnus/a, 1/1999-5/2002, September 2003

Many employers come to campus to recruit. The business school and the engineering students almost always have a job before graduation. Arts and science students are not often as lucky. Career fairs are held once a semester, and the career services office is open every day to help students and alumni alike. Additionally, alumni are more than happy to help out whenever possible. Alumni even come to campus to do mock interviews with students to help them prepare for an interview in their field. Overall, the school wants the students to succeed. They will do whatever needs to be done to help them.

Quality of Life

Alumnus/a, 8/2002-5/2006, September 2006

In terms of campus housing, the way campus is set up is that freshmen mostly reside on south campus, sophomores primarily reside on main campus, and juniors primarily reside on west campus. Seniors are not guaranteed housing unless they are scholarship athletes, nurses, female engineers, or presidential scholares. It's more fun to live off campus senior year anyhow; it's a transition period as you start to wean yourself off campus life and onto living in the "real world."

Housing is OK freshman and sophomore years as long as you don't have a triple. The best places to live are Stanford for freshman and either the quad (in terms of being in a prime locale, but it is loud and it has small rooms) or Good Council (big rooms, sinks in the rooms, sucky locale) for sophomore year.

As long as you score an apartment for junior year, you are in luck—they are gorgeous!

Villanova is located on the Main Line. There are plenty of small shops, restaurants (Minilla's 24-hour diner is a campus fav and there is a Chili's, a Bertucci's, and several others).

Current student, 8/2005-Submit Date, April 2006

The facilities and dining are some of the best in the country. The area is a very safe area. The local police are always patrolling the surrounding area and there is plenty of campus safety patrolling the campus. They even offer personal escorting if desired during the night. The dormitories are some of the more bigger ones out of the dorms that I have seen. They are rather nice. Overall, there are not that many issues that negatively affect quality of life.

Current student, 8/2003-Submit Date, May 2006

The housing is not that great unless you are a junior. There is no guaranteed housing for seniors. Crime and safety are fine. Dining services are OK. Compared to some local schools, it is good. Compared to other prominent schools, it is just OK. The student body is not diverse.

Alumnus/a, 8/1995-5/1999, January 2004

Quality of life at Villanova is close to the ideal one imagines when picturin traditional college experience. Housing has improved dramatically over the decade, with the addition of upperclassman apartments, which are new, spacio and pleasant. Some dorms are now coed, and there are a few specialized dorr including the Freshman Experience Dorm, which creates a living/learning/soc environment in which students integrate all these aspects of college life with group of 15 to 20 students. Dining options have also increased, with more atte tion to diversity in diet. Food plans are versatile enough to allow varied dini options from the traditional dining hall to convenience store settings. The ca pus is remarkably beautiful, something out of a movie. The campus is gre grassy and tree-filled. The buildings are old and stately. The Main Line outs Philadelphia plays gracious host to the campus with its idyllic, safe atmosphe

Social Life

Current student, 9/2003-Submit Date, December 2006

Villanova is mostly a bar school, but it is close enough to Philadelphia to hav city feel. One could take a train into Philadelphia, which is approximately minutes, and the train stop is located right on the university's campus, which very convenient. 33 percent of the student body participates in the Greek life. is nice because it is not too overwhelming that those who do not participate Greek life feel left out.

Alumnus/a, 8/2002-5/2006, September 2006

There are plenty of parties and things to do on campus. Nova is also pretty cl to Philly with two trains that run through campus going into Center City; unf tunately, most Nova students don't take full advantage of the city's proximity

There are tons of bars on the main line that pretty much cater to Nova, prima ly, and then also to the smaller schools in the area (of which there are severa Brownie's, Erin's, Kelly's are the most fun with a variety of others also f quented by the Nova student body. Manayunk is another happening area.

Greek system is available and has plenty of parties and off-campus housi Nova does not provide frat or sorority houses so as not to isolate this group.

Nova's a damp campus meaning that if you are 21 you can drink, but if y aren't you can't (obviously because this is a U.S. law). That doesn't mean t there aren't parties on campus and that there isn't underage drinking.

Current student, 8/2005-Submit Date, April 2006

The social life is really good. There are plenty of campus-supported groups tl plan many activities during the week and for the weekend. There are sever bars that are rather close to the campus that students over 21 go to in order enjoy. Greek life is very popular although no Greek housing exist. What is re ly nice is that Villanova is rather close to Philadelphia, so all of its bar and cl scenes are available to the students. Furthermore, the King of Prussia Mall also a short drive away, and weekend buses are provided to transport students and from the mall.

Current student, 8/2003-Submit Date, May 2006

The student body is not that diverse; however, this is slowly starting to chang Villanova is not located near a city but there is access by having trains on ca pus. There are a few good bars and restaurant nearby. To go to clubs, you ha to go into the city (Philadelphia). A lot of the student body is involved in a fi or sorority.

Brown University

Admissions Office
Brown University
Providence, RI 02912
Admissions phone: (401) 863-2378
Admissions e-mail: admission_undergraduate@brown.edu
Admissions URL:
www.brown.edu/Administration/Admission/

Note: The school has chosen not to review the student surveys submitted.

Admissions

Current student, 9/2003-Submit Date, August 2006

The application includes a personal statement and a few shorter essays, all of which must be written in your own handwriting, so write neatly! There is also a mandatory interview that can do a lot to get you in if your interviewer really takes a liking to you. Brown likes to see passion, dedication, ambition and self-reflection. It is a very selective university with an admissions process that is not really predictable. It may seem random who gets in and who doesn't. They want personality, originality and spark. Be yourself and be different. Stand out in your essay and in your interview.

Current student, Engineering, 9/2003-Submit Date, November 2006

The admission essay is probably the most important factor in the admissions process. With every applicant demonstrating strong academic record and extracurriculars, what could distinguish you is the essay. I spent hours crafting my admissions essay—show your perspective, depth and intelligence.

Current student, 8/2005-Submit Date, October 2006

I applied through the Early Acceptance program. Applications were due November 1st, and applicants were notified in mid-December. This process allowed me to avoid filling out many other tedious applications and is highly recommended. The Brown application for admission is fairly standard, but grants quite a bit of freedom in writing submissions, giving several specific questions as well as on open-ended option. Interviews are optional, and while I actively had to request and seek out an interviewer, it was a great experience. The selectivity at Brown is quite high, but matriculating classes are continually growing with increased applicant pools.

Current student, 9/2002-Submit Date, January 2006

Brown University became a hot commodity when it began rejecting kids who had excellent overall scores and activities, but lacked that certain special Brown something: quirkiness, coolness, a commitment to social justice or whatnot. (I worked at the admissions office for my freshman and sophomore years.) Many of those kids were forced to settle for New Haven instead and will carry a chip on their shoulders for the rest of their lives. Essays about coming to understand one's heritage or identity, essays that show creativity and initiative rather than pure academic skills, and essays that show how quirky and cool you are are all positives. The interview is not very important. The essays used to be mandatory hand-written, but they are no longer, due to the encroachment of the Internet. The admissions officers are cool people. I was once told by a former Brown admissions officer that an essay reader doesn't want to see an essay full of B.S.—(s)he wants to see an essay full of exquisite B.S. After all, the ability to B.S. really makes Brown students what we are.

Current student, 9/2003-Submit Date, November 2005

Admissions process is comparable to other Ivy League universities. I filled out my application, but did not have an in-person interview. My application also included an essay portion that was required to be hand-written. In addition, a picture was asked to be included in the application (at school, we consistently joke that the reason why our campus has such good-looking people is because of

our admissions process). I would suggest that you focus on things that set you apart from the average person. Brown is definitely not a school for cookie cut outs. We like people to be bright, different, passionate and interested in new things.

Alumnus/a, 9/2000-5/2004, October 2005

I started by sending in my completed application. The application to Brown is a bit unique, as it requires the essay be completely hand-written on the application form. After sending in the application, I got an interview in my hometown. The interview was very informal, and not very important in the selection process. Basically, it was a chance for a Brown alumnus/a to see if you have any freakish, completely anti-social tendencies that make it difficult for you to interact with society. If not, you get a pass. The interview was also a chance to get more of a feel about Brown, although my interviewer had graduated 30 or 40 years previously, so his impressions were likely not the most accurate. Brown is a ridiculously selective university, with an admissions rate in the neighborhood of 16 percent.

Academics

Current student, 9/2003-Submit Date, August 2006

Brown students benefit from attending a smaller, private school. It is rare to not get into a class of your choice. Even with the most popular, limited enrollment classes, all students should be able to get in over the course of their four years. There are no requirements at Brown, besides those of your chosen major. Thus it is completely up to you to shape your liberal education by giving yourself both breadth and depth in you curriculum. Most majors require only 10 to 15 courses, while you need to complete 30 courses to graduate. There is much left up for you to decide. There are many extremely popular "must take" classes that everyone talks about and are excellent courses. They are easy to get into. Almost all classes are well-liked and a magazine called *Critical Review* gives you honest reviews on courses and professors, helping guide your course selection. Grading is fair, and getting A's is not too difficult. Professors are accessible, and for the most part excited to talk with students.

Current student, Engineering, 9/2003-Submit Date, November 2006

Professors are very accessible. While I've built a mentoring relationship with only one professor, those who are more aggressive often get to know a few professors well. Also, they are very accessible outside of classes—I feel extremely comfortable e-mailing them and dropping by their office hours asking questions.

As an engineering major, the workload could be hard. With the open curriculum, however, I almost never get stressed because I know I have the control. I could take a class S/NC anytime. Alternatively, there was a semester when I really wanted to dive into the humanities, and I had the absolute freedom to do so. The culture is take whatever you want to learn at the moment, and when you really want to learn something, you'll never feel burnt out despite the workload. Finally, students are extremely supportive. We care about what we learn, but people always go out of their way to help you understand/do the work. It's about collaborating, not competing.

Current student, 8/2005-Submit Date, October 2006

Brown's unique New Curriculum allows students to spread their studies across disciplines as they wish and more easily explore new disciplines. There are no core requirements or distribution requirements. Students are also allowed to take as many courses pass/fail as they choose. This option is rarely used for particularly challenging courses (and especially rarely within one's major) but rather for classes students have no prior experience in or ones they are experimenting with (e.g., an engineering major in an art history class.) Brown's small graduate school lends great emphasis to undergraduate teaching, and the quality of classes is usually regarded as very high. Popular classes can be difficult to get into if they have capped enrollment, but persistence and contact with professors usually yield successful results. While grade inflation is an issue discussed across all

Read all of Vault's College Surveys at www.vault.com/college—get complete surveys on 100s of colleges and universities, expert advice on applicaton essays and more.

VAULT CAREER LIBRARY 653

Ivy League schools, most students believe their grades to be fairly given. Most students have close personal contact with at least one professor, and almost always find accessing their professors easy. The workload depends highly on the department and particular class, but Brown's shopping period (the first two weeks of the semester in which students can freely add or drop new courses) usually allows them to balance their workload by getting an early idea of just how their classes will be.

Current student, 9/2002-Submit Date, January 2006

The open curriculum allows you to choose your classes flexibly, doesn't force you into core classes, and allows you to make your own way in life. This can be good or bad. You can take all brain-rotting classes or you can give yourself an excellent, well-rounded education. Some classes are large, and some are small. You have two weeks at the beginning of the semester to choose which ones you wish to take. Small classes are limited enrollment, but you can always get in if you show loyalty to the teacher during shopping period and continue going every day and doing the homework. The IR program is highly flexible and interdisciplinary. The MCM program is filled with Foucault and deconstructionist mishmash. The history program is excellent. The comp lit program is excellent. The engineering and science programs are excellent.

Current student, 9/2003-Submit Date, November 2005

The undergraduate programs at Brown are incredible. A student can do anything from choose his/her own major to taking any class pass/fail. This supports a student's ability to take challenging courses, without being fearful of the manner in which that grade could affect his or her overall ranking. In addition, Brown does not calculate a GPA, and does not require that any general ed classes be taken. Grades are single letter (A, B, C) and there are no pluses or minuses. I did biomedical engineering, so the flexibility in courses was less relevant for me. For others, though, they had a major that required only eight courses, and so 24 courses were available for anything they wanted. That's amazing—never will you be able to take a class about something you're interested in, without having to worry about requirements.

Current student, 8/2000-Submit Date, April 2004

The sciences at Brown are as challenging as can be, but students can skate by in the humanities with little effort. You really can get a great education here, but you have to be willing to go beyond what little work is required to get the grade. Possibly the worst thing about Brown is that every class here has to be "different" in a progressive and enlightening way. The traditional canon is disregarded to the point where many Brown students couldn't have an intelligent conversation about literature with the average community college freshman. We have only one Shakespeare class between the theatre and English departments, and four classes that focus primarily on the works of Hannah Arendt. (Our school's humor magazine just put out an issue with a segment entitled "New Additions to the Course Announcement Bulletin." Two of the classes listed were: American Civ115—Issues of Race, Gender and Class, and Physics 145—Issues of Race, Gender and Class in Thermodynamics.) This about captures it. Ever wanted to take a course called "Black Lavender: Gay and Lesbian African-American Playwrights of the 1960s and 70s"? Come to Brown and you can.

 ## Employment Prospects

Current student, 9/2003-Submit Date, August 2006

Brown attracts all the most prestigious recruiters in the highly competitive investment banking and consulting fields. A larger Career Development Office and staff are extremely helpful, providing weekly workshops for all classes, not just seniors and juniors. They give workshops on choosing a career, résumé and cover letter building, interviewing skills and more. They also put together numerous career fairs and receptions over the course of the year. A large alumni network and database allow students to contact alumni all over the world. Also, Brown's job link online has up-to-date information on all jobs offered and all interviews taking place on campus. Brown is a great place to find a job.

Current student, 8/2003-Submit Date, October 2005

The biggest employers are the Peace Corps and Goldman Sachs. Career services can revise your résumé and give you some basic info. But, I believe the key to getting jobs is who you end up knowing and how well you can present your-

self in an interview. Any place you go should have an alumni database. If [...] spend a weekend getting dozens of names for industries in which you're in [...] ested—you can probably come up with enough contacts to get career info, [...] internship offers or ask for more names for more job offers. Career services [...] helped me make my résumé look good. But, from family, friends and my t[...] ative personality, I have gotten more internship offers the other way arou[...] Granted, a Brown degree will probably carry more weight 10 years from now[...] with grad school admissions. But, no college will get me or anyone else a [...] You need to get that yourself. Please don't let that control what kind of coll[...] you want to go to.

Current student, 9/2003-Submit Date, November 2005

Sure, major top employers hit up Brown when recruiting, but it is not viewe[...] high as other Ivy League universities. The alumni network is spectacular, ar[...] have received plenty of offers via this method of communication. Not m[...] Brown kids go into finance, but a large portion are interested in the environm[...] and politics, and so D.C. is naturally a place that many students feed into[...] found that most of the people I knew at Brown went overseas or did teaching[...] pursued another degree.

Current student, 8/2003-Submit Date, November 2004

Brown students are diverse enough that the top four employers after gradua[...] are Goldman Sachs, Teach for America, Morgan Stanley and the Peace Co[...] The alumni network is very active, with people from every major I-bank com[...] back and interviewing. The career services people are very nice, helping[...] absolutely any circumstance. On-campus recruiting, done through e-recr[...] ing.com, is probably one of the most comprehensive sites out there. The p[...] tige of the employers coming to Brown is second to none (actually, proba[...] Harvard and Yale). Internships are a big deal to most students during their j[...] ior year. For example, a recent survey of Brown sophomores said that merel[...] percent actually thought an internship was a necessity. On the other hand, sc[...] 63 percent of Brown juniors consider a summer internship to be worthy of t[...] attention.

 ## Quality of Life

Current student, 9/2003-Submit Date, August 2006

Students live on campus for three years and can choose to stay on campus [...] senior year. Thus, the dorms are the center of campus life. They are well-ma[...] tained with spacious rooms. There are many possible living configurations fr[...] singles and doubles to seven-person suites with living rooms. Dining consist[...] two large dining halls with excellent salad bars and healthy options, as well a[...] variety of snack bars where you can use your meal credit. A pizza place, a b[...] rito bar and a fast food hangout are all such places. Campus facilities are ex[...] lent, with many 24-hour study spaces in libraries and residence halls. There[...] wireless Internet on most of the campus. There are two large fitness centers [...] a few smaller satellite fitness rooms with many cardio machines and f[...] weights. There are also recreation areas with video games and pool tables. [...] on-campus bar hosts live music and open-mic nights for students. The nei[...] borhood is full of restaurants, bars and fun stores, however crime can be an is[...] and students should be careful walking around alone at night.

Current student, 8/2005-Submit Date, October 2006

The quality of life at Brown is generally regarded highly. There are often ho[...] ing shortages, but students are guaranteed housing for all four years of und[...] graduate study. Freshman housing is assigned randomly. Upperclassmen er[...] a housing lottery individually or by group and select any available room on ca[...] pus based on a lottery number randomly assigned by class. The campus is loc[...] ed on College Hill, a short walk from downtown Providence and E[...] Providence. It is utterly beautiful. Recent major renovations include a new L[...] Sciences Building, and a giant pedestrian passage way is in the works that [...] connect the whole campus. Two main dining halls provide decent food ([...] Verner-Wooley Dining Hall is strongly preferred over Sharpe Refectory) a[...] smaller eateries offer coffee and so on at various times throughout the d[...] Athletic facilities abound, with the main sports center offering just about a[...] thing desired, and smaller gyms dispersed throughout campus, which are v[...] nice. The neighborhood tends to be upper-middle class—off-campus housing[...] affordable in groups, and most residences are large houses dating back to [...]

th or 18th centuries. Recent crime has prompted the arming of Brown Police
ficers, and issues of police brutality and racial discrimination have been taken
between university students and the Providence Police Dept lately, but most
gard the campus as very safe. SafeWalk—a program where students escort
ers at night—and SafeRide—a 24-hour shuttle—offer much comfort and sup-
rt.

rrent student, 9/2002-Submit Date, January 2006

own is consistently cited as the one place where everyone loves their school.
e housing is sometimes a bit shoddy, and one must go through an utterly
achiavellian housing lottery each year in order to acquire a living space. The
npus is beautiful except for several major concrete eyesores created during
e mid 1960s, unfortunately including some of the main libraries. Muggings
e not very dangerous but somewhat frequent, though the police have recently
en armed so they will now be able to actually pursue muggers. Dining con-
ues to improve in variety and flexibility.

rrent student, 9/2003-Submit Date, November 2005

solutely amazing—never will you be in a school with students who have such
liversity in their interests, thinking and cultures. The engineers in my cours-
were also some of the best poets I have ever met. Students are required to live
campus three of the four years, and then 85 percent of the students move off
ir fourth year. Each of the dorms has its own charm, but some are definitely
tter than others. The housing lottery can work either for you or against you—
my case, it worked against me (every single year!).

Social Life

rrent student, 9/2003-Submit Date, August 2006

ere are some great bars around campus. Viva hosts the European crowd with
ig dance floor that gets crowded. Paragon is a fusion restaurant with a bar
a that fills up in the later hours. Liquid Lounge is an underground, more mel-
v bar that also hosts Providence locals. Spats is the new sports bar that has
come very popular. Every Wednesday night a bar called Fish Co. throws a
rty for Brown students with drink specials and dancing that is infamous on
npus. Providence is also home to many fine restaurants. Student favorites
clude two very affordable BYOB sushi spots, and a huge selection of Italian
staurants in the Italian neighborhood, Federal Hill. The frat scene is very
iall, but still provides occasional parties. Most large parties are held at hous-
and can be really fun. If you're looking to go out five nights a week, it def-
tely can be done at Brown.

Current student, 8/2005-Submit Date, October 2006

Social life at Brown is fantastic. Nearby Thayer Street offers a myriad of bars,
clubs, and restaurants (of many ethnicities) that are always regarded as some of
Providence's best (East Side Pockets, Kabob and Curry, Antonio's Pizza are all
immensely popular). Throughout the year this is the place to socialize off campus. Also nearby is the Wickendon St. area, a little less lively but cozier and
quaint (the Coffee Exchange roasts its own beans). Few people date, but most
enjoy meeting people and going out frequently. There are weekly college nights
at local clubs (especially Fish Co.) that are popular. Greek life is present but not
dominating (five or so fraternities, two sororities, two co-ed literary societies)
and program housing groups—ranging from Technology to Cooking groups—
offer other events. A cappella is very popular, with campus favorites ranging
from the pirate choir, ARGHH!!! to the whistling choir Lip Service. Midnight
organ concerts are given in the university's old chapel, and students bundle up
in sleeping bags to watch.

Current student, 9/2004-Submit Date, September 2005

The social life at Brown is varied, ranging from alcohol-free get-togethers (a
cappella concerts) to hard-core drinking and drug use. It's probably not remarkable in that regard, except that it is probably one of the few schools where you
will regularly hear two drunk kids arguing over Kierkegaard. The Greek scene
is relatively small, but lively.

Current student, 8/2003-Submit Date, November 2004

Not much of a social life unless you look for it. Restaurants are very good
around the area. The dating scene is not very good, with attractive people
everywhere wanting to hook up but nothing really serious. Greek life at Brown
is practically nonexistent compared to other Ivy League schools like Dartmouth.
Some 7 percent of all students are in a fraternity or sorority, and their parties are
usually attended by the same 15 percent of students. Most students find their
social life in private parties hosted by seniors off campus, by parties by organizations on campus (Democrats, Lesbian Gay Transexual Bisexual Organization,
French House).

Current student, 8/2000-Submit Date, April 2004

Social life here is pretty low-key. Frats are a small phenomenon, and they offer
parties that only freshmen and sophomores with no better alternatives attend.
People basically spend evenings and weekends hanging out with a few friends
in dormrooms. There are some clubs and bars around campus, but generally they
are only frequented by certain well-defined segments of the student population.
Mainly athletes, party girls and the international jet-setters.

Providence College

ovidence College
49 River Avenue
ovidence, RI 02918-0001
dmissions phone: (401) 865-2535 or (800) 721-6444
dmissions fax: (401) 865-2826
dmissions e-mail: pcadmiss@providence.edu
dmissions URL: www.providence.edu/Admission/

Admissions

rrent student, Biology, 5/2003-Submit Date, April 2007

e tours they give at Providence College are among the best in the nation. I
red a lot of schools, but nowhere else were the tour guides so engaging and
en to questions. The school is hard to get into, but below the best Ivy League
iools of the nation. If this is your top choice, I recommend applying Early
tion. Also SAT scores are no longer required for admittance.

Current student, Political Science, 9/2003-Submit Date, April 2007

The admissions process was fairly easy since the school was on the Common
Application. No additional application was needed. Also, Providence College
doesn't do interviews (or at least they didn't while I was applying). As for selectivity, the school is constantly making itself better and better, so it is getting
harder and harder to gain admission year after year.

Current student, Psychology, 9/2006-Submit Date, April 2007

Providence has grown increasingly selective over the past five years, yet, has
recently (for the Class of 2011) decided to omit the SAT, which was required for
my class year (2010). There is no interview offered. Essays, as with any other
school, are used (with the hope) to introduce a unique side of the student.
Moreover, it is plausible that the significance placed on the essay has increased
due to the removal of the previously required SAT and SAT Subject Tests.
Strong recommendations and challenging classes in high school (APs and honors courses) separate the student by increasing his or her potential acceptance to
PC.

Read all of Vault's College Surveys at **www.vault.com/college**—get complete surveys on 100s of colleges and universities, expert advice on applicaton essays and more.

VAULT CAREER LIBRARY **655**

Current student, Business, 9/2004-Submit Date, April 2007

No interview is required for admission. SATs are no longer required, but when they were I believe the average was around 1100. I don't have much advice for getting in except to write an original essay that will stay in the reader's mind.

Current student, Mathematics, 9/2006-Submit Date, April 2007

Providence just recently stopped accepting SAT scores, and instead looks for well-rounded students and something that makes them stand out above all (juggling swords in Europe). Admissions here is extremely helpful. You receive a call once you have been admitted.

Current student, Chemistry, 9/2005-Submit Date, April 2007

The admissions process is fairly typical of other schools across the nation. Providence College uses the Common Application. In addition to the Common Application, an essay, letters of recommendation and high school transcripts are required. In 2007, Providence College went test optional, which means that SAT scores are no longer required. I would suggest submitting them if you are a particularly strong candidate because very high scores can increase your chances of securing one of the many academic scholarships the school gives out. If you don't submit SAT scores, it will not hurt you in any way. Most students at Providence College were very well-rounded in high school. It is not uncommon for a student on campus to have been in the top 10 percent of their class, been captain of a varsity sport, and to have volunteered 10 hours a week in high school.

Current student, Business, 9/2004-Submit Date, April 2007

Interview process was pretty simple. Common Application with a supplement, if I recall properly. I did Early Action. Good SAT scores, grades and teacher recommendations will generally do it, and if your essays are well-written you are golden. From what I'm told, applying has become more selective since I applied, but if you scored 1280+ on your SATs and have a 3.4 GPA or better in high school, you have as good a shot as anyone.

Current student, Business, 10/2006-Submit Date, April 2007

PC takes a different caliber of student. I think the applicant needs to separate him or herself from the crowd by participating in numerous extracurriculars, community service and really accomplishing something in those organizations or service. This is not your average school; you have to show them you're different.

Current student, Cultural Studies, 9/2006-Submit Date, April 2007

I did not visit Providence or really know anything about it prior to applying. I sent in an application because I applied to many similar schools and Providence was on the Common Application. Interviews were not required here but I did interview at several other schools. Two essays were required for Providence but I was able to use each of them at other schools as well. I did not feel that the school was very selective.

Alumnus/a, Political Science, 9/2001-5/2005, April 2007

Now that SATs are no longer required for admission, extracurricular activities are crucial, especially a strong investment in one or two. Similarly, be sure to make the essay truly personal. The admissions counselors take a great deal of time reviewing applications and the essay is a great way to allow the counselors to learn more about you. Finally, all of the GPAs are recalculated to create a standard system of comparison. Therefore, taking a greater number of honors and AP courses is very helpful for a higher recalculated GPA.

 **Academics**

Current student, Political Science, 9/2003-Submit Date, April 2007

PC has a fantastic core curriculum, including the Development of Western Civilization Program, which meets five days a week for the first two years of college. It approaches the development of Western civilization from the four-pronged perspective of theology, literature, philosophy and history. It is team taught by four professors, and the class is a lecture four times a week and breaks down into a 20-person seminar once per week.

The political science program is wonderful. The professors are extremely accommodating to students, while at the same time, hold them to the highest aca-

demic standards. It is a very writing-intensive program, with excellent supp also for internships and independent research. Upper-level courses genera expect at least 20 pages of writing per semester, along with vigorous class d cussion based on readings.

Current student, Biology, 5/2003-Submit Date, April 2007

The biology major is one of the most demanding at the college. The classes this department are all pretty good, but it is not easy to get into the ones y want, even as a senior. The workload is intense your first three years, but eas in your fourth as you start applying to grad schools.

Current student, Business, 9/2004-Submit Date, April 2007

The classes are tough, and the Western Civilization program takes up a lot time. There is about an even split of really good professors to just OK prof sors. And as you become an upperclassman, it becomes increasingly easier get desired classes; however, there isn't a wide selection of classes to take.

Current student, Business, 9/2004-Submit Date, April 2007

One thing that sets Providence College apart from other colleges is the man tory Development of Western Civilization four semester long progra Freshmen and sophomores choose a "team" of two to four professors who sp cialize in literature, philosophy, theology, and history. Most students dread t course because it is five days a week and an additional two theology and two p losophy courses are required to fulfill the core. Once you have completed course though, the knowledge attained is worth the torture. Core classes (cla es that need to be completed before graduating) tend to have 20 to 30 stude in them. Once you get more concentrated into your major class sizes drop about five to 15 students. Getting popular professors is difficult for freshm The workload depends entirely on your major. Sciences expect a lot of study for exams. Business majors expect to spend a lot of time out of class worki on group projects and presentations. Art majors will spend a lot of time in studio.

Current student, Political Science, 9/2004-Submit Date, April 20(

Providence College is not the easy safety school that some people make it out be. The workload is demanding, and I have personally seen transfer stude struggle with the change from their other schools. The Western Civ Program t is required of freshmen and sophomores does not seem like a good program you're going through it, but afterwards you will understand the significance it. I highly recommend the Honors Program for all those invited into it. T Western Civ classes are much smaller and you get to know your classmates a teachers a lot better. Civ can be overwhelming, but going through it in a sma er setting is helpful. Getting the classes you want gets easier as you advan through the years. As a freshman, you obviously have last choice so sometim you're left without any great options. The administration has recently re-do the way our schedule works, so it provides more options for students. On whole, professors are well liked. Ratemyprofessors.com is an excelle resource, so definitely take advantage of it. Most of them grade pretty fai although as with all schools, you will come across a few sticklers.

Current student, Biology, 9/2004-Submit Date, April 2007

Registration day is probably one of the most frustrating and stressful days of semester. As an underclassman, it is sometimes difficult to get the classes y want, with the professors you want. The teachers know you by name, which my book is a good thing. I would say that 90 percent of my teachers knew name and still know it today when I see them in passing. Workload is manag able so long as you get a routine down for time management.

Alumnus/a, Political Science, 9/2002-5/2006, April 2007

I loved the Political Science Dept. Even though I was assigned to one profess as my advisor, I could go to any of the professors for advice on classes and h to arrange my schedule. The core curriculum at PC is quite extensive and d give you a good insight into other fields of study but at the same time it d become a bit redundant and takes away from flexibility and freedom to take el tive classes outside of your major. I had a major and a minor and I only to maybe one class that had nothing to do with my minor, major or core. Also w the theology requirements on top of those taught in the Development of West Civilization series, you get bored with theology. Moreover, due to the fact t theology, to Providence, really means Catholicism, the classes can cover simi material. I didn't take any classes on other religions or religious though Besides that, the classes are great. All of the professors I have had are incre

well versed in their fields, but at the same time they are very approachable
and willing to help all of their students. Some professors are easier or more difficult then others but overall they are all pretty fair. As long as you give it effort
you can do very well. Also there are enough class offerings to get what you
want. You may not get the professor you want, but if two professors are teaching the same class, the classwork and grading is very similar and in many cases
the professors work together on the class. The workload isn't too bad either.
There is a lot of reading, especially for a liberal arts major like Political Science.
As a Political Science major I wrote at least one 10- to 15-page paper per class
after the two introductory courses. By your senior year multiple 10- to 15-page
papers are expected of you and your Senior Capstone Paper is expected to be
about 20 pages or more, but by the time you get to that point you are well-trained
in how to conduct research and write an extensive paper.

Looking back on it the smaller papers in my freshman and sophomore year were
more difficult because I hadn't developed a system or style of my own. After
meeting with professors time after time to discuss papers and research it got easier because I had developed a system to organize my thoughts and write a good
research paper. In my experience there were times I had more work then others
but overall, it never got to the point where I couldn't do extracurricular activities
or go to events on campus every once in a while because I had too much work.
With good time management you can do a little bit of everything while still getting the work done.

 Employment Prospects

Current student, Business, 9/2003-Submit Date, April 2007

eFriars is a great web site Career Services offers that has many prestigious
employers. I was able to get an internship with one of the Big Four accounting
firms for the summer entering into my senior year, in which case I was offered
a job in August before senior year even began, which was very nice.

Current student, Political Science, 9/2003-Submit Date, April 2007

I'm not sure if employers see PC grads as having "prestige" but they seem eager
to at least interview us. The school provides us with many job opportunities
through web sites and job fairs. They also have a good program in place to help
with résumés and other related topics. Internships are also available, but you
are not required to take them in most majors. I think most graduates get decent
jobs when they enter the workforce. Also, alumni have high regard for PC, so
they are willing to go out of the way to help fellow alumni.

Current student, Psychology, 9/2006-Submit Date, April 2007

I believe PC provides a solid educational background/status that gains the attention of prospective employers. For those in the psychology program (set up
specifically for students who want to get a PhD in psychology), many opportunities are available for those applying to grad school.

Current student, Business, 9/2004-Submit Date, April 2007

PC has a large network of alumni throughout the Northeast in a variety of positions. This is one of the school's biggest assets. These alumni will generally be
very helpful in networking while trying to land internships and job offers.
Additionally, Career Services sponsors good programs to aid with résumés and
cover letters, interview tactics, dress attire and formal dining.

However, a glaring weakness in the school's employment prospects occurs in the
limited scope of its reach. The school is very active and well-known among
employers in Massachusetts and Rhode Island, but surprisingly, a few states
away, in New Jersey, New York and Pennsylvania this is not the case. The vast
majority of internships made available through Career Services are in these two
states. Furthermore, if you are not from the Northeast, utilizing alumni to network will be of little consequence if you don't desire to work in the Northeast.

On-campus recruiting opportunities are generally made known through academic departments, although Career Services does keep a list of upcoming events as
well. These are helpful, but again are limited to the scope of the Northeast, particularly MA and RI.

Current student, Political Science, 9/2004-Submit Date, April 2007

There is a sense of prestige that comes along with a Providence College diploma, and employers do like to see the name. Since Providence is located in a capital city, there are plenty of internships to come by, especially if you're interested in law or government. However, finding internships for all majors is relatively easy.

 Quality of Life

Current student, Chemistry, 9/2005-Submit Date, April 2007

The quality of life here at Providence College is very good. Our dorms tend to
be a little congested, and the food is average, but the community spirit on campus is very strong. This is a school where students frequently hold doors open
for each other, and we look out for each other.

Current student, Political Science, 9/2003-Submit Date, April 2007

I have had an overwhelmingly positive experience, and over the course of my
four-year career, I have noticed nothing but improvements in quality of life
issues. The housing process is based on a lottery and while the process itself
may be a bit hectic, in the end, from my experience, most students end up being
accommodated. A brand-new, multi-million dollar fitness center will be open in
the fall.

Current student, Biology, 5/2003-Submit Date, April 2007

The apartment and suite-style housing options are phenomenal. The regular dormitories leave much to be desired. The dining services are both really good and
the cafeteria staff becomes like surrogate grandmothers to you because they are
so nice. Alumni Hall cafeteria is definitely the better of the two and the brand-
new Jazzman's coffee shop is excellent. PC is not located in the best of neighborhoods though.

Current student, Political Science, 9/2003-Submit Date, April 2007

Housing is good, but slightly overpriced. The college has been accepting more
students than it can handle, so they have been crowding some of the dorms but
not offering a discount in price. I found the cable/Internet to be pretty bad,
although it seems to have improved this year. The neighborhood is an urban one,
so it is not wise to walk alone at night. On campus, however, crime is pretty low.

Current student, Mathematics, 9/2006-Submit Date, April 2007

Curfews and parietals exist here, which means that those of the opposite sex
must be out of the dorms by 12 a.m., Sunday through Thursday, and 2 a.m.,
Friday and Saturday. PC is in a rough area of town but security does an outstanding job making it safe on campus. Off campus, don't walk alone after sunset. Housing is pretty spacious. However many upperclassmen opt to stay on
campus living in suites and apartments, which were newly renovated. This
means that it can be hard for underclassmen to get their first choices.

Current student, Education, 9/2006-Submit Date, April 2007

The campus is a little bit old, but they are working to modernize it and update its
facilities. They recently installed wireless Internet in almost all of the buildings
and are building a state-of-the-art gym that should be done in Fall, 2007.
Housing selection can be stressful, as most students prefer to live on campus.

Alumnus/a, History, 9/2002-5/2006, April 2007

Quality of life at PC is very good. The campus is very pretty and small enough
that it is never a long walk to get to anything on campus. The housing choices
PC offers are some of the best I have seen. Freshmen live in traditional dorms.
Sophomores, juniors and seniors can pick from a variety of on-campus housing
options, including four- and six-person suites and four- and six-person apartments. A significant percentage of students used to live off campus as upperclassmen but that percentage has been on the decline since these new (and really nice) housing options have become available. The dining is pretty much standard college fare, nothing to write home about.

Read all of Vault's College Surveys at www.vault.com/college—get complete surveys on 100s of colleges and universities, expert advice on applicaton essays and more.

VAULT CAREER LIBRARY 657

Social Life

Current student, Political Science, 9/2003-Submit Date, April 2007

I have had an amazing social experience. Much of the social scene is based on the off-campus bars, which underclassmen use fake IDs to get into. However, both PC and the City of Providence are working to crack down on this. For upperclassmen, the on-campus bar, McPhail's, is a wonderful social outlet. Live music is provided nearly every Thursday, Friday and Saturday night, and there is a nice mix of student bands and bigger name local favorites. Once per month, the junior and senior classes hold Class Nights at McPhail's to promote class camaraderie.

Social life is very important at PC, and many students are of the mentality: "work hard, play harder." During the week, throughout the day and early evening, the library and computer labs are packed with students pouring over their work, but at the same time, any night of the week, those same students can be found stumbling out of local bars.

Current student, Business, 9/2004-Submit Date, April 2007

The biggest problem on campus is that there are no locations on campus, except residence halls, open 24 hours a day so it makes it difficult to socialize without going off campus. But, being in Providence (a small city) is very conducive to the students' social lives as it allows opportunities to go out and explore without feeling overwhelmed.

Current student, Political Science, 9/2003-Submit Date, April 2007

The social life is good, although the school [is trying to reduce drinking]. The nearby bars are decent, but the best place is the on-campus bar, McPhail's. It is safe, on campus and cheap. The dating scene does not really exist. The school has many events going on all the time, especially service projects through Campus Ministry. They do events such as Habitat for Humanity and going to local soup kitchens. There is no Greek life on campus, although the school has Friars Club, which is a selective group that seems to think it is a co-ed Greek club.

Current student, Business, 9/2004-Submit Date, April 2007

This is a bar school. Don't expect many house parties unless you have some upperclassman friends who live off campus. Most students have a fake ID, even if they don't drink because the bar is the place to socialize. We also have an on-campus bar, McPhail's, that anyone can go into and there are usually local bands playing or a DJ. If your parents are in town and paying for dinner, have them take you to Federal Hill, there are a lot of great Italian restaurants there. Thayer Street and the mall have a lot of good places too. There is no Greek life; more emphasis is put on application to popular clubs on campus, like Board of Programmers, Friar Club, and Intramural Athletic Board. There isn't much of a dating scene here either. Most people are single and having fun or have a boyfriend/girlfriend at home. There are a few couples on campus, though.

 The School Says

Be transformed. That's the invitation and promise offered by Providence College to 3,800 undergraduates each year.

It's an invitation for students to find themselves and their direction in life, and to thrive in an environment that challenges them on every level: mind and body, heart and soul.

It's a promise inspired by the Dominican Friars, a Catholic religious order dedicated to the pursuit of truth and to a spirituality that embraces the whole person.

This spirit permeates a rigorous liberal arts curriculum and sustains a vibrant campus community. The result is an education in success and values that transforms students and, ultimately, the society in which they live.

This is Providence College—the only college or university in the nation operated by the Dominican Friars—offering an education that challenges and transforms.

Providence College recently introduced two initiatives that reinforce its founding mission as a Catholic and Dominican college: to provide a comprehensive liberal arts education to first-generation immigrant and multicultural students who might otherwise be unable to obtain a college degree.

Providence College no longer requires undergraduate applicants to submit SAT or ACT scores as part of the admission application. Prospective students who choose not to submit standardized test scores will receive full consideration, without penalty, for admission. Students who have taken a standardized test and choose to enroll at Providence College will be required to submit their test scores upon enrollment so they may receive appropriate academic advisement.

The college also has shifted a greater portion of its resources away from exclusively merit-based scholarships and towards need-based financial aid.

Since 1997, Providence has been recognized in *U.S. News'* America's Best Colleges as one of the Top Two master's level universities in the North region. Providence's graduation and retention rates are recognized as among the highest in the country; its service learning programs are widely cited as among the best nationwide.

University of Rhode Island

ndergraduate Admission Office
ewman Hall
4 Upper College Rd.
ngston, RI 02881
dmissions phone:(401) 874-7000
dmissions e-mail: admission@uri.edu
dmissions URL: www.uri.edu/admission/

Admissions

rrent student, 12/2003-Submit Date, January 2006

e University of Rhode Island has an excellent communication process
oughout enrollment. High school grades with an average GPA of 3.0 for out-
state students are a must. The college essay is very important and can help
t significantly if your GPA is below a 3.0. You have a much better chance of
ng enrolled if you are a resident of Rhode Island. If, for any reason, the
ool is not happy with any of your grades, they will notify you and allow you
bring your grade up to still have a second chance to be admitted into the uni-
rsity.

rrent student, 9/2003-Submit Date, July 2004

a transfer student there wasn't an interview, so you don't have to worry about
t. For admittance I would look for an over-1000 SAT and GPA over 2.7. Just
k about yourself or something that defines who you are in your essay.

rrent student, 9/2001-Submit Date, May 2004

pplied a few years ago so the details are somewhat vague. The application
s somewhat standard, including questions on academics, background infor-
tion on the student and his family, current activities and sports and interest in
rsuing them at the college level. There were also a few essays.

I am a Rhode Island resident, I did not have to have an interview, and I'm
tty sure not many people do. The school is somewhat selective, although less
ective for its residents. I was not particularly concerned with getting into the
ool therefore I did not seek any advice on getting in, although I'm sure it
uld have been there had I wanted it.

Academics

rrent student, 12/2003-Submit Date, January 2006

e engineering program at the University of Rhode Island is intense. The pro-
m is intended to filter out the students who are not serious about their engi-
ering careers. Freshman year involves very large lecture classes, no matter
at major you are.

e biggest problem with the University of Rhode Island is getting the classes
u want/need. Classes fill up very quickly and usually involve needing to get
rmission to be forced into the class. The ratio between the number of classes
take and students needing them is very low. Once you become involved in
ur major during your second and third year, the size of the classes slowly
ninishes and the relationships between students and teachers begin to grow.

rrent student, 9/2003-Submit Date, July 2004

e classes at URI are becoming increasingly more intense over the time I have
n here. Professors are always there for extra help, even though a few are for-
n and hard to understand. E-campus (online registration of classes) is a pain
get onto and classes fill up very quickly, especially for freshmen.

ading is based on a typical 4.0 scale, some professors grade easier than oth-
. A 15-credit semester (if you want to graduate in four years) is tough here at

URI but doable. The library is extensive and has a computer lab with over 100
computers on the bottom floor.

Current student, 9/2001-Submit Date, May 2004

The average workload is a bit demanding, although not impossibly so. It is challenging to the student without taking up too much time. Classes are generally
harder to get into when you are younger, as seniors are allowed to sign up for
classes first, juniors second and so on. Popular classes often have many sections
in order to keep up with the demand, although they are still quite hard to get into
sometimes.

The quality of the classes varies depending upon the subject, the professor and
the level of the course (intro courses are much larger and taught in lecture format, while senior-level courses are often small and there is more student-teacher
interaction and participation). Many of the introductory courses are graded on
things like attendance and homework, whereas the higher-level courses are graded on performance and participation. The majority of the professors I have had
are friendly and enthusiastic.

Employment Prospects

Current student, 12/2003-Submit Date, January 2006

The University of Rhode Island has a great program for internships. For the field
that you choose at the University of Rhode Island, your professors are very helpful with letting students know which internships are available. Every year, there
is also a job fair that allows students to get a look at which jobs are available for
their major. As for the engineering program, they are very good at preparing students for the real world and most students are offered jobs right after graduation.

Current student, 9/2003-Submit Date, July 2004

Career Day happens once a semester on the quad, where employers have a booth
and eager students learn about internships and career paths they may or may not
like to follow.

Current student, 9/2001-Submit Date, May 2004

The university offers many programs to help with jobs. There is an annual career
and internship job fair held at the union and open to all students.

Advisors hold regular office hours and are very helpful in assisting students find
internships or decide which career path they would like to take. Advisors also
have a lot of information on career placement, how to achieve your career goals,
which programs will get you ahead and what types of extracurriculars will help
you on your way.

Quality of Life

Current student, 12/2003-Submit Date, January 2006

Recently, there has been a lot of construction on campus, with new housing facilities and dining halls. The biggest problem with campus is the lack of campus.
The parking services department gives out more parking passes than there are
parking spots. The university also loves to ticket the many students who are ille-
gally parked because of the lack of parking.

The university is in a very nice location in Rhode Island were crime and safety
is not an issue.

Current student, 9/2003-Submit Date, July 2004

URI is placing new dorms all over campus and there are many dining halls
including take-out. Police and fire departments are on campus just a hop, skip
and jump away. And emergency blue lights are all over the place as well—very
safe campus.

Read all of Vault's College Surveys at **www.vault.com/college**—get complete surveys on 100s of colleges and universities, expert advice on applicaton essays and more.

VAULT CAREER LIBRARY **659**

Current student, 9/2001-Submit Date, May 2004

Quality of life, as a whole, is quite good. There are lots of things for students to do on and off campus. The dorms are currently being renovated and the newly built and renovated ones are bright, roomy and quite comfortable. The old dorms that have not been renovated are a bit cramped, but hopefully they'll be improved soon. There are four major dining halls on campus that serve a wide variety of good food.

There is also a shopping center at one end of campus that has a Dunkin' Donuts, Spike's Hot Dogs, Bess Eaton, Cumberland Farms, CVS, hair salon, coffee shop, Chinese restaurant, breakfast place and pizza parlor. There is also a video rental store and a laundromat on the other side of the street.

Parking is a big issue in that there is not nearly enough. However, this is partly due to the fact that freshmen are allowed cars on campus, something that many schools do not allow.

The gym is quite large with many free programs. The first week of each semester is Free Week when all aerobics classes are free to try so students can decide whether they want to sign up for them. After Free Week the classes are only for those who pay. The gym, itself, is pretty small and near spring break it gets very crowded, to the point of a line 20 to 30 people long. The pool is open most of the time, although there are times when the swim team practices or there are lessons. There is an ice rink that is generally open to the public next door to the gym. On the other side of the gym there is the Ryan Center, which hosts all URI home basketball games, as well as concerts and other events.

 ## Social Life

Current student, 12/2003-Submit Date, January 2006

Most of the URI social life is composed of the Greek system and off-campus life. Most students move off campus their second year to live in beach houses, while all of the Greek houses are on campus. Even though the beach houses are about a half-hour commute to school, it is worth it when your house is walking distance from the beautiful beaches of Rhode Island.

Off-campus life primarily involves two locations. Down the Line, which is a location in Narragansett, RI and Bonnet Shores in Southern Narragansett. The social life is the best part of attending URI. What is there not to love about living close to all of your friends in multi-million dollar houses walking distance from the beach?

Current student, 9/2003-Submit Date, July 2004

Dry campus (no bars or alcohol on campus unless you are 21 and then you have a limit as to how much you can have with you at any time). The Emporium is located at the top of the campus, with International House of Pizza, Subway, Cumberland Farms, Pizza Pockets and many more. In the Memorial Union (heart of the campus) there are events such as concerts or hypnotists, and also Ronzio's Pizza downstairs.

There is a dating service online for URI students. The student senate sponsors student-run organizations that anyone can join, and if there isn't a club that you would like to join start one of your own by standing in front of the senate. You get a budget and on office.

The Greek scene isn't too big on campus, mostly off-campus houses. URI located in the country, so there isn't too much to do off campus. Most part are located in Narragansett on a strip we call Down the Line. This is like a 3 minute drive from campus. Along with parties, there are many bars and plac for college students to hang out and get together for a night out.

Current student, 9/2001-Submit Date, May 2004

There are many things to do on and off campus. We have a rather large Gre system with nine sororities and 10 fraternities. Currently, all the sororities a on campus and have houses as do six of the fraternities. The best fraternity pa ties, I think, are thrown at Chi Phi and Phi Kappa Psi. Tau Epsilon Phi and B Theta Pi are also quite good party houses.

There aren't many bars near campus, most of them are between 10 and 20 mi utes away. The popular bars are Casey's on Sunday for karaoke and Tuesday 10¢ wings, Black Point on Wednesdays and Fridays, Okies on Thursdays, a Charlie O's on Saturdays. There is also a number of other bars students freque on various nights, although they are a lot smaller. Bobby G's and summ favorites Coast Guard House, Bon Vue, Pancho O'Malley's, George's a Finback's are a few.

I don't know much about the dating scene because I am in a sorority and tend meet people through that, but most people meet each other at frat parties, at bars or in class. There are quite a few restaurants people go to. Casey's is al popular for this, as well as New Dragon, where people go to eat and drink th famous Scorpion Bowls.

The many student senate-recognized clubs include a variety of sports and oth clubs. These clubs are very well represented in the student body. The girls a boys lacrosse clubs are very popular, as well as the newest club recognized, Knitting Club.

Clemson University

Admissions Office
05 Sikes Hall
ox 345124
lemson, SC 29634-5124
dmissions phone: (864) 656-2287
dmissions URL: www.clemson.edu/attend/undrgrd

Admissions

rrent student, 8/2003-Submit Date, July 2006

e admissions process is fairly straightforward, requiring timely submissions
transcripts, test scores and the completed application. As a university aiming
r Top 20 in the nation, however, admission selectivity has increased signifi-
ntly, particularly for more popular engineering, science, agriculture and busi-
ss majors, as well as for out-of-state applicants. Be sure to include extracur-
ular activities and leadership potential.

umnus/a, 8/1999-8/2003, May 2006

ere was not an interview or essays. The best advice for getting into this school
any other school would be to work very hard at a minimum of your junior and
nior year of high school to maintain good grades. Also, join a few volunteer
oups.

rrent student, 8/2004-Submit Date, April 2005

emson University utilizes two methods of admissions. Students may either
ply on paper or through the Internet. However, given the amount of prodding
e admissions office does in pushing its applicants towards using the online sys-
m, it appears that admissions will soon be entirely electronic. The actual
ocess is quite simple, as it does not require any essays. The only time students
tually have to write anything in essay format is a section at the end of the
plication, in which they are given the option to add anything they feel admis-
ns counselors may benefit from knowing.

ere is no separate application for the Calhoun Honors College. Rather, an
missions board from the Honors College sends acceptance letters to worthy
dents upon review of the original application sent to the university. Finally,
mission to the university is becoming increasingly difficult for a number of
asons, not least of which include Clemson's continuing rise towards becoming
Top 20 public institution and a growing applicant pool in the face of a capped
eshman class (approximately 2,000 freshman students are admitted each fall).

> **The school says:** "We actually admit over 6,600 students in our
> attempt to enroll approximately 2,800 new freshmen."

rrent student, 8/2004-Submit Date, April 2005

e admissions process at Clemson is awesome. If you apply by the December
adline, you will be notified of your admission status the week of February 15.
ere is no interview for general admission, but some of the top scholarships
quire an interview. An essay is also not required for general admission. On
e application, there is an optional personal statement, but it is not required.
e only advice I have for getting into Clemson is to challenge yourself in high
hool by taking AP and IB classes and also to keep your GPA up during high
hool. Also, it is good to participate in extracurriculars and do your best on the
T or ACT.

rrent student, 8/2002-Submit Date, March 2005

e admissions process is relatively painless as the application takes about 15
inutes to complete, with no essay involved. However, Clemson is becoming
ore and more competitive to get into and many students are shocked when they
ceive rejection letters or are waitlisted. Make sure to take a challenging
urseload.

Current student, 8/2002-Submit Date, March 2005

Clemson University's application for admission is very simple. It asks for your
general information and some details on extracurricular activities and honors and
awards from high school. A full transcript and SAT scores were required, and at
the end of the application, the applicants had the option to write a short paragraph explaining why they wanted to go to Clemson. Clemson did not require
any essays or interviews during the admissions process. Selectivity was fairly
high, although it didn't seem extremely difficult for me personally to get in. As
long as a student has decent grades and a decent SAT score, he/she will get
accepted to Clemson. Those who didn't make the grades, however, aren't
accepted.

Alumnus/a, 8/1998-5/2002, July 2004

The admissions process is fairly easy, however the requirements are getting
much more strenuous than when I applied in 1998 and even more so than when
my brother applied in 2001. There is no interview or essay requirement for
admission. However, the average SAT score is now over 1200. I also believe
that something very important in gaining admissions is class rank. My brother-
in-law applied last year (from in state) with nearly a 4.0 GPA and 1200 SAT,
however he went to a private school and was not in the top 20 percent of his
class. He did not get admitted. There is an appeal process if you do not get
accepted. He went through that process and was asked to take two summer
school courses. With a passing grade of C or better, he will gain full-time admission for the fall. So, in a nutshell, admission to Clemson is becoming very competitive.

> **Clemson University says:** "The average SAT in fall 2004 was
> 1204. In the case of marginal applicants that go before the
> Appeals Committee, everything in the student's record is con-
> sidered."

Academics

Current student, 8/2003-Submit Date, July 2006

The Biological Science program is fairly intense with a wide scope that attracts
many medical school hopefuls despite the separate pre-med program. A very
competitive major, some popular classes may be difficult to get, but with early
upperclassman registration it's not too difficult. Professors in this major are usually fair, very knowledgeable and willing to help.

The workload is usually the student's responsibility, i.e., not usually frivolous
group projects with those investing more time into their studies doing better than
those investing less. Often, grades are determined simply with exam performance although some professors assign occasional projects that provide a small
cushion, though they're hardly freebies.

Current student, 8/2004-Submit Date, April 2005

While some freshman class sizes can reach numbers around 150 students, numbers of this size are typically only limited to the courses every freshman in an
engineering and science degree must take, such as biology or chemistry. Even
with these large sizes, the university has extra measures to ensure that students
have the opportunity to receive personal attention if they so desire. Professors
are also required to have at least six hours of office time for their students, and
many are willing to meet outside of these office hours if need be. Most professors, especially those in the courses students take in their upperclassman years,
are very accessible and willing to help students achieve the goals they have set
for themselves.

> **The school says:** "We are best known for our engineering and
> business programs."

Read all of Vault's College Surveys at **www.vault.com/college**—get complete surveys on 100s of colleges and universities, expert advice on applicaton essays and more.

VAULT CAREER LIBRARY **661**

Alumnus/a, 8/1995-5/2000, January 2006

When I fist entered Clemson, I was involved in their animal science degree. The classes were very challenging for me. I stuck with it for two years and then decided that it was not right for me. I was very impressed with the program. They have you working with animals and vets right from the beginning in order weed out weak students.

So, I then decided to change my major to special education. This worked very well for me. The professors were great. Except for [one] teacher, I had great professors. The classes were small. The professors were willing to meet with me whenever I needed help. The professors worked well to make sure that the workload was not too heavy on one particular day. The ability to do a practicum and then student teach was extremely helpful my last year.

Current student, 8/2004-Submit Date, April 2005

I am a business major at Clemson and have thus far enjoyed my program of study. The professors have been nothing but amazing and I've enjoyed all of my classes. At Clemson, the classes are not all structured the same way, but I have found that the professors really want to design each class so it meets the current students' needs. They understand that what may have been an effective teaching style one semester may not always work for the next class. It is really comforting to know that my professors want my feedback and they want the class to work for me!

All of the professors at Clemson are required to have six posted office hours a week. During this time, students can go in and talk to the professor, whether it is for homework help or just to get to know them. The professors are always more than happy to develop relationships with their students.

Current student, 8/2002-Submit Date, April 2005

Because I am a member of the Honors College, I have always had priority registration, so I have never had difficulty getting into classes. I find my classes to be of a very high quality, with professors from varied backgrounds. The grading system is difficult without being too much. The workload is what you make it, a minimum of 12 hours being required each semester, but being able to take up to 21.

Current student, 8/2004-Submit Date, April 2005

Classes are about 30 to 200 people depending on which classes and which college you attend. The professors here are very thorough and fast-paced. Popular classes are sometimes harder for freshmen to get than seniors because freshmen have last pick of their schedules. Clemson has a lot of professors who teach the popular classes to increase the students' chances of getting in that particular class. Workload at Clemson varies, but is, overall, very challenging and heavy!

Current student, 8/2002-Submit Date, March 2005

The registration process is done very fairly, too. Those in the honors program and seniors register first, followed by juniors, then sophomores and so on. It is not very difficult to get popular classes because there seems to be enough sections of classes to meet demand for what students need. As for my workload, it is moderate. I have enough work to keep me diligent, but I am not overly stressed all the time and I have sufficient time to have fun. Grading is moderate to hard, as well. If you put in the effort, you'll get the grades to show for it, but hard work is required.

Current student, 8/2002-Submit Date, March 2005

I have been really pleased with my classes at Clemson. The average class size here is small (though, of course, there might be 150 people in a freshman biology class) and all of the professors make themselves extremely available, sometimes even offering their home phone numbers with the syllabus. I find that the workload definitely has periods of high and low stress levels because the professors tend to assign projects and papers right around midterm, breaks and finals, but other than that it's very manageable and challenging.

Current student, 8/2003-Submit Date, March 2005

Civil engineering is an intense program, it is easy to get the classes you need for your major. It is somewhat difficult to get fun classes that everyone wants to take, grading is fair, the professors have no problem meeting after class and getting you set up with a tutor. The workload for civil engineering is a lot, but not so much for many other majors.

Current student, 8/2002-Submit Date, March 2005

The quality of classes is great. The student-to-faculty ratio is 15:1 and the ave age class size is 29. We do online registration. It is usually possible to get all your classes, and we have a request log so you are able to get in right away. T professors are great. They have open-door office hours each week. That is ti when they are sure to be in their offices, and you can come visit them. The pr fessors' offices are always close to the buildings they teach in. The professo are also good at knowing names. I have had a class of 14 and of 100+, but bo ways, they have made an effort to get to know us. In addition, we have the ac demic support center. They offer free tutoring. They also do supplemen instruction (or SI sessions). That is where the top students in the class serve tutors for that class the next year. All of these programs are free.

Employment Prospects

Alumnus/a, 8/1999-8/2003, May 2006

I joined the co-op program at school and it worked out very well. I got to ge little taste of what it was like to work in my field. The last semester was stru tured well in that it allowed local companies to come in and discuss their wo and allowed you to interact with them. Also, a career fair was held for you talk with prospective employers. The last semester before graduation is a hec time. With concentration on classes while on the side, putting in résumés companies and scheduling interviews.

Current student, 8/2004-Submit Date, April 2005

Having been a major part of the economy of upstate South Carolina since the la 1800s, it is not surprising to note that Clemson has established reputable bu ness relationships with many manufacturing, agricultural, engineering and oth major corporations located within and around the state of South Carolina. Tho who major in the traditional majors of Clemson, such as agriculture, engineeri or textiles, will have little to no trouble finding a job after graduation. There a a number of on-campus programs designed to help students ease into a care such as job fairs, a career center and more. There is also a co-op and internsh department that helps students find these types of jobs while they are still school, so they can gain valuable work experience.

Current student, 8/2002-Submit Date, March 2005

The Michelin Career Center has helped a ton of students to get employment aft graduation from Clemson. Employers come to campus to recruit, and Clems has made a very good name for itself, which means our degrees are worth a l to employers. The alumni network is extremely helpful. We have a progra made specifically for students to log onto the web site that has a number of alur ni in our field who are willing to answer questions and help in any way they ca Alumni stay extremely involved with Clemson, and we have a family Clemson Tigers who all work together.

Current student, 8/2001-Submit Date, March 2005

Employment prospects include GE, Bank of America, Wachovia, VanGuar Ernst & Young, Goldman Sachs, Citigroup, Citibank, Prudential and Gra Thorton. They are entry-level and above positions. Networking with alumni huge at Clemson. The recruitment on campus is great. The career center hel you find the job that is right for you. There is also a career fair where comp nies participate in recruitment.

Current student, 8/2003-Submit Date, March 2005

Clemson is very dedicated to finding its students great jobs. We have a care center on campus that allows you to do mock interviews (that can be videotap so you can see what mistakes you make) and gives you tips on how to make great résumé. Many employers, such as GE and BMW, pair up with the care center to do on-campus interviews. There is also a network called Tigers f Tigers, which allows current students to be connected with alumni in their care fields, so they can use that network to find a job. The engineering programs particular have great co-oping and internship programs, and it is not hard to g set up with one of these if you want to. One neat fact is that our graphics con munications major has a 100 percent job placement.

Quality of Life

Current student, 8/2003-Submit Date, July 2006

Clemson works to provide a high quality of life. Approximately 6,500 students live in 21 furnished residence halls (just bring items to personalize), four apartment areas and the Clemson House. There are both single sex and co-ed areas. Clemson also offers convenient and accessible housing for the physically challenged. Each room contains a high-speed data port for each student. There are also full computer labs located in 10 residence areas on campus. [All halls have] resident assistants and directors trained in counseling, crisis management and aiding in the transition into college life. Holmes is one of the best residence halls, but reserved for honors students.

Current student, 8/2004-Submit Date, April 2005

There are very few reports of campus crime here at Clemson. Despite this fact, there are many safeguards that are implemented on campus to ensure the safety of students, including key card entry to all dorms, limited visitation hours for members of the opposite sex in most dorms, late-night escort shuttles that pick people up on request and more. There are approximately 21 on-campus housing facilities from which to choose ranging from suites to traditional dorms all the way to apartment-style housing. There are three dining halls that are aptly suited to serve the number of students who attend this university, and there is also a wide variety of other food options available when the dining hall food just doesn't cut it (which is rare!).

Current student, 8/2004-Submit Date, April 2005

On-campus housing at Clemson is great. The housing department is so open to new ideas and really tries to facilitate bonding within the residence halls.

The library is the very center of campus or the bull's eye. The next ring is all of the academic buildings, the next ring is composed of residence halls and dining facilities, and the outer ring is parking and athletic facilities. Safety is also a big issue at Clemson that hasn't been overlooked. I have never felt unsafe on this campus even if I'm walking around alone at night. There are measures in place though if one does feel uncomfortable. For example, we have the escort system that runs from 7 p.m. until 7 a.m. every day. What you do if you need a ride somewhere is call the escort, who comes to where you are whether it be your dorm or a parking lot, picks you up, brings you to where you need to go and makes sure you get in safely.

Current student, 8/2002-Submit Date, March 2005

Clemson is the ideal college life!! The city's focus is the college, so everything within miles of campus is very Clemson spirited. The campus is a walking campus, which is wonderful because Clemson's campus is beautiful! Facilities are always being renovated or improved! Recently, a dining hall, basketball arena, student recreation facilities, fraternity quad, student center, genetics and bioengineering building and computer science building were renovated or created! Buildings are constantly being altered to become more state-of-the-art. Dining options are abundant on campus and good! The Clemson community is very friendly and there is little crime.

Current student, 8/2002-Submit Date, March 2005

As an RA who works for housing on campus at Clemson, I know that Clemson only provides the best for its students. There are resident assistants for every floor in dormitories, resident directors for every on-campus housing, and resident area coordinators that reach the specific areas. Clemson provides safety and a clean environment for all its students. The campus is absolutely gorgeous with a policy of seeing green everywhere you look, so there is lots of grass, trees, gardening and landscaping around. Clemson is a pedestrian-friendly campus that is well lit and organized to meet every students need. The dining facilities are well spread out throughout the campus. Dining provides fresh food with wide variety.

Social Life

Current student, 8/2003-Submit Date, July 2006

80 percent of Clemson's undergraduate population participates as members of one of the many national [Greek] organizations. There is a huge number of student organizations with which to get involved, including Clemson Dancers, Multicultural Organization, Sailing, Sky-diving, Student Senate, Tigers Who Care, Karate and so many more. Clemson sports are huge part of university life, therefore another social highlight includes tailgating during football season with solid orange filling Death Valley stadium. Running down the hill is said to be the most exciting entrance in college football. In addition, events such as Tiger Gras, Greek Week, First Friday, Welcome Back, Latin Fest and various concerts promise something for everyone. Clemson University strives to include everyone in the Clemson family.

Alumnus/a, 8/1995-5/2000, January 2006

I had a great social life. The Greek life is very big at Clemson. I was able to meet very good friends through the Greek system. I joined the Kappa Kappa Gamma sorority. It provided great social activities (mixers and socials) and philanthropy projects. I was also able to meet my husband. The restaurant scene was not very extensive in Clemson but I had not money so that really wasn't a problem. Football is the best time of year at Clemson. The fans are incredible. There is nothing like going to a Clemson football game. My husband and I still attend all of the home games. We even named our dog after the coach. I loved my experience at Clemson and hope that my daughter will want to attend one day.

Current student, 7/2004-Submit Date, April 2005

Clemson students are known to work hard and play hard. Social life is very important here. We have numerous bars and restaurants within a five- to 10-minute walk from campus. There are also numerous organizations and events to meet new people with interests similar to your own. Only a fifth of the university is Greek, but Greek life has a huge impact on on-campus life. Many people go to fraternity and sorority parties and events. Greeks are also known for their charity work around the area.

Current student, 8/2004-Submit Date, April 2005

Many students and alumni are particularly fond of the places in Clemson that have been there for many years, including Mac's Drive-In, the Esso Club restaurant, Knickerbocker, Judge Keller's and more. Clemson is steeped in tradition, and this extends to its social life as well. On warm spring/summer days, many students can be found sunbathing or tossing the frisbee around on any number of the wide open green spaces spread throughout the campus. The most popular hangout is Bowman Field, located at the heart of the campus and formerly the parade grounds for cadets when the university was a military school. Greek life is also a major tradition here on campus, as there are 10 Panhellenic sororities and an almost equal number of fraternities.

Current student, 8/2004-Submit Date, April 2005

The restaurants downtown all have their own atmosphere and personality. We have Mac's, which is a drive-in hamburger joint and a favorite of many students. Also, Ancheaux's with their huge burritos is a great choice. My personal favorite is Acropolis, which serves both Greek and Italian food. There are numerous bars downtown but you have to be 21 to get into most of them, which stinks. Some of the bars host musicians (both local and non) and on those nights, usually you only have to be only 18 for entrance. In the fall, the social scene revolves around FOOTBALL SATURDAYS!! Football here at Clemson is more than just a sport, it's a tradition and a religion!

Current student, 8/2002-Submit Date, April 2005

There is one bar on campus with a bowling alley and billiard room, and the downtown strip is a conglomeration of bars and spirit stores selling university paraphernalia. The sororities and fraternities are huge here, about 40 percent of students participate. Football games are the biggest deal in Clemson, the stadium seating over 86,000 screaming fans dressed in orange. There are over 700 clubs on campus and events, such as concerts happen monthly. Kelly Clarkson is coming this month!

Current student, 8/2002-Submit Date, March 2005

Clemson's Greek system is very good in that it doesn't dominate social life. Students who are not Greek, like me, do not feel set apart or excluded. There are plenty of opportunities to get involved outside of the Greek system. Those who are Greek, however, love it. It's all personal preference, and whatever the choice, the students are happy. Clemson also provides a ton of events, clubs, and opportunities outside of the classroom. Downtown Clemson has a lot of neat

Read all of Vault's College Surveys at **www.vault.com/college**—get complete surveys on 100s of colleges and universities, expert advice on applicaton essays and more.

VAULT CAREER LIBRARY **663**

local restaurants, bars and shops. There is never a lack of things to do at Clemson, especially during football season!

The School Says

Clemson University, one of the country's top research universities, combines the best of small-college teaching and big-time science, engineering and technology.

With nearly half of classes at Clemson having fewer than 20 students, Clemson professors get to know their students and explore innovative ways of teaching. It's one reason Clemson's retention and graduation rates rank among the highest in the country among public schools. It's why Clemson continues to attract some of the country's best students who seek intellectual challenge.

Clemson provides education and enrichment opportunities to create leaders, thinkers and entrepreneurs solving real-world problems through research, outreach and public service. Clemson's Academic Success Center earned international acclaim as the Outstanding Supplemental Instruction Program in 2006.

The university's 17,000 students can select from 70 undergraduate and 100 graduate degree programs offered by five colleges: Agriculture, Forestry and Life Sciences; Architecture, Arts and Humanities; Business and Behavioral Science; Engineering and Science; and Health, Education and Human Development.

Clemson is well known for its prominent athletic programs and for the spirit of its fans. Another important aspect of Clemson is its dedication to improving the world through public service, which is why the University encourages faculty to engage their classes through service learning. Recently, Clemson was recognized by The Princeton Review as one of a few select American universities as a "Campus With a Conscience" for its work in community service.

With its college town, lakefront setting against a backdrop of mountains and forests, Clemson is characterized by a strong sense of community, a commitment to service and a love of winning—in academics, in athletics and in life.

Furman University

Office of Admissions
Furman University
3300 Poinsett Highway
Greenville, SC 29613
Admissions phone: (864) 294-2034
Admissions fax: (864) 294-2018
Admissions e-mail: admissions@furman.edu
Admissions URL: www.engagefurman.com/

Admissions

Alumnus/a, English, 9/2002-6/2006, December 2006

Furman was my first choice, so I applied early. The great thing about this is that you find out your status by December 15, so if you don't get in, there is still plenty of time to fill out applications for other schools. Back when I applied, the requirements were not as tough. Upon graduating this past June, rumors were going around that the average SAT score of the class of 2010 was 1450. What I noticed about Furman is that they might not care as much about SAT as they do about creating an interesting and well-rounded group of freshmen. This is an ongoing change that is happening at the school as it used to be primarily white, wealthy Southerners. The institution is committed to diversifying the school, which is something I really appreciated. If you really want to go to Furman, I suggest making a name for yourself early in your high school career by visiting and talking with counselors.

Alumnus/a, 9/2000-6/2004, September 2005

I applied Early Decision to Furman. I would recommend applying early to anyone who knows that FU is his/her first choice. I think it enhances your chances for admission, especially now that admission is getting more competitive.

Current student, 9/2001-Submit Date, June 2004

Furman's application is medium-length; not as long as an Ivy League school, but longer than that of a state school. Not just anyone with a pulse can get in, but it is by no means impossible; if you're in the top quarter of your high school class, you've probably a got a pretty good shot.

The application contains one relatively short (two or three paragraphs) essay which is of a pretty typical nature. I simply modified one of my other essays fit the specific direction of the question. There are no mandatory interviews anything of that sort, although an official visit is recommended.

Alumnus/a, 9/2001-5/2005, July 2005

Furman sent information to me based on my SAT score, and the institution waived my application fee. Furthermore, they selected me for a scholarship program. The application involved basic information and a few essays. All in a it was fairly easy to be admitted to the school.

Alumnus/a, 9/1999-5/2003, October 2004

The process at Furman is handled pretty well and you can get help at any time That is one advantage about Furman, it is so small that you are not forced to r around to all the different departments trying to get an answer. Furman is ve selective about whom it accepts and the acceptance rate gets smaller and sma er every year. So I suggest that you put as much effort into your essays a application as possible. Not many have to do any interviews for this college, that is somewhat of a relief, but I definitely suggest visiting the school and sta ing with a student to help you get some perspective.

Academics

Alumnus/a, 9/2000-6/2004, September 2005

I was a business administration major. It was a 12-class major with gene classes. Professors are wonderful, and they were very willing to give help those who sought it out.

Classes were small (15 to 20), so there were a lot of hands-on projects and inte action in class. Workload was intense but not overwhelming. Each class m every day, so you had to make sure that you were always prepared. Classes we fairly easy to get as long as kept up your CLPs (Cultural Life Program Students had to attend 36 CLPs over their career at FU. You had to stay curre on them or else you registered later than everyone else.

Alumnus/a, English, 9/2002-6/2006, December 2006

s I went to a Georgia public school, it's safe to say that I was not as prepared
r Furman as many of my peers. During orientation week when I met with my
lvisory group, the professor said, "Don't expect A's. C's are good grades here."
While I definitely made A's and B's, it really was difficult. However, it was a
eat experience. I was an English major and generally had between five and 10
ople in my classes. I always got the class and class time I wanted. Professors
enerally go above and beyond to help you out. The thing I appreciate most
oout Furman is that I feel comfortable in any conversation. No matter what the
pic is, from literature to environmental science, to art history, Furman molds
u into a well-informed and well-spoken individual.

urrent student, 9/2001-Submit Date, June 2004

ifficulty varies widely by major. Psychology and chemistry majors are typi-
lly found in the library. If you major in economics, business or political sci-
ice (the two largest departments in the university) you can have a life most of
e time.

lost of the professors are pretty decent and with only about 2,700 students you
n usually find out which ones to avoid. We are on a trimester system, which
me love and some hate. You take three classes in fall and spring terms that
ich meet for 50 minutes, five days a week. In winter term you take two class-
that each meet for 75 minutes, five days a week.

etting popular classes isn't hard, particularly if you're a sophomore or higher.
ven if you don't get in through the normal registration, many professors will let
u in anyway. Most classes are worthwhile, although I've certainly had a few
ho were not.

rading, even in so-called "easy A" classes is usually tough. In most core and
troductory classes, you can expect a moderately heavy reading load and a few
quisite relatively short essays, with little or no daily work to be turned in. In
ost classes, grades consist of three or four tests, a small participation grade and
erhaps a couple essays. Most professors simply go by the university attendance
olicy—freshmen may miss up to 15 percent of classes and upperclassmen may
iss up to 25 percent.

Alumnus/a, 9/2001-5/2005, July 2005

urman was excellent academically. I could always get the classes that I want-
l, and I found them to be challenging and rewarding. The grading system is the
andard 4.0 system, but grading is such that it is difficult to receive a 4.0 in a
ass.

rofessors are fair, open-minded and intelligent. They invest a lot in their stu-
ents and truly care about the students' progress. Workload is moderately heavy
ut still reasonable. The work is necessary to receive the quality education that
demanded of the institution.

Alumnus/a, 9/1999-5/2003, October 2004

he academics are the best at Furman. Because it is a small, private school, you
re able to get a lot of attention and you are offered many kinds of opportunities
at you might not get anywhere else. The classes are rigorous and the profes-
ors expect a lot out of you, but they give their best too and have an open-door
olicy. So it is definitely not a school where you can just slide by.

ou can more than likely get into classes, especially as you get into your major,
y talking to the professors whom you usually get to know because of the school
mosphere. They don't have quite the range of majors that bigger universities
ave, but if you check into it before hand you should be safe. The strongest
ajors are chemistry, biology, business, policy and education.

> **Regarding academics, the school says:** "Beginning in 2008-09,
> the university will adopt a new curriculum and academic calen-
> dar. Instead of the current three-term system (12-week fall and
> spring terms and an eight-week winter term), Furman will move
> to a calendar of two 14-week semesters and an optional, three-
> week 'Maymester.'"

Employment Prospects

Current student, 9/2001-Submit Date, June 2004

There is a joint Office of Student Employment/Office of Career Services that
assists students in finding employment while at the university and for after graduation, respectively. There are various internship and job fairs held on campus
throughout the year. Furman is a pretty big name in the Southeast, so if you plan
on living in Atlanta or Charlotte or anywhere else in the area, you have a good
shot at getting a job.

Alumnus/a, English, 9/2002-6/2006, December 2006

I am a fairly recent graduate. Right after leaving Furman I moved to Tucson
where I was helped tremendously by other alumni. The alumni network is very
close. I got in touch with Alumni Services at Furman and they sent me a spread-
sheet of every alumni living in Tucson: 25 of them! At least 12 of them bought
me lunch and gave me advice, and one woman got me my current job. I'm waiting for the opportunity to help out a fellow grad. One thing I will say, most people in Tucson don't know of Furman, but if you stay in the South, WHOA!
People compare it to Harvard and will really think highly of you for going to the
school.

Alumnus/a, 9/2000-6/2004, September 2005

Furman is in the same league as Vanderbilt, UVA and Duke academically, but
they really get no one to come on campus to interview students. Most of the
interviews I attended were more for me to get interviewing experience. I will
say that FU is very good if you want to go straight to a grad school of any kind.
Schools, especially in the South, look very highly upon FU graduates and most
students have no problem getting into the schools that they want.

Alumni network is smaller because of the size of the school, but they are helpful when asked.

Alumnus/a, 9/2001-5/2005, July 2005

Furman graduates have a wide network of opportunities and are thoroughly
equipped to handle any job they pursue. The school is well known throughout
the Southeast, and its reputation is spreading throughout the rest of the U.S.

Graduates go on to do work in the government, in business, NGOs, hospitals and
other places. Post-graduate work is typical of the Furman student, and it is needed because Furman seeks to provide a well-rounded, liberal arts education
instead of specific, technical skills.

Alumnus/a, 9/1999-5/2003, October 2004

Depending on your major, most people recognize the Furman name. Furman is
willing to help students while they are at school and even when they get out of
school. There are plenty of recruiting [opportunities,] but again it depends on
your major. Most graduates seem to go into politics, science or on to graduate
school.

Quality of Life

Alumnus/a, English, 9/2002-6/2006, December 2006

Everything in this category seemed great to me. Juniors and seniors live in really nice apartments. (You can apply to live off campus, but why bother? These
are nice and cheap, as well.) The dining hall is good and has a variety of options.
I remember once I was watching my carbohydrates and so I requested spinach
pasta. They served it a few days later.

Alumnus/a, 9/2000-6/2004, September 2005

People always refer to Furman as "the bubble" because it is almost not the real
world. The campus is beautiful, students are all well off, facilities are topnotch
and there is virtually no crime. I can honestly say that I never locked my on-
campus apartment. Students are required to live on campus, but the apartments
are very nice. It almost makes graduating difficult because FU students have it
so great while they are there.

Current student, 9/2001-Submit Date, June 2004

Campus housing is above average judging from the other schools I've visited.
Most of the dormrooms are a decent size, considering that they are, in fact,

Read all of Vault's College Surveys at **www.vault.com/college**—get complete surveys on 100s of colleges and universities, expert advice on applicaton essays and more.

VAULT CAREER LIBRARY **665**

dormrooms. Housing is kept in good condition. All rooms have T1 Internet access, central air, phone jacks and plenty of electric outlets.

Freshmen and sophomores live in traditional dormrooms, while juniors and seniors live in four-person apartments with a kitchen, a living room and two bathrooms—most of the apartments have four bedrooms, but some have two larger bedrooms that are each shared by two people.

The campus is actually quite beautiful and is consistently ranked as one of the best looking college campuses in the country. The academic campus (that is, not counting the golf course and other school properties) is about 750 acres. The current campus is only about 50 years old (although the school was founded in 1826) so none of the buildings are ancient. Within the past decade, the school has been building and renovating nearly continuously.

Campus dining consists of the dining hall and the Paladen (a food court). There is also a coffee shop that serves Starbucks products. The area surrounding the school is a good, safe area. I've never been the victim of any sort of crime on campus or known anyone who has. I've never heard of any violent crimes at all. Most areas are well lit at night and campus police are on patrol 24 hours a day.

Alumnus/a, 9/2001-5/2005, July 2005

Housing facilities are excellent. The university does not permit much off-campus living, so it invests a great deal in its housing program. Many students, however, would prefer the ability to live off campus.

The campus is consistently voted one of the most beautiful in the U.S. and the facilities are clean and up-to-date. The campus has a new library and is in the process of renovating its two primary education halls. Dining services are excellent, providing a dining hall with three meals a day and a food court that stays open relatively late. The campus is safe, even though it is open to the Greenville community.

 ## Social Life

Alumnus/a, 9/2000-6/2004, September 2005

There is a mixed bag as far as social life is concerned. Being that FU is a very conservative school, there are many people who don't partake in the party scene. But at the same time, there is a good number of students who do enjoy partying and going out. So there is something for everyone.

I was a member of a fraternity, and I found the social life to be quite enjoyable. Everyone is very friendly and, due to the smaller size of school, I knew everyone. This is a good or bad depending on who you are, but I liked it. Rush is done differently at FU than at other schools. Rush takes places over the course of the fall term, and students accept their bids in January. I liked this because it gives you time to really make an informed decision based on friendships rather than first impressions.

Downtown Greenville is great. They have built it up quite a bit over the last few years. There is a number of bars and really good restaurants downtown. There are also all the chain restaurants out by the mall.

Alumnus/a, English, 9/2002-6/2006, December 2006

Greenville was my least favorite thing about Furman. The downtown is really cute and fun, but it's only one street. People who live elsewhere in SC consider it to be a big city, but coming from Atlanta, I thought that was ridiculous. The dating scene is awful, particularity at Furman. There is very little casual dating at the school.

Current student, 9/2001-Submit Date, June 2004

Furman is definitely not a big party school. I have been to some pretty good p[ar]ties, but they don't happen every weekend. A lot of people fill their social li[fe] by getting involved in clubs and organizations of various types. Furman is pr[et]ty close to downtown Greenville, which you will not mistake for Manhatt[an]. Nonetheless, it has some pretty decent bars, including Blue Ridge Brewing [Co.] (which is actually a microbrewery with pretty good food), Barley's (good piz[za] and beer, but the service is crappy sometimes), Wild Wing (good beer and [hot] wings); there is also the Bait Shack, which isn't nearly yuppy enough to be re[al]ly popular with Furman students, but it does have $1 drafts and all the f[ree] peanuts you can eat. Other popular places include the Gathering Spot and T[ime] Bob's.

I usually eat at one of the bars when I go downtown with friends, but when o[n a] date there are some pretty good restaurants that cost only a small fortune. O[ne] of my favorites is Trio (Italian). Other good restaurants in the area inclu[de] California Dreaming (not really sure what the cuisine is classified as, but i[t's] casual/dressy casual, and they have excellent ribs, salads and rolls and they [get] cheesecake in daily from the Carnegie Deli in NYC), Chophouse '47, and Ren[o's] Steakhouse (high-end steakhouses).

The dating scene at Furman is kind of weird because the school is so small, [as] well as because of the relatively even divide between students who are religio[us] and those who aren't (the two groups don't mix terribly often). Supposedly [X] percent of Furman students end up marrying another Furman student, so it ca[n't] be all that bad.

There are occasional concerts by well-known groups on campus (Da[ve] Matthews, Jump Little Children), free movies every weekend in the campus th[e]ater, a carnival every spring and a junior/senior formal. The biggest social eve[nt] of the year is Homecoming. Besides the game and dance, which a lot of peo[ple] don't go to, there is the float-building competition, skit and spirit competiti[on] that [all the fraternities, sororities and other campus groups compete in]. Alm[ost] everyone, even those not competing in the float building, are out on the camp[us] mall Friday and Saturday nights to socialize.

There are clubs of just about every type, from sports teams to political grou[ps]. There are something like eight fraternities and six sororities on campus an[d I] think about 30 percent of students go Greek. Unfortunately, the university do[es] not provide fraternity houses (sororities are supposedly not allowed to ha[ve] houses because of some antiquated South Carolina law) and the fraternit[ies] aren't big enough to get good houses.

Alumnus/a, 9/2001-5/2005, July 2005

The social life at Furman is excellent as well. Lasting friendships are commo[n-]place. Many of the students are highly religious, and they tend to sociali[ze] through their various religious organizations. The Greek life is very popul[ar], involving almost a third of the students. It is probably the best dating scene.

Most students are hardworking and dedicated to their studies. Greenville has [a] quaint, clean downtown that is approx. 10 minutes from campus. The downtow[n] is very safe, and it is very popular with the students. Downtown Greenville h[as] a variety of restaurants and art shops, as well as a performance arts facility call[ed] the Peace Center. The Bi-Lo Center hosts large concerts and events. Favori[te] restaurants are Soby's, Spill the Beans, Coffee Underground, Barley's Taproo[m] and the Wild Wing Cafe. Intramural sports are very popular at Furman, and o[ne] can find a club for just about any sport.

Upstate South Carolina also has some of the state's finest hiking and kayakin[g], and many students are involved in outdoor recreation. Cycling is also a popu[lar] sport, and Greenville is home to Discovery Channel rider George Hincapie wh[o] hosts a cycling event each year downtown. Furman has an excellent social li[fe] that is fueled by the creativity and talents of its students and faculty.

University of South Carolina

SC Office of Undergraduate Admissions
eber College
02 Sumter St. Access
olumbia, SC 29208
dmissions phone: (803) 777-7700 or (800) 868-5872
dmissions fax: (803) 777-0101
dmissions e-mail: admissions-ugrad@sc.edu
dmissions URL: www.sc.edu/admissions/

 ## Admissions

urrent student, 1/2006-Submit Date, January 2006

applied online using the USC web site, and got my confirmation letter in the
ail about a month later. I applied late, so I was sort of rushed to get everything
ady on time. I did not have an interview or an essay. If you have a B average
d extracurricular activities, it is fairly easy to get accepted here. The staff was
so very helpful with getting everything ready in time for me.

lumnus/a, 8/2001-6/2005, November 2005

dmissions process is now completely online. GPA and prestige of high school
e the most important criteria for admissions. Additionally, a heavy weight is
aced on SAT score and diversity. I was an international student and was given
nsiderable incentives to attend the program. For in-state students who quali-
for the state LIFE Scholarship, a university education can be a huge bargain.
ut the program focuses intensely on out-of-state and international students
der to promote diversity and a better quality of student.

urrent student, 8/2004-Submit Date, September 2005

he admissions process for the University of South Carolina was very extensive
d helpful. When I first considered the school, I decided to take a trip and visit
e campus. Everyone at the visitors center was extremely helpful. After leav-
g the campus, I received a great deal of information regarding the admissions
rocess for the school. The school gave me some great advice on how success-
lly to get into their institution. The first advice was to send in my transcripts
early. They also recommended that I apply eight months in advance. The
ssays that were required were very clear and easy to comprehend, however they
lso allowed me to think a great deal about why this institution should choose
e. The school was also very selective with my incoming class. We had the
ighest academic [achievements] of any incoming freshman class.

urrent student, 8/2001-Submit Date, March 2005

here was not a difficult process for applying. My best friend and I applied at
e same time, and within a few weeks we were both accepted as transfer stu-
ents from technical colleges. His GPA was not what it should have been, but
e still got accepted. It seems like GPA is not as important once you leave [high
chool]. I only know one person who was not accepted and his GPA and previ-
us school record were horrible. It seems like being a transfer student almost
uarantees entry.

urrent student, 9/2003-Submit Date, November 2004

got in with a 3.4 GPA and a 1150 on my SAT. The essay wasn't very difficult
complete and didn't take me very much time. It is not very hard to get into.
you work hard, you can get anywhere.

lumnus/a, 9/1999-5/2003, November 2004

ince this is a state school, admissions was quite simple. An easy-to-read appli-
ation was mailed in, along with my transcripts of my high school grades and my
AT score. The only problem I had with the entire process is that I felt the deci-
ion was made too late. Even though the University of South Carolina was my
irst choice, I was accepted by two other schools before USC accepted me. I was
omewhat concerned about what my decision would be if for some reason USC
hose not to accept me. I did not have to interview for the school. Once I was

accepted, the school had me down for a two-day orientation session that I found
invaluable. The fall semester had not started, so our group was able to tour the
entire campus in an uncrowded environment. It was nice to be able to go to
school in the fall and already know where everything was. The orientation session was also helpful to allay the fears and rumors about the horrors of registration and the size of some of the freshman classes.

 ## Academics

Current student, 1/2004-Submit Date, February 2006

Really enjoyed my time here at USC. My majors are in management and
finance. I've had some amazing professors in both programs. The international business program is the school's baby, but the other programs continue to get
better year after year. I've also never had a problem getting into particular classes. The business school is definitely not for slackers—a lot is expected of the
students. Overall, simply a great place.

Alumnus/a, 8/1999-5/2003, November 2005

I was in the business school, and I had a very good experience. Lower-level
classes and general ed. classes tended to be large (approximately 100 to 200 students). Upper-level classes were much smaller and professors were always
accessible. I never had much trouble getting the classes I needed. Registration
was done based on the number of credit hours you had. The courseload was fairly rigorous.

I joined the Honors College after my freshman year, and I enjoyed these classes
the most. The classes were small, and there was a wide range of courses from
which to choose, some as a means to satisfy a major requirement and some just
for fun or interest.

Alumnus/a, 8/2000-8/2002, November 2005

USC has a very wide range of courses but they are most well-known for their
international business and their sciences. The program I focused on was the
Marine Science Program. It is a great program because it allows you to get the
in-classroom experience, as well as the field experience necessary to further
your career. A lot of the courses actually correspond with pre-med, therefore this
field gives you the opportunity to take it in many directions if your major field
changes before you graduate. Most classes are fairly small, especially as they
get more specific. Most general classes hold about 100 to 150 students, then the
specialized classes are from eight to 30.

Most of the professors are more than helpful. Nearly all of them have open-door
policies, which is great when you are having trouble. There is also a lot of diversity between the professors. Also, if for any reason you cannot get to your professors, nearly all of them have graduate assistants who are more than willing to
step in and tutor or just point you in the right direction. Finally, workload is
completely dependent on the professor and the type of class. For instance, if you
are taking a class with a lab, you may consider the workload to be more because
you have the in-class work as well as the lab homework and reports. Also, if you
end up enjoying the class, the workload will also seem very small even if you
have a lab because you will finish it more quickly and have a good time doing
the work.

Current student, 8/2004-Submit Date, February 2006

Each school will vary depending on what you study, but most all general education requirements are the same. The School of Hospitality, Restaurant and
Tourism at the University of South Carolina is nationally ranked in the Top 100
and is very competitive. At most schools you will be required to retain a certain
GPA just to remain in that college. For example, at the University of South
Carolina Moore School of Business you are required to maintain a 3.0 GPA. So,
being sure your heart and mind are into what you are studying is essential. If so,
make sure you check out the professors you take before you take them.

Read all of Vault's College Surveys at **www.vault.com/college**—get complete surveys on 100s of colleges and universities, expert advice on applicaton essays and more.

VAULT CAREER LIBRARY 667

Current student, 8/2004-Submit Date, September 2005

The academics at the University of South Carolina are fair but difficult. The professors at the university are very helpful and make themselves extremely available to the students after class. The size of some basic classes is large; however, the school makes students feel comfortable with a suitable number of TAs per class. Many of my professors focus on real-world application rather than focusing on increasing the workload to great lengths. Many of my professors have also been fair with their grading. They provided a curve when they felt it necessary. The workload of these courses is not overwhelming, however it does keep you challenged and busy. I spend about two hours per day doing homework and two hours per day studying for my 15-hour classload.

Current student, 8/2001-Submit Date, March 2005

The business school is difficult to get into. It's one of the best schools in the nation. I had no trouble getting into my major. The English classes that everyone needs fill up very fast, so it's important to sign up early. Overrides are possible, but students who stay on the ball don't usually need them. Grading varies according to the teachers. The workload is not light, but it is manageable, even while working full time. The classes are good, and all the professors I have had were knowledgeable and helpful during class and after (even after the semester was over). Most of my classes have had under 30 students, with some popular classes occasionally having a couple hundred. The English classes have fewer students, as do the specific courses in political science. Classes such as Intro to Poli Sci are always larger classes designed to weed out students who aren't really there for the education.

Alumnus/a, 9/1999-9/2003, November 2004

I thought the academic nature of the program was excellent. Quality of classes was high and encouraged independent thought and analysis of the materials being studied. Once I got past the freshman courses and into my major area of study, getting into the classes I wanted was simple. Generally, an interview with the professor beforehand would get me pre-approved for those classes that I wanted to take, but were outside my major course of study.

 Employment Prospects

Current student, 1/2004-Submit Date, February 2006

Employment prospects are pretty good for graduates. Alumni are working in everything from small companies to the top banks and consulting companies. The career center does a lot to try and help students find the right internships and full-time jobs. A good many banks and other national companies do on-campus interviews. The school also holds a few big job fairs each year. They are nicely organized and you can look up the participants online and get plenty of research done in advance. Be quick to go to the career center and sign up for Career Link in order to interview on campus with many of the companies that participate.

Alumnus/a, 8/1999-5/2003, November 2005

Being a low-profile school, I do not feel like graduates have easy access to high-profile business jobs. However, many solid Fortune 500 companies recruit at USC, and I thought the career center did a great job coordinating events. As a graduate, I was able to win a prestigious scholarship for study abroad, and I was accepted into a competitive teaching service initiative.

Current student, 8/2004-Submit Date, February 2006

At the University of South Carolina, the career center offers help for alumni and students alike. The services offered include: résumé writing workshops, mock interviews, career counseling and many other services that can aid in the employment process.

There are also many on-campus workshops and career days that bring potential employers into the school to interact with the students. Many Fortune 100 companies routinely recruit at universities for future graduates. The students who actively immerse themselves into this process generally reap the rewards of their hard work and land wonderful internships/job opportunities.

Current student, 8/2001-Submit Date, March 2005

With a wide variety of majors and a large student body, everyone's experiences differ. Those planning on going to law school at USC have found that the price

has recently gone up along with the level of difficulty in entering. There is ple[...]ty of available on-campus recruiting, internship and job orientations, but th[...] are typically under-attended and under-announced.

Current student, 9/2003-Submit Date, November 2004

They can help with job placement. They have great internships that offer y[...] jobs after college. There job salaries can range from $50,000 on up.

Alumnus/a, 9/1999-9/2003, November 2004

Employment prospects were very good. I interviewed with more than a doz[...] companies and got job offers from five. Interviews were held on campus. I w[...] also coached by my professors as to how to handle myself during job intervie[...] and they helped me fill out applications. The placement office provided with [...] with a lot of details about the prospective employers allowing me to make[...] much more informed decision about which position I would select.

 **Quality of Life**

Current student, 1/2006-Submit Date, January 2006

I live off campus, and there are lots of places that are nice if you choose to li[...] off campus. There are many places to eat on campus and you can use your st[...] dent ID for most campus purchases, so it's easy, too. They have a shuttle fr[...] the parking lots to different campus buildings, so it's easy to get around. T[...] campus police are among some of the best in the country and are equal with sta[...] troopers. Plus there are many help stations all over the campus where you c[...] just press a button and help will come.

Alumnus/a, 8/2000-8/2002, November 2005

The dorms are set up basically to keep people with similar interests near ea[...] other. There are athletic dorms, called the Roost, that have great access to t[...] gyms and baseball fields, there are honors dorms for students in honors class[...] there are Greek dorms that for all those involved in Greek life and, finally, the[...] are apartment suites for upperclassmen who are ready for more responsibili[...] All facilities have access to the many different cafeterias and eateries, and sor[...] dorms actually have there own cafeteria inside. Within the cafeterias there a[...] buffets and other branded restaurants, such as Taco Bell, Subway, Pizza Hut a[...] Smoothie King. All the dorms are also within walking distance of other resta[...] rants and bookstores.

Other facilities of interest may be the library that is five stories, where only t[...] first story is above ground and the rest of the library is below ground. It is, [...] course, fully Internet accessible with a beautiful view. In front of the library [...] a reflection pool and benches where you can sit and relax between classes [...] while studying. In my opinion, the best facilities are the gyms. There are se[...] eral gym and recreational facilities. The oldest is one called the PE cent[...] There are [two weight rooms,] five full basketball courts and an Olympic-siz[...] pool. There are also cycling classrooms, as well as yoga and martial arts room[...]

Current student, 8/2004-Submit Date, September 2005

The University of South Carolina provides a high quality of life. Many of th[...] dorms have been renovated over the past couple of years. The dorms in whi[...] I have lived were renovated over the summer. The dorms are kept clean a[...] alcohol-free. West Quad is the most environmentally-friendly dorm in the enti[...] United States. The [West Quad] dorm has contests to conserve energy. Th[...] campus is also very clean and pretty. There are trees and brick pathwa[...] throughout the entire campus. Many of our buildings are historical, and there a[...] also large grass areas for outdoor activities. There are also state-of-the-art faci[...] ities on the campus. The dining facilities pride themselves in providing clea[...] healthy and delicious food. We also have many fast-food places available to st[...] dents.

Current student, 8/2001-Submit Date, March 2005

There are, of course, dangerous areas [in Columbia] but, for the most part, the[...] can be avoided by simply asking around and taking the advice of people wh[...] live in the area. The campus is set between two big spots for nightlife (The Vis[...] and Five Points) and so there are plenty of things to do if you decide to lea[...] campus. There are several dining options on campus and plenty of places wit[...] in walking or short driving distance. There are two well-equipped gyms, and lo[...] of activities on campus and in the area for every type of person. The school read out, but most of the classes a student takes are in a particular area. important buildings that everyone uses, such as the library and the Russel House where the food is), are located in the center of the campus.

lumnus/a, 9/1999-9/2003, November 2004

was the best four years of my life. Campus life was tremendous. I never felt ke I was in danger. Stayed in three different dormitories and lived off campus ne year. The dorms were excellent, although there was a trade-off. The older orms had much larger rooms, but at that time, had no air conditioning (a prob- m in Columbia, SC during the hot months). The newer dorms were air condi- oned, but the rooms were much smaller and most halls had common bath- ooms. In the older dorms, every two dormrooms shared a bathroom.

Social Life

urrent student, 1/2004-Submit Date, February 2006

here are plenty of bars very close to campus. Five Points (bar central) is with- walking distance. Plenty of restaurants (just not enough are open 24/7). lenty of events, clubs and frats from which to choose. And, of course, what amecock doesn't love its football! Tailgating for a game all day is simply a ust. Intramurals are also a big thing if you want to get some play time in your- elf.

lumnus/a, 8/2000-8/2002, November 2005

he social life has a has huge range of activities. Starting from the academic and point you would want to get involved in clubs. Many clubs have their own vens and/or outings. For instance, I was involved in the Marine Science Club nd for three days twice a semester we would go to Pritchards Island, SC. Other lubs will take ski trips, cruises and go to other events to socialize.

urrent student, 8/2004-Submit Date, February 2006

he Greek system at USC consists of well over 30 fraternities and sororities. he newly-designed Greek village at USC consists of some 20 houses built

specifically for the Greek members who wish to live together. The Greek hous- es are all grouped together and offer a unique way of living for student life, not to mention all include a short-order cook. Of course, the price to live in a Greek house may include additional college expenses; e.g., Greek membership costs and [more for] student campus housing.

The Greek village is located on campus and right next door to the newly built Strom Thurmond PE Center and Carolina Coliseum. This might make the cost of living in the Greek village well worth it for most. This geographic advantage makes the Greek village a favorite among most the students who choose to live there.

Current student, 8/2004-Submit Date, September 2005

The social life at the university resembles many other colleges'. There is a downtown area where there are many bars and nightclubs. That area is known as Five Points. This area has restaurants, bars, nightclubs, coffee shops and shopping areas. There is also a restaurant at the top of one of our dormitories that offers fine dining on Sunday for brunch. The name of that restaurant is The Top of Carolina. Many people casually date and hook up the same as many other colleges. The school hosts many special events, such as Late Night Carolina. This is where a number of fun events are held in one building such as hosting hypnotists and dance parties. The Greek life is very prevalent and popular at USC. We have something known as the Greek village, which is the collection of sorority and fraternity houses. Each house is a multi-million dollar home. These frats and sororities throw many mixers.

Current student, 8/2001-Submit Date, March 2005

USC has all the major fraternities and sororities, and I could not even begin to count all the student clubs and organizations. As I mentioned before, there are plenty of clubs, bars and restaurants that cater to the college life and are within close proximity of the school. The Vista and Five Points are the two main areas and students can find live music, good food and drink specials every night of the week. There is usually visible security around, keeping serious problems to a minimum.

Read all of Vault's College Surveys at **www.vault.com/college**—get complete surveys on 100s of colleges and univer- sities, expert advice on applicaton essays and more.

VAULT CAREER LIBRARY **669**

The University of South Dakota

U. Admissions
414 E Clark
Vermillion, SD 57069
Admissions phone: (877) COYOTES (269-6837)
Admissions fax: (605) 677-6323
Admissions e-mail: admissions@usd.edu
Admissions URL: www.usd.edu/future/

 ## Admissions

Current student, 8/2004-Submit Date, July 2006

The admissions process was really simple. I sent in my application, which was very straightforward, and within a couple of weeks I received a response. Because it's a state university, you don't have to stress out about interviews or admissions essays.

The only essays you really have to write for USD are for scholarships. After you receive your admittance letter, they will send you packet of information on scholarships and have one due date for the whole lot. It makes it easy to get all your scholarships applied for and sent in on one date.

As for advice on getting in, USD is very strict about its ACT requirement. Although it's a state university, it is somewhat selective. It is currently trying to increase its ACT requirement from 18 to 21.

> **The school says:** "Students submit their application, an official high school transcript and their ACT or SAT scores in order to be considered for admission."

Current student, 8/2003-Submit Date, July 2006

The school offers a great opportunity to experience college life before even making a commitment to USD. Students have the chance to visit campus and tour the campus accompanied by a current student at USD, sit in during any class, visit with professors and stay overnight at the dorms or a Greek house.

As far as the application, make sure to emphasize community involvement and high school achievements. USD prides itself on extracurricular activities such as research and club activities, so if you can show potential in either of those categories, you're sure to get a boost in your scholarship chance.

> **USD says:** "The scholarship application is separate from the admissions application and is due in mid-December."

Current student, 8/2006-Submit Date, July 2006

The admissions process is easy. All you have to do is fill out an application and then send it in. The application is self-explanatory; there are no tricky questions and if you don't know the answer, don't sweat it, you can ask someone or fill it in later. If you go to one of the tour days, you can apply for free, which makes the process a lot less difficult. You will also have to have your high school transcripts sent to the school.

Current student, 9/2003-Submit Date, July 2006

You need to send in the general application around February. If you plan on trying for scholarships you also need to send in an essay. Try writing the essay well in advance and contacting the university to see if there are more scholarship opportunities for your particular major/interests.

> **Regarding application deadlines, the school says:** "USD has a rolling application deadline; applications will be accepted until school capacity is reached. The scholarship application is due in mid-December."

Current student, 1/2003-Submit Date, July 2006

To be accepted to the nursing program, there was a test required and an interview process. The interview was new and I think it was a great addition to the program. Some people just don't test well and to interview and see them face-to-face gives a more accurate picture of who they are.

Current student, 8/2003-Submit Date, July 2006

FastTrack, a detailed introduction process to all aspects of USD, is a great way to get acquainted with the faculty and campus of USD. Meeting new students, getting advice from faculty in your chosen field, and taking a campus tour, contribute to a positive first experience at USD. Admissions processes are pretty straightforward, with the usual test scores and grades being evaluated. The majority of students are admitted, then are helped by professors and advisors in their specific field.

Current student, 8/2003-Submit Date, July 2006

Right now, all that is needed is to meet one of these three requirements: rank in the top 60 percent of your graduating class, have an ACT composite score of or higher, or have a minimum grade point average of at least 2.6 on a 4.0 scale in all high school courses.

> **Regarding admissions requirement, the school says:** "Students applying for Fall 2008 need to have either a 2.6 GPA (4-point scale), be in the top 50 percent of their class or have a 20 on the ACT. Students entering in Fall 2009 will have need to have either a 2.6 GPA (4-point scale), be in the top 50 percent of their class or have a 21 on the ACT."

The application is fairly easy to fill out, and there is the option to apply to all the other state schools also with one application. There are no interviews, essays or other extra requirements, just watch the mailbox for the acceptance letter if least one of the aforementioned requirements are met.

 ## Academics

Current student, 8/2004-Submit Date, July 2006

Since attending USD, I have been able to get into every class required for my program. Professors are available and communication is accessible. Grading has been consistent in all 100- and 200-level courses. When you get into your program classes, the grading scales are higher and set the bar for other universities with similar programs. Workload has steadily increased, and several courses seem to require busywork.

Current student, 8/2004-Submit Date, July 2006

Classes are good. The 10-point grading scale helps a lot in trying to achieve better grades with ease. Professors are generally good about helping outside of class and answering questions in e-mail. The homework changes depending on the course, obviously, so you'll just have to take the courses to find out.

> **The school says:** "Each instructor has his/her own grading scale for his/her classes; grade point averages are calculated using a 4.0 scale."

Current student, 8/2004-Submit Date, July 2006

It can be hard to get the classes you want, especially if they're popular, like the Psych of Sex class at USD. The more credits you've completed, the earlier you can register; so the older you get, the easier it is. But getting into required courses is easy, there are usually plenty of seats.

Ease of classes is hard to say—some generals are a breeze for some, even up to the point where they don't have to take the final to get an A! Other people can barely make it through. It just depends on what your learning style is. And some professors don't make any sense—they give you a bad grade on a paper, let you do it, and even if you follow all your suggestions they won't raise it more than half a letter grade! Others are just amazing—so much fun and so engaging.

Current student, 8/2004-Submit Date, July 2006

The academics are really good here. They definitely work to keep students on their toes and really help us get prepared for the real world. High grades can be achieved but you definitely have to work for them. The professors love to work with students, which helps out in the learning process a lot.

Getting into popular classes is difficult freshman and sophomore years, but as upperclassmen it is relatively easy to get into any class you wish. The grading is pretty standard across the board and workload is fairly simple, always depending on which class you take. This university has a huge emphasis on writing, so both small and large papers make up the majority of outside work, save for reading assignments.

Current student, 1/2005-Submit Date, July 2006

Although I have been reluctant to take a few core classes that aren't my forté, all has gone well. Graduate assistants, tutors and faculty are almost always available to offer additional assistance. Some courses have additional class hours set up as a regular schedule to assist students in grasping a better understanding of the material while attaining the necessary reviews to perform to the greatest of each student's ability. Study groups are encouraged in many classes.

For students a little less outgoing, I've witnessed faculty assist in securing positions in study group or with one-on-one tutors. Students have access to the course schedules for each semester as much as a year ahead.

Current student, 8/2003-Submit Date, July 2006

The workload and difficulty of a college do not really depend on its name or reputation but rather on the classes and professors. Each degree at the U offers more challenging classes and contrasting ones that are somewhat easier. This allows the student to choose exactly how difficult of a workload he or she wants during a particular semester.

If you're looking for a challenging schedule throughout your entire college career, the honors program is the way to go. The honors curriculum is spread out over four years and consists of at least one class per semester and concludes with an honors thesis. With several Goldwater and Truman Scholarship winners and extraordinary research opportunities, the honors program is sure to skyrocket your career in whatever discipline. If you can do it, do it!

Current student, 8/2003-Submit Date, July 2006

The professors here are excellent because our student-to-faculty ratio is 15:1, so there is a lot of individualized attention. Class sizes are small enough that students do not feel like numbers, but large enough that there are many people with whom to work in groups, study or have great discussions. There are many opportunities outside of the classroom to study abroad, do internships or do research. Classes at the U can be difficult since many professors have graduated or taught at prestigious schools.

Current student, 8/2003-Submit Date, July 2006

The University of South Dakota is a liberal arts institution with a strong emphasis on social sciences and the humanities. While the biology and chemistry departments are strong, the other science departments (like physics, geology and ecology) are lacking. USD has the only medical school and law school in the state. Therefore, many of the stronger undergraduate programs fall within those fields.

The quality of classes varies. Some required classes, such as Speech and Introduction to Literature, are treated as just that, requirements, by both students and faculty and thus are of a lower quality than other classes. However, many classes, especially upper-level, are of a very good quality. Most of these classes are easy to get into.

All of the professors whom I have taken have been of excellent quality. Since USD is smaller, there is more focus from the faculty on teaching than research compared to the massive research-driven state schools.

While the workload is too class dependent to make any good generalizations, most classes that I have taken have been very reasonable in the workload. While

taking 15 to 18 credits every semester, I have never had to pull an all-nighter or ask for an extension.

 Employment Prospects

Current student, 8/2004-Submit Date, July 2006

We actually have a Career Development Center where you can go at any time while you're on campus. They can help with careers after college, part-time jobs while you're in college or internships. They offer each student a chance to sit down with them for practice interviews and will critique résumés to help tweak them.

Current student, 1/2005-Submit Date, July 2006

The U holds several workshops and recruiting seminars throughout each year. Internships are encouraged and sought out to provide the practical work experience the best employers demand. The U has attracted students of such high caliber that they have not just one internship offer but several, some climbing into extreme levels of prestige.

From my department, students are being recruited into positions with local, state and federal government agencies. One graduate left graduation and almost immediately embarked upon a campaign for a position in the state legislature. He won the election. After years of attending college I'm finally able to see positions that I'm not only interested in but qualify for. I'm encourage by what I'm seeing for future prospects and have little doubt I'll be able to leave graduation and walk almost immediately into the beginning of a career.

Current student, 8/2003-Submit Date, July 2006

The school organizes several job fairs and exhibits through the year. It also offers a Career Development Center filled with expert job hunters who can help you perfect your résumé, cover letter or find the job you're looking for. One of the most beneficial employment opportunities comes from the many research projects with which the U is involved.

Current student, 8/2003-Submit Date, July 2006

Many employers are impressed with the perceived work ethic of Midwestern students. Students usually obtain jobs in professional fields, such as medicine and law; however, the majority of USD graduates enter into fields of business. There are numerous on-campus job fairs throughout the year, with prospective employers offering job and internship opportunities.

Current student, 8/2006-Submit Date, July 2006

The key to success is to get involved. It will be unnerving to go to a possible organization without any friends there for support, but everyone is in the same boat. You will make friends with these people. The organizations with which I am involved have allowed me to go to the National Conference for Undergraduate Research in North Carolina, meet Warren Buffet, invest thousands of dollars of the university's money and be a part of a national brothership in Delta Sigma Pi. In all of these situations, I have been able to network and I am only going to be a sophomore.

Current student, 8/2003-Submit Date, July 2006

My knowledge of employment opportunities is merely second-hand. Many of my fellow students are currently working in internships in Washington, D.C. Within my department, political science, the alumni connections are strong. The University of South Dakota presents many opportunities for alumni to come back and connect with current students. The political science department also has a mentor program. One student in the program who recently graduated is now working for the United Nations in Sudan.

 **Quality of Life**

Current student, 8/2004-Submit Date, July 2006

With a small campus, it's quite easy to feel safe. Even walking from one end of campus to another, it's probably an easy 15-minute walk. Public Safety is on hand 24 hours a day if there's ever an emergency, or even if you want an officer to walk you back to the dorms.

Read all of Vault's College Surveys at **www.vault.com/college**—get complete surveys on 100s of colleges and universities, expert advice on applicaton essays and more.

VAULT CAREER LIBRARY **671**

Dining was an issue in past years with pricing and quality, but we recently got a new catering manager, and they now offer vegetarian options and better prices. Our dining hall features your average college food—burgers, fries and pizza. But there's also a salad bar and a Chinese line where you create your own dinner.

Current student, 1/2005-Submit Date, July 2006

Quality of life is very safe. Housing is being updated on campus and there is a great variety of options for off-campus housing. New Wal-Mart in town has made basics more available and has supplemented great small-town service of local grocery stores. Restaurant dining is also varied: Chinese, Mexican, several pizza places, hamburger joints and cafe-type eateries. For a nontraditional, this is a great place to go to college.

Current student, 8/2004-Submit Date, July 2006

Housing isn't the greatest—they're currently remodeling dorms right now, and even though they look nicer, the rooms are still pretty small. It's a pretty safe campus. There are a couple buildings that are really nice—Old Main and the Al Neuharth Media Center come to mind. But my very first class was in the basement of an older building with no windows, hardly any lights, an old-school blackboard and no technology to speak of whatsoever. But most of the classrooms are decent; there is always access to a TV, computer, Internet and projector. They may not look the prettiest, but they get the job done.

Current student, 8/2004-Submit Date, July 2006

Dorm life is dorm life. You really cannot guess what your floor will be like or who your neighbors will be. The dorms are comfortable and you really take out what you put in. If you choose to be a bad neighbor, your whole floor will take offense and you probably won't have a very fun year. If you choose to be social and have fun, chances are you will enjoy the dorm life very much. The campus is so gorgeous and not too big.

Current student, 1/2005-Submit Date, July 2006

Facilities are offered for both traditional and nontraditional students. Dorms have been refurbished and updated. Family housing is offered for married couples and students with children. The Coyote Student Center is being totally rebuilt to maintain a comfortable but progressive atmosphere for students who make the U their home. Normally the home of several dining facilities, the dining options have all been relocated to the commons until the new Coyote Student Center is completed.

 ## Social Life

Current student, 1/2004-Submit Date, July 2006

USD has stuff going on all the time. From plays to football, Dakota Days to poetry readings, there is something for everyone. There is a really nifty coffee shop on campus with live music at least once a week. There is also a park that is perfect for picnic lunches and studying. The new super Wal-Mart really makes it easy to have everything you need without having to go far. USD Theater productions are almost always packed—and for good reason. Vermillion is right in the middle of Sioux City and Sioux Falls—both excellent venues for shopping and dining out.

Current student, 9/2003-Submit Date, July 2006

There are plenty of parties and bars to attend. With all of the fraternities and houses, there is a party just about every night. The bars are nicely located and are really close to one another. Plus with the SafeRide program, you don't have to worry about walking home or driving drunk.

Current student, 8/2003-Submit Date, July 2006

While the university is located in a small town, the Program Council does manage to bring in entertainment, such as concerts, movies and comedians. There are several popular restaurants around town that provide decent options. Mexican, Italian, Chinese and American diners are the basics, and along with fast-food restaurants, provide students with a limited but diverse choice of where to eat. Especially close to campus are Mexico Viejo and Little Italy's, two student favorites that are reasonably priced.

The bar scene in Vermillion is a strange sight. The relatively small historic downtown area is brimming with students on any given weekend night. Nigh deals and specialty nights such as jazz night, karaoke and local performances Open Mike's make it a favorite. However, Carey's is, and has been since 19[?] the big name in the downtown bar scene. These and others make downtown bustling center of nighttime activity in an otherwise calm and quiet town. fact, "downtown" has become synonymous with going out to the bars.

Current student, 8/2003-Submit Date, July 2006

Vermillion is a town of 10,000 people and has approximately 15 bars. The soc life is amazing because we are a big college town. Students make this tov great. There are many places to go on dates and the Missouri River along w[ith] Lewis and Clark Reservoir are within 30 miles of the campus. This offers f[or] recreation and beaches for students to attend and party.

There are four sororities and nine fraternities, making the Greek system stro[ng] here at USD. Greek students tend to get really involved in campus activities a[nd] have a higher GPA than non-Greeks. USD has a Program Council that hosts sp[e] cial events like concerts, jello wrestling, After Hours (which includes activiti[es] such as grocery bingo, a hypnotist, a mentalist, comedians and improv group[s.] Traveling shops/craftsmen frequent our student center to sell unique poste[rs,] jewelry, purses and other interesting artifacts. There are also lots of opportu[ni] ties for philanthropic events like Habitat for Humanity, giving blood and SERV[E] (which includes Adopt a School, Adopt a Grandparent, Big Pal/Little P[al,] Campus Cleanup, Into the Streets and Heroes, which works with middle scho[ol] students).

 ## The School Says

The University of South Dakota has everything you'll need to find your place in the fast paced, ever-changing professional world. The U is home of the state's only law and medical schools as well as the only College of Fine Arts in the region. Entrepreneurs and accountants will attend our professionally accredited School of Business, and students studying disciplines ranging from biology to sociology will experience cutting edge courses in our College of Arts and Sciences. Choose from more than 130 majors and minors and thousands of course offerings. Our Graduate School offers master's degrees in more than 50 areas and doctorates are available in 12 fields.

At The U, we match our commitment to academic excellence with the personal attention and welcoming atmosphere necessary for a successful transition into college life. As the only South Dakota public university The Princeton Review named in its 2008 edition of "The Best 366 Colleges," it is the perfect fit for students looking for a smart educational investment.

Extraordinary professors not only provide students with world class instruction, but also with the knowledge and skills needed to compete for some of the nation's most prestigious scholarships. In the past three years, students from The U have received three of the nation's top scholarships—Fulbright, Truman and Goldwater. The awards put The University of South Dakota among a select group of colleges and universities across the country. The University of South Dakota is also a Truman Honor Institution for sustained success in student recipients of Harry S. Truman Scholarships. In addition to scholarship opportunities, many students from The U earn grant funding to pursue their studies.

Maintain your active lifestyle and enjoy heart pounding athletics at The U's multipurpose DakotaDome. The DakotaDome is a 145,000 square-foot facility featuring an indoor football field, five basketball courts, a 25-meter swimming pool, an eight-lane 200-meter track, and racquetball, volleyball and tennis courts, in addition to a large, newly renovated weight room. The

Coyotes have provided decades of quality athletics in 17 inter-collegiate programs. The U is in the process of moving its athletic program to the NCAA Division I level, with 2007-08 doubling as the exploratory year and the first year in the five-year reclassification process.

Don't miss out on the extraordinary possibilities waiting for you at The University of South Dakota. With so much going on, isn't it time you scheduled a visit to find out where you fit in?

Read all of Vault's College Surveys at **www.vault.com/college**—get complete surveys on 100s of colleges and universities, expert advice on applicaton essays and more.

VAULT CAREER LIBRARY   673

East Tennessee State University

Admissions Office
P. O. Box 70731
Johnson City, TN 37614
Admissions phone: (423) 439-4213 or (800) 462-3878
Admissions e-mail: GO2ETSU@mail.etsu.edu
Admissions URL: www.etsu.edu/admissions/

 ## Admissions

Current student, 8/2003-Submit Date, May 2006

The admissions process was a cinch, and took just a couple of minutes to fill out the application form. ETSU's requirements are a 19 on the ACT and something like a 2.5 or 2.75 high school GPA, and as long as you meet those, there's really not much to the application. My scores and GPA were much higher than required, so I can't attest to how difficult it is to be admitted if you're marginal, but I don't know anybody who met those requirements who wasn't accepted here. At least at the time I applied, admissions were done on a rolling basis, so when I applied in September, I got my acceptance letter just a couple of weeks later. It was very nice to have that in hand and not have to be waiting on an acceptance at the same time as I was trying to juggle scholarship offers from other schools in March; I did have to wait on an acceptance from a big-name school, and it was so off-putting after my pleasant no-hassle experience with ETSU that the wait in itself weighed heavily on my turning down that other school. The application needed (I believe) simply test scores, GPA, a statement that you'd taken the classes that are required of college-prep high school curricula in this state and a signature, little more. There were not any competitive essays or interviews for admission to the university, but those things are very common in the competitions for several of the valuable scholarship programs.

> **ETSU says:** "For undergraduate admission, ETSU requires a 19 ACT (or 900 SAT not including the writing portion) or a 2.3 high school GPA and 14 specific high school units."

Current student, 9/2002-Submit Date, May 2006

The admissions process is very straightforward. The application for admittance and for various scholarships is simple and painless to fill out. Additionally, the admissions department and staff are extremely friendly, knowledgeable and willing to help students in any way possible.

Current student, 8/2004-Submit Date, April 2006

The admissions process here is pretty simple. There is no formal interview. You fill out the application and wait for the reply. We are not an extremely hard school to get into, but do not let that make you think we don't have exceptional programs. We have several programs here that even though you get accepted to our campus, you must then go through another application process to get into these programs.

Current student, 8/2003-Submit Date, April 2006

I really appreciated the campus tour that was given to me. The tour guides honestly answered my questions regarding social activities, parties and how professors interacted with their students. The admissions team is so diverse that there was always somebody there who could answer questions about different programs. Moreover, ETSU offers this program called Preview. It was, in my opinion, the best transition from high school life to college. The program allowed us to move in a couple of days early and our leaders showed us around town, interacted with us, educated us about the differences that we would experience on a college campus, and it started me off with a small group of 30 friends.

Current student, 8/2003-Submit Date, April 2005

When applying for college, high ACT or SAT scores are a plus. Getting into ETSU was actually a less stressful process than any other school's enrollment process of which I've heard. All you have to do is enroll through ETSU's online web site, wait for a response and send in your transcript. It's easy and exactly how enrolling in college should be. It was the least stressful application proce that I encountered.

Regarding admissions, The school says: "The goal at ETSU is to make the in-person and online application process as user friendly as possible. We encourage students to schedule visits to our beautiful tree-shaded campus [(800) GO2-ETSU] and to seek information on our up-to-date web site www.etsu.edu. Transfer students are provided a complete analysis of their transfer work upon admission. A special web site for transfer students answers key questions www.etsu/admissions/transfer.asp. ETSU is also a campus friendly to adult students. We have an office specially designed to assist adult and commuting students with their sometimes unique situations at www.etsu.edu/students/acts."

 ## Academics

Current student, 8/2003-Submit Date, May 2006

I love academic life at ETSU. I'm an honors scholar here, so the majority of n core classes have been honors classes rather than the usual university classe and they have been wonderful. The non-honors courses I've taken have al been great, just a little different (as could be expected). I've completed 1: hours so far and have only had one class with a graduate assistant; every oth teacher I've had has been a full-time tenure-track faculty member, which impressive for a public university of our size. Registration has been a breez It's all done online, and you can change your courses as many times as you wan whenever you want, before each semester starts. The departments tend to l small enough that they'll make sure there's room for you in classes that you nee for your major, and there are lots of sections of the general classes you take f the core, so getting the classes you want is pretty accessible. The only probler I've had with workload and grading have been mostly personal conflicts with couple of particular professors, and the majority of people I've worked with ha been very fair about those things.

Alumnus/a, Digital Media, 9/2003-Submit Date, September 200

The classes aren't as difficult as assumed, due to the fact that I really enjoyed t classes and my major. Luckily, I had fairly good professors who were usual willing to help. Due to the class types I had a lot of projects to do, resulting late-night work. All in all, I loved doing college work. Making whatever pro ects I could conjure up, without true clients to sell our work to, we could do an thing, no matter how unusual.

Current student, 9/2002-Submit Date, May 2006

As one of many students on this campus pursuing a career in the health profe sions, I can say that while many lower-level classes and general education clas es are very easy or don't require a lot of work to still get good grades, uppe level courses, particularly science courses, can be very demanding and difficu Classes vary considerably in terms of workload. Some courses may require ve little outside studying or work, while others require and consume the majority your time to get high grades. In terms of grading criteria, again this vari according to different professors. I would say the majority are very fair and ma even be on the easier side, but there are certainly exceptional professors who a very tough and may seem nearly impossible to please.

ETSU is a great place for taking unique courses. A lot of courses are on a rota ing schedule and may be offered only every other semester or year, so they ca be tough to fit into your schedule when trying to get all the requirements yo need for your specific major. ETSU does offer a lot of special topics course particularly during the summer sessions. In years past, there have been classe centered around Asian culture, coastal biology field study, society of the 60s, well as a host of other special courses in a variety of majors and minors.

though there are bound to be a few bad professors on a campus this large, in general, professors are very nice. In my four years here, I only had one whom I really could not stand on both an academic and personal level. Professors have regularly scheduled office hours, but they are all always happy to meet with students pretty much any time if the student shows an interest or makes the effort. I have had a diverse group of professors here and have found mentors and friends in many of them. For the most part, the professors here are really great in that they don't try to position themselves as dominant over the students. They really treat students like peers and as equals, and they don't try to put students down to make themselves feel superior. This fosters an environment where I think we can all learn from each other and makes students feel much more comfortable talking with their professors and asking questions.

Alumnus/a, 8/1997-5/2001, April 2006

One of the strong points of ETSU is the class size and intimacy. Granted, the core classes I was enrolled in my first year had anywhere from 50 to 200 students. However, once I got into my degree classes, the average size was around . My professors knew me by name and took great interest in my education. Regarding registration for classes, upperclassmen (i.e., seniors and juniors) get preference. However, I always was able to register for my first choices. You can now register online or by phone, so the standing in line that I had to do during my freshman year is a thing of the past! You will have an advisor in your area study that helps with your class choices, so you never feel like you're in the dark. The graduation office does a marvelous job of keeping you up to date on where you are in regard to meeting your graduation requirements, so there's no bad surprises on graduation day.

Current student, 8/2003-Submit Date, April 2006

The professors are very good educators and exhibited signs of interest in the students' learning. My Organic Chemistry teacher gave us his home phone number, personal e-mail address and instant messenger name, in case we needed to contact him outside of his office hours or needed to ask questions. The popular classes tend to fill up very quickly, but the professors are really good with allowing students to be cut into the class. The grading scale, similarly, was very fair in evaluating my performance.

Current student, 8/2004-Submit Date, April 2006

Most of the programs we have here are high quality programs. Each college has its specialty programs. We are no different. Getting into the classes you want is usually not difficult to do. If you are an entering freshman, then it all depends on which orientation you go to. Orientation is where you register for your classes, so if you wait until the end, then it's your own fault. As far as grading and workload goes, that is all up to the professor. You will have some tough professors no matter where you go. That is just part of it. The best thing to do is to research each professor before taking him/her. Ask around and get suggestions from others.

Current student, 8/2002-Submit Date, April 2006

In my time at ETSU I have had no trouble getting into the classes I have wanted. I have had all wonderful professors who were concerned with how well I did in their class. I have chosen to take heavy courseloads while here, however, my workload has not been that bad. In the classes I have taken professors only give meaningful work, it is not just items to get grades with, the assignments have a purpose. All the grade scales are fair, with some of the most difficult courses having slightly altered grading scales. There are multiple offerings for all classes, so it is easy to get the classes you need needed and the professors you want.

Current student, 8/2003-Submit Date, April 2005

At ETSU, popular classes are easy to get into as long as you are a sophomore or higher. Freshmen have a much tougher time with the selection of classes pertaining to certain favorite easy classes such as Geography or Sociology with the easiest teachers. Most upperclassmen wait until their junior year to enroll for those types of classes to finish their core requirements. The classes are genuine and well-taught.

The school says: "ETSU has an orientation program for all new students where they meet with an academic advisor who assists with course scheduling and the registration process. Every semester, academic advisors help keep students on track with course selection. A telephone helpline is available to ensure ease of registration through the online process. Many support services are in place to assist with academic success. Tutoring, a writing and communications lab, a math lab and peer mentoring are examples of services available to all. Additional services are provided to assist students who have not made a decision regarding a major field of study. Our university advisement center is available to introduce students to the over 100 fields of study and assist with defining personal goals at www.etsu.edu/univadvctr/uac/."

Employment Prospects

Current student, 8/2003-Submit Date, April 2006

There is a wall of jobs available and employers post ads for positions they are seeking. I was recently browsing the flyers and stumbled across one for an internship at a hospital this summer. I called and followed the procedure and now I have an internship at a hospital.

Alumnus/a, 8/1997-5/2001, April 2006

After completing my undergraduate career, I pursued training in professional school. I was received as a well-rounded applicant with an excellent undergraduate experience, both in and out of the classroom. My colleagues who did not pursue any further education found jobs quickly after graduation and now are very successful in the business world.

Current student, 8/2003-Submit Date, May 2006

ETSU is mostly a regional school, with the great majority of students coming from in state, and a lot of the graduates go on to jobs that are pretty local. ETSU grads are very well-reputed in the area, as far as I know (and I've lived in the city my whole life so I've seen a lot in the working world in this area). There are several job fairs every year, and there's a great job placement and internship office on campus that can help students find work experience. Graduates do a little of everything, and they're well-prepared either to go straight into the workforce or to go into grad school for every in which I've known students.

Current student, 8/2003-Submit Date, April 2005

Each department has a club that helps students obtain internships with surrounding companies. These jobs help students obtain strong experience for their future job search. One particular student service offered to students is the career and placement service that allows students to sign up and browse documents entered into the ETSU database in order to find a job.

Alumnus/a, 8/1991-12/1996, September 2004

I majored in computer science and information technology. A lot of jobs were available at the time I graduated, but 80 percent of them were outside of the area where I lived. The computer science department always had postings for internships and campus recruiting was available a few times a year. There was a career placement office on campus, and getting advice and help with résumé writing was always available. Many workshops were also offered to help students prepare for interviews and résumé writing.

Regarding employment prospects, The school says: "The Office of Career Planning and Placement provides services related to internships, co-op programs with various companies and agencies and job placement, as well as résumé building and interview skills at www.etsu.edu/careers/carlinks/htm."

Quality of Life

Current student, 8/2003-Submit Date, May 2006

I've never had trouble with the dorms, but I'm not too picky. Some of the rooms are pretty small, but some of them are made for three people and they only put two in them, so there's a lot of extra space there. Lots of people tell me they've visited a lot of other schools and that ETSU has the biggest dormrooms that they've seen. The campus-owned apartments are gorgeous, with tons of space and hardwood floors. The campus is beautiful year-round, set in the mountains with all kinds of different trees, and it stays really clean. Facilities are largely 60s- and 70s-vintage, so sort of old, but we're starting a big building and reno-

Read all of Vault's College Surveys at **www.vault.com/college**—get complete surveys on 100s of colleges and universities, expert advice on applicaton essays and more.

675

vating campaign all over campus that's fixing up a lot of things. The food is really good, with a lot of choices and really flexible meal plans (that you don't have to purchase to live on campus if you don't want to). We're set pretty close to some nice residential areas, so you can live off campus in a house or apartment and still be close enough to walk to class if you want. ETSU is really low-crime (as is all of Johnson City), and public safety is usually helpful if you call. They're bad about parking tickets, but if you need to be walked to your car in the dark, they'll come pick you up.

Current student, 9/2002-Submit Date, May 2006

Although ETSU may be known as a typical suitcase campus, it is still a great place. Housing is available for those who choose to live on campus. The dorms here are much nicer and the rooms are larger than most I have seen when visiting other colleges. They are also in the process of building a brand-new dorm on campus, set to open fall of 2007. We do not have mega-sized dorms here, so students can really get to know most the people living in their dorms. There are lots of commuting students here, and there is ample housing available very close to campus. This is a college town, and there are apartments and condos everywhere. There are also houses for rent, and the cost of living in Johnson City is very low.

The crime rate on campus is almost nothing. This is a very safe campus and a safe city in general. Just doing the common sense things like locking your doors and not leaving valuables in plain sight is more than enough. Violent crime here is almost totally unheard of. ETSU and Johnson City are safe places with a welcoming family and friendly atmosphere where you can feel safe walking by yourself or jogging along the historic tree streets or hiking or biking along one of the many trails all over the area.

The facilities are pretty typical. Sure there could be updates in some buildings, but overall the campus is well maintained, and they are constantly making improvements (as is evident by a lot of construction all over campus). The new center for physical activity is a topnotch workout facility for all students. It has an Olympic length swimming pool, rock climbing walls, aerobic rooms, racquetball courts, three basketball courts, free weights and machines, with TVs to watch while you use the treadmills and other cardio machines, and a jogging track. The new Sherrod Library is also very, very nice. It has desktop computers, printers, copiers and lots of small study rooms with white boards, which are great for study groups. Students can bring laptops since the library has wireless access or they can check out laptops to work on for free while in the library. The new digital media center is immaculate. It is really a premier facility. They are getting set to build new, first rate soccer and softball complexes and have plans for many new athletic facilities in the coming years. They have already completed a golf complex that is second to none in the entire country.

Current student, 9/2004-Submit Date, April 2006

I love living in Johnson City and on ETSU campus. The dorms are much better here than I have seen elsewhere in my college search. The campus is a great size and is very compact. The university is set up somewhat by itself and is not in the middle of a huge city. They are in the process of major renovations all over campus so many of our facilities are getting facelifts. ETSU has one of the lowest crime rates of a college campus. I have always felt safe and at home here.

Current student, 8/2003-Submit Date, April 2005

Housing on campus has a big variety, from private rooms to shared rooms, all over campus. Most buildings are very old but remodeling is in process. Dining has extensive hours up until 10 p.m. with everything a student could want including meats, veggies, hamburgers, hotdogs, ice cream with cakes and puddings, 24-hour waffle stations, pasta, and rice with mixed meat and vegetables. The campus is one of the most beautiful I've seen yet and encourage any student looking at this school to go ahead and apply—it is a collegiate heaven for any student.

> **The school says:** "Governors Hall, a recently completed residence hall with a capacity of 542 students, opened for the fall 2007 semester. A lobby with a fireplace and grand stairway, study rooms on each floor, and wiring for data access, cable, and telephones are among the amenities in the new facility. Modern apartment-style housing with all the extras is also a popular feature on the ETSU campus. Further information is available at www.etsu.edu/students/housing/housing.htm."

ETSU prides itself on being a warm and friendly campus with an impressive record of security in a safe region of the country."

 ## Social Life

Current student, 8/2003-Submit Date, May 2006

Greek life is very active in homecoming activities and charitable fundraisers, not so active that you can't have a social life if you're not in a fraternity or sorority. They throw parties and stuff sometimes, always off campus, and sometimes they do things like free formal dances to which the whole school is invited. They also hold competitions like the all-sing, where Greeks and non-Greeks form musical performing groups and compete for prizes to raise money for the Ronald McDonald House. There are clubs on campus for about every interest imaginable, including special-interest Greek organizations. Outdoors clubs are pretty active, since we're in a great location in the Appalachian Mountains to hike, bike, ski and kayak. Mostly, what you do for a social life here is eat. Johnson City has one of the highest restaurants per capita rates in the whole Southeast and so there are tons of places to eat and hang out. Poor Richard's next to campus is a favorite with students; it's a pretty nice restaurant during the day and turns to more of a bar at night. Buck's Pizza, also near campus, is another place like that. There are several well-attended clubs nearby, and there are a bunch of places you can go to hear live music in Johnson City and nearby.

Current student, 8/2004-Submit Date, April 2006

The social life here at ETSU is excellent. Involvement on campus is one of the keys to making your college life fun and exciting. Our campus has over 180 different organizations which covers everything from service organizations to Greeks, to campus ministries. There is something on this campus for everyone. As far as social life off campus—our campus is in a central location to many hotspots. We are surrounded by restaurants that range from fast-food chains to steakhouses. We are less than 10 minutes from the Johnson City Mall, which is a fairly decent sized mall for this area. We are surrounded by the mountains which allows us to be on a ski slope in about two hours. If you are into dancing and socially drinking, then we also have two clubs just right off of campus. Thursday night is the night to go out. Our campus only has about 12,000 students, but we have something here for everyone. Make your college life exciting by being involved.

> **ETSU says:** "Enrollment for fall 2007 exceeds 13,000."

Current student, 9/2002-Submit Date, May 2006

The social scene at ETSU is whatever you want to make it. If you want to party, there are lots of popular little bars and a few clubs really close to campus, each with its own unique atmosphere. If you are into the outdoors, this is the place for you. ETSU is in the best possible location for outdoor adventurers. Lots of people here love to hike, climb, ski, kayak, ride bike trails, among many other outdoor activities. The Appalachian Trail is right here and skiing can be found at several locations within an hour's driving time. There are innumerable trails, rivers, streams and parks right here for our enjoyment.

With over 200 organizations on campus, you can find people who share your same interests, whatever they may be. There are several volunteer and religious organizations that are very active on campus. Greek life is apart of ETSU, but it is not such a big part that you feel like you have to be in a sorority or fraternity to have a social life or fit in. If you are into Greek life, we have a very active Greek system here, but it doesn't dominate campus social life.

Johnson City isn't a huge place, but you can find lots to do, no matter what interests you may have. There are lots of plays and musical performances. This is a great place for music lovers. There are many music festivals that come to the close surrounding area throughout the year. Good music can also be found in many of the bars and hangouts all around town. Johnson City has the most restaurants per capita of any city in the nation, so needless to say, there are lots of restaurants and places to eat. Somehow, even with all our restaurants, they are all still packed every Friday and most Saturday nights, so expect to wait at most places those nights. But overall Johnson City is a really friendly town. People here are happy to have students around and businesses and residents here support the university in many ways. Many of the fast food places across town and near campus, along with lots of small businesses in the area provide student scounts. Johnson City is a great little place, not too big, not too small. There plenty to do here, you just have to get out there and take advantage of it.

urrent student, 8/2003-Submit Date, April 2005

hile living on campus, you will become accustomed to a party life that starts . Thursday night. Most students hang out at Poor Richard's, a local pub with er starting at 25¢ a cup. Some hang out at The Planet or Second Level for club ncing. Others go see movies or shop at the Johnson City Mall. Every day ere is something new going on around campus. Just check the flyers.

The school says: "Campus life is active at ETSU. We have over 200 student organizations ranging from national honor societies to sororities and fraternities. Our Student Organizations Resource Center (SORC) coordinates the diverse efforts of these service and social entities that enrich lives both on and off campus. SORC also brings a full calendar of exciting programs and activities to ETSU at www.etsu.edu/students/sorc/index/htm."

The School Says

Since the doors first opened in 1911, East Tennessee State University has provided quality educational opportunities and exciting career options for traditional-aged students as well as working adults.

With over 13,000 undergraduate, graduate students and professionals pursuing studies in over 100 academic degree programs, ETSU continues to add facilities and degree programs to meet the expectations of students and the demands of employers in business and industry. Our new Center of Excellence in Mathematics and Science Education is a reflection of this commitment to improve the nation's endeavors in these high-demand fields. A vital, vibrant partner throughout the region, state and nation, we also offer study abroad mutual exchange opportunities with various universities around the world.

The university provides traditional day and evening classes, plus a number of courses offered entirely online, as well as special cohort degree opportunities in various locations, and the

Regents Online Degree program with bachelor's and master's degree options.

ETSU students follow their dreams in one-of-a-kind initiatives within these colleges and schools: College of Arts and Sciences, College of Business and Technology, Claudius G. Clemmer College of Education, Honors College, James H. Quillen College of Medicine, College of Nursing, College of Pharmacy, College of Public and Allied Health, School of Continuing Studies and School of Graduate Studies.

Doctoral degrees include: Doctor of Medicine (M.D.); Doctor of Education (Ed.D.); Doctor of Philosophy (Ph.D.) in Biomedical Sciences, Environmental Health Sciences, Nursing, and Psychology; Doctorate of Audiology (Au.D.); Doctor of Physical Therapy (D.P.T.); Doctor of Pharmacy (Pharm.D.); and Doctor of Public Health (Dr.P.H.).

ETSU has the caring atmosphere of a small school, but the complexity of a much larger one, and the university has a number of unique programs, such as the world's only master's degree in storytelling and reading. Our three-dimensional animation graphics design program is recognized throughout the video game and film industries. ETSU also has a vital service-learning initiative that is an essential part of campus life at ETSU and is embedded across the curriculum. Recently opened, the interactive ETSU and General Shale Brick Natural History Museum and Visitor Center at the Gray Fossil Site is situated on one of the country's richest Miocene Epoch finds, with an estimated age of between 4.5 million and 7 million years. With less than one percent of the site actually explored, to date, thousands of fossils have been uncovered from more than 20 different large mammals such as the saber-toothed cat, short-faced bear, ground sloth, rhino, red panda and shovel-tusked elephant. Numerous smaller mammals and fossilized plant remains are among the finds.

Plan a visit to ETSU by calling the Office of Admissions at (423) 439-4213, toll free at (800) 462-3878 or online at www.etsu.edu.

Rhodes College

ffice of Admissions
hodes College
000 North Parkway
Memphis, TN 38112-1690
dmissions phone: (800) 844-5969 or (901) 843-3700
dmissions e-mail: adminfo@rhodes.edu
dmissions URL: www.rhodes.edu/Admissions/

Admissions

urrent student, Chemistry, 8/2004-Submit Date, June 2007

he admissions process is really simple. Everyone who applies is automatical- considered for most scholarships. An interview is not necessary except for ne or two extremely competitive scholarships.

urrent student, English, 8/2004-Submit Date, June 2007

am proud of the admissions process at Rhodes. It focuses on accepting a iverse student body, and therefore, is open to people of all backgrounds and life xperiences. The only advice I could give about the interview and essay is to be

yourself, which of course sounds cliché. Although this is true, it is definitely the best way to go in order to have the best chances at getting accepted, because Rhodes will accept you if you are unique. This means they are looking for you to be yourself, and that means that there is something about you that is different from everyone else.

Alumnus/a, Liberal Arts, 8/2002-5/2006, June 2007

An admissions counselor came to my high school to talk about Rhodes. She gave us advice about applying, scheduling an interview, and choosing a college. I visited Rhodes on a tour and loved the small class sizes and the faculty involvement. I applied, interviewed, and received more financial aid and scholarships than I would have received had I applied at a state university.

Current student, History, 8/2006-Submit Date, June 2007

The Rhodes admissions process is amazing. I visited 16 schools and I definitely felt the most welcome at Rhodes. The admissions officers are very interested in you and they make it very easy to talk with teachers, sit in on classes, and stay over night. Current students are also always happy to talk with students.

Rhodes is always seeking to add diversity to campus. They are really trying to make the minority population bigger. As far as advice goes on interviews, I

Read all of Vault's College Surveys at **www.vault.com/college**—get complete surveys on 100s of colleges and universities, expert advice on application essays and more.

VAULT CAREER LIBRARY 677

would say just be yourself. They want to see who you are and what you are truly interested in, not just what you did in order to get into a school like Rhodes.

Current student, Religion, 8/2003-Submit Date, March 2007

From what I remember, there were two essays. The college is pretty selective but I was a valedictorian so I thought that I was hot stuff to all colleges. I did not get the top scholarship but got a pretty good academic scholarship and the opportunity to interview for a community service-based scholarship. They paid for my flight to Memphis. The weekend was amazing. Participating in college student planned activities was an awesome experience. The scholarship interview was intense and forced me to be more reflective than I had been at that point. I remember not wanting to write the essays but that they were short enough to do it.

Current student, Liberal Arts, 8/2004-Submit Date, March 2007

The admissions process at Rhodes is what initially attracted me to the college; it's extremely personable. I received several handwritten postcards and notes from admissions officers congratulating me on my acceptance and encouraging me to call with questions. The only advice I have is visit and interview. With an interview you're 50 times more likely to get scholarships and aid and there's no way to know if Rhodes is right for you without a visit.

Current student, Economics, 8/2003-Submit Date, March 2007

I've worked in recruiting, and I know that Rhodes specifically targets ethnically diverse students as well as athletes. Generally, though, if you've got good grades and any sort of extracurricular activity, you'll get in.

Current student, 8/2003-Submit Date, April 2006

I applied for the top scholarship to the school, did not get selected, but was entered into a pool for another group of scholarships. The interviews were not too bad. The essays were about average. I'm not sure about the selectivity. I knew that one needed a 1200 or better on the SAT and really good grades to be considered for scholarships. I had that, so I didn't worry about anything else.

Current student, 8/2003-Submit Date, April 2006

If Rhodes does not admit you, you shouldn't be here. Overall, our admissions department is too lax. This is a very difficult school, and you shouldn't want to be here unless you want to work.

Current student, 8/2002-Submit Date, April 2006

The best advice I can give is to be yourself and to make sure that shows in your application during the admissions process. Rhodes is pretty selective, so be sure to spend time on your essays. Good writing is expected while at Rhodes, so the admissions office seeks applicants with strong writing skills and a record of past achievement.

Current student, 8/2005-Submit Date, April 2006

Overall, the application process is pretty easy, and they give you really interesting essay topics. I wrote mine about my favorite movie.

One thing that the admissions office likes to see is interest in the school. If you visit the school, it can give you a leg up in admissions. Also, apply for academic scholarships, even if you don't think that you have a chance of getting one. They are really looking for people who are well rounded, not just brains. Because Rhodes is a small private school, they give out a lot of financial aid. Rhodes is getting more selective every year, but they do let a lot of people in off of the waitlist.

 ## Academics

Current student, English, 8/2004-Submit Date, June 2007

Academics, of course, are the main focus at Rhodes. The classes are small so students get a lot of one-on-one attention from the professor, which ensures their mastery of the material. Getting into classes is not a big problem, because of the small size of the school. The professors at Rhodes are all genuinely interested in the students not only as students, but also as individual people. If there is a problem that you encounter that interferes with your ability to perform in the classroom, the professor will do everything he or she can to assist you and to make sure you are a success in the class. The key is communication.

Current student, Chemistry, 8/2004-Submit Date, June 2007

The academics at Rhodes are pretty tough, but not impossible. Because of small class sizes, professors are easily approachable outside of the classroom help. The professors do expect a lot of the students. Approximately, one spe[nds] three hours doing work outside the class for each hour of class.

Current student, History, 8/2006-Submit Date, June 2007

Rhodes classes are amazing! If you like small classes and like discussion-ba[sed] teaching, then you will love what is offered here. Teachers have open-d[oor] polices and are always happy to have you in their office, even when it's not th[e] normal hours. Teachers also respond to e-mails really quickly. I had some qu[es]tions about study-abroad over winter break, and all my teachers responded wi[thin] in a day. Professors at Rhodes really care about their students and are willing [to] help in anyway to make sure they succeed.

Rhodes has a lottery for classes. Seniority dictates who gets which class[es]. Although I have never had a problem getting the classes I have wanted, some [of] my friends have. All you have to do though is go talk to the teacher and ask [to] be added.

Workload is pretty heavy and for most students, you either sink or swim. A[nd] most Rhodes students are pretty driven, so they usually do just fine. You [do] work for your grade though. If you want an A it is definitely possible; it j[ust] might be a lot of work.

Current student, Religion, 8/2003-Submit Date, March 2007

In the first two years, a student takes "Life" or "Search." These are courses t[hat] cover a wide range of information and essentially assess values in Western so[ci]ety and culture. They are good courses, but many people don't find them exc[it]ing.

The academic rigor is strong in every major or field. The fine arts are the wo[rst] because it is as if the professors have a chip on their shoulders, or something [to] prove. The workload is heavy: there is a lot of reading and writing. For [the] math/science/business folks, there is a lot of quantitative analysis, and thus a [lot] of detailed exhaustive (and exhausting) work. You will know who the go[od] teachers are and what the good classes are by their popularity. I have not h[ad] any trouble getting into the classes that I have wanted; most professors will p[ut] you on a waitlist and work with you even if their class has filled its registrati[on] quota. Grading is different for every prof.

Current student, Liberal Arts, 8/2004-Submit Date, March 200[7]

Don't let anyone lie to you. Classes are tough here, and while I'm sure you c[an] wiggle your way without taking the hardest classes, few succeed in doing so. [Be] prepared to work, but also understand that the professors are more than happy [to] meet you halfway. If you demonstrate work effort and commitment, then yo[ur] professors will work with you and offer you any help you need. I cannot emph[a]size enough the doors that have been opened for me because of the faculty, sta[ff] and academic life at Rhodes.

Current student, Economics, 8/2003-Submit Date, March 200[7]

Rhodes is a liberal arts school, so you can expect a well-rounded repertoire. [I] love my major, my professors and the interaction between students. The ac[a]demics are difficult but not impossible. Basically, if you show up, you can g[et] a C pretty easily. A's, however, you really have to bust your butt to earn. A [lot] of my friends haven't been able to get their bachelor of science due to cla[ss] unavailability, and we're seniors. It's never been a problem for me, but I'[ve] heard it's a big issue in the sciences.

Current student, 8/2003-Submit Date, April 2006

All our classes are fairly small, but most are easy to get into. The business a[nd] economics professors are very good, and you will learn a lot, but only if you c[an] put up with their personalities. Biology has a few difficult professors as we[ll] but for the most part, all our professors are reasonable and compassionate.

Current student, 8/2002-Submit Date, April 2006

Professors expect a lot of their students, and that's exactly what I wanted out [of] my college experience. The workload is heavy, but by no means unbearabl[e]. The liberal arts program at Rhodes creates an environment in which it is easy f[or] students to draw connections between different courses and to express those co[n]nections in different classes. In fact, professors expect us to do so.

Employment Prospects

Current student, History, 8/2006-Submit Date, June 2007

I chose Rhodes because of the very high percentage of students who get into graduate school. I really want to go to an Ivy League law school and this is the place to be. Rhodes really helps its students find internships and make connections.

Alumnus/a, Liberal Arts, 8/2002-5/2006, June 2007

Career Services and the Alumni Office are very involved in post-graduate success of students. They hold networking events and organize trips to visit alumni from other cities, or bring them to us. There are also plenty of internships in the business, art and music worlds. We have job fairs and graduate school information sessions. My work study job led to my current post-graduate position. I was the assistant to the events coordinator as a student. After her departure, Rhodes hired me to coordinate campus events, such as commencement, homecoming and student programs. Some of my classmates are in Teach for America, which is a national teaching association based out of Memphis that allows students to work in different locations impacting students in need. We also have St. Jude Children's Medical Center five minutes from Rhodes, where many pre-med students are now employed or participating in internship programs. Memphis is a great place to start out after college.

Current student, Liberal Arts, 8/2003-Submit Date, April 2007

Rhodes has great connections with St. Jude's Hospital, Morgan Keegan, Fed Ex, Teach for America, and other large firms in the Memphis area. Employment prospects for a Rhodes graduation are pretty high, so long as the student pursues a job and has applied himself during college life. I have found networking to be the best tool in establishing employment prospects: alumni, friends, family members, internships and so on. We host tons of recruiting and internship events on campus throughout the year to promote networking, job interests and prospects. I imagine half of graduates attend a graduate school (law, med and so on) immediately after graduation. Many take time off to travel, relax, do non-traditional exciting jobs, teach ESL classes in Europe and Asia, and so on. Employment opportunities are limitless; networking is the key, and I have found those connections on this campus for every career I am considering.

Current student, Religion, 8/2003-Submit Date, March 2007

A lot of people get into med school and law school, including many of my friends. I've heard mention of schools like UAB, Vanderbilt and so on. I heard about companies like Morgan Keegan and Coca Cola. The alumni network has proven invaluable already. I am looking to stay in Memphis and I have already applied to several positions through alumni help. The internship opportunities are really good. Most orgs in the city want to get students from Rhodes.

Quality of Life

Current student, Chemistry, 8/2004-Submit Date, June 2007

Housing at Rhodes is considered to be great, with palatial dorms. All students have access to excellent work-out facilities and two meal plan options. Campus safety is very good at keeping the crime level at Rhodes remarkably low. Students are immediately notified of any crimes that do take place on campus.

Current student, English, 8/2004-Submit Date, June 2007

The food at Rhodes is some of the best that I have encountered and the campus is one of the most beautiful. I definitely feel safe while I am on campus, because the campus is gated and campus safety checks out any visitors that attempt to gain entry to the campus.

Alumnus/a, Liberal Arts, 8/2002-5/2006, June 2007

The housing is great. Many students stay on campus all four years. The proximity to our huge new library, research labs, the dining hall and gym facilities cannot be beat. The food is top-quality. There are multiple workout rooms, gyms, fields, tennis courts and tracks for exercise. The pool is always fun! The neighborhood is very safe. Students walk at night. Most of the faculty and staff live within a five-mile radius of campus and walk, as well. When the individuals who could live farther away choose to stay close, it's a good sign. I never understood what quality of life meant until I came to Rhodes.

Current student, History, 8/2006-Submit Date, June 2007

Housing is a win-lose situation for freshmen. You either get really nice rooms or really bad rooms. It gets much better after freshman year though. The campus is gorgeous. Upkeep is definitely very important to Rhodes. When you walk around, you really feel like you are at a collegiate setting. All the buildings are stone and almost all the windows have stained glass.

Although Rhodes is not in the best neighborhood in Memphis, security, like upkeep, is one of Rhodes top priorities. Our campus is gated and there are always officers driving around to make sure everything is OK. Students can also call campus security anytime there is a problem.

Current student. 8/2002-Submit Date, April 2006

One of my absolute favorite qualities about Rhodes is that it's so easy for students to become immersed in extracurricular activities. That's what has made the quality of life here, for me, so outstanding. Housing is great. In the past, Rhodes has been categorized as having dorms like palaces. And I've never heard anyone step onto the Rhodes campus and say it was anything less than beautiful.

Social Life

Alumnus/a, Liberal Arts, 8/2002-5/2006, June 2007

The social scene on campus is lively, with lots of Greek and club events. There are ice-breakers and interest groups, video game tournaments, and study breaks sponsored by the Rhodes Activities Board. Being in Memphis is also great because it has the feel of a big city but the familiarity of a small town, especially Midtown, where Rhodes is located. There are lots of restaurants within walking distance, but the Memphis Zoo and the Brooks Museum of Art are the most exciting attractions, only two blocks away!

Current student, History, 8/2006-Submit Date, June 2007

The Greek system is very big. Your house signifies the type of person you are. Campus parties are usually open though, so non-Greeks can find a way to have fun. Rhodes is very close to Memphis, so there is always somewhere to go to get away from all the stress. Redbirds games, picnics by the Mississippi river on Mud Island, dinner at Hue's, and of course Beele Streat are all favorites of Rhodes students.

Current student, Economics, 8/2003-Submit Date, April 2007

The social scene at Rhodes is very intertwined with the Greek system; with more than half the campus being Greek, that's just how it goes. The Greeks throw lots of all-campus parties though, keeping the social scene inclusive. Recently though, the college has cracked down on drinking in fraternity houses, so most of the underage drinking now takes place off campus.

As far as bars and clubs, during the week students usually avoid downtown by going to Midtown bars like Zinnies and the Blue Monkey; on the weekend though most start the night at a house or fraternity party, then go downtown, and on a really good night: Raiford's until 4 a.m. Downtown Memphis is about a 10-minute drive from campus. The place to be on the weekend (after a house or frat party) is Beale Street. This street closed to traffic but filled with nightlife—from blues music, to dueling pianos, to Memphis rap. The drinks will add up, but most of the bars don't charge cover.

One really good thing Memphis has going for itself is its selection of eclectic restaurants. Some Midtown favorites include Fino's, Fresh Slices, The Bar-B-Q Shop, The Beauty Shop, Blue Fish, and Alex's Tavern (for late-night chicken fingers). Downtown favorites are Automatic Slims, Sawaddi, The Butcher Shop, and The Happy Mexican.

Current student, Economics, 8/2003-Submit Date, March 2007

The Memphis social scene is awesome. For the partiers, Beale Street has a plethora of bars and clubs that are always open. For the artsy kids, the Cooper-Young district is full of little shops, foreign food, and eccentric places to hang out. And there are plenty of parks, the Zoo, malls, restaurants, it's all here. If you come to Rhodes, be sure to eat a burger at Huey's and get some of Alex's chicken fingers. They are student staples!

Read all of Vault's College Surveys at **www.vault.com/college**—get complete surveys on 100s of colleges and universities, expert advice on applicaton essays and more.

VAULT CAREER LIBRARY **679**

Current student, 8/2003-Submit Date, April 2006

There are not any bars on campus. One dining facility sells beer on special occasions. In my opinion, you don't come to Rhodes to have fun—you come for an education.

I like that we have a student activities fund and allocations board to give student groups funds. I know that some schools don't have that. I don't think that I've dated here at all. One person. Three years. I'm graduating soon. Clubs are usually friend based and have an underlying political agenda. If you don't have a vested interest in the identity or goal that a certain club is promoting, chances are you won't join. There aren't one or two clubs that cover the whole campus—students don't seem, [to me], to be into "unity."

 ## The School Says

Rhodes students are passionate about learning, effecting change in their communities and the world, and exemplifying leadership and service with integrity.

The college has incorporated its mission into an outcomes-based curriculum that encourages students to take classroom skills into the community where they connect knowledge with practice and learn effective leadership through service, internships, international travel and research. The applied learning approach continues when students return to the classroom with the discoveries, problem-solving skills, contextualization, engagement and motivation they gained through their experiences. Through a variety of programs Rhodes offers practical opportunities for students to learn about themselves and the broader world.

We believe that learning is a life-long pursuit. Our academic programs combine the best of the classroom and the outside world, involving our students in the larger Rhodes and Memphis communities through a variety of intellectual, service, social and cultural opportunities. Our students study, play and serve others with a determination to grow personally and to improve the quality of life within their communities.

University of Tennessee

Admissions Office
320 Student Services Building
Knoxville, TN 37996-0230
Admission phone: (865) 974-2184
Admission e-mail: admissions@utk.edu
Admissions URL: www.utk.edu/admissions/

 ## Admissions

Current student, 1/2004-Submit Date, December 2006

The admissions process at UT is fairly easy. The application is not difficult; the essays are pretty generic, meaning you could probably use essay answers from other applications for UT's. Even better, you can use the Common Application. There are no interviews, but I recommend scheduling a campus visit and making a connection with as many faculty members as possible. As far as selectivity is concerned, when I applied, UT was not very selective at all. However, with the HOPE lottery scholarship, more and more in-state students are applying and admissions standards are going up every year. Extraordinary grades still aren't necessary, but you must be at least average in terms of high school GPA and test scores. I think the big thing that will weigh on applications now are demonstrations of involvement outside the classroom, like leadership roles or volunteer work. These things will set you apart from the thousands of cookie-cutter in-state students applying. Overall, getting in should not be difficult if you have decent grades and are moderately involved with your community. The key is to demonstrate ability, engagement and a willingness to commit to UT.

Current student, Accounting, 8/2003-Submit Date, December 2006

The admissions process was very simple when I was applying. Applying for scholarships was also simple and effective. UT covers all my tuition plus an $1,100 per semester stipend for books/living expenses. I thought that orientation was a waste of time. In my opinion, anyone who can use the school's web site can find whatever information they need without going.

Alumnus/a, 1/1999-12/2003, May 2006

The selection process is standard for a state school. Standard tests (SAT an ACT) are looked at, as well as high school transcripts. No essay is required f admittance. There is a personal interview required for the acting classes as it one of the best acting schools in the Southeast. I also minored in business, whi held no requirements except to maintain a C or above.

Current student, 8/2005-Submit Date, November 2005

I applied the fall of my senior year in high school. I applied before the first dea line, which was November 1, to ensure my entry. The application was about fi pages long. It included clubs I was in, out-of-school activities, a transcript se from the school, and then, of course, my personal information. They also inclu ed a section in which you could write about the reasons why you should get in the school if you thought that the grades and clubs you had were not enoug This section is helpful for anyone; and I think anyone who encounters this in college application should fill it out because it is just one more chance to pro your worth. There was a separate section completely for scholarship applic tions. It included references by teachers and then by other adults not scho related. You had to attach a two-page essay on why you deserve the schola ships.

Current student, 8/2003-Submit Date, March 2005

I filled out the undergraduate application, and sent it in with everything that w required. After a short period of time, I got in. Then in the summer of 2003 went to the required two-day orientation. At the orientation, I learned a lot abo the school, what the programs offered, campus life and where everything w located. I did not write any essays or do any interviews to get in. The selecti ity of getting into UTK is becoming higher and higher every year. This curre year's admissions received 12,000 applications and is growing, and they ca only let around 4,000 people in. The average GPA to get in to UTK this year around 3.49. The lottery scholarship is now available, which explains the rise the number of applicants.

Alumnus/a, 8/1999-5/2000, December 2004

I recall the admissions process being very simple. I don't think there were a essays—you just fill out basic information. It's extremely easy for in-state st dents to get accepted, but I don't it's that hard for anyone out of state to get i

dents who are good enough for top undergraduate schools will be very com-itive in terms of scholarships. UTK is very interested in recruiting minorities, cifically African-Americans. I heard from UTK in no time after sending in application, and I think they were the first school from which I heard. They e a ridiculously long and tiring orientation, which we had to attend during the mer. You pick a time slot when you can come to campus, and you spend two s being bombarded with information. You get a taste of what attending UTK l be like before actually enrolling.

lumnus/a, 8/1998-5/2003, November 2004

e admissions process is not very difficult, especially for a Tennessee residents. ere are a few forms to fill out, and it usually takes a little while to hear back. e application includes some essays, but it's not too stringent. Selectivity has ne up, but it still is not too difficult to get in for the average student. There lly is no interview, just the forms to send in. The average student really has worries about getting in.

rrent student, 8/2001-Submit Date, December 2003

e admissions process was not very difficult, even if you were from out of te. In the last years there has been a push towards recruiting students with her ACT scores, and it has been reported that standards have gone up. I don't nk they really read the essays and that they mostly rely on the numbers. Any dent with a 3.0 and a 23 or higher on their ACT should get in with flying col-

Academics

rrent student, 1/2004-Submit Date, December 2006

e academics at UT vary greatly by major. As a Psychology major, I've found st classes to be fairly easy. The major thing for all classes is the understand-; that you do not have to be super-smart to get good grades; you simply have be willing to do the work. It really is as easy as that. Class quality varies as ll. Generally, the more upper-level you get, the better the classes and teach-are. However, I haven't had any experiences of a totally incompetent/insane fessor. I have never been unable to get myself into a "closed" section. The y is to e-mail the teacher as soon as you realize you want to add the class, even classes haven't started yet; they'll often write down your name, remember u, and add you before everyone else on the first day of class. If you e-mail the cher beforehand and show up to class on the first day with a drop/add slip, u should be fine. Throwing in some story about how you really need the class ps too!

orkload and grading vary like crazy. The workload in most of my classes has ied from ridiculously easy (tennis class) to somewhat overwhelming (anato-and physiology). But as long as you manage your time wisely and stay on of the syllabus, you'll be OK. Grading is reasonable, and every professor e ever had has been awesome about offering extra credit opportunities or er ways to raise your grade if you prove that you're involved in the class and ing hard.

lumnus/a, 1/1999-12/2003, May 2006

tudied acting with a minor in business. My favorite classes were the acting sses because they didn't require sitting at a desk the entire time. Another orite was Sociology of Religion because it really required you to think and derstand different views and cultures. It was interesting to read about how dif-ent religions were created during different social times. The teacher gave cellent passionate lectures that kept you on the edge of your seat. The teacher lly does make all the difference in the class. If the teacher sucks, so does the ss. It is a simple equation. All of my classes were based in A, B, C, D grad-; format based on tests and class participation. The business classes such as ance, accounting and statistics were pretty dull, however, I really enjoyed siness ethics and small business management because you were required to sign your own business from start to finish. You started with an idea and a ssion statement and then ran the virtual business until the course was over. In end, you were graded on how well your business did.

rrent student, 8/2005-Submit Date, November 2005

m currently taking 14 hours of class. Those include Chemistry 120, English 1, Finite Math 123, Political Science 101 and Business Administration 100.

My chemistry class is the most difficult. It involves two lecture classes a week, a three-hour lab session and a discussion class once a week. The lab is very easy to follow and the instructor does a good job of making us understand. The lec-ture, however, is basically just a reading of PowerPoint notes. The discussion is used for quiz-taking and review. My math class is three times a week and the teaching is good. My political science class is a small lecture class and it easy to follow. My BA class is just for freshman business majors, and it just an intro-duction to a lot of assets that are available to freshmen that they may not know about. None of these classes were hard to get into, and the advising class at ori-entation made it very easy to schedule all of them.

Current student, Accounting, 8/2003-Submit Date, December 2006

Many first- or second-year classes are taught by TAs, which some people are annoyed with, but it personally didn't bother me. Do you expect tenured pro-fessors to teach college algebra or English 101?

After getting into third- and fourth-year major-specific classes, the pace picks up quite a bit. All my accounting professors have been very well-qualified in their subjects and presented extremely challenging projects and tests.

Current student, 8/2003-Submit Date., March 2005

Academics at UTK are very good. The classes are very hard. Most classes are large in number (100 to 600 people). Usually you have four exams a semester in each class, and possibly quizzes or papers. The grading scale starts off with a 90 as an A.

Registration is important. You have to meet with an advisor in your field of study before you can register. Classes do go very fast, so it is best to make sure you register on the first day possible. One of the most popular classes, the History of Rock, is very hard to get into; nearly impossible for freshmen. I am in the class and on the first day, every seat in the auditorium was taken. Around 50 people were standing or sitting on the stairs, and he still said that he would add anyone who wanted to attemd.

The workload is generally hard. You definitely have to put forth effort. The best way to make A's is to read every chapter and make a detailed outline of every-thing important, and then study that. This seems to work for every class. Just know everything, and you will do well.

Alumnus/a, 8/1998-5/2003, November 2004

Some programs are better than others, of course. Engineering, business and nursing are rated very well. Science classes are usually taught pretty well. Most students find difficulty with the math, since they either cannot understand the accent of the professor, or they can't understand how it is taught. Humanities are very popular here, and easiest to pass. These classes fill up very fast, and class-rooms are becoming overcrowded. You definitely have to register as early as possible to get the classes you want, even some science courses. Grading is harsher for the sciences, but there is grade inflation throughout most depart-ments. The science workload is much greater than humanities, as expected. The humanities courses have a lot of paper writing, though, which can become tiring for incoming freshmen.

Employment Prospects

Current student, 1/2004-Submit Date, December 2006

I don't have much direct experience with obtaining a job after graduation, but I do know that every single person I know in the school of business has obtained an internship with a big organization upon graduation. Kids majoring in accounting do the best; most sign contracts with Big Four firms and end up with ridiculously high-paying internships before they even graduate, not to mention a guaranteed high-paying job later. The Career Services Office is great about set-ting students up with part-time jobs, internships, and jobs after graduation. They have listings for every field you could ever want, and they hold career fairs twice a year where companies come and set up booths to give information to potential employees.

Current student, Accounting, 8/2003-Submit Date, December 2006

For accounting majors, UT has an excellemt career placement program. More than enough events are planned for networking with potential employers and

Read all of Vault's College Surveys at **www.vault.com/college**—get complete surveys on 100s of colleges and univer-sities, expert advice on applicaton essays and more.

VAULT CAREER LIBRARY **681**

landing a job. The interviewing process for accounting majors starts usually the fall of senior year. I was able to get an internship with a major public accounting firm without too much difficulty for the following summer, which will undoubtedly lead to a full-time position upon completing the MAcc program at UT.

I know people in logistics and finance who have also been able to find jobs without difficulty through UT's career services department. I cannot say the same for people of other majors. There are hundreds of unemployed UT grads with psychology or creative writing degrees. I'm sure that follows suit at every university, though.

Alumnus/a, 1/1999-12/2003, May 2006

I acquired a job with Merck Pharma right after graduation. Then I moved to NY and acquired representation with an elite commercial agency. I am currently acting. There were several job fairs on campus and tons of help when it came to creating and distributing my résumé through the college after graduation.

Current student, 8/2003-Submit Date, March 2005

Employment prospects for graduates of my school are good as far as I know. Nursing is an excellent prospect; everyone who graduated for the College of Nursing gets offered multiple jobs. The nursing school and law school are very prestigious. I am not sure, but I think the law school is one of the Top 10. As far as I know, recruiting is good as well as internships. UTK is the most prestigious school in East Tennessee, and probably second in the state next to Vanderbilt.

Alumnus/a, 8/1999-5/2000, December 2004

Many of my friends at UTK got jobs upon graduation. One of them is now working in Florida, and another one is working in Texas. Neither of them is from those locations. I think this is very interesting considering the fact that the economy is in trouble right now and that UTK is a second-tier school with a more regional academic reputation (sports is a different story). However, I'm pretty sure their GPAs were of cum laude status or higher. So if you don't want to go to graduate or professional school but want a good job coming straight from UTK, make the grades. Other than that, UTK is golden in Knoxville. This school is very much loved there—Knoxville basically revolves around UTK. I know people who were not from Knoxville who now live and work there after getting their UTK degree. Even if you don't necessarily have a high GPA, you probably can still get something decent in the area.

Current student, 8/2001-Submit Date, December 2003

The annual career fairs are very helpful if you are a business major. Within the different departments there is a lot of help for those who want it. Our accounting program has one of the strongest programs, frequently placing their students in prestigious internships (Coca-Cola, FedEx).

Quality of Life

Current student, Accounting, 8/2003-Submit Date, December 2006

I lived in student housing my first year at UT. The experience was not unbearable, and the facilities were at least relatively new and in good condition. Dorms are small, but everything works. Campus is large and a new student might have to spend some time figuring out where everything is and what the fastest way to get there is. UT has a bus system that runs throughout campus and in the Fort Sanders neighborhood directly north of the campus, which is really useful for tired students. I lived in an apartment at the very edge of the bus route and a decent walk from campus, so catching the bus from time to time was nice.

My first year I was on the student meal plan, which was OK. The food definitely got old, but there is at least one cafeteria at the university center that always had fresh, good food.

Alumnus/a, 1/1999-12/2003, May 2006

The campus is safe and clean. However, there are quite a bit of homeless people around, but they are harmless. There is a mission near the school where they come to eat and get rest. Housing is good and plentiful. The buildings are old but constantly undergoing upgrades and updating. From observance, the campus has quite a bit of budget money to do these restorations. The food in the

cafeterias is great. They have a great credit card program for kids that pare can put money on for food only, thus requiring kids to have to provide their o earned money from part-time jobs in order to pay for extracurricular items. T campus is dry, so if you want to drink you have to go to the Strip to do so. T keeps the dorms safe and quiet at night.

Current student, 8/2005-Submit Date, November 2005

The campus living for freshmen is very nice. Although the dorms are small, th are kept clean by a once-a-week cleaning service. Our RAs are very easy access and question about any problems we might have. Dining is very close us. There are two facilities outside of the dorms. One is a grill that has seve fast-food companies in it, and another is a cafeteria. Although the cafeteria is you can eat, it has odd dinner hours. It is only open 4:30 to 7:30, which son times isn't very helpful for fitting in with a lot of people's schedules. The ca pus police constantly walking around the campus especially at night. It see fairly safe, although crime still happens, and it is logged in the on-campus nev paper daily.

Current student, 8/2003-Submit Date, March 2005

The quality of life is fantastic at UTK. I love it. The environment is great.

Everyone I have met there is so nice and laid-back. Not to mention that a f years ago it was named the Number One party school in the U.S. That fact dra a lot of people here. Alcohol is very prevalent on this campus, as well as at le 20 clubs and bars very nearby. I live off campus, but the housing is OK, like a other college. They are always building new facilities, especially for spo Most of the facilities are nice. There are so many dining options. There around six or seven university dining places, that look like food courts—so even have real fast food. It is towards downtown Knoxville. Crime and saf are mostly an issue at night, and usually it involves drinking.

Social Life

Current student, 1/2004-Submit Date, December 2006

One thing about UT that is always fun is the social life. On any given ni (especially Thursday, Friday and Saturday), students can choose to party on F Row on campus, go to the bars and restaurants on the Strip or in the Old City, go to apartment parties in the Fort or several off-campus apartment complex There are always concerts going on; the Velcro Pygmies (an 80s cover band) a Trotline (a country cover band) are favorites. As far as restaurants go, Chili's popular, and everyone goes to Copper Cellar on Wednesdays because their bu ers are only $3.99 every week. For bars, the popular ones are Tap Room, O Cool Beans, Bar Knoxville, Half Barrel, and the Cube, all of which are on t Strip. People also go to New Amsterdam if there's a good band there, wh there often is; fraternities usually rent it out for their parties.

Speaking of fraternities, Greek life at UT is somewhat big, especially for gu I personally am not in a sorority and have never been unable to participate what I want to because of it; I still go to fraternity parties sometimes and nobo thinks it's weird. The Greek scene seems to be more important to those involv in it than to everyone else. Fraternities seem to have a bigger visibility on ca pus because they're the ones who rent out bars for live bands and have t events; every spring semester, SAE or its alumni put on a huge weekend-lo boxing tournament that's really popular and fun. But for people totally unint ested in Greek life, there are many more organizations on campus to get involv in. UT literally has hundreds of student clubs catering to every interest possib I'm in a service sorority and an honors society, and they both provide aweso opportunities.

Current student, 8/2005-Submit Date, November 2005

There are social events nearly every day. Football is a big deal on our camp and is probably the number one social event. There are many active sororit and fraternities on campus that hold band parties, mixers and formals quite oft For those not involved in the Greek lifestyle, there are many activities to atte There are lots of on-campus movies, bands, speakers and other types of even

Current student, 8/2003-Submit Date, March 2005

The Greek scene is huge here. You go to a class, and a third of the people in are wearing Greek t-shirts. There are very many bars, a few clubs on the act ip. In walking distance, there are many more bars and clubs also. The Strip where all the food is and a majority of bars. It is a common place to hang out night. The dating scene in good, due to the number of clubs and bars. There a restaurant for everyone, and it seems like new ones are being added. It is finitely a testament to the famous freshman 15 saying.

have a ton of events at this university, and an organization to join for every-e. I personally belong to Clinic Vols, in which I volunteer in the nurse's office an inner-city elementary school. It is very rewarding. It is very easy to make ends here, considering there are 28,000 students in attendance. My favorite d place is probably Sawyers, which is all about chicken, and they have a spe-l sauce that is awesome. UTK is huge when it comes to sports. We have the dy Vols, one of the top female college basketball teams. Football is probably most popular sport. People go crazy for UT football. We are usually ranked h in the SEC, and we won the national title in 1998. We are also popular for r track—one person on it went to the Olympics this past summer.

The School Says

From ever-increasing research dollars to affordability and value, the University of Tennessee is recognized for academic quality and programs that best prepare students to compete in a global economy.

As the state's flagship, research-intensive university, the University of Tennessee continues in its unique role of promoting education, research and public service to enhance its national reputation as a top-tier institution of higher education and to ensure the region's strong economic growth into the future.

UT's student body is a strong sign of the university's academic quality:

- Fully one-third of the nearly 4,100 entering freshmen admitted in fall 2007 had a core high school GPA of 4.0.

- The new class has an average ACT score of 26, up from 25.8 the previous year and 25.6 in 2005.

- The percentage of black students at UT jumped 1.9 percentage points between 2001 and 2004, the largest increase of any of the nation's flagship state universities, according to the Journal of Blacks in Higher Education.

To further enhance its accessibility to all students, the Knoxville campus has added $1 million to support its new Tennessee Pledge and Promise scholarship programs, which focus on improving access and success to Tennessee students.

The lab's exciting new facility, its "crown jewel," is the Spallation Neutron Source (SNS) research facility. SNS will allow researchers from the United States and all over the world to use neutrons to understand the most fundamental structures and processes of matter, transforming it for uses that were unimaginable even a few short years ago.

UT and ORNL will manage a new $125 million bioenergy research center that will search for ways to produce alternatives to gasoline. The Bioenergy Science Center, to be located at the Joint Institute for Biological Sciences, will study how to more efficiently extract cellulose from plants such as switchgrass and poplar trees. The results of this research will be used at the Tennessee Biofuels Initiative, a 5 million-gallon-per-year pilot plant for demonstration of switchgrass-to-ethanol conversion.

UT continues to forge partnerships around the region and the nation. The Center for Transportation Research is a hub connecting universities across the Southeast in conducting vital research to improve the nation's transportation safety through new approaches and new technologies. The UT Research Foundation is partnering with local, state and national agencies to construct the Innovation Valley Center for Entrepreneurship, a 15,000 square-foot, $2.5 million facility that will house, develop and promote new technology businesses.

The University of Tennessee is moving forward in its mission to be the preeminent public research and teaching university linking the people of Tennessee to the nation and the world.

The University of the South (Sewanee)

ffice of Admission
35 University Ave.
ewanee, TN 37383-1000
dmissions phone: (800) 522-2234
dmissions e-mail: admiss@sewanee.edu
dmissions URL: admission.sewanee.edu/

Admissions

urrent student, 8/2005-Submit Date, May 2006

you qualify for Merit Weekend you get to stay in a student's dormroom and mpete with round table group discussion/interviews and private interviews. is stay can be anywhere from one to three nights depending on your schedule. is particular weekend made me make my choice to attend Sewanee. And I am w best friends and the future roommate of the girl who hosted me. I'm sure e same life changing experience can occur at the other experience weekends. lefinitely suggest that prospective students stay over for a Sewanee weekend!!!

Multicultural Experience Weekend and Sewanee Experience Weekend are a couple of them.

Current student, 8/2005-Submit Date, May 2006

Sewanee is very proud of its campus and traditions and I made sure to mention both of those in the essay I wrote for my application; however, most importantly, my essay came from the heart and really said a lot about who I was, what I wanted out of Sewanee and what I was ready to contribute to the community.

I also applied early, which I'm sure helped me a little bit more. Sewanee was the first stop on my first college visit and I immediately fell in love. There are similar stories all over campus, as it seems that you either love Sewanee or you hate it—there's no iffy middle ground. This is all to say that it seems many current students applied early or had Sewanee as their first choice in schools.

I visited so many times that the secretary in the admissions office jokingly offered me a job giving tours, but I don't feel this is necessary for making you stand out to the admissions staff. The admissions officers here are looking for enthusiastic, conscientious and honest students who are low-maintenance. Though I am the quintessential city girl, I am still able to chill out and focus on

Read all of Vault's College Surveys at **www.vault.com/college**—get complete surveys on 100s of colleges and universities, expert advice on applicaton essays and more.

VAULT CAREER LIBRARY **683**

what's important. Because the admissions officers want to choose people who will stay, they look for potential students who will be able to cut it and are sincere in their desire to attend Sewanee.

Current student, 8/2005-Submit Date, May 2006

The admissions process included an application and several essays. I believe I may have used the Common App. Visiting Sewanee is key for understanding the community feeling that the university has, and pictures will not do the beautiful campus justice. It is small enough where interviewers will remember you, and they have great relationships with most of the athletic coaches, so it is important to set up a meeting with the coach if you are thinking of playing college sports.

Current student, 9/2005-Submit Date, May 2006

Sewanee really encourages visiting the school. The campus is truly the selling point, so before you send in your application they try to host you as a prospective. There are only 1,200 students currently enrolled so the process is clearly selective. Association with alumni helps. Sewanee prides itself on academics, so almost all of the students who get in are quality students with great writing skills and top of class status.

The essays are pretty straighforward, but the only advice I have is make sure you take the question and make it your own. They don't want average Joes and Janes here, they want individuals who will make a difference on campus. Sewanee has so much to offer and it is mainly because its students offer so much.

Current student, 9/2002-Submit Date, May 2006

The admissions process was pretty straightforward and typical. There are several weekend opportunities for students to come check out the school while other high schoolers are visiting. Getting into Sewanee requires more than good grades—extracurriculars, church involvement, athletics all help. The interview isn't very important, its more of an opportunity for the high schooler to ask questions. Students will be very honest with their answers if you have any questions about life at Sewanee.

Current student, 8/2002-Submit Date, April 2006

My admissions process was fairly simple. I believe that I sent in the Common Application, my SAT score and my ACT score. Sewanee is very competitive academically and my GPA was a 3.8, which was great because my SAT score was not that high, an 1100.

My tour was given by a faculty member as it was the beginning of August and school was not in session. It was informative and honest. My interview was also good. My representative wrote a personal letter afterwards and visited my small boarding school in northeastern Connecticut just to visit it. I had to leave school unexpectedly during his visit and when I returned he had left another note just to see how my senior year was going.

Sewanee has steadily grown more and more difficult to get into and I sincerely wonder if I would be accepted applying four years later, however they are totally committed to making Sewanee the best liberal arts school it can possibly be. My college counselor was pretty confident that I would be accepted and when I was, it was the seriously one of the happiest days of my life. Where I decided to go to school would depend on how much financial aid I was awarded and luckily for me, Sewanee gave me the most.

Current student, 8/2005-Submit Date, April 2006

The admissions process, like everything at Sewanee, is warm and personalized. From the first call I made to find out about the school, I was greeted by individuals honestly excited about the university and ready to make my application process as easy and stress-free as possible. Once accepted, my admissions counselor was ready to answer any questions or concerns I may have had at any time. I could not imagine or ask for a better admissions experience.

 **Academics**

Current student, 8/2005-Submit Date, May 2006

The majority of my professors have been absolutely amazing human beings and professors. The classes have also been fabulous. Chemistry 102 was a lot of fun

and I learned a lot and am having my lecture prof for that class as my lab p for Organic Chemistry. My French prof is actually from France.

My classes have been extremely informative and enjoyable. English 1 involved lots of round table discussions, which really allowed me truly to und stand the works we read. History 100 was involved in the same way as Engl 101. Biology 132 also gave me a deeper insight into subjects about whicl desired to learn more.

Current student, 8/2005-Submit Date, May 2006

Something very special to Sewanee is its FYP: First Year Program. This allo incoming freshmen to choose a class (most FYPs offered go toward graduati requirements) that will double as an advisory in the first semester. While ev freshman student is given an advisor, students in the FYPs have the add advantage of having this advisor in the classroom. The FYPs help students get to know one another and foster a strong bond between students and their p fessors/advisors who usually will have the students over for dinner a cou times at their homes.

The classes you take are divided into three sections: a third is core requiremen another third is for your major and the last third is for electives. This allows s dents to experiment and explore while still getting the basic academic foun tion needed to succeed in life. Class sign-up is a bit of a hassle, as students a allowed to register in sections. Senior gownsmen (with the highest grades) a allowed to go first, then regular seniors, junior gownsmen and so on until it g to the end. Many spots are saved for incoming freshmen, so sophomores end having it the worst. However, because it is a small school, students are enco aged to talk to their advisors and e-mail professors whose classes they wish get into, a tactic that often works (I e-mailed my way into a calc class—I'll ne know why I was so adamant about that!).

Professors are always very understanding and will work with you up to a cert extent. The Honor Code, which all students sign at the beginning of the year, highly regarded above everything else and this allows professors and stude the freedom to take tests under trees or with the professor in their office. Hor Code violations are taken very seriously and can result in expulsion.

Workload varies according to year and major, but expect to spend a significa amount of time studying if you want your gown! Potential students should worry too much, however; we often play just as hard as we work. We earn it

Current student, 9/2005-Submit Date, May 2006

The classes are very small compared to most universities; however, this mea total interaction. Even lecture courses are intimate and integrate class discu sions and lectures. The intimacy of the classes allows students to get to kne one another academically and socially as well as wonderful student/profess interaction. Sewanee has the most unique student/professor relationship becau most of the professors live right on campus and it is not unusual to get invited dinner with a professor and his/her spouse.

The workload is a challenge and the grading is not that easy but nothing impossible. Sewanee makes you work hard, but the outcome of every class worth the long hours.

Current student, 7/2002-Submit Date, May 2006

Sewanee boasts one of the best student/teacher relations in the country. We ha the privilege of dropping by a professor's house for a drink and political chat, advice on different classes. The quality of education is far above average, a while the workload is intense during the week, the students let loose during t weekends.

Grades are given according to effort; the harder you work, the higher marks y will receive. Class sizes are extremely small, allowing for an intimate relatic ship with the instructor. Students show respect for their professors by dressi nicely for class, lovingly referred to as class dress. Classes become easier to g into once you become an upperclassman.

Current student, 9/2005-Submit Date, May 2006

The classes are very small and intimate. Relationships with professors are ge erally very close; I have had dinner at my professors' houses several times a go to them whenever I have trouble with my work. They are usually very unde standing and know what the life of a Sewanee student is like. Like any scho

re are better professors than others, but as a whole, Sewanee has some of the
st amazing professors in the world. Just about all of them have their PhDs,
ne have more than one. They are all extremely intelligent. You are never
ght by a TA, the professors always teach their classes.

e problem with academics is the difficulty of getting into classes. To keep the
fessor-to-student ratio low, the classes must be small and there are not enough
fessors. Registration is really frustrating, but honestly it all works out in the
l. Everyone usually ends up getting the classes they want.

e workload is tough. I'm only speaking for myself, but honestly if you want
stay in Sewanee, you have to do a lot of work. There are a lot of people who
get by without doing much for their classes, but I am not one of them.
atever work you have to do on the weekdays is more than made up for in fun
the weekends, though!

rrent student, 8/2005-Submit Date, May 2006

ademics are difficult here and the workload is strenuous. Every semester, you
e four classes. While this seems to be a small workload, the amount of work
uired for each course makes up for the fact that you only have to take four
arses a semester. It is said that for every hour spent in class, you should spend
ee or four hours in preparation for that class.

ce this is a liberal arts school, there are core requirements including one reli-
n/philosophy/humanities, one political science/economics/anthropology, one
music/theater, one lab science, two PEs, one history, one math and one
glish.

fessors are extremely intelligent and have high expectations for students.
gh grades are not given out casually. A C average is considered average, while
B is above average, and an A is exceptional. Making an A is rare, though it is
ainable through hard work. Students often form close relationships with their
fessors. Professors have office hours and encourage the students to come
et with them to discuss papers or projects, or even just to chat. It is not unusu-
for a student or entire class to be invited to dinner at a professor's house.
ough the work here can be a daunting task, the quality of the classes is excel-
t, and the amount that you learn from each and every course makes the time
ent in preparation for each class worth the effort.

Employment Prospects

rrent student, 8/2003-Submit Date, May 2006

e school's name carries a fair bit of weight, particularly in Washington, D.C.,
lanta, Nashville, Chattanooga, Charlotte and others in the region. The alum-
network in these cities is generally pretty good, with networking trips twice a
ar to the bigger ones. Career services does a pretty good job of helping you
d, if not a job, at least connections that can lead you there.

rrent student, 7/2002-Submit Date, May 2006

e alumni network has set up a Sewanee Gateway that allows you to look up
d contact previous students. Internships are widely publicized and available—
it takes is a quick trip to career services.

rrent student, 8/2002-Submit Date, May 2006

e Sewanee network is tight and surprisingly far-reaching. It is not a problem
find a job (especially in the Southeast) with a Sewanee degree. There is also
arge constituency in New York and Boston. Many graduates go west after
ir studies, and some even abroad. The school is small enough to ensure a
rm welcome anywhere graduates cross paths, giving us an edge in certain
ches of the professional world (especially law and publishing/editorial).

rrent student, 8/2002-Submit Date, April 2006

though career services is extremely helpful in connecting you with people,
rking on résumés, cover letters and securing internships, these connections
 limited to Sewanee graduates. However, these graduates will do anything for
ellow Sewanee student, anything at all. They are helpful, reliable and enthu-
stic about current students.

reer services offers a program called Beyond the Gates, which brings alumni
d other professionals to the mountain for a long weekend in January when they

conduct mock interviews, information sessions and offer helpful hints in attaining a job or internship.

Sewanee is highly regarded in the South as a respectable and prestigious university. It is not so well known in other parts of the country. Jobs vary according
to the motivation of the student, but if you work hard, rewards will certainly
come. Because Sewanee is so small and in a remote area, there are not many
recruiters that come and there are certainly no recruiting fairs available. We are
encouraged to join in Vanderbilt's fairs though. Like jobs, internships are attainable if the student is motivated to apply and there is funding available through
career services for unpaid internships.

Current student, 8/2003-Submit Date, April 2006

Sewanee has an amazing alumni database that is open to all students and graduates. You can search for jobs offered by alumni or simply have them as are
source to life after Sewanee. Career services has an extensive web site that
offers internships as well as how to information. They also host weekly workshops on résumé writing and interview skills as well as other events and trips
throughout the year to help students develop a solid network with Sewanee
alumni and parents. Some of our most esteemed graduates are now the editors
of *Newsweek* or working on Capitol Hill.

 # Quality of Life

Current student, 8/2005-Submit Date, May 2006

Sewanee is a super safe community as the school and the town are one in the
same. Students operate the Fire Department and EMS. The police department
is in the middle of main campus. There are dorms spread out all over campus so
depending on your interests you can live in different parts of campus.

McClurg is the main campus meal plan cafeteria that actually serves delicious
food in wide variety. Cereal, pasta, pizza, wonderful deserts, Asian noodles and
hamburgers/hot dogs are always available in addition to many other foods, both
vegan and meat-containing. Most profs live on campus in houses between all
the dorms.

Current student, 8/2002-Submit Date, May 2006

The campus is referred to affectionately as a bubble—we are far removed from
the urban world, but still hold traces of urban culture. The campus is the second
largest in the nation (I think) at just over 10,000 acres, and must be one of the
safest. Everyone knows the local police, and they are even known to give rides
home late at night upon request. Most everyone lives in dorms, which are much
nicer than average, but after three years the priviledge to live off campus is coveted.

The network of communal living provides a forced environment of fellowship
that can be both good (especially freshman year) and bad (esp. junior year)
because it is somewhat forced and therefore less sincere. Everyone has a slightly different take on residential life on the mountain. Some dorms are better than
others for peace and quiet, but on the whole students learn to use their rooms less
and enjoy everything else here more—the domain caters to almost every outdoor
sport, the indoor facility is as nice as the Ramsey Center at UGA when you consider the per-capita differences, and everything is centralized so walking is usually the best option.

The dining hall is impressive for almost a year and then it gets redundant—it is
architecturally magnificent and otherwise sufficient, more than anything it is
convenient. Very few people decide against the meal plan, and that says a lot.

Current student, 8/2002-Submit Date, April 2006

Sewanee is a very old university and the buildings reflect that in a charming
Gothic style. I would say half of the dorms are air conditioned. All are clean,
safe and well maintained. The maintenance staff respond quickly with any problems and are extremely friendly. As are the cleaning staff. All facilities are well
maintained and technologically up to date.

The food at Sewanee is amazing! I cannot say enough good things about it.
There are tons of options and all of them are delicious. All of the students love
the food and going to McClurg is a highlight of my day. Sewanee is in a rural
area but the university itself is 100 percent safe. I feel safe in the middle of the

Read all of Vault's College Surveys at www.vault.com/college—get complete surveys on 100s of colleges and universities, expert advice on applicaton essays and more.

VAULT CAREER LIBRARY 685

day or the middle of the night. You can walk safely anywhere on campus, there is a sober ride on all weekends, and if you still don't feel safe, the police will drive you anywhere. The Sewanee police officers are one of the best things about the school. They always wave when they drive by, come whenever you need, talk to you at parties, and are fair. They even gave me a ride to class one morning when it was pouring down rain.

 ## Social Life

Current student, 9/2002-Submit Date, May 2006

This is very much an alcohol campus. It is a safe campus because of precautionary steps taken by the administration. The administration maintains a policy that you cannot stop people from drinking but you can make them safe while they do it. I feel that the university should at least make an attempt to discourage drinking while maintaining the precautionary measures for safety.

Current student, 8/2002-Submit Date, May 2006

Being on top of a mountain in rural Tennessee, there is a limited number of things to do, including restaurants and bars. Greek life is an important factor in the social scene, but those who are not involved are not left out because all the parties are open and everyone is friends between groups, though at times it can be cliquey.

Alcohol plays a big role in the social life here and sometimes those who don't drink might have problems finding things to do, but they form their own group and they are not excluded. There isn't really a dating scene—it is either random hooking up or practically engaged, not too much in between.

Because we are in the middle of nowhere and we have so much to do, the outdoor program is amazing with lots of hiking trails, spelunking, canoeing and other things. It is a great place to be when the weather is good. People try to bring events here, with is a nice change of pace, but even if there is nothing Chattanooga and Nashville are not to far away and it is nice just to be on the mountain.

Current student, 8/2005-Submit Date, May 2006

As the nearest real bars and clubs are probably an hour away in Chattanooga, the Sewanee party scene stays in Sewanee. This proves to be ideal, as students are able to bond truly with one another in a safe environment. Police are found at every official party on campus and are able to carry on conversations with the more outgoing (or inebriated) students while simultaneously looking out for their safety. Last weekend at a big concert I introduced myself to the chief of Sewanee police and was promised that if I kept introducing myself that he would know my name by the time I graduated.

Bacchus—a fleet of 15-passenger vans—is available on the weekends to dr students to dorms and events, so drinking and driving is a big no-no. Safety first at Sewanee and because of the Honor Code, special relationship with police and special community and bond between the students, students are a to enjoy themselves with little or no fear of something bad happening.

Greek life is big up here but not very talked about (if that makes sense). Wh a huge percent of the student population is a part of Greek life, it is conside taboo to ask an upperclassman to which Greek organization he/she belon Like everything else up on the mountain, Greek life and the rush process pretty chill and simply add to the fun up here. Greek parties are open to eve one on campus. While there are many fraternities (all national) on campus, th is only one national sorority, KD, which is not very popular. Many of the ternities up here are nothing like their brothers at other campuses, though SA KA and ATO are the most popular.

Every aspect of social life up here (from Residential Life's numerous ho logged matching up the perfect freshman roommates to the lively Greek sce is simply there to add more to the Sewanee experience and help bring stude even closer together. We are all very close up here and it is like one big fam (I love it!). The only downside to this big family is the lack of a dating sce as it is thought a bit strange for two people to want to spend time not hang out with the rest of the tribe. People who date are either in it for the long run in it very casually—there seem to be very few exceptions to that.

 ## The School Says

The University of the South, popularly known as Sewanee, is an independent liberal arts college and school of theology owned by 28 Southeastern dioceses of the Episcopal Church. It is consistently ranked among the nation's very best liberal arts colleges as a direct result of the care and devotion of faculty who work closely with their students to yield an unmatched educational experience. Since its founding, the College of Arts and Sciences at the university has graduated 25 Rhodes Scholars, 34 Watson Fellows and 25 NCAA Postgraduate Scholars, while the institution's School of Theology has added to its alumni ranks countless bishops, including three of the last four presiding bishops of the Episcopal Church.

Vanderbilt University

fice of Undergraduate Admissions
805 West End Avenue
ashville, TN 37203-1727
dmissions phone: (615) 322-2561 or (800) 288-0432
dmissions e-mail: admissions@vanderbilt.edu

Admissions

rrent student, Management, 8/2004-Submit Date, June 2007

eceived advice on getting in from my guidance counselor in high school who
ected Vanderbilt as best fit for me, from my parents who both attended dif-
ent colleges and universities, and from my sisters who had graduated and still
ended college. I was not interviewed. I wrote an essay. They were very selec-
e because it is a Top 20 school with only about 6,000 undergrads. They
oose from students all across the country and have a wide range of applicants.
elieve they focus on well-rounded students who have a variety of interests and
very well academically.

rrent student, 8/2003-Submit Date, May 2006

nderbilt is a very selective school. It is extremely important to make sure that
ery part of your application is the absolute best it can be. Spend a lot of time
the essays—the admissions counselors really read these! Also, make your-
f stand out. Write about something different, showcase a unique talent—the
ancellor is always impressed when he can say that our new freshman class is
arter and has higher SATs than ever before, but also that the students are well
nded. We have captains of sports teams and SGA presidents, but we also
ve jugglers and students who speak five languages. When selling yourself to
nderbilt, make sure you find a way to stand out; show them what you will
ng that will make our school better.

umnus/a, 8/2002-5/2006, May 2006

eceived the application to Vanderbilt from my high school guidance counselor.
stened to many teachers and my counselor for advice on what to write on my
plication and what Vanderbilt would be looking for. I did my own research on
nderbilt also. I applied Regular Decision and applied for financial aid. As far
my essays go, I was completely honest. I wrote about what was important to
e. I knew I wanted to be a teacher so I applied to Peabody School of Education
d declared secondary education as my major. I already knew I wanted to teach
gh school students. I felt Peabody was the perfect fit for me. I did not inter-
w at Vanderbilt when I visited. In fact, I did not even know interviewing was
option until I was admitted. I feel that an interview would have helped my
plication even more.

> **Regarding interviews, the school says:** "While Vanderbilt does
> not offer interviews with admissions officers, interviews with
> alumni are available all across the country. These are an option-
> al part of the application process."

nderbilt is a very selective university. I was in the top 3 percent of my class
d most of my friends at Vanderbilt were also at the top of their class. While
y test scores were not the highest, I was very involved in my community and
y school. I believe this helped me to be the well-rounded student Vanderbilt
s looking for.

rrent student, 8/2004-Submit Date, May 2006

dmissions at Vanderbilt is extremely efficient. It contains a structured and
ganized admissions team with a caring and personal touch. I've worked with
e admissions office recently and found on both sides of the process that apply-
g is taken extremely seriously. Every person is argued for at this selective uni-
rsity. My best advice for getting in is being a good, well-rounded person for
ts and sciences, a great musician for Blair, an extremely good science and math
dent for engineering, and specialized in service for Peabody. There are no

interviews but that doesn't matter. Take a tour, meet professors and meet admissions. Networking will do wonders for you.

Alumnus/a, 8/2002-5/2006, May 2006

Admissions application includes an Early Decision (ED) I, EDII and a Regular
Decision component. Early Decision is binding and the difference between the
two ED applications is the due date. Vanderbilt accepts the Common
Application and also asks for a supplemental application. Interviews are not
required and are informational for the prospective student and a chance to meet
with his/her admissions counselor (assigned by geographical location) face-to-
face. The essay is important, but Vanderbilt emphasizes the applicant as a whole
person. Involvement in high school activities is looked at as well as SAT/ACT
scores (SAT Subject Tests not required, but suggested). It is recommended that
you visit campus and do an overnight visit and campus tour to get a real feel for
Vanderbilt first-hand. The overall admissions process is very rigorous and
Vanderbilt is looking for students who will contribute to Vanderbilt's campus, as
well as students who excel in their studies. Call the Office of Undergraduate
Admissions with any further questions.

> **The school says:** "The Office of Undergraduate Admissions now
> offers the 'Dore for a Day Program' instead of overnight visits.
> Students can spend a day shadowing a current student, attend-
> ing classes, eating in the dining hall, and attending on-campus
> events."

Current student, 8/2003-Submit Date, January 2006

Vanderbilt is climbing in the rankings as I speak, so high school GPA and test
scores matter more now than a few years ago. Even though the overwhelming
majority of applicants are well-qualified when it comes to these statistical measures of success, Vandy seems to look most at what you've done in high school.
Real commitment and success to one activity is enough to set you apart.
Résumé-padding is frowned upon in the student body, and I assume the same is
true in admissions; most people I know who go here have done one or two things
extraordinarily well in high school (e.g., sports, debate, philanthropy). In this
respect, the admissions committee seems to look for depth of involvement rather
than breadth of involvement.

Academics

Current student, 9/2004-Submit Date, February 2007

The classes are difficult. When you come to a Top 20 school, you have to be
ready to work and work hard. It's not a cake-walk but it's also not impossible.
Just be committed and know that even though it may be a tough four years, it
pays big dividends over the next 50. The workload is certainly enough to keep
you busy, but the great thing is that there is also a large number of students who
work just as hard as you do that will form study groups to help make assignments more manageable.

Alumnus/a, Engineering, 8/1999-5/2003, January 2007

Great teachers. Very supportive, and truly care about the students. I was in
Engineering and really had to earn the A's and B's. Workload is tough, but classes are enjoyable so it makes those all nighters not so bad. One of my favorite
things about Vandy is that the students work together and are not as cutthroat as
I hear they are at some of those New England schools. Everyone wants everyone else to succeed.

Alumnus/a, Engineering, 8/2002-5/2006, June 2007

The faculty at Vanderbilt does a great job of motivating students to work hard. I
can't think of one professor who wasn't enthusiastic to meet for discussions outside of class or actively offering his/her help to students. As expected, the workload is quite demanding; if you work hard, you will do well academically.
Vanderbilt is known for its great balance of strong academics and social life. It

Read all of Vault's College Surveys at **www.vault.com/college**—get complete surveys on 100s of colleges and universities, expert advice on applicaton essays and more.

VAULT CAREER LIBRARY **687**

doesn't get better than Vandy. This is something I realized after visiting all of my friends at other colleges across the country.

Current student, Management, 8/2004-Submit Date, June 2007

My major's official name is Human and Organizational Development, which is specific to Vanderbilt. We do a lot of hands-on work learning what it's like to work out in the real world. We are most closely related to Human Resources. We have a required student internship that we must complete in one of five major U.S. cities or England during one semester. Some classes are somewhat repetitive but we learn self-development, group development and business development at which point we choose a more specific path. Mine was leadership.

Grading varies among teachers but is known to be a little bit easier than other majors at Vanderbilt. Vanderbilt is known to have harder grading than other universities in the nation. Getting popular classes is easier with a higher standing (senior or junior with senior credits). We do not do it on a first come, first serve basis. I have never been dropped from a class that I wanted. Workload requires a lot of long paper writing and response papers. We also have a lot of quizzes and reading. Professors, for the most part, are pretty understanding of workload from other classes but the occasional professor believes that his/her class is the only one you're taking, so the workload is hard to keep up with.

Alumnus/a, 8/2002-5/2006, June 2006

The quality of the classes is incredible. I never thought I would learn as much as I did. The professors are amazing—really knowledgeable, engaging and helpful. The workload, however, is a little much. But as long as you're good at time managing, you'll be fine. I was in many activities and still balanced everything. But it takes time and a hard work ethic.

Current student, 8/2004-Submit Date, June 2006

Classes are challenging, but not so difficult that you can't have a great social life. Professors all hold office hours and are incredibly accessible and will almost always work with you or give you advice. I've only gotten bumped from a really popular class once, and usually, if you go talk to the professor or shoot them an e-mail, you can get in. Grading standards depend on the professor and the school.

Current student, 8/2003-Submit Date, May 2006

Academics are very challenging at Vanderbilt. The workload is heavy, but the classes, subject matter and professors are so interesting, that it's worth the work. If you have (or quickly develop) good time management skills, you will be able to manage the average courseload (15 credit hours) and the homework (30 to 45 hours outside of class per week). The professors are topnotch in their fields, but are also really interested in college life. It is not uncommon to go to lunch with a professor or see him/her at a school event or sporting event.

Alumnus/a, 8/2002-5/2006, May 2006

Vanderbilt is known to be an academic institution. I attended a college preparatory high school so I was somewhat prepared for the coursework. Freshmen at Vanderbilt are allowed to apply to any class but upperclassmen do have priority, so I was bumped from a class I had signed up for every semester until my senior year. I never had a problem enrolling in my education classes. Vanderbilt makes sure that you are able to take the classes in your major that are required to graduate. Professors are very accessible. Office hours are offered at least twice a week and students take full advantage of these times to ask questions and get answers. The grading system here at Vanderbilt is what I expected. An A in Peabody starts at a 94. My English classes were amazing. Starting out with a writing course allowed me to re-write papers and understand my mistakes. My professors were always there to offer advice and answer questions. The workload for a student depends on what his or her major is. My workload was not difficult. Student teaching was time consuming but it allowed me to grow as a teacher.

Alumnus/a, 8/2002-5/2006, May 2006

The workload at Vanderbilt is very rigorous and difficult. There is no grade inflation and even the athletes get the same treatment as the rest of the student body. No special academic perks for anyone. All majors are equally difficult in their own right. The two programs that are slightly more competitive than the others are the pre-med track and the engineering programs. Most of the classes

are discussion based (sciences aside) and you will have much contact with y[ ] professors and teaching assistants. Accessibility of professors is very help and an awesome resource. Professors are required to hold weekly office ho[ ] to answer any questions a student may have. Also, appointments to see prof[ ] sors outside of class are almost always available. Registration for classes online and there is never a problem getting into a class. Almost all students gra[ ] uate within four years and there are very few who stay an extra year or sem[ ] ter. Workload is difficult, but Vanderbilt students do have a balance betwe[ ] their academic studies, their extracurriclar activities and fun. Classes challe[ ] you intellectually and demand much of your time. Most professors make [ ] effort to bring class material in an interesting and creative way, which makes[ ] class experience more enjoyable.

Employment Prospects

Current student, Communications, 8/2004-Submit Date, June 20[ ]

My major is the top major for employment after graduation. Types of j[ ] include, work in advertising, marketing, investment, the music industry, a entrepreneurial ventures. We have a program called Dore-2-Dore, an online s that connects you to alumni who are VERY helpful in helping you find jobs. [ ] the internship search, my major brings in companies for an internship fair, wh[ ] I used and received all the internships I applied to, choosing my favorite one [ ]

Alumnus/a, Engineering, 8/1999-5/2003, July 2007

Vanderbilt Career Center: One huge mistake I made, as undoubtedly did ma others, is that I neglected to visit the Career Center until my junior year. T Career Center does a great job of helping you figure out your career interests a this is one of those things I wish I had done earlier. Also, you can find out [ ] list of companies coming to recruit on campus early. There are also spring a fall career fairs that cater to both internships and full-time positions. I gradu[ ] ed in a year with a decent economy and job prospects and yet, I was surprised[ ] the number of students who spent no time at the Career Center researching co[ ] panies coming to campus and connecting with alumni already working there a then were surprised at not having the job offer they wanted at the end of the ye[ ]

I had three job offers at the end of my senior year and the one I accepted with consulting firm was one that I came to know about due to my very close re[ ] tionship with a member of the Career Center staff. She forwarded me the j[ ] opening in an e-mail and let me know that the firm was still interested in inte viewing even though they would not be able to come to campus. They want[ ] to video interview as a first step and although I was not too sure how it wou[ ] turnout. I'm glad I took the chance and got the job that I could only ha[ ] dreamed of. In addition, I would not underestimate the openness of the alum[ ] network. As an alumnus now, I still receive requests from alumni and stude[ ] whom I try to assist as best I can.

Alumnus/a, 8/2002-5/2006, May 2006

Vanderbilt's Career Center truly helped me through the job interviewing proce[ ] As a student, I cannot miss class to go out of town to interview. The Care Center brought the employers to campus and I was able to interview here and [ ] miss class. It was convenient and I was comfortable. The alumni office has be[ ] very helpful in providing information about alumni chapters where I will [ ] moving in August. They also offer alumni e-mail addresses and informati[ ] about Vandy alumni in your specific area. Most of my friends have either g[ ] ten into the graduate school to which they applied or have gotten a job. This w mostly done before graduation. The jobs range from teachers to consultan[ ] Many are moving to larger cities and many are staying here in Nashville.

Current student, 8/2004-Submit Date, May 2006

Vanderbilt features a wonderful Career Center that guides you on your internsh[ ] and job search. The center is extremely helpful and allows you to log-in onli[ ] to personalize your search. This center helps all graduates get the very best jo[ ] in the nation. Many of my senior friends are moving on into the top law scho[ ] in the nation or top jobs on Wall Street. Alumni are helpful as well in the esta[ ] lished alumni network. You've got resources all around you at this prestigio[ ] institution.

Quality of Life

rrent student, Economics, 1/2004-Submit Date, July 2007

e campus is absolutely beautiful—it is a national arboretum. The housing
cess can be frustrating because Vanderbilt recently moved to a residential col-
e system, which means that students are supposed to live on campus for all
r years. The facilities are great—especially on Peabody where all of the com-
ers are brand-new Mac computers. The dining on campus is not bad and
re are plenty of options (except for when you're on the Peabody campus in
ich the dining options are very limited—or completely nonexistent).

> **The school says:** "The new Commons Dining Center opened on
> the Peabody side of campus in the fall of 2007; its offerings are
> available to all students. The Peabody library also houses the
> Iris Café where students can grab coffee and a quick snack."

rrent student, 9/2004-Submit Date, February 2007

e campus is beautiful. One of the best kept landscapes of any school that I
ted anywhere. The crime rate is the same as any other college. I feel per-
ly safe here with various stations located around campus that provide a direct
k to the police in the event of an emergency (a pole with a very bright blue
nt with a speaker directly to Vandy police). Housing is just the same as any
er college: average. Some dorms are better than others, but it is safe to say
t you live in much better places as a senior than you do as a frosh—no shock-
There is a wide availability of off-campus housing (apartments), but there is
culation that Vanderbilt may end that option in the very near future.

> **Regarding housing, the school says:** "With the opening of the
> new Commons residential area, Vanderbilt now requires all
> undergraduates to live on campus."

umnus/a, 8/2002-5/2006, February 2007

aranteed housing all four years. Stayed in a single in Kissam Quad freshman
r, single in Towers sophomore year, six-person suite in Towers junior year,
l double in Morgan senior year. Seems to be a lot of cinderblock walls for
ut 70 percent of the housing areas. There are new residential colleges that I
ven't seen. I found the cafeteria to be awful: food is bad, prices are high, and
meal plan is required for freshmen. Gym is pretty good, but a walk from
ere most freshmen live. Campus is beautiful; most of the classrooms are
nfortable. Lately there has been an explosion of building on campus, so facil-
s are improving. Wireless connection covers most of campus.

rrent student, 8/2004-Submit Date, May 2006

most 84 percent of students live on campus, so there is a really great atmos-
ere on campus. There is a variety of options (singles, doubles, double and
le apartments, suites and lodges) with increasing choice and availability with
reasing seniority since our housing is based on a points system. Dorms are
t palaces, however, there is plenty of room and we have over 80 cable chan-
s plus very fast Internet connections in the rooms. There are so many food
tions on the meal plan, including a [kosher] vegetarian café (the only one in
shville), right on campus. Vanderbilt is in downtown Nashville, however, it's
o far enough away that we have a real campus that is gorgeous. There is a lit-
crime due to the urban setting, but I feel safe walking at night as long as I
ve a friend with me (this coming from a girl). We have our own police depart-
nt and they have a strong presence on campus. We also have Dore Walks,
ich is a student escort system that is available on the weekends so you don't
ve to walk anywhere alone. Vandy vans run from dusk until 5 a.m., so that is
ways a safe option to travel around campus.

Social Life

rrent student, Economics 1/2004-Submit Date, July 2007

e social life is very entertaining. This goes along with Vanderbilt's theme:
Work hard, Play hard." The Greek system is very popular, where about 45 to
percent of the campus is involved in either a fraternity or sorority. This offers
ot of theme parties every weekend. The fall semester is incredible, with foot-
ll games every weekend, and plenty of tailgates. Students come to the game
essed to impress, girls in dresses and guys in ties. For the first couple of games

guys tend to ask girls to go as dates. Tuesday night at Sportsman's is somewhat
of a tradition. Thursday night is another big night (usually downtown) although
the location is not as consistent as Sportsman's.

Current student, Communication, 8/2004-Submit Date, June 2007

[30] percent of guys are involved in Greek life and 50 percent of girls are. I am
not, but most of my friends are. There are four bar options. The first being "college bar" options, which have deals on different week nights that anyone who
goes to Vanderbilt knows what day what bar is popular (Sportsman's on
Tuesdays, Flying Saucer on Monday). The second option is downtown where
the honky-tonk bars play and you are bound to run into locals (The Stage,
Roberts, Tootsies). The third option is Demonbreun, which is a row of bars (Dan
McGuiness, Tin Roof), a quick cab away that feature live music. The last option
is the weekend clubs that students promote across campus that either offer specials or a music group. The dating scene involves hooking up for the most part
and then dating. People don't casually date.

Current student, 8/2004-Submit Date, May 2006

Vanderbilt is known for its incredible balance of work and play. Organizations
are key here as most students find a unique home in the myriad of opportunities.
Most likely, that strange hobby you have will have its own club here (and you
can start one if there isn't one). Restaurants are plentiful all around campus and
Nashville, and the bar scene downtown is incredible and fun (Lonnie's Karaoke
Bar is a huge hit). Greeks are a big part of the social life here as 40 percent of
the campus is Greek, but its an open Greek scene (meaning all parties are open
to all of campus). You won't feel excluded if you're not Greek, and I even
rushed a year late and could have gone either way. You'll most likely find another organization outside of the Greek scene to invest your social life in and it'll
be just as fulfilling. There's no shortage of great times and incredible friends at
Vanderbilt and in Nashville. Come here if you're looking for an incredibly fulfilling social and academic life.

Current student, 8/2003-Submit Date, May 2006

There are so many different lives to lead at Vanderbilt. I wish I could experience
all of them. On campus, social life revolves around athletic events, Greek life
and student organizations. The Greek scene is open to all Greeks and non-
Greeks, so frat-hopping is a popular Friday and Saturday night activity for
underclassmen. Each fraternity has a party that is really looked forward to each
year, such as Sigma Chi's Paint Party during Derby Week, ZBT Tahiti, SAE's
American Pride, Beta 54, and KA 80s and 70s parties. All of these parties are
open to the entire campus and are crazy. Upperclassmen tend to prefer bar-hopping in Nashville's famous Broadway area downtown or in the newly developed
Demonbreun area. Other popular upperclassman scenes are the restaurants
Cabana, McDougal's and Virago. The music scene has a huge influence on
social life both on and off campus. The most popular concerts on Vanderbilt's
campus are probably Greek Week and Rites of Spring. This year Greek Week
hosted All American Rejects and last year hosted Nickel Creek and Howie Day.
Rites of Spring is a two-day long music festival the weekend before finals begin.
The dating scene is pretty much nonexistent, with the exception of the Vanderbilt
tradition of getting dressed up for football games and taking a date. Student
organizations are always hosting events during the week and on weekends.

The School Says

Vanderbilt, an internationally recognized research university, is
located just five minutes from downtown Nashville, Tennessee,
on a gorgeous 330-acre campus that is also a national arboretum. Buildings on the original campus date to its founding in
1873 and the Peabody section of campus has been a registered
National Historic Landmark since 1966.

One of America's Top 20 universities, Vanderbilt is home to just
over 11,000 undergraduate and professional students. We
offer 66 major fields of study in the arts and sciences, engineering, music, education, and human development, as well as
a full range of graduate and professional degrees. Our 10
schools, public policy institute, distinguished medical center and
The Freedom Forum First Amendment Center provide opportu-

Read all of Vault's College Surveys at www.vault.com/college—get complete surveys on 100s of colleges and universities, expert advice on applicaton essays and more.

VAULT CAREER LIBRARY 689

nities to know some of the most talented students and faculty on earth.

We believe a university advances through its faculty, and Vanderbilt professors are at the forefront of their academic disciplines. They have held virtually every major fellowship and won countless prestigious awards, including the Nobel, Fulbright, Guggenheim, MacArthur, Mellon, National Endowment for the Humanities, National Science Foundation and Presidential Young Investigators. At Vanderbilt, professors and students often work together as research partners and share authorship of professional papers. Faculty advisers work closely with students to create academic programs that meet individual aspirations. Through the Faculty in Residence Program, some faculty members live in the residence halls, adding another element to the interesting mix of residence hall life.

Our students are also an integral, involved part of the campus community, belong to well over 200 student-run clubs, publications and organizations as well as serving on our Board of Trust and administering hundreds of thousands of dollars worth of programming money used to bring today's most popular musical acts and most engaging speakers to campus. Academically,

our students find their classroom experiences challenging and rewarding. The average student to faculty ratio is 9:1, our average class size is 19, and 78 percent of our undergraduate classes have fewer than 25 students.

Though the appeal of Nashville is great, our campus is something of a world unto itself—with modern classrooms, labs and residence halls; coffee shops and bookstores; and facilities for concerts, plays, lectures, films, sports and recreation. You can easily walk across the campus within 15 minutes. All of our buildings—including four undergraduate and six graduate and professional schools, residential halls and supporting facilities—stand shoulder to shoulder, evidence that Vanderbilt is a common enterprise, a varied but cohesive community.

Vanderbilt alumni can be found in Congress, on the judicial bench, heading corporations, conducting innovative medical research, writing for and appearing on the stage and screen, and playing in the NFL and NBA.

Our university continues to carefully preserve important traditions while maintaining a new trajectory that embraces interdisciplinary scholarship, encourages a renewed sense of involvement in and dedication to Nashville and the world, and celebrates an institution better than ever.

Baylor University

Admissions Office
ne Bear Place, #97056
aco, TX 76798-7056
dmissions phone: (800) BAYLOR-U, menu option 1-1
or (254) 710-3435
dmissions fax: (254) 710-3436

 Admissions

lumnus/a, 8/2002-12/2005, November 2006

like many topnotch universities, Baylor's selectivity process is unique; while
ey do hold high standards for admissions, they also factor in student potential
d other personal attributes that they feel are equally (if not more) important in
termining student success. So, while SAT/ACT scores and high school
A/rank are taken seriously, they aren't the sole determinants of admission.
oreover, if they feel you have potential as demonstrated through unique per-
nal accomplishments: that is also held in high regard. For the admissions
cess, SAT/ACT scores need to be sent directly to Baylor (which can be
coded at time of testing). Secondly, an official transcript has to be sent direct-
to the office of admissions. Lastly, the formal admissions packet along with
admissions essay needs to be submitted. For admissions into general curric-
, an interview usually isn't necessary, but some programs (e.g., the Honors
ogram, University Scholars, BIC) may require a personal or phone interview.
terms of advice for getting in: I would say that having a well diversified high
hool record (plenty of variation in classes), a fairly large repertoire of extracur-
ulars, and AP/honors level courses would be a great start. And, of course,
od to excellent grades.

urrent student, 1/2005-Submit Date, December 2005

e admissions process was fairly easy, though Baylor is a selective institution.
aylor University is a private university, but they, of course, do not discriminate
ainst anyone. One look at the diversity on campus will tell you that. I trans-
rred in with more than enough credit hours, a pretty good GPA, and pretty
od SAT and ACT scores. If you have those, I imagine you can get in without
y problems. I have been pretty busy, so I actually do not remember my inter-
ew, but I know for my essay I did the best I could with the prompted essay
estion in the application. You can do the application and the essay online to
ve time. I strongly recommend saving from page to page, though if I remem-
r right the web site does that automatically. There are some forms you have
fill out, such as health forms, but that is pretty much a standard with any col-
ge or university.

e best advice I can give to an applicant is to be yourself. True, they are selec-
e, but if you are not being yourself, you will never know whether you got in
r did not get in) because you were not being who you truly are. I have a friend
ho did that at another place, and he regrets not just being honest. Plus, if you
e not being honest, Baylor probably will not like that one bit.

verall, the admissions process is pretty painless. If you are transferring in with
edit hours, as with any college or university, be prepared for some things not
transfer in, or to have to talk it over with academic advisors and the office of
dent records to get things as you want them—or as close as you can get them,
any rate. On that note, Baylor only accepts 70 hours of transferred hours, the
st have to be completed at Baylor.

urrent student, 8/2003-Submit Date, November 2005

he admissions process is not too hard. The application requires a well thought
t essay. There is no interview process, but further acceptance into the honors
ogram and Baylor Interdisciplinary Core depends on your grades and SAT
ores. If your SAT score is above 1200, then you should have no problem get-
ng in. But the higher your grades and the higher your SAT scores, the better
ur chances of getting a good scholarship.

Current student, 8/2004-Submit Date, February 2006

The online application is very easy. The application does not have an essay, but
Baylor is looking for a wide variety of students who will do great in life and in
school. They can only take so many students and usually 20,000 apply, so send
your application in early. The way you get scholarships is through your scores.
There are no interviews and I actually worked with one lady and she helped me
through the whole process and called me the day she found out I was in. They
do the scholarships by scores, so the higher the more you get. You want as much
as you can get. Baylor is very expensive.

Current student, 5/2003-Submit Date, October 2005

Right now Baylor is taking many people. To be competitive you probably only
need a 1000 on the SAT or the equivalent on the ACT. And grades just have to
be passing, although many have to go to the Summer Challenge Program if their
grades or SAT are too low. No one knows what those too-low limits are. It helps
if you have a relative who went here before, but it is definitely not a necessity.
There is one essay on the application, and you can usually use the big essay that
you turned into every other school. It's usually a broad topic like, "What influences have you had in your life that made you select your goals?" Finally, selectivity is down right now because Baylor needs the money to fund the new buildings around campus, but there are pretty new buildings to look at.

 **Academics**

Current student, 8/2004-Submit Date, February 2007

Make no mistake: though Baylor is a fairly easy school to get into, it is not a
cakewalk. The attrition rate is really high around here. However challenging
classes and grading systems are, though, you will surely get your money's worth
at Baylor. At an internship interview with a financial firm in Dallas recently, I
was able to answer more questions than any other applicant about the financial
sector. You will learn. You'll just work a lot to learn it all.

Alumnus/a, 8/2002-12/2005, November 2006

The academics are the highlight of Baylor University. Baylor continually strives
to give each of its students a quality education. By quality, I mean below surface level/conceptual learning, excellent professors who are dedicated to assisting their students, small class sizes, and a social environment that is bar none.
Although I graduated through the Honors College, I know for a fact (through
many friends) that the general curriculum in any program is rigorous and thorough. Grading is done with a A, B+, B, C+, C, D, F format. Like nearly all
schools, the rigor by which standards are met are determined by the individual
professor. From my personal experience, Baylor professors are fair with their
grading procedures—just don't expect to be babied. Do a B job and get a B; do
an A job and get an A, slack and get a D or F. It pretty much boils down to motivation and work ethic; have a decent amount of both and you should be just fine.

As for workload, that would depend on your major and/or time requirements of
individual courses. While any major takes a lot of time and commitment, some
require more actual hours than others. For example, while a 3000-level soci-
ogy course would normally take three hours of actual class time and two hours
a day of studying, a 3000-level music class would require the same amount of
class time but could potentially call for more outside hours. So, judge your
courseload based on how many actual hours each of your classes require. Don't
overdo it; been there, done that, don't want any more. As for getting into popular classes, it's usually pretty easy to get into the classes that you need/want. If
you really want the benefit of early registration, join the Honors College.

Alumnus/a, English, 8/2000-5/2004, April 2007

Baylor does a very thorough weeding-out in the first year. Classes are difficult,
but I suppose they should be. Religious courses are required upon graduating.
They enforce/request you have them completed your first year, which adds some
pressure, along with the strict attendance rules.

Read all of Vault's College Surveys at www.vault.com/college—get complete surveys on 100s of colleges and universities, expert advice on applicaton essays and more.

VAULT CAREER LIBRARY 691

Alumnus/a, 8/2002-12/2004, March 2007

I only had two classes with more than 100 student in them. They were required classes with popular professors. In general, the classes are smaller (less than 50 students) but to get the most popular classes you must register the first/second day they open. In general, the professors are in love with their jobs and their fields. In my department, I only had one professor who felt it was his mission to weed out less serious students. The workload is manageable but if you have to work hard at school (not a natural) don't take more than 12 hours your first few semesters so you don't get overwhelmed. The flip side of that issue is if you want to graduate in four years, you need to take closer to 15 hours a semester and/or take several summer classes.

Current student, 8/2003-Submit Date, November 2005

The academics at Baylor University are very good. Classes are small and teachers are very interested in what they teach. Each class is very thorough and thought-provoking. There are also opportunities to do research projects with teachers in subjects in which you are interested. Workload for classes is not bad. Reading the text and doing the homework assigned assures that you will get a good grade in the class. You cannot pass by just sitting in class.

Current student, 8/2004-Submit Date, February 2006

Baylor has a huge core curriculum that takes up your first year or two. Once you get past that, it is all major from there. Some classes are easy and some are ridiculous but very rewarding. Teachers really care about how you do and what you are doing in accordance with class. We actually have a web site that tells you which classes to take with the best teachers. Workload is good; it allows for extracurricular activities and other stuff. Class can sometimes be long and boring but then you get some classes that are fun and you want to go to them.

Current student, 5/2003-Submit Date, October 2005

Academic rigor completely depends on the programs you select. The easiest known major on campus is the Family and Consumer Science degree, which includes the Fashion Design, Interior Design, nutrition, and just a general FCS degree. There are many classes required, but these are the people who never study. Education is also known to be somewhat easy, but most people want to be preschool and elementary teachers coming out of this school. The business school is where everyone who has no idea what they want to do is, and it is somewhat easier than a liberal arts degree, but still challenging. The arts and science degree also varies across its offered majors as to difficulty, but the sciences are probably the hardest major on campus and classics is another hard major.

Most classes are taught by a professor who really cares about the student's learning and well-being. They work with students regularly, and the class goals and deadlines are usually laid out clearly. As long as you sign up on your registration day and do not wait until the last minute, a popular class should be open. I have had semesters when I did not get one popular class, but another one I also needed was open. I have never had a bad schedule here.

Grading varies from teacher to teacher. Avoid the ones with a reputation for the bell curve, and opt for the ones who will just give the grade you earn no matter how the class does. The workload usually ebbs and flows. Most of the tests are scheduled around the same time so that you have a week or two of lots of work and then a week or two with little to do. I guess you are supposed to be working ahead, but for most college students they just let it pile into the "hard week." Workload is definitely manageable, though.

Employment Prospects

Alumnus/a, English, 8/2000-5/2004, April 2007

Waco is one of the poorest cities in the nation, work is scarce and hard to find—most graduates are sent to nearby bigger cities, like Dallas and Houston. Most graduates though are continuing graduate school at Baylor's law school or medical schools, which are properly located in the Houston/Dallas/Austin area.

Most education majors will do their student teaching at the nearby school districts like Waco ISD or Lorena, Gatesville, Robinson, possibly Hillsboro and so on. There are two hospitals in Waco as well to gain residency hours, but most students prefer elsewhere. Baylor also exceeds in the Ministry/Theology department; there are several churches around helping those students out and the uni-

versity provides special vocational and missionary opportunities in ot[h] states/countries.

Current student, 8/2004-Submit Date, February 2007

Baylor is a surprisingly connected school. The school of business, in particul[ar] has some stunning connections and tons of opportunities. There is never a ti[me] when someone isn't either recruiting in the business school lobby, or throu[gh] Hire-a-Bear, or through some other medium. Tons of special speakers from s[ur] rounding companies come from Dallas/Fort Worth and Houston, which are b[oth] booming business areas. The Finance department boasts a couple of Whart[on] MBAs and a former President of the CFP Board. Alumni network is rea[lly] strong, and major firms from big cities (including all of the Big Four firms) re[al] ly target Baylor grads (esp. KPMG). Average salary for graduating undergrad[u] ate business class in 2006 was $45,000, average signing bonus being alm[ost] $4,000. Average starting salaries for Baylor grads is above average across [the] board, though, and Baylor carries a reputation for being the school to look to [for] ethical employees. Definitely helps you get connected with places that resp[ect] your values.

Current student, 8/2002-Submit Date, November 2005

Many companies prefer hiring Baylor graduates over other programs, especia[lly] students from the business school and computer science and engineering depa[rt] ments. There are job fairs held at least once a year, and there are free progra[ms] like MonsterTRAK to help students find a job. There is also a department t[hat] helps students prepare their résumé and gives mock interviews.

Current student, 8/2004-Submit Date, February 2006

Baylor sets students up with many job fairs and also many companies come [to] Baylor to look for students. Baylor allows students to have internships throug[h] out the four years they are here, ranging from different countries to up in Dall[as.] These internships are very helpful in getting a job in the future. Starting salar[ies] are really high for graduates because it is Baylor University. Alumni relatio[ns] are very good; they love to hire new graduates and are fun to talk with also.

Current student, 5/2003-Submit Date, October 2005

I graduate in December and I already have a physical therapy tech job lined [up] for the spring. I plan to take the MCAT and go to medical school, so I am n[ot] that worried about the job I get right now. People I know have gone to work [in] Washington, D.C., New York and Los Angeles, but most go to Dallas, Austin [or] Houston. The in-state networking in Texas from Baylor is amazing. If you wa[nt] to stay in Texas, this is the school to go to. I haven't talked to anyone who d[id] not get the job he/she desired out of Baylor. Some teachers, some financi[al] advising, some research positions and many go to graduate school. Somethi[ng] like 90 percent go to graduate school at some point after Baylor. The on-cam pus recruiting is good for the business jobs and internships, but struggles to [be] very diverse when doing workshops or career days. If you go into them wi[th] specifics they will keep an eye out for you.

Quality of Life

Current student, 8/2004-Submit Date, February 2007

You can live two blocks from campus in a safe, well-furnished apartment for t[he] same price as living in the dorms, which are still largely heated/cooled b[y] Baylor's 80-year-old heating system. Cafeteria food is tolerable, but way ove[r] priced. No curfews, but opposite gender have to be out of most dorms by [1] p.m. on weekends, 8 p.m. on weeknights. There are strict rules about having co[f] fee machines, microwaves and even extension chords in the rooms. It is, how ever, a great way to meet people, and if nothing else, at least living in the sam[e] crappy (or, if it's nice, overpriced) dorm gives you a common experience to bor over. I lived in the Honors College Living-learning Center, and it was a blast. [I] moved out middle of sophomore year, though, when I realized the network [of] friends I'd made there had all moved off campus. Campus is beautiful. Most [of] Baylor's facilities are well cared for (great maintenance staff at Baylor—def[i] nitely a plus) and new, if not ridiculously nice ($103 million science building[).] Chili's Too is the only one of its kind on a college campus, next door to a pop[u] lar and very chic neighborhood Starbucks. Crime and safety are good on cam pus, and not too bad one or two blocks from campus. Waco is kind of known f[or] being sketchy, but thankfully, Baylor's terf is a relieving exception.

lumnus/a, English, 8/2000-5/2004, April 2007

...using on campus is required first year. It helps to get to know fellow class-...tes, however the visitation hours for the opposite sex were difficult to get ...und. Dining facilities on campus are good, there is a wide range of food to ...k from and many meal plans from which to choose too, just don't get too hun-... on Sundays, everything is closed. No need to worry though, every fast food ...ce known to man is right along I-35. Housing off campus is cheap and there ...tons of programs on campus, like the Community Living and Leadership ...m, to help with the adjustment. If you choose to live "on the other side of I-..." it's expected you'll encounter some crime. The City of Waco isn't too par-... to Baylor students, generally for good reason.

lumnus/a, 8/2002-12/2004, March 2007

...t about everything at Baylor is beautiful (although directly west of campus is ...n-down area—but lately all the houses are being bought and renovated). The ...ldings and campus areas are well maintained and pleasing. In addition to ...ms (some of which have been recently rebuilt) there is upperclassman on-...npus housing and they are like nice apartments. The dining halls are fantas-...—just about anything you'd like to eat—but if you live in campus housing, ...u are required to buy a meal plan. Even with a nearby lower income area, ...re is low criminal activity and students feel safe—you can see people running ...two and a half mile track that surround campus at any time of night.

rrent student, 8/2003-Submit Date, November 2005

...-campus housing is available for students and required for freshmen. Most ...-campus housing is very close to campus. Affordable housing is also avail-...e. Cars are not needed for campus due to its small size. Three dining halls ...located on campus and two cafes are located in other buildings. Restaurants ...located close to campus. The neighborhood around campus is safe, although ...with any other campus, safety lessens the farther you get from campus.

rrent student, 8/2004-Submit Date, February 2006

...ry nice. Many places to eat on campus. Waco isn't that big, so everything is ...t too far. Campus is the prettiest I have seen anywhere. Love it. Waco is kind ...ghetto, though. You have to watch where you are and who is around you, but ...u get used to the bums asking for money. But overall safe. Waco is fun, you ...t have to get used to it. Lots of fun things to do you just have to find them. ...enty of housing not far from campus, so don't worry about housing.

 Social Life

rrent student, 8/2004-Submit Date, February 2007

...cial life is abundant on campus—lots of activities with which to get involved, ...m swing dance (personal plug) to fencing to 20+ Greek organizations. No ...lly good bars or clubs, though (and the modestly decent ones are in really ...etchy areas), no frat/sorority houses on campus (though there's a strong net-...ork of unofficial Greek housing off campus), classy/big money productions on

campus, and for the more commitment-phobic people, lots of random events to go to throughout the year. Dating scene is hot. Not to mention that Baylor has been ranked, in an unofficial national survey, as the most Beautiful College Campus in America (they're not talking about the quad).

Alumnus/a, 8/2002-12/2005, November 2006

Cream of the crop. If you're an extreme liberal, it may not be as entertaining for you, but you should still have a pretty good time.

Alumnus/a, 8/2002-12/2004, March 2007

Even with a strong Christian atmosphere, there is a strong vein of fun running through campus life. Parties on most weekends—some exclusively Greek, others open to anyone. Last time I was on campus, a very popular place was the hookah bar (low lighting, exotic music, fat floor cushions for sitting and reclining, hot teas and so on) and the Vietnamese restaurant. There are clubs for dancing (ballroom, swing, salsa and so on), bicycling, horseback riding, martial arts, outdoor hiking/camping/canoeing, extensive intramural sports teamsand so on. A favorite bar in town for students is Treff's. It started as an upscale bar for single 20- to 30-somethings in town and was quickly taken over by Baylor students. Has an almost classy atmosphere upstairs and an awesome piano guy.

Current student, 8/2002-Submit Date, November 2005

There is an atmosphere at Baylor commonly known as the "Baylor bubble." Students here seem to be very sheltered from the poverty of surrounding Waco. The Greek system at Baylor is huge, with a large percentage of students joining a fraternity or sorority. Men are in luck; there are typically two women to every man, and they're generally all very nice. The nightlife of Waco seems to be decent, and Thursday is a very popular bar/club night around campus.

Current student, 8/2003-Submit Date, November 2005

The social life at Baylor is good. There is a big Greek system consisting of all types of fraternities and sororities. Although the city of Waco is small, you can find everything you need to have a good time. There are lots of bars and pool halls, bowling alleys and movie theaters. There is a little bit of everything.

Current student, 5/2003-Submit Date, October 2005

The Greek system is only [25] percent of the students, but its presence is much larger. They run homecoming floats, Pigskin Review (a song and dance show), and have many of the still-involved alumni. Legacies are strong here. The school is big enough to be split by not only the Greek system, but by athletes vs. non-athletes, and drinkers vs. non-drinkers. There is no drinking allowed on campus, but there are several bars that are frequented by students: Scruffy Murphy's on Speight, Treft's on Austin Ave, and Crickets and Bogarts right next to each other on Franklin. Otherwise, parties take place at people's houses off campus. The restaurants are spread out from around campus to valley mills out to Highway 84. The dating scene is basically either church or fraternities. Group hangs go to one-on-one hang outs, go to boyfriend/girlfriend. Of course there are exceptions to that stereotype. Clubs are not extremely popular on campus, but they are there if you have a niche and want to join.

Read all of Vault's College Surveys at www.vault.com/college—get complete surveys on 100s of colleges and univer-sities, expert advice on applicaton essays and more.

VAULT CAREER LIBRARY 693

Rice University

Rice University
Office of Admission-MS 17
P.O. Box 1892
Houston, TX 77251-1892
Admissions phone: (713) 348-RICE (7423) or
  (800) 527-OWLS (6957)
Admissions e-mail: admi@rice.edu
Admissions URL: futureowls.rice.edu/futureowls

Admissions

Current student, 8/2003-Submit Date, April 2006

From what I have heard from the admissions office, Rice is very big on people showing interest in coming. No matter how good your grades or SAT scores are, you need to visit Rice or attend the information sessions to prove that you are truly interested. Likewise, if you are a mediocre candidate, conversations with the recruiters and attending the information sessions can really add to your application and qualifications. In addition, every year Rice asks applicants to fill a box on the application with "something that appeals to you." As an undergraduate here, other students and professors will constantly ask what you put in your box as a get-to-know-you icebreaker activity—so choose wisely!

> The school says: "Rice does not admit mediocre candidates. Our admit rate is 25 percent, middle 50 percent on the SAT is 1340 to 1510 and 88 percent ranked in the top 10 percent of their senior class."

Current student, 8/2003-Submit Date, April 2006

The admissions process included an application with general information, a couple of essays, an optional interview which could be completed at or away from Rice, and two or three recommendations. The process is pretty much like another university except the unique Rice box which is a blank box in which students are asked to fill it in any way they like. They are asked to make the box representative of themselves in some way and creative. The interview is like a conversations. Selectivity is very competitive although not quite as competitive as Ivy League, but I think Rice attracts a different kind of crowd than Ivy Leagues—more of a middle-class setting rather than stratified between upper and lower.

Current student, 8/2003-Submit Date, April 2006

For me the admissions process was quite different. I visited Rice, toured the campus, and met with the dean of engineering. I did not interview with Rice, though this was probably a big mistake since I was deferred. Definitely interview. Rice puts lots of emphasis on creating a culture at the University and the only way they can fill it is by knowing the students before they accept them.

Current student, 9/2003-Submit Date, November 2005

I didn't do an interview. The essay included a creative portion and a more traditional essay. I had a 1530 on the SAT and I'm toward the high end here but there are quite a few around me. I transferred here from [an Ivy League school] with a 3.2 GPA in engineering. Most of the people here seem to be very smart but not too many are incredibly amazing extracurricularly. We get a few of those all around people.

Current student, 8/2001-Submit Date, April 2005

The school is extremely selective. Even with great numbers, you are not guaranteed admission. They pride themselves on turning away perfect SAT scores. More than many others schools, they seem to be looking for unique individuals. Make sure your essay and what you put in "the box" is uniquely you. The interview is highly recommended. It is more for your benefit than for theirs, I think, but it shows interest and can help your application.

Academics

Alumnus/a, 8/1999-5/2003, September 2006

You are required to take distribution classes in three different areas: social s_ences, humanities and math/natural sciences. Some of these classes are v_good, some aren't. Getting into some of the more interesting classes, l_Welding or Lego Lab, can be difficult, but with enough perseverance, very p_sible. Grading seems rather abstract. Some professors give almost entirely _and B's, others grade on a mean curve. The quality of professors is fairly hi_It is cool to read about research that your professors are doing in popular ma_zines. Also there can be a good deal of out of class interaction with professe_even as an undergraduate.

Current student, Engineering, 8/2003-Submit Date, September 20_

Classes are very large for freshman science and engineering classes, especia_Orgo, Calc 101 and 102, Phys 101 and 102. I have been very pleased with _professors within the mechanical engineering classes. The workload can be h_rendous and really cramps the social aspect of college during November a_April. Grading is not on a curve toward the upper levels because the classes _too small usually to get a good distribution. Straight A's are very difficult to _however.

Engineers will find that their curriculum is heavily biased toward the theoreti_aspects of the discipline. In talking with my friends at other Texas engineeri_programs, their classes are much more applied toward real-world engineeri_practice. Also there is more pressure from professors and the administration h_than at other schools to go on to graduate school.

Alumnus/a, 8/2002-5/2006, October 2006

Great profs in most departments. The highlight of the Rice experience is _quality of the professors, who are mostly excellent and very teaching-oriente_This does not necessarily apply to science and engineering classes; howev_where professors may be less responsive. A lot of Rice students over-stre_themselves by not managing their time well and consequently missing out _opportunities to do something outside of school. With good time managemen_was able to spend three hours, six days a week on my favorite hobby and st_complete a triple major. The key to being successful in the classroom and o_side is managing your time well and not feeling pressured into spending mo_time than necessary on schoolwork. Don't be made to feel guilty if you want _make time for things that are important to you other than school.

Current student, 8/2003-Submit Date, April 2006

Because Rice is so small, getting the classes you want is rarely a problem, esp_cially for upperclassmen. The professors are very accommodating, and th_usually will let more students in if you talk to them and show a sincere intere_Rice has distinct groups of people academically, the main two being Academ_(humanities and social science majors) or S/Es (science and engineering major_Each has its stereotype, with S/Es being labeled as nerds and S/Es complaini_that Academs are lazy and don't do enough work. The workload comes as qu_a shock, especially to all the ridiculously smart people who breezed through hi_school. Our interaction with professors is unique since they participate in life _the residential colleges, with some living at the colleges and some go to eat wi_students frequently. Everyone is readily approachable and always willing to he_you with material from classes or finding jobs and research opportunities.

Current student, 8/2003-Submit Date, April 2006

The academic nature is very uptight. The students are very very focused _their studies—save a few of course! Thus, the quality of classes is topnotc_The professors expect their students to work hard and oftentimes know materi_just as well as they do. It's definitely a challenge. Getting into popular class_can also be a challenge sometimes but usually if you really want to take the cla_you can just show up, and the professor will usually let you in someho_Grading is oftentimes very harsh—especially in the sciences when the avera_has to be set in the 60s! Workload is really hard. Overall, it's really hard to ke_

with everything on top of all the extracurriculars people have (because every-
~~l~~y does everything here especially since it's a small school). So students
~~s~~ly extremely hard and almost all the time. Oftentimes, free time is feeling
~~gui~~lty that you should be working!

~~Cu~~rrent student, 8/2003-Submit Date, January 2006

~~Th~~e curriculum is as hard as you make it. In general, the classes are tough—
~~plu~~s, there are so many smart people, it's not easy getting on the right side of the
~~cur~~ve. There is no way that the Ivy League has a better group of students than
~~Ri~~ce. Everyone here is really driven and competitive. There are easy classes,
~~bu~~t for the most part, the classes are challenging and require a lot of work.
~~Ho~~wever, there is a great tutoring system. It is possible to get good grades but
~~yo~~u have to work for them. Most classes are taught by professors, which is
~~goo~~d. Only the lowest of lower-level classes are taught by TAs. The student
~~faci~~lities are great for computing. The library is undergoing huge renovations.
~~It i~~s one of the more pleasant places to study on campus.

Employment Prospects

~~Cu~~rrent student, 8/2003-Submit Date, September 2006

~~A~~ Rice degree is very, very prestigious among employers. However, because of
~~the~~ size of our school not very many recruiters come. For engineers, the only
~~on-~~campus recruiting opportunities are in oil and gas. If you are an engineer and
~~yo~~u want to do something besides oil and gas, your options are doing a lot of
~~yo~~ur own legwork, grad school or business.

~~Al~~umnus/a, 8/1999-5/2003, September 2006

~~Al~~most everyone in my chemical engineering class got a good job. That said, it
~~is~~ considerably harder for other majors to find work. The on-campus career fair
~~co~~nsists of many Houston-area businesses that are in the energy, oil/gas, chemi-
~~ca~~ls and financial businesses. This means that chemical and mechanical engi-
~~ne~~ers get jobs and there are also many consulting jobs, and trading jobs available
~~to~~ economics-ish majors. Electrical engineers also seem to find jobs at places
~~lik~~e TI and comp sci majors can usually find work.

~~Cu~~rrent student, 8/2003-Submit Date, April 2006

~~Si~~nce Rice is such a small school, not a lot of companies outside of Houston
~~co~~me to recruit at Rice. That being said, because of its size, a Rice alumnus at
~~an~~y company or organization will usually be more than willing to bend over
~~ba~~ckwards to help out a fellow Rice graduate. Career Services is trying to set up
~~mo~~re programs and make it easier for students to find jobs in other companies
~~be~~sides the usual sectors of oil and gas, investment banking and consulting. Rice
~~stu~~dents are able to obtain great jobs with people who recognize the name and
~~kn~~ow how quickly Rice students learn, but students do have problems securing
~~jo~~bs outside of Texas where Rice is lesser known.

~~Cu~~rrent student, 8/2003-Submit Date, April 2006

~~Ou~~r employment office could use a little development. But overall, Rice is real-
~~ly~~ good about getting people in post undergrad schools (e.g., medical school, law
~~sc~~hool, graduate school). The percentage is extremely high in these areas. We
~~al~~so do really well with engineering jobs, consulting jobs and investment bank-
~~in~~g jobs. On-campus recruiting could be better but for our size and location; it's
~~pr~~etty good although students often complain about the lack of options besides
~~co~~nsulting, investment banking and engineering companies. The alumni net-
~~wo~~rk is OK, but only helpful occasionally in finding jobs.

~~Cu~~rrent student, 8/2001-Submit Date, April 2005

~~T~~he alumni network is very strong. The school has a strong sense of communi-
~~ty~~, so Rice loyalty is powerful and can be very helpful in looking for a job. All
~~T~~exas employers, and many others elsewhere, recognize Rice as a topnotch
~~sc~~hool and treat the graduates accordingly. The on-campus recruiting program
~~is~~ strong. I managed to find internships every summer without looking beyond
~~on~~-campus recruiting.

> **The school says:** "As of graduation day (typically the first
> Sunday of May) 75 percent of the bachelor degree candidates
> at Rice had already accepted jobs, been admitted to graduate or
> professional school, or had other definite plans. 51 percent

went directly into the workforce, 41 percent went to graduate
school, and 6 percent had other plans like travel scholarships."

Quality of Life

Alumnus/a, 8/1999-5/2003, September 2006

Housing varies in quality across campus according to the residential college to
which you are randomly assigned as a freshman. I was assigned to the newest
college, so life was good. There are two dining halls on campus about which
everyone likes to complain, but the food is actually pretty good. Rice is going
to build a new recreational facility pretty soon so that should be much better.
Also, for students living off campus, the neighborhood of Houston right around
Rice is very nice. It is residential to the north and to the west.

Alumnus/a, 8/2000-5/2004, November 2006

It's a very insular and clique-y scene. The college system encourages a kind of
pointless, artificial fealty to your college and equally pointless and artificial
antagonism toward the other colleges. You find out very quickly that anyone
with any personality tries to move off campus ASAP. Living off campus is moderately expensive, but doable. And worth it.

Alumnus/a, 8/2002-5/2006, October 2006

Insulated but mostly really good. Colleges (dorms) vary in their age and condition, but most have good facilities and amenities. The campus is small and self-
contained, so it never takes more than 15 minutes to get anywhere, and you don't
have to worry about navigating city streets. The neighborhood immediately
around Rice is very ritzy, though sketchy areas are only a few minutes away (this
is true throughout Houston). The campus is well-lit and patrolled by Rice's own
police force (not just a campus security department). Overall it feels safe even
late at night, though of course normal precautions should be taken. Food is considered very good for college fare, and freshmen are usually very pleased.
However, by the time you graduate you will be thoroughly sick of it and may
find yourself living off instant noodles. If you move off campus, commuting is
easy and housing is cheap in Houston.

Current student, 8/2003-Submit Date, April 2006

Rice is unique in that the majority of the students want to live on campus all four
years. The housing is broken up into nine residential colleges, to which you are
randomly assigned before your freshman year and are a part of all four years.
Each college has its own dining facilities, which most people eat at because of
the convenience and the company of other people from your college. Campus is
small enough that you can walk around everywhere with no problem, and there
is only one road that goes around campus, separating the residential colleges
from the main quad and classroom areas. The neighborhood surrounding Rice
is very nice, and there is a village with shops and restaurants that is just a two-
minute drive or pleasant walk away. There is also a light rail stop across the
street, which provides easy access to the downtown area.

Current student, 8/2003-Submit Date, April 2006

Overall, Rice has an amazing housing system. Students love the college system,
and each college is forced to hold a lottery for spaces on campus because the
demand for on-campus housing is so high. The campus is beautiful and actually very large for such a small student body. The facilities and dining are OK.
There aren't a whole lot of options since we're so small, and I think that frustrates a lot of students. The neighborhood is one of the best areas. Overall quality of life is good—if you're a partier. Rice is a wet campus, which is great for
drinkers because it keeps all the students on campus. Very very rarely do students go off campus or even think about driving drunk. So that's great, and fortunately we have an amazing police staff, EMS staff and student body willing to
help each other out all the time. For non-drinkers, campus life is fun and certain
weekends can be extremely enjoyable, but many of the parties do revolve around
the drinkers so it can be hard. But the facilities offer many nice TVs, relaxation
areas, a coffee house and a theatre. So finding other options, although sometimes hard, is pretty good for being such a small school. Support for varsity athletics could definitely use some improvement.

Read all of Vault's College Surveys at **www.vault.com/college**—get complete surveys on 100s of colleges and universities, expert advice on applicaton essays and more.

VAULT CAREER LIBRARY **695**

Social Life

Alumnus/a, 8/1999-5/2003, September 2006

Social life on campus revolves heavily around alcohol and large parties. There is no Greek system, but the residential college system is a lot of fun. It makes it easy to meet people and categorize them. For example, its common to hear someone say, "You know that chick from Hansen (one of the colleges)." Since the college selection is random, people know that these groupings don't mean anything, but it makes for a good social "handle." Also it makes it easier to identify people's social circles and helps build friendships.

Off campus, Houston is a very vibrant and layered city. There are areas of town that are pretty ritzy, and areas that are artsy/liberal and then areas that are super industrial. The food scene is amazing with everything from Texas BBQ to Thai, to French deli within two blocks. Downtown Houston has really picked up a night since the installation of the light rail that happily goes directly from Rice to the clubs downtown and runs until 2 a.m. on weekends.

Alumnus/a, 8/2002-5/2006, October 2006

Good opportunities on and off campus. Rice is close to lots of great restaurants, bars and clubs. Houston's public transportation is almost nonexistent, however, so anywhere farther than Rice Village (within walking distance) or not along the light rail line requires a car. You will never be short of opportunities off campus. On campus, social life centers around the colleges (there is no Greek system), where you will probably make most of your friends. Public parties with lots of drinking are popular, as are private parties (also with lots of drinking). Many Rice students do not drink, however, and are able to find friends with whom to do other things on weekends. General Rice philosophy seems to be "work hard, party hard."

Current student, 8/2003-Submit Date, April 2006

Because Rice is situated in a great spot in the fourth largest city in America, there are tons of restaurants, bars and clubs that are easily accessible. Besides the regular dining options, there are many great cultural options, and many times the residential colleges will sponsor group outings to go eat different types of food. The social scene is pretty much contained in the colleges. Because of the alcohol policy that makes Rice a wet campus, there are usually on-campus parties every weekend, complete with different themes that Rice students love to get excited for, such as Bacchanalia (toga party), NOD (Night of Decadence, where students wear practically nothing), 80s party and many more. Since there is no Greek system, the colleges play a similar role, but include everyone and provide a large variety of opportunities for student government, different activities and a social network. There are always tons of events going on besides parties in both the colleges and on the university level, and some Rice students rarely venture "beyond the hedges," as the larger task of going off campus is referred to.

Current student, 8/2003-Submit Date, April 2006

Dating scene is hard because of the college system. Oftentimes people end up practically married because they date within the college and therefore hang out all of the time. It's hard to balance. Also, since so much of the social interaction is on campus, you end up hanging out with the same people all of the time. There is no Greek system because of the residential college, which most students love about the school. It makes students come here. The Rice Village is great since it's so close and students go off campus there. Most students don't have cars and since Houston, as a whole, has a terrible transportation system, off-campus activities are not as important as at other schools. Overall though, the type of student who comes to Rice is a little different from the rest. I think of us as smart shoppers—we could have done the Ivy League thing, but we wanted less snobiness and a better price and better financial aid.

 ## The School Says

Rice University is a private, comprehensive research university located in the nation's fourth largest city, Houston, TX. Distinguished for its collaborative culture, the university is made up of six schools: humanities, social sciences, natural sciences, engineering, architecture, and music. The Jesses Jones School of Business at Rice grants graduate degrees exclusively. In addition, there are over 40 interdisciplinary research institutes, centers and consortia.

2,900 undergraduates enjoy a 1:5 faculty-to-student ratio and median class size of 13 students. 90 percent of Rice's classes are taught by faculty, 6 percent by staff, and 4 percent by graduate students. All undergraduates have access to research, study abroad, internships and independent study. Need and merit aid can be applied to study abroad.

The Residential College System is at the heart of student life. Every student is a member of one of nine residential colleges. These units are small communities where students live, dine and interact with faculty, staff and alumni. The colleges are self governing. Leadership development and networking thrive within this system. Each college administers its own budget (approximately $40,000) for student entertainment and selected activities.

Outside of the college system, students enjoy over 200 clubs and organizations. 80 percent of Rice students participate in community service. Rice competes in NCAA Division I-A sports through Conference USA. Men's sports include basketball, baseball, cross country, football, golf, tennis, track and field. Women's sports include basketball, cross country, soccer, swimming, tennis, track and field. Rice's baseball team has won its conference championship for the last nine years in row. The 2003 baseball team were National Champions.

Houston plays an important role for experiential learning experiences such as the Texas Medical Center (the world's largest medical center), NASA, and 23 Fortune 500 companies. All Rice students are given a "Passport to Houston," which provides free and unlimited access to the light rail, bus system, the Museum of Fine Arts, and the Zoo. In addition, Rice students enjoy deep discounts for attending the symphony, opera and ballet—all permanent companies in Houston.

Admission to Rice is highly selective. It is also need-blind and we guarantee to meet 100 percent of need eligibility. Merit awards are also available.

We believe that diversity advances the educational experience for every student. Rice students come from all 50 states and over 30 foreign countries. 46 percent of the 2007-2008 freshmen are students of color.

Rice enjoys one of the highest endowments per student in the nation. As of the time of this publication the endowment stood at $4.6 billion.

Southern Methodist University

SMU Division of Enrollment Services
Office of Undergraduate Admission
P.O. Box 750181
Dallas, TX 75275-0181
Admissions phone: (214) 768-2058 or (800) 323-0672
Admissions e-mail: ugadmission@smu.edu
Admissions URL: www.smu.edu/admission/home.asp

 ## Admissions

Current student, 8/2003-Submit Date, October 2006

I had to write an essay about a hard experience in my life and how I have changed according to that. I just really made sure to read over it many times and let at least two people to double check it. An interview was not required for admission. I would not say it is extremely hard to get into school here unless you are an arts student, but they do look for students who show leadership abilities. If your SAT scores are high enough, you might be eligible for the President's Scholarship, which is full tuition and pays for a study abroad program among other perks. I was accepted for the second highest scholarship (half tuition) after matriculation, so they do reward you for hard work here!

Current student, 8/2004-Submit Date, January 2006

The best advice I can give about applying to SMU is to do early admissions! This way, you can be looked at more closely to receive scholarships. The admissions office is wonderful! They are very organized and keep you very up to date. Visiting SMU was what sealed the deal for me to go there. Attend Mustang Mondays and sit in on classes if you can. This will definitely persuade you!

> **The school says:** "The best way to see if SMU is right for you is to visit. Find out about campus life, academics, merit-based scholarships and financial aid and tour the campus. There are several ways to visit SMU, including SpringFest, Mustang Mondays and other special programs. Visit smu.edu/out&about to learn more."

Current student, 8/2004-Submit Date, November 2005

The Common Application is accepted here. So online application is possible. Early Decision is one choice and increases your chances of getting in, but if you get in, you must come. Not a very hard school to get into, but it is very expensive.

> **SMU says:** "The Early Action deadline is Nov. 1. Regular Decision deadline is Jan. 15. If you use the National Common Application, don't forget to include SMU's Common Application supplement. Nearly 80 percent of first-year students receive some form of financial assistance through merit- and need-based scholarships, grants, part-time jobs, payment plans and/or loans."

Current student, 8/2005-Submit Date, October 2005

SMU has an approximately 70 percent acceptance rate, and an average (old) SAT score of 1200. Good grades, extracurricular activities and community service help. Essays are required both for admission and for scholarships.

> **Regarding selectivity, the school says:** "The average combined SAT score of first-year undergraduates was 1223 in 2006. SMU's acceptance rate for the same year was 54 percent."

Current student, 8/2004-Submit Date, September 2006

The admissions process is not complicated and much like other universities to which I applied. Selectivity is apparent, but nothing to be worried about if you

were a good student in high school. I was accepted into the Honors Program and I was worried about even getting into SMU.

Current student, 8/2005-Submit Date, October 2005

This school is looking for students of moral, academic and extracurricular quality. The application process in online. An interview is not needed (I did not have one) but if a representative is in your area, it is recommended that you get an interview. The selectivity is above average. There is a wide range of intelligence here. But most students come from well-educated backgrounds. Most students here are on scholarships or financial aid of some kind.

Current student, 8/2005-Submit Date, September 2005

The admissions process at SMU is wonderful; they do a very fair job on evaluating each of the prospective students. It is getting harder to get in and I suggest that you apply Early Action and not Regular Decision. Also, for the essay I suggest that you show ambition (a lot of it), courage, cleverness, good use of language (but don't over do it), and something that will keep the reader interested. Also, make sure that the essay will pertain to what you want or are capable of doing in your life. In any interview I suggest getting personal with the interviewer, really show who you are and do not be fake.

Current student, 8/2003-Submit Date, April 2004

Take a rigorous courseload in high school; SMU likes to see students in leadership positions and students who take an active interest in the community around them. To apply, one must take either the SAT or ACT (though both are recommended). The application can be obtained by contacting SMU's admissions office or by using the Common Application (an application viable at numerous universities). If an interview is requested or offered, it is in the best interest of the applicant to participate, for it can greatly increase your chances of admission. All universities like to see an essay that is unique, rather than your average run-of-the-mill college application essay. Individuality is key.

Current student, 8/2002-Submit Date, January 2004

General admission to SMU is hassle-free: the application involves filling out the standard name, address and extracurricular activities, and submitting a teacher recommendation and an essay either of your choice or following a topic, such as "the role heritage plays in your life." Fortunately, these files can be accessed and filled out on their web site, www.smu.edu, or sent in via snail mail. SMU looks for the well-rounded student. GPA doesn't have to be outstanding if your extracurricular involvement looks good, and visa versa. The school will offer you scholarship money based on GPA and SAT scores, though, so the better you do, the less you pay. Those students matriculating with a 1,350 or over, and with a high-end GPA, are considered for the Presidential Scholarship, a free ride that includes one fully paid year abroad and one summer. Another tip: If applying to study within the Meadows School of the Arts, be wary. It takes more than a great GPA to get in here. There selectivity can be as slim as 6 percent a year! Come to your auditions well prepared and ready to improvise within your art form. Meadows interviewers are looking for energetic and passionate people who maintain other interests while still being dedicated to their discipline.

 ## Academics

Current student, 8/2003-Submit Date, October 2006

The most valuable thing about an education at a smaller school would have to be the smaller student-teacher ratio. I have gotten to know almost all of my professors very well and have been grateful for their honest interest in my learning. Some of my classes have been extremely challenging, but this has encouraged me to really learn the information and become interested in what I'm doing. But as at every school, you can find blow off classes, in which the teachers usually try to make it harder by giving you busywork, which serves for nothing. Workload will really depend on your path of study; I had about 16 to 17 hours freshman through junior year, now I'm at 13 with five hours of PE-type classes. Getting into the most popular classes just requires being an upperclassmen and

Read all of Vault's College Surveys at **www.vault.com/college**—get complete surveys on 100s of colleges and universities, expert advice on applicaton essays and more.

VAULT CAREER LIBRARY 697

keeping your eyes open daily for someone who drops the class for whatever reason before the semester starts. Most of my professors seem to spend an incredible amount of time grading and are excellent about giving partial credit, which keeps me from getting discouraged while prompting me to fix my mistakes in the future.

> **The school says:** "SMU's student-to-faculty ratio is 12:1. In fall 2006, the average SMU class size was 21 students, and TAs taught 1 percent of courses."

Alumnus/a, 8/2002-5/2006, September 2006

Great classes! Best ones go to students with the most credit hours so take AP tests. Professors care about students and have open-door policies.

Current student, 8/2004-Submit Date, September 2006

Classes and personal relationships with professors make SMU a true "bang for the buck." I've had two classes with about 200 people, but all the rest average out to around 25 to 30 students. I've never had a TA teach a course. Professors have required office hours, love to talk with you, and are extremely professional and helpful. Classes are more difficult to get as a freshman and sophomore, so I would highly recommend coming in with credit because you'll get to register sooner. The Temerlin Advertising Institute is the only privately endowed program in the nation. I am an advertising major and love it! Classes are great; professors are incredibly dedicated and love what they are teaching and want to see you succeed. We also have very strong ties with The Richards Group, the largest private agency in the U.S., which is located only five minutes down the road. Workload overall at SMU is manageable, but more challenging starting junior year.

Current student, 8/2004-Submit Date, January 2006

SMU is a very competitive institute. Classes tend to be small (about 30 to 50 people), which is wonderful! With small classes like this, you really get to know your professors. All the programs at SMU are rated as excellent programs in the country, but the two most popular and well known programs are the business program and the political science programs. These two programs are very competitive and most everyone around knows of their prestige.

Current student, 8/2004-Submit Date, November 2005

The business school here is very highly regarded. I am in the engineering program, which is also a very good program here. The workload for the engineering program is multiple times that of the business program. Classes all depend on the teacher you pick. Some hard classes are made easy by great professors, and likewise, bad/inexperienced professors can turn an easy class into one of your hardest. Getting into the classes I've wanted to here has been a breeze, if the class is full usually all you have to do is talk to the teacher and he/she will let you in.

Current student, 8/2005-Submit Date, October 2005

I am in the honors program at SMU. So far I have been more than satisfied with the intensity of the courses and the qualification of the teachers. At SMU, like many colleges, you can tailor your classes to be as difficult or easy as you want.

> **Regarding the honors program, SMU says:** "Participants in the University Honors Program are challenged in small classes. They are encouraged to conduct independent research and explore individual interests through special projects and interdisciplinary studies. Members of the Hilltop Scholars Program live in the same residence hall and take some of the same courses. These courses allow for personal interaction with classmates and instructors both in and out of the classroom. Additionally, for students who want an additional intellectual challenge, there opportunities to participate in the honors track within academic majors."

Current student, 8/2005-Submit Date, October 2005

The classes are great! The professors here are very well qualified. My largest class is only 80 and my smallest class is nine. The academics are challenging. SMU is known for its business and arts programs, but there is a wide variety of other programs and majors. There is definitely something here for everyone. Popular classes usually go to upperclassmen. The workload depends on the student. I am in the honors program and the workload is slightly more rigorous than

a non-honors program. I have six classes a week. Some students only have fo At SMU you are required to take cultural formations classes, which are classes meant to enhance your education.

Current student, 8/2005-Submit Date, September 2005

Academics at SMU are getting harder and harder, the classes are always enging and professors do do a wonderful job of keeping college students attent while also challenging each of his or her students. It is not that hard to get pe ular classes because there are so many sections of each class that SMU make easy for students to take what they want to take. SMU professor generally tough graders and they grade on a numerical percentage. The professors understanding and kind and enjoy helping their students. There is a pretty hea workload no matter how many classes you take, each professor assigns son thing each night.

Current student, 8/2003-Submit Date, April 2004

At SMU, one can take as difficult or as easy classes as one desires. The univ sity is best known for its business program, though all are adequate to stro academically. Workload generally corresponds to the number of hours and typ of courses you take; however, I find that the workload is never excessive. majority of the professors here are quite good, though there are always exce tions. As a freshman, it's not always easy to get the popular classes, since re istration is ranked by student status, that is, the number of hours you have co pleted toward graduation. A downside of grading is that there is a +/- scale (i. instead of a 90 and up being an A, 93 and up is an A, while 90 to 92 is an A Grading style also varies from professor to professor.

Employment Prospects

Current student, 8/2003-Submit Date, October 2006

Especially around the Dallas area, SMU carries a lot of prestige. Most of n friends who have graduated found work right away after college. Employe know that SMU graduates are serious and are generally known as great leade With the business school here, many students go into marketing, business finances and usually find work within top companies. My friend, for examp began working with the nationally-known company Nokia immediately aft graduating. As many SMU graduates stay around Dallas, alumni can be ve helpful. I would say SMU has a much, much larger network than any oth school of its size. Advisors and the career center are excellent about informi students of internships and job opportunities.

> **The school says:** "The Hegi Family Career Development Center has a staff of counselors who assist students with career counseling and exploration, as well as individual guidance for developing an effective job search. The Center offers a series of workshops and online guides including résumé and cover letter development, interviews, networking and job search planning, in addition to job fairs."

Alumnus/a, 8/2002-5/2006, September 2006

Tons of companies recruit on campus: students placed with all major consultin firms and investment banks as well as smaller private research firms (sell si and buy side). The Career Development Center does a great job getting comp nies on campus and providing opportunities, although they are not always t best at helping a student with interview skills or résumé critiques. Alumni ne work is great; most SMU alumni hire SMU alumni.

> **SMU says:** "Established relationships with companies in the Dallas region provide a platform for launching careers through internship and mentoring opportunities. And with nearly 40,000 alumni living in the Dallas-Fort Worth area, students have several resources for networking and career exploration and development."

urrent student, 8/2004-Submit Date, September 2006

1U is very well-regarded within the Dallas area and in the South. I feel we are t as well known on the East Coast. Business and engineering and advertising ids have no problem getting jobs. We have an incredible Career Development nter for no additional cost. There are multiple job fairs each semester, on-npus interviews and company showcases on a weekly basis.

urrent student, 8/2004-Submit Date, November 2005

1U is a great place to come if you want to have great connections after grad-ting. Many alumni are highly esteemed businesspeople who would give a job another alum before another candidate. The engineering program has a great -op program in which a student has an opportunity to use half of his/her mesters working, and half in school—this provides useful contacts when grad-ting and shows the student if this line of work is really for him/her.

urrent student, 8/2005-Submit Date, September 2005

ie employment offerings for students who graduate are very good, normally ey are matched with a corporate mentor and students get help through them, .o there is a huge alumni response for obtaining jobs, as well.

urrent student, 8/2003-Submit Date, April 2004

ie SMU Cox School of Business has a very strong alumni base, and alumni are ry involved in campus activities, facilitating student access to internships, jobs d other opportunities. There is also a Career Development Center, which aids students in building their résumé and preparing for life after college. Many umni that have matriculated at SMU are very successful, and they in turn lend hand to current students.

Quality of Life

urrent student, 8/2003-Submit Date, October 2006

was very happy with my experience in the dorms here at SMU. The un-reno-ited ones are cheaper, but aren't gross or anything. The on-campus food real-isn't bad; of course if you eat there everyday, you will get sick of it, but com-iratively (with other universities) it's good food. But I have to say both the orms and especially the meal plan are extremely overpriced. I don't think any-ie eats $1,800 worth of food in one semester! The fitness center is brand-new id absolutely amazing, with an indoor swimming pool, outdoor volleyball ourts and wading pool, there are plenty of basketball courts, a little soccer rink, cquetball, yoga/martial arts studio, workout machines and free weights, rock-imbing wall, indoor track and locker rooms with showers.

he SMU PD are excellent for safety but sticklers for parking tickets, so make ire you only park where you're allowed to and pay your meters, unless you ant your tickets to mount up (as they do for many students). They will escort ou around campus after dark if you are alone, drunk, or just feel unsafe.

> **Regarding dorms, the school says:** "Nearly 90 percent of rooms will be renovated by fall 2008. Renovations are currently under-way and some have been completed."

Current student, 8/2004-Submit Date, September 2006

MU is in the perfect location: the center of a city, but within one of the most restigious towns/neighborhoods in America: Highland Park. Campus is very afe, facilities are gorgeous, grounds very well-kept and landscaped, dining ecently renovated and the library just became 24/7. Beautiful campus, breath-iking actually—a landmark in Dallas.

Current student, 8/2004-Submit Date, November 2005

MU campus is one of the most beautiful I have ever stepped foot on. All of the uildings are gorgeous brick. On-campus housing is required for all first years. he dorms are incredible and up to the SMU standards. Some of the biggest ooms I have seen. The new Dedman Health Center, brand-new 2005, is incred-ile, with basketball courts, indoor track/pool/rock climbing, the gym area is the lost impressive though. Provided for the aerobic machines are seven huge plas-na screens with different channels playing constantly. But if you would rather vatch something of your own liking, they also provide about 15 machines with maller LCD screens on them for personal use. And the gym, every machine you ould possibly think of and some you couldn't. It is perfect. They are going to

build an extension on the cafeteria this summer and if it is going to be how they show it, it will be one of the best cafeterias ever.

Current student, 8/2005-Submit Date, October 2005

SMU is a wealthy school due to its wealthy alumni and patrons. The buildings are beautiful and the landscape is green with lots of trees. The dormitories are very nice as well. The rooms are larger than the average dorm. The students in Virginia-Snyder hall live like royalty with all suit-style rooms, a large lounge and the newest building on campus. SMU is located in the wealthiest neighbor-hood in Dallas: Highland Park. It is a very safe and very beautiful neighbor-hood. There are Highland Park police around, as well as the SMU police. I have never felt unsafe here.

> **SMU says:** "SMU residence halls include special theme commu-nities. Students can choose from halls that are tailored to a spe-cific major, academic goals or even lifestyle. Community options include fine arts, wellness, multicultural and honors res-idence halls, among others."

Current student, 8/2005-Submit Date, September 2005

SMU has been typically known as one of the happiest campuses in America. The housing here is phenomenal, buildings are clean and very spacious. All the facilities are state-of-the art. The neighborhood is very friendly although Dallas is not one of the safest cities in America and crime does happen.

> **The school says:** "According to the 2007 Princeton Review, SMU ranks Number Six for Great College Towns and Number 20 for Happiest Students."

Social Life

Current student, 8/2003-Submit Date, October 2006

The Greek system here is huge. But if, like me, you're not into that, you can find a life for yourself also. Tailgating is a big event before all home football games—this is where it comes in handy to know someone in a frat/sorority to have a tent to hang out at and score some free food and/or booze.

> **The school says:** "SMU has 29 Greek organizations on campus. Approximately 65 percent of SMU's students choose not to join a sorority or fraternity."

There are tons of great restaurants in Dallas and the nightlife is descent. There are a few different districts with clubs and bars, depending on what your style/preference is: local music, alternative, uptown, hip-hop, techno. I haven't been much into the dating scene (except I met my boyfriend when I was study-ing abroad in Spain, and he has now moved to Dallas), but it seems that every-one is on the market, so if you're looking, you can find it here. The girls are beautiful here, but not so many hot guys; there are some, but you have to look a bit harder. There are so many social/extracurricular events here that are really quite interesting: famous speakers, movie screenings and, of course, sports. Intramurals are very popular here and club sports for things like rugby, lacrosse, rowing, hockey and so on. There is lots of great shopping around and two inde-pendent movie theaters really close by.

Current student, 8/2004-Submit Date, November 2005

SMU has a very large Greek system. This large Greek system makes the social scene here one of the best in the nation. There is always something going on either on or off campus. The only downside to the bars around here is that they all close at 2 a.m. The on-campus tailgate is one of the most amazing parties every game. People line the Boulevard, grilling, drinking, just having a good time. Although our football team isn't all that good anymore, the tailgate is incredible. The dating scene at SMU is what I would imagine just like every other school. Girls here love to be wined and dined. There is someone for everyone here though. And it doesn't take much of a look to see the SMU girls, are more then average, they are gorgeous.

> **SMU says:** "In addition to 29 Greek organizations, SMU offers approximately 180 student groups ranging from academic clubs to multicultural, religious, political and sports clubs, among oth-ers."

Read all of Vault's College Surveys at www.vault.com/college—get complete surveys on 100s of colleges and univer-sities, expert advice on applicaton essays and more.

VAULT CAREER LIBRARY **699**

Current student, 8/2004-Submit Date, January 2006

SMU could not be in a better city! Dallas has the most restaurants per capita in the country. Dallas' nightlife and arts district are very well known. SMU is mainly Greek, but there are quite a few people who decide not to go Greek.

Current student, 8/2005-Submit Date, October 2005

The fraternities rent out clubs/bars and will bus anyone who wants to go to the bar. This is nice because it prevents drunk driving. These bus parties happen nearly every weekend. Also, parties at fraternity houses are common. There are some local bars that most students go to. They require a 10-minute walk, or use of public transportation if you don't have a car. Most students like to go to Jack's or Margarita Ranch. Both are across the freeway but not too far away. There is a shopping center nearby called Mockingbird Station. There is a movie theater, shops and restaurants. Mockingbird Station is also a hub of the DART system. I have taken the light-rail at Mockingbird to downtown Dallas for nightlife in Deep Ellum. Deep Ellum is my personal favorite. There are clubs, bars, art, restaurants, music venues and shops. It is very urban.

Current student, 8/2005-Submit Date, September 2005

SMU is very social, there are tons of bars both ranging from pubs to nightclubs. There are a wide range of restaurants (the range is selection and price). Never have I had better food than at the restaurants in the greater Dallas area. There are many events such as football games, tailgating, BBQs and formals. There are always lots of people who attend and it is typically seen as the thing to do around campus. The Greek system is very competitive here and it is a major part of the social scene and the day to day life at SMU.

The School Says

As SMU approaches the centennial of its founding in 2011 and its opening in 2015, the University continues its rise in national prominence. We aspire to the highest level of achievement among private universities in the country.

SMU educates leaders and thinkers by providing a strong liberal arts foundation and nationally competitive professional programs. More than 80 majors are offered through four undergraduate colleges: Dedman College of Humanities and Sciences, Cox School of Business, Meadows School of the Arts and the School of Engineering. SMU offers graduate and professional degrees in these schools, as well as the Dedman School of Law, Perkins School of Theology, and the School of Education and Human Development.

The SMU experience includes small classes taught by professors for personal attention and mentoring. Students can take part in real-world research projects, study abroad through 24 programs in 13 countries, gain job experience through internships and learn good citizenship through community involvement. World leaders visit SMU on a regular basis, thanks to a distinguished guest lecture series, and students have the opportunity to interact with them. Close ties with alumni ensure a strong network for career exploration and development both in Dallas and beyond.

Located five miles north of the vibrant city center of Dallas, the main campus is known for its graceful Neo-Georgian architecture and expansive green quads. SMU offers some programs in its facilities in Plano, near several international corporate headquarters. Unique to SMU is its campus near Taos, New Mexico, which offers summer courses and archaeological dig sites.

SMU is racially, economically and religiously diverse. Minority enrollment numbers 21 percent, and nearly 80 percent of first-year students receive some form off financial aid. SMU's 11,000 students come from all 50 states, the District of Columbia and 86 foreign countries. SMU is nonsectarian in its teaching and committed to free and open inquiry.

SMU offers the education of your life because of its vibrant academic environment, and you'll enjoy the life of your education through a well-rounded campus experience in a dynamic, global city.

Texas A&M University

Texas A&M University
Office of Admission
P.O. Box 30014
College Station, TX 77842-3014
Admissions phone: (979) 845-3741
Admissions e-mail: admissions@tamu.edu
Admissions: admissions.tamu.edu/

Admissions

Current student, 8/2003-Submit Date, November 2006

To apply, I filled out the general application to Texas state schools, which included two essays. I was accepted automatically because I was in the top 10 percent of my class. To get in, I would advise people to be in the top 10 percent of their class because even if the top 10 percent rule is capped at 50 percent of admissions, this will not drastically change TAMU's admissions.

Current student, Communications, 8/2003-Submit Date, May 2007

The admissions process to Texas A&M University was fairly simple when I attended. I was in the top 3 percent of my high school graduating class and had no trouble being admitted on early admission status. I believe at that time all people in the top 10 percent of their classes were automatic admits. Over th years, I've become aware that the admissions process is a bit tougher. I wou say it is much more important now to be in the very top tier of your high scho class and have as many extracurriculars as possible. Being a state school, Tex A&M is a top choice for many high school graduates because of the tuition. A private school tuition continues to rise, I am sure more and more high scho graduates will apply to top state schools. I believe it will become ever mo challenging to be accepted in the future.

Current student, Engineering, 8/2005-Submit Date, June 2007

Like many people, I came from a highly competitive high school and had over 4.0 but was in the bottom quarter, so I was a little on edge about getting int TAMU. My SATs weren't ideal, but I apparently had no problem getting in. Ju make sure you have a good balance between grades and extra activities. U your English teachers or someone to [help edit] your essays. TAMU is compe itive to get into but it's not as hard as many high school seniors make it out be. I was very worried about getting in, but now I look back and realize I had made early on.

Current student, 8/2002-Submit Date, March 2006

The admissions process requires the completion of the ApplyTexas Applicatio and a couple of essays. SAT or ACT scores are also required, and from my expe rience, it appears that ACT scores tend to be a higher, so I would definitely tak at test. If you go to a Texas school and are in the top 10 percent of your grad-ting class, you are a lock for acceptance. They also have automatic acceptance r students with high test scores and high class ranks (the exact figures have anged recently with the new SAT). If you don't fit in those two groups, ugh, don't worry. A large number of students at TAMU come from what they ll the review admissions process. Apply as early as you can make sure they've ceived all your materials before the deadline. Also, if you're an automatic mit and you apply early in the fall, you'll get your acceptance letter faster and ll then be able to apply for housing earlier, giving you a much better shot at ur ideal dorm!

urrent student, 1/2004-Submit Date, January 2006

pplied as a transfer student. My application included an essay and transcript m a community college. No interview was required. Once I received my ceptance letter, I visited the campus on transfer students orientation day. gistration for classes was completed that same day, and I applied for financial d immediately. All of that went pretty flawlessly. My department had reserved me class spots for transfer student, otherwise all the classes would have been ll by the time our registration went through. The application essay carries a lot weight, especially for transfer students. Also, showing an interest in the col-ge by regular visits, keeping track of names of people you see. Financial aid utinely comes in late so that I have to take out a short-term loan to cover reg-tration and books. Sorting through all the financial stuff has been the biggest ssle.

lumnus/a, 9/2002-12/2004, April 2005

you are a resident of Texas and are in the top 10 percent of your graduating ass, you are automatically granted admission to any Texas public college. The dmissions standards for Texas A&M are getting higher and higher every year. xtracurricular activities will help you out a lot with admissions. TAMU seeks admit the best leaders for the future so any possible leadership roles you have ld are important. A good essay is key because they really will read each essay d this helps them to know you beyond your grades and stats. Texas A&M has plan that is has started recently called Vision 2020, which basically wants to ramatically increase the minority enrollment and also attempt to make the hool more Ivy League.

urrent student, 1/2004-Submit Date, April 2005

he admissions process is just like any other admissions. You can fill out an pplication online and send it in with a charge for the application process. You an pay this charge online using a check or credit card. As this is a public col-ge in Texas, if you are in the top 10 percent of your class you automatically get . If not, I recommend writing a really good essay on the application. I would lso recommend applying early. If you are transferring in visit the web site and nd out when they start taking applications. Start filling it out as soon as possi-le.

Academics

urrent student, Pre-med, 8/2006-Submit Date, January 2007

lasses are great, and the professors really do care and provide a lot of help. My urrent classes are known as clusters and we have great team interaction on proj-cts and other team tasks. The workload is a lot but you just do it and everything sually turns out great.

urrent student, 8/2003-Submit Date, November 2006

AMU has a good undergraduate program that strives to offer many majors with wide variety of classes for each one. In my experience, classes have ranged in ize from eight to 500 people, which is expected from a university of this size. s far as required classes go, it is not too difficult getting in, but the more pop-lar, non-required classes can be very difficult to get into.

lumnus/a, 8/2003-5/2006, October 2006

etting the classes you want is easy if you are in the honors program, otherwise 'm not so sure. Intro classes are very large, impersonal and have multiple hoice tests. I preferred to skip those (I considered them a waste of my time) nd took smaller, advanced classes where I got to know my professors and there was more flexibility within the curriculum. Those classes were more work but

they were much more rewarding (I mean we're in college to learn, aren't we?) and much better preparation for graduate school.

Current student, Engineering, 8/2005-Submit Date, June 2007

I am in the engineering school, and the freshman and sophomore classes are annoying. The professors are great if you go talk to them, so if you go to their office several times you may end up with a much better grade than you expect-ed. Also, tutoring at one of the two tutoring companies, A+ or 4.0 and Go, are amazing for calculus and physics. Getting the schedule/professors/class times you want depends on what time you get to register, then if that doesn't work just go to your advisor and they can force you in. The workload is heavy but not unbearable. It makes you learn; all I can say is that it is worth it in the end.

Alumnus/a, 8/2000-5/2005, December 2006

TAMU is a great engineering and business school. Liberal arts are an after-thought by the university and the funding and class availability reflects this fact. Most of the major specific classes are offered every other semester (if not less) and are almost impossible to enroll in if you are not a senior or honors student. Grading is fair and I never received a grade I didn't deserve. The professors are (for the most part) very encouraging and accessible. I was very happy with my experiences concerning the faculty at TAMU. The workload I found to be com-pletely normal. It wasn't overbearing, but you did have to work an hour or two every night and preparation for a test or major paper usually involved around 20 hours the week before.

Current student, 8/2005-Submit Date, September 2006

Getting into classes really isn't bad. The only part that may seem bad is that freshmen are on the bottom of the list to sign up, but it gets better every year. There will be more classes available and more times. My sophomore year I got a schedule for only Tuesday and Thursday classes, which is awesome.

Current student, 8/2002-Submit Date, March 2006

I can only speak to my personal experience, because at a university of this size, there is a lot of fluctuation in how classes are structured and what profs are like. Overall, my classes have been quite good. Many of them were both challenging and interesting. My department is not one of TAMU's headline programs, but they have been making a conscious effort to build it up; and in my four years here, I've seen it grow in leaps and bounds. I have had many professors I have absolutely loved. They (along with the TA, if you have one) have weekly office hours. It is never a bad idea to go to those and get to know the professor if you're struggling in class, or if you are in one of the freshman lecture courses of 200 students. If the professor knows you, it will probably be beneficial to you.

The other great way to get help if you need in those core classes is SIs, or sup-plemental instruction. They are structured study groups run by a student who has taken the course before and performed really well in it. He or she works with the professor, comes to class, and three times a week holds study sessions. It's totally free and you can participate in it to the extend that you would like, whether that be every single sessions, just the review for one particular lecture that you didn't quite understand, or for test reviews.

Current student, 9/2002-Submit Date, January 2006

Getting really popular classes is tough, but if you take the sludge classes as an underclassman, you get to take some really fun stuff as an upperclassman. For instance, I'm in my last semester, and I'm taking 13 hours of electives. I'm in Women Writers, Ballet, Floral Design, a book club worth three hours, and Entomology and Society.

Current student, 1/2004-Submit Date, January 2006

I am an English major, minoring in journalism. I completed all my basic course-work at a community college, so my choices for classes were limited. Getting the classes I want has not been easy, although some preference is given to stu-dents who are employed. I am finding that I need to take some filler classes because the ones I need or want are full. For instance, I need another year of Spanish, but every Spanish class has been full for the last two semesters. I had to take a Shakespeare and a Faulker at the same time (an enormous amount of reading) because they were the only classes left open by the time I was allowed to register. Most of the professors have been decent. However, I was having trouble with one particular class (Logic). I met with my SI (student instructor) for several hours each week for tutoring, and did everything I could to study. I still ended up failing the class. I feel that I could have been given other options,

Read all of Vault's College Surveys at www.vault.com/college—get complete surveys on 100s of colleges and univer-sities, expert advice on applicaton essays and more.

VAULT CAREER LIBRARY 701

or a different SI, or some other advice to keep that F from being on my permanent record. I have not been assertive enough in seeking help from counselors. When I have asked for help everyone in my own department has been very willing to assist me. I am beginning to learn the system.

Employment Prospects

Alumnus/a, 8/2003-5/2006, October 2006

Employment prospects vary dramatically. People at the top of their class with lots of impressive work and volunteer experience are often recruited by prestigious companies and graduate schools, but for people at the lower end of their class, I'm not so sure, especially the liberal arts majors with no extracurricular experience and poor GPAs.

Current student, 8/2003-Submit Date, November 2006

Employment prospects are very good. There is a high prestige regarding this university. Graduates obtain all sorts of jobs. Very strong network of alumni support. On-campus recruitment and internships are very accessible.

Current student, Communications, 8/2003-Submit Date, May 2007

Employment prospect overall for graduates of Texas A&M University are great if residing in the state of Texas. It has a well-deserved excellent reputation within the state. However, out of state is another story. I was a military wife and left the state right after graduation. Most prospective employers had never even heard of Texas A&M. The alumni network is very strong there and maintains a good database of job prospects.

Current student, Pre-med, 8/2006-Submit Date, January 2007

Employers love TAMU engineering students! We had the largest student-run career fair here last semester and we had 350+ companies and we only had that many because we couldn't fit anymore. The alumni networks are great as Aggies help Aggies. The Career Center is a great help for students looking for internships and co-ops and I plan to use their services next semester.

Current student, 8/2002-Submit Date, March 2006

The Aggie Network is quite possibly the most valuable tool a former student has at his or her disposal. There are countless tales of applicants getting jobs because the interviewer, an TAMU grad as well, recognized the Aggie Ring. I've heard of the Ring also getting people free meals, places to stay in distant cities and so on. You wear that ring forever, and it will always be a benefit to you. Bottom line is, Aggies take care of their own.

The Career Center is excellent. Besides all of their resources for internship searches, résumé writing, business dress and graduate school searches, they set up something like 30,000 interviews a year between companies coming to TAMU to recruit and students. They actually arrange more interviews per student than any other university career center in the country.

Thousands of companies come to TAMU to recruit. TAMU graduates have a reputation of being hard working individuals with good characters to back that up, so the career fairs are always full of companies eager to hire Aggies. If you are a business or engineering student, you will have tons of opportunities open to you because of this. Some of the other majors will probably find that they have less resources to work with, but the Career Center does try very hard to give them the same great opportunities.

Quality of Life

Current student, 8/2003-Submit Date, November 2006

TAMU works hard to offer a good living environment. Residence halls on campus try to build community through programs put on by hall councils. The university offers many good dining facilities, fairly nice classrooms, and a campus that is very open, avoiding the tight, compactness of many other campuses.

Current student, Communications, 8/2003-Submit Date, May 200[

Quality of life at Texas A&M was the reason I chose to attend school here. T campus is beautiful, easy to navigate and very safe. All of the facilities are to notch and I have only good things to say about the traditions and quality of l at TAMU.

Current student, Engineering, 8/2005-Submit Date, June 2007

Housing on campus depends on what you get. Corps housing is small but li able, then you have a little bigger suites, then there are module dorms. Northsi is more open and more social. It's also closer to Northgate. Southside is com monly referred to as the quiet side, but I just know that there were a lot of soro ity girls that lived there so they were always gone. Just depends on where y want to live or be close to. Off-campus living is great for students. Most apa ment complexes are student communities. I moved into a house and it's aw some, I found it randomly on a roommates web site. Do meet your potenti roommates beforehand, and be cooperative. The crime is almost nothing, an live closer to the "bad part of Bryan," which is a joke coming from a metropo itan city. It's College Station—everyone is helpful and nice.

Current student, 8/2002-Submit Date, March 2006

Campus is huge, but manageable. It feels overwhelming at first, but once y adjust, it isn't bad. Some the classes on West Campus do require some mo work to get to, but the TAMU bus system is extremely helpful in that area. Mo of the older buildings are on main campus, while the vast majority of expansio has taken place "across the tracks" on West Campus. Personally, I prefer ma campus, even though the facilities aren't as modern. It's pretty and has tons trees. I've found I actually do my best studying outside in some of those area

Living on campus isn't required as a freshman, but it is definitely recommend ed. I loved campus life. There are two clusters of residence halls, one on eac end of campus. Southside tends to be a bit more quiet and reserved (my person theory is that this is because the Corps of Cadets resides on Southside, and the are the focal point of that particular area). Northside, on the other hand, is mo centered around the individual dorms. For that reason, they tend to be mo social, a bit louder, and a bit more rambunctious. Both are fun places to live; you ask a Northsider which is better, they'll tell you Northside, and it's the oppo site for Southside.

The other great thing about Northside in particular is Sbisa Dining Hall, th largest cafeteria on campus. It is famous for Sbisa cookies and Sbisa balls (or of the many little traditions the dorms have there), and always has a huge selec tion of food. I recently counted, out of curiosity, and they were offering 30 di ferent entrees on one night. You can also use your meal plans at a bunch of th little eatery places we have on campus. These are everything from smooth stands to delis, to pizza places, to Chick-fil-a, and come in the form of an ou bound meal. You get a combination of food (example: sandwich, chips, cook ies, a drink, with the option of substituting in fruit or soup) that counts as a mea on your plan. The greatest piece of advice for incoming freshmen: howeve many meals a week you think you are going to use, get the plan below that one Freshmen are notorious for having too many meals. If you run out, you ca always get more, but if they're left over at the end of the semester, they are gone You don't want to be one of those people who buys 40 rice bowls at the C[onve nience]-store at the end of the year just to use up your meals.

Social Life

Current student, Communications, 8/2003-Submit Date, May 200[

Social life at TAMU is anything you want it to be. Everyone usually hangs ou at the clubs on Northgate. The dating scene is great with plenty of guys (gott love the Senior Boots in the Corps!) and lots of fun things to do. Traditiona activities are a big part of life on campus. Everyone looks forward to things lik Fish Camp, Midnight Yell, Silver Taps, Aggie Muster, Elephant Walk and so on The traditions acquired at Texas A&M live on in its graduates long after the leave College Station.

Current student, 8/2003-Submit Date, November 2006

TAMU boasts having over 800 student organizations in which students can b involved. Surrounding TAMU are many bars, a few dance halls, and man restaurants. There are fraternities and sororities at TAMU, but they are not a ominent as they are at many other schools. Personally, I do not go to any bars, t I have fun with people from the Christ United Methodist Church and enjoy ting at places such as Jonny Carino's, Longhorn Tavern, Cheddar's, Fazoli's, d Frittella.

urrent student, Engineering, 8/2005-Submit Date, June 2007

sically, since the town is small, the only way to meet a lot of people is to join mething, whether that be a club, frat/sorority, church and so on. Take time out studying to go somewhere, even it's by yourself, and meet people. Northgate popular for everyone, whether you like to drink, dance, or hangout and play ol, it's all there within two blocks. Antonio's Pizza is a great place to go grab mething to eat with a couple of friends. Fitswilly's is good. The bars are all od; most people bar hop when they go on Thursdays or Fridays. Also, the xas Hall of Fame is fun to go and dance, or Harry's. Cheddars and Texas oadhouse are very popular restaurants. Then there is Freebird's. You have not ten in College Station if you haven't had Freebird's. It's good for anyone.

ggies have countless traditions, too many to keep listing. But the best time is the fall when everything is new and exciting. Football is a major thing and

everyone participates whether you like it or not. We have so much respect for the traditions and keep them going, with help from the Yell leaders, which are five elected guys. They lead the crowd; some of them are kind of funny, but it's tradition. You also have to pull out if you do the wildcat for the class above yours. A wildcat is what a class does for good things or at the end of a yell. There are different ones and everyone wants to whoop but can't until you are a junior. Then we have silver taps once a month to honor the Aggies who have passed in the past month. Everyone gathers in the academic plaza and waits for a special group of corps guys to march up and fire their rifles. At the end of the year, all around the world, all Aggies gather together and honor all the Aggies who have fallen, which is called Muster. It is the most honored and revered tradition.

Alumnus/a, 8/2000-5/2005, December 2006

TAMU has a massive social scene, including a famous bar scene (Northgate), a variety of restaurants, and several hundred student organizations ranging from cigar appreciation to Old Testament studies, to ultimate frisbee. There is a large Greek system, but with TAMU's corps system and military history, the student body is not as Greek as most universities.

Texas Christian University

dmissions Office
CU Box 297013
ort Worth, TX 76129
dmissions phone: (800) 828-3764 or (817) 257-7490
dmissions fax: (817) 257-7268
dmissions e-mail: frogmail@tcu.edu
dmissions URL: www.admissions.tcu.edu/

 Admissions

ormer student, 8/2005-12/2006, April 2006

ne application is comprehensive. In addition to the application, applicants ust submit a résumé according to a specified format, several teacher recom- endations, and an essay on a specific topic. Interviews are optional. Despite e application process, TCU is not very difficult to get into as long as you are le to pay for it. I think the average GPA is above a 3.0; however, there are AP udents with 4.0s as well as very average students.

> **The school says:** "About 70 percent of TCU students receive financial assistance from TCU, and a wide range of scholar- ships, grants, and loans are available for those eligible."

urrent student, 8/2000-Submit Date, March 2005

hen I came in 2000, you needed a decent GPA, a good SAT score (1100), and me involvement in either volunteer work, sports, or clubs I personally think aving a family member that is a TCU grad or knowing a current student is very elpful. I would say it is more selective now than when I came.

> **The school says:** "All prospective students are evaluated according to the same criteria. The 75th to 25th percentile range of test scores for accepted freshmen is 1080 to 1260 on the SAT and 23 to 28 on the ACT."

urrent student, 8/2001-Submit Date, February 2004

CU has gotten more and more selective in the past three years, as administra- on has attempted to maintain a limited enrollment. As I do some part-time ork in the admissions office, I have noticed minorities have been getting the od a little more, as have males. This is most likely due to the fact that TCU is credibly white and females outnumber males three to one.

The school says: "TCU aims to keep enrollment small, yet selec- tive and in 2005, had a 67 percent acceptance rate for incom- ing freshmen. The student population at TCU is 19 percent minority, 41 percent male and 59 percent female."

An essay is required, although I do not think they carry much weight, and inter- views are available. Really class rank, test scores (1060 to 1260 SAT) and extracurriculars catch admissions officers' eyes the most. Recommendations also are important; make sure the person actually knows you instead of knowing of you!

Alumnus/a, 9/1997-5/1998, June 2004

I went to visit the college for an overnight dorm stay and orientation for the full next day. I did this in the spring semester before enrolling in any program. This was to determine if I was interested in the college. I had to take an entrance test to determine if I had to take the SATs or any other test required for the program course I was interested in. There was no interview process for this program.

> **The school says:** "Through personal campus visits and Monday at TCU, prospective students are encouraged to discover the TCU experience through sitting in on a class, interest sessions, campus and residence hall tours."

 Academics

Current student, 8/2000-Submit Date, March 2005

Many of the classes are fairly difficult and require a good amount of studying if you want an A or B (in the business school), others are not that difficult. The professors are good overall—some are terrible and give you a huge workload and others are great teachers who are interesting and really teach you something. The classes are larger in your first two years but once you get into your major, the classes are only 15 to 30 students. You can normally get into whichever classes you need, and if the classes are closed, someone will help you get into a class (teacher, advisors, department head) although you may not get the exact class time you wanted. Grading is done by letter only, no plus or minus.

> **Regarding grading, the school says:** "TCU is currently making the transition to a plus/minus system of grading."

Read all of Vault's College Surveys at **www.vault.com/college**—get complete surveys on 100s of colleges and univer- sities, expert advice on applicaton essays and more.

VAULT CAREER LIBRARY 703

Former student, 8/2005-12/2006, April 2006

TCU is excellent academically. Most of the classes are small. Many of the classes are between 30 and 60 students. TAs do not teach classes or grade papers at all. The professors are experts in their field, and have very interesting backgrounds. Most professors are very available to help you outside of class. Most classes offer extra credit for perfect attendance. Tests are easy as long as you go to class and study the night before. The workload is very manageable.

> **The school says:** "TCU offers a personal academic experience with an average class size of 25 students and a 14 to one average student to faculty ratio. Each student is assigned an advisor from their particular college to assist with scheduling decisions and other academic needs."

Current student, 8/2001-Submit Date, February 2004

I have found my major classes in political science to be much more difficult than my major classes in business (TCU's most popular major). In my experience, the teaching quality has been generally excellent and the small class sizes make the professors very accessible. This comes in handy when your grade is on the borderline or you need a letter of recommendation.

I would say the workload is tough but not unmanageable. If you keep up with reading and homework and put in a little extra effort on the side, there is no reason you should make less than a B. Our entrepreneurial business program is rated in the Top 50 in the country by *BusinessWeek*, as is our undergraduate engineering program.

> **The school says:** "The M.J. Neeley School of Business is ranked Number 33 of 1,400 undergraduate business school programs in a 2006 survey by *BusinessWeek*. The Princeton Review also ranked Neeley Number Two in 'Campus facilities' and Number Nine in 'opportunities for Women' in the 2006 *237 Top Business Schools.*"

Alumnus/a, 9/1997-5/1998, June 2004

I was never interested in the most popular classes; I just took the offered courses that allowed me to complete my program. The courses were challenging, but that's what made all the quality of the class better. The workload was not too demanding of me; however, others might see it differently. The grading system was fair. You got graded on what the work you did and on your performance on tests. Certain items counted at different levels. The professors were always willing to help in any way possible. Each one had after class hours to help if you did not understand a certain item or point during any of the lectures and activities.

 Employment Prospects

Former student, 8/2005-12/2006, April 2006

TCU offers help with résumés, help practicing for interviews, and help getting internships. The alumni are very helpful in getting jobs. Graduates get jobs at prestigious companies; however, most students continue to a graduate program before entering the workforce. Students are able to get into top graduate schools. Many continue on into law school or MBA programs at ivy league schools.

> **The school says:** "TCU's University Career Services provides many helpful tools for students including a resource center, online job search engine and two career nights each year featuring several of the nation's top companies. In addition to the career nights, each year over 50 prospective employers conduct on-campus interviews at TCU."

Current student, 8/2000-Submit Date, March 2005

Almost all employers are impressed with TCU graduates. The teachers and the alumni are very helpful with finding jobs. TCU does some on-campus recruiting, and has several large companies come to recruit.

Current student, 8/2001-Submit Date, February 2004

TCU seems to have a solid rep within Texas. While we don't fare too well in *U.S. News & World Report* rankings (tier two), that is due mainly to our lack of

a law or medical school. The administration makes no excuses for focusing the undergrad experience instead of catering to research and grad work.

> **The school says:** "TCU ranks in the first tier of *U.S. News & World Report* rankings."

Alumnus/a, 9/1997-5/1998, June 2004

Upon completion of this course I have been with this career for which I went school going on 10 years now. It puts me in a higher bracket as for as pay a experience with the job that I perform. Compared to employees that do not ha the education or the experience that I have, my pay is higher. I do recomme this course to any person seeking to become a private school teacher or to beg a teaching career.

 Quality of Life

Alumnus/a, 9/1997-5/1998, June 2004

I never ended up staying on campus for my course of study; however the ca pus was always clean. The neighborhood were the campus is located at w quiet not any crime of which I was aware. The lunchroom was always clean a quiet.

Former student, 8/2005-12/2006, April 2006

Most of the dorms are really small. There are no single rooms. Although the are cleaning ladies, the bathrooms tend to get really dirty and gross.

> **The school says:** "TCU recently opened two new residence halls as part of the Campus Commons project consisting of suite-style rooms, full beds and baths within each suite. Two more suite-style residence halls will open for the Spring 2008 semester. 46 percent of undergraduate students live in on-campus residences, including all female, all male and co-ed residence halls as well as on-campus apartments. While most students have roommates, single rooms may be requested."

The campus is really pretty. There are plants, trees, flowers, and fountai everywhere. The campus is also really small and easy to get around. On-ca pus dining includes a cafeteria, a sandwich place, a Subway and a stir fry plac

> **Texas Christian says:** "From the gourmet sandwiches of Deco Deli to the Italian dishes in the Main, students can choose from nine dining locations on campus, offering full menus or snacks to go."

Off campus there are good restaurants within walking distance. The campus very safe. Escorts on golf carts drive girls around campus after it gets dark that girls do not have to walk around alone.

Current student, 8/2000-Submit Date, March 2005

TCU provides a great quality of life. The Fort Worth area is nice, the people a friendly, the campus is always kept up and new flowers are planted almost eve other week. The dorms are old but they are OK—some of the dining servic are good—the campus is very safe.

> **The school says:** "The Campus commons project is underway and will include the new Brown-Lupton University Union, which will include a new dining facility, and four new, suite-style residence halls for students classified as sophomores and above."

Current student, 8/2001-Submit Date, February 2004

TCU's freshman dorms are livable, although not great. There are some very ni dorms that have been renovated, and the on-campus apartments are a great add tion. Safety does not seem to be an issue outside of the occasional car-break i perhaps due to TCU's vigilant police force who ride around in Durango's, wri ing parking tickets en masse. The food is good with Pizza Hut and an abundanc of Starbucks facilities on campus and in the library.

Social Life

Current student, 8/2000-Submit Date, March 2005

TCU students love to go out. There are a few school bars close to campus that we go to, but we mostly go to bars downtown. There are always people going out Thursday through Sunday, if you want to go one or more of those nights. There are many different school clubs and organizations. The Greek thing is really big! It seems that almost everyone is in a fraternity or sorority, in fact when you are a freshman and sophomore, and you meet someone new they will normally ask your name followed by what sorority or fraternity you are in.

Former student, 8/2005-12/2006, April 2006

There are a few bars within walking distance of campus. There is a ton of restaurants nearby. Dating is an important part of life and most students are very marriage oriented. There are a ton of events, including pep rallies, sporting events, spirit groups, concerts, intramural sports, religious functions and events at the dorms. The school newspaper, intramurals, working out at the rec center, volunteering, student government, academic/honors groups, and fraternities/sororities are all popular activities. The Greek system is huge. Fraternities and sororities have exclusive parties, BBQs and fundraisers.

> **The school says:** "There are more than 200 student organizations of campus, offering numerous opportunities for community service, academic, athletic and social involvement. Through student government, programming council, the leadership center, and many other organizations, all students have the chance to be involved and become a leader. 43 percent of students are involved in the Greek system, made up of 14 fraternities and 15 sororities."

Alumnus/a, 9/1997-5/1998, June 2004

I was never apart of a club or organization, so I am not familiar with that part of the school. I went to school during the day. So were no night-time outings for me. My favorite place to go in between classes was Student Hall. It was always quiet, and you could always study there [without] loud noises or anything of that nature. The cafeteria was next to it, so there was not to far to walk for a snack when trying to study.

Current student, 8/2001-Submit Date, February 2004

Everyone here is good looking and never seems to go to class. The typical student is rich, white, Greek and conservative. Diversity at TCU arrives primarily in the form of international students, who mostly associate among themselves. Most students are devout Christians who manage to reconcile their beliefs on weekends when they head out to The Pub, Scooners, or the ironically named Library downtown. In my opinion, I don't know how non-Greeks have friends. TCU also gets behind the football team a good bit, especially following our near breaking into the BCS this past year. Most other sports are sparsely attended unless some incentive is being offered.

> **The school says:** "TCU students come from all 50 states, more than 70 countries and more than 40 faiths. With a diverse background, the student population is 19 percent minority."

The School Says

The mission of TCU—to educate individuals to think and act as ethical leaders and responsible citizens in the global community—impacts every area of this person-centered, private university. With a total enrollment of 8,749, TCU is large enough to offer the choices of a major university yet small enough for students to take advantage of them.

Academic programs and co-curricular opportunities emphasize leadership development. TCU offers 100 undergraduate programs and 20 graduate degrees within seven colleges and schools: AddRan College of Humanities and Social Sciences, M.J. Neeley School of Business, College of Communication, School of Education, College of Fine Arts, College of Health and Human Sciences and the College of Science and Engineering.

TCU faculty members are recognized leaders in their fields, but their main focus is on teaching and mentoring; 98 percent teach undergraduates. The university offers study abroad programs in more than 25 countries, and TCU ranks seventh in the nation in the percentage of students who study abroad.

Reflective of our historic tie to the Christian Church (Disciples of Christ), a mainstream Protestant denomination, TCU encourages respect for faith traditions. Instead of imposing a particular religious point of view, TCU challenges students to consider their own beliefs. Students of more than 40 faiths (and of none) call TCU home.

TCU has completed more than $200 million in campus improvements, including new buildings for science, engineering, business and a new recreation center. In addition, the $100 Campus Commons project will add four new residence halls and a new University Union and a $10.2 million campaign will provide a complete restoration to the School of Education building. High-speed Internet access is available in every residence hall room and in more than 30 campus computer labs, and wireless networking is available in the library, select academic buildings and outdoor areas.

There are more than 200 student organizations, from the Programming Council (behind the scenes of homecoming and campus-wide activities) to the Horned Frog Yearbook. TCU competes with some of the best-known universities in the country as a member of NCAA's Division I, and offers multiple intramural sports programs.

TCU's tuition is several thousand dollars lower than most institutions of comparable quality and selectivity, but the university doesn't stop there. About 70 percent of TCU students receive financial assistance from TCU, and a wide range of scholarships, grants and loans are available for eligible students.

Read all of Vault's College Surveys at **www.vault.com/college**—get complete surveys on 100s of colleges and universities, expert advice on applicaton essays and more.

VAULT CAREER LIBRARY 705

Texas Tech University

Office of Admissions
Box 45005
Lubbock, TX 79409-5005
Admissions phone: (806) 742-1480
Admissions fax: (806) 742-0062
Admissions URL: www.depts.ttu.edu/gototexastech/

 Admissions

Current student, 1/2004-Submit Date, January 2006

The admissions process is very smooth. You submit your application documents to the admissions office and specify the program in which you are interested. Your paperwork is sent to the appropriate department, and a visit or tour is scheduled to show and interact with the prospective student in a more personal level. Essays may be required with the application package, but are usually basic and intended to give the student an opportunity to tell about him/herself and his/her goals. Student are selected easily; all they need is the minimum requirements and if they don't have those minimum requirements, advisors usually find the best way to help the student get into the program in question and fulfill his/her goals.

Current student, 8/2003-Submit Date, January 2006

The admissions process was through the ApplyTexas Application. I recommend trying to provide a lot of extra detail and even providing a high school résumé that includes a picture of you and all of your extracurricular activities and jobs held. Activities that were a longer commitment always look better than having been in a lot of various clubs for only a short period of time. The essay was common. It was basically describing an important time/person/event in your life that was the most influencing. Texas Tech looks for students who will bring in a good name for university. It is a research school among other things and it seems as if the university loves to admit people with colorful backgrounds.

Current student, 8/2003-Submit Date, April 2005

I was in the top quarter of my high school class and had above an 1140 on my SAT, which assured me admission to the school. I used to think that getting in to Texas Tech was easy, but many of my high school friends have been denied admission to Tech and accepted to other prestigious schools.

Current student, 8/2004-Submit Date, April 2005

The admissions process is very detailed and worded in a manner that is easy to understand. You first go to www.applytexas.org. You fill out the general application for the university and then you move on to the essay portion. The essay can be optional if you meet the certain criteria that Tech has for test scores. My advice on the whole admissions process is to allow enough time and don't procrastinate. This is a very time consuming process and you don't want to feel rushed. The earlier you apply, the higher your chances for acceptance are.

Current student, 8/2002-Submit Date, July 2005

It is recommended that an application for admission be submitted in the early part of senior year so that if not accepted the first time around, the student can re-apply. It is important to have a competitive GPA and SAT. The lower a GPA, the more important SAT scores are. If in the lower half of the graduating class, a SAT score of at least 1180 is necessary. An interview and essay are normally not required. The selectivity is based on academic achievement and testing schools and would be considered to be about average.

Current student, 8/2003-Submit Date, May 2005

To get into Texas Tech, I would advice you to get at least a 1100 on the SAT and get mostly A's and B's. You don't have to have any interviews or write any essays depending on the program. The school isn't too selective, so if you apply you can get in with little problem. Apply early to avoid getting waitlisted or rejected. As long as you have a well-rounded application, you are already half way in. Once you do get accepted, make sure to choose a meal plan that is a step above what you normally eat during the fall semester so you don't run out points before the end of the year.

Current student, 8/2003-Submit Date, April 2005

For the most part, the admissions process was fairly simple. I sent in three l ters of recommendation, two essays on my life experience so far and what attr utes I think that I have, and transcripts from the college that I was attending the time. The best thing for prospective students to do is apply as early as p sible. Go visit the campus before applying, and really research the field that y plan on majoring in. I was told that on average a typical student changes his her major at least four times.

 **Academics**

Current student, 1/2004-Submit Date, January 2006

The academic nature of the program is great; it's a very academic-orien school. Most of the classes have a low student-to-professor ratio. It's easier returning students to get popular classes, but even if you are a new or trans student, you can still get into the class you would like because of there are ple ty of sessions for the most popular classes. Grading procedures are good a usually favorable to students because professors adjust to their classes and t demands or accommodations that the students may need. The workload appropriate for the classes in question and the professors are very approacha and usually keep track of the performance of the individual students.

Current student, 8/2003-Submit Date, January 2006

It's a large university, so the ease of getting popular classes isn't very high. T quality of the education is excellent for a public school. I applied to all priva universities and Texas Tech matched up with some of the best, including an I League. You do need to be prepared to work; all of the professors take th classes to be very important and you won't run across to much of an easy cla or one that doesn't require time outside of it. It isn't the easiest school to atte you do have to know how to manage your time and organize your studies. T professors treat you like an adult and only you are responsible for your gra There is an entire building dedicated to tutoring and other academic help campus and is used virtually by every student on campus. Most professors, matter what the class size, make themselves available if you prefer a more p sonal relationship and want more insight on the class.

Alumnus/a, Civil Engineering, 8/2001-5/2006, September 200

I was pursuing an undergraduate degree in civil engineering. I feel tha received a fairly decent quality of education during my attendance. The profe sors were all pretty sharp and many of them went to world-renowned Ivy Leag institutions for their PhDs. As in all engineering the workload was rather larg The ease of getting classes is dependent upon your classification (i.e., juni senior and so on).

Current student, 7/2003-Submit Date, May 2005

I would highly recommend sending an application into the Honors College you wish to be challenged academically. I have really enjoyed all of my hono classes thus far and have learned far more from them than from the regular clas es. Grading, workload and quality of classes are very mediocre, at best. Gettin popular classes is very difficult unless you are in the Honors College that reg ters first, even before seniors.

Current student, 8/2004-Submit Date, May 2005

Classes are hard, but not if you study. The professors are willing to help yo earn the grade you think you deserve; you simply have to be willing to try a show effort. The workload is not too bad as long as you learn to manage yo time because it's not like high school, you have a very different schedule and i all up to you to make time to get things done.

Current student, 8/2003-Submit Date, April 2005

ost of the lower-level classes are quite large, but with smaller lab classes and scussion classes. If you want to be in a class that is full, all you have to do is talk to the professor and he/she will let you into the class. The workload is propriate for the classes and the professors are always willing to listen to your mments and questions.

Current student, 8/2004-Submit Date, April 2005

ave enjoyed all my classes that I have taken so far. I have found many of the asses very useful, not only to my major but also my everyday life. All of my ofessors have been very personal and willing to help with whatever I need. y professors are all very understanding with the workload of the class and try make it as fair as possible. The only downfall I have found in the past is get-g to register for good classes. If you register on the last day, it will be harder find classes you want and some may even be closed.

Current student, 8/2003-Submit Date, April 2004

really was not what I had expected. Many of my professors have been laid-ck kind of guys. The tests are not super-hard, nor are the classes. Some pro-ssors try to give students as much attention as possible, while others brush off. Depending on the professor and the nature of the course, the tests have been r and relatively harmless. Getting into the classes has been a bit of a challenge the semesters went by. I found that the classes I needed either were not being fered at the semester that I needed them, or they were not in more time slots. ave had to miss a lot of work because of my schedule. Fewer instructors eans fewer classes available for the number of students at the university.

The school says: "The student-to-faculty ratio at TTU is 21:1."

Current student, 8/2001-Submit Date, March 2004

m a senior majoring in accounting. The courses that I took my first two years re varied greatly regarding professors. Sometimes I had really great profes-rs who clearly knew what they were talking about; other times I had teaching sistants (TAs) who didn't seem to care. Your academic experience during ose early years will depend largely on which you get.

ound the coursework to be very manageable. Nearly every course I've taken ed multiple-choice exams. I would prefer something more challenging than l-in-the-bubble, but I still feel that I've gotten a lot out of my courses. Most the professors are really generous in that they will curve the exams if students not do well.

terms of my business courses, many of them are set in a lecture hall that seats 0+ students, so you will probably not speak to your professor and he/she will ver notice if you are attending or not. If you prefer a smaller classroom set-g, Tech may not be the place for you. I've found every accounting professor 1om I've had to be excellent, and all very good at doing their jobs.

 # Employment Prospects

umnus/a, 8/2001-5/2006, September 2006

ere is a significant amount of recruiting on the campus. Most people secure ternships during their undergraduate studies. Graduates from Texas Tech (in gineering) are employed by the same companies who hire people from "bet-r" schools in the state (based on rankings). The alumni network is rather rong. Many companies try to hire Tech grads exclusively. The more Tech ads at a company, the more likely you are to get hired.

Current student, 1/2004-Submit Date, January 2006

raduates from Texas Tech University find jobs easily because of the multiple b fairs that the school organizes throughout the year. The different depart-ents constantly bring employers for on-campus recruitment to search for full-ne employees, interns, co-ops and conduct interviews. Employers respect ch grads because it's a very academics-oriented school. The alumni network lps by representing Tech in the industry and providing support by sharing their periences with students.

Current student, 8/2003-Submit Date, April 2005

I really like that Tech usually brings in Tech graduates as job recruiters and employers to recruit students for jobs. They like to hire Tech graduates and that's really good for the students. Every major has some sort of internship that is a part of your degree plan—this right here pretty much assures you a job some-where. We also have an excellent career center that brings in recruiters, lectures, provides résumé help, mock interviews, and will pretty much do whatever they can to help get you a good job after college.

Current student, 8/2001-Submit Date, June 2005

Employment prospects for graduates of my school range from small local firms to large Fortune 500 companies. Large government contractors, such as Lockheed Martin, along with leading industry leaders in technology, including IBM and Texas Instruments, are just a few employers of graduates of Texas Tech. With a helpful and supportive career center responsible for employment and recruitment internships and co-ops are readily available.

Current student, 8/2002-Submit Date, April 2005

Texas Tech has a wonderful reputation in the work force. We have graduates working for Fortune 500 companies across the globe, as well as numerous vice presidents and CEOs of major American corporations. The alumni from our uni-versity are amazing and have proven to be very beneficial for my friends when it came to finding a job. They are very strong and united world wide. Texas Tech also has a very large presence and alumni base on Capitol Hill in Washington, D.C. Any student looking for future connections in politics need not look any further than Texas Tech.

 # Quality of Life

Current student, 8/2003-Submit Date, January 2006

Housing on campus is better than I've ever seen before. Each dorm is kept up and you never run across power/water outages. Each dorm also has its own restaurant or dining hall. If you want to stay off campus, there is a multitude of apartment living as well as houses that students can rent for low prices. All of these are a five-minute walk to the campus. They meet the needs of living for all of their students. Texas Tech is located in a smaller city so you don't hear much about the big city crimes. It's a really quiet town as far as crime. You have your normal neighborhood theft, but never anything that occurs on campus or even close to campus. Texas Tech's web site provides a crime report for events on campus and around Lubbock for interested students and their parents.

Alumnus/a, 8/2001-5/2006, September 2006

The crime in Lubbock is not bad when compared to other major metropolitan areas in the state. The cost of living is very low compared to other major cities in the state (about half as much as in Dallas, Austin or Houston). The campus looks very nice. All the buildings have a nice Southwest architecture theme.

Current student, 8/2003-Submit Date, May 2005

The quality of life here at Texas Tech University is amazing. I lived on campus for two years and enjoyed every moment; I felt safe and at home. The dining halls on campus are impressive; I have never had a problem with the food or the service. The neighborhood here in Lubbock is amazing, as well; the communi-ty really gets involved with the college students, and supports us as a whole uni-versity.

Current student, 8/2004-Submit Date, April 2005

One of my favorite aspects of my first year at Tech has been on-campus hous-ing. I have made so many friends and have become so close with all of the girls in my hall. I believe this is the best way to get settled in during your first year because you have a large support system and everyone else is in the exact same situation. Tech has many different dining halls on campus, so whether you like fast food or a typical dining hall meal, you can get what you want.

Current student, 8/2003-Submit Date, April 2004

The facilities at Tech are getting so much better. Just recently, they purchased new computers for the computer lab. All of which run much faster, and with less trouble. You can tell how old the business school is next to the other buildings. But over the past few semesters you can really see a difference. They have been

Read all of Vault's College Surveys at www.vault.com/college—get complete surveys on 100s of colleges and univer-sities, expert advice on applicaton essays and more.

VAULT CAREER LIBRARY 707

remodeling some of the floors, and are really putting forth the effort to make it look updated.

Current student, 8/2001-Submit Date, March 2004

Several options are available for on-campus housing. One option is living in a traditional dorm. The dorms have two people to every room, with one community restroom/shower for each floor. The space is limited, though comfortable, assuming you do not bring a crazy amount of stuff with you. You can pick your roommate if you wish or live with a random person. They have you fill out a survey so that you are placed with someone with whom you will be able to get along. The food in the dining halls, in my personal opinion, is awful. The one real benefit is Sam's Place and The Market.

Sam's Place is a convenience store and fast-food restaurant all in one. You can use your meal plan to make purchases, so you do not need actual money to go there. They give you a discount (30 percent) if you use a meal plan, though the prices are quite high. The Market is similar to a food court. You can use your meal plan to make purchases.

Social Life

Alumnus/a, 8/2001-5/2006, September 2006

There is always something to do in Lubbock. You can typically get a beer for under a quarter every night of the week (if you go to the right bars). Some of the places with cheap drinks are the Daiquiri Lounge and Bash Riprocks. There are tons of beautiful women at Texas Tech! More than I have seen in most cities in the U.S. They have a large Greek system but I never wanted to be a part of that. Football is everything at Texas Tech! There are concerts and BBQs before every home game.

Current student, 1/2004-Submit Date, January 2006

The school's social life is great in the sense that you can always find something to do when not in class, and you can always run into your friends in the most popular locations. If you would like, you could go out and have fun every day of the week and weekend. There are always cultural, social and sports celebrations on campus, which make it more and more entertaining. Bars and restaurants are within a decent radius of the school, not too far or too close. There are always events in the city and off campus. When it come to dating, you cannot resist the joy of walking around the beautiful campus and enjoying the fresh evenings in some of the isolated and romantic areas on campus with your date.

Current student, 8/2003-Submit Date, January 2006

Social life is excellent. It's one of the advantages of going to a large university. Businesses try to meet the demands of all students and there is never just a few choices for dining or nightlife. Events and clubs are never-ending and you can almost overwhelm yourself trying to make a decision as to which you want to join. Greek life is one of the greatest with over a third of the campus being Greek. There are tons of concerts, great sports events, wonderful bars (with awesome drink specials!) and events for every walk of life, no matter race, creed or religion.

Current student, 8/2003-Submit Date, April 2005

I love living in Lubbock. Many people may think that we are a small town in the middle of nowhere, and we are! However, there is so much more to Tech than that. Everyone is so friendly, and since we are in the middle of nowhere, it makes the student body even closer. We are like one huge extended family. Since we can't travel to other Big 12 schools every weekend, it forces you to stay here and make a home at Tech! It's a safe school—very friendly—and there is plenty to do and there are certainly plenty of places to eat and shop. Nightlife is excellent too, especially if you like Texas country. You can pretty much find a Texas country concert every weekend for cheap. That's something else that is great about Lubbock, almost everything can be free. The community embraces the Tech community so much that they help the college students out and feed us and entertain us for free! The center for campus life is an awesome place for this. There is something going on every weekend.

Current student, 8/2002-Submit Date, April 2005

The social scene at Texas Tech is amazingly diverse. Lubbock has everything offer for which a college student might be looking. To begin, there is the De District. In the Depot, you can find tons of bars and clubs, ranging from lc breweries and pubs to the old honky-tonk saloon. The Depot is also filled w live music galore.

You can hear an up-and-coming artist playing in the Depot any night of week. Lubbock has produced numerous major recording artists such as Bu Holly, Mac Davis, Pat Green, Natalie Maines of the Dixie Chicks, and ma more. You never know who the next major star from Lubbock, TX will be.

The School Says

Texas Tech University, founded in 1923, is a residential state university with a population of more than 28,500 students who come from all 50 states and 99 countries. Students at Texas Tech have the opportunity to study from more than 300 graduate and undergraduate degree programs. Academics are the top priority at Texas Tech, and students find admission standards comparable to other state institutions.

Texas Tech is one of the country's top universities to offer such diverse academic programs on one campus. The university is built around 10 colleges: Agricultural Sciences and Natural Resources, Architecture, Arts and Sciences, Business Administration, Education, Engineering, Honors, Human Sciences, Mass Communications and Visual and Performing Arts. The graduate school and law school, which has one of the highest number of students passing the bar exam in Texas, are conveniently located on the main campus. Also present is the Texas Tech University Health Sciences Center with its Schools of Medicine, Nursing, Pharmacy, Allied Health and a Graduate School of Biomedical Sciences.

Texas Tech has become a leader in academic programs ranging from pioneering research with the U.S. Department of Agriculture to improving alternative fuel capabilities for the nation's leading automakers. Wind engineering research has led to the creation of shelters that withstand some of the nation's most deadly tornadoes. Students also find opportunities to master the arts with instruction from classically trained musicians. Unique study abroad programs are also available.

Admission criteria for all students are designed to ensure academic success. For freshmen, admission decisions are based primarily on test scores and class rank. Additional factors such as leadership experience and extracurricular activities, community or volunteer service, talents and special honors, awards and achievements, and employment and internships are considered.

Admission requirements for transfer students differ, depending on the number of college hours a student has earned.

Trinity University

Admissions office
One Trinity Place
San Antonio, TX 78212-7200
Admissions phone: (210) 999-7011
Admissions e-mail: admissions@trinity.edu
Admissions URL: www.trinity.edu/departments/admissions

Admissions

Current student, Physical Sciences, 8/2004-Submit Date, April 2007

Trinity is a highly selective university, enrolling somewhere around 640 students each year. Taking the SAT and ACT early to see what your scores are like compared to the averages of the schools at which you are looking is always a good idea, and Trinity is no exception to this. During my admissions process, I chose the Early Action application. This was a non-binding agreement that showed the school I was serious about attending. Early Decision is a binding agreement that if accepted, you will attend that school. There were no interviews that I went through. The essay is a critical piece that should have some valid thought put in because the admissions people like to see creative applicants. Don't use the same essay for different schools if possible.

Current student, Visual Arts, 8/2003-Submit Date, April 2007

Trinity has become and continues to become a very selective school. It is getting harder and harder to get in. My advice for getting it would really be to show yourself as an active part of of your high school community. Trinity values individuals who not only succeed academically, but who are also well-rounded, showing involvement in student government, extracurricular activities and volunteer efforts. Also, keep your grades up and do well on your SAT or ACT, as these are important, as well.

Current student, Economics, 8/2003-Submit Date, April 2007

The admissions process at Trinity was relatively painless. The Common Application is accepted online, which is very convenient. For the essays, I would suggest choosing a subject of personal interest about which you are passionate. When visiting Trinity, I would suggest interviewing or meeting faculty, coaches and admissions counselors. Since Trinity is a pretty small school, it is easy to get to know people very personally, and most care immensely about attracting talented students. Selectivity seems moderately difficult. The SAT score ranges seem to increase every year, and probably will continue to increase as Trinity gains more national recognition.

Alumnus/a, Psychology, 8/2001-5/2005, April 2007

The admissions process was painless and somewhat fun. I interviewed with a couple of professors the day I had the campus tour, but that was more for my benefit than for theirs. Trinity is vigilant in keeping potential student's interest. They sent postcards and letters, and really did a great job in selling the school.

Current student, Communications, 8/2004-Submit Date, April 2007

Being able to use the Common Application was helpful in applying to Trinity. Also, the fee for submitting an application is waived if students complete it online. The majority of students at Trinity is from Texas, so I feel that applying from out of state gave me a leg up on the competition. Trinity is selective in choosing from the pool of applicants, but the competition to get in is not cutthroat by any means. Although I applied early in the fall semester, the selection committee was extremely quick in making a decision and sending me an acceptance e-mail. Trinity is such a small, close knit community that I often still see my admissions counselor who visited my high school during my senior year to recruit students. Also, as a potential athlete, I was able to stay on campus with current athletes, which was one of the deciding factors in my decision to attend Trinity. Interviews are not typically conducted for prospective students, though I did meet with my possible future coach. After I made the decision to attend Trinity, the school was very helpful in keeping me updated on happenings and helping me work through freshman anxieties, which was much appreciated.

Current student, Liberal Arts, 8/2003-Submit Date, April 2007

I used the Common Application, which was an easy process, but Trinity is becoming more and more selective. In regards to the essay, take a personal anecdote and demonstrate how it has helped you understand the world in which you live, or whatever aspect of the essay question you are trying to answer. Don't make sweeping generalizations, but be as specific as possible, focusing on something you find paradigmatic for understanding the world.

Current student, 8/2002-Submit Date, April 2006

Trinity is a fantastic school, but because of its size and selectivity its name remains somewhat obscure to the general public. Because of this, there seem to be fewer applicants than at some bigger-name schools of similar size and rigor. This has three distinct consequences: first, it allows a wider range of applicants to be accepted—one need not have a perfect high school transcript or stellar SAT/ACT scores to apply. Second, it allows much more flexibility to those participating in the selection process—they are more free to pick and choose a more diverse, interesting and personable group of students than institutions worried about maintaining a certain average test score among their incoming class. And third, the smaller applicant pool allows a higher level of financial aide to be given to each prospective student.

There is no fee for applying if the application is submitted online using the Common Application. On the application there is one essay question in which, though several prompts are suggested, the applicant may write whatever he or she chooses. There is an optional interview that typically can only help the applicant.

The theme of the application process is for the university to get to know the applicant and understand him/her as an individual. Only then can the decision-makers decide whether or not the applicant would be a good fit with the university and its community. The most successful applicants are those who have demonstrated strong academic success, gained interesting life experiences, and who possess friendly and outgoing personalities.

Academics

Current student, Biology, 8/2003-Submit Date, April 2007

I think that Trinity academics are excellent. The classes I have taken here have prepared me to be competitive for entrance to graduate programs. The workload in science course can be intense, but not unreasonable. The professor-student relationships, in general, are excellent. Professors make themselves available to students and take interest in their students' well-being. Usually, getting into classes is not a p.roblem and students can explore classes outside of their majors.

Current student, Visual Arts, 8/2003-Submit Date, April 2007

Academically, Trinity is very challenging. The professors are amazing, but they also expect a lot out of you. You will get out of class as much as you put in, and it is worth it to do so. Of course there are some classes that are duds, but for the most part, I have really enjoyed the classes I have taken and have learned a lot. The workload varies from class to class—entry-level courses being much easier, and upper-division courses, once you get into your major, are much more demanding. My one complaint is that classes can be difficult to get into, especially the popular common curriculum classes. It gets easier the older you get, so it's best just to wait to take these classes as a junior or senior.

Current student, Communications, 8/2004-Submit Date, April 2007

The workload is intensive and constant, most of the time. The grading is fair but only if the professors can tell if you've put effort into the work/test/project. The professors are personable, helpful, and they have high expectations of their students. The classes are not extremely easy to get into during registration, but you

Read all of Vault's College Surveys at **www.vault.com/college**—get complete surveys on 100s of colleges and universities, expert advice on applicaton essays and more.

VAULT CAREER LIBRARY **709**

can usually campaign the professors to get into a popular class, especially if the class is a part of your major or concentration.

Current student, Economics, 8/2003-Submit Date, April 2007

Academics are important and quality of teaching is heavily stressed. Professors are not only great authorities in their subjects, they are also engaging and personable, making classes high quality and enjoyable with few exceptions.

Popular classes are often difficult to register for since classes are capped at a small size, but for the most part, professors are flexible about adding students and/or you will get into the class before you graduate.

Grading varies by professor and by department. For the most part there is some control for grade inflation but professors generally want students to be successful.

Depending again on your academic program, the workload is pretty moderate. Most students double major, and take five or six classes a semester, which can get overwhelming during peak times of the semester.

Alumnus/a, Business, 8/2001-5/2005, April 2007

My management and marketing classes were great! The final business course is extremely difficult and taught by an infamous professor. That said, he truly challenged you in class. The academic rigor in most of my classes was strenuous. Of course, you get what you put in to the course.

Alumnus/a, Communications, 8/2002-5/2006, April 2007

I always wondered how the academics fared at Trinity. I figured they were just like any other college. That is, until I came to graduate school at a large public university. I then realized how challenging the Trinity courses were, but how much I really got out of them and learned from them. My preparedness comes from the challenging courses, but also from the involved professors and positive attitude around campus.

Current student, Communications, 8/2003-Submit Date, April 2007

It is really hard to get some of the popular classes because the registration process is really frustrating; however, whatever class you end up taking, it is only going to enhance your liberal arts education, so you might as well take it. Grading is hard, but it makes you a better student, if you want to succeed. Workloads vary from course to course, but are never unmanageable. The professors are the greatest asset to the university. They are incredibly knowledgeable and extremely renowned in the academic community. They are so eager to help and are very accessible.

Current student, Physical Sciences, 8/2004-Submit Date, April 2007

Trinity is known for being a great academic institution. There are very few classes at this school that will not force the student to work and manage time well. All the classes are taught by professors, not by TAs or graduate assistants. While there are opportunities for research here, the focus of Trinity is the students and ensuring that they learn. Trinity recently added an electronic waitlist feature that goes along with the registration process. This allows those who don't get into a class at the time of registration an opportunity to get into the class based on when they got on the waitlist. Professors can still let you into a class though if you talk to them.

Current student, Liberal Arts, 8/2003-Submit Date, April 2007

The classes are phenomenal. Professors are always accessible and take the time to challenge all of their students. Some classes are difficult to get into, but if you plan correctly you can get into any class except the Astronomy Lab. Grading varies, but is typically fair, and professors are always clear with what they expect and responsive to students who are concerned about the evaluation of work. The workload varies by course, but there is typically a substantial amount of reading with minimal assignments excluding two to four exams and a few papers.

Alumnus/a, English, 8/2001-5/2005, July 2007

The English program is really good. Professors are extremely easy to talk to, and easy to contact between classes. Popular classes are only hard to get into if you're in one of the newer classes. Juniors and seniors generally have no problem getting their picks.

Employment Prospects

Current student, Liberal Arts, 8/2003-Submit Date, April 2007

Our Career Services Office is great and is constantly working with Alum Relations and companies around the world to have job fairs and foster prof sional relationships. There are several on-campus employment fairs eve semester, but all graduates who start the job search early find something they happy with. As for graduate schools, you are as prepared as you would like be. There are great students from Trinity with busy social lives who are goi to Harvard, Princeton, University of Chicago, University of Texas, Colum University, USC and so on.

Current student, Visual Arts, 8/2003-Submit Date, April 2007

Trinity has a good Career Services Office, with someone always there to he review your résumé and cover letters. They are active in programming eve like career fairs, interview practice days, résumé review days and so on. Trin graduates do not have much difficulty finding jobs in the San Antonio area, because we are such a small university and located in Texas, it can be a challer (but in no way impossible) to find jobs in many cities. Many have done so, it may not be done with the ease that one might have if attending a larger u versity. The alumni network can be helpful.

Current student, Economics, 8/2003-Submit Date, April 2007

Within Texas, Trinity has an excellent reputation. Business students are qua fied to work at many well-known companies. The school has a program wh students are given a large amount of money to invest as they wish. It is one the largest programs—Student Managed Fund—for a small liberal arts schoo

Current student, Biology, 8/2003-Submit Date, April 2007

There are lots of opportunities to meet with potential grad schools, employ and so on. Career Services on campus is very proactive about preparing stude for interviews, helping with résumés and so on. I'm a biology major and a of students either take a year off before applying to medical school or gradua school, or go straight into graduate school. Professors are the most helpful pe ple with helping get internships and letting students know about different opp tunities that arise.

Current student, Biology, 8/2003-Submit Date, April 2007

Trinity has a great alumni network that helps student get connected in the j market. Having a Trinity degree has meaning. I know many graduates who ha gotten prestigious jobs directly after graduating, such as JP Morgan Bank a Matrix Engineering Firm. Trinity is also helpful in getting into graduate p gram. I know students going to Princeton, University of Chicago, University Florida, Southwestern and Duke next year.

Current student, Physical Sciences, 8/2004-Submit Date, April 20

As a junior, I plan on attending a graduate school when I graduate from Trin next year. I have worked as an intern at an oil and gas company in Houston two years now and most of the people whom I meet recognize Trinity as a gr academic institution. Trinity is especially known for its Health C Administration program and has graduates working as the COO's for many la hospitals across the nation.

Alumnus/a, English, 8/2001-5/2005, July 2007

Employment prospects are very good in San Antonio and in Texas, but outsi of the state, things get very difficult. Not may employers have heard of school. However, once they've done the research, they're generally impress with what they find.

Quality of Life

Current student, Economics, 8/2003-Submit Date, April 2007

Housing is very comfortable on campus. You must live on campus for thr years, and all housing is suite-style, with double rooms. The facilities at Trin are great. The library is very nice, and athletic fields and facilities are some the best I've seen at Division III schools. Academic buildings are generally ni though some need to be updated (and will be in the next few years). Dining good—all meals are a la carte, so there are a lot of options and you can eat fro a.m. to midnight on campus. There is crime in the City of San Antonio. ough Trinity tries to police its campus, there is a certain amount of crime that unavoidable.

urrent student, Visual Arts, 8/2003-Submit Date, April 2007

ousing is great: we are known for our large and comfortable dorm rooms, ich are situated in a suite-style, with your own bathrooms and in some, a com- n living area. I really enjoyed not having to share a bathroom with an entire or of women, but instead just three other people. The campus feels very safe d I have never been worried about and crime or security issues. Dining is also tter than most schools, although many students complain. I feel that there is ood variety of options, but as with any campus, you do grow tiresome of the ne stations. The food plans can also be overpriced due to the school's con- ct with Aramark. Overall, the quality of life at Trinity is high!

urrent student, Communications, 8/2004-Submit Date, April 2007

e dorms are very nice, especially since a lot of them have been re-done recent- but by the end of the three-year living requirement, you are ready to live off mpus! The food on campus is also really good compared to other schools, but e anything, having it over and over for three years it does get old. The dining ff has recently been trying new food options, which I think have been work- out great and making dining on campus a lot more enjoyable.

urrent student, Physical Sciences, 8/2004-Submit Date, April 2007

nity is located adjacent to the Monte Vista historical district and only five to minutes from downtown San Antonio. It is set in a beautiful part of town ere students have no need to worry about their safety. To add to this, the partment of Campus Safety is always patrolling and with a campus that is not large, they can get to you in a moment's notice should you ever need assis- ce. Trinity's student housing is considered to be some the best in the coun- . The rooms are all suite style, so you have your own bathroom and not a mmunity bath, which is very nice. The Bell Athletic Center houses several ight rooms and an aerobics room for those who like to keep in shape. There also a track that is open to all students that encircles the football field as well a jogging trail on upper campus.

urrent student, Liberal Arts, 8/2003-Submit Date, April 2007

r dorms are Number One according to *CosmoGirl*. The campus is beautiful ough sometimes the weather is too warm and humid. We are one of the most nwired" campuses in the country (wireless Internet), the food is great (they st introduced fresh sushi and BBQ), we are in an optimal place of San Antonio th very little crime on campus.

urrent student, Biology, 8/2003-Submit Date, April 2007

r dorms are some of the best college dorms available. We have suite bath- oms and cleaning services. Dining facilities and selections are limited but ve student needs. Like any city, San Antonio has crime and walking around 2 a.m. by yourself is not a good idea. Campus security is good and friendly, ough.

 Social Life

urrent student, Visual Arts, 8/2003-Submit Date, April 2007

a member of the Trinity Greek system, most of my social life stems from my perience in a sorority. I attend fraternity parties as well as parties and mixers onsored by my sorority. My life would definitely not be as exciting socially if ad not become part of the Greek system, but that is not necessarily true for all dents. I think that Trinity has a very lively social scene. The motto here is: ork hard, play hard," with students being very focused on academic achieve- nt, but also allowing time to relax and have fun. As far as dating, Trinity stu- nts do not really date as much as other schools. We are small and everyone ows everyone, making it seem like high school at times. It can get harder to et new people, but you really just have to force yourself out there and meet w people. This is usually when dating happens, when you branch out and ng out with a different crowd. There are some fun college bars around the area ere students hang out, but it's typically a 21-and-up crowd, with the exception a couple of places. There are tons and tons of good restaurants in San tonio! Mexican food is great and there are lots of cheap options in the area.

Current student, Communications, 8/2004-Submit Date, April 2007

Campus life is pretty good. I am in a sorority and I love it. There are tons of great restaurants around town (Demos Greek food, Madhatters, J Alexanders, Cheesecake Factory) and also lots of swanky bars (V Bar, Davenport); the fun usually begins once you are 21. Then you really get to experience San Antonio and all it has to offer.

Current student, Communications, 8/2003-Submit Date, April 2007

Incredible social life. Who says smart kids can't party? Greek like is an amaz- ing social network and very different from big state schools. The sororities/frats are small, local and very involved. San Antonio is a great city to go out in but most kids frequent some of the local bars around campus, such as Bombay's Bicycle Club and the downtown Pat O'Brien's scene. There's so much to do in the city whether it's sports, festivals, concerts, shows, bars and so on.

Current student, Economics, 8/2003-Submit Date, April 2007

The Greek system represents approximately 30 percent of the campus. They have a strong presence and are very active. It's not difficult to be a Greek and involved in other activities. Nor are students limited in their friendships. The campus is very outgoing and warm. There isn't much dating at Trinity; we always have a few students who get married, but I feel that it isn't a priority of the students to find their spouses.

Alumnus/a, English, 8/2001-5/2005, July 2007

Social life can be fun, but it's mostly composed of Greek life. About 25 percent of campus is Greek, and it's local, not national. So, the best social activities are during Greek rush, when there are plenty of parties. Other than that, the sports activities are entertaining, and no student should make it through without going tubing at some point. There's nothing better than riding down a river for four hours, with beer and inner tubes.

 The School Says

Since our founding in 1869, Trinity University has been dedi- cated to helping talented, motivated students hone their skills, define their goals, and follow their dreams. Our academic pro- grams allow you to pursue almost any interest and Trinity's practical spin on the liberal arts ensures that the skills and knowledge you acquire will have endless professional applica- tions. Trinity offers unparalleled opportunities for personal growth both in and outside the classroom, so if you are a bright and enthusiastic student with a passion for learning then Trinity may be the perfect choice for you.

Trinity attracts a remarkably diverse, smart, and active group of students from almost every state in the nation and over 60 countries. They are drawn to our unique combination of small class sizes with individual attention from faculty, and our high quality resources and facilities which are usually only found at much larger universities. Trinity's rigorous, flexible curriculum is the optimal blend of science, liberal arts, and professional pro- grams. Outside the classroom there are over 130 social, aca- demic, service, political, and recreational student organizations, not to mention numerous campus festivals, lectures, concerts, dramatic performances, and celebrations. In addition, the uni- versity's hometown, San Antonio, is the seventh largest city in America, and offers all the urban amenities a college student could want, ranging from the shops and restaurants of the famed River Walk to the excitement of a Spurs game, a hike down the historic Mission Trail, or the thrill rides at Six Flags Fiesta Texas.

Trinity's emphasis on a personalized education begins with the application process. We take a holistic approach to undergrad- uate admissions, and strongly consider each prospective stu- dent's GPA, test scores, academic preparation, course rigor, application supplement, personal statement, extracurricular and community involvement, and teacher and counselor recommen- dations. We also encourage students to visit our beautiful sky-

Read all of Vault's College Surveys at **www.vault.com/college**—get complete surveys on 100s of colleges and univer- sities, expert advice on applicaton essays and more.

VAULT CAREER LIBRARY   **711**

line campus to tour our facilities, check our spacious residence halls, talk to students, faculty, and admissions representatives, and even grab a bite in Mabee Dining Hall. The university offers

several comprehensive Saturday preview programs as well as individual visits, which all can be scheduled at www.trinity.edu/visit or by calling (800) TRINITY.

University of North Texas

Admissions Office
University of North Texas
P.O. Box 311277
Denton, TX 76203
Admissions phone: (800) UNT-8211 or (940)565-2681
Admissions e-mail: undergrad@unt.edu
Admissions URL: www.unt.edu/admissions.htm

 ## Admissions

Current student, Journalism, 8/2004-Submit Date, January 2007

I was a transfer student, so there was the general hassle of transferring and the credits you lose out on for not being at the university starting with your freshman year. Overall, it wasn't that hard. No essays were required, whether or not I attended junior college to raise my grades to make the university's eligibility requirements. Advertising, for some reason, falls under the department of journalism at UNT. There was no interview, just an orientation day. As far as selectivity, the University of North Texas highly target transfer students from other schools and welcomes them as many other schools are notorious for rejecting transfer students.

Alumnus/a, Computer Science, 8/2002-8/2006, May 2007

Admissions process was easy. I filled out an application online and they responded very fast. Not to mention, I lived in the United Arab Emirates at the time and I received my acceptance letter within one month of application. I had no trouble with the admissions staff. They have one standard essay asking you to outline your goals, previous experience and what you hope to get out of your degree at UNT and so on. As long as they have all your test scores, i.e., TOEFL, SAT and so on, you should be good. I didn't think it was hard to get in at all. They didn't have an interview for undergraduate students. I did however have a 3.75 GPA with which I was transferring to UNT. That did help!

Current student, 9/2004-Submit Date, January 2007

The admissions process for applying to UNT was simple. There is one application for all University of Texas universities throughout the state. The application fee is $40 and can be found at www.unt.edu or any of the other University of Texas web sites. I later received a letter informing me of to which schools I was accepted and which did not accept me. Over 6,000 students apply to UNT each year and about 70 percent are accepted. Some things that help very much in the acceptance process are having good letters of recommendation from previous teachers, professors or mentors; also it seems to be an advantage to apply to the school early rather than waiting until the last minute. Other important factors for admission are class rank and scores on standardized tests, such as the SAT and ACT.

Alumnus/a, 8/2000-5/2004, January 2006

The University of North Texas is not that hard to get into. Write a well-constructed essay. If you are applying to the school of music, that is a different story. Be aware that if they accept you to the school of music, it doesn't necessarily mean they accepted you as a major status. You may have to audition again to be accepted into your specific department so that you can declare your major. This is the major pitfall of the University of North Texas music program. Most

applicants don't realize they weren't accepted as a piano major, voice major whatever and just float around in the system without a declared degree.

Current student, 1/2003-Submit Date, February 2005

UNT is a school that is fairly easy to get into. I believe you only need a 2.0 get in, and that is coming from a community college or another university. Y can still be accepted with that GPA, but will be subject to probation status. Y probably don't need any interviews to get in, essays are optional, the selecti process is fairly broad, and there are really no barriers that one must fit as far ethnicity, race and religion. Of course, they like diversity like any university anyone who wants to go can as long as his/her GPA is congruent to the univ sity's standards for admission.

Current student, 8/2003-Submit Date, July 2004

There are minimum test requirements for automatic admission to the univers Should one fail the test requirements, certain essays are required for submissi Admission is not difficult, but should not be dismissed as easy. One must st on top of various issues, such as financial aid and other deadlines. UNT is growing university with a new Dallas campus soon to open. As a result, the u versity is frequently looking for new students and an aspiring applicant sho not have a problem getting in.

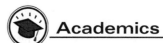 ## Academics

Alumnus/a, Social Work, 8/1999-8/2004, February 2007

The social work program is one of the best programs available. They provi hands-on experience in the community, which allows you the opportunity make community connections. The classes are small in size and provide y with one-on-one attention by the professors. The program is tight knit and wh in it you get to know the people in your courses as well as the professors. T workload is manageable and professors are readily available for assistance.

Current student, Journalism, 8/2004-Submit Date, January 200

The quality of classes, as is true with any school, varies along with each profe sor and the opinion of the student. To get a popular class, early registration nearly the only way. Grading is more varied than I've seen it, although I'm ve glad that other students, including myself, voted against the plus/minus syste Some professors go with the calculation of 1,000 points totaled from ea assignment over a semester, others use the average of all grades totaled at the e of the semester. Some professors are still employed due to their respectal work done in their field, despite complaints of ineffective teaching methoc Workload varies with each professor, just as much so as grading polic Generally, the workload does depend on necessity: the amount of work need for the class and professor to meet the goals as stated in the syllabus.

Alumnus/a, Computer Science, 8/2002-8/2006, May 2007

As an international student, I found myself really at ease in the classroon maybe because I had gone to an American college in UAE. I thought the cla es were hard. My major was Business Computer Information Systems and th had pretty tough projects in some of the classes but lots of projects in just abc every class. You need to manage time very well or you wouldn't finish the The exams were fair but could be really tough. There were easy going class mainly depending on the professor who was teaching. But if you take the tou professors, they really make you learn and you come out a winner (and possib a very high grade—that's the tradeoff). There was a lot of diversity in my [ma]jor with enough classes in both business and IT. The popular classes may not [nec]essarily be the best ones but always better to register during the early regis[tra]tion period if you want the right professor for the right class.

[Du]ring senior year, the class sizes were about 15 to 30 students. But I did have [so]me classes like Marketing, Economics and so on, during my junior year where [the]y had up to 100 students. But this is generally not the case in your senior year. [Gra]ding is fair. Some classes are tough. Sometimes they let you walk away [fro]m writing the finals if you have already got an A in the class. Most of the [cla]sses involve teamwork and group projects.

[Cu]rrent student, Geography, 9/2004-Submit Date, January 2007

[I a]m an undergraduate student majoring in geography. The geography depart[me]nt at the University of North Texas is relatively small with regard to student [po]pulation. However, the professors are extremely knowledgeable and experi[enc]ed in their fields. Many are known throughout the nation as experts, such as [Dr.] Joseph Oppong who is regarded as a leading Medical Geographer in the [Un]ited States. The program is rigorous and rewarding. Because of the quality [of] professors, classes are interesting and well structured. Classes at UNT that [ful]fill the core curriculum for all students are great in number. There is usually [a l]arge number of different professors and different times during the week that [the]se classes are offered. Major-specific classes should be registered for during [ear]ly registration times because there is often only one time it is offered during [a s]emester or a year. These classes fill up quickly.

[Al]umnus/a, 8/2001-12/2005, January 2006

[Ma]ny of my classes (Criminal Justice, Sociology, Human Services) were taught [by] adjunct professors and grad students. The quality did not seem to be a major [fac]tor; they lectured and then you were tested over about four chapters of infor[ma]tion, but most material was not in the book. If you did not memorize the info, [yo]u did not do well on the test, no other means of knowing whether you knew [the] material was ever provided. The professors did not seem to care whether you [pas]sed with a good grade or not; they seem to care more about getting a large [num]ber of students into the classes. I took a five-week summer course last [sem]ester and the teacher gave out work like it was a regular 20-week course. It [wa]s essays, assignments, research paper, tests, movie reviews, guest speakers [rev]iews, just total chaos.

[Al]umnus/a, 8/2000-5/2004, January 2006

[Th]e courses for core classes are not difficult if you show up to class and do the [req]uired readings. Music classes can be rigorous, especially the theory classes [tha]t all music majors are required to take. In my experience, there are many [gre]at professors at UNT. I've never had a problem getting the courses I request[ed] as long as I register for classes as early as possible. Most classes have strong [att]endance policies, which will penalize you if you do not attend class. The [wo]rkload is somewhat moderate. As you get into higher-level courses, more is [exp]ected as far as workload and effort. Most class sizes are large (100 or more) [in] lower-level music classes and core classes. I had very small sized classes as [wel]l, especially with junior and senior level.

Employment Prospects

[Al]umnus/a, Computer Sciences, 8/2002-8/2006, May 2007

[Be]st part about UNT is the location. There's plenty of big companies in the [Da]llas Metroplex area that recruit at UNT. Sabre, American Airlines, Fidelity [In]vestments, Citibank just to name a few.

[Ev]eryone in my graduating class had a job in hand during their last semester. I [am] not kidding. For international students, an internship is a great way to obtain [ful]l-time employment later and there are plenty of internships and job listings. [Ap]art from the Career Center, there's also the Cooperative Education Office that [hel]ps with internships and co-op opportunities. There are also job fairs all [thr]ough the semester. Career Center aids with job interviews and résumé work[sho]ps. Everyone's eager to help.

[Al]umnus/a, Social Work, 8/1999-8/2004, February 2007

[Wh]ile in the social work program you are required to complete community serv[ice] hours and volunteer with various agencies in the community—this provides

you with wonderful connections. There is a required practicum that provides you with an internship in a local agency and provides you with hands-on experience. The school offers a program to graduates to assist with finding employment. However I found that due to the connections I was able to make while in school and the various hands-on experiences I gained through my community service, I did not need it. I was able to get a job before graduating at a local agency at which I have volunteered previously through one of my courses.

Current student, 9/2004-Submit Date, January 2007

Professors, the alumni network, the UNT web site, librarians and groups across campus are extremely helpful with providing prospective graduates with career ideas for after graduation. Students must take initiative on their own in this respect. This information is not freely offered, however students who actively seek will find that help and prospective are readily available and that people are very willing to guide them. Visiting the Career Center at the University of North Texas can be extremely helpful. They provide help alumni and current students in making career decisions and exploring their options through career development programs and other assistance.

Quality of Life

Current student, 9/2004-Submit Date, January 2007

Campus is full of activities at all times. There are many clubs, lectures, multicultural events and other organized events to provide ways for any type of person to get involved with others in their area of interest. We even have a radio and television station and the *North Texas Daily Newspaper*. The Recreation Center has an outdoor activity planning center where you can rent equipment, such as tents, backpacks, even kayaks. They also organize group camping and outdoor activities that can be a lot of fun and a good way to meet interesting people. Students here are generally helpful and friendly to one another. Many students live on campus and find it a great environment. I never had that opportunity but I have friends who do and who have made life long friends that way. On-campus housing means there are always students walking throughout the campus in the evening and on holidays, which makes the school feel lively.

Alumnus/a, Social Work, 8/1999-8/2004, February 2007

Before coming to school, they offer a tour of the campus that helps you decide where you would like to live. All of the dorms are located close to each other and provide different food options. If you choose the meal plan, you can eat at any of the various dorm facilities and choose what you would like to eat. If you choose to live off campus, you can find an apartment close by that allows you to walk to class if you choose. The streets on campus and around the campus are well-lit and police security patrol the campus on a regular basis. The campus has a book store located where they also offer food from various fast food restaurants, including Chick-fil-A and a buffet. At the beginning of the year there is a week full of activities provided to all students to help provide a sense of community and introduce new students to college life. Each floor of the dorms has a resident assistant who helps make sure that the transition into college life is made easy.

Alumnus/a, 8/2000-5/2004, January 2006

There is plenty of on-campus housing very close to the school. The campus has been improved dramatically in the last four years as far aesthetics. The university has built many new buildings, including a fantastic recreational facility. Denton offers very cheap food and apartments and is a safe town. It is also a small town and manageable.

Current student, 8/2003-Submit Date, July 2004

Quality of life is excellent on and around campus. Housing is simple and high quality. There are plenty of places to go for amusement on campus and in the surrounding areas. The people are always nice and crime is minimal. There are plenty of people to meet and plenty of events at which to meet them. One only needs to attend different school functions to become involved with the community and its people.

Last year, I attended school Monday through Friday, and worked in my hometown during the weekends. I found myself more anxious to get back to school than I was to go home for the weekend despite home cooked meals and free laundry. The University of North Texas is a very desirable place to be.

Read all of Vault's College Surveys at **www.vault.com/college**—get complete surveys on 100s of colleges and universities, expert advice on applicaton essays and more.

VAULT CAREER LIBRARY   **713**

Social Life

Alumnus/a, Computer Science, 8/2002-8/2006, May 2007

UNT is right next to the famous Fry Street, which is famous for its bars and nightlife. Denton is part of the dry county system, so bars close at 2 a.m. But the place is alive until late most nights and can get pretty crazy during the weekends. The restaurants here are popular for their cheap food—you can get huge Texas size burgers and a basket of fries for around $3 to $5. The Tomato's are famous for their pizzas. Gotta' try 'em. There's also Subway and Jack in the Box in the area. Lots of choices. Two local Italian places are very popular and there is also a very popular bubble tea place.

There are plenty of student organizations and club. My personal fav was World Echoes, an organization that catered to international students and locals. They used to organize trips to Dallas, which was a rare treat for those of us with no mode of transport. There are also a lot of activities every semester for students to get involved. The International Student Week is very popular.

Alumnus/a, Social Work, 8/1999-8/2004, February 2007

Denton is a wonderful community. The town is known for its amazing music and there are many different social activities available. They have several different types of coffee shops that provide music on some nights and school clubs on other nights. There is a local pizza parlor that has excellent food and is located next to the campus. The campus is surrounded by various restaurants, local eclectic stores and a wonderful ambiance. The school provides a paper that assists with finding housing and provides information on local activities. The school also shows movies on specific nights and has various clubs to join. There is also a new health facility, which is provided to all students free of charge. This facility has an inside track, a pool, wall climbing and offers several classes. The school has on-campus police and there are phones located all over campus to contact police in case of an emergency. The town is very safe and there always seems to be people around due to the location of the school. Fry Street is located on the edge of campus and has various bars, restaurants and a coffee shop that is well known for its excellent food and low prices.

Current student, 9/2004-Submit Date, January 2007

UNT is in the middle of a relatively small city, Denton. Within walking distance of campus are several restaurants, shops, bars and coffee shops, dry cleaners and any other necessary business. I was surprised at how I fell in love with living here almost immediately. I did not expect to enjoy such a small town, but I love it here. Most people I have met who did not grow up in Denton feel the same way. Dating at UNT is fun and interesting and because there is such a great variety of activities, students have the opportunity to meet people with similar interests while doing things they both love. There are many clubs on campus, including sports, academics, community service, religious, spiritual, political and other special interest groups. Also popular are Greek councils, fraternities and sororities. These organizations are great ways to make friends who are into similar things and to make the changes we would like to see on campus and in the world.

Alumnus/a, 8/2000-5/2004, January 2006

There are plenty of bars on Fry Street within walking distance of campus. Denton offers a lively music scene, and good cheap ethnic restaurants such as Thai, Korean, Greek, Japanese, Chinese and Middle Eastern cuisine. There are plenty of sororities and fraternities, if that is what you are looking for. The Green House is a popular place on Mondays and Thursdays because of great jazz music and cheap drinks. Haley's is a new club and rated the best in the Metroplex. There are theme nights and a big dance floor and excellent sound system. There are numerous shows from DJs to hip hop, or Indie music at Haley's

 ## The School Says

The University of North Texas is a student-centered public research university and is the flagship of the UNT System.

One of the largest universities in Texas with 34,000 students, UNT is located in the fast-growing Dallas-Fort Worth region, the fifth largest metropolitan area in the United States. It continues to increase in enrollment despite higher admission standards. A state-of-the-art student health and wellness center opened in January 2007 and two new residence halls—one just for students in the Honors College—opened in Fall 2007. A life sciences building and a new business building are being planned.

UNT offers many nationally and internationally recognized programs:

- 96 bachelor's degree programs
- 111 master's degree programs
- 50 doctoral degree programs

In 2007, UNT was one of only seven U.S. universities with the maximum number of Goldwater Scholarships in math and science.

Founded in 1890, UNT takes pride in its outstanding faculty, high academic standards and diverse student body. Offering a traditional college experience at an affordable cost, UNT boasts a 19:1 student-faculty ratio and Division 1-A athletics.

UNT's library system, with 5.9 million cataloged holdings in five libraries, is designated a major research library by the U.S. Department of Education.

UNT takes pride in its outstanding faculty that includes many professors who are widely known as experts in their fields.

The university has many programs that have been recognized around the world—for example, the philosophy department's program in environmental ethics; the jazz studies program, which is the first of its kind in the nation; and the psychology department's Center for Collaborative Organizations. Nationally ranked programs include public administration, counseling, music, art, and library and information sciences.

In nearly every field of study, students get hands-on experience by participating in internships through UNT's accredited cooperative education program. UNT prepares its graduates for today's technology-oriented workplace by providing more computers per student than any public university in the region.

UNT's eCampus has the largest online enrollment in Texas and includes distance learning through web-based courses and videoconferencing.

The university provides abundant opportunities for students to discover the power of ideas. For more information, go to www.unt.edu/yourfuture.

University of Texas at Austin

Office of Admissions
The University of Texas at Austin
P.O. Box 8058
Austin, TX 78713-8058
Admissions phone: (512) 475-7399
Admissions fax: (512) 475-7478
Admissions URL: www.utexas.edu/prospective/

 Admissions

Current student, Biology, 6/2004-Submit Date, June 2007

The admissions process is a typical application with two personal essays. Essays are important insights into the qualities of a student beyond his/her academic abilities. My advice is having the strongest personal essay possible and strong letters of recommendation. There was not an interview process for UT. Selectivity depends on your desired major; some degree options are harder to get into due to the number of students applying for that degree. For example, if you are interested in biology, you many not want to apply for the Human Biology option because this is a very popular yet misleading degree options for incoming freshmen. Instead apply under Cellular and Molecular Biology, to which however students initially apply. You can always change you major once you are at a university.

> **The school says:** "Undergraduate applicants no longer apply to specific major options in the College of Natural Sciences. All applicants interested in a biology major apply simply to Biology and select an option at some point after enrolling."

Also, Texas currently uses a policy where students graduating in the top 10 percent of their high school class are guaranteed admittance to a Texas public university.

> **UT Austin says:** "Top 10 percent automatic admission guarantees admission only to graduates of Texas high schools."

Current student, Health, 8/2003-Submit Date, June 2007

In order to get into the University of Texas, one must fill out the Texas Common Application found at www.utexas.edu. While applying for admittance, prospective students are also advised to fill out a preference for student housing that will be entered into a lottery, applications for financial aid, and any honors programs in which they may be interested. Certain scholarships, grants and honors programs require interviews, essays and letters of recommendation, but the university only requires that the Texas Common Application is completely filled out.

> **The school says:** "The Texas Common Application is now officially known as the ApplyTexas Application."

Alumnus/a, History, 8/2003-5/2007, June 2007

I recommend that prospective students fill out the application for scholarships. The student will need to submit the application to the university in the fall (rather than the last deadline in the spring) for this option, but it is worth it if s/he gets a scholarship. The application process is not difficult, but right now the majority of students is admitted under Texas' top 10 percent law. There are no interviews.

Current student, Cultural Studies, 1/2006-Submit Date, May 2007

Admission to UT, like all Texas schools, begins with applying online at applytexas.org. It is a straightforward application that takes you step by step through the process. If you have graduated in the top 10 percent of a Texas high school, then you get automatic acceptance right after high school graduation. For everyone else, getting in is a more competitive ordeal; however, it is not impossible.

Just make sure that you have good grades as a high school student or as a transfer student. As a transfer student, you will need to have a cumulative GPA of around 3.4 to make it; this varies slightly depending on the college to which you are applying, but is a good guideline to go by. Once you've applied, you get assigned an Electronic ID (called an EID) and password to get into the UT web site. From there you can monitor your application status and see if you got in or not. If you have any questions, I have found that calling admissions is very helpful.

Alumnus/a, Liberal Arts, 1/2004-5/2007, May 2007

The undergraduate admissions process for UT-Austin was relatively straightforward and expedient: submit application (including short essay and all supporting documents) and receive response in timely manner. Selectivity for admissions depends upon the college (department). Architecture, engineering, psychology, pharmacy and law are quite selective; other programs do not seem to be quite so much (though it's not a breeze to get in, either, as UT is a good school in general).

> **The school says:** "Some of the most selective undergraduate programs are omitted from the list, such as business, communications, kinesiology, Plan II, and nursing."

GPA and test scores are probably the most important factors for undergraduates trying to get in.

Current student, Cultural Studies, 6/2006-Submit Date, May 2007

In-state students use the [ApplyTexas Application] found at www.applytexas.org. The application is fairly simple and straightforward. Students need all relevant information, such as GPA and activities. Admissions rate is about 50 percent, with all in-state students in the top 10 percent automatically accepted. No interview is needed. It is good to have a couple very strong points in your profile in areas such as senior year schedule, GPA, AP classes taken and passed, extracurricular clubs and such. I was not in the top 10 percent and feel that I was accepted because of a Sister Cities International Cultural Exchange trip as well as six years in Boy Scouts, a solid GPA and a strong senior year schedule.

> **UT Austin says:** "AP classes are not required and do not affect admission decisions."

Current student, Liberal Arts, 8/2004-Submit Date, May 2007

I was admitted through the top 10 percent rule. All I had to do was maintain my rank in high school, fill out the [ApplyTexas Application], and send in a transcript. There were no interviews, but I had to write two essays for the McCombs business school, which usually only admits top three percent. (They admit top 1 percent, then top 2 percent and so on.)

Current student, Music, 9/2004-Submit Date, November 2006

The applications process started with the [ApplyTexas Application], which is a standard for public colleges and universities in Texas. The application process was fairly long, but could be applied to multiple colleges, which saved time in the end. Each college has different essays required for admission, which could also be submitted through the [ApplyTexas Application]. Essays included writing about how you could contribute to campus, meaningful life events, and goals for your college career.

I went through an audition process to gain entry into the School of Music. This is done through the playing of solos and other excerpts of music, which demonstrate ability. Selection was very exclusive, as I was one of a very small number of incoming freshmen. For entrance into the School of Natural Science, I really only needed to express interest and declare a major. Hundreds get into the college with no problems.

Read all of Vault's College Surveys at **www.vault.com/college**—get complete surveys on 100s of colleges and universities, expert advice on applicaton essays and more.

VAULT CAREER LIBRARY 715

Academics

Current student, Health, 8/2003-Submit Date, June 2007

The classes offered at the University of Texas are of a rigorous nature and assume that three hours will be dedicated to studying outside of class for every hour that is spent in class. Popular classes often require persistence on the parts of the students trying to register. Grading is typically done by TAs in large classes, with the criteria determined by the professor; but the grading in classes with less students enrolled may be accomplished by the professors themselves. The professors generally have high expectations, but can be very understanding when warranted, and the workloads are usually on the heavy side.

Current student, Biology, 8/2005-Submit Date, June 2007

My first year here I mostly took large introductory classes with 500 other students. It wasn't the best experience. Once you get into your upper-division classes, it dies down to about 40 or less. I felt much more comfortable as I progressed into my major.

Current student, 8/2005-Submit Date, June 2007

At UT, it is difficult to get into popular classes. The registration process is almost a competition. In order to get the best professors, you have to stay on top of the add/drop period, constantly refreshing the page to see if anyone has dropped the class so that you may add it. Because there are so many professors for each class, the research process of finding the best professor is time consuming. Also, because many classes are offered at many times, it also is time consuming just figuring out your class schedule in general. The classes themselves are always beneficial. You leave the class at the end of the semester always learning something. The workload is usually average. In writing classes, math, science and engineering classes, there is naturally a higher workload.

Current student, Communications, 8/2006-Submit Date, June 2007

I happen to be one of the lucky ones. I was accepted into the Gateway Program in which I get to register with the upperclassmen and I'm guaranteed the classes I want! My classes tend to be smaller than other classes because the program is for small town kids to adapt to a bigger place and still feel like they can get the one-on-one time with professors. I would say the grading is fair. The professors let you know how it's going to be the first day of class, so if you have any issues with it you can address it then. I happen to like the professors I had except one. As far as the workload, it just depends on the professor you get, but UT is just as big on academics as it is on sports, so be prepared to study. (Don't worry, there's still time to party on Sixth Street!)

Alumnus/a, History, 8/2003-5/2007, June 2007

Like most large state institutions, the quality of classes varies greatly. I participated in the Liberal Arts Honors Program; the professors who teach in this program are generally very good and the classes are interesting. The workload in these classes is moderate to extensive, but the students are usually more committed, so the environment is more conducive to learning. I really enjoyed these classes and recommend any of UT's many honors programs. For general classes, one can look up the course instructor surveys for professors who have taught before. Many students also look at Pick-A-Prof to see grade distributions. There are many excellent professors at UT who care about their students and try to make their classes educationally valuable. I never really had trouble getting the classes I wanted, but registration times are determined by the number of hours a student has.

Alumnus/a, Cultural Studies, 6/2002-12/2006, May 2007

Academics at UT are what you make of them. If you are committed to searching out the best classes and teachers, you will more than likely be able to take these courses at some point in your university career. The same applies to special programs such as Liberal Arts Honors, Departmental Honors, Longhorn Scholars, Texas Interdisciplinary Plan, and Connexus. While it is true that as a freshman it is hard to get the exact class schedule that you desire, the fact that most freshman classes number in the 100s means that you will be able to find a spot in one of the sections. As your seniority increases, it becomes much easier to register for the classes that you want. A piece of advice that I always give to incoming students is that if you are choosing between a large major, such as economics, and a smaller major, such as Asian studies, choose the smaller major; you will get more attention and will definitely have a better experience. Even if you choose the larger major, make sure to carve out a space for yourself. Visit

your advisor, talk to your professors, try to take classes with common themes professors. At UT you can sail through without working very hard, but this a means that you will sail through without anyone every taking notice of you. a school as large as UT, you make what you will of the school and you can eit get a great education for your money or get lost in the shuffle. Assertive a driven students do best at a university such as UT.

Alumnus/a, Pre-med, 8/2003-5/2007, May 2007

I was a student in the College of Liberal Arts, as a Spanish major and Plan major (UT specific program). I was also a pre-med student, and these clas were part of the College of Natural Sciences. All my science classes were r orous and well-organized. Usually only the top 20 to 25 percent get A's, but fluctuates some. These classes are also very large. Liberal arts classes, wh are much, much smaller, are usually not as difficult or require as much work. many cases, the areas in Liberal Arts offer honors programs that include gra ate level professors and more demanding classes. Plan II Honors is one s program.

Employment Prospects

Current student, Communications, 1/2003-Submit Date, June 20

UT has a great reputation, in and out of Texas, for its graduating students a their ability to compete in the work force. The alumni center is huge, and c give you connections all over the world. There are recruiting fairs for every c lege within UT. They couldn't be a more helpful organization in that ser Where UT lacks in personal attention, it makes up for it in quantity of job fa advisors and recruiting outlets.

Current student, Biology, 6/2004-Submit Date, June 2007

Most students who graduate with a BS in Biology do not immediately purs employment but instead continue their education either in graduate school medical school. However, during your undergraduate career there are am opportunities to seek part-time employment through the university or at lo business. Students who do attempt to find jobs immediately after graduat usually seek laboratory technician positions at the university or nearby ind tries.

Current student, Health, 8/2003-Submit Date, June 2007

The alumni association on campus, called the Texas Exes, is active in checki up on alumni and pressing them for donations in order to fund scholarshi Camp Texas for freshmen and opportunities to network with possible futu employers. Each college has a Career Services Department offering stude information on employment prospects for their respective fields. Each colle also organizes biannual career fairs where companies looking for recent colle grads have the opportunity to recruit. Large corporations often set up inform tional booths on campus and recruit sporadically throughout the academic ye Internships are also available in certain departments.

Current student, 8/2005-Submit Date, June 2007

The UT career services department does a great job. There are many da throughout the semester when fairs are held for job recruiters to come and app to the students. I know specifically through the McCombs School of Busine the students who graduate are always receiving high offers from well-kno companies. Once again, the career services centers do a great job in helping s dents get internships. No student is usually disappointed with their internsh which they gained with the help of the UT career services.

Alumnus/a, Liberal Arts, 1/2004-5/2007, May 2007

The undergraduate advisor is fantastic, forwarding dozens of job opportunit on a weekly basis and keeping students up-to-date with internship and recruit information. The liberal arts college at UT is also really good at getting stude involved with job fairs on campus, recruiting efforts, career counseling and on.

Quality of Life

Current student, Physical Sciences, 6/2006-Submit Date, May 2007

The campus is equipped with numerous libraries of substantial quality and size, and there's nothing more exciting than stumbling randomly across a library nestled away into a building. There are numerous places where students can access the Internet, and most outdoor areas of campus have wireless connections for those sunny days when you just want to be outside.

Current student, Biology, 6/2004-Submit Date, June 2007

If you want to live in a dorm, there are a few from which to choose, including the most expensive at San Jacinto (you and your roommate share a bathroom) or the more budget-friendly Jester, which is more community oriented. There are three major dining halls for students and many surrounding business off campus take BEVO-Bucks, a method of payment that is provided by the Division of Housing and food meal plan if you are living in a dorm. UT is unique because there are many academic and research resources on campus. There are multiple libraries and museums and study areas.

Current student, Biology, 8/2005-Submit Date, June 2007

I live off campus like most other students and it is great! UT does an excellent job in providing transportation for off-campus students. There is a bus for every area surrounding campus. I live off Riverside, and there are at least five different bus lines that pick students up and take them straight to campus. The rent is cheap and the neighborhood is very safe because everywhere you look there are students just like you.

Current student, Health, 8/2003-Submit Date, June 2007

UT offers a variety of housing options. The campus is pretty and big with lots of trees and squirrels. Facilities are nice and state-of-the-art (for the most part). Dining is OK, offering both fast food and sit down services. Nearby neighborhoods are nice, but costly to live in. Crime is minimal and UT has emergency call buttons set up to alert campus police of any unscrupulous activity. I feel safe walking alone on campus, both night and day.

Alumnus/a, Communications, 8/2003-5/2007, June 2007

Housing opportunities are plentiful around the campus area, but the prices are way-high now that giant apartment complexes are taking over west campus. There is a severe lack of parking now due to all the construction. If you walk around west campus long enough, you'll have a thin coat of dust all over yourself. This severely hinders the quality of life directly surrounding campus. Other than that, in the Hyde Park area, the quality of life is fantastic. Everything is lush and green and quiet. You really get a sense of community living outside the busy campus-centric areas of Austin. We have had some crime issues, but mainly it's been public intoxication and alcohol related due to the number of frat parties that go on.

Alumnus/a, Liberal Arts, 1/2004-5/2007, May 2007

Austin is a great college town and there are lots of things to do, in and around campus. Excellent nightlife with amazing live music, hundreds of amazing restaurants and coffee shops, lots of outdoor activities, lots of cultural and fine arts resources. That being said, it's a large campus with lots of students. Housing on campus seems limited (I never stayed in a UT dorm, but this is what I've seen and heard), and housing off campus is either nice but expensive or cheap but rundown. If you're willing to live outside of a five to seven mile radius of campus, apartments become much more plentiful land affordable. One thing to note is that there aren't any major grocery stores within walking distance of main campus. You have to take a bus to access one. The campus itself is nice, large and spread out, but nice. Good recreational facilities, lots of bike racks, lots of restaurants and museums and walkable neighborhoods off the main campus.

Social Life

Current student, Cultural Studies, 1/2006-Submit Date, May 2007

The City of Austin is renowned for its live music scene. It has a small town feel with a plethora of mom-and-pop stores. Not to mention it is the capital, so it has its fair share of political drama. It is a happening town and the locals (and students) love it.

Current student, Biology, 6/2004-Submit Date, June 2007

The University of Texas campus has a large, student-oriented social structure. If you want to go work out, stop by the three-story Gregory Gym or the Rec Center. If you want to catch a movie (sometimes even special previews) try the Dobie Theater. If you want to join a club or be part of a Greek society, there is plenty of opportunity to join whether your interest be in research (SYNAPSE and SURGE), drama (Theater Guild), or even the AnimeClub. But the most important part of the UT social life is the close interaction with the City of Austin. The surrounding City of Austin prides itself on providing numerous sources of social entertainment. Live music is a popular pastime for the city and can be found at restaurants, bars and frequent festivals. Austin's popular party attraction is Sixth Steet, which is the home to clubs, bars including Coyote Ugly, and restaurants. Austin also interacts closely with local businesses and local farmers and has a Farmer's Market every Saturday. Austin is also health oriented with cancer support groups including Lance Armstrong's Cancer Foundation and year-round marathons and walks to create awareness for other diseases and disorders. Another quality of Austin is its outdoor hiking and biking trails and parks. An individual can take a early morning run around the four-mile Town Lake trail or a group can enjoy an afternoon at Zilker Park or canoeing. The capital city has so many places to see including museums, theaters and many more activities.

Current student, Health, 8/2003-Submit Date, June 2007

Austin offers many bars that are targeted at college students (namely Sixth Street) as well as more upscale bars for graduate students and young professionals (Fourth and Fifth streets and the warehouse district). Coffeehouses are all over the place, and a popular study cafe is Spider House, which offers I like beer and wet t-shirt contests with a laidback environment, great coffee, indoor and outdoor seating, cool music and great people-watching. Austin has a variety of restaurants that'll suit any palate.

Current student, Communications, 1/2003-Submit Date, June 2007

The school's social scene is what makes UT the best. The Greek life is huge. Sixth Street is huge. Mexican food is amazing. With over 50,000 students there are always new people to meet, date and be friends with. Trudy´s on Thursday night. Hula Hut on Friday evening. Float the River on Saturday. Pick up a breakfast taco in any taco shack East of 35 on Sunday and head toward South Congress for lunch and shopping. Best life you could ever imagine.

The School Says

The University of Texas at Austin is one of the world's leading public research universities and one of the largest universities in the United States. Founded in 1883, the university has a 350-acre main campus in the Texas state capital with 21,000 faculty and staff, 16 colleges and schools and almost 50,000 students.

The university's reach goes far beyond the borders of the main campus with satellite campuses and research centers across Texas, including the J.J. Pickle Research Campus, the Marine Science Institute, the McDonald Observatory, the Montopolis Research Center and the Brackenridge tract.

With an enrollment of 11,000 students and more than 3,500 master's and doctor's degrees awarded annually, the Graduate School is a national leader in graduate degrees awarded and one of the largest graduate schools in the nation.

The university's renowned faculty, which includes Nobel and Pulitzer prize winners, annually generates more than $400 million in research funding. Through its research and its commitment to entrepreneurship, The University of Texas at Austin is a major catalyst for economic development in Texas.

The university's major academic units include nationally noted colleges of Communication, Education, Engineering, Fine Arts,

Read all of Vault's College Surveys at **www.vault.com/college**—get complete surveys on 100s of colleges and universities, expert advice on applicaton essays and more.

VAULT CAREER LIBRARY   **717**

Liberal Arts, Natural Sciences and Pharmacy and schools of Architecture, Business, Geosciences, Information, Law, Nursing, Public Affairs and Social Work. More than 8,700 bachelor's degrees are awarded annually in more than 170 fields of study and 100 majors.

Few universities can match the vast collection of artifacts, art, manuscripts, photographs, musical recordings and historical documents housed on the university's campus in the Ransom Center, the Blanton Museum of Art, the Center for American History, the Lyndon B. Johnson Library and Museum, and the Texas Memorial Museum

The university has one of the most diverse student populations in the country and is a national leader in the number of undergraduate degrees awarded to minority students.

For more information about The University of Texas at Austin visit www.utexas.edu/.

Brigham Young University

YU Admissions Office
153 ASB
ovo, UT 84602
dmissions phone: (801) 422-2507
dmissions fax: (801) 422-0005
dmissions e-mail: admissions@byu.edu
dmissions URL: saas.byu.edu/depts/admissions/

 Admissions

urrent student, 9/2003-Submit Date, September 2005

YU requires high standardized test scores, very well-written essays and com-
unity services from its applicants. The form is standard compared to other uni-
rsities across the nation. There are about three essays that you have to write
300 words or less. The topics include leadership, community service and
urch service (BYU is a private university under The Church of Jesus Christ of
tter-day Saints). Students must display that they have been active in their reli-
on and community in order to enhance their ability to get accepted into the uni-
rsity.

> **The school says:** "Essay requirements may change from year to
> year. For the current admissions application, one essay is
> required."

lumnus/a, 9/1999-9/2003, May 2006

ey needed my SAT/ACT scores, letters of recommendation and a few essays.
n not sure how much they look at the essays, but basically if you have good
ores on your SATs, you are in! One of my friends had terrible grades in high
hool, but did very well on his SATs. He was admitted very easily. It is much
sier to get into BYU if you are part of a minority.

> **The school says:** "BYU implements a holistic review of the appli-
> cation when making admissions decisions. As such, the essay
> is an integral part of the admissions review. Good grades and
> a high ACT/SAT score are advantageous, but do not guarantee
> admission. Additionally, multicultural students are reviewed
> with the same holistic philosophy as every other student."

urrent student, 8/2004-Submit Date, January 2006

pplied online. I was not required to write any essays, except for a short essay
about 300 words. The admissions process itself is quite simple, but it is chal-
nging to get into this school. The process is so easy because many students
ply from all over the country. It would be unreasonable and difficult if inter-
ews were required. Many fewer students would come if it were necessary to
 out to Utah to be interviewed.

is a wonderful school. Advice I would give on getting into this university
uld be to have as many extracurriculars as possible without appearing too
sy—BYU values the family relationship. You don't want to appear as if you
ent all of your time away from home. Also, do your best to keep your grades
gh, and work hard to get a good ACT/SAT score.

lumnus/a, 9/1995-12/2001, April 2005

e admissions process at BYU is fairly rigorous as it requires you not only to
ve an account of your academic and extracurricular activities but also of your
iritual ones. In addition to the basic information on your application, you will
ed to submit essays and an ecclesiastical endorsement from your bishop if you
 a member of the Church of Jesus Christ of Latter-day Saints. Even if you are
t a member of the Church, you will be required to commit to the Honor Code
at includes standards set by the Church of personal morality about dating, liv-
g conditions (no boy/girl roommates), the basic morals of honesty and mod-
ty in dress, and refraining from alcohol and drugs.

There are no interviews apart from the one with your ecclesiastical leader, so I
suggest you really try to show the admissions office who you are through your
essays. That is where your voice will be heard. They like hearing about life lessons you have learned or poignant experiences that have effected your person.
They respond best to sincerity. You will need high ACT scores as well as a good
GPA and a variety of extracurricular activities. Community service is also very
highly valued in your application.

Alumnus/a, 8/2000-8/2004, May 2005

BYU is selective, but not in the ordinary ways. BYU requires more in the area
of moral fiber for admission. This is the subject of the essays that are required.
There are no interviews for admission, though they are required for the best
scholarships.

> **BYU states:** "All applicants must have ecclesiastical inter-
> views."

Current student, 9/2000-Submit Date, March 2005

BYU uses the ACT as their standard test, so I took that when I was a high school
junior and received a 27. I had about a 3.5 GPA from high school when I
applied, which is just good enough with the 27 on the ACT. I play the cello, so
I auditioned for the music department and ended up getting a $1,000 a semester
musical performance scholarship, which was great and hard to get. It is quite
difficult to get an academic scholarship. For the music department, I also had to
take an easy test to show my simple musical knowledge. I was definitely helped
by my musical skills.

> **The school says:** "BYU uses either the ACT or the SAT exam.
> No preference is given to either exam."

Current student, 9/2001-Submit Date, April 2004

BYU requires an interview by an ecclesiastical leader before entrance. The
school has one of the most extensive Honor Codes out there, so you must agree
to adhere to all of the rules therein. You do not have to be of the official religion, but it's easier to abide by the code if you are, because it's something you're
used to. You have to fill out an application, which includes a section about your
past school experience, an essay (that changes every year), and the question,
"Why do you want to come to BYU?" Selectivity is pretty competitive. It's not
that everyone in the world wants to go there, it's just that everyone in the world
who's Mormon does.

Current student, 8/2003-Submit Date, May 2004

Entrance is based primarily on ACT scores, GPA and AP classes. Foreign students also have a good chance of acceptance. Extracurricular activities and
accomplishments are not weighted as heavily as at most other schools. The best
way to secure admission is to score over 20 on the ACT and maintain a high
school GPA of 3.8 or higher with a heavy sampling of AP classes. Students at
schools that don't offer AP classes are at a disadvantage, I would say an unfair
disadvantage. My school did not offer AP classes but had several college-level
advanced classes. Because they were not AP, they were not weighted in my
favor.

The application essays are the only real opportunity you have to sell yourself to
the admissions office. I don't think they are used unless there is a tie in academic
statistics, because of the automated system. I think interviews and a heavier
reliance on essays would be a huge improvement for BYU's admissions process.
However, because of the number of applicants, BYU feels this is impractical.

> **Brigham Young University states:** "In the evaluation of new
> freshman applicants, the GPA and ACT each count for approxi-
> mately one-third of the overall review. Extracurricular activities,
> special talents, leadership and other subjective factors count for
> the remaining one-third of the evaluation. While the number of
> AP courses a student takes is considered, grades are not
> weighted. While foreign students are welcome to apply, they
> receive no special consideration in the admissions process. The

Read all of Vault's College Surveys at **www.vault.com/college**—get complete surveys on 100s of colleges and universities, expert advice on applicaton essays and more.

VAULT CAREER LIBRARY **719**

average GPA for new freshmen entering fall 2004 is approximately 3.7. The average ACT for these same students is approximately 27."

Academics

Current student, Independent, 6/2003-Submit Date, June 2007

The school is highly academic and challenging. There were few, if any classes I took that were not challenging in some way and with few exceptions the professors were excellent. Many classes were so large that it was difficult to get the attention needed, so speak up and don't be afraid to contact the professors personally after class for help or work with the assistants. I was in a language program for one of the most difficult languages. As a result, classes in my major were small and were not as difficult.

Alumnus/a, 6/1999-4/2005, January 2006

I studied philosophy, which if you're looking for something like that, BYU's a great place to be. The professors are excellent and there's a good feeling within the department—something not all philosophy departments have. Classes were varied. I took the standard history of philosophy courses, but also nontraditional courses such as one on J.H. Newman and the Philosophy of Religion (focusing mainly on French Philosophy). There were some classes I didn't like in the major, but for the most part all of them were challenging, but not too challenging. I feel I learned a lot of skills that are turning out to be beneficial.

One thing I did was audit classes. I worked during school, so it was hard to take a huge load and still do well. Still, I wanted to learn things so I audited classes so I could learn, but not fuss over the grade. I'd recommend that to anyone.

The other aspect of BYU is the religion requirement. I had a couple of good classes, but for the most part they were bad. Most of my classes suffered from poor-quality teaching or over-zealous teachers.

Current student, 9/2004-Submit Date, January 2006

I find BYU to be very intense and competitive academically. Every student is highly motivated and more focused on good grades than partying, something you might not find at a non-religious school. Grading is fair, but beware of the sliding scale where A-'s no longer will get you a 4.0. You can use add/drop cards to get into any class you want, if you can't get in by the normal online registration process.

Current student, 9/2003-Submit Date, September 2005

[In the Marriott School of Business,] students must also complete a mentor program in which they actively participate in talking with a BYU alumnus/a who works in the business field. The workload demands a lot of your time as well. The coursework is very structured and specific to your emphasis. The classes are also focused to real-life business world applications and assignments are given to express this. There is a large focus on groupwork, too. The program requires two full semesters of eight classes where you work in the same groups for all of the classes. Teachers assign group, as well as individual projects.

Current student, 8/2004-Submit Date, January 2006

The classes are wonderful and I love almost all of the professors I've had so far. The workload is rather difficult, but not too terrible. The university has been getting increasingly more difficult in the past few years as more and more students have wanted to attend. They have had to make it more difficult and rigorous. It is rather difficult to get into popular classes because there are now over 30,000 students at BYU. Seniors get first choice in classes, then juniors and so on. So, as a freshman, it's very hard to get into popular classes. But on the other hand, when I am a senior, it will definitely be a lot easier!

The classes are a lot of fun, even though they are demanding. Because this is a church school, the professors bring religion into class discussion, which makes the classes more interesting and meaningful, and also adds spiritual depth to our education. There are numerous required religion classes, which have easily become my favorites.

Current student, 9/2000-Submit Date, March 2005

The general education classes at BYU are the toughest. They are almost always large classes with 200 to 400 students per class and divided up into 30 student labs taught by teaching assistants. The classes are very good, the professors [are] very knowledgeable and usually quite likeable but have to be pretty strict ab[out] grading so that they don't get taken advantage of by the class.

The student advisors are great and will answer any questions you have and [do] their best to help you out with any problems.

Current student, 9/2001-Submit Date, April 2004

The classes are pretty good. They are always sure to tie in how the issues fit i[n] the real world. Getting into popular classes is tough if you don't have a lot [of] credit hours under your belt; seniors and juniors are given big-time prior[ity]. Grading is tough as well, especially in certain departments where professors [are] only allowed to give a certain number of A's. At BYU that's hard, because m[ost] people are really focused on school and are there to get good grades, not to g[et] off. The workload is big as well, or so I'm told from friends who have a[lso] attended other universities.

> **The school says:** "At BYU, some faculty choose to grade on curves, but faculty are not given any limit on 'a certain number of A's.'"

Current student, 8/2003-Submit Date, May 2004

Most classes try to offer students as much hands-on experience as possible. T[he] science professors encourage students to participate in internships and resear[ch] projects as well as requiring projects as part of the course curriculum. Oth[er] fields incorporate hands-on learning as much as possible.

Alumnus/a, 1/2000-4/2003, September 2003

Regardless of major, BYU requires all students to take general elective cour[ses] covering a broad range of topics, such as biological, natural and social scienc[e], writing, foreign language or advanced math. The general classes are very lar[ge], some had up to 900 students. However, the large classes have excellent teac[hing] aides. That is, the class is broken into sections that meet weekly to review [the] lecture material. Grades depend on the teacher and the department. E[ach] seemed to grade objectively. I had excellent professors. In big classes, a k[ey] difference for me was to stop by the professor's office during his or her hou[rs]. Workload varies. My first semester I was on campus in classes or studying fr[om] 8 a.m. to 8 p.m. Not that I didn't do my share of talking with friends or surfi[ng], but I needed a lot of hours to do well. My last semester I had classes just th[ree] days and averaged about 30 hours of studying a week.

Employment Prospects

Current student, 9/2004-Submit Date, January 2006

This is a definite selling point to BYU. Many firms come to the two career fa[irs] BYU puts on. BYU uses eRecruiting, which is very easy and helpful. I have [an] interview with a Top 10 consulting firm this coming Thursday, if that's any in[di]cation of BYU's employment prospects.

Alumnus/a, 8/1998-5/2000, January 2006

It's important to be employment-minded all through college, and get as mu[ch] experience as possible through going to job fairs, networking activities a[nd] spending time with your advisor getting advice and leads on how you can be [the] most marketable after you graduate. It's best to spend much of your senior y[ear] lining up a satisfactory job. BYU offers all these resources and has an excelle[nt] counseling and career center, as well as internship opportunities. Many emplo[y]ers are impressed with hearing you are a BYU graduate because they assume y[ou] are clean cut, hard-working and honest, which is an immediate advantage.

Alumnus/a, 9/1987-5/1993, October 2005

My employment prospects were great! The head of the actuarial program h[ad] contacts with the insurers in Utah. The insurers would contact him looking [for] candidates, either for full-time employment or internships. That is how I got [my] first job. He referred me for an interview. The faculty sincerely helps stude[nts] as they try to find employment. They stay in contact with former stude[nts] around the country and help students establish contacts, which are a key part [of] finding employment. I work with or around several students who went thro[ugh] the actuarial program at BYU.

umnus/a, 8/1999-8/2003, October 2005

ere are a lot of aids on campus for finding jobs and job placement post grad-
ion. There is a job board in the administration building and each school
ajor) has other information on finding jobs. A lot of employers see BYU and
nk honesty, so it is a real plus. Graduates get entry-level positions in their
pected fields, and some are given higher positions based on GPA, internships
l experience.

e alumni network was wonderful for me when I graduated. Everyone I spoke
h was more than willing to help, to network with others and encourage me
ough the job hunting process. When I was at BYU, I also took a class specif-
ly designed to help locate internships and evaluate them. I had three intern-
ps my senior year. It gave me a lot of work experience to use when I gradu-
d.

umnus/a, 8/2000-8/2004, May 2005

cepted an offer from Bain & Company out of undergraduate at BYU. First I
s an intern, then I accepted a full-time position. Personally, I turned down
ers from McKinsey & Company, Boston Consulting Group, Monitor Group,
rcer Management Consulting, Mercer HR, Goldman Sachs, JP Morgan
ase, Morgan Stanley and several other companies. I have many friends from
dergraduate who now work at several of those firms, as well as many others
economics consulting (Charles River, LECG). I also have friends who graded from BYU who have gone to work in private equity firms, like KKR, Bain
pital, Golden Gate Capital, Hicks Muse, Sorenson Capital and others. I don't
ieve any doors were not open in fields I considered.

rrent student, 9/2001-Submit Date, April 2004

YU political science program is a good program. There is an internship called
shington Seminar where students go to D.C. for a semester and can intern
h senators, law firms, interest groups or whatever. Employment prospects are
d for BYU students in government, especially law enforcement and intelli-
nce, because BYU students usually pass the background checks, and almost
of them a have a foreign language skill of some kind. The career placement
good as well, as university alumni are networked around the country, espe-
ly in Utah, Southern California, Arizona and Washington, D.C.

Quality of Life

umnus/a, 6/1999-12/2004, April 2006

e best thing about BYU is the Honor Code. The rules are in place to provide
lean and safe atmosphere. There are good people who attend BYU. I would
ommend on-campus housing for all incoming freshmen. It is great because
u become friends with first-time college students. On-campus housing is also
e because of the proximity to campus—it is very close.

e dining program for on-campus housing is also great, and I think good for
shmen so that they can focus on their studies rather than cooking. When
u're a sophomore, off-campus housing is great. There are several options
und and most are also pretty close to campus. Provo is very student-friend-
Crime is minimal, but it is important to be watchful and careful just as you
uld anywhere else!

rrent student, 8/2004-Submit Date, January 2006

mpus is beautiful and kept immaculately clean and lovely. On-campus hous-
g is nice, but I definitely wouldn't want to stay on campus more than one year.
ovo is a very safe city with a lot of fun things to do. Most residents of this
ea are Mormons, which contributes to a friendly and welcoming atmosphere.
is is a beautiful area with a lot of friendly people. My only complaint would
that people can be too trusting of each other—not locking your door when
u leave is never a good idea.

rrent student, 9/2003-Submit Date, November 2005

u must sign and live the Honor Code in order to go to BYU. The Honor Code
cludes rules such as dressing modestly, being moral, abstaining from drugs,
cohol and coffee, living the law of chastity, being honest and so on. Housing
les state that members of the opposite sex must live in separate buildings, and
nnot go past the living room and kitchen into the other bedrooms. Also, mem-
rs of the opposite sex must be out of the apartment by 12 a.m. Facilities are

beautiful and of the finest quality. Crime is fairly low compared to other places,
but it still exists.

Current student, 9/2000-Submit Date, March 2005

Depending on the kind of person you are, BYU will either be perfect or a difficult place to go to school because of the rules of the school, which are very strict
compared to most higher education institutions. There is no drinking, no smoking and no sex allowed unless you are married. There are also grooming and
dress standards that are pretty easy to follow. These rules will either work great
for you or could be very annoying if misunderstood.

Current student, 1/2003-Submit Date, March 2005

This is a great town with good people. There are always activities going on on
campus because there is not a lot to do in the town. They have lots of intramural sports. There is a lot of really nice housing and it is very affordable. Most
of the time it is with six other people, but the apartments are huge and you get
your own room. The campus is the nicest one that I have ever seen and most of
the buildings are brand new. It is not that big, either and so you can walk just
about anywhere.

Social Life

Current student, Independent, 6/2003-Submit Date, June 2007

The social life here can be amazing. There are so many beautiful people here.
Lots of social activities and clubs on and off campus, dances are to be found on
campus almost every weekend with attendance from the hundreds to thousands.
Lots of people date and marry very young here, so always watch for rings before
you make your move; many students marry from 18 to their early 20s, so don't
let it catch you off guard. Cheap eats abound in Utah county and nicer establishments and nightclubs can be found in Salt Lake City, less than an hour's
drive away. Chain restaurants abound and there are more international choices
in the small but cute Downtown Provo at State and Center Street, but for the
most part it's just hometown American and Mexican restaurants. Some will
frown if you go out to nightclubs even just to dance because drugs, drinking, pre-
marital sex, wearing any kind of revealing clothing (we're talking tank tops and
shorts shorter than the knees) [are not allowed].

Alumnus/a, 6/1999-12/2004, April 2006

The social life in Provo is the best! BYU offers so many free activities for students. You should never be bored in Provo! The athletic events are always fun!
I recommend buying an all-sports pass at the beginning of the semester. This
gives you tickets to every home football game, and gives you a pass into every
sporting event at BYU, all for the one-time fee for the sports pass. It is worth it,
and so much fun!

Current student, 9/2003-Submit Date, November 2005

There are no bars; it is against the Honor Code to drink and doing so [is prohib-
ited]. The school holds a devotional every Tuesday afternoon in the Marriott
Center. The whole school shuts down for the devotional. Most stores and dining places on campus close around 6 p.m. Most people prefer to go on group
dates and activities. They include creative and fun activities as well as the usual:
bowling, hiking the Y, movies, eating out, playing sports, concerts, comedy
clubs, going to the nutty putty caves, taking weekend trips to St. George, Vegas
or Moab.

One unique thing about BYU is that about half (or more) of the student body is
married. Also, a lot of these married individuals have children already while
they are attending school. It is not uncommon to have a mother bring her baby
to class.

The school says: "The married students comprise about 25 percent of the student body. A parent bringing his/her baby to
class is rare, although it does happen."

The school has various clubs and organizations, however sororities are not
allowed. The clubs range from karate to swing dance, to Spanish.

Read all of Vault's College Surveys at www.vault.com/college—get complete surveys on 100s of colleges and universities, expert advice on applicaton essays and more.

VAULT CAREER LIBRARY   721

Current student, 8/2004-Submit Date, January 2006

The dating scene at BYU has a reputation for being incredibly lively. Some places that people love to go on dates are to Movies 8, and restaurants like Fat Cats, Tucano's, Fazoli's and Cold Stone. The social life here is unbelievable—I went on dates almost every weekend last semester. BYU is famous for students getting married unusually often, but that's part of the fun! My roommates is getting proposed to right now, probably is already engaged. Not that marriage should be taken lightly, not at all, I'm just saying that the dating is one of the best parts of BYU.

Alumnus/a, 8/2000-8/2004, May 2005

Since BYU students don't consume alcohol, bars are pretty much a non-issue. Restaurants abound, as the dating scene at BYU may well be the most active in America. Most people go on at least one date a week, with more than that being quite common. The university has many events with which many students are always involved. These include Spring Fling and a fall event that is similar. During these events the campus is opened with free food, events and recognizable bands. They are always well-attended. The dances are also well-attended, though more so by freshmen.

Students are forever getting into groups to go into the mountains and canyons to go sledding, make fires, go skiing (slopes are 20 minutes away at the closest), or just hang out together. The atmosphere is amazingly accepting. You can really just strike up a conversation with anyone on campus, and it's acceptable, expect-

ed, and nothing out of the ordinary. People help each other out when there need that's observed. This includes academic needs, emotional needs, or just occasional apartment-to-apartment move.

Alumnus/a, 9/1995-12/2001, April 2005

There are no official fraternities or sororities at BYU, though there are a clubs that resemble the Greek organizations. Most of the social life happen on-campus dances, comedy routines, and other activities as well as at which er student "ward" (students are grouped by where they live into congregati called wards) you are in. Wards not only make up sunday meetings but a come together for smaller group activities every Monday night like bowling some kind of game, BBQs, hikes and dances.

Students especially enjoy what the outdoors has to offer in Utah. Some of best skiing in the world is no more than an hour away with the closest be within 20 minutes. You can use the Olympic ice skating rink or other Olym facilities. Or you can just visit Park City where the Sundance Film Festival ta place. It offers great shopping, outlets and a picturesque small mountain to feel, as well as Deer Valley, one of the most exclusive ski resorts in the wo For those who prefer the warmer weather, many students go south to Moab mountain bike or camp in Zion's National Park. And of course, many stude drive to Vegas occasionally (it's about a six-hour drive from Provo) for the we end. You never run out of things to do between the on-campus social life and outdoor opportunities all around you.

The University of Utah

Admissions Office
201 S 1460 E
Rm. 250 S
Salt Lake City, UT 84112-9057
Admissions phone: (801) 581-7281
Admissions e-mail: admissions@sa.utah.edu
Admissions URL: www.sa.utah.edu/admiss/

 Admissions

Current student, 9/2001-Submit Date, February 2007

The admissions process was very straightforward. The school I transferred from helped me with most of the work. Being a transfer student, I did not have to have an interview. They just went by test scores and GPA.

Alumnus/a, 8/2000-5/2003, February 2006

You can fill out the application online, there are no essays or interviews. There is also a scholarship application online that asks for your GPA and ACT score. The University of Utah is not highly selective, and it is fairly easy to be accepted.

Alumnus/a, 6/1990-6/1996, October 2005

I started summer quarter after graduation. The classes were small and I felt that this would be to my best benefit as I was so new to the college world. I went to admissions, registered and they had a brief synopsis of the registering process, very advisable to ask if one is available. I chose my classes, went to registrars office and signed up. Paid tuition that was due immediately and got books list. Also check out parking on campus, see if it is easier or available to use mass transit, and figure out that aspect for your scheduling.

Current student, 8/2003-Submit Date, September 2005

I applied online and it was relatively easy. I had about a 3.7 GPA and attended the university during my senior year through a concurrent enrollment program.

The University of Utah was the only school to which I really applied. I was s I was going to get in, and it was the most logical choice for my financial sit tion. Because I was responsible for paying for all my tuition and fees, I dec ed to live at my parent's house and commute. The University of Utah offer great education, interesting classes and degree options, and affordable tuit that is all nearby local attractions and entertainment.

Current student, 8/2005-Submit Date, July 2006

Moderately selective. High school transcript (classes, grades) and standardi test scores are all that is considered. Essays required for scholarship appli tions.

Current student, 1/2005-Submit Date, February 2005

The admissions process was very straightforward and easy to complete. I did have any troubles being admitted, and found the process to be very user-frie ly. I applied and got accepted in about two weeks.

Current student, 8/2003-Submit Date, October 2004

To get admitted to the University of Utah, students are evaluated by their hi school GPA, ACT or SAT score and by how involved they were in their h school and the community (for example, student government, athletics and v unteering). By taking Advanced Placement (AP) classes in high school, stude can, if they scored high enough, transfer their AP scores as credit to the univ sity. This will allow a student to waive or skip some level of classes that th would otherwise have to take.

ACT or SAT scores determine into which level of math and English/writ classes a student will be placed. If they score high enough, students are plac into higher levels of such classes, and if they score poorly, they will have to st from the beginning writing and math levels. Overall, ACT and SAT scores alc with a student's GPA matter greatly, however commitment in school clubs a volunteering can definitely boost a student's chance of getting admitted at University of Utah.

Current student, 1/2003-Submit Date, May 2005

...lled out an application to get accepted into the U. As long as you have a min-...um GPA of 2.0 they, generally, allow you in. I didn't have to submit an essay ...participate in an interview to be accepted to the University of Utah.

Current student, 8/2003-Submit Date, May 2004

...e admissions process is fairly simple at the University of Utah. No essay is ...quired. The admissions is pretty open, meaning that if one applies [and meets ...e guidelines] and is willing to pay [the admissions fee], one will get in. The ...ice of a full-time semester is near $1,600 for in-state students, but over $9,000 ...r out-of-state students.

Academics

Alumnus/a, 8/2000-5/2003, February 2006

...e University of Utah is best known for its nursing program, anthropology ...partment and ballet program. These programs are some of the best in the ...tion. Class sizes are varied. You can find a class of 12 all the way up to a class ...400. It is not too difficult to get into the popular classes, simply because they ...ake the enrollment cap fairly high to meet the demands of the students. ...eshmen receive priority registration when they attend orientation, so that is ...ur best chance at getting into a popular class because you register before all ...her students. Definitely take advantage of that opportunity. The professors ...em very approachable and are willing to help you out when you need it. The ...orkload is not overwhelming, but of course it depends on the classes you take. ...my experience, grading seemed fair in most of my classes. If you do the ...ork, you will not have a problem receiving an A or a B in the class.

Alumnus/a, 8/1998-5/2000, September 2005

...vas in the finance program. I felt the professors were all of very high quality. ...e class sizes were quite large so it was not much of a problem to get into any ...asses I needed. The only problem with a huge class size is getting individual-...ed help or attention from the professors. The best thing to do is form study ...oups with other students to work through and understand problems. Grading ...based primarily on tests and quizzes. Workload was not severe, as I was able ...work full time and attend school full time.

Current student, 8/2005-Submit Date, July 2006

...everal outstanding programs; particularly excellent ones are sciences, business, ...nce (ballet and modern), music, architecture, health (including exercise and ...orts science), humanities (excellent English and communication departments), ...litical science and engineering. I got into several elite schools and chose the ...over the more prestigious schools based on value. The U's honors program is ...e of the best in the nation, providing students with the opportunities one might ...d in an Ivy League university. See www.honors.utah.edu for more informa-...on.

Current student, 1/2003-Submit Date, May 2005

...e quality of classes is excellent, with demanding coursework to strengthen ...udents' study skills. Your student status (e.g., sophomore, junior) determines ...hen you register for classes, the earlier you register the easier it is to get into ...e popular classes. The grading varies from professor to professor and overall, ...believe I have been treated fairly.

Current student, 8/2003-Submit Date, October 2004

...e University of Utah provides a great variety of classes, whether art or sci-...ce. The University of Utah has a particularly strong science department where ...udents can major in engineering, medicine and such. The business department ...also strong, ranked in the Top 30 in the nation.

...e size of classes and the quality of professors become better and better as a ...udent gets more into a specific major. The higher the level of classes, the bet-...r the teachers and size of classrooms. Most of the general ed classes are big, ...ometimes with up to 300 people in a class. The teachers in such classes are also ...ss likely to be interested in the well-being of an individual student because ...ch classes are so tightly packed.

Current student, 8/2001-Submit Date, April 2004

I am a history major. The nature of my program is very academic. The history department focuses on a wide range of classes. I have to take classes in every area of world history. To be considered for the honors program, you have to maintain a 3.6 GPA or higher. The requirements for graduation include a senior seminar. Seniors are required to complete a comprehensive primary research project. This includes a minimum of a 30-page research paper with 10 primary sources, and also secondary sources complete with footnotes and bibliography. It is a semester-long class that is very academic. This requirement gives you an idea of the types of classes we take each semester of the program.

If you work hard and do all your assignments, you will get A's. Teachers are not afraid of A's; they give them out frequently. If you meet with your teachers, talk about your papers and ask questions about the class, you have a better chance of getting A's. These teachers love proactive students. I am good friends with many of my teachers, and it helps. History teachers never grade on a scale. In fact, there are typically never any multiple choice and true-false tests. Everything you do is written. There is no curve. You are graded on how well you understand the topic and how well you can express that in written form.

Alumnus/a, 8/2000-5/2004, May 2004

As a student in the David Eccles School of Business, I was afforded many supe-rior educational opportunities, but only because I was careful when selecting classes. I always tried to take classes from the most challenging professors and took all the business honors classes. Any student who is less selective will receive a mediocre education. Any student who takes the honors classes from the most difficult professors will receive an Ivy League education. The quality of classes and professors is exceptional if you are selective.

Employment Prospects

Alumnus/a, 8/2000-5/2003, February 2006

There is a career department on campus that is open to current students and alumni. They have applications and job listings across the State of Utah and the nation. There are also job fairs each semester.

Alumnus/a, 6/1990-6/1996, October 2005

This is another area where your counselors come in handy—it is their job to counsel you, to help you. They know the ropes; it's their job, so let them help you!

Alumni, 8/1998-5/2000, September 2005

The University of Utah has very many programs and networks for graduates to make contacts in the business world. The business school is gaining more and more prestige every year. There is heavy on-campus recruiting and many intern-ship opportunities. You must put in some effort and legwork to make these var-ious opportunities work for you.

Current student, 8/2003-Submit Date, September 2004

Currently, I am working as a financial planner for Beneficial Financial Group. I am working on applying to several companies in the East Coast and I would truly enjoy getting a few years experience before jumping into an MBA program. The U's business school is ranked in the Top 30 in the nation so it helps when trying to begin a career. The only downfall is no big companies recruit on cam-pus. You have to go to them.

Current student, 8/2003-Submit Date, May 2004

In the field of political science, the number of careers is not extremely high, but the ability to enter graduate schools is very high. A high number of internships is offered at the Utah capital and the nation's capital. The counselors at the University of Utah are very concerned with career placement of the students and have a great number of opportunities and lists. Also, career fairs are frequent on campus.

Current student, 8/2001-Submit Date, April 2004

A history major has a lot of career options. The program does a great job of let-ting you know what your opportunities are. They constantly have postings for positions, internships and fellowships. A history major can also use the degree to go into various other fields or a master's program. A large percentage of our

Read all of Vault's College Surveys at www.vault.com/college—get complete surveys on 100s of colleges and univer-sities, expert advice on applicaton essays and more.

VAULT CAREER LIBRARY   723

students go into law. Some of the career options the department boasts are teacher, research assistant, work in museums, libraries and colleges, historical preservation, law researcher, film historian, government positions and so forth.

Alumnus/a, 8/2000-5/2004, May 2004

If you are an honors business student, the school is fairly successful in placing students with top firms and schools. Some of my classmates were hired by various top-tier investment banks in NY. Another student was offered deferred enrollment at Harvard Business School. Other classmates have received employment at Goldman Sachs in the local operations division. In general, career prospects are solid only if the student actively works to obtain his or her dream job. The job will not be handed to you, even if you have stellar grades.

Quality of Life

Alumnus/a, 8/2000-5/2003, February 2006

The quality of life is very high at the University of Utah. New dorm buildings were built for the 2002 Salt Lake Olympics, which are very nice and include all the amenities a student could hope for. There is also graduate student housing. The campus is large, but you can walk from one end to the other in 15 minutes if necessary. The campus is located in the foothills of the Wasatch Mountains and is only 20 to 30 minutes from several world-class ski resorts.

Current student, 8/2003-Submit Date, September 2005

I love living in the Salt Lake Valley because it has all the benefits of a metropolis, while having the quaint feeling of a small town. There are a lot of things to do while it is also very easy to get away to a quiet spot. The campus hosts large parties every other month or so with free entertainment and fun activities. The area itself could not be any safer. The Salt Lake Valley was founded by highly religious individuals, and this historic feel resonates throughout it. The streets of downtown are safe to walk on in the middle of the night, and you can trust almost anyone you might bump into at the mall or a bank. The people are all friendly overall, and as long as you don't mind meeting with missionaries, you will be fine.

Alumni, 8/1998-5/2000, September 2005

Quality of life is very high in Salt Lake City. There is available on-campus housing, but this school is a known as a commuter school so the majority of students live off campus and commute. There is a lightrail system the goes right through campus and is very convenient for any student living anywhere in the valley. It is very easy to find off-campus housing for a very reasonable price. I was able to rent a room in a home only three miles from campus for $225 a month. Crime and safety is low compared to other universities. The university has its own dedicated police force and they have safety programs, such as escorts to vehicles when it is late at night or dark out.

Current student, 8/2005-Submit Date, July 2006

The dorms are very nice. The campus is really booming in the fall term, and I made hundreds of friends my first semester here. In the spring, things tend to die down a bit, but that just makes fall all the more fun. Many students ski and snowboard in the wintertime, and academics keep students busy as well. Excellent neighborhood—set in the foothills of the beautiful Salt Lake Valley.

Current student, 8/2003-Submit Date, October 2004

I believe that the University of Utah is a pretty safe campus. I haven't had many night classes but for the ones that I did have, I had no problem walking alone to and from the classroom. The campus is generally easy to get around once you get a hang of it; it is pretty large in size but there are also many transportation utilities that can ease and shorten the path. The University of Utah is very diverse and a student has an opportunity to join many clubs of all sorts of interests. I have, along with three other Bosnian friends of mine, established a Bosnian and Herzegovinian Student Organization this year and it has been a great experience.

Current student, 1/2003-Submit Date, May 2005

I live a block away from the University of Utah and I love it. I am within walking distance of the U and feel comfortable walking back and forth in safety. The campus is well kept, with beautiful landscaping in the summer, shoveled walks in the winter, and clean buildings year round. The temperature inside is always

comfortable, winter and spring. There are many facilities to enjoy activities They have a swimming pool, gym (which includes a sauna, hot tub [private women], indoor track, weight machines and cardio machines), basketball cour volleyball courts, you name it, it is available. The Union hosts a dining facil with many options for vegetarian and ethnic cuisines, with reasonable prices.

Social Life

Alumnus/a, 8/2000-5/2003, February 2006

There is a bowling alley and pool hall on campus. There is also a Greek syste including five sororities and five fraternities. There are numerous clubs on ca pus and encouragement to start your own if can't find one that fits your nee The beauty of Utah is that you are rarely any farther than 20 minutes from a local hotspot. Downtown Salt Lake is 10 minutes away and has plenty of resta rants and bars. Just 20 minutes away is Park City, home of the Sundance Fi Festival, which contains more great bars, restaurants and skiing.

Alumnus/a, 6/1990-6/1996, October 2005

I loved it! Everything in walking distance, and if you wanted to go clubbing go out there are several options. Greek system is great very active on camp A lot of school spirit. The University of Utah provides a lot of packages to spo ing functions for cheep tickets for students and alumni. University ranks well football, basketball, gymnastics, and has wonderful facilities for players a spectators.

Current student, 8/2005-Submit Date, July 2006

Excellent in the fall. OK Greek system with nice chapter houses. Being Gre at the U is like being in a small college within the large university. Lots of gre restaurants near campus or accessible through the lightrail TRAX trains, free students. Some big-name concerts throughout the year, free to students. Dati scene—pretty much the LDS students date the other LDS students they meet the Institute, and the dorm crowd dates the dorm crowd, while Greeks da Greeks.

Current student, 1/2003-Submit Date, May 2005

Shaggy's and the Vortex are really popular clubs at which to hang out. Th have excellent restaurants that provide Indian and Thai cuisine. There are handful of events to choose from monthly to participate in—sporting even plays at Pioneer Theatre and ballets at Kingsbury Hall.

Current student, 8/2003-Submit Date, May 2004

Salt Lake City is home to a large number of restaurants, bars, clubs, concerts a a large group of fraternities and sororities. Furthermore, the dating scene is ve popular. A close campus favorite is a pizza joint called The Pie Pizzeria, w live bands and microbrews and root beer. There are two large malls in dow town Salt Lake City with a wide variety of stores and theatres. Brigham Your University, Utah Valley State College, Salt Lake Community College, Web State College and Utah State University are all within an hour's drive of t University of Utah, so activities that are focused on students and young adu are plentiful.

Current student, 8/2001-Submit Date, April 2004

The University of Utah is a great place to go to school. They have very acti student councils that provide many opportunities for leisure and entertainme Concerts, bands and dances are going on all the time. Around campus or jus 10-minute train ride downtown, there are multitudes of bars, clubs and resta rants.

The dating scene is great; I met my husband on campus. We also have a lot dating lines and services. Students take advantage of our for-credit Outdo Adventure classes. These include skiing, snowboarding, snowshoeing, cros country skiing, snowmobiling and ice-fishing in the winter, and biking, hikin camping, fishing, canoeing, rafting, kayaking, rock climbing and water skiing the summer. It is so great you can earn college credit for all these activities. is fun to go to school here in any season.

Alumnus/a, 8/2000-5/2004, May 2004

This is definitely a commuter campus, but the university's administration a student government are working actively to change that. The new universi sident was recently hired based [in part] on his commitment to change the ool's [sense of community]. Progress is underway. Greek life is very excit-, and any student who comes to the University of Utah should try to join a ternity or sorority. There are all types of Greeks!

ere are hundreds of clubs on campus. Whatever your fancy is, you can find a ıb that makes sense for you. The business school clubs are definitely a mendous opportunity for students. The most active participation can be found in the business school clubs, including the Student Investment Fund, Students in Free Enterprise, the University Venture Fund and the American Marketing Association.

The school says: "Although exact statistics are not known, the student population is approximately 50 percent Mormon, 50 percent non-Mormon."

Utah State University

dmissions Office
aggart Student Center 102
160 Old Main Hill
gan, UT 84322-0160
dmissions phone: (435) 797-1079 or (800) 488-8108
dmissions e-mail: admit@usu.edu
dmissions URL: www.usu.edu/admissions/

Admissions

urrent student, History, 8/2004-Submit Date, May 2007

hat I really liked about the application process to Utah State was the fact that lid not need to fill out a separate scholarship application. Once my admissions plication was received, the university processed my information and realized ualified for their Presidential Transfer Scholarship (a full-tuition scholarship). quickly received my acceptance letter to Utah State, along with another letter ting that I qualified for a scholarship.

order to decide if I really wanted to go to Utah State, I decided I should visit e campus since I had never really been there before. I went to the admissions ıb site, and signed up for a date and time that I could visit the campus. I ceived a letter in the mail that included an outline of the day's activities and a ıp of how to get to the university. I was able to meet with my advisor, and dis-ıs my program of interest. My academic advisor was extremely helpful in ıswering my questions, and understanding the workings of the program. I also ceived a campus tour from an ambassador, and tasted some free Aggie ice 2am! I appreciated the friendly and helpful atmosphere I found at Utah State. y favorite part about that visit, is that I was able to remain in contact with the 1bassador (who was a current student) to ask him any questions that came up ter. He was great to reply back quickly to my e-mails, and was extremely help-.

urrent student, Psychology, 8/2005-Submit Date, May 2007

lid a paper application that counted as my application to the university and an plication for any available scholarships. Then I turned it in to the Admissions ffice at the university and was sent a letter informing me of my acceptance.

lumnus/a, English, 8/2002-5/2007, May 2007

ie admissions process was prompt and succinct. I receive all the information eeded through forms and documents in the mail and browsing the USU web e.

urrent student, Communications, 8/2005-Submit Date, May 2007

was a transfer student and decided to transfer to Utah State University after mpletion of a two-year college. Getting admitted was a pretty simple process. ust had to fill out a form with my GPA and give them a current transcript. Also ey have the scholarship application tied into their admission form. The best lvice I could give would be to make sure you get to know the people with ıom you are working in the offices, like admissions or financial aid, as they :come your greatest tool when you need help or anything.

Current student, 9/2003-Submit Date, October 2006

The admissions process was very quick and simple. They responded within a month, I believe. Do well on your ACT/SAT and they may have a scholarship available, which was great for me as an out-of-state student.

Alumnus/a, Art, 8/2000-5/2004, November 2005

I believe getting in has gotten harder since I went to USU. What is really impor-tant is a good SAT or ACT score. Now getting into your major is another thing. I was an Art major, and at the time they didn't have any pre-reqs to register as one. They do now, however. When you apply you need to make sure you have a good portfolio. It could be drawing, painting, photography, whatever, but a combination is best. You cannot start taking classes for your major until they let you in, so having a good portfolio is important.

Current student, 8/2001-Submit Date, February 2005

Admissions was fairly simple. My high school had a college fair for juniors and seniors to start looking for continuing education. Utah State had a booth with applications. I had wanted to attend that school since I was 12 and joined 4-H, which is associated with it because it is the state agricultural school. I had to apply for the bioveterinary program separately and had to be accepted into that and the school to get into my program of choice. I did not have an interview; my high school grades were in the top 10 percent and that made it fairly simple, it also helped earn me a couple of scholarships there. I also had a high ACT score, which is more commonly used for the admissions index in Utah. Because my index score was so high, there did not seem to be any trouble getting admit-ted. I believe it was $35 to apply, which I had from my part-time job. I was real-ly excited about the scholarships and my acceptance into the bioveterinary pro-gram.

The school says: Two entrance essays are required and there is a $40 application fee.

Academics

Current student, History, 8/2004-Submit Date, May 2007

My education has definitely been challenged at Utah State. Since my degree is History Education, I actually experienced an education through two different colleges. With history and political science, I had professor who helped my to take an analytical view to the past and challenge some of the things that I had previously learned. They also did a good job trying to help me understand how to write effectively, and do research. With education, I had many opportunities not only to learn theory, but also to apply what I was learning. As I took my edu-cation classes, I also worked for 30 hours a semester in a regular school class-room observing and teaching lessons. This helped me to cement the material I was learning. The professors are great to work with. It is a smaller university, so it is easier to get to know the professors. They also do a great job answering e-mails, proof reading papers, and offering advice for furthering our education. I felt that my professors were all very fair in their grading. They were straight-forward about what they wanted, and if I ever had a question, I could go to them and talk about it.

My history and political science classes had a more challenging workload, because there was a lot of reading. Sometimes I was unable to get through

Read all of Vault's College Surveys at **www.vault.com/college**—get complete surveys on 100s of colleges and universities, expert advice on applicaton essays and more.

V∧ULT CAREER LIBRARY   **725**

everything, so I would just have to kind of skim it to get by. I sometimes felt like I was doing busywork in some of my education classes, but a large percentage of the coursework was creating lesson plans that I will be able to use when I start teaching. As far as getting into popular classes, I would usually just need to speak with the professor and explain why I wanted to get into the class. They would usually work with me.

Current student, Psychology, 8/2005-Submit Date, May 2007

Getting in to the classes that you want/need is relatively easy. Most registration occurs online, which makes it so much more convenient to see which classes are available and which classes are full. Plus, no long lines at the Registrar's Office when you add/drop classes online! Although popular classes fill up quickly, if you check back every once in a while, you're bound to find a spot. The best thing is to wait until after the "purge" when people who haven't paid for their tuition and fees lose their classes—most all of the classes open up so you can squeeze right in.

Every class that I've taken at Utah State has been excellent. I attended another university before coming here and those classes don't stack up to the ones that I've taken here. Every professor is concerned about your success and is always available if you need extra help.

Alumnus/a, Communications, 1/2003-12/2005, May 2007

I never had a problem getting into classes, and really enjoyed most of my classes. My professors were always very available. I transferred to Utah State from a very small liberal arts school that I loved, and felt right at home at Utah State. Although it's a large school with over [15,000] students, I felt like my professors knew me well and cared about me as a student. I also felt very in touch with the student leadership, and felt like I had a voice on campus.

Current student, Communications, 8/2005-Submit Date, May 2007

I really like USU's journalism and communications department, they are, what I feel, some of the most diverse individuals. One of the best things about my classes is that they are small. My biggest class is a class of 60 and my smallest was 12. I really got to know my professors and the skills I will need in the public relations field. I really enjoyed my Research Methods class because we got to work on a real campaign with a real client that my own group picked; it rocked!

Alumnus/a, English, 8/2002-5/2007, May 2007

I attended the English department's program for Professional and Technical Writing. As one of the 10 largest academic programs of its kind in the nation, it was academically intense but had a consistent sense of community and professionalism due to the congenial professors. Ease of getting popular classes was high and the ease of getting goods grades in my classes was high as long as I remained hardworking, energetic and prompt. The program was ultimately a wonderful learning experience that taught me versatility for the vast field of professional writing.

Alumnus/a, 8/2000-5/2004, November 2005

USU has a really great art program and it is getting more and more popular, which means it is harder and harder to get into the classes. It also means that when you do get in, there is lots of competition and you have to stay on top of things. Register as soon as you can every semester, and if you don't get in initially, keep checking, including going to the professor whose class you want to take. Sometimes he/she will sign you in on the first or second day of class. These classes are intense, but so much fun. You will not meet a greater set of professors anywhere. I had a graphic design emphasis and it was a lot of hard work, but I learned so much. More than my counterparts at other UT schools. Though professors can be lax about due dates, get things in on time; you do not want to get behind, because most people who do, never catch up. These classes are hard enough to get into, you do not want to have to take them twice.

Current student, 8/2004-Submit Date, November 2004

The Constitutional Legal Studies Program is basically set up to cover the same stuff you would in your first year of law school. It is a smaller major as far as required core classes (under 40 hours), but the classes are more intense than a lot of the other majors. You must maintain a 3.0 to stay in the program also. I have only been here shortly, but the classes seem pretty good—the professors seem willing to work with you. The workload is pretty heavy, if you want to succeed. The one thing about USU I don't like is that they are not too flexible with class-

es and class times. It seems like they don't have enough classes, and the tim are not too flexible. (Adding block classes could help this, I believe.)

Current student, 8/2001-Submit Date, February 2005

Freshmen always have a difficult time getting into the classes that they need I followed my advisor's directions and took fairly general easy-to-get-into cla es except for my program's intro course, which was very specific. My progr required extremely specific courses with very few electives. I was also in honors program for my first year and a half, which allowed general courses w smaller classes and I think a more enjoyable curriculum. The honors course was required to take for the program were great and had maybe 40 stude instead of 200 or 18 instead of 35. It was nice. I definitely recommend gett into an honors program.

Employment Prospects

Current student, History, 8/2004-Submit Date, May 2007

The university provides a great program called Career Aggie, which helps s dents build their résumés, network, find jobs, and gain paid and unpaid inte ships. The also do a career fair every year where companies from all over state and country come to recruit. So, there are plenty of opportunities for g ting applicable jobs while you're a student, and finding a great career when y graduate.

Current student, Psychology, 8/2005-Submit Date, May 2007

The Career Center at Utah State is invaluable. They hold a career fair each ye that brings employers from all over so students can network and make great co nections with people currently in their field. The Career Center also offers mc interviews, résumé assistance, and a web site called Career Aggie, which lets y put your résumé out there for employers.

Alumnus/a, Political Science, 9/1997-5/2000, May 2007

I was so close to my professors, through their connections I had interviews w top governmental agencies. However, after the interviews and looking at direction I wanted to pursue, I decided on non-governmental, nonprofit agenci Within a couple of months of graduation, I was hired by The American R Cross; from my internship experience I had already established a reputation w the Red Cross.

Current student, Communications, 8/2005-Submit Date, May 200

Utah State University gives students great opportunities for employment af graduation. When you tell people that you have graduated from USU they excited; it is famous for its research and they know that you have worked han on. Many students in public relations go on to work for PR firms locally a around the world. Just to name a couple, NASA and Microsoft.

Alumnus/a, English, 8/2002-5/2007, May 2007

The employment prospects for USU students are bountiful due to the incredib active on-campus recruiting and internship programs. While working as a s dent, I obtained job opportunities as a computer lab consultant, newspap columnist, art museum tour guide, and technical writer. As long as I was wi ing to extend myself into new territory, I easily got hired for new jobs due to r professionalism and passion for new experiences. I think most USU gradua move on to full-time, professional positions in the business administratic accounting and education fields.

Alumnus/a, 8/2001-8/2003, July 2004

I was surprised at how many job offers I received after I graduated. Utah Sta conducted two job fairs during my senior year. The Career Center is topnotc providing career advice, internship opportunities and assistance in preparing the job market. Seminars in résumé preparation and job interviews are routin ly provided by the career center.

The economics program provided a well-rounded background that prepared for almost any job in the business world. As an economics major, I was offer and accepted a job offer in public finance. I feel confident that the educatior obtained at Utah State University has prepared me to excel at any career tha may decide to pursue.

Alumnus/a, 9/1999-9/2003, July 2004

...elt that USU was helpful in the career process, but not to the point they land... me the job. One of the classes I took was all about what I could do with my ...gree and what agencies I could work for. There is a job fair every year and a ...o placement center on campus. Several employers are aware of USU and ...ow the high quality grads that it puts out. There are several majors that offer ...ernship programs and will help you find an internship. They also make rec... ...mmendations of companies you may be cut out for. This was a huge help to ...e.

Quality of Life

...urrent student, History, 8/2004-Submit Date, May 2007

...ogan has a great quality of life for college students. It is definitely a college ...wn, so much of what exists here is for college students. There is a lot of dif... ...rent housing options to fit the various needs of different personalities. Much ...f the housing is very close to campus, so you can walk or take the Aggie Shuttle ...his is the university's bus system that runs five routes surrounding campus). ...here is also a local transit system called the LTD, which is free for everyone. ...o it is really easy to get around. Logan is a smaller university, so its main cam... ...us is also smaller. You can walk from one end to campus to the other in about ...0 to 15 minutes. This is a nice feature when planning classes, because you do ...t need to worry if 10 minutes will be enough time to get to your next class. ...n campus there is also a large recreation facility. There is what we call the ...eld House, which contains an indoor track, treadmills, elliptical, bikes, weight ...ting equipment, indoor tennis and pool tables for people work out. There is ...other building, HPER, which contains courts for basketball, volleyball, bad... ...inton, racquetball, as well as two swimming pools. This building also contains ...couple of dance rooms for dance classes. As far as dining is concerned, there ...all the regular fast-food restaurants (McDonald's, Burger King, Wendy's), as ...ell as mid-range restaurants. There is a lot of really cool, inexpensive local ...staurants that do deals for students. Logan is also one of the safest cities in the ...untry. I have never felt unsafe walking around campus at night; many students ...n even leave their doors unlocked and not worry about theft. It is a great envi... ...nment for college students.

...urrent student, Psychology, 8/2005-Submit Date May 2007

...here is a multitude of choices for housing that suit every need. If you want a ...cial atmosphere, on-campus housing holds a lot of activities and puts you right ...the middle of the action with regard to sports, intramurals and clubs. Campus ...cilities range from historic buildings built in 1890, like Old Main, to brand... ...w facilities, such as the engineering building, all of which are structurally ...eautiful and functional. With regard to safety, last year Logan was voted the ...fest metropolitan area in the U.S. due to its low crime rate. We also ranked ...ry high on the list this year. Campus is also very safe. If you want someone ...o walk you to your car or dorm, campus police are on call to do so for free.

...lumnus/a, English, 8/2002-5/2007, May 2007

...he quality of life in Logan, Utah was clean, peaceful and full of nature. The ...eighborhoods are safe and have a strong sense of community. Quality of life at ...SU is diverse, like any university, but it's mostly quite clean and responsible. ...ogan, being a comparatively active city, is a perfect outlet for hiking, camping, ...king, skiing and sports.

...lumnus/a, 8/2000-5/2004, November 2005

...ogan is a great college town. USU has a fantastic campus. It is small enough ...ot to be overwhelming, but big enough to have a true college feel. There are so ...any activities going on all of the time, it is hard to get bored, and too easy to ...et distracted from your studies. It is also a safe place, with hardly any crime. ...he housing is also great. Snow Hall is the best for dorms, Aggie Village for a ...ore studious experience.

> **Regarding housing, the school says:** "USU opened a new student living/learning center in fall 2007...and it's located right next to the student center on campus!"

This university is amazing. There are tons of places to live, both on and off campus. They have an awesome variety of dining services to fit each individual student's needs. Everything is really close to campus, so you are always close by to classes or anything else you need. Utah State University is located in the heart of Logan, Utah and there is very little crime.

Social Life

Current student, History, 8/2004-Submit Date, May 2007

There is a lot to do at Utah State. Since the campus is set right up against the mountains, there are plenty of opportunities for hiking, mountain biking, rock climbing, kayaking, camping, and in the winter, snowshoeing, sledding, skiing and snowboarding. There is actually a ski resort about 45 minutes from campus. If the outdoors is not your thing, there are other activities. Many students love to go clubbing at NVO; it is dominated by college students. There are also places to go bowling, rollerblading and play the arcades. There is one major bar in town called the White Owl.

The university provides many events for the students to enjoy, including concerts, plays and parties. Two of the biggest events that bring people from all over the state are the Howl (the Halloween Dance) and our Mardi Gras celebration. For Mardi Gras, the student center is turned into a casino with poker tables, palm readers and more. They are a ton of fun. There are over 200 clubs to get involved with, everything from the Ugly Dancing Club to the Insomniac Club, to the Longboarding Club, to the Ballroom Dance Club. There are also several intramural sports that you can participate in by yourself or with a group of friends. There are six fraternities, and four sororities on campus. They each have a house located on or near campus. The Greek system is very service orientated at Utah State, and does a lot to improve the community and the university. Some of my favorite memories of Utah State are floating the canal (use a big tube to float down a river), eating at Cafe Sabor (local favorite), dancing at Club NVO, and hanging out with my friends. It is a great place to be!

Current student, Psychology, 8/2005-Submit Date, May 2007

The social scene on campus is always busy. We host the Howl every year, which is the biggest Halloween party in the state of Utah. We also have Mardi Gras, which is another student favorite. Almost every student you ask will tell you that he/she loves to go to men's basketball games! The Dee Glen Smith Spectrum is one of the most feared places for other teams to play due to our insane student section!

Alumnus/a, Political Science, 9/1997-5/2000, May 2007

There are so many things to do in Logan, with a beautiful canyon five miles behind campus. Students can enjoy snow sports, including downhill skiing and ice fishing. During summer and spring and fall there are still so many recreational things to do like hiking, fishing, mountain biking, camping, water skiing and so on. The restaurant scene is fun and intimate. There are many famous chain restaurants and there are home grown restaurants, as well. Both are recommend and so good. I love the Blue Bird, Coppermill and Famosa. Utah State always had scheduled on-campus activities, such as parties. Our Halloween party, the Howl, is so well know that other schools would rent activity buses and travel to Utah State so their students could participate. I was involved in many student government organizations and felt very involved. We are also know for breaking the world record for the most kissing couples kissing in one place at the same time (I was part of that record). The are legends and school traditions that are fun to participate in as well, for example becoming a true Aggie. In order to be considered a true Aggie, you must kiss on an appointed night on the Aggie letter A on campus or kiss a true Aggie under a full moon. You get a "True Aggie Card" that proves your "true Aggieness." There are an assortment of events and activities at Utah State and all the Greek clubs that you would find at every university.

Current student, 9/2003-Submit Date, October 2006

There is always something going on, be it a basketball, football or hockey game, a play, a dance, a party, intramurals, concerts, art gallery, bonfires up the canyon, or just relaxing watching a movie, you can always have fun. Just leave your

Read all of Vault's College Surveys at www.vault.com/college—get complete surveys on 100s of colleges and univer-sities, expert advice on applicaton essays and more.

VAULT CAREER LIBRARY 727

dorm room sometime and you'll find something to do. Don't lock yourself up in your room all semester!

Alumnus/a, 8/1999-8/2003, April 2005

Socially, there are lots of get-to-know-you events, including Greek dances and other club dances. Every week, there are swing and country dances where you can learn how to dance. The on-campus gyms are also a great place to meet people. They have lacrosse, soccer, tennis and other teams you can join, too. There are lots of restaurants nearby. The Coppermill, Cafe Sabor, Chili's, Olive Garden and Cafe Ibis are just a few favorites. Lots of dating, and there is so much to do. There is a canyon about five minutes from campus where students enjoy camping, fishing, hiking, swimming and lots more. There are several movie theatres, bowling alleys, a skate park, rock wall, golf and skiing at Bea[v] Mountain in Logan Canyon. Salt Lake City is fun to visit and close by.

Current student, 8/2001-Submit Date, February 2005

First tip: if joining a sorority or fraternity, make sure you really want to be acti[ve] and that you have some money going into it. Great fun, and nice people, but y[ou] have to be dedicated. Not many bars in town. Students more likely to go [to] Chili's than the "controversial" bar. A couple of fun dancing clubs. The sch[ool] always had social events like theatre, sports, music and Student Associat[ion] activities. It really did not get very boring unless you really wanted to lock yo[ur]self away. A ton of clubs available and the service opportunities are great.

Bennington College

Bennington College
Office of Admissions
One College Drive
Bennington, VT 05201
Admissions phone: (800) 833-6845
Admissions fax: (802) 440-4320
Admissions e-mail: admissions@bennington.edu
Admissions URL: www.bennington.edu

 ## Admissions

Current student, Mathematics, 9/2005-Submit Date, May 2007

A big part of applying is actually coming to visit. You get to meet students on campus as well as faculty if you choose to sit in on the courses. Also, if you send in a reply card, a student worker (tour guide) will send you an e-mail to serve as a resource. While this is you finding out information about Bennington, it lets the office know that you're interested.

You go through an interview, either a phone interview or in person if you're on campus. These are more conversations than attempts to grill you, so be relaxed and take this opportunity to share something interesting about yourself.

The application is the same way. Of course you need to fill out the application and the Common Application essays, but on the Bennington essay, just be honest and yourself.

Current student, English, 9/2005-Submit Date, May 2007

The admissions process at Bennington relies heavily on the interview and the essays. Sell yourself and make the college know, understand and believe that you want to be here and that you'll work hard once you are. The essays change every year, but you are always allowed and encouraged to send in "supplemental material"—basically anything: visual art, music, someone once sent in a pair of decorated pants, and this material really helps the school to know more about you and what you are about. The process is fairly selective, but because of it, we end up with such a high concentration of determined, passionate, creative and talented students, and that in turn creates the energy of this place that is unlike anywhere else.

Current student, Cultural Studies, 8/2004-Submit Date, May 2007

The admissions office at Bennington is incredibly personal, and base most of the acceptances on personal experiences and one-on-one interactions with potential students. Without being required to submit the SAT, students can better display who they are personally—through the interview, supplemental work and essays. Be yourself, be creative, and give a good display of your work, and you'll be fine.

Current student, Education, 9/2005-Submit Date, May 2007

Bennington does not require test scores, so the admissions process is much more personal than most schools. Because we're so small, we are able to look at students individually and get to know the students. The best way to approach Bennington is to visit, have an interview, and focus on the essay.

Current student, English, 9/2003-Submit Date, May 2007

Bennington doesn't have a formula or anything when it comes to admissions, everything is taken into consideration equally. More than anything, Bennington wants to see that the applicant is enthusiastic about learning. Lots of things can reflect that enthusiasm, not just grades. This means that the interview and supplemental materials are probably more important here than at other schools. Anything a student wants to send us that they think will give the admissions office a better idea of who they are is welcome. The essay questions reflect that approach, as well. Generally, the Bennington essay will ask the applicant to solve some sort of problem, or ask a question that's as much about the process of answering as the answer itself. Things like, "Design an experiment to prove whether or not toads can hear." or, "How might you envision a library of the future?" The best thing about the admissions process here is that it treats applicants as individuals, not just numbers. We really take the time to get to know our applicants and make them a part of the Bennington community before they even arrive.

Alumnus/a, 9/2002-6/2005, April 2006

When I applied, the admissions process at Bennington was structured in a typical liberal arts college fashion but also very open-ended. For example, I had to submit my high school and previous college transcripts, teacher recommendations and I had to write the all-important essay. However, while my SAT scores were good, I didn't have to submit them (so I didn't).

The essay questions didn't seem as stuffy as those from other schools either. There was nothing lame like "explain both your greatest strengths and weaknesses," but rather, "describe the biology experiment for answering the questions about nature that you have always pondered." Upon reading the application I knew that Bennington was for me, mostly because it didn't seem typical or shallow.

Another aspect of this openness in the Bennington admissions process is the school's willingness to accept whatever else you submit with your application. I remember one student who created an elaborate board game as her application and got into a major magazine as a result.

> **Regarding admissions, the school says:** "Bennington College uses the Common Application and a Bennington Supplement, which includes and additional essay, a critical writing sample, and the opportunity to submit supplemental materials. Submission of standardized test scores is optional. While interviews are not required, students are strongly encouraged to visit campus-to meet current Bennington students, sit in on classes, and talk with an admissions counselor. In addition, upon receipt and review of a student's application, the Office of Admissions may schedule a telephone interview to discuss the student's application materials and ongoing work."

 ## Academics

Current student, 8/2004-Submit Date, May 2007

The quality of the professors is unparalleled because they are all practicing professionals in the field that they teach. My dance teacher runs his own dance company in NYC. Thus the classes are of a high quality as well. There are a few classes that are always very hard to get into, but if you persist, you will. The workload can be very heavy, but that's largely self-determined. How hard are you going to push yourself?

Current student, English, 9/2003-Submit Date, May 2007

Instead of following a pre-determined major, students design their own programs at Bennington through a Plan process focusing on what they really want out of their college experience. This allows them to focus on programs that may otherwise be very broad; for instance, a music concentrator could be focusing on recording, jazz drumming, and composition, while another could be singing and playing the guitar. The Plan also allows students to combine multiple interests such as biology or dance, and there is plenty of room for flexibility. Each Plan is approved by a committee of faculty that points students in the right direction as far as their interests, or suggests classes that the student might be overlooking. Classes here are excellent, all small, all taught by faculty who are practitioners in their fields, whose real experience is invaluable for learning. Most classes, except for the most popular in a few areas, are easy to get into, especially for upperclassmen with prior experience in that area. The focus is on a student becoming personally invested in the work they're doing through projects in that area, not just passive lectures and assignments. There are no grades here, unless

Read all of Vault's College Surveys at **www.vault.com/college**—get complete surveys on 100s of colleges and universities, expert advice on applicaton essays and more.

VAULT CAREER LIBRARY 729

the student requests them for graduate school; the focus is instead on a narrative evaluation system that specifies on the work a student has done in the class, as well as constructive criticism and other feedback that can help the student improve.

Current student, 9/2003-Submit Date, May 2007

You have to be very self-motivated at Bennington because there are no core requirements. You design your plan of study with a group of faculty members and your advisor each year and you write an essay each year discussing your plan of study (i.e., concentration) that has to be approved by the dean's office. You do not choose a major, you design one. For example, even if you are concentrating in mathematics, you are choosing which courses suit your interest in mathematics most effectively. Grades are optional at Bennington. Students receive written evaluations. However, about a third of the students at Bennington also request to receive grades. Classes are interactive, discussion-based, hands-on, innovative, energetic, serious and require a lot of work outside of class time. All the professors are working professionals in their fields, so they bring their own interests and current work into the classroom setting. They are equally active participants in the areas that we study.

Current student, Education, 9/2005-Submit Date, May 2007

Bennington is what you make of it. The Plan structure allows you to create your own education; thus, you have students who concentrate in something rather than major in it. We are not bound by major discipline requirements, which allows Bennington students to follow their interests and passions. Because of the size of the school, 600, classes average at about 12 people. This means that professors are readily available to work one-on-one with students. Again, because students are creating their own education, the quality of classes, ease of getting in and workload will all vary depending on the individual.

Current student, 9/2004-Submit Date, May 2007

The quality of my classes has been exquisite. A number of faculty members have become personal mentors and professional advisors. The academic structure of Bennington is set by individualized personal essays dictating our academic plans. Because of my relationships with my faculty and the specificity of my Plan, I've been able to get all of the classes I've wanted.

Current student, 2/2005-Submit Date, April 2006

Students at Bennington are in control of their own education. The classes are small and provide each student with individual attention from the professors. Professors here are all practitioners; literature professors are poets and novelists, science professors do field research but also teach right in the classrooms (no TAs). The workload is what you make of it. I love the work I'm doing and I'm constantly doing work here, and a general rule about Bennington is you get out what you put in.

Current student, 9/2006-Submit Date, April 2006

Bennington College is able to offer its students strong academics along with a strong visual arts program. Classes are kept extremely small (very rarely more than 30 students), with an emphasis on discussion. Students do not receive grades unless they specifically request them. Students do receive evaluations from teachers at the end of each term.

Unlike other schools, Bennington does not have online registration. Students sign up for classes with their professors, often explaining their reasoning behind wanting to join the class. While it can be difficult to get into popular classes, waitlists always exist. If a student expresses a great enough interest in a class, it should be possible for that student to join that class.

The workload of a Bennington student varies—students can take 16 credits or more. Visual arts classes tend to be extremely intense and time-consuming. However, academic classes can be equally rigorous. The number and type of classes each student chooses determines his or her workload.

> **Regarding grades, the school says:** "Students may request letter grades (A,B,C,D,F) for any and all courses they take. In addition to the optional grades, all students receive written narrative evaluations at the end of each term for each course they have taken. Faculty summarize the student's progress, appraise his/her work, and often make suggestions for further develop-

ment. A narrative evaluation is issued whether or not the student elects to receive a letter grade.

"All students are encouraged to consider requesting grades for at least two years (or 64 credits) of their study at Bennington so that a GPA might be produced upon graduation, particularly if the student thinks s/he might study abroad, apply for certain scholarships, or apply to graduate school. All international students are recommended to request grades as well."

 Employment Prospects

Current student, Liberal Arts, 2/2005-Submit Date, May 2007

A Bennington grad can go on to do whatever he/she wants. This school m impart the most open-ended education anywhere. We have a wide alumni ba for such a young institution. The alumni are always more than willing to he other Bennington grads, especially right after graduating. What is so satisfy about the grads is that they usually search for jobs doing what they love. Th take the time to explore what meant most to them in college and now can re the benefits of taking the time to really look at themselves and ask the right que tions. We have alumni who go on to all walks of life and do what they love.

Current student, Education, 9/2005-Submit Date, May 2007

Bennington students are required to complete seven-week internships every ye in between the fall and spring terms. These internships provide a great oppor nity to add to your résumé. By the time you leave Bennington, you'll have least four jobs under your belt. There is an office dedicated to the FWT with to of resources for students—these resources can also be used to find summer jo and to find employment after graduation.

Current student, 1/2003-Submit Date, April 2006

A Bennington education is pretty unique in that it requires what is called a Fie Work Term (FWT) every year. This term is taken during January throu February. Classes are not in session and students are required to work 210 hou doing some sort of job, internship or, during upperclassman years, an indepen ent project. While a very small handful of students stay in Bennington, Vermo most go off into the world traveling all over the country as well as abroad. Th is an amazing opportunity just at face value, but also when it comes to gradu tion—to have four additional real world jobs already on your résumé.

Students do all sorts of things from building motorcycles to working at Nation Public Radio, to flying hot air balloons, to teaching children about AIDS Nigeria. The opportunities are endless and FWT is certainly one of my ve favorite parts about the Bennington education. I'm really seeing its value no (as a senior), because looking at my résumé I have four professional jobs wi tons of references already lined up.

FWT affords networking opportunities like no other and also gives students tl experience of finding housing, planning a budget, cooking and dealing wi problems in the workplace before hitting graduation day. I feel so much mo prepared for the real world than my peers at other schools just because of FW

Current student, 9/2004-Submit Date, April 2006

Graduates from Bennington go on to do numerous and varying things, fro working in large business corporations in New York City to writing for sitcom in Los Angeles, or even becoming successful performers in Las Vegas. One the best benefits that Bennington offers to its students is the Field Work Term helping the students to graduate with a BA as well as an extensive resum Students are able to go into the world with references and intern experienc galore, finding it easier to move on after Bennington than most other schools.

Our Field Work Term Office also helps students to prepare for the technic aspects of moving on. With resumé writing workshops, workshops on findin summer jobs, full-time jobs and internships, the FWT assistants aid in unde standing the technical aspects of finding a job. They even offer a workshop c Not Selling Out: How to Be an Artist in the Real World. These unique class/di cussion groups help students trying to move from college artist to a respectabl member of the artistic community.

Quality of Life

Current student, English, 9/2006-Submit Date, May 2007

The school is somewhat isolated and insular at times. Housing is great; we live in actual houses, not dorms, and each one has its own personality so that anyone could find one in which they feel at home. We are guaranteed single rooms our junior and senior years. The campus is beautiful but somewhat cut off from the town surrounding it.

Current student, Social Sciences, 9/2005-Submit Date, May 2007

Houses are amazing, mainly because they are houses and not dorms. About 30 students live in each of the 18 houses on campus and a few live off campus in the Welling Townhouse. The houses are open 24/7 and students can come and go into whatever house they like as they please. We have full kitchens, so you can cook a meal for friends and some houses have laundry facilities. Every Sunday at 10 p.m., we have coffee hour, which really brings each house together as a community. Crime is a non-issue at Bennington, although food does go missing from the kitchen on a fairly consistent basis. Students leave their doors unlocked and let people borrow their cars and we have a lot of trust and respect for one another.

Current student, English, 9/2003-Submit Date, May 2007

Housing here is awesome. It's my favorite thing about Bennington. The rooms are huge and most are in colonial style houses, not huge cinderblock complexes. Each one has its own feel and community. We throw great house parties, have cookouts, and just hang out as a house on a regular basis. For me, most of my social network consists of people with whom I live.

The food is OK. They make most of it fresh on campus and there are plenty of vegetarian and vegan options.

Current student, 9/2005-Submit Date, April 2006

Housing is great here! We have three sets of houses, the 12 colonial houses, the three 70s houses and the three new houses. All houses are 35 to 40 students and are co-class and co-ed. Houses are divided into smoking or non-smoking, and quiet hours, extended quiet hours or none at all. Two house chairs manage the residential issues and also participate in committees that serve the campus, such as the residential committee and the food committee.

Each house as a certain character—some houses are known for crazy parties, and some houses contain many people who want to study in their houses. The house chairs facilitate discussions and announcements at our weekly coffee hours, where the house hangs out, talks about what's happening around campus, and eat snacks together.

Security is not really an issue. Most students leave their doors unlocked and feel fine about leaving their belongings while they attend to business elsewhere. Also, our post office has open boxes, meaning anyone can put mail in the box, and we don't need a special key to pick up mail. Dance studios, drama spaces, art studios and practice rooms are all open to any student, regardless of interest or courses.

The dining hall is amazing! We have a salad bar, a soup of the day, fresh baked bread, cereal, fruit, sandwich bar, hot food line and amazing desserts, like chocolate raspberry bars and amazing pineapple upside-down cake. The dining hall is very conscious of vegetarians and vegans and many dishes accommodate those preferences. We do have meat dishes for those who enjoy meat. Our dining hall has omelets on Sundays, we have sundae Sunday, and the dining hall will accept any recipes. They baked 170 pounds of a teriyaki recipe my mom sent from home.

Social Life

Current student, 8/2004-Submit Date, May 2007

There's a bar in our student center. There's Pangaea, the fancy restaurant/lounge/grill/bar that's a 15-minute walk from campus. Several more bars in that vicinity. You will definitely not see "young people" at the bar. You'll see middle-aged Vermont men and women. And if you do, they'll be your classmates. The dating scene is restricted, generally, although there are no rules or anything. It's intense to date someone on campus, because it's so small, and campus life is generally very intense as far as interpersonal relationships go. Everyone knows your business.

Current student, Cultural Studies, 8/2004-Submit Date, May 2007

Social life is awesome. Dance parties every weekend, and most of them are themed. Whether it's the "Dress to Get Laid" party, or one of the famous versus parties (e.g., Pirates versus Ninjas, Hiltons versus Hillbillys). There are also tons of bands, and every spring term there's an event called Sunfest where bands come all day, a 24-hour music festival. There is no Greek system.

Current student, English, 9/2003-Submit Date, May 2007

The social life here is pretty campus-centered. Every weekend there are bands playing, house dance parties, movies and performances. There's an on-campus bar, and some good restaurants and bars in town (Kevin's at Mike's Place, Gimme Pizza). It's a friendly place. I've made some really great friends here and always feel like I can count on the community for anything I need.

Current student, 9/2006-Submit Date, April 2006

Activities are constantly going on to make up for our more isolated campus. Our Outing Club takes students skiing, ice skating, hiking and river rafting. Our Campus Activities Board brings different bands to school each weekend. Professors give poetry readings. Our Community Outreach Leadership Team coordinates tutoring at nearby elementary schools and volunteer activities, both on campus and in Bennington.

Meanwhile, students are always performing. Plays and readings and galleries are constantly going up. Student musicians perform at acoustic and open-mic nights. Houses frequently host dance parties and annual parties.

There are no sororities or fraternities on campus. The down-caf is our campus bar for students over 21, although all students are allowed inside. As far as dating goes, students tend to have marriage-like relationships if they choose to date.

The School Says

A Bennington education is characterized by cross-disciplinary learning, the close working relationship between student and teacher, the self-direction of its academic planning process, and the connection to the world through its winter internship term. Under the thoughtful guidance of faculty advisors, students progress through Bennington by integrating different areas of the curriculum around central ideas or questions, newly discovered and ongoing. In this way, Bennington's academic structure enables students to take increasing responsibility for their education, their work, and their lives.

Founded in 1932, Bennington was, and remains, an invitation to learn through experience. Committed to the belief that the best teachers do what they teach, Bennington faculty members bring their experience to the classroom. This spirit continues to animate a faculty of working scientists, writers, scholars, politicians, and artists who are eager to teach, in the words of one, "what keeps them awake at night." Because both students and teachers are actively engaged in the work at hand, the relationship between teacher and student is richly collaborative, more like coach to athlete, mentor to apprentice, and ultimately colleague to colleague than expert to non-expert.

Each academic year consists of three terms: two 15-week on-campus terms and a seven-week winter Field Work Term (FWT). During FWT, students take their academic interests to the world beyond campus and complete internships in fields that complement their studies, clarify their interests, and prepare them for their future. Bennington is grounded in the conviction that as a college education develops students' professional capacities, it should also prepare them to be deeply thoughtful and actively engaged citizens of the world.

Read all of Vault's College Surveys at **www.vault.com/college**—get complete surveys on 100s of colleges and universities, expert advice on application essays and more.

VAULT CAREER LIBRARY   **731**

Bennington offers a full range of study, with programs in the humanities, natural sciences, mathematics, social sciences, and visual and performing arts, as well as a five-year Bachelor's/Master's degree in Teaching. Additional graduate programs include a low-residency Master of Fine Arts in Writing, a Master of Fine Arts in Performing Arts, and a Master of Arts in Teaching a Second Language.

Middlebury College

Admissions Office
The Emma Willard House
Middlebury College
Middlebury, VT 05753
Admissions phone: (802) 443-3000
Admissions e-mail: admissions@middlebury.edu
Admissions URL: www.middlebury.edu/admissions/

 Admissions

Alumnus/a, English, 9/2003-5/2007, June 2007

I had to do both SAT and an SAT Subject Test—got really good scores on both—I'm sure that really helped my application. Middlebury is big on diversity so feel free to emphasize the particularities of your ethnic, cultural, religious, academic, sporting and so on background—it's a small college so they are very interested in individuals. As Middlebury's reputation increases the selectivity has also increased—easily a Top 10 liberal arts college in the U.S. Midd is also an amazing school for athletes so if you play any sport from rugby to soccer, to American football, to water polo, to crew—emphasize it, contact coaches and meet with them.

Alumnus/a, Pre-med, 10/2002-7/2006, March 2007

Midd was very selective and it was one of the few liberal arts schools to which I applied. I felt the process was detailed and in-depth; I received a few letters from the admissions office after turning in my app saying that the acceptance rate would be the lowest ever.

Alumnus/a, 2/2001-2/2005, March 2006

The admissions process at Middlebury is essentially like any other elite small liberal arts college. I think, however, that they're really interested in students who are well-rounded, active and leaders, especially for their February admissions.

Current student, 9/2001-Submit Date, March 2005

Very Selective. Early Decision was a key for me. There are a lot of athletes here, so playing a sport helps.

Current student, 9/2003-Submit Date, November 2004

The admissions process is similar to that of most other schools of its caliber, and is highly selective. 99 percent selectivity rating in the Princeton Review. Past involvement in extracurriculars and the essay are both key factors in gaining admission. It is extremely helpful to visit the college, attend courses and go on interviews. The college also appreciates students who write about how Middlebury is different from other liberal arts colleges of its caliber, and what they think they would add to the Middlebury community.

Current student, 9/2001-Submit Date, June 2004

The admissions process was fairly standard. I chose to complete the Common Application, which meant that I only had to do one extra essay for Middlebury. Middlebury does not require SATs, which is a bonus—the school does, however, require that you submit three SAT Subject Tests. The interviews supposedly play no role in the admissions process, but making the effort to go and see the school certainly does reflect well upon students. If you want to go to Middlebury, make that desire clear to the admissions staff and show interest throughout the process.

Current student, 9/2000-Submit Date, February 2004

The admissions process was rigorous. They do not look at your SAT scores; th care more about what kind of student you were in high school and what kind interesting things can you bring to Middlebury College and its constituents.

Middlebury College states: "Candidates must submit standardized tests and may select from a menu of three different test options. The requirement may be met by submitting either the ACT; or the SAT I administered on or after March 12, 2005; or three SAT II exams in different areas of study."

 Academics

Alumnus/a, English, 9/2003-5/2007, June 2007

Small classes—you'll get to know profs well if you put in the effort and the should definitely know you—participation is a big part of your grade in mc classes. Most profs require tons of reading (but you can get away with skimmi some to get the general idea). Science majors live in labs; comp sci kids live the computer lab. Some profs at Midd are leading authorities on their subjects—my advisor is one of the, if not the leading critic on George Bernard Shaw. Pro doors are open to anyone at least twice a week so take advantage of that—sor of the greatest minds in the U.S.

Juniors and seniors get whatever classes they want. Freshmen and sophomor have a harder time to get popular classes first try but if you keep on pushing (i. just go to the class and get there early for a week), others will lose hope, chan their minds and drop out—you'll be there to fill their spot. If you plan ahea classes should not be a problem—if you don't it may be.

Take at least a semester abroad (in a warm climate or city if you can)—rur Vermont is great but if you are a city kid or a tropics kid you will miss the hu tle and bustle and the warmth. Take a language—language classes at Midd a incredible. Grading totally depends on profs but with the two or three midterm two or three papers, quizzes and problem sets, you are always aware of how we you are doing throughout the semester so if you do poorly it will not be a su prise. Workload is not easy but that is mainly because most Midd kids are ove achievers (I mean that as a compliment). They have their major, a minor, pla to go abroad, play a sport at its highest level or are part of a performing grou on campus, sit on several boards, pursue hobbies and have crazy social lives—their energy is infectious—you will learn to do all-nighters (which will pay o in the real world).

Alumnus/a, 2/2001-2/2005, March 2006

Middlebury has some phenomenal professors, particularly in geography, polit cal science, English and some of the languages. Despite being known for its lar guage programs, the Spanish department is pretty weak. It's relatively easy get into your top choice classes, you just have to contact the professors, who a interested in having motivated, proactive students in their classrooms. There a smattering of easy or gut classes at Middlebury, some in-between and som really challenging ones—like most colleges, you can basically choose the lev of difficulty you want. The more interesting classes are, no surprise, the harde It can be frustrating to see some students graduate with honors when you've ha much more difficult classes. Grade inflation is a problem in some department

Current student, 9/2003-Submit Date, November 2004

The professors here are absolutely amazing. They are consistently ranked in the top Five for liberal arts colleges, and you get to know each one on a personal level, whether it is having a meal with them or just chatting over office hours. The classes and workload are strenuous, but the result is an incredible amount of knowledge that you learn without ever being bored. A wide variety of classes is available for a wide variety of majors. The quality of these classes exceeds that of many colleges due to the professors and lack of grad-students teaching the courses. Grading is pretty standard, and popular classes are easy to get. Deans and advisors are incredible resources in both academic and extracurricular issues, and are always readily available to help. Middlebury is known for its students studying and working hard. Students are committed to succeeding, and it is evident in their work habits.

Current student, 9/2001-Submit Date, June 2004

Middlebury just adopted a new system of registration for classes, which gives priority based on seniority. It is a fair system, though it means that more of the popular classes will be filled with juniors and seniors. Classes are generally amazing. Most professors are very friendly and extremely approachable. Professors are generally more than happy to meet with you outside of class for whatever reason and truly do act as a support system for the students. There is quite a bit of work, but the amount really varies by class.

Alumnus/a, 9/1997-5/2001, February 2004

Middlebury students receive a liberal arts education in the true sense of the term. Although the requirements are fairly easy to fulfill, each student must complete distribution requirements in seven out of eight academic areas in order to graduate. It's not uncommon for a physics major to take a class in art, or a student to double in English and math. Very few classes fill during registration, but professors are often very flexible. Show up for the first day of class, and they'll often let you in. If not, the college has a very advanced, computer-based registration system that tries to spread the wealth. You are likely to get a class the next time around if you are not enrolled with your first try.

Classes are generally intense—you can expect to read several hundred pages a week for each class, although you can get away with doing much less than that. Teachers try to vary content as much as possible. Outside classes and outdoor labs are common. Most students will get at least a B- or B if they put half effort into a class, but I don't think Middlebury has the grade inflation problem with which other schools are wrestling. Professors are generally accessible and seem to enjoy teaching. I found them very friendly and obviously intelligent. I recall wading through a Vermont stream on a rainy November day with a professor in order to collect stream data when he began quoting from Henry V: "We few / We happy few / Into the breach once more..."

> **Regarding academics, the school says:** "With students from 77 countries, Middlebury College brings a distinctly international focus to the liberal arts. The C.V. Starr-Middlebury Schools Abroad offer 30 programs in 12 countries. Nearly two thirds of Middlebury students spend a semester or year abroad. Middlebury hosts world-renowned summer language schools and the college is affiliated with the Monterey Institute of International Studies."

Employment Prospects

Alumnus/a, English, 9/2003-5/2007, June 2007

In the Northeast—particularly Boston, NYC, CT and Washington, D.C.—Middlebury has an incredible reputation. Alumni network is invaluable during job search—just send them an e-mail and they will get back to you ASAP—and it's easy to find their e-mail addresses. Recommendations from certain profs and admin on campus are great ways to get in the door for an interview. Loads of economics majors (and some non-majors) are actively recruited by Wall Street (Lehman, CSFB, Morgan Stanley, Goldman and so on). Loads of CX majors actively recruited by Wall Street for their tech people. Every two weeks or so, there are companies coming to give presentations or conduct interviews. Teach for America is a popular choice. Many humanities majors work in advertising.

Alumnus/a, 2/2001-2/2005, March 2006

There is a good Career Services Office with a strong alumni network, but students have to be proactive about utilizing those services. Employers do come to campuses to do recruiting, and investment banking firms tend to be the most ubiquitous that come because of Middlebury's strong alumni community in I-banking.

Current student, 9/2003-Submit Date, November 2004

Due to the extensive alumni network, job placement at this school is one of the top in the country. It is extremely easy to get good internships (I will be going to Costa Rica this winter) because of the J-term scheduling. Graduates are able to obtain jobs in every field, and the prestige that comes with the name Middlebury is very helpful in placement.

Current student, 9/2000-Submit Date, February 2004

People who leave Middlebury either end up teaching for a couple of years or go off to work on some Wall Street firm for a couple of years. The school seems to breed a lot of people who are interested in nonprofit or environmentally friendly organizations.

Alumnus/a, 9/1997-5/2001, February 2004

Midd grads leave college with so-called "unemployable" liberal arts degrees, but this problem is mitigated by the growing prestige of the Middlebury name. Middlebury grads generally end up with interesting and varied careers, ranging from investment banking to avalanche for casting. Although the Middlebury name might not be as well known as some Ivy League schools, top employers and grad schools certainly appreciate the school, as evidenced by the long line of recruiters on campus each fall. Middlebury's extensive Career Services apparatus is complemented by a loyal and extended alumni network that is always looking out for fellow Midd grads. I got my first job out of college at a Middlebury alumni event at a baseball game, and Midd's web site has a section where Midd grads can post jobs open only to Middlebury students—the list is quite long!

Quality of Life

Alumnus/a, English, 9/2003-5/2007, June 2007

Everyone lives on campus or five minutes away, which is great in terms of getting to know people very well but hard to find new faces. Beautiful campus. Facilities are second to none—new library is a spaceship on the outside (good and bad) but inside the resources from media viewing rooms to Bloomberg terminal, to IT support, to books are incredible. Science labs are great; the sports complex has climbing wall, heated pool and ice hockey rink; Midd has its own snow ball! Adirondacks and other mountains make for great hikes. Crime is almost nonexistent. Workload does limit taking advantage of some of the great guest lecturers and performers who visit.

Alumnus/a, 2/2001-2/2005, March 2006

The quality of life at Middlebury was pretty amazing—the campus is the most stunning I've seen in the Northeast; the facilities are like that of a large university; crime is virtually nonexistent and housing is great

Current student, 9/2001-Submit Date, March 2005

The physical infrastructure is very impressive. I am a senior and have seen about 10 new buildings completed in my time here. Housing is very good and the campus is very safe.

Current student, 9/2003-Submit Date, November 2004

The quality of life is indicative of a rural college. It is absolutely beautiful (we own our own mountain to ski on), and crime is not an issue. The campus is gorgeous, and every aspect of the landscape is clean and groomed. Housing is pretty average. The buildings are spectacular, but they are college dormrooms, although the newer dorms have tremendous living conditions. The food here is locally and organically grown, as they try to support local farmers. It is easy for vegetarians to have healthy meals here as well, and even the salmon is non-farmed Alaskan salmon. You can watch your food be cooked and they will cook to order. The college provides one of the most secure, homey atmospheres I have ever experienced.

Read all of Vault's College Surveys at **www.vault.com/college**—get complete surveys on 100s of colleges and universities, expert advice on applicaton essays and more.

VAULT CAREER LIBRARY   **733**

Current student, 9/2000-Submit Date, February 2004

The quality of life at Middlebury is very high. Tuition is high, so all activities are usually paid for. The school's activities board caters to mostly the wider whiter public, so there are few events that the school's white students put on for diversity. To offset that, student organizations of color put on events with sizable budgets. Living is great. Most housing on campus is newly built and tailored to what the students want. Food is very good. There are at least three dining halls open at any given time.

> **Regarding quality of life, Middlebury says:** "Middlebury was ranked second in the nation by Grist on its list of green colleges and universities. Well known for its emphasis on campus sustainability, the college has the oldest undergraduate environmental studies program in the country and has pledged to be carbon neutral by 2016. Among its many carbon-reducing initiatives, the college offers students the use of Zipcars—highly efficient Toyota hybrids—with the aim of reducing the number of vehicles on campus."

 Social Life

Alumnus/a, English, 9/2003-5/2007, June 2007

There are five bars within walking distance—everyone goes to the same two on Thursday nights. Great food at the three different dining halls. No Greek system—but there are co-ed social houses—not the same thing and not for everyone, but they do sponsor a lot of campus events and parties. Party scene declined over the past few years but if you're a freshman, you enjoy anything because it's all new; if you're a senior you can go to the bar; if you're a junior you should spend at least a semester abroad. Great performances come through on the weekends but they need more, way more—especially high-profile musicians.

Talented students put on good shows throughout the week at the Grille. If yo are into a cappella, you will be very satisfied.

Current student, 9/2003-Submit Date, November 2004

The social life at Middlebury definitely revolves around on-campus activitie Because it is located in the middle of Vermont, there are few bars and clubs the surrounding area. Some students choose to go to Burlington or Montreal f the weekend if they are looking for scenes such as those. On campus, there a numerous events going on every weekend. Student shows, dance troups, mus cal artists, movies and dance parties are always present. In addition to activiti such as these, the college has a social house system, rather than the common fr ternities and sororities. Social houses are co-ed and provide the club-like atmo phere that the town lacks. There are frequent themed parties, dances and alc hol is available. The social houses on campus have something happening eve weekend and provide a great atmosphere for meeting up with friends or meetir new people.

Current student, 9/2001-Submit Date, June 2004

Social houses are a source of entertainment for many on campus. Off-camp parties (for which buses are generally rented) have become an increasingly po ular option for students. There is one bar in town that serves as a student han out on Thursday nights. The restaurant selection in and around Middlebury surprisingly good—we have an amazing bakery in town as well as an amazir sandwich shop. For dinner options, there are a few casual options, though the are also a number of excellent upscale options.

Current student, 9/2000-Submit Date, February 2004

The social life on campus is mostly what you make of it. In the wintertime seems as if everyone at the school is off skiing. The weekends are usually fu of social house parties, minority organization events and cultural dinner Throughout all those events there are also high numbers of drinking partie however, there are always non-alcoholic events going on every week at campu for those that do not use any substances.

University of Vermont

Undergraduate Admissions Office
194 S. Prospect St.
Burlington, VT 05401
Admissions phone: (802) 656-3370
Admissions fax: (802) 656-8611
Admissions e-mail: admissions@uvm.edu
Admissions URL:
www.uvm.edu/admissions/undergraduate/

 Admissions

Current student, English, 8/2005-Submit Date, June 2007

UVM [accepts] the Common App, which made it really easy to apply. I came to Burlington, did a campus tour and an interview, and mailed a paper application. My best advice for getting into UVM (i.e., essays, interviews and so on) is to be completely honest and real. Burlington is an incredible town, and UVM is full of people who are very passionate and driven. The best way to show that you want to be a part of a community such as that is to show yourself to the counselor, the tour guide, or with whomever it is you're meeting.

Current student, 8/2004-Submit Date, May 2007

As a Vermont student, UVM had always been an obvious choice when deciding on schools. After taking a tour of campus, I knew UVM was the place I wanted

to spend the next four years of my life, so I decided to apply. What helps in th admissions process is to figure out what sets you apart from other applicants an show that off, either in the interview or in the application or essay. In past years due to tremendous popularity, UVM has become a selective institution, so yo must take yourself out of the crowd and show why you will be a benefit to UVM

Current student, 9/2003-Submit Date, September 2005

As a transfer student, the admissions process was tedious. However, tedious a it was, the staff here at UVM is always very helpful with any questions that may arise during the process.

Tips on getting in: good letters of recommendation (more is better), high SAT scores, high GPA from previous college is better then a good high school GPA keep in touch with the heads of the department of interest, make appointment for interviews and most importantly show that you are willing to do anything Colleges are looking for devoted students; it looks good when a university ha low drop-out rates and high GPA average.

Current student, 9/2003-Submit Date, May 2005

I had to fill out an application and submit an essay. No interview was required I received my letter of acceptance a few months later. The university is not ter ribly selective, so I didn't have many doubts as to whether I would get in. I wa sent a lot of information about the university through the mail, and I attended tour and orientation.

Current student, 8/2004-Submit Date, November 2005

e admissions process is pretty standard. Must fill out the application and the FSA, write an essay. The school has about 8,500 people here and is expanding.

> **Regarding admissions, The school says:** "Last year, 65 percent of first-year applicants were admitted to the University of Vermont. Admission to each of UVM's seven undergraduate schools closely follows this average. Applicants should be aware that some academic programs, including business, engineering and health sciences, recommend or require additional math and science preparation beyond the minimum necessary for admission to the university. Application criteria are listed at www.uvm.edu/admissions/undergraduate/applying."

Academics

Current student, Engineering, 8/2004-Submit Date, May 2007

a mechanical engineering student, I have gotten the pleasure of enjoying aller classes and developing strong relationships with my professors. This ows for professors really to push you to your potential, but also to be there if u happen to fall behind. Usually getting into the larger, more popular classes 't too hard, and if it is a required class for your major, you are pretty much aranteed a spot.

Current student, English, 8/2005-Submit Date, June 2007

eally felt as though I'd found a home in the English department during my phomore year. I started taking more specific classes that were smaller, more ding intensive, and more discussion based, and I found that my professors re valuable tools whom I'd been taking for granted. They have so much to fer and are entirely open and willing to help. I chose English because it's what m naturally good at, but they consistently push me and as a result I've devel ed with each passing semester. Additionally, I've fostered relationships with ofessors outside of the classroom, which I've found to be invaluable. They ve just as much to teach about life as they do about literature, and I am grate l to have come across a faculty that influences all aspects of my life.

Current student, 8/2006-Submit Date, May 2007

ourses are very easy to get into, especially if they're required for your major. y advisors and teachers are also very encouraging. Whenever I talk to an advi r or go to a teacher for help, I always walk away feeling like I am capable of ing anything. Classes also aren't too large, and if they are (like 200 people) s easy to get to know your teacher during office hours. They are always more an happy to talk to students.

Current student, 9/2003-Submit Date, May 2005

m a women's studies major. The classes are good; we have competent profes rs and class size is usually no more than 30. Some classes are more, but they e usually introductory classes.

he grading system is normal, A through F. Unfortunately, there is not a large lection of classes offered in my field. Our workload is normal, I think; for ch class about two hours of homework a night.

ometimes it's difficult to register for some classes, especially for freshmen and nall majors. For example, it is impossible to take an art class unless you are an t major—there just isn't any availability.

> **The school says:** "Some courses do fill up quickly each year. Flexible students generally are able to enroll in any course of interest for which they meet requirements, though not always in the semester desired."

Current student, 8/2004-Submit Date, November 2005

he professors here are very good. Even if there is a class size of 200 people, 's easy to stand out and have a personal relationship with the professor. The asses are very challenging but not impossible. The workload isn't too bad. I n an athlete and work, and I still had a 3.53 GPA last year. Grading is very fair re.

Alumnus/a, 9/1999-6/2003, December 2004

School of Business Administration deserves a second look from employees and critics. The program is very difficult and prepares you for the real world. The professors are very down to earth but do not let anything slide. I have heard of students handing reports in late at other schools, this would not fly at UVM's BSAD.

Workload is normal, various semester projects, test, quizzes and homework assignments. Each teacher has his/her own grading style, some a lot harder than others, but always fair. Expect to learn more from professors than your grade reflects.

Classes are offered on first come, first serve basis. If a student needs a class to complete a requirement, he/she can get the teacher and advisors to sign off on an override form. Use your academic advisor. Mine never knew my name and was not of much help my first two years. Make the most out of every service the school offers because they are there to help you. The program is very well-rounded, though it also separates students into their desired fields.

> **Regarding academics, The school says:** "With more than 90 undergraduate majors, 53 master's degree and 22 doctoral programs, UVM offers exceptional academic breadth in most disciplines, serving undergraduate and graduate students alike. More than 2,200 courses are offered to undergraduates. A self-designed major option allows motivated students to pursue courses of study beyond existing program offerings. Outstanding opportunities also exist to combine interests in different fields of study, for instance business with foreign language, engineering with environmental studies."

Employment Prospects

Current student, 9/2003-Submit Date, September 2005

Most graduates get a job right out of college. Molecular genetics is a widely diversified field. Jobs can range from stem cell research to the creation and testing of pharmaceuticals. Remember, the harder majors more often land the highest paying jobs and are most readily available for employment right out of college. Don't expect to find a job with a degree in psychology right out of college.

Current student, English, 8/2005-Submit Date, June 2007

UVM Career Services is a strong program with a real will to help students, whether they're still undergraduates or have just graduated. They offer job fairs, coaching, networking and support. In addition, UVM is a research university with a very small graduate school; this leaves a lot of research and internship opportunities for undergrad students, which can only help after graduation.

Current student, 8/2004-Submit Date, November 2005

There are always internships available, many students do student teaching and work in the hospital located right on campus. There are always guest speakers coming to help with résumés and internships and helping seniors find jobs.

Alumnus/a, 9/1999-6/2003, December 2004

A new Career Connection Center was recently added [to the business school]. The staff continues to network with alumni and organize trips for the various business school clubs to meet with them. Make the most of the career center. Unfortunately, many employers overlook UVM's BSAD School.

Alumni, on the other hand, are great. Graduates can land any job they want except for the highly recruited positions, due to employers' relationships with other schools. The Business School is getting better every year. Jobs range from the biggest banks to "boiler room" firms, from the best marketing companies to marketing for major corporations. My friends all have jobs at very well-respected investment banks.

> **Regarding career opportunities, The school says:** "UVM has excellent recruiting relationships with leading employers around the country. General Electric, Burton Snowboards, IBM, PricewaterhouseCoopers and Duff & Phelps are but a few examples of the many firms recruiting business students, as well as

Read all of Vault's College Surveys at **www.vault.com/college**—get complete surveys on 100s of colleges and universities, expert advice on applicaton essays and more.

VAULT CAREER LIBRARY 735

other majors. Our career network continues to grow in size and activity through the success of UVM graduates and expansion of University Career Services. Currently, more than 3,000 companies listed on our employer database encourage applications from UVM students and graduates for permanent positions, internships and seasonal employment."

Quality of Life

Current student, English, 8/2005-Submit Date, June 2007

Students at UVM are entirely happy to be here. 33 percent of our student body is from Vermont, but 33 percent of our student body doesn't pack up to go home on the weekends. People like to be here because they feel comfortable and because there is something for everyone. We have all different program housing (themed suite-style living, the Slade House, the live music floor, community service floors, the Green House, and on and on), 11 different dining facilities, and our own accredited police force. We're also right up the hill from downtown Burlington, and in between Lake Champlain and the Green Mountains—a perfect location.

Current student, 8/2004-Submit Date, May 2007

Housing on campus is required for the first two years of school, after that most students move off campus to downtown Burlington. There is a multitude of apartments for students and they provide a great way to see Burlington in a new light. The campus is currently under construction, but it is slated to complete by fall 2007, which will provide students with a large number of new facilities. The gym at UVM is also great; I love to go because you can choose to look out over the mountains or watch TV while you run. There is really something for everyone at the gym, from varsity sports to intramurals, or just people getting together to play basketball on a Sunday night, or even free ballroom dance lessons with the Dance Club—it is all there.

Current student, 9/2003-Submit Date, September 2005

The campus has nearly no crime, it is a very safe in which community to live. On-campus housing is convenient for getting to and from class because of UVM's bus system and in most cases class is just a short walk from the dorms. Dining is always readily available with dining areas around every corner on campus.

Currently, however, the campus is adding new dorms and research buildings. Therefore, the campus is a mess in some areas and detours are needed. But students can check the online campus map and it will show a detailed map of where the construction is.

Current student, 9/2003-Submit Date, May 2005

Campus life is good. Food is very expensive, but usually nutritious. Unfortunately, it's not the best cooking, and you get pretty tired of it after a while. One problem is there is not enough of a selection of vegan/vegetarian food. I lived this entire semester on veggie burgers and salad. Another problem is there's nowhere to get food after 11 p.m. on weekdays and 9 p.m. on weekends. This leads to a lot of hungry students.

Regarding quality of life, The school says: "First- and second-year students are required to live on campus. Most thank us for it! On-campus living promotes academic success as well as connection to the UVM community. In their junior and senior years, many students take a step toward greater independence and move off campus into apartments throughout Burlington's hill section, between campus and downtown.

"University Heights, an attractive new residential complex featuring leading environmental design, added 800 beds to UVM's residential capacity in Spring, 2006. Nearly all existing residence halls have recently been renovated, further enhancing campus living options."

Social Life

Current student, 8/2006-Submit Date, May 2007

There isn't too much Greek influence on the social life. The male-to-female ratio is fairly equal and can even be distracting. In my experience, you meet people mostly through the activities with which you're involved and with who is on your floor. In the first-year classes, due to the size, I generally don't meet many people through classes, unless it's a lab partner.

Current student, 8/2004-Submit Date, May 2007

I am heavily involved in the Ski and Snowboard Club on campus, which offers lots of trips, as well as buses to local ski mountains on the weekends. The trips have always proved to lots of fun, and a great way to meet tons of UVM students who like to get out and be active. Downtown Burlington is also a great place to go hangout. There are tons of little coffee shops, stores and lots of bars, some that are even open to 18+ for dancing and listening to local bands.

Current student, 9/2003-Submit Date, September 2005

The social life is great (if you have time). Downtown Burlington is beautiful with many great places to dine out, including a great nightlife with hopping bars (I recommend RJ's). Lots of dating going on; you won't go a day without meeting someone new if you put yourself out there.

UVM always has great events from comedians (Dane Cook!!!) to concerts, and don't forget the varsity sports. The Greek system is small in comparison to other universities'. However, the majority of the Greek system is very respectable and have a huge impact on campus life for those who are involved.

Current student, 9/2003-Submit Date, May 2005

There's no campus bar, but the walk downtown is very short. There is a good number of bars and clubs downtown, but you have to be 21 to get in, so otherwise it can get a bit boring. Along with the bars and clubs there is an excellent restaurant scene, but they are a bit expensive for a college budget, so eating out is a treat but not a regular habit. There are a lot of school-hosted events, but sometimes they're expensive. There are a lot of free events, though. All lectures and movies are free.

The Greek system exists on campus, but usually for partying—I'm not familiar with it outside of frat parties. There are many clubs, ranging from a variety of interests from athletic to political. These clubs are very active but largely under funded.

Current student, 8/2004-Submit Date, November 2005

Burlington is a college town. Church Street is a street blocked off to traffic with tons of shops and vendors and restaurants. It is a college favorite. It is within walking distance from campus although the bus does travel there. There is also a mall in the opposite direction as Church Street from campus. Three Tomatoes, American Flatbread and Sweetwaters are just a few of the amazing restaurants to try.

Regarding social life, The school says: "UVM students are exceptionally active, both inside and outside the classroom. The recreational options available in the city (music, theaters, shops, restaurants) and in the surrounding area (hiking, biking, boating, skiing, snowboarding) have earned Burlington distinctions as one of the nation's top college towns and best places to live. Campus organizations help students get to the mountains, theater, French-speaking Montreal (100 miles north) and other attractions.

"Those looking for a 'party school' atmosphere likely won't make it past the first year, and need not apply. UVM, the City of Burlington and the Greek system (8 percent of the student body) have stepped-up enforcement and penalties associated with underage drinking: all residence halls are now substance-free."

College of William & Mary

ffice of Undergraduate Admission
O. Box 8795
illiamsburg, VA 23187-8795
dmissions phone: (757) 221-4223
dmissions fax: (757) 221-1242
dmissions e-mail: admission@wm.edu
dmissions URL: www.wm.edu/admission/

 Admissions

lumnus/a, Biology, 8/2001-5/2005, May 2007

&M is more focused on well-rounded students than some other programs. s, you must have good grades and test scores, but the essays are most impor- it. The admissions staff definitely looks for students who will add to the com- unity, not just students at the top of high school classes. I recommend taking ery opportunity to get your name noticed by the admissions committee: attend urs (make sure to sign up for the mailing list!), get an interview, spend a night ith students. Each time your name passes by for one of these events, the admis- ons committee takes notice! And if waitlisted, don't stop. Those who are entually let in showed they wanted to be at the school: sending in extra essays creative projects or showing up on campus to promote themselves.

> **The school says:** "While making oneself stand out as an appli- cant is an important part of the admissions process, William and Mary does not use demonstrated interest as a factor in admis- sions decisions."

urrent student, 8/2005-Submit Date, May 2006

illiam & Mary requires the Common Application and then has an additional pplement. Unlike some of its competitors, William & Mary does not have ultiple essays and short answer questions. There is an optional essay, though any reasonable applicant it would seem a good idea to complete this essay as can be on any topic and provides the admissions staff with a more personal and mplete picture of the applicant. William & Mary looks at a range of factors to termine admission for applicants. There is no single, must-have factor— ough taking challenging courses in high school and being active in your com- unity (sports, a club or service) are among the most important factors.

now also that the admissions staff is not frightening and they actually are iman; call them with a question or for advice and they will be helpful. William Mary does not do interviews—they have optional interviews during the sum- er in which a rising senior interviews students. This information is not a make- -break situation for the applicant—you can definitely get in without an inter- ew (I didn't have one) but it is another way to set yourself apart and give the Imissions office a more personal view of yourself and talents.

or selectivity, William & Mary is a highly selective institution but among those elected each year there is a unique mix of personalities, interests and talents. /illiam & Mary's new president, Gene Nichol, has made increasing minority umbers within the college a top priority and so that should begin to be reflect- I in the admissions numbers in the coming years.

urrent student, 8/2003-Submit Date, May 2006

ith approximately only 33 percent of students being admitted, the process is efinitely competitive. Solid advice: use your personal essay. You've heard it a t, but get creative. Don't write about your lame experiences helping people ecause nearly 5,000 of the applications say that). Feel free to be different and low some personality! Shake things up!

urrent student, 8/2004-Submit Date, May 2006

visited William & Mary twice to make sure I was really going to fit in. I used e Common Application with supplement and did not have an interview. I was

told of my acceptance early because I was a Monroe Scholar. That extra honor really cemented my decision to come; I felt particularly wanted by the school.

Current student, 8/2002-Submit Date May 2006

From my experience, William & Mary values life experiences, involvement and leadership in the admissions process more than just about any other four-year college. Of course, class rank and test scores are important too, but not more so than involvement and breadth of experiences prior to college.

Current student, 8/2004-Submit Date, May 2005

William & Mary uses the Common Application. Interviews are not typically part of the application process. The university is highly selective for out-of-state applicants; I went to a very competitive public high school north of Detroit, and our valedictorian, who was also a National Merit semi-finalist, was not accept- ed. This type of situation occurs because two-thirds of accepted applicant must be from Virginia, resulting in a noticeable difference between the qualifications of Virginia students and out-of-state students.

> **The school says:** "There is not a noticeable difference between the qualifications of in-state versus out-of-state students; it is just a more selective process for the non-VA residents."

As for essays, the admissions officers really do read them, and the optional sub- mission, which is supposed to describe yourself, is very important. Don't just slap in another essay you wrote for another college; you can make a collage or draw a picture, but just do something interesting and unique. Even if you are already qualified, the optional selection seems to influence the awarding of Monroe Scholarships, which carry multiple perks in addition to money.

> **The school says:** "The optional submission does not impact the awarding of the Monroe Scholars distinction."

Current student, 1/2003-Submit Date, September 2003

I applied Early Decision to William & Mary. I filled out the normal application, got recommendations from high school teachers, and wrote essays. The essays are also weighted heavily here, so be sure to put in special effort into those. Having a science and math background has been helpful in the past—as a liber- al arts school, it tries to attract people with those types of backgrounds; so if you are concerned about your application, try to emphasize any experience you have there.

 Academics

Alumnus/a, History, 8/2001-5/2005, May 2006

I always felt prepared for classes and tests if I just followed the simple rule of showing up. There aren't many curveballs thrown at you as the professors have a great course of study lined up no matter the class and want to see you succeed and contribute to the class.

Workload was never beyond my abilities—I usually took around 16 credits a semester, with no more than two classes that really challenged me time-wise or mental capacity-wise. Always try to take a class that lets you relax and enjoy yourself—either a kinesiology or a music class a semester really levels things out against in-depth science, history or economics.

I never came across a professor who was out of reach—in fact, almost all were very approachable and loved to help out. As a history major, professors loved to chat with you and help you find angles to write about and research.

Like any public school in VA, recent budget cuts have forced classloads to be diminished, thereby making it harder to get into certain classes. As a psycholo- gy minor, it was very tough to get into classes needed for a minor as very few were options and they were snagged up by students with majors in psychology prior to anyone else getting a shot. This was felt in certain higher-level history

Read all of Vault's College Surveys at **www.vault.com/college**—get complete surveys on 100s of colleges and univer- sities, expert advice on applicaton essays and more.

VAULT CAREER LIBRARY **737**

classes as well as the music department. It's recommended to come in with college credits via AP or IB to make your registration time slot as early as possible to get the leg up on your classmates.

Alumnus/a, Biology, 8/2001-5/2005, May 2007

The focus is definitely on academics. You will be challenged in class. But this isn't a bad thing. Instead it makes you take an active role in your education. Participation is required in pretty much all classes, from the 10-person freshman seminars to the large intro lectures. The professors are dedicated to providing a topnotch education and are equally involved in making sure students reach their potentials. You can easily approach them out of class for added help or just a coffee to get to know them better (key for when you want them to write a recommendation). While the workload can seem daunting at times, keep up and you'll be fine. There has been a problem with getting in to certain classes (kinesiology, English and small-sized classes for the first two years), but if you keep looking to register for them, you can get in before graduation. The biggest shock academically will be grades. Inflation is rare and standards are high. For most students, they will receive their first D or F. Don't expect all A's. Then again, that's not the point of academics here. Students work hard to get a B and are satisfied with that because of the amount of knowledge they obtain from courses. The success you achieve here is not in a GPA; it's in the education you've received.

Current student, 8/2004-Submit Date, May 2006

I found the coursework to be the appropriate next step up from my very competitive high school. I greatly enjoy my classes, both lecture and discussion oriented. Even in my large intro science classes my professor knows everyone by name and makes the class feel really intimate. I find that I use my scholar status as a tool to get into classes but even regular students often get into classes through e-mailing professors early or showing up on the first day anyway. Grading is fair but students certainly work for a good grade. I tend to balance my courseload with one lighter class to keep me sane. Professors are always available to talk both academically and as advisors for other areas of life. I have become incredibly close with several professors not including my advisor. We often have coffee and discuss personal and academic life. I certainly work a lot here, but it's my job as a student to do, so if you don't want to learn and aren't passionate, don't come here.

Current student, 8/2002-Submit Date, May 2006

Every class I took at William & Mary was a new experience. Professors are usually at the very top of their fields and incredibly dedicated to the work they do and to making sure that every student in class can relate to the topic and its importance. Getting popular classes is rarely difficult—a student's sincere interest in a topic overrules course capacity for the majority of professors here. Workload is very substantial—doing five or six hours per day of work every weekday is not unheard of, and grading is stringent. There is absolutely no grade inflation here—one professor told me that that is the first thing professors are told when they are hired.

Alumnus/a, 9/1999-5/2003, May 2006

W&M offers a very strong academic environment. Professors have a genuine interest in teaching. If they weren't interested in teaching, they would be working at a major research university and getting twice as much. But time and time again, the professors "profess" it's the students who keep them at W&M. Perhaps it's the small classes and interactions between the professors and students who make the learning environment so special. The famous freshman seminar where all freshmen must take a seminar with 15 or less students is testament to the university's commitment of keeping small class sizes and fostering strong professor-student relationships.

As for the workload, this can be quite heavy at times across most majors. That being said, not many people get to W&M and are able to breeze by. Achieving A's is not the status quo.

Alumnus/a, 7/1999-5/2003, September 2005

William & Mary is a liberal arts university that is known for its ability to produce great thinkers. Look at how many past presidents graduated from the school. Thomas Jefferson, to name one, is a graduate. Very competitive and challenging courses. You cannot just master the academic material and expect to excel. You must be able to interpret information and apply it to various situations. Great faculty. Very knowledgeable and approachable. The school has

an outstanding reputation that aids in further education if desired by student. grade inflation. One of the hardest workloads in the country. Very difficult rewarding. It will allow you to reach your professional goals.

Employment Prospects

Current student, 8/2003-Submit Date, May 2006

The business school has strong numbers (95 percent have a job within months of graduation). Not sure about the general numbers. About 40 perc of students go straight on to graduate school. The alumni network is strong. T into this. Career services is useful only for résumé/cover letter writing and mo interviews. Otherwise, they are limited.

Alumnus/a, Biology, 8/2001-5/2005, May 2007

There is a lot of recruitment on campus, especially for government positio Alumni are very successful in obtaining jobs or entering higher-level stud (med school, law school, graduate school) with all degrees. Alumni are a everywhere, in every job sector you can think of, as are people who know a respect the name. Additionally, many graduates pursue service opportuniti such as Teach for America or Peace Corps. It is well known that W&M grad ates are academically strong and, almost more importantly, well-grounded people. Students are socially conscious, hardworking and motivated, all qua ties eagerly sought by employers. The name might not be as flashy as an I League school, but it opens up just as many doors.

Alumnus/a, 9/1999-5/2003, May 2006

People often smile and say, "oh, yes, that's a good school," when you tell the you went to William & Mary; however, I can't say that the school is inundat with big-name companies that are looking to hire prized W&M grads. It ha good name, but perhaps it is its location that is the biggest barrier for getti Fortune 500 companies to recruit on campus. On the other hand, if you are loo ing to work in the D.C. Metropolitan area, W&M has a strong pipeline wi employers in the area. Many grads end up working in the D.C. area after th graduate. But once you start moving outside the middle states area, recruite tend to divert their focus to other more accessible and bigger name schoo Unlike the Ivy League schools, the onus lies predominantly on the W&M st dent to find a job outside the realm of regional companies/institutions th actively recruit on the campus.

Alumnus/a, 8/2000-5/2005, October 2005

At William & Mary, they tell you that they have a great reputation and that it w open doors for you when you graduate. What they do not tell you is the who truth. It will open doors for you if: (1) you plan on furthering your degree; (you plan on staying in Virginia or Washington, D.C. area; and (3) you are accounting or finance major. Do not get sucked into the rhetoric. Start appl ing for jobs early, make contacts, and do internships. It will pay off later.

Alumnus/a, 8/1999-5/2003, June 2005

William & Mary is the gold standard when applying for local jobs and gradua schools. Its prestige is known far beyond Williamsburg—most people on t East Coast, I think, give a William & Mary grad an immediate boost in respec Employers know what an academic boot camp W & M is, and know the streng and dedication of its students. Graduates go all over, some volunteering for t Peace Corps and Americorps, some going straight into business, and others co tinuing on to graduate school. Many W & M students go to law school, or on get their MBA or PhD. Students work far and wide—and there are extreme active alumni associations in D.C. and New York. No matter where you ar you'll find W & M alumni to be incredibly friendly and welcoming, and willi to help their own. I've found this an invaluable resource in the years since graduated. While there are the standard on-campus recruiting opportuniti found at any top school, William & Mary also offers its students incredib internship opportunities, whether through alumni connections or simply W M's good name worldwide. Getting a William & Mary education is the first st to a successful and rewarding professional life, no matter where you may wa to go—or what you want to do.

Quality of Life

Current student, 8/2004-Submit Date, May 2006

While housing leaves a little to be desired, the college is making a conscious effort to improve with the new dorms being built. Personally, I have enjoyed living on campus and will do so all four years. The college is so campus oriented that I want to stay in the heart of things. I love Williamsburg as a college town. There's enough tourist money to keep safety and dining options but enough student pull that prices at most places are low to fair.

Alumnus/a, Biology, 8/2001-5/2005, May 2007

Students take it upon themselves to get things done and improve the quality of life on campus. When there was a need for recycling, a group coordinated the campus-wide program. Students lobbied for increased rights in the area, such as easier local voting registration and changes to housing laws. The administration has supported students 100 percent. Housing is available for anyone who wants it. Freshmen live on campus. A large percentage continues to live on campus for the remaining years, though housing in the area is also cheap and available. Food isn't bad but isn't amazing either. The campus and area are very safe. Campus police are approachable and understanding but still keep firm control. The campus itself is beautiful. New housing has just been finished and even the older buildings are being renovated to keep up with student needs. Really, anything that is needed to make student life better is done.

Current student, 8/2005-Submit Date, May 2006

The housing on campus is excellent. A large majority of students choose to live on campus all four years. Freshmen are required to live on campus—of the freshman dorms available, Barrett Hall and Dupont Hall are the best choices. Barrett went co-ed this year and is the showcase dorm. It is situated right on old campus and has tall ceilings, has air conditioning and a gorgeous parlor. This coming fall a brand-new set of dorms is opening that will be really really nice. As for upperclassman dorms you have lots of choices as far as location and type of dorm. Housing lottery occurs every spring and there are traditionally a couple hundred rising sophomores who are bumped.

The campus is absolutely gorgeous. There are two main parts of campus—Old Campus and New Campus. Old Campus borders Colonial Williamsburg and includes the Wren Building (the oldest academic building still in use today in the U.S.), the president's home and office, the academic buildings that line the Sunken Gardens, and some dorms. On warm days, students sunbathe in the Sunken Gardens, play frisbee and football. Various philanthropy events, King and Queens Ball, fairs, school-sponsored fairs, concerts and movies all occur on the Sunken Gardens.

As for the rec center—it is somewhat on the far reaches of campus—but think of its distance as part of your workout and you feel better about yourself for going! The rec center is almost done being completely rebuilt. As for the dining, there are three main dining halls—the Marketplace, the U.C. and the Caf.

As for safety—I have never felt unsafe on campus, even walking across campus at midnight. That said, there are blue-lights scattered throughout campus and the police and student escort service are available to drive students home if they are out late. In general, there is really very little crime on campus. I feel comfortable leaving my computer and books in the library while I get a meal and know that no one will take it. I leave my door unlocked and have never worried or felt unsafe when I wasn't there.

Finally, the surrounding neighborhood, Colonial Williamsburg, is a wonderful place to go. There are lots of shops and restaurants and it is simply beautiful. The bookstore has a Starbucks and is a great place to study. Running down the main street (Duke of Gloucester Street) is lots of fun and the green in front of the Governor's palace is a really nice place to study. Overall, Colonial Williamsburg is a really nice place to study, enjoy a relaxing afternoon, or get a quick meal!

Social Life

Current student, 8/2003-Submit Date, October 2006

The Green and Gold Affair (a fundraising campus-wide dance) was a highlight of the fall. The alcohol task force made parties illegal three years ago, but the social life has grown back quite heavily. I mean, it's a blast, [and] I love my friends.

> **The school says:** "On-campus parties are not illegal, but they are regulated to ensure that students have fun safely. William & Mary students effectively balance academic and social life on campus, but this does not mean that the majority of students spend their weekends studying."

Alumnus/a, 8/2001-5/2005, May 2006

There will always be a stigma or a bad social scene, few parties and generally nerdy people associated with William & Mary. Truth of the matter is, like any other undergraduate institution in the world, the party and social scene is what you want it to be. If you want to rely on other people providing you the fun, there's a lot of options, but they won't always be tailor fitted to you. UCAB, the campus activities board, does a whole lot with the money they receive each year to bring a wide variety of activities, bands, speakers, and general nonsense for the students.

The fraternities are a rite of passage for freshmen too scared to throw a party in their dorms, but there isn't much variety here and really should only be a last resort for people eager for a party.

Once you're of age (or know the bouncer pretty well) the delis are an isolated, yet very fun, time. Essentially they're bars, with great alcohol and tons of people on the weekends.

Throw your own parties if you have a dorm conducive to it. It's really a blast and after a night of drinking (or not drinking), the size of layout of the campus affords a ton of late night activities (frisbee, kickball).

Other than that, Richmond and VA Beach aren't that far away if you need to retreat from campus for a night or so.

Just be creative and have fun somehow—you'll be much more fun to hang out with if you're not constantly complaining about how there's nothing to do, because there seriously is tons to do.

Current student, 8/2004-Submit Date, May 2006

While the delis (the Green Leafe is far and away the top favorite) are hit or miss with letting students in, Greek life and small gatherings satisfy many students socially. Students participate in the whole dating spectrum from casual hookups to formalized dating. Tequila Rose is the cheap place to drink margueritas and have fantastic drunk food and IHOP caters to the campus. The great thing about the social life here is pretty much everyone is connected by some mutual friends but there are enough people so you're not always dating your friends' exes.

Current student, 1/2003-Submit Date, September 2003

Only three real bars exist—the Green Leafe, Paul's and College Delly—but they are frequented heavily by the students (especially in the business school). College Delly is filled with freshmen and sophomores; by the time you're a senior you hang out at The Leafe for their wide selection of beer and Sunday Mug Nights. About one third of undergrad students are in Greek organizations. There are lots of restaurants in the area (Colonial Williamsburg is, after all, a tourist destination). Favorites are The Cheese Shop, which has a new location in CW on DOG Street (student references to Colonial Williamsburg and Duke of Gloucester Street), Mongolian Barbecue, Sno To Go (summers only—snowball/ice cream place), and Sal's. Also good ethnic food—Nawab Indian and Chez Trinh Vietnamese. Williamsburg is a big shopping destination, and the outlets are close by. Virginia Beach and Norfolk are 45 minutes to an hour away.

Read all of Vault's College Surveys at **www.vault.com/college**—get complete surveys on 100s of colleges and universities, expert advice on applicaton essays and more.

VAULT CAREER LIBRARY 739

Of course, you have to participate in the W&M Triathlon as an undergrad—jump, streak, swim—in which you jump over the CW Governor's Palace wall to run through the maze before the security guards catch you, swim the Crim Dell pond, and streak the school's Sunken Gardens. As the oldest continuously used university in the country, the school has a lot of tradition, this being one of them, and you'll find a lot of the social events surround the idea of keeping with those traditions.

Regarding social life, The school says: "William & Mary offers a wide range of extracurricular activities. Whatever your personal passion, political persuasion or preferred pastime may be, William & Mary has a club to match your interests. At last count, there were about 380 campus organizations, ranging from the African Cultural Society to Animal Protection, from Classical Studies to the Cleftomaniacs, from Improvisational Theatre to the Investment Club, and from the Sign Language Club to the Surfing Club to the Seventh Grade Comedy Club.

"The school also has 23 varsity sports teams that compete in NCAA Division I against the likes of Notre Dame, University of North Carolina, Duke, Georgetown and UVA. Intramural sports offerings range from tennis and floor hockey to mini-golf and billiards."

 ## The School Says

The College of William & Mary is a prestigious public university steeped in history and tradition, boasting distinguished alumni from Thomas Jefferson to Jon Stewart, and is lead by charismatic figures like President Gene Nichol and Chancellor Sandra Day O'Connor. But most importantly, the College of William & Mary offers its students an engaging community atmosphere in which students thrive on experience, socially and academically. William & Mary has approximately 380 student organizations on a very residential campus, including the African Cultural Society, a cappella groups such as the Stairwells, Accidentals and Cleftomaniacs, comedy groups such as IT (Improvisational Theater) and Seventh Grade Sketch Comedy, a Surfing Club, the three-time world champion Model United Nations team, and of course the all-important Homer Simpson Appreciation Society. Over 75 percent of the student body participates in volunteer activities and 85 percent of the student body participates in athletic programs at the varsity, club or intramural level.

The college has 23 varsity teams competing in Division I of NCAA athletics, 41 club sport teams, and 22 intramural programs. Add all that activity together and factor in the charming backdrop of Colonial Williamsburg, it's a wonder that W&M students find the time to become such accomplished academia, but they certainly do.

The College of William & Mary is a liberal arts university certainly known for its strong programs in History, Government, and English, but also offers exceptional programs in Business Administration, International Relations, Education, Biology, Psychology and other sciences. With an 11:1 student-to-teacher ratio and a strong commitment to teaching at the undergraduate level, William & Mary students benefit from close interactions with faculty across all academic departments. Undergraduate students at the College of William & Mary are offered opportunities to conduct meaningful academic research usually reserved for graduate students at other institutions. Working closely with faculty and peers strengthens the academic experience at the college and is a trademark of its enduring success. A degree from the College of William & Mary represents well-roundedness as a student and a person that serves graduates in an impressive variety of professional and academic endeavors.

In its efforts to enroll the best and brightest students to the college, the Office of Undergraduate Admission conducts an extensive and holistic review of each and every application we receive. William & Mary is now an exclusive user of the Common Application for both freshmen and transfer applicants. Our top priority is to add to the depth and richness of the invigorating campus community that exists at William & Mary. Maintaining the college's impressive geographic diversity, increasing its racial and cultural diversity, ensuring that our student body represents different socio-economic backgrounds, and bringing together young adults with a plethora of impressive credentials and interesting experiences to share with one another are at the forefront of our mission.

Show us what outstanding qualities you can add to the Tribe!

But first, feel free to visit our web site and learn more about the College of William & Mary at www.wm.edu.

George Mason University

dmissions Office
SN 3A4
400 University Drive
airfax, VA 22030-4444
dmissions phone: (703) 993-2400
dmissions fax: (703) 993-2392

Admissions

urrent student, 1/2003-Submit Date, February 2007

e easiest way to get into GMU is to go through Northern Virginia Community
ollege. If you get your associates degree at NVCC with a C average or better,
MU pretty much has to accept you. You can, however, bypass the extra use-
s credits needed for the associate's degree and just take the important classes
NOVA and do well. I had a 3.9 after one year at NOVA and got in to GMU
 problem. The other standard way to get in is to apply as a high school stu-
nt. This process has become very competitive over the last few years and is
ich more difficult than going through NOVA.

urrent student, Economics, 9/2003-Submit Date, April 2007

 has gotten a lot harder to get into since I applied because of Northern
rginia's population increasing and proximity to D.C. The school also gained
lot of exposure nationwide due to NCAA final four basketball, which also
racted more students. The application fee was expensive. I actually trans-
rred so it took me a while to get all my credits transferred. Just have to keep
 with the admissions staff. At the end I got more credits than I wanted or
served, which I was happy about. The process is still not as selective as other
hools, but in a few years, with so many people applying to college from high
hool, it will be very tough to get into Mason with a low GPA and low extracur-
ulars. I anticipate Mason climbing the rankings with so many building proj-
ts going on and funding coming in.

lumnus/a, 1/2003-5/2004, May 2006

e admissions process is quite simple. All you need are your transcripts (from
gh school or any other college you have attended), to fill out the form, write
 essay and submit. I did not even have an interview. I do not think the school
highly selective. However, I did have a high GPA (4.0) and several extracur-
ular activities. From my understanding and common knowledge among
tive Virginians, Mason accepts just about anyone. Receiving in-state tuition
om Mason is a major pain. I moved away from Virginia for a few years,
turned to VA and worked there for at least one year, and still could not get inte tuition. Over the summer, I took classes at the local community college and
t in-state tuition in a flash. Not sure why it is so difficult at Mason.

urrent student, 1/2003-Submit Date, February 2005

e admissions process at George Mason University is very simple. First, you
ust submit your SAT scores and high school transcript along with your appli-
tion and application fee. The application is composed of education back-
ound and an essay. The essay is about 500 words or less and should describe
ur biggest accomplish and/or role model. Once you have submitted your
plication and all other materials, you are then selected on how balanced your
PA and SAT are; usually the minimum GPA is 3.3 and the minimum SAT is
00. There is no interview process; George Mason does all of the selecting
sed on a prospect's application.

lumnus/a, 9/1998-12/2000, September 2003

ne admissions process is very easy and straightforward. As long as you meet
e minimum requirement, your chance of getting in is big. You do have to write
 essay to submit with the application, but there is no interview required.
eorge Mason has a very close relationship with Northern Virginia Community
ollege (NOVA). That said, if for some reason, your qualifications don't meet
ason's minimum requirements, whether it's SAT, TOEFL or GPA, you can also

try to get into NOVA and take some 100- and 200-level courses. As long as you
do well at NOVA (GPA of around 3.5 or above), your chance of getting into
Mason is very high. Make sure that you do well at NOVA, though. You really
have no chance of getting into Mason if you do poorly at NOVA.

Getting admitted to Mason doesn't mean that you're admitted to the School of
Management (SOM). In order to be admitted to SOM, you have to have a GPA
of at least 2.5 for certain required courses. If you don't get at least 2.5 GPA for
these courses, there is no way you can get into SOM. Your alternative would be
a BA in Economics, which is not one of SOM's programs.

Alumnus/a, 8/1999-5/2003, November 2003

The admissions at George Mason University is the standard application, evaluation and interview process. You are evaluated on a balance between scholastic
and extracurricular activities. Leadership positions and experience are a definite
plus, when reflected in the interviews and essays. George Mason University is
becoming increasingly selective, especially admittance for the individual
schools: the School of Management and School of Information Technology and
Engineering.

Academics

Current student, Economics, 9/2003-Submit Date, April 2007

You don't have to kill yourself. Just do the homework and attend classes and
that guarantees you at least a B+. In most of the classes in which I didn't do
well, I didn't attend boring lectures. Difficulty varies by major and professor but
undergrad economics was pretty painless in retrospect.

Current student, 1/2003-Submit Date, February 2007

The quality of classes varies greatly at GMU. Depending on the teacher you can
have a great informative class or you can have a really lousy class. Grading at
GMU is pretty fair so long as you show up for class and do the assigned work.
If you do end up in class with a foreign professor whose English skills are lacking, you need to take the initiative and get extra help. Workload is relatively
light for most classes; however, the upper-level business classes increase the
workload dramatically.

Current student, 1/2003-Submit Date, October 2006

The economics program is much more challenging and intellectually honest than
other departments. Nearly all of their professors are privately funded, so if one
cares about the quality of education, it's much higher than at the average state
school. Also, you get a great deal of personal attention within the department,
which contrasts with, say, an Ivy where undergrads are treated poorly. The support staff is helpful, and the registrar's office is saintly.

Alumnus/a, 1/2003-5/2004, May 2006

The course descriptions are quite accurate. I think the quality of classes was
high too, except for the professors who are on tenure. They seem to be a little
more difficult for no reason. Many of the upper-level courses are overcrowded
(200+). Like any other college, you have some classes from which you learn and
some that are not any more helpful if you never stepped foot in the class. Getting
popular classes and professors is fairly easy. Grading should be standardized
though. Some professors use +/- grading, while others just give A's, B's and C's
with no in between. Workload is moderate. I suggest balancing your workload
with a few lower-level and a few higher-level courses. Best schedule is being
able to tailor classes to be on just Monday through Thursday. Mason is popular
for that, and it's awesome for everyone all around. If you want out by Thursday,
you get it; but if you like Friday classes, the campus is nice and quiet on Fridays
(always).

Current student, 1/2003-Submit Date, February 2005

Academics vary at George Mason depending on your major and/or minor. They
have a wide variety of different programs including: nursing, business manage-

Read all of Vault's College Surveys at **www.vault.com/college**—get complete surveys on 100s of colleges and universities, expert advice on applicaton essays and more.

VAULT CAREER LIBRARY **741**

ment, arts, mathematics and biology. I have really enjoyed the classes I have taken; they are challenging but if you prepare for them beforehand, you will do well. There are so many classes at the university, which makes it very easy when selecting your classes; they have one subject that is taught at several times during the day so it's easier to find a class time that fits your schedule.

Professors can differ between classes, as do the grades because one class might have 200 students while another may only have 25. There are fewer options when you have a bigger class, so grading has to be quite simple for the professor mainly by having multiple choice tests. The workload is up to you; an individual can take five classes and do just fine if he or she is dedicated to taking on all the classes and the work that goes along with it. If an individual seems to be carrying a heavy load, I suggest either dropping one or two classes or squeezing in more time for studying by either socializing less or spending fewer hours at work.

Current student, 8/2003-Submit Date, January 2005

GMU has some of the top-ranked programs in the nation. However, that does not necessarily mean these programs are tailored to what students want or need. Registration is a joke and graduate professors are often arrogant. The workload is relatively easy.

Current student, 8/2001-Submit Date, April 2004

I have had teachers here at Mason who have changed my life. I started without any idea of what I would be doing after college, and it is because, and only because, I had such inspiring teachers that I know what I want to do. Of course there are difficult teachers, but I've never had an impossible one. The key is to make sure the teacher knows who you are. If you become a real person to him/her, not just a face in the crowd, then you matter and he/she is willing to help you.

Often classes fill up early, but it has been my experience that everyone on the waiting list gets in the class during the first week. If you ask the teacher and make an effort to prove that you will be a productive member of the class, he/she is sure to let you in!

Current student, Marketing, 8/1998-Submit Date, October 2003

I am a business major, marketing to be specific. The program is really up and coming, and we are in the top 20 percent of business programs in the nation. Very impressive. The professors are getting harder, and they put us in groups a lot. It is a great school, though. I didn't really like the first two years of school, since that was basically two years of taking classes I didn't care about, like biology and Spanish. But by the third year, things were rocking.

Current student, History, 9/2002-Submit Date, September 2003

As a history major in my senior year, I find the reading workload very heavy. However, the professors are generally excellent. The grading is usually very fair. GMU does teacher evaluations every semester, and these are available online (from campus PCs only, though).

It's fairly easy to get classes you need. They have waitlists, and I've been able to get into all the classes I've needed. The online library offers access to Georgetown University, Catholic University and other colleges in the D.C. area.

Employment Prospects

Current student, 1/2003-Submit Date, February 2007

GMU is not a top school yet. Some top employers don't actively recruit at Mason. However, with good grades and some initiative, a student can go wherever he/she pleases after graduating. The school has a lot of on-campus recruiting events.

Alumnus/a, 1/2003-5/2004, May 2006

Employment after graduation is competitive for higher paying/quality jobs, especially in the NOVA area. Mason isn't seen as very prestigious, but they're really trying to change their image. The school has Georgetown, George Washington and UVA to contend with. So if you have an undergraduate degree from Mason, I would definitely pursue more education. Undergrads receive typical entry-level job offers (sales, recruiting), but the alumni network is not that

helpful, in my opinion. You have to be extremely involved and doing m activities to network well around here, but many students don't have time that.

Current student, 1/2003-Submit Date, October 2006

There is a fairly surprising range of options for a state school, including c sulting firms and finance companies. Alumni network is limited because school is relatively young, but getting larger. Career office is surprisingly he ful, with many events and genuinely interested staff. On-campus recruiting very streamlined and organized.

Current student, Economics, 9/2003-Submit Date, April 2007

They have a great career services center that offers plenty of internship oppo nities. My brother, friends and myself all got full-time positions with benefit IT, management and accounting fields.

Current student, 1/2003-Submit Date, February 2005

George Mason does a wonderful job of trying to help students and graduates f job opportunities; there are career services that are offered to give advice to s dents who are interested in entering the working field and there are many eve where employers come and give on-the-spot interviews and jobs. George Mas wants its students to be very successful in the business world; it sets up mo interviews so that students can work on their interviewing skills and possibly able to win a job because of their interview. George Mason offers a lot of r working events and on-campus recruiting so that students have several oppor nities to find a career that's suited for them.

Alumnus/a, 8/1999-5/2003, November 2003

Although George Mason University may not yet be as recognized as Harvard Yale or its sister school, University of Virginia, GMU is well known in Northern Virginia-D.C. metro area. The nation's top strategy consulting fir financial firms and high-tech firms all know GMU and the quality and divers of students and their education that come from George Mason University. T nation's federal government agencies also recruit the best from George Mas The FBI and CIA, General Accounting Office, Securities and Exchar Commission, Department of Defense and numerous think tanks and governm contract agencies avail themselves to George Mason graduates.

Internship opportunities are numerous but competitive. George Mason stude have an advantage in internships, since they can intern with a nearby firm agency during the whole school year, not only during the summer season. T career center counselors are knowledgeable and helpful when finding resour and companies that match a students particular needs—however, more work needed on the student's part to find the jobs and to contact the firms.

Quality of Life

Current student, 1/2003-Submit Date, February 2007

I never lived on campus, and rarely ever ate there. However, the food is pre much typical college fare. Nothing great, most of it isn't good, but all edibl Quality of life is good, facilities are adequate, nothing special, nothing rea bad. The campus is generally very safe, I never felt nervous walking around any hour of the night.

Current student, Economics, 9/2003-Submit Date, April 2007

Crime is low. Safety is great because of a lot of police and being located Fairfax suburbs. Housing is limited because there are so many students who commuters, but they are building more and more dorms. The new ones are pr ty amazing looking. Traffic and parking are a major issue and population of school is increasing very rapidly and more educational as well recreational/housing buildings continue to go up. Campus is very modern a well equipped with labs, Wi-Fi, gyms, aquatic center, PE building, field ho and the gem is the Johnson Center in the middle of the campus.

Current student, 1/2003-Submit Date, October 2006

Commuter school syndrome still plagues student life. Finding a social life tal a great deal of effort unless one is into the frat scene.

using is limited and of low quality, though this is improving. Off-campus ousing is higher quality, though expensive (if easy to find).

mpus is trying to grow, but this is tough to pull of aesthetically because it is island in a suburb. Buildings are mostly brick, and not terribly easy on the es.

umnus/a, 1/2003-5/2004, May 2006

ver go on campus alone at night if you can help it. New gym is really nice. me of the buildings are old, but that's typical of older college campuses. erall, housing and campus are just fine. Most students live off campus and ve in. The drive in is always crowded but you get use to it. If you have a end, it's nice to just stay over at their dorm, because parking is terrible. You ve to park out so far and walk in. The parking surrounds the parameter of the nool and there isn't a transit system that will take you around the school. Be epared to walk in rain, sleet or snow!

rrent student, 1/2003-Submit Date, February 2005

o not stay on campus, but from what I have observed, George Mason is in a ry nice location. The neighborhood is very lovely and quiet. The crime rate the neighborhood is not fairly high, in fact there are on-campus policemen and curity who are on duty all night so that if something were to happen it would taken care of by an official. George Mason offers housing, gym membership d dining to all students; they try to accommodate in any way they can so that idents' needs are taken care of.

rrent student, 8/2001-Submit Date, April 2004

ave been living on campus for three years now, and I don't regret a moment. course sometimes I miss having my own kitchen and laundry facilities, but I uldn't give this up for anything. Nothing compares to having your friends wn the hall from you, and knowing that there will always be someone else ake at 3 a.m. to talk with you. I love it. The facilities are great and continu- y improving. New dorms and dining services have been opening each year ice I've been here. I can't believe the options I have here, especially compared schools some of my high school friends attend. The campus groups put on s of programs over the weekends for the on-campus students; there is never thing going on here.

Social Life

rrent student, Economics, 9/2003-Submit Date, April 2007

ere are tons of frats and sororities to join. Hot girls are everywhere. Mason the most diverse school in America, and there is a great social and dating

scene. There are plenty of clubs from which to choose, as well. Most people do house parties or go to D.C. to party. There are a few bars in Fairfax, as well.

Current student, 1/2003-Submit Date, February 2007

Mason is still very much a commuter school. Most students live off campus. This is changing; however, the majority still live off campus. This puts a strain on the school's social scene. Mason's campus is dry, and there are no fraternity houses. If you're over age you can have a reasonable amount of alcohol in your dorm room; however, the Mason police enforce the drinking age strictly. This all puts a huge damper on the party scene, which I think is basically nonexistent. However once you are 21, there are many bars in the area that cater to the college crowd. This makes for some excellent Thursday and Friday nights. Additionally, Washington, D.C. is about 15 minutes away and there are many places to enjoy the night in the city. If you're outgoing and of age, there is a lot of fun to be had at Mason. If you're underage and shy, then it may not be the best place to open up.

The dating scene is sort of weak. Since a lot of people don't hang out on campus and many live off campus, it's hard to meet people who aren't in your classes. However if you're sociable you can make a lot of friends.

Alumnus/a, 1/2003-5/2004, May 2006

Bars are really fun around the campus, but by Thursday and Friday, almost everyone leaves the school. The campus feels completely dead, but it's nice to get away. Dating scene is fun and relaxed. It's really easy to meet nice people/students here.

Current student, 1/2003-Submit Date, February 2005

George Mason has many social events that take place throughout the year. The university offers several different sports related events including women's and men's basketball, softball/baseball and soccer. George Mason is located in Fairfax, VA, which is located by all the excitement; top malls are in the area and there are many different restaurants that serve a wide variety of foods. George Mason has so many Greek organizations, there are events usually at the beginning of each semester for individuals who are interested in joining. The dating scene is pretty good at the university; there are many females and males who are looking for a good time and a possible love interest.

Current student, 8/2001-Submit Date, April 2004

Mason Day has got to be the student favorite of the year. Each spring the school brings in bands, food, games, moon walks, cotton candy and all kinds of crazy things we loved as kids and refuse to admit we still love! Here in Fairfax there is a ton to do, the city is nearby, especially the old City of Fairfax where you can walk around and enjoy everything. We are also almost on top of Washington, D.C., and there is always something going on there, a new club, new bars, concerts, everything from local people to the big bands in the country.

Read all of Vault's College Surveys at www.vault.com/college—get complete surveys on 100s of colleges and univer- sities, expert advice on applicaton essays and more.

VAULT CAREER LIBRARY   743

Hollins University

Admissions Office
Hollins University
Roanoke, VA 24020
Admissions phone: (800) 456-9595 or (540) 362-6401
Admissions e-mail: huadm@hollins.edu
Admissions URL:
www.hollins.edu/admissions/admissions.htm

 ## Admissions

Current student, Biology, 9/2003-Submit Date, April 2007

Hollins isn't that selective in the admissions process, but they give very good merit-based scholarships, which tend to bring up the caliber of students at Hollins. The admissions counselors are friendly and helpful. When I received my acceptance letter, there were congratulations confetti in the envelope.

Current student, Visual Arts, 8/2005-Submit Date, April 2007

In order to get into Hollins, I had to send in a transcript, SAT scores and a résumé plus a short essay and short answers to questions they ask to get a general idea of who you are as a student. Then you are interviewed by an admissions counselor, but this really is more like an informal chat with a friend because the admissions counselors are so nice.

Grades are not as important as are your extracurricular activities and your essay. You get to choose an essay topic, and it's very important to show in this essay your knowledge of grammar as well as your creativity as a writer. As a previous member of the scholarship committee, I was able to read incoming students' essays, and I realized that creativity can't entirely mask the lack of grammatical knowledge. Write in complete sentences and paragraphs! Make it easy for your evaluator to read your paper, so pick a topic (if you can) that would be interesting to both you and the readers. Also, don't make your essays too long. They aren't looking for a novel, just a short excerpt that shows your personality and knowledge.

The interview is really, like I said, an informal chat with a nice person who wants you at Hollins. Because Hollins is very liberal in taking students, students are given the opportunity to choose Hollins. It's more like students choose Hollins, and not like Hollins chooses its students, which can be quite different from other colleges, especially more prestigious institutions that act like it's a privilege that they are allowing you to come the their institutions. I mean really it should be about the students, since we are paying them! This is how it is at Hollins. Once accepted (which most applicants are), you are given the opportunity to have overnight stays and find out if Hollins is the right place for you, not if you are right for Hollins.

Alumna, 8/2001-5/2005, May 2006

The admissions staff at Hollins is extremely dedicated to its students. By the time a student enrolls, a counselor has more than likely personally visited her high school, arranged a visit to campus including a tour, class visits, meetings with faculty and coaches, and a financial aid session, as well as spoken to her and her parents multiple times on the phone.

Hollins operates on a rolling admission basis and usually turns around decisions in three weeks. Interviews and well-written essays are essential for "borderline" students. The admissions office is more concerned with a student's enthusiasm and fit at Hollins than grades and SATs.

Alumna, 8/1999-5/2003, May 2006

An admissions rep came to my high school. I was so impressed with her and what she had to say about Hollins that I knew I had to apply. In fact, Hollins was the only college to which I applied. I didn't know much about the admissions process—I'm the first in my family to go to college—at the time, nor did I talk to anyone, nor did I even visit the campus. Outside of meeting an admissions

representative and sending my application, I had nothing to do with the admissions process.

Alumna, 8/1998-5/2002, May 2006

Hollins consistently sent me personal, hand-written notes from the time I took the PSATs until I arrived to start my first year. The admissions staff knew what I was looking for, which wasn't Hollins. They never tried to convince me that Hollins was better than the other colleges to which I applied by showing me things Hollins had to offer. When I came to visit during a large prospective weekend, they knew who I was before I introduced myself.

Alumna, 8/1997-5/2001, May 2006

The admissions office was an incredible help. Not only did it provide me with information on clubs, activities and academic interests, but it also was very helpful with finding financial aid. It also connected me with a variety of students who were very candid with me about what Hollins life was like.

I interviewed over the phone since I lived across the country and since the admissions staff was so personable I felt totally at ease. The scholarships were pretty competitive but the admissions folks did a good job of pointing me in the right direction in terms of what to apply for, and I got one heck of a financial aid package with grants, scholarships and two small loans.

 ## Academics

Current student, Biology, 9/2003-Submit Date, April 2007

Hollins has very small classes and very accessible professors. Most of the programs are rigorous, but help is available for students from professors and other academic resources. Most of my classes have been really fantastic, with only a few exceptions. However, a Hollins education is what you put into it. If you choose to take rigorous classes, you'll learn a lot. If you choose to take Blah classes, you can squeak by and not learn much.

Current student, Visual Arts, 8/2005-Submit Date, April 2007

The program at Hollins is very unique and was adapted from a larger institution to work as a small, private, women's college. We have a general education program called ESP, which stands for Education through Skills and Perspectives. It gives students the opportunity to experience a wide range of different classes to enhance the overall experience at college as well as gives students the depth needed to succeed in the workplace and in life.

Classes are very small in size. The most students in one of my classes was fewer than 50, but most classes max out at 13 to 15. This way students and professors know each other, which helps facilitate class discussions and relationships between students and professors.

Because of the small size, most popular classes are filled very fast, but again since most students know the professors, all one has to do is ask the professor if she can be in the class. More than likely the teacher won't have a problem putting her in the class. This is what's so nice about a small school: you have the opportunity to develop a rapport with the teacher before class even starts!

Grading is very much suited to helping the student achieve full potential. Ask for help and the teacher will help facilitate for any learning disabilities and so on. The workload is manageable since you take an average of four classes, but lots of girls do take five classes.

Alumna, 8/2001-5/2005, May 2006

Hollins has a very unique general education program. Rather than requiring classes, Hollins requires students to fulfill certain Skills and Perspectives that range from Oral Presentation to Global Knowledge, to Quantitative Reasoning with the idea that classes in nearly every discipline can fulfill these requirements. Students can end up filling their math requirements with an art class or science labs through the psychology department.

...s do not exist at Hollins. Every class is taught by a full professor. All of the ...ulty members welcome students' questions and are anxious to see their stu-...ts do well. Many of the faculty live on or near campus, which makes the ...mmunity feel very inclusive.

...ere is a wide variety of classes offered for such a small school. They range ...m very basic and general, like Intro to Psychology, to very off beat and spe-...c, like Arab Women Writers or Philosophy and *Star Trek*. It's very easy to get ... classes you want, if a class is full usually a student can show up on the first ... and have the professor sign her in.

...erall, Hollins is a very laid-back campus, students are serious about their aca-...nics but not competitive with one another. The student-run Writing and ...oring Center is a great place to get feedback on papers and extra help with ...nework. Professors are generally flexible with paper and exam deadlines. ...st exams are given on the Independent Exam System, which is also run by ...dents. Students have a week to take all their exams and are free to pick them ... and take them anytime during the week, students can finish all their exams in ...ay or stretch their studying out over five.

...umna, 8/2001-5/2005, May 2006

...oved the academic climate at Hollins. Classes were small enough that you ...ld get into any class with a little effort and persistence. The professors are ...llins' greatest asset. Students take academics seriously, but not too seriously. ...eryone still loves to have fun (even the professors). Prime example—the infa-...us history department party at the end of each semester. It's one of the best ...ties on campus.

...umna, 8/1998-5/2002, May 2006

...l of the professors were fantastic and easily accessible. I loved calling the pro-...sors (most of them) by their first names. A lot of the professors invited stu-...ts to their homes or had meals together—I never had a close relationship like ...t with a professor while I was a student, but have developed that with some ...my professors as an alumna.

...e profs genuinely cared about students and were always available—even at ...me—to answer questions. I had a student with a learning disability in one of ... classes and it was nice to see how the professor helped my classmate with-...t embarrassing her. Certain classes were really popular, but I managed to talk ... way into some of them—the professors cared more about having attentive, ...erested students in their classes than if someone was at the head of the regis-...tion line or not. I definitely did a lot of work and studying, but not too much ...that I felt like I was always bogged down.

Employment Prospects

...rrent student, Biology, 9/2003-Submit Date, April 2007

...e connections I've made at Hollins really helped me when I was looking for ...ernships and applying to graduate school. A member of the board of trustees ...om I'd never met helped me get my dream internship at a nonprofit. The rela-...nships I formed with professors got me good recommendations for applica-...ns.

...rrent student, Visual Arts, 8/2005-Submit Date, April 2007

...cause of Hollins' amazing network of alumni and the internships available, ...ent graduates almost always get a job right out of college. I recently did a ...e-month internship with Sotheby's in New York City because of the connec-...ns with alumni. Depending on the major, most students who apply for grad-...te school are accepted.

...e Career Development Center is working hard to keep the alumnae network ...-to-date, which helps students find internships, housing opportunities and see ...at Hollins graduates are up to now.

...hink Hollins is the kind of school where you are given the tools to make job ...portunities happen, but you have to want it and work for it. For example, I ...nted an internship at Sotheby's so I sent résumés and called people, but I just ...sn't getting through. Then, I talked to the president of Hollins who hooked ...e up with an alumna who had friends who worked at Sotheby's. Next thing I ...ow, I'm e-mailing and talking to a real person at Sotheby's who wants me as

their department intern for that January. It really was amazing how just that lit-tle bit of connection sets you apart from the rest, just so people can see how real-ly amazing you are.

Alumna, 8/2001-5/2005, May 2006

The Career Development Center on campus is very helpful with writing résumés and contacting alumnae. The school's January short term is an ideal time for internships and the CDC can help students find them in a particular field or loca-tion or with a specific alumna. Alumnae are eager to help out current students or recent graduates.

Everyone I know of with whom I graduated had a job within months of gradu-ating. Because Hollins is small, employers may not recognize the name, but they are sure to be impressed with internships, research opportunities and coursework that racks up on Hollins' résumés.

Alumna, 8/1997-5/2001, May 2006

After graduation I joined the Peace Corps along with six other classmates. At that time, it was one of the schools with the highest percentage of students who joined the Peace Corps. That's what I'm talking about—Hollins inspires you to do more—to take what you've learned and test it and find your own truth.

Alumna, 8/1997-5/2001, May 2006

Through the school, I had an internship with the New York Stock Exchange between my junior and senior years of college. There are other similarly presti-gious internships available in different fields of study, and I really believe that the strength of the internship programs is one of Hollins' greatest assets. I had a job immediately after graduation with a large law firm in Washington, D.C., and I'm still working there five years later (and with one year of law school left).

Quality of Life

Current student, Biology, 9/2003-Submit Date, April 2007

The housing and whole campus at Hollins is really beautiful. There are no dorms with cinder block walls here. The student government at Hollins has more power than student governments at most schools, so students have a lot of say over how the campus is run. Our concerns are really listened to. The food is pretty good as far as college food goes.

Current student, Visual Arts, 8/2005-Submit Date, April 2007

The small scale of Hollins offers accessibility to buildings on campus that's not found at a larger institution. Most buildings are open for student use after hours, some are even open all day! Housing is a bit pricey given the small nature of the dorm rooms and the shared bathrooms, but they are working on improving this along with the food selection (since the dining package is included in room and board). Our food provider has diligently worked to give us many options.

Hollins really is a very enclosed campus. Many people don't feel the need to venture far from campus or don't have a car to do so. Since Roanoke is a small city, there's really not much happening, which makes Hollins a very safe place. Petty theft does occur though, but not muggings.

Alumna, 8/2001-5/2005, May 2006

While I was a student, Hollins was voted Number One for quality of life by the Princeton Review two years in a row. The freshman dorms are significantly larg-er than the typical cinder block box, the campus is beautiful, cafeteria food is up to par, most importantly, everyone on campus has a friendly attitude, loves Hollins and goes out of their way to help others.

Alumna, 8/1998-5/2002, May 2006

Quality of life was excellent. Campus housing was fantastic—one of the things that attracted me to Hollins in the first place. Not all of the dorms have air con-ditioning, though, and they really need it since Roanoke gets hot. Otherwise, everything is beautiful and all of the accommodations are fantastic.

The campus itself is prettier than the photos Hollins sends out—no photo can capture just how magnificent things are there! The new library (which was new when I was there, it isn't so new now) was a great addition to the university. The look alone helps propel the university toward a better status academically. Roanoke is completely safe—no crime on campus or even in the city. I always

Read all of Vault's College Surveys at **www.vault.com/college**—get complete surveys on 100s of colleges and univer-sities, expert advice on applicaton essays and more.

VAULT CAREER LIBRARY **745**

felt safe no matter where I was walking or what time it was. Most students didn't even lock their doors.

Food was delicious—not many universities can say that! We had our own chef and even had meals like steak and lobster—and not just on parents' weekend! We also had special meals with cloth table cloths for special holidays, which was a really nice touch. The dining hall people were extremely accommodating. I had a milk allergy and they bought me Lactaid milk and kept it in a special fridge for me so I didn't have to miss out on the cereal. I volunteered with Big Brothers Big Sisters and wanted to make Rice Krispie treats with my little sister one time and the dining hall gave me everything I needed so I didn't have to go out and spend my own money.

 Social Life

Current student, Biology, 9/2003-Submit Date, April 2007

Hollins is kind of an isolated campus, so there's not much to do within walking distance. Students usually go to downtown Roanoke on the weekends, where there are quite a few fun bars, a good coffee shop and an independent movie theater. Students also head to other schools, such as Virginia Tech, Hampden-Sydney and University of Virginia for parties on the weekends. Everyone's favorite restaurants are Hollywoods, which is walking distance from campus, and the Veranda Bistro, which is just a mile down the road and has amazing pizza. There are lots of clubs on campus, although they sometimes struggle for participation because there are so few students. There are always lots of events happening on campus, such as bands or DJs, movies or other club parties.

Current student, Visual Arts, 8/2005-Submit Date, April 2007

There's always something happening on campus, from new release movie showings in the new Visual Arts Center theatre to events planned by one of the many student-run organizations. And if there's not a club you would like to see on campus, you can easily start one. Hollins Activities Board works hard bringing in local bands to play here, and we have joint concerts where students from neighboring colleges are invited.

Bars and restaurants that are enjoyable are located in downtown, but you have to be 21 for clubs here (and of course, bars too). There is one club that people do go to frequently called The Park, which is always an adventure. But be forwarned: it is a gay club. People like to go for the dancing. Some good restaurants are: Nawab, which is great Indian food, In d-town, a good Thai restaurant. Great pizza place called Grace's Pizza, which is in a cute area of Roanoke near the Grand in Theatre and Co-Op food store.

There's no Greek life on campus, and it really isn't necessary. Hollins is small enough for most people to know each other, or know the people in your dorm hall. Another way to get to know people is to join a sports team. Since it's not very competitive, it's a good way to bond and form friendships.

Dating could pose a problem since it is all girls, unless you're into that. It's a very open environment. But girls like to go to VMI, Hampton-Sydney or VT for boyfriends and other places to party. Roanoke College is just down the road also, but for some reason, we don't really hang out with those kids much.

Another really awesome thing to do here is drive or hike the Blueridge Parkway. It is so amazing especially when the seasons are changing. Roanoke is located in a valley so we are serenely surrounded by great beautiful mountains. There are lots of hiking trails that have fun streams to swim in also.

Alumna, 8/1998-5/2002, May 2006

The school's social life does leave something to be desired. Because the school is not co-ed, many students go off campus in search of dating opportunities and events, and there is no Greek system on campus. There are various activities organizations within the Student Government Association, and they coordinate events such as Cotillion, the Spring Formal and smaller concerts throughout the year. They are all fun events. Downtown Roanoke has some bars, clubs and restaurants that students frequent, such as Billy's Ritz (restaurant), Carlos' Brazilian Restaurant and Chico & Billy's (pizza place), especially on the weekends.

Alumna, 8/1999-5/2003, May 2006

The social life at Hollins is interesting. There is always a niche that one can into, and the sisterhood quality is amazing. I never had a sister, so going Hollins was a new experience for me and, as it turns out, I now have th Hollins is a traveling school, which means a good portion of Hollins girls' soc izing is done elsewhere—Hampden-Sydney College, VMI and Washington Lee.

The local bar, restaurant, and club scene lacks, which means Hollins women to work compensating for it by creating their own social scenes. There is Greek system, which is perfect because it doesn't allow for factionalism on ca pus, and because Hollins is so small anyway we're like one giant sorority rega less.

 The School Says

Hollins University in Roanoke, VA, has been a motivating force for women to go places since it was founded in 1842.

This women's college's approach to education is to teach students to think and encourage exploration and discovery. The academic experience stresses the benefits of interaction and support from both professors and fellow students.

Students are as much colleagues with their professors as they are pupils. One of the hallmarks of the Hollins faculty is their accessibility; many professors include students in their research and writing and have open-door office policies. Hollins' student-to-faculty ratio is 10:1.

Hollins offers majors in 29 fields of study. While perhaps best known for its creative writing program, the university also features strong disciplines in the visual and performing arts and the social and physical sciences.

To complement its majors, Hollins features an innovative general education program called Education through Skills and Perspectives, designed to help students see the world in different ways and apply knowledge in practical ways.

In the fall of 2007, the university launched two new co-curricular programs. First, the university is offering seminars to first-year students with a goal of making each student's first academic experience a distillation of the best the university has to offer. Seminars are experiential, experimental and cross-disciplinary, and are designed to acquaint students with applied research techniques that they will use throughout their college years.

Second, a Certificate in Leadership Studies builds on Hollins' long-standing tradition of preparing women to become leaders in their chosen fields.

Hollins encourages its students to pursue learning opportunities outside the U.S. The university was among the nation's first colleges to offer an international study abroad program, recognizing that the global nature of business, technology and international affairs makes learning in another country an increasingly vital component of education. Today, 52 percent of Hollins students enjoy an international learning experience.

Extensive internship opportunities are another of Hollins' distinctions. Thanks to a dedicated network of alumnae and friends of the university, 80 percent of Hollins students put their education to work through internships with a diverse group of organizations.

The university is committed to making the Hollins experience affordable, having developed a strong financial assistance program that combines merit and need-based aid. 98 percent of Hollins students receive some form of financial assistance.

Hollins' admissions process is selective, but not exclusive. The university looks for strengths both in and out of the classroom. Academic performance, class rank, a balanced program of courses, test scores, and academic recommendations are all important. Participation in extracurricular activities, volunteer and work-related experiences, and dedication and promise in the performing arts, if applicable, are also considered.

Hollins founder Charles Lewis Cocke once said, "This school recognizes the principle that young women require the same thorough and rigid training as that afforded to young men." Through the years, the school has remained committed to this goal, upholding a mission of "preparing students for lives of active learning, fulfilling work, personal growth, achievement and service to society."

James Madison University

ffice of Admissions
SC 0101
arrisonburg, VA 22807
dmissions phone: (540) 568-5681
dmissions fax: (540) 568-3332
dmissions e-mail: admissions@jmu.edu

Admissions

lumnus/a, 8/2002-5/2006, November 2006

e application was pretty straightforward; I liked that the essay question was en ended so I could write about whatever I wanted to.

lumnus/a, 8/2001-5/2005, August 2006

IU takes a very holistic approach to admissions. Classes taken, grades eived, SATs, extracurriculars, essays and recommendations are all consid- d. Your program of study and grades in high school are definitely the most portant things. Take challenging courses! Interviews are not offered. Above , if you are unsure of something: call admissions! Do not rely on word of uth from guidance counselors or current students.

lumnus/a, 8/2002-5/2006, May 2006

y advice? Apply Early Admission. Take a tour. Talk to students after the tour. interview necessary. School is becoming much more selective. Essay was a ndard question of "Who do you admire and why?"

rrent student, 8/2004-Submit Date, May 2005

om what I've seen, there is no clear cut method to being the perfect JMU stu- nt. I've seen people get in, who in my opinion shouldn't, and vice versa. I nk when it comes right down to it, JMU is taking more and more of a num- r's oriented approach. SATs and GPAs do matter, and being vice-president of Spanish club isn't going to change that. The personal statement is now tional, but very effective I believe. JMU admissions are motivated by the adison community in which they live; if you can creatively and effectively nvey your love to surround yourself with others in a learning community to ke the most of the undergraduate experience.

rrent student, 8/2004-Submit Date, May 2005

e admissions process at JMU begins with the tour. This is JMU's first effort allow kids and their parents to be aware of the great atmosphere at JMU. The udent Ambassadors (tour guides) are budgeted into the university's program so at Ambassadors are allotted a sum of money each year to improve their tours, d other activities they work on. Once prospective students have gone on a tour become interested in JMU, they can fill out an application. The application n be submitted online, however, it is not required to be submitted that way. IU is currently trying to move from hard-copy applications to soft-copy appli- tions that won't use as much paper, and avoid the possible risks and mis- acement of mail through the post office. The application is simple, with stan- rd info (name, birthdate, address) and also includes extracurricular activities d/or jobs. The optional essay is where students have a chance to describe

themselves further or explain something about themselves. I used my essay to share a dark secret of my past. It was a change in my life, and made me a different person. I knew with college approaching I would be changing as well. So I decided to write about my first major change as a person in my essay.

These applications, along with the essay, have to be turned in mid-November for Early Action or mid-January for Regular Decision. Early Action is a really great program because it allows students to know in January whether they were admitted. Most schools do this, however JMU's Early Action is non-binding. So if a student is admitted he/she is are not required to go there. It's important for JMU to be flexible like this because it allows only those who want to come to JMU to come. There is no benefit in "trapping" kids into a school who don't want to go there. I wasn't admitted Early Action. JMU has higher standards to be admitted early than on Regular Decision. I was immediately deferred to Regular Decision. Even after being so upset by not getting into JMU at first try, I did not give up and was so excited when my phone call came in the spring. JMU makes phone calls to accepted out-of-state students. This is another thing that Ambassadors do. It's a wonderful feeling to get a call from a university just to know that they are pleased you have been admitted and are inviting you to come to the school. JMU is proud of their university, but have not become cocky. They want others to experience the university because they see each new class as a group of 350+ students who can change JMU for the better. The admissions process overall tries to get prospective students excited about JMU and once they've selected a group of diverse students they are grateful for their hard work, time and effort. Every year the JMU admissions office is pleased and more excited than the year before to meet the incoming freshmen.

Current student, 8/2003-Submit Date, May 2004

The selectivity is starting to get a little higher, because JMU is gaining a lot of popularity very fast—so it is very important that you have an interesting personal statement in addition to a stable record behind you. A total of 1400 on your SATs is not a must-have for this place (which gives regular students a breather), but I believe the key to getting in is just presenting yourself in a way that is different from everyone else and talking about not only how you can use the help of the university, how you can help the university as well. Talk about why they could use you!

Academics

Alumnus/a, 8/2002-5/2006, November 2006

The faculty at JMU is so great. Most of the professors I had were so approachable and nice. As long as you put in effort, they will help you. It was not always easy to get into the popular classes; everyone uses RateMyProfessor.com to find out which teachers to get. Some advice is to come in with some credits so you are ahead of your peers, because the way they rank your scheduling is by credits. You will register before other people if you have more credits and be able to get better classes.

Read all of Vault's College Surveys at **www.vault.com/college**—get complete surveys on 100s of colleges and univer- sities, expert advice on applicaton essays and more.

VAULT CAREER LIBRARY 747

Alumnus/a, 8/2002-5/2006, May 2006

The required general education classes are a pain in the butt, but like any other college or university they are requirements to make the student more well-rounded. There are a lot of classes from which to choose, which is nice.

The business school was recently ranked 35th in the country by *Business Week* and as a recent grad I can say it was well deserved. The professors are extremely helpful and will get to know you on a first name basis. I still talk to a majority of my business professors via e-mail. The professors at JMU are here for the student not for grants from the school to work on their own research and projects like most big name universities. Class size range from 90 to 100. GenEd classes are larger and as you progress through your degree they become smaller.

Getting the class and the professor you want goes by the number of credits you have. You receive a registration date by the number of credits you have under your belt. The more credits you have, the earlier your registration.

Grading is fair, and every professor has his or her own grading scale. The workload is up to you. The gen ed class workload is more busywork, while your major and minor class workload is more hefty. As you progress through the years, you will become more proficient with managing your time and organizing your workload.

Current student, 8/2005-Submit Date, January 2006

JMU's academic program is very expansive and diverse. The quality of the classes and buildings at JMU is excellent and the landscape is beautiful. It is harder for freshmen to get some of the classes that they want because of the 15,000 or so students. Registering is based on the number of credits you have, so the more credits, the earlier you get to register for classes and get the ones that you want. Most of the professors here are very knowledgeable about what they are doing. There is a web site called ratemyprofessor.com that you can go to and see what other people think of the professor before you sign up for his/her class. The workload here is very demanding and you must study and read a lot, but in the end it is worth it.

Current student, 9/2003-Submit Date, October 2005

I am pleased with the classes. There are all different levels, some easy and some very difficult. I have had good professors and a pretty demanding workload. There is a web site that helps students pick out the best professors for their classes called ratemyprofessor.com. It is very helpful and most students use it and are usually pleased with their professors and classes.

Current student, 8/2004-Submit Date, May 2005

The program is set up as having many general education classes, which everyone is required to take ranging from math to literature to some kind of art. This is to make sure students have a broad base of general knowledge so they can live life well, even if they don't need it for their degree. Professors are very available to students, holding many office hours and willing to meet with students even after their office hours if needed. There is a system that JMU uses to let students know of their grades, Blackboard; many professors post grades and if they don't, many e-mail you your grades for large assignments that are turned in. The honor code is very strictly enforced at JMU and all students are aware of what the honor code is and how seriously it is taken.

Current student, 8/2003-Submit Date, May 2005

The quality of classes is definitely exceptional. The material is interesting and presented in an interesting manner and the faculty is always accessible. Grading is hard but never set in stone. Be sure to build relationships with your professors because if they know that you are genuinely interested in learning the material but are still having problems, they will definitely take that into consideration when grades are about to be set. The workload is intense so be sure not to overwhelm yourself with too many extracurriculars. I have found that it is difficult to get into popular classes but some professors grant overrides if you ask them.

Current student, 8/2003-Submit Date, May 2005

The professors here at JMU the best. You always hear horror stories about professors in college and how all they want to do is flunk you. Well, it is exactly the opposite here at JMU. Every single professor I have had has whole-heartedly wanted his/her students to do well. They extend office hours before an exam or come in at 8 p.m. Sunday night before the Organic Chemistry final just

so that students can ask some final questions. The professors here are one of kind.

Employment Prospects

Alumnus/a, Business, 8/2002-5/2006, November 2006

JMU has a great career center. They will help you with your résumé. They a bring many employers to campus and have job fairs. You just have to take i tiative. I was a business major and the faculty also was willing to he Professors were willing to serve as references and look at student résumés. teachers also often brought back former students as guest speakers to sp about their jobs. I actually got my current job because of someone in my depa ment helping me and linking me to the company. JMU has a strong emphasis helping people get a job after they leave.

Internships were another thing. It was way too competitive. I went to the inte ship fair most of the year and never got an internship. I also searched a lot a applied to the companies that came to campus. It seemed like the only peo who got internships were people with connections. But in the end, it was nc big deal not having one.

Alumnus/a, 8/2001-5/2005, August 2006

JMU has a great career center with career fairs, internship fairs, mock int views, and on campus recruiting. Take advantage of it!

Alumnus/a, 8/2002-5/2006, May 2006

James Madison has multiple career fairs during the year, which attract we known employers, such as Bearing Point, PricewaterhouseCoopers, Ernst a Young and Lockheed Martin. As the university is rapidly growing, more a more big-name companies are showing up each year. The employment opp tunities are increasing daily.

Current student, 8/2005-Submit Date, January 2006

Employment prospects from JMU graduates is very high, especially in the co puter technology, business and arts areas. The alumni are very helpful and off give donations through a system called the Madison Connection. On-camp recruiting and internships are available but you have to look for them and be a to fight to get them because of the limited number offered.

Alumnus/a, 8/2001-5/2005, May 2005

I just graduated from JMU in May 2005 and had my job lined up in Novem 2004. JMU graduates get jobs! I believe that JMU is perceived to be a pres gious school by all employers in the State of Virginia. Now more and more o of-state employers are coming on campus to recruit JMU students. JMU p fessors and faculty members truly try hard to help their students obtain jo JMU provides a department known as MadisonTrak. MadisonTrak does excellent job of connecting students with a countless numbers of potenti employers on a weekly basis. MadisonTrak also offers mock interviews, résu building classes and a career development center.

Current student, 1/2004-Submit Date, May 2005

JMU has its own personal alumni network and works extremely hard to keep alumni up to date on all events on JMU's campus, as well as any opportuniti off campus, in which they may be interested. Each undergraduate college h seminars where firms come and scout students to join their firms. Either on or twice a year, JMU puts on an internship fair, where many companies come advertise their internship programs available to those students who are intere ed. It's a great way to learn more about the company's programs and let the see the students in a more personal manner.

Current student, 8/2003-Submit Date, February 2004

JMU offers many fairs with companies looking for interns, and really urges st dents to pursue internships. The university has a good name that seems to go long way, and the business program is highly regarded. They have a great sy tem set up through Monster to help students submit résumés to prospecti employers. There is an extensive career development center on campus, with plethora of information on thousands of companies. All students, regardless GPA, can find a job if they utilize this resource.

Quality of Life

mnus/a, 8/2002-5/2006, November 2006

U is located in a very safe area. My friends and I were never afraid to walk
e late at night on the weekends after going to parties. Housing is OK; the
ms are relatively nice and decent. The off-campus apartments are hit or miss.
chase, Stone Gate, and some of the newer apartments are nice. Hunter's
e and Ashby are the apartments to live in if you want your place to get trashed
vant to have parties a lot.

dining on campus is excellent. I miss the food at JMU; that is how good it
Top Dog Cafe is probably the best. D-Hall is the main dining hall and it is
d all you can eat food. Ms. Greens is a good salad bar and good if you want
at healthly. There were many good dining options on campus.

mnus/a, 8/2001-5/2005, August 2006

ould say that the quality of life at JMU is higher than at most other schools I
e encountered. It's a beautiful campus and people are incredibly friendly.
ms are pretty typical, but off-campus apartments are amazing! The food is
great; we are very spoiled!

mnus/a, 8/2002-5/2006, May 2006

npus is beautiful! Go see it!

risonburg is a developing city, which has its ups and downs. The students
e up a majority of the activity in Harrisonburg. Housing is unique. It is very
y to tell who the students are and who the townies are in Harrisonburg. I have
had a problem with crime.

rrent student, 8/2005-Submit Date, January 2006

best aspect of the JMU quality of life is food, which is ranked sixth in the
ion. The newer dorms (in which I live) are very nice because they contain air
ditioning; the older ones do not. We also have a kitchen and laundry room
t is readily available. The campus, itself, is beautiful and has the Number
ee landscape in the nation and its neighborhood is filled with kind and car-
people. The crime and safety force here is excellent. JMU has its own police
ce and whenever there is an incident, a bulletin is sent out to every JMU stu-
t so that everyone knows what is going on.

rrent student, 9/2003-Submit Date, October 2005

quality of life is great. Traffic can be horrible when classes are getting out
ause of the highway that cuts through our campus. A lot of long lights; it's
er to just take the bus. I feel like the campus is getting over-crowded and
y need to start cutting down the inflow of students. Parking sucks! Everyone
s off campus after their first year. The food is great! There are so many dif-
nt places to eat on campus, but I think they should make an off-campus meal
n also. There are break-ins from time to time in the apartments, and have
n some peepers in the dorms.

rrent student, 8/2003-Submit Date, May 2005

st-year housing is guaranteed to freshmen. 50 percent move off sophomore
r, but I still loved my sophomore year experience on campus. JMU's cam-
is beautiful and surrounded by gorgeous mountains. The sunsets are amaz-
. Our facilities are excellent including our student recreation center (UREC),
ich was built just for students (not varsity athletes). I feel safe here at JMU,
ever I do take certain common sense precautions (don't walk alone late at
ht by yourself).

Social Life

mnus/a, 8/2002-5/2006, November 2006

U is a very social school. People are always out doing things. If you are a
et person, going to JMU could make you more outgoing. There is always
ff to do on campus, various free programs going on. There is a campus movie
ater (Grafton-Stovall) and there are tons of student organizations. JMU also
a "Student Organization Night" each semester where students can find out
ich clubs are on campus.

As for bars, the main one is Highlawn. (It has since been re-named or changed
into a restaurant, though.) People like to go to The Pub and Main Street Bar and
Grill as well. Buffalo Wild Wings is also popular; it is right across from the
Quad.

Most of the social stuff is at off-campus parties though. There are buses that go
to all the apartment complexes and to campus so no one has to worry about
drunk driving. And the bus runs till 2 or 3 a.m. on weekends. Even if you don't
drink, go party and mingle with people. I did that at first and still had fun without alcohol.

Alumnus/a, 8/2001-5/2005, August 2006

There is always something going on at JMU! We are definitely not a bar school,
but you will save a lot of money by going to all the free apartment parties. There
are plenty of restaurants around town. If parties aren't your thing, we have an
on-campus movie theatre, Division I sports, concerts, coffee houses and so on.
It's great!

Current student, 8/2005-Submit Date, January 2006

I do not know anything about bars here myself, but I have been told that they
host good bands and provide a lot of good entertainment. The restaurants surrounding JMU are vast, including Applebee's, Outback, Cracker Barrel and
IHOP. We also have a wide host of fast-food places including Wendy's,
McDonalds, Burger King, KFC, Hardees, Pizza Hut, Dominoes, Subway and
others. In addition, we have a nice restaurant on campus called the Madison
Grill. We have an events calender on our home web site that contains many
diverse activities and events available to everyone. JMU is home to over 600
clubs (even a Crocheting Club). My personal favorite clubs are the Tai Kwon
Do Club and Fencing Club.

Current student, 9/2003-Submit Date, October 2005

We need more bars! Seriously, there are a few good bars but not enough.
Students only really go to the bars during the week. There are never good deals
or promos on the weekends. The restaurants are good, a lot of them. But most
of the restaurants are chain restaurants. I think the dating scene is no different
than any other college, many couples, but I think a greater majority would be
called casual dating. Great parties, block parties are the best, but cops are starting to get really strict. The parties take place is apartments. This town is full of
apartment complexes and students are this town.

Current student, 8/2004-Submit Date, May 2005

Welcome to farm country. If you're looking for a college town, Harrisonburg is
it. With a student population that doubles the population of the town, the university is pretty much the only thing to do. But that's what makes JMU all that
it is. Madison is a community, they are the people with whom you learn and
interact on a daily basis. In many ways, they become much more than your
peers, but your family. While fine dining is scarce and there aren't many clubs,
JMU is renowned for its dance parties and apartment get-togethers. Smaller
scale memories that you wind up cherishing the most. Greek life represents
approximately 14 percent of the population, not an overbearing presence.
Sororities are on campus, fraternities (those that haven't had their charters
revoked) are off.

The School Says

James Madison University is a public, comprehensive university
and is the only university in America named for U.S. President
James Madison. JMU's mission statement is "We are a community committed to preparing students to be educated and
enlightened citizens who lead productive and meaningful lives."

At JMU, students benefit from exceptional opportunities to participate in undergraduate and interdisciplinary research and to
contribute to emerging studies and practices in environmental
sustainability and stewardship.

The university is observing its centennial during the 2007-08
year and will mark its 100th anniversary March 14, 2008.

Read all of Vault's College Surveys at www.vault.com/college—get complete surveys on 100s of colleges and universities, expert advice on applicaton essays and more.

VAULT CAREER LIBRARY   749

The university offers programs on the bachelor's, master's and doctoral levels with its primary emphasis on the undergraduate student. JMU provides total education to students—one that has a broad range of the liberal arts as its foundation and encompasses an extensive variety of professional and pre-professional programs

JMU offers the following undergraduate degrees: Bachelor of Arts, Bachelor of Business Administration, Bachelor of Fine Arts, Bachelor of Individualized Studies, Bachelor of Music, Bachelor of Science, Bachelor of Science in Nursing and Bachelor of Social Work.

JMU offers the following graduate degrees: Doctor of Audiology, Doctor of Musical Arts, Doctor of Philosophy, Doctor of Psychology, Educational Specialist, Master of Arts, Master of Arts in Teaching, Master of Business Administration, Master of Education, Master of Fine Arts, Master of Music, Master of Occupational Therapy, Master of Public Administration, Master of Physician Assistant Studies, Master of Science, Master of Science in Education and Master of Science in Nursing.

Academic coursework is augmented by a multitude of learning experiences outside the classroom. Students can choose from 300 clubs and organizations for membership to pursue new interests or to maintain favorite activities.

JMU has been identified as the South's top public, master's-level university in the annual *U.S. News & World Report* America's Best Colleges guide for 14 consecutive years. The 2008 edition of the guide cited JMU on its national recognitions segments for outstanding first-year experiences, learning communities and service learning.

JMU currently enrolls more than 18,000 students. Approximately 61 percent of the undergraduate student body is female. The 2007-08 freshman class is made up of more than 3,900 students.

All freshmen live in university-sponsored housing. After freshman year, students may remain on or move off campus.

Radford University

Admissions Office
Martin Hall
P.O. Box 6903
Radford, VA 24142
Admissions phone: (540) 831-5371 or (800) 890-4265
Admissions fax: (540) 831-5038
Admissions e-mail: ruadmiss@radford.edu
Admissions URL: www.radford.edu/admissions/

 Admissions

Current student, 8/2003-Submit Date, May 2006

Radford has now turned to a set deadline admissions process. Early Action, which is non-binding, takes place in December. RU does not require a personal statement or letters of recommendation, but the admissions office does recommend them. They help them see who you are and if you would fit in well at RU. If you want to be considered for scholarships, you must apply by December. If you qualify, they will notify you of the further information they need. This usually includes an essay and letters of recommendation. They then select students to visit RU in the spring and compete through an interview for the scholarships.

Current student, 8/2004-Submit Date, May 2006

I applied online after taking a tour of the school. Radford isn't very hard to get into. I don't know anyone who hasn't been accepted, but I do know people who have been kicked out for academic reasons.

Current student, 8/2004-Submit Date, May 2006

I first made contact with Radford University during my junior year of high school. RU sent me a packet of information about academics, the students and the area. My mother and I visited RU for the first time during the summer following my junior year. I lucked out because my cousin is an alumna of Radford and she gave me a personal tour. Visit campus! You need to see it, feel it and speak face-to-face with some key people. It's the best way for you to decide if Radford is right for you. During the fall of my junior year, I visited Radford again during Homecoming weekend. I met more people and went on an official guided tour. The second visit cemented my decision to apply to RU. The more you visit, the better!

By the time I applied I knew my admissions very well! I was still decid[ing] between theatre and nursing as majors. I know those are two very differ[ent] fields, but I love both areas. I e-mailed, called and met the directors of b[oth] departments. I made sure they knew my name and got a lot of information ab[out] the programs from them. I recommend contacting the director of the departm[ent] in which you're interested before you apply and after, as well.

I decided to pursue nursing. I chose to apply online, but you can also apply snail-mail. The online application is easy to use because you can save your w[ork] and come back to it. Make sure you have your parents' personal information[as] well as your own. If you don't have your social security number memorized[,] memorize it now. You'll need it again and again! When it's time to dish out y[our] extracurricular activities, don't leave anything out. I know you hear this all [the] time, but you never know what's going to make you stand out to the admissi[ons] board. Volunteer work, summer camp work, any clubs, religious activities a[nd] more. During the summer after my sophomore year of high school, I went o[n a] mission trip to Bulgaria to teach English at an English camp and to help lead [an] international Christian camp. It was an exciting time in my life. I chose to w[rite] about it in my admissions essay. The essay is optional, but you should mak[e it] a personal requirement. I think that my essay may have been the line-and-h[ook] for my application!

I sent my application in before December 15th because that's the deadline [for] applicants competing for scholarships. I received my acceptance letter in [the] mail on December 24th, Christmas Eve. I also received the School of Nurs[ing] Deans' Scholarship. The admissions process didn't end there! I still had [to] accept the invitation to attend Radford. Radford was my number one choice, [but] I had applied to other good schools. Some of which were closer to home and [my] mom was rooting for them. I made another visit to Radford in April [for] Highlander Day. It was a special day for accepted applicants to learn more ab[out] RU before making their decision. We had a lot of fun and I won a candy bar [play]ing a game. RU's nursing school seemed tough, which I liked, but I also wa[nt]ed to have fun during college. So I confirmed my attendance to RU! Fina[lly] the admissions process was over!

Alumnus/a, 8/1999-8/2003, April 2005

The admissions process required a written essay, meeting quotas for out-of-to[wn] students, the specific availability of the program a candidate was trying to [get] into, as well as a basic application and SAT scores. The most useful advice i[s] keep your scores and grades as high as possible to keep yourself competiti[ve] s, if you are waitlisted, make a personal phone call. Every school should nk they are your first choice!

The school says: "RU does not have quotas for any group of students. There is no waitlist program."

rrent student, 8/2003-Submit Date, January 2005

dford University is not as easy to get into as some may think. Your grade int average and SAT scores do count. Minimum of 900 on SAT, and a mini- im of 2.5 GPA are recommended. Anything less and they will almost defi- ely count you out. Be sure to get the application from the admissions office. me programs such as art and music require an extra application form. Be are that your acceptance may also require letters of recommendation, slides r art), or a special interview (for music). You will be judged by your experi- es thus far, as well as your academic profile. Scholarships also require rec- mmendations, interviews, slides and applications as well. Do not forget to fill t your FAFSA on time, or you will definitely be in hot water.

Radford University says: "There is no specific minimum SAT score."

Academics

rrent student, 8/2003-Submit Date, May 2006

J provides a wonderful academic environment. Every RU student comments the helpfulness of the professors. Because classes are relatively small, with :1:1 ratio, so students and professors are able to get to know each other. Most J classes are taught by PhD professors; very few are taught by graduate stu- nts. RU provides a choice of over 106 majors, and has support services for dents who come in undecided on a major. We are a liberal arts institution, so dents take a variety of classes as part of their general education. You have ny choices to fulfill these areas, which allows you to explore interests outside your major. If a student is struggling in a class and needs extra help, the arning Assistance and Resource Center (LARC) provides free tutoring for any ss. There is always a variety of academic enriching programs and lectures on npus, also. Each year, the International Education Center hosts a cultures fes- al, highlighting a specific region of the world. Many departments host lec- es in their fields throughout the year also.

rrent student, 8/2004-Submit Date, May 2006

n a nursing major. I'm proud to say that because I earned acceptance into the rsing program this spring; I was only a pre-nursing major before. I start clin- ls this fall. The nursing school told us to plan on not having a life for the next o years as we work our way through upper-division nursing school. I can't you much about upper-division nursing because I'm only just beginning. I pass the required math skills test! Passing means 85 percent or higher. I've nt the last two years meeting gen ed and prerequisite requirements. If you n a 3.5 or higher your freshman year, you're guaranteed acceptance into the rsing program.

ost professors deliver their material in a way that students not only remember, also understand. Every professor I've had remembers my name and actual- got to know me a little. If you give their class some of your time, they'll give u all the time you need from them to do well in the class. Many professors l meet with you at any time if you can't make their regular office hours. I en see professors having lunch with students on campus. They write amazing erence letters to help you land scholarships. My best advice about interacting th your professors: introduce yourself the very first day of class. Just walk up, ke hands, and tell them your name. They'll take notice in a good way. At the ne time, don't view your professors as an obstacle. At RU, the professor ches the class—not a TA. The professor is also more interested in teaching u than in research. The better your relationship with your professor, the bet- you'll do in the class.

e never had any problems registering for classes that I've wanted. If you real- need a class and you can't get into it, you can have the department head write u in to the class. Last semester, there were a lot of pre-nursing students who ded chemistry and not enough sections available. In response, the nursing

school created another section of chemistry. I'm glad because it was the class I needed to take before entering upper-division nursing.

Current student, 8/2004-Submit Date, May 2006

I have been very satisfied with all of the classes that I have taken there so far. I think that the grading and workload are pretty good. I have had really good pro- fessors who love what they teach and really care about their students.

Alumnus/a, 8/1999-5/2003, October 2005

Overall, I was pleased with my experience at Radford. I graduated with a bach- elor's degree in Statistics. The workload was heavy. Out-of-class work was time consuming. Most of my concentration classes were smaller in size ranging around 10 students per class. General education class sizes were much larger ranging from 25 to 100+ students. I never had any difficulty registering for classes. I always got in the classes for which I registered. Overall, the profes- sors were knowledgeable and brought a wealth of work experience to the class- rooms.

Alumnus/a, 8/1999-5/2002, March 2005

Workload is pretty typical in comparison to other institutions to which I have had exposure. The one major difference is the quality of education that I received from Radford. I wasn't "just a number," I received plenty of individual attention and I was able to meet with professors any time. We were also given more dif- ficult testing because our professors did not just cop out and give us a multiple choice test because they would have too many tests to grade to give anything dif- ferent. Speaking of professors: very high quality and always available to stu- dents.

Current student, 8/2003-Submit Date, November 2004

The programs here at RU are small and focused. Classes are of a high caliber; while it sometimes may be a struggle to get the class you want, the registrar is usually there to help you. The professors are, for the most part, great! They love what they do and it shows in how they run their classrooms. As an English major, I seem to have the de rigger workload, but from speaking to my friends, the workload they are under seems reasonable. RU is well known for its great speciality programs, such as its nursing program and five-year master's teaching program.

Employment Prospects

Current student, 8/2003-Submit Date, May 2006

The Center for Experimental Learning and Career Development aids students in finding jobs and internships, writing résumés and [developing] interviewing skills. RU has a very high rate of employment after graduation, and few students struggle to find jobs in their fields after graduation. Some programs, including our teaching and nursing programs, are sought-after for jobs after graduation because of the excellence of the program. Alumni, especially in the Commonwealth of Virginia, are able to help students find jobs in different regions of the state. Since many majors now require an internship prior to grad- uation, many students obtain jobs this way.

Current student, 8/2004-Submit Date, May 2006

As a nursing student, I know that I won't have a hard time finding a job after graduation. There is a nursing shortage that RU nurses will be able to fill. Radford nursing grads also have more clinical experience than some of the other programs available. My cousin graduated from RU with a degree in education. When she applied for her first job teaching at an elementary school, the school told her that they offered her the job because she was an RU grad. She actually got the offer in a call on her cell phone while she was driving home from the interview.

Current student, 1/2003-Submit Date, November 2005

Radford is very good about providing opportunities for employment, but mostly just in the surrounding areas of Radford. For those who are graduating soon or have already graduated, weekly e-mails are sent out for jobs that have become available. There are also job fairs for most business majors and others a couple of times a year. As for me, I was a music therapy major and most of that infor- mation was received from my professor and through the Internet. In the music therapy department, if you want an internship (which is required to get certified)

Read all of Vault's College Surveys at **www.vault.com/college**—get complete surveys on 100s of colleges and univer- sities, expert advice on applicaton essays and more.

VAULT CAREER LIBRARY   **751**

you can get one; 100 percent of students who want internships get them in this department.

Alumnus/a, 8/1999-5/2003, October 2005

The alumni network tried to be helpful in providing a general base for jobs available across the U.S. After graduating, I immediately relocated out of state and found a job on my own. After relocating, I continued to receive correspondence from the alumni association and they were helpful in finding other alumni in my newly relocated area.

Current student, 8/2003-Submit Date, January 2005

Graduates have plenty of choices when they go looking for their careers. Radford has ties with companies in Virginia, and will e-mail information to upcoming graduates as they receive it. Career services supplies information on creating a winning résumé, and keeps the student population notified about special events and job fairs. Computer and business related jobs seem to be the favorites, but there is a wide selection of companies within different fields of study. On-campus recruiting and internships are excellent. Radford will work with you and try to settle you in a program or internship that fits your specific field. If you need an internship, this is the place.

Current student, 8/2003-Submit Date, November 2004

The employment rate of RU is amazingly high from what I understand. While I cannot quote an exact percentage, I know that a graduate from RU will do very well in the competitive job market. I know that while there may not be many jobs around the Radford area, I do know that the Radford job system is very effective in aiding students on job searches. Radford also has a great work study program while you are enrolled here.

 ## Quality of Life

Current student, 8/2003-Submit Date, May 2006

RU residence halls are co-ed by suite. Two girls' rooms will share a bathroom, but across the hall could be guys. This is great for meeting new people, especially as a freshman. The halls are scattered throughout campus, so you are never far away from academic buildings. After sophomore year, many students move off campus into apartments; however, these are all one or two blocks off campus. RU is very safe; we have a full police force that monitors campus safety at all times. We have two traditional dining halls and two food courts with Chick-fil-A, Au Bon Pain and Sbarro, which provide a great variety of food choices.

Current student, 8/2004-Submit Date, May 2006

The quality of life at RU is awesome! I always feel safe. I have loved living on campus in Floyd Hall. You really get to know your fellow residences. My closest friend was actually my suitemate during my first year at RU. There are programs in the dorm all the time, ranging from ethical discussions to movie nights on the roof. If you don't feel like dining at Dalton or Muse Marketplace, you can use your flex dollars at the terrace shops or in the Bonnie. I love Chick-fil-A, Starbucks coffee and soup from Au Bon Pain. We have an auditorium that serves as a movie theatre Thursday through Sunday. It really feels like you're at the movies with the cushioned seats and the big screen playing current movies. The only difference is the price—it's a lot cheaper. If you don't want to see a movie, you can always play pool or go bowling. The new bowling lanes are really nice, especially at night!

Your parents are going to want to know you're safe, especially for the ladies. Residence Halls lock at 10 p.m. every night and you must have an ID card on hand to gain access to the building. We also heavy room doors that lock. They can only be opened with the key you and your roommate have. Campus police are everywhere, all the time. They make regular rounds at night in the parking lots and on campus. Emergency buttons that call the campus police are positioned around campus. The local neighborhood is safe. I've never had any trouble and I rarely hear about crime in the news.

Current student, 1/2003-Submit Date, November 2005

Because Radford is a small town, there is very little trouble with crime. Because it is a college campus, there are several students becoming intoxicated every weekend, but that is to be expected. There is enough housing on and off cam-

pus available for whoever wants/needs it. There are also a few dining are throughout campus that provide a good variety of food.

Alumnus/a, 8/1999-8/2003, April 2005

Quality of life was high, even beyond campus life. You cannot beat spring in southwest corner of Virginia. The mountains are incredible and everythi blooms a couple of weeks early. Dorms were very nice, and not too crowde There were four people to a suite and people tended to be comfortable consid ing the close quarters. Some older residents often moved out of their homes town and rented them to students. There are beautiful structures and a qua feel to the college town. Student life was nourished and a ton of truly nice pe ple. Crime was nothing to speak of and safety was monitored at all hours. believe there were mostly alcohol-related incidents.

Current student, 8/2003-Submit Date, January 2005

Housing can be crowded. Muse is the largest residence hall on campus, housi over 900 students. Other smaller residence halls house between 150 and 200 st dents each. Radford rotates renovations on these halls, so just about the ti they really need fixing up, they get it. The rooms are big enough to live in co fortably, only with two people in them each. Two rooms share a bathroo There are two sinks in each bathroom, a toilet and a shower.

Dining has improved a great deal. Dalton dining hall not only offers a cafeter but a Freshen's, Sbarro, Au Bon Pain, Chick-fil-A and Mean Gene's Burge There are plenty of options for the hungry student. Meal plans are decided number of meals a week, or overall food dollars. Meals per week does r include the fast food. You get so many meals a week and $125 in food dolla to be used for any of the choices. The flex plan is based on a dollar amou which you can use at any of the restaurants or dining facilities, including t Ritazza in the library, Muse cafeteria or any of the Dalton areas.

 ## Social Life

Current student, 8/2003-Submit Date, May 2006

Radford has a great social scene. There are many restaurants, shops and thin to do around town. We also have a strong Greek community. There is alwa something to do on campus. We have a 10-lane bowling alley, game room a movie theater that are open and running every day. Campus activities always h an event for students; also, many clubs and organizations will have campus-wi events for all students during the week and on weekends. We have over 2 clubs and organizations, which makes it easy to get involved. We also have a of intramural sports and club sports in which to participate.

Current student, 8/2004-Submit Date, May 2006

If you want to go to school in the big city, Radford is not the place for you. you like small Southern college towns, Radford is the place for you. We've a beautiful main street, train tracks, the New River and more. We've also g every fast food restaurant known to America. Come for a visit and you'll fi them! This might be essential news for some off you: yes, Radford has a 2 hour Wal-Mart. I highly suggest that anyone merely passing through Radfo stop in at Troy's for a Philly Cheese Steak. Christiansburg is a short drive awa That's where we keep the mall which has a Deb, Bath and Body Work Victoria's Secret and more. We also keep Target, Goodies, TJ MAXX, Kma Barnes & Noble, Payless Shoe Source, Red Lobster and an even bigger Wa Mart in Christiansburg. New to Christiansburg are a new roller skati rink/laser tag, Starbucks Coffee and Cold Stone Creamery (great ice cream).

There are lots of outdoor activities around RU. Drive down 460 for a day vis ing the cascades! The long walk up the trail leads to a beautiful waterfall. The are a lot of trails to ride your bike on also. If you don't feel like driving, just for a walk by the New River. If you want to get wet, you can go tubing in t New River! It's my favorite thing to do at the beginning of the fall semest The River Walk leads to Bisset Park where people cook out, play frisbee a girls go to lay out in the sun.

Radford has the typical college party scene and an even bigger reputation f being a party school. As a student who actually attends Radford, I'd just like say that Radford isn't as big of a party school as everyone thinks. Lots of pa tying goes on, but no more than at any other school. Your social life at Radfo what you make of it. You can choose the crowd with which you hang out! ne people go to parties every night and others have never been to a party with hol. Radford is co-ed. It's inevitable that people date! I've been dating the e guy for about three years. He goes to Virginia Tech. That's common at . A lot of people at RU, guys and girls, date people at Tech. We believe in ating a mixed culture. While some folks prefer long-term relationships, oth-just casually date.

ek life is huge at Radford. I can't even name all of them! APO is a service ternity and it's great for your résumé. There are a lot of clubs at RU. There's Ultimate Frisbee Club, College Republicans, College Democrats, Honors ademy, Residence Hall Association, Red Cross Club and various clubs asso-ted with academic departments. There are also many religious organizations. mpus Crusade for Christ, is very popular.

rrent student, 1/2003-Submit Date, November 2005

ere are plenty of Greek frats and sororities at Radford University. The one I ociated with the most because of my major was SAI, because I majored in sic. There is a club fair at the beginning of every school year that all the clubs ne to and there is something for everyone. In the City of Radford there are y a couple of bars but about 15 minutes away is Christiansburg, Virginia ere most people go for entertainment and food. Blackburg, Virginia is also se, which is where Virginia Tech is located. They have several bars and ces to party and attend football games.

rrent student, 8/2003-Submit Date, January 2005

ties, bars, restaurants, Greek societies, you name it. We've got it here in dford or within a half an hour of driving. 15 or 20 minutes from school is the y of Christiansburg. Christiansburg has a mall, restaurants, Va Tech, supply res, bookstores, clothing shops and other shopping. It's where you go to do get what you can't in Radford. Greek societies are rampant, and they all want ι. Take your pick, and beware the rush. Parties are mostly frats or sororities.

For $3 or $5, you get to party with all the beer you can drink. If you like to drink, that is. Dance, drink and try to wobble on home.

The School Says

Nestled in the scenic Blue Ridge Mountains of Virginia, Radford University is a premier teaching and learning university focused on providing outstanding academic programs. Well-known for its strong faculty/student bonds, innovative use of technology in the learning environment and vibrant student life on a beautiful campus, RU offers many opportunities to get involved and succeed in and out of the classroom.

Throughout its history, Radford University has been visionary, embracing new concepts and technologies that put the institution at the forefront of national trends. Today, the university's wireless campus and technologically savvy faculty demonstrate RU's commitment to staying ahead of the curve and offering its students the best possible learning environment.

The university welcomes more than 9,200 students from across the country and around the world each year. Its seven colleges offer 106 undergraduate and 38 graduate program options with minors in most fields and pre-professional programs in law, medicine, physical therapy and pharmacy. Student life thrives on RU's campus with more than 200 clubs and organizations, NCAA Division I athletics, special events, performances and lectures each year.

To learn more about Radford University, visit us online at www.radford.edu.

University of Richmond

dmissions Office
Westhampton Way
niversity of Richmond, VA 23173
dmissions phone: (800) 700-1662 or (804) 289-8640
dmissions fax: (804) 287-6003
dmissions e-mail: admissions@richmond.edu
dmissions URL: www.richmond.edu/prospective/

Admissions

rrent student, 8/2003-Submit Date, February 2006

e admissions process is obviously key to getting into the school. I encourage u to spend time on the application and then continue to follows up the appli-ion through phone calls, visits to the univer sity and e-mails. The staff that iews the applications is small—and it can be critical to show how interested the university you are. They want people who will want to be there. The ectivity is higher for girls than boys. They try to keep a 50/50 ratio of men to men, and more women apply to the university than men. If you're a woman, ke sure your essay says how you are unique. Also, they are looking for diver-y at this time, so show why you add to their diversity!

umnus/a, 8/2002-5/2006, October 2006

e admissions process is pretty standard. There were no interviews. As far as tting in, you are going to need to be in the top 15 percent of a competitive pub-school, or top 25 percent from a prestigious private school. UR is doing its st to bring more diversity to campus and brings in a lot of international stu-

dents from South America and Europe. If you are an international student or a minority with good grades and test scores, you have a good chance of getting accepted. As far as the essay goes, I was asked to write about somebody who has inspired me. I wrote about my great uncle and his leadership skills. UR has a school of leadership studies and I feel like emphasizing my interest and under-standing of leadership ability helped me gain the admissions director's attention. I also had letters of recommendation from my guidance counselor, two high school teachers, and the director of a nonprofit organization for which I volun-teered. (He coincidentally used to be the head of the psychology department at UR.)

Alumnus/a, 8/2001-5/2005, February 2006

Very selective school, very hard to get into, standards have increased dramati-cally over the years. Need-blind acceptance, but tuition is $40,000+.

Alumnus/a, 8/1999-5/2003, April 2004

The University of Richmond looks at a combination of test scores, grades and extracurricular activities, roughly in that order of importance. SAT Subject Tests are especially important. The school becomes more selective every year, which is great for alumni, but not so great for children of alumni.

Alumnus/a, 8/1995-5/1999, September 2003

The admissions process to the University of Richmond is not that complicated. The required materials were the application forms, including the essay, SAT and SAT Subject Test scores, high school transcript, financial aid forms and recom-mendation letters (which may have been optional). Interviews are not required for admission, but they are recommended so that you can learn more about the school while the school learns about you. A campus visit is highly recommend-ed, to determine whether the university has the elements of campus living that

Read all of Vault's College Surveys at **www.vault.com/college**—get complete surveys on 100s of colleges and univer-sities, expert advice on applicaton essays and more.

VAULT CAREER LIBRARY 753

are most important to you. Try to make an appointment with department heads to speak with them in depth about the program, the intensity of the program and the type of students that succeed in their departments.

The essay is straightforward, especially if the Common Application is used. The university gives equal weight to the Common Application and the school's own paper application. Whatever the topic, be sure to organize the essay before writing. Spending at least two weeks developing the essay and two weeks revising it is highly recommended. Have at least two people review your essay, and try to obtain as much feedback as possible.

The university accepts people from many backgrounds and geographical areas. Generally, Richmond attracts a large population of people from the Northeast, some from the West Coast and some from Virginia. There was a small group of international students as well. For a university its size, the population was fairly diverse. The students came from a wide variety of academic backgrounds, including some of the brightest students to average students. Be sure to check the academic requirements on the school's web site to make sure that you meet the requirements.

Academics

Alumnus/a, 8/2002-5/2006, October 2006

UR may have a reputation for having the country club lifestyle, but don't let the beautiful campus fool you. If you do decide to go to UR, prepare to work. Classes are challenging and have rigorous workloads. Even my second semester of senior year, I was still pulling at least three all-nighters a month. The teachers are great, class sizes are small, and I never once had a TA. Getting into the class of your choice is pretty easy. If you don't get into the class of your choice, you can always e-mail the professor and ask for an override. UR is definitely known more for its business school than anything else. Last May, the Robins School of Business was ranked 25th in the world for undergraduate business schools. However, the first two years most students are encouraged to take generic courses in the school of arts and sciences, the school of leadership studies, and the business school. Grading really depends on the professor. There are very few classes that are available (especially in the business school) that are considered "easy A's."

Current student, 8/2003-Submit Date, February 2006

Going to the university is for serious students. The quality of the faculty is amazing and the class sizes are all under 40 people and very often you will have around 20 in a class. The professors are all highly qualified and many are happy to be working at a university with a class of students who all strive to be the best. Grading is difficult—rumor has it with a good amount of work you'll get a B in most classes; it's very difficult to get the A, however. And workload varies. It's pretty serious only because of all the other commitments you have in addition to school (organizations, Greek life and work, friends).

Alumnus/a, 8/1999-5/2003, April 2004

Small class sizes. Excellent professors. Professors go out of their way to help students (make themselves available outside of class and office hours). Getting popular classes can be difficult for underclassmen. Grading is fair. Workload can be heavy, depending on the major.

Alumnus/a, 8/1999-5/2003, April 2004

Almost all teachers have their doctorates. Classes range in difficulty depending on the level, and there are a few courses in every discipline that strike fear in those striving for summa cum laude. Popular courses, professors and times for classes often fill up fast, but the Dean's Office is accommodating enough to allow students to get into classes that they need. The workload depends on the course, with general requirements usually requiring less work than upper-level major classes.

Alumnus/a, 8/1995-5/1999, September 2003

The university offers good programs in the humanities and science departments. Richmond requires core classes that are requirements for all first-year students as a part of the liberal arts education credits. Reputedly, the strongest departments are English, philosophy, religion, art and foreign languages. These departments have very accessible department heads and professors, whose doors

are always open during and sometimes outside of office hours. The classes generally small, and even the most popular classes in these departments are larger than 25 or so students. Because the class sizes are small, Richmond tr to offer more sessions for them so that registering for them can be done with ative ease.

The sciences (biology, chemistry, physics), mathematics and business depa ments are good programs. The introductory science courses, usually for majo are generally large (over 30 students). The courses tend to be smaller for more advanced courses, and the labs are on the small and crowded side. T mathematics department is also small with smaller class sizes. The busin school has a large department, and there are a lot of business school majors. T classes are large, regardless of whether they are introductory or advanced cou es. It is difficult to get into any business course, especially if it is a popu course.

As for the workload, the science courses have the highest volume of work c to the work associated with labs. Although most of the courses have a reaso able amount of work, it is a much greater workload than high school cours Most courses all have a lot of required reading, as well as papers, examinatic and class participation. While it is difficult to generalize the workload for courses across departmental borders, it is fair to say that there is a lot of mate al covered in the courses. Each student gets what he or she puts into the cou es, and it is possible to be very academically successful at Richmo Cultivating relationships with professors and fellow students is important an significant part of one's education, and students should definitely take advanta of that.

Employment Prospects

Alumnus/a, 8/2002-5/2006, October 2006

Anybody who has a major in accounting or finance ends up with a job right c of college. Richmond has a better reputation amongst employers on the Ea Coast than in the Midwest and the West Coast. Many students go off to grac ate school or law school. The Career Development Center does a decent job helping students find employment opportunities, but more can be done. I hea a rumor that they are going to start working with Phillip Morris and a few tec nology companies and financial institutions to combine internship progra with actual classes. I don't know of anyone who graduated from UR who end up with a job flipping burgers or serving coffee. There is a career fair that is he at the beginning of first semester and that is one way of networking for a jc The school does need to do a better job of working together with companies develop internship programs for the students.

Current student, 8/2003-Submit Date, February 2006

Employers love our graduates. They are known for being wonderful and knov edgeable about what an employer wants. The Career Development Center amazing at preparing for an interview, the résumé and finding internships a jobs. There is a very active alumni network willing to help undergraduates fi jobs and internships. In addition, there are several prestigious companies th pull from us—Phillip Morris, Goldman Sachs, Genworth Financial (Former GE), JP Morgan and Target.

Alumnus/a, 8/1992-5/1996, January 2005

Employment prospects were probably best for graduates of the business scho at the University of Richmond. Most business or leadership majors are able obtain lucrative jobs before graduating. Students graduating with a bachelo degree in science face a more difficult time getting a good paying job. Most the science majors whom I knew did not have jobs lined up before graduatic Those not going on to medical school generally obtained jobs working in sor sort of biology or chemistry research and development lab within a few mont of graduation.

Alumnus/a, 8/1999-5/2003, April 2004

Excellent job and internship opportunities. UR brings a ton of employers campus for interviews and job fairs. High prestige with employers on the Ea Coast. Wonderful job opportunities and connections for business school grad ates, too.

Alumnus/a, 8/1999-5/2003, April 2004

University of Richmond's Career Development Center is a huge success. Any student who makes a serious attempt at finding an internship or a job can do so with the help of the CDC. The school attracts a diverse group of employers to job and internship fairs and arranges on-campus interviews through online scheduling. The online system is easy to use and highly effective. UofR remains one of the most prestigious Virginia schools, on par with Washington and Lee and University of Virginia. Certain majors attract more employers, and the well-known accounting and finance programs probably draw the most.

Quality of Life

Alumnus/a, 8/2002-5/2006, October 2006

The campus is beautiful. It's 10 minutes away from downtown Richmond, which has a respectable nightlife scene. 50 percent of the female population joins a sorority, while only about 30 percent of the male population joins a fraternity. The facilities, for the most part, are topnotch. The dorms, while beautiful on the outside, are starting to show some wear and tear on the inside. The on-campus apartments for upperclassmen should have been torn down decades ago. The food at the dining hall is pretty typical for a college campus, however a Mongolian Grill is going in this fall. The gym facilities are also under construction and should be completely state-of-the-art when they finish. There are also plans to put a mock trading floor in the business school, when they start construction on their addition within the next five years. UR is located in a very upscale suburban part of West Richmond and has basically no crime. There is a bus that will pick up students after 8 o'clock anywhere on campus and drop them off wherever they need to go.

Current student, 8/2003-Submit Date, February 2006

Everyone is busy on campus. Everyone is involved in at least two organizations and tends to be heavily involved in them. Most students live on campus; juniors and seniors can live in on-campus apartments. It's wonderful to be living in this environment with everyone else—it makes you very close. Dining is improving next year with a new D Hal that will be amazing!

Alumnus/a, 8/1999-5/2003, April 2004

Quality of life is a strong point for Richmond. The school's housing, academic facilities, dining options and security are all topnotch. The campus is always perfectly groomed and looks better than a lot of country clubs. There are plenty of activities around campus, and the school is located on the border of the City of Richmond limits. Many students take advantage of an extensive study abroad program, which is one of the best around. Students have opportunities to study all over the world, and almost 50 percent of students take advantage of this.

Alumnus/a, 8/1995-5/1999, September 2003

The overall quality of life is good at Richmond. The campus is situated in one of Richmond's most prestigious neighborhoods, and it is a beautiful campus. The architecture is nice, there is a lake in the middle of campus and a large student center, and the buildings in which classes take place are all a short distance away from the dormitories. Upperclassmen have the option of moving into the university's own apartments, situated on campus but a longer distance away from the academic buildings than the dormitories. The apartments have two bedrooms, two people to a room, with a living room, kitchen and parking spaces. The male and female apartments are situated near each other, but each apartment is single-sex.

There is one dining hall on campus, which is connected to the student center. The school has reasonable food, but it is not considered fantastic. The cafeteria offered a variety of foods, with weekly international menus, but it was not vegetarian or vegan-friendly. Different meal plans could be purchased depending on how many times a student eats in the cafeteria each week. There were several options for takeout and delivery near campus.

Approximately 15 to 30 minutes away is downtown Richmond, which offers a host of restaurants, cafes, shops and cultural activities. Students with cars could do some grocery shopping at Ukrops, which is a high-end grocery store, but the students in dormitories have limited cooking facilities. There are also approximately three shopping malls within a hour radius of campus, as well as the historic shopping district, Carytown. While downtown Richmond is a bit more

dangerous, especially at night, the immediate area of the university is quiet, clean and very safe. Campus police are also on duty to provide additional security for students. A campus van is provided in the evening hours to transport students from academic buildings to residence halls for additional security and comfort. Very few security issues arose during most students' four-year tenures at Richmond.

Social Life

Alumnus/a, 8/2002-5/2006, October 2006

The typical student works hard and plays hard. There is an on-campus bar called the Cellar, which has typical pub food with a limited beer and wine selection. Most nights the Cellar has live music as well. There are also a couple of nearby bars and great restaurants that are no more than a few minute car ride from campus. There are also three malls within 10 minutes of campus. Downtown Richmond has a thriving nightlife scene with lots of bars, clubs and restaurants. Greek life is prominent on campus but is quite different than Greek life at other schools. Sororities at UR don't have houses, and fraternities have lodges that throw weekly parties with free beer.

Most students live on campus in the dorms or on-campus apartments. Very few people decide to live off campus. The Campus Activities Board is a very important organization on campus. In the past they have brought bands like Guster, Maroon 5, Dave Matthews Band, Filter, Yellow Card, and a variety of comedians. They also show movies every week in the Commons. Some favorite student events on campus are Homecoming, tailgating at football games, Ring Dance and Pig Roast in the spring (now called Festivus). Due to the fact that it's almost a 50/50 ratio of guys to girls—you can definitely find your match at Richmond. Some people want serious relationships, some want to have fun and have random hookups, and some decide to be celibate—it really depends on the person. A lot of partying takes place in the dorms and in the on-campus apartments. Occasionally the on-campus police or an RA will break up the party, but it's never really that big of a deal.

Current student, 8/2003-Submit Date, February 2006

Richmond has a huge social outlet. The downtown area is great—Carytown is another great place to hang out. Many chic and many cheap places to have a good time. Greek life involvement is heavy on campus—providing many parties each weekend on campus. There is a bar on campus that students enjoy hanging out at.

> The school says: "The accurate percentages for our undergraduates who join the Greek system are as follows: 46 percent of our female undergraduates and 29 percent of our male undergraduates."

Alumnus/a, 8/1999-5/2003, April 2004

The social life is centered around the Greek system; however, the administration is making concerted efforts to change that. Fraternities provide parties for all students and soak up the financial responsibility involved. The school is tightening up the already strict policies regarding Greek activities. The Richmond bar scene is fun for juniors and seniors. There is a multitude of bars in the Fan and Schockoe Bottom, which students frequent Monday through Saturday. Dating is essentially nonexistent at Richmond because the school is so small that after the first semester, you know everyone in your class who parties. There are plenty of activities for those who choose not to imbibe, from on-campus concerts in the Cellar to an on-campus eatery and bar, to religious and environmental meetings. Overall, there is plenty to keep one occupied for three and a half years, and the last semester requires some creativity.

Alumnus/a, 8/1995-5/1999, September 2003

Richmond's social life is ruled by the Greek system. A large percentage of first-years participate in the rush process with sororities and fraternities. The majority of the fraternities and sororities are social, but there are a few service fraternities. A significant part of Richmond's social life is dictated by the Greek system, so this is something to be considered if social life outside of the Greek system is important.

Read all of Vault's College Surveys at www.vault.com/college—get complete surveys on 100s of colleges and universities, expert advice on applicaton essays and more.

VAULT CAREER LIBRARY   755

The bottom line is that most of the students' lives are conducted on campus. Over 95 percent of the students live on campus, either in dormitories or campus apartments. Partying is done on campus, usually at the fraternity houses or the upperclassman apartments, and it is usually related to the Greek system or the athletes. The student population is mostly comprised of people from affluent or upper-middle-class backgrounds, and it shows in how students dress, what they own, the cars they drive and the attitudes they have about their world and beyond.

 The School Says

The University of Richmond is a nationally ranked liberal arts institution for students who seek both the intimacy of a small college and the academic, research and cultural opportunities of a large university. With fewer than 3,500 full-time students, the latest technology and stellar facilities, Richmond offers outstanding undergraduate and graduate degree programs in arts and sciences, business, leadership studies, law and continuing studies. The nation's first school of leadership studies and a Top 25 business school enhance a strong liberal arts curriculum and make Richmond an institution unlike any other.

Student-centered teaching, discovery-based learning and a global perspective are the cornerstones of a Richmond education. A low student-to-faculty ratio of 10:1 (with zero teaching assistants), an emphasis on undergraduate research, numerous internships and service-learning opportunities provide the hands-on academic and professional experiences necessary to succeed in today's complex world. Additionally, more than half of Richmond students study abroad during their time at the university, and two-thirds of them participate in community service projects each year.

For those students requiring financial assistance—which 69 percent of our students receive—Richmond offers one of the most generous financial aid programs in the country. One out of every 15 incoming undergraduate students receives a full-tuition merit scholarship. And, the average need-based aid package awarded to entering students in fall 2006 was $30,640. Plus, partial scholarships are available in areas ranging from art to community service, and many of our nearly 400 student-athletes come to the university on scholarships as well.

No matter who you are, where you come from or what you believe, you'll find an environment at Richmond that values diversity in all of its forms including racial, ethnic, socioeconomic, geographic and religious. Through a continued emphasis on diversity through the university-wide Common Ground Initiative, Richmond is an institution that values and understands differences as key to a dynamic and transforming environment for work and education. Of our current full-time undergraduate students, 12 percent are American students of color and 6 percent are international students from over 70 countries. In addition, 7 percent of our first-year students are members of the first generation of their family to attend college, and more than 60 percent come from public schools.

For more information on the University of Richmond, call (804) 289-8000 or visit www.richmond.edu.

University of Virginia

Office of Admission
P.O. Box 400160
Charlottesville, VA 22904
Admissions phone: (434) 982-3200
Admissions fax: (434) 924-3587
Admissions e-mail: undergradadmission@virginia.edu
Admissions URL: www.virginia.edu/OfStud.html

 Admissions

Current student, 8/2003-Submit Date, December 2006

UVA's application centers heavily on essays and extracurricular involvement. There was a choice of many thought-provoking and creative questions, such as, "What is your favorite word and why?" I found the application to be more interesting than some of the other schools to which I applied. My advice would be to answer these as honestly and candidly as possible. There were no interviews, which was a relief. In addition to my application materials, I also sent in some musical performance recordings I had made. UVA values well-roundedness very highly so this was a plus. I do not find UVA to be impossibly selective in-state. Many of my high school classmates who were on the same "level" as me had also gotten in, so I was confident I would be accepted. If a student does well in high school and takes all the AP classes that are offered, I do think it is easy or at least achievable to get in.

Current student, 8/2005-Submit Date, November 2006

Essays were a critical part of the application process for UVA. I selected three essay questions of the six offered and spent about three days making my essays powerful. I answered one question asking me to respond to a statement Martin Luther King said, "Life begins to end the moment we become silent about things that matter." I found this to be a complex question to answer, but it struck me that if I found questions like this on an application for entrance into the university, I would be challenged even more once I got in.

Current student, 8/2004-Submit Date, November 2006

The university accepts a Common Application and does not require an interview. If applying in-state your chances are increased if you live south of the Roanoke area, and decreased if you are coming from prestigious northern schools, such as TJ. It is good to come and stay with a prospective student to get a feel for the campus because it really is unique; but it will not aid you in the actual admissions process. Out-of-state admittance is arguably harder because this is a public school, with most out-of-state students coming from New Jersey and the surrounding areas. Every incoming class seems to have better numbers than the last class, and thus the prestige should soon outrank Berkeley.

Current student, 9/2003-Submit Date, October 2006

From what I remember, UVA used to require three SAT Subject Tests and SAT scores. Now, the SAT Subject Tests are optional (lucky applicants). My SAT score was on the lower end of the ever-popular "25 to 75" SAT range, so it led me to believe that the admissions office has a very holistic approach when it comes to admitting students. A lot of school say that scores aren't everything and here at UVA I think it is actually true.

We had to do three essays, I think. There was some choice as to the ones we wanted to do—"What's your favorite word and why?" and "What do you see outside your window?" and "How would you describe yourself—technophile or technophobe?" and, my favorite, "What piece of art, idea and the like, has challenged you and why?" There were some other choices, but those are the ones that I remember. It was a good variety of questions and none of them were passive.

larly long. Interviews are not required. Selectivity is pretty high, especially a public university. I think the acceptance rate for applicants is around the to 35 percent range. I'm not sure how many of those actually end up accepting their offers here, but I imagine it being in the high 80th percentiles. Quotase, UVA will have its incoming class be one-third out of state, two-thirds in te. That is the only hard and fast rule they abide by.

Current student, 8/2005-Submit Date, October 2006

e university is a very selective school that looks at all aspects of an individual's application, but it is by no means dependent on one or two features. You st present yourself as a whole person with all of your attributes and highlight ur passion for the things in which you are most interested; those are the quals they are looking for, rather than a high score on some test.

Academics

Current student, 9/2004-Submit Date, December 2006

e University of Virginia is composed of many undergraduate programs, which included in its Commerce School, Nursing School, College of Arts and iences, Architecture School, Education and Engineering Schools. Required tures for freshmen tend to be large classes, ranging from 100 to 300 students. wever, as students become more focused and select a major, classes do get aller, with a teacher-to-student ratio of 1:15. Upperclassmen also tend to be le to get the most sought after classes. Grading tends to be fair, professors are ways available and glad to meet with students and most students have a maneable workload and tend to party as hard as they work.

Current student, 8/2003-Submit Date, December 2006

VA is very academically rigorous. You will have to study hard and do lots of search to succeed, but it is not impossible. The smaller, upper-level classes re are very rewarding, but you must first take almost mind-numbing large lece classes, especially in the sciences. Popular classes fill up first, but can be ainable if you have enough pre-requisites. I would say grading is reasonable. is depends on the professor, of course. Sometimes you will study for days and ll get a B, sometimes you will put in minimal effort and get an A. Grading on urve usually only happens in large classes. The workload, then, can be overelming. Expect to do at least two hours of preparation for each lecture. ojects, exams, and papers take much more time. The professors are always lling to talk over a problem with you. They are not always the most personle, but they do to help.

Current student, 8/2005-Submit Date, November 2006

e McIntire School of Commerce at UVA is filled with challenges. The first mester of a student's third year is submersion into the world of business. The rd-year program in business is called I.C.E. for Integrated Core Experience, t I like to think of it as being pushed into a frozen pond—a real wake-up call.

udents are organized into teams and taught to work with one another while aling with complex issues facing business today. Student teams were spon- red by a business during the first semester and presented with a project requir- g strong analysis. The workload of this project included staying up all night metimes to prepare and learn about the sponsor and in preparation for a final esentation to 10 executives from the sponsoring business.

Current student, 8/2004-Submit Date, November 2006

ecause so many of the programs here are nationally ranked, there is a great aura superiority, especially held by pre-comm and comm school students. All of e professors are superb, and make the most out of unpleasant situations, such the sometimes cramped and outdated rooms of Cabell Hall. Grading policies ry between professors and departments, with GUT science classes providing ceptional curves yet their brother major-oriented programs are strenuously own for curving downward, much to several students' undeniable chagrin. e workload itself is really what you make of it, but effort will certainly shine rough in the grading. A strong presence in class will not make up for poor tan- ble work, but the opposite may certainly take precedence.

Current student, 9/2003-Submit Date, October 2006

y main pet peeve about UVA is the difficulty in getting the classes you want. eing a politics major is so hard; it's a great department with great professors,

but so many people here are Government majors/minors, that it is rare someone will get every class he/she wants without some maneuvering. Grading is not too bad. As long as you do all the work and turn in assignments on time, I think you are guaranteed a B in most classes. That being said, most people actually put a lot of effort into their studies, so don't let the "guaranteed B" fool you. Workload fluctuates. Everyone is busy at the mid point of the semester (midterms) and at the end of a semester (finals). In the midst of all that, work-load ebbs and flows depending on papers and other homework you may have. I heard a statistic coming in that the average UVA student spends four hours a day on homework. That's a crock; however, there are points in time where all-nighters may occur, so maybe it averages out to a couple of hours daily (not sure though).

Current student, 9/2000-Submit Date, September 2004

The quality of classes is on par with the best institutions in the country. There are many famous professors who happen to be decent lecturers. Many are large lectures that may not fit every style of learning but it is a state school and thus 250-person lecture classes are par for the course. Arts and Sciences and McIntyre (undergraduate commerce school) are the more highly regarded pro-grams as an undergrad. If you want to be an engineer, go somewhere else with a higher ranking to justify the amount of work that you'd have to do here. Grading is relatively easy here to allow high GPAs for future trips to grad school and career opportunities. The most difficult adjustment is the difficulty of the classes, which can be quite high for those who never studied in high school. Many classes are not intuitive and require work to get good grades.

Employment Prospects

Current student, 9/2004-Submit Date, December 2006

UVA students tend to be very successful at gaining employment after graduation. The Commerce and Engineering Schools hold various job fairs throughout the year, some of which are aimed specifically for minority and international stu-dents. Advisors and the university's career services are always willing to help students in preparing their résumés as well as seeking employment. The UVA Alumni Association is also an important network, which can easily be accessed by current students.

Current student, 8/2004-Submit Date, November 2006

UCS keeps students informed with weekly programs jam-packed for student awareness. The problem arises in that the university's students are sometimes too involved to partake in these opportunities. Still, even average UVA students seek out positions at top-rated firms and companies. UVA was recently rated the Number One provider of Peace Corps volunteers and Teach for America stu-dents, as well. Recruiters can be found in Newcomb, at JPJ Career Fairs (includ-ing a Diversity Career Day) or taking students out en masse to dinners at popu-lar Corner hot-spots like Biltmore Bar and Grill. If you are lucky and the recruiter happens to be a UVA alum or connected to your fraternity or sorority, your position is as good as gold.

Current student, 9/2003-Submit Date, October 2006

If you are in the Commerce School and don't screw up, you are pretty much guaranteed a good paying job after graduation. They have such great connec-tions with companies. That being said, the career center facilities for everyone are great. The on-campus interviewing here is marvelous, and makes the job search and interviewing process much easier. Many recruiters from all over the U.S. will come here and interview students for internships and full-time posi-tions, so students should definitely take advantage of that. Alumni Hall is a great place for more information on alumni options.

Alumnus/a, Business, 1/2004-5/2007, June 2007

Employment prospects are great. There is a strong focus on consulting and investment banking, and nearly all, if not all, top consulting firms and banks show up every year, throwing on-grounds recruiting events and interviewing dozens of candidates. The same companies also come to recruit interns.

Advice? Keep your GPA above a 3.5+ and you will have a good shot at almost all of the top employers. Above a 3.0, you will still have a chance, especially if you have a relevant internship.

Read all of Vault's College Surveys at **www.vault.com/college**—get complete surveys on 100s of colleges and univer-sities, expert advice on applicaton essays and more.

VAULT CAREER LIBRARY **757**

I slacked off, ended up with a 3.15, but I still had six to eight (can't remember exactly) on-grounds interviews, set up through career fairs or the online career recruiting system. And I ended up with three job offers. I'm headed to a consulting firm. I expect to make approximately $70K my first year.

Quality of Life

Current student, 9/2004-Submit Date, December 2006

Freshmen are required to live in on-grounds housing. However, many students after their first year often move to off-campus housing. The transportation system at the university is excellent, consisting of reliable buses and trolleys. The layout of the university also makes it easy for students to walk to classes, no matter where they choose to live. The university has four gymnasiums and three dining halls. Meal plans are available to students all four years. The university also has 14 libraries, which is good for finding quiet and isolated study spots during midterms and finals. The campus is relatively safe, equipped with a system of safety phones around the campus with direct access to 911. The citizens of Charlottesville tend to be friendly, and mind their own business. There are many restaurants and bars near to the campus, at which students often hang out. Overall, UVA students tend to be very satisfied with the quality of life.

Current student, 8/2004-Submit Date, November 2006

With real estate values in Charlottesville sky-rocketing as the city maintains its "Number One place to live" status, it is surprising that students can find places readily available to live. They really can, though, with options ranging from a variety of on-grounds dorms and apartments, to off-grounds houses and condominiums. The campus itself is as gorgeous as the accommodations, and students can cook for themselves out of the local grocery stores, catch some fast food along Barracks or dine with friends at the Corner District or Downtown Mall. Police are readily available as a help, not a hindrance, and campus blue phones and well-lighted shops and alleyways provide a feeling of security.

Current student, 9/2003-Submit Date, October 2006

You are guaranteed on-grounds housing all four years should you choose to live on grounds. That being said, about half the student body lives off grounds as well. The university does not help much with off-grounds options, but many student-run sites help out with those prospects. Safety-wise is a little tricky. The university makes it a top priority, but there has been recent "streak of crime" as I call it. For example, for many weeks we had robberies and assaults just outside the campus that involved students and Charlottesville residents.

The dining hall is good: I believe we have one of the highest percentage of upperclassmen who retain their meal plans after their first year (I guess we don't mind the food!). But, all things considered, Charlottesville is great. It's a great balance of things—you can find places to relax, you can find busier places, and overall the area is not some big urban hub or some shanty farm town. It's great.

Current student, Business, 8/2003-Submit Date, October 2006

Life in Charlottesville is great. The thing about UVA is that during the week people do work and actually try to learn. But everyone here is a real person and wants to have fun too, so there is always something going onto help you relax and enjoy life a little. Work hard, play hard is definitely a reality at UVA.

Current student, 8/2003-Submit Date, December 2004

Too many fraternities, but life in Charlottesville is still nice. The city is very safe and the standard of living is cheap. Housing is plentiful, however driving can be a hassle. Not enough bike lanes. There are also four recreation centers on campus, which are very nice. There are plenty of things to do in the city and at school, so anyone can find his/her niche. With its classic red brick buildings, ancient oaks and sloping green lawns, Jefferson's "academical village" has inspired many a case of perpetual-student syndrome. Inside the Rotunda, modeled after Rome's Pantheon, climb the stairs to what has been called the most beautiful room in America—the light-filled Dome Room, with its series of double 15-foot columns cleverly hiding a series of bookcases.

Social Life

Current student, 9/2004-Submit Date, December 2006

The social scene at UVA mostly consists of bars and frat parties. The Greek L at UVA is made up by a large number of fraternities and 16 sororities. 30 p cent of students are affiliated with the Greek system. Students not involved Greek life still attend frat parties on the weekends, hit the bar scene, join vario clubs and host parties of their own at their apartments or houses. Many stude enjoy eating out and discovering new restaurants on the pedestrian Downto Mall area of Charlottesville after their first year, when they are permitted to ha cars on campus.

Current student, 8/2003-Submit Date, December 2006

There are so many bars and restaurants here. It would be impossible to run of nice places to go in the evening and on weekends. The bar scene is vibra and always exciting. They are usually pretty crowded though. UVA tries ve hard to offer events like concerts, film festivals, comedy shows, fairs, carniva volunteering opportunity to the students. Everything is well-funded. The st dents take a lot of personal responsibility for these events as well, and form rel ed clubs. Some popular ones are Madison House, UPC, UGuides, various th ater groups, and the outdoors club.

Greek life is about one third of the student body. I myself am in a sorority, a I have had a good experience with it in general. I like the fact that you do have to rush until second semester of first year. While I think there is a certa "stereotype" that revolves around the Greek system, I think it is still possible everyone to find their niche.

Current student, 8/2004-Submit Date, November 2006

First-year is rank with Rugby Road's frat scene, and Greek life essentia smothers second semester. As students grow accustomed to the university ho ever, they begin to burst forth from the bubble and venture to the Corner with array of bars and restaurant for every taste, or even the Downtown Mall with very eclectic college feel. With Charlottesville Pavilion and John Paul Jon Arena bringing in top-name bands, the music scene is rockin' and student clu (all 500+ of them) provide everything from dances and social activities to ph anthropies and community service work.

Current student, 8/2005-Submit Date, October 2006

Student life and social life are also important to students at the university. Wh many participate in the Greek system, it is by no means the dominant social el ment. There are many restaurants, movie theatres and fun events in which participate while at school. Charlottesville is a great college town that offers lot to do; however, most students choose to stay near the university because it so active. Probably the greatest element of it is that students can make their ov social life and choose what they and their friends want to do. It is sometim difficult to balance this with schoolwork but most students can find free leisu time

Virginia Tech

Admissions Office
01 Burruss Hall
acksburg, VA 24061
dmissions phone: (540) 231-6267
dmissions fax: (540) 231-3242
dmissions URL: www.admiss.vt.edu

 Admissions

urrent student, 8/2003-Submit Date, December 2006

ne admissions process was very thorough. VT's was the quickest application I
led out and part of it was a very user-friendly online application. The essay
sociated with the application was optional and more of a personal statement. It
gives you the opportunity to provide Virginia Tech with whatever you think
ould be the most important extra information. The admissions representative
ho visited my high school was very informative and gave straight answers to
estions such as, "What's the minimum SAT score you typically accept?" or,
Can I be accepted to the university but not a certain program? And if so, is it
ssible to transfer in later?" I was always receiving little postcards highlight-
g upcoming prospective events throughout my junior and senior years of high
hool. It made me excited to come to VT.

urrent student, 8/2004-Submit Date, November 2006

rginia Tech was my first choice school. It's amazing! I recommend going
rly Decision if this is where your heart is. There are so many people who
ply here, the extra effort looks good. The essay in the application did not even
atter—in fact I did not even do one. They mainly are looking for how involved
u were in high school, and the standards you set for yourself.

urrent student, Engineering, 8/2003-Submit Date, September 2006

rom what I understand, if you apply for Early Decision, you have a better
ance of being accepted. I got accepted Early Decision, without any compli-
tions. I did fill out the optional essay portion on the application, and in high
hool I took five AP courses. I took the SAT once, only because I knew it would
e good enough to get me in Early Decision into the engineering program.

urrent student, 7/2002-Submit Date, February 2006

rginia Tech has a fairly moderate selectivity. Engineering applicants are given
ore consideration than other majors. I am currently a senior in computer engi-
eering and have seen the selectivity for engineering become more selective
hereas other majors have remained the same. You can complete the admissions
ocess online. Admissions does not require the submission of an essay, but sub-
itting one, I believe, improves your chances. The average SAT score of incom-
g freshmen in engineering is 1200.

urrent student, 8/2004-Submit Date, June 2006

he admissions process is all online and is very simple. Because it is such a
rge school, there are no essays or interviews required. The admissions com-
ittee still strives to be selective, however, as only those students who prove
erit through academics, extracurriculars and leadership are offered admission.
ased on my high school classmates, I would estimate the mean GPA of those
ccepted is approximately 3.5 weighted.

urrent student, 9/2001-Submit Date, February 2006

he admissions process has gotten considerably more competitive since I have
een here. Back when I got in the average accepted GPA was a 3.5, now it is a
.8. The personal statement that was on the application was fairly optional four
ears ago, now I recommend filling it out. Taking the highest level classes pos-
ble and also taking three or four years of a foreign language is helpful, as well.
ech is a huge school and admissions gets tons of applications; try to stick out
o guarantee entry. The nice thing is, despite its competitive nature, it's a big
chool and there are lots of spots for worthy students! One other side note, the
amplin College of Business can be hard to get into—if you have the grades in

high school and think you might be remotely interested in majoring in business,
state that on the application. If you do not have the grades, wait until you get
here to try to become a business major.

 Academics

Current student, 8/2003-Submit Date, December 2006

The quality of classes I've taken at VT is exceptional. I would say far more
intense and difficult than originally anticipated; however, I've found professors
to be very accommodating for the most part. Getting into the classes you want
or need is another story. The course request process is in need of serious
revamping. Every semester, except one, I've had to force-add a class or take
alternative classes to make a full schedule. I'm actually taking an extra semester and graduating late due to classes only offered in the fall and an inability to
take them at the time I needed. The workload varies greatly among majors.
Obviously, the most competitive programs, architecture and engineering typically, have the most demanding workload. My major, Urban Studies, typically
requires 25 to 30 hours a week or reading, paper writing or research. Other
majors, such as Communications or Human Nutrition Foods and Exercise
(HNFE), are less demanding.

Current student, Business, 8/2001-Submit Date, November 2006

I started out in Pamplin, which is our business school, and I am about to graduate with a degree in Business Information Technology with a concentration in
Decision Support Systems. The first two years are very hard weed-out classes,
such as Accounting, Econ and Statistics. To make sure you get the best teachers, visit ratevtteachers.com. Trust me, most of the teacher evaluations are accurate or will at least give you an idea of what to expect from each teacher. After
the first two years, most of your classes will only be Tuesdays and Thursdays,
which gives you a lot of free time. Overall, you have to work hard to get
through, but once you are a senior and realize how good the teachers are, you
will be glad you went to Tech.

Current student, 8/2004-Submit Date, November 2006

The academics at Tech are usually good. The only problem is the size of classes. I am a junior, and I have never met one of my professors one-on-one. That's
fine with me because I still get good grades, but to other students, an intimate
relationship with a teacher is a must.

So far, all of my professors have been phenomenal. The professors are very
interested in making sure the students learn the material throughout. As for
grades, all of my teachers have turned out to be pretty fair. However, I'd say the
workload here is pretty difficult. It's definitely a change from high school.

Alumnus/a, Biology, 8/2001-5/2006, October 2006

If you got into Virginia Tech, chances are you have what it takes to make it
through the biology program. This is especially true because the biology department is very diverse and you can pick and choose which classes you want to take
(rather than having to pass a standard set of classes in order to graduate). If
Toxicology isn't your thing, you can just as easily focus on Ecology. However,
it's wise not to underestimate the difficulty of this flexibility, as I have seen a
number of people drop out because they didn't apply themselves. There will be
classes in which most people fail, and sometimes these are, in fact, required
classes.

Recent budget cuts have made it so that it's become harder to get the classes you
want, when you want them. Have a four-year plan for which classes you're
going to take, but make it as flexible as possible to avoid being stuck taking an
extra year at VT because you didn't get that physics class back in sophomore
year (which is a requirement for a wide range of biology/chemistry classes).

The course quality is decent. Most professors are knowledgeable and full of all
kinds of useful information. However, due to its ambition to be a Top 20

Read all of Vault's College Surveys at **www.vault.com/college**—get complete surveys on 100s of colleges and universities, expert advice on applicaton essays and more.

VAULT CAREER LIBRARY **759**

research university, Virginia Tech has a lot of professors who are not meant to be teaching (and yet, do). Most professors teach because they are made to, in order to continue their research with the university. This has led to a lot of very bad professors trying to teach their students things that are just way above their level of understanding (and the eventual frustration of both student and professor).

Current student, Engineering, 8/2003-Submit Date, September 2006

The first year of engineering is basically a lot of busywork to weed out the people who are not willing to sit through the workload of engineering classes. There is a joke that freshman engineering classes are also known as "pre-business" classes. Sophomore and junior years are when you do the bulk of the coursework for your degree. Junior year was by far the hardest year I had at school, especially the fall semester taking Thermodynamics and Fluid Mechanics at the same time. I'm currently in my fall semester of my senior year and the workload has been reduced a lot, and most of the work I do is in group projects and labs. They reduce the work (I think) because we're applying for jobs and having to go through the interview process and that requires a lot of your time. To graduate in four years, you are more than likely going to have to spend a summer session or two in Blacksburg taking classes.

Current student, 8/2003-Submit Date, February 2006

I love classes here at VT. Most are smaller classes. The only big classes are easier classes where you don't need a professor's help. The professors here are always there to help you but they will not come to you if you need help, you have to go to them. Getting popular classes is difficult. Seniors get first choice in getting classes so as a freshman you don't have much luck at getting a popular class. Freshman year is the time to get your basic classes done.

Some majors have less work than others. Engineering and physics give you a lot of workload while communication and history don't. One problem with academics is the math department. I have had problems with professors in math. There will be about three to five people teaching a certain subject once you get past basic math. The problem with this is that they all teach differently. So you might get the easier professor who you understand or you might get the professor who only confuses you. It is just the luck of the draw.

Employment Prospects

Current student, 8/2003-Submit Date, December 2006

VT graduates seem to be widely respected in the job world. Majors in Business, Engineering, and Building Construction usually get the lion's share of jobs and career fairs. I know some major employers that typically hire VT students include Boeing, Lockheed Martin, NASA, IBM, Google, Ferguson Enterprises, SAIC, Booz Allen, Marriott, Hilton and so on. There is an entire building dedicated solely to Career Services. They offer résumé building workshops, mock interviews, and set up job prospects based on major. I'm yet to utilize the alumni network but I've heard, "Hokies respect fellow Hokies."

Current student, 8/2001-Submit Date, November 2006

I have received offers from Booz Allen Hamilton (Federal IT Consultant), KPMG (Federal IT Auditor), and Ventera Corporation (IT Consultant). The best thing to do to obtain a great job is to get at least two internships or co-op with someone who will give you a security clearance. We have a connections fair that will help you meet employers hiring strictly for internships. Fellow Hokies do take care of their own so there are a lot of companies who hire a lot of Hokies. All you have to do is go to our experience web site and contact them.

Alumnus/a, Business, 8/1999-5/2003, April 2006

On-campus career fairs were abundant. I got a job in the first semester of my senior year. I interviewed on campus and then from there was taken to an onsite interview paid for by the company. Very helpful career center helped us work on résumés and look for companies that interested us. I was a business information technology major out of the Pamplin College of Business. It was a quite a demanding major but when I was accepted to the school a lot of alumni told me that the job outlook for a BIT major was very optimistic. The only thing to be careful of is understanding the nature and the role of the job before settling on what you think you might want. The working world is nothing like the college world.

Current student, 8/2004-Submit Date, June 2006

While Virginia Tech is still working its way up in the world to have stude[nts] recruited from top-tier companies, it has employers come from all over the E[ast] Coast to interview students on campus. As a sophomore, I was able to obt[ain] one of the Top 10 internships in the country by visiting the Business Horizo[ns] Career Fair and speaking with a recruiter. The school also has a system cal[led] e-recruiting set up. Using this system, students can post their résumés online a[nd] essentially ask many different companies to be considered for an intervie[w]. There is also a strong bond between students and alumni, many willing to go [out] of their way to help a student who takes the initiative to call him/her and expr[ess] interest in the alumnus' field.

Alumnus/a, 8/2001-5/2005, February 2006

Campus has a very helpful career center, as well as many prestigious employ[ers] who recruit at Blacksburg. The only thing is that they are mostly VA employe[rs] so being out of state will not be as useful for you. There are on-campus int[er]views offered, and many students obtain jobs right out of school. There are al[so] several seminars offered by the career center on choosing your major, career a[nd] how to interview.

Quality of Life

Current student, 8/2003-Submit Date, December 2006

Blacksburg is one of the safest towns anywhere. There is virtually no crime [at] all and I have always felt safe walking around the town in the day or night. [It's] 70 percent college students so the town really thrives around the university. O[ff]-campus housing was above average compared to other schools I've visite[d]. Students are encouraged to live on campus beyond their freshman year and i[t's] certainly convenient. The dining halls at VT are amazing!! They win natio[nal] awards every year and the numerous theme dinners are great. You can get fi[let] mignon, lobster, burgers, pizza, Chinese, Mexican and so on, all over camp[us]. Many off-campus students have some sort of meal plan because the food is [so] good.

Current student, 8/2001-Submit Date, November 2006

The housing is good, the food is great. If you're a freshman, try to get into o[ne] of the large dorms so you can meet people. We have a beautiful campus esp[e]cially when it snows and it will snow. It might snow from December to Marc[h,] maybe late April. The dining program is excellent. I've been to other campu[s]es and their food is terrible. Steak and lobster are included in the meal plan. W[e] also have Sbarro, Au Bon Pain, Chick-fil-A, Pizza Hut, Cinnabun and a BB[Q] place included in the meal plan. They provided a wide variety of healthy optio[ns] and have special meals plan every other month, such as a Chili Cook-off a[nd] Customer Appreciation Day. There isn't much crime, mostly drunk in pub[lic] because everyone here believes this is a "drinking town, with a football prob[]lem." Parking is horrible here but I hear they are trying to improve that.

Current student, Engineering, 8/2003-Submit Date, September 200[6]

We are definitely spoiled with the food. I've visited other schools and their cam[]pus food is some of the grossest food I've ever seen. I think Virginia Tech is co[n]sistently in the Top 10 of food quality in the U.S. The campus is huge, and [I] think it's gorgeous. The worst thing people will tell you about Blacksburg is t[he] weather. During the winter it is cold and windy, and they never cancel class[es] here, so you have to hike across campus in the snow.

Alumnus/a, Engineering, 8/2001-5/2006, September 2006

This is one of the best parts about Virginia Tech and I challenge anyone to fin[d] a better quality of life and college atmosphere than the one Virginia Tech has [to] offer. The dining facilities are topnotch and I believe we have won some natio[n]al awards for them. There are a lot of different housing options from which [to] choose and even though the buildings are old, the staff does a good job of keep[]ing them clean. The campus is beautiful and you couldn't ask for a better su[r]rounding community of which to be a part. The people of Blacksburg an[d] Virginia Tech have a great relationship and you definitely have the support of n[ot] only your campus community but of the town community as well. Blacksbur[g] is a small town and definitely has that feeling.

Social Life

Current student, 8/2003-Submit Date, December 2006

VT certainly has party-school potential. Being a huge football school, it dominates the social scene fall semester. Main Street has numerous bars all within walking distance of campus and each has a unique quirk about them. They include Hokie House's pool tables, TOTS's karaoke Tuesdays, Sharkey's famous wings, and Champs' live bands to name a few. If you're underage many people go to apartment or fraternity parties. Oftentimes there is a charge to get into these parties and you never know how it could go. Some nights could be awesome and others a bust. The campus is about 20 percent Greek with 13 sororities and 30+ fraternities. Greeks hold most of the leadership positions on campus and Homecoming and Greek Week are highlights of the year. For restaurants, VT students love El Rod's (El Rodeo) Mexican restaurant for its cheap good food, huge margaritas and friendly service. Macadoos is famous for its extensive sandwich list. The best Chinese in Blacksburg is Hunan King and it's probably one of the cheapest Chinese restaurants around. The Cellar has great calzones and pasta, and Boston Beanery is a great bar/American fare menu.

Current student, 8/2001-Submit Date, November 2006

Anything you want to do here you can do. Tech offers free salsa and belly dancing. We have all the sororities and fraternities and what we don't have you can create. Tech allows anyone to create a student organization and provides funding through budget board to get your student organization started. Major dancing bars are Oge Chi and Cinco de Mayo. Major drinking places are Sharkeys, Top of the Stairs and Big Al's. The closet major city is Roanoke. It's only 45 mins away and they have a good mall, great places to eat, and all the major stores you would need.

Current student, 8/2004-Submit Date, November 2006

Social life is a must at any college. Our social life revolves around the downtown area where everything is located (bars, restaurants). It's a good, fun, safe college environment.

There are so many extracurricular activities here at Tech. There is a club for everyone. $10 and a few students can start any kind of club a kid can imagine. We even have a SAW club (Students Against Winter—they only were shorts and flip flops). Clubs here at Tech are a good way to get involved and meet new people.

My favorite is intramural sports. It's a rec league for students. There's co-rec and single-sex teams for things like inter tube water polo, flag football, soccer, softball, basketball, dodge ball, kickball and so on. I love getting together with friends and having a good time on the field. Two other club favorites are the YMCA, a service organization, and SAA, Student Alumni Association. Both clubs are ways to give back to Tech through volunteering. By doing this I have gained a sense of Hokie pride!

Alumnus/a, Engineering, 8/2001-5/2006, September 2006

The people are the best part about Virginia Tech. Virginia Tech has a great social life and there is something for everyone. Blacksburg is loaded with bars that offer many different scenes. The restaurants in downtown Blacksburg are good too. The thing I like most is that there are hardly any chain restaurants so they are all unique. As for school clubs, there is just about anything and everything you can think of. If there happens to be something that no one has thought of yet, Virginia Tech does a great job of working with you to starting new clubs. Virginia Tech has a very active Greek scene if you are interested and there are constantly Greek events going on.

The School Says

Founded in 1872 as a land-grant college, Virginia Tech is a comprehensive, innovative research university with more than 27,000 students from all 50 states and more than 100 countries. Through a combination of its three missions of instruction, research, and public service, Virginia Tech continually strives to accomplish the charge of its motto: *Ut Prosim* ("That I May Serve").

The university offers more than 70 undergraduate majors through its seven undergraduate academic colleges: Agriculture and Life Sciences, Architecture and Urban Studies, Engineering, Liberal Arts and Human Sciences, Natural Resources, Pamplin College of Business, and Science. Virginia Tech's College of Engineering is ranked 7th and the Pamplin College of Business is ranked 37th in *U.S. News & World Report's America's Best Colleges* 2007 survey. *DesignIntelligence*, the only national college ranking survey focused exclusively on design, ranked Virginia Tech's undergraduate architecture program seventh nationwide and the university's undergraduate landscape architecture eighth in the nation. *Kiplinger's Personal Finance* magazine ranks Virginia Tech in the Top 20 among institutions where students can receive a first-class educational experience at a bargain price.

Virginia Tech students use technology to learn better and faster and prepare themselves for success in tomorrow's workplace. Each student is required to bring a laptop or tablet computer to campus and has access to high-speed Ethernet connections in all residence halls, laboratories, and lecture rooms, as well as wireless access in all academic buildings.

With so much to do in such a beautiful setting, life as a Hokie is never dull. The area offers an abundance of outdoor activities, as well as plenty of indoor entertainment. With more than 600 student organizations, a culturally diverse student body, 21 NCAA athletic teams, and themed residential communities, students have endless opportunities to meet new people and enjoy life outside the classroom. Blacksburg's newly renovated and lively downtown area provides restaurants, music clubs, and stores within walking distance of campus. Many students choose to take advantage of Tech's award-winning dining centers, which include all-you-care-to-eat facilities, a la carte food courts, and a gourmet coffee and ice cream shop. The 2008 Princeton Review's *Best 366 Colleges* ranked Virginia Tech Number One in its "Best Campus Food" category.

Students in any major can spend one or two semesters—or a whole summer—in a foreign country with Tech's foreign exchange and study abroad programs. There are also plenty of opportunities for students to earn money AND gain on-the-job experience through the university's co-op, internship, and work-study options. The Career Services Building at Virginia Tech houses a team of knowledgeable professionals dedicated to preparing students for the workplace. Hundreds of top companies actively pursued Virginia Tech students last year, and, of graduates reporting employment, more than 90 percent found field-related employment.

Read all of Vault's College Surveys at **www.vault.com/college**—get complete surveys on 100s of colleges and universities, expert advice on applicaton essays and more.

VAULT CAREER LIBRARY   761

Washington and Lee University

Admissions Office
Gilliam House
Lexington, VA 24450
Admissions phone: (540) 458-8710
Admissions fax: (540) 458-8062

 Admissions

Alumnus/a, Biology, 9/2003-5/2007, June 2007

Admissions is tougher than ever. The school cares very much about legacies and interviews, while not required, are strongly encouraged. W&L seeks well-rounded individuals and they make up the majority of the student body. Many were varsity athletes and members of student government. Excellent recommendation letters go a long way here, as do high SAT scores. AP tests are a must.

Alumnus/a, Political Science, 9/2001-6/2005, May 2007

My first visit to campus was during winter break, so there were no students around and I took a self-guided tour and interviewed, as well. I must admit that at the time I didn't realize how selective the institution was and only realized that after spending some time there as a student and even more so after I graduated. For me the process was very fluid and there weren't many issues. I had a very pleasant and productive interview. What was more grueling for me was the application process for the Honors Scholarship Program. It involved an initial paper application and then an on-campus application process after you were selected as a finalist from your region. My advice for surviving the process is to personalize yourself throughout the process and make yourself stand out in some capacity.

Alumnus/a, Business, 9/2002-6/2006, May 2007

I flew to Virginia for the prospective student weekend. We sat in classes, attended forums and did an admissions interview. Prior to my first visit, I wrote several essays and learned that Washington and Lee has a very small student body and likes to keep it that way. So they were extremely selective on who they chose to accept.

Current student, 9/2003-Submit Date, April 2007

Washington and Lee is quite selective in their admissions process. You are required to write an essay, take three SAT Subject Tests, and you are supposed to participate in a on-campus interview. The interview is very liberal in the sense that you (the interviewee) are able to direct the conversation and talk about your strengths or any random interest you have that you think is relevant to distinguishing yourself from the other applicants.

Current student, 9/2004-Submit Date, December 2006

If you know you want to come here, definitely apply Early Decision. The acceptance rates are much higher for Early Decision applicants. Definitely have an interview, on-campus if at all possible. The selectivity is high. I used the same essay I used for all other schools and I got in Regular Decision.

Current student, 9/2003-Submit Date, February 2005

Applying Early Decision greatly increases your chances of getting in. Getting in regular admission is much tougher. Your admissions chances are also increased if you plan to play a sport. The interview is virtually meaningless. If you are interviewed, it is probably because you are up for one of the honors scholarship, which are full rides.

 **Academics**

Current student, Business, 9/2003-Submit Date, April 2007

Close student-professor relationships are required for most upper-level course It is not uncommon for one-on-one meetings to be mandated weekly for semin type courses. With rare exception, attendance is a part of the final grad whether explicitly or through participation. There are no TAs and most class and professors are of a high caliber.

Alumnus/a, Political Science, 9/2001-6/2005, May 2007

I rarely had difficulty getting into any of the classes I wanted. Sometimes heard from my friends about not getting into a class during registration b through the drop-add period, they were able to find their way into the class sin ply by talking to the professor personally and demonstrating their interest. A of my professors, save one or two, were all incredibly accessible and supportiv I never had trouble meeting with them if I needed help or had some questions pose. I think the academics at Washington and Lee are very strong and cha lenging. My only critique with the overall curriculum is that it was a little ol fashioned in the sense that there wasn't much of a focus on things outside of th theoretical. I would have liked to have seen more diverse classes that foster cu tural and international learning. For example, within the political science depa ment, there weren't many offerings that exposed students to international affair As I work currently at another liberal arts school that has a very internation approach to its academics, I see this as a weakness that W&L needs to addres in order to compete in an increasingly global society. The workload vari depending on the classes you're taking and the major you have. I would say th for my double major in journalism and politics, I had a reasonable amount work. I was neither bored nor was I overwhelmed by the workload.

Alumnus/a, Business, 9/2002-6/2006, May 2007

The classes were great, typically small so we received a lot of attention from pr fessors. I can't recall ever having trouble getting into a class that I wanted take and usually if the class was full you could show up of the first day and ad it. Grading was fairly hard but objective. The professors were nice and alway available. And the workload was very heavy. I did exchange programs an study abroad and no place had a workload the size of Washington and Lee's.

Current student, 9/2003-Submit Date, April 2007

Most of the classes here are of high quality and help contribute to acquiring th education for which you pay. Grading varies from professor to professor, whic creates the incentive for us students to take the easier classes. However, unt being an upperclassman, getting into popular classes is not particularly eas Each term, there are many students who are not able to take the classes they hop to. The workload varies depending on the type of class you take. Ultimatel there is a fair to large amount of work in any class you take depending on how well you want to do in the course.

Current student, 9/2004-Submit Date, December 2006

Academics are superb! Class quality is high, and classes are very small. Th grading is hard and the workload is heavy, but the professors are absolutel excellent. I can't say enough about the professors. They love it here, the ar extremely friendly and accessible. My sorority hosts a professors' dinner ever semester and they absolutely love to come. It is pretty easy to get in a popula class if you e-mail the prof a lot and go to the class on the first day. The gene al education requirements are not too bad, and are essential to getting a true lib eral arts education. There is a trimester system (12 weeks, 12 weeks, six weeks which most students really like. A lot of students study abroad for the six-wee semester.

Current student, 9/2003-Submit Date, February 2005

The quality of academics is fantastic. Small classes, great professors who ar there to teach (not research), and top facilities make the academic experienc excellent. Classes are hard—not much grade inflation. It isn't hard to get int pular classes, especially as you get older. The workload is not too bad as long you don't wait until the last minute to complete assignments.

Employment Prospects

urrent student, 9/2003-Submit Date, April 2007

mployment opportunities for C-School majors (business, accounting and eco- mics) are very good. The alumni network is strong at many top firms (such JP Morgan) and they recruit heavily at W&L. If you have a 3.5 GPA or high- you have the opportunity to get any job depending on your knowledge of the mpany your interviewing with as well as your interviewing skills. The Career enter helps with that to provide mock interviews to help students acquire the cessary skills to thrive in interviews. The popular career for business/account- g/econ majors is investment banking. To my knowledge, practically every vestment bank makes a trip to W&L to interview potential candidates. If u're not a C-School major, then you better be going to graduate school or law hool if you are hoping for a high paying job in the future. Otherwise, the tions you have are very limited unless you have a very high GPA.

lumnus/a, Political Science, 9/2001-6/2005, May 2007

think that W&L does a good job with placing students in the corporate and ancial sectors. The alumni network is supposedly strong but I was never real- taught how to use the alumni network to my advantage. I think guidance of me sort needs to be provided for that kind of networking. I was also concerned at the alumni network mainly served students who were in the Greek system cause of the bonds that are created there. For someone like me who was not part of the Greek system (out of choice and lack of economic resources), I was t of the loop and I imagine that many other students in my position were left t of the mix as well. Career counseling took place mostly during junior and nior years. I did three different internships during my three summers as an dergrad.

urrent student, Business, 9/2003-Submit Date, April 2007

he alumni network is phenomenal. Through the alumni network I was able to cure an internship at a bulge bracket investment bank in November of my jun- r year for that summer, with the almost guarantee of a job offer. Alumni are tremely responsive and actively recruit students. The school has a good rep- ation with employers. There is a full calendar of on-campus events. This pect is highly related to the alumni network. There is an overweighting of vestment banking/financial services jobs obtained by students, yet many stu- nts also pursue graduate programs at prestigious institutions or work in other elds.

urrent student, 9/2004-Submit Date, December 2006

xcellent employment prospects. I got an internship with Goldman Sachs cause of the extremely helpful alumni. On-campus recruiting is very preva- nt. Most grads go to grad school or get very good jobs. Investment banking very popular. Employers are impressed by W&L students and hire them year ter year. Washington and Lee has a very good name, even though it is small d few people know about it.

urrent student, 9/2003-Submit Date, February 2005

st about everyone I know has a job at some I-bank. Personally, I'm going to arvard Law School, so I have to say it is pretty good. There is a great online atabase of alumni that is really helpful in networking. Accounting majors are e most sought after group of students. It is hard not to get a job with one of e Big Four accounting firms or with a boutique in Washington or Atlanta. The cruiting is basically confined to the South, e.g., Washington, D.C., Atlanta and harlotte. Some kids get jobs with investment banks in New York, but you have have either some good connections or good grades for this.

lumnus/a, 9/1998-6/2002, February 2004

areer prospects vary with the major a student chooses. The commerce/business chool has a very good network of recruiters and often places students in jobs efore graduation. Other courses of study are feeders for post-graduate studies. he journalism school, from which I graduated, is a tight-knit group, and pro- essors will do what they can to get a student a job. However, there are no set ecruiters, and students are responsible for setting up interviews and job search-

es. The department has a few sources and contacts at different media organiza- tions, but it is up to the student to take advantage of those.

Quality of Life

Alumnus/a, Political Science, 9/2001-6/2005, May 2007

The town of Lexington is a small and quaint college town that doesn't offer a whole lot but did meet my needs. There are some great restaurants and fun cafes and coffee shops that are great for gatherings with friends and family. The cam- pus itself is very safe. I never felt that my life was in any kind of danger and I was always able to get in touch with a security officer to walk with me or give me a lift. All of the facilities at W&L are topnotch and incredibly up to date and beautiful. The student commons and the fitness center were the two main new structures that were erected while I was at W&L and both are very impressive. I would say that the quality of life at W&L is very good overall. It's a beautiful campus that is supportive and nurturing.

Current student, 9/2003-Submit Date, April 2007

Housing is not quite as good as you would expect for the money you pay. The facilities are also not great on average. However, much of this can be attributed to maintaining the historical look of the campus. Additionally, the school has been building new facilities that are quite nice. The Lexington community is deceivingly safe. The cops are very active and do a good job of preventing crime from occurring. On average, the students are safe and basically need to lock their doors if they live off campus. On campus, you can leave your wallet, your books, and anything you own somewhere and come back an hour or day later and still see your possessions where you left them. In my opinion, it's the nicest feature of the Honor Code.

Current student, Business, 9/2003-Submit Date, April 2007

On-campus housing is guaranteed/mandated freshman and sophomore years, after which time most students elect to live off campus. The freshman year liv- ing situation provides for a close-knit class. Some of the biggest perks to the school are the innumerable outdoor activities provided by the natural surround- ings. The Outing Club is the largest club on campus and experienced or inex- perienced students hike, kayak, fly fish, and overall just enjoy the opportunities provided by the Blue Ridge Mountains. Tubing is a frequent springtime activi- ty.

Current student, 9/2004-Submit Date, December 2006

Housing is excellent; you live on campus freshman and sophomore years. The campus is one of the most beautiful in the country—on the historic registry. The climate here is average—hot summers, mild winters but you definitely get snow in December/January/February. Facilities are cutting-edge, especially for busi- ness/commerce/journalism/science majors. Lexington is super safe. Dining is pretty good. Lexington has some good restaurants including The Bistro, Sheridan Livery, Southern Inn and Cafe Michel. There is a Mexican restaurant, Chinese, fast food and several very good bakeries. Sophomores usually eat at the fraternity and sorority houses and the cooks are overall pretty good.

Alumnus/a, 8/1998-6/2002, November 2005

W&L is a very social, Greek-oriented school. Campus life is the center of every freshman's and many sophomores' experience, as they live on campus. Dining hall food rates pretty average, but hopefully it has improved in the last six years. Athletics are particularly popular, and most students with athletic skills are able to try out for the varsity teams or participate on a club level. The field hockey, tennis and baseball facilities are without peer in the Old Dominion Athletic Conference, and probably compared to all other D-II schools, as well.

Social Life

Current student, 9/2003-Submit Date, April 2007

There is one bar that student go to in Lexington—the Palms. Other than that, there is no social scene outside of the Greek system. Therefore, the Greek sys- tem provides all of the parties and entertainment for the student body. If you don't join a Greek house, you may feel alienated from the social scene, but you are still able to attend just about any Greek event. The great thing about W&L

Read all of Vault's College Surveys at **www.vault.com/college**—get complete surveys on 100s of colleges and univer- sities, expert advice on applicaton essays and more.

VAULT CAREER LIBRARY **763**

is that parties are open to everyone and the fraternities that throw parties provide the alcohol for everyone without requiring non-members to be on a list or pay for admission. The dating scene exists, but due to the large amount of alcohol consumption and party atmosphere, the hook-up scene is much more prevalent. The social life here may be the most distinctive feature of the school. There are parties in the fraternity houses, and parties off campus that can be 20 to 30 minutes away and are somehow largely successful. The popular off-campus parties are usually in the country, which means out in an open area/field by someone's off-campus house. There are usually a ton of people, kegs and other various tasty treats. Whether positive or negative, these parties can be quite an experience.

Alumnus/a, Business, 9/2002-6/2006, May 2007

The social life on campus was great if you were a white fraternity or sorority student. However, minorities and international students would probably say that there was very little to no social outlets. There were only a few bars but the students didn't typically go there. Dating was awful especially if things didn't work out because the environment is so small and everyone knows everything. There were no clubs. But the Greek system was huge—about 80 percent of the student body.

Current student, Business, 9/2003-Submit Date, April 2007

Washington & Lee is not a bar school. There is one local bar frequented by many juniors and seniors, but the predominance of the social scene revolves around the Greek system. Around 75 percent of the school is Greek, but it serves as a unifying force instead of a dividing force. There are no lists at the doors and all are welcome. Fraternities hire bands and are required to follow school safety guidelines. The system provides a better controlled environment and does not involve exclusion.

Current student, 9/2004-Submit Date, December 2006

Greek system is huge. There are parties almost every Monday, Wednesday, Friday and Saturday nights. Of course, people here work extremely hard and care a lot about classes and grades so less people go out during the week. Most parties are in the frat houses or off-campus country homes. There is a safe ride system, called Traveller (named after Robert E. Lee's horse) that runs from 10 to 2 a.m. every Monday, Wednesday, Friday and Saturday night and almost all students take advantage of that. It is great. There are only two bars in Lexington. Dating isn't very popular. I am definitely not bored here, but a lot of students study abroad for a semester their junior years to get a taste of the rest of the world. While it is an isolated campus, it is only an hour from Charlottesville and two and a half hours from D.C. I go there a lot to go shopping.

Alumnus/a, 8/1998-6/2002, November 2005

Social life is still dominated by the Greek scene, as the two or three bars Lexington are open only to those 21 years and older. (No one risks going the with a fake ID because that would be an honor violation with near-immedi grounds for dismissal from the school.) There are some nice restaurants arou the historical downtown section.

Current student, 9/2003-Submit Date, February 2005

Frat parties until you turn 21, and then bars are the norm. The social life is gre as a freshman, but diminishes in quality the older you get. The school is tryi to get people to do more non-drinking activities by showing movies and havi speakers and performers, but it's still a pretty hard-core drinking scho Everyone is a member of the Greek system, and Pi Phi is the best fraternity campus, so get a bid there if possible. The Palms is the best bar and only bar Lexington, so make sure to get acquainted. There are some decent restaurants town, but if you're looking for something different you have to drive an hour so to Charlottesville or Roanoke. People usually have a girlfriend or boyfrie during their senior year, but there isn't really official one-on-one dating. I more of the group activity that is described in *I am Charlotte Simmons* by o awesome alumnus, Tom Wolfe.

Alumnus/a, 9/1998-6/2002, February 2004

Social life at W&L is topnotch. Not only do we get an amazing education, b we have a lot of fun doing it. There is a great camaraderie between students, a the fraternity and sorority life is also very active. Not all students go Greek, b the Greek life is a great way to have a fun, active social life. The town Lexington is a beautiful, trusting, warm town that also enhances students' sen of security and love for the school. There is a favorite bar in town called T Palms, legendary to all Lexington students, that provides great food and fun f students 21 and older (no underage drinking here due to the honor code). W& is definitely one of the most fun schools in the country, in addition to being on of the top educational institutions. I cannot think of many other schools provi ing both fun and education with such extensive opportunities.

Gonzaga University

Admissions Office
102 E. Boone Avenue
Spokane, WA 99258-0102
Admissions phone: (800) 322-2584 or (509) 323-6572
Admissions fax: (509) 323-5780
Admissions e-mail: mcculloh@gu.gonzaga.edu
Admissions URL: www.gonzaga.edu/Admissions/

Admissions

Current student, 8/2004-Submit Date, May 2006

Well, being almost certain that I was going to attend Gonzaga University, I did not go through the normal admissions process such as tours or meeting with counselors. However, now being an ambassador of Gonzaga and helping majorly in the admissions process, I truly value the way Gonzaga organizes and handles these things. Our tours are very organized and are accessible almost all of the time, going out twice a day, five days a week. After every tour almost half of the students have planned meetings with advisors or counselors and the counselor or advisor even meets them outside of the Admissions Office, following their tour. They are given huge, informative folders including discounts at the bookstore along with an area map of downtown. We have programs for prospective students to stay the night in a host dormroom, so they can really be immersed into the college life and see what it's like from the inside. Our tours even tour dormrooms. If I wasn't set on Gonzaga attending, I sure would have been after visiting and touring.

Current student, 8/2002-Submit Date, May 2006

The admissions process is pretty routine. I did happen to work in the admissions office freshman year and I know that they award points for different parts of the application. Your test scores and GPA do not define who you are! Let your creativity shine through! A good letter of reference is always nice too! As far as selectivity, Gonzaga selects the best students for the university. Sometimes that might not be the valedictorian or the girl with all the right community service—sure those people will get in—but they look at what you can do at the university in broader terms of getting an A in philosophy or biochem.

Current student, 8/2002-Submit Date, May 2006

The one thing that I can say is to make sure you get all your paperwork in on time. You do not want people following up with you making sure you have all your paperwork in. I think it is a good idea to come in and have an interview with an admissions representative because it allows them to put a face with an application instead of just trying to go from what is on paper. It also helps to come visit the school to make sure that it is a place where you could see yourself spending four years studying, and if the people there are people you would be interested in meeting.

Current student, 9/2003-Submit Date, February 2006

The admissions process is really quite easy. You can do it with either a mail-in application, or an online application. I applied using the online application and found it to be very easily done. Included in the application, there is an essay that you can choose from three different topics, all having to do with your character or similar. They also say that an interview is required for admission, but I never went through any sort of interview process. They might be utilizing this process as of late because of the huge numbers of applicants they have had recently.

> **The school says:** "We do NOT require interviews—it is an option—more so for borderline students."

Current student, 8/2003-Submit Date, July 2006

The admissions process is, in all honesty, a piece of cake. I recently helped my brother with his application and discovered that his essay has the same prompt that mine had. Provided that you have reasonably high grades, mediocre SAT/ACT scores, and at least a medium level of participation in extracurriculars,

you'll have no problem receiving an admission offer. I will say that Gonzaga has raised its admissions standards in recent years, largely as a result of the increasing number of applications due to the men's basketball team's national recognition.

Current student, 8/2001-Submit Date, March 2005

The admissions process is similar to many other colleges. At Gonzaga, it does not only help to get good grades in high school and on the SAT and ACT, but to be well-rounded gains a lot of ground. In your application, include all the groups, clubs, and teams that you were on. Also, a big thing is to include all the community service that you did during high school. Gonzaga is accepting more and more freshmen every year, so the selectivity is getting broader and they aren't as selective as they used to be. Write original essays! Tell stories or things that they do not hear all the time. This will not only catch their eye, but they will remember you better! Also, I would recommend getting your application in early, so that you are sure that they received it—call to make sure—and make sure you are not waitlisted.

> **The school says:** "We are now more selective than we have ever been—we accepted 67 percent of our applicants last year—that is down from 73 percent the year before."

Current student, 8/2003-Submit Date, July 2004

The admissions process at Gonzaga was very smooth. I had to write an essay on a work of literature and explain the significance it held in my life. There was no interview required, but selectivity was rather high. I got in based on my high grades (3.87), the difficult classes I took in high school (11 AP and honors classes), and my volunteer work throughout high school.

Academics

Current student, 8/2004-Submit Date, May 2006

The academics here at Gonzaga are absolutely awesome. Our average class size is [23]; student-to-professor ratio is [14]:1; professors teach 100 percent of classes. It doesn't get much better than that. All of our professors are so open and willing to help inside as well as outside of class time. A lot of them even give their home phone number or home e-mail, just to make sure we can get a hold of them no matter what. Since our classes are so small and intimate, it is so easy and encouraged that we form friendships with our professors. They know all their students. It makes us get involved in class discussions. If when registering a student does not get into one of their classes, if they go to the teacher and talk to him/her, the teacher will let them in. All it takes are some signatures and you are in. The workload is great, although it does vary. Since the classes are smaller it seems easier because you are encouraged to go visit professors and ask them questions and you really get to know the people in your class so it's always very easy to find help when need be. Professors are also required to have at least four office hours a week.

Current student, 8/2002-Submit Date, May 2006

I believe that Gonzaga is a very good academic institution. It excels in many different areas. The class quality is high. The professors are very knowledgeable in their fields and bring that to the classroom. Even though the quality of classes is high, it is getting more difficult to get into classes, which makes it frustrating as a student who is trying to sign up for a class that he/she really wants to take. The grading in the classes depends on the professor, but from my experience it is a difficult grading scale in upper-division classes because they want to challenge you. The professors are great; they make themselves available for office hours and are good about giving contact information out so you can reach them even when they are at home. The workload is standard; I would not say it is anything too much, but it definitely keeps you busy throughout the semester.

Read all of Vault's College Surveys at **www.vault.com/college**—get complete surveys on 100s of colleges and universities, expert advice on applicaton essays and more.

VAULT CAREER LIBRARY 765

Current student, 8/2002-Submit Date, May 2006

Academically, the university is pretty tough. You'll find classes that are pretty easy and you'll have classes that you think will legitimately kill you long before finals week. But a general overtone I've found in my classes is that, regardless of the material, all the classes are taught by excellent professors who love what they are teaching. Additionally, the students at Gonzaga bring to the table their own beliefs, experience and opinions to every class, which takes any course up a notch or two. Registration is a dreaded time of year. However, we all make it through and chances are you will get into the classes you wanted/needed. Sure, it may take a few trips around campus and a paper trail, but I've never been denied entrance into a class. Our professors are awesome. They are so dedicated to the success of their students. I have had a history professor meet a group of us at Starbucks on a Sunday morning to help us review for a final on Monday. They are accessible and most importantly, they want to help. Most students take between 16 and 18 credits a semester. It all depends on the combination of your classes. I think it is safe to say that the general attitude of most students at GU is work hard, play hard. We get our stuff in the week and we have fun on the weekends.

Current student, 9/2003-Submit Date, February 2006

Gonzaga University, although mainly known for basketball, is a very good academic school. The business and engineering schools are very well known in industry. All of my professors in the engineering department have all worked at least 10 years in the engineering industry, rather than just went to grad school and straight to teaching. This gives a great variety of experiences with each different professor you meet. All the classes I've taken have been really interesting and well beyond what I expected. My favorite thing about classes is the size. I haven't had a class with more than 35 students. This helps the professor get to know each student and help each person individually, if needed. The only downside to the small class size is that popular classes fill up very quickly and can be difficult to get into.

Current student, 8/2003-Submit Date, July 2006

The College of Arts and Sciences seems to be unreasonably easy. My major courses demand a good deal of my time, but I'm in the minority when it comes to academic discipline here. Engineering and pre-med workloads are unsurprisingly heavy, whereas many BA programs are undemanding in nature. Grading here is extremely fair, and most professors are genuinely interested in their students' opinions and intellectual development, most likely because research productivity isn't weighted heavily (and student ratings of professors are) when tenure decisions are made. Popular classes are also easy for enrollment; I haven't known a student who couldn't approach a professor and get into a class even after its only section had been closed.

Current student, 8/2001-Submit Date, March 2005

Gonzaga is very good academically. The classes are small and have anywhere from eight in the upper-division classes, to 30ish in the core classes. There isn't much to choose from compared to large state schools, but there are the common majors. The quality of the classes improves as they go from lower-division and core classes to upper-division classes. There is a religion requirement at Gonzaga because it is a Jesuit school. There are priests who teach, which gives the courses a different viewpoint. Because the classes are so small, it is often hard to get the popular classes. Teachers are pretty nice about letting you e-mail them to ask if you can join if a class is closed. Some teachers will allow students in, some don't. Seniors usually get most of the classes that they want.

The grading is pretty hard. 93 and above is an A, so you have to work pretty hard. Upperclassmen are usually really willing to offer suggestions to new students about which classes and teachers are good and which are not. The workload depends on the class and the teacher. For the most part, it is a substantial workload, but I play for the soccer team and it wasn't too much for me, so I think that although it is substantial, it is not overwhelming.

The school says: An A does not necessarily constitute a 93 and up.

Alumnus/a, 9/1999-5/2003, October 2004

The liberal arts are Gonzaga's strong suit and this institution does it right. I've personally only had one professor who was less than completely in touch with the needs of my class. Faculty is topnotch; classes possess excellent student-to-

teacher ratios, and nowhere to be found are the auditorium size classes comm[on] to state schools.

Classloads are challenging and the core requirements of four semesters of ph[i]losophy and three of religion will challenge even the most responsible stude[nt]. The best thing I can say on behalf of Gonzaga is that after graduating, I real[ly] feel like I learned how to think, communicate my ideas and beliefs, and exam[ine] my world critically. This is a great school for anyone looking to build a sol[id] foundation of humanistic knowledge in the great Western tradition.

The real question just over the horizon is whether Gonzaga will stick with t[he] tenured professors who have helped it garner such a stellar reputation. The oth[er] option is a move to adjunct professors who divide their time between Gonzag[a] and Washington State, a few miles down the road in Cheney.

The school says: The current student-to-faculty ratio is 14:1, with the average class size at 23.

Current student, 8/2003-Submit Date, July 2004

The program I am currently involved in (pre-med) is rather vigorous. I have [a] minimum of two science classes every semester that usually include at least o[ne] lab a piece. These classes are in very high demand, due to the increasing size [of] the student body and the limited number of professors, so it is often difficult [to] get the best teachers and classes at the best times. The professors are general[ly] very good, and usually very willing to help students succeed. Grading is fair f[or] the most part, but Gonzaga is not known for being an easy school. It is ve[ry] tough to get A's in many of the courses. Workload is pretty extreme at times, b[ut] I always take the maximum of 18 credits, so I am just asking for it I guess.

 # Employment Prospects

Current student, 8/2004-Submit Date, May 2006

Only being a sophomore, I am not really sure how easy or hard it is to get a jo[b] following undergraduate graduation. However, I do know that Gonzaga has a l[ot] of programs and clubs to join that help this process of finding a job after colleg[e]. We have GAMP, which is Gonzaga Alumni Mentoring Program. This progra[m] pairs you up with Gonzaga alumni who majored or are working in the same fiel[d] that you are studying. This way you can ask them how they got to where the[y] are and what they did, with whom they spoke and internships they got. This pro[gram] is very useful and really helps with networking. There are also bi-weekl[y] lectures where Gonzaga alumni will come lecture about their success and ho[w] they got there. They will also drop names of helpful, useful sources.

Current student, 8/2002-Submit Date, May 2006

I graduate in 11 days. I have no idea what I am doing after college. I do no[t] have a job lined up. Now, if I was an accounting major or engineering major, [I] would have the next three to four years of my life planned. Gonzaga student[s] are sought after for certain degrees like those, but for someone like me—a pub[lic] relations major—we are really on our own. They do have a few program[s] that help establish relationships and get your feet wet, but when push comes t[o] shove, you have to do your own work to get a job.

Current student, 9/2002-Submit Date, May 2006

Internships are a vital and encouraged part of the School of Business course-work. On-campus recruiting for the accounting majors is one of the bes[t] processes in the area. Easily found a job before graduation.

Current student, 9/2003-Submit Date, February 2006

I'm not sure about the business school or other schools, but with the engineering school, job placement among graduates is somewhere near 97 percent right ou[t] the door. This is due to how closely the program works with many differen[t] companies in industry. The professors also bring their own networking abilities to help graduates get a job. The alumni network is great; they have a gathering once a year for different schools to help students get contacts and jobs. Recruiting and internships are both taken care of by the internship office. Almost once a week, there are companies on campus for recruiting and such.

Current student, 8/2003-Submit Date, July 2006

...dents in the liberal arts program have a notoriously difficult time finding jobs. ...nkly, many deserve the hardship, as they fail to use the school's career cen-...or build relationships with their professors or with alumni. Those who find ...mselves unemployed after graduation lack the initiative that Gonzaga claims ...rly all of its students have. Consequently, many employers do not bother to ...it campus, as many students do not present themselves in a very dignified ...nner to potential employers. The prestigious companies that do seek out ...nzaga students (e.g., Accenture, Deloitte, Amazon, Boeing, Microsoft) do so ...ough the school's excellent alumni network. As long as you've worked hard ...ring your tenure at Gonzaga and have a high GPA and leadership experiences ...show for it, Gonzaga alumni will bend over backwards to help you out.

...umnus/a, 8/1999-5/2003, October 2003

...ave found that students from the accounting program and almost all of the ...gineers have easily gotten a good job. Recruiting for accounting majors is ...ne early in the school year and is generally with the Big Four as well as a few ...ers. I know many who have had multiple offers from accredited firms. A ...od GPA can be key here, and if you have it there isn't much question as to ...ether you will be offered a job. Engineers also seem to have quite an easy ...ne finding good jobs. While I am not an engineer, I know many who have ...duated and gone on to good, high paying jobs.

...ernships and the career center are still gaining steam. While both are not bad, ...y can be very frustrating to work with at times. The career center especially. ...hile they want to see everyone get a good job and work fairly hard at it, they ...ify with returning phone calls and are known to give students a hard time for ...t coming in sooner. Because of this, many students prefer not to go in because ...y don't want to be lectured as though the department were their parents.

...nally, the prestige of the university is really starting to come around. Almost ...yone in the NW and Northern CA thinks highly of the university. (Speaking ...m a business standpoint.) Personally, I have not found, nor heard of anyone ...t getting the same consideration that schools like Stanford receive (on the ...est Coast).

Quality of Life

...rrent student, 9/2004-Submit Date, May 2006

...ere are new residence halls sprouting up across campus and the quality of the ...oms and buildings is great! Housing staff is available when you need it and ...es to get involved with its respective halls as much as possible. The sur-...unding Logan neighborhood is not the safest neighborhood—especially at ...ght—but there is a wide variety of charities and nonprofit organizations to ...ork with. Gonzaga prides itself in the number of service hours students per-...m each year.

...rrent student, 8/2002-Submit Date, May 2006

...nzaga is a beautiful campus located in a not-so-beautiful neighborhood. The ...ogan neighborhood is no Beverly Hills, but the nice thing is that the five blocks ...rth of campus are, for the most part, composed of houses of students. I've ...ved off campus for two years and we've only have two "situations," so for the ...ost part, I have felt very safe. Our facilities have definitely been upgraded dur-...g my past four years here and they are amazing. The university has done a ...onderful job of taking care of each different aspect of the school to make sure ...erything is getting the attention it deserves. We have a new basketball arena, ...new fitness center, an upgraded science center, an upgraded business center, an ...graded engineering center, a brand-new broadcast studio, in addition to build-...g new dorms, fixing up the age old administration building and great plans in ...e works.

...rrent student, 8/2002-Submit Date, May 2006

...would have to say that the overall quality of life here at Gonzaga is good. The ...using on campus is reasonable and the housing off campus is good. The cam-...us itself is very welcoming and kept in good condition throughout the year. In ...rm of facilities, there are some older building, mostly dorms, that need some ...ork; however, the academic buildings are being brought up to date with both ...nstruction and technology. The campus dining is good. They have three dif-...rent options for meal plans so for those students who like to eat on campus

more, they can have more meals on campus and those who like to eat off cam-pus do not have to purchase as many meals on campus if they do not wish to. The neighborhood surrounding the campus is not bad, but it is not the best either. There are some small crimes, such as cars getting broken into, but a lot of times it is because students are not careful about leaving things in their cars that attract people to break into them. As a student, I feel safe in the surrounding neighbor-hood, especially when going from place to place in a group.

Current student, 8/2001-Submit Date, March 2005

The quality of life is pretty good. The housing is old dorms for the freshmen with community bathrooms unless you choose to live in a positive choice dorm that restricts alcohol and drugs in any way! There are really nice dorms and apartments that can be obtained through the lottery system after freshman year. The campus is really small, but very pretty. It has a small lake and is right next to the Spokane River. There is a trail called Centennial Trail that runs from Idaho and through Gonzaga's campus to downtown Spokane, which is about a 10-minute walk on the trail from the campus. There are great athletic facilities. A new fitness center was built last year, and they just finished building a new arena for the men's and women's basketball teams. The dining is good. There are three on-campus food restaurants—Pandini's is Italian, Sub Connection is sandwiches, and Spikes is like a grill. There is also the COG, which is the gen-eral cafeteria. They hired new management this year, so the food has been bet-ter and it is open until 11 p.m. on weekdays, which is nice. The neighborhood is a low income neighborhood so there tends to be crime. The most common is breaking into cars and car theft. The campus is safe with a good campus secu-rity system, but the surrounding area is not as safe.

Social Life

Current student, 9/2004-Submit Date, May 2006

There are two favorite bars right next to campus—Star Bar and Jack and Dan's. These are the places to be if you are over 21. Parties are at all different houses next to campus and tend to be less than five minutes walking from wherever you are located. There are two malls in Spokane. Also, rivers and the beautiful Centennial Trail, which runs alongside campus and all the way into Idaho. There is currently no Greek system, however, there is a service organization for soph-omores called Knights and Setons. 30 sophomore girls and boys spend the entire year fundraising for a charity of their choice within Spokane. There are also thousands of clubs on campus for all different areas of interest.

Current student, 8/2002-Submit Date, May 2006

Gonzaga students work hard, play hard. The social life at GU is awesome. We have the party oasis known as the Triangle. The Triangle consists of three bars that are located a stone's throw from campus. Jack and Dan's is the bar most frequented followed closely by The Bulldog, which is located across the street. The Star Bar is adjacent to the Bulldog and is the Thursday night hotspot.

Spokane has some great restaurants. For a college kid, nothing is better than Ionic Burrito—a little burrito shop located two blocks away from campus. 10 feet from campus is the complex that has a Starbucks, the most amazing bagel shop—Ultimate Bagel—and the newly opened Pita Pit (which is open until 3 a.m. to accommodate those late night bar cravings). And when the parents are in town, places like Anthony's not only has great food and a great view—it is sit-uated right on the Spokane Falls. Clinkerdagger's is a personal favorite and it sits right along the Spokane River. There are two great sushi bars in town—sushi.com is my favorite.

Gonzaga has a variety of annual events that are looked forward to every year. Madonna Stock is a daylong musical extravaganza on campus, which happens in late April. April's Angels is a day long community service event that includes about 500 undergraduates volunteering their time to help fix up a local elemen-tary school. Basketball season is one continuous event, from the ticket distribu-tions to the games themselves, campus is a buzz whenever it comes to our Zags.

Current student, 8/2002-Submit Date, May 2006

I believe Gonzaga has a good social life. The bars around campus are always full with students and locals. Every time you go out you know you are going to run into a group of friends even if they aren't the ones you went out with that night. The Triangle is always a favorite for GU students. This includes Jack and

Read all of Vault's College Surveys at **www.vault.com/college**—get complete surveys on 100s of colleges and univer-sities, expert advice on applicaton essays and more.

VAULT CAREER LIBRARY   **767**

Dan's, The Bulldog and The Star. The dating scene I would have to say is all right. There are many opportunities to get to know people and that helps when it comes to dating. There are many events that go on in Spokane throughout the year that students attend. There are concerts, sporting events, and other things like musicals, plays and opera. Gonzaga does have many clubs on campus ranging from club sports teams to diversity clubs, to dance teams. Gonzaga does not have a Greek system, and I think not having one fits our campus better than if we did have one.

Current student, 9/2003-Submit Date, February 2006

The social life at GU is pretty good, especially during basketball season. During basketball season, the Kennel Club has great get-togethers before and after games where you can go and most likely celebrate another Bulldog win. Those over 21 can attend the Northern Lights Kennel Club party at the Northern Lights bar near campus. This is a great place for both students and alumni to mingle and meet. The party scene and bar scene is good all year around as well. My only gripe about the Gonzaga is the lack of Greek system.

Current student, 8/2001-Submit Date, March 2005

There are many bars within walking distance from campus including Jack a Dan's rated Number Six in *Sports Illustrated*'s Top 10 Sports Bars. Downto is also a 10 to 15 minute walk to bars. There have been the opening of the F Club and The Big Easy (bar/concert hall) and a couple new bars that attract a of the college students. There are also two gay bars downtown. There are ma good restaurants. A college favorite is Red Robin downtown. There are me expensive restaurants, such as Mizuna, Moxie, Clinkerdaggers and The Pal that are also very good and all downtown. The dating scene is not hu; Gonzaga only has about 4,000 plus undergraduates. Many people date, but the is no dating service per se for Gonzaga students. Spokane is a small city, so th do not receive many large events. There have been some concerts and plays the Spokane Arena and Opera House. The main events that attract Gonzaga s dents as well as the Spokane community are the men's basketball games. Tick are pretty easy to obtain if you are a student. You don't have to pay—there ticket distribution days when you take your student ID with you and wait in li They provide pizza, food, and drinks while you wait. There is no Greek syst at Gonzaga since it is a private university. There are a lot of house parties, most all of them are list parties, where you have to be on the list to get in.

University of Washington

Office of Admissions
1410 NE Campus Parkway
Box 355852
Seattle, WA 98195-5852
Admissions phone: (206) 543-9686
Admissions fax: (206) 543-5150
Admissions URL: admit.washington.edu/admission/

 ## Admissions

Alumnus/a, 9/2002-6/2006, November 2006

I think the selection process is tougher than a few years ago, but I got in with a 3.91 GPA and SAT score of 1320. I believe that placed me in the 98th percentile for automatic admission into the school.

My advice is to apply early (I applied in November and heard back the first or second week of December) because you never know what problems may come up with your application. For example, my fine arts credit for high school graduation requirements was journalism, but that didn't count for my fine arts admission requirements for UW. Good thing I heard back in December because then I had time to switch my schedule for the following semester and make sure I took a graphics design class for my fine arts admissions requirements.

Current student, 9/2003-Submit Date, May 2006

Because I am an in-state student with a good GPA and high SAT score, my admissions index level was in the 99 percentile. Getting in was fairly easy—I didn't even have to submit an essay. I had friends, though, at the same high school who had decent GPAs and SAT scores who had trouble getting in. One of my friends had about a 3.2 and I think around an 1100 on the SAT and didn't get in at all.

> **The school says:** "The university no longer uses an Admission Index; instead, to take into account many aspects of an applicant's achievements and personal history, we use an individualized application review more typically found at smaller private universities and colleges."

With holistic admissions, though, getting into the UW might be a little tough for those students who only have good grades and test scores. The UW has be very focused on diversifying the student body and encouraging students from backgrounds to apply. This means that they are looking at more than just GP, and test scores and will be placing more importance on who you are as an ind vidual and what you can contribute to campus (which I think is brilliant!).

Current student, 9/2003-Submit Date, November 2005

The admissions process at the University of Washington is simple and ea: When I was admitted, the UW did everything online—filled out forms, wrote personal essay, a goal essay and one other. The university used to use a gradi rubric for giving out admissions, which was based on GPA and SAT scor They have since changed it, and the university no longer uses the rubric, but completely subjective based on academic performance, extracurricular activiti and your future goals. My advice to incoming students is to find at least of extracurricular activity at which you succeed. This will be an important fact in admission to the university.

> **The school says:** "The individualized admission review looks at many factors; please check out admit.washington.edu/ BeforeYouApply/Freshman/Trends."

Current student, 9/2002-Submit Date, December 2004

Applying was a breeze. Essays were required. Interviews are neither requir or recommended. Admission favors certain people. Non-residents will find more difficult to get into the school than Washington residents. The scho recruits underrepresented minority groups (African-American, American India Hispanic).

Getting into the undergraduate business program is a painful process. There a three ways to get admitted. The most common way by far is UAG; it requir applicants to take a half-dozen specific classes, some of which will not be us ful to unsuccessful applicants, and a two hour writing test. 80 percent of adm ted students are admitted based on college grades (including those earned taki university level classes in high school), the writing test, and their applicatio The other 20 percent are chosen largely based on their personal essays (inclu ed in the application). About 50 percent of applicants are admitted to the bu ness school and the average GPA of an admit is about a 3.4.

Academics

∣umnus/a, 9/2002-6/2006, November 2006

∣ople say it's hard to get into classes as a freshman. I agree but only to some ∣tent. There are measures you can take to increase your chances of getting the ∣hedule of your choice. E-mailing the instructor to get an add code for a full ∣ass is the first step someone should take when he or she can't get into a class. ∣e second step is to check online constantly for an opening to come up in the ∣ass. Check through your break and even through the first week of the quarter. ∣ople always change their schedules.

∣efore picking classes, you should always check the instructor ratings. That ∣ways helped me determine whether I should take a class or not. The best ∣structor can make any class interesting and worthwhile. Sometimes though ∣u have to go with a less highly-rate instructor because you need the class to ∣fill a certain requirement. Most instructors though are pretty good, and even ∣they're not, most are helpful during their office hours.

∣umnus/a, 9/2003-6/2006, September 2006

∣ definitely depends on your major! Generally, pre-meds have tons of work. ∣gineering students spend lots of time in the lab. Liberal arts majors vary in ∣fficulty, with communication regarded on the easier end and political science, ∣glish and history majors loaded with reading. Most, if not all, departments ∣ve Departmental Honors Programs for students who want to challenge them-∣lves intellectually. Departmental Honors usually involves a thesis or extend-∣ research project and looks great on graduate school applications!

∣asses are a mixed bag, but you can find amazing professors if you scrutinize ∣e Course Evaluations online and rely on word of mouth among students. I had ∣handful of outstanding, approachable, life-changing professors and am lucky ∣ have been able to take several classes with them! There are also several ∣search opportunities, for both science and liberal arts majors, with professors ∣d departments. If you're an underclassman, getting into popular classes can ∣ tough, but juniors and seniors should have no problems. Great selection and ∣riety of classes, including quirky ones like Anthropology of Death and Asian ∣merican Cinema.

∣urrent student, 9/2003-Submit Date, May 2006

∣e department in which I am currently majoring (and hopefully receiving hon-∣s in) has competitive admission, like many of the departments on campus. The ∣w, Societies and Justice (LSJ) major consists of three categories of classes: ∣man rights and resistance; crime, social control and justice; comparative legal ∣stitutions and politics. The courses that fall into these categories come from ∣ different departments, including political science, international studies, ∣merican ethnic studies, women studies, geography, history, sociology and ∣thropology. I love my major partly because of the diverse classes I can take ∣at apply to it, but also because many of the courses I've taken through the ∣partment have been taught by excellent professors and have literally changed ∣y world and political views. The only downside to being an LSJ major is that ∣is a relatively small department with few actual LSJ professors, so trying to get ∣to the core classes you have to take in order to apply for the major is a chal-∣nge. However, the adviser is very nice and always eager to help students get ∣to the classes they need—especially if they show a lot of enthusiasm for the ∣partment.

∣orkload all depends on the type of person and what department you are in at ∣e UW. I've had classes (Chem 120, Stat 220) that I only showed up for the two ∣idterms and finals and section (the smaller TA-led part of big lectures) and was ∣le to be successful. I've also had classes that I showed up to every day and ∣d all the reading and assignments and only received a mediocre grade (Phil ∣5). Overall, though, if you show up to class most of the time and actually ∣bsorb what professors are saying, you'll do all right. Your grade increases sig-∣ficantly when you do the readings for a course. And, crazy at it may seem, the ∣ore you contribute to courses, the more rapport you'll have with professors and ∣e higher marks you'll receive (since they know that you know the material).

∣urrent student, 9/2003-Submit Date, November 2005

∣e undergraduate program at Washington is competitive. There are lots of ∣mpetitive students all trying to enter majors that are hard to get in. Thousands ∣ undergrads choose to go the pre-medical track until classes start. Mean grades

in competitive classes are set low, intentionally trying to weed out students who don't feel fit to continue. The professors are of high quality, and most conduct their own research in the field they are lecturing. They make time to meet with students in office hours and other small groups, making the large lectures feel small. Workload for these classes is standard. Most professors require about two hours of outside study for each hour spent in the classroom. Popular class-es are hard to get into freshman year, as the registration system needs to be redesigned. Currently, all 5,000 freshmen register at the same time, so if you're not the first person up, it's hard to get classes you want.

> **The school says:** "New freshmen register in small groups throughout the summer, while continuing freshmen register over two days."

Current student, 9/2002-Submit Date, December 2004

The UW is based on the quarter system, with each quarter being 10 weeks long. It offers a pretty broad array of classes, although access to classes beyond the introductory level is sometimes barred by requirements that students enroll in particular majors—good luck taking American Press and Politics if you're not a poly sci or communications major. To get a good idea of the workload, consid-er that the introductory level composition class (Engl 131) required about three five-page essays with a few one- or two-page essays on top. Nothing too demanding. Access to math classes may be hindered by a placement test, which can sometimes be circumvented by scoring a five on the AP calculus test or tak-ing a college-level calculus course elsewhere. Really popular classes can be dif-ficult to get into. Signup is tiered by seniority—graduating seniors register first, freshmen last. You can often count on a couple people to drop in a full class, but if the class is really popular, you can probably count on a long waitlist, too.

The undergrad business program is decent. Although all students graduate with a BA in business, they can choose to concentrate in specific business fields, e.g., marketing and information systems. Accounting is unofficially considered the most difficult concentration and finance is presently the most popular. TAs teach a fair number of the upper-level courses. Quality and workload varies. Few business classes meet Friday and a fair number of students manage to do intern-ships or work part-time while enrolled at school full-time. The average GPA at the UW is about a 3.1.

Employment Prospects

Alumnus/a, Business, 8/2002-6/2006, November 2006

Most students stay within the Pacific Northwest. Good campus recruiting with regional companies/firms, including Microsoft, Google, Amazon, Starbucks, Boeing. Best school in the region thus has very good outlook for job opportu-nities and internships.

Alumnus/a, 9/2002-6/2006, November 2006

The UW Career Center is very active in attracting employers, hosting career fairs and offering career help (résumé, interviewing). I wouldn't solely rely on it though. You have to motivate yourself as well to research, talk to people and figure out what you want to do. There are so many opportunities for internships and other experiences offered by UW and the student organizations.

Current student, 8/2005-Submit Date, December 2005

I see many on-campus recruiting events every month. Career Services Office in our school help students with looking for a job. They also often hold workshops teach students how to write a résumé and how to do during an interview. Our school also has a only job system. This makes both employers and students eas-ier to connect with each other and all the interview schedule, requests are processed in the online system.

> **The school says:** "Each year about 350 employers conduct campus interviews to select candidates for entry-level career positions, internships or summer jobs."

Current student, 9/2002-Submit Date, December 2004

A lot of UW grads end up in the Northwest. The school does not have much prestige in the East. It can be very difficult to jump to a big-name investment bank with only a UW diploma, and some leading consulting firms do not recruit

Read all of Vault's College Surveys at **www.vault.com/college**—get complete surveys on 100s of colleges and univer-sities, expert advice on applicaton essays and more.

VAULT CAREER LIBRARY   **769**

from the UW at all. On-campus recruiting for industry positions seems to be improving. Some bigger names such as Pepsi and Ford have come to campus in large numbers for the first time in a while. It seems like the College of Arts and Sciences is more of a crapshoot than business or engineering departments. GPA seems to matter a lot. One friend with an econ degree and good grades ended up at the Bureau of Labor and Statistics, another with an econ degree and bad grades ended up a cashier at a hardware store. Partner programs, such as INROADS, seem to give some UW students access to bigger name firms such as Deloitte and Pfizer.

Quality of Life

Alumnus/a, Business, 8/2002-6/2006, November 2006

UW campus is close to Seattle. It is a laidback, but a good mid-size city, which allows for plenty of outdoor activities and a very pleasant living environment. Safe and relaxed neighborhood, with a good mix of student and community members. Out-dated business school building and facilities. Need upgrade (in planning).

Alumnus/a, 9/2002-6/2006, November 2006

Living on campus is a lot of fun. There are Resident Advisors who live on every floor. They help build community in the dorms by planning activities, helping residents resolve issues and so on. There's also a student council of sorts in every dorm. It's a great way to get involved.

Right by campus is the Ave, where all kinds of foods and services are available to students for a cheap price. The buses also run along that street and along 15th Ave. It is very easy to get anywhere from UW riding the bus. For example, any of the buses numbered in the 70s will get you to downtown Seattle in 20 minutes or so.

Alumnus/a, 9/2003-6/2006, September 2006

Excellent! The campus is gorgeous, with brick buildings and Gothic architecture, situated amidst leafy trees, mini-gardens and flowers. It's especially beautiful in the spring, when the Quad is filled with blooming pink cherry blossoms.

The U-District is great as well—tons of cheap food, arguably the fastest and cheapest ethnic food in Seattle concentrated in one area. At night, certain areas of campus are deserted and sketchy, with some homeless people, but if you walk in groups and use common sense, you should be fine. For athletes, the UW has an incredible gym and miles of running trails—the Burke-Gilman, the Arboretum and Greenlake nearby—many of which have stunning views of the lake.

Current student, 9/2003-Submit Date, May 2006

I lived on campus my freshman year and had a great experience. The rooms are nice enough, the people are great, and the location is the most convenient of all living situations for being a full-time student. You are a hop and skip away from central campus, have food facilities either in your building or a two minute walk away, are about five to 10 minutes away from the IMA/gym, and essentially have the opportunity to get involved in campus affairs that most commuter students either don't or can't.

> **The school says:** "The Intramural Activities building (IMA), home to dozens of recreational activities on campus, recently underwent a $44 million expansion and renovation."

Because of recent remodels of both the north and south campus dining halls, the food is gourmet and exceptionally good for dorm food. The only downside is that it is expensive and you don't have the option of not purchasing a food plan unless you live in one of the upperclassman dorms or the student apartments. I didn't gain the freshman 15 because I was obsessed with exercising and training for a half-marathon for most of the year (the dorms are about a 10 minute walk from the IMA), but many people do—portion size is out of control at the campus residence halls!

Current student, 9/2003-Submit Date, November 2005

The quality of life in the Seattle area is excellent. There are plenty of parks, restaurants, bars and shopping centers within walking distance of the campus. There are opportunities to maintain an active lifestyle, whether it is with the free

membership to the Intramural Athletics Building or by riding bikes on Burke-Gilman Trail around beautiful Lake Washington. The University Distr also is home to many cultural restaurants and shops, which offer cuisine fro India, China, France or Israel. Police presence is above normal (they ride bikes, horseback, walk and drive), as they work to keep the University Distr safe for the thousands of students who live there.

Social Life

Alumnus/a, 9/2002-6/2006, November 2006

UW is a big school, so there is so much going on all the time. There are movi playing at the Husky Union Building twice a week (very popular, especia when they show movies before they are actually released in the theaters There's probably a student organization for everything you can think of, and not, you can create your own. There's even ample opportunity to get involv with the student government.

There are a couple of popular bars on the Ave, like Earl's and Big Time Brewe It's usually pretty tame and safe. I wouldn't recommend though walking arou on the Ave by yourself past 9 or 10 p.m., especially if you're a girl. Sor sketchy people hang around (mostly homeless), but be assured that the police a also roaming around the streets. The Ave has cleaned up a lot, so there's not ing really to fear.

Alumnus/a, 9/2003-6/2006, September 2006

As a freshman, it's sometimes quite easy to feel lost among the crowds. If y don't bond well in your dorm, it can be difficult to make tons of friends rig away. Joining the Greek system, clubs, intramural sports or writing for t newspaper are great ways to meet new people. Also, joining a Freshman Intere Group can help you feel part of a smaller learning community. However, I know several people who made very few new friends at UW and ended up han ing with their high school pals most of the time.

Current student, 9/2003-Submit Date, November 2005

The social life around campus is great. As a member of the Greek system, I c tell you first hand that fraternity-sorority relations are great, parties are huge, a the busiest nights are Wednesday and Thursday nights. Because of the camp location in the heart of Seattle, most undergrads live closeby and Friday a Saturday nights are pretty lame. The bar scene is nice, as there are opportuniti for anything. The frat party is at Tommy's on Tuesday and Thursday, hangin out at the pub on Monday's means free trivia and cheap microbrews at Fi MacCools, and the Duchess provides free shuffleboard. All are located with walking distance of each other on the Ave.

Current student, 9/2002-Submit Date, December 2004

The sports facilities are great and the fitness center was renovated in 200 Football is always popular to watch on fall Saturdays. The popularity of oth sports (including basketball) depends on the team's success. Bars and Asi restaurants line the Ave. There are a few Mexican options, and only one fa food place (Jack in the Box) within walking distance. Pizza is available until a.m. at some places. Greeks make up about 10 percent of the student bod Expect drinking, shared adversity, and lots of police on patrol (since the fa 2003 riot). Parties are usually on Thursday, Friday and Saturday nights and determined student can always find one. There are lots of clubs, some of whic have hundreds of members. To browse the available clubs, go to the Stude Activities Office's page at: depts.washington.edu/sao/search_alpha.php.

The School Says

Why Washington? Because There Are No Limits.

"The opportunities for students at the UW are unparalleled. Whatever you wish to pursue, there are people there to help you reach your goals." —Sariah Khormaee '06, Marshall Scholar

Lux sit is the University of Washington's motto. It means, "let there be light" and it expresses the heart of the UW. We are a community of learners striving to create and share new knowledge. The UW is so accomplished at bringing new knowledge to light that it is considered one of the world's premiere research universities. It's an amazing place to be a student—and therefore in high demand.

Lux sit is our communal quest: we collect spacedust from comets, discover a 3.5 billion-year-old microfossil, find new ways to think about cancer vaccines, interpret ancient Buddhist manuscripts, create new dance forms.

UW students are an integral part of lux sit. Every year, 7,000 undergraduates participate in research—in labs, archives, in the field and the community. One of those researchers could be you, presenting your findings at the Annual Undergraduate Research Symposium. Or join the hundreds of students who choose one of 60 study abroad programs to expand their perspectives as global citizens. In 2006, UW graduates won three of the world's most prestigious scholarships—the Rhodes, Gates Cambridge, and Marshall. Each award gives the student a full ride to a top university in the United Kingdom.

Why Washington? Because We're Here.

"You have virtually everything here! The city offers great music venues and food of course. And there are a lot of outdoor activities because the geology here is amazingly beautiful. Seattle has the entertainment that comes with a city, but it has gorgeous surroundings that make it different than anywhere else."
—UW Sophomore

As a UW student, you'll call two cities your second home: the university community and the buzzing, comfortable Emerald City of Seattle. Step off campus and grab an espresso or catch a movie on "the Ave." Ready to explore? You're 15 minutes and one bus away from downtown, where UW students make the most of big city life: internships, theater, nightlife, shopping, restaurants, and arts and film festivals. The weather never stops anyone from playing outdoors. Hike at Mount Rainier, hop into a kayak for a trip around Lake Washington, snowboard at Snoqualmie (less than an hour away), or play volleyball at Alki Beach. It's all about location.

Did You Know?

- The University of Washington was founded in 1861, one of the first public universities on the West Coast.

- UW's outstanding faculty includes six Nobel Prize winners, 53 members in the National Academy of Sciences, 54 members in the American Academy of Arts and Sciences, and 39 members in the Institute of Medicine. The UW faculty have received nine fellowships from the MacArthur Foundation—the so-called "genius awards."

- The UW is located on a spectacular 643-acre campus, five miles from downtown Seattle.

- Seattle's average annual rainfall is 36"—compare it to 15" in LA, 34.5" in Chicago, 39" in Washington, D.C., and 40" in New York City.

Whitman College

Office of Admission
45 Boyer Avenue
Walla Walla, WA 99362
Admissions phone: (509) 527-5176
Admissions fax: (509) 527-4967
Admissions e-mail: admission@whitman.edu
Admissions URL: www.whitman.edu/admission

 Admissions

Alumnus/a, Visual Arts, 1/2000-5/2002, April 2007

Transferred to Whitman during my second year and they did a lot to make sure the transition was smooth. They're really looking for people who delve into a lot of areas. They don't look for straight A's and four-year varsity athletes as much as they look for people who led clubs and organized activities and wrote for the school paper and found an interesting part-time job. Breadth of interest and experience is a hallmark of the Whitman community, so in essays you need to express what unique qualities you have that will enrich the other students around you. Whitman is becoming more and more selective every year, but the emphasis on uniqueness and diversity remains very important.

Current student, 8/2006-Submit Date, March 2007

I was sent information from Whitman with all of the rest of college mail that I received. I wasn't really interested, but something made me go visit Walla Walla the summer before senior year of high school. I loved it. That fall I filled out the Common Application along with Whitman's supplement, which called for an essay on diversity as well as for a graded high school paper. Sometime in the fall, I also attended an informational session in downtown Seattle where George

Bridges, President of Whitman College, and Tony Cabasco, Dean of Admission and Financial Aid at Whitman College, highlighted their favorite aspects of the Whitman experience. I was hooked and decided then an there to apply Early Decision. In October I took a formal visit to campus, attended Whitman's unique CORE class for first-year students, ate lunch with a student and had an interview. During the interview, which is highly recommended but not required (it is very informal and more like a conversation), I handed the admissions officer my application. Shortly after December 15th, I received my acceptance letter along with a letter notifying me of my merit scholarship. I sent in the response card and that was that.

Current student, 8/2006-Submit Date, March 2007

Whitman looks for the whole package. The admissions officers are wonderful people who are looking to bring wonderful people to the school. SAT scores and GPA are helpful, but by no means get you accepted or rejected. Try to show on your application what makes you tick, what makes you unique. Students at Whitman are extremely passionate, so passion is a must to show. It doesn't matter much what you care about, just care about something! My friends and I joke that the interviews are personality screenings, because it's so rare to find a Whittie whom everybody doesn't love.

Current student, Pre-med, 8/2005-Submit Date, March 2007

I feel like the admissions process at Whitman is very personal. They officers take their time, reviewing each applicant individually. The staff in the office knew me by name when I arrived for my interview and made me feel very comfortable. It was unnerving to hear students say that admissions was getting more selective each year, but I felt like everyone really cared about my application individually. The selectiveness is to make sure that each student they admit will fit in well and succeed at Whitman.

Read all of Vault's College Surveys at **www.vault.com/college**—get complete surveys on 100s of colleges and universities, expert advice on applicaton essays and more.

VAULT CAREER LIBRARY   771

Current student, 8/2006-Submit Date, March 2007

Whitman is hard, but not impossible to get in. Admission officers look for passion and a sincere desire to attend Whitman. Fit is very important. So, one must be able to convey why Whitman and "why me." Naturally, this also means go and interview so that you can convey all of your excitement to go to Whitman. While Whitman is a top liberal arts college, if you don't articulate why there is a good fit, your chances decrease regardless of your stats—I even know of a person with a 4.0, and a pretty high SAT who got rejected. But, yeah, in a word: passion.

Current student, 8/2003-Submit Date, March 2007

Whitman has a very active admissions program for interested prospective students, affectionately called "prospies" by current students. Call ahead, and the visit coordinator can arrange for you to visit classes (in departments that interest you), stay overnight with a student (Sunday through Thursday), take a tour, have an interview or info session, eat in the dining halls, and/or meet with professors and coaches.

Admissions is getting more competitive every year; Whitties often joke that by the time they graduate, they wouldn't have been able to get in (don't worry—this is a joke). The admissions committee looks for students who can handle the academic rigor of Whitman, but also bring something of their own to the college. The applicant fills out the Common Application and a Whitman supplement (consisting of a graded essay from junior or senior year in high school and a diversity statement). You must take either the SAT or the ACT; no SAT Subject Tests required. There are Early Decisions I and II, but no Early Action.

In addition to your test scores, Whitman's admissions committee looks at your courses—the rigor, the grades, and how much you've challenged yourself given what your high school offers. [They also consider] the extracurriculars you've participated in—looking for passion, longevity, leadership—and recommendations from teachers and guidance counselors (and any others you send in!), and your writing sample.

And remember, contacting Whitman helps you! As you're applying, be sure to keep yourself known to the admissions staff—thank you cards for visits and interviews, e-mails, phone calls. If you have a question, don't hesitate to ask. Don't just be interested—show you're interested!

> **The school says:** "Whitman uses the Common Application exclusively. Deadlines for Early Decision I and II are November 15 and January 1. Deadline for Regular Decision is January 15, and for Transfer Applicants, March 1."

 # Academics

Alumnus/a, 9/2002-5/2006, May 2007

Whitman entails a great deal of heavy intellectual lifting, which can, at times, feel overwhelming. However, it is my experience that the intellectual rigors and stern grading practices serve to improve the quality of one's thinking. It prepares students in ways that are otherwise unachievable.

Alumnus/a, Physical Sciences, 9/1998-5/2002, April 2007

You can be a complete library junkie, but that is not the type of student that Whitman attracts. Many people start off pre-med, but a much smaller number finish their Whitman career that way. Classes are very demanding. Of course, with more popular classes, it can occasionally be difficult to get in as an underclassman, but unlike bigger schools, I never heard of anyone not graduating or having graduation delayed because he/she couldn't get the classes he/she needed. The professors, since there are no graduate programs, are 100 percent focused on supporting students and providing high quality classes. Doors are always open. Professors have office hours, but they are largely irrelevant most of the time as they are almost always easily available without an appointment. Learning opportunities outside of the classroom abound. As a geology student, during my time at Whitman, I took trips to the Oregon Coast, Yellowstone, the Galapagos, Andes, Canadian Rockies and regional locations. What more could I ask for? I was able to find a passion, and am still working in that field today. I know that similar opportunities exist for students studying in the humanities and life sciences.

Current student, 8/2006-Submit Date, March 2007

Academics at Whitman are very rigorous and the students here are serious ab school. At the same time, the learning atmosphere is very collaborative. have small, seminar-style classes, all taught by professors (no TAs) who eager and excited to involve students in class and in their own resear Whitman provides a liberal arts education, which means that we are require take classes in all subject areas. This is accentuated by Core, a course enti Antiquity and Modernity, which is year-long and is required of all first-year s dents. This class is meant to deepen our understanding of the development Western Civilization. We read primary texts and discuss them in a small cla room environment, and the students and professor remain the same through the two semesters. Core, in addition to those classes required for distributi provides the ultimate foundation for all of our education in the future—prese ing us with themes, ideas, skills and materials that are pertinent to all of major fields of study. Students tend to have large workloads, consisting of re ing, writing and problem solving in the maths and sciences. To be honest, f time is not something that readily available, but Whitman students do make ti for activities, events and other things that are important to them. Grading Whitman varies, however we are all held to high standards, with participat being very important. The professors are intelligent and knowledgeable in th fields, articulate and most of all, they have a tremendous understanding of liberal arts.

Current student, 8/2006-Submit Date, March 2007

Academics at Whitman are as difficult (or as easy) as you're willing to m them. There are definitely easy classes that you can ride by on, but the majo ty take real dedication. The professors will do anything and everything for y (including lengthy extensions, inviting you to their house, and giving out th cell phone number in case you have trouble with homework), and they appre ate and respect the same in exchange. They are extremely driven and kno edgeable in their fields. The most popular classes fill up quickly, but you c usually beg your way into anything, because everyone at Whitman is so acco modating. They want to make you happy! You are also expected to s engaged and participate; many classes are under 15 or even 10 students, you've got to pull your fair share of weight. You have tons of freedom in cl selection because the requirements are so easy to cover. There is only c required course, Core for freshmen, and even that is generally pretty fun.

Current student, 8/2003-Submit Date, March 2007

Whitman is an academically rigorous school; there's no way around that! Fo lot of first-years (at Whitman, you're a "first year," not a "freshman"), the wake-up call class is Core. Officially called Antiquity and Modernity, Core the only required class at Whitman. It's a year-long course, and a variety profs teach it (from English to art, to physics, to classics, to psychology). Y start the year with *The Odyssey* (Homer) and end with *Beloved* (Toni Morriso and sort of read your way through the development of Western Civilizatio between. It is a reading, writing and discussion intensive class, and it gi every single Whitman student the same foundation, which is really handy.

Also, since Whitman is a liberal arts school, there are distribution requireme (so you come out of this as a "well-rounded individual"). In other words, y have to take approximately two classes in each of these fields: humanities, f arts, social sciences and sciences (at least one of your science courses must ha a lab component). You also have to take at least one course in quantitative ana sis (a math class), but you can take something more like psych stats if calcu et al. is not your thing. Finally, you must take at least two classes in "alter tive voices," which is loosely defined as "a non-Western-based thought clas so Asian history/studies/religion counts, as do upper-level language classes, a a third semester extension of the Core class.

Current student, 8/2004-Submit Date, October 2006

A+ in every way: easy to get into classes due to the small nature of the scho the professors make classes very challenging but they are not out to get you; a lots of studying is required to earn A's. I am a mathematics-physics major, a it is much harder to earn good grades in the hard sciences and mathematics th the social sciences and humanities especially.

Employment Prospects

lumnus/a, Sociology, 9/1997-5/2001, April 2007

e Career Center is very accessible and always willing to help with résumés or
b searches. They also have a program where you can do personality and voca-
nal tests to see what you're best suited for. The prestige of Whitman is quite
ong, though mostly in the Pacific Northwest. Once you find another Whittie,
ough, there seems to be an automatic bond wherever it's found. I work for a
rge university in New York State doing grants administration.

lumnus/a, 9/2002-5/2006, May 2007

ind Whitman alumni sprinkled throughout powerful institutions nationwide.
hitman connections, for example, helped me land two topnotch internships
ile a student and an extremely competitive job after graduation. Furthermore,
hitman's intellectual rigor has proven exceedingly beneficial in my workplace,
en that I spar with graduates from Yale, Dartmouth and Tufts.

lumnus/a, Physical Sciences, 9/1998-5/2002, April 2007

hitman does not have the name recognition of an Ivy League, but that is a good
ing. Everybody who knows the name of Whitman is familiar with the quality
students it produces. It might not be a big name with employers, but in aca-
mic circles, Whitman is highly respected. Whitman prepares its students well
r graduate programs in the sciences, medicine, law and humanities. Whitman
dents get into grad school.

ere is no typical Whitman graduate; the commonality is that they follow their
ssion, whether it is being a cowboy for a few years on a Watson fellowship,
king the Pacific Crest Trail, or leading backpacking trips for teenagers.

lumnus/a, Visual Arts, 1/2000-5/2002, April 2007

e average Whitman graduate tends to pursue nontraditional career paths
mediately after undergrad. Many go work for nonprofits or work on grass-
ots political campaigns or volunteer with the Peace Corps or AmeriCorps. I
cured a job well in advance of my graduation, which was very unique. Most
d to gain additional experience before going on to further study. To my
owledge there is virtually no on-campus recruiting, but there is an extremely
ong alumni network that many use for employment purposes. I have hired a
mber of Whitman graduates in recent years and have advised many others on
reer options in my field.

urrent student, 8/2003-Submit Date, March 2007

great deal of Whitties go on to grad school, but certainly not all. Whitman is
nerally seen as a prestigious college, but it is best-known in Washington state
d throughout the Northwest—employers back east are less likely to know of
hitman. The alumni office is very active, and an extremely high percentage of
hitman alumni donate back to Whitman.

e Career Center is available to Whitties both during their time at Whitman and
terward. Alumni are more than welcome to use the college's services in look-
g for a (new) career. There is also an active alumni network available to other
hitties—this is a database of alumni who are willing to talk to fellow Whitties
out their jobs and fields, which provides a very helpful networking system for
rrent and former students. If you're interested in fellowships or grants, there
a very good advisor at Whitman who specializes in these and will support you
rough your application process; every year, a respectable number of Whitties
garner big-name grants and fellowships.

Quality of Life

lumnus/a, Visual Arts, 1/2000-5/2002, April 2007

hitman is a very safe place and can at times feel very insular, but the commu-
ty support is what drives people to succeed. Because each person's studies are
individualized there is little competition on campus and anyone can find any
rt of outlet for exploration or experimentation. Housing on campus is only
quired during the first two years. Interest houses allow you to live with peo-
e who have similar passion for a language or the arts, or environmental issues.
y semester in the Fine Arts House was very important to me and I made sev-

eral lasting relationships from my various living situations. Off-campus housing
options are abundant and are usually multi-bedroom houses shared by students.

Current student, Pre-med, 8/2005-Submit Date, March 2007

It is a well-known fact around campus that Whitman is rated as one of the colleges with the "happiest students." Students take pride in this, and everyone
agrees. Freshmen are met with a first-year program that upperclassmen lovingly refer to as Camp Whitman. The first week is packed with interesting speakers, and plenty of time to get to know the enthusiastic residence staff and fellow
students. Dorms are not great, but everyone ends up loving it by the end of the
first semester. Food in the dining halls is well above average, and even the juniors and seniors come back to be "swiped in." Since the campus is in a small
city, it is always safe to walk around at night, or even to wander around the
neighboring streets.

Current student, 8/2006-Submit Date, March 2007

Walla Walla is very safe and very friendly, as is the Whitman campus. The town
and the college are beautiful, green and full of smiling faces. The residence halls
are comfortable, cozy, safe and well-maintained, as are all of the academic buildings. We just opened a new fitness center complete with a [30-meter] pool and
a vast array of cardio and weight machines. The food on campus is surprisingly tasty for a college setting, with many different kinds of food as well as vegetarian and vegan options at all meals. Because Whitman students and faculty are
so environmentally conscience, our food is fresh, sometimes organic, locally
grown when applicable and generally very socially aware.

Current student, 8/2006-Submit Date, March 2007

All freshmen and sophomores live on campus in residence halls and interest
houses. Upperclassmen tend to live in houses that surround campus, which
aren't hard to find to rent. Both on- and off-campus housing is pretty good, especially if you want to be in close proximity with your friends. Students tend to
stay on campus because Walla Walla doesn't have much to offer. It's sometimes
referred to as the "Whitman Bubble." This does mean that the school brings in
tons of entertainment; there is never enough time to do everything you want to
do. We get really famous speakers and bands pretty often. Walla Walla is quaint,
and safe enough to take night walks and wander through town without ever feeling threatened. The campus is absolutely beautiful, with three trees for every
student and a wandering stream. Lakum Duckum is, of course, always full of
ducks, and we have a pretty huge squirrel population. The food, especially for
a college, is very good, with lots of variety and vegetarian/vegan/healthy
options. In general, Whitman is a very happy place and students are energized
and in love with their lives.

Current student, 8/2003-Submit Date, March 2007

Whitman's dorms are extremely nice. Compared with many other colleges'
dorm rooms, Whitman's are more likely to be renovated and are often larger.
You're required to live on campus for your first two years at least, and you are
more than welcome to live on campus for all four years if you'd like. There are
two first-year halls, one all-woman hall (which also houses the three sororities;
the four frats are in houses on the other side of campus), and one coed, first-year
through senior hall. After your first year, there are a couple of other dorms open
to you, as well as the Interest House community; these are a living option starting your sophomore year. They are houses that cater to a specific interest. So
there's the French House, the German House, the Spanish House, the Japanese
House, the Asian Studies House, the Multi-Ethnic Center for Cultural
Awareness, the Writing House, the Fine Arts House, the Community Service
House, the Outhouse (environmentally friendly house), and the Global
Awareness House. There are also—for your junior and senior years—many
apartments and houses available to rent near campus.

You're required to be on a meal plan for as long as you live on campus, and the
food is really not that bad. The trick is that there are lots of options—there is
always a vegetarian option, a vegan option, a meat option, and pizza or a grill
(depending on which dining hall you're at). There's always a salad bar (a fruit
bar replaces this at breakfast), and the dining halls stagger their hours of operation so you can find a time that works well for you. The Reid Campus Center
boasts a grill, pizza, and a third specialty section that changes out week by week
(Mongolian grill, fajitas).

Read all of Vault's College Surveys at www.vault.com/college—get complete surveys on 100s of colleges and universities, expert advice on applicaton essays and more.

VAULT CAREER LIBRARY **773**

Social Life

Alumnus/a, Physical Sciences, 9/1998-5/2002, April 2007

While the Greek system is big on campus (about half of the students are involved, at least when I was there), social life does not center around, nor is limited to the Greek houses.

> **The school says:** "32 percent of Whitman students are affiliated with the Greek system."

The campus does a great job of bringing speakers to campus on all topics. While I was attending, I saw Howard Zinn, Christopher Hitchens and Steph Davis (world-class rock climber). Events that bring the whole campus together are Dragfest, Visitors Weekend, the annual Beer Mile on the campus green (which I helped organize for four years as a member of the cross country team), Sweet Onion Crank (climbing competition), and an annual music festival.

Current student, 8/2006-Submit Date, March 2007

The entire social scene takes place on campus and at off-campus houses. CAB (Campus Activities Board) throws all kinds of events, including outdoor movies with projectors, Casino Night and various dances. The bi-annual BSU dance is always popular and has the best music selection. The Greek system is not at all stereotypical. It is pretty laid-back and not exclusive. The parties and functions they hold are often open to the whole campus. Alcohol is very popular, both at Greek and independent parties, but drugs are almost nonexistent. Freshman year there is not much dating, and people tend to complain that even hookups are difficult because you're bound to see the person the next day on Ankeny Field or in bio lab. Long term relationships do happen, especially in older years, and it isn't uncommon for Whitties to marry each other after graduation. Overall, the social life is pretty buzzing, especially for a tiny college in a tiny town. Students are good at making their own fun.

Current student, 8/2003-Submit Date, March 2007

Whitman is located in Walla Walla, Washington (Small Town, USA), so a lot [of] the entertainment is brought directly to campus (translation: is free to student[s]). In the 2006-2007 school year, we had Flogging Molly and Guster come give p[er]formances on campus and a stellar lecture from Jane Elliott (of the bro[wn] eyes/blue eyes experiment fame); in the past, we've had visits from Ben Ste[in,] Maya Angelou, Ben Folds, Death Cab for Cutie and many more big names.

If parties are not your thing, that's absolutely fine! Campus is always offering[a] variety of events during the week and throughout the weekend. There is [a] Visiting Writers Reading Series, which brings authors to campus to hold rea[d]ings and Q&As; a number of film series go on throughout the year; speakers a[nd] bands come constantly; dances are held every once in a while; and there is li[ve] music in the campus center every Friday night. It is not uncommon to have [to] pick and choose which events to attend, but there is honestly something [for] everyone!

Current student, 8/2004-Submit Date, October 2006

Most of the social scene takes place at house parties and fraternity houses. The[re] is a strong Greek scene as well as a strong independent scene. There are a co[u]ple of good bars in town that Whitman students frequent, but none are soc[ial] hubs. Because Walla Walla is a small town of 40,000 inhabitants, there is [not] much of a social scene on the town besides wine tasting. The wine tasting [is] great as there are over 50 wineries within 15 minutes drive, but tasting is o[nly] good as a daytime activity, and only some students enjoy it enough to regular[ly] partake. As far as the night social scene goes, Whitman students have learned [to] make their own fun on campus, at fraternity houses, and mainly at off-camp[us] house parties. Luckily, almost all off-campus houses are within a five-min[ute] walk of campus so there is no real concern with drinking and driving. Becau[se] of the limited nature of Walla Walla's social scene, I think that Whitman stude[nts] are especially adept at creating their own fun and having a goodtime regardl[ess] of the circumstances.

Marshall University

Marshall University Office of Recruitment
One John Marshall Drive
Huntington, WV 25755
Phone: 1-877-GOHERD1 or 1-304-696-6833
Email: recruitment@marshall.edu
URL: www.marshall.edu

Admissions

Current student, 8/2003-Submit Date, November 2006

In-state admission is extremely simple. My high school guidance counselor gave me an application (which can be downloaded from the Marshall University web site at www.marshall.edu). Even if you are from out of state, you can download this application and submit it online, and then mail in your signature and any necessary fees. For Marshall University, there is a $25 application fee for in-state, and increases for metro student applications and non-metro student applications.

What Marshall wants to see most is which classes you took your senior year in high school. No slackers! Your GPA and ACT score are both important, as well. There is no interview, and Marshall generally will only reject an application if the ACT score is too low (below an 18) or the prospective student has a discouraging GPA.

Alumnus/a, 8/1998-5/2003, September 2005

I found the admissions process to be very easy. Marshall University was partnering with my local high school to provide dual-credit classes, and so many of the initial enrollment steps, including picture IDs, were taken care of as part of that process. Because of the dual-credit classes, I never felt that there would be any problem with being admitted to the university.

Alumnus/a, 7/1997-12/2001, March 2005

There is an application you can receive by mail as well as an online application. There is no essay or interview. Admission is based on your ACT scores. The application is easy to understand and fill out. As I recall it is only two pages long. MU also has a program for people who do not meet the requirements of the ACT scores in the way of a community college and the HELP program for people with learning disabilities.

Alumnus/a, 8/1995-5/1998, November 2004

The application is typical—fill it out and send your transcripts plus the application fee, all your activities and awards accumulated in high school, your ACT or SAT scores and three letters of reference and your immunization records. You will be sent a letter stating whether you've been accepted or not. Once you are, you will have orientation and an interview with your advisor and register for your classes. Marshall has a reputation of building bright futures for their graduates. They require a 19 on the ACTs and a C or above average high school GPA. The orientation process was a great experience, you are split up into groups and give a list of programs and activities offered. They show you around campus and give the history of the school.

Academics

Current student, 8/2003-Submit Date, November 2006

Marshall University has what it calls the Marshall Plan. With this Plan, a student takes a well-rounded schedule of courses, including ones such as electives in sociology, psychology, geography, biology, geology, economics and English. Once you have declared a major, you can begin taking the core classes for that major. For example, in the Lewis College of Business this will involve taking Accounting 215 and 216, Micro- and Macro-economics, Management 360, Marketing 340 and Finance 323.

Popular classes are difficult to get into unless you by chance get an early scheduling date. Scheduling dates are assigned by last name, with graduate students and seniors going first. A schedule of courses is released at least one week prior to scheduling and it will contain the scheduling dates.

Grading is done generally on a 100-point scale, so that 90 to 100 is an A, an 80 to 89 is a B and so on. Marshall has its fair share of easy professors and difficult ones. It is best to join an organization and seek friendships with those with the same major you are interested in so you can find out which professors will help you, and which ones will not.

Workload again depends on several factors: the professor, the level of difficulty of the class (100-level, 200-level and so on) and how good the student is in school. A student's study habits will play a role in how difficult the workload seems. Work and get it done and no matter how much there is, it won't seem that bad. Procrastination will not let you excel in college. You may get C's and B's, but you are paying to get this education, so earn the better grade!

Alumnus/a, 8/1998-5/2003, September 2005

I felt that most of the classes I attended at Marshall University were stimulating and thought-provoking. The professors were almost exclusively helpful and guidelines were generally clearly spelled out and carefully followed. Grading was also generally fair and clearly explained, with generally enough assignments to balance the weight of the courseload and grade determination. The admissions process improved when the online/telephone access program MILO became available for class enrollment. The rotation of enrollment days seemed fair, and classes were usually available, or professors would often give overloads if asked. It is university policy that graduating seniors must be given overloads into classes that they need, which eliminated a lot of stress the last two semesters.

Alumnus/a, 7/1997-12/2001, March 2005

I have a degree in music education, which, although not recognized as such, is essentially a double major. Even with taking 21 hours a semester (a full courseload is 18 and you must take 12 to be considered full time), I had to take three summer courses to allow me to graduate in four and a half years. The degree is listed as a four-year degree, but that is with taking several more summer sessions than I took. I found the majority of my music classes to be challenging and fulfilling, but the education classes were of no difficulty what so ever. Registration at MU is much the same as most other universities, senior get first pick of classes and freshmen get last pick. There are always ample basic classes available but the electives fill up quickly.

Alumnus/a, 8/1995-5/1998, November 2004

Marshall offers over 40 different undergraduate programs and 51 different graduate programs. They also offer associate programs from their on campus community college. The programs are fairly hard—you must study and be prepared. The professors I had were willing to help you if you ask for it, the classes are 25 to 35 students, the classes were detailed and fairly intimate as far as student/teacher relationships go. As long as you register for classes early you will have no problem getting the classes you need, once you have completed your first freshman semester you can use the MILO system to register for classes this allows you to register for classes over the phone. The grading is fair—some grade on a curve, most don't. The teachers expect you to learn so you will have much homework. The professors tend to care and want to see you succeed; they are more than willing to help where needed.

Read all of Vault's College Surveys at **www.vault.com/college**—get complete surveys on 100s of colleges and universities, expert advice on applicaton essays and more.

VAULT CAREER LIBRARY 775

Employment Prospects

Current student, 8/2003-Submit Date, November 2006

Marshall University's Career Center is extremely helpful in assisting you with finding a job. By registering with the Career Center, you can go to their web site online and download your résumé. The Center will then post it under the category of your major, and you will receive e-mails if a job opportunity becomes available. If an e-mail address is included in your résumé, employers will contact you.

All colleges offer several internships with local businesses, or you can apply for an out-of-state and summer internship. The career fairs held both in the fall and the spring give students the perfect opportunity to present themselves to employers. This past fall, there were over 75 business organizations represented at the fair.

Alumnus/a, 8/1998-5/2003, September 2005

The employment prospects differed from college to college within my university. There seemed to be more emphasis on jobs and internships among my peers in the business, science and teaching colleges, as well as for those enrolled in the associate programs. I was aware that a job-placement service existed, but I never personally visited the facility. Job fairs were hosted fairly regularly in the student center, but I never found much of interest in them, though one of my friends did get a job from one such job fair.

Alumnus/a, 7/1997-12/2001, March 2005

There are many on-campus job fairs set up every semester. I am still receiving e-mails about the job fairs. Some are job-specific and some are mass fairs incorporating several different job fields at the same time.

Alumnus/a, 8/1995-5/1998, November 2004

Marshall has many connections with employers: St. Mary's Hospital, Cabell Huntington Hospital and its new medical wing. Many graduates have gone on to become news anchors, professors at the college, even professional football players. Marshall alumni hold dinners where local business can meet and recruit future graduates for their business. The mayor of Huntington, WV was elected directly after graduating from Marshall, and has been elected to his second term. Huntington is a booming city and has been creating new jobs daily. There are many opportunities for those who chose to stay in the Huntington area. Marshall also holds career expos and job fairs every semester.

Quality of Life

Current student, 8/2003-Submit Date, November 2006

Marshall University is working to develop itself into a bigger and more attractive university. A Health and Wellness Center is in the plans to be built in the near future. There are several new dormitories and apartments on campus.

Some of the dormitories are in need of renovations, such as the Twin Towers. The housing office will let you select your roommate or at least put you with someone of similar tastes. There are private rooms available, but it will cost more.

The Marshall University Police Department has 75 employees who are on duty around the clock. The station is behind the Welcome Center. There are several Emergency Call Buttons on campus that can be used if a student feels he/she is in danger, or if the student would like to be escorted to his/her car (if it is night time, this is a safe task to do).

There are three dining halls on campus. The cafeteria in the Student Center has several eating alternatives—Chik-Fil-A, a deli, Pizza Hut, grilled food, and to-go choices. The student dining halls (one in Twin Towers and a separate building, called the Harless Dining Hall) offer all you can eat buffets with a variety of food choices, including a salad bar and desserts. Items that appear on the menus generally all the time are pizza, hamburgers, grilled cheese and french fries. Both dining halls offer other food items every day, and a monthly menu is available.

Alumnus/a, 8/1998-5/2003, September 2005

I commuted to college and did not live in a dorm, which made parking, not hou ing, my primary concern. Parking was inconvenient at best and expensive more than doubling during my enrollment time to several hundred dollars p year. There are quite a few apartment complexes within walking distance of t university, and the dorms seem livable, though crowded, with the university one time temporarily housing freshmen in nearby hotels because a sudd increase in enrollment caused them to have fewer dormrooms available th needed. Although crime did exist, I never felt vulnerable.

Alumnus/a, 7/1997-12/2001, March 2005

Housing has recently increased in quality at MU due to two new residences campus. The rooms are nice most with overhead lighting and air conditionir The new dorms offer each resident a cellphone as opposed to an in-room lar line. All rooms have Internet connections as well as cable hook-ups at no ex charge. There are three dining rooms and the cafe in the student center. Crir is not really a problem at MU, they have campus police that are actually train police officers who carry guns rather than the usual rent-a-cop. They patrol foot, bike, motorcycle and car. Huntington is a rather low crime area in and itself, so I felt no danger at all while on campus.

Current student, 8/2003-Submit Date, January 2005

The campus is small, which is good because no car is needed to get to class staying on campus. The dorms could use a little work, or at least be less stiff rules and procedures. The cafeteria leaves much to be desired. Breakfast, lun and dinner need longer hours, or at least quit giving us classes that are or available during these meals (sometimes to the exact second of the beginni and end of dinner or lunch).

Alumnus/a, 8/1995-5/1998, November 2004

I lived off campus, but I had some friends who lived on campus and their dorr were nice, mostly double occupancy but also single. The community showe are nice and well taken care of. The lounges at Marshall have pool tables a ping pong tables, pinball games and many of them hold dorm tournaments. Lc crime on and around campus. The campus police were always available. I liv across from the campus so I was fortunate enough to take advantage of many the activities they offered. Marshall University has many clubs and activities f the students to have an active college life.

Social Life

Current student, 8/2003-Submit Date, November 2006

There are over 100 student-led organizations at Marshall. These range fro common interests (skiing, chess, language) to community service (Circle APO). There is Greek life at Marshall, led by the Inter-Greek Communi (IGC). Please check out Marshall University's Student Activities web site www.marshall.edu/studentactivities for more information.

Most bars and nightclubs are not within walking distance of campus, but a b is available to take for free to downtown Huntington and Pullman Squar Pullman Square is a new facility featuring Starbucks, a multi-cinema, a boo store and small shops. Some of the favored bars are ICON and The Union. new western bar has recently opened on 3rd Avenue, and on 4th Avenue anot er new Christian nightclub has opened called the House of David (above t upperclassman apartments).

Restaurants of choice are Applebee's, which offers half-price appetizers a drinks after 9 p.m., from Sunday to Thursday. The Hall of Fame Cafe, Rc Lobster, Moe's, Chili Wili's, and Giovanni's Pub are other favored restaurant Fast-food chains are close to campus, as well.

The Huntington Mall is another social scene with several shops (The Gap, Aer AE, JC Penney, Sears, Talbot's, New York & Co., Lerner's and others) ar places to eat (Chinese, Japanese, Ruby Tuesday and so on).

Alumnus/a, 8/1998-5/2003, September 2005

Once again, as an off-campus student, I was not intimate with much of the soci life of the students living on campus. For whatever reason, Thursday night seeme to be the night most of the students hit the bars, making Friday morning classes ha

many to attend. There are at least 10 bars within walking distance of the cam-
, and probably close to 20 restaurants, including McDonald's, Wendy's, Pizza
, Shoney's, Fazoli's, Captain D's, Subway and Burger King. There are many
erent Greek societies, including a few honorary fraternities such as Gamma Beta
and others associated with specific collages.

Alumnus/a, 7/1997-12/2001, March 2005

There are several bars surrounding the campus and a plethora of restaurants.
There are social activities provided by the Greek system, as well as other campus organizations. There is something to do every day. There are three movie
theaters within walking distance and there are always plays, bands and well-
known acts being brought in by the university. In the past, Carrot Top, Bill
Cosby, touring Broadway shows and many more have visited.

West Virginia University

est Virginia University
lmissions & Records
O. Box 6009
organtown, WV 26506-6009
lmissions phone: (304) 293-2121 or (800) 344-WVU1
lmissions fax: (304) 293-3080
lmissions e-mail: go2wvu@mail.wvu.edu
lmissions URL: admissions.wvu.edu/undergraduate/

 ## Admissions

irrent student, 8/2002-Submit Date, May 2006

e admissions process was typical. I filled out an application and had high
ool transcripts sent to WVU. Because I am a music major I did have to audi-
1 and take a theory exam.

lmnus/a, 8/1999-8/2003, April 2005

e credentials for West Virginia University are average. You have to have a
ent GPA and an average score on the SAT or ACT. Make sure you visit the
npus before making your decision. I do not recall having an interview here,
the essays are long! Be very honest in your essay and you should be fine!

irrent student, 8/2000-Submit Date, February 2005

mission is easy. Pretty much everyone gets accepted into this school. It helps
have a good score on SATs and ACTs. There were no interviews or essays
uired to get into WVU. It's a large school, so they accept almost everyone.

lmnus/a, 8/1999-8/2003, November 2004

ere are no essays to compete for general admissions. The application process
airly easy. When I applied I had no idea what I was doing and got approved.
is is a fairly easy college to get admitted into. If your high school scores are
high enough, try attending a community college for a year or two before
nding the university.

irrent student, 9/2003-Submit Date, September 2004

sonally, I mailed in an application and was accepted as a transfer student from
maller private college, so no papers, essays or interviews were required of me
hat time. WVU isn't known for being particularly selective of its incoming
dents. The best part of applying was the opportunity for many different schol-
hips, and this school gave me quite a substantial academic scholarship

irrent student, 8/2000-Submit Date, June 2004

st Virginia University is one of the top schools for the program I entered. For
mission to the university you have to take the ACT or SAT. Once you take
m you are on your way into the university. Once in the university, you have
apply to the program you want. I went into communication studies. You have
have 2.5 GPA and pass Comm 200 and 201 with a B average. People think
ting into the communication department is easy. I had a focus group, and

most of the people were coming from the business school because they could not
get into the department of business. But little did they know that Comm 200 and
201 are not that easy to pass. My advice is to stay ahead and on top of your
work. Do not get behind!

Current student, 8/2000-Submit Date, March 2004

To get into the WVU Child Development and Family Studies Program, you need
to apply go to Allen Hall on the Evansdale campus. You can visit wvu.edu to get
more information on the school and program. After you get into WVU you can
go straight into the program. The only requirement is to maintain a C or better
in your CDFS classes. At WVU, if you get a 19 or better on your ACT, you are
probably going to get in.

> WVU states: "The average WVU freshman from in state has a
> 23 ACT."

 ## Academics

Alumnus/a, 8/2001-12/2005, November 2006

I graduated with a degree in Public Relations; I found the Journalism school to
be a great place to learn. Registering for classes is quick and easy. If you are at
the undergraduate advising center, which you will be until you get into your program, read the handbook for your major! You can save yourself time and
headaches by knowing exactly what you need to take; those advisers do not
know you.

Current student, 8/2002-Submit Date, May 2006

Classes were, for the most part, very straightforward. I had no problem getting
into the classes I needed and the grading was more than fair. All of my professors have gone above and beyond the call of duty. At times I felt the workload
was a little overbearing, but I feel that just toughened me up for the real world.

Alumnus/a, 8/1999-8/2003, April 2005

The classes at West Virginia University are usually not difficult to get into once
you are in your classes for your major. They have made it easier by allowing
you to register for classes online. The education program is one of the top programs in the U.S. and is not easy. It is a lot of work, but the professors are wonderful and you can go to them with any problems. The workload is not extreme,
but can be if you do not follow a schedule and get behind. Popular classes can
be difficult to get into before you are an upperclassman. Take the classes you
have to the first two years and then take the classes you might find interesting!

Current student, 8/2000-Submit Date, February 2005

The classes are quality. I feel like I'm getting just as good of an education as
people who go to school out of state or to an expensive university. There is also
a variety of programs and classes offered. Getting into classes depends on your
status—seniors register first, followed by juniors, sophomores, then freshmen.
So, whether or not you get into a class just depends. If you really need to get
into a class, you can see an advisor for a pink slip. Then, you show up on the

Read all of Vault's College Surveys at www.vault.com/college—get complete surveys on 100s of colleges and universities, expert advice on applicaton essays and more.

VAULT CAREER LIBRARY 777

first day of that class, and if the professor feels there is adequate space for you, then you can be enrolled for the class. Grading is on a 100-point scale (90 through 100 is an A). The professors are all people who are very educated, with some people who are known for a lot of prestigious accomplishments. Workload depends on your dedication to school. I would say you could pass as long as you attend classes and don't skip. I studied all the time, and have been a straight-A student. I've also been able to work part time since I started college.

Current student, 9/2003-Submit Date, September 2004

Classes are of excellent quality; much of the student body is unmotivated, but teachers are great and very, very helpful in almost every instance.

Current student, 8/2000-Submit Date, June 2004

My best advice is to stay ahead of the game. If you have questions, ask your advisors. They are there to help you through your college experience. Your first year, you should enter into an orientation class. This is where you get used to using the facilities on campus and get to know where everything is.

Current student, 8/2000-Submit Date, March 2004

The classes are not too bad. They are easy to get in and schedule. WVU now offers online registration, which makes the process a lot easier. The professors, for the most part, are fair, but every now and then you get a difficult one. They are all unbiased. For the CDFS classes, the workload is pretty simple. Just go at a steady pace.

Alumnus/a, Engineering, 8/1986-6/1991, May 2004

WVU has nearly anything you would want. They're a full-service university, with colleges in each area of study, such as engineering, arts and sciences, fine arts and forestry.

Freshman core classes are rather large, but with robust graduate student aids, the process is well run. Once you get into higher-level classes, class size is nearly always very small.

The faculty at WVU is very good. Many are leaders in their fields. For example, the Computer Engineering Fepartment has a program where industry leaders are invited to teach for a designated number of years, in conjunction with the company. For example, one of my professors was a transfer from Bell Labs where he invented the newest generation of microchip. Very cool for an engineer like me.

Alumnus/a, 9/1995-5/1998, October 2003

Because of the relatively small size of each class, there is seldom an issue with not getting a class or not getting a particular professor. Required courses tend to have 60 to 70 people generally, and electives may have as few as five people. The size of classes makes a tremendous difference with respect to the learning experience.

Employment Prospects

Alumnus/a, 8/2001-12/2005, November 2006

WVU gets a bad rap for being a party school, which it is, but we are no different than any other college I have visited. Employers are usually impressed to see a school of WVU's caliber on your résumé.

Current student, Music, 8/2002-Submit Date, May 2006

In my particular field (music), employment is most contingent on auditions, but my professors at the College of Creative Arts are very experienced professional musicians as well. They are all required to maintain their status as professional musicians throughout their tenure at WVU. Thus, they are more than qualified to help us prepare for the toughest audition.

Alumnus/a, 8/1999-8/2003, April 2005

I cannot really tell about other programs, but the education program makes searching for a job very easy. There is a job fair usually in March or April, where you can interview with school districts from all around. If you want to stay in West Virginia, however, jobs are scarce. As far as I know, most programs will help you find a job in your field. There are job fairs at least twice a year for the entire campus.

Current student, 8/2000-Submit Date, February 2005

Employers are enthusiastic about hiring WVU graduates. This school has a v good name for graduating highly qualified students every year. Graduates obt all kinds of jobs, like marketing careers (drug reps), different types of engine ing (mechanical, civil), lawyers (graduates from the law school), doctors a other medical fields (medical school graduates), and entrepreneurs (busin graduates). On-campus recruiting makes it easy for soon-to-be graduates obtain employment. The school holds a job fair before every graduation a invites hundreds of potential employers who will interview and accept appli tions right on the spot! There are also a lot of internship possibilities in the a no matter what your major. There are a lot of professors and advisors who very willing to help you obtain internships by making calls or writing a letter recommendation for you.

Alumnus/a, 8/1986-6/1991, May 2004

The career center is very robust, helpful and effective. They really reach ou employers and work with you to find a job. They have a list of services incl ing simple researching of prospective employers, personal surveys, résumé he job hunting skills and development. You can choose what you need.

Quality of Life

Current student, 8/2002-Submit Date, May 2006

The first three years at WVU were spent in the dorms. I would say the qua of life at the dorms was typical. I never felt I was in danger during my stay the The dining was adequate by dorm food standards.

Current student, 8/2000-Submit Date, February 2005

The dorms are nice. All freshmen are required to live in the dorms for the fi year. Each dorm has a dining hall, offering a variety of foods at different tin of the day. There are also several fast food and desert restaurants located in student center (called the Mountainlair). The campus is divided into two se tions—the downtown campus and the Evansdale campus. A transit syste which is like a little train, is provided free for students to get from one camp to the other. The facilities offered to students are pretty nice. For example huge rec center was built just about two years ago, offering many activiti Some things included in the rec center are: indoor pool with hot tubs, indoor r ning track, indoor climbing wall, free weights, cardio equipment, aerobics cla es, tennis courts, racquetball courts, basketball courts, intramural sports, stu rooms and a healthy snack bar. The facility is free for students to use! Cri rate is low.

Alumnus/a, 8/1999-8/2003, November 2004

I lived in the Towers for two years and loved it. It was a big adjustment fo small town girl, but fun as well. The staff plans activities to help the floor get know each other. Off-campus housing is a different story. I lived in Pierpo and liked that I could fix my own meals, but maid service was provided. T apartments were big enough to live in, but nothing extravagant. Private apa ments are tough. Most landlords do not keep up the units or if they do, th charge an enormous amount for rent.

Current student, 8/2004-Submit Date, October 2004

The campus area is up-and-coming. Several well-known chains such as Pane are moving into the area. A big drawback is that there is as of yet no Starbuc present on campus. There are several jobs available for students. The area very safe, with police active in the area. Fun-loving area. Many nice, up-ke apartments/complexes available for students of all levels. Driving around area is easy. One drawback is that parking is not readily available on camp The school does provide public transportation to all campus sites for studen which is very reliable.

Current student, 9/2003-Submit Date, September 2004

Campus facilities, dining and neighborhood are all fantastic, but the place sometimes covered in college garbage. It feels like a safe campus, though, a there is very little legitimate crime. I don't worry about walking alone at nig and it doesn't bother me to have my door unlocked through the day.

Social Life

umnus/a, 8/2001-12/2005, November 2006

cial life is by far the greatest asset WVU has to offer. From the dorms to the
sses, you will definitely meet friends with whom you will keep in contact for
e rest of you life.

rrent student, 8/2002-Submit Date, May 2006

organtown is very much a college town, with plenty of bars, restaurants and
er attractions aimed toward the student population. We are a very sports-ori-
ed campus. Our football and basketball teams are topnotch and provide
ensive entertainment during the fall and winter months.

umnus/a, 8/1999-8/2003, April 2005

you want a social life, this is the place to attend! West Virginia University is
own above all for its parties. The Mountainlair has activities on weekends for
dents who do not prefer the club scene and there are dozens of clubs (espe-
lly on High St.). There is a program called Mountaineer Singles where you
n find dates. There are plenty of restaurants, my favorite being Rose's Italian
staurant. There are also many extracurricular activities you can join. The
eek system is very powerful here and many students pledge a fraternity or
rority. The bars and clubs in town vary in taste. There are some low key clubs
ere you can just hang out and have a beer with your friends and then there are
nce clubs for ages 18 and up. There is plenty of shopping and activities to
ep you busy when you aren't busy with school!

rrent student, 8/2000-Submit Date, February 2005

VU has been previously named the Number One party school! There are tons
sororities and fraternities to join, as well as an extensive nightlife on the
wntown campus. There are many, many bars to go to, which are all good
ces to meet people. There are bars for those who are under 21 also. Some
rs only allow those who are over 21. Bent Willy's is one of the most popular
rs. It has about seven different bars in the entire building, with an up and
wnstairs. There are also two outdoor decks, which are really nice when it's
rm! Chicken Bones is another good bar to go to if you're 21 and over. It
ently expanded, so it's one of the newer places. There are always specials
ing on at the bars. Every night, some bar is offering a special. Which bar to
to on what night becomes pretty obvious! There's a big variety of restaurants
the area, with some that are privately owned and some that are national chains.

ting is not a problem! With such an extensive nightlife, it's impossible to go
t and not meet people. But, if you don't like going out, then there is a web site
lled mountaineersingles.com, which is a place where you can meet other stu-
nts. Also, for people who don't like the bar scene, a program called Up-All-
ght is offered on Friday and Saturday nights in the Mountainlair. They have
kinds of free food, games and activities offered. There is something different
ery weekend. Some of the things they've had before include virtual simula-
s, caricature artists, photo booths, laser tag, laser bowling, comedians, movies
cluding Float 'n' Flick, where you go to the pool and watch a movie on a huge
een while relaxing in the pool or hot tub), and game shows like *Mountaineer
l* (operated like *American Idol*) where you can win cash and other nice prizes.
is goes on every weekend and is completely free to students and one guest.
VU also does fall fest at the beginning of the fall semester and spring fest at
e beginning of the spring semester. It's a huge concert with several well-
own artists. Some people who have come in the past were X-zibit, Kanye
est and Wyclef, just to mention a few.

Current student, 8/2000-Submit Date, March 2004

There are a few good bars and clubs to go to. Morgantown is small but very
social, and there is a bar for everyone. Some of the bars are: Bent Willies,
Chicken Bones, Elements, The Alley, Vice Versa, Mario's Fish Bowl, The Press
Box, Crockets and Keglers. WVU has a number of frats for guys and gals.
Alpha Phi Omega is one of the volunteer frats. The dating scene is slim pickins,
but there are some hotties running around. There are a number of restaurants to
pick from and a lot of fast food, too.

The School Says

West Virginia University combines the hands-on, personal attention of a small school with the countless opportunities of a
major public institution.

Offering 179 degree programs, WVU's student-centered philosophy ensures that its graduates are prepared for personal and
professional success. Outstanding, caring faculty, excellent
academic programs, and innovative new facilities (including a
new library) all make a WVU education the affordable investment of a lifetime.

Our tradition of academic achievement includes 25 Rhodes
Scholars, 30 Goldwater Scholars, and 18 Truman Scholars. A
cutting-edge general education curriculum and $150 million in
annual research funding ensure that hundreds of Fortune 500
companies recruit on the campus of this Carnegie Research
University (High Research Activity) school.

Building a strong community of young scholars is a top priority
at WVU. A student-centered first-year experience allows faculty to live side-by-side with students, serving as teachers and
mentors. WVU All Night, an award-winning program, provides
free food, fun, and socializing on weekends.

The Mountaineer Parents Club connects 17,000 families. More
than 300 student organizations and a new state-of-the-art
Recreation Center (with a 50-foot indoor climbing wall) create
shared interests that help our students grow academically and
socially.

Students from all 50 states (and DC) and nearly 100 countries
create an environment in which diversity thrives. WVU is located 70 miles south of Pittsburgh, PA, in Morgantown, WV, a
safe community ranked as the Number One Small City in
America, and the Best Small City in the East. A vibrant downtown and miles of scenic trails are close to campus, and opportunities for hiking, skiing, rock climbing, whitewater rafting and
mountain biking are nearby.

There is no other college or university in the state that matches
the breadth, depth, or mission of WVU. In fact, institutions
from all over the country visit us to replicate our award-winning
programs. I urge you to give yourself the best possible future,
and start on your path to greatness with us.

Read all of Vault's College Surveys at **www.vault.com/college**—get complete surveys on 100s of colleges and universities, expert advice on applicaton essays and more.

VAULT CAREER LIBRARY   779

Beloit College

Office of Admissions/Office of Financial Aid
700 College Street
Beloit, WI 53511
Admissions phone: (800) 9-BELOIT (923-5648)
Admissions fax: (608) 363-2075
Admissions e-mail: admiss@beloit.edu
Admissions URL: www.beloit.edu/~admiss/

Note: The school has chosen not to comment on the student surveys submitted.

 Admissions

Alumnus/a, 8/2001-5/2005, March 2006

Admissions is increasingly selective, but great grades alone won't get you in. That said, mediocre grades could still get you admitted if you demonstrate intellectual interest, creativity or other activity.

Don't be afraid to talk to the admissions counselors personally and often. Showing informed interest in Beloit will help a lot on your application. They actually decline offers of admission to people who are good students but whom they don't think will like Beloit. Make sure you get all the information you can from current students (you can chat with them online), alumni (you can meet them in your area) and the admissions officers. Getting into Beloit doesn't require "beating out" other students; it requires showing that you have the interest and abilities to thrive at Beloit—this is measured by many things, including grades, test scores, recommendations and essays, but also less tangible things, like your interests and enthusiasm.

Alumnus/a, 8/2000-5/2004, October 2004

The greatest advice I can give to any Beloit College prospective student is be yourself. Beloit College thrives on this most basic principle. Indeed, while Beloit College can be very selective in its choice of its students based on the variety of its student body, if you can demonstrate that you are willing to reinvent yourself, during the admissions process, your chances if getting in are great.

Alumnus/a, 8/1993-5/1997, September 2003

In order to be admitted in 1993 when I applied, you had to fill out an application and write an essay, as well as provide either ACT or SAT scores. Beloit College seemed to be looking for students who were individuals, not the typical well-rounded student whom high school counselors often touted. I think at that time, Beloit was considered "very selective" but given the various terms, I am not sure what that meant. Beloit was moderately selective, i.e., not everyone was going to get in, but at the same time Beloit took a chance on a lot of interesting students who may not have been accepted at comparable liberal arts schools.

There were lots of admissions events, including a weekend for high school students to come and stay on campus and meet students and attend classes. I would highly recommend attending such an event because it settled for me that I wanted to attend Beloit College. I do not recall that I had an interview with anyone, but I did start my trip at the admissions office and met with someone, I believe.

 **Academics**

Alumnus/a, 8/2001-5/2005, March 2006

The quality of academics you'll experience at Beloit depends on how much you are willing to put into your classes and other academic experiences. If you just want to squeak by, you'll be able to find classes where you can do little and get mediocre grades. However, if you are intellectually curious, you'll find the academic environment to be demanding, invigorating and fascinating. Professors are highly available to talk to you about your coursework, their research, current events, career guidance or whatever else. Research programs are in place those students who most want to pursue certain areas. Plenty of other students are also engaged in classes, other campus lectures and current events, providing you with eager classmates for lively discussions inside and outside the classroom. There are those at Beloit who choose to leave the learning at the classroom door, but there many others who continue the class discussions far beyond the classroom and continue to engage with the ideas and each other in other social and studious settings.

In terms of nontraditional academics, Beloit has strong study abroad program opportunities and several on-campus programs that stand out, such as CELEB, a center for entrepreneurship where students can run their own businesses, and Gallery Abba, a student-run art gallery. Programs such as The Duffy Community Partnerships assign students to an internship with a community group and has weekly seminars to discuss students' experiences and reflect topics of social change and social policy.

Alumnus/a, 8/2000-5/2004, October 2004

The Beloit College student thrives on selecting classes from all disciplines before he/she graduates. Indeed, while you might eventually pick a major your sophomore year, you are still allowed time to decide on that right through your senior year. The classes are small, which is always a plus and there is great emphasis on writing. Be prepared for that. The professors are generally tough but fair with respect to their grading. As for the workload, be prepared a long four years.

Alumnus/a, Literary Studies, 8/1993-5/1997, September 2003

Beloit College is a liberal arts school. There was a requirement of taking two classes in each discipline, I believe, but other than that, students were encouraged to take whatever classes were of interest to them. My last year at Beloit College, there was even some sort of interdisciplinary major created where students who had not concentrated in one area could still have a major and graduate.

I can only really speak about the quality of the classes and professors in the English department since I majored in Literary Studies. The English department is filled with extraordinary professors who love teaching the classes that they teach and are available for students who want to discuss anything after or before class. Additionally, the classes offered ranged from the traditional British Literature to the not so traditional Cross-Dressed Gender Bending where we read Peter Pan and Myra Breckenridge and Orlando to look at gender in literature. Although it was possible to get closed out of certain classes, for example Expository Writing, which every student wanted to take, most professors would allow you into the class if there was any way to arrange it.

I never had any issues with the way things were graded, except in the Education department at Beloit College where it appeared as though in order to get a good grade, students were required to regurgitate a particular professor's stance of what constituted a good education. The workload was always reasonable every class that I took, and professors were always available to discuss assignments and offer help if needed.

 Employment Prospects

Alumnus/a, 8/2001-5/2005, March 2006

If you are dead-set on getting a high-powered investment banking job after graduation, Beloit College is not the place for you. If, however, you are interested developing your analytical and critical thinking skills such that you are capable of continuing to learn on and off the job as your career develops, Beloit is the place to be. The skills set you will develop at this liberal arts college will prepare you for future jobs in many fields.

alumni network is strong and full of interesting, capable people willing to
 and advise recent graduates. I am currently working at a well-paying, intel-
ually-interesting job at a consulting firm—a job that I heard about from a
nt alumnus.

mnus/a, 8/2000-5/2004, October 2004

ere is no question about it, employers love Beloit College students primarily
ause of our strong liberal arts background. There is also a continuous alum-
network that is always willing to help you fit into the real world easier and as
 on-campus recruiting and internships, there are tons of them so you will get
ed of them. If you are focused and know what you want, this will not be a
blem. And as for jobs graduates obtain, it is remarkable the kind of things
oit College graduates do, from engineering to law. We do it all.

mnus/a, 8/1993-5/1997, September 2003

 Career Services Office was small with a pretty small library of career
urces, but students had the opportunity to speak with counselors in the office
rding careers and to the director of career services, as well as use computer
grams to determine what sort of careers matched their interests and skills. I
not recall whether there was a whole lot of campus recruiting, other than by
 Peace Corps, but they did have a fair every year where alumni would come
k and discuss where they were working and answer questions.

Quality of Life

mnus/a, 8/2001-5/2005, March 2006

oit, Wisconsin is not a teeming metropolis, so if you are looking for big city
, keep looking. The Beloit College campus is vibrant, tight-knit and a lot of
, in part because of the lack of an [off-campus] city life that draws away stu-
ts. There are some interesting things going on in downtown Beloit, such as
Arts Incubator and widespread river front/urban planning. In the town and
rounding areas are abundant examples of Midwest quirkiness, if you ever feel
 need to get off campus.

oit is filled with interesting things to some but seems dull to others. Make
e you visit and like what you see. If bowling alleys, farm fields, small Swiss
ns with breweries and cheese, great thrift stores and ex-industrial architec-
e don't appeal to you, make sure you like the campus a lot or consider look-
 elsewhere.

mnus/a, 8/2000-5/2004,October 2004

y on campus. Because Beloit College is really the only attraction the City of
oit has, there is no point in living off campus. Housing, dining and all the
 will cost one approximately $2,500 a semester, but I will say it is worth it.
re is really nothing much to say about the neighborhood, but there are cheap-
houses close to the college that you can live in and you don't have to worry
ut your safety. I have never encountered any crimes in all my years there. It
efinitely a safe place to go to college.

mnus/a, 8/1993-5/1997, September 2003

 years at Beloit College were the best of my life. There was always some-
g going on on campus, whether it was a movie in Wilson Theatre or a band
he C-Haus or a singer brought by the Cafe Series. There was never a week-
 where my friends and I did not have numerous entertainment options above
 beyond the various Greek houseparties.

campus was extremely safe no matter the time, and I never had an issue off
npus either, but would recommend not wandering around by oneself late at
ht.

 on-campus housing was fine, and there were always renovations being done
 the residence halls and the other buildings. Commons (the cafeteria) and
's were the food service facilities on campus and both were adequate but
hing special. However, there were a number of dining options both within
king distance and in the surrounding areas.

Social Life

Alumnus/a, 8/2001-5/2005, March 2006

As a whole, people at Beloit work hard and play hard. There is a vast spectrum
of social activities at Beloit and it's really quite acceptable to participate in any
of them.

There are lots of school-funded events, and you can get your events funded at
the student government meetings. Besides formal events, such as concert series,
film series and campus parties, there are also hosts of informal and spontaneous
events that can be just a blast. People get really creative.

We have a limited Greek life. If you join, fine; if you don't, fine. Those who
are in it enjoy it, but if you aren't Greek, you won't feel like you're missing out
on anything.

The alcohol philosophy is liberal. The school administration and security expect
that you will behave responsibly, and allow you to make your own decisions.
Basically, what that means is that you can drink almost anywhere on campus
without having to hide it, whether you are 21 or not, as long as you are responsible about it. That means no drinking games, but it also means not having to
chug hard liquor behind closed doors before you go to a party. You can just bring
your drinks to the party. It means people look out for each other and aren't afraid
to call security for help if someone's in bad shape. You aren't allowed to supply
alcohol at parties, so no kegs or "jungle juice," which means the likelihood of
getting drugged is lower (I've never heard of it happening at Beloit), and freshman girls don't get liquored up at strange parties by strange older guys, as happens at some schools.

Drinking is not a big deal at Beloit precisely because it is not forbidden. People
drink to have a good time, but it is a secondary, not primary focus to social activities. If you don't drink at all, that is also fine. Plenty of people don't, and it
doesn't necessarily put a damper on their social life. There are a couple bars in
town that people go to, but campus doesn't empty out by any means, because
people often stay on campus to drink and socialize. There is also a campus bar
that serves to those 21 and older.

If you are looking for a big clubbing scene, Beloit is not the place to be. But if
you like having good times on campus with creative people, this is the place to
be. Beloit is just an all-around fun place to be with people who are fun to be
around.

Alumnus/a, 8/2000-5/2004, October 2004

There is an relentless efforts by the residential life program in Beloit to make
your stay there eventful. From about 60 clubs that you can join to extracurricular activities like soccer, basketball, tennis, you are guaranteed that you will not
be bored. The bar scene does not really apply to the students until you reach 21
and by then you are leaving college. However, the Greek system on campus
lightens up campus life with their parties on Fridays or Saturdays. As for dating, most students date other students on campus.

Alumnus/a, 8/1993-5/1997, September 2003

Clubs were available for any interest whatsoever, and if there wasn't a club on
campus it was moderately easy for students to get a club created or an intramural sport. For example, lacrosse wasn't a sport on campus until some guys got
together and decided that they were interested in starting a lacrosse team.

Additionally, there were so many activities to become involved in on campus.
On the weekend, many different clubs were always sponsoring activities, and the
on-campus bar had a band scheduled to play. In addition to the on-campus
events, there were numerous bars in Beloit within walking distance.

Read all of Vault's College Surveys at **www.vault.com/college**—get complete surveys on 100s of colleges and universities, expert advice on applicaton essays and more.

VAULT CAREER LIBRARY   781

Marquette University

Admissions Office
P.O. Box 1881
Milwaukee, WI 53201-1881
Admissions phone: (800) 222-6544 or (414) 288-7302
Admissions fax: (414) 288-3764
Admissions URL: www.marquette.edu/student/

 ## Admissions

Alumnus/a, Engineering, 1/2003-12/2006, May 2007

The admissions staff is amazing and very personable. They are willing to help in any way that they can. The application was pretty standard, nothing too different from other schools of the same caliber. Since 2003 when we went to the Final Four, Marquette's selectivity has been increasing, making it harder to get in now.

Current student, 8/2003-Submit Date, November 2005

Getting into Marquette is honestly quite easy. My experience was different as I applied as a transfer student to this school. Being that transfer student applications are looked at separately than undergrads, I can't necessarily speak for general applicants, but to my knowledge as long as your high school GPA is decent and you didn't bomb your ACT/SAT, you'll have no problem getting in. The school claims to be getting more selective. Mention that you are Catholic and are attracted to the Jesuit identity if you want some extra bonus points. High school community service is also a plus.

Alumnus/a, 8/1998-5/2002, November 2004

Marquette congratulated me on my 200+ community service hours completed in high school. As a Jesuit institution, Marquette focuses on being a person for others. Students are encouraged to give back to the community in any way possible. As a student with community service in my background, I fulfilled one characteristic of the school's ideal candidates. In addition to the community service, I completed many honors and AP courses in high school. I earned a GPA above 3.6, while working between 10 and 20 hours a week. Participation in several school sports and organization contributed to the well-rounded image for which Marquette looks. These were all summarized in the application essay, which was only one of three factors that shaped the admissions process at Marquette. The second factor contributing to the admissions process was shaking hands with the university's West Coast representative. Once I became interested in the university, I planned a trip. The undergraduate programs fulfilled all my expectations. With solid grades while balancing the requirements of maintaining a part-time job, participating in school organizations and participating in community outreach programs, Marquette recognized my qualifications as matching candidacy requirements. Marquette granted me admission and complemented the acceptance with a scholarship.

Alumnus/a, 8/2000-5/2004, February 2005

I had an easy application with few essays and no interviews since I met several preliminary requirements with grades and alumni parents. There were several essay options for qualifying for additional scholarships.

Alumnus/a, 8/1997-12/2001, February 2004

Admissions really was no big deal. If you have a good GPA and a good ACT/SAT you should be fine. For those who are on the border, MU provides a Freshman Frontier Program during the summer. From what I hear, it is a great way to meet people and get a feel for a college class or two, and after completing the program you gain admittance into Marquette.

I also thought that MU was very thorough during their application process and provided many scholarships for various things. Many of my friends had scholarships, which definitely helped with the high tuition. I received one for leadership, having attended a military academy prior to MU.

Alumnus/a, 5/1997-5/2000, November 2003

The admissions process was not overly rigorous. Pretty good ACT, SAT GPA will get you admitted to the university. An essay with a theme related community service is what the university looks for as well, considering it Jesuit institution that emphasizes social activism. It may be more difficult, he ever, to be accepted to the college of your choice. The more difficult undergraduate programs are business, nursing and engineering. Communications, and sciences are not as challenging, and this can become apparent when you applying for high-paying jobs.

Alumnus/a, 8/1995-12/1999, November 2003

Marquette is selective, but being a private Jesuit school, it looks subjectively each candidate's record and not just at test scores. Demonstrated academ growth throughout high school will be noticed. Write a good admissions ess

 ## Academics

Current student, 8/2003-Submit Date, November 2005

I am currently enrolled in the college of communications as a pub relations/broadcasting student. The broadcasting department is very good, nationally recognized. There are many internship/professional opportuni available as well as an on-campus television station that is very active. As the public relations aspect, no matter what school you'll go to—it'll be ess tially the same thing. A couple of good professors with a few lousy ones. and all, I felt that Marquette was challenging enough for my tastes, and I have heard too many people complaining that classes are overly easy. Just watch for the theology and philosophy courses as Marquette really tries students those.

Alumnus/a, Engineering, 1/2003-12/2006, May 2007

As an engineering student I found most of the coursework very relevant to major. Almost every professor I had was willing to (and encouraged) meet outside of class if necessary in order to clarify or help students with the inf mation. Class registration is based on randomly-assigned sign-up dates/tim but if you really need or want a certain class, I've never had a professor c department that didn't let me into a full class. The workload is definitely tou if you're in engineering, but manageable.

Alumnus/a, 8/1998-5/2002, November 2004

I originally signed up for a double major in business and political philosop Both colleges focused on class sizes between 20 and 40 students, allow everyone a chance to know the professor and participate in classroom disc sions. Because of the school size you could get your classes each semester. grading was a bit stringent and the workload between 10 to 20 hours a week class.

Alumnus/a, 8/2000-5/2004, February 2005

Most upper-division courses are tough, but for the most part, worthwhile. Ev semester you are randomly assigned a registration date, so classes are easy to into if you get an early date. However, many profs will let you into their classes if you actually meet with them and ask.

Alumnus/a, 5/1997-5/2000, November 2003

Being accepted to quality classes is not very difficult. This is based on the l tery of registration times and it usually is not that difficult. At Marquette greater strategy is learning the names of the best professors and registering their specific classes.

Within the business school the professors are pretty good. They are knowledg able in their respective fields, but be aware Marquette is not a research insti tion. The teachers are paid to teach, not to publish articles. This makes the generally available for questions during office hours for people to ask questio They definitely are academic individuals who develop personalities.

most of the business school classes, the grading is usually determined by a
[num]ber of papers, projects, tests and quizzes versus one or two exams a semes-
[...]. This enables students to take more control of their final grades. This can
[ad]d to the workload, however. It seems that every week, students have multiple
[me]asures of knowledge. If a student decides to relax for a week and not open
[the] books, it will show.

[cl]asses are small. After freshman year I had very few lecture classes. You begin
[to] feel that you know your classmates and professors, and they will know if you
[do]n't show up for class as well. Attendance can be taken formally or informal-

[Al]umnus/a, 8/1997-12/2001, February 2004

[M]U is academically challenging. You will have to put in your time here, but
[re]member this is a great party school too, so the key is balancing both. MU has
[str]ong engineering, business and health science classes and many renowned arts
[an]d sciences professors. I really enjoyed the classes I took here. They were not
[on]ly challenging, but also very rewarding. There are the so-called popular or
[ea]sy classes, but these are usually pretty hard to get into. Grading is fair, but
[so]metimes it is very hard to get an A rather than an a B. You really have to work
[fo]r that A. Workload was pretty much normal, I guess. Usually it consisted of
[a fe]w small projects, lots of reading, midterm, paper and a final.

[Al]umnus/a, 8/1995-12/1999, November 2003

[M]arquette is a quality education. Most of the professors teach the classes; there
[wa]s only one class where I had the TA as the instructor. The focus of most of
[m]y professors was teaching the concept and critical thinking rather than just the
[ru]le or fact. Most professors care about their students and are accessible outside
[of] class. Grading is competitive, especially in the higher-level classes. Many
[stu]dents come from private high schools and ranked high in their graduating
[cla]ss.

Employment Prospects

[Cu]rrent student, 8/2003-Submit Date, November 2005

[I k]now Marquette has a very strong reputation in Milwaukee and Wisconsin. If
[yo]u are from the Midwest and are looking for a job in business, Marquette would
[be] good. There are several major corporations in Milwaukee that are affiliated
[wi]th MU. The school also utilizes alumni in mentorship programs across the
[na]tion.

[A]lumnus/a, 8/1998-5/2002, November 2004

[Em]ployment prospects center their efforts within the local Milwaukee commu-
[nit]y and distant, Chicago. The school's prestige become less know the farther
[yo]u travel, unless people are aware of college basketball. The excellent Les
[As]pin Center for Government program offered by Marquette in the heart of
[W]ashington, D.C. is the best facilitating program for jobs on Capitol Hill.

> **The school says:** "Marquette's Les Aspin Center for
> Government in Washington, D.C., is a nationally recognized
> educational program that offers students an opportunity to live,
> learn and work for a semester in the heart of our nation's capi-
> tal. Offering one of the premier Congressional internship pro-
> grams, the center helps students learn how government works
> through specialized courses in public policy, foreign policy and
> interest group politics. Students work as interns in Congress,
> the Department of State, Secret Service and other government
> agencies."

[A]lumnus/a, 8/1997-12/2001, February 2004

[M]arquette has a lot of connections all over, but particularly in the Midwest. The
[na]me carries a lot of weight, and I had no trouble finding jobs after graduation.
[Th]ey have dozens of internship opportunities, including the Les Aspin Program,
[a] program in which you live, work and take classes on Capitol Hill in
[W]ashington, all through MU. It's a blast, and I highly recommend it. It's also
[op]en to all majors, not just poli sci. Biomed engineers go and work at the FDA
[in]stead. There is a lot of opportunity if you look for it.

Alumnus/a, 8/2000-5/2004, February 2005

There are several resources for employment, both during and after college. The
Career Services Center is very helpful and will work with you to put together a
good résumé and practice interviews. There are many alumni connections to
prestigious employers.

> **Marquette says:** "The Marquette University Career Services
> Center strives to assist all students and alumni in discerning,
> developing and pursuing meaningful traditional and nontradi-
> tional career paths. This is achieved through teaching students
> and alumni to develop lifelong job search skills and use online
> and traditional career resources and developing positive rela-
> tionships with employers resulting in student and employer con-
> nections."

Alumnus/a, 8/1995-12/1999, November 2003

For those in downtown Milwaukee, internship and job opportunities are plentiful. To the local community, Marquette is known as a prestigious school, but it
gets less well known the farther away one goes. Many companies recruit on
campus; the school has a strong job placement program.

Alumnus/a, 5/1997-5/2000, November 2003

The more difficult undergraduate programs are business, nursing and engineering. These students will have opportunities to obtain work experience in internships. This can be essential for finding the job after school. For this reason,
many undergraduates work in downtown Milwaukee during their junior or senior year to line up jobs.

Quality of Life

Current student, 8/2003-Submit Date, November 2005

Let's face facts—Milwaukee isn't the prettiest of cities and Marquette is in a
pretty sketchy neighborhood. However, over my three years at the school, the
campus has improved vastly as has the neighborhood. My guess is that within
five years, the campus and surrounding area will have been completely re-done
and modernized. Housing is moderately expensive (as it is close to downtown)
but there is never a shortage of housing. Parking will be your big problem as the
City of Milwaukee is very strict with on-street parking. Safety is always a concern; however, MU does a very good job protecting its students and providing
free rides wherever a student wants to go.

Alumnus/a, 8/1998-5/2002, November 2004

The campus housing is affordable and good for a college student. The gym facilities are great! The neighborhood is surrounded by the impoverished areas of
Milwaukee; however, campus police make the area relatively safe.

Alumnus/a, 8/2000-5/2004, February 2005

The popular freshman dorm has very tiny rooms and is loud. Because it is a city
campus, students must check all guests in at a guarded entrance. I always felt
safe in the dorms even though it was a pain sometimes to always scan in and
have friends from other schools or even other dorms over.

Alumnus/a, 8/1997-12/2001, February 2004

MU is beautiful. The campus is great. Although you are in downtown
Milwaukee, when you are in the classroom area, you really cannot tell. It has a
lot of character, and it's only getting better with all the new additions in the past
couple of years.

Housing requirements are that you live in the dorms for at least two years, and
then you can seek off-campus housing. Dorms are fine, depending on which
ones you get into. Off-campus housing is abundant and cheap! The neighborhood is OK. It borders some bad parts, but MU provides a shuttle service anywhere on campus, and there are always public safety services. Never had a problem.

When you are in the dorm, you think the food is horrible. However, in hindsight
it's really not that bad. Especially when you no longer live in the dorms and are
starving! It sounds pretty good then.

Read all of Vault's College Surveys at **www.vault.com/college**—get complete surveys on 100s of colleges and universities, expert advice on applicaton essays and more.

VAULT CAREER LIBRARY **783**

Alumnus/a, 8/1995-12/1999, November 2003

Marquette is an urban campus, located in the inner city of Milwaukee. If you do not like city life, even a smaller city like Milwaukee, then Marquette is not for you. The campus has a strong public safety program and plenty of awareness events; still, incidents do happen. Its location gives way to plenty of opportunity for volunteering and service learning, which Marquette is big on.

The dorms are typical, and so is the food. The RAs are very involved with their floor-mates, and there are social events on campus throughout the year. Recently there has been a crackdown on drinking in the dorms. I would say the quality of life is pretty good. Being Jesuit creates a warm, community feel on campus, even for those who are not Catholic (like myself).

Alumnus/a, 5/1997-5/2000, November 2003

The quality of life is mixed. The campus is in the inner city of Milwaukee, but there are some beautiful parts of campus. Some of the student dorms and campus housing is very good, but some is bleak. Interested students should do what they can to be placed in preferred housing. If you want to save money, you can find very cheap housing in less desirable neighborhoods, but I wouldn't recommend it for women. Every year there is an incident, but it usually (not always) involves careless students. There is student transportation, university-employed students on public safety foot-patrol, and public safety in police-type cars.

Social Life

Current student, 8/2003-Submit Date, November 2005

MU is no Big 10 school; but there are still plenty of parties on campus. In addition, because of its close proximity to downtown, there is always something to do at a relatively cheap price. There are only three campus bars and few restaurants, but as I said, everything downtown is within walking distance.

Alumnus/a, 8/1998-5/2002, November 2004

The social life is restricted within the small confines of downtown Milwaukee. However, students often travel to Chicago on the weekends, where there is everything under the sun! A small Greek systems exists.

Alumnus/a, 8/1997-12/2001, February 2004

Social life is awesome! I guarantee you will have a blast at this school. Tons of bars in Milwaukee, great campus parties, small but solid Greek life. Truly a blast, no matter if you join an organization or just roam the streets looking for a good party!

Alumnus/a, 8/1995-12/1999, November 2003

The Greek system is not big at Marquette, and therefore there is no separation between Greeks and non-Greeks. The social scene is active with plenty to do, both on campus and off. Bars and restaurants are within walking distance of campus, and some bars are quite strict about being of age. Murphy's is a popular hangout. Frequent social events and activities make it easy to meet people and to get involved in campus life. I'd say 60 percent of the student body is Catholic. Mass is popular, but not required. Many Marquette grads marry soon after graduation and stay in the Milwaukee/Green Bay/Chicago area.

Alumnus/a, 5/1997-5/2000, November 2003

The social life is very mixed. I think there is almost something for everyo Most students drink on the weekends. However, in recent years the student bo has been much more health conscious.

The usual establishments are bars near campus and certain favorites in dov town Milwaukee. Nightclubs are attended less frequently, because the stud body is very casual.

Dating happens, but not too much. There is more hanging out-type dating. Greek system exists, but it is not the in-crowd.

The all-school dance in January, Winter-Flurry, is a drunken affair that is v fun, especially for undergraduates. When the basketball team is playing well overshadows everything. March Madness will engulf the school.

If you don't drink and like to get involved in campus activities outside the b there are many opportunities: plays, movies, sporting events, philanthropy more. Many students graduate in four years without ever being a regular at the b

The School Says

Founded in 1881, Marquette University delivers nationally recognized programs for more than 11,000 undergraduate and graduate students in the Catholic, Jesuit tradition. *U.S. News & World Report* places Marquette among the nation's Top 100 colleges, and *Kiplinger's Personal Finance* magazine lists Marquette 38th among private universities that offer the best values. Students from more than 80 countries and all 50 states seek this education that challenges their abilities and encourages a deepening of faith. Located in Milwaukee, students connect with the city through transformational service-learning programs and outstanding internships. With a mission that fosters excellence, faith, leadership and service, Marquette students are challenged to use what they learn to make the world a better place.

The University Core of Common Studies is the foundation of each student's undergraduate educational experience. The 36-hour core includes courses in nine areas—Rhetoric, Mathematical Reasoning, Individual and Social Behavior, Diverse Culture, Literature/Performing Arts, Histories of Cultures and Societies, Science and Nature, Human Nature and Ethics, and Theology. Marquette offers more than 100 majors. With a student-to-faculty ratio of 15:1, students get plenty of individual attention. Nearly 250 student organizations provide students with an opportunity to explore their interests and gain leadership skills outside the classroom.

Marquette University is a place where you will find not just what you want to do, but who you want to become; where you will learn how to think, not what to think; where you will be prepared not only for your first job, but for the rest of your life; where you will learn to be a leader in your profession and your community; where you will realize you can make the world a better place.

University of Wisconsin—Madison

W—Madison
Office of Admissions
Armory and Gymnasium
16 Langdon Street
Madison, WI 53706-1481
Admissions phone: (608) 262-3961
Admissions e-mail: onwisconsin@admissions.wisc.edu
Admissions URL: www.admissions.wisc.edu/

Admissions

Current student, 9/2004-Submit Date, June 2006

apply, I first had my ACT scores sent directly to the university. Like most Midwestern colleges, the UW prefers the ACT. Once I did that, I went to the UW web site and applied for admissions online; it is a very simple process and not too time consuming. And, best of all, it is free. The majority of the application is information that is easily available, such as address and GPA. There is essay portion, which may vary as to what the question is, but when I applied, simply asked why I felt I would be a good addition to the university. It is not very long essay, however I did have my high school English teacher look it over. This is not a bad idea, as this is the primary way in which they differentiate students based on anything other than grades and test scores. What you can if you don't get in is go through an appeals process, which first requires other essay, and if taken as far is it can go, requires a hearing with the admissions board, I believe. Try to make yourself stand out in your essay, this is the most important thing to do!

> **The school says:** "We accept both the SAT and the ACT and do not prefer one over the other. Regarding the application fee, there is a $35 nonrefundable application fee that is applied to both print and online applications. As far as an admission decision appeal, students can appeal a decision by submitting a letter explaining the grounds for the appeal. That appeal is considered by our admissions committee and the student is notified of the final decision. An appeals hearing is not part of the process."

Current student, 8/2004-Submit Date, October 2004

worked very hard throughout high school, especially in my early years, in order be able to attend the college of my choice. I applied and within one or two months, I was accepted. I think one very important factor in my admission to the university was my early application. Although I did apply very early, I didn't write an essay or send a letter of recommendation. I believe that UW-Madison does a great job of selecting a wide range of students from different ethnic and social backgrounds. Extracurricular activities are very important to UW because they want to be sure and get the most well-rounded individuals to attend the college. I think the admissions process at UW is great, but it could be improved just a little bit.

Alumnus/a, 8/2001-5/2003, March 2005

Admission to UW—Madison has become increasingly harder over the past few years. I was initially put on the waiting list with a 3.6 GPA and a 26 on my ACT. That was four years ago, and I don't think you would get in with that today. I think GPA and ACT/SAT scores are the most important. Letters of recommendation, a good essay and lots of community involvement will help.

> **The school says:** "Our admission counselors review each application individually and are looking for students who demonstrate strong academic ability, as well as leadership, community service, creativity, talent and enthusiasm. We also consider personal characteristics that will contribute to the strength and diversity of our university."

Current student, 9/2001-Submit Date, May 2004

I found that the university looks at class rank a lot. I also can say that the essay portion of the application is important, because the university reads those when they have to decide which students should be admitted when they are at the same level of academics. I think that volunteering is a necessity, but it should apply to some special interest or field in which you would like to be. I also can say that the University of Wisconsin—Madison is very up to date. You may call a number to check on the status of your application. If you are put on a waiting list, they will inform you on what is going on and how long you can expect to wait. All of this information is given in the letter that is mailed to you. This letter states that they have received your application and provides answers to the questions may have. Their selectivity is somewhat difficult. So my advice would be to concentrate on those focus areas and form your identity. However, be versatile and universal in your interests.

> **The school says:** "Our online Application Status Check web site allows students to follow their application through our review process. Features include a checklist of application items received and yet required, as well as the ability to view the admission decision when available."

Current student, 8/2003-Submit Date, March 2004

The process of getting accepted to Madison was fairly simple to complete. All there was to do was fill out the standard state application and send a copy of my high school transcripts into the school for review. There were no essays involved in the process or interviews. It is also nice to have lots of extracurriculars on your application. Selectivity to get into Madison is not extreme, but it is very selective. Last year, many valedictorians of their classes who applied here did not receive acceptance to the university.

> **The school says:** "While a personal statement and/or recommendations are not required, they are highly recommended and very important components of a competitive application for admission. Academic preparation and success are the primary considerations for admission, but there is not a minimum GPA, test score, or class rank above which admission is guaranteed."

Current student, 9/2003-Submit Date, November 2003

The University of Wisconsin used to be a slam dunk for most aspiring high school grads, but now that's not the case. Particularly from high performing schools in Minnesota and the Chicago area, the requirements for entrance have increased drastically. However, if you are in state, while it has become much more difficult to get in, it's not bad.

Academics

Alumnus/a, Business, 8/1999-5/2003, March 2007

Finance and Real Estate program, some classes were difficult to get into, but generally speaking availability was excellent and scheduling was convenient. Professors were generally very good, although I felt they could have been more involved in the business student organizations and more available as advisers/mentors. Workload and grading were reasonable and what one would expect from a top quality university

Current student, 9/2004-Submit Date, June 2006

The university is a topnotch university, and the professors often display this. However, like all universities, many entry-level classes are taught primarily through TAs often of varying experience, and often your grade relies on them. Nevertheless, I have never had much trouble with this. Getting into entry-level courses is simple, as there are hundreds of open spots. In gateway classes like psychology, the grading is often done on a bell curve to weed out students who are going for business or other psych related fields, and therefore are harder to get a good grade. Most classes, however, are graded on simple point systems

Read all of Vault's College Surveys at **www.vault.com/college**—get complete surveys on 100s of colleges and universities, expert advice on application essays and more.

VAULT CAREER LIBRARY 785

and if one does the work, which is admittedly heavy in science and math courses, one should get a decent grade.

Current student, 9/2001-Submit Date, September 2005

The academic process is fairly standard. The school is Big 10, which means that the funding is high and so is tuition. In my school (there are seven separate schools), the students are the cream of the crop, and competition to be the best in any particular class is always underlying. Grades are primarily test based but a full third of the grade is reliant on the papers and various presentations. Usually 20 percent of the overall grade is from in-class participation. Attendance is rarely taken. Most instructors have at least one doctoral degree. The workload can be heavy at first, but as one progresses through the program, the assignments become more real-world oriented and seem to flow easily enough.

> **The school says:** "We have nine undergraduate schools and colleges offering 160 majors among them."

Current student, 8/2004-Submit Date, October 2004

The academic reputation of UW—Madison is very good for a public school, one of the best in the nation at that. Class sizes vary from 15 to 300. It is a very large university with about 41,000 total students, which means there are always tons of new people to meet. The professors here are super friendly and always willing to meet your needs to better your education.

Workload obviously depends on the quantity and quality of classes you're taking, but for the most part, the workload here is just right. The professors know that there is so much to do around campus and that most students are very involved, so they don't give you an overwhelming amount. Grading is great here because the professors give out occasional homework assignments, which if you do a good job on, will raise your grades. Sometimes it is difficult to get the exact classes you want because there are so many students, but UW offers such a great variety of classes that there is always an interesting class you'll be able to take instead.

Alumnus/a, 8/2001-5/2003, March 2005

UW—Madison has a prestige to hold, so this oftentimes doesn't help students. Lots of the freshman classes are weed-out classes designed to only let the best of the best move on. Lots are graded on a bell curve, so no matter how well the class did, only a certain percentage can get an A. It is very tough to get into classes you want when you are an undergraduate.

Grading is done on an A, AB, B, BC and so on scale. Most large classes have a professor who lectures, then you have a discussion with a TA. These TAs either make or break your grade and experience in the class. These are usually upperclassmen or graduate students in the program. Some are great and help you a lot, and some are [not as good].

Current student, 9/2001-Submit Date, May 2004

The beginning classes are in large lecture halls, and these classes are mostly requirements. Once you get through the survey classes, it seems to be easier to focus and obtain stronger grades. The programs are somewhat difficult to get in depending on the interest. Most advisors will tell you if you have an honest shot of getting in. Many classes, especially the lecture halls of 500 to 600 people, grade on a bell curve. This curve can make it difficult to get an A in the class and is very competitive.

As you get to be in smaller classes, your input, no matter how big it may be, is looked upon and will reflect your grade of the course. Professors' main means of communication are Internet and talks after class. You are going to have to be the facilitator and not them. This may make your workload more because of all the individual office hours or appointments that you may attend to talk to your professors.

> **UW—Madison says:** "The average undergraduate class size is 29 students. 10 percent of classes have more than 100 students and 10 percent of classes have fewer than 10 students. When students are enrolled in the larger lecture classes, they almost always will be in a smaller discussion section that will consist of 15 to 20 students."

 Employment Prospects

Alumnus/a, Business, 8/1999-5/2003, March 2007

Many prospects, even in a down market. The business career center did a gr[eat] job of helping to place students. Alumni network is topnotch—especially in [the] real estate program and the school is held in high esteem in the business co[m]munity.

Alumnus/a, 8/1990-12/1994, November 2005

The College of Engineering at the University of Wisconsin—Madison has gr[eat] prestige with employers in many fields. Chemical engineers and civil engine[ers] usually receive multiple job offers upon graduation, even in lean yea[rs.] Graduates often land positions at blue chip companies in their fields of stu[dy;] electrical and computer engineers are highly sought after by companies such [as] Microsoft, Sun and IBM; chemical engineers are sought by companies such [as] Dow Corning, and mechanical engineers are often hired by major automob[ile] manufacturers such as Ford and General Motors.

Alumnus/a, 9/1995-5/1999, December 2005

I didn't really take advantage of all the university had to offer in this regard[. I] only went to on-campus recruiting for summer jobs, but had no problems fi[nd]ing a good job there. I did the legwork myself in finding a job after I gradua[ted,] but had a job lined up before graduation doing what I wanted. I'm not a me[m]ber of the alumni network.

Alumnus/a, 4/1999-4/2003, April 2005

The Midwest does not have many prestigious private schools and a busin[ess] degree from Wisconsin can get you in on the ground floor at many Midw[est] companies. Don't be afraid to contact top-tier Chicago companies either. [I] worked at a mid-market investment banking firm and believed my educatio[n at] Wisconsin was as good or better than other analysts' from different Big [10] schools.

The on-campus recruiting center is fairly good. The staff was very friendly a[nd] helpful considering all the students/recruiters they had to put up with. I got [on] most "closed lists" that I wanted to, but knew of smart people who did n[ot.] Many recruiters have long-term relationships with UW—Madison and plu[ck] away at least one graduate per year.

Alumnus/a, 8/2001-5/2003, March 2005

The prestige is pretty high for UW—Madison. A degree from here will help y[ou] in the job market. There are lots of programs to help you meet employers, ta[ke] part in internships and co-ops. UW—Madison's most popular departments, [in] terms of the number of degrees granted to undergraduate students are politi[cal] science, history and psychology. The electrical engineering program granted [the] most master's degrees of any UW—Madison department in 2003-04, while el[ec]trical engineering and English produced the most new PhDs.

Current student, 9/2001-Submit Date, May 2004

Many undergraduate programs require you to have at least one internship dur[ing] your undergraduate years. This is very easy to do, and many advisors have pag[es] of places that are looking for help. I found that the community thrives off [of] internships in Madison. Thus, internships can be a great way into establishing [a] career with that company. The university also has many job fairs in which pe[o]ple come from all over to see students and try to hire graduates for careers or al[so] for the semester internships. The university provides a well-rounded educatio[n,] leaving you with many options when you finish school. People prefer to do v[ol]unteering services to enhance their résumé when they graduate. Teach [for] America has many recruiting meetings for students. Finally, being a researc[h] based college, there are a lot of opportunities for students to work in resear[ch.] This is an important way to show a future employer that you do have hands[-on] experience. It gives you an edge over other prospective employees.

 **Quality of Life**

Alumnus/a, Business, 8/1999-5/2003, March 2007

Excellent quality of life—the campus is beautiful, everything is accessible a[nd] the city is rated one of the best in America in which to live.

Current student, 9/2004-Submit Date, June 2006

...dison is easily one of the safest campuses and cities in America, with a low ...me rate, its own campus police force, and plenty of services for ensuring safe-... Nevertheless, things do happen, as anywhere else, and students must take ...tion to prevent such things as theft. The dining facilities are decent, the selec-...n is not bad but the quality of food is sub par. The dorms are a little old in ...ne parts, but in other parts new and impressive, but the activities they all offer ...xtensive.

Current student, 9/2001-Submit Date, September 2005

...e quality of life at campus is high. Incentives are routinely given out in the ...idence halls pertaining to model behavior. The city is geared to the college. ...dents receive discounts everywhere in town. Some students are from New ...rk and Chicago, others are international. We have more restaurants per cap-...n in Madison than in any other city.

Alumnus/a, 8/2001-5/2003, March 2005

...ere are weight rooms, cardio rooms, basketball courts, racquetball courts, a ...ol, an indoor track, and probably lots of other stuff. It was just renovated, and ...s many new amenities. Madison is located between three beautiful lakes. The ...efront Memorial Union is considered the living room of campus, where stu-...nts, faculty, staff and members of the community mingle and socialize. In the ...mmer there are concerts almost every night of the week on the terrace.

Current student, 8/2004-Submit Date, October 2004

...e UW campus is one of the most beautiful campuses around and it's nudged ...tween two big lakes, Monona and Mendota. These provide for wonderful ...ter activities such as sailing, boating, fishing, and much more. Housing here ...UW is good, and is going through a renovation to become even better! Within ... next few years, there will be brand spankin' new freshman housing. Other ...cilities such as the fitness and recreational facilities are well-maintained.

...ive across the street from a very new and expansive fitness center. The foot-...ll stadium, which is home to one of the best football programs in the nation, ...newly remodeled as well. There isn't much crime here on campus thanks to ... university's own police force. It is a very safe place to be. In addition to the ...WPD, the university has programs such as SAFE, which sends out escorts free ... charge to whomever feels it is unsafe to walk home at night or just doesn't ...el comfortable.

Current student, 9/2001-Submit Date, May 2004

...e university is a safe and enriching environment. They have a campus police ...partment and many programs such as a Safewalk or Saferide. These programs ...ck you up and bring you to where you have to be so that you do not have to ...lk alone in the dark. You also get a fee bus pass so that you may venture off ...mpus. Housing is all around campus, and depending on your interests and ...ea of residence, there is something for everyone. In the dorms, there is often ...shortage of space, forcing students to live in private residence halls or apart-...ents. So my advice would be to fill out your housing application for the dorms ...ht away. The dorms have computer labs in most of them, and the cafeterias ... always close by.

Current student, 9/2003-Submit Date, November 2003

...od on campus is sub par, but palatable. Sub on State Street (slightly off cam-...s) is great! The campus itself ranges from dingy in the winter to beautiful in ... fall and summer. The quality of facilities also ranges greatly: some really ...ol new buildings and some really old space-race era relics (mechanical engi-...ering). I definitely suggest visiting the campus once in February and then ...ain in June to get a taste of what Madison is like.

Social Life

Alumnus/a, Business, 8/1999-5/2003, March 2007

...s UW—Madison. It's the best social life in the nation! Football, basketball, ...ckey, and the Memorial Union Terrace are all student favorites. The bar scene ...fantastic. The Greek system is there, but not as prevalent as it is in other parts ... the country, such as the South. Still house parties abound and people are hav-...g fun (and learning) seven days a week. Students are very active and there is ... shortage of social opportunities.

Current student, 9/2004-Submit Date, June 2006

Madison is named the top party school in America for good reason, and the bar scene is active. There are also tons of unique restaurants, and more small business ethnic places on and near campus than there are chains, which is nice. I enjoy the intramural sports, which offers sports from soccer to dodgeball, to frisbee, and is well organized with its own web site for statistics and schedules. The campus sports are great as well, and it is one of the few schools that can boast a top level hockey, basketball, football, track, cross country and rowing team, among others which escape me. Every sport has a huge following and performs well.

Alumnus/a, 9/1995-5/1999, December 2005

The social life is what you make of it. The UW has a reputation as a party school, and it is if you want it to be. If that's not your scene, then you won't be bothered by it, either. Campus is big enough that you'll find your niche, whatever it may be. There are all kinds of clubs in which to take part, including sports clubs for athletes who maybe weren't Division I quality but still want to participate competitively in sports. There's always something going on on campus. Plays, musicals, sporting events, concerts, you name it. As far as dating goes, I was lucky enough to find my husband the second month I was there, so I didn't have to worry about it too much. Friends who were on the dating scene didn't really have a problem finding as many dates as they wanted.

Current student, 9/2001-Submit Date, September 2005

The Kollege Klub, The Klinic, Dotty Dumpling's Dowery, The Nitty Gritty (free drinks on your b-day), BW-3, The Plaza, Bullfeathers, Stillwaters and The Annex (alternative crowd) are just the main bars out of literally over a hundred that are popular drinking/hang-out spots for students. The students are always out in full force on Saturday night. The Greek system generally keeps to itself and is most involved/visible in the community at large around homecoming.

Alumnus/a, 41999-4/2003, April 2005

State Street will always be the place to be, but there are also plenty of good neighborhood bars. I wasn't a big drinker at Madison (I know, it's hard to believe that anyone wasn't a big drinker at Madison) but the bar scene was still great. I would encourage any business student to join as many professional frats as possible. They frequently host guest speakers and it always looks good on the résumé.

Current student, 8/2004-Submit Date, October 2004

The social life here at UW is unbelievable. Because the campus is so big and there are so many nice students, it makes for a wonderful atmosphere. Clubs and intramural sports are a great way to meet people and can make for a really fun time. The sports teams here are very successful and have a great tradition to go along with the school's wonderful sense of team spirit. For example, after every home football game the band stays after and the whole student section participates in "the fifth quarter."

There are tons of bars around town and even if you don't want to go the bars, there's always a bangin' party somewhere. The favorite restaurant of students at UW is most definitely Ian's Pizza. The toppings are crazy and at 2 in the morning after a Friday or Saturday night, Ian's is packed full of exhausted students. Greek life at UW is amazing and very successful in the community. It's a very large and strong tradition. As for meeting that dream guy/girl, [I think that] the UW library was rated by *Playboy* one of the top places in America to meet that lucky one.

Current student, 9/2001-Submit Date, May 2004

Your social life is what you make of it. I mean that there is a variety of interest offered, and your job is to decide which one you want to go to. Many organizations and special interest groups are always looking for more people. Belly dancing to intramural sports, from house parties to bars, there is something for everyone.

The dating scene is diverse in which homosexuals, transvestites and bisexuals are all accepted. The Greek system is very active in the community and university. They all are well organized and provide multiple benefits to students who want to join.

Read all of Vault's College Surveys at **www.vault.com/college**—get complete surveys on 100s of colleges and universities, expert advice on applicaton essays and more.

VAULT CAREER LIBRARY 787

University of Wyoming

UW Admissions
Department 3435
1000 E. University Ave
Laramie, WY 82071
Admissions phone: (307) 766-5160 or (800) DIAL-WYO
Admissions e-mail: why-wyo@uwyo.edu
Admissions URL: uwadmnweb.uwyo.edu/ADMISSIONS/

 Admissions

Current student, Engineering, 8/2003-Submit Date, May 2007

Because the University of Wyoming (UW) is the only four-year academic institution in the state, plenty of money is provided by the state and university for students to attend. Consequently, I received a four-year scholarship upon high school graduation to attend, which made my decision to attend UW relatively easy. Once I made my decision, the application process was a snap.

Current student, Communications, 5/2003-Submit Date, April 2007

If you are interested in attending the school keeps incredible contact with you before sending you all kinds of information about the school. The process of admissions was fairly easy and self explanatory. Once you got accepted they continued to send information on the things that needed to be done before arriving to school. Overall, there were no surprises.

Current student, Engineering, 8/2006-Submit Date, April 2007

The admissions process here at the University of Wyoming is relatively simple. You can come take tours of the campus, but all that is required is to turn in an application. The application is relatively short and no essays or interviews are required. The university is easy to get into as long as a person has a decent GPA. Anything at or above a 2.5 GPA is usually good enough and people with lower GPAs might still have a chance at getting in.

> **The school says:** "See below for correct admissions requirements. The application must be followed up or sent with an official high school transcript and test scores, and the $40 fee."

Current student, Business, 8/2005-Submit Date, April 2007

The admissions department is very helpful. They provide information and advice on entrance, financial aid, college life and general questions. There are no essays unless you have been suspended, then I do believe you have to write a letter to the admissions director. As long as your GPA is above a 3.0 admittance is almost guaranteed. Very easy and quick.

Current student, Engineering, 8/2006-Submit Date, April 2007

Don't miss the early deadlines. Being accepted to the University of Wyoming as an undergraduate is relatively easy. The application is simple, there are no interviews, and generally everyone that applies is accepted. However, their scholarship deadlines are extremely early. Most are February 1, and everyone admitted to the university and college is automatically considered for scholarships. So, be accepted before the deadlines or you will miss out on any scholarships!

> **Regarding selectivity, the school says:** "UW is a selective institution, and has minimum requirements for admission. For assured admission, Wyoming residents must have a 2.75 cumulative unweighted high school GPA, nonresidents must have a 3.0 unweighted cumulative high school GPA. n addition, students must have at least a 20 on the ACT, or a combined Math/Verbal score of 960 on the SAT, and must have completed the required college prep courses. See www.uwyo.edu/admissions for more information on these requirements, or for information on admission with conditions or admission by exception."

Current student, Health, 8/2004-Submit Date, March 2007

Admissions is pretty easy. No essay was needed, no real interviews. Just fill the form and send in the cash. They do a little interview after you are accepted but it's nothing that will make or break your chance of college here. The Honor Program only requires a 3.0 GPA also, so anyone can graduate with honors.

> **The school says:** "There is no interview required for admission to UW, but visiting campus is encouraged, and includes a one-on-one meeting with an admissions professional. Freshman applicants to the Honors Program must have one of the following: a composite ACT score of 28, a minimum combined Math and Verbal SAT score of 1240, or an unweighted high school GPA of 3.7 or better. Transfer applicants to the Honors Program must have a transfer GPA of 3.25, and expect to be on campus for four or more semesters."

Current student, Communications, 8/2006-Submit Date, March 2007

The admissions process is relatively easy, and you can do the application either on paper or online. There is a small fee of $40 (cheaper than a lot of other schools I looked at) for applying, and they ask only needed information. They do like out-of-state students (like me), and they even have a good scholarship out-of-state students with good GPAs and ACT scores. There is no interview essay, or anything of the sort. In my opinion, it is easy to get into this school. Don't let that fool you, however, they do challenge you.

Current student, Biology, 8/2005-Submit Date, March 2007

The admissions process at the University of Wyoming is simple. The application is very straightforward, requiring basic information and academic records. There are no essays. There is no interview process. For select programs and scholarships more involved applications are required. I wouldn't say that it fair to judge the quality of the university based on their application. The simple application isn't to say that the programs and quality of the university are worthwhile. It is a state school, and I think that is part of the reason for the application format.

Current student, Social Sciences, 8/2006-Submit Date, March 2007

The admissions process at UW is very simple. Being an in-state student, there is lots of attention put on UW since it is the only major university in the state. You can submit either a paper application or an online one. UW is looking for diversity, as well as all bright students. For me, the admissions process was very smooth. After submitting my application, I was getting scholarship offers within two weeks. The university may not have the highest requirements for admission as compared to other major universities, but it offers nothing less in terms of education. In the application itself, I was only asked to submit a short essay only about 200 words. It is your standard college essay question, and they are looking to for competitiveness, will to learn, a goal oriented person, and competent writing skills. The university is not very selective, and there is not a whole lot of competition to get into the university. After getting accepted, the university is very good at keeping you informed on what you need to do to finalize your admission and prepare yourself for college at UW.

> **The school says:** "There is no essay required for those students who meet assured admissions standards. Students who do not meet the minimum admissions requirements may provide a personal essay, and letters of recommendation to be considered for admission with conditions. Depending upon a student's answer to specific academic honesty and/or background questions, they may be required to provide more information or an explanation of their answer. UW is a selective institution, but does not have to cap admissions, so if a student meets minimum requirements, they need do nothing further."

Current student, Cultural Studies, 8/2006-Submit Date, March 2007

e application is available online and is easy to understand and fill out. The ay was an interesting but not difficult prompt, so it was easy to write. The ff is knowledgeable and was able to answer any questions I had about the uni-sity.

Academics

Current student, Communications, 8/2006-Submit Date, March 2007

e University of Wyoming, as a whole, has good academics. The classes ered are challenging, without being too difficult. The teachers whom I have countered are amazing, and if they aren't, there are faculty reviews done by ery student every semester, so you have a chance to have your say then.

gistration for classes can be tough, but they open registration in segments. st, the athletes, honors and special needs students register. After that come iors, then juniors, then freshmen, then sophomores. That way, when you ve up (except sophomore year), you register earlier. I highly recommend the nors Program for its priority registration and the caliber of the classes.

e workload isn't drastic (being an English and Journalism major, I really only ve to do a lot of reading and a few assignments). My friends in engineering d nursing, however, tell me that they have a pretty balanced workload. You n't be staying up till 3 a.m. doing assignments.

Current student, Engineering, 8/2003-Submit Date, May 2007

e College of Engineering at UW is topnotch. The classes are very challeng-g, but class sizes are limited anywhere from 40 students to seven students, pending on the level of class. This allows for excellent student-teacher inter-tion. Very rarely, if ever, are engineering courses at UW are taught by gradu-students. Academic advisors for the college prepare their students very well, d students rarely have problems with conflicting classes or getting into desired urses. Although the workload for UW's College of Engineering is very manding and stringent, the quality of education is outstanding. In fact, UW's chitectural Engineering program is leading the region by incorporating the ilding Information Modeling program (BIM), Revit, into its design curricu-n. This is a cutting-edge design program that is quickly replacing programs e AutoCAD in major firms for design work.

Current student, Engineering, 9/2002-Submit Date, April 2007

e mechanical engineering program at the University of Wyoming is very ensive. That being said, the quality of education obtained here is no better n any other state school. Grading is varied depending on the professor and ges from impossible to please to hard but fair. Workload is entirely out of ntrol. One of my professors stated that she expected six hours out of class for ery hour in class in work time.

> **The University of Wyoming says:** "UW's Engineering program has national, and in some cases, international recognition. UW engineering students consistently score above the national aver-age on their initial licensing exam. 100 percent of classes are taught by faculty, and undergraduate students have the oppor-tunity to work side-by-side with professors on cutting-edge research."

Current student, Engineering, 8/2006-Submit Date, April 2007

e University of Wyoming has really high quality classes, many of which are p in the country. The majority of classes, especially upper-level classes, are all in size, so interactions between professors and students are relatively easy. ost classes have an environment where the professors and students can have scussions on a more personal level than in classes of 200 or more. The small ass size sometimes makes it difficult to get into more popular classes and it is t always possible to get the professor a person may want. The professors are me of the top in the world and are readily available to help students. The grad-g is as fair as it can be in most classes although there are a few teachers who ade more difficulty than others. The workload is reasonable and is much lower an some other universities even though there is still quite a bit of work to be ne sometimes. Overall the University of Wyoming is a great school, but the glish and education departments leave something to be desired.

Current student, Engineering, 8/2001-Submit Date, April 2007

Freshman and sophomore year you take common classes with all other engi-neers, math, sciences and intro engineering classes. Then you choose what type of engineer you want to be, if you haven't yet. Each type of engineer stays in a specific curriculum. You get close to a group of people, and it's easy to get into the classes. The workload is the usual engineering workload.

Current student, Business, 8/2005-Submit Date, April 2007

The program itself is good. Sometimes it is difficult to get into the classes that everyone needs but you only run into that your freshman and senior years. The College of Business tries to anticipate the number of students and is really good about adding classes or increasing enrollment to make it happen. Professors, for the most part, are good; most are tenured, which in my opinion is not good. Workload and classes are fair though.

Current student, Engineering, 8/2005-Submit Date, April 2007

Freshman year, I took more small classes than auditorium classes. Most of these classes were to get the student introduced into the college world with research, interviews with professors, and getting to know some fellow students. There were some huge classes, mainly general physics, chemistry and Intro to Object Programming. All the classes up to this year have been high quality with good lab sections and professors who will go out of their way to help you understand the material. All the professors and TAs I know try to get to know the student on a personal level.

Current student, Environment, 8/2004-Submit Date, April 2007

My major is Agroecology and UW was the first university to offer this degree. It is a very broad program with the option to specialize in whatever you think are the most interesting fields. Even though you get a good overall picture you can study and get a minor in things like: plant science, weed science, soil science, plant pathology, watershed management and so on. There are so many options from which to choose, it makes it hard to pick just one!

The classes are great! They are the best classes I have ever taken, and the same goes for the instructors. In three years there has only been one class for which I was not able to register, due to a time conflict with another class. The staff is amazing! The classes are reasonably small and professors are so willing to help you with anything. The workload is very appropriate, I had only one class that was hard to stay ahead of, and the grading has always been fair.

Current student, Cultural Studies, 8/2004-Submit Date, March 2007

UW has a wonderful diversity when it comes to classes and majors. UW has tried very hard to expand all areas of research as well as attract a very established international student community. Like with every university, you will inevitably find good and bad teachers. However at UW the teachers, in general, are pas-sionate about the topics they teach and the community in which they live. As attendance rises it has become harder to get into specific classes but UW is con-stantly working to help staff people in these areas.

> **The school says:** "UW received over $70 million in external con-tracts and research grants in 2006, breaking its own record for the 20th consecutive year."

Employment Prospects

Current student, Cultural Studies, 8/2004-Submit Date, March 2007

UW has a large number of its students who partake in progressive internships on the state and federal level. Also the travel abroad program is huge and allows for many students to be able to partake in such an important and life changing experience. Because UW has such a prestigious reputation many students move on to excellent jobs and permanent internships.

> **The school says:** "Thanks to a generous $1.8 million donation (matched by the state) from Dick and Lynne Cheney, UW now has the largest single-university endowment in the U.S. dedi-cated to study abroad scholarships and support."

Read all of Vault's College Surveys at www.vault.com/college—get complete surveys on 100s of colleges and univer-sities, expert advice on applicaton essays and more.

VAULT CAREER LIBRARY 789

Current student, Engineering, 8/2003-Submit Date, May 2007

There is an absolute wealth of internship and recruiting opportunities on campus, especially for the College of Engineering. Employers tend to like Wyoming graduates because they are generally friendly and down-to-earth with excellent communication skills, which is the key to success for today's working world. Examples of employers who regularly recruit on campus include: DCI-Engineers headquartered in Bellevue, Washington; Raytheon; Halliburton; EchoStar Communications Corp.; EnCana Oil and Gas; and Micron Technology. Additionally, many students, including myself, have the opportunity through the Wyoming Space Grant Consortium to perform research at various NASA locations through grants and such programs as NASA's Undergraduate Student Research Program (USRP), NASA Academy, and the Jet Propulsion Laboratory (JPL) in Pasadena, CA.

Current student, Education, 8/2006-Submit Date, April 2007

For a small town, Laramie has a large number of job opportunities. Hailing from a large city, I thought the town would be boring and lack employment prospects, but this is not the case. Laramie has many small businesses, as well as government/university jobs available for all ages. If you are interested in graduate research work, then this is the place for you!

Current student, Engineering, 8/2005-Submit Date, April 2007

The university is great with sending out notices about companies coming to campus or internships that are fairly new. They include companies ranging from local small firms to Microsoft and Raytheon and others. Graduates get decent starting jobs. A lot of the jobs come from references of professors and alumni the student knows. It's a good idea to be active on campus in registered student organizations like the Greek community.

Current student, Environment, 8/2004-Submit Date, April 2007

For my program, we are required to complete an internship. The agroecology advisors generally set up a government related job for the internship that will be offered as a full-time job upon graduation. There are numerous graduate assistantships available.

Current student, Engineering, 8/2006-Submit Date, April 2007

The engineering college is always sending employment notices to the students. Whether it's for graduates, or undergraduate intern positions, they are really good about it.

 ## Quality of Life

Current student, Biology, 1/2006-Submit Date, March 2007

Laramie is a wonderful town in which to live. The worst thing about it is the winter weather. I feel totally safe walking home at night by myself. It's pretty cheap to live here and housing is always available. The campus is great. Parts of ag and animal science are spread out but main campus is pretty compact. Dining is OK in the town. It is comprised of a lot of small independent places. If you are craving a chain restaurant, Fort Collins or Cheyenne are not very far away.

Current student, Engineering, 8/2003-Submit Date, May 2007

The University of Wyoming is nestled in a very friendly and safe community among nearby hiking, ski and snowshoeing trails. People from this region are genuinely caring and considerate. Unlike many places where I've lived and visited, people at UW do not hesitate to smile and say, "hi," to complete strangers or offer to hold doors open for others who may be still be 20 feet away from the entrance of a building. The university administration and student senate take very active roles in promoting student health, happiness and wellness on campus. As a testament to this, the dining facility, Washakie Dining Center, was completely remodeled four years ago to provide healthy meal options, including a Mongolian grill, smoothie bar and sushi bar among regularly provided menu items. Additionally, the university has plans for a multi-million dollar renovation and expansion of the campus recreational facility, which houses an infield area for cardio and strength training, campus intramural sports programs, climbing wall, swimming pool, basketball and racquetball courts, outdoor adventure program, and health and wellness center.

With regard to housing, UW's residential area on campus consists of a clos knit community of six residence halls and an adjacent row of Greek houses (f ternities and sororities). All campus housing is located within a half of a mile the farthest end of campus, which is a very scenic walk across campus. T years ago, the university made great strides in campus beautification efforts convert UW's campus into a more scenic walking campus. Finally, as a boos campus morale, this year the UW Cowgirls basketball team won the Wome National Invitational Tournament (WNIT), the men's football team defea UCLA in the Las Vegas Pure Vision bowl two years ago, and a UW footb player was recently drafted to the NFL—a testament to the university's comm ment to athletics.

Current student, Engineering, 8/2006-Submit Date, April 2007

The Laramie area has a very low crime rate and it's quite safe to go for a str past midnight. The difficulty is housing. Though there is a lot of housing ava able around town and on campus, it can be very expensive. The restaurants great—there are both chain and locally-owned restaurants. The campus is o but the university is renovating and constructing like mad! The technology great, you can always find a computer on campus, and most of campus is set for wireless access for students.

> **The University of Wyoming says:** "UW has just completed, or has in progress, over $200 million in capitol construction and improvements, with many more plans in the works."

Current student, Business, 8/2004-Submit Date, March 2007

Laramie, Wyoming is a very small community, with little to do. If you enjoy t outdoors that would be a bonus since we are right on the edge of the Roc Mountains and less than an hour from Colorado. Snow sports are very popu and ski resorts are very easy to get to. Off-campus living is overpriced but t student housing is very well-priced and gives transportation to the campus.

 ## Social Life

Current student, Education, 8/2006-Submit Date, April 2007

It's easy to make friends at the University of Wyoming. Whether you meet pe ple through the dorms, major-specific activities or the bars and restaurants abo town, meeting people is a breeze. The Greek system is alive and well, but I pr fer to live off campus. Major events that really incorporate the students are t Weeks of Welcome, Friday Night Fever and all football and basketball game My favorite restaurant is Chelo's in West Laramie and favorite bar is Thi Street.

Current student, Engineering, 8/2003-Submit Date, May 2007

Laramie, Wyoming could definitely be considered a college town. Popular sp to hang out include downtown bars like Lovejoy's, Third Street, Tommy Jack and the ever popular and historic Buckhorn Bar. The ASUW Stude Government even sponsors a SafeRide program to provide free rides to studer anywhere in the town of Laramie on Thursday, Friday and Saturday nights. C campus, the newly remodeled student union also provides students with b liards, ping pong and beer gardens. In the same area of the student union, pe ple can watch any number of free musical entertainment acts nearly every wee The Student Activity Center on campus also sponsors musical acts every seme ter, which have included performers like Wyclef Jean, Chris Ledoux, BB Kin Switchfoot, Hootie and the Blowfish and Real Big Fish. Another opportunity f social interaction includes the Greek community on campus, which includes fo women's sororities and six men's fraternities each with its own large and histor house located on either Fraternity or Sorority Row, as well as a number of oth nontraditional Greek letter organizations. In addition to this, many studer choose to utilize the outdoor recreational opportunities in the area by joinir organizations like the Outdoor Adventure Program (OAP) and Nordic ski tea There is no shortage of opportunities on the UW campus for social interactio exploration, and development.

Current student, Communications, 5/2003-Submit Date, April 200

The bars in Laramie are pretty busy on the weekends. There are lots of thin that bars do to bring in people. There is a local band, The Younger Brothe Band, that is very popular in this town. It's nice because you can walk into a b and know a lot of people there, making it feel like a safe place. The restaura good; there are lots of different options for food and the atmosphere at those staurants is really good. Our school offers many different clubs to join that er to almost every possible interest. If there isn't a club that caters to your erest, you just need 12 people and you can make your own club. Greek sys- m is OK here; it is not as big as some campuses. But they do try and get very volved with the school and the community. The dating here is really fun, at ist for girls. There are a lot of guys here. So you have a lot of different tions. The university also puts on a Friday Night Fever that puts on different ents to bring students something to do. They bring in bands, comedians and t on movies. The other thing that is big is sporting events. The school really es to put on activities to encourage students to go. It is getting bigger and big- r each year. The student support for some of the sports team is very amazing.

urrent student, Engineering, 8/2005-Submit Date, April 2007

e school's social life is its blood, metaphorically. There are two places on mpus that serve alcoholic beverages, The Union and the College of Law. All e restaurants in town are enjoyable, with good food and great atmospheres! ating is a minor part to social life, but does occur with the help of Facebook. ents and clubs always occur with each other. Everyone, or over half the stu- nt body, attends major sporting events and club events. The Greek system is a rebound, and is strongly encouraged to at least go through fall recruitment meet people who have been in your shoes.

> **The school says:** "No alcohol is served anywhere on campus other than at The Gardens in the Union, and ID must be provid- ed. If specific College events/receptions, such as the Law School Ball, do serve alcohol, a special permit is required, and all students must show I.D. Alcohol is not normally permitted at campus special events if students under the age of 21 will be in attendance."

The School Says

Established as a land-grant institution in 1886, the University of Wyoming is found among the top research universities in the U.S. and offers a long history of academic excellence as well as a future made bright by generous funding from the state. In a recent national study, UW was found to spend more per student on higher education than any school in the nation. The scenic Rocky Mountain environment is a draw for students from all 50 states and more than 65 foreign countries every year.

Outside Magazine has recognized UW's hometown, Laramie, as one of the "40 Coolest College Towns" and the University as one of the top adventure schools in the country. And on cam- pus, in addition to newly renovated residence halls, dining hall, student union, athletic, and wellness facilities, UW currently has over $200 million in capitol construction projects in progress.

UW offers more than 80 undergraduate degree programs (many nationally recognized), through our Colleges of Agriculture, Arts and Sciences, Business, Education, Engineering, Health Sciences, as well as the School of Environment and Natural Resources, and the newly established School of Energy Resources.

Each year, more than 1,500 undergraduates have the opportu- nity to work on cutting-edge research with their professors. The University of Wyoming has a low 15:1 student-to-faculty ratio, and is very proud that 89 percent of the classes are taught by faculty.

The University of Wyoming has been recognized by the Princeton Review in *The Best 366 Colleges*, and also in their list of 165 of "America's Best Value Colleges." With low nonresi- dent tuition ("America's 100 Best College Buys" for nine con- secutive years) and competitive scholarship programs for stu- dents from all states, the University of Wyoming offers a high quality education at an extremely reasonable price.

Read all of Vault's College Surveys at **www.vault.com/college**—get complete surveys on 100s of colleges and univer- sities, expert advice on applicaton essays and more.

VAULT CAREER LIBRARY **791**

Canadian
College Profiles

Acadia University

dmissions Office
cadia University
ayward House
1 Acadia Street
Volfville, NS B4P 2R6
dmissions phone: (902) 585-1016
dmissions fax: (902) 585-1092
dmissions e-mail: admissions@acadiau.ca
RL: www.acadiau.ca

 Admissions

lumnus/a, Business, 1/2003-10/2005, May 2007

raightforward admissions process requires: high school transcript and univer-
y transcript (if currently studying at other university). Application for entry
holarship is in a separate form. If your GPA is over 3.85, you are likely to get
is award.

lumnus/a, 9/2000-5/2005, May 2007

s a high school student in the U.S., I was relieved to see paragraph answers
eded in the Acadia application rather than the usual essays for American col-
ges. That said, I think it's important for a university to have a more personal
nnection to applicants than what can be expressed in demographics and short
swers. That's where the interview comes in. Unfortunately, Acadia didn't do
 interview with me. I also liked the later application deadlines for Acadia
mpared to U.S. colleges, but I guess that has to do with Canadian universities
general. Admissions wrote personal notes on their letters to me, and general-
kept in better touch!

lumnus/a, 9/2001-5/2005, May 2007

he admissions process at Acadia is very easy, the same process you go through
ith most Canadian universities. The difference with Acadia is that you choose
ur major when you apply. This allows the programs to be much more focused
nce you are working towards your major right from day one. This is a great
ature if you know what you want, but may be a little less desirable if you want
 take some time to figure out your direction. The majority of people are very
eased with this option.

lumnus/a, 9/2000-5/2004, May 2007

dmissions was easy. I went to the open house in October and was able to apply
r free (usually there is a $60 charge). I just had to see that they received my
gh school transcript and then around March I heard back that I had been
ccepted.

lumnus/a, Nutrition and Dietetics, 8/2000-5/2004, May 2007

enjoyed the ease of application through the online form. There was also sig-
ificant over-the-phone support both during and after I submitted my applica-
on. I found the questions on the application to be relevant and offered appro-
riate insight as to my motivation for applying to the school.

lumnus/a, Music, 9/2001-5/2005, May 2007

dmission is pretty standard. Having good marks helps a lot. There was no
ssay when I went there. I did, however, have an audition (as I was a music
ajor). Along with the audition was a theory and ear-training test. I recom-
end, if this is not something you spent much time on in past lessons or music
lasses (I find vocalists and guitarists are generally the most likely to be "defi-
ient"), that you try to get a few theory lessons in there. Depending on your
core, you'll be put in either first-year theory and ear training or the rudimenta-
y class. I was in the rudiments class, and though it was an extra course I had to
ke, it didn't affect me graduating on time or anything. There will also be an
iterview. Most questions are pretty basic (why do you want to study music,

why would you choose Acadia and so on). Just prepare yourself so you're not
stumbling over your words.

Current student, 9/2005-Submit Date, April 2006

Applications for the Acadia education program were easy to follow, fill out and
complete. Once I applied, I was sent a letter acknowledging my application and
given instructions on how to check my status and what to do if I hadn't heard
back right away. When I came down for the day of the interview I also booked
a tour of the campus and was greeted by friendly staff and current students. I
had already had one interview for the same program but at a different school and
felt at ease after entering the university grounds. Not only is Acadia a beautiful
school, but the staff in the School of Education is very helpful in directing where
to go and what to know for the interview. During the interview, both the man
and woman who interviewed me made me feel at home, relaxed and welcome.
I was impressed from start to finish and, within a week, was eager to know if I
was going to be able to attend the university. When I phoned the administration
about the status of my file, they not only told me to call back, but they also
explained the process as to why it took so long and what to expect. Within three
days of calling, they phoned back to let me know I had been offered a position.
Within a week a letter was sent asking me to reply on my decision and within a
month I had all the information needed to register, apply for residence and pick
my courses. It was a easy, quick and stress-free process; I am glad I was accepted to Acadia.

Current student, 9/2003-Submit Date, April 2006

The admissions process was online, which was different than any other school
to which I applied. This was kind of neat because you could actually see what
process your admissions request was in pending or accepted. To apply online
was a very simple process, a few questions and then all you had to do was mail
in your most current transcript. You were allowed to pick the top three faculties
to which you were interested in applying (and only had to pay one price!) and
heard back from each of these faculties within a few days of your acceptance.
The university had a great web site available for prospective students with
answers to most of their questions. If you couldn't find something, it was super
to e-mail someone from the university to get an answer. The selectivity didn't
seem that difficult, I was able to get into all three faculties without hesitation;
however, it was when I was applying for some of the courses that I realized I did-
n't actually have the pre-reqs to get in. This was super frustrating, especially
considering I would have had enough time to get the pre-reqs prior to starting
my program in the summer.

 Academics

Alumnus/a, 9/2001-5/2005, May 2007

One of the major advantages at Acadia is the small class sizes. It provides a truly
unique educational experience because your professors really care about you.
It's the kind of school where if you e-mail a professor in the morning, you will
likely have a response from him/her by that night. The professors are extremely approachable and hands-on, and I really appreciated that. The workload was
heavy in most cases, but manageable and definitely prepared students for future
employment or further education. The grading was generally very fair and professors were often very reasonable, offering alternate marking schemes to help
you get the best grade possible. They were also very good about helping you out
outside of the classroom. It was sometimes difficult to get into popular classes,
especially due to the small class sizes, but you were definitely rewarded for your
years at Acadia since the upper-year students usually got to register first.

Alumnus/a, 9/2002-4/2006, May 2007

In both the faculty of pure and applied science and the faculty of arts, I found
classes to be small and professors to know me by name and interact with me outside of classes. The workload was fair and grading was also fair. Professors
were available for questions or extra help outside of class time. The popular
classes did not always interest me. However, in my third year my complete plan

Read all of Vault's College Surveys at **www.vault.com/college**—get complete surveys on 100s of colleges and universities, expert advice on applicaton essays and more.

VAULT CAREER LIBRARY **795**

was messed up because of lack of availability of a few courses in my traditional science department.

Alumnus/a, 9/2002-4/2006, May 2007

Popular classes can be difficult to get because the class sizes are so small at Acadia. However, if you are in good standing with your professors it is sometimes a little easier to get "what you want." It was a very good transition from high school. With the classes being small, it was easy to keep up with material and you could feel comfortable asking questions in a classroom setting. Grading is not on a curve, and so there is very little competition within the school and classes/faculty. Also, Acadia has a great Intranet where teachers can post grades and so on. Almost all professors respond to e-mail and prefer that as a method of getting their attention.

Alumnus/a, 9/2001-5/2005, May 2007

I find that as long as you do your work, you should be fine. Most profs offer extensive office hours if you are having problems, and there are opportunities for tutors, as well. In smaller programs like music, for example, class sizes are very small (five to 30), but even in larger courses, the class sizes don't get bigger than 200 or so. Acadia is known for many programs, including music, theatre, business, kinesiology, recreation management and education, just to name a few. Once you get to know some upperclassmen in your program, they'll let you know which profs are the greatest and which to try to stay clear from. I've heard of great profs in all faculties, and very few bad ones.

Alumnus/a, Business Administration, 9/2001-5/2005, May 2007

I felt the business administration program was good. It was structured but gave you freedom to choose classes in other areas of interest. The quality of classes were very good, the professors passionate about their work and always willing to help students who had questions. I loved the fact that all of my business professors were in one building because I easily met 10 professors I knew every time I went in there. Online registration was always nice, as well, because you could constantly check the status of your classes if need be. Workload was manageable in my classes, lots of groupwork for business, which actually took up most of the time. Professors were always listening to student concerns. Grading is fair and competitive, but if you go and do your work to your full potential, you will be graded on that.

Current student, Sociology, 9/2003-Submit Date, April 2006

I am a sociology major in honors. My program is not that difficult, but there is a lot of reading and essays that you need to do to keep up good grades. Since the reading is so heavy, some days are homework ridden. That said, my professors are extremely easy to talk to. Each professor has at least four office hours a week (which is the bare minimum and none of my professors have not been around when I needed them). Furthermore, if you are having trouble, they'll let you know. Many of my professors offer extra help (not just their TAs). If you can't meet on a certain day or need to talk, our community is so small that it's not uncommon to go and discuss school stuff at the local coffee shop. I have found that all of the professors are very keen on the honors program and if you're interested in doing it, they will do everything in their power to make sure you're prepared. The required courses for my program are challenging and sometimes boring, but the professors here make such programs interesting. You want to come to class. From this, there is a high attendance rate to the classes, but because the school is so small, my third-year classes that are packed have 28 students. The small class size does give a little bit of problem for getting into popular classes. However, there are tricks of the trade that most people use to squeeze themselves in. Also, if you don't get in your first year, you have more opportunity in your second, as our sign-up for classes is done by year (highest year first, lowest last).

Employment Prospects

Alumnus/a, 9/2002-4/2006, May 2007

It is a very well-known school throughout Canada. For science students, like myself, it is a great school to complete an undergraduate degree in order to continue on to do more research or go into the medical field (as I did).

Alumnus/a, Business, 9/2001-5/2005, May 2007

My fellows are in Europe, the U.K., the U.S., the Bahamas and all over Canada. Acadia strongly encourages this type of networking, recognizing as they do that Wolfville is relatively out of the way and not on the tour that large firms undertake to find employees. Therefore, professors are heavily involved in helping their students place in good positions. It's hard to comment on internships and on-campus recruiting because I came to university with a good network already established. I will say, however, that arts students seem to have great difficulty finding good positions immediately after school.

Alumnus/a, 9/2001-5/2006, May 2007

Acadia computer science bachelor graduates typically have a relatively easy time finding entry-level programming positions due to the reputation of Acadia's program as being demanding and challenging. The alumni network's effectiveness will rely largely on your own ability to network once you're at the school though. Not much unity after graduation, as people disperse all over the world and alumni events are scarce (but do pop up from time to time).

Alumnus/a, 9/2002-5/2004, May 2007

Acadia provided us with a job fair specifically for teachers in the area. This gave us a place to meet people and make connections. Many people were hired even before graduation. Acadia grads always have an advantage because of our experience with computers.

Alumnus/a, 9/2001-5/2007, May 2007

Acadia University grads hold an advantage over many universities because of our technology. I believe employers recognize this as a huge advantage in our society. However, it is not only the laptops that make us esteemed employees. At a small school, students are forced to work hard and are noticed by faculty. You gain close relationships with all your professors, which greatly helps when you are looking for jobs and need ideas or reference letters. Many companies come to our school from all over to recruit.

Current student, Education, 9/2003-Submit Date, April 2006

Acadia University has consistently ranked in the Top Three in Canada in *Maclean's* magazine ratings for undergraduate universities. As such, Acadia grads are highly regarded. Our education program is a two-year program on which schools look very favorably. It includes two months of practicum teaching per year so we will be well prepared when it comes time to beginning work. Both of my sisters have graduated from this program and both have wonderful jobs.

Current student, 9/2002-Submit Date, April 2006

Acadia University is a well-known institution and has been recognized as one of the best schools in Canada for undergraduate education. In addition, if an employer is unfamiliar with the school, Acadia's detailed web site provides a great amount of information regarding the school's goals and student life. There are a number of services on campus available to students looking for jobs and certain faculties host guest speakers on a regular basis, allowing student's to see possibilities in their field. Co-op programs are also available to students who are interested and are highly recommended.

Quality of Life

Alumnus/a, 9/2002-4/2006, May 2007

Campus life is alive and vibrant. The residences have distinct personalities and many social activities. I felt safe on Acadia's campus. The dining hall is superb and facilities on campus, like the athletics complex and chapel, are welcoming.

Alumnus/a, 9/2001-5/2005, May 2007

Living on campus was one of the best things you can do. You meet your best friends there; the ones with whom you study, hang out, procrastinate and party. I had a roommate my first year, and if you're lucky, it can be really great. If you don't want to take that chance of having a roomie with whom you don't particularly mesh, there are lots of single rooms to be had. Most residences have been remodeled. Meal hall has its hits and misses, but that could be said about just about any university. Wolfville is an incredibly safe town, but the university does take extra precautions to ensure its students' safety (U-Hall shuttle, blue

...emergency phones, walk home service). Living off campus is also a lot of fun, and the housing varies from big old Victorian style houses to more modern apartment buildings. Everything is walking distance, but if you don't like hills, stay away from places on Pleasant St.

Alumnus/a, Business Administration, 9/2001-5/2005, May 2007

Acadia has recently upgraded a lot of its student residences to very beautiful dorms. You almost don't feel you are living in a dorm, it's so nice. The campus is beautiful and I love driving through it when I return for visits. It's one of my favorite places to be. The facilities are good and always being upgraded. The gym needed work when I was there, including new equipment and facilities, but I think they were improving that dramatically when I was graduating. There is a dining hall on campus, which is actually quite good. It gets a lot of complaints because eating at the same place is annoying after a while. They have a snack shop and there are tons of pizza places downtown, as well as a Subway and Tim Hortons and several great sit-down restaurants, all within a five- to 10-minute walk from campus. The town is 3,000 people and it literally doubles to 6,000 when the students are there. The town is very accepting and there is constant collaboration between the town and the university. They are very serious about keeping Wolfville and the campus safe. There are drive home programs, and shuttles to get people home safely. Also plenty of lighting and there are always people around to walk home with you. The security is very tight and I never ran into a problem, and I walked to friends houses off campus and home to my house off campus all the time late at night.

Alumnus/a, 9/2001-5/2007, May 2007

If you are from the city, you will initially be shocked in our little community of Wolfville. However, it is a close-knit area that prides on the university. Growing up in the area, I felt privileged to be so close to the university and everyone who lives here and in the surrounding communities feels the same way. It is a small town where the population doubles once the students come in every September. Residences at Acadia are amazing. They have all been renovated or built within the past five years. As for crime and safety, I can't think of another place where you would feel safer. The security at Acadia is always around and easily reachable and the town police are always around, too.

Social Life

Alumnus/a, 9/2004-4/2004, May 2007

Although there were only two bars in the town (one on campus for students only and one in town), it felt like that was all you needed. Halifax was only an hour away if you wanted a bigger bar scene. There were plenty of events held by the Acadia Students Union. Dating was good but got monotonous because you knew everyone and knew who they were with. However, there did seem to be enough members of the opposite sex that it wasn't boring. There was no Greek system at Acadia.

Alumnus/a, 9/2001-5/2005, May 2007

Wolfville is a small town, so there are limited choices for entertainment. There are two bars, the Axe (on campus) and the 'Vil. Two popular restaurants, Paddy's and Joe's both serve drinks and Paddy's is well known for its Jug'n'Jam night on Wednesdays (Pitchers of Paddy's brewed beer and traditional Irish music). There are lots of opportunities to get involved on campus, with the many clubs to pique just about anyone's interest. New Minas, the next town over, has a cinema and a mall and is only a short bus ride away. Chill out or meet for a study group at the Coffee Merchant, or have a pint of Guinness upstairs at the Library Pub. I found that the dating scene was through friends because everyone knows everyone at Acadia.

Alumnus/a, 9/2001-5/2007, May 2007

Social life at Acadia is quite limited to the few places where you can go, but it is not lacking at all. Everyone knows everyone and wherever you go, you fit in! There is an on-campus bar that is always busy and a lot of fun. With a room upstairs that residences, clubs and so on usually rent for parties. Restaurants in Wolfville are great. You have an Irish pub with great food, the Library Pub with great beer, the local restaurant with great potato skins and two higher class restaurants for those fine dining occasions you may wish to have. You are also only a 10-minute drive away from all the fast food you could want and a shop-

ping mall. The school is also only an hour away from the capital of Nova Scotia, so whenever you need to get away or have more options, you are never that far away! We do not have a Greek system here, as is the case at most Canadian schools.

Current student, 9/2002-Submit Date, April 2006

The university has its own bar called the Axe, which is a favorite among students. There are frequent contests and events going on at the Axe, as well as cheap drink nights and karaoke at times. The Mackeen Room upstairs in the same building is also the home to many concerts and special events that attract a number of students. There are many opportunities for student bands to play on campus, as well during that Coffee Haus that Acadia hosts. In town, there are plenty of restaurants to choose from, as well as some great take-out menus. Mere minutes away is New Minas, which has a shopping mall and plenty of other places to eat, such as Chinese, Pizza Hut, KFC, Harvey's and Swiss Chalet, as well as fine dining.

Acadia has also recently acquired a new building, the KC Irving Centre, which has also hosted numerous events and concerts. Bands, such as Treble Charger, Sloan, The Trews and others, have come to play at Acadia. As for dating, it is a small school with small classes, so it is easy to meet new people from class, residence or the local bars and pubs. There are also plenty of opportunities for other activities, such as sports (varsity and intramural), as well as extensive gym equipment, walking trails along a scenic route, which are a favorite in the spring and summer months, and a pond for skating.

Current student, 9/2003-Submit Date, April 2006

The social life is what you make it. We live in a very small community, so there isn't a lot in the way of bars (only two), restaurants (only four) or hang-out spots. As mentioned before, Halifax is only an hour away and there is a ton of stuff to do. Or about 15 minutes down the road is a bigger (small) town that has a movie theatre, pool rooms and a mall. As for Wolfville, many of the students are active in intramurals and clubs. There are tons of clubs and everyone has access (even if you've never been on a horse, you can still join the equestrian team, for example). There are tons of volunteer opportunities, as well, and it's not uncommon to have the school participate. We're a very small campus (4,000 students), so there is more of a hook-up scene than a dating scene. With this in mind, because we're so small, everyone knows your business. It keeps people friends, though, and when you do go out to one of our local bars, you know everyone on the dance floor. There is no Greek system (technically) but the major sports teams are a system of their own. The rugby boys, in particular, throw the best parties throughout the year and they're usually themed and ridiculously fun. The locals always love when 2,000 students are running around town in their 70s wear.

The School Says

ACADIA UNIVERSITY, founded in 1838, is located in the town of Wolfville, Nova Scotia, approximately 100 kilometres northwest of Halifax, the provincial capital. Acadia is a topnotch research university, but teaching is at the heart of all that we do. Learning at Acadia happens in a stimulating environment that extends beyond our state-of-the-art classrooms into our labs, coffee shops, and spills out into the surrounding community. Acadia's average class has 26 students, which helps to maintain an intimate learning environment for students. Our faculty's commitment to their students means they are continuously exposed to nationally and internationally recognized research initiatives.

Acadia has embarked on the next educational evolution in learning with the Acadia Advantage program, an initiative that integrates the use of notebook computers into the undergraduate curriculum. All of Acadia's undergraduate students use laptop computers as an important part of their learning experience.

Why choose Acadia when there are so many other options available? The answer is simple: Acadia students earn a degree from one of Canada's most respected universities and learn in a way

Read all of Vault's College Surveys at **www.vault.com/college**—get complete surveys on 100s of colleges and universities, expert advice on applicaton essays and more.

VAULT CAREER LIBRARY **797**

that is unique among post-secondary institutions. Acadia grad-uates are poised for success whatever path they choose.

Acadia's small classes insure that professors are more than teachers; they are also mentors and advisors, who open doors to career opportunities and academic post-graduate program. In this setting, Acadia students "learn by doing," gaining valuable knowledge and research experience that they can apply imme-diately after they graduate. This hands-on approach, combined with Acadia's unique technology-rich environment and curricu-lum, gives graduates a competitive advantage when they enter the workforce or continue with their studies in graduate schools and professional programs.

Students enrolled in an honours program choose a faculty advi-sor and perform academic research while completing their the-sis. Our graduates tell us that their experience at Acadia allows them to excel in their graduate programs. Acadia is an impor-

tant stepping stone for those who go on to professional pro-grams in fields from law to medicine, to business. As an Acadia alumnus/a, your opportunities are endless.

Acadia University has an excellent reputation. For the past 13 years, *Maclean's* magazine survey has consistently ranked Acadia as one of the top undergraduate universities in Canada in the reputational category (Leaders of Tomorrow, Highest Quality, Most Innovative and Best Overall).

The small-town setting and predominantly residential character encourages personal growth through close contacts with stu-dents and professors, through participation in intramural and intercollegiate activities, and through a wide variety of cultural programs. Acadia's 3,000 students form a close relationship with the small, safe, and friendly town of Wolfville. Acadia has more than 30,000 alumni worldwide and currently has students from over 60 countries around the globe.

McGill University

Admissions, Recruitment and Registrar's Office (ARR)
James Administration Building
845 Sherbrooke Street West
Montreal, QC H3A 2T5
Admissions phone: (514) 398-3910
Admissions fax: (514) 398-4193
Admissions e-mail: admissions@mcgill.ca
Admissions URL: www.mcgill.ca/applying

 Admissions

Alumnus/a, 9/2001-6/2005, December 2006

I was applying as an international student. The application process was really quite simple. I filled out an online application, paid $60 and that's all. No SAT, references or essay required. That was the good part.

Current student, Business, 9/2003-Submit Date, April 2007

The admissions process is very easy, as it does not require any references or essays. It is suggested that you send your SAT score if you achieve at least a 1200 (out of 1600 on the older SAT version). It is much more difficult to get in as an international student, where rate of acceptance is around 15 percent. You will need to have a high grades, since they do not look at anything else.

Current student, 9/2003-Submit Date, September 2005

The admissions process is fairly straightforward. Applications are available electronically and can be filled out completely online. Transcripts are required; however, they were sent directly from my local school board to the university. There were no interviews and the application process did not require the sub-mission of essays. Having said this, McGill is one of the toughest schools in the country to get into. The entrance average increase annually, so high school marks count!

Alumnus/a, 9/2001-6/2004, March 2006

Admissions process was incredibly painless. Unless you're looking a financial aid package, all you really have to do is run through the standard online back-ground questions and input a few numbers (standardized test scores, GPA). There wasn't any essay to write back when I applied in winter 2001. From start to finish, the application couldn't have taken more than 45 minutes. They seemed to only evaluate the basic numbers—e.g., GPA and standardized test scores. There was no interview necessary and McGill sent back the acceptance letter after a mere three weeks. I think that if you have a strong GPA and SATs (AP scores that are four or five are seen very positively there and they will later

translate into six full credits), you'll be in great shape. This isn't a great choic if you're looking to compensate for weak board scores with wonderful recom mendations, extracurriculars and essays.

Current student, 8/2004-Submit Date, May 2005

McGill is a very prestigious university that does not have an extensive, annoy ing application process. It does not require an essay or an interview. I applie online in a matter of minutes and made an easy online payment for the applica tion fee, which is also cheaper than most other schools. All you need to appl online are standardized testing scores and a high school transcript. Though th application process is simple, the selectivity is still competitive and thus the stu dious and diverse environment of McGill is created.

Current student, Engineering, 9/2003-Submit Date, March 2005

There was no interview to get into mechanical engineering at McGill. The appli cation was simple and I was notified rather quickly. It was a pretty satisfactor process. You might need to write an essay if you apply for a full entrance scho arship. Otherwise, it's very simple.

Current student, 9/2004-Submit Date, January 2005

The official university web site is extremely helpful in directing prospective stu dents in the direction they want to go. It provides links to the various facultie and available courses, along with the basic requirements needed for acceptanc into each course. When the prospective student knows the faculty for which h or she wishes to apply, he or she can apply directly online by filling out th online application that takes around an hour to complete.

The application requires basic information and asks for grade 11 and 12 classe and marks. Beyond this, there are a few short questions that ask about the stu dent's involvement in and out of school and any notable achievements or award the student has won. The student may also pay the required application fe directly online with a credit card. The management program at McGill is fairl selective, as it looks for individuals with not only good graduating grades, bu also good extracurricular involvement, as the faculty seeks well-rounded indi viduals who are the potential business leaders of the future. Generally, appli cants are notified of acceptance anywhere from mid July to early August.

Current student, 9/2003-Submit Date, September 2004

Application is either through the Internet registration, or handwritten applicatio forms. There is no essay or interview required to apply. Selection for the pro gram is based solely on academic standings. However, the university does tak into account circumstances that may have resulted in a lower GPA than expect ed. In such a case, a letter must be submitted to the university upon hearing tha one was not accepted or in conjunction with a handwritten application.

Academics

rrent student, Health, 1/2005-Submit Date, May 2007

is is variable depending not only on your department but also on the type of dent you are. If you are proactive and interested in your field, you will find ple opportunity to interact with researchers who are generally friendly and ling to help. Some classes are less interesting and like any educational insti- ion some of the teachers are not friendly. All in all, your experience will be at you make of it. McGill has all the resources, along with topnotch profes- s and researchers, to make your experience exactly what you want it but you ve to do it, don't expect anybody else to make sure that you have a good expe- nce.

rrent student, Business, 9/2003-Submit Date, April 2007

e bachelor's program is organized around core courses, and then you are fered the choice of majors (10 classes) or concentrations (five classes) in any siness related subject. Class sizes are bigger than those at elite American uni- rsities, but you can get adequate help from TAs and professors outside of class ne. They have a curve, requiring class averages to be a B, which creates a mpetitive environment, and some extra hard exams just to get the average wn. It requires a lot of work, but you can choose to what extent you wish to well.

umnus/a, 9/2000-6/2003, September 2005

vas enrolled in an inter-faculty program that was a combination of the arts and anagement faculties. I studied industrial relations. The curriculum is struc- red with many mandatory courses. This makes for a small group that moves m class to class. Class size ranges from 20 to 35 students, with no problem gistering for each class. The professors are caring and due to the small class- , very attentive to the students' needs. Workload can be difficult, depending one's schedule; however, it is most definitely manageable. A characteristic of e school that is often overlooked is the composition of the student body. cGill has one of the largest international populations in the country. Students me from all over Canada and the United States. There is also a large number students from Europe, Africa, Latin America and Southeast Asia.

umnus/a, 9/2001-6/2004, March 2006

er since they changed over to Minerva (they started my first year), the course lection process has been made remarkably easy. McGill is notorious for its red e and bureaucracy (it can actually be difficult to meet and talk with someone o can help you if you have a very specific problem), so the transparency in e class selection process is certainly a welcome change.

> **The school says:** "Over the last few years, McGill has vastly
> improved the efficiency of its student services. For example,
> signing up for an ID card used to require long waiting times; the
> wait in the last two years has been reduced to 10 or 15 min-
> utes, and students can set up their e-mail accounts and sign up
> for orientations at the same time they get their ID. 'Ask Me'
> volunteers—armed with maps, goodies bags and lot of informa-
> tion—are on campus during frosh week to guide new students
> and their parents. The Principal's Task Force on Student Life
> and Learning made recommendations in late 2006 on how to
> further streamline bureaucracy, and the university is developed
> a plan to implement the suggestions, under the guidance of the
> new Deputy Provost, Student Life and Learning."

ademics are obviously very strong. Top professors from Canada and occa- nally some second- and (rarely) first-tier professors from the States make up e core. The workload is very much dependent upon your program. For exam- e, the school of engineering is notoriously brutal. Many arts programs, such psychology, anthropology and sociology, are (this I can personally vouch for) atively easy and you can easily get B's doing minimal work or A's if you do the work and attend all the classes. Getting straight A's is a very rare feat, wever. Only eight people during my freshman year had 4.0s in the faculty of ts and the number above 3.8 was around 90. I don't know what the statistics re in subsequent years; I was never above 3.8 again.

ne more thing: the academics at McGill are whatever you make of them. If you e very interested in the subject matter and are inclined to really learn, then pro-

fessors are incredibly helpful, welcoming and available. If you're there to party and get a diploma, that works, too, just don't expect straight A's or that profs will be particularly receptive to a kid whom they haven't seen in class until two days before the midterm.

Current student, 7/2003-Submit Date, March 2005

I am currently enrolled in a BA program. I am double-majoring in English lit- erature and psychology. I have been blessed with amazing professors and have learned a lot. The classes are competitive and thus grading is often difficult. There are lots of reading material and assignments in all of my classes.

I am currently taking a full courseload, five classes per semester. Consequently, I am extremely busy with a heavy workload. The smaller classes are more dif- ficult to get. But I always register on the first possible date, and therefore have not encountered any problems. McGill is a very challenging but rewarding uni- versity.

Current student, 9/2004-Submit Date, January 2005

The McGill management program is consistently ranked in the Top Three busi- ness schools in Canada by *Maclean's* magazine, and the school itself is consid- ered one of the Top 10 universities in the world. Management students take core classes in all areas of management during their first two years at McGill before declaring their major or concentration and selecting classes in that specific field of study. All management classes are of high quality, with class sizes that do not surpass 100 students, and these large classes are normally only the core classes required in freshman year.

It is extremely easy to register for classes, as it is all done online, and popular classes always have more than one section, allowing more students to take them. Classes can be taken on the standard grading scale and getting a grade of B or higher is easy provided the student does the required assignments and partici- pates in class discussions.

The professors in the management faculty are excellent because they all want students to succeed not only in school but also in the future. All maintain office hours every week and are normally available at any time when appointments are made to meet with them. Professors are very receptive to students who put in the extra effort and go to office hours when they have questions. In addition to this, there are many groups in the faculty that run mass tutorials for various pop- ular classes at exam time, which are extremely helpful when preparing for exams.

The workload varies from class to class, some have no required assignments and grades are based on the midterm and final exams, while others are based on major group projects (especially marketing classes). The management faculty in general creates a workload that is easily handled, even with playing an intercol- legiate sport and being part of a fraternity, sorority or any other group on cam- pus.

Employment Prospects

Current student, 9/2003-Submit Date, March 2005

There are many ways to get employed when you are in mechanical engineering at McGill. The MECC career centre is the most obvious way. They can help you find summer employment or one-year internships or full- or part-time jobs, career related or not. You can also apply for a NSERC USRA undergraduate summer research award if your GPA is high enough. There are on-campus tech fairs and info sessions where many companies recruit students usually once per semester.

Current student, Health, 1/2005-Submit Date, May 2007

The university is very theoretical/research-focused. You have to work hard to get a more practical experience. Some programs, like science and engineering, are easier but others are harder. The health-related professional degrees like medicine, OT/PT, nursing have a very good balance of both.

Current student, Business, 9/2003-Submit Date, April 2007

McGill is very well known, but for international students, it was nearly impos- sible to have access to summer internships in Canada until they changed the law. Approximately 20 percent of students go international, 50 percent the rest of

Read all of Vault's College Surveys at **www.vault.com/college**—get complete surveys on 100s of colleges and univer- sities, expert advice on applicaton essays and more.

VAULT CAREER LIBRARY **799**

Canada and 30 percent stay in Quebec. The top companies come, but I found that McGill's Career Services was not helpful at all when looking outside Canada.

Current student, 9/2004-Submit Date, January 2005

The management program is great for getting employment after graduation. It has an extensive alumni list, many of whom are more than willing to offer jobs to graduates of the faculty. Jobs with accounting firms, stock brokers and marketing companies (or marketing jobs) are extremely popular for graduates.

The faculty has a career center that is open from 9 a.m. to 5 p.m., Monday to Friday with an extremely helpful staff. They will help a student perfect his or her résumé, do mock job interviews and set up interviews with prospective employers. They also hold career days that are great for meeting with different companies and developing a network (and you get free stuff).

There are also many internship opportunities with major businesses in Montreal, as McGill has a very well-developed and well-maintained internship program. Applying for internships is very easy with the help of the career center. The is also the marketing network that allows students to develop their own networks with prospective employers though various seminars and guest speakers. It is generally very easy for a management graduate to get a fairly prestigious job upon graduation. The management faculty is also home to the Alpha Kappa Psi professional business fraternity that provides members with an alumni network of over 300,000 business men and women.

Quality of Life

Current student, Business, 9/2003-Submit Date, April 2007

The campus is in downtown Montreal, so you have access to everything. You get to live off campus second year with plenty of adequate housing. The facilities are improving greatly, especially in management.

Current student, Health, 1/2005-Submit Date, May 2007

Montreal is great, arguably one of the best cities to live in for school. It is safe and affordable. Don't be afraid to live a little out of the "McGill Ghetto." The 20 minutes Metro or bus ride will be worth it. The campus is very beautiful but is in dire need of an upgrade. Housing is very expensive in the Ghetto and decreases as you get away. There are many places to live outside the Ghetto and that is a good thing. Food in the city is great and diversified. The city is very vibrant.

Alumnus/a, 9/2001-6/2004, March 2006

The quality of life is outstanding: Montreal is the safest city I had ever been to (until I went to Ottawa, and then there's Halifax, too). Live near campus if you can—you'll meet so many students just living in the McGill Ghetto (don't worry, it's not actually a ghetto). Living in the dorms first year was the best year of my life. During that first year is when everybody forms their core group of friends, so it's important to be outgoing and build a broad social network. The McGill facilities, particularly for arts students, are really in need of renovation. The money has gone into the amazing new music building and some new med building and one new science building. But arts is pretty run down. In terms of dorms, you really can't go wrong with any of them, so take your pick. I recommend the new ones on Park Ave. The truth behind them (and you'll notice this if you ever see them) is that all of the housing on Park consists of buildings that were formerly hotels that McGill bought to meet the housing demands of its ever-growing student body. They haven't changed them that much since, so you get by far the nicest dorm room (for a little extra dough, however).

Current student, 8/2004-Submit Date, May 2005

McGill is located in downtown Montreal but is relatively safe. There are also services like Drive Safe and Walk Safe to ensure the safety of the students. On-campus housing is guaranteed for the first year. There are many different types of dorms that cater to the interests and preferences of every individual.

The dorms are all well-supplied, organized and good for socializing. There is an on-campus gym that is cheap for students to join. The cafeterias are decent but the food is repetitive. There are many other options for dining, such as eating

out or ordering in. Though safety and crime is less of a concern, McGill nonetheless in a city and students should apply common sense and caution.

Current student, 9/2003-Submit Date, September 2004

The McGill residence halls located to the east of the school are in an area ove flowing with students. It creates a small community within a big city that allo one to get to know several people in similar classes or in the party scer Nearby, there is not only a wide variety of grocery stores, entertainment such theatres and bars, but also all the necessary stores, such as a drugstore or p office.

Being mostly students, crime is minimal. The downtown McGill campus magnificent, with a collection of both old and new structures that form a uniq atmosphere that compliments the unique mix of students who attend. McG possesses a wonderful variety of students and a combination of Anglo a Francophone students.

Social Life

Current student, Health, 1/2005-Submit Date, May 2007

Everything is close in Montreal, nightlife is great and there are ample opport nities to volunteer, view cultural exhibits/shows, travel in the Northeast US Ontario, Maritimes and Quebec (make sure that you explore the province, do just live on the island). Finally, the winters are cold so make sure you rewa yourself and spend at least one summer in Montreal, you can work easily in t summer in the city (even if your French is only passable) or on campus (do need French).

Current student, Businesst, 9/2003-Submit Date, April 2007

Montreal is a vibrant and young city, with close to 300,000 students between t ages 18 to 25, out of a total population of 3 million. This city is truly a great st dent city, with the legal drinking age of 18 in Quebec. Montreal is a very op and diverse melting pot, so no matter your preferences (sexual, musical, dining you will find something. There are plenty of clubs and bars, so there is litt need for a Greek system. There are some fraternities and sororities, but they a more about networking than anything else.

Alumnus/a, 9/2001-6/2004, March 2006

Greek life is virtually nonexistent. There are a few frats that struggle mighti for relevance. Sororities are somewhat more popular in terms of sheer number but are still very much marginalized.

The SSMU (student society of McGill) is very active and does an amazing j of helping people who want to be involved in some sort of activity find oth like-minded students (hell, they even had a knitting society while I was there Be sure to attend club night—it's once a semester about two weeks in, in t Shatner building (the student center on MacTavish).

The nightlife is tops in North America in terms of appeal for college student You have everything at your disposal in Montreal. There is a scene for ever individual. My personal favorites were the dive bars on St. Catherine's, thoug living it up on Lower St. Laurent is always fun on a Friday or Saturday nigh And don't underestimate the appeal of being in such a multicultural cit Whenever you like, you can take the Metro out east from your comfort zone the downtown core and feel as if you've suddenly been dropped onto a differe continent.

Current student, 7/2003-Submit Date, March 2005

McGill has its own campus bar that is open most nights of the week. This ba Gerts, is the host of various events throughout the year to promote student socia ization in the university community, such as McGill Idol and charity auctions o days like Valentine's Day. Gerts is also the venue for three large university pa ties per year, in which all four floors of the McGill student building are open fo different varieties of music and dance.

In addition, Montreal is a wonderful nightlife city. There are seemingly endles bars and clubs for all students and Montreal locals to attend. Student hotspo include Saint Laurent and Crescent Street.

urrent student, 9/2004-Submit Date, January 2005

ontreal has a very popular social scene, with McGill right in the middle of it. is very easy to get socially involved in the community through all the clubs d groups offered by the faculties or by the students union. All faculties have ny popular events like frosh week and winter carnival. McGill is situated tween two of the most popular bar and club streets in Montreal, and they are vays packed with students on the weekends.

e students building also has Gerts, the campus pub, where students can always ax and play pool or have a drink with friends. Occasionally, professors drop the pub and mingle with students. There is a strong Greek community at cGill that is overseen by a very capable Inter-Greek Letter Council (IGLC). ere is a fraternity or sorority for every student, depending on what he or she looking for. There is also a co-ed fraternity. McGill is ranked very high in the cial aspect by *Maclean's* and any student can be as involved as he or she likes!

The School Says

Founded in 1821 with a bequest by Montreal merchant James McGill, McGill University has earned an international reputation for scholarly achievement and scientific discovery. The only Canadian university ranked in the Top 25 universities in the world by the *Times Higher Education Supplement* for three years running, McGill was also picked as the top medical-doctoral school in the country by *Maclean's* magazine in 2006.

Innovative research programs and cutting-edge facilities attract internationally respected faculty and the best students, who have the highest average entering grade of any university in Canada. With a reputation built on teaching and research excellence, McGill offers its 33,000 students unparalleled opportunities to enrich their educational experience through hands-on research opportunities, international exchanges, internships, field-study and study-abroad programs.

McGill's 21 faculties and professional schools offer degrees in more than 300 fields of study. McGill offers a full range of bachelor's, master's and doctoral programs, as well as professional degrees in law, dentistry, business and medicine. The world-renowned Faculty of Medicine has four affiliated teaching hospitals and graduates more than 1,000 health care professionals each year.

Under the leadership of Principal Heather Munroe-Blum, McGill is committed to providing the best services and support to students. The Principal's Task Force on Student Life and Learning made recommendations in late 2006 to improve the availability and quality of academic advising, as well as to increase funding and financial aid to graduate and undergraduate students.

With almost 20 percent of its students coming from 150 countries around the globe, McGill has the most internationally diverse student body of any medical-doctoral university in Canada. The ability to balance academic excellence with extracurricular activities is another hallmark of students at McGill. In addition to a rich athletic tradition that includes many Olympians, thousands of McGill students participate in the hundreds of clubs, associations and community groups that enrich Montreal and contribute to a vibrant campus life.

Lively and sophisticated, yet safe and affordable, the bilingual and multicultural city of Montreal boasts four universities and one of the highest number of university students per capita in North America. McGill's main campus, a mosaic of heritage and modern buildings laid out around an oasis of green space, is set in the heart of Montreal's vibrant downtown core. A short drive west of downtown, the Macdonald campus occupies 650 hectares of woods and waterfront property, providing unique opportunities for fieldwork and research activities.

Approximately 2,400 housing places are available for eligible students, including apartments, shared facilities/houses, and co-ed and women's residences. Many McGill students who live in residence in their first academic year move into their own apartments in subsequent years.

Our web site, www.mcgill.ca, provides an excellent introduction to McGill, including descriptions of academic programs and links to major publications, resources and events. An annual open house for prospective students is held in January each year, and our Welcome Centre arranges walking tours and the student-for-a-day program, information about accommodation close to campus and much more in the way of support for prospective students and their families.

For information on applying to McGill University, go to www.mcgill.ca/applying.

Queen's University

.dmission Services
ueen's University
ordon Hall
4 Union Street
ingston, ON K7L 3N6
.dmissions phone: (613) 533-2218
.dmissions fax: (613) 533-6810
.dmissions e-mail: admission@queensu.ca
.dmissions URL: www.queensu.ca/admission/

Admissions

urrent student, Commerce, 9/2003-Submit Date, June 2005

he commerce program weights the personal information form very heavily. ou must have a high average to get in (last year's cutoff was 89), but you must lso have a very good résumé. Get a part-time job, volunteer in the community nd get involved in extracurriculars at school.

You must take English and a calculus course for Ontario high schools. Check the admissions web site for information from other schools. Don't expect to be admitted first round to the commerce program. And also don't expect to get in if you have a 95 average with no extracurriculars or a job.

Current student, Engineering, 9/2004-Submit Date, July 2007

Besides grades, the admissions process for Queen's University required a Personal Statement of Experience (PSE). This form required prospective students to fill out their academic achievements, as well as their community achievements, since Queen's strongly believes in community involvement. Showing a great deal of leadership within both school and community gives an individual strong consideration from the enrollment board.

Alumnus/a, 9/1999-5/2003, April 2005

When you apply to the undergraduate program at Queen's University, you must apply separately to each school. For example, I applied to the School of Arts and Science, as well as to Applied Science. I was accepted to each one separately. At the time of my application, they required a high school transcript and information about extracurricular activities. I don't recall having to write any essays

Read all of Vault's College Surveys at **www.vault.com/college**—get complete surveys on 100s of colleges and universities, expert advice on applicaton essays and more.

VAULT CAREER LIBRARY **801**

or obtain any letters of recommendation aside from the those I needed for the scholarships for which I applied.

The course prerequisites for Applied Science were very specific (e.g., calculus, algebra, chemistry, physics, English) but those for Arts and Science were less specific. There was no interview in the selection process. I believe that my acceptance to Queen's was based almost exclusively on my high school transcript. Queen's is highly selective in terms of grades.

Current student, 9/2003-Submit Date, September 2005

Being admitted was only a matter of applying and having high enough grades to make the cut. A personal statement of experience was optional but helps chances of being admitted. If you are not admitted right away, there is a waitlist that often opens up. You may get a letter of denial but then receive a phone call or a letter saying that a place has opened up for you. There are no interviews or essays. Marks are the major factor upon applying to an undergraduate program; however, graduate schools take into account other things, such as experience that you have with the field, on par with marks.

Current student, 9/2004-Submit Date, July 2004

Students apply through the Ontario Universities' Application Centre. Grade 11 and 12 marks are submitted, and the top six grade 12 courses are used to calculate an admissions average, which must be approximately 82 percent or higher for admission to Arts and Science, higher for some other programs.

Commerce is the most selective program, requiring a minimum average of 87 percent for consideration as well as strong extracurriculars. For all programs, students must submit a short personal statement of experience outlining their extracurricular activities. Queen's is arguably the most selective university in Canada.

Alumnus/a, 9/1995-5/1999, September 2004

The admissions process is done through the Ontario Universities' Application Centre. If you want to get in to Queen's, you need to have a stellar academic record (at least 85 percent in high school; check www.ouac.on.ca or www.queensu.ca for current requirements). At the same time, you have to have extracurricular experiences to show that you are a well-rounded individual.

 **Academics**

Current student, Engineering, 9/2004-Submit Date, July 2007

The nature of Queen's engineering is challenging yet rewarding. The classes offered are excellent and provide a solid background in engineering principles. All first-year engineering students take the same classes thus exposing them to various fields of engineering, such as mechanical, chemical, electrical and geological. The grading by the professors is fair. If there are any problems with the marking scheme, the professors are very approachable and will work through the problem with the students. The workload in general is quite substantial although managing your time effectively and wisely can lead to a successful year.

Current student, 1/2000-Submit Date, June 2004

School has turned out to be excellent in all aspects. A great deal of emphasis is put on academics over athletics at the school, which creates a perfect environment for those who want to learn. With only 16,000 students, entry into most classes is of no difficulty. Professors have their office hours and sometimes go above and beyond the call to aid a student over the course of the program.

Alumnus/a, 9/1999-5/2003, April 2005

Applied Science is a very difficult program with limited flexibility. In the first year, every engineering student takes the same classes, which span all the disciplines (e.g., mechanical, geological, chemical, computer, math, physics) for the purpose of getting everyone up to the same level and allowing students to determine with which discipline they wish to continue at the end of first year.

You spend your next three years specializing in a particular discipline, with very specific course requirements (e.g., you may choose one or two non-engineering electives per year, out of a total of approximately 12 to 14 courses). Within your discipline, there are different options you can choose, sort of equivalent to a minor. For example, I was in engineering physics (electrical option), which

means that approximately 60 percent of my courses were in eng phys, 30 perce were in electrical eng and 10 percent were electives.

There are approximately 35 hours of class per week in first year, consisting lectures, tutorials and labs. This dropped slightly in later years, but generally was always taking at least six classes per semester. When you're not in cla you're bogged down with a huge amount of work (weekly assignments, tests a projects). If you are the type who needs to get everything done, you will r have time for a social life here. They really do pile on more than anyone c possibly handle. You have to learn how to pick and choose what is important do.

The grading in engineering at Queen's is not designed to stroke any eg. Typically, students find their grades drop 15 to 20 percent from high scho Often midterm averages are in the 50s and even lower. But there is much talk the bell curve, so if you can just make sure you're keeping up with everyone el then you'll be fine. I had some truly excellent professors at Queen's and son truly dismal ones. Generally the teaching was pretty good, but a few bad appl did leave some negative impressions.

Current student, 9/2003-Submit Date, September 2005

Academics are excellent; Queen's is an excellent school and makes sure that y are challenged. Lecture courses and first- and second-year classes tend to quite large without opportunity to get to know your professor in class. Studer can easily change this by going to office hours and participating as much as po sible in the lectures. Seminars and third- and fourth-year classes are very d ferent; they usually have no more then 30 students, and this number is even qui high.

Grading is different, at Queen's a 50 percent to 64 percent is a C, a 65 percent 79 percent is a B and 80 percent and above is an A. This is because the gradi is often quite difficult and this is the school's way of compensating for that.

Current student, 9/2003-Submit Date, June 2005

The workload is heavy, but it is worth it. The quality of the classes, professo and facilities is among the best in the country. I have had no problem getting tl classes I want. The first two years of the program are already set out for you. third year, you pick the stream that you want to go into. Some choices inclu finance, marketing, accounting, human resources, MIS and so on. Mostly all the professors are PhDs and many are recruited from around the world.

Current student, 9/2003-Submit Date, June 2005

Classes are relatively large first year but I don't find it bad at all. Lecture th atres have good projection screens and speakers so you can hear and see we Also notes are often online for convenience. Classes are no problem to enroll i although as an engineering student I only get to choose a few. Courses are ch sen online making it easy and quick to get your choice. Professors are real good and have fair assignments and tests with a reasonable workload for the pr gram.

 Employment Prospects

Alumnus/a, 9/1999-5/2003, April 2005

Although not as well-known outside Canada, Queen's has a very prestigious rep utation. A Queen's graduate has better employment prospects than most. In pa ticular, Queen's is known far and wide as an engineering school. There is a po ular engineering internship program that extends your program to five year while allowing you to work in industry for one year.

Out of my friends who have graduated from Queen's, most went on to do pos graduate degrees in a variety of fields (public health, education, occupation therapy and engineering), either staying at Queen's or moving on to other pres tigious schools (Cornell and Yale). Those who started work immediately aft graduating had little trouble finding jobs, depending on their fields (the high tech industry seems to think highly of Queen's graduates).

Current student, 1/2000-Submit Date, June 2004

Queen's holds a very high reputation in Canada for its academics and any degre from this school is somewhat equivalent to an Ivy League in the U.S. (but obv sly not in the rest of the world). Careers can be found easily upon leaving the institution.

urrent student, Engineering, 9/2004-Submit Date, July 2007

e Queen's name runs high among Canadian universities. An Ivy League hool of Canada if you will. Employment among graduates is high, attracting ny prestigious companies such as IBM, Shell-Canada, Imperial Oil, AMD, search In Motion, General Motors, Honda, Bombardier, Pratt-Whitney and octor & Gamble, to name a few. The Queen's alumni are well known to net-rk with current students. Their involvement reaches as far down as first-year urses. Companies keep a close eye on Queen's graduates, which is a result of ong on-campus presence as well as heavy involvement with providing intern-ips.

urrent student, 9/2003-Submit Date, September 2005

een's is a very respected university and hosts many job fairs for graduating dents of all degree types. Engineers and other specialty programs often find emselves a career in their first year of graduating, while arts and science grees often go on to do more specialized post-graduate work.

urrent student, 9/2003-Submit Date, June 2005

any companies recruit right from the Queen's School of Business. The siness Career Centre is very good at helping you find a job. As long as you well in the program and stay involved, employment will not be an issue. any accounting firms sponsor events right inside the school. *BusinessWeek* cently rated Queen's School of Business one of the best business schools in the rld outside of the U.S. Our name and reputation speak for themselves among ployers across the world.

urrent student, 9/2004-Submit Date, July 2004

e Globe newspaper's University Report Card ranked Queen's first for Career rvices, and the institution has a very good reputation with employers.

urrent student, 9/2003-Submit Date, June 2005

een's is high up in the prestige list and is looked highly upon by employers. ere are on-campus recruiting days and interviews, which is convenient, and so internship opportunities. Faculties send e-mail about jobs specific for you, ich helps a lot. Graduates can obtain decent jobs easily right after graduation.

Quality of Life

urrent student, 1/2000-Submit Date, June 2004

verything at this school was ideal. Crime was almost nonexistent, an eight-uare-block radius around the campus was solely student housing (the ghetto, it is called), being downtown there are plenty of opportunities for employment d night and social life.

urrent student, Engineering, 9/2004-Submit Date, July 2007

ingston is one of the safest cities in Canada, which leads to a safe environment r both the students and residents of the Kingston community. Since Queen's one of the smaller universities, housing is not a problem for most students. een's has more than 10 student residences. Many facilities have been recent-renovated thus providing quality to be matched with the top universities in anada. There are three dining halls on campus as well as satellite food shops ound campus. Queen's proudly displays its history with breathtaking archi-cture composed of limestone with a terrific view of Lake Ontario just steps way.

lumnus/a, 9/1999-5/2003, April 2005

lmost all (90 percent) first-year students live in residences (either on main mpus or west campus, which is a 15-minute walk). Students are required to e on a meal plan. The food, at least when I attended, was horrendous. This is well-known fact. I didn't gain the freshman 15; I lost it because I couldn't omach the food. There was very little choice, and most of what was available as tasteless or unsavory.

side from the food, the residences were pretty nice. The rooms weren't huge at adequate and it wasn't too hard to get a single if you wanted one. After first ear, most students move off campus into neighborhood houses, usually in

groups of three or more. Unfortunately, most affordable student housing near campus is atrocious. Many of the houses are old and require significant renova-tions that landlords aren't willing to provide. Nice places go quickly, so students start looking as early as January for a May lease.

It is a reasonably safe area. There is a campus walk-home service, but I never felt the need to use it while I was there. I never felt uncomfortable walking around alone at night.

Current student, 9/2003-Submit Date, September 2005

Crime is low; there is lots of off-campus housing available for upper-year stu-dents, which the university makes available. Rent is not too steep, and first-year students can count on a room in residence. There are many restaurants from fast food to fine dining within a 15-minute walking radius; everything you need is with in that same radius.

Security alerts are sent out via e-mail to warn students of any dangerous people in the neighborhood. Throughout campus is a blue light system, which is sim-ply a series of lights that are easy to spot with an emergency button on them; if you feel you are in trouble, you can go from light to light and security will trace your pattern and find you. The school also offers programs like Walk Home, where if you call them two people (a girl and boy) will come to meet you where you are and walk you home safely. This is doubly beneficial, as it provides employment opportunities as well as a safety feature.

Current student, 9/2003-Submit Date, June 2005

Kingston is a small, safe town. Housing is not the best in Kingston, but the stu-dent atmosphere is comforting and enjoyable. You'll have no problems eating around here, as the selection of restaurants is excellent. The campus is beautiful and not very large. It is easy to get around and the commerce building looks like a large Toronto law firm's office. The building has wireless Internet throughout, a lounge with a big screen TV and leather couches, and classrooms fitted with large projection screens.

Current student, 9/2004-Submit Date, July 2004

Kingston is a nice neighborhood and mid-sized city. It has a vibrant downtown with restaurants and shopping located close to campus. The campus itself is beautiful, borders on the lake and is confined to a fairly small area. Housing is readily available and not too expensive, but is often not in excellent condition. Academic facilities are excellent, with state-of-the-art libraries and science labs, but athletic facilities are out of date.

The campus has a blue light security system that allows students to contact secu-rity easily if they feel uncomfortable on campus, as well as a walk home serv-ice. The school is known for its trademark spirit.

Current student, 9/2003-Submit Date, June 2005

The campus is gorgeous, the nicest around I feel with beautiful buildings and trees. On campus, residences are really nice and close to everywhere, the cafe-teria is nice with fairly good food for a café. I think Queen's has all you really need on the campus. Downtown is also very close, which is extremely conven-ient and there're good stores, groceries and bars/clubs to go to.

The student housing is really close to campus and downtown as well and pro-vides an excellent community—although the houses are pretty old and known for not being that nice, it is an experience you cannot do without and a lot of fun in the student ghetto. I feel safe on and off campus, even at night, as there are lots of students around and security. There isn't much crime really and you can get a walk home or take taxis very easily for safety.

Social Life

Current student, Engineering, 9/2004-Submit Date, July 2007

Since Queen's is a small campus, the average student will run into familiar faces more often than not. Queen's has three on-campus bars that are run by students. Downtown Kingston is just a short five-minute walk from campus where most of the nightlife takes place with several clubs and bars sprinkling the main street. Queen's also provides many events and clubs to offer students a way to network as well as to have fun. Some favorites include: Queen's Model Parliament, Queen's Bands and Queen's Players.

Read all of Vault's College Surveys at **www.vault.com/college**—get complete surveys on 100s of colleges and univer-sities, expert advice on applicaton essays and more.

VAULT CAREER LIBRARY **803**

Current student, 9/2003-Submit Date, September 2005

There are at least four on-campus bars, and many more within short walking distance, there are also clubs of all different types, from religious to entertainment. Students frequent bars like The Brass, Stages, Elixer, Alfie's and the QP. Many restaurants off campus are so close by that students eat there instead of on campus.

There are countless opportunities for people to get involved with student council and charity organizations to meet new people. First-year students, for the most part, stay in residence where it is impossible not to meet people, and Frosh Week also helps integrate the new students into the school by grouping students by faculty so that they meet others in the same classes.

Current student, 9/2003-Submit Date, June 2005

The nightlife is great here while school is in session. There is one main street with all the bars and clubs on it. You can always find it jammed on Thursday, Friday and Saturday nights. There are plenty of on- and off-campus events to keep you busy every night of the week. Queen's has a large number of clubs and it is easy to get involved. Whether you want to join a religious club, sporting

club or just a special interest, we most likely have it. And if we don't, it's ea to start up your own club.

Current student, 9/2004-Submit Date, July 2004

There are a number of shows offered by the university, including two perfor ances per year by each of the Student Opera, Musical Theatre, Queen's Play and drama department. Cheap movies are shown on Sunday nights, and there also a regular movie theatre closeby.

The university has over 200 clubs and a variety of athletics for all leve Restaurants, shopping and coffee shops are located within a 10-minute walk campus. Although Kingston is not a large city, there is still a strong social li

Current student, 9/2003-Submit Date, June 2005

Queen's is very social. There are several events showing extreme school spi such as the Frosh Week and Homecoming. The downtown is very convenie for going out and has tons of restaurants to meet anyone's needs or cultu desires. There are also several bars and clubs off campus that are popular, su as The Brass, Peel Pub, Stages and Elixer, and on campus there are several b as well, including Clark Hall, Alfie's and Queen's Pub, which are all a lot of f

Simon Fraser University

Admissions Office
8888 University Drive
Burnaby, BC V5A 1S6
Admissions phone: (604) 291-3224
Admissions fax: (604) 291-4969
Admissions URL: students.sfu.ca/adm/

 ## Admissions

Alumnus/a, 8/2000-10/2003, June 2005

The admissions process at SFU is pretty straightforward for undergraduates. You may choose which faculties you prefer, and then depending on your high school marks or college GPA (if you are on transfer), you will be assigned to one of your preferred faculties. For business faculty students, there is actually no difference whether you are in the faculty already or not in the first and second year of your study. However, the cut-off GPA for admission to the business faculty is quite high. The recent cut-off GPA is 3.01 (for students transferring from another college, their college GPA will be deducted by 0.30 for the faculty admission criteria) so the best advice is that once you have a high enough GPA and take some required courses, get in there as soon as possible. The cut-off mark has been increasing gradually in recent years, from 2.90 to 3.01. Requirement for TOEFL for foreign students is not that high. TOEFL may be waived if the student receives a B or better in his/her first-year English course in college.

Current student, 1/2003-Submit Date, March 2005

The admissions process was pretty straightforward for Simon Fraser University (SFU). All I had to do was apply via mail, and was immediately returned with admissions notification and a reference number for my own purposes. I applied to the business administration program, for which students need at least an 88 percent average in high school for their final year to receive direct entry. Otherwise, you'll have to duel it out for an opening come the second year. I was so lucky to receive direct entry, so I had no real problems.

Current student, 1/2004-Submit Date, November 2004

I transferred to the third-year business administration [program] at Simon Fraser University. The admission office first checked my GPA from another post-secondary institute and phoned with the result of their decision on my admission. Later on, my files were transferred to the business administration faculty for further evaluation.

Current student, 1/2000-Submit Date, September 2004

SFU requires no interviews or essays for general entry; the only programs th use this are the contemporary arts or programs with limited seating. In the ca of the former, you'll be required to submit a portfolio prior to your registrati to the satisfaction of professions. I highly recommend compiling this advance; most high schools and colleges recommend building up your portfol up to a year in advance. SFU isn't known as a strong fine arts college, but th do take in a good portion of BC's student body interested in the discipline.

The application process is straightforward. I cannot stress how important it is have all of your transcripts in order. The application form itself is easy. Be ho est. The application requirements go up every year; percentiles for general a and science students hovers around an average of 75 percent, though for cor puter science and business, it can go upwards of 90 percent. Note that SFU h English language proficiency scores (you have to score an A, 86 percent, English in order to avoid taking a first-year English placement test) and if you an ESL student, be sure to take a TOEFL test to ensure you've got what it take It's also very valuable to have a second language up to your junior year (gra 11). SFU requires a grade 11 language course for students to get in from B and this applies to other Canadian students, as well.

The best tip: apply early. This is true for most institutions. If you apply early SFU, it's very likely that you'll have a chance to make up any errors or comp the information needed. Transfer students from British Columbia shou absolutely reference the BCCAT (BC College Transfer Guide) in advance and prepared to contest a few of the courses with SFU.

Talk to the department advisor and the department chair long before you con here, and if you can secure equivalency in writing, by all means, do it! I al suggest that you keep and gather up your course outlines, because that's a p mary way SFU determines compatibility between one course and another, ev if it looks obvious.

 ## Academics

Alumnus/a, 8/2000-10/2003, June 2005

The courses offered in the faculty of business administration are actually pret broad. On your third- and fourth-year studies, you are required to choose yo specialization, e.g., finance, accounting, international business, human resour or management science. Students who are already admitted in the faculty w get preference when choosing which courses to take. The favorite courses (no

lly in accounting and finance) are usually full before the course registration
opened for non-faculty students. Grading in business faculty is very harsh.
e faculty decided to grade using a so-called bell-curve marking, meaning that
you get a 85 percent mark for your exam while the average of the class is 85
rcent too, you will only get a B- or C+. Only the top 10 percent will get A- to
. With this kind of marking, if you happen to take a course with many bright
dents, you can basically predict your mark will be in the C region. This mark-
g puts SFU students at a disadvantage when they later try to look for a job for
ich the employer would want to take a look on their university transcript.

ere are many full-time professors in the faculty. Class workload normally
pends on the lecturer although, personally, I believe the class workload is just
out fine. SFU is ranked first for a couple of years as the best comprehensive
iversity in Canada (by *Maclean's*) although recently it dropped to second
ace.

rrent student, 1/2003-Submit Date, March 2005

was enrolled in the Honors Bachelor's of Business Administration Program.
U is extremely well-known in Western Canada for its rigorous BBA program,
hough this is not really the case outside of British Columbia. The program can
st be described as competitive. Well, and cutthroat too. All marks are curved
every class, so that you'll always find yourself competing against others for
ose precious A grades. In addition, the school is very much a commuter cam-
s, which means you're competing against a bunch of kids who do nothing but
home and study. I excelled, but at the cost of my social life.

rrent student, 1/2004-Submit Date, November 2004

e quality of class is on an average level. Some are quite good, some are so-
. It's not so easy to get popular classes because the date of choosing class is
based on your current credit hours. If you have more credit hours, then you
ll register ahead of others. The grading system is quite fair but hard. The
ding of all major business classes is based on statistical curving system. This
ans you will get a C for 75 percent of the total mark if the average of your
ss is 85 percent. The professors are qualified in their fields. However, some
them are not quite good at teaching. Therefore, some lectures are quite bor-
g. The workload is somewhere higher than the average level. This is mainly
cause of the high competitive study environment around you.

rrent student, 1/2000-Submit Date, September 2004

aclean's magazine, a major news magazine in Canada, has consistently rated
U amongst the Top Five comprehensive undergraduate universities in Canada.
n aggressive advertising campaign in the past five years (since I've been there)
s increased the student body. SFU is actively pursuing business majors since
taining TechBC, a technical institution specializing in information technology
urses. They're trying to woo [IT students] away from their main rivals, the
niversity of British Columbia and the British Columbia Institute of
chnology. Both these schools offer a lot of competition.

ut let's talk academics, shall we? SFU follows a traditional format for its arts
urses, consisting of a lecture usually held once, twice or three times a week
vice is the norm; once for the upper-division courses at the 300- and 400-
vel). This follows a format where the professor speaks on a topic. Once per
eek, you may have a tutorial where further matters, often readings, are dis-
ssed. Lectures can range from 50 to 300 people, the average probably 60 at
cond and third year, and 25 to 40 at fourth year. First year really does range.
ll distance education courses, unless specially specified, accept 100 people.
ur tutorials, applying only to non-distance courses, usually have no more than
people and they're led by either the professor or the TA.

can be hard to get into all the courses you need, especially the introductory
urses. But] let's assume you've actually got the course. How high a quality
it? Www.ratemyprofessor.ca is a popular resource to determine it. There are
any gifted professors in SFU but there are also very poor ones. A problem
aguing arts students is the limited office hours of professors, especially those
aching at more than one institution.

rading is not too bad, although too many professors are using marking software
sending away papers. This really frustrates many students because it's an
fort to stop plagiarism but makes the marking process very impersonal.
ocument everything!

Employment Prospects

Alumnus/a, 8/2000-10/2003, June 2005

For employment prospects (for business faculty students), SFU's co-op program
is very helpful in finding a job for you while you are still at SFU. The co-op job
normally pays a slightly lower salary [than a normal, full-time position,] but it
gives good exposure to the real work. The downside, however, is that the co-op
jobs posted are not many. You will be competing with at least 30 students for a
good co-op job, for which the employer will most likely pick up the brightest
students for interviews.

Current student, 1/2003-Submit Date, March 2005

Personally, I found that most of the jobs were for small companies, in really what
amounted to glorified administrative positions. What did I hope for? Getting
consulting firms to recruit on campus, and so on. But again, this I think was really more of an issue with Vancouver itself, not the school.

Current student, 1/2000-Submit Date, September 2004

The career center offers plenty of weekly and monthly information sessions
about how to hone job hunting skills, develop networking skills and write winning résumés. SFU uses workopoliscampus.com for all job postings except
internal, which you can still access by contacting the registrar.

SFU offers co-op programs and with the size of Vancouver, placements should-
n't be difficult. Documents are rather difficult to find about the co-op program,
however, and I advise you to talk to the people in the department.

Alumnus/a, 6/1990-4/1993, October 2003

Compared to the other major universities on the lower mainlands, SFU has made
great strides in terms of prestige; especially the business program. At the time I
attended, the norm was that UBC was much better. However, by the time I had
left, SFU was gaining ground, and today I have even heard that SFU has sur-
passed UBC due to the intensive use of the co-op program and the usage of case
studies in senior level courses. Furthermore, the increased popularity of the
downtown campus has contributed to the awareness of SFU within the business
community.

Quality of Life

Alumnus/a, 8/2000-10/2003, June 2005

SFU is located on the top of Burnaby Mountain, making it very secluded from
city life. Housing on campus is very limited, although I heard they have recently built new housing. Campus facilities are quite complete. SFU is planning to
build so-called UniverCity. UniverCity will provide broader options of foods (or
fast food) from which to choose and also an increase in the number of housing
and stores. It boasts that SFU will become a city of its own. Crime is very low
there even though it is located in a secluded area. Security officers can normally be seen patrolling on a bike in places less traveled.

Current student, 1/2004-Submit Date, November 2004

I'm not living on campus. But the housing on campus looks good. The school
provides several building options for each student. The campus is not fully covered by grassland and there is a lack of sports facilities. There are several alarm
terminals at some points on campus, which can be used to make emergency calls.
The teaching facilities are not quite sufficient.

Current student, 1/2000-Submit Date, September 2004

SFU is located atop Burnaby Mountain east of Vancouver, BC. At this altitude,
SFU's main campus on the mountain does have cooler weather than down below.
This doesn't make commuting a problem because rarely does it snow (even at
SFU) and they're good about posting conditions on the web site.

But with regards to cars, parking here is expensive ($2 an hour) and parking
passes are done through a lottery so they're very hard to get. You pay a premium for that vehicle. Car break-ins seems to be somewhat problematic and
though there is campus security all over the place, it's really negligible to suggest how much good they do if you're all the way over in the far C parking lot.

Read all of Vault's College Surveys at **www.vault.com/college**—get complete surveys on 100s of colleges and universities, expert advice on applicaton essays and more.

VAULT CAREER LIBRARY **805**

Dining facilities on the mountain are very limited. You'll find no grocery store, a major minus because the only place you can find snacks after things close is down the hill at Safeway in the Kensington Plaza, which is a well-stocked shopping plaza. There's not a lot of healthy choices; on site you'll find Mr. Sub, Koya of Japan, White Spot (hamburgers) and two cafeterias usually in service. Quality of food varies and you're paying a premium.

The campus facilities themselves aren't bad, and the gym is a great deal. However, here's a fact SFU students have to get used to: You're living in a concrete building in a place where it gets dark and dreary from late autumn until early spring. Summer is beautiful, winter rains are not. The health center is adequate and modern, with a BC Biomed on site, but its rotating doctors make it hard to get a regular physician and they are not worth it for dispensing prescriptions. Go to the youth clinics prevalent all over Burnaby, Coquitlam and Vancouver.

Social Life

Alumnus/a, 8/2000-10/2003, June 2005

Social life on campus is not that promising. There is only one bar on campus and it is quite small. For dating, there aren't many romantic places, though you can always go to the top of the buildings (normally in the Academic Q area) and sit facing to the mountains, which have very beautiful scenery. In the beginning of each semester, they normally held so-called Club Days, where you can take a look and choose which clubs you would like to join. For students who are new to western Canada or are from overseas, it is best to join a skiing club or snowboarding club. Vancouver is located very close to probably the best skiing and snowboarding place, Whistler. Whistler is only a couple of hours away on a drive and it is a place for the future Winter Olympic in 2010.

Current student, 1/2003-Submit Date, March 2005

One bar, commuter campus, and not too much to do. I nevertheless enjoyed education but, be warned, not a fun school by any means. I had a few opportunities to attend conferences and case competitions at neighboring schools, a from this experience I can speak to the true university experience that I miss out on.

Current student, 1/2000-Submit Date, September 2004

It's been said Vancouver is a "no fun" city. If that's the case, then SFU is the " fun" university. The community spirit you expect at the post-secondary le isn't here. Clubs here are limited in number and many cater to ethnic or religic groups.

Intramural sports are present on campus but not at the campus at Harbour Cent They offer a fairly limited selection through the year and you're often going feel outmatched by nearly Olympic-class athletes. SFU has one of the very f scholarship programs and support of NAIA athletics, so there are a number very talented, accomplished athletes here. The facilities are quite good but often feels like you're sort of locked out of them.

Sports teams here are focused mostly around swimming, basketball, football a rugby. There's not a continuous event that people really get behind; we do have a fully fledged stadium on the hill. For that, you need to go to UBC.

So what is there to do? The SFU contemporary arts students put on a number free performances at the theatre, which is centrally located across from t library in Convocation Square. It's a great deal if you like contemporary a modern performances, like dance and music, although mainstream Canadian a international musicians usually don't make it up except during the first week autumn or spring term. SFU has three semesters, be aware: fall, spring and sur mer (intercession).

University of Alberta

Prospective Student Office
Augustana Faculty, University of Alberta
4901 46th Avenue
Camrose, AB T4V 2R3
Admissions phone: (780) 679-1132
Admissions fax: (780) 679-1164
Admissions e-mail: admissions@augustana.ca
Admissions URL: ww.ualberta.ca/~publicas/uofa/prospective/undergrad_admissions.html

Note: The school has chosen not to comment on the student surveys submitted.

Admissions

Alumnus/a, 9/1999-6/2003, January 2007

Entrance was fairly easy. I filled out the application forms and sent in my records from high school. I studied overseas but was a Canadian citizen. The university didn't bring up any issues whatsoever with my application. Advice: Make sure you fill it out correctly and you know what you are applying for.

Alumnus/a, Computer Science, 9/2002-6/2006, September 2006

When I entered the school you could not be directly admitted to the computer science program, which has now changed. It seemed a lot harder to get into than it really was for a high school student. You just had to fill out the forms and pay your deposit, then wait. The wait wasn't too bad for me; I found out in late

June/early July that I was enrolled, however other years have had to wait as lo as mid-August for their admissions. Admission is based solely on grades.

Current student, 9/2004-Submit Date, April 2006

All I had to do was fill out the application form in February and send curre high school marks to get conditional acceptance. Then once I got my final hi school transcript, I had to send it to them for confirmation. I also had to pay confirmational deposit of about $150, which later goes toward your tuition fe I applied to get into the Bachelor's of Science program for which you needed 80 percent. If you are an international student, then you might have to do TOEFL exam, as well.

Alumnus/a, 9/2000-4/2003, April 2005

The University of Alberta's engineering program is a well-regarded and soug after program. Admission it is done on an purely academic system, based final grades out of high school or equivalent. Applications are taken in the fa of the year prior and transcripts are sent out over the summer. Since the first ye of engineering is general and specializing doesn't take place till the second ye there are no complicated selection processes. The University of Alberta offe 10 different engineering departments: chemical, materials, civil, environment electrical, compute, engineering physics, mechanical, mining and petroleu with different specialties and both co-ops (work terms mixed in with norm class semesters) and traditional (only summer work terms) options.

The selection process into the second-year disciplines is again done on an ac demic basis. Each student fills out a preference list of the specialties that he/sl would like to be in, usually the top five or six choices. From that, each depar ment is filled based on academic performance from the first year and prefe ences. The only issue with this system is that if a person is toward the botto of the academic pile, it can take well into the summer before he/she knows whi cipline he/she is accepted into and may only get his/her fourth or fifth choice. e University of Alberta also accepts transfer students into the second year of program from seven different colleges around Alberta and these students are ated and ranked exactly the same as the first-year University of Alberta stu-nts. This is the route that I personally took, doing my first year at Red Deer llege. I recommend this approach to prospective students as it is a cheaper tion and I found Red Deer College to be an excellent place for the first year. ce in a specific discipline, some transferring is possible but after more than second year would require a year or more extra (after your originally sched-d graduation date) to complete the degree.

umnus/a, 9/2000-12/2004, February 2005

ere is a pre-selection process during which university representatives visit al high schools and review applying students' current marks in the early nths of each year. If the student is pre-accepted by the representative, then he she does not have to worry about whether he or she will be accepted when he she applies to the school. This process gives a reassuring feeling to the appli-nt. Entering the general science or art program is recommended, unless you ply straight for the engineering program. By completing a general first year art or science, students can choose to stay in those programs or to apply to er programs, such as business.

rrent student, 9/2003-Submit Date, August 2004

order to be admitted to the University of Alberta, grades were the only decid-g factor. There were no interviews or essays required but admission grades re high and become higher almost every year. Some faculties do not accept ry many students so grades needed to be even higher in those cases.

most everything is done online here but telephone, in-person and snail mail plications are possibilities. The best advice for getting in is to apply early and end a lot of time checking out the web site for help and information.

Academics

umnus/a, 9/1999-6/2003, January 2007

tudied civil engineering. Getting into the courses was relatively easy as there ually was enough room in the classes I wanted. Some morning classes of the neral first-year courses would fill up. Usually, courses were graded as fol-ws: 10 to 20 percent homework, 10 to 15 percent lab, 25 to 35 percent dterm, 50 percent final. Homework was fairly straightforward and an easy ay to raise your grades. Teachers were OK. The courses were somewhat dry, t that is generally the case for most engineering courses. I found there were many math courses and not enough civil engineering courses.

umnus/a, Computer Science, 9/2002-6/2006, September 2006

e computing science program is very demanding and not for the faint of heart. pect to be coding for several hours each day and (unless you are really good working ahead) many late night coding sessions as deadlines approach. urses are almost all graded on a curve, or a modified curve, and you can check ur grades and standing in the class (e.g., 15th out of 30 students) online, which n help you infer your grade. The classes range from amazing to total duds, but ere is effort being made to improve the duds, and any suggestions are strong-appreciated by profs and administration. There are spots available in almost courses right up to the add/drop deadline. The chair is amazing and very ergetic at being involved with all levels of the program. The undergraduate gram is receiving a lot of attention and TLC.

rrent student, 9/2004-Submit Date, April 2006

rst year is always tough so never take it for granted. The workload felt like a t compared to high school but I learned to organize myself and be ahead of the me at all times. Most of my first-year classes were big; the biggest class I was had about 400 students. The only small class I had was English, which had out 30 students, while the rest were 100 and up. I personally did not find it rd to be in classes that were this big. The professors can sometimes turn out etty bad. I always ask around for people who have had good profs and try to t into their classes. It's always wise to register as soon as you can so that you ll have a better chance of getting into popular classes. The grades are on the rve, in that you get a grade according to what your class average is. The class erage is said to be a B-.

Alumnus/a, 9/2000-4/2003, April 2005

The academic portion of the University of Alberta is very good. It is now grad-ed on a 4.0 scale, similar to most post-secondary schools. The quality of the instructors and classes is also very good with some cutting-edge research being done at the University of Alberta. The core classes are easily obtained and both traditional and co-operative programs are offered. The workload is about nor-mal for an engineering discipline, and fairly heavy when compared to other degrees. The professors are very accommodating and open to student inquiries for the most part. I have not had any significant issues finding a professor out of class or obtaining help from him/her. There is some difficulty with enrolling in some outside courses for the complementary study electives as they either do not fit in the engineering time table or else are reserved for other faculties.

Current student, 9/2003-Submit Date, January 2005

The education program is highly recommended, and is one of the best in Canada. *Maclean's* magazine ranked the University of Alberta fifth in the "best overall" category, out of 47 universities across Canada and third overall for "leaders of tomorrow." Many of my professors are the authors of our class textbook. The classes are interactive and innovative. First-year classes are still large, but sec-ond-, third- and fourth-year classes are small, approximately 32 people per class due to there being many sections. I always got into the classes I needed, even my option class. Workload is moderate. It's university—you have to study and there is a lot of reading. But it is doable; I still partied and I had a part-time job, as well.

Current student, 9/2003-Submit Date, August 2004

Classes are very big at the university. There are great classes with a lot of won-derful professors, as well. Online registration makes it easy to get the courses you want and you are able to pick your favorite professors based on the com-ments from other students in previous classes. Grades are fairly assigned on a curve and there is a grade challenge opportunity as well in case you feel that you were unfairly graded. Most courses have a large workload but many have few or no exams and are graded mostly on participation.

Current student, 7/1999-Submit Date, June 2004

The business program is fairly competitive. After one year of general studies, you need a GPA of around 3.5 to get into the business school. From there class-es are generally of high caliber and there are a few excellent professors in first-year business. After your required classes are fulfilled, workload increases. Profs have always proven helpful, if not in class then in office hours. Workload, in general, is manageable but not simple; grading is fair and I find it fairly easy to do well.

Employment Prospects

Alumnus/a, 9/1999-6/2003, January 2007

Most of the jobs are in western Canada, and most of the offers come from com-panies related in the oil industry. This may be different for other careers, other than engineering, but I doubt it. If you want get into the oil industry and don't mind working in northern Canada or Alberta, then this is a good school to study at. The school offers petroleum engineering, which has turned out to be in extremely high demand around the world.

Alumnus/a, Computer Science, 9/2002-6/2006, September 2006

The computer industry is not easy to break into these days: everyone is looking for experience (though that is the same in most industries). Saying that, I am four months out of my degree and making $45K/year with no previous industry experience. However, I highly recommend that you either get summer jobs in the field or do the internship after third year, if only for the confidence it will give you in your programming ability.

The UoA's Computing Science program is the best CS program in western Canada and one of the Top Three in the country. You can often find postings on the university's job posting site (CaPS) for programmers.

Alumnus/a, 9/2000-12/2004, February 2005

There is a career fair on campus for all students at the beginning of each school year. Prospective employers from all around the country will come and demon-strate their company at the fair. The University of Alberta has a prestigious name

Read all of Vault's College Surveys at **www.vault.com/college**—get complete surveys on 100s of colleges and univer-sities, expert advice on applicaton essays and more.

VAULT CAREER LIBRARY **807**

in the local area, beating out local colleges. Many employers seem to like graduates from this university.

Current student, 9/2003-Submit Date, January 2005

Throughout the third and fourth year in the program, students are sent out to schools around Alberta to complete a four-week student-teaching practicum and a nine-week practicum. These are compulsory but also a great way to make contacts in the teaching profession. The faculty of education also puts on a job fair every year. This year, 69 different school boards came to recruit teachers to teach everywhere from around Canada, to the U.S., the U.K., Australia and New Zealand. Résumés were accepted on the spot, and personal interviews were granted as well. Employment prospects are high right now for teachers all around the world.

Current student, 7/1999-Submit Date, June 2004

Internships are plentiful for accounting students especially if you get into the co-op program. (Interview and grades are used to select co-op students for the popular and invaluable program.) Jobs are mostly limited to western Canada with a few opportunities outside the region. The UofA is a topnotch school that is not respected at the level it should be. Employers outside the region are unfamiliar with the school and recruitment can be difficult if you don't want to be in western Canada.

Quality of Life

Alumnus/a, 9/1999-6/2003, January 2007

There is barely any crime in Edmonton, especially around the university area. This can be said for pretty much all universities in Canada. The school has very good gym facilities. Food courts are usually the typical mall type: fast food and not very good. Western Canada is not a place to expect much in the food quality or variety. The city itself (pop: 800,000) is fairly unexciting as it is a relatively new city in the middle of nowhere but is large enough not to feel isolated. Housing facilities are OK.

Alumnus/a, Computer Science, 9/2002-6/2006, September 2006

For comp sci majors, the workload is very demanding, and if you aren't careful, you can forget what a real life is like. However, the UoA offers many good distractions, and the department is working on adding some into the building. The common area on the main floor has three microwaves and an XBox connected to a projector for times you just want to get away from the CRT screen. Campus rec offers may active diversions, and UACS (undergraduate association of computing science) has weekly bar outings, LAN parties every semester, and many other events.

Current student, 9/2004-Submit Date, April 2006

The campus is huge! There are all sorts of activities and opportunities for students. It's free to use the gym or the swimming pools or play any sports. There are lots of clubs you could join as well like dance, squash and art, there are just too many to count! You can find all sorts of food around campus. There are about four food courts and lots of other places to go eat around campus. It's pretty safe around campus. At night, if you are scared of walking alone you can always call Safewalk, a student union group, and they will walk with you and also take the LRT with you.

Alumnus/a, 9/2000-4/2003, April 2005

The University of Alberta has a high quality of life. Living costs are fairly reasonable; $800 per month for a decent two-bedroom apartment. There are residence places available as well as several apartment buildings and houses in the area. The busy workload that is common to engineering does require some time at the school outside of regular class hours but also provides a great opportunity to interact and meet classmates. The campus is clean, well-kept and very safe. The university is very close to Whyte Avenue, which is know in the area for its shopping as well as for the many restaurants and pubs located along it.

Alumnus/a, 9/2000-12/2004, February 2005

There are many facilities to accommodate students of the university. In the student union building (SUB), there exists a large food court, fireplace with lots of couches, a bubble studying area and other food concessions as well as the main bookstore. Other buildings include HUB, which provides more food vendors

and housing opportunities. The housing opportunities are pretty good at the u[ni]versity as there are many facilities off campus for families. Crime and safety a[re] not a problem at the university; there are on-campus security officers availa[ble] all the time and all the university staff is very helpful.

Current student, 9/2003-Submit Date, January 2005

The quality of life on campus is great. The campus is architecturally beautif[ul] with lots of open space and trees. It is located in the trendy South Side of [the] city, close to shopping, restaurants and Whyte Ave (shopping and bar strip). [It] is very safe, and the campus offers 24-hour safe walk. This is a program offer[ed] by the student union so you can be escorted to your car, home, or bus by t[wo] other people. Campus housing is spacious, but you may share with two or th[ree] others. There are single rooms available but are quickly taken up. You can li[ve] right on campus, in HUB, where there are also many eating areas, a booksto[re,] a tanning and hair salon, gym, and other shops all in the same building. T[he] campus pharmacy is located in the main bookstore in SUB, with a school d[is]count on all prescriptions, fast service and great employees. SUB also conta[ins] eateries, instant teller machines, silent and open study areas, a Ticket Mast[er,] Travel Cuts and other student services, all run by students. There are also gr[eat] concerts going on in the theatres for great prices! We have a huge indoor tra[ck,] the Butterdome, and gym facilities. Membership is included in tuition! Lock[er] fee for the year is $50. We also have a great university sports program and of[fer] student prices to home games.

Social Life

Alumnus/a, 9/1999-6/2003, January 2007

I was not involved in any fraternities: this is an American thing so they are n[ot] as popular or common in Canada. The bar scene is relatively close and there a[re] two bars on campus, although more would be appreciated, especially in the wi[n]ter. Edmonton is in the middle of nowhere and the only other city nearby, i.[e.] driving distance, is Calgary. The Rocky Mountains, which are beautiful a[nd] offer plenty of skiing opportunities, are unfortunately about three and a h[alf] hours away. The city does not have much history or culture. The downto[wn] core is dead after 5 p.m. and the bar area is near the university, both on the oth[er] side of the downtown area. There are no malls in or near the university are[a.] The big mall, West Edmonton mall, is about an hour away by bus, which [is] annoying in winter. The downtown area is connected by the single subway lin[e.] The frequencies after peak hours are not very good (15+ minutes).

Alumnus/a, Computer Science, 9/2002-6/2006, September 200[6]

What is a comp sci social life? I am slowly discovering now that I can actua[lly] do things again! It's amazing. Be prepared to give up on many extracurricula[rs] unless you make specific effort to engage in them during the term. Your spa[re] time is limited, so enjoy it.

Alumnus/a, 9/1994-4/1998, December 2005

UofA, like any university, is abuzz with social activity, but due to the nature [of] these specialized programs, a person will more than likely find their soci[al] refuge amongst the ensembles to which he/she is a part. The province of Alber[ta] is easily the wealthiest in Canada, attracting singles and young professiona[ls] from across the country. Calgary, only a three-hour drive to the south, is regard[ed] as the singles capital of Canada. Whyte Avenue hosts many clubs and cafe[s,] art supply shops and some extremely funky shops. The entire Strathcona com[m]munity in which the UofA is settled is abuzz with cultural activity from yoga stu[dios] to bowling alleys, to meditation classes, pool halls, art house movie th[e]atres, second hand books, awesome pizza at the Wicked Wedge! For readi[ng] week, a sweet two-hour car drive to the mountains awaits you.

Alumnus/a, 9/2000-4/2003, April 2005

The social life is fairly active. There are several clubs and on-campus event[s.] Being very close to Whyte Ave in Edmonton provides several bars and pubs an[d] restaurants within easy walking distance or else a short cab ride away. There a[re] two restaurants and pubs on campus that see their fair share of students an[d] events alike. A short ride on the LRT (light rail transit) system, for $2, gets [a] person downtown to access more restaurants, shopping opportunities and bar[s.] There is also the world's largest mall, West Edmonton Mall (if it isn't still, [it] once was) a short drive from the university that provides just about anything o[ne]

imagine. There is a water park, amusement park, shooting range, restau-
ts, a hotel, bars and, of course, hundreds of stores. Typical campus favorites
bars are the Iron Horse (Whyte Ave), Cook County Saloon (Whyte Ave) as
ll as the many bars in West Edmonton Mall. The dating scene is fairly active
th several people coming from other provinces and cities to attend university.

rrent student, 9/2003-Submit Date, January 2005

ere are many different frats and sororities from which to choose, with beauti-
old character houses located near campus (a five-minute walk). The Power
nt is located on campus and packed every Thursday and Saturday, offering

great music and fun. You're bound to run into someone you know any day of
the week! There are at least 40 clubs offered from chess to religious clubs.
Whyte Ave is about a 15-minute walk from campus. This is about six blocks of
pubs, dance and cocktail bars, boutiques, salons, shops and coffee shops all in
one spot! Great time and bar hopping! For the after-hours snack, the Funky
Pickle (pizza shop) is packed and worth every bite! The dating scene is out there
and Edmontonians are very friendly!

University of British Columbia

r prospective students in Canada:

BC Student Recruitment and Advising Office
ock Hall Welcome Centre
374 East Mall, Rm 1200
ancouver, BC V6T 1Z1
dmissions phone: (604 822-9836, (877) 272-1422
dmissions fax: (604) 822-6943

r prospective students outside Canada:

ternational Student Recruitment Office
ock Hall Welcome Centre
200 - 1874 East Mall
ancouver, BC V6T 1Z1
t'l Admissions phone: 604-822-8999, (877) 272-1422
t'l Admissions fax: 604-822-9888
t'l online questions and e-mail: http://askme.ubc.ca
ain URL: https://you.ubc.ca

 ## Admissions

rrent student, Chemistry, 9/2005-Submit Date, July 2007

BC is very proactive in providing information for prospective students. Free
mpus tours led by student ambassadors are available Monday through
turday. UBC Spring Break Focus Days are an initiative to provide opportuni-
s for secondary school students to experience UBC through a guided campus
r, as well as workshops and student-run activities. Info sessions are also held
schools and communities for out-of-province prospective students. UBC held
ture Student Receptions to welcome students and families to get to know UBC
tter. Admissions office is also very helpful; and UBC's web site is also easy
navigate in order to search for information about the admissions process.

rrent student, Engineering, 9/2004-Submit Date, June 2007

e application process is very straightforward and I had no difficulties finding
the information I needed online. It is definitely important to begin the appli-
tion process well before the deadline, particularly if you are applying from
road because all the forms have to be mailed. I also found that the staffs at the
cruitment Office and at enrollment services were extremely helpful and very
ompt at answering questions by e-mail.

The school says: "Applications are made online, and certain
supporting material such as broad-based admission information
can be provided online at the time of application. Other supporting documents must be received by UBC by March 15 (for
a decision by May 1) or June 30 (final date)."

Current student, Economics, 9/2004-Submit Date, June 2007

It is best to make sure [you know] the procedures involved for the admissions
process. High school counselors can only assist you in the process, but they cannot remind you of every deadline and document that you need. For UBC, there
are no interviews or essays required for admission. However, the deadlines are
relatively early, as they usually take place in February, and you need to make
sure your transcripts and other documents are sent to UBC before the deadlines.
(If you study within BC, they are automatically sent to the university, though it
is always a good idea to double-check with your counselor.) If your first language is not English, you will have to take TOEFL test and obtain a certain
score. As you can take the test only once a month, it is better to start preparing
early! Once you finish your application, you should look into what you want to
study because different programs have different prerequisites. Also, in order to
take first-year English, which is required in most programs, you have to have a
good mark from English grade 12 or you have to take a test called LPI and obtain
a certain grade.

Current student, 9/2003-Submit Date, June 2006

Selectivity is primarily based on academic merit, although my understanding is
that students are now selected according to much more broad-based metrics,
including leadership, participation in extracurricular activities and sports. Try to
maintain a high school average of greater than 86 percent, and you should be
considered a serious applicant. Seats are limited and can be subject to competition, especially at the Sauder School of Business (UBC's own business program), in which the ratio of applicants to accepted is getting larger every year.

The school says: "Admission to the Bachelor of Commerce program in the Sauder School of Business is based on academic
performance and overall records of leadership and accomplishment. All applicants must complete the BCom Supplemental
Application Form: www.sauder.ubc.ca/bcom/admissions"

Current student, 1/2003-Submit Date, May 2006

The admissions process was fairly easy, although finding out information on the
school for out-of-province students was difficult. Most of the work was already
done for me through databases and such, all I really needed to do was fill out
some forms and send them away. To be accepted, however, the school required
a high academic average.

Current student, 9/2002-Submit Date, March 2006

The admissions process is done online through the Pasbc (www.pas.bc.ca), then
you'll receive a student number and password that are used to upload interim
grades through the Student Services Center (ssc.adm.ubc.ca).

You can select up to two faculties of your choice but early admission only considers the first choice. My first choice was commerce and second was arts;
apparently my grades weren't high enough for commerce so I had to wait until
early August to receive my admission letter.

The application deadline usually is Feb. 28 and UBC visits almost all secondary
schools in Lower Mainland before then to answer questions. The self-admission

Read all of Vault's College Surveys at **www.vault.com/college**—get complete surveys on 100s of colleges and universities, expert advice on applicaton essays and more.

VAULT CAREER LIBRARY **809**

deadline is sometime in March. A list of materials that need to be submitted can be found at students.ubc.ca/welcome/apply.cfm?page=bba.

UBC says: "Self admission is only for high school students in BC or Yukon. All other applicants will be evaluated as their file is completed (official transcripts, test scores, and other required documents are all received at UBC)."

The admission fee is CDN $60 for Canadian citizens and residents, otherwise it's CDN $100.

The school says: "The Application fee for all undergraduate applicants (Canadian and international) is now CDN $100."

 ## Academics

Current student, Engineering, 9/2004-Submit Date, June 2007

The class size is a little bit big in the first and second years, but it gets smaller in the third and fourth years as you become more specialized. It is easy to get classes you want if you have good grades as course registration time is ordered by students' grades. Workload is OK. There are some very good professors.

Current student, Chemistry, 9/2005-Submit Date, July 2007

Being a great university, UBC provides excellent academic life. Some of the classes vary from 20 to 200 students, depending on the program and the student's year. However, webCT initiative at UBC makes student academic life easier. Students can log into their webCT in order to access professor lecture notes, chat with other students in the same class to form study group or discuss any topics, and do some of their online quizzes. Every professor has office hours where students can be guaranteed to be able to meet their professors during those hours.

UBC is trying to encourage students to be self-led. Instead of having a regular lecture, some of UBC classes are held in Problem Based Learning, where students are divided into groups to solve specific problems/projects through their own research related to the topic discussed. Known as a research university, UBC provides research opportunities for students. In some programs, students are allowed to choose to write a thesis for their undergraduate experience. Speaking from my experience; I am involved in my prof's research project that allows me to gain valuable research experience prior to graduate school.

The laboratories, museum and technology on campus (e.g., earthquake simulator, robotic development, anthropology museum, plant research and so on) are amazingly incredible and provide students with the best and advanced research opportunities. Over 99 percent of UBC professors hold a PhD degree, and they are very involved with research projects. Some topics discussed in lecture originate in their own research.

Current student, Psychology, 5/2006-Submit Date, June 2007

I think grading is pretty fair. By that I mean the effort and time you spend on your studies are well-reflected by the outcomes. Most of the UBC professors are very experienced and knowledgeable teachers. Especially profs in zoology and psychology departments are nice and encouraging. I think they gave me the motivation to specialize and go deeper in these fields. All in all, UBC has a lot to offer to students.

Current student, Independent, 8/2005-Submit Date, June 2007

As I did IB in high school, the workload at UBC does not seem very hard. There are some challenges from time to time. About half my classes were very small (15 students) as they are fine arts and hence the quality was amazing. Getting into popular classes doesn't seem to be a problem either. Grading seems fair, apart from classes, such as Economics, where the percentage of students that fail and do poorly is very high. I usually find classes that have around 300 students boring and it is hard to pay attention.

Current student, 6/2005-Submit Date, August 2006

I aim for an undergraduate arts degree, with a major in Spanish. I took classes in third- and fourth-year Spanish. The classes were all full, in fact the professors in each of the seven courses allowed at least one more student into the class. I did not notice any impact on the quality of the course because of extra students. The professors were skilled at using small groups to enhance the learning

process. They were from all parts of Latin America and Spain, very eclectic areas of interest and manners of teaching. Students became quite close and supportive of each other; it was a benefit to organization and prioritization assignments. I found the grading to be fair, considering that the learning curve was very steep for me. The drop-out rate was almost nonexistent.

Current student, 9/2004-Submit Date, May 2006

I am enrolled in the faculty of applied science, in the geological engineering department. Most of the first-year classes are fairly large (100 to 200 students) but it is easy to get one-on-one help from professors and teaching assistants during office hours and tutorials. Engineering students have to declare their major at the end of first year, and therefore second-year class sizes tend to be smaller. All engineering programs have large workloads, and most students take between five and seven courses per term. Most engineering courses have integrated lab and/or tutorial components, and most courses involve weekly assignments and/or lab reports.

Current student, 9/2003-Submit Date, June 2006

Quality of classes is superb, though first-year courses are quite generic. At the 300 and 400 level, there tends to be a bigger focus on cross-enterprise education whereby students actually get the big picture when it comes to managing a business. Functional specializations can sometimes make students feel cubby-holed. Classes are not entirely difficult. As in everything else, students must put in the effort and the results will speak for themselves. Selection of professors is critical to getting the most out of this educational experience, and I recommend using ratemyprofessor.ca for this assessment.

Current student, 1/2003-Submit Date, May 2006

The workload is a lot only if you don't like the classes that you are taking. There is a huge selection of classes, which is nice because it means that likely there's something that you want to take. Most professors I find are either amazing or horrible, there is no in between.

 ## Employment Prospects

Current student, Engineering, 9/2004-Submit Date, June 2007

The employment prospects are quite good. Almost every friend I know who has graduated recently has found a good job with a prestigious employer. There are many on-campus recruiting sessions with famous companies. And internship opportunities abound. For computer engineering/science majors, many go to work with Microsoft, Google, Electronic Arts and Business Objects.

Current student, Economics, 9/2004-Submit Date, June 2007

UBC has a great reputation in BC. It has great co-op programs in each faculty of which students definitely should take advantage. Many students are hired by their co-op employers, and if not, you still make connections and get to know about your future options. There are many on-campus recruiting events that are helpful in gaining information about various companies. There are career services around UBC that are very resourceful. They help you prepare résumé and cover letters, and have workshops where they teach you how to prepare for interviews. Many of UBC alumni come back to UBC to hire students too. Although UBC students have good reputation, it is always better to look into internship and career services. For international students, the International House will help you prepare for obtaining post-graduation work permits.

Current student, Engineering, 9/2004-Submit Date, June 2007

UBC provides career fairs and many opportunities for networking with industry members every year. At the moment, employment prospects for geological engineering graduates are excellent. Everyone I know from my program who was looking for a summer job this year was able to find one. The co-op program also provides students with the opportunity to gain valuable work experience before graduating.

Current student, 9/2003-Submit Date, June 2006

Prestige with employers is limited to a few. There tends to be a very top-heavy focus at the school, with tremendous resources devoted to the top-tier students and almost nothing devoted to those who are deemed academically unable or not professionally marketable. Recruiters all aim at the same "cream of the crop" and positions do not filter down to less capable students; employers simply leave other schools in the east. That said, motivated, intelligent and career-minded students should have no trouble excelling in this environment.

The school says: "UBC is not responsible for external company hiring practices, but it does seek to ensure that all undergraduates are fully supported throughout their program with access to career advising and guidance services. UBC Career Services offer a full range of preparation programs, and several Faculties have dedicated career offices, all aimed at ensuring students are well prepared for their future after graduation."

Quality of Life

Current student, Psychology, 5/2006-Submit Date, June 2007

UBC (and Vancouver in general) has a lovely environment with lots of places to sit, eat, shop and so on. It's nature-rich but also highly modern. But some people find Vancouver a bit boring after several months of stay.

Current student, Chemistry, 9/2005-Submit Date, July 2007

There are seven residences on campus, including for single student or student family housings. We have various on-campus housing styles: dormitory, apartment and townhouse styles. Many events are organized in every residence organized by residence advisors. Some residences have a pool table, gym, study areas, a cafeteria and so on. Full wireless service is available on campus for free.

The campus has a great facilities, including indoor and outdoor Olympic-size swimming pools, large student recreation centre (three full-sized gyms, fitness centre, martial arts studio and dance studio), tennis centre, winter sport centre (three ice rinks) and so on.

There are various dining place on campus, include fast food, pub, cafe, coffee shop (five Starbucks on campus) and upscale dining. Public transportation is also very convenient to get students go outside the campus to get foods.

The campus is considered a safe and secure environment. UBC Safewalk is available to accompany students between locations on campus at no cost. Campus security is also very helpful; not only that they take care of the safety of campus, but they are also willing to drive students around campus if we are not willing to walk by ourselves. Campus bus also has various stops at on-campus residences.

Current student, Engineering, 9/2004-Submit Date, June 2007

On-campus housing is affordable and very convenient. Personally, I have had a very positive experience living on campus, and some of my closest friends are people I met in first-year residence.

Current student, Independent, 8/2005-Submit Date, June 2007

Quality of life at UBC is amazing. It seems as the most beautiful campus in the world. With a national park surrounding it, beautiful beaches and parks, UBC provides a very green, relaxing, and healthy environment. Housing however is not that great. First-year residence rooms are tiny and all the facilities are very worn out. Many areas are also very dark and almost depressing. Cafeteria food at UBC is nothing to be proud of. Rarely healthy or tasty, I highly recommend cooking for oneself. It is very handy to come home and not have to worry about making food; however, many times you'd rather skip the food that is provided. The neighborhood is amazing. UBC is a small town of its own with students everywhere making it easy to fit in and make many good friends. There are numerous things that UBC offers, such as clubs, sport facilities, sport activities and so on, making it easy for everyone to keep busy. The libraries and studying facilities are amazing as well. Crime is very low here, a bike stolen here and there is all, and safety is amazing.

Regarding housing, the school says: "UBC Housing has eleven major residential complexes across Vancouver and Okanagan campuses, including several newly constructed buildings. A program of refurbishment is always underway, and although every building block can't be in mint condition, the standard of student accommodation at UBC is generally of high quality."

Social Life

Current student, Economics, 9/2004-Submit Date, June 2007

UBC is building many new places to spend your time. They recently opened a new bar/restaurant, and the University Village has many stores, such as Staples, grocery stores and restaurants. Sororities and fraternities are very active too, and they have great residence and social events. Many events are happening around UBC and outside UBC all year long, and you can easily make friends and have fun. Club activities are very active too, and you can join them at the beginning of the school year when they have club days. A lot of students like to participate in sports events, and UBC has the biggest sporting event in Canada and/or North America, in which hundreds of students participate every year. UBC is definitely a fun university as long as you get out there.

Alumnus/a, Liberal Arts, 8/2002-5/2007, June 2007

The number and range of events offered on campus is incredible—athletic, social, music, cultural, academic, professional and so on—there is so much going on all the time. However, there is no real central place to access information on what's being offered on campus. University has its own, student societies have their own, so do the clubs and various campus organizations (i.e., International House, First Nations Long House, Residences and so on).

Current student, 9/2003-Submit Date, May 2006

We have a great social life on campus and lots of tight student bonding. There are only about three pubs on campus, and they fill up each weekend. There is always something to do on campus no matter what. There are tons of sports events, social get togethers, and sometimes fraternity parties that involve many students on campus. We have over 220 clubs at UBC, which gives students hundreds of opportunities to find something that they like to do or get involved in. Every event ends up being such an extraordinary bonding experience for everyone.

Current student, Engineering, 9/2004-Submit Date, June 2007

UBC is like a small self-contained city in itself, and you can find a variety of restaurants, pubs, shops and grocery stores right on campus. Students are very active and a large number of social events are organized throughout the year. There are also over 200 clubs that range from sports, music and theatre, to community service and environmental conservation. One of the things I like best about UBC is that I never get bored: there is always something to do, every day of the week, so it is easy to keep a healthy balance between your academic and your social life.

The School Says

The University of British Columbia (1908), is one of Canada's premier universities with a global reputation for excellence in teaching and research. Outstanding students from 135 countries choose UBC for our wide selection of programs of study, expert faculty, world-class facilities for learning, international perspectives, and vibrant student life.

Two Great Campuses

UBC's choice of campus locations is unrivaled. The Vancouver campus is located on 1000 acres of parkland, just 20 minutes from downtown Vancouver. The city of Vancouver—host of the 2010 Winter Olympic Games—is consistently rated one of the world's most livable urban environments. The Okanagan campus, in Kelowna, is ideal for students who prefer a more intimate setting with a strong sense of community.

Both Vancouver and Kelowna enjoy pleasantly temperate climates, with warm summers and mild winters. With nearby mountains, beaches, parks, and trails, UBC students have access to numerous outdoor activities year-round.

Read all of Vault's College Surveys at **www.vault.com/college**—get complete surveys on 100s of colleges and universities, expert advice on applicaton essays and more.

VAULT CAREER LIBRARY   811

Innovative, Interdisciplinary, and International program options

With 18 facilities and 13 schools across two major campuses, UBC provides undergraduate students with hundreds of options. UBC's four-year undergraduate program lead to globally-recognized degrees in the visual and performing arts, humanities, social sciences, life and physical sciences, computer science, engineering, education, forestry, land and food systems, human kinetics, and business.

First-year students benefit from interdisciplinary teaching programs pioneered at UBC such as the Science One program which blends biology, chemistry, mathematics, and physics in an integrated format, or the Arts One program that integrates themes from English literature, philosophy, and history and organizes classes into small learning communities.

UBC Okanagan offers a community-oriented cross-disciplinary approach to learning, including region-centered research and international learning opportunities. Innovative curricula and creative methodologies encourage students to traverse traditional boundaries between arts, sciences, fine arts, languages, and social sciences.

Co-op programs allow students to combine their academics with paid work experience, and are available in selected programs at both campuses. Undergraduate students may also study or volunteer abroad at any one of UBC's 155 partner institutions in 42 countries.

Admission is Competitive

UBC welcomes applications from students who demonstrate superior academic ability. Both international and domestic students may compete for merit-based scholarships and academic awards. A limited number of awards specifically for international students are available to academically outstanding students who demonstrate leadership and financial need.

University of Guelph

Admissions Office
50 Stone Road East
Guelph, ON N1G 2W1
Admissions phone: (519) 824-4120, ext. 58721
Admissions e-mail: admission@registrar.uoguelph.ca
Admissions URL: www.uoguelph.ca/admissions/

 ## Admissions

Current student, 9/2005-Submit Date, November 2005

For acceptance to this university, I filled out a form and then monitored everything online. Unfortunately, I did not get a chance to tour the campus prior to arriving here as it was a bit far from my place of residence. To get accepted, one needed a minimal 70 percent average as well as six grade 12 university courses (including English). I received some brochures through the mail, but most of the information was sent through e-mail or could be found online at the university web site.

Current student, 9/2001-Submit Date, March 2005

I applied through my high school during my OAC year, but one can also directly contact the university or visit its web site to apply. Selectivity for undergraduate programs is based mainly on academic performance in high school. No interviews or essays were needed for my program.

Alumnus/a, 11/1990-6/1995, December 2005

I found the admissions process to be very helpful. The counselors at the University of Guelph treated my like an individual and didn't group me in with anyone else. I got good advice from my soccer coach and other student athletes because I was trying out for the varsity soccer team.

Alumnus/a, 9/1999-9/2003, November 2004

I filled out the application form and sent it in through the college application service in Ontario. I had to earn a specific average to be automatically accepted into the co-op degree. I then had to get the faculty's permission to add another major. They had a good program for the co-op students and a very detailed program that helped me to get the job I wanted after graduation

Current student, 9/2004-Submit Date, March 2005

Advice to get into any Ontario university would be just to apply for a general BA and not specifically to the program in which you are interested. This way you can explore other subject areas to be sure you are really interested in pursuing career or further education in your intended field. For a general BA, you do have to worry about having a high average from high school in order to accepted for a specific program, especially a highly-competitive program. I didn't have an interview or have to write an essay. All I had to do was fill out personal information about what high school I attended and what universitie wanted to attend and OUAC did the rest. Also, don't limit yourself to applyi to just one university or college; pick a couple so that if you don't get accep into the one you really want, you still have other options.

Alumnus/a, 9/1997-6/2000, January 2005

Admission was allowed to students who held an 80 percent average or higher their final year of high school. There were no interviews, but they have a pr gram where you can live with people from your program that were all hi achievers in high school. To get into this program you have to have higher th an 80 percent average.

 ## Academics

Current student, 9/2005-Submit Date, November 2005

The classes that I am currently taking have not been too difficult, only a bit d and I am questioning their relativity to my program of choice (however, I a told, that this gets better in the following years). The professors are all well qu ified and many of them have completed work for which they are recognize Getting popular classes can be difficult—they tend to fill up quickly, so depends when one has one's time slot when one may choose classes. The wor load is bearable, although much worse for the science and math courses. As f as grading goes, so far I have been surprised to be able to say that I am doi fairly well.

Current student, 9/2001-Submit Date, March 2005

The first year and a half is a generalized science program and includes introdu tory biology, chemistry, statistics, calculus, physics, biochemistry and geneti Following that, the focus is on animal biology courses, with an emphasis comparison between groups. The program requires a lot of memorization a the ability to grasp concepts. Classes are easier to get into when you are in yo final couple of years, but this is a popular program here so it can sometim depend on luck. Your student number determines the day on which you can re ister for your next semester's classes. Professors vary; I've had some excelle ones and others who were somewhat less than desirable, but this really happe where. Grading depends on the professors and TAs, but is generally fair. n't expect class grades to be bell-curved or modified later on, though. If you /e any discrepancies, bring them up right away with the appropriate person. ur professor or the dean, if necessary. Workload can be heavy, but it isn't easonable.

umnus/a, 11/1990-6/1995, December 2005

iversity of Guelph is rated Number One in the country for academics. The gram is Bachelor of Arts, which is a very general program. First-year cours- were the same for many first-year students. We had to complete a number of uired courses and a few elective courses. It was pretty easy to work a sched- around popular courses. Most courses were available several times a day and east two to three times a week, so getting into a popular course in the semes- that I needed it usually wasn't a problem. Grading was on a percentage basis. would have both midterm and final exams. We had semester courses that ran ce a year, so if you couldn't get into a course the first semester because it was l, your counselor could register you for the course the next semester in the ne calendar year. The professors were excellent; I never had a problem with / of them. They were all very clear on what they expected from us and what s going to be on the exams come the end of the year. The workload first year s pretty difficult, it definitely was an adjustment from high school. Once you tled into the first semester you knew what was expected of you and how to ndle the workload with good time management skills.

umnus/a, 9/1999-9/2003, November 2004

me professors are scary and some are quite good. There is a big range in pro- ms. I was able to focus my criminal justice courses to focus on youth and e to fit the BA requirements through program electives. The workload was ndard: two midterms and lots of multiple choice and essay exams.

rrent student, 9/2004-Submit Date, March 2005

e University of Guelph is pretty good at making sure there are enough class- and seats available for all students. The web advisor makes it easy to choose l drop classes. About 50 percent of my classes consist of two midterms and inal exam. This method simply tests how much I can memorize and not what ctually know. I do have one class, however, that consists of nine assignments l a final, which really not only helps me learn the material but also tests me e what I know and how well I can use the tools that I am learning in class.

me professors teach directly from the text, which makes it easier to refer to text if I missed something, but some teachers use the text simply as a refer- ce and you really have to be careful not to miss anything important because information won't be repeated. Some professors post classnotes, which is an esome tool for those of us who like to print out the material before class and l to the notes. I don't get hand cramps when teachers offer this and it is a lot sier for me to absorb the information instead of rushing to write it all down. e workload can get pretty heavy because there is a lot of reading. For those us who are slow readers, the readings assigned for one class may take a cou- e days to go through, especially when the material is boring.

umnus/a, 9/1997-6/2000, January 2005

ok biology with a specialization in fisheries and wildlife. This program was ry demanding. First year was definitely not an indicator of what was to come. cond year is when they weed out students and your average will drop at least percent. The classes were all excellent and testing is very demanding. Only best biologists graduate from Guelph. The workload is demanding but not the way of homework. There are few assignments unless you are taking a urse with a laboratory. Most classes have a midterm and final. The split is ually 50/50 or 40/60. For classes with a laboratory, the split is normally 10 rcent for the lab, and 45/45 for midterms and exams. A lot of the tests are mul- le choice because of the sizes of some of the classes. Do not be fooled, these very difficult multiple choice questions and are often worth a percent or two your final mark. Everyone fits in well in this school and the dress code is mfy. We were ranked the Worst Dressed School in Ontario. What is wrong th wearing PJs to class?

umnus/a, 9/1994-6/1998 , November 2004

ality of classes was very generic for the first two years of the program. ecializing in the third and fourth years helped create the type of program that vanted to be in. Getting classes was never an issue; I was able to get whatev- I applied for. Grading was very fair, rarely did I have issue with a grade I was

given. The majority of the professors were very good, specifically in the third- and fourth-year classes. Their ability to explain and speciality in their fields was very useful. Supervisors of a specific area of the program proved to be the most impressive as they have a great amount of experience and passion for their work.

Employment Prospects

Alumnus/a, 11/1990-6/1995, December 2005

Most people graduate from the University of Guelph with a good understanding of what employment opportunities are available. There are several on-campus job boards and employment counselors to help you when it's time to go out into the real world and look for the perfect job. They hold job fairs twice a year where the students of the University of Guelph are invited to a fair where sever- al popular employers are gathered to accept résumés from up-and-coming grad- uates. You get the opportunity to go to one location and meet several employers and see where you'd like to possibly work and what type of jobs each company has to offer.

The alumni network is extremely helpful, you can have easy access to several alumni and ask other graduates of the same program as you their opinion or sug- gestions on employment opportunities. Co-op student opportunities are also offered at the University of Guelph and they have a great success rate in terms of finding you a job in your field upon graduation.

Current student, 9/2001-Submit Date, March 2005

A large proportion of people in my program aim to apply to the veterinary col- lege here either part way through their degree, or after they have completed it. They [will] enjoy high employment rates after graduation from the vet college. Many of the zoology graduates carry on to graduate school. Preparation for this can be obtained via research courses done in the school or abroad.

Alumnus/a, 9/1999-9/2003, November 2004

Co-op was good at getting me the job I have had for the past three years. It assisted me in finding a career field that I enjoy. I needed to take an extra col- lege degree to get more specific intervention training that I wanted for working with kids. The degree is a lot of theory. Many choices for co-op jobs and staff are extremely helpful. There is a big job fair held every year and free trans- portation is provided by the school.

Alumnus/a, 9/1997-6/2000, January 2005

Most employers know Guelph. They love to hire students from here because they know only the best graduate and most of the employers graduated from Guelph as well. Graduates in most fields are in demand. Fisheries is not one of the demanding fields. A lot of courses are offered with a co-op option that helps you to gain experience while you are attending school. The alumni network is great.

Alumnus/a, 9/1994-6/1998, November 2004

Some of the co-op work that I arranged my fourth year helped with my job expe- rience when I was first applying for jobs in the human kinesics field.

Quality of Life

Current student, 9/2005-Submit Date, November 2005

The Guelph campus is a mixture of modern and ancient architecture—it's quite scenic. There are greenhouses and trees, which are that not likely to be found in, for example, Toronto, in any reasonable number. I live in residence and that has proven to work well. My room is a single but it's not too small and has every- thing I need (desk, lamp, bed, furniture, phone, high-speed Internet). There are always involvement opportunities going on for one to participate in if one so chooses. Most facilities can be found directly on campus but, for those that aren't, it is easy to get into town via the bus and our free bus passes (paid in our tuition). Related to crime, our campus is supposed to be one of the safest around. We also have a program called Safe Walk that provides escorts for students com- ing home from night classes if they wish.

Read all of Vault's College Surveys at **www.vault.com/college**—get complete surveys on 100s of colleges and univer- sities, expert advice on applicaton essays and more.

VAULT CAREER LIBRARY 813

Current student, 9/2001-Submit Date, March 2005

The majority of the people are very pleasant and the neighborhood is safe, as a general rule. The campus isn't too big; one can comfortably walk from one end to the other in 15 or 20 minutes. This makes for a closer knit community than many of the larger campuses. Off-campus housing is plentiful, houses, townhouses and apartments are available. A student-hosted web site (The Cannon) provides classified ads and is extremely helpful in looking for a place to live, roommates, buying or selling textbooks or other items. Several dining areas both on and off campus, many off-campus restaurants accept university meal-cards for payment, which makes it easy to enjoy an impromptu dinner out with friends or family. An athletic centre provides gym facilities, sports and clubs; and a health centre is available to all students and any dependents.

Current student, 9/2004-Submit Date, March 2005

The library is an excellent resource, there are always people there who can help you even if it's completely unrelated. They also offer a program called the Learning Commons, which is another excellent resource. There are drop-in sessions or you can book an appointment to have senior students review your work before you hand it in for class. I used this service for one of my essays and I found it excellent. I really learned a lot from the student who helped me; she gave me some excellent tips. As for crime and safety, Guelph is a very safe campus. There are emergency polls all over campus where, if you feel something is wrong, you can call for help and there is a walk home program for those who study late and don't want to walk back to their room unattended.

Alumnus/a, 9/1997-6/2000, January 2005

The best time of my life! The residences in the North End are beautiful. There is one building designated to first-year students, which makes the transition to university not too bad. They have an excellent security service for each building and the campus has its own police force. There is a program known as Safe Walk that allows students to call for someone to walk them home at night if they are alone. There is an amazing recreational complex, with physiotherapy, physicians and food. You never even have to leave the world of Guelph. The city is great and offers a wide variety of cultural places to eat and hang out. And the police in the city of Guelph like to make sure all the students get home safe at night. There is also a bus that picks up students from 12 to 3 a.m. and brings them home safely.

 **Social Life**

Current student, 9/2005-Submit Date, November 2005

There are a number of eateries located directly on campus, however, off cam[pus] there are many more things to do, including fast-food restaurants, several b[ars] and clubs, a mall and cinemas. Students usually go to any of the things lis[ted] whenever they want a break from studying or have spare time on their hands.

Current student, 9/2001-Submit Date, March 2005

The main university centre features a very popular restaurant and bar for[merly] referred to as The Keg by students. Gryph's is another popular restaurant [on] campus and Creelman's is a market-style restaurant. There is a lot to cho[ose] from. Off campus, there are bars and clubs downtown as well as the pop[ular] Ranch just a 10-minute drive away. The CSA holds regular events and a w[ide] array of clubs can be found through the athletic centre, everything from b[elly] dancing and hip hop to martial arts. Choirs and bands are open to auditions fr[om] all students. They, along with a theatre group, hold concerts on occasion.

Alumnus/a, 11/1990-6/1995, December 2005

Social life is great; the University of Guelph has one of the highest rates of [on-]campus bars in Ontario, Canada. There is also a great downtown area that a[lso] has several bars. There are several restaurants located both on campus [and] throughout the city. The dating scene is good; although there is a ratio of 70 p[er]cent women to 30 percent men at the University of Guelph, there's a surprisi[ng]ly good outcome of dating for women. The students' favorite event is always [the] Homecoming weekend in September where past and present students gather [to] watch the big football game and then celebrate over the weekend with differ[ent] social events. Events also include the Bullring event and The Keg.

Alumnus/a, 9/1999-9/2003, November 2004

All the favorite restaurants are located in same area. The pizza place deliv[ers] and can be paid for on the meal plan, along with some other restaurants. Th[ere] are many, many bars.

Current student, 9/2004-Submit Date, March 2005

The famous bar at the university is The Keg or also known as The Bass Ta[vern.] Guelph doesn't seem to have much of a dating scene and all the events offe[red] are academic related. My friends and I specifically like to go and play pool, a[nd] The Keg is really the place to do that.

University of Toronto

Admissions and Awards
315 Bloor Street West
Toronto, ON M5S 1A3
Admissions phone: (416) 978-2190
Admissions fax: (416) 978-7022
Admissions e-mail: admissions.help@utoronto.ca
Admissions URL: www.adm.utoronto.ca/

Note: The school has chosen not to review the student surveys submitted.

 Admissions

Alumnus/a, 9/1999-5/2003, March 2006

I applied to University of Toronto from the U.S., so SAT scores were important, as was GPA. The school has a large number of applicants and heavily weights these two numbers in evaluation of students.

There are opportunities to discuss additional qualifications, such as spo[rts,] extracurriculars, community service and other "rounding" skills, in the sho[rt-] answer section of the application. As with many of the schools utilizing [the] Ontario Common Application, free-response questions seem to be minimiz[ed.] This is in sharp contrast to the type of applications one would experience w[ith] private schools in the U.S. where essays are weighed so heavily.

Current student, Commerce, 1/2003-Submit Date, April 2007

University of Toronto is composed of different colleges, such as Victoria Colle[ge] or Trinity College or University College, each with its own traditions and its o[wn] admission requirements. For more information, check their web si[tes.] Requirements for each college differ dramatically, so make sure you apply [to] the one that suits you the most because when you apply, you choose both, [the] program and the college. And if you meet the program requirements but do[n't] meet the college admissions criteria, you simply do not get admitted into [the] University of Toronto.

The reason the admission criteria differs for each college has to do with [the] number applicants for the commerce program in each college, number of co[m-]merce students that each college may admit, the types of scholarships they off[er,] the traditions that each college has, the facilities and so on. For instan[ce,]

ctoria College offers by far the highest scholarships yet Trinity has amazing
ilities, such as castle-like dorms and tennis courts.

other thing to note about admissions, most colleges of the University of
ronto have their own additional application processes, on top of the procedure
applying through the governmental agency. The majority of these colleges
l explicitly ask you if any of your relatives attended University of Toronto and
at they do (their occupation). This also plays a factor in your admission, since
ny of the colleges have strong traditions.

portant note one: once you get your admission (even if it says "Guaranteed
mission into the Commerce Program") it does not mean that you are in the
gram. Actual Commerce program starts in the second year. The first year
y try to accept more people than they need and then "weed" the weak ones
t. The ones who were weeded out usually go on to pursue general arts and sci-
ce (politics, literature and so on). Commerce faculty accepted around 450
ple in my year and only 300 graduated. Now, it does not imply that all 150
not meet admissions requirements for the second year. Some of them might
have liked the program and transferred to a different faculty, but the majori-
just didn't meet the criteria (no marks below 65 percent in your first year uni-
sity).

rrent student, 9/2005-Submit Date, November 2005

mission forms can be filled online or through regular application process. For
gineering, the cut-off high school grade 12 average revolves around 85 per-
t, for some other courses, the admission requirements also include submis-
n of portfolio and essays. Being involved in high school life also helps in the
missions process. U of T usually looks for all-rounders with academic, co-
ricular and also extracurricular experience and knowledge.

rrent student, 9/2005-Submit Date, November 2005

a mature student without the proper prerequisites, I had to go through an aca-
mic bridging program that was offered by U of T. It involved completing an
ensive university course in a period of six months. After finishing this pro-
m, I was automatically admitted to the university as a full-time student.

rrent student, 1/2003-Submit Date, January 2005

e university has instituted a Transitional Year Program, which allows mature
dents with extraordinary life circumstances (circumstances, usually, which
evented them from completing or doing well in high school) to transition into
iversity with a lot of support. It's a great program and worth looking into by
ose without a high school diploma who want to pursue post-secondary educa-
n.

rrent student, 9/2004-Submit Date, May 2005

tting into the University of Toronto is largely dependent on high school grades
d community involvement. High grades are needed, but there is no interview
ocess. There are several different colleges within the university that offer dif-
ent programs and scholarships, some of them require essays and are selective
en it comes to admitting new students. Although very good grades are
uired, admission to the university is readily available.

Academics

rrent student, Commerce, 1/2003-Submit Date, April 2007

mmerce program is a joint program by the faculty of Arts and Sciences and
Rotman School of Management. Thus, as a student, you get access to the
st of what the University of Toronto may offer. Your business courses are
ght by professors from Rotman and all other courses, such as math, econom-
and your electives, are taught by the faculty of Arts and Sciences. Keep in
nd that as a commerce student you have exclusive access to the courses and
ources of Rotman School of Management, unlike other students in the Arts
d Sciences. For instance, there are two finance courses that are similar in what
y cover. One is offered by Rotman for commerce students only, and another
is offered by Arts and Sciences under their actuary program. You learn many
the same things in the two courses, but the way they are taught, the exams and
professors are completely different. Thus, finance for commerce students
m Rotman is taught by some leading business professors with huge emphasis
cases, whereas another finance course offered by Arts and Sciences are taught

jointly by actuarial and economics professors and their exams are not cases, but
rather concrete questions and multiple choice questions. Perhaps, this is what
distinguishes the program the most.

In the undergraduate program there is a huge emphasis on accounting. However,
in recent years they started paying more attention to finance and other disciplines. With new professors and new courses, they are significantly improving
the finance program.

In the first two years of the program, most of the material and exams are general standardized tests with some cases. The last two years (the third- and fourth-
year courses) are almost all cases-based. Most cases are bought from Harvard,
yet I have seen some from Ivey.

Professors are good. The University of Toronto is very picky when it comes to
professors. There are very strong faculty traditions. You get some of the top,
world-renowned professors, as well as some who are just starting their careers.
I had professors who taught at Harvard, HEC, Kellogg and Wharton, and I also
had professors who were less known and coming from Canadian Universities,
such as Laurier or McMaster. They also come from different backgrounds, many
international professors. For instance one of the profs, before teaching, was
holding a middle rank position in the Ministry of Finance of Israel. Another professor taught for several years at HEC Paris (French business school) and
worked closely with one of the investment banks. Yet another professor held a
senior position overseeing accounting and finance for one of the major North
American manufacturing firms. On the downside, they would often send less
experienced professors/instructors to teach the second-year courses (especially
courses like marketing). Many students thought that they could gain more from
more experienced and more qualified instructors. However, in later years when
you get super star professors, it balances out.

Alumnus/a, 9/1999-5/2003, March 2006

Grading is stringent with class averages around 70 percent (many times a curve
is applied when averages rise above 70 percent that re-normalized grades around
the 70 percent mark).

The quality of the professors varies and students must make an effort to approach
professors and establish one-on-one connections. Professors are available and
very willing to meet with students and create personal relationships; however,
the impetus lies on the student to initiate and maintain these connections.

Workload is high. Students are expected to work hard and to keep up with a fast-
paced rigorous class schedule. Slipping behind can create problems as the
midterm and final tests typically account for 65 to 90 percent of the final grade.

Current student, 9/2005-Submit Date, November 2005

Since the university is quite large, most of the more popular courses are offered
in many different sessions and are thus not impossible to secure a spot in. The
grading is quite difficult but not unreasonable for such a respected university. As
for the professors and workload, that obviously changes from course to course
and program to program, but I am quite pleased with all of my first-year profs,
as they are all very passionate about the courses and subjects that they are teaching—this enthusiasm tends to rub off on the students. And the workload is not
as bad as I had anticipated, as many of my courses rely on several heavily
weighted exams rather than assignments. However, in order to stay on top of the
course, the readings are very important, something that takes up the majority of
my time.

Current student, 9/2003-Submit Date, March 2006

The program focuses on the science-based material relating to the human body.
Popular classes are hard to get into and one must be patient to get in before the
last date to enroll. The workload is pretty heavy for first-years because the transition from high school to university is huge. The grading is fair, but at times,
students feel that the professors are out to fail them. The classes are of utmost
importance and so they are of high quality.

Current student, 9/2003-Submit Date, October 2004

Once you're in the commerce program, you shouldn't have too much trouble
finding space in the classes if you do this promptly, i.e., don't leave registration
until the day before classes begin, otherwise they will be full. The classes are of
good quality and getting better. A new building has been made specially for
commerce students with up-to-date everything as far as technology goes and a

Read all of Vault's College Surveys at **www.vault.com/college**—get complete surveys on 100s of colleges and universities, expert advice on applicaton essays and more.

VAULT CAREER LIBRARY **815**

nice atmosphere. The professors are also of good quality, all of which come from the Rotman School of Management, which is one of the prime graduate business schools in the country and recognized worldwide. The workload seems to increase year after year. Lots of reading can be expected, which becomes hard to stay on top of as deadlines approach and midterms need writing.

Current student, 5/2003-Submit Date, July 2005

Some of the first-year classes are overly large, with more than 1,000 students. This leads to a sense of being quite disconnected from the lecturer and does not allow the lecturer to attend to questions. In overly large classes, generally evaluation takes the form of multiple-choice tests and exams which are not a particularly good way of gauging whether a student can re-contextualize the information that they've learned.

It is somewhat difficult to get in to the most popular courses, but even if I missed out on a course I wanted, I usually got my second choice. Teaching assistants do most of the grading and tend to grade somewhat more harshly than is warranted by the level of the course; they don't seem to be able to take into account that students in a first-year course won't have the scholastic maturity and knowledge that a second-year PhD student has. Many professors quite rigidly refuse to re-grade papers that have been marked by a TA. The workload is moderate and it is easy to keep up with the work but it's deadly to let weekly readings slide for more than a week because then it becomes very difficult to catch up. The school holds to a fairly rigid grade curve, so the average of most large classes has to be C+; otherwise the professor has to make a case to the department that the class was an exceptionally bright one.

Employment Prospects

Current student, 1/2001-Submit Date, October 2005

Employment prospects for graduates of the University of Toronto are above average in Canada and the United States. This is due to the high recognition of the university name, as well as the quality of the program offered. The University of Toronto offers annual recruitment and internship opportunities through alumni networks, on-campus recruiting and career fairs. This fair gives students a chance to mingle with prospective employees and also to submit their résumés.

Current student, Commerce, 1/2003-Submit Date, April 2007

University of Toronto Career Center is really well-organized and provides a lot of help and guidance to students. Almost all of the major employers recruit from University of Toronto. There is an increasing number of international recruiters (outside of North America). Once in a while you see postings for Europe and quite a lot from Asia and Hong Kong, to be precise.

Commerce program has its own career web site, exclusive for commerce students and alumni, with additional access to various resources that could be useful in job search. Relative to what students from other schools have, it seems that the U of T career center is doing a good job. All major firms from the business community come to U of T. There is a lot going on around the campus. Everyone in Canada knows U of T. It seems to have a good reputation in Asia and the U.S.

Alumnus/a, 9/1999-5/2003, March 2006

There are one or two U of T job fairs and one or two engineering-specific job fairs. These are useful for applying to Canadian businesses and include all of the top players in Canada (as well as large U.S. outfits such as Microsoft), but for those looking for employment in the U.S., they are on their own for the most part.

U of T offers a PEY (Professional Experience Year) program that allows students to take a year off between third and fourth year to join a related business and experience working. This greatly enhances a student's attractiveness to potential employers, but the loss of a year (with PEY, undergrad takes five years) must also be taken into consideration. Also PEY is less applicable to students intent on leaving the engineering field for careers in consulting or law.

Alumnus/a, 9/1998-12/2002, June 2004

The management program, which is another term for business degree, provi undergraduates with great flexibility. Many jobs do require a business degr As noted earlier, a top school like the U of T offers undergraduates with comp tition from other top schools. Job searching is competitive, but having a deg from U of T BBA does give one the opportunity. Career placement sources a provide a comprehensive resource for students if they take advantage of Nothing is handed on a platter, but if you take the initiative, make the eff there is ample ways to make the most out of your opportunity.

Current student, 9/2004-Submit Date, May 2005

The employment prospects are excellent; the University of Toronto alumni distinguished and successful. Many go on to teach in Ivy League schools or r for office. The career centre on campus is very helpful in finding part-time jc for students, as well as full-time jobs for graduates. The alumni network is la and extremely helpful, making employment prospects even brighter. It extremely easy to get a job in Canada or the U.S. The University of Toront a world-class, post-secondary education.

Quality of Life

Alumnus/a, 9/1999-9/2003, June 2006

Very safe city life. Great restaurants. Housing was great, especially University College where we were offered single rooms. Food is reasona tasty. Despite the prevalence of a wide variety of student interest groups a related organizations (the 340 student clubs and organizations are probably m than any other Canadian university), U of T suffers from the same imperso atmosphere as other large universities. Most students live off campus, and many the U of T experience is limited solely to attending classes. This resulted in a general lack of school spirit and the disconnection many of its s dents feel from the school and other students. Student government is headed the Students' Administrative Council, and votes for student council genera gets a turnout of below 10 percent.

The school has two main newspapers: *The Varsity* and *The Newspaper*. E college, faculty and many other groups also publish newspapers. It has a ra station, CIUT.

Current student, Commerce, 1/2003-Submit Date, April 2007

Facilities are great, and every year U of T seems to be adding more facilities improving the existing ones: very safe and very friendly.

Resources that the school has are truly impressive. There are over 40 librari the third largest collection of books and articles in North America. There are t gyms (athletic centers) and one stadium.

Quality of residence really depends on the college. Best ones, based on the s tings, furniture, the kinds of buildings and facilities would be Trinity, Victo Innis, Woodsworth.

Current student, 9/2003-Submit Date, March 2006

Residence on campus is very convenient. There are many study areas, such libraries and study halls. The lighting is great, making the facilities look n and spacious. There's a low crime rate on campus.

Current student, 1/2003-Submit Date, January 2005

What makes student life here so special? The people. You can expect to fi common rooms alive with conversation or heated debate, or fourth-year stude helping out frosh with first-year calculus. And we attract all kinds of peo from all over the place: from inside of Toronto, outside of Toronto, outside Canada, and outside of the Western Hemisphere. The diversity of people a interests found within our faculty is one of our great strengths. In fact, University of Toronto as a whole reflects the greater Toronto community: a pla where almost every corner of the world is represented—it's a cultural mosaic

rrent student, 5/2003-Submit Date, July 2005

of T is located in the heart of Toronto. The neighborhood is vibrant, the ath- ic facilities are good. There is not a lot of student housing (especially not for dents with families) and off-campus housing for students is somewhat expen- e (more so than in most Canadian cities). There are not a lot of restaurants, rs, clubs on campus but one doesn't have to travel far for all of the above. ronto is amazingly safe for a large urban centre, and is very clean.

rrent student, 9/2004-Submit Date, May 2005

e University of Toronto campus is located in downtown Toronto. It is tremely safe, especially with the addition of several security groups on cam- s that walk students to their dorms at night if they are afraid. There is a great nosphere at U of T, quality of dining is superb and there is a wonderful ghtlife available to all students. Housing is readily available and the dorms are and new. The quality of life is above average by comparison to many other iversities that I have personally seen.

Social Life

rrent student, Commerce, 1/2003-Submit Date, April 2007

you live on campus, it really makes a difference in which college you are. nity and Victoria have strong traditions and tend to organize more activities its students than say Woodsworth college. Check their web sites to find re.

any of the students are commuters, so there are not as many parties and activ- es as maybe in universities that are of smaller size and in smaller towns. This iversity is too academics oriented. It's too much concentration on the study- and the marks.

ain, it makes a huge difference if you are a commuter or living at rez. Rez rties are great. But again this school is all about its studying. At times there a sense that there is a bit too much competition.

orts life exists and is relatively strong. The school is known for its swimmers. t because the school is so academically oriented, it does not have very good ms (like a football team or a hockey team).

umni, 9/1999-5/2003, March 2006

cial life seems to revolve around the residential spaces for students. fortunately there is limited space in residence for students, particularly for se from the GTA who don't receive extra points for distance from the school. gardless, everyone should apply to residence as it is the center of on-campus cial life; this means that students applying to the Engineering program must mplete a separate application for the residential colleges. Students entering A or BS programs (arts and science programs) will apply to a residential col- ge as part of their main U of T application. For those not in residence, the

Engineering program in particular offers a variety of social opportunities from extracurricular programs to bar events.

Alumnus/a, 9/1999-9/2003, November 2005

One bar and that's it. Events were organized but not really exciting. Dating scene was hot. But no time to actually go out and date too much due to pres- sures of study. I do not think there was something wrong with it but still I would have liked to have more fun at school than I really did.

Current student, 9/2003-Submit Date, October 2004

The social life is as can be expected from a big school that really does not have any set campus boundaries. This makes for a less campus-like feeling when it comes to parties that you may expect to be taking place at university. I find most nights are spent off campus in downtown Toronto. Having said this, there have been some memorable parties held on campus or very nearby in frat houses or local pubs. Overall, it is a fun time but for a more closed feeling when it come to campuses and their parties, a school like Queens or Western in the smaller towns would be ideal.

Current student, 5/2003-Submit Date, July 2005

Each student enrolls in a college within the University of Toronto and the most organized social events occur within the student's college. There is something for every taste, but most students tend to head to bars and clubs on their own rather than to an organized event. There are multiple student organizations rep- resenting every possible interest, background and lifestyle. There are newspa- pers and a radio station.

Current student, 9/2003-Submit Date, February 2005

Many clubs available with a facility just for clubs called Hart House. Campus is located in downtown Toronto, where many clubs and bars are. Annual balls and parties are organized. School sport teams are available and well-supported.

Current student, 9/2001-Submit Date, July 2005

Because the university is downtown, it is surrounded by a large variety of clubs, bars and social activities. Popular spots are found along Bloor Street and along College Street. Throughout the year, pub nights are organized which allows stu- dents to meet each other and to experience the city. Extracurriculars are easy to join and many times are free.

Read all of Vault's College Surveys at **www.vault.com/college**—get complete surveys on 100s of colleges and univer- sities, expert advice on applicaton essays and more.

V/\ULT CAREER LIBRARY **817**

University of Waterloo

Admissions Office
200 University Avenue West
Waterloo, ON N2L 3G1
Admissions phone: (519) 888-4567 ext. 3777
Admissions e-mail: askus@uwaterloo.ca
Admissions URL: www.findoutmore.uwaterloo.ca

 Admissions

Alumnus/a, Computer Science, 9/2001-4/2006, November 2006

The admissions process was pretty straightforward. They required an application package that consisted of the following. Your official transcript from high school, a short one-page essay describing yourself and explaining why you have selected this school and program, why you are a good candidate and deem yourself fit and a reference section. The reference section included contacts of teachers/coaches and other professionals who know you well. Also, it was required that one of the contacts write a reference letter on your behalf, describing you as a person and how you may fit into the program. Actually, now that I think about it, it wasn't that straightforward! In addition, the University of Waterloo heavily looks upon the Descartes Math Contest result, which is a senior-level standardized mathematics examination (similar to the SATs, yet no verbal section and much more difficult mathematics). All that is taken into consideration while selecting candidates. During my year, the accepted averages were as low as 93 percent cumulative, depending on the extracurricular activities.

Current student, 9/2002-Submit Date, August 2006

I personally didn't find the admission process for University of Waterloo to be very rigorous. Basically, all you need is good academic transcripts and good recommendations. However, for some of the programs such as Software Engineering or Mathematics-Business (Double Degree), extracurricular and other activities related to your career of choice are very important.

Current student, Engineering, 9/2004-Submit Date, December 2006

The application process is very simple. High marks are required, minimum of 80 percent, and they also consider other aspects of the student, such as extracurricular involvement and volunteer activities. It is not as hard to get into as it once was. In the past they only accepted one class (about 150 students) into the Electrical Engineering program, but now they accept two classes, so the chances of getting in are much higher.

Current student, 9/2006-Submit Date, October 2006

Applying to the Honors Arts and Business programs required higher marks than expected. It said you need mid to high 70s, and I had a 78 and did not get admitted to the program initially. We spoke with them and that changed. But this year (for students starting fall 2007) it specifically says for regular-mid 70s, co-op high 70s to low 80s.

Current student, 10/2004-Submit Date, January 2006

Getting into the university was not a big problem. I was required to have a 75 percent or higher average from high school, with certain necessary courses such as the Calculus and English. I had to sign up to get into this university just like I did for others, via OSAP online. It's a very easy way to sign up, but you have to pay about $300 to sign up for around six universities. I wasn't required to do any essays or interviews whatsoever.

Alumnus/a, 9/2001-6/2005, September 2005

Being accepted to University of Waterloo is not as difficult as most people may think. Most undergrad programs offered by the school involve no interviews or essays. For all engineering programs, a standard application form with short-answer questions is involved. It serves the purpose of an interview so some typical interview questions such as your strengths and weaknesses, will be asked. However, from experience, grades are essentially what the admission considers.

If you do not meet the minimum grade requirement, don't bother apply becau the school care more about academics than extracurriculars.

Alumnus/a, 9/1996-4/2000, October 2004

Depending on for which program you applied within the university, you need to submit six prerequisite OACs (Ontario Academic Credit) from an Onta high school. For example, if applying to a science program you must submit OAC in English, two sciences (physics, chemistry or biology), two maths (fin algebra and geometry or calculus), and one more credit. The credits are av aged (percentages) and depending on the cut-off marks for that entering cla you are offered acceptance based on whether you meet this average. For b derline cases (people right at the cut-off and spaces pending) extracurricu activities are looked at. However, acceptance mostly comes down to marks. F more specific programs (programs like engineering or applied health scienc the prerequisites are more strict, as well as the competition to get in so stude looking to get into these programs better have good marks from high school a be well-rounded.

Current student, 9/2003-Submit Date, February 2005

The application process was done through the Provincial Association Universities. The process allowed me to apply to any school (or schools) in province from one convenient location.

The only advice regarding getting into the university would be to apply early a complete the required information essay on time. Certain programs requ higher grades and extracurricular activities, while others, such as general ar are not as picky.

Current student, 8/2003-Submit Date, April 2004

The school is rated Number One by *Maclean's* magazine. The admissio process was fairly easy but required an average of 90 percent or above for mo than half of the programs available. Letters of reference from teachers we required along with a questionnaire booklet inquiring about extracurricu activities, interests, hobbies, and community service. The booklet was compl ed by each individual student and reviewed as the school not only placed impo tance on academics, but on other activities in which the student was involved

There was no formal interview process, but the selectivity of the students w great. For every spot that was offered, there were approximately 30 candidat depending on the faculty, with greater emphasis on the mathematics and en neering faculties.

> **The school says:** "This information has not been reviewed by the University of Waterloo. For accurate details about UW, visit www.findoutmore.uwaterloo.ca."

 **Academics**

Alumnus/a, Computer Science, 9/2001-4/2006, November 20(

Computer Engineering at Waterloo is a rigorous program with respect to workload. The first term is an easy transition from high school with a lot repeated material. It works well that way because most students are getti adjusted to living alone and figuring out the school/party life balance. Class take place from 9 to 5, Monday to Friday and have extra mandatory tutorial s sions. The first few years are mandatory courses so you will be with your cl clique most of the time, but during the last two years there is only a select set compulsory courses and you can branch out to select the courses that interest y the most. Professors are knowledgeable and the workload is fair. At tim (especially term 2B) the workload increases and the due dates overlap so y will need strong time management skills.

Current student, 9/2002-Submit Date, August 2006

The program I was enrolled in was Statistics and Operations Research (Dou Honors). I would say that the program is quite challenging due the nature

ntent that I studied and the workload. You do need extremely good time man-
ement and organizational skills. The workload is quite a bit compared to some
the other schools in Canada.

ost of the professors are quite nice and always welcoming. There are always
e or two exceptions, but in general, I really liked all my professors. They were
lpful and available the majority of the time when I needed help.

urrent student, Engineering, 9/2004-Submit Date, December 2006

ost classes are very good, with excellent professors. There are always some
o do not do an exceptional job of teaching, but for the most part, the teaching
very good. The professors are very knowledgeable, approachable and helpful.
ere is not much choice as far as course selection because in the first six of
ght terms in which you are required to be in school, the timetable and classes
e predetermined. Occasionally students get to choose an elective, but for most
rms, all classes are pre-scheduled. The grading is fair, but there are a lot of
justments made to ensure that a certain number of students pass the course.
r example, a class average of 60 percent may be adjusted to 70 percent by
creasing everyone's mark. The workload varies. Some terms it is very easy,
d others it is horrible. It is definitely manageable though.

urrent student, Engineering, 9/2002-Submit Date, October 2006

ystems Design Engineering is one of the most challenging but unique programs
the world. It requires over a 90 high school average, good extracurriculars
d interests in everything from physics to computing to user interface design to
ectronics. Good overall background about engineering. A third of the gradu-
ng class gets their master's (in engineering, law and medicine), another third
es into business, finance and consulting, and the other third works in the high-
ch industry.

lumnus/a, 9/2001-6/2005, September 2005

niversity of Waterloo is not known for its excellence in math and engineering
r nothing. It demands a lot from the students, both time commitment and intel-
gence. Assignments are lengthy and challenging so it will eat up a lot of your
ne. Do expect to have a very little social life if you actually put effort into get-
g good grades. For math faculty only, some first-year assignment questions
e meant to be IQ tests. Do not get overly frustrated with them if you don't
ow how to solve them on your own. There is a first- and second-year Math
torial Centre for a reason. TAs are usually very helpful, despite some lan-
age barriers. However, they are usually not the markers for your assignments
they usually hire an undergrad "marker" to grade your assignments. That
id, try to keep your assignment answers neat and legible. Each marker has to
ade around 100 assignments, so they will not be looking in detail at every step
u take. As always, everything in math is very clear-cut; so is the grading.
on't expect to b.s. your way through exams or assignments because you will
t nothing in return. You can skip a few steps in your solution (as the profs
ways do in class) as long as the marker can follow your progress.

urrent student, 9/2003-Submit Date, February 2005

he classes are a good size in second year; first year's are quite large. Popular
asses are quite difficult to get unless you are in upper years when you have
ore credits and choose courses earlier.

ne professors are quite good, but there are some to watch out for because they
e more into the research aspect of their job than the teaching. You can go on-
ne to look at past rankings of the teacher to see how he/she was liked by past
udents. The workload is not too difficult. Just keep up regarding examinations
d assignments (as with all post-secondary institutions) because it a very
emanding school regarding grades.

urrent student, 9/2000-Submit Date, June 2004

he quality of classes is good, but not spectacular as many professors are sim-
y researchers for the school, and would rather be doing research. I would say
ost profs are average in quality, with some being poor and a select few being
eat. It is easy to get into the classes you want in general, even if classes are
ll. The key is to decide early and pre-register. The grading is fair on most
xams and assignments. There is nothing bad in this area.

The school says: "This information has not been reviewed by
the University of Waterloo. For accurate details about UW, visit
www.findoutmore.uwaterloo.ca."

Employment Prospects

Alumnus/a, Computer Science, 9/2001-4/2006, November 2006

Waterloo is known for its spectacular co-op placement program. From your first
term you are required to put together your resume and start applying for co-op
jobs. The first few are lower-end positions but as you progress and develop your
experience, you will be applying to better companies such as Google, Microsoft,
Morgan Stanley, Bear Sterns, McKinsey, RIM, NVidia, ATI, CIBC, RBC,
Deloitte and Accenture. Computer engineering students moved around to a lot
of U.S. placements, which gave them good experience. Microsoft was the top
company that students aspired for but I believe that changed to Google near
graduation time. Many big corporations went on to offer their co-op students
full-time positions upon graduation. I have colleagues all over USA and Canada
as well as some in Japan currently pursuing their full-time career. Waterloo has
a wonderful network of employees looking to hire the cream of the crop engineering students, for which Waterloo is known.

Current student, 9/2002-Submit Date, August 2006

The University of Waterloo offers the best co-op program in the world. Thus,
most of the students (who are enrolled in the co-op program) graduate in five
years with two years of work experience before taking their first step into the
industry. The employment prospects are quite decent for graduates. Most of the
top technology firms like RIM, Motorolla, Qualcomm, Microsoft, Google and so
on recruit on our campus because of the reputation of our Engineering,
Computer Science, and Mathematics Programs.

For those entering the finance industry, all of Canada's top banks post co-
op,summer internships, and graduating job postings regularly. Lately, I have
also seen quite a few job postings and info sessions from Mackenzie &
Company, Morgan Stanley, UBS and Goldman Sachs.

Since our alumni network has the reputation to be the best one in Canada and our
alumni do hold top managerial positions in quite a few prestigious corporations
around the world, that is why we have recruiters coming not only from Canada
and United States, but from UK as well.

Current student, Engineering, 9/2004-Submit Date, December 2006

Waterloo has the best co-op system in the world. I think the employment rate
for the students is around 95 percent for the first co-op term, which is four
months after the beginning of university in some situations. Graduate jobs are
also very good as students get to network with employers for five or six co-op
terms before graduation. There is no difficulty in getting employed if you are a
University of Waterloo engineering student.

Current student, Engineering, 9/2002-Submit Date, October 2006

Very good. 100 percent co-op placement for work terms other than the first one.
After graduation, most people end up being very successful and get financially
rewarded for all the hard work and sleepless nights.

Current student, 10/2004-Submit Date, January 2006

My university is known to be one of the best for graduating computer science,
accounting, engineering, math and even economics students. All the best and
well-known companies usually recruit Waterloo students. For example, Deloitte
(the top accounting firm) recruits almost exclusively from Waterloo. Same for
the other three in the Big Four accounting firms, KMPG,
PricewaterhouseCoopers, Deloitte, Ernst and Young. For computer science, all
the top companies come here as well, such as Microsoft, which hires 15 percent
of Waterloo students. Google is now also interested in Waterloo students, as
well. Mercers, Sunlife and especially RIM hire CS students from Waterloo, as
well. For business/finance, I've known companies like Royal Bank, Bank of
Montreal, TD BANK, AGF, among others hiring Waterloo students.

The school says: "This information has not been reviewed by
the University of Waterloo. For accurate details about UW, visit
www.findoutmore.uwaterloo.ca."

Read all of Vault's College Surveys at **www.vault.com/college** — get complete surveys on 100s of colleges and universities, expert advice on applicaton essays and more.

VAULT CAREER LIBRARY **819**

Quality of Life

Alumnus/a, Computer Science, 9/2001-4/2006, November 2006

It's a very safe, fun loving neighborhood at Waterloo. The first year you will be placed in on-campus housing and can enjoy the benefits of the gym, recreational rooms, meal plans and all the facilities. From second year onwards, it is up to you to find your way with the vast selection of near-campus housing. Tons of people are looking to sublet because of the co-op style education system, so finding a place is not a hassle, just need to find something about one or two months in advance. Waterloo has great gym facilities, including pick-up basketball, squash courts, public swim times, outdoor volleyball courts, on campus arcade and intramural sports teams. Students and neighborhood residents are kind and friendly, similar to the administrative employees at Waterloo University. Very nice and enjoyable place to be.

Current student, 9/2002-Submit Date, August 2006

Housing can be a bit of an issue since on-campus housing is only available to first-year students and most of the upper-years are not accommodated. However, since Waterloo is a very small town with two universities in town, there is a lot of off-campus housing available for students.

Since it's mostly a student town, there is hardly any crime other than just the student troubles, which are quite rare as well. The quality of life is very good in my opinion. While it is a small student town, there are malls, cinemas and lots of club and pubs to go around. In short, it's the perfect town for student lifestyle.

Current student, 10/2004-Submit Date, January 2006

University of Waterloo is really on top of everything. Housing is not an issue whatsoever. The campus is one of the biggest I've seen, with so many free facilities such as gym, health care and guidance counseling. There are programs like Safe Walk at night to ensure that everyone is safe. There are also police vehicles roaming around the campus at all times ensuring safety.

Current student, 8/2003-Submit Date, April 2004

The school offers housing for all students in their first year and can accommodate several thousand upper-year students. There are seven different housing facilities, which range from single rooms, double rooms, townhouses, complex buildings and regular dorm-style apartments. Half of these facilities include dining cafeterias, while some are equipped with kitchens for home cooking. The city has a low crime rate and the majority of the residences around the school are occupied by students.

Current student, 9/2000-Submit Date, June 2004

The campus is very large and lush, however the buildings aren't the most aesthetically pleasing. However, the money was spent in the right places as most labs are equipped with very good computers, a student card can be used to purchase many things electronically, and there are two good quality gym facilities on campus as well. There are many places to eat at the main plaza near the university, with foods ranging from hamburgers, Chinese, Italian and East Indian.

> **The school says:** "This information has not been reviewed by the University of Waterloo. For accurate details about UW, visit www.findoutmore.uwaterloo.ca."

Social Life

Current student, Engineering, 9/2002-Submit Date, October 2006

Prepare to work hard. But you will be with smart, motivated and interesting people like you who are great to spend time with. Systems classes typically work in tight-knit groups. You will be best friends with at least a quarter of the class (very unusual in most other engineering schools in the world). Competitive, but people want you to succeed so people help each other with job interviews and school work. Great people.

Alumnus/a, Computer Science, 9/2001-4/2006, November 20[06]

It's a quieter town than most people would expect. Laurier University is ab[out] five to 10 minutes down the road, so there is a combination of students from b[oth] universities enjoying the nightlife. It's a party town if you get into the ri[ght] crowd with big parties at bars like Philthy's, Caesers and on-campus bars, su[ch] as Turret and the Bomber. Rev is the closest non-university affiliated club t[hat] is always packed at the beginning of the term. First Rev is the most popular a[nd] you must be there by 9:30 p.m. that night if you plan on getting in before [12] a.m.—yes, that's how crazy it is! Tons of students your age are there in a mix[ed] culture so it's a great place to have fun and meet new people. Some believe t[hat] it's a "study only" school, which is incorrect. People work hard and party ha[rd] also, but like any other university, it depends on the crowd you're with.

Current student, 9/2002-Submit Date, August 2006

I personally think that campus life is very good. There are lots of clubs and oth[er] activities through which you do get a chance to meet a lot of people from d[if]ferent cultures and ethnicities. There are lots of clubs and events are happen[ing] on campus all the time. Even summer terms here are better than other scho[ols] since some of the co-op students come back in summer and the campus is st[ill] lively. The school does have a few Greek societies as well; however, they a[re] not very big. There are two fraternities (Sigma Chi and Zeta PSI) and one soro[r]ity (Kappa Kappa Gamma).

As for campus clubs: the list just goes on and on and I haven't met anyone [who] who doesn't fit anywhere in that list. (You name the activity/interest/ethni[ci]ty/religion/voluntary organization, it has an on-campus club.)

The university has big plaza right next to it (literally right next to it) that ha[s a] lot of hotspots for eating. So you're hardly ever out of choices.

Current student, 9/2006-Submit Date, October 2006

Social life on campus is one of the great things about Waterloo. It is a quiet ca[m]pus during the week but come Friday, everything changes. Students here wo[rk] hard during the week, and reward themselves on the weekends. Some peo[ple] study so much that you never see them, while others socialize more oft[en.] Overall, a good balance!

Current student, 10/2004-Submit Date, January 2006

Social life is also great in Waterloo. There is a free club within the student l[ife] centre. There are many, many restaurants, at least seven across the camp[us.] There are tons of clubs to join, and a lot of events take place. Bill Gates rece[nt]ly visited University of Waterloo, the only university he visited in Canad[a I] believe, on his last tour. Social life here is average, it's not a party school. B[ut] there are still weekly parties held in the student life center, as well as in a pla[ce] called Feds.

Current student, 9/2003-Submit Date, November 2004

The school's social life is improving. The Bomber, our bar, is probably one [of] the student favorites on campus. There are always specials on. The clubs a[re] quite good in the area but are quite a distance away from campus and requi[re] either a car or transit. There are well over 50 clubs on campus affiliated with t[he] Undergrad Student Government. On top of that, you have the two sororities a[nd] two fraternities in the area, undergrad program societies, and those not affilia[ted] with the government.

Current student, 9/2003-Submit Date, November 2004

There are two on-campus bars, one is a dance club and one is a bar with occ[a]sional bands playing. There are a large number of clubs that students can jo[in,] such as sports teams and clubs. There are restaurants in almost every buildi[ng] and the new 24-hour Tim Horton's is a great addition to the campus for la[te] nights at the library.

> **The school says:** "This information has not been reviewed by the University of Waterloo. For accurate details about UW, visit www.findoutmore.uwaterloo.ca."

The University of Western Ontario

Admissions Office
Undergraduate Recruitment and Admissions Room 165
Stevenson-Lawson Building
London, ON N6A 5B8
Admissions phone: (519) 661-2100
Admissions fax: (519) 850-2590
Admissions URL:
welcome.uwo.ca/en/secondlevel/admissions.html

Admissions

Current student, Business, 9/2004-Submit Date, January 2007

Getting into UWO is about having over an 80 percent average. Depending on the year, 80 isn't necessarily safe, but an 83/84 and you're set.

The Ivey admissions process is significantly more selective. I was not an AEO (pre-Ivey), but I can safely say that 80 to 90 percent of my classmates had averages over 80 percent in their last two years of university. And of course, an excellent grade in the only required course (BUS 257) and at least a reasonable number of extracurriculars.

Current student, History, 9/2004-Submit Date, April 2007

Admissions at Western is based solely on high school grades for entry into the faculty of Social Science. Once accepted into the faculty, one chooses general courses and does not declare one's major/minor until registering for one's second year. This gives students flexibility is choosing first-year courses and in deciding which field or fields they are interested in progressing. I started out with the intention of entering psychology, but liked my history course so much that I switched into history.

Current student, 9/2003-Submit Date, October 2006

The process began with an online application to register with the universities. The online application was very simple and came with step-by-step instructions. Here I listed all the universities to which I intended to apply. This is also the time when you have to pay for the application process. This can be done by credit card. There is a base charge that allows you to apply for three universities, then an additional charge for more. Once this is complete, the universities will send you applications to be filled out. I recommend filling them out as soon as you get them but take the time to have them proofread. This way you avoid missing the cutoff date and any errors in the application. Then it is just a matter of waiting until the responses arrive.

Current student, History, 9/2006-Submit Date, June 2007

Applying was very easy. If you live in Ontario applying to Western is only a matter of using the OUAC web site. Admissions standards are high, around an 80 to 90, depending on your program. If you have an average over 85 coming out of high school you will automatically receive a $1,500 scholarship. You can check your application status both through the Western web site and the OUAC web site. Or you could wait for the letter to come in the mail. Once you gain admission, you must begin the process of selecting a residence (if that's what you choose to do). For new students the university offers a summer academic orientation. If you are geographically close enough to attend I would recommend it. However it is important to do independent research into what courses you will talked in first year. Blindly taking the advice of the professor that is assigned to be your academic advisor is not a wise decision. Several of my friends and I ended up in courses we hated (and as result got less than fantastic marks).

Current student, 9/2003-Submit Date, November 2005

The university requires a high academic standing of at least 80 percent to apply. Along with grades, be sure to include extracurriculars while applying. The university also has many subdivisions of colleges and it prefers that students apply to specific colleges and programs.

Current student, 9/2003-Submit Date, January 2005

I have returned to school as a mature student. My application was treated a little differently than if I were coming right from high school. Because I was returning as a mature student, I had to get both my high school and college transcripts and send them to the registrar's office. I then had a personal interview with a counselor at the registrar's office and had to wait about two weeks before I received my letter of acceptance.

Current student, 9/2003-Submit Date, May 2004

The admissions process at the University of Western Ontario went very smoothly for me. In Ontario you must complete an online form called OUAC that is very simple. You choose the universities to which you wish to apply, the individual programs, and send in your high school transcript and extracurricular activities. That is your application. For the program I applied to, you had to have at least an 83 percent average to get in, so the advice that was given to me was never to slack off in my last year of high school, just work my hardest. The university gathered all applications and transcripts and would frequently send me tons of pamphlets and books about everything you could possibly want to know about the university as well as letters letting you know how the process was going and when you could expect to hear from them. The University of Western Ontario didn't have an interview or essay, and I was very comfortable with the process and how I was admitted.

Academics

Current student, History, 9/2004-Submit Date, April 2007

For first-year students, Western can be overwhelming academically. The academic standards are high in order to be accepted into honors programs and for continuation at Western. The history program at Western involves mandatory classes and a heavy amount of reading and writing. A history student at Western will generally take three essay courses a year, which can be daunting. Getting into classes in history is not difficult as the classroom demands can be accommodated to the demand for the particular course. Professors can seem uninterested at times with undergraduate affairs, but one-on-one they are extremely helpful and accommodating. Grading at Western is difficult and generally consistent. Retaining an average in the 70s is impressive at Western as many course averages hover around the high 60s. Receiving an 80 percent on an assignment or paper should be taken as quite an accomplishment, equivalent to at least a 90 percent on a major exam in a science course. The workload is hard but not when managed efficiently. Advice that I would give is always to stay on top of readings and to work ahead on major essays as they all compound and are usually due at the same time.

Current student, Business, 9/2004-Submit Date, January 2007

Excellent profs, heavy workload, high quality class discussions. Grades are all bell curved to a 78 average and the range is typically anywhere from 70 to 85. HBA1 (third year of university) classes are mandatory and are scheduled for you. You get into popular HBA2 classes through a lottery system, so it's safe to say it can be challenging to get what you want.

Current student, 9/2003-Submit Date, October 2006

In my program the popular classes fill up very quickly. Since you are given a date and time that you can begin to register, it is important to do so at that time. Try to figure out all the classes that you want to take before beginning the online sign up. Psychology does not have a large number of class hours but it does have a lot of reading, so if you are able to motivate yourself to do work you should be fine. As for grades all profs grade differently. Talk to the TAs or the profs directly if you are unsure of their expectations. Get to know your profs. The better you know them the more likely they are to be flexible when you need a little extra help or time on an assignment.

Read all of Vault's College Surveys at **www.vault.com/college**—get complete surveys on 100s of colleges and universities, expert advice on applicaton essays and more.

VAULT CAREER LIBRARY **821**

Current student, 9/2003-Submit Date, November 2005

I am enrolled in the psychology program. The program is very intensive with a high number of applicants after first year. The classes and professors are of very high standing and it is considered one of the best psychology programs. Popular classes are fairly hard to get into and need to be taken ahead of time. The grading is fairly strict. The workload is fairly heavy but manageable. The program also offers fourth-year independent studies where students can work closely with professors for an entire semester of research.

Current student, History, 9/2006-Submit Date, June 2007

Workload, for me, was a big shock. As a social science student in four essay courses, the reading and essay writing was overwhelming. Don't take the stance that the work ethic that got you in the university will keep you there. For the most part, this isn't true. Take the time to meet your professors and your TAs. They grade your work, so make sure they know your name and they know you care about the work you do and the course material. This will help in getting better grades and learning more from the assignments and lectures. This will also give you an idea of what the environment is like in your department or faculty.

Alumnus/a, 9/2002-5/2006, June 2006

Amazing profs, amazing classes, no competition for enrollment. Small class environments excellent for discussion and accelerated achievement.

Current student, 9/2003-Submit Date, January 2005

I am currently in a three-year undergraduate program called childhood and family relations. I find Western very accommodating for classes; being a part-time student, I need my classes to accommodate my work schedule. There are lots of options from which to choose for courses. The workload has been manageable, with lots of reading, but that is to be expected. The exams have been multiple choice only but that depends on the professor and the course. I have found the professors to be very fair. They give you the feeling that they really care how you do and want to help you as much as possible to do to well in their class. They are always available if you need extra help or have questions. If you attend the smaller colleges affiliated with the university, the classes are smaller and this can give you an advantage to do well in the course.

Current student, 9/2003-Submit Date, May 2004

The academic nature of my program is very science-based and not easy! The class sizes for most of my first-year courses were very large, around 1,000 people, but I found no difficulty in getting the popular courses that I wanted. The quality of the classes and the professors is amazing at Western. I couldn't be happier with the opportunities I've had this year and I will miss them next year. Grading was very effective, the profs made use of teaching assistants so all work would be graded in about a week and exams in about three days or so depending on the course. The workload is heavy, I do approximately six hours of homework a night and no classes on Fridays.

 ## Employment Prospects

Current student, Business, 9/2004-Submit Date, January 2007

Recruitment is one of Ivey's performance metrics, so we get a lot of corporate events and on campus recruiting. Right now, I'm in the middle of trying to secure a summer internship in investment banking, but other companies (marketing, consulting and so on) also recruit here.

Current student, History, 9/2006-Submit Date, June 2007

Western alumni are like no other. They are proud and, for the most part, are willing to do anything for their former school. People love Western that much. You will soon learn this if you decide to spend the next four years of your life in the purple heaven. Do research and look for companies or offices run by Western grads, you have a connection with these people and they will be eager to chat about your life at Western.

Current student, 9/2003-Submit Date, October 2006

The University of Western Ontario has a great reputation and many people find work easily after graduation. This of course varies with the degree completed.

There are many on-campus job fairs that allow you to get in tough with employers. There is also a student employment service at the school that can help get

you in touch with employers, help you with you resume or help you dec which specific job may be best for you.

Current student, 9/2003-Submit Date, November 2005

Our university has the highest standing in our community. A lot of our progra offer help in final years to obtain jobs after graduation. The mayor of our city an alumnus, thereby having a strong alumni influence. Many of our progra have on-campus recruiting sessions for graduating students. The career cen also has many internships and summer jobs available in prospective progra and fields.

Current student, 9/2003-Submit Date, January 2005

Employment prospects with my degree would be to apply to teacher's colle for one year. I would also qualify to work with children as a counselor. I co also work on my own as a family counselor or life coach. This degree wou also allow me to work for the government as a childcare or social worker.

Current student, 9/2003-Submit Date, May 2004

This program is amazing for career prospects; it's oriented toward paving t way to medical school and easing that transition and the recruiting for the p gram is amazing. Since it's only my first year I am not too sure on any car placement resources but will know later on in my educational career.

 ## Quality of Life

Current student, History, 9/2006-Submit Date, June 2007

I always felt safe when walking the campus at night. The campus is always we maintained. Walking to classes is always a nice walk; buildings around the ca pus are gorgeous. I caught myself staring at Middlesex or University Colleg few times. Residences are OK. The living conditions are certainly not luxu ous, but the lifestyle and experience is worth it. Whatever you have heard abc the infamous Saugeen Maitland Hall is not true. I lived there for my first ye I partied my fair share but I also slept and studied in peace.

Current student, Political Science, 1/2003-Submit Date, July 200

The University of Western Ontario is considered one of the finest all arou environments for academics in Canada. The housing and campuses are exc lent, and the neighborhood is focused around the school. The nightlife and par scene are considered one of the best in North America.

Current student, Business, 9/2004-Submit Date, January 2007

I didn't go to residence, but I've heard very few complaints about the residenc or their food. There is a new upper-year residence, as well (London Hall). I lived in this neighborhood for 10 years or more, so I can say that it's fairly sa and relatively crime free.

Current student, 9/2003-Submit Date, October 2006

Housing near the university in fairly inexpensive and well maintained. It is ea to find housing just by walking around the neighborhood or checking the onli database of housing rentals. The campus is beautiful. The buildings are all w kept and so is the landscape. It is not uncommon to see people stopped on ca pus taking pictures. The campus has a walk home program that is free of char if anyone ever feels uncomfortable walking home at night, however the camp is well lit and as a young woman walking on campus I have never felt threaten or scared.

Alumnus/a, 9/2001-4/2004, November 2005

Western has quite possibly the most beautiful campus in North America. It is own little community in the city and is surrounded by walls, making it sort of enclosed fortress. There is plenty of on-campus housing, as well as through t city, although London is known to be an expensive place to live in terms of hou ing. On campus, I was not thrilled with the food—it was either cafeteria Swiss Chalet or Tim Horton's. Off campus, London has amazing restaura which didn't help the freshman 15!

Current student, 9/2003-Submit Date, January 2005

The facilities are very good. There are lots of extracurricular activities with tv large buildings for physical fitness, including a swimming pool, and a skati rink. There are lots of chances to join either academic or recreational clubs. T

iversity is located in the upper-middle class area of London. Security guards
e plentiful and I always feel safe. Western is a fairly large university but has
few independent colleges so you are able to take classes in a smaller, more inti-
ate environment if that is preferred. This allows for you to get more personal
th your classmates and the professor. Relationships can be on a name basis
ther than number only.

urrent student, 9/2003-Submit Date, May 2004

ur campus rocks! It has to be the best campus around, there isn't a more spir-
ed and friendly atmosphere than Western. Each faculty has its own student
ounsel separate from the main campus student counsel and makes you feel very
home! There are lots of sports for students to participate and get involved.
ousing on campus is by far extremely exceptional. Many are new and even the
d ones are great. They all have their own dining hall and there are also many
eat places to eat in each faculty building as well as in our community center
ilding. We have a crime and safety committee on campus called Foot Patrol
d they escort students wherever they need to go across campus at late hours.
lso, we have our own campus police.

 ## Social Life

urrent student, Political Science, 1/2003-Submit Date, July 2007

ne social life at Western is ranked Number One in *MacLean's* university study.
ven David Letterman once ranked the school Number Two for partying a cou-
e of years ago.

urrent student, History, 9/2004-Submit Date, April 2007

ondon's social scene is exploding at this very moment. London's heralded
ichmond Row boasts dozens of bars, ranging form dance clubs to Irish pubs.
lso on campus, the Spoke and the Wave offer both a club and pub atmosphere.
ondon's downtown features a wide variety of dining establishments all with
asonable prices for their food. For theatre, the Grand is a Class A profession-
theatre and Stratford (World Famous) is less than one hour's drive from the
niversity. The London music scene is fabulous as on any given night; you can
oose from multiple venues where live music ranging from indie rock, jazz and
etal can be found. Also, the John Labatt Centre draws the biggest names in
usic (Metallica, Pearl Jam, Elton John to name just a few). The John Labatt
entre is also home to the London Knights, Canada's most successful junior
ockey franchise of the past five years. Western itself offers over 100 clubs and
rganizations that are open to students to join at minimal costs. The Greek sys-
m is also represented well at Western, as there are numerous fraternities and
rorities that operate at Western. Western has gotten a reputation as a party
chool and London's features certainly add to this mentality.

Current student, 9/2003-Submit Date, October 2006

Western has an incredible number of clubs that can be joined. During the first
month of school there is a display of all the clubs and an opportunity to join any
number of them. It is a great way to meet people and to get involved. As for
nightlife, London is a great place to go out. There are countless bars for every
taste. If you are into martinis, there is the Barking Frog; if you are more into
dance, then try The Phoenix. Like sitting out on a patio? Barney's is for you.
If you are more into a classic pub, try Molly Blooms. If you like to mix a little
of every thing then Jack's or the Ceeps are great places to go. All of these bars
are located within a $10 cab ride from campus and most of the restaurants are
located in the same area.

Current student, 9/2003-Submit Date, November 2005

The school has great diversity and ethnicity. One is able to celebrate all cultures
and indulge in other cultures. There isn't a great number of food options but the
student community is close knit. Students enjoy hanging out and usually end up
knowing everyone by their junior/senior years. There is a campus bar but the
rest are cafeteria-style food places. The dating scene is pretty nonexistent as it
is such a close-knit community. Most people either end up going stable in relationships or go off campus to find people. There are many events going on all
the time, ranging from clubbing to movie nights, to small social gatherings. One
is able to find everything one would like to do available through clubs. Students
who get involved through councils and clubs tend to have a better social life and
enjoy their university experience more.

Current student, 9/2003-Submit Date, January 2005

I have visited the popular bars and restaurants. The City of London and Western
offer lots of opportunities to join in clubs and socialize at local pubs and restaurants. I have found the students to be very friendly and welcoming of newcomers. This school is also very progressive in multiculturism. There are students
from all across the world. It is highly respected as a university.

Current student, 9/2003-Submit Date, May 2004

Western is known as the party place. We have two bars on campus, one called
the Wave, a student favorite throughout frosh week, and then makes an excellent
restaurant for the rest of the year. And we have the Spoke, the pub on campus
and it's also a favorite where we get many bands and great events going on in
there. The dating scene is crazy at Western, you can meet people everywhere
and anywhere and it always seems to be happy. We have over 100 clubs on campus and many different events that are run by all sorts.

Read all of Vault's College Surveys at www.vault.com/college—get complete surveys on 100s of colleges and universities, expert advice on applicaton essays and more.

VAULT CAREER LIBRARY 823

About the Editors

Stephanie Hauser

Stephanie is the Education Editor at Vault. Born and raised in Miami, FL, she ventured up north to Boston College to earn her degree in English Literature and Communication before settling in New York City.

Carolyn C. Wise

Carolyn is the Senior Education Editor at Vault. Born and raised in Brooklyn, NY, she graduated from Princeton University with a degree in English Literature. Carolyn is a volunteer firefighter in Saltaire, NY.

Vault Editors

Vault is the leading media company for career information. *The College Buzz Book* is part of a series of books on educational programs based on surveys of students and alumni. Other titles in the series include *The Law School Buzz Book* and *The Business School Buzz Book*.

Our team of industry-focused editors takes a journalistic approach in covering news, employment trends and specific employers in their industries. We annually survey 10,000s of employees to bring readers the inside scoop on industries and specific employers. Our guides for college students and recent grads include the *College Career Bible, Vault Guide to Top Internships, Vault Guide to Resumes, Cover Letters and Interviews,* Vault guides to industries such as accounting, biotech, consulting, fashion, investment banking, media, real estate, and many more. To see a complete list of Vault's more than 120 career and education titles, go to www.vault.com.

Read all of Vault's college surveys at **www.vault.com/college** – get complete surveys on 100's of colleges and universities, get expert advice on applicaton essays and and more.

VAULT CAREER LIBRARY 824